Oxford

English-English-Malay
DICTIONARY

THIRD EDITION

Happy reading!
Happy marriage life!
Love you both!
Cheers & Jul.

OXFORD FAJAR

Oxford Fajar Sdn. Bhd. (008974-T)

Oxford Fajar Sdn. Bhd. (00897-T)
4, Jalan Pemaju U1/15, Seksyen U1
Hicom-Glenmarie Industrial Park
40150 Shah Alam
Selangor Darul Ehsan

© Oxford Fajar Sdn. Bhd. (008974-T) 2003, 2005, 2009, 2012, 2015
First published 2003
Updated first edition 2004 (19 impressions)
Second edition 2009 (6 impressions)
Updated second edition 2012 (5 impressions)
Third edition 2015

ISBN 978 983 47 1563 2 (L)
ISBN 978 983 47 1562 5 (B)

Original copy in English published by
Oxford University Press, Great Clarendon Street, Oxford as
Oxford Wordpower Dictionary 4th Edition
(ISBN: 978 0 19 439798 8)

© Oxford University Press 2012

This Edition is licensed for sale in Malaysia, Brunei
and Singapore only and not for export thereafter.

All right reserved.
No part of this publication may be reproduced,
stored in a retrieval system, or transmitted, in any form or
by any means, electronic, mechanical, photocopying, recording
or otherwise, without the prior permission of
Oxford Fajar Sdn. Bhd. (008974-T)

Perpustakaan Negara Malaysia   Cataloguing-in-Publication Data

Oxford English - English - Malay DICTIONARY - THIRD EDITION
 ISBN 978-983-47-1563-2
 1. English language--Dictionaries--Malay. 2. Malay language--Dictionaries--English.
 423.9923

Impression: 10 9 8 7 6 5 4 3 2

Text set in 7 point ITC Stone Sans
by Far East Offset & Engraving Sdn. Bhd.
Printed in Malaysia by
Vivar Printing Sdn. Bhd., Selangor Darul Ehsan

Contents

iv	Guide to the dictionary
vi	Abbreviations
vii	Labels and symbols used in the dictionary
viii	Phonetic spelling
ix	Guide to Common Errors
1 – 989	**The Dictionary**
	Study section
WT1 – WT16	Writing Tutor
P1 – P16	Colour pages
R1 – R41	Reference section
R42 – R59	Wordpower Workout
R60	List of illustrations in the dictionary
R62	List of notes in the dictionary

Guide to the dictionary

Pronunciation in phonetic spelling | **Part of speech** (= noun, verb, adjective, etc.)

teacher /ˈtiːtʃə(r)/ noun [C] a person whose job is to teach, especially in a school or college □ *guru; cikgu*: He's a teacher at a primary school. ♦ a chemistry/music teacher

Definition (= the meaning of the word) in simple English

Malay equivalent enhances understanding of the English word

Words with the same spelling divided into nouns, verbs, etc.

swot¹ /swɒt/ noun [C] (*informal*) a person who studies too hard □ *kaki belajar/studi*

swot² /swɒt/ verb [I,T] (*informal*) swot (up) (swotting; swotted) swot (up) (for/on sth); swot sth up to study sth very hard, especially to prepare for an exam □ *belajar/menelaah dgn tekun*: She's swotting for her final exams.

Irregular spelling and **irregular forms** clearly shown

study² /ˈstʌdi/ verb (studying; studies; pt, pp studied) **1** [I,T] study (sth/for sth) to spend time learning about sth □ *menelaah; mempelajari; belajar*: Leon has been studying hard for his exams. ♦ to study French at university **2** [T] to look at sth very carefully □ *meneliti*: to study a map

I = intransitive verb
T = transitive verb

Patterns that the word is used in

exam /ɪgˈzæm/ (also formal examination) noun [C] a written, spoken or practical test of what you know or can do □ *peperiksaan*: an English exam ♦ the exam results ♦ to do/take/sit an exam ♦ to pass/fail an exam ♦ to revise for an exam ⊃ note at pass, study

This word is used in **formal** English

Collocations (= words that go together) in bold

extra-curricular /ˌekstrə kəˈrɪkjələ(r)/ adj not part of the **curriculum** (= the normal course of studies in a school or college) □ *luar kurikulum*: The school offers many extra-curricular activities such as sport, music, drama, etc.

Difficult words in definitions are explained for you

The Oxford 3000™ marked with a key to show the most useful and important words in English

language /ˈlæŋɡwɪdʒ/ noun
▸OF A COUNTRY **1** [C] the system of communication in speech and writing that is used by people of a particular country □ *bahasa*: How many languages can you speak? ♦ What is your first language (= your mother tongue)? ♦ They fell in love in spite of **the language barrier** (= having different first languages).
▸COMMUNICATION **2** [U] the system of sounds and writing that people use to express their thoughts, ideas and feelings □ *bahasa*: written/spoken language

C = countable noun
U = uncountable noun

Short cuts take you quickly to the meaning you want

truant /ˈtruːənt/ noun [C] a child who stays away from school without permission □ *budak yg ponteng sekolah*
IDM play truant; (*AmE*) play hooky to stay away from school without permission □ *ponteng sekolah*

Idioms in a separate section

AmE shows **American English**

Stress marks show you how to pronounce compound words

ballpoint /ˈbɔːlpɔɪnt/ (also **ballpoint ˈpen**, BRE ALSO Biro™) noun [C] a pen with a very small metal ball at the end that rolls ink onto paper □ *pena mata bulat* ⇒ picture at **stationery**

Illustrations build your vocabulary and help with confusing words

vowel /ˈvaʊəl/ noun [C] a letter that represents a **vowel** sound. In English the vowels are *a, e, i, o* or *u*. □ *vokal* ⇒ look at **consonant**

Look at related words to build your vocabulary

compulsory /kəmˈpʌlsəri/ adj that must be done, by law, rules, etc. □ *wajib*: Maths and English are compulsory subjects on this course. ♦ It is compulsory to wear a hard hat on the building site. **SYN** obligatory **OPP** optional, voluntary

Opposite (= a word with the opposite meaning)

Synonym (= a word with the same meaning)

clever /ˈklevə(r)/ adj (**cleverer**; **cleverest**) [You can also use **more clever** and **most clever**.] **1** able to learn, understand or do sth quickly and easily; intelligent □ *pandai; cerdik; pintar*: a clever student ♦ How clever of you to mend my watch! ⇒ note at **intelligent 2** (used about things, ideas or sb's actions) showing skill or intelligence □ *bijak; bagus*: a clever device ♦ We made a clever plan. ▸ **cleverly** adv ▸ **cleverness** noun [U]

Comparatives and superlatives of adjectives and adverbs are shown

Examples show you how to use the word

Derivative (= a word formed from another word)

note² /nəʊt/ verb [T] **1** to notice or pay careful attention to sth □ *memerhatikan; perasan*: He noted a slight change in her attitude towards him. ♦ Please note that this office is closed on Tuesdays. **2** to mention sth □ *menyebut*: I'd like to note that the project has so far been extremely successful.
PHR V note sth down to write sth down so that you remember it □ *mencatat*

Phrasal verbs in a separate section

Topic notes give you the words you need to talk about everyday topics

Exam tips give you helpful advice on how to prepare for and do exams

TOPIC

E-books

You can buy an e-book **over the Internet** and read it on an **e-reader/e-book reader** (= a small electronic device that you carry with you). You can keep many books on one e-reader. It is also possible to buy an **app** (= computer application) that will allow you to **download** e-books **onto** your computer, smartphone, iPod™, etc.

EXAM TIP

Paragraphs

When you write an essay, it is important to organize your writing into paragraphs to show how your ideas develop. Each paragraph should contain a separate idea and include at least two sentences that relate to this idea. You start each paragraph on a new line.

Other types of note

HELP	to avoid mistakes	GRAMMAR	for difficult grammar points
MORE	to build your vocabulary	WRITING TIP	to help you improve your writing
CULTURE	for information about Britain and America	OTHER WORDS FOR	for help choosing exactly the right word

v

Abbreviations used in the dictionary

English

abbr	abbreviation		*pp*	past participle
adj	adjective		*prep*	preposition
adv	adverb		*pron*	pronoun
BrE	British English		*pt*	past tense
C	countable noun		*sb*	somebody
conj	conjunction		*sing*	singular
etc.	and so on		*sth*	something
excl	exclamation		T	transitive verb
fem	feminine form		™	trademark
I	intransitive verb		U	uncountable noun
masc	masculine form		*AmE*	American English
pl	plural			

Malay

AS	Amerika Syarikat	*dsb*	dan sebagainya	*sst* sesuatu
dgn	dengan	*kk*	kata kerja	*tdk* tidak
dll	dan lain-lain	*kn*	kata nama	*ttg* tentang
dlm	dalam	*kpd*	kepada	*UK* United Kingdom
dpt	dapat	*pd*	pada	*utk* untuk
dr	dari	*spt*	seperti	*yg* yang
drpd	daripada	*sso*	seseorang	

Labels used in the dictionary

formal   used in serious or official language (for example, *extinguish, nevertheless*)

informal   used between friends, or in a relaxed or an unofficial situation (for example, *mum, snooze*)

written   used in books, letters, reports, etc. (for example, *circa, abode*)

spoken   used especially in informal conversation (for example, *I must say, You're joking*)

slang   very informal language, sometimes used only by a particular group of people, such as teenagers (for example, *awesome, buff*)

technical   used by people who specialize in particular subject areas (for example, *affidavit, diagnostic*)

figurative   not used with its exact meaning but in a way that is different to give a special effect (for example, *infectious laughter, a murky past*)

old-fashioned   usual in the past, but not now (for example, *ado, slovenly*)

Symbols used in the dictionary

- **SYN** synonym
- **OPP** opposite
- **IDM** idioms section
- **PHR V** phrasal verbs section
- ▶ derivatives section

- 🔑 Oxford 3000™ word

  For more information about **The Oxford 3000™** and to download a copy of the list, visit the website:

  www.oup.com/elt/oxford3000

Phonetic spelling

Vowels

iː	see /siː/	ʊ	put /pʊt/	aɪ	five /faɪv/
i	any /ˈeni/	uː	too /tuː/	aʊ	now /naʊ/
ɪ	sit /sɪt/	u	usual /ˈjuːʒuəl/	ɔɪ	join /dʒɔɪn/
e	ten /ten/	ʌ	cup /kʌp/	ɪə	near /nɪə/
æ	hat /hæt/	ɜː	fur /fɜː/	eə	hair /heə/
ɑː	arm /ɑːm/	ə	ago /əˈɡəʊ/	ʊə	pure /pjʊə/
ɒ	got /ɡɒt/	eɪ	pay /peɪ/		
ɔː	saw /sɔː/	əʊ	home /həʊm/		

Consonants

p	pen /pen/	f	fall /fɔːl/	h	how /haʊ/
b	bad /bæd/	v	van /væn/	m	man /mæn/
t	tea /tiː/	θ	thin /θɪn/	n	no /nəʊ/
d	did /dɪd/	ð	then /ðen/	ŋ	sing /sɪŋ/
k	cat /kæt/	s	so /səʊ/	l	leg /leɡ/
ɡ	got /ɡɒt/	z	zoo /zuː/	r	red /red/
tʃ	chin /tʃɪn/	ʃ	she /ʃiː/	j	yes /jes/
dʒ	June /dʒuːn/	ʒ	vision /ˈvɪʒn/	w	wet /wet/

Guide to Common Errors

Section 1: Alphabetical list of some common errors

A

a
- ► You need a friends. (✗)
- ► You need **friends**. (✓)

A means 'one'. Do not use it with a plural noun.

- ► I enjoy listening to a music. (✗)
- ► I enjoy listening to **music**. (✓)

Do not use **a** with uncountable nouns like *music*.

- ► A best way to do this is ... (✗)
- ► **The** best way to do this is ... (✓)

Use **the**, not **a**, before *best*.

a/an
- ► He is an university student. (✗)
- ► He is **a** university student. (✓)

Use **a**, not **an**, before 'uni-' words (e.g. *university, unit, unilateral*).

absent/ absence
- ► I was not absence on Tuesday. (✗)
- ► I was not **absent** on Tuesday. (✓)

The adjective form is **absent**. **Absence** is a noun (e.g. *His absence is noticed by the Director*).

advance/ advanced
- ► We are using advance techniques. (✗)
- ► We are using **advanced** techniques. (✓)

Advance is a verb. Before a noun, use the adjective form **advanced**.

advice
- ► He gave me an advice./He gave me some advices. (✗)
- ► He gave me **some** advice. (✓)

Advice is uncountable. Do not use it with a plural *-s*, or with *an*. Say **some advice** or **a piece of advice**.

advise
- ► I advised her don't go. (✗)
- ► I advised her **not to** go. (✓)

A negative idea after **advise** uses **not to** + infinitive.

afraid
- ► We shouldn't afraid. (✗)
- ► We shouldn't **be** afraid. (✓)

Afraid is not a verb. Before **afraid**, use the verb *be* (*am/are/is/was/were*).

after
- ► After saw the film, we ... (✗)
- ► After **we** saw the film, we ... (✓)

After is not directly followed by a verb (except an '-ing' verb, as in *After seeing the film, we ...*).

ix

agree	▶ *I agree the people who say that ...* (✗) ▶ I agree **with** the people who say that ... (✓) **agree WITH somebody**
all	▶ *All of students may use the library.* (✗) ▶ **All students** may use the library. (✓) *Of* is wrong here. Use it only if *the* follows: *All of the students ...*
alphabet	▶ *There are six alphabets in this word.* (✗) ▶ There are six **letters** in this word. (✓) **Alphabet** means the whole series of letters from A to Z.
already	▶ *He did it already.* (✗) ▶ He **has done** it already. (✓) **Already** is not used with the simple past tense (e.g. *did, went*). It is mainly used with the present perfect (*has ...*).
also	▶ *The children also can help.* (✗) ▶ The children **can also** help. (✓) **Also** goes before one-word verbs (e.g. *helps* in *Suria also helps*. But it is placed AFTER the verbs *be, have, can/could, must, may/might, will/would*).
although	▶ *Although Farid was ill, but he played well.* (✗) ▶ Although Farid was ill, he played well. (✓) Do not use **although** and **but** together. ▶ *Although they are poor, men can be happy.* (✗) ▶ **Even if** they are poor, men can be happy. (✓) Using **although** suggests that all men are poor. If you wish to describe just an extreme case (as in this example), use **even if**.
always	▶ *She knows always the cheapest shops.* (✗) ▶ She **always knows** the cheapest shops. (✓) **Always** is used BEFORE a one-word verb (e.g. *knows*). However, it is placed after the verbs *be, have, must, can/could, will/would, may/might* (e.g. *She has always known*).
answer	▶ *The answer for this question is ...* (✗) ▶ The answer **to** this question is ... (✓) **the answer TO** (not *for*) **a question**
any	▶ *I have any good friends in Taiping.* (✗) ▶ I have **some** good friends in Taiping. (✓) **Any** is used only in negative sentences and questions, unless you mean 'any one of' (e.g. *Give me a book, any book*.)

appreciate	▶ *I would appreciate if ...* (**✗**) ▶ I would appreciate **it** if ... (**✓**) **Appreciate + IT + if/when ...**
as	▶ *There is no other person as my mother.* (**✗**) ▶ There is no other person **like** my mother. (**✓**) A thing can be **like** (= similar to) something, not *as* something. ▶ *Our school needs equipment, as desks and chairs.* (**✗**) ▶ Our school needs equipment, **such as** desks and chairs. (**✓**) **As** does not mean 'for example'. Use **such as**. ▶ *He became as a drug addict.* (**✗**) ▶ He became a drug addict. (**✓**) **As** is not used after *become, be called, be named*.
as such	▶ *It is raining, and as such I shall stay indoors.* (**✗**) ▶ It is raining, (and) **so** I shall stay indoors. (**✓**) **As such** does not mean 'because of this'. An example of the correct meaning is *I am your teacher: as such* (= as your teacher) *I expect you to work hard*.
aspect	▶ *From the economic aspect, ...* (**✗**) ▶ From the economic **point the view**, ... (**✓**) An **aspect** is something you look AT (*Let us consider the economic aspect*), not a place you look *from*.
at	▶ *I came here at 1988.* (**✗**) ▶ I came here **in** 1988. (**✓**) **In**, not **at**, is used with years.
athletics	▶ *Subra is good at athletic.* (**✗**) ▶ Subra is good at **athletics**. (**✓**) ▶ *Athletics are important in our education.* (**✗**) ▶ Athletics is important in our education. (**✓**) **Athletics** (always spelt with -s) is a *singular* word.
avoid	▶ *We cannot avoid this from happening.* (**✗**) ▶ We cannot **prevent** this from happening. (**✓**) **avoid** a problem; **prevent** something from happening

B

before
- *Before went out, he ...* (✗)
- Before **he** went out, he ... (✓)

Before is not directly followed by a verb (except an '-ing' verb, as in *Before going out, he ...*).

behind
- *The lorry was in behind the workshop.* (✗)
- The lorry was **behind** the workshop. (✓)

Do not use *in* with **behind**.

believe
- *Some people are believing that ...* (✗)
- Some people **believe** that ... (✓)

Do not use **believe** in continuous tenses.

better
- *You better follow my advice.* (✗)
- You **had better** follow my advice. (✓)

The correct expression is **had better**. It can be used in both the present and the past.

between
- *In the city we are always between people.* (✗)
- In the city we are always **among** people. (✓)

between two things only; **among** several things

- *Between 1945 to 1957, ...* (✗)
- Between 1945 **and** 1957, ... (✓)

Do not confuse **between ... and ...**
from ... to ...

bored/ boring
- *I am boring with doing the same things every day.* (✗)
- I am **bored** with doing the same things every day. (✓)

The things you do may be **boring**; but *you* are **bored**.

borrow/ lend
- *Can I lend your book, please?* (✗)
- Can I **borrow** your book, please? (✓)

If you **lend** a book, you give it; if you **borrow** a book, you take it.

bread
- *I bought a bread/six breads.* (✗)
- I bought a **loaf of** bread/six **loaves of** bread. (✓)

Bread is uncountable. You cannot say *a bread*; use **a loaf of bread**.

bring
- *Please can you bring me to the station?* (✗)
- Please can you **take** me to the station? (✓)

Bring contains the idea of '*towards* the place where we are now'. **Take** = *away* from where we are now.

but	▶ *Although Farid was ill, but he played well.* (✗) ▶ Farid was ill, but he played well. (✓) Do not use **but** and **although** together.
by	▶ *She did it by saved a lot of money.* (✗) ▶ She did it by **saving** a lot of money. (✓) **by** + *-ing* verb ▶ *We went to Kuantan by the bus.* (✗) ▶ We went to Kuantan **by bus**. (✓) In the expressions **by car, by bus** etc., do not use *the*.

C

call	▶ *Let's call Maniam for the party.* (✗) ▶ Let's **invite** Maniam for the party. (✓) to **invite** someone = ask him to come to **call** someone = speak from far away (e.g. by telephone)
can	▶ *She can swimming very well.* (✗) ▶ She can **swim** very well. (✓) **can** + **infinitive verb** (not *-ing*) ▶ *We can healthy if we exercise.* (✗) ▶ We can **be** healthy if we exercise. (✓) Adjectives (e.g. *healthy*, *famous*) must not follow **can** directly. Use **can be**.
care	▶ *We must take care about our parents.* (✗) ▶ We must take care **of** our parents. (✓) take care **OF** somebody (but **care ABOUT** a problem)
cheap price	▶ *I paid a very cheap price for this dress.* (✗) ▶ I paid a very **low** price for this dress. (✓) Goods can be cheap (*a cheap dress*) but prices are *low* or *high*.
chop	▶ *Please chop this receipt for me.* (✗) ▶ Please **stamp** this receipt for me. (✓) The correct meaning of **chop** is 'cut', as in *chop the chilli*.
cinema names	▶ *I went to Moviemax cinema.* (✗) ▶ I went to **the** Moviemax cinema. (✓) Use **the** before cinema names.

xiii

close	▶ *Zul closed the TV and went to bed.* (✗) ▶ Zul **turned off/switched off** the TV and went to bed. (✓) We *close* a door or a window, but we **turn off** or **switch off** electrical equipment.
colour	▶ *a blue colour car* (✗) ▶ a **blue car** (✓) The word *colour* is unnecessary after **blue, green, red,** etc.
compared/ comparing	▶ *Comparing to other models, this is cheap.* (✗) ▶ **Compared** to other models, this is cheap. (✓) One thing can be **compared** (not *comparing*) to another.
comprise	▶ *The house comprises of six rooms.* (✗) ▶ The house **comprises** six rooms/**consists of** six rooms. (✓) **consist of** something *but* **comprise something** (without *of*)
conclusion	▶ *As a conclusion, we can say ...* (✗) ▶ **In conclusion,** we can say ... (✓) **In conclusion** is a fixed expression and cannot be changed.
confident/ confidence	▶ *I am confidence that ...* (✗) ▶ I am **confident** that ... (✓) **Confidence** is a noun: *Farid has a lot of confidence*. The adjective, used to describe somebody, is **confident**.
could	▶ *We could see beautiful buildings if we go to KL.* (✗) ▶ We **can** see beautiful buildings if we go to KL. (✓) Could is a past tense verb. Use it only to refer to the past, or to express great doubt about the present: *I could be a millionaire if I were lucky.*
country	▶ *My country is Perlis Indera Kayangan.* (✗) ▶ My **state** is Perlis Indera Kayangan. (✓) **country** = 'negara'; **state** = 'negeri'
cover up/ cover-up	▶ *The action taken was a cover up to hide his mistake.* (✗) ▶ The action taken was a **cover-up** to hide his mistake. (✓) *Cover up* is a phrasal verb. The two words are joined with a hyphen to form the noun **cover-up**.

D

dead

- ▶ *My cousin dead in that accident.* (✗)
- ▶ My cousin **died** in that accident. (✓)

The verb is **die** (past tense **died**).
Dead is an adjective, as in: *a dead snake*.

despite

- ▶ *I went to the graveyard despite of my father's warning.* (✗)
- ▶ I went to the graveyard **despite** my father's warning. (✓)
- ▶ I went to the graveyard **in spite of** my father's warning. (✓)

Despite and **in spite of** have the same meaning. Do not mix the two forms.

develop

- ▶ *France is a development country.* (✗)
- ▶ France is a **developed** country. (✓)

Before a noun, use the adjective form **developed**.

different/difference

- ▶ *You and I have difference ideas.* (✗)
- ▶ You and I have **different** ideas. (✓)

The adjective, used to describe something, is **different**.
Difference is the noun.

discuss

- ▶ *We discussed about our problems.* (✗)
- ▶ We **discussed** our problems. (✓)

Discuss is NOT followed by *about*.

downstairs

- ▶ *My mother was in downstairs.* (✗)
- ▶ My mother **was downstairs**. (✓)

Do not use *in* or *at* with **downstairs**.

during

- ▶ *During he was in Kedah Darul Aman, he ...* (✗)
- ▶ **While** he was in Kedah Darul Aman, he ... (✓)

During must be followed by a noun, e.g. *during the war*.
Before a sentence (e.g. *he was in Kedah Darul Aman*) use **while**

dynamic/dynamics

- ▶ *This topic is about fluid dynamic.* (✗)
- ▶ This topic is about fluid **dynamics**. (✓)

Dynamic (without an -s) is an adjective, as in *dynamic process*.
In the sentence above, it should be **dynamics** (a noun).

E

Economics
- *I study Economic.* (✗)
- I study **Economics**. (✓)

Economic (without -s) is an adjective, as in *economic policies*. The academic subject is **Economics**.

embarrass(ed)
- *I felt very embarrass.* (✗)
- I felt very **embarrassed**. (✓)

Embarrass is a verb (*His bad manners embarrass us all*). The adjective is **embarrassed**.

enjoy
- *At the waterfall we can enjoy together.* (✗)
- At the waterfall we can enjoy **ourselves** together. (✓)

enjoy + myself/yourself/himself (etc.)

- *Children enjoy to visit a museum.* (✗)
- Children enjoy **visiting** a museum. (✓)

enjoy + -ing verb

enter
- *She entered into the room.* (✗)
- She **entered** the room. (✓)

Do not use *into* with **enter** (except in the expression *enter into an agreement*).

equipment
- *We use a special equipment for this job.* (✗)
- We use a special **piece of equipment** for this job. (✓)

- *The sports equipments are in the storeroom.* (✗)
- The sports **equipment is** in the storeroom. (✓)

Equipment is NOT a countable noun. It cannot take a plural -s, and it cannot be used with *a*. For a single item, say **a piece of equipment**.

even
- *Anybody can succeed even they are poor.* (✗)
- Anybody can succeed **even if** they are poor. (✓)

Before a sentence like *they are poor*, use **even if**.

every
- *Every schools in Malaysia has a canteen.* (✗)
- Every **school** in Malaysia has a canteen. (✓)

Use a *singular* word after **every**.

everybody/everything
- *Everybody were waiting to eat.* (✗)
- Everybody **was** waiting to eat. (✓)

Surprisingly, the words **everybody, everyone, everything** are used with *singular* verbs, even though their meaning is plural.

excited/ exciting	▶ *I felt very exciting when I heard the news.* (✗) ▶ I felt very **excited** when I heard the news. (✓) Events can be **exciting**. A person feels **excited**.

F

few	▶ *I had only a few money.* (✗) ▶ I had only a **little** money. (✓) Use **few** + **countable** noun; **little** + **uncountable** noun. ▶ *A few of children don't obey their parents.* (✗) ▶ **A few children** don't obey their parents. (✓) *Of* is wrong here. Use it only if *the* follows: *A few of the children ...*
first	▶ *At first, I want to say ...* (✗) ▶ **Firstly**, I want to say ... (✓) **At first** means first *in time*. **Firstly** introduces a series of reasons or arguments.
fish	▶ *Meena bought some fishes for her cat.* (✗) ▶ Meena bought some **fish** for her cat. (✓) The plural form *fishes* can be used to refer to different kinds of fish. Modern English uses **fish** for both singular and plural.
follow	▶ *Why don't you follow Aziz to Penang?* (✗) ▶ Why don't you **go with** Aziz to Penang? (✓) **follow** = go AFTER somebody.
food	▶ *I like a spicy food.* (✗) ▶ I like spicy food. (✓) **Food** is normally uncountable. Do not use it with *a*.
foot	▶ *Auntie May always goes shopping by foot.* (✗) ▶ Auntie May always goes shopping **on** foot. (✓) We go *by* taxi, car, bus, etc., but **on foot**.
for	▶ *I went to town for buy something.* (✗) ▶ I went to town **to** buy something. (✓) **For** + **verb** does not mean *in order to*. Use **to** + **infinitive**.

friend	▶ *That boy won't friend me!* (✗) ▶ That boy won't **be friends with** me! (✓)
	Friend is not a verb.

frighten(ed)	▶ *Rosnani became very frighten.* (✗) ▶ Rosnani became very **frightened**. (✓)
	Frighten is a verb: *That man frightens me.* The adjective is **frightened**.

fruit	▶ *Are we having fruits for dessert.* (✗) ▶ Are we having **fruit** for dessert. (✓)
	Fruit is usually uncountable. You can use **fruit** or **fruits** when talking about different types of fruit. Add an *-s* if there is a number before the word: *There are six fruits on the branch.*

furniture	▶ *My furnitures are old and broken.* (✗) ▶ My **furniture is** old and broken. (✓)
	Furniture is uncountable. It cannot take a plural *-s*, and it cannot be used with *a*. For a single item, say **a piece of furniture**.

H

had	▶ *These are the best shoes I had.* (✗) ▶ These are the best shoes I **have**. (✓)
	Do not use the past tense **had** to refer to the present.

hair	▶ *Mei Lin has a black hair.* (✗) ▶ Mei Lin **has black hair**. (✓)
	Use *a hair* only if you mean that she has one hair on her head!

happen	▶ *This incident was happened in my village.* (✗) ▶ This incident **happened** in my village. (✓)
	Happen cannot have a passive form. *Is happened* and *was happened* are wrong.

happy/ happily	▶ *Shamsul is a happily person.* (✗) ▶ Shamsul is a **happy** person. (✓)
	The adjective is **happy**. Use *happily* to say HOW something is done: *He is singing happily.*

hardly	▶ *If we study hardly we will succeed.* (✗) ▶ If we study **hard** we will succeed. (✓)
	Hardly means 'very little': *I hardly know him.*

have to	▶ *You haven't to worry about little things.* (✗) ▶ You **mustn't** worry about little things. (✓) The negative of *have to* is **mustn't**. *Haven't to* does not exist.
he	▶ *Encik Azman he is a kind man.* (✗) ▶ Encik Azman is a kind man. (✓) You cannot use **he** or **she** to 'repeat' the subject of a sentence in this way.
health	▶ *I hope you are in a good health.* (✗) ▶ I hope you are **in good health**. (✓) **In good health** is a fixed expression. Do not add *a*.
help	▶ *If you need a help, just call me.* (✗) ▶ If you need **help**, just call me. (✓) **Help** is uncountable. You cannot use it with *a*.
her/ hers	▶ *She said the purse was her.* (✗) ▶ She said the purse was **hers**. (✓) ▶ *Those are not hers children.* (✗) ▶ Those are not **her** children. (✓) **Her** is the adjective form (used only *before a noun*). **Hers** is the form which stands alone.
high	▶ *I am 1.6 metres high.* (✗) ▶ I am 1.6 metres **tall**. (✓) Use **high** for mountains and things above the ground. Use **tall** for people or trees.
his/her	▶ *Mr Tan took her daughter to the temple.* (✗) ▶ Mr Tan took **his** daughter to the temple. (✓) **His** means 'belonging to a man'. **Her** means 'belonging to a woman'.
home	▶ *After school I go to home.* (✗) ▶ After school I **go home**. (✓) ▶ *Some women prefer to stay in home.* (✗) ▶ Some women prefer to stay **at home**. (✓) *To* and *in* are not used before **home**.

homework, housework	▶ *I had a homework/some homeworks.* (✗) ▶ I had **some** homework. (✓) Like work, **homework** and **housework** are uncountable. They cannot be used with *a*; they cannot take a plural *-s*.
horn	▶ *The driver horned loudly.* (✗) ▶ The driver **sounded his horn** loudly. (✓) **Horn** is a noun. There is no verb *to horn*.
hour	▶ *It was a two hours drive to the lake.* (✗) ▶ It was a **two-hour** drive to the lake. (✓) Note the correct way to form an adjective from **hour**.
how	▶ *The man asked me how could he help me.* (✗) ▶ The man asked me how **he could** help me. (✓) Note the correct word order after **how**. The 'question form' of the verb is NOT used in 'indirect' questions like this.

I

if	▶ *You can drive if pass your test.* (✗) ▶ You can drive if **you** pass your test. (✓) **If** is not followed directly by a verb.
important/ importance	▶ *Mr Rajan is an importance man.* (✗) ▶ Mr Rajan is an **important** man. (✓) ▶ *You do not realise the important of this work.* (✗) ▶ You do not realise the **importance** of this work. (✓) **Important** is the adjective form, used before a noun. **Importance** is a noun (e.g. *the importance of …*).
independent/ independence	▶ *Luckily, we are an independence country.* (✗) ▶ Luckily, we are **independent** country. (✓) Before a noun, use the adjective form **independent**.
inform	▶ *I wish to inform that …* (✗) ▶ I wish to inform **you** that … (✓) **inform SOMEBODY that…; inform SOMEBODY about** something

information	▶ I have a useful information for you. (✗) ▶ I have **some** useful information for you. (✓) **Information** is uncountable, so it cannot be used with *a*. Say **some information** or **a piece of information**.
interested/ interesting	▶ Mrs Fong is interesting in aerobics. (✗) ▶ Mrs Fong is **interested** in aerobics. (✓) **interested** (not *interesting*) in something ▶ I am interested to apply for that job. (✗) ▶ I am interested **in applying** for that job. (✓) **interested IN** + *-ing* verb
involve	▶ Students should not involve in drugs. (✗) ▶ Students should not **be involved/get involved** in drugs. (✓) **BE** or **GET involved in** something
isn't it?	▶ You have visited Lake Toba, isn't it? (✗) ▶ You have visited Lake Toba, **haven't you**? (✓) A 'question tag' at the end of a sentence MUST follow the form of the main verb, e.g. *He has ..., hasn't he? I can ..., can't I? They will ..., won't they?*
it	▶ My house it is very pretty. (✗) ▶ My house is very pretty. (✓) You cannot use **it** to 'repeat' the subject of a sentence in this way.
its/it's	▶ The elephant lay on it's side. (✗) ▶ The elephant lay on **its** side. (✓) **it's** = it is; **its** = belonging to it

J

Japan	▶ Japan spare parts are expensive. (✗) ▶ **Japanese** spare parts are expensive. (✓) Before a noun, use the adjective form **Japanese**.
just	▶ Ismail just can carry the box. (✗) ▶ Ismail **can just** carry the box. (✓) **Just** must FOLLOW the verbs *be, have, can/could, will/would, may/might*.

xxi

K

know
- ► *Everybody is knowing that ...* (✗)
- ► Everybody **knows** that ... (✓)

> **Know** is not normally used in continuous tenses.

L

last
- ► *At last, we can conclude that ...* (✗)
- ► **Finally**, we can conclude that ... (✓)

> **At last** expresses relief after a long wait: *At last the train arrived, six hours late.* It does NOT mean 'My last point is ...'

last time
- ► *Last time, cars were much cheaper.* (✗)
- ► **In the past**, cars were much cheaper. (✓)

> **Last time** = on ONE previous occasion. It cannot refer to the past in general.

lay/lie
- ► *The goalkeeper was laying on the ground.* (✗)
- ► The goalkeeper was **lying** on the ground. (✓)

> **Lie (lay, lain)** is the correct verb here. Note the irregular spelling of **lying**.
> **To lay (laid, laid)** = put something down: *She laid her book on the table.*

learn/study
- ► *Johan is learning for his exams.* (✗)
- ► Johan is **studying** for his exams. (✓)

> Use **study** for academic subjects. Use **learn** for a skill: *Johan is learning to play the guitar.*

lend/borrow
- ► *Can I lend your car, please?* (✗)
- ► Can I **borrow** your car, please? (✓)

> **lend** = GIVE for a short time
> **borrow** = TAKE for a short time

let
- ► *She sometimes lets me helping her.* (✗)
- ► She sometimes lets me **help** her. (✓)

> **let** + **me, him** etc. + **infinitive verb** WITHOUT *to*

little
- ► *Careful people have a little to worry about.* (✗)
- ► Careful people have **little** to worry about. (✓)

> **a little** = some; **little** (without *a*) = not much

luck	► Yesterday I had a bad luck. (✗) ► Yesterday I had **some** bad luck. (✓) **Luck** is uncountable. You cannot have *a luck*, but you can have **some luck** or **a piece of luck**.
luggage	► *Please leave your luggages here.* (✗) ► Please leave your **luggage** here. (✓) **Luggage** is uncountable, so it cannot take a plural -*s*.

M

make	► *He made me explaining everything.* (✗) ► He made me **explain** everything. (✓) **make + me, him** etc. + **infinitive verb** WITHOUT *to*
Malaysia	► *I prefer to buy Malaysia products.* (✗) ► I prefer to buy **Malaysian** products. (✓) Before a noun, use the adjective form **Malaysian**.
many	► *He does not have many success.* (✗) ► He does not have **much** success. (✓) **Many** is used with countable nouns only. With uncountable nouns like *success*, use **much**. ► *Many of people watch TV nowadays.* (✗) ► **Many people** watch TV nowadays. (✓) *Of* is wrong here. Use it only together with *the*: *Many of the people ...*
marketing	► *Mrs Ng went marketing.* (✗) ► Mrs Ng went **shopping in the market**. (✓) **Marketing** does NOT mean 'buying in the market'. It means 'selling', as in: *a marketing executive*.
mature(d)	► *She is a matured woman of 45.* (✗) ► She is a **mature** woman of 45. (✓) There is no *d* at the end of the adjective **mature**.
minutes	► *It is a ten minutes job.* (✗) ► It is a **ten-minute** job. (✓) Note the correct way to form an adjective from **minute**.

mistake	▶ Chong did a serious mistake. (✗) ▶ Chong **made** a serious mistake. (✓) **make** (not do) a mistake
most	▶ Most interesting essays was Aisha's. (✗) ▶ **The** most interesting essay was Aisha's. (✓) Use **the** before *most* + adjective. ▶ Most of people prefer a quiet life. (✗) ▶ **Most people** prefer a quiet life. (✓) *Of* is wrong here. Use it only together with *the*: Most of the people ...
much	▶ That car uses much petrol. (✗) ▶ That car uses **a lot of** petrol. (✓) Normally, **much** is used only in negative sentences, e.g. *That car doesn't use much petrol.*
must	▶ You must visiting us soon. (✗) ▶ You must **visit** us soon. (✓) **must + infinitive verb** without *to*
my/mine	▶ The black shoes are my. (✗) ▶ The black shoes are **mine**. (✓) **My** can only be used before a noun, e.g. *my shoes*. **Mine** is the form which stands alone.

N

need	▶ You need not to do that. (✗) ▶ You **don't need to** do that/You **needn't** do that. (✓) **don't need + to + infinitive verb** or **needn't + infinitive verb** without *to*
never	▶ She never has visited Penang. (✗) ▶ She **has never** visited Penang. (✓) **Never** is used before a one-word verb (e.g. *went, says*). But use it AFTER the verb *have, be, will/would, can/could, must, may/might*.

xxiv

news	▶ *I have a good news for you.* (✗) ▶ I have **some** good news for you. (✓) **News** is uncountable. You cannot say *a news*, but you can say **some news** or **a piece of news**.
newspaper names	▶ *I have read in Malay Mail that ...* (✗) ▶ I have read in **the** Malay Mail that ... (✓) Use **the** before the name of an English language newspaper. (The rule applies to *newspapers*, not magazines such as *Asiaweek* or *Time*.)

O

off	▶ *Please off the light.* (✗) ▶ Please **turn off** the light. (✓) *Off* is not a verb. Use **turn off**.
often	▶ *We often can see these things.* (✗) ▶ We **can often** see these things. (✓) **Often** is used before a one-word verb (e.g. *went, eats*). But it goes AFTER the verbs *have, be, can/could, will/would, may/might*.
on	▶ *Now you can on the switch.* (✗) ▶ Now you can **turn on** the switch. (✓) *On* is not a verb. Use **turn on**.
one	▶ *He has one house in Subang.* (✗) ▶ He has **a** house in Subang. (✓) Use **one** only when the *number* is important: *He has one house in Subang and two others in Sentul.* Otherwise use **a**.
open	▶ *I cannot open this screw/this tap.* (✗) ▶ I cannot **loosen** this screw/**turn on** this tap. (✓) We **open** a window or a door, but we **loosen** a screw, and **turn on** a tap or a switch.
or	▶ *My village is called or named Pantai Lama.* (✗) ▶ My village is called Pantai Lama. (✓) It is bad style to use two words joined by **or** when they have almost the same meaning. One word is enough.

P

pain
- ► My leg is paining. (✗)
- ► My leg is **hurting**. (✓)

Pain is not a verb, except in the expression *It pains me to say that ...*

---

people
- ► I am a people who likes to work. (✗)
- ► I am a **person** who likes to work. (✓)

Differentiate between singular: **a person** and plural: **people** (without *a*).

---

personnel
- ► Chandran is a personnel at the airport. (✗)
- ► Chandran **works** at the airport. (✓)

Personnel is a *plural* word meaning '*all* the people who work in a certain place'. You cannot talk about *a personnel*.

Philippines
- ► My uncle has visited Philippines. (✗)
- ► My uncle has visited **the** Philippines. (✓)

The correct name is **the Philippines**. *The* is also used for many other groups of islands: *the Maldives, the Falklands*.

---

piece
- ► I bought 12 pieces of cushion covers. (✗)
- ► I bought **12 cushion covers**. (✓)

It is bad style to use *piece* before a countable noun, because it suggests something broken or torn.

---

police
- ► A police was waiting by the door. (✗)
- ► A **policeman** was waiting by the door. (✓)

Police (a plural word, although it has no *-s*) refers to a *group* of policemen or to the police force in general: *The police set up a road block*. One officer is **a policeman**.

---

pollution
- ► There are a lot of pollutions in our towns. (✗)
- ► There **is** a lot of **pollution** in our towns. (✓)

Pollution is uncountable. It cannot take a plural *-s*.

Q

quite
- ► Lee bought a quite expensive car. (✗)
- ► Lee bought **quite an** expensive car. (✓)

Use **quite** before **a/an**.

R

rob
- ▶ *The thief robbed her necklace.* (✗)
- ▶ The thief **stole** her necklace. (✓)

A thief **robs** a person or a place (e.g. a bank), but he **steals** things.

research
- ▶ *He is doing a research into orchids.* (✗)
- ▶ He is **doing research** into orchids. (✓)

Research is uncountable. You cannot use it with *a*. Say **research, some research** or **a piece of research**.

return
- ▶ *I shall never return back to that place.* (✗)
- ▶ I shall never **return to** that place. (✓)

Return is NOT followed by *back*.

S

safe
- ▶ *Luckily we all safe now.* (✗)
- ▶ Luckily we **are** all safe now. (✓)

Safe is not a verb. Use it after *be*, or before a noun: *a safe place*.

same
- ▶ *Your bicycle is same like Mat's.* (✗)
- ▶ *Your bicycle is same as Mat's.* (✗)
- ▶ Your bicycle is **the same as Mat's**. (✓)

The same as is a fixed expression. It cannot be changed.

scenery
- ▶ *There is a beautiful scenery near this town.* (✗)
- ▶ There is **some** beautiful scenery near this town. (✓)

Scenery is uncountable. You cannot make it plural (*sceneries*); you cannot use it with *a*.

scissors
- ▶ *You need a scissors for this job.* (✗)
- ▶ You need **scissors/a pair of scissors** for this job. (✓)

Scissors is a plural word. It cannot be used with *a*.

search
- ▶ *I searched my friend everywhere.* (✗)
- ▶ I **searched for** my friend everywhere. (✓)

Use **search for** when you mean *look for*. **Search** (without *for*) means *look through* or *examine carefully*: The customs officers *searched* our luggage.

send
- ▶ *She sends her son to school in the car.* (✗)
- ▶ She **takes** her son to school in the car. (✓)

If you **send** somebody or something (e.g. *send a letter*), you do not go yourself. If you go WITH a person, you **take** him.

shock(ed)	▶ *I was shock when ... (✗)* ▶ I was **shocked** when .. (✓) Something **shocks** us, but we are **shocked**.
shop	▶ *a books shop, a shoes shop (✗)* ▶ a **bookshop**, a **shoe shop** (✓) In a noun + noun compound, the first noun is usually singular. However, there are exceptions, e.g. a **clothes** shop, a **customs** officer and the **accounts** department.
shorts	▶ *He was wearing a short. (✗)* ▶ He was wearing **shorts/a pair of shorts**. (✓) **Shorts** are *always plural*.
sleep	▶ *I usually sleep at 11.30 p.m. (✗)* ▶ I usually **go to bed** at 11.30 p.m. (✓) **Sleep** refers to the time when we are actually asleep (*I sleep for eight hours every night*), not to the moment when we go to bed.
so	▶ *He is a so foolish boy. (✗)* ▶ He is a **very** foolish boy. (✓) Do not use **so** after *a*. Use **very**. ▶ *I was so interested in the film. (✗)* ▶ I was **very** interested in the film. (✓) Use **so + adjective** only when *that* follows, e.g. : *I was so interested that I saw the film twice.*
some	▶ *He didn't have some free time. (✗)* ▶ He didn't have **any** free time. (✓) In negative sentences, use **any** instead of *some*. ▶ *Some of villages have no electricity. (✗)* ▶ Some villages have no electricity. (✓) *Of* is wrong here. Use it only together with *the*: *Some of the villages ...*
staff	▶ *He is a staff. (✗)* ▶ He is **a member of** staff. (✓) **Staff** refers to *all* people who work in a certain place. One person is a **member of staff**.
statistics	▶ *Statistic is my best subject. (✗)* ▶ *Statistics are my best subject. (✗)* ▶ **Statistics is** my best subject. (✓) **Statistics** (although spelt with an *-s*) is a singular word.

stay	▶ *Justin stays in Kampung Baru.* (✗) ▶ Justin **lives** in Kampung Baru. (✓) Use **stay** for temporary residence only, e.g.: *He is staying in a hotel.*
still	▶ *We still can see many traditional customs.* (✗) ▶ We **can still** see many traditional customs. (✓) **Still** is used before a one-word verb (e.g. *goes, ate*). But it goes AFTER the verbs *be, have, can/could, will/would, must, may/might*.
stress	▶ *Encik Zakaria stressed on the need for exports.* (✗) ▶ Encik Zakaria stressed the need for exports. (✓) **stress something** (WITHOUT *on*)
suit	▶ *He wore a pair of blue suit.* (✗) ▶ He wore a blue suit (✓) **A suit** consists of two items: jacket and trousers. Do not use *a pair of* with *suit*.
suppose(d)	▶ *We are suppose to wait here.* (✗) ▶ We are **supposed** to wait here. (✓) We **suppose that** … We **are supposed to** do something.

T

tell	▶ *He told to me his sad story.* (✗) ▶ He **told me** his sad story. (✓) You **tell** somebody something (without *to*) but you **tell** something **to** somebody. ▶ *Tell Puan Zaleha don't go.* (✗) ▶ Tell Puan Zaleha **not to** go. (✓) A negative command after **tell** uses **not to** + infinitive.
these	▶ *These problem is serious.* (✗) ▶ **This** problem is serious. (✓) Do not confuse **this**: singular and **these**: plural.
time	▶ *When I have a free time …* (✗) ▶ When I have **some** free time … (✓) **Time** is uncountable, except in fixed expressions like *Have a good time*.

too	▶ *I am too happy when I go home.* (✗) ▶ I am **very** happy when I go home. (✓) **Too** always suggests that something is wrong (e.g. *He is too ill to walk*). If there is no problem, use **very**.
trousers	▶ *He was wearing a grey trousers.* (✗) ▶ He was wearing **grey trousers/a pair of grey trousers**. (✓) **Trousers** is a plural word. It cannot be used with *a*.
true/truth	▶ *The truth story is ...* (✗) ▶ The **true** story is ... (✓) The adjective (used before a noun) is **true**. **Truth** is a noun: *The truth is ...*

U

UK, United States, USA, USSR	▶ *This came from UK.* (✗) ▶ This came from **the** UK. (✓) These countries, whose names begin with *U* (= 'united'), always take ***the***.
units	▶ *We have sold six units of air-conditioner.* (✗) ▶ We have sold **six air-conditioners**. (✓) It is bad style to use *units of* after a number, except in lists or inventories.
upstairs	▶ *I ran to upstairs.* (✗) ▶ I ran **upstairs**. (✓) Do not use *to* with **upstairs**.
used to/ am used to	▶ *He was used to be my teacher.* (✗) ▶ He **used to** be my teacher. (✓) Use **used to** + **infinitive verb** for a past habit. Use **be used to** + **noun** or **-ing verb** to mean 'accustomed to': *After ten years in Canada, he was used to the cold weather.*

V

very	▶ *Motorbikes are very faster than bicycles.* (✗) ▶ Motorbikes are **much** faster than bicycles. (✓) Do not use *very* before *-er* adjectives. Use **much**.

W

wait
- *I waited my friend.* (✗)
- I waited **for** my friend. (✓)

wait FOR somebody or something

want
- *Emily wants buying a dress.* (✗)
- Emily wants **to buy** a dress. (✓)

want to + infinitive verb

was
- *I think Malaysia was a beautiful country.* (✗)
- I think Malaysia **is** a beautiful country. (✓)

Do not use the past tense *was* when you are talking about the present!

way
- *He buys sweets in the way to school.* (✗)
- He buys sweets **on** the way to school. (✓)

Use **on** (not *in*) the way to a place.

week
- *a two weeks holiday* (✗)
- a **two-week** holiday (✓)

Note the correct way to form an adjective from **week**.

when
- *When saw the thief, she screamed.* (✗)
- When **she** saw the thief, she screamed. (✓)

When is not directly followed by a verb.

when, where, which, who, why
- *She told me why was she crying.* (✗)
- She told me why **she was** crying. (✓)

- *I wonder where does he work?* (✗)
- I wonder where **he works**. (✓)

Note the correct word order after **when, where,** etc. The 'question form' of the verb is NOT used in 'indirect' questions like the examples above.

which, who
- *He is a friend who he helps everyone.* (✗)
- He is a friend who helps everyone. (✓)

- *These are things which we should avoid them.* (✗)
- These are things which we should avoid. (✓)

After **who** and **which**, do not use *he, she, it, them*, etc. to repeat a word already used. In the examples above, *he* repeats *a friend*; *them* repeats *things*. This is wrong.

will	▶ *One day she will famous.* (✗) ▶ One day she will **be** famous. (✓) **will** + **infinitive verb** (e.g. *go, have*) **will** + **BE** + **adjective** (e.g. *famous, successful*) *Famous* is not a verb; it is an adjective.
wish	▶ *I wish I am rich.* (✗) ▶ I wish I **was** rich. (✓) **Wish** is always followed by a past tense verb, whether it refers to the past or the present.
without	▶ *He left without said goodbye.* (✗) ▶ He left without **saying** goodbye. (✓) **without** + **noun** or **-ing verb** only
work	▶ *I have a work for you.* (✗) ▶ I have a **job** for you. (✓) **Work** is uncountable: you cannot say *a work*. Use **a job** or **some work**.
world	▶ *This is the famous mosque in a world.* (✗) ▶ This is the **most** famous mosque in **the** world. (✓) Use **the**, not **a**, with **world**. Note also the correct expression using **most**.
worry	▶ *Sometimes I worry for my children.* (✗) ▶ Sometimes I worry **about** my children. (✓) You **worry about** something or somebody.
worse/worst	▶ *If worse comes to worse ...* (✗) ▶ If **the worst** comes **to the worst** ... (✓) This is a fixed expression and cannot be changed.
would	▶ *The inspector would arrive tomorrow.* (✗) ▶ The inspector **will** arrive tomorrow. (✓) ▶ *He is kind and would always help me.* (✗) ▶ He is kind and always **helps** me. (✓) **Would** is a past tense verb. Unless you wish to express uncertainty (*If I were you, I would ...*) or politeness (*Would you please ...?*), do not use **would** to refer to the present or the future.

Y

year
- ▶ *a sixteen years old girl* (✗)
- ▶ a **sixteen-year-old** girl (✓)

> Note the correct way of forming an adjective with **year**.

- ▶ *I am aged 26 years old.* (✗)
- ▶ I **am 26** years old./I am 26. (✓)

> *Aged* is not necessary in this expression.

your/yours
- ▶ *I think this pen is your.* (✗)
- ▶ I think this pen is **yours**. (✓)

> **Your** is used only before a noun, e.g. *your pen*. **Yours** is the form which stands alone.

Section 2: Common Mistakes in Verb Use

1 Simple and continuous verbs
Present tenses

- ▶ *Every week I going to Ipoh.* (✗)
- ▶ *Every week I am go to Ipoh.* (✗)
- ▶ Every week I **go** to Ipoh. (✓)

The forms of the two English present tenses are often confused. Taking the verb *go* as an example, the correct forms are:

> **Simple present:** *go; goes*
> (the 'general purpose' present tense)

Simple present verbs consist of **one word only**.

> **Present continuous:** *am going; are going; is going*
> (for actions happening right now)

Present continuous verbs (also known as *present progressive*) consist of **two** words. The first is part of the verb *be*; the second ends in *-ing*.

Past tenses

- ▶ *Jamil was went to the market.* (✗)
- ▶ *Jamil was go to the market.* (✗)
- ▶ Jamil **went** to the market. (✓)   (*simple past*)   OR
- ▶ Jamil **was going** to the market. (✓) (*past continuous*)

In the same way, the forms of the two past tenses – the *simple past* and the *past continuous* – are also confused. Taking *go* as an example, the correct forms are **went** (simple past) and **was** (or **were**) **going** (past continuous).

Mixed-up forms such as *I going*, *She was went* or *We are go* have no meaning and are not English.

2 Subject/verb agreement

> ▶ *My arm feel weak and I cannot write.* (✗)
> ▶ My arm **feels** weak and I cannot write. (✓)

A simple present verb must end in *-s* if it has a singular subject.

The simple present tense and the verb *be* (both present and past) have different singular and plural forms. These verbs must always 'agree' with the subject of the sentence: a singular subject takes a singular verb, and a plural subject takes a plural verb.

> Singular forms of *be*: **is** (present) and **was** (past).
> Plural forms of *be*: **are** (present) and **were** (past).

Is the subject singular or plural?

> ▶ *The students in the hostel near the gate is from Sabah.* (✗)
> ▶ The students in the hostel near the gate **are** from Sabah. (✓)

Sometimes it is not easy to know whether the subject of a sentence is singular or plural. Look at the **main** word of the subject. In the example above, the main word of the subject is *students* (plural); so the verb must also be plural.

> ▶ *Good public transport are very important.* (✗)
> ▶ Good public transport **is** very important. (✓)

Uncountable nouns (such as *transport*) always take a **singular** verb.

> ▶ *Everybody have the chance to go to school.* (✗)
> ▶ Everybody **has** the chance to go to school. (✓)

Everybody, **everyone** and **everything**, as well as other expressions beginning with **every** (e.g. *every village*), also take a **singular** verb.

3 Negative forms

> ▶ *I was not made any mistake.* (✗)
> ▶ *I did not made any mistake.* (✗)
> ▶ *I did not making any mistake.* (✗)
> ▶ I **did not** (or *didn't*) **make** any mistake. (✓)   (*simple past*)

Mistakes in negative forms are particularly common in the simple present and simple past tenses. The negative forms of these tenses are made from: **do** (does, did) + **not** + **infinitive**.

The difference between simple present and simple past negative verbs lies in the FIRST word of the verb only. *Don't* and *doesn't* are used for the present; *didn't* is used for the past. The last word of the negative verb is always the **infinitive** form, with no *-s*, *-ed* or *-ing* ending. Forms such as *He didn't expected* are WRONG.

4 Question forms

> ▶ *Are we want our country to be poor?* (✗)
> ▶ **Do we want** our country to be poor? (✓)

Correct questions in the simple present and simple past are formed in the same way as negatives, using *do/does/did* and the infinitive:

Does he want ...? Do they want ...?	(*present*)
Did he/they want ...?	(*past*)

5 Verbs which must be followed by an infinitive

> ▶ *We must all going to the ceremony.* (✗)
> ▶ We must all **go** to the ceremony. (✓)

> ▶ *Too much smoking will damaged your health.* (✗)
> ▶ Too much smoking will **damage** your health. (✓)

The 'auxiliary' or 'modal' verbs *must*, *can/could*, *will/would*, *shall/should* and *may/might* are ALWAYS followed by an infinitive verb without *to*. Any other form is wrong.

The same rule applies to *do/does/did* (when they are used in negatives and questions – see Point 3) and to the irregular negative forms *needn't, daren't*:

> *You needn't buy it if you don't want to.*
> *They daren't insult us now.*

6 Passive verbs

> ▶ *The palace has built in 1865.* (✗)
> ▶ The palace **was built** in 1865. (✓) (*simple past*)

Has + present participle does not give a passive meaning. Instead, it gives an (active) present perfect, as in *The Sultan has built a palace*.

English passive verbs always have the form:

part of the verb be + past participle

The **tense** of a passive verb is shown by the first word. So a simple past passive begins with the simple past of *be*: *was* or *were*.

> ▶ *My writing needs to be improve.* (✗)
> ▶ My writing needs to **be improved**. (✓)

After *to* or any verbs which is followed by an infinitive (see Point 5), the correct passive form is:

be + past participle

> ▶ *This incident was occurred in India.* (✗)
> ▶ This incident **occurred** in India. (✓)

The verbs *occur* and *happen* NEVER take a passive form.

7 Tenses and time

> ▶ *His kindness makes me happy when I was with him.* (✗)
> ▶ His kindness **makes** me happy when I **am** with him. (✓) (*present*)   OR
> ▶ His kindness **made** me happy when I **was** with him. (✓) (*past*)

English verb tenses fall into two main groups: present and past. The simple present, present continuous and present perfect are present tenses; the simple past, past continuous and past perfect are past tenses. *Will* and *can* are present; *would* and *could* are past.

The basic rule for tense use is: *Do not mix past and present tenses without good reason.*

In the example above, there is no reason to change from present tense *makes* to past tense *was*. If the sentence refers to the present, both verbs must be in the present tense. If it refers to the past, both verbs must be in the past tense.

> ► *We do not recommend this tool, as it had not been approved by SIRIM.* (✗)
> ► We do not recommend this tool, as it **has** not been approved by SIRIM. (✓)
> ► *I am sure that we would make a profit soon.* (✗)
> ► I am sure that we **will** make a profit soon. (✓)

A very common mistake is to use **had** and **would** to refer to the present. Both of these are PAST tense verbs.

> ► *I will be surprised if I saw a flying bicycle.* (✗)
> ► I **would** be surprised if I **saw** a flying bicycle. (✓) (*an unlikely event*)

Past tense verbs (including *would*) can refer to the present ONLY if you wish to express doubt, or to suggest that something is unreal. An *if-* sentence (like the example above) describes a doubtful or unlikely event if BOTH verbs are past tense.

8 *-ing* and *-ed* participles

> ► *I am interesting in this job.* (✗)
> ► I am **interested** in this job. (✓)

Participles are adjectives formed from verbs.

> *-ed* participles are used to describe how we feel about something (*interested, worried,* etc.)
> *-ing* participles (*interesting, worrying*, etc.) describe the thing which affects us

So if a job is **interesting**, we are **interested** in it; if a person's action is **shocking**, we feel **shocked**.

> ► *Anybody wanted to come should contact ...* (✗)
> ► Anybody **wanting** to come should contact ... (✓)

-ed participles usually have a **passive** meaning, while *-ing* participles have an **active** meaning. So *Anybody wanted* means 'Anybody who is wanted (by somebody) ...' and *Anybody wanting* means 'Anybody who wants ...'.

Section 3: Common Mistakes in Sentence Structure

1 Omission of the verb 'be'

> ► *Even a small school can famous.* (✗)
> ► Even a small school can **be** famous. (✓)

You cannot use an adjective (e.g. *famous, successful, happy*) directly after the verbs *can, must* or *will*. The correct form is:

can/must/will + BE + adjective

> ► *Unfortunately his uncle still not satisfied.* (✗)
> ► Unfortunately his uncle **was** still not satisfied. (✓)

Some writers wrongly use the words **always, also, definitely, just, not, never, often, probably, sometimes, still** or **usually** instead of the verb *be*. These words must be used AS WELL AS (*not* instead of) the appropriate part of *be*:

Part of 'be'	+always/still (etc.)	+adjective or noun
e.g. Shamsul **was**	always	happy.
Mohan **is**	also	my friend.

2 Omission of the subject or object of a verb
Missing subject

- ▶ *We cannot work when become old.* (✗)
- ▶ We cannot work when **we** become old. (✓)

A sentence with two parts joined by *before, after, when, while, if, because* or *so* must have **two subjects** – one in each part.

This rule does not apply if the verb following *when* (etc.) is in the *-ing* form. So we say **After we washed** *our hands, we ate* but **After washing** *our hands, we ate*.

Missing object

- ▶ *I wish to inform that …* (✗)
- ▶ I wish to inform **you** that … (✓)

Several common verbs MUST take an object. Among them are:

appreciate	base	believe	enjoy	feed	give
have	inform	like	tell	thank	use

To find out whether a verb needs an object, look in the main part of the dictionary. Verbs needing an object are marked *vt*.

3 Singular/plural agreement

- ▶ *Most housewives are a hard-working person.* (✗)
- ▶ Most housewives are **hard-working people**. (✓)

Clearly, many *housewives* (plural) cannot be one *person* (singular). It is very easy to make this kind of mistake out of carelessness. Always check your writing for singular/plural problems.

- ▶ *Please return these books after you have finished it.* (✗)
- ▶ Please return these books after you have finished **them**. (✓)

Remember that **he/him, she/her** and **it** refer to a single person or thing. **They** and **them** refer to several people or things.

4 Pronoun use
Confusion between subject and object pronouns

- ▶ *I told she to speak softly.* (✗)
- ▶ I told **her** to speak softly. (✓)

Most pronouns have different *subject* and *object* forms:

Subject forms (used before the verb)	Object forms (used after the verb and after prepositions)
I	me
we	us
you	you
he	him
she	her
it	it
they	them

Unnecessary repetition of the subject

- *The test it was very difficult.* (✗)
- The test was very difficult. (✓)

Do not use a pronoun to give a sentence a 'double subject', like *The test it* in the example above. English does not use pronouns for emphasis in this way.

Unnecessary pronouns in relative clauses

A *relative clause* is an expression which follows *who, which, whom, whose* or *that*, and which describes a word used earlier in the sentence. In relative clauses, you MUST NOT use a pronoun to repeat the word described by the clause.

- *Muthu has an uncle who he is very rich.* (✗)
- Muthu has an uncle who is very rich. (✓)

The relative clause *who is very rich* describes the word *uncle*. The pronoun *he* also refers to *uncle*; it must not be used here.

- *Melaka is a town that I like to visit it.* (✗)
- Melaka is a town that I like to visit. (✓)

In this sentence, *that I like to visit* describes *Melaka*. The world *it* also refers to *Melaka*. It is not necessary; leave it out.

5 Comparative and superlative constructions

'More' used together with '-er'

- *Our services are more better.* (✗)
- Our services are **better**. (✓)

Use either *more* OR *-er* to make a comparison – NOT both together.

Superlative adjectives without 'the'

- *This team is strongest and most experienced in Asia.* (✗)
- This team is **the strongest** and **the most experienced** in Asia. (✓)

The must be used before superlative adjectives with *most* or *-est*.

Incorrect pairs of comparative words

- *My life is not that hard as a farmer's.* (✗)
- My life is not **as** (or **so**) hard **as** a farmer's. (✓)
- *Talking is very civilised than fighting.* (✗)
- Talking is **more** civilised **than** fighting. (✓)

In comparisons, **as** ... and **so** ... must go together with ... **as**.
More ... or **-er** (NOT *very, as* or *so*) go together with **than**.

6 Order of adjectives

- *She gave me a red beautiful rose.* (✗)
- She gave me a **beautiful red** rose. (✓)

Opinion adjectives (like *beautiful*) are placed before **fact adjectives** (like *red*).

If several fact adjectives are used together, the order is:

size + age + colour + nationality + type (+ noun)

e.g. *a little old red British sports car*

7 Position of adverbs
Adverb between a verb and its object

▶ *He counted carefully his money.* (✗)
▶ He counted his money **carefully**. (✓)

Adverbs must never be placed between a verb and its object. Most adverbs go either:
– at the end of the sentence (if it is a short one); *or*
– before the verb (if it is a one-word verb); *or*
– in the middle of the verb (if the verb has two or more words).

Adverb before a 2-word verb

▶ *They never have been to Bangkok.* (✗)
▶ They **have never been** to Bangkok. (✓)

When the verb consists of two words, the adverb is placed BETWEEN the words of the verb, *not* before it.

8 Indirect questions

▶ *He asked her how could she be so angry?* (✗)
▶ He asked her **how she could be** so angry. (✓)

An 'indirect question' is a question which is **not** *the main part* of the sentence, as in the example above (where the main idea is *He asked her*). There are two mistakes here.

Firstly, an indirect question does NOT have a question mark.

Secondly, indirect questions do NOT use the question form of the verb. *Could she be* (the question form) is wrong here.

▶ *I don't know where does she live.* (✗)
▶ I don't know where **she lives**. (✓)

This is another kind of indirect question. Again the question form of the verb should **not** be used.

9 Use of commas
Comma pairs

▶ *Some people, however prefer town life.* (✗)
▶ Some people, however, prefer town life. (✓)

Often, words and short expressions like *however*, *by the way* or *according to the newspaper* are 'dropped into' the basic sentence. In this case, commas must be used BEFORE AND AFTER the 'dropped in' word or words. One comma is not enough.

Comma between subject and verb

▶ *Most of the teams, are not ready for the tournament.* (✗)
▶ Most of the teams are not ready for the tournament. (✓)

Even when the subject is a long one, you should NOT use a comma to separate it from its verb.

A a

A, a /eɪ/ noun [C,U] (pl **As**; **A's**; **a's**/eɪz/) **1** the first letter of the English alphabet □ *A, a (huruf)*: 'Andy' begins with (an) 'A'. **2** the highest grade given for an exam or piece of work □ *A (gred)*: I got an 'A' for my essay. **3 A** (used about music) the sixth note in the scale of C major: *A major/minor* ◆ *A flat/sharp*

a /ə/; *strong form* eɪ/ (*also* **an** /ən; *strong form* æn/) *indefinite article*

> **HELP** The form **an** is used before a vowel sound: *an apple* ◆ *an hour* ◆ *an MP*

1 one □ *se; satu*: *A cup of coffee, please.* ◆ *We've got an apple, a banana and two oranges.* **2** used when you talk about one example of sth for the first time □ *se-*: *I saw a dog chasing a cat this morning. The cat climbed up a tree.* ◆ *Have you got a dictionary* (= any dictionary)? **3** used for saying what kind of person or thing sb/sth is □ *se-; seorang, dsb*: *He's a doctor.* ◆ *She's a Muslim.* ◆ *You are a clever boy.* ◆ *'Is that an eagle?' 'No, it's a falcon.'* **4** (used when you are talking about a typical example of sth) any; every □ *digunakan utk menyatakan contoh lazim*: *An elephant can live for up to eighty years.*

> **HELP** You can also use the plural in this sense: *Elephants can live for up to eighty years.*

5 (used with prices, rates, measurements) each □ *se-; setiap*: *I usually drink two litres of water a day.* ◆ *twice a week* ◆ *He was travelling at about 80 miles an hour.* **SYN per 6** used with some expressions of quantity □ *digunakan utk menyatakan kuantiti tertentu*: *a lot of money* ◆ *a few cars* ❶ For more information about the indefinite article, look at the **Reference Section** at the back of this dictionary.

A2 (level) /ˌeɪ ˈtuː (ˌlevl)/ noun [C,U] a British exam usually taken in Year 13 of school or college (= the final year) when students are aged 18. Students must first have studied a subject at AS level before they can take an A2 exam. Together AS and A2 level exams form the A-level qualification, which is needed for entrance to universities □ *pangkat A2*: *A2 exams* ◆ *She's doing an A2 (level) in History.* ➔ look at **A level, AS (level)**

the AA /ˌeɪ ˈeɪ/ abbr (in Britain) the **Automobile Association**; an organization for drivers. If you are a member of the AA and your car breaks down, they will send sb to help you □ *Persatuan Automobil*: *My car wouldn't start so I called the AA.*

A & E /ˌeɪ ənd ˈiː/ abbr = accident and emergency

aback /əˈbæk/ adv
PHR V take sb aback ➔ take

abacus /ˈæbəkəs/ noun [C] a frame with small balls which slide along wires. It is used as a tool or toy for counting. □ *sempoa; dekak-dekak*

abandon /əˈbændən/ verb [T] **1** to leave sb/sth that you are responsible for, usually permanently □ *meninggalkan*: *The bank robbers abandoned the car just outside the city.* **2** to stop doing sth without finishing it or without achieving what you wanted to do □ *menghentikan*: *The search for the missing sailors was abandoned after two days.* ▶ **abandonment** noun [U]

abandoned /əˈbændənd/ adj **1** left and no longer wanted, used or needed □ *terbiar; ditinggalkan*: *an abandoned car/house* ◆ *The child was found abandoned but unharmed.* **2** (of people or their behaviour) wild; not following accepted standards □ *liar; tdk bermaruah*

abashed /əˈbæʃt/ adj [not before a noun] feeling guilty and embarrassed because of sth that you have done □ *malu; tersipu-sipu*: *'I'm sorry,' said Ali, looking abashed.*

abate /əˈbeɪt/ verb [I,T] (formal) to become less strong; to make sth less strong □ *reda; menjadi (kan) kurang*: *The storm showed no signs of abating.*

abattoir /ˈæbətwɑː(r)/ (BrE) = slaughterhouse

abbey /ˈæbi/ noun [C] a large church together with a group of buildings where **monks** or **nuns** (= religious men or women who live away from other people) live or lived in the past □ *gereja*

abbreviate /əˈbriːvieɪt/ verb [T] to make sth shorter, especially a word or phrase □ *memendekkan*: *'Kilometre' is usually abbreviated to 'km'.* **SYN** shorten ➔ look at **abridge**

abbreviation /əˌbriːviˈeɪʃn/ noun [C] a short form of a word or phrase □ *singkatan*: *In this dictionary 'sth' is the abbreviation for 'something'.*

ABC /ˌeɪ biː ˈsiː/ noun [sing] **1** the alphabet; the letters of English from A to Z □ *ABC (abjad)* **2** the simple facts about sth □ *perkara asas*: *an ABC of Gardening*

abdicate /ˈæbdɪkeɪt/ verb **1** [I] to give up being king or queen □ *turun dr takhta*: *The Queen abdicated in favour of her son* (= her son became king). **2** [T] to give sth up, especially power or a position □ *melepaskan*: *to abdicate responsibility* (= to refuse to be responsible for sth) ▶ **abdication** /ˌæbdɪˈkeɪʃn/ noun [C,U]

abdomen /ˈæbdəmən/ noun [C] a part of your body below the chest, in which the stomach is contained □ *abdomen* ▶ **abdominal** /æbˈdɒmɪnl/ adj

abduct /æbˈdʌkt/ verb [T] to take hold of sb and take them away illegally □ *melarikan*: *He has been abducted by a terrorist group.* ▶ **abduction** noun [C,U]

CONSONANTS p **p**en b **b**ad t **t**ea d **d**id k **c**at g **g**ot tʃ **ch**in dʒ **J**une f **f**all v **v**an θ **th**in

aberration /ˌæbəˈreɪʃn/ noun [C,U] (formal) a fact, an action or a way of behaving that is not usual, and that may be unacceptable □ *aberasi; perlakuan di luar kebiasaan*

abet /əˈbet/ verb (abetting; abetted)
IDM aid and abet ⊃ aid²

abhor /əbˈhɔː(r)/ verb [T] (abhorring; abhorred) to hate sth very much □ *sangat membenci*: *All civilized people abhor the use of torture.*

abhorrence /əbˈhɒrəns/ (AmE also) / noun [U] a strong feeling of hate; disgust □ *kebencian yg amat sangat*: *Protesters expressed their abhorrence of war.*

abhorrent /əbˈhɒrənt/ (AmE also) / adj that makes you feel hate or disgust □ *sangat dibenci*: *The idea of slavery is abhorrent to us nowadays.*

abide /əˈbaɪd/ verb
IDM can't/couldn't abide sb/sth/doing sth to hate sb/sth; to not like sb/sth at all □ *benci akan sso/sst; tdk suka akan sso/sst* **SYN** stand
PHR V abide by sth to obey a law, etc.; to do what sb has decided □ *mematuhi; mengikut (apa yg telah ditentukan)*

ability /əˈbɪləti/ noun [C,U] (pl abilities) the ability to do sth the mental or physical power or skill that makes it possible to do sth □ *kebolehan; kemampuan*: *the ability to make decisions* ♦ *students of mixed abilities* **OPP** inability

abject /ˈæbdʒekt/ adj (formal) 1 terrible and without hope □ *melarat; teruk*: *abject poverty* 2 without any pride or respect for yourself □ *hina; tiada maruah*: *an abject apology*

ablaze /əˈbleɪz/ adj [not before a noun] burning strongly; completely on fire □ *terbakar; dijilat api*: *Soldiers used petrol to set the building ablaze.*

able /ˈeɪbl/ adj (abler; ablest) [You can also use more able and most able.] 1 [used as a modal verb] be able to do sth to have the ability, power, opportunity, time, etc. to do sth □ *dpt; boleh; mampu*: *Will you be able to come to a meeting next week?* ♦ *I was able to solve the problem quickly.* ♦ *Many men don't feel able to express their emotions.* **OPP** unable

HELP In the passive can/could are used, not be able: *The arrangement can't be changed.*

ℹ For more information about modal verbs, look at the Reference Section at the back of this dictionary. 2 clever; doing your job well □ *berkebolehan; pandai*: *one of the ablest/most able students in the class* ♦ *an able politician* ▶ably /ˈeɪbli/ adv

able-bodied adj physically healthy and strong; having full use of your body □ *tegap dan sihat*

abnormal /æbˈnɔːml/ adj different from what is normal or usual, in a way that worries you or that is unpleasant □ *abnormal; tak normal; luar biasa*: *abnormal weather conditions* **OPP** normal ▶abnormally /-məli/ adv: *abnormally high temperatures*

abnormality /ˌæbnɔːˈmæləti/ noun (pl abnormalities) something that is not normal, especially in sb's body □ *keabnormalan; ketaknormalan*: *He was born with an abnormality of the heart.*

aboard /əˈbɔːd/ adv, prep on or onto a train, a ship, an aircraft or a bus □ *naik atau berada di dlm (kereta api, bas, dsb)*: *The plane crashed, killing all 158 people aboard.* ♦ *We climbed aboard the train and found a seat.*

abode /əˈbəʊd/ noun [C, usually sing] (written) the place where you live □ *tempat tinggal*
IDM (of) no fixed abode/address ⊃ fixed

abolish /əˈbɒlɪʃ/ verb [T] to end a law or system officially □ *memansuhkan; menghapuskan*: *When was capital punishment abolished here?*

abolition /ˌæbəˈlɪʃn/ noun [U] the act of ending a law or system officially □ *pemansuhan; penghapusan*: *the abolition of slavery in the US*

abominable /əˈbɒmɪnəbl/ adj very bad; shocking □ *keji; teruk* **SYN** appalling ▶abominably /-əbli/ adv

Aboriginal /ˌæbəˈrɪdʒənl/ (also Aborigine /ˌæbəˈrɪdʒəni/) noun [C] a member of the race of people who were the first people to live in a country, especially Australia □ *kaum peribumi Australia* ▶aboriginal adj: *aboriginal traditions*

abort /əˈbɔːt/ verb [T] 1 to make a foetus (= a baby that is developing in its mother's body) die before it is born □ *menggugurkan anak dlm kandungan* 2 to end sth before it is complete □ *membatalkan; membantutkan*: *The company aborted the project when they realized it was costing too much.*

abortion /əˈbɔːʃn/ noun [C,U] a medical operation that causes a baby to die inside its mother before it is fully developed □ *pengguguran anak dlm kandungan*: *to have an abortion* ♦ *Abortion is illegal in some countries.* ⊃ look at miscarriage

abortive /əˈbɔːtɪv/ adj not completed successfully; failed □ *gagal; terbantut*: *He made two abortive attempts to escape from prison.* **SYN** unsuccessful

abound /əˈbaʊnd/ verb [I] to exist in large numbers □ *banyak sekali*: *Animals and birds abound in the forest.* ♦ *Rumours abound about the actor's arrest.*
PHR V abound with sth to contain large numbers of sth □ *penuh dgn; banyak*: *The lake abounds with fish.*

about¹ /əˈbaʊt/ adv 1 (also around) a little more or less than □ *kira-kira; lebih kurang*: *It's about three miles from here to the city centre.* ♦ *I got home at about half past seven.* **SYN** approximately 2 (informal) almost; nearly □ *hampir*: *Dinner's just about ready.* 3 (also around) in many directions or places □ *ke/di sana sini*: *I could hear people moving about upstairs.* ♦ *Don't leave your clothes lying about all over the floor.* **4** (also around) [used after certain verbs] without doing anything in particular □ *tdk membuat apa-apa yg tertentu*: *The kids spend most evenings sitting about, bored.* **5** (also around) present in a place; existing □ *ada; wujud*: *It was very late and there were few people about.* ♦ *There isn't much good music about these days.*

IDM **be about to do sth** to be going to do sth very soon □ *akan; baru saja hendak*: *The film's about to start.* ♦ *I was just about to explain when she interrupted me.*

about² /əˈbaʊt/ *prep* **1** on the subject of □ *ttg; berkenaan dgn*: *Let's talk about something else.* ♦ *What's your book about?* ♦ *He told me all about his family.* ♦ *I don't like it, but there's nothing I can do about it.* **2** in the character of sb/sth □ *ttg; berkenaan dgn*: *There's something about him that I don't quite trust.* ♦ *I like the food, the climate and everything else about this country.* **3** busy with sth; doing sth □ *sibuk atau asyik dgn sst*: *Everywhere people were going about their daily business.* **4** (also around) (*especially BrE*) in many directions or places; in different parts of sth □ *ke sana sini; di sana sini*: *We wandered about the town for an hour or two.* ♦ *Lots of old newspapers were scattered about the room.*

IDM **how/what about...?** **1** used when asking for information about sb/sth or for sb's opinion or wish □ *bagaimana dgn/pula*: *How about Ruth? Have you heard from her lately?* ♦ *I'm going to have chicken. What about you?* **2** used when making a suggestion □ *bagaimana kalau*: *What about going to a film tonight?*

a,bout-ˈturn (*AmE* **a,bout-ˈface**) *noun* [C] a complete change of opinion, plan or behaviour □ *perubahan haluan*: *The government did an about-turn over tax.* ⊃ look at **U-turn**

above /əˈbʌv/ *prep, adv*
▶HIGHER PLACE **1** in a higher place □ *di atas*: *The coffee is in the cupboard above the sink.* ♦ *The people in the flat above make a lot of noise.* **OPP** below
▶MORE THAN **2** more than a number, an amount, a price, etc □ *ke atas; lebih drpd*: *children aged 11 and above* ♦ *A score of 70 and above will get you a grade B.* ♦ *You must get above 50% to pass.* ♦ *above-average temperatures* **OPP** below ⊃ look at **over**
▶AT WORK **3** with a higher position in an organization, etc □ *lebih tinggi; lebih kanan*: *The person above me is the department manager.* **OPP** below
▶PROUD **4** too proud to do sth □ *enggan melakukan sst yg tdk sepadan dgn darjat sso*: *He seems to think he's above helping with the cleaning.*
▶EARLIER PART **5** in an earlier part (of sth written) □ *di atas*: *Contact me at the above address/the address above.* **OPP** below

IDM **above all** (used to emphasize the main point) most importantly □ *paling penting sekali*: *Above all, stay calm!*

above board (used especially about a business deal, etc.) honest and open □ *jujur dan telus*

abrasive /əˈbreɪsɪv/ *adj* **1** rough and likely to scratch □ *kasap; (yg) melelaskan*: *abrasive kitchen cleaners* **2** (used about a person) rude and rather aggressive □ *kasar*

abreast /əˈbrest/ *adv* **abreast (of sb/sth)** next to or level with sb/sth and going in the same direction □ *seiring; sebaris*: *The soldiers marched two abreast.*

IDM **be/keep abreast of sth** to have all the most recent information about sth □ *mengikuti (perkembangan sst)*

abridge /əˈbrɪdʒ/ *verb* [T] to make sth (usually a book) shorter by removing parts of it □ *meringkaskan; menyingkatkan* ⊃ look at **abbreviate**

abroad /əˈbrɔːd/ *adv* in or to another country or countries □ *di/ke luar negara*: *They found it difficult to get used to living abroad.* ♦ *My mother has never been abroad.* ♦ *She often goes abroad on business.*

abrupt /əˈbrʌpt/ *adj* **1** sudden and unexpected □ *tiba-tiba; mendadak*: *an abrupt change of plan* **2** seeming rude and unfriendly □ *tdk mesra*
▶**abruptly** *adv* ▶**abruptness** *noun* [U]

abscess /ˈæbses/ *noun* [C] a swelling on or in the body, containing **pus** (= a poisonous yellow liquid) □ *abses; bengkak bernanah*

abscond /əbˈskɒnd/ *verb* [I] (*formal*) **abscond (from sth) (with sth)** to run away from a place where you should stay, sometimes with sth that you should not take □ *melarikan diri*: *to abscond from prison* ♦ *She absconded with all the company's money.*

abseil /ˈæbseɪl/ (*AmE* **rappel**) *verb* [I] **abseil (down, off, etc. sth)** to go down the side of a very steep, high rock or a building while you are tied to a rope, pushing against the surface with your feet □ *menuruni lereng atau cerun bukit bangunan dgn bantuan tali* ⊃ picture on page P5

absence /ˈæbsəns/ *noun* **1** [C,U] a time when sb is away from somewhere; the fact of being away from somewhere □ *ketidakhadiran; ketiadaan*: *Frequent absences due to illness meant he was behind with his work.* ♦ *I have to make all the decisions in my boss's absence.* **2** [U] the fact of sth/sb not being there; lack □ *ketiadaan; tdk ada*: *In the absence of a doctor, try to help the injured person yourself.* **OPP** for both meanings **presence**

absent /ˈæbsənt/ *adj* **1** **absent (from sth)** not present somewhere □ *tdk hadir*: *He was absent from work because of illness.* **OPP** present **2** thinking about sth else; not paying attention □ *melamun; tdk menumpukan perhatian*: *an absent stare* ▶**absently** *adv*

absentee /ˌæbsənˈtiː/ *noun* [C] a person who is not in the place where they should be □ *orang yg tdk hadir*

VOWELS iː **see** i **any** ɪ **sit** e **ten** æ **hat** ɑː **father** ɒ **got** ɔː **saw** ʊ **put** uː **too** u **usual**

absenteeism → abuse

absenteeism /ˌæbsənˈtiːɪzəm/ *noun* [U] the problem of workers or students often not going to work or school □ *ketidakhadiran; perbuatan ponteng kerja atau sekolah*

absent-ˈminded *adj* often forgetting or not noticing things, because you are thinking about sth else □ *pelupa* **SYN** forgetful ▶ **absent-mindedly** *adv*

absolute /ˈæbsəluːt/ *adj* **1** complete; total □ *sepenuhnya; sama sekali; betul-betul*: *a course for absolute beginners* ♦ *The whole trip was an absolute disaster.* ♦ *None of the political parties had an absolute majority* (= more votes, etc. than all the other parties together). **2** [only before a noun] used, especially in spoken English, to give emphasis to what you are saying □ *sesungguhnya*: *There's absolute rubbish on television tonight!* **3** not measured in comparison with sth else □ *(secara) mutlak*: *Spending on the Health Service has increased in absolute terms.*

absolutely *adv* **1** /ˈæbsəluːtli/ completely □ *sepenuhnya; betul-betul; sama sekali; langsung*: *It's absolutely freezing outside!* ♦ *I absolutely refuse to believe that.* ♦ *He made absolutely no effort* (= no effort at all) *to help me.* **2** /ˌæbsəˈluːtli/ (used when you are agreeing with sb) yes; certainly □ *betul; tentu sekali*: *'It is a good idea, isn't it?' 'Oh, absolutely!'*

absolve /əbˈzɒlv/ *verb* [T] **absolve sb (from/of sth)** to say formally that sb does not have to take responsibility for sth □ *membebaskan (sso drpd tuduhan, dsb)*: *The driver was absolved of any blame for the train crash.*

absorb /əbˈsɔːb; -ˈzɔːb/ *verb* [T]
▶LIQUID/HEAT **1 absorb sth (into sth)** to take in and hold sth (a liquid, heat, etc.) □ *menyerap*: *a drug that is quickly absorbed into the bloodstream* ♦ *Black clothes absorb the sun's heat.*
▶INTO STH LARGER **2 absorb sth (into sth)** to take sth into sth larger, so that it becomes part of it □ *bercantum*: *Over the years many villages have been absorbed into the city.*
▶INFORMATION **3** to take sth into the mind and understand it □ *menyerap; memahami*: *I found it impossible to absorb so much information so quickly.*
▶INTEREST SB **4** to hold sb's attention completely or interest sb very much □ *menarik seluruh perhatian atau minat sso*: *History is a subject that absorbs her.*
▶A HIT **5** to reduce the effect of a sudden violent knock, hit, etc □ *menyerap; mengurangkan kesan (hentaman, dsb)*: *The front of the car is designed to absorb most of the impact of a crash.*
▶ **absorption** /əbˈsɔːpʃn; -ˈzɔːp-/ *noun* [U]

absorbed /əbˈsɔːbd; -ˈzɔːbd/ *adj* **absorbed (in sth)** giving all your attention to sth □ *asyik; leka*: *He was absorbed in his work and didn't hear me come in.*

absorbent /əbˈsɔːbənt; -ˈzɔːb-/ *adj* able to take in and hold liquid □ *dpt menyerap*: *an absorbent cloth*

absorbing /əbˈsɔːbɪŋ; -ˈzɔːb-/ *adj* holding all your interest and attention □ *mengasyikkan*: *an absorbing book*

abstain /əbˈsteɪn/ *verb* [I] **1** (in a vote) to say that you are not voting either for or against sth □ *tdk mengundi; berkecuali*: *Two people voted in favour, two voted against and one abstained.* ⊃ *noun* **abstention 2** (formal) **abstain (from sth/doing sth)** to stop yourself from doing sth that you enjoy □ *menahan diri drpd menikmati perkara yg menyeronokkan*: *The doctor said he should abstain from (eating) fatty foods until he was better.* ⊃ *noun* **abstinence**

abstention /əbˈstenʃn/ *noun* [C,U] the act of not voting either for or against sth □ *tindakan utk berkecuali; tdk mengundi*

abstinence /ˈæbstɪnəns/ *noun* [U] (formal) stopping yourself from having or doing sth that you enjoy □ *perihal menahan diri drpd melakukan sst yg disukai*: *The doctor advised total abstinence from dairy products.* ⊃ *verb* **abstain**

abstract¹ /ˈæbstrækt/ *adj* **1** existing only as an idea, not as a physical thing □ *abstrak; mujarad*: *It is hard to imagine an abstract idea like 'eternity'.* **OPP** concrete **2** (used about art) not showing people and things as they really look □ *abstrak*: *an abstract painting*

abstract² /ˈæbstrækt/ *noun* [C] **1** an example of abstract art □ *karya abstrak* **2** a short piece of writing that tells you the main contents of a book, speech, etc. □ *ikhtisar; ringkasan; abstrak* **SYN** summary
IDM **in the abstract** only as an idea, not in real life □ *pada teorinya; secara abstrak*

absurd /əbˈsɜːd/ *adj* not at all logical or sensible □ *tdk munasabah; tdk masuk akal*: *It would be absurd to spend all your money on one pair of shoes.* ♦ *Don't be absurd! I can't possibly do all that in one day.* **SYN** ridiculous ▶ **absurdity** /əbˈsɜːdəti/ *noun* [C,U] (*pl* absurdities) ▶ **absurdly** *adv*

abundance /əˈbʌndəns/ *noun* [sing, U] a very large quantity of sth □ *jumlah yg banyak sekali*: *There is an abundance of wildlife in the forest.* ♦ *These flowers grow here in abundance.* **SYN** profusion

abundant /əˈbʌndənt/ *adj* existing in very large quantities; more than enough □ *(yg) banyak*: *abundant supplies of food* ♦ *Fish are abundant in the lake.* **SYN** plentiful ▶ **abundantly** *adv*

abuse¹ /əˈbjuːs/ *noun* **1** [C,U] using sth in a bad or dishonest way □ *penyalahgunaan*: *an abuse of power* ♦ *the dangers of drug abuse* **2** [U] bad, usually violent treatment of sb □ *penganiayaan; penderaan*: *He subjected his children to verbal and physical abuse.* ♦ *a victim of sexual abuse* **3** [U] rude words, used to insult another person □ *caci maki*: *The other driver leaned out of the car and hurled abuse at me.* ♦ *racial abuse*

abuse² /əˈbjuːz/ verb [T] **1** to use sth in a bad or dishonest way □ *menyalahgunakan*: *The politician was accused of abusing his position in order to become rich.* **2** to treat sb badly, often violently □ *menganiayai; mendera*: *The girl had been physically abused.* **3** to say rude things to sb □ *memaki hamun*: *The goalkeeper got a red card for abusing the referee.* **SYN** insult

abusive /əˈbjuːsɪv/ adj using rude language to insult sb □ *(kata-kata yg) kesat atau menghina*: *an abusive remark*

abysmal /əˈbɪzməl/ adj very bad; of very poor quality □ *teruk sekali* ▶ **abysmally** /-məli/ adv

abyss /əˈbɪs/ noun [C] a very deep hole that seems to have no bottom □ *jurang yg sangat dlm*

a/c abbr = **account¹**(1)

academic¹ /ˌækəˈdemɪk/ adj **1** connected with education, especially in schools and universities □ *akademik; ilmiah*: *The academic year begins in September.* **2** connected with subjects of interest to the mind rather than technical or practical subjects □ *akademik; ilmiah*: *academic subjects such as History* **OPP** non-academic **3** not connected with reality; not affecting the facts of a situation □ *akademik; ilmiah*: *It's academic which one I prefer because I can't have either of them.* ▶ **academically** /-kli/ adv

academic² /ˌækəˈdemɪk/ noun [C] a person who teaches and/or does research at a university or college □ *ahli akademik; ilmiawan*

academy /əˈkædəmi/ noun [C] (pl **academies**) **1** a school for special training □ *akademi; maktab*: *a military academy* **2** Academy an official group of people who are important in art, science or literature □ *Akademi*: *the Royal Academy of Arts* **3** a school in England which has some independence from local authority control □ *sebuah sekolah di England yg tdk tertakluk kpd kawalan pihak berkuasa tempatan sepenuhnya*

accelerate /əkˈseləreɪt/ verb [I,T] to go faster; to make sth go faster or happen more quickly □ *mencepatkan*: *The driver slowed down for the bend then accelerated away.* ◆ *The government plans to accelerate the pace of reform.* ▶ **acceleration** /əkˌseləˈreɪʃn/ noun [U]

accelerator /əkˈseləreɪtə(r)/ noun [C] the control in a vehicle that you press with your foot in order to make it go faster □ *pemecut* ➔ picture at **car**

accent /ˈæksent; -sənt/ noun **1** [C,U] a particular way of pronouncing words that is connected with the country, area or social class that you come from □ *telor; loghat*: *He speaks with a strong Scottish accent.* **2** [C] the greater force that you give to a particular word or part of a word when you speak □ *tekanan*: *In the word 'because' the accent is on the second syllable.* **SYN** stress **3** [C] (in writing) a mark, usually above a letter, that shows that it has to be pronounced in a certain way □ *aksen; tanda tekanan (bunyi)*: *Séance has an accent on the first 'e'.* **4** [C, usually sing] the particular importance that is given to sth □ *tumpuan; penekanan*: *In all our products the accent is on quality.* **SYN** emphasis

accentuate /əkˈsentʃueɪt/ verb [T] to make sth easier to notice □ *menyerlahkan; menonjolkan*: *She uses make-up to accentuate her beautiful eyes.*

accept /əkˈsept/ verb **1** [I,T] to say yes to sth or to agree to sth willingly □ *menerima; bersetuju*: *Thank you for your invitation. I am happy to accept.* ◆ *He asked her to marry him and she accepted.* ◆ *She has accepted the job.* **OPP** refuse **2** [T] to agree to sth or approve of sth □ *menerima; mengambil*: *Do I have to pay in cash or will you accept a credit card?* ◆ *Why won't you accept my advice?* **3** [T] to admit or recognize that sth difficult or unpleasant is true □ *menerima (hakikat); mengaku*: *They refused to accept responsibility for the accident.* ◆ *She didn't accept that I was telling the truth.* **4** [T] to make sb feel welcome or to allow sb to join a group or an organization □ *menerima*: *The university has accepted me on the course.* ◆ *All children want to be accepted.* **OPP** reject

acceptable /əkˈseptəbl/ adj **1** that can be allowed □ *boleh diterima*: *One or two mistakes are acceptable but no more than that.* **2** good enough □ *dpt diterima*: *We hope that you will consider our offer acceptable.* ◆ *The food was acceptable, but no more* (= not very good, but good enough). **SYN** satisfactory **OPP** for both meanings **unacceptable** ▶ **acceptability** /əkˌseptəˈbɪləti/ noun [U] ▶ **acceptably** /əkˈseptəbli/ adv

acceptance /əkˈseptəns/ noun [C,U] the act of accepting or being accepted □ *penerimaan*: *His ready acceptance of the offer surprised me.* ◆ *He quickly gained acceptance in the group* (= the other people thought of him as equal to them).

access¹ /ˈækses/ noun [U] **1** access (to sth) a way of entering or reaching a place □ *jalan masuk*: *Access to the garden is through the kitchen.* **2** access (to sth) the chance or right to use or have sth □ *peluang atau hak menggunakan atau memiliki sst*: *Do you have access to a personal computer?* **3** access (to sb) permission, especially legal or official, to see sb □ *kebenaran utk menemui sso*: *They are divorced, but he has regular access to the children.*

access² /ˈækses/ verb [T] to find information on a computer □ *mengakses; mendapatkan maklumat*: *Click on the icon to access a file.*

accessible /əkˈsesəbl/ adj **1** possible to be reached or entered □ *boleh sampai (ke situ); dpt didatangi*: *The island is only accessible by boat.* **2** easy to get, use or understand □ *mudah didapati, digunakan atau difahami*: *This TV programme aims to make history more accessible to children.* **OPP** for both meanings **inaccessible** ▶ **accessibility** /əkˌsesəˈbɪləti/ noun [U]: *Computers have given people greater accessibility to information.*

accession /ækˈseʃn/ noun [U] the act of taking a very high position, especially as ruler of a country or head of sth □ *perbuatan menaiki takhta atau menyandang jawatan tinggi*

accessory /əkˈsesəri/ noun [C] (pl accessories) **1** an extra item that is added to sth and is useful or attractive but not of great importance □ *aksesori; alat tambahan*: *a wide range of car accessories, such as alloy wheels and roof racks* **2** [usually pl] a thing that you wear or carry that matches your clothes, for example a piece of jewellery, a bag, etc. □ *aksesori; hiasan tambahan* **3** **an accessory (to sth)** (in law) a person who helps sb to do sth illegal □ *subahat; orang yg turut serta melakukan perkara yg menyalahi undang-undang*

accident /ˈæksɪdənt/ noun [C] an unpleasant event that happens unexpectedly and causes damage, injury or death □ *kemalangan; kecelakaan*: *I hope they haven't had an accident.* ◆ *a car accident* ◆ *a fatal accident* (= when sb is killed) ◆ *I didn't mean to kick you, it was an accident.*
IDM **by accident** by chance; without intending to □ *dgn tdk sengaja; secara kebetulan*: *I knocked the vase over by accident as I was cleaning.* **OPP** **deliberately**

accidental /ˌæksɪˈdentl/ adj happening by chance; not planned □ *secara tdk sengaja*: *Police do not know if the explosion was accidental or caused by a bomb.* ▶ **accidentally** /-təli/ adv: *As I turned around, I accidentally hit him in the face.*

ˌaccident and eˈmergency (also **casualty**) (BrE) noun [U] (abbr **A & E**) (AmE **eˈmergency room**) the part of a hospital where people who have been injured in accidents are taken for immediate treatment □ *unit kemalangan dan kecemasan*

ˈaccident-prone adj often having accidents □ *mudah kemalangan*

acclaim /əˈkleɪm/ verb [T, usually passive] **acclaim sb/sth (as sth)** to express a very high opinion of sb/sth □ *menyanjung; memuji*: *a highly acclaimed new film* ◆ *The novel has been acclaimed as a modern classic.* ▶ **acclaim** noun [U]: *The film received widespread critical acclaim.*

acclimatize (also **-ise**) /əˈklaɪmətaɪz/ verb [I,T] **acclimatize (yourself/sb/sth) (to sth)** to get used to a new climate, situation, place, etc. so that it is not a problem any more □ *menyesuaikan diri dgn iklim, keadaan, dsb yg baharu* ▶ **acclimatization** (also **-isation**) /əˌklaɪmətaɪˈzeɪʃn/ noun [U] ▶ **acclimatized** (also **-ised**) adj

accolade /ˈækəleɪd/ noun [C] a comment, prize, etc. that you receive which shows people's high opinion of sth you have done □ *sanjungan; penghormatan*

accommodate /əˈkɒmədeɪt/ verb [T] **1** to provide sb with a place to stay, live or work □ *menyediakan penginapan*: *During the conference, you will be accommodated in a nearby hotel.* **2** to have enough space for sb/sth, especially for a certain number of people □ *muat; menampung*: *Each apartment can accommodate up to six people.* **3** (formal) to do or provide what sb wants or needs □ *membuat penyesuaian*

accommodating /əˈkɒmədeɪtɪŋ/ adj (used about a person) agreeing to do or provide what sb wants □ *mudah bertolak ansur*: *My boss is very accommodating when I need time off work.*

accommodation /əˌkɒməˈdeɪʃn/ noun [U] a place for sb to live or stay □ *tempat tinggal; penginapan*: *We lived in rented accommodation before buying this house.* ◆ *The price of the holiday includes flights and accommodation.*

> **GRAMMAR** **Accommodation** is uncountable, so you CANNOT say 'an accommodation'. Sometimes it is better to use a different phrase instead: *I need to find somewhere to live.* ◆ *I'll help you find a place to stay.*

accompaniment /əˈkʌmpənimənt/ noun [C] something that goes together with another more important thing □ *iringan; hidangan sampingan*: *He only drinks wine as an accompaniment to food.*

accompany /əˈkʌmpəni/ verb [T] (**accompanying**; **accompanies**; pt, pp **accompanied**) **1** to go together with sb/sth □ *menemani; mengiringi*: *He went to America accompanied by his wife and three children.* ◆ *Massive publicity accompanied the film's release.* **2** **accompany sb (on sth)** to play music for a singer or another instrument □ *mengiringi*: *She accompanied him on the guitar.*

accomplice /əˈkʌmplɪs/ noun [C] **an accomplice (to/in sth)** a person who helps sb to do sth bad, especially a crime □ *subahat*: *She was charged with being an accomplice to the murder.*

accomplish /əˈkʌmplɪʃ/ verb [T] to succeed in doing sth difficult that you planned to do □ *mencapai (kejayaan)*: *I managed to accomplish my goal of sending twenty emails in an evening.*

accomplished /əˈkʌmplɪʃt/ adj highly skilled at sth □ *mahir; ulung*: *an accomplished actor*

accomplishment /əˈkʌmplɪʃmənt/ noun **1** [C] something difficult that sb has succeeded in doing or learning □ *pencapaian; kejayaan* **SYN** **achievement** **2** [U] (formal) the act of completing sth successfully □ *penyempurnaan*: *the accomplishment of a plan*

accord¹ /əˈkɔːd/ noun [C] an agreement, especially between countries □ *perjanjian; persetujuan*: *the Helsinki accords on human rights*
IDM **in accord (with sth/sb)** in agreement with sth/sb □ *bersetuju; selaras dgn*
of your own accord without being forced or asked □ *dgn kehendak atau kerelaan sendiri*: *He wasn't sacked from his job—he left of his own accord.*

accord² /əˈkɔːd/ verb (formal) **1** [T] to give sth to sb □ *memberi* **2** [I] **accord (with sth)** to match; to agree with □ *selaras; bertepatan*

accordance /əˈkɔːdns/ noun

IDM **in accordance with sth** in a way that follows or obeys sth □ *menurut atau selaras dgn sst*: *to act in accordance with instructions*

accordingly /əˈkɔːdɪŋli/ adv **1** in a way that is suitable □ *sewajarnya*: *I realized that I was in danger and acted accordingly.* **2** (formal) therefore; for that reason □ *oleh itu; dgn demikian*

according to /əˈkɔːdɪŋ tə/ prep **1** as stated by sb; as shown by sth □ *menurut*: *According to Mick, it's a brilliant film.* ◆ *Standards of living are improving, according to the statistics.* **2** in a way that matches, follows or depends on sth □ *mengikut*: *Everything went off according to plan* (= as we had planned it). ◆ *The salary will be fixed according to experience.*

accordion   concertina

accordion /əˈkɔːdiən/ noun [C] a musical instrument that you hold in both hands and play by pulling the two sides apart and then pushing them together, while pressing the keys and/or buttons with your fingers □ *akordion*

accost /əˈkɒst/ (AmE also) / verb [T] to go up and talk to sb in a way that is surprising or rude □ *mendekati dan menegur sso secara kasar atau mengancam*

account¹ /əˈkaʊnt/ noun [C] **1** (abbr a/c) the arrangement by which a bank looks after your money for you □ *akaun*: *a current/deposit account* ◆ *to open/close an account* ◆ *I have an account with/at Barclays.* ◆ *My salary is paid into my bank account every month.* ⊃ note at **money 2** [usually pl] a record of all the money that a person or business has received or paid out □ *kira-kira; akaun*: *If you are self-employed you have to keep your own accounts.* **3** an arrangement with a shop, etc. that allows you to pay for goods or services at a later date □ *akaun*: *Most customers settle/pay their account in full every month.* **4** sb's report or description of sth that has happened □ *pemerian; perihalan*: *She gave the police a full account of the robbery.*

IDM **by all accounts** according to what everyone says □ *(menurut) kata orang*: *By all accounts, she's a very good doctor.*
by your own account according to what you say yourself □ *menurut kata sso itu sendiri*: *By his own account, Peter was not very good at his job.*
on account of because of □ *disebabkan oleh*: *Our flight was delayed on account of bad weather.*
on no account; not on any account not for any reason □ *jangan sekali-kali*: *On no account should you walk home by yourself.*
take account of sth; take sth into account to consider sth, especially when deciding or judging sth □ *mengambil kira akan sst*: *We'll take account of your comments.* ◆ *We'll take your comments into account.*

account² /əˈkaʊnt/ verb

PHR V **account for sth 1** to explain or give a reason for sth □ *memberikan sebab*: *How can we account for these changes?* **2** to form the amount that is mentioned □ *mewakili*: *Sales to Europe accounted for 80% of our total sales last year.*

accountable /əˈkaʊntəbl/ adj expected to give an explanation of your actions, etc.; responsible □ *bertanggungjawab; dipertanggungjawabkan*: *She is too young to be held accountable for what she did.* ▶**accountability** /əˌkaʊntəˈbɪləti/ noun [U]

accountancy /əˈkaʊntənsi/ noun [U] the work or profession of an **accountant** □ *ilmu perakaunan*

accountant /əˈkaʊntənt/ noun [C] a person whose job is to keep or examine the financial accounts of a business, etc. □ *akauntan*

accredited /əˈkredɪtɪd/ adj officially recognized or approved □ *diiktiraf; diakui secara rasmi*: *a fully accredited course*

accumulate /əˈkjuːmjəleɪt/ verb **1** [T] to collect a number or quantity of sth over a period of time □ *mengumpulkan*: *Over the years, I've accumulated hundreds of books.* **2** [I] to increase over a period of time □ *menimbun; terkumpul*: *Dust soon accumulates if you don't clean the house for a week or so.* ▶**accumulation** /əˌkjuːmjəˈleɪʃn/ noun [C,U]

accurate /ˈækjərət/ adj exact and correct; without mistakes □ *tepat*: *He gave the police an accurate description of the robbers.* ◆ *That clock isn't very accurate.* **OPP** **inaccurate** ▶**accuracy** /ˈækjərəsi/ noun [U] **OPP** **inaccuracy** ▶**accurately** adv: *It is difficult to estimate the age of these bones accurately.*

accusation /ˌækjuˈzeɪʃn/ noun [C,U] a statement saying that sb has done sth wrong □ *tuduhan; dakwaan*

accuse /əˈkjuːz/ verb [T] **accuse sb (of sth/doing sth)** to say that sb has done sth wrong or broken the law □ *menuduh; mendakwa*: *I accused her of cheating.* ◆ *He was accused of murder.* ▶**accuser** noun [C]

the accused /əˈkjuːzd/ noun [C] (pl **the accused**) (used in a court of law) the person who is said to have broken the law □ *orang yg dituduh*

accusing /əˈkjuːzɪŋ/ adj showing that you think sb has done sth wrong □ *(yg) menuduh*: *He gave me an accusing look.* ▶**accusingly** adv

accustom /əˈkʌstəm/ verb [T] **accustom yourself/sb/sth to sth** to make yourself/sb/sth get used to sth □ *membiasakan (diri)*: *It took him a while to accustom himself to the idea.*

accustomed /əˈkʌstəmd/ adj **1 accustomed to sth** if you are **accustomed** to sth, you are used to it and it is not strange for you □ *sudah biasa*

ace → acquisition

dgn; menjadi biasa: *She's accustomed to travelling a lot with her parents.* ♦ *It took a while for my eyes to get accustomed to the dark room.* **SYN** **used 2** (*formal*) usual; regular □ *(yg) biasa*

ace /eɪs/ *noun* [C] **1** a playing card which has a single shape on it. An **ace** has either the lowest or the highest value in a game of cards □ *daun sat*: *the ace of spades* ➔ note at **card** ➔ picture at **card 2** (in the sport of **tennis**) a **service** (= the first hit of the ball) that the person playing against you cannot hit back because it is too fast □ *servis cemerlang*: *to serve an ace*

ache¹ /eɪk/ *verb* [I] to feel a continuous pain □ *sakit; berasa sakit*: *His legs ached after playing football.* ♦ *She was aching all over.*

ache² /eɪk/ *noun* [C] a pain that lasts for a long time □ *sakit*: *to have toothache/earache/backache/stomach ache* ➔ note at **pain**

> **HELP** **Ache** is often used in compounds. In British English it is usually used without 'a' or 'an': *I've got toothache*. But we always use 'a' with 'headache': *I've got a bad headache*. In American English, **ache** is usually used with 'a' or 'an', especially when talking about a particular attack of pain: *I have an awful stomach ache*.

achieve /əˈtʃiːv/ *verb* [T] **1** to gain sth, usually by effort or skill □ *mencapai; memperoleh*: *You have achieved the success you deserve.* **2** to complete sth by hard work and skill □ *menyudahkan; menyiapkan*: *They have achieved a lot in a short time.*

achievement /əˈtʃiːvmənt/ *noun* [C,U] something that you have done successfully, especially through hard work or skill □ *pencapaian; kejayaan*: *She felt that winning the gold medal was her greatest achievement.* ♦ *He enjoys climbing mountains because it gives him **a sense of achievement**.*

Achilles heel /əˌkɪliːz ˈhiːl/ *noun* [C] a weak point or fault in sb/sth □ *kelemahan*

acid¹ /ˈæsɪd/ *noun* [C,U] (in chemistry) a liquid substance that can dissolve metal and may burn your skin or clothes. **Acids** have a **pH** (= a measurement of the level of acid or alkali in sth) value of less than 7 □ *asid*: *sulphuric acid* ➔ look at **alkali**

acid² /ˈæsɪd/ *adj* **1** (also **acidic** /əˈsɪdɪk/) containing an **acid** □ *berasid*: *an acid solution* **OPP** **alkaline 2** (used about a fruit, etc.) with a sour taste □ *masam*

acidity /əˈsɪdəti/ *noun* [U] the quality of being **acid** □ *keasidan*: *to measure the acidity of soil*

acid rain *noun* [U] rain that has chemicals in it from factories, etc. and that causes damage to trees, buildings and rivers □ *hujan asid* ➔ note at **environment**

acknowledge /əkˈnɒlɪdʒ/ *verb* [T] **1** to accept or admit that sth is true or exists □ *meng-*

akui; mengiktiraf: *He acknowledged (the fact) that he had made a mistake.* ♦ *He is acknowledged to be the country's greatest writer.* **2** to show that you have seen or noticed sb/sth or received sth □ *mengaku telah nampak sso/sst atau telah menerima sst*: *I would be grateful if you could acknowledge my application* (= tell me that you have received it).

acknowledgement /əkˈnɒlɪdʒmənt/ *noun* **1** [U] the act of showing that you have seen or noticed sb/sth □ *pengakuan bahawa telah nampak sso/sst*: *The president gave a smile of acknowledgement to the photographers.* **2** [C,U] a letter, etc. that says that sth has been received or noticed □ *akuan terima (surat, dsb)*: *I haven't received (an) acknowledgement of my job application yet.* **3** [C] a few words of thanks that an author writes at the beginning or end of a book to the people who have helped them □ *penghargaan*

acne /ˈækni/ *noun* [U] a skin disease that usually affects young people. When you have **acne** you get a lot of spots on your face and neck. □ *akne; jerawat batu*

acorn /ˈeɪkɔːn/ *noun* [C] the small nut of the **oak** (= a large tree with hard wood), that grows in a base shaped like a cup □ *buah oak*

acoustic /əˈkuːstɪk/ *adj* **1** connected with sound or the sense of hearing □ *akustik* **2** (of a musical instrument) not electric □ *akustik*: *an acoustic guitar* ➔ picture at **music**

acoustics /əˈkuːstɪks/ *noun* [pl] the qualities of a room, etc. that make it good or bad for you to hear music, etc. in □ *akustik*: *The theatre has excellent acoustics.*

acquaintance /əˈkweɪntəns/ *noun* **1** [C] a person that you know but who is not a close friend □ *kenalan* **2** [C,U] **acquaintance with sb/sth** a slight knowledge of sb/sth □ *perkenalan; pengetahuan*

acquainted /əˈkweɪntɪd/ *adj* [not before a noun] (*formal*) **1 acquainted with sth** knowing sth □ *tahu; biasa dgn*: *I went for a walk to get acquainted with my new neighbourhood.* **2 acquainted (with sb)** knowing sb, but usually not very closely □ *kenal*

acquiesce /ˌækwiˈes/ *verb* [I] (*written*) **acquiesce in/to sth** to accept sth without argument, although you may not agree with it □ *akur; bersetuju* ▶ **acquiescence** *noun* [U]

acquire /əˈkwaɪə(r)/ *verb* [T] (*formal*) to obtain or buy sth □ *mendapat; memperoleh*: *She has acquired a good knowledge of English.* ♦ *He's acquired a reputation for being difficult to work with.* ♦ *The company has acquired shares in a rival business.*

acquisition /ˌækwɪˈzɪʃn/ *noun* (*formal*) **1** [U] the act of obtaining or buying sth □ *pemerolehan*: *a study of language acquisition in children* **2** [C] something that you have obtained or bought □ *perolehan*: *This sculpture is the museum's latest acquisition.*

ð **then**   s **so**   z **zoo**   ʃ **she**   ʒ **vi**sion   h **how**   m **man**   n **no**   ŋ **sing**   l **leg**   r **red**   j **yes**   w **wet**

acquit /əˈkwɪt/ verb [T] (acquitting; acquitted)
1 acquit sb (of sth) to state formally that a person is not guilty of a crime □ *membebaskan (sso drpd tuduhan)*: *The jury acquitted her of murder.* **OPP** convict **2** (*formal*) acquit yourself ... to behave in the way that is mentioned □ *berkelakuan spt yg disebutkan*: *He acquitted himself well in his first match as a professional.*
▶ **acquittal** /əˈkwɪtl/ *noun* [C,U]

acre /ˈeɪkə(r)/ *noun* [C] a measure of land; 0.405 of a **hectare** (= 10 000 square metres) □ *ekar*: *a farm of 20 acres/a 20-acre farm*

acrid /ˈækrɪd/ *adj* having a strong, bitter smell or taste that is unpleasant □ *(bau) tajam; kuat; (rasa) pekat; tengik*: *acrid smoke*

acrimonious /ˌækrɪˈməʊniəs/ *adj* (*formal*) angry and full of strong feelings and words □ *pedih; getir*: *His parents went through an acrimonious divorce.* **SYN** bitter

acrobat /ˈækrəbæt/ *noun* [C] a person who performs difficult movements of the body, especially in a **circus** (= a show that travels to different towns) □ *akrobat*

acrobatic /ˌækrəˈbætɪk/ *adj* performing or involving difficult movements of the body □ *akrobatik*: *an acrobatic dancer* ♦ *an acrobatic leap*
▶ **acrobatically** /-kli/ *adv*

acrobatics /ˌækrəˈbætɪks/ *noun* [U] (the art of performing) difficult movements of the body □ *akrobatik; gerak badan yg sukar dilakukan*

acronym /ˈækrənɪm/ *noun* [C] an acronym (for sth) a short word that is made from the first letters of a group of words □ *akronim*: *TEFL is an acronym for Teaching English as a Foreign Language.*

across /əˈkrɒs/ *adv, prep* **1** from one side of sth to the other □ *merentang*: *The stream was too wide to jump across.* ♦ *He walked across the field.* ♦ *A smile spread across his face.* ♦ *The river was about 20 metres across.* ♦ *The bank has 800 branches across* (= in all parts of) *the country.* **2** on the other side of sth □ *di seberang*: *There's a bank just across the road.* ♦ *The house across the road from us is for sale.*

> **HELP** Across or over? We can use **across** or **over** to mean 'on or to the other side': *I ran across/over the road.* But when we talk about crossing something high, we usually use **over**: *I can't climb over that wall.* With 'room' we usually use **across**: *I walked across the room to the door.*

IDM across the board involving or affecting all groups, members, cases, etc. □ *menyeluruh*

acrylic /əˈkrɪlɪk/ *noun* [C,U] an artificial material that is used in making clothes and paint □ *akrilik*

act¹ /ækt/ *noun* [C]
▶ STH YOU DO **1** a thing that you do □ *perbuatan; tindakan*: *In a typical act of generosity they refused to accept any money.* ♦ *to commit a violent act*

> **HELP** Act, action or activity? Act and action can have the same meaning: *It was a brave act/action.* Act, not action can be followed by of: *It was an act of bravery.* Activity is used for something that is done regularly: *I like outdoor activities such as cycling and camping.*

▶ LAW **2** *often* Act a law made by a government □ *Akta*: *The government passed an act protecting the rights of tenants.*
▶ BEHAVIOUR **3** behaviour that hides your true feelings □ *pura-pura*: *She seems very happy but she's just putting on an act.*
▶ IN PLAY **4** *often* Act one of the main divisions of a play or an **opera** (= a musical play) □ *babak*: *How many scenes are there in Act 4?*
▶ ENTERTAINMENT **5** a short piece of entertainment, especially as part of a show □ *persembahan*: *Did you enjoy the clowns' act?*

IDM be/get in on the act become involved in an activity that is becoming popular □ *turut sama terlibat*
get your act together to organize yourself so that you can do sth properly □ *membuat sst dgn baik*: *If he doesn't get his act together he's going to lose his job.*
a hard act to follow ⊃ hard¹
in the act (of doing sth) while doing sth, especially sth wrong □ *ketika sedang (melakukan sst)*: *She caught him in the act of looking through the papers on her desk.*

act² /ækt/ *verb* **1** [I] act (on sth) to do sth; to take action □ *bertindak; ambil peduli*: *The doctor knew he had to act quickly to save the child.* ♦ *I'm always giving my brother advice but he never acts on* (= as a result of) *it.* **2** [I] to behave in the way that is mentioned □ *berkelakuan; berpura-pura*: *Stop acting like a child!* ♦ *Although she was trying to act cool, I could see she was really upset.* ♦ *Ali's acting strangely today—what's wrong with him?* **3** [I,T] to perform in a play or film □ *berlakon*: *I acted in a play at school.* ♦ *He's always wanted to act the part of Hamlet.* ♦ *He hasn't really hurt himself—he's just acting* (= pretending)*!*
4 [I] act as sth to perform a particular function □ *bertindak; berfungsi*: *The man we met on the plane to Tokyo was kind enough to act as our guide.* ♦ *The elephant's trunk acts as a nose, a hand and an arm.*

acting¹ /ˈæktɪŋ/ *noun* [U] the art or profession of performing in plays or films □ *seni lakon*
⊃ picture on page P3

acting² /ˈæktɪŋ/ *adj* [only before a noun] doing the job mentioned for a short time □ *pemangku*: *Jane Green will be the acting director while Henry King is away.*

action /ˈækʃn/ *noun*
▶ DOING STH **1** [U] doing things, often for a particular purpose □ *tindakan*: *Now is the time for action.* ♦ *If we don't take action quickly it'll be too late!* **OPP** inaction **2** [C] something that you do □ *tindakan; perbuatan*: *The doctor's quick action saved the child's life.* ♦ *They should*

activate → adage

be judged by their actions, not what they say. ◆ note at **act**
▸IN COURT **3** [C,U] the process of settling an argument in a court of law □ *tindakan*: *He is going to take legal action against the hospital.*
▸IN WAR **4** [U] fighting in a war □ *pertempuran*: *Their son was killed in action.*
▸IN STORY/FILM/PLAY **5** [sing] the most important events in a story, film or play □ *peristiwa penting atau bahagian utama*: *The action takes place in London.*
▸EXCITING EVENTS **6** [U] exciting things that happen □ *perkara atau kegiatan menarik; aksi*: *There's not much action in this boring town.* ◆ *I like films with lots of action.* ◆ *an action-packed film*
▸EFFECT **7** [sing] the effect that one substance has on another □ *tindakan*: *They're studying the action of sunlight on the skin.*
IDM **in action** in operation; while working or doing sth □ *beroperasi; sedang melakukan sst*: *We shall have a chance to see their new team in action next week.*
into action into operation □ *melaksanakan; menjalankan*: *We'll put the plan into action immediately.*
out of action not able to do the usual things; not working □ *rosak*: *The coffee machine's out of action again.*

activate /ˈæktɪveɪt/ verb [T] to make sth start working □ *mengaktifkan; menghidupkan*: *A slight movement can activate the car alarm.*

active /ˈæktɪv/ adj **1** involved in activity □ *cergas; aktif*: *My grandfather is very active for his age.* ◆ *I have a very active social life.* ◆ *I was at the meeting but I didn't take an active part in the discussion.* **SYN** **lively** **OPP** **inactive** **2** that produces an effect; that is in operation □ *aktif*: *an active volcano* (= one that can still explode). **3** used about the form of a verb or a sentence when the subject of the sentence performs the action of the verb □ *aktif (kk)*: *In the sentence 'The dog bit him', the verb is active.*

HELP You can also say: 'The verb is in the active'.

◆ look at **passive** ▶**actively** adv: *She is actively looking for a job.*

activist /ˈæktɪvɪst/ noun [C] a person who takes action to cause political or social change, usually as a member of a group □ *aktivis*: *a protest by environmental activists*

activity /ækˈtɪvəti/ noun (pl **activities**) **1** [U] a situation in which there is a lot of action or movement □ *kesibukan; aktiviti*: *The house was full of activity on the morning of the wedding.* **OPP** **inactivity** **2** [C] something that you do, usually regularly and for enjoyment □ *kegiatan*: *The hotel offers a range of leisure activities.* ◆ note at **act**

actor /ˈæktə(r)/ noun [C] a person whose job is to act in a play, film or on TV □ *pelakon; seniman* ◆ note at **theatre**: *one of the country's leading actors*

actress /ˈæktrəs/ noun [C] a woman whose job is to act in a play, film or on TV □ *pelakon wanita; seniwati*: *In 1940 he married actress Jane Wyman.*

MORE Many women now prefer to be called **actors**.

◆ note at **theatre**

actual /ˈæktʃuəl/ adj [only before a noun] real; that happened □ *sebenar*: *The actual damage to the car was not as great as we had feared.* ◆ *They seemed to be good friends but in actual fact they hated each other.*

actually /ˈæktʃuəli/ adv **1** really; in fact □ *benar-benar*: *You don't actually believe her, do you?* ◆ *I can't believe that I'm actually going to America!* **2** although it may seem strange □ *betul-betul*: *He actually expected me to cook his meal for him!*

HELP **Actually** is often used in conversation to get somebody's attention or to correct somebody politely: *Actually, I wanted to show you something. Have you got a minute?* ◆ *We aren't married, actually.* ◆ *I don't agree about the book. I think it's rather good, actually.*

HELP In English **actually** does not mean 'at the present time'. We use **currently**, **at present** or **at the moment** instead: *He's currently working on an article about China.* ◆ *I'm studying for my exams at present.*

acumen /ˈækjəmən/ noun [U] the ability to understand and decide things quickly and well □ *acumen; kepintaran; ketajaman (fikiran)*: *business/commercial/financial acumen*

acupuncture /ˈækjupʌŋktʃə(r)/ noun [U] a way of treating an illness or stopping pain by putting thin needles into parts of the body □ *akupunktur*

acute /əˈkjuːt/ adj **1** very serious; very great □ *genting; runcing*: *an acute shortage of food* ◆ *acute pain* **2** (used about an illness) becoming dangerous very quickly □ *akut; mendadak*: *acute appendicitis* ◆ look at **chronic** **3** (used about feelings or the senses) very strong □ *tajam*: *Dogs have an acute sense of smell.* ◆ *acute hearing* **4** showing that you are able to understand things easily □ *tajam*: *The report contains some acute observations.* ▶**acutely** adv

a͵cute ˈangle noun [C] an angle of less than 90° □ *sudut tirus* ◆ look at **obtuse angle**, **right angle**

AD /ˌeɪ ˈdiː/ abbr (from Latin) **anno domini**; used in dates to show the number of years after the time when Christians believe Jesus Christ was born □ *TM (Tahun Masihi)*: *in (the year) AD 44* ◆ *in 44 AD* ◆ look at **BC**

ad /æd/ (informal) = **advertisement** □ *iklan*: *I saw your ad in the local paper.*

adage /ˈædɪdʒ/ noun [C] a common phrase expressing sth that is always true about people or the world □ *pepatah*

adamant /ˈædəmənt/ adj (formal) very sure; refusing to change your mind □ *tegas; berkeras*: *She was adamant that she would not come.* ▶**adamantly** adv

Adam's apple /ˌædəmz ˈæpl/ noun [C] the lump at the front of the throat that sticks out, particularly in men, and moves up and down when you swallow □ *halkum*

adapt /əˈdæpt/ verb **1** [T] **adapt sth (for sth)** to change sth so that you can use it in a different situation □ *mengubah suai; mengadaptasi*: *The bus was adapted for disabled people.* ◆ *The teacher adapts the coursebook to suit the needs of her students.* **2** [I,T] **adapt (yourself) (to sth)** to change your behaviour because the situation you are in has changed □ *menyesuaikan diri*: *They were quick to adapt (themselves) to the new system.*

adaptable /əˈdæptəbl/ adj able to change to suit new situations □ *dpt menyesuaikan diri*

adaptation /ˌædæpˈteɪʃn/ noun **1** [C] a play or film that is based on a novel, etc □ *pengubahsuaian; pengadaptasian*: *a screen adaptation of Jane Austen's 'Pride and Prejudice'* **2** [U] the state or process of changing to suit a new situation □ *penyesuaian*

adapted /əˈdæptɪd/ adj having all the necessary qualities to do sth □ *sesuai*: *Chickens are poorly adapted for flight.*

adaptor (also **adapter**) /əˈdæptə(r)/ noun [C] **1** a device that allows you to connect more than one piece of electrical equipment to a **socket** (= an electricity supply point) □ *penyesuai palam* **2** a device for connecting pieces of electrical equipment that were not designed to be fitted together □ *penyesuai; adaptor*

add /æd/ verb **1** [I,T] **add (sth) (to sth)** to put sth together with sth else, so that you increase the size, number, value, etc □ *menambah*: *I added a couple more items to the shopping list.* ◆ *The noise of the crowd added to the excitement of the race.* **2** [I,T] to put numbers or amounts together so that you get a total □ *campur; mencampur; menjumlah*: *If you add 3 and 3 together, you get 6.* ◆ *Add £8 to the total, to cover postage and packing.* ◆ *Ronaldo cost more than all the other players added together.* ◆ *Don't ask me to work it out—I can't add.* **OPP** subtract

> **MORE** We often use the word **plus** when we add two numbers: *2 plus 2 is 4.*

3 [T] to say sth more □ *tambah*: *'By the way, please don't tell anyone I phoned you,' she added.*

PHR V **add sth on (to sth)** to include sth □ *ditambah*: *10% will be added on to your bill as a service charge.*

add up to seem to be a true explanation □ *munasabah*: *I'm sorry, but your story just doesn't add up.*

add (sth) up to find the total of several numbers □ *menjumlahkan*: *The waiter hadn't added up the bill correctly.*

add up to sth to have as a total □ *berjumlah*: *How much does all the shopping add up to?*

added /ˈædɪd/ adj in addition to what is usual; extra □ *tambahan*: *milk with added vitamins*

ˈadded to prep in addition to sth; as well as □ *selain (itu)*

adder /ˈædə(r)/ noun [C] a small poisonous snake □ *ular kapak*

addict /ˈædɪkt/ noun [C] a person who cannot stop taking or doing sth harmful □ *penagih*: *a drug addict* ▶**addicted** /əˈdɪktɪd/ adj **addicted (to sth)**: *He is addicted to computer games.* **SYN** hooked ▶**addiction** noun [C,U]: *the problem of teenage drug addiction*

addictive /əˈdɪktɪv/ adj difficult to stop taking or doing □ *yg menyebabkan ketagihan*: *Jogging is highly addictive.* ◆ *an addictive game*

addition /əˈdɪʃn/ noun **1** [U] adding sth, especially two or more numbers □ *penjumlahan; kira-kira campur*: *children learning addition and subtraction* ⊃ look at **subtraction 2** [C] **an addition (to sth)** a person or thing that is added to sth □ *tambahan*: *They've got a new addition to the family* (= another child).
IDM **in addition (to sth)** as well as □ *selain drpd*: *She speaks five foreign languages in addition to English.*

additional /əˈdɪʃənl/ adj added □ *tambahan*: *a small additional charge for the use of the swimming pool* **SYN** extra ▶**additionally** /-ʃənəli/ adv

additive /ˈædətɪv/ noun [C] a substance that is added to sth in small amounts for a special purpose □ *bahan tambahan*: *food additives* (= to add colour or flavour)

address[1] /əˈdres/ noun [C] **1** the number of the building and the name of the street and place where sb lives or works □ *alamat*: *Let me give you my home/business address.* ◆ *She no longer lives at this address.* ◆ *Please inform the office of any change of address.* ◆ *an address book* (= a small book where you keep the addresses of people you know or a computer file where you store email and Internet addresses) ⊃ picture at **letter 2** a series of words and/or numbers that tells you where you can find sth using a computer □ *alamat*: *What's your email address?* **3** a formal speech that is given to an audience □ *ucapan*: *tonight's televised presidential address*

IDM **(of) no fixed abode/address** ⊃ **fixed**

address[2] /əˈdres/ verb [T]
▶WRITE ON LETTER **1 address sth (to sb/sth)** to write the name and address of the person you are sending a letter, etc. to □ *mengalamatkan; membubuh alamat*: *The package was returned because it had been wrongly addressed.*
▶MAKE SPEECH **2** to make an important speech to an audience □ *berucap*: *to address a meeting*
▶COMMUNICATE **3** (formal) **address sth to sb** to make a comment, etc. to sb □ *mengemukakan*: *Kindly address any complaints you have to the manager.*

adept → admiration

▶USE NAME **4 address sb as sth** to talk or write to sb using a particular name or title □ *memanggil*: *She prefers to be addressed as 'Ms'.*
▶DEAL WITH PROBLEM **5** (*formal*) **address (yourself to) sth** to try to deal with a problem, etc. □ *memberikan perhatian kpd*: *The government is finally addressing the question of corruption.*

adept /əˈdept/ *adj* **adept (at sth)** very good or skilful at sth □ *mahir; cekap* **SYN** skilful **OPP** inept

adequate /ˈædɪkwət/ *adj* **1** enough for what you need □ *cukup*: *Make sure you take an adequate supply of water with you.* **2** just good enough; acceptable □ *memadai*: *Your work is adequate but I'm sure you could do better.* **OPP** for both meanings **inadequate** ▶**adequacy** /ˈædɪkwəsi/ *noun* [U] ▶**adequately** *adv*: *The mystery has never been adequately explained.*

adhere /ədˈhɪə(r)/ *verb* [I] (*formal*) **adhere (to sth)** to stick firmly to sth □ *melekat*: *Wash the wall first, or the paint will not adhere to the surface.*
PHR V adhere to sth to continue to support an idea, etc.; to follow a rule □ *berpegang teguh pada sst*

adherent /ədˈhɪərənt/ *noun* [C] a person who supports a particular idea □ *penyokong; pengikut* **SYN** supporter ▶**adherence** *noun* [U]

adhesive¹ /ədˈhiːsɪv/ *noun* [C,U] a substance that makes things stick together □ *perekat*: *a fast-drying adhesive*

adhesive² /ədˈhiːsɪv/ *adj* that can stick, or can cause two things to stick together □ *berperekat*: *He sealed the parcel with adhesive tape.* **SYN** sticky

ad hoc /ˌæd ˈhɒk/ *adj* made or done suddenly for a particular purpose □ *ad hoc; sst yg dibuat tanpa rancangan utk memenuhi keperluan tertentu*: *They set up an ad hoc committee to discuss the matter.* ♦ *Staff training takes place occasionally on an ad hoc basis.*

adjacent /əˈdʒeɪsnt/ *adj* **adjacent (to sth)** (used about an area, a place or a building) next to or close to sth □ *bersebelahan; berdekatan*: *She works in the office adjacent to mine.* ♦ *There was a fire in the adjacent building.*

adjectival /ˌædʒekˈtaɪvl/ *adj* that contains or is used like an adjective □ *(berkenaan dgn) adjektif*: *The adjectival form of 'smell' is 'smelly'.*

adjective /ˈædʒɪktɪv/ *noun* [C] a word that tells you more about a noun, for example *big* and *clever* in *a big house* and *a clever idea* □ *adjektif; kata sifat*

adjoining /əˈdʒɔɪnɪŋ/ *adj* next to or nearest to sth □ *bersebelahan*: *A scream came from the adjoining room.*

adjourn /əˈdʒɜːn/ *verb* [I,T] to stop a meeting, trial, etc. for a short time and start it again later □ *menghentikan sementara; menunda*: *The meeting adjourned for lunch.* ♦ *The trial was adjourned until the following week.* ▶**adjournment** *noun* [C,U]

adjudicate /əˈdʒuːdɪkeɪt/ *verb* [I,T] (*written*) to act as an official judge in a competition or to decide who is right when two people or groups disagree about sth □ *menghakimkan*

adjudicator /əˈdʒuːdɪkeɪtə(r)/ *noun* [C] a person who acts as a judge, for example in a competition □ *hakim; pengadil*

adjust /əˈdʒʌst/ *verb* **1** [T] to change sth slightly, especially because it is not in the right position □ *melaraskan; membetulkan*: *The brakes on my bicycle need adjusting.* ♦ *The seat can be adjusted to different positions.* **2** [I] **adjust (to sth)** to get used to new conditions or a new situation □ *menyesuaikan diri*: *She found it hard to adjust to working at night.* ▶**adjustment** *noun* [C,U]: *We'll just make a few minor adjustments and the room will look perfect.*

adjustable /əˈdʒʌstəbl/ *adj* that can be adjusted □ *dpt dilaraskan*: *an adjustable chair*

ad lib /ˌæd ˈlɪb/ *adj, adv* done or spoken without preparation □ *secara spontan; tanpa persediaan*: *She had to speak ad lib because she couldn't find her notes.* ▶**ad lib** *verb* [I] (**ad libbing; ad libbed**): *The singer forgot the words so he had to ad lib.*

administer /ədˈmɪnɪstə(r)/ *verb* [T] (*formal*) **1** to control or manage sth □ *mentadbir; mengurus* **2** to give sb sth, especially medicine □ *memberi*

administration /ədˌmɪnɪˈstreɪʃn/ *noun* **1** (*BrE also informal* **admin** /ˈædmɪn/) [U] the process or act of managing sth, for example a system, an organization or a business □ *pengurusan*: *The administration of a large project like this is very complicated.* ♦ *A lot of the teachers' time is taken up by admin.* **2** [sing] the group of people or part of a company that organizes or controls sth □ *pentadbiran*: *the hospital administration* **3** *often* **the Administration** [C] the government of a country, especially the US □ *pentadbiran*: *the Obama Administration*

administrative /ədˈmɪnɪstrətɪv/ *adj* connected with the organization of a country, business, etc., and the way in which it is managed □ *pentadbiran; tadbir*: *London is still the most important administrative centre in Britain.*

administrator /ədˈmɪnɪstreɪtə(r)/ *noun* [C] a person whose job is to organize or manage a system, business, etc. □ *pentadbir*

admirable /ˈædmərəbl/ *adj* (*formal*) that you admire; excellent □ *(yg) mengagumkan* ▶**admirably** /-əbli/ *adv*: *She dealt with the problem admirably.*

admiral /ˈædmərəl/ *noun* [C] the most important officer in the navy □ *laksamana*

admiration /ˌædməˈreɪʃn/ *noun* [U] **admiration (for/of sb/sth)** a feeling of liking and respecting sb/sth very much □ *kekaguman*: *I have great admiration for what he's done.*

[I] **intransitive**, a verb which has no object: *He laughed.*   [T] **transitive**, a verb which has an object: *He ate an apple.*

admire /əd'maɪə(r)/ verb [T] **admire sb/sth (for sth/doing sth)** to respect or like sb/sth very much; to look at sb/sth with pleasure □ *mengagumi; menikmati (pemandangan, dsb)*: Everyone admired the way he dealt with the problem. ♦ I've always admired her for being such a wonderful mother. ♦ We stopped at the top of the hill to admire the view.

admirer /əd'maɪərə(r)/ noun [C] a person who admires sb/sth □ *peminat*: I've always been a great admirer of her books.

admiring /əd'maɪərɪŋ/ adj feeling or expressing admiration □ *terasa kagum atau minat* ▶**admiringly** adv

admissible /əd'mɪsəbl/ adj that can be allowed or accepted, especially in a court of law □ *yg boleh diterima; yg dibenarkan*: admissible evidence **OPP** inadmissible

admission /əd'mɪʃn/ noun 1 [C,U] **admission (to sth)** the act of allowing sb to enter a school, club, public place, etc □ *kemasukan*: Admissions to British universities have increased by 15% this year. ⊃ look at **entrance** 2 [C] a statement that admits that sth is true □ *pengakuan* 3 [U] the amount of money that you have to pay to enter a place □ *bayaran masuk*: The museum charges half-price admission on Mondays.

admit /əd'mɪt/ verb (admitting; admitted) 1 [I,T] **admit sth; admit to sth/doing sth; admit (that …)** to agree that sth unpleasant is true or that you have done sth wrong □ *mengaku*: You should admit your mistake. ♦ After trying four times to pass the exam, I finally **admitted defeat**. ♦ She admitted having broken the computer. ♦ He refused to admit to the theft. ♦ I have to admit (that) I was wrong. **OPP** deny 2 [T] **admit sb/sth (into/to sth)** to allow sb/sth to enter; to take sb into a place □ *membenarkan atau menerima masuk; dimasukkan*: He was admitted to hospital with suspected appendicitis.

admittance /əd'mɪtns/ noun [U] (formal) being allowed to enter a place; the right to enter □ *kebenaran masuk*: The journalist tried to gain admittance to the minister's office.

admittedly /əd'mɪtɪdli/ adv it must be admitted (that …) □ *(namun) diakui*: The work is very interesting. Admittedly, I do get rather tired.

ado /ə'duː/ noun
IDM without further/more ado (old-fashioned) without delaying; immediately □ *tanpa melengahkan masa*

adolescence /ˌædə'lesns/ noun [U] the period of sb's life between being a child and becoming an adult, between the ages of about 13 and 17 □ *zaman remaja* **SYN** puberty

adolescent /ˌædə'lesnt/ noun [C] a young person who is no longer a child and not yet an adult, between the ages of about 13 and 17 □ *remaja*: the problems of adolescents ♦ an adolescent daughter ⊃ look at **teenager**

adopt /ə'dɒpt/ verb [I,T] 1 to take a child into your family and treat them as your own child by law □ *mengambil anak angkat*: They couldn't have children so they adopted. ♦ They're hoping to adopt a child. 2 [T] to take and use sth □ *mengambil dan menggunakan*: What approach did you adopt when dealing with the problem? ▶**adopted** adj: an adopted child ▶**adoption** noun [C,U]: The number of adoptions has risen in the past year (= the number of children being adopted). ⊃ note at **child**

adoptive /ə'dɒptɪv/ adj (used about parents) having legally taken a child to live with them as part of their family □ *(ibu atau bapa) angkat*: the baby's adoptive parents

adorable /ə'dɔːrəbl/ adj (used about children or animals) very attractive □ *menawan* **SYN** lovely

adore /ə'dɔː(r)/ verb [T] 1 to love and admire sb/sth very much □ *sayang; menyayangi*: Kim adores her older sister. 2 to like sth very much □ *sangat suka*: I adore his music! ▶**adoration** /ˌædə'reɪʃn/ noun [U] ▶**adoring** adj: his adoring fans

adorn /ə'dɔːn/ verb [T] **adorn sth (with sth)** to add sth in order to make a thing or person more attractive or beautiful □ *menghiasi* ▶**adornment** noun [C,U]

adrenaline (also **adrenalin**) /ə'drenəlɪn/ noun [U] a substance that your body produces when you are very angry, frightened or excited and that makes your heart go faster □ *adrenalin*

adrift /ə'drɪft/ adj [not before a noun] (used about a boat) not tied to anything or controlled by anyone □ *hanyut*

adulation /ˌædju'leɪʃn/ noun [U] (formal) admiration for sb, especially when this is greater than is necessary □ *penyanjungan; pemujian (secara berlebih-lebihan)*

adult /'ædʌlt; ə'dʌlt/ noun [C] a person or an animal that is fully grown □ *orang dewasa*: This film is suitable for both adults and children. **SYN** grown-up ▶**adult** adj: She was born in America but has spent her adult life in Chile.

adultery /ə'dʌltəri/ noun [U] (formal) sex between a married person and sb who is not their wife/husband □ *zina (hubungan seks antara sso suami atau isteri dgn orang yg bukan pasangannya)*: He was accused of committing adultery. ▶**adulterous** /ə'dʌltərəs/ adj: an adulterous relationship

adulthood /'ædʌlthʊd; ə'dʌlt-/ noun [U] the time in your life when you are an adult □ *zaman dewasa*

advance[1] /əd'vɑːns/ noun 1 [C, usually sing] forward movement □ *kemaraan*: the army's advance towards the border **OPP** retreat 2 [C,U] progress in sth □ *kemajuan*: advances in computer technology 3 [C] an amount of money that is paid to sb before the time when it is usually paid □ *wang pendahuluan*: She asked for an advance on her salary.

CONSONANTS p **p**en b **b**ad t **t**ea d **d**id k **c**at g **g**ot tʃ **ch**in dʒ **J**une f **f**all v **v**an θ **th**in

advance → advice columnist

IDM **in advance (of sth)** before a particular time or event □ *dahulu*: *You should book tickets for the concert well in advance.*

advance² /əd'vɑːns/ *verb* 1 [I] to move forward □ *mara*: *The army advanced towards the city.* **OPP** **retreat** 2 [I,T] to make progress or help sth make progress □ *maju; meningkat*: *Our research has not advanced much recently.*

advance³ /əd'vɑːns/ *adj* [only *before* a noun] that happens before sth □ *awal; terdahulu*: *There was no advance warning of the earthquake.*

advanced /əd'vɑːnst/ *adj* 1 highly developed □ *maju*: *a country that is not very advanced industrially* 2 of a high level □ *lanjutan*: *an advanced English class*

ad'vanced level (*formal*) = **A level**

advancement /əd'vɑːnsmənt/ *noun* (*formal*) 1 [U,C] the process of helping sth to make progress or succeed; the progress that is made □ *kemajuan; perkembangan; pembangunan*: *the advancement of knowledge/education/science* 2 [U] progress in a job, social class, etc. □ *peningkatan*: *There are good opportunities for advancement if you have the right skills.*

advantage /əd'vɑːntɪdʒ/ *noun* 1 [C] **an advantage (over sb)** something that may help you to do better than other people □ *kelebihan*: *Her experience gave her an advantage over the other applicants.* ◆ *Living abroad means* **he has the advantage** *of being fluent in two languages.* ◆ *Some runners try to gain an unfair advantage by taking drugs.* 2 [C,U] something that helps you or that will bring you a good result □ *kebaikan; manfaat; faedah*: *Each of these systems has its advantages and disadvantages.* ◆ *The traffic is so bad here that* **there is no advantage in** *having a car.* ⊃ look at **pro** **OPP** for both meanings **disadvantage**

IDM **take advantage of sb/sth** 1 to make good or full use of sth □ *menggunakan (peluang, kesempatan, dsb)*: *We should take full advantage of these low prices while they last.* 2 to make use of sb/sth in a way that is unfair or dishonest in order to get what you want □ *mempergunakan; mengeksploitasi*: *You shouldn't let him take advantage of you like this.*

advantageous /ˌædvən'teɪdʒəs/ *adj* that will help you or bring you a good result □ *menguntungkan; berfaedah*

advent /'ædvent/ *noun* 1 [sing] (*formal*) **the advent of sth/sb** the coming of an important event, person, new technology, etc. □ *kedatangan; ketibaan* 2 **Advent** [U] (in the Christian year) the period that includes the four Sundays before Christmas □ *Advent*

adventure /əd'ventʃə(r)/ *noun* [C,U] an experience or event that is very unusual, exciting or dangerous □ *pengalaman atau peristiwa yg menguja, luar biasa atau berbahaya*: *Our journey through the jungle was quite an adventure!* ◆ *She left home to travel, hoping for excitement and adventure.*

adventurous /əd'ventʃərəs/ *adj* 1 (used about a person) liking to try new things or have adventures □ *suka mencuba sst yg baharu*: *I'm not an adventurous cook—I like to stick to recipes I know.* 2 involving adventure □ *melibatkan aktiviti yg menguja atau mendebarkan*: *For a more adventurous holiday try mountain climbing.*

adverb /'ædvɜːb/ *noun* [C] a word that adds more information about place, time, manner, cause or degree to a verb, an adjective, a phrase or another adverb □ *adverba; kata keterangan*: *In 'speak slowly', 'extremely funny', 'arrive late' and 'too quickly', 'slowly', 'extremely', 'late', 'too' and 'quickly' are adverbs.* ▸**adverbial** /æd'vɜːbiəl/ *adj*: *'Very quickly indeed' is an adverbial phrase.* ⊃ note at **sudden**

adversary /'ædvəsəri/ *noun* [C] (*pl* adversaries) (*formal*) an enemy, or an opponent in a competition □ *musuh; lawan*

adverse /'ædvɜːs/ *adj* (*formal*) making sth difficult for sb □ *buruk; menyukarkan*: *Our flight was cancelled because of adverse weather conditions.* **OPP** **favourable** ⊃ look at **unfavourable** ▸**adversely** *adv*

adversity /əd'vɜːsəti/ *noun* [C,U] (*pl* adversities) (*formal*) difficulties or problems □ *kesusahan*

advert /'ædvɜːt/ (*BrE informal*) = **advertisement** □ *iklan*: *adverts on television*

advertise /'ædvətaɪz/ *verb* 1 [I,T] **advertise sth (as sth)** to put information in a newspaper, on the Internet, in a public place, on TV, etc. in order to persuade people to buy sth, to interest them in a new job, etc. □ *mengiklankan*: *a poster advertising a new type of biscuit* ◆ *The job was advertised in the local newspapers.* ◆ *It's very expensive to advertise on TV.* 2 [I] **advertise (for sb/sth)** to say publicly in a newspaper, on a sign, etc. that you need sb to do a particular job, want to buy sth, etc □ *mengiklan utk mendapatkan sso/sst*: *The shop is advertising for a part-time sales assistant.* ▸**advertiser** *noun* [C] ▸**advertising** *noun* [U]: *The magazine gets a lot of money from advertising.* ◆ *an advertising campaign*

advertisement /əd'vɜːtɪsmənt/ (also *informal* **ad, advert**) *noun* [C] a piece of information in a newspaper, on TV, a picture on a wall, etc. that tries to persuade people to buy sth, to interest them in a new job, etc □ *iklan*: *an advertisement for a new brand of shampoo* ◆ *to put an advertisement in a newspaper*

advice /əd'vaɪs/ *noun* [U] an opinion that you give sb about what they should do □ *nasihat*: *She took her teacher's advice and worked hard for the exam.* ◆ *Let me give you some advice …*

GRAMMAR Advice is uncountable. We say **a piece of advice** (not 'an advice') and **a lot of advice** (not 'advices').

ad'vice columnist (*AmE*) = **agony aunt/uncle**

advisable /əd'vaɪzəbl/ adj (formal) that is a good thing to do; sensible □ *lebih baik; ada baiknya*: *It is advisable to reserve a seat.* **OPP** inadvisable

advise /əd'vaɪz/ verb 1 [I,T] advise sb (to do sth); advise (sb) (against sth/against doing sth) to tell sb what you think they should do □ *menasihatkan*: *I would strongly advise you to take the job.* ◆ *They advised us not to travel on a Friday.* ◆ *The newspaper article advised against eating too much meat.* ◆ *He did what the doctor advised.* ◆ *She advises the Government on economic affairs.* 2 [T] to officially tell sb sth □ *memberitahu; memaklumkan*: *We would like to advise you that the goods are now ready for collection.* **SYN** inform

adviser (*AmE* advisor) /əd'vaɪzə(r)/ noun [C] a person who gives advice to a company, government, etc □ *penasihat*: *an adviser on economic affairs*

advisory /əd'vaɪzəri/ adj giving advice only; not having the power to make decisions □ *(sebagai) penasihat*

advocate¹ /'ædvəkeɪt/ verb [T] (formal) to recommend or say that you support a particular plan or action □ *mengesyorkan; menyokong*

advocate² /'ædvəkət/ noun [C] 1 an advocate (of sth) a person who supports a particular plan or action, especially in public □ *penyokong* 2 a lawyer who defends sb in a court of law □ *peguam bela*

aerial¹ /'eəriəl/ (*AmE* antenna) noun [C] a long metal stick on a building, car, etc. that receives radio or TV signals □ *aerial* ⊃ picture on **page P8**

aerial² /'eəriəl/ adj from or in the air □ *(dr atau di) udara*: *an aerial photograph of the town*

aerobics /eə'rəʊbɪks/ noun [U] physical exercises that people do to music □ *aerobik*: *I do aerobics twice a week to keep fit.*

aerodynamics /ˌeərəʊdaɪ'næmɪks/ noun [U] the scientific study of the way that things move through the air □ *aerodinamik* ▶ **aerodynamic** adj: *the aerodynamic design of a racing car*

aeroplane /'eərəpleɪn/ noun [C] = plane¹(1) □ *kapal terbang*: *the noise of an aeroplane flying overhead*

aerosol /'eərəsɒl/ noun [C] a container in which a liquid substance is kept under pressure. When you press a button the liquid comes out in a fine spray. □ *aerosol* ⊃ picture at **spray**

aerospace /'eərəʊspeɪs/ noun [U] the industry of building aircraft, vehicles and equipment to be sent into space □ *aeroangkasa*

aesthetic (*AmE* also esthetic) /iːs'θetɪk; es-/ adj concerned with beauty or art □ *estetik*: *The columns are there for purely aesthetic reasons* (= only to look beautiful). ▶ **aesthetically** (*AmE* also esthetically) /-kli/ adv: *The design is aesthetically pleasing as well as practical.*

aesthetics (*AmE* also esthetics) /iːs'θetɪks; /- noun [U] the study of beauty, especially in art □ *estetik*

afar /ə'fɑː(r)/ adv
IDM from afar (*written*) from a long distance away □ *dr jauh*

affable /'æfəbl/ adj pleasant, friendly and easy to talk to □ *peramah; mudah mesra* **SYN** genial ▶ **affably** /-əbli/ adv

affair /ə'feə(r)/ noun 1 affairs [pl] important personal, business, national, etc. matters □ *hal ehwal; urusan*: *the minister for foreign affairs* ◆ *current affairs* (= the political and social events that are happening at the present time) 2 [C] an event or a situation □ *hal; perkara*: *The whole affair has been extremely unpleasant.* 3 [C] a sexual relationship between two people, usually when at least one of them is married to sb else □ *hubungan sulit*: *She's having an affair with her boss.* 4 [sing] something private that you do not want other people to know about □ *urusan*: *What happened between us is my affair. I don't want to discuss it.*
IDM state of affairs ⊃ state¹

affect /ə'fekt/ verb [T] 1 make sb/sth change in a particular way; to influence sb/sth □ *mempengaruhi; menjejaskan*: *Her personal problems seem to be affecting her work.* ◆ *This disease affects the brain.* ⊃ note at **influence** 2 to make sb feel very sad, angry, etc □ *terkilan; terharu*: *The whole community was affected by the tragedy.*

> **HELP** Affect or effect? Notice that **affect** is a verb and **effect** is a noun: *Smoking can affect your health.* ◆ *Smoking can have a bad effect on your health.*

affected /ə'fektɪd/ adj (used about a person or their behaviour) not natural or sincere □ *dibuat-buat; tdk ikhlas* **OPP** unaffected ▶ **affectation** /ˌæfek'teɪʃn/ noun [C,U]

affection /ə'fekʃn/ noun [C,U] (an) affection (for/towards sb/sth) a feeling of loving or liking sb/sth □ *kasih; sayang*: *Mark felt great affection for his sister.*

affectionate /ə'fekʃənət/ adj showing that you love or like sb very much □ *penyayang; mesra*: *a very affectionate child* **SYN** loving ▶ **affectionately** adv

affidavit /ˌæfə'deɪvɪt/ noun [C] (technical) a written statement that you swear is true, and that can be used as evidence in court □ *afidavit*

affiliate /ə'fɪlieɪt/ verb [T, usually passive] affiliate sth (to sth) to connect an organization to a larger organization □ *bergabung*: *Our local club is affiliated to the national association.* ▶ **affiliated** adj ▶ **affiliation** /əˌfɪli'eɪʃn/ noun [C,U]

affinity /ə'fɪnəti/ noun [C,U] (pl affinities) 1 (an) affinity (for/with sb/sth) a strong feeling that you like and understand sb/sth, usually because you feel similar to them or it in some way □ *kecenderungan*: *He had always had an affinity for wild and lonely places.* 2 (an) affinity (with sb/sth); (an) affinity (between A and B) a

| VOWELS | iː see | i any | ɪ sit | e ten | æ hat | ɑː father | ɒ got | ɔː saw | ʊ put | uː too | u usual |

affirm → after-effect

similar quality in two or more people or things □ *kesamaan*

affirm /əˈfɜːm/ *verb* [T] (*formal*) to say formally or clearly that sth is true or that you support sth strongly □ *mengaskan; mengesahkan* ▸**affirmation** /ˌæfəˈmeɪʃn/ *noun* [C,U]

affirmative /əˈfɜːmətɪv/ *adj* (*formal*) meaning 'yes' □ *bermaksud 'ya'*: *an affirmative answer*

HELP We can also say: *an answer in the affirmative*

OPP negative

affix /ˈæfɪks/ *noun* [C] a letter or group of letters added to the beginning or end of a word to change its meaning. The **prefix** *un-* in *unhappy* and the **suffix** *-less* in *careless* are both **affixes**. □ *imbuhan*

afflict /əˈflɪkt/ *verb* [T, usually passive] (*formal*) **afflict sb/sth (with sth)** to cause sb/sth to suffer pain, sadness, etc. □ *menderitai*: *He had been afflicted with the illness since childhood.* ▸**affliction** *noun* [C,U]

affluent /ˈæfluənt/ *adj* having a lot of money □ *kaya; mewah*: *Edward comes from a very affluent family.* **SYN** wealthy ▸**affluence** *noun* [U]: *Increased exports have brought new affluence.*

afford /əˈfɔːd/ *verb* [T] (usually after *can, could* or *be able to*) **afford sth/to do sth 1** to have enough money or time to be able to do sth □ *mampu*: *We couldn't afford a car in those days.* ◆ *I've spent more than I can afford.* ⊃ note at **loan 2** to not be able to do sth or let sth happen because it would have a bad result for you □ *boleh*: *The other team is very good so we can't afford to make any mistakes.* ▸**affordable** *adj*: *affordable prices*

affront /əˈfrʌnt/ *noun* [C] **an affront (to sb/sth)** something that you say or do that is insulting to sb/sth □ *penghinaan* ▸**affront** *verb* [T, usually passive]: *She was affronted by his remarks.*

afield /əˈfiːld/ *adv*

IDM **far/farther/further afield** far away, especially from where you live or from where you are staying □ *jauh dr tempat tinggal*: *We decided to hire a car in order to explore further afield.*

afloat /əˈfləʊt/ *adj* [not before a noun] **1** on the surface of the water; not sinking □ *terapung*: *A life jacket helps you stay afloat if you fall in the water.* **2** (used about a business, an economy, etc.) having enough money to survive □ *mampu meneruskan perniagaan, dsb*

afoot /əˈfʊt/ *adj* [not before a noun] being planned or prepared □ *sedang dirancang*: *There are plans afoot to increase taxation.*

afraid /əˈfreɪd/ *adj* [not before a noun] **1 afraid (of sb/sth); afraid (of doing sth/to do sth)** feeling fear; frightened □ *takut*: *Are you afraid of dogs?* ◆ *Ben is afraid of going out after dark.* ◆ *I was too afraid to answer the door.* **2 afraid (that ...); afraid (of doing sth)** worried about sth □ *khuatir; takut*: *We were afraid that you would be angry.* ◆ *to be afraid of offending somebody* **3 afraid for sb/sth** worried that sb/sth will be harmed, lost, etc □ *bimbang*: *When I saw the gun I was afraid for my life.*

HELP **Afraid** or **frightened**? You can only use **afraid** after a verb such as 'be', but you can use **frightened** before a noun or after a verb: *a frightened animal* ◆ *The animal was afraid/frightened.*

IDM **I'm afraid (that ...)** used for saying politely that you are sorry about sth □ *ungkapan bersopan yg bermaksud kesal ttg sst*: *I'm afraid I can't come on Sunday.* ◆ *'Is the factory going to close?' 'I'm afraid so.'* ◆ *'Is this seat free?' 'I'm afraid not/it isn't.'*

afresh /əˈfreʃ/ *adv* (*formal*) again, in a new way □ *semula*: *to start afresh*

African A'merican *noun* [C] an American citizen whose family was originally from Africa □ *orang Afrika-Amerika* ▸**African American** *adj*

Afro-Caribbean /ˌæfrəʊ kærəˈbiːən/ *noun* [C] a person whose family came originally from Africa, and who was born or whose parents were born in the Caribbean □ *orang Afrika-Caribbean* ▸**Afro-Caribbean** *adj*

after /ˈɑːftə(r)/ *prep, conj, adv* **1** at a later time; following sth □ *selepas*: *Ian phoned just after 6 o'clock.* ◆ *the week after next* ◆ *I hope to arrive some time after lunch.* ◆ *They arrived at the station after the train had left.* ◆ *After we had finished our dinner, we went into the garden.* ◆ *I went out yesterday morning, and* **after that** *I was at home all day.* ◆ *That was in April. Soon after, I heard that he was ill.*

HELP It is more common to use **afterwards** at the end of a sentence: *We played tennis and went to Angela's house afterwards.*

⊃ note at **then 2 ... after ...** repeated many times or continuing for a long time □ *demi; berkali-kali*: *day after day of hot weather* ◆ *I've told the children time after time not to do that.* **3** following or behind sb/sth □ *selepas; di belakang*: *Shut the door after you.* ◆ *C comes after B in the alphabet.* **4** as a result of sth □ *setelah; selepas*: *After the way he behaved, I won't invite him here again.* **5** looking for or trying to catch or get sb/sth □ *mencari; mengejar*: *The police were after him.* ◆ *Nicky is after a job in advertising.* **6** used when sb/sth is given the name of another person or thing □ *bersempena dgn*: *We called our son William after his grandfather.*

IDM **after all 1** used when sth is different in reality to what sb expected or thought □ *akhirnya; ... rupanya!*: *So you decided to come after all!* (= I thought you weren't going to come) **2** used for reminding sb of a certain fact □ *lagipun*: *She can't understand. After all, she's only two.*

'after-effect *noun* [C] an unpleasant result of sth that comes some time later □ *akibat susulan*

aftermath /ˈɑːftəmæθ; -mɑːθ/ noun [sing] a situation that is the result of an important or unpleasant event □ *akibat*

afternoon /ˌɑːftəˈnuːn/ noun [C,U] the part of a day between midday and about 6 o'clock □ *tengah hari*: I'll see you tomorrow afternoon. ◆ What are you doing this afternoon? ◆ I studied all afternoon. ◆ I usually go for a walk *in the afternoon*. ◆ He goes swimming every afternoon. ◆ She arrived at 4 o'clock in the afternoon. ◆ Tom works two afternoons a week. ◆ Are you busy *on Friday afternoon*? ⊃ note at **morning**
IDM **good afternoon** (*formal*) used when you see sb for the first time in the afternoon □ *selamat tengah hari*

HELP Often we just say **Afternoon**: 'Good afternoon, Mrs Davies.' 'Afternoon, Jack.'

aftershave /ˈɑːftəʃeɪv/ noun [C,U] a liquid with a pleasant smell that men put on their faces after shaving □ *losen lepas cukur*

afterthought /ˈɑːftəθɔːt/ noun [C, usually sing] something that you think of or add to sth else at a later time □ *sst yg difikirkan kemudian; tambahan*

afterwards /ˈɑːftəwədz/ (*AmE* also **afterward**) *adv* at a later time □ *selepas itu; kemudian*: He was taken to hospital and died shortly afterwards. ◆ Afterwards, I realized I'd made a terrible mistake.

again /əˈgen; əˈgeɪn/ *adv* **1** once more; another time □ *sekali lagi; semula; lagi*: Could you say that again, please? ◆ She's out at the moment, so I'll phone again later. ◆ Don't ever do that again! **2** in the place or condition that sb/sth was in before □ *semula; kembali*: It's great to be home again. ◆ I hope you'll soon be well again. **3** in addition to sth □ *lagi*: 'Is that enough?' 'No, I'd like *half as much again*, please' (= one-and-a-half times the original amount).
IDM **again and again** many times □ *berkali-kali*: He said he was sorry again and again, but she wouldn't listen.
then/there again used to say that sth you have just said may not happen or be true □ *tetapi*: She might pass her test, but then again she might not.
yet again ⊃ **yet**

against /əˈgenst; əˈgeɪnst/ *prep* **1** being an opponent to sb/sth in a game, competition, etc., or an enemy of sb/sth in a war or fight □ *melawan; menentang*: We played football against a school from another district. **2** not agreeing with or supporting sb/sth □ *menentang*: Are you for or against the plan? ◆ She felt that everybody was against her. **OPP** **for** **3** what a law, rule, etc. says you must not do □ *melanggar*: It's against the law to buy cigarettes before you are sixteen. **4** in order to protect yourself from sb/sth □ *mencegah*: Take these pills as a precaution against malaria. **5** in the opposite direction to sth □ *melawan; menyongsong*: We had to cycle against the wind. **6** touching sb/sth for support □ *bersandar pada*: I put the ladder against the wall.

17   **aftermath → agency**

age¹ /eɪdʒ/ noun **1** [C,U] the length of time that sb has lived or that sth has existed □ *umur; usia*: Ali is seventeen *years of age*. ◆ She left school *at the age of* sixteen. ◆ Children of all ages will enjoy this film. ◆ He needs some friends of his own age.

HELP When you want to ask about somebody's age, you usually say: How old is she? and the answer can be: She's eighteen or: She's eighteen years old ◆ (but NOT She's eighteen years). Here are some examples of other ways of talking about age: I'm nearly nineteen. ◆ a girl of eighteen ◆ an eighteen-year-old girl ◆ The robber is of medium height and aged about 16 or 17.

2 [C,U] a particular period in sb's life □ *peringkat umur; masa*: a problem that often develops *in middle age* ◆ Her sons will look after her in her old age. **3** [C] a particular period of history □ *zaman*: the computer age ◆ the history of art through the ages **4** [U] the state of being old □ *tua; berumur*: a face lined with age ◆ The doctor said she *died of old age*. ⊃ look at **youth** **5 ages** [pl] (*informal*) a very long time □ *lama benar*: We had to wait (for) ages at the hospital. ◆ It's ages since I've done any exercise.
IDM **the age of consent** the age at which sb can legally agree to have sex □ *cukup dewasa*
at a tender age; at the tender age of ... ⊃ **tender¹**
come of age the age at which sb has an adult's rights and responsibilities in law □ *menjadi dewasa*: My father gave me a watch when I came of age.
feel your age ⊃ **feel¹**
under age not old enough by law to do sth □ *bawah umur*

age² /eɪdʒ/ *verb* [I,T] (**ageing** or **aging**; *pt, pp* **aged** /eɪdʒd/) to become or look old; to cause sb to look old □ *menjadi tua; kelihatan berumur*: My father seems to have aged a lot recently. ◆ I could see her illness had aged her. ◆ an ageing aunt

aged 1 /eɪdʒd/ *adj* [not before a noun] of the age mentioned □ *berumur*: The woman, aged 26, was last seen at Victoria Station. **2 the aged** /ˈeɪdʒɪd/ *noun* [pl] very old people □ *warga tua*: services for the sick and the aged

ˈage group *noun* [C] people of about the same age □ *kumpulan umur*: This club is very popular with the 20-30 age group.

ageism ((*AmE* also **agism**) /ˈeɪdʒɪzəm/ *noun* [U] unfair treatment of people because they are considered too old □ *memperlakukan sso secara tdk adil disebabkan usia tua mereka*: ageism in job advertisements ▶ **ageist** /-ɪst/ *adj*: ageist and sexist remarks ▶ **ageist** *noun* [C]

agency /ˈeɪdʒənsi/ *noun* [C] (*pl* **agencies**) **1** a business or an organization that provides a particular service □ *agensi*: an advertising agency ◆ aid agencies caring for refugees **2** (especially

[C] **countable**, a noun with a plural form: *one book, two books*   [U] **uncountable**, a noun with no plural form: *some sugar*

AmE) a government department □ *jabatan*: *the Central Intelligence Agency* (= the CIA)

agenda /əˈdʒendə/ *noun* [C] a list of matters that need to be discussed or dealt with □ *agenda*: *The first item **on the agenda** at the meeting will be security.* ♦ *The government have **set an agenda** for reform over the next ten years.*

agent /ˈeɪdʒənt/ *noun* [C] **1** a person whose job is to do business for a company or for another person □ *ejen*: *Our company's agent in Rio will meet you at the airport.* ♦ *Most actors and musicians have their own agents.* ♦ *a travel agent* ♦ *an estate agent* **2** = **secret agent**

aggravate /ˈæɡrəveɪt/ *verb* [T] **1** to make sth worse or more serious □ *menjadikan lebih buruk; menerukkan*: *She aggravated her bad back by lifting a table.* **2** (*informal*) to make sb angry or annoyed □ *membangkitkan kemarahan*: *What aggravates me is that she never listens.* ▶ **aggravation** /ˌæɡrəˈveɪʃn/ *noun* [C,U]

aggregate /ˈæɡrɪɡət/ *noun*
IDM on aggregate in total □ *jumlah; agregat*: *Our team won 3-1 on aggregate.*

aggression /əˈɡreʃn/ *noun* [U] **1** angry feelings or behaviour that make you want to attack other people □ *perasaan marah; sikap agresif*: *People often react to this kind of situation with fear or aggression.* **2** the act of starting a fight or war without reasonable cause □ *serangan; pencerobohan*

aggressive /əˈɡresɪv/ *adj* **1** ready or likely to fight or argue □ *galak; ganas*: *an aggressive dog* ♦ *Some people get aggressive after drinking alcohol.* **2** using or showing force or pressure in order to succeed □ *agresif; memaksa-maksa*: *an aggressive salesman* ▶ **aggressively** *adv*: *The boys responded aggressively when I asked them to make less noise.*

aggressor /əˈɡresə(r)/ *noun* [C] a person or country that attacks sb/sth or starts fighting first □ *penyerang; penceroboh*

aggrieved /əˈɡriːvd/ *adj* (*formal*) upset or angry □ *sakit hati; terkilan*

aghast /əˈɡɑːst/ *adj* [not before a noun] **aghast (at sth)** filled with great fear and shock when you see or hear sth □ *terkejut; tergamam*: *She stared aghast at the amount of blood.* **SYN** **horrified**

agile /ˈædʒaɪl/ *adj* able to move quickly and easily □ *tangkas; cekatan*: *Monkeys are extremely agile.* ▶ **agility** /əˈdʒɪləti/ *noun* [U]: *This sport is a test of both physical and mental agility.*

agism (*AmE*) = **ageism**

agitate /ˈædʒɪteɪt/ *verb* [I] **agitate (for/against sth)** to make other people feel very strongly about sth so that they want to help you achieve it □ *menggesa; mendesak*: *to agitate for reform*

agitated /ˈædʒɪteɪtɪd/ *adj* worried or nervous □ *gelisah; resah* ▶ **agitation** /ˌædʒɪˈteɪʃn/ *noun* [U]

AGM /ˌeɪ dʒiː ˈem/ *abbr* (*BrE*) **Annual General Meeting**; an important meeting which the members of an organization hold once a year □ *Mesyuarat Agung Tahunan*

agnostic /æɡˈnɒstɪk/ *noun* [C] a person who is not sure whether God exists or not □ *agnostik*

ago /əˈɡəʊ/ *adv* in the past; back in time from now □ *tadi; lalu; dahulu*: *Paul left ten minutes ago* (= if it is 12 o'clock now, he left at ten to twelve). ♦ *That was a long time ago.* ♦ *How long ago did it happen?* ⊃ note at **for**

> **GRAMMAR** Ago is used with the past simple tense and not the present perfect tense: *I arrived in Britain three months ago.* Compare **ago** and **before**. **Ago** means 'earlier than now' and **before** means 'earlier than then' (that is earlier than a particular time in the past): *Anne married Simon two years ago.* ♦ *They had been at school together ten years before* (= ten years before she married Simon).

agonize (also **-ise**) /ˈæɡənaɪz/ *verb* [I] to worry or think about sth for a long time □ *lama memikirkan ttg sst (yg sukar utk diputuskan, dsb)*: *to agonize over a difficult decision*

agonized (also **-ised**) /ˈæɡənaɪzd/ *adj* showing extreme pain or worry □ *(yg menunjukkan) derita atau kesakitan*: *an agonized cry*

agonizing (also **-ising**) /ˈæɡənaɪzɪŋ/ *adj* causing extreme worry or pain □ *(yg) amat menyukarkan atau menyeksa*: *an agonizing choice* ♦ *an agonizing headache*

agony /ˈæɡəni/ *noun* [C,U] (*pl* **agonies**) great pain or suffering □ *azab; sengsara*: *to be/scream in agony*

ˈagony aunt (*masc* **ˈagony uncle**) (*AmE* **adˈvice columnist**) *noun* [C] a person who writes in a newspaper or magazine giving advice in reply to people's questions about their personal problems □ *penulis ruangan nasihat*

agoraphobia /ˌæɡərəˈfəʊbiə/ *noun* [U] fear of being in public places where there are a lot of people □ *agorafobia* ▶ **agoraphobic** *adj*

agree /əˈɡriː/ *verb*
▶SHARE OPINION **1** [I] **agree (with sb/sth)**; **agree (that ...)** to have the same opinion as sb/sth □ *bersetuju*: *'I think we should talk to the teacher about this.' 'Yes, I agree.'* ♦ *I agree with Paul.* ♦ *Do you agree that we should travel by train?* ♦ *I'm afraid I don't agree.* **OPP** **disagree**

> **HELP** Note that we say: *I agree* and: *I don't agree* NOT 'I am agree' or 'I am not agree'. This is incorrect.

▶SAY YES **2** [I] **agree (to sth/to do sth)** to say yes to sth □ *setuju*: *I asked my boss if I could go home early and she agreed.* ♦ *Alkis has agreed to lend me his car for the weekend.* **OPP** **refuse**
▶ARRANGE **3** [I,T] **agree (to do sth)**; **agree (on sth)** to make an arrangement or decide sth with sb

□ *bersetuju*: *They agreed to meet the following day.* ♦ *Can we agree on a price?* ♦ *We agreed a price of £500.*
▶APPROVE OF **4** [I] **agree with sth** to think that sth is right □ *bersetuju*: *I don't agree with experiments on animals.* **OPP** **disagree**
▶BE THE SAME **5** [I] to be the same as sth □ *sama*: *The two accounts of the accident do not agree.* **OPP** **disagree**
IDM **not agree with sb** (used about food) to make sb feel ill □ *tdk serasi bagi sso*: *I like spicy food but it doesn't agree with me.*

agreeable /əˈgriːəbl/ *adj* **1** pleasant; nice □ *menyenangkan; baik* **OPP** **disagreeable** **2** [not before a noun] (*formal*) ready to agree □ *bersetuju*: *If you are agreeable, we would like to visit your offices on 21 May.* ▶**agreeably** /-əbli/ *adv*: *I was agreeably surprised by the film.*

agreement /əˈgriːmənt/ *noun* **1** [C] a contract or decision that two or more people have made together □ *perjanjian; persetujuan*: *Please sign the agreement and return it to us.* ♦ *The leaders reached an agreement after five days of talks.* ♦ *We never break an agreement.* **2** [U] the state of agreeing with sb/sth □ *persetujuan*: *She nodded her head in agreement.* ♦ *We are totally in agreement with what you have said.* **OPP** **disagreement**

agriculture /ˈægrɪkʌltʃə(r)/ *noun* [U] keeping animals and growing crops for food; farming □ *pertanian*: *the Minister of Agriculture* ▶**agricultural** /ˌægrɪˈkʌltʃərəl/ *adj*

agritourism /ˈægrɪtʊərɪzəm/ (*BrE also*) -tɔːr-/ *noun* [U] holidays in which tourists stay with local people who live in the countryside □ *pelancongan tani*

aground /əˈɡraʊnd/ *adv* if a ship **runs/goes aground**, it touches the ground in water that is not deep enough and it cannot move □ *terkandas (kapal); di dasar air cetek*: *The oil tanker ran/went aground off the Spanish coast.* ▶**aground** *adj* [not before a noun]

ah /ɑː/ *exclam* used for expressing surprise, pleasure, understanding, etc □ *ah; eh*: *Ah, there you are.*

aha /ɑːˈhɑː/ *exclam* used when you suddenly find or understand sth □ *aha*: *Aha! Now I understand.*

ahead /əˈhed/ *adv* **ahead (of sb/sth)** **1** in front of sb/sth □ *di hadapan; ke depan*: *I could see the other car about half a mile ahead of us.* ♦ *The path ahead looked narrow and steep.* ♦ *Look straight ahead and don't turn round!* **2** before or more advanced than sb/sth □ *lebih awal; mendahului*: *Inga and Nils arrived a few minutes ahead of us.* ♦ *London is about five hours ahead of New York.* ♦ *The Japanese are way ahead of us in their research.* **3** into the future □ *masa depan; lebih dahulu*: *He's got a difficult time ahead of him.* ♦ *We must think ahead and make a plan.* **4** winning in a game, competition, etc □ *mendahului*: *The goal put Italy 2-1 ahead at half-time.* ⊃ look at **behind**

agreeable → aimless

IDM **ahead of your time** so modern that people do not understand you □ *mendahului zaman* **streets ahead** ⊃ **street**

aid[1] /eɪd/ *noun* **1** [U] money, food, etc. that is sent to a country or to people in order to help them □ *bantuan*: *We sent aid to the earthquake victims.* ♦ *economic aid* **2** [U] help □ *bantuan*: *to walk with the aid of a stick* ♦ *He had to go to the aid of a child in the river.* ⊃ look at **first aid 3** [C] a person or thing that helps you □ *pembantu; alat bantuan*: *a hearing aid* ♦ *dictionaries and other study aids*
IDM **in aid of sb/sth** in order to collect money for sb/sth, especially for a charity □ *(mengutip derma) utk membantu sso/sst*: *a concert in aid of Children in Need*

aid[2] /eɪd/ *verb* [T] (*formal*) to help sb/sth □ *membantu*: *Sleep aids recovery from illness.*
IDM **aid and abet** to help sb to do sth that is not allowed by law □ *bersubahat*

aide /eɪd/ *noun* [C] a person who helps another person, especially a politician, in their job □ *pembantu; penolong*

AIDS (also **Aids**) /eɪdz/ *noun* [U] **Acquired Immune Deficiency Syndrome**; an illness caused by **HIV** (= a virus which destroys the body's ability to fight infection) □ *penyakit Aids*: *He was HIV positive for three years before developing full-blown AIDS.* ♦ *to contract AIDS* ♦ *the AIDS virus*

ailing /ˈeɪlɪŋ/ *adj* not in good health; weak □ *uzur; lemah*: *an ailing economy*

ailment /ˈeɪlmənt/ *noun* [C] (*formal*) any illness that is not very serious □ *penyakit*

aim[1] /eɪm/ *noun* **1** [C] something that you intend to do; a purpose □ *cita-cita; tujuan; matlamat*: *Our aim is to open offices in Paris and Rome before the end of the year.* ♦ *His only aim in life is to make money.* **2** [U] the act of pointing sth at sb/sth before trying to hit them or it with it □ *bidikan*: *She picked up the gun, took aim and fired.* ♦ *Jo's aim was good and she hit the target.*

aim[2] /eɪm/ *verb* **1** [I] **aim to do sth**; **aim at/for sth** to intend to do or achieve sth □ *bertujuan; berhasrat*: *We aim to leave after breakfast.* ♦ *The company is aiming at a 25% increase in profit.* ♦ *You should always aim for perfection in your work.* **2** [I,T] **aim (sth) (at sb/sth)** to point sth at sb/sth before trying to hit them or it with it □ *mengacukan; membidikkan*: *She aimed (the gun) at the target and fired.* **3** [T] **aim sth at sb/sth** to direct sth at a particular person or group □ *menujukan; ditujukan*: *The advertising campaign is aimed at young people.*
IDM **be aimed at sth/doing sth** to be intended to achieve sth □ *bertujuan utk*: *The new laws are aimed at reducing heavy traffic in cities.*

aimless /ˈeɪmləs/ *adj* having no purpose □ *tanpa tujuan*: *an aimless discussion* ▶**aimlessly** *adv*

ain't → airy

ain't /eɪnt/ (*informal*) short for **am not; is not; are not; has not; have not** □ *tdk; bukan*

HELP Ain't is NOT considered to be correct English.

air¹ /eə(r)/ *noun* **1** [U] the mixture of gases that surrounds the earth and that people, animals and plants breathe □ *udara*: *the pure mountain air* ♦ *Open a window—I need some fresh air.* ♦ *The air was polluted by smoke from the factory.* **2** [U] the space around and above things □ *angkasa; udara; luar*: *to throw a ball high into the air* ♦ *in the open air* (= outside) **3** [U] travel or transport in an aircraft □ *perjalanan dgn kapal terbang*: *to travel by air* ♦ *an air ticket* **4** [sing] **an air (of sth)** the particular feeling or impression that is given by sb/sth □ *lagak; suasana*: *She has a confident air.*

IDM **a breath of fresh air** ➔ **breath**
clear the air ➔ **clear²**
in the air probably going to happen soon □ *dpt dirasakan*: *A feeling of change was in the air.*
in the open air ➔ **open¹**
on/off (the) air (not) sending out programmes on the radio or TV □ *membuat siaran*: *This radio station is on the air 24 hours a day.*
vanish, etc. into thin air ➔ **thin¹**

air² /eə(r)/ *verb* **1** [I,T] to put clothes, etc. in a warm place or outside in the fresh air to make sure they are completely dry; to become dry in this way □ *menganginkan; menjemur*: *Put the sheets on the washing line to air.* **2** [I,T] to make a room, etc. fresh by letting air into it; to become fresh in this way □ *menganginkan*: *Open the window to air the room.* **3** [T] to tell people what you think about sth □ *mengemukakan*: *The discussion gave people a chance to air their views.*

airbag /'eəbæg/ *noun* [C] a device in a car that fills with air if there is an accident. It protects the people sitting in the front. □ *beg udara/ keselamatan*

airbase /'eəbeɪs/ *noun* [C] an airport for military aircraft □ *pangkalan tentera udara*

airborne /'eəbɔːn/ *adj* flying in the air □ *berada di udara*

air conditioning *noun* [U] the system that keeps the air in a room, building, etc. cool and dry □ *(sistem) penyaman udara* ▶ **air-conditioned** *adj*: *air-conditioned offices*

aircraft /'eəkrɑːft/ *noun* [C] (*pl* **aircraft**) any vehicle that can fly in the air, for example a plane □ *pesawat terbang* ➔ picture on page P6

aircraft carrier *noun* [C] a ship that carries military aircraft and that has a long flat area where they can take off and land □ *kapal induk pesawat terbang*

airfare /'eəfeə(r)/ *noun* [C] the money that you pay to travel by plane □ *tambang kapal terbang*: *high/low/cheap airfares* ➔ look at **fare**

airfield /'eəfiːld/ *noun* [C] an area of land where aircraft can land or take off. An **airfield** is smaller than an airport. □ *padang terbang*

air force *noun* [C, with sing or pl verb] the part of a country's military organization that fights in the air □ *tentera udara* ➔ note at **war** ➔ look at **army, navy**

air hostess *noun* [C] (*old-fashioned*) a woman who looks after the passengers on a plane □ *pramugari* ➔ look at **cabin crew, flight attendant**

airing cupboard *noun* [C] a warm cupboard that you put clothes, etc. in to make sure they are completely dry after being washed □ *almari penganginan*

airless /'eələs/ *adj* not having enough fresh air □ *pengap; tdk berangin*: *The room was hot and airless.*

airlift /'eəlɪft/ *noun* [C] an operation to take people, soldiers, food, etc. to or from an area by aircraft, especially in an emergency or when roads are closed or dangerous □ *pengangkutan udara* ▶ **airlift** *verb* [T]: *Two casualties were airlifted to safety.*

airline /'eəlaɪn/ *noun* [C] a company that provides regular flights for people or goods in aircraft □ *syarikat penerbangan*

airliner /'eəlaɪnə(r)/ *noun* [C] a large plane that carries passengers □ *kapal terbang penumpang*

airmail /'eəmeɪl/ *noun* [U] the system for sending letters, packages, etc. by plane □ *mel udara*: *I sent the parcel (by) airmail.*

airplane /'eəpleɪn/ (*AmE*) = **plane¹**(1)

airport /'eəpɔːt/ *noun* [C] a place where aircraft can land and take off and that has buildings for passengers to wait in □ *lapangan terbang* ➔ note at **plane**: *Bologna airport* ♦ *waiting in the airport lounge*

air raid *noun* [C] an attack by military aircraft □ *serangan udara*

airsick /'eəsɪk/ *adj* feeling sick or **vomiting** (= bringing up food from the stomach) as a result of travelling on a plane □ *mabuk udara* ➔ look at **carsick, seasick, travel-sick**

airspace /'eəspeɪs/ *noun* [U] the part of the sky that is above a country and that belongs to that country by law □ *ruang udara*

airstrip /'eəstrɪp/ (also **landing strip**) *noun* [C] a narrow piece of land where aircraft can take off and land □ *landasan kapal terbang*

airtight /'eətaɪt/ *adj* that air cannot get into or out of □ *kedap udara*

air traffic con'troller *noun* [C] a person whose job is to organize routes for aircraft, and to tell pilots by radio when they can land and take off □ *pengawal lalu lintas udara*

airy /'eəri/ *adj* (**airier; airiest**) having a lot of fresh air inside □ *berangin*

aisle /aɪl/ *noun* [C] a passage between the rows of seats in a church, theatre, etc., or between rows of shelves in a large shop □ *lorong*

ajar /əˈdʒɑː(r)/ *adj* [not before a noun] (used about a door) slightly open □ *renggang; terbuka sedikit*

akin /əˈkɪn/ *adj* (*formal*) **akin to sth** similar to sth □ *sama; serupa*

à la carte /ˌɑː lɑː ˈkɑːt/ *adj, adv* (used about a meal in a restaurant) where each dish that is available has a separate price and there is not a fixed price for a complete meal □ *'a la carte'*

alarm¹ /əˈlɑːm/ *noun* **1** [U] a sudden feeling of fear or worry □ *perasaan cemas; kebimbangan*: *He jumped up in alarm.* **2** [sing] a warning of danger □ *amaran bahaya*: *A small boy saw the smoke and raised the alarm.* **3** [C] a machine that warns you of danger, for example by ringing a loud bell □ *(alat) penggera*: *The burglars set off the alarm when they broke the window.* ◆ *The fire/burglar alarm went off at 4 a.m.* **4** [C] = **alarm clock**
IDM **a false alarm** ➔ **false**

alarm² /əˈlɑːm/ *verb* [T] to make sb/sth feel suddenly frightened or worried □ *mencemaskan; membimbangkan*: *The news of the escaped prisoner alarmed the local people.*

a'larm clock (also **alarm**) *noun* [C] a clock that you can set to make a noise at a particular time to wake you up □ *jam loceng*: *She set the alarm clock for half past six.* ➔ picture at **clock**

alarmed /əˈlɑːmd/ *adj* [not before a noun] **alarmed (at/by sth)** frightened or worried □ *cemas; takut*: *She was alarmed at the thought of staying alone in the house.*

alarming /əˈlɑːmɪŋ/ *adj* that makes you frightened or worried □ *(yg) mencemaskan atau menakutkan*: *The population of the world is increasing at an alarming rate.* ▶ **alarmingly** *adv*

alas /əˈlæs/ *exclam* (*formal*) used for expressing sadness about sth □ *aduhai; sayang sekali*

albeit /ˌɔːlˈbiːɪt/ *conj* (*formal*) although □ *walaupun*: *He finally agreed to come, albeit unwillingly.*

albino /ælˈbiːnəʊ/ *noun* [C] (*pl* **albinos**) a person or an animal with very white skin, white hair and pink eyes □ *balar*

album /ˈælbəm/ *noun* [C] **1** a book in which you can keep stamps, photographs, etc. that you have collected □ *album* **2** a collection of songs on a CD or on the Internet □ *album*: *The band are about to release a new album.* ➔ note at **pop** ➔ look at **single**

alcohol /ˈælkəhɒl/ *noun* [U] **1** drinks such as beer, wine, etc. that can make people drunk □ *alkohol*: *He never drinks alcohol.* **2** the clear liquid in drinks such as beer and wine that can make you drunk □ *minuman keras; arak*: *low-alcohol beer*

alcoholic¹ /ˌælkəˈhɒlɪk/ (*AmE* also) / *adj* containing alcohol □ *beralkohol*: *alcoholic drinks*
OPP **non-alcoholic**
MORE Drinks without alcohol are also called **soft drinks**.

alcoholic² /ˌælkəˈhɒlɪk/ (*AmE* also) / *noun* [C] a person who regularly drinks too much alcohol and cannot easily stop drinking □ *penagih arak; kaki botol*
MORE A person who does not drink alcohol at all is a **teetotaller**.

alcoholism /ˈælkəhɒlɪzəm/ (*AmE* also) / *noun* [U] a medical condition that is caused by regularly drinking a large amount of alcohol and not being able to stop □ *ketagihan arak; alkoholisme*

alcove /ˈælkəʊv/ *noun* [C] a small area in a room where one part of the wall is further back than the rest of the wall □ *serokan; ruang kecil*

ale /eɪl/ *noun* [U,C] a type of beer □ *ale; sejenis bir*

alert¹ /əˈlɜːt/ *adj* **alert (to sth)** watching, listening, etc. for sth with all your attention □ *berwaspada; menumpukan penuh perhatian*: *Security guards must be alert at all times.* ◆ *to be alert to possible changes*

alert² /əˈlɜːt/ *verb* [T] **alert sb (to sth)** to warn sb of danger or a problem □ *memberi amaran ada bahaya*

alert³ /əˈlɜːt/ *noun* [C] a warning of possible danger □ *amaran*: *a bomb alert*
IDM **on the alert (for sth)** ready or prepared for danger or an attack □ *dlm keadaan berjaga-jaga*

'A level (also **ad'vanced level**) *noun* [C,U] a British exam taken in a particular subject, usually in the final year of school at the age of 18 □ *(peperiksaan) A Level*: *How many A levels have you got?* ◆ *I'm doing my A levels this summer.* ◆ *You need two passes at A level to get onto this course.* ➔ look at **A2, AS, GCSE**

algae /ˈældʒiː; ˈælɡiː/ *noun* [pl, with sing or pl verb] very simple plants that grow mainly in water □ *alga*

algebra /ˈældʒɪbrə/ *noun* [U] a type of mathematics in which letters and symbols are used to represent numbers □ *algebra*

alias¹ /ˈeɪliəs/ *adv* used for giving sb's false name □ *alias; atau*: *Norma Jean Baker, alias Marilyn Monroe*

alias² /ˈeɪliəs/ *noun* [C] a false name, for example one that is used by a criminal □ *nama palsu*: *Castorri is known to the police under several aliases.*

alibi /ˈæləbaɪ/ *noun* [C] (*pl* **alibis**) **an alibi (for sth)** a statement by sb that says you were in a different place at the time of a crime and so cannot be guilty of the crime □ *alibi*: *He had a good alibi for the night of the robbery.*

alien → the all-clear

alien¹ /ˈeɪliən/ *adj* **1 alien (to sb)** very strange and completely different from your normal experience □ *asing; ganjil* **2** of another country; foreign □ *asing*: *an alien land*

alien² /ˈeɪliən/ *noun* [C] **1** (*formal*) a person who comes from another country □ *rakyat asing* **2** a creature that comes from another planet □ *makhluk asing*

alienate /ˈeɪliəneɪt/ *verb* [T] **1** to make people feel that they cannot share your opinions any more □ *merenggangkan*: *The Prime Minister's new policies on defence have alienated many of his supporters.* **2 alienate sb (from sb/sth)** to make sb feel that they do not belong somewhere or are not part of sth □ *menyisihkan* ▶**alienation** /ˌeɪliəˈneɪʃn/ *noun* [U]

alight¹ /əˈlaɪt/ *adj* [not before a noun] on fire; burning □ *menyala; terbakar*: *A cigarette set the petrol alight.*

> **HELP Alight** or **burning**? You can only use **alight** after a verb such as 'be' but you can use **burning** before a noun: *The whole building was alight.* ◆ *a burning building*

alight² /əˈlaɪt/ *verb* [I] (*formal*) **alight (from sth)** to get off a bus, train, etc. □ *turun (bas, dsb)*

align /əˈlaɪn/ *verb* [T] **align sth (with sth)** to arrange things in a straight line or so that they are parallel to sth else □ *menyebariskan; menjajarkan*: *The mechanic aligned the wheels of the car.*

PHR V align yourself with sb/sth to say that you support the opinions of a particular group, country, etc. □ *bersekutu; bersepakat*

alignment /əˈlaɪnmənt/ *noun* **1** [U] arrangement in a straight line or parallel to sth else □ *penyebarisan; penjajaran* **2** [C,U] an agreement between political parties, countries, etc. to support the same thing □ *penyekutuan; persepakatan*

alike¹ /əˈlaɪk/ *adj* [not before a noun] very similar □ *serupa*: *The two children are very alike.*

alike² /əˈlaɪk/ *adv* in the same way; equally □ *sama*: *We try to treat women and men alike in this company.* ◆ *The book is popular with adults and children alike.*

alimony /ˈælɪməni/ *noun* [U] money that you have to pay by law to your former wife or husband after getting divorced □ *alimoni*

ˈA-list *adj* used to describe a group of people who are famous, successful or important □ *senarai orang penting*: *He only invited A-list celebrities to his party.*

alive /əˈlaɪv/ *adj* [not before a noun] **1** not dead; living □ *hidup; bernyawa*: *The young woman was still alive when the ambulance reached the hospital.* ◆ *The quick action of the doctors kept the child alive.*

> **HELP Alive** or **living**? **Alive** can only be used after a noun or a verb such as 'be', but you can use **living** before a noun: *Are her parents still alive?* ◆ *Does she have any living relatives?*

2 continuing to exist. □ *hidup; masih ada*: *Many old traditions are very much alive in this area of the country.* **3** full of life □ *cergas; rancak*: *In the evening the town really comes alive.*

alkali /ˈælkəlaɪ/ *noun* [C,U] a chemical substance that can burn skin when it is dissolved in water. An **alkali** has a pH (= a measurement of the level of acid or alkali in sth) value of more than 7. □ *alkali* ◯ look at **acid** ▶**alkaline** *adj*

all¹ /ɔːl/ *determiner, pron* **1** every one of a group □ *semua; kesemua*: *All (of) my children can swim.* ◆ *My children can all swim.* ◆ *She's read all (of) these books.* ◆ *She's read them all.* ◆ *The people at the meeting all voted against the plan.* ◆ *All of them voted against the plan.* **2** the whole of a thing or of a period of time □ *semua; sepanjang*: *All (of) the food has gone.* ◆ *They've eaten all of it.* ◆ *They've eaten it all.* ◆ *This money is all yours.* ◆ *All of it is yours.* ◆ *all week/month/year* ◆ *He worked hard all his life.* **3** everything that; the only thing that □ *semua; itu sahaja; hanya*: *I wrote down all I could remember.* ◆ *All I've eaten today is one banana.*

IDM above all ◯ **above**
after all ◯ **after**
for all 1 in spite of □ *walaupun*: *For all her wealth and beauty, she was never very happy.* **2** used to show that sth is not important or of no interest or value to you □ *entah-entah*: *For all I know, he's probably remarried by now.* ◯ note at **altogether**
in all in total □ *semuanya*: *There were ten of us in all.*
not all that ... not very □ *tdk pun sangat*: *The film wasn't all that good.*
(not) at all in any way □ *langsung tdk*: *I didn't enjoy it at all.*
not at all used as a polite reply when sb thanks you for sth □ *sama-sama*: *'Thanks very much for your help.' 'Not at all, it was a pleasure.'*

all² /ɔːl/ *adv* **1** completely; very □ *semuanya; sangat; semata-mata; langsung*: *He has lived all alone since his wife died.* ◆ *I didn't watch that programme—I forgot all about it.* ◆ *They got all excited about it.* **2** (in sport) for each side □ *sama*: *The score was two all.*

IDM all along from the beginning □ *dr mula lagi*: *I knew you were joking all along.*
all the better, harder, etc. even better, harder, etc. than before □ *lebih baik, sukar, dll*: *It will be all the more difficult with two people missing.*
all/just the same ◯ **same**

Allah /ˈælə/ *noun* [sing] the Muslim name for God □ *Allah*

allay /əˈleɪ/ *verb* [T] (*formal*) to make sth less strong □ *mengurangkan; meredakan*

the ˌall-ˈclear *noun* [sing] a signal telling you that a situation is no longer dangerous □ *isyarat menandakan keadaan tdk bahaya lagi*

ʌ cup ɜː bird ə ago eɪ pay əʊ go aɪ my aʊ now ɔɪ boy ɪə near eə hair ʊə pure

allege /ə'ledʒ/ verb [T] (formal) to say that sb has done sth wrong, but without having any proof that this is true □ *mendakwa; menuduh*: *The woman alleged that Williams had attacked her with a knife.* ▶**allegation** /ˌælə'geɪʃn/ noun [C]: *to make allegations of police corruption* ▶**alleged** /ə'ledʒd/ adj [only before a noun] ▶**allegedly** /ə'ledʒɪdli/ adv: *The man was allegedly shot while trying to escape.*

allegiance /ə'liːdʒəns/ noun [U,C] (formal) support for a leader, government, belief, etc □ *sokongan; kesetiaan*: *Many people switched allegiance and voted against the government.* **SYN** loyalty

allegory /'æləgəri/ noun [C,U] (pl **allegories**) a story, play, picture, etc. in which each character or event is a symbol representing an idea or a quality, such as truth, evil, death, etc.; the use of such symbols □ *kiasan; ibarat* ▶**allegorical** /ˌælə'ɡɒrɪkl/ (AmE also) / adj: *an allegorical figure/novel*

allergic /ə'lɜːdʒɪk/ adj 1 allergic (to sth) having an **allergy** □ *alah*: *I can't drink cow's milk. I'm allergic to it.* 2 caused by an **allergy** □ *(disebabkan oleh) alahan*: *an allergic reaction to house dust*

allergy /'ælədʒi/ noun [C] (pl **allergies**) an allergy (to sth) a medical condition that makes you ill when you eat, touch or breathe sth that does not normally make other people ill □ *alergi; alahan*: *an allergy to cats/shellfish/pollen* ➔ note at **ill** ➔ look at **hay fever**

alleviate /ə'liːvieɪt/ verb [T] to make sth less strong or bad □ *mengurangkan*: *The doctor gave me an injection to alleviate the pain.* ▶**alleviation** /əˌliːvi'eɪʃn/ noun [U]

alley /'æli/ (also **alleyway** /'æliweɪ/) noun [C] a narrow passage between buildings □ *lorong* ➔ picture on page P11

alliance /ə'laɪəns/ noun [C] an agreement between groups, countries, etc. to work together and support each other □ *perikatan; persekutuan*: *The two parties formed an alliance.* ➔ look at **ally**

allied adj 1 /'ælaɪd/ [only before a noun] (used about organizations, countries, etc.) having an agreement to work together and support each other □ *berikat; bersekutu*: *allied forces* 2 /ə'laɪd/ allied (to sth) connected with; existing together with □ *berkaitan; berhubungan*: *The newspaper is closely allied to the government.*

alligator /'ælɪɡeɪtə(r)/ noun [C] a large animal with a hard skin covered in scales, a long tail and a big mouth with sharp teeth. **Alligators** live in the lakes and rivers of America and China. □ *aligator* ➔ look at **crocodile**

ˌall-'in adj [only before a noun] including everything □ *termasuk semua*: *an all-in price*

alliteration /əˌlɪtə'reɪʃn/ noun [U] (technical) the use of the same letter or sound at the beginning of words that are close together, as in *sing a song of sixpence* □ *aliterasi*

---

allege → allowance

allocate /'æləkeɪt/ verb [T] allocate sth (to/for sb/sth) to give sth to sb as their share or to decide to use sth for a particular purpose □ *menguntukkan*: *The government has allocated half the budget for education.* ▶**allocation** /ˌælə'keɪʃn/ noun [C,U]

allot /ə'lɒt/ verb [T] (**allotting**; **allotted**) allot sth (to sb/sth) to give a share of work, time, etc. to sb/sth □ *membahagi-bahagikan; memperuntukkan*: *Different tasks were allotted to each member of the class.* ◆ *We all finished the exam in the allotted time.*

allotment /ə'lɒtmənt/ noun [C] (BrE) a small area of land in a town that you can rent for growing vegetables on □ *tanah peruntukan*

ˌall 'out adj, adv using all your strength, etc □ *sedaya upaya*: *We're going all out for victory.* ◆ *an all-out effort*

allow /ə'laʊ/ verb [T] 1 allow sb/sth to do sth; allow sth to give permission for sb/sth to do sth or for sth to happen □ *membenarkan*: *You are not allowed to eat or drink on this bus.* ◆ *I'm afraid we don't allow people to bring dogs into this restaurant.* ◆ *Photography is not allowed inside the cathedral.* ◆ *You are allowed to bring two guests to the ceremony.* 2 allow sb sth to let sb have sth □ *membenarkan*: *My contract allows me four weeks' holiday a year.* 3 to give permission for sb/sth to be or go somewhere □ *dibenarkan*: *No dogs allowed.* ◆ *I'm only allowed out on Friday and Saturday nights.* 4 to make sth possible □ *membolehkan*: *Working part-time would allow me to spend more time with my family.* 5 allow sth (for sb/sth) to provide money, time, etc. for sb/sth □ *memberikan; menguntukkan*: *You should allow about 30 minutes for each question.*

PHR V allow for sb/sth to think about possible problems when you are planning sth and include extra time, money, etc. for them □ *mengambil kira ttg*: *The journey should take about two hours, allowing for heavy traffic.*

OTHER WORDS FOR

allow

Compare **allow**, **permit** and **let**. **Allow** can be used in both formal and informal English. The passive form **be allowed to** is especially common. **Permit** is a formal word and is usually used only in written English. **Let** is an informal word, and very common in spoken English. You **allow sb to do sth** but **let sb do sth** (no 'to'). **Let** cannot be used in the passive: *Visitors are not allowed/permitted to smoke in this area.* ◆ *Smoking is not allowed/permitted.* ◆ *I'm not allowed to smoke in my bedroom.* ◆ *My dad won't let me smoke in my bedroom.*

---

allowable /ə'laʊəbl/ adj that is allowed, especially by law or by a set of rules □ *yg dpt dibenarkan/diizinkan*

allowance /ə'laʊəns/ noun [C] 1 an amount of money that you receive regularly to help you

alloy → aloud

pay for sth that you need □ *elaun* **2** an amount of sth that you are allowed □ *peruntukan*: *Most flights have a 20 kg baggage allowance.* **3** (*especially AmE*) = **pocket money**
IDM **make allowances for sb/sth** to judge a person or their actions in a kinder way than usual because they have a particular problem or disadvantage □ *memberi kelonggaran; mengambil kira*

alloy /ˈælɔɪ/ *noun* [C,U] a metal that is formed by mixing two types of metal together, or by mixing metal with another substance □ *aloi*: *Brass is an alloy of copper and zinc.*

all ˈright // (also *informal* **alright**) *adj, adv, exclam* [not before a noun] **1** good enough □ *memuaskan; baik*: *Is everything all right?* **2** safe and well □ *selamat; tdk apa-apa*: *I hope the children are all right.* ◆ *Do you feel all right?* **3** showing you agree to do what sb has asked □ *baiklah*: '*Can you get me some stamps?*' '*Yes, all right.*' **SYN** *for all meanings* **OK**

> **HELP** You say '*That's all right,*' when sb thanks you for sth or when sb says sorry for sth he/she has done: '*Thanks for the lift home.*' '*That's (quite) all right.*' ◆ '*I'm so sorry I'm late.*' '*That's all right. We haven't started yet anyway.*'

ˈall-round *adj* [only *before* a noun] able to do many different things well; good in many different ways □ *serba boleh; menyeluruh*: *a superb all-round athlete* ◆ *The school aims at the all-round development of the child.*

ˌall-ˈrounder *noun* [C] a person who can do many different things well □ *orang yg serba boleh*

allude /əˈluːd/ *verb* [I] (*formal*) **allude to sb/sth** to speak about sb/sth in an indirect way □ *mengiaskan* ▶ **allusion** /əˈluːʒn/ *noun* [C,U]: *He likes to make allusions to the size of his salary.*

alluring /əˈlʊərɪŋ/ *adj* attractive in an exciting way □ *sangat menarik; menawan; memikat*: *an alluring smile* ▶ **alluringly** *adv*

ally¹ /ˈælaɪ/ *noun* [C] (*pl* **allies**) **1** a country that has an agreement to support another country, especially in a war □ *sekutu*: *France and its European allies* ➪ *look at* **alliance** **2** a person who helps and supports you, especially when other people are against you □ *penyokong*: *the Prime Minister's political allies*

ally² /əˈlaɪ/ *verb* [T] (**allying; allies**; *pt, pp* **allied**) **ally (yourself) with sb/sth** to give your support to another group or country □ *bersekutu*: *The prince allied himself with the Scots.*

almighty /ɔːlˈmaɪti/ *adj* **1** having the power to do anything □ *maha kuasa*: *Almighty God* **2** [only *before* a noun] (*informal*) very great □ *amat; sangat*: *Suddenly we heard the most almighty crash.*

almond /ˈɑːmənd/ *noun* [C] a flat pale nut □ *badam* ➪ *picture at* **nut**

almost /ˈɔːlməʊst/ *adv* nearly; not quite □ *hampir*: *By 9 o'clock almost everybody had arrived.* ◆ *Careful! I almost fell into the water then!* ◆ *The film has almost finished.* ◆ *She almost always cycles to school.* ◆ *There's almost nothing left.* ◆ *Almost all the students passed the exam.* **SYN** **nearly**

alone /əˈləʊn/ *adj* [not before a noun] *adv* **1** without any other person □ *seorang diri; sendirian*: *The old man lives alone.* ◆ *Are you alone? Can I speak to you for a moment?* ◆ *I don't like walking home alone after dark.* **2** [after a noun or pronoun] only □ *hanya; sahaja*: *You alone can help us.* **3** [after a noun or pronoun] used to emphasize one particular thing □ *sahaja*: *The rent alone takes up most of my salary.*
IDM **go it alone** to start working on your own without the usual help □ *sendirian*
leave sb/sth alone ➪ **leave¹**
let alone and certainly not □ *apatah lagi*: *We haven't decided where we're going yet, let alone booked the tickets.*

> **OTHER WORDS FOR**
>
> **alone**
>
> **Alone** and **lonely** both mean that you are not with other people. **Lonely** (*AmE* **lonesome**) means that you are unhappy about this, but **alone** does not usually suggest either happiness or unhappiness. **Alone** cannot be used before a noun. You can also use **on your own** and **by yourself** to mean 'alone'. These expressions are more informal and very common in spoken English.

along /əˈlɒŋ/ *prep, adv* **1** from one end to or towards the other end of sth □ *sepanjang*: *I walked slowly along the road.* ◆ *David looked along the corridor to see if anyone was coming.* **2** on or beside sth long □ *di sepanjang; di*: *Wild flowers grew along both sides of the river.* ◆ *Our house is about halfway along the street.* **3** forward □ *ke hadapan*: *We moved along slowly with the crowd.* **4** (*informal*) with sb □ *ikut sama*: *We're going for a walk. Why don't you come along too?*
IDM **all along** ➪ **all²**
along with sb/sth together with sb/sth □ *bersama-ma dgn sso/sst*
go along with sb/sth to agree with sb's ideas or plans □ *bersetuju dgn sso/sst*

alongside /əˌlɒŋˈsaɪd/ *prep, adv* **1** next to sb/sth or at the side of sth □ *di tepi*: *The boat moored alongside the quay.* ◆ *Nick caught up with me and rode alongside.* **2** together with sb/sth □ *bersama-sama*: *the opportunity to work alongside experienced musicians*

aloof /əˈluːf/ *adj* not friendly or interested in other people □ *tdk mesra; dingin*: *Her shyness made her seem aloof.* **SYN** **distant**

aloud /əˈlaʊd/ (also ˌout ˈloud) *adv* in a normal speaking voice that other people can hear □ *kuat-kuat*: *to read aloud from a book* **OPP** **silently**

[I] **intransitive**, a verb which has no object: *He laughed.*

[T] **transitive**, a verb which has an object: *He ate an apple.*

alphabet /ˈælfəbet/ noun [C] a set of letters in a fixed order that you use when you are writing a language □ *abjad*: There are 26 letters in the English alphabet.

alphabetical /ˌælfəˈbetɪkl/ adj arranged in the same order as the letters of the alphabet □ *menurut abjad*: The names are listed in alphabetical order. ▶**alphabetically** /-kli/ adv: arranged/stored alphabetically

alpine /ˈælpaɪn/ adj of or found in high mountains □ *berkenaan dgn atau terdapat di pergunungan tinggi*: alpine flowers

already /ɔːlˈredi/ adv 1 used for talking about sth that has happened before now or before a particular time in the past □ *sudah*: 'Would you like some lunch?' 'No, I've already eaten, thanks.' ♦ We got there at 6.30 but Marsha had already left. ♦ Sita was already awake when I went into her room. 2 (used in negative sentences and questions for expressing surprise) so early; as soon as this □ *sudahkah; sudah*: Have you finished already? ♦ Surely you're not going already!

alright /ɔːlˈraɪt/ adv (*informal*) = **all right**

also /ˈɔːlsəʊ/ adv [not with negative verbs] in addition; too □ *juga*: He plays several instruments and also writes music. ♦ Bring summer clothing and also something warm to wear in the evenings. ♦ The food is wonderful, and also very cheap.
IDM not only … (but) also ⊃ **not**

OTHER WORDS FOR

also

Too and **as well** are less formal than **also** and are very common in spoken English. **Also** usually goes before a main verb or after 'is', 'are', 'were', etc: He also enjoys reading. ♦ He has also been to Australia. ♦ He is also intelligent. **Too** and **as well** usually go at the end of a phrase or sentence: I really love this song, and I liked the first one too/as well.

altar /ˈɔːltə(r)/ noun [C] a high table that is the centre of a religious ceremony □ *altar*

alter /ˈɔːltə(r)/ verb [I,T] to make sth different in some way, but without changing it completely; to become different □ *menukar; mengubah*: We've altered our plan, and will now arrive at 7.00 instead of 8.00. ♦ The village seems to have altered very little in the last twenty years.

alteration /ˌɔːltəˈreɪʃn/ noun [C,U] (an) alteration (to/in sth) a small change in sb/sth □ *perubahan*: We want to **make a few alterations** to the house before we move in.

alternate¹ /ˈɔːltəneɪt/ verb 1 [T] alternate A with B to cause two types of events or things to happen or follow regularly one after the other □ *bersilih ganti; berselang-seli*: He alternated periods of work with periods of rest. 2 [I] alternate with sth; alternate between A and B (used about two types of events, things, etc.) to happen or follow regularly one after the other □ *menyelang-nyeli*: Busy periods in the hospital alternate with times when there is not much to do. ♦ She seemed to alternate between hating him and loving him. ▶**alternation** /ˌɔːltəˈneɪʃn/ noun [C,U]

alternate² /ɔːlˈtɜːnət/ adj 1 (used about two types of events, things, etc.) happening or following regularly one after the other □ *bersilih ganti; berselang-seli*: There will be alternate periods of sun and showers tomorrow. 2 one of every two □ *selang se-(hari, minggu, dsb)*: He works alternate weeks (= he works the first week, he doesn't work the second week, he works again the third week, etc.). ▶**alternately** adv: The bricks were painted alternately white and red.

alternative¹ /ɔːlˈtɜːnətɪv/ noun [C] an alternative (to sth) one of two or more things that you can choose between □ *pilihan; gantian*: What can I eat as an alternative to meat? ♦ There are several alternatives open to us at the moment.

alternative² /ɔːlˈtɜːnətɪv/ adj [only before a noun] 1 that you can use, do, etc. instead of sth else □ *lain; alternatif*: The motorway was closed so we had to find an alternative route. 2 different to what is usual or traditional □ *alternatif*: alternative medicine ▶**alternatively** adv

although /ɔːlˈðəʊ/ conj 1 in spite of the fact that □ *sungguhpun*: Although she was tired, she stayed up late watching TV. ⊃ note at **despite** 2 and yet; but □ *namun demikian; tetapi*: I love dogs, although I wouldn't have one as a pet. **SYN** for both meanings **though**

HELP **Though** and **although** are the same, but at the end of a sentence it is only possible to use **though**: She knew all her friends would be at the party. She didn't want to go, though. **Even though** can be used for emphasis: She didn't want to go, although/though/even though she knew all her friends would be there.

altitude /ˈæltɪtjuːd/ noun 1 [sing] the height of sth above sea level □ *ketinggian; altitud*: The plane climbed to an altitude of 10 000 metres. 2 [C, usually pl] a place that is high above sea level □ *tempat tinggi*: You need to carry oxygen when you are climbing at high altitudes.

alto /ˈæltəʊ/ noun [C] (pl altos) the lowest normal singing voice for a woman, the highest for a man; a woman or man with this voice □ *alto*

altogether /ˌɔːltəˈgeðə(r)/ adv 1 completely □ *sepenuhnya; betul-betul; sama sekali*: I don't altogether agree with you. ♦ At the age of 55 he stopped working altogether. ♦ This time the situation is altogether different. 2 including everything; in total □ *semuanya*: How much money will I need altogether? ♦ Altogether there were six of us. 3 when you consider everything; generally □ *(pd) keseluruhannya*: Altogether, this town is a pleasant place to live.

HELP **Altogether** or **all together**? **All together** means 'everything or everybody together': Put your books all together on the table. ♦ Let's sing. All together now!

altruistic /ˌæltruˈɪstɪk/ adj (formal) caring about the needs and happiness of other people more than your own □ *altruistik; sikap mengutamakan kesenangan orang lain*: altruistic behaviour ▶**altruism** /ˈæltruɪzəm/ noun [U]

aluminium /ˌæljəˈmɪniəm; æləˈ-/ (AmE **aluminum** /əˈluːmɪnəm/) noun [U] (symbol Al) a light silver-coloured metal that is used for making cooking equipment, etc. □ *aluminium*: aluminium saucepans

always /ˈɔːlweɪz/ adv 1 at all times; regularly □ *sentiasa; selalu*: I always get up at 6.30. ◆ Why is the train always late when I'm in a hurry? 2 all through the past until now □ *selamanya; sentiasa*: Tony has always been shy. ◆ I've always liked music. 3 for ever □ *sentiasa; selama-lamanya*: I shall always remember this moment. 4 [only used with continuous tenses] again and again, usually in an annoying way □ *selalu; sentiasa*: She's always complaining about something. 5 used with 'can' or 'could' for suggesting sth that sb could do, especially if nothing else is possible □ *boleh saja*: If you haven't got enough money, I could always lend you some.

> **GRAMMAR** Always does not usually go at the beginning of a sentence. It usually goes before the main verb or after 'is', 'are', 'were', etc: He always wears those shoes. ◆ I have always wanted to visit Egypt. ◆ Fiona is always late. However, **always** can go at the beginning of a sentence when you are telling somebody to do something: Always stop and look before you cross the road.

Alzheimer's disease /ˈæltshaɪməz dɪziːz/ noun [sing] a disease that affects the brain and makes you become more and more confused as you get older □ *penyakit Alzheimer*

AM /ˌeɪ ˈem/ abbr amplitude modulation; one of the systems of sending out radio signals □ *AM*

a.m. (AmE **A.M.**) /ˌeɪ ˈem/ abbr (from Latin ante meridiem; before midday □ *pagi*: 10 a.m. (= 10 o'clock in the morning) ⊃ look at **p.m.**

am /əm; strong form æm/ ⊃ look at **be**

amalgamate /əˈmælgəmeɪt/ verb [I,T] (used especially about organizations, groups, etc.) to join together to form a single organization, group, etc. □ *bergabung* **SYN** merge ▶**amalgamation** /əˌmælgəˈmeɪʃn/ noun [C,U]

amass /əˈmæs/ verb [T] to collect or put together a large quantity of sth □ *mengumpulkan*: We've amassed a lot of information on the subject.

amateur[1] /ˈæmətə(r)/ noun [C] 1 a person who takes part in a sport or an activity for pleasure, not for money as a job □ *amatur*: Only amateurs can take part in the tournament. **OPP** professional 2 (usually used in a critical way) a person who does not have skill or experience when doing sth □ *amatur*

amateur[2] /ˈæmətə(r)/ adj 1 done, or doing sth, for pleasure (not for money as a job) □ *amatur*: an amateur production of a play ◆ an amateur photographer **OPP** professional 2 (also **amateurish** /-rɪʃ/) done without skill or experience □ *tdk mahir; tdk pakar*: The painting was an amateurish fake.

amaze /əˈmeɪz/ verb [T] to surprise sb very much; to be difficult for sb to believe □ *sungguh menghairankan*: Sometimes your behaviour amazes me! ◆ It amazes me that anyone could be so stupid!

amazed /əˈmeɪzd/ adj amazed (at/by sb/sth); amazed (to do sth/that ...) very surprised □ *amat hairan*: I was amazed by the change in his attitude. ◆ She was amazed to discover the truth about her husband.

amazement /əˈmeɪzmənt/ noun [U] a feeling of great surprise □ *kehairanan*: He looked at me in amazement. ◆ To my amazement, he remembered me.

amazing /əˈmeɪzɪŋ/ adj very surprising and difficult to believe □ *yg menakjubkan; yg sukar dipercayai*: She has shown amazing courage. ◆ I've got an amazing story to tell you. **SYN** incredible ▶**amazingly** adv ⊃ note at **sudden**

ambassador /æmˈbæsədə(r)/ noun [C] an important person who represents their country in a foreign country □ *duta*: the Spanish Ambassador to Britain ⊃ look at **consul**

> **MORE** An ambassador lives and works in an **embassy**.

amber /ˈæmbə(r)/ noun [U] 1 a hard clear yellowish-brown substance used for making jewellery or objects for decoration □ *ambar* 2 a yellowish-brown colour □ *kuning jingga; kuning*: The three colours in traffic lights are red, amber and green. ▶**amber** adj

ambidextrous /ˌæmbiˈdekstrəs/ adj able to use the left hand and the right hand equally well □ *ambidekstrus; dwicakat*

ambiguity /ˌæmbɪˈɡjuːəti/ noun [C,U] (pl ambiguities) the possibility of being understood in more than one way; something that can be understood in more than one way □ *ketaksaan*

ambiguous /æmˈbɪɡjuəs/ adj having more than one possible meaning □ *taksa*: That's a rather ambiguous remark—what exactly do you mean? ▶**ambiguously** adv

ambition /æmˈbɪʃn/ noun 1 [C] ambition (to do/be sth); ambition (of doing sth) something that you want to do or achieve very much □ *cita-cita*: It has always been her ambition to travel the world. ◆ He finally achieved his ambition of becoming a doctor. 2 [U] a strong desire to be successful, to have power, etc □ *keinginan (utk berjaya, berkuasa, dsb)*: One problem of young people today is their lack of ambition.

ambitious /æmˈbɪʃəs/ adj 1 ambitious (to be/do sth) having a strong desire to be success-

ambivalent → amoral

ful, to have power, etc □ *bercita-cita tinggi*: I'm not particularly ambitious—I'm content with my life the way it is. ◆ We are ambitious to succeed. **2** difficult to achieve or do because it takes a lot of work or effort □ *mencabar*: The company have announced ambitious plans for expansion.

ambivalent /æmˈbɪvələnt/ *adj* having or showing a mixture of feelings or opinions about sb or sth □ *berbelah bagi; ambivalen* ▶**ambivalence** *noun* [C,U]

amble /ˈæmbl/ *verb* [I] to walk at a slow relaxed speed □ *berjalan perlahan-lahan*: We ambled down to the beach. **SYN** stroll

ambulance /ˈæmbjələns/ *noun* [C] a special vehicle for taking ill or injured people to and from hospital □ *ambulans*: the ambulance service ◆ Call an ambulance! ➔ note at **hospital**

ambush /ˈæmbʊʃ/ *noun* [C,U] a surprise attack from a hidden position □ *serang hendap*: He was killed in an enemy ambush. ◆ The robbers were waiting in ambush. ▶**ambush** *verb* [T]

ameba (*AmE*) = amoeba

amen /ɑːˈmen, eɪˈmen/ *exclam* a word used at the end of prayers by Christians and Jews □ *amin*

amenable /əˈmiːnəbl/ *adj* happy to accept sth □ *sudi menerima*: I'm amenable to any suggestions you may have.

amend /əˈmend/ *verb* [T] to change sth slightly in order to make it better □ *meminda*

amendment /əˈmendmənt/ *noun* **1** [C] a part that is added or a small change that is made to a piece of writing, especially to a law □ *pindaan* **2** [U] an act of amending sth □ *pemindaan*

amends /əˈmendz/ *noun*
IDM **make amends** to do sth for sb, that shows that you are sorry for sth bad that you have done before □ *menebus (kesalahan, dsb)*

amenity /əˈmiːnəti/ *noun* [C] (*pl* **amenities**) something that makes a place pleasant or easy to live in □ *kemudahan*: Among the town's amenities are two cinemas and a sports centre.

American /əˈmerɪkən/ *adj* from or connected with the US □ *(dr atau berkaitan dgn) Amerika*: Have you met Bob? He's American. ◆ an American accent ▶**American** *noun* [C]: Millions of Americans visit Britain each year.

A͵merican ˈfootball (*AmE* **football**) *noun* [U] a game that is played in the US by two teams of eleven players with a ball shaped like an egg. The players wear **helmets** (= hard hats) and other protective clothing and try to carry the ball to the end of the field. □ *bola sepak Amerika* ➔ note at **football** ➔ picture at **football**

A͵merican ˈIndian = Native American

amethyst /ˈæməθɪst/ *noun* [C,U] a purple stone, used in making jewellery □ *ametis; batu kecubung*: an amethyst ring

amiable /ˈeɪmiəbl/ *adj* friendly and pleasant □ *mesra; baik* ▶**amiably** /-əbli/ *adv*

amicable /ˈæmɪkəbl/ *adj* made or done in a friendly way, without argument □ *secara baik* ▶**amicably** /-əbli/ *adv*

amid /əˈmɪd/ (also **amidst** /əˈmɪdst/) *prep* (written) in the middle of; among □ *di tengah-tengah*

amiss /əˈmɪs/ *adj* [not before a noun] *adv* wrong; not as it should be □ *tdk kena*: When I walked into the room I could sense that something was amiss.
IDM **not come/go amiss** to be useful or pleasant □ *elok juga*: Things are fine, although a bit more money wouldn't come amiss.
take sth amiss to be upset by sth, perhaps because you have understood it in the wrong way □ *berkecil hati*: Please don't take my remarks amiss.

ammonia /əˈməʊniə/ *noun* [U] (*symbol* NH_3) a gas with a strong smell; a clear liquid containing **ammonia** used for cleaning □ *ammonia*

ammunition /ˌæmjuˈnɪʃn/ *noun* [U] **1** the supply of bullets, etc. that you need to fire from a weapon □ *bekalan peluru, dsb*: The troops surrendered because they had run out of ammunition. **2** facts or information that can be used against sb/sth □ *perkara yg boleh digunakan utk menyerang sso*

amnesia /æmˈniːziə/ *noun* [U] loss of memory □ *amnesia*

amnesty /ˈæmnəsti/ *noun* [C] (*pl* **amnesties**) **1** a time when a government forgives political crimes □ *pengampunan*: The government has announced an amnesty for all political prisoners. **2** a time when people can give in illegal weapons without being arrested □ *amnesti; pengampunan*

amoeba (*AmE* also **ameba**) /əˈmiːbə/ *noun* [C] (*pl* **amoebas** or **amoebae** /-biː/) a very small living creature that consists of only one cell □ *ameba*

amok /əˈmɒk/ *adv*
IDM **run amok** to suddenly become very angry or excited and start behaving violently, especially in a public place □ *mengamuk* **SYN** run riot

among /əˈmʌŋ/ (also **amongst** /əˈmʌŋst/) *prep* **1** surrounded by; in the middle of □ *di tengah-tengah; dlm kalangan*: I often feel nervous when I'm among strangers. ◆ I found the missing letter amongst a heap of old newspapers. ➔ note at **between** ➔ picture at **between 2** in or concerning a particular group of people or things □ *sesama; dlm kalangan; antara*: Discuss it amongst yourselves and let me know your decision. ◆ There is a lot of anger among students about the new law. ◆ Among other things, the drug can cause headaches and sweating. **3** to each one of (a group) □ *antara*: On his death, his money will be divided among his children.

amoral /ˌeɪˈmɒrəl/ (*AmE* also) / *adj* (used about people or their behaviour) not following any moral rules; not caring about right or wrong

VOWELS iː see i any ɪ sit e ten æ hat ɑː father ɒ got ɔː saw ʊ put uː too u usual

amorous → anagram 28

□ *tdk mengikuti prinsip-prinsip moral* ⊃ look at **moral, immoral**

amorous /ˈæmərəs/ *adj* showing sexual desire and love towards sb □ *penuh berahi*: *She rejected his amorous advances.* ▶**amorously** *adv*

amount[1] /əˈmaʊnt/ *noun* [C] **1** total or sum of money □ *jumlah; amaun*: *You are requested to pay the full amount within seven days.* **2** the amount of sth is how much of it there is; quantity □ *kuantiti; banyak*: *I spent an enormous amount of time preparing for the exam.* ♦ *I have a certain amount of sympathy with her.* ♦ *a large amount of money*

amount[2] /əˈmaʊnt/ *verb* [I] **amount to sth 1** to add up to; to total □ *berjumlah*: *The cost of the repairs amounted to £5 000.* **2** to be the same as □ *sama saja*: *Whether I tell her today or tomorrow, it amounts to the same thing.*

amp /æmp/ *noun* [C] **1** (also *formal* **ampere** /ˈæmpeə(r)/ *AmE also* /) a measure of electric current □ *amp* **2** (*informal*) = **amplifier**

amphetamine /æmˈfetəmiːn/ *noun* [C,U] a drug, sometimes taken illegally, that makes you feel excited and full of energy □ *amfetamina*

amphibian /æmˈfɪbiən/ *noun* [C] an animal with cold blood that can live on land and in water □ *amfibia*: *Frogs, toads and newts are all amphibians.* ⊃ look at **reptile** ⊃ picture on **page P13**

amphibious /æmˈfɪbiəs/ *adj* able to live or be used both on land and in water □ *amfibia; dpt hidup atau berfungsi di darat dan di air*: *Frogs are amphibious.* ♦ *amphibious vehicles*

amphitheatre (*AmE* **amphitheater**) /ˈæmfɪθɪətə(r)/ *noun* [C] a round building without a roof and with rows of seats that rise in steps around an open space. **Amphitheatres** were used in ancient Greece and Rome for public entertainment. □ *amfiteater*

ample /ˈæmpl/ *adj* **1** enough or more than enough □ *cukup; lebih drpd cukup*: *We've got ample time to make a decision.* ♦ *I'm not sure how much the trip will cost, but I should think £1 000 will be ample.* **2** large □ *besar; luas*: *There is space for an ample car park.* ▶**amply** /ˈæmpli/ *adv*

amplifier /ˈæmplɪfaɪə(r)/ *noun* (also *informal* **amp**) *noun* [C] a piece of electrical equipment for making sounds louder or signals stronger □ *amplifier; pembesar suara* ⊃ picture at **music**

amplify /ˈæmplɪfaɪ/ *verb* [T] (**amplifying**; **amplifies**; *pt, pp* **amplified**) **1** to increase the strength of a sound, using electrical equipment □ *menguatkan* **2** to add details to sth in order to explain it more fully □ *memperjelas* ▶**amplification** /ˌæmplɪfɪˈkeɪʃn/ *noun* [U]

amputate /ˈæmpjuteɪt/ *verb* [I,T] to cut off sb's arm, leg, etc. for medical reasons □ *memotong (tangan, kaki, dsb)*: *His leg was so badly injured that it had to be amputated from the knee down.* ▶**amputation** /ˌæmpjuˈteɪʃn/ *noun* [C,U]

amuse /əˈmjuːz/ *verb* [T] **1** to make sb laugh or smile; to seem funny to sb □ *menggelikan hati*: *Everybody laughed but I couldn't understand what had amused them.* **2** to make time pass pleasantly for sb; to stop sb from getting bored □ *menghiburkan*: *I did some crosswords to amuse myself on the journey.* ♦ *I've brought a few toys to amuse the children.*

amused /əˈmjuːzd/ *adj* thinking that sth is funny and wanting to laugh or smile □ *geli hati*: *I was amused to hear his account of what happened.*
IDM **keep sb/yourself amused** to do sth in order to pass time pleasantly and stop sb/yourself getting bored □ *menghabiskan masa membuat sst supaya tdk bosan*

amusement /əˈmjuːzmənt/ *noun* **1** [U] the feeling caused by sth that makes you laugh or smile, or by sth that entertains you □ *rasa geli hati*: *Much to the pupils' amusement, the teacher fell off his chair.* **2** [C] something that makes time pass pleasantly; an entertainment □ *hiburan*: *The holiday centre offers a wide range of amusements, including golf and tennis.*

a'musement arcade = **arcade**(2)

a'musement park *noun* [C] a large park which has a lot of things that you can ride and play on and many different activities to enjoy □ *taman hiburan*

amusing /əˈmjuːzɪŋ/ *adj* causing you to laugh or smile □ *(yg) menghiburkan atau menggelikan hati*: *He's a very amusing person and he makes me laugh a lot.* ♦ *The story was quite amusing.* ⊃ note at **humour**

an ⊃ **a**

anaemia (*AmE* **anemia**) /əˈniːmiə/ *noun* [U] a medical condition in which there are not enough red cells in the blood □ *anemia* ▶**anaemic** (*AmE* **anemic**) *adj*

anaesthetic (*AmE* **anesthetic**) /ˌænəsˈθetɪk/ *noun* [C,U] a substance that stops you feeling pain, for example when a doctor is performing a medical operation on you □ *ubat bius; anestetik*: *The dentist gave me a **local anaesthetic** (= one that only affects part of the body and does not make you unconscious).* ♦ *You'll need to be **under anaesthetic** for the operation.* ♦ *Did you have a **general anaesthetic** (= one that makes you unconscious) for your operation?*

anaesthetist (*AmE* **anesthetist**) /əˈniːsθətɪst/ *noun* [C] a person with the medical training necessary to give **anaesthetics** to patients □ *pakar bius*

anaesthetize (also **-ise**; *AmE* **anesthetize**) /əˈniːsθətaɪz/ *verb* [T] to give an **anaesthetic** to sb □ *membius*

anagram /ˈænəɡræm/ *noun* [C] a word or phrase that is made by arranging the letters of another word or phrase in a different order □ *anagram*: *'Worth' is an anagram of 'throw'.*

analogous /əˈnæləgəs/ adj (formal) **analogous (to/with sth)** similar in some way; that you can compare □ *seakan-akan sama; sebagai perbandingan*

analogue (AmE **analog**) /ˈænəlɒg/ (AmE also) / adj **1** (used about an electronic process) using a continuously changing range of physical quantities to measure or store data □ *analog: an analogue circuit/computer/signal* **2** (BRE ALSO **analog**) (used about a clock or watch) showing the time using hands on a **dial** (= the round part) and not with a display of numbers □ *analog* ⊃ look at **digital**

analogy /əˈnælədʒi/ noun [C] (pl **analogies**) **an analogy (between A and B)** a comparison between two things that shows a way in which they are similar □ *analogi: You could make an analogy between the human body and a car engine.*
IDM **by analogy** by comparing sth to sth else and showing how they are similar □ *dgn menggunakan analogi*

⚡ **analyse** (AmE **analyze**) /ˈænəlaɪz/ verb [T] to look at or think about the different parts or details of sth carefully in order to understand or explain it □ *menganalisis: The water samples are now being analysed in a laboratory.* ♦ *to analyse statistics* ♦ *She analysed the situation and then decided what to do.*

⚡ **analysis** /əˈnæləsɪs/ noun (pl **analyses** /-siːz/) **1** [C,U] the careful examination of the different parts or details of sth □ *penganalisisan; analisis: Some samples of the water were sent to a laboratory for analysis.* **2** [C] the result of a careful examination of sth □ *analisis: Your analysis of the situation is different from mine.* **3** [U] = **psychoanalysis**

analyst /ˈænəlɪst/ noun [C] a person whose job is to examine sth carefully as an expert □ *juruanalisis: a food analyst* ♦ *a political analyst*

analytical /ˌænəˈlɪtɪkl/ (also **analytic** /ˌænəˈlɪtɪk/) adj using careful examination in order to understand or explain sth □ *analitis*

analyze (AmE) = **analyse**

anarchic /əˈnɑːkɪk/ adj without rules or laws □ *berunsur anarki*

anarchism /ˈænəkɪzəm/ noun [U] the political belief that there should be no government or laws in a country □ *anarkisme* ▶ **anarchist** /-ɪst/ noun [C]

anarchy /ˈænəki/ noun [U] a situation in which people do not obey rules and laws; a situation in which there is no government in a country □ *anarki: While the civil war went on, the country was in a state of anarchy.*

anatomy /əˈnætəmi/ noun (pl **anatomies**) **1** [U] the scientific study of the structure of human or animal bodies □ *anatomi* **2** [C] the structure of a living thing □ *anatomi: the anatomy of the frog* ▶ **anatomical** /ˌænəˈtɒmɪkl/ adj

ancestor /ˈænsestə(r)/ noun [C] a person in your family who lived a long time before you □ *nenek moyang/leluhur: My ancestors settled in this country a hundred years ago.* ⊃ look at **descendant** ▶ **ancestral** /ænˈsestrəl/ adj: *her ancestral home* (= that has belonged to her family for many years)

ancestry /ˈænsestri/ noun [U,C, usually sing] (pl **ancestries**) all of sb's **ancestors** □ *keturunan: He is of Scottish ancestry.*

anchor¹ /ˈæŋkə(r)/ noun [C,U] a heavy metal object at the end of a chain that you drop into the water from a boat in order to stop the boat moving □ *sauh*

anchor² /ˈæŋkə(r)/ verb **1** [I,T] to drop an **anchor**; to stop a boat moving by using an **anchor** □ *melabuhkan sauh; berlabuh* **2** [T] to fix sth firmly so that it cannot move □ *mengukuhkan*

anchovy /ˈæntʃəvi/ noun [C,U] (pl **anchovies**) a small fish that has a strong taste of salt □ *ikan bilis*

⚡ **ancient** /ˈeɪnʃənt/ adj **1** belonging to a period of history that is thousands of years in the past □ *kuno; purba: ancient civilizations* ♦ *an ancient tradition* **OPP** **modern** **2** very old □ *sangat tua: I can't believe he's only 30—he looks ancient!*

⚡ **and** /ənd; ən; strong form ænd/ conj **1** (used to connect words or parts of sentences) also; in addition to □ *dan: a boy and a girl* ♦ *Do it slowly and carefully.* ♦ *We were singing and dancing all evening.* ♦ *Come in and sit down.*

HELP When the two things are closely linked, you do not need to repeat the 'a', etc: *a knife and fork* ♦ *my father and mother*

2 (used when you are saying numbers in sums) in addition to □ *dgn; campur: Twelve and six is eighteen.* **SYN** **plus**

HELP When you are saying large numbers *and* is used after the word 'hundred': We say 2 264 as *two thousand, two hundred and sixty-four*.

3 used instead of 'to' after certain verbs, for example 'go', 'come', 'try' □ *dan: Go and answer the door for me, will you?* ♦ *Why don't you come and stay with us one weekend?* ♦ *I'll try and find out what's going on.* **4** used between repeated words to show that sth is increasing or continuing □ *bertambah; semakin: The situation is getting worse and worse.* ♦ *I shouted and shouted but nobody answered.*

anecdote /ˈænɪkdəʊt/ noun [C] a short interesting story about a real person or event □ *anekdot*

anemia (AmE) = **anaemia**

anesthetic (AmE) = **anaesthetic**

anesthetist (AmE) = **anaesthetist**

anesthetize (AmE) = **anaesthetize**

anew /əˈnjuː/ adv (written) again; in a new or different way □ *semula: I wish I could start my life anew!*

angel → annexe 30

angel /'eɪndʒl/ noun [C] **1** a spirit who is believed to carry messages from God. In pictures **angels** are often dressed in white, with wings. □ *malaikat* **2** a person who is very kind □ *orang yg sangat baik hati*

angelic /æn'dʒelɪk/ adj looking or acting like an angel □ *spt malaikat* ▶ **angelically** /-kli/ adv

anger[1] /'æŋɡə(r)/ noun [U] the strong feeling that you have when sth has happened or sb has done sth that you do not like □ *kemarahan*: *He could not hide his anger at the news.* ◆ *She was shaking with anger.*

anger[2] /'æŋɡə(r)/ verb [T] to make sb become angry □ *menimbulkan kemarahan*

angle[1] /'æŋɡl/ noun [C] **1** the space between two lines or surfaces that meet, measured in degrees □ *sudut*: *a right angle* (= an angle of 90°) ◆ *at an angle of 40°* ◆ *The three angles of a triangle add up to 180°.* **2** the direction from which you look at sth □ *sudut*: *Viewed from this angle, the building looks bigger than it really is.*

IDM at an angle not straight □ *senget; condong*

angles

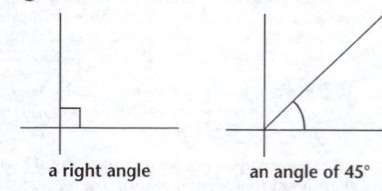

a right angle   an angle of 45°

angle[2] /'æŋɡl/ verb [T] **1** to put sth in a position that is not straight □ *condongkan; serongkan*: *Angle the lamp towards the desk.* **2 angle sth (at/to/towards sb)** to show sth from a particular point of view; to aim sth at a particular person or group □ *ditujukan*: *The new magazine is angled at younger viewers.*

PHR V angle for sth to try to make sb give you sth, without asking for it in a direct way □ *memancing (undangan, pujian, dsb)*: *She was angling for an invitation to our party.*

angler /'æŋɡlə(r)/ noun [C] a person who catches fish as a hobby □ *pengail* ➲ look at **fisherman**

Anglican /'æŋɡlɪkən/ noun [C] a member of the Church of England or of a related church in another English-speaking country □ *Anglikan* ▶ **Anglican** adj

angling /'æŋɡlɪŋ/ noun [U] fishing as a sport or hobby □ *mengail*: *He goes angling at weekends.* ➲ look at **fishing**

Anglo- /'æŋɡləʊ/ [in compounds] connected with England or Britain (and another country or countries) □ *Inggeris-; Anglo-*: *Anglo-American relations*

Anglo-Saxon /ˌæŋɡləʊ 'sæksn/ noun **1** [C] a person whose family originally came from England □ *orang Inggeris-Saxon* **2** [C] a person who lived in England before the Norman Conquest (= the year 1066 when people originally from northern Europe defeated the English and then ruled the country) □ *Inggeris-Saxon* **3** (also **Old English**) [U] the English language before about 1150 □ *bahasa Inggeris kuno* ▶ **Anglo-'Saxon** adj

angry /'æŋɡri/ adj (**angrier; angriest**) **angry (with sb) (at/about sth)** feeling or showing anger □ *marah*: *Calm down, there's no need to get angry.* ◆ *My parents will be angry with me if I get home late.* ◆ *He's always getting angry about something.* ▶ **angrily** adv

angst /æŋst/ noun [U] a feeling of worry about a situation, or about your life □ *kebimbangan; kegelisahan (yg amat sangat)*: *teenage angst*

anguish /'æŋɡwɪʃ/ noun [U] (*written*) great mental pain or suffering □ *kesakitan mental; azab* ▶ **anguished** adj

angular /'æŋɡjələ(r)/ adj with sharp points or corners □ *tajam; berbucu-bucu*

animal /'ænɪml/ noun [C] a living creature that can move and feel □ *haiwan; binatang*: *the animal kingdom* ◆ *Humans are social animals.* ◆ *farm animals* ◆ *He studied the animals and birds of Southern Africa.* ➲ picture on **page P12**

HELP Animal is sometimes used to talk about only mammals.

animate /'ænɪmət/ adj (*formal*) living; having life □ *animat; hidup/bernyawa*: *animate beings* **OPP inanimate**

animated /'ænɪmeɪtɪd/ adj **1** interesting and full of energy □ *rancak; bersemangat*: *an animated discussion* **2** (used about films) using a process or method which makes pictures or models appear to move □ *animasi*: *an animated cartoon*

animation /ˌænɪ'meɪʃn/ noun [U] **1** the state of being full of energy and enthusiasm □ *(keadaan) rancak atau penuh semangat* **2** the method of making films, computer games, etc. with pictures or models that appear to move □ *animasi*: *computer animation*

animosity /ˌænɪ'mɒsəti/ noun [C,U] (pl **animosities**) **animosity (toward(s) sb/sth); animosity (between A and B)** a strong feeling of disagreement, anger or hatred □ *permusuhan; perasaan marah atau benci yg amat sangat* **SYN hostility**

ankle /'æŋkl/ noun [C] the part of your body where your foot joins your leg □ *pergelangan*: *The water only came up to my ankles.* ➲ picture at **body**

annex /ə'neks/ verb [T] to take control of another country or region by force □ *merampas* ▶ **annexation** /ˌænek'seɪʃn/ noun [C,U]

annexe (*especially AmE* **annex**) /'æneks/ noun [C] a building that is joined to a larger one □ *bangunan tambahan*

[I] **intransitive**, a verb which has no object: *He laughed.*   [T] **transitive**, a verb which has an object: *He ate an apple.*

annihilate /əˈnaɪəleɪt/ verb [T] to destroy or defeat sb/sth completely ▫ *memusnahkan* ▶**annihilation** /ˌənaɪəˈleɪʃn/ noun [U]

anniversary /ˌænɪˈvɜːsəri/ noun [C] (pl **anniversaries**) a day that is exactly a year or a number of years after a special or an important event ▫ *(hari) ulang tahun*: the hundredth anniversary of the country's independence ♦ a wedding anniversary ➲ note at **birthday**, **jubilee**

annotated /ˈænəteɪtɪd/ adj (used about a book, etc.) with notes added to it that explain and give extra information about the contents ▫ *beranotasi*

announce /əˈnaʊns/ verb [T] 1 to make sth known publicly and officially ▫ *mengumumkan*: They announced that our train had been delayed. ♦ The winners will be announced in next week's paper. 2 to say sth in a firm or serious way ▫ *menyatakan dgn keras*: She stormed into my office and announced that she was leaving.

announcement /əˈnaʊnsmənt/ noun 1 [C] a statement that tells people about sth ▫ *pengumuman*: Ladies and gentlemen, I'd like to make an announcement. 2 [U] the act of telling people about sth ▫ *pengumuman*

announcer /əˈnaʊnsə(r)/ noun [C] a person who introduces or gives information about programmes on radio or TV ▫ *juruhebah*

annoy /əˈnɔɪ/ verb [T] to make sb angry or slightly angry ▫ *menyakitkan hati; menyebabkan rasa meradang*: It really annoys me when you act so selfishly. ♦ Close the door if the noise is annoying you. **SYN** irritate

annoyance /əˈnɔɪəns/ noun 1 [U] the feeling of being annoyed ▫ *rasa marah atau meradang* 2 [C] something that annoys sb ▫ *hal yg mengganggu*

annoyed /əˈnɔɪd/ adj **annoyed (with sb) (at/about sth); annoyed that ...** slightly angry ▫ *meradang*: I shall be extremely annoyed if he turns up late again. ♦ She's annoyed with herself for making such a stupid mistake. ♦ He's annoyed that nobody believes him. ♦ He got annoyed with me for being late. **SYN** irritated

annoying /əˈnɔɪɪŋ/ adj making you feel angry or slightly angry ▫ *(yg) menyebabkan rasa meradang; benci betul!*: It's so annoying that I can't come with you! ♦ His most annoying habit is always arriving late.

annual¹ /ˈænjuəl/ adj 1 happening or done once a year or every year ▫ *tahunan*: the company's annual report ♦ an annual festival 2 for the period of one year ▫ *tahunan*: What's the average annual salary for a nurse? ♦ the annual sales figures ▶**annually** /-juəli/ adv

annual² /ˈænjuəl/ noun [C] a book, especially one for children, that is published once each year ▫ *terbitan tahunan*: the 2013 Football Annual

annul /əˈnʌl/ verb [T] (**annulling**; **annulled**) to state officially that sth is no longer legally valid ▫ *membatalkan, memansuhkan*: Their marriage was annulled after just six months. ▶**annulment** noun [C,U]

anomalous /əˈnɒmələs/ adj (formal) different from what is normal ▫ *luar drpd biasa*: In a few anomalous cases, these drugs have made people ill.

anomaly /əˈnɒməli/ noun [C] (pl **anomalies**) something that is different from what is normal or usual ▫ *anomali*: We discovered an anomaly in the sales figures for August.

anon /əˈnɒn/ abbr **anonymous**; used to show that we do not know who did a piece of writing ▫ *tanpa nama*

anonymity /ˌænəˈnɪməti/ noun [U] the situation where sb's name is not known ▫ *ketanpanamaan*

anonymous /əˈnɒnɪməs/ adj 1 (used about a person) whose name is not known or made public ▫ *(orang) yg namanya tdk diketahui*: An anonymous caller told the police that a robbery was going to take place. 2 done, written, etc. by sb whose name is not known or made public ▫ *tanpa nama*: He received an anonymous letter. ▶**anonymously** adv

anorak /ˈænəræk/ noun [C] (BrE) 1 a short coat with a covering for your head that protects you from rain, wind and cold ▫ *anorak* 2 (slang) a person who enjoys learning boring facts ▫ *orang yg suka mengetahui perkara-perkara yg membosankan*: He's a real anorak—he can name every player in the World Cup.

anorexia /ˌænəˈreksiə/ (also **anorexia nervosa** /ˌænəˌreksiə nɜːˈvəʊsə/) noun [U] an illness, especially affecting young women, that makes them so afraid of being fat that they do not eat ▫ *anoreksia* ➲ look at **bulimia** ▶**anorexic** adj, noun [C]

another /əˈnʌðə(r)/ determiner, pron 1 one more person or thing of the same kind ▫ *satu lagi*: Would you like another drink? ♦ They've got three children already and they're having another. 2 a different thing or person ▫ *yg lain*: I'm afraid I can't see you tomorrow. Could we arrange another day? ♦ If you've already seen that film, we can go and see another.
IDM **another/a different matter** ➲ **matter¹**
one after another/the other ➲ **one¹**
yet another ➲ **yet**

answer¹ /ˈɑːnsə(r)/ noun [C] **an answer (to sb/sth)** 1 something that you say, write or do as a reply ▫ *jawapan; balasan*: The answer to your question is that I don't know. ♦ They've made me an offer and I have to give them an answer by Friday. ♦ I wrote to them two weeks ago and I'm still waiting for an answer. ♦ I knocked on the door and waited but there was no answer. **SYN** reply 2 a solution to a problem ▫ *penyelesaian; jalan keluar*: I didn't have any money so the only answer was to borrow some. 3 the correct reply to a question in a test or exam ▫ *jawapan*: What was the answer to question 4? 4 a reply to a question in a

answer → anticipation 32

test or exam □ *jawapan*: *My answer to question 5 was wrong.* ♦ *How many answers did you get right?* **IDM** **in answer (to sth)** as a reply (to sth) □ *sebagai jawapan*

answer² /'ɑːnsə(r)/ *verb* [I,T] **1** to say or write sth back to sb who has asked you sth or written to you □ *jawab; menjawab*: *I asked her what the matter was but she didn't answer.* ♦ *I've asked you a question, now please answer me.* ♦ *Answer all the questions on the form.* ♦ *He hasn't answered my email yet* (= written an email back to me). ♦ *When I asked him how much he earned, he answered that it was none of my business.* ♦ *'No!' he answered angrily.* **2** to do sth as a reply □ *jawab*: *to answer the phone* (= to pick up the phone when it rings) ♦ *I rang their doorbell but nobody answered.*

PHR V **answer back** to defend yourself against sth bad that has been written or said about you □ *membela diri*
answer (sb) back to reply rudely to sb □ *menjawab (balik); melawan*
answer for sb/sth 1 to accept responsibility for sth/sb □ *bertanggungjawab*: *Somebody will have to answer for all the damage that has been caused.* **2** to speak in support of sb/sth □ *menyokong*: *I can certainly answer for her honesty.*

OTHER WORDS FOR

answer

Answer and **reply** are the most common verbs used for speaking or writing in reaction to questions, letters, etc: *I asked him a question but he didn't answer.* ♦ *I sent my application but they haven't replied yet.* Note that you **answer** a person, a question, an email or a letter (no 'to') but you **reply to** an email or a letter. **Respond** is less common and more formal with this meaning: *Applicants must respond within seven days.* It is more commonly used with the meaning of 'reacting in a way that is desired': *Despite all the doctor's efforts the patient did not respond to treatment.*

---

answerable /'ɑːnsərəbl/ *adj* [not before a noun] **answerable to sb (for sth)** having to explain and give good reasons for your actions to sb; responsible to sb □ *bertanggungjawab*

'answering machine (*BrE* also **answerphone** /'ɑːnsəfəʊn/) *noun* [C] a machine that answers the telephone and records messages from the people who call □ *mesin jawab panggilan telefon*: *I rang him and left a message on his answering machine.*

ant /ænt/ *noun* [C] a very small insect that lives in large groups and works very hard □ *semut* ⊃ picture on **page P13**

antagonism /æn'tægənɪzəm/ *noun* [C,U] **antagonism (towards sb/sth); antagonism (between A and B)** a feeling of hate and of being against sb/sth □ *permusuhan* ▶ **antagonistic** /æn,tægə'nɪstɪk/ *adj*

antagonize (also **-ise**) /æn'tægənaɪz/ *verb* [T] to make sb angry or to annoy sb □ *membangkitkan kemarahan; memarahkan*

the Antarctic /æn'tɑːktɪk/ *noun* [sing] the most southern part of the world □ *kawasan Antartik* ⊃ look at **the Arctic** ⊃ picture at **earth**

Antarctic /æn'tɑːktɪk/ *adj* [only *before* a noun] connected with the coldest, most southern parts of the world □ *Antartik*: *an Antarctic expedition* ⊃ look at **Arctic**

antelope /'æntɪləʊp/ *noun* [C] (*pl* **antelope** or **antelopes**) an African animal with horns and long, thin legs that can run very fast □ *antelop*

antelope

antenatal /,æntɪ'neɪtl/ *adj* [only *before* a noun] connected with the care of pregnant women □ *antenatal*: *an antenatal clinic* ♦ *antenatal care*

antenna /æn'tenə/ *noun* [C] **1** (*pl* **antennae** /-niː/) one of the two long thin parts on the heads of insects and some animals that live in shells. Antennae are used for feeling things. □ *sesungut* **SYN** **feeler** ⊃ picture on **page P13** **2** (*pl* **antennas**) (*AmE*) = **aerial¹**

anthem /'ænθəm/ *noun* [C] a song, especially one that is sung on special occasions □ *lagu yg dinyanyikan dlm peristiwa tertentu*: *the national anthem* (= the special song of a country)

anthology /æn'θɒlədʒi/ *noun* [C] (*pl* **anthologies**) a book that contains pieces of writing or poems, often on the same subject, by different authors □ *antologi*: *an anthology of love poetry*

anthrax /'ænθræks/ *noun* [U] a serious disease that affects sheep, cows and sometimes people, and can cause death □ *antraks*

anthropology /,ænθrə'pɒlədʒi/ *noun* [U] the study of humans, especially of their origin, development, customs and beliefs □ *antropologi* ▶ **anthropological** /,ænθrəpə'lɒdʒɪkl/ *adj* ▶ **anthropologist** /,ænθrə'pɒlədʒɪst/ *noun* [C]

anti- /'ænti/ [in compounds] **1** against □ *menentang*: *anti-tank weapons* ⊃ look at **pro- 2** the opposite of □ *berlawanan dgn*: *anticlimax* **3** preventing □ *mencegah*: *antifreeze*

antibiotic /,æntibaɪ'ɒtɪk/ *noun* [C, usually *pl*] a medicine which is used for destroying bacteria and curing infections □ *antibiotik*

antibody /'æntibɒdi/ *noun* [C] (*pl* **antibodies**) a substance that the body produces in the blood to fight disease, or as a reaction when certain substances are put into the body □ *antibodi*

anticipate /æn'tɪsɪpeɪt/ *verb* [T] to expect sth to happen and prepare for it □ *menjangka*: *to anticipate a problem* ♦ *I anticipate that the situation will get worse.*

anticipation /æn,tɪsɪ'peɪʃn/ *noun* [U] **1** the state of expecting sth to happen (and preparing for it) □ *jangkaan*: *The government has reduced tax **in anticipation of** an early general election.* **2** excited feelings about sth that is going to happen □ *(perasaan) penuh harapan*: *happy/eager/excited anticipation*

anticlimax /ˌænti'klaɪmæks/ *noun* [C,U] an event, etc. that is less exciting than you had expected or than what has already happened □ *antiklimaks*: *When the exams were over, we all had a sense of anticlimax.*

anticlockwise /ˌænti'klɒkwaɪz/ (*AmE* **counterclockwise**) *adv, adj* in the opposite direction to the movement of the hands of a clock □ *lawan arah jam*: *Turn the lid anticlockwise/in an anticlockwise direction.* **OPP** **clockwise**

antics /'æntɪks/ *noun* [pl] funny, strange or silly ways of behaving □ *telatah*

antidepressant /ˌæntidɪ'presnt/ *noun* [C] a drug used to treat depression (= unhappiness that lasts for a long time) □ *antidepresan*

antidote /'æntidəʊt/ *noun* [C] **1** a medical substance that is used to prevent a poison or a disease from having an effect □ *penawar*: *an antidote to snake bites* **2** anything that helps you to deal with sth unpleasant □ *penawar; ubat*

antifreeze /'æntifriːz/ *noun* [U] a chemical that you add to the water in cars, etc. to stop it from freezing □ *antibeku*

antipathy /æn'tɪpəθi/ *noun* [C,U, usually sing] (*pl* **antipathies**) (*formal*) **antipathy (to/towards sb/sth)** a strong feeling of not liking sb/sth □ *antipati; rasa benci* **SYN** **dislike**

antiperspirant /ˌænti'pɜːspərənt/ *noun* [C,U] a substance that people use, especially under the arms, to prevent or reduce sweat □ *antipeluh*

antiquated /'æntikweɪtɪd/ *adj* old-fashioned and not suitable for the modern world □ *kolot; lapuk*

antique /æn'tiːk/ *adj* very old and therefore unusual and valuable □ *antik*: *an antique vase/table* ♦ *antique furniture/jewellery* ▶ **antique** *noun* [C]: *an antique shop* (= one that sells antiques) ♦ *That vase is an antique.*

antiquity /æn'tɪkwəti/ *noun* (*pl* **antiquities**) **1** [U] the ancient past, especially the times of the ancient Greeks and Romans □ *zaman purba* **2** [U] the state of being very old or ancient □ *kepurbaan* **3** [C, usually pl] a building or object from ancient times □ *bangunan atau barang-barang purba*: *Greek/Roman antiquities*

anti-Semitism /ˌænti 'semətɪzəm/ *noun* [U] unfair treatment of Jewish people □ *anti-Yahudi* ▶ **anti-Semitic** /ˌænti sə'mɪtɪk/ *adj*

antiseptic /ˌænti'septɪk/ *noun* [C,U] a liquid or cream that prevents a cut, etc. from becoming infected □ *antiseptik*: *Put an antiseptic/some antiseptic on that scratch.* **SYN** **disinfectan** ▶ **antiseptic** *adj*: *antiseptic cream*

antisocial /ˌænti'səʊʃl/ *adj* **1** harmful or annoying to other people □ *antisosial*: *antisocial behaviour* **2** not liking to be with other people □ *tdk suka bergaul; antisosial*

antithesis /æn'tɪθəsɪs/ *noun* [C, usually sing] (*pl* **antitheses** /æn'tɪθəsiːz/) (*formal*) **1** the opposite of sth □ *lawan; sst yg bertentangan*: *Love is the antithesis of hate.* **2** a difference between two things □ *antitesis*

antivirus /ˌænti'vaɪrəs/ *adj* (used of software) designed to find and destroy computer viruses □ *antivirus* ⊃ note at **cybercrime**

antler /'æntlə(r)/ *noun* [C, usually pl] a horn shaped like a branch on the head of some adult male animals □ *tanduk rusa*: *a pair of antlers* ⊃ picture at **deer, elk, reindeer** ⊃ picture on **page P12**

antonym /'æntənɪm/ *noun* [C] (*technical*) a word that means the opposite of another word □ *antonim; kata lawan* **SYN** **opposite** ⊃ look at **synonym**

anus /'eɪnəs/ *noun* [C] the hole through which solid waste substances leave the body □ *dubur; anus*

¶ **anxiety** /æŋ'zaɪəti/ *noun* [C,U] (*pl* **anxieties**) a feeling of worry or fear, especially about the future □ *kebimbangan*: *a feeling/state of anxiety* ♦ *There are anxieties over the effects of unemployment.*

¶ **anxious** /'æŋkʃəs/ *adj* **1 anxious (about/for sb/sth)** worried and afraid □ *risau; bimbang; cemas*: *I'm anxious about my exam.* ♦ *I began to get anxious when they still hadn't arrived at 9 o'clock.* ♦ *an anxious look/expression* **2** causing worry and fear □ *(yg) mencemaskan*: *For a few anxious moments we thought we'd missed the train.* **3 anxious to do sth; anxious for sth** wanting sth very much □ *ingin sekali*: *Police are anxious to find the owner of the white car.* ▶ **anxiously** *adv*: *'Are you all right?' he asked anxiously.*

¶ **any** /'eni/ *determiner, pron, adv* **1** used instead of *some* in negative sentences and in questions □ *sebarang; mana-mana; apa-apa; langsung*: *We didn't have any lunch.* ♦ *I speak hardly any* (= almost no) *Spanish.* ♦ *Do you have any questions?* ♦ *I don't like any of his books.* ⊃ note at **some** **2** used for saying that it does not matter which thing or person you choose □ *mana-mana; bila-bila*: *Take any book you want.* ♦ *Come round any time—I'm usually in.* ♦ *I'll take any that you don't want.* **3** [used in negative sentences and questions] at all; to any degree □ *lebih (laju, baik, dsb)*: *I can't run any faster.* ♦ *Is your father any better?*

IDM **any moment, day, minute, second, etc. (now)** very soon □ *bila-bila masa saja*: *She should be home any minute now.*

¶ **anybody** /'enibɒdi/ (*AmE* also) / (also **anyone**) *pron* **1** [usually in questions or negative statements] any person □ *sesiapa*: *I didn't know anybody at the party.* ♦ *Is there anybody here who can speak Japanese?* ♦ *Would anybody else* (= any other person) *like to come with me?* ⊃ note at **some, somebody**

anyhow → aperitif

HELP The difference between **somebody** and **anybody** is the same as the difference between **some** and **any**.

2 any person, it does not matter who □ *sesiapa pun*: **Anybody** (= all people) can learn to swim. ◆ Can **anybody** come, or are there special invitations?

anyhow /ˈenihaʊ/ adv **1** = **anyway 2** in a careless way; with no order □ *secara sembarangan*: Don't throw your clothes down just **anyhow**!

any ˈmore (BrE) (also **anymore**) adv often used at the end of negative sentences and at the end of questions, to mean 'any longer' □ *lagi*: She doesn't live here **any more**. ◆ Why doesn't he speak to me **any more**?

anyone /ˈeniwʌn/ = **anybody**

anyplace /ˈenipleɪs/ (AmE) = **anywhere**

anything /ˈeniθɪŋ/ pron **1** [usually in negative sentences and questions] one thing (of any kind) □ *apa-apa pun; apa-apa*: It was so dark that I couldn't see **anything** at all. ◆ There isn't **anything** interesting in the newspaper today. ◆ Did you buy **anything**? ◆ 'I'd like a kilo of apples please.' '**Anything** else?' (= any other thing?) ➔ note at **some**

HELP The difference between **something** and **anything** is the same as the difference between **some** and **any**.

2 any thing or things: it does not matter what □ *sst; apa-apa saja; apa saja*: I'm very hungry—I'll eat **anything**! ◆ I'll do **anything** you say.

IDM anything but not at all □ *sama sekali tdk*: Their explanation was **anything but** clear.
anything like sb/sth at all similar to sb/sth; nearly □ *serupa dgn; sama*: She isn't **anything like** her sister, is she? ◆ This car isn't **anything like** as fast as mine.
as happy, quick, etc. as anything (spoken) very happy, quick, etc. □ *benar-benar gembira, pantas, dsb*
do nothing/not do anything by halves ➔ **half¹**
like anything ➔ **like¹**
not come to anything ➔ **come**

anyway /ˈeniweɪ/ (also **anyhow**) adv **1** (used to add an extra point or reason) in any case □ *lagipun*: I don't want to go out tonight, and **anyway** I haven't got any money. **SYN** besides **2** used when saying or writing sth which contrasts in some way with what has gone before □ *walau bagaimanapun*: I don't think we'll succeed, but **anyway** we can try. ◆ I'm afraid I can't come to your party, but thanks **anyway**. **3** used after a pause in order to change the subject or go back to a subject being discussed before □ *bagaimanapun*: **Anyway**, that's enough about my problems. How are you? **4** (used for correcting sth you have just said and making it more accurate) at least □ *sekurang-kurangnya*: Everybody wants to be rich—well, most people **anyway**.

anywhere /ˈeniweə(r)/ (AmE also **anyplace**) adv **1** [usually in negative sentences or in questions] in, at or to any place □ *di mana-mana; ke mana-mana*: I can't find my keys **anywhere**. ◆ Is there a post office **anywhere** near here? ◆ You can't buy the book **anywhere else** (= in another place). ➔ note at **some**

HELP The difference between **somewhere** and **anywhere** is the same as the difference between **some** and **any**.

2 any place; it does not matter where □ *di mana pun*: You can sit **anywhere** you like.

aorta /eɪˈɔːtə/ noun [C] the main **artery** that carries blood from the heart to the rest of the body □ *aorta*

apart /əˈpɑːt/ adv **1** away from sb/sth or each other; not together □ *renggang; jarak; terpisah; jauh berbeza, dsb*: The doors slowly slid **apart**. ◆ Stand with your feet **apart**. ◆ The houses are ten metres **apart**. ◆ I'm afraid our ideas are too far **apart**. ◆ I can't tell the twins **apart**. (= I can't see the difference between them.) ➔ look at **tell**(7) **2** into pieces □ *berkecai; berderai*: The material was so old that it just fell/came **apart** in my hands.
IDM take sth apart to separate sth into pieces □ *menanggalkan; mencerai-ceraikan*: He took the whole bicycle **apart**.

aˈpart from (especially AmE **aˈside from**) prep **1** except for □ *melainkan; kecuali*: I've answered all the questions **apart from** the last one. ◆ There's nobody here **apart from** me. **2** as well as; in addition to □ *selain*: **Apart from** music, she also loves painting.

apartheid /əˈpɑːtaɪt/ (AmE also) / noun [U] the former official government policy in South Africa of separating people of different races and making them live apart □ *aparteid*

apartment /əˈpɑːtmənt/ noun [C] **1** (especially AmE) = **flat²**(1) **2** a set of rooms rented for a holiday □ *apartmen; pangsapuri*: a self-catering **apartment**

aˈpartment block noun [C] (AmE) (also **aˈpartment building**) a large building containing several apartments □ *blok pangsapuri*

apathetic /ˌæpəˈθetɪk/ adj lacking interest or desire to act □ *bersikap acuh tak acuh*: Many students are **apathetic** about politics.

apathy /ˈæpəθi/ noun [U] the feeling of not being interested in or enthusiastic about anything □ *sikap acuh tak acuh; apati*: There is widespread **apathy** towards the elections.

ape¹ /eɪp/ noun [C] a type of animal like a large **monkey** (= an animal that lives in hot countries and can climb trees) with no tail or only a very short tail □ *mawas*: Chimpanzees and gorillas are **apes**.

ape² /eɪp/ verb [T] to copy sb/sth, especially in a ridiculous way □ *meniru; mengajuk*: The children were **aping** the teacher's way of walking.

aperitif /əˌperəˈtiːf/ noun [C] an alcoholic drink that you have before a meal □ *aperitif*

ʌ **cup**   ɜː **bird**   ə **ago**   eɪ **pay**   əʊ **go**   aɪ **my**   aʊ **now**   ɔɪ **boy**   ɪə **near**   eə **hair**   ʊə **pure**

aperture /ˈæpətʃə(r)/ noun [C] (formal) a small opening in sth, especially one that allows light into a camera □ *apertur; bukaan; lubang*

apex /ˈeɪpeks/ noun [C, usually sing] (pl **apexes**) the top or highest part of sth □ *apeks; puncak; titik tertinggi*: *the apex of the roof*

apiece /əˈpiːs/ adv [used after a noun or number] each □ *setiap (seorang/satu)*: *Rooney and Walcott scored a goal apiece.*

apologetic /əˌpɒləˈdʒetɪk/ adj feeling or showing that you are sorry for sth you have done □ *meminta maaf; menyatakan kesal*: *He was most apologetic about his son's bad behaviour.* ◆ *I wrote him an apologetic letter.* ▶ **apologetically** /-kli/ adv

apologize (also **-ise**) /əˈpɒlədʒaɪz/ verb [I] **apologize (to sb) (for sth)** to say that you are sorry for sth that you have done □ *meminta maaf*: *You'll have to apologize to your teacher for being late.*

> **MORE** When you apologize, the actual words you use are usually '**I'm sorry**'.

apology /əˈpɒlədʒi/ noun [C,U] (pl **apologies**) **(an) apology (to sb) (for sth)** a spoken or written statement that you are sorry for sth you have done, etc □ *(kenyataan) meminta maaf*: *Please accept our apologies for the delay.* ◆ *a letter of apology*

apostrophe /əˈpɒstrəfi/ noun [C] **1** the sign (') used for showing that you have left a letter or letters out of a word as in *I'm, can't* or *we'll* □ *koma di atas (utk menandakan pengguguran huruf)* **2** the sign (') used for showing who or what sth belongs to, as in *John's chair, the boy's room* or *Russia's President* □ *koma di atas (utk menunjukkan milik)*

app /æp/ (also **application**) noun [C] a computer program that is designed to do a particular job, especially one that lets you see information about a particular subject, play games, etc. on your mobile phone □ *aplikasi*: *I've got an English dictionary app on my phone.*

appal (*AmE* **appall**) /əˈpɔːl/ verb [T] (**appalling; appalled**) [usually passive] to shock sb very much □ *mengejutkan*: *We were appalled by the poverty and starvation we saw everywhere.* ▶ **appalling** adj ▶ **appallingly** adv

apparatus /ˌæpəˈreɪtəs/ noun [U] the set of tools, instruments or equipment used for doing a job or an activity □ *perkakas; radas; alat*

apparent /əˈpærənt/ adj **1 apparent (to sb)** clear; easy to see □ *jelas; ketara*: *It quickly became apparent to us that our teacher could not speak French.* **SYN** **obvious** **2** [only before a noun] that seems to be real or true but may not be □ *nampaknya*: *His apparent interest in the proposal didn't last very long.*

apparently /əˈpærəntli/ adv according to what people say or to how sth appears, but perhaps not true □ *nampaknya; dengarnya*: *Apparently, he's already been married twice.* ◆ *He was apparently undisturbed by the news.*

apparition /ˌæpəˈrɪʃn/ noun [C] the image of a dead person that a living person believes they can see □ *penjelmaan; lembaga*

appeal¹ /əˈpiːl/ noun **1** [C] a formal request to sb in authority to change a decision □ *rayuan*: *The judge turned down the defendant's appeal.* **2** [U] the attraction or interesting quality of sth/sb □ *daya tarikan*: *I can't understand the appeal of stamp collecting.* **3** [C] a serious request for sth you need or want very much □ *rayuan*: *The police have made an urgent appeal for witnesses to come forward.* **4** [C] **an appeal to sth** a suggestion that tries to influence sb's feelings or thoughts so that they will do what you want □ *rayuan*: *an appeal to our sense of national pride*

appeal² /əˈpiːl/ verb [I] **1 appeal (against/for sth)** to ask sb in authority to make or change a decision □ *membuat rayuan (bantahan)*: *He decided to appeal against his conviction.* ◆ *The player fell down and appealed for a penalty.* **2 appeal (to sb)** to be attractive or interesting to sb □ *menarik hati*: *The idea of living in the country doesn't appeal to me at all.* **3 appeal to sb (for sth); appeal for sth** to make a serious request for sth you need or want very much □ *merayu*: *She appealed to the kidnappers to let her son go.* ◆ *Relief workers in the disaster area are appealing for more supplies.* **4 appeal to sth** to influence sb's feelings or thoughts so that they will do sth you want □ *merayu*: *We aim to appeal to people's generosity.*

appealing /əˈpiːlɪŋ/ adj **1** attractive or interesting □ *menarik*: *The idea of a lying on a beach sounds very appealing!* **2** showing that you need help, etc □ *(yg) memerlukan bantuan*: *an appealing look* ▶ **appealingly** adv

appear /əˈpɪə(r)/ verb [I] **1 appear to be/do sth; appear (that)…** to seem □ *nampaknya*: *She appears to be very happy in her job.* ◆ *It appears that you were given the wrong information.* ⊃ *adjective* **apparent** **2** to suddenly be seen; to come into sight □ *muncul; kelihatan*: *The bus appeared from round the corner.* **OPP** **disappear** **3** to begin to exist □ *mula timbul*: *The disease is thought to have appeared in Africa.* **4** to be published or printed □ *diterbitkan*: *The article appeared in this morning's paper.* **5** to perform or speak where you are seen by a lot of people □ *muncul*: *to appear on TV/in a play*

appearance /əˈpɪərəns/ noun **1** [U] the way that sb/sth looks or seems □ *rupa*: *A different hairstyle can completely change your appearance.* ◆ *He gives the appearance of being extremely confident.* **2** [sing] the coming of sb/sth □ *kemunculan*: *the appearance of TV in the home in the 1950s* **3** [C] an act of appearing in public, especially on stage, TV, etc. □ *kemunculan*: *His last appearance before his death was as Julius Caesar.*

[C] **countable**, a noun with a plural form: *one book, two books*   [U] **uncountable**, a noun with no plural form: *some sugar*

appease → appraise

appease /əˈpiːz/ verb [T] (formal) to give sb what they want in order to make them less angry or to give a country what it wants in order to avoid a war □ *menenangkan; memujuk* ▶**appeasement** noun [U]

appendicitis /əˌpendəˈsaɪtɪs/ noun [U] an illness in which your **appendix** becomes extremely painful and usually has to be removed □ *apendisitis*

appendix /əˈpendɪks/ noun [C] 1 (pl appendixes) a small organ inside your body near your stomach. In humans, the **appendix** has no real function. □ *apendiks* 2 (pl appendices /-dɪsiːz/) a section at the end of a book, etc. that gives extra information □ *lampiran*

appetite /ˈæpɪtaɪt/ noun [C,U] a strong desire for sth, especially food □ *selera; keinginan*: *Some fresh air and exercise should give you an appetite* (= make you hungry). • *He has a great appetite for work/life.* • *loss of appetite*
IDM whet sb's appetite ⊃ whet

appetizer (also -iser) /ˈæpɪtaɪzə(r)/ (especially AmE) = starter

appetizing (also -ising) /ˈæpɪtaɪzɪŋ/ adj (used about food, etc.) that looks or smells attractive; making you feel hungry □ *menyelerakan*: *an appetizing smell*

applaud /əˈplɔːd/ verb 1 [I,T] to hit your hands together many times in order to show that you like sb/sth □ *memberi tepukan; bertepuk tangan*: *The audience applauded loudly.* • *The team was applauded as it left the field.* 2 [T, usually passive] to express approval of sth □ *memuji*: *The decision was applauded by everybody.*

applause /əˈplɔːz/ noun [U] the noise made by a group of people hitting their hands together to show their approval and enjoyment □ *tepukan*: *Let's all give a big round of applause to the cook!*

apple /ˈæpl/ noun [C,U] a hard, round fruit with a smooth green, red or yellow skin □ *(buah) epal*: *apple juice* • *an apple pie* • *three apple trees* ⊃ picture on **page P14**

appliance /əˈplaɪəns/ noun [C] a piece of equipment for a particular purpose in the house □ *alat*: *washing machines and other domestic appliances*

applicable /əˈplɪkəbl; ˈæplɪkəbl/ adj applicable (to sb/sth) that concerns sb/sth □ *berkenaan/berkaitan dgn*: *This part of the form is only applicable to married women.* **SYN** relevant

applicant /ˈæplɪkənt/ noun [C] a person who applies for sth, especially for a job, a place at a college, university, etc. □ *pemohon*: *There were over 200 applicants for the job.*

application /ˌæplɪˈkeɪʃn/ noun 1 [C,U] (an) application (to sb) (for sth) a formal written request, especially for a job or a place in a school, club, etc □ *permohonan*: *Applications for the job should be made to the Personnel Manager.* • *To become a member, fill in the application form.* • *Further information is available on application to the principal.* ⊃ note at **job** 2 [C,U] the practical use (of sth) □ *penggunaan*: *the application of technology in the classroom* 3 [C] a computer program designed to do a particular job □ *aplikasi*: *a database application* 4 [C] = app 5 [U] hard work; effort □ *ketekunan; usaha*: *Success as a writer demands great application.*

applied /əˈplaɪd/ adj (used about a subject) studied in a way that has a practical use □ *gunaan* **OPP** pure

apply /əˈplaɪ/ verb (applying; applies; pt, pp applied)
▶FOR JOB/COURSE **1** [I] apply (to sb) (for sth) to ask for sth in writing □ *memohon*: *I've applied to that company for a job.* • *She's applying for a place at university.*
▶USE **2** [T] apply sth (to sth) to make practical use of sth □ *menggunakan; digunakan*: *new technology which can be applied to solving problems in industry*
▶CREAM **3** [T] apply sth (to sth) to put or spread sth onto sth □ *membubuh*: *Apply the cream to the infected area twice a day.*
▶BE RELEVANT **4** [I] apply (to sb/sth) to concern or involve sb/sth □ *ada kaitan*: *This information applies to all children born after 2007.*
▶DESCRIBE **5** [T, usually passive] to use a word, a name, etc. to describe sb/sth □ *digunakan*: *I don't think the term 'music' can be applied to that awful noise.*
▶WORK HARD **6** [T] apply yourself/sth (to sth/doing sth) to make yourself give all your attention to sth □ *menumpukan (perhatian)*: *to apply your mind to something*

appoint /əˈpɔɪnt/ verb [T] **1** appoint sb (to sth) to choose sb for a job or position □ *melantik*: *The committee have appointed a new chairperson.* • *He's been appointed (as) assistant to Dr McMullen.* **2** (formal) appoint sth (for sth) to arrange or decide on sth □ *menentukan; menetapkan*: *the date appointed for the next meeting*

appointment /əˈpɔɪntmənt/ noun **1** [C,U] an appointment (with sb) an arrangement to see sb at a particular time □ *janji temu*: *I have an appointment with Dr Sula at 3 o'clock.* • *I'd like to make an appointment to see the manager.* • *I realized I wouldn't be able to keep the appointment so I cancelled it.* • *Visits are by appointment only* (= at a time that has been arranged in advance). **2** [U] appointment (to sth) the act of choosing sb for a job □ *pelantikan*: *Many people criticized the appointment of such a young man to the post.* **3** [C] a job or a position of responsibility □ *jawatan*: *a temporary/permanent appointment*

appraisal /əˈpreɪzl/ noun [C,U] (formal) a judgement about the value or quality of sb/sth □ *penilaian*

appraise /əˈpreɪz/ verb [T] (formal) to judge the value or quality of sb/sth □ *menilai*

[I] **intransitive**, a verb which has no object: *He laughed.*   [T] **transitive**, a verb which has an object: *He ate an apple.*

appreciable /ə'priːʃəbl/ adj noticeable or important □ *agak ketara*

appreciate /ə'priːʃieɪt/ verb 1 [T] to enjoy sth or to understand the value of sb/sth □ *menilai; menghargai; menghayati*: My boss doesn't appreciate me. ◆ I don't appreciate good coffee—it all tastes the same to me. 2 [T] to be grateful for sth □ *menghargai*: Thanks very much. I really appreciate your help. 3 [T] to understand a problem, situation, etc □ *faham; sedar*: I appreciate your problem but I'm afraid I can't help you. 4 [I] to increase in value □ *bertambah nilai*: Houses in this area have appreciated faster than elsewhere.

appreciation /ə,priːʃi'eɪʃn/ noun [U] 1 understanding and enjoyment of the value of sth □ *tahu menikmati*: I'm afraid I have little appreciation of modern architecture. 2 understanding of a situation, problem, etc. □ *kesedaran; menyedari* 3 the feeling of being grateful for sth □ *penghargaan*: We bought him a present to show our appreciation for all the work he had done. 4 an increase in value □ *kenaikan nilai*

appreciative /ə'priːʃətɪv/ adj 1 appreciative (of sth) grateful for sth □ *menghargai; berterima kasih*: He was very appreciative of our efforts to help. 2 feeling or showing pleasure or admiration □ *(yg) menunjukkan penghargaan*: an appreciative audience

apprehend /,æprɪ'hend/ verb [T] (formal) (used about the police) to catch sb and arrest them □ *menangkap; memberkas*

apprehensive /,æprɪ'hensɪv/ adj worried or afraid that sth unpleasant may happen □ *khuatir; risau*: I'm feeling apprehensive about tomorrow's exam. ▶**apprehension** /,æprɪ'henʃn/ noun [C,U]

apprentice /ə'prentɪs/ noun [C] a young person who works for a fixed period of time, in order to learn the skills needed in a particular job □ *perantis*: an apprentice electrician/chef/plumber

apprenticeship /ə'prentɪʃɪp/ noun [C,U] the state or time of being an **apprentice** □ *perantisan*: He served a two-year apprenticeship as a carpenter.

approach¹ /ə'prəʊtʃ/ verb 1 [I,T] to come near or nearer to sb/sth □ *menjelang; mendekati*: The day of the exam approached. ◆ When you approach the village you will see a garage on your left. 2 [T] to speak to sb usually in order to ask for sth □ *berjumpa (dgn sso utk meminta sst)*: I'm going to approach my bank manager about a loan. 3 [T] to begin to deal with a problem, a situation, etc □ *mula menghadapi atau mengatasi sst (keadaan, masalah, dsb)*: What is the best way to approach this problem?

approach² /ə'prəʊtʃ/ noun 1 [C] a way of dealing with sb/sth □ *pendekatan*: Parents don't always know what approach to take with teenage children. 2 [sing] the act of coming nearer (to sb/sth) □ *(perbuatan) mendekati; menjelang*: the approach of winter 3 [C] a request for sth □ *permintaan*: The club has **made an approach to** us for financial assistance. 4 [C] a road or path leading to sth □ *jalan masuk*: the approach to the village

approachable /ə'prəʊtʃəbl/ adj 1 friendly and easy to talk to □ *mudah didekati; tdk sombong* 2 [not before a noun] that can be reached □ *dpt sampai* **SYN** accessible

appropriate¹ /ə'prəʊpriət/ adj appropriate (for/to sth) suitable or right for a particular situation, person, use, etc □ *wajar; sesuai*: The matter will be dealt with by the appropriate authorities. ◆ I don't think this film is appropriate for young children. **OPP** inappropriate ▶appropriately adv

appropriate² /ə'prəʊprieɪt/ verb [T] (formal) to take sth to use for yourself, usually without permission □ *mengambil* ▶appropriation /ə,prəʊpri'eɪʃn/ noun [U, sing]

approval /ə'pruːvl/ noun [U] feeling, showing or saying that you think sth is good; agreement □ *persetujuan; kebenaran*: Everybody gave their approval to the proposal. **OPP** disapproval

approve /ə'pruːv/ verb 1 [I] approve (of sb/sth) to be pleased about sth; to like sb/sth □ *berkenan; suka*: His father didn't approve of him becoming a dancer. ◆ Her parents don't approve of her friends. **OPP** disapprove 2 [T] to agree formally to sth or to say that sth is correct □ *mengesahkan; meluluskan*: We need to get an accountant to approve these figures.

approving /ə'pruːvɪŋ/ adj showing support or admiration for sth □ *menunjukkan berkenan atau setuju*: 'I agree entirely,' he said with an approving smile. ▶approvingly adv

approx abbr (written) = approximate, approximately

approximate /ə'prɒksɪmət/ adj (abbr approx) almost correct but not completely accurate □ *kira-kira; lebih kurang; anggaran*: The approximate time of arrival is 3 o'clock. ◆ I can only give you an approximate idea of the cost. **OPP** exact

approximately /ə'prɒksɪmətli/ adv (abbr approx) about □ *kira-kira; lebih kurang*: It's approximately fifty miles from here. **SYN** roughly

approximation /ə,prɒksɪ'meɪʃn/ noun [C] a number, an answer, etc which is nearly, but not exactly, right □ *anggaran*

Apr. abbr = **April**: 2 Apr. 2009

apricot /'eɪprɪkɒt/ noun [C] a small, round, yellow or orange fruit with a large stone inside □ *aprikot* ⊃ picture on page P14

April /'eɪprəl/ noun [U,C] (abbr Apr.) the 4th month of the year, coming after March □ *April* ⊃ note at **January**

April Fool's Day → architecture

April Fool's Day noun [sing] 1 April □ *Hari April Fool*

> **CULTURE**
> On this day it is traditional for people to play tricks on each other, especially by inventing silly stories and trying to persuade other people that they are true. If somebody believes such a story, they are called an **April Fool**.

apron /'eɪprən/ noun [C] a piece of clothing that you wear over the front of your usual clothes in order to keep them clean, especially when cooking □ *apron* ⇒ picture at **overall**

apt /æpt/ adj 1 suitable in a particular situation □ *sesuai*: *I thought 'difficult' was an apt description of the book.* 2 **apt to do sth** often likely to do sth □ *besar kemungkinannya*

aptitude /'æptɪtjuːd/ noun [U,C] **aptitude (for sth/for doing sth)** natural ability or skill □ *kebolehan; bakat*: *She has an aptitude for learning languages.*

aptly /'æptli/ adv in an appropriate way □ *wajar*: *The winner of the race was aptly named Alan Speedy.* **SYN** *suitably*

aquamarine /ˌækwəmə'riːn/ noun 1 [C,U] a pale greenish-blue **precious** (= rare and valuable) stone □ *(batu) akuamarin* 2 [U] a pale greenish-blue colour □ *(warna) akuamarin* ▶**aquamarine** adj: *the aquamarine sea*

aquarium /ə'kweəriəm/ noun [C] (pl **aquariums** or **aquaria** /-riə/) 1 a glass container filled with water, in which fish and water animals are kept □ *akuarium* 2 a building where people can go to see fish and other water animals □ *akuarium*

Aquarius /ə'kweəriəs/ noun [C,U] the 11th sign of the **zodiac** (= 12 signs which represent the positions of the sun, moon and planets), the Water Carrier; a person born under this sign □ *Aquarius*: *I'm an Aquarius.* ⇒ picture at **zodiac**

aquatic /ə'kwætɪk/ adj living or taking place in, on or near water □ *akuatik*: *aquatic plants* ♦ *windsurfing and other aquatic sports*

Arab /'ærəb/ noun [C] a member of a people who lived originally in Arabia and who now live in many parts of the Middle East and North Africa □ *orang Arab* ▶**Arab** adj: *Arab countries*

Arabic /'ærəbɪk/ noun [sing] the language of Arab people □ *bahasa Arab* ▶**Arabic** adj

arable /'ærəbl/ adj (in farming) connected with growing crops for sale, not keeping animals □ *berkaitan dgn pertanian*: *arable land/farmers*

arbitrary /'ɑːbɪtrəri/ adj not seeming to be based on any reason or plan □ *sewenang-wenang; sembarangan*: *The choice of players for the team seemed completely arbitrary.* ▶**arbitrarily** /ˌɑːbɪ'treərəli/ adv

arbitrate /'ɑːbɪtreɪt/ verb [I,T] to officially settle an argument between two people or groups by finding a solution that both can accept □ *menimbang tara* ▶**arbitration** /ˌɑːbɪ'treɪʃn/ noun [U] ▶**arbitrator** /'ɑːbɪtreɪtə(r)/ noun [C]

arc /ɑːk/ noun [C] a curved line, part of a circle □ *lengkok*

arcade /ɑː'keɪd/ noun [C] 1 a large covered passage or area with shops along one or both sides □ *arked*: *a shopping arcade* 2 (also **a'musement arcade**) a large room with machines and games that you put coins into to play □ *arked*

arch[1] /ɑːtʃ/ noun [C] 1 a curved structure with straight sides, often supporting a bridge or the roof of a large building, or it may be above a door or window □ *gerbang* ⇒ look at **archway** 2 the curved part of the bottom of your foot □ *lengkung tapak kaki*

arch[2] /ɑːtʃ/ verb [I,T] to make a curve □ *melengkungkan*

archaeological (*AmE* **archeological**) /ˌɑːkiə'lɒdʒɪkl/ adj connected with **archaeology** □ *(berkenaan dgn) arkeologi*

archaeologist (*AmE* **archeologist**) /ˌɑːki'ɒlədʒɪst/ noun [C] an expert in **archaeology** □ *ahli arkeologi*

archaeology (*AmE* **archeology**) /ˌɑːki'ɒlədʒi/ noun [U] the study of the past, based on objects or parts of buildings that are found in the ground □ *arkeologi*

archaic /ɑː'keɪɪk/ adj very old-fashioned; no longer used □ *arkaik; kuno*

archbishop /ˌɑːtʃ'bɪʃəp/ noun [C] a priest with a very high position, in some branches of the Christian Church, who is responsible for all the churches in a large area of a country □ *ketua biskop*: *the Archbishop of Canterbury* (= the head of the Church of England) ⇒ look at **bishop**

archeological (*AmE*) = **archaeological**

archeologist (*AmE*) = **archaeologist**

archeology (*AmE*) = **archaeology**

archer /'ɑːtʃə(r)/ noun [C] a person who shoots arrows through the air by pulling back a tight string on a **bow** (= a curved piece of wood) and letting go. In the past this was done in order to kill people, but it is now done as a sport. □ *pemanah*

archery /'ɑːtʃəri/ noun [U] the sport of shooting arrows □ *(sukan) memanah*

architect /'ɑːkɪtekt/ noun [C] a person whose job is to design buildings □ *arkitek; jurubina*

architectural /ˌɑːkɪ'tektʃərəl/ adj connected with the design of buildings □ *(berkenaan dgn) seni bina*

architecture /'ɑːkɪtektʃə(r)/ noun [U] 1 the study of designing and making buildings *(ilmu) seni bina* **2** the style or design of a building or buildings □ *(gaya) seni bina*: *modern architecture*

archive /'ɑːkaɪv/ *noun* [C] (also **archives** [pl]) a collection of historical documents, etc. which show the history of a place or an organization; the place where they are kept □ *arkib*: *archive material on the First World War* ▶ **archive** *verb* [T]: *Do you want to archive these documents now?*

archway /'ɑːtʃweɪ/ *noun* [C] a passage or entrance with an **arch** (= a curved structure) over it □ *pintu gerbang*

the Arctic /'ɑːktɪk/ *noun* [sing] the area around the North Pole □ *kawasan Artik* ⊃ look at **the Antarctic**

Arctic /'ɑːktɪk/ *adj* [only before a noun] **1** connected with the region around the North Pole (the most northern point of the world) □ *(berkenaan dgn) Artik* ⊃ look at **Antarctic 2 arctic** extremely cold □ *sangat sejuk*

the Arctic Circle *noun* [sing] a line that we imagine going around the cold area at the top of earth; the line of **latitude** (= a measurement of distance north or south) 66° 30' North □ *Garisan Artik* ⊃ picture at **earth**

ardent /'ɑːdnt/ *adj* showing strong feelings, especially a strong liking for sb/sth □ *ghairah; penuh semangat*: *an ardent supporter of the local football team* ▶ **ardently** *adv*

arduous /'ɑːdjuəs, -dʒu-/ *adj* full of difficulties; needing a lot of effort □ *sukar dan berat*: *an arduous journey* ♦ *arduous work*

are /ə(r); strong form ɑː(r)/ ⊃ **be**

ℓ area /'eəriə/ *noun* **1** [C] a part of a town, a country or the world □ *kawasan*: *Housing is very expensive in the Tokyo area.* ♦ *The wettest areas are in the West of the country.* ♦ *built-up areas* (= where there are a lot of buildings) ♦ *Forests cover a large area of the country.* **2** [C] a space used for a particular activity □ *bahagian*: *The shop has a children's play area.* **3** [C] a particular part of a subject or an activity □ *bidang*: *Training is one area of the business that we could improve.* **4** [C,U] the size of a surface, that you can calculate by multiplying the length by the width □ *luasnya*: *The area of the room is 35 square metres.* ♦ *The room is 35 square metres in area.* ⊃ look at **volume**

> **OTHER WORDS FOR**
>
> **area**
> A **district** may be part of a town or country, and it may have fixed boundaries: *the district controlled by a council.* A **region** is larger, usually part of a country only and may not have fixed boundaries: *the industrial regions of the country.* An **area** is the most general term and is used with the same meaning as both **district** and **region**: *the poorer areas of a town* ♦ *an agricultural area of the country.* We use **part** more often when we are talking about a section of a town: *Which part of Paris do you live in?*

39   **archive → aristocracy**

arena /ə'riːnə/ *noun* [C] **1** an area with seats around it where public entertainments (sports events, concerts, etc.) are held □ *gelanggang*; *arena* **2** an area of activity that concerns the public □ *arena*

aren't /ɑːnt/ short for **are not**

arguable /'ɑːgjuəbl/ *adj* **1** probably true; that you can give reasons for □ *ada benarnya*: *It is arguable that all hospital treatment should be free.* **2** probably not true; that you can give reasons against □ *dpt dipertikaikan* ▶ **arguably** /-əbli/ *adv*: *'King Lear' is arguably Shakespeare's best play.*

ℓ argue /'ɑːgjuː/ *verb* **1** [I] **argue (with sb) (about/over sth)** to say things, often angrily, that show that you do not agree with sb about sth □ *bertengkar; bertelingkah*: *The couple next door are always arguing.* ♦ *I never argue with my parents about money.* ⊃ look at **fight, quarrel** **2** [I,T] **argue that ...; argue (for/against sth)** to give reasons that support your opinion about sth □ *berhujah*: *She argued that they needed more time to finish the project.* ♦ *He argued against buying a new computer.* ♦ *They argued for the right to strike.*

ℓ argument /'ɑːgjumənt/ *noun* **1** [C,U] **an argument (with sb) (about/over sth)** an angry discussion between two or more people who disagree with each other □ *pertengkaran; pertelingkahan*: *Sue had an argument with her father about politics.* ♦ *He accepted the decision without argument.*

> **MORE** A noisy, serious argument is a **row** /raʊ/. A **quarrel** is usually about something less serious.

2 [C] the reason(s) that you give to support your opinion about sth □ *alasan*: *What are the arguments for/against lower taxes?*

argumentative /ˌɑːgjuː'mentətɪv/ *adj* often involved in or enjoying arguments □ *suka bertengkar*

aria /'ɑːriə/ *noun* [C] a song for one voice, especially in an **opera** (= a musical play) □ *aria; nyanyian solo dlm opera*

arid /'ærɪd/ *adj* (used about land or climate) very dry; with little or no rain □ *gersang*

Aries /'eəriːz/ *noun* [C,U] the 1st of the 12 signs of the **zodiac** (= 12 signs which represent the positions of the sun, moon and planets), the Ram; a person born under this sign □ *Aries*: *I'm an Aries.* ⊃ picture at **zodiac**

ℓ arise /ə'raɪz/ *verb* [I] (*pt* **arose** /ə'rəʊz/; *pp* **arisen** /ə'rɪzn/) to begin to exist; to appear □ *timbul; muncul*: *If any problems arise, let me know.* ♦ *A storm arose during the night.*

aristocracy /ˌærɪ'stɒkrəsi/ *noun* [C, with sing or pl verb] (*pl* **aristocracies**) the people of the highest social class who often have special

VOWELS   iː **see**   i **any**   ɪ **sit**   e **ten**   æ **hat**   ɑː **father**   ɒ **got**   ɔː **saw**   ʊ **put**   uː **too**   u **usual**

titles □ *aristokrat; golongan bangsawan* **SYN** **nobility**

aristocrat /ˈærɪstəkræt/ *noun* [C] a member of the highest social class, often with a special title □ *aristokrat* ▶**aristocratic** /ˌærɪstəˈkrætɪk/ *adj*

arithmetic /əˈrɪθmətɪk/ *noun* [U] the kind of mathematics which involves counting with numbers (adding, **subtracting** (= taking away), multiplying and dividing) □ *aritmetik; ilmu hisab*: *I'm not very good at mental arithmetic.*

arm

arm in arm

arms folded/crossed

arm¹ /ɑːm/ *noun* [C] **1** the long part at each side of your body connecting your shoulder to your hand □ *lengan*: *He was carrying a newspaper under his arm.* ⊃ picture at **body 2** the part of a piece of clothing that covers your arm; a sleeve □ *lengan baju*: *He had a hole in the arm of his jumper.* **3** the part of a chair where you rest your arms □ *tempat letak tangan*
IDM arm in arm with your arm folded around sb else's arm □ *berganding tangan*: *The friends walked arm in arm.*
cross/fold your arms to cross your arms in front of your chest □ *berpeluk tubuh*: *She folded her arms and waited.* ♦ *James was sitting with his arms crossed.*
twist sb's arm ⊃ **twist¹**
with open arms ⊃ **open¹**

arm² /ɑːm/ *verb* [I,T] to prepare sb/yourself to fight by supplying or getting weapons □ *melengkapi dgn senjata*: *The country is beginning to arm itself for war.* ⊃ look at **armed, arms**

armaments /ˈɑːməmənts/ *noun* [pl] weapons and military equipment □ *persenjataan*

armband /ˈɑːmbænd/ *noun* [C] **1** a piece of cloth that you wear around your arm □ *simpai lengan*: *The captain of the team wears an armband.* **2** a plastic ring filled with air which you can wear on each of your arms when you are learning to swim □ *boya lengan*

armchair /ˈɑːmtʃeə(r)/ (*AmE* also) / *noun* [C] a soft comfortable chair with sides which support your arms □ *kerusi malas* ⊃ picture at **chair**

armed /ɑːmd/ *adj* carrying a gun or other weapon; involving weapons □ *bersenjata*: *All the terrorists were armed.* ♦ *armed robbery* ♦ *the armed forces* (= the army, navy and air force) **OPP** **unarmed**

armful /ˈɑːmfʊl/ *noun* [C] the amount that you can carry in your arms □ *serangkum*

armhole /ˈɑːmhəʊl/ *noun* [C] the opening in a piece of clothing where your arm goes through □ *lubang lengan*

armistice /ˈɑːmɪstɪs/ *noun* [C] an agreement between two countries who are at war that they will stop fighting □ *perjanjian gencatan senjata*

armour (*AmE* **armor**) /ˈɑːmə(r)/ *noun* [U] clothing, often made of metal, that soldiers wore in earlier times to protect themselves □ *baju besi*: *a suit of armour*

armoured (*AmE* **armored**) /ˈɑːməd/ *adj* (used about a vehicle) covered with metal to protect it in an attack □ *berperisai*

armpit /ˈɑːmpɪt/ *noun* [C] the part of the body under the arm at the point where it joins the shoulder □ *ketiak* ⊃ picture at **body**

arms /ɑːmz/ *noun* [pl] **1** weapons, especially those that are used in war □ *senjata*: *a reduction in nuclear arms* **2** = **coat of arms**
IDM up in arms protesting angrily about sth □ *membantah dgn keras*: *The workers were up in arms over the news that the factory was going to close.*

army /ˈɑːmi/ *noun* [C, with sing or pl verb] (*pl* **armies**) **1** the military forces of a country which are trained to fight on land □ *angkatan tentera darat*: *the British Army* ♦ *She joined the army at the age of eighteen.* ♦ *The army is/are advancing towards the border.* ♦ *an army officer* ⊃ note at **war** ⊃ look at **air force, navy 2** a large number of people, especially when involved in an activity together □ *kumpulan besar*: *An army of children was helping to pick up the rubbish.*

ˈA-road *noun* [C] (in Britain) a main road, usually not as wide as a **motorway** (= a wide road for fast traffic) □ *jalan utama*

aroma /əˈrəʊmə/ *noun* [C] a smell, especially a pleasant one □ *bau sedap* ⊃ note at **smell²** ▶**aromatic** /ˌærəˈmætɪk/ *adj* **SYN** **fragrant**

aromatherapy /əˌrəʊməˈθerəpi/ *noun* [U] the use of natural oils with a pleasant smell in order to control pain or make sb feel relaxed □ *aromaterapi*: *an aromatherapy massage* ▶**aromatherapist** /-pɪst/ *noun* [C]

arose past tense of **arise**

around /əˈraʊnd/ *adv, prep* **1** (also **round**) in or to various places or directions □ *ke sana sini*: *This is our office—Victoria will show you around* (= show you the different parts of it). ♦ *They wandered around the town, looking at the shops.* **2** (also **round**) moving so as to face in the opposite direction □ *pusing balik*: *Turn around and go back the way you came.* **3** (also **round**) on all sides; forming a circle □ *di sekeliling*: *The park has a wall all around.* ♦ *Gather around so that you can all see.* ♦ *We sat down around the table.*

arouse → art

4 (also **round**) near a place □ *dekat*: *Is there a bank around here?* **5** (also **about**) present or available □ *ada di situ*: *I went to the house but there was nobody around.* **6** (also **about**) approximately □ *kira-kira*: *I'll see you around seven* (= at about 7 o'clock). **7** (also **about**) used for activities with no real purpose □ *bermaksud membuat sst tanpa tujuan*: *'What are you doing?' 'Nothing, just lazing around.'*

arouse /əˈraʊz/ *verb* [T] to cause a particular reaction in people □ *menimbulkan; membangkitkan*: *to arouse somebody's curiosity/interest* ▶ **arousal** /əˈraʊzl/ *noun* [U]

arr. *abbr* **arrives**: *arr. York 07.15*

arrange /əˈreɪndʒ/ *verb* **1** [I,T] **arrange (for) sth; arrange to do sth; arrange (sth) with sb** to make plans and preparations so that sth can happen in the future □ *mengatur; merancang*: *We're arranging a surprise party for Mark.* ◆ *She arranged for her mother to look after the baby.* ◆ *He arranged to meet Stuart after work.* **2** [T] to put sth in order or in a particular pattern □ *mengatur; menyusun*: *The books were arranged in alphabetical order.* ◆ *Arrange the chairs in a circle.* ◆ *She arranged the flowers in a vase.*

arrangement /əˈreɪndʒmənt/ *noun* **1** [C, usually pl] plans or preparations for sth that will happen in the future □ *rancangan; persiapan*: *Come round this evening and we'll make arrangements for the party.* **2** [C,U] an agreement with sb to do sth □ *persetujuan*: *They have an arrangement to share the cost of the food.* ◆ *We both need to use the computer so we'll have to come to some arrangement.* **3** [C] a group of things that have been placed in a particular pattern □ *gubahan; susunan*: *a flower arrangement*

array /əˈreɪ/ *noun* [C] a large collection of things, especially one that is impressive and is seen by other people □ *susunan; kumpulan*

arrears /əˈrɪəz/ *noun* [pl] money that sb owes that they should have paid earlier □ *tunggakan*

IDM **be in arrears; fall/get into arrears** to be late in paying money that you owe □ *menunggak; tertunggak*: *I'm in arrears with the rent.*
in arrears if money or a person is paid **in arrears** for work, the money is paid after the work has been done □ *dibayar kemudian*: *You will be paid monthly in arrears.*

arrest¹ /əˈrest/ *verb* [T] when the police arrest sb, they take them prisoner in order to question them about a crime □ *menangkap; menahan*: *The man was arrested for carrying a weapon.* ⊃ note at **crime**

arrest² /əˈrest/ *noun* [C,U] the act of arresting sb □ *penangkapan; penahanan*: *The police made ten arrests after the riot.* ◆ *The wanted man is now under arrest* (= has been arrested).

arrival /əˈraɪvl/ *noun* **1** [U] reaching the place to which you were travelling □ *ketibaan*: *On our arrival we were told that our rooms had not been reserved.* **OPP** **departure** **2** [C] people or things that have arrived □ *orang atau barang yg baru tiba*: *We brought in extra chairs for the late arrivals.*

arrive /əˈraɪv/ *verb* [I] **1 arrive (at/in ...)** to reach the place to which you were travelling □ *tiba; sampai*: *We arrived home at about midnight.* ◆ *What time does the train arrive in Newcastle?* ◆ *They arrived at the station ten minutes late.*

HELP Be careful. We use **arrive in** with the name of a town, country, etc. and **arrive at** with a place, building, etc.

2 to come or happen □ *tiba; sampai*: *The day of the wedding had finally arrived.*
PHR V **arrive at** to decide on or find sth, especially after discussion or thought □ *mencapai*: *We finally arrived at a decision.*

arrogant /ˈærəgənt/ *adj* thinking that you are better and more important than other people □ *angkuh; sombong; bongkak* **SYN** **self-important** ▶ **arrogance** *noun* [U] ▶ **arrogantly** *adv*

arrow /ˈærəʊ/ *noun* [C] **1** a thin piece of wood or metal, with one pointed end and feathers at the other end, that is shot by pulling back the string on a **bow** (= a curved piece of wood) and letting go □ *anak panah*: *to fire an arrow at a target* ⊃ look at **archer** **2** the sign (→) which is used to show direction □ *tanda anak panah*: *The arrow is pointing left.*

arsenal /ˈɑːsənl/ *noun* [C] a large collection of weapons, or a building where they are made or stored □ *kilang atau gudang senjata dan peluru*

arsenic /ˈɑːsnɪk/ *noun* [U] (*symbol* **As**) a type of very strong poison □ *arsenik*

arson /ˈɑːsn/ *noun* [U] the crime of setting fire to a building on purpose □ *(jenayah) membakar*

arsonist /ˈɑːsənɪst/ *noun* [C] a person who deliberately sets fire to a building □ *orang yg melakukan jenayah membakar*

art /ɑːt/ *noun* **1** [U] the activity or skill of producing things such as paintings, designs, etc.; the objects that are produced □ *(kegiatan atau kemahiran) seni; kesenian*: *an art class* ◆ *modern art* ◆ *I've never been good at art.* **2** [C,U] a skill or sth that needs skill □ *seni; kemahiran*: *There's an art to writing a good letter.* **3 the arts** [pl] art, literature, music, theatre, etc. when you think of them as a group □ *seni; bidang seni*: *The government has agreed to spend twice as much on the arts next year.* **4 arts** [pl] the subjects that you study at school or university that are not scientific, such as history or languages □ *(bidang) sastera*: *an arts degree*

MORE We usually contrast **arts** (or **arts subjects**) with **sciences** (or **science subjects**).

[C] **countable**, a noun with a plural form: *one book, two books*   [U] **uncountable**, a noun with no plural form: *some sugar*

artefact → as 42

> **TOPIC**
> **Art**
> An **artist** works in a **studio**. A **painter** paints **pictures**, for example **portraits** (= pictures of people), **landscapes** (= pictures of the countryside) or **abstract paintings** (= pictures that do not show people or things as they really look). A picture might be a **watercolour** or an **oil painting**. You put a picture in a **frame** and hang it on the wall. A **sculptor** makes **sculptures** of figures or objects in materials such as **marble** (= a type of stone) or **bronze** (= a type of metal). An **exhibition** is a collection of **works of art** which the public can go and see in an **art gallery**. A great work of art is called a **masterpiece**.

artefact /ˈɑːtɪfækt/ noun [C] an object that is made by a person □ *artifak*

artery /ˈɑːtəri/ noun [C] (pl arteries) one of the tubes which take blood from the heart to other parts of the body □ *arteri; salur darah* ➔ look at **vein**

artful /ˈɑːtfl/ adj clever at getting what you want, sometimes by not telling the truth □ *licik; penuh muslihat* **SYN** crafty

arthritis /ɑːˈθraɪtɪs/ noun [U] a disease which causes swelling and pain when you bend your arms, fingers, etc. □ *artritis* ▶**arthritic** /ɑːˈθrɪtɪk/ adj

artichoke /ˈɑːtɪtʃəʊk/ (also ˌglobe ˈartichoke) noun [C] a green vegetable with a lot of thick pointed leaves. You can eat the bottom part of the leaves and its centre. □ *articok* ➔ picture on page P15

article /ˈɑːtɪkl/ noun [C] **1** an object, especially one of a set □ *barang*: *articles of clothing* **2** a piece of writing in a newspaper or magazine □ *artikel; rencana; makalah*: *There's an article about Mexico in today's paper.* **3** The words *a*, *an* (= the indefinite article) or *the* (= the definite article) □ *kata sandang* ❶ For more information about articles, look at the **Reference Section** at the back of this dictionary.

articulate¹ /ɑːˈtɪkjuleɪt/ verb [I,T] to say sth clearly or to express your ideas or feelings □ *menyatakan/melahirkan/meluahkan dgn jelas*: *She struggled to articulate her thoughts.* ▶**articulation** /ɑːˌtɪkjuˈleɪʃn/ noun [U] (formal)

articulate² /ɑːˈtɪkjələt/ adj good at expressing your ideas clearly □ *petah* **OPP** inarticulate

articulated /ɑːˈtɪkjuleɪtɪd/ adj (BrE) (used about a large vehicle such as a lorry) made of two sections which are joined together □ *bersambung; bersendi*

artificial /ˌɑːtɪˈfɪʃl/ adj not genuine or natural but made by people □ *tiruan; buatan*: *artificial flowers* ◆ *an artificial lake* ▶**artificially** /-ʃəli/ adv

ˌartificial inˈtelligence noun [U] (the study of) the way in which computers can be made to copy the way humans think □ *kecerdasan buatan*

artillery /ɑːˈtɪləri/ noun [U] large, heavy guns that are moved on wheels; the part of the army that uses them □ *meriam; artileri*

artisan /ˌɑːtɪˈzæn/ noun [C] (formal) a person who makes things in a skilful way, especially with their hands □ *artisan; tukang; pekerja mahir* **SYN** craftsman

artist /ˈɑːtɪst/ noun [C] a person who produces art, especially paintings or drawings □ *pelukis; seniman*: *I like that picture—who is the artist?* ◆ *a graphic artist* ◆ *Monet was a famous French artist.*

artiste /ɑːˈtiːst/ (also **artist**) noun [C] a person whose job is to perform, for example a singer or a dancer □ *artis; seniman*

artistic /ɑːˈtɪstɪk/ adj **1** [only before a noun] connected with art □ *(berkaitan dgn) seni*: *a work of great artistic merit* ◆ *the artistic director of the theatre* **2** showing a skill in art □ *berseni*: *Elizabeth is very artistic—her drawings are excellent.* ▶**artistically** /-kli/ adv

artistry /ˈɑːtɪstri/ noun [U] the skill of an artist □ *kemahiran seni*

artwork /ˈɑːtwɜːk/ noun **1** [U] photographs, drawings, etc. that have been prepared for a book or magazine □ *kerja seni*: *a piece of artwork* **2** [C] a work of art, especially one in a museum or a show □ *karya seni*

arty /ˈɑːti/ adj (informal) seeming or wanting to be very artistic or interested in the arts □ *pura-pura (berjiwa seni); mempamerkan bakat/ minat artistik*: *He can't really like all those boring arty films.*

as /əz; strong form æz/ prep, adv, conj **1** used for talking about sb/sth's job, role or function □ *sebagai*: *Think of me as your friend, not as your boss.*

> **HELP** As or like? Before a noun, **as** refers to a job or function: *She works as a scientist.* ◆ *I used the jar as a vase.* **Like** means 'similar to': *He has blue eyes like his father.* **Like** (or formally, **such as**) also means 'for example': *I love sweet food, like chocolate.*

2 as … as used for comparing people or things □ *sama*: *Lenka's almost as tall as me.* ◆ *Lenka's almost as tall as I am.* ◆ *It's not as cold as it was yesterday.* ◆ *I'd like an appointment as soon as possible.* ◆ *She earns twice as much as her husband.* ◆ *I haven't got as many books as you have.* ➔ note at **similarity** **3** while sth else is happening □ *ketika; sewaktu; sambil*: *The phone rang just as I was leaving the house.* ◆ *As she walked along the road, she thought about her father.* **4** in a particular way, state, etc.; like □ *spt*: *Please do as I tell you.* ◆ *Leave the room as it is. Don't move anything.* **5** because □ *kerana*: *I didn't buy the dress, as I decided it was too expensive.* ➔ note at **because** **6** used at the beginning of a comment about what you are saying □ *spt; sebagaimana*: *As you know, I've decided to leave at the end of the month.*

[I] **intransitive**, a verb which has no object: *He laughed.*   [T] **transitive**, a verb which has an object: *He ate an apple.*

IDM as for used when you are starting to talk about a different person or thing □ *ttg*: *Gianni's upstairs. As for Tino, I've no idea where he is.*

as if; as though used for saying how sb/sth appears □ *spt; seolah-olah*: *She looks as if/though she's just got out of bed.*

as it were used for saying that sth is only true in a certain way □ *seolah-olah*: *She felt, as it were, a stranger in her own house.*

as of; as from starting from a particular time □ *mulai*: *As from next week, Tim Shaw will be managing this department.*

as to about a particular thing; concerning □ *ttg; berkenaan dgn*: *I was given no instructions as to how to begin.*

asap /ˌeɪ es eɪ ˈpiː/ *abbr* as soon as possible □ *singkatan yg bermaksud secepat mungkin*

asbestos /æsˈbestəs/ *noun* [U] a soft grey material that does not burn and was used in the past to protect against heat □ *asbestos*

ascend /əˈsend/ *verb* [I,T] (*formal*) to go up □ *naik* OPP **descend** ▶**ascending** *adj*: *The questions are arranged in ascending order of difficulty* (= the most difficult ones are at the end).

ascent /əˈsent/ *noun* [C] **1** the act of climbing or going up □ *pendakian*: *the ascent of Everest* **2** a path or hill leading upwards □ *laluan ke atas*: *There was a steep ascent before the path became flat again.* OPP for both meanings **descent**

ascertain /ˌæsəˈteɪn/ *verb* [T] (*formal*) to find sth out □ *memastikan*

ascribe /əˈskraɪb/ *verb* [T] **ascribe sth to sb/sth** **1** to say that sth was written by or belonged to sb □ *menganggap sst itu dibuat oleh sso*: *Many people ascribe this play to Shakespeare.* **2** to say what caused sth □ *berpunca drpd*: *He ascribed his forgetfulness to old age.*

asexual /ˌeɪˈsekʃuəl/ *adj* **1** (*technical*) not involving sex; not having sexual organs □ *aseks; tanpa jantina atau organ seks*: *asexual reproduction* **2** not having sexual qualities; not interested in sex □ *tdk berminat terhadap hubungan seks*

ash /æʃ/ *noun* **1** [U, pl] the grey or black powder which is left after sth has burned □ *abu*: *cigarette ash* ♦ *the ashes of a fire* **2 ashes** [pl] what is left after a dead person has been burned □ *abu mayat* **3** [C] a type of forest tree that grows in cool countries □ *pokok ash*

ashamed /əˈʃeɪmd/ *adj* [not before a noun] **ashamed (of sth/sb/yourself); ashamed that ...; ashamed to do sth** feeling guilty or embarrassed about sb/sth or because of sth you have done □ *malu*: *She was ashamed of her old clothes.* ♦ *How could you be so rude? I'm ashamed of you!* ♦ *She felt ashamed that she hadn't helped him.* OPP **unashamed**

ashen /ˈæʃn/ *adj* (used about sb's face) very pale; without colour because of illness or fear □ *pucat lesi*

ashore /əˈʃɔː(r)/ *adv* onto the land from the sea, a river, etc □ *ke darat*: *The passengers went ashore for an hour while the ship was in port.*

ashtray /ˈæʃtreɪ/ *noun* [C] a small dish for collecting ash (= the powder that is made as a cigarette is burned) □ *tempat habuk rokok*

Asian /ˈeɪʃn; ˈeɪʒn/ *noun* [C] a person from Asia or whose family was originally from Asia □ *orang Asia* ▶**Asian** *adj*

aside /əˈsaɪd/ *adv* **1** on or to one side; out of the way □ *ke tepi*: *We stood aside to let the man go past.* **2** to be kept separately, for a special purpose □ *menyimpan; mengasingkan*: *I try to set aside a little money each month.*

aˈside from (*especially AmE*) = **apart from** □ *selain*: *Aside from a few scratches, I'm OK.*

ask /ɑːsk/ *verb*
▶QUESTION **1** [I,T] **ask (sb) (about sb/sth); ask sth** to put a question to sb in order to find out some information □ *bertanya*: *We need to ask about tickets.* ♦ *Can I ask you a question?* ♦ *Ask him how old he is.* ♦ *She asked if I wanted tea or coffee.* ♦ *'What's the time?' he asked.* ♦ *He asked what the time was.* ♦ *He asked me the time.*
▶REQUEST **2** [I,T] **ask (sb) for sth; ask sth (of sb); ask sb to do sth** to request that sb gives you sth or does sth for you □ *meminta*: *She sat down and asked for a cup of coffee.* ♦ *Don't ask Joe for money—he hasn't got any.* ♦ *You are asking too much of him—he can't possibly do all that!* ♦ *Ring this number and ask for Mrs Khan.* ♦ *I asked him if he would drive me home.* ♦ *I asked him to drive me home.*
▶PERMISSION **3** [I,T] to request permission to do sth □ *minta izin*: *I'm sure she'll let you go if you ask.* ♦ *Theo asked to use our phone.* ♦ *We asked the teacher if we could go home early.*
▶INVITE **4** [T] **ask sb (to sth)** to invite sb □ *mengajak; mempelawa*: *They asked six friends to dinner.*
▶MONEY **5** [T] to say the price that you want for sth □ *(harga yg) diminta*: *How much are they asking for your car?*

IDM ask for trouble/it to behave in a way that will almost certainly cause you problems □ *memang mencari pasal*: *Driving when you're tired is just asking for trouble.*

if you ask me if you want my opinion □ *pd pendapat sayalah*

PHR V ask after sb to ask about sb's health or to ask for news of sb □ *bertanya khabar ttg sso*: *Tina asked after you today.*

ask sb out to invite sb to go out with you, especially as a way of starting a romantic relationship □ *mengajak; mempelawa*: *Harry's too shy to ask her out.*

ask sb round/over to invite sb to your home for a meal, to watch a DVD, etc. □ *mengundang*

askew /əˈskjuː/ *adv, adj* [not before a noun] not in a straight or level position □ *senget; herot*

asleep /əˈsliːp/ *adj* [not before a noun] not awake; sleeping □ *tidur*: *The baby is fast/sound asleep* (= very deeply asleep). ♦ *It didn't take me*

AS (level) → assist 44

long to **fall asleep** last night. **OPP** awake ⊃ note at **sleep**¹

HELP **Asleep** or **sleeping**? Notice that you can only use **asleep** after a noun or a verb such as 'be'. **Sleeping** can be used before the noun: *a sleeping child*

AS (level) /ˌeɪ ˈes levl/ *noun* [C,U] Advanced Subsidiary (level); a British exam usually taken in the year before the final year of school or college when students are aged 17. Together with A2 levels, AS levels form the A-level qualification, which is needed for entrance to universities □ *peperiksaan Peringkat Subsidiari Lanjutan yg diambil di England dan Wales*: *Students will normally take four or five AS subjects.* ♦ *She's doing an AS (level) in French.* ⊃ look at **A2 (level), A level**

asparagus /əˈspærəgəs/ *noun* [U] a plant with green or white **stems** (= the long thin parts) that you cook and eat as a vegetable □ *asparagus* ⊃ picture on **page P15**

⸸ aspect /ˈæspekt/ *noun* [C] one of the qualities or parts of a situation, an idea, a problem, etc. □ *aspek; segi*: *What are the main aspects of your job?*

asphalt /ˈæsfælt/ *noun* [U] a thick black substance that is used for making the surface of roads □ *asfalt*

asphyxiate /əsˈfɪksieɪt/ *verb* [I,T] to make sb unable to breathe or to be unable to breathe □ *menjadi lemas*: *He was asphyxiated by the smoke while he was asleep.* ▶ **asphyxiation** /əsˌfɪksiˈeɪʃn/ *noun* [U]

aspire /əˈspaɪə(r)/ *verb* [I] (*formal*) aspire to sth/to do sth to have a strong desire to have or do sth □ *bercita-cita; berhasrat*: *She aspired to become managing director.* ♦ *an aspiring actor* ▶ **aspiration** /ˌæspəˈreɪʃn/ *noun* [C,U]

aspirin /ˈæsprɪn; ˈæspərɪn/ *noun* [C,U] a drug used to reduce pain and a high temperature □ *aspirin*

ass /æs/ = donkey

assailant /əˈseɪlənt/ *noun* [C] (*formal*) a person who attacks sb □ *penyerang*

assassin /əˈsæsɪn/ *noun* [C] a person who kills a famous or important person for money or for political reasons □ *pembunuh (orang kenamaan)* ▶ **assassinate** /əˈsæsɪneɪt/ *verb* [T] ⊃ note at **kill** ▶ **assassination** /əˌsæsɪˈneɪʃn/ *noun* [C,U]

assault /əˈsɔːlt/ *noun* [C,U] assault (on sb/sth) a sudden attack on sb/sth □ *serangan* ▶ **assault** *verb* [T]: *He was charged with assaulting a police officer.*

assemble /əˈsembl/ *verb* **1** [I,T] to come together or bring sb/sth together in a group □ *mengumpulkan*: *I've assembled all the information I need for my essay.* **2** [T] to fit the parts of sth together □ *memasang*: *We spent hours trying to assemble our new bookshelves.*

assembly /əˈsembli/ *noun* (*pl* **assemblies**) **1** [C,U] a large group of people who come together for a particular purpose □ *perhimpunan*: *school assembly* (= a regular meeting for all the students and teachers of a school) **2** [U] the act of fitting the parts of sth together □ *pemasangan*

asˈsembly line *noun* [C] a line of people and machines in a factory that fit the parts of sth together in a fixed order □ *barisan pemasangan*

assent /əˈsent/ *noun* [U] (*formal*) assent (to sth) official agreement to sth □ *persetujuan*: *The committee gave their assent to the proposed changes.* ▶ **assent** *verb* [I] assent (to sth)

assert /əˈsɜːt/ *verb* [T] **1** to say sth clearly and firmly □ *menegaskan* **2** to behave in a determined and confident way to make people listen to you or to get what you want □ *menegaskan; memperlihatkan*: *You ought to assert yourself more.* ♦ *to assert your authority*

assertion /əˈsɜːʃn/ *noun* **1** [C] a statement that says you strongly believe that sth is true □ *kenyataan yg tegas* **2** [U] the act of showing, using or stating sth strongly □ *penegasan*

assertive /əˈsɜːtɪv/ *adj* expressing your opinion clearly and firmly so that people listen to you or do what you want □ *bertegas* ▶ **assertively** *adv* ▶ **assertiveness** *noun* [U]

assess /əˈses/ *verb* [T] **1** to judge or form an opinion about sth □ *menilai*: *It's too early to assess the effects of the price rises.* **2** assess sth (at sth) to guess or decide the amount or value of sth □ *menaksir*: *to assess the cost of repairs* ▶ **assessment** *noun* [C,U]: *I made a careful assessment of the risks involved.*

asset /ˈæset/ *noun* [C] **1** an asset (to sb/sth) a person or thing that is useful to sb/sth □ *orang/barang yg berharga*: *She's a great asset to the organization.* **2** [usually pl] something of value that a person, company, etc. owns □ *aset; harta*

assign /əˈsaɪn/ *verb* [T] **1** assign sth to sb/sth to give sth to sb for a particular purpose □ *memberikan; menguntukkan*: *We assigned 20% of our budget to the project.* **2** assign sb to sth to give sb a particular job to do □ *menugaskan*

assignment /əˈsaɪnmənt/ *noun* [C,U] a job or type of work that you are given to do □ *tugas; tugasan*: *The teacher gave us an assignment to do during the holidays.*

assimilate /əˈsɪməleɪt/ *verb* **1** [T] to learn and understand sth □ *menyerap*: *to assimilate new facts/information/ideas* **2** [I,T] assimilate (sb/sth) (into sth) to become or allow sb/sth to become part of a country, a social group, etc. □ *berasimilasi; menyerap* ▶ **assimilation** /əˌsɪməˈleɪʃn/ *noun* [U]

⸸ assist /əˈsɪst/ *verb* [I,T] (*formal*) assist (sb) in/with sth; assist (sb) in doing sth to help □ *membantu*: *Ben pays a student to assist him with his research.* ♦ *Volunteers assisted in searching for the boy.*

ð **th**en   s **s**o   z **z**oo   ʃ **sh**e   ʒ vi**s**ion   h **h**ow   m **m**an   n **n**o   ŋ si**ng**   l **l**eg   r **r**ed   j **y**es   w **w**et

assistance /əˈsɪstəns/ noun [U] (formal) help or support □ *bantuan*: financial assistance for poorer families ◆ She shouted for help but nobody came to her assistance.

assistant /əˈsɪstənt/ noun [C] (abbr Asst) **1** a person who helps sb in a more important position □ *pembantu*: The director is away today. Would you like to speak to her assistant? ◆ He's assistant to the Sales Manager. **2** (AmE **clerk**) a person who sells things to people in a shop □ *pembantu jualan*: a shop/sales assistant ▶assistant adj [only before a noun]: the assistant manager

Assoc. abbr = association

associate¹ /əˈsəʊʃieɪt/ verb **1** [T] associate sb/sth (with sb/sth) to make a connection between people or things in your mind □ *mengaitkan*: I always associate the smell of the sea with my childhood. **2** [I] associate with sb to spend time with sb □ *bergaul*: I prefer not to associate with colleagues outside work. **3** [T] associate yourself with sth to say that you support sth or agree with sth □ *mengaitkan diri dgn sst*: I do not wish to associate myself with any organization that promotes violence. **OPP** for all meanings **dissociate**

associate² /əˈsəʊʃiət/ noun [C] a person that you meet and get to know through your work □ *rakan; sekutu*: a business associate

association /əˌsəʊʃiˈeɪʃn; əˌsəʊsiˈeɪ-/ noun **1** [C] (abbr Assoc.) a group of people or organizations that work together for a particular purpose □ *persatuan*: the National Association of Language Teachers **2** [U] joining or working with another person or group □ *bersama dgn*: We work in association with our New York office. **3** [C,U] the act of connecting one thing or thing with another in your mind □ *perkaitan*: The cat soon made the association between human beings and food.

assorted /əˈsɔːtɪd/ adj of different types; mixed □ *aneka jenis; pelbagai*: a bowl of assorted fruit

assortment /əˈsɔːtmənt/ noun [C] a group of different things or of different types of the same thing □ *kepelbagaian; beraneka jenis*: You'll find a wide assortment of gifts in our shop. **SYN** mixture

Asst abbr = assistant

assume /əˈsjuːm/ verb [T] **1** to accept or believe that sth is true even though you have no proof; to expect sth to be true □ *menganggap*: I assume that you have the necessary documents. ◆ Everyone assumed Ralph was guilty. ◆ Everyone assumed Ralph to be guilty. **2** to begin to use power or to have a powerful position □ *menyandang; mengambil alih*: to assume control of something **SYN** take **3** to pretend to have or be sb/sth □ *menyamar*: to assume a false name

assumption /əˈsʌmpʃn/ noun **1** [C] something that you accept is true even though you have no proof □ *anggapan; andaian*: We'll work on the assumption that guests will be hungry when they arrive. ◆ It's unfair to make assumptions about somebody's character before you know them. ◆ a reasonable/ false assumption **2** [U] **the assumption of sth** the act of taking power or of starting an important job □ *perihal mula menyandang jawatan; pengambilalihan*

assurance /əˈʃʊərəns (BrE also) əˈʃɔːr-/ noun **1** [C] a promise that sth will certainly happen or be true □ *jaminan; janji*: They gave me an assurance that the work would be finished by Friday. **2** (also ˌself-asˈsurance) [U] the belief that you can do or succeed at sth; confidence □ *keyakinan (diri)*

assure /əˈʃʊə(r) (BrE also) əˈʃɔː(r)/ verb [T] **1** to promise sb that sth will certainly happen or be true, especially if they are worried □ *menjanjikan; meyakinkan*: I assure you that it is perfectly safe. ◆ Let me assure you of my full support. **2** to make sb sure or certain □ *menjamin*: The success of the new product assured the survival of the company.

assured /əˈʃʊəd (BrE also) əˈʃɔːd/ (also ˌself-asˈsured) adj believing that you can do sth or succeed at sth; confident □ *berkeyakinan*: The doctor had a calm and assured manner.

asterisk /ˈæstərɪsk/ noun [C] the symbol (*) that you use to make people notice sth in a piece of writing □ *asterisk*

asteroid /ˈæstərɔɪd/ noun [C] one of the very large rocks or small planets which go around the sun □ *asteroid*

asthma /ˈæsmə/ noun [U] a medical condition that makes breathing difficult □ *asma; penyakit lelah*

asthmatic /æsˈmætɪk/ noun [C] a person who has **asthma** □ *orang yg menghidap asma* ▶asthmatic adj

astonish /əˈstɒnɪʃ/ verb [T] to surprise sb very much □ *mengejutkan; menghairankan*: She astonished everybody by announcing her engagement. **SYN** amaze ▶astonished adj: I was astonished by the decision.

astonishing /əˈstɒnɪʃɪŋ/ adj very surprising □ *(yg) menghairankan* **SYN** amazing ▶astonishingly adv

astonishment /əˈstɒnɪʃmənt/ noun [U] very great surprise □ *kehairanan*: He stared in astonishment. **SYN** amazement

astound /əˈstaʊnd/ verb [T, usually passive] to surprise sb very much □ *menghairankan*: We were astounded by how well he performed. **SYN** amaze

astounded /əˈstaʊndɪd/ adj feeling or showing great surprise □ *hairan; kagum*: We sat in astounded silence.

astounding /əˈstaʊndɪŋ/ adj causing sb to feel extremely surprised □ *yg menghairankan*: an astounding success

astray /əˈstreɪ/ adv
IDM **go astray** to become lost or be stolen □ *sesat; dicuri*
lead sb astray ➔ **lead¹**

astride /əˈstraɪd/ prep, adv with one leg on each side of sth □ *bercelapak; mengangkang*: *to sit astride a horse*

astrologer /əˈstrɒlədʒə(r)/ noun [C] a person who is an expert in **astrology** □ *ahli astrologi; ahli nujum*

astrology /əˈstrɒlədʒi/ noun [U] the study of the positions and movements of the stars and planets and the way that some people believe they affect people and events □ *ilmu astrologi; ilmu nujum* ➔ note at **zodiac** ➔ look at **horoscope**

astronaut /ˈæstrənɔːt/ noun [C] a person who works and travels in space □ *angkasawan*

astronomer /əˈstrɒnəmə(r)/ noun [C] a person who studies **astronomy** □ *ahli astronomi; ahli falak*

astronomical /ˌæstrəˈnɒmɪkl/ adj 1 connected with **astronomy** □ *(berkenaan dgn) astronomi* 2 extremely large □ *terlalu (mahal, besar, dsb)*: *astronomical house prices*

astronomy /əˈstrɒnəmi/ noun [U] the scientific study of the sun, moon, stars, etc. □ *astronomi; ilmu falak*

astute /əˈstjuːt/ adj very clever; good at judging people or situations □ *pintar; bijak*

asylum /əˈsaɪləm/ noun [U] protection that a government gives to people who have left their own country for political reasons □ *perlindungan*: *to give somebody political asylum*

aˈsylum seeker noun [C] a person who has been forced to leave their own country because they are in danger and who arrives in another country asking to be allowed to stay there □ *pemohon suaka*

at /ət; strong form æt/ prep 1 used to show where sb/sth is or where sth happens □ *di*: *at the bottom/top of the page* ♦ *He was standing at the door.* ♦ *Change trains at Chester.* ♦ *We were at home all weekend.* ♦ *Are the children at school?* ♦ *'Where's Peter?' 'He's at Sue's.'* (= at Sue's house) 2 used to show when sth happens □ *pd*: *I start work at 9 o'clock.* ♦ *at the weekend* ♦ *at night* ♦ *at Easter* ♦ *She got married at 18* (= when she was 18). 3 in the direction of sb/sth □ *bermaksud ke arah sso/sst*: *What are you looking at?* ♦ *He pointed at the child with his pen.* ♦ *Don't shout at me!* 4 used to show what sb is doing or what is happening □ *sedang*: *They were hard at work.* ♦ *The two countries were at war.* 5 used to show the price, rate, speed, etc. of sth □ *dgn (harga, kadar, dsb); se-(laju, banyak, dsb)*: *We were travelling at about 50 miles per hour.* 6 because of sth □ *akan; apabila (mendengar, melihat, dsb sst)*: *I was surprised at her behaviour.* ♦ *We laughed at his jokes.* 7 used with adjectives that show how well sb/sth does sth □ *pandai (membuat sst)*: *She's not very good at French.* 8 the symbol (@) used in email addresses □ *simbol @*

ate past tense of **eat**

atheism /ˈeɪθiɪzəm/ noun [U] the belief that there is no God □ *ateisme* ▶ **atheist** /-ɪst/ noun [C]

athlete /ˈæθliːt/ noun [C] a person who can run, jump, etc. very well, especially one who takes part in sports, competitions, etc. □ *olahragawan; olahragawati; atlet*

athletic /æθˈletɪk/ adj 1 (used about a person) having a fit, strong and healthy body □ *kuat dan cergas* 2 [only before a noun] connected with **athletes** or **athletics** □ *(berkenaan dgn) olahraga*: *athletic ability*

athletics /æθˈletɪks/ noun [U] sports such as running, jumping, throwing, etc. □ *olahraga* ➔ note at **sport** ➔ picture on page P4

atishoo /əˈtɪʃuː/ exclam used to represent the sound that you make when you suddenly **sneeze** (= blow air out of your nose, for example because you have a cold) □ *bunyi bersin*

atlas /ˈætləs/ noun [C] a book of maps □ *atlas; buku peta*: *a road atlas of Europe* ➔ note at **book**

ATM /ˌeɪ tiː ˈem/ = **cash machine**

ˌATM card (AmE) = **cash card**

atmosphere /ˈætməsfɪə(r)/ noun 1 **the atmosphere** [C, usually sing] the mixture of gases that surrounds the earth or any other star, planet, etc □ *atmosfera*: *the earth's atmosphere* 2 [sing] the air in a place □ *udara*: *a smoky atmosphere* 3 [sing] the mood or feeling of a place or situation □ *suasana*: *The atmosphere of the meeting was relaxed.*

atmospheric /ˌætməsˈferɪk/ adj 1 [only before a noun] connected with the earth's **atmosphere** □ *(berkenaan dgn) atmosfera* 2 creating a particular feeling or emotion □ *menimbulkan suasana tertentu*: *atmospheric music*

atom /ˈætəm/ noun [C] the smallest part into which a chemical element can be divided □ *atom*: *the splitting of the atom* ♦ *(figurative) There isn't an atom of* (= there is no) *truth in these rumours.* ➔ look at **molecule**

ˈatom bomb = **atomic bomb**

atomic /əˈtɒmɪk/ adj connected with an atom or atoms □ *(berkenaan dgn) atom*: *atomic physics* ➔ look at **nuclear**

aˌtomic ˈbomb (also **ˈatom bomb**) noun [C] a bomb that explodes using the energy that is produced when an atom or atoms are split □ *bom atom*

aˌtomic ˈenergy noun [U] the energy that is produced when an atom or atoms are split. **Atomic energy** can be used to produce electricity. □ *tenaga atom*

atrocious /əˈtrəʊʃəs/ adj extremely bad □ *sangat teruk; dahsyat*: *atrocious weather* **SYN terrible** ▶ **atrociously** adv

atrocity /əˈtrɒsəti/ noun [C,U] (pl atrocities) (an action of) very cruel treatment of sb/sth □ *kekejaman*: Both sides were accused of committing atrocities during the war.

attach /əˈtætʃ/ verb [T] 1 attach sth (to sth) to fasten or join sth to sth □ *melekatkan; memasang*: I attached a label to each bag. **OPP** detach 2 attach sth to sb/sth to think that sth has a particular quality □ *menganggap*: Don't attach too much importance to what they say. 3 [usually passive] attach sb/sth to sb/sth to make sb/sth join or belong to sb/sth □ *merupakan sebahagian drpd*: The research centre is attached to the university.

IDM (with) no strings attached; without strings ⊃ string¹

attached /əˈtætʃt/ adj 1 [not before a noun] attached to sb/sth liking sb/sth very much □ *sayang akan*: He's become very attached to you. 2 attached to sth joined to sth □ *yg dilampirkan*: Please complete the attached application form.

attachment /əˈtætʃmənt/ noun 1 [C,U] attachment (to/for sb/sth) the feeling of liking sb/sth very much □ *perihal sayang akan*: emotional attachment 2 [C] something that you can fit on sth else to make it do a different job □ *alat tambahan*: an electric drill with a range of attachments 3 [C] a document that you send to sb using email □ *lampiran*

attack¹ /əˈtæk/ noun 1 [C,U] (an) attack (on sb/sth) trying to hurt or defeat sb/sth by using force □ *serangan*: The rebel forces launched an attack on the capital. ♦ The town was under attack from all sides. 2 [C,U] (an) attack (on sb/sth) an act of saying strongly that you do not like or agree with sb/sth □ *kecaman*: an outspoken attack on government policy 3 [C] a short period when you suffer badly from a disease, medical condition, etc. □ *serangan (penyakit, dsb)*: an attack of asthma/flu/nerves 4 [C] the act of trying to score a point in a game of sport □ *serangan*: The home team went on the attack again.

attack² /əˈtæk/ verb 1 [I,T] to try to hurt or defeat sb/sth by using force □ *menyerang*: The child was attacked by a dog. 2 [T] to say strongly that you do not like or agree with sb/sth □ *mengecam; membidas*: Steffi attacked Guy's right-wing political views. 3 [T] to damage or harm sb/sth □ *menyerang*: a virus that attacks the nervous system 4 [I,T] to try to score a point in a game of sport □ *menyerang*: This team attacks better than it defends.

attacker /əˈtækə(r)/ noun [C] a person who tries to hurt sb using force □ *penyerang*: The victim of the assault didn't recognize his attackers.

attain /əˈteɪn/ verb [T] to succeed in getting or achieving sth, especially after a lot of effort □ *mencapai*

attainable /əˈteɪnəbl/ adj that can be achieved □ *dpt dicapai*: realistically attainable targets

attainment /əˈteɪnmənt/ noun 1 [C] a skill or sth you have achieved □ *pencapaian* 2 [U] the act of achieving sth □ *pencapaian*: the attainment of the government's objectives

attempt¹ /əˈtempt/ noun [C] 1 an attempt (to do sth/at doing sth) an act of trying to do sth □ *percubaan*: The thief made no attempt to run away. ♦ I failed the exam once but passed at the second attempt. ♦ They failed in their attempt to reach the North Pole. 2 an attempt (on sb/sth) trying to attack or beat sb/sth □ *percubaan; mencuba*: an attempt on somebody's life (= to try to kill sb)

IDM a last-ditch attempt ⊃ last¹

attempt² /əˈtempt/ verb [T] attempt (to do) sth to try to do sth that is difficult □ *mencuba*: Don't attempt to make him change his mind.

attempted /əˈtemptɪd/ adj [only before a noun] (used about a crime, etc.) that sb has tried to do but without success □ *percubaan (yg tdk berjaya)*: attempted rape/murder/robbery ♦ She was accused of attempted murder (= she didn't succeed).

attend /əˈtend/ verb 1 [I,T] to go to or be present at a place □ *menghadiri*: The children attend the local school. ♦ We'd like as many people as possible to attend. 2 [I] (formal) attend to sb/sth to give your care, thought or attention to sb/sth or look after sb/sth □ *mengurus*: Please attend to this matter immediately.

attendance /əˈtendəns/ noun 1 [U] being present somewhere □ *kedatangan*: Attendance at lectures is compulsory. 2 [C,U] the number of people who go to or are present at a place □ *kedatangan*: There was a poor attendance at the meeting.

attendant¹ /əˈtendənt/ noun [C] a person whose job is to serve or help people in a public place □ *atendan; pelayan*: a car park attendant

attendant² /əˈtendənt/ adj [only before a noun] (formal) that goes together with or results from sth □ *yg berkaitan*: unemployment and all its attendant social problems

attention¹ /əˈtenʃn/ noun [U] 1 watching, listening to or thinking about sb/sth carefully □ *perhatian*: I shouted in order to attract her attention. ♦ Shy people hate to be the centre of attention (= the person that everyone is watching). ♦ to hold somebody's attention (= to keep them interested in sth) 2 special care or action □ *perhatian; rawatan*: The hole in the roof needs urgent attention. ♦ to require medical attention 3 a position in which a soldier stands up straight and still □ *berdiri tegak*: to stand/come to attention

IDM catch sb's attention/eye ⊃ catch¹
draw (sb's) attention to sth ⊃ draw¹
get/have sb's undivided attention; give your undivided attention (to sb/sth) ⊃ undivided
pay attention ⊃ pay¹

attention² /əˈtenʃn/ exclam used for asking people to listen to sth carefully □ *minta*

attentive → Aug.

perhatian: Attention, please! The boat will be leaving in five minutes.

attentive /əˈtentɪv/ *adj* **attentive (to sb/sth)** watching, listening to or thinking about sb/sth carefully □ *memberi penuh perhatian*: The hotel staff were very attentive to our needs. **OPP** **inattentive** ▶**attentively** *adv*: to listen attentively to something

attest /əˈtest/ *verb* [I] (*formal*) **attest (to sth)** to show or prove that sth is true □ *membuktikan*: Her long fight against cancer attests to her courage.

attic /ˈætɪk/ *noun* [C] the space or room under the roof of a house □ *loteng* ➔ look at **loft** ➔ picture on **page P8**

attitude /ˈætɪtjuːd/ *noun* [C] **an attitude (to/towards sb/sth)** the way that you think, feel or behave □ *sikap*: People's attitude to marriage is changing. ◆ She has a positive attitude to her work.

attn (also **attn.**) *abbr* (in writing) **for the attention of** □ *utk perhatian*: Sales Dept, attn C Biggs

attorney /əˈtɜːni/ *noun* [C] (*AmE*) = **lawyer**

attract /əˈtrækt/ *verb* [T] **1** [usually passive] to cause sb to like sb/sth □ *tertarik*: She was attracted by his sense of humour. **2** to cause sb/sth to go to sth or give attention to sth □ *menarik perhatian*: I waved to attract the waiter's attention. ◆ Moths are attracted to light. ◆ The new film has attracted a lot of publicity.

attraction /əˈtrækʃn/ *noun* **1** [U] a feeling of liking sb/sth □ *tarikan; daya penarik*: sexual attraction **2** [C] something that is interesting or enjoyable □ *tarikan; sst yg menarik*: The city offers all kinds of tourist attractions.

attractive /əˈtræktɪv/ *adj* **1** (used about a person) beautiful or nice to look at □ *menarik; menawan*: He found her very attractive. ➔ note at **beautiful 2** that pleases or interests you; that you like □ *menarik*: an attractive part of the country ◆ an attractive idea **OPP** for both meanings **unattractive** ▶**attractively** *adv* ▶**attractiveness** *noun* [U]

attribute¹ /əˈtrɪbjuːt/ *verb* [T] **attribute sth to sb/sth** to believe that sth was caused or done by sb/sth □ *mempercayai; meyakini*: Mustafa attributes his success to hard work. ◆ a poem attributed to Shakespeare

attribute² /ˈætrɪbjuːt/ *noun* [C] a quality of sb/sth □ *sifat; ciri*: physical attributes **SYN** **feature**

attributive /əˈtrɪbjətɪv/ *adj* (used about an adjective or a noun) used before a noun to describe it □ *atribut; sifatan*: In 'the blue sky' and 'a family business', 'blue' and 'family' are attributive. ➔ look at **predicative** ▶**attributively** *adv*: Some adjectives can only be used attributively.

atypical /ˌeɪˈtɪpɪkl/ *adj* (*formal*) not typical of a particular type, group, etc □ *atipikal*: atypical behaviour **OPP** **typical** ➔ look at **untypical**

aubergine /ˈəʊbəʒiːn/ (*AmE* **eggplant**) *noun* [C,U] a long vegetable with dark purple skin □ *terung* ➔ picture on **page P15**

auburn /ˈɔːbən/ *adj* (used about hair) reddish-brown □ *coklat kemerah-merahan*

auction¹ /ˈɔːkʃn/ *noun* [C,U] a public sale at which items are sold to the person who offers to pay the most money □ *jualan lelong*: The house was sold **at/by auction**.

auction² /ˈɔːkʃn/ *verb* [T] **auction sth (off)** to sell sth at an **auction** □ *melelong*

auctioneer /ˌɔːkʃəˈnɪə(r)/ *noun* [C] a person who organizes the selling at an **auction** □ *jurulelong*

audacious /ɔːˈdeɪʃəs/ *adj* (*formal*) willing to take risks or to do sth shocking □ *berani; lancang*: an audacious decision **SYN** **daring** ▶**audaciously** *adv*

audacity /ɔːˈdæsəti/ *noun* [U] behaviour that shows courage but that is also rude or shocking □ *keberanian; kelancangan*: He had the audacity to say I was too fat. **SYN** **nerve**

audible /ˈɔːdəbl/ *adj* that can be heard □ *dpt didengar*: Her speech was barely audible. **OPP** **inaudible** ▶**audibly** /-əbli/ *adv*

audience /ˈɔːdiəns/ *noun* [C] **1** [with sing or pl verb] all the people who are watching or listening to a play, concert, speech, the TV, etc. □ *audiens; penonton; hadirin*: The audience was/were wild with excitement. ◆ There were only about 200 people in the audience. ➔ note at **theatre 2** a formal meeting with a very important person □ *menghadap; menemui (ketua negara, dsb)*: He was granted an audience with the President.

audio /ˈɔːdiəʊ/ *adj* [only before a noun] connected with the recording of sound □ *audio*: audio equipment ◆ audio and video cassettes

audio-ˈvisual *adj* using both sound and pictures □ *pandang dengar*

audit /ˈɔːdɪt/ *noun* [C] an official examination of the present state of sth, especially of a company's financial records □ *audit*: to carry out an audit ▶**audit** *verb* [T]

audition¹ /ɔːˈdɪʃn/ *noun* [C] a short performance by a singer, an actor, etc. to find out if they are good enough to be in a play, show, etc. □ *uji bakat*

audition² /ɔːˈdɪʃn/ *verb* [I,T] **audition (sb) (for sth)** to do or to watch sb do an **audition** □ *menguji bakat*: I auditioned for a part in the play. ◆ They're auditioning singers for the band.

auditor /ˈɔːdɪtə(r)/ *noun* [C] a person whose job is to examine a company's financial records □ *juruaudit*

auditorium /ˌɔːdɪˈtɔːriəm/ *noun* [C] (*pl* **auditoriums** or **auditoria** /-riə/) the part of a theatre, concert hall, etc. where the audience sits □ *auditorium*

Aug. *abbr* = **August** □ *Ogos*: 10 Aug. 1957

[I] **intransitive**, a verb which has no object: He laughed. [T] **transitive**, a verb which has an object: He ate an apple.

augment /ɔːɡˈment/ verb [T] (formal) to increase the amount, value, size, etc. of sth □ *menambah* ▶**augmentation** /ˌɔːɡmenˈteɪʃn/ noun [C,U]

augur /ˈɔːɡə(r)/ verb
IDM **augur well/ill for sb/sth** (formal) to be a good/bad sign of what will happen in the future □ *merupakan pertanda baik/buruk bagi sso/sst*

August /ˈɔːɡəst/ noun [U,C] (abbr **Aug.**) the 8th month of the year, coming after July □ *Ogos* ➔ note at **January**

aunt /ɑːnt/ (also informal **auntie**, **aunty** /ˈɑːnti/) noun [C] the sister of your father or mother; the wife of your uncle □ *ibu saudara; mak cik*: *Aunt Ellen* ♦ *My aunt lives in Australia.*

au pair /ˌəʊ ˈpeə(r)/ noun (BrE) [C] a person, usually a girl, from another country who comes to live with a family in order to learn the language. An **au pair** helps to clean the house and look after the children. □ *'au pair'*

aura /ˈɔːrə/ noun [C] (formal) the quality that sb/sth seems to have □ *aura*

aural /ˈɔːrəl/ adj connected with hearing and listening □ *berkaitan dgn mendengar*: *an aural comprehension test* ➔ look at **oral**

auspices /ˈɔːspɪsɪz/ noun
IDM **under the auspices of sb/sth** with the help and support of sb/sth □ *di bawah naungan*

auspicious /ɔːˈspɪʃəs/ adj that seems likely to be successful in the future □ *bertuah; baik*: *She made an auspicious start to her professional career when she won her first race.* **OPP** **inauspicious**

austere /ɒˈstɪə(r)/ adj **1** very simple; without decoration □ *sangat sederhana* **2** (used about a person) very strict and serious □ *serius* **3** not having anything that makes your life more comfortable □ *sangat sederhana, tanpa kemewahan*: *The nuns lead simple and austere lives.* ▶**austerity** /ɒˈsterəti/ noun [U]

authentic /ɔːˈθentɪk/ adj **1** that you know is real or genuine □ *tulen; asli; sebenar*: *an authentic Van Gogh painting* **2** true or accurate □ *sebenar*: *an authentic model of the building* ▶**authenticity** /ˌɔːθenˈtɪsəti/ noun [U]

author /ˈɔːθə(r)/ noun [C] a person who writes a book, play, etc. □ *pengarang; penulis*: *a well-known author of detective novels* ♦ *Who's your favourite author?* ▶**authorship** noun [U]

authoritarian /ɔːˌθɒrɪˈteəriən/ adj not allowing people the freedom to decide things for themselves □ *autoritarian; kuku besi*: *authoritarian parents*

authoritative /ɔːˈθɒrətətɪv/ adj **1** having authority; demanding or expecting that people obey you □ *berkuasa; memerintah*: *an authoritative tone of voice* **2** that you can trust and respect as true and correct □ *(yg) boleh dipercayai*: *They will be able to give you authoritative advice on the problem.*

authority /ɔːˈθɒrəti/ noun (pl **authorities**)
▶POWER **1** [U] the power and right to give orders and make others obey □ *kuasa; orang yg ada kuasa*: *Children often begin to question their parents' authority at a very early age.* ♦ *You must get this signed by a person in authority* (= who has a position of power).
▶PERMISSION **2** [U] **authority (to do sth)** the right or permission to do sth □ *hak; kebenaran*: *The police have the authority to question anyone they wish.* ♦ *He was sacked for using a company vehicle without authority.*
▶OFFICIAL GROUP **3** [C, usually pl] a person, group or government department that has the power to give orders, make official decisions, etc. □ *pihak berkuasa*: *I have to report this to the authorities.*
▶KNOWLEDGE **4** [U] the power to influence people because they respect your knowledge or official position □ *kewibawaan*: *He spoke with authority and everybody listened.*
▶EXPERT **5** [C] **an authority (on sth)** a person with special knowledge □ *pakar; ahli*: *He's an authority on criminal law.*

authorize (also **-ise**) /ˈɔːθəraɪz/ verb [T] to give official permission for sth or for sb to do sth □ *memberi kebenaran atau kuasa*: *He authorized his secretary to sign letters in his absence.* ▶**authorization** (also **-isation**) /ˌɔːθəraɪˈzeɪʃn/ noun [U]

autistic /ɔːˈtɪstɪk/ adj having a serious mental illness which makes it very difficult to form relationships with other people □ *autistik*

autobiography /ˌɔːtəbaɪˈɒɡrəfi/ noun [C,U] (pl **autobiographies**) the story of a person's life, written by that person □ *autobiografi* ➔ note at **book** ➔ look at **biography** ▶**autobiographical** /ˌɔːtəˌbaɪəˈɡræfɪkl/ adj

autograph /ˈɔːtəɡrɑːf/ noun [C] a famous person's name, written by that person and given to sb □ *autograf*: *The players stopped outside the stadium to sign autographs.* ▶**autograph** verb [T]: *The whole team have autographed the football.*

automate /ˈɔːtəmeɪt/ verb [T, usually passive] to make sth operate by machine, without needing people □ *mengautomasikan*

automatic[1] /ˌɔːtəˈmætɪk/ adj **1** (used about a machine) that can work by itself without direct human control □ *automatik*: *an automatic washing machine* **2** done without thinking □ *tanpa berfikir*: *Practise this exercise until it becomes automatic.* **3** always happening as a result of a particular action or situation □ *secara automatik*: *All the staff have an automatic right to a space in the car park.* ▶**automatically** /-kli/ adv: *The lights will come on automatically when it gets dark.* ♦ *You will automatically receive a reminder when your next payment is due.*

automatic[2] /ˌɔːtəˈmætɪk/ noun [C] an **automatic** machine, gun or car □ *(mesin, kereta, dsb) automatik*: *This car is an automatic* (= has automatic gears).

automation /ˌɔːtəˈmeɪʃn/ noun [U] the use of machines instead of people to do work □ *automasi*

automobile /ˈɔːtəməbiːl/ (AmE) = **car**(1)

autonomy /ɔːˈtɒnəmi/ noun [U] the right of a person, an organization, a region, etc. to govern or control their or its own affairs □ *autonomi* ▶**autonomous** /ɔːˈtɒnəməs/ adj: *The people in this region want to be completely autonomous.*

autopsy /ˈɔːtɒpsi/ noun [C] (pl **autopsies**) an examination of a dead body to find out the cause of death □ *autopsi*

autumn /ˈɔːtəm/ (AmE usually **fall**) noun [C,U] the season of the year that comes between summer and winter □ *musim luruh*: *In autumn the leaves on the trees begin to fall.* ▶**autumnal** /ɔːˈtʌmnəl/ adj

auxiliary /ɔːɡˈzɪliəri/ adj [only before a noun] giving extra help □ *tambahan*: *auxiliary nurses/troops/staff*

auˈxiliary ˈverb noun [C] a verb (for example *be, do* or *have*) that is used with a main verb to show tense, etc. or to form questions □ *kata kerja bantu*

avail /əˈveɪl/ noun
IDM **of little/no avail** not helpful; having little or no effect □ *tdk berguna; sia-sia*
to little/no avail without success □ *tdk berhasil; hampa*: *They searched everywhere, but to no avail.*

availability /əˌveɪləˈbɪləti/ noun [U] the state of being available □ *ketersediaan*: *You will receive the colour you order, subject to availability* (= if it is available).

available /əˈveɪləbl/ adj **1 available (to sb)** (used about things that you can get, buy, use, etc □ *boleh didapati*: *This information is easily available to everyone at the local library.* ◆ *Refreshments are available at the snack bar.* **2** (used about people) free to be seen, talked to, etc □ *dpt ditemui, dihubungi, dsb*: *The minister was not available for comment.*

avalanche /ˈævəlɑːnʃ/ noun [C] a very large amount of snow that slides quickly down the side of a mountain □ *runtuhan salji*: *Two skiers are still missing after yesterday's avalanche.*

the avant-garde /ˌævɒn ˈɡɑːd/ noun [sing] extremely modern works of art, music or literature, or the artists who create these □ *avant-garde; progresif* ▶**avant-garde** adj

avarice /ˈævərɪs/ noun [U] (formal) extreme desire to be rich □ *ketamakan; kehalobaan* **SYN** greed ▶**avaricious** /ˌævəˈrɪʃəs/ adj

avatar /ˈævətɑː(r)/ noun [C] **1** (in Hinduism and Buddhism) a god appearing in a physical form □ *avatar; tuhan yg muncul dlm bentuk fizikal* **2** a picture of a person or an animal that represents a particular user on a computer screen □ *avatar; gambar yg mewakili pengguna dlm skrin komputer*

Ave. abbr = **avenue** □ *Lebuh*: 26 Elm Ave.

avenge /əˈvendʒ/ verb [T] **avenge sth; avenge yourself on sb** to punish sb for hurting you, your family, etc. in some way □ *menuntut bela; membalas dendam*: *He wanted to avenge his father's murder.* ◆ *He wanted to avenge himself on his father's murderer.* ⊃ look at **revenge**

avenue /ˈævənjuː/ noun [C] **1** (abbr **Ave.**) a wide street, especially one with trees or tall buildings on each side □ *lebuh*: *I live on Kingsdown Avenue.* **2** a way of doing or getting sth □ *jalan; cara*: *We must explore every avenue open to us* (= try every possibility).

average¹ /ˈævərɪdʒ/ adj **1** [only before a noun] (used about a number) found by calculating the **average²**(1) □ *purata*: *What's the average age of your students?* **2** normal or typical □ *biasa; sederhana*: *children of above/below average intelligence*

average² /ˈævərɪdʒ/ noun **1** [C] the number you get when you add two or more figures together and then divide the total by the number of figures you added □ *purata*: *The average of 14, 3 and 1 is 6* (= 18 divided by 3 is 6). ◆ *He has scored 93 goals at an average of 1.55 per game.* **2** [sing, U] the normal standard, amount or quality □ *biasanya; pukul rata*: *On average, I buy a newspaper about twice a week.*

average³ /ˈævərɪdʒ/ verb [T] to do, get, etc. a certain amount as an average □ *mencari purata*: *If we average 50 miles an hour we should arrive at about 4 o'clock.*

PHR V **average out (at sth)** to result in an average (of sth) □ *pukul rata*

averse /əˈvɜːs/ adj [not before a noun] (formal) [often with a negative] **averse to sth** against or not in favour of sth □ *enggan; keberatan*: *He is not averse to trying out new ideas.*

aversion /əˈvɜːʃn/ noun [C, usually sing] **an aversion (to sb/sth)** a strong feeling of not liking sb/sth □ *benci; tdk suka*: *Some people have an aversion to spiders.*

avert /əˈvɜːt/ verb [T] to prevent sth unpleasant □ *menghindarkan*: *The accident could have been averted.*

aviary /ˈeɪviəri/ noun [C] (pl **aviaries**) a large cage (= a box made of bars) or area in which birds are kept □ *lau burung*

aviation /ˌeɪviˈeɪʃn/ noun [U] the designing, building and flying of aircraft □ *penerbangan*

avid /ˈævɪd/ adj **1** very enthusiastic about sth (usually a hobby) □ *sangat suka*: *an avid collector of antiques* **SYN** keen **2 avid for sth** wanting to get sth very much □ *ingin sekali; rakus*: *Journalists crowded round the entrance, avid for news.* ▶**avidly** adv: *He read avidly as a child.*

avocado /ˌævəˈkɑːdəʊ/ noun [C] (pl **avocados**) a tropical fruit that is wider at one end than the other, with a hard green skin and a large stone inside □ *avokado* ⊃ picture on **page P14**

avoid /əˈvɔɪd/ *verb* [T] **1 avoid sth/doing sth** to prevent sth happening or to try not to do sth □ *menghindari; mengelak drpd*: *He always tried to avoid an argument if possible.* ♦ *She has to avoid eating fatty food.* **2** to keep away from sb/sth □ *mengelakkan; mengelak drpd*: *I leave home early to avoid the rush hour.* ▶ **avoidance** *noun* [U]

avoidable /əˈvɔɪdəbl/ *adj* that can be prevented; unnecessary □ *dpt dielakkan* **OPP** **unavoidable**

await /əˈweɪt/ *verb* [T] (*formal*) to wait for sb/sth □ *menunggu*: *We sat down to await the arrival of the guests.*

awake¹ /əˈweɪk/ *adj* [not before a noun] not sleeping □ *jaga; tdk tidur*: *I was sleepy this morning but I'm wide awake now.* ♦ *They were so tired that they found it difficult to stay awake.* ♦ *I hope our singing didn't keep you awake last night.* **OPP** **asleep**

awake² /əˈweɪk/ *verb* [I,T] (*pt* **awoke** /əˈwəʊk/; *pp* **awoken** /əˈwəʊkən/) to wake up; to make sb/sth wake up □ *terjaga; bangun tidur*: *I awoke to find that it was already 9 o'clock.* ♦ *A sudden loud noise awoke us.* ⊃ A more common expression is **wake up**.

awaken /əˈweɪkən/ *verb* **1** [I,T] (*written*) to wake up; to make sb/sth wake up □ *terjaga; bangun tidur*: *We were awakened by a loud knock at the door.* ⊃ A much more common expression is **wake up**. **2** [T] (*formal*) to produce a particular feeling, attitude, etc. in sb □ *membangkitkan*: *The film awakened memories of her childhood.*

PHR V **awaken sb to sth** to make sb notice or realize sth for the first time □ *menyedarkan sso akan sst*: *The letter awakened me to the seriousness of the situation.*

awakening /əˈweɪkənɪŋ/ *noun* [C, usually sing] **1** a moment when sb notices or realizes sth for the first time □ *kesedaran; tersentak*: *It was a rude (= unpleasant) awakening when I suddenly found myself unemployed.* **2** the act of starting to feel or understand sth; the start of a feeling, etc □ *kesedaran; mula (menyedari, merasai, dsb)*: *the awakening of an interest in the opposite sex*

award¹ /əˈwɔːd/ *noun* [C] **1** a prize, etc. that sb gets for doing sth well □ *hadiah; anugerah*: *This year the awards for best actor and actress went to two Americans.* **2** an amount of money given to sb as the result of a court decision □ *award; pampasan*: *She received an award of £5 000 for damages.*

award² /əˈwɔːd/ *verb* [T] **award sth (to sb)** to give sth to sb as a prize, payment, etc □ *memberi hadiah; menghadiahkan; memberi pampasan*: *She was awarded first prize in the gymnastics competition.* ♦ *The court awarded £10 000 each to the workers injured in the accident.*

aware /əˈweə(r)/ *adj* **1** [not before a noun] **aware (of sb/sth); aware (that)** knowing about or realizing sth; conscious of sb/sth □ *sedar akan; menyedari; tahu*: *I am well aware of the problems you face.* ♦ *I suddenly became aware that someone was watching me.* ♦ *There is no other entrance, as far as I am aware.* **OPP** **unaware** **2** interested in and knowing about sth □ *mempunyai kesedaran*: *Many young people are very politically aware.*

awareness /əˈweənəs/ *noun* [U] knowledge or interest □ *kesedaran*: *People's awareness of healthy eating has increased in recent years.* **SYN** **consciousness**

awash /əˈwɒʃ/ (*AmE* also) / *adj* [not before a noun] **awash (with sth)** covered with water □ *kebanjiran; dibanjiri; dipenuhi*: (*figurative*) *The city was awash with rumours.*

away /əˈweɪ/ *adv* **1 away (from sth)** at a particular distance from a place □ *jauhnya dr (sst tempat)*: *The village is two miles away from the sea.* ♦ *My parents live five minutes away.* **2** in the future □ *lagi*: *Our summer holiday is only three weeks away.* **3 away (from sb/sth)** to a different place or in a different direction □ *pergi dr; ke arah lain*: *Go away! I'm busy!* ♦ *I called his name, but he just walked away from me.* **4** into a place where sth is usually kept □ *simpan; angkat (mengalihkan ke tempat lain)*: *Put your books away now.* ♦ *They cleared the dishes away* (= off the table). ♦ *I'm going to throw my old clothes away* (= put them in the rubbish). **5 away (from sth)** (used about people) not present □ *tdk ada; tdk hadir*: *My neighbours are away on holiday at the moment.* ♦ *Aki was away from school for two weeks with measles.* **SYN** **absent** **6** continuously, without stopping □ *terus-menerus*: *They chatted away for hours.* **7** until sth disappears □ *sehingga habis, lenyap, dsb*: *The crash of thunder slowly died away.* ♦ *He's given most of his money away.* **8** (used about a football, etc. match) on the other team's ground □ *di tempat lawan*: *Our team's playing away on Saturday.* ♦ *an away match/game* **OPP** **home** ❶ For special uses with many verbs, for example **give away**, look at the verb entries.

IDM **do away with sb/sth** to get rid of sb/sth □ *menghapuskan*: *The government are going to do away with the tax on fuel.*

right/straight away immediately; without any delay □ *sekarang juga*: *I'll phone the doctor right away.*

awe /ɔː/ *noun* [U] feelings of respect and either fear or admiration □ *rasa segan/kagum/takut*: *We watched in awe as the rocket took off.*

IDM **be in awe of sb/sth** to admire sb/sth and be slightly afraid of them or it □ *berasa segan, kagum atau takut*: *As a young boy he was very much in awe of his uncle.*

ˈ**awe-inspiring** *adj* causing a feeling of respect and fear or admiration □ *mengagumkan*

awesome /ˈɔːsəm/ *adj* **1** impressive and sometimes frightening □ *(yg) sangat mengagumkan;*

awful → baby

menggerunkan, dsb: *an awesome task* **2** (*AmE slang*) very good; excellent □ *bagus sekali*

awful /'ɔ:fl/ *adj* **1** very bad or unpleasant □ *teruk*: *We had an awful holiday. It rained every day.* ♦ *I feel awful—I think I'll go to bed.* ♦ *What an awful thing to say!* **SYN** **terrible** ⇨ note at **bad 2** [only *before* a noun] (*informal*) very great □ *sangat; amat*: *We've got an awful lot of work to do.* **3** terrible; very serious □ *buruk; dahsyat*: *I'm afraid there's been some awful news.*

awfully /'ɔ:fli/ *adv* (*informal*) very; extremely □ *sangat; amat*: *I'm awfully sorry.* **SYN** **terribly**

awkward /'ɔ:kwəd/ *adj* **1** embarrassed or embarrassing □ *canggung; kekok; tdk selesa*: *I often feel awkward in a group of people.* ♦ *There was an awkward silence.* **2** difficult to deal with □ *sukar (dijawab, dilayani, dsb)*: *That's an awkward question.* ♦ *You've put me in an awkward position.* ♦ *an awkward customer* ♦ *The box isn't heavy but it's awkward to carry.* **SYN** **difficult 3** not convenient □ *tdk sesuai; sukar*: *My mother always phones at an awkward time.* ♦ *This tin-opener is very awkward to clean.* **SYN** **difficult 4** not using the body in the best way; not elegant or comfortable □ *kekok; tdk selesa*: *I was sitting with my legs in an awkward position.* ▶ **awkwardly** *adv* ▶ **awkwardness** *noun* [U]

awning /'ɔ:nɪŋ/ *noun* [C] a sheet of strong cloth that spreads out above a door or window to protect it from the sun or rain □ *sengkuap; kajang; pelindung kanvas atau plastik spt atap*

awoke *past tense* of **awake**²

awoken *past participle* of **awake**²

awry /ə'raɪ/ *adv, adj* [not before a noun] wrong, not in the way that was planned; untidy □ *herot; tdk keruan*

axe¹ (*especially AmE* **ax**) /æks/ *noun* [C] a tool with a wooden handle and a heavy metal head with a sharp edge, used for cutting wood, etc. □ *kapak*

axe² (*especially AmE* **ax**) /æks/ *verb* [T] **1** (used especially in newspapers) to reduce sth by a great amount □ *memotong; mengurangkan*: *Budgets are to be axed.* **2** to remove sb/sth □ *dibuang (kerja, dsb)*: *Hundreds of jobs have been axed.*

axis /'æksɪs/ *noun* [C] (*pl* **axes** /'æksi:z/) **1** a line we imagine through the middle of an object, around which the object turns □ *paksi*: *The earth rotates on its axis.* ⇨ picture at **earth 2** a fixed line used for marking measurements on a **graph** (= a diagram with lines on it to show the relationship between two sets of numbers) □ *paksi*: *the horizontal/vertical axis*

axle /'æksl/ *noun* [C] a bar that connects a pair of wheels on a vehicle □ *gandar*

azure /'æʒə(r)/ (*BrE also*) /'æʒjʊə(r)/ *adj, noun* [U] (of) a bright blue colour like the sky □ *biru cerah*

B, b /biː/ *noun* [C,U] (*pl* **Bs; B's; b's** /biːz/) **1** the second letter of the English alphabet □ *B; b* (*huruf*): *'Bicycle' begins with (a) 'B'.* **2 B** (used about music) the seventh note in the scale of C major □ *not ketujuh dlm skala C major*: *B major/minor* ♦ *B flat*

b. *abbr* = **born**¹ □ *dilahirkan*: *J S Bach, b. 1685*

BA /ˌbiː'eɪ/ *abbr* **Bachelor of Arts**; the degree that you receive when you complete a university or college course in an arts subject □ *ijazah Sarjana Muda Sastera* ⇨ look at **BSc, MA**

baa /baː/ *noun* [sing] the sound that a sheep makes □ *embek; bunyi kambing biri-biri*

babble¹ /'bæbl/ *noun* [sing] **1** the sound of many voices talking at the same time □ *bunyi banyak orang bercakap yg tdk jelas butirnya; bebelan*: *a babble of voices* **2** talking that is confused or silly and is difficult to understand □ *bebelan; racauan; raban*: *I can't bear his constant babble.*

babble² /'bæbl/ *verb* [I] **1** to talk quickly or in a way that is difficult to understand □ *membebel* **2** to make the sound of water running over stones □ *mendesir*

babe /beɪb/ *noun* [C] **1** (*old-fashioned*) a baby □ *bayi* **2** (*especially AmE slang*) used when talking to sb, especially a girl or young woman □ *cik adik; sayang*: *It's OK, babe.* **3** (*slang*) an attractive young woman □ *wanita muda yg cantik*

baboon /bə'buːn/ *noun* [C] a large African or Asian **monkey** (= an animal that lives in hot countries and can climb trees) with a long face like a dog's □ *babun*

baby /'beɪbi/ *noun* [C] (*pl* **babies**) **1** a very young child □ *bayi; anak; cahaya mata*: *I'm going to have a baby.* ♦ *She's expecting a baby early next year.* ♦ *When's the baby due?* (= when will it be born?) ♦ *a baby boy/girl* **2** a very young animal or bird □ *anak binatang atau burung*: *a baby rabbit* **3** (*AmE slang*) a person, especially a girl or young woman, that you like or love □ *buah hati*

> **TOPIC**
>
> **Babies**
> A **pregnant** woman has a baby growing inside her; you can also say: *She's having/expecting a baby*. She **gives birth** and the baby **is born**, usually with the help of a **midwife**. If a baby is born early, it is **premature**. If a mother gives birth to two babies at the same time, they are **twins**. Parents **take care of** their baby by feeding it, bathing it and changing its **nappy**. A woman whose job is to look after other people's babies and children is a **nanny**. A baby sleeps in a **cot** and you take it outside in a **pram**. As a baby grows up and starts to walk it is called a **toddler**.

ʌ **c**up   ɜː **b**ir**d**   ə **a**go   eɪ **p**ay   əʊ **g**o   aɪ **m**y   aʊ **n**ow   ɔɪ **b**oy   ɪə **n**ear   eə **h**air   ʊə **p**ure

'baby boom noun [C, usually sing] a time when more babies are born than usual □ *zaman bayi banyak dilahirkan*

'baby carriage (AmE) = pram

babyish /'beɪbiɪʃ/ adj suitable for or behaving like a baby □ *sesuai utk bayi; berkelakuan spt bayi*: This book is a bit too babyish for Faruk now.

babysit /'beɪbɪsɪt/ verb [I] (**babysitting**; pt, pp **babysat**) to look after a child for a short time while the parents are out □ *menjaga budak*: I sometimes babysit for our neighbours' children at weekends. ▶**babysitter** noun [C]

bachelor /'bætʃələ(r)/ noun [C] 1 a man who has not yet married □ *bujang* ➲ look at **spinster**

> **MORE** Nowadays **single** is the most usual word for describing a man who is not married: *a single man*.

2 a person who has a first university degree □ *(orang yg memiliki ijazah) Sarjana Muda*: a Bachelor of Arts/Science

back

back to front   inside out

back¹ /bæk/ noun [C] 1 the part of a person's or an animal's body between the neck and the bottom □ *belakang*: Do you sleep **on your back** or on your side? ◆ She was standing **with her back to** me so I couldn't see her face. ◆ A camel has a hump on its back. 2 [usually sing] the part or side of sth that is furthest from the front □ *bahagian belakang*: I sat **at the back of** the class. ◆ The answers are **in the back of** the book. ◆ Write your address **on the back of** the cheque. 3 the part of a chair that supports your upper body when you sit down □ *sandaran kerusi*: He put his coat over the back of the chair.

IDM **at/in the back of your mind** if sth is at the back of your mind, it is in your thoughts but is not the main thing that you are thinking about □ *dlm fikiran; teringat-ingat*: With next week's exam at the back of my mind, I couldn't relax and enjoy the film.

back to front with the back where the front should be □ *terbalik (depan ke belakang)*: Wait a minute—you've got your jumper on back to front. ➲ look at **way¹** (3)

behind sb's back without sb's knowledge or agreement □ *tanpa pengetahuan sso*: They criticized her behind her back. **OPP** **to sb's face**

get off sb's back (*informal*) to stop annoying sb, for example when you keep asking them to do sth □ *jangan mengganggu*: I've told her I'll do the job by Monday, so I wish she'd get off my back!

know sth like the back of your hand ➲ **know¹**

a pat on the back ➲ **pat²**

turn your back on sb/sth to refuse to be involved with sb/sth □ *tdk mempedulikan; meninggalkan*: He turned his back on his career and went to live in the country.

back² /bæk/ adj [only before a noun] 1 furthest from the front □ *belakang*: Have you locked the back door? ◆ the back row of the theatre ◆ back teeth 2 owed from a time in the past □ *tunggakan*: back pay/rent

IDM **take a back seat** to allow sb to play a more important or active role than yourself in a particular situation □ *mengambil peranan yg kurang penting*

back³ /bæk/ adv 1 away from the direction you are facing or moving in □ *ke belakang*: She walked away without **looking back**. ◆ Could everyone **move back** a bit, please? **OPP** **forward** 2 away from sth; under control □ *menahan*: The police were unable to **keep** the crowds **back**. ◆ She tried to **hold back** her tears. 3 in or to a place or state that sb/sth was in before □ *balik; pulang*: I'm going out now—I'll **be back** about 6 o'clock. ◆ It started to rain so I **came back** home. ◆ **Go back** to sleep. ◆ Could I **have** my pen **back**, please? ◆ I've got to **take** these books **back** to the library. 4 in or into the past; ago □ *kembali (ke masa lalu); dahulu*: I met him a few years back, in Madrid. ◆ **Think back** to your first day at school. 5 in return or in reply □ *kembali*: He said he'd phone me back in half an hour.

IDM **back and forth** from one place to another and back again, all the time □ *pergi balik; ulang-alik*: Travelling back and forth to work takes up a lot of time.

back⁴ /bæk/ verb 1 [I,T] to move backwards or to make sth move backwards □ *mengundur*: She backed into her office and closed the door. ◆ He backed the car into the parking space. 2 [T] to give help or support to sb/sth □ *menyokong*: We can go ahead with the scheme if the bank will agree to back us. 3 [T] to bet money that a particular horse, team, etc. will win in a race or game □ *bertaruh pd*: Which horse are you backing in the 2 o'clock race? 4 [I] to face sth at the back □ *membelakangi*: Many of the colleges back onto the river.

PHR V **back away (from sb/sth)** to move backwards because you are afraid, shocked, etc □ *mengundur (menjauhi sso/sst)*: He began to back slowly away from the snake.

back down to stop saying that you are right □ *mengalah; menarik balik*: I think you are right to demand an apology. Don't back down now.

back out (of sth) to decide not to do sth that you had promised to do □ *menarik diri (drpd sst)*: You promised to come with me. You just can't back out of it now!

back bench → backward 54

back sb/sth up to support sb; to say or show that sth is true □ *menyokong sso/sst*: *I'm going to say exactly what I think at the meeting. Will you back me up?* ♦ *All the evidence backed up what she had said.*

back (sth) up to move backwards, especially in a vehicle □ *berundur; mengundurkan*: *Back up a little so that the other cars can get past.*

back sth up to make a copy of a computer file, etc. that can be used if the original one is lost or damaged □ *membuat salinan*

back bench *noun* [C, usually pl] (in Britain) a seat in the House of Commons for an ordinary member of Parliament □ *kerusi ahli parlimen biasa*: *to sit on the back benches* ♦ *back-bench MPs* ▶**backbencher** *noun* [C]

backbone /'bækbəʊn/ *noun* **1** [C] the row of small bones that are connected together down the middle of your back □ *tulang belakang* **SYN** spine ᗧ picture at **body** **2** [sing] the most important part of sth □ *tulang belakang; tunjang*: *Agriculture is the backbone of their economy.*

backcloth /'bækklɒθ/ = **backdrop**

backdate /ˌbæk'deɪt/ *verb* [T] to make a document, cheque or payment take effect from an earlier date □ *mengundurkan tarikh*: *The pay rise will be backdated to 1 April.*

backdrop /'bækdrɒp/ (also **backcloth**) *noun* [C] a painted piece of cloth that is hung at the back of the stage in a theatre □ *tirai latar*

backer /'bækə(r)/ *noun* [C] a person, an organization or a company that gives support to sb, especially financial support □ *penyokong; pembiaya*

backfire /ˌbæk'faɪə(r)/ *verb* [I] to have an unexpected and unpleasant result, often the opposite of what was intended □ *berkesudahan sebaliknya*

backgammon /'bækgæmən/ *noun* [U] a game for two people played by moving pieces around a board marked with long thin triangles □ *sejenis permainan yg menggunakan papan dan buah dadu*

background /'bækgraʊnd/ *noun* **1** [C] the type of family and social class you come from and the education and experience you have □ *latar belakang*: *We get on very well together in spite of our different backgrounds.* **2** [sing, U] the facts or events that are connected with a situation □ *latar*: *The talks are taking place against a background of increasing tension.* ♦ *I need some background information.* **3** [sing] the part of a view, scene, picture, etc. which is furthest away from the person looking at it □ *latar belakang*: *You can see the mountains in the background of the photo.* **OPP** foreground **4** [sing] a position where sb/sth can be seen/heard, etc. but is not the centre of attention □ *tdk menonjolkan diri; latar*: *The film star's husband prefers to stay in the background.* ♦ *All the time I was speaking to her,* *I could hear a child crying in the background.* ♦ *I like to have background music when I'm studying.*

backhand /'bækhænd/ *noun* [sing] a way of hitting the ball in sports such as **tennis** that is made with the back of your hand facing forward □ *pukulan kilas* **OPP** forehand

backing /'bækɪŋ/ *noun* [U] help or support to do sth, especially financial support □ *sokongan*: *financial backing* ♦ *a backing group/singer/track* (= one that accompanies the main singer or tune)

backlash /'bæklæʃ/ *noun* [sing] a strong negative reaction against a political or social event or development □ *tindak balas negatif*

backlog /'bæklɒg/ (AmE also) / *noun* [C, usually sing] an amount of work, etc. that has not yet been done and should have been done already □ *tunggakan (kerja, dsb)*: *Because I've been off sick, I've got a backlog of work to catch up on.*

backpack¹ /'bækpæk/ (also **pack**, BRE ALSO **rucksack**) *noun* [C] a large bag, often on a metal frame, that you carry on your back when you are travelling □ *beg galas belakang* ᗧ picture at **bag** ᗧ picture on page P1

backpack² /'bækpæk/ *verb* [I] to go walking or travelling with your clothes, etc. in a **backpack** □ *mengembara dgn membawa beg galas belakang* ᗧ note at **holiday**

HELP Go backpacking is used when you are talking about spending time backpacking: *We went backpacking round Europe last summer.*

▶**backpacker** *noun* [C]

backside /'bæksaɪd/ *noun* [C] (*informal*) the part of your body that you sit on □ *punggung; buntut* **SYN** bottom

backslash /'bækslæʃ/ *noun* [C] a mark (\ ), used in computer commands □ *garis miring belakang* ᗧ look at **forward slash**

backstage /ˌbæk'steɪdʒ/ *adv* in the part of a theatre where the actors get dressed, wait to perform, etc. □ *di belakang pentas*

backstroke /'bækstrəʊk/ *noun* [U] a style of swimming that you do on your back □ *kuak lentang*: *Can you do backstroke?* ᗧ picture at **swim**

backtrack /'bæktræk/ *verb* [I] **1** to go back the same way you came □ *berpatah balik*: *We got lost in the wood and had to backtrack.* **2 backtrack (on sth)** to change your mind about a plan, promise, etc. that you have made □ *menarik diri*: *Unions forced the company to backtrack on its plans to close the factory.*

backup /'bækʌp/ *noun* **1** [U] extra help or support that you can get if necessary □ *bantuan tersedia*: *The police officer requested urgent back-up from the rest of the team.* **2** [C] a copy of a computer file, etc. that you can use if the original one is lost or damaged □ *salinan*: *Always make a backup of your files.*

backward /'bækwəd/ *adj* **1** [only *before* a noun] directed towards the back □ *ke belakang*:

[I] **intransitive**, a verb which has no object: *He laughed.*   [T] **transitive**, a verb which has an object: *He ate an apple.*

a backward step/glance **OPP** *forward* **2** slow to develop or learn □ *terkebelakang; mundur*: *Our teaching methods are backward compared to some countries.*

backwards /'bækwədz/ (*especially AmE* **backward**) *adv* **1** towards a place or a position that is behind □ *ke belakang*: *Could everybody take a step backwards?* **2** in the opposite direction to usual □ *terbalik; menyongsang*: *Can you say the alphabet backwards?* **OPP** for both meanings **forwards**
IDM **backward(s) and forward(s)** first in one direction and then in the other, many times □ *mundar-mandir; pergi balik*: *The dog ran backwards and forwards, barking loudly.*

backwater /'bækwɔːtə(r)/ *noun* [C] a place that is away from the places where most things happen and so is not affected by new ideas or outside events □ *terpencil; ulu*

backyard /ˌbækˈjɑːd/ *noun* [C] **1** (*BrE*) an area behind a house, with a hard surface and a wall or fence around it □ *kawasan belakang rumah* **2** (*AmE*) the whole area behind the house including the grass area and the garden □ *kawasan belakang rumah termasuk laman belakang*

bacon /'beɪkən/ *noun* [U] meat from the back or sides of a pig that has been **cured** (= treated with salt or smoke to keep it fresh), usually served in thin slices □ *bakon* ➲ note at **meat** ➲ look at **gammon, ham, pork**

bacteria /bækˈtɪəriə/ *noun* [pl] very small living things that can only be seen with a **microscope** (= a piece of equipment that makes small objects look bigger). Bacteria exist in large numbers in air, water, soil, plants and the bodies of people and animals. Some bacteria cause disease. □ *bakteria* ➲ look at **virus** ▶**bacterial** *adj*: *bacterial infections*

bad /bæd/ *adj* (**worse** /wɜːs/, **worst** /wɜːst/)
▶UNPLEASANT **1** not good; unpleasant □ *tdk baik; buruk*: *bad weather* ♦ *I'm afraid I've got some bad news for you.* ♦ *It's bad enough losing your job, but to lose your house as well is awful.*
▶POOR QUALITY **2** of poor quality; of a low standard □ *tdk baik; kurang baik*: *Many accidents are caused by bad driving.* ♦ *This isn't as bad as I thought.*
▶NOT SKILFUL **3 bad (at sth/at doing sth)** not able to do sth well or easily □ *tdk berapa pandai*: *a bad teacher/driver/cook* ♦ *I've always been bad at sport.* **SYN** **poor**
▶SERIOUS **4** serious □ *teruk*: *The traffic was very bad on the way to work.* ♦ *She went home with a bad headache.* ♦ *That was a very bad mistake!*
▶NOT SUITABLE **5** [only before a noun] difficult or not suitable □ *sukar; tdk sesuai; tdk wajar*: *This is a bad time to phone—everyone's out to lunch.*
▶PERSON/BEHAVIOUR **6** not good; morally wrong □ *jahat*: *He was not a bad man, just rather weak.*
▶HARMFUL **7** [not before a noun] **bad for sb/sth** likely to damage or hurt sb/sth □ *tdk baik; menjejaskan (kesihatan, dsb)*: *Sugar is bad for your teeth.*
▶PART OF THE BODY **8** not healthy; painful □ *sakit*: *He's always had a bad heart.* ♦ *Keith's off work with a bad back.*
▶FOOD **9** not fresh or suitable to eat □ *basi; busuk*: *These eggs will go bad if we don't eat them soon.*
IDM **not bad** (*informal*) quite good □ *agak baik*: *'What was the film like?' 'Not bad.'*
too bad (*informal*) used to show that nothing can be done to change a situation □ *apa boleh buat; nasiblah*: *'I'd much rather stay at home.' 'Well that's just too bad. We've said we'll go.'*
ℹ For other idioms containing **bad**, look at the entries for the nouns, adjectives, etc. For example, **go through a bad patch** is at **patch**.

OTHER WORDS FOR

bad

You can say **awful, dreadful** or **terrible** instead of 'very bad'. **Horrible** describes somebody or something that is unpleasant or somebody who is unkind: *He's always saying horrible things to me.* We also say: **poor** *quality* ♦ *an* **unpleasant** *experience* ♦ *a* **disgusting** *smell* ♦ *a* **serious** *accident/illness/problem*

---

baddy /'bædi/ *noun* [C] (*pl* **baddies**) (*informal*) a bad person in a film, book, etc. □ *orang jahat* **OPP** **goody**

badge /bædʒ/ *noun* [C] a small piece of metal, cloth or plastic with a design or words on it that you wear on your clothing □ *lencana*: *The players all have jackets with the club badge on.*

badger /'bædʒə(r)/ *noun* [C] an animal with black and white lines on its head that lives in holes in the ground and comes out at night □ *badger*

bad 'language *noun* [U] words that are used for swearing □ *bahasa kesat*: *You'll get into trouble if you use bad language.*

badly /'bædli/ *adv* (**worse** /wɜːs/, **worst** /wɜːst/) **1** in a way that is not good enough; not well □ *teruk; tdk berapa baik*: *'Can you speak French?' 'Only very badly.'* ♦ *She did badly in the exams.* **OPP** **well 2** very much □ *sangat (memerlukan, dsb)*: *He badly needed a holiday.* **3** seriously; in a terrible way □ *teruk; parah*: *He was very badly hurt in the accident.*
IDM **well/badly off** ➲ **off**

badminton

badminton /ˈbædmɪntən/ noun [U] a game for two or four people in which players hit a **shuttlecock** (= a type of light ball with feathers) over a high net, using a **racket** (= a piece of equipment that is held in the hand) ▢ *badminton*

badminton: shuttlecock, rackets

bad-ˈtempered adj often angry or impatient ▢ *panas baran*: *a bad-tempered old man* ♦ *Don't be so bad-tempered!*

baffle /ˈbæfl/ verb [T] to be impossible to understand; to confuse sb very much ▢ *membingungkan*: *His illness baffled the doctors.* ▶**baffled** adj: *The instructions were so complicated that I was absolutely baffled.* ▶**baffling** adj: *I find it baffling how people can enjoy computer magazines.*

bag¹ /bæg/ noun **1** [C] a container made of paper or thin plastic that opens at the top ▢ *kampit; beg (plastik/kertas)*: *She brought some sandwiches in a plastic bag.* ⊃ picture at **container 2** [C] a strong container made from cloth, plastic, leather, etc. usually with one or two handles, used to carry things in when travelling, shopping, etc ▢ *beg (tangan, pakaian, dsb)*: *a shopping bag* ♦ *Have you packed your bags yet?* ♦ *She took her purse out of her bag* (= handbag). ♦ *Don't forget your school bag.* **3** [C] the amount contained in a bag ▢ *se-(kampit, paket, dsb)*: *She's eaten a whole bag of sweets!* ♦ *a bag of crisps/sugar/flour* **4** [pl] (BrE) **bags (of sth)** a lot (of sth); plenty (of sth) ▢ *banyak*: *There's no hurry—we've got bags of time.* **5 bags** [pl] folds of skin under the eyes, often caused by lack of sleep ▢ *sembap bawah mata*: *I've got terrible bags under my eyes.*

bag² /bæg/ verb [T] (**bagging**; **bagged**) (informal) to try to get sth for yourself so that other people cannot have it ▢ *mengambil*: *Somebody's bagged the seats by the pool!*

bagel /ˈbeɪgl/ noun [C] a type of bread roll in the shape of a ring ▢ *bagel*

baggage /ˈbægɪdʒ/ noun [U] bags, suitcases, etc. used for carrying sb's clothes and things on a journey ▢ *bagasi*: *excess baggage* (= baggage weighing more than the airline's allowed limit) ♦ *I went to wait for my suitcase at baggage reclaim* (= the area in an airport where baggage goes after being unloaded from a plane). **SYN** **luggage** ⊃ note at **plane**

ˈbaggage room (AmE) = **left-luggage office**

baggy /ˈbægi/ adj (**baggier**; **baggiest**) (used about a piece of clothing) big; hanging on the body in a loose way ▢ *gedoboh*: *a baggy sweater* **OPP** **tight**

bagpipes /ˈbægpaɪps/ noun [pl] a musical instrument, popular in Scotland, that is played by blowing air through a pipe into a bag and then pressing the bag so that the air comes out of other pipes ▢ *begpaip*

baguette /bæˈget/ noun [C] a type of bread in the shape of a long thick stick ▢ *baguette; roti Perancis*

bagpipes

bail¹ /beɪl/ noun [U] money that sb agrees to pay if a person accused of a crime does not appear in court on the day they are called. When **bail** has been arranged, the accused person can go free until that day ▢ *ikat jamin; jaminan*: *She was released on bail of £2 000.* ♦ *The judge set bail at £10 000.* ♦ *The judge felt that he was a dangerous man and refused him bail.* ♦ *She was granted bail.*

bail² /beɪl/ verb [T] to free sb on **bail¹** ▢ *diberi ikat jamin*

PHR V **bail sb out 1** to obtain sb's freedom by paying money to the court ▢ *membayar ikat jamin utk sso*: *Her parents went to the police station and bailed her out.* **2** to rescue sb or sth from a difficult situation (especially by providing money) ▢ *membantu; menyelamatkan*: *If you get into trouble, don't expect me to bail you out again!*

bailiff /ˈbeɪlɪf/ noun [C] an officer whose job is to take the possessions and property of people who cannot pay money that they owe ▢ *bailif*

bailout /ˈbeɪlaʊt/ noun [C] an act of giving money to a company, a foreign country, etc. that has very serious financial problems ▢ *perihal memberikan wang kpd pihak yg dilanda masalah kewangan yg serius*

bait /beɪt/ noun [U] **1** food or sth that looks like food that is put onto a hook to catch fish, or to catch animals or birds ▢ *umpan* **2** something that is used for persuading or attracting sb ▢ *umpan*: *Free offers are often used as bait to attract customers.*

bake /beɪk/ verb [I,T] **1** to cook in an oven in dry heat ▢ *membakar*: *I could smell bread baking in the oven.* ♦ *On his birthday she baked him a cake.* ⊃ note at **cook 2** to become or to make sth hard by heating it ▢ *menjadi keras*: *The hot sun baked the earth.*

ˌbaked poˈtato = **jacket potato**

baker /ˈbeɪkə(r)/ noun **1** [C] a person who bakes bread, cakes, etc. to sell in a shop ▢ *pembuat roti* **2 the baker's** [sing] (BrE) a shop that sells bread, cakes, etc ▢ *kedai roti*: *Get a loaf at the baker's.*

bakery /ˈbeɪkəri/ noun [C] (pl **bakeries**) a place where bread, cakes, etc. are baked and/or sold ▢ *kilang roti; kedai roti*

baking /ˈbeɪkɪŋ/ adj very hot ▢ *sangat panas*: *The workers complained of the baking heat in the office.*

baking powder *noun* [U] a mixture of powders that is used to make cakes rise and become light as they are baked □ *serbuk penaik*

balance¹ /ˈbæləns/ *noun* **1** [sing] **(a) balance (between A and B)** a situation in which different or opposite things are of equal importance, size, etc. □ *perimbangan; keseimbangan*: *The course provides a good balance between academic and practical work.* ♦ *Tourism has upset the delicate balance of nature on the island.* **2** [U] the ability to keep steady with an equal amount of weight on each side of the body □ *keseimbangan*: *to lose your balance* ♦ *It's very difficult to keep your balance when you start learning to ski.* ♦ *You need a good sense of balance to ride a motorbike.* **3** [C, usually sing] the amount that still has to be paid; the amount that is left after some has been used, taken, etc. □ *baki*: *You can pay a 10% deposit now, with the balance due in one month.* ♦ *to check your bank balance* (= to find out how much money you have in your account) **4** [C] (technical) an instrument used for weighing things □ *penimbang; neraca*
IDM in the balance uncertain □ *belum pasti*: *Following poor results, the company's future hangs in the balance.*
(catch/throw sb) off balance (to find or put sb) in a position that is not safe and from which it is easy to fall □ *menyebabkan hilang keseimbangan*: *A strong gust of wind caught me off balance and I nearly fell over.*
on balance having considered all sides, facts, etc. □ *setelah mempertimbangkan segala-galanya*: *On balance, I've had a pretty good year.*
strike a balance (between A and B) ➔ **strike¹**

balance² /ˈbæləns/ *verb* **1** [I,T] to be or to put sb/sth in a steady position so that their/its weight is not heavier on one side than on the other □ *mengimbangkan*: *I had to balance on the top step of the ladder to paint the ceiling.* ♦ *Carefully,* *she balanced a glass on top of the pile of plates.* **2** [I,T] **balance (sth) (out) (with sth)** to have or give sth equal value, importance, etc. in relation to other parts □ *mengimbangi*: *The loss in the first half of the year was balanced out by the profit in the second half.* **3** [T] **balance sth against sth** to consider and compare one matter in relation to another □ *mempertimbangkan*: *In planning the new road, we have to balance the benefit to motorists against the damage to the environment.* **4** [I,T] to have equal totals of money spent and money received □ *seimbang*: *I must have made a mistake—the accounts don't balance.* ♦ *She is always very careful to balance her weekly budget.*

balanced /ˈbælənst/ *adj* keeping or showing a balance so that different things, or different parts of things, exist in equal or correct amounts □ *seimbang*: *I like this newspaper because it gives a balanced view.* ♦ *A balanced diet plays an important part in good health.* **OPP unbalanced**

balance of ˈpayments *noun* [sing] the difference between the amount of money one country receives from other countries for things it sells and the amount it pays other countries for things it buys, in a particular period of time □ *imbangan pembayaran*

balance of ˈpower *noun* [sing] **1** a situation in which political power or military strength is divided between two countries or groups of countries □ *imbangan kuasa* **2** the power that a smaller political party has when the larger parties need its support because they do not have enough votes on their own □ *kuasa penentu*

ˈbalance sheet *noun* [C] a written statement showing the amount of money and property that a company has, and how much has been received and paid out □ *kunci kira-kira*

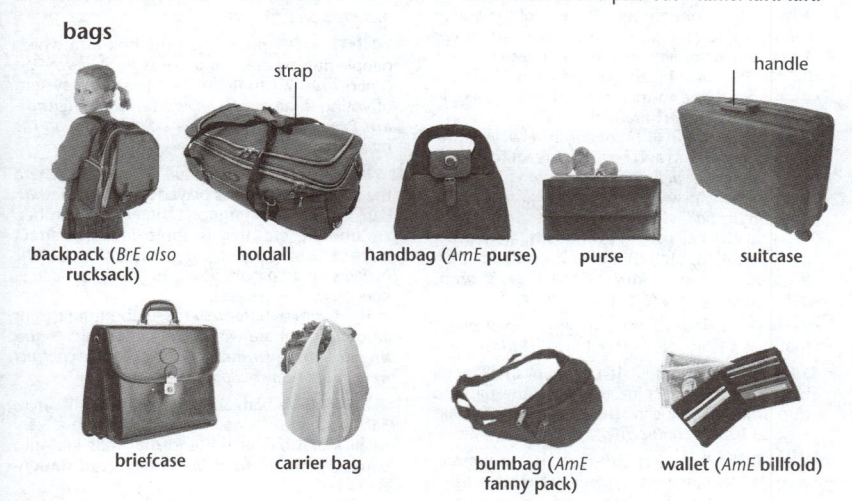

bags

backpack (BrE also rucksack) holdall handbag (AmE purse) purse suitcase

briefcase carrier bag bumbag (AmE fanny pack) wallet (AmE billfold)

VOWELS iː see i any ɪ sit e ten æ hat ɑː father ɒ got ɔː saw ʊ put uː too u usual

balcony /'bælkəni/ noun [C] (pl **balconies**) 1 a platform built on an upstairs outside wall of a building, with a wall or rail around it □ *balkoni; anjung* 2 (*especially AmE*) = **circle**[1](3)

bald /bɔːld/ adj 1 (used about people) having little or no hair on your head □ *botak*: *I hope I don't go bald like my father did.* ♦ *He has a bald patch on the top of his head.* ⊃ picture at **hair** 2 (used about sth that is said) simple; without extra words □ *tanpa tokok tambah; semata-mata*: *the bald truth*

balding /'bɔːldɪŋ/ adj starting to lose the hair on your head □ *sudah mula botak*: *a balding man in his fifties*

baldly /'bɔːldli/ adv in a few words with nothing extra or unnecessary and without trying to be polite □ *dgn terus terang*: '*You're lying*,' *he said baldly.*

bale /beɪl/ noun [C] a large quantity of sth pressed tightly together and tied up □ *bandela*: *a bale of hay/cloth/paper*

balk (*especially AmE*) = **baulk**

⚑ **ball** /bɔːl/ noun [C]
▸ROUND OBJECT 1 a round object that you hit, kick, throw, etc. in games and sports □ *bola*: *a tennis/golf/rugby ball* ♦ *a football* ⊃ picture at **pool** 2 a round object or a thing that has been formed into a round shape □ *bola; bebola*: *a ball of wool* ♦ *The children threw snowballs at each other.* ♦ *We had meatballs and pasta for dinner.*
▸THROW/KICK 3 one throw, kick, etc. of the ball in some sports □ *(tendangan atau pukulan) bola*: *That was a great ball from the defender.*
▸PART OF THE BODY 4 (*slang*) = **testicle**
▸DANCE 5 a large formal party at which people dance □ *majlis tari-menari*
IDM **be on the ball** (*informal*) to always know what is happening and be able to react to or deal with it quickly □ *peka terhadap apa yg berlaku*: *With so many new developments, you really have to be on the ball.*
set/start the ball rolling to start sth (an activity, a conversation, etc.) that involves or is done by a group □ *memulakan (aktiviti, perbualan, dsb)*: *I told a joke first, to set the ball rolling.*

ballad /'bæləd/ noun [C] a long song or poem that tells a story, often about love □ *balada*

'**ball** '**bearing** noun [C] a ring of small metal balls used in a machine to enable the parts to turn smoothly; one of these small metal balls □ *galas bebola; bolbering*

ballerina /,bælə'riːnə/ noun [C] a woman who dances in **ballets** □ *penari balet wanita*

ballet /'bæleɪ/ noun 1 [U] a style of dancing that tells a story with music but without words □ *(tarian) balet*: *He wants to be a ballet dancer.* 2 [C] a performance or work that consists of this type of dancing □ *(pertunjukan) balet*

'**ball** **game** noun [C] 1 any game played with a ball □ *permainan bola* 2 (*AmE*) a **baseball** match □ *perlawanan besbol*
IDM **a (whole) new/different ball game** something completely new or different □ *keadaan yg serba baharu atau jauh berbeza drpd yg sebelumnya*: *I'm used to working outside, so sitting in an office all day is a whole new ball game for me.*

ballistic /bə'lɪstɪk/ adj
IDM **go ballistic** (*informal*) to become very angry □ *balistik; menjadi sangat marah*: *He went ballistic when I told him.*

balloon /bə'luːn/ noun [C] 1 a small coloured object that you blow air into and use as a toy or for decoration □ *belon*: *to blow up/burst/pop a balloon* 2 (*also* **hot-**'**air balloon**) a large **balloon** made of cloth that is filled with gas or hot air so that it can fly through the sky, carrying people in a **basket** (= a container) underneath it □ *belon udara panas*

ballot /'bælət/ noun 1 [C,U] a secret written vote □ *undi sulit*: *The union will hold a ballot on the new pay offer.* ♦ *The committee are elected by ballot every year.* 2 (*BrE also* '**ballot paper**) [C] the piece of paper on which sb marks who they are voting for □ *kertas undi* ▸**ballot** verb [T] **ballot sb (about/on sth)**: *The union is balloting its members on strike action.*

'**ballot box** noun 1 [C] the box into which people put the piece of paper with their vote on □ *peti undi* 2 **the ballot box** [sing] the system of voting in an election □ *peti undi; pengundian*: *People will express their opinion through the ballot box.*

ballpark /'bɔːlpɑːk/ noun [C] a place where the sport of **baseball** is played □ *padang besbol*
IDM **a ballpark figure/estimate** a number, an amount, etc. that is approximately correct □ *lebih kurang tepat; anggaran*: *We asked the builders for a ballpark figure, to give us an idea of how much it would cost.*
in the ballpark (*informal*) (used about figures or amounts) that are within the same limits □ *dlm lingkungan yg sama*: *All the bids for the contract were in the same ballpark.*

ballpoint /'bɔːlpɔɪnt/ (*also* ,**ballpoint** '**pen**, *BRE ALSO* **Biro**™) noun [C] a pen with a very small metal ball at the end that rolls ink onto paper □ *pena mata bulat* ⊃ picture at **stationery**

ballroom /ˈbɔːlruːm; -rʊm/ noun [C] a large room used for dancing on formal occasions □ *dewan tari-menari*

ballroom ˈdancing noun [U] a formal type of dance in which couples dance together using particular steps and movements □ *berdansa*

balm /bɑːm/ noun [U,C] a liquid, cream, etc. with a pleasant smell, used to make wounds less painful or skin softer □ *salap; balsam*: *lip balm*

baloney /bəˈləʊni/ noun [U] (*AmE informal*) nonsense; lies □ *karut; bohong*: *Don't give me that baloney!*

bamboo /ˌbæmˈbuː/ noun [C,U] (pl **bamboos**) a tall tropical plant of the grass family. **Bamboo**, **shoots** (= young bamboo plants) can be eaten and the hard parts of the plant are used for making furniture, etc □ *buluh*: *a bamboo chair*

❡ **ban** /bæn/ verb [T] (**banning**; **banned**) **ban sth**; **ban sb (from sth/from doing sth)** to officially say that sth is not allowed, often by law □ *mengharamkan; melarang (secara rasmi)*: *The government has banned the import of products from that country.* ♦ *He was fined £2 000 and banned from driving for a year.* **SYN** **prohibit** ▶**ban** noun [C] **a ban (on sth)**: *There is a ban on mobile phones in the classroom.* ♦ *to impose/lift a ban*

banal /bəˈnɑːl/ adj not original or interesting □ *biasa; hambar; basi*: *a banal comment*

banana /bəˈnɑːnə/ noun [C,U] a curved fruit with yellow skin that grows in hot countries □ *pisang*: *a bunch of bananas* ➩ picture on **page P14**
IDM **go bananas** (*slang*) to become angry, crazy or silly □ *naik angin*

❡ **band** /bænd/ noun [C]
▶MUSICIANS **1** [with sing or pl verb] a small group of musicians who play popular music together, often with a singer or singers □ *pancaragam; kugiran*: *a rock/jazz band* ♦ *He plays the drums in a band.* ♦ *The band has/have announced that it/they is/are going to split up.* ➩ note at **pop**
▶GROUP OF PEOPLE **2** [with sing or pl verb] a group of people who do sth together or have the same ideas □ *kumpulan; gerombolan*: *A small band of rebels is/are hiding in the hills.*
▶FOR FASTENING **3** a long thin piece or circle of material that is put round things to hold them together □ *jalur; gelang*: *She rolled up the papers and put an elastic band round them.*
▶COLOUR **4** a line of colour or material on sth that contrasts with the background □ *jalur*: *She wore a red pullover with a green band across the middle.*
▶RADIO WAVES **5** = **waveband**

bandage /ˈbændɪdʒ/ noun [C] a long piece of soft white cloth that you tie round a wound or an injury □ *pembalut (luka, dsb)* ▶**bandage** verb [T] **bandage sth/sb (up)**: *The nurse bandaged my hand up.* ➩ picture at **plaster**

bandanna /bænˈdænə/ noun [C] a piece of brightly coloured cloth worn around the neck or head □ *skarf bandana*

---

59   **ballroom → banish**

B and B (also **B & B**) /ˌbiː ən ˈbiː/ abbr **bed and breakfast** □ *inapan dan sarapan*

bandit /ˈbændɪt/ noun [C] a member of an armed group of thieves who attack people who are travelling □ *penyamun; penjahat*

bandwagon /ˈbændwæɡən/ noun
IDM **climb/jump on the bandwagon** to copy what other people are doing because it is fashionable or successful □ *meniru apa-apa yg dibuat oleh orang lain kerana perkara itu popular atau berjaya*

bandwidth /ˈbændwɪdθ/ noun [C,U] a measure of the amount of information that a group of connected computers or an Internet connection can send in a particular time □ *lebar jalur*

bang¹ /bæŋ/ verb [I,T] **1** to make a loud noise by hitting sth hard; to close sth or to be closed with a loud noise □ *berdentum; menghentam*: *He banged his fist on the table and started shouting.* ♦ *Somewhere in the house, I heard a door bang.* **SYN** **slam 2** to knock against sth by accident; to hit a part of the body against sth by accident □ *terhantuk; melanggar*: *As I was crossing the room in the dark I banged into a table.* ♦ *Be careful not to bang your head on the ceiling. It's quite low.*

bang² /bæŋ/ noun [C] **1** a sudden, short, very loud noise □ *dentuman; letupan*: *There was an enormous bang when the bomb exploded.* **2** a short, strong knock or hit, especially one that causes pain and injury □ *hantukan; hentaman*: *a nasty bang on the head* **3 bangs** (*AmE*) = **fringe¹(1)**
IDM **with a bang** in a successful or exciting way □ *dgn berjaya*: *Our team's season started with a bang when we won our first five matches.*

bang³ /bæŋ/ adv (*especially BrE informal*) exactly; directly; right □ *betul-betul*: *Our computers are bang up to date.* ♦ *The shot was bang on target.*
IDM **bang goes sth** (*informal*) used for expressing the idea that sth is now impossible □ *habislah*: *'It's raining!' 'Ah well, bang goes our picnic!'*

bang⁴ /bæŋ/ exclam used to sound like the noise of a gun, etc. □ *beng (bunyi letupan)*

banger /ˈbæŋə(r)/ noun [C] (*BrE informal*) **1** a **sausage** (= meat formed in a long thin shape) □ *sosej* **2** an old car that is in very bad condition □ *kereta cabuk*: *I'm tired of driving around in that old banger.* **3** a small, noisy **firework** (= a device that burns or explodes, used for entertainment) □ *mercun*

bangle /ˈbæŋɡl/ noun [C] a circle of metal that is worn round the arm or wrist for decoration □ *gelang* ➩ picture at **jewellery**

banish /ˈbænɪʃ/ verb [T] (*formal*) **1** to send sb away (especially out of the country), usually as a punishment □ *dibuang negeri*: *They were banished from the country for demonstrating against the government.* **SYN** **exile 2** to make sb/sth go away; to get rid of sb/sth □ *mengusir*;

[C] **countable**, a noun with a plural form: *one book, two books*   [U] **uncountable**, a noun with no plural form: *some sugar*

meluputkan: *She banished all hope of winning from her mind.*

banister (also **bannister**) /ˈbænɪstə(r)/ noun [C, often plural] the posts and rail at the side of a set of stairs □ *selusur tangga*: *The children loved sliding down the banister at the old house.* ⊃ picture on **page P8**

banjo /ˈbændʒəʊ/ noun [C] (pl **banjos**) a musical instrument like a **guitar**, with a long thin neck, a round body and four or more strings □ *banjo* ⊃ picture at **music**

bank¹ /bæŋk/ noun [C]
▶FOR MONEY **1** an organization which keeps money safely for its customers; the office or building of such an organization. You can take money out, save, borrow or exchange money at a bank □ *bank*: *My salary is paid directly into my bank.* ♦ *I need to go to the bank to get some money out.* ♦ *a bank account/loan* ⊃ note at **money**
▶STORE **2** a store of things, which you keep to use later □ *bank; tabung*: *a databank* ♦ *a blood bank in a hospital*
▶BESIDE A RIVER **3** the ground along the side of a river or **canal** (= an artificial river) □ *tebing; tambak*: *People were fishing along the banks of the river.*
▶HIGHER GROUND **4** a higher area of ground that goes down or up at an angle, often at the edge of sth or dividing sth □ *tebing; batas*: *There were grassy banks on either side of the road.*
▶CLOUD/SNOW **5** a mass of cloud, snow, etc □ *timbunan; kepulan*: *The sun disappeared behind a bank of clouds.*

bank² /bæŋk/ verb [I] **bank (with/at ...)** to have an account with a particular bank □ *mempunyai akaun bank*: *I've banked with HSBC for years.*
PHR V **bank on sb/sth** to expect and trust sb to do sth, or sth to happen □ *meletakkan harapan pd sso/sst*: *Our boss might let you have the morning off but I wouldn't bank on it.*

banker /ˈbæŋkə(r)/ noun [C] a person who owns or has an important job in a bank □ *pemilik, pengarah atau pengurus bank*

bank holiday noun [C] (*BrE*) a public holiday (not a Saturday or Sunday) □ *cuti awam/umum*

banking /ˈbæŋkɪŋ/ noun [U] the type of business done by banks □ *perbankan*: *She decided on a career in banking.*

banknote /ˈbæŋknəʊt/ = **note¹** (4)

bankrupt /ˈbæŋkrʌpt/ adj not having enough money to pay what you owe □ *muflis; bankrap*: *The company must cut its costs or it will go bankrupt.* ▶**bankrupt** verb [T]: *The failure of the new product almost bankrupted the firm.*

bankruptcy /ˈbæŋkrʌptsi/ noun [C,U] (pl **bankruptcies**) the state of being **bankrupt** □ *kemuflisan; kebankrapan*: *The company filed for bankruptcy* (= asked to be officially bankrupt) *in 2011.*

bank statement (also **statement**) noun [C] a printed list of all the money going into or out of your bank account during a certain period □ *penyata bank*

banner /ˈbænə(r)/ noun [C] a long piece of cloth with words or signs on it, which can be hung up or carried on two poles □ *sepanduk*: *The demonstrators carried banners saying 'Stop the War'.* ⊃ picture at **placard**

bannister = **banister**

banquet /ˈbæŋkwɪt/ noun [C] a formal meal for a large number of people, usually as a special event at which speeches are made □ *bankuet; jamuan formal*

banter /ˈbæntə(r)/ noun [U] friendly comments and jokes □ *gurau senda* ▶**banter** verb [I]

baptism /ˈbæptɪzəm/ noun [C,U] a ceremony in which a person becomes a member of the Christian Church by being held underwater for a short time or having drops of water put onto their head. Often they are also formally given a name. □ *pembaptisan* ⊃ look at **christening** ▶**baptize** (also **-ise**) /bæpˈtaɪz/ verb [T] ⊃ look at **christen**

Baptist /ˈbæptɪst/ noun [C], adj (a member) of a Protestant Church that believes that **baptism** should only be for people who are old enough to understand the meaning of the ceremony and should be done by placing the person fully underwater □ *Baptis*

bars

a bar of soap   a bar of chocolate

bar¹ /bɑː(r)/ noun [C]
▶FOR DRINKS/FOOD **1** a place where you can buy and drink alcoholic and other drinks □ *bar*: *They had a drink in the bar before the meal.* **2** a long, narrow, high surface where drinks, etc. are served □ *bar*: *She went to the bar and ordered a drink.* ♦ *We sat on stools at the bar.* **3** [in compounds] a place where a particular type of food or drink is the main thing that is served: *a wine/coffee/sandwich bar*
▶SOAP/CHOCOLATE **4 a bar (of sth)** a small block of solid material, longer than it is wide □ *buku; ketul*: *a bar of soap/chocolate*
▶ON A WINDOW **5** a long, thin, straight piece of metal, often placed across a window or door to stop sb from getting through it □ *palang*: *They escaped by sawing through the bars of their prison cell.*
▶THAT PREVENTS YOU **6 a bar (to sth)** a thing that prevents you from doing sth □ *penghalang; rin-*

tangan: *Lack of education is not always a bar to success in business.*
▶IN MUSIC **7** one of the short, equal units of time into which music is divided □ *bar*: *If you sing a few bars of the song I might recognize it.*
IDM **behind bars** (*informal*) in prison □ *dlm penjara*: *The criminals are now safely behind bars.*

bar² /bɑː(r)/ *verb* [T] (**barring**; **barred**) **1** (usually passive) to close sth with a bar or bars □ *memalang*: *All the windows were barred.* **2** to block a road, path, etc. so that nobody can pass □ *merintangi*; *menghalangi*: *A line of police officers barred the entrance.* **3 bar sb from sth/from doing sth** to say officially that sb is not allowed to do, use or enter sth □ *menghalang*: *He was barred from the club for fighting.*

bar³ /bɑː(r)/ *prep* except □ *melainkan*; *kecuali*: *All the seats were taken, bar one.*

barbarian /bɑːˈbeəriən/ *noun* [C] a wild person with no culture, who behaves very badly □ *orang yg tdk beradat atau beradab*

barbaric /bɑːˈbærɪk/ *adj* very cruel and violent □ *kejam dan ganas*: *barbaric treatment of prisoners* ▶**barbarism** /ˈbɑːbərɪzəm/ *noun* [U]: *acts of barbarism committed in war* ▶**barbarity** /bɑːˈbærəti/ *noun* [C,U] (*pl* **barbarities**)

barbecue /ˈbɑːbɪkjuː/ *noun* [C] (*abbr* **BBQ**) **1** a metal frame on which food is cooked outdoors over an open fire □ *(dapur) barbeku* **2** an outdoor party at which food is cooked in this way □ *(majlis) barbeku*: *Let's have a barbecue on the beach.* ⊃ look at **roast** ▶**barbecue** *verb* [T]: *barbecued steak* ⊃ note at **cook**

barbed wire /ˌbɑːbd ˈwaɪə(r)/ *noun* [U] strong wire with sharp points on it □ *kawat berduri*: *a barbed-wire fence*

barber /ˈbɑːbə(r)/ *noun* **1** [C] a man whose job is to cut men's hair and sometimes to shave them □ *tukang gunting* ⊃ look at **hairdresser** **2 the barber's** [sing] (*BrE*) a shop where men go to have their hair cut □ *kedai gunting*

'bar code *noun* [C] a pattern of thick and thin lines that is printed on things you buy. It contains information that a computer can read. □ *kod bar*

bare /beə(r)/ *adj* (**barer**; **barest**) **1** (used about part of the body) not covered by clothing □ *terdedah*: *bare arms/feet/shoulders* ⊃ look at **naked**, **nude 2** without anything covering or in it □ *gondol*; *tdk beralas, dsb*: *They had taken the pictures down, so the walls were bare.* **3** [only before a noun] just enough; the most basic or simple □ *asas*; *paling*: *You won't pass your exams if you just do the bare minimum.* ♦ *I don't take much luggage when I travel, just the bare essentials.*
IDM **with your bare hands** without weapons or tools □ *dgn tangan semata-mata (tanpa senjata atau alat)*: *She killed the snake with her bare hands.*

barefoot /ˈbeəfʊt/ *adj*, *adv* with nothing (for example shoes, socks, etc.) on your feet □ *kaki*

61 **bar → barley**

ayam; *tdk berkasut, dsb*: *We walked barefoot along the beach.*

barely /ˈbeəli/ *adv* [used especially after *can* and *could* to emphasize that sth is difficult to do] only just; almost not □ *hanya*; *hampir tdk*: *I was so tired I could barely stand up.* ♦ *I earn barely enough money to pay my rent.* ⊃ look at **hardly**

bargain¹ /ˈbɑːɡən/ *noun* [C] **1** something that is cheaper or at a lower price than usual □ *(barang, tawaran, dsb) murah*: *At that price, it's an absolute bargain!* ♦ *I found a lot of bargains in the sale.* **2** an agreement between people or groups about what each of them will do for the other or others □ *perjanjian*: *Let's make a bargain—I'll lend you the money if you'll help me with my work.* ♦ *I lent him the money but he didn't keep his side of the bargain.*
IDM **into the bargain** (used for emphasizing sth) as well; in addition; also □ *di samping itu*: *They gave me free tickets and a free meal into the bargain.*
strike a bargain (with sb) ⊃ **strike¹**

bargain² /ˈbɑːɡən/ *verb* [I] **bargain (with sb) (about/over/for sth)** to discuss prices, conditions, etc. with sb in order to reach an agreement that suits each person □ *menawar*; *tawar-menawar*: *I'm sure that if you bargain with him, he'll drop the price.* ♦ *They bargained over the price.*
PHR V **bargain for/on sth** [usually in negative sentences] to expect sth to happen and be ready for it □ *menduga*: *When I agreed to help him I didn't bargain for how much it would cost me.*

barge¹ /bɑːdʒ/ *noun* [C] a long narrow boat with a flat bottom that is used for carrying goods or people on a **canal** (= an artificial river) or river □ *baj*; *tongkang*

barge² /bɑːdʒ/ *verb* [I,T] to push people out of the way in order to get past them □ *merempuh*: *He barged (his way) angrily through the crowd.*

baritone /ˈbærɪtəʊn/ *noun* [C] a male singing voice that is fairly low; a man with this voice □ *bariton*

MORE Baritone is between **tenor** and **bass**.

bark¹ /bɑːk/ *noun* **1** [U] the hard outer covering of a tree □ *kulit kayu* ⊃ picture at **tree 2** [C] the short, loud noise that a dog makes □ *salakan anjing*: *The dog next door has a very loud bark.*

bark² /bɑːk/ *verb* **1** [I] **bark (at sb/sth)** (used about dogs) to make a loud, short noise or noises □ *menyalak* **2** [I,T] **bark (sth) (out) (at sb)** to speak to sb in a loud voice in an angry or aggressive way □ *menengking*; *membentak*: *The boss came in, barked out some orders and left again.*

barley /ˈbɑːli/ *noun* [U] **1** a plant that produces grain that is used for food or for making beer and other drinks □ *barli* **2** the grain produced by this plant □ *bijian barli*

CONSONANTS p **p**en b **b**ad t **t**ea d **d**id k **c**at g **g**ot tʃ **ch**in dʒ **J**une f **f**all v **v**an θ **th**in

barman /ˈbɑːmən/ (*pl* -men /-mən/) (*fem* **barmaid** /ˈbɑːmeɪd/) (*AmE* **bartender**) *noun* [C] a person who serves drinks from behind a bar in a pub, etc. □ *pelayan bar (lelaki)*

bar mitzvah /ˌbɑː ˈmɪtsvə/ *noun* [C] a ceremony in the Jewish religion for a boy who is about 13 years old. After the ceremony, he is considered an adult. □ *upacara Yahudi yg menandakan balighnya sso budak lelaki* ➔ look at **bat mitzvah**

barn /bɑːn/ *noun* [C] a large building on a farm in which crops or animals are kept □ *bangsal* ➔ picture on **page P11**

barometer /bəˈrɒmɪtə(r)/ *noun* [C] **1** an instrument that measures air pressure and indicates changes in the weather □ *barometer* **2** something that indicates the state of sth (a situation, a feeling, etc.) □ *barometer; pengukur*: *Results of local elections are often a barometer of the government's popularity.*

baron /ˈbærən/ *noun* [C] **1** a man of a high social position □ *baron; bangsawan* **2** a person who controls a large part of a particular industry or type of business □ *taikun; ahli perniagaan yg amat berkuasa*: *drug/oil barons*

baroness /ˈbærənəs/ *noun* [C] a woman of a high social position; the wife of a **baron** □ *baroness; isteri baron*

baroque (also **Baroque**) /bəˈrɒk/ *adj* used to describe the highly decorated style of European art, buildings and music of the 17th and early 18th centuries □ *barok; baroque*: *baroque churches/music*

barracks /ˈbærəks/ *noun* [C, with sing or pl verb] (*pl* **barracks**) a building or group of buildings in which soldiers live □ *berek; tangsi*: *Guards were on duty at the gate of the barracks.*

barrage /ˈbærɑːʒ/ *noun* [C] **1** a continuous attack on a place with a large number of guns □ *serangan bertalu-talu* **2** a large number of questions, comments, etc., directed at a person very quickly □ *soalan, komen dsb, yg bertalu-talu*: *The minister faced a barrage of questions from reporters.*

barrel /ˈbærəl/ *noun* [C] **1** a large, round, wooden, plastic or metal container for liquids, that has a flat top and bottom and is wider in the middle □ *tong*: *a beer/wine barrel* ◆ *The price of oil is usually given per barrel.* **2** the long metal part of a gun like a tube through which the bullets are fired □ *laras*

barren /ˈbærən/ *adj* **1** (used about land or soil) not good enough for plants to grow on □ *tandus; tdk subur* **2** (used about trees or plants) not producing fruit or seeds □ *mandul*

barrette /bæˈret/ (*AmE*) = **hairslide**

barricade /ˌbærɪˈkeɪd/ *noun* [C] an object or line of objects that is placed across a road, an entrance, etc. to stop people getting through □ *perintang; penyekat; halangan*: *The demonstrators put up barricades to keep the police away.*

PHR V **barricade yourself in** to defend yourself by putting up a **barricade** □ *bertahan dgn menggunakan sst tempat sebagai kubu*: *Demonstrators took over the building and barricaded themselves in.* ▶**barricade** *verb* [T]

barrier /ˈbæriə(r)/ *noun* [C] **1** an object that keeps people or things separate or prevents them moving from one place to another □ *sekatan; sempadan*: *The crowd were all kept behind barriers.* ◆ *The mountains form a natural barrier between the two countries.* ➔ look at **crash barrier** **2** **a barrier (to sth)** something that causes problems or makes it impossible for sth to happen □ *halangan; rintangan*: *When you live in a foreign country, the language barrier can be a difficult problem to overcome.*

barring /ˈbɑːrɪŋ/ *prep* except for; if there is not/are not □ *kecuali*: *Barring any unforeseen problems, we'll be moving house in a month.*

barrister /ˈbærɪstə(r)/ *noun* [C] (in English law) a lawyer who is trained to speak for you in the higher courts □ *peguam bela* ➔ note at **lawyer**

barrow /ˈbærəʊ/ *noun* [C] **1** (*BrE*) a small thing on two wheels on which fruit, vegetables, etc. are moved or sold in the street, especially in markets □ *kereta sorong (roda dua)* **2** = **wheelbarrow**

bartender /ˈbɑːtendə(r)/ (*AmE*) = **barman**

barter /ˈbɑːtə(r)/ *verb* [I,T] **barter sth (for sth)**; **barter (with sb) (for sth)** to exchange goods, services, property, etc. for other goods, etc. without using money □ *saling menukar (barang, perkhidmatan, dsb)*: *The farmer bartered his surplus grain for machinery.* ◆ *The prisoners bartered with the guards for writing paper and books.* ▶**barter** *noun* [U]

base¹ /beɪs/ *noun* [C] **1** the lowest part of sth, especially the part on which it stands or at which it is fixed or connected to sth □ *kaki; dasar*: *the base of a column/glass* ◆ *I felt a terrible pain at the base of my spine.* **2** an idea, a fact, etc. from which sth develops or is made □ *asas*: *With these ingredients as a base, you can create all sorts of interesting dishes.* ◆ *The country needs a strong economic base.* **3** a place used as a centre from which activities are done or controlled □ *pangkalan; pusat kegiatan atau operasi*: *This hotel is an ideal base for touring the region.* **4** a military centre from which the armed forces operate □ *pangkalan*: *an army base* **5** (in baseball) one of the four points from which a runner must touch □ *tapak*

base² /beɪs/ *verb* [T, usually passive] **base sb/sth in ...** to make one place the centre from which sb/sth can work or move around □ *menempatkan; ditempatkan; bertempat*: *I'm based in New York, although my job involves a great deal of travel.* ◆ *a Cardiff-based company*

PHR V **base sth on sth** to form or develop sth from a particular starting point or source □ *berdasarkan*: *This film is based on a true story.*

baseball /'beɪsbɔːl/ noun [U] a team game that is popular in the US in which players hit the ball with a **bat** (= a piece of wood or metal) and run around the four **bases** to score points □ *besbol* ➲ picture on **page P4**

basement /'beɪsmənt/ noun [C] a room or rooms in a building, partly or completely below ground level □ *tingkat bawah tanah*: *a basement flat* ➲ look at **cellar**

bases 1 *plural of* **basis 2** *plural of* **base¹**

bash¹ /bæʃ/ verb (*informal*) **1** [I,T] to hit sb/sth very hard □ *menghentam; melanggar*: *I didn't stop in time and bashed into the car in front.* **2** [T] to criticize sb/sth strongly □ *mengecam*: *The candidate continued to bash her opponent's policies.*

bash² /bæʃ/ noun [C] **1** a hard hit □ *hentaman; hantukan*: *He gave Alex a bash on the nose.* **2** (*informal*) a large party or celebration □ *parti; majlis keraian*: *Are you going to Gary's birthday bash?*
IDM **have a bash (at sth/at doing sth)** (*BrE spoken*) to try □ *mencuba; (sst/membuat sst)*: *I'll get a screwdriver and have a bash at mending the light.*

bashful /'bæʃfl/ adj shy and embarrassed □ *malu-malu; pemalu*

basic /'beɪsɪk/ adj **1** forming the part of sth that is most necessary and from which other things develop □ *asas; dasar; pokok*: *The basic question is, can we afford it?* ◆ *basic information/facts/ideas* **2** of the simplest kind or level; including only what is necessary without anything extra □ *asas*: *This course teaches basic computer skills.* ◆ *The basic pay is £300 a week—with extra for overtime.*

basically /'beɪsɪkli/ adv used to say what the most important or most basic aspect of sb/sth is □ *pd dasarnya*: *The two designs are basically the same.* **SYN** **essentially**

basics /'beɪsɪks/ noun [pl] the simplest or most important facts or aspects of sth; things that you need the most □ *asas; perkara-perkara penting atau asas*: *So far, I've only learnt the basics of computing.*

basil /'bæzl/ noun [C] a **herb** (= a type of plant) with shiny green leaves that smell sweet and are used in cooking □ *daun selasih* ➲ picture on **page P14**

basin /'beɪsn/ noun [C] **1** = **washbasin 2** a round open bowl often used for mixing or cooking food □ *besen* **3** an area of land from which water flows into a river □ *lembangan; lembah*: *the Amazon Basin*

basis /'beɪsɪs/ noun (*pl* **bases** /'beɪsiːz/) **1** [sing] the principle or reason which lies behind sth □ *asas; berasaskan; dasar*: *We made our decision on the basis of the reports which you sent us.* **2** [sing] the way sth is done or organized □ *secara*: *They meet on a regular basis.* ◆ *to employ somebody on a temporary/voluntary/part-time basis* **3** [C] a starting point, from which sth can develop □ *asas*: *She used her diaries as a basis for her book.*

63 **baseball → bat**

bask /bɑːsk/ verb [I] **bask (in sth) 1** to sit or lie in a place where you can enjoy the warmth □ *berjemur*: *The snake basked in the sunshine on the rock.* **2** to enjoy the good feelings you have when other people admire you, give you a lot of attention, etc □ *menikmati (pujian, dsb)*: *The team was still basking in the glory of winning the cup.*

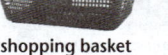

baskets

shopping basket   wicker basket

basket /'bɑːskɪt/ noun [C] **1** a container for carrying or holding things, made of thin pieces of material that bends easily, such as wood, plastic or wire □ *bakul*: *a waste-paper basket* ◆ *a shopping basket* ◆ *a clothes/laundry basket* (= in which you put dirty clothes before they are washed) **2** (in **basketball**) a net that hangs from a metal ring high up at each end of a court □ *jaring (tempat memasukkan bola)* ➲ picture on **page P4 3** (in **basketball**) a score of one, two or three points, made by throwing the ball through one of the nets □ *kiraan mata (dlm permainan bola keranjang)*
IDM **put all your eggs in one basket** ➲ **egg¹**

basketball /'bɑːskɪtbɔːl/ noun [U] a game for two teams of five players in which you score points by throwing a large ball through the other team's **basket** (2) □ *bola keranjang* ➲ picture on **page P4**

bass /beɪs/ noun **1** [U] the lowest part in music □ *bes* **2** [C] the lowest male singing voice; a singer with this kind of voice □ *suara bes* ➲ look at **tenor, baritone 3** [C] (*also* **bass gui'tar**) an electric **guitar** (= a musical instrument with strings) which plays very low notes □ *gitar bes* ➲ note at **music 4** = **double bass** ▶ **bass** adj [only before a noun]: *a bass drum* ◆ *Can you sing the bass part?*

bassoon /bə'suːn/ noun [C] a musical instrument that you blow which makes a very deep sound □ *basun* ➲ picture at **music**

baste /beɪst/ verb [T] to pour liquid, such as sauce, juice or wine, over meat, etc. while it is cooking □ *melumuri; menuang*

bat¹ /bæt/ noun [C] **1** a piece of wood for hitting the ball in sports such as **table tennis, cricket** or **baseball** □ *pemukul bola*: *a cricket bat* ➲ picture on **page P4**

MORE Some sports have special words for the type of bat that is used to hit the ball. In **tennis** and **badminton** you use a **racket**, in **hockey** you use a **stick** and in **golf** you use a **club**. In **snooker, pool** and **billiards** you hit the ball with a **cue**.

VOWELS   iː see   i any   ɪ sit   e ten   æ hat   ɑː father   ɒ got   ɔː saw   ʊ put   uː too   u usual

bat → battle

2 a small animal, like a mouse with wings, which flies and hunts at night □ *kelawar* ➲ picture on **page P12**
IDM **off your own bat** without anyone asking you or helping you □ *sendiri-sendiri; pandai-pandai*

bat² /bæt/ *verb* [I] (**batting; batted**) (used about one player or a whole team) to have a turn hitting the ball in sports such as **cricket** or **baseball** □ *(giliran) memukul bola* ➲ look at **field**
IDM **not bat an eyelid**; (*AmE*) **not bat an eye** to show no surprise or embarrassment when sth unusual happens □ *tdk menunjukkan rasa hairan atau agak malu, dsb*

batch /bætʃ/ *noun* [C] a number of things or people which belong together as a group □ *kumpulan; kelompok*: *The bus returned to the airport for the next batch of tourists.*

bated /ˈbeɪtɪd/ *adj*
IDM **with bated breath** excited or afraid, because you are waiting for sth to happen □ *dgn penuh perhatian, kebimbangan, dsb*

bath¹ /bɑːθ/ *noun* **1** [C] (*especially AmE* **bathtub**, *informal* **tub**) a large container for water in which you sit to wash your body □ *tab mandi*: *Can you answer the phone? I'm in the bath!* ➲ picture on **page P8** **2** [sing] an act of washing the whole of your body when you sit or lie in a bath filled with water □ *mandi berendam (dlm tab mandi)*: **to have a bath** ◆ (*especially AmE*) Would you prefer to **take a bath** or a shower? **3 baths** [pl] (*BrE old-fashioned*) a public building where you can go to swim; a public place where people went in past times to have a wash or a bath □ *kolam mandi awam*: *Roman baths*

bath² /bɑːθ/ *verb* **1** [T] to give sb a bath □ *memandikan*: *bath the baby* **2** [I] (*old-fashioned*) to have a bath □ *mandi (dgn berendam dlm kolam mandi)*: *I prefer to bath in the mornings.*

bathe /beɪð/ *verb* **1** [T] to wash or put part of the body in water, often for medical reasons □ *mencuci atau merendam (bahagian tubuh yg luka, dsb)*: *She bathed the wound with antiseptic.* **2** [I] (*old-fashioned*) to swim in the sea or in a lake or river □ *berenang* ➲ look at **sunbathe**

bathed /beɪðd/ *adj* (*written*) [not before a noun] **bathed in sth** covered with sth □ *bermandikan*: *The room was bathed in moonlight.*

bathrobe /ˈbɑːθrəʊb/ = **dressing gown**

bathroom /ˈbɑːθruːm; -rʊm/ *noun* [C] **1** a room where there is a bath and/or a shower, a **washbasin** (= a place to wash your hands) and often a toilet □ *bilik mandi*: *Go and wash your hands in the bathroom.* ➲ picture on **page P8 2** (*AmE*) a room with a toilet □ *bilik air; tandas*: *I have to go to the bathroom* (= use the toilet). ➲ note at **toilet**

bathtub /ˈbɑːθtʌb/ = **bath¹**(1)

bat mitzvah /ˌbæt ˈmɪtsvə/ *noun* [C] a ceremony in the Jewish religion for a girl who is about 13 years old □ *upacara Yahudi yg* *menandakan balighnya sso budak perempuan* ➲ look at **bar mitzvah**

baton /ˈbætɒn/ *noun* [C] **1** = **truncheon 2** a short thin stick used by the person who directs an **orchestra** (= a large group of musicians who play together) □ *baton* **3** a stick which a runner in a **relay** (= a race in which each member of the team runs one part of the race) passes to the next person in the team □ *baton*

batsman /ˈbætsmən/ *noun* [C] (*pl* **-men** /-mən/) (in the sport of **cricket**) one of the two players who hit the ball to score **runs** (= points scored by running from one end to the other) □ *pemukul bola* ➲ note at **cricket** ➲ picture on **page P4**

battalion /bəˈtæliən/ *noun* [C] a large unit of soldiers that forms part of a larger unit in the army □ *batalion*

batter¹ /ˈbætə(r)/ *verb* [I,T] to hit sb/sth hard, many times □ *menghentam bertalu-talu*: *The wind battered against the window.* ◆ *He battered the door down.*

batter² /ˈbætə(r)/ *noun* [U,C] a mixture of flour, eggs and milk used to cover food such as fish, vegetables, etc. before frying them □ *bater; tepung salut*

battered /ˈbætəd/ *adj* no longer looking new; damaged or out of shape □ *lusuh; kopak-kapik*: *a battered old hat*

battery /ˈbætəri; -tri/ *noun* (*pl* **batteries**) **1** [C] a device which provides electricity for a toy, radio, car, etc. □ *bateri*: *to recharge a battery* ◆ *a flat battery* (= one that is no longer producing electricity) **2** [C] (*BrE*) a large number of very small **cages** (= boxes made of bars) in which chickens, etc. are kept on a farm □ *deretan sangkar kecil utk menternak ayam*: *a battery hen/farm* ➲ look at **free-range 3** [U] the crime of attacking sb physically □ *serangan sentuh*: *He was charged with assault and battery.*

battle¹ /ˈbætl/ *noun* **1** [C,U] a fight, especially between armies in a war □ *pertempuran*: *the battle of Trafalgar* ◆ *to die/be killed in battle* **2** [C] **a battle (with sb) (for sth)** a competition, an argument or a fight between people or groups of people trying to win power or control □ *perlawanan; pertarungan*: *a legal battle for custody of the children* **3** [C, usually sing] **a battle (against/for sth)** a determined effort to solve a difficult problem or to succeed in a difficult situation □ *perjuangan; usaha melawan*: *After three years she lost her battle against cancer.*
IDM **a losing battle** ➲ **lose**

battle² /ˈbætl/ *verb* [I,T] **battle (with/against sb/sth); battle (on)** to try very hard to achieve sth difficult or to deal with sth unpleasant or dangerous □ *bertungkus-lumus; berusaha dgn gigih; bergelut; melawan*: *Mark is battling with his maths homework.* ◆ *The little boat battled against the wind.* ◆ *The two brothers were battling for control of the family business.* ◆ *Life is hard at the moment but we're battling on.* ◆ *The teams will* **battle it out** *in the final next week.*

battlefield /'bætlfi:ld/ (also **battleground** /'bætlgraʊnd/) noun [C] the place where a battle is fought □ *medan pertempuran*

battlements /'bætlmənts/ noun [pl] a low wall around the top of a castle with spaces in it that people inside could shoot through □ *baluarti; benteng; dinding tembok tempat menembak; kekota*

battleship /'bætlʃɪp/ noun [C] a very large ship with big guns used in war □ *kapal perang*

bauble /'bɔ:bl/ noun [C] **1** a piece of cheap jewellery □ *barang perhiasan yg murah* **2** a decoration in the shape of a ball that is hung on a Christmas tree □ *hiasan bebola utk pokok Krismas*

baulk (especially AmE **balk**) /bɔ:k/ verb [I] **baulk (at sth)** to not want to do or agree to sth because it seems too difficult, dangerous or unpleasant □ *enggan; keberatan*: *She liked horses, but she baulked at riding one.*

bawl /bɔ:l/ verb [I,T] to shout or cry loudly □ *memekik; melaung; meraung*

bay /beɪ/ noun [C] **1** a part of the coast where the land goes in to form a curve □ *teluk*: *the Bay of Bengal* ♦ *The harbour was in a sheltered bay.* ➲ picture on **page P10 2** a part of a building, an aircraft or an area which has a particular purpose □ *ruang*: *a parking/loading bay*
IDM **hold/keep sb/sth at bay** to stop sb dangerous from getting near you; to prevent a situation or problem from getting worse □ *menghalang (musuh, dsb) drpd mendekati; menghalang sst keadaan drpd menjadi lebih buruk*

bayonet /'beɪənət/ noun [C] a knife that can be fixed to the end of a gun □ *bayonet*

bay window noun [C] a window in a part of a room that sticks out from the wall of a house □ *tingkap unjur* ➲ picture on **page P9**

bazaar /bə'zɑ:(r)/ noun [C] **1** (in some eastern countries) a market □ *bazar* **2** (BrE) a sale where the money that is made goes to charity □ *jualan amal*: *The school held a bazaar to raise money for the hospital.*

BBC /ˌbi: bi: 'si:/ abbr **the British Broadcasting Corporation**; one of the national radio and TV companies in Britain □ *BBC (Badan Penyiaran British)*: *a BBC documentary* ♦ *watch a programme on BBC1*

BBQ abbr = **barbecue**

BC /ˌbi: 'si:/ abbr **before Christ**; used in dates to show the number of years before the time when Christians believe Jesus Christ was born □ *SM (Sebelum Masihi)*: *in (the year) BC 300* ➲ look at **AD**

be[1] /bi; strong form bi:/ verb ❶ For the forms of 'be', look at the irregular verbs section at the back of this dictionary. **1** [T] **there is/are** to exist; to be present □ *ada*: *I tried phoning them but there was no answer.* ♦ *There are some people outside.* ♦ *There are a lot of trees in our garden.* **2** [I] used to give the position of sb/sth or the place where sb/sth is □ *di; berada di; terletak di*: *Paula's in her office.* ♦ *Where are the scissors?* ♦ *The bus stop is five minutes' walk from here.* ♦ *St Tropez is on the south coast.* **3** [I] used to give the date or age of sb/sth or to talk about time □ *digunakan utk menyatakan tarikh atau umur sso/sst atau utk bercakap ttg masa*: *My birthday is on April 24th.* ♦ *It's 6 o'clock.* ♦ *It was Tuesday yesterday.* ♦ *Sue'll be 21 in June.* ♦ *He's older than Miranda.* ♦ *It's ages since I last saw him.* **4** [I] used when you are giving the name of people or things, describing them or giving more information about them □ *digunakan utk memberikan nama orang atau benda, memerihalkan atau memberikan maklumat lanjut ttg mereka*: *This is my father, John.* ♦ *I'm Alison.* ♦ *He's Italian. He's from Milan.* ♦ *He's a doctor.* ♦ *What's that?* ♦ *A lion is a mammal.* ♦ *'What colour is your car?' 'It's green.'* ♦ *How much was your ticket?* ♦ *The film was excellent.* ♦ *She's very friendly.* ♦ *'How is your wife?' 'She's fine, thanks.'* **5** [I] (only used in the perfect tenses) to go to a place (and return) □ *digunakan utk membawa maksud pergi ke sst tempat (dan kembali)*: *Have you ever been to Japan?* ➲ look at **been**
IDM **be yourself** to act naturally □ *(buat) spt biasa*: *Don't be nervous; just be yourself and the interview will be fine.*
-to-be [in compounds] future □ *bakal*: *his bride-to-be* ♦ *mothers-to-be* (= pregnant women)

be[2] /bi; strong form bi:/ auxiliary verb **1** used with a past participle to form the passive; used with a present participle to form the continuous tenses □ *kk bantu utk membentuk kk pasif dan kala berterusan*: *He was killed in the war.* ♦ *Where were they made?* ♦ *The house was still being built.* ♦ *You will be told what to do.* ♦ *I am studying Italian.* ♦ *What have you been doing?* ❶ For more information, look at the **Reference Section** at the back of this dictionary. **2 be to do sth** used to show that sth must happen or that sth has been arranged □ *digunakan utk menyatakan sst yg mesti berlaku atau yg telah diatur*: *You are to leave here at 10 o'clock at the latest.* **3 if sb/sth were to do sth** used to show that sth is possible but not very likely □ *digunakan utk menyatakan sst yg boleh berlaku (tetapi besar kemungkinan tdk akan berlaku)*: *If they were to offer me the job, I'd probably take it.*

beach /bi:tʃ/ noun [C] an area of sand or small stones beside the sea □ *pantai*: *to sit on the beach* ➲ picture on **page P10**

beacon /'bi:kən/ noun [C] a fire or light on a hill or tower, often near the coast, which is used as a signal □ *suar; api atau lampu isyarat*

bead /bi:d/ noun [C] **1** a small round piece of wood, glass or plastic with a hole in the middle for putting a string through to make jewellery, etc. □ *manik*: *a string of glass beads* ➲ picture at **jewellery 2** a drop of liquid □ *titis; titik*: *There were beads of sweat on his forehead.*

[C] **countable**, a noun with a plural form: *one book, two books* [U] **uncountable**, a noun with no plural form: *some sugar*

beady /ˈbiːdi/ *adj* (used about eyes) small, round and bright; watching everything closely □ *(berkenaan dgn mata) kecil, bulat dan bersinar*

beak /biːk/ *noun* [C] the hard pointed part of a bird's mouth □ *paruh*: *The gull held the fish in its beak.* ⊃ picture on **page P12**

beaker /ˈbiːkə(r)/ *noun* [C] **1** a plastic or paper drinking cup, usually without a handle □ *bikar; cawan* **2** a glass container used in scientific experiments, etc. for pouring liquids □ *bikar*

beam¹ /biːm/ *noun* [C] **1** a line of light □ *pancaran; sinar; alur*: *the beam of a torch* ♦ *The car's headlights were on full beam* (= giving the most light possible and not directed downwards). ♦ *a laser beam* **2** a long piece of wood, metal, etc. that is used to support weight, for example in the floor or ceiling of a building □ *rasuk; alang; galang* **3** a happy smile □ *senyuman yg berseri-seri*

beam² /biːm/ *verb* **1** [I] **beam (at sb/sth)** to smile happily □ *tersenyum riang*: *I looked at Sam and he beamed back at me.* **2** [T] to send out radio or TV signals □ *menyiarkan*: *The programme was beamed live by satellite to many different countries.* **3** [I] to send out light and warmth □ *memancarkan; menyinarkan*: *The sun beamed down on them.*

bean /biːn/ *noun* [C] **1** the seed or **pod** (= long thin seed container) from a climbing plant that is eaten as a vegetable □ *kacang*: *soya beans* ♦ *a tin of baked beans* (= beans in a tomato sauce) ♦ *green beans* ⊃ picture on **page P15** **2** similar seeds from other plants □ *biji*: *coffee beans*
IDM full of beans/life ⊃ **full¹**
spill the beans ⊃ **spill**

bear¹ /beə(r)/ *verb* (*pt* **bore** /bɔː(r)/; *pp* **borne** /bɔːn/)
▶ACCEPT **1** [T] [used with *can/could* in negative sentences or in questions] to be able to accept and deal with sth unpleasant □ *sanggup; tahan; larat*: *I can't bear spiders.* ♦ *She couldn't bear the thought of anything happening to him.* ♦ *How can you bear to listen to that music?* ♦ *The pain was almost more than he could bear.* **SYN** **stand, endure**
▶NOT BE SUITABLE **2** [T] **not bear sth/doing sth** to not be suitable for sth; to not allow sth □ *tdk wajar; tdk dpt dipakai; tdk sanggup*: *These figures won't bear close examination* (= when you look closely you will find mistakes). ♦ *What I would do if I lost my job doesn't bear thinking about* (= is too unpleasant to think about).
▶BE RESPONSIBLE **3** [T] (*formal*) to take responsibility for sth □ *menanggung; memikul*: *Customers will bear the full cost of the improvements.*
▶FEEL **4** [T] to have a feeling, especially a negative feeling □ *menaruh*: *Despite what they did, she bears no resentment towards them.* ♦ *He's not the type to bear a grudge against anyone.*
▶SUPPORT **5** [T] to support the weight of sth □ *menahan; menopang*: *Twelve pillars bear the weight of the roof.*
▶SHOW/CARRY **6** [T] (*formal*) to show sth; to carry sth so that it can be seen □ *membawa; menunjukkan*: *He still bears the scars of his accident.* ♦ *She bore a strong resemblance to her mother* (= she looked like her). ♦ *The waiters came in bearing trays of food.*
▶HAVE A CHILD **7** [T] (*formal*) to give birth to children □ *beranak*: *She bore him four children, all sons.*

HELP A much more common expression is **have children**: *She had four children.* When you talk about sb's own birth you use **be born**: *Robert was born in 1996.*

▶TURN **8** [I] to turn or go in the direction that is mentioned □ *belok; ikut arah*: *Where the road forks, bear left.*
IDM bear the brunt of sth to suffer the main force of sth □ *menanggung sst*: *Her sons usually bore the brunt of her anger.*
bear fruit to be successful; to produce results □ *berhasil*: *At last our hard work is beginning to bear fruit.*
bear in mind (that); bear/keep sb/sth in mind ⊃ **mind¹**
bear witness (to sth) to show evidence of sth □ *menunjukkan/membuktikan (sst)*: *The burning buildings and empty streets bore witness to a recent attack.*
PHR V bear down (on sb/sth) 1 to move closer to sb/sth in a frightening way □ *meluru ke arah (sso/sst)*: *We could see the hurricane bearing down on the town.* **2** to push down hard on sb/sth □ *menekan; meneran*
bear sb/sth out to show that sb is correct or that sth is true □ *membuktikan atau menyokong sso/sst*: *The evidence bears out my theory.*
bear up to be strong enough to continue at a difficult time □ *menghadapi; mengatasi*: *How is he bearing up after his accident?*
bear with sb/sth to be patient with sb/sth □ *bersabar dgn sso/sst*: *Bear with me—I won't be much longer.*

bear² /beə(r)/ *noun* [C] a large, heavy wild animal with thick fur and sharp teeth □ *beruang*: *a polar/grizzly/brown bear* ⊃ look at **teddy bear**

bearable /ˈbeərəbl/ *adj* that you can accept or deal with, although unpleasant □ *dpt ditahan*: *It was extremely hot but the breeze made it more bearable.* **OPP unbearable**

beard /bɪəd/ *noun* [C,U] the hair which grows on a man's cheeks and chin □ *janggut*: *I'm going to grow a beard.* ⊃ look at **goatee, moustache** ⊃ picture at **hair**

bearded /ˈbɪədɪd/ *adj* with a beard □ *berjanggut*

bearer /ˈbeərə(r)/ *noun* [C] a person who carries or brings sth □ *pembawa*: *I'm sorry to be the bearer of bad news.*

bearing /'beərɪŋ/ noun **1** [U, sing] (a) bearing on sth a relation or connection to the subject being discussed □ *kaitan; kena-mengena*: *Her comments had no bearing on our decision.* **2** [U, sing] the way in which sb stands or moves □ *perawakan*: *a man of dignified bearing* **3** [C] a direction measured from a fixed point using a **compass** (= an instrument that shows direction) □ *kedudukan*

IDM get/find your bearings to become familiar with where you are □ *mengetahui apa atau di mana kedudukan sso*

lose your bearings ⊃ lose

beast /biːst/ noun [C] (*formal*) an animal, especially a large one □ *haiwan besar; binatang*: *a wild beast*

beat[1] /biːt/ verb (*pt* beat; *pp* beaten /'biːtn/) **1** [T] beat sb (at sth) to defeat sb; to be better than sth □ *mengalahkan*: *He always beats me at tennis.* ♦ *We're hoping to beat the world record.* ♦ *If you want to keep fit, you can't beat swimming.* **2** [I,T] to hit many times, usually very hard □ *memukul; memalu-malu*: *The rain was beating on the roof of the car.* ♦ *The man was beating the donkey with a stick.* ⊃ note at **hit** **3** [I,T] to make a regular sound or movement □ *berdegup; mengeluarkan bunyi sekata; mengepak-ngepakkan*: *Her heart beat faster as she ran to pick up her child.* ♦ *We could hear the drums beating in the distance.* ♦ *The bird beat its wings* (= moved them up and down quickly). **4** [T] to mix quickly with a fork, etc. □ *memukul; membancuh*: *Beat the eggs and sugar together.*

IDM beat about/around the bush to talk about sth for a long time without mentioning the main point □ *bercakap berbelit-belit*: *Stop beating about the bush and tell me how much money you need.*

(it) beats me (*spoken*) I do not know □ *saya tdk tahu; hairan saya*: *It beats me where he's gone.* ♦ *'Why is she angry?' 'Beats me!'*

off the beaten track in a place where people do not often go □ *terpencil*

PHR V beat sb/sth off to fight until sb/sth goes away □ *mematahkan serangan/melawan/ menangkis (sso/sst)*: *The thieves tried to take his wallet but he beat them off.*

beat sb to sth to get somewhere or do sth before sb else □ *mengalahkan/mendahului sso dlm sst*: *She beat me back to the house.* ♦ *I wanted to ring him first but Kate beat me to it.*

beat sb up to attack sb by hitting or kicking them many times □ *membelasah sso*: *He was badly beaten up at the bus stop last night.*

beat[2] /biːt/ noun **1** [C] a single hit on sth such as a drum or the movement of sth, such as your heart; the sound that this makes □ *paluan; pukulan; degup*: *Her heart skipped a beat when she saw him.* **2** [sing] a series of regular hits on sth such as a drum, or of movements of sth; the sound that this makes □ *bunyi pukulan; degupan*: *the beat of the drums* ⊃ look at **heartbeat** **3** [C] the strong rhythm that a piece of music has □ *rentak*: *This type of music has a strong beat to it.* **4** [sing] the route along which a police officer regularly walks □ *laluan rondaan*: *Having more policemen on the beat helps reduce crime.*

beating /'biːtɪŋ/ noun [C] **1** a punishment that you give to sb by hitting them □ *pukulan*: *The boys got a beating when they were caught stealing.* **2** a defeat □ *kekalahan*

IDM take a lot of/some beating to be so good that it would be difficult to find sth better □ *sukar ditandingi*: *Mary's cooking takes some beating.*

beautician /bjuː'tɪʃn/ noun [C] a person whose job is to improve the way people look with beauty treatments, etc. □ *jurusolek; pakar kecantikan*

beautiful /'bjuːtɪfl/ adj very pretty or attractive; giving pleasure to the senses □ *cantik; jelita; indah; merdu; amat bagus, harum, dsb*: *The view from the top of the hill was really beautiful.* ♦ *What a beautiful day—the weather's perfect!* ♦ *He has a beautiful voice.* ♦ *A beautiful perfume filled the air.* ♦ *a beautiful woman*
▶ **beautifully** /-fli/ *adv*: *He plays the piano beautifully.* ♦ *She was beautifully dressed.*

> **OTHER WORDS FOR**
> **beautiful**
> **Beautiful** and **pretty** are usually used about women and girls. **Pretty** is especially used about young women or girls. **Good-looking** and **attractive** can be used for both men and women. **Handsome** is used most often to describe men. **Gorgeous** is an informal word for **very attractive**.

beauty /'bjuːti/ noun (*pl* beauties) **1** [U] the quality which gives pleasure to the senses; the state of being beautiful □ *keindahan; kejelitaan; kemerduan*: *I was amazed by the beauty of the mountains.* ♦ *music of great beauty* **2** [C] a beautiful woman □ *wanita jelita*: *She grew up to be a beauty.* **3** [C] a particularly good example of sth □ *(sst yg) bagus sekali*: *Look at this tomato—it's a beauty!*

'beauty spot noun [C] (*BrE*) a place in the countryside which is famous because it is beautiful □ *tempat yg indah*

beaver /'biːvə(r)/ noun [C] an animal with brown fur, a wide, flat tail and sharp teeth. It lives in water and on land and uses branches to build **dams** (= walls across rivers to hold back the water). □ *beaver*

became past tense of **become**

because /bɪ'kɒz/ *conj* for the reason that □ *kerana*: *They didn't go for a walk, because it was too cold.* ♦ *I did it because he told me to.*

because of → bedclothes

WRITING TIP

Giving a reason

As, **because** and **so** are all words that you can use to give a reason for something: *I'm taking an umbrella, because it's starting to rain.* ◆ *As it was raining, I took an umbrella.* ◆ *It started to rain, so we decided to go back home.*

ⓘ For more help with writing, look at **Wordpower Writing Tutor** at the back of this dictionary.

be·cause of *prep* as a result of; on account of □ *disebabkan oleh*: *They didn't go for a walk because of the rain.* ◆ *They are here because of us.*

beck /bek/ *noun*
IDM **at sb's beck and call** always ready to obey sb's orders □ *ikut telunjuk*

beckon /ˈbekən/ *verb* [I,T] to show sb with a movement of your finger or hand that you want them to come closer □ *menggamit; memberi isyarat*: *She beckoned me over to speak to her.*

become /bɪˈkʌm/ *verb* [I] (*pt* **became** /bɪˈkeɪm/; *pp* **become**) to begin to be sth □ *menjadi*: *Mr Saito became Chairman in 2008.* ◆ *She wants to become a pilot.* ◆ *They became friends.* ◆ *She became nervous as the exam date came closer.* ◆ *He is becoming more like you every day.*

> **MORE** **Get** s also used with adjectives in this sense: *She got nervous as the exam date came closer.* ◆ *He's getting more like you every day.* It is very common in conversation and is less formal than **become**.

PHR V **become of sb/sth** to happen to sb/sth □ *terjadi kpd sso/sst*: *What became of Alima? I haven't seen her for years!*

BEd /ˌbiː ˈed/ *abbr* **Bachelor of Education**; a degree in education for people who want to be teachers □ *ijazah Sarjana Muda Pendidikan*

bed¹ /bed/ *noun* **1** [C,U] a piece of furniture that you lie on when you sleep □ *katil*: **to make the bed** (= to arrange the sheets, etc. so that the bed is tidy and ready for sb to sleep in) ◆ *What time do you usually* **go to bed**? ◆ *She was lying* **on the bed** (= on top of the covers). ◆ *When he rang I was already* **in bed** (= under the covers). ◆ *It's late. It's* **time for bed**. ◆ **to get into bed** ◆ **to get out of bed** ⊃ note at **sleep** ⊃ picture on page P8 **2** **-bedded** having the type or number of beds mentioned □ *berkatil*: *a twin-bedded room* **3** [C] the ground at the bottom of a river or the sea □ *dasar*: *the seabed* **4** [C] = **flower bed**

IDM **bed and breakfast**; **B and 'B**; **'B & 'B** a place to stay in a private house or small hotel that consists of a room for the night and breakfast; a place that provides this □ *inapan dan sarapan* ⊃ note at **hotel**

go to bed with sb (*informal*) to have sex with sb □ *tidur dgn sso*

TOPIC

Beds

A bed for one person is called a **single bed** and a bed for a couple to share is a **double bed**. Two single beds next to each other in the same room are called **twin beds**. Rooms in hotels are called **double**, **single** or **twin-bedded/twin** rooms. Two single beds built as a unit with one above the other, used especially by children, are called **bunk beds**. A **futon** is a kind of mattress that can be used for sitting on or rolled out to make a bed.

bed² /bed/ *verb* [T] (**bedding; bedded**) to fix sth firmly in sth □ *menanam; membenamkan*

PHR V **bed down** to sleep in a place where you do not usually sleep □ *tidur*: *We couldn't find a hotel so we bedded down for the night in the van.*

bedclothes /ˈbedkləʊðz/ (*BrE also* **ˈbed-covers**) *noun* [pl] the sheets, covers, etc. that you put on a bed □ *cadar, selimut, dsb*

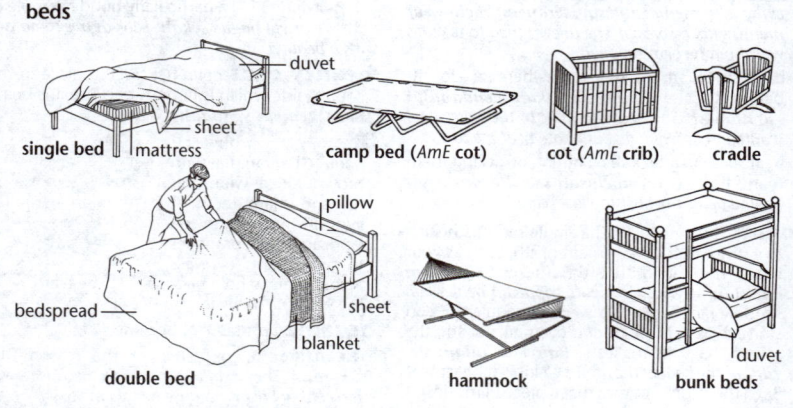

beds

— duvet — sheet
single bed | mattress

camp bed (*AmE* **cot**)

cot (*AmE* **crib**)

cradle

bedspread — pillow — sheet — blanket
double bed

hammock

duvet
bunk beds

ð **then** s **so** z **zoo** ʃ **she** ʒ **vi**sion h **how** m **man** n **no** ŋ si**ng** l **leg** r **red** j **yes** w **wet**

bedding /ˈbedɪŋ/ noun [U] everything that you put on a bed and need for sleeping □ *kelengkapan tempat tidur*

bedraggled /bɪˈdrægld/ adj very wet and untidy or dirty □ *basah kuyup dan tdk kemas atau comot*: bedraggled hair

bedridden /ˈbedrɪdn/ adj being too old or ill to get out of bed □ *terlantar di katil*

bedroom /ˈbedruːm; -rʊm/ noun [C] a room which is used for sleeping in □ *bilik tidur*: You can sleep in the spare bedroom. ♦ a three-bedroom house ➔ picture on **page P8**

bedside /ˈbedsaɪd/ noun [sing] the area that is next to a bed □ *sisi katil*: She sat at his bedside all night long. ♦ A book lay open on the bedside table. ➔ picture on **page P8**

bedsit /ˈbedsɪt/ (also ˈbedsitter) noun [C] (BrE) a room that a person rents which is used for both living and sleeping in □ *bilik sewa (tempat tinggal dan tidur)*

bedspread /ˈbedspred/ noun [C] an attractive cover for a bed that you put on top of the sheets and other covers □ *cadar* ➔ picture at **bed**

bedtime /ˈbedtaɪm/ noun [U] the time that you normally go to bed □ *waktu tidur*

bee /biː/ noun [C] a black and yellow insect that lives in large groups and that makes **honey** (= a sweet substance that we eat) □ *lebah* ➔ look at **beehive, wasp** ➔ picture on **page P13**

> **MORE** A large number of bees together is a **swarm**. Bees **buzz** or **hum** when they make a noise. They may **sting** if they are angry.

beech /biːtʃ/ noun 1 (also ˈbeech tree) [C] a large tree that produces small nuts with three sides □ *pokok bic* 2 [U] the wood from the beech tree □ *kayu bic*

beef /biːf/ noun [U] the meat from a cow □ *daging lembu*: a joint of beef ♦ a slice of roast beef ➔ note at **meat** ➔ picture on **page P16**

beefburger /ˈbiːfbɜːɡə(r)/ (also **burger**, especially AmE **hamburger**) noun [C] beef that has been cut up small and pressed into a flat round shape □ *burger lembu*

beefy /ˈbiːfi/ adj (**beefier; beefiest**) having a strong body with big muscles □ *tegap dan berotot*

beehive /ˈbiːhaɪv/ (also **hive**) noun [C] a type of box that people use for keeping **bees** (= black and yellow insects) in □ *sarang lebah*

been /biːn; bɪn/ past participle of **be, go¹**

> **GRAMMAR** Been is used as the past participle of both **be** and **go**: I've never been seriously ill. ♦ I've never been to Lisbon. **Gone** is also a past participle of **go**. Note the difference in meaning: I'm cold because I've just been outside (= I'm here now). ♦ Jim's not here, I'm afraid—he's just gone out (= he's not here now).

beep /biːp/ noun [C] a short high noise, for example made by the horn of a car □ *bunyi bip* ▶ **beep** verb [I,T]: I beeped my horn at the dog, but it wouldn't get off the road.

beeper /ˈbiːpə(r)/ (AmE) = **bleeper**

beer /bɪə(r)/ noun 1 [U] a type of alcoholic drink that is made from grain □ *bir*: a barrel/bottle/glass of beer ➔ look at **wine** 2 [C] a type or glass of beer □ *sejenis atau segelas bir*: We went out for a couple of beers.

> **MORE** Lager is a type of light-coloured beer, which is drunk cold. **Bitter** is a darker beer, which is drunk at room temperature. **Shandy** is beer mixed with lemonade.

beet /biːt/ (AmE) = **beetroot**

beetle /ˈbiːtl/ noun [C] an insect, often large, shiny and black, with a hard case on its back covering its wings. There are many different types of beetle. □ *kumbang* ➔ picture on **page P13**

beetroot /ˈbiːtruːt/ (AmE **beet**) noun [C,U] a dark red vegetable which is the root of a plant. Beetroot is cooked and can be eaten hot or cold. □ *ubi bit*

befall /bɪˈfɔːl/ verb [T] (pt **befell** /bɪˈfel/; pp **befallen** /bɪˈfɔːlən/) (written) (used about sth bad) to happen to sb □ *menimpa*

before¹ /bɪˈfɔː(r)/ prep, conj 1 earlier than sb/sth; earlier than the time that □ *sebelum; dahulu*: You can call me any time before 10 o'clock. ♦ the week before last ♦ They should be here before long (= soon). ♦ Turn the lights off before you leave. 2 (formal) in a position in front of sb/sth □ *di hadapan*: They knelt before the altar. ♦ You will appear before the judge tomorrow. 3 in front of sb/sth (in an order) □ *di hadapan*: 'H' comes before 'N' in the alphabet. ♦ A very difficult task lies before us. ♦ a company that puts profit before safety (= thinks profit is more important than being safe) 4 rather than □ *lebih rela*: I'd die before I apologized to him!

before² /bɪˈfɔː(r)/ adv at an earlier time; already □ *dahulu; sebelumnya*: I think we've met somewhere before. ♦ It was fine yesterday but it rained the day before. ➔ note at **ago**

beforehand /bɪˈfɔːhænd/ adv at an earlier time than sth □ *terlebih dahulu*: If you visit us, phone beforehand to make sure we're in.

befriend /bɪˈfrend/ verb [T] to become sb's friend; to be kind to sb □ *memperkawan; berbaik-baik (dgn sso)*

beg /beɡ/ verb [I,T] (**begging; begged**) 1 beg (sb) for sth; beg sth (of/from sb); beg (sb) to do sth to ask sb for sth strongly, or with great emotion □ *merayu*: He begged for forgiveness. ♦ Can I beg a favour of you? ♦ We begged him to lend us the money. **SYN** entreat, implore ➔ look at **plead** 2 beg (for) sth (from sb) to ask people for food, money, etc. because you are very poor

began → belie

□ *meminta sedekah*: *People were begging for food in the streets.*

IDM **I beg your pardon** (*formal*) **1** I am sorry □ *maaf*: *I beg your pardon. I picked up your bag by mistake.* **2** used for asking sb to repeat sth because you did not hear it properly □ *maaf, tolong ulang*

began past tense of **begin**

beggar /ˈbegə(r)/ *noun* [C] a person who lives by asking people for money, food, etc. on the streets □ *peminta sedekah; pengemis*

begin /bɪˈɡɪn/ *verb* (**beginning**; *pt* **began** /bɪˈɡæn/; *pp* **begun** /bɪˈɡʌn/) **1** [I,T] to start doing sth; to do the first part of sth □ *mula; mulakan*: *Shall I begin or will you?* ♦ *I began (= started reading) this novel last month and I still haven't finished it.* ♦ *When did he begin his lesson?* ♦ *When do you begin work?* ♦ *We began writing to each other in 1992.* ♦ *The carpet is beginning to look dirty.* **2** [I] to start to happen or exist, especially from a particular time □ *mula; bermula*: *What time does the concert begin?* **3** [I] **begin (with sth)** to start in a particular way, with a particular event, or in a particular place □ *bermula*: *My name begins with 'W' not 'V'.* ♦ *The fighting began with an argument about money.* ♦ *This is where the footpath begins.*

HELP **Begin** or **start**? **Begin** and **start** are very similar in meaning but **start** is more often used in informal speech. They can be followed by *to* or by the *-ing* form of a verb: *The baby began/started crying/to cry.* When **begin** or **start** are themselves in the *-ing* form they must be followed by *to*: *The baby was just beginning/starting to cry.* In some meanings only **start** can be used: *I couldn't start the car.* ♦ *We'll have to start (= leave) early if we want to be in Dover by 8 o'clock.*

IDM **to begin with 1** at first □ *pd mulanya*: *To begin with they were very happy.* **2** used for giving your first reason for sth or to introduce your first point □ *pertamanya*: *We can't possibly go. To begin with it's too far and we can't afford it either.* ▶ **beginner** *noun* [C]

beginning /bɪˈɡɪnɪŋ/ *noun* [C] the first part of sth; the time when or the place where sth starts □ *mula; permulaan*: *I've read the article from beginning to end.* ♦ *We're going away at the beginning of the school holidays.*

begrudge /bɪˈɡrʌdʒ/ *verb* [T] **begrudge (sb) sth 1** to feel angry or upset because sb has sth that you think that they should not have □ *berasa iri hati*: *He's worked hard. I don't begrudge him his success.* **2** to be unhappy that you have to do sth □ *mengesali; berasa tdk puas hati*: *I begrudge paying so much money in tax each month.*

begun past participle of **begin**

behalf /bɪˈhɑːf/ *noun*

IDM **on behalf of sb; on sb's behalf** for sb; instead of sb □ *bagi pihak sso*: *I would like to thank you all on behalf of my colleagues and myself.* ♦ *Emma couldn't be present so her husband accepted the prize on her behalf.*

behave /bɪˈheɪv/ *verb* **1** [I] **behave well, badly, etc. (towards sb)** to act in a particular way □ *berkelakuan; bertindak*: *Don't you think that Ellen has been behaving very strangely recently?* ♦ *I think you behaved very badly towards your father.* ♦ *He behaves as if/though he was the boss.* **2** [I,T] **behave (yourself)** to act in the correct or appropriate way □ *berkelakuan baik*: *I want you to behave yourselves while we're away.* **OPP** **misbehave** **3** **-behaved** [in compounds] behaving in the way mentioned □ *berkelakuan*: *a well-behaved child* ♦ *a badly-behaved class*

behaviour (*AmE* **behavior**) /bɪˈheɪvjə(r)/ *noun* [U] the way that you act or behave □ *kelakuan*: *Her behaviour has been very strange recently.* ♦ *He was sent out of the class for bad behaviour.*

behead /bɪˈhed/ *verb* [T] to cut off sb's head, especially as a punishment □ *(kepala) memancung; memenggal; memotong* **SYN** **decapitate**

behind /bɪˈhaɪnd/ *prep, adv* **1** in, at or to the back of sb/sth □ *di belakang*: *There's a small garden behind the house.* ♦ *The sun went behind a cloud.* ♦ *You go on ahead. I'll follow on behind.* ♦ *Look behind you before you drive off.* ♦ *He ran off but the police were close behind.* **2** **behind (in/with) (sth)** later or less good than sb/sth; making less progress than sb/sth □ *lambat; ketinggalan*: *The train is twenty minutes behind schedule.* ♦ *Jane is behind the rest of the class in maths.* ♦ *We are a month behind with the rent.* ⊃ look at **ahead** **3** supporting or agreeing with sb/sth □ *menyokong*: *Whatever she decides, her family will be behind her.* **4** responsible for causing or starting sth □ *(sebab) di sebalik*: *What is the reason behind his sudden change of opinion?* **5** used to say that sth is in sb's past □ *sudah berlalu; lupakan*: *It's time you put your problems behind you (= forgot about them).* **6** in the place where sb/sth is or was □ *tertinggal*: *Oh no! I've left the tickets behind (= at home).*

beige /beɪʒ/ *adj, noun* [U] (of) a light brown colour □ *warna kuning air*: *a beige coat*

being¹ ⊃ **be**

being² /ˈbiːɪŋ/ *noun* **1** [U] the state of existing □ *wujud*: *When did the organization come into being?* **SYN** **existence** **2** [C] a living person or thing □ *manusia; makhluk*: *a human being*

belated /bɪˈleɪtɪd/ *adj* coming late □ *terlambat*: *a belated apology* ▶ **belatedly** *adv*: *They have realized, rather belatedly, that they have made a mistake.*

belch /beltʃ/ *verb* **1** [I] to let gas out from your stomach through your mouth with a sudden noise □ *bersendawa* **SYN** **burp** **2** [T] to send out a lot of smoke, etc. □ *meluahkan*: *The volcano belched smoke and ash.* ▶ **belch** *noun* [C]

belie /bɪˈlaɪ/ *verb* [T] (**belying**; **belies**; *pt, pp* **belied**) to give an idea of sth that is false □ *tdk* *memperlihatkan; menyembunyikan*: *His smiling face belied his true feelings.*

belief /bɪˈliːf/ *noun* **1** [sing, U] **belief in sb/sth** a feeling that sb/sth is true, morally good or right, or that sb/sth really exists □ *kepercayaan*: *She has lost her belief in God.* ⊃ look at **disbelief 2** [sing, U] (*formal*) **belief (that ...)** something you accept as true; what you believe □ *kepercayaan; pendapat*: *It's my belief that people are basically good.* ◆ *There is a general belief that things will soon get better.* ◆ **Contrary to popular belief** (= in spite of what many people think) *the north of the country is not poorer than the south.* **3** [C] an idea about religion, politics, etc □ *kepercayaan; fahaman*: *Divorce is contrary to their religious beliefs.*
IDM **beyond belief** (in a way that is) too great, difficult, etc. to be believed □ *sukar dipercayai; menakjubkan*: *The amount of money we owe has increased beyond belief.*

believable /bɪˈliːvəbl/ *adj* that can be believed □ *dpt dipercayai* **OPP** **unbelievable**

believe /bɪˈliːv/ *verb* [not used in the continuous tenses] **1** [T] to feel sure that sth is true or that sb is telling the truth □ *percaya; mempercayai*: *I don't believe you!* ◆ *He said he hadn't taken any money but I didn't believe him.* **2** [T] **believe (that)...** to think that sth is true or possible, although you are not certain □ *percaya; rasa; dipercayai*: *I believe they have moved to Italy.* ◆ *'Does Pat still work there?' 'I believe so.'* ◆ *The escaped prisoner is believed to be in this area.* ◆ *Four people are still missing, believed drowned.* **3** [T] **believe (that)...** to have the opinion that sth is right or true □ *percaya; rasa; berpendapat*: *The party believes (that) education is the most important issue facing the government.* ⊃ note at **think** **4** [T] **don't/can't believe sth** used to show anger or surprise at sth □ *takkanlah*: *I can't believe (that) you're telling me to do it again!* **5** [I] to have religious beliefs □ *percaya (pd Tuhan)*: *The god appears only to those who believe.*

HELP Although this verb is not used in the continuous tenses, it is common to see the present participle (= *-ing* form): *Believing the house to be empty, she quietly let herself in.*

IDM **believe it or not** it may be surprising but it is true □ *percaya tak*: *Believe it or not, English food can sometimes be quite good.*
give sb to believe/understand (that) [often passive] to give sb the impression or idea that sth is true □ *(saya, dsb) difahamkan bahawa*: *I was given to believe that I had got the job.*
PHR V **believe in sb/sth** to be sure that sb/sth exists □ *percaya akan adanya (sso/sst)*: *Do you believe in God?* ◆ *Most young children believe in Father Christmas.*
believe in sb/sth; believe in doing sth to think that sb/sth is good or right □ *percaya sso/sst itu baik atau benar*: *They need a leader they can believe in.* ◆ *He doesn't believe in killing animals for their fur.*

believer /bɪˈliːvə(r)/ *noun* [C] a person who has religious beliefs □ *orang yg percaya; penganut*
IDM **be a (great/firm) believer in sth** to think that sth is good or right □ *percaya betul*: *He is a great believer in getting things done on time.*

belittle /bɪˈlɪtl/ *verb* [T] to make sb or the things they do seem unimportant or not very good □ *memperkecil-kecil*

bell /bel/ *noun* [C] **1** a metal object, often shaped like a cup, that makes a ringing sound when it is hit by a small piece of metal inside it □ *loceng*: *the sound of church bells* ◆ *Her voice came back clear as a bell.* ◆ *an animal with a bell round its neck* ⊃ picture at **goat 2** an electrical device that makes a ringing sound when the button on it is pushed; the sound that it makes □ *loceng elektrik*: *Ring the doorbell and see if they're in.*
IDM **ring a bell** ⊃ **ring²**

belligerent /bəˈlɪdʒərənt/ *adj* unfriendly and aggressive □ *agresif; sifat suka bergaduh/ berkelahi* ▶ **belligerence** *noun* [U]

bellow /ˈbeləʊ/ *verb* **1** [I,T] **bellow (sth) (at sb)** to shout in a loud deep voice, especially because you are angry □ *menempik; bertempik*: *They bellowed at her to stop.* **2** [I] to make a deep low sound, like a **bull** (= an adult male cow) □ *mendenguh* ▶ **bellow** *noun* [C]

belly /ˈbeli/ *noun* [C] (*pl* **bellies**) the stomach or the front part of your body between your chest and your legs □ *perut*

ˈbelly button (*informal*) = **navel**

belong /bɪˈlɒŋ/ *verb* [I] to have a right or usual place □ *menjadi sebahagian drpd*: *The plates belong in that cupboard.* ◆ *It took quite a long time before we felt we belonged in the village* (= until we felt comfortable).
PHR V **belong to sb** to be owned by sb □ *kepunyaan; milik*: *Who does this pen belong to?* ◆ *Don't take anything that doesn't belong to you.*
belong to sth to be a member of a group or an organization □ *menganggotai*: *Do you belong to any political party?*

belongings /bɪˈlɒŋɪŋz/ *noun* [pl] the things that you own that can be moved, that is, not land and buildings □ *barang-barang kepunyaan*: *They lost all their belongings in the fire.*

beloved /bɪˈlʌvd; bɪˈlʌvɪd/ *adj* (*formal*) much loved □ *dikasihi; tercinta*: *They had always intended to return to their beloved Ireland.*

HELP When 'beloved' comes before a noun, the pronunciation is /bɪˈlʌvɪd/.

below /bɪˈləʊ/ *prep, adv* at or to a lower position or level than sb/sth □ *di bawah; ke bawah*: *Do not write below this line.* ◆ *The temperature fell below freezing during the night.* ◆ *Her marks in the exam were below average.* ◆ *I don't live on the top floor. I live on the floor below.* ◆ *temperatures of 30° and below* **OPP** **above** ⊃ note at **under**

belt¹ /belt/ noun [C] **1** a thin piece of cloth, leather, etc. that you wear around your waist □ *tali pinggang*: I need a belt to keep these trousers up. ➔ look at **seat belt** ➔ picture on **page P1 2** a long narrow piece of rubber, cloth, etc. in a circle, that is used for carrying things along or for making parts of a machine move □ *tali sawat*: The suitcases were carried round on a conveyor belt. ♦ **the fan belt** of a car (= that operates the machinery that keeps a car engine cool) **3** an area of land that has a particular quality or where a particular group of people live □ *kawasan*: the green belt around London (= an area of countryside where you are not allowed to build houses, factories, etc.) ♦ the commuter belt

IDM **below the belt** (*informal*) unfair or cruel □ *tdk adil; kejam*: That remark was rather below the belt.

tighten your belt ➔ **tighten**

under your belt (*informal*) that you have already done or achieved □ *memperoleh; mempunyai*: She's already got four tournament wins under her belt.

belt² /belt/ verb (*informal*) **1** [T] to hit sb hard □ *memukul* **2** [I] to run or go somewhere very fast □ *bergerak laju; memecut*: I was belting along on my bicycle.

PHR V **belt sth out** to sing, shout or play sth loudly □ *mengumandangkan*: In the restaurant, loudspeakers were belting out Spanish pop music.

belt up (*slang*) used to tell sb rudely to be quiet □ *diamlah(!)*: Belt up! I can't think with all this noise.

bemused /bɪˈmjuːzd/ adj confused and unable to think clearly □ *bingung*

bench /bentʃ/ noun [C] **1** a long wooden or metal seat for two or more people, often outdoors □ *bangku*: a park bench ➔ picture at **chair 2** (in the British parliament) the seats where a particular group of politicians sit □ *kerusi ahli parlimen*: the Government front bench ♦ the Labour back benches ➔ look at **back bench 3** a long narrow table that people work at, for example in a factory □ *meja kerja*

benchmark /ˈbentʃmɑːk/ noun [C] a standard that other things can be compared to □ *tanda aras*: These new safety features set a benchmark for other manufacturers to follow.

bend

bending down
(*also* **bending over**)

bending a spoon

bend¹ /bend/ verb (*pt, pp* **bent** /bent/) **1** [I] to move your body forwards and downwards □ *membongkok*: He bent down to tie up his shoelaces. **2** [T] to make sth that was straight into a curved shape □ *membengkokkan*: to bend a piece of wire into an S shape ♦ It hurts when I bend my knee. **3** [I] to be or become curved □ *melentur; membengkok; membelok*: The road bends to the left here.

IDM **bend the rules** to do sth that is not normally allowed by the rules □ *memesong sedikit drpd apa-apa yg dibenarkan oleh peraturan*

bend² /bend/ noun [C] a curve or turn, for example in a road □ *selekoh; lengkok*: a sharp bend in the road

IDM **round the bend** ➔ **round²**

beneath /bɪˈniːθ/ prep, adv **1** in, at or to a lower position than sb/sth; under □ *di bawah; di sebalik*: The ship disappeared beneath the waves. ♦ His calm exterior hid the anger beneath. ➔ note at **under 2** not good enough for sb □ *di bawah taraf; jatuh maruah*: She felt that cleaning for other people was beneath her.

benefactor /ˈbenɪfæktə(r)/ noun [C] a person who helps or gives money to a person or an organization □ *penderma*

beneficial /ˌbenɪˈfɪʃl/ adj **beneficial (to sb/sth)** having a good or useful effect □ *bermanfaat; berfaedah*: A good diet is beneficial to health.

beneficiary /ˌbenɪˈfɪʃəri/ noun [C] (*pl* **beneficiaries**) **beneficiary (of sth) 1** a person who gains as a result of sth □ *orang yg mendapat faedah/manfaat drpd sst*: Who will be the main beneficiary of the cuts in income tax? **2** a person who receives money or property when sb dies □ *benefisiari; orang yg menerima sst spt wang atau harta apabila sso mati*

benefit¹ /ˈbenɪfɪt/ noun **1** [U,C] an advantage or useful effect that sth has □ *manfaat; faedah*: A change in the law would be to everyone's benefit. ♦ I can't see the benefit of doing things this way. ♦ the benefits of modern technology **2** [U,C] (*BrE*) money that the government gives to people who are ill, poor, unemployed, etc. □ *faedah*: child/sickness/housing benefit ♦ I'm not entitled to unemployment benefit. ♦ to claim benefits **3** [C, usually pl] advantages that you get from your company in addition to the money you earn □ *kelebihan*: a company car and other benefits

IDM **for sb's benefit** especially to help, please, etc. sb □ *utk faedah*: For the benefit of the newcomers, I will start again.

give sb the benefit of the doubt to believe what sb says although there is no proof that it is true □ *memberi faedah kesangsian*

benefit² /ˈbenɪfɪt/ verb (**benefiting**; **benefited** or **benefitting**; **benefitted**) **1** [T] to produce a good or useful effect □ *mendatangkan faedah; menguntungkan*: The new tax laws will benefit people on low wages. **2** [I] **benefit (from sth)** to receive an advantage from sth □ *mendapat kelebihan*: Small businesses have benefited from the changes in the law.

benevolent /bəˈnevələnt/ *adj* (*formal*) kind, friendly and helpful to others □ *baik hati* ▶**benevolence** *noun* [U]

benign /bɪˈnaɪn/ *adj* **1** (used about people) kind or gentle □ *bersifat baik hati dan lembut*: *a benign influence* **2** (used about a disease, etc.) not dangerous □ *tdk berbahaya*: *a benign tumour* OPP **malignant**

bent[1] past tense, past participle of **bend**[1]

bent[2] /bent/ *adj* **1** not straight □ *bengkok; bongkok*: *Do this exercise with your knees bent.* ◆ *This knife is bent.* ◆ *It was so funny we were bent double with laughter.* **2** (BrE *informal*) (used about a person in authority) dishonest □ *tdk jujur*: *a bent policeman* SYN **corrupt**
IDM **bent on sth/on doing sth** wanting to do sth very much; determined □ *bertekad atau berazam ttg sst/utk melakukan sst*: *They seem bent on moving house, whatever the difficulties.*

bent[3] /bent/ *noun* [sing] **a bent for sth/doing sth** a natural skill at sth or interest in sth □ *kecenderungan; minat*: *She has a bent for music.*

bequeath /bɪˈkwiːð/ *verb* [T] (*formal*) **bequeath sth (to sb)** to arrange for sth to be given to sb after you have died □ *mewariskan*: *He bequeathed £1 000 to his favourite charity.* ⊃ A much more common word is **leave**.

bequest /bɪˈkwest/ *noun* [C] (*formal*) something that you arrange to be given to sb after you have died □ *warisan*: *He left a bequest to each of his grandchildren.*

bereaved /bɪˈriːvd/ *adj* **1** having lost a relative or close friend who has recently died □ *(yg) mengalami kematian* **2 the bereaved** *noun* [pl] the people whose relative or close friend has died recently □ *orang yg kematian (sso)*

bereavement /bɪˈriːvmənt/ *noun* (*formal*) **1** [U] the state of having lost a relative or close friend who has recently died □ *keadaan kehilangan sso kerana kematian* **2** [C] the death of a relative or close friend □ *kematian*: *There has been a bereavement in the family.*

bereft /bɪˈreft/ *adj* [not before a noun] (*formal*) **1 bereft of sth** completely lacking sth; having lost sth □ *kehilangan*: *bereft of ideas/hope* **2** (used about a person) sad and lonely because you have lost sth □ *sedih dan kesepian*: *He was utterly bereft when his wife died.*

beret /ˈbereɪ/ *noun* [C] a soft flat round hat □ *beret* ⊃ picture at **hat**

berry /ˈberi/ *noun* [C] (*pl* **berries**) a small soft fruit with seeds □ *(buah) beri*: *Those berries are poisonous.* ◆ *a raspberry/strawberry/blueberry*

berserk /bəˈzɜːk, -ˈsɜːk/ *adj* [not before a noun] very angry; crazy □ *mengamuk*: *If the teacher finds out what you've done he'll go berserk.*

berth /bɜːθ/ *noun* [C] **1** a place for sleeping on a ship or train □ *tempat tidur (dlm kapal, dsb)*: *a cabin with four berths* **2** a place where a ship can stop and stay □ *tempat berlabuh; pelabuhan*

beset /bɪˈset/ *verb* [T] (**besetting**; *pt, pp* **beset**) (*formal*) to affect sb/sth in a bad way □ *menimpa; dilanda*: *The team has been beset by injuries all season.*

beside /bɪˈsaɪd/ *prep* at the side of, or next to sb/sth □ *di sisi; di sebelah*: *Come and sit beside me.* ◆ *He kept his bag close beside him at all times.*
IDM **beside the point** not connected with the subject you are discussing □ *tdk ada kenamengena*
beside yourself (with sth) not able to control yourself because of a very strong emotion □ *lupa diri*: *Emily was almost beside herself with grief.*

besides /bɪˈsaɪdz/ *prep, adv* in addition to or as well as sb/sth; also □ *selain; lagipun*: *There will be six people coming, besides you and David.* ◆ *I don't want to go out tonight. Besides, I haven't got any money.* ⊃ look at **anyway**

besiege /bɪˈsiːdʒ/ *verb* [T] **1** to surround a place with an army □ *mengepung* **2** [usually passive] (used about sb unpleasant or annoying) to surround sb/sth in large numbers □ *mengerumuni; dikerumuni*: *The actor was besieged by fans and reporters.*

besotted /bɪˈsɒtɪd/ *adj* [not before a noun] **besotted (with/by sb/sth)** so much in love with sb/sth that you cannot think or behave normally □ *mabuk asmara*

best[1] /best/ *adj* [the superlative of **good**] of the highest quality or level; most suitable □ *terbaik; paling (bagus, karib, dll)*: *His latest book is by far his best.* ◆ *I'm going to wear my best shirt to the interview.* ◆ *Who in the class is best at maths?* ◆ *It's best to arrive early if you want a good seat.* ◆ *Who's your best friend?* ◆ *What's the best way to get to York from here?*
IDM **your best bet** (*informal*) the most sensible or appropriate thing for you to do in a particular situation □ *lebih baik; yg bagus*: *There's nowhere to park in the city centre. Your best bet is to go in by bus.*
the best/better part of sth ⊃ **part**[1]

best[2] /best/ *adv* [the superlative of **well**] to the greatest degree; most □ *paling (baik, suka, disukai, dll)*: *He works best in the morning.* ◆ *Which of these dresses do you like best?* ◆ *one of Britain's best-loved TV stars*
IDM **as best you can** as well as you can even if it is not perfectly □ *sebaik mungkin*

best[3] /best/ **the best** *noun* [sing] the person or thing that is of the highest quality or level or better than all others □ *(sso/sst yg) paling baik*: *When you pay that much for a meal you expect the best.* ◆ *Even the best of us make mistakes sometimes.* ◆ *I think James is the best!* ◆ *They are the best of friends.* ◆ *The best we can hope for is that the situation doesn't get any worse.* ⊃ look at **second best**
IDM **all the best** (*informal*) used when you are saying goodbye to sb or ending a letter, to give

sb your best wishes □ *selamat maju jaya, dsb*: *All the best! Keep in touch, won't you?*

at best if everything goes as well as possible; taking the most positive view □ *paling-paling (awal, dll)*: *We won't be able to deliver the goods before March, or, at best, the last week in February.*

at its/your best in its/your best state or condition □ *yg paling baik/bagus*: *This is an example of Beckett's work at its best.* ◆ *No one is at their best first thing in the morning.*

be (all) for the best used to say that although sth appears bad now, it will be good in the end □ *ada hikmahnya*: *I didn't get the job, but I'm sure it's all for the best.*

bring out the best/worst in sb to show sb's best/worst qualities □ *memperlihatkan kelebihan/kekurangan sso*: *The crisis really brought out the best in Tony.*

do/try your best to do all or the most that you can □ *berusaha sedaya upaya*: *I did my best to help her.*

look your best ➔ **look¹**

make the best of sth/a bad job to accept a difficult situation and try to be as happy as possible □ *menerima sst keadaan yg sukar dgn sebaik-baiknya*

best 'man *noun* [sing] a man who helps and supports the **bridegroom** (= the man who is getting married) at a wedding □ *pengapit pengantin lelaki* ➔ note at **wedding**

bestow /bɪˈstəʊ/ *verb* [T] (*formal*) **bestow sth (on/upon sb)** to give sth to sb, especially to show how much they are respected □ *menganugerahkan; mengurniakan; menghadiahkan*: *It was a title bestowed upon him by the king.*

bestseller /ˌbestˈselə(r)/ *noun* [C] a book or other product that is bought by large numbers of people □ *buku, dll yg paling laris* ▶ **bestselling** *adj* [only *before* a noun]: *a bestselling novel*

bet¹ /bet/ *verb* [I,T] (**betting**; *pt, pp* **bet** *or* **betted**) **1 bet (sth) (on sth)** to risk money on a race or an event by trying to predict the result. If you are right, you win money □ *bertaruh*: *I wouldn't bet on them winning the next election.* ◆ *I bet him £50 he couldn't beat me at tennis.* **SYN gamble, put money on sth 2** (*informal*) used to say that you are almost certain that sth is true or that sth will happen □ *pasti; tentu*: *I bet he arrives late—he always does.* ◆ *I bet you're worried about your exam, aren't you?*

IDM I/I'll bet (*spoken*) **1** used to show that you can understand what sb is feeling, describing, etc □ *memahami apa-apa yg dirasai, dinyatakan dsb oleh sso*: *'I nearly died when he told me.' 'I bet!'* **2** used to tell sb that you do not believe what they have just said □ *tdk mempercayai apa-apa yg dinyatakan oleh sso*: *'I'm going to tell her what I think of her.' 'Yeah, I bet!'*
you bet (*spoken*) a way of saying 'Yes, of course!' □ *tentu sekali*: *'Are you coming too?' 'You bet (I am)!'*

bet² /bet/ *noun* [C] **1** an act of betting □ *pertaruhan*: *Did you have a bet on that race?* ◆ *to win/lose a bet* **2** an opinion □ *pendapat; agakan*: *My bet is that he's missed the train.*

IDM your best bet ➔ **best¹**
hedge your bets ➔ **hedge²**

betide /bɪˈtaɪd/ *verb*
IDM woe betide sb ➔ **woe**

betray /bɪˈtreɪ/ *verb* [T] **1** to give information about sb/sth to an enemy; to make a secret known □ *mengkhianati; membelot*: *She betrayed all the members of the group to the secret police.* ◆ *He refused to betray their plans.* ◆ *to betray your country* ➔ note at **traitor 2** to hurt sb who trusts you, especially by not being loyal or faithful to them □ *mengkhianati*: *If you take the money you'll betray her trust.* ◆ *When parents get divorced the children often feel betrayed.* **3** to show a feeling or quality that you would like to keep hidden □ *mendedahkan*: *Her steady voice did not betray the emotion she was feeling.* ▶ **betrayal** /bɪˈtreɪəl/ *noun* [C,U]

better¹ /ˈbetə(r)/ *adj* **1** [the comparative of **good**] **better than sb/sth** of a higher quality or level or more suitable than sb/sth □ *lebih baik*: *I think her second novel was much better than her first.* ◆ *He's far better at English than me.* ◆ *It's a long way to drive. It would be better to take the train.* ◆ *You'd be better getting the train than driving.* **2** [the comparative of **well**] less ill; completely healthy again after an illness □ *sihat sedikit; sembuh*: *You can't go swimming until you're better.*

IDM the bigger, smaller, faster, slower, etc. the better used to say that sth should be as big, small, etc. as possible □ *sebesar, sekecil dsb yg mungkin*: *I love giving parties, the bigger the better.*

better² /ˈbetə(r)/ *adv* [the comparative of **well**] in a better way; to a greater or higher degree □ *lebih baik*: *I think you could have done this better.* ◆ *Sylvie speaks English better than I do.*

IDM (be) better off [the comparative of *well off*] with more money □ *lebih berada*: *We're much better off now I go out to work too.*
(be) better off (doing sth) to be in a more pleasant or suitable situation □ *lebih baik lagi*: *You look terrible. You'd be better off at home in bed.*
you, etc. had better you should; you ought to □ *lebih baik awak, dsb*: *I think we'd better go before it gets dark.* ◆ *You'd better take a pen and paper—you might want to take notes.* ❶ For other idioms containing **better**, look at the entries for the nouns, adjectives, etc. For example **think better of (doing) sth** is at **think**.

better³ /ˈbetə(r)/ *noun* [sing] something that is of higher quality □ *sst yg lebih baik*: *The hotel wasn't very good. I must say we'd expected better.*

IDM a change for the better/worse ➔ **change²**
get the better of sb/sth to defeat or be stronger than sb/sth □ *mengalahkan sso/sst*: *When we have an argument she always gets the better of me.*

betting shop noun [C] a shop where you can go to put money on a race or an event □ *kedai judi* ⊃ look at **bookmaker**

between /bɪˈtwiːn/ prep, adv **1 between A and B; in between** in the space in the middle of two things, people, places etc. □ *di antara*: *I was sitting between Sam and Charlie.* ◆ *a village between Cambridge and Ely* ◆ *She was standing in between the desk and the wall.* **2 between A and B; in between** (used about two amounts, distances, ages, times, etc.) at a point that is greater or later than the first and smaller or earlier than the second; somewhere in the middle □ *antara*: *They said they would arrive between 4 and 5 o'clock.* ◆ *They've got this shirt in size 10 and size 16, but nothing in between.* **3** from one place to another and back again □ *(berulang-alik) antara*: *There aren't any direct trains between here and Manchester.* **4** involving or connecting two people, groups or things □ *sesama; antara*: *There's some sort of disagreement between them.* ◆ *There may be a connection between the two crimes.* **5** choosing one and not the other (of two things) □ *antara*: *to choose between two jobs* ◆ *What's the difference between 'some' and 'any'?* **6** giving each person a share □ *antara*: *The money was divided equally between the two children.* ◆ *We ate all the chocolates between us.*

between

a small house **between** two large ones

a house **among** some trees

> **HELP** **Between** or **among**? **Between** is usually used of two people or things: *sitting between her mother and father* ◆ *between the ages of 12 and 14.* However, **between** can sometimes be used of more than two when the people or things are being considered as individuals, especially when the meaning is that of number 6 (above): *We drank a bottle of wine between the three of us.* **Among** is always used of more than two people or things considered as a group rather than as individuals: *You're among friends here.*

7 by putting together the actions, efforts, etc. of two or more people □ *sesama; sama-sama*: *Between us we saved up enough money to buy a car.*

beverage /ˈbevərɪdʒ/ noun [C] (written) a drink □ *minuman*: *hot and cold beverages*

beware /bɪˈweə(r)/ verb [I] [only in the imperative or infinitive] **beware (of sb/sth)** (used for giving a warning) to be careful □ *awas; jaga-*

jaga: *Beware of the dog!* (= written on a sign) ◆ *We were told to beware of strong currents in the sea.*

bewilder /bɪˈwɪldə(r)/ verb [T] to confuse and surprise □ *menjadi hairan; menghairankan*: *I was completely bewildered by his sudden change of mood.* ▶ **bewildered** *adj*: *a bewildered expression* ▶ **bewildering** *adj*: *a bewildering experience* ▶ **bewilderment** *noun* [U]: *to stare at somebody in bewilderment*

bewitch /bɪˈwɪtʃ/ verb [T] to attract and interest sb very much □ *mempesona*

beyond /bɪˈjɒnd/ prep, adv **1** on or to the other side of □ *di sebalik*: *beyond the distant mountains* ◆ *We could see the mountains and the sea beyond.* **2** further than; later than □ *melampaui; melepasi*: *Does the motorway continue beyond Birmingham?* ◆ *Most people don't go on working beyond the age of 65.* **3** more than sth □ *lebih drpd; selain*: *The house was far beyond what I could afford.* ◆ *I haven't heard anything beyond a few rumours.* **4** used to say that sth is not possible □ *tdk mungkin*: *The car was completely beyond repair* (= too badly damaged to repair). ◆ *The situation is beyond my control.* **5** too far or too advanced for sb/sth □ *di luar; melebihi*: *The activity was beyond the students' abilities.*

IDM **be beyond sb** (*informal*) to be impossible for sb to understand or imagine □ *entah kenapa; tdk faham*: *Why she wants to go and live there is quite beyond me.*

bias¹ /ˈbaɪəs/ noun **1** [C,U] a strong feeling of favour towards or against one group of people, or on one side in an argument, often not based on fair judgement or facts □ *sikap berat sebelah; prasangka*: *a bias against women drivers* ◆ *The BBC has been accused of political bias.* **2** [C, usually sing] an interest in one thing more than others; a special ability □ *kecenderungan*: *a course with a strong scientific bias*

bias² /ˈbaɪəs/ verb [T] (**biasing**; **biased** or **biassing**; **biassed**) to influence sb/sth, especially unfairly; to give an advantage to one group, etc □ *bersikap berat sebelah; berprasangka*: *Good newspapers should not be biased towards a particular political party.* ▶ **biased** *adj*: *a biased report*

bib /bɪb/ noun [C] a piece of cloth or plastic that a baby or small child wears under the chin to protect its clothes while it is eating □ *lapik dada*

the Bible /ˈbaɪbl/ noun [sing] the book of great religious importance to Christian and Jewish people □ *Kitab Injil* ▶ **biblical** /ˈbɪblɪkl/ *adj*

bibliography /ˌbɪbliˈɒɡrəfi/ noun [C] (*pl* **bibliographies**) **1** a list of the books and articles that a writer used when they were writing a particular book or article □ *bibliografi; daftar bacaan* **2** a list of books on a particular subject □ *bibliografi*

bicentenary /ˌbaɪsen'tiːnəri/ noun [C] (*pl* **bicentenaries**) (*AmE* **bicentennial** /ˌbaɪsen'teniəl/) the day or the year two hundred years after sth happened or began □ *ulang tahun ke-200*: *the bicentenary of the French Revolution*

biceps /'baɪseps/ noun [C] (*pl* biceps) the large muscle at the front of the upper part of your arms □ *biseps*

bicker /'bɪkə(r)/ verb [I] to argue about unimportant things □ *bertengkar*: *The children are always bickering about something.*

bicycle /'baɪsɪkl/ (*also* **bike**) noun [C] a vehicle with two wheels, which you sit on and ride by moving your legs □ *basikal*: *Did you COME BY bicycle?* ◆ *He got on his bicycle and rode off.* ◆ *We went for a bicycle ride on Sunday.* ➜ note at **bike**

bid¹ /bɪd/ verb (**bidding**; *pt, pp* **bid**) **1** bid (sth) (for sth) [I,T] to offer to pay a particular price for sth, especially at an **auction** (= a public sale where things are sold to the person who offers the most money) □ *membuat tawaran; menawarkan*: *Somebody bid £5 000 for the painting.* ◆ *I wanted to buy the vase but another man was bidding against me.* **2** [I] to offer to do work or provide a service for a particular price, in competition with other companies, etc. □ *(a) membida; menawarkan harga utk sst (b) membida; menawarkan harga utk melakukan sst*: *A French firm will be bidding for the contract.*

bid² /bɪd/ noun [C] **1** an offer by a person or a business company to pay a certain amount of money for sth □ *bida; tawaran*: *Granada mounted a hostile* **takeover bid** (= when one company tries to buy another company) *for Forte.* ◆ *At the auction we* **made a bid** *of £100 for the chair.* **2** (*especially AmE*) = **tender²** **3** a bid (for sth); a bid (to do sth) an effort to do, obtain, etc. sth □ *percubaan*: *His bid for freedom had failed.* ◆ *Tonight the Ethiopian athlete will* **make a bid** *to break the world record.* **SYN** attempt **bidder** noun [C]: *The house was sold to the highest bidder* (= the person who offered the most money).

bide /baɪd/ verb
IDM **bide your time** to wait for a good opportunity □ *menunggu (peluang baik)*: *I'll bide my time until the situation improves.*

bidet /'biːdeɪ/ noun [C] a large bowl in the bathroom that you can sit on in order to wash your bottom □ *bidet*

biennial /baɪ'eniəl/ adj happening once every two years □ *dua tahun sekali*

bifocals /ˌbaɪ'fəʊklz/ noun [pl] a pair of glasses with each **lens** (= a piece of glass) made in two parts. The upper part is for looking at things at a distance, and the lower part is for looking at things that are close to you. □ *kaca mata berkanta dwifokus* ▶ **bifocal** adj

big /bɪg/ adj (**bigger**; **biggest**) **1** large; not small □ *besar*: *a big house/town/salary* ◆ *This dress is too big for me.* **OPP** small **2** [only *before* a noun] (*informal*) older □ *lebih tua; abang; kakak*: *a big brother/sister* **OPP** little **3** great or important □ *besar; penting*: *They had a big argument yesterday.* ◆ *That was the biggest decision I've ever had to make.* ◆ *some of the big names in Hollywood*
IDM **Big deal!** (*informal*) used to say that you think sth is not important or interesting □ *tak hairan pun*: *'Look at my new bike!' 'Big deal! It's not as nice as mine.'*
a big deal/no big deal (*informal*) something that is (not) very important or exciting □ *penting /tdk penting*: *Birthday celebrations are a big deal in our family.* ◆ *A 2% pay increase is no big deal.*
give sb a big hand to hit your hands together to show approval, enthusiasm, etc. □ *memberikan sso tepukan gemuruh*: *The audience gave the girl a big hand when she finished her song.*
in a big/small way ➜ **way¹**

bicycle

handlebar
seat/saddle
brake
water bottle
front brake
crossbar
tyre (AmE tire)
wheel
rear brake
helmet
frame
lock
spoke
pedal
chain
valve
gears
stand
pump

ʌ cup ɜː bird ə ago eɪ pay əʊ go aɪ my aʊ now ɔɪ boy ɪə near eə hair ʊə pure

OTHER WORDS FOR

big

Big and **large** can both be used when talking about size or number: *a big/large house* ♦ *a big baby*. **Large** is more formal and should be used in writing, unless it is in an informal style. **Large** is not usually used to describe people, except to avoid saying 'fat'. **Great** suggests importance, quality, etc: *a great occasion/musician*. In formal English, it is often used with uncountable nouns to mean 'a lot of': *great happiness/care/sorrow*. In informal English, **great** can be used to emphasize an adjective of size or quantity. Note also the phrases: *a large amount of* ♦ *a large number of* ♦ *a large quantity of* ♦ *a great deal of* ♦ *in great detail*.

bigamy /ˈbɪɡəmi/ *noun* [U] the crime of being married to two people at the same time □ *bigami; kesalahan berkahwin dua (bagi orang bukan Islam)* ➲ look at **monogamy, polygamy** ▸ **bigamist** /-mɪst/ *noun* [C] ▸ **bigamous** /ˈbɪɡəməs/ *adj*: *a bigamous relationship*

ˈbig-head *noun* [C] (*informal*) a person who thinks they are very important or clever because of sth they have done □ *(orang yg) besar kepala* ▸ **ˌbig-ˈheaded** *adj*

ˌbig ˈmouth *noun* [C] (*informal*) a person who talks too much and cannot keep a secret □ *(orang yg) banyak mulut*

bigot /ˈbɪɡət/ *noun* [C] a person who has very strong and unreasonable opinions and refuses to change them or listen to other people □ *pentaasub: a religious/racial bigot* ▸ **bigoted** *adj* ▸ **bigotry** /ˈbɪɡətri/ *noun* [U]

the ˈbig time *noun* [sing] success; fame □ *kejayaan; kemasyhuran: This is the role that could help her make it to the big time in Hollywood.*

ˈbig time¹ *adv* (*especially AmE slang*) very much □ *teruk: You screwed up big time, Wayne!*

ˈbig time² *adj* [only *before* a noun] important or famous □ *penting; terkenal: a big time politician/actor*

bike /baɪk/ *noun* [C] a bicycle or a motorbike □ *basikal atau motosikal: Hasan's just learnt to ride a bike.* ➲ picture at **bicycle**

> **MORE** Note that you **go on a/your bike** or **by bike**. You can also use the verbs **ride** and **cycle**. A **cyclist** is a person who rides a bike and a **motorcyclist** is a person who rides a motorbike.

bikini /bɪˈkiːni/ *noun* [C] (*pl* **bikinis**) a piece of clothing, in two pieces, that women wear for swimming □ *bikini*

bilateral /ˌbaɪˈlætərəl/ *adj* **1** involving two groups of people or two countries □ *dua hala/dwipihak; melibatkan dua pihak: bilateral relations/agreements/trade/talks* **2** involving both sides of the body or brain □ *bilateral/dwisisi* ➲ look at **multilateral, unilateral** ▸ **bilaterally** /-rəli/ *adv*

bile /baɪl/ *noun* [U] **1** a greenish brown liquid with a bitter unpleasant taste that is produced by your **liver** (= one of the body's main organs) to help your body break down the fats you eat □ *hempedu* **2** (*formal*) anger or hatred □ *kemarahan atau kebencian: The critic's review of the play was just a paragraph of bile.*

bilingual /ˌbaɪˈlɪŋɡwəl/ *adj* **1** able to speak two languages equally well □ *dwibahasa: Our children are bilingual in English and Spanish.* **2** having or using two languages □ *dwibahasa: a bilingual dictionary* ➲ look at **monolingual**

bill¹ /bɪl/ *noun* **1** [C] a piece of paper that shows how much money you owe for goods or services □ *bil: an electricity bill* ♦ *to pay a bill* **2** (*AmE* **check**) [C] a piece of paper that shows how much you have to pay for the food and drinks you have had in a restaurant □ *bil: Can I have the bill, please?* ➲ note at **restaurant 3** [C] (*AmE*) = **note¹**(4): *a ten-dollar bill* **4** [C] a plan for a possible new law □ *rang undang-undang: The bill was passed/defeated.* **5** [sing] the programme of entertainment offered in a show, concert, etc. □ *rancangan persembahan: Which bands are on the bill at the festival?* **6** [C] a bird's beak □ *paruh* ➲ picture on page P12
IDM **foot the bill** ➲ **foot²**

bill² /bɪl/ *verb* [T, usually passive] **bill sb/sth as sth** to describe sb/sth to the public in an advertisement, etc □ *diiklankan; dikatakan: This young player is being billed as 'the new Beckham'.*

billboard /ˈbɪlbɔːd/ (*BrE also* **hoarding**) *noun* [C] a large board near a road where advertisements are put □ *papan iklan*

billfold /ˈbɪlfəʊld/ (*AmE*) = **wallet**

billiards /ˈbɪliədz/ *noun* [U] a game played on a big table covered with cloth. You use a **cue** (= a long thin stick) to hit three balls against each other and into pockets at the corners and sides of the table □ *biliard: to have a game of/play billiards* ➲ look at **pool, snooker**

> **HELP** Note that when **billiard** comes before another noun it has no 's': *a billiard table*

billion /ˈbɪljən/ *number* 1 000 000 000 □ *bilion: billions of dollars*

> **HELP** Formerly, 'billion' was used with the meaning 'one million million'. We now say **trillion** for this. When you are counting, use billion without 's': *three billion yen*

ℹ For more information about numbers, look at the section on using numbers at the back of this dictionary.

billionaire /ˌbɪljəˈneə(r)/ *noun* [C] a person who has a billion pounds, dollars, etc.; an extremely rich person □ *jutawan; bilionair*

billow /ˈbɪləʊ/ *verb* [I] **1** to fill with air and move in the wind □ *menggelembung: curtains billowing in the breeze* **2** to move in large clouds through the air □ *berkepul-kepul: Smoke billowed from the chimneys.*

bin → biological

bins

litter bins

dustbin (AmE **garbage can**)

bin /bɪn/ noun [C] **1** a container that you put rubbish in □ *tong sampah*: *to throw something in the bin* ♦ *a litter bin* ♦ *The dustmen come to empty the bins on Wednesdays.* **2** a container, usually with a lid, for storing bread, flour, etc □ *bekas bertutup*: *a bread bin*

binary /ˈbaɪnəri/ adj using only 0 and 1 as a system of numbers, used especially by computers □ *perduaan; binari; sistem perduaan*: *the binary system*

bin bag noun [C] (*informal*) (*BrE*) a large plastic bag for putting rubbish in □ *beg sampah* ⊃ look at **liner**

bind¹ /baɪnd/ verb [T] (*pt, pp* **bound** /baʊnd/) **1 bind sb/sth (to sb/sth); bind A and B (together)** to tie or fasten with string or rope □ *mengikat*: *They bound the prisoner's hands behind his back.* **2 bind A to B; bind A and B (together)** to unite people, organizations, etc. so that they live or work together more happily or with better effect □ *mengikat; terikat*: *The two countries are bound together by a common language.* **3 bind sb (to sth)** to force sb to do sth by making them promise to do it or by making it their duty to do it □ *mengikat; terikat*: *to be bound by a law/an agreement* ♦ *The contract binds you to completion of the work within two years.* **4** [usually passive] to fasten sheets of paper into a cover to form a book □ *menjilid; dijilid*: *The book was bound in leather.*

bind² /baɪnd/ noun [sing] (*BrE informal*) something that you find boring or annoying □ *(sst yg) menyusahkan atau membosankan*: *I find housework a real bind.* **SYN** nuisance

binder /ˈbaɪndə(r)/ noun [C] a hard cover for holding sheets of paper, magazines, etc. together □ *penjilid; perekat*: *a ring binder* ⊃ picture at **stationery**

binding¹ /ˈbaɪndɪŋ/ adj making it necessary for sb to do sth they have promised or to obey a law, etc. □ *mengikat*: *This contract is legally binding.*

binding² /ˈbaɪndɪŋ/ noun **1** [C] a cover that holds the pages of a book together □ *kulit jilid* **2** [C,U] material that you fasten to the edge of sth to protect or decorate it □ *kulit jilid* **3 bindings** [pl] (in the activity of **skiing**) a device that fastens your boot to your **ski** (= a long, flat, narrow piece of wood or plastic) □ *pengikat ski*

binge¹ /bɪndʒ/ noun [C] (*informal*) a period of eating or drinking too much □ *tempoh makan atau minum keterlaluan*: *to go on a binge*

binge² /bɪndʒ/ verb [I] (**bingeing** or *AmE* also **binging**) (*informal*) **binge (on sth)** to eat or drink too much, especially without being able to control yourself □ *makan atau minum keterlaluan*: *When she's depressed, she binges on chocolate.*

bingo /ˈbɪŋɡəʊ/ noun [U] a game in which each player has a different card with numbers on it. The person in charge of the game calls numbers out and the winner is the first player to have all the numbers on their card called out. □ *permainan bingo*

binoculars

telescope

binoculars /bɪˈnɒkjələz/ noun [pl] an instrument with two **lenses** (= pieces of glass) which you look through in order to make objects in the distance seem nearer □ *binokular; teropong*: *a pair of binoculars*

biochemist /ˌbaɪəʊˈkemɪst/ noun [C] a person who studies **biochemistry** □ *ahli biokimia*

biochemistry /ˌbaɪəʊˈkemɪstri/ noun [U] the study of the chemistry of living things □ *biokimia*

biodegradable /ˌbaɪəʊdɪˈɡreɪdəbl/ adj that can be absorbed back into the earth naturally and so not harm the environment □ *biorosot*

biodiversity /ˌbaɪəʊdaɪˈvɜːsəti/ noun [U] the state of having a large number of different kinds of animals and plants which make a balanced environment □ *biokepelbagaian*

biofuel /ˈbaɪəʊfjuːəl/ noun [C,U] fuel made from plant or animal sources and used in engines □ *bahan api yg dibuat drpd tumbuhan atau haiwan*

biogas /ˈbaɪəʊɡæs/ noun [U] gas produced by natural waste, that can be used as fuel □ *biogas*

biographer /baɪˈɒɡrəfə(r)/ noun [C] a person who writes the story of sb else's life □ *penulis biografi*

biography /baɪˈɒɡrəfi/ noun [C,U] (*pl* **biographies**) the story of sb's life written by sb else □ *biografi*: *a biography of Napoleon* ♦ *I enjoy reading science fiction and biography.* ⊃ note at **book** ⊃ look at **autobiography** ▶ **biographical** /ˌbaɪəˈɡræfɪkl/ adj

biological /ˌbaɪəˈlɒdʒɪkl/ adj **1** connected with the scientific study of animals, plants and other living things □ *(berkenaan dgn) biologi*:

[I] **intransitive**, a verb which has no object: *He laughed.*

[T] **transitive**, a verb which has an object: *He ate an apple.*

biological research **2** involving the use of living things to destroy or damage other living things □ *(menggunakan kaedah) biologi*: *biological weapons*

biology /baɪˈɒlədʒi/ *noun* [U] the scientific study of living things □ *biologi*: *Biology is my favourite subject.* ⊃ note at **science** ⊃ look at **botany**, **zoology** ▶**biologist** /-dʒɪst/ *noun* [C]

birch /bɜːtʃ/ *noun* **1** (also ˈbirch tree) [C] a type of tree with smooth thin branches □ *pokok birch* **2** [U] the wood from the **birch** tree □ *kayu birch*

bird /bɜːd/ *noun* [C] a creature that is covered with feathers and has two wings and two legs. Most birds can fly □ *burung*: *Gulls and sparrows are birds.* ◆ *I like to feed the birds in winter.* ⊃ picture on **page P12**

> **MORE** Birds **fly** and **sing**. They build **nests** and **lay eggs**.

> **IDM** kill two birds with one stone ⊃ **kill¹**

bird of ˈprey *noun* [C] a bird that kills and eats other birds or small animals □ *burung pemangsa*

birdwatcher /ˈbɜːdwɒtʃə(r)/ (*AmE* also) / *noun* [C] a person who studies birds in their natural surroundings □ *pengkaji burung* ⊃ The formal word is **ornithologist**. ▶**birdwatching** *noun* [U]

Biro™ /ˈbaɪrəʊ/ *noun* [C] (*pl* Biros) (*BrE*) = **ballpoint**

birth /bɜːθ/ *noun* **1** [C,U] being born; coming out of a mother's body □ *kelahiran; lahir*: *It was a difficult birth.* ◆ *The baby weighed 3 kilos at birth* (= when it was born). ◆ *What's your date of birth?* (= the date on which you were born) **2** [sing] the beginning of sth □ *kemunculan*: *the birth of an idea* **3** [U] the country you belong to □ *keturunan*: *She's always lived in England but she's British by birth.*

> **IDM** give birth (to sb) to produce a baby □ *melahirkan (anak)*: *She gave birth to her second child at home.* ⊃ note at **baby**

ˈbirth certificate *noun* [C] an official document that states the date and place of sb's birth and the names of their parents □ *surat beranak; sijil kelahiran*

ˈbirth control *noun* [U] ways of limiting the number of children you have □ *pencegahan kehamilan* ⊃ look at **contraception**, **family planning**

birthday /ˈbɜːθdeɪ/ *noun* [C] the day in each year which is the same date as the one when you were born □ *hari jadi; hari lahir*: *My birthday's on November 15th.* ◆ *my eighteenth birthday* ◆ *a birthday present/card/cake*

> **TOPIC**
>
> **Birthdays**
> When it is somebody's birthday, we say **Happy Birthday!** If we know a person well, we send a special card to them or give them a present. They might have a birthday **party**, and a birthday **cake** with candles, one to represent each year of their age. Your 18th birthday is an important occasion when you legally become an adult. An **anniversary** is not the same as a **birthday**. It is the day in each year which is the same date as an important past event: *our wedding anniversary* ◆ *the anniversary of the end of the war*

birthmark /ˈbɜːθmɑːk/ *noun* [C] a red or brown mark on sb's body that has been there since they were born □ *tanda lahir*

birthplace /ˈbɜːθpleɪs/ *noun* **1** [C] the house or town where a person was born □ *tempat lahir* **2** [sing] the place where sth began □ *tempat bermulanya*: *Greece is the birthplace of the Olympic Games.*

ˈbirth rate *noun* [C] the number of babies born in a particular group of people during a particular period of time □ *kadar kelahiran*

biscuit /ˈbɪskɪt/ *noun* [C] **1** (*AmE* cookie) a type of small cake that is thin, hard and usually sweet □ *biskut*: *a chocolate biscuit* ◆ *a packet of biscuits* ⊃ picture at **cake 2** (*AmE*) a type of small simple cake that is not sweet □ *sejenis kuih* (spt roti)

bisexual /ˌbaɪˈsekʃuəl/ *adj* sexually attracted to both men and women □ *dwiseksual* ⊃ look at **heterosexual**, **homosexual**

bishop /ˈbɪʃəp/ *noun* [C] **1** a priest with a high position in some branches of the Christian Church, who is responsible for all the churches in a city or a district □ *biskop; uskup* ⊃ look at **archbishop 2** a piece used in the game of **chess** that is shaped like a **bishop's** hat □ *gajah (permainan catur)*

bison /ˈbaɪsn/ *noun* [C] (*pl* bison) a large wild animal that looks like a cow and is covered with hair □ *bison*

bistro /ˈbiːstrəʊ/ *noun* [C] (*pl* bistros) a small informal restaurant □ *bistro*

bit¹ /bɪt/ *noun*

➤SMALL AMOUNT **1** a bit [sing] slightly, a little □ *sedikit*: *I was a bit annoyed with him.* ◆ *I'm afraid I'll be a little bit late tonight.* ◆ *Could you be a bit quieter, please?* **2** a bit [sing] a short time or distance □ *sedikit; sekejap*: *Could you move forward a bit?* ◆ *I'm just going out for a bit.*

➤A LOT **3** a bit [sing] (*informal*) a lot □ *agak banyak (lama, lebat, dll)*: *It must have rained quite a bit during the night.*

➤SMALL PART **4** [C] a bit of sth a small piece, amount or part of sth □ *serpihan; cebisan*: *There were bits of broken glass all over the floor.* ◆ *Could you give me a bit of advice?* ◆ *Which bit of the film did you like best?*

➤COMPUTING **5** [C] the smallest unit of information that is stored in a computer's memory □ *bit*

➤FOR A HORSE **6** [C] a metal bar that you put in a horse's mouth when you ride it □ *kekang* ⊃ picture at **horse**

IDM **bit by bit** slowly or a little at a time □ *sedikit demi sedikit*: *Bit by bit we managed to get the information we needed.*

a bit much (*informal*) annoying or unpleasant □ *melampau*: *It's a bit much expecting me to work on Sundays.*

a bit of a (*informal*) rather a □ *agak sedikit*: *I've got a bit of a problem …*

bits and pieces (*informal*) small things of different kinds □ *keropas-kerapis; itu ini*: *I've finished packing except for a few bits and pieces.*

do your bit (*informal*) to do your share of sth; to help with sth □ *membantu*: *It won't take long to finish if we all do our bit.*

not a bit not at all □ *tdk sedikit pun*: *The holiday was not a bit what we had expected.*

to bits 1 into small pieces □ *hingga berkecai*: *She angrily tore the letter to bits.* **2** very much □ *seronok sangat*: *I was thrilled to bits when I won the competition.*

bit² *past tense of* **bite¹**

bitch¹ /bɪtʃ/ *verb* [I] (*informal*) **bitch (about sb/sth)** to say unkind and critical things about sb/sth, especially about sb who is not there □ *bersungut; mengomel; suka mengata*: *She's not the kind of person who would bitch about you behind your back.*

bitch² /bɪtʃ/ *noun* [C] a female dog □ *anjing betina*

bitchy /ˈbɪtʃi/ *adj* (**bitchier**; **bitchiest**) talking about other people in an unkind way □ *(yg) suka mengata*: *a bitchy remark*

ˈbite¹ /baɪt/ *verb* (*pt* **bit** /bɪt/; *pp* **bitten** /ˈbɪtn/) **1** [I,T] **bite (into sth); bite (sb/sth)** to cut or attack sb/sth with your teeth □ *menggigit*: *He picked up the bread and bit into it hungrily.* ♦ *Don't worry about the dog—she never bites.* ♦ *The cat bit me.* ⇒ picture at **lick 2** [I,T] (used about some insects and animals) to push a sharp point into your skin and cause pain □ *menyengat; memagut*: *He was bitten by a snake/mosquito/spider.*

HELP Wasps, bees and jellyfish do not **bite** you. They **sting** you.

3 [I] to begin to have an unpleasant effect □ *terasa; terkesan*: *In the South the job losses are starting to bite.*

IDM **bite sb's head off** to answer sb in a very angry way □ *menengking sso*

bite your ˈtongue to stop yourself from saying sth that might upset sb or cause an argument, although you want to speak □ *menahan diri drpd bercakap*

ˈbite² /baɪt/ *noun* **1** [C] a piece of food that you can put into your mouth □ *gigitan*: *She took a big bite of the apple.* **2** [sing] (*informal*) a a small meal □ *sedikit makanan*: *Would you like a bite to eat before you go?* **SYN** **snack 3** [C] a painful place on the skin made by an insect, a snake, a dog, etc. □ *gigitan*: *I'm covered in mosquito bites.*

bitten *past participle of* **bite¹**

ˈbitter¹ /ˈbɪtə(r)/ *adj* [**More bitter** and **most bitter** are the usual comparative and superlative forms, but **bitterest** can also be used.] **1** caused by anger or hatred □ *pahit; getir*: *a bitter quarrel* **2** **bitter (about sth)** (used about a person) very unhappy or angry about sth that has happened because you feel you have been treated unfairly □ *kecewa; sakit hati*: *She was very bitter about not getting the job.* **3** causing unhappiness or anger for a long time; difficult to accept □ *pahit*: *Failing the exam was a bitter disappointment to him.* ♦ *I've learnt from bitter experience not to trust him.* **4** having a sharp, unpleasant taste; not sweet □ *pahit*: *bitter coffee* ⇒ look at **sour 5** (used about the weather) very cold □ *sangat sejuk; menusuk ke tulang*: *a bitter wind* ▶ **bitterness** *noun* [U]

bitter² /ˈbɪtə(r)/ *noun* [U,C] (*BrE*) a type of dark beer that is popular in Britain □ *bir pahit*: *A pint of bitter, please.* ⇒ note at **beer**

ˈbitterly /ˈbɪtəli/ *adv* **1** in an angry and disappointed way □ *marah dan penuh kecewa*: *'I've lost everything,' he said bitterly.* **2** (used for describing strong negative feelings or cold weather) extremely □ *sangat (kecewa, sakit hati, sejuk, dsb)*: *bitterly disappointed/resentful* ♦ *a bitterly cold winter/wind*

bitty /ˈbɪti/ *adj* (**bittier**; **bittiest**) (*informal*) made up of a lot of parts which do not seem to be connected □ *tdk bersepadu*: *Your essay is rather bitty.*

bizarre /bɪˈzɑː(r)/ *adj* very strange □ *sangat pelik*: *The story had a most bizarre ending.* **SYN** **weird** ▶ **bizarrely** *adv*: *bizarrely dressed*

bk *abbr* (*pl* **bks**) = **book¹**(1) □ *buku*

ˈblack¹ /blæk/ *adj* (**blacker**; **blackest**) **1** having the darkest colour, like night or coal □ *hitam*: *a shiny black car* **2** belonging to a race of people with dark skins □ *kulit hitam*: *the black population of Britain* ♦ *black culture* **3** (used about coffee or tea) without milk or cream □ *o; tanpa susu atau krim*: *black coffee with sugar* **4** very angry □ *sangat marah*: *to give somebody a black look* **5** (used about a situation) without hope □ *gelap; muram*: *The economic outlook for the coming year is rather black.* **SYN** **depressing 6** funny in a cruel or unpleasant way □ *hitam*: *The film was a black comedy.*

IDM **black and blue** covered with **bruises** (= purple marks on the body) because you have been hit by sb/sth □ *lebam-lebam*

black and white (used about TV, photographs, etc.) showing no colours except black, white and grey □ *hitam putih*: *a film made in black and white*

ˈblack² /blæk/ *noun* **1** [U] the darkest colour, like night or coal □ *warna hitam*: *People often wear black* (= black clothes) *at funerals.* **2** usually **Black** [C] a person who belongs to a race of people with dark skin □ *orang kulit hitam*

HELP Be careful. In this meaning **black** is more common in the plural. It can sound offensive in the singular.

black → blanch

IDM **be in the black** (*informal*) to have some money in the bank □ *ada wang dlm akaun bank* **OPP** **be in the red**
in black and white in writing or in print □ *bertulis; secara hitam putih*: *I won't believe I've passed the exam till I see it in black and white.* ▶ **blackness** *noun* [U]

black³ /blæk/ *verb*
PHR V **black out** to become unconscious for a short time □ *pitam* **SYN** **faint**

BlackBerry™ /ˈblækbəri/ (*pl* **BlackBerrys**) *noun* [C] a very small computer that you hold in your hand and that you can use for phone calls, emails, looking at the Internet, etc: *While I'm away I'll check my emails on my BlackBerry.*

blackberry /ˈblækbəri/ (*pl* **blackberries**) *noun* [C] a small black fruit that grows wild on bushes □ *beri hitam* ➲ picture on **page P14**

blackbird /ˈblækbɜːd/ *noun* [C] a common European bird. The male is black with a yellow beak and the female is brown. □ *burung hitam*

blackboard /ˈblækbɔːd/ (*AmE* **chalkboard**) *noun* [C] a large dark board that teachers write on with **chalk** (= a small white or coloured stick) □ *papan hitam*

blackcurrant /ˌblækˈkʌrənt; ˈblækk-/ *noun* [C] a small round black fruit that grows on bushes □ *'blackcurrant'; sejenis beri hitam*

blacken /ˈblækən/ *verb* 1 [I,T] to become black; to make sth black □ *menghitamkan* 2 [T] to make sb seem bad, by saying unpleasant things about them □ *memburukkan; mencemarkan*: *to blacken somebody's name*

ˌblack ˈeye *noun* [C] an area of dark-coloured skin around sb's eye where they have been hit □ *mata lebam*: *He got a black eye in the fight.*

blackhead /ˈblækhed/ *noun* [C] a small spot on the skin with a black centre □ *bintik hitam*

ˌblack ˈhole *noun* [C] an area in outer space that pulls everything into it and from which nothing can escape □ *lubang hitam; kawasan di angkasa lepas yg menarik semua benda ke dlmnya*

blacklist /ˈblæklɪst/ *noun* [C] a list of people, companies, etc. who are considered bad or dangerous □ *senarai hitam*: *to be on somebody's blacklist* ▶ **blacklist** *verb* [T]: *She was blacklisted by all the major Hollywood studios.*

ˌblack ˈmagic *noun* [U] a type of magic that is used for evil purposes □ *sihir*

blackmail /ˈblækmeɪl/ *noun* [U] the crime of forcing a person to give you money or do sth for you, usually by threatening to make known sth which they want to keep secret □ *peras ugut; ugutan* ▶ **blackmail** *verb* [T] **blackmail sb (into doing sth)** ▶ **blackmailer** *noun* [C]

ˌblack ˈmarket *noun* [C, usually sing] the buying and selling of goods or foreign money in a way that is not legal □ *pasar gelap*: *to buy/sell something on the black market*

blackout /ˈblækaʊt/ *noun* [C] 1 a period of time during a war, when all lights must be turned off or covered so that the enemy cannot see them □ *perbuatan menggelapkan sst kawasan* 2 a period when you are unconscious for a short time □ *pitam*: *to have a blackout*

blacksmith /ˈblæksmɪθ/ *noun* [C] a person whose job is to make and repair things made of iron □ *tukang besi*

bladder /ˈblædə(r)/ *noun* [C] the part of your body where **urine** (= waste liquid) collects before leaving your body □ *pundi kencing* ➲ picture at **body**

blade /bleɪd/ *noun* [C] 1 the flat, sharp part of a knife, etc. □ *mata (pisau, dsb)* ➲ picture at **garden, penknife, scissors, tool** 2 one of the flat, wide parts that turn round very quickly on an aircraft, etc □ *kipas (helikopter, dsb)*: *the blades of a propeller* ➲ picture on **page P6** 3 the flat, wide part of an **oar** (= one of the long poles that you use to move a boat through water) □ *daun dayung* 4 a long, thin leaf of grass □ *helai (rumput)*: *a blade of grass*

blag /blæg/ *verb* [T] (**blagging; blagged**) (*BrE informal*) to persuade sb to give you sth, or to let you do sth, by talking to them in a clever or amusing way □ *memujuk; meyakinkan*: *I blagged some tickets for the game.*

blame¹ /bleɪm/ *verb* [T] **blame sb (for sth); blame sth on sb/sth** to think or say that a certain person or thing is responsible for sth bad that has happened □ *menyalahkan*: *The teacher blamed me for the accident.* ♦ *Some people blame the changes in the climate on pollution.*
IDM **be to blame (for sth)** to be responsible for sth bad □ *patut disalahkan (kerana sst)*: *The police say that careless driving was to blame for the accident.*
I don't blame you/her, etc. (for doing) to think that sb is not wrong to do sth; to understand sb's reason for doing sth □ *tdk menyalahkan*: *I don't blame you for feeling fed up.*
shift the blame/responsibility (for sth) (onto sb) ➲ **shift¹**

blame² /bleɪm/ *noun* [U] **blame (for sth)** responsibility for sth bad □ *dipersalahkan; dipertanggungjawabkan*: *The government must take the blame for the economic crisis.* ♦ *The report put the blame on rising prices.* ♦ *Why do I always get the blame?*

blameless /ˈbleɪmləs/ *adj* (*written*) not guilty; that should not be **blamed** □ *tdk bersalah*: *He insisted that his wife was blameless and hadn't known about his crimes.* **SYN** **innocent**

blanch /blɑːntʃ/ *verb* 1 [I] (*formal*) **blanch (at sth)** to become pale because you are shocked or frightened □ *menjadi pucat* 2 [T] to prepare food, especially vegetables, by putting it in boiling water for a short time □ *mencelur*

VOWELS iː **see** i **any** ɪ **sit** e **ten** æ **hat** ɑː **father** ɒ **got** ɔː **saw** ʊ **put** uː **too** u **usual**

bland /blænd/ *adj* (**blander**; **blandest**) **1** ordinary or not very interesting □ *biasa sahaja; tdk menarik*: *a rather bland style of writing* **2** (used about food) mild or lacking in taste □ *hambar* **3** not showing any emotion □ *bersahaja* ▶**blandly** *adv*

blank¹ /blæŋk/ *adj* **1** empty, with nothing written, printed or recorded on it □ *kosong; tdk bertulis, dirakam, dsb*: *a blank CD/piece of paper/page* **2** without feelings, understanding or interest □ *kosong; tanpa perasaan, kefahaman, dsb*: *a blank expression on his face* ♦ *My mind went blank when I saw the exam questions* (= I couldn't think properly or remember anything). ▶**blankly** *adv*: *She stared at me blankly, obviously not recognizing me.*

blank² /blæŋk/ *noun* [C] an empty space □ *tempat kosong; kosong*: *Fill in the blanks in the following exercise.* ♦ (*figurative*) *I couldn't remember his name—my mind was a complete blank.*
IDM **draw a blank** ➔ **draw¹**

blank cheque *noun* [C] a cheque that has been signed but that has an empty space so that the amount to be paid can be written in later □ *cek kosong*

blanket¹ /'blæŋkɪt/ *noun* [C] **1** a cover made of wool, etc. that is put on beds to keep people warm □ *selimut* ➔ picture at **bed 2** a thick layer or covering of sth □ *litupan; liputan*: *a blanket of snow*
IDM **a wet blanket** ➔ **wet¹**
▶**blanket** *verb* [T, often passive] **blanket sth (in/with sth)**: *The countryside was blanketed in snow.*

blanket² /'blæŋkɪt/ *adj* [only *before* a noun] affecting everyone or everything □ *menyeluruh*: *There is a blanket ban on journalists reporting the case.*

blare /bleə(r)/ *verb* [I,T] **blare (sth) (out)** to make a loud, unpleasant noise □ *membingar; berbunyi bising*: *Car horns were blaring in the street outside.* ♦ *The loudspeaker blared out pop music.* ▶**blare** *noun* [sing]: *the blare of a siren*

blasphemy /'blæsfəmi/ *noun* [U] writing or speaking about God in a way that shows a lack of respect □ *nistaan terhadap Tuhan* ▶**blasphemous** /'blæsfəməs/ *adj*

blast¹ /blɑːst/ *noun* [C] **1** an explosion, especially one caused by a bomb □ *letupan* **2** a sudden strong current of air □ *hembusan; tiupan kencang*: *a blast of cold air* **3** a loud sound made by a musical instrument, etc □ *bunyi kuat*: *The driver gave a few blasts on his horn.*

blast² /blɑːst/ *verb* [T] **1** to make a hole, a tunnel, etc. in sth with an explosion □ *membuat lubang, terowong, dsb dengan letupan*: *They blasted a tunnel through the mountainside.* **2** to criticize sth very strongly □ *mengecam; mengkritik*: *Union leaders last night blasted the government's proposals.*
PHR V **blast off** (used about a **spacecraft**) to leave the ground; to take off □ *dilancarkan*

'blast-off *noun* [U] the time when a **spacecraft** (= a vehicle that travels in space) leaves the ground □ *pelancaran*

blatant /'bleɪtnt/ *adj* (used about actions which are considered bad) done in an obvious and open way without caring if people are shocked □ *terang-terangan*: *a blatant lie* ▶**blatantly** *adv*

blaze¹ /bleɪz/ *verb* [I] **1** to burn with bright strong flames □ *memarak* **2 blaze (with sth)** to be extremely bright; to shine brightly □ *bersinar terang-benderang; berapi-api (kerana marah, dsb)*: *I woke up to find that the room was blazing with sunshine.* ♦ (*figurative*) *'Get out!' she shouted, her eyes blazing with anger.*

blaze² /bleɪz/ *noun* **1** [C] a large and often dangerous fire □ *api yg marak; api kebakaran*: *It took firefighters four hours to put out the blaze.* **2** [sing] **a blaze of sth** a very bright show of light or colour □ *bersemarak; gilang-gemilang*: *In the summer the garden was a blaze of colour.* ♦ *The new theatre was opened in a blaze of publicity* (= newspapers, etc. gave it a lot of attention).

blazer /'bleɪzə(r)/ *noun* [C] a jacket, especially one that has the colours or symbol of a school, club or team on it □ *blazer*: *a school blazer*

bleach¹ /bliːtʃ/ *verb* [T] to make sth white or lighter in colour by using a chemical or by leaving it in the sun □ *memutihkan; melunturkan*

bleach² /bliːtʃ/ *noun* [C,U] a strong chemical substance used for making clothes, etc. whiter or for cleaning things □ *bahan pemutih/peluntur*

bleak /bliːk/ *adj* (**bleaker**; **bleakest**) **1** (used about a situation) bad; without much hope □ *suram; gelap*: *a bleak future for the next generation* **2** (used about the weather) cold and grey □ *sejuk dan suram*: *a bleak winter's day* **3** (used about a place) cold, empty and grey □ *tandus; sejuk serta suram*: *the bleak Arctic landscape* ▶**bleakly** *adv* ▶**bleakness** *noun* [U]

bleary /'blɪəri/ *adj* (used about the eyes) red, tired and unable to see clearly □ *(mata) buram*: *We were all rather bleary-eyed after the overnight journey.* ▶**blearily** *adv*

bleat /bliːt/ *verb* **1** [I] to make the sound of a sheep □ *mengembek* **2** [I,T] to speak in a weak or complaining voice □ *merungut-rungut* ▶**bleat** *noun* [C]

bleed /bliːd/ *verb* [I] (*pt, pp* **bled** /bled/) to lose blood □ *berdarah; mengeluarkan darah* ▶**bleeding** *noun* [U]: *He wrapped a scarf around his arm to stop the bleeding.*

bleep¹ /bliːp/ *noun* [C] a short, high sound made by a piece of electronic equipment □ *bunyi blip*

bleep² /bliːp/ *verb* **1** [I] (used about machines) to make a short high sound □ *berbunyi blip*: *Why is the computer bleeping?* **2** (*AmE* also **beep**) [T] to attract sb's attention using an electronic machine □ *memanggil (dgn alat keloi)*: *Please bleep the doctor on duty immediately.*

bleeper /ˈbliːpə(r)/ (*AmE* **beeper**) *noun* [C] a small piece of electronic equipment that **bleeps** to let a person (for example a doctor) know when sb is trying to contact them □ *alat keloi* **SYN pager**

blemish /ˈblemɪʃ/ *noun* [C] a mark that spoils the way sth looks □ *tompok; cacat* ▶**blemish** *verb* [T] (*figurative*): *The defeat has blemished the team's perfect record.*

blend¹ /blend/ *verb* [T] **blend A with B; blend A and B (together)** to mix □ *mencampurkan; mengadunkan*: *First blend the flour and the melted butter together.*
PHR V blend (in) with sth to combine with sth in an attractive or suitable way □ *berpadu; secocok; sesuai*: *The new room is decorated to blend in with the rest of the house.*
blend (into sth) to match or be similar to the surroundings sb/sth is in □ *bersepadu; kelihatan sama dgn*: *These animals' ability to blend into their surroundings provides a natural form of defence.*

blend² /blend/ *noun* [C] a mixture □ *campuran; paduan*: *He had the right blend of enthusiasm and experience.*

blender /ˈblendə(r)/ (*BrE also* **liquidizer**) *noun* [C] an electric machine that is used for making food into liquid □ *pengisar* ⊃ picture at **mixer**

bless /bles/ *verb* [T] (*pt, pp* **blessed** /blest/) to ask for God's help and protection for sb/sth □ *memohon berkat*
IDM be blessed with sth/sb to be lucky enough to have sth/sb □ *beruntung kerana dikurniai sst/sso*: *The West of Ireland is an area blessed with many fine sandy beaches.*
Bless you! what you say to a person who has just **sneezed** (= blown air noisily out of their nose, for example because they have a cold) □ *ungkapan balas apabila mendengar orang bersin*

blessed /ˈblesɪd/ *adj* **1** having God's help and protection □ *(yg) dirahmati Tuhan*: *the Blessed Virgin Mary* **2** (in religious language) lucky □ *beruntung; bertuah*: *Blessed are the pure in heart.* **SYN fortunate 3** [only before a noun] (*formal*) giving great pleasure □ *(yg) menggembirakan/ disyukuri*: *The cool breeze brought blessed relief from the heat.*

blessing /ˈblesɪŋ/ *noun* [C] **1** a thing that you are grateful for or that brings happiness □ *syukur; rahmat*: *It's a great blessing that we have two healthy children.* ♦ *Not getting that job was a blessing in disguise* (= sth which does not seem lucky but is a good thing in the end). **2** [usually sing] (a prayer asking for) God's help and protection □ *doa selamat*: *The priest said a blessing.* **3** [usually sing] approval or support □ *restu; persetujuan*: *They got married without their parents' blessing.*

blew past tense of **blow¹**

blight¹ /blaɪt/ *verb* [T] to spoil or damage sth □ *merosakkan*: *His career has been blighted by injuries.*

blight² /blaɪt/ *noun* **1** [U,C] any disease that kills plants, especially crops □ *hawar*: *potato blight* **2** [sing, U] **blight (on sb/sth)** something that has a bad effect on a situation, sb's life or the environment □ *perosak*

blind¹ /blaɪnd/ *adj* (**blinder; blindest**) **1** unable to see □ *buta*: *a blind person* ♦ *to be completely/ partially blind*

> **HELP** People who cannot see very well are sometimes described as **partially sighted** or **visually impaired** rather than **blind**.

2 blind (to sth) not wanting to notice or understand sth □ *buta; tdk nampak*: *He was completely blind to her faults.* **3** without reason or thought □ *membabi buta; tanpa fikiran waras*: *He drove down the motorway in a blind panic.* **4** impossible to see round □ *terselindung*: *You should never overtake on a blind corner.*
IDM turn a blind eye (to sth) to pretend not to notice sth bad is happening so that you do not have to do anything about it □ *berpura-pura tdk nampak (sst)* ▶**blindly** *adv* ▶**blindness** *noun* [U]

blind² /blaɪnd/ *verb* [T] **1** to make sb unable to see □ *menjadi buta; menjadi silau*: *Her grandfather had been blinded in an accident* (= permanently). ♦ *Just for a second I was blinded by the sun* (= for a short time). **2 blind sb (to sth)** to make sb unable to think clearly or behave in a sensible way □ *mengaburkan*

blind³ /blaɪnd/ *noun* **1** [C] a piece of cloth or other material that you pull down to cover a window □ *bidai* ⊃ picture at **curtain 2 the blind** *noun* [pl] people who are unable to see □ *orang buta*

blind 'date *noun* [C] an arranged meeting between a man and a woman who have never met before to see if they like each other enough to begin a romantic relationship □ *janji temu dgn orang yg belum dikenali*

blindfold /ˈblaɪndfəʊld/ *noun* [C] a piece of cloth, etc. that is used for covering sb's eyes □ *kain (dsb) penutup mata* ▶**blindfold** *verb* [T]

'blind spot *noun* [C] **1** the part of the road just behind you that you cannot see when driving a car □ *titik buta* **2** if you have a **blind spot** about sth, you cannot understand or accept it □ *sst yg sukar difahami atau diterima*

bling /blɪŋ/ (also ˌbling-ˈbling) *noun* [U] (*informal*) expensive shiny jewellery and fashionable clothes □ *barang kemas mahal dan pakaian yg mengikut fesyen* ▶**bling** (also ˌbling-ˈbling) *adj*

blink /blɪŋk/ *verb* **1** [I,T] to shut your eyes and open them again very quickly □ *mengelipkan*

blinker → blog

mata: Oh dear! You blinked just as I took the photograph! ➲ look at **wink** 2 [I] (used about a light) to come on and go off again quickly □ *berkelip-kelip* ▶**blink** *noun* [C]

blinker /'blɪŋkə(r)/ *noun* 1 [C] (*informal*) = **indicator**(2) 2 **blinkers** [pl] pieces of leather that are placed at the side of a horse's eyes to stop it from looking sideways □ *tuntun mata*

blinkered /'blɪŋkəd/ *adj* not considering every aspect of a situation; not willing to accept different ideas about sth □ *berfikiran sempit*: *a blinkered policy/attitude/approach* **SYN** narrow-minded

blip /blɪp/ *noun* [C] 1 a light flashing on the screen of a piece of equipment, sometimes with a short high sound □ *cahaya yg memancar-mancar pd skrin sst peralatan* 2 a small problem that does not last for long □ *masalah kecil*

bliss /blɪs/ *noun* [U] perfect happiness □ *kebahagiaan* ▶**blissful** /'blɪsfl/ *adj* ▶**blissfully** /-fəli/ *adv*

blister¹ /'blɪstə(r)/ *noun* [C] a small painful area of skin that looks like a bubble and contains clear liquid □ *lecur; lepuh*. Blisters are usually caused by rubbing or burning.

blister² /'blɪstə(r)/ *verb* [I,T] 1 to get or cause blisters □ *melecur; melepuh* 2 to swell and break open or to cause sth to do this □ *bergelembung-gelembung*: *The paint is starting to blister.*

blistering /'blɪstərɪŋ/ *adj* very strong or extreme □ *sangat (panas, laju, dll)*: *the blistering midday heat* ♦ *The runners set off at a blistering pace.*

blitz /blɪts/ *noun* [C] **a blitz (on sth)** a sudden effort or attack on sb/sth □ *serbuan kilat*: *The police are planning a blitz on vandalism.*

blizzard /'blɪzəd/ *noun* [C] a very bad storm with strong winds and a lot of snow □ *ribut salji* ➲ note at **storm**

bloated /'bləʊtɪd/ *adj* unusually large and uncomfortable because of liquid, food or gas inside □ *kembung*: *I felt a bit bloated after all that food.*

blob /blɒb/ *noun* [C] a small piece of a thick liquid □ *tompok; tepek*: *a blob of paint/cream/ink*

bloc /blɒk/ *noun* [C, with sing or pl verb] a group of countries that work closely together because they have the same political interests □ *blok*

block¹ /blɒk/ *noun* [C]
▶PIECE OF STH **1** a large, heavy piece of sth, usually with flat sides □ *bongkah; ketul*: *a block of wood* ♦ *huge concrete blocks*
▶BUILDING **2** a large building that is divided into separate flats or offices □ *blok*: *a block of flats* ➲ look at **apartment block, office block** ➲ picture on **page P9**
▶STREETS **3** a group of buildings in a town which has streets on all four sides □ *blok*: *The restaurant is three blocks away.*
▶AMOUNT **4** a quantity of sth or an amount of time that is considered as a single unit □ *kelompok; blok*: *The class is divided into two blocks of fifty minutes.*
▶THAT STOPS YOU **5** [usually sing] a thing that makes movement or progress difficult or impossible □ *sekatan*: *a block to further progress in the talks* ➲ look at **roadblock**

IDM **have a block (about sth)** to be unable to think or understand sth properly □ *kebuntuan fikiran (ttg sst)*: *I had a complete mental block. I just couldn't remember his name.*

block² /blɒk/ *verb* [T] 1 **block sth (up)** to make it difficult or impossible for sb/sth to pass □ *menyekat; tersekat; merintangi*: *Many roads are completely blocked by snow.* 2 to prevent sth from being done □ *menyekat; menghalang*: *The management tried to block the deal.* 3 to prevent sth from being seen by sb □ *melindung; menghalang*: *Get out of the way, you're blocking the view!*

PHR V **block sth off** to separate one area from another with sth solid □ *menyekat; menutup*: *This section of the motorway has been blocked off by the police.*

block sth out to try not to think about sth unpleasant □ *melenyapkan; melupakan*: *She tried to block out the memory of the crash.*

blockade /blɒ'keɪd/ *noun* [C] a situation in which a place is surrounded by soldiers or ships in order to prevent goods or people from reaching it □ *pengepungan* ▶**blockade** *verb* [T]

blockage /'blɒkɪdʒ/ *noun* [C] a thing that is preventing sth from passing; the state of being blocked □ *sekatan; keadaan tersumbat*: *a blockage in the drainpipe* ♦ *There are blockages on some major roads.*

blockbuster /'blɒkbʌstə(r)/ *noun* [C] a book or film with an exciting story which is very successful and popular □ *buku atau filem yg amat berjaya dan popular*

block 'capital *noun* [C, usually pl] a big letter such as 'A' (not 'a') □ *huruf besar*: *Please write your name in block capitals.*

blog /blɒg/ (also **weblog**) *noun* [C] a personal record that sb puts on their website □ *blog*: *Have you seen his blog from the festival?* ▶**blog** *verb* [I] (**blogging; blogged**): *I'll be blogging again on Tuesday.* ▶**blogger** *noun* [C]

TOPIC

Blogs

A **blogger** is someone who writes a **blog** (or **weblog**) about things that interest them and about websites that they have visited. You visit someone's blog to read their **posts** (= messages) and you can **post comments** (= add messages) about what they have said. A popular **microblogging** site (= a service for very short blogs) is **Twitter™**, where you **follow** the people whose **tweets** (= short messages) you want to read.

[I] **intransitive**, a verb which has no object: *He laughed.* [T] **transitive**, a verb which has an object: *He ate an apple.*

bloke /bləʊk/ noun [C] (BrE slang) a man □ *orang (lelaki)*: *He's a really nice bloke.*

blonde (also **blond**) /blɒnd/ adj with fair or yellow hair □ *(orang yg) berambut perang muda*: *Both my sisters have blonde hair.* ♦ *a small, blond boy* ▶ **blonde** noun [C]: *She's a blonde.* ⊃ look at **brunette**

> **MORE** When describing men the spelling **blond** is used: *He's tall and blond.* The noun is usually only used of women and is spelled **blonde**. It is sometimes considered offensive to refer to a woman in this way.

blood /blʌd/ noun [U] the red liquid that flows through your body □ *darah*: *The heart pumps blood around the body.* ⊃ look at **bleed**
IDM **in your blood** a strong part of your character □ *sudah menjadi darah daging*: *A love of the countryside was in his blood.*
in cold blood ⊃ **cold¹**
shed blood ⊃ **shed²**
your (own) flesh and blood ⊃ **flesh**

bloodbath /ˈblʌdbɑːθ/ noun [sing] an act of violently killing many people □ *pembunuhan beramai-ramai; mandi darah*

blood-curdling adj very frightening □ *mengerikan*: *a blood-curdling scream*

blood donor noun [C] a person who gives some of their blood for use in medical operations □ *penderma darah*

blood group (also **blood type**) noun [C] any of several different types of human blood □ *kumpulan darah*: *'What blood group are you?' 'Blood group/type O.'*

bloodless /ˈblʌdləs/ adj **1** without killing or violence □ *tanpa pertumpahan darah*: *a bloodless revolution* **2** (used about a part of the body) very pale □ *pucat lesi*

blood pressure noun [U] the force with which the blood travels round the body □ *tekanan darah*: *to have high/low blood pressure*

bloodshed /ˈblʌdʃed/ noun [U] the killing or harming of people □ *pertumpahan darah*: *Both sides in the war want to avoid further bloodshed.*

bloodshot /ˈblʌdʃɒt/ adj (used about the white part of the eyes) full of red lines, for example when sb is tired □ *mata merah*

blood sport noun [C] a sport in which animals or birds are killed □ *sukan berburu*

bloodstain /ˈblʌdsteɪn/ noun [C] a mark or spot of blood on sth □ *kesan darah* ▶ **bloodstained** adj

bloodstream /ˈblʌdstriːm/ noun [sing] the blood as it flows through the body □ *aliran darah*: *drugs injected straight into the bloodstream*

bloodthirsty /ˈblʌdθɜːsti/ adj wanting to use violence or to watch scenes of violence □ *suka menggunakan atau melihat keganasan*

blood transfusion noun [C] the process of putting new blood into sb's body □ *pemindahan/transfusi darah*

blood type = **blood group**

blood vessel noun [C] any of the tubes in your body which blood flows through □ *saluran darah* ⊃ look at **artery, vein**

bloody /ˈblʌdi/ adj (**bloodier; bloodiest**) **1** involving a lot of violence and killing □ *melibatkan pertumpahan darah*: *a bloody war* **2** covered with blood □ *berlumuran darah*: *a bloody knife* **3** [only before a noun] also adv (BrE slang) a swear word used for emphasizing a comment or an angry statement □ *sial; celaka; betul-betul*: *What a bloody stupid thing to say!*

> **HELP** Be careful. Many people find this word offensive.

bloom¹ /bluːm/ noun [C] a flower □ *bunga*
IDM **in bloom** with its flowers open □ *mekar*: *All the wild plants are in bloom.*

bloom² /bluːm/ verb [I] to produce flowers □ *berbunga*: *This shrub blooms in May.*

blossom¹ /ˈblɒsəm/ noun [C,U] a flower or a mass of flowers, especially on a fruit tree in the spring □ *bunga; jambak bunga*: *The apple tree is in blossom.* ⊃ picture at **tree**

blossom² /ˈblɒsəm/ verb [I] **1** (used especially about trees) to produce flowers □ *berbunga* **2 blossom (into sth)** to become more healthy, confident or successful □ *berkembang atau meningkat menjadi (sst)*: *This young runner has blossomed into a top-class athlete.*

blot¹ /blɒt/ verb [T] (**blotting; blotted**) **1** to remove liquid from a surface by pressing soft paper or cloth on it □ *memedap* **2** to make a spot or a mark on sth, especially ink on paper □ *membuat tompok/titik*
PHR V **blot sth out** to cover or hide sth □ *menutup; melindungi; melenyapkan*: *Fog blotted out the view completely.* ♦ *She tried to blot out the memory of what happened.*

blot² /blɒt/ noun [C] **1** a spot of sth, especially one made by ink on paper □ *tompok* **SYN** **stain** **2 a blot on sth** a thing that spoils your happiness or other people's opinion of you □ *tompok hitam; sst yg menjejaskan nama baik sso*

blotch /blɒtʃ/ noun [C] a temporary mark or an area of different colour on skin, plants, cloth, etc. □ *tompok; belak*: *The blotches on her face showed that she had been crying.* ▶ **blotchy** (also **blotched**) adj

blotting paper noun [U] soft paper that you use for drying wet ink after you have written sth on paper □ *kertas pedap*

blouse /blaʊz/ noun [C] a piece of clothing like a shirt, that women wear □ *blaus*

blow¹ /bləʊ/ verb (pt **blew** /bluː/; pp **blown** /bləʊn/)

blow → blue-collar 86

blow¹
- ▶WITH MOUTH **1** [I] to send air out of the mouth □ *meniup; menghembus*: *The policeman asked me to blow into the breathalyser.*
- ▶WIND/AIR **2** [I,T] (used about wind, air, etc.) to be moving or to cause sth to move □ *bertiup*: *A gentle breeze was blowing.* **3** [I] to move because of the wind or a current of air □ *ditiup angin; berterbangan*: *The balloons blew away.* ◆ *My papers blew all over the garden.*
- ▶INSTRUMENT **4** [I,T] to produce sound from a musical instrument, etc. by blowing air into it □ *meniup*: *The referee's whistle blew for the end of the match.* ◆ *He blew a few notes on the trumpet.*
- ▶MAKE STH **5** [T] to make or shape sth by blowing air out of your mouth □ *meniup*: *to blow bubbles/smoke rings* ◆ *to blow (somebody) a kiss* (= to kiss your hand and pretend to blow the kiss towards sb)
- ▶ELECTRICITY **6** [I,T] when a **fuse** (= a thin piece of wire in an electrical system) stops working suddenly because the electric current is too strong □ *terbakar*: *A fuse has blown.* ◆ *I think the kettle's blown a fuse.*
- ▶MONEY **7** [T] (*informal*) **blow sth (on sth)** to spend or waste a lot of money on sth □ *memboroskan; menjolikan wang*: *She blew all her savings on a trip to China.*
- ▶OPPORTUNITY **8** [T] (*informal*) to waste an opportunity □ *mensia-siakan peluang*: *I think I've blown my chances of promotion.* ◆ *You had your chance and you blew it.*

IDM **blow your nose** to clear your nose by blowing strongly through it into a **handkerchief** (= a piece of cloth) or a **tissue** (= a piece of paper) □ *menghembuskan hingus*

PHR V **blow sth apart** to completely destroy sth in an explosion □ *meletupkan*

blow over to disappear without having a serious effect □ *reda; berlalu*: *The scandal will soon blow over.*

blow up 1 to explode or to be destroyed in an explosion □ *meletup*: *The car blew up when the door was opened.* **2** to start suddenly and strongly □ *membadai*: *A storm blew up in the night.* ◆ *A huge row blew up about money.*

blow sth up 1 to make sth explode or to destroy sth in an explosion □ *meletupkan*: *The terrorists tried to blow up the plane.* **2** to fill sth with air or gas □ *mengisi angin*: *to blow up a balloon* **3** to make a photograph bigger □ *membesarkan*

blow up (at sb) (*informal*) to become very angry □ *memberang; mengamuk*: *The teacher blew up when I said I'd forgotten my homework.*

blow

blowing   sucking

blow² /bləʊ/ *noun* [C] **1** a hard hit from sb's hand, a weapon, etc □ *pukulan*: *She aimed a blow at me.* **2** **a blow (to sb/sth)** a sudden shock or disappointment □ *kejutan; tamparan; bencana*: *It was a blow when I didn't get the job.* **3** an act of blowing □ *perbuatan menghembus*: *Give your nose a blow!*

IDM **a blow-by-blow account, description, etc. (of sth)** an account, etc. of an event that gives all the exact details of it □ *laporan, cerita, dsb (ttg sst) detik demi detik*

come to blows (with sb) (over sth) to start fighting or arguing (about sth) □ *mula bergaduh (dgn sso) (kerana sst)*

deal sb/sth a blow; deal a blow to sb/sth ➔ **deal¹**

blow-dry *verb* [T] (**blow-drying**; **blow-dries**; *pt, pp* **blow-dried**) to dry and shape sb's hair using a **hairdryer** (= a machine that produces hot air) and a brush □ *meniupkeringkan (rambut)*

blown *past participle* of **blow¹**

blowout /ˈbləʊaʊt/ *noun* [C] (*informal*) **1** a burst tyre □ *(tayar) meletup; pancit*: *We had a blowout on the motorway.* **SYN** **puncture** **2** a very large meal at which people eat too much; a large party or social event □ *hidangan makan yg besar; majlis keramaian*

blubber /ˈblʌbə(r)/ *noun* [U] the fat of sea animals, such as whales □ *blubber; lemak binatang laut spt ikan paus*

bludgeon /ˈblʌdʒən/ *verb* [T] **1** to hit sb several times with a heavy object □ *memukul berulang kali dgn objek berat; membelantan* **2** **bludgeon sb (into sth/into doing sth)** to force sb to do sth, especially by arguing with them □ *memaksa sso berbuat sst; mendesak berulang kali*: *They tried to bludgeon me into joining their protest.*

blue¹ /bluː/ *adj* (**bluer**; **bluest**) **1** having the colour of a clear sky when the sun shines □ *biru*: *His eyes were bright blue.* ◆ *light/dark blue* **2** (*informal*) (often used in songs) sad □ *sedih; sugul*: *He'd been feeling blue all week.*

IDM **black and blue** ➔ **black¹**

once in a blue moon ➔ **once**

blue² /bluː/ *noun* **1** [C,U] the colour of a clear sky when the sun shines □ *warna biru*: *a deep blue* ◆ *dressed in blue* (= blue clothes) **2** **the blues** [pl] a type of slow sad music □ *muzik blues*: *a blues singer* **3** **the blues** [pl] (*informal*) feelings of sadness □ *rasa sugul atau murung*: *to have the blues*

IDM **out of the blue** suddenly; unexpectedly □ *tiba-tiba; tanpa disangka*: *I didn't hear from him for years and then this email came out of the blue.*

blue-ˈchip *adj* [only *before* a noun] a blue-chip investment is thought to be safe and likely to make a profit □ *cip biru*: *blue-chip companies*

blue-ˈcollar *adj* [only *before* a noun] doing or involving physical work with the hands rather than office work □ *kolar biru* ➔ look at **white-collar**

ð **then** s **so** z **zoo** ʃ **she** ʒ **vi**s**ion** h **how** m **man** n **no** ŋ **si**n**g** l **leg** r **red** j **yes** w **wet**

blueish = bluish

blueprint /ˈbluːprɪnt/ noun [C] a photograph of a plan, or a description of how to make, build or achieve sth □ *cetak biru*

bluff¹ /blʌf/ verb [I,T] to try to make people believe that sth is true when it is not, usually by appearing very confident □ *menemberang: Don't take any notice of him, he's just bluffing.*
IDM bluff your way in, out, through, etc. sth to trick sb in order to get into, out of a place, etc. □ *menemberang supaya dpt masuk, keluar, melalui, dsb sst: We managed to bluff our way into the stadium by saying we were journalists.*

bluff² /blʌf/ noun [U,C] making sb believe that you will do sth when you really have no intention of doing it, or that you know sth when, in fact, you do not know it □ *temberang*
IDM call sb's bluff ➔ **call¹**

bluish (also **blueish**) /ˈbluːɪʃ/ adj (informal) slightly blue □ *kebiru-biruan: bluish green*

blunder¹ /ˈblʌndə(r)/ noun [C] a stupid mistake □ *kesilapan (yg tdk sepatutnya): I'm afraid I've made a terrible blunder.*

blunder² /ˈblʌndə(r)/ verb [I] to make a stupid mistake □ *membuat kesilapan (yg tdk sepatutnya)*
PHR V blunder about, around, etc. to move in an uncertain or careless way, as if you cannot see where you are going □ *meraba-raba (kerana gelap atau tdk nampak): We blundered about in the dark, trying to find the light switch.*

blunt /blʌnt/ adj (**blunter**; **bluntest**) **1** (used about a knife, pencil, tool, etc.) without a sharp edge or point □ *tumpul: blunt scissors* **OPP** sharp **2** (used about a person, comment, etc.) very direct; saying what you think without trying to be polite □ *terus terang: I'm sorry to be so blunt, but I'm afraid you're just not good enough.* ▶ blunt verb [T] ▶ bluntly adv ▶ bluntness noun [U]

blur¹ /blɜː(r)/ noun [C, usually sing] something that you cannot see clearly or remember well □ *kabur; samar-samar: Without my glasses, their faces were just a blur.*

blur² /blɜː(r)/ verb [I,T] (**blurring**; **blurred**) to become or to make sth less clear □ *menjadi kabur; mengaburi: The words on the page blurred as tears filled her eyes.* ▶ blurred adj

blurt /blɜːt/ verb
PHR V blurt sth out to say sth suddenly or without thinking □ *mengatakan sst dgn tiba-tiba: We didn't want to tell Mum but Ann blurted the whole thing out.*

blush /blʌʃ/ verb [I] to become red in the face, especially because you are embarrassed or feel guilty □ *menjadi merah (muka): She blushed with shame.* ▶ blush noun [C, usually sing]

blusher /ˈblʌʃə(r)/ (AmE also **blush**) noun [U,C] a coloured cream or powder that some people put on their cheeks to give them more colour □ *pemerah pipi*

blustery /ˈblʌstəri/ adj (used to describe the weather) with strong winds □ *berangin kencang: The day was cold and blustery.*

BO /ˌbiː ˈəʊ/ abbr = **body odour**

boa constrictor /ˌbəʊə kənˈstrɪktə(r)/ (also **boa**) noun [C] a large South American snake that kills animals for food by wrapping its body around them and crushing them □ *ular boa*

boar /bɔː(r)/ noun [C] (pl boar or boars) **1** a wild pig □ *babi hutan* **2** a male pig □ *babi jantan* ➔ note at **pig**

board¹ /bɔːd/ noun **1** [C] a long, thin, flat piece of wood used for making floors, walls, etc. □ *papan: The old house needed new floorboards.* **2** [C] a thin flat piece of wood, etc. used for a particular purpose □ *papan: an ironing board ♦ a surfboard ♦ a noticeboard ♦ board games* (= games you play on a board) **3** [C, with sing or pl verb] a group of people who control an organization, company, etc □ *lembaga: The board of directors is/are meeting to discuss the firm's future. ♦ a board meeting* **4** [U] the meals that are provided when you stay in a hotel, etc □ *makanan: The prices are for a double room and full board* (= all the meals).
IDM above board ➔ **above**
across the board ➔ **across**
on board on a ship or an aircraft □ *atas kapal atau kapal terbang: All the passengers were safely on board.*

board² /bɔːd/ verb **1** [I,T] to get on a plane, ship, bus, etc. □ *menaiki (kapal, bas, dll): We said goodbye and boarded the train.* **2** [I] be boarding when a plane or ship **is boarding**, it is ready for passengers to get on □ *sedia utk dinaiki (kapal terbang atau kapal): Flight LH7059 to Hamburg is now boarding at Gate 27.*
PHR V board sth up to cover with boards □ *menutup sst dgn papan: Nobody lives there now—it's all boarded up.*

boarder /ˈbɔːdə(r)/ noun [C] (BrE) **1** a child who lives at school and goes home for the holidays. □ *murid yg tinggal di asrama* **2** a person who pays to live at sb's house □ *penyewa bilik (di rumah sso)* ➔ look at **lodger**

'boarding house noun [C] a private house where you can pay to stay and have meals for a period of time □ *rumah tumpangan*

'boarding pass (also **'boarding card**) noun [C] a document that you must show in order to get on a plane or ship □ *kad berlepas; pas masuk*

'boarding school noun [C] a school that children live at while they are studying, going home only in the holidays □ *sekolah berasrama*

boardroom /ˈbɔːdruːm; -rʊm/ noun [C] the room where the **board of directors** (= the group of people in charge of a company or an organization) meets □ *bilik lembaga*

boast /bəʊst/ verb **1** [I] to talk with too much pride about sth that you have or can do

VOWELS   iː see   i any   ɪ sit   e ten   æ hat   ɑː father   ɒ got   ɔː saw   ʊ put   uː too   u usual

boastful → body odour 88

□ *bermegah-megah; bercakap besar*: *I wish she wouldn't boast about her family so much.* **2** [T] (used about a place) to have sth that it can be proud of □ *mempunyai sst yg boleh dimegahkan*: *The town boasts over a dozen restaurants.* ▶ boast *noun* [C]

boastful /ˈbəʊstfl/ *adj* (used about a person or the things that they say) showing too much pride □ *suka bermegah-megah*

boat /bəʊt/ *noun* [C] **1** a small vehicle that is used for travelling across water □ *bot; perahu; sampan*: *The cave can only be reached by boat/in a boat.* ♦ *a rowing/fishing boat* ➪ picture on **page P6 2** any ship □ *kapal*: *When does the next boat to France sail?*
IDM rock the boat ➪ rock²

TOPIC

Boats

A boat is smaller than a **ship**. A **liner** is used to carry people for long distances, called **voyages** or, if they are for pleasure, **cruises**. A **ferry** is used to carry people and sometimes cars for short distances, called **crossings**. A ship that carries goods from one place to another is a **freighter**. A large boat with sails is a **yacht**. **Lifeboat** has two meanings: it is a special boat that is used to rescue people who are in danger at sea, or it is a small boat that is kept on a ship and is used by people to escape if the ship is going to sink. A boat that you move by rowing with oars is a **rowing boat**. The front of a boat is the **bow**, the back is the **stern**. When you are facing the front of a boat the side on the right is called **starboard**, the side on the left is called **port**. The people who work on a boat are its **crew**. The person in command is the **captain**.

---

boats

rowing boat (*AmE* rowboat) — oar

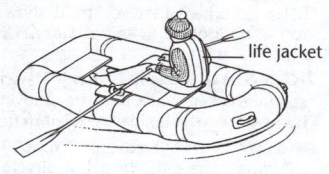

dinghy — life jacket

bob /bɒb/ *verb* [I,T] (**bobbing**; **bobbed**) to move quickly up and down; to make sth do this □ *terumbang-ambing; turun naik*: *The boats in the harbour were bobbing up and down in the water.* ♦ *She bobbed her head down below the top of the wall.*
PHR V **bob up** to appear suddenly from behind or under sth □ *timbul; muncul*: *He disappeared and then bobbed up again on the other side of the pool.*

bobsleigh /ˈbɒbsleɪ/ (*AmE* **bobsled** /ˈbɒbsled/) *noun* [C] a racing vehicle for two or more people that slides over snow along a track □ *kereta lumba luncur salji* ➪ look at **sleigh, sledge, toboggan**

bode /bəʊd/ *verb*
IDM **bode well/ill (for sb/sth)** to be a sign that sb/sth will have a good/bad future □ *pertanda baik/buruk (utk sso/sst)*

bodily¹ /ˈbɒdɪli/ *adj* [only *before* a noun] of the human body; physical □ *jasmani*: *First we must attend to their bodily needs* (= make sure that they have a home, enough to eat, etc.).

bodily² /ˈbɒdɪli/ *adv* by taking hold of the body □ *dgn memegang badan*: *She picked up the child and carried him bodily from the room.*

body /ˈbɒdi/ *noun* (*pl* **bodies**)
▶PERSON/ANIMAL **1** [C] the whole physical form of a person or an animal □ *tubuh*: *the human body* **2** [C] the part of a person that is not their legs, arms or head □ *badan*: *She had injuries to her head and body.* **3** [C] a dead person □ *mayat*: *The police have found a body in the canal.*
▶MAIN PART **4** [sing] the main part of sth □ *bahagian utama*: *We agree with the body of the report, although not with certain details.*
▶GROUP OF PEOPLE **5** [C, with sing or pl verb] a group of people who work or act together, especially in an official way □ *badan; perkumpulan*: *The governing body of the college meets/meet once a month.*
▶OBJECT **6** [C] (*formal*) an object □ *benda*: *The doctor removed a foreign body from the child's ear.*
IDM **in a body** all together □ *bersama-sama; semua sekali*

bodyboard /ˈbɒdibɔːd/ *noun* [C] a short light type of **surfboard** that you ride lying on your front □ *sejenis papan luncur* ▶ **bodyboarding** *noun* [U]

bodybuilding /ˈbɒdibɪldɪŋ/ *noun* [U] making the muscles of the body stronger and larger by exercise □ *bina badan* ▶ **bodybuilder** *noun* [C] □ *ahli bina badan*

bodyguard /ˈbɒdigɑːd/ *noun* [C] a person or group of people whose job is to protect sb □ *pengawal peribadi*

ˈbody language *noun* [U] showing how you feel by the way you move, stand, sit, etc., rather than by what you say □ *bahasa gerak-geri*: *I could tell by his body language that he was scared.*

ˈbody odour *noun* [U] (*abbr* **BO**) the unpleasant smell from sb's body, especially of sweat □ *bau badan*

ʌ **c**u**p**   ɜː **b**i**rd**   ə **a**go   eɪ **p**a**y**   əʊ **g**o   aɪ **m**y   aʊ **n**ow   ɔɪ **b**o**y**   ɪə **n**ear   eə **h**air   ʊə **p**ure

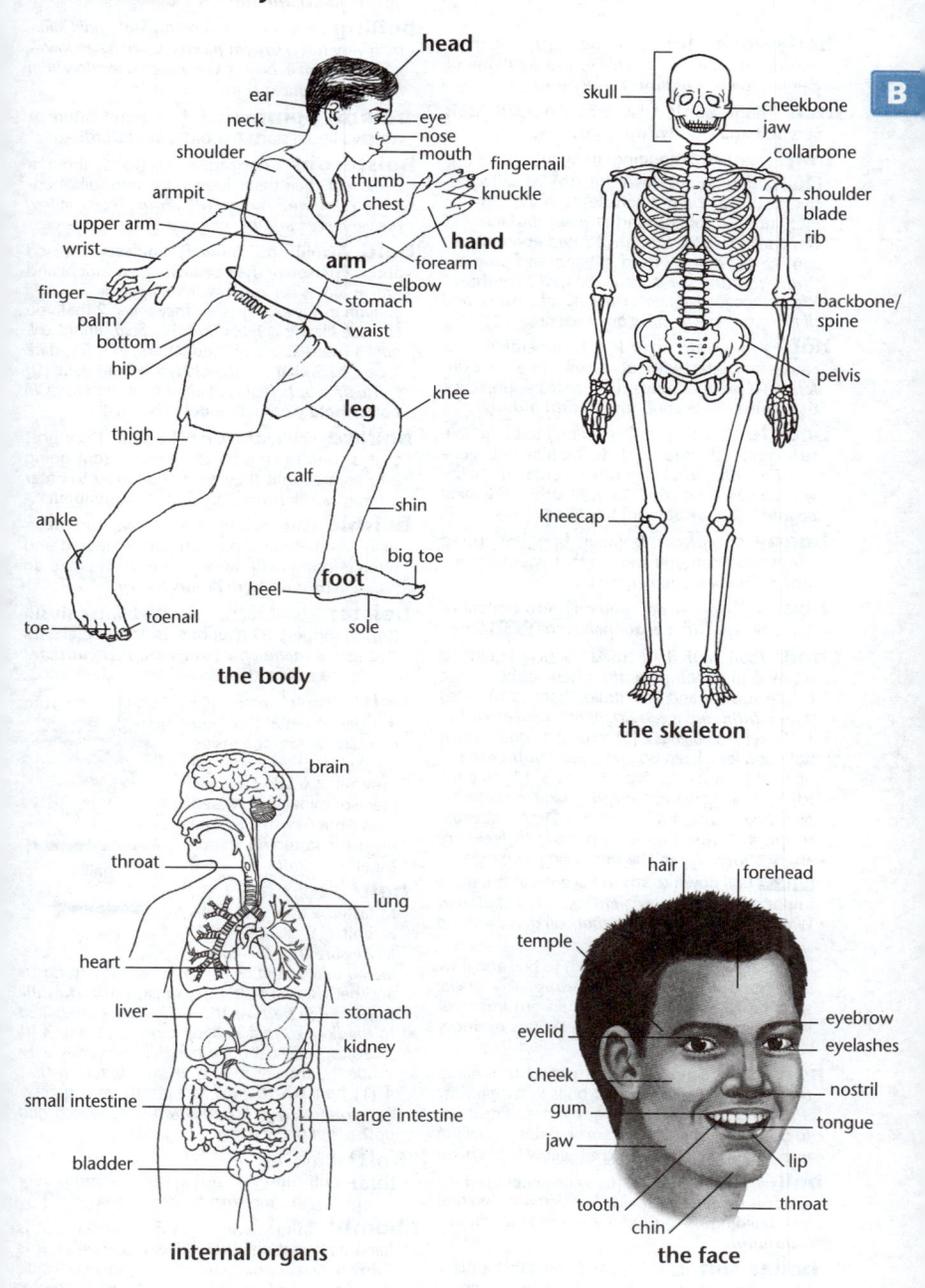

The Human Body

the body

- head
- ear
- neck
- shoulder
- armpit
- upper arm
- wrist
- finger
- palm
- bottom
- hip
- thigh
- ankle
- toe
- eye
- nose
- mouth
- fingernail
- thumb
- knuckle
- chest
- arm
- hand
- forearm
- elbow
- stomach
- waist
- leg
- knee
- calf
- shin
- big toe
- foot
- heel
- sole
- toenail

the skeleton

- skull
- cheekbone
- jaw
- collarbone
- shoulder blade
- rib
- backbone/spine
- pelvis
- kneecap

internal organs

- brain
- throat
- lung
- heart
- liver
- stomach
- kidney
- small intestine
- large intestine
- bladder

the face

- hair
- forehead
- temple
- eyelid
- cheek
- gum
- jaw
- tooth
- chin
- eyebrow
- eyelashes
- nostril
- tongue
- lip
- throat

[C] **countable**, a noun with a plural form: *one book, two books* [U] **uncountable**, a noun with no plural form: *some sugar*

bodywork /ˈbɒdiwɜːk/ noun [U] the main outside structure of a vehicle, usually made of painted metal □ *badan (kenderaan)*

bog¹ /bɒg/ noun [C,U] an area of ground that is very soft and wet □ *rawa*: *a peat bog*

bog² /bɒg/ verb (**bogging**; **bogged**)
PHR V **bog sb/sth down (in sth)** [usually passive] **1** (used about a vehicle) to make sth sink into mud or soft ground □ *menyebabkan sst terbenam ke dlm lumpur* **2** (used about a person) to prevent sb from making any progress □ *menghalang sso drpd mencapai kemajuan*: *We got bogged down in a long discussion and didn't have time to make any decisions.*

bogey /ˈbəʊgi/ noun [C] **1** something that causes fear, often without reason □ *momok* **2** (informal) a piece of **mucus** (= the sticky substance that forms inside your nose) □ *tahi hidung*

boggle /ˈbɒgl/ verb [I] (informal) to be unable to imagine sth; impossible to imagine or believe □ *sukar dibayangkan atau dipercayai*: '*What will happen if his plan doesn't work?*' '*The mind boggles!*' ⊃ look at **mind-boggling**

boggy /ˈbɒgi/ adj (**boggier**; **boggiest**) (used about land) soft and wet, so that your feet sink into it □ *berbencah; berpaya*

bogus /ˈbəʊgəs/ adj pretending to be real or genuine □ *palsu*: *a bogus policeman* **SYN** **false**

boil¹ /bɔɪl/ verb **1** [I] (used about a liquid) to reach a high temperature where bubbles rise to the surface and the liquid changes to a gas □ *mendidih; menggelegak*: *Water boils at 100°C.* ♦ *The kettle's boiling.* **2** [T] to heat a liquid until it boils and let it keep boiling □ *mendidihkan*: *Boil all drinking water for five minutes.* **3** [I,T] to cook (sth) in boiling water □ *merebus*: *Put the potatoes on to boil, please.* ♦ *to boil an egg* ⊃ note at **cook**, **recipe 4** [I] (used about a person) to feel very angry □ *meradang*: *She was boiling with rage.*
PHR V **boil down to sth** to have sth as the most important point □ *yg pentingnya; pokoknya*: *What it all boils down to is that you don't want to spend too much money.*
boil over 1 (used about a liquid) to boil and flow over the sides of a pan □ *meruap*: *You let the soup boil over.* **2** (used about an argument or sb's feelings) to become more serious or angry □ *meluap-luap*

boil² /bɔɪl/ noun **1** [sing] a period of boiling; the point at which a liquid boils □ *tempoh sst dididihkan*: *You'll have to give those shirts a boil to get them clean.* **2** [C] a small, painful swelling under your skin, with a red or yellow top □ *bisul*

boiler /ˈbɔɪlə(r)/ noun [C] a container in which water is heated to provide hot water or heating in a building or to produce steam in an engine □ *dandang*

'boiler suit noun [C] (*AmE* **coveralls**) a piece of clothing that you wear over your normal clothes to protect them when you are doing dirty work □ *baju luar*

boiling /ˈbɔɪlɪŋ/ (also **boiling 'hot**) adj (informal) very hot □ *sangat panas*: *Open a window—it's boiling hot in here.* ♦ *Can I open a window? I'm boiling.* ⊃ note at **cold**

'boiling point noun [C] the temperature at which a liquid starts to boil □ *takat didih*

boisterous /ˈbɔɪstərəs/ adj (used about a person or their behaviour) noisy and full of energy □ *riuh dan cergas; tdk diam*: *Their children are very nice but they can get a bit too boisterous.*

bold /bəʊld/ adj (**bolder**; **boldest**) **1** (used about a person or their behaviour) confident and not afraid □ *berani*: *Not many people are bold enough to say exactly what they think.* **2** that you can see clearly □ *jelas; ketara*: *bold, bright colours* **3** (used about printed letters) in thick, dark type □ *berhuruf tebal*: *bold type* ▶ **bold** noun [U] □ *huruf tebal*: *Highlight the important words in bold.* ▶ **boldly** adv ▶ **boldness** noun [U]

bollard /ˈbɒlɑːd/ noun [C] a short thick post that is used to stop motor vehicles from going into an area that they are not allowed to enter □ *tonggak sekatan* ⊃ picture at **roundabout**

bolshie (also **bolshy**) /ˈbɒlʃi/ adj (*BrE informal*) (used about a person) bad-tempered and often refusing to do what people ask them to do □ *perengus dan degil; panas baran*

bolster /ˈbəʊlstə(r)/ verb [T] **bolster sb/sth (up)** to support or encourage sb/sth; to make sth stronger □ *memberangsangkan; menguatkan*: *His remarks did nothing to bolster my confidence.*

bolt¹ /bəʊlt/ noun [C] **1** a bar of metal that you can slide across the inside of the door in order to fasten it □ *selak* **2** a small piece of metal that is used with a **nut** (= a small metal ring) for fastening things together □ *bolt*

bolt² /bəʊlt/ verb **1** [T] to fasten a door, etc. with a **bolt¹(1)** □ *menyelak*: *Make sure that the door is locked and bolted.* **2** [T] to fasten one thing to another using a **bolt¹(2)** □ *dilekatkan atau ditambat dgn bolt*: *All the tables have been bolted to the floor so that nobody can steal them.* **3** [I] (used especially about a horse) to run away very suddenly, usually in fear □ *lari dgn tiba-tiba* **4** [T] **bolt sth (down)** to eat sth very quickly □ *memolok*: *She bolted down a sandwich and dashed out of the house.*

bolt³ /bəʊlt/ adv
IDM **bolt upright** sitting or standing very straight □ *(duduk atau berdiri) tegak*

bomb¹ /bɒm/ noun **1** [C] a container that is filled with material that will explode when it is thrown or dropped, or when a device inside it makes it explode □ *bom*: *Fortunately, the car* bomb failed to go off. **2 the bomb** [sing] nuclear weapons □ *senjata nuklear*: *How many countries have the bomb now?* **3 a bomb** [sing] (*informal*) a lot of money □ *banyak wang; mahal*: *That car must have cost you a bomb!*

bomb² /bɒm/ *verb* **1** [T] to attack a city, etc. with bombs □ *mengebom*: *Enemy forces have bombed the bridge.* **2** [I] (*BrE informal*) **bomb along, down, up, etc.** to move along very fast in the direction mentioned, especially in a vehicle □ *memecut*: *He was bombing along at 100 miles an hour when the police stopped him.*

bombard /bɒmˈbɑːd/ *verb* [T] to attack a place with bombs or guns □ *mengebom; membedil*: *They bombarded the city until the enemy surrendered.* ◆ (*figurative*) *The reporters bombarded the minister with questions.* ▶ **bombardment** *noun* [C,U]: *The main radio station has come under enemy bombardment.*

bomb disposal *noun* [U] the removing or exploding of bombs in order to make an area safe □ *pemusnahan bom*: *a bomb disposal expert*

bomber /ˈbɒmə(r)/ *noun* [C] **1** a type of plane that drops bombs □ *kapal terbang pengebom* **2** a person who makes a bomb explode in a public place □ *pengebom*

bombshell /ˈbɒmʃel/ *noun* [C, usually sing] an unexpected piece of news, usually about sth unpleasant □ *sst yg menggemparkan*: *The head teacher dropped a bombshell when he said he was resigning.*

bona fide /ˌbəʊnə ˈfaɪdi/ *adj* real or genuine □ *sebenarnya; memang ada*: *This car park is for the use of bona fide customers only.*

bond /bɒnd/ *noun* **1** [C] something that joins two or more people or groups of people together, such as a feeling of friendship □ *ikatan*: *Our two countries are united by bonds of friendship.* **2** [C] a certificate that you can buy from a government or company that promises to pay you interest on the money you have given □ *bon*: *government bonds*

bone¹ /bəʊn/ *noun* **1** [C] one of the hard parts inside the body of a person or an animal that are covered with muscle, skin, etc □ *tulang*: *He's broken a bone in his hand.* ◆ *This fish has got a lot of bones in it.* **2** [U] the substance that bones are made of □ *tulang*: *knives with bone handles*
IDM **have a bone to pick with sb** to have sth that you want to complain to sb about □ *ada sst yg hendak dipersoalkan dgn sso*
make no bones about (doing) sth to do sth in an open honest way without feeling nervous or worried about it □ *tdk teragak-agak (membuat sst)*: *She made no bones about telling him exactly what she thought about him.*

bone² /bəʊn/ *verb* [T] to take the bones out of fish or meat □ *menulangi*

bone dry *adj* completely dry □ *kering betul*: *Give that plant some water—it's bone dry.*

bone marrow (also **marrow**) *noun* [U] the soft substance that is inside the bones of a person or an animal □ *tulang sumsum*

bonfire /ˈbɒnfaɪə(r)/ *noun* [C] a large fire that you build outside to burn rubbish, as part of a festival, etc. □ *unggun api*

Bonfire Night *noun* [C,U] in Britain, the night of 5 November □ *Pesta Unggun Api*

> **CULTURE**
>
> On this day people in Britain light fireworks and burn a model of a man called a **guy** on top of a bonfire, to celebrate the failure of Guy Fawkes to blow up the Houses of Parliament in the 17th century.

bonkers /ˈbɒŋkəz/ *adj* [not before a noun] (*slang*) crazy □ *gila*: *I'd go bonkers if I worked here full-time.* **SYN** **mad**

bonnet /ˈbɒnɪt/ *noun* [C] **1** a type of hat which covers the sides of the face and is fastened with strings under the chin □ *(topi) bonet* **2** (*AmE* **hood**) the front part of a car that covers the engine □ *bonet* ⊃ picture on **page P7**

bonus /ˈbəʊnəs/ *noun* [C] **1** a payment that is added to what is usual □ *bonus*: *All our employees receive an annual bonus.* **2** something good that you get in addition to what you expect □ *(sst) kelebihan*: *I enjoy my job, and having my own office is an added bonus.*

bony /ˈbəʊni/ *adj* (**bonier; boniest**) so thin that you can see the shape of the bones □ *kurus; cengkung*: *long bony fingers*

boo /buː/ *exclam, noun* [C] (*pl* **boos**) **1** a sound you make to show that you do not like sb/sth □ *ejekan*: *The band's act was met with boos from the audience.* **2** a sound you make to frighten or surprise sb □ *seruan utk memeranjatkan sso*: *He jumped out from behind the door and said 'boo'.* ▶ **boo** *verb* [I,T]

boob /buːb/ *noun* [C] **1** (*slang*) a woman's breast □ *tetek* **2** (*informal*) a silly mistake □ *kesilapan yg memalukan* ▶ **boob** *verb* [I] (*informal*): *I'm afraid I've boobed again.*

booby prize /ˈbuːbi praɪz/ *noun* [C] a prize that is given as a joke to the person or team that comes last in a competition □ *hadiah si corot*

booby trap /ˈbuːbi træp/ *noun* [C] a device that will kill, injure or surprise sb when they touch the object that it is connected to □ *jerangkap* ▶ **booby-trap** *verb* [T]

book¹ /bʊk/ *noun* **1** [C] (*abbr* **bk**) a written work that is published as printed pages fastened together inside a cover, or in electronic form □ *buku*: *I'm reading a book on astrology.* ◆ *She's writing a book about her life abroad.* ◆ *Do you have any books by William Golding?* ◆ *hardback/paperback books* ⊃ look at **e-book 2** [C] a number of pieces of paper, fastened together inside a cover, for people to write or draw on □ *buku (tulis, lukis, dsb)*: *Please write down all the new vocabulary in your exercise books.* ◆ *a notebook*

book → boost 92

♦ *a sketch book* **3** [C] a number of things fastened together in the form of a book □ *buku*: *a book of stamps* ♦ *a chequebook* **4 books** [pl] the records that a company, etc. keeps of the amount of money it spends and receives □ *buku akaun*: *We employ an accountant to keep the books.*
IDM **be in sb's good/bad books** (*informal*) to have sb pleased/angry with you □ *menyebabkan sso suka/marah akan sso itu*: *He's been in his girlfriend's bad books since he forgot her birthday.* **by the book** exactly according to the rules □ *betul-betul mengikut peraturan*: *A policeman must always do things by the book.* **(be) on sb's books** (to be) on the list of an organization □ *dlm senarai sso*: *The employment agency has hundreds of qualified secretaries on its books.*

TOPIC

Books
An **author** is a person who writes a book. The name of a book is its **title**. A **novel** is a book that tells a story, usually divided into **chapters**. The story of sb's life is called a **biography**, or an **autobiography** if a person writes their own life story. You use a **reference book**, for example a **dictionary**, an **atlas** or an **encyclopedia**, to look up information. Reference books usually have a **list of contents** at the front and an **index** at the back, to show you what information the book contains. A **hardback** has a hard **cover** and a **paperback** has a soft cover. Do you prefer reading **fiction** (= stories) or **non-fiction** (= facts)?

---

book² /bʊk/ *verb* **1** [I,T] to arrange to have or do sth at a particular time □ *menempah*: *Have you booked a table, sir?* ♦ *to book a seat on a plane/train/bus* ♦ *I've booked a hotel room for you/I've booked you a hotel room.* ♦ *I'm sorry, but this evening's performance is fully booked* (= there are no seats left). ♦ *I forgot to book.* **2** [T] (*informal*) to officially write down the name of a person who has done sth wrong □ *menyaman, mendenda*: *The police booked her for* (= charged her with) *dangerous driving.* ♦ *The player was booked for a foul and then sent off for arguing.*
PHR V **book in** to say that you have arrived at a hotel, etc., and sign your name on a list □ *mendaftar masuk*
book sb in to arrange a room for sb at a hotel, etc. in advance □ *menempahkan bilik utk sso*: *I've booked you in at the George Hotel.*

bookcase /'bʊkkeɪs/ *noun* [C] a piece of furniture with shelves to keep books on □ *almari buku* ⊃ picture on **page P8**

bookie /'bʊki/ (*informal*) = **bookmaker**

booking /'bʊkɪŋ/ *noun* [C,U] the arrangement you make in advance to have a hotel room, a seat on a plane, etc. □ *tempahan*: *Did you manage to make a booking?* ♦ *No advance booking is necessary.*

booking office *noun* [C] an office where you buy tickets □ *pejabat tempahan*

bookkeeping /'bʊkkiːpɪŋ/ *noun* [U] keeping the accounts of the money that a company, etc. spends or receives □ *simpan kira*

booklet /'bʊklət/ *noun* [C] a small thin book, usually with a soft cover, that gives information about sth □ *buku kecil*

bookmaker /'bʊkmeɪkə(r)/ (also *informal* **bookie**) *noun* **1** [C] a person whose job is to take bets on horse races, etc. □ *penerima taruhan* **2 the bookmaker's** [sing] a shop, etc. where you can bet money on a race or an event □ *kedai tempat membeli taruhan; kedai judi* ⊃ look at **betting shop**

bookmark /'bʊkmɑːk/ *noun* [C] **1** a narrow piece of card, etc. that you put between the pages of a book so that you can find the same place again easily □ *penanda buku* **2** (also **favorite**) a file from the Internet that you have stored on your computer □ *penanda buku*

bookseller /'bʊkselə(r)/ *noun* [C] a person whose job is selling books □ *penjual buku*

bookshelf /'bʊkʃelf/ (*pl* **bookshelves** /'bʊkʃelvz/) *noun* [C] a shelf that you keep books on □ *rak buku*

bookshop /'bʊkʃɒp/ (*AmE* **bookstore**) *noun* [C] a shop that sells books □ *kedai buku* ⊃ look at **library**

bookstall /'bʊkstɔːl/ (*AmE* **'news-stand**) *noun* [C] a type of small shop, which is open at the front, selling newspapers, magazines and books, for example at a station □ *gerai buku*

bookstore /'bʊkstɔː(r)/ (*AmE*) = **bookshop**

bookworm /'bʊkwɜːm/ *noun* [C] a person who likes reading books very much □ *kutu buku*

boom¹ /buːm/ *noun* [C] **1** a period in which sth increases or develops very quickly □ *pertambahan pesat*: *a boom in car sales* ⊃ look at **slump** **2** [usually sing] a loud deep sound □ *dentuman*: *the distant boom of thunder*

boom² /buːm/ *verb* **1** [I,T] **boom (sth) (out)** to make a loud deep sound □ *berdentum*: *The loudspeaker boomed out instructions to the crowd.* **2** [I] to grow very quickly in size or value □ *berkembang pesat*: *Business is booming in the computer industry.*

boomerang /'buːməræŋ/ *noun* [C] a curved piece of wood that returns to you when you throw it in a particular way □ *bumerang*

boon /buːn/ *noun* [C] a thing that is very helpful and that you are grateful for □ *rahmat; manfaat*

boost¹ /buːst/ *verb* [T] to increase sth in number, value or strength □ *meningkatkan; menambahkan*: *If we lower the price, that should boost sales.* ♦ *The good exam result boosted her confidence.*

boost² /buːst/ *noun* [C] something that encourages people; an increase □ *merangsangkan; menggalakkan*: *The president's visit gave a*

ð **then**   s **so**   z **zoo**   ʃ **she**   ʒ **vi**sion   h **how**   m **man**   n **no**   ŋ **sing**   l **leg**   r **red**   j **yes**   w **wet**

boost to the soldiers' morale. ♦ *The fall in the value of the pound has led to a boost in exports.*

boot¹ /buːt/ noun [C] **1** a type of shoe that covers your foot and ankle and often part of your leg □ *but (kasut)*: *ski boots* ♦ *walking/climbing boots* ♦ *football boots* ⮕ picture at **shoe 2** (*AmE* **trunk**) the part of a car where you put luggage, usually at the back □ *but (kereta)*: *I'll put the luggage in the boot.* ⮕ picture on **page P7**

boot² /buːt/ verb (*informal*) **1** [T] to kick sth/sb hard □ *menendang kuat*: *He booted the ball over the fence.* **2** [I,T] to make a computer ready for use when it is first switched on □ *but*

PHR V **boot sb/sth out** to force sb/sth to leave a place □ *menendang sso/sst keluar*: *The boys were booted out of the club for fighting.*

booth /buːð/ noun [C] a small place with thin walls that divide it from the rest of the room or area, where you can do sth that is private □ *pondok; gerai*: *a phone booth*

booty /ˈbuːti/ noun [U] things that are taken by thieves or captured by soldiers in a war □ *harta rampasan*

booze¹ /buːz/ noun [U] (*informal*) alcohol □ *arak*

booze² /buːz/ verb [I] (*informal*) to drink a lot of alcohol □ *minum arak*: *He went out boozing with some friends on Saturday.*

border¹ /ˈbɔːdə(r)/ noun [C] **1** a line that divides two countries, etc.; the land close to this line □ *sempadan*: *The refugees escaped across/over the border.* ♦ *the Moroccan border* ♦ *the border between France and Italy* ♦ *Italy's border with France* **2** a band or narrow line around the edge of sth, often for decoration □ *tepi; sibar-sibar*: *a white tablecloth with a blue border*

> **OTHER WORDS FOR**
> **border**
> We use **border** and **frontier** to talk about the line that divides two countries or states. We usually use **border** to talk about natural divisions: *The river forms the border between the two countries.* **Boundary** is usually used for the line that divides smaller areas: *the county boundary*

border² /ˈbɔːdə(r)/ verb [T] to form a border to an area; to be on the border of an area □ *menyempadani; disempadani*: *The road was bordered with trees.*

PHR V **border on sth 1** to be almost the same as sth □ *hampir merupakan*: *The dictator's ideas bordered on madness.* **2** to be next to sth □ *bersebelahan dgn*: *Our garden borders on the railway line.*

borderline /ˈbɔːdəlaɪn/ noun [sing] the line that marks a division between two different cases, conditions, etc. □ *pinggiran*: *He's a borderline case—he may pass the exam or he may fail.*

bore¹ /bɔː(r)/ verb **1** [T] to make sb feel bored, especially by talking too much □ *membosan-*

kan: *I hope I'm not boring you.* **2** [I,T] to make a long deep hole with a tool □ *menebuk lubang*: *This drill can bore (a hole) through solid rock.* **3** past tense of **bear¹**

bore² /bɔː(r)/ noun **1** [C] a person who talks a lot in a way that is not interesting □ *orang yg membosankan* **2** [sing] (*informal*) something that you have to do that you do not find interesting □ *perkara yg membosankan*: *It's such a bore having to learn these lists of irregular verbs.*

bored /bɔːd/ adj **bored (with sth)** feeling tired and perhaps slightly annoyed because sth is not interesting or because you do not have anything to do □ *bosan*: *I'm bored with eating the same thing every day.* ♦ *The children get bored on long journeys.* ♦ *He gave a bored yawn.* ♦ *The play was awful—we were bored stiff* (= extremely bored).

> **HELP** If you have nothing to do, or if what you are doing does not interest you, then you are **bored**. The person or thing that makes you feel like this is **boring**.

boredom /ˈbɔːdəm/ noun [U] the state of being bored □ *kebosanan*: *I sometimes eat out of boredom.*

boring /ˈbɔːrɪŋ/ adj not at all interesting □ *(yg) membosankan*: *a boring film/job/speech/man*
SYN dull

born¹ /bɔːn/ verb (abbr **b.**) **be born** to come into the world by birth; to start existing □ *dilahirkan*: *Where were you born?* ♦ *I was born in London, but I grew up in Leeds.* ♦ *I'm going to give up work after the baby is born.* ♦ *The idea of free education for all was born in the 19th century.* ♦ *His unhappiness was born out of a feeling of frustration.*

born² /bɔːn/ adj **1** [only before a noun] having a natural ability to do sth □ *ada bakat semula jadi*: *She's a born leader.* **2** **-born** [in compounds] born in the place or state mentioned □ *(yg) dilahirkan di*: *This Kenyan-born athlete now represents Denmark.*

born-aˈgain adj [only before a noun] having found new, strong religious belief □ *lahir semula*: *a born-again Christian*

borne past participle of **bear¹**

borough /ˈbʌrə/ noun [C] a town, or an area inside a large town, that has some form of local government □ *kawasan berpentadbiran tempatan*

borrow /ˈbɒrəʊ/ (*AmE also* /) verb [I,T] **borrow (sth) (from/off sb/sth) 1** to take or receive sth from sb/sth that you intend to give back, usually after a short time □ *meminjam*: *I had to borrow from the bank to pay for my car.* ♦ *We'll have to borrow a lot of money to buy a car.* ♦ *Could I borrow your pen for a minute?* ♦ *He's always borrowing off his mother.* ♦ *I borrowed a book from the library.*

borrow/lend

She's **lending** her son some money.

He's **borrowing** some money from his mother.

HELP Be careful not to confuse **borrow** with its opposite **lend**.

2 to take sth and use it as your own; to copy sth □ *meminjam; meniru*: *That idea is borrowed from another book.*

borrower /ˈbɒrəʊə(r)/ (*AmE* also /) *noun* [C] a person who borrows sth □ *peminjam*

bosom /ˈbʊzəm/ *noun* [sing] (*formal*) sb's chest, especially a woman's breasts □ *dada*: *She clutched the child to her bosom.*

IDM **in the bosom of sth** close to; with the protection of □ *dlm pangkuan (keluarga, dsb)*: *He was glad to be back in the bosom of his family.*

bosom friend *noun* [C] a very close friend □ *sahabat karib*

boss¹ /bɒs/ *noun* [C] (*informal*) **1** a person whose job is to give orders to others at work; an employer; a manager □ *bos; majikan*: *I'm going to ask the boss for a day off work.* ◆ *OK. You're the boss* (= you make the decisions). **2** a person who is in charge of a large organization □ *bos; ketua*: *the new boss at IBM* ◆ *Hospital bosses protested at the government's decision.*

boss² /bɒs/ *verb* [T] **boss sb (about/around)** to give orders to sb, especially in an annoying way □ *mengarahkan*: *I wish you'd stop bossing me around.*

bossy /ˈbɒsi/ *adj* (**bossier**; **bossiest**) liking to give orders to other people, often in an annoying way □ *suka mengarahkan*: *Don't be so bossy!* ▶ **bossily** *adv* ▶ **bossiness** *noun* [U]

botanist /ˈbɒtənɪst/ *noun* [C] a person who studies plants □ *ahli botani*

botany /ˈbɒtəni/ *noun* [U] the scientific study of plants □ *botani* ➔ look at **biology**, **zoology** ▶ **botanical** /bəˈtænɪkl/ *adj*: *botanical gardens* (= a type of park where plants are grown for scientific study)

botch /bɒtʃ/ *verb* [T] (*informal*) **botch sth (up)** to do sth badly □ *membuat sst kerja dgn tdk senonoh; merosakkan*: *I've completely botched up this typing, I'm afraid.* **SYN** **mess sth up**

both /bəʊθ/ *determiner, pron* **1** the two; the one as well as the other □ *kedua-dua*: *Both women were French.* ◆ *Both the women were French.* ◆ *Both of the women were French.* ◆ *I liked them both.* ◆ *We were both very tired.* ◆ *Both of us were tired.* ◆ *I've got two sisters. They both live in London/Both of them live in London.*

HELP Note that we CANNOT say: *the both women* or: *my both sisters.*

2 both ... and ... not only ... but also ... □ *kedua-duanya*: *Both he and his wife are vegetarian.* ➔ note at **similarity**

bother¹ /ˈbɒðə(r)/ *verb* **1** [I] [usually negative] **bother (to do sth/doing sth)**; **bother (about/with sth)** to make the effort to do sth □ *susah-susah (membuat sst); (tdk) langsung pun*: *'Shall I make you something to eat?' 'No, don't bother—I'm not hungry.'* ◆ *He didn't even bother to say thank you.* ◆ *Don't bother waiting for me—I'll catch you up later.* ◆ *Don't bother about the washing-up. I'll do it later.* **2** [T] to disturb, annoy or worry sb □ *mengganggu*: *I'm sorry to bother you, but could I speak to you for a moment?* ◆ *Don't bother Geeta with that now—she's busy.* **SYN** **trouble**

IDM **be bothered (about sth)** (*especially BrE informal*) to think that sb/sth is important □ *peduli (akan sst)*: *'What would you like to do this evening?' 'I'm not bothered really.'* ◆ *Sam doesn't seem too bothered about losing his job.*

can't be bothered (to do sth) used to say that you do not want to spend time or energy doing sth □ *malas atau tdk hendak (membuat sst)*: *I can't be bothered to do my homework now. I'll do it tomorrow.*

bother² /ˈbɒðə(r)/ *noun* [U] trouble or difficulty □ *susah payah*: *Thanks for all your help. It's saved me a lot of bother.*

Botox™ /ˈbəʊtɒks/ *noun* [U] a substance that makes muscles relax. It is sometimes put under the skin around sb's eyes using a needle, in order to remove lines and make the skin look younger. □ *botoks*

bottle¹ /ˈbɒtl/ *noun* [C] **1** a glass or plastic container with a narrow neck for keeping liquids in □ *botol*: *a beer bottle* ◆ *an empty bottle* ➔ picture at **bicycle** **2** the amount of liquid that a bottle can hold □ *sebotol (ukuran)*: *a bottle of lemonade* ➔ picture at **container**

bottle² /ˈbɒtl/ *verb* [T] to put sth into bottles □ *membotolkan; dibotolkan*: *After three or four months the wine is bottled.* ◆ *bottled water* (= that you can buy in bottles)

PHR V **bottle sth up** to not allow yourself to express strong emotions □ *memendam perasaan*: *You'll make yourself ill if you keep your feelings bottled up.*

bottle bank *noun* [C] a large container in a public place where people can leave their empty bottles so that the glass can be **recycled** (= used again) □ *tong kumpul botol kosong*

bottleneck /ˈbɒtlnek/ noun [C] **1** a narrow piece of road that causes traffic to slow down or stop □ *jalan sempit yg menjadi punca kesesakan lalu lintas* **2** something that makes progress slower, especially in business or industry □ *sst yg melambatkan proses kerja*

bottom¹ /ˈbɒtəm/ noun **1** [C, usually sing] the lowest part of sth □ *bahagian bawah; kaki; dasar*: *The house is at the bottom of a hill.* ♦ *I think I've got a pen in the bottom of my bag.* ♦ *The sea is so clear that you can see the bottom.* **OPP top 2** [C] the flat surface on the outside of an object, on which it stands □ *sebelah bawah; belakang*: *There's a label on the bottom of the box.* **OPP top 3** [sing] the far end of sth □ *hujung*: *The bus stop is at the bottom of the road.* **OPP top 4** [sing] the lowest position in relation to other people, teams, etc □ *bawah; corot*: *I started at the bottom and now I'm the Managing Director.* **OPP top 5** [C] the part of your body that you sit on □ *punggung*: *He fell over and landed on his bottom.* ⊃ picture at **body 6 bottoms** [pl] the lower part of a piece of clothing that is in two parts □ *pakaian bahagian bawah (seluar, skirt, dsb)*: *pyjama bottoms* ♦ *track suit bottoms*

IDM **be at the bottom of sth** to be the cause of sth □ *punca*: *I'm sure Molly Potter is at the bottom of all this.*

from the (bottom of your) heart ⊃ **heart**
get to the bottom of sth to find out the real cause of sth □ *mencari sebab sebenar sst*

bottom² /ˈbɒtəm/ adj [only before a noun] in the lowest position □ *bawah sekali*: *the bottom shelf* ♦ *I live on the bottom floor.*

bottomless /ˈbɒtəmləs/ adj very deep; without limit □ *sangat dlm; tdk ada hadnya*

bottom line noun [sing] **1 the bottom line** the most important thing to consider when you are discussing or deciding sth, etc □ *yg penting sekali*: *A musical instrument should look and feel good, but the bottom line is how it sounds.* **2** the final profit or loss that a company has made in a particular period of time □ *jumlah untung rugi* **3** the lowest price that sb will accept for sth □ *harga paling rendah*

bough /baʊ/ noun [C] one of the main branches of a tree □ *dahan*

bought past tense, past participle of **buy¹**

boulder /ˈbəʊldə(r)/ noun [C] a very large rock □ *batu besar*

boulevard /ˈbuːləvɑːd/ noun [C] a wide street in a city often with trees on each side □ *lebuh*

bounce /baʊns/ verb **1** [I,T] (used about a ball, etc.) to move away quickly after it has hit a hard surface; to make a ball do this □ *melantun; memantul*: *The stone bounced off the wall and hit her on the head.* ♦ *A small boy came down the street, bouncing a ball.* **2** [I] to jump up and down continuously □ *meloncat-loncat*: *The children were bouncing on their beds.* ⊃ picture at **hop 3** [I,T] (used about a cheque) to be returned by a bank without payment because there is not enough money in the account □ *(berkenaan dgn cek) melambung* **4** [I,T] **bounce (sth) (back)** (used about an email) to be returned to the person who sent it because the system cannot deliver it □ *melantun*

PHR V bounce back to become healthy, successful or happy again after an illness, a failure, or a disappointment □ *pulih kembali* ▶ **bounce** noun [C]

bouncer /ˈbaʊnsə(r)/ noun [C] a person who is employed to stand at the entrance to a club, pub, etc. to stop people who are not wanted from going in, and to throw out people who are causing trouble inside □ *orang yg diupah utk mengusir pengacau*

bouncy /ˈbaʊnsi/ adj (**bouncier**; **bounciest**) **1** that bounces well or that can make things bounce □ *boleh melantun atau melantunkan*: *a bouncy ball/surface* **2** (used about a person) full of energy □ *lincah*: *She's a very bouncy person.* **SYN** lively

bound¹ /baʊnd/ adj [not before a noun] **1 bound to do sth** certain to do sth □ *pasti; tentu*: *You've done so much work that you're bound to pass the exam.* **2 bound (by sth)(to do sth)** having a legal or moral duty to do sth □ *terikat; terpaksa (membuat sst)*: *The company is bound by UK employment law.* ♦ *She felt bound to refuse the offer.* **3 bound (for …)** travelling to a particular place □ *menuju ke*: *a ship bound for Australia* **IDM** **bound up with sth** closely connected with sth □ *berkait rapat*

bound² /baʊnd/ verb [I] to run quickly with long steps □ *berlari sambil melompat; melompat-lompat*: *She bounded out of the house to meet us.* ▶ **bound** noun [C]: *With a couple of bounds he had crossed the room.*

bound³ past tense, past participle of **bind¹**

boundary /ˈbaʊndri/ noun [C] (pl **boundaries**) a real or imagined line that marks the limits of sth and divides it from other places or things □ *sempadan*: *national boundaries* ♦ *The road is the boundary between the two districts.* ♦ *Scientists continue to push back the boundaries of human knowledge.* ⊃ note at **border**

boundless /ˈbaʊndləs/ adj having no limit □ *tdk terhingga; tdk terhad*: *boundless energy*

bounds /baʊndz/ noun [pl] limits that cannot or should not be passed □ *batas; batasan*: *Price rises must be kept within reasonable bounds.*
IDM **out of bounds** (used about a place) where people are not allowed to go □ *tdk boleh dimasuki*: *This area is out of bounds to all staff.*

bouquet /buˈkeɪ/ noun [C] a bunch of flowers that is arranged in an attractive way □ *jambak bunga*

bourbon /ˈbɜːbən/ noun [C,U] a type of whisky (= a strong alcoholic drink) that is made mainly in the US □ *sejenis wiski*

bourgeois /ˈbʊəʒwɑː/ adj 1 belonging to the middle class □ *borjuis; tergolong dlm kelas pertengahan* 2 (disapproving) interested mainly in having more money and a higher social position □ *borjuis; mementingkan wang atau taraf sosial*: *bourgeois attitudes/ideas/values*

the bourgeoisie /ˌbʊəʒwɑːˈziː/ noun [sing, with sing or pl verb] the middle classes in society □ *borjuis*

bout /baʊt/ noun [C] 1 a short period of great activity □ *tempoh membuat sst kegiatan*: *a bout of hard work* 2 a period of illness □ *serangan penyakit*: *I'm just recovering from a bout of flu.*

boutique /buːˈtiːk/ noun [C] a small shop that sells fashionable clothes or expensive presents □ *butik* ▸**boutique** adj [only before a noun] (used about a business) small and offering products or services of a high quality to a small number of customers: *a boutique hotel in the old part of the city*

bovine /ˈbəʊvaɪn/ adj (technical) connected with cows □ *(berkenaan dgn) lembu*: *bovine diseases*

bow¹ /baʊ/ verb [I,T] **bow (sth) (to sb)** to bend your head or the upper part of your body forward and down, as a sign of respect □ *tunduk; menundukkan*: *The speaker bowed to the guests and left the stage.* ♦ *He bowed his head respectfully.*

PHR V **bow out (of sth/as sth)** to leave an important position or stop taking part in sth □ *mengundurkan diri (dr sst/sebagai sst)*: *After a long and successful career, she has decided to bow out of politics.* ♦ *He finally bowed out as chairman after ten years.*

bow to sb/sth to accept sth □ *tunduk; akur*: *They finally bowed to pressure from the public.*

bow² /baʊ/ noun [C] 1 an act of bowing¹ □ *(perbuatan) tunduk menerima penghargaan*: *The director of the play came on stage to take a bow.* 2 the front part of a ship □ *haluan* **OPP** stern ◆ note at **boat** ◆ picture on **page P6**

bow³ /bəʊ/ noun [C] 1 a weapon for shooting arrows. A bow is a curved piece of wood that is held in shape by a tight string. □ *busur* 2 a knot with two loose round parts and two loose ends that you use when you are tying shoes, etc. □ *simpul kupu-kupu*: *He tied his laces in a bow.* ◆ picture at **loop** 3 a long thin piece of wood with hair stretched across it that you use for playing some musical instruments □ *penggesek (biola, dsb)*: *a violin bow* ◆ picture at **music**

bowel /ˈbaʊəl/ noun [C, usually pl] one of the tubes that carries waste food away from your stomach to the place where it leaves your body □ *usus*

bowl¹ /bəʊl/ noun [C] 1 a deep round dish without a lid that is used for holding food or liquid □ *mangkuk*: *a soup bowl* ◆ look at **plate** ◆ picture on **page P16** 2 a large plastic container that is used for washing dishes, washing clothes, etc. □ *besen*: *a washing-up bowl* 3 the amount of sth that is in a bowl □ *semangkuk (ukuran)*: *I usually have a bowl of cereal for breakfast.*

bowl² /bəʊl/ verb [I,T] (in games such as **cricket**) to throw the ball in the direction of the person with the **bat** (= a piece of wood or metal) □ *membaling/melontar bola*

PHR V **bowl sb over** 1 to knock sb down when you are moving quickly □ *melanggar sso* 2 to surprise sb very much in a pleasant way □ *menakjubkan sso*: *I was absolutely bowled over by the beautiful scenery.*

bow legs /ˌbəʊ ˈlegz/ noun [pl] legs that curve out at the knees □ *kaki pengkar* ▸**bow-legged** /ˌbəʊ ˈlegɪd/ adj

bowler /ˈbəʊlə(r)/ noun [C] 1 (in the sport of **cricket**) the player who throws the ball in the direction of the person with the **bat** (= a piece of wood or metal) □ *pembaling (bola)* ◆ note at **cricket** ◆ picture on **page P4** 2 (also **bowler 'hat**; *AmE* **derby**) a round hard black hat, usually worn by men □ *topi bowler* ◆ picture at **hat**

bowling /ˈbəʊlɪŋ/ noun [U] a game in which you roll a heavy ball down a **lane** (= a special track) towards a group of **pins** (= wooden objects shaped like bottles) and try to knock them all down □ *boling*: *to go bowling*

'bowling alley noun [C] a building or part of a building where people can go **bowling** □ *lorong boling*: *The complex contains a bowling alley, pool hall and indoor tennis courts.*

bowls /bəʊlz/ noun [U] a game in which you try to roll large wooden balls as near as possible to a smaller ball □ *bola golek*: *to play bowls*

bow tie /ˌbəʊ ˈtaɪ/ noun [C] a tie in the shape of a **bow³** (2), that is worn by men, especially on formal occasions □ *tali leher kupu-kupu*

box¹ /bɒks/ noun
▸CONTAINER 1 [C] a container made of wood, cardboard, metal, etc. with a flat stiff base and sides and often a lid □ *kotak*: *a cardboard box* ♦ *a shoebox* ◆ picture at **container** 2 [C] a box and the things inside it □ *sekotak*: *a box of chocolates/matches/tissues*
▸SMALL AREA 3 [C] a small area with walls on all sides that is used for a particular purpose □ *petak*: *a telephone box* ♦ *the jury/witness box* (= in a court of law)
▸ON A FORM 4 [C] an empty square on a form in which you have to write sth □ *petak*: *Write your full name in the box below.*
▸TV 5 **the box** [sing] (*BrE informal*) TV □ *televisyen*: *What's on the box tonight?*

box² /bɒks/ verb 1 [I,T] to fight in the sport of **boxing** □ *bertinju* 2 [T] **box (sth) up** to put sth into a box □ *meletakkan dlm kotak*

PHR V **box sb/sth in** to prevent sb from getting out of a small space □ *menghalang sso/sst*: *Someone parked behind us and boxed us in.*
▸**boxed** adj: *a boxed set of DVDs*

[I] **intransitive**, a verb which has no object: *He laughed.*   [T] **transitive**, a verb which has an object: *He ate an apple.*

boxer /'bɒksə(r)/ noun [C] a person who does **boxing** as a sport □ *petinju* ➔ picture on **page P5**

boxer shorts (also **boxers**, AmE **shorts**) noun [pl] short trousers that men use as underwear □ *seluar dlm boxer*

boxing /'bɒksɪŋ/ noun [U] a sport in which two people fight by hitting each other with their hands inside large gloves □ *tinju*: the world middleweight boxing champion ♦ boxing gloves ➔ picture on **page P5**

Boxing Day noun [C,U] (BrE) the day after Christmas Day, 26 December □ *hari selepas Krismas*

box number noun [C] a number used as an address, especially in newspaper advertisements □ *nombor peti surat*

box office noun [C] the place in a cinema, theatre, etc. where the tickets are sold □ *tempat tiket*

boy /bɔɪ/ noun [C] a male child or a young man □ *anak/budak lelaki*: They've got three children—two boys and a girl. ♦ I used to play here when I was a boy. ♦ Her eldest boy is at college.

boycott /'bɔɪkɒt/ verb [T] to refuse to buy things from a particular company, take part in an event, etc. because you do not approve of it □ *memboikot*: Several countries boycotted the Olympic Games in protest. ♦ We ask people to boycott companies that use child labour. ▶ **boycott** noun [C]: a boycott of the local elections

boyfriend /'bɔɪfrend/ noun [C] a man or boy that sb has a romantic or sexual relationship with □ *teman lelaki*: She has had a lot of boyfriends.

boyhood /'bɔɪhʊd/ noun [U] the time of being a boy □ *zaman budak-budak*: My father told me some of his boyhood memories.

boyish /'bɔɪɪʃ/ adj like a boy □ *kebudak-budakan*: a boyish smile

bra /brɑː/ noun [C] a piece of clothing that women wear under their other clothes to support their breasts □ *coli; baju dlm perempuan*

brace¹ /breɪs/ noun 1 [C] (AmE **braces** [pl]) a metal frame that is fixed to a child's teeth in order to make them straight □ *pendakap (gigi)* 2 **braces** (AmE **suspenders**) [pl] a pair of narrow pieces of **elastic** (= material that can stretch) that go over your shoulders to hold your trousers up □ *tali bawat*

brace² /breɪs/ verb [T] **brace sth/yourself (for sth)** to prepare yourself for sth unpleasant □ *bersedia (utk menghadapi sst)*: You'd better brace yourself for some bad news.

bracelet /'breɪslət/ noun [C] a piece of jewellery, for example a metal chain or band, that you wear around your wrist or arm □ *rantai tangan* ➔ picture at **jewellery**

bracing /'breɪsɪŋ/ adj making you feel healthy and full of energy □ *menyegarkan*: bracing sea air

---

97 **boxer** → **brainless**

bracket¹ /'brækɪt/ noun [C] 1 (especially AmE **parenthesis**) [usually pl] one of two marks, () or [ ], that you put round extra information in a piece of writing □ *tanda kurung*: A translation of each word is given in brackets. 2 **age, income, price, etc. bracket** ages, prices, etc. which are between two limits □ *golongan; kumpulan*: to be in a high income bracket 3 a piece of metal or wood that is fixed to a wall and used as a support for a shelf, lamp, etc. □ *pendakap*

bracket² /'brækɪt/ verb [T] 1 to put a word, number, etc. between **brackets¹**(1) □ *meletakkan dlm tanda kurung* 2 **bracket A and B (together); bracket A with B** to think of two or more people or things as similar in some way □ *menggolongkan*

brag /bræg/ verb [I] (**bragging**; **bragged**) **brag (to sb) (about/of sth)** to talk in a very proud way about sth □ *bercakap besar; bermegah*: She's always bragging to her friends about how clever she is.

braid /breɪd/ noun 1 [U] thin coloured rope that is used to decorate military uniforms, etc. □ *pita brid (tentera)* 2 (AmE) = **plait** 3 (AmE) = **pigtail**

Braille /breɪl/ noun [U] a system of printing, using little round marks that are higher than the level of the paper they are on and which people who cannot see can read by touching them □ *Braille*: The signs were written in Braille.

brain /breɪn/ noun 1 [C] the part of your body inside your head that controls your thoughts, feelings and movements □ *otak*: damage to the brain ♦ a brain tumour ♦ a brain surgeon ➔ picture at **body** 2 [C,U] the ability to think clearly; intelligence □ *akal; otak; kepintaran*: She has a very quick brain and learns fast. ♦ He hasn't got the brains to be a doctor. 3 [C, usually pl] (informal) a very clever person □ *orang yg pandai*: He's one of the best brains in the country. 4 **the brains** [sing] the person who plans or organizes sth □ *orang yg merancang*: She's the real brains in the organization.

IDM **have sth on the brain** (informal) to think about sth all the time □ *asyik berfikir ttg sst; asyik teringat akan sst*: I've had that song on the brain all day.
rack your brains ➔ **rack²**

brainchild /'breɪntʃaɪld/ noun [sing] the idea, plan, design, etc. of a particular person □ *gagasan; buah fikiran*: The music festival was the brainchild of a young teacher.

brain-dead adj 1 having serious brain damage and needing a machine to stay alive □ *mati otak* 2 (informal) unable to think clearly; stupid □ *mati otak; mamai*: He's brain-dead from watching too much TV.

brainless /'breɪnləs/ adj (informal) very silly; stupid □ *tdk berotak; bodoh*

brainstorm¹ /ˈbreɪnstɔːm/ noun [C] **1** a moment of sudden confusion □ *kebingungan; mamai*: *I had a brainstorm in the exam and couldn't answer any questions.* **2** (AmE) = **brainwave**

brainstorm² /ˈbreɪnstɔːm/ verb [I,T] to solve a problem or make a decision by thinking of as many ideas as possible in a short time □ *sumbang saran*: *We'll spend five minutes brainstorming on how we can raise money.* ♦ *Brainstorm as many ideas as possible before you start to write your answer.* ➔ note at **mind map**

brainwash /ˈbreɪnwɒʃ/ (AmE also) / verb [T] **brainwash sb (into doing sth)** to force sb to believe sth by using strong mental pressure □ *mempengaruhi fikiran sso (melalui tekanan jiwa)*: *TV advertisements try to brainwash people into buying things that they don't need.* ▶ **brainwashing** noun [U]

brainwave /ˈbreɪnweɪv/ (AmE **brainstorm**) noun [C] (*informal*) a sudden clever idea □ *ilham; mendapat idea*: *If I have a brainwave, I'll let you know.*

brainy /ˈbreɪni/ adj (**brainier**, **brainiest**) (*informal*) intelligent □ *pandai; pintar; cerdik*

braise /breɪz/ verb [T] to cook meat or vegetables slowly in a little liquid in a covered dish □ *menumis reneh*

brake¹ /breɪk/ noun [C] **1** the part of a vehicle that makes it go slower or stop □ *brek*: *She put her foot on the brake and just managed to stop in time.* ➔ picture at **bicycle**, **car** **2** something that makes sth else slow down or stop □ *menahan*: *The Government must try to put a brake on inflation.*

brake² /breɪk/ verb [I] to make a vehicle go slower or stop by using the **brakes** □ *membrek*: *If the driver hadn't braked in time, the car would have hit me.*

bran /bræn/ noun [U] the brown outer covering of grains that is left when the grain is made into flour □ *bran; dedak*

branch¹ /brɑːntʃ/ noun [C] **1** one of the main parts of a tree that grows out of the **trunk** (= the thick central part) □ *dahan; cabang*: *He climbed the tree and sat on a branch.* ➔ picture at **tree** **2** an office, a shop, etc. that is part of a larger organization □ *cawangan*: *The company I work for has branches in Paris, Milan and New York.* **3** a part of an academic subject □ *cabang*: *Psychiatry is a branch of medicine.*

branch² /brɑːntʃ/ verb

PHR V **branch off** (used about a road) to leave a larger road and go off in another direction □ *bercabang; menyimpang*: *A bit further on, the road branches off to the left.*

branch out (into sth) to start doing sth new and different from the things you usually do □ *meluaskan kegiatan; bercabang*: *The band has recently branched out into acting.*

brand¹ /brænd/ noun [C] **1** the name of a product that is made by a particular company □ *jenama*: *a well-known brand of coffee* **2** a particular type of sth □ *jenis*: *a strange brand of humour*

brand² /brænd/ verb [T] **1 brand sb (as sth)** to say that sb has a bad character so that people have a bad opinion of them □ *mengecap; mencela*: *She was branded as a troublemaker after she complained about her long working hours.* **2** to mark an animal with a hot iron to show who owns it □ *menyelar*

branding /ˈbrændɪŋ/ noun [U] the activity of giving a particular name and image to goods and services so that people will be attracted to them and want to buy them □ *penjenamaan*

brandish /ˈbrændɪʃ/ verb [T] to wave sth in the air in an aggressive or excited way □ *mengayun-ayunkan; mengacaukan*: *The robber was brandishing a knife.*

brand ˈnew adj completely new □ *betul-betul baharu*

brandy /ˈbrændi/ noun [U,C] (*pl* **brandies**) a strong alcoholic drink that is made from wine □ *brandi*

brash /bræʃ/ adj too confident and direct □ *agak lancang*: *Her brash manner makes her unpopular with strangers.* ▶ **brashness** noun [U]

brass /brɑːs/ noun **1** [U] a hard yellow metal that is a mixture of **copper** (= a reddish-brown metal) and **zinc** (= a silver-grey metal) □ *loyang*: *brass buttons on a uniform* **2** [U, sing, with sing or pl verb] the group of musical instruments that are made of **brass** □ *bras; alat muzik loyang*: *the brass section in an orchestra* ➔ note at **instrument** ➔ picture at **music**

brat /bræt/ noun [C] a child who behaves badly and annoys you □ *budak nakal*

bravado /brəˈvɑːdəʊ/ noun [U] a confident way of behaving that is intended to impress people, sometimes as a way of hiding a lack of confidence □ *keberanian yg ditunjuk-tunjuk atau dibuat-buat*

brave¹ /breɪv/ adj (**braver**, **bravest**) **1** ready to do things that are dangerous or difficult without showing fear □ *berani*: *the brave soldiers who fought in the war* ♦ *'This may hurt a little, so try and be brave,' said the dentist.* **2** needing or showing courage □ *(yg memerlukan) keberanian; berani*: *a brave decision* ♦ *a brave fight against cancer* ▶ **bravely** adv: *The men bravely defended the town for three days.*

brave² /breɪv/ verb [T] to face sth unpleasant, dangerous or difficult without showing fear □ *menghadapi (tanpa takut)*: *She braved the rain and went out into the street.*

bravery /ˈbreɪvəri/ noun [U] actions that are **brave** □ *keberanian*: *After the war he received a medal for bravery.* **SYN** **courage**

bravo /ˌbrɑːˈvəʊ/ exclam a word that people shout to show that they have enjoyed sth that sb has done, for example a play □ *bravo; syabas*

brawl /brɔːl/ noun [C] a noisy fight among a group of people, usually in a public place ▫ *pergaduhan* ►**brawl** verb [I]: *We saw some football fans brawling in the street.*

brawn /brɔːn/ noun [U] physical strength ▫ *kekuatan jasmani*: *To do this kind of job you need more brawn than brain (= you need to be strong rather than clever).* ►**brawny** adj: *He folded his brawny arms across his chest.*

brazen /ˈbreɪzn/ adj without embarrassment, especially in a way which shocks people ▫ *tdk tahu malu*: *Don't believe a word she says—she's a brazen liar!* ►**brazenly** adv: *He brazenly admitted he'd been having an affair.*

brazil /brəˈzɪl/ (also **braˈzil nut**) noun [C] a nut that we eat, with a very hard shell that has three sides ▫ *kacang Brazil* ◆ picture at **nut**

breach¹ /briːtʃ/ noun 1 [C,U] **breach (of sth)** an act that breaks an agreement, a law, etc. ▫ *pelanggaran; melanggar; mungkir*: *Giving private information about clients is a breach of confidence.* ◆ *The company was found to be in breach of contract.* 2 [C] a break in friendly relations between people, groups, etc ▫ *terputusnya (hubungan)*: *The incident caused a breach between the two countries.* 3 [C] an opening in a wall, etc. that defends or protects sb/sth ▫ *retakan; rekahan*: *The waves made a breach in the sea wall.*

breach² /briːtʃ/ verb [T] 1 to break an agreement, a law, etc. ▫ *melanggar (undang-undang, dsb); mungkir*: *He accused the Government of breaching international law.* 2 to make an opening in a wall, etc. that defends or protects sb/sth ▫ *menembusi; menerobos*

bread /bred/ noun [U] a type of food made from flour, water and usually **yeast** (= a substance which makes the bread rise) mixed together and baked in an oven ▫ *roti*: *We had cheese and bread for lunch.* ◆ *Would you like some bread and butter?*

> **GRAMMAR** Bread is uncountable, so we say **a piece/slice of bread** or **some bread** (not 'a bread').

bread

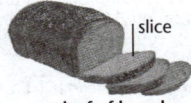

slice

a loaf of bread   a bread roll

> **MORE** A **loaf** of bread is bread that has been shaped and cooked in one piece. A **roll** is bread baked in a round shape for one person to eat. **Wholemeal** bread is made from flour that contains all the grain.

breadcrumbs /ˈbredkrʌmz/ noun [pl] very small pieces of bread that are used in cooking ▫ *serbuk roti*

breadth /bredθ/ noun [U] 1 the distance between the two sides of sth ▫ *lebar*: *We measured the length and breadth of the garden.* **SYN width** 2 the wide variety of things, subjects, etc. that sth includes ▫ *keluasan; luasnya*: *I was amazed by the breadth of her knowledge.* ◆ adjective **broad**

IDM the length and breadth of sth ◆ **length**

breadwinner /ˈbredwɪnə(r)/ noun [C, usually sing] the person who earns most of the money that their family needs ▫ *pencari nafkah*: *When his dad died, Steve became the breadwinner.*

break¹ /breɪk/ verb (pt **broke** /brəʊk/; pp **broken** /ˈbrəʊkən/)

▸IN PIECES 1 [I,T] to separate, or make sth separate, into two or more pieces ▫ *memecahkan; pecah; patah*: *She dropped the vase onto the floor and it broke.* ◆ *He broke his leg in a car accident.* ◆ picture at **chip**

▸STOP WORKING 2 [I,T] (used about a machine, etc.) to stop working; to stop a machine, etc. working ▫ *merosakkan*: *The photocopier has broken.* ◆ *Be careful with my camera—I don't want you to break it.*

▸LAW/PROMISE 3 [T] to do sth that is against the law, or against what has been agreed or promised ▫ *melanggar (undang-undang, dsb); memungkiri*: *to break the law/rules/speed limit* ◆ *Don't worry—I never break my promises.*

▸STOP 4 [I,T] to stop doing sth for a short time ▫ *berhenti*: *Let's break for coffee now.* ◆ *We decided to break the journey and stop for lunch.*

▸END STH 5 [T] to make sth end: *Once you start smoking it's very difficult to break the habit.* ▫ *menghentikan; memecahkan* ◆ *Suddenly, the silence was broken by the sound of a bird singing.*

▸BEGIN 6 [I] to begin ▫ *bermula; (fajar) menyingsing; mula membadai*: *Day was breaking as I left the house.* ◆ *We ran indoors when the storm broke.*

▸OF NEWS 7 [I] if a piece of news **breaks**, it becomes known ▫ *mula tersiar*: *When the story broke in the newspapers, nobody could believe it.* ◆ look at **break the news**

▸OF A WAVE 8 [I] to reach its highest point and begin to fall ▫ *memecah; menghempas*: *I watched the waves breaking on the rocks.*

▸OF THE VOICE 9 [I] to change suddenly ▫ *pecah suara*: *Most boys' voices break when they are 13 or 14 years old.* ◆ *His voice was breaking with emotion as he told us the awful news.*

▸OF A RECORD 10 [T] to do sth better, faster, etc. than anyone has ever done it before ▫ *memecahkan; mengatasi*: *She had broken the world 100 metres record.* ❶ For idioms containing **break**, look at the entries for the nouns, adjectives, etc. For example, **break even** is at **even**.

PHR V break away (from sb/sth) 1 to escape suddenly from sb who is holding you ▫ *melepaskan diri (drpd sso/sst)* 2 to leave a political party, state, etc. in order to form a new one ▫ *keluar dari*

break down 1 (used about a vehicle or machine) to stop working ▫ *rosak*: *Akram's car broke down on the way to work this morning.* ◆ note at **car**

2 (used about a system, discussion, etc.) to fail □ *gagal*: *Talks between the two countries have completely broken down.* **3** to lose control of your feelings and start crying □ *tdk dpt menahan perasaan*: *He broke down in tears when he heard the news.*

break sth down 1 to destroy sth by using force □ *memecahkan/mengopak sst*: *The police had to break down the door to get into the house.* **2** to make a substance separate into parts or change into a different form in a chemical process □ *memecah/menguraikan sst*: *Food is broken down in our bodies by the digestive system.*

break in to enter a building by force, usually in order to steal sth □ *memecah masuk*: *Burglars broke in and stole cash, credit cards and a laptop.*

break in (on sth) to interrupt when sb else is speaking □ *mengganggu; mencelah*: *She longed to break in on their conversation but didn't want to appear rude.*

break into sth 1 to enter a place that is closed □ *memecah masuk/memasuki sst*: *Thieves broke into his car and stole the radio.* ◆ (*figurative*) *The company is trying to break into the Japanese market.* **2** to start doing sth suddenly □ *mula (menyanyi, berlari, dll)*: *to break into song/a run*

break off to suddenly stop doing or saying sth □ *berhenti (bercakap, dsb) dgn tiba-tiba*: *He started speaking and then broke off in the middle of a sentence.*

break (sth) off to remove a part of sth by force; to be removed in this way □ *mematahkan (sst)*: *Could you break off another bit of chocolate for me?*

break sth off to end a relationship suddenly □ *memutuskan (hubungan, dsb) dgn tiba-tiba*: *After a bad argument, they decided to break off their engagement.*

break out (used about fighting, wars, fires, etc.) to start suddenly □ *bermula; meletus*: *They left the city when war broke out in 1939.*

break out in sth to suddenly have a skin problem □ *keluar bintik, ruam, dsb*: *to break out in spots/a rash*

break out (of sth) to escape from a prison, etc. □ *melepaskan diri/lari (dr sst)*

break through (sth) to manage to get past sth that is stopping you □ *merempuh (sst)*: *The protesters were trying to break through the line of police.*

break up 1 to separate into smaller pieces □ *pecah; berkecai*: *The ship broke up on the rocks.* **2** (used about events that involve a group of people) to end or finish □ *bersurai*: *The meeting broke up just before lunch.* **3** (*BrE*) to start school holidays □ *mula cuti; tutup (sekolah)*: *When do you break up for the summer holidays?* **4** when a person who is talking on a mobile phone **breaks up**, you can no longer hear them clearly because the signal has been interrupted □ *menjadi kabur*

break sth up 1 to make sth separate into smaller pieces □ *memecahkan*: *The ship was broken up for scrap metal.* **2** to make people leave sth or stop doing sth, especially by using force □ *meleraikan/menghentikan sst*: *The police arrived and broke up the fight.*

break up (with sb) to end a relationship with sb □ *berpisah (dgn sso)*: *She's broken up with her boyfriend.*

break with sth to end a relationship or connection with sb/sth □ *memutuskan hubungan/pertalian dgn sso/sst*: *to break with tradition/the past*

break² /breɪk/ *noun* [C]
▶SHORT REST **1** a short period of rest □ *rehat*: *We worked all day without a break.* ◆ *to take a break* ⊃ note at **interval**
▶HOLIDAY **2** a short holiday □ *istirahat; cuti*: *a weekend break in Prague*
▶CHANGE **3** break (in sth); break (with sb/sth) a change from what usually happens or an end to sth □ *terputusnya; perubahan*: *The incident led to a break in diplomatic relations.* ◆ *She wanted to make a complete break with the past.*
▶SPACE **4** an opening or a space in sth □ *ruang; sela; reda*: *Wait for a break in the traffic before you cross the road.*
▶BROKEN PART **5** a place where sth has been broken □ *tempat pecah*: *The X-ray showed there was no break in his leg.*
▶GOOD LUCK **6** (*informal*) a piece of good luck □ *kesempatan; peluang baik*: *to give somebody a break* (= to help sb by giving him/her a chance to be successful)

IDM **break of day** (*written*) the time when light first appears in the morning □ *fajar menyingsing* **SYN** **dawn**

give sb a break 1 used to tell sb to stop saying things that are annoying or not true □ *sudahlah; cukuplah*: *Give me a break and stop nagging, OK!* **2** (*especially AmE*) to be fair to sb □ *adillah sedikit (!)*

breakage /ˈbreɪkɪdʒ/ *noun* [C, usually pl] something that has been broken □ *benda-benda yg pecah*: *Customers must pay for any breakages.*

breakaway /ˈbreɪkəweɪ/ *adj* [only before a noun] (used about a political group, an organization, or a part of a country) that has separated from a larger group or country □ *(yg) memisahkan diri* ▶**breakaway** *noun* [C]

breakdown /ˈbreɪkdaʊn/ *noun* [C] **1** a time when a vehicle, machine, etc. stops working □ *kerosakan*: *I hope we don't have a breakdown on the motorway.* **2** the failure or end of sth □ *terputusnya; kegagalan*: *The breakdown of the talks means that a strike is likely.* **3** a list of all the details of sth □ *huraian*: *I would like a full breakdown of how the money was spent.* **4** = **nervous breakdown**

breakfast /ˈbrekfəst/ *noun* [C,U] the meal which you have when you get up in the morning □ *sarapan*: *to have breakfast* ◆ *What do you usually have for breakfast?* ◆ *to eat a big breakfast* ⊃ note at **meal**

CULTURE

In a hotel, an **English** breakfast means cereal, fried eggs, bacon, sausages, tomatoes, toast, etc. A **Continental** breakfast means bread and jam with coffee.

IDM bed and breakfast ⊃ bed¹

break-in noun [C] the act of entering a building by force, especially in order to steal sth □ *kejadian pecah masuk*: *The police say there have been several break-ins in this area.*

breakneck /'breɪknek/ adj [only before a noun] very fast and dangerous □ *terlalu laju hingga membahayakan*: *He drove her to the hospital at breakneck speed.*

breakthrough /'breɪkθruː/ noun [C] a breakthrough (in sth) an important discovery or development □ *penemuan/perkembangan penting (dlm sst)*: *Scientists are hoping to make a breakthrough in cancer research.*

break-up noun [C] 1 the end of a relationship between two people □ *perpisahan*: *the break-up of a marriage* 2 the process or result of a group or an organization separating into smaller parts □ *keruntuhan; perpecahan*: *the break-up of the Soviet Union*

breast /brest/ noun [C] 1 one of the two soft round parts of a woman's body that can produce milk □ *buah dada; payudara*: *She put the baby to her breast.* ◆ *breast cancer* ◆ *breast milk* 2 a word used especially in literature for the top part of the front of your body, below the neck □ *dada*: *to clasp somebody to your breast* **SYN** chest 3 the front part of the body of a bird □ *dada burung*: *breast feathers* ◆ *The robin has a red breast.* ⊃ picture on **page P12**

breastfeed /'brestfiːd/ verb [I,T] (pt, pp breastfed) to feed a baby with milk from the breast □ *menyusui anak dgn susu badan; meneteki*

breaststroke /'breststrəʊk/ noun [sing, U] a style of swimming on your front in which you start with your hands together, push both arms forward and then move them out and back through the water □ *kuak dada*: *to do (the) breaststroke* ⊃ look at **backstroke, butterfly, crawl** ⊃ picture at **swim**

breath /breθ/ noun 1 [U] the air that you take into and blow out of your lungs □ *nafas*: *His breath smelt of garlic.* ◆ *to have bad breath* (= breath which smells unpleasant) 2 [C] an act of taking air into or blowing air out of your lungs □ *nafas*: *Take a few deep breaths before you start running.*

IDM a breath of fresh air the clean air which you breathe outside, especially when compared to the air inside a room or building □ *udara segar; sst/sso yg dialu-alukan atau menyegarkan*: *Let's go for a walk. I need a breath of fresh air.* ◆ (figurative) *The child's happy face was like a breath of fresh air on that miserable day.*
catch your breath ⊃ **catch**¹
get your breath (again/back) to rest after physical exercise so that your breathing returns to normal □ *berhenti mencungap; tdk termengah-mengah lagi*
hold your breath to stop breathing for a short time, for example when you are swimming or because of fear or excitement □ *menahan nafas*: *We all held our breath as we waited for her reply.*
(be/get) out of/short of breath (to be/start) breathing very quickly, for example after physical exercise □ *termengah-mengah*: *She was out of breath after climbing the stairs.*
say sth, speak, etc. under your breath to say sth very quietly, usually because you do not want people to hear you □ *mengatakan sst dsb, perlahan-lahan*
take your breath away to be very surprising or beautiful □ *membuat sso terpegun; mengagumkan*: *The spectacular view took our breath away.*
⊃ adjective **breathtaking**
take a deep breath ⊃ **deep**¹
with bated breath ⊃ **bated**

breathalyse (AmE breathalyze) /'breθəlaɪz/ verb [T] to test the breath of a driver with a breathalyser □ *menguji nafas (dgn menggunakan alat penguji nafas)*

breathalyser (also Breathalyzer™) /'breθəlaɪzə(r)/ noun [C] a device used by the police to measure the amount of alcohol in a driver's breath □ *alat penguji nafas (alkohol)*

breathe /briːð/ verb [I,T] to take air, etc. into your lungs and blow it out again □ *bernafas; (sedut/hembus) nafas*: *Breathe out as you lift the weight and breathe in as you lower it.* ◆ *None of us want to breathe (in) exhaust fumes from heavy traffic.*

IDM (not) breathe a word (of/about sth) (to sb) to (not) tell sb about sth that is secret □ *tdk memberitahu (ttg sst) (kpd sesiapa pun)*: *If you breathe a word of this to my mother, I'll never speak to you again!* ▶ breathing noun [U]: *heavy/irregular breathing* ◆ *These deep breathing exercises will help you relax.*

breather /'briːðə(r)/ noun [C] (informal) a short rest □ *berehat sebentar; melepaskan lelah*: *to have/take a breather*

breathless /'breθləs/ adj 1 having difficulty breathing □ *termengah-mengah*: *I was hot and breathless when I got to the top of the hill.* 2 not able to breathe because you are so excited, frightened, etc □ *menahan/tertahan nafas*: *to be breathless with excitement* ▶ breathlessly adv

breathtaking /'breθteɪkɪŋ/ adj extremely surprising, beautiful, etc □ *menakjubkan*: *breathtaking scenery*

breath test noun [C] a test by the police on the breath of a driver to measure how much alcohol he or she has drunk □ *ujian nafas (alkohol)* ⊃ look at **breathalyse**

breed¹ /briːd/ verb (pt, pp bred /bred/) 1 [I] (used about animals) to have sex and produce

[C] **countable**, a noun with a plural form: *one book, two books*   [U] **uncountable**, a noun with no plural form: *some sugar*

breed → briefly

young animals □ *membiak; beranak*: *Many animals won't breed in zoos.* **SYN** **mate** **2** [T] to keep animals or plants in order to produce young from them □ *membiak baka; menternak*: *These cattle are bred to produce high yields of milk.* **3** [T] to cause sth □ *menimbulkan*: *This kind of thinking breeds intolerance.* ▶ **breeding** noun [U]

breed² /briːd/ noun [C] a particular variety of an animal □ *baka; jenis*: *a breed of cattle/dog*

breeder /ˈbriːdə(r)/ noun [C] a person who breeds animals or plants □ *pembiak baka*: *a dog breeder*

'breeding ground noun [C] **1** a place where wild animals go to breed □ *tempat pembiakan* **2** a place where sth can develop □ *tempat membiaknya*: *a breeding ground for crime*

breeze¹ /briːz/ noun [C] a light wind □ *bayu; angin sepoi-sepoi bahasa*: *A warm breeze was blowing.*

breeze² /briːz/ verb [I] **breeze along, in, out,** etc. to move in a confident and relaxed way □ *bergerak dgn lincah dan bersahaja*: *He just breezed in twenty minutes late without a word of apology.*

breezy /ˈbriːzi/ adj (breezier; breeziest) **1** with a little wind □ *agak berangin* **2** happy and relaxed □ *riang; ceria*: *You're bright and breezy this morning!*

brevity /ˈbrevəti/ noun [U] the state of being short or quick □ *keringkasan; singkatnya* ⊃ adjective **brief**

brew /bruː/ verb **1** [T] to make beer □ *membuat bir* **2** [T] to make a drink of tea or coffee by adding hot water □ *membuat teh atau kopi*: *to brew a pot of tea* **3** [I] (used about tea) to stand in hot water before it is ready to drink □ *membiarkan daun teh kembang*: *Leave it to brew for a few minutes.*
IDM **be brewing** (used about sth bad) to develop or grow □ *mula berlaku/bergolak*: *There's trouble brewing.*

brewery /ˈbruːəri/ noun [C] (*pl* breweries) a place where beer is made □ *kilang bir*

bribe /braɪb/ noun [C] money, etc. that is given to sb such as an official to persuade them to do sth to help you that is wrong or dishonest □ *rasuah; sogokan*: *to accept/take bribes* ▶ **bribe** verb [T] **bribe sb (with sth)**: *They got a visa by bribing an official.* ▶ **bribery** /ˈbraɪbəri/ noun [U]

bric-a-brac /ˈbrɪk ə bræk/ noun [U] small items of little value, for decoration in a house □ *keropas-kerapis*

brick /brɪk/ noun [C,U] a hard block of baked clay (= a type of earth) that is used for building houses, etc □ *batu bata*: *a lorry carrying bricks* ♦ *a house built of red brick*

bricklayer /ˈbrɪkleɪə(r)/ noun [C] a person

[I] **intransitive**, a verb which has no object: *He laughed.*

whose job is to build walls with bricks □ *penurap batu bata*

brickwork /ˈbrɪkwɜːk/ noun [U] the part of a building that is made of bricks □ *binaan batu bata*

bridal /ˈbraɪdl/ adj [only before a noun] connected with a **bride** □ *(berkenaan dgn) pengantin perempuan*

bride /braɪd/ noun [C] a woman on or just before her wedding day □ *pengantin perempuan*: *a bride-to-be* (= a woman whose wedding is soon) ♦ *the bride and groom* ⊃ note at **wedding**

bridegroom /ˈbraɪdɡruːm/ (also **groom**) noun [C] a man on or just before his wedding day □ *pengantin lelaki* ⊃ note at **wedding**

bridesmaid /ˈbraɪdzmeɪd/ noun [C] a woman or girl who helps the **bride** on her wedding day □ *pengiring pengantin perempuan* ⊃ note at **wedding**

bridge¹ /brɪdʒ/ noun **1** [C] a structure that carries a road or railway across a river, valley, road or railway □ *jambatan*: *a bridge over the River Danube* ⊃ picture on **page P10** **2 the bridge** [sing] the high part of a ship where the captain and the people who control the ship stand □ *anjungan kapal* **3** [U] a card game for four people □ *bridge*

bridge² /brɪdʒ/ verb [T] to build a bridge over sth □ *membina jambatan merentangi*
IDM **bridge a/the gap** to fill a space between two people, groups or things or to bring them closer together □ *merapatkan jurang*: *Baby food bridges the gap between milk and solid food.*

bridle /ˈbraɪdl/ noun [C] the narrow pieces of leather that you put around a horse's head so that you can control it when you are riding it □ *tali kekang* ⊃ picture at **horse**

brief¹ /briːf/ adj (briefer; briefest) short or quick □ *ringkas; singkat*: *a brief description* ♦ *Please be brief. We don't have much time.* ⊃ noun **brevity**
IDM **in brief** using only a few words □ *ringkasnya*: *In brief, the meeting was a disaster.*

brief² /briːf/ noun [C] instructions or information about a job or task □ *arahan; taklimat*: *He was given the brief of improving the image of the organization.*

brief³ /briːf/ verb [T] to give sb information or instructions about sth □ *memberi taklimat/arahan*: *The minister has been fully briefed on what questions to expect.*

briefcase /ˈbriːfkeɪs/ noun [C] a flat case that you use for carrying papers, etc., especially when you go to work □ *beg dokumen/bimbit* ⊃ picture at **bag** ⊃ picture on **page P1**

briefing /ˈbriːfɪŋ/ noun [C,U] instructions or information that you are given before sth happens □ *taklimat*: *a press/news briefing* (= where information is given to journalists)

briefly /ˈbriːfli/ adv **1** for a short time; quickly □ *sebentar; dlm masa yg singkat*: *She glanced briefly at the letter.* **2** using only a few words

[T] **transitive**, a verb which has an object: *He ate an apple.*

□ *secara ringkas; pendeknya*: I'd like to comment very briefly on that last statement.

briefs /briːfs/ noun [pl] men's or women's underwear □ *seluar dlm*: a pair of briefs

brigade /brɪˈɡeɪd/ noun [C] **1** a large group of soldiers that forms a unit in the army □ *briged* **2** a group of people who work together for a particular purpose □ *pasukan*: the fire brigade

brigadier /ˌbrɪɡəˈdɪə(r)/ noun [C] an important officer in the army □ *brigadier*

bright /braɪt/ adj (brighter; brightest)
▸FULL OF LIGHT **1** having a lot of light □ *terang; bercahaya*: a bright, sunny day ◆ eyes bright with happiness
▸OF A COLOUR **2** strong and easy to see □ *terang; cerah*: a bright yellow jumper
▸HAPPY **3** happy □ *ceria; riang*: to feel bright and cheerful
▸INTELLIGENT **4** intelligent; able to learn things quickly □ *pandai; cerdas*: a bright child ◆ a bright idea ⊃ note at **intelligent**
▸POSITIVE **5** likely to be pleasant or successful □ *cerah*: The future looks bright.
IDM look on the bright side ⊃ **look¹** ▸**brightly** adv: brightly coloured clothes ▸**brightness** noun [U]

brighten /ˈbraɪtn/ verb [I,T] brighten (sth) (up) to become brighter or happier; to make sth brighter □ *menjadi cerah; berseri*: His face brightened when he saw her. ◆ to brighten up somebody's day (= make it happier)

brilliant /ˈbrɪliənt/ adj **1** very clever, skilful or successful □ *bijak*: a brilliant young scientist ◆ That's a brilliant idea! **2** having a lot of light; very bright □ *terang-benderang; bersinar-sinar*: brilliant sunshine **3** (informal) very good □ *cemerlang*: That was a brilliant film! ⊃ note at **good** ▸**brilliance** noun [U] ▸**brilliantly** adv

brim¹ /brɪm/ noun [C] **1** the top edge of a cup, glass, etc. □ *bibir (cawan, gelas, dsb)*: The cup was full to the brim. **2** the bottom part of a hat that is wider than the rest □ *tepi* ⊃ picture at **hat**

brim² /brɪm/ verb [I] (brimming; brimmed) brim (with sth) to be full of sth □ *penuh (dgn sst); digenangi*: His eyes were brimming with tears.
PHR V brim over (with sth) (used about a cup, glass, etc.) to have more liquid than it can hold □ *melimpah; penuh dgn*: The bowl was brimming over with water. ◆ (figurative) to be brimming over with health/happiness

brine /braɪn/ noun [U] salt water that is used especially to keep food in good condition □ *air garam*

bring /brɪŋ/ verb [T] (pt, pp brought /brɔːt/)
▸CARRY **1** to carry or take sb/sth to a place with you □ *membawa; bawakan*: Is it all right if I bring a friend to the party? ◆ Could you bring us some water, please? ◆ My sister went to Spain on holiday and brought me back a T-shirt. ◆ (figurative) He will bring valuable skills and experience to the team.

briefs → bring

▸CAUSE **2** to cause or result in sth □ *membawa; menyebabkan*: The sight of her brought a smile to his face. ◆ Money doesn't always bring happiness. **3** to cause sb/sth to be in a certain place or condition □ *menyebabkan*: Their screams brought people running from all directions. ◆ Add water to the mixture and bring it to the boil. ◆ An injury can easily bring an athlete's career to an end.
▸MOVE **4** to move sth somewhere □ *mengalihkan; mengeluarkan*: She brought the book down off the shelf. ◆ Louis brought a photo out of his wallet and showed it to us.
▸FORCE YOURSELF **5** bring yourself to do sth to force yourself to do sth □ *sanggup*: The film was so horrible that I couldn't bring myself to watch it. ❶ For idioms containing **bring**, look at the entries for the nouns, adjectives, etc. For example **bring up the rear** is at **rear**.

PHR V bring sth about to cause sth to happen □ *menyebabkan*: to bring about changes in people's lives

bring sth back **1** to cause sb to remember sth □ *membawa kembali*: The photographs brought back memories of his childhood. **2** to cause sth that existed before to be introduced again □ *memperkenalkan semula*: Nobody wants to bring back the days of child labour.

bring sb/sth down to defeat sb/sth; to make sb/sth lose a position of power □ *menjatuhkan sso/sst*: to bring down the government

bring sth down to make sth lower in level □ *menurunkan; mengurangkan*: to bring down the price of something

bring sth forward **1** to move sth to an earlier time □ *mencepatkan*: The date of the meeting has been brought forward by two weeks. **OPP** put sth back **2** to suggest sth for discussion □ *mengemukakan*

bring sb in to ask or employ sb to do a particular job □ *mengambil sso masuk*: A specialist was brought in to set up the new computer system.

bring sth in to introduce sth □ *memperkenalkan sst*: The government have brought in a new law on dangerous dogs.

bring sth off to manage to do sth difficult □ *berjaya (melakukan sst yg sukar)*: The team brought off an amazing victory.

bring sth on to cause sth □ *menyebabkan sst; disebabkan oleh*: Her headaches are brought on by stress.

bring sth out to produce sth or cause sth to appear □ *mengeluarkan*: When is the company bringing out its next new model?

bring sb round (also bring sb to) to make sb become conscious again □ *menyedarkan sso*: I splashed cold water on his face to try to bring him round.

bring sb round (to sth) to persuade sb to agree with your opinion □ *meyakinkan/memujuk sso (ttg sst)*: After a lot of discussion we finally brought them round to our point of view.

CONSONANTS p **p**en b **b**ad t **t**ea d **d**id k **c**at ɡ **g**ot tʃ **ch**in dʒ **J**une f **f**all v **v**an θ **th**in

bring/fetch/take

Bring the newspaper.

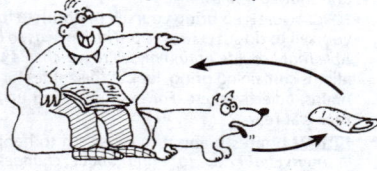

Fetch the newspaper.

Take the newspaper.

bring sth round to sth to direct a conversation to a particular subject □ *mengarahkan sst; mengubah hala sst*: I finally brought the conversation round to the subject of money.

bring sb up to look after a child until they are an adult and to teach them how to behave □ *membesarkan/memelihara/mendidik sst*: After her parents were killed the child was brought up by her uncle. ♦ a well-brought-up child

bring sth up 1 to introduce sth into a discussion or conversation □ *mengemukakan sst*: I intend to bring the matter up at the next meeting. **2** to be sick so that food comes up from the stomach and out of the mouth □ *memuntahkan sst* **SYN** vomit

brink /brɪŋk/ *noun* [sing] **the brink (of sth)** if you are on the **brink** of sth, you are almost in a very new, exciting or dangerous situation □ *tepi; pinggir; hampir-hampir*: Just when the band were **on the brink** of becoming famous, they split up.

brisk /brɪsk/ *adj* (**brisker** no superlative) **1** quick or using a lot of energy; busy □ *cergas; giat*: They set off **at a brisk pace**. ♦ Trading has been brisk this morning. **2** confident and practical; wanting to get things done quickly □ *lincah; cergas* ▶ **briskly** *adv* ▶ **briskness** *noun* [U]

bristle¹ /ˈbrɪsl/ *noun* [C] **1** a short thick hair □ *bulu kejur; tunggul janggut*: The bristles on my chin hurt the baby's face. **2** one of the short thick hairs of a brush □ *bulu*

bristle² /ˈbrɪsl/ *verb* [I] **1 bristle (with sth) (at sb/sth)** to show that you are angry □ *melenting (marah)* **2** (used about hair or an animal's fur) to stand up straight because of fear, anger, cold, etc. □ *meremang*

PHR V bristle with sth to be full of sth □ *penuh dgn sst*

Brit /brɪt/ *noun* [C] (*informal*) a British person □ *orang British*

Britain /ˈbrɪtn/ = Great Britain

British /ˈbrɪtɪʃ/ *adj* **1** of the United Kingdom (= Great Britain and Northern Ireland) □ *British*: British industry ♦ to hold a British passport **2 the British** *noun* [pl] the people of the United Kingdom □ *orang British*

the ˌBritish ˈIsles *noun* [pl] Great Britain and Ireland with all the islands that are near their coasts □ *Kepulauan Britain*

HELP Note that the British Isles is only a geographical unit, not a political unit. ⊃ note at **United Kingdom**

Briton /ˈbrɪtn/ *noun* [C] a person who comes from Great Britain □ *orang British*

MORE This is normally only used in newspapers, or when talking about the inhabitants of Britain in earlier times: *Three Britons killed in air crash.* ♦ *the Ancient Britons.* Otherwise we say 'a British man', 'a British woman'.

brittle /ˈbrɪtl/ *adj* hard but easily broken □ *rapuh*: The bones become brittle in old age.

broach /brəʊtʃ/ *verb* [T] to start talking about a particular subject, especially one which is difficult or embarrassing □ *menimbulkan (sst perkara)*: How will you **broach the subject** of the money he owes us?

ˈB-road *noun* [C] (in Britain) a road that is not as wide or important as an **A-road** (= a main road) or a **motorway** (= a wide road for fast traffic) □ *jalan gred B*: We drove the whole way on B-roads.

broad /brɔːd/ *adj* (**broader**; **broadest**) **1** wide □ *lebar*: a broad street/river ♦ broad shoulders ♦ a broad smile ⊃ *noun* **breadth** **OPP** narrow

HELP Wide is more often used than broad when you are talking about the distance between one side of something and the other: *The gate is four metres wide.*

2 including many different people or things □ *luas; pelbagai*: We sell a **broad range** of products. **3** [only before a noun] without a lot of detail; general □ *secara umum*: I'll explain the new system **in broad terms**. **4** (used about the way sb speaks) very strong □ *pekat*: She has a broad Somerset accent.

IDM (in) broad daylight during the day, when it is easy to see □ *siang hari*: He was attacked in broad daylight.

broadband /ˈbrɔːdbænd/ noun [U] a way of connecting a computer to the Internet, which allows you to receive information, including pictures, etc., very quickly □ *jalur lebar*: We have broadband at home now.

broad ˈbean noun [C] a type of large flat green bean (= seed from a plant) that can be cooked and eaten as a vegetable □ *sejenis kacang*

broadcast /ˈbrɔːdkɑːst/ verb [I,T] (pt, pp broadcast) to send out radio or TV programmes □ *menyiarkan*: The Olympics are broadcast live around the world (= at the same time as they take place). ▶**broadcast** noun [C]: We watched a live broadcast of the speech (= one that was made at the same time as the speech was made).

broadcaster /ˈbrɔːdkɑːstə(r)/ noun [C] a person who speaks on the radio or on TV □ *penyiar*

broaden /ˈbrɔːdn/ verb [I,T] broaden (sth) (out) to become wider; to make sth wider □ *melebar; melebarkan; meluaskan*: The river broadens out beyond the bridge. ♦ (figurative) Travel broadens the mind (= it makes you understand other people better).

broadly /ˈbrɔːdli/ adv 1 generally □ *secara umum*: Broadly speaking, the scheme will work as follows ... 2 (used to describe a way of smiling) with a big, wide smile □ *dgn lebar*: He smiled broadly as he shook everyone's hand.

broad-ˈminded adj happy to accept beliefs and ways of life that are different from your own □ *berfikiran luas* **OPP** narrow-minded

broccoli /ˈbrɒkəli/ noun [U] a thick green plant with green or purple flower heads that can be cooked and eaten as a vegetable □ *brokoli* ➔ picture on page P15

brochure /ˈbrəʊʃə(r)/ noun [C] a small book with pictures and information about sth □ *brosur; risalah*

broil /brɔɪl/ (especially AmE) = grill²(1)

broke¹ past tense of break¹

broke² /brəʊk/ adj [not before a noun] (informal) having no money □ *pokai; tdk berduit*: I can't come out tonight—I'm absolutely broke.

broken¹ past participle of break¹

broken² /ˈbrəʊkən/ adj 1 damaged or in pieces; not working □ *rosak; pecah; patah*: The washing machine's broken. ♦ Watch out! There's broken glass on the floor. ♦ a broken leg ♦ How did the window get broken? ➔ picture at chip²(1) 2 (used about a promise or an agreement) not kept □ *mungkir* 3 not continuous; interrupted □ *terputus-putus*: a broken line ♦ a broken night's sleep 4 [only before a noun] (used about a foreign language) spoken slowly with a lot of mistakes □ *tdk fasih; banyak kesilapannya*: to speak in broken English

broken-ˈdown adj 1 in a very bad condition □ *usang; dlm keadaan buruk*: a broken-down old building 2 (used about a vehicle) not working □ *(kenderaan) rosak*: A broken-down bus was blocking the road.

broken-ˈhearted = heartbroken

broken ˈhome noun [C] a family in which the parents do not live together, for example because they are divorced □ *rumah tangga yg berpecah belah*: Many of the children came from broken homes.

broker /ˈbrəʊkə(r)/ noun [C] a person who buys and sells things, for example shares in a business, for other people □ *broker*: an insurance broker ➔ look at stockbroker

brolly /ˈbrɒli/ (pl brollies) (BrE informal) = umbrella

bronchitis /brɒŋˈkaɪtɪs/ noun [U] an illness of the bronchial tubes (= tubes leading to the lungs) that causes a very bad cough □ *bronkitis*

bronze /brɒnz/ noun 1 [U] a dark brown metal that is made by mixing tin with copper (= a reddish-brown metal) □ *gangsa* 2 = bronze medal ▶**bronze** adj

bronzed /brɒnzd/ adj having skin that has been turned brown, in an attractive way, by the sun □ *berkulit perang* ➔ look at tan

bronze ˈmedal (also bronze) noun [C] a round piece of bronze that you get as a prize for coming third in a race or a competition □ *pingat gangsa* ➔ look at gold medal, silver medal

brooch /brəʊtʃ/ noun [C] a piece of jewellery with a pin at the back that women wear on their clothes □ *kerongsang* ➔ picture at jewellery

brood¹ /bruːd/ verb [I] 1 brood (on/over/about sth) to worry, or to think a lot about sth that makes you worried or sad □ *merisaukan*: to brood on a failure 2 (used about a female bird) to sit on her eggs □ *mengeram*

brood² /bruːd/ noun [C] all the young birds that belong to one mother □ *anak-anak seperinduk*

broody /ˈbruːdi/ adj 1 (used about a woman) wanting to have a baby □ *inginkan anak* 2 (used about a female bird) ready to have or sit on eggs □ *hendak mengeram*: a broody hen

brook /brʊk/ noun [C] a small narrow river □ *anak sungai* **SYN** stream

broom /bruːm/ noun [C] a brush with a long handle that you use for removing dirt from the floor □ *penyapu* ➔ picture at brush

broomstick /ˈbruːmstɪk/ noun [C] the handle of a broom □ *batang penyapu*

Bros abbr Brothers (used in the name of companies) □ *Bersaudara; Adik-beradik*: Wentworth Bros Ltd

broth /brɒθ/ noun [U] thick soup □ *sup pekat*: chicken broth

brothel /ˈbrɒθl/ (AmE also) / noun [C] a place where men can go and pay to have sex with a prostitute (= a woman who earns money in this way) □ *rumah pelacuran*

brother /ˈbrʌðə(r)/ *noun* [C] **1** a man or boy who has the same parents as another person □ *abang; adik lelaki*: *Michael and Jim are brothers.* ♦ *Michael is Jim's brother.* ♦ *a younger/older brother* ♦ *brothers and sisters* ♦ *Michael and Jim are Maria's brothers.* ⊃ look at **half-brother**, **stepbrother**

HELP Siblings means 'both brothers and sisters' but it is very formal, so we usually say: *Have you got any brothers and sisters?* ♦ *I haven't got any brothers or sisters.*

2 a man who is a member of a Christian religious community □ *Brother*: *Brother Luke* **3** (*informal*) a man who you feel close to because he is a member of the same society, group, etc. as you □ *saudara*: *He was greatly respected by his brother officers.*

brotherhood /ˈbrʌðəhʊd/ *noun* **1** [U] a feeling of great friendship and understanding between people □ *persaudaraan*: *the brotherhood of man* (= a feeling of friendship between all the people in the world) **2** [C, with sing or pl verb] an organization which is formed for a particular, often religious, purpose □ *persatuan*

ˈbrother-in-law *noun* [C] (*pl* **brothers-in-law**) **1** the brother of your husband or wife □ *abang/adik ipar* **2** the husband of your sister □ *abang/adik ipar*

brotherly /ˈbrʌðəli/ *adj* showing feelings of love and kindness that you would expect a brother to show □ *sebagai saudara*: *brotherly love/advice*

brought *past tense, past participle* of **bring**

brow /braʊ/ *noun* [C] **1** = **forehead 2** [usually pl] = **eyebrow 3** [sing] the top part of a hill □ *puncak*: *Suddenly a car came over the brow of the hill.*

brown¹ /braʊn/ *adj* (**browner**; **brownest**) *noun* **1** [C,U] (of) the colour of earth or wood □ *warna coklat/perang*: *brown eyes/hair* ♦ *the yellows and browns of the trees in autumn* ♦ *You don't look nice in brown* (= in brown clothes). **2** having skin that the sun has made darker □ *kulit perang*: *Although I often sunbathe, I never seem to go brown.*

brown² /braʊn/ *verb* [I,T] to become or make sth become brown □ *menjadi perang*: *First, brown the meat in a frying pan.*

brownie /ˈbraʊni/ *noun* [C] **1** a type of heavy chocolate cake that often contains nuts □ *brownie* **2 Brownie** a young girl who is a member of the lowest level of the Girl Guides organization □ *Tunas Puteri*

ˌbrown ˈpaper *noun* [U] strong, thick paper used for putting round packages, etc. □ *kertas kuning*: *I wrapped the books in brown paper and tied the package with string.*

browse /braʊz/ *verb* **1** [I] to spend time pleasantly in a shop, looking at a lot of things rather than looking for one particular thing □ *melihat-lihat*: *I spent hours browsing in the local bookshop.* **2** [I] **browse through sth** to look through a book or magazine without reading every part or studying it carefully □ *membelek-belek buku, majalah, dsb*: *I enjoyed browsing through the catalogue but I didn't order anything.* **3** [T] to look for and read information on a computer □ *menyemak seimbas*: *I've just been browsing the Internet for information on Iceland.*
▶ **browse** *noun* [sing]

browser /ˈbraʊzə(r)/ *noun* [C] a computer program that lets you look at words and pictures from other computer systems by receiving information through telephone wires □ *penyemak seimbas*: *an Internet browser*

bruise /bruːz/ *noun* [C] a blue, brown or purple mark that appears on the skin after sb has fallen, been hit, etc. □ *lebam*

MORE A bruise around your eye is a **black eye**.

▶ **bruise** *verb* [I,T]: *I fell over and bruised my arm.* ♦ *Handle the fruit carefully or you'll bruise it.* ♦ *I've got the sort of skin that bruises easily.*

brunette /bruːˈnet/ *noun* [C] a white woman with dark brown hair □ *wanita kulit putih berambut coklat tua* ⊃ look at **blonde**

brunt /brʌnt/ *noun*
IDM **bear the brunt of sth** ⊃ **bear¹**

brushes

nail brush

toothbrush hairbrush

dustpan

broom paintbrushes brush

brush¹ /brʌʃ/ *noun* **1** [C] an object that is used for cleaning things, painting, tidying your hair, etc. □ *berus*: *I took a brush and swept the snow from the path.* ♦ *a toothbrush* ♦ *a paintbrush* ♦ *a hairbrush* **2** [sing] an act of cleaning, tidying the hair, etc. with a brush □ *(perbuatan) memberus/diberus*: *The floor needs a brush.*

IDM **(have) a brush with sb/sth** (to have or almost have) an unpleasant meeting with sb/sth □ *perselisihan dgn sso/sst*: *My only brush with the law was when I was stopped for speeding.*

brush² /brʌʃ/ *verb* [T] to clean, tidy, etc. sth with a brush □ *memberus; merapikan rambut* *dgn berus*: Make sure you **brush** your **teeth** twice a day. ♦ **Brush** your **hair** before you go out. ➲ note at **clean²** **2** [I,T] to touch sb/sth lightly when passing ▫ *menyentuh; menggesel*: *Her hand brushed his cheek.* ♦ *Leaves brushed against the car as we drove along the narrow road.*

PHR V **brush sb/sth aside** **1** to refuse to pay attention to sb/sth ▫ *tdk mengendahkan (atau mengetepikan) sso/sst*: *She brushed aside the protests and continued with the meeting.* **2** to push past sb/sth ▫ *menolak sso/sst ke tepi*: *He hurried through the crowd, brushing aside the reporters and photographers who tried to stop him.*
brush sth off (sth)/away to remove sth with a brush or with the hand, as if using a brush ▫ *menyapu dgn berus atau tangan utk membuang sst*: *I brushed the dust off my jacket.*
brush sth up/brush up on sth to study or practise sth in order to get back knowledge or skill that you had before and have lost ▫ *mempelajari atau berlatih semula sst*: *She took a course to brush up her Spanish.*

'brush-off *noun*
IDM **give sb the brush-off** (*informal*) to refuse to be friendly to sb ▫ *menolak; tdk melayan*: *I'd ask her to go out with me but I'm scared she'd give me the brush-off.*

brusque /bru:sk/ *adj* using very few words and sounding rude ▫ *kasar*: *He gave a brusque 'No comment!' and walked off.* ▶ **brusquely** *adv*

Brussels sprout /ˌbrʌslz ˈspraʊt/ (also **sprout**) *noun* [C, usually pl] a round green vegetable that looks like a very small **cabbage** (= a large round vegetable with thick green leaves) ▫ *kubis Brussels* ➲ picture on **page P15**

brutal /ˈbruːtl/ *adj* very cruel and/or violent ▫ *kejam*: *a brutal murder* ♦ *a brutal dictatorship* ▶ **brutally** /-təli/ *adv*: *He was brutally honest and told her that he didn't love her any more.*

brutality /bruːˈtæləti/ *noun* [C,U] (*pl* **brutalities**) very cruel and violent behaviour ▫ *kekejaman*

brute¹ /bruːt/ *noun* [C] **1** a cruel, violent man ▫ *orang yg kejam* **2** a large strong animal ▫ *binatang besar*: *That dog of theirs is an absolute brute.*

brute² /bruːt/ *adj* [only *before* a noun] using strength to do sth rather than thinking about it ▫ *kekuatan jasmani; kekerasan*: *I think you'll have to use brute force to get this window open.*

BSc /ˌbiː es ˈsiː/ *abbr* **Bachelor of Science**; the degree that you receive when you complete a university or college course in a science subject ▫ *ijazah Sarjana Muda Sains* ➲ look at **BA, MSc**

BSE /ˌbiː es ˈiː/ (also *informal* ˌmad ˈcow disˌease) *noun* [U] **bovine spongiform encephalopathy**; a disease of cows which affects their brains and usually kills them ▫ *BSE; penyakit lembu gila* ➲ look at **CJD**

BST /ˌbiː es ˈtiː/ *noun* [U] **British Summer Time**; the time used in Britain between March and October, which is one hour ahead of GMT ▫ *Waktu Musim Panas British*

BTEC /ˈbiːtek/ *noun* [C] an exam for young people who have left secondary school and are training in commercial or technical subjects ▫ *peperiksaan BTEC*: *She's doing a BTEC in design.*

BTW *abbr* used in emails, etc. to mean 'by the way' ▫ *'oh ya'*

bubble¹ /ˈbʌbl/ *noun* [C] a ball of air or gas, in liquid or floating in the air ▫ *buih; gelembung*: *You can blow bubbles with washing-up liquid.* ♦ *We knew where there were fish because of the bubbles on the surface.*

bubble² /ˈbʌbl/ *verb* [I] **1** to produce bubbles or to rise with bubbles ▫ *berbuih; membobok*: *Cook the pizza until the cheese starts to bubble.* ♦ *The clear water bubbled up out of the ground.* **2** **bubble (over) (with sth)** to be full of happy feelings ▫ *meluap-luap (dgn kegembiraan, dsb)*

'bubble bath *noun* [U] a liquid that you can add to the water in a bath to produce a mass of white bubbles ▫ *mandian buih*

bubblegum /ˈbʌblgʌm/ *noun* [U] a sticky sweet that you eat but do not swallow and that can be blown into bubbles out of the mouth ▫ *gula-gula getah* ➲ look at **chewing gum**

bubbly /ˈbʌbli/ *adj* (**bubblier; bubbliest**) **1** full of bubbles ▫ *penuh buih* **2** (used about a person) happy and full of energy ▫ *periang*

buck¹ /bʌk/ *noun* [C] **1** (*AmE informal*) a US dollar ▫ *dolar*: *Could you lend me a few bucks?* **2** (*pl* **buck** or **bucks**) a male **rabbit** (= a small animal with long ears) or **deer** (= a large wild animal that eats grass) ▫ *jantan (bagi rusa, arnab dan haiwan tertentu yg lain)* ➲ note at **deer** ➲ picture at **deer** ➲ picture on **page P12**
IDM **pass the buck** ➲ **pass¹**

buck² /bʌk/ *verb* [I] (used about a horse) to jump into the air or to kick the back legs in the air ▫ *(kuda) melompat atau mengangkat kaki belakang ke atas*
PHR V **buck (sb/sth) up** (*informal*) to feel or to make sb feel better or happier ▫ *menggembirakan/menceriakan (sso/sst)*: *Drink this—it'll buck you up.* ♦ *Unless you buck your ideas up* (= become more sensible and serious), *you'll never pass the exam.*

bucket /ˈbʌkɪt/ *noun* [C] **1** a round, open container, usually made of metal or plastic, with a handle, that is used for carrying sth ▫ *baldi* **2** (also **bucketful** /-fʊl/) the amount that a bucket contains ▫ *sebaldi*: *How many buckets of water do you think we'll need?*
IDM **a drop in the bucket** ➲ **drop²**

buckle¹ /ˈbʌkl/ *verb* [I,T] **1** to fasten or be fastened with a **buckle** ▫ *melekapkan dgn gancu; mengancing* **2** to become crushed or bent

buckle → bug

[Illustration labels: bucket, polish, duster, mop, rubber gloves, cloth, sponge]

because of heat, force, weakness, etc.; to crush or bend sth in this way □ *membengkok: Some railway lines buckled in the heat.*

buckle² /ˈbʌkl/ *noun* [C] a piece of metal or plastic at the end of a belt or other narrow piece of material that is used for fastening it □ *gancu* ⊃ picture at **button** ⊃ picture on **page P1**

bud /bʌd/ *noun* [C] a small lump on a tree or plant that opens and develops into a flower or leaf □ *tunas; kudup: rosebuds* ⊃ picture at **plant, tree**
IDM nip sth in the bud ⊃ nip

Buddhism /ˈbʊdɪzəm/ *noun* [U] an Asian religion that was started in India by Siddharta Gautama (Buddha) □ *agama Buddha*

Buddhist /ˈbʊdɪst/ *noun* [C] a person whose religion is Buddhism □ *penganut agama Buddha* ▶ **Buddhist** *adj*: *a Buddhist temple*

budding /ˈbʌdɪŋ/ *adj* [only before a noun] wanting or starting to develop and be successful □ *mula meningkat: Have you got any tips for budding young photographers?*

buddy /ˈbʌdi/ *noun* [C] (pl **buddies**) (*informal*) a friend □ *kawan; teman: an old college buddy of mine*

budge /bʌdʒ/ *verb* [I,T] **1** to move or make sth move a little □ *menganjak; menganjakkan: I tried as hard as I could to loosen the screw but it simply wouldn't budge.* ♦ *We just couldn't budge the car when it got stuck in the mud.* **2** to change or make sb change a firm opinion □ *berganjak: Neither side in the dispute is prepared to budge.*

budgerigar /ˈbʌdʒərɪɡɑː(r)/ (also *informal* **budgie**) *noun* [C] a small, brightly coloured bird that people often keep as a pet in a **cage** (= a box made of bars) □ *budgerigar* ⊃ note at **pet**

budget¹ /ˈbʌdʒɪt/ *noun* **1** [C,U] a plan of how to spend an amount of money over a particular period of time; the amount of money that is mentioned □ *peruntukan belanja; belanjawan; bajet: What's your monthly budget for food?* ♦ *a country's defence budget* ♦ *The work was finished on time and within budget.* ♦ *The builders are already 20% over budget.* **2 Budget** [C, usually sing] a statement by a government saying how much money it plans to spend on particular things in the next year and how it plans to collect money □ *belanjawan: Do you think taxes will go up in this year's budget?*

budget² /ˈbʌdʒɪt/ *verb* [I,T] **budget (sth) (for sth)** to plan carefully how much money to spend on sth □ *menyediakan belanjawan; membuat peruntukan: The government has budgeted £10 billion for education.*

budget³ /ˈbʌdʒɪt/ *adj* [only before a noun] (*informal*) (used in advertisements) very cheap □ *jimat; murah: budget holidays*

budgie /ˈbʌdʒi/ (*informal*) = **budgerigar**

buff¹ /bʌf/ *noun* [C] (*informal*) a person who knows a lot about a particular subject and is very interested in it □ *peminat: a film/computer buff*

buff² /bʌf/ *adj* (*slang*) physically fit and attractive with big muscles □ *tegap*

buffalo /ˈbʌfələʊ/ *noun* [C] (pl **buffalo** or **buffaloes**) a large wild animal that looks like a cow with long curved horns □ *kerbau: a herd of buffalo*

buffer /ˈbʌfə(r)/ *noun* [C] **1** a thing or person that reduces the unpleasant effects of sth or prevents violent contact between two things, people, etc □ *penampan: UN forces are acting as a buffer between the two sides in the war.* **2** a flat round piece of metal with a spring behind it that is on the front or back of a train or at the end of a railway track. **Buffers** reduce the shock when sth hits them. □ *penimbal*

buffet¹ /ˈbʊfeɪ; ˈbʌfeɪ/ *noun* [C] **1** a meal (usually at a party or a special occasion) at which food is placed on a long table and people serve themselves □ *bufet; jamuan berselerak: Lunch was a cold buffet.* ♦ *a buffet lunch* **2** part of a train or a place at a station where passengers can buy food and drinks □ *gerabak bufet*

buffet² /ˈbʌfɪt/ *verb* [T] to knock or push sth in a rough way from side to side □ *memukul; mengoleng-oleng: The boat was buffeted by the rough sea.*

bug¹ /bʌɡ/ *noun* **1** [C] (*especially AmE*) any small insect □ *serangga* **2** [C] an illness that is not very serious and that people get from each other □ *penyakit: I don't feel very well—I think I've got the bug that's going round.* **3** usually **the … bug** [sing] (*informal*) a sudden interest in sth □ *gila; amat meminati: They've been bitten by the golf bug.* **4** [C] a very small **microphone** (= a device used for recording sounds) that is hidden and used to secretly listen to and record people's conversations □ *peranti pepijat* **5** [C] something wrong in a system or machine, especially a computer □ *pepijat; kesilapan: There's a bug in the software.*

[I] **intransitive**, a verb which has no object: *He laughed.*

[T] **transitive**, a verb which has an object: *He ate an apple.*

bug² /bʌg/ verb [T] (bugging; bugged) **1** to hide a very small **microphone** (= a device used for recording sounds) somewhere so that people's conversations can be recorded secretly □ *memasang peranti pepijat*: Be careful what you say. This room is bugged. **2** (informal) to annoy or worry sb □ *menyakitkan hati; merunsingkan*: It bugs him that he's not as successful as his brother.

buggy /'bʌgi/ (pl buggies) (BrE) = pushchair

build¹ /bɪld/ verb (pt, pp built /bɪlt/) **1** [T] to make sth by putting pieces, materials, etc. together □ *membina*: They've built a new bridge across the river. ◆ The house is built of stone. **2** [I] to use land for building on □ *mendirikan bangunan*: There's plenty of land to build on around here. **3** [T] to develop or increase sth □ *membina; membangunkan*: The government is trying to build a more modern society. ◆ This book claims to help people to build their self-confidence.

PHR V build sth in/on; build sth into/onto sth to make sth a part of sth else □ *memasukkan/menyertakan sst ke dlm sst; membina/membentuk sst pd sst*: They've made sure that a large number of checks are built into the system. ◆ We're planning to build two more rooms onto the back of the house.

build on sth to use sth as a base from which you can make further progress □ *menggunakan sst sebagai asas utk pembangunan seterusnya*: Now that we're beginning to make a profit, we must build on this success.

build sth on sth to base sth on sth □ *mengasaskan sst pd sst*: a society built on the principle of freedom and democracy

build up (to sth) to become greater in amount or number; to increase □ *semakin meningkat*: The traffic starts to build up at this time of day.

build sth up 1 to make sth seem more important or greater than it really is □ *membesar-besarkan sst*: I don't think it's a very serious matter, it's just been built up in the newspapers. **2** to increase or develop sth over a period □ *meningkatkan/membangunkan sst*: You'll need to build up your strength again slowly after the operation.

build² /bɪld/ noun [C,U] the shape and size of sb's body □ *bentuk badan*: She has a very athletic build.

> **HELP** Build or figure? **Build** usually describes size in connection with strength and muscle and is used for both men and women. **Figure** usually describes shape, especially whether it is attractive or not, and is usually used only for women.

builder /'bɪldə(r)/ noun [C] a person whose job is to build houses and other buildings □ *pembina*

building /'bɪldɪŋ/ noun **1** [C] a structure, such as a house, shop or school, that has a roof and walls □ *bangunan; binaan*: There are a lot of very old buildings in this town. **2** [U] the process or business of making buildings □ *binaan; pembinaan*: the building of the school ◆ building materials ◆ the building industry

'building site noun [C] an area of land on which a building is being built □ *tapak binaan*

'building society noun [C] (BrE) an organization like a bank with which people can save money and which lends money to people who want to buy a house □ *syarikat pinjaman perumahan*

'build-up noun [C, usually sing] **1 a build-up (of sth)** an increase of sth over a period □ *bertambahnya; meningkatnya*: The build-up of tension in the area has made war seem more likely. **2 a build-up (to sth)** a period of preparation or excitement before an event □ *tempoh persediaan atau rasa penuh semangat menjelang sst peristiwa*: The players started to get nervous in the build-up to the big game.

built¹ /bɪlt/ [in compounds] made in the particular way that is mentioned □ *mengikut cara yg dinyatakan*: a newly built station ◆ The man was tall and well built.

built² past tense, past participle of **build**

,built-'in adj [only before a noun] that is a part of sth and cannot be removed □ *sebahagian drpd struktur keseluruhan*: built-in cupboards

,built-'up adj covered with buildings, roads, etc. □ *berbangunan*: a built-up area

bulb /bʌlb/ noun [C] **1** (also 'light bulb) the glass part of an electric lamp that gives out light □ *mentol*: The bulb's gone (= it no longer works) in this lamp. ⊃ picture at **lamp 2** the round root of certain plants □ *bebawang*: a tulip bulb ⊃ picture at **plant**

bulbous /'bʌlbəs/ adj fat, round and ugly □ *bulat dan dempak*: a bulbous red nose

bulge¹ /bʌldʒ/ verb [I] **1 bulge (with sth)** to be full of sth □ *membonjol; penuh dgn*: His bags were bulging with presents for the children. **2** to stick out in a lump from sth that is usually flat □ *membonjol; menjadi buncit*: My stomach is starting to bulge. I must get more exercise.

bulge² /bʌldʒ/ noun [C] a round lump that sticks out on sth □ *benjol*

bulging /'bʌldʒɪŋ/ adj sticking out □ *(yg) membonjol*: He had a thin face and rather bulging eyes.

bulimia /bu'lɪmiə/ (also bulimia nervosa /bu,lɪmiə nɜː'vəʊsə/) noun [U] an illness in which a person eats too much and then forces himself or herself to **vomit** (= bring up food from the stomach) □ *bulimia* ⊃ look at **anorexia**
▶ **bulimic** adj, noun [C]

bulk /bʌlk/ noun **1** [sing] **the bulk (of sth)** the main part of sth; most of sth □ *bahagian utama; sebahagian besar*: The bulk of the work has been done, so we should finish this week. **2** [U] the size, quantity or weight of sth large □ *besarnya;*

bulky → bumper

besar: *The cupboard isn't especially heavy—what makes it hard to move is its bulk.* ♦ *He slowly lifted his vast bulk out of the chair.*
IDM **in bulk** in large quantities □ *banyak-banyak; secara pukal*: *If you buy in bulk, it's 10% cheaper.*

bulky /'bʌlki/ *adj* (**bulkier**; **bulkiest**) large and heavy and therefore difficult to move or carry □ *besar dan berat*: *a bulky parcel*

bull /bʊl/ *noun* [C] **1** an adult male of the cow family □ *lembu jantan* ⊃ note at **cow** ⊃ picture at **cow 2** a male **whale** (= a very large sea animal) or **elephant** (= a large grey animal with a long nose) □ *jantan (bagi paus, gajah dan haiwan tertentu yg lain)*

bulldog /'bʊldɒɡ/ *noun* [C] a strong dog with short legs, a large head and a short, thick neck □ *(anjing) buldog*

'Bulldog clip™ *noun* [C] (*BrE*) a metal device for holding papers together □ *klip Bulldog* ⊃ picture at **stationery**

bulldoze /'bʊldəʊz/ *verb* [T] to make ground flat or to knock down a building with a **bulldozer** □ *meratakan dgn jentolak*: *The old buildings were bulldozed and new ones were built.*

bulldozer

bulldozer /'bʊldəʊzə(r)/ *noun* [C] a large, powerful vehicle with a wide piece of metal at the front, used for clearing ground or knocking down buildings □ *jentolak*

bullet /'bʊlɪt/ *noun* [C] a small metal object that is fired from a gun □ *peluru*: *The bullet hit her in the arm.* ♦ *a bullet wound*

bulletin /'bʊlətɪn/ *noun* [C] **1** a short news report on TV or radio; an official statement about a situation □ *buletin; berita ringkas*: *The next news bulletin on this channel is at 9 o'clock.* **2** a short newspaper that a club or an organization produces □ *buletin; risalah*: *As a member of the fan club, she receives a monthly bulletin.*

'bulletin board *noun* [C] **1** (*AmE*) = **noticeboard 2** a place in a computer system where you can write or read messages □ *tapak buletin* ⊃ note at **netiquette**

bulletproof /'bʊlɪtpruːf/ *adj* made of a strong material that stops bullets from passing through it □ *kalis peluru*

bullfight /'bʊlfaɪt/ *noun* [C] a traditional public entertainment, especially in Spain, Portugal and Latin America, in which a **bull** (= an adult male cow) is fought and usually killed □ *sukan lawan lembu* ▶**bullfighter** *noun* [C] ▶**bullfighting** *noun* [U]

bullion /'bʊliən/ *noun* [U] bars of gold or silver □ *bulion; jongkong*: *The dollar price of gold bullion has risen by more than 10%.*

bullseye /'bʊlzaɪ/ *noun* [C] the centre of the round object that you shoot or throw things at in certain sports; a shot that hits this □ *pusat sasaran*

bully¹ /'bʊli/ *noun* [C] (*pl* **bullies**) a person who uses their strength or power to hurt or frighten people who are weaker □ *orang yg suka membuli*

bully² /'bʊli/ *verb* [T] (**bullying**; **bullies**; *pt, pp* **bullied**) **bully sb (into doing sth)** to use your strength or power to hurt or frighten sb who is weaker or to make them do sth □ *membuli*: *Don't try to bully me into making a decision.* ▶**bullying** *noun* [U]: *Bullying is a serious problem in many schools.*

bum /bʌm/ *noun* [C] (*informal*) **1** (*BrE*) the part of your body on which you sit □ *buntut; punggung* **SYN** **bottom 2** (*especially AmE*) an insulting word for a person who lives on the street □ *orang gelandangan* **3** (*especially AmE*) a lazy or useless person □ *pemalas*

bumbag /'bʌmbæɡ/ (*AmE* '**fanny pack**) *noun* [C] (*informal*) a small bag worn around the waist to keep money, etc. in □ *beg pinggang* ⊃ picture at **bag**

bump¹ /bʌmp/ *verb* **1** [I] **bump against/into sb/sth** to hit sb/sth by accident when you are moving □ *terlanggar*: *She bumped into a lamp post because she wasn't looking where she was going.* **2** [T] **bump sth (against/on sth)** to hit sth against or on sth by accident □ *terhantuk*: *I bumped my knee on the edge of the table.* **3** [I] to move along over a rough surface □ *terhinggut-hinggut*: *The car bumped along the track to the farm.*
PHR V **bump into sb** to meet sb by chance □ *terserempak dgn sso*: *I bumped into an old friend on the bus today.*
bump sb off (*slang*) to murder sb □ *membunuh sso*
bump sth up (*informal*) to increase or make sth go up □ *meningkatkan/menaikkan sst*: *All this publicity will bump up sales of our new product.*

bump² /bʌmp/ *noun* [C] **1** the action or sound of sth hitting a hard surface □ *kejadian atau bunyi terhantuk*: *She fell and hit the ground with a bump.* **2** a lump on the body, often caused by a hit □ *benjol* **3** a part of a surface that is higher than the rest of it □ *bonggol*: *There are a lot of bumps in the road, so drive carefully.*

bumper¹ /'bʌmpə(r)/ *noun* [C] the bar fixed to the front and back of a motor vehicle to protect it if it hits sth □ *bampar* ⊃ picture on page P7

bumper² /'bʌmpə(r)/ *adj* [only before a noun] larger than usual □ *lebih banyak, baik, dsb drpd biasa*: *The unusually fine weather has produced a bumper harvest this year.*

ð **then**   s **so**   z **zoo**   ʃ **she**   ʒ **vi**sion   h **how**   m **man**   n **no**   ŋ **si**ng   l **leg**   r **red**   j **yes**   w **wet**

bumpy /ˈbʌmpi/ adj (bumpier; bumpiest) not flat or smooth □ berbonggol-bonggol; lekak-lekuk; terenjut-enjut; melambung-lambung: *a bumpy road* ◆ *Because of the stormy weather, it was a very bumpy flight.* **OPP** smooth

bun /bʌn/ noun [C] **1** a small round sweet cake □ *ban: a currant bun* ⊃ picture at **cake 2** a small soft bread roll □ *roti ban: a hamburger bun* **3** hair fastened tightly into a round shape at the back of the head □ *sanggul; siput: She wears her hair in a bun.* ⊃ picture at **hair**

bunch¹ /bʌntʃ/ noun **1** [C] a number of things, usually of the same type, fastened or growing together □ *jambak; sikat; gugus; rangkai: He bought her a bunch of flowers.* ◆ *a bunch of bananas/grapes* ◆ *a bunch of keys* **2** [C, with sing or pl verb] (*informal*) a group of people □ *kumpulan: My colleagues are the best bunch of people I've ever worked with.* **3** bunches [pl] long hair that is tied on each side of the head □ *rambut yg diikat: She wore her hair in bunches.* ⊃ picture at **hair**

bunch² /bʌntʃ/ verb [I,T] bunch (sth/sb) (up/together) to stay together in a group; to form sth into a group or bunch □ *berkumpul; memulun: The runners bunched up as they came round the final bend.* ◆ *He kept his papers bunched together in his hand.*

bundle¹ /ˈbʌndl/ noun [C] **1** a number of things tied or folded together □ *berkas; ikat: a bundle of letters with an elastic band round them* **2** a number of things that belong, or are sold together □ *bungkusan: a bundle of graphics packages for your PC*

bundle² /ˈbʌndl/ verb [T] to put or push sb or sth quickly and in a rough way in a particular direction □ *menolak cepat-cepat; menggesa: He was arrested and bundled into a police car.*

PHR V bundle sth up; bundle sth together to make or tie a number of things together □ *mengikat; mengumpul: I bundled up the old newspapers and threw them away.*

bung¹ /bʌŋ/ verb [T] (*BrE informal*) to put or throw sth somewhere in a rough or careless way □ *mencampakkan; menyumbat: We bunged the suitcases into the car and drove away.*

bung² /bʌŋ/ noun [C] a round piece of wood or rubber that is used for closing the hole in a container such as a **barrel** □ *penyumbat*

bungalow /ˈbʌŋɡələʊ/ noun [C] (*BrE*) a house that is all on one level, without stairs □ *banglo* ⊃ picture on **page P9**

bunged ˈup adj (*informal*) blocked, so that nothing can get through □ *tersumbat: I feel terrible—I've got a cold and my nose is all bunged up.*

bungee jumping /ˈbʌndʒi dʒʌmpɪŋ/ noun [U] a sport in which you jump from a high place, for example a bridge, with a thick elastic (= material that can stretch) rope tied round your feet □ *terjun lelabah* ⊃ picture on **page P5**

bungle /ˈbʌŋɡl/ verb [T] to do sth badly or fail to do sth □ *membuat sst dgn tdk sempurna: a bungled robbery*

bunk /bʌŋk/ noun [C] **1** a bed that is fixed to a wall, especially on a ship or train □ *tempat tidur (dlm kapal, kereta api, dsb)* **2** (also ˈbunk bed) one of a pair of single beds built as a unit with one above the other □ *katil dua tingkat* ⊃ note at **bed** ⊃ picture at **bed**
IDM do a bunk (*BrE informal*) to run away or escape; to leave without telling anyone □ *cabut; melarikan diri*

bunker /ˈbʌŋkə(r)/ noun [C] **1** a strong underground building that gives protection in a war □ *kubu bawah tanah* **2** a hole filled with sand on a **golf course** (= the large area of land on which you hit a small ball into a number of holes) □ *bunker*

bunny /ˈbʌni/ noun [C] (*pl* bunnies) a child's word for **rabbit** (= a small animal with long ears) □ *arnab*

Bunsen burner /ˌbʌnsn ˈbɜːnə(r)/ noun [C] an instrument used in scientific work that produces a hot gas flame □ *penunu Bunsen*

buoy¹ /bɔɪ/ noun [C] an object that floats on the sea or a river that shows the places where it is dangerous for boats to go □ *boya*

buoy² /bɔɪ/ verb [T] buoy sb/sth (up) **1** to keep sb happy and confident □ *memberi semangat; menggembirakan: His encouragement buoyed her up during that difficult period.* **2** to keep sth at a high level □ *mengapung; kekal pd tahap yg tinggi: Share prices were buoyed by news of a takeover.*

buoyant /ˈbɔɪənt/ adj **1** (used about prices, business activity, etc.) staying at a high level or increasing, so that people make more money □ *berada pd tahap tinggi atau meningkat: Despite the recession, the property market remained buoyant.* **2** happy and confident □ *periang: The team were in buoyant mood after their win.* **3** (used about a material) floating or able to float □ *dpt mengapung* ▶ buoyancy /-ənsi/ noun [U]: *the buoyancy of the German economy*

burden¹ /ˈbɜːdn/ noun [C] **1** a responsibility or difficult task that causes a lot of work or worry □ *beban: Having to make all the decisions is a terrible burden for me.* ◆ *I don't want to be a burden to my parents.* **2** something that is heavy and difficult to carry □ *beban*

burden² /ˈbɜːdn/ verb [T] burden sb/yourself (with sth) to give sb/yourself a responsibility or task that causes a lot of work or worry □ *membebankan*

bureau /ˈbjʊərəʊ/ noun [C] (*pl* bureaux or bureaus /-rəʊz/) **1** (*BrE*) a writing desk with drawers and a lid □ *meja tulis berlaci* **2** an organization that provides information □ *biro: a tourist information bureau* **3** (*especially AmE*) one

bureaucracy → burning 112

of certain government departments □ *biro; jabatan*: *the Federal Bureau of Investigation*

bureaucracy /bjʊəˈrɒkrəsi/ noun (pl **bureaucracies**) **1** [U] (often used in a critical way) the system of official rules that an organization has for doing sth, that people often think is too complicated □ *birokrasi; peraturan-peraturan rasmi yg rumit*: *Getting a visa involves a lot of unnecessary bureaucracy.* **2** [C,U] a system of government by a large number of officials who are not elected; a country with this system □ *birokrasi* ▶ **bureaucratic** /ˌbjʊərəˈkrætɪk/ adj: *You have to go through a complex bureaucratic procedure if you want to get your money back.*

bureaucrat /ˈbjʊərəkræt/ noun [C] (often used in a critical way) an official in an organization or government department □ *birokrat*

bureau de change /ˌbjʊərəʊ də ˈʃɑːnʒ/ noun [C] (pl **bureaux de change**) an office at an airport, in a hotel, etc. where you can change the money of one country to the money of another country □ *kedai urup*

burger /ˈbɜːɡə(r)/ **1** (also **beefburger**, especially *AmE* **hamburger**) beef that has been cut up small, pressed into a flat round shape and cooked. A **burger** is often eaten in a bread roll. □ *burger* **2** something that is cooked like and looks like a **burger**, but is made of sth else □ *burger*: *a veggie burger*

burglar /ˈbɜːɡlə(r)/ noun [C] a person who enters a building illegally in order to steal □ *pencuri (yg memecah masuk)*: *The burglars broke in by smashing a window.* ➔ note at **thief** ▶ **burgle** /ˈbɜːɡl/ (*AmE* **burglarize** /ˈbɜːɡləraɪz/) verb [T]: *Our flat was burgled while we were out.*

'burglar alarm noun [C] a piece of equipment, usually fixed on a wall, that makes a loud noise if a thief enters a building □ *penggera kecurian*

burglary /ˈbɜːɡləri/ noun [C,U] (pl **burglaries**) the crime of entering a building illegally in order to steal □ *kejadian mencuri*: *There was a burglary next door last week.* ◆ *He is in prison for burglary.*

burgundy /ˈbɜːɡəndi/ noun **1** Burgundy [U,C] (pl **Burgundies**) a red or white wine from the Burgundy area of eastern France □ *Burgundy (wain)* **2** [U] a dark red colour □ *(warna) merah manggis* ▶ **burgundy** adj

burial /ˈberiəl/ noun [C,U] the ceremony when a dead body is buried in the ground □ *pengebumian*: *The burial took place on Friday.* ➔ note at **funeral**

burka (also **burkha**) /ˈbʊəkə; ˈbɜːkə/ noun [C] a long loose piece of clothing that covers the whole body and that is worn by Muslim women in some countries □ *burka*

burly /ˈbɜːli/ adj (**burlier**; **burliest**) (used about a person or their body) strong and heavy □ *tegap sasa*

ʔ burn¹ /bɜːn/ verb (pt, pp **burnt** /bɜːnt/ or **burned** /bɜːnd/) **1** [I] to be on fire □ *terbakar*: *Firemen raced to the burning building.* ➔ note at **alight 2** [T] to destroy, damage or injure sb/sth with fire or heat □ *membakar; terbakar*: *We took all the rubbish outside and burned it.* ◆ *It was a terrible fire and the whole building was burnt to the ground* (= completely destroyed). ◆ *If you get too close to the fire you'll burn yourself.* ◆ *The people inside the building couldn't get out and they were all burnt to death.* **3** [I] to be destroyed, damaged or injured by fire or heat □ *hangus; terselar; terbakar*: *If you leave the cake in the oven for much longer, it will burn.* ◆ *I can't spend too much time in the sun because I burn easily.* ◆ *They were trapped by the flames and they burned to death.* **4** [T] to produce a hole or mark in or on sth by burning □ *berlubang atau bertanda kerana terbakar*: *He dropped the match and it burned a hole in the carpet.* **5** [T] to use sth as fuel □ *menggunakan sst sebagai bahan api*: *an oil-burning lamp* **6** [I] to feel very hot and painful □ *membahang; menjadi panas*: *You have a temperature—your forehead's burning.* **7** [I] to produce light □ *menyala*: *I don't think he went to bed at all—I could see his light burning all night.* **8** [T] to put information onto a CD, etc. □ *menyalin maklumat* **9** [I] **burn (with sth)** to be filled with a very strong feeling □ *membara; meluap-luap*: *She was burning with indignation.*

IDM **sb's ears are burning** ➔ **ear**

PHR V **burn down** (used about a building) to be completely destroyed by fire □ *musnah dijilat api*: *The fire could not be brought under control and the school burned down.*

burn sth down to completely destroy a building by fire □ *terbakar; hangus*: *The house was burnt down in a fire some years ago.*

burn (sth) off to remove sth or to be removed by burning □ *membuang/menanggalkan (sst) dgn membakar*

burn sth out [usually passive] to completely destroy sth by burning □ *musnah/hangus terbakar*: *the burnt-out wreck of a car*

burn (yourself) out to work, etc., until you have no more energy or strength and feel extremely tired □ *kehabisan tenaga*: *I've been studying so hard recently I feel completely burned out.*

burn (sth) up to destroy or to be destroyed by fire or strong heat □ *membakar; terbakar*: *The space capsule burnt up on its re-entry into the earth's atmosphere.*

burn² /bɜːn/ noun [C] damage or an injury caused by fire or heat □ *luka terbakar; melecur*: *He was taken to hospital with minor burns.* ◆ *There's a cigarette burn on the carpet.*

burner /ˈbɜːnə(r)/ (*AmE*) = **ring¹(5)**

burning /ˈbɜːnɪŋ/ adj [only before a noun] **1** (used about a feeling) extremely strong □ *(yg) berkobar-kobar*: *a burning ambition/desire* **2** very important or urgent □ *sangat penting; mendesak*: *a burning issue/question* **3** feeling very hot □ *panas membahang*: *the burning sun*

burnt *past tense, past participle of* **burn**

burp /bɜːp/ *verb* [I] to make a noise with the mouth when air rises from the stomach and is forced out □ *bersendawa*: *He sat back when he had finished his meal and burped loudly.* ▶**burp** *noun* [C]

burrow¹ /ˈbʌrəʊ/ *verb* [I] to dig a hole in the ground, to make a tunnel or to look for sth □ *mengorok; menyeluk*: *These animals burrow for food.* ♦ (*figurative*) *She burrowed in her handbag for her keys.*

burrow² /ˈbʌrəʊ/ *noun* [C] a hole in the ground made by certain animals, for example **rabbits** (= small animals with long ears), in which they live □ *korok*

bursar /ˈbɜːsə(r)/ *noun* [C] the person who manages the financial matters of a school, college or university □ *bendahari*

bursary /ˈbɜːsəri/ *noun* [C] (*pl* bursaries) a sum of money given to a specially chosen student to pay for his or her studies at a college or university □ *dermasiswa* ➔ look at **scholarship**

burst¹ /bɜːst/ *verb* (*pt, pp* burst) **1** [I,T] to break open suddenly and violently, usually because there is too much pressure inside; to cause this to happen □ *pecah; meletup*: *The ball burst when I kicked it.* ♦ *You'll burst that tyre if you blow it up any more.* ♦ (*figurative*) *If I eat any more I'll burst!* ♦ *If it rains much more, the river will burst its banks.* **2** [I] **burst into, out of, through, etc. (sth)** to move suddenly in a particular direction, often using force □ *menerpa atau merempuh (masuk/keluar/melalui sst)*: *She burst into the manager's office and demanded to speak to him.*
IDM be bursting (with sth) to be very full of sth □ *penuh dgn (sst)*: *I packed so many clothes that my suitcase was bursting.* ♦ *She was bursting with pride when she won the race.*
be bursting to do sth to want to do sth very much □ *sangat ingin atau tdk sabar-sabar lagi utk membuat sst*: *I'm bursting to tell someone the news but it's a secret.*
burst (sth) open to open or make sth open suddenly or violently □ *membuka (sst) dgn tiba-tiba atau ganas; merempuh (sst)*: *Suddenly the doors burst open and five police officers rushed in.*
PHR V burst in on sb/sth to interrupt sb/sth by arriving suddenly □ *muncul dgn tiba-tiba*: *The police burst in on the gang as they were counting the money.*
burst into sth to start doing sth suddenly □ *tiba-tiba (menangis, terbakar, dll)*: *On hearing the news she burst into tears* (= started crying). ♦ *The lorry hit a wall and burst into flames* (= started burning).
burst out 1 to start doing sth suddenly □ *tiba-tiba (tertawa, menyanyi, dll)*: *He looked so ridiculous that I burst out laughing.* **2** to say sth suddenly and with strong feeling □ *membentak*: *She burst out, 'I can't stand it any more!'*

burst² /bɜːst/ *noun* [C] **1** a short period of a particular activity, that often starts suddenly □ *cetusan; pecutan; ledakan; sekejap-sekejap*: *a burst of energy/enthusiasm/speed* ♦ *a burst of applause/gunfire* ♦ *He prefers to work in short bursts.* **2** an occasion when sth bursts or explodes; a crack or hole caused by this □ *pecah*: *a burst in a water pipe*

bury /ˈberi/ *verb* [T] (burying; buries; *pt, pp* buried) **1** to put a dead body in the ground □ *mengebumikan*: *She was buried in Highgate Cemetery.* **2** to put sth in a hole in the ground and cover it □ *menanam*: *Our dog always buries its bones in the garden.* **3** [usually passive] to cover or hide sth/sb □ *tertimbus; tersembunyi; leka*: *At last I found the photograph, buried at the bottom of a drawer.* ♦ (*figurative*) *Aisha was buried in a book and didn't hear us come in.*

bus /bʌs/ *noun* [C] a big public vehicle which takes passengers along a fixed route and stops regularly to let people get on and off □ *bas*: *Where do you usually get on/off the bus?* ♦ *We'll have to hurry up if we want to catch the 9 o'clock bus.* ♦ *We'd better run or we'll miss the bus.*
➔ picture on **page P7**

> **TOPIC**
>
> **Travelling by bus**
> You can get on or off a bus at a **bus stop** and the place where most bus routes start is the **bus station**. The **bus driver** will probably take the money (your **fare**) and give you your **ticket**, or there may be a **conductor** who collects the fares. You can buy a **single** (= to your destination but not back) or a **return** ticket (= to your destination and back). A bus **pass** allows you to travel in a particular area for a fixed period of time. In British English a comfortable bus used for long journeys is called a **coach**. Note that we travel **on the bus** or **by bus**: 'How do you get to work?' 'On the bus.'

bush /bʊʃ/ *noun* **1** [C] a plant like a small, thick tree with many low branches □ *pokok rimbun/bangkut*: *a rose bush* ♦ *The house was surrounded by thick bushes.* ➔ picture on **page P11** **2** often **the bush** [U] wild land that has not been cleared, especially in Africa and Australia □ *belukar; hutan kecil*
IDM beat about/around the bush ➔ **beat¹**

bushy /ˈbʊʃi/ *adj* (bushier; bushiest) growing closely together in large numbers; thick □ *lebat*: *bushy hair/eyebrows*

busier, busiest, busily ➔ **busy¹**

business /ˈbɪznəs/ *noun*
▶TRADE **1** [U] buying and selling as a way of earning money □ *perniagaan; urus niaga*: *She's planning to set up in business as a hairdresser.* ♦ *I'm going to go into business with my brother.* ♦ *They are very easy to do business with.*
▶WORK **2** [U] the work that you do as your job □ *urusan; urusan perniagaan*: *The manager will be away on business next week.* ♦ *a business trip*

businesslike → but

▶CUSTOMERS **3** [U] the number of customers that a person or company has had □ *perniagaan*: *Business has been good for the time of year.*
▶COMPANY **4** [C] a firm, a shop, a factory, etc. which produces or sells goods or provides a service □ *perniagaan*: *She aims to start a business of her own.* ♦ *Small businesses are finding it hard to survive at the moment.*
▶RESPONSIBILITY **5** [U] something that concerns a particular person □ *urusan*: *The friends I choose are my business, not yours.* ♦ *Our business is to collect the information, not to comment on it.* ♦ *'How much did it cost?' 'It's none of your business!'* (= I don't want to tell you. It's private.)
▶IMPORTANT MATTERS **6** [U] important matters that need to be dealt with or discussed □ *perkara*: *First we have some unfinished business from the last meeting to deal with.*
▶EVENT **7** [sing] a situation or an event, especially one that is strange or unpleasant □ *perkara; hal; kejadian*: *The divorce was an awful business.* ♦ *I found the whole business very depressing.*

IDM **get down to business** to start the work that has to be done □ *mula membuat kerja yg perlu dilakukan*: *Let's just have a cup of coffee before we get down to business.*
go out of business to have to close because there is no more money available □ *tutup kedai; gulung tikar*: *The shop went out of business because it couldn't compete with the new supermarket.*
have no business to do sth/doing sth to have no right to do sth □ *tdk berhak melakukan sst*: *You have no business to read/reading my letters without asking me.*
mind your own business ⊃ **mind²**
monkey business ⊃ **monkey**

businesslike /ˈbɪznəslaɪk/ *adj* dealing with matters in a direct and practical way, without trying to be friendly □ *membuat sst dgn cekap (tanpa meluangkan masa utk beramah-tamah, dsb*: *She has a very businesslike manner.*

businessman /ˈbɪznəsmæn; -mən/, **businesswoman** /ˈbɪznəswʊmən/ *noun* [C] (*pl* **-men** /-men/, **-women** /-wɪmɪn/) **1** a person who works in business, especially in a top position □ *ahli perniagaan (lelaki)*: *a millionaire businessman* **2** a person who is skilful at dealing with money □ *orang (lelaki) yg cekap berurus niaga*: *I should have got a better price for the car, but I'm not much of a businessman.*

business person *noun* [C] (*pl* **-people** /-piːpl/) a person who works in business, especially in a top position □ *ahli perniagaan* ⊃ look at **businessman**

business studies *noun* [U] the study of how to control and manage a company □ *kajian perniagaan*: *a course in business studies*

busk /bʌsk/ *verb* [I] to sing or play music in the street so that people will give you money □ *berhibur-hibur di jalanan*

busker /ˈbʌskə(r)/ *noun* [C] a street musician □ *seniman jalanan* ⊃ picture on page P11

[I] **intransitive**, a verb which has no object: *He laughed.*

bust¹ /bʌst/ *verb* (*pt, pp* **bust** or **busted**) (*informal*) **1** [T] to break or damage sth so that it cannot be used □ *memecahkan; merosakkan* **2** [T] to arrest sb □ *menangkap*: *He was busted for possession of heroin.*

bust² /bʌst/ *noun* [C] **1** a model in stone, etc. of a person's head, shoulders and chest □ *patung (paras dada)* **2** a woman's breasts; the measurement round a woman's chest □ *buah dada; ukuran dada*: *This blouse is a bit too tight around the bust.* **3** (*informal*) an unexpected visit by the police in order to arrest people for doing sth illegal □ *serbuan*: *a drugs bust*

bust³ /bʌst/ *adj* [not before a noun] (*informal*) broken or not working □ *pecah; rosak*: *The zip on these trousers is bust.*

IDM **go bust** (*informal*) (used about a business) to close because it has lost so much money □ *jatuh bankrap*: *During the recession thousands of businesses went bust.* **SYN** **go bankrupt**

bustle¹ /ˈbʌsl/ *verb* **1** [I,T] to move in a busy, noisy or excited way; to make sb move somewhere quickly □ *bersibuk-sibuk; menggegas*: *He bustled about the kitchen making tea.* ♦ *They bustled her out of the room before she could see the body.* **2** [I] **bustle (with sth)** to be full of people, noise or activity □ *penuh dgn (orang, bunyi bising, kegiatan, dsb)*: *The streets were bustling with shoppers.*

bustle² /ˈbʌsl/ *noun* [U] excited and noisy activity □ *kesibukan*: *She loved the bustle of city life.*

ˈbust-up *noun* [C] (*informal*) an argument □ *pertengkaran*: *He had a bust-up with his boss over working hours.*

busy¹ /ˈbɪzi/ *adj* (**busier**; **busiest**) **1 busy (with sth); busy (doing sth)** having a lot of work or tasks to do; not free; working on sth □ *sibuk*: *Mr Khan is busy until 4 o'clock but he could see you after that.* ♦ *Don't disturb him. He's busy.* ♦ *She's busy with her preparations for the party.* ♦ *We're busy decorating the spare room before our visitors arrive.* **2** (used about a period of time) full of activity and things to do □ *sibuk*: *I've had rather a busy week.* **3** (used about a place) full of people, movement and activity □ *sangat sibuk*: *The town centre was so busy that you could hardly move.* **4** (*especially AmE*) (used about a telephone) being used □ *sedang digunakan*: *The line's busy at the moment. I'll try again later.*

IDM **get busy** to start working □ *mulai bekerja*: *We'll have to get busy if we're going to be ready in time.* ▶ **busily** *adv*: *When I came in, she was busily writing something at her desk.*

busy² /ˈbɪzi/ *verb* [T] (**busying**; **busies**; *pt, pp* **busied**) **busy yourself with sth; busy yourself doing sth** to keep yourself busy; to find sth to do □ *bersibuk-sibuk (membuat sst)*

busybody /ˈbɪzibɒdi/ *noun* [C] (*pl* **busybodies**) a person who is too interested in other people's private lives □ *penyibuk*

but¹ /bət; *strong form* bʌt/ *conj* **1** used for introducing an idea which contrasts with or is different from what has just been said □ *tetapi*:

[T] **transitive**, a verb which has an object: *He ate an apple.*

The weather will be sunny but cold. ♦ *Theirs is not the first but the second house on the left.* ♦ *James hasn't got a car but his sister has.* **2** however; and yet □ *namun begitu; akan tetapi*: *By the end of the day we were tired but happy.* ♦ *I'd love to come but I can't make it till 8 o'clock.* **3** used when you are saying sorry for sth □ *digunakan apabila meminta maaf ttg sst*: *Excuse me, but is your name David Harries?* ♦ *I'm sorry, but I can't stay any longer.* **4** used for introducing a statement that shows that you are surprised or annoyed or that you disagree □ *tetapi*: *'Here's the book you lent me.' 'But it's all dirty and torn!'* ♦ *'But that's not possible!'*

IDM **but then** however; on the other hand □ *walau bagaimanapun; namun demikian*: *We could go swimming. But then perhaps it's too cold.* ♦ *He's brilliant at the piano. But then so was his father* (= however, this is not surprising because …).

but² /bət; strong form bʌt/ prep except □ *melainkan; kecuali*: *I've told no one but you about this.* ♦ *We've had nothing but trouble with this washing machine.*

IDM **but for sb/sth** except for or without sb/sth □ *kalaulah tdk kerana sso/sst*: *We wouldn't have managed but for your help.*

butcher¹ /ˈbʊtʃə(r)/ noun [C] **1** a person who sells meat □ *penjual daging*: *The butcher cut me four lamb chops.* ◯ note at **meat 2 the butcher's** [sing] a shop that sells meat □ *penjual daging*: *She went to the butcher's for some sausages.* **3** a person who kills a lot of people in a cruel way □ *pembunuh yg kejam*

butcher² /ˈbʊtʃə(r)/ verb [T] to kill a lot of people in a cruel way □ *membunuh dgn kejam*

butchery /ˈbʊtʃəri/ noun [U] **1** cruel killing □ *pembunuhan kejam* **2** the work of preparing meat to be sold □ *penyediaan daging utk jualan*

butler /ˈbʌtlə(r)/ noun [C] a person who works in a very large house, whose duties include organizing and serving food and wine □ *butler*

butt¹ /bʌt/ verb [T] to hit sb/sth with the head □ *menyondol; menghantuk dgn kepala*

PHR V **butt in (on sb/sth)** to interrupt sb/sth or to join in sth without being asked □ *menyela/mengganggu (sso/sst)*: *I'm sorry to butt in but could I speak to you urgently for a minute?*

butt² /bʌt/ noun [C] **1** the thicker, heavier end of a weapon or tool □ *pangkal; buntut*: *the butt of a rifle* **2** a short piece of a cigarette which is left when it has been smoked □ *puntung* **3** (especially AmE informal) the part of your body that you sit on; your bottom □ *punggung; buntut*: *Get up off your butt and do some work!* **4** the act of hitting sb with your head □ *sondolan*

IDM **be the butt of sth** a person who is often laughed at or talked about in an unkind way □ *bahan ketawa; sasaran*: *Fat children are often the butt of other children's jokes.*

‡ **butter¹** /ˈbʌtə(r)/ noun [U] a soft yellow fat that is made from cream and used for spreading on bread, etc. or in cooking □ *mentega*: *Do you prefer butter or low-fat spread?* ♦ *First, melt a little butter in the pan.* ◯ look at **margarine**

butter² /ˈbʌtə(r)/ verb [T] to spread butter on bread, etc □ *menyapukan mentega*: *I'll cut the bread and you butter it.* ♦ *hot buttered toast*

butterfly /ˈbʌtəflaɪ/ noun [C] (pl butterflies) an insect with a long, thin body and four brightly coloured wings □ *kupu-kupu*: *Caterpillars develop into butterflies.* ◯ picture on page P13 **2** [sing, U] a style of swimming in which both arms are brought over the head at the same time, and the legs move up and down together □ *gaya kupu-kupu* ◯ picture at **swim**

IDM **have butterflies (in your stomach)** (informal) to feel very nervous before doing sth □ *kecut perut*

buttermilk /ˈbʌtəmɪlk/ noun [U] the liquid that is left when butter is separated from milk □ *susu mentega*

buttock /ˈbʌtək/ noun [C, usually pl] one of the two parts of your body which you sit on □ *punggung; buntut*

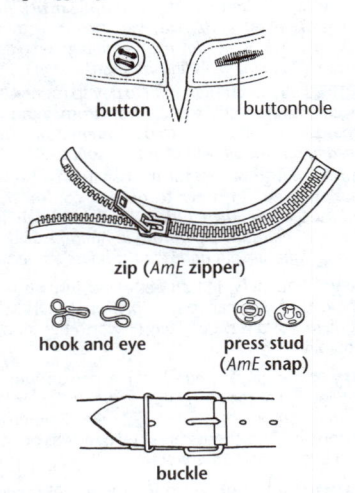

button | buttonhole

zip (*AmE* zipper)

hook and eye   press stud (*AmE* snap)

buckle

‡ **button** /ˈbʌtn/ noun [C] **1** a small, often round, piece of plastic, wood or metal that you use for fastening your clothes □ *butang*: *One of the buttons on my jacket have come off.* ♦ *This blouse is too tight—I can't fasten the buttons.* ◯ picture on page P1 **2** a small part of a machine, etc. that you press in order to operate sth □ *butang*: *Press the button to ring the bell.* ♦ *To dial the same number again, push the 'redial' button.* ♦ *Which button turns the volume down?* ♦ *Double click the right mouse button.* ◯ picture at **handle 3** a small area on a computer screen that you click on in order to do sth □ *butang*: *To print a file, simply click on the 'print' button.*

buttonhole /ˈbʌtnhəʊl/ *noun* [C] **1** a hole in a piece of clothing that you push a button through in order to fasten it □ *lubang butang* ⊃ picture at **button 2** (*BrE*) a flower worn in the **buttonhole** of a coat or jacket □ *bunga yg diselit di kelepet kot atau jaket*

buttress¹ /ˈbʌtrəs/ *noun* [C] a stone or brick structure that supports a wall □ *penyangga, sagang*

buttress² /ˈbʌtrəs/ *verb* [T] (*formal*) to support or give strength to sb/sth □ *menyokong, memperkuat*: *The sharp increase in crime seems to buttress the argument for more police officers on the street.*

buy¹ /baɪ/ *verb* [T] (*pt, pp* **bought** /bɔːt/) **buy sth (for sb); buy sb sth** to get sth by paying money for it □ *membeli*: *I'm going to buy a new dress for the party.* ◆ *We bought this book for you in London.* ◆ *Can I buy you a coffee?* ◆ *He bought the car from a friend.* ◆ *Did you buy your car new or second-hand?* ◆ *He bought the necklace as a present for his wife.* ⊃ note at **shopping** **OPP** **sell** **IDM** **buy time** to do sth in order to delay an event, a decision, etc. □ *membuat sst utk melengahkan sst peristiwa, keputusan, dsb*: *He took a few days' holiday in order to buy some time before giving them his final decision.*

PHR V **buy sb off** (*informal*) to pay sb money, especially dishonestly, to stop them from doing sth you do not want them to do □ *menyogok*: *They tried to buy me off with a large discount.*

buy sb out to pay sb for their share in a house, business, etc. in order to get full control of it yourself □ *membeli bahagian harta, dsb sso supaya memiliki sepenuhnya*: *After the divorce, she bought him out and kept the house for herself.*

buy² /baɪ/ *noun* [C] an act of buying sth or a thing that you can buy □ *belian*: *I think your camera was a very good buy* (= worth the money you paid).

buyer /ˈbaɪə(r)/ *noun* [C] **1** a person who is buying sth or may buy sth □ *pembeli*: *I think I've found a buyer for my car.* **OPP** **seller** **2** a person whose job is to choose and buy goods to be sold in a large shop □ *jurubeli*

buyout /ˈbaɪaʊt/ *noun* [C] the act of buying enough or all of the shares in a company in order to get control of it □ *beli habis*

buzz¹ /bʌz/ *verb* **1** [I] to make the sound that a bee (= a black and yellow insect) makes when flying □ *berdengung*: *A large fly was buzzing against the windowpane.* ◆ *The doorbell buzzed loudly.* **2** [I] **buzz (with sth)** to be full of excitement, activity, thoughts, etc. □ *penuh dgn (perasaan seronok, pelbagai fikiran, dll); sibuk*: *Her head was buzzing with questions that she wanted to ask.* ◆ *The room was buzzing with activity.* **3** [I,T] to call sb by using an electric bell, etc. □ *memanggil (sso) dgn loceng elektrik*: *The doctor will buzz for you when he's ready.*

buzz² /bʌz/ *noun* **1** [C, usually sing] the sound that a **bee** (= a black and yellow insect), etc. makes when flying □ *dengung*: *the buzz of insects* **2** [sing] the low sound made by many people talking at the same time □ *bunyi percakapan*: *I could hear the buzz of conversation in the next room.* **3** [sing] (*informal*) a strong feeling of excitement or pleasure □ *perasaan seronok atau ghairah*: *a buzz of expectation* ◆ *Parachuting gives me a real buzz.* ◆ *She gets a buzz out of shopping for expensive clothes.*

buzzer /ˈbʌzə(r)/ *noun* [C] a piece of equipment that makes a **buzzing** sound □ *pembaz*: *Press your buzzer if you know the answer to a question.*

buzzword /ˈbʌzwɜːd/ *noun* [C] a word or phrase, especially one connected with a particular subject, that has become fashionable and popular □ *kata atau rangkai kata popular*: *Empowerment is the current buzzword.*

by /baɪ/ *prep, adv* **1** beside; very near □ *di sisi; di tepi; dekat*: *Come and sit by me.* ◆ *We stayed in a cottage by the sea.* ◆ *The shops are close by.* **2** used after a passive verb for showing who or what did or caused sth □ *oleh*: *She was knocked down by a car.* ◆ *The event was organized by local people.* ◆ *I was deeply shocked by the news.* ◆ *Who was the book written by?/Who is the book by?* **3** through doing or using sth; by means of sth □ *dgn; melalui*: *You can get hold of me by phoning this number.* ◆ *Will you be paying by cash or card?* ◆ *The house is heated by electricity.* ◆ *'How do you go to work?' 'By train, usually.'* ◆ *by bus/car/plane/bicycle* ◆ *We went in by the back door.* **4** as a result of sth □ *kerana; secara*: *I got on the wrong bus by mistake/accident.* ◆ *I met an old friend by chance.* **5** not later than; before □ *selewat-lewatnya; sebelum*: *I'll be home by 7 o'clock.* ◆ *He should have telephoned by now/by this time.* **6** past □ *lalu; melewati*: *He walked straight by me without speaking.* ◆ *We stopped to let the ambulance get by.* **7** [usually without *the*] during a period of time; in a particular situation □ *pd*: *By day we covered about thirty miles and by night we rested.* ◆ *The electricity went off so we had to work by candlelight.* **8** to the amount mentioned □ *sebanyak; (kadangkala tdk diterjemahkan)*: *Prices have gone up by 10 per cent.* ◆ *I missed the bus by a few minutes.* **9** according to sth; concerning sth □ *mengikut; menurut*: *It's 8 o'clock by my watch.* ◆ *By law you have to attend school from the age of five.* ◆ *She's French by birth.* ◆ *He's a doctor by profession.* **10** (used with a part of the body or an article of clothing) holding □ *digunakan dgn maksud memegang bahagian pakaian atau badan sso/sst*: *He grabbed me by the arm.* **11** [often used with *the*] in the quantity or period mentioned □ *mengikut; selama; sebanyak; demi*: *You can rent a car by the day, the week or the month.* ◆ *Copies of the book have sold by the million.* ◆ *They came in one by one.* ◆ *Day by day she was getting better.* **12** used for showing the measurements of an area □ *kali*: *The table is six feet by three feet* (= six feet long and three feet wide). **13** used for multiplying or

dividing □ *dgn*: 4 multiplied by 5 is 20. ♦ 6 divided by 2 is 3.
IDM by and large ➜ **large**
by the way ➜ **way¹**

bye /baɪ/ (also ˌbye-ˈbye) exclam (informal) goodbye □ *selamat tinggal*: Bye! See you tomorrow. ♦ She waved bye-bye and got into the car.

by-election noun [C] an election to choose a new Member of Parliament for a particular **constituency** (= town or area). It is held when the former member has died or left suddenly. □ *pilihan raya kecil* ➜ note at **election**

bygone /ˈbaɪɡɒn (AmE also) / adj [only before a noun] that happened a long time ago □ *lampau; lalu; dahulu*: a bygone era

bygones /ˈbaɪɡɒnz (AmE also) / noun
IDM let bygones be bygones to decide to forget disagreements or arguments that happened in the past □ *yg sudah itu sudahlah*

bypass¹ /ˈbaɪpɑːs/ noun [C] 1 a road which traffic can use to go round a town, instead of through it □ *jalan pirau/lencongan* ➜ look at **ring road** 2 an operation on the heart to send blood along a different route so that it does not go through a part which is damaged or blocked □ *pembedahan pintasan*: a triple bypass operation ♦ heart bypass surgery

bypass² /ˈbaɪpɑːs/ verb [T] to go around or to avoid sth using a **bypass** □ *memirau; melencong*: Let's try to bypass the city centre. ♦ (figurative) It's no good trying to bypass the problem.

by-product noun [C] 1 something that is formed during the making of sth else □ *hasil sampingan* 2 something that happens as the result of sth else □ *akibat sampingan*

bystander /ˈbaɪstændə(r)/ noun [C] a person who is standing near and sees sth that happens, without being involved in it □ *orang yg menyaksikan sst tanpa terlibat*: Several innocent bystanders were hurt when the two gangs attacked each other.

byte /baɪt/ noun [C] a unit of information stored in a computer, equal to 8 **bits**. Computer memory is measured in bytes. □ *bait*

byword /ˈbaɪwɜːd/ noun [C, usually sing] 1 a **byword for sth** a person or a thing that is a typical or well-known example of a particular quality □ *lambang*: A limousine is a byword for luxury. 2 (especially AmE) a word or phrase that is often used □ *kata-kata yg selalu digunakan*

C

C, c /siː/ noun [C,U] (pl **Cs**; **C's**; **c's** /siːz/) 1 the third letter of the English alphabet □ *C, c (huruf)*: 'Car' begins with (a) 'C'. 2 C (used about music) the first note in the scale of C major □ *not pertama dlm skala C major*: C major/minor ♦ C sharp

c /siː/ abbr 1 C = **Celsius, centigrade** □ *Celsius; centigrade*: Water freezes at 0°C. 2 = **cent(s)** 3 = **circa**: c 1770

cab /kæb/ noun [C] 1 (especially AmE) = **taxi¹** □ *teksi*: Let's take a cab/go by cab. 2 the part of a lorry, train, bus, etc. where the driver sits □ *ruang pemandu*

cabaret /ˈkæbəreɪ/ noun [C,U] entertainment with singing, dancing, etc. in a restaurant or club □ *pertunjukan kabaret*

cabbage /ˈkæbɪdʒ/ noun [C,U] a large round vegetable with thick green, dark red or white leaves □ *kubis*: Cabbages are easy to grow. ♦ Do you like cabbage? ➜ picture on **page P15**

cabin /ˈkæbɪn/ noun [C] 1 a small room in a ship or boat, where a passenger sleeps □ *kabin* 2 the part of a plane where the passengers sit □ *kabin* 3 a small wooden house □ *pondok*: a log cabin

ˈcabin crew noun [C, with sing or pl verb] the people whose job is to take care of passengers on a plane □ *anak kapal kabin*

cabinet /ˈkæbɪnət/ noun [C] 1 **the Cabinet** [with sing or pl verb] the most important ministers in a government, who decide and advise on policy and have regular meetings □ *kabinet; jemaah menteri*: The Cabinet is/are meeting today to discuss the crisis. 2 a cupboard with shelves or drawers, used for storing things □ *kabinet; almari*: a medicine cabinet ♦ a filing cabinet ➜ picture on **page P8**

cable /ˈkeɪbl/ noun 1 [C] a thick strong metal rope □ *kabel* 2 [C,U] a set of wires covered with plastic, etc., for carrying electricity or signals □ *kabel; wayar*: underground/overhead cables ♦ a telephone cable ♦ two metres of cable 3 = **cable television**

ˈcable car noun [C] a vehicle like a box that hangs on a moving metal **cable** and carries passengers up and down a mountain □ *kereta kabel*

ˌcable ˈtelevision (also **cable**) noun [U] a system of sending out TV programmes along wires instead of by radio signals □ *televisyen kabel*

cache¹ /kæʃ/ noun [C] 1 a hidden store of things such as weapons □ *simpanan tersembunyi benda-benda*: an arms cache 2 a part of a computer's memory that stores copies of data that is often needed while a program is running. This data can be found very quickly. □ *storan data sementara dlm komputer*

cache² /kæʃ/ verb [T] 1 to store things in a secret place, especially weapons □ *menyembunyikan; menyorokkan* 2 to store data in a **cache¹** on a computer □ *menyimpan data dlm storan data sementara*: This page is cached.

cackle /ˈkækl/ verb [I] to laugh in a loud, unpleasant way □ *ketawa terkekeh-kekeh* ▶ **cackle** noun [C]

cactus /ˈkæktəs/ noun [C] (pl **cactuses** or **cacti** /ˈkæktaɪ/) a type of plant that grows in hot, dry areas, especially deserts. A **cactus** has a thick **stem** (= the central part) and sharp points but no leaves. □ *kaktus*

cadet /kəˈdet/ noun [C] a young person who is training to be in the army, navy, air force or police □ *kadet*

cadge /kædʒ/ verb [I,T] (informal) **cadge (sth) (from/off sb)** to try to persuade sb to give or lend you sth □ *mengecek*: *He's always trying to cadge money off me.*

Caesarean (also **Caesarian**; AmE also **cesarean, cesarian**) /sɪˈzeərɪən/ noun [C] a medical operation in which an opening is cut in a mother's body in order to take out the baby when a normal birth would be impossible or dangerous □ *pembedahan Caesarean*: *to have a Caesarean*

> **MORE** This operation is also called a **Caesarean section** or in American English a **C-section**.

cafe /ˈkæfeɪ/ noun [C] a small restaurant that serves drinks and light meals □ *kafe* ⊃ picture on **page P11**

> **CULTURE**
>
> In Britain a cafe does not normally serve alcoholic drinks. People go to a **pub** or **bar** to drink wine, beer etc.

cafeteria /ˌkæfəˈtɪərɪə/ noun [C] a restaurant, especially one for workers, where people collect their meals themselves and carry them to their tables □ *kafeteria* ⊃ look at **canteen**

caffeine /ˈkæfiːn/ noun [U] the substance found in coffee and tea that makes you feel more active □ *kafeina* ⊃ look at **decaffeinated**

cage /keɪdʒ/ noun [C] a box made of bars or wire, or a space surrounded by wire or metal bars, in which a bird or an animal is kept so that it cannot escape □ *sangkar; kurungan*: *a birdcage* ▶ **cage** verb [T] ▶ **caged** adj: *He felt like a caged animal in the tiny office.*

cagey /ˈkeɪdʒi/ adj (**cagier**; **cagiest**) (informal) **cagey (about sth)** not wanting to give information or to talk about sth □ *berselindung-selindung*

cagoule /kəˈguːl/ noun [C] a long jacket with a **hood** (= a part that covers your head) that protects you from the rain or wind □ *jaket cagoule*

cajole /kəˈdʒəʊl/ verb [T,I] **cajole sb (into sth/into doing sth)**; **cajole sth out of sb** to persuade sb to do sth by talking to them and being very nice □ *memujuk*: *He cajoled me into agreeing to do the work.* ♦ *I managed to cajole their address out of him.* ♦ *Her voice was soft and cajoling.* **SYN** **coax**

cake¹ /keɪk/ noun 1 [C,U] a sweet food made by mixing flour, eggs, butter, sugar, etc. together and baking the mixture in the oven □ *kek; kuih*: *to make/bake a cake* ♦ *a wedding cake* ♦ *a piece/slice of birthday cake* ♦ *Would you like some more cake?* 2 [C] a mixture of other food, cooked in a round, flat shape □ *kek; ketulan*: *fish/potato cakes*

IDM **have your cake and eat it** to enjoy the advantages of sth without its disadvantages; to have both things that are available □ *menikmati kelebihan dua perkara yg lazimnya hanya satu pilihan yg mungkin*: *You can't go out every night and pass your exams. You can't have your cake and eat it.*
a piece of cake ⊃ **piece¹**

cake² /keɪk/ verb [T, usually passive] **cake sth (in/with sth)** to cover sth with a thick layer of sth that becomes hard when it dries □ *bersalut*: *boots caked in mud*

calamity /kəˈlæməti/ noun [C,U] (pl **calamities**) a terrible event that causes a lot of damage or harm □ *malapetaka* **SYN** **disaster**

calcium /ˈkælsiəm/ noun [U] (symbol **Ca**) a chemical element that is found in food such as milk or cheese. It helps to make teeth and bones strong. □ *kalsium*

calculate /ˈkælkjuleɪt/ verb [T] 1 to find sth out by using mathematics; to work sth out □ *mengira*: *It's difficult to calculate how long the project will take.* 2 to consider or expect sth □ *menimbang; menjangka*: *We calculated that the advantages would be greater than the disadvantages.*
IDM **be calculated to do sth** to be intended or designed to do sth □ *bertujuan utk melakukan sst*: *His remark was clearly calculated to annoy me.*

calculating /ˈkælkjuleɪtɪŋ/ adj planning things in a very careful way in order to achieve what you want, without considering other people □ *licik*: *Her cold, calculating approach made her many enemies.*

calculation /ˌkælkjuˈleɪʃn/ noun 1 [C,U] finding an answer by using mathematics □ *kiraan*;

hitungan: *I'll have to do a few **calculations** before telling you how much I can afford.* ◆ *Calculation of the exact cost is impossible.* **2** [U] (*formal*) careful planning in order to achieve what you want, without considering other people □ ***kelicikan***: *His actions were the result of deliberate calculation.*

calculator /'kælkjuleɪtə(r)/ *noun* [C] a small electronic machine used for calculating figures □ ***kalkulator***: *a pocket calculator*

caldron (*especially AmE*) = **cauldron**

calendar /'kælɪndə(r)/ *noun* [C] **1** a list that shows the days, weeks and months of a particular year □ ***kalendar***

HELP **Calendar** or **diary**? A **calendar** is often hung on a wall and may have a separate page for each month, sometimes with a picture or photograph. A **diary** is a little book which you can carry around with you and which has spaces next to the dates so that you can write in appointments, etc.

2 a list of dates and events in a year that are important in a particular area of activity □ ***kalendar***: *Wimbledon is a major event in the sporting calendar.* **3** a system for dividing time into fixed periods and for marking the beginning and end of a year □ ***takwim; kalendar***: *the Muslim calendar*

ˌcalendar ˈmonth = month(1)
ˌcalendar ˈyear = year(1)

calf /kɑːf/ *noun* [C] (*pl* **calves** /kɑːvz/) **1** the back of your leg, between your ankle and your knee □ ***betis***: *I've strained a calf muscle.* ➲ picture at **body** **2** a young cow □ ***anak lembu*** ➲ note at **cow, meat** ➲ picture at **cow** **3** the young of some other animals, for example **elephants** (= large grey animals with long noses) □ ***anak haiwan tertentu (misalnya gajah)***

calibre (*AmE* **caliber**) /'kælɪbə(r)/ *noun* [sing, U] the quality or ability of a person or thing □ ***kaliber***: *The company's employees are of (a) high calibre.*

CALL /kɔːl/ *abbr* computer-assisted language learning □ ***pembelajaran bahasa berbantu komputer***

call¹ /kɔːl/ *verb*

▸NAME **1** **be called** to have as your name □ ***bernama; dinamai***: *His wife is called Silvia.* ◆ *What was that village called?* **2** [T] to name or describe a person or thing in a certain way □ ***memanggil; menggelar***: *They called the baby Freddie.* ◆ *It was very rude to call her fat.* ◆ *Are you calling me a liar?*

▸SHOUT **3** [I,T] **call (out) to sb; call (sth) (out)** to say sth loudly or to shout in order to attract attention □ ***berteriak; memanggil***: *'Hello, is anybody there?' she called.* ◆ *He called out the names and the winners stepped forward.* ◆ *I could hear a man calling his dog.* ◆ *She called out to her father for help.*

▸TELEPHONE **4** [I,T] (*especially AmE*) = **ring²**(1) □ ***menelefon***: *Who's calling, please?* ◆ *I'll call you tomorrow.* ◆ *We're just in the middle of dinner. Can I call you back later?* ➲ note at **telephone**

[C] **countable**, a noun with a plural form: *one book, two books*

calculator → call

▸ORDER SB TO COME **5** [T] to order or ask sb to come to a certain place □ ***panggil; memanggil***: *Can you call everybody in for lunch?* ◆ *I think we had better call the doctor.*

▸VISIT **6** [I] **call (in/round) (on sb/at ...)** to make a short visit to a person or place □ ***mengunjungi; singgah***: *I called in on Mike on my way home.* ◆ *We called at his house but there was nobody in.*

▸STOP **7** [I] **call at ...** (used about a train, ship, etc.) to stop at the places mentioned □ ***singgah***: *This is the express service to London, calling at Manchester and Birmingham.*

▸MEETING **8** [T] to arrange for sth to take place at a certain time □ ***mengaturkan; mengadakan***: *to call a meeting/an election/a strike*

IDM **bring/call sb/sth to mind** ➲ **mind¹**

call sb's bluff to tell sb to actually do what they are threatening to do (believing that they will not risk doing it) □ ***mencabar sso membuat apa-apa yg diancamnya (kerana percaya dia sebenarnya tdk berani membuatnya)***

call it a day (*informal*) to decide to stop doing sth □ ***menghentikan sst kerja***: *Let's call it a day. I'm exhausted.*

call sb names to use insulting words about sb □ ***mencela sso***

call the shots/tune (*informal*) to be in a position to control a situation and make decisions about what should be done □ ***berkuasa***

PHR V **call by** (*informal*) to make a short visit to a place or person as you pass □ ***singgah***: *I'll call by to pick up the book on my way to work.*

call for sb (*BrE*) to collect sb in order to go somewhere together □ ***menjemput sso***: *I'll call for you when it's time to go.*

call for sth to demand or need sth □ ***meminta; memerlukan sst***: *The crisis calls for immediate action.* ◆ *This calls for a celebration!*

call sth off to cancel sth □ ***membatalkan sst***: *The football match was called off because of the bad weather.*

call sb out to ask sb to come, especially to an emergency □ ***memanggil sso (supaya datang)***: *We had to call out the doctor in the middle of the night.*

call sb up **1** (*especially AmE*) to telephone sb □ ***menelefon***: *He called me up to tell me the good news.* **2** to order sb to join the army, navy or air force □ ***mengerah memasuki tentera***: *All men under 30 were called up to fight in the war.*

call sth up to look at sth that is stored in a computer □ ***memaparkan maklumat yg tersimpan dlm komputer***: *The bank clerk called up my account details on screen.*

call² /kɔːl/ *noun*

▸TELEPHONE **1** (also **ˈphone call**) [C] an act of telephoning or a conversation on the telephone □ ***panggilan (telefon)***: *Were there any calls for me while I was out?* ◆ *I'll give you a call at the weekend.* ◆ *to make a local call* ◆ *a long-distance call*

▸SHOUT **2** [C] a loud sound that is made to attract attention; a shout □ ***teriakan; bunyi***: *a call for help* ◆ *That bird's call is easy to recognize.*

[U] **uncountable**, a noun with no plural form: *some sugar*

call box → camp

▶VISIT **3** [C] a short visit, especially to sb's house □ *kunjungan*: *The doctor has several calls to make this morning.* ♦ (old-fashioned) *We could pay a call on Dave on our way home.*

▶DEMAND **4** [C] a request, demand for sth □ *permintaan*: *There have been calls for the President to resign.* **5** [C,U] **call for sth** a need for sth □ *keperluan*: *The doctor said there was no call for concern.*

IDM at sb's beck and call ⇒ beck
(be) on call to be ready to work if necessary □ *bertugas*: *Dr Young will be on call this weekend.*

'**call box** = telephone box

'**call centre** (*AmE* '**call center**) *noun* [C] an office in which many people work using telephones, for example taking customers' orders or answering questions □ *pusat panggilan*

caller /ˈkɔːlə(r)/ *noun* [C] a person who telephones or visits sb □ *orang yg menelefon atau melawat sso*

callous /ˈkæləs/ *adj* not caring about the suffering of other people □ *tdk berperasaan* **SYN** cruel

calm¹ /kɑːm/ *adj* (**calmer**; **calmest**) **1** not excited, worried or angry; quiet □ *tenang; tenteram*: *Try to keep calm—there's no need to panic.* ♦ *She spoke in a calm voice.* ♦ *The city is calm again after last night's riots.* **2** without big waves □ *tenang*: *a calm sea* **OPP** rough **3** without much wind □ *tenang*: *calm weather* ▶ **calmly** *adv* ▶ **calmness** *noun* [U]

calm² /kɑːm/ *verb* [I,T] **calm (sb/sth) (down)** to become or to make sb quieter or calm □ *bertenang; menenangkan*: *Calm down! Shouting at everybody won't help.* ♦ *I did some breathing exercises to calm my nerves.*

calm³ /kɑːm/ *noun* [C,U] a period of time or a state when everything is peaceful □ *ketenangan*: *After living in the city, I enjoyed the calm of country life.*

Calor gas™ /ˈkælə gæs/ *noun* [U] gas that is kept in special bottles and used for cooking, heating, etc. □ *gas Calor*™

calorie /ˈkæləri/ *noun* [C] a measure of the energy value of food □ *kalori*: *A fried egg contains about 100 calories.* ♦ *a low-calorie drink/yogurt/diet*

calves *plural of* calf

camcorder /ˈkæmkɔːdə(r)/ *noun* [C] a camera that you can carry around and use for recording pictures and sound on a video □ *kamkorder* ⇒ *picture at* **camera**

came *past tense of* **come**

camel /ˈkæml/ *noun* [C] an animal that lives in the desert and has a long neck and either one or two **humps** (= large masses of fat) on its back.

camel

It is used for carrying people and goods. □ *unta*

cameo /ˈkæmiəʊ/ *noun* [C] (*pl* **cameos**) **1** a small part in a film or play that is usually played by a famous actor □ *(watak) kameo*: *Sean Connery plays a cameo role as the dying king.* **2** a piece of jewellery that has a design in one colour and a background in a different colour □ *kameo*

camera

flash | zoom lens

digital camera

screen

camcorder   tripod

camera /ˈkæmərə/ *noun* [C] a piece of equipment that you use for taking photographs or moving pictures □ *kamera*: *Just point the camera and press the button.* ♦ *a video/TV camera*

> **TOPIC**
>
> **Cameras**
> You use a camera to **take photos** (formal **photographs**). You adjust the **lens** to make sure that the image is **in focus** (= clear and sharp), not **out of focus** (= not clear). You need a **zoom lens** to take pictures of things that are a long distance away. If there is not much light or you are indoors you will probably need to use the **flash**. **Digital cameras** allow you to take digital photos which you can download and store on your computer. Some people like to put their photos into **albums** to look at them, others prefer to just view them on their computer. If you want to **pose** for a photo and ask sb to take it with you camera, you can say 'Could you take a photo of me, please?'

cameraman /ˈkæmrəmæn/ *noun* [C] (*pl* -men /-men/) a person whose job is to operate a camera for a film or a TV company □ *juru-kamera* ⇒ *look at* **photographer**

camouflage /ˈkæməflɑːʒ/ *noun* [U] **1** materials or colours that soldiers use to make themselves and their equipment difficult to see □ *pakaian samaran* **2** the way in which an animal's colour or shape matches its surroundings and makes it difficult to see □ *samaran* ▶ **camouflage** *verb* [T]

camp¹ /kæmp/ *noun* [C,U] a place where people live in tents or simple buildings away from their usual home □ *kem; khemah; perkhemahan*: *a holiday camp* ♦ *a refugee camp* ♦ *an army training camp* ♦ *The climbers set up camp at the foot of the mountain.*

[I] **intransitive**, a verb which has no object: *He laughed.*

[T] **transitive**, a verb which has an object: *He ate an apple.*

camp² /kæmp/ verb [I] **camp (out)** to sleep without a bed, especially outside in a tent □ *berkhemah*: *We camped next to a river.*

> **HELP** **Go camping** is a common way of talking about camping for pleasure: *They went camping in France last year.*

campaign¹ /kæm'peɪn/ noun [C] **1** a plan to do a number of things in order to achieve a special aim □ *kempen*: *to launch an advertising/election campaign* ♦ *a campaign to reduce road accidents* **2** a planned series of attacks in a war □ *kempen*

campaign² /kæm'peɪn/ verb [I] **campaign (for/against sb/sth)** to take part in a planned series of activities in order to make sth happen or to prevent sth □ *berkempen*: *Local people are campaigning for lower speed limits in the town.* ▶ **campaigner** noun [C]: *an animal rights campaigner*

'camp bed (*AmE* **cot**) noun [C] a light, narrow bed that you can fold up and carry easily □ *katil lipat* ⊃ picture at **bed**

camper /'kæmpə(r)/ noun [C] **1** a person who stays in a tent on holiday □ *orang yg berkhemah* **2** (also **'camper van**, *AmE* **RV**; **recreational vehicle**) a motor vehicle in which you can sleep, cook, etc. when you are on holiday □ *van kamper* ⊃ picture at **camping**

camping /'kæmpɪŋ/ noun [U] sleeping or having a holiday in a tent, **camper**, etc. □ *berkhemah*: *Camping is cheaper than staying in hotels.* ♦ *to go on a camping holiday*

camping

camper

caravan (*AmE* trailer)

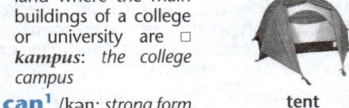

tent

campsite /'kæmpsaɪt/ noun [C] a place where you can stay in a tent □ *tapak perkhemahan*

campus /'kæmpəs/ noun [C,U] the area of land where the main buildings of a college or university are □ *kampus*: *the college campus*

can¹ /kən; strong form kæn/ modal verb (negative **cannot** /'kænɒt/; short form **can't** /kɑːnt/; pt **could** /kəd/; strong form kʊd/; negative **could not**; short form **couldn't** /'kʊdnt/)

▶ ABILITY **1** used for showing that it is possible for sb/sth to do sth or that sb/sth has the ability to do sth □ *boleh; dpt*: *Can you ride a bike?* ♦ *He can't speak French.*

> **GRAMMAR** **Can** has no infinitive or participle forms. To make the future and perfect tenses, we use **be able to**: *One day people will be able to travel to Mars.* **Could have** is used when we say that somebody had the ability or opportunity to do something but did not do it: *She could have passed the exam but she didn't really try.*

▶ SENSES **2** used with the verbs 'feel', 'hear', 'see', 'smell', 'taste' □ *digunakan dgn beberapa kk tertentu*: *I can smell something burning.*
▶ PERMISSION **3** used to ask for or give permission □ *boleh(kah)*: *Can I have a drink, please?* ♦ *He asked if he could have a drink.*

> **GRAMMAR** When we are talking about general permission in the past **could** is used: *I could do anything I wanted when I stayed with my grandma.* When we are talking about one particular occasion we do not use **could**: *They were allowed to visit him in hospital yesterday.*

▶ OFFER **4** used for offering to do sth □ *bolehkah*: *Can I help at all?*
▶ REQUEST **5** used to ask sb to do sth □ *bolehkah*: *Can you help me carry these books?*
▶ PROBABILITY **6** used in the negative for saying that you are sure sth is not true □ *(tdk) mungkin*: *That can't be Maria—she's in London.* ♦ *Surely you can't be hungry. You've only just had lunch.*
▶ POSSIBILITY **7** used to talk about sb's typical behaviour or of a typical effect □ *memang*: *You can be very annoying.* ♦ *Wasp stings can be very painful.* ❶ For more information about modal verbs, look at the **Reference Section** at the back of this dictionary.

can² /kæn/ noun [C] **1** a metal or plastic container that is used for holding or carrying liquid □ *bekas logam atau plastik*: *an oil can* ♦ *a watering can* **2** a metal container in which food or drink is kept without air so that it stays fresh □ *tin*: *a can of sardines* ♦ *a can of coke* ⊃ picture at **container**

> **HELP** **Can** or **tin**? In British English we usually use the word **tin** when it contains food. **Can** is used for drinks.

can³ /kæn/ verb [T] (**canning**; **canned**) to put food, drink, etc. into a can in order to keep it fresh for a long time □ *mengetin; ditinkan*: *canned fruit*

canal /kə'næl/ noun [C] **1** a deep cut that is made through land and filled with water for boats or ships to travel along; a smaller cut used for carrying water to fields, crops, etc. □ *terusan*: *the Panama Canal* **2** one of the tubes in the body through which food, air, etc. passes □ *saluran*

ca'nal boat noun [C] a long narrow boat used on canals □ *bot terusan*

canary /kə'neəri/ noun [C] (pl **canaries**) a small yellow bird that sings and is often kept in a **cage** (= a box made of bars) as a pet □ *burung kenari*

cancel /'kænsl/ verb [T] (**cancelling**; **cancelled**, *AmE* **canceling**; **canceled**) **1** to decide that sth that has been planned or arranged will not happen □ *membatalkan*: *All flights have been* *cancelled because of the bad weather.* ➲ look at **postpone 2** to stop sth that you asked for or agreed to □ *membatalkan*: *to cancel a reservation* ◆ *I wish to cancel my order for these books.*

PHR V cancel (sth) out to be equal to or have an equal effect □ *saling membatalkan*: *What I owe you is the same as what you owe me, so our debts cancel each other out.*

cancellation /ˌkænsəˈleɪʃn/ *noun* [C,U] the act of cancelling sth □ *pembatalan*: *We had to make a last-minute cancellation.*

Cancer /ˈkænsə(r)/ *noun* [C,U] the 4th sign of the **zodiac** (= 12 signs which represent the positions of the sun, moon and planets), the Crab; a person born under this sign □ *bintang Kanser*: *I'm a Cancer.* ➲ picture at **zodiac**

cancer /ˈkænsə(r)/ *noun* [C,U] a very serious disease in which lumps grow in the body □ *barah; kanser*: *She has lung cancer.* ◆ *He died of cancer.*

cancerous /ˈkænsərəs/ *adj* (used especially about a part of the body or sth growing in the body) having cancer □ *berbarah*: *a cancerous growth* ◆ *cancerous cells*

candid /ˈkændɪd/ *adj* saying exactly what you think □ *terus terang*: *a candid interview* **SYN** **frank** ▶ *noun* **candour** ▶ **candidly** *adv*

candidacy /ˈkændɪdəsi/ *noun* [U] the fact of being a **candidate** □ *pencalonan*

candidate /ˈkændɪdət/ *noun* [C] **1** a person who makes a formal request to be considered for a job or wants to be elected to a particular position □ *calon*: *We have some very good candidates for the post.* ➲ note at **election 2** a person who is taking an exam □ *calon*: *There are 12 candidates for FCE this month.*

candle /ˈkændl/ *noun* [C] a round stick of **wax** (= solid oil or fat) with a **wick** (= a piece of string) through the middle that you can burn to give light □ *lilin*: *to light/blow out a candle*

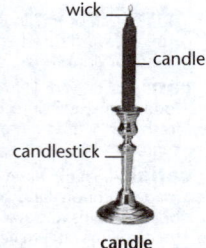

candlelight /ˈkændllaɪt/ *noun* [U] light that comes from a **candle** □ *cahaya lilin*: *They had dinner by candlelight.*

candlestick /ˈkændlstɪk/ *noun* [C] an object for holding a **candle** or **candles** □ *kaki lilin*: *a silver candlestick*

candour (*AmE* **candor**) /ˈkændə(r)/ *noun* [U] the quality of being honest; saying exactly what you think □ *sifat terus terang* ➲ *adjective* **candid**

candy /ˈkændi/ *noun* [C,U] (*pl* **candies**) (*AmE*) = **sweet**[2](1): *You eat too much candy.*

cane /keɪn/ *noun* **1** [C,U] the long central part of certain plants, for example **bamboo** (= a tall tropical plant), that is like a tube and is used as a material for making furniture, etc. □ *batang (buluh, tebu, dsb); rotan*: *sugar cane* ◆ *a cane chair* **2** [C] a stick that is used to help sb walk □ *tongkat*

canine /ˈkeɪnaɪn/ *adj* connected with dogs □ *(berkenaan dgn) anjing; kanin*

canister /ˈkænɪstə(r)/ *noun* [C] a small round metal container □ *kanister*: *a gas canister*

cannabis /ˈkænəbɪs/ *noun* [U] a drug made from **hemp** (= a type of plant) that some people smoke for pleasure, but which is illegal in many countries □ *kanabis*

cannibal /ˈkænɪbl/ *noun* [C] a person who eats human flesh □ *kanibal* ▶ **cannibalism** /ˈkænɪbəlɪzəm/ *noun* [U]

cannon /ˈkænən/ *noun* [C] (*pl* **cannon** or **cannons**) **1** a large, simple gun that was used in the past for firing **cannon balls** (= large stone or metal balls) □ *meriam* **2** a large gun on a ship, an army vehicle, an aircraft, etc. □ *meriam*

cannot ➲ **can**[1]

canoe /kəˈnuː/ *noun* [C] a light, narrow boat for one or two people that you can move through the water using a **paddle** (= a flat piece of wood) □ *kanu; jalur* ➲ look at **kayak** ➲ picture at **kayak** ▶ **canoe** *verb* [I] (**canoeing**; **canoes**; *pt, pp* **canoed**): *They canoed down the river.*

HELP When we are talking about spending time in a canoe it is more usual to say **go canoeing**: *We're going canoeing on the river tomorrow.*

canon /ˈkænən/ *noun* [C] a Christian priest who works in a **cathedral** (= a large church) □ *canon (paderi)*

'can opener (*especially AmE*) = **tin opener**

canopy /ˈkænəpi/ *noun* [C] (*pl* **canopies**) a cover that hangs or spreads above sth □ *langit-langit; tenda; sudur*: *The highest branches of the rainforest form a dense canopy.* ◆ *a parachute canopy*

can't short for **cannot**

canteen /kænˈtiːn/ *noun* [C] the place in a school, a factory, an office, etc. where the people who work there can get meals □ *kantin*: *the staff canteen* ➲ look at **cafeteria**

canter /ˈkæntə(r)/ *verb* [I] (used about a horse and its rider) to run fairly fast but not very fast □ *meligas*: *We cantered along the beach.* ➲ look at **gallop**, **trot** ▶ **canter** *noun* [sing]

canvas /ˈkænvəs/ *noun* **1** [U] a type of strong cloth that is used for making sails, bags, tents, etc. □ *kain kanvas* **2** [C] a piece of strong cloth for painting a picture on □ *kanvas*

canvass /ˈkænvəs/ *verb* **1** [I,T] **canvass (sb/sth) (for sth)** to try to persuade people to vote for a particular person or party in an election or to support sb/sth □ *memancing undi*: *to canvass for votes* ◆ *He's canvassing for the Conservative*

Party. ♦ *She's been to trying to canvass support for the plan.* **2** [T] to find out what people's opinions are about sth □ *mendapatkan pendapat orang ramai*

canyon /ˈkænjən/ *noun* [C] a deep valley with very steep sides □ *ngarai; lembah*

cap¹ /kæp/ *noun* [C] **1** a hat that has a part sticking out at the front □ *kep*: *a baseball cap* ➔ picture at **hat 2** a soft hat that is worn for a particular purpose □ *topi*: *a shower cap* ➔ picture on page **P1 3** a hat that is given to a player who is chosen to play for their country □ *kep*: *He won his first cap against France.* **4** a covering for the end or top of sth □ *tutup*: *Please put the cap back on the bottle.* ➔ note at **top¹** ➔ picture at **container**

cap² /kæp/ *verb* [T] (**capping**; **capped**) **1** to cover the top of sth □ *melitupi; dilitupi; menutup*: *mountains capped with snow* **2** to limit the amount of money that can be spent on sth □ *mengehadkan perbelanjaan* **3** to follow sth with sth bigger or better □ *mengatasi* **4** to choose a player to represent their country in a sport □ *memilih pemain utk mewakili negara* **IDM to cap it all** (*informal*) as a final piece of bad luck □ *paling teruk sekali*: *I had a row with my boss, my bike was stolen, and now to cap it all I've lost my keys!*

capability /ˌkeɪpəˈbɪləti/ *noun* [C,U] (*pl* **capabilities**) **capability (to do sth/of doing sth)** the quality of being able to do sth □ *keupayaan; kebolehan*: *Animals in the zoo have lost the capability to catch/of catching food for themselves.* ♦ *I tried to fix the computer, but it was beyond my capabilities.*

capable /ˈkeɪpəbl/ *adj* **1 capable of (doing) sth** having the ability or qualities necessary to do sth □ *boleh; berupaya; mampu*: *He's capable of passing the exam if he tries harder.* ♦ *That car is capable of 180 miles per hour.* ♦ *I do not believe that she's capable of stealing.* **2** having a lot of skill; good at doing sth □ *berkebolehan*: *She's a very capable teacher.* **OPP incapable** ▶ **capably** /-əbli/ *adv*

capacity /kəˈpæsəti/ *noun* (*pl* **capacities**) **1** [sing, U] the amount that a container or space can hold □ *muatan; isian*: *The tank has a capacity of 1 000 litres.* ♦ *The stadium was filled to capacity.* **2** [sing] **a capacity (for sth/for doing sth); a capacity (to do sth)** the ability to understand or do sth □ *keupayaan*: *That book is beyond the capacity of young children.* ♦ *a capacity for hard work/for learning languages* ♦ *Babies are born with the capacity to swim underwater.* **3** [C] the official position that sb has □ *tugas*: *In his capacity as chairman of the council …* **SYN role 4** [U, sing] the amount that a factory or machine can produce □ *keupayaan maksimum*: *The power station is working at full capacity.*

cape /keɪp/ *noun* [C] **1** a piece of clothing with no sleeves that hangs from your shoulders □ *mantel* ➔ look at **cloak 2** a piece of high land that sticks out into the sea □ *tanjung*: *the Cape of Good Hope*

canyon → capsule

capital¹ /ˈkæpɪtl/ *noun* **1** (also ˌcapital ˈcity) [C] the town or city where the government of a country is □ *ibu negara*: *Rome is the capital of Italy.* **2** [C] a place that is well known for a particular thing □ *tempat yg popular*: *Niagara Falls is the honeymoon capital of the world.* **3** [U] an amount of money that you use to start a business or to put in a bank, etc. so that you earn interest on it □ *modal*: *When she had enough capital, she bought a shop.* **4** (also ˌcapital ˈletter) [C] the large form of a letter of the alphabet □ *huruf besar*: *Write your name in capitals.* ➔ note at **letter**

capital² /ˈkæpɪtl/ *adj* [only *before* a noun] **1** connected with punishment by death □ *(berkenaan dgn) hukuman mati*: *Murder is a capital offence in some countries.* **2** (used about letters of the alphabet) written in the large form □ *huruf besar*: *'David' begins with a capital 'D'.*

ˌcapital inˈvestment *noun* [U] money that a business spends on buildings, equipment, etc. □ *pelaburan modal*

capitalism /ˈkæpɪtəlɪzəm/ *noun* [U] the economic system in which businesses are owned and run for profit by individuals and not by the state □ *kapitalisme* ➔ look at **communism**, **Marxism**, **socialism** ▶ **capitalist** /-ɪst/ *noun* [C], *adj*

capitalize (also **-ise**) /ˈkæpɪtəlaɪz/ *verb*
PHR V capitalize on sth to use sth to your advantage □ *memanfaatkan; mempergunakan*: *We can capitalize on the mistakes that our rivals have made.*

ˌcapital ˈletter = **capital¹ (4)**

ˌcapital ˈpunishment *noun* [U] punishment by death for serious crimes □ *hukuman bunuh* ➔ look at **corporal punishment**, **death penalty**

capitulate /kəˈpɪtʃuleɪt/ *verb* [I] (*formal*) to stop fighting and accept that you have lost; to give in to sb □ *menyerah (kalah)* ▶ **capitulation** /kəˌpɪtʃuˈleɪʃn/ *noun* [C,U]

capricious /kəˈprɪʃəs/ *adj* changing behaviour suddenly in a way that is difficult to predict □ *kerap mengubah perilaku*: *a capricious actor* **SYN unpredictable**

Capricorn /ˈkæprɪkɔːn/ *noun* [C,U] the 10th sign of the **zodiac** (= 12 signs which represent the positions of the sun, moon and planets), the Goat; a person born under this sign □ *bintang Kaprikorn/Jadi*: *I'm a Capricorn.* ➔ picture at **zodiac**

capsize /kæpˈsaɪz/ *verb* [I,T] (used about boats) to turn over in the water □ *terbalik*: *The canoe capsized.* ♦ *A big wave capsized the yacht.*

capsule /ˈkæpsjuːl/ *noun* [C] **1** a very small closed tube of medicine that you swallow □ *kapsul (ubat)* ➔ picture at **medicine 2** a container that is closed so that air, water, etc. cannot enter □ *kapsul*

VOWELS iː **see** i **any** ɪ **sit** e **ten** æ **hat** ɑː **father** ɒ **got** ɔː **saw** ʊ **put** uː **too** u **usual**

captain¹ /ˈkæptɪn/ noun [C] (abbr capt.) **1** the person who is in command of a ship or an aircraft ▫ *kapten*: *The captain gave the order to abandon ship.* ◆ *Captain Cook* ➲ note at **boat 2** a person who is the leader of a group or team ▫ *kapten; ketua pasukan*: *Who's (the) captain of the French team?* **3** an officer at a middle level in the army or navy ▫ *kapten*

captain² /ˈkæptɪn/ verb [T] to be the captain of a group or team ▫ *mengetuai; menjadi kapten*

caption /ˈkæpʃn/ noun [C] the words that are written above or below a picture, photograph, etc. to explain what it is about ▫ *kapsyen; keterangan*

captivate /ˈkæptɪveɪt/ verb [T] to attract and hold sb's attention ▫ *menawan hati; mempesona* ▶ **captivating** adj

captive¹ /ˈkæptɪv/ adj kept as a prisoner; (used about animals) kept in a **cage** (= a box made of bars), etc. ▫ *dlm tawanan/kurungan; asyik; leka*: *(figurative) a captive audience* (= listening because they cannot leave)
IDM **hold/take sb captive/prisoner** to keep sb as a prisoner and not allow them to escape ▫ *menahan sso sebagai tawanan*

captive² /ˈkæptɪv/ noun [C] a prisoner ▫ *(orang) tawanan*

captivity /kæpˈtɪvəti/ noun [U] the state of being kept in a place that you cannot escape from ▫ *dlm tawanan/kurungan*: *Wild animals are often unhappy when kept in captivity.*

captor /ˈkæptə(r)/ noun [C] a person who takes or keeps a person as a prisoner ▫ *penawan*

capture¹ /ˈkæptʃə(r)/ verb [T] **1** to take a person or an animal prisoner ▫ *menawan; menangkap*: *The lion was captured and taken back to the zoo.* **SYN** **catch 2** to take control of sth ▫ *menawan; menguasai*: *The town has been captured by the rebels.* ◆ *The company has captured 90% of the market.* **3** to make sb interested in sth ▫ *menarik minat*: *The story captured the children's imagination/interest/attention.* **SYN** **catch 4** to succeed in representing or recording sth in words, pictures, etc. ▫ *merakamkan*: *This poem captures the atmosphere of the carnival.* ◆ *The robbery was captured on video.*

capture² /ˈkæptʃə(r)/ noun [U] the act of capturing sth or being captured ▫ *penangkapan; penawanan*: *the capture of enemy territory* ◆ *data capture*

car /kɑː(r)/ noun [C] **1** (AmE also **automobile**) a road vehicle with four wheels that can carry a small number of people ▫ *kereta; motokar*: *a new/second-hand car* ◆ *Where can I park the car?* ◆ *They had a car crash.* ◆ *to get into/out of a car* ➲ note at **driving, parking, road** ➲ picture on **page P7**

HELP Note that we go **in the car** or **by car**. You can also use the verb **drive**: *I come to work in the car/by car.* ◆ *I drive to work.*

car

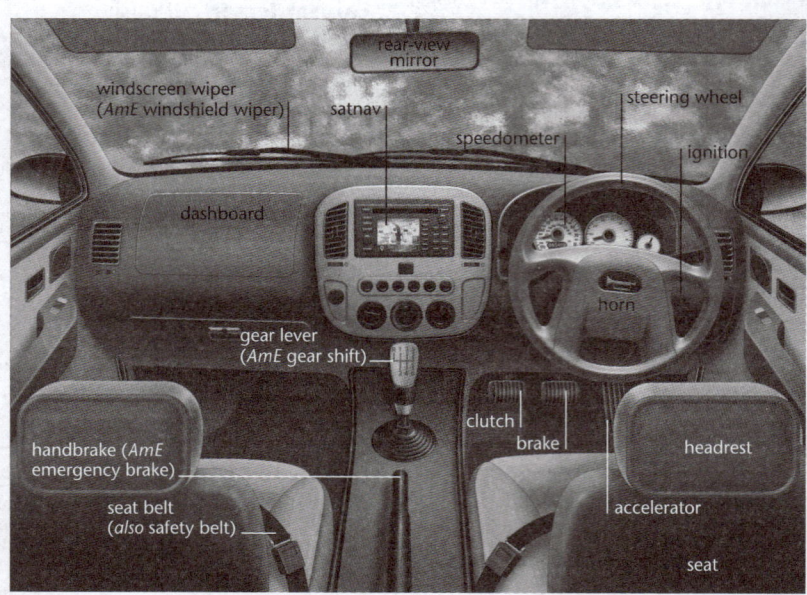

Labels: rear-view mirror, windscreen wiper (AmE windshield wiper), satnav, steering wheel, speedometer, ignition, dashboard, horn, gear lever (AmE gear shift), clutch, brake, headrest, handbrake (AmE emergency brake), seat belt (also safety belt), accelerator, seat

ʌ c**u**p ɜː b**ir**d ə **a**go eɪ p**ay** əʊ g**o** aɪ m**y** aʊ n**ow** ɔɪ b**oy** ɪə n**ear** eə h**air** ʊə p**ure**

2 (*BrE*) a section of a train that is used for a particular purpose □ *gerabak*: *a dining/sleeping car* **3** (*AmE*) = **carriage** (1) **4** (*AmE*) = **truck**

> **TOPIC**
> **Cars**
> You **fill up** your car with **petrol** or **diesel** at a **petrol station**. Many cars run on **unleaded** petrol. If your car **breaks down** (= stops working), it might need to be **towed** (= pulled by another vehicle) to a **garage** so that you can **have it repaired** by a **mechanic**.

carafe /kəˈræf/ *noun* [C] a glass container like a bottle with a wide neck, in which wine or water is served □ *karaf* ⮕ picture at **jug**

caramel /ˈkærəməl/ *noun* **1** [C,U] a type of sticky sweet that is made from boiled sugar, butter and milk □ *gula-gula karamel* **2** [U] burnt sugar that is used to add flavour and colour to food □ *karamel; gula hangus*

carat (*AmE* **karat**) /ˈkærət/ *noun* [C] a measure of how pure gold is or how heavy **jewels** (= valuable stones) are □ *karat*: *a 20-carat gold ring*

caravan /ˈkærəvæn/ *noun* [C] **1** (*AmE* **trailer**) a large vehicle that is pulled by a car or a horse. You can sleep, cook, etc. in a **caravan** when you are travelling or on holiday. □ *karavan* ⮕ picture at **camping**

> **HELP** When we are talking about using a caravan for holidays we say **go caravanning**.

2 a group of people and animals that travel together, for example across a desert □ *kafilah*

carbohydrate /ˌkɑːbəʊˈhaɪdreɪt/ *noun* [C,U] one of the substances in food, for example sugar, that gives your body energy □ *karbohidrat*: *Athletes need a diet that is high in carbohydrate.*

carbon /ˈkɑːbən/ *noun* [U] (*symbol* C) a chemical substance that is found in all living things, and also in diamonds, coal, petrol, etc. □ *karbon*

carbon copy *noun* [C] **1** a copy of a letter, etc. that was made using **carbon paper** □ *salinan karbon* **2** a person or a thing that is very similar to sb/sth else □ *sso/sst yg serupa; salin tak tumpah*

carbon credit *noun* [C] a measure of the amount of **carbon dioxide** and other gases that a country or an organization is allowed to produce and that can be traded □ *had pengeluaran karbon* ⮕ look at **carbon trading**

carbon dioxide /ˌkɑːbən daɪˈɒksaɪd/ *noun* [U] (*symbol* CO_2) a gas that has no colour or smell that people and animals breathe out of their lungs □ *karbon dioksida*

carbon footprint *noun* [C] a measure of the amount of **carbon dioxide** that is produced by the daily activities of a person or company □ *jejak karbon*: *Companies are looking at ways to reduce their carbon footprints.*

[C] **countable**, a noun with a plural form: *one book, two books*

carafe → card

carbon monoxide /ˌkɑːbən məˈnɒksaɪd/ *noun* [U] (*symbol* CO) a poisonous gas. Motor vehicles produce a lot of **carbon monoxide**. □ *karbon monoksida*

carbon neutral *adj* producing no **carbon dioxide** or an amount that is balanced by actions that protect the environment □ *tanpa karbon*: *We need to use more fuels that are renewable and carbon neutral.* **SYN** **zero-carbon**

carbon offset *noun* [C,U] a way for a company or person to reduce the level of **carbon dioxide** (= a gas) for which they are responsible. They pay money to a company that works to reduce the total amount produced in the world, for example by planting trees □ *imbangan karbon*: *Wind energy companies sell carbon offsets.*

carbon paper *noun* [U] thin paper with a dark substance on one side that you put between two sheets of paper to make a copy of what you are writing □ *kertas karbon*

carbon trading *noun* [U] a system that gives countries and organizations the right to produce a particular amount of **carbon dioxide** and other gases that cause **global warming** (= the increase in the temperature of the earth's atmosphere), and allows them to sell this right □ *perdagangan karbon* ⮕ look at **carbon credit**

car boot sale *noun* [C] (*BrE*) an outdoor sale where people sell things they do not want from the back of their cars □ *jualan barang (dr but kereta)*

carburettor (*AmE* **carburetor**) /ˌkɑːbəˈretə(r)/ *noun* [C] the piece of equipment in a car's engine that mixes petrol and air □ *karburetor*

carcass /ˈkɑːkəs/ *noun* [C] the dead body of an animal □ *bangkai; karkas* ⮕ look at **corpse**

cards

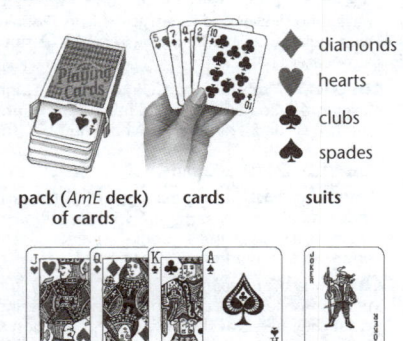

pack (*AmE* deck) of cards   cards   suits

♦ diamonds
♥ hearts
♣ clubs
♠ spades

jack   queen   king   ace   joker

card /kɑːd/ *noun* **1** [U] thick stiff paper □ *kad; kertas keras*: *a piece of card* **2** [C] a small piece of

[U] **uncountable**, a noun with no plural form: *some sugar*

cardboard → career

card or plastic that has information on it □ *kad*: *Here is my business card in case you need to contact me.* ♦ *a membership/an identity/a credit card* ➲ picture at **money 3** (also 'greetings card) [C] a piece of card with a picture on it that you use for sending a special message to sb □ *kad ucapan*: *a Christmas/birthday card* ♦ *a get-well card* (= one that you send to sb who is ill) ➲ picture at **letter 4** [C] = **postcard 5** (also 'playing card) [C] one of a set of 52 small pieces of card with shapes or pictures on them that are used for playing games □ *daun terup*: *a pack of cards* **6 cards** [pl] games that are played with cards □ *permainan daun terup*: *Let's play cards.* ♦ *Let's have a game of cards.* ♦ *I never win at cards!*

IDM **on the cards**; (*AmE* **in the cards**) (*informal*) likely to happen □ *besar kemungkinan berlakunya*: *Their marriage break-up has been on the cards for some time now.*

TOPIC

Playing cards
A **pack** of cards is divided into four **suits**, two red (**hearts** and **diamonds**) and two black (**clubs** and **spades**). Each suit has an **ace**, a **king**, a **queen**, a **jack** and nine other cards, numbered from 2 to 10. Before we play cards we **shuffle**, **cut** and **deal** the cards. A popular card game, often played for money, is **poker**.

---

cardboard /ˈkɑːdbɔːd/ *noun* [U] very thick paper that is used for making boxes, etc. □ *kadbod*: *The goods were packed in cardboard boxes.*

cardiac /ˈkɑːdiæk/ *adj* [only before a noun] (*formal*) connected with the heart □ *(berkenaan dgn) jantung*: *cardiac surgery* ♦ *a cardiac arrest* (= when the heart stops temporarily or permanently)

cardigan /ˈkɑːdɪɡən/ *noun* [C] a warm piece of clothing, often made of wool, which you wear on the top half of your body. Cardigans have long sleeves and fasten at the front, usually with buttons. □ *kardigan; baju sejuk* ➲ note at **sweater**

cardinal /ˈkɑːdɪnl/ *noun* [C] **1** a priest at a high level in the Roman Catholic Church □ *kardinal* **2** (also ˌcardinal 'number) a whole number, for example 1, 2, 3, that shows quantity □ *nombor kardinal* ➲ look at **ordinal**

'**card index** (also **index**) *noun* [C] (*pl* **card indexes**) a box of cards with information on them, such as names, books, subjects, etc., arranged in order from A-Z □ *indeks kad*

care¹ /keə(r)/ *noun* **1** [U] **care (for sb)** the process of looking after sb/sth and providing what they need for their health or protection □ *jagaan*: *All the children in their care were healthy and happy.* ♦ *This hospital provides free medical care.* ♦ *She's in intensive care* (= the part of the hospital for people who are very seriously ill). ♦ *skin/hair care products* **2** [U] **care (over sth/in doing sth)** thinking about what you are doing so

that you do it well or do not make a mistake □ *berhati-hati; cermat*: *You should take more care over your homework.* ♦ *This box contains glasses—please handle it with care.* **3** [C,U] something that makes you feel worried or unhappy □ *beban; tanggungan*: *Since Charlie retired he doesn't have a care in the world.* ♦ *It was a happy life, free from care.*

IDM **in care** (used about children) living in a home which is organized by the government, and not with their parents □ *diletakkan dlm rumah kebajikan kanak-kanak*: *They were taken into care after their parents died.*
take care (that …/to do sth) to be careful □ *hati-hati; jaga-jaga; jaga diri*: *Goodbye and take care!* ♦ *Take care that you don't spill your tea.* ♦ *He took care not to arrive too early.*
take care of sb/sth to deal with sb/sth; to organize or arrange sth □ *menguruskan sso/sst*: *I'll take care of the food for the party.* ➲ note at **care²**
take care of yourself/sb/sth to keep yourself/sb/sth safe from injury, illness, damage, etc.; to look after sb/sth □ *jaga diri; menjaga sso/sst*: *My mother took care of me when I was ill.* ♦ *She always takes great care of her books.*

care² /keə(r)/ *verb* [I,T] **care (about sb/sth)** to be worried about or interested in sb/sth □ *ambil peduli; menghiraukan*: *Money is the thing that she cares about most.* ♦ *He really cares about his staff.* ♦ *I don't care what you do.*

HELP **Care about** or **take care of**?: *She really cares about the environment* (= she is interested in it and thinks it is important). ♦ *He has to take care of/look after his sick wife* (= be with her and help her). ♦ *You can borrow my camera, but please take care of/look after it* (= keep it in good condition). **Take care of** can also mean 'be responsible for': *I'll take care of the travel arrangements.*

IDM **I, etc. couldn't care less** (*informal*) it does not matter to me, etc. at all □ *saya, dsb, tdk peduli*: *I couldn't care less what Barry thinks.*
not care/give a damn (about sb/sth) ➲ **damn³**
who cares? (*informal*) nobody is interested; it is not important to anyone □ *peduli apa*: '*I wonder who'll win the match.*' '*Who cares?*'
would you care for …/to do sth (*formal*) a polite way to ask if sb would like sth or would like to do sth □ *sudikah/mahukah anda sst …/membuat sst*

PHR V **care for sb** to look after sb □ *menjaga sso*: *Who cared for her while she was ill?*
care for sb/sth to like or love sb/sth □ *suka/sayang akan sso atau sst*: *She still cares for Liam, although he married someone else.* ♦ *I don't care for that colour very much.*

career¹ /kəˈrɪə(r)/ *noun* [C] **1** the series of jobs that sb has in a particular area of work □ *kerjaya*: *Sarah is considering a career in engineering.* ♦ *a successful career in politics* **2** the period of your life that you spend working □ *kerjaya; tempoh bekerja*: *She spent most of her career working in India.*

[I] **intransitive**, a verb which has no object: *He laughed.*   [T] **transitive**, a verb which has an object: *He ate an apple.*

career² /kəˈrɪə(r)/ verb [I] to move quickly and in a dangerous way □ *meluru*: *The car careered off the road and crashed into a wall.*

carefree /ˈkeəfriː/ adj with no problems or worries □ *ceria; senang hati*

careful /ˈkeəfl/ adj **1 careful (of/with sth); careful (to do sth)** thinking about what you are doing so that you do not have an accident or make mistakes, etc. □ *berhati-hati; waspada*: *Be careful! There's a car coming.* ◆ *Please be very careful of the traffic.* ◆ *Be careful with that knife—it's very sharp.* ◆ *That ladder doesn't look very safe. Be careful you don't fall.* ◆ *I was careful not to say anything about the money.* ◆ *a careful driver* **OPP careless 2** giving a lot of attention to details to be sure sth is right □ *teliti*: *I'll need to give this matter some careful thought.* ◆ *a careful worker* ▶ **carefully** /-fəli/ adv: *Please listen carefully. It's important that you remember all this.*

caregiver /ˈkeəɡɪvə(r)/ (AmE) = **carer**

careless /ˈkeələs/ adj **1 careless (about/with sth)** not thinking enough about what you are doing so that you make mistakes □ *cuai; kurang hati-hati*: *Jo's very careless.* ◆ *The accident was caused by careless driving.* **OPP careful 2** resulting from a lack of thought or attention to detail □ *(yg) disebabkan oleh kecuaian*: *a careless mistake* ▶ **carelessly** adv: *She threw her coat carelessly on the chair.* ▶ **carelessness** noun [U]

carer /ˈkeərə(r)/ (AmE **caregiver**) noun [C] a person who regularly looks after a sick or an old person at home □ *penjaga (orang sakit, tua, dsb)*

caress /kəˈres/ verb [T] to touch sb/sth in a gentle and loving way □ *membelai; mengelus* ▶ **caress** noun [C]

caretaker /ˈkeəteɪkə(r)/ (AmE **janitor**) noun [C] a person whose job is to look after a large building, for example a school or a block of flats □ *penjaga (bangunan sekolah, rumah pangsa, dsb)*

cargo /ˈkɑːɡəʊ/ noun [C,U] (pl **cargoes**, (AmE also) **cargos**) the goods that are carried in a ship or an aircraft □ *kargo; barang muatan*: *Luggage is carried in the cargo hold of the plane.* ◆ *a cargo ship*

cargo pants (also **cargoes**, Bre also **combats**) noun [pl] loose trousers that have pockets in various places, for example on the side of the leg above the knee □ *seluar panjang kargo* ➔ picture on **page P1**

the Caribbean /ˌkærɪˈbiːən; kəˈrɪbiːən/ noun [sing] the area in the Caribbean Sea where the group of islands called the West Indies is found □ *(kawasan) Caribbean* ▶ **Caribbean** adj

caricature /ˈkærɪkətʃʊə(r)/ (AmE also) / noun [C] a picture or description of sb that makes their appearance or behaviour funnier and more extreme than it really is □ *karikatur*: *Many of the people in the book are caricatures of the author's friends.*

caring /ˈkeərɪŋ/ adj showing that you care about other people □ *penyayang*: *We must work towards a more caring society.*

carnage /ˈkɑːnɪdʒ/ noun [U] the violent killing of a large number of people □ *pembunuhan beramai-ramai; pembunuhan besar-besaran*: *a scene of carnage* **SYN slaughter**

carnation /kɑːˈneɪʃn/ noun [C] a white, pink or red flower with a pleasant smell □ *bunga teluki*

carnival /ˈkɑːnɪvl/ noun [C] a public festival that takes place in the streets with music and dancing □ *karnival; pesta*: *the carnival in Rio*

carnivore /ˈkɑːnɪvɔː(r)/ noun [C] any animal that eats meat □ *karnivor; haiwan maging* ▶ **carnivorous** /kɑːˈnɪvərəs/ adj: *Tigers are carnivorous animals.*

carol /ˈkærəl/ (also ˌChristmas ˈcarol) noun [C] a Christian religious song that people sing at Christmas □ *lagu karol*

carousel /ˌkærəˈsel/ noun [C] **1** (AmE) = **merry-go-round 2** a moving belt at an airport that carries luggage for passengers to collect □ *karusel*

ˈcar park (AmE ˈparking lot) noun [C] an area or building where you can leave your car □ *tempat letak kereta*: *a multi-storey car park*

carpenter /ˈkɑːpəntə(r)/ noun [C] a person whose job is to make things from wood □ *tukang kayu* ➔ note at **house** ➔ look at **joiner** ➔ picture on **page P2**

carpentry /ˈkɑːpəntri/ noun [U] the skill or work of a **carpenter** □ *pertukangan kayu*

carpet /ˈkɑːpɪt/ noun **1** [C,U] (a piece of) thick material that is used for covering floors and stairs □ *hamparan; permaidani*: *a fitted carpet* (= one that is cut to the exact shape of a room) ◆ *a square metre of carpet* ➔ look at **rug** ➔ picture on **page P8 2** [C] a thick layer of sth that covers the ground □ *litupan; hamparan*: *a carpet of snow* ▶ **carpeted** adj: *The rooms are carpeted.*

carriage /ˈkærɪdʒ/ noun [C] **1** (also **coach**; AmE **car**) one of the separate parts of a train where people sit □ *gerabak*: *a first-class carriage* ➔ picture on **page P7 2** a vehicle with wheels that is pulled by horses □ *pedati; kereta kuda* ➔ look at **coach**

carriageway /ˈkærɪdʒweɪ/ noun [C] (BrE) one of the two sides of a **motorway** (= a wide road for fast traffic) or main road, used by vehicles travelling in one direction only □ *laluan (lebuh raya)*: *the southbound carriageway of the motorway* ➔ look at **dual carriageway**

carrier /ˈkæriə(r)/ noun [C] **1** (in business) a company that transports people or goods □ *syarikat pengangkutan (perkapalan, penerbangan)*: *the Dutch carrier, KLM* **2** a military vehicle or ship that is used for transporting

carrier bag → cascade

soldiers, planes, weapons, etc. □ *kapal pengangkut*: *an aircraft carrier* **3** a person or an animal that can give an infectious disease to others but does not show the signs of the disease □ *pembawa*: *Some insects are carriers of tropical diseases.* **4** (BrE) = carrier bag

'carrier bag (BrE also **carrier**) *noun* [C] a plastic or paper bag for carrying shopping □ *beg plastik/kertas* ⊃ picture at **bag**

carrot /'kærət/ *noun* **1** [C,U] a long thin orange vegetable that grows under the ground □ *lobak merah*: *A pound of carrots, please.* ♦ *grated carrot* ⊃ picture on **page P15 2** [C] something attractive that is offered to sb in order to persuade them to do sth □ *ganjaran*: *The management have offered them the carrot of a £500 bonus if they agree to work extra hours.*

carry /'kæri/ *verb* (**carrying**; **carries**; *pt, pp* **carried**) **1** [T] to hold sb/sth in your hand, arms or on your back while you are moving from one place to another □ *membawa; mengangkat; memikul*: *Could you carry this bag for me? It's terribly heavy.* ♦ *She was carrying a rucksack on her back.*

> **HELP Carry or wear?** You use **wear**, not **carry**, to talk about having clothes, jewellery, etc. on your body: *He was wearing a black jacket.*

2 [T] to have sth with you as you go somewhere □ *membawa*: *I never carry much money with me when I go to London.* ♦ *Do the police carry guns in your country?* **3** [T] to transport sb/sth from one place to another □ *mengangkut; membawa*: *A train carrying hundreds of passengers crashed yesterday.* ♦ *Strong winds carried the boat off course.* **4** [T] to have an infectious disease that can be given to others, usually without showing any signs of the disease yourself □ *membawa*: *Rats carry all sorts of diseases.* **5** [I] (used about a sound) to reach a long distance □ *dpt didengar dr jauh*: *You'll have to speak louder if you want your voice to carry to the back of the room.* **6** [T, usually passive] to officially approve of sth in a meeting, etc., because the largest number of people vote for it □ *disokong*: *The motion was carried by 12 votes to 9.*

IDM be/get carried away to be so excited that you forget what you are doing □ *terbawa-bawa*: *I got so carried away watching the race that I forgot how late it was.*

carry weight to have influence on the opinion of sb else □ *berpengaruh*: *Nick's views carry a lot of weight with our manager.*

PHR V carry it/sth off to succeed in doing sth difficult □ *berjaya (melakukan sst yg sukar)*: *He felt nervous before he started his speech but he carried it off very well.*

carry on (with sth/doing sth) to continue □ *meneruskan (membuat sst)*: *They ignored me and carried on with their conversation.* ♦ *She intends to carry on studying after the course has finished.*

carry on sth to do an activity □ *melakukan sst*: *to carry on a conversation/a business*

carry sth out 1 to do sth that you have been ordered to do □ *melaksanakan/menjalankan (perintah, tugas, dsb)*: *The soldiers carried out their orders without question.* **2** to do a task, repair, etc. □ *menjalankan*: *to carry out tests/an investigation*

carrycot /'kærikɒt/ *noun* [C] a small bed, like a box with handles, that you can carry a baby in □ *katil bimbit*

'carry-on bag *noun* [C] (AmE) = **hand luggage**

'carry-out (AmE) = **takeaway**

carsick /'ka:sɪk/ *adj* feeling sick or **vomiting** (= bringing up food from the stomach) as a result of travelling in a car □ *mabuk kereta*: *to get/feel/be carsick* ⊃ look at **airsick, seasick, travel-sick**

cart¹ /ka:t/ *noun* [C] **1** a vehicle with wheels that is used for transporting things □ *kereta sorong*: *a horse and cart* **2** = **trolley**(1)

cart² /ka:t/ *verb* [T] (*informal*) to take or carry sth/sb somewhere, often with difficulty □ *mengangkut*: *We left our luggage at the station because we didn't want to cart it around all day.*

cartilage /'ka:tɪlɪdʒ/ *noun* [C,U] a strong substance in the places where your bones join □ *rawan*

carton /'ka:tn/ *noun* [C] a small container made of cardboard or plastic □ *karton*: *a carton of milk/orange juice* ⊃ picture at **container**

cartoon /ka:'tu:n/ *noun* [C] **1** a funny drawing, especially in a newspaper or magazine □ *kartun* **2** a film that tells a story by using moving drawings instead of real people and places □ *filem kartun*

cartoonist /ka:'tu:nɪst/ *noun* [C] a person who draws **cartoons** □ *pelukis kartun*

cartridge /'ka:trɪdʒ/ *noun* [C] **1** a small tube that contains powder that can explode and a bullet. You put a **cartridge** into a gun when you want to fire it. □ *kartrij; patrum* **2** a closed container that holds sth that is used in a machine, for example film for a camera, ink for printing, etc. **Cartridges** can be removed and replaced when they are finished or empty. □ *kartrij*

cartwheel /'ka:twi:l/ *noun* [C] a fast physical movement in which you turn in a circle sideways by putting your hands on the ground and bringing your legs, one at a time, over your head □ *putar roda*: *to do/turn cartwheels*

carve /ka:v/ *verb* **1** [I,T] **carve (sth) (out of sth)** to cut wood or stone in order to make an object or to put a pattern or writing on it □ *mengukir*: *The statue is carved out of marble.* ♦ *He carved his name on the desk.* **2** [T] to cut a piece of cooked meat into slices □ *memotong; menghiris*: *to carve a chicken*

carving /'ka:vɪŋ/ *noun* [C,U] an object or a design that has been **carved** □ *ukiran*: *There are ancient carvings on the walls of the cave.*

cascade¹ /kæ'skeɪd/ *noun* [C] **1** a small waterfall (= water that falls down the side of a mountain, etc.) □ *air terjun* **2** a large quantity of sth that falls or hangs down □ *juraian*: *a cascade of blond hair*

cascade² /kæˈskeɪd/ *verb* [I] to fall or hang down, especially in large amounts or in stages □ *mencurah turun; mengurai*: *Water cascaded from the roof.*

case /keɪs/ *noun*
▸SITUATION **1** [C] a particular situation or example of sth □ *hal; kejadian*: *In some cases, people have had to wait two weeks for a doctor's appointment.* ♦ *Most of us travel to work by tube—or, in Jim's case, by train and tube.* ♦ *Cases of the disease are very unusual in this country.* **2 the case** [sing] the true situation □ *keadaan/hal sebenar*: *The man said he worked in Cardiff, but we discovered later that this was not the case.*
▸LEGAL MATTER **3** [C] a crime or legal matter □ *kes*: *The police deal with hundreds of murder cases a year.* ♦ *The case will come to court in a few months.*
▸REASONS **4** [C, usually sing] the facts and reasons that support one side in a discussion or legal matter □ *alasan; sebab-sebab*: *She tried to make a case for shorter working hours, but the others disagreed.*
▸CONTAINER **5** [C] [in compounds] a container or cover for sth □ *sarung; bekas*: *a pencil case* ♦ *a pillowcase* ♦ *a bookcase* ♦ *She put her glasses back in the case.* **6** = **suitcase** □ *beg pakaian*: *Would you like me to carry your case?*
IDM (be) a case of sth/doing sth a situation in which sth is needed □ *keadaan yg memerlukan sst*: *There's no secret to success in this business. It's just a case of hard work.*
in any case whatever happens or has happened □ *walau bagaimanapun*: *I don't care how much the tickets cost, I'm going in any case.* **SYN anyway**
(just) in case because sth might happen □ *kalau; sekiranya; manalah tahu*: *I think I'll take an umbrella in case it rains.* ♦ *I wasn't intending to buy anything but I took my credit card just in case.*

> **HELP** **In case** or **if**? In British English, **in case** and **if** have a different meaning. Compare: *You should buy insurance, in case you are robbed.* ♦ *If you are robbed, you should call the police.*

in case of sth (*formal*) if sth happens □ *sekiranya berlaku*: *In case of fire, break this glass.*
in that case if that is the situation □ *kalau begitu*: 'I'm busy on Tuesday.' 'Oh well, in that case we'll have to meet another day.'

'case study *noun* [C] a detailed study of a person, group, situation, etc. over a period of time □ *kajian kes*

cash¹ /kæʃ/ *noun* [U] **1** money in the form of coins or notes and not cheques, plastic cards, etc. □ *wang tunai*: *Would you prefer me to pay in cash or by credit card?* ♦ *How much cash have you got with/on you?* ⊃ note at **money**

> **HELP** We use **cash** when we are talking about coins and notes, but **change** when we are talking about coins only.

2 (*informal*) money in any form □ *wang*: *I'm a bit short of cash this month so I can't afford to go out much.* ⊃ picture at **money**

cash² /kæʃ/ *verb* [T] to exchange a cheque, etc. for coins and notes □ *menunaikan (cek, dsb)*: *I'm just going to the bank to cash a cheque.*
PHR V cash in (on sth) to take advantage of a situation □ *mengambil kesempatan*

cashback /ˈkæʃbæk/ *noun* [U] **1** if you ask for **cashback** when you are paying for goods in some shops with a **debit card** (= a plastic card that takes money directly from your bank account), you get a sum of money in cash, that is added to your bill □ *tunai balik* **2** an offer of money as a present that is made by some banks, companies selling cars, etc. in order to persuade customers to do business with them □ *tunai balik*

'cash card (*AmE* ˌATˈM **card**) *noun* [C] a plastic card given by a bank to its customers so that they can get money from a **cash machine** (= a special machine in or outside a bank) □ *kad tunai* ⊃ look at **cheque card**, **credit card**

'cash desk *noun* [C] the place in a large shop where you pay for things □ *tempat membayar*

'cash dispenser = **cash machine**

cashew /ˈkæʃuː; kæˈʃuː/ (also ˈcashew nut) *noun* [C] a small curved nut that we eat □ *biji gajus* ⊃ picture at **nut**

'cash flow *noun* [sing] the movement of money into and out of a business as goods are bought and sold □ *aliran tunai*: *The company had cash-flow problems and could not pay its bills.*

cashier /kæˈʃɪə(r)/ *noun* [C] the person in a bank, shop, etc. that customers pay money to or get money from □ *juruwang*

'cash machine (also **'cash dispenser**, **Cashpoint™**) *noun* [C] a machine inside or outside a bank, etc., that you can get money from at any time of day by putting in a **cash card** (= a special card that is given to you by your bank) □ *mesin tunai* ⊃ note at **money**

cashmere /ˈkæʃmɪə(r)/ (*AmE* also /) *noun* [U] a type of wool that is very fine and soft □ *(kain bulu) kashmir*

Cashpoint™ /ˈkæʃpɔɪnt/ = **cash machine**

'cash register = **till²**

casing /ˈkeɪsɪŋ/ *noun* [C,U] a cover that protects sth □ *sarung/bekas barang*: *a camera with a waterproof casing*

casino /kəˈsiːnəʊ/ *noun* [C] (*pl* **casinos**) a place where people play card games, etc. in which you can win or lose money □ *kasino*

cask /kɑːsk/ *noun* [C] a large wooden container in which alcoholic drinks, etc. are stored □ *tong kayu*

casket /ˈkɑːskɪt/ (*AmE*) = **coffin**

cassava /kəˈsɑːvə/ (also **manioc**) *noun* [U] **1** a tropical plant with many branches and long

casserole → catalogue

roots that you can eat □ *sejenis tumbuhan tropika* **2** the roots of this plant, which can be cooked or made into flour □ *ubi kayu*

casserole /ˈkæsərəʊl/ *noun* **1** [C,U] a type of food made by cooking meat and vegetables in liquid for a long time in the oven □ *kaserol*: *chicken casserole* **2** [C] (also ˈcasserole dish) a large dish with a lid for cooking **casseroles** in □ *mangkuk kaserol*

cassette /kəˈset/ *noun* [C] a small flat plastic case containing tape for playing or recording music or sound □ *kaset*: *to put on/play/listen to a cassette* ♦ *a cassette player/recorder* ➲ look at **video**

cast¹ /kɑːst/ *verb* (*pt, pp* cast) **1** [I,T] to throw a fishing line or net into the water □ *melemparkan tali pancing; menebar jala*: *He cast his line into the river and waited.* **2** [T, often passive] to choose an actor for a particular role in a play, film, etc. □ *memberi peranan*: *She always seems to be cast in the same sort of role.*

IDM **cast doubt on sth** to make people less sure about sth □ *menimbulkan keraguan ttg sst*: *New evidence casts doubt on the truth of the Prime Minister's statement.*

cast an eye/your eye(s) over sb/sth to look at sb/sth quickly □ *melihat sso/sst sepintas lalu*

cast light on sth to help to explain sth □ *memberi penjelasan ttg sst*: *Can you cast any light on the problem?*

cast your mind back to make yourself remember sth □ *mengingat kembali*: *She cast her mind back to the day she met her husband.*

cast a shadow (across/over sth) to cause an area of shade to appear somewhere □ *menimbulkan bayang-bayang; mendatangkan kesan*: (*figurative*) *The accident cast a shadow over the rest of the holiday* (= stopped people enjoying it fully).

cast a/your vote to vote □ *membuang undi*: *Cast your vote for the winner by calling this phone number now.*

PHR V **cast around/about for sth** to try to find sth □ *mencari-cari sst*: *Jack cast around desperately for a solution to the problem.*

cast² /kɑːst/ *noun* **1** [C, with sing or pl verb] all the actors in a play, film, etc. □ *barisan pelakon*: *The entire cast was/were excellent.* **2** [C] a container that you use to make an object in a particular shape by pouring hot liquid metal, etc. into it; an object that is made in this way □ *acuan* **SYN** **mould**

castaway /ˈkɑːstəweɪ/ *noun* [C] a person who is left alone somewhere after their ship has sunk □ *orang yg terdampar*

caste /kɑːst/ *noun* [C,U] a social class or group based on your position in society, how much money you have, family origin, etc.; the system of dividing people in this way □ *kasta*: *Hindu society is based on a caste system.*

ˌcast ˈiron *noun* [U] a hard type of iron that is shaped by pouring the hot liquid metal into a mould (= a specially shaped container) □ *(yg diperbuat drpd) besi tuang; kuat; tdk boleh digugat*: *a bridge made of cast iron* ♦ (*figurative*) *a cast-iron alibi* (= one that people cannot doubt) ➲ look at **wrought iron**

castle /ˈkɑːsl/ *noun* [C] **1** a large building with high walls and towers that was built in the past to defend people against attack □ *istana kota; kastil*: *a medieval castle* ♦ *Edinburgh Castle* **2** (in the game of **chess**) any of the four pieces placed in the corner squares of the board at the start of the game, usually made to look like a castle □ *benteng; tir*

castle

ˈcast-off *noun* [C, usually pl] a piece of clothing that you no longer want and that you give to sb else or throw away □ *(pakaian dsb) yg tdk dikehendaki lagi*: *When I was little I had to wear my sister's cast-offs.*

castrate /kæˈstreɪt/ *verb* [T] to remove part of the sexual organs of a male animal so that it cannot produce young □ *mengembiri* ➲ look at **neuter** ▶ **castration** /kæˈstreɪʃn/ *noun* [U]

casual /ˈkæʒuəl/ *adj* **1** relaxed and not worried; not showing great effort or interest □ *bersahaja; sambil lewa*: *I'm not happy about your casual attitude to your work.* ♦ *It was only a casual remark so I don't know why he got so angry.* **2** (used about clothes) not formal □ *santai; kasual*: *I always change into casual clothes as soon as I get home from work.* **3** (used about work) done only for a short period; not regular or permanent □ *sambilan; sementara*: *Most of the building work was done by casual labour.* ♦ *a casual job* ▶ **casually** /ˈkæʒuəli/ *adv*: *She walked in casually and said, 'I'm not late, am I?'* ♦ *Dress casually—it won't be a formal party.*

casualty /ˈkæʒuəlti/ *noun* (*pl* casualties) **1** [C] a person who is killed or injured in a war or an accident □ *orang yg terkorban/cedera*: *After the accident the casualties were taken to hospital.* **2** [C] a person or thing that suffers as a result of sth else □ *mangsa*: *Many small companies became casualties of the economic crisis.* **SYN** **victim** **3** [C,U] (also ˈcasualty department) = **accident and emergency**

cat /kæt/ *noun* [C] **1** a small animal with soft fur that people often keep as a pet □ *kucing*: *cat food* ➲ note at **pet** **2** a wild animal of the cat family □ *haiwan keluarga kucing*: *the big cats* (= lions, tigers, etc.)

MORE A young cat is called a **kitten**. A male cat is called a **tom**, although **cat** is often used for both males and females. When a cat makes a soft sound of pleasure, it **purrs**. When it makes a louder sound, it **miaows**.

catalogue (*AmE* catalog) /ˈkætəlɒg/ (*AmE usually*) / *noun* [C] **1** a list of all the things that you can buy, see, etc. somewhere □ *katalog* **2** a series, especially of bad things □ *rentetan*: *a* catalogue of disasters/errors/injuries ▶ **catalogue** (AmE **catalog**) verb [T]: *She started to catalogue all the new library books.*

catalyst /ˈkætəlɪst/ noun [C] **1** (in chemistry) a substance that makes a reaction happen faster without being changed itself □ *mangkin* **2 catalyst (for sth)** a person or thing that causes a change □ *pemangkin; orang atau sst yg menyebabkan perubahan*: *I see my role as being a catalyst for change.*

catalytic converter /ˌkætəˌlɪtɪk kənˈvɜːtə(r)/ noun [C] a device used in motor vehicles to reduce the damage caused to the environment by poisonous gases □ *penukar bermangkin*

catamaran /ˌkætəməˈræn/ noun [C] a fast sailing boat with two **hulls** (= bottom parts that go in the water) □ *katamaran*

catapult¹ /ˈkætəpʌlt/ (AmE **slingshot**) noun [C] a Y-shaped stick with a piece of **elastic** (= material that can stretch) tied to each side that is used by children for shooting stones □ *lastik*

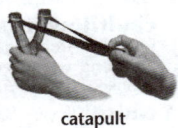

catapult

catapult² /ˈkætəpʌlt/ verb [T] to throw sb/sth suddenly and with great force □ *memelantingkan; terhumban; melambungkan*: *When the car crashed the driver was catapulted through the windscreen.* ◆ (figurative) *The success of his first film catapulted him to fame.*

cataract /ˈkætərækt/ noun [C] a white area that grows over the eye as a result of disease □ *katarak*

catarrh /kəˈtɑː(r)/ noun [U] a thick liquid that forms in the nose and throat when you have a cold □ *katar; hingus*

catastrophe /kəˈtæstrəfi/ noun [C] **1** a sudden disaster that causes great suffering or damage □ *malapetaka; bencana*: *major catastrophes such as floods and earthquakes* **2** an event that causes great difficulty, disappointment, etc. □ *sst yg menyukarkan/mengecewakan; musibah*: *It'll be a catastrophe if I fail the exam again.* ▶ **catastrophic** /ˌkætəˈstrɒfɪk/ adj: *The war had a catastrophic effect on the whole country.*

catch¹ /kætʃ/ verb (pt, pp **caught** /kɔːt/)
▶HOLD **1** [T] to take hold of sth that is moving, usually with your hand or hands □ *menangkap*: *The dog caught the ball in its mouth.*
▶CAPTURE **2** [T] to capture sb/sth that you have been following or looking for □ *menangkap*: *Two policemen ran after the thief and caught him at the end of the street.* ◆ *to catch a fish*
▶DISCOVER **3** [T] to notice or see sb doing sth bad □ *nampak*: *I caught her taking money from my purse.*
▶BE IN TIME **4** [T] to be in time for sth; not to miss sb/sth □ *sempat*: *We arrived just in time to catch the beginning of the film.* ◆ *I'll phone her now. I might just catch her before she leaves the office.*
▶GET BUS, ETC. **5** [T] to get on a bus, train, plane, etc. □ *menaiki*: *I caught the train from Bari to Lecce.* **OPP miss**
▶ILLNESS **6** [T] to get an illness □ *mendapat; dijangkiti*: *to catch a cold/flu/measles*
▶GET STUCK **7** [I,T] to become or cause sth to become accidentally connected to or stuck in sth □ *tersangkut*: *His jacket caught on a nail and ripped.* ◆ *If we leave early we won't get caught in the traffic.*
▶HIT **8** [T] to hit sb/sth □ *kena; terkena*: *The branch caught him on the head.*
▶HEAR/UNDERSTAND **9** [T] to hear or understand sth that sb says □ *menangkap; memahami*: *I'm sorry, I didn't quite catch what you said. Could you repeat it?*

IDM catch sb's attention/eye to make sb notice sth □ *menarik perhatian sso*: *I tried to catch the waiter's eye so that I could get the bill.*
catch your breath 1 to breathe in suddenly because you are surprised □ *tersentak nafas* **2** to rest after physical exercise so that your breathing returns to normal □ *menghilangkan mengah*: *I had to sit down at the top of the hill to catch my breath.*
catch your death (of cold) to get very cold □ *sangat kesejukan*: *Don't go out without a coat—you'll catch your death!*
catch fire to start burning, often accidentally □ *terbakar; disambar api*: *Nobody knows how the building caught fire.*
catch sb red-handed to find sb just as they are doing sth wrong □ *menangkap sso (ketika dia sedang melakukan sst kesalahan)*: *The police caught the burglars red-handed with the stolen jewellery.*
catch sight of sb/sth to see sb/sth for a moment □ *nampak kelibat sso/sst*: *I caught sight of the man at the end of the street.*
catch the sun (informal) (used about people) to become red or brown because of spending time in the sun □ *diselar matahari*: *Your face looks red. You've really caught the sun, haven't you?*

PHR V be/get caught up in sth to be or get involved in sth, usually without intending to □ *terlibat dlm sst*: *I seem to have got caught up in a rather complicated situation.*
catch on (informal) **1** to become popular or fashionable □ *menjadi popular*: *The idea has never really caught on in this country.* **2** to understand or realize sth □ *menangkap/memahami sst*: *She's sometimes a bit slow to catch on.*
catch sb out to cause sb to make a mistake by asking a clever question □ *memerangkap (sso)*: *Ask me anything you like—you won't catch me out.*
catch up (with sb); catch sb up to reach sb who is in front of you □ *menyaingi; mengejar*: *Sharon's missed so much school she'll have to work hard to catch up with the rest of the class.* ◆ *Go on ahead, I'll catch you up in a minute.*
catch up on sth to spend time doing sth that you have not been able to do for some time □ *menyiapkan sst*: *I'll have to go into the office at the weekend to catch up on my work.*

[C] **countable**, a noun with a plural form: *one book, two books*   [U] **uncountable**, a noun with no plural form: *some sugar*

catch → caution 132

catch² /kætʃ/ noun [C] **1** an act of catching sth, for example a ball □ *penangkapan; (perbuatan) menangkap* **2** the amount of fish that sb has caught □ *tangkapan*: *The fishermen brought their catch to the harbour.* **3** a device for fastening sth and keeping it closed □ *kancing*: *I can't close my suitcase—the catch is broken.* ♦ *a window catch* **4** a hidden disadvantage or difficulty in sth that seems attractive □ *muslihat*: *It looks like a good offer, but I'm sure there must be a catch in it.*

catching /'kætʃɪŋ/ adj [not before a noun] (used about a disease or an emotion) passing easily or quickly from one person to another □ *berjangkit* **SYN** infectious

catchment area /'kætʃmənt eəriə/ noun [C] the area from which a school gets its students, a hospital gets its patients, etc. □ *kawasan tadahan/tampungan*

catchphrase /'kætʃfreɪz/ noun [C] a phrase that becomes famous for a while because it is used by a famous person □ *ungkapan popular*

catchy /'kætʃi/ adj (**catchier; catchiest**) (used about a tune or song) easy to remember □ *mudah diingat*

categorical /ˌkætə'gɒrɪkl/ adj very definite □ *mutlak; pasti*: *The answer was a categorical 'no'.* ▶**categorically** /-kli/ adv: *The Minister categorically denied the rumour.*

categorize (also -**ise**) /'kætəgəraɪz/ verb [T] to divide people or things into groups; to say that sb/sth belongs to a particular group □ *mengkategorikan*

category /'kætəgəri/ noun [C] (pl **categories**) a group of people or things that are similar to each other □ *kategori*: *This painting won first prize in the junior category.* ♦ *These books are divided into categories according to subject.*

cater /'keɪtə(r)/ verb [I] **1 cater (for sb/sth)** to provide and serve food and drink at an event or in a place that a lot of people go to □ *menyediakan/menyajikan makanan*: *Our firm caters for the 5 000 staff and visitors at the festival.* **2 cater for sb/sth; cater to sth** to provide what sb/sth needs or wants □ *memenuhi keperluan, cita rasa, dsb sso/sst*: *We need a hotel that caters for small children.* ♦ *The menu caters to all tastes.*

caterer /'keɪtərə(r)/ noun [C] a person or business that provides food and drink at events or in places that a lot of people go to □ *penyaji makanan; katerer*

catering /'keɪtərɪŋ/ noun [U] the activity or business of providing food and drink at events or in places that a lot of people go to □ *penyajian; katering*: *the hotel and catering industry* ♦ *Who's going to do the catering at the wedding?*

caterpillar /'kætəpɪlə(r)/ noun [C] a small animal with a long body and a lot of legs, which eats the leaves of plants. □ *beluncas; ulat bulu*. A **caterpillar** later becomes a **butterfly** (= an insect with large brightly coloured wings) or a **moth** (= an insect similar to a butterfly). ⊃ picture on page P13

cathedral /kə'θi:drəl/ noun [C] a large church that is the most important one in a district □ *gereja besar; katedral*

Catholic /'kæθlɪk/ = **Roman Catholic** □ *Katolik* ▶**Catholicism** /kə'θɒləsɪzəm/ = **Roman Catholicism**

cattle /'kætl/ noun [pl] male and female cows that are kept as farm animals for their milk or meat □ *lembu*: *a herd* (= a group) *of cattle* ⊃ note at **cow**

caught past tense, past participle of **catch¹**

cauldron (especially AmE **caldron**) /'kɔ:ldrən/ noun [C] a large, deep, metal pot that is used for cooking things over a fire □ *kawah*

cauliflower /'kɒliflaʊə(r)/ (AmE also) / noun [C,U] a large vegetable with green leaves and a round white centre that you eat when it is cooked □ *kubis bunga* ⊃ picture on page P15

cause¹ /kɔ:z/ noun **1** [C] a thing or person that makes sth happen □ *sebab; punca*: *The police do not know the cause of the accident.* ♦ *Smoking is one of the causes of heart disease.* **2** [U] **cause (for sth)** reason for feeling sth or behaving in a particular way □ *sebab*: *The doctor assured us that there was no cause for concern.* ♦ *I don't think you have any real cause for complaint.* **3** [C] an idea or organization that a group of people believe in and support □ *tujuan; perjuangan*: *We are all committed to the cause of racial equality.*
IDM be for/in a good cause to be worth doing because it will help other people □ *utk tujuan yg baik*
a lost cause ⊃ **lost²**

cause² /kɔ:z/ verb [T] to make sth happen □ *menyebabkan; disebabkan*: *The fire was caused by an electrical fault.* ♦ *High winds caused many trees to fall during the night.* ♦ *Is your leg causing you any pain?*

'cause (BrE informal) = **cos**

causeway /'kɔ:zweɪ/ noun [C] a raised road or path across water or wet ground □ *tambak*

caustic /'kɔ:stɪk/ adj **1** (used about a substance) able to burn or destroy things by chemical action □ *kaustik* **2** critical in a cruel way □ *pedas; tajam*: *a caustic remark*

caution¹ /'kɔ:ʃn/ noun **1** [U] great care, because of possible danger □ *berhati-hati*: *Any advertisement that asks you to send money should be treated with caution.* **2** [C] a spoken warning that a judge or police officer gives to sb who has committed a crime that is not too serious □ *amaran*

caution² /'kɔ:ʃn/ verb **1** [I,T] **caution (sb) against sth** to warn sb not to do sth □ *memberi peringatan; menasihatkan*: *The president's advisers have cautioned against calling an election too early.* **2** [T] to give sb an official warning □

[I] **intransitive**, a verb which has no object: *He laughed.*

[T] **transitive**, a verb which has an object: *He ate an apple.*

memberi/diberi amaran: *Dixon was cautioned by the referee for wasting time.*

cautionary /ˈkɔːʃənəri/ *adj* [only before a noun] giving a warning □ *(yg) memberi peringatan atau amaran*: *The teacher told us a cautionary tale about a girl who cheated in her exams.*

cautious /ˈkɔːʃəs/ *adj* taking great care to avoid possible danger or problems □ *berhati-hati*: *I'm very cautious about expressing my opinions in public.* ▶ **cautiously** *adv*

cavalry /ˈkævlri/ *noun* [sing, with sing or pl verb] the part of the army that fought on horses in the past; the part of the modern army that uses heavily protected vehicles □ *pasukan askar berkuda; pasukan kereta perisai*

cave¹ /keɪv/ *noun* [C] a large hole in the side of a **cliff** (= a high steep area of rock) or hill, or under the ground □ *gua*: *When it started to rain, we ran to shelter in a cave.*

cave² /keɪv/ *verb*
PHR V cave in 1 to fall in □ *runtuh; roboh*: *The roof of the tunnel had caved in and we could go no further.* **2** to suddenly stop arguing or being against sth □ *beralah; menyerah*: *He finally caved in and agreed to the plan.*

cavern /ˈkævən/ *noun* [C] a large, deep hole in the side of a hill or under the ground; a big **cave¹** □ *gua besar*

caviar (also **caviare**) /ˈkævɪɑː(r)/ *noun* [U] the eggs of a **sturgeon** (= a large fish) that you can eat. Caviar is usually very expensive. □ *kaviar*

cavity /ˈkævəti/ *noun* [C] (*pl* **cavities**) an empty space inside sth solid □ *rongga; lubang*: *a cavity in a tooth* ♦ *a wall cavity*

CBI /ˌsiː biː ˈaɪ/ *abbr* **the Confederation of British Industry**; an employers' association □ *CBI (Persekutuan Perusahaan British)*

cc /ˌsiː ˈsiː/ *abbr* **1 carbon copy** (used on business letters and emails to show that a copy is being sent to another person) □ *pendua; salinan (karbon)* **2 cubic centimetre(s)** □ *cc (sentimeter padu)*: *a 1200cc engine*

CCTV /ˌsiː siː tiː ˈviː/ *abbr* = **closed-circuit television**

CD /ˌsiː ˈdiː/ (also ˌcompact ˈdisc) *noun* [C] a small, round, flat piece of hard plastic on which sound or information is recorded □ *CD (cakera padat)* ⊃ look at **CD player**.

ˌ**CD ˈburner** (also ˌ**CD ˈwriter**) *noun* [C] a piece of equipment used for copying sound or information from a computer onto a CD □ *pembakar CD*

ˌ**CD ˈplayer** *noun* [C] a piece of equipment that you use for playing CDs □ *pemain CD*

CD-ROM /ˌsiː diː ˈrɒm/ *noun* [C] a CD on which large amounts of information, sound and pictures can be stored, for use on a computer □ *CD-ROM (Cakera Padat – Ingatan Baca Sahaja)* ⊃ picture at **computer**

133 **cautionary → cellar**

cease /siːs/ *verb* [I,T] (*formal*) to stop or end □ *berhenti; tdk lagi berlaku*: *Fighting in the area has now ceased.* ♦ *That organization has ceased to exist.*

ceasefire /ˈsiːsfaɪə(r)/ *noun* [C] an agreement between two groups to stop fighting each other □ *gencatan senjata* ⊃ look at **truce**

ceaseless /ˈsiːsləs/ *adj* continuing for a long time without stopping □ *tdk berhenti-henti* ▶ **ceaselessly** *adv*

cedar /ˈsiːdə(r)/ *noun* **1** [C] a tall tree that has hard red wood and wide spreading branches and that stays green all year □ *pokok cedar* **2** [U] the wood from the **cedar** tree □ *kayu cedar*

cede /siːd/ *verb* [T] (*written*) to give land or control of sth to another country or person □ *menyerahkan hak/milik*

ceiling /ˈsiːlɪŋ/ *noun* [C] **1** the top surface of the inside of a room □ *siling*: *a room with a high/low ceiling* **2** a top limit □ *had paling tinggi*: *The Government has put a 10% ceiling on wage increases.*

celeb /səˈleb/ (*informal*) = **celebrity**

celebrate /ˈselɪbreɪt/ *verb* [I,T] to do sth to show that you are happy about sth that has happened or because it is a special day □ *meraikan; merayakan*: *When I got the job we celebrated by going out for a meal.* ♦ *Gloria celebrated her 18th birthday yesterday.* ▶ **celebratory** /ˌseləˈbreɪtəri/ *adj*: *We went out for a celebratory meal after the match.*

celebrated /ˈselɪbreɪtɪd/ *adj* (*formal*) famous □ *terkenal*: *a celebrated poet*

celebration /ˌselɪˈbreɪʃn/ *noun* [C,U] the act or occasion of doing sth enjoyable because sth good has happened or because it is a special day □ *perayaan; keraian*: *birthday celebrations* ♦ *I think this is an occasion for celebration!*

celebrity /səˈlebrəti/ (also *informal* **celeb**) *noun* [C] (*pl* **celebrities**) a famous person □ *selebriti*: *a TV celebrity* **SYN personality**

celery /ˈseləri/ *noun* [U] a vegetable with long green and white sticks that can be eaten without being cooked □ *saderi*: *a stick of celery* ⊃ picture on page P15

celibate /ˈselɪbət/ *adj* (*formal*) never having sexual relations, often because of religious beliefs □ *menjauhi hubungan seks* ▶ **celibacy** /ˈselɪbəsi/ *noun* [U]

cell /sel/ *noun* [C] **1** a small room in a prison or police station in which a prisoner is locked □ *bilik penjara; sel* **2** the smallest living part of an animal or a plant □ *sel*: *The human body consists of millions of cells.* ♦ *red blood cells*

cellar /ˈselə(r)/ *noun* [C] an underground room that is used for storing things □ *bilik bawah tanah* ⊃ look at **basement** ⊃ picture on page P8

| CONSONANTS | p **p**en | b **b**ad | t **t**ea | d **d**id | k **c**at | g **g**ot | tʃ **ch**in | dʒ **J**une | f **f**all | v **v**an | θ **th**in |

cellist → centre 134

cellist /ˈtʃelɪst/ noun [C] a person who plays the **cello** □ *pemain selo*

cello /ˈtʃeləʊ/ noun [C] (pl cellos) a large musical instrument with strings. You sit down to play it and hold it between your knees. □ *selo* ⮕ note at **music** ⮕ picture at **music**

Cellophane™ /ˈseləfeɪn/ noun [U] a transparent plastic material used for wrapping things □ *Cellophane*™ *(selofan)*

cellphone /ˈselfəʊn/ (also ˌcellular ˈphone) (especially AmE) = **mobile phone**

cellular /ˈseljələ(r)/ adj consisting of cells □ *bersel: cellular tissue*

Celsius /ˈselsiəs/ (also centigrade) adj (abbr C) the name of a scale for measuring temperatures, in which water freezes at 0° and boils at 100° □ *Celsius: The temperature tonight will fall to 7°C (= 'seven degrees Celsius').* ⮕ look at **Fahrenheit**

Celtic /ˈkeltɪk/ adj connected with the Celts (= the people who lived in Wales, Scotland, Ireland and Brittany in ancient times) or with their culture □ *(berkaitan dgn) kaum Celt*

cement[1] /sɪˈment/ noun [U] a grey powder, that becomes hard after it is mixed with water and left to dry. It is used in building for sticking bricks or stones together or for making very hard surfaces. □ *simen*

cement[2] /sɪˈment/ verb [T] 1 to join two things together using **cement**[1], or a strong sticky substance □ *menyimen* 2 to make a relationship, an agreement, etc. very strong □ *mengeratkan: This agreement has cemented the relationship between our two countries.*

cemetery /ˈsemətri/ noun [C] (pl cemeteries) a place where dead people are buried, especially a place that does not belong to a church □ *(tanah) perkuburan* ⮕ look at **graveyard, churchyard**

censor[1] /ˈsensə(r)/ noun [C] an official who censors[2] books, films, etc. □ *penapis: All films have to be examined by the board of film censors.*

censor[2] /ˈsensə(r)/ verb [T] to remove the parts of a book, film, etc. that might offend people or that are considered to be immoral or a political threat □ *menapis: News reports from the area have been censored.* ▶ **censorship** noun [U]: *state censorship of radio and TV programmes*

censure /ˈsenʃə(r)/ verb [T] (written) to tell sb, in a strong and formal way, that they have done sth wrong □ *menegur dgn keras: The attorney was censured for not revealing the information earlier.* ▶ **censure** noun [U]

census /ˈsensəs/ noun [C] an official count of the people who live in a country, including information about their ages, jobs, etc. □ *banci*

cent /sent/ noun [C] (abbr c, ct) a unit of money that is worth 100th part of the main unit of money in many countries, for example of the US dollar or of the euro □ *sen: The price of a stamp goes up by 10 cents today.* ⮕ look at **per cent**

centenary /senˈtiːnəri/ noun [C] (pl centenaries) (AmE centennial /senˈteniəl/) the year that comes exactly one hundred years after an important event or the beginning of sth □ *ulang tahun keseratus: 2001 was the centenary of Disney's birth.*

center (AmE) = **centre**

centigrade /ˈsentɪɡreɪd/ = **Celsius**

centilitre (AmE centiliter) /ˈsentɪliːtə(r)/ noun [C] (abbr cl) a measure of liquid. There are 100 centilitres in a litre. □ *sentiliter*

centimetre (AmE centimeter) /ˈsentɪmiːtə(r)/ noun [C] (abbr cm) a measure of length. There are 100 centimetres in a metre □ *sentimeter: The insect was about two centimetres long.*

centipede /ˈsentɪpiːd/ noun [C] a small creature like an insect, with a long thin body and many legs □ *lipan*

central /ˈsentrəl/ adj 1 most important; main □ *utama; teras: The film's central character is a fifteen-year-old girl.* 2 [only before a noun] having control over all other parts □ *pusat: central government* (= the government of a whole country, not local government) ♦ *the central nervous system* 3 in the centre of sth □ *tengah; di tengah-tengah: a map of central Europe* ♦ *Our flat is very central* (= near the centre of the city and therefore very convenient).

ˌcentral ˈheating noun [U] a system for heating a building from one main point. Air or water is heated and carried by pipes to all parts of the building. □ *sistem pemanasan pusat*

centralize (also -ise) /ˈsentrəlaɪz/ verb [T, usually passive] to give control of all the parts of a country or an organization to a group of people in one place □ *memusatkan; dipusatkan; terpusat: Our education system is becoming increasingly centralized.* ▶ **centralization** (also -isation) /ˌsentrəlaɪˈzeɪʃn/ noun [U]

centrally /ˈsentrəli/ adv in or from the centre □ *di/dari tengah: a centrally located hotel* (= near the centre of the town)

centre[1] (AmE **center**) /ˈsentə(r)/ noun 1 [C, usually sing] the middle point or part of sth □ *bahagian tengah; pusat: I work in the centre of London.* ♦ *Which way is the town centre, please?* ♦ *She hit the target dead centre* (= exactly in the centre). ⮕ note at **middle** 2 [C] a place where sb/sth is collected together; the point towards which sth is directed □ *pusat; tumpuan: major urban/industrial centres* ♦ *She always likes to be **the centre of attention**.* ♦ *You should bend your legs to keep a low **centre of gravity**.* 3 [C] a building or place where a particular activity or service is based □ *pusat: a sports/health/shopping centre* ♦ *This university is a centre of excellence for medical research.* 4 [sing, with sing or pl verb] a political position that is not extreme □ *kedudukan tengah/sederhana: a party of the centre*

ð **then** s **so** z **zoo** ʃ **she** ʒ **vision** h **how** m **man** n **no** ŋ **sing** l **leg** r **red** j **yes** w **wet**

centre² (*AmE* center) /ˈsentə(r)/ *verb*
PHR V **centre on/around sb/sth** to have sb/sth as its centre □ *berpusatkan/tertumpu pd sso/sst*: *My aunt's life centres on the home and family.*

-centric /ˈsentrɪk/ [in compounds] concerned with or interested in the thing mentioned □ *berpusatkan*: *Eurocentric policies* (= concerned with Europe)

century /ˈsentʃəri/ *noun* [C] (*pl* **centuries**) **1** a particular period of 100 years that is used for giving dates □ *abad; kurun*: *We live in the 21st century* (= the period between the years 2000 and 2099). **2** any period of 100 years □ *abad*: *People have been making wine in this area for centuries.*
IDM **the turn of the century/year** ⊃ **turn²**

ceramic /səˈræmɪk/ *adj* made of clay (= a type of earth) that has been baked □ *seramik; tembikar*: *ceramic tiles* ▶ **ceramic** *noun* [C, usually pl]: *an exhibition of ceramics by Picasso*

cereal /ˈsɪəriəl/ *noun* [C,U] **1** any type of grain that can be eaten or made into flour, or the grass that the grain comes from □ *bijian*: *Wheat, barley and rye are cereals.* **2** a food that is made from grain, often eaten for breakfast with milk □ *bijirin*: *a bowl of cereal* ⊃ picture on **page P16**

cerebral /ˈserəbrəl/ *adj* of the brain □ *(ttg) otak*

ceremonial /ˌserɪˈməʊniəl/ *adj* connected with a ceremony □ *(berkaitan dgn) istiadat*: *a ceremonial occasion* ▶ **ceremonially** /-niəli/ *adv*

ceremony /ˈserəməni/ *noun* (*pl* **ceremonies**) **1** [C] a formal public or religious event □ *istiadat; upacara majlis*: *the opening ceremony of the Olympic Games* ♦ *a wedding ceremony* **2** [U] formal behaviour, speech, actions, etc. that are expected on special occasions □ *adat istiadat; beradat-adat*: *The new hospital was opened with great ceremony.*

certain /ˈsɜːtn/ *adj* **1** **certain (that ...); certain (to do sth)** sure to happen or to do sth; definite □ *pasti; tentu*: *It is almost certain that unemployment will increase this year.* ♦ *The director is certain to agree.* ♦ *We must rescue them today, or they will face certain death.* ⊃ note at **sure 2** [not before a noun] **certain (that ...); certain (of sth)** completely sure; without any doubts □ *pasti*: *I'm absolutely certain that there was somebody outside my window.* ♦ *We're not quite certain what time the train leaves.* ♦ *I'm certain of one thing—he didn't take the money.* **OPP** **uncertain 3** [only before a noun] used for talking about a particular thing or person without naming it or them □ *tertentu*: *You can only contact me at certain times of the day.* ♦ *There are certain reasons why I'd prefer not to meet him again.* **4** [only before a noun] (*formal*) used before sb's name to show that you do not know them □ *sso*: *I received a letter from a certain Mrs Berry.* **5** [only before a noun] some, but not very much □ *sedikit*: *I suppose I have a certain amount of respect for Mr Law.* **6** [only before a noun] noticeable but difficult to describe □ *tertentu*: *There was a certain feeling of autumn in the air.*

IDM **for certain** without doubt □ *dgn pasti*: *I don't know for certain what time we'll arrive.*
make certain (that ...) **1** to do sth in order to be sure that sth else happens □ *memastikan (bahawa...)*: *They're doing everything they can to make certain that they win.* **2** to do sth in order to be sure that sth is true □ *utk memastikan*: *We'd better phone Akram before we go to make certain he's expecting us.*

certainly /ˈsɜːtnli/ *adv* **1** without doubt; definitely □ *pastinya; sudah tentu*: *The number of students will certainly increase after 2015.* **2** (used in answer to questions) of course □ *tentu sekali*: *'Do you think I could borrow your notes?' 'Certainly.'*

certainty /ˈsɜːtnti/ *noun* (*pl* **certainties**) **1** [U] the state of being completely sure about sth □ *penuh kepastian*: *We can't say with certainty that there is life on other planets.* **OPP** **uncertainty 2** [C] something that is sure to happen □ *pastinya*: *It's now almost a certainty our team will win the league.*

certificate /səˈtɪfɪkət/ *noun* [C] **1** an official piece of paper that says that sth is true or correct □ *sijil*: *a birth/marriage/medical certificate* **2** an official document that students gain by successfully completing a course of study or by passing an exam □ *sijil*: *First Certificate in English* ⊃ note at **degree**

certify /ˈsɜːtɪfaɪ/ *verb* [T] (**certifying; certifies**; *pt, pp* **certified**) **1** to say formally that sth is true or correct □ *mengesahkan; memperakui*: *We need someone to certify that this is her signature.* **2** to give sb a certificate to show that they have successfully completed a course of training for a particular profession □ *diperakui; bertauliah*: *a certified accountant*

cesarean (*AmE*) = **Caesarean**

cf. *abbr* **compare**

CFC /ˌsiː ef ˈsiː/ *noun* [C,U] **chlorofluorocarbon**; a type of gas, found for example in cans of spray, which is harmful to the earth's atmosphere □ *CFC (klorofluorokarbon)* ⊃ look at **ozone layer**

ch *abbr* = **chapter**

chador /ˈtʃɑːdɔː(r)/ *noun* [C] a large piece of cloth that covers a woman's head and upper body so that only the face can be seen, worn by some Muslim women □ *cadur*

chain¹ /tʃeɪn/ *noun* **1** [C,U] a line of metal rings that are joined together □ *rantai*: *a bicycle chain* ♦ *She was wearing a silver chain round her neck.* ♦ *a length of chain* ⊃ picture at **bicycle, jewellery, key, padlock 2** [C] a series of connected things or people □ *banjaran; rangkaian; rentetan*: *a chain of mountains/a mountain chain* ♦ *The book examines the complex chain of events that led to the Russian Revolution.* ♦ *The Managing Director is at the top of the chain of command.* **3** [C] a group of shops, hotels, etc. that are owned by the same company □ *rangkaian*: *a chain of supermarkets* ♦ *a fast-food chain*

chain → champagne

chain² /tʃeɪn/ verb [T] **chain sb/sth (to sth); chain sb/sth (up)** to fasten sb/sth to sth else with a chain □ *merantaikan sso/sst (kpd sst); merantaikan sso/sst*: The dog is kept chained up outside.

chainsaw /'tʃeɪnsɔː/ noun [C] a tool for cutting wood that has a chain with sharp teeth □ *gergaji rantai*

'chain-smoke verb [I] to smoke continuously, lighting one cigarette after another □ *merokok tanpa henti* ▶ **'chain-smoker** noun [C]

'chain store noun [C] one of a number of similar shops that are owned by the same company □ *kedai rantaian*

chairs

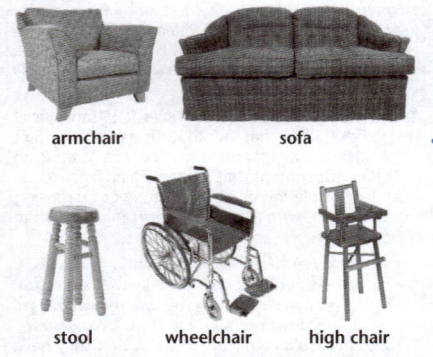

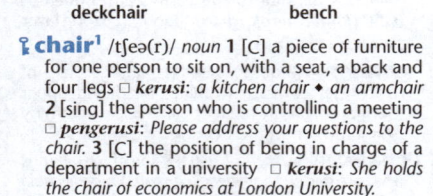

armchair **sofa**

stool **wheelchair** **high chair**

deckchair **bench**

chair¹ /tʃeə(r)/ noun **1** [C] a piece of furniture for one person to sit on, with a seat, a back and four legs □ *kerusi*: a kitchen chair ♦ an armchair **2** [sing] the person who is controlling a meeting □ *pengerusi*: Please address your questions to the chair. **3** [C] the position of being in charge of a department in a university □ *kerusi*: She holds the chair of economics at London University.

chair² /tʃeə(r)/ verb [T] to be the chairperson of a meeting □ *mempengerusikan*: Who's chairing today's meeting?

chairman /'tʃeəmən/, **chairwoman** /'tʃeəwʊmən/, **chairperson** /'tʃeəpɜːsn/ (*pl* **-persons**) noun [C] (*pl* **-men** /-mən/, **-women** /-wɪmɪn/) **1** a person who controls a meeting □ *pengerusi* **2** the head of a company or other organization □ *pengerusi* ▶ **chairmanship** noun [sing]

chalet /'ʃæleɪ/ noun [C] a wooden house, especially one built in a mountain area or used by people on holiday □ *chalet*

chalk¹ /tʃɔːk/ noun **1** [U] a type of soft white rock □ *batu kapur*: chalk cliffs **2** [C,U] a small stick of soft white or coloured rock that is used for writing or drawing □ *kapur tulis*

chalk² /tʃɔːk/ verb [I,T] to write or draw sth with **chalk** □ *menulis/melukis dgn kapur*: Somebody had chalked a message on the wall.
PHR V **chalk sth up** to succeed in getting sth □ *mendapat*: The team has chalked up five wins this summer.

chalkboard /'tʃɔːkbɔːd/ (*AmE*) = **blackboard**

challenge¹ /'tʃælɪndʒ/ noun [C] **1** something new and difficult that forces you to make a lot of effort □ *cabaran*: Rob found his new job an exciting challenge. ♦ The school will have to face many **challenges** in the coming year. ♦ How will this government **meet the challenge** of rising unemployment? **2 a challenge (to sb) (to do sth)** an invitation from sb to fight, play, argue, etc. against them □ *cabaran*: The school team accepted the challenge and fixed a match for the following week.

challenge² /'tʃælɪndʒ/ verb [T] **1** to question if sth is true, right, etc. or not □ *mencabar; mempersoalkan*: She hates anyone challenging her authority. **2 challenge sb (to sth/to do sth)** to invite sb to fight, play, argue, etc. against you □ *mencabar*: They've challenged us to a football match this Saturday.

challenger /'tʃælɪndʒə(r)/ noun [C] a person who invites you to take part in a competition, because they want to win a title or position that you hold □ *pencabar*

challenging /'tʃælɪndʒɪŋ/ adj forcing you to make a lot of effort □ *(yg) mencabar*: a challenging job

chamber /'tʃeɪmbə(r)/ noun [C] **1** an organization that makes important decisions, or the room or building where it meets □ *dewan*: a council chamber ♦ Parliament consists of an upper chamber and a lower chamber. **2** a room that is used for a particular purpose □ *kamar; ruang*: a burial chamber **3** a closed space in the body, a machine, etc. □ *kebuk; rongga; ruang*: the four chambers of the heart

chambermaid /'tʃeɪmbəmeɪd/ noun [C] a woman whose job is to clean and tidy hotel bedrooms □ *pengemas bilik*

'chamber music noun [U] a type of **classical, music** (= traditional Western music) that is written for a small group of instruments □ *muzik kamar*

chameleon /kə'miːliən/ noun [C] a small lizard (= an animal with four legs, dry skin and a long tail) that can change colour according to its surroundings □ *kameleon; sumpah-sumpah*

champagne /ʃæm'peɪn/ noun [U,C] a French white wine which has a lot of bubbles in it and is often very expensive □ *champagne*

ʌ **cup** ɜː **bird** ə **ago** eɪ **pay** əʊ **go** aɪ **my** aʊ **now** ɔɪ **boy** ɪə **near** eə **hair** ʊə **pure**

champion¹ /'tʃæmpiən/ noun [C] **1** a person, team, etc. that has won a competition □ *johan; juara*: *a world champion* ◆ *a champion swimmer* **2** a person who speaks for and fights for a particular group, idea, etc. □ *pejuang*: *a champion of free speech*

champion² /'tʃæmpiən/ verb [T] to support or fight for a particular group or idea □ *memperjuangkan*: *to champion the cause of human rights*

championship /'tʃæmpiənʃɪp/ noun [C, often plural] a competition or series of competitions to find the best player or team in a sport or game □ *kejohanan; kejuaraan*: *the World Hockey Championships*

chance¹ /tʃɑːns/ noun **1** [C] a chance of (doing) sth; a chance (that …) a possibility □ *kemungkinan*: *Is there any chance of getting tickets for tonight's concert?* ◆ *I think we stand a good chance of winning the competition.* ◆ *I think there's a good chance that she'll be the next team manager.* ◆ *to have a slim/an outside chance of success* **2** [C] chance (of doing sth/to do sth) an opportunity □ *peluang*: *If somebody invited me to America, I'd jump at the chance* (= accept with enthusiasm). ◆ *Be quiet and give her a chance to explain.* ◆ *I think you should tell him now. You may not get another chance.* ⊃ note at **occasion 3** [C] a risk □ *risiko*: *We may lose some money but we'll just have to take that chance.* ◆ *Fasten your seat belt—you shouldn't take (any) chances.* ◆ *I didn't want to take a chance on anyone seeing me, so I closed the curtains.* **4** [U] luck; the way that some things happen without any cause that you can see or understand □ *nasib*: *We have to plan every detail—I don't want to leave anything to chance.* ◆ *We met by chance* (= we had not planned to meet) *as I was walking down the street.*
IDM **by any chance** (used for asking sth politely) perhaps or possibly □ *secara kebetulan*: *Are you, by any chance, going into town this afternoon?*
the chances are (that)… (*informal*) it is probable that … □ *mungkin*: *The chances are that it will rain tomorrow.*
no chance (*informal*) there is no possibility of that happening □ *tdk mungkin; jangan harap*: '*Perhaps your mother will give you the money.*' '*No chance!*'
on the off chance in the hope that sth might happen, although it is not very likely □ *kalau-kalau*: *I didn't think you'd be at home, but I just called in on the off chance.*

chance² /tʃɑːns/ verb **1** [T] (*informal*) chance sth/doing sth to risk sth □ *mengambil risiko*: *It might be safe to leave the car here, but I'm not going to chance it.* **2** [I] (*formal*) chance to do sth to do sth without planning or trying to do it □ *kebetulan*: *I chanced to see the letter on his desk.*

chance³ /tʃɑːns/ adj [only before a noun] not planned □ *secara kebetulan*: *a chance meeting*

chancellor /'tʃɑːnsələ(r)/ noun [C] **1** the head of the government in some countries □ *canselor; ketua kerajaan*: *the German chancellor* **2** (also ˌChancellor of the Exˈchequer) (*BrE*) the government minister who makes decisions about taxes and government spending □ *menteri kewangan*

chandelier /ˌʃændəˈlɪə(r)/ noun [C] a large round frame with many branches for lights or candles (= tall sticks that you burn to give light), that hangs from the ceiling and is decorated with small pieces of glass □ *candelier*

change¹ /tʃeɪndʒ/ verb
▶BECOME/MAKE DIFFERENT **1** [I,T] to become different or to make sb/sth different □ *berubah*: *This town has changed a lot since I was young.* ◆ *Our plans have changed—we leave in the morning.* ◆ *His lottery win has not changed him at all.* **SYN** alter **2** [I,T] change (sb/sth) to/into sth; change (from A) (to/into B) to become a different thing; to make sb/sth take a different form □ *bertukar; mengubah*: *to change from a caterpillar into a butterfly* ◆ *They changed the spare bedroom into a study.* ◆ *The traffic lights changed from green to red.*
▶REPLACE **3** [T] change sth (for sth) to take, have or use sth instead of sth else □ *menukar*: *Could I change this shirt for a larger size?* ◆ *to change jobs* ◆ *to change a wheel on a car* ◆ *to change direction* ◆ *Can I change my appointment from Wednesday to Thursday?*
▶EXCHANGE **4** [T] [used with a plural noun] to change sth (with sb) to exchange sth with sb, so that you have what they had, and they have what you had □ *bertukar(-tukar)*: *The teams change ends at half-time.* ◆ *If you want to sit by the window I'll change seats with you.* **SYN** swap
▶CLOTHES **5** [I,T] change (out of sth) (into sth) to take off your clothes and put different ones on □ *menyalin pakaian*: *He's changed his shoes.* ◆ *I had a shower and changed before going out.* ◆ *She changed out of her work clothes and into a clean dress.*

HELP **Get changed** is a common expression meaning 'to change your clothes': *You can get changed in the bedroom.*

▶CLEAN THINGS **6** [T] to put clean things onto sb/sth □ *menyalin; menukar*: *The baby's nappy needs changing.* ◆ *to change the bed* (= to put clean sheets on)
▶MONEY **7** [T] change sth (for/into sth) to give sb money and receive the same amount back in money of a different type □ *menukar; mengurup*: *Can you change a ten-pound note for two fives?* ◆ *I'd like to change fifty pounds into US dollars.*
▶BUS/TRAIN/PLANE **8** [I,T] to get out of one bus, train, etc. and get into another □ *bertukar*: *Can we get to London direct or do we have to change (trains)?*
IDM **change hands** to pass from one owner to another □ *bertukar tangan*
change your mind to change your decision or opinion □ *mengubah fikiran*: *I'll have the green one. No, I've changed my mind—I want the red one.*
change/swap places (with sb) ⊃ **place¹**

[C] **countable**, a noun with a plural form: *one book, two books*   [U] **uncountable**, a noun with no plural form: *some sugar*

change → character 138

change the subject to start talking about sth different □ *tukar tajuk perbualan; buka cerita lain*

change your tune (*informal*) to change your opinion or feelings about sth □ *berubah sikap, pendapat, dsb*

change your ways to start to live or behave in a different and better way from before □ *berubah (perangai, dsb menjadi lebih baik)*

chop and change ⇒ **chop¹**

PHR V change over (from sth) (to sth) to stop doing or using one thing and start doing or using sth else □ *bertukar kpd*: *The theatre has changed over to a new booking system.*

change² /tʃeɪndʒ/ *noun* **1** [C,U] **change (in/to sth)** the process of becoming or making sth different □ *perubahan*: *There was little change in the patient's condition overnight.* ◆ *After two hot summers, people were talking about a change in the climate.* **2** [C] **a change (of sth)** something that you take, have or use instead of sth else □ *pertukaran*: *We must notify the bank of our change of address.* ◆ *I packed my toothbrush and a change of clothes.* **3** [U] the money that you get back if you pay more than the amount sth costs □ *duit baki*: *If a postcard costs 60p and you pay with a pound coin, you will get 40p change.* **4** [U] coins of low value □ *duit kecil*: *He needs some change for the phone.* ◆ *Have you got change for a twenty-pound note?* (= coins or notes of lower value that together make 20 pounds) ⇒ note at **cash**

IDM a change for the better/worse a person, thing or situation that is better/worse than the one before □ *perubahan menjadi lebih baik/buruk*

a change of heart a change in your opinion or the way that you feel □ *mengubah fikiran, pendapat, dsb*

for a change in order to do sth different from usual □ *supaya lain sedikit (drpd kebiasaan)*: *I usually cycle to work, but today I decided to walk for a change.*

make a change used to say that an activity is enjoyable or pleasant because it is different from what you usually do □ *satu perubahan (yg baik)*

changeable /'tʃeɪndʒəbl/ *adj* likely to change; often changing □ *(mudah) berubah-ubah*: *English weather is very changeable.*

changeover /'tʃeɪndʒəʊvə(r)/ *noun* [C] a change from one system to another □ *pertukaran*

'changing room *noun* [C] a room for changing clothes in, for example before or after playing sport □ *bilik salin pakaian* ⇒ look at **fitting room**

channel¹ /'tʃænl/ *noun* [C] **1** a TV station □ *saluran*: *Which channel is the film on?* ⇒ look at **station 2** a band of radio waves used for sending out radio or TV programmes □ *saluran; rangkaian*: *digital/satellite channels* **3** a way or route along which news, information, etc. is sent

□ *saluran*: *a channel of communication* ◆ *You have to order new equipment through the official channels.* **4** an open passage along which liquids can flow □ *saluran; alur*: *drainage channels in the rice fields* **5** the part of a river, sea, etc. which is deep enough for boats to pass through □ *terusan* **6 the Channel** (also **the English 'Channel**) the sea between England and France □ *Selat Inggeris*: *a cross-channel ferry*

channel² /'tʃænl/ *verb* [T] (**channelling**; **channelled**, (*AmE* also) **channeling**; **channeled**) to make sth move along a particular path or route □ *menyalurkan; disalurkan*: *Water is channelled from the river to the fields.* ◆ (*figurative*) *You should channel your energies into something constructive.*

the ˌChannel 'Tunnel *noun* [sing] the tunnel under the sea that connects England and France □ *Terowong Selat Inggeris*

chant¹ /tʃɑːnt/ *noun* **1** [C] a word or phrase that is sung or shouted many times □ *teriakan yg diulang-ulang*: *A chant of 'we are the champions' went round the stadium.* **2** [C,U] a religious song with only a few notes that are repeated many times □ *lagu; dikir*

chant² /tʃɑːnt/ *verb* [I,T] to sing or shout a word or phrase many times □ *bernyanyi atau berteriak berulang-ulang*: *The protesters marched by, chanting slogans.*

chaos /'keɪɒs/ *noun* [U] a state of great confusion and lack of order □ *keadaan huru-hara/kelam-kabut*: *The country was in chaos after the war.* ◆ *The heavy snow has caused chaos on the roads.*

chaotic /keɪ'ɒtɪk/ *adj* in a state of **chaos** □ *(dlm keadaan) huru-hara/kelam-kabut*: *With no one in charge the situation became chaotic.*

chap /tʃæp/ *noun* [C] (*especially BrE old-fashioned informal*) a man or boy □ *orang/budak lelaki*

chapel /'tʃæpl/ *noun* [C,U] a small building or room that is used by some Christians as a church or for prayer □ *gereja kecil; capel*: *a Methodist chapel*

chaperone /'ʃæpərəʊn/ *noun* [C] in the past, an older person, usually a woman, who went to public places with a young woman who was not married, to look after her and to make sure that she behaved correctly □ *caperon* ▶ **chaperone** *verb* [T]

chaplain /'tʃæplɪn/ *noun* [C] a Christian priest who is responsible for the religious needs of people in prison, hospital, the army, etc. □ *paderi* ⇒ look at **priest**

chapter /'tʃæptə(r)/ *noun* [C] (*abbr* **ch**) one of the parts into which a book is divided □ *bab; babak*: *Please read Chapter 2 for homework.* ◆ (*figurative*) *The last few years have been a difficult chapter in the country's history.*

character /'kærəktə(r)/ *noun*
▶QUALITIES **1** [C,U] the qualities that make sb/sth different from other people or things; the nature of sb/sth □ *watak; sifat; ciri*: *The new shopping*

[I] **intransitive**, a verb which has no object: *He laughed.*   [T] **transitive**, a verb which has an object: *He ate an apple.*

139 **characteristic → charity shop**

centre has changed the character of the town. ◆ Although they are twins, their characters are quite different. ◆ These two songs are very different **in character**. 2 [U] strong personal qualities □ *keperibadian*: The match developed into a test of character rather than just physical strength. 3 [U] qualities that make sb/sth interesting □ *ciri tersendiri/istimewa*: Modern houses often seem to lack character.

▶GOOD OPINION 4 [U] the good opinion that people have of you □ *nama baik*: The article was a vicious attack on the president's character.

▶PERSON 5 [C] (*informal*) an interesting or amusing person; a strange or an unpleasant person □ *orang (yg menarik, pelik, tdk disenangi, dsb)*: Neil's quite a character—he's always making us laugh. ◆ I saw a suspicious-looking character outside the bank, so I called the police. 6 [C] a person in a book, story, etc. □ *watak*: The main character in the film is a boy who meets an alien.

▶SYMBOL/LETTER 7 [C] a letter or sign that you use when you are writing or printing □ *aksara*: Chinese characters

IDM **in/out of character** typical/not typical of sb/sth □ *biasa/ganjil bagi sso*: Emma's rude reply was completely out of character.

characteristic¹ /ˌkærəktəˈrɪstɪk/ *adj* **characteristic of (sb/sth)** very typical of sb/sth □ *yg biasa bagi sso/sst*: The flat landscape is characteristic of this part of the country. **OPP** **uncharacteristic** ▶ **characteristically** /-kli/ *adv*: 'No' he said, in his characteristically direct manner.

characteristic² /ˌkærəktəˈrɪstɪk/ *noun* [C] **a characteristic of (sb/sth)** a quality that is typical of sb/sth and that makes them or it different from other people or things □ *sifat; ciri*: The chief characteristic of fish is that they live in water.

characterize (also **-ise**) /ˈkærəktəraɪz/ *verb* [T] (*formal*) 1 [often passive] to be typical of sb/sth □ *mencirikan*: the tastes that characterize Indian cooking 2 **characterize sb/sth (as sth)** to describe what sb/sth is like □ *menyifatkan*: The president characterized the meeting as friendly and positive.

charade /ʃəˈrɑːd/ *noun* 1 [C] a situation or an event that is clearly false but in which people pretend to do or be sth □ *kepura-puraan*: They pretend to be friends but it's all a charade. Everyone knows they hate each other. 2 **charades** [U] a party game in which people try to guess the title of a book, film, etc. that one person must represent using actions but not words □ *teka lakon*

charcoal /ˈtʃɑːkəʊl/ *noun* [U] a black substance that is produced from burned wood. It can be used for drawing or as a fuel. □ *arang*

charge¹ /tʃɑːdʒ/ *noun*

▶MONEY 1 [C,U] the price that you must pay for sth □ *bayaran*: The hotel makes a small charge for changing currency. ◆ We deliver **free of charge**. ⇨ note at **price**

▶CRIME 2 [C,U] a statement that says that sb has done sth illegal or bad □ *tuduhan*: He was arrested **on a charge of** murder. ◆ She was released **without charge**. ◆ The writer dismissed the charge that his books were childish.

▶RESPONSIBILITY 3 [U] a position of control over sb/sth; responsibility for sb/sth □ *jagaan; tanggungjawab*: Who is **in charge of** the school while Mrs Webb's away? ◆ The assistant manager had to **take charge of** the team when the manager resigned.

▶ELECTRICITY 4 [C] the amount of electricity that is put into a battery or carried by a substance □ *cas*: a positive/negative charge

▶ATTACK 5 [C] a sudden attack where sb/sth runs straight at sb/sth else □ *serbuan; serangan*: He led the charge down the field.

IDM **bring/press charges (against sb)** to formally accuse sb of a crime so that there can be a trial in a court of law □ *mengemukakan tuduhan (terhadap sso)*

reverse the charges ⇨ **reverse¹**

charge² /tʃɑːdʒ/ *verb* 1 [T,I] **charge (sb/sth) for sth** to ask sb to pay a particular amount of money □ *mengenakan bayaran*: We charge £65 per night for a single room. ◆ They forgot to charge us for the drinks. ◆ Do you charge for postage and packing? ⇨ look at **overcharge** 2 [T] **charge sb (with sth)** to accuse sb officially of doing sth which is against the law □ *menuduh; dituduh*: Three men have been charged with attempted robbery. 3 [I,T] to run straight at sb/sth, or in a particular direction, in an aggressive or noisy way □ *menyerbu; menyerang*: The bull put its head down ready to charge (us). ◆ The children charged into the room. 4 [T] to put electricity into sth □ *mengecas*: to charge a battery ⇨ look at **recharge**

IDM **charge/pay the earth** ⇨ **earth¹**

charger /ˈtʃɑːdʒə(r)/ *noun* [C] a piece of equipment for loading a battery with electricity □ *alat pengecas*: a mobile phone charger

chariot /ˈtʃæriət/ *noun* [C] an open vehicle with two wheels that was pulled by a horse or horses in ancient times □ *rata; kereta kuda*

charisma /kəˈrɪzmə/ *noun* [U] a powerful personal quality that some people have to attract and influence other people □ *karisma*: The president is not very clever, but he has great charisma. ▶ **charismatic** /ˌkærɪzˈmætɪk/ *adj*

charitable /ˈtʃærətəbl/ *adj* 1 connected with a charity □ *(berkenaan dgn) amal/kebajikan* 2 kind; generous □ *pemurah; baik hati*: Some people accused him of lying, but a more charitable explanation was that he had made a mistake.

charity /ˈtʃærəti/ *noun* (*pl* charities) 1 [C,U] an organization that collects money to help people who are poor, sick, etc. or to do work that is useful to society □ *pertubuhan amal*: We cycled round Africa to **raise money for charity**. ⇨ note at **money** 2 [U] kindness towards other people □ *(sifat) belas kasihan*: to act out of charity

'charity shop *noun* [C] a shop that sells clothes, books, etc. given by people to make money for charity □ *kedai amal*

CONSONANTS p **p**en b **b**ad t **t**ea d **d**id k **c**at g **g**ot tʃ **ch**in dʒ **J**une f **f**all v **v**an θ **th**in

charlatan /ˈʃɑːlətən/ *noun* [C] a person who pretends to have knowledge or skills that they do not really have □ *penyemu*

charm¹ /tʃɑːm/ *noun* **1** [C,U] a quality that pleases and attracts people □ *daya tarikan*: *The charm of the island lies in its unspoilt beauty.* ♦ *Alison still finds it hard to resist Frank's charms.* **2** [C] something that you wear because you believe it will bring you good luck □ *tangkal; azimat*: *a lucky charm* ➔ picture at **jewellery**

charm² /tʃɑːm/ *verb* [T] **1** to please and attract sb □ *memikat; menawan hati*: *Her drawings have charmed children all over the world.* **2** to protect sb/sth as if by magic □ *terlindung seolah-olah dgn kuasa ajaib*: *He has led a charmed life, surviving serious illness and a plane crash.*

charming /ˈtʃɑːmɪŋ/ *adj* very pleasing or attractive □ *menawan*: *a charming old house* ▶ **charmingly** *adv*

charred /tʃɑːd/ *adj* burnt black by fire □ *hangus; rentung*

chart¹ /tʃɑːt/ *noun* **1** [C] a drawing which shows information in the form of a diagram, etc. □ *carta*: *a temperature chart* ♦ *This chart shows the company's sales for this year.* ➔ look at **pie chart, flow chart** **2** [C] a map of the sea or the sky □ *carta*: *navigation charts* **3 the charts** [pl] an official list of the songs or CDs, etc. that have sold the most in a particular week □ *senarai lagu-lagu popular*: *The album went straight into the charts at number 1.*

chart² /tʃɑːt/ *verb* [T] **1** to follow or record sth carefully and in detail □ *mengikuti/merakam setiap detik*: *This TV series charts the history of the country since independence.* **2** to make a map of one area of the sea or sky □ *mencartakan; memetakan*: *Cook charted the coast of New Zealand in 1768.*

charter¹ /ˈtʃɑːtə(r)/ *noun* [C,U] **1** a written statement of the rights, beliefs and purposes of an organization or a particular group of people □ *piagam*: *The club's charter does not permit women to become members.* **2** the renting of a ship, plane, etc. for a particular purpose or for a particular group of people □ *sewaan khas*: *a charter airline*

charter² /ˈtʃɑːtə(r)/ *verb* [T] to rent a ship, plane, etc. for a particular purpose or for a particular group of people □ *menyewa khas; carter*: *As there was no regular service to the island we had to charter a boat.*

chartered /ˈtʃɑːtəd/ *adj* [only before a noun] (used about people in certain professions) fully trained; having passed all the necessary exams □ *berkanun*: *a chartered accountant*

'charter flight *noun* [C] a flight in which all seats are paid for by a travel company and then sold to their customers, usually at a lower price than normal □ *penerbangan sewa khas/carter*: *Is it a charter flight or a scheduled flight?*

chase¹ /tʃeɪs/ *verb* **1** [I,T] **chase (after) sb/sth** to run after sb/sth in order to catch them or it □ *mengejar*: *The dog chased the cat up a tree.* ♦ *The police car chased after the stolen van.* **2** [I] to run somewhere fast □ *berkejar(-kejaran)*: *The kids were chasing around the park.*

chase² /tʃeɪs/ *noun* [C] the act of following sb/sth in order to catch them or it □ *pengejaran; (perbuatan) kejar-mengejar*: *an exciting car chase*

IDM give chase to begin to run after sb/sth in order to try to catch them or it □ *mengejar*: *The robber ran off and the policeman gave chase.*

chasm /ˈkæzəm/ *noun* [C] **1** a deep hole in the ground □ *gegaung; jurang* **2** a wide difference of feelings, interests, etc. between two people or groups □ *jurang*

chassis /ˈʃæsi/ *noun* [C] (*pl* **chassis** /-siz/) the metal frame of a vehicle onto which the other parts fit □ *casis*

chaste /tʃeɪst/ *adj* (*old-fashioned*) **1** not having sex with anyone; only having sex with your husband/wife □ *suci* **2** not involving thoughts and feelings about sex □ *suci; murni*: *a chaste kiss on the cheek* ▶ **chastity** /ˈtʃæstəti/ *noun* [U]

chastise /tʃæˈstaɪz/ *verb* [T] (*formal*) **chastise sb (for sth/for doing sth)** to criticize or punish sb for doing sth wrong □ *memarahi atau menghukum dgn keras* ▶ **chastisement** *noun* [U]

chat¹ /tʃæt/ *verb* [I] (**chatting; chatted**) **chat (with/to sb) (about sth)** **1** to talk to sb in an informal, friendly way □ *bersembang*: *The two grandmothers sat chatting about the old days.* ♦ *Helen chats away for hours on the phone to her friends.* **2** to exchange messages with other people on the Internet, especially in a **chat room** □ *bersembang (melalui Internet)*: *He's been on the computer all morning, chatting with his friends.*

PHR V chat sb up (*BrE informal*) to talk to sb in a friendly way because you are sexually attracted to them □ *mengurat sso*

chat² /tʃæt/ *noun* [C,U] **1** a friendly informal conversation □ *perbualan; (perbuatan) berbual-bual*: *I'll have a chat with Jim about the arrangements.* **2** communication between people on the Internet □ *sembang*: *Fans are invited to an online chat.* ♦ *Internet chat services*

'chat room *noun* [C] an area on the Internet where you can join in a discussion □ *ruang chat (Internet)* ➔ note at **Internet**

TOPIC

Chat room

You can take part in an **online discussion** in a **chat room** by **posting a message** or **following a thread** (= adding your comments). You can use chat rooms to communicate with people that share your interests. **Online chat** is a way of communicating by exchanging messages with people in the same chat room as you **in real time** (= at the same time as the messages are sent). When you take part in online chat, you can sometimes use **webcams** (= video cameras connected to the Internet) to see other people in the chat room. Chat rooms usually have rules that their users should follow. In some chat rooms **moderators** check that the comments are appropriate and respond to complaints. Messages that people deliberately send to make other users angry are called **trolls**.

'chat show noun [C] a TV or radio programme on which well-known people are invited to talk about themselves □ *bicarawara*

chatter /'tʃætə(r)/ verb [I] **1** to talk quickly or for a long time about sth unimportant □ *berceloteh*: *The children were all laughing and chattering excitedly.* **2** (used about your teeth) to knock together because you are cold or frightened □ *menggelatuk* ▶ **chatter** noun [U]

chatty /'tʃæti/ adj (**chattier**; **chattiest**) **1** talking a lot in a friendly way □ *suka berbual* **2** in an informal style □ *secara tdk formal serta ramah mesra*: *a chatty letter*

chauffeur /'ʃəʊfə(r)/ noun [C] a person whose job is to drive a car for sb else □ *drebar; pemandu*: *a chauffeur-driven limousine* ▶ **chauffeur** verb [T]

chauvinism /'ʃəʊvɪnɪzəm/ noun [U] **1** the belief that your country is better than all others □ *cauvinisme* **2** (also **male 'chauvinism**) the belief that men are better than women □ *cauvinisme lelaki* ▶ **chauvinist** /-ɪst/ noun [C]

ℰ cheap¹ /tʃiːp/ adj (**cheaper**; **cheapest**) **1** low in price, costing little money □ *murah*: *Oranges are cheap at the moment.* ♦ *Computers are getting cheaper all the time.* **SYN** **inexpensive** **OPP** **dear, expensive** **2** charging low prices □ *tdk mahal; ekonomi*: *a cheap hotel/restaurant* **SYN** **inexpensive** **OPP** **expensive** **3** low in price and quality and therefore not attractive □ *murah; picisan*: *The clothes in that shop look cheap.*
IDM **dirt cheap** ⊃ **dirt**

cheap² /tʃiːp/ adv (*informal*) for a low price □ *dgn harga yg murah*: *I got this coat cheap in the sale.*
IDM **be going cheap** (*informal*) be on sale at a lower price than usual □ *dijual dgn harga yg murah*

cheapen /'tʃiːpən/ verb [T] **1** to make sb lose respect for himself or herself □ *merendahkan harga diri; menurunkan rasa hormat*: *She felt cheapened by their treatment of her.* **2** to make sth lower in price □ *menurunkan harga* **3** to make sth appear to have less value □ *membuat sst kelihatan lebih murah atau hina*: *The film was accused of cheapening human life.*

ℰ cheaply /'tʃiːpli/ adv for a low price □ *dgn harga yg murah*: *You can travel quickly and cheaply all over the town by bus.*

ℰ cheat¹ /tʃiːt/ verb **1** [T] to trick sb, or to make them believe sth that is not true, especially when

141　　　　　　　　　　　　**chat show → check**

that person trusts you □ *menipu*: *The shopkeeper cheated customers by giving them too little change.* **2** [I] **cheat (at sth)** to act in a dishonest or unfair way in order to get an advantage for yourself □ *menipu; meniru*: *Paul was caught cheating in the exam.* ♦ *to cheat at cards* **3** [I] **cheat (on sb)** to not be faithful to your husband, wife or regular partner by having a secret sexual relationship with sb else □ *tdk setia*
PHR V **cheat sb (out) of sth** to take sth from sb in a dishonest or unfair way □ *menipu sso utk mendapatkan sst*: *They tried to cheat the old lady out of her savings.*

ℰ cheat² /tʃiːt/ noun [C] a person who cheats □ *penipu*: *The man's a liar and a cheat!*

ℰ check¹ /tʃek/ verb **1** [I,T] **check (sth) (for sth)** to examine or test sth in order to make sure that it is safe or correct, in good condition, etc. □ *menyemak; memeriksa*: *Check your work for mistakes before you hand it in.* ♦ *The doctor X-rayed me to check for broken bones.* **2** [I,T] **check (sth) (with sb)** to find out if sth/sb is there, correct or true, or if sth is how you think it is □ *memastikan (sst) (dgn sso)*: *You'd better check with Tim that it's OK to borrow his bike.* ♦ *I'll phone and check what time the bus leaves.* ♦ *I need to check my email.* **3** [T] to stop or make sb/sth stop or go more slowly □ *menahan; mengurangkan*: *She almost told her boss what she thought of him, but checked herself in time.* ♦ *Phil checked his pace as he didn't want to tire too early.* **4** [T] (*AmE*) = **tick¹(2)**
PHR V **check in (at ...); check into ...** to go to a desk in a hotel or an airport and tell an official that you have arrived □ *mendaftar masuk*: *Passengers should check in two hours before their departure time.* ⊃ note at **hotel, plane**
check sth off to mark names or items on a list □ *menyemak senarai*: *The boxes were all checked off as they were unloaded.*
check (up) on sb/sth to find out how sb/sth is □ *menyiasat, menyelidik, dsb utk mengetahui keadaan sso/sst*: *We call my grandmother every evening to check up on her.*
check out (of ...) to pay for your room, etc. and leave a hotel □ *mendaftar keluar* ⊃ note at **hotel**: *What time do we need to check out in the morning?*
check sb/sth out **1** to find out more information about sb/sth, especially to find out if sth is true or not □ *menyiasat sso/sst*: *We need to check out these rumours of possible pay cuts.* **2** (*slang*) to look at sb/sth, especially to find out if you like them or it □ *melihat; menengok*: *I'm going to check out that new club tonight.*
check up on sb/sth to make sure that sb/sth is working correctly, behaving well, etc., especially if you think he/she/it is not □ *memeriksa sama ada sso itu berkelakuan baik atau sst itu berfungsi dgn betul*: *My mother's always checking up on me to see if I've done my homework.*

VOWELS iː **see** i **any** ɪ **sit** e **ten** æ **hat** ɑː **father** ɒ **got** ɔː **saw** ʊ **put** uː **too** u **usual**

check → cheers

> **EXAM TIP**
>
> **Checking your work**
> Before the exam, practise checking your work before you hand it in. Read it through several times: once to look at spellings, once to check that you have used the correct grammatical constructions and that the forms of the verbs and plurals of nouns are correct, and once to make sure that you have not missed anything out that you wanted to say. Use your dictionary to help you check. Make a note of useful points and add them to your **last-minute list** (= a list that you check just before your exam).

check² /tʃek/ noun 1 [C] **a check (on sth)** a close look at sth to make sure that it is safe, correct, in good condition, etc. □ *pemeriksaan; (perbuatan) menyemak atau mengawasi*: We carry out/do regular **checks** on our products to make sure that they are of high quality. ◆ I don't go to games, but I like to **keep a check** on my team's results. **2** [C,U] a pattern of squares, often of different colours □ *corak dam/kotak-kotak*: a check jacket ◆ a pattern of blue and red checks **3** [U] the position in **chess** (= a game for two players played on a black and white board) in which a player's king (= the most important piece) can be directly attacked by the other player's pieces □ *sekat*: There, you're in check. ⊃ look at **checkmate**. **4** (AmE) = **bill¹**(2) **5** (AmE) = **cheque 6** (AmE) = **tick²**(1) ⊃ look at **rain check**

IDM **hold/keep sth in check** to keep sth under control so that it does not get worse □ *mengawal sst*: government measures to keep inflation in check

checkbook (AmE) = **chequebook**

checked /tʃekt/ adj with a pattern of squares □ *bercorak kotak-kotak*: a red-and-white checked tablecloth ⊃ picture at **page P1**

checkers /'tʃekəz/ (AmE) = **draught¹**(2)

'check-in noun [C,U] **1** the place where you go first when you arrive at an airport to show your ticket, etc. □ *kaunter daftar masuk* **2** the act of checking in at an airport □ *daftar masuk*: Our check-in time is 10.30 a.m.

'checking account (AmE) = **current account**

checklist /'tʃeklɪst/ noun [C] a list of things that you must remember to do □ *senarai semak*

'check mark (AmE) = **tick²**(1)

checkmate /,tʃek'meɪt/ (also **mate**) noun [U] the position in **chess** (= a game for two players played on a black and white board) in which one player cannot prevent their king (= the most important piece) from being captured and so loses the game □ *mat* ⊃ look at **check²**(3)

checkout /'tʃekaʊt/ noun [C] the place in a large shop or on a website where you pay □ *kaunter bayaran*

checkpoint /'tʃekpɔɪnt/ noun [C] a place where all people and vehicles must stop and be checked □ *tempat pemeriksaan*: an army checkpoint

'check-up noun [C] a general medical examination to make sure that you are healthy □ *pemeriksaan doktor*: to go for/have a check-up

Cheddar /'tʃedə(r)/ noun [U] a type of hard yellow cheese □ *keju cedar*

cheek /tʃiːk/ noun **1** [C] either side of the face below your eyes □ *pipi*: Tears rolled down her cheeks. ⊃ picture at **body 2** [U, sing] (BrE) rude behaviour; lack of respect □ *sikap biadab; kurang asam*: He's got a cheek, asking to borrow money again!

IDM **(with) tongue in cheek** ⊃ **tongue**

cheekbone /'tʃiːkbəʊn/ noun [C] the bone below your eye □ *tulang pipi* ⊃ picture at **body**

cheeky /'tʃiːki/ adj (**cheekier**; **cheekiest**) (BrE) not showing respect; rude □ *tdk hormat; agak biadab*: Don't be so cheeky! Of course I'm not fat!
▶ **cheekily** adv

cheer¹ /tʃɪə(r)/ noun [C] a loud shout to show that you like sth or to encourage sb who is taking part in a competition, sport, etc. □ *sorakan*: The crowd **gave a cheer** when the team scored. ⊃ look at **hip**

cheer² /tʃɪə(r)/ verb **1** [I,T] to shout to show that you like sth or to encourage sb who is taking part in competition, sport, etc. □ *bersorak*: Everyone cheered the winner as he crossed the finishing line. **2** [T] to make sb happy or to give hope □ *berasa gembira*: They were all cheered by the good news.

PHR V **cheer sb on** to shout in order to encourage sb in a race, competition, etc. □ *bersorak memberikan semangat kpd sso*: As the runners started the last lap, the crowd cheered them on.
cheer (sb/sth) up to become or to make sb happier; to make sth look more attractive □ *bergembiralah; menggembirakan; menceriakan*: Cheer up! Things aren't that bad. ◆ A few pictures would cheer this room up a bit.

cheerful /'tʃɪəfl/ adj **1** feeling happy; showing that you are happy □ *riang; girang*: Caroline is always very cheerful. ◆ a cheerful smile **2** giving you a feeling of happiness □ *ceria*: walls painted in cheerful colours ⊃ note at **happy** ▶ **cheerfully** /-fəli/ adv: to laugh/nod/whistle cheerfully ▶ **cheerfulness** noun [U]

cheerio /,tʃɪəri'əʊ/ exclam (BrE informal) goodbye □ *selamat tinggal*: Cheerio! See you later.

cheerleader /'tʃɪəliːdə(r)/ noun [C] (in the US) one of a group of girls or women at a sports match who wear special uniforms and shout, dance, etc. in order to encourage people to support the players □ *kumpulan penyorak*

cheers /tʃɪəz/ exclam (informal) **1** used to express good wishes before having an alcoholic drink □ *digunakan sebagai ucap selamat semasa minum minuman keras*: 'Cheers,' she said, raising her wine glass. **2** (BrE) goodbye □

ʌ c**u**p   ɜː b**ir**d   ə **a**go   eɪ p**ay**   əʊ g**o**   aɪ m**y**   aʊ n**ow**   ɔɪ b**oy**   ɪə n**ear**   eə h**air**   ʊə p**ure**

selamat tinggal **3** (BrE) thank you □ *terima kasih*

cheery /'tʃɪəri/ adj (**cheerier**; **cheeriest**) happy and smiling □ *riang; ria*: *a cheery remark/wave/smile* ▶ **cheerily** adv

cheese /tʃiːz/ noun **1** [U] a type of food made from milk. Cheese is usually white or yellow in colour and can be soft or hard □ *keju*: *a piece of cheese* ◆ *a cheese sandwich* ◆ *a chunk/piece/slice of cheese* ⊃ picture on **page P16 2** [C] a type of cheese □ *jenis keju*: *a wide selection of cheeses*

cheesecake /'tʃiːzkeɪk/ noun [C,U] a type of cake that is made from soft cheese and sugar on a **pastry** (= a mixture of flour, fat and water) or biscuit base, often with fruit on top □ *kek keju*

cheesy /'tʃiːzi/ adj (**cheesier**; **cheesiest**) (*informal*) of low quality and without style □ *rendah mutu dan tanpa gaya*: *an incredibly cheesy love song*

cheetah /'tʃiːtə/ noun [C] a large wild cat with black spots that can run very fast □ *citah* ⊃ picture at **lion**

chef /ʃef/ noun [C] a professional cook, especially the head cook in a hotel, restaurant, etc. □ *jurumasak; cef*

chemical[1] /'kemɪkl/ adj connected with chemistry; involving changes to the structure of a substance □ *(berkenaan dgn) kimia*: *a chemical reaction* ◆ *the chemical industry* ◆ *chemical weapons/warfare* ▶ **chemically** /-kli/ adv

chemical[2] /'kemɪkl/ noun [C] a substance that is used or produced in a chemical process □ *bahan kimia*: *Sulphuric acid is a dangerous chemical.*

chemist /'kemɪst/ noun [C] **1** (also **pharmacist**, *AmE* also **druggist**) a person who prepares and sells medicines □ *ahli farmasi* **2 the chemist's** (*AmE* **drugstore**) [sing] a shop that sells medicines, soap, camera film, etc. □ *kedai ubat dan benda-benda lain; farmasi*: *I got my tablets from the chemist's.* ◆ *Take this prescription to the chemist's.* **3** a person who studies chemistry □ *ahli kimia*: *My daughter is a research chemist.*

chemistry /'kemɪstri/ noun [U] **1** the scientific study of the structure of substances and what happens to them in different conditions or when mixed with each other □ *(ilmu) kimia*: *We did an experiment in the chemistry lesson.* ⊃ note at **science 2** the structure of a particular substance □ *kimia*: *The patient's blood chemistry was monitored regularly.*

cheque (*AmE* **check**) /tʃek/ noun [C,U] a piece of paper printed by a bank that you sign and use to pay for things □ *cek*: *She wrote out a cheque for £50.* ◆ *I went to the bank to cash a cheque.* ◆ *Can I pay by cheque?* ⊃ picture at **money**

chequebook (*AmE* **checkbook**) /'tʃekbʊk/ noun [C] a book of cheques □ *buku cek* ⊃ picture at **money**

'**cheque card** noun [C] (*BrE*) a small plastic card that you show when you pay with a cheque to prove that your bank will pay the amount on the cheque □ *kad cek* ⊃ look at **cash card, credit card, debit card**

cherish /'tʃerɪʃ/ verb [T] **1** to love sb/sth and look after them or it carefully □ *menyayangi; menjaga dgn baik*: *The ring was her most cherished possession.* **2** to keep a thought, feeling, etc. in your mind and think about it often □ *menghargai; menaruh (harapan, perasaan, dll)*: *She cherished the memory of those days in Paris.*

cherry /'tʃeri/ noun [C] (*pl* **cherries**) **1** a small round black or red fruit that has a stone inside it □ *(buah) ceri* ⊃ picture on **page P14 2** (also '**cherry tree**) the tree that produces **cherries** □ *pokok ceri*

cherub /'tʃerəb/ noun [C] (in art) a type of **angel** (= a being who is believed to live in heaven), shown as an attractive child with wings □ *sejenis malaikat yg digambarkan sebagai kanak-kanak yg montel dan bersayap* ▶ **cherubic** /tʃə'ruːbɪk/ adj (*formal*): *a cherubic face* (= looking round and innocent, like a small child's)

chess /tʃes/ noun [U] a game for two people that is played on a **chessboard** (= a board with 64 black and white squares). Each player has 16 pieces which can be moved according to fixed rules □ *catur*: *Can you play chess?*

chessboard

chess

chest /tʃest/ noun [C] **1** the top part of the front of your body □ *dada*: *a muscular chest* ◆ *a chest infection* ⊃ picture at **body 2** a large strong box that is used for storing or carrying things □ *peti*: *We packed all our books into a chest.* ◆ *a treasure chest*

IDM **get sth off your chest** (*informal*) to talk about sth that you have been thinking or worrying about □ *meluahkan perasaan*

chestnut /'tʃesnʌt/ noun [C] **1** (also '**chestnut tree**) a tree with large leaves that produces smooth brown nuts in shells with sharp points on the outside □ *pokok berangan* **2** a smooth brown nut from the chestnut tree. You can eat some types of chestnut. □ *buah berangan* ⊃ look at **horse chestnut** ⊃ picture at **nut**

chest of 'drawers (AmE **dresser**) noun [C] a piece of furniture with drawers in it that is used for storing clothes, etc. □ *almari berlaci* ⊃ picture on **page P8**

chew /tʃuː/ verb [I,T] **1** to break up food in your mouth with your teeth before you swallow it □ *mengunyah*: *You should chew your food thoroughly.* **2 chew (on) sth** to bite sth continuously with the back teeth □ *menggigit-gigit*: *The dog was chewing on a bone.*

'chewing gum (also **gum**) noun [U] a sweet sticky substance that you **chew** in your mouth but do not swallow □ *gula-gula getah* ⊃ look at **bubblegum**

chewy /'tʃuːi/ adj (**chewier**; **chewiest**) (used about food) difficult to break up with your teeth before it can be swallowed □ *liat; kenyal*: *chewy meat/toffee*

chic /ʃiːk/ adj fashionable and elegant □ *anggun dan bergaya* SYN **stylish** ▶ **chic** noun [U]

chick /tʃɪk/ noun [C] **1** a baby bird, especially a young chicken □ *anak ayam/burung* ⊃ picture at **chicken 2** (old-fashioned, slang) a way of referring to a young woman □ *gadis*

chickens

cock **chick** **hen**
(AmE **rooster**)

chicken¹ /'tʃɪkɪn/ noun **1** [C] a bird that people often keep for its eggs and its meat □ *ayam*: *free-range chickens* **2** [U] the meat of this bird □ *daging ayam*: *chicken soup*

> **MORE** Chicken is the general word for the bird and its meat. A male chicken is called a **cock** (*US* **rooster**), a female is called a **hen** and a young bird is called a **chick**.

IDM Don't count your chickens (before they're hatched) ⊃ **count¹**

chicken² /'tʃɪkɪn/ verb
PHR V chicken out (of sth) (*informal*) to decide not to do sth because you are afraid □ *menarik diri kerana takut*: *Mark chickened out of swimming across the river when he saw how far it was.*

chickenpox /'tʃɪkɪnpɒks/ noun [U] a disease, especially of children. When you have **chickenpox** you feel very hot and get red spots on your skin that make you want to scratch. □ *cacar air*

chickpea /'tʃɪk piː/ (AmE usually **garbanzo**) noun [C] a round brown seed that can be dried and used in cooking □ *kacang kuda*: *leek and chickpea stew*

chicory /'tʃɪkəri/ (AmE **endive**) noun [U] a small pale green plant with bitter leaves that can be eaten cooked or not cooked □ *cikori*

chief¹ /tʃiːf/ adj [only before a noun] **1** most important; main □ *utama*: *One of the chief reasons for his decision was money.* **2** of the highest level or position □ *ketua*: *the chief executive of a company*

chief² /tʃiːf/ noun [C] **1** the person who has command or control over an organization □ *ketua*: *the chief of police* **2** the leader of a **tribe** (= a group of people with the same language and customs) □ *ketua; penghulu*: *African tribal chiefs*

chiefly /'tʃiːfli/ adv mostly □ *terutamanya*: *His success was due chiefly to hard work.* SYN **mainly**

chiffon /'ʃɪfɒn/ noun [U] a very thin, transparent type of cloth used for making clothes, etc. □ *sifon*

chilblain /'tʃɪlbleɪn/ noun [C] a painful red area on your foot, hand, etc. that is caused by cold weather □ *bengkak sejuk*

child /tʃaɪld/ noun [C] (pl **children** /'tʃɪldrən/) **1** a young boy or girl who is not yet an adult □ *kanak-kanak*: *A group of children were playing in the park.* ♦ *a six-year-old child* **2** a son or daughter of any age □ *anak*: *She has two children but both are married and have moved away.*

> **TOPIC**
> **Children**
> An **only child** is a child who has no brothers or sisters. A child whose parents have died is an **orphan**. A person may **adopt** a child who is not his/her own son or daughter. A **foster child** is looked after for a certain period of time by a family that is not his/her own. If your husband or wife has children from a previous marriage, they are your **stepchildren**. Parents are responsible for **bringing up** their children (= looking after them until they are adults and teaching them how to behave).

childbirth /'tʃaɪldbɜːθ/ noun [U] the act of giving birth to a baby □ *(perbuatan) melahirkan anak/bersalin*: *His wife died in childbirth.*

childcare /'tʃaɪldkeə(r)/ noun [U] the job of looking after children, especially while the parents are at work □ *penjagaan anak*: *Some employers provide childcare facilities.*

childhood /'tʃaɪldhʊd/ noun [C,U] the time when you are a child □ *zaman kanak-kanak*: *Harriet had a very unhappy childhood.* ♦ *childhood memories*

childish /'tʃaɪldɪʃ/ adj like a child □ *keanak-anakan* SYN **immature** OPP **mature**

> **HELP Childish** or **childlike**? If you say that people or their behaviour are **childlike**, you mean that they are like children in some way: *His childlike enthusiasm delighted us all.* If you

say that an adult's behaviour is **childish**, you are criticizing it because you think it is silly: *Don't be so childish! You can't always have everything you want.*

▶ **childishly** *adv*

childless /ˈtʃaɪldləs/ *adj* having no children □ *tdk mempunyai anak*

childlike /ˈtʃaɪldlaɪk/ *adj* like a child □ *spt kanak-kanak* ⊃ note at **childish**

childminder /ˈtʃaɪldmaɪndə(r)/ *noun* [C] (*BrE*) a person whose job is to look after a child while his or her parents are at work □ *penjaga anak* ⊃ look at **babysitter**

children plural of **child**

'children's home *noun* [C] an institution where children live whose parents cannot look after them □ *rumah kebajikan kanak-kanak*

chili (*AmE*) = **chilli**

chill¹ /tʃɪl/ *noun* **1** [sing] an unpleasant cold feeling □ *kesejukan; rasa sejuk*: *There's a chill in the air.* ♦ (*figurative*) *A chill of fear went down my spine.* **2** [C] (*informal*) a common illness that affects your nose and throat; a cold □ *selesema*: *to catch a chill*

chill² /tʃɪl/ *verb* **1** [I,T] to become or to make sb/ sth colder □ *menyejukkan*: *Let the pudding chill for an hour in the fridge.* **2** *verb* [I] (*informal*) to spend time relaxing □ *bersantai*: *We went home and chilled in front of the television.*

PHR V **chill out** (*informal*) to relax and stop feeling angry or nervous about sth □ *bertenang*: *Sit down and chill out!*

chilli (*AmE* **chili**) /ˈtʃɪli/ *noun* [C,U] (*pl* **chillies**, *AmE* **chilies**) a small green or red vegetable that has a very strong hot taste □ *cili; lada*: *chilli powder* ⊃ picture on **page P15**

chilling /ˈtʃɪlɪŋ/ *adj* frightening □ *seram; menakutkan*: *a chilling ghost story*

chilly /ˈtʃɪli/ *adj* (**chillier**; **chilliest**) (used about the weather but also about people) too cold to be comfortable □ *sejuk; dingin*: *It's a chilly morning. You need a coat on.* ♦ *They gave us a very chilly* (= unfriendly) *reception.*

chime /tʃaɪm/ *verb* [I,T] (used about a bell or clock) to ring □ *berbunyi (loceng/jam)*

PHR V **chime in (with sth)** (*informal*) to interrupt a conversation and add your own comments □ *mencelah; menyampuk*

▶ **chime** *noun* [C]

chimney /ˈtʃɪmni/ *noun* [C] a structure through which smoke or steam is carried up and out through the roof of a building □ *serombong*: *Smoke poured out of the factory chimneys.* ⊃ picture on **page P8**

'chimney pot *noun* [C] a short wide pipe that is placed on top of a chimney □ *pepasu serombong*

'chimney sweep *noun* [C] a person whose job is to clean the inside of **chimneys** with long brushes □ *pencuci serombong*

childless → chip

chimpanzee /ˌtʃɪmpænˈziː/ (also *informal* **chimp** /tʃɪmp/) *noun* [C] a small intelligent **ape** (= an animal that lives in hot countries and can climb trees) □ *cimpanzi* ⊃ look at **monkey**

chin /tʃɪn/ *noun* [C] the part of your face below your mouth □ *dagu*: *He sat listening, his chin resting on his hand.* ♦ *a strong/weak/pointed chin* ♦ *a double chin* (= fat under sb's chin that looks like another chin) ⊃ picture at **body**

IDM **(keep your) chin up** (*informal*) used to tell sb to try to stay cheerful even though they are in a difficult or unpleasant situation □ *bergembiralah*

china /ˈtʃaɪnə/ *noun* [U] **1** white **clay** (= a type of earth) of good quality that is used for making cups, plates, etc. □ *tanah liat putih; porselin*: *a china vase* **2** cups, plates, etc. that are made from china □ *pinggan mangkuk porselin*

chink /tʃɪŋk/ *noun* [C] a small narrow opening □ *celah; sela*: *Daylight came in through a chink between the curtains.*

chintz /tʃɪnts/ *noun* [U] a shiny cotton cloth with a printed design, usually of flowers, which is used for making curtains, covering furniture, etc. □ *kain cita (utk langsir, dsb)*

chips (*esp AmE* **French fries**)   **crisps** (*AmE* **chips**)

chip¹ /tʃɪp/ *noun* [C] **1** the place where a small piece of stone, glass, wood, etc. has broken off sth □ *sumbing*: *This dish has a chip in it.* **2** a small piece of stone, glass, wood, etc. that has broken off sth □ *serpihan*: *chips of wood* **3** (*especially AmE* **French 'fry**, **fry**) [usually pl] a thin piece of potato that is fried in hot fat or oil □ *kentang goreng*: *Would you prefer boiled potatoes or chips?* ⊃ note at **fish 4** (*AmE*) = **crisp² 5** = **microchip 6** a flat round piece of plastic that you use instead of money when you are playing some games □ *cip; tagan*

IDM **have a chip on your shoulder (about sth)** (*informal*) to feel angry about sth that happened a long time ago because you think it is unfair □ *menyimpan perasaan marah (ttg sst)*: *My dad still has a chip on his shoulder about being thrown out of school.*

chip² /tʃɪp/ *verb* [I,T] (**chipping**; **chipped**) **1** to break a small piece off the edge or surface of sth

chip

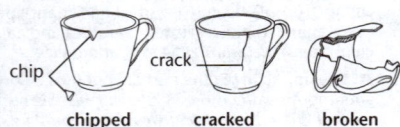

chip — crack
chipped — cracked — broken

□ *menyebabkan sumbing; menyerpihkan*: *They chipped the paint trying to get the table through the door.* **2** (in sport) to kick or hit a ball a short distance through the air □ *pukulan/tendangan sungkit*

PHR V **chip in (with sth)** (*informal*) **1** to interrupt when sb else is talking □ *mencelah; menyampuk* **2** to give some money as part of the cost of sth □ *memberikan sumbangan*: *We all chipped in and bought him a present when he left.*

'chip shop (*BrE informal* **chippy** /'tʃɪpi/; *pl* **chippies**) *noun* [C] (in Britain) a shop that cooks and sells fish and chips and other fried food to take away and eat □ *kedai makanan goreng*

chiropodist /kɪˈrɒpədɪst/ (also **podiatrist**) *noun* [C] a person whose job is to look after people's feet □ *kiropodis* ▶ **chiropody** (also **podiatry**) *noun* [U]

chirp /tʃɜːp/ *verb* [I] (used about small birds and some insects) to make short high sounds □ *menciap*

chisel /'tʃɪzl/ *noun* [C] a tool with a sharp end that is used for cutting or shaping wood or stone □ *pahat* ⊃ picture at **tool**

chivalry /'ʃɪvəlri/ *noun* [U] polite and kind behaviour by men which shows respect towards women □ *sifat bersopan santun (berkenaan dgn lelaki)* ▶ **chivalrous** /'ʃɪvlrəs/ *adj*

chives /tʃaɪvz/ *noun* [pl] the long thin leaves of a plant that tastes like onion and is used in cooking □ *kucai*

chlorine /'klɔːriːn/ *noun* [U] (*symbol* **Cl**) a greenish-yellow gas with a strong smell, that is used for making water safe to drink or to swim in □ *klorin*

chlorophyll /'klɒrəfɪl/ *noun* [U] the green substance in plants that absorbs light from the sun to help them grow □ *klorofil*

chock-a-block /ˌtʃɒk ə 'blɒk/ *adj* (*BrE informal*) [not before a noun] completely full □ *penuh sesak*: *The High Street was chock-a-block with shoppers.*

chocoholic /ˌtʃɒkəˈhɒlɪk/ (*AmE also*) / *noun* [C] (*informal*) a person who loves chocolate and eats a lot of it □ *orang yg sangat suka makan coklat*

chocolate /'tʃɒklət/ *noun* **1** [U] a sweet brown substance made from **cocoa**, **beans** (= seeds of a tropical tree) that you can eat as a sweet or use to give flavour to food and drinks □ *coklat*: *a bar of milk/plain chocolate* ♦ *a chocolate milkshake* ⊃ picture at **bar 2** [C] a small sweet that is made from or covered with chocolate □ *coklat*: *a box of chocolates* **3** [C,U] a drink made from chocolate powder with hot milk or water □ *minuman coklat*: *a mug of hot chocolate* **4** [U] a dark brown colour □ *warna coklat*

choice¹ /tʃɔɪs/ *noun* **1** [C] **a choice (between A and B)** an act of choosing between two or more people or things □ *pemilihan; pilihan*: *David was forced to make a choice between moving house and losing his job.* **2** [U] the right or chance to choose □ *pilihan*: *There is a rail strike so we have no choice but to cancel our trip.* ♦ *to have freedom of choice* ⊃ look at **option 3** [C] a person or thing that is chosen □ *pilihan*: *Barry would be my choice as team captain.* **4** [C,U] two or more things from which you can or must choose □ *pilihan*: *This cinema offers a choice of six different films every night.* ⊃ *verb* **choose**

IDM **out of/from choice** because you want to; of your own free will □ *atas pilihan (sendiri)*: *I wouldn't have gone to London out of choice. I was sent there on business.*

choice² /tʃɔɪs/ *adj* (**choicer**; **choicest**) [only before a noun] of very good quality □ *pilihan; sangat baik*: *choice beef*

choir /'kwaɪə(r)/ *noun* [C, with sing or pl verb] a group of people who sing together in churches, schools, etc. □ *koir*

choke¹ /tʃəʊk/ *verb* **1** [I,T] **choke (on sth)** to be or to make sb unable to breathe because sth is stopping air getting into the lungs □ *tercekik; melemaskan*: *She was choking on a fish bone.* ♦ *The smoke choked us.* ⊃ look at **strangle 2** [T, usually passive] **choke sth (up) (with sth)** to fill a passage, space, etc., so that nothing can pass through □ *tersumbat; penuh dgn*: *The roads to the coast were choked with traffic.*

PHR V **choke sth back** to hide or control a strong emotion □ *menahan*: *to choke back tears/anger*

choke² /tʃəʊk/ *noun* [C] **1** the device in a car, etc. that controls the amount of air going into the engine. If you pull out the **choke** it makes it easier to start the car. □ *pencekik* **2** an act or the sound of sb **choking** □ *perbuatan atau bunyi tercekik*: *A tiny choke of laughter escaped her.*

cholera /'kɒlərə/ *noun* [U] a serious disease that causes stomach pains and **vomiting** (= bringing up food from the stomach) and can cause death. **Cholera** is most common in hot countries and is carried by water. □ *kolera*

cholesterol /kəˈlestərɒl/ *noun* [U] a substance that is found in the blood, etc. of people and animals. Too much **cholesterol** can cause heart disease. □ *kolesterol*

choose /tʃuːz/ *verb* [I,T] (*pt* **chose** /tʃəʊz/; *pp* **chosen** /'tʃəʊzn/) **1 choose (between A and/or B); choose (A) (from B); choose sb/sth as sth** to decide which thing or person you want out of the ones that are available □ *pilih; memilih*: *Choose carefully before you make a final decision.* ♦ *Amy had to choose between getting a job or going to college.* ♦ *The viewers chose this programme as*

ð **then** s **so** z **zoo** ʃ **she** ʒ **vision** h **how** m **man** n **no** ŋ **sing** l **leg** r **red** j **yes** w **wet**

their favourite. **2** choose (to do sth) to decide or prefer to do sth □ *membuat keputusan; lebih suka (dlm menentukan sst pilihan)*: *You are free to leave whenever you choose.* ♦ *They chose to resign rather than work for the new manager.* ➲ noun choice

IDM pick and choose ➲ pick¹

choosy /ˈtʃuːzi/ *adj* (choosier; choosiest) (*informal*) (used about a person) difficult to please □ *memilih*

chop¹ /tʃɒp/ *verb* [T] (chopping; chopped) chop sth (up) (into sth) to cut sth into pieces with a knife, etc. □ *memotong; mencencang*: *finely chopped herbs* ♦ *Chop the onions up into small pieces.*

IDM chop and change to change your plans or opinions several times □ *berubah-ubah*

PHR V chop sth down to cut a tree, etc. at the bottom so that it falls down □ *menebang*: *It's a shame to chop a cherry tree down.*

chop sth off (sth) to remove sth from sth by cutting it with a knife or a sharp tool □ *memotong; mencantas*: *to chop a branch off a tree*

chop² /tʃɒp/ *noun* [C] **1** a thick slice of meat with a piece of bone in it □ *potongan daging bertulang*: *a pork/lamb chop* ➲ look at steak **2** an act of chopping sth □ *tetakan*: *a karate chop*

chopper /ˈtʃɒpə(r)/ (*informal*) = **helicopter**

ˈchopping board *noun* [C] a piece of wood or plastic used for cutting meat or vegetables on □ *papan cencang* ➲ picture at kitchen

choppy /ˈtʃɒpi/ *adj* (choppier; choppiest) (used about the sea) with a lot of small waves; not calm □ *berombak*

chopsticks /ˈtʃɒpstɪks/ *noun* [pl] two thin sticks made of wood or plastic, that people use for picking up food to eat, especially in some Asian countries □ *sepit; penyepit*

choral /ˈkɔːrəl/ *adj* (used about music) that is written for or involves a choir (= a group of singers) □ *koral*

chord /kɔːd/ *noun* [C] two or more musical notes that are played at the same time □ *kord*

chore /tʃɔː(r)/ *noun* [C] a job that is not interesting but that you must do □ *kerja yg leceh*: *household chores*

choreograph /ˈkɒriəɡrɑːf/ *verb* [T] to design and arrange the movements of a dance □ *mereka tari; koreograf* ▶ **choreographer** /ˌkɒriˈɒɡrəfə(r)/ *noun* [C]

choreography /ˌkɒriˈɒɡrəfi/ *noun* [U] the arrangement of movements for a dance performance □ *reka tari; koreografi*

chorus¹ /ˈkɔːrəs/ *noun* **1** [C] the part of a song that is repeated □ *korus; baris ulang* **SYN** refrain ➲ look at verse **2** [C] a piece of music, usually part of a larger work, that is written for a large choir (= a group of singers) □ *korus; muzik koir* **3** [C, with sing or pl verb] a large group of people who sing together □ *koir* **4** [C, with sing or pl verb] the singers and dancers in a musical show who do not play the main parts □ *barisan korus* **5** [sing] a chorus of sth something that a lot of people say together □ *sst yg dikatakan beramai-ramai dgn serentak*: *a chorus of cheers/criticism/disapproval*

chorus² /ˈkɔːrəs/ *verb* [T] (used about a group of people) to sing or say sth together □ *menyanyi/mengatakan (sst) dgn serentak*: *'That's not fair!' the children chorused.*

chose past tense of **choose**

chosen past participle of **choose**

Christ /kraɪst/ (also Jesus, Jesus ˈChrist) *noun* [sing] the man who Christians believe is the son of God and on whose ideas and beliefs the Christian religion is based □ *Jesus Christ*

christen /ˈkrɪsn/ *verb* [T] **1** to give a person, usually a baby, a name during a Christian ceremony in which they are made a member of the Church □ *menamakan bayi (upacara di gereja)*: *The baby was christened Simon Mark.* ➲ look at baptize **2** to give sb/sth a name □ *menggelar*: *The area has been christened 'Britain's last wilderness'.*

christening /ˈkrɪsnɪŋ/ *noun* [C] the church ceremony in the Christian religion in which a baby is given a name □ *upacara penamaan bayi (di gereja)* ➲ look at baptism

Christian /ˈkrɪstʃən/ *noun* [C] a person whose religion is Christianity □ *orang Kristian* ▶ **Christian** *adj*

Christianity /ˌkrɪstiˈænəti/ *noun* [U] the religion that is based on the ideas taught by Jesus Christ □ *agama Kristian*

Christmas /ˈkrɪsməs/ *noun* [C,U] **1** ˌChristmas ˈDay a public holiday on 25 December. It is the day on which Christians celebrate the birth of Christ each year. □ *Hari Krismas* **2** the period of time before and after 25 December □ *musim Krismas*: *We wish you a merry Christmas.* ♦ *Where are you spending Christmas this year?*

MORE Christmas is sometimes written as **Xmas** in informal English.

ˈChristmas card *noun* [C] a card with a picture on the front and a message inside that people send to their friends and relatives at Christmas □ *kad Krismas*

ˌChristmas ˈcarol = **carol**

ˌChristmas ˈcracker = **cracker**(2)

ˌChristmas ˈdinner *noun* [C,U] the traditional meal eaten on Christmas Day □ *makan besar Hari Krismas*: *We had a traditional Christmas dinner that year, with roast turkey, Christmas pudding and all the trimmings.*

ˌChristmas ˈEve *noun* [C,U] 24 December, the day before Christmas Day □ *hari sebelum Krismas*

Christmas pudding noun [C,U] a sweet dish made from dried fruit and eaten hot with sauce at Christmas □ *puding Krismas*

Christmas tree noun [C] a real or an artificial tree, which people bring into their homes and cover with coloured lights and decorations at Christmas □ *pokok Krismas*

chrome /krəʊm/ (also **chromium** /ˈkrəʊmiəm/) noun [U] (symbol **Cr**) a hard shiny metal that is used for covering other metals □ *krom*

chromosome /ˈkrəʊməsəʊm/ noun [C] a part of a cell in living things that decides the sex, character, shape, etc. that a person, an animal or a plant will have □ *kromosom*

chronic /ˈkrɒnɪk/ adj (used about a disease or a problem) that continues for a long time □ *kronik; teruk*: *chronic bronchitis* ♦ *There is a chronic shortage of housing in the city.* ⊃ look at **acute** ▶ **chronically** /-kli/ adv

chronicle /ˈkrɒnɪkl/ noun [C, often plural] a written record of historical events describing them in the order in which they happened □ *riwayat*

chronological /ˌkrɒnəˈlɒdʒɪkl/ adj arranged in the order in which the events happened □ *mengikut kronologi*: *This book describes the main events in his life in chronological order.* ▶ **chronologically** /-kli/ adv

chrysalis /ˈkrɪsəlɪs/ noun [C] the form of a **butterfly** (= an insect with large brightly coloured wings) or a **moth** (= an insect similar to a butterfly) while it is changing into an adult inside a hard case, which is also called a chrysalis □ *krisalis; kepompong* ⊃ picture on **page P13**

chrysanthemum /krɪˈsænθəməm/ noun [C] a large garden flower which is brightly coloured and shaped like a ball □ *bunga kekwa*

chubby /ˈtʃʌbi/ adj (**chubbier**; **chubbiest**) slightly fat in an attractive way □ *montel; tembam*: *a baby with chubby cheeks* ⊃ note at **fat**

chuck /tʃʌk/ verb [T] (informal) to throw sth in a careless way □ *mencampakkan*: *You can chuck those old shoes in the bin.*

PHR V **chuck sth in** to give sth up □ *meninggalkan*: *He's chucked his job in because he was fed up.*

chuck sb out (of sth) to force sb to leave a place □ *mengusir; menghalau*: *They were chucked out of the cinema for making too much noise.*

chuckle /ˈtʃʌkl/ verb [I] to laugh quietly □ *tertawa kecil*: *Bruce chuckled to himself as he read the letter.* ▶ **chuckle** noun [C]

chug /tʃʌɡ/ verb [I] (**chugging**; **chugged**) to move making the sound of an engine running slowly □ *bergerak dgn bunyi 'cag-cag'*: *The train chugged out of the station.*

chunk /tʃʌŋk/ noun [C] a large or thick piece of sth □ *ketul*: *chunks of bread and cheese*

chunky /ˈtʃʌŋki/ adj (**chunkier**; **chunkiest**) 1 thick and heavy □ *tebal dan besar; bungkal*: *chunky jewellery* 2 (used about a person) short and strong □ *dempak*: *He was a short man with chunky legs.* 3 (used about food) containing thick pieces □ *berketul-ketul*: *chunky banana milkshake*

church /tʃɜːtʃ/ noun 1 [C,U] a building where Christians go to worship □ *gereja*: *Services are held in this church every Sunday morning at 10.* ♦ *Do you go to church regularly?*

HELP Notice that when you are talking about going to a ceremony (a service) in a church you say 'in church', 'to church' or 'at church' without 'a' or 'the': *Was Mrs Stevens at church today?*

2 **Church** [C] a particular group of Christians □ *mazhab (Kristian)*: *the Anglican/Catholic/Methodist/Church* 3 **(the) Church** [sing] the ministers or the institution of the Christian religion □ *gereja (institusi agama)*: *the conflict between Church and State*

churchgoer /ˈtʃɜːtʃɡəʊə(r)/ noun [C] a person who goes to church regularly □ *orang yg selalu ke gereja*

the Church of England (abbr **C. of E.**) noun [sing] the Protestant Church, which is the official church in England, whose leader is the Queen or King □ *Gereja Inggeris* ⊃ look at **Anglican**

churchyard /ˈtʃɜːtʃjɑːd/ noun [C] the area of land that is around a church □ *kawasan gereja* ⊃ look at **cemetery**, **graveyard**

churn /tʃɜːn/ verb 1 [I,T] **churn (sth) (up)** to move, or to make water, mud, etc. move around violently □ *berpusar-pusar*: *The dark water churned beneath the huge ship.* ♦ *Vast crowds had churned the field into a sea of mud.* 2 [I,T] if your stomach **churns** or sth makes it **churn**, you feel sick because you are disgusted or nervous □ *memulas*: *Reading about the murder in the newspaper made my stomach churn.* 3 [T] to make butter from milk or cream □ *menggodak*

PHR V **churn sth out** (informal) (often disapproving) to produce large numbers of sth very quickly □ *mengeluarkan sst dgn banyak dan cepat*

chute /ʃuːt/ noun [C] a tube or passage down which people or things can slide: *a laundry/rubbish chute* (= from the upper floors of a high building) ♦ *a water chute* (= at a swimming pool) □ *pelongsor*

chutney /ˈtʃʌtni/ noun [U,C] a thick sweet sauce that is made from fruit or vegetables. You eat **chutney** cold with cheese or meat. □ *cutni; sejenis sos*

CIA /ˌsiː aɪ ˈeɪ/ abbr **the Central Intelligence Agency**; the US government organization that tries to discover secret information about other countries □ *CIA (Agensi Perisikan Pusat)*

ciabatta /tʃəˈbætə; -ˈbɑːtə/ noun [U,C] a type of Italian bread made in a long flat shape; a **loaf** (= a whole piece of baked bread) of this ▫ *sejenis roti Itali*

cider /ˈsaɪdə(r)/ noun [U,C] **1** (*BrE*) an alcoholic drink made from apples ▫ *sider (arak)*: *dry/sweet cider* **2** (*AmE*) a drink made from apples that does not contain alcohol ▫ *sider (minuman epal)*

cigar /sɪˈɡɑː(r)/ noun [C] a thick roll of **tobacco** (= a type of dried leaf) that people smoke. **Cigars** are larger than cigarettes ▫ *cerut*

cigarette /ˌsɪɡəˈret/ noun [C] a thin tube of white paper filled with **tobacco** (= a type of dried leaf) that people smoke ▫ *rokok*: *a packet/pack of cigarettes*

ciˈgarette lighter (also **lighter**) noun [C] an object which produces a small flame for lighting cigarettes, etc. ▫ *pemetik api*

cinder /ˈsɪndə(r)/ noun [C] a very small piece of burning coal, wood, etc. ▫ *bara api*

cinema /ˈsɪnəmə/ noun **1** [C] (*BrE*) a place where you go to see a film ▫ *pawagam*: *What's on at the cinema this week?*

> **HELP** In American English, you use **movie theater** to talk about the building where films are shown but **the movies** when you are talking about going to see a film there: *There are five movie theaters in this town.* ♦ *Let's go to the movies this evening.*

2 [U] films in general; the film industry ▫ *wayang gambar; filem; bidang perfileman*: *one of the great successes of British cinema* ➔ note at **film**

cinnamon /ˈsɪnəmən/ noun [U] a sweet brown powder that is used as a spice in cooking ▫ *(serbuk) kayu manis* ➔ picture on **page P14**

circa /ˈsɜːkə/ prep (abbr **c**) (*written*) (used with dates) about; approximately ▫ *kira-kira*: *The vase was made circa 600 AD.*

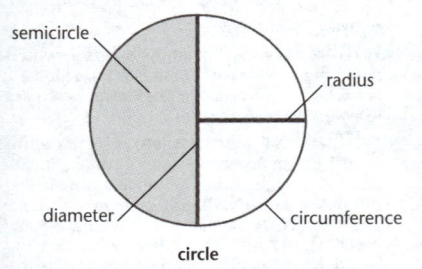

[diagram labeled: semicircle, radius, diameter, circumference — **circle**]

circle¹ /ˈsɜːkl/ noun **1** [C] a flat, round area ▫ *bulatan*: *She cut out a circle of paper.* ➔ picture at **shape 2** [C] A round shape like a ring ▫ *bulatan*: *The children were drawing circles and squares on a piece of paper.* ♦ *We all stood in a circle and held hands.* **3 the (dress) circle** (also **balcony**) [sing] an area of seats that is upstairs in a cinema, theatre, etc. ▫ *tempat duduk utama*: *We've booked seats in the front row of the circle.* **4** [C]

a group of people who are friends, or who have the same interest or profession ▫ *lingkungan*: *He has a large circle of friends.* ♦ *Her name was well known in artistic circles.*
IDM a vicious circle ➔ **vicious**

circle² /ˈsɜːkl/ verb **1** [I,T] to move, or to move round sth in, a circle ▫ *mengelilingi*: *The plane circled the town several times before it landed.* **2** [T] to draw a circle round sth ▫ *bulatkan*: *There are three possible answers to each question. Please circle the correct one.*

circuit /ˈsɜːkɪt/ noun **1** [C] a journey, route or track that forms a circle ▫ *pusingan*: *The cars have to complete ten circuits of the track.* **2** [C] the complete path of wires and equipment that an electric current flows around ▫ *litar* **3** [sing] a series of sports competitions, meetings or other organized events that are regularly visited by the same people ▫ *pertandingan litar*: *She's one of the best players on the tennis circuit.*

circular¹ /ˈsɜːkjələ(r)/ adj **1** round and flat; shaped like a circle ▫ *bulat*: *a circular table* **2** (used about a journey, etc.) moving round in a circle ▫ *berkeliling*: *a circular tour of Munich*

circular² /ˈsɜːkjələ(r)/ noun [C] a printed letter, notice or advertisement that is sent to a large number of people ▫ *surat pekeliling*

circulate /ˈsɜːkjəleɪt/ verb [I,T] **1** (used about a substance) to move or make sth move round continuously ▫ *mengedari; mengelilingi*: *Blood circulates round the body.* **2** to go or be passed from one person to another ▫ *tersebar; mengedarkan*: *Rumours were circulating about the Minister's private life.* ♦ *We've circulated a copy of the report to each department.*

circulation /ˌsɜːkjəˈleɪʃn/ noun **1** [U] the movement of blood around the body ▫ *peredaran*: *If you have bad circulation, your hands and feet get cold easily.* **2** [U] the passing of sth from one person or place to another ▫ *penyebaran; edaran*: *the circulation of news/information/rumours* ♦ *Those coins are no longer in circulation* (= being used by people). **3** [C] the number of copies of a newspaper, magazine, etc. that are sold each time it is produced ▫ *edaran*: *This newspaper has a circulation of over a million.*

circumcise /ˈsɜːkəmsaɪz/ verb [T] **1** to remove the skin at the end of the **penis** (= the male sexual organ) of a boy or man for religious or medical reasons ▫ *mengkhatankan (lelaki)* **2** to cut off part of the sex organs of a girl or woman ▫ *mengkhatankan (perempuan)* ▸ **circumcision** /ˌsɜːkəmˈsɪʒn/ noun [C,U]

circumference /səˈkʌmfərəns/ noun [C,U] the distance round a circle or sth in the shape of a circle ▫ *lilitan*: *The Earth is about 40 000 kilometres in circumference.* ➔ look at **diameter, radius** ➔ picture at **circle**

circumspect /ˈsɜːkəmspekt/ adj (*formal*) thinking very carefully about sth before doing it,

[C] **countable**, a noun with a plural form: *one book, two books*   [U] **uncountable**, a noun with no plural form: *some sugar*

circumstance → civilize

because there may be risks involved □ *berhati-hati; waspada* SYN **cautious**

circumstance /'sɜːkəmstəns/ *noun*
1 [C, usually pl] the facts and events that affect what happens in a particular situation □ *keadaan*: *Police said there were no suspicious circumstances surrounding the boy's death.* ♦ *In normal circumstances I would not have accepted the job, but at that time I had very little money.* **2 circumstances** [pl] (*formal*) the amount of money that you have □ *keadaan hidup; kedudukan (kewangan)*: *The company has promised to repay the money when its financial circumstances improve.*
IDM in/under the circumstances as the result of a particular situation □ *dlm keadaan demikian*: *It's not an ideal solution, but it's the best we can do in the circumstances.* ♦ *My father was ill at that time, so under the circumstances I decided not to go on holiday.*
in/under no circumstances never; not for any reason □ *jangan sekali-kali*: *Under no circumstances should you enter my office.*

circumstantial /ˌsɜːkəmˈstænʃl/ *adj* (used in connection with the law) containing details and information that strongly suggest sth is true but are not actual proof of it □ *berdasarkan keadaan*: *They had only circumstantial evidence.*

circus /'sɜːkəs/ *noun* [C] a show performed in a large tent by a company of people and animals □ *sarkas*

CIS /ˌsiː aɪ 'es/ *abbr* **the Commonwealth of Independent States** (a group of independent countries that were part of the Soviet Union until 1991) □ *CIS (Komanwel Negara-negara Merdeka)*

cistern /'sɪstən/ *noun* [C] a container for storing water, especially one that is connected to a toilet □ *tangki*

cite /saɪt/ *verb* [T] (*formal*) to mention sth or use sb's exact words as an example to support, or as proof of, what you are saying □ *memetik; menyebut*: *She cited a passage from the president's speech.* ▶ **citation** /saɪˈteɪʃn/ *noun* [C,U]

citizen /'sɪtɪzn/ *noun* [C] **1** a person who is legally accepted as a member of a particular country □ *warganegara; rakyat*: *She was born in Japan, but became an American citizen in 1981.* **2** a person who lives in a town or city □ *warga; penduduk*: *the citizens of Paris* ⊃ look at **senior citizen**

citizenship /'sɪtɪzənʃɪp/ *noun* [U] the state of being a citizen of a particular country □ *kewarganegaraan; kerakyatan*: *After living in Spain for twenty years, he decided to apply for Spanish citizenship.*

citrus /'sɪtrəs/ *adj* used to describe fruit such as oranges and lemons □ *sitrus*

city /'sɪti/ *noun* (*pl* **cities**) **1** [C] a large and important town □ *bandar raya; kota; bandar*: *Venice is one of the most beautiful cities in the world.* ♦ *Many people are worried about housing conditions in Britain's inner cities* (= the central parts where there are often social problems). ♦ *the city centre* ♦ *the country's capital city* ⊃ picture on **page P11 2 the City** [sing] the oldest part of London, which is Britain's financial centre □ *gelaran pusat kewangan (di kota London)*: *a City stockbroker*

> **TOPIC**
>
> **City life**
> Life in the **city** can be **hectic** (= very busy). People are often **in a hurry** and the **streets** are **crowded** and **noisy**. There is a lot of **traffic** (= cars, buses, etc.) so the air is **polluted**. Many people live in **flats**, and if you live in the **suburbs** (= areas outside the city), you spend a lot of time **commuting** (= travelling to and from work). But cities are also **lively** places (= full of energy). There are restaurants, shops, theatres, museums and **sports facilities** (such as stadiums and swimming pools). Many cities are **cosmopolitan** (= full of people from all over the world).

civic /'sɪvɪk/ *adj* officially connected with a city or town □ *sivik*: *civic pride* (= feeling proud because you belong to a particular town or city) ♦ *civic duties* ♦ *the civic centre* (= the area where the public buildings are in a town)

civil /'sɪvl/ *adj* **1** [only *before* a noun] connected with the people who live in a country □ *awam*: *civil disorder* (= involving groups of people within the same country) **2** [only *before* a noun] connected with the state, not with the army or the Church □ *awam; sivil*: *a civil wedding* (= not a religious one) ♦ *civil engineering* (= the designing and building of roads, railways, bridges, etc.) **3** [only *before* a noun] (in law) connected with the personal legal matters of ordinary people, and not criminal law □ *sivil*: *civil courts* **4** polite, but not very friendly □ *sopan*: *I know you don't like the director, but do try and be civil to him.* ▶ **civilly** /'sɪvəli/ *adv*

civilian /səˈvɪliən/ *noun* [C] a person who is not in the army, navy, air force or police force □ *preman*: *Two soldiers and one civilian were killed when the bomb exploded.*

civilization (also **-isation**) /ˌsɪvəlaɪˈzeɪʃn/ *noun* **1** [U] an advanced state of social and cultural development, or the process of reaching this state □ *pentamadunan; pemeradaban*: *the civilization of the human race* **2** [C,U] a society which has its own highly developed culture and way of life □ *tamadun; peradaban*: *the civilizations of ancient Greece and Rome* ♦ *Western civilization* **3** [U] all the people in the world and the societies they live in considered as a whole □ *dunia*: *Global warming poses a threat to the whole of civilization.*

civilize (also **-ise**) /'sɪvəlaɪz/ *verb* [T] to educate and improve a person or a society; to make sb's manners or behaviour better □ *mentamadunkan*

civilized (also -ised) /ˈsɪvəlaɪzd/ *adj* **1** (used about a society) well organized; having a high level of social and cultural development □ *bertamadun* **2** polite and reasonable □ *bersopan santun*: *a civilized conversation*

civil ˈrights (also **civil ˈliberties**) *noun* [pl] sb's legal right to freedom and equal treatment in society, whatever their sex, race or religion □ *hak awam*: *the civil rights leader Martin Luther King*

civil ˈservant *noun* [C] a person who works for **the civil service** □ *kakitangan awam*

the ˌcivil ˈservice *noun* [sing] all the government departments, except for the armed forces, and all the people who work in them □ *perkhidmatan awam*

civil ˈwar *noun* [C,U] a war between groups of people who live in the same country □ *perang saudara*

CJD /ˌsiː dʒeɪ ˈdiː/ *abbr* **Creutzfeldt-Jakob disease**; a disease of the brain caused by eating infected meat □ *(penyakit) CJD* ➲ look at **BSE**

cl *abbr* = **centilitre** □ *cl (sentiliter)*

clad /klæd/ *adj* [not before a noun] (*formal*) dressed (in); wearing a particular type of clothing □ *berpakaian*: *The children were warmly clad in coats, hats and scarves.*

claim¹ /kleɪm/ *verb* **1** [T] **claim (that)**; **claim (to be sth)** to say that sth is true, without having any proof □ *mendakwa; mengatakan*: *Colin claims (that) the book belongs to him.* ♦ *The woman claims to be the oldest person in Britain.* **2** [I,T] **claim (for sth)** to ask for sth from the government, a company, etc. because you think it is your legal right to have it, or it belongs to you □ *menuntut*: *The police are keeping the animal until somebody claims it.* ♦ *Don't forget to claim for your travel expenses when you get back.* ♦ (*figurative*) *No one has claimed responsibility for the bomb attack.* **3** [T] to cause death □ *meragut*: *The earthquake claimed thousands of lives.*

claim² /kleɪm/ *noun* [C] **1 a claim (that)** a statement that sth is true, which does not have any proof □ *dakwaan*: *I do not believe the Government's claim that they can reduce unemployment by the end of the year.* **2 a claim (to sth)** the right to have sth □ *tuntutan (atas hak milik)*: *You will have to prove your claim to the property in a court of law.* **3 a claim (for sth)** a demand for money that you think you have a right to, especially from the government, a company, etc. □ *tuntutan*: *to make an insurance claim* ♦ *After the accident he decided to put in a claim for compensation.*
IDM stake a/your claim ➲ **stake²**

claimant /ˈkleɪmənt/ *noun* [C] a person who believes they have the right to have sth □ *pihak yg menuntut*: *The insurance company refused to pay the claimant any money.*

clairvoyant /kleəˈvɔɪənt/ *noun* [C] a person who some people believe has special mental powers and can see what will happen in the future □ *peramal*

clam¹ /klæm/ *noun* [C] a **shellfish** (= a creature with a shell that lives in water) that you can eat □ *remis* ➲ picture at **shellfish**

clam² /klæm/ *verb* (**clamming**; **clammed**)
PHR V clam up (on sb) (*informal*) to stop talking and refuse to speak, especially when sb asks you about sth □ *membungkam*

clamber /ˈklæmbə(r)/ *verb* [I] **clamber up, down, out etc.** to move or climb with difficulty, usually using both your hands and feet □ *memanjat dgn bersusah payah*: *She managed to clamber up and over the wall.*

clammy /ˈklæmi/ *adj* (**clammier**; **clammiest**) cold, slightly wet and sticky in an unpleasant way □ *berlengas; lembap*: *clammy hands*

clamour (*AmE* **clamor**) /ˈklæmə(r)/ *verb* [I] **clamour for sth** to demand sth in a loud or angry way □ *mendesak kuat-kuat atau dgn marah*: *The public are clamouring for an answer to all these questions.* ▶ **clamour** (*AmE* **clamor**) *noun* [sing]: *the clamour of angry voices*

clamp¹ /klæmp/ *verb* [T] **1 clamp A and B (together)**; **clamp A to B** to fasten two things together with a **clamp** □ *mengapit*: *The metal rods were clamped together.* ♦ *Clamp the wood to the table so that it doesn't move.* **2** to hold sth very firmly in a particular position □ *mencengkam; mengetap*: *Her lips were clamped tightly together.* **3** (*BrE*) to fix a metal object to the wheel of a vehicle that has been parked illegally, so that it cannot move □ *mengunci roda kereta*: *Oh no! My car's been clamped.*
PHR V clamp down on sb/sth (*informal*) to take strong action in order to stop or control sth □ *mengetatkan kawalan*: *The police are clamping down on people who drink and drive.* ➲ look at **clampdown**

clamp² /klæmp/ *noun* [C] **1** a tool that you use for holding two things together very tightly □ *penyepit* **2** (also **ˈwheel clamp**) (*BrE*) a metal object that is fixed to the wheel of a car that has been parked illegally, so that it cannot drive away □ *kunci roda kereta*

clampdown /ˈklæmpdaʊn/ *noun* [C] strong action to stop or control sth □ *kawalan ketat*: *a clampdown on tax evasion*

clan /klæn/ *noun* [C, with sing or pl verb] a group of families who are related to each other, especially in Scotland □ *kaum kerabat*

clandestine /klænˈdestɪn; ˈklændəstaɪn/ *adj* (*formal*) secret and often not legal □ *secara rahsia/diam-diam*: *a clandestine meeting*

clang /klæŋ/ *verb* [I,T] to make or cause sth metal to make a loud ringing sound □ *berdentang*: *The iron gates clanged shut.* ▶ **clang** *noun* [C]

clank → classified advertisement

clank /klæŋk/ *verb* [I,T] to make or cause sth metal to make a loud unpleasant sound □ *berdentang-dentang*: *The lift clanked its way up to the seventh floor.* ▶ **clank** *noun* [C]

clap¹ /klæp/ *verb* (**clapping**; **clapped**) **1** [I,T] to hit your hands together many times, usually to show that you like sth □ *bertepuk tangan*: *The audience clapped as soon as the singer walked onto the stage.* ◆ *Everybody was clapping their hands in time to the music.* **2** [T] to put sth onto sth quickly and firmly □ *menepuk*: *'Oh no, I shouldn't have said that,' she said, clapping a hand over her mouth.* ▶ **clapping** *noun* [U]

clap² /klæp/ *noun* [C] **1** an act of clapping □ *tepukan*: *Let's have a big clap for our next performer!* **2** a sudden loud noise □ *dentuman*: *a clap of thunder*

claret /'klærət/ *noun* **1** [C,U] a red wine from Bordeaux in France □ *klaret* **2** [U] a dark red colour □ *merah tua*

clarification /ˌklærəfɪ'keɪʃn/ *noun* [U,C] an act of making sth clear and easier to understand □ *penjelasan*: *We'd like some clarification of exactly what the new exam will be like.* ⊃ look at **clarity**

clarify /'klærəfaɪ/ *verb* [T] (*formal*) (**clarifying**; **clarifies**; *pt, pp* **clarified**) to make sth become clear and easier to understand □ *menjelaskan*: *I hope that what I say will clarify the situation.* ⊃ *adjective* **clear**

clarinet /ˌklærə'net/ *noun* [C] a musical instrument that is made of wood. You play a **clarinet** by blowing through it. □ *klarinet* ⊃ look at **woodwind** ⊃ note at **music** ⊃ picture at **music**

clarity /'klærəti/ *noun* [U] the quality of being clear and easy to understand □ *kejelasan*: *clarity of expression* ⊃ look at **clarification**

clash¹ /klæʃ/ *verb* **1** [I] **clash (with sb) (over sth)** to fight or disagree seriously about sth □ *bertempur; bertelingkah*: *A group of demonstrators clashed with police outside the Town Hall.* **2** [I] **clash (with sth)** (used about two events) to happen at the same time □ *bertembung*: *It's a pity the two concerts clash. I wanted to go to both of them.* **3** [I] **clash (with sth)** (used about colours, etc.) to not match or look nice together □ *tak kena*: *I don't think you should wear that tie—it clashes with your shirt.* **4** [I,T] (used about two metal objects) to hit together with a loud noise; to cause two metal objects to do this □ *berkelentangan*: *She clashed the cymbals.*

clash² /klæʃ/ *noun* [C] **1** a fight or serious disagreement □ *pertempuran; pertelingkahan*: *a clash between police and demonstrators* **2** a big difference □ *pertentangan*: *a clash of opinions* ◆ *There was a personality clash between the two men* (= they did not get on well together or like each other). **3** a loud noise, made by two metal objects hitting each other □ *bunyi kelentang*: *the clash of cymbals*

clasp¹ /klɑːsp/ *verb* [T] to hold sb/sth tightly □ *memeluk; memegang erat-erat*: *Kevin clasped the child in his arms.*

clasp² /klɑːsp/ *noun* [C] an object, usually of metal, which fastens or holds sth together □ *kancing*: *the clasp on a necklace/brooch/handbag* ⊃ picture at **jewellery**

class¹ /klɑːs/ *noun*
►SCHOOL **1** [C, with sing or pl verb] a group of students who are taught together □ *kelas*: *Jane and I are in the same class at school.* ◆ *The whole class is/are going to the theatre tonight.* **2** [C,U] a lesson □ *kelas; pelajaran*: *Classes begin at 9 o'clock in the morning.* ◆ *We watched an interesting video in class* (= during the lesson) *yesterday.*
►SOCIETY **3** [U,C] the way people are divided into social groups; one of these groups □ *kelas; golongan*: *The idea of class still divides British society.* ◆ *class differences* ◆ *the working/middle/upper class*
►GROUP **4** [C] (*technical*) a group of animals, plants, words, etc. of a similar type □ *kelas (jenis)*: *There are several different classes of insects.*
►QUALITY **5** [U] (*informal*) high quality or style □ *kelas (bergaya/bermutu)*: *Pele was a football player of great class.* **6** [C] [in compounds] of a certain level of quality □ *kelas*: *a first-class carriage on a train* ◆ *Are you travelling economy class or business class on this flight?*
►UNIVERSITY DEGREE **7** [C] [in compounds] (*BrE*) a mark that you are given when you pass your final university exam □ *kelas*: *a first-/second-/third-class degree*

class² /klɑːs/ *verb* [T] **class sb/sth (as sth)** to put sb/sth in a particular group or type □ *mengelaskan; dikelaskan*: *Certain animals and plants are now classed as 'endangered species'.*

classic¹ /'klæsɪk/ *adj* **1** (used about a book, play, etc.) important and having a value that will last □ *klasik*: *the classic film 'Gone With The Wind'* **2** typical □ *tipikal*: *It was a classic case of bad management.* **3** elegant but traditional in style or design □ *klasik; anggun*: *a classic grey suit*

classic² /'klæsɪk/ *noun* **1** [C] a famous book, play, etc. which has a value that will last □ *karya klasik*: *All of Charles Dickens' novels are classics.* **2 Classics** [U] the study of ancient Greek and Roman language and literature □ *Pengajian Klasik*: *a degree in Classics* ⊃ note at **literature**

classical /'klæsɪkl/ *adj* **1** traditional, not modern □ *klasik; tradisional*: *classical ballet* ◆ *the classical theory of unemployment* **2** connected with ancient Greece or Rome □ *Klasik*: *classical architecture* **3** (used about music) serious and having a value that lasts □ *klasik*: *I prefer classical music to pop.* ◆ *a classical composer/violinist* ⊃ note at **music** ▶ **classically** /-kli/ *adv*

classified /'klæsɪfaɪd/ *adj* officially secret □ *sulit; rahsia*: *classified information*

classified ad'vertisement (*BrE informal* ˌ**classified 'ad**, ˌ**small 'ad**) *noun* [C, usually pl]

classify /ˈklæsɪfaɪ/ verb [T] (classifying; classifies; pt, pp classified) classify sb/sth (as sth) to put sb/sth into a group with other people or things of a similar type □ *mengelaskan*: *Would you classify it as an action film or a thriller?* ▶ classification /ˌklæsɪfɪˈkeɪʃn/ noun [C,U]: *the classification of the different species of butterfly*

classmate /ˈklɑːsmeɪt/ noun [C] a person who is in the same class as you at school or college □ *rakan sekelas*

classroom /ˈklɑːsruːm; -rʊm/ noun [C] a room in a school, college, etc. where lessons are taught □ *bilik darjah*: *classroom activities* ♦ *technology in the classroom*

classy /ˈklɑːsi/ adj (classier; classiest) (informal) of high quality or style; expensive and fashionable □ *ada kelas*: *a classy restaurant*

clatter /ˈklætə(r)/ verb [I,T] to make or cause sth hard to make a series of short loud repeated sounds □ *berkeletak-keletuk*: *The horses clattered down the street.* ▶ clatter noun [usually sing]

clause /klɔːz/ noun [C] 1 a group of words that includes a subject and a verb. A **clause** is usually only part of a sentence □ *klausa*: *The sentence 'After we had finished eating, we watched a film.' contains two clauses.* 2 one of the sections of a legal document that says that sth must or must not be done □ *fasal*

claustrophobia /ˌklɔːstrəˈfəʊbiə/ noun [U] fear of being in a small space with walls on all sides □ *klaustrofobia*

claustrophobic /ˌklɔːstrəˈfəʊbɪk/ adj 1 extremely afraid of small spaces with walls on all sides □ *menimbulkan klaustrofobia*: *Hilary always feels claustrophobic in lifts.* 2 used about sth that makes you feel afraid in this way □ *(mengalami) klaustrofobia*: *a claustrophobic little room*

clavicle /ˈklævɪkl/ (formal) = **collarbone**

claw¹ /klɔː/ noun [C] 1 one of the long curved nails on the end of an animal's or a bird's foot □ *cakar; kuku* ⊃ picture on **page P12** 2 one of a pair of long, sharp fingers that certain types of **shellfish** (= creatures with shells that live in water) have. They use them for holding things or picking things up □ *sepit*: *the claws of a crab* ⊃ picture at **shellfish**

claw² /klɔː/ verb [I,T] claw (at) sb/sth to scratch or tear sb/sth with claws or with your nails □ *mencakar*: *The cat was clawing at the furniture.*

clay /kleɪ/ noun [U] heavy earth that is soft and sticky when it is wet and becomes hard when it is baked or dried □ *tanah liat*: *clay pots*

clean¹ /kliːn/ adj (cleaner; cleanest) 1 not dirty □ *bersih*: *The whole house was beautifully clean.* ♦ *Cats are very clean animals.* **OPP** dirty ⊃ noun cleanliness 2 free from harmful or unpleasant substances □ *bersih*: *clean air* ♦ *clean drinking water* 3 (used about humour) not about sex □ *sopan; tdk lucah*: *a clean joke* **OPP** dirty 4 having no record of offences or crimes □ *bersih*: *a clean driving licence*

IDM a clean sweep a complete victory in a sports competition, an election, etc. that you get by winning all the different parts of it □ *memenangi semua; sapu bersih*: *The Russians made a clean sweep of all the gymnastics events.*

clean² /kliːn/ verb [I,T] to make sth free from dust or dirt by washing or rubbing it □ *membersihkan*: *to clean the windows* ♦ *Don't forget to clean your teeth!* ♦ *Linda comes in to clean after office hours.* ⊃ look at **dry-clean**, **spring-clean**

HELP Do the cleaning is often used instead of clean: *I do the cleaning once a week.*

PHR V clean sth out to clean the inside of sth □ *mengemas*: *I'm going to clean out all the cupboards next week.*

clean (sth) up to remove all the dirt from a place that is particularly dirty □ *membersihkan*: *I'm going to clean up the kitchen before Mum and Dad get back.* ♦ *Oh no, you've spilt coffee on the new carpet! Can you clean it up?*

OTHER WORDS FOR

clean

Clean is a general word for removing dirt from something. If you **wash** something you clean it with water and often soap. You can **wipe** a surface by rubbing it with a wet cloth; you **dust** a surface by rubbing it with a dry cloth. If you **brush** something you clean it with a brush that has a short handle; if you **sweep** the floor you use a brush with a long handle. When you clean or tidy your home, you **do the housework**.

clean³ /kliːn/ adv (informal) completely □ *betul-betul; sama sekali; langsung*: *I clean forgot it was your birthday.*

IDM come clean (with sb) (about sth) (informal) to tell the truth about sth that you have been keeping secret □ *mendedahkan keadaan sebenarnya*: *She decided to come clean with her father about the money she owed.*

go clean out of your mind to be completely forgotten □ *langsung tdk ingat*

cleaner /ˈkliːnə(r)/ noun 1 [C] a person whose job is to clean the rooms and furniture inside a house or other building □ *tukang cuci; pencuci*: *an office cleaner* 2 [C] a substance or a special machine that you use for cleaning sth □ *pembersih; pencuci*: *liquid floor cleaners* ♦ *a carpet cleaner* ⊃ look at **vacuum cleaner** 3 the cleaner's = **dry-cleaner's**

cleanliness /ˈklenlinəs/ noun [U] being clean or keeping things clean □ *kebersihan*: *High standards of cleanliness are important in a hotel kitchen.*

cleanly → clear-cut

cleanly /ˈkliːnli/ *adv* easily or smoothly in one movement □ *dgn licin*: *The knife cut cleanly through the rope.*

cleanse /klenz/ *verb* [T] to clean your skin or a wound □ *membersihkan* ⊃ look at **ethnic cleansing**

cleanser /ˈklenzə(r)/ *noun* [C,U] a substance that you use for cleaning your skin, especially your face □ *bahan pembersih*

clean-ˈshaven *adj* a man who is **clean-shaven** does not have a beard or other hair growing on his face □ *bercukur bersih*

ℹ clear¹ /klɪə(r)/ *adj* (**clearer; clearest**)
▶WITHOUT DOUBT **1 clear (to sb)** easy to understand and not causing any confusion □ *jelas; nyata*: *There are clear advantages to the second plan.* ♦ *It was clear to me that he was not telling the truth.* ♦ *She gave me clear directions on how to get there.* ⊃ *verb* **clarify**
▶SURE **2 clear (about/on sth)** sure or definite; without any doubts or confusion □ *jelas; pasti*: *I'm not quite clear about the arrangements for tomorrow.* ⊃ *verb* **clarify**
▶EASY TO HEAR, ETC. **3** easy to see or hear □ *jelas; terang*: *His voice wasn't very clear on the telephone.*
▶TRANSPARENT **4** easy to see through □ *jernih*: *The water was so clear that we could see the bottom of the lake.*
▶NOT MARKED **5** free from marks □ *cerah; mulus*: *a clear sky* (= without clouds) ♦ *a clear skin* (= without spots)
▶NOT BLOCKED **6 clear (of sth)** free from things that are blocking the way □ *bersih; tdk terhalang*: *The police say that most roads are now clear of snow.*
▶NOT GUILTY **7** not guilty □ *tdk berasa bersalah*: *It wasn't your fault. You can have a completely clear conscience.*
IDM **make yourself clear**; **make sth clear/plain (to sb)** to speak so that there can be no doubt about what you mean □ *menyatakan sst dgn tegas*: *'I do not want you to go to that concert,' said my mother. 'Do I make myself clear?'* ♦ *He made it quite clear that he was not happy with the decision.*

ℹ clear² /klɪə(r)/ *verb*
▶REMOVE **1** [T] to remove sth that is not wanted or needed □ *membersihkan*: *to clear the roads of snow/to clear snow from the roads* ♦ *It's your turn to clear the table* (= to take away the dirty plates, etc. after a meal). **2** [T] to make people leave a place □ *menyuraikan*: *After the bomb warning, police cleared the streets.*
▶OF WEATHER/WATER **3** [I] (used about smoke, etc.) to disappear □ *hilang; lenyap; menyingsing*: *The fog slowly cleared and the sun came out.* **4** [I] (used about the sky, the weather or water) to become free of clouds, rain or mud □ *menjadi cerah/jernih*: *After a cloudy start, the weather will clear during the afternoon.*
▶FIND SB NOT GUILTY **5** [T] **clear sb (of sth)** to provide proof that sb is innocent of sth □ *membebaskan; dibebaskan*: *The man has finally been cleared of murder.*
▶GIVE PERMISSION **6** [T] to give official permission for a plane, ship, etc. to enter or leave a place □ *memberi kebenaran*: *At last the plane was cleared for take-off.* **7** [T] **clear sth (with sb)** to get official approval for sth to be done □ *mendapat kelulusan*: *I'll have to clear it with the manager before I can refund your money.*
▶MONEY **8** [I] (used about a cheque) to go through the system that moves money from one account to another □ *menjelaskan; dijelaskan*: *The cheque will take three days to clear.*
▶GET OVER/PAST **9** [T] to jump over or get past sth without touching it □ *melompat melepasi*: *The horse cleared the first jump but knocked down the second.*
IDM **clear the air** to improve a difficult or tense situation by talking honestly about worries, doubts, etc. □ *menjernihkan suasana*: *I'm sure if you discuss your feelings with her it will help to clear the air between you.*
clear your throat to cough slightly in order to make it easier to speak □ *berdeham; mendeham*
PHR V **clear off** (*informal*) used to tell sb to go away □ *pergi*
clear sth out to tidy sth and throw away things that you do not want □ *mengemaskan sst (dgn membuang apa yg tdk dikehendaki lagi)*: *I really must clear out the kitchen cupboards.*
clear up (used about the weather or an illness) to get better □ *menjadi cerah; sembuh*: *We can go out for a walk if it clears up later on.* ♦ *The doctor told him to stay at home until his cold cleared up.*
clear (sth) up to make sth tidy □ *membersihkan; mengemaskan*: *Make sure you clear up properly before you leave.*
clear sth up to find the solution to a problem, cause of confusion, etc. □ *menyelesaikan*: *There's been a slight misunderstanding but we've cleared it up now.*

clear³ /klɪə(r)/ *adv* **1** in a way that is easy to see or hear □ *dgn jelas*: *We can hear the telephone loud and clear from here.* **2 clear (of sth)** away from sth; not touching sth □ *jauhkan; jangan dekat*: *Stand clear of the doors* (= on a train).
IDM **keep/stay/steer clear (of sb/sth)** to avoid sb/sth because they or it may cause problems □ *elakkan/jauhkan (drp sst)*: *It's best to keep clear of the town centre during the rush hour.*

clearance /ˈklɪərəns/ *noun* [U] **1** the removing of sth that is old or not wanted □ *pembersihan; perabis*: *The shop is having a clearance sale* (= selling everything quickly by offering it at a low price). **2** the distance between an object and something that is passing under or beside it, for example a ship or vehicle □ *kelegaan*: *There was not enough clearance for the bus to pass under the bridge safely.* **3** official permission for sb/sth to do sth □ *izin; kelulusan*: *She was given clearance to work at the nuclear research establishment.*

ˌclear-ˈcut *adj* definite and easy to see or understand □ *jelas*

ʌ **cup** ɜː **bird** ə **ago** eɪ **pay** əʊ **go** aɪ **my** aʊ **now** ɔɪ **boy** ɪə **near** eə **hair** ʊə **pure**

clear-headed *adj* able to think clearly, especially if there is a problem □ *berfikiran waras*

clearing /ˈklɪərɪŋ/ *noun* [C] a small area without trees in the middle of a wood or forest □ *cerang*

clearly /ˈklɪəli/ *adv* **1** in a way that is easy to see, hear or understand □ *dgn jelas*: *It was so foggy that we couldn't see the road clearly.* **2** in a way that is not confused □ *dgn jelas*: *I'm so tired that I can't think clearly.* **3** without doubt □ *jelas sekali*: *She clearly doesn't want to speak to you any more.* **SYN obviously**

clear-sighted *adj* understanding or thinking clearly; able to make good decisions and judgements □ *tajam fikiran; bijaksana*

cleavage /ˈkliːvɪdʒ/ *noun* [C,U] the space between a woman's breasts □ *lurah dada*

clef /klef/ *noun* [C] (in music) a sign (𝄞, 𝄢) at the beginning of a line of written music that shows the area of sound that the notes are in □ *klef*: *the bass/treble clef*

clementine /ˈkleməntiːn/ *noun* [C] a type of fruit like a small orange □ *sejenis oren kecil*

clench /klentʃ/ *verb* [T] to close or hold tightly □ *menggenggam; mengetap*: *She clenched her fists and looked as if she was going to hit him.*

clergy /ˈklɜːdʒi/ *noun* [pl] the people who perform religious ceremonies in the Christian church □ *golongan paderi*: *a member of the clergy*

clergyman /ˈklɜːdʒimən/ *noun* [C] (*pl* **-men** /-mən/) a male member of the **clergy** □ *paderi (lelaki)*

clergywoman /ˈklɜːdʒiwʊmən/ *noun* [C] (*pl* **-women** /-wɪmɪn/) a female member of the **clergy** □ *paderi (wanita)*

clerical /ˈklerɪkl/ *adj* **1** connected with the work of a **clerk** in an office □ *perkeranian*: *clerical work* **2** connected with the **clergy** □ *(berkenaan dgn) paderi*

clerk /klɑːk/ *noun* [C] **1** a person whose job is to do written work or look after records or accounts in an office, a bank, a court of law, etc. □ *kerani*: *an office clerk* ◆ *a Town Clerk* **2** (*AmE*) = **shop assistant**

clever /ˈklevə(r)/ *adj* (**cleverer**; **cleverest**) [You can also use **more clever** and **most clever**.] **1** able to learn, understand or do sth quickly and easily; intelligent □ *pandai; cerdik; pintar*: *a clever student* ◆ *How clever of you to mend my watch!* ➔ note at **intelligent 2** (used about things, ideas or sb's actions) showing skill or intelligence □ *bijak; bagus*: *a clever device* ◆ *We made a clever plan.* ▶ **cleverly** *adv* ▶ **cleverness** *noun* [U]

cliché /ˈkliːʃeɪ/ *noun* [C] a phrase or an idea that has been used so many times that it no longer has any real meaning or interest □ *klise; ungkapan/idea basi*: *She trotted out the old cliché that 'a problem shared is a problem halved'.*

click¹ /klɪk/ *verb* **1** [I,T] to make a short sharp sound; to cause sth to do this □ *berbunyi klik/kertik; mengertik*: *The door clicked shut.* ◆ *He clicked his fingers at the waiter.* **2** [I,T] **click (on sth)** to press one of the buttons on a computer mouse □ *klik; mengklik*: *To open a file, click on the menu.* ◆ *Position the pointer and double click the left-hand mouse button* (= press it twice very quickly). **3** [I] (*informal*) (used about a problem, etc.) to become suddenly clear or understood □ *menjadi jelas; faham*: *Once I'd found the missing letter, everything clicked into place.* **4** [I] (*BrE informal*) (used about two people) to become friendly immediately □ *secocok; serasi*: *We met at a party and just clicked.*

click² /klɪk/ *noun* [C] **1** a short sharp sound □ *bunyi klik/kertik*: *the click of a switch* **2** the act of pressing the button on a computer mouse □ *klik*

client /ˈklaɪənt/ *noun* [C] **1** a person who receives a service from a professional person, for example a lawyer □ *klien*: *to act on behalf of a client* **2** a computer that is connected to a **server** (= the main computer that stores shared information) □ *pelanggan; klien*

> **HELP Client** or **customer**? **Client** cannot be used for people in shops or restaurants. Those people are **customers**.

clientele /ˌkliːənˈtel/ *noun* [U] all the customers, guests or **clients** who regularly go to a particular shop, hotel, organization, etc. □ *kumpulan pelanggan* ➔ Less formal words are **customers** or **guests**.

cliff /klɪf/ *noun* [C] a high, very steep area of rock, especially one next to the sea □ *cenuram*: *the white cliffs of Dover* ➔ picture on **page P10**

climate /ˈklaɪmət/ *noun* [C] **1** the normal weather conditions of a particular region □ *iklim*: *a dry/humid/tropical climate* **2** an area with particular weather conditions □ *tempat beriklim tertentu*: *They wanted to move to a warmer climate.* **3** the general opinions, etc. that people have at a particular time □ *suasana*: *What is the current climate of opinion regarding the death penalty?* ◆ *the political climate*

climate change *noun* [U] changes in the earth's weather, including changes in temperature, wind patterns and **rainfall** (= the total amount of rain that falls in a particular place during a month, year, etc.), especially the increase in the temperature of the earth's atmosphere that is caused by the increase of particular gases, especially **carbon dioxide** □ *perubahan iklim*: *the threat of global climate change* ➔ look at **global warming**

climatic /klaɪˈmætɪk/ *adj* [only *before* a noun] connected with the climate □ *(berkenaan dgn) iklim*

climax /ˈklaɪmæks/ *noun* [C] the most important and exciting part of a book, play, piece of music, an event, etc. □ *klimaks; kemuncak*:

climb → cloak

The novel reaches a dramatic climax in the final chapter. ▶ **climax** *verb* [I]

climb¹ /klaɪm/ *verb* **1** [I,T] **climb (up) (sth)** to move up towards the top of sth □ *memanjat; mendaki; menaiki*: *to climb a tree/mountain/rope* ◆ *She climbed the stairs to bed.* ◆ *to climb up a ladder* **2** [I] to move, with difficulty or effort, in the direction mentioned □ *bergerak dgn susah payah ke arah yg disebutkan*: *I managed to climb out of the window.* ◆ *The prisoners climbed over the wall.* **3** [I] to go up mountains, etc. as a sport □ *mendaki gunung*

> **HELP Go climbing** is a common way of talking about climbing for pleasure: *I go climbing in the Alps most summers.*

4 [I] to rise to a higher position □ *mendaki; meningkat; naik*: *The plane climbed steadily.* ◆ *The road climbed steeply up the side of the mountain.* ◆ (*figurative*) *The value of the dollar climbed against the pound.*

IDM **climb/jump on the bandwagon** ⊃ **bandwagon**

PHR V **climb down (over sth)** (*informal*) to admit that you have made a mistake; to change your opinion about sth in an argument □ *mengaku tersilap; mengalah* ⊃ look at **climbdown**

climb² /klaɪm/ *noun* [C] an act of climbing or a journey made by climbing □ *pendakian; (perbuatan) mendaki*: *The monastery could only be reached by a three-hour climb.*

climbdown /ˈklaɪmdaʊn/ *noun* [C] an act of admitting you have been wrong; a change of opinion in an argument □ *pengakuan telah tersilap*: *a government climbdown*

climber /ˈklaɪmə(r)/ *noun* [C] a person who climbs mountains as a sport □ *pendaki*

climbing /ˈklaɪmɪŋ/ *noun* [U] the sport or activity of climbing rocks or mountains □ *pendakian*: *to go climbing* ◆ *a climbing accident* ⊃ picture on **page P3**

clinch /klɪntʃ/ *verb* [T] (*informal*) to finally manage to get what you want in an argument or a business agreement □ *mencapai penyelesaian/apa yg dikehendaki*: *to clinch a deal*

cling /klɪŋ/ *verb* [I] (*pt, pp* **clung** /klʌŋ/) **1 cling (on) to sb/sth; cling together** to hold on tightly to sb/sth □ *memegang kuat-kuat; berpaut; berpelukan*: *She clung to the rope with all her strength.* ◆ *They clung together for warmth.* **2 cling to sb/sth** to stick firmly to sth □ *melekap*: *Her wet clothes clung to her.* **3 cling (on) to sth** to continue to believe sth, often when it is not reasonable to do so □ *menaruh harapan*: *They were still clinging to the hope that the girl would be found alive.* ▶ **clingy** *adj*: *a clingy child* (= that does not want to leave its parents) ◆ *a clingy sweater*

ˈcling film *noun* [U] thin transparent plastic used for covering food to keep it fresh □ *plastik lekap*

clinic /ˈklɪnɪk/ *noun* [C] **1** a small hospital or a part of a hospital where you go to receive special medical treatment □ *klinik*: *He's being treated at a private clinic.* **2** a time when a doctor sees patients and gives special treatment or advice □ *klinik*: *Dr Greenall's clinic is from 2 to 4 on Mondays.* ◆ *An antenatal clinic is held every Friday.*

clinical /ˈklɪnɪkl/ *adj* **1** [only before a noun] connected with the examination and treatment of patients at a **clinic** or hospital □ *klinikal*: *Clinical trials of the new drug have proved successful.* **2** (used about a person) cold and not emotional □ *dingin; tdk beremosi* ▶ **clinically** /-kli/ *adv*: *clinically dead* (= judged to be dead from the condition of the body)

clink /klɪŋk/ *noun* [sing] the short sharp ringing sound that objects made of glass, metal, etc. make when they touch each other □ *dentingan*: *the clink of glasses* ▶ **clink** *verb* [I,T]

clip¹ /klɪp/ *noun* [C] **1** a small object, usually made of metal or plastic, used for holding things together □ *klip; sepit*: *a paper clip* ◆ *a hair clip* ⊃ picture at **stationery** **2** an act of cutting sth □ *(perbuatan) memotong* **3** a small section of a film that is shown so that people can see what the rest of the film is like □ *sedutan filem* ⊃ look at **trailer** **4** (*informal*) a quick hit with the hand □ *(perbuatan) menampar*: *She gave the boy a clip round the ear.*

clip² /klɪp/ *verb* (**clipping**; **clipped**) **1** [I,T] to be fastened with a **clip**; to fasten sth to sth else with a **clip** □ *mengklipkan*: *Clip the photo to the letter, please.* **2** [T] to cut sth, especially by cutting small parts off □ *memotong; mencantas; memangkas*: *Andy will clip the hedge tomorrow.* **3** [T] to hit sb/sth quickly □ *melanggar*: *My wheel clipped the pavement and I fell off my bike.*

clipboard /ˈklɪpbɔːd/ *noun* [C] **1** a small board with a **clip** at the top for holding papers, used by sb who wants to write while standing or moving around □ *papan klip* ⊃ picture at **stationery** **2** a place where information from a computer file is stored for a time until it is added to another file □ *papan keratan*

clippers /ˈklɪpəz/ *noun* [pl] a small metal tool used for cutting things, for example hair or nails □ *gunting; ketam; pengetip (kuku, dsb)*: *a pair of nail clippers* ⊃ picture at **scissors**

clipping /ˈklɪpɪŋ/ (*AmE*) = **cutting¹** (1)

clique /kliːk/ *noun* [C] a small group of people with the same interests who do not want others to join their group □ *klik* ▶ **cliquey** *adj*: *The office can be a very cliquey place.*

clitoris /ˈklɪtərɪs/ *noun* [C] the small part of the female sex organs which becomes larger when a woman is sexually excited □ *kelentit*

cloak /kləʊk/ *noun* **1** [C] a type of loose coat without sleeves that was more common in former times □ *mantel* ⊃ look at **cape** **2** [sing] a thing that hides sth else □ *selubung; sst yg menyembunyikan sst yg lain*: (*figurative*) *a cloak of mist*

[I] **intransitive**, a verb which has no object: *He laughed.*   [T] **transitive**, a verb which has an object: *He ate an apple.*

cloakroom /ˈkləʊkruːm/ noun [C] a room near the entrance to a building where you can leave your coat, bags, etc. □ *bilik gantungan kot, dll*

clobber /ˈklɒbə(r)/ verb [T] (*BrE informal*) to hit sb hard □ *menghentam*

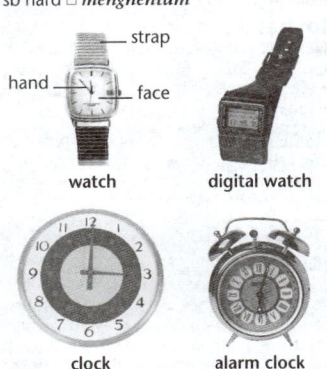

watch — strap, hand, face

digital watch

clock

alarm clock

clock¹ /klɒk/ noun [C] **1** an instrument that shows you what time it is □ *jam*: an alarm clock ◆ a church clock ➔ look at **watch 2** (*informal*) = **milometer**: My car has only 10 000 miles on the clock.
IDM against the clock to do sth fast in order to finish it before a certain time □ *mengejar masa*: It was a race against the clock to get the building work finished on time.
around/round the clock all day and all night □ *siang malam*: They are working round the clock to repair the bridge.
put the clock/clocks forward/back to change the time, usually by one hour, at the beginning/end of summer □ *mencepatkan/melambatkan jam*

clock² /klɒk/ verb
PHR V clock in/on; clock off to record the time that you arrive at or leave work, especially by putting a card into a type of clock □ *mencatat masa masuk/keluar tempat kerja*
clock sth up to achieve a certain number or total □ *mendapat; mencapai; mencatat (masa, jarak, dsb)*: Our car clocked up over 2 000 miles while we were on holiday.

clockwise /ˈklɒkwaɪz/ adv, adj in the same direction as the hands of a clock □ *ikut arah jam*: Turn the handle clockwise. ◆ to move in a clockwise direction **OPP** **anticlockwise, counterclockwise**

clockwork /ˈklɒkwɜːk/ noun [U] a type of machinery found in certain toys, etc. that you operate by turning a key □ *sawat jam; berjalan dgn lancar*: a clockwork toy ◆ The plan went like clockwork (= smoothly and without any problems).

clog¹ /klɒg/ verb [I,T] (**clogging; clogged**) **clog (sth) (up) (with sth)** to block or become blocked □ *tersumbat; sesak*: The drain is always clogging up. ◆ The roads were clogged with traffic.

clog² /klɒg/ noun [C] a type of shoe made completely of wood or with a thick wooden base □ *terompah; kasut kayu*

cloister /ˈklɔɪstə(r)/ noun [C, usually pl] a covered passage around a square garden, usually forming part of a religious building □ *serambi gereja; biara*

clone¹ /kləʊn/ noun [C] an exact copy of a plant or an animal that is produced from one of its cells by scientific methods □ *klon*

clone² /kləʊn/ verb [T] **1** to produce an exact copy of a plant or an animal from one of its cells □ *mengklon (haiwan)*: A team from the UK were the first to successfully clone an animal. **2** to illegally copy information from sb's credit card or mobile phone so that you can use it but the owner of the card or phone receives the bill □ *mengklon; membuat pendua*

close¹ /kləʊz/ verb [I,T] **1** to shut □ *menutup; memejamkan; pejamkan*: The door closed quietly. ◆ to close a door/window ◆ Close your eyes—I've got a surprise. ◆ Close your books. **2** to be, or to make sth, not open to the public □ *ditutup; menutup*: What time do the shops close? ◆ The police have closed the road to traffic. **3** to end or to bring sth to an end □ *ditamatkan; berakhir; menutup*: The meeting closed at 10pm. ◆ Detectives have closed the case on the missing girl. **OPP** for all meanings **open**
PHR V close (sth) down to stop all business or work permanently at a shop or factory □ *menutup; ditutup*: The factory has had to close down. ◆ Health inspectors have closed the restaurant down.
close in (on sb/sth) to come nearer and gradually surround sb/sth, especially in order to attack □ *menghampiri dan mengepung (sso/sst)*: The army is closing in on the enemy troops.
close sth off to prevent people from entering a place or an area □ *menutup*: The police closed off the city centre because of a bomb alert.

close² /kləʊz/ noun [sing] the end, especially of a period of time or an activity □ *penghujung; berakhirnya*: the close of the 20th century ◆ The speaker brought the lecture **to a close**. ◆ The guests began to leave as the evening **drew to a close**.

close³ /kləʊs/ adj, adv **1** [not before a noun] **close (to sb/sth); close (together)** near □ *dekat; rapat-rapat*: Is our hotel close to the beach? ◆ The tables are quite close together. ◆ to follow close behind someone ◆ I held her close (= tightly). **2** (used about a friend, etc.) known very well and liked □ *karib; rapat; akrab*: They invited only close friends to the wedding. **3** [only before a noun] near in a family relationship □ *rapat; dekat*: a close relative **OPP** **distant 4** careful; thorough □ *teliti; rapi*: On close examination, you could see that the banknote was a forgery. **5** (used about a competition, etc.) only won by a small amount □ *sengit*: a close match ➔ note at **near¹** **6** (used about the weather, etc.) heavy and with little movement of

close → cloud

air □ *pengap; cuaca lembap dan tdk berangin*: *It's so close today that there might be a storm.*
IDM **at close quarters** at or from a position that is very near □ *dr dekat; sangat dekat*
close by (sb/sth) at a short distance from sb/sth □ *berdekatan*: *She lives close by.*
close on nearly; almost □ *hampir*: *He was born close on a hundred years ago.*
a close shave/thing a bad thing that almost happened □ *nyaris-nyaris; sipi-sipi*: *I wasn't injured, but it was a close shave.*
close/dear/near to sb's heart ⊃ **heart**
close up (to sb/sth) at or from a very short distance to sb/sth □ *sangat dekat; dekat-dekat*: *You can't tell it's a forgery until you look at it close up.*
come close (to sth/to doing sth) to almost do sth □ *hampir-hampir*: *We didn't win but we came close.*
▶ **closely** adv: *to watch somebody closely* ◆ *The insect closely resembles a stick.*
▶ **closeness** noun [U]

close⁴ /kləʊs/ noun [C] a street that is closed at one end □ *solok*: *5 Devon Close*

closed /kləʊzd/ adj not open; shut □ *tutup*: *Keep your mouth closed.* ◆ *The supermarket is closed.* ◆ *The museum is closed on Mondays.* ◆ (figurative) *a closed mind* **OPP** **open**

ˌclosed-ˈcircuit teleˈvision (abbr **CCTV**) noun [C,U] a television system used in a limited area, for example a shopping centre, to protect it from crime □ *televisyen litar tertutup*

closet /ˈklɒzɪt/ noun [C] (especially AmE) a large cupboard that is built into a room □ *almari*: *a walk-in closet*

close-up /ˈkləʊs ʌp/ noun [C] a photograph or film of sb/sth that you take from a very short distance away □ *gambar/filem jarak dekat*: *Here's a close-up of Mike.*

ˈclosing time noun [C] the time when a shop, pub, etc. closes □ *waktu tutup*

closure /ˈkləʊʒə(r)/ noun [C,U] the permanent closing, for example of a business □ *penutupan; perihal ditutup*: *The firm is threatened with closure.*

clot¹ /klɒt/ noun [C] a lump formed by blood as it dries □ *darah beku*: *They removed a blood clot from his brain.*

clot² /klɒt/ verb [I,T] (**clotting; clotted**) to form or cause blood to form thick lumps □ *(darah) menjadi beku*: *a drug that stops blood from clotting during operations*

cloth /klɒθ/ noun (pl **cloths** /klɒθs/) **1** [U] a material made of cotton, wool, etc. that you use for making clothes, curtains, etc. □ *kain*: *a metre of cloth* **SYN** **fabric 2** [C] a piece of material that you use for a particular purpose □ *kain*: *a tablecloth* ◆ *Where can I find a cloth to wipe this water up?* ⊃ picture at **bucket**

clothe /kləʊð/ verb [T] to provide clothes for sb □ *menyediakan pakaian*: *to feed and clothe a child*

clothed /kləʊðd/ adj **clothed (in sth)** dressed; wearing sth □ *berpakaian*: *He was clothed in black from head to foot.*

clothes /kləʊðz/ noun [pl] the things that you wear, for example trousers, shirts, dresses, coats, etc. □ *pakaian*: *to put on/take off your clothes* ◆ *She was wearing new clothes.* ⊃ picture on **page P1**

> **GRAMMAR** There is no singular form of **clothes**. An **article** /an **item** /a **piece of clothing** is used to describe a single thing that you wear: *A kilt is an item of clothing worn in Scotland.*

> **TOPIC**
> **Clothes**
> Before buying new clothes, you can **try them on** to see if they **fit** (= are the right shape and **size** for you). **Well-dressed** people **wear** clothes which **suit** them (= make them look good). When we say that a **style** of clothing is **in fashion**, **fashionable** or **trendy** we mean that it is popular at the moment. Many people wear **smart** clothes, such as a suit, at work. Others wear a **uniform**: *a police/school uniform*. People usually **get changed** into **casual** (= comfortable, informal) clothes when they come home from work or school.

ˈclothes line noun [C] a thin rope that you hang clothes on so that they can dry □ *ampaian (kain)*

ˈclothes peg (AmE **clothespin**) = **peg¹**(3)

clothing /ˈkləʊðɪŋ/ noun [U] the clothes that you wear, especially for a particular activity □ *pakaian*: *You will need waterproof/outdoor/winter clothing.* ⊃ **Clothing** is a more formal word than **clothes**.

ˌclotted ˈcream noun [U] a type of thick rich cream □ *sejenis krim pekat*

cloud¹ /klaʊd/ noun **1** [C,U] a mass of very small drops of water that floats in the sky and is usually white or grey □ *awan*: *The sun disappeared behind a cloud.* ◆ *A band of thick cloud is spreading from the west.* ⊃ picture on **page P10 2** [C] a mass of smoke, dust, sand, etc. □ *kepulan*: *Clouds of smoke were pouring from the burning building.*
IDM **every cloud has a silver lining** even a very bad situation has a positive side □ *ada cerah di sebalik gelap*
under a cloud with the disapproval of the people around you □ *dlm keadaan yg memalukan/dicurigai*: *She left her job under a cloud because she'd been accused of stealing.*

cloud² /klaʊd/ verb **1** [T] to make sth less clear or easy to understand □ *mengaburkan*: *Her personal involvement in the case was beginning to cloud her judgement.* **2** [T] to make sth less enjoyable; to spoil □ *menyuramkan*: *Illness has clouded the last few years of his life.* **3** [I,T] to become or make sth difficult to see through □ *menjadi kabur*: *His eyes clouded with tears.*

PHR V **cloud over** (used about the sky) to become full of clouds □ *menjadi mendung*

cloudburst /ˈklaʊdbɜːst/ *noun* [C] a sudden heavy fall of rain □ *hujan lebat tiba-tiba*

cloudless /ˈklaʊdləs/ *adj* (used about the sky, etc.) clear; without any clouds □ *cerah*

cloudy /ˈklaʊdi/ *adj* (**cloudier**; **cloudiest**) 1 (used about the sky, etc.) full of clouds □ *mendung* 2 (used about liquids, etc.) not clear □ *keruh*: *cloudy water*

clout /klaʊt/ *noun* (*informal*) 1 [U] influence and power □ *pengaruh dan kuasa*: *He's an important man—he has a lot of clout in the town.* 2 [C] a hard hit, usually with the hand □ *pukulan*: *to give somebody a clout*

clove /kləʊv/ *noun* [C] 1 the small dried flower of a tropical tree, used as a spice in cooking □ *bunga cengkih* ⮕ picture on page P14 2 one of the small separate sections of **garlic** (= a vegetable of the onion family with a strong taste and smell) □ *ulas*

clover /ˈkləʊvə(r)/ *noun* [U] a small plant with pink or white flowers and leaves with three parts to them □ *klover*

> **CULTURE**
>
> Sometimes clover leaves have four parts and it is thought to be very lucky if you find one of these.

clown¹ /klaʊn/ *noun* [C] 1 a person who wears funny clothes and a big red nose and does silly things to make people (especially children) laugh □ *badut; pelawak* 2 a person who makes jokes and does silly things to make the people around them laugh □ *orang yg suka membuat kelakar*: *At school, Jan was always the class clown.*

clown² /klaʊn/ *verb* [I] **clown (about/around)** to act in a funny or silly way □ *melawak*: *Stop clowning around and get some work done!*

cloze test /ˈkləʊz test/ *noun* [C] a type of test in which you have to put suitable words in spaces in a text where words have been left out □ *ujian kloze*

> **EXAM TIP**
>
> **Doing a cloze test**
> To find the correct word, look very carefully at the words on either side of the gap. Think about which words **collocate** (= go with) each other. Try to hear natural speech patterns in your head. When you know which word to use, make sure it is in the right tense and form. When you are practising for this type of exam, you can use the grammatical information and example sentences in your dictionary to help you.

club¹ /klʌb/ *noun* 1 [C] a group of people who meet regularly to share an interest, do sport, etc.; the place where they meet □ *kelab*: *to join a club* ♦ *to be a member of a club* ♦ *a tennis/football/golf club* 2 (also **nightclub**) [C] a place where you can go to dance and drink late at night □ *kelab malam*: *the club scene in Ibiza* 3 [C] a heavy stick, usually with one end that is thicker than the other, used as a weapon □ *belantan* 4 [C] = **golf club** 5 **clubs** [pl] in a pack of playing cards, the **suit** (= one of the four sets) with black three-leafed shapes on them □ *(set daun terup) kelawar*: *the two/ace/queen of clubs* ⮕ note at **card** ⮕ picture at **card** 6 [C] one of the cards from this suit □ *daun (terup) kelawar*: *I played a club.*

club² /klʌb/ *verb* (**clubbing**; **clubbed**) 1 [T] to hit sb/sth hard with a heavy object □ *membelasah* 2 [I] **go clubbing** to go dancing and drinking in a club □ *pergi berdansa dan minum-minum di kelab malam*: *She goes clubbing every Saturday.*

PHR V **club together (to do sth)** to share the cost of sth, for example a present □ *berkongsi (membuat sst)*: *We clubbed together to buy him a leaving present.*

cluck /klʌk/ *noun* [C] the noise made by a chicken □ *bunyi ayam berketak* ▸ **cluck** *verb* [I]

clue /kluː/ *noun* [C] **a clue (to sth)** a piece of information that helps you solve a problem or a crime, answer a question, etc. □ *petunjuk; maklumat*: *The police were looking for clues to his disappearance.* ♦ *the clues for solving a crossword puzzle*

IDM **not have a clue** (*informal*) to know nothing about sth □ *tdk tahu langsung*

clued-up /ˌkluːd ˈʌp/ (*AmE also* ˌclued-ˈin) *adj* **clued-up (on sth)** knowing a lot about sth □ *tahu; pandai*: *I'm not really clued-up on the technical details.*

clueless /ˈkluːləs/ *adj* (*informal*) not able to understand; stupid □ *tdk tahu-menahu; dungu*: *Many politicians are clueless about the lives of ordinary people.*

clump /klʌmp/ *noun* [C] a small group of plants or trees, growing together □ *rumpun; kelompok*

clumsy /ˈklʌmzi/ *adj* (**clumsier**; **clumsiest**) 1 (used about a person) careless and likely to knock into, drop or break things □ *kekok; cemerkap*: *I spilt your coffee. Sorry—that was clumsy of me.* 2 (used about a comment, etc.) likely to upset or offend people □ *tdk berhalus; agak menyinggung*: *He made a clumsy apology.* 3 large, difficult to use and not attractive in design □ *besar dan tdk menarik*: *a clumsy piece of furniture* ▸ **clumsily** *adv* ▸ **clumsiness** *noun* [U]

clung *past tense, past participle of* **cling**

cluster¹ /ˈklʌstə(r)/ *noun* [C] a group of people, plants or things that stand or grow close together □ *kelompok; gugus*: *a cluster of schoolchildren*

cluster² /ˈklʌstə(r)/ *verb*

clutch → coax

PHR V **cluster around sb/sth** to form a group around sb/sth □ *berkelompok; berkerumun*: *The tourists clustered around their guide.*

clutch[1] /klʌtʃ/ verb [T] to hold sth tightly, especially because you are in pain, afraid or excited □ *memegang sst erat-erat*: *He clutched his mother's hand in fear.*

PHR V **clutch at sth** to try to take hold of sth □ *menggapai*: *She clutched at the money but the wind blew it away.*

clutch[2] /klʌtʃ/ noun 1 [C] the part of a vehicle, etc. that you press with your foot when you are driving in order to change the **gear** (= the machinery that changes engine power into movement); the part of the engine that it is connected to □ *klac; cekam*: *to press/release the clutch* ➲ picture at **car** 2 **clutches** [pl] power or control over sb □ *cengkaman*: *He fell into the enemy's clutches.*

clutter[1] /ˈklʌtə(r)/ verb [T] **clutter sth (up)** to cover or fill sth with a lot of objects in an untidy way □ *menyemakkan; menyepahkan*: *Don't leave those books there—they're cluttering up the table.*

clutter[2] /ˈklʌtə(r)/ noun [U] things that are where they are not wanted or needed and make a place untidy □ *benda-benda yg berserak/bersepah-sepah*: *Who left all this clutter on the floor?* ▶ **cluttered** adj: *a cluttered desk*

cm abbr = **centimetre**

Co. /kəʊ/ abbr **1** = **company** □ *Rakan; syarikat*: *W Smithson & Co.* **2** (written) = **County** □ *kaunti*: *Co. Down*

c/o abbr (used for addressing a letter to sb who is staying at another person's house); **care of** □ *di alamat*: *Andy Kirkham, c/o Mrs Potter*

coach[1] /kəʊtʃ/ noun [C] **1** a person who trains people to compete in certain sports □ *jurulatih*: *a tennis coach* **2** (BrE) a comfortable bus used for long journeys □ *koc; bas persiaran*: *It's cheaper to travel by coach than by train.* ➲ note at **bus** ➲ picture on **page P7 3** = **carriage 4** a large vehicle with four wheels pulled by horses, used in the past for carrying passengers □ *kereta kuda* ➲ look at **carriage, car**

coach[2] /kəʊtʃ/ verb [T] **coach sb (in/for sth)** to train or teach sb, especially to compete in a sport or pass an exam □ *melatih; membimbing*: *She is being coached for the Olympics by a former champion.*

coal /kəʊl/ noun **1** [U] a type of black mineral that is dug from the ground and burnt to give heat □ *arang batu*: *a lump of coal* ◆ *a coal fire* ◆ *a coal mine* **2** a piece of coal □ *bara*: *A hot coal fell out of the fire and burnt the carpet.* ➲ picture at **fireplace**

coalition /ˌkəʊəˈlɪʃn/ noun [C, with sing or pl verb] a government formed by two or more political parties working together □ *kerajaan campuran*: *to form a coalition* ◆ *a coalition government*

ˈcoal mine (also **pit**) noun [C] a place, usually underground, where coal is dug from the ground □ *lombong arang batu* ➲ look at **colliery**

ˈcoal miner (also **miner**) noun [C] a person whose job is to dig coal from the ground □ *pelombong arang batu*

coarse /kɔːs/ adj (**coarser**; **coarsest**) **1** consisting of large pieces; rough, not smooth □ *kasar; kasap*: *coarse salt* ◆ *coarse cloth* **OPP** **fine, smooth 2** (used about a person or their behaviour) rude, likely to offend people; having bad manners □ *kasar*: *His coarse remarks about women offended her.* ▶ **coarsely** adv: *Chop the onion coarsely* (= into pieces which are not too small). ◆ *He laughed coarsely.*

coarsen /ˈkɔːsn/ verb [I,T] to become or to make sth **coarse** □ *menjadi kasar*

coast[1] /kəʊst/ noun [C] the area of land that is next to or close to the sea □ *pantai*: *After sailing for an hour we could finally see the coast.* ◆ *Ancona is on the east coast.* ➲ picture on **P10**

coast[2] /kəʊst/ verb [I] **1** to travel in a car, on a bicycle, etc. (especially down a hill) without using power □ *meluncur* **2** to achieve sth without much effort □ *mendapat sst dgn mudah*: *They coasted to victory.*

coastal /ˈkəʊstl/ adj on or near a coast □ *(di dekat dgn) pantai*: *a coastal path*

coastguard /ˈkəʊstɡɑːd/ noun [C] a person or group of people whose job is to watch the sea near the coast in order to help people or ships that are in danger or to stop illegal activities □ *pengawal pantai*

coastline /ˈkəʊstlaɪn/ noun [C] the edge or shape of a coast □ *tepi pantai*: *a rocky coastline*

coat[1] /kəʊt/ noun [C] **1** a piece of clothing that you wear over your other clothes to keep warm when you are outside □ *kot*: *Put your coat on—it's cold outside.* ➲ look at **overcoat, raincoat** ➲ picture on **page P1 2** the fur or hair covering an animal's body □ *bulu*: *a dog with a smooth coat* ➲ picture on **page P12 3** a layer of sth covering a surface □ *lapisan*: *The walls will probably need two coats of paint.*

coat[2] /kəʊt/ verb [T] **coat sth (with/in sth)** to cover sth with a layer of sth □ *menyalut; menyapu (dgn cat, dsb)*: *biscuits coated with milk chocolate*

ˈcoat hanger = **hanger**

coating /ˈkəʊtɪŋ/ noun [C] a thin layer of sth that covers sth else □ *lapisan nipis*: *wire with a plastic coating*

ˌcoat of ˈarms (also **arms**) noun [C] a design that is used as the symbol of a family, a town, a university, etc. □ *jata*

coax /kəʊks/ verb [T] **coax sb (into/out of sth/doing sth); coax sth out of/from sb** to persuade sb gently □ *memujuk*: *The child wasn't hungry, but his mother coaxed him into eating a little.* ◆ *At last he coaxed a smile out of her.*

cobalt /ˈkəʊbɔːlt/ noun [U] **1** (symbol Co) a hard silver-white metal that is often mixed with other metals and used to give a deep bluish-green colour to glass □ *kobalt* **2** (also ˌcobalt ˈblue) a deep bluish-green colour □ *(warna) biru kobalt*

cobble /ˈkɒbl/ verb
PHR V **cobble sth together** to make sth or put sth together quickly and without much care □ *membuat/mengumpulkan sst dgn cepat dan tdk berapa teliti*

cobbler /ˈkɒblə(r)/ noun [C] (old-fashioned) a person who repairs shoes □ *tukang kasut*

cobbles /ˈkɒblz/ (also **cobblestones** /ˈkɒblstəʊnz/) noun [pl] small round stones used (in the past) for covering the surface of streets □ *batu bulat* ▶ **cobbled** adj

cobra /ˈkəʊbrə/ noun [C] a poisonous snake that can spread out the skin at the back of its neck. Cobras live in India and Africa. □ *ular tedung*

cobweb /ˈkɒbweb/ noun [C] a net of threads made by a spider in order to catch insects □ *sarang labah-labah*

cocaine /kəʊˈkeɪn/ (also informal **coke**) noun [U] a dangerous drug that some people take for pleasure but which is **addictive** (= difficult to stop using) □ *kokaina*

cock¹ /kɒk/ noun [C] **1** (AmE **rooster**) an adult male chicken □ *ayam jantan* ⇒ note at **chicken** ⇒ picture at **chicken** **2** an adult male bird of any type □ *burung jantan*

cock² /kɒk/ verb [T] to hold up a part of the body □ *menegakkan; mengangkat; menelengkan; menyerengetkan*: *The horse cocked its ears on hearing the noise.*
PHR V **cock sth up** (BrE slang) to do sth very badly and spoil sth □ *merosakkan* ⇒ look at **cock-up**

cock-a-doodle-doo /ˌkɒk ə ˌduːdl ˈduː/ noun [sing] the noise made by an adult male chicken □ *bunyi kokok ayam*

cockerel /ˈkɒkərəl/ noun [C] a young male chicken □ *ayam jantan muda*

cockney /ˈkɒkni/ noun **1** [C] a person who was born and grew up in the East End of London □ *orang Cockney* **2** [U] the way of speaking English that is typical of people living in this area □ *loghat Cockney*: *a cockney accent*

cockpit /ˈkɒkpɪt/ noun [C] the area in a plane, boat or racing car where the pilot or driver sits □ *kokpit*

cockroach /ˈkɒkrəʊtʃ/ (AmE **roach**) noun [C] a large dark brown insect, usually found in dirty or slightly wet places □ *lipas*

cocktail /ˈkɒkteɪl/ noun [C] **1** a drink made from a mixture of alcoholic drinks and fruit juices □ *koktel* **2** a mixture of small pieces of food that is served cold □ *koktel*: *a prawn cocktail*

[C] **countable**, a noun with a plural form: *one book, two books*

cobalt → C. of E.

ˈ**cock-up** noun [C] (slang) something that was badly done; a mistake that spoils sth □ *sst yg merosakkan; kesilapan*

cocoa /ˈkəʊkəʊ/ noun **1** [U] a dark brown powder made from the seeds of a tropical tree and used in making chocolate □ *serbuk koko* **2** [C,U] a hot drink made from this powder mixed with milk or water; a cup of this drink □ *minuman koko/coklat*: *a cup of cocoa*

coconut /ˈkəʊkənʌt/ noun [C,U] a large tropical fruit with a hard shell that is covered with hair □ *kelapa* ⇒ picture on **page P14**

cocoon¹ /kəˈkuːn/ noun [C] **1** a covering of silk threads that some insects make to protect themselves before they become adults □ *kokun* **2** a soft covering that wraps all around sb/sth and keeps them safe □ *balutan; bedungan*: (figurative) *the cocoon of a caring family*

cocoon² /kəˈkuːn/ verb [T] **cocoon sb/sth (in sth)** to surround sb/sth completely with sth for protection □ *menutup atau membalut utk melindungi sst*

cod /kɒd/ noun [C,U] (pl **cod**) a large sea fish with white flesh that you can eat □ *ikan kod*

code¹ /kəʊd/ noun **1** [C,U] a system of words, letters, numbers, etc. that are used instead of the real letters or words to make a message or information secret □ *kod*: *They managed to break/crack the enemy code* (= find out what it means). ◆ *a security code* ◆ *They wrote letters to each other in code.* ⇒ look at **decode 2** [C] a group of numbers, letters, etc. that is used for identifying sth □ *kod*: *What's the code* (= the telephone number) *for Stockholm?* ⇒ look at **bar code 3** [U] a system of computer programming instructions □ *kod* **4** [C] a set of rules for behaviour □ *tata; peraturan*: *a code of practice* (= a set of standards agreed and accepted by a particular profession) ◆ *the Highway Code* (= the rules for driving on the roads)

code² /kəʊd/ verb [T] **1** to use a particular system for identifying things □ *berkod*: *The files are colour-coded: blue for Europe, green for Africa.* **2** (also **encode**) to put or write sth in code □ *mengekodkan*: *coded messages* **OPP** **decode**

ˌ**co-edu**ˈ**cational** (also informal **coed** /ˌkəʊˈed/) adj (used about a school) where girls and boys are taught together □ *campuran lelaki dan perempuan (ttg sekolah)* **SYN** **mixed**

coerce /kəʊˈɜːs/ verb [T] (formal) **coerce sb (into sth/doing sth)** to force sb to do sth, for example by threatening them □ *memaksa* ▶ **coercion** /kəʊˈɜːʃn/ noun [U]

coexist /ˌkəʊɪɡˈzɪst/ verb [I] to live or be together at the same time or in the same place as sb/sth □ *wujud/hidup bersama* ▶ **coexistence** noun [U]

C. of E. /ˌsiː əv ˈiː/ abbr = Church of England □ *Gereja Inggeris*

[U] **uncountable**, a noun with no plural form: *some sugar*

coffee /ˈkɒfi (AmE usually) / noun 1 [U] coffee, beans (= seeds of a tropical bush) that are cooked, made into powder and used for making a drink □ *(biji/serbuk) kopi*: *Coffee is the country's biggest export.* ♦ *a jar of coffee* 2 [U] a drink made by adding hot water to this powder □ *(air) kopi*: *Would you prefer tea or coffee?* ♦ *a cup of coffee* 3 [C] a cup of this drink □ *secawan kopi*: *Two coffees please.* ⮕ picture on **page P16**

TOPIC

Coffee

Black coffee is made without milk; **white coffee** is with milk. **Decaffeinated coffee** has had the **caffeine** (= the substance that makes you feel more awake and full of energy) taken out. Coffee can be **weak** or **strong**. **Instant coffee** is sold in a jar and made by pouring hot water or milk onto coffee powder in a cup. **Fresh coffee** is made in a coffee pot from coffee beans that have just been **ground** (= crushed into a powder). **Filter coffee** is made in a special machine. You can buy different kinds of coffee ready to drink at a **coffee bar/shop**.

coffee bar (also **coffee shop**) noun [C] (*BrE*) a place in a hotel, a large shop, etc. where simple food, coffee, tea and other drinks without alcohol are served □ *kaunter minuman disajikan*

coffee pot noun [C] a container in which coffee is made and served □ *teko kopi*

coffee table noun [C] a small low table for putting magazines, cups, etc. on □ *meja kopi* ⮕ picture on **page P8**

coffin /ˈkɒfɪn/ noun [C] (*AmE* **casket**) a box in which a dead body is buried in the ground or **cremated** (= burnt) □ *keranda* ⮕ note at **funeral**

cog /kɒɡ/ noun [C] 1 one of a series of teeth on the edge of a wheel that fit between the teeth on the next wheel and cause it to move □ *gigi roda* 2 = **cogwheel**

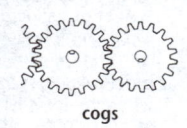

cogs

cognac /ˈkɒnjæk/ noun 1 [U] a type of **brandy** (= a strong alcoholic drink made from wine) that is made in France □ *cognac (sejenis arak)* 2 [C] a glass of this drink □ *segelas cognac*

cogwheel /ˈkɒɡwiːl/ (also **cog**) noun [C] a wheel with a series of teeth on its edge that fit into the teeth in the next wheel and cause it to move □ *roda bergear*

cohabit /kəʊˈhæbɪt/ verb [I] (*formal*) (used about a couple) to live together as if they are married □ *bersekedudukan*

coherent /kəʊˈhɪərənt/ adj clear and easy to understand □ *jelas; koheren* OPP **incoherent** ▶ **coherence** noun [U] ▶ **coherently** adv

cohesion /kəʊˈhiːʒn/ noun [U] the ability to stay or fit together well □ *kepaduan*: *What the team lacks is cohesion—all the players play as individuals.*

coil¹ /kɔɪl/ verb [I,T] to make sth into a round shape □ *melingkar; berlingkar*: *a snake coiled under a rock*

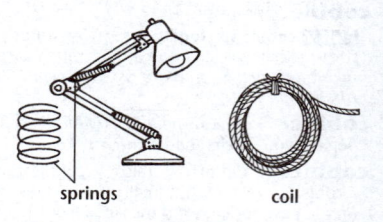

springs   *coil*

coil² /kɔɪl/ noun [C] a length of rope, wire, etc. that has been made into a round shape □ *gelung*: *a coil of rope*

coin¹ /kɔɪn/ noun [C] a piece of money made of metal □ *duit syiling*: *a pound coin* ⮕ picture at **money**

coin² /kɔɪn/ verb [T] to invent a new word or phrase □ *mencipta*: *Who was it who coined the phrase 'less is more'?*

coincide /ˌkəʊɪnˈsaɪd/ verb [I] **coincide (with sth) 1** (used about events) to happen at the same time as sth else □ *berbetulan; serentak*: *The Queen's visit is timed to coincide with the country's centenary celebrations.* **2** to be exactly the same or very similar □ *sama; serupa*: *Our views coincide completely.*

coincidence /kəʊˈɪnsɪdəns/ noun [C,U] two or more similar things happening at the same time by chance, in a surprising way □ *kebetulan*: *We hadn't planned to meet, it was just coincidence.*

coincidental /kəʊˌɪnsɪˈdentl/ adj resulting from two similar or related events happening at the same time by chance □ *(merupakan satu) kebetulan* ▶ **coincidentally** /-təli/ adv

coke /kəʊk/ noun [U] **1** (*informal*) = **cocaine 2** a solid black substance produced from coal and used as a fuel □ *kok*

Col. abbr = **Colonel**

cola /ˈkəʊlə/ noun [C,U] a sweet brown drink that does not contain alcohol; a glass or can of this □ *kola*

colander /ˈkʌləndə(r)/ noun [C] a metal or plastic bowl with a lot of small holes in it that is used for removing water from food that has been boiled or washed □ *penapis* ⮕ picture at **kitchen**

cold¹ /kəʊld/ adj (**colder; coldest**) **1** having a low temperature; not hot or warm □ *sejuk*: *Shall we put the heating on? I'm cold.* ♦ *Take your coat. It's cold outside.* ♦ *I'm not going into the sea—the water's too cold.* **2** (used about food or drink) not heated or cooked; having become cold after being heated or cooked □ *sejuk*: *a cold drink* ♦ *Have your soup before it gets cold.* **3** (used about a person or sb's behaviour) very unfriendly; not

showing kindness, understanding, etc. □ *dingin*: *She gave him a cold, hard look.*
IDM **cold turkey** suddenly and completely, without getting used to sth gradually □ *(berhenti menghisap rokok, dsb) secara mendadak*: *I gave up smoking cold turkey.*
get/have cold feet (*informal*) to become/be afraid to do sth □ *takut; kecut perut*: *She started to get cold feet as her wedding day approached.*
in cold blood in a cruel way and without pity □ *dgn kejam*: *to kill somebody in cold blood*

OTHER WORDS FOR

temperature
Compare **cold** with **hot**, **warm** and **cool**.

Hot describes a high temperature: *I can't drink this tea yet, it's too hot.* **Warm** means 'fairly hot, especially in a pleasant way': *Come and sit by the fire, you'll soon get warm again.* **Boiling** is an informal word for 'very hot': *Could you turn the heating down? It's boiling in here!*

Cool means 'fairly cold, especially in a pleasant way': *It's hot outside but it's nice and cool in here.* **Freezing** means 'extremely cold': *It's absolutely freezing outside.* It can mean that the temperature is below 0° Celsius.

---

cold² /kəʊld/ *noun* **1** [sing, U] lack of heat; low temperature; cold weather □ *kedinginan; kesejukan*: *We walked home in the snow, shivering with cold.* ♦ *Come on, let's get out of the cold and go indoors.* **2** [C,U] a common illness of the nose and throat. When you have a cold you have a sore throat and often cannot breathe through your nose □ *selesema*: *I think I'm getting a cold.* ♦ *Wear some warm clothes when you go out or you'll catch cold.* ⊃ note at **ill**

ˌcold-ˈblooded *adj* **1** cruel; having or showing no pity □ *kejam*: *cold-blooded killers* **2** (used about animals, for example fish or snakes) having a blood temperature that changes with the temperature of the surroundings □ *berdarah sejuk*: *Reptiles are cold-blooded.* ⊃ look at **warm-blooded**

ˌcold-ˈhearted *adj* unkind; showing no kindness, understanding, etc. □ *tanpa perasaan (simpati, sayang, dll)*

coldly /ˈkəʊldli/ *adv* in an unfriendly way; in a way that shows no kindness or understanding □ *dgn dingin*: *'Stop crying immediately,' she said coldly.*

coldness /ˈkəʊldnəs/ *noun* [U] the lack of warm feelings; unfriendly behaviour □ *kedinginan; dinginnya*

colic /ˈkɒlɪk/ *noun* [U] severe pain in the stomach area, which especially babies get □ *kembung (bayi)*

collaborate /kəˈlæbəreɪt/ *verb* [I] **1 collaborate (with sb) (on sth)** to work together (with sb), especially to create or produce sth □ *bekerjasama*: *She collaborated with another author on the book.* **2 collaborate (with sb)** (*disapproving*) to help the enemy forces who have taken control of your country □ *bersubahat*

▶ **collaboration** /kəˌlæbəˈreɪʃn/ *noun* [U] ▶ **collaborator** /kəˈlæbəreɪtə(r)/ *noun* [C]

collage /ˈkɒlɑːʒ/ *noun* [C,U] a picture made by fixing pieces of paper, cloth, photographs, etc. onto a surface; the art of making a picture like this □ *kolaj*

collapse¹ /kəˈlæps/ *verb* [I] **1** to fall down or break into pieces suddenly □ *runtuh; roboh*: *A lot of buildings collapsed in the earthquake.* **2** (used about a person) to fall down and often become unconscious, usually because you are very ill □ *rebah*: *The winner collapsed at the end of the race.* **3** (used about a business, plan, etc.) to fail suddenly or completely □ *lingkup; runtuh*: *The company collapsed, leaving hundreds of people out of work.* **4** to fold sth or be folded into a shape that uses less space □ *melipatkan*: *a chair that collapses for easy storage*

collapse² /kəˈlæps/ *noun* **1** [C,U] the sudden or complete failure of sth, such as a business, plan, etc. □ *kegagalan*: *The peace talks were on the brink/verge of collapse.* **2** [sing, U] (used about a building) a sudden fall □ *keruntuhan; robohnya*: *the collapse of the motorway bridge* **3** [sing, U] (used about a person) a medical condition when a person becomes very ill and suddenly falls down □ *keadaan apabila sso itu tiba-tiba rebah kerana sakit teruk*: *She was taken to hospital after her collapse at work.*

collapsible /kəˈlæpsəbl/ *adj* that can be folded into a shape that makes sth easy to store □ *boleh lipat*: *a collapsible bed*

collar¹ /ˈkɒlə(r)/ *noun* [C] **1** the part of a shirt, coat, dress, etc. that fits round the neck and is often folded over □ *kolar*: *a coat with a fur collar* ⊃ look at **blue-collar**, **dog collar**, **white-collar** ⊃ picture at **lace** ⊃ picture on **page P1** **2** a band of leather that is put round an animal's neck (especially a dog) □ *relang leher*

collar² /ˈkɒlə(r)/ *verb* [T] (*informal*) to catch hold of sb who does not want to be caught □ *menahan*: *The police officer collared the thief.*

collarbone /ˈkɒləbəʊn/ (also *formal* **clavicle**) *noun* [C] one of the two bones that connect your chest bones to your shoulder □ *tulang selangka* ⊃ picture at **body**

collateral /kəˈlætərəl/ *noun* [U] property or sth valuable that you agree to give if you cannot pay back money that you have borrowed □ *sandaran; cagaran*

colleague /ˈkɒliːg/ *noun* [C] a person who works at the same place as you □ *rakan sekerja*: *We were friends and colleagues for many years.*

collect¹ /kəˈlekt/ *verb* **1** [T] to bring a number of things together □ *memungut; mengutip; dikutip*: *All the exam papers will be collected at the end.* **2** [T] to get and keep together a number of objects of a particular type over a period of time as a hobby □ *mengumpul*: *He used to collect stamps.* ⊃ picture on **page P3** **3** [I] to come

collect → colloquialism

together □ *berkumpul*: *A crowd collected to see what was going on.* **SYN gather** 4 [T] (*especially BrE*) to go and get sb/sth from a particular place; to pick sb/sth up □ *mengambil; menjemput*: *to collect the children from school* 5 [I,T] to ask for money from a number of people □ *mengutip*: *to collect for charity* ◆ *The landlord collects the rent at the end of each month.* 6 [T] **collect yourself/sth** to get control of yourself, your feelings, thoughts, etc. □ *menenangkan fikiran*: *She collected herself and went back into the room as if nothing had happened.* ◆ *I tried to collect my thoughts before the exam.*

collect² /kəˈlekt/ *adj, adv* (*AmE*) (used about a telephone call) to be paid for by the person who receives the call □ *panggilan pindah bayaran*: *a collect call* ◆ *She called me collect.*

> **HELP** In British English, we **make a reverse-charge call** or **reverse the charges**.

collected /kəˈlektɪd/ *adj* [not before a noun] calm and in control of yourself, your feelings, thoughts, etc. □ *tenang*: *She felt cool, calm and collected before the interview.*

collection /kəˈlekʃn/ *noun* 1 [C] a group of objects of a particular type that sb has collected as a hobby □ *himpunan; koleksi*: *a stamp collection* 2 [C,U] the act of getting sth from a place or from people □ *pemungutan; pengambilan*: *rubbish collections* 3 [C] a group of people or things □ *kumpulan; himpunan; timbunan*: *a large collection of papers on the desk* 4 [C] a number of poems, stories, letters, etc. published together in one book □ *koleksi*: *a collection of modern poetry* 5 [C] the act of asking for money from a number of people (for charity, in church, etc.) □ *pungutan*: *a collection for the poor* 6 [C] a variety of new clothes or items for the home that are specially designed and sold at a particular time □ *koleksi; himpunan*: *Armani's stunning new autumn collection*

collective¹ /kəˈlektɪv/ *adj* shared by a group of people together; not individual □ *bersama*: *collective responsibility* ▶ **collectively** *adv*: *We took the decision collectively at a meeting.*

collective² /kəˈlektɪv/ *noun* [C, with sing or pl verb] an organization or a business that is owned and controlled by the people who work in it □ *usaha sama*

collector /kəˈlektə(r)/ *noun* [C] [in compounds] a person who collects things as a hobby or as part of their job □ *pengumpul; pengutip*: *a stamp collector* ◆ *a ticket/rent/tax collector*

college /ˈkɒlɪdʒ/ *noun* 1 [C,U] an institution where you can study after you leave school (at the age of 16) □ *kolej; maktab*: *an art college* ◆ *a sixth-form college* (= an institution where students aged 16 to 18 can prepare for A Levels) ◆ *She's studying Spanish at the college of further education* (= a college that provides education and training for people over 16).

> **HELP** We talk about **college**, without **the**, when we mean that somebody is attending a college or university as a student: *He's at college in York.* ◆ *She's going to college in October.* We use **the** if somebody goes there for any other reason: *I went to an art exhibition at the college last night.*

2 [C] (in the US) a university, or part of one, where students can study for a degree □ *universiti* 3 [C] (in Britain) one of the separate institutions into which certain universities are divided □ *kolej*: *King's College, London* ◆ *a tour of Oxford colleges*

collide /kəˈlaɪd/ *verb* [I] **collide (with sb/sth)** to crash; to hit sb/sth very hard while moving □ *berlanggar*: *He ran along the corridor and collided with his music teacher.*

colliery /ˈkɒliəri/ *noun* [C] (*pl* **collieries**) (*especially BrE*) a coal mine and its buildings □ *lombong arang batu*

collision /kəˈlɪʒn/ *noun* [C,U] an occasion when things or people **collide** □ *perlanggaran*: *It was a head-on collision and the driver was killed instantly.*

IDM be on a collision course (with sb/sth) 1 to be in a situation which is certain to end in a disagreement or an argument □ *menjurus ke arah pertentangan*: *I'm not surprised they're arguing—they've been on a collision course over money all week.* 2 to be moving in a direction which is certain to cause a crash □ *bergerak ke arah yg pasti mengakibatkan perlanggaran*: *The ship was on a collision course with an iceberg.*

collocation /ˌkɒləˈkeɪʃn/ *noun* [C,U] a combination of words in a language, that happens very often and more frequently than would happen by chance; the fact that these combinations happen □ *kolokasi; gandingan kata*: *'Resounding success' and 'crying shame' are English collocations.* ◆ *Students need to be aware of the importance of collocation.*

> **EXAM TIP**
>
> **Collocations**
>
> When you learn a new word, learn the words that go with it. This expands your vocabulary and helps you to write and speak natural English. For example, if you look at the entry for **fashion**, you will find sentences that include the expressions *the latest fashion*, *in fashion*, *come back into fashion* and *out of fashion*. You can even learn more by looking up familiar words. For example, is it better to say 'strong rain' or 'heavy rain'?

colloquial /kəˈləʊkwiəl/ *adj* (used about words, phrases, etc.) used in spoken conversation, not in formal situations □ *bahasa basahan; kolokial* ▶ **colloquially** /-kwiəli/ *adv*

colloquialism /kəˈləʊkwiəlɪzəm/ *noun* [C] a colloquial word or phrase □ *kata atau ungkapan basahan; frasa*

ð **th**en   s **s**o   z **z**oo   ʃ **sh**e   ʒ vi**s**ion   h **h**ow   m **m**an   n **n**o   ŋ si**ng**   l **l**eg   r **r**ed   j **y**es   w **w**et

collusion /kəˈluːʒn/ noun [U] (formal) secret agreement, especially in order to do sth dishonest □ *pakatan sulit; komplot*: *The police were corrupt and were acting in collusion with the criminals.*

cologne /kəˈləʊn/ = eau de cologne

colon /ˈkəʊlən/ noun [C] the mark (:) used before a list, an explanation, an example, etc. □ *titik bertindih*

colonel /ˈkɜːnl/ noun [C] (abbr Col.) an officer of a high level in the army □ *kolonel*

colonial /kəˈləʊniəl/ adj connected with or belonging to a **colony** (= a country that is controlled by another country) □ *(berkenaan dgn) penjajahan; kolonial*: *Spain used to be a major colonial power.*

colonialism /kəˈləʊniəlɪzəm/ noun [U] the practice by which a powerful country controls another country or countries, in order to become richer □ *dasar penjajahan; kolonialisme*

colonist /ˈkɒlənɪst/ noun [C] a person who goes to live in a country that has become a **colony** □ *kolonis*

colonize (also **-ise**) /ˈkɒlənaɪz/ verb [T] to take control of another country or place and make it a **colony** □ *menjajah* ▶ **colonization** (also **-isation**) /ˌkɒlənaɪˈzeɪʃn/ noun [U]

colony /ˈkɒləni/ noun [C] (pl **colonies**) **1** a country or an area that is ruled by another, more powerful country □ *tanah jajahan; koloni* **2** [with sing or pl verb] a group of people who go to live permanently in another country but keep their own habits and customs □ *koloni; perkampungan* **3** a group of the same type of animals, insects or plants living or growing in the same place □ *koloni; kumpulan*: *a colony of ants*

colossal /kəˈlɒsl/ adj extremely large □ *amat besar/banyak*: *a colossal building* ♦ *a colossal amount of money*

colour¹ (AmE **color**) /ˈkʌlə(r)/ noun **1** [C,U] the fact that sth is red, green, yellow, blue, etc. □ *warna*: *'What colour is your car?' 'Red.'* ♦ *What colours do the Swedish team play in?* ♦ *a dark/deep colour* ♦ *a bright colour* ♦ *a light/pale colour* ♦ *Those flowers certainly give the room a bit of colour.*

> **HELP** We say 'I like the colour blue' NOT 'I like blue colour'. Also, we say that a thing **is** a certain colour, not that it **has** a colour.

2 [U] the use of all the colours, not just black and white □ *warna; berwarna*: *All the pictures in the book are in colour.* ♦ *colour printing* **3** [U] a red or pink colour in your face, particularly when it shows how healthy you are or that you are embarrassed □ *warna merah (pd muka tanda sihat atau malu)*: *You look much better now, you've got a bit more colour.* ♦ *Colour flooded her face when she thought of what had happened.* **4** [U] interesting or exciting details □ *butir-butir menarik*: *It's a busy area, full of activity and colour.*

IDM **off colour** ill □ *tdk sihat*
with flying colours ⊃ **flying**

colour² (AmE **color**) /ˈkʌlə(r)/ verb [T] **1** to put colour on sth, for example by painting it □ *mewarnakan; diwarnakan*: *Colour the picture with your crayons.* ♦ *The area coloured yellow on the map is desert.* **2** to influence thoughts, opinions, etc. □ *mempengaruhi; menjejaskan*: *You shouldn't let one bad experience at school colour your attitude to education.*

PHR V **colour sth in** to fill a shape, a picture, etc. with colour using pencils, paint, etc. □ *mewarnakan*: *The children were colouring in pictures of animals.*

'colour-blind adj unable to see certain colours, especially red and green □ *buta warna*

coloured (AmE **colored**) /ˈkʌləd/ adj **1** having colour or a particular colour □ *berwarna*: *a coffee-coloured dress* ♦ *brightly coloured lights* **2** (used about a person) belonging to a race that does not have white skin □ *bukan orang kulit putih*

> **HELP** This word is considered offensive nowadays. To refer to a person belonging to a particular racial group, you should use black, Asian, etc. as appropriate.

colourful (AmE **colorful**) /ˈkʌləfl/ adj **1** with bright colours; full of colour □ *berwarna-warni*: *Gary wore a colourful shirt.* **2** full of interest or excitement □ *menarik*: *a colourful story* ♦ *He has a rather colourful past.*

colouring (AmE **coloring**) /ˈkʌlərɪŋ/ noun **1** [C,U] a substance that is used to give a particular colour to sth, especially food □ *pewarna* **2** [U] the colour of a person's hair, skin, etc. □ *warna rambut, kulit, dsb*: *to have fair/dark colouring*

colourless (AmE **colorless**) /ˈkʌlələs/ adj **1** without any colour □ *tdk berwarna*: *a colourless liquid, like water* **2** not interesting or exciting □ *tdk menarik; membosankan* **SYN** dull

'colour scheme noun [C] the way in which colours are arranged, especially in a room □ *skema warna*

colt /kəʊlt/ noun [C] a young male horse □ *anak kuda jantan*

column /ˈkɒləm/ noun [C]
▶STONE **1** a tall solid vertical post made of stone, supporting or decorating a building or standing alone □ *tiang*: *Nelson's Column is a monument in London.* ⊃ picture at **arch**
▶SHAPE **2** something that has the shape of a column □ *kepulan; pancutan*: *a column of smoke* (= smoke rising straight up)
▶ON PAGE **3** one of the vertical sections into which a printed page, especially in a newspaper, is divided □ *lajur; ruang*: *a column of text*
▶IN NEWSPAPER **4** a piece of writing in a newspaper or magazine that is part of a regular series or always written by the same writer □ *ruang*: *the travel/gossip column*

columnist → come

▶ NUMBERS **5** a series of numbers written one under the other □ *lajur*: *to add up a column of figures*
▶ PEOPLE/VEHICLES **6** a long line of people, vehicles, etc., one following behind another □ *barisan*: *a column of troops*

columnist /ˈkɒləmnɪst/ *noun* [C] a journalist who writes regular articles in a newspaper or magazine □ *penulis ruang*: *a gossip columnist*

coma /ˈkəʊmə/ *noun* [C] a deep unconscious state, often lasting for a long time and caused by serious illness or injury □ *keadaan koma*

comatose /ˈkəʊmətəʊs/ *adj* **1** deeply unconscious; in a **coma** □ *berada dlm keadaan koma* **2** (*informal*) deeply asleep □ *tidur nyenyak*: *After a large dinner, Mum was comatose on the sofa.*

comb¹ /kəʊm/ *noun* [C] **1** a flat piece of metal or plastic with teeth that you use for making your hair tidy □ *sikat* **2** [usually sing] an act of **combing** the hair □ *(perbuatan) menyikat*: *Give your hair a comb before you go out.*

comb² /kəʊm/ *verb* [T] **1** to make your hair tidy using a **comb** □ *menyikat* **2 comb sth (for sb/sth)** to search an area carefully □ *menggeledah*: *Police are combing the woodland for the murder weapon.*

combat¹ /ˈkɒmbæt/ *noun* [C,U] a fight, especially in war □ *pertempuran; pertarungan*: *unarmed combat* (= without weapons)

combat² /ˈkɒmbæt/ *verb* [T] to fight against sth; to try to stop or defeat sth □ *memerangi; melawan*: *to combat terrorism* ♦ *new medicines to combat heart disease*

combatant /ˈkɒmbətənt/ *noun* [C] a person who takes part in fighting, especially in war □ *orang yg terlibat dlm pertempuran*

combats /ˈkɒmbæts/ (also ˈcombat trousers) *noun* [pl] (*BrE*) = cargo pants

combination /ˌkɒmbɪˈneɪʃn/ *noun* [C,U] a number of people or things mixed or joined together; a mixture □ *gabungan; kombinasi*: *The team manager still hasn't found the right combination of players.* ♦ *On this course, you may study French in combination with Spanish or Italian.*

combine /kəmˈbaɪn/ *verb* **1** [I,T] **combine (sth) (with sb/sth)** to join or mix two or more things together □ *bergabung*: *The two organizations combined to form one company.* ♦ *Bad weather, combined with illness, led to the picnic being cancelled.* **2** [T] **combine A and/with B** to do or have two or more things at the same time □ *menggabungkan*: *to combine business with pleasure* ♦ *This car combines speed and reliability.*

combined /kəmˈbaɪnd/ *adj* done by a number of people joining together, resulting from the joining of two or more things □ *bersama-sama; paduan*: *The combined efforts of the emergency services prevented a major disaster.*

combine harvester /ˌkɒmbaɪn ˈhɑːvɪstə(r)/ (also **combine**) *noun* [C] a large farm machine that both cuts a crop and separates the grain from the rest of the plant □ *mesin penuai kombin* ⊃ look at **harvest**

combustible /kəmˈbʌstəbl/ *adj* able to begin burning easily □ *sangat mudah terbakar*: *combustible material/gases* **SYN** inflammable

combustion /kəmˈbʌstʃən/ *noun* [U] the process of burning □ *pembakaran*

ℹ come /kʌm/ *verb* [I] (*pt* **came** /keɪm/; *pp* **come**) **1** to move to or towards the person who is speaking or the place that sb is talking about □ *mari; datang*: *Come here, please.* ♦ *Come and see what I've found.* ♦ *I hope you can come to my party.* ♦ *They're coming to stay for a week.* ♦ *The children came running into the room.* **2 come (to …)** to arrive somewhere or reach a particular place or time □ *sampai; tiba*: *What time are you coming home?* ♦ *Has the newspaper come yet?* ♦ *After a few hours in the jungle, we came to a river* ♦ *Her hair comes down to her waist.* ♦ *The water in the pool came up to our knees.* ♦ *The time has come to say goodbye.* **3** to be in a particular position in a series □ *digunakan utk menyatakan kedudukan dlm sst siri; berikut; sebelum*: *March comes after February.* ♦ *Charlie came second in the exam.* ♦ *I can't wait to find out what comes next in the story.* **4 come in sth** to be available □ *terdapat*: *This blouse comes in a choice of four colours.* ♦ *Do these trousers come in a larger size?* **5** to be produced by or from sth □ *datang drpd; didapati*: *Wool comes from sheep.* **6** to become open or loose □ *menjadi terbuka/terurai*: *Your blouse has come undone.* ♦ *Her hair has come untied.* **7 come to do sth** used for talking about how, why or when sth happened □ *digunakan apabila bercakap ttg bagaimana, mengapa atau bila sst itu berlaku*: *How did you come to lose your passport?* **8 come to/into sth** to reach a particular state □ *sampai pd sst kedudukan*: *We were all sorry when the holiday came to an end.* ♦ *The military government came to power in a coup d'état.*

IDM **come and go** to be present for a short time and then go away □ *datang dan pergi; sekejap ada, sekejap tdk*: *The pain in my ear comes and goes.*

come easily, naturally, etc. to sb to be easy, natural, etc. for sb to do □ *mudah bagi sso*: *Apologizing does not come easily to her.*

come to nothing; not come to anything to fail; to not be successful □ *tdk menjadi; gagal*: *Unfortunately, all his efforts came to nothing.*

How come? (*informal*) why or how □ *macam mana…?; kenapa…?*: *'I think you owe me some money.' 'How come?'* ♦ *How come you're back so early?*

to come [used after a noun] in the future □ *akan datang; pd masa depan*: *You'll regret it in years to come.*

when it comes to sth/to doing sth when it is a question of sth □ *kalau dr segi…*: *When it comes to value for money, these prices are hard to beat.*
ⓘ For other idioms containing **come**, look at the entries for the nouns, adjectives, etc. For example **come to a head** is at **head**.

ʌ **cup**   ɜː **bird**   ə **ago**   eɪ **pay**   əʊ **go**   aɪ **my**   aʊ **now**   ɔɪ **boy**   ɪə **near**   eə **hair**   ʊə **pure**

PHR V **come about** to happen □ *berlaku*: How did this situation come about?

come across/over (as sth) to make an impression of a particular type □ *nampaknya seperti*: Elizabeth comes across as being rather shy.

come across sb/sth to meet or find sb/sth by chance □ *terserempak dgn; terjumpa*: I came across this book in a second-hand shop.

come along 1 to arrive or appear □ *tiba; muncul*: An old man was coming along the road. 2 = **come on**(2) 3 = **come on**(3)

come apart to break into pieces □ *berkecai; koyak*: This old coat is coming apart at the seams.

come away (from sth) to become separated from sth □ *tertanggal; lekang*: The wallpaper is coming away from the wall in the corner.

come away with sth to leave a place with a particular opinion or feeling □ *meninggalkan sst tempat (dgn sst perasaan, kesan, dll)*: We came away with a very favourable impression of Lisbon.

come back 1 to return □ *pulang*: I don't know what time I'll be coming back. 2 to become popular or fashionable again □ *kembali popular*: Flared trousers are coming back again.

come back (to sb) to be remembered □ *ingat semula*: When I went to Italy again, my Italian started to come back to me.

come before sb/sth to be more important than sb/sth else □ *lebih penting drpd sso/sst*: Mark feels his family comes before his career.

come between sb and sb to damage the relationship between two people □ *menjejaskan hubungan antara sso dgn sso lain*: Arguments over money came between the two brothers.

come by sth to manage to get sth □ *mendapat; didapati*: Fresh vegetables are hard to come by in the winter.

come down 1 to fall down □ *tumbang*: The power lines came down in the storm. 2 (used about an aircraft, etc.) to land □ *mendarat*: The helicopter came down in a field. 3 (used about prices) to become lower □ *turun*: The price of land has come down in the past year.

come down to sth/to doing sth (*informal*) to be able to be explained by a single important point □ *berpokok pada*: It all comes down to having the right qualifications.

come down with sth to become ill with sth □ *diserang/kena sst (penyakit)*: I think I'm coming down with flu.

come forward to offer help □ *tampil ke depan (utk membantu)*: The police are asking witnesses to come forward.

come from ... to live in or have been born in a place □ *berasal dr...*: Where do you come from originally?

come from (doing) sth to be the result of sth □ *akibat*: 'I'm tired.' 'That comes from all the late nights you've had.'

come in 1 to enter a place □ *masuk*: Come in and sit down. 2 (used about the **tides** (= the regular movements of the sea)) to move towards the land and cover the beach □ (*air*) *pasang* ➔ look at table 3 to become popular or fashionable □ *menjadi popular*: Punk fashions came in during the seventies. 4 (used about news or information) to be received □ *diterima*: Reports are coming in of fighting in Beirut.

come in for sth to receive sth, especially sth unpleasant □ *mendapat; menerima*: The government came in for a lot of criticism.

come of sth/of doing sth to be the result of sth □ *hasil atau akibat drpd sst/membuat sst*: We've written to several companies asking for help but nothing has come of it yet.

come off 1 to be able to be removed □ *dibuka; tanggal*: Does the hood come off? 2 (*informal*) to be successful □ *berjaya*: The deal seems unlikely to come off. 3 [before an adverb] (*informal*) to be in a good, bad, etc. situation as a result of sth □ *berada dlm sst kedudukan (baik, teruk, dsb)*: Unfortunately, Dennis came off worst in the fight.

come off (sth) 1 to fall off sth □ *jatuh dr (sst)*: Kim came off her bicycle and broke her leg. 2 to become removed from sth □ *tertanggal; tercabut*: One of the legs has come off this table.

come off it (*spoken*) used to say that you do not believe sb/sth or that you strongly disagree with sb □ *sudahlah*: 'I thought it was quite a good performance.' 'Oh, come off it—it was awful!'

come on 1 to start to act, play in a game of sport, etc. □ *muncul*: The audience jeered every time the villain came on. ♦ The substitute came on in the second half. 2 (also **come along**) to make progress or to improve □ *bertambah baik*: Your English is coming on nicely. 3 (also **Come along!**) used to tell sb to hurry up, try harder, etc. □ *cepatlah; ayuh!*: Come on or we'll be late! 4 to begin □ *hendak mula (kena)*: I've got a cold coming on.

come out 1 to appear; to be published □ *muncul; keluar; diterbitkan*: The rain stopped and the sun came out. ♦ The report came out in 1998. 2 to become known □ *diketahui*: It was only after David's death that the truth came out. 3 if a person **comes out**, they tell family, friends, etc. that they are **homosexual** (= sexually attracted to people of the same sex) □ *mengaku sebagai homoseksual*

come out (of sth) to be removed from sth □ *tanggal/hilang (drpd sst)*: Red wine stains don't come out easily.

come out against sth to say in public that you do not like or agree with sth □ *menentang sst*: The Prime Minister came out against capital punishment.

come out in sth to become covered in spots, etc. □ *tumbuh/timbul (ruam, dsb)*: Heat makes him come out in a rash.

come out with sth to say sth unexpectedly □ *mengatakan/cakap sst*: The children came out with all kinds of stories.

come over = **come across/over**

come over (to ...) (from ...) to visit people or a place a long way away □ *pergi/datang (ke...); datang (dr...)*: They've invited us to come over to Australia for a holiday.

come over sb (used about a feeling) to affect sb □ *melanda sso*: A feeling of despair came over me.

[C] **countable**, a noun with a plural form: *one book, two books*   [U] **uncountable**, a noun with no plural form: *some sugar*

come round 1 (also **come to**) to become conscious again □ *sedar semula*: *She hasn't come round from the anaesthetic yet.* **OPP** **pass out** **2** (used about an event that happens regularly) to happen □ *tiba; datang*: *The end of the holidays always comes round very quickly.*

come round (to ...) to visit a person or place not far away □ *datang*: *Do you want to come round for lunch on Saturday?*

come round (to sth) to change your opinion so that you agree with sb/sth □ *mengubah fikiran; bersetuju*: *They finally came round to our way of thinking.*

come through (used about news, information, etc.) to arrive □ *sampai; diterima*: *The football results are just coming through.*

come through (sth) to escape injury or death in a dangerous situation, illness, etc. □ *selamat (drpd sst)*: *She was lucky to come through the operation.*

come to = **come round** (1)

come to sth 1 to equal or total a particular amount □ *berjumlah*: *The bill for the meal came to £35.* **2** to result in a bad situation □ *sampai ke (sst keadaan, kedudukan, dsb)*: *We will sell the house to pay our debts if we have to but we hope it won't come to that.*

come under sth to be included in a particular section, department, etc. □ *termasuk di bawah (sst tajuk, kategori, dsb)*: *Garages that sell cars come under 'car dealers' in the telephone book.*

come up 1 (used about a plant) to appear above the soil □ *tumbuh* **2** (used about the sun and moon) to rise □ *terbit; naik* **3** to happen or be going to happen in the future □ *berlaku; timbul; hal (yg terjadi)*: *Something's come up at work so I won't be home until late tonight.* **4** to be discussed or mentioned □ *timbul; dibangkitkan*: *The subject of religion came up.*

come up against sb/sth to find a problem or difficulty that you have to deal with □ *berhadapan dgn atau menghadapi sso/sst*: *We came up against a very strong team in the first match.*

come up to sth to be as good as usual or as necessary □ *sampai ke (taraf, peringkat, dll) tertentu; spt*: *This piece of work does not come up to your usual standard.*

come up with sth to find an answer or a solution to sth □ *mendapat (jawapan, penyelesaian, dsb)*: *Engineers have come up with new ways of saving energy.*

comeback /ˈkʌmbæk/ *noun* [C] a return to a position of strength or importance that you had before □ *(cuba) kembali ke tahap (kekuatan, kepentingan, dsb) yg sebelumnya*: *The former world champion is hoping to make a comeback.*

comedian /kəˈmiːdiən/ (also **comic**) *noun* [C] a person whose job is to entertain people and make them laugh, for example by telling jokes □ *pelawak*

comedown /ˈkʌmdaʊn/ *noun* [sing] (*informal*) a loss of importance or social position □ *jatuh martabat*: *It's a bit of a comedown for her having to move to a smaller flat.*

comedy /ˈkɒmədi/ *noun* (*pl* **comedies**) **1** [C] an amusing play, film, etc. that has a happy ending □ *drama/filem komedi*: *a romantic comedy* ⊃ look at **tragedy 2** [U] the quality of being amusing or making people laugh □ *kelucuan*: *There is a hint of comedy in all her novels.* **SYN** **humour**

comet /ˈkɒmɪt/ *noun* [C] an object in space that looks like a bright star with a tail and that moves around the sun □ *komet*

comfort¹ /ˈkʌmfət/ *noun* **1** [U] the state of having everything your body needs, or of having a pleasant life □ *selesa*: *Most people expect to live in comfort in their old age.* ♦ *to travel in comfort* **2** [U] the feeling of being physically relaxed and in no pain □ *keselesaan*: *This car has been specially designed for extra comfort.* **OPP** **discomfort 3** [U] help or kindness to sb who is suffering □ *sst yg melegakan*: *I tried to offer a few words of comfort.* **4** [sing] **be a comfort (to sb)** a person or thing that helps you when you are very sad or worried □ *sso/sst yg membawa rasa lega*: *You've been a real comfort to me.* **5** [C] something that makes your life easier or more pleasant □ *keselesaan; kemudahan*: *the comforts of home*

comfort² /ˈkʌmfət/ *verb* [T] to try to make sb feel less worried or unhappy □ *melegakan; menenangkan hati*: *to comfort a crying child*

comfortable /ˈkʌmftəbl/ *adj* **1** (also *informal* **comfy** /ˈkʌmfi/) that makes you feel physically relaxed and in no pain; that provides you with everything your body needs □ *selesa*: *a comfortable temperature* (= not too hot or too cold) ♦ *Sit down and make yourselves comfortable.* ♦ *a comfortable pair of shoes* **OPP** **uncomfortable 2** not having or causing worry, difficulty, etc. □ *selesa*: *He did not feel comfortable in the presence of so many women.* **3** having or providing enough money for all your needs □ *hidup selesa*: *My parents are not wealthy but they're quite comfortable.* ▶ **comfortably** /-əbli/ *adv*: *Jon was sitting comfortably in the armchair.* ♦ *You can't live comfortably on such low wages.*

comic¹ /ˈkɒmɪk/ *adj* that makes you laugh; connected with amusing entertainment □ *lucu*: *a comic scene in a play*

comic² /ˈkɒmɪk/ *noun* [C] **1** = **comedian 2** (especially *AmE* **ˈcomic book**) a magazine for children that tells stories through pictures □ *(buku) komik*

comical /ˈkɒmɪkl/ *adj* that makes you laugh; funny □ *(yg) melucukan* ▶ **comically** /-kli/ *adv*

ˈcomic book (especially *AmE*) = **comic²** (2)

ˈcomic strip (also **ˈstrip cartoon**) *noun* [C] a short series of pictures that tell a funny story, for example in a newspaper □ *komik*

coming /ˈkʌmɪŋ/ noun [sing] the moment when sth new arrives or begins □ *kedatangan*: *The coming of the computer meant the loss of many jobs.* ▶ **coming** adj [only before a noun]: *We've got a lot of plans for the coming year.*

comma /ˈkɒmə/ noun [C] the mark (,) used for dividing parts of a sentence or items in a list □ *koma*

command¹ /kəˈmɑːnd/ noun **1** [C] an order □ *perintah*: *The captain's commands must be obeyed without question.* **2** [C] an instruction given to a computer □ *arahan* **3** [U] control over sb/sth □ *kuasa memerintah/mengetuai*: *Who is in command of the expedition?* ◆ *to take command of a situation* **4** [sing] the state of being able to do or use sth well □ *penguasaan*: *She has a good command of French.*

IDM at/by sb's command (formal) because you were ordered by sb □ *atas arahan sso*: *At the command of their officer the troops opened fire.* **be at sb's command** to be ready to obey sb □ *bersedia menurut perintah sso*: *I'm completely at your command.*

command² /kəˈmɑːnd/ verb [T] **1** (formal) **command (sb to do sth)** to tell or order sb to do sth □ *memerintah*: *I command you to leave now!* **2 command sb/sth** to control or be in charge of sb/sth □ *mempunyai kuasa di atas sso/sst*: *to command an army/a regiment/a ship* **3** to deserve and get sth □ *mendapat*: *The old man commanded great respect.*

commandant /ˈkɒməndænt/ noun [C] the officer in charge of a particular group of people or institution □ *komandan*

commandeer /ˌkɒmənˈdɪə(r)/ verb [T] to take control or possession of sth for military or police use □ *merampas*

commander /kəˈmɑːndə(r)/ noun [C] **1** a person who controls or is in charge of a military organization or group □ *komander; ketua* **2** (BrE) an officer at a fairly high level in the navy □ *komander*

commanding /kəˈmɑːndɪŋ/ adj **1** [only before a noun] in charge of or having control of sb/sth □ *(yg) memerintah*: *Who is your commanding officer?* **2** strong or powerful □ *kuat; memerintah*: *to speak in a commanding tone of voice*

commandment (also **Commandment**) /kəˈmɑːndmənt/ noun [C] (formal) one of the ten important laws that Christian people should obey □ *rukun*

commando /kəˈmɑːndəʊ/ noun [C] (pl **commandos**) one of a group of soldiers who is trained to make sudden attacks in enemy areas □ *komando*

commemorate /kəˈmeməreɪt/ verb [T] to exist or take place in order to make people remember a special event □ *utk memperingati*: *a statue commemorating all the soldiers who died in the last war* ▶ **commemoration** /kəˌmeməˈreɪʃn/ noun [C,U]: *The concerts were held in commemoration of the 200th anniversary of Mozart's death.*

commence /kəˈmens/ verb [I,T] (formal) **commence sth/doing sth** to start or begin □ *bermula* ▶ **commencement** noun [C,U]

commend /kəˈmend/ verb [T] (formal) to say officially that sb/sth is very good □ *memuji; dipuji*: *Dean was commended for his excellent work.*

commendable /kəˈmendəbl/ adj (formal) that people think is good □ *patut dipuji*: *She acted with commendable honesty and fairness.*

comment¹ /ˈkɒment/ noun [C,U] **comment (on sth)** something that you say or write that gives your opinion or feeling about sth □ *komen; ulasan*: *The chancellor was not available for comment.* ◆ *I heard someone make a rude comment about my clothes.* ➔ look at **observation**, **remark**

IDM no comment used in reply to a question when you do not want to say anything at all □ *tdk ada komen*: *'Mr President, how do you feel about these latest developments?' 'No comment.'*

comment² /ˈkɒment/ verb [I] **comment (on sth)** to say what you think or feel about sth □ *membuat komen/ulasan; mengatakan*: *Several people commented on how ill David looked.* ◆ *He refused to comment until after the trial.*

commentary /ˈkɒməntri/ noun (pl **commentaries**) **1** [C,U] a spoken description on the radio or TV of sth as it is happening □ *ulasan*: *a sports commentary* **2** [C] a written explanation or discussion of sth such as a book or play □ *ulasan; komentar* **3** [C] something that shows what sth is like □ *gambaran*: *This drug scandal is a sad commentary on the state of the sport.* ◆ *These petty quarrels are a sad commentary on the state of the government.*

commentate /ˈkɒmənteɪt/ verb [I] **commentate (on sth)** to give a spoken description on the radio or TV of sth as it is happening □ *mengulas*

commentator /ˈkɒmənteɪtə(r)/ noun [C] **1** a person who gives their opinion about sth on the radio, on TV or in a newspaper □ *pengulas*: *a political commentator* **2** a person who gives a spoken description on radio or TV of sth as it is happening □ *pengulas*: *a sports commentator*

commerce /ˈkɒmɜːs/ noun [U] the business of buying and selling things □ *perdagangan*

commercial¹ /kəˈmɜːʃl/ adj **1** connected with buying and selling goods and services □ *(berkenaan dgn) perdagangan*: *commercial law* **2** selling sth or sold in large quantities to the public □ *komersial; perdagangan*: *commercial airlines* ◆ *commercial products* **3** [only before a noun] making or trying to make money □ *komersial; meraih keuntungan*: *Although it won a lot of awards, the film was not a commercial success.* ▶ **commercially** /-ʃəli/ adv: *The factory was closed down because it was no longer commercially viable.*

commercial → commonly 170

commercial² /kəˈmɜːʃl/ noun [C] an advertisement on TV or the radio □ *iklan*: *a commercial break* (= a space between TV programmes when commercials are shown)

commercialism /kəˈmɜːʃəlɪzəm/ noun [U] the attitude that making money is more important than anything else □ *sikap terlalu mementingkan keuntungan; komersialisme*

commercialize (also -ise) /kəˈmɜːʃəlaɪz/ verb [T] to try to make money out of sth, even if it means spoiling it □ *memperdagangkan; diperdagangkan*: *Christmas has become very commercialized over recent years.* ▶ **commercialization** (also -isation) /kəˌmɜːʃəlaɪˈzeɪʃn/ noun [U]

commiserate /kəˈmɪzəreɪt/ verb [I] (formal) **commiserate (with sb) (on/over/for sth)** to feel sorry for and show understanding towards sb who is unhappy or in difficulty □ *turut bersimpati dgn*: *I commiserated with Debbie over losing her job.*

¶ commission¹ /kəˈmɪʃn/ noun **1** often Commission [C] an official group of people who are asked to find out about sth □ *suruhanjaya*: *A Commission was appointed to investigate the causes of the accident.* **2** [C,U] money that you get for selling sth □ *komisen; dalal*: *Agents get 10% commission on everything they sell.* **3** [C,U] money that a bank, etc. charges for providing a particular service □ *komisen*: *The bureau de change charges 5% commission.* **4** [C] a formal request to an artist, a writer, etc. to produce a piece of work □ *kerja; tempahan*: *He received a commission to write a play for the festival.*

¶ commission² /kəˈmɪʃn/ verb [T] **commission sb (to do sth); commission sth (from sb)** to ask an artist, a writer, etc. to do a piece of work □ *meminta sso (seniman, dsb) menghasilkan sst karya; menempah*: *to commission an architect to design a building*

commissioner /kəˈmɪʃənə(r)/ noun [C] the head of the police or of a government department in some countries □ *pesuruhjaya*

¶ commit /kəˈmɪt/ verb [T] (**committing; committed**) **1** to do sth bad or illegal □ *melakukan*: *to commit a crime* **2** to kill yourself deliberately □ *bunuh diri*: *to commit suicide* **3 commit sb/yourself (to sth/to doing sth)** to make a definite agreement or promise to do sth □ *menjanjikan; berjanji*: *I can't commit myself to helping you tomorrow.* **4 commit yourself (on sth)** to make a decision or give an opinion publicly so that it is then difficult to change it □ *menyatakan pendapat ttg sst*: *I'm not going to commit myself on who will win the election.* ➔ look at **non-committal 5** (formal) to decide to use money or time in a certain way □ *memperuntukkan*: *The government has committed £2 billion to education.* **6** (formal) **commit sb to sth** to send sb to a prison, mental hospital, etc. □ *memasukkan*: *She was committed to a psychiatric hospital.*

¶ commitment /kəˈmɪtmənt/ noun **1** [C,U] a promise or an agreement to do sth; a responsibility □ *komitmen; tugas; tanggungjawab*: *When I make a commitment I always stick to it.* ♦ *Helen now works fewer hours because of family commitments.* **2** [U] **commitment (to sth)** being prepared to give a lot of your time and attention to sth because you believe it is right or important □ *komitmen; iltizam*: *I admire Gary's commitment to protecting the environment.*

committed /kəˈmɪtɪd/ adj **committed (to sth)** prepared to give a lot of your time and attention to sth because you believe it is right or important □ *komited; beriltizam*: *The company is committed to providing quality products.*

¶ committee /kəˈmɪti/ noun [C, with sing or pl verb] a group of people who have been chosen to discuss sth or decide sth □ *jawatankuasa*: *to be/sit on a committee* ♦ *The planning committee meets/meet twice a week.*

commodity /kəˈmɒdəti/ noun [C] (pl **commodities**) a product or material that can be bought and sold □ *komoditi; barangan*: *Salt was once a very valuable commodity.*

¶ common¹ /ˈkɒmən/ adj (**commoner; commonest**) [More common and most common are more frequent.] **1** happening or found often or in many places; usual □ *biasa; lazim*: *Pilot error is the commonest/most common cause of plane crashes.* ♦ *The daisy is a common wild flower.* **OPP uncommon 2 common (to sb/sth)** shared by or belonging to two or more people or groups; shared by most or all people □ *sama; umum; biasa*: *This type of behaviour is common to most children of that age.* ♦ *We have a common interest in gardening.* **3** [only before a noun] not special; ordinary □ *biasa*: *The officers had much better living conditions than the common soldiers.* **4** (BrE informal) having or showing a lack of education □ *spt orang kebanyakan; drpd kelas bawahan*: *Don't speak like that. It's common!*
IDM be common/public knowledge ➔ **knowledge**

common² /ˈkɒmən/ noun [C] an area of open land that anyone can use □ *padang (awam)*
IDM have sth in common (with sb/sth) to share sth with sb/sth else □ *mempunyai persamaan (dgn sso/sst)*: *to have a lot in common with somebody*
in common with sb/sth (formal) in the same way as sb/sth else; like sb/sth □ *spt juga yg lain*: *This company, in common with many others, is losing a lot of money.*

ˌcommon ˈground noun [U] beliefs, interests, etc. that two or more people or groups share □ *titik persamaan*

ˌcommon ˈlaw noun [U] laws in England that are based on decisions that judges have made, not laws that were made by Parliament □ *'common law'; undang-undang lazim*

¶ commonly /ˈkɒmənli/ adv normally; usually □ *biasanya*: *commonly held opinions* ♦ *Christopher is commonly known as Kit.*

commonplace /ˈkɒmənpleɪs/ adj not exciting or unusual; ordinary □ *biasa; lazim*: *Foreign travel has become commonplace in recent years.*

ˈ**common room** noun [C] a room in a school, university, etc. where students or teachers can go to relax when they are not in class □ *bilik rehat*

the Commons /ˈkɒmənz/ = The House of Commons

ˌ**common ˈsense** noun [U] the ability to make good sensible decisions or to behave in a sensible way □ *akal*

the Commonwealth /ˈkɒmənwelθ/ noun [sing] the group of countries that once formed the British Empire and that work together in a friendly way □ *Negara-negara Komanwel*

commotion /kəˈməʊʃn/ noun [sing, U] great noise or excitement □ *kekecohan*

communal /kəˈmjuːnl; ˈkɒmjənl/ adj shared by a group of people □ *komunal; bersama; umum*: *a communal kitchen*

commune /ˈkɒmjuːn/ noun [C, with sing or pl verb] a group of people, not from the same family, who live together and share their property and responsibilities □ *kumpulan; masyarakat*

⚡ **communicate** /kəˈmjuːnɪkeɪt/ verb 1 [I,T] to share and exchange information, ideas or feelings with sb □ *berhubung; berkomunikasi*: *Parents often have difficulty communicating with their teenage children.* ♦ *Our boss is good at communicating her ideas to the team.* 2 [T, usually passive] (*formal*) to pass a disease from one person or animal to another □ *menjangkitkan; merebakkan*: *The disease is communicated though dirty drinking water.* 3 [I] to lead from one place to another □ *bersambung*: *two rooms with a communicating door*

⚡ **communication** /kəˌmjuːnɪˈkeɪʃn/ noun 1 [U] the act of sharing or exchanging information, ideas or feelings □ *perhubungan; komunikasi*: *Radio is the only means of communication in remote areas.* ♦ *We are in regular communication with our head office in New York.* 2 [pl] **communications** [pl] the methods that are used for travelling to and from a place or for sending messages between places □ *perhubungan; komunikasi*: *The telephone lines are down so communications are very difficult.* 3 [C] (*formal*) a message □ *mesej*: *a communication from head office*

communicative /kəˈmjuːnɪkətɪv/ adj willing and able to talk and share ideas, etc. □ *berkomunikasi*: *Paolo has excellent communicative skills.*

communion /kəˈmjuːniən/ noun [U] 1 **Communion** a Christian church ceremony in which people share bread and wine □ *Perjamuan Suci* 2 (*formal*) the sharing of thoughts or feelings □ *perihal berkongsi fikiran atau perasaan*

communiqué /kəˈmjuːnɪkeɪ/ noun [C] an official statement, especially from a government, a political group, etc. □ *kenyataan*

communism /ˈkɒmjunɪzəm/ noun [U] the political system in which the state owns and controls all factories, farms, services, etc. and aims to treat everyone equally □ *komunisme* ➲ look at **capitalism, Marxism, socialism**

communist (also **Communist**) /ˈkɒmjənɪst/ noun [C] a person who believes in or supports **communism**; a member of the **Communist** Party □ *komunis* ▶ **communist** (also **Communist**) adj: *communist sympathies*

⚡ **community** /kəˈmjuːnəti/ noun (pl **communities**) 1 **the community** [sing] all the people who live in a particular place, area, etc. when considered as a group □ *masyarakat*: *Recent increases in crime have disturbed the whole community.* 2 [C, with sing or pl verb] a group of people who have sth in common □ *komuniti; golongan*: *the Asian community in Britain* ♦ *the business community* 3 [U] the feeling of belonging to a group in the place where you live □ *sikap muhibah*: *There is a strong sense of community in the neighbourhood.*

comˈmunity centre (*AmE* **comˈmunity center**) noun [C] a building that local people can use for meetings, classes, sports, etc. □ *balai raya*

commute /kəˈmjuːt/ verb [I] to travel by bus, train, car, etc. from home to work and back every day □ *berulang-alik*: *A lot of people commute to London from nearby towns.* ▶ **commuter** noun [C]

compact /kəmˈpækt/ adj small and easy to carry □ *kecil dan mudah dibawa; kompak*: *a compact camera*

ˌ**compact ˈdisc** = CD

companion /kəmˈpæniən/ noun [C] a person or an animal who you spend a lot of time or go somewhere with □ *teman*: *a travelling companion*

companionship /kəmˈpæniənʃɪp/ noun [U] the pleasant feeling of having a friendly relationship with sb and not being alone □ *persahabatan; perihal berteman*

⚡ **company** /ˈkʌmpəni/ noun (abbr **Co.**) (pl **companies**) 1 [C, with sing or pl verb] a business organization selling goods or services □ *syarikat*: *The company is/are planning to build a new factory.*

HELP In names, **company** is written with a capital letter. The abbreviation is **Co.**: *the Walt Disney Company* ♦ *Milton & Co.*

2 [C, with sing or pl verb] a group of actors, singers, dancers, etc □ *kumpulan*: *a ballet company* ♦ *the Royal Shakespeare Company* 3 [U] being with a person □ *bertemankan sso; teman*: *I always enjoy Rachel's company.* ♦ *Jeffrey is very good company* (= pleasant to be with). 4 [U] a

VOWELS iː see   i any   ɪ sit   e ten   æ hat   ɑː father   ɒ got   ɔː saw   ʊ put   uː too   u usual

visitor or visitors □ *tamu*: *Sorry, I wouldn't have called if I'd known you had company.*
IDM **keep sb company** to go or be with sb so that they are not alone □ *menemankan sso*: *She was nervous, so I went with her to keep her company.*
part company ⊃ **part²**

comparable /ˈkɒmpərəbl/ *adj* **comparable (to/with sb/sth)** of a similar standard or size; that can be compared with sth □ *berbandingan*: *The population of Britain is comparable to that of France.* ♦ *A comparable flat in my country would be a lot cheaper.*

comparative¹ /kəmˈpærətɪv/ *adj* **1** that compares things of the same kind □ *perbandingan*: *a comparative study of systems of government* **2** compared with sth else or with what is usual or normal □ *jika dibandingkan; agak*: *He had problems with the written exam, but passed the practical exam with comparative ease.* **3** (used about the form of an adjective or adverb) expressing a greater amount, quality, size, etc. □ *perbandingan*: *'Hotter' and 'more quickly' are the comparative forms of 'hot' and 'quickly'.*

comparative² /kəmˈpærətɪv/ *noun* [C] the form of an adjective or adverb that expresses a greater amount, quality, size, etc. □ *bentuk perbandingan*: *'Bigger' is the comparative of 'big'.*

comparatively /kəmˈpærətɪvli/ *adv* when compared with sth else or with what is usual; fairly □ *secara perbandingan; agak*: *Fortunately, the disease is comparatively rare nowadays.*

⸮ compare /kəmˈpeə(r)/ *verb* **1** [T] (abbr cf.) **compare A and B; compare A with/to B** to consider people or things in order to see how similar or how different they are □ *membandingkan; dibandingkan*: *When the police compared the two letters, they realized that they had been written by the same person.* ♦ *I'm quite a patient person, compared with him.* ♦ *Compared to the place where I grew up, this town is exciting.* **2** [I] **compare (with/to sb/sth)** to be as good as sb/sth □ *setanding; sebaik*: *Her last film was brilliant but this one simply doesn't compare.* ♦ *There is nothing to compare with the taste of bread fresh from the oven.* **3** [T] **compare A to B** to say that sb/sth is similar to sb/sth else □ *menyamakan; menyifatkan*: *When it was built, people compared the stadium to a spaceship.*
IDM **compare notes (with sb)** to discuss your opinions, ideas, experiences, etc. with sb else □ *bertukar-tukar pendapat*: *At the beginning of term we met and compared notes about the holidays.*

⸮ comparison /kəmˈpærɪsn/ *noun* [C,U] an act of comparing; a statement in which people or things are compared □ *perbandingan*: *Put the new one and the old one side by side, for comparison.* ♦ *It's hard to make comparisons between two athletes from different sports.*
IDM **by/in comparison (with sb/sth)** when compared □ *jika dibandingkan (dgn sso/sst)*: *In comparison with many other people, they're quite well off.*

compartment /kəmˈpɑːtmənt/ *noun* [C] **1** one of the separate sections which railway carriages (= the parts of a train) are divided into □ *kompartmen; bahagian*: *a first-class compartment* **2** one of the separate sections into which certain containers are divided □ *bahagian; petak*: *the glove compartment* (= the space where you can keep maps, etc. in a car)

compasses

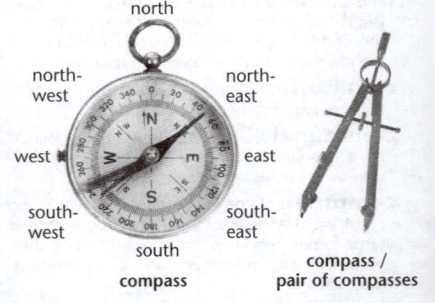

compass

compass / pair of compasses

compass /ˈkʌmpəs/ *noun* [C] **1** an instrument for finding direction, with a needle that always points north □ *kompas*: *the points of the compass* (= North, South, East, West, etc.) ♦ *They had to find their way back to the camp using a map and a compass.* **2** **compasses** [pl] a V-shaped instrument that is used for drawing circles □ *kompas; jangka lukis*: *Use a pair of compasses.*

compassion /kəmˈpæʃn/ *noun* [U] **compassion (for sb)** understanding or pity for sb who is suffering □ *belas kasihan*: *to have/feel/show compassion* ▶ **compassionate** /kəmˈpæʃənət/ *adj*

compatible /kəmˈpætəbl/ *adj* **compatible (with sb/sth)** able to be used together, or to live or exist together □ *serasi; bersesuaian*: *These two computer systems are not compatible.* ♦ *Lee's diet is not compatible with his active lifestyle.* **OPP** **incompatible** ▶ **compatibility** /kəmˌpætəˈbɪləti/ *noun* [U]

compatriot /kəmˈpætriət/ *noun* [C] a person who comes from the same country as you □ *teman senegeri*

compel /kəmˈpel/ *verb* [T] (**compelling; compelled**) (*formal*) **compel sb to do sth** to force sb to do sth □ *memaksa*: *I felt compelled to tell her what I really thought of her.*

compelling /kəmˈpelɪŋ/ *adj* that forces or persuades you to do or to believe sth □ *amat menarik; meyakinkan*: *compelling evidence* ⊃ *noun* **compulsion**

compensate /ˈkɒmpenseɪt/ *verb* **1** [I] **compensate (for sth)** to remove or reduce the bad effect of sth □ *menyilih; menggantikan*;

mengimbangi: *His willingness to work hard compensates for his lack of skill.* **2** [I,T] **compensate (sb) (for sth)** to pay sb money because you have injured them or lost or damaged their property □ *mengganti rugi; membayar pampasan*: *The airline offered to compensate me for losing my luggage.*

compensation /ˌkɒmpenˈseɪʃn/ *noun* **1** [U] **compensation (for sth)** money that you pay to sb because you have injured them or lost or damaged their property □ *pampasan*: *I got £5 000 (in) compensation for my injuries.* **2** [C,U] a fact or an action that removes or reduces the bad effect of sth □ *kelebihannya*: *City life can be very tiring but there are compensations* (= good things about it).

compère /ˈkɒmpeə(r)/ *noun* [C] (*BrE*) a person who entertains the audience and introduces the different people who perform in a show □ *pengacara/juruacara* ▸ **compère** *verb* [T]: *Who compèred the show?*

compete /kəmˈpiːt/ *verb* [I] **compete (in sth) (against/with sb) (for sth)** to try to win or achieve sth, or to try to be better than sb else □ *bertanding; berlumba; bersaing*: *The world's best athletes compete in the Olympic Games.* ◆ *We'll be competing against seven other teams for the trophy.* ◆ *As children, they always used to compete with each other.* ◆ *Supermarkets have such low prices that small shops just can't compete.*

competence /ˈkɒmpɪtəns/ *noun* [U] the fact of having the ability or skill that is needed for sth □ *kecekapan*: *She quickly proved her competence in her new position.* **OPP** **incompetence**

competent /ˈkɒmpɪtənt/ *adj* **1** having the ability or skill needed for sth □ *cekap*: *a highly competent player* ◆ *Isobel is competent at her job.* **OPP** **incompetent** **2** good enough, but not excellent □ *agak memuaskan*: *The singer gave a competent, but not particularly exciting, performance.* ▸ **competently** *adv*

competition /ˌkɒmpəˈtɪʃn/ *noun* **1** [U] a situation where two or more people or organizations are trying to achieve, obtain, etc. the same thing or to be better than sb else □ *persaingan*: *He is in competition with three other people for promotion.* ◆ *There was fierce competition among the players for places in the team.* **2** [C] an organized event in which people try to win sth □ *pertandingan*: *to take part in/go in for/enter a competition* ◆ *They hold a competition every year to find the best young artist.* ◆ *He came second in an international piano competition.* **3 the competition** [sing, with sing or pl verb] the other people, companies, etc. who are trying to achieve the same as you □ *saingan; bersaing*: *If we are going to succeed, we must offer a better product than the competition.*

competitive /kəmˈpetətɪv/ *adj* **1** involving people or organizations competing against each other □ *(berkenaan dgn) persaingan/ pertandingan*: *The travel industry is a highly competitive business.* ◆ *competitive sports* **2** able to be as successful as or more successful than

others □ *dpt bersaing*: *They are trying to make the company competitive in the international market.* ◆ *Our prices are highly competitive* (= as low as or lower than those of the others). **3** (used about people) wanting very much to win or to be more successful than others □ *suka persaingan*: *She's a very competitive player.* ▸ **competitively** *adv*: *Their products are competitively priced.* ▸ **competitiveness** *noun* [U]

competitor /kəmˈpetɪtə(r)/ *noun* [C] a person or an organization that is competing against others □ *pesaing; peserta*: *There are ten competitors in the first race.* ◆ *Two local companies are our main competitors.*

compilation /ˌkɒmpɪˈleɪʃn/ *noun* **1** [C] a collection of pieces of music, writing, film, etc. that are taken from different places and put together □ *susunan; himpunan*: *A compilation CD of the band's greatest hits.* **2** [U] the act of compiling □ *penyusunan*

compile /kəmˈpaɪl/ *verb* [T] to collect information and arrange it in a list, book, etc. □ *menyusun*: *to compile a dictionary/a report/a list*

complacent /kəmˈpleɪsnt/ *adj* feeling too satisfied with yourself or with a situation, so that you think that there is no need to worry □ *berpuas hati*: *He had won his matches so easily that he was in danger of becoming complacent.* ▸ **complacency** /kəmˈpleɪsnsi/ *noun* [U] ▸ **complacently** *adv*

complain /kəmˈpleɪn/ *verb* [I] **complain (to sb) (about sth/that …)** to say that you are not satisfied with or happy about sth □ *merungut; membuat aduan*: *We complained to the hotel manager that the room was too noisy.* ◆ *People are always complaining about the weather.* ⊃ note at **protest**

PHR V **complain of sth** to say that you have a pain or illness □ *mengadu; mengatakan ada (sakit)*: *He went to the doctor, complaining of headaches.*

complaint /kəmˈpleɪnt/ *noun* **complaint (about sth); complaint (that …)** **1** [C] a statement that you are not satisfied with sth □ *aduan*: *You should make a complaint to the company that made the machine.* **2** [U] the act of complaining □ *pengaduan; rungutan*: *I wrote a letter of complaint to the manager about the terrible service I had received.* ◆ *Jim's behaviour never gave the teachers cause for complaint.* **3** [C] an illness or a disease □ *penyakit*: *a serious heart complaint*

complement¹ /ˈkɒmplɪmənt/ *noun* [C] (*formal*) **1** a thing that goes together well with sth else □ *pelengkap*: *A cream sauce is the perfect complement to this dessert.* **2** the total number that makes a group complete □ *bilangan yg cukup*: *Without a full complement of players, the team will not be able to take part in the match.* **3** a word or words, especially a noun or an adjective, used after a verb such as 'be' or 'become' and describing the subject of that verb □ *pelengkap*:

In 'I'm angry' and 'He became a teacher', 'angry' and 'teacher' are complements.

complement² /ˈkɒmplɪment/ verb [T] to go together well with □ *melengkap; bersesuaian*: *The colours of the furniture and the carpet complement each other.*

complementary /ˌkɒmplɪˈmentri/ adj going together well with sb/sth; adding sth which the other person or thing does not have □ *saling melengkapi*: *They work well together because their skills are complementary: he's practical and she's creative.*

complete¹ /kəmˈpliːt/ adj 1 [only before a noun] as great as possible; in every way □ *betul-betul*: *It was a complete waste of time.* ◆ *The room is a complete mess.* ◆ *We were in complete agreement.* SYN **total** 2 having or including all parts; with nothing missing □ *lengkap; sempurna; sepenuhnya*: *I gave a complete list of the stolen items to the police.* ◆ *The book explains the complete history of the place.* OPP **incomplete** 3 [not before a noun] **complete (with sth)** including sth extra, in addition to what is expected □ *lengkap*: *The computer comes complete with instruction manual and printer.* 4 [not before a noun] finished or ended □ *siap; sudah*: *The repair work should be complete by Friday.* OPP **incomplete** ▶ **completeness** noun [U]

complete² /kəmˈpliːt/ verb [T] 1 to finish sth; to bring sth to an end □ *menyiapkan; siap; tamat*: *When the building has been completed, it will look impressive.* ◆ *He completed his teacher training course in June 2005.* 2 to write all the necessary information on sth (for example a form) □ *mengisi; isikan*: *Please complete the following in capital letters.* 3 to make sth whole □ *melengkapkan*: *We need two more players to complete the team.*

completely /kəmˈpliːtli/ adv in every way; fully □ *seluruhnya; betul-betul; sama sekali*: *The building was completely destroyed by fire.* ◆ *I've completely forgotten her name.* SYN **totally**

completion /kəmˈpliːʃn/ noun [U] (formal) the act of finishing sth or the state of being finished □ *penyiapan; siap*: *You will be paid on completion of the work.* ◆ *The new motorway is due for completion within two years.*

complex¹ /ˈkɒmpleks/ adj made up of several connected parts and often difficult to understand □ *rumit; kompleks*: *a complex system of taxation* ◆ *a complex problem/subject* SYN **complicated**

complex² /ˈkɒmpleks/ noun [C] 1 a group of connected things, especially buildings □ *kompleks*: *a shopping/sports complex* 2 **a complex (about sth)** a mental problem that makes sb worry a lot about sth □ *kompleks; gangguan jiwa*: *He's got a complex about his height.* ◆ *an inferiority complex*

complexion /kəmˈplekʃn/ noun [C] 1 the natural colour and quality of the skin on your face □ *kulit muka*: *a dark/fair complexion* ◆ *a healthy complexion* 2 [usually sing] the general nature or character of sth □ *wajah; rupa atau keadaan*: *These recent announcements put a different complexion on our situation.*

complexity /kəmˈpleksəti/ noun (pl **complexities**) 1 [U] the state of being **complex** and difficult to understand □ *kompleksiti; kekompleksan*: *an issue of great complexity* 2 [C] one of the many details that make sth complicated □ *kerumitan; butir-butir yg rumit*: *I haven't time to explain the complexities of the situation now.*

compliant /kəmˈplaɪənt/ adj (formal) **compliant (with sth)** working or done in agreement with particular rules, orders, etc □ *mematuhi; menepati*: *All new products must be compliant with EU specifications.* ▶ **compliance** noun [U]: *A hard hat must be worn at all times in compliance with safety regulations.*

complicate /ˈkɒmplɪkeɪt/ verb [T] to make sth difficult to understand or deal with □ *merumitkan; menyulitkan*: *Let's not complicate things by adding too many details.*

complicated /ˈkɒmplɪkeɪtɪd/ adj made of many different things or parts that are connected; difficult to understand □ *rumit*: *a novel with a very complicated plot* ◆ *The instructions look very complicated.* SYN **complex**

complication /ˌkɒmplɪˈkeɪʃn/ noun [C] 1 something that makes a situation hard to understand or to deal with □ *kerumitan; keadaan rumit*: *Unless there are any unexpected complications, I'll be arriving next month.* 2 a new illness that you get when you are already ill □ *komplikasi*: *She developed complications after the operation.*

complicity /kəmˈplɪsəti/ noun [U] (formal) the fact of being involved with sb else in a crime □ *persubahatan*

compliment¹ /ˈkɒmplɪmənt/ noun 1 [C] **a compliment (on sth)** a statement or action that shows admiration for sb □ *pujian*: *People often pay her compliments on her piano playing.* 2 **compliments** [pl] (formal) used to say that you like sth or to thank sb for sth □ *ihsan; pemberian*: *Tea and coffee are provided with the compliments of the hotel management* (= without charge).

compliment² /ˈkɒmplɪment/ verb [T] **compliment sb (on sth)** to say that you think sb/sth is very good □ *memuji*: *She complimented them on their smart appearance.*

complimentary /ˌkɒmplɪˈmentri/ adj 1 given free of charge □ *percuma*: *a complimentary theatre ticket* 2 showing that you think sb/sth is very good □ *pujian; bersifat memuji*: *He made several complimentary remarks about her work.*

comply /kəmˈplaɪ/ verb [I] (complying; complies; pt, pp complied) (formal) comply (with sth) to obey an order or a request □ *mematuhi*: *All school buildings must comply with the fire and safety regulations.*

component /kəmˈpəʊnənt/ noun [C] one of several parts of which sth is made □ *bahagian; komponen*: *The human eye has two main components.* ♦ *the components of a machine/system* ▶ **component** *adj* [only before a noun]: *the component parts of an engine*

compose /kəmˈpəʊz/ verb 1 [T] to be the parts that together form sth □ *membentuk*: *the parties that compose the coalition government* 2 [I,T] to write music □ *menggubah*: *Mozart composed forty-one symphonies.* 3 [T] to produce a piece of writing, using careful thought □ *mengarang; menulis*: *I sat down and composed a letter of reply.* 4 [T] to make yourself, your feelings, etc. become calm and under control □ *menenangkan*: *The news came as such a shock that it took me a while to compose myself.*

composed /kəmˈpəʊzd/ *adj* 1 composed of sth made or formed from several different parts, people, etc. □ *terdiri drpd*: *The committee is composed of politicians from all parties.* 2 calm, in control of your feelings □ *tenang*: *Although he felt very nervous, he managed to appear composed.*

composer /kəmˈpəʊzə(r)/ *noun* [C] a person who writes music □ *penggubah*

composite /ˈkɒmpəzɪt/ *adj* [only before a noun] consisting of different parts or materials □ *komposit; (yg terdiri drpd) gabungan* ▶ **composite** *noun* [C]

composition /ˌkɒmpəˈzɪʃn/ *noun* 1 [U] the parts that form sth; the way in which the parts of sth are arranged □ *komposisi; kandungan*: *the chemical composition of a substance* ♦ *the composition of the population* 2 [C] a piece of music that has been written by sb □ *gubahan*: *Chopin's best-known compositions* ⊃ note at **music** 3 [U] the act or skill of writing a piece of music or text □ *penggubahan; mengarang*: *She studied both musical theory and composition.* 4 [C] a short piece of writing done at school, in an exam, etc. □ *karangan*: *Write a composition of about 300 words on one of the following subjects.*

compost /ˈkɒmpɒst/ *noun* [U] a mixture of dead plants, old food, etc. that is added to soil to help plants grow □ *kompos* ▶ **compost** *verb* [T]

composure /kəmˈpəʊʒə(r)/ *noun* [U] the state of being calm and having your feelings under control □ *ketenangan*: *The goalkeeper couldn't regain his composure after his mistake.*

compound¹ /ˈkɒmpaʊnd/ *noun* [C] 1 something that consists of two or more things or substances combined together □ *sebatian*: *a chemical compound* 2 a word or phrase consisting of two or more parts that combine to make a single meaning □ *kata majmuk*: *'Car park' and 'bad-tempered' are compounds.* 3 an area of land with a group of buildings on it, surrounded by a wall or fence □ *kawasan; pekarangan*

compound² /kəmˈpaʊnd/ *verb* [T] to make sth such as a problem worse □ *memburukkan lagi*

comprehend /ˌkɒmprɪˈhend/ *verb* [T] (formal) to understand sth completely □ *memahami*: *She's too young to comprehend what has happened.*

comprehensible /ˌkɒmprɪˈhensəbl/ *adj* easy to understand □ *dapat difahami*: *The book is written in language that is clear and comprehensible.* **OPP** incomprehensible

comprehension /ˌkɒmprɪˈhenʃn/ *noun* 1 [U] (formal) the ability to understand □ *pemahaman*: *The horror of war is beyond comprehension.* **OPP** incomprehension 2 [C,U] an exercise that tests how well you understand spoken or written language □ *kefahaman*: *a listening comprehension* ⊃ note at **skim**

comprehensive¹ /ˌkɒmprɪˈhensɪv/ *adj* 1 including everything or nearly everything that is connected with a particular subject □ *menyeluruh; komprehensif*: *a guide book giving comprehensive information on the area* 2 (BrE) (used about education) teaching children of all levels of ability in the same school □ *komprehensif*: *a comprehensive education system*

comprehensive² /ˌkɒmprɪˈhensɪv/ (also compre'hensive school) *noun* [C] (BrE) a secondary school in which children of all levels of ability are educated □ *sekolah komprehensif*: *My sister went to the local comprehensive.*

comprehensively /ˌkɒmprɪˈhensɪvli/ *adv* completely □ *secara menyeluruh/komprehensif* **SYN** thoroughly

compreˈhensive school (BrE) = comprehensive²

compress /kəmˈpres/ *verb* [T] compress sth (into sth) to make sth fill less space than usual □ *memampatkan; dimampat; meringkaskan*: *Divers breathe compressed air from tanks.* ♦ *He found it hard to compress his ideas into a single page.* ▶ **compression** /kəmˈpreʃn/ *noun* [U]

comprise /kəmˈpraɪz/ *verb* [T] 1 to consist of; to have as parts or members □ *terdiri drpd; mempunyai*: *a house comprising three bedrooms, kitchen, bathroom and a living room* 2 to form or be part of sth □ *membentuk*: *Women comprise 62% of the staff.*

compromise¹ /ˈkɒmprəmaɪz/ *noun* [C,U] a compromise (between/on sth) an agreement that is reached when each person gets part, but not all, of what they wanted □ *kompromi; kata sepakat*: *to reach a compromise* ♦ *Both sides will have to be prepared to make compromises.*

compromise² /ˈkɒmprəmaɪz/ *verb* 1 [I] compromise (with sb) (on sth) to accept less than you want or are aiming for, especially in order to reach an agreement □ *berkompromi*: *Unless both sides are prepared to compromise,*

compulsion → computer

there will be no peace agreement. ♦ *The company never compromises on the quality of its products.* **2** [T] compromise sb/sth/yourself to put sb/sth/yourself in a bad or dangerous position, especially by doing sth that is not very sensible □ *menjelaskan*: *He compromised himself by accepting money from them.*

compulsion /kəmˈpʌlʃn/ *noun* **1** [U] the act of forcing sb to do sth or being forced to do sth □ *paksaan*: *There is no compulsion to take part. You can decide yourself.* ⊃ *verb* compel **2** [C] a strong desire that you cannot control, often to do sth that you should not do □ *keinginan*: *Though I knew it was wrong, I felt a strong compulsion to laugh.* **SYN** urge

compulsive /kəmˈpʌlsɪv/ *adj* **1** (used about a bad or harmful habit) caused by a strong desire that you cannot control □ *kerana desakan nafsu; kuat*: *compulsive eating* **2** (used about a person) having a bad habit that they cannot control □ *suka; kaki (judi, dll)*: *a compulsive gambler/shoplifter* **3** so interesting or exciting that you cannot take your attention away from it □ *sangat menarik*: *This book makes compulsive reading.* ► **compulsively** *adv*

compulsory /kəmˈpʌlsəri/ *adj* that must be done, by law, rules, etc. □ *wajib*: *Maths and English are compulsory subjects on this course.* ♦ *It is compulsory to wear a hard hat on the building site.* **SYN** obligatory **OPP** optional, voluntary

compute /kəmˈpjuːt/ *verb* [T] (*formal*) to calculate sth □ *menghitung*

computer /kəmˈpjuːtə(r)/ *noun* [C] an electronic machine that can store, find and arrange information, calculate amounts and control other machines □ *komputer*: *The bills are all done by computer.* ♦ *a computer program* ♦ *a home/personal computer* ♦ *computer software/games* ♦ *First of all, the details are fed into a computer.* ⊃ note at **Internet**

TOPIC

Computers
Most people use their **computers** for sending and receiving **emails** and for **word processing** (= writing letters, reports, etc.). You can also use **the Internet**, play **computer games** or watch **DVDs**. You **log in/on** with your

computer

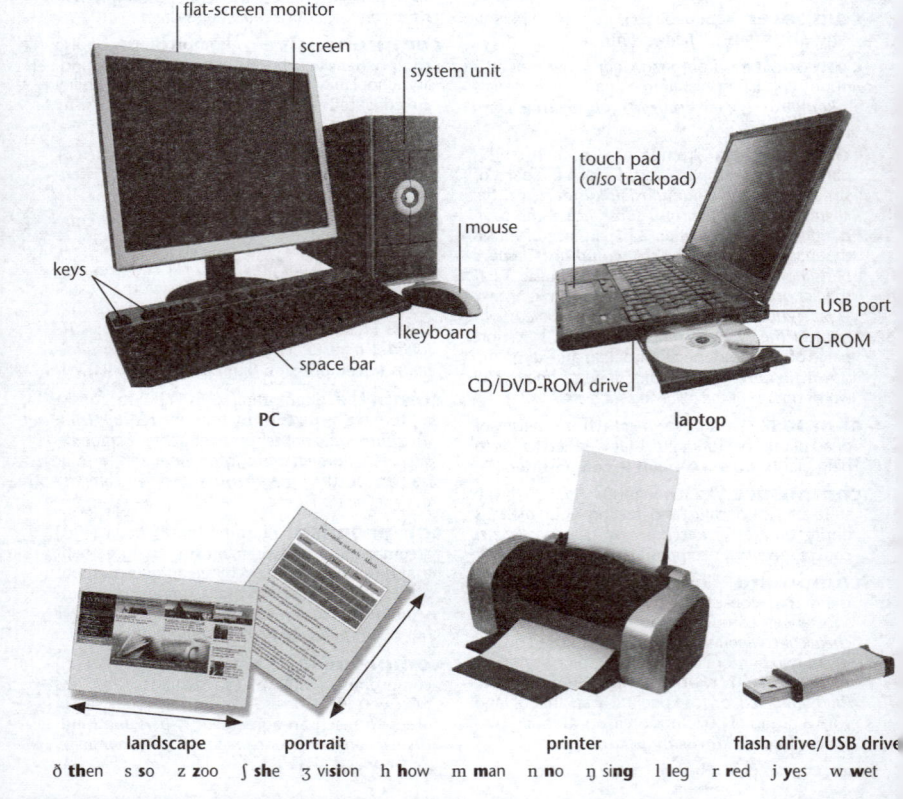

- flat-screen monitor
- screen
- system unit
- touch pad (*also* trackpad)
- mouse
- USB port
- CD-ROM
- keys
- keyboard
- space bar
- CD/DVD-ROM drive

PC   **laptop**

landscape   portrait   printer   flash drive/USB drive

ð **th**en   s **s**o   z **z**oo   ʃ **sh**e   ʒ vi**s**ion   h **h**ow   m **m**an   n **n**o   ŋ si**ng**   l **l**eg   r **r**ed   j **y**es   w **w**et

username and **password**. You **type in** words on a **keyboard** and **print out** documents on a **printer**. Information is displayed on the **screen** and you select the **icons** (= small pictures or symbols) using a **mouse**. **Data** (= information) is stored in **files** on the **hard disk**, on a **flash drive** or **CD-ROM**. The **programs** that are used to operate a computer are called **software**. A computer that you use at work or home is a **PC** or **desktop**. A **laptop** is a small computer that you can carry around with you and a **tablet** is a very small, flat computer that you work by touching the screen.

computerize (also **-ise**) /kəmˈpjuːtəraɪz/ verb [T] to use computers to do a job or to store information □ *mengkomputerkan; dikomputerkan*: *The whole factory has been computerized.* ♦ *We have now computerized the library catalogue.* ▶ **computerization** (also **-isation**) /kəmˌpjuːtəraɪˈzeɪʃn/ noun [U]

com,puter-'literate adj able to use a computer □ *celik komputer*

computing /kəmˈpjuːtɪŋ/ noun [U] the use of computers □ *pengkomputeran; penggunaan komputer*: *She did a course in computing.*

comrade /ˈkɒmreɪd/ noun [C] **1** a person who is a member of the same political party as the person speaking □ *komrad* **2** (old-fashioned) a friend or other person that you work with, especially as soldiers during a war □ *sahabat*: *They were old army comrades.* ▶ **comradeship** noun [U]

Con abbr = Conservative² (2)

con¹ /kɒn/ noun [C] (informal) a trick, especially in order to cheat sb out of some money □ *penipuan*
IDM the pros and cons ⊃ pro

con² /kɒn/ verb [T] (**conning**; **conned**) (informal) **con sb (into doing sth/out of sth)** to cheat sb, especially in order to get money □ *menipu; ditipu*: *He conned her into investing in a company that didn't really exist.* ♦ *The old lady was conned out of her life savings.*

concave /kɒnˈkeɪv/ (AmE also) / adj having a surface that curves towards the inside of sth, like the inside of a bowl □ *cekung* ⊃ look at **convex**

conceal /kənˈsiːl/ verb [T] (formal) **conceal sth/sb (from sb/sth)** to hide sb/sth; to prevent sb/sth from being seen or discovered □ *menyembunyikan*: *She tried to conceal her anger from her friend.* ▶ **concealment** noun [U]: *the concealment of the facts of the case*

concede /kənˈsiːd/ verb [T] (formal) **1** to admit that sth is true although you do not want to □ *mengakui; menerima hakikat*: *When it was clear that he would lose the election, he conceded defeat.* ♦ *She conceded that the problem was mostly her fault.* **2 concede sth (to sb)** to allow sb to take sth although you do not want to □ *menyerahkan*: *They lost the war and had to concede territory to their enemy.* ⊃ noun **concession**

conceit /kənˈsiːt/ noun [U] too much pride in yourself and your abilities and importance □ *keangkuhan; sikap bongkak* ▶ **conceited** adj: *He's so conceited—he thinks he's the best at everything!*

conceivable /kənˈsiːvəbl/ adj possible to imagine or believe □ *dpt difikirkan/dipercayai; (yg) mungkin*: *I made every conceivable effort to succeed in my new career.* **SYN** possible **OPP** inconceivable ▶ **conceivably** /-əbli/ adv: *She might just conceivably be telling the truth.*

conceive /kənˈsiːv/ verb **1** [T] (formal) to think of a new idea or plan □ *memikirkan*: *He conceived the idea for the novel during his journey through India.* **2** [I,T] (formal) **conceive (of) sb/sth (as sth)** to think about sb/sth in a particular way; to imagine □ *membayangkan; memikirkan*: *He started to conceive of the world as a dangerous place.* **3** [I,T] to become pregnant □ *mengandung; hamil* ⊃ noun **conception**

concentrate /ˈkɒnsntreɪt/ verb [I,T] **concentrate (sth) (on sth/doing sth)** to give all your attention or effort to sth □ *menumpukan (perhatian, usaha, dsb)*: *I need to concentrate on passing this exam.* ♦ *I tried to concentrate my thoughts on the problem.* **2** to come together or to bring people or things together in one place □ *tertumpu*: *Most factories are concentrated in one small area of the town.*

concentrated /ˈkɒnsntreɪtɪd/ adj **1** showing determination □ *bersungguh-sungguh*: *With one concentrated effort we can finish the work by tonight.* **2** made stronger by removing some liquid □ *pekat*: *This is concentrated orange juice. You have to add water before you drink it.*

concentration /ˌkɒnsnˈtreɪʃn/ noun **1** [U] **concentration (on sth)** the ability to give all your attention or effort to sth □ *daya penumpuan*: *This type of work requires total concentration.* ♦ *Don't lose (your) concentration or you might make a mistake.* **2** [C] **concentration (of sth)** a large amount of people or things in one place □ *penumpuan; kepekatan*: *There is a high concentration of chemicals in the drinking water here.*

concen'tration camp noun [C] a prison (usually a number of buildings inside a high fence) where political prisoners are kept in very bad conditions □ *kem tahanan*

concentric /kənˈsentrɪk/ adj (used about circles of different sizes) having the same centre point □ *sepusat*

concept /ˈkɒnsept/ noun [C] **the concept (of sth/that ...)** an idea; a basic principle □ *konsep*:

concentric circles

convex   concave

*It is difficult to **grasp the concept** of eternity.* ▶ **conceptual** /kənˈseptʃuəl/ *adj*

conception /kənˈsepʃn/ *noun* **1** [U] the process of forming an idea or a plan □ *pemikiran* **2** [C,U] **(a) conception (of sth)** an understanding of how or what sth is □ *konsepsi; tanggapan; pengertian*: *We have no real conception of what people suffered during the war.* **3** [C,U] the moment when a woman or female animal becomes pregnant □ *penghamilan* ⊃ *verb* **conceive**

concern¹ /kənˈsɜːn/ *verb* [T] **1** [often passive] to affect or involve sb/sth □ *melibatkan; kenamengena; dr segi*: *This does not concern you. Please go away.* ♦ *It is important that no risks are taken where safety is concerned.* **2** [often passive] to be about sth □ *mengenai; berkenaan dgn*: *The main problem concerns the huge cost of the project.* ♦ *Tonight's programme is concerned with the effects of the law on ordinary people.* **3** to worry sb □ *merisaukan*: *What concerns me is that we have no long-term plan.* **4 concern yourself with sth** to give your attention to sth □ *memberi perhatian; susah-susahkan (diri)*: *You needn't concern yourself with the hotel booking. The travel agent will take care of it.*

concern² /kənˈsɜːn/ *noun* **1** [C,U] **concern (for/about/over sb/sth); concern (that ...)** a feeling of worry; something that causes worry □ *perasaan risau; perkara yg merisaukan*: *The safety officer assured us that there was no **cause for concern**.* ♦ *My main concern is that we'll run out of money.* **2** [C] something that is important to you or that involves you □ *urusan*: *Financial matters are not my concern.* **3** [C] a company or business □ *syarikat; perniagaan*: *a large industrial concern*
IDM a going concern ⊃ **going²**

concerned /kənˈsɜːnd/ *adj* **concerned (about/for sth); concerned (that ...)** worried and feeling concern about sth □ *risau; bimbang*: *If you are concerned about your baby's health you should consult a doctor immediately.* **OPP** **unconcerned**

concerning /kənˈsɜːnɪŋ/ *prep* about; on the subject of □ *berkenaan/berkaitan dgn*: *She refused to answer questions concerning her private life.*

concert /ˈkɒnsət/ *noun* [C] a performance of music □ *konsert*: *The band is on tour doing concerts all over the country.* ♦ *a concert of music by Bach* ♦ *a concert hall/pianist* ⊃ look at **recital**
IDM in concert (with sb/sth) (*formal*) working together with sb/sth □ *bersama-sama (dgn sso/sst)*

concerted /kənˈsɜːtɪd/ *adj* [only before a noun] done by a group of people working together □ *bersama; bersepadu*: *We must all **make a concerted effort** to finish the work on time.*

concertina /ˌkɒnsəˈtiːnə/ *noun* [C] a musical instrument that you hold in your hands and play by pressing the ends together and pulling them apart □ *konsertina* ⊃ look at **accordion** ⊃ picture at **accordion**

concerto /kənˈtʃɜːtəʊ/ *noun* [C] (*pl* **concertos**) a piece of music for an **orchestra** (= a large group of musicians who play together) and one instrument playing a **solo** (= an important part on its own) □ *konserto*: *Mozart's second piano concerto*

concession /kənˈseʃn/ *noun* **1** [C,U] **(a) concession (to sb/sth)** something that you agree to do in order to end an argument □ *konsesi; tolak ansur*: *Employers have been forced to **make concessions** to the union.* ⊃ *verb* **concede** **2** [C] a lower price for certain groups of people □ *konsesi; pengurangan harga*: *Concessions are available for students and pensioners.*

concessionary /kənˈseʃənəri/ *adj* having a lower price for certain groups of people □ *konsesi*: *a concessionary fare*

conciliation /kənˌsɪliˈeɪʃn/ *noun* [U] the process of ending an argument or a disagreement □ *pendamaian; berdamai*: *All attempts at conciliation have failed and civil war seems inevitable.*

conciliatory /kənˈsɪliətəri/ *adj* that tries to end an argument or a disagreement □ *pendamai; utk berdamai*: *a conciliatory speech/gesture*

concise /kənˈsaɪs/ *adj* giving a lot of information in a few words □ *ringkas dan padat*: *He gave a clear and concise summary of what had happened.* **SYN** **brief** ▶ **concisely** *adv* ▶ **conciseness** *noun* [U]

conclude /kənˈkluːd/ *verb* **1** [T] **conclude sth from sth** to form an opinion as the result of thought or study □ *membuat kesimpulan; menyimpulkan*: *From the man's strange behaviour I concluded that he was drunk.* **2** [I,T] (*formal*) to end or to bring sth to an end □ *mengakhiri; menamatkan*: *The prince concluded his tour by attending a charity concert.* **3** [T] **conclude sth (with sb)** to formally arrange or agree to sth □ *mencapai persetujuan*: *conclude a business deal/treaty*

conclusion /kənˈkluːʒn/ *noun* **1** [C] **the conclusion (that ...)** an opinion that you reach after thinking about sth carefully □ *kesimpulan*: *After trying to phone Bob for days, I **came to the conclusion** that he was on holiday.* ♦ *Have you **reached** any **conclusions** from your studies?* **2** [C, usually sing] (*formal*) an end to sth □ *kesudahan; berakhir*: *Let us hope the peace talks **reach a successful conclusion**.* **3** [U] an act of arranging or agreeing to sth formally □ *pencapaian persetujuan*: *The summit ended with the conclusion of an arms-reduction treaty.*
IDM a foregone conclusion ⊃ **foregone**
in conclusion finally □ *akhir sekali*: *In conclusion, I would like to wish you continued success in the future.*
jump to conclusions ⊃ **jump¹**

conclusive /kənˈkluːsɪv/ *adj* that shows sth is definitely true or real □ *kukuh; yg meyakinkan*:

The blood tests gave conclusive proof of Roy's guilt. **OPP** **inconclusive** ▶ **conclusively** adv

concoct /kən'kɒkt/ verb [T] **1** to make sth unusual by mixing different things together □ *membuat campuran yg luar biasa* **2** to make up or invent sth (an excuse, a story, etc.) □ *mereka-reka* ▶ **concoction** noun [C]

concourse /'kɒŋkɔːs/ noun [C] a large hall or space inside a building such as a station or an airport □ *dataran; ruang legar*

concrete[1] /'kɒŋkriːt/ adj **1** made of concrete □ *dibuat drpd konkrit*: *a concrete floor/bridge* **2** based on facts, not on ideas or guesses □ *konkrit; maujud*: *concrete evidence/proposals/proof* ◆ *Can you give me a concrete example of what you mean?* **OPP** **abstract** ▶ **concretely** adv

concrete[2] /'kɒŋkriːt/ noun [U] a hard substance made from **cement** (= a grey powder) mixed with sand, water and small stones, which is used in building □ *konkrit*: *a modern office building of glass and concrete*

concrete[3] /'kɒŋkriːt/ verb [T] **concrete sth (over)** to cover sth with concrete □ *menutup/menurap dgn konkrit*

concur /kən'kɜː(r)/ verb [I] (**concurring**; **concurred**) (*formal*) to agree □ *bersetuju*

concurrent /kən'kʌrənt/ adj existing or happening at the same time as sth else □ *serentak* ▶ **concurrently** adv: *The semi-finals are played concurrently, so it is impossible to watch both.*

concuss /kən'kʌs/ verb [T, usually passive] to injure sb's brain by hitting their head □ *mendapat kecederaan pd otak; terkonkus*: *I was slightly concussed when I fell off my bicycle.* ▶ **concussion** /kən'kʌʃn/ noun [U]

condemn /kən'dem/ verb [T] **1** **condemn sb/sth (for/as sth)** to say strongly that you think sb/sth is very bad or wrong □ *mengutuk*: *A government spokesman condemned the bombing as a cowardly act of terrorism.* **2** **condemn sb (to sth/to do sth)** to say what sb's punishment will be; to sentence sb □ *menghukum; dihukum; terpaksa*: *The murderer was condemned to death.* ◆ (*figurative*) *Their poor education condemns them to a series of low-paid jobs.* **3** **condemn sth (as sth)** to say officially that sth is not safe enough to use □ *mengisytiharkan (sst) tdk selamat*: *The building was condemned as unsafe and was demolished.*

condemnation /ˌkɒndem'neɪʃn/ noun [C,U] the act of **condemning** sth; a statement that condemns □ *kecaman*: *The bombing brought condemnation from all around the world.*

condensation /ˌkɒnden'seɪʃn/ noun [U] small drops of liquid that are formed when warm air touches a cold surface □ *pemeluwapan*

condense /kən'dens/ verb **1** [I,T] to change or make sth change from gas to liquid □ *memeluwap*: *Steam condenses into water when it touches a cold surface.* ⊃ look at **evaporate 2** [T] **condense sth (into sth)** to make sth smaller or shorter so that it fills less space □ *meringkaskan*: *We'll have to condense these three chapters into one.*

condescend /ˌkɒndɪ'send/ verb [I] **1** **condescend (to do sth)** to do sth that you believe is below your level of importance □ *membuat sst yg dianggap mengurangkan darjat sso*: *Celia only condescends to speak to me when she wants me to do something for her.* **2** **condescend (to sb)** to behave towards sb in a way that shows that you think you are better or more important than them □ *bersikap meninggikan diri* **SYN** **patronize** ▶ **condescending** adj: *a condescending smile* ▶ **condescension** /ˌkɒndɪ'senʃn/ noun [U]

condition[1] /kən'dɪʃn/ noun **1** [U, sing] the state that sb/sth is in □ *keadaan*: *to be in poor/good/excellent condition* ◆ *He looks really ill. He is certainly not in a condition to drive home.* **2** [C] a medical problem that you have for a long time □ *sakit; penyakit*: *to have a heart/lung condition* **3** **conditions** [pl] the situation or surroundings in which people live, work or do things □ *keadaan*: *The prisoners were kept in terrible conditions.* ◆ *poor living/housing/working conditions* **4** [C] something that must happen so that sth else can happen or be possible □ *syarat*: *One of the conditions of the job is that you agree to work on Sundays.* ◆ *He said I could borrow his bike on one condition—that I didn't let anyone else ride it.* ◆ *I agreed to help on condition that I got half the profit.*

IDM **on no condition** (*formal*) not for any reason □ *jangan sekali-kali*: *On no condition must the press find out about this.*

out of condition not physically fit □ *tdk berapa sihat*

condition[2] /kən'dɪʃn/ verb [T] to affect or control the way that sb/sth behaves □ *melatih; dilatih; dibiasakan*: *Boys are conditioned to think that they are stronger than girls.*

conditional /kən'dɪʃənl/ adj **1** **conditional (on/upon sth)** that only happens if sth else is done or happens first □ *bergantung pd; bersyarat*: *My university place is conditional on my getting good marks in the exams.* **OPP** **unconditional 2** [only *before* a noun] describing a situation that must exist before sth else can happen. A **conditional** sentence often contains the word 'if' □ *bersyarat*: *'If you don't study, you won't pass the exam' is a conditional sentence.* ❶ For more information about conditional sentences, look at the **Reference Section** at the back of this dictionary. ▶ **conditionally** /-ʃənəli/ adv

conditioner /kən'dɪʃənə(r)/ noun [C,U] a substance that keeps sth in a good condition □ *(bahan) perapi*: *Do you use conditioner on your hair?*

condo /'kɒndəʊ/ (*informal*) = **condominium**

condolence /kən'dəʊləns/ noun [pl, U] an expression of how sorry you feel for sb whose

condom → confident

relative or close friend has just died □ *takziah*: *offer your condolences* ◆ *a message of condolence*

condom /ˈkɒndɒm/ (also informal **rubber**) noun [C] a thin rubber covering that a man wears over his sexual organ during sex to prevent the woman from becoming pregnant or as protection against disease □ *kondom*

condominium /ˌkɒndəˈmɪniəm/ (also informal **condo**) noun [C] (AmE) a flat or block of flats owned by the people who live in them □ *kondominium*

condone /kənˈdəʊn/ verb [T] to accept or agree with sth that most people think is wrong □ *membiarkan*: *I can never condone violence—no matter what the circumstances are.*

conducive /kənˈdjuːsɪv/ adj (formal) **conducive (to sth)** helping or making sth happen □ *membantu; mewujudkan keadaan yg sesuai*: *This hot weather is not conducive to hard work.*

ℹ conduct¹ /kənˈdʌkt/ verb [T] 1 (formal) to organize and do sth, especially research □ *menjalankan; mengendalikan*: *to conduct tests/a survey/an inquiry* 2 to stand in front of an **orchestra** (= a large group of musicians who play together) and direct the musicians □ *memimpin orkestra*: *a concert by the Philharmonic Orchestra, conducted by Sir Colin Davis* 3 (formal) **conduct yourself well, badly, etc.** to behave in a particular way □ *berkelakuan*: *He conducted himself far better than expected.* 4 to allow heat or electricity to pass along or through sth □ *mengalirkan*: *Rubber does not conduct electricity.*

ℹ conduct² /ˈkɒndʌkt/ noun [U] 1 sb's behaviour □ *kelakuan*: *His conduct has always been of the highest standard.* ◆ *a code of conduct* (= a set of rules for behaviour) 2 (formal) **conduct of sth** the act of controlling or organizing sth □ *pengendalian*: *She was criticized for her conduct of the bank's affairs.*

conductor /kənˈdʌktə(r)/ noun [C] 1 a person who stands in front of an **orchestra** (= a large group of musicians who play together), a group of singers, etc. and directs their performance □ *pemimpin orkestra* 2 (AmE) = **guard¹**(5) 3 (BrE) a person whose job is to collect money from passengers on a bus or to check their tickets □ *konduktor* 4 a substance that allows heat or electricity to pass through or along it □ *pengalir; konduktor*

cone /kəʊn/ noun [C] 1 a shape or an object that has a round base and a point at the top □ *kon*: *traffic cones* ◆ *an ice cream cone* ⊃ adjective **conical** ⊃ picture at **cube** 2 the hard fruit of a **pine** tree or a **fir** tree (= trees with thin sharp leaves which stay green all through the year) □ *kon* ⊃ look at **conifer** ⊃ picture at **tree**

confectionery /kənˈfekʃənəri/ noun [U] sweets, cakes, chocolates, etc. □ *konfeksi; manis-manisan*

confederacy /kənˈfedərəsi/ noun [C] a group of people, states or political parties with the same aim □ *gabungan*

confederation /kənˌfedəˈreɪʃn/ noun [C,U] an organization of smaller groups which have joined together □ *gabungan*: *a confederation of independent republics*

confer /kənˈfɜː(r)/ verb (**conferring**; **conferred**) 1 [I] **confer (with sb) (on/about sth)** to discuss sth with sb before making a decision □ *berbincang; berunding*: *The president is conferring with his advisers.* 2 [T] (written) **confer sth (on sb)** to give sb a special right or advantage □ *mengurniakan; menganugerahkan*

ℹ conference /ˈkɒnfərəns/ noun [C] a large official meeting, often lasting several days, at which members of an organization, a profession, etc. meet to discuss important matters □ *persidangan*: *Political parties usually hold a conference once a year.* ◆ *an international conference on climate change* ◆ *a conference room/centre/hall*

confess /kənˈfes/ verb [I,T] **confess (to sth/to doing sth); confess (sth) (to sb)** to admit that you have done sth bad or wrong □ *mengaku*: *The young woman confessed to the murder of her boyfriend/to murdering her boyfriend.* ◆ *They confessed to their mother that they had spent all the money on sweets.* ⊃ A less formal expression is **own up (to sth)**.

confession /kənˈfeʃn/ noun [C,U] an act of admitting that you have done sth bad or wrong □ *pengakuan*: *The police persuaded the man to make a full confession.*

confetti /kənˈfeti/ noun [U] small pieces of coloured paper that people throw over a man and woman who have just got married □ *konfeti*

confide /kənˈfaɪd/ verb [T] **confide sth to sb** to tell sb sth that is secret □ *meluahkan (sst yg rahsia)*: *She did not confide her love to anyone—not even to her best friend.*

PHR V confide in sb to talk to sb that you trust about sth secret or private □ *menceritakan (sst yg rahsia) kpd sso (yg boleh dipercayai)*

ℹ confidence /ˈkɒnfɪdəns/ noun [U] 1 **confidence (in sb/sth)** trust or strong belief in sb/sth □ *keyakinan; kepercayaan*: *The public is losing confidence in the present government.* ◆ *I have every confidence in Emily's ability to do the job.* 2 the feeling that you are sure about your own abilities, opinion, etc. □ *keyakinan*: *I didn't have the confidence to tell her I thought she was wrong.* ◆ *to be full of confidence* ◆ *'Of course we will win,' the team captain said with confidence.* ⊃ look at **self-confidence** 3 a feeling of trust in sb to keep sth a secret □ *kepercayaan; secara rahsia*: *The information was given to me in strict confidence.* ◆ *It took a while to win/gain her confidence.*

ˈconfidence trick noun [C] a way of getting money by cheating sb □ *penipuan*

ℹ confident /ˈkɒnfɪdənt/ adj **confident (of sth/that …); confident (about sth)** feeling or showing that you are sure about your own abilities, opinions, etc. □ *yakin*: *Kate feels* *confident of passing/that she can pass the exam.* ♦ *to be confident of success* ♦ *You should feel confident about your own abilities.* ♦ *Dillon has a very confident manner.* ⊃ look at **self-confident** ▶ **confidently** *adv*: *She stepped confidently onto the stage and began to sing.*

confidential /ˌkɒnfɪˈdenʃl/ *adj* secret; not to be shown or told to other people □ *rahsia; sulit*: *The letter was marked 'private and confidential'.* ▶ **confidentiality** /ˌkɒnfɪˌdenʃiˈæləti/ *noun* [U] ▶ **confidentially** /-ʃəli/ *adv*

configuration /kənˌfɪɡəˈreɪʃn/ *noun* [C,U] **1** (*formal*) the way in which the parts of sth, or a group of things, are arranged □ *tatarajah* **2** the equipment and programs that form a computer system and the particular way that these are arranged □ *konfigurasi*

configure /kənˈfɪɡə(r)/ *verb* [T, usually passive] to arrange sth in a particular way, especially computer equipment □ *menyusun atur*

⁊ confine /kənˈfaɪn/ *verb* [T] **1 confine sb/sth/yourself to sth** to stay within the limits of sth □ *membatasi; batasi*: *Please confine your questions to the topic we are discussing.* **SYN restrict 2 confine sb/sth (in/to sth)** to keep a person or an animal in a particular, usually small, place □ *mengurung; dikurung*: *The prisoners are confined to their cells for long periods at a time.*

⁊ confined /kənˈfaɪnd/ *adj* (used about a space) very small □ *sempit*: *Sailors on submarines must get used to living in confined spaces.*

confinement /kənˈfaɪnmənt/ *noun* [U] being kept in a small space □ *pengurungan*: *to be kept in solitary confinement* (= in a prison and separated from other people)

confines /ˈkɒnfaɪnz/ *noun* [pl] (*formal*) the limits of sth □ *batas; lingkungan; had*: *Patients are not allowed beyond the confines of the hospital grounds.*

⁊ confirm /kənˈfɜːm/ *verb* [T] **1** to say or show that sth is true; to make sth definite □ *mengesahkan*: *Seeing the two of them together confirmed our suspicions.* ♦ *Can you confirm that you will be able to attend?* **2** to accept sb as a full member of a Christian Church in a special ceremony □ *mengesahkan/menerima sebagai ahli sst mazhab Kristian*: *He was confirmed at the age of thirteen.* ▶ **confirmation** /ˌkɒnfəˈmeɪʃn/ *noun* [C,U]: *We are waiting for confirmation of the report.* ♦ *You will receive a written confirmation of your reservation.* ♦ (*formal*): *We are awaiting confirmation.*

confirmed /kənˈfɜːmd/ *adj* [only before a noun] fixed in a particular habit or way of life □ *tetap (dlm sst tabiat atau cara hidup)*: *a confirmed bachelor*

confiscate /ˈkɒnfɪskeɪt/ *verb* [T] to take sth away from sb as a punishment □ *merampas*: *Any cigarettes found in school will be confiscated.* ▶ **confiscation** /ˌkɒnfɪˈskeɪʃn/ *noun* [C,U]

⁊ conflict¹ /ˈkɒnflɪkt/ *noun* [C,U] **1 (a) conflict with sb/sth (over sth)** a fight or an argument

□ *pertikaian; pertentangan*: *an armed conflict* ♦ *The new laws have brought the Government into conflict with the unions over pay increases.* **2** a difference between two or more ideas, wishes, etc. □ *konflik; percanggahan*: *Many women have to cope with the conflict between their career and their family.* ♦ *a conflict of interests*

⁊ conflict² /kənˈflɪkt/ *verb* [I] **A and B conflict; A conflicts with B** to disagree with or be different from sb/sth □ *bercanggah; bertentangan*: *The statements of the two witnesses conflict.* ♦ *John's statement conflicts with yours.* ♦ *conflicting results*

conform /kənˈfɔːm/ *verb* [I] **conform (to sth) 1** to behave in the way that other people and society expect you to behave □ *mengikut apa yg telah ditentukan atau diterima umum; menyesuaikan diri*: *Children are under a lot of pressure to conform when they first start school.* **2** to obey a rule or law □ *mematuhi*: *This building does not conform to fire regulations.* ▶ **conformity** /kənˈfɔːməti/ *noun* [U] (*formal*)

conformist /kənˈfɔːmɪst/ *noun* [C] a person who behaves in the way that people are expected to behave by society □ *orang yg mengikut apa yg telah ditentukan atau diterima umum* **OPP** nonconformist

⁊ confront /kənˈfrʌnt/ *verb* [T] **1 confront sth; confront sb (with sb/sth)** to think about, or to make sb think about, sth that is difficult or unpleasant □ *menghadapi; dihadapkan; berhadapan; disemukakan*: *to confront a problem/a difficulty/an issue* ♦ *When the police confronted him with the evidence, he confessed.* **2** to stand in front of sb, for example because you want to fight them □ *berhadapan*: *The unarmed demonstrators were confronted by a row of soldiers.*

confrontation /ˌkɒnfrʌnˈteɪʃn/ *noun* [C,U] a fight or an argument □ *pertentangan; konfrontasi*

⁊ confuse /kənˈfjuːz/ *verb* [T] **1** to make sb unable to think clearly or to know what to do □ *mengelirukan*: *He confused everybody with his pages of facts and figures.* **2 confuse A and/with B** to mistake sb/sth for sb/sth else □ *keliru antara*: *I often confuse Lee with his brother. They look very much alike.* **3** to make sth complicated □ *menjadi lebih rumit/sukar*: *The situation is confused by the fact that so many organizations are involved.*

⁊ confused /kənˈfjuːzd/ *adj* **1** not able to think clearly □ *keliru; bingung*: *When he regained consciousness he was dazed and confused.* **2** difficult to understand □ *bercelaru; tdk jelas*: *The article is very confused—I don't know what the main point is.* ▶ **confusedly** /kənˈfjuːzɪdli/ *adv*

⁊ confusing /kənˈfjuːzɪŋ/ *adj* difficult to understand □ *mengelirukan*: *Her instructions were contradictory and confusing.* ▶ **confusingly** *adv*

confusion /kənˈfjuːʒn/ noun [U] **1** the state of not being able to think clearly or not understanding sth □ *kebingungan; keliruan*: He stared **in confusion** at the exam paper. ♦ There is still a great deal of confusion as to the true facts. **2** the act of mistaking sb/sth for sb/sth else □ *keliruan; kesilapan*: To avoid confusion, all luggage should be labelled with your name and destination. **3** a lack of order □ *kacau-bilau; kucar-kacir; kekacauan*: Their unexpected visit threw all our plans into confusion.

congeal /kənˈdʒiːl/ verb [I,T] (used about a liquid) to become solid; to make a liquid solid □ *membeku; menjadi beku*: congealed blood

congenial /kənˈdʒiːniəl/ adj (formal) pleasant □ *menyenangkan*: We spent an evening in congenial company.

congenital /kənˈdʒenɪtl/ adj (used about a disease) beginning at and continuing since birth □ *sejak lahir; kongenital*

congested /kənˈdʒestɪd/ adj so full of sth that nothing can move □ *penuh sesak*: The streets of London are congested with traffic. ▶ **congestion** /kənˈdʒestʃən/ noun [U]: severe traffic congestion

conglomerate /kənˈɡlɒmərət/ noun [C] a large firm made up of several different companies □ *konglomerat*

conglomeration /kənˌɡlɒməˈreɪʃn/ noun [C] a group of many different things that have been brought together □ *gabungan; campuran*

congratulate /kənˈɡrætʃuleɪt/ verb [T] **congratulate sb (on sth)** to tell sb that you are pleased about sth they have done □ *mengucapkan tahniah*: Colin congratulated Sue on passing her driving test.

congratulations /kənˌɡrætʃuˈleɪʃnz/ noun [pl] used for telling sb that you are pleased about sth they have done □ *tahniah*: Congratulations on the birth of your baby boy! ♦ Congratulations! Your painting has won first prize. ♦ to offer/send your congratulations

congregate /ˈkɒŋɡrɪɡeɪt/ verb [I] to come together in a crowd or group □ *berhimpun*

congregation /ˌkɒŋɡrɪˈɡeɪʃn/ noun [C, with sing or pl verb] the group of people who attend a particular church □ *jemaah*

congress /ˈkɒŋɡres/ noun [C] **1** a large formal meeting or series of meetings □ *kongres*: a medical congress **2 Congress** the name in some countries (for example the US) for the group of people who are elected to make the laws □ *kongres*: Congress will vote on the proposals tomorrow.

CULTURE

The US Congress consists of the **Senate** and the **House of Representatives**.

congressional /kənˈɡreʃənl/ adj [only before a noun] connected with a **congress** or **Congress** □ *(berkenaan dgn) kongres/Kongres*

Congressman /ˈkɒŋɡresmən/, **Congresswoman** /ˈkɒŋɡreswʊmən/ noun [C] (pl -men /-mən/, -women /-wɪmɪn/) (also **Congressperson** /-pɜːsn/) a member of Congress in the US, especially the House of Representatives □ *ahli kongres*

conical /ˈkɒnɪkl/ adj having a round base and getting narrower towards a point at the top □ *berbentuk kon; runjung* ➔ noun **cone**

conifer /ˈkɒnɪfə(r)/ noun [C] a tree with needles that stays green all through the year and that has **cones** (= hard brown fruit) □ *konifer* ▶ **coniferous** /kəˈnɪfərəs/ adj

conjecture /kənˈdʒektʃə(r)/ verb [I,T] (formal) to guess about sth without real proof or evidence □ *meneka; menduga* ▶ **conjecture** noun [C,U]

conjugal /ˈkɒndʒəɡl/ adj [only before a noun] (formal) connected with marriage □ *berkenaan dgn perkahwinan atau hubungan antara suami dgn isteri*

conjugate /ˈkɒndʒəɡeɪt/ verb [T] to give the different forms of a verb □ *berkonjugat; mengkonjugat* ▶ **conjugation** /ˌkɒndʒuˈɡeɪʃn/ noun [C,U]

conjunction /kənˈdʒʌŋkʃn/ noun [C] a word that is used for joining other words, phrases or sentences □ *kata penghubung*: 'And', 'but' and 'or' are conjunctions.

IDM in conjunction with sb/sth together with sb/sth □ *bersama dgn sso/sst*

conjure /ˈkʌndʒə(r)/ verb [I] to do tricks by clever, quick hand movements, that appear to be magic □ *main silap mata*

PHR V conjure sth up 1 to cause an image to appear in your mind □ *menimbulkan dlm fikiran; menggambarkan*: Hawaiian music conjures up images of sunshine, flowers and sandy beaches. **2** to make sth appear quickly or suddenly □ *menyediakan sst*: Mum can conjure up a meal out of almost anything.
▶ **conjuring** noun [U]

conjuror (also **conjurer**) /ˈkʌndʒərə(r)/ noun [C] a person who does clever tricks that appear to be magic □ *ahli silap mata* ➔ look at **magician**

conker /ˈkɒŋkə(r)/ noun (BrE informal) = **horse chestnut** (2) □ *berangan kuda*

connect /kəˈnekt/ verb **1** [I,T] **connect (sth) (up) (to/with sth)** to be joined to sth; to join sth to sth else □ *menyambung; bersambung; menghubungkan*: The tunnels connect (up) ten metres further on. ♦ The printer is connected to the computer. ♦ This motorway connects Cadiz with Seville. ➔ look at **disconnect 2** [T] **connect sb/sth (with sb/sth)** to have an association with sb/sth else; to realize or show that sb/sth is involved with sth else □ *mengaitkan; dikaitkan*: There was no evidence that she was connected with the crime. **3** [I] **connect (with sth)** (used about a bus,

connection /kəˈnekʃn/ noun 1 [C,U] a connection between A and B; a connection with/to sth an association or a relationship between two or more people or things □ *hubungan; kaitan*: *Is there any connection between the two organizations?* ♦ *What's your connection with Brazil? Have you worked there?* ♦ *I'm having problems with my Internet connection.* 2 [C] a place where two wires, pipes, etc. join together □ *sambungan*: *The radio doesn't work. There must be a loose connection somewhere.* 3 [C] a bus, train, plane, etc. that leaves soon after another arrives □ *(bas, kereta api, dll) sambungan*: *Our bus was late, so we missed our connection.*

IDM **in connection with sb/sth** (*formal*) about or concerning □ *berkaitan dgn sso/sst*: *I am writing to you in connection with your application.* **in this/that connection** (*formal*) about or concerning this/that □ *berhubung dgn (sst perkara); mengenai*

connive /kəˈnaɪv/ verb [I] connive at sth; connive (with sb) (to do sth) to work secretly with sb to do sth that is wrong; to do nothing to stop sb doing sth wrong □ *bersubahat; membiarkan sahaja*: *The two parties connived to get rid of the president.*

connoisseur /ˌkɒnəˈsɜː(r)/ (*AmE* also) / noun [C] a person who knows a lot about art, good food, wine, music, etc. □ *pakar; ahli*

connotation /ˌkɒnəˈteɪʃn/ noun [C] an idea expressed by a word in addition to its main meaning □ *konotasi*: *'Spinster' means a single woman, but it has negative connotations.*

conquer /ˈkɒŋkə(r)/ verb [T] 1 to take control of a country or city and its people by force, especially in a war □ *menakluk*: *Napoleon's ambition was to conquer Europe.* ♦ (*figurative*) *The young singer conquered the hearts of audiences all over the world.* 2 to succeed in controlling or dealing with a strong feeling, problem, etc. □ *mengatasi*: *She's trying to conquer her fear of flying.*

conqueror /ˈkɒŋkərə(r)/ noun [C] a person who has **conquered**(1) sth □ *penakluk*

conquest /ˈkɒŋkwest/ noun 1 [C,U] an act of **conquering** sth □ *penaklukan*: *the Norman conquest* (= of England in 1066) ♦ *the conquest of Mount Everest* 2 [C] an area of land that has been taken in a war □ *taklukan*

conscience /ˈkɒnʃəns/ noun [C,U] the part of your mind that tells you if what you are doing is right or wrong □ *hati kecil; suara hati; sanubari*: *a clear/a guilty conscience*
IDM **have sth on your conscience** to feel guilty because you have done sth wrong □ *rasa bersalah*

conscientious /ˌkɒnʃiˈenʃəs/ adj (used about people) careful to do sth correctly and well □ *hemat dan tekun*: *He's a conscientious worker.* ▶ **conscientiously** adv

conscientious objector noun [C] a person who refuses to join the army, etc. because they believe it is morally wrong to kill other people □ *pembantah khidmat tentera*

conscious /ˈkɒnʃəs/ adj 1 [not before a noun] conscious (of sth/that ...) noticing or realizing that sth exists □ *sedar; perasan*: *She didn't seem conscious of the danger.* ♦ *Bill suddenly became conscious that someone was following him.* **SYN** **aware** 2 able to see, hear, feel, etc. things; awake □ *sedar*: *The injured driver was still conscious when the ambulance arrived.* **OPP** **unconscious** 3 that you do on purpose or for a particular reason □ *secara sedar; sengaja*: *We made a conscious effort to treat both children equally.*

MORE **Deliberate** has a similar meaning.

▶ **consciously** adv

consciousness /ˈkɒnʃəsnəs/ noun 1 [U] the state of being able to see, hear, feel, etc. □ *keadaan sedar*: *As he fell, he hit his head and lost consciousness.* ♦ *She regained consciousness after two weeks in a coma.* 2 [U, sing] consciousness (of sth) the state of realizing or noticing that sth exists □ *kesedaran*: *There is (a) growing consciousness of the need to save energy.*

conscript¹ /kənˈskrɪpt/ verb [T] to make sb join the army, navy or air force □ *mengerah masuk tentera* ▶ **conscription** noun [U]

conscript² /ˈkɒnskrɪpt/ noun [C] a person who has been **conscripted** □ *tentera kerahan*
➲ look at **volunteer**

conscription /kənˈskrɪpʃn/ noun (*especially AmE* **the draft**) noun [U] the system of making sb join the army, etc. □ *kerahan/pengerahan*

consecrate /ˈkɒnsɪkreɪt/ verb [T] to state formally in a special ceremony that a place or an object can be used for religious purposes □ *mentahbiskan* ▶ **consecration** /ˌkɒnsɪˈkreɪʃn/ noun [C,U]

consecutive /kənˈsekjətɪv/ adj coming or happening one after the other □ *berturut-turut*: *This is the team's fourth consecutive win.* ▶ **consecutively** adv

consensus /kənˈsensəs/ noun [sing, U] (a) consensus (among/between sb) (on/about sth) agreement among a group of people □ *kata sepakat; sepersetujuan*: *to reach a consensus* ♦ *There is no consensus among experts about the causes of climate change.*

consent¹ /kənˈsent/ verb [I] consent (to sth) to agree to sth; to allow sth to happen □ *bersetuju; mengizinkan*

consent² /kənˈsent/ noun [U] agreement; permission □ *persetujuan; izin*: *The child's parents had to give their consent to the operation.*
IDM **the age of consent** ➲ **age¹**

consequence /ˈkɒnsɪkwəns/ noun 1 [C] something that happens or follows as a result of sth else □ *akibat*: Many people may lose their jobs *as a consequence of* recent poor sales. 2 [U] (formal) importance □ *kepentingan*: It is of no consequence.

consequent /ˈkɒnsɪkwənt/ adj [only before a noun] (formal) following as the result of sth else □ *akibatnya*: The lack of rain and consequent poor harvests have led to food shortages. ▶ **consequently** adv: She didn't work hard enough, and consequently failed the exam. ⊃ note at **therefore**

conservation /ˌkɒnsəˈveɪʃn/ noun [U] 1 the protection of the natural world □ *pemuliharaan*: Conservation groups are protesting against the plan to build a road through the forest. 2 not allowing sth to be wasted, damaged or destroyed □ *penjimatan*: the conservation of energy ⊃ verb **conserve**

conservationist /ˌkɒnsəˈveɪʃənɪst/ noun [C] a person who believes in protecting the natural world □ *penyokong pemuliharaan*

conservatism /kənˈsɜːvətɪzəm/ noun [U] 1 the disapproval of new ideas and change □ *sikap konservatif* 2 usually **Conservatism** the beliefs of the Conservative Party □ *prinsip-prinsip Parti Konservatif; konservatisme*

conservative¹ /kənˈsɜːvətɪv/ adj 1 **Conservative** connected with the British Conservative Party □ *(berkenaan dgn) Parti Konservatif*: Conservative voters 2 not liking change; traditional □ *konservatif; tdk suka perubahan*: This design is too modern for them. They have very conservative tastes. 3 (used when you are guessing how much sth costs) lower than the real figure or amount □ *secara konservatif; (anggaran) rendah*: Even a conservative estimate would put the damage at about £4 000 to repair. ▶ **conservatively** adv

conservative² /kənˈsɜːvətɪv/ noun [C] 1 a person who does not like change □ *orang yg bersikap konservatif* 2 usually **Conservative** (abbr **Con**) a member of the British Conservative Party □ *ahli Parti Konservatif*

the Conˈservative Party noun [sing, with sing or pl verb] one of the main political parties in Britain. The Conservative Party supports a free market and is against the state controlling industry. □ *Parti Konservatif* ⊃ note at **party** ⊃ look at **the Labour Party, the Liberal Democrats**

conservatory /kənˈsɜːvətri/ noun [C] (pl **conservatories**) (BrE) a room with glass walls and a glass roof that is built onto the outside of a house □ *bangsal/rumah kaca*

conserve /kənˈsɜːv/ verb [T] to avoid wasting sth □ *menjimatkan*: to conserve water ⊃ noun **conservation**

consider /kənˈsɪdə(r)/ verb [T] 1 consider sb/sth (for/as sth); consider doing sth to think about sth carefully, often before making a decision □ *mempertimbangkan; memikirkan*: They are considering him for the part of Romeo. ◆ She had never considered nursing as a career. ◆ We're considering going to Spain for our holidays. 2 consider sb/sth (as/to be) sth; consider that … to think about sth in a particular way □ *menganggap*: He considered the risk (to be) too great. ◆ He considered that the risk was too great. ◆ Jane considers herself an expert on the subject. 3 to remember or pay attention to sth, especially sb's feelings □ *memikirkan; mengambil kira*: I can't just move abroad. I have to consider my family.

considerable /kənˈsɪdərəbl/ adj great in amount or size □ *banyak; besar*: A considerable number of people preferred the old building to the new one. ▶ **considerably** /-əbli/ adv (formal): This flat is considerably larger than our last one. **SYN** significantly

considerate /kənˈsɪdərət/ adj considerate (of sb) (to do sth); considerate (towards sb) careful not to upset people; thinking of others □ *bertimbang rasa*: It was very considerate of you to offer to drive me home. **SYN** thoughtful **OPP** inconsiderate

consideration /kənˌsɪdəˈreɪʃn/ noun 1 [U] (formal) an act of thinking about sth carefully or for a long time □ *pertimbangan*: I have given some consideration to the idea but I don't think it would work. 2 [C] something that you think about when you are making a decision □ *pertimbangan*: If he changes his job, the salary will be an important consideration. 3 [U] consideration (for sb/sth) the quality of thinking about what other people need or feel □ *sikap timbang rasa*: Most drivers show little consideration for cyclists.
IDM take sth into consideration to think about sth when you are forming an opinion or making a decision □ *mengambil kira sst*

considering /kənˈsɪdərɪŋ/ prep, conj (used for introducing a surprising fact) when you think about or remember sth □ *memandangkan*: Considering you've only been studying for a year, you speak English very well.

consign /kənˈsaɪn/ verb [T] (formal) consign sb/sth to sth to put or send sb/sth somewhere, especially in order to get rid of them or it □ *meletakkan (di sst tempat); membuang*: I think I can consign this junk mail straight to the bin.

consignment /kənˈsaɪnmənt/ noun [C] goods that are being sent to sb/sth □ *pengiriman barang-barang; konsainan*: a new consignment of books

consist /kənˈsɪst/ verb [not used in the continuous tenses]
PHR V consist in sth (formal) to have sth as its main point □ *adalah; ciri yg paling penting*: Her job consisted in welcoming the guests as they arrived.

consist of sth to be formed or made up of sth □ *terdiri drpd*: The band consists of a singer, two guitarists and a drummer.

HELP Although this verb is not used in the continuous tenses, it is common to see the present participle (= *-ing* form): *It's a full-time course consisting of six different modules.*

consistency /kənˈsɪstənsi/ *noun* (*pl* **consistencies**) **1** [U] the quality of always having the same standard, opinions, behaviour, etc. □ *sifat konsisten*: *Your work lacks consistency. Sometimes it's excellent but at other times it's full of mistakes.* **OPP** **inconsistency** **2** [C,U] how thick or smooth a liquid substance is □ *kepekatan*: *The mixture should have a thick, sticky consistency.*

consistent /kənˈsɪstənt/ *adj* **1** always having the same opinions, standard, behaviour, etc.; not changing □ *konsisten* **2 consistent (with sth)** agreeing with or similar to sth □ *selaras; sama dgn*: *I'm afraid your statement is not consistent with what the other witnesses said.* **OPP** for both meanings **inconsistent** ▸ **consistently** *adv*: *We must try to maintain a consistently high standard.*

consolation /ˌkɒnsəˈleɪʃn/ *noun* [C,U] a thing or person that makes you feel better when you are sad □ *sst atau sso yg menyenangkan hati* **SYN** **comfort**: *It was some consolation to me to know that I wasn't the only one who had failed the exam.*

console¹ /kənˈsəʊl/ *verb* [T] to make sb happier when they are very sad or disappointed □ *menyenangkan hati* **SYN** **comfort**

console² /ˈkɒnsəʊl/ *noun* [C] a flat surface which contains all the controls and switches for a machine, a piece of electronic equipment, etc. □ *konsol*: *a games console*

consolidate /kənˈsɒlɪdeɪt/ *verb* [I,T] to become or to make sth firmer or stronger □ *mengukuhkan; memperkukuhkan*: *We're going to consolidate what we've learnt so far by doing some revision exercises today.* ▸ **consolidation** /kənˌsɒlɪˈdeɪʃn/ *noun* [U]

consonant /ˈkɒnsənənt/ *noun* [C] any of the letters of the English alphabet except *a*, *e*, *i*, *o* and *u* □ *(huruf) konsonan*: *The letters 't', 'm', 's' and 'b' are all consonants.* ➔ look at **vowel**

consortium /kənˈsɔːtiəm/ *noun* [C] (*pl* **consortiums** or **consortia** /-tiə/) a group of companies that work closely together for a particular purpose □ *konsortium*

conspicuous /kənˈspɪkjuəs/ *adj* easily seen or noticed □ *ketara* **OPP** **inconspicuous** ▸ **conspicuously** *adv*

conspiracy /kənˈspɪrəsi/ *noun* [C,U] (*pl* **conspiracies**) a secret plan by a group of people to do sth bad or illegal □ *komplot; pakatan sulit*: *a conspiracy against the president*

conspirator /kənˈspɪrətə(r)/ *noun* [C] a member of a group of people who are planning to do sth bad or illegal □ *pengkomplot*

conspire /kənˈspaɪə(r)/ *verb* [I] **1 conspire (with sb) (to do sth)** to plan to do sth bad or illegal with a group of people □ *berkomplot*: *A group of terrorists were conspiring to blow up the plane.* **2 conspire (against sb/sth)** (used about events) to seem to work together to make sth bad happen □ *bergabung*: *When we both lost our jobs in the same week, we felt that everything was conspiring against us.*

constable /ˈkʌnstəbl/ = **police constable**

constabulary /kənˈstæbjələri/ *noun* [C] (*pl* **constabularies**) the police force of a particular area □ *pasukan polis sst tempat*: *the West Yorkshire Constabulary*

constant /ˈkɒnstənt/ *adj* **1** happening or existing all the time or again and again □ *sentiasa; tdk henti-henti; berkali-kali*: *The constant noise gave me a headache.* **2** that does not change □ *malar*: *You use less petrol if you drive at a constant speed.*

constantly /ˈkɒnstəntli/ *adv* always; again and again □ *sentiasa; acap kali*: *The situation is constantly changing.*

constellation /ˌkɒnstəˈleɪʃn/ *noun* [C] a group of stars that forms a pattern and has a name □ *buruj*

consternation /ˌkɒnstəˈneɪʃn/ *noun* [U] a feeling of shock or worry □ *kegugupan; terkejut*: *We stared at each other in consternation.*

constipated /ˈkɒnstɪpeɪtɪd/ *adj* not able to empty waste from your body □ *sembelit* ▸ **constipation** /ˌkɒnstɪˈpeɪʃn/ *noun* [U]: *to suffer from/have constipation*

constituency /kənˈstɪtjuənsi/ *noun* [C] (*pl* **constituencies**) a district and the people who live in it that a politician represents □ *para pengundi; kawasan pilihan raya* ➔ note at **election**

constituent /kənˈstɪtjuənt/ *noun* [C] **1** a person who lives in the district that a politician represents □ *pengundi* **2** one of the parts that form sth □ *juzuk; bahagian*: *Hydrogen and oxygen are the constituents of water.*

constitute /ˈkɒnstɪtjuːt/ *verb* [T] [not used in the continuous tenses] (*formal*) **1** to be considered as sth; to be equal to sth □ *merupakan*: *The presence of the troops constitutes a threat to peace.* **2** to be one of the parts that form sth □ *membentuk; terdiri drpd*: *Women constitute a high proportion of part-time workers.*

HELP Although this verb is not used in the continuous tenses, it is common to see the present participle (= *-ing* form): *Management has to fix a maximum number of hours as constituting a day's work.*

constitution /ˌkɒnstɪˈtjuːʃn/ *noun* **1** [C] the basic laws or rules of a country or an organization □ *perlembagaan*: *the United States constitution* **2** [U] the way the parts of sth are put together; the structure of sth □ *pembentukan; susunan*: *the constitution of DNA*

constitutional /ˌkɒnstɪˈtjuːʃənl/ *adj* connected with or allowed by the **constitution** of

constrain → contact

a country, etc □ *(berkenaan dgn atau dibenarkan oleh) perlembagaan*: *It is not constitutional to imprison a person without trial.*

constrain /kənˈstreɪn/ *verb* [T] (*formal*) **constrain sb/sth (to do sth)** to limit sb/sth; to force sb/sth to do sth □ *menyekat; mengekang; memaksa*: *The company's growth has been constrained by high taxes.*

constraint /kənˈstreɪnt/ *noun* [C,U] something that limits you □ *sekatan; kekangan* SYN **restriction**: *There are always some financial constraints on a project like this.*

constrict /kənˈstrɪkt/ *verb* [I,T] **1** to become or make sth tighter, narrower or less □ *menjerut; menyempitkan*: *She felt her throat constrict with fear.* ♦ *The valve constricts the flow of air.* **2** to limit sb's freedom to do sth □ *mengekang; menyekat* ▶ **constriction** *noun* [C,U]

construct /kənˈstrʌkt/ *verb* [T] **1** to build or make sth □ *membina*: *Early houses were constructed out of mud and sticks.* ⊃ **Construct** is more formal than **build**. **2** to form sth by putting different things together □ *menggubah*: *You must learn how to construct a logical argument.*

construction /kənˈstrʌkʃn/ *noun* **1** [U] the act or method of building or making sth □ *pembinaan*: *A new bridge is now under construction.* ♦ *He works in the construction industry.* **2** [C] (*formal*) something that has been built or made; a building □ *binaan*: *The new pyramid was a construction of glass and steel.* **3** [C] the way that words are used together in a phrase or sentence □ *konstruksi*: *a difficult grammatical construction*

constructive /kənˈstrʌktɪv/ *adj* useful or helpful □ *membina*: *constructive suggestions/criticisms/advice* ▶ **constructively** *adv*

construe /kənˈstruː/ *verb* [T] (*formal*) **construe sth (as sth)** to understand the meaning of sth in a particular way □ *mentafsirkan*: *Her confident manner is sometimes construed as arrogance.* ⊃ look at **misconstrue**

consul /ˈkɒnsl/ *noun* [C] an official who works in a foreign city helping people from his or her own country who are living or visiting there □ *konsul; kuasa usaha*: *the British consul in Miami* ⊃ look at **ambassador** ▶ **consular** /ˈkɒnsjələ(r)/ *adj*

consulate /ˈkɒnsjələt/ *noun* [C] the building where a **consul** works □ *konsulat; pejabat konsul* ⊃ look at **embassy**

consult /kənˈsʌlt/ *verb* **1** [T] **consult sb/sth (about sth)** to ask sb for some information or advice, or to look for it in a book, etc □ *merujuk kpd; meminta nasihat*: *If the symptoms continue, consult your doctor.* **2** [I] **consult (with sb)** to discuss sth with sb □ *berunding dgn; membincangkan*: *Harry consulted with his sisters before selling the family business.* ♦ *I expect to be consulted on major issues.*

[I] **intransitive**, a verb which has no object: *He laughed.*

consultancy /kənˈsʌltənsi/ *noun* (*pl* **consultancies**) **1** [C] a company that gives expert advice on a particular subject □ *syarikat perunding* **2** [U] expert advice that sb is paid to provide on a particular subject □ *kepakaran runding*

consultant /kənˈsʌltənt/ *noun* [C] **1** a person who gives advice to people on business, law, etc □ *pakar perunding; perunding*: *a firm of management consultants* **2** (*BrE*) a hospital doctor who is an expert in a particular area of medicine □ *doktor pakar*: *a consultant psychiatrist*

consultation /ˌkɒnslˈteɪʃn/ *noun* [C,U] **1** a discussion between people before a decision is taken □ *perundingan*: *Diplomats met for consultations on the hostage crisis.* ♦ *The measures were introduced without consultation.* **2** (*formal*) meeting sb to get information or advice, or looking for it in a book □ *rundingan; rujukan*: *a consultation with a doctor*

consume /kənˈsjuːm/ *verb* [T] (*formal*) **1** to use sth such as fuel, energy or time □ *menggunakan*: *This car consumes a lot of petrol.* **2** to eat or drink sth □ *makan; minum*: *Wrestlers can consume up to 10 000 calories in a day.* ⊃ *noun* **consumption 3** (used about an emotion) to affect sb very strongly □ *melanda; dilanda*: *She was consumed with rage after he left her.* ♦ *consumed with anger/curiousity/grief/rage* **4** (used about fire) to destroy sth □ *membinasakan*

consumer /kənˈsjuːmə(r)/ *noun* [C] a person who buys things or uses services □ *pengguna*: *Consumers should complain if they are not satisfied with the service they receive.*

consuming /kənˈsjuːmɪŋ/ *adj* [only before a noun] that takes up a lot of your time and attention □ *yg mengambil banyak masa dan tumpuan perhatian*: *Sport is her consuming passion.*

consummate¹ /ˈkɒnsəmət/ *adj* [only before a noun] (*formal*) extremely skilled; a perfect example of sth □ *handalan; cukup pandai*: *a consummate performer/performance/professional*

consummate² /ˈkɒnsəmeɪt/ *verb* [T] (*formal*) to make a marriage or relationship complete by having sex □ *bersatu; bersetubuh* ▶ **consummation** /ˌkɒnsəˈmeɪʃn/ *noun* [C,U]

consumption /kənˈsʌmpʃn/ *noun* [U] **1** the act of using, eating, etc. sth □ *(perbuatan) menggunakan, memakan, dsb sst*: *The meat was declared unfit for human consumption* (= for people to eat). **2** the amount of fuel, etc. that sth uses □ *penggunaan*: *a car with low fuel consumption* ⊃ *verb* **consume**

cont. (*also* **contd**) *abbr* continued □ *bersambung*: *cont. on p 9*

contact¹ /ˈkɒntækt/ *noun* **1** [U] **contact (with sb/sth)** meeting, talking to or writing to sb else □ *hubungan; berhubung*: *They are trying to make contact with the kidnappers.* ♦ *We keep in contact with our office in New York.* ♦ *It's a pity to lose contact with old school friends.* **2** [U] **contact (with**

[T] **transitive**, a verb which has an object: *He ate an apple.*

sb/sth) the state of touching sb/sth □ *bersentuhan; perihal menyentuh*: *This product should not come into contact with food.* **3** [C] a person that you know who may be able to help you □ *kenalan*: *business contacts*

contact² /ˈkɒntækt/ *verb* [T] to telephone or write to sb □ *menghubungi*: *Is there a phone number where I can contact you?* ▶ **contactable** /ˈkɒntæktəbl/ *adj*: *I'll be contactable on this number …*

'**contact lens** *noun* [C] a small piece of plastic that fits onto your eye to help you to see better □ *kanta sentuh* ⊃ picture at **glasses**

contagious /kənˈteɪdʒəs/ *adj* (used about a disease) that you can get by touching sb/sth □ *berjangkit*: *Measles is a highly contagious disease.* ♦ (*figurative*) *Her laugh is contagious.* ⊃ look at **infectious** ▶ **contagion** /kənˈteɪdʒən/ *noun* [U]

contain /kənˈteɪn/ *verb* [T] [not used in the continuous tenses] **1** to have sth inside or as part of itself □ *mengandungi*: *Each box contains 24 tins.*

> **HELP** Although this verb is not used in the continuous tenses, it is common to see the present participle (= *-ing* form): *food containing nuts*

2 to keep sth within limits; to control sth □ *membendung; menahan; mengawal*: *efforts to contain inflation* ♦ *She found it hard to contain her anger.*

187 **contact → contemplate**

> **HELP Contain** or **include**? We use **contain** to talk about objects which have other things inside them: *a jar containing olives* ♦ *This film contains violent scenes.* We use **include** to show that sb/sth forms part of a whole or belongs to something: *a team of seven people including a cameraman and a doctor* ♦ *The price of the holiday includes accommodation.*

container /kənˈteɪnə(r)/ *noun* [C] **1** a box, bottle, bag, etc. in which sth is kept □ *bekas*: *a plastic container* **2** a large metal box that is used for transporting goods by sea, road or rail □ *kontena*: *a container lorry/ship*

contaminate /kənˈtæmɪneɪt/ *verb* [T] to add a substance which will make sth dirty or harmful □ *mencemari; dicemari*: *The town's drinking water was contaminated with poisonous chemicals.* ▶ **contamination** /kənˌtæmɪˈneɪʃn/ *noun* [U]

contd = continued

contemplate /ˈkɒntəmpleɪt/ *verb* [T] **1** to think carefully about sth or the possibility of doing sth □ *berfikir dlm-dlm*: *Before her illness she had never contemplated retiring.* **SYN consider 2** to look at sb/sth, often quietly or for a long time □ *merenung* ▶ **contemplation** /ˌkɒntəmˈpleɪʃn/ *noun* [U]

containers

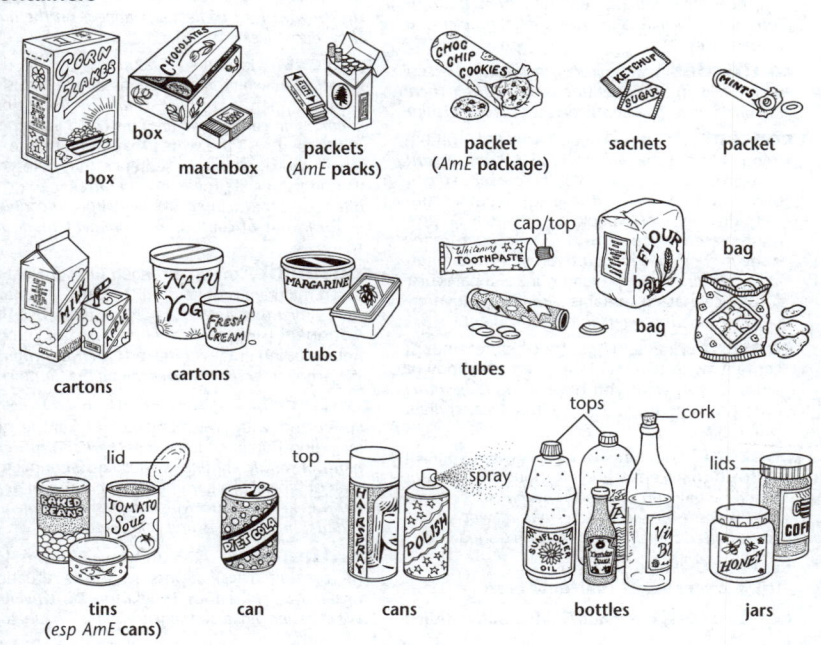

box
box
matchbox
packets (*AmE* packs)
packet (*AmE* package)
sachets
packet

cartons
cartons
tubs
cap/top
tubes
bag
bag

lid
tins (*esp AmE* cans)
top
can
cans
tops
cork
spray
bottles
lids
jars

CONSONANTS p **p**en b **b**ad t **t**ea d **d**id k **c**at g **g**ot tʃ **ch**in dʒ **J**une f **f**all v **v**an θ **th**in

contemporary → contingency

contemporary¹ /kənˈtemprəri/ adj **1** belonging to the same time as sb/sth else □ *sezaman*: *The programme includes contemporary film footage of the First World War.* **2** of the present time □ *kontemporari; semasa*: *contemporary music/art/society* **SYN** modern

contemporary² /kənˈtemprəri/ noun [C] (pl **contemporaries**) a person who lives or does sth at the same time as sb else □ *orang yg sezaman atau sebaya dgn sso*: *The Beatles and their contemporaries changed popular music in the 60s.*

contempt /kənˈtempt/ noun [U] **contempt (for sb/sth)** the feeling that sb/sth does not deserve any respect or is without value □ *rasa benci; kebencian*: *The teacher treated my question with contempt.* ▶ **contemptuous** /kənˈtemptʃuəs/ adj: *The boy just gave a contemptuous laugh when I asked him to be quiet.*

contemptible /kənˈtemptəbl/ adj (formal) not deserving any respect at all □ *layak dihina; hina; patut dibenci*: *contemptible behaviour* **SYN** despicable

contend /kənˈtend/ verb **1** [T] (formal) to say or argue that sth is true □ *menegaskan; berkeras mengatakan*: *The young man contended that he was innocent.* **2** [I] **contend (for sth)** to compete against sb to win or gain sth □ *bertanding*: *Two athletes are contending for first place.* **3** [I] **contend with/against sb/sth** to have to deal with a problem or a difficult situation □ *menghadapi; dihadapi; diatasi*: *She's had a lot of problems to contend with.*

contender /kənˈtendə(r)/ noun [C] a person who may win a competition □ *petanding*: *There are only two serious contenders for the leadership.*

content¹ /ˈkɒntent/ noun **1 contents** [pl] the thing or things that are inside sth □ *kandungan; muatan*: *Add the contents of this packet to a pint of cold milk and mix well.* **2** [sing] the main subject, ideas, etc. of a book, an article, a TV programme, etc □ *kandungan*: *The content of the essay is good, but there are too many grammatical mistakes.* **3** [sing] the amount of a particular substance that sth contains □ *kandungan*: *Many processed foods have a high sugar content.*

content² /kənˈtent/ adj [not before a noun] **content (with sth); content to do sth** happy or satisfied with what you have or do □ *berpuas hati*: *I don't need a new car—I'm perfectly content with this one.*

content³ /kənˈtent/ verb [T] **content yourself with sth** to accept sth even though it was not exactly what you wanted □ *terpaksa berpuas hati menerima sst*: *The restaurant was closed, so we had to content ourselves with a sandwich.*

content⁴ /kənˈtent/ noun
IDM to your heart's content ➔ heart

contented /kənˈtentɪd/ adj happy or satisfied □ *puas hati; bahagia*: *The baby gave a contented chuckle.* ▶ **contentedly** adv

contention /kənˈtenʃn/ noun **1** [U] (formal) arguing; disagreement □ *perbahasan; pertelingkahan* **2** [C] (formal) your opinion; something that you say is true □ *pendapat*: *The government's contention is that unemployment will start to fall next year.*
IDM in contention (for sth) having a chance of winning a competition □ *bertanding; berpeluang memenangi*: *Four teams are still in contention for the cup.*

contentious /kənˈtenʃəs/ adj likely to cause argument □ *yg menimbulkan perbalahan*: *a contentious issue*

contentment /kənˈtentmənt/ noun [U] a feeling of happiness and satisfaction □ *rasa puas hati*

contest¹ /ˈkɒntest/ noun [C] **1** a competition to find out who is the best, strongest, most beautiful, etc. □ *pertandingan*: *I've decided to enter that writing contest.* **2** a struggle to gain control or power □ *persaingan*: *a contest for the leadership of the party*

contest² /kənˈtest/ verb [T] **1** to take part in a competition or try to win sth □ *bertanding*: *Twenty-four teams will contest next year's World Cup.* **2** to say that sth is wrong or that it was not done properly □ *mempertikaikan*: *They contested the decision, saying that the judges had not been fair.*

contestant /kənˈtestənt/ noun [C] a person who takes part in a **contest** □ *peserta pertandingan*: *Four contestants appear on the quiz show each week.*

context /ˈkɒntekst/ noun [C,U] **1** the situation in which sth happens or that caused sth to happen □ *konteks; keadaan*: *To put our company in context, we are now the third largest in the country.* **2** the words that come before or after a word, phrase or sentence that help you to understand its meaning □ *konteks*: *You can often guess the meaning of a word from its context.* ◆ *Taken out of context, his comment made no sense.*

continent /ˈkɒntɪnənt/ noun **1** [C] one of the seven main areas of land on the Earth □ *benua*: *Asia, Africa and Antarctica are continents.* **2 the Continent** [sing] (BrE) the main part of Europe not including Britain or Ireland □ *benua Eropah*: *We're going to spend a weekend on the Continent.*

continental /ˌkɒntɪˈnentl/ adj **1** (BrE) connected with the main part of Europe not including Britain or Ireland □ *(berkenaan dgn) benua Eropah*: *continental holidays* **2** connected with or typical of a continent □ *(berkenaan dgn) benua; kebenuaan*: *Moscow has a continental climate: hot summers and cold winters.*

contingency /kənˈtɪndʒənsi/ noun [C] (pl **contingencies**) a possible future situation or event □ *(hal) luar jangkaan; kontingensi*: *We'd better make contingency plans just in case*

ð **then** s **so** z **zoo** ʃ **she** ʒ vi**s**ion h **h**ow m **m**an n **n**o ŋ si**ng** l **l**eg r **r**ed j **y**es w **w**et

something goes wrong. ♦ *We've tried to prepare for every possible contingency.*

contingent /kənˈtɪndʒənt/ *noun* [C, with sing or pl verb] **1** a group of people from the same country, organization, etc. who are attending an event □ *kontinjen; pasukan*: *the Irish contingent at the conference* **2** a group of armed forces forming part of a larger force □ *kontinjen*

continual /kənˈtɪnjuəl/ *adj* [only before a noun] happening again and again □ *tdk henti-henti*: *His continual phone calls started to annoy her.* ⊃ look at **incessant** ▶ **continually** /-jʊəli/ *adv*

continuation /kənˌtɪnjuˈeɪʃn/ *noun* [sing, U] something that continues or follows sth else; the act of making sth continue □ *penerusan; berterusan; sambungan*: *The team are hoping for a continuation of their recent good form.* ♦ *Continuation of the current system will be impossible.*

continue /kənˈtɪnju:/ *verb* **1** [I] to keep happening or existing without stopping □ *berterusan*: *If the pain continues, see your doctor.* **2** [I,T] **continue (doing/to do sth); continue (with sth)** to keep doing sth without stopping □ *meneruskan*: *They ignored me and continued their conversation.* ♦ *He continued working/to work late into the night.* ♦ *Will you continue with the lessons after the exam?* **3** [I,T] to go further in the same direction □ *meneruskan*: *The next day we continued our journey.* **4** [I,T] to begin to do or say sth again after you had stopped □ *menyambung; disambung; meneruskan; diteruskan*: *The meeting will continue after lunch.* ♦ *I'm sorry I interrupted. Please continue.* ♦ *We'll continue the meeting later.*

continued /kənˈtɪnju:d/ (*abbr* cont.; contd) *adj* [only before a noun] going on without stopping □ *berterusan; berlarutan*: *We are grateful for your continued support.*

continuity /ˌkɒntɪˈnju:əti/ *noun* [U] the fact of continuing without stopping or of staying the same □ *kesinambungan*: *The pupils will have the same teacher for two years to ensure continuity.*

continuous /kənˈtɪnjuəs/ *adj* **1** happening or existing without stopping □ *berterusan*: *There was a continuous line of cars stretching for miles.* **2** (*informal*) repeated many times □ *bertubi-tubi*: *For four days the town suffered continuous attacks.* ▶ **continuously** *adv*: *It has rained continuously here for three days.*

the conˈtinuous tense (also **the proˈgressive tense**) *noun* [C] the form of a verb such as 'I am waiting', 'I was waiting' or 'I have been waiting' which is made from a part of 'be' and a verb ending in '-ing' and is used to describe an action that continues for a period of time □ *kala berlanjutan* ℹ For more information about the continuous tense, look at the **Reference Section** at the back of this dictionary.

contort /kənˈtɔ:t/ *verb* [I,T] to move or to make sth move into a strange or unusual shape □ *berkernyut; meliut*: *His face contorted/was contorted with pain.* ▶ **contortion** *noun* [C]

contour /ˈkɒntʊə(r)/ *noun* [C] **1** the shape of the outer surface of sth □ *garis bentuk*: *I could just make out the contours of the house in the dark.* **2** (also **ˈcontour line**) a line on a map joining places of equal height □ *kontur*

contra- /ˈkɒntrə/ [in nouns, verbs and adjectives] against; opposite □ *kontra*: *contraflow* ♦ *contradict*

contraband /ˈkɒntrəbænd/ *noun* [U] goods that are illegally taken into or out of a country □ *barangan seludup*: *contraband cigarettes* ♦ *to smuggle contraband*

contraception /ˌkɒntrəˈsepʃn/ *noun* [U] the ways of preventing a woman from becoming pregnant □ *pencegahan kehamilan*: *a reliable form of contraception* ⊃ look at **birth control**, **family planning**

contraceptive /ˌkɒntrəˈseptɪv/ *noun* [C] a drug or a device that prevents a woman from becoming pregnant □ *ubat/alat pencegah kehamilan* ▶ **contraceptive** *adj* [only before a noun]

contract¹ /ˈkɒntrækt/ *noun* [C] a written legal agreement □ *kontrak*: *They signed a three-year contract with a major record company.* ♦ *a temporary contract*

contract² /kənˈtrækt/ *verb* **1** [I,T] to become or to make sth smaller or shorter □ *mengecutkan*: *Metals contract as they cool.* **OPP** expand **2** [T] to get an illness or disease, especially a serious one □ *mendapat (penyakit)*: *to contract pneumonia* **3** [I,T] to make a written legal agreement with sb to do sth □ *membuat/mengikat kontrak*: *His firm has been contracted to supply all the furniture for the new building.*

PHR V **contract sth out (to sb)** to arrange for work to be done by sb outside your own company □ *mengkontrakkan.sst (kpd sso)*

contraction /kənˈtrækʃn/ *noun* **1** [U] the process of becoming or of making sth become smaller or shorter □ *pengecutan*: *the expansion and contraction of a muscle* **2** [C] a strong movement of the muscles that happens to a woman as her baby is born □ *kontraksi; pengecutan* **3** [C] a shorter form of a word or words □ *singkatan*: *'Mustn't' is a contraction of 'must not'.*

> **EXAM TIP**
>
> **Using contractions**
>
> Think carefully before you use a contraction in an exam, as they are not usually used in formal writing. You can use contractions in some types of writing, for example a letter or an email to a friend, or an article for a student magazine, but be careful. Make sure you are still using proper English. You should never use words like 'gonna' or 'wanna', which are only used in spoken English.

VOWELS iː see i any ɪ sit e ten æ hat ɑː father ɒ got ɔː saw ʊ put uː too u usual

contractor /kənˈtræktə(r)/ noun [C] a person or company that has a contract to do work or provide goods or services for another company □ *kontraktor*

contractual /kənˈtræktʃuəl/ adj connected with or included in a contract □ *berdasarkan kontrak; kontraktual*

contradict /ˌkɒntrəˈdɪkt/ verb [T] to say that sth is wrong or not true; to say the opposite of sth □ *menyanggah; menyangkal; bertentangan*: *These instructions seem to contradict previous ones.*

contradiction /ˌkɒntrəˈdɪkʃn/ noun [C,U] a statement, a fact or an action that is opposite to or different from another one □ *percanggahan; perihal bertentang*: *There were a number of contradictions in what he told the police.* ♦ *This letter is in complete contradiction to their previous one.*

contradictory /ˌkɒntrəˈdɪktəri/ adj being opposite to or not matching sth else □ *(yg) bertentangan/bercanggah*: *Contradictory reports appeared in the newspapers.*

contraflow /ˈkɒntrəfləʊ/ noun [C] (BrE) the system that is used when one half of a wide road is closed for repairs, and traffic going in both directions has to use the other side □ *(laluan) lawan arus*

contralto /kənˈtræltəʊ/ noun [C,U] (pl contraltos) the lowest female singing voice; a woman with this voice □ *kontralto*

contraption /kənˈtræpʃn/ noun [C] a strange or complicated piece of equipment □ *alat yg agak pelik*: *The first aeroplanes were dangerous contraptions.*

contrary[1] /ˈkɒntrəri/ adj 1 [only before a noun] completely different □ *bertentangan; berlawanan*: *I thought it was possible, but she took the contrary view.* **OPP opposite** 2 **contrary to** completely different from; opposite to; against □ *bertentangan dgn*: *Contrary to popular belief* (= to what many people think), *not all boxers are stupid.*

contrary[2] /ˈkɒntrəri/ noun
IDM on the contrary the opposite is true; certainly not □ *sebaliknya*: *'You look as if you're not enjoying yourself.' 'On the contrary, I'm having a great time.'*
to the contrary (formal) saying the opposite □ *sebaliknya*: *Unless I hear anything to the contrary, I shall assume that the arrangements haven't changed.*

contrast[1] /ˈkɒntrɑːst/ noun 1 [U] comparison between two people or things that shows the differences between them □ *perbandingan; berbanding*: *In contrast to previous years, we've had a very successful summer.* 2 [C,U] (a) contrast (to/with sb/sth); (a) contrast (between A and B) a clear difference between two things or people that is seen when they are compared □ *per-*

bezaan: *There is a tremendous contrast between the climate in the valley and the climate in the hills.* 3 [C] something that is clearly different from sth else when the two things are compared □ *perbezaan; berbeza*: *The work you did today is quite a contrast to what you did last week.*

WRITING TIP

How to show contrast 1
To show contrast between positive and negative aspects of a subject, we often use **however**, **nevertheless**, **nonetheless** or **on the one hand … on the other hand**: *Smartphones are very useful.* **However**, *they are very expensive.* ♦ *Smartphones are very expensive.* **Nevertheless/Nonetheless**, *they are very useful.* ♦ **On the one hand** *smartphones are very useful, but* **on the other hand**, *they are very expensive.* ⊃ note at **despite**

ℹ For more help with writing, look at **Wordpower Writing Tutor** at the back of this dictionary.

contrast[2] /kənˈtrɑːst/ verb 1 [T] contrast (A and/with B) to compare people or things in order to show the differences between them □ *membandingkan*: *The film contrasts his poor childhood with his later life as a millionaire.* 2 [I] contrast with sb/sth to be clearly different when compared □ *berbeza*: *This comment contrasts sharply with his previous remarks.*

contrasting /kənˈtrɑːstɪŋ/ adj very different in style, colour or attitude □ *sangat berbeza*: *bright, contrasting colours* ♦ *contrasting opinions*

contravene /ˌkɒntrəˈviːn/ verb [T] (formal) to break a law or a rule □ *melanggar/menyalahi undang-undang, dsb* ▸ **contravention** /ˌkɒntrəˈvenʃn/ noun [C,U]

contribute /kənˈtrɪbjuːt; ˈkɒntrɪbjuːt/ verb contribute (sth) (to/towards sth) 1 [I,T] to give a part of the total, together with others □ *menyumbang; memberi sumbangan*: *Would you like to contribute towards our collection for famine relief?* ♦ *The research has contributed a great deal to our knowledge of cancer.* 2 [I] to be one of the causes of sth □ *merupakan sebab*: *It is not known whether the bad weather contributed to the accident.* 3 [I,T] to write articles for a magazine or newspaper □ *menyumbang*: *She contributed a number of articles to the magazine.*

contribution /ˌkɒntrɪˈbjuːʃn/ noun [C] a contribution (to/towards sth) something that you give, especially money or help, or do together with other people □ *sumbangan*: *If we all make a small contribution, we'll be able to buy Ray a good present.* ♦ *I'd like to thank everyone for their contribution towards clearing up after the party.*

contributor /kənˈtrɪbjətə(r)/ noun [C] a person who **contributes** to sth □ *penyumbang*

contributory /kənˈtrɪbjətəri/ adj helping to cause or produce sth □ *merupakan sebab*: *Tiredness is a contributory factor in many road accidents.*

contrive /kənˈtraɪv/ verb [T] **1** to manage to do sth, although there are difficulties □ *dpt*: *If I can contrive to get off work early, I'll see you later.* **2** to plan or invent sth in a clever and/or dishonest way □ *merancangkan*: *He contrived a scheme to cheat insurance companies.*

contrived /kənˈtraɪvd/ adj hard to believe; not natural or realistic □ *mustahil; tdk munasabah*: *The ending of the film seemed rather contrived.*

control¹ /kənˈtrəʊl/ noun **1** [U] **control (of/ over sb/sth)** power and ability to make sb/sth do what you want □ *kuasa; kawalan; mengawal*: *Rebels managed to take control of the radio station.* ♦ *Some teachers find it difficult to keep control of their class.* ♦ *He lost control of the car and crashed.* ♦ *I was late because of circumstances beyond my control.* **2** [C,U] **(a) control (on/over sth)** a limit on sth; a way of keeping sb/sth within certain limits □ *kawalan*: *price controls* ♦ *The faults forced the company to review its quality control procedures.* **3** [C] one of the parts of a machine that is used for operating it □ *alat kawalan*: *the controls of an aeroplane/a TV* ♦ *a control panel* ♦ *Hold down the control key* (= a key on a computer keyboard used for performing a particular operation) *and click.* ♦ *a control pad* (= used for playing computer games) **4** [sing] the place from which sth is operated or where sth is checked □ *pusat kawalan*: *We went through passport control and then got onto the plane.*
IDM **be in control (of sth)** to direct or manage a situation □ *menguasai*: *The police are again in control of the area following last night's violence.*
be/get out of control to be/become impossible to deal with □ *tdk dpt dikawal*: *The demonstration got out of control and fighting broke out.*
under control being dealt with successfully □ *dpt dikawal*: *It took several hours to bring the fire under control.*

control² /kənˈtrəʊl/ verb [T] (**controlling; controlled**) **1** to have power and ability to make sb/sth do what you want □ *menguasai; mengawal*: *One family controls the company.* ♦ *Police struggled to control the crowd.* ♦ *I couldn't control myself any longer and burst out laughing.* **2** to keep sth within certain limits □ *mengawal*: *measures to control price rises* ▶ **controller** noun [C]: *air traffic controllers*

conˈtrol freak noun [C] (*informal*) (used in a critical way) a person who always wants to be in control of their own and other people's lives, and to organize how things are done □ *pengongkong*

controlled /kənˈtrəʊld/ adj **1** done or arranged in a very careful way □ *teratur*: *a controlled explosion* **2** limited, or managed by law or by rules □ *terhad*: *controlled airspace* **3** **-controlled** [in compounds] managed by a particular group or in a particular way □ *dikawal*: *a British-controlled company* ♦ *computer-controlled systems* **4** remaining calm and not getting angry or upset □ *terkawal*: *She remained quiet and controlled.* ⊃ look at **uncontrolled**

controversial /ˌkɒntrəˈvɜːʃl/ adj causing public discussion and disagreement □ *menimbulkan kontroversi/perbalahan*: *a controversial issue/decision/plan*

controversy /ˈkɒntrəvɜːsi; kənˈtrɒvəsi/ noun [C,U] (*pl* **controversies**) public discussion and disagreement about sth □ *kontroversi*: *The plans for changing the city centre caused much controversy.*

conurbation /ˌkɒnɜːˈbeɪʃn/ noun [C] a very large area of houses and other buildings where towns have grown and joined together □ *bandar gabungan*

convalesce /ˌkɒnvəˈles/ verb [I] to rest and get better over a period of time after an illness □ *berehat sesudah sembuh drpd penyakit* ▶ **convalescence** noun [sing, U] ▶ **convalescent** /ˌkɒnvəˈlesnt/ adj

convene /kənˈviːn/ verb [I,T] (*formal*) to come together or to bring people together for a meeting, etc. □ *bersidang*

convenience /kənˈviːniəns/ noun **1** [U] the quality of being easy, useful or suitable for sb □ *kemudahan; kesenangan*: *a building designed for the convenience of disabled people* ♦ *For convenience, you can pay for everything at once.* **2** [C] something that makes things easier, quicker or more comfortable □ *kemudahan*: *houses with all the modern conveniences* (= central heating, hot water, etc.) **3** [C] (*BrE*) a public toilet □ *tandas awam*

conˈvenience food noun [C,U] food that you buy frozen or in a box or can, that you can prepare very quickly and easily □ *makanan mudah*

convenient /kənˈviːniənt/ adj **1** suitable or practical for a particular purpose; not causing difficulty □ *sesuai; senang*: *I'm willing to meet you on any day that's convenient for you.* ♦ *It isn't convenient to talk at the moment, I'm in the middle of a meeting.* **OPP** **inconvenient** **2** close to sth; in a useful position □ *dekat; berhampiran*: *Our house is convenient for the shops.* ▶ **conveniently** adv

convent /ˈkɒnvənt/ (*AmE* also) / noun [C] a place where **nuns** (= religious women) live together in a community □ *konven* ⊃ look at **monastery**

convention /kənˈvenʃn/ noun **1** [C,U] a traditional way of behaving or of doing sth □ *kebiasaan; amalan biasa; adat*: *A speech by the bride's father is one of the conventions of a wedding.* ♦ *The film shows no respect for convention.* **2** [C] a large meeting of the members of a profession, political party, etc. □ *persidangan*: *the Democratic Party Convention* **SYN** **conference** **3** [C] a formal agreement, especially between different countries □ *konvensyen; persetujuan*: *the Geneva Convention*

[C] **countable**, a noun with a plural form: *one book, two books*   [U] **uncountable**, a noun with no plural form: *some sugar*

conventional → convulsion 192

conventional /kən'venʃənl/ *adj* **1** always behaving in a traditional or normal way □ *bersikap konvensional*: *conventional attitudes* ♦ *I quite like him but he's so conventional* (= boring, because of this). **2** following what is traditional or the way sth has been done for a long time □ *secara konvensional*: *You can cook it in a microwave or in a conventional oven.* ► **conventionally** /-ʃənəli/ *adv*

converge /kən'vɜːdʒ/ *verb* [I] **converge (on sb/sth)** (used about two or more people or things) to move towards each other or meet at the same point from different directions □ *bertemu; bertumpu; berkumpul*: *Fans from all over the country converge on the village during the annual music festival.* **OPP** **diverge**

conversant /kən'vɜːsnt/ *adj* (*formal*) **conversant with sth** knowing about sth; familiar with sth □ *mengetahui/maklum ttg sst*: *All employees should be conversant with basic accounting.*

conversation /ˌkɒnvə'seɪʃn/ *noun* [C,U] a talk between two or more people □ *perbualan*: *I had a long conversation with her about her plans for the future.* ♦ *His job is his only topic of conversation.* ♦ *She finds it difficult to make conversation* (= to think of things to say).
IDM **deep in thought/conversation** ⇒ **deep¹**
► **conversational** /-ʃənl/ *adj*

converse /kən'vɜːs/ *verb* [I] (*formal*) to talk to sb; to have a conversation □ *berbual*

conversely /'kɒnvɜːsli/ *adv* (*formal*) in a way that is opposite to sth □ *sebaliknya*: *People who earn a lot of money have little time to spend it. Conversely, many people with limitless time do not have enough money to do what they want.*

conversion /kən'vɜːʃn/ (*AmE* also) / *noun* [C,U] **(a) conversion (from sth) (into/to sth)** **1** the act or process of changing from one form, system or use to another □ *penukaran*: *a conversion table for miles and kilometres* **2** becoming a member of a different religion □ *perihal memeluk agama lain*

convert¹ /kən'vɜːt/ *verb* [I,T] **1** **convert (sth) (from sth) (into/to sth)** to change from one form, system or use to another □ *menukarkan; mengubah suai*: *a sofa that converts into a double bed* ♦ *How do you convert pounds into kilos?* **2** **convert (sb) (from sth) (to sth)** to change or to persuade sb to change to a different religion □ *menukar/masuk agama*: *As a young man he converted to Islam.* ♦ *to convert people to Christianity*

convert² /'kɒnvɜːt/ *noun* [C] **a convert (to sth)** a person who has changed their religion □ *orang yg bertukar agama*

convertible¹ /kən'vɜːtəbl/ *adj* able to be changed into another form □ *dpt ditukarkan*: *convertible currencies* (= ones that can be exchanged for those of other countries)

convertible² /kən'vɜːtəbl/ *noun* [C] a car with a roof that can be folded down or taken off □ *kereta berhud*

convex /'kɒnveks/ *adj* having a surface that curves towards the outside of sth, like an eye □ *cembung*: *a convex lens* ⇒ look at **concave** ⇒ picture at **concave**

convey /kən'veɪ/ *verb* [T] **1** **convey sth (to sb)** to make ideas, thoughts, feelings, etc. known to sb □ *menyampaikan*: *The film conveys a lot of information but in an entertaining way.* ♦ *Please convey my sympathy to her at this sad time.* **2** (*formal*) to take sb/sth from one place to another, especially in a vehicle □ *membawa*

con'veyor belt *noun* [C] a moving belt that carries objects from one place to another, for example in a factory □ *tali sawat penyampai*

convict¹ /kən'vɪkt/ *verb* [T] **convict sb (of sth)** to say officially in a court of law that sb is guilty of a crime □ *disabitkan bersalah*: *He was convicted of armed robbery and sent to prison.* **OPP** **acquit**

convict² /'kɒnvɪkt/ *noun* [C] a person who has been found guilty of a crime and put in prison □ *banduan*

conviction /kən'vɪkʃn/ *noun* **1** [C,U] the act of finding sb guilty of a crime in a court of law □ *sabitan*: *He has several previous convictions for burglary.* **2** [C] a very strong opinion or belief □ *kepercayaan*: *religious convictions* **3** [U] the feeling of being certain about what you are doing □ *keyakinan*: *He played without conviction and lost easily.*

convince /kən'vɪns/ *verb* [T] **1** **convince sb (of sth/that ...)** to succeed in making sb believe sth □ *meyakinkan; membuat sso percaya*: *She convinced him of the need to go back.* ♦ *I couldn't convince her that I was right.* **2** **convince sb (to do sth)** to persuade sb to do sth □ *meyakinkan (dgn memujuk)*: *I tried to convince him to see a doctor.*

convinced /kən'vɪnst/ *adj* [not before a noun] completely sure about sth □ *yakin*: *He's convinced of his ability to win.*

convincing /kən'vɪnsɪŋ/ *adj* **1** able to make sb believe sth □ *meyakinkan*: *Her explanation for her absence wasn't very convincing.* **2** (used about a victory) complete; clear □ *mutlak; jelas*: *a convincing win* ► **convincingly** *adv*

convoy /'kɒnvɔɪ/ *noun* [C,U] a group of vehicles or ships travelling together □ *konvoi*: *a convoy of lorries* ♦ *warships travelling in convoy*

convulse /kən'vʌls/ *verb* [I,T] to make sudden violent movements that you cannot control; to cause sb to move in this way □ *terkokol-kokol*: *He was convulsed with pain.*

convulsion /kən'vʌlʃn/ *noun* [C, usually pl] a sudden violent movement that you cannot control □ *konvulsi; sawan*: *Children sometimes have convulsions when they are ill.* ► **convulsive** /kən'vʌlsɪv/ *adj*: *Her breath came in convulsive gasps.*

[I] **intransitive**, a verb which has no object: *He laughed.*   [T] **transitive**, a verb which has an object: *He ate an apple.*

coo /ku:/ verb [I] **1** to make a soft low sound like a dove (= a white bird, often used as a sign of peace) □ *mendekut* **2** to speak in a soft, gentle voice □ *berbisik lembut*: *He went to the cot and cooed over the baby.*

cook¹ /kʊk/ verb **1** [I,T] to prepare food for eating by heating it □ *memasak; dimasak*: *My mother taught me how to cook.* ◆ *The sauce should be cooked on low heat for twenty minutes.* ◆ *He cooked us a meal.* **2** [I] (used about food) to be prepared for eating by being heated □ *sedang dimasak*: *I could smell something delicious cooking in the kitchen.* ➔ note at **recipe** ➔ picture on page P11

PHR V **cook sth up** (*informal*) to invent sth that is not true □ *mereka-reka sst*: *She cooked up an excuse for not arriving on time.*

TOPIC

Cooking
Food can be cooked in various ways. You can **boil** or **steam** vegetables with water in a **saucepan** and you can **fry** meat, fish and vegetables in oil in a **frying pan**. You **roast** meat or **bake** bread and cakes in the **oven**. You can **grill** meat or fish under the **grill**, but **toast** is usually made in a **toaster**. If you want an easy meal you can **microwave** a **ready meal** (= a complete meal bought from a supermarket) in a special oven called a **microwave**. In the summer you can **barbecue** burgers, etc. on an outside grill, also called a **barbecue**.

---

cook² /kʊk/ noun [C] a person who cooks □ *tukang masak*: *My sister is an excellent cook.* ➔ picture on page P2

cookbook /'kʊkbʊk/ (*BrE also* **'cookery book**) *noun* [C] a book that gives instructions on cooking and contains **recipes** (= instructions on how to cook individual dishes) □ *buku masakan* ➔ note at **recipe**

cooker /'kʊkə(r)/ (*especially AmE* **stove**) *noun* [C] a large piece of kitchen equipment for cooking using gas or electricity. It consists of an oven, a flat top on which pans can be placed and often a **grill** (= a device which heats the food from above). □ *dapur (gas, elektrik)* ➔ picture on page P8

cookery /'kʊkəri/ noun [U] the skill or activity of preparing and cooking food □ *masak-memasak*: *Chinese/French/Italian cookery*

'cookery book = **cookbook**

cookie /'kʊki/ (*AmE*) = **biscuit 2** a computer file with information that shows the user's preferences and that is stored each time that person uses the Internet □ *kuki*

cooking /'kʊkɪŋ/ noun [U] **1** the preparation of food for eating □ *memasak*: *Cooking is one of her hobbies.* ◆ *In our house, I do the cleaning and my husband does the cooking.* **2** food produced by cooking □ *masakan*: *He missed his mother's cooking when he left home.*

---

cool¹ /ku:l/ adj **1** fairly cold; not hot or warm □ *agak sejuk*: *It was a cool evening so I put on a pullover.* ◆ *What I'd like is a long cool drink.* ➔ note at **cold¹** **2** calm; not excited or angry □ *tenang*: *She always manages to remain cool under pressure.* **3** unfriendly; not showing interest □ *dingin*: *When we first met, she was rather cool towards me, but later she became friendlier.* **4** (*informal*) very good or fashionable □ *bagus; bergaya*: *Those are cool shoes you're wearing!* **5** (*informal*) people say **Cool!** or **That's cool** to show that they approve of sth or agree to a suggestion □ *baguslah*: *'We're meeting in town and then going to see a film.' 'Cool!'*

cool² /ku:l/ verb **1** [I,T] **cool (sth/sb) (down/off)** to lower the temperature of sth; to become cool □ *menjadi sejuk; menyejukkan*: *Let the soup cool (down).* ◆ *After the game we needed to cool off.* ◆ *A nice cold drink will soon cool you down.* **2** [I] (used about feelings) to become less strong □ *berkurang; menjadi dingin*: *Relations between them have definitely cooled.*

PHR V **cool (sb) down/off** to become or make sb calmer □ *meredakan; menenangkan*

cool³ /ku:l/ noun **the cool** [sing] a cool temperature or place; the quality of being cool □ *tempat sejuk/teduh*: *We sat in the cool of a cafe, out of the sun.*

IDM **keep/lose your cool** to stay calm/to stop being calm and become angry, nervous, etc. □ *kekal tenang/menjadi marah, gugup, hilang sabar, dsb*

cooling-'off period noun [C] a period of time when sb can think again about a decision that they have made □ *tempoh bertenang*

coolly /'ku:lli/ adv in a calm way; without showing much interest or excitement □ *dgn tenang*: *At first she was very angry; then she explained the problem coolly.*

coolness /'ku:lnəs/ noun [U] the quality or state of being cool □ *kesejukan; sejuknya; ketenangan; sikap dingin*: *the coolness of the water* ◆ *his coolness under stress* ◆ *their coolness towards strangers*

coop /ku:p/ verb

PHR V **coop sb/sth up (in sth)** to keep sb/sth inside a small space □ *mengurung; terkurung*: *The children were cooped up indoors all day because the weather was so terrible.*

cooperate (*BrE also* **co-operate**) /kəʊˈɒpəreɪt/ verb [I] **cooperate (with sb/sth)** **1** to work with sb else to achieve sth □ *bekerjasama*: *Our company is cooperating with an Italian firm on this project.* **2** to be helpful by doing what sb asks you to do □ *bekerjasama*: *If everyone cooperates by following the instructions, there will be no problem.*

cooperation (*BrE also* **co-operation**) /kəʊˌɒpəˈreɪʃn/ noun [U] **1 cooperation (with sb)** working together with sb else to achieve sth □ *kerjasama*: *Schools are working in close cooperation with parents to improve standards.* **2** help that you give by doing what sb asks you to do □ *kerjasama*: *The police asked the public for their cooperation in the investigation.*

cooperative¹ (BrE also **co-operative**) /kəʊˈɒpərətɪv/ *adj* **1** done by people working together □ *kerjasama*: *a cooperative business venture* **2** helpful; doing what sb asks you to do □ *memberikan kerjasama; bekerjasama*: *My firm were very cooperative and allowed me to have time off.*

cooperative² (BrE also **co-operative**) /kəʊˈɒpərətɪv/ *noun* [C] a business or an organization that is owned and run by all of the people who work for it □ *koperasi; syarikat kerjasama*: *a workers' cooperative*

coordinate¹ (BrE also **co-ordinate**) /kəʊˈɔːdɪneɪt/ *verb* [T] to organize different things or people so that they work together □ *menyelaraskan*: *It is her job to coordinate the various departments.*

coordinate² (BrE also **co-ordinate**) /kəʊˈɔːdɪnət/ *noun* [C] one of the two sets of numbers and/or letters that are used for finding the position of a point on a map □ *koordinat*

Co-ordinated Universal Time *noun* [U] (*abbr* **UTC**) the time based on **atomic**, **clocks** (= very accurate and scientific clocks), used as the basis of legal time in most countries □ *Waktu Universal Selaras* ⊃ look at **GMT**

coordination (BrE also **co-ordination**) /kəʊˌɔːdɪˈneɪʃn/ *noun* [U] **1** the organization of different things or people so that they work together □ *penyelarasan* **2** the ability to control the movements of your body properly □ *koordinasi*: *Children's coordination improves as they get older.*

coordinator (BrE also **co-ordinator**) /kəʊˈɔːdɪneɪtə(r)/ *noun* [C] a person who is responsible for organizing different things or people so that they work together □ *penyelaras*

cop¹ /kɒp/ (also **copper**) *noun* [C] (*informal*) a police officer □ *polis*

cop² /kɒp/ *verb* (**copping**; **copped**)

PHR V **cop out (of sth)** (*informal*) to avoid sth that you should do, because you are afraid or lazy □ *mengelak (drpd membuat sst)*: *She was going to help me with the cooking but she copped out at the last minute.*

cope /kəʊp/ *verb* [I] **cope (with sb/sth)** to deal successfully with a difficult matter or situation □ *menangani (sst hal atau keadaan)*: *She finds it difficult to cope with the pressure of exams.* **SYN** **manage**

copier /ˈkɒpiə(r)/ (*especially AmE*) = **photocopier**

copious /ˈkəʊpiəs/ *adj* in large amounts □ *banyak sekali*: *She made copious notes at the lecture.* ▶ **copiously** *adv*

cop-out *noun* [C] (*informal*) a way of avoiding sth that you should do □ *pengelakan*

copper /ˈkɒpə(r)/ *noun* **1** [U] (*symbol* **Cu**) a common reddish-brown metal □ *tembaga*: *water pipes made of copper* **2** [C] (*BrE*) a coin of low value made of brown metal □ *syiling tembaga*: *I only had a few coppers left.* **3** = **cop¹**

copse /kɒps/ *noun* [C] a small area of trees or bushes □ *belukar*

copulate /ˈkɒpjuleɪt/ *verb* [I] (*formal*) (used especially about animals) to have sex □ *mengawan; bersanggama* ▶ **copulation** /ˌkɒpjuˈleɪʃn/ *noun* [U]

copy¹ /ˈkɒpi/ *noun* [C] (*pl* **copies**) **1** something that is made to look exactly like sth else □ *salinan*: *I kept a copy of the letter I wrote.* ♦ *the master copy* (= the original piece of paper from which copies are made) ♦ *to make a copy of a computer file* ⊃ look at **photocopy** **2** one book, newspaper, record, etc. of which many have been printed or produced □ *naskhah*: *I managed to buy the last copy of the book left in the shop.*

copy² /ˈkɒpi/ *verb* (**copying**; **copies**; *pt, pp* **copied**) **1** [T] to make sth exactly the same as sth else □ *menyalin; membuat salinan*: *The children copied pictures from a book.* ♦ *It is illegal to copy videos.* **2** [T] **copy sth (down/out)** to write down sth exactly as it is written somewhere else □ *menyalin*: *I copied down the address on the brochure.* ♦ *I copied out the letter more neatly.* **3** [T] to do or try to do the same as sb else □ *meniru*: *She copies everything her friends do.* **SYN** **imitate** **4** [I] **copy (from sb)** to cheat in an exam or a test by writing what sb else has written □ *meniru*: *He was caught copying from another student in the exam.* **5** [T] = **photocopy**

EXAM TIP

Copying

When you are doing a written exam, try not to copy the words exactly as they are used in the instructions. You will gain marks if you use your own words and expressions instead.

You should never copy anyone else's work in an exam. This is cheating, and, if you are caught, you will get no marks for that exam.

---

copyright /ˈkɒpiraɪt/ *noun* [C,U] the legal right to be the only person who may print, copy, perform, etc. a piece of original work, such as a book, a song or a computer program □ *hak cipta*: *Who owns the copyright?*

coral /ˈkɒrəl/ (*AmE* also /ˈkɔːrəl/) *noun* [U] a hard red, pink or white substance that forms in the sea from the bones of very small sea animals □ *batu karang*: *a coral reef* (= a line of rock in the sea formed by coral)

cord /kɔːd/ *noun* **1** [C,U] (a piece of) strong, thick string ⊃ picture at **rope** **2** (*especially AmE*) = **flex²** **3 cords** [pl] trousers made of **corduroy** (= a thick soft cotton cloth with raised lines on it) □ *seluar korduroi*

cordial /ˈkɔːdiəl/ adj (formal) pleasant and friendly □ *mesra*: *a cordial greeting/smile* ▶ **cordially** /-diəli/ adv

cordless /ˈkɔːdləs/ adj not connected to its power supply by wires □ *tanpa wayar*: *a cordless phone/kettle/iron*

cordon¹ /ˈkɔːdn/ noun [C] a line or ring of police or soldiers that prevents people from entering an area □ *kepungan*

cordon² /ˈkɔːdn/ verb
PHR V **cordon sth off** to stop people entering an area by surrounding it with a ring of police or soldiers □ *mengepung*: *The street where the bomb was discovered was quickly cordoned off.*

corduroy /ˈkɔːdərɔɪ/ noun [U] a thick soft cotton cloth with lines on it, used for making clothes □ *korduroi*: *a corduroy jacket*

core /kɔː(r)/ noun **1** [C] the hard centre of certain fruits, containing seeds □ *empulur*: *an apple core* ⊃ picture on **page P14 2** [C] the central part of a planet □ *teras*: *the earth's core* **3** [sing] the central or most important part of sth □ *teras*: *the core curriculum* (= the subjects that all students have to study) ♦ *What's the core issue here?*
IDM **to the core** completely; in every way □ *sepenuhnya; betul-betul*: *The news shook him to the core* (= shocked him very much).

cork /kɔːk/ noun **1** [U] a light soft material which comes from the outside of a type of tree □ *gabus*: *cork floor tiles* **2** [C] a round piece of **cork** that you push into the end of a bottle to close it, especially a bottle of wine □ *gabus* ⊃ picture at **container**

corkscrew /ˈkɔːkskruː/ noun [C] a tool that you use for pulling **corks** out of bottles □ *skru pencungkil gabus* ⊃ picture at **kitchen**

corn /kɔːn/ noun **1** [U] (*especially BrE*) any plant that is grown for its grain, such as **wheat**; the seeds from these plants □ *biji-bijian*: *a field of corn* ♦ *a cornfield* **2** [U] (*AmE*) = **maize 3** [U] (*AmE*) = **sweetcorn 4** [C] a small, painful area of hard skin on the foot, especially the toe □ *kematu*

corners

The lamp is **in** the corner.

The bank is **on** the corner.

corner¹ /ˈkɔːnə(r)/ noun [C] **1** a place where two lines, edges, surfaces or roads meet □ *penjuru; sudut; bucu*: *Put the lamp in the corner of the room.* ♦ *Write your address in the top right-hand corner.* ♦ *The shop is on the corner of Wall Street and Long Road.* ♦ *He went round the corner at top speed.* **2** a quiet or secret place or area □ *ceruk*: *a remote corner of Scotland* **3** a difficult situation from which you cannot escape □ *keadaan sukar*: *to get yourself into a corner* **4** (in football) a free kick from the corner of the field □ *tendangan penjuru*: *to take a corner*
IDM **cut corners** to do sth quickly and not as well as you should □ *mengambil jalan mudah* **(just) round the corner** very near □ *dekat saja*: *There's a phone box just round the corner.*

corner² /ˈkɔːnə(r)/ verb [T] **1** to get a person or an animal into a position from which they or it cannot escape □ *mengepung*: *He cornered me at the party and started telling me all his problems.* **2** to get control in a particular area of business so that nobody else can have any success in it □ *menguasai (pasaran)*: *That company's really cornered the market in health foods.*

cornflakes /ˈkɔːnfleɪks/ noun [pl] food made of small pieces of dried **corn** and eaten with milk for breakfast □ *emping jagung*

cornflour /ˈkɔːnflaʊə(r)/ noun [U] very fine flour often used to make sauces, etc. thicker □ *tepung jagung*

corn on the cob noun [U] **sweetcorn** (= a type of vegetable) that is cooked with all the yellow grains still on the inner part and eaten □ *jagung tongkol* ⊃ picture on **page P15**

corny /ˈkɔːni/ adj (**cornier**; **corniest**) (*informal*) too ordinary or familiar to be interesting or amusing □ *biasa; sudah basi*: *a corny joke*

coronary¹ /ˈkɒrənri/ adj connected with the heart □ *koronari*

coronary² /ˈkɒrənri/ noun [C] (*pl* **coronaries**) a type of heart attack □ *serangan sakit jantung*

coronation /ˌkɒrəˈneɪʃn/ noun [C] an official ceremony at which sb is made a king or queen □ *pertabalan*

coroner /ˈkɒrənə(r)/ noun [C] a person whose job is to find out the causes of death of people who have died in violent or unusual ways □ *koroner*

Corp. *abbr* (*AmE*) = **corporation**(1) □ *syarikat besar; perbadanan*: *West Coast Motor Corp.*

corporal /ˈkɔːpərəl/ noun [C] a person at a low level in the army or air force □ *koperal*

corporal punishment noun [U] the punishment of people by hitting them, especially of children by parents or teachers □ *hukuman dera* ⊃ look at **capital punishment**

corporate /ˈkɔːpərət/ adj [only before a noun] of or shared by all the members of a group or an organization □ *bersama*: *corporate responsibility*

corporation /ˌkɔːpəˈreɪʃn/ noun [C, with sing or pl verb] **1** (abbr **Corp.**) a large business company □ *syarikat besar; perbadanan*: multinational corporations ◆ the British Broadcasting Corporation **2** (BrE) a group of people elected to govern a particular town or city □ *majlis (perbandaran)*

corps /kɔː(r)/ noun [C, with sing or pl verb] (pl **corps** /kɔːz/) **1** a part of an army with special duties □ *kor*: the medical corps **2** a group of people involved in a special activity □ *kor*: the diplomatic corps

corpse /kɔːps/ noun [C] a dead body, especially of a person □ *mayat* ⊃ look at **carcass**

ʔ correct¹ /kəˈrekt/ adj **1** with no mistakes; right or true □ *betul; tepat*: Well done! All your answers were correct. ◆ Have you got the correct time, please? **2** (used about behaviour, manners, dress, etc.) suitable, proper or right □ *betul; sesuai; bersopan*: What's the correct form of address for a judge? **OPP** for both meanings **incorrect** ▶ **correctly** adv ▶ **correctness** noun [U]

ʔ correct² /kəˈrekt/ verb [T] **1** to make a mistake, fault, etc. right or better □ *membetulkan; menanda*: to correct a spelling mistake ◆ to correct a test (= mark the mistakes in it) **2** to tell sb what mistakes they are making or what faults they have □ *membetulkan; menegur*: He's always correcting me when I'm talking to people.

correction /kəˈrekʃn/ noun **1** [C] a change that makes a mistake, fault, etc. right or better □ *pembetulan*: I've made a few small corrections to your report. ◆ The paper had to publish a correction to the story. **2** [U] the act or process of correcting sth □ *dibetulkan*: There are some programming errors that need correction.

corrective /kəˈrektɪv/ adj intended to make sth right that is wrong □ *pembetulan; pemulihan*: to take corrective action

correlate /ˈkɒrəleɪt/ (AmE also) / verb [I,T] to have or to show a relationship or connection between two or more things □ *menghubungkaitkan; berhubung kait* ▶ **correlation** /ˌkɒrəˈleɪʃn/ (AmE also) / noun [C,U]: There is a correlation between a person's diet and height.

correspond /ˌkɒrəˈspɒnd/ (AmE also) / verb [I] **1** **correspond (to/with sth)** to be the same as or equal to sth; to match □ *selaras; sama*: Does the name on the envelope correspond with the name inside the letter? **2** (formal) **correspond (with sb)** to write letters to and receive them from sb □ *berkirim-kiriman surat*: They corresponded for a year before they got married.

correspondence /ˌkɒrəˈspɒndəns/ (AmE also) / noun **1** [U, sing] (formal) the act of writing letters; the letters themselves □ *surat-menyurat*: There hasn't been any correspondence between them for years. **2** [C,U] a close connection or relationship between two or more things □ *persamaan; kesepadanan*: There is no correspondence between the two sets of figures.

correspondent /ˌkɒrəˈspɒndənt/ (AmE also) / noun [C] **1** a person who provides news or writes articles for a newspaper, etc., especially from a foreign country □ *wartawan; koresponden*: our Middle East correspondent **2** a person who writes letters to sb □ *penulis surat*

corresponding /ˌkɒrəˈspɒndɪŋ/ (AmE also) / adj [only before a noun] related or similar to sth □ *sama*: Sales are up 10% compared with the corresponding period last year. **SYN** **equivalent** ▶ **correspondingly** adv

corridor /ˈkɒrɪdɔː(r)/ (AmE also) / noun [C] a long narrow passage in a building or train, with doors that open into rooms, etc. □ *koridor*

corroborate /kəˈrɒbəreɪt/ verb [T] (formal) to support a statement, an idea, etc. by providing new evidence □ *menyokong*: The witness corroborated Mr Patton's statement about the night of the murder. ▶ **corroboration** /kəˌrɒbəˈreɪʃn/ noun [U]

corrode /kəˈrəʊd/ verb [I,T] (used about metals) to become weak or to be destroyed by chemical action; to cause a metal to do this □ *mengakis*: Parts of the car were corroded by rust. ▶ **corrosion** /kəˈrəʊʒn/ noun [U] ▶ **corrosive** /kəˈrəʊsɪv/ adj

corrugated /ˈkɒrəɡeɪtɪd/ (AmE also) / adj (used about metal or cardboard) shaped into folds □ *beralun-alun*

corrugated iron

corrupt¹ /kəˈrʌpt/ adj **1** doing or involving illegal or dishonest things in exchange for money, etc. □ *korup; menerima rasuah*: corrupt officials who accept bribes ◆ corrupt business practices **2** containing changes or faults, and no longer in the original state □ *rosak*: corrupt software

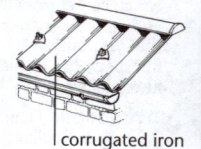

corrupt² /kəˈrʌpt/ verb **1** [T] to cause sb/sth to start behaving in a dishonest or an immoral way □ *menjadi tdk jujur/tdk bermoral*: Too many people are corrupted by power. **2** [I,T] [often passive] to change the original form of sth or to cause mistakes to appear, especially in a computer file □ *merosakkan*: The program has somehow corrupted the system files. ◆ corrupted data

corruption /kəˈrʌpʃn/ noun [U] **1** dishonest or immoral behaviour or activities □ *amalan rasuah; korupsi*: There were accusations of corruption among senior police officers. **2** the process of making sb/sth corrupt □ *perihal merosakkan (akhlak, moral, dsb)*

corset /ˈkɔːsɪt/ noun [C] a piece of clothing worn especially in the past to make a woman's waist look smaller □ *korset*

cos (also **'cos, 'cause, coz**) /kəz/ (BrE also) kɒz/ conj (BrE informal) because □ *kerana*: *I can't come to the party cos I've got too much homework.*

> **HELP** Do NOT use **cos** in formal written English.

cosmetic[1] /kɒzˈmetɪk/ noun [C, usually pl] a substance that you put on your face or hair to make yourself look more attractive □ *alat solek; kosmetik* ⊃ look at **make-up**

cosmetic[2] /kɒzˈmetɪk/ adj **1** done in order to improve only the appearance of sth, without changing it in any other way □ *kosmetik; luaran*: *changes in government policy which are purely cosmetic* **2** used or done in order to make your face or body more attractive □ *kosmetik*: *cosmetic products* ◆ *cosmetic surgery*

cosmic /ˈkɒzmɪk/ adj connected with space or the universe □ *kosmos*

cosmonaut /ˈkɒzmənɔːt/ noun [C] an **astronaut** (= a person who works and travels in space) from the former Soviet Union □ *angkasawan*

cosmopolitan /ˌkɒzməˈpɒlɪtən/ adj **1** containing people from all over the world □ *kosmopolitan*: *a cosmopolitan city* **2** influenced by the culture of other countries □ *kosmopolitan*: *a cosmopolitan and sophisticated young woman*

the cosmos /ˈkɒzmɒs/ noun [sing] the universe □ *kosmos; alam semesta*

cost[1] /kɒst/ noun **1** [C,U] the money that you have to pay for sth □ *kos*: *The cost of petrol has gone up again.* ◆ *The hospital was built at a cost of £10 million.* ◆ *The damage will have to be repaired regardless of cost.* ⊃ note at **price 2** [sing, U] what you have to give or lose in order to obtain sth else □ *kerugian; pengorbanan*: *He achieved great success but only at the cost of a happy family life.* **3** **costs** [pl] the amount of money that the losing side has to pay for lawyers, etc. in a court of law □ *kos*: *a £2 500 fine and £1000 costs*
IDM **at all costs/at any cost** using whatever means are necessary to achieve sth □ *dgn apa cara sekalipun*: *We must win at all costs.*
cover the cost (of sth) ⊃ **cover**[1]
to your cost in a way that is unpleasant or bad for you □ *drpd (pengalaman pahit, dsb) yg pernah dirasai/dialami*: *Life can be lonely at university, as I found out to my cost.*

cost[2] /kɒst/ verb [T] (pt, pp **cost**) **1** to have the price of □ *berharga*: *How much does a return ticket to London cost?* ◆ *We'll take the bus—it won't cost much.* ◆ *(informal) How much did your bike cost you?* **2** to make you lose sth □ *menyebabkan kerugian; mengorbankan*: *That one mistake cost him his job.*
IDM **cost the earth/a fortune** to be very expensive □ *sangat mahal*

co-star /ˈkəʊstɑː(r)/ verb (**co-starring; co-starred**) **1** [T] (used about a film, play, etc.) to have two or more famous actors as its stars □ *dibintangi bersama*: *a film co-starring Ryan Gosling and Emma Stone* **2** [I] (used about actors) to be one of two or more stars in a film, play, etc. □ *berlakon bersama*: *Emma Stone co-stars with Ryan Gosling in the film.* ▶ **co-star** noun [C]: *His co-star was Marilyn Monroe.*

costly /ˈkɒstli/ adj (**costlier; costliest**) **1** costing a lot of money; expensive □ *mahal; menelan belanja yg besar*: *a costly repair bill* **2** involving great loss of time, effort, etc. □ *melibatkan kerugian besar (masa, tenaga, dll)*: *a costly mistake*

costume /ˈkɒstjuːm/ noun [C,U] **1** a set or style of clothes worn by people in a particular country or in a particular historical period □ *pakaian*: *17th-century costume* ◆ *Welsh national costume* **2** clothes that an actor, etc. wears in order to look like sth else □ *kostum*: *One of the children was dressed in a pirate's costume.* ◆ *The last rehearsal of the play will be done in costume.* **3** (BrE) = **swimsuit**

cosy (AmE **cozy**) /ˈkəʊzi/ adj (**cosier; cosiest**) warm and comfortable □ *nyaman dan selesa*: *The room looked cosy and inviting in the firelight.*

cot /kɒt/ noun [C] **1** (AmE **crib**) a bed with high sides for a baby □ *katil anak* **2** (AmE) = **camp bed** ⊃ picture at **bed**

cottage /ˈkɒtɪdʒ/ noun [C] a small and usually old house, especially in the country □ *rumah kecil*: *a country cottage with roses round the door* ◆ *We rented a holiday cottage by the sea.* ⊃ picture on **page P9**

cottage cheese noun [U] a type of soft white cheese in small wet lumps □ *keju kotej*

cotton /ˈkɒtn/ noun [U] **1** a natural cloth or thread made from the thin white hairs of the cotton plant □ *kain/benang kapas*: *a cotton shirt* ◆ *a reel of cotton* **2** (AmE) = **cotton wool**

cotton wool noun [U] a soft mass of cotton, used for cleaning the skin, cuts, etc. □ *kapas*

couch[1] /kaʊtʃ/ noun [C] a long seat, often with a back and arms, for sitting or lying on □ *kerusi panjang*: *They were sitting on the couch in the living room.*

couch[2] /kaʊtʃ/ verb [T, usually passive] (formal) to express a thought, an idea, etc. in the way mentioned □ *mengungkapkan dgn cara tertentu*: *His reply was couched in very polite terms.*

couch potato noun [C] (informal) a person who spends a lot of time sitting and watching television □ *sso yg membazirkan masa dgn duduk dan menonton televisyen*

cough[1] /kɒf/ verb **1** [I] to send air out of your throat and mouth with a sudden loud noise, especially when you have a cold, have sth in your throat, etc. □ *batuk*: *The smoke from the fire made me cough.* ⊃ note at **ill 2** [T] **cough (up) sth** to send sth out of your throat and mouth with a sudden loud noise □ *membatukkan; batuk keluar (sst)*: *When I started coughing (up) blood I called the doctor.*

cough

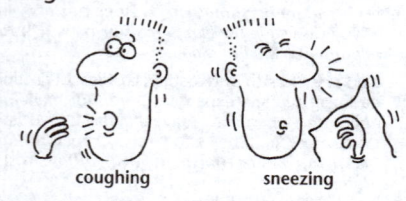

coughing | **sneezing**

PHR V **cough (sth) up** (*informal*) to give money when you do not want to □ *(terpaksa) mengeluarkan wang*: *Come on, cough up what you owe me!*

▶ **coughing** noun [U]: *a fit of coughing*

cough² /kɒf/ noun [C] **1** an act or the sound of coughing □ *(perbuatan/bunyi) batuk*: *He gave a nervous cough before he started to speak.* **2** an illness or infection that makes you cough a lot □ *penyakit batuk*: *Kevin's got a bad cough.*

could /kəd; strong form kʊd/ modal verb (negative **could not**; short form **couldn't** /'kʊdnt/)
▶ABILITY/PERMISSION **1** used as the past tense of **can** □ *dpt; boleh*: *I could run three miles without stopping when I was younger.* ◆ *Elena said we could stay at her house.*

> **GRAMMAR** If something was possible on one occasion in the past, use **was/were able to** or **managed to**: *The firemen were able to/managed to rescue the children.* But in negative sentences **could not** can be used, too: *The firemen couldn't rescue the children.*

▶REQUEST **2** used for asking permission politely □ *bolehkah*: *Could I possibly borrow your car?* **3** used for asking sb politely to do sth for you □ *bolehkah tolong*: *Could you open the door? My hands are full.*
▶POSSIBILITY **4** used for saying that sth may be or may have been possible □ *dpt; boleh; mungkin; patutnya*: *I could do it now if you like.* ◆ *She could be famous one day.* ◆ *He could have gone to university but he didn't want to.* ◆ *You could have said you were going to be late!* (= I'm annoyed that you didn't)
▶SUGGESTION **5** used for making a suggestion □ *boleh*: *'What do you want to do tonight?' 'We could go to the cinema or we could just stay in.'*
▶SENSES **6** used with the verbs 'feel', 'hear', 'see', 'smell', 'taste' □ *dpt*: *We could hear/see children playing outside.* ❶ For more information about modal verbs, look at the **Reference Section** at the back of this dictionary.

IDM **could do with sth** to want or need sth □ *perlu*: *I could do with a holiday.*

council (also **Council**) /'kaʊnsl/ noun [C, with sing or pl verb] **1** a group of people who are elected to govern an area such as a town, city, etc. □ *majlis (perbandaran, tempatan, dsb)*: *The county council has/have decided to build a new road.* ◆ *a council house* (= one that a council owns and lets to people who do not have much money) ◆ *My father's on the local council.* **2** a group of people chosen to give advice, manage affairs, etc. for a particular organization or activity □ *majlis*: *the Arts Council*

councillor /'kaʊnsələ(r)/ noun [C] a member of a **council** □ *anggota/ahli majlis*: *to elect new councillors*

counsel¹ /'kaʊnsl/ noun [C,U] (*formal*) **1** advice □ *nasihat* **2** a lawyer who speaks in a court of law □ *peguam bela*: *the counsel for the defence/prosecution*

counsel² /'kaʊnsl/ verb [T] (**counselling**; **counselled**, (*AmE*) **counseling**; **counseled**) **1** to give professional advice and help to sb with a problem □ *memberikan kaunseling* **2** (*formal*) to tell sb what you think they should do; to advise □ *menasihatkan*: *Mr Dean's lawyers counselled him against making public statements.*

counselling (*AmE* **counseling**) /'kaʊnsəlɪŋ/ noun [U] professional advice and help given to people with problems □ *kaunseling*: *Many students come to us for counselling.*

counsellor (*AmE* **counselor**) /'kaʊnsələ(r)/ noun [C] a person whose job is to give advice □ *kaunselor*: *a marriage counsellor*

count¹ /kaʊnt/ verb **1** [I] to say numbers one after another in order □ *membilang*: *Close your eyes and count (up) to 20.* **2** [T] **count sth** to calculate the total number or amount of sth □ *mengira; menghitung*: *The teacher counted the children as they got on the bus.* **3** [T] to include sb/sth when you are calculating an amount or a number □ *termasuk*: *There were thirty people on the bus, not counting the driver.* **4** [I] **count (for sth)** to be important or valuable □ *dianggap penting; dihargai*: *I sometimes think my opinion counts for nothing at work.* **5** [I] **count (as sth)** to be valid or accepted □ *mengambil kira; diterima*: *The referee had already blown his whistle so the goal didn't count.* ◆ *Will my driving licence count as identification?* **6** [I,T] to consider sb/sth in a particular way □ *mengira; dikira; menganggap; dianggap*: *You should count yourself lucky to have a good job.* ◆ *On this airline, children over 12 count/are counted as adults.*

IDM **Don't count your chickens (before they're hatched)** used to say that you should not be too confident that sth will be successful because sth might still go wrong □ *jangan angan-angan Mat Jenin*

PHR V **count against sb** to be considered as a disadvantage □ *menjejaskan (peluang, dll) sso*: *Do you think my age will count against me?*
count on sb/sth to expect sth with confidence; to depend on sb/sth □ *mengharapkan sso/sst*: *Can I count on you to help me tonight?*
count sb/sth out 1 to count things slowly, one by one □ *mengira satu per satu*: *She carefully counted out the money into my hand.* **2** (*informal*) to not include sb/sth □ *jangan mengira atau memasukkan sso/sst*: *If you're going swimming, you can count me out!*

[I] **intransitive**, a verb which has no object: *He laughed.* | [T] **transitive**, a verb which has an object: *He ate an apple.*

count² /kaʊnt/ noun [C] **1** [usually sing] an act of counting or a number that you get after counting □ *pengiraan; kiraan*: *At the last count, there were nearly 2 million unemployed.* ♦ *Raise your leg and hold for a count of ten.* **2** [usually pl] a point that is made in a discussion, an argument, etc. □ *hal; poin*: *I proved her wrong on all counts.* **IDM** **keep/lose count (of sth)** to know/not know how many there are of sth □ *mengira/tdk terkira lagi*: *I've lost count of the number of times he's told that joke!*

countable /ˈkaʊntəbl/ adj that can be counted □ *(kn) hitung*: *'Chair' is a countable noun, but 'sugar' isn't.* ♦ *Countable nouns are marked '[C]' in this dictionary.* **OPP** **uncountable**
ⓘ For more information about countable nouns, look at the **Reference Section** at the back of this dictionary.

countdown /ˈkaʊntdaʊn/ noun [C] the act of saying numbers backwards to zero just before sth important happens □ *kira detik*: *the countdown to the lift-off of a rocket* ♦ *(figurative) The countdown to this summer's Olympic Games has started.*

countenance¹ /ˈkaʊntənəns/ noun [C] (formal) sb's face or expression □ *air muka sso atau ekspresi*

countenance² /ˈkaʊntənəns/ verb [T] (formal) to support sth or agree to sth happening □ *menyokong; menyetujui*: *The committee refused to countenance Harding's proposals.*

counter- /ˈkaʊntə(r)/ [in compounds] **1** against; opposite □ *berlawanan, bertentangan*: *counterterrorism* ♦ *counter-argument* **2** related or similar to sth □ *yg sama atau berkaitan dgn sst*: *counterpart/countersign*

counter¹ /ˈkaʊntə(r)/ noun [C] **1** a long, flat surface in a shop, bank, etc. where customers are served □ *kaunter*: *The man behind the counter in the bank was very helpful.* **2** a small object (usually round and made of plastic) that is used in some games to show where a player is on the board □ *gundu* **3** an electronic device for counting sth □ *pembilang*: *The needle on the rev counter soared.* **4** (AmE) = **worktop**

counter² /ˈkaʊntə(r)/ verb **1** [I,T] to reply or react to criticism □ *membalas*: *He countered our objections with a powerful defence of his plan.* **2** [T] to try to reduce or prevent the bad effects of sth □ *mencegah; mengurangkan*: *The shop has installed security cameras to counter theft.*

counter³ /ˈkaʊntə(r)/ adv **counter to sth** in the opposite direction to sth □ *bertentangan*: *The results of these experiments run counter to previous findings.*

counteract /ˌkaʊntərˈækt/ verb [T] to reduce the effect of sth by acting against it □ *mengurangkan*: *measures to counteract traffic congestion*

ˈcounter-attack noun [C] an attack made in reaction to an enemy or opponent's attack □ *serangan balas* ▶ **counter-attack** verb [I,T]

199　　　**count → countryman**

counterclockwise /ˌkaʊntəˈklɒkwaɪz/ (AmE) = **anticlockwise**

counterfeit /ˈkaʊntəfɪt/ adj not genuine, but copied so that it looks like the real thing □ *palsu*: *counterfeit money*

counterfoil /ˈkaʊntəfɔɪl/ noun [C] the part of a cheque, ticket, etc. that you keep when you give the other part to sb else □ *keratan*

counterpart /ˈkaʊntəpɑːt/ noun [C] a person or thing that has a similar position or function in a different country or organization □ *rakan sejawat; sso/sst yg setara*: *the French president and his Italian counterpart (= the Italian president)*

counterproductive /ˌkaʊntəprəˈdʌktɪv/ adj having the opposite effect to the one you want □ *mempunyai kesan bertentangan dgn yg diingini*: *It can be counterproductive to punish children.* ⊃ look at **productive**

countless /ˈkaʊntləs/ adj [only before a noun] very many □ *banyak; sangat; tdk terkira banyaknya*: *I've tried to phone him countless times but he's not there.*

country /ˈkʌntri/ noun (pl countries) **1** [C] an area of land with its own people, government, etc □ *negara*: *France, Spain and other European countries* ♦ *There was snow over much of the country during the night.* **2** [U] an area of land □ *kawasan*: *We looked down over miles of open country.* ♦ *hilly country* **SYN** **terrain** **3** **the country** [sing] the people who live in a country □ *rakyat; negeri; negara*: *a survey to find out what the country really thinks* **4** **the country** [sing] land which is away from towns and cities □ *desa*: *Do you live in a town or in the country?* ⊃ note at **scenery** ⊃ look at **countryside** **5** [U] = **country and western**

OTHER WORDS FOR

country

Nation is another word for country, or the people who live in a country: *The entire nation, it seemed, was watching TV.* **State** is used for talking about a country as an organized political community controlled by one government. It can also mean the government itself: *a politically independent state* ♦ *the member states of the EU* ♦ *You get a pension from the state when you retire.* ♦ *state education* **Land** is more formal or literary: *explorers who set out to discover new lands*

ˌcountry and ˈwestern (also **country**) noun [U] a type of music based on traditional music from the southern and western US □ *'country and western'; lagu rakyat Amerika*

countryman /ˈkʌntrimən/ noun [C] (pl -men /-mən/) a person from your own country □ *orang senegeri/senegara*: *The Italian Castorri beat his fellow countryman Rossi in the final.*

the countryside → court

the countryside /ˈkʌntrisaɪd/ noun [U, sing] land which is away from towns and cities, where there are fields, woods, etc. □ *kawasan desa*: From the hill there is a magnificent view of the surrounding countryside. ➔ look at **country** ➔ note at **nature, scenery** ➔ picture on page P11

county /ˈkaʊnti/ noun [C] (abbr **Co.**) (pl **counties**) an area in Britain, Ireland or the US which has its own local government □ *daerah; wilayah*: the county of Nottinghamshire ◆ Orange County, California ➔ look at **province, state**

coup /kuː/ noun [C] 1 (also **coup d'état** /ˌkuː deɪˈtɑː/) a sudden, illegal and often violent change of government □ *rampasan kuasa; kudeta*: a coup to overthrow the President ◆ an attempted coup (= one which did not succeed) 2 a clever and successful thing to do □ *tindakan cemerlang*: Getting that promotion was a real coup.

couple¹ /ˈkʌpl/ noun [C, with sing or pl verb] two people who are together because they are married or in a relationship □ *pasangan*: a married couple ◆ Is/Are that couple over there part of our group? ➔ look at **pair**
IDM a couple of people, things, etc. 1 two people, things, etc. □ *dua*: I need a couple of plates. **2** a few □ *beberapa*: I last saw her a couple of months ago.

couple² /ˈkʌpl/ verb [T, usually passive] to join or connect sb/sth to sb/sth else □ *berserta; bersama-sama*: The fog, coupled with the amount of traffic on the roads, made driving very difficult.

coupon /ˈkuːpɒn/ (AmE also) / noun [C] **1** a small piece of paper which you can use to buy goods at a lower price, or which you can collect and then exchange for goods □ *kupon*: a coupon worth 10% off your next purchase **2** a printed form in a newspaper or magazine which you use to order goods, enter a competition, etc. □ *kupon*

courage /ˈkʌrɪdʒ/ noun [U] the ability to control fear in a situation that may be dangerous or unpleasant □ *keberanian*: It took real courage to go back into the burning building. ◆ She **showed great courage** all through her long illness. **SYN** bravery
IDM pluck up courage ➔ **pluck¹** ▶ **courageous** /kəˈreɪdʒəs/ adj

courgette /kʊəˈʒet/ (BrE also) kɔː-/ (AmE **zucchini**) noun [C] a long vegetable with dark green skin that is white inside □ *zukini* ➔ picture on page P15

courier /ˈkʊriə(r)/ noun [C] **1** a person whose job is to carry letters, important papers, etc., especially when they are urgent □ *kurier; penghantar*: The package was delivered by motorcycle courier. **2** a person whose job is to look after a group of tourists □ *pengiring pelancong*

course /kɔːs/ noun [C] **1** a course (in/on sth) a complete series of lessons or studies □ *kursus*: I've decided to **enrol on** a computer course. ◆ I'm going to **take/do a course** in French. **2** [C,U] the route or direction that sth, especially an aircraft, a ship or a river, takes □ *laluan; haluan; arah*: The hijackers forced the captain to **change course** and head for Cuba. ◆ to be **on/off course** (= going in the right/wrong direction) ◆ (figurative) I'm **on course** (= making the right amount of progress) to finish this work by the end of the week. ◆ The road follows the course of the river. **3** (also **course of 'action**) [C] a way of dealing with a particular situation □ *jalan tindakan*: In that situation, resignation was the only course open to him. **4** [sing] the development of sth over a period of time □ *perjalanan; arus masa*: events that changed the course of history ◆ In the normal course of events (= the way things normally happen) such problems do not arise. **5** [C] any of the separate parts of a meal □ *jenis sajian*: a three-course lunch ◆ I had chicken for the **main course**. ➔ note at **restaurant 6** [C] an area where **golf** (= a game in which you hit a small ball into a number of holes) is played or where certain types of race take place □ *padang*: a golf course ◆ a racecourse **7** [C] a course (of sth) a series of medical treatments □ *siri rawatan*: The doctor put her on a course of tablets.
IDM be on a collision course (with sb/sth) ➔ **collision**
in the course of sth during sth □ *semasa; dlm masa*: He mentioned it in the course of conversation.
in the course of time when enough time has passed □ *lambat-laun* **SYN** eventually
in due course ➔ **due¹**
a matter of course ➔ **matter¹**
of course naturally; certainly □ *tentu sekali; sudah tentu*: Of course, having children has changed their lives a lot. ◆ 'Can I use your phone?' 'Of course (you can).' ◆ 'You're not annoyed with me, are you?' 'Of course (I'm) not.'

coursebook /ˈkɔːsbʊk/ noun [C] a book for studying from that is used regularly in class □ *buku kursus*

course of 'action = **course**(3)

coursework /ˈkɔːswɜːk/ noun [U] work that students do during a course of study, not in exams, that is included in their final grade □ *kerja kursus*: Coursework accounts for 40% of the final marks.

court¹ /kɔːt/ noun **1** [C,U] (also **court of 'law**, BrE also **law court**) the place where legal trials take place and crimes, etc. are judged □ *mahkamah*: the civil/criminal courts ◆ A man has been charged and will **appear in court** tomorrow. ◆ Bill's company are refusing to pay him so he's decided to **take them to court**. **2 the court** [sing] the people in a court, especially those taking part in the trial □ *mahkamah*: Please tell the court exactly what you saw. **3** [C,U] an area where certain ball games are played □ *gelanggang*: a tennis/squash/badminton court ➔ look at **pitch** ➔ picture on page P4

ð **then** s **so** z **zoo** ʃ **she** ʒ **vision** h **how** m **man** n **no** ŋ **sing** l **leg** r **red** j **yes** w **wet**

TOPIC

Court

The **accused** (= a person charged with a crime) has the right to a **trial** which is held in a **court**. All trials have a **judge** and some have a **jury** (= a group of members of the public), who **try the case**. One group of lawyers (the **prosecution**) tries to prove the guilt of the accused (= to show that he did it), while another group (the **defence**) tries to defend him. They examine the **evidence** to see if there is **proof** that he committed the crime. They may hear evidence from **witnesses** (= people who saw the crime being committed). At the end of the trial the judge or the jury will reach a **verdict** and decide if he is **guilty** or **not guilty**. If the accused is found guilty he will receive a **sentence**. He may be **fined** (= forced to pay money) or sent to **jail/prison**.

court² /kɔːt/ verb [T] (formal) **1** to try to gain sb's support by paying special attention to them □ *cuba memikat/mengambil hati/memancing*: *Politicians from all parties will be courting voters this week.* **2** to do sth that might have a very bad effect □ *menempah; mencari*: *Britain is courting ecological disaster if it continues to dump waste in the North Sea.*

courteous /ˈkɜːtiəs/ adj polite and pleasant, showing respect for other people □ *berbudi bahasa* OPP **discourteous** ▶ **courteously** adv

courtesy /ˈkɜːtəsi/ noun (pl **courtesies**) **1** [U] polite and pleasant behaviour that shows respect for other people □ *budi bahasa; sopan santun*: *She didn't even have the courtesy to say that she was sorry.* **2** [C] (formal) a polite thing that you say or do when you meet people in formal situations □ *basa-basi; bermanis mulut*: *The two presidents exchanged courtesies before their meeting.*

IDM **(by) courtesy of sb** (formal) with the permission or because of the kindness of sb □ *(dgn) ihsan sso*: *These pictures are being shown by courtesy of BBC TV.*

,court ˈmartial noun [C,U] (pl **courts martial**) a military court that deals with matters of military law; a trial that takes place in such a court □ *mahkamah tentera*: *His case will be heard by a court martial.*
▶ **court-martial** verb [T]

,court of ˈlaw noun [C] (pl **courts of law**) = **court¹**(1)

courtship /ˈkɔːtʃɪp/ noun [C,U] (old-fashioned) the relationship between a man and a woman before they get married □ *hubungan cinta sebelum berkahwin*

courtyard /ˈkɔːtjɑːd/ noun [C] an area of ground, without a roof, that has walls or buildings around it, for example in a castle or between houses or flats □ *laman*

cousin /ˈkʌzn/ (also **,first ˈcousin**) noun [C] the child of your aunt or uncle □ *sepupu*: *Paul and I are cousins.*

court → cover

MORE The same word is used for both male and female cousins. A **second cousin** is the child of your mother's or father's cousin.

cove /kəʊv/ noun [C] a small area of the coast where the land curves round so that it is protected from the wind, etc. □ *suak; teluk kecil*: *a sandy cove*

cover¹ /ˈkʌvə(r)/ verb
▶HIDE/PROTECT **1** [T] **cover sb/sth (up/over) (with sth)** to put sth on or in front of sth to hide or protect it □ *menutup; mengalas*: *Could you cover the food and put it in the fridge?* ♦ *She couldn't look any more and covered her eyes.* ♦ *I covered the floor with newspaper before I started painting.* ♦ (figurative) *Paula laughed to cover* (= hide) *her embarrassment.* OPP **uncover**
▶SPREAD OVER SURFACE **2** [T] **cover sb/sth in/with sth** to be on the surface of sth; to make sth do this □ *meliputi; memercikkan*: *A car went through the puddle and covered me with mud.* ♦ *Graffiti covered the walls.* ♦ *The eruption of the volcano covered the town in a layer of ash.* **3** [T] to fill or spread over a certain area □ *meliputi*: *The floods cover an area of about 15 000 square kilometres.*
▶INCLUDE **4** [T] to include or to deal with sth □ *membuat liputan; meliputi; mencakupi*: *All the papers covered the election in depth.* ♦ *The course covered both British and European naval history.*
▶MONEY **5** [T] to be enough money for sth □ *cukup utk menampung*: *We'll give you some money to cover your expenses.*
▶TRAVEL **6** [T] to travel a certain distance □ *meliputi jarak*: *We covered about 500 kilometres that day.*
▶DO SB'S JOB **7** [I] **cover (for sb)** to do sb's job while they are away from work □ *menggantikan (sso)*: *Matt's phoned in sick today so we'll have to find someone to cover (for him).*
▶INSURANCE **8** [T] **cover sb/sth against/for sth** to protect sb/sth with insurance □ *melindungi*: *The insurance policy covers us for any damage to our property.*

IDM **cover the cost (of sth)** to have or make enough money to pay for sth □ *cukup utk membiayai kos (sst)*: *We made so little money at our school dance that we didn't even cover the cost of the band.*

PHR V **cover sth up** to prevent people hearing about a mistake or sth bad □ *menutup/menyembunyikan (sst)*: *The police have been accused of trying to cover up the facts of the case.*
cover up for sb to hide sb's mistakes or crimes in order to protect them □ *menyelindungi sso*: *His wife covered up for him to the police.*

cover² /ˈkʌvə(r)/ noun
▶PROTECTION **1** [C] something that is put on or over sth, especially in order to protect it □ *penutup; tutup; alas; sarung; tudung*: *a plastic cover for a computer* ♦ *a duvet cover* **2** [U] protection from the weather, damage, etc. □ *perlindungan*: *When the storm started we had to*

coverage → crab 202

take cover *in a shop doorway.* ♦ *When the gunfire started everyone ran for cover.* **SYN** shelter
▶OF BOOK, ETC. **3** [C] the outside part of a book or magazine □ *kulit*: *I read the magazine from cover to cover* (= from beginning to end).
▶INSURANCE **4** [U] **cover (against sth)** insurance against sth □ *insurans; perlindungan*: *The policy provides cover against theft.*
▶ON BED **5 the covers** [pl] the sheets, etc. on a bed □ *cadar, alas tilam, dsb*: *She threw back the covers and leapt out of bed.*
▶HIDING STH **6** [C,U] **a cover (for sth)** something that hides what sb is really doing □ *topeng; sst yg menyelindung*: *The whole company was just a cover for all kinds of criminal activities.* ♦ *police officers working under cover*
▶OF JOB **7** [U] doing sb's job for them while they are away from work □ *ganti*: *Joe's off next week so we'll have to arrange cover.*
IDM **under (the) cover of sth** hidden by sth □ *diselindung oleh sst*: *They attacked under cover of darkness.*

coverage /ˈkʌvərɪdʒ/ *noun* [U] **1** the act or amount of reporting on an event in newspapers, on TV, etc. □ *liputan*: *TV coverage of the Olympic Games was excellent.* **2** the amount or quality of information included in a book, magazine, etc. □ *liputan*: *The grammar section provides coverage of all the most problematic areas.*

coveralls /ˈkʌvərɔːlz/ *noun* [pl] (*AmE*) **1** = overall²(2) **2** = boiler suit

covered /ˈkʌvəd/ *adj* **1 covered in/with sth** having a layer or a large amount of sth on sb/sth □ *diliputi; diselaputi*: *She was covered in mud/sweat/dust.* ♦ *nuts covered with chocolate* **2** having a cover, especially a roof □ *berbumbung*: *a covered shopping centre*

covering /ˈkʌvərɪŋ/ *noun* [C] something that covers the surface of sth □ *litupan; lapisan; alas*: *There was a thick covering of dust over everything.*

ˌcovering ˈletter (*AmE* **ˈcover letter**) *noun* [C] a letter containing extra information that you send with sth □ *surat iringan*: *To apply for the job, send your CV with a covering letter.*

covert /ˈkʌvət; ˈkəʊvɜːt/ *adj* (*formal*) done secretly □ *terselindung; secara rahsia*: *a covert police operation* **OPP** overt ▶ **covertly** *adv*

ˈcover-up *noun* [C] an act of preventing sth bad or dishonest from becoming known □ *perbuatan menutup/menyembunyikan (sst)*: *Several newspapers have claimed that there has been a government cover-up.*

covet /ˈkʌvət/ *verb* [T] (*formal*) to want to have sth very much (especially sth that belongs to sb else) □ *sangat menginginkan*

cow /kaʊ/ *noun* [C] **1** a large female animal that is kept on farms to produce milk or beef □ *lembu betina*: *to milk a cow* ♦ *dairy cows* (= cows kept for their milk) ⊃ note at **meat**

udder
cow
bull
calf

MORE Cow is often used for both the male and female animal. A male cow is called a **bull** and a young cow is a **calf**. A group of cows is a **herd**. An **ox** is a male that cannot produce young and which is used for pulling heavy loads. Cows and bulls that are kept as farm animals can be called **cattle**. The noise that cows make is **moo**.

2 the adult female of certain large animals, for example **elephants** (= large grey animals with a long nose) □ *haiwan betina* **3** (*slang*) an insulting word for a woman □ *betina*

coward /ˈkaʊəd/ *noun* [C] a person who has no courage and is afraid in dangerous or unpleasant situations □ *pengecut*: *I hate going to the dentist's because I'm a terrible coward.* ▶ **cowardly** *adj*

cowardice /ˈkaʊədɪs/ *noun* [U] a lack of courage; behaviour that shows that you are afraid □ *sifat pengecut*

cowboy /ˈkaʊbɔɪ/ *noun* [C] **1** a man whose job is to look after cows (usually on a horse) in certain parts of the US □ *koboi* **2** (*BrE informal*) a person in business who is not honest or who does work badly □ *ahli perniagaan yg tdk jujur atau kerjanya tdk bagus*: *a cowboy builder*

cower /ˈkaʊə(r)/ *verb* [I] to move back or into a low position because of fear □ *meromok*: *The dog cowered under the table when the storm started.*

coy /kɔɪ/ *adj* **1** pretending to be shy or innocent □ *pura-pura malu*: *She lifted her head a little and gave him a coy smile.* **2** not wanting to give information about sth or to answer questions that tell people too much about you □ *malu-malu*: *Don't be coy, tell me how much you earn.* ▶ **coyly** *adv*

coz (*BrE informal*) = cos

cozy (*AmE*) = cosy

crab /kræb/ *noun* **1** [C] a sea animal with a flat shell and ten legs that moves sideways. The front two legs have **pincers** (= long curved points) on them. ⬜ *ketam* ⮕ picture on **page P13 2** [U] the meat from a crab ⬜ *daging ketam*

crack → crafty

crack¹ /kræk/ *verb*
►BREAK **1** [I,T] to break or to make sth break so that a line appears on the surface, but without breaking into pieces ⬜ *meretakkan; retak*: *Don't put boiling water into that glass—it'll break.* ♦ *The stone cracked the windscreen but didn't break it.* ⮕ picture at **chip 2** [T] to break sth open ⬜ *memecahkan*: *Crack two eggs into a bowl.*
►HIT **3** [T] to hit a part of your body against sth; to hit sb with sth ⬜ *terhantuk; memukul*: *She stood up and cracked her head on the cupboard door.* ♦ *She cracked the thief over the head with her umbrella.*
►MAKE SOUND **4** [I,T] to make a sudden loud, sharp sound; to cause sth to make this sound ⬜ *mengeluarkan bunyi letusan, lecutan, dsb*: *to crack a whip/your knuckles*
►VOICE **5** [I] (used about sb's voice) to suddenly change in a way that is not controlled ⬜ *menjadi serak; pecah (suara)*: *Her voice cracked as she spoke about her father's death.*
►UNDER PRESSURE **6** [I] to no longer be able to deal with pressure and so lose control ⬜ *mendapat sakit jiwa*: *He cracked under the strain of all his problems.*
►FIND SOLUTION **7** [T] (*informal*) to solve a problem ⬜ *menyelesaikan; memecahkan; menghuraikan*: *to crack a code* ♦ *The police have cracked an international diamond-smuggling ring.*
►JOKE **8** [T] to tell or make a joke ⬜ *berjenaka*: *Stop cracking jokes and do some work!*
IDM **get cracking** (*BrE informal*) to start doing sth immediately ⬜ *cepat mula*: *I have to finish this job today so I'd better get cracking.*
PHR V **crack down (on sb/sth)** (used about people in authority) to start dealing strictly with bad or illegal behaviour ⬜ *bertindak keras terhadap (sso/sst)*: *The police have started to crack down on street crime.*
crack up 1 (*informal*) to be unable to deal with pressure and so lose control and become mentally ill ⬜ *mendapat sakit jiwa*: *He cracked up when his wife left him.* **2** (*slang*) to suddenly start laughing, especially when you should be serious ⬜ *terketawa*

crack² /kræk/ *noun*
►BREAK **1** [C] a line on the surface of sth where it has broken, but not into separate pieces ⬜ *retak; rekahan*: *a pane of glass with a crack in it* ♦ (*figurative*) *They had always seemed happy together, but then cracks began to appear in their relationship.* ⮕ picture at **chip²(1)**
►OPENING **2** [C] a narrow opening ⬜ *rekahan; celah*: *a crack in the curtains*
►SOUND **3** [C] a sudden loud, sharp sound ⬜ *bunyi letusan, dsb*: *There was a loud crack of thunder as the storm broke.*
►HIT **4** [C] a hard hit on a part of the body ⬜ *hantukan; pukulan*: *Suddenly a golf ball gave him a nasty crack on the head.*
►DRUG **5** [U] a dangerous and illegal drug that some people take for pleasure and cannot then stop taking ⬜ *sejenis dadah haram*: *a crack addict*
►JOKE **6** [C] (*informal*) an amusing, often critical, comment; a joke ⬜ *jenaka*: *She made a crack about his bald head and he got angry.*
IDM **the crack of dawn** very early in the morning ⬜ *subuh-subuh lagi*
have a crack (at sth/at doing sth) (*informal*) to try to do sth ⬜ *mencuba (sst/membuat sst)*: *I'm not sure how to play but I'll have a crack at it.*

crack³ /kræk/ *adj* [only *before* a noun] (used about soldiers or sports players) very well trained and skilful ⬜ *sangat mahir/cekap*: *crack troops* ♦ *He's a crack shot* (= very accurate at shooting) *with a rifle.*

crackdown /'krækdaʊn/ *noun* [C] action to stop bad or illegal behaviour ⬜ *tindakan keras*: *Fifty people have been arrested in a police crackdown on street crime.*

cracked /krækt/ *adj* damaged with lines in its surface but not completely broken ⬜ *retakan*: *a cracked mirror/mug* ♦ *He suffered cracked ribs and bruising.* ⮕ picture at **chip**

cracker /'krækə(r)/ *noun* [C] **1** a thin dry biscuit that is often eaten with cheese ⬜ *biskut tawar* **2** (also ˌChristmas ˈcracker) a cardboard tube covered in coloured paper and containing a small present. Crackers are pulled apart by two people, each holding one end, at Christmas parties. They make a loud noise as they break. ⬜ *letup-letup Krismas* **3** (*BrE informal*) a very good example of sth ⬜ *sangat bagus*: *That story he told was a real cracker.*

crackle /'krækl/ *verb* [I] to make a series of short, sharp sounds ⬜ *detas-detus; bunyi gemersik*: *The radio started to crackle and then it stopped working.* ► **crackle** *noun* [sing]: *the crackle of dry wood burning*

cradle¹ /'kreɪdl/ *noun* [C] a small bed for a baby. Cradles can often be moved from side to side. ⬜ *buaian* ⮕ picture at **bed**

cradle² /'kreɪdl/ *verb* [T] to hold sb/sth carefully and gently in your arms ⬜ *mendukung*

craft /krɑːft/ *noun* **1** [C,U] a job or an activity for which you need skill with your hands ⬜ *kraf; ketukangan*: *an arts and crafts exhibition* ♦ *I studied craft and design at school.* ⮕ look at **handicraft 2** [C] any job or activity for which you need skill ⬜ *seni*: *He regards acting as a craft.* **3** [C] (*pl* **craft**) (*formal*) a boat, an aircraft or a **spacecraft** (= a vehicle that travels in space) ⬜ *bot; kapal; pesawat*: *a pleasure craft*

craftsman /'krɑːftsmən/ *noun* [C] (*pl* **-men** /-mən/) a person who makes things in a skilful way, especially with their hands ⬜ *tukang*

craftsmanship /'krɑːftsmənʃɪp/ *noun* [U] the skill used by sb to make sth of high quality with their hands ⬜ *kemahiran ketukangan*

crafty /'krɑːfti/ *adj* (**craftier**; **craftiest**) clever at getting or achieving things by using unfair or dishonest methods ⬜ *licik* ► **craftily** *adv*

[C] **countable**, a noun with a plural form: *one book, two books*   [U] **uncountable**, a noun with no plural form: *some sugar*

crag /kræg/ noun [C] a steep, rough mass of rock on a hill or mountain □ *(batuan) terjal; batu cancang*

craggy /ˈkrægi/ adj **1** having a lot of steep rough rock □ *bercancang*: *a craggy coastline* **2** (used about a man's face) strong and with deep lines, especially in an attractive way □ *(ttg lelaki) mempunyai raut muka yg agak kasar tetapi menarik*

cram /kræm/ verb (**cramming**; **crammed**) **1** [T] **cram sb/sth in (sth)**; **cram sb/sth into/onto sth** to push people or things into a small space □ *memperosok; menyumbatkan*: *We only spent two days in Dublin but we managed to cram a lot of sightseeing in.* ♦ *I managed to cram all my clothes into the bag but I couldn't close it.* **2** [I] **cram in (sth)**; **cram into/onto sth** to move, with a lot of other people, into a small space □ *mengasakkan; menyumbat*: *He only had a small car but they all managed to cram in.* **3** [I] to study very hard and learn a lot in a short time before an exam □ *belajar dgn bertungkus-lumus*: *She's cramming for her exams.*

crammed /kræmd/ adj very or too full □ *penuh sesak; padat*: *That book is crammed with useful information.*

cramp /kræmp/ noun [U,C] a sudden pain that you get in a muscle, that makes it difficult to move □ *kejang urat*

cramped /kræmpt/ adj not having enough space □ *sempit*: *The flat was terribly cramped with so many of us living there.*

cranberry /ˈkrænbəri/ noun [C] (pl **cranberries**) a small round red fruit that tastes sour and is used in cooking □ *kranberi*: *cranberry sauce*

crane¹ /kreɪn/ noun [C] a large machine with a long metal arm that is used for moving or lifting heavy objects □ *kren* ⊃ picture on **page P11**

crane² /kreɪn/ verb [I,T] to stretch your neck forward in order to see or hear sth □ *memanjangkan leher; menjulurkan kepala*: *We all craned forward to get a better view.*

crank /kræŋk/ noun [C] a person with strange ideas or who behaves in a strange way □ *orang yg aneh*: *Lots of cranks phoned the police confessing to the man's murder.*

cranny /ˈkræni/ noun [C] (pl **crannies**) a small opening in a wall, rock, etc. □ *rekahan*
IDM every nook and cranny ⊃ **nook**

crap /kræp/ noun [U] (*slang*) a rude word meaning nonsense or rubbish □ *(sst yg) karut/bukan-bukan* ▶ **crappy** /ˈkræpi/ adj (**crappier**; **crappiest**) [usually before a noun] (*slang*)

  HELP Be careful. Some people find this word offensive.

crash¹ /kræʃ/ noun [C] **1** an accident when a car or other vehicle hits sth and is damaged □ *perlanggaran; nahas*: *a car/plane crash* **2** a sudden loud noise made by sth breaking, hitting sth, etc. □ *dentuman*: *I heard a crash and ran outside.* **3** (used about money or business) a sudden fall in the value or price of sth □ *kejatuhan*: *the Stock Market crash of 1987* **4** a sudden failure of a machine, especially a computer □ *kegagalan berfungsi*

crash² /kræʃ/ verb **1** [I,T] to have an accident in a vehicle; to drive a vehicle into sth □ *berlanggar; terlanggar*: *He braked too late and crashed into the car in front.* **2** [I] to hit sth hard, making a loud noise □ *terhempas*: *The tree crashed to the ground.* **3** [I] to make a loud noise □ *berdentum*: *I could hear thunder crashing outside.* **4** [I] (used about money or business) to suddenly lose value or fail □ *jatuh; runtuh*: *Share prices crashed to an all-time low yesterday.* **5** [I] (used about a computer) to suddenly stop working □ *tdk berfungsi; tergendala*: *We lost the data when the computer crashed.*

crash³ /kræʃ/ adj [only before a noun] done in a very short period of time □ *(kursus, dll) kilat*: *She did a crash course in Spanish before going to work in Madrid.*

ˈ**crash barrier** noun [C] a strong low fence or wall at the side of a road or between two halves of a major road □ *pengadang kemalangan*

ˈ**crash helmet** noun [C] a hard hat worn by motorbike riders, racing drivers, etc. □ *topi keledar* ⊃ picture at **hat**

ˌ**crash-ˈland** verb [I,T] to land a plane in a dangerous way in an emergency □ *membuat pendaratan kecemasan* ▶ **crash ˈlanding** noun [C]: *to make a crash landing*

crass /kræs/ adj stupid, showing that you do not understand sth □ *sangat bodoh*: *It was a crass comment to make, when he knew how upset she was.*

crate /kreɪt/ noun [C] a large box in which goods are carried or stored □ *tong*

crater /ˈkreɪtə(r)/ noun [C] **1** the hole in the top of a **volcano** (= a mountain that explodes), through which hot gases and liquid rock are forced □ *genahar gunung berapi* ⊃ picture at **volcano** **2** a large hole in the ground □ *lubang besar; kawah*: *The bomb left a large crater.* ♦ *craters on the moon*

cravat /krəˈvæt/ noun [C] a wide piece of cloth that some men tie around their neck and wear inside the **collar** (= the folded part around the neck) of their shirt □ *kravat*

crave /kreɪv/ verb [I,T] **crave (for) sth** to want and need to have sth very much □ *sangat mengingini*: *Sometimes I really crave for some chocolate.* ♦ *He craves attention from other people.*

craving /ˈkreɪvɪŋ/ noun [C] a strong desire for sth □ *keinginan yg amat sangat*: *When she was pregnant she used to have cravings for all sorts of peculiar food.*

crawl¹ /krɔːl/ verb [I] **1** to move slowly with your body on or close to the ground, or on your hands and knees □ *merangkak; menyu-*

sup; merayap: Their baby has just started to crawl. ♦ *An insect crawled across the floor.* **2** (used about vehicles) to move very slowly □ *merangkak: The traffic crawls through the centre of town in the rush hour.* **3** (*informal*) **crawl (to sb)** to be very polite or pleasant to sb in order to be liked or to gain sth □ *mengampu: He only got promoted because he crawled to the manager.* **IDM** **be crawling with sth** to be completely full of or covered with unpleasant animals □ *dikerumuni/penuh dgn sst: The kitchen is crawling with insects.* ♦ (*figurative*) *The village is always crawling with tourists at this time of year.*

The baby is crawling.

crawl² /krɔːl/ *noun* **1** [sing] a very slow speed □ *bergerak perlahan-lahan; merangkak: The traffic slowed to a crawl.* **2** often **the crawl** [sing, U] a style of swimming which you do on your front. When you do the **crawl**, you move first one arm and then the other over your head, turn your face to one side so that you can breathe and kick up and down with your legs. □ *gaya rangkak* ➲ picture at **swim**

crayon /ˈkreɪən/ *noun* [C,U] a soft, thick, coloured pencil that is used for drawing or writing, especially by children □ *krayon* ▶ **crayon** *verb* [I,T]

craze /kreɪz/ *noun* [C] **a craze (for sth) 1** a strong interest in sth, that usually only lasts for a short time □ *kegilaan: There was a craze for that kind of music last year.* **2** something that a lot of people are very interested in □ *kegilaan: Knitting is the latest craze among Hollywood celebrities.*

crazy /ˈkreɪzi/ *adj* (**crazier**; **craziest**) (*informal*) **1** not sensible; stupid □ *gila: You must be crazy to turn down such a wonderful offer.* **2** very angry □ *naik berang: She goes crazy when people criticize her.* **3** showing great excitement □ *terlampau sangat suka: The fans went crazy when their team scored the first goal.* **4 crazy about sb/sth** liking sb/sth very much □ *sangat suka; gila (akan) sso; gila (akan) sst: He's always been crazy about horses.* ▶ **crazily** *adv* ▶ **craziness** *noun* [U]

creak /kriːk/ *verb* [I] to make the noise of wood bending or of sth not moving smoothly □ *berkeriang-keriut: The floorboards creaked when I walked across the room.* ▶ **creak** *noun* [C] ▶ **creaky** *adj: creaky stairs*

cream¹ /kriːm/ *noun* **1** [U] the thick yellowish-white liquid that rises to the top of milk □ *krim: coffee with cream* ♦ *whipped cream* (= cream that has been beaten) ➲ picture on **page P16 2** [C,U] a substance that you rub into your skin to keep it soft □ *krim* **3** = ointment: *(an) antiseptic cream* **4 the cream** [sing] the best part of sth or the best people in a group □ *(sst/orang) yg terbaik: the cream of New York society*

cream² /kriːm/ *adj, noun* [U] (of) a yellowish-white colour □ *warna putih kekuning-kuningan: cream linen trousers*

cream³ /kriːm/ *verb*
PHR V **cream sb/sth off** to take away the best people or part from sth for a particular purpose □ *mengambil sso/sst yg terbaik: The big clubs cream off the country's best young players.*

creamy /ˈkriːmi/ *adj* (**creamier**; **creamiest**) **1** containing cream; thick and smooth like cream □ *berkrim; spt krim: a creamy sauce* **2** having a light colour like cream □ *berwarna putih kekuning-kuningan: creamy skin*

crease¹ /kriːs/ *noun* [C] **1** an untidy line on paper, material, a piece of clothing, etc. that should not be there □ *kedut; kesan renyuk: Your shirt needs ironing, it's full of creases.* ♦ *When I unrolled the poster, there was a crease in it.* **2** a tidy straight line that you make in sth, for example when you fold it □ *kesan lipatan: He had a sharp crease in his trousers.*

crease² /kriːs/ *verb* [I,T] to get **creases**; to make sth get **creases** □ *menjadi ronyok; berkedut; membuat kesan lipat: Hang up your jacket or it will crease.* ♦ *Crease the paper carefully down the middle.*

create /kriˈeɪt/ *verb* [T] **1** to cause sth new to happen or exist □ *menghasilkan; mencipta: a plan to create new jobs in the area* **2** to produce a particular feeling □ *menghasilkan: William created a bad impression at the interview.*

creation /kriˈeɪʃn/ *noun* **1** [U] the act of causing sth new to happen or exist □ *penghasilan; pewujudan: the creation of new independent states* **2** [C] something new that sb has made or produced □ *ciptaan: This dish is a new creation—I didn't use a recipe.* **3** usually **the Creation** [sing] the act of making the whole universe, as described in the Bible □ *penciptaan alam*

creative /kriˈeɪtɪv/ *adj* **1** using skill or imagination to make or do new things □ *kreatif; berdaya cipta: She's a fantastic designer—she's so creative.* **2** connected with producing new things □ *kreatif: the company's creative team* ▶ **creatively** *adv*

creativity /ˌkriːeɪˈtɪvəti/ *noun* [U] the ability to make or produce new things using skill or imagination □ *kreativiti; daya cipta: We want teaching that encourages children's creativity.*

creator /kriˈeɪtə(r)/ *noun* [C] a person who makes or produces sth new □ *pencipta: He was the creator of some of the best-known characters in literature.*

creature /ˈkriːtʃə(r)/ *noun* [C] a living thing such as an animal, a bird, a fish or an insect, but not a plant □ *makhluk: a living creature* ♦ *sea creatures*

crèche /kreʃ/ *noun* [C] a place where small children are looked after while their parents are working, shopping, etc. □ *pusat jagaan bayi*

credentials → cremate

credentials /krəˈdenʃlz/ noun [pl] **1** the qualities, experience, etc. that make sb suitable for sth □ *kelayakan*: *He has the perfect credentials for the job.* **2** a document that is proof that you have the training, education, etc. necessary to do sth, or proof that you are who you say you are □ *bukti kelayakan; surat tauliah*

credibility /ˌkredəˈbɪləti/ noun [U] the quality that sb has that makes people believe or trust them □ *kebolehpercayaan; kredibiliti*: *The Prime Minister had lost all credibility and had to resign.*

credible /ˈkredəbl/ adj **1** that you can believe □ *boleh dipercayai*: *It's hardly credible that such a thing could happen without him knowing it.* **OPP** incredible **2** that seems possible □ *boleh diterima; yg mungkin*: *We need to think of a credible alternative to nuclear energy.*

credit¹ /ˈkredɪt/ noun
▶PAYING LATER **1** [U] a way of buying goods or services and not paying for them until later □ *kredit*: *I bought the TV on credit.*
▶MONEY BORROWED **2** [U] a sum of money that a bank, etc. lends to sb □ *kredit*: *The company was not able to get any further credit and went bankrupt.*
▶MONEY IN ACCOUNT **3** [U] having money in an account **3** □ *ada wang dlm akaun bank*: *No bank charges are made if your account remains in credit.* ♦ *I've run out of credit on my mobile phone.* **4** [C] a payment made into an account □ *bayaran masuk*: *There have been several credits to her account over the last month.* **OPP** debit
▶PRAISE **5** [U] an act of saying that sb has done sth well □ *penghargaan; pujian*: *He got all the credit for the success of the project.* ♦ *I can't take any credit; the others did all the work.* ♦ *She didn't do very well but at least give her credit for trying.*
▶PERSON **6** [sing] **a credit to sb/sth** a person or thing that you should be proud of □ *kebanggaan*: *She is a credit to her school.*
▶IN FILM/ON TV **7** **the credits** [pl] the list of the names of the people who made a film or TV programme, shown at the beginning or end of the film/programme □ *senarai karyawan*
▶AT UNIVERSITY **8** [C] (AmE) a part of a course at a college or university that a student has completed successfully □ *kredit*
IDM **do sb credit** (used about sb's qualities or successes) to be so good that people should be proud of them □ *sangat membanggakan*: *His courage and optimism do him credit.*
have sth to your credit to have finished sth that is successful □ *berjaya menghasilkan*: *He has three best-selling novels to his credit.*
(be) to sb's credit used for showing that you approve of sth that sb has done, although you have criticized them for sth else □ *patut dipuji*: *The company, to its credit, apologized and refunded my money.*

credit² /ˈkredɪt/ verb [T] **1** to add money to an account □ *mengkreditkan*: *Has the payment been credited to my bank account yet?* **2 credit sb/ sth with sth; credit sth to sb/sth** to believe or say that sb/sth has a particular quality or has done sth well □ *menganggap; percayalah (yg sso/ sst itu...)*: *Of course I wouldn't do such a stupid thing—credit me with a bit more sense than that!* **3** [usually in negative sentences and questions] to believe sth □ *mempercayai; percaya*: *I simply cannot credit that he has made the same mistake again!*

creditable /ˈkredɪtəbl/ adj of a quite good standard that cannot be criticized, though not excellent □ *memuaskan*: *It was a creditable result considering that three players were injured.*

credit card // noun [C] a small plastic card that you can use to buy goods or services and pay for them later □ *kad kredit*: *Can I pay by credit card?* ⊃ look at **cash card, cheque card, debit card** ⊃ picture at **money**

credit crunch noun [usually sing] a time when it suddenly becomes difficult to borrow money from a bank □ *luluh kredit*

creditor /ˈkredɪtə(r)/ noun [C] a person or company from whom you have borrowed money □ *pemiutang; pemberi hutang*: *He went abroad to avoid his creditors.*

creed /kriːd/ noun [C] a set of beliefs or principles (especially religious ones) that strongly influence sb's life □ *fahaman; kepercayaan*

creek /kriːk/ noun [C] **1** (BrE) a narrow piece of water where the sea flows into the land □ *caruk* **2** (AmE) a small river □ *anak sungai* **SYN** stream

creep¹ /kriːp/ verb [I] (pt, pp **crept** /krept/) **1** to move very quietly and carefully so that nobody will notice you □ *menyusup*: *She crept into the room so as not to wake him up.* **2** to move forward slowly □ *merangkak; merayap*: *The traffic was only creeping along.*
IDM **make your flesh creep** ⊃ **flesh**
PHR V **creep in** to begin to appear □ *mula masuk/timbul*: *All sorts of changes are beginning to creep into the education system.*

creep² /kriːp/ noun [C] (informal) a person that you do not like because they try too hard to be liked by people in authority □ *si pengampu; kaki bodek*
IDM **give sb the creeps** (informal) to make sb feel frightened or nervous □ *meremangkan bulu roma; menimbulkan rasa tdk senang*: *There's something about him that gives me the creeps.*

creeper /ˈkriːpə(r)/ noun [C] a plant that grows up trees or walls or along the ground □ *tumbuhan menjalar*

creepy /ˈkriːpi/ adj (**creepier**; **creepiest**) (informal) that makes you feel nervous or frightened □ *menyeramkan* **SYN** spooky

cremate /krəˈmeɪt/ verb [T] to burn the body of a dead person as part of a funeral service □ *membakar (mayat)* ⊃ note at **funeral** ▶ **cremation** /krəˈmeɪʃn/ noun [C,U]

crematorium /ˌkreməˈtɔːriəm/ noun [C] (pl **crematoria** /-ˈtɔːriə/ or **crematoriums**) a building in which the bodies of dead people are burned □ *krematorium*

Creole (also **creole**) /ˈkriːəʊl/ noun **1** [C] a person of mixed European and African race, especially one who lives in the West Indies □ *orang Kreol* **2** [C] a person whose relatives were among the first Europeans to live in the West Indies and South America, or among the first French or Spanish people to live in the southern states of the US □ *orang Kreol*: *the Creole cooking of New Orleans* **3** [C,U] a language that was originally a mixture of a European language and a local, especially African, language □ *bahasa Kreol*

crept past tense, past participle of **creep**[1]

crescendo /krəˈʃendəʊ/ noun [C] (pl **crescendos**) a noise or piece of music that gets louder and louder □ *kresendo*

crescent /ˈkresnt/ noun [C] **1** a curved shape that is pointed at both ends, like the moon in its first and last stages □ *(bentuk) bulan sabit* ⊃ picture at **shape 2** a street that is curved □ *lengkok*

cress /kres/ noun [U] a small plant with very small green leaves that does not need to be cooked and is eaten in salads and **sandwiches** (= two slices of bread with food between them) □ *kres; selada*

crest /krest/ noun [C] **1** the top of a hill or a wave □ *puncak; mercu; rabung* **2** a design used as a symbol of a particular family or organization □ *lambang; lencana*: *the university crest* **3** a group of feathers on the top of a bird's head □ *jambul*

crestfallen /ˈkrestfɔːlən/ adj disappointed or sad because you have failed and did not expect to □ *sugul; kecewa*

crevasse /krəˈvæs/ noun [C] a deep crack in a very thick layer of ice □ *jurang glasier; krevas*

crevice /ˈkrevɪs/ noun [C] a narrow crack in a rock, wall, etc. □ *rekahan*

crew /kruː/ noun [C, with sing or pl verb] **1** all the people who work on a ship, an aircraft, etc. □ *anak kapal* ⊃ note at **boat 2** a group of people who work together □ *krew; pasukan*: *a camera crew* (= people who film things for TV, etc.)

crib[1] /krɪb/ (AmE) = **cot**

crib[2] /krɪb/ verb [I,T] (**cribbing**; **cribbed**) **crib (sth) (from/off sb)** to copy sb else's work and pretend it is your own □ *meniru; mencedok*

crick /krɪk/ noun [sing] a pain in your neck, back, etc. that makes it difficult for you to move easily □ *sakit tegang urat* ▶ **crick** verb [T]: *I've cricked my neck.*

cricket /ˈkrɪkɪt/ noun **1** [U] a game that is played with a ball and a **bat** (= a piece of wood) on a large area of grass by two teams of eleven players □ *kriket* ⊃ picture on **page P4**

MORE In cricket, the **bowler** bowls (= throws) the ball to the **batsman** who tries to hit it with a **bat** and then score a **run** by running from one **wicket** to the other.

2 [C] an insect that makes a loud noise by rubbing its wings together □ *cengkerik*

cricketer /ˈkrɪkɪtə(r)/ noun [C] a person who plays **cricket** □ *pemain kriket*

crime /kraɪm/ noun **1** [U] illegal behaviour or activities □ *jenayah*: *There has been an increase in car crime recently.* ◆ *to fight crime* **2** [C] something which is illegal and which people are punished for, for example by being sent to prison □ *(perbuatan) jenayah*: *to commit a crime* ⊃ look at **cybercrime 3** usually **a crime** [sing] something that is morally wrong □ *kesalahan*: *It is a crime to waste food when people are starving.*

TOPIC

Crime

A crime is **illegal** or **against the law**. A person who **commits** a crime is a **criminal**. There are different words for particular crimes and the people who commit them. A **murderer** commits **murder** (= kills sb). A **kidnapper kidnaps** sb (= takes sb away by force and asks for money for them to be returned). **Terrorists** use violence for political reasons and commit acts of **terrorism**. For example, they sometimes **hijack** planes (= take control of them using violence). **Vandals** commit **vandalism** (= destroy people's property for no reason).

It is the job of the police to **investigate** crimes and try to catch the criminal. If the police think sb may have committed a crime, that person is a **suspect**. When they have enough **evidence** the police can **arrest** and **charge** them **with** the crime (= officially accuse them). If the suspect **confesses** to the crime, they admit that they did it. If they **deny** the charge, they say that they did not do it.

criminal[1] /ˈkrɪmɪnl/ adj **1** [only before a noun] connected with crime □ *(berkaitan dgn) jenayah*: *Deliberate damage to public property is a criminal offence.* ◆ *criminal law* **2** morally wrong □ *yg salah*: *a criminal waste of taxpayers' money* ▶ **criminally** /-nəli/ adv: *criminally insane*

criminal[2] /ˈkrɪmɪnl/ noun [C] a person who has done sth illegal □ *penjenayah*: *CCTV in the city centre has helped to deter criminals.*

crimson /ˈkrɪmzn/ adj, noun [U] (of) a dark red colour □ *merah lembayung*

cringe /krɪndʒ/ verb [I] **1** to move away from sb/sth because you are frightened □ *mengekot*: *The dog cringed in terror when the man raised his arm.* **2** to feel embarrassed □ *berasa malu*: *awful family photographs which make you cringe*

crinkle /ˈkrɪŋkl/ verb [I,T] **crinkle (sth) (up)** to have, or to make sth have, thin folds or lines

VOWELS iː see i any ɪ sit e ten æ hat ɑː father ɒ got ɔː saw ʊ put uː too u usual

folded

crumpled

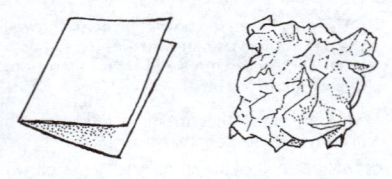

crinkled

in it □ *merenyukkan*: *He crinkled the silver paper up into a ball.* ▶ **crinkly** /ˈkrɪŋkli/ *adj*: *crinkly material*

cripple /ˈkrɪpl/ *verb* [T] to damage sth badly □ *merosakkan; melumpuhkan*: *The recession has crippled the motor industry.*

crippling /ˈkrɪplɪŋ/ *adj* that causes very great damage or has a very bad effect □ *(yg) melumpuhkan*: *They had crippling debts and had to sell their house.*

crisis /ˈkraɪsɪs/ *noun* [C,U] (*pl* **crises** /-siːz/) a time of great danger or difficulty; the moment when things change and either improve or get worse □ *krisis; kemelut*: *the international crisis caused by the invasion* ♦ *a friend you can rely on in times of crisis*

crisp¹ /krɪsp/ *adj* (**crisper**; **crispest**) **1** pleasantly hard and dry □ *rangup*: *Store the biscuits in a tin to keep them crisp.* **2** firm and fresh or new □ *segar; rangup*: *a crisp salad/apple* ♦ *a crisp cotton dress* **3** (used about the air or weather) cold and dry □ *sejuk dan kering*: *a crisp winter morning* **4** (used about the way sb speaks) quick, clear but not very friendly □ *ringkas dan tegas*: *a crisp reply* ▶ **crisply** *adv*: *'I disagree,' she said crisply.* ▶ **crispy** *adj* (*informal*) = **crisp**

crisp² /krɪsp/ (*BrE* also **po̱tato ˈcrisp**, *AmE* **chip**, **po̱tato chip**) *noun* [C] a very thin piece of potato that is fried in oil, then dried and eaten cold. Crisps are sold in small plastic bags and usually have salt or another flavouring on them □ *kerepek kentang*: *a packet of crisps* ⊃ picture at **chip**

criss-cross /ˈkrɪs krɒs/ *adj* [only before a noun] with many straight lines that cross over each other □ *silang-menyilang*: *a criss-cross pattern* ▶ **criss-cross** *verb* [I,T]: *Many footpaths criss-cross the countryside in Suffolk.*

criterion /kraɪˈtɪəriən/ *noun* [C] (*pl* **criteria** /-riə/) the standard that you use when you make a decision or form an opinion about sb/sth □ *kriteria; ukuran*: *The main criterion is value for money.* ♦ *What are the criteria for deciding who gets a place on the course?*

critic /ˈkrɪtɪk/ *noun* [C] **1** a person whose job is to give their opinion about a play, film, book, work of art, etc. □ *pengkritik*: *a film/restaurant/art critic* **2** a person who says what is bad or wrong with sb/sth □ *pengkritik*: *He is a long-standing critic of the council's transport policy.*

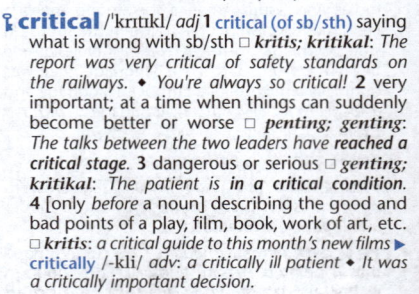

critical /ˈkrɪtɪkl/ *adj* **1** **critical (of sb/sth)** saying what is wrong with sb/sth □ *kritis; kritikal*: *The report was very critical of safety standards on the railways.* ♦ *You're always so critical!* **2** very important; at a time when things can suddenly become better or worse □ *penting; genting*: *The talks between the two leaders have reached a critical stage.* **3** dangerous or serious □ *genting; kritikal*: *The patient is in a critical condition.* **4** [only before a noun] describing the good and bad points of a play, film, book, work of art, etc. □ *kritis*: *a critical guide to this month's new films* ▶ **critically** /-kli/ *adv*: *a critically ill patient* ♦ *It was a critically important decision.*

criticism /ˈkrɪtɪsɪzəm/ *noun* **1** [C,U] (an expression of) what you think is bad about sb/sth □ *kritikan*: *The council has come in for severe criticism over the plans.* **2** [U] the act of describing the good and bad points of a play, film, book, work of art, etc □ *kritikan*: *literary criticism*

criticize (also **-ise**) /ˈkrɪtɪsaɪz/ *verb* [I,T] **criticize (sb/sth) (for sth)** to say what is bad or wrong with sb/sth □ *mengkritik*: *The doctor was criticized for not sending the patient to hospital.* **OPP** **praise**

critique /krɪˈtiːk/ *noun* [C] a piece of writing that describes the good and bad points of sb/sth □ *kritik*

croak /krəʊk/ *verb* [I] to make a rough low sound like a **frog** (= a small animal that lives in or near water, with long back legs that it uses for jumping) □ *menguak; mengeluarkan bunyi garuk* ▶ **croak** *noun* [C]

crochet /ˈkrəʊʃeɪ/ *noun* [U] a way of making clothes, cloth, etc. by using wool or cotton and a needle with a hook at one end □ *kait jarum satu; krusye* ▶ **crochet** *verb* [I,T] (*pt*, *pp* **crocheted** /-ʃeɪd/) ⊃ look at **knit**

crockery /ˈkrɒkəri/ *noun* [U] cups, plates and dishes □ *pinggan mangkuk* ⊃ look at **cutlery**

crocodile /ˈkrɒkədaɪl/ *noun* [C] a large animal with a hard skin covered in scales, a long tail and a big mouth with sharp teeth. Crocodiles live in rivers and lakes in hot countries. □ *buaya* ⊃ look at **alligator**

crocus /ˈkrəʊkəs/ *noun* [C] a small yellow, purple or white flower that grows in early spring □ *bunga krokus*

croissant /ˈkrwæsɒ̃/ *noun* [C] a type of bread roll, shaped in a curve, that is often eaten with butter for breakfast □ *kroisan*

ʌ **cup**   ɜː **bird**   ə **ago**   eɪ **pay**   əʊ **go**   aɪ **my**   aʊ **now**   ɔɪ **boy**   ɪə **near**   eə **hair**   ʊə **pure**

crony /ˈkrəʊni/ noun [C] (pl **cronies**) (informal) (often used in a critical way) a friend □ *kawan; kroni; konco*

crook /krʊk/ noun [C] 1 (informal) a dishonest person; a criminal □ *penyangak* 2 a bend or curve in sth □ *kelok; liku; lengkok*: the crook of your arm (= the inside of your elbow)

crooked /ˈkrʊkɪd/ adj 1 not straight or even □ *bengkok; senget; tak rata*: That picture is crooked. ◆ crooked teeth 2 (informal) not honest □ *tdk jujur*: a crooked accountant

crop¹ /krɒp/ noun 1 [C, usually pl] plants that are grown on farms for food □ *tanaman*: Rice and soya beans are the main crops here. 2 [C] all the grain, fruit, vegetables, etc. of one type that are grown on a farm at one time □ *hasil tanaman*: a crop of apples 3 [sing] a number of people or things which have appeared at the same time □ *kumpulan*: the recent crop of movies about aliens

crop² /krɒp/ verb (**cropping**; **cropped**) 1 [T] to cut sth very short □ *memotong pendek*: cropped hair 2 [T] to cut off part of a photograph or picture □ *memotong* 3 [I] to produce a crop □ *mengeluarkan hasil*
PHR V **crop up** to appear suddenly, when you are not expecting it □ *muncul; timbul*: We should have finished this work yesterday but some problems cropped up.

cropper /ˈkrɒpə(r)/ noun
IDM **come a cropper** (informal) 1 to fall over or have an accident □ *jatuh; mendapat kemalangan* 2 to fail □ *gagal*

croquet /ˈkrəʊkeɪ/ noun [U] a game that you play on grass. When you play **croquet** you use **mallets** (= long wooden hammers) to hit balls through **hoops** (= curved pieces of metal). □ *kroket; sejenis permainan*

cross¹ /krɒs/ noun [C] 1 a mark that you make by drawing one line across another (×). The sign is used for showing the position of sth, for showing that sth is not correct, etc. □ *tanda pangkah*: I drew a cross on the map to show where our house is. ◆ Incorrect answers were marked with a cross. ➲ look at **noughts and crosses** ➲ picture at **tick** 2 often **the Cross** the two pieces of wood in the shape of a cross on which people were killed as a punishment in the past, or sth in this shape that is used as a symbol of the Christian religion □ *salib*: She wore a gold cross round her neck. ➲ look at **crucifix** 3 [usually sing] **a cross (between A and B)** something (especially a plant or an animal) that is a mixture of two different types of thing □ *kacukan*: a fruit which is a cross between a peach and an apple 4 (in sports such as football) a kick or hit of the ball that goes across the front of the goal □ *tendangan/pukulan melintasi depan gol*: Silva's cross was headed into the goal by Tevez.

cross² /krɒs/ verb
▶GO/PUT ACROSS 1 [I,T] **cross (over) (from sth/ to sth)** to go from one side of sth to the other □ *melintas; menyeberang*: to cross the road ◆ Where did you cross the border? ◆ We crossed from Dover to Calais. ◆ I waved and she crossed over. 2 [I] (used about lines, roads, etc.) to pass across each other □ *bersilang*: The two roads cross just north of the village. 3 [T] to put sth across or over sth else □ *menyilang*: to cross your arms/legs
▶OPPOSE 4 [T] to make sb angry by refusing to do what they want you to do □ *menentang; melawan*: He's an important man. It could be dangerous to cross him.
▶MIX 5 [T] **cross sth with sth** to produce a new type of plant or animal by mixing two different types □ *mengacukkan*: If you cross a horse with a donkey, you get a mule.
▶IN SPORT 6 [I,T] (in sports such as football and **hockey**) to pass the ball across the front of the goal □ *menghantar bola melintasi depan gol*: Owen crossed (the ball) for Cole to head into the goal.
IDM **cross/fold your arms** ➲ **arm¹** ➲ picture at **arm**
cross your fingers; keep your fingers crossed ➲ **finger¹**
cross my heart (and hope to die) (spoken) used for emphasizing that what you are saying is true □ *sumpah (betul apa yg dikatakan)*: I won't tell a soul. Cross my heart!
cross your mind (used about a thought, an idea, etc.) to come into your mind □ *terlintas di fikiran*: It never once crossed my mind that she was lying.
PHR V **cross sth off (sth)** to remove sth from a list, etc. by drawing a line through it □ *memotong*: Cross Dave's name off the guest list—he can't come.
cross sth out to draw a line through sth that you have written because you have made a mistake, etc. □ *memotong*: to cross out a spelling mistake

cross³ /krɒs/ adj (informal) **cross (with sb) (about/for sth)** angry or annoyed □ *marah*: I was really cross with her for leaving me with all the work. ➲ **Cross** is less formal than **angry**. ▶ **crossly** adv: 'Be quiet,' Dad said crossly.

crossbar /ˈkrɒsbɑː(r)/ noun [C] 1 the piece of wood over the top of a goal in football, etc. □ *palang gol* 2 the metal bar that joins the front and back of a bicycle □ *palang basikal* ➲ picture at **bike**

ˌcross-ˈcountry adj, adv across fields and natural land; not using roads or tracks □ *rentas desa*: We walked 10 miles cross-country before we saw a village.

ˌcross-eˈxamine verb [T] to ask sb questions in a court of law, etc. in order to find out the truth about sth □ *menyoal balas*: The witness was cross-examined for an hour. ▶ **ˌcross-exˌamiˈnation** noun [C,U]

ˌcross-ˈeyed adj having one or both your eyes looking towards your nose □ *juling*

crossfire /ˈkrɒsfaɪə(r)/ noun [U] a situation in which guns are being fired from two or more different directions □ *tembak-menembak*: *The journalist was killed in crossfire.* ♦ (figurative) *When my parents argued, I sometimes got* **caught in the crossfire**.

crossing /ˈkrɒsɪŋ/ noun [C] **1** a place where you can cross over sth □ *lintasan; tempat melintas*: *You should cross the road at the pedestrian crossing.* ♦ *a border crossing* ➲ look at **level crossing 2** a journey from one side of a sea or river to the other □ *perjalanan menyeberangi sungai, laut, dsb*: *We had a rough crossing.*

with her legs crossed    cross-legged

cross-legged /ˌkrɒs ˈlegd; ˈlegɪd/ adj, adv sitting on the floor with your legs pulled up in front of you and with one leg or foot over the other □ *bersila*: *to sit cross-legged*

cross purposes noun
IDM **at cross purposes** a state of confusion between people who are talking about different things but think they are talking about the same thing □ *keadaan salah faham*: *I think we're talking at cross purposes; that's not what I meant at all.*

cross reference noun [C] a note in a book that tells you to look in another place in the book for more information □ *rujuk silang*

crossroads /ˈkrɒsrəʊdz/ noun [C] (pl **crossroads**) a place where two or more roads cross each other □ *persimpangan*: *When you come to the next crossroads turn right.* ➲ picture at **roundabout**

cross section noun [C] **1** a picture of what the inside of sth would look like if you cut through it □ *keratan rentas*: *a cross section of the human brain* **2** a number of people, etc. that come from the different parts of a group, and so can be considered to represent the whole group □ *keratan lintang*: *The families we studied were chosen to represent a cross section of society.*

crosswalk /ˈkrɒswɔːk/ (AmE) = **pedestrian crossing**

crossword /ˈkrɒswɜːd/ (also **crossword puzzle**) noun [C] a word game in which you have to write the answers to **clues** (= questions) in square spaces, which are arranged in a pattern □ *teka silang kata*: *Every morning I try to do the crossword in the newspaper.*

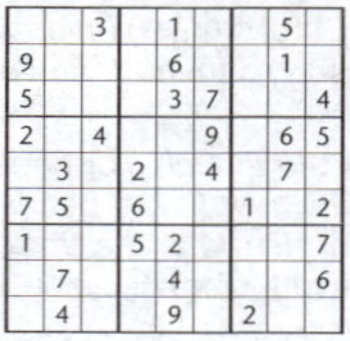

crotch /krɒtʃ/ (also **crutch**) noun [C] the place where your legs, or the legs of a pair of trousers, join at the top □ *kelangkang*

crouch /kraʊtʃ/ verb [I] **crouch (down)** to bend your legs and body so that you are close to the ground □ *bercangkung; mendekam*: *He crouched down behind the sofa.* ➲ picture at **kneel**

crow¹ /krəʊ/ noun [C] a large black bird that makes a loud noise □ *gagak*
IDM **as the crow flies** (used for describing distances) in a straight line □ *mengikut garis lurus*: *It's a kilometre as the crow flies but three kilometres by road.*

crow² /krəʊ/ verb [I] **1** to make a loud noise like a **cock** (= an adult male chicken) □ *berkokok* **2** (informal) to speak in a very proud way about sth □ *berkokok; bermegah-megah* **SYN** **boast**

crowbar /ˈkrəʊbɑː(r)/ noun [C] a long iron bar that is used for forcing sth open □ *tuil besi; alabangka*

crowd¹ /kraʊd/ noun **1** [C, with sing or pl verb] a large number of people in one place □ *kumpulan orang ramai*: *The crowd was/were extremely noisy.* ♦ *He pushed his way through the crowd.* ♦ *I go shopping early in the morning to avoid the crowds.* **2** [C, with sing or pl verb] (informal) a group of people who know each other □ *kumpulan; geng; klik*: *John, Linda and Barry will be there—all the usual crowd.* **3** **the crowd** [sing] ordinary people □ *orang ramai*: *He wears weird clothes because he wants to* **stand out from the crowd**.

crowd² /kraʊd/ verb [T] (used about a lot of people) to fill an area □ *memenuhi; membanjiri; melanda*: *Groups of tourists crowded the main streets.* ♦ (figurative) *Memories crowded her mind.*
PHR V **crowd around/round (sb)** (used about a lot of people) to stand in a large group around sb/sth □ *berkerumun*: *Fans crowded round the singer hoping to get his autograph.*
crowd into sth; crowd in to go into a small place and make it very full □ *berhimpit-himpit*: *Somehow we all crowded into their small living room.*
crowd sb/sth into sth; crowd sb/sth in to put a lot of people into a small place □ *mengasak/diasak masuk ke dlm sst tempat*: *Ten prisoners were crowded into one small cell.*
crowd sth out; crowd sb out (of sth) to completely fill a place so that nobody else can enter

☐ *memenuhi sst tempat hingga orang lain tdk dpt masuk; meminggirkan*: Students crowd out the cafe at lunchtimes. ◆ Smaller companies are being crowded out of the market.

crowded /ˈkraʊdɪd/ adj full of people ☐ *penuh sesak*: a crowded bus ◆ people living in poor and crowded conditions

crown¹ /kraʊn/ noun **1** [C] a circle made of gold and **jewels** (= valuable stones), that a king or queen wears on his or her head on official occasions ☐ *mahkota* **2** the Crown [sing] the state as represented by a king or queen ☐ *negeri; kerajaan*: an area of land belonging to the Crown **3** [sing] the top of your head or of a hat ☐ *mercu kepala; bahagian atas* ⊃ picture at **hat 4** [sing] the top of a hill ☐ *puncak; mercu*

crown² /kraʊn/ verb [T] **1** to put a crown on the head of a new king or queen in an official ceremony ☐ *memahkotai; dimahkotai*: Elizabeth was crowned in 1953. ◆ (figurative) the newly crowned British champion

MORE The ceremony at which someone is made king or queen is called a **coronation**.

2 [often passive] crown sth (with sth) to have or put sth on the top of sth ☐ *meliputi puncak; merupakan kemuncak*: The mountain was crowned with snow. ◆ (figurative) Her years of hard work were finally crowned with success.

crowning /ˈkraʊnɪŋ/ adj [only before a noun] the best or most important ☐ *paling baik/penting*: Winning the World Championship was the crowning moment of her career.

crucial /ˈkruːʃl/ adj crucial (to/for sth) extremely important ☐ *sangat penting*: Early diagnosis of the illness is crucial for successful treatment. **SYN** vital ▶ crucially /-ʃəli/ adv

crucifix /ˈkruːsəfɪks/ noun [C] a small model of a cross with a figure of Jesus on it ☐ *patung salib*

crucifixion /ˌkruːsəˈfɪkʃn/ noun [C,U] the act of killing sb by fastening them to a cross ☐ *penyaliban*: the Crucifixion of Christ

crucify /ˈkruːsɪfaɪ/ verb [T] (crucifying; crucifies; pt, pp crucified) to kill sb by fastening them to a cross ☐ *menyalib*

crude /kruːd/ adj (cruder; crudest) **1** simple and basic, without much detail, skill, etc. ☐ *kasar*: The method was crude but very effective. ◆ She explained how the system worked **in crude terms**. **2** referring to sex or the body in a way that would offend many people ☐ *tdk sopan*: He's always telling crude jokes. **3** in its natural state, before it has been treated with chemicals ☐ *mentah*: crude oil ▶ crudely adv: a crudely drawn face

cruel /ˈkruːəl/ adj (crueller; cruellest) causing physical or mental pain or suffering to sb/sth ☐ *zalim; kejam*: I think it's cruel to keep animals in cages. ◆ a cruel punishment **OPP** kind ▶ cruelly /ˈkruːəli/ adv

cruelty /ˈkruːəlti/ noun (pl cruelties) **1** [U] cruelty (to sb/sth) cruel behaviour ☐ *kezaliman;*

211 **crowded → crush**

kekejaman: cruelty to children **OPP** kindness **2** [C, usually pl] a cruel act ☐ *kekejaman*: the cruelties of war

cruise¹ /kruːz/ noun [C] a holiday in which you travel on a ship and visit a number of different places ☐ *pelayaran persiaran*: They're planning to go on a cruise.

cruise² /kruːz/ verb [I] **1** to travel by boat, visiting a number of places, as a holiday ☐ *belayar makan angin*: to cruise around the Caribbean ⊃ note at **holiday, journey 2** to stay at the same speed in a car, plane, etc. ☐ *bergerak dgn kelajuan sekata*: cruising at 80 kilometres an hour

cruiser /ˈkruːzə(r)/ noun [C] **1** a large fast ship used in a war ☐ *penjajap; kruiser* **2** a motorboat which has room for people to sleep in it ☐ *kapal persiaran*

crumb /krʌm/ noun [C] a very small piece of bread, cake or biscuit ☐ *serbuk; cebisan*

crumble /ˈkrʌmbl/ verb [I,T] crumble (sth) (up) to break or make sth break into very small pieces ☐ *runtuh; hancur; menghancurkan*: The walls of the church are beginning to crumble. ◆ We crumbled up the bread and threw it to the birds. ◆ (figurative) Support for the government is beginning to crumble. ▶ crumbly /ˈkrʌmbli/ adj: This cheese has a crumbly texture.

crumple /ˈkrʌmpl/ verb [I,T] crumple (sth) (into sth); crumple (sth) (up) to be pressed or to press sth into an untidy shape ☐ *remuk; merenyukkan*: The front of the car crumpled when it hit the wall. ◆ She crumpled the letter into a ball and threw it away. ⊃ picture at **crinkle, squeeze**

crunch¹ /krʌntʃ/ noun [sing] an act or the noise of crunching ☐ *bunyi derap*: the crunch of feet on gravel

IDM if/when it comes to the crunch if/when you are in a difficult situation and must make a difficult decision ☐ *apabila tiba masanya/saat penentuan*: If it comes to the crunch, I'll stay and fight.

crunch² /krʌntʃ/ verb **1** [T] crunch sth (up) to make a loud noise when you are eating sth hard ☐ *mengunyah kerap-kerup*: to crunch an apple **2** [I] to make a loud noise like the sound of sth being crushed ☐ *berderap-derap*: We crunched through the snow. ▶ crunchy adj: a crunchy apple

crusade /kruːˈseɪd/ noun [C] **1** a fight for sth that you believe to be good or against sth that you believe to be bad ☐ *perjuangan/usaha menentang sst*: a crusade for justice ◆ a crusade against drugs **SYN** campaign **2** Crusade one of the wars fought in Palestine by European Christians against Muslims in the Middle Ages ☐ *Perang Salib* ▶ crusader noun [C]

crush¹ /krʌʃ/ verb [T] **1** to press sb/sth hard so that he/she/it is broken, damaged or injured ☐ *pecah; remuk; ditimpa; dihempap; digelek*: She sat on my hat and crushed it. ♦ He was crushed to death by a lorry. **2 crush sth (up)** to break sth into very small pieces or a powder □ *menghancurkan*: *Crush the garlic and fry in oil.* ➔ picture at **squeeze 3** to defeat sb/sth completely □ *mengalahkan; menewaskan*: *The army was quickly sent in to crush the rebellion.*

crush² /krʌʃ/ *noun* **1** [sing] a large group of people in a small space □ *kumpulan orang ramai yg bersesak-sesak*: *There was such a crush that I couldn't get near the bar.* **2** [C] (*informal*) **a crush (on sb)** a strong feeling of love for sb that only usually lasts for a short time □ *jatuh hati*: *Maria had a huge crush on her teacher.*

crushing /ˈkrʌʃɪŋ/ *adj* [only before a noun] that defeats sb/sth completely; very bad □ *teruk*: *a crushing defeat*

crust /krʌst/ *noun* [C,U] **1** the hard part on the outside of a piece of bread, a **pie** (= a type of baked food), etc. □ *kulit roti* **2** a hard layer on the outside of sth □ *kerak bumi*: *the earth's crust*

crustacean /krʌˈsteɪʃn/ *noun* [C] (*technical*) a creature with a hard shell and a soft body that is divided into sections, such as a **crab**, **lobster** or **shrimp**. Most **crustaceans** live in water. □ *krustasia* ➔ look at **shellfish**

crusty /ˈkrʌsti/ *adj* (**crustier**; **crustiest**) **1** (used about food) having a hard part on the outside □ *berkulit rangup*: *crusty bread* **2** (*informal*) bad-tempered and impatient □ *perengus*: *a crusty old man*

crutch /krʌtʃ/ *noun* [C] **1** a type of stick that you put under your arm to help you walk when you have hurt your leg or foot □ *topang tongkat ketiak*: *She was on crutches for two months after she broke her ankle.* ➔ look at **walking stick** ➔ picture at **plaster 2** = **crotch**

crux /krʌks/ *noun* [sing] the most important or difficult part of a problem □ *pokok; (hal) paling penting*: *The crux of the matter is how to stop this from happening again.*

ʔcry¹ /kraɪ/ *verb* (**crying**; **cries**; *pt*, *pp* **cried**) **1** [I] to make a noise and produce tears in your eyes, for example because you are unhappy or have hurt yourself □ *menangis*: *The baby never stops crying.* ♦ *The child was crying for* (= because she wanted) *her mother.* ♦ *'It's all right. Don't cry.'* **2** [I,T] **cry (out)** to shout or make a loud noise □ *berteriak; menjerit*: *We could hear someone crying for help.* ♦ *'Look,' he cried, 'There they are.'*
IDM **cry your eyes out** to cry a lot for a long time □ *menangis lama*
a shoulder to cry on ➔ **shoulder¹**
PHR V **cry out for sth** to need sth very much □ *sangat memerlukan*: *Birmingham is crying out for a new transport system.*

ʔcry² /kraɪ/ *noun* (*pl* **cries**) **1** [C] a shout or loud high noise □ *teriakan; sorakan*: *the cries of the children in the playground* ♦ *We heard Adam give a cry of pain as the dog bit him.* ♦ (*figurative*) *Her* suicide attempt was really *a cry for help.* **2** [sing] an act of crying □ *menangis*: *After a good cry I felt much better.*
IDM **a far cry from sth/from doing sth** ➔ **far¹**
hue and cry ➔ **hue**

crying /ˈkraɪɪŋ/ *adj* [only before a noun] (used to talk about a bad situation) very great □ *amat; mendesak; sangat; sungguh*: *There's a crying need for more doctors.* ♦ *It's a crying shame that so many young people can't find jobs.*

crypt /krɪpt/ *noun* [C] a room that is under a church, where people were sometimes buried in the past □ *bilik di bawah gereja*

cryptic /ˈkrɪptɪk/ *adj* having a hidden meaning that is not easy to understand □ *rahsia*: *a cryptic message/remark/smile* **SYN** **mysterious** ▶ **cryptically** /-kli/ *adv*

crystal /ˈkrɪstl/ *noun* **1** [C] a regular shape that some mineral substances form when they become solid □ *hablur*: *salt crystals* **2** [U] a clear mineral that can be used in making jewellery □ *hablur; kristal* **3** [U] glass of very high quality □ *kristal*: *a crystal vase*

ˌcrystal ˈball *noun* [C] a glass ball in which some people say you can see what will happen in the future □ *bola kaca tukang tilik*

ˌcrystal ˈclear *adj* **1** (used about water, glass, etc.) that you can see through perfectly □ *jernih* **2** very easy to understand □ *jelas*: *The meaning is crystal clear.*

crystallize (also **-ise**) /ˈkrɪstəlaɪz/ *verb* [I,T] **1** (used about thoughts, plans, etc.) to become or to make clear and fixed □ *memperjelas; menjadi jelas dan nyata*: *Our ideas began to crystallize into a definite plan.* ♦ *The final chapter crystallizes all the main issues.* **2** (*technical*) to form or to make sth form into **crystals** □ *membentuk menjadi hablur*: *The salt crystallizes as the water evaporates.*

ct *abbr* = **cent**

cu. *abbr* = **cubic** □ *padu*: *a volume of 3 cu. ft*

cub /kʌb/ *noun* **1** [C] a young animal, for example a bear, lion, etc. □ *anak beruang, singa, dll* ➔ note at **fox** ➔ picture at **lion 2 the Cubs** [pl] the part of the Boy Scout organization that is for younger boys □ *Anak Serigala (pengakap)* **3 Cub** (also **Cub ˈScout**) [C] a member of the **Cubs** □ *ahli Anak Serigala*

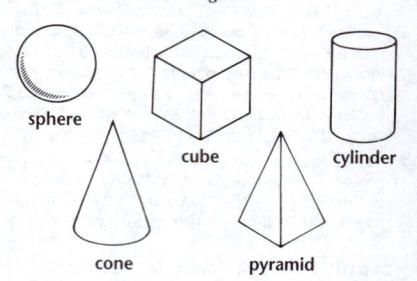

sphere

cube

cylinder

cone

pyramid

cube¹ /kju:b/ noun [C] **1** a solid shape that has six equal square sides □ *kiub; kubus* **2** the number that you get if you multiply a number by itself twice □ *kuasa tiga*: *The cube of 5 (5³) is 125 (= 5 x 5 x 5).*

cube² /kju:b/ verb [T, usually passive] to multiply a number by itself twice □ *menguasatigakan*: *Four cubed (4³) is 64 (= 4 x 4 x 4).*

cubic /ˈkju:bɪk/ adj [only before a noun] (abbr **cu.**) used to show that a measurement is the **volume** (= the amount of space that sth contains or fills) of sth, that is the height multiplied by the length and the width □ *padu*: *If a box is 4cm long, 4cm wide and 4cm high, its volume is 64 cubic centimetres.* ♦ *The lake holds more than a million cubic metres of water.*

cubicle /ˈkju:bɪkl/ noun [C] a small room that is made by separating off part of a larger room □ *bilik kecil; kubikel*: *There are cubicles at the swimming pool for changing your clothes.*

Cub Scout = cub(3)

cuckoo /ˈkuku:/ noun [C] (pl **cuckoos**) a bird which makes a sound like its name and which leaves its eggs in another bird's nest □ *burung sewah tekukur*

cucumber /ˈkju:kʌmbə(r)/ noun [C,U] a long, thin vegetable with a dark green skin that does not need to be cooked □ *timun* ➔ picture on **page P15**

cuddle /ˈkʌdl/ verb [I,T] to hold sb/sth closely in your arms □ *memeluk; mendakap*: *The little girl was cuddling her favourite doll.*
PHR V **cuddle up (to/against sb/sth)**; **cuddle up (together)** to move close to sb and sit or lie in a comfortable position □ *berpelukan; berdakapan*: *They cuddled up together for warmth.*
▶ **cuddle** noun [C]: *He gave the child a cuddle and kissed her goodnight.*

cuddly /ˈkʌdli/ adj (**cuddlier**; **cuddliest**) soft and pleasant to hold close to you □ *enak didakap*: *a cuddly toy*

cue /kju:/ noun [C] **1** a word or movement that is the signal for sb else to say or do sth, especially in a play □ *kiu; isyarat*: *When Julia puts the tray on the table, that's your cue to come on stage.* **2** a long, thin wooden stick used to hit the ball in the games of **snooker**, **billiards** or **pool** (= similar games where players try to hit balls into pockets around a special table) □ *kiu* ➔ picture at **pool**
IDM **(right) on cue** at exactly the moment expected □ *tepat pd masanya*: *Just as I was starting to worry about Stan, he phoned right on cue.*
take your cue from sb/sth to copy what sb/sth else does as an example of how to behave □ *contoh; (perbuatan) meneladani*: *I'm not sure how to behave at a Japanese wedding, so I'll take my cue from the hosts.*

cuff /kʌf/ noun [C] **1** the end part of a sleeve, which often fastens at the wrist □ *manset* ➔ picture on **page P1** **2** **cuffs** [pl] = **handcuffs** **3** a light hit with the open hand □ *tamparan perlahan*

IDM **off the cuff** (used about sth you say) without thought or preparation before that moment □ *secara spontan*: *I haven't got the figures here, but, off the cuff, I'd say the rise is about 10%.*

cufflink /ˈkʌflɪŋk/ noun [C, usually pl] one of a pair of small objects used instead of a button to fasten a shirt sleeve together at the wrist □ *kafling; kancing lengan baju*

cuisine /kwɪˈzi:n/ noun [U] the style of cooking of a particular country, restaurant, etc. □ *masakan*: *Italian cuisine*

cul-de-sac /ˈkʌl də sæk/ noun [C] (pl **cul-de-sacs**) a street that is closed at one end □ *'cul-de-sac'; jalan mati*

culinary /ˈkʌlɪnəri/ adj [only before a noun] (formal) connected with cooking □ *(berkaitan dgn) masak-memasak*

cull¹ /kʌl/ verb [T] to kill a number of animals in a group to prevent the group from becoming too large □ *menakai; pilih bunuh; membunuh sejumlah binatang utk mengurangkan jumlahnya*
PHR V **cull sth from sth** to collect information, ideas, etc., from different places □ *mendapatkan maklumat, idea dsb drpd pelbagai sumber*: *I managed to cull some useful addresses from the Internet.*

cull² /kʌl/ noun [C] the act of killing some animals in order to stop a group becoming too large □ *penakaian; perbuatan pilih bunuh*: *a deer cull*

culminate /ˈkʌlmɪneɪt/ verb [I] (formal) **culminate in sth** to reach a final result □ *berakhir dgn; mencapai kemuncak*: *The team's efforts culminated in victory in the championships.* ▶ **culmination** /ˌkʌlmɪˈneɪʃn/ noun [sing]: *The joint space mission was the culmination of years of research.*

culpable /ˈkʌlpəbl/ adj (formal) responsible for sth bad that has happened □ *bersalah*

culprit /ˈkʌlprɪt/ noun [C] a person who has done sth wrong □ *orang yg bersalah*

cult /kʌlt/ noun [C] **1** a person or thing that has become popular with a particular group of people □ *kegilaan*: *cult movies* **2** a type of religion or religious group, especially one that is considered unusual □ *kultus*

cultivate /ˈkʌltɪveɪt/ verb [T] **1** to prepare and use land for growing plants for food or to sell □ *mengusahakan tanah utk bercucuk tanam*: *to cultivate the soil* **2** to grow plants for food or to sell □ *menanam; ditanam*: *Olives have been cultivated for centuries in Mediterranean countries.* **3** to try to develop a friendship with sb □ *mencuba memupuk*: *He cultivated links with colleagues abroad.* ▶ **cultivation** /ˌkʌltɪˈveɪʃn/ noun [U]

cultivated /ˈkʌltɪveɪtɪd/ adj **1** well educated, with good manners □ *berpelajaran dan halus* *budi pekertinya* **2** (used about land) used for growing plants for food or to sell □ *diusahakan (utk bercucuk tanam)* **3** (used about plants) grown on a farm, not wild □ *ditanam*

cultural /ˈkʌltʃərəl/ *adj* **1** connected with the customs, ideas, beliefs, etc. of a society or country □ *(berkaitan dgn) kebudayaan*: *The country's cultural diversity is a result of taking in immigrants from all over the world.* ⊃ look at **multicultural** **2** connected with art, music, literature, etc. □ *(berkaitan dgn) seni budaya*: *The city has a rich cultural life, with many theatres, concert halls and art galleries.* ▶ **culturally** /-rəli/ *adv*

culture /ˈkʌltʃə(r)/ *noun* **1** [C,U] the customs, ideas, beliefs, etc. of a particular society, country, etc. □ *kebudayaan; budaya*: *the language and culture of the Aztecs* ♦ *people from many different cultures* **2** [U] art, literature, music, etc. □ *kebudayaan*: *London has always been a centre of culture.*

cultured /ˈkʌltʃəd/ *adj* well educated and showing a good knowledge of art, music, literature, etc. □ *berbudaya tinggi*

ˈculture shock *noun* [U] a feeling of confusion, etc. that you may have when you go to live in or visit a country that is very different from your own □ *kejutan budaya*

cumbersome /ˈkʌmbəsəm/ *adj* **1** heavy and difficult to carry, use, wear, etc. □ *berat dan menyusahkan* **2** (used about a system, etc.) slow and complicated □ *lembap dan tdk cekap*: *cumbersome legal procedures*

cumulative /ˈkjuːmjələtɪv/ *adj* increasing steadily in amount, degree, etc. □ *kumulatif*: *a cumulative effect*

cunning /ˈkʌnɪŋ/ *adj* clever in a dishonest or bad way □ *licik*: *He was as cunning as a fox.* ♦ *a cunning trick* SYN **sly, wily** ▶ **cunning** *noun* [U] ▶ **cunningly** *adv*

cups

cup | handle

saucer

cup and saucer   **mug**

cup¹ /kʌp/ *noun* [C] **1** a small container usually with a handle, used for drinking liquids □ *cawan*: *a teacup* ♦ *a cup of coffee* **2** an object shaped like a cup □ *mangkuk*: *an eggcup* **3** (in sport) a large metal cup given as a prize; the competition for such a cup □ *piala*: *Our team won the cup in the basketball tournament.* ♦ *the World Cup* ⊃ picture at **medal**
IDM **not sb's cup of tea** not what sb likes or is interested in □ *bukan apa yg digemari oleh sso*: *Horror films aren't my cup of tea.*

cup² /kʌp/ *verb* [T] (**cupping; cupped**) to form sth, especially your hands, into the shape of a cup; to hold sth with your hands shaped like a cup □ *meraup; memungkumkan; menadah (tangan)*: *I cupped my hands to take a drink from the stream.*

cupboard /ˈkʌbəd/ *noun* [C] a piece of furniture, usually with shelves inside and a door or doors at the front, used for storing food, clothes, etc. □ *almari*: *a kitchen cupboard* ♦ *built-in cupboards* ⊃ picture on **page P8**

cupful /ˈkʌpfʊl/ *noun* [C] the amount that a cup will hold □ *secawan penuh*: *two cupfuls of water*

curable /ˈkjʊərəbl/ *adj* (used about a disease) that can be made better □ *dpt diubati; boleh sembuh* OPP **incurable**

curate /ˈkjʊərət/ *noun* [C] (in the Church of England) an assistant to a priest □ *paderi pembantu*

curator /kjʊəˈreɪtə(r)/ *noun* [C] a person whose job is to look after the things that are kept in a museum □ *kurator*

curb¹ /kɜːb/ *verb* [T] to limit or control sth, especially sth bad □ *mengekang; mengawal*: *He needs to learn to curb his anger.*

curb² /kɜːb/ *noun* [C] **a curb (on sth)** a control or limit on sth □ *kawalan*: *a curb on local government spending* **2** (*especially AmE*) = **kerb**

curdle /ˈkɜːdl/ *verb* [I,T] (used about liquids) to turn sour or to separate into different parts; to make sth do this □ *mengental menjadi dadih*: *She heated the sauce for too long and it curdled.* ⊃ look at **blood-curdling**

cure¹ /kjʊə(r)/ *verb* [T] **1 cure sb (of sth)** to make sb healthy again after an illness □ *menyembuhkan*: *The treatment cured him of cancer.* **2** to make an illness, injury, etc. end or disappear □ *mengubati; membaiki*: *It is still not possible to cure the common cold.* ♦ (*figurative*) *The plumber cured the problem with the central heating.* **3** to make certain types of food last longer by drying them, or treating them with smoke or salt □ *mengawetkan*: *cured ham*

cure² /kjʊə(r)/ *noun* [C] **a cure (for sth)** **1** a medicine or treatment that can cure an illness, etc. □ *ubat*: *There is no cure for this illness.* **2** a return to good health; the process of being cured □ *penyembuhan*: *The new drug brought about a miraculous cure.*

curfew /ˈkɜːfjuː/ *noun* [C] **1** a time after which people are not allowed to go outside their homes, for example during a war □ *perintah berkurung*: *The government imposed a dusk-to-dawn curfew.* **2** (*AmE*) a time when children must arrive home in the evening □ *waktu mesti pulang ke rumah*: *She has a 10 o'clock curfew.*

curiosity /ˌkjʊəriˈɒsəti/ *noun* (*pl* **curiosities**) **1** [U] a desire to know or learn □ *sifat ingin tahu*: *I was full of curiosity about their plans.* ♦ *Out of curiosity, he opened her letter.* **2** [C] an unusual and interesting person or thing □ *sso/sst yg* *aneh*: *The museum was full of historical curiosities.*

curious /ˈkjʊəriəs/ *adj* **1 curious (about sth); curious (to do sth)** wanting to know or learn sth □ *ingin tahu*: *They were very curious about the people who lived upstairs.* ◆ *He was curious to know how the machine worked.* **2** unusual or strange □ *aneh*: *It was curious that she didn't tell anyone about the incident.* ▶ **curiously** *adv*

curl¹ /kɜːl/ *verb* **1** [I,T] to form or to make sth form into a curved or round shape □ *menjadi gelungan; keriting; mengeriting*: *Does your hair curl naturally?* **2** [I] to move round in a curve □ *melilit; bergulung-gulung*: *The snake curled around his arm.* ◆ *Smoke curled up into the sky.*
PHR V curl up to pull your arms, legs and head close to your body □ *berlingkar*: *The cat curled up in front of the fire.*

curl² /kɜːl/ *noun* [C] **1** a piece of hair that curves round □ *rambut keriting*: *Her hair fell in curls round her face.* **2** a thing that has a curved round shape □ *gelungan; kepulan*: *a curl of blue smoke*

curler /ˈkɜːlə(r)/ *noun* [C] a small plastic or metal tube that you roll your hair around in order to make it curly □ *penggulung rambut*

curly /ˈkɜːli/ *adj* (**curlier; curliest**) full of **curls**; shaped like a **curl** □ *keriting*: *He's got curly hair.* ◆ *a dog with a curly tail* **OPP straight** ⊃ picture at **hair**

currant /ˈkʌrənt/ *noun* [C] **1** a very small dried grape (= a small fruit that grows in bunches) used to make cakes, etc. □ *kismis* **2** [in compounds] a small black, red or white fruit that grows in bunches on bushes □ *buah jenis beri*: *blackcurrants*

currency /ˈkʌrənsi/ *noun* (*pl* **currencies**) **1** [C,U] the system or type of money that a particular country uses □ *mata wang*: *The currency of Argentina is the peso.* ◆ *foreign currency* ◆ *a weak/strong/stable currency* **2** [U] the state of being believed, accepted or used by many people □ *tersebar luas; diterima ramai; popular*: *The new ideas soon gained currency.*

current¹ /ˈkʌrənt/ *adj* **1** [only *before* a noun] of the present time; happening now □ *sekarang; kini; semasa*: *current fashions/events* **2** generally accepted; in common use □ *diterima umum; dipakai*: *Is this word still current?*

current² /ˈkʌrənt/ *noun* **1** [C] a continuous flowing movement of water, air, etc. □ *arus*: *to swim against/with the current* ◆ (*figurative*) *a current of anti-government feeling* **2** [C,U] the flow of electricity through a wire, etc. □ *arus elektrik; karan*: *Turn off the current before cleaning the machine.*

current ac·count (*AmE* **ˈchecking account**) *noun* [C] a bank account that you can take money out of at any time, and that provides you with a cheque book and **cash card** (= a special card that is given to you by your bank) □ *akaun semasa* ⊃ look at **deposit account**

current af·fairs *noun* [pl] important political or social events that are happening at the present time □ *hal ehwal semasa*

currently /ˈkʌrəntli/ *adv* at present; at the moment □ *pd masa ini*: *He is currently working in Spain.* ⊃ note at **actually**

curriculum /kəˈrɪkjələm/ *noun* [C] (*pl* **curriculums** or **curricula** /-lə/) all the subjects that are taught in a school, college or university; the contents of a particular course of study □ *kurikulum*: *Latin is not on the curriculum at our school.* ⊃ look at **syllabus**

curriculum vitae /kəˌrɪkjələm ˈviːtaɪ/ = **CV**

curry /ˈkʌri/ *noun* [C,U] (*pl* **curries**) an Indian dish of meat, vegetables, etc. containing a lot of spices, usually served with rice □ *kari*: *a hot/mild curry* ▶ **curried** *adj*: *curried chicken*

ˈcurry powder *noun* [U] a fine mixture of strongly flavoured spices that is used to make **curry** □ *serbuk rempah kari*

curse¹ /kɜːs/ *noun* [C] **1** a word used for expressing anger; a swear word □ *caci maki* **2** a word or words expressing a wish that sth terrible will happen to sb □ *sumpahan*: *The family seemed to be under a curse* (= a lot of bad things happened to them). **3** something that causes great harm □ *musibat*: *the curse of poverty*

curse² /kɜːs/ *verb* **1** [I,T] **curse (sb/sth) (for sth)** to swear at sb/sth; to use rude language to express your anger □ *memaki; menyumpah seranah*: *He dropped the box, cursing himself for his clumsiness.* **2** [T] to use a magic word or phrase against sb because you wish them harm □ *menyumpah*: *She cursed his family.*

cursor /ˈkɜːsə(r)/ *noun* [C] a small sign on a computer screen that shows the position you are at □ *kursor*

cursory /ˈkɜːsəri/ *adj* quick and short; done in a hurry □ *sepintas lalu*: *a cursory glance*

curt /kɜːt/ *adj* short and not polite □ *ringkas dan kasar*: *He gave him a curt reply and slammed the phone down.* ▶ **curtly** *adv* ▶ **curtness** *noun* [U]

curtail /kɜːˈteɪl/ *verb* [T] (*formal*) to make sth shorter or smaller; to reduce sth □ *mengurangkan; memendekkan*: *I had to curtail my answer as I was running out of time.* ▶ **curtailment** *noun* [C,U]

curtain /ˈkɜːtn/ *noun* [C] **1** (*AmE also* **drape**) a piece of cloth that you can move to cover a window, etc. □ *langsir; tabir; tirai*: *Could you draw the curtains, please?* (= Could you open/close the curtains?) ◆ *a pair of curtains* ◆ *lace curtains* ◆ *a shower curtain* ◆ *The curtain goes up at 7pm* (= in a theatre, the play begins). **2** a thing that covers or hides sth □ *tabir*: *a curtain of mist*

[C] **countable**, a noun with a plural form: *one book, two books* [U] **uncountable**, a noun with no plural form: *some sugar*

curtsy → cut

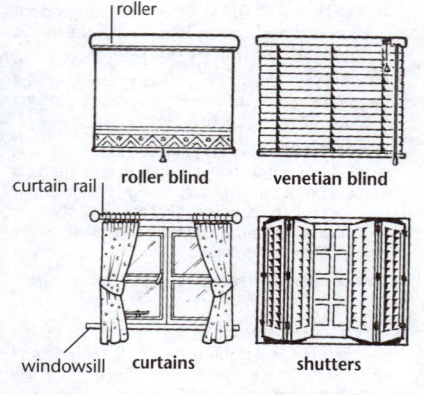

roller
curtain rail — **roller blind** — **venetian blind**
windowsill — **curtains** — **shutters**

curtsy (also **curtsey**) /ˈkɜːtsi/ noun [C] (pl **curtsies** or **curtseys**) a movement made by a woman as a sign of respect, done by bending the knees, with one foot behind the other □ *tunduk sambil membengkokkan lutut sebagai tanda hormat* ▶ **curtsy** (also **curtsey**) verb [I]: *She curtsied to the Queen.*

curve¹ /kɜːv/ noun [C] a line that bends round □ *lengkok; lengkung; kelok*: *a curve on a graph* ◆ *a pattern of straight lines and curves* ⇨ picture at **line**

curve² /kɜːv/ verb [I,T] to bend or to make sth bend in a curve □ *melengkok; melengkung*: *The bay curved round to the south.* ▶ **curved** adj: *a curved blade* ⇨ picture at **line**

cushion¹ /ˈkʊʃn/ noun [C] 1 a bag filled with soft material, for example feathers, which you put on a chair, etc. to make it more comfortable □ *kusyen* ⇨ picture on **page P8**

> **MORE** A cushion on a bed is a **pillow**.

2 something that acts or is shaped like a **cushion** □ *kusyen; alas; lapisan*: *A hovercraft rides on a cushion of air.* ⇨ picture at **pool**

cushion² /ˈkʊʃn/ verb [T] 1 to make a fall, hit, etc. less painful □ *mengurangkan kesan; mengampu*: *The snow cushioned his fall.* 2 to reduce the unpleasant effect of sth □ *melindungi*: *She spent her childhood on a farm, cushioned from the effects of the war.*

cushy /ˈkʊʃi/ adj (**cushier**; **cushiest**) (*informal*) too easy, needing little effort (in a way that seems unfair to others) □ *senang dan selesa*: *a cushy job*

custard /ˈkʌstəd/ noun [U] a sweet yellow sauce made from milk, eggs and sugar. In Britain it is eaten hot or cold with sweet dishes □ *kastard*: *apple pie and custard*

custodian /kʌˈstəʊdiən/ noun [C] 1 (*formal*) a person who looks after or protects sth, such as a museum, library, etc. □ *penjaga; penyimpan* 2 (*AmE*) = **caretaker**

custody /ˈkʌstədi/ noun [U] 1 the legal right or duty to take care of sb/sth □ *jagaan*: *After the divorce, the mother had custody of the children.* 2 the state of being guarded, or kept in prison temporarily, especially by the police □ *(dlm) tahanan*: *The man was kept in custody until his trial.*

custom /ˈkʌstəm/ noun 1 [C,U] a way of behaving which a particular group or society has had for a long time □ *adat*: *It's the custom in Britain for a bride to throw her bouquet to the wedding guests.* ◆ *according to local custom* ⇨ note at **habit** 2 [sing] (*formal*) something that a person does regularly □ *kebiasaan*: *It was her custom to rise early in the morning.* 3 [U] (*BrE*) commercial activity; the practice of people buying things regularly from a particular shop, etc. □ *langganan*: *The local shop lost a lot of custom when the new supermarket opened.* ⇨ look at **customs**

customary /ˈkʌstəməri/ adj according to custom; usual □ *kebiasaan*: *Is it customary to send cards at Christmas in your country?*

customer /ˈkʌstəmə(r)/ noun [C] 1 a person who buys goods or services in a shop, restaurant, etc. □ *pelanggan*: *a regular customer* ◆ *The shop assistant was serving a customer.* ⇨ note at **client** 2 (*informal, old-fashioned*) [after certain adjectives] a person □ *orang*: *a tough/an awkward/an odd customer*

customs (also **Customs**) /ˈkʌstəmz/ noun [pl] 1 the government department that collects taxes paid on goods from other countries □ *kastam*: *a customs officer* 2 the place at a port or an airport where your bags are checked to make sure you are not bringing goods into the country illegally □ *kastam*: *to go through customs and passport control* ⇨ look at **excise**

cut¹ /kʌt/ verb (**cutting**; pt, pp **cut**)
▶ HOLE **1** [I,T] to make an opening, a wound or a mark in sth using a sharp tool, for example a pair of scissors or a knife □ *memotong; melukai*: *Be careful not to cut yourself on that broken glass!* ◆ *This knife doesn't cut very well.*
▶ REMOVE **2** [T] **cut sth (from sth)** to remove sth or a part of sth, using a knife, etc. □ *memotong*: *She cut two slices of bread (from the loaf).*
▶ DIVIDE **3** [T] **cut sth (in/into sth)** to divide sth into pieces with a knife, etc. □ *memotong; membahagikan; mengerat*: *She cut the cake into eight (pieces).* ◆ *He cut the rope in two.*
▶ MAKE SHORTER **4** [T] to make sth shorter by using scissors, etc. □ *memotong; menggunting*: *I cut my own hair.* ◆ *to have your hair cut* (= at the hairdresser's) ◆ *to cut the grass*
▶ SHAPE/FORM **5** [T] to make or form sth by removing material with a sharp tool □ *membuat; menebuk*: *She cut a hole in the card and pushed the string through.* ◆ *They cut a path through the jungle.*
▶ REDUCE/REMOVE **6** [T] to reduce sth or make it shorter; to remove sth □ *mengurangkan*;

dipotong: *to cut taxes/costs/spending* ♦ *Several violent scenes in the film were cut.*
▸COMPUTING **7** [T] to remove a piece of text from the screen □ *potong*: *Use the cut and paste buttons to change the order of the paragraphs.*
▸GO ACROSS **8** [I] **cut across, along, through, etc. (sth)** to go across, etc. sth, in order to make your route shorter □ *merentasi; memintas*: *It's much quicker if we cut across the field.*
▸STOP **9** [T] (*spoken*) to stop sth □ *menghentikan; hentikan*: *Cut the chat and get on with your work!*
▸UPSET **10** [T] to deeply offend sb or hurt their feelings □ *melukakan perasaan*: *His cruel remarks cut her deeply.* ❶ For idioms containing **cut**, look at the entries for the nouns, adjectives, etc. For example **cut corners** is at **corner**.

PHR V **be cut out for sth**; **be cut out to be sth** to have the qualities needed to do sth; to be suitable for sth/sb □ *sesuai utk menjadi sst*: *You're not cut out to be a teacher.*
cut across sth to affect or be true for different groups that usually remain separate □ *merentasi; menjangkau; mendatangkan kesan kpd semua pihak*: *The question of aid for the earthquake victims cuts across national boundaries.*
cut sth back; **cut back (on sth)** to reduce sth □ *mengurangkan*: *to cut back on public spending*
cut sth down 1 to make sth fall down by cutting it □ *menebang*: *to cut down a tree* **2** to make sth shorter □ *memendekkan*: *I have to cut my essay down to 2 000 words.*
cut down; **cut down (on sth)** to reduce the quantity or amount of sth; to do sth less often □ *mengurangkan*: *You should cut down on fatty foods.*
cut in (on sb/sth) to interrupt sb/sth □ *mencelah; menyampuk*: *She kept cutting in on our conversation.*
cut sb off [often passive] to stop or interrupt sb's telephone conversation □ *sambungan/talian (telefon) terputus*: *We were cut off before I could give her my message.*
cut sb/sth off [often passive] to stop the supply of sth to sb □ *dipotong; menghentikan bekalan*: *The electricity/gas/water has been cut off.*
cut sth off to block a road, etc. so that nothing can pass □ *menyekat*: *We must cut off all possible escape routes.*
cut sth off (sth) to remove sth from sth larger by cutting □ *memotong hingga putus; terputus*: *Be careful you don't cut your fingers off using that electric saw.*
cut sb/sth off (from sb/sth) [often passive] to prevent sb/sth from moving from a place or contacting people outside □ *terpisah; putus hubungan; terpencil*: *The farm was cut off from the village by heavy snow.*
cut sth open to open sth by cutting □ *membelah; mendapat luka*: *She fell and cut her head open.*
cut sth out 1 to remove sth or to form sth into a particular shape by cutting □ *memotong/menggunting sst*: *He cut the job advertisement out of the newspaper.* **2** to not include sth □ *memotong; buang*: *Cut out all the boring details!* **3** (*especially AmE informal*) to stop saying or doing sth that

cut → cutters

annoys sb □ *berhenti (membuat/mengatakan sst yg menyakitkan hati)*: *Cut that out and leave me alone!* **4** (*informal*) to stop doing or using sth □ *berhenti (membuat/menggunakan sst)*: *You'll only lose weight if you cut out sweet things from your diet.*
cut sth up to cut sth into small pieces with a knife, etc □ *memotong-motong; mencencang*: *He cut up the meat on his plate.*

cut² /kʌt/ *noun* [C]
▸INJURY **1** an injury or opening in the skin made with a knife, etc. □ *luka*: *He had a deep cut on his forehead.*
▸OF HAIR **2** an act of cutting □ *(perbuatan) memotong*: *to have a cut and blow-dry* (= at the hairdresser's)
▸REDUCTION **3 a cut (in sth)** a reduction in size, amount, etc. □ *pemotongan; pengurangan; terputusnya*: *a cut in government spending* ♦ *a power cut* (= when the electric current is stopped temporarily)
▸MONEY **4** (*informal*) a share of the profits from sth, especially sth dishonest □ *bahagian; habuan*: *They were rewarded with a cut of 5% from the profits.*
▸MEAT **5** a piece of meat from a particular part of an animal □ *potongan*: *cheap cuts of lamb* ⇨ look at **short cut**

cutback /ˈkʌtbæk/ *noun* [C] a reduction in amount or number □ *pengurangan*: *The management were forced to make cutbacks in staff.*

cute /kjuːt/ *adj* (**cuter**; **cutest**) attractive; pretty □ *comel; molek*: *Your little girl is so cute!* ♦ *a cute smile*

cutlery /ˈkʌtləri/ **cutlery** (*AmE* **silverware**) *noun* [U] the knives, forks and spoons that you use for eating food □ *pisau, sudu dan garpu* ⇨ look at **crockery**

cutlet /ˈkʌtlət/ *noun* [C] a small, thick piece of meat, often with bone in it, that is cooked □ *kutlet*

fork knife spoon

ˈcut-off *noun* [C] the level or time at which sth stops □ *tahap/tempoh akhir*: *The cut-off date is 12 May. After that we'll end the offer.*

ˈcut-price (*AmE* **ˈcut-rate**) *adj* [only *before* a noun] sold at a reduced price; selling goods at low prices □ *harga potongan; harga rendah*: *cut-price offers* ♦ *a cut-price store*

cutters /ˈkʌtəz/ *noun* [pl] a tool that you use for cutting through sth, for example metal □ *pemotong*: *a pair of wire cutters*

cut-throat *adj* caring only about success and not worried about hurting anyone □ *(perniagaan, persaingan, dsb) sembelih; cekik darah*: *cut-throat business practices*

cutting[1] /ˈkʌtɪŋ/ *noun* [C] (*AmE* clipping) a piece cut out from a newspaper, etc. □ *potongan; keratan*: *press cuttings* **2** a piece cut off from a plant that you use for growing a new plant □ *keratan*

cutting[2] /ˈkʌtɪŋ/ *adj* (used about sth you say) unkind; meant to hurt sb's feelings □ *tajam; menyakitkan hati*: *a cutting remark*

cutting edge *noun* [sing] **1 the cutting edge (of sth)** the newest, most advanced stage in the development of sth □ *tercanggih; termaju; terbaharu*: *working at the cutting edge of computer technology* **2** an aspect of sth that gives it an advantage □ *kelebihan; aspek sst yg memberi manfaat kpdnya*: *We're relying on him to give the team a cutting edge.*

CV /ˌsiː ˈviː/ (*AmE* résumé) *noun* [C] **curriculum vitae**; a formal list of your education and work experience, often used when you are trying to get a new job □ *keterangan peribadi* ➔ note at **job**

cwt. *abbr* = hundredweight

cyanide /ˈsaɪənaɪd/ *noun* [U] a poisonous chemical □ *sianida*

cyberbully /ˈsaɪbəbʊli/ *noun* [C] (*pl* cyberbullies) a person who uses the Internet to threaten and frighten sb else with unpleasant messages □ *pembuli siber* ➔ look at **bully** ▸ cyberbullying *noun* [U]

cybercafe /ˈsaɪbəkæfeɪ/ *noun* [C] a place with computers where customers can pay to use the Internet □ *kafe siber* ➔ note at **Internet**

cybercrime /ˈsaɪbəkraɪm/ *noun* [U,C] crime that is committed using the Internet, for example by stealing sb's bank details or sending a virus to sb's computer □ *jenayah siber*

> **TOPIC**
>
> **Cybercrime**
> Be careful when you **download** (= copy) a file, as it may **contain a virus**. It is important that you install **antivirus software** (= a program that finds and destroys viruses) and a **firewall** (= a program that prevents people from making changes to your computer without your permission). Your **email account** should have **a filter** to stop any **junk emails/spam** reaching your inbox. There is also the danger of **phishing**. This is when criminals send emails to try to make you give them information that will allow them to steal money from you.

cyberspace /ˈsaɪbəspeɪs/ *noun* [U] a place that is not real, where electronic messages exist while they are being sent from one computer to another □ *ruang siber*

cycle[1] /ˈsaɪkl/ *noun* [C] **1** a bicycle or motorbike □ *basikal; motosikal*: *a cycle shop* **SYN** bike **2** a series of events, etc. that happen again and again in the same order □ *kitar*: *the life cycle of a frog*

cycle[2] /ˈsaɪkl/ *verb* [I] to ride a bicycle □ *berbasikal*: *Leonie usually cycles to work.*

> **HELP** Go cycling is a common way of talking about cycling for pleasure: *We go cycling most weekends.*

cyclic /ˈsaɪklɪk/ (also cyclical /ˈsɪklɪkl/) *adj* following a repeated pattern □ *berkitar*

cyclist /ˈsaɪklɪst/ *noun* [C] a person who rides a bicycle □ *penunggang basikal*

cyclone /ˈsaɪkləʊn/ *noun* [C] a large, violent storm in which strong winds move in a circle □ *siklon* ➔ note at **storm**

cygnet /ˈsɪɡnət/ *noun* [C] a young swan (= a large white bird with a long neck) □ *anak burung undan*

cylinder /ˈsɪlɪndə(r)/ *noun* [C] **1** an object shaped like a tube □ *silinder* ➔ picture at **cube** **2** a part of an engine shaped like a tube, for example in a car □ *silinder* ▸ cylindrical /səˈlɪndrɪkl/ *adj*

cymbal /ˈsɪmbl/ *noun* [C, usually pl] one of a pair of round metal plates used as a musical instrument. Cymbals make a loud ringing sound when you hit them together or with a stick. □ *simbal* ➔ picture at **music**

cynic /ˈsɪnɪk/ *noun* [C] a person who believes that people only do things for themselves, rather than to help others □ *orang yg sinis*: *Don't be such a cynic. He did it to help us, not for the money.* ▸ cynical /-kl/ *adj*: *a cynical remark* ▸ cynically /-kli/ *adv* ▸ cynicism /ˈsɪnɪsɪzəm/ *noun* [U]

Cyrillic /səˈrɪlɪk/ *noun* [U] the alphabet that is used in languages such as Russian □ *(abjad) Cyril*

cyst /sɪst/ *noun* [C] a swelling or a lump filled with liquid in the body or under the skin □ *sista*

czar, czarina = tsar, tsarina

D d

D, d /diː/ *noun* [C,U] (*pl* Ds; D's; d's /diːz/) **1** the fourth letter of the English alphabet □ *D, d (huruf)*: *'December' begins with (a) 'D'.* **2 D** (used about music) the second note in the scale of C major □ *not kedua dlm skala C major*: *D major/minor* ♦ *D flat/sharp*

d. *abbr* died □ *mati; meninggal dunia*: *W A Mozart, d. 1791*

dab[1] /dæb/ *verb* [I,T] (dabbing; dabbed) to touch sth lightly, usually several times □ *memedap; menekap*: *He dabbed the cut with some cotton wool.*

PHR V **dab sth on/off (sth)** to put sth on or to remove sth lightly □ *membubuh; memalit; mengesat; mengelap*: *to dab some antiseptic on a wound*

dab² /dæb/ *noun* [C] **1** a small quantity of sth that is put on a surface □ *secalit; sedikit*: *a dab of paint/perfume* **2** a light touch □ *(perbuatan) menyentuh sedikit*: *She gave her eyes a dab with a handkerchief.*

dabble /ˈdæbl/ *verb* **1** [I] to become involved in sth in a way that is not very serious □ *berkecimpung*: *to dabble in politics* **2** [T] to put your hands, feet, etc. in water and move them around □ *berkecimpung; mengocak-ngocak air*: *We sat on the bank and dabbled our toes in the river.*

dad /dæd/ *noun* [C] (*informal*) father □ *bapa; ayah*: *Is that your dad?* ♦ *Come on, Dad!*

daddy /ˈdædi/ *noun* [C] (*pl* **daddies**) (*informal*) (used by children) father □ *bapa; ayah*: *I want my daddy!*

daffodil /ˈdæfədɪl/ *noun* [C] a tall yellow flower that grows in the spring □ *dafodil*

daft /dɑːft/ *adj* (**dafter**; **daftest**) (*informal*) silly □ *bodoh*: *Don't be daft.* ♦ *a daft idea*

dagger /ˈdægə(r)/ *noun* [C] a type of knife used as a weapon, especially in past times □ *pisau belati; badik* ➲ picture at **sword**

daily¹ /ˈdeɪli/ *adj* [only *before* a noun] *adv* done, made or happening every day □ *harian; sehari-hari*: *a daily routine/delivery/newspaper* ♦ *Our airline flies to Japan daily.* ➲ note at **routine**

daily² /ˈdeɪli/ *noun* [C] (*pl* **dailies**) (*informal*) a newspaper that is published every day except Sunday □ *akhbar harian*

dainty /ˈdeɪnti/ *adj* (**daintier**; **daintiest**) **1** small and pretty □ *kecil molek; comel*: *a dainty lace handkerchief* **2** (used about sb's movements) very careful in a way that tries to show good manners □ *lemah gemalai*: *Veronica took a dainty bite of her cucumber sandwich.* ▸ **daintily** *adv*

dairy¹ /ˈdeəri/ *noun* [C] (*pl* **dairies**) **1** a place on a farm where milk is kept and butter, cheese, etc. are made □ *tempat menyimpan hasil tenusu* **2** a company which sells milk, butter, eggs, etc. □ *syarikat yg menjual hasil tenusu*

dairy² /ˈdeəri/ *adj* [only *before* a noun] **1** made from milk: *dairy products/produce* (= milk, butter, cheese, etc.) □ *diperbuat drpd susu; hasil tenusu* **2** connected with the production of milk □ *(berkaitan dgn) tenusu*: *dairy cattle* ♦ *a dairy farm*

daisy /ˈdeɪzi/ *noun* [C] (*pl* **daisies**) a small white flower with a yellow centre, which usually grows wild in grass □ *bunga daisi*

dam /dæm/ *noun* [C] a wall built across a river to hold back the water and form a **reservoir** (= lake) behind it □ *empangan* ▸ **dam** *verb* [T] (**damming**; **dammed**)

damage¹ /ˈdæmɪdʒ/ *noun* **1** [U] **damage (to sth)** harm or injury caused when sth is broken or spoiled □ *kerosakan; kemusnahan*: *Earthquakes can cause terrible damage in urban areas.* ♦ *It will take weeks to repair the damage done by the vandals.* **2 damages** [pl] money that you can ask for if sb damages sth of yours or hurts you □ *bayaran ganti rugi*: *Mrs Rees, who lost a leg in the crash, was awarded damages of £100 000.*

damage² /ˈdæmɪdʒ/ *verb* [T] to spoil or harm sth, for example by breaking it □ *merosakkan*: *The roof was damaged by the storm.* ▸ **damaging** *adj*: *These rumours could be damaging to her reputation.*

dame /deɪm/ *noun* **Dame** [C] (*BrE*) a title given to a woman as an honour because of sth special that she has done □ *(gelaran) Dame*: *Dame Agatha Christie*

damn¹ /dæm/ (*also* **damned** /dæmd/) *adj, adv* (*slang*) **1** a swear word that people use to show that they are angry □ *sial betul! celaka betul*: *Some damn fool has parked too close to me.* **2** (a swear word that people use for emphasizing what they are saying) very □ *sangat; betul-betul*: *Read it! It's a damn good book.*

damn² /dæm/ *verb* [I,T] (*slang*) a swear word that people use to show that they are angry □ *sial; jahanam*: *Damn (it)! I've left my money behind.*

damn³ /dæm/ *noun*
IDM **not care/give a damn (about sb/sth)** (*slang*) not care at all □ *tdk peduli langsung*: *I don't give a damn what he thinks about me.*

damning /ˈdæmɪŋ/ *adj* that criticizes sth very much □ *yg membidas teruk; yg menyelar*: *There was a damning article about the book in the newspaper.*

damp¹ /dæmp/ *adj* (**damper**; **dampest**) a little wet □ *lembap*: *The house had been empty and felt rather damp.* ▸ **damp** *noun* [U]: *She hated the damp and the cold of the English climate.* ➲ note at **wet**

damp² /dæmp/ *verb* [T] **damp sth (down)** **1** to make sth less strong or urgent □ *memalapkan; mengurangkan; meredakan*: *He tried to damp down their expectations in case they failed.* **2** to make a fire burn less strongly or stop burning □ *memalapkan/memadamkan api*: *He tried to damp (down) the flames.*

dampen /ˈdæmpən/ *verb* [T] **1** to make sth a little wet □ *melembapkan; membasahkan sedikit*: *He dampened his hair to try to stop it sticking up.* **2** to make sth less strong or urgent □ *memalapkan; mengurangkan; meredakan*: *Even the awful weather did not dampen their enthusiasm for the trip.*

dance¹ /dɑːns/ *noun* **1** [C] a series of steps and movements which you do to music □ *tarian*: *The only dance I can do is the tango.* **2** [U] dancing as a form of art or entertainment □ *seni tari*: *She's very interested in modern dance.* **3** [C] (*old-fashioned*) a social meeting at which people dance with each other □ *majlis tari-menari*: *My parents met at a dance.*

dance² /dɑːns/ *verb* **1** [I,T] to move around to the rhythm of music by making a series of steps □ *menari*: *I can't dance very well.* ◆ *to dance the samba* **2** [I] to jump and move around with energy □ *melonjak-lonjak*: *She was dancing up and down with excitement.*

dancer /ˈdɑːnsə(r)/ *noun* [C] a person who dances, often as a job □ *penari*: *a ballet dancer* ◆ *She's a good dancer.* ⊃ picture at **ballet**

dancing /ˈdɑːnsɪŋ/ *noun* [U] the act of moving to music □ *menari; tarian*: *I'm hopeless at dancing—I've got no sense of rhythm.* ◆ *Will there be dancing at the party?*

dandelion /ˈdændɪlaɪən/ *noun* [C] a small wild plant with a bright yellow flower □ *dandelion*

dandruff /ˈdændrʌf/ *noun* [U] small pieces of dead skin in the hair, that look like white powder □ *kelemumur*

danger /ˈdeɪndʒə(r)/ *noun* **1** [U,C] the chance that sb/sth may be hurt, killed or damaged or that sth bad may happen □ *bahaya*: *When he saw the men had knives, he realized his life was in danger.* ◆ *The men kept on running until they thought they were out of danger.* ◆ *If things carry on as they are, there's a danger that the factory may have to close.* **2** [C] a danger (to sb/sth) a person or thing that can cause injury, pain or damage to sb □ *sst yg membahayakan*: *Drunk drivers are a danger to everyone on the road.*

dangerous /ˈdeɪndʒərəs/ *adj* likely to cause injury or damage □ *berbahaya*: *a dangerous animal/road/illness* ◆ *Police warn that the man is highly dangerous.* ▶ **dangerously** *adv*: *He was standing dangerously close to the cliff edge.*

dangle /ˈdæŋɡl/ *verb* [I,T] to hang freely; to hold sth so that it hangs down in this way □ *terjuntai; menjuntaikan*: *She sat on the fence with her legs dangling.* ◆ *The police dangled a rope from the bridge and the man grabbed it.*

dank /dæŋk/ *adj* wet, cold and unpleasant □ *lembap, sejuk dan tdk selesa*

dare¹ /deə(r)/ *verb* **1** [I] [usually in negative sentences] dare (to) do sth to have enough courage to do sth □ *berani*: *Nobody dared (to) speak.* ◆ *I daren't ask her to lend me any more money.* ◆ *We were so frightened that we didn't dare (to) go into the room.*

> **GRAMMAR** The negative is **dare not** (usually **daren't** /deənt/) or **do not/does not** (= **don't/doesn't**) **dare**. In the past tense it is **did not** (**didn't**) **dare**. In the present tense the negative is used without *to*: *I daren't move.*

2 [T] dare sb (to do sth) to ask or tell sb to do sth in order to see if they have the courage to do it □ *mencabar; cabar*: *Can you jump off that wall? Go on, I dare you!* ◆ *He dared his friend to put a mouse in the teacher's bag.*

IDM **don't you dare** used for telling sb very strongly not to do sth □ *jangan sekali-kali*: *Don't you dare tell my parents about this!*

how dare you used when you are angry about sth that sb has done □ *berani kau*: *How dare you speak to me like that!*

I dare say used when you are saying sth is probable □ *mungkin*: *'I think you should accept the offer.' 'I dare say you're right.'*

dare² /deə(r)/ *noun* [C, usually sing] something dangerous that sb asks you to do, to see if you have the courage to do it □ *cabaran*: *'Why did you try to swim across the river?' 'For a dare.'*

daredevil /ˈdeədevl/ *noun* [C] a person who likes to do dangerous things □ *orang yg suka membuat sst yg berbahaya*

daring /ˈdeərɪŋ/ *adj* involving or taking risks □ *berani*: *a daring attack* **SYN** **brave** ▶ **daring** *noun* [U]: *The climb required skill and daring.*

dark¹ /dɑːk/ *adj* (darker; darkest) **1** with no light or very little light □ *gelap*: *It was a dark night, with no moon.* ◆ *What time does it get dark in winter?* **2** (used about a colour) not light; nearer black than white □ *tua*; *dark blue* **OPP** **light, pale** **3** (*especially BrE*) (used about sb's hair, skin or eyes) brown or black; not fair □ *berwarna coklat atau hitam (bukan perang)*: *She was small and dark with brown eyes.* **OPP** **fair** ⊃ look at **skin¹** (2) **4** [only before a noun] hidden and frightening □ *tersembunyi; misteri*: *He seemed friendly, but there was a dark side to his character.* **SYN** **mysterious** **5** [only before a noun] sad; without hope □ *gelap; kelam*: *the dark days of the recession*

dark² /dɑːk/ *noun* the dark [sing] the state of having no light □ *(keadaan) gelap*: *He's afraid of the dark.* ◆ *Why are you sitting alone in the dark?*

IDM **before/after dark** before/after the sun goes down in the evening □ *sebelum/selepas gelap (malam)*

(be/keep sb) in the dark (about sth) (be/keep sb) in a position of not knowing about sth □ *tdk tahu (ttg sst)*: *Don't keep me in the dark. Tell me!*

darken /ˈdɑːkən/ *verb* [I,T] to become or to make sth darker □ *menjadi gelap; menggelapkan*: *The sky suddenly darkened and it started to rain.*

dark ˈglasses = **sunglasses**

darkly /ˈdɑːkli/ *adv* **1** in a threatening or an unpleasant way □ *secara mengugut*: *He hinted darkly that all was not well.* **2** showing a dark colour □ *berwarna gelap*

darkness /ˈdɑːknəs/ *noun* [U] the state of being dark □ *kegelapan*: *We sat in total darkness, waiting for the lights to come back on.*

darkroom /ˈdɑːkruːm, -rʊm/ *noun* [C] a room that can be made completely dark so that film can be taken out of a camera and photographs can be produced there □ *bilik gelap*

darling /ˈdɑːlɪŋ/ noun [C] a word that you say to sb you love □ *sayang*

darn /dɑːn/ verb [I,T] to repair a hole in clothes by sewing across it in one direction and then in the other □ *menjerumat*: I hate darning socks.

dart¹ /dɑːt/ noun 1 [C] an object like a small arrow. It is thrown in a game or shot as a weapon □ *dart; damak*: The keeper fired a tranquillizer dart into the tiger to send it to sleep. 2 **darts** [U] a game in which you throw **darts** at a **dartboard** □ *baling dart/damak*

dart² /dɑːt/ verb [I,T] to move or make sth move suddenly and quickly in a certain direction □ *meluru; melontarkan*: A rabbit darted across the field. ◆ She darted an angry glance at me.

dartboard /ˈdɑːtbɔːd/ noun [C] a round board used in the game of **darts** □ *papan baling damak*

dash¹ /dæʃ/ noun 1 [sing] an act of going somewhere suddenly and quickly □ *(perbuatan) meluru*: Suddenly the prisoner made a dash for the door. 2 [C, usually sing] a small amount of sth that you add to sth else □ *sedikit*: Add a dash of lemon juice. 3 [C] a small horizontal line (–) used in writing, especially for adding extra information □ *tanda sengkang* ⊃ look at **hyphen**

dash² /dæʃ/ verb 1 [I] to go somewhere suddenly and quickly □ *meluru; berlari*: We all dashed for shelter when it started to rain. ◆ I must dash—I'm late. 2 [I,T] to hit sth with great force; to throw sth so that it hits sth else very hard □ *menghempaskan*: She dashed her racket to the ground.

IDM **dash sb's hopes (of sth/of doing sth)** to completely destroy sb's hopes of doing sth □ *menghancurkan harapan sso (utk sst/membuat sst)*: The accident dashed his hopes of becoming a pianist.

PHR V **dash sth off** to write or draw sth very quickly □ *menulis/melukis sedikit lebih kurang*: I dashed off a note to my boss and left.

dashboard /ˈdæʃbɔːd/ noun [C] the part in a car in front of the driver where most of the switches, etc. are □ *papan pemuka* ⊃ picture at **car**

data /ˈdeɪtə (BrE also)/ ˈdɑːtə (AmE also) / noun [U, pl] facts or information □ *data*: to gather/collect data ◆ data capture/retrieval (= ways of storing and looking at information on a computer)

database /ˈdeɪtəbeɪs/ noun [C] a large amount of data that is stored in a computer and can easily be used, added to, etc. □ *pangkalan data*

date¹ /deɪt/ noun 1 [C] a particular day of the month or year □ *tarikh; hari bulan*: What's the date today?/What date is it today?/What's today's date? ◆ What's your **date of birth**? ◆ We'd better **fix a date** for the next meeting. 2 [sing] a particular time □ *masa*: We can discuss this **at a later date**. ⊃ look at **sell-by date** 3 [C] an arrangement to meet sb, especially a boyfriend or girlfriend □ *janji temu*: Shall we **make a date** to have lunch together? ◆ I've got a date with her on Friday night. ⊃ look at **blind date** 4 [C] a small, sweet, dark brown fruit that comes from a tree which grows in hot countries □ *kurma*

IDM **out of date** 1 not fashionable; no longer useful □ *ketinggalan zaman; sudah lapuk*: out-of-date methods/machinery 2 no longer able to be used □ *sudah mati; sudah tamat tempohnya*: I must renew my passport. It's out of date.

to date (formal) until now □ *setakat ini; hingga kini*: We've had very few complaints to date.

up to date 1 completely modern □ *moden; terkini*: The new kitchen will be right up to date, with all the latest gadgets. 2 with all the most recent information; having done everything that you should □ *kemas kini*: In this report we'll bring you up to date with the latest news from the area.

date² /deɪt/ verb 1 [T] to write the day's date on sth □ *bertarikh*: The letter is dated 24 March, 2012. 2 [T] to discover or guess how old sth is □ *mentarikhkan; menentukan tarikh*: The skeleton has been dated at about 3 000 BC. 3 [I] to seem, or to make sb/sth seem old-fashioned □ *kelihatan ketinggalan zaman*: We chose a simple style so that it wouldn't date as quickly.

PHR V **date back to …; date from …** to have existed since … □ *telah wujud sejak…; bermula sejak..*: The house dates back to the 17th century. ◆ We found photographs dating from before we were born.

dated /ˈdeɪtɪd/ adj not fashionable □ *ketinggalan zaman; lapuk; usang*: This sort of jacket looks rather dated now.

daub /dɔːb/ verb [T] **daub A on B; daub B with A** to spread a lot of a substance such as paint, mud, etc. carelessly onto sth □ *memalit; mencalit; menurap*: The walls of the building were daubed with red paint.

daughter /ˈdɔːtə(r)/ noun [C] a female child □ *anak perempuan*: I have two sons and one daughter. ◆ Janet's daughter is a doctor.

ˈdaughter-in-law noun [C] (pl daughters-in-law) the wife of your son □ *menantu perempuan*

daunt /dɔːnt/ verb [T, usually passive] to frighten or to worry sb by being too big or difficult □ *menakutkan*: Don't be daunted by all the controls—in fact it's a simple machine to use. ▶ **daunting** adj: a daunting task

dawdle /ˈdɔːdl/ verb [I] to go somewhere very slowly □ *berlengah-lengah*: Stop dawdling! We've got to be at school by eight.

dawn¹ /dɔːn/ noun 1 [U,C] the early morning, when light first appears in the sky □ *subuh*: before/at dawn ◆ Dawn was breaking (= it was starting to get light) as I set off to work. ⊃ look at **daybreak** 2 [sing] the beginning □ *bermulanya*: the dawn of civilization

IDM the crack of dawn ⇒ crack²

dawn² /dɔːn/ verb [I] **1** (formal) to begin to grow light, after the night □ *fajar menyingsing*: *The day dawned bright and cold.* ◆ (figurative) *A new era of peace is dawning.* **2 dawn (on sb)** to become clear (to sb) □ *mula menyedari/teringat*: *Suddenly it dawned on her. 'Of course!' she said. 'You're Mike's brother!'*

day /deɪ/ noun **1** [C] a period of 24 hours. Seven days make up a week □ *hari*: *'What day is it today?' 'Tuesday.'* ◆ *We went to Italy for ten days.* ◆ *We're meeting again the day after tomorrow/in two days' time.* ◆ *The next/following day I saw Mark again.* ◆ *I'd already spoken to him the day before/the previous day.* ◆ *I have to take these pills twice a day.* ◆ *I work six days a week. Sunday's my day off* (= when I do not work). **2** [C,U] the time when the sky is light; not night □ *waktu siang*: *The days were warm but the nights were freezing.* ◆ *It's been raining all day (long).* ◆ *Owls sleep by day* (= during the day) *and hunt at night.* **3** [C] the hours of the day when you work □ *sehari*: *She's expected to work a seven-hour day.* **4** [C] often **days** a particular period of time in the past □ *zaman*: *in Shakespeare's day* ◆ *There weren't so many cars in those days*
IDM at the end of the day ⇒ end¹
break of day ⇒ break²
call it a day ⇒ call¹
day by day every day; as time passes □ *hari demi hari*: *Day by day, she was getting a little bit stronger.*
day in, day out every day, without any change □ *setiap hari*: *Frank sits at his desk working, day in, day out.*
day-to-day happening as a normal part of each day; usual □ *harian; biasa*
from day to day; from one day to the next within a short period of time □ *dr sehari ke sehari*: *Things change so quickly that we never know what will happen from one day to the next.*
have a field day ⇒ field day
it's early days (yet) ⇒ early
make sb's day (informal) to make sb very happy □ *menggembirakan sso*
one day; some day at some time in the future □ *satu hari nanti*: *One day we'll go back and see all our old friends.*
the other day, morning, week, etc. ⇒ other
the present day ⇒ present¹
these days in the present age □ *sekarang ini* **SYN nowadays**

daybreak /'deɪbreɪk/ noun [U] the time in the early morning when light first appears □ *waktu subuh* **SYN dawn**

daydream /'deɪdriːm/ noun [C] thoughts that are not connected with what you are doing; often pleasant scenes in your imagination □ *angan-angan*: *The child stared out of the window, lost in a daydream.* ▶ **daydream** verb [I] *Don't just sit there daydreaming—do some work!*

daylight /'deɪlaɪt/ noun [U] the light that there is during the day □ *cahaya waktu siang*: *The colours look quite different in daylight.* ◆ *daylight hours*
IDM (in) broad daylight ⇒ broad

day re'turn noun [C] (BrE) a train or bus ticket for going somewhere and coming back on the same day. It is cheaper than a normal return ticket. □ *tiket ulang-alik sama hari*

daytime /'deɪtaɪm/ noun [U] the time when it is light; not night □ *siang hari*: *These flowers open in the daytime and close again at night.* ◆ *daytime TV*

daze /deɪz/ noun
IDM in a daze unable to think or react normally; confused □ *kebingungan*

dazed /deɪzd/ adj unable to think or react normally; confused □ *bingung*: *He had a dazed expression on his face.*

dazzle /'dæzl/ verb [T, usually passive] **1** (used about a bright light) to make sb unable to see for a short time □ *menyilaukan; silau*: *She was dazzled by the other car's headlights.* **2** to impress sb very much □ *mempesona; terpesona*: *He had been dazzled by her beauty.* ▶ **dazzling** adj: *a dazzling light*

dead¹ /ded/ adj **1** no longer alive □ *mati; (daun) kering*: *My father's dead. He died two years ago.* ◆ *Police found a dead body under the bridge.* ◆ *The man was shot dead by a masked gunman.* ◆ *dead leaves* ⇒ noun **death**, verb **die 2** no longer used; finished □ *pupus; lapuk*: *Latin is a dead language.* **OPP living 3** [not before a noun] (used about a piece of equipment) no longer working □ *mati; rosak*: *I picked up the telephone but the line was dead.* ◆ *This battery's dead.* **4** without movement, activity or interest □ *mati; lengang; sepi*: *This town is completely dead after 11 o'clock at night.* **5** [not before a noun] (used about a part of the body) no longer able to feel anything □ *kebas*: *Oh no, my foot's gone dead. I was sitting on it for too long.* **SYN numb 6** [only before a noun] complete or exact □ *betul-betul*: *a dead silence/calm* ◆ *The arrow hit the dead centre of the target.*
IDM a dead end 1 a street that is only open at one end □ *jalan mati* **2** a point, situation, etc. from which you can make no further progress □ *buntu; tdk memberi harapan utk maju*: *a dead-end job* (= one that offers no chance of moving to a higher position)
drop dead ⇒ drop¹

dead² /ded/ **the dead** noun [pl] people who have died □ *orang yg mati*: *A church service was held in memory of the dead.*
IDM in/at the dead of night in the middle of the night, when it is very dark and quiet □ *malam-malam buta; larut malam*

dead³ /ded/ adv completely, exactly or very □ *betul-betul; sangat; amat*: *The car made a strange noise and then stopped dead.* ◆ *He's dead keen to start work.*

deaden /ˈdedn/ verb [T] to make sth less strong, painful, etc. □ *mengurangkan; meredamkan; melalikan*: They gave her drugs to try and deaden the pain.

dead 'heat noun [C] the result of a race when two people, etc. finish at exactly the same time □ *keputusan tergantung*

deadline /ˈdedlaɪn/ noun [C] a time or date before which sth must be done or finished □ *tarikh akhir; tempoh masa*: I usually **set** myself a deadline when I have a project to do. ◆ A journalist is used to having to **meet deadlines**.

deadlock /ˈdedlɒk/ noun [sing, U] a situation in which two sides cannot reach an agreement □ *jalan buntu; kebuntuan*: Talks have reached (a) deadlock. ◆ to try to break the deadlock

deadly /ˈdedli/ adj, adv (deadlier; deadliest) 1 causing or likely to cause death □ *boleh membawa maut*: a deadly poison/weapon/disease 2 [adjective only before a noun] very great; complete □ *sangat; (musuh) ketat*: They're deadly enemies. 3 extremely accurate, so that no defence is possible □ *sangat tepat*: That player is deadly when he gets in front of the goal. 4 completely; extremely □ *benar-benar; betul*: I'm not joking. In fact I'm deadly serious.

deadpan /ˈdedpæn/ adj without any expression on your face or in your voice □ *selamba; bersahaja*: He told the joke with a completely deadpan face.

deaf /def/ adj (deafer; deafest) 1 unable to hear anything or unable to hear very well □ *pekak*: You'll have to speak louder. My father's a bit deaf. ◆ to go deaf 2 the deaf noun [pl] people who cannot hear □ *orang pekak*: sign language for the deaf 3 deaf to sth not wanting to listen to sth □ *tdk mahu mendengar; memekakkan telinga*: I've told her what I think but she's deaf to my advice. ▶ **deafness** noun [U]

deafen /ˈdefn/ verb [T, usually passive] to make sb unable to hear by making a very loud noise □ *memekakkan; bingit telinga*: We were deafened by the loud music. ▶ **deafening** adj: deafening music

deal¹ /diːl/ verb (pt, pp dealt /delt/) 1 [I,T] deal (sth) (out); deal (sth) (to sb) to give cards to players in a game of cards □ *membahagikan daun terup*: Start by dealing seven cards to each player. ◆ Whose turn is it to deal? 2 [I,T] (informal) to buy and sell illegal drugs □ *berjual beli dadah* **IDM** deal sb/sth a blow; deal a blow to sb/sth 1 to give sb a shock, etc. □ *merupakan satu kejutan besar*: This news dealt a terrible blow to my father. 2 to hit sb/sth □ *memukul sso/sst; merupakan satu tamparan/pukulan*: He was dealt a nasty blow to the head in the accident.
PHR V deal in sth to buy and sell a particular product □ *berniaga*: He deals in second-hand cars.

deal sth out to give sth to a number of people □ *membahagi-bahagikan*: The profits will be dealt out among us.

deal with sb/sth 1 to do business with a person or an organization □ *berurusan*: Our firm deals with customers all over the world. 2 to take suitable action in a particular situation in order to solve a problem, etc. □ *menguruskan/menangani sst*: He's a difficult man. Nobody quite knows how to deal with him. ◆ My secretary will deal with my correspondence while I'm away. 3 to have sth as its subject □ *membicarakan/memperkatakan ttg sst*: This chapter deals with letter-writing.

deal² /diːl/ noun [C] 1 an agreement or arrangement, especially in business □ *urus niaga; urus janji; persetujuan; setuju*: We're hoping to **do a deal** with an Italian company. ◆ Let's **make a deal** not to criticize each other's work. ◆ 'I'll help you with your essay if you'll fix my bike.' 'OK, **it's a deal**!' 2 the way that sb is treated □ *layanan*: With high fares and unreliable services, rail users are **getting a raw deal**. ◆ The new law aims to give pensioners **a fair deal**. 3 the act of giving cards to players in a card game □ *(perbuatan) membahagikan daun terup*
IDM a big deal/no big deal ➔ **big**
a good/great deal (of sth) a lot (of sth) □ *banyak*: I've spent a great deal of time on this report.

dealer /ˈdiːlə(r)/ noun [C] 1 a person whose business is buying and selling things □ *peniaga; pengedar (dadah)*: a dealer in gold and silver ◆ an art dealer 2 the person who gives the cards to the players in a game of cards □ *pembahagi (daun terup)*

dealing /ˈdiːlɪŋ/ noun 1 dealings [pl] relations, especially in business □ *urusan*: We had some dealings with that firm several years ago. 2 [U] buying and selling □ *urus niaga*: share dealing

dealt past tense, past participle of **deal¹**

dean /diːn/ noun [C] 1 a priest who is responsible for a large church or a number of small churches □ *paderi* 2 an important official at some universities or colleges □ *dekan*

dear¹ /dɪə(r)/ adj (dearer; dearest) 1 dear (to sb) loved by or important to sb □ *yg dikasihi; yg penting*: It was a subject that was very dear to him. ◆ She's one of my dearest friends. 2 Dear used at the beginning of a letter before the name or title of the person you are writing to □ *digunakan sebagai bentuk sapaan pd permulaan surat*: Dear Sarah, … ◆ Dear Mr. Dawson, … ◆ Dear Sir or Madam, …

MORE Use **Dear Sir or Madam** if you do not know the name of the person you are writing to, and end your letter with **Yours faithfully**.

➔ note at **sincere** 3 (BrE) expensive □ *mahal*: How can people afford to drive when petrol is so dear?
IDM close/dear/near to sb's heart ➔ **heart**

dear² /dɪə(r)/ exclam 1 used for expressing disappointment, sadness, surprise, etc. □ *alamak*: Dear me! Aren't you ready? 2 (old-fashioned) used when speaking to sb you know well □ *sayang*: Would you like a cup of tea, dear?

dearly → decay

dearly /ˈdɪəli/ adv **1** very much □ *sangat*: I'd dearly like to go there again. **2** (*formal*) in a way that causes damage or suffering, or costs a lot of money □ *mengakibatkan kerugian atau pengorbanan besar*: I've already paid dearly for that mistake.

dearth /dɜːθ/ noun [sing] a dearth (of sb/sth) a lack of sth; not enough of sth □ *kekurangan*: There's a dearth of young people in the village.

death /deθ/ noun **1** [C,U] the end of sb/sth's life; dying □ *kematian; mati*: There were two deaths and many other people were injured in the accident. ◆ The police do not know the **cause of death**. ◆ There was no food and people were **starving to death**. ⊃ adjective **dead**, verb **die 2** [U] the end (of sth) □ *berakhirnya*: the death of communism

IDM catch your death (of cold) ⊃ catch¹
a matter of life and/or death ⊃ matter¹
put sb to death [usually passive] (*formal*) to kill sb as a punishment, in past times □ *dihukum bunuh*
sick to death of sb/sth ⊃ sick¹
sudden death ⊃ sudden

deathly /ˈdeθli/ adj, adv like death □ *spt mayat; sangat (senyap, sunyi, dll)*: There was a deathly silence.

death penalty noun [sing] the legal punishment of being killed for a crime □ *hukuman mati* ⊃ look at **capital punishment**

death toll noun [C] the number of people killed in a disaster, a war, an accident, etc. □ *bilangan mangsa yg terkorban*

debase /dɪˈbeɪs/ verb [T, usually passive] (*formal*) to reduce the quality or value of sth □ *menjatuhkan mutu atau nilai sst*

debatable /dɪˈbeɪtəbl/ adj not certain; that you could argue about □ *boleh dipersoalkan/ dibahaskan*: It's debatable whether people have a better lifestyle these days.

debate¹ /dɪˈbeɪt/ noun **1** [C] a formal argument or discussion of a question at a public meeting or in Parliament □ *perbahasan; perdebatan*: a debate on educational reform **2** [U] general discussion about sth expressing different opinions □ *perbincangan*: There's been a lot of debate about the cause of acid rain.

debate² /dɪˈbeɪt/ verb **1** [I,T] to discuss sth in a formal way or at a public meeting □ *membahaskan; mendebatkan*: Politicians will be debating the bill later this week. **2** [T] to think about or discuss sth before deciding what to do □ *menimbang-nimbangkan; berbincang*: They debated whether to go or not.

debauched /dɪˈbɔːtʃt/ adj a debauched person is immoral in their sexual behaviour, drinks a lot of alcohol, takes drugs, etc. □ *(orang) tdk berakhlak, tdk bermoral* **SYN** depraved
▶ **debauchery** /dɪˈbɔːtʃəri/ noun [U]

debit¹ /ˈdebɪt/ noun [C] an amount of money paid out of a bank account □ *debit* **OPP** credit ⊃ look at **direct debit**

debit² /ˈdebɪt/ verb [T] to take an amount of money out of a bank account, etc. usually as a payment; to record this □ *mendebitkan*

debit card noun [C] a plastic card that can be used to take money directly from your bank account when you pay for sth □ *kad debit* ⊃ look at **credit card**

debris /ˈdebriː/ noun [U] pieces from sth that has been destroyed, especially in an accident □ *puing*

debt /det/ noun **1** [C] an amount of money that you owe to sb □ *hutang*: Teresa borrowed a lot of money and she's still paying off the debt. ⊃ note at **loan 2** [U] the state of owing money □ *berhutang*: After he lost his job, he **got into debt**. **3** [C, usually sing] (*formal*) something that you owe sb, for example because they have helped or been kind to you □ *rasa terhutang budi*: In his speech he acknowledged his debt to his family and friends for their support.

IDM be in/out of debt to owe/not owe money □ *berhutang/tdk berhutang*
be in sb's debt (*formal*) to feel grateful to sb for sth that they have done for you □ *terhutang budi kpd sso*

debtor /ˈdetə(r)/ noun [C] a person who owes money □ *penghutang*

debug /ˌdiːˈbʌɡ/ verb [T] (**debugging**; **debugged**) to look for and remove the faults in a computer program □ *nyahpepijat*

debut (also **début**) /ˈdeɪbjuː/ noun [C] a first appearance in public of an actor, etc. □ *debut; kemunculan kali pertama*: She made her debut in London in 1989.

Dec. abbr = **December** □ *Disember*: 5 Dec. 2012

decade /ˈdekeɪd; dɪˈkeɪd/ noun [C] a period of ten years □ *dekad; dasawarsa*: the last decade of the 20th century

decadence /ˈdekədəns/ noun [U] behaviour, attitudes, etc. that show low moral standards □ *kemerosotan* ▶ **decadent** /ˈdekədənt/ adj: a decadent society

decaffeinated /ˌdiːˈkæfɪneɪtɪd/ adj (used about coffee or tea) with most or all of the **caffeine** (= the substance that makes you feel awake) removed □ *nyahkafeina* ⊃ note at **coffee**

decapitate /dɪˈkæpɪteɪt/ verb [T] (*formal*) to cut off sb's head □ *memancung kepala* **SYN** behead

decay¹ /dɪˈkeɪ/ noun [U] the process or state of being slowly destroyed □ *pereputan; kerosakan; kemerosotan; usang*: tooth decay ◆ The old farm was in a terrible state of decay.

decay² /dɪˈkeɪ/ verb [I] **1** to go bad or be slowly destroyed □ *menjadi busuk/reput*: the decaying carcass of a dead sheep **SYN** rot **2** to become weaker or less powerful □ *merosot*: His business empire began to decay. ▶ **decayed** adj: a decayed tooth

the deceased /dɪˈsiːst/ noun [sing] (formal) a person who has died, especially one who has died recently □ *si mati*: Many friends of the deceased were present at the funeral. ▶ **deceased** adj

deceit /dɪˈsiːt/ noun [U] dishonest behaviour; trying to make sb believe sth that is not true □ *penipuan; tipu daya*: Their marriage eventually broke up because she was tired of his lies and deceit.

deceitful /dɪˈsiːtfl/ adj dishonest; trying to make sb believe sth that is not true □ *suka menipu* ▶ **deceitfully** /-fəli/ adv ▶ **deceitfulness** noun [U]

deceive /dɪˈsiːv/ verb [T] deceive sb/yourself (into doing sth) to try to make sb believe sth that is not true □ *menipu*: He deceived his mother into believing that he had earned the money, not stolen it. ♦ You're deceiving yourself if you think there's an easy solution to the problem. ⊃ noun **deception** or **deceit**

December /dɪˈsembə(r)/ noun [U,C] (abbr **Dec.**) the 12th month of the year, coming after November □ *Disember* ⊃ note at **January**

decency /ˈdiːsnsi/ noun [U] moral or correct behaviour □ *kesopanan*: She had the decency to admit that it was her fault.

decent /ˈdiːsnt/ adj 1 of a good enough standard □ *agak bagus*: All she wants is a decent job with decent wages. 2 (used about people or behaviour) honest and fair; treating people with respect □ *jujur; bersopan santun; baik* 3 not likely to offend or shock sb □ *sopan; seronok; berpakaian senonoh*: I can't come to the door, I'm not decent (= I'm not dressed). **OPP** indecent ▶ **decently** adv

deception /dɪˈsepʃn/ noun [C,U] making sb believe or being made to believe sth that is not true □ *penipuan*: He had obtained the secret papers by deception. ⊃ verb **deceive**

deceptive /dɪˈseptɪv/ adj likely to make you believe sth that is not true □ *mengelirukan*: The water is deceptive. It's much deeper than it looks. ▶ **deceptively** adv: She made the task sound deceptively easy.

decibel /ˈdesɪbel/ noun [C] a measure of how loud a sound is □ *desibel*

decide /dɪˈsaɪd/ verb 1 [I,T] decide (to do sth); decide against (doing) sth; decide about/on sth; decide that ... to think about two or more possibilities and choose one of them □ *membuat keputusan; memutuskan*: There are so many to choose from—I can't decide! ♦ We've decided not to invite Isabel. ♦ She decided against borrowing the money. ♦ They decided on a name for the baby. ♦ He decided that it was too late to go. ♦ The date hasn't been decided yet. 2 [T] to influence sth so that it produces a particular result □ *menentukan*: Your votes will decide the winner. 3 [T] to cause sb to make a decision □ *menyebabkan sso*

225 **the deceased → declaration**

membuat keputusan: What finally decided you to leave? ⊃ noun **decision**, adjective **decisive**

decided /dɪˈsaɪdɪd/ adj [only before a noun] clear; definite □ *jelas; nyata*: There has been a decided improvement in his work. ▶ **decidedly** adv

deciduous /dɪˈsɪdjuəs/ adj (used about a tree) of a type that loses its leaves every autumn □ *(ttg pokok) daun luruh* ⊃ look at **evergreen**

decimal[1] /ˈdesɪml/ adj based on or counted in units of ten □ *(berdasarkan) perpuluhan*: decimal currency

decimal[2] /ˈdesɪml/ noun [C] part of a number, written after a **decimal**, **point** (= a small round mark) □ *perpuluhan*: A quarter expressed as a decimal is 0.25.

decimate /ˈdesɪmeɪt/ verb [T] to destroy or badly damage a large number of people or things □ *memusnahkan; menghapuskan; mengorbankan*: The rabbit population was decimated by the disease.

decipher /dɪˈsaɪfə(r)/ verb [T] to succeed in reading or understanding sth that is not clear □ *memahami; membaca*: It's impossible to decipher his handwriting.

decision /dɪˈsɪʒn/ noun 1 [C,U] a decision (to do sth); a decision on/about sth; a decision that ... a choice or judgement that you make after thinking about various possibilities □ *keputusan*: Have you made a decision yet? ♦ I realize now that I made the wrong decision. ♦ There were good reasons for his decision to leave. ♦ I took the decision that I believed to be right. 2 [U] being able to decide clearly and quickly □ *kebolehan membuat keputusan dgn tegas*: We are looking for someone with decision for this job. ⊃ verb **decide**

decisive /dɪˈsaɪsɪv/ adj 1 making sth certain or final □ *muktamad; penentuan*: the decisive battle of the war 2 having the ability to make clear decisions quickly □ *tegas*: It's no good hesitating. Be decisive. **OPP** indecisive ⊃ verb **decide** ▶ **decisively** adv ▶ **decisiveness** noun [U]

deck /dek/ noun [C] 1 one of the floors of a ship or bus □ *geladak; dek; tingkat* 2 (AmE) = **pack**[2](6): a deck of cards 3 part of a machine that records and/or plays sounds □ *dek*

IDM on deck on the part of a ship which you can walk on outside □ *di dek*: I'm going out on deck for some fresh air.

deckchair /ˈdektʃeə(r)/ noun [C] a chair that you use outside, especially on the beach. You can fold it up and carry it. □ *kerusi malas* ⊃ picture at **chair**

declaration /ˌdekləˈreɪʃn/ noun 1 [C,U] an official statement about sth □ *pengisytiharan; pengumuman; penegasan*: In his speech he made a strong declaration of support for free education. ♦ the declaration of war 2 [C] a written statement giving information on goods or money you

VOWELS iː see i any ɪ sit e ten æ hat ɑː father ɒ got ɔː saw ʊ put uː too u usual

declare → deed

have earned, on which you have to pay tax □ *pengakuan; penyataan*: *a customs declaration*

declare /dɪˈkleə(r)/ *verb* [T] **1** to state sth publicly and officially or to make sth known in a firm, clear way □ *mengisytiharkan; mengumumkan*: *to declare war on another country* ♦ *I declare that the winner of the award is Jenni Taylor.* **2** to give information about goods or money you have earned, on which you have to pay tax □ *menyatakan; membuat pengakuan*: *You must declare all your income on this form.*

decline¹ /dɪˈklaɪn/ *noun* [C,U] (a) decline (in sth) a process or period of becoming weaker, smaller or less good □ *kemerosotan*: *a decline in sales* ♦ *As an industrial power, the country is in decline.*

decline² /dɪˈklaɪn/ *verb* **1** [I] to become weaker, smaller or less good □ *merosot*: *declining profits* ♦ *The standard of education has declined in this country.* **2** [I,T] (*formal*) to refuse, usually politely □ *menolak*: *Thank you for the invitation but I'm afraid I have to decline.*

decode /ˌdiːˈkəʊd/ *verb* [T] to find the meaning of a secret message □ *menyahkod* **OPP** encode

decoder /ˌdiːˈkəʊdə(r)/ *noun* [C] a device that changes electronic signals into a form that can be understood □ *penyahkod; pentafsir kod*: *a satellite/video decoder*

decompose /ˌdiːkəmˈpəʊz/ *verb* [I,T] to slowly be destroyed by natural chemical processes □ *reput; menjadi busuk*: *The body was so badly decomposed that it couldn't be identified.* ▶ decomposition /ˌdiːkɒmpəˈzɪʃn/ *noun* [U]

decor /ˈdeɪkɔː(r)/ *noun* [U, sing] the style in which the inside of a building is decorated □ *gaya hiasan; dekor*

decorate /ˈdekəreɪt/ *verb* **1** [T] decorate sth (with sth) to add sth in order to make a thing more attractive to look at □ *menghias*: *Decorate the cake with cherries and nuts.* **2** [I,T] (*especially BrE*) to put paint and/or coloured paper onto walls, ceilings and doors in a room or building □ *mengecat dan/atau memasang kertas dinding*: *I think it's about time we decorated the living room.*

decoration /ˌdekəˈreɪʃn/ *noun* **1** [C,U] something that is added to sth in order to make it look more attractive □ *perhiasan*: *Christmas decorations* ♦ *the elaborate decoration on the carved wooden door* **2** [U] the process of decorating a room or building; the style in which sth is decorated □ *kerja menghias; dihias; gaya hiasan*: *The house is in need of decoration.*

decorative /ˈdekərətɪv/ *adj* attractive or pretty to look at □ *merupakan hiasan; cantik; menarik*: *The cloth had a decorative lace edge.*

decorator /ˈdekəreɪtə(r)/ *noun* [C] a person whose job is to paint and decorate houses and buildings □ *juruhias*

decoy /ˈdiːkɔɪ/ *noun* [C] a person or an object that is used in order to trick sb/sth into doing what you want, going where you want, etc. □ *denak; umpan* ▶ decoy *verb* [T]

decrease¹ /dɪˈkriːs/ *verb* [I,T] to become or to make sth smaller or less □ *mengurangkan; berkurang; menyusut*: *Profits have decreased by 15%.* ♦ *Decrease speed when you are approaching a road junction.* **OPP** increase

decrease² /ˈdiːkriːs/ *noun* [C,U] (a) decrease (in sth) the process of becoming or making sth smaller or less; the amount that sth is reduced by □ *pengurangan; berkurangnya*: *a 10% decrease in sales*

decree /dɪˈkriː/ *noun* [C] an official order given by a government, a ruler, etc. □ *dekri* ▶ decree *verb* [T] (*pt, pp* decreed)

decrepit /dɪˈkrepɪt/ *adj* (used about a thing or person) old and in very bad condition or poor health □ *tua dan uzur*

dedicate /ˈdedɪkeɪt/ *verb* [T] **1** dedicate sth to sth to give all your energy, time, efforts, etc. to sth □ *membaktikan*: *He dedicated his life to helping the poor.* **2** dedicate sth to sb to say that sth is specially for sb □ *mendedikasikan*: *He dedicated the book he had written to his brother.*

dedicated /ˈdedɪkeɪtɪd/ *adj* giving a lot of your energy, time, efforts, etc. to sth that you believe to be important □ *berdedikasi*: *dedicated nurses and doctors*

dedication /ˌdedɪˈkeɪʃn/ *noun* **1** [U] wanting to give your time and energy to sth because you feel it is important □ *dedikasi; pembaktian*: *I admire her dedication to her career.* **2** [C] a message at the beginning of a book or piece of music saying that it is for a particular person □ *dedikasi*

deduce /dɪˈdjuːs/ *verb* [T] to form an opinion using the facts that you already know □ *membuat kesimpulan*: *From his name I deduced that he was Polish.* ➔ *noun* deduction

deduct /dɪˈdʌkt/ *verb* [T] deduct sth (from sth) to take sth such as money or points away from a total amount □ *memotong*: *Marks will be deducted for untidy work.*

deduction /dɪˈdʌkʃn/ *noun* [C,U] **1** something that you work out from facts that you already know; the ability to think in this way □ *kesimpulan; penyimpulan*: *It was a brilliant piece of deduction by the detective.* ➔ *verb* deduce **2** deduction (from sth) taking away an amount or number from a total; the amount or number taken away from the total □ *pemotongan; potongan*: *What is your total income after deductions?* (= when tax, insurance, etc. are taken away) ➔ *verb* deduct

deed /diːd/ *noun* [C] **1** (*formal*) something that you do; an action □ *perbuatan; tindakan*: *a brave/good/charitable deed* **2** a legal document that shows that you own a house or building □ *surat ikatan*: *The deeds of our house are kept at the bank.*

deem /diːm/ verb [T] (formal) to have a particular opinion about sth □ *menganggap*: He did not even deem it necessary to apologize.

deep¹ /diːp/ adj (**deeper**, **deepest**)
▸TOP TO BOTTOM **1** going a long way down from the surface □ *dlm*: to dig a deep hole ◆ That's a deep cut. ◆ a coat with deep pockets ⊃ noun **depth** ⊃ picture at **shallow**
▸FRONT TO BACK **2** going a long way from front to back □ *lebar ke dlm*: deep shelves
▸MEASUREMENT **3** measuring a particular amount from top to bottom or from front to back □ *dlm*: The water is only a metre deep at this end of the pool. ◆ shelves 40 centimetres deep
▸SOUNDS **4** low □ *dlm*; *garuk*: a deep voice
▸COLOURS **5** dark; strong □ *tua*; *gelap*: a deep red **OPP** light
▸SLEEP **6** not easy to wake from □ *lena*; *nyenyak*: I was in a deep sleep and didn't hear the phone ringing for ages. **OPP** light
▸EMOTION **7** strongly felt □ *mendlm*: He felt a very deep love for the child.
▸THOROUGH **8** dealing with difficult subjects or details □ *mendlm*: His books show a deep understanding of human nature. **SYN** profound
IDM deep in thought/conversation thinking very hard or giving sb/sth your full attention □ *tekun*; *asyik*
take a deep breath to breathe in a lot of air, especially in preparation for doing sth difficult □ *menarik nafas dlm-dlm*: He took a deep breath then walked on stage.
▸ the deep noun [U]: She awoke in the deep of the night (= in the middle of the night). ◆ the deep (= a way in literature of referring to the sea)
▸ **deeply** adv: a deeply unhappy person ◆ to breathe deeply

deep² /diːp/ adv a long way down or inside sth □ *jauh ke dlm*: He gazed deep into her eyes. ◆ He dug his hands deep into his pockets.
IDM deep down in what you really think or feel □ *jauh di lubuk hati*: I tried to appear optimistic but deep down I knew there was no hope.
dig deep ⊃ **dig¹**

deepen /ˈdiːpən/ verb [I,T] to become or to make sth deep or deeper □ *menjadi semakin dlm*; *mendlmkan*: The river deepens here.

deep ˈfreeze = freezer

deep-ˈrooted (also ˌdeep-ˈseated) adj strongly felt or believed and therefore difficult to change □ *berakar umbi*: deep-rooted fears

deep vein thromˈbosis noun [C,U] (abbr DVT) a serious condition caused by a **clot** (= a thick mass of blood) forming in a tube that carries blood to the heart □ *trombosis vena dlm*: Passengers on long-haul flights are being warned about the risks of deep vein thrombosis.

deer /dɪə(r)/ noun [C] (pl deer) a large wild animal that eats grass. The male has **antlers** (= large horns shaped like branches) on its head. □ *rusa*

MORE A male deer is called a **buck** or, especially if it has fully-grown antlers, a **stag**. The female is a **doe** and a young deer is a **fawn**. **Venison** is the meat from deer.

---

227   deem → defeatism

deer

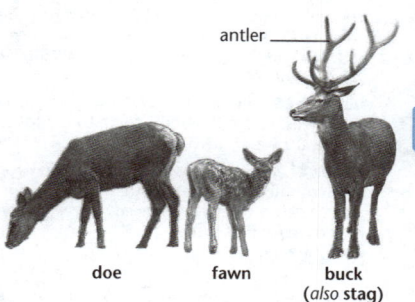

antler

doe   fawn   buck
                (also stag)

deface /dɪˈfeɪs/ verb [T] to spoil the way sth looks by writing on or marking its surface □ *merosakkan*; *mencacatkan*

defamation /ˌdefəˈmeɪʃn/ noun [U,C] (formal) the act of damaging the opinion that people have of sb by saying or writing bad or false things about them □ *fitnah*: He sued for defamation of character.

default¹ /dɪˈfɔːlt/ noun [sing] a course of action taken by a computer when it is not given any other instruction □ *(fungsi) lalai*
IDM by default because nothing happened, not because of successful effort □ *kerana (pihak lain yg terlibat gagal hadir, mungkir, dsb)*: They won by default, because the other team didn't turn up.

default² /dɪˈfɔːlt/ verb [I] **1** default (on sth) to not do sth that you should do by law □ *gagal*; *mungkir*; *ingkar*: If you default on the credit payments (= you don't pay them), the car will be taken back. **2** default (to sth) (used about a computer) to take a particular course of action when no other command is given □ *melalai (ke sst)*

defeat¹ /dɪˈfiːt/ verb [T] **1** to win a game, a fight, a vote, etc. against sb □ *mengalahkan*: The army defeated the rebels after three days of fighting. ◆ In the last match France defeated Wales. **SYN** beat **2** to be too difficult for sb to do or understand □ *tdk membingungkan*; *tdk berjaya membuat atau memahami sst*: I've tried to work out what's wrong with the car but it defeats me. **3** to prevent sth from succeeding □ *menggagalkan*; *menghalang*: The local residents are determined to defeat the council's building plans.

defeat² /dɪˈfiːt/ noun **1** [C] an occasion when sb fails to win or be successful against sb else □ *kekalahan*: This season they have had two victories and three defeats. **2** [U] the act of losing or not being successful □ *kalah*; *gagal*: She refused to admit defeat and kept on trying.

defeatism /dɪˈfiːtɪzəm/ noun [U] the attitude of expecting sth to end in failure □ *sikap mudah berputus asa atau menyerah kalah*

[C] **countable**, a noun with a plural form: *one book, two books*   [U] **uncountable**, a noun with no plural form: *some sugar*

defeatist → deficit

defeatist /dɪˈfiːtɪst/ adj expecting not to succeed □ *bersikap mudah berputus asa atau menyerah kalah*: *a defeatist attitude/view* ▶ **defeatist** noun [C]: *Don't be such a defeatist, we haven't lost yet!*

defecate /ˈdefəkeɪt/ verb [I] (formal) to get rid of waste from the body; to go to the toilet □ *buang air besar; berak*

defect¹ /ˈdiːfekt/ noun [C] sth that is wrong with or missing from sb/sth □ *kecacatan*: *a speech defect* ◆ *defects in the education system* ▶ **defective** /dɪˈfektɪv/ adj

defect² /dɪˈfekt/ verb [I] to leave your country, a political party, etc. and join one that is considered to be the enemy □ *membelot; berpaling tadah* ▶ **defection** noun [C,U] ▶ **defector** /dɪˈfektə(r)/ noun [C]

defence (*AmE* **defense**) /dɪˈfens/ noun
▶IN PROTECTION **1** [U] something that you do or say to protect sb/sth from attack, bad treatment, criticism, etc. □ *(perbuatan) mempertahankan/membela*: *Would you fight in defence of your country?* ◆ *When her brother was criticized she leapt to his defence.* ◆ *I must say in her defence that I have always found her a very reliable employee.* ◯ look at **self-defence 2** [C] **a defence (against sth)** something that protects sb/sth from sth, or that is used to fight against attack □ *pertahanan; perlindungan*: *the body's defences against disease* **3** [U] the military equipment, forces, etc. for protecting a country □ *pertahanan*: *Spending on defence needs to be reduced.*
▶IN LAW **4** [C] an argument in support of the accused person in a court of law □ *pembelaan; alasan (utk membela diri)*: *His defence was that he was only carrying out orders.* **5** **the defence** [sing, with sing or pl verb] the lawyer or lawyers who are acting for the accused person in a court of law □ *pihak pembela*: *The defence claims/claim that many of the witnesses were lying.* ◯ note at **court** ◯ look at **the prosecution**
▶IN SPORT **6** usually **the defence** [sing, U] action to prevent the other team scoring; the players who try to do this □ *pertahanan*: *She plays in defence.*

defenceless /dɪˈfensləs/ adj unable to defend yourself against attack □ *tdk berupaya mempertahankan diri*

defend /dɪˈfend/ verb
▶PROTECT **1** [T] **defend sb/sth/yourself (against/from sb/sth)** to protect sb/sth from harm or danger □ *mempertahankan*: *Would you be able to defend yourself if someone attacked you in the street?*
▶SUPPORT **2** [T] **defend sb/sth/yourself (against/from sb/sth)** to say or write sth to support sb/sth that has been criticized □ *mempertahankan*: *The minister went on TV to defend the government's policy.*
▶IN SPORT **3** [I,T] to try to stop the other team or player scoring □ *mempertahankan*: *They defended well and managed to hold onto their lead.*
▶IN COMPETITIONS **4** [T] to take part in a competition that you won before and try to win it again □ *mempertahankan*: *She successfully defended her title.* ◆ *He is the defending champion.*
▶IN LAW **5** [T] to speak for sb who is accused of a crime in a court of law □ *membela*: *He has employed one of the UK's top lawyers to defend him.*

defendant /dɪˈfendənt/ noun [C] a person who is accused of a crime in a court of law □ *defendan; pihak yg didakwa*

defender /dɪˈfendə(r)/ noun [C] a person who defends sb/sth, especially in sport □ *pembela; barisan pertahanan*

defense (*AmE*) = **defence**

defensive¹ /dɪˈfensɪv/ adj **1** that protects sb/sth from attack □ *(utk) pertahanan*: *The troops took up a defensive position.* **OPP** **offensive** **2** showing that you feel that sb is criticizing you □ *bersikap mempertahankan diri*: *When I asked him about his new job, he became very defensive and tried to change the subject.*

defensive² /dɪˈfensɪv/ noun
IDM **on the defensive** acting in a way that shows that you expect sb to attack or criticize you □ *bersikap mempertahankan diri kerana menjangka akan diserang atau dikecam*: *My questions about her past immediately put her on the defensive.*

defer /dɪˈfɜː(r)/ verb [T] (**deferring**; **deferred**) (formal) to leave sth until a later time □ *menangguhkan*: *She deferred her place at university for a year.*

deference /ˈdefərəns/ noun [U] polite behaviour that you show towards sb/sth, usually because you respect them □ *(sikap) hormat; menghormati*
IDM **in deference to sb/sth** because you respect and do not wish to upset sb □ *sebagai menghormati sso/sst*: *In deference to her father's wishes, she didn't mention the subject again.*

defiance /dɪˈfaɪəns/ noun [U] open refusal to obey sb/sth □ *keingkaran; (perbuatan) mengingkari*: *an act of defiance* ◆ *She married Jack in defiance of her parents' wishes.* ◯ verb **defy**

defiant /dɪˈfaɪənt/ adj showing open refusal to obey sb/sth □ *ingkar* ◯ verb **defy** ▶ **defiantly** adv

deficiency /dɪˈfɪʃnsi/ noun (pl **deficiencies**) **deficiency (in/of sth) 1** [C,U] the state of not having enough of sth; a lack □ *kekurangan*: *a deficiency of vitamin C* **2** [C] a fault or a weakness in sb/sth □ *kekurangan; kecacatan*: *The problems were caused by deficiencies in the design.*

deficient /dɪˈfɪʃnt/ adj **1** **deficient (in sth)** not having enough of sth □ *kurang*: *food that is deficient in minerals* **2** not good enough or not complete □ *kurang*

deficit /ˈdefɪsɪt/ noun [C] the amount by which the money you receive is less than the money you have spent □ *defisit; kurangan*: *a trade deficit*

[I] **intransitive**, a verb which has no object: *He laughed.*   [T] **transitive**, a verb which has an object: *He ate an apple.*

define /dɪˈfaɪn/ verb [T] **1** to say exactly what a word or an idea means □ *mentakrifkan; memberikan makna*: How would you define 'happiness'? **2** to explain the exact nature of sth clearly □ *menjelaskan*: We need to define the problem before we can attempt to solve it.

defining /dɪˈfaɪnɪŋ/ adj **1** (used about clauses) explaining which particular person or thing you are talking about rather than giving extra information about them □ *yg mentakrifkan* ❶ For more information, look at the Reference Section at the back of this dictionary. **2** a set of carefully chosen words used to write the explanations in some dictionaries □ *yg menjelaskan*: This dictionary uses a **defining vocabulary** of 3 000 words.

definite /ˈdefɪnət/ adj **1** fixed and unlikely to change; certain □ *pasti; tentu*: I'll give you a definite decision in a couple of days. **OPP** **indefinite 2** clear; easy to see or notice □ *jelas; nyata; tentu*: There has been a definite change in her attitude recently.

the definite article noun [C] the name used for the word 'the' □ *kata sandang pasti "the"* ➲ look at the **indefinite article** ❶ For more information about the definite article, look at the **Reference Section** section at the back of this dictionary.

definitely /ˈdefɪnətli/ adv certainly; without doubt □ *pasti; tentu; benar-benar*: I'll definitely consider your advice.

definition /ˌdefɪˈnɪʃn/ noun [C,U] a description of the exact meaning of a word or an idea □ *takrif; definisi; makna*: Wordpower is a dictionary with clear, simple definitions.

definitive /dɪˈfɪnətɪv/ adj in a form that cannot be changed or that cannot be improved □ *muktamad; paling sahih; terbaik*: This is the definitive version. ◆ the definitive performance of Hamlet ▸ **definitively** adv

deflate /dɪˈfleɪt ˌdiː-/ verb **1** [I,T] to become or to make sth smaller by letting the air or gas out of it □ *mengempis*: The balloon slowly deflated. **OPP** **inflate 2** [T] to make sb feel less confident, proud or excited □ *berasa kecewa atau tawar hati*: I felt really deflated when I got my exam results.

deflect /dɪˈflekt/ verb **1** [I,T] to change direction after hitting sb/sth; to make sth change direction in this way □ *melencong; melencongkan; terpesong*: The ball deflected off a defender and into the goal. **2** [T] to turn sb's attention away from sth □ *memesongkan*: Nothing could deflect her from her aim.

deflection /dɪˈflekʃn/ noun [C,U] a change of direction after hitting sb/sth □ *pemesongan*

deforestation /ˌdiːˌfɒrɪˈsteɪʃn/ (*AmE* also) / noun [U] cutting down trees over a large area □ *pembasmian hutan* ➲ note at **environment**

deform /dɪˈfɔːm/ verb [T] to change or spoil the natural shape of sth □ *mencacatkan; merosakkan*

deformed /dɪˈfɔːmd/ adj having a shape that is not normal because it has grown wrongly □ *cacat*

deformity /dɪˈfɔːməti/ noun [C,U] (pl **deformities**) the condition of having a part of the body that is an unusual shape because of disease, injury, etc. □ *kecacatan*: The disease causes facial deformities.

defraud /dɪˈfrɔːd/ verb [T] **defraud sb (of sth)** to get sth from sb in a dishonest way □ *menipu*: He defrauded the company of millions.

defrost /ˌdiːˈfrɒst/ verb **1** [I,T] (used about frozen food) to return to a normal temperature; to make food do this □ *mencairbekukan*: Defrost the chicken thoroughly before cooking. **2** [T] to remove the ice from sth □ *menyahfroskan*: to defrost a fridge ➲ look at **de-ice**

deft /deft/ adj (used especially about movements) skilful and quick □ *cekap* ▸ **deftly** adv

defunct /dɪˈfʌŋkt/ adj no longer existing or in use □ *tdk wujud/berfungsi lagi*

defuse /ˌdiːˈfjuːz/ verb [T] **1** to make a situation calmer or less dangerous □ *meredakan*: She defused the tension by changing the subject. **2** to remove part of a bomb so that it cannot explode □ *menanggalkan fius (bom)*: Army experts defused the bomb safely.

defy /dɪˈfaɪ/ verb [T] (**defying; defies**; pt, pp **defied**) **1** to refuse to obey sb/sth □ *mengingkari*: She defied her parents and continued seeing Brendan. ➲ adjective **defiant**, noun **defiance 2** to make sth impossible or very difficult □ *tdk dpt; sukar*: It's such a beautiful place that it defies description.

IDM defy sb to do sth to ask sb to do sth that you believe to be impossible □ *mencabar*: I defy you to prove me wrong.

degenerate¹ /dɪˈdʒenəreɪt/ verb [I] to become worse, lower in quality, etc. □ *merosot atau menurun (kualiti, dll)*: The calm discussion degenerated into a nasty argument. ▸ **degeneration** /dɪˌdʒenəˈreɪʃn/ noun [U]

degenerate² /dɪˈdʒenərət/ adj having moral standards that have fallen to a very low level □ *rosak akhlaknya; tdk bermaruah*

degradation /ˌdegrəˈdeɪʃn/ noun [U] **1** the act of making sb be less respected; the state of being less respected □ *kehinaan; menjatuhkan maruah*: the degradation of being in prison **2** causing the condition of sth to become worse □ *kemerosotan; degradasi*: environmental degradation

degrade /dɪˈɡreɪd/ verb [T] to make people respect sb less □ *menjatuhkan maruah; menghina*: It's the sort of film that really degrades women. ▸ **degrading** adj

degree /dɪˈɡriː/ noun **1** [C] a measurement of angles □ *darjah*: a forty-five degree (45°) angle ◆ An angle of 90 degrees is called a right angle.

dehydrate → delicate

2 [C] a measurement of temperature □ *darjah*: *Water boils at 100 degrees Celsius (100°C).* ♦ *three degrees below zero/minus three degrees (-3°)* **3** [C,U] (used about feelings or qualities) a certain amount or level □ *sedikit sebanyak; tahap; tingkat*: *There is always a* **degree** *of risk involved in mountaineering.* ♦ *I sympathize with her* **to some degree**. **4** [C] an official document that students gain by successfully completing a course at university or college □ *ijazah*: *Michael's got a* **degree in** *Philosophy.* ♦ *to do a Chemistry* **degree** ♦ *a first-class* **degree**

> **TOPIC**
>
> **Qualifications**
> In Britain **degree** is the usual word for the qualification you get when you complete and pass a university course. You can study for a **diploma** or a **certificate** at other types of college. The courses may be shorter and more practical than degree courses. The best result you can get in a British university degree is a **first**, followed by a **two-one**, a **two-two**, a **third**, a **pass** and a **fail**.

dehydrate /diːˈhaɪdreɪt; ˌdiːhaɪˈdreɪt/ *verb* **1** [T, usually passive] to remove all the water from sth □ *menyahhidratkan; mengeringkan*: *Dehydrated vegetables can be stored for months.* **2** [I,T] to lose or make sb lose too much water from the body □ *kekurangan air*: *If you run for a long time in the heat, you start to dehydrate.* ▶ **dehydration** /ˌdiːhaɪˈdreɪʃn/ *noun* [U]: *Several of the runners were suffering from severe dehydration.*

de-ice /ˌdiːˈaɪs/ *verb* [T] to remove the ice from sth □ *menyahais*: *The car windows need de-icing.* ⊃ look at **defrost**

deign /deɪn/ *verb* [T] **deign to do sth** to do sth although you think you are too important to do it □ *sudi*: *He didn't even deign to look up when I entered the room.*

deity /ˈdeɪəti/ *noun* [C] (*pl* **deities**) (*formal*) a god □ *dewa; dewi*

dejected /dɪˈdʒektɪd/ *adj* very unhappy, especially because you are disappointed □ *kecewa*: *The fans went home dejected after watching their team lose once more.* ▶ **dejectedly** *adv* ▶ **dejection** /dɪˈdʒekʃn/ *noun* [U]

delay¹ /dɪˈleɪ/ *noun* [C,U] a situation or period of time where you have to wait □ *kelewatan; penangguhan; (perbuatan) berlengah-lengah*: *Delays are likely on the roads because of heavy traffic.* ♦ *If you smell gas, you should report it* **without delay** (= immediately).

delay² /dɪˈleɪ/ *verb* **1** [T] to make sb/sth slow or late □ *melambatkan; melewatkan; terlewat*: *The plane was delayed for several hours because of bad weather.* **2** [I,T] **delay (sth/doing sth)** to decide not to do sth until a later time □ *menangguhkan*: *I was forced to delay the trip until the following week.*

delegate¹ /ˈdelɪɡət/ *noun* [C] a person who has been chosen to speak or take decisions for a group of people, especially at a meeting □ *wakil*

delegate² /ˈdelɪɡeɪt/ *verb* [I,T] to give sb with a lower job or position a particular task to do □ *menugaskan kerja kpd orang lain*: *You can't do everything yourself. You must learn how to delegate.*

delegation /ˌdelɪˈɡeɪʃn/ *noun* **1** [C, with sing or pl verb] a group of people who have been chosen to speak or take decisions for a larger group of people, especially at a meeting □ *perwakilan*: *The British delegation walked out of the meeting in protest.* **2** [U] the process of giving sb work or responsibilities that would usually be yours □ *penugasan*

delete /dɪˈliːt/ *verb* [T] to remove sth that is written □ *memotong; menghapuskan*: *Your name has been deleted from the list.* ▶ **deletion** /dɪˈliːʃn/ *noun* [C,U]

deliberate¹ /dɪˈlɪbərət/ *adj* **1** done on purpose; planned □ *dibuat dgn sengaja; sengaja*: *Was it an accident or was it deliberate?* **SYN** **intentional** **2** done slowly and carefully, without hurrying □ *perlahan-lahan dan berhati-hati*: *She spoke in a calm, deliberate voice.*

deliberate² /dɪˈlɪbəreɪt/ *verb* [I,T] (*formal*) to think about or discuss sth fully before making a decision □ *mempertimbangkan*: *The judges deliberated for an hour before announcing the winner.*

deliberately /dɪˈlɪbərətli/ *adv* **1** in a way that was planned, not by chance □ *dgn sengaja*: *I didn't break it deliberately, it was an accident.* **SYN** **purposely** **OPP** **by accident** **2** slowly and carefully, without hurrying □ *dgn perlahan-lahan dan berhati-hati*: *He packed up his possessions slowly and deliberately.*

deliberation /dɪˌlɪbəˈreɪʃn/ *noun* (*formal*) **1** [C,U] discussion or thinking about sth in detail □ *perbincangan/pertimbangan yg teliti*: *After much deliberation I decided to reject the offer.* **2** [U] the quality of being very slow and careful in what you say and do □ *sifat membuat sst dgn perlahan-lahan dan berhati-hati; ketelitian*: *He spoke with great deliberation.*

delicacy /ˈdelɪkəsi/ *noun* (*pl* **delicacies**) **1** [U] the quality of being easy to damage or break □ *keadaan mudah rosak atau pecah* **2** [U] great care; a gentle touch □ *sikap berhati-hati atau berhalus*: (*figurative*) *Be tactful! It's a matter of some delicacy.* **3** [C] a type of food that is considered particularly good □ *makanan istimewa*: *Try this dish, it's a local delicacy.*

delicate /ˈdelɪkət/ *adj* **1** easy to damage or break □ *mudah rosak/pecah; halus*: *delicate skin* ♦ *the delicate mechanisms of a watch* **2** often ill or hurt □ *selalu sakit*: *He was a delicate child and often in hospital.* **3** needing skilful treatment and care □ *memerlukan kemahiran dan ketelitian*: *Repairing this is going to be a very delicate operation.* **4** (used about colours, flavours, etc.) light and pleasant; not strong □ *lembut*: *a* *delicate shade of pale blue* ▶ **delicately** *adv*: *She stepped delicately over the broken glass.*

delicatessen /ˌdelɪkəˈtesn/ *noun* [C] a shop that sells special, unusual or foreign foods, especially cold cooked meat, cheeses, etc. □ *deli; delikatesen; kedai yg menjual makanan istimewa*

delicious /dɪˈlɪʃəs/ *adj* having a very pleasant taste or smell □ *lazat; sedap*: *This soup is absolutely delicious.*

delight¹ /dɪˈlaɪt/ *noun* **1** [U] great pleasure □ *kegembiraan; gembira; seronok*: *She laughed with delight as she opened the present.* **SYN** joy **2** [C] something that gives sb great pleasure □ *(sst yg) menggembirakan menyeronokkan*: *The story is a delight to read.* ▶ **delightful** /-fl/ *adj*: *a delightful view of the sea* ▶ **delightfully** /-fəli/ *adv*

delight² /dɪˈlaɪt/ *verb* [T] to give sb great pleasure □ *menggembirakan*: *She delighted the audience by singing all her old songs.*
PHR V **delight in sth/in doing sth** to get great pleasure from sth □ *suka akan sst/membuat sst*: *He delights in playing tricks on people.*

delighted /dɪˈlaɪtɪd/ *adj* **delighted (at/with/about sth); delighted to do sth/that ...** extremely pleased □ *sangat gembira*: *She was delighted at getting the job/that she got the job.* ◆ *They're absolutely delighted with their baby.* ➲ note at **happy**

delinquency /dɪˈlɪŋkwənsi/ *noun* [U] (*formal*) bad or criminal behaviour, especially among young people □ *kelakuan jahat atau jenayah (remaja)*

delinquent /dɪˈlɪŋkwənt/ *adj* (*formal*) (usually used about a young person) behaving badly and often breaking the law □ *delinkuen; berkelakuan jahat dan melanggar undang-undang* ▶ **delinquent** *noun* [C]: *a juvenile delinquent*

delirious /dɪˈlɪriəs/ *adj* **1** speaking or thinking in a crazy way, often because of illness □ *meracau* **2** extremely happy □ *sangat gembira*: *I was absolutely delirious when I passed the exam.* ▶ **deliriously** *adv*

deliver /dɪˈlɪvə(r)/ *verb* **1** [I,T] to take sth (goods, letters, etc.) to the place requested or to the address on it □ *menghantar; dihantar*: *Your order will be delivered within five days.* ◆ *We deliver free within the local area.* **2** [T] (*formal*) to say sth formally □ *menyampaikan; memberi*: *to deliver a speech/lecture/warning* **3** [I] (*informal*) **deliver (on sth)** to do or give sth that you have promised □ *menunaikan janji*: *The new leader has made a lot of promises, but can he deliver on them?* **4** [T] to help a mother to give birth to her baby □ *menyambut bayi; membidani*: *to deliver a baby*
IDM **come up with/deliver the goods** ➲ **goods**

delivery /dɪˈlɪvəri/ *noun* (*pl* **deliveries**) **1** [U] the act of taking sth (goods, letters, etc.) to the place or person who has ordered it or whose address is on it □ *penghantaran; serahan*: *Please allow 28 days for delivery.* ◆ *a delivery van* **2** [C] an occasion when sth is delivered □ *penghantaran*: *Is there a delivery here on Sundays?* **3** [C] something (goods, letters, etc.) that is **delivered** □ *hantaran*: *The shop is waiting for a new delivery of apples.* **4** [C] the process of giving birth to a baby □ *bersalin*: *an easy/difficult delivery*

delta /ˈdeltə/ *noun* [C] an area of flat land shaped like a triangle where a river divides into smaller rivers as it goes into the sea □ *delta*

delude /dɪˈluːd/ *verb* [T] to make sb believe sth that is not true □ *memperdaya; menipu*: *If he thinks he's going to get rich quickly, he's deluding himself.* ➲ *noun* **delusion**

deluge¹ /ˈdeljuːdʒ/ *noun* [C] **1** a sudden very heavy fall of rain □ *hujan lebat; banjir* **2** **a deluge (of sth)** a very large number of things that happen or arrive at the same time □ *banjiran*: *The programme was followed by a deluge of complaints from the public.* **SYN** flood

deluge² /ˈdeljuːdʒ/ *verb* [T, usually passive] to send or give sb/sth a very large quantity of sth, all at the same time □ *dibanjiri*: *They were deluged with applications for the job.* **SYN** flood

delusion /dɪˈluːʒn/ *noun* [C,U] a false belief □ *kepercayaan palsu; delusi*: *He seems to be under the delusion that he's popular.* ➲ *verb* **delude**

de luxe /də ˈlʌks/ *adj* of extremely high quality and more expensive than usual □ *mewah*: *a de luxe hotel*

delve /delv/ *verb* [I] **delve into sth** to search inside sth □ *mencari (dlm sst); menyelongkar; menyelidiki*: *She delved into the bag and brought out a tiny box.* ◆ (*figurative*) *We must delve into the past to find the origins of the custom.*

Dem *abbr* = **democrat**(2), **Democratic Party**

demand¹ /dɪˈmɑːnd/ *noun* **1** [C] **a demand (for sth/that ...)** a strong request or order that must be obeyed □ *desakan; tuntutan*: *a demand for changes in the law* ◆ *I was amazed by their demand that I should leave immediately.* **2** **demands** [pl] something that sb/sth makes you do, especially sth that is difficult or tiring □ *(perihal) menghendaki/memerlukan*: *Running a marathon makes huge demands on the body.* **3** [U, sing] **demand (for sth/sb)** the desire or need for sth among a group of people □ *permintaan*: *We no longer sell that product because there is no demand for it.*
IDM **in demand** wanted by a lot of people □ *popular; dikehendaki ramai*: *I'm in demand this weekend—I've had three invitations!*
on demand at any time that you ask for it □ *apabila dikehendaki*: *This treatment is available from your doctor on demand.*

demand² /dɪˈmɑːnd/ *verb* [T] **1 demand to do sth/that ...; demand sth** to ask for sth in an extremely firm or aggressive way □ *menuntut; mendesak; mahu; hendak*: *I walked into the office and demanded to see the manager.* ◆ *She demanded that I pay her immediately.* ◆ *Your* *behaviour was disgraceful and I demand an apology.* **2** to need sth □ *memerlukan: a sport that demands skill as well as strength*

demanding /dɪˈmɑːndɪŋ/ *adj* **1** (used about a job, task, etc.) needing a lot of effort, care, skill, etc. □ *memerlukan banyak tenaga, ketelitian, kemahiran, dll: It will be a demanding schedule—I have to go to six cities in six days.* **2** (used about a person) always wanting attention or expecting very high standards of people □ *banyak kerenah; cerewet: Young children are very demanding.* ♦ *a demanding boss*

demise /dɪˈmaɪz/ *noun* [sing] **1** the end or failure of sth □ *kegagalan; berakhirnya: Poor business decisions led to the company's demise.* **2** (formal) the death of a person □ *kematian*

demo /ˈdeməʊ/ *noun* [C] (*pl* demos) (*informal*) **1** (*especially BrE*) = **demonstration**(1): *They all went on the demo.* **2** = **demonstration**(2): *I'll give you a demo.* **3** a record or tape with an example of sb's music on it □ *pita ragaan: a demo tape*

democracy /dɪˈmɒkrəsi/ *noun* (*pl* democracies) **1** [U] a system in which the government of a country is elected by the people □ *demokrasi* **2** [C] a country that has this system □ *negara berdemokrasi* **3** [U] the right of everyone in an organization, etc. to be treated equally and to vote on matters that affect them □ *demokrasi: There is a need for more democracy in the company.*

democrat /ˈdeməkræt/ *noun* [C] **1** a person who believes in and supports **democracy** □ *demokrat* **2 Democrat** (*abbr* Dem) a member of, or sb who supports, the Democratic Party of the US □ *ahli Parti Demokrat* ➔ look at **Republican**

democratic /ˌdeməˈkrætɪk/ *adj* **1** based on the system of **democracy** □ *demokratik: democratic elections* ♦ *a democratic government* ➔ note at **politics 2** having or supporting equal rights for all people □ *demokratik: a democratic decision* (= made by all the people involved) ▶ **democratically** /-kli/ *adv: a democratically elected government*

the Democratic Party *noun* [sing] (*abbr* Dem) one of the two main political parties of the US □ *Parti Demokrat* ➔ look at **the Republican Party**

demographics /ˌdeməˈɡræfɪks/ *noun* [pl] data relating to the population and different groups within it □ *demografik: the demographics of radio listeners* ▶ **demographic** *adj: demographic changes/trends/factors* ▶ **demographically** /-kli/ *adv*

demolish /dɪˈmɒlɪʃ/ *verb* [T] to destroy sth, for example a building □ *merobohkan; meruntuhkan: The old shops were demolished and a supermarket was built in their place.* ♦ (*figurative*) *She demolished his argument in one sentence.* ▶ **demolition** /ˌdeməˈlɪʃn/ *noun* [C,U]

demon /ˈdiːmən/ *noun* [C] an evil spirit □ *hantu; setan*

demonic /diˈmɒnɪk/ *adj* connected with, or like, a **demon** □ *berkaitan hantu, setan; spt hantu, setan*

¶ demonstrate /ˈdemənstreɪt/ *verb* **1** [T] **demonstrate sth (to sb)** to show sth clearly by giving proof □ *menunjukkan; membuktikan: Using this chart, I'd like to demonstrate to you what has happened to our sales.* **2** [I,T] **demonstrate sth (to sb)** to show and explain to sb how to do sth or how sth works □ *menunjuk cara; mendemonstrasikan: The crew demonstrated the use of life jackets just after take-off.* ♦ *I'm not sure what you mean—could you demonstrate?* **3** [I] **demonstrate (against/for sb/sth)** to take part in a public protest for or against sb/sth □ *menunjuk perasaan; berdemonstrasi: Enormous crowds have been demonstrating against the government.* **SYN** protest

demonstration /ˌdemənˈstreɪʃn/ *noun* **1** (*especially BrE informal* demo) [C] **a demonstration (against/for sb/sth)** a public protest for or against sb/sth □ *tunjuk perasaan; demonstrasi: demonstrations against a new law* **2** (*also informal* demo) [C,U] an act of showing or explaining to sb how to do sth or how sth works □ *demonstrasi; tunjuk cara: The salesman gave me a demonstration of what the computer could do.* **3** [C,U] something that shows clearly that sth exists or is true □ *pembuktian: This accident is a clear demonstration of the system's faults.*

demonstrative /dɪˈmɒnstrətɪv/ *adj* (used about a person) showing feelings, especially loving feelings, in front of other people □ *mudah menunjukkan rasa hati, misalnya kasih sayang*

demonstrator /ˈdemənstreɪtə(r)/ *noun* [C] a person who takes part in a public protest □ *penunjuk perasaan* **SYN** protester

demoralize (*also* -ise) /dɪˈmɒrəlaɪz/ (*AmE also*) /-ˈmɔːr-/ *verb* [T] to make sb lose confidence or the courage to continue doing sth □ *mematahkan semangat: Repeated defeats completely demoralized the team.* ▶ **demoralization** (*also* -isation) /dɪˌmɒrəlaɪˈzeɪʃn/ *noun* [U] ▶ **demoralizing** (*also* -ising) *adj: Constant criticism can be extremely demoralizing.*

demote /ˌdiːˈməʊt/ *verb* [T] **demote sb (from sth) (to sth)** to move sb to a lower position or less important job, often as a punishment □ *menurunkan pangkat* **OPP** promote ▶ **demotion** /ˌdiːˈməʊʃn/ *noun* [C,U]

demure /dɪˈmjʊə(r)/ *adj* (used especially about a girl or young woman) shy, quiet and polite □ *pemalu, pendiam dan bersopan*

den /den/ *noun* [C] **1** the place where certain wild animals, such as **lions** live □ *jerumun* **2** a secret place, especially for illegal activities □ *sarang: a gambling den*

denial /dɪˈnaɪəl/ *noun* **1** [C] a statement that sth is not true □ *penafian; penyangkalan: The* minister issued a denial that he was involved in the scandal. **2** [C,U] **(a) denial (of sth)** refusing to allow sb to have or do sth ▫ *keengganan memberi kebenaran; enggan membenarkan*: *a denial of personal freedom* **3** [U] a refusal to accept that sth unpleasant or painful has happened ▫ *keengganan menerima sst kenyataan*: *He's been in denial ever since the accident.* ➔ verb **deny**

denim /'denɪm/ noun [U] a thick cotton cloth (often blue) that is used for making clothes, especially jeans ▫ *denim*: *a denim jacket* ➔ picture on **page P1**

denomination /dɪˌnɒmɪ'neɪʃn/ noun [C] one of the different religious groups that you can belong to ▫ *mazhab*

denote /dɪ'nəʊt/ verb [T] to mean or be a sign of sth ▫ *bermakna; menandakan*: *In algebra the sign x always denotes an unknown quantity.*

denounce /dɪ'naʊns/ verb [T] to say publicly that sth is wrong; to be very critical of a person in public ▫ *mengecam; mengutuk*: *The well-known actor has been denounced as a bad influence on young people.* ➔ noun **denunciation**

dense /dens/ adj (**denser**; **densest**) **1** containing a lot of things or people close together ▫ *tebal; padat*: *dense forests* ♦ *areas of dense population* **2** difficult to see through ▫ *tebal*: *dense fog* **3** (*informal*) not intelligent; stupid ▫ *bodoh*
▶ **densely** adv: *densely populated areas*

density /'densəti/ noun (pl **densities**) **1** [U] the number of things or people in a place in relation to its area ▫ *kepadatan*: *There is a high density of wildlife in this area.* **2** [C,U] (*technical*) the relation of the weight of a substance to its size ▫ *ketumpatan*: *Lead has a high density.*

dent¹ /dent/ verb [T] to damage a flat surface by hitting it but not breaking it ▫ *mengemikkan*: *I hit a wall and dented the front of the car.*

dent² /dent/ noun [C] a place where a flat surface, especially metal, has been hit and damaged but not broken ▫ *kemik*: *This tin's got a dent in it.*

dental /'dentl/ adj [only before a noun] connected with teeth ▫ *pergigian; gigi*: *dental care/ treatment*

dental floss noun [U] a type of thread that is used for cleaning between the teeth ▫ *flos gigi*

dentist /'dentɪst/ noun **1** [C] a person whose job is to look after people's teeth ▫ *doktor gigi*: *an appointment with the dentist* ➔ note at **tooth** ➔ picture on **page P2 2 the dentist's** [sing] the place where a dentist works ▫ *klinik gigi*: *I have to go to the dentist's today.*

dentistry /'dentɪstri/ noun [U] **1** the medical study of the teeth and mouth ▫ *(jurusan) pergigian* **2** the work of a dentist ▫ *pekerjaan doktor gigi*

dentures /'dentʃəz/ = **false teeth**

denunciation /dɪˌnʌnsi'eɪʃn/ noun [C,U] an expression of strong disapproval of sb/sth in public ▫ *pengecaman; pengutukan* ➔ verb **denounce**

deny /dɪ'naɪ/ verb [T] (**denying**; **denies**; pt, pp **denied**) **1 deny sth/doing sth; deny that …** to state that sth is not true; to refuse to admit or accept sth ▫ *menafikan; menyangkal*: *In court he denied all the charges.* ♦ *She denied telling lies/ that she had told lies.* **OPP** **admit 2** (*formal*) **deny sb sth; deny sth (to sb)** to refuse to allow sb to have sth ▫ *tdk membenarkan/mengizinkan*: *She was denied permission to remain in the country.* ➔ noun **denial**

deodorant /di'əʊdərənt/ noun [C,U] a chemical substance that you put onto your body to prevent bad smells ▫ *deodoran; penyahbau*

dep. abbr **departs** ▫ *berlepas*: *dep. London 15.32*

depart /dɪ'pɑːt/ verb [I,T] (*formal*) to leave a place, usually at the beginning of a journey ▫ *bertolak; berlepas*: *Ferries depart for Spain twice a day.* ♦ *The next train to the airport departs from platform 2.* ➔ note at **leave¹** ➔ noun **departure**

department /dɪ'pɑːtmənt/ noun [C] (abbr **Dept**) **1** one of the sections into which an organization, for example a school or a business, is divided ▫ *bahagian*: *the Modern Languages department* ♦ *She works in the accounts department.* **2** a division of the government responsible for a particular subject ▫ *jabatan*: *the Department of Health* ➔ look at **ministry**

departmental /ˌdiːpɑːt'mentl/ adj [only before a noun] connected with a department ▫ *(berkenaan dgn) bahagian/jabatan*: *There is a departmental meeting once a month.*

de'partment store noun [C] a large shop that is divided into sections selling different types of goods ▫ *gedung serbaneka*

departure /dɪ'pɑːtʃə(r)/ noun [C,U] **1** leaving or going away from a place ▫ *pemergian; berlepas*: *Helen's sudden departure meant I had to do her job as well as mine.* ♦ *Passengers should check in at least one hour before departure.* **OPP** **arrival** ➔ verb **depart 2 a departure (from sth)** an action which is different from what is usual or expected ▫ *penyimpangan*: *a departure from normal practice*

depend /dɪ'pend/ verb

IDM **that depends; it (all) depends** [used alone or at the beginning of a sentence] used to say that you are not certain of sth until other things have been considered ▫ *bergantung pd; tengoklah*: *'Can you lend me some money?' 'That depends. How much do you want?'* ♦ *I don't know whether I'll see him. It depends what time he gets here.*

PHR V **depend on sb/sth** to be able to trust sb/ sth to do sth ▫ *bergantung kpd; mengharapkan; berharap*: *If you ever need any help, you know you can depend on me.* ♦ *You can't depend on the trains. They're always late.* ♦ *I was depending on getting the money today.* **SYN** **rely on**

dependable → depress

depend on sb/sth (for sth) to need sb/sth to provide sth □ *bergantung pd sso/sst (utk sst)*: *Our organization depends on donations from the public.*

depend on sth to be decided or influenced by sb/sth □ *bergantung pd sst*: *His whole future depends on these exams.*

dependable /dɪˈpendəbl/ *adj* that can be trusted □ *boleh diharap*: *The bus service is very dependable.* **SYN** reliable

dependant (*especially AmE* **dependent**) /dɪˈpendənt/ *noun* [C] a person who depends on sb else for money, a home, food, etc. □ *tanggungan*: *insurance cover for you and all your dependants*

dependence /dɪˈpendəns/ *noun* [U] **dependence on sb/sth** the state of needing sb/sth □ *pergantungan*: *The country wants to reduce its dependence on imported oil.* **OPP** independence

dependency /dɪˈpendənsi/ *noun* [U] the state of being **dependent** on sb/sth; the state of being unable to live without sth, especially a drug □ *kebergantungan*

dependent /dɪˈpendənt/ *adj* **1 dependent (on sb/sth)** needing sb/sth to support you □ *bergantung*: *The industry is heavily dependent on government funding.* ◆ *Do you have any dependent children?* **2 dependent on sb/sth** influenced or decided by sth □ *bergantung*: *The price you pay is dependent on the number in your group.* **OPP** for both meanings **independent**

depict /dɪˈpɪkt/ *verb* [T] **1** to show sb/sth in a painting or drawing □ *menggambarkan*: *a painting depicting a country scene* **2** to describe sb/sth in words □ *menggambarkan; menceritakan*: *The novel depicts rural life a century ago.*

deplete /dɪˈpliːt/ *verb* [T] to reduce the amount of sth so that there is not much left □ *menghabiskan; mengurangkan*: *Wealthy nations are depleting the world's natural resources.* ▶ **depletion** /dɪˈpliːʃn/ *noun* [U]

deplorable /dɪˈplɔːrəbl/ *adj* (*formal*) morally bad and deserving disapproval □ *amat buruk; teruk*: *They are living in deplorable conditions.* ▶ **deplorably** /-əbli/ *adv*

deplore /dɪˈplɔː(r)/ *verb* [T] (*formal*) to feel or say that sth is morally bad □ *mengecam; mengesali*: *I deplore such dishonest behaviour.*

deploy /dɪˈplɔɪ/ *verb* [T] **1** to put soldiers or weapons in a position where they are ready to fight □ *menghantar; menempatkan (askar dan senjata)* **2** to use sth in a useful and successful way □ *menggunakan* ▶ **deployment** *noun* [U,C]: *the deployment of troops*

deport /dɪˈpɔːt/ *verb* [T] to force sb to leave a country because they have no legal right to be there □ *mengusir; diusir*: *A number of illegal immigrants have been deported.* ▶ **deportation** /ˌdiːpɔːˈteɪʃn/ *noun* [C,U]

depose /dɪˈpəʊz/ *verb* [T] to remove a ruler or leader from power □ *menggulingkan*: *There was a revolution and the dictator was deposed.*

deposit¹ /dɪˈpɒzɪt/ *noun* [C] **1 a deposit (on sth)** a sum of money which is the first payment for sth, with the rest of the money to be paid later □ *cengkeram; wang muka*: *Once you have paid a deposit, the booking will be confirmed.* **2** [usually sing] **a deposit (on sth)** a sum of money that you pay when you rent sth and get back when you return it without damage □ *cagaran*: *Boats can be hired for £15 an hour, plus £30 deposit.* **3** a sum of money paid into a bank account □ *simpanan* **4** a substance that has been left on a surface or in the ground as the result of a natural or chemical process □ *mendapan; longgokan*: *mineral deposits*

deposit² /dɪˈpɒzɪt/ *verb* [T] **1** to put sth down somewhere □ *meletakkan*: *He deposited his bags on the floor and sat down.* **2** (used about liquid or a river) to leave sth lying on a surface, as the result of a natural or chemical process □ *memendapkan*: *mud deposited by a flood* **3** to put money into an account at a bank □ *menyimpan; memasukkan (ke dlm bank)*: *He deposited £20 a week into his savings account.* **4 deposit sth (in sth); deposit sth (with sb/sth)** to put sth valuable in an official place where it is safe until needed again □ *menyimpan; meletakkan*: *Valuables can be deposited in the hotel safe.*

deˈposit account *noun* [C] (*BrE*) a type of bank account where your money earns interest. You cannot take money out of a **deposit account** without arranging it first with the bank. □ *akaun deposit* ➲ look at **current account**

depot /ˈdepəʊ/ *noun* [C] **1** a place where large amounts of food, goods or equipment are stored □ *depot* **2** a place where large numbers of vehicles (buses, lorries, etc.) are kept when not in use □ *depot* **3** (*AmE*) a small bus or railway station □ *stesen*

depraved /dɪˈpreɪvd/ *adj* (*formal*) morally bad □ *rosak akhlak dan moral*: *This is the work of a depraved mind.* **SYN** wicked, evil ▶ **depravity** /dɪˈprævəti/ *noun* [U] **SYN** wickedness

depreciate /dɪˈpriːʃieɪt/ *verb* [I] to become less valuable over a period of time □ *susut nilai*: *New cars start to depreciate the moment they are on the road.* ▶ **depreciation** /dɪˌpriːʃiˈeɪʃn/ *noun* [C,U]

depress /dɪˈpres/ *verb* [T] **1** to make sb unhappy and without hope or enthusiasm □ *menyedihkan; memuramkan*: *All this wet weather really depresses me.* **2** (used about business) to cause sth to become less successful □ *meleset; melembapkan*: *The reduction in the number of tourists has depressed local trade.* **3** (*formal*) to press sth down on a machine, etc. □ *menekan*: *To switch off the machine, depress the lever.* ▶ **depressing** *adj*: *The thought of growing old alone is very depressing.* ▶ **depressingly** *adv*

[I] **intransitive**, a verb which has no object: *He laughed.*

[T] **transitive**, a verb which has an object: *He ate an apple.*

depressed /dɪˈprest/ *adj* **1** very unhappy, often for a long period of time □ *murung; sedih; muram*: *He's been very depressed since he lost his job.* ➲ note at **sad 2** (used about a place or an industry) without enough businesses or jobs □ *meleset*: *an attempt to create employment in depressed areas*

depression /dɪˈpreʃn/ *noun* **1** [U] a feeling of unhappiness that lasts for a long time. **Depression** can be a medical condition and may have physical signs, for example being unable to sleep, etc. □ *kemurungan; kesedihan; kemuraman*: *clinical/post-natal depression* **2** [C,U] a period when the economic situation is bad, with little business activity and many people without a job □ *kemelesetan*: *The country was in the grip of (an) economic depression.* **3** [C] a part of a surface that is lower than the parts around it □ *lekukan*: *Rainwater collects in shallow depressions in the ground.*

deprive /dɪˈpraɪv/ *verb* [T] **deprive sb/sth of sth** to prevent sb/sth from having sth; to take away sth from sb □ *menghalang; tdk membenarkan; tdk diberi*: *The prisoners were deprived of food.* ▶ **deprivation** /ˌdeprɪˈveɪʃn/ *noun* [U]

deprived /dɪˈpraɪvd/ *adj* not having enough of the basic things in life, such as food, money, etc. □ *serba kekurangan*: *He came from a deprived background.*

Dept *abbr* = **department** □ *jabatan; bahagian*: *the Sales Dept*

depth /depθ/ *noun* **1** [C,U] the distance down from the top to the bottom of sth □ *kedlman; dlmnya*: *The hole should be 3 cm in depth.* **2** [C,U] the distance from the front to the back of sth □ *dlmnya*: *the depth of a shelf* ➲ picture at **length 3** [U] the amount of emotion, knowledge, etc. that a person has □ *dlmnya*: *He tried to convince her of the depth of his feelings for her.* **4** [C, usually pl] the deepest, most extreme or most serious part of sth: *in the depths of winter* (= when it is coldest) □ *bahagian paling (dlm, jauh, dll); tengah-tengah* ➲ *adjective* **deep**
IDM in depth looking at all the details; in a thorough way □ *dgn/secara mendlm*: *to discuss a problem in depth* ♦ *an in-depth report*
out of your depth 1 (*BrE*) in water that is too deep for you to stand up in □ *dlm air yg terlalu dlm*: *If you're not a very strong swimmer, don't go out of your depth.* **2** in a situation that is too difficult for you □ *tdk faham*: *When they start discussing politics I soon get out of my depth.*

deputation /ˌdepjuˈteɪʃn/ *noun* [C, with sing or pl verb] a group of people sent to sb to act or speak for others □ *perwakilan*

deputize (also -**ise**) /ˈdepjutaɪz/ *verb* [I] **deputize (for sb)** to act for sb in a higher position, who is away or unable to do sth □ *diberi tugas sebagai pengganti/wakil; menggantikan*

deputy /ˈdepjuti/ *noun* [C] (*pl* **deputies**) the second most important person in a particular organization, who does the work of their manager if the manager is away □ *timbalan*: *the deputy head of a school*

derail /dɪˈreɪl/ *verb* [T] to cause a train to come off a railway track □ *tergelincir drpd landasan*

derailment /dɪˈreɪlmənt/ *noun* [C,U] an occasion when sth causes a train to come off a railway track □ *kejadian kereta api tergelincir*

deranged /dɪˈreɪndʒd/ *adj* thinking and behaving in a way that is not normal, especially because of mental illness □ *tdk siuman*

derby /ˈdɑːbi/ *noun* [C] (*pl* **derbies**) **1** (*BrE*) a race or sports competition □ *perlumbaan; perlawanan*: *a motorcycle derby* **2** **the Derby** (*BrE*) a horse race which takes place every year at Epsom □ *(Lumba Kuda) Derby* **3** (*AmE*) = **bowler**(2)

derelict /ˈderəlɪkt/ *adj* no longer used and in bad condition □ *terbiar; kopak-kapik*: *a derelict house*

deride /dɪˈraɪd/ *verb* [T] to say that sb/sth is ridiculous; to laugh at sb/sth in a cruel way □ *memperolokkan; mentertawakan* ▶ **derision** /dɪˈrɪʒn/ *noun* [U]: *Her comments were met with derision.* ▶ **derisive** /dɪˈraɪsɪv/ *adj*: *'What rubbish!' he said with a derisive laugh.*

derisory /dɪˈraɪsəri/ *adj* too small or of too little value to be considered seriously □ *terlalu kecil atau tdk bernilai sangat utk dipertimbangkan secara serius*: *Union leaders rejected the derisory pay offer.*

derivation /ˌderɪˈveɪʃn/ *noun* [C,U] the origin from which a word or phrase has developed □ *berasal; penerbitan*

derivative /dɪˈrɪvətɪv/ *noun* [C] a form of sth (especially a word) that has developed from the original form □ *terbitan*: *'Sadness' is a derivative of 'sad.'*

derive /dɪˈraɪv/ *verb* **1** [T] (*formal*) **derive sth from sth** to get sth (especially a feeling or an advantage) from sth □ *mendapat*: *I derive great satisfaction from my work.* **2** [I,T] (used about a name or word) to come from sth; to have sth as its origin □ *mendapat; berasal*: *The town derives its name from the river on which it was built.*

derogatory /dɪˈrɒɡətri/ *adj* expressing a lack of respect for, or a low opinion of, sth □ *menghina*: *derogatory comments about the standard of my work*

descend /dɪˈsend/ *verb* [I,T] (*formal*) to go down to a lower place; to go down sth □ *turun*: *The plane started to descend and a few minutes later we landed.* ♦ *She descended the stairs slowly.* **OPP** **ascend**
IDM be descended from sb to have sb as a relative in past times □ *drpd keturunan*: *He says he's descended from a Russian prince.*

descendant /dɪˈsendənt/ *noun* [C] a person who belongs to the same family as sb who lived a long time ago □ *keturunan*: *Her family are*

descent /dɪˈsent/ noun 1 [C] a movement down to a lower place □ *(gerakan) turun*: *The pilot informed us that we were about to begin our descent.* **OPP** ascent 2 [U] sb's family origins □ *keturunan*: *He is of Italian descent.* **SYN** ancestry

describe /dɪˈskraɪb/ verb [T] describe sb/sth (to/for sb); describe sb/sth (as sth) to say what sb/sth is like, or what happened □ *menceritakan; menggambarkan; memerihalkan*: *Can you describe the bag you lost?* ◆ *It's impossible to describe how I felt.* ◆ *The thief was described as tall, thin, and aged about twenty.*

description /dɪˈskrɪpʃn/ noun 1 [C,U] a picture in words of sb/sth or of sth that happened □ *gambaran; pemerihalan; huraian*: *The man gave the police a detailed description of the burglar.* 2 [C] a type or kind of sth □ *jenis*: *It must be a tool of some description, but I don't know what it's for.*

descriptive /dɪˈskrɪptɪv/ adj that describes sb/sth, especially in a skilful or an interesting way □ *(yg merupakan) huraian; perihalan; gambaran; deskriptif*: *a piece of descriptive writing* ◆ *She gave a highly descriptive account of the journey.*

desecrate /ˈdesɪkreɪt/ verb [T] to damage a thing or place of religious importance or to treat it without respect □ *memperlakukan (benda atau tempat suci) dgn cara yg tdk hormat, keji*: *desecrated graves* ▶ desecration /ˌdesɪˈkreɪʃn/ noun [U]

desert¹ /ˈdezət/ noun [C,U] a large area of land, usually covered with sand, that is hot and has very little water and very few plants □ *padang pasir; gurun*: *the Gobi Desert*

desert² /dɪˈzɜːt/ verb 1 [T] to leave sb/sth, usually for ever □ *meninggalkan*: *Many people have deserted the countryside and moved to the towns.* 2 [I,T] (used especially about sb in the armed forces) to leave without permission □ *meninggalkan tugas (tentera)*: *He deserted because he didn't want to fight.* ▶ desertion noun [C,U]

deserted /dɪˈzɜːtɪd/ adj empty, because all the people have left □ *lengang; kosong; ditinggalkan*: *a deserted house* ◆ *deserted streets* **SYN** abandoned

deserter /dɪˈzɜːtə(r)/ noun [C] a person who leaves the armed forces without permission □ *pembolos (tentera)*

desert island noun [C] an island, especially a tropical one, where nobody lives □ *pulau yg tdk dihuni*

deserve /dɪˈzɜːv/ verb [T] [not used in the continuous tenses] to earn sth, either good or bad, because of sth that you have done □ *patut; sepatutnya*: *We've done a lot of work and we deserve a break.* ◆ *He deserves to be punished severely for such a crime.*

HELP Although this verb is not used in the continuous tenses, it is common to see the present participle (= *-ing* form): *There are other aspects of the case deserving attention.*

deservedly /dɪˈzɜːvɪdli/ adv in a way that is right because of what sb has done □ *memang sepatutnya/wajar*: *He deservedly won the Best Actor award.*

deserving /dɪˈzɜːvɪŋ/ adj deserving (of sth) that you should give help, money, etc. to □ *patut menerima*: *This charity is a most deserving cause.*

design¹ /dɪˈzaɪn/ noun 1 [U] the way in which sth is planned and made or arranged □ *reka bentuk*: *Design faults have been discovered in the car.* 2 [U] the process and skill of making drawings that show how sth should be made, how it will work, etc. □ *seni reka bentuk*: *to study industrial design* ◆ *graphic design* 3 [C] a design (for sth) a drawing or plan that shows how sth should be made, built, etc. □ *pelan*: *The architect showed us her design for the new theatre.* 4 [C] a pattern of lines, shapes, etc. that decorate sth □ *corak*: *a T-shirt with a geometric design on it* **SYN** pattern

design² /dɪˈzaɪn/ verb 1 [I,T] to plan and make a drawing of how sth will be made □ *mereka bentuk*: *to design cars/dresses/houses* 2 [T] to invent, plan and develop sth for a particular purpose □ *direka bentuk; dibuat*: *The bridge wasn't designed for such heavy traffic.*

designate /ˈdezɪɡneɪt/ verb [T, often passive] (*formal*) 1 designate sth (as) sth to give sth a name to show that it has a particular purpose □ *menamai; dikhaskan*: *This has been designated (as) a conservation area.* 2 designate sb (as) sth to choose sb to do a particular job or task □ *melantik; diberi tugas*: *Who has she designated (as) her deputy?* 3 to show or mark sth □ *menandakan; melambangkan*: *These arrows designate the emergency exits.*

designer /dɪˈzaɪnə(r)/ noun [C] a person whose job is to make drawings or plans showing how sth will be made □ *pereka*: *a fashion designer* ▶ designer adj [only before a noun]: *designer jeans*

desirable /dɪˈzaɪərəbl/ adj 1 wanted, often by many people; worth having □ *menjadi idaman; elok jika dimiliki*: *Experience is desirable but not essential for this job.* **OPP** undesirable 2 sexually attractive □ *menggiurkan; mengghairahkan*

desire¹ /dɪˈzaɪə(r)/ noun [C,U] (a) desire (for sth/to do sth) 1 the feeling of wanting sth very much; a strong wish □ *keinginan*: *the desire for a peaceful solution to the crisis* ◆ *I have no desire to visit that place again.* 2 the wish for a sexual relationship with sb □ *nafsu berahi*: *She felt a surge of love and desire for him.*

desire² /dɪˈzaɪə(r)/ verb [T] 1 [not used in the continuous tenses] (*formal*) to want; to wish for □ *mengingini; ingini*: *They have everything they* *could possibly desire.* ♦ *The service in the restaurant left a lot to be desired* (= was very bad). **2** to find sb/sth sexually attractive □ *berasa ghairah terhadap sso/sst*: *He still desired her.*

> **HELP** Although this verb is not used in the continuous tenses, it is common to see the present participle (= -ing form): *Not desiring another argument, she turned away.*

desk /desk/ *noun* [C] **1** a type of table, often with drawers, that you sit at to write or work □ *meja tulis*: *The students put their books on their desks.* ♦ *He used to be a pilot but now he has a desk job* (= he works in an office). **2** a table or place in a building where a particular service is provided □ *meja; kaunter*: *an information desk* ♦ *Take your suitcases and tickets to the check-in desk.*

desktop /'desktɒp/ *noun* [C] **1** the top of a desk □ *bahagian atas meja* **2** a computer screen on which you can see **icons** (= symbols) showing the programs, information, etc. that are available to be used □ *paparan ikon*; *desktop* **3** (also ˌdesktop com'puter) a computer that can fit on a desk □ *komputer meja* ➲ look at **laptop**

ˌdesktop 'publishing *noun* [U] (*abbr* **DTP**) the use of a small computer and a machine for printing, to produce books, magazines and other printed material □ *(sistem) penerbitan meja*

desolate /'desələt/ *adj* **1** (used about a place) empty in a way that seems very sad □ *lengang dan terbiar; gersang*: *desolate wasteland* **2** (used about a person) lonely, very unhappy and without hope □ *sepi dan sedih* ▶ **desolation** /ˌdesə'leɪʃn/ *noun* [U]: *a scene of desolation.* ♦ *He felt utter desolation when his wife died.*

despair¹ /dɪ'speə(r)/ *noun* [U] the state of having lost all hope □ *putus asa*: *I felt like giving up in despair.* ▶ **despairing** *adj*: *a despairing cry* ➲ look at **desperate**

despair² /dɪ'speə(r)/ *verb* [I] **despair (of sb/sth)** to lose all hope that sth will happen □ *berputus asa*: *We began to despair of ever finding somewhere to live.*

despatch (*BrE*) = **dispatch**

desperate /'despərət/ *adj* **1** out of control and ready to do anything to change the situation you are in because it is so terrible □ *terdesak*: *She became desperate when her money ran out.* **2** done with little hope of success, as a last thing to try when everything else has failed □ *terakhir*: *I made a desperate attempt to persuade her to change her mind.* **3 desperate (for sth/to do sth)** wanting or needing sth very much □ *betul-betul ingin; sangat memerlukan*: *Let's go into a cafe. I'm desperate for a drink.* **4** terrible, very serious □ *genting; serius*: *There is a desperate shortage of skilled workers.* ▶ **desperately** *adv*: *She was desperately* (= extremely) *unlucky not to win.* ▶ **desperation** /ˌdespə'reɪʃn/ *noun* [U]

despicable /dɪ'spɪkəbl/ *adj* very unpleasant or evil □ *keji; hina*: *a despicable act of terrorism*

despise /dɪ'spaɪz/ *verb* [T] to hate sb/sth very much □ *membenci*: *I despise him for lying to me.*

despite /dɪ'spaɪt/ *prep* without being affected by the thing mentioned □ *walaupun*: *Despite having very little money, they enjoy life.* ♦ *The scheme went ahead despite public opposition.* ♦ *She was good at physics, despite the fact that she found it boring.* **SYN in spite of**

> **WRITING TIP**
>
> **How to show contrast 2**
> To show that there is something surprising or unexpected in the contrast between the two points, we can use **despite**, **in spite of** or **although**: *In spite of/Despite knowing about the dangers of smoking, large numbers of young people continue to smoke.* ♦ *In spite of/ Despite the fact that smoking is dangerous, large numbers of young people continue to smoke.* ♦ *Although smoking is dangerous, large numbers of young people continue to smoke.*

➲ note at **contrast** ❶ For more help with writing, look at Wordpower Writing Tutor at the back of this dictionary.

despondent /dɪ'spɒndənt/ *adj* **despondent (about/over sth)** without hope; expecting no improvement □ *putus asa*: *She was becoming increasingly despondent about finding a job.* ▶ **despondency** /dɪ'spɒndənsi/ *noun* [U]

despot /'despɒt/ *noun* [C] a ruler with great power, especially one who uses it in a cruel way □ *pemerintah kuku besi* ▶ **despotic** /dɪ'spɒtɪk/ *adj*

dessert /dɪ'zɜːt/ *noun* [C,U] something sweet that is eaten after the main part of a meal □ *(hidangan) pencuci mulut*: *What would you like for dessert—ice cream or fresh fruit?* ➲ note at **restaurant** ➲ look at **pudding**

dessertspoon /dɪ'zɜːtspuːn/ *noun* [C] a spoon used for eating sweet food after the main part of a meal □ *sudu sedang* ➲ picture at **spoon**

destabilize (also **-ise**) /ˌdiː'steɪbəlaɪz/ *verb* [T] to make a system, government, country, etc. become less safe and successful □ *menggugat kestabilan*: *Terrorist attacks were threatening to destabilize the government.* ➲ look at **stabilize**

destination /ˌdestɪ'neɪʃn/ *noun* [C] the place where sb/sth is going □ *destinasi*: *I finally reached my destination two hours late.* ♦ *popular holiday destinations like the Bahamas*

destined /'destɪnd/ *adj* **1 destined for sth/to do sth** having a future that has been decided or planned at an earlier time □ *ditakdirkan*: *I think she is destined for success.* ♦ *He was destined to become one of the country's leading politicians.* **2 destined for ...** travelling towards a particular place □ *menuju ke*: *I boarded a bus destined for New York.*

destiny /ˈdestəni/ noun (pl **destinies**) 1 [C] the things that happen to you in your life, especially things that you cannot control □ *nasib; untung; takdir*: She felt that it was her destiny to be a great singer. 2 [U] a power that people believe controls their lives □ *takdir* **SYN** for both meanings **fate**

destitute /ˈdestɪtjuːt/ adj without any money, food or a home □ *papa kedana; melarat* ▶ **destitution** /ˌdestɪˈtjuːʃn/ noun [U]

destroy /dɪˈstrɔɪ/ verb [T] 1 to damage sth so badly that it can no longer be used or no longer exists □ *memusnahkan; membinasakan*: The building was destroyed by fire. ◆ The defeat destroyed his confidence. 2 to kill an animal, especially because it is injured or dangerous □ *membunuh*: The horse broke its leg and had to be destroyed.

destroyer /dɪˈstrɔɪə(r)/ noun [C] 1 a small ship that is used in war □ *kapal pembinasa* 2 a person or thing that destroys sth □ *pembinasa; pemusnah*

destruction /dɪˈstrʌkʃn/ noun [U] the act of destroying sth □ *kemusnahan; pembinasaan*: The war brought death and destruction to the city. ◆ the destruction of the rainforests

destructive /dɪˈstrʌktɪv/ adj causing a lot of harm or damage □ *(yg) merosakkan/membinasakan; pembinasa*: destructive weapons ◆ the destructive effects of a poor diet

detach /dɪˈtætʃ/ verb [T] **detach sth (from sth)** to separate sth from sth it is connected to □ *menanggalkan; tanggalkan*: Detach the form at the bottom of the page and send it to this address … **OPP** **attach**

detachable /dɪˈtætʃəbl/ adj that can be separated from sth it is connected to □ *boleh ditanggalkan*: a coat with a detachable hood

detached /dɪˈtætʃt/ adj 1 (used about a house) not joined to any other house □ *(rumah) sebuah* ⊃ picture on **page P9** 2 not being or not feeling personally involved in sth; without emotion □ *tdk terlibat; berkecuali; tanpa emosi*

detachment /dɪˈtætʃmənt/ noun 1 [U] the fact or feeling of not being personally involved in sth □ *sikap berkecuali; sikap tdk beremosi* 2 [C] a group of soldiers who have been given a particular task away from the main group □ *detasmen; pasukan tentera yg diberi tugas khas*

detail¹ /ˈdiːteɪl/ noun [C,U] one fact or piece of information □ *butir-butir; perincian*: Just give me the basic facts. Don't worry about the details. ◆ On the application form you should give details of your education and experience. ◆ The work involves close attention to detail.
IDM **go into detail(s)** to talk or write about the details of sth; to explain sth fully □ *membincangkan secara terperinci; menjelaskan sepenuhnya*: I can't go into detail now because it would take too long.

in detail including the details □ *dgn terperinci; sepenuhnya*: We haven't discussed the matter in great detail yet. **SYN** **thoroughly**
▶ **detailed** adj: a detailed description

detail² /ˈdiːteɪl/ verb [T] to give a full list of sth; to describe sth completely □ *memperincikan*: He detailed all the equipment he needed for the job.

detain /dɪˈteɪn/ verb [T] to stop sb from leaving a place; to delay sb □ *menahan; melengahkan*: A man has been detained by the police for questioning (= kept at the police station). ◆ Don't let me detain you if you're busy. ⊃ look at **detention**

detainee /ˌdiːteɪˈniː/ noun [C] a person who is kept in prison, usually because of his or her political opinions □ *(orang) tahanan; tahanan politik*

detect /dɪˈtekt/ verb [T] to notice or discover sth that is difficult to see, feel, etc. □ *mengesan; menjumpai*: I detected a slight change in his attitude. ◆ Traces of blood were detected on his clothes. ▶ **detection** noun [U]: The crime escaped detection (= was not discovered) for many years.

detective /dɪˈtektɪv/ noun [C] a person, especially a police officer, who tries to solve crimes □ *detektif; mata-mata gelap*

deˈtective story noun [C] a story about a crime in which sb tries to find out who the guilty person is □ *cerita detektif*

detector /dɪˈtektə(r)/ noun [C] a machine that is used for finding or noticing sth □ *pengesan*: a smoke/metal/lie detector

detention /dɪˈtenʃn/ noun [U,C] 1 the act of stopping a person leaving a place, especially by keeping them in prison □ *penahanan*: They were kept in detention for ten days. 2 the punishment of being kept at school for a time after other students have gone home □ *hukuman kena tahan di sekolah* ⊃ verb **detain**

deter /dɪˈtɜː(r)/ verb [T] (**deterring**; **deterred**) **deter sb (from doing sth)** to make sb decide not to do sth, especially by telling them that it would have bad results □ *menghalang*: The council is trying to deter visitors from bringing their cars into the city centre. ⊃ noun **deterrent**

detergent /dɪˈtɜːdʒənt/ noun [C,U] a chemical liquid or powder that is used for cleaning things □ *bahan pencuci; detergen*

deteriorate /dɪˈtɪəriəreɪt/ verb [I] to become worse □ *menjadi semakin buruk/teruk; merosot*: The political tension is deteriorating into civil war. ▶ **deterioration** /dɪˌtɪəriəˈreɪʃn/ noun [C,U]

determination /dɪˌtɜːmɪˈneɪʃn/ noun [U] 1 **determination (to do sth)** the quality of having firmly decided to do sth, even if it is very difficult □ *keazaman; tekad*: her determination to win ◆ You need great determination to succeed in business. 2 (formal) the process of deciding sth officially □ *penentuan; penetapan*: the determination of future government policy

determine /dɪˈtɜːmɪn/ verb [T] (formal) 1 to discover the facts about sth □ *menentukan; memastikan*: We need to determine what *happened immediately before the accident.* **2** to make sth happen in a particular way or be of a particular type □ *menentukan*: *The results of the tests will determine what treatment you need.* ◆ *Age and experience will be determining factors in our choice of candidate.* **3** to decide sth officially □ *menentukan; menetapkan*: *A date for the meeting has yet to be determined.*

determined /dɪˈtɜːmɪnd/ *adj* **determined (to do sth)** having firmly decided to do sth or to succeed, even if it is difficult □ *berazam*: *He is determined to leave school, even though his parents want him to stay.* ◆ *She's a very determined athlete.*

determiner /dɪˈtɜːmɪnə(r)/ *noun* [C] a word that comes before a noun to show how the noun is being used □ *kata penentu*: *'Her', 'most' and 'those' are all determiners.*

deterrent /dɪˈterənt/ *noun* [C] something that should stop you doing sth □ *pencegahan*: *Their punishment will be a deterrent to others.* ⊃ *verb* **deter** ▶ **deterrent** *adj*

detest /dɪˈtest/ *verb* [T] to hate or not like sb/sth at all □ *membenci; sangat membenci*: *They absolutely detest each other.* **SYN** **loathe**

detonate /ˈdetəneɪt/ *verb* [I,T] to explode or to make a bomb, etc. explode □ *meletup; meletupkan*

detonator /ˈdetəneɪtə(r)/ *noun* [C] a device for making a bomb explode □ *(bom) peledak; peletup; peletus*

detour /ˈdiːtʊə(r)/ *noun* [C] **1** a longer route from one place to another that you take in order to avoid sth/sb or in order to see or do sth □ *lencongan*: *Because of the accident we had to make a five-kilometre detour.* **2** (*AmE*) = **diversion** (3)

detox /ˈdiːtɒks/ *noun* [U] (*informal*) **1** the process of removing harmful substances from your body by only eating and drinking particular things □ *detoks* **2** = **detoxification** ▶ **detoxify** /ˌdiːˈtɒksɪfaɪ/ *verb* [I,T]

detoxification /ˌdiːˌtɒksɪfɪˈkeɪʃn/ (also *informal* **detox**) *noun* [U] treatment given to people to help them stop drinking alcohol or taking drugs □ *penyahtoksikan*

detract /dɪˈtrækt/ *verb* [I] **detract from sth** to make sth seem less good or important □ *mengurangkan*: *These criticisms in no way detract from the team's achievements.*

detriment /ˈdetrɪmənt/ *noun*

IDM **to the detriment of sb/sth** harming or damaging sb/sth □ *menjejaskan sso/sst*: *Doctors claim that the changes will be to the detriment of patients.* ▶ **detrimental** /ˌdetrɪˈmentl/ *adj*: *Too much sugar is detrimental to your health.*

deuce /djuːs/ *noun* [U] a score of 40 points to each player in a game of **tennis** □ *dius*

devalue /ˌdiːˈvæljuː/ *verb* [T] **1** to reduce the value of the money of one country in relation to the value of the money of other countries □ *menurunkan nilai*: *The pound has been devalued against the dollar.* **2** to reduce the

239 determined → development

value or importance of sth □ *memperkecil; mengurangkan taraf*: *The refusal of the top players to take part devalues this competition.* ▶ **devaluation** /ˌdiːˌvæljuˈeɪʃn/ *noun* [U]

devastate /ˈdevəsteɪt/ *verb* [T] **1** to destroy sth or damage it badly □ *memusnahkan; dimusnahkan*: *a land devastated by war* **2** to make sb extremely upset and shocked □ *terkejut besar dan menyedihkan*: *This tragedy has devastated the community.* ▶ **devastation** /ˌdevəˈsteɪʃn/ *noun* [U]: *a scene of total devastation*

devastated /ˈdevəsteɪtɪd/ *adj* extremely shocked and upset □ *sangat terkejut dan sedih*: *They were devastated when their baby died.*

devastating /ˈdevəsteɪtɪŋ/ *adj* **1** that destroys sth completely □ *yg mengakibatkan kemusnahan teruk*: *a devastating explosion* **2** that shocks or upsets sb very much □ *yg amat mengejutkan*: *The closure of the factory was a devastating blow to the workers.*

develop /dɪˈveləp/ *verb*
▶GROW **1** [I,T] to grow slowly, increase, or change into sth else; to make sb/sth do this □ *berkembang; mengembangkan; membesar; menghasilkan*: *to develop from a child into an adult* ◆ *a scheme to help pupils develop their natural talents* ◆ *Scientists have developed crops that are resistant to disease.* ◆ *Over the years, she's developed her own unique singing style.*
▶PROBLEM/DISEASE **2** [I,T] to begin to have a problem or disease; to start to affect sth □ *mendapat; bermula*: *to develop cancer/AIDS* ◆ *Trouble is developing along the border.*
▶BUILD HOUSES **3** [T] to build houses, shops, factories, etc. on a piece of land □ *membangunkan; memajukan*: *This site is being developed for offices.*
▶IDEA/STORY **4** [T] to make an idea, a story, etc. clearer or more detailed by writing or talking about it more □ *mengembangkan*: *She went on to develop this theme later in the lecture.*
▶PHOTOGRAPHS **5** [T] to make pictures from a piece of film by using special chemicals □ *mencuci filem*: *to develop a film*

developed /dɪˈveləpt/ *adj* of a good level or standard □ *maju*: *a highly developed economy*

developer /dɪˈveləpə(r)/ (also **property developer**) *noun* [C] a person or company that builds houses, shops, etc. on a piece of land □ *pemaju*

developing /dɪˈveləpɪŋ/ *adj* [only before a noun] (used about a poor country) that is trying to develop or improve its economy □ *(yg) membangun*: *a developing country* ◆ *the developing world*

development /dɪˈveləpmənt/ *noun* **1** [U] the process of becoming bigger, stronger, better, etc., or of making sb/sth do this □ *kemajuan*: *a child's intellectual development* ◆ *the development of tourism in Cuba* **2** [U,C] the process of creating sth more advanced; a more advanced product

deviate → diagram 240

□ *pembangunan*: She works in **research and development** for a software company. ◆ the latest developments in space technology **3** [C] a new event that changes a situation □ *perkembangan*: This week has seen a number of new developments in the Middle East. **4** [C,U] a piece of land with new buildings on it; the process of building on a piece of land □ *pembangunan*: a new housing development ◆ The land has been bought for development.

deviate /ˈdiːvieɪt/ *verb* [I] **deviate (from sth)** to change or become different from what is normal or expected □ *menyimpang; menyeleweng*: He never once deviated from his original plan.

deviation /ˌdiːviˈeɪʃn/ *noun* [C,U] a difference from what is normal or expected, or from what is approved of by society □ *penyimpangan; penyelewengan*: a deviation from our usual way of doing things

device /dɪˈvaɪs/ *noun* [C] **1** a tool or piece of equipment made for a particular purpose □ *peranti*: a security device which detects any movement ◆ labour-saving devices such as washing machines and vacuum cleaners ⊃ note at **tool 2** a clever method for getting the result you want □ *cara; muslihat*: Critics dismissed the speech as a political device for winning support.

devil /ˈdevl/ *noun* [C] **1 the Devil** the most powerful evil being, according to the Christian, Jewish and Muslim religions □ *Iblis* ⊃ look at **Satan 2** an evil being; a spirit □ *syaitan; hantu* **3** (*spoken*) a word used to show pity, anger, etc. when you are talking about a person □ *orang yg (dikasihani, nakal dll)*: The poor devil died in hospital two days later. ◆ Those kids can be little devils sometimes.
IDM **be a devil** used to encourage sb to do sth that they are not sure about doing □ *digunakan sebagai ungkapan menggalak*: Go on, be a devil—buy both of them.
speak/talk of the devil used when the person who is being talked about appears unexpectedly □ *panjang umur*

devious /ˈdiːviəs/ *adj* clever but not honest or direct □ *licik; tdk jujur*: I wouldn't trust him—he can be very devious. ◆ a devious trick/plan ▶ **deviously** *adv*

devise /dɪˈvaɪz/ *verb* [T] to invent a new way of doing sth □ *merekakan; mencipta*: They've devised a plan for keeping traffic out of the city centre.

devoid /dɪˈvɔɪd/ *adj* (*formal*) **devoid of sth** not having a particular quality; without sth □ *tdk mempunyai; tanpa*: devoid of hope/ambition/imagination

devolution /ˌdiːvəˈluːʃn/ *noun* [U] the movement of political power from central to local government □ *pemindahan kuasa*

devote /dɪˈvəʊt/ *verb* [T] **devote yourself/sth to sb/sth** to give a lot of time, energy, etc. to sb/sth □ *menumpukan; memberi*: She gave up work to devote herself full-time to her music. ◆ Schools should devote more time to science subjects.

devoted /dɪˈvəʊtɪd/ *adj* **devoted (to sb/sth)** loving sb/sth very much; completely loyal to sb/sth □ *sangat menyayangi; setia*: Neil's absolutely devoted to his wife.

devotee /ˌdevəˈtiː/ *noun* [C] **a devotee (of sb/sth)** a person who likes sb/sth very much □ *peminat; pemuja*: Devotees of science fiction will enjoy this new film.

devotion /dɪˈvəʊʃn/ *noun* [U] **devotion (to sb/sth) 1** great love for sb/sth □ *kasih sayang*: a mother's devotion to her children **SYN** dedication **2** the act of giving a lot of your time, energy, etc. to sb/sth □ *kebaktian; penumpuan*: devotion to duty **SYN** dedication **3** very strong religious feeling □ *kesolehan*

devour /dɪˈvaʊə(r)/ *verb* [T] **1** to eat sth quickly because you are very hungry □ *melahap* **2** to do or use sth quickly and completely □ *membuat atau melakukan sst dgn rakus*: Lisa devours two or three novels a week.

devout /dɪˈvaʊt/ *adj* very religious □ *soleh; warak*: a devout Muslim family ▶ **devoutly** *adv*

dew /djuː/ *noun* [U] small drops of water that form on plants, leaves, etc. during the night □ *embun*

dexterity /dekˈsterəti/ *noun* [U] skill at doing things, especially with your hands □ *kecekatan*

diabetes /ˌdaɪəˈbiːtiːz/ *noun* [U] a serious disease in which sb's body cannot control the level of sugar in the blood □ *kencing manis*

diabetic¹ /ˌdaɪəˈbetɪk/ *adj* connected with **diabetes** or **diabetics** □ *(berkenaan dgn) kencing manis*: diabetic chocolate (= safe for diabetics)

diabetic² /ˌdaɪəˈbetɪk/ *noun* [C] a person who suffers from **diabetes** □ *pesakit kencing manis*

diagnose /ˈdaɪəgnəʊz/ *verb* [T] **diagnose sth (as sth); diagnose sb as/with sth** to find out and say exactly what illness a person has or what the cause of a problem is □ *mendiagnosiskan*: His illness was diagnosed as bronchitis. ◆ I've been diagnosed as (a) diabetic/with diabetes. ◆ After a couple of minutes I diagnosed the trouble—a flat battery.

diagnosis /ˌdaɪəgˈnəʊsɪs/ *noun* [C,U] (*pl* **diagnoses** /-siːz/) the act of saying exactly what illness a person has or what the cause of a problem is □ *diagnosis*: to make a diagnosis

diagnostic /ˌdaɪəgˈnɒstɪk/ *adj* (*technical*) connected with identifying sth, especially an illness □ *diagnostik*: to carry out diagnostic tests

diagonal /daɪˈægənl/ *adj* (used about a straight line) joining two sides of sth at an angle that is not 90° or vertical or horizontal □ *pepenjuru*: Draw a diagonal line from one corner of the square to the opposite corner. ⊃ picture at **line** ▶ **diagonally** /-nəli/ *adv*

diagram /ˈdaɪəɡræm/ *noun* [C] a simple picture that is used to explain how sth works or what sth looks like □ *gambar rajah*: a diagram of the body's digestive system

[I] **intransitive**, a verb which has no object: *He laughed.* [T] **transitive**, a verb which has an object: *He ate an apple.*

dial¹ /ˈdaɪəl/ noun [C] **1** the round part of a clock, watch, control on a machine, etc. that shows a measurement of time, amount, temperature, etc □ *muka jam; dail*: *a dial for showing air pressure* **2** the round control on a radio, cooker, etc. that you turn to change sth □ *dail* **3** the round part with holes in it on some older telephones that you turn to call a number □ *dail*

dial² /ˈdaɪəl/ verb [I,T] (**dialling**; **dialled**, (AmE) **dialing**; **dialed**) to push the buttons or move the **dial** on a telephone in order to call a telephone number □ *mendail*: *You can now dial direct to Singapore.* ♦ *to dial the wrong number*

dialect /ˈdaɪəlekt/ noun [C,U] a form of a language that is spoken in one part of a country □ *loghat; dialek*: *a local dialect*

ˈdialog box (BRE ALSO ˈdialogue box) noun [C] a box that appears on a computer screen asking the user to choose what they want to do next □ *kotak dialog*

dialogue (AmE **dialog**) /ˈdaɪəlɒg (AmE usually) / noun [C,U] **1** (a) conversation between people in a book, play, etc. □ *dialog; perbualan*: *This movie is all action, with very little dialogue.* ♦ *On the tape you will hear a short dialogue between a shop assistant and a customer.* **2** (a) discussion between people who have different opinions □ *dialog; perbincangan*: *(a) dialogue between the major political parties*

diameter /daɪˈæmɪtə(r)/ noun [C] a straight line that goes from one side to the other of a circle, passing through the centre □ *diameter; garis pusat* ⊃ look at **circumference**, **radius** ⊃ picture at **circle**

diamond /ˈdaɪəmənd/ noun **1** [C,U] a hard, bright **precious** (= rare and valuable) stone which is very expensive and is used for making jewellery. A diamond usually has no colour □ *berlian*: *a diamond ring* **2** (also **lozenge**) [C] a flat shape that has four sides of equal length and points at two ends □ *bentuk potong wajik* ⊃ picture at **shape 3 diamonds** [pl] in a pack of playing cards, the **suit** (= one of the four sets) with red shapes like diamonds(2) on them □ *daiman*: *the seven of diamonds* ⊃ note at **card** ⊃ picture at **card 4** [C] one of the cards from this suit □ *daiman*: *I haven't got any diamonds.* **5** [U] celebrating the 60th anniversary of sth □ *ulang tahun ke-60*: *This year's their diamond wedding.* ⊃ look at **golden**, **silver**

diaper /ˈdaɪəpə(r)/ (AmE) = **nappy**

diaphragm /ˈdaɪəfræm/ noun [C] **1** the muscle between your lungs and your stomach that helps you to breathe □ *diafragma* **2** a rubber device that a woman puts inside her body before having sex to prevent her from becoming pregnant □ *diafragma*

diarrhoea (AmE **diarrhea**) /ˌdaɪəˈrɪə/ noun [U] an illness that causes you to get rid of **faeces** (= solid waste) from your body very often and in a more liquid form than usual □ *cirit-birit; diarea*

diary /ˈdaɪəri/ noun [C] (pl **diaries**) **1** a book in which you write down things that you have to do, remember, etc. □ *diari; buku harian*: *I'll just check in my diary to see if I'm free that weekend.* ⊃ note at **calendar 2** a book in which you write down what happens to you each day □ *diari*: *Do you keep a diary?*

dice /daɪs/ noun [C] (pl **dice**) a small solid square object with six sides and a different number of spots (from one to six) on each side, used in certain games □ *dadu*: *Throw the dice to see who goes first.*

dice

dictate /dɪkˈteɪt/ verb **1** [I,T] **dictate (sth) (to sb)** to say sth in a normal speaking voice so that sb else can write or type it □ *merencanakan; mengimlakkan*: *to dictate a letter to a secretary* **2** [I,T] **dictate (sth) (to sb)** to tell sb what to do in a way that seems unfair □ *mengarahkan*: *Parents can't dictate to their children how they should run their lives.* **3** [T] to control or influence sth □ *menentukan; ditentukan*: *The kind of house people live in is usually dictated by how much they earn.*

dictation /dɪkˈteɪʃn/ noun [C,U] spoken words that sb else must write or type □ *imlak*: *We had a dictation in English today* (= a test in which we had to write down what the teacher said).

dictator /dɪkˈteɪtə(r)/ noun [C] a ruler who has total power in a country, especially one who rules the country by force □ *diktator* ▶ **dictatorship** noun [C,U]: *a military dictatorship* ▶ **dictatorial** /ˌdɪktəˈtɔːriəl/ adj: *dictatorial behaviour*

dictionary /ˈdɪkʃənri/ noun [C] (pl **dictionaries**) **1** a book that contains a list of the words in a language in the order of the alphabet and that tells you what they mean, in the same or another language □ *kamus*: *to look up a word in a dictionary* ♦ *a bilingual/monolingual dictionary* **2** a book that lists the words connected with a particular subject and tells you what they mean □ *kamus*: *a dictionary of idioms* ♦ *a medical dictionary* ⊃ note at **book**

did /dɪd/ past tense of **do**

didn't /ˈdɪdnt/ short for **did not**

die /daɪ/ verb (**dying**; **dies**; pt, pp **died**) **1** [I,T] **die (from/of sth)** to stop living □ *mati*: *My father died when I was three.* ♦ *Thousands of people have died from this disease.* ♦ *to die of hunger* ♦ *to die for what you believe in* ♦ *to die a natural/violent death* ⊃ adjective **dead**, noun **death 2** [I] to stop existing; to disappear □ *luput; lenyap*: *The old customs are dying.* ♦ *Our love will never die.*

IDM **be dying for sth/to do sth** (spoken) to want sth/to do sth very much □ *ingin sangat akan sst/membuat sst*: *I'm dying for a cup of coffee.*

| CONSONANTS | p **p**en | b **b**ad | t **t**ea | d **d**id | k **c**at | g **g**ot | tʃ **ch**in | dʒ **J**une | f **f**all | v **v**an | θ **th**in |

die hard to change or disappear only slowly or with difficulty □ *sukar berubah; sukar utk ditinggalkan*: *Old attitudes towards women die hard.*

die laughing to find sth very funny □ *ketawa setengah mati*: *I thought I'd die laughing when he told that joke.*

to die for (*informal*) if you think that sth is to die for, you really want it and would do anything to get it □ *amat diingini; cukup bagus*: *She was wearing a dress to die for.*

PHR V die away to slowly become weaker before stopping or disappearing □ *semakin lemah/perlahan*: *The sound of the engine died away as the car drove into the distance.*

die down to slowly become less strong □ *mengurang; mereda*: *Let's wait until the storm dies down before we go out.*

die off to die one by one until there are none left □ *mati satu per satu*

die out to stop happening or disappear □ *pupus; lenyap*: *The use of horses on farms has almost died out in this country.*

diesel /ˈdiːzl/ *noun* **1** [U] a type of heavy oil used in some engines instead of petrol □ *diesel*: *a diesel engine* ◆ *a taxi that runs on diesel* **2** [C] a vehicle that uses **diesel** □ *kenderaan diesel*: *My new car's a diesel.* ⊃ look at **petrol**

ᵩ diet¹ /ˈdaɪət/ *noun* **1** [C,U] the food that a person or an animal usually eats □ *makanan*: *They live on a diet of rice and vegetables.* ◆ *I always try to have a healthy, balanced diet* (= including all the different types of food that the body needs). ◆ *Poor diet is a cause of ill health.* **2** [C] certain foods that a person who is ill or who wants to lose weight is allowed to eat □ *diet*: *a low-fat diet* ◆ *a sugar-free diet*

IDM be/go on a diet to eat only certain foods or a small amount of food because you want to lose weight □ *berdiet*

▶ **dietary** /ˈdaɪətəri/ *adj*: *dietary habits/requirements*

diet² /ˈdaɪət/ *verb* [I] to try to lose weight by eating less food or only certain kinds of food □ *berdiet; menjaga makan*: *You've lost some weight. Have you been dieting?*

differ /ˈdɪfə(r)/ *verb* [I] **1 differ (from sb/sth)** to be different □ *berbeza*: *How does this car differ from the more expensive model?* **2 differ (with sb) (about/on sth)** to have a different opinion □ *tdk sependapat*: *I'm afraid I differ with you on that question.*

ᵩ difference /ˈdɪfrəns/ *noun* **1** [C] **a difference (between A and B)** the way that people or things are not the same or the way that sb/sth has changed □ *perbezaan*: *What's the difference between this computer and that cheaper one?* ◆ *From a distance it's hard to **tell the difference** between the twins.* **OPP** **similarity 2** [C,U] **difference (in sth) (between A and B)** the amount by which people or things are not the same or by which sb/sth has changed □ *perbezaan; beza*: *There's an age difference of three years between the two children.* ◆ *There's very little difference in price since last year.* ◆ *We gave a 30% deposit and must **pay the difference** when the work is finished* (= the rest of the money). **3** [C] a disagreement that is not very serious □ *perselisihan/perbezaan pendapat*: *All couples **have** their **differences** from time to time.* ◆ *There was a **difference of opinion** over how much we owed.*

IDM make a, some, etc. difference (to sb/sth) to have an effect (on sb/sth) □ *mendatangkan kesan; membawa perubahan*: *Marriage made a big difference to her life.*

make no difference (to sb/sth); not make any difference to not be important (to sb/sth); to have no effect □ *tdk ada bezanya*: *It makes no difference to us if the baby is a girl or a boy.*

split the difference ⊃ **split¹**

WRITING TIP

How to compare different things

To show how two things, people, etc. are different, we can use comparative adjectives: *Australia is bigger than England.* ◆ *Enthusiasm is more important than experience.* You can also use the following expressions; **Unlike X, Y ...** : *Unlike Jim, Mike likes playing sports* (= Mike likes playing sports, but Jim does not), **X is different from Y (in that) ...** : *A tablet computer is different from a laptop in that a tablet has a touchscreen* (= a tablet has a touchscreen, but a laptop does not), **While X ..., Y ...** : *While Brian enjoys going out with his friends, Simon prefers to stay at home* or **X ..., while Y ...** : *Brian enjoys going out with his friends, while Simon prefers to stay at home* (= Brian is very sociable, but Simon is not).

⊃ note at **similarity** ❶ For more help with writing, look at **Wordpower Writing Tutor** at the back of this dictionary.

ᵩ different /ˈdɪfrənt/ *adj* **1 different (from/to sb/sth)** not the same □ *berbeza; berlainan*: *The play was different from anything I had seen before.* ◆ *The two houses are very different in style.* ◆ *You'd look completely different with short hair.* ◆ *When Ulf started school in this country, the other kids were cruel to him because he was different.* **OPP** **similar**

HELP In American English **different than** is also used.

2 [only *before* a noun] separate; individual □ *lain*: *This coat is available in three different colours.*

IDM another/a different matter ⊃ **matter¹**
a (whole) new/different ball game ⊃ **ball game**

▶ **differently** *adv*: *I think you'll feel differently about it tomorrow.*

differentiate /ˌdɪfəˈrenʃieɪt/ *verb* **1** [I,T] **differentiate between A and B; differentiate A (from B)** to see or show how things are different □ *membezakan*: *It is hard to differentiate between these two types of seed.* **2** [T] **differentiate sth (from sth)** to make one thing different from another □ *membezakan*: *The coloured feathers differentiate the male bird from the plain brown female.* **3** [T] to treat one person or group differently from another □ *membeza-bezakan*: *We don't differentiate between the two groups—we treat everybody alike.* **SYN** distinguish ▸ differentiation /ˌdɪfəˌrenʃiˈeɪʃn/ *noun* [U]

difficult /ˈdɪfɪkəlt/ *adj* **1** difficult (for sb) (to do sth) not easy to do or understand □ *susah; sukar; payah*: *a difficult test/problem* ♦ *I find it difficult to get up early in the morning.* ♦ *It was difficult for us to hear the speaker.* ♦ *I'm in a difficult situation. Whatever I do, somebody will be upset.* **2** (used about a person) not friendly, reasonable or helpful □ *cerewet; sukar*: *a difficult customer* **SYN** awkward

difficulty /ˈdɪfɪkəlti/ *noun* (*pl* difficulties) **1** [U,C] difficulty (in sth/in doing sth) a problem; a situation that is hard to deal with □ *kesusahan; kesukaran; kesulitan; susah payah*: *I'm sure you won't have any difficulty getting a visa for America.* ♦ *We had no difficulty selling our car.* ♦ *We found a hotel without difficulty.* ♦ *With difficulty, I managed to persuade Alice to lend us the money.* ♦ *I could see someone in difficulty in the water so I went to help them.* ♦ *If you borrow too much money you may get into financial difficulties.* **2** [U] how hard sth is to do or to deal with □ *kesukaran; sukar*: *The questions start easy and then increase in difficulty.*

diffident /ˈdɪfɪdənt/ *adj* not having confidence in your own strengths or abilities □ *malu-malu; kurang keyakinan diri*: *He has a very diffident manner.* ▸ diffidence *noun* [U]

dig¹ /dɪɡ/ *verb* [I,T] (digging; *pt, pp* dug /dʌɡ/) to move earth and make a hole in the ground □ *menggali*: *The children are busy digging in the sand.* ♦ *to dig a hole*
IDM dig deep to try harder, give more, go further, etc. than is usually necessary □ *mencuba/memberi/mencari lebih drpd biasa*: *Charities for the homeless are asking people to dig deep into their pockets in this cold weather.*
dig your heels in to refuse to do sth or to change your mind about sth □ *tdk berganjak; enggan beralah/membuat sst*: *The union dug its heels in and waited for a better pay offer.*
PHR V dig (sth) in; dig sth into sth to push or press (sth) into sb/sth □ *menekan sst; memasukkan sst ke dlm sst*: *My neck is all red where my collar is digging in.* ♦ *He dug his hands deep into his pockets.*

spade — dig

dig sb/sth out (of sth) **1** to get sb/sth out of sth by moving the earth, etc. that covers them or it □ *menggali keluar sso/sst*: *Rescue workers dug the survivors out of the rubble.* **2** to get or find sb/sth by searching □ *mencari atau menemui sso/sst*: *I dug out some old photos from the attic.*
dig sth up **1** to remove sth from the earth by digging □ *menggali; mengorek*: *to dig up potatoes* **2** to make a hole or take away soil by digging □ *menggali*: *Workmen are digging up the road in front of our house.* **3** to find information by searching or studying □ *mengorek; mencungkil*: *Newspapers have dug up some embarrassing facts about his private life.*

dig² /dɪɡ/ [C], *noun* **1** a hard push □ (*perbuatan*) *menyiku/mencucuk*: *to give somebody a dig in the ribs* (= with your elbow) **2** something that you say to upset sb □ *sindiran*: *The others kept making digs at him because of the way he spoke.* **3** an occasion or a place where a group of people try to find things of historical or scientific interest in the ground in order to study them □ *penggalian*: *an archaeological dig*

digest /daɪˈdʒest/ *verb* [T] **1** to change food in your stomach so that it can be used by the body □ *menghadamkan; dihadam*: *I'm not going to go swimming until I've digested my lunch.* **2** to think about new information so that you understand it fully □ *memahami*: *The lecture was interesting, but too much to digest all at once.*

digestion /daɪˈdʒestʃən/ *noun* [C,U] the process of changing food in your stomach so that it can be used by the body □ *penghadaman* ▸ digestive /daɪˈdʒestɪv/ *adj*: *the digestive system*

digit /ˈdɪdʒɪt/ *noun* [C] any of the numbers from 0 to 9 □ *digit*: *a six-digit telephone number*

digital /ˈdɪdʒɪtl/ *adj* **1** using an electronic system that uses the numbers 1 and 0 to record sound or store information, and that gives results of a high quality □ *digital*: *a digital camera* ♦ *digital television/radio* **2** showing information by using numbers □ *digital; berdigit*: *a digital watch* ⊃ picture at **clock**

dignified /ˈdɪɡnɪfaɪd/ *adj* behaving in a calm, serious way that makes other people respect you □ *menimbulkan rasa hormat*: *dignified behaviour* **OPP** undignified

dignity /ˈdɪɡnəti/ *noun* [U] **1** calm, serious behaviour that makes other people respect you □ *maruah; martabat*: *to behave with dignity* **2** the quality of being serious and formal □ *sifat yg serius dan formal*: *the quiet dignity of the funeral service*

digress /daɪˈɡres/ *verb* [I] (*formal*) to stop talking or writing about the main subject under discussion and start talking or writing about another less important one □ *menyimpang* ▸ digression /daɪˈɡreʃn/ *noun* [C,U]

dike = dyke

dilapidated → dip

dilapidated /dɪˈlæpɪdeɪtɪd/ adj (used about buildings, furniture, etc.) old and broken ▫ *kopak-kapik* ▶ **dilapidation** /dɪˌlæpɪˈdeɪʃn/ noun [U]

dilate /daɪˈleɪt/ verb [I,T] to become or to make sth larger, wider or more open ▫ *mengembang; menjadi luas*: Her eyes dilated with fear. ♦ dilated pupils/nostrils **OPP** contract ▶ **dilation** /daɪˈleɪʃn/ noun [U]

dilemma /dɪˈlemə/ noun [C] a situation in which you have to make a difficult choice between two or more things ▫ *dilema; keadaan serba salah*: Doctors **face a** moral **dilemma** of when to keep patients alive artificially and when to let them die. ♦ to be in a dilemma

diligent /ˈdɪlɪdʒənt/ adj (formal) showing care and effort in your work or duties ▫ *rajin; tekun; teliti*: a diligent student/worker ▶ **diligently** adv

dilute /daɪˈluːt/ verb [T] **dilute sth (with sth)** to make a liquid weaker by adding water or another liquid ▫ *mencairkan* ▶ **dilute** adj

dim¹ /dɪm/ adj (**dimmer; dimmest**) **1** not bright or easy to see; not clear ▫ *malap; kabur; samar-samar*: The light was too dim to read by. ♦ a dim shape in the distance ♦ My memories of my grandmother are quite dim. **2** (informal) not very clever; stupid ▫ *bodoh*: He's a bit dim. **3** (informal) (used about a situation) without much hope ▫ *malap*: The prospects of the two sides reaching an agreement look dim. ▶ **dimly** adv

dim² /dɪm/ verb [I,T] (**dimming; dimmed**) to become or make sth less bright or clear ▫ *menjadi malap; memalapkan*: The lights dimmed. ♦ to dim the lights

dime /daɪm/ noun [C] a coin used in the US and Canada that is worth ten cents ▫ *sepuluh sen*

dimension /daɪˈmenʃn; dɪ-/ noun **1** [C,U] a measurement of the length, width or height of sth ▫ *ukuran* ♦ **dimensions** [pl] the size of sth including its length, width and height ▫ *dimensi; saiz*: to measure the dimensions of a room ♦ (figurative) The full dimensions of this problem are only now being recognized. **3** [C] something that affects the way you think about a problem or situation ▫ *dimensi; segi*: to add a new dimension to a problem/situation **4** -dimensional /-ʃənl/ [in compounds] having the number of **dimensions** mentioned ▫ *dimensi; matra*: a three-dimensional model

diminish /dɪˈmɪnɪʃ/ verb [I,T] (formal) to become or to make sth smaller or less important ▫ *mengurangkan; berkurang*: The world's rainforests are diminishing fast. ♦ The bad news did nothing to diminish her enthusiasm for the plan. **SYN** decrease

diminutive /dɪˈmɪnjətɪv/ adj (formal) much smaller than usual ▫ *kecil; kenit*

dimple /ˈdɪmpl/ noun [C] a round area in the skin on your cheek, etc. which often only appears when you smile ▫ *lesung pipit*

din /dɪn/ noun [sing] a lot of unpleasant noise that continues for some time ▫ *hingar-bingar; bunyi bising*

dine /daɪn/ verb [I] (formal) to eat a meal, especially in the evening ▫ *makan malam*: We dined at an exclusive French restaurant.
PHR V **dine out** to eat in a restaurant ▫ *makan malam di luar*

diner /ˈdaɪnə(r)/ noun [C] **1** a person who is eating at a restaurant ▫ *orang yg sedang makan di restoran* **2** (AmE) a restaurant that serves simple, cheap food ▫ *restoran kecil*

dinghy /ˈdɪŋi/ noun [C] (pl **dinghies**) **1** a small boat that you sail ▫ *perahu layar* ⊃ look at **yacht** **2** a small open boat, often used to take people to land from a larger boat ▫ *perahu kecil; dingi* ⊃ picture at **boat**

dingy /ˈdɪndʒi/ adj (**dingier; dingiest**) dirty and dark ▫ *kotor dan suram*: a dingy room/hotel

'dining room noun [C] a room where you eat meals ▫ *bilik makan* ⊃ picture on **page P8**

dinner /ˈdɪnə(r)/ noun **1** [C,U] the main meal of the day, eaten either at midday or in the evening ▫ *waktu makan utama; makan malam*: Would you like to **go out for/to dinner** one evening? ♦ I never eat a big dinner. ♦ What's for dinner, Mum? ⊃ note at **meal 2** [C] a formal occasion in the evening during which a meal is served ▫ *majlis makan malam*: The club is holding its annual dinner next week.

'dinner jacket (AmE **tuxedo**) noun [C] a black or white jacket that a man wears on formal occasions. A **dinner jacket** is usually worn with a **bow tie** (= a special kind of tie). ▫ *jaket makan malam*

dinosaur /ˈdaɪnəsɔː(r)/ noun [C] one of a number of very large animals that became **extinct** (= disappeared from the earth) millions of years ago ▫ *dinosaur*: dinosaur fossils

Dip abbr = **diploma**

dip¹ /dɪp/ verb (**dipping; dipped**) **1** [T] **dip sth (into sth); dip sth (in)** to put sth into liquid and immediately take it out again ▫ *mencelupkan*: Julie dipped her toe into the pool to see how cold it was. **2** [I,T] to go down or make sth go down to a lower level ▫ *menurun; menjunam*: The road suddenly dipped down to the river. ♦ Sales have dipped disastrously this year.
PHR V **dip into sth** **1** to use part of an amount of sth that you have ▫ *menggunakan simpanan*: Tim had to dip into his savings to pay for his new car. **2** to read parts, but not all, of sth ▫ *membaca sepintas lalu*: I've only dipped into the book. I haven't read it all the way through.

dip² /dɪp/ noun **1** [C] (informal) a short swim ▫ *berenang sekejap*: We went for a dip before breakfast. **2** [C] a fall to a lower level, especially for a short time ▫ *penurunan*: a dip in sales/

temperature **3** [C] an area of lower ground □ *cerun*: *The cottage was hidden in a dip in the hills.* **4** [C,U] a thick sauce into which you **dip** biscuits, vegetables, etc. before eating them □ *cecahan*: *a cheese/chilli dip*

diphtheria /dɪfˈθɪəriə (*AmE* also) / *noun* [U] a serious disease of the throat that makes it difficult to breathe □ *difteria*

diphthong /ˈdɪfθɒŋ; ˈdɪp-/ *noun* [C] two vowel sounds that are pronounced together to make one sound, for example the /aɪ/ sound in 'fine' □ *diftong*

diploma /dɪˈpləʊmə/ *noun* [C] (*abbr* Dip) a diploma (in sth) a certificate that you receive when you complete a course of study, often at a college □ *diploma*: *I'm studying for a diploma in hotel management.* ⊃ note at **degree**

diplomacy /dɪˈpləʊməsi/ *noun* [U] **1** the activity of managing relations between different countries □ *diplomasi*: *If diplomacy fails, there is a danger of war.* **2** skill in dealing with people without upsetting or offending them □ *diplomasi*: *He handled the tricky situation with tact and diplomacy.*

diplomat /ˈdɪpləmæt/ *noun* [C] an official who represents their country in a foreign country □ *diplomat*: *a diplomat at the embassy in Rome*

diplomatic /ˌdɪpləˈmætɪk/ *adj* **1** connected with **diplomacy**(1) □ *diplomatik*: *to break off diplomatic relations* **2** skilful at dealing with people □ *diplomatik; berdiplomasi*: *He searched for a diplomatic reply so as not to offend her.* **SYN** tactful ▶ **diplomatically** /-kli/ *adv*

dire /ˈdaɪə(r)/ *adj* (**direr; direst**) (*formal*) very bad or serious; terrible □ *dahsyat; teruk*: *dire consequences/poverty*
IDM **be in dire straits** to be in a very difficult situation □ *dlm kesulitan*: *The business is in dire straits financially and may go bankrupt.*

direct¹ /dəˈrekt; dɪ-; daɪ-/ *adj, adv* **1** with nobody/nothing in between; not involving anyone/anything else □ *terus; langsung*: *The British Prime Minister is in direct contact with the US President.* ◆ *a direct attack on the capital* ◆ *As a direct result of the new road, traffic jams in the centre have been reduced.* ◆ *You should protect your skin from direct sunlight.* **OPP** **indirect** **2** going from one place to another without turning or stopping; straight □ *terus*: *a direct flight to Hong Kong* ◆ *This bus goes direct to London.* **OPP** **indirect** **3** saying what you mean; clear □ *terus terang*: *She sometimes offends people with her direct way of speaking.* ◆ *Politicians never give a direct answer to a direct question.* **OPP** **indirect** **4** [only *before* a noun] complete; exact □ *betul-betul; sama sekali*: *What she did was in direct opposition to my orders.*

direct² /dəˈrekt; dɪ-; daɪ-/ *verb* [T] **1** direct sth to/towards sb/sth; direct sth at sb/sth to point or send sth towards sb/sth or in a particular direction □ *mengarahkan; menghalakan; menujukan*: *In recent weeks the media's atten-* tion has been directed towards events abroad. ◆ *The advert is directed at young people.* ◆ *The actor directed some angry words at a photographer.* **2** to manage or control sb/sth □ *mengarahkan; mengawal*: *A policeman was in the middle of the road, directing the traffic.* ◆ *to direct a play/film* **3** (*formal*) to tell or order sb to do sth □ *mengarahkan; menyuruh*: *Take the medicine as directed by your doctor.* **4** direct sb (to …) to tell or show sb how to get somewhere □ *mengarahkan; menyuruh*: *I was directed to an office at the end of the corridor.* ⊃ note at **lead¹**

di‚rect ˈdebit *noun* [C,U] an order to your bank that allows sb else to take a particular amount of money out of your account on certain dates □ *debit terus*

direction /dəˈrekʃn; dɪ-; daɪ-/ *noun* **1** [C,U] the path, line or way along which a person or thing is moving, looking, pointing, developing, etc. □ *arah; hala*: *A woman was seen running in the direction of the station.* ◆ *We met him coming in the opposite direction.* ◆ *I think the new speed limit is still too high, but it's a step in the right direction.* ◆ *I think the wind has changed direction.* ◆ *I've got such a hopeless sense of direction—I'm always getting lost.* **2** [C,U] a purpose; an aim □ *haluan*: *I want a career that gives me a (sense of) direction in life.* **3** [usually pl] information or instructions about how to do sth or how to get to a place □ *arahan*: *I'll give you directions to my house.* **4** [U] the act of managing or controlling sth □ *arahan; perihal mengetuai*: *This department is under the direction of Mrs Walters.*

TOPIC

Asking for and giving directions

Excuse me, is there a bank near here?

Can you tell me the way to the (nearest) station?

Turn right at the T-junction.

Turn left at the crossroads.

Go straight on at the traffic lights.

Take the third exit at the roundabout.

Take the second left.

It's on the right, next to the museum.

It's opposite the library.

You can't miss it!

---

directive /dəˈrektɪv; dɪ-; daɪ-/ *noun* [C] an official order to do sth □ *arahan rasmi*: *an EU directive on safety at work*

directly¹ /dəˈrektli; dɪ-; daɪ-/ *adv* **1** in a direct line or way □ *secara langsung; betul-betul*: *The bank is directly opposite the supermarket.* ◆ *He refused to answer my question directly.* ◆ *Lung cancer is directly related to smoking.* **2** immediately; very soon □ *segera; sebentar lagi*: *Wait where you are. I'll be back directly.*

directly² /dəˈrektli; dɪ-; daɪ-/ conj as soon as □ *sebaik sahaja*: I phoned him directly I heard the news.

diˌrect ˈobject noun [C] a noun or phrase that is affected by the act of a verb □ *objek langsung*: In the sentence 'Anna bought a record', 'a record' is the direct object. ⊃ look at **indirect object** ❶ For more information about direct objects, look at the **Reference Section** at the back of this dictionary.

director /dəˈrektə(r); dɪ-; daɪ-/ noun [C] **1** a person who manages or controls a company or an organization □ *pengarah*: the managing director of Rolls Royce ♦ She's on the board of directors (= the group of directors) of a large computer company. **2** a person who is responsible for a particular activity or department in a company, a college, etc. □ *pengarah*: He's the director of studies of a language school. **3** a person who tells the actors, etc. what to do in a film, play, etc. □ *pengarah*: a film/theatre director

directory /dəˈrektəri; dɪ-; daɪ-/ noun [C] (pl **directories**) **1** a list of names, addresses and telephone numbers in the order of the alphabet □ *buku panduan*: the telephone directory ♦ I tried to look up Joe's number but he's ex-directory (= he has chosen not to be listed in the telephone directory). **2** a file containing a group of other files or programs in a computer □ *direktori*

diˌrect ˈspeech noun [U] the actual words that a person said □ *cakap ajuk* ⊃ look at **reported speech** ❶ For more information about direct speech, look at the **Reference Section** at the back of this dictionary.

dirt /dɜːt/ noun [U] **1** a substance that is not clean, such as dust or mud □ *kotoran*: His face and hands were covered in dirt. **2** earth or soil □ *tanah*: a dirt track **3** damaging information about sb □ *maklumat yg boleh menjelaskan nama baik sso*: The press are always trying to **dig up dirt** on the minister's love life.
IDM **dirt cheap** extremely cheap □ *sangat murah*

dirty¹ /ˈdɜːti/ adj (**dirtier**; **dirtiest**) **1** not clean □ *kotor*: Your hands are dirty. Go and wash them! ♦ Gardening is dirty work (= it makes you dirty). **OPP** **clean** **2** referring to sex in a way that may upset or offend people □ *lucah; kotor*: to tell a dirty joke **3** unpleasant or dishonest □ *tdk jujur; keji*: He's a dirty player. ♦ I'm not going to tell her you don't want to go. You **do** your own **dirty work**.
IDM **a dirty word** an idea or thing that you do not like or agree with □ *sst yg tdk disukai*: Work is a dirty word to Frank.
play dirty (*informal*) to behave or to play a game in an unfair or a dishonest way □ *mengelat; main kotor*
▶ **dirty** adv

dirty² /ˈdɜːti/ verb [I,T] (**dirtying**; **dirties**; pt, pp **dirtied**) to become or to make sth dirty □ *menjadi kotor; mengotorkan* **OPP** **clean**

disability /ˌdɪsəˈbɪləti/ noun (pl **disabilities**) **1** [C] something that makes you unable to use a part of your body properly □ *kecacatan; ketakupayaan*: Because of his disability, he needs constant care. **2** [U] the state of being unable to use a part of your body properly, usually because of injury or disease □ *kehilangan upaya; kecacatan*: physical/mental disability

disable /dɪsˈeɪbl/ verb [T, often passive] to make sb unable to use part of their body properly, usually because of injury or disease □ *hilang upaya; menjadi cacat*: Many soldiers were disabled in the war.

disabled /dɪsˈeɪbld/ adj **1** unable to use a part of your body properly □ *cacat; hilang upaya*: A car accident left her permanently disabled. **2** **the disabled** noun [pl] people who are **disabled** □ *orang cacat*: The hotel has improved facilities for the disabled.

disadvantage /ˌdɪsədˈvɑːntɪdʒ/ noun [C] **1** something that may make you less successful than other people □ *kekurangan; kelemahan*: Your qualifications are good. Your main disadvantage is your lack of experience. **2** something that is not good or that causes problems □ *keburukan*: The main disadvantage of the job is the long hours. ♦ What are the advantages and disadvantages of nuclear power? **OPP** for both meanings **advantage**
IDM **put sb/be at a disadvantage** to put sb or be in a situation where they or you may be less successful than other people □ *merugikan; menyukarkan*: The fact that you don't speak the language will put you at a disadvantage in France.
to sb's disadvantage (*formal*) not good or helpful for sb □ *merugikan*: The agreement will be to your disadvantage—don't accept it.

disadvantaged /ˌdɪsədˈvɑːntɪdʒd/ adj in a bad social or economic situation; poor □ *yg kurang bernasib baik*: disadvantaged groups/children

disadvantageous /ˌdɪsædvɑːnˈteɪdʒəs/ adj causing sb to be in a worse situation compared to other people □ *(yg) merugikan*

disagree /ˌdɪsəˈɡriː/ verb [I] **1** **disagree (with sb/sth) (about/on sth)** to have a different opinion from sb/sth; to not agree □ *berlainan pendapat; tdk bersetuju*: Stephen often disagrees with his father about politics. ♦ They strongly disagreed with my idea. ♦ 'We have to tell him.' 'No, I disagree. I don't think we should tell him at all.' **2** to be different □ *berlainan*: These two sets of statistics disagree. **OPP** for both meanings **agree**
PHRV **disagree with sb** (used about sth you have eaten or drunk) to make you feel ill; to have a bad effect on you □ *tdk sesuai/serasi*

disagreeable /ˌdɪsəˈɡriːəbl/ adj (*formal*) unpleasant □ *tdk menyenangkan* **OPP** **agreeable**
▶ **disagreeably** /-əbli/ adv

disagreement /ˌdɪsəˈɡriːmənt/ noun [C,U] **disagreement (with sb) (about/on/over sth)** a situation in which people have a different opinion about sth and often also argue □ *pertelingkahan; perselisihan pendapat*: *It's normal for couples to have disagreements.* ◆ *Mandy resigned after a disagreement with her boss.* ◆ *The conference ended in disagreement.* **OPP** agreement

disallow /ˌdɪsəˈlaʊ/ *verb* [T] to not allow or accept sth □ *tdk membenarkan/menolak*: *The goal was disallowed because the player was offside.*

disappear /ˌdɪsəˈpɪə(r)/ *verb* [I] **1** to become impossible to see or to find □ *hilang*: *He walked away and disappeared into a crowd of people.* ◆ *My purse was here a moment ago and now it's disappeared.* **2** to stop existing □ *lenyap; pupus*: *Plant and animal species are disappearing at an alarming rate.* **SYN** for both meanings **vanish** **OPP** for both meanings **appear** ▶ **disappearance** *noun* [C,U]: *The mystery of her disappearance was never solved.*

disappoint /ˌdɪsəˈpɔɪnt/ *verb* [T] to make sb sad because what they had hoped for has not happened or is less good, interesting, etc. than they had hoped □ *mengecewakan; menghampakan*: *I'm sorry to disappoint you but I'm afraid you haven't won the prize.*

disappointed /ˌdɪsəˈpɔɪntɪd/ *adj* disappointed (about/at sth); disappointed (in/with sb/sth); disappointed that ... sad because you/ sb/sth did not succeed or because sth was not as good, interesting, etc. as you had hoped □ *kecewa*: *Lucy was deeply disappointed at not being chosen for the team.* ◆ *We were disappointed with our hotel.* ◆ *I'm disappointed in you. I thought you could do better.* ◆ *They are very disappointed that they can't stay longer.* ◆ *I was disappointed to hear that you can't come to the party.*

disappointing /ˌdɪsəˈpɔɪntɪŋ/ *adj* making you feel sad because sth was not as good, interesting, etc. as you had hoped □ *(yg) mengecewakan*: *It has been a disappointing year for the company.* ▶ **disappointingly** *adv*

disappointment /ˌdɪsəˈpɔɪntmənt/ *noun* **1** [U] the state of being disappointed □ *rasa kecewa*: *To his great disappointment he failed to get the job.* **2** [C] a disappointment (to sb) a person or thing that disappoints you □ *kekecewaan*: *She has suffered many disappointments in her career.*

disapproval /ˌdɪsəˈpruːvl/ *noun* [U] a feeling that sth is bad or that sb is behaving badly □ *rasa tdk suka/tdk berkenan*: *She shook her head in disapproval.*

disapprove /ˌdɪsəˈpruːv/ *verb* [I] disapprove (of sb/sth) to think that sb/sth is bad, silly, etc. □ *tdk bersetuju; tdk berkenan*: *His parents strongly disapproved of his decision to leave college before he had finished his course.* **OPP** approve

disapproving /ˌdɪsəˈpruːvɪŋ/ *adj* showing that you think sth is bad, silly, etc. □ *tdk bersetuju*: *After he had told the joke there was a disapproving silence.* ▶ **disapprovingly** *adv*: *David frowned disapprovingly when I arrived late.*

247 **disallow → discharge**

disarm /dɪsˈɑːm/ *verb* **1** [T] to take weapons away from sb □ *melucutkan senjata*: *The police caught and disarmed the terrorists.* **2** [I] (used about a country) to reduce the number of weapons it has □ *mengurangkan senjata* **3** [T] to make sb feel less angry □ *melembutkan hati*: *Jenny could always disarm the teachers with a smile.*

disarmament /dɪsˈɑːməmənt/ *noun* [U] reducing the number of weapons that an army or a country has □ *perlucutan senjata*: *nuclear disarmament*

disassociate /ˌdɪsəˈsəʊʃieɪt; -ˈsəʊs-/ = **dissociate**

disaster /dɪˈzɑːstə(r)/ *noun* **1** [C] an event that causes a lot of harm or damage □ *bencana; malapetaka*: *earthquakes, floods and other natural disasters* **2** [C,U] a terrible situation or event □ *bencana; kecelakaan*: *Losing your job is unfortunate, but it's not a disaster.* ◆ *This year's lack of rain could spell disaster for many farmers.* **3** [C,U] (*informal*) a complete failure □ *kegagalan; gagal sama sekali*: *The school play was an absolute disaster. Everything went wrong.*

disastrous /dɪˈzɑːstrəs/ *adj* terrible, harmful or failing completely □ *teruk; dahsyat; membawa kecelakaan*: *Our mistake had disastrous results.* ▶ **disastrously** *adv*: *The plan went disastrously wrong.*

disband /dɪsˈbænd/ *verb* [I,T] to stop existing as a group; to separate □ *membubarkan; berpecah*

disbelief /ˌdɪsbɪˈliːf/ *noun* [U] the feeling of not believing sb/sth □ *rasa tdk percaya*: *'It can't be true!' he shouted in disbelief.*

disbelieve /ˌdɪsbɪˈliːv/ *verb* [T] to think that sth is not true or that sb is not telling the truth □ *tdk mempercayai*: *I have no reason to disbelieve her.* **OPP** believe

disc (*especially AmE* **disk**) /dɪsk/ *noun* [C] **1** a round flat object □ *cakera; ceper*: *He wears an identity disc around his neck.* **2** = **CD 3** = **disk**(2) **4** one of the pieces of **cartilage** (= thin strong material) between the bones in your back □ *cakera*: *a slipped disc* (= one that has moved from its correct position, causing pain)

discard /dɪsˈkɑːd/ *verb* [T] (*formal*) to throw sth away because it is not useful □ *membuang*

discern /dɪˈsɜːn/ *verb* [T] (*formal*) to see or notice sth with difficulty □ *nampak; terasa*: *I discerned a note of anger in his voice.* ▶ **discernible** *adj*: *The shape of a house was just discernible through the mist.*

discerning /dɪˈsɜːnɪŋ/ *adj* able to recognize the quality of sb/sth □ *pandai menilai; arif*: *The discerning music lover will appreciate the excellence of this recording.*

discharge¹ /dɪsˈtʃɑːdʒ/ *verb* [T] **1** to allow sb officially to leave; to send sb away □

CONSONANTS   p **p**en   b **b**ad   t **t**ea   d **d**id   k **c**at   g **g**ot   tʃ **ch**in   dʒ **J**une   f **f**all   v **v**an   θ **th**in

discharge → discourse

membenarkan sso meninggalkan atau keluar dr: *to discharge somebody from hospital* **2** to send sth out (a liquid, gas, etc.) □ *mengeluarkan; membuang*: *Smoke and fumes are discharged from the factory.* **3** to do sth that you have to do □ *melaksanakan; menjalankan*: *to discharge a duty/task*

discharge² /ˈdɪstʃɑːdʒ/ *noun* [C,U] **1** a substance that has come out of somewhere □ *lelehan*: *yellowish discharge from a wound* **2** the act of sending sb/sth out or away □ *buangan; luahan; keluarnya; penamatan perkhidmatan; kebenaran keluar*: *The wounded soldier was given a medical discharge.* ♦ *The discharge of oil from the leaking tanker could not be prevented.*

disciple /dɪˈsaɪpl/ *noun* [C] a person who follows a teacher, especially a religious one □ *pengikut* **SYN** follower

disciplinary /ˈdɪsəplɪnəri; ˌdɪsəˈplɪnəri/ *adj* connected with punishment for breaking rules □ *(berkenaan dgn) disiplin/tatatertib*

discipline¹ /ˈdɪsəplɪn/ *noun* **1** [U] the practice of training people to obey rules and behave well □ *disiplin; tatatertib*: *A good teacher must be able to maintain discipline in the classroom.* **2** [U] the practice of training your mind and body so that you control your actions and obey rules; a way of doing this □ *disiplin*: *It takes a lot of self-discipline to study for three hours a day.* ♦ *Having to get up early every day is good discipline for a child.* **3** [C] a subject of study □ *disiplin; bidang*: *academic disciplines*

discipline² /ˈdɪsəplɪn/ *verb* [T] **1** to train sb to obey and to behave in a controlled way □ *mendisiplinkan*: *You should discipline yourself to practise the piano every morning.* **2** to punish sb □ *mengenakan tindakan disiplin*: *The player was disciplined for using racist language.*

ˈdisc jockey = DJ

disclaim /dɪsˈkleɪm/ *verb* [T] to say that you do not have sth □ *menafikan; tdk mengaku*: *to disclaim responsibility/knowledge* **SYN** deny

disclose /dɪsˈkləʊz/ *verb* [T] (*formal*) to tell sth to sb or to make sth known publicly □ *memberitahu; mendedahkan*: *The newspapers did not disclose the victim's name.* **SYN** reveal

disclosure /dɪsˈkləʊʒə(r)/ *noun* [C,U] making sth known; the facts that are made known □ *pendedahan*: *the disclosure of secret information* ♦ *He resigned following disclosures about his private life.* **SYN** revelation

disco /ˈdɪskəʊ/ *noun* [C] (*pl* **discos**) (*old-fashioned*) a place, party, etc. where people dance to recorded music □ *disko*: *Are you going to the school disco?* ➔ look at **club**

discolour (*AmE* **discolor**) /dɪsˈkʌlə(r)/ *verb* [I,T] to change or to make sth change colour (often by the effect of light, age or dirt) □ *berubah warna*

discomfort /dɪsˈkʌmfət/ *noun* [U] **1** a slight feeling of pain □ *rasa sakit sedikit; ketidakselesaan*: *There may be some discomfort after the operation.* **2** a feeling of embarrassment □ *rasa kurang senang; rasa malu*: *I could sense John's discomfort when I asked him about his job.*

disconcert /ˌdɪskənˈsɜːt/ *verb* [T, usually passive] to make sb feel confused or worried □ *rasa kurang senang/agak bingung*: *She was disconcerted when everyone stopped talking and looked at her.* ▶ **disconcerting** *adj* ▶ **disconcertingly** *adv*

disconnect /ˌdɪskəˈnekt/ *verb* [T] **1** to stop a supply of water, gas or electricity going to a piece of equipment or a building □ *memotong; memberhentikan*: *If you don't pay your gas bill your supply will be disconnected.* **2** to separate sth from sth □ *terpisah; tercabut; tertanggal; terputus*: *The brake doesn't work because the cable has become disconnected from the lever.*

discontent /ˌdɪskənˈtent/ (also **discontentment** /ˌdɪskənˈtentmənt/) *noun* [U] the state of being unhappy with sth □ *rasa tdk puas hati*: *The management could sense growing discontent among the staff.* ▶ **discontented** *adj*: *to be/feel discontented*

discontinue /ˌdɪskənˈtɪnjuː/ *verb* [T] (*formal*) to stop sth or stop producing sth □ *menghentikan; menamatkan*

discord /ˈdɪskɔːd/ *noun* [U] (*formal*) disagreement or argument □ *perselisihan; perbalahan*

discordant /dɪsˈkɔːdənt/ *adj* that spoils a general feeling of agreement □ *(yg) bercanggahan; sumbang*: *Her criticism was the only discordant note in the discussion.*

discount¹ /ˈdɪskaʊnt/ *noun* [C,U] a lower price than usual □ *diskaun; potongan harga*: *Staff get 20% discount on all goods.* ♦ *Do you give a discount for cash?* **SYN** reduction

discount² /dɪsˈkaʊnt/ *verb* [T] to consider sth not true or not important □ *tdk mengambil kira; mengetepikan*: *I think we can discount that idea. It's just not practical.*

discourage /dɪsˈkʌrɪdʒ/ *verb* [T] **discourage sb (from doing sth)** to stop sb doing sth, especially by making them realize that it would not be successful or a good idea □ *tdk menggalakkan*: *I tried to discourage Jake from giving up his job.* ♦ *Don't let these little problems discourage you.* **OPP** encourage ▶ **discouraged** *adj*: *After failing the exam again Paul felt very discouraged.* ▶ **discouraging** *adj*: *Constant criticism can be very discouraging.*

discouragement /dɪsˈkʌrɪdʒmənt/ *noun* [C,U] a thing that makes you not want to do sth; the act of trying to stop sb from doing sth □ *rasa tawar hati; perihal tdk menggalakkan; penghalang*: *the government's discouragement of smoking* ♦ *the government's discouragement of political protest*

discourse /ˈdɪskɔːs/ *noun* [C,U] (*formal*) a long and serious discussion of a subject in speech or writing □ *wacana*

discourteous /dɪsˈkɜːtiəs/ *adj* not polite or showing respect for people □ *biadab, tdk sopan, tdk menghormati* SYN **impolite** OPP **courteous**

discover /dɪˈskʌvə(r)/ *verb* [T] **1** to find or learn sth that nobody had found or knew before □ *menemukan*: *Who discovered the lost city of Machu Picchu?* ◆ *Scientists are hoping to discover the cause of the epidemic.* **2** to find sb/sth that was hidden and that you did not expect to find □ *mendapati; berjumpa dgn*: *The police discovered the painting hidden under the floor.* **3** to find out about sth; to find some information about sth □ *mendapat tahu*: *I think I've discovered why the computer won't print out.* ▶ **discoverer** *noun* [C]: *Parkinson's disease was named after its discoverer.*

discovery /dɪˈskʌvəri/ *noun* (*pl* **discoveries**) **1** [U] the act of finding sth □ *penemuan; perihal mendapat tahu*: *The discovery of X-rays changed the history of medicine.* **2** [C] something that has been found or learnt about for the first time □ *penemuan; jumpaan*: *scientific discoveries*

discredit /dɪsˈkredɪt/ *verb* [T] to make people stop respecting or believing sb/sth □ *mencemarkan nama baik*: *Journalists are trying to discredit the president by inventing stories about his love life.* ▶ **discredit** *noun* [U]

discreet /dɪˈskriːt/ *adj* careful in what you say and do so as not to cause embarrassment or difficulty for sb □ *berhati-hati (dlm percakapan atau perbuatan)*: *I don't want anyone to find out about this, so please be discreet.* OPP **indiscreet** ↪ *noun* **discretion** ▶ **discreetly** *adv*

discrepancy /dɪsˈkrepənsi/ *noun* [C,U] (*pl* **discrepancies**) a difference between two things that should be the same □ *percanggahan*: *Something is wrong here. There is a discrepancy between these two sets of figures.*

discretion /dɪˈskreʃn/ *noun* [U] **1** the freedom and power to make decisions by yourself □ *budi bicara*: *You must decide what is best. Use your discretion.* **2** care in what you say and do so as not to cause embarrassment or difficulty for sb □ *sikap berhati-hati (dlm percakapan atau perbuatan)*: *This is confidential but I know I can rely on your discretion.* ↪ *adjective* **discreet**
IDM **at sb's discretion** depending on what sb thinks or decides □ *atas budi bicara sso*: *Pay increases are awarded at the discretion of the director.*

discriminate /dɪˈskrɪmɪneɪt/ *verb* **1** [I,T] **discriminate (between A and B)** to see or make a difference between two people or things □ *membezakan*: *The immigration law discriminates between political and economic refugees.* **2** [I] **discriminate (against sb)** to treat one person or group worse than others □ *membeza-bezakan; pilih kasih*: *It is illegal to discriminate against any ethnic or religious group.*

discriminating /dɪˈskrɪmɪneɪtɪŋ/ *adj* able to judge the good quality of sth □ *bijak menilai*: *a discriminating audience/customer* SYN **discerning**

249 **discourteous → disentangle**

discrimination /dɪˌskrɪmɪˈneɪʃn/ *noun* [U] **1** **discrimination (against sb)** treating one person or group worse than others □ *diskriminasi; perihal pilih kasih*: *sexual/racial/religious discrimination* ◆ *Discrimination against disabled people is illegal.* **2** (*formal*) the state of being able to see a difference between two people or things □ *pembezaan*: *discrimination between right and wrong*

discus /ˈdɪskəs/ *noun* **1** [C] a heavy round flat object that is thrown as a sport □ *cakera* **2** **the discus** [sing] the sport or event of throwing a discus as far as possible □ *acara lempar cakera*

discuss /dɪˈskʌs/ *verb* [T] **discuss sth (with sb)** to talk or write about sth seriously or formally □ *membincangkan*: *I must discuss the matter with my parents before I make a decision.* ◆ *The article discusses the need for a change in the law.*

discussion /dɪˈskʌʃn/ *noun* [C,U] the process of talking about sth seriously or deeply □ *perbincangan*: *We had a long discussion about art.* ◆ *After much discussion we all agreed to share the cost.*
IDM **under discussion** being talked about □ *sedang dibincangkan*: *Plans to reform the Health Service are under discussion in Parliament.*

disdain /dɪsˈdeɪn/ *noun* [U] the feeling that sb/sth is not good enough to be respected □ *sikap menghina*: *Monica felt that her boss always treated her ideas with disdain.* ▶ **disdainful** /-fl/ *adj* ▶ **disdainfully** /-fəli/ *adv*

disease /dɪˈziːz/ *noun* [C,U] an illness of the body in humans, animals or plants □ *penyakit*: *an infectious/contagious disease* ◆ *These children suffer from a rare disease.* ◆ *Rats and flies spread disease.* ◆ *Smoking causes heart disease.* ◆ *Obesity causes heart disease.* ▶ **diseased** *adj*: *His diseased kidney had to be removed.* ↪ note at **ill**

HELP **Disease or illness?** A **disease** is a medical problem which has a name and may be caused by bacteria, viruses, etc. Diseases can often be caught and passed on to other people. An **illness** can be either a medical problem or a period of ill health.

disembark /ˌdɪsɪmˈbɑːk/ *verb* [I] (*formal*) to get off a ship or an aircraft □ *turun* OPP **embark** ▶ **disembarkation** /ˌdɪsˌembɑːˈkeɪʃn/ *noun* [U]

disenchanted /ˌdɪsɪnˈtʃɑːntɪd/ *adj* having lost your good opinion of sb/sth □ *kecewa; menjadi tawar hati*: *Fans are already becoming disenchanted with the new team manager.* ▶ **disenchantment** *noun* [U]

disentangle /ˌdɪsɪnˈtæŋgl/ *verb* [T] to free sb/sth that had become connected to sb/sth else in a confused and complicated way □ *melepaskan; mengasingkan; memisahkan*: *My coat got caught up in some bushes and I couldn't disentangle it.* ◆ (*figurative*) *Listening to her story, I found it hard to disentangle the truth from the lies.*

VOWELS   iː **see**   i **any**   ɪ **sit**   e **ten**   æ **hat**   ɑː **father**   ɒ **got**   ɔː **saw**   ʊ **put**   uː **too**   u **usual**

disfigure /dɪsˈfɪɡə(r)/ verb [T] to spoil the appearance of sb/sth □ *mencacati*: *His face was permanently disfigured by the fire.*

disgrace¹ /dɪsˈɡreɪs/ noun 1 [U] the state of not being respected by other people, usually because you have behaved badly □ *keaiban; aib*: *She left the company in disgrace after admitting stealing from colleagues.* 2 [sing] a disgrace (to sb/sth) a person or thing that gives a very bad impression and makes you feel sorry and embarrassed □ *sst/sso yg memalukan; penghinaan*: *The streets are covered in litter. It's a disgrace!* ♦ *Politicians who tell lies are a disgrace to their profession.*

disgrace² /dɪsˈɡreɪs/ verb [T] to behave badly in a way that makes you or other people feel sorry and embarrassed □ *memalukan*: *My brother disgraced himself by starting a fight at the wedding.*

disgraceful /dɪsˈɡreɪsfl/ adj very bad, making other people feel sorry and embarrassed □ *(yg) memalukan; sangat teruk*: *The behaviour of the team's fans was absolutely disgraceful.* ▶ **disgracefully** /-fəli/ adv

disgruntled /dɪsˈɡrʌntld/ adj disappointed and annoyed □ *tdk puas hati; meradang*

disguise¹ /dɪsˈɡaɪz/ verb [T] disguise sb/sth (as sb/sth) to change the appearance, sound, etc. of sb/sth so that people cannot recognize them or it □ *menyamar; menyembunyikan*: *They disguised themselves as fishermen and escaped in a boat.* ♦ *(figurative) His smile disguised his anger.*

disguise² /dɪsˈɡaɪz/ noun [C,U] a thing that you wear or use to change your appearance so that nobody recognizes you □ *samaran; perihal menyamar*: *The robbers were wearing heavy disguises so that they could not be identified.* ♦ *She is so famous that she has to go shopping in disguise.*

⸸ disgust¹ /dɪsˈɡʌst/ noun [U] disgust (at sth) a strong feeling of not liking or approving of sth/sb that you feel is unacceptable, or that looks, smells, etc. unpleasant □ *rasa menyampah, meluat, benci, tdk suka, jijik atau geli*: *The film was so bad that we walked out in disgust.* ♦ *Much to my disgust, I found a hair in my soup.*

⸸ disgust² /dɪsˈɡʌst/ verb [T] 1 to cause a strong feeling of not liking or approving of sb/sth □ *menimbulkan rasa menyampah, meluat atau benci*: *Cruelty towards animals absolutely disgusts me.* 2 to make sb feel ill □ *menimbulkan rasa geli atau jijik; berasa hendak muntah*: *The way he eats with his mouth open completely disgusts me.*

⸸ disgusted /dɪsˈɡʌstɪd/ adj disgusted (at/with sb/sth) not liking or approving of sb/sth at all □ *berasa benci atau tdk suka*: *We were disgusted at the standard of service we received.*

⸸ disgusting /dɪsˈɡʌstɪŋ/ adj very unpleasant □ *(yg) menimbulkan rasa meluat, benci, jijik, dsb*: *What a disgusting smell!* **SYN** revolting

disgustingly /dɪsˈɡʌstɪŋli/ adv 1 extremely (often used to show that you would like to have what sb else has) □ *sangat; terlalu*: *Our neighbours are disgustingly rich.* 2 in a way that you do not like or approve of or that makes you feel sick □ *dgn cara yg menjijikkan*: *The kitchen was disgustingly dirty.*

⸸ dish¹ /dɪʃ/ noun 1 [C] a round container for food that is deeper than a plate □ *bekas; pinggan mungkum*: *Is this dish ovenproof?* 2 the dishes [pl] all the plates, cups, etc. that you use during a meal □ *pinggan mangkuk*: *I'll cook and you can wash the dishes.* 3 [C] a type of food prepared in a particular way □ *hidangan; masakan*: *The main dish was curry. It was served with a selection of side dishes.* ♦ *Paella is a typical Spanish dish, made with rice and shellfish.* 4 = satellite dish

dish² /dɪʃ/ verb
PHR V dish sth out (informal) to give away a lot of sth □ *memberikan*: *to dish out advice*

dish sth up (informal) to serve food □ *menghidangkan*

dishcloth /ˈdɪʃklɒθ/ noun [C] a cloth for washing dishes □ *kain membasuh pinggan*

dishearten /dɪsˈhɑːtn/ verb [T, usually passive] to make sb lose hope or confidence □ *hilang harapan atau keyakinan; mengecewakan* **OPP** hearten **SYN** discourage ▶ **disheartened** /dɪsˈhɑːtnd/ adj ▶ **disheartening** /dɪsˈhɑːtnɪŋ/ adj: *a disheartening experience*

dishevelled (AmE **disheveled**) /dɪˈʃevld/ adj (used about sb's appearance) very untidy □ *tdk kemas* **SYN** unkempt

⸸ dishonest /dɪsˈɒnɪst/ adj that you cannot trust; likely to lie, steal or cheat □ *tdk jujur*: *Beware of dishonest traders in tourist areas.* **OPP** honest ▶ **dishonestly** adv ▶ **dishonesty** noun [U] **OPP** honesty

dishonour¹ (AmE **dishonor**) /dɪsˈɒnə(r)/ noun [U,sing] (formal) the state of no longer being respected, especially because you have done sth bad □ *keaiban; aib*: *Her cheating in exams has brought dishonour on the school.* **OPP** honour ▶ **dishonourable** adj **OPP** honourable

dishonour² (AmE **dishonor**) /dɪsˈɒnə(r)/ verb [T] (formal) to do sth bad that makes people stop respecting you or sb/sth close to you □ *membawa aib; mengaibkan*

dishwasher /ˈdɪʃwɒʃə(r)/ (AmE also) / noun [C] a machine that washes plates, cups, knives, forks, etc. □ *mesin basuh pinggan mangkuk* ⊃ picture on page P8

disillusion /ˌdɪsɪˈluːʒn/ verb [T] to destroy sb's belief in or good opinion of sb/sth □ *mengecewakan* ▶ **disillusion** (also **disillusionment**) noun [U]: *I feel increasing disillusion with the government.*

disillusioned /ˌdɪsɪˈluːʒnd/ *adj* disappointed because sb/sth is not as good as you first thought □ *kecewa*: *She's disillusioned with nursing.*

disillusionment /ˌdɪsɪˈluːʒnmənt/ = disillusion

disinfect /ˌdɪsɪnˈfekt/ *verb* [T] to clean sth with a liquid that destroys bacteria □ *menyahjangkit; membasmi kuman*: *to disinfect a wound* ▶ **disinfection** *noun* [U]

disinfectant /ˌdɪsɪnˈfektənt/ *noun* [C,U] a substance that destroys bacteria and is used for cleaning □ *bahan penyahjangkitan/pembasmi kuman*

disintegrate /dɪsˈɪntɪɡreɪt/ *verb* [I] to break into many small pieces □ *hancur berkecai; bersepai*: *The plane disintegrated as it fell into the sea.* ▶ **disintegration** /dɪsˌɪntɪˈɡreɪʃn/ *noun* [U]: *the gradual disintegration of traditional values*

disinterested /dɪsˈɪntrəstɪd/ *adj* fair, not influenced by personal feelings □ *berkecuali*: *Let me give you some disinterested advice.*

> **HELP** Be careful. **Uninterested** has a different meaning.

disjointed /dɪsˈdʒɔɪntɪd/ *adj* (used especially about ideas, writing or speech) not clearly connected and therefore difficult to follow □ *terputus-putus* ▶ **disjointedly** *adv*

disk /dɪsk/ *noun* [C] **1** (*especially AmE*) = **disc** **2** a flat piece of plastic that stores information for use by a computer □ *cakera* ⊃ note at **computer** ⊃ look at **floppy disk**, **hard disk**

'disk drive *noun* [C] a piece of electrical equipment that passes information to or from a computer disk □ *pemacu cakera*

diskette /dɪsˈket/ = **floppy disk**

dislike¹ /dɪsˈlaɪk/ *verb* [T] (*formal*) **dislike (doing) sth** to not like sb/sth □ *tdk suka*: *I really dislike flying.* ♦ *What is it that you dislike about living here?* **OPP** **like**

OTHER WORDS FOR

dislike

Dislike is rather formal, so in conversation we use **don't like**: *I don't like (doing) sport.* You can also say 'I don't **spend much time** doing sport', 'I'm **not** very **keen on** (doing) sport', or 'I'm **not** very **interested in** sport'. If you dislike sth very much, you can use **hate**, **really don't like** or **can't stand**: *I hate/really don't like/can't stand (doing) sport.*

---

dislike² /dɪsˈlaɪk/ *noun* [U, sing] **(a) dislike (of/ for sb/sth)** the feeling of not liking sb/sth □ *rasa tdk suka*: *She couldn't hide her dislike for him.* ♦ *He seems to have a strong dislike of hard work.* **IDM take a dislike to sb/sth** to start **disliking** sb/ sth □ *mula tdk suka*: *He took an instant dislike to his boss.*

dislocate /ˈdɪsləkeɪt/ *verb* [T] to put sth (usually a bone) out of its correct position □ *terkehel*: *He dislocated his shoulder during the game.* ▶ **dislocation** /ˌdɪsləˈkeɪʃn/ *noun* [C,U]

dislodge /dɪsˈlɒdʒ/ *verb* [T] **dislodge sth (from sth)** to make sb/sth move from its correct fixed position □ *mengajakkan; mencungkil keluar*: *The strong wind dislodged several tiles from the roof.*

disloyal /dɪsˈlɔɪəl/ *adj* **disloyal (to sb/sth)** not supporting your friends, family, country, etc.; doing sth that will harm them □ *tdk setia*: *It was disloyal to your friends to repeat their conversation to Peter.* **OPP** **loyal** ▶ **disloyalty** /-ˈlɔɪəlti/ *noun* [C,U] (*pl* **disloyalties**)

dismal /ˈdɪzməl/ *adj* **1** causing or showing sadness □ *menyedihkan; suram*: *dismal surroundings* **SYN** **miserable** **2** (*informal*) of low quality; poor □ *teruk*: *a dismal standard of work*

dismantle /dɪsˈmæntl/ *verb* [T] to take sth to pieces; to separate sth into the parts it is made from □ *merungkai; membuka*: *The photographer dismantled his equipment and packed it away.*

dismay /dɪsˈmeɪ/ *noun* [U] a strong feeling of disappointment and sadness □ *rasa kecewa dan sedih*: *I realized to my dismay that I was going to miss the plane.* ▶ **dismay** *verb* [T]: *Their reaction dismayed him.* ▶ **dismayed** *adj* **dismayed (at/by sth); dismayed to find, hear, see, etc**: *I was dismayed to find that the train had already left.*

dismember /dɪsˈmembə(r)/ *verb* [T] to cut a dead body into pieces □ *mengerat-ngerat*

dismiss /dɪsˈmɪs/ *verb* [T] **1** **dismiss sb/sth (as sth)** to decide not to think about sth/sb □ *mengetepikan; melupakan*: *He dismissed the idea as nonsense.* **2** **dismiss sb (from sth)** to order an employee to leave his or her job □ *memecat*: *He was dismissed from his post for refusing to obey orders.* **SYN** **fire, sack** ⊃ note at **job 3** to send sb away □ *menyuraikan; bersurai*: *The lesson ended and the teacher dismissed the class.* **4** (used in law) to say that a trial or court case should not continue, usually because there is not enough evidence □ *membuang (kes)*: *The case was dismissed.* ▶ **dismissal** /dɪsˈmɪsl/ *noun* [C,U]: *She was hurt at their dismissal of her offer of help.* ♦ *a case of unfair dismissal*

dismissive /dɪsˈmɪsɪv/ *adj* **dismissive (of sb/ sth)** saying or showing that you think that sb/ sth is not worth considering seriously □ *bersikap acuh tak acuh; tdk menganggap penting*: *The boss was dismissive of all the efforts I had made.* ▶ **dismissively** *adv*

dismount /dɪsˈmaʊnt/ *verb* [I] to get off sth that you ride (a horse, a bicycle, etc.) □ *turun* **OPP** **mount**

disobedient /ˌdɪsəˈbiːdiənt/ *adj* refusing or failing to obey □ *ingkar* **OPP** **obedient** ▶ **disobedience** *noun* [U]

disobey /ˌdɪsəˈbeɪ/ verb [I,T] to refuse to do what you are told to do □ *mengingkari*: *He was punished for disobeying orders.* **OPP** obey

disorder /dɪsˈɔːdə(r)/ noun 1 [U] an untidy, confused or badly organized state □ *keadaan berserak/bercelaru*: *His financial affairs are in complete disorder.* **OPP** order 2 [U] violent behaviour by a large number of people □ *kekacauan*: *Disorder broke out on the streets of the capital.* 3 [C,U] an illness in which the mind or a part of the body is not working properly □ *gangguan; penyakit*: *treatment for eating disorders such as anorexia* ♦ *a kind of mental disorder*

disordered /dɪsˈɔːdəd/ adj untidy, confused or badly organized □ *berserak; bercelaru*

disorderly /dɪsˈɔːdəli/ adj 1 (used about people or behaviour) out of control and violent; causing trouble in public □ *tdk senonoh; tdk terkawal*: *They were arrested for being drunk and disorderly.* 2 untidy □ *berserak* **OPP** orderly

disorganization (also -isation) /dɪsˌɔːɡənaɪˈzeɪʃn/ noun [U] a lack of careful planning and order □ *perihal tdk teratur; kecelaruan* **OPP** organization

disorganized (also -ised) /dɪsˈɔːɡənaɪzd/ adj badly planned; not able to plan well □ *tdk teratur; bercelaru* **OPP** organized

disorientate /dɪsˈɔːriənteɪt/ (especially AmE **disorient** /dɪsˈɔːrient/) verb [T] to make sb become confused about where they are □ *menjadi keliru; mengelirukan; membingungkan*: *The road signs were very confusing and I soon became disorientated.* ▶ **disorientation** /dɪsˌɔːriənˈteɪʃn/ noun [U]

disown /dɪsˈəʊn/ verb [T] to say that you no longer want to be connected with or responsible for sb/sth □ *tdk mengaku sebagai (anak, dsb)*: *When he was arrested, his family disowned him.*

disparage /dɪˈspærɪdʒ/ verb [T] (formal) to talk about sb/sth in a critical way; to say that sb/sth is of little value or importance □ *merendah-rendahkan; memperkecil* ▶ **disparaging** adj: *disparaging remarks*

disparity /dɪˈspærəti/ noun [U,C] (pl **disparities**) (formal) a difference, especially one connected with unfair treatment □ *perbezaan; ketidaksamaan*: *the wide disparity between rich and poor*

dispatch (BRE ALSO **despatch**) /dɪˈspætʃ/ verb [T] (formal) to send sb/sth to a place □ *menghantar; dihantar*: *Your order will be dispatched within 7 days.*

dispel /dɪˈspel/ verb [T] (**dispelling**; **dispelled**) to make sth, especially a feeling or a belief, disappear □ *melenyapkan; menghilangkan*: *His reassuring words dispelled all her fears.*

dispensable /dɪˈspensəbl/ adj not necessary □ *tdk perlu*: *I suppose I'm dispensable. Anybody could do my job.* **OPP** indispensable

dispense /dɪˈspens/ verb [T] (formal) to give or provide people with sth □ *memberi; mengeluarkan*: *a machine that dispenses hot and cold drinks*
PHR V **dispense with sb/sth** to get rid of sb/sth that is not necessary □ *mengetepikan atau tdk membenarkan sso/sst*: *They decided to dispense with luxuries and live a simple life.*

dispenser /dɪˈspensə(r)/ noun [C] a machine or container from which you can get sth □ *dispenser*: *a cash dispenser at a bank* ♦ *a soap dispenser* ⊃ picture at **stationery**

disperse /dɪˈspɜːs/ verb [I,T] to separate and go in different directions; to make sb/sth do this □ *bersurai*: *When the meeting was over, the group dispersed.* ♦ *The police arrived and quickly dispersed the crowd.* ▶ **dispersal** /dɪˈspɜːsl/ noun [U,C]

dispirited /dɪˈspɪrɪtɪd/ adj having lost confidence or hope □ *tdk bersemangat; murung* **SYN** depressed

displace /dɪsˈpleɪs/ verb [T] 1 to remove and take the place of sb/sth □ *menggantikan; mengambil tempat*: *She hoped to displace Seles as the top tennis player in the world.* 2 to force sb/sth to move from the usual or correct place □ *terkeluar drpd tempatnya; terpaksa berpindah*: *refugees displaced by the war* ▶ **displacement** noun [U]

display¹ /dɪˈspleɪ/ verb [T] 1 to put sth in a place where people will see it or where it will attract attention □ *mempamerkan; dipamerkan*: *Posters for the concert were displayed throughout the city.* 2 to show signs of sth (for example a feeling or a quality) □ *menunjukkan*: *She displayed no interest in the discussion.*

display² /dɪˈspleɪ/ noun [C] 1 an arrangement of things in a public place for people to see □ *peragaan; pameran*: *a window display in a shop* 2 a public event in which sth is shown in action □ *pertunjukan*: *a firework display* 3 behaviour that shows a particular feeling or quality □ *perihal menunjukkan*: *a sudden display of aggression* 4 words, pictures, etc. that can be seen on a computer screen □ *paparan*
IDM **on display** in a place where people will see it and where it will attract attention □ *dipamerkan*: *Treasures from the sunken ship were put on display at the museum.*

displease /dɪsˈpliːz/ verb [T] (formal) to annoy sb or to make sb angry or upset □ *menggusarkan; tdk menyenangkan hati* ▶ **displeased** adj **OPP** pleased

displeasure /dɪsˈpleʒə(r)/ noun [U] (formal) the feeling of being annoyed or not satisfied □ *kegusaran; rasa tdk senang hati*: *I wrote to express my displeasure at not having been informed sooner.*

disposable /dɪˈspəʊzəbl/ adj made to be thrown away after being used once or for a short time □ *pakai buang*: *a disposable razor*

disposal /dɪˈspəʊzl/ noun [U] the act of getting rid of sth or throwing sth away □ *pem-*

buangan; pelupusan: *the disposal of dangerous chemical waste* ◆ *bomb disposal*
IDM **at sb's disposal** available for sb to use at any time □ *boleh digunakan oleh sso pd bila-bila masa sahaja*: *They put their house at my disposal.*

dispose /dɪˈspəʊz/ *verb*
PHR V **dispose of sb/sth** to throw away or sell sth; to get rid of sb/sth that you do not want □ *membuang/menjual sst; menghapuskan; menyingkirkan sso*

disposition /ˌdɪspəˈzɪʃn/ *noun* [C, usually sing] the natural qualities of sb's character or the way they usually behave □ *sifat semula jadi atau tabii seseorang*: *to have a cheerful disposition* ◆ *people of a nervous disposition* **SYN** **temperament**

disproportionate /ˌdɪsprəˈpɔːʃənət/ *adj* **disproportionate (to sth)** too large or too small when compared to sth else □ *tdk seimbang*: *Her salary is disproportionate to the amount of work she has to do.* ▶ **disproportionately** *adv*

disprove /ˌdɪsˈpruːv/ *verb* [T] to show that sth is not true □ *membuktikan salah* **OPP** **prove**

dispute¹ /dɪˈspjuːt/ *noun* [C,U] **(a) dispute (between A and B) (over/about sth)** a disagreement or argument between two people, groups or countries □ *perbalahan; pertikaian*: *a pay dispute* ◆ *There was some dispute between John and his boss about whose fault it was.*
IDM **in dispute** in a situation of arguing or being argued about □ *sedang dipertikaikan/dipersoalkan*: *He is in dispute with the tax office about how much he should pay.*

dispute² /dɪˈspjuːt/ *verb* [T] to argue about sth and to question if it is true or right □ *mempertikaikan; mempersoalkan*: *The player disputed the referee's decision.*

disqualify /dɪsˈkwɒlɪfaɪ/ *verb* [T] **(disqualifying; disqualifies;** *pt, pp* **disqualified) disqualify sb (from sth/doing sth); disqualify sb (for sth)** to officially prevent sb from doing sth or taking part in sth, usually because they have broken a rule or law □ *tdk dibenarkan; diisytiharkan tdk layak*: *He was disqualified from driving for two years.* ◆ *The team were disqualified for cheating.* ▶ **disqualification** /dɪsˌkwɒlɪfɪˈkeɪʃn/ *noun* [C,U]

disregard /ˌdɪsrɪˈɡɑːd/ *verb* [T] to take no notice of sb/sth; to treat sth as unimportant □ *tdk mempedulikan; tdk menghiraukan*: *These are the latest instructions. Please disregard any you received before.* ▶ **disregard** *noun* [U, sing] **disregard (for sb/sth)**: *He rushed into the burning building with complete disregard for his own safety.*

disrepair /ˌdɪsrɪˈpeə(r)/ *noun* [U] the state of being in bad condition because repairs have not been made □ *keadaan kopak-kapik*: *Over the years the building fell into disrepair.*

disreputable /dɪsˈrepjətəbl/ *adj* not to be trusted; well known for being bad or dishonest □ *tdk boleh dipercayai; mempunyai nama buruk*: *disreputable business methods* **OPP** **respectable**

dispose → dissociate

disrepute /ˌdɪsrɪˈpjuːt/ *noun* [U] the situation when people no longer respect sb/sth □ *nama buruk*: *The players' bad behaviour* **brings the game into disrepute**.

disrespect /ˌdɪsrɪˈspekt/ *noun* [U] **disrespect (for/to sb/sth)** a lack of respect for sb/sth that is shown in what you do or say □ *sikap tdk menghormati* **OPP** **respect** ▶ **disrespectful** /-fl/ *adj* **OPP** **respectful** ▶ **disrespectfully** /-fəli/ *adv*

disrupt /dɪsˈrʌpt/ *verb* [T] to stop sth happening as or when it should □ *mengganggu; menggendalakan*: *The strike severely disrupted flights to Spain.* ▶ **disruption** *noun* [C,U] ▶ **disruptive** /dɪsˈrʌptɪv/ *adj*

dissatisfaction /ˌdɪsˌsætɪsˈfækʃn/ *noun* [U] **dissatisfaction (with/at sb/sth)** the feeling of not being satisfied or pleased □ *rasa tdk puas hati*: *There is some dissatisfaction among teachers with the plans for the new exam.* **OPP** **satisfaction**

dissatisfied /dɪsˈsætɪsfaɪd/ *adj* **dissatisfied (with sb/sth)** not satisfied or pleased □ *tdk puas hati*: *complaints from dissatisfied customers* **OPP** **satisfied**

dissect /dɪˈsekt/ *verb* [T] to cut up a dead body, a plant, etc. in order to study it □ *membedah* ▶ **dissection** *noun* [C,U]

dissent¹ /dɪˈsent/ *noun* [U] (*formal*) disagreement with official or generally agreed ideas or opinions □ *pertentangan pendapat*: *There is some dissent within the Labour Party on these policies.*

dissent² /dɪˈsent/ *verb* [I] (*formal*) **dissent (from sth)** to have opinions that are different to those that are officially held □ *menentang; tdk bersetuju* ▶ **dissenting** *adj*: *dissenting groups/opinions/views*

dissertation /ˌdɪsəˈteɪʃn/ *noun* [C] a long piece of writing on sth that you have studied, especially as part of a university degree □ *disertasi* ⊃ look at **thesis**

disservice /dɪsˈsɜːvɪs/ *noun*
IDM **do (a) disservice to sb/sth** to do sth that harms sb and the opinion other people have of them □ *menjejaskan (kedudukan, nama baik, dll) sso/sst; merugikan*: *The minister's comments do the teaching profession a great disservice.*

dissident /ˈdɪsɪdənt/ *noun* [C] a person who strongly disagrees with and criticizes their government, especially in a country where it is dangerous to do this □ *penentang*: *left-wing dissidents* ▶ **dissidence** /ˈdɪsɪdəns/ *noun* [U]

dissimilar /dɪˈsɪmɪlə(r)/ *adj* **dissimilar (from/to sb/sth)** not the same; different □ *tdk sama; berbeza*: *Your situation is not dissimilar* (= is similar) *to mine.* **OPP** **similar**

dissociate /dɪˈsəʊsieɪt; -ˈsəʊs-/ (also **disassociate**) *verb* [T] **dissociate sb/sth/yourself (from sth)** to show that you are not connected with or do not support sb/sth; to show that

dissolve → distinguishable 254

two things are not connected with each other □ *memisahkan diri (drpd sst); tdk menyokong sso/sst; menunjukkan tdk ada kaitan*: *She dissociated herself from the views of the extremists in her party.* **OPP** associate

dissolve /dɪˈzɒlv/ *verb* [I,T] (used about a solid) to become or to make sth become part of a liquid □ *larut; melarutkan*: *Sugar dissolves in water.* ♦ *Dissolve two tablets in cold water.*

dissuade /dɪˈsweɪd/ *verb* [T] **dissuade sb (from doing sth)** to persuade sb not to do sth □ *memujuk/menasihati supaya jangan (membuat sst)*: *I tried to dissuade him from spending the money, but he insisted.* **OPP** persuade

distance¹ /ˈdɪstəns/ *noun* **1** [C,U] the amount of space between two places or things □ *jarak; jauh*: *The map tells you the distances between the major cities.* ♦ *We can walk home from here; it's no distance* (= it isn't far). ♦ *The house is within walking distance of the shops.* **2** [sing] a point that is a long way from sb/sth □ *jarak; jauh*: *At this distance I can't read the number on the bus.* ♦ *From a distance the village looks quite attractive.* **IDM** **in the distance** far away □ *nun jauh; di kejauhan*: *I could just see Paul in the distance.* **keep your distance** to stay away from sb/sth □ *menjauhkan diri dr sso/sst*: *Rachel's got a bad cold, so I'm keeping my distance until she gets better.* **within striking distance** ➔ **strike¹**

distance² /ˈdɪstəns/ *verb* [T] **distance yourself from sb/sth** to become less involved or connected with sb/sth □ *menjauhkan diri; tdk melibatkan diri*: *She was keen to distance herself from the views of her colleagues.*

distant /ˈdɪstənt/ *adj* **1** a long way away in space or time □ *jauh*: *travel to distant parts of the world* ♦ *in the not-too-distant future* (= quite soon) **2** [only *before* a noun] (used about a relative) not closely related □ *jauh*: *a distant cousin* **3** not very friendly □ *dingin; tdk mesra*: *He has a rather distant manner and it's hard to get to know him well.* **4** seeming to be thinking about sth else □ *jauh; spt memikirkan sst yg lain*: *She had a distant look in her eyes and clearly wasn't listening to me.*

distaste /dɪsˈteɪst/ *noun* [U, sing] not liking sth; the feeling that sb/sth is unpleasant or offends you □ *rasa jijik/tdk suka*: *He looked at the dirty room with distaste.*

distasteful /dɪsˈteɪstfl/ *adj* (*formal*) unpleasant or causing offence □ *yg jijik/tdk disukai*: *a distasteful remark*

distil (*AmE* **distill**) /dɪˈstɪl/ *verb* [T] (**distilling**; **distilled**) to make a liquid pure by heating it until it becomes a gas and then collecting the liquid that forms when the gas cools □ *menyuling* ▸ **distillation** /ˌdɪstɪˈleɪʃn/ *noun* [C,U]

distillery /dɪˈstɪləri/ *noun* [C] (*pl* **distilleries**) a factory where strong alcoholic drink is made by the process of **distilling** □ *kilang arak*

distinct /dɪˈstɪŋkt/ *adj* **1** clear; easily seen, heard or understood □ *jelas; nyata; ketara*: *There has been a distinct improvement in your work recently.* ♦ *I had the distinct impression that she was lying.* **2 distinct (from sth)** clearly different □ *berbeza; berlainan*: *Her books fall into two distinct groups: the novels and the travel stories.* ♦ *This region, as distinct from other parts of the country, relies heavily on tourism.* **OPP** indistinct

distinction /dɪˈstɪŋkʃn/ *noun* **1** [C,U] **(a) distinction (between A and B)** a clear or important difference between things or people □ *perbezaan*: *We must make a distinction between classical and popular music here.* **2** [U] the quality of being excellent; fame for what you have achieved □ *cemerlang; unggul*: *a violinist of distinction* **3** [C,U] the highest mark that is given to students in some exams for excellent work □ *(markah) cemerlang*: *James got a distinction in maths.* ➔ *verb* ➔ **distinguish**
IDM **draw a distinction between sth and sth** ➔ **draw¹**

distinctive /dɪˈstɪŋktɪv/ *adj* clearly different from others and therefore easy to recognize □ *tersendiri*: *The soldiers were wearing their distinctive red berets.* ▸ **distinctively** *adv*

distinctly /dɪˈstɪŋktli/ *adv* **1** clearly □ *dgn jelas*: *I distinctly heard her say that she would be here on time.* **2** very; particularly □ *amat; sangat; begitu*: *His behaviour has been distinctly odd recently.*

distinguish /dɪˈstɪŋgwɪʃ/ *verb* **1** [I,T] **distinguish between A and B**; **distinguish A from B** to recognize the difference between two things or people □ *membezakan*: *He doesn't seem able to distinguish between what's important and what isn't.* ♦ *People who are colour-blind often can't distinguish red from green.* **SYN** differentiate **2** [T] **distinguish A (from B)** to make sb/sth different from others □ *membezakan*: *distinguishing features* (= things by which sb/sth can be recognized) ♦ *The power of speech distinguishes humans from animals.* **3** [T] to see, hear or recognize with effort □ *nampak; mendengar; mengenali*: *I listened carefully but they were too far away for me to distinguish what they were saying.* **4** [T] **distinguish yourself** to do sth which causes you to be noticed and admired □ *mendapat nama*: *She distinguished herself in the exams.* ➔ *verb* ➔ **distinction**

distinguishable /dɪˈstɪŋgwɪʃəbl/ *adj* **1** possible to recognize as different from sb/sth else □ *dpt dibezakan*: *The male bird is distinguishable from the female by the colour of its beak.* **2** possible to see, hear or recognize with effort □ *dpt dilihat, didengar atau dikenali*: *The letter is so old that the signature is barely distinguishable.* **OPP** for both meanings **indistinguishable**

distinguished /dɪˈstɪŋgwɪʃt/ adj important, successful and respected by other people □ *ternama*: *a distinguished guest*

distort /dɪˈstɔːt/ verb [T] 1 to change the shape or sound of sth so that it seems strange or is not clear □ *mengherotkan; menjadi herot*: *Her face was distorted with grief.* ♦ *The kidnapper used a device to distort his voice over the telephone.* 2 to change sth and show it in a way that is not correct or true □ *memesongkan; memberi, menunjukkan, dsb gambaran yg tdk benar*: *Foreigners are often given a distorted view of this country.* ▶ distortion noun [C,U]

distract /dɪˈstrækt/ verb [T] distract sb (from sth) to take sb's attention away from sth □ *memesongkan/mengalih perhatian (sso); mengganggu*: *Could you stop talking please? You're distracting me from my work.*

distracted /dɪˈstræktɪd/ adj unable to give your full attention to sth because you are worried or thinking about sth else □ *(fikiran) terganggu*

distraction /dɪˈstrækʃn/ noun [C,U] something that takes your attention away from what you were doing or thinking about □ *gangguan*: *I find it hard to work at home because there are so many distractions.*
IDM to distraction with the result that you become upset, excited or angry and unable to think clearly □ *(mengganggu sso) hingga bagai nak gila*: *The noise of the traffic outside at night is driving me to distraction.*

distraught /dɪˈstrɔːt/ adj extremely upset and anxious □ *tdk keruan*

distress¹ /dɪˈstres/ noun [U] 1 the state of being very upset or of suffering great pain or difficulty □ *kesedihan; penderitaan; kesakitan*: *She was in such distress that I didn't want to leave her on her own.* 2 the state of being in great danger and needing immediate help □ *dlm bahaya/kesusahan*: *The ship's captain radioed that it was in distress.*

distress² /dɪˈstres/ verb [T] to make sb very upset or unhappy □ *menyedihkan; menyusahkan hati*: *Try not to say anything to distress the patient further.* ▶ distressed adj: *She was too distressed to talk.* ▶ distressing adj: *a distressing experience/illness*

distribute /dɪˈstrɪbjuːt; ˈdɪstrɪbjuːt/ verb [T] 1 distribute sth (to/among sb/sth) to give things to a number of people □ *mengedarkan*: *Tickets will be distributed to all club members.* ♦ *They distributed emergency food supplies to the areas that were most in need.* 2 to transport and supply goods to shops, companies, etc. □ *mengedarkan*: *Which company distributes this product in your country?* 3 to spread sth equally over an area □ *mengagihkan; membahagi-bahagikan*: *Make sure that the weight is evenly distributed.*

distribution /ˌdɪstrɪˈbjuːʃn/ noun 1 [C,U] the way sth is shared out; the pattern in which sth is found □ *pembahagian; pengagihan; taburan*: *a map to show the distribution of rainfall in Africa* 2 [U] the act of giving sth to a number of people □ *pengedaran*: *the distribution of food parcels to the refugees* 3 [U] the system of transporting and delivering goods □ *pengedaran*: *worldwide distribution systems*

distributor /dɪˈstrɪbjətə(r)/ noun [C] a person or company that transports and supplies goods to a number of shops and companies □ *pengedar*

district /ˈdɪstrɪkt/ noun [C] 1 a part of a town or country that is special for a particular reason or is of a particular type □ *kawasan*: *rural districts* ♦ *the financial district of the city* 2 an official division of a town or country □ *daerah*: *the district council* ♦ *postal districts* ➔ note at **area**

distrust /dɪsˈtrʌst/ noun [U, sing] (a) distrust (of sb/sth) the feeling that you cannot believe sb/sth; a lack of trust □ *rasa tdk percaya; kecurigaan* ▶ distrust verb [T]: *She distrusts him because he lied to her once before.* ➔ look at **mistrust** ▶ distrustful /-fl/ adj

disturb /dɪˈstɜːb/ verb [T] 1 to interrupt sb while they are doing sth or sleeping; to spoil a peaceful situation □ *mengganggu*: *I'm sorry to disturb you but there's a phone call for you.* ♦ *Their sleep was disturbed by a loud crash.* 2 to move sth or change its position □ *mengusik; terusik*: *I noticed a number of things had been disturbed and realized that there had been a burglary.* 3 to cause sb to worry □ *membimbangkan*: *It disturbed her to think that he might be unhappy.*

disturbance /dɪˈstɜːbəns/ noun [C,U] something that makes you stop what you are doing, or that upsets the normal condition of sth □ *gangguan; kekacauan*: *They were arrested for causing a disturbance (= fighting) in the town centre.* ♦ *emotional disturbance*

disturbed /dɪˈstɜːbd/ adj 1 having mental or emotional problems □ *fikiran terganggu*: *a school for disturbed young people* 2 very anxious and unhappy about sth □ *cemas*: *I was deeply disturbed by the news of his accident.*

disturbing /dɪˈstɜːbɪŋ/ adj making you worried or upset □ *(yg) membimbangkan*: *I found the film about AIDS very disturbing.*

disuse /dɪsˈjuːs/ noun [U] the state of not being used any more □ *tdk digunakan lagi*: *The farm buildings had been allowed to fall into disuse.*

disused /ˌdɪsˈjuːzd/ adj not used any more □ *(yg) tdk digunakan lagi*: *a disused railway line*

ditch¹ /dɪtʃ/ noun [C] a long narrow hole that has been dug into the ground, especially along the side of a road or field for water to flow along □ *parit; longkang*
IDM a last-ditch attempt ➔ **last¹**

ditch² /dɪtʃ/ verb [T] (informal) to get rid of or leave sb/sth □ *meninggalkan*: *She ditched her old friends when she became famous.*

dither → diving board

dither /'dɪðə(r)/ verb [I] to be unable to decide sth □ *teragak-agak*: *Stop dithering and make up your mind!* **SYN** hesitate

ditto /'dɪtəʊ/ noun [C] (symbol ") the same; used, especially in a list, underneath a particular word or phrase, to show that it is repeated and to avoid having to write it again □ *sama* ▶ **ditto** *adv*: *'I'm starving.' 'Ditto (= me too).'*

divan /dɪ'væn/ noun [C] (BrE) a type of bed with a thick base and a mattress □ *katil dipan*

dive¹ /daɪv/ verb [I] (pt **dived**, AmE also **dove** /dəʊv/; pp **dived**) **1 dive (off/from sth) (into sth); dive in** to jump into water with your arms and head first □ *terjun menjunam; terjun*: *In Acapulco, men dive off the cliffs into the sea.* ◆ *A passer-by dived in and saved the drowning man.* **2** to swim under the surface of the sea, a lake, etc. □ *menyelam*: *people diving for pearls* ◆ *I'm hoping to go diving on holiday.* **3** to move quickly and suddenly downwards □ *menyelinap; meluru; menerpa*: *He dived under the table and hid there.* ◆ *The engines failed and the plane dived.*

PHR V **dive into sth** to put your hand quickly into a pocket or bag in order to find or get sth □ *menyeluk pantas*: *She dived into her bag and brought out an old photograph.*

dive² /daɪv/ noun [C] **1** the act of **diving** into water □ *junaman* **2** a quick and sudden downwards movement □ *terpaan*: *Despite a desperate dive, the goalkeeper couldn't stop the ball.*

diver /'daɪvə(r)/ noun [C] **1** a person who swims under the surface of water using special equipment □ *penyelam; juruselam* **2** a person who jumps into water with their arms and head first □ *orang yg terjun menjunam*

diverge /daɪ'vɜːdʒ/ verb [I] (formal) **diverge (from sth) 1** (used about roads, lines, etc.) to separate and go in different directions □ *bercabang; menyimpang; berpisah*: *The paths suddenly diverged and they didn't know which one to take.* **2** to be or become different □ *berbeza*: *Attitudes among teachers diverge on this question.* **OPP** *for both meanings* **converge**

diverse /daɪ'vɜːs/ adj very different from each other □ *berbeza; berlainan; pelbagai*: *people from diverse social backgrounds* ◆ *My interests are very diverse.* ⊃ noun **diversity**

diversify /daɪ'vɜːsɪfaɪ/ verb [I,T] (**diversifying; diversifies**; pt, pp **diversified**) **diversify (sth) (into sth)** to increase or develop the number or types of sth □ *mempelbagaikan; menjadi pelbagai*: *To remain successful in the future, the company will have to diversify.* ◆ *Latin diversified into several different languages.* ▶ **diversification** /daɪˌvɜːsɪfɪ'keɪʃn/ noun [C,U]

diversion /daɪ'vɜːʃn/ noun **1** [C,U] the act of changing the direction or purpose of sth, especially in order to solve or avoid a problem □ *penyimpangan; perubahan haluan; pemindahan*: *We made a short diversion to go and look at the castle.* ◆ *the diversion of government funds to areas of greatest need* **2** [C] something that takes your attention away from sth □ *sst yg mengalih perhatian*: *Some prisoners created a diversion while others escaped.* **3** [C] (AmE **detour**) a different route which traffic can take when a road is closed □ *lencongan*: *For London, follow the diversion.*

diversity /daɪ'vɜːsəti/ noun [C,U] the wide variety of sth □ *perbezaan; kelainan; kepelbagaian*: *cultural and ethnic diversity*

divert /daɪ'vɜːt/ verb [T] **divert sb/sth (from sth) (to sth); divert sth (away from sth)** to change the direction or purpose of sb/sth, especially to avoid a problem □ *melencongkan; memindahkan; mengalihkan perhatian*: *During the road repairs, all traffic is being diverted.* ◆ *Government money was diverted from defence to education.* ◆ *Politicians often criticise each other to divert attention away from their own mistakes.*

divide¹ /dɪ'vaɪd/ verb
▶SEPARATE INTO PARTS **1** [I,T] **divide (sth) (up) (into sth)** to separate into different parts □ *membahagi; dibahagi-bahagikan*: *The egg divides into two cells.* ◆ *Where the path divides, keep right.* ◆ *The house was divided up into flats.* **2** [T] **divide sth (out/up) (between/among sb)** to separate sth into parts and give a part to each of a number of people □ *membahagi-bahagikan*: *The robbers divided the money out between themselves.* ◆ *When he died, his property was divided up among his children.* **3** [T] **divide sth (between A and B)** to use different parts or amounts of sth for different purposes □ *membahagikan*: *They divide their time between their two homes.* **4** [T] to separate two places or things □ *memisahkan; mengasingkan*: *The river divides the old part of the city from the new.*
▶CAUSE DISAGREEMENT **5** [T] to cause people to disagree □ *memecahbelahkan*: *The question of immigration has divided the country.* **SYN** split
▶MATHEMATICS **6** [T] **divide sth by sth** to calculate how many times a number will go into another number □ *membahagikan*: *10 divided by 5 is 2.* **OPP** multiply

divide² /dɪ'vaɪd/ noun [C, sing] **a divide (between A and B)** a difference between two groups of people that separates them from each other □ *jurang*: *a divide between the rich and the poor*

diˌvided ˈhighway (AmE) = **dual carriageway**

dividend /'dɪvɪdend/ noun [C] a part of a company's profits that is paid to the people who own shares in the company □ *dividen*

divine /dɪ'vaɪn/ adj connected with God or a god □ *(berkenaan dgn) Tuhan/tuhan*

diving /'daɪvɪŋ/ noun [U] the activity or sport of jumping into water or swimming under the surface of the sea, a lake, etc. □ *(sukan) junam* ⊃ picture at **swim**

ˈdiving board noun [C] a board at the side of a swimming pool from which people can jump into the water □ *papan junam*

divisible /dɪˈvɪzəbl/ adj [not before a noun] that can be divided □ *boleh dibahagikan*: *12 is divisible by 3.*

division /dɪˈvɪʒn/ noun
▸INTO SEPARATE PARTS **1** [U, sing] **division (of sth) (into sth); division (of sth) (between A and B)** the process or result of separating sth into different parts; the sharing of sth between different people, groups, places, etc. □ *pembahagian*: *an unfair division of the profits* ◆ *There is a growing economic division between the north and south of the country.*
▸MATHEMATICS **2** [U] dividing one number by another □ *pembahagian; bahagi*: *the teaching of multiplication and division*
▸DISAGREEMENT **3** [C,U] **a division (in/within sth); a division (between A and B)** a disagreement or difference of opinion between sb/sth □ *perbezaan pendapat*: *deep divisions within the Labour Party*
▸PART OF ORGANIZATION **4** [C] a part or section of an organization □ *bahagian; divisyen*: *the company's sales division* ◆ *the First Division* (= one of the groups of teams in a sports competition)
▸BORDER **5** [C] a line that separates sth; a border □ *pemisah*: *The river marks the division between the two counties.*

divisive /dɪˈvaɪsɪv/ adj (formal) likely to cause disagreements or arguments between people □ *(yg) memecahbelahkan*: *a divisive policy*

divorce¹ /dɪˈvɔːs/ noun [C,U] the legal end of a marriage □ *perceraian; cerai*: *to get a divorce* ◆ *Two in five marriages end in divorce.*

divorce² /dɪˈvɔːs/ verb **1** [I,T] to legally end your marriage to sb □ *menceraikan; bercerai*: *My parents got divorced when I was three.* ◆ *She divorced him a year after their marriage.* **2** [T] **divorce sb/sth from sth** to separate sb/sth from sth □ *memisahkan; terpisah*: *Sometimes these modern novels seem completely divorced from everyday life.* ▶ **divorced** adj

> **MORE** If a couple are still legally married but not living together any more, they are **separated**.

divorcee /dɪˌvɔːˈsiː/ noun [C] a person who is divorced, especially a woman □ *janda; duda*

divulge /daɪˈvʌldʒ/ verb [T] (formal) to tell sth that is secret □ *mendedahkan*: *The phone companies refused to divulge details of their costs.*

Diwali /diːˈwɑːli/ noun [sing] a Hindu festival that takes place in October or November, in which people decorate their homes with lights □ *Deepavali*

DIY /ˌdiː aɪ ˈwaɪ/ abbr **do-it-yourself**; the activity of making, repairing or decorating things in the home yourself, instead of paying sb to do it □ *buat sendiri*: *a DIY store* (= where you can buy materials for DIY) ⊃ note at **house**

dizzy /ˈdɪzi/ adj (**dizzier**; **dizziest**) **1** feeling as if everything is turning round and that you might fall □ *pening*: *I feel/get dizzy in high places.* **2** very great; extreme □ *sangat; amat*: *the dizzy pace of life in London* ◆ *The following year, the band's popularity reached dizzy heights.* ▶ **dizziness** noun [U]

DJ /ˈdiː dʒeɪ/ (also **disc jockey**) noun [C] a person who plays and talks about recorded music on radio or television or at a club □ *pengacara lagu; DJ*

DNA /ˌdiː en ˈeɪ/ noun [U] the chemical in the cells of animals and plants that controls what characteristics that animal or plant has □ *asid deoksiribonukleik*: *a DNA test*

do¹ /duː/ verb ❶ For the forms of 'do', look at the **Reference section** at the back of this dictionary. **1** [T] to perform an action, activity or job □ *membuat; buat; lakukan*: *What are you doing?* ◆ *What is the government doing about pollution* (= what action are they taking)? ◆ *What do you do* (= what is your job)? ◆ *Have you done your homework?* ◆ *I do twenty minutes' exercise every morning.* ◆ *to do the cooking/cleaning/ironing* ◆ *to do judo/aerobics/windsurfing* ◆ *What did you do with the keys* (= where did you put them)? **2** [I,T] to make progress or develop; to improve sth □ *membawa maksud maju atau berkembang; memperbaiki sst*: *'How's your daughter doing at school?' 'She's doing well.'* ◆ *Last week's win has done wonders for the team's confidence.* ◆ *This latest scandal will do nothing for* (= will harm) *this government's reputation.* **3** [T] to make or produce sth □ *membuat/menghasilkan sst*: *The photocopier does 60 copies a minute.* ◆ *to do a painting/drawing* **4** [T] to study sth or find the answer to sth □ *mempelajari atau mencari jawapan bagi sst*: *to do French/a course/a degree* ◆ *I can't do question three.* **5** [T] to travel a certain distance or at a certain speed □ *berjalan sejauh; bergerak selaju*: *I normally do about five miles when I go running.* ◆ *This car does 120 miles per hour.* **6** [T] to provide a service □ *membekalkan sst perkhidmatan*: *Do you do eye tests here?* **7** [I,T] to be enough or suitable □ *cukup; sesuai; memadai*: *If you haven't got a pen, a pencil will do.* ◆ *This room will do me nicely.* **8** [T] to have a particular effect □ *menimbulkan/ mendatangkan sst kesan*: *A holiday will do you good.* ◆ *The storm did a lot of damage.*

IDM **be/have (got) (sth) to do with sb/sth** to be connected with sb/sth □ *ada kena-mengena dgn sso/sst*: *I'm not sure what Paola's job is, but I think it's got something to do with animals.* ◆ *'How much do you earn?' 'It's nothing to do with you!'*
that does it (informal) used to show that you will not accept sth any longer □ *cukuplah*: *That does it—I'm leaving! I won't put up with you swearing at me any longer.*
that's done it (informal) used to say that an accident, a mistake, etc. has spoiled or ruined sth □ *habislah*: *That's done it. You've broken it now.* ❶ For other idioms containing **do**, look at the entries for the nouns, adjectives, etc. For example, **do sb credit** is at **credit**.

PHR V **do away with sth** to get rid of sth □ *menghapuskan sst*: *Most European countries have done away with their royal families.*

do sb out of sth to prevent sb having sth in an unfair way; to cheat sb □ *menipu sso supaya dia tdk mendapat sst*: They've done me out of my share of the money!

do sth up 1 to fasten a piece of clothing □ *mengancing pakaian (dgn butang, zip, dsb)*: Hurry up. Do up your jacket and we can go! **OPP undo 2** to repair a building and make it more modern □ *mengubah suai sst*: They're doing up the old cottage. ⊃ note at **house**

do without (sth) to manage without having sth □ *tanpa*: If there isn't any coffee left, we'll just have to do without.

do² /də; strong form du:/ auxiliary verb **1** used with other verbs to form questions and negative sentences, also in short answers and **question tags** (= short questions at the end of a sentence) □ *digunakan dgn kk lain utk membentuk ayat tanya dan ayat nafi, juga dlm jawapan dan soalan ringkas*: I don't like fish. ♦ Does she speak Italian? ♦ He doesn't work here, does he? ❶ For more information, look at the Reference section at the back of this dictionary. **2** used to avoid repeating the main verb □ *digunakan utk mengelak drpd mengulangi kk utama*: He earns a lot more than I do. ♦ She's feeling much better than she did last week. **3** used for emphasizing the main verb □ *digunakan utk menekankan kk utama*: I can't find the receipt now but I'm sure I did pay the phone bill.

do³ /du:/ noun [C] (pl **dos** /du:z/) (informal) a party or other social event □ *parti; majlis*: We're having a bit of a do to celebrate Tim's birthday. **IDM dos and don'ts** things that you should and should not do □ *peraturan; perkara-perkara yg patut dan tdk patut dibuat*: the dos and don'ts of mountain climbing

docile /ˈdəʊsaɪl/ adj (used about a person or an animal) quiet and easy to control □ *mengikut kata; jinak (binatang)*

dock¹ /dɒk/ noun **1** [C,U] an area of a port where ships stop to be loaded, repaired, etc. □ *dok; limbungan* **2 docks** [pl] a group of **docks** with all the buildings, offices, etc. that are around them □ *kawasan limbungan*: He works down at the docks. **3** (AmE) = **jetty** **4** [C, usually sing] the place in a court of law where the person who is accused sits or stands □ *kandang orang salah*

dock² /dɒk/ verb **1** [I,T] (used about a ship) to sail into a port and stop at the **dock** □ *berlabuh*: The ship had docked/was docked at Lisbon. **2** [T] to take away part of the money sb earns, especially as a punishment □ *memotong*: They've docked £20 off my wages because I was late.

ˈdocking station noun [C] a device to which you can connect a small computer in order to use it like a larger one; a device with speakers that you can connect to some types of small equipment for listening to music □ *peranti penyambung* ⊃ note at **iPod™**, **smartphone**

doctor¹ /ˈdɒktə(r)/ noun (abbr Dr) **1** [C] a person who has been trained in medicine and who treats people who are ill □ *doktor*: Our family doctor is Dr Laing. ♦ I've got a doctor's appointment at 10 o'clock. ⊃ note at **disease**, **hospital**, **ill** ⊃ picture on page P2 **2 the doctor's** [sing] a doctor's **surgery** (= the place where a doctor sees patients) □ *klinik*: I'm going to the doctor's today. **3** [C] a person who has a **doctorate** (= the highest degree from a university) □ *doktor*: a Doctor of Philosophy

---

TOPIC

Going to the doctor

In Britain a **doctor** who looks after general health problems is called a **GP** (/ˌdʒiːˈpiːcolon; ˈpiːæpcolon;/). He/She works in **a surgery**. When you **go to the doctor's**, you describe your **symptoms**: My head hurts. ♦ I've got stomach ache. The doctor may **prescribe** a particular **medicine**. This is written on an official piece of paper called a **prescription**, which you take to a **chemist's** and show when you buy the medicine. If you are feeling very **ill** or if you are in a lot of **pain**, the doctor may send you to **hospital** for more **treatment**.

---

doctor² /ˈdɒktə(r)/ verb [T] **1** to change sth that should not be changed in order to gain an advantage □ *memalsukan*: The results of the survey had been doctored. **2** to add sth harmful to food or drink □ *membubuh sst yg berbahaya pd makanan atau minuman*

doctorate /ˈdɒktərət/ noun [C] the highest university degree □ *ijazah kedoktoran*

doctrine /ˈdɒktrɪn/ noun [C,U] a set of beliefs that is taught by a church, political party, etc. □ *doktrin*

document /ˈdɒkjumənt/ noun [C] **1** an official piece of writing which gives information, proof or evidence □ *dokumen*: Her lawyer asked her to read and sign a number of documents. **2** a computer file that contains writing, etc. □ *dokumen*: Save the document before closing.

documentary /ˌdɒkjuˈmentri/ noun [C] (pl **documentaries**) a film or TV or radio programme that gives facts or information about a particular subject □ *dokumentari*: Did you see that documentary on Sri Lanka?

doddle /ˈdɒdl/ noun [sing] (BrE informal) something that is very easy to do □ *sangat senang; mudah sekali*: The exam was an absolute doddle!

dodge¹ /dɒdʒ/ verb **1** [I,T] to move quickly in order to avoid sb/sth □ *mengelak*: I had to dodge between the cars to cross the road. **2** [T] to avoid doing sth that you should do □ *mengelak*: Don't try to dodge your responsibilities!

dodge² /dɒdʒ/ noun [C] (informal) a clever way of avoiding sth □ *elakan; pengelakan*: The man had been involved in a massive tax dodge.

dodgy /ˈdɒdʒi/ adj (**dodgier**; **dodgiest**) (BrE informal) involving risk; not honest or not to be

---

[I] **intransitive**, a verb which has no object: He laughed.   [T] **transitive**, a verb which has an object: He ate an apple.

trusted □ *tdk boleh dipercayai; tdk baik*: *This meat looks a bit dodgy—when did we buy it?* ♦ *a dodgy business deal*

doe /dəʊ/ *noun* [C] a female **deer** (= a large wild animal that eats grass) or **rabbit** (= a small animal with long ears) □ *rusa/arnab betina* ⊃ note at **deer** ⊃ picture at **deer**

does /dʌz/ ⊃ **do**

doesn't /'dʌznt/ short for **does not**

dog¹ /dɒg/ *noun* [C] **1** an animal that many people keep as a pet, or for working on farms, hunting, etc □ *anjing*: *dog food* ⊃ note at **pet** **2** a male dog or male **fox** (= a wild animal like a dog with reddish fur and a thick tail) □ *anjing jantan; binatang jantan (rubah, dsb)*: *If you're getting a puppy, bitches are gentler than dogs.*

> **TOPIC**
>
> **Dogs**
> When you **take** your dog **for a walk**, you control it with a long piece of leather, rope, etc. called a **lead**. You might put a **muzzle** over its nose and mouth so that it cannot **bite**. When a dog makes a noise it **barks** (written as **woof**) and when it is excited, it **wags** its **tail**. A young dog is called a **puppy**. Dogs that are **trained** to help the blind (= people who cannot see) are called **guide dogs**.

dog² /dɒg/ *verb* [T] (**dogging; dogged**) to follow sb closely □ *mengekori; memburu*: *A shadowy figure was dogging their every move.* ♦ (*figurative*) *Bad luck and illness have dogged her career from the start.*

'dog collar *noun* [C] (*informal*) a white band that is worn around the neck by some priests in the Christian church □ *kolar paderi*

'dog-eared *adj* (used about a book or piece of paper) in bad condition with untidy corners and edges because it has been used a lot □ *berkelepet; lusuh*

dogged /'dɒgɪd/ *adj* refusing to give up even when sth is difficult □ *gigih; penuh azam*: *I was impressed by his dogged determination to succeed.* ▶ **doggedly** *adv*: *She doggedly refused all offers of help.*

dogma /'dɒgmə/ *noun* [C,U] a belief or set of beliefs that people are expected to accept as true without questioning □ *dogma*

dogmatic /dɒg'mætɪk/ *adj* being certain that your beliefs are right and that others should accept them, without considering other opinions or evidence □ *dogmatik* ▶ **dogmatically** /-kli/ *adv*

dogsbody /'dɒgzbɒdi/ *noun* [C] (*pl* **dogsbodies**) (*BrE informal*) a person who has to do the boring or unpleasant jobs that nobody else wants to do and who is considered less important than other people □ *orang suruhan*

the doldrums /'dɒldrəmz/ *noun*
IDM **in the doldrums 1** unhappy □ *muram; sedih*: *He's been in the doldrums ever since she left him.* **2** not active or busy □ *tdk giat; lembap; malap*: *Business has been in the doldrums recently.*

the dole /dəʊl/ *noun* [sing] (*BrE informal*) money that the State gives every week to people who are unemployed □ *elaun pengangguran*: *I lost my job and had to go on the dole.*

dole /dəʊl/ *verb*
PHR V **dole sth out** (*informal*) to give sth, especially food, money, etc. in small amounts to a number of people □ *membahagikan seorang sedikit*

doleful /'dəʊlfl/ *adj* sad or unhappy □ *suram; sedih*: *She looked at him with large doleful eyes.* ▶ **dolefully** /-fəli/ *adv*

doll /dɒl/ *noun* [C] a child's toy that looks like a small person or a baby □ *anak patung*

dollar /'dɒlə(r)/ *noun* **1** [C] (*symbol* $) a unit of money in some countries, for example the US, Canada and Australia □ *dolar*: *Can I pay in US dollars?*

> MORE There are 100 **cents** in a dollar.

2 [C] a note or coin that is worth one dollar □ *satu dolar*: *a dollar bill* **3 the dollar** [sing] the value of the US dollar on international money markets □ *dolar*: *The dollar fell against the pound.*

dollop /'dɒləp/ *noun* [C] (*informal*) a lump of sth soft, especially food □ *longgok*: *a dollop of ice cream*

dolphin

shark

dolphin /'dɒlfɪn/ *noun* [C] an animal that lives in the sea and looks like a large fish. **Dolphins** usually swim in **schools** (= large groups). □ *dolfin; ikan lumba-lumba*

domain /də'meɪn; dəʊ-/ *noun* [C] **1** an area of knowledge or activity □ *bidang*: *I don't know— that's outside my domain.* ♦ *This issue is now in the public domain* (= the public knows about it). **2** a set of websites on the Internet which end with the same group of letters, for example '.com', '.org' □ *domain*

dome /dəʊm/ *noun* [C] a round roof on a building □ *kubah*: *the dome of St Paul's in London* ⊃ picture on **page P11** ▶ **domed** *adj*: *a domed roof/forehead*

domestic /dəˈmestɪk/ *adj* **1** not international; only within one country □ *dlm negeri*: *domestic affairs/flights/politics* **2** [only before a noun] connected with the home or family □ *(berkenaan dgn) rumah tangga atau keluarga*: *domestic chores/tasks* ♦ *the growing problem of* **domestic violence** (= violence between members of the same family) ♦ *domestic water/gas/electricity supplies* **3** (used about a person) enjoying doing things in the home, such as cooking and cleaning □ *suka kehidupan di rumah*: *I'm not a very domestic sort of person.* **4** (used about animals) kept as pets or on farms; not wild □ *jinak; peliharaan*: *domestic animals such as cats, dogs and horses*

domesticated /dəˈmestɪkeɪtɪd/ *adj* **1** (used about animals) happy being near people and being controlled by them □ *jinak* **2** (used about people) to be good at cleaning the house, cooking, etc. □ *biasa atau pandai dlm kerja-kerja rumah*: *Men are expected to be much more domesticated nowadays.*

dominance /ˈdɒmɪnəns/ *noun* [U] control or power □ *penguasaan; dominans*: *Japan's dominance of the car industry*

dominant /ˈdɒmɪnənt/ *adj* more powerful, important or noticeable than others □ *paling berkuasa; dominan*: *His mother was the dominant influence in his life.*

dominate /ˈdɒmɪneɪt/ *verb* **1** [I,T] to be more powerful, important or noticeable than others □ *menguasai*: *The Italian team dominated throughout the second half of the game.* ♦ *She always tends to dominate the conversation.* **2** [T] (used about a building or place) to be much higher than everything else □ *paling tinggi; menguasai pemandangan*: *The cathedral dominates the area for miles around.* ▶ **domination** /ˌdɒmɪˈneɪʃn/ *noun* [U]

domineering /ˌdɒmɪˈnɪərɪŋ/ *adj* having a very strong character and wanting to control other people □ *suka menguasai/menindas* SYN **overbearing**

dominion /dəˈmɪniən/ *noun* (*formal*) **1** [U] the power to rule and control □ *kuasa memerintah; penguasaan*: *to have dominion over an area* **2** [C] an area controlled by one government or ruler □ *kawasan yg dikuasai; dominion*: *the dominions of the Roman empire*

domino /ˈdɒmɪnəʊ/ *noun* [C] (*pl* **dominoes**) one of a set of small flat pieces of wood or plastic, marked on one side with two groups of spots representing numbers, that are used for playing a game called **dominoes** □ *domino*

donate /dəʊˈneɪt/ *verb* [T] **donate sth (to sb/ sth)** **1** to give money or goods to an organization, especially one for people or animals who need help □ *mendermakan*: *She donated a large sum of money to Cancer Research.* **2** to allow doctors to remove blood or a body organ in order to help sb who needs it □ *mendermakan darah*

donation /dəʊˈneɪʃn/ *noun* [pl] money, etc. that is given to a person or an organization such as a charity, in order to help people or animals in need □ *derma*

done¹ *past participle of* **do¹**

done² /dʌn/ *adj* [not before a noun] **1** finished □ *siap; selesai*: *I've got to go out as soon as this job is done.* **2** (used about food) cooked enough □ *cukup masak*: *The meat's ready but the vegetables still aren't done.*
IDM **over and done with** completely finished; in the past □ *habis selesai; sudah lepas*

done³ /dʌn/ *exclam* used for saying that you accept an offer □ *setuju*: *'I'll give you twenty pounds for it.' 'Done!'*

donkey /ˈdɒŋki/ (*AmE* also) / *noun* [C] (also **ass**) an animal like a small horse, with long ears □ *keldai*
IDM **donkey's years** (*BrE informal*) a very long time □ *lama betul*: *We've known each other for donkey's years.*

donkey

donor /ˈdəʊnə(r)/ *noun* [C] **1** a person who gives money or goods to an organization that helps people or animals □ *penderma* **2** a person who gives blood or a part of their own body for medical use □ *penderma*: *a blood/kidney donor*

don't /dəʊnt/ *short for* **do not**

donut (*AmE*) = **doughnut**

doodle /ˈduːdl/ *verb* [I] to draw lines, patterns, etc. without thinking, especially when you are bored □ *mencoreng* ▶ **doodle** *noun* [C]

doom /duːm/ *noun* [U] death or a terrible event in the future which you cannot avoid □ *ajal, maut, nasib malang, malapetaka, dsb yg pasti akan berlaku; selalu menjangkakan yg tdk baik*: *a sense of impending doom* (= that sth bad is going to happen) ♦ *Don't listen to her. She's always full of* **doom and gloom** (= expecting bad things to happen). ▶ **doomed** *adj*: *The plan was doomed from the start.*

door /dɔː(r)/ *noun* [C] **1** a piece of wood, glass, etc. that you open and close to get in or out of a room, building, car, etc. □ *(daun) pintu*: *to open/shut/close the door* ♦ *to answer the door* (= to open the door when sb knocks or rings the bell) ♦ *There's somebody at the door. Could you see who it is?* ♦ *Have you bolted/locked the door?* ♦ *I could hear someone knocking on the door.* ♦ *the* front/back door ♦ *the fridge door* ➔ picture on page P7 **2** the entrance to a building, room, car, etc. □ *pintu*: *I looked through the door and saw her sitting there.*

IDM **(from) door to door** (from) house to house □ *dr rumah ke rumah*: *The journey takes about five hours, door to door.* ♦ *a door-to-door salesman* (= a person who visits people in their homes to try and sell them things)

next door (to sb/sth) in the next house, room, etc □ *(di) sebelah rumah*: *Do you know the people who live next door?*

out of doors outside □ *(di) luar rumah*: *Shall we eat out of doors today?* **SYN** **outdoors** **OPP** **indoors**

doorbell /'dɔːbel/ *noun* [C] a bell with a button outside a house that you push to let the people inside know that you are there □ *loceng pintu*

doorman /'dɔːmən/ *noun* [C] (*pl* **-men** /-mən/) a man, often in uniform, whose job is to stand at the entrance to a large building such as a hotel or a theatre, and open the door for visitors, find them taxis, etc. □ *penjaga pintu*

doormat /'dɔːmæt/ *noun* [C] **1** a piece of material on the floor in front of a door which you can clean your shoes on before going inside □ *alas/pengesat kaki* **2** (*informal*) a person who allows other people to treat them badly without complaining □ *orang yg sanggup ditindas tanpa merungut*

doorstep /'dɔːstep/ *noun* [C] a step in front of a door outside a building □ *anak tangga depan pintu*

IDM **on your/the doorstep** very near to you □ *sangat dekat*: *The sea was right on our doorstep.*

doorway /'dɔːweɪ/ *noun* [C] an opening filled by a door leading into a building, room, etc. □ *muka/ambang pintu*: *She was standing in the doorway.*

dope¹ /dəʊp/ *noun* (*informal*) **1** [U] an illegal drug, such as **cannabis** □ *dadah* **2** [C] a stupid person □ *(si) bodoh/tongong*: *What a dope!*

dope² /dəʊp/ *verb* [T] to give a drug secretly to a person or an animal, especially to make them sleep □ *memberi dadah*

dopey /'dəʊpi/ *adj* (**dopier**; **dopiest**) (*informal*) **1** stupid; not intelligent □ *bodoh*; *tongong* **2** tired and not able to think clearly, especially because of drugs, alcohol or lack of sleep □ *mamai*

dormant /'dɔːmənt/ *adj* not active for some time □ *tdk aktif*; *pendam*: *a dormant volcano*

dormitory /'dɔːmətri/ *noun* [C] (*pl* **dormitories**) (also **dorm** /dɔːm/) **1** a large bedroom with a number of beds in it, especially in a school, etc. □ *bilik asrama* **2** (*AmE*) = **hall of residence**

dosage /'dəʊsɪdʒ/ *noun* [C, usually *sing*] the amount of a medicine you should take over a period of time □ *dos*: *The recommended dosage is one tablet every four hours.*

dose¹ /dəʊs/ *noun* [C] **1** an amount of medicine that you take at one time □ *sukatan ubat*: *Take a dose of the medicine before going to bed.* ➔ look at **overdose** **2** an amount of sth, especially sth unpleasant □ *banyaknya sst (selalunya sst yg tdk menyenangkan)*: *a dose of the flu* ♦ *I can only stand him in small doses.*

dose² /dəʊs/ *verb* [T] to give sb/yourself some medicine or a drug □ *makan ubat*: *She dosed herself with aspirin and went to work.*

doss /dɒs/ *verb* (BrE *informal*)

PHR V **doss about/around** to waste time not doing very much □ *melepak*: *We just dossed about in class yesterday.*

doss (down) to lie down to sleep, without a proper bed □ *tidur*: *Do you mind if I doss down on your floor tonight?*

dot¹ /dɒt/ *noun* [C] **1** a small, round mark, like a full stop □ *titik*; *bintik*: *a white dress with black dots* ♦ *The letters i and j have dots above them.*

HELP We use **dot** when we say a person's email address. For the address written as ann@smithuni.co.uk we would say 'Ann **at** smithuni **dot** co **dot** uk'.

2 something that looks like a **dot** □ *titik*: *He watched until the aeroplane was just a dot in the sky.*

IDM **on the dot** (*informal*) at exactly the right time or at exactly the time mentioned □ *tepat pd waktunya*: *Lessons start at 9 o'clock on the dot.*

dot² /dɒt/ *verb* [T] (**dotting**; **dotted**) **1** to mark with a **dot** □ *membubuh titik* **2** [usually passive] to spread things or people over an area; to be spread over an area □ *berselerak*; *bertaburan*: *The countryside was dotted with small villages.* ♦ *There are restaurants dotted about all over the centre of town.* ♦ *Small villages dot the countryside.*

dot-com (also **dotcom**) /,dɒt 'kɒm/ *noun* [C] a company that sells products and services on the Internet □ *syarikat yg menjual produk dan perkhidmatan di Internet*: *The weaker dot-coms have collapsed.* ♦ *a dot-com millionaire*

dote /dəʊt/ *verb* [I] **dote on sb/sth** to have or show a lot of love for sb/sth and ignore their faults □ *sangat sayang/memanjakan*: *He's always doted on his eldest son.* ▸ **doting** *adj*: *doting parents*

dotted line *noun* [C] a line of **dots** which show where sth is to be written on a form, etc. □ *garis titik*: *Sign on the dotted line.* ➔ picture at **line**

double¹ /'dʌbl/ *adj, determiner* **1** twice as much or as many (as usual) □ *sekali ganda*: *His income is double his wife's.* ♦ *We'll need double the amount of wine.* **2** having two equal or similar parts □ *kembar*; *dua*: *double doors* ♦ *Does 'necessary' have (a) double 's'?* ♦ *My phone number is two four double three four* (= 24334). **3** made for or used by two people or things □ *kelamin*; *utk dua orang*: *a double garage* ➔ note at **bed¹** ➔ picture at **bed**

double² /'dʌbl/ adv in pairs or two parts □ *berdua; dua*: When I saw her with her twin sister I thought I was seeing double.

double³ /'dʌbl/ noun 1 [U] twice the (usual) number or amount □ *dua kali lebih banyak; sekali ganda*: When you work overtime, you get paid double. **2** [C] a glass of strong alcoholic drink containing twice the usual amount □ *segelas arak yg mengandungi dua kali sukatan arak drpd biasa* **3** [C] a person who looks very much like another □ *orang yg serupa*: I thought it was you I saw in the supermarket. You must have a double. **4** [C] an actor who replaces another actor in a film to do dangerous or other special things □ *pelakon gantian* **5** [C] a bedroom for two people in a hotel, etc. □ *bilik kelamin*: Would you like a single or a double? ⊃ look at **single 6 doubles** [U, with sing or pl verb] (in some sports, for example **tennis**) with two pairs playing □ *permainan beregu*: the Men's Doubles final ⊃ look at **single**

double⁴ /'dʌbl/ verb 1 [I,T] to become or to make sth twice as much or as many; to multiply by two □ *berganda; menggandakan*: The price of houses has almost doubled. ♦ Think of a number and double it. **2** [I] **double (up) as sth** to have a second use or function □ *juga digunakan sebagai*: The small room doubles (up) as a study.

PHR V double (sb) up/over (to cause sb) to bend the body □ *terbongkok-bongkok*: to be doubled up with pain/laughter

double 'bass (also **bass**) *noun* [C] the largest musical instrument with strings, that you can play either standing up or sitting down □ *dabal bes* ⊃ picture at **music**

double-'breasted *adj* (used about a coat or jacket) having two rows of buttons down the front □ *berbutang dua baris*

double-'check *verb* [I,T] to check sth again, or with great care □ *menyemak/memeriksa sekali lagi*

double-'click *verb* [I,T] ~ **(on sth)** to choose a particular function or item on a computer screen by pressing one of the buttons on a mouse twice quickly □ *klik dua kali*: To run an application, just double-click on the icon.

double-'cross *verb* [T] to cheat sb who believes that they can trust you after you have agreed to do sth dishonest together □ *mengkhianati; membelot*

double-'decker *noun* [C] a bus with two floors □ *bas dua tingkat*

double 'Dutch *noun* [U] (BrE) conversation or writing that you cannot understand at all □ *perbualan atau tulisan yg tdk difahami*: The listening comprehension in the exam was really hard. It all sounded like double Dutch to me!

double 'figures (AmE **double ˌdigits**) *noun* [U] (BrE) a number that is more than nine and less than 100 □ *dua digit*: Inflation is in double figures.

double 'glazing *noun* [U] two layers of glass in a window to keep a building warm or quiet □ *kaca dua lapis* ▸ **double-'glazed** *adj*

doubly /'dʌbli/ adv 1 more than usually □ *betul-betul*: Pete made doubly sure that the door was locked. **2** in two ways □ *dua kali; berganda*: He was doubly blessed with both good looks and talent.

doubt¹ /daʊt/ noun [C,U] **doubt (about sth); doubt that …; doubt as to sth** a feeling of being uncertain about sth □ *keraguan*: If you have any doubts about the job, feel free to ring me and discuss them. ♦ There's some doubt that Jan will pass the exam.

IDM cast doubt on sth ⊃ **cast¹**
give sb the benefit of the doubt ⊃ **benefit¹**
in doubt not sure or definite □ *ragu-ragu; tdk pasti*
no doubt 1 used when you are saying sth is probable □ *mungkin sekali*: No doubt she'll write when she has time. **2** used when you are saying that sth is certainly true □ *memang benar*: He's made some great movies. There's no doubt about it.
without (a) doubt definitely □ *tentu sekali*: It was, without doubt, the coldest winter for many years.

doubt² /daʊt/ verb [T] to think sth is unlikely or to feel uncertain (about sth) □ *meragui*: She never doubted that he was telling the truth. ♦ I doubt whether/if I'll have time to go to the shops today. ♦ He had never doubted her support.

doubtful /'daʊtfl/ adj 1 doubtful (about sth/about doing sth) (used about a person) not sure □ *berasa ragu-ragu*: John still felt doubtful about his decision. **2** unlikely or uncertain □ *belum tentu lagi; tdk mungkin*: It's doubtful whether/if we'll finish in time. ♦ It was doubtful that he was still alive. ▸ **doubtfully** /-fəli/ *adv*: 'I suppose it'll be all right,' she said doubtfully.

doubtless /'daʊtləs/ adv almost certainly □ *sudah tentu*: Doubtless she'll have a good excuse for being late!

dough /dəʊ/ noun [U] **1** a mixture of flour, water, etc. used for baking into bread, etc. □ *doh* **2** (slang) money □ *duit*

doughnut (AmE **donut**) **/'dəʊnʌt/ noun** [C] a small cake in the shape of a ball or a ring, often filled with jam, etc., made from a sweet **dough** cooked in very hot oil □ *donut* ⊃ picture at **cake**

dour /dʊə(r)/ adj (used about sb's manner or expression) cold and unfriendly □ *(muka) masam; (sikap) dingin*

douse /daʊs/ (also **dowse /daʊz/**) *verb* [T] **1 douse sth (with sth)** to stop a fire from burning by pouring liquid over it □ *memadamkan (api)*: The firefighters managed to douse the flames. **2 douse sb/sth (in/with sth)** to cover sb/sth with liquid □ *menyimbah*: to douse yourself in perfume (= wear too much of it)

dove¹ /dʌv/ noun [C] a type of white bird, often used as a sign of peace □ *merpati putih*

dove² /dəʊv/ (*AmE*) past tense of **dive¹**

dowdy /'daʊdi/ adj (**dowdier**; **dowdiest**) (used about a person or the clothes they wear) not attractive or fashionable □ *tdk bergaya; tdk menarik*

down¹ /daʊn/ adv, prep **1** to or at a lower level or place; from the top towards the bottom of sth □ *ke/di bawah; turun; menuruni*: Can you get that book down from the top shelf? ♦ 'Where's Mary?' 'She's down in the basement.' ♦ Her hair hung down her back. ♦ The rain was running down the window. **2** from a standing or vertical position to a sitting or horizontal one □ *baring; jatuh*: I think I'll sit/lie down. **3** used for showing that the level, amount, strength, etc. of sth is less or lower □ *kurang; turun*: Do you mind if I turn the heating down a bit? **4** to or in the south □ *ke/di selatan; turun*: We went down to Devon for our holiday. **5** on paper □ *tuliskan; catatkan*: Put these dates down in your diary. **6** along □ *sepanjang*: We sailed down the river towards the sea. ♦ 'Where's the nearest garage?' 'Go down this road and take the first turning on the right.' **7 down to sb/sth** even including □ *hinggakan*: We had everything planned down to the last detail.

IDM be down to sb to be sb's responsibility □ *bergantung pd sso*: When my father died it was down to me to look after the family's affairs.

be down to sth to have only the amount mentioned left □ *hanya tinggal*: I need to do some washing—I'm down to my last shirt.

down and out having no money, job or home □ *hidup melarat*

down in the dumps unhappy or sad □ *sedih*

down under (*informal*) (in) Australia □ *(di) Australia*

down² /daʊn/ verb [T] (*informal*) to finish a drink quickly □ *meneguk; menggogok*: She **downed** her drink in one (= she drank the whole glass without stopping).

down³ /daʊn/ adj [not before a noun] **1** sad □ *muram; sugul*: You're looking a bit down today. **2** (used about computers) not working □ *tdk berfungsi*: I can't access the file as our computers have been down all morning. **3** lower than before □ *turun; kurang; susut*: Unemployment figures are down again this month.

down⁴ /daʊn/ noun [U] very soft feathers □ *bulu lembut*: a duvet filled with duck down

IDM ups and downs ⊃ **ups**

down-and-out noun [C] a person who has got no money, job or home □ *orang yg hidup melarat*

downcast /'daʊnkɑːst/ adj **1** (used about a person) sad and without hope □ *sugul; sedih* **2** (used about eyes) looking down □ *memandang ke bawah*

downfall /'daʊnfɔːl/ noun [sing] a loss of sb's money, power, social position, etc.; the thing that causes this □ *kejatuhan*: The government's downfall seemed inevitable. ♦ Greed was her downfall.

downgrade /ˌdaʊn'greɪd/ verb [T] **downgrade sb/sth (from sth) (to sth)** to reduce sb/sth to a lower level or position of importance □ *menurunkan pangkat/taraf*: Tom's been downgraded from manager to assistant manager.

downhearted /ˌdaʊn'hɑːtɪd/ adj [not before a noun] sad □ *sedih; bersedih hati*

downhill /ˌdaʊn'hɪl/ adj, adv (going) downwards; towards the bottom of a hill □ *menuruni bukit*: It's an easy walk. The road runs downhill most of the way. **OPP** uphill

IDM go downhill to get worse □ *semakin teruk; merosot*: Their relationship has been going downhill for some time now.

download /ˌdaʊn'ləʊd/ verb [T] to copy a computer file, etc. from a large computer system to a smaller one □ *muat turun* **OPP** upload ▶ **download** /'daʊnləʊd/ noun [C]

downmarket /ˌdaʊn'mɑːkɪt/ adj cheap and of low quality □ *murah; picisan*: a downmarket newspaper **OPP** upmarket ▶ **downmarket** adv

down 'payment noun [C] a sum of money that is given as the first part of a larger payment □ *bayaran pendahuluan; cengkeram*: We're saving to **make a down payment on** a new car.

downpour /'daʊnpɔː(r)/ noun [C] a heavy, sudden fall of rain □ *hujan lebat*

downright /'daʊnraɪt/ adj [only before a noun] (used about sth bad or unpleasant) complete □ *betul-betul*: The holiday was a downright disaster. ▶ **downright** adv: The way he spoke to me was downright rude!

downside /'daʊnsaɪd/ noun [C, usually sing] the disadvantages or negative aspects of sth □ *kekurangan*: All good ideas have a downside.

Down's syndrome /'daʊnz sɪndrəʊm/ noun [U] a medical condition in which a person is born with a flat, wide face and lower than average intelligence □ *sindrom Down*

downstairs /ˌdaʊn'steəz/ adv, adj towards or on a lower floor of a house or building □ *ke/di tingkat bawah*: He fell downstairs and broke his arm. ♦ Dad's downstairs, in the kitchen. ♦ a downstairs toilet **OPP** upstairs ▶ **downstairs** noun [sing]: We're painting the downstairs. **OPP** upstairs

downstream /ˌdaʊn'striːm/ adv in the direction in which a river flows □ *ke hilir*: We were rowing downstream. **OPP** upstream

down to 'earth adj (used about a person) sensible, realistic and practical □ *praktikal; bersifat realistik*

downtrodden /'daʊntrɒdn/ adj (used about a person) made to suffer bad treatment or living conditions by people in power, but being too tired, poor, ill, etc. to change this □ *(yg) tertindas*

[C] **countable**, a noun with a plural form: *one book, two books*   [U] **uncountable**, a noun with no plural form: *some sugar*

downturn → drain

downturn /ˈdaʊntɜːn/ noun [C, usually sing] a downturn (in sth) a drop in the amount of business that is done; a time when the economy becomes weaker □ *kemerosotan*: *a downturn in sales/trade/business* **OPP** upturn

downward /ˈdaʊnwəd/ adj [only before a noun] towards the ground or a lower level □ *ke bawah; menurun*: *a downward movement* ▶ **downwards** /ˈdaʊnwədz/ adv: *She laid the picture face downwards on the table.* **OPP** upward(s)

dowry /ˈdaʊri/ noun [C] (pl dowries) money and/or property which, in some countries, a woman's family gives to the man she is marrying, or that a husband must pay to his wife's family □ *hantaran kahwin*

dowse = douse

doze /dəʊz/ verb [I] to sleep lightly and/or for a short time □ *terlelap; terlena*: *He was dozing in front of the TV.*
PHR V **doze off** to go to sleep, especially during the day □ *terlelap*: *I'm sorry—I must have dozed off for a minute.*
▶ **doze** noun [sing]

dozen /ˈdʌzn/ noun [C] (abbr doz.) (pl dozen) twelve or a group of twelve □ *dozen*: *A dozen eggs, please.* ♦ *half a dozen (= six)* ♦ *two dozen sheep*
IDM **dozens (of sth)** (informal) very many □ *banyak*: *I've tried phoning her dozens of times.*

dozy /ˈdəʊzi/ adj 1 wanting to sleep; not feeling awake □ *mengantuk*: *The wine had made her rather dozy.* 2 (BrE informal) stupid; not intelligent □ *bodoh; bongok*: *You dozy thing—look what you've done!*

Dr abbr = **Doctor**[1] □ *doktor*: *Dr Ruchira Paranjape*

drab /dræb/ adj (drabber; drabbest) not interesting or attractive □ *suram; tdk menarik*: *a drab grey office building*

draft[1] /drɑːft/ noun 1 [C] a piece of writing, etc. which will probably be changed and improved; not the final version □ *draf*: *the first draft of a speech/essay* 2 [C] a written order to a bank to pay money to sb □ *draf bank*: *All payments must be made by bank draft.* 3 **the draft** [sing] (especially AmE) = **conscription** 4 [C] (AmE) = **draught**[1](1)

draft[2] /drɑːft/ verb [T] 1 to make a first or early copy of a piece of writing □ *mendraf*: *I'll draft a letter and show it to you before I send it.* 2 to choose people and send them somewhere for a special task □ *mengerah*: *Extra police are being drafted in to control the crowds.* 3 [usually passive] (AmE) to force sb to join the armed forces □ *dikerah*: *He was drafted into the army.*

draftsman /ˈdrɑːftsmən/ (AmE) = **draughtsman**

drafty (AmE) = **draughty**

drag[1] /dræg/ verb (dragging; dragged) 1 [T] to pull sb/sth along with difficulty □ *menyeret*: *The box was so heavy we had to drag it along the floor.* 2 [T] to make sb come or go somewhere □ *mengheret; mengajak*: *She's always trying to drag me along to museums, but I'm not interested.* 3 [I] **drag (on)** to be boring or to seem to last a long time □ *meleret-leret; berlarutan*: *The speeches dragged on for hours.* 4 [T] to move sth across the screen of the computer using the mouse □ *seret*: *Click on the file and drag it into the new folder.*
PHR V **drag sth out** to make sth last longer than necessary □ *meleret-leretkan*: *Let's not drag this decision out—shall we go or not?*
drag sth out (of sb) to force or persuade sb to give you information □ *mencungkil maklumat (drpd sso)*

drag[2] /dræg/ noun 1 [sing] (informal) a person or thing that is boring or annoying □ *sst yg membosankan atau menyusahkan*: *'The car's broken down.' 'Oh no! What a drag!'* 2 [C] an act of breathing in cigarette smoke □ *(perbuatan) menyedut asap rokok*: *He took a long drag on his cigarette.* 3 [U] women's clothes worn by a man, especially as part of a show, etc. □ *pakaian perempuan yg dipakai oleh lelaki*: *men in drag*

drag-and-ˈdrop adj relating to the moving of **icons** (= small pictures or symbols that represents programs), etc. on a screen using the mouse □ *seret dan lepas*

dragon /ˈdrægən/ noun [C] (in stories) a large animal with wings, which can breathe fire □ *naga*

dragonfly /ˈdrægənflaɪ/ noun [C] (pl dragonflies) an insect with a long thin body and two pairs of wings, often seen near water □ *pepatung, patung-patung* ➔ picture on **page P13**

drain[1] /dreɪn/ verb 1 [I,T] to become empty or dry as liquid flows away and disappears; to make sth dry or empty in this way □ *menyalirkan; mengeringkan; mengetuskan*: *Leave the dishes to drain.* ♦ *The whole area will have to be drained before it can be used for farming.* ♦ *Drain the pasta and add the sauce.* 2 [I,T] **drain (sth) (from/out of sth); drain (sth) (away/off)** to flow away; to make a liquid flow away □ *mengalirkan*: *The sink's blocked—the water won't drain away at all.* ♦ *The plumber had to drain the water from the heating system.* ♦ *(figurative) He felt all his anger begin to drain away.* 3 [T] to drink all the liquid in a glass, cup, etc. □ *menghabiskan (minuman)*: *He drained his glass in one gulp.* 4 [T] **drain sb/sth (of sth)** to make sb/sth weaker, poorer, etc. by slowly using all the strength, money, etc. available □ *melemahkan; menyusutkan*: *Her hospital expenses were slowly draining my funds.* ♦ *The experience left her emotionally drained.*

drain[2] /dreɪn/ noun [C] a pipe or hole in the ground that dirty water, etc. goes down to be carried away □ *parit; longkang*
IDM **(go) down the drain** (informal) (to be) wasted □ *sia-sia*: *All that hard work has gone down the drain.*

a drain on sb/sth something that uses up time, money, strength, etc. □ *(sst yg) menyusutkan/ melemahkan sst/sso*: *The cost of travelling is a great drain on our budget.*

drainage /ˈdreɪnɪdʒ/ *noun* [U] a system used for making water, etc. flow away from a place □ *saliran*

draining board (*AmE* **drain board**) *noun* [C] the place in the kitchen where you put plates, cups, knives, etc. to dry after washing them □ *bod pengetus*

drainpipe /ˈdreɪnpaɪp/ *noun* [C] a pipe which goes down the side of a building and carries water from the roof into a **drain** □ *paip salir* ⇒ picture on **page P8**

drake /dreɪk/ *noun* [C] a male **duck** (= a bird that lives on or near water) □ *itik jantan* ⇒ note at **duck** ⇒ picture at **duck**

drama /ˈdrɑːmə/ *noun* 1 [C] a play for the theatre, radio or TV □ *drama*: *a contemporary drama* 2 [U] plays as a form of writing; the performance of plays □ *seni drama; seni lakon*: *He wrote some drama, as well as poetry.* ⇒ note at **literature** 3 [C,U] an exciting event; exciting things that happen □ *seni*: *a real-life courtroom drama*

dramatic /drəˈmætɪk/ *adj* 1 noticeable or sudden and often surprising □ *mendadak*: *a dramatic change/increase/fall/improvement* 2 exciting or impressive □ *dramatik; menarik*: *the film's dramatic opening scene* 3 connected with plays or the theatre □ *(berkenaan dgn) drama/seni lakon*: *Shakespeare's dramatic works* 4 (used about a person or their behaviour) showing feelings, etc. in a very obvious way because you want other people to notice you □ *berdrama*: *Calm down. There's no need to be so dramatic about everything!* ▶ **dramatically** /-kli/ *adv*

dramatist /ˈdræmətɪst/ *noun* [C] a person who writes plays for the theatre, radio or TV □ *dramatis; penulis drama* SYN **playwright**

dramatize (also **-ise**) /ˈdræmətaɪz/ *verb* 1 [T] to make a book, an event, etc. into a play □ *mendramakan*: *The novel has been dramatized for TV.* 2 [I,T] to make sth seem more exciting or important than it really is □ *membesar-besarkan*: *The newspaper was accused of dramatizing the facts.* ▶ **dramatization** (also **-isation**) /ˌdræmətaɪˈzeɪʃn/ *noun* [C,U]

drank *past tense of* **drink**[1]

drape /dreɪp/ *verb* [T] 1 **drape sth round/over sth** to put a piece of cloth, clothing, etc. on sth in a loose way □ *menyangkut; menggantung*: *He draped his coat over the back of his chair.* 2 [usually passive] **drape sb/sth (in/with sth)** to cover sb/sth (with cloth, etc.) □ *ditutup*: *The furniture was draped in dust sheets.* ▶ **drape** *noun* (*AmE*) = **curtain**(1)

drastic /ˈdræstɪk/ *adj* extreme, and having a sudden very strong effect □ *keras; drastik; mendadak*: *a drastic rise in crime* ▶ **drastically** /-kli/ *adv*

drainage → draw

draught[1] /drɑːft/ *noun* 1 (*AmE* **draft**) [C] a flow of cold air that comes into a room □ *angin sejuk*: *Can you shut the door? There's a draught in here.* 2 **draughts** (*AmE* **checkers**) [U] a game for two players that you play on a black and white board using round black and white pieces □ *permainan dam* ▶ **draughty** (*AmE* **drafty**) *adj* (**draughtier**; **draughtiest**)

draught[2] /drɑːft/ *adj* (*BrE*) (used about beer, etc.) served from a **barrel** (= a large round container) rather than a bottle □ *bir yg dihidangkan drpd tong*: *draught beer*

draughtsman (*AmE* **draftsman**) /ˈdrɑːftsmən/ *noun* [C] (*pl* **-men** /-mən/) a person whose job is to do technical drawings □ *pelukis pelan*

draw[1] /drɔː/ *verb* (*pt* **drew** /druː/; *pp* **drawn** /drɔːn/)

▶PICTURE **1** [I,T] to make a picture or diagram of sth with a pencil, pen, etc. but not paint □ *melukis*: *I'm good at painting but I can't draw.* ◆ *Shall I draw you a map of how to get there?*

▶PULL **2** [T] to pull sth/sb into a new position or in the direction mentioned □ *menarik*: *She drew the letter out of her pocket and handed it to me.* ◆ *to draw* (= open or close) *the curtains* ◆ *He drew me by the hand into the room.*

▶MOVE **3** [I] to move in the direction mentioned □ *bergerak; mendekati; semakin hampir*: *The train drew into the station* ◆ *I became more anxious as my exams drew nearer.*

▶GET/TAKE **4** [T] **draw sth (from sb/sth)** to get or take sth from sb/sth □ *mendapat; memperoleh*: *He draws the inspiration for his stories from his family.*

▶ATTRACT **5** [T] **draw sth (from sb)**; **draw sb (to sb/ sth)** to make sb react to or be interested in sb/sth □ *menarik*: *The advertisement has drawn criticism from people all over the country.* ◆ *The musicians drew quite a large crowd.*

▶LEARN **6** [T] **draw sth (from sth)** to learn or decide sth as a result of study, research or experience □ *membuat (kesimpulan, dsb); mengambil (iktibar, dsb)*: *Can we draw any conclusions from this survey?* ◆ *There are important lessons to be drawn from this tragedy.*

▶GAME **7** [I,T] to finish a game, competition, etc. with equal scores so that neither person or team wins □ *berakhir dgn kedudukan seri*: *The two teams drew.* ◆ *The match was drawn.*

IDM bring sth/come/draw to an end ⇒ **end**[1]

draw (sb's) attention to sth to make sb notice sth □ *menarik perhatian (sso) kpd sst*: *The article draws attention to the problem of homelessness.*

draw a blank to get no result or find no answer □ *tdk mendapat apa-apa; tdk berhasil sama sekali*: *Detectives investigating the case have drawn a blank so far.*

draw a distinction between sth and sth to show how two things are different □ *menunjukkan perbezaan antara sst dgn sst*

draw the line at sth/doing sth to say 'no' to sth even though you are happy to help in other ways

---

CONSONANTS   p **p**en   b **b**ad   t **t**ea   d **d**id   k **c**at   g **g**ot   tʃ **ch**in   dʒ **J**une   f **f**all   v **v**an   θ **th**in

□ *enggan membuat sst*: I do most of the cooking but I draw the line at washing up as well!
draw lots to decide sth by chance □ *mengundi*: They drew lots to see who should stay behind.
PHR V draw in to get dark earlier as winter arrives □ *semakin awal sudah mula gelap*: The days/nights are drawing in.
draw out to become lighter in the evening as summer gets nearer □ *semakin panjang*
draw sth out to take money out of a bank account □ *mengeluarkan*: How much cash do I need to draw out?
draw up (used about a car, etc.) to drive up and stop in front of or near sth □ *berhenti*: A police car drew up outside the building.
draw sth up to prepare and write a document, list, etc. □ *membuat (kontrak, dll)*: Our solicitor is going to draw up the contract.

draw² /drɔː/ *noun* [C] **1** an act of deciding sth by chance by pulling out names or numbers from a bag, etc. □ *cabutan*: a prize draw **2** a result of a game or competition in which both players or teams got the same score so that neither of them wins □ *seri*: The match ended in a draw.

drawback /'drɔːbæk/ *noun* [C] a disadvantage or problem □ *kelemahan*: His lack of experience is a major drawback. **SYN** disadvantage

drawbridge /'drɔːbrɪdʒ/ *noun* [C] a bridge that can be pulled up, for example to stop people from entering a castle □ *jambatan angkat*: to raise/lower the drawbridge

drawer /drɔː(r)/ *noun* [C] a container which forms part of a piece of furniture such as a desk, that you can pull out to put things in □ *laci*: There's some paper in the top drawer of my desk.

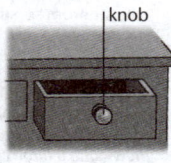

drawer

drawing /'drɔːɪŋ/ *noun* **1** [C] a picture made with a pencil, pen, etc. but not paint □ *lukisan*: He did a drawing of the building. ⊃ note at **painting 2** [U] the art of drawing pictures □ *seni lukis*: She's good at drawing and painting.

'**drawing pin** (*AmE* **thumbtack**) *noun* [C] a short pin with a flat top, used for fastening paper, etc. to a board or wall □ *paku tekan* ⊃ picture at **pin, stationery**

'**drawing room** *noun* [C] (*old-fashioned*) a living room, especially in a large house □ *bilik tamu*

drawl /drɔːl/ *verb* [I,T] to speak slowly, making the vowel sounds very long □ *menarik panjang kata-kata* ▶ **drawl** *noun* [sing]: *to speak with a drawl*

drawn¹ *past participle* of **draw¹**

drawn² /drɔːn/ *adj* (used about a person or their face) looking tired, worried or ill □ *kelihatan letih; risau atau sakit*: He looked pale and drawn after the long journey.

,**drawn-'out** *adj* lasting longer than necessary □ *berpanjangan*: long drawn-out negotiations

dread¹ /dred/ *verb* [T] to be very afraid of or worried about sth □ *sangat takut/bimbang*: I'm dreading the exams. ◆ She dreaded having to tell him what had happened. ◆ I **dread to think** what my father will say. ▶ **dreaded** *adj*

dread² /dred/ *noun* [U, sing] great fear □ *rasa takut*: He lived **in dread of** the same thing happening to him.

dreadful /'dredfl/ *adj* very bad or unpleasant □ *sangat teruk; dahsyat*: We had a dreadful journey—traffic jams all the way! ◆ I'm afraid there's been a dreadful (= very serious) mistake. **SYN** terrible ⊃ note at **bad**

dreadfully /'dredfəli/ *adv* **1** very; extremely □ *sangat; terlalu*: I'm dreadfully sorry, I didn't mean to upset you. **2** very badly □ *(dgn) teruk*: The party went dreadfully and everyone left early.

dreadlocks /'dredlɒks/ *noun* [pl] hair worn in long thick pieces, especially by some black people □ *gaya rambut 'dreadlock'*

dream¹ /driːm/ *noun* **1** [C] a series of events or pictures which happen in your mind while you are asleep □ *mimpi*: I had a strange dream last night. ◆ That horror film has given me bad dreams. ⊃ look at **nightmare 2** [C] something that you want very much to happen, although it is not likely □ *impian; idaman*: His dream was to give up his job and live in the country. ◆ My dream house would have a huge garden and a swimming pool. ◆ Becoming a professional dancer was **a dream come true** for Nicola. **3** [sing] a state of mind in which you are not thinking about what you are doing □ *khayalan*: You've been in a dream all morning!

dream² /driːm/ *verb* (*pt, pp* **dreamt** /dremt/ or **dreamed**) **1** [I,T] **dream (about sb/sth)** to see or experience pictures and events in your mind while you are asleep □ *bermimpi*: I dreamt about the house that I lived in as a child. ◆ I dreamed that I was running but I couldn't get away. ⊃ look at **daydream 2** [I] **dream (about/of sth/doing sth)** to imagine sth that you would like to happen □ *mengimpikan*: I've always dreamt about winning lots of money. **3** [I] **dream (of doing sth/that ...)** to imagine that sth might happen □ *termimpi akan*: I wouldn't dream of telling Stuart that I don't like his music. ◆ When I watched the Olympics on TV, I never dreamt that one day I'd be here competing!

PHR V dream sth up (*informal*) to think of a plan, an idea, etc., especially sth strange □ *mereka-reka sst*: Which of you dreamt up that idea?

dreamer /'driːmə(r)/ *noun* [C] a person who thinks a lot about ideas, plans, etc. which may never happen instead of thinking about real life □ *orang yg suka berangan-angan; mat jenin*

dreamt *past tense, past participle* of **dream**

dreamy /ˈdriːmi/ adj (dreamier; dreamiest) looking as though you are not paying attention to what you are doing because you are thinking about sth else □ *dgn fikiran yg melayang jauh*: *a dreamy look/expression* ▶ **dreamily** adv

dreary /ˈdrɪəri/ adj (drearier; dreariest) not at all interesting or attractive; boring □ *suram; membosankan*: *His dreary voice sends me to sleep.*

dredge /dredʒ/ verb [T] to clear the mud, etc. from the bottom of a river, **canal** (= an artificial river), etc. using a special machine □ *mengorek (dgn kapal korek)*

PHR V **dredge sth up** to mention sth unpleasant from the past that sb would like to forget □ *membangkitkan*: *The newspaper had dredged up all sorts of embarrassing details about her private life.*

dregs /dregz/ noun [pl] **1** the last drops in a container of liquid, containing small pieces of solid waste □ *keladak* **2** the worst and most useless part of sth □ *sampah*: *These people were regarded as the dregs of society.*

drench /drentʃ/ verb [T, usually passive] to make sb/sth completely wet □ *basah kuyup*: *Don't go out while it's raining so hard or you'll get drenched.*

dress¹ /dres/ noun **1** [C] a piece of clothing worn by a girl or a woman. It covers the body from the shoulders to the knees or below □ *gaun*: *a wedding dress* **2** [U] clothes for either men or women □ *pakaian*: *formal/casual dress* ♦ *He was wearing Bulgarian national dress.*

dress² /dres/ verb **1** [I,T] to put clothes on sb or yourself □ *memakai(kan) baju*: *He dressed quickly and left the house.* ♦ *My husband dressed the children while I got breakfast ready.* ♦ *Hurry up! Aren't you dressed yet?* **OPP** **undress** ➔ note at **routine** ➔ **Get dressed** is more common than **dress**. **2** [I] to put or have clothes on, in the way or style mentioned □ *berpakaian*: *to dress well/badly/casually* ♦ *to be well dressed/badly dressed/casually dressed* **3** [T] to put a clean covering on the place on sb's body where they have been hurt □ *membalut luka*: *to dress a wound*

IDM **(be) dressed in sth** wearing sth □ *berpakaian*: *The people at the funeral were all dressed in black.*

PHR V **dress up 1** to put on special clothes, especially in order to look like sb/sth else □ *berpakaian*: *The children decided to dress up as pirates.* **2** to put on formal clothes, usually for a special occasion □ *berpakaian formal*: *You don't need to dress up for the party.*

dresser /ˈdresə(r)/ noun [C] **1** (BrE) a piece of furniture with cupboards at the bottom and shelves above. It is used for holding dishes, cups, etc. □ *gerobok tetingkat* **2** (AmE) = **chest of drawers**

dressing /ˈdresɪŋ/ noun **1** [C,U] a sauce for food, especially for salads □ *kuah salad* **2** [C] a covering that you put on a part of sb's body that has been hurt to protect it and keep it clean □ *pembalut (luka)*

267   **dreamy → drily**

ˈdressing gown (AmE **bathrobe**; **robe**) noun [C] a piece of clothing like a loose coat with a belt, which you wear before or after a bath, before you get dressed in the morning, etc. □ *jubah santai*

ˈdressing table noun [C] a piece of furniture in a bedroom, which has drawers and a mirror □ *meja solek*

drew past tense of **draw¹**

dribble /ˈdrɪbl/ verb **1** [I] to allow **saliva** (= liquid that is produced in the mouth) to run out of the mouth □ *air liur meleleh*: *Small children often dribble.* **2** [I,T] (used about a liquid) to move downwards in a thin flow; to make a liquid move in this way □ *meleleh*: *The paint dribbled slowly down the side of the pot.* **3** [I] (used in ball games) to make a ball move forward by using many short kicks or hits □ *menggelecek*: *Ronaldo dribbled round the goalkeeper and scored.*

dried¹ past tense, past participle of **dry²**

dried² /draɪd/ adj (used about food) with all the liquid removed from it □ *kering*: *dried milk/fruit*

drier = **dryer**

drift¹ /drɪft/ noun **1** [C] a slow movement towards sth □ *aliran; penghanyutan*: *the country's drift into economic decline* **2** [C] a pile of snow or sand that was made by wind or water □ *hanyutan; endapan* **3** [sing] the general meaning of sth □ *maksud*: *I don't understand all the details of the plan but I get the drift.*

drift² /drɪft/ verb [I] **1** to move slowly or without any particular purpose □ *berjalan perlahan-lahan; hanyut*: *He drifted from room to room.* ♦ *Helena drifted into acting almost by accident.* **2** (used about snow or sand) to be moved into piles by wind or water □ *menimbun; berlonggok*: *The snow drifted up to two metres deep in some places.* **3** to be carried or moved along by wind or water □ *hanyut; dihanyutkan; melayang-layang*: *The boat drifted out to sea.*

PHR V **drift apart** to slowly become less close or friendly with sb □ *menjadi renggang*

drill¹ /drɪl/ noun **1** [C] a tool or machine that is used for making holes in things □ *gerudi*: *a dentist's drill* ➔ picture at **tool** **2** [C] something that you repeat many times in order to learn sth □ *latih tubi* **3** [C,U] practice for what you should do in an emergency □ *latihan*: *a fire drill* **4** [U] exercise in marching, etc. that soldiers do □ *latihan berkawat, dll*

drill² /drɪl/ verb **1** [I,T] to make a hole in sth with a **drill** □ *menggerudi*: *to drill for oil* ♦ *to drill a hole in something* **2** [T] to teach sb by making them repeat sth many times □ *melatih tubi*

drily (also **dryly**) /ˈdraɪli/ adv (used about the way sb says sth) in an amusing way that sounds serious □ *berjenaka secara serius; agak sinis*: *'I can hardly contain my excitement,' Peter said drily* (= he was not excited at all).

VOWELS   iː **see**   i **any**   ɪ **sit**   e **ten**   æ **hat**   ɑː **father**   ɒ **got**   ɔː **saw**   ʊ **put**   uː **too**   u **usual**

drink → drive-through 268

drink¹ /drɪŋk/ noun [C,U] **1** liquid for drinking □ *minuman*: *Can I have a drink please?* ◆ *a drink of milk* ◆ *soft drinks* (= cold drinks without alcohol) ◆ *food and drink* ⊃ picture on **page P16** **2** (an) alcoholic drink □ *minuman keras*: *Shall we go for a drink?*

drink² /drɪŋk/ verb (pt **drank** /dræŋk/; pp **drunk** /drʌŋk/) **1** [I,T] to take liquid into your body through your mouth □ *minum*: *Would you like something to drink?* ◆ *We sat drinking coffee and chatting for hours.* ◆ *Sam stopped drinking and put the cup down.* **2** [I,T] to drink alcohol □ *minum arak*: *I never drink and drive so I'll have an orange juice.* ◆ *What do you drink—beer or wine?* ◆ *Her father used to drink heavily but he's teetotal now.*
PHR V **drink to sb/sth** to wish sb/sth good luck by holding your glass up in the air before you drink □ *minum ucap selamat*: *We all drank to the future of the bride and groom.* ⊃ look at **toast**
drink (sth) up to finish drinking sth □ *habiskan minum*: *Drink up your tea—it's getting cold.*

ˌdrink-ˈdriver (*AmE* **ˌdrunk ˈdriver**) noun [C] a person who drives after drinking too much alcohol □ *pemandu yg minum arak* ▸ **ˌdrink-ˈdriving** (*AmE* **ˌdrunk ˈdriving**) noun [U]: *He was convicted of drink-driving and was banned for two years.* ⊃ note at **driving**

drinker /ˈdrɪŋkə(r)/ noun [C] a person who drinks a lot of sth, especially alcohol □ *peminum; kaki botol*: *a heavy drinker* ◆ *I'm not a big coffee drinker.*

drinking /ˈdrɪŋkɪŋ/ noun [U] drinking alcohol □ *tabiat suka minum arak*: *Her drinking became a problem.*

ˈdrinking water noun [U] water that is safe to drink □ *air minuman*

drip¹ /drɪp/ verb (**dripping; dripped**) **1** [I] (used about a liquid) to fall in small drops □ *menitis; menitik*: *Water was dripping down through the roof.* **2** [I,T] to produce drops of liquid □ *menitis*: *The tap is dripping.* ◆ *Her finger was dripping blood.*

drip² /drɪp/ noun **1** [sing] the act or sound of water dripping □ *titisan* **2** [C] a drop of water that falls down from sb/sth □ *titisan*: *We put a bucket under the hole in the roof to catch the drips.* **3** [C] a piece of medical equipment, like a tube, that is used for putting liquid food or medicine straight into sb's blood □ *drip*: *She's on a drip.*

drive¹ /draɪv/ verb (pt **drove** /drəʊv/; pp **driven** /ˈdrɪvn/)
▸VEHICLE **1** [I,T] to control or operate a car, train, bus, etc. □ *memandu*: *Can you drive?* ◆ *to drive a car/train/bus/lorry* **2** [I,T] to go or take sb somewhere in a car, etc. □ *membawa kereta; menghantar dgn kereta*: *I usually drive to work.* ◆ *We drove Maki to the airport.*
▸MACHINE **3** [T] to make a machine work, by giving it power □ *menjalankan; menggerakkan*: *What drives the wheels in this engine?*
▸MAKE SB DO STH **4** [T] to cause sb to be in a particular state or to do sth □ *menyebabkan; membuat*: *His constant stupid questions drive me mad.* ◆ *to drive somebody to despair* **5** [T] to make sb/sth work very hard □ *memaksa (sso/sst) bekerja keras*: *You shouldn't drive yourself so hard.*
▸MAKE SB/STH MOVE **6** [T] to force people or animals to move in a particular direction □ *menggiring*: *The dogs drove the sheep into the field.*
▸HIT STH **7** [T] to force sth into a particular position by hitting it □ *mengetuk; memukul*: *to drive a post into the ground*
IDM **be driving at** (*informal*) to want to say sth; to mean □ *yg dimaksudkan*: *I'm afraid I don't understand what you're driving at.*
drive sth home (to sb) to make sth clear so that people understand it □ *membuat sso faham (sst)*
PHR V **drive off** (used about a car, driver, etc.) to leave □ *pergi*
drive sb/sth off to make sb/sth go away □ *mengusir*: *They kept a large dog outside to drive off burglars.*

drive² /draɪv/ noun
▸IN VEHICLE **1** [C] a journey in a car □ *perjalanan dgn kereta*: *The supermarket is only a five-minute drive away.* ◆ *Let's go for a drive.* **2** [U] the equipment in a vehicle that takes power from the engine to the wheels □ *pemacu*: *a car with four-wheel drive*
▸OUTSIDE HOUSE **3** (also **driveway**) [C] a wide path or short road that leads to the door of a house □ *jalan masuk rumah*: *We keep our car on the drive.*
▸EFFORT **4** [C] a big effort by a group of people in order to achieve sth □ *kempen; usaha*: *The company is launching a big sales drive.*
▸ENERGY **5** [U] the energy and determination you need to succeed in doing sth □ *dorongan; semangat*: *You need lots of drive to run your own company.*
▸DESIRE **6** [C,U] a strong natural need or desire □ *desakan*: *a strong sex drive*
▸IN SPORT **7** [C] a long hard hit □ *pukulan*: *This player has the longest drive in golf.*
▸COMPUTING **8** [C] the part of a computer that reads and stores information □ *pemacu*: *a 200 GB hard drive* ◆ *a CD drive* ⊃ look at **disk drive** ⊃ picture at **computer**
▸ROAD **9** [C] a street, usually where people live □ *jalan*: *They live at 23 Woodlands Drive.*

ˈdrive-by adj [only before a noun] (*AmE*) (used about a shooting) done from a moving car □ *tembakan dr kereta yg bergerak*: *drive-by killings*

ˈdrive-in noun [C] a place where you can eat, watch a film, etc. in your car □ *pandu masuk*

driven past participle of **drive¹**

driver /ˈdraɪvə(r)/ noun [C] a person who drives a vehicle □ *pemandu; drebar*: *a bus/train driver*

ˈdrive-through noun [C] (*especially AmE*) a restaurant, bank, etc. where you can be served without getting out of your car □ *pandu lalu*

driving¹ /ˈdraɪvɪŋ/ noun [U] the action or skill of controlling a car, etc. □ *memandu*: *She was arrested for dangerous driving.* ◆ *Joe's having driving lessons.* ◆ *She works as a driving instructor.* ◆ *a driving school* ⊃ note at **car**, **road**

IDM **be in the driving seat** to be the person, group, etc. that has the most powerful position in a particular situation □ *pemandu; pengemudi*

TOPIC

Driving

You cannot **drive** unless you have passed your **driving test** and have a **driving licence**. Motorists should not **break the speed limit** (= drive too fast) or **drink and drive** (= drive a car after drinking alcohol). You can offer to take a person somewhere in your car by asking: *'Can I give you a lift?'* The **driver** and **passengers** (= people travelling in a **vehicle**) should wear **seatbelts**, in case there is an **accident** /a **crash**. If the road is **congested**, for example during **rush hour**, you will probably find yourself stuck in a **traffic jam**.

---

driving² /ˈdraɪvɪŋ/ adj [only before a noun] very strong □ *sangat kuat, lebat, mendesak, dll*: *driving rain* ◆ *driving ambition* ◆ *Who's the driving force behind this plan?*

driving licence (AmE ˈdriver's license) noun [C] an official document that shows that you are allowed to drive □ *lesen memandu*

drizzle /ˈdrɪzl/ noun [U] light rain with very small drops □ *hujan renyai-renyai* ▸ **drizzle** verb [I] ⊃ note at **weather**

drone /drəʊn/ verb [I] to make a continuous low sound □ *berdengung; mendengung*: *the sound of the tractors droning away in the fields*

PHR V **drone on** to talk in a flat or boring voice □ *bercakap dgn suara yg membosankan*: *We had to listen to the chairman drone on about sales for hours.*

▸ **drone** noun [sing]

drool /druːl/ verb [I] **1** to let **saliva** (= liquid) come out from the mouth, usually at the sight or smell of sth good to eat □ *meleleh air liur* **2 drool (over sb/sth)** to show in a silly or exaggerated way that you want sth or admire sb/sth very much □ *tergila-gilakan*: *teenagers drooling over photographs of their favourite pop stars*

droop /druːp/ verb [I] to bend or hang downwards, especially because of weakness or because you are tired □ *melentok; terkulai; melentur ke bawah*: *The flowers were drooping without water.* ▸ **drooping** adj: *a drooping moustache*

drop¹ /drɒp/ verb (**dropping**; **dropped**) **1** [T] to let sth fall □ *jatuh; menjatuhkan; terjatuh*: *That vase was very expensive. Whatever you do, don't drop it!* **2** [I] to fall □ *rebah; jatuh; gugur*: *The parachutist dropped safely to the ground.* ◆ *At the end of the race she dropped to her knees exhausted.* **3** [I,T] to become lower; to make sth lower □ *turun; menurunkan*: *The temperature will drop to minus 3 overnight.* ◆ *They ought to drop their prices.* ◆ *to drop your voice* (= speak more quietly) **4** [T] **drop sb/sth (off)** to stop your car, etc. so that sb can get out, or in order to take sth out □ *menurunkan*: *Drop me off at the traffic lights, please.* ◆ *I'll drop the parcel at your house.* **5** [T] **drop sb/sth (from sth)** to no longer include sb/sth in sth □ *menggugurkan*: *Joe has been dropped from the team.* **6** [T] to stop doing sth □ *meninggalkan; tdk mengambil*: *I'm going to drop geography next term* (= stop studying it).

IDM **drop dead** (*informal*) to die suddenly □ *mati tiba-tiba*

drop sb a line (*informal*) to write a letter or an email to sb □ *menulis surat*: *Do drop me a line when you've time.*

PHR V **drop back**; **drop behind (sb)** to move into a position behind sb else, because you are moving more slowly □ *tinggal di belakang; ketinggalan*: *Towards the end of the race she dropped behind the other runners.*

drop by; **drop in (on sb)** to go to sb's house on an informal visit or without having told them you were coming □ *datang; singgah; menjengah (sso)*: *We were in the area so we thought we'd drop in and see you.*

drop off (*informal*) to fall into a light sleep □ *tertidur*: *I dropped off in front of the TV.*

drop out (of sth) to leave or stop doing sth before you have finished □ *menarik diri; keluar; tercicir*: *His injury forced him to drop out of the competition.*

drop² /drɒp/ noun **1** [C] a very small amount of liquid that forms a round shape □ *titis; titik*: *a drop of blood/rain* **2** [C, usually sing] a small amount of liquid □ *sedikit*: *I just have a drop of milk in my coffee.* **3** [sing] a fall to a smaller amount or level □ *kejatuhan; kekurangan*: *The job is much more interesting but it will mean a drop in salary.* ◆ *a drop in prices/temperature* **4** [sing] a distance down from a high point to a lower point □ *jarak jatuh*: *a sheer drop of 40 metres to the sea* **5 drops** [pl] liquid medicine that you put into your eyes, ears or nose □ *ubat titis*: *The doctor prescribed me drops to take twice a day.*

drop

IDM **at the drop of a hat** immediately; without having to stop and think about it □ *dgn segera; serta-merta*

a drop in the ocean; (AmE **a drop in the bucket**) an amount of sth that is too small or unimportant to make any real difference to a situation □ *amat sedikit*: *The money we made was a drop in the ocean compared to the amount we need.*

drop-dead adv (*informal*) used before an adjective to emphasize how attractive sb/sth is □ *sangat (jelita, kacak, dsb)*: *She's drop-dead gorgeous.*

[C] **countable**, a noun with a plural form: *one book, two books*   [U] **uncountable**, a noun with no plural form: *some sugar*

drop-down menu → dry

drop-down 'menu noun [C] a list which appears on your computer screen and that stays there until you choose one of the functions on it □ *menu ke bawah*

dropout /ˈdrɒpaʊt/ noun [C] **1** a person who leaves school, university, etc. before finishing their studies □ *penuntut yg tercicir*: *a university with a high dropout rate* **2** a person who does not accept the ideas and ways of behaving of the rest of society □ *orang yg meminggirkan diri drpd masyarakat*

droppings /ˈdrɒpɪŋz/ noun [pl] waste material from the bodies of small animals or birds □ *tahi (burung, tikus, dll)*

drought /draʊt/ noun [C,U] a long period without rain □ *kemarau*: *two years of severe drought*

drove past tense of **drive**[1]

drown /draʊn/ verb **1** [I,T] to die in water because it is not possible to breathe; to make sb die in this way □ *mati lemas; membenamkan ke dlm air sehingga mati*: *The girl fell into the river and drowned.* ♦ *Twenty people were drowned in the floods.* **2** to make sth very wet; to completely cover sth in water or another liquid □ *mencelup*: *The fruit was drowning in cream.* **3** [T] **drown sb/sth (out)** (used about a sound) to be so loud that you cannot hear sb/sth else □ *menenggelamkan*: *His answer was drowned out by the music.*

drowsy /ˈdraʊzi/ adj (**drowsier**; **drowsiest**) tired and almost asleep □ *mengantuk*: *The heat made me feel drowsy.* ▶ **drowsily** adv ▶ **drowsiness** noun [U]

drudgery /ˈdrʌdʒəri/ noun [U] hard and boring work □ *kerja keras yg membosankan*

ʔ drug[1] /drʌɡ/ noun [C] **1** a chemical which people use to give them pleasant or exciting feelings. It is illegal in many countries to use drugs □ *dadah*: *He doesn't drink or take drugs.* ♦ *She suspected her son was on drugs.* ♦ **hard drugs** such as heroin and cocaine ♦ **soft drugs** **2** a chemical which is used as a medicine □ *drug; ubat*: *drug companies* ♦ *Some drugs can only be obtained with a prescription from a doctor.*

drug[2] /drʌɡ/ verb [T] (**drugging**; **drugged**) **1** to give a person or an animal a chemical to make them or it go to sleep or become unconscious □ *memberi ubat/drug*: *The lion was drugged before the start of the journey.* **2** to put a drug into food or drink □ *memasukkan dadah/drug ke dlm makanan atau minuman*: *I think his drink was drugged.*

'drug addict noun [C] a person who cannot stop taking drugs □ *penagih dadah* ▶ **'drug addiction** noun [U]

druggist /ˈdrʌɡɪst/ (AmE) = **chemist**(1)

ʔ drugstore /ˈdrʌɡstɔː(r)/ (AmE) = **chemist**(2)

[I] **intransitive**, a verb which has no object: *He laughed.*

ʔ drum[1] /drʌm/ noun [C] **1** a musical instrument like an empty container with plastic or skin stretched across the ends. You play a drum by hitting it with your hands or with sticks □ *dram; gendang*: *She plays the drums in a band.* ➔ note at **music** ➔ picture at **music 2** a round container □ *tong*: *an oil drum*

drum[2] /drʌm/ verb (**drumming**; **drummed**) **1** [I] to play a drum or drums □ *bermain dram/gendang* **2** [I,T] to make a noise like a drum by hitting sth many times □ *bergendang; menggendang*: *to drum your fingers on the table* (= because you are annoyed, impatient, etc.)
PHR V drum sth into sb to make sb remember sth by repeating it many times □ *memberitahu sst perkara kpd sso dgn banyak kali supaya dpt diingatnya*: *The importance of road safety should be drummed into children from an early age.*
drum sth up to try to get support or business □ *melobi (sokongan, dsb)*: *to drum up more custom*

drummer /ˈdrʌmə(r)/ noun [C] a person who plays a drum or drums □ *pemain dram; pemukul gendang*

drumstick /ˈdrʌmstɪk/ noun [C] **1** a stick used for playing the drums □ *kayu dram* **2** the lower part of the leg of a chicken or similar bird that we cook and eat □ *paha (ayam, itik, dsb)*

ʔ drunk[1] /drʌŋk/ adj [not before a noun] having drunk too much alcohol □ *mabuk*: *to get drunk* **OPP sober** ▶ **drunk** (also old-fashioned **drunkard** /ˈdrʌŋkəd/) noun [C]: *There was a drunk asleep on the bench.*

drunk[2] past participle of **drink**[2]

drunk 'driver = **drink-driver**

drunken /ˈdrʌŋkən/ adj [only before a noun] **1** having drunk too much alcohol □ *mabuk*: *drunken drivers* **2** showing the effects of too much alcohol □ *dlm keadaan mabuk*: *drunken singing* ▶ **drunkenly** adv ▶ **drunkenness** noun [U]

ʔ dry[1] /draɪ/ adj (**drier**; **driest**)
▶NOT WET **1** without liquid in it or on it □ *kering*: *The washing isn't dry yet.* ♦ *The paint is dry now.* ♦ *Rub your hair dry with a towel.* **OPP wet**
▶WITHOUT RAIN **2** having little or no rain □ *kering; tdk hujan; kurang hujan*: *a hot, dry summer* ♦ *a dry climate* **OPP wet**
▶HAIR/SKIN **3** not having enough natural oil □ *kering*: *a shampoo for dry hair*
▶WINE **4** not sweet □ *tdk manis*: *a crisp dry white wine*
▶HUMOUR **5** (used about what sb says, or sb's way of speaking) amusing, although it sounds serious □ *berjenaka tetapi bunyinya serius*: *a dry sense of humour*
▶BORING **6** not interesting □ *biasa; tdk menarik*: *dry legal documents*
▶WITHOUT ALCOHOL **7** where no alcohol is allowed □ *minuman keras diharamkan*: *a dry country/state*
IDM be left high and dry ➔ **leave**[1]
▶ **dryness** noun [U]

[T] **transitive**, a verb which has an object: *He ate an apple.*

dry² /draɪ/ *verb* [I,T] (**drying**; **dries**; *pt, pp* **dried**) to become dry; to make sth dry □ *menjadi kering; mengeringkan*: *I hung my shirt in the sun to dry.* ◆ *to dry your hands on a towel*

PHR V **dry (sth) out** to become or make sth become completely dry □ *menjadi kering; dibiarkan kering*: *Don't allow the soil to dry out.*

dry up 1 (used about a river, etc.) to have no more water in it □ *menjadi kering* **2** to stop being available □ *habis; tdk ada lagi*: *Because of the recession, offers of work have begun to dry up.* **3** to forget what you were going to say, for example because you are very nervous □ *terbungkam*: *When he came on stage and saw the audience, he dried up completely.*

dry (sth) up (*BrE*) to dry plates, knives, forks, etc. with a small piece of cloth after they have been washed □ *mengelap dgn kain supaya kering*

dry-ˈclean *verb* [T] to clean clothes using special chemicals, without using water □ *mencuci kering*

dry-ˈcleaner's (also **cleaner's**) *noun* [C] the shop where you take your clothes to be cleaned □ *kedai cucian kering*

dryer (also **drier**) /ˈdraɪə(r)/ *noun* [C] [often in compounds] a machine that you use for drying sth □ *pengering*: *a hairdryer*

dry ˈland *noun* [U] land, not the sea □ *darat; tanah*: *I was glad to be back on dry land again.*

dryly = **drily**

DTP /ˌdiː tiː ˈpiː/ *abbr* = **desktop publishing**

dual /ˈdjuːəl/ *adj* [only before a noun] having two parts □ *dwi; dua*: *to have dual nationality*

dual ˈcarriageway (*AmE* **diˌvided ˈhighway**) *noun* [C] a wide road that has an area of grass or a fence in the middle to separate the traffic going in one direction from the traffic going in the other direction □ *jalan berkembar*

dub /dʌb/ *verb* [T] (**dubbing**; **dubbed**) **1** to give sb/sth a new or amusing name □ *menggelar; digelar*: *Margaret Thatcher was dubbed 'the Iron Lady'.* **2 dub sth (into sth)** to change the sound in a film so that what the actors said originally is spoken by actors using a different language □ *mengalih suara*: *I don't like foreign films when they're dubbed into English. I prefer subtitles.* ➲ look at **subtitle 3** to make a piece of music by mixing different pieces of recorded music together □ *mengalih sunting*

dubious /ˈdjuːbiəs/ *adj* **1** **dubious (about sth/ about doing sth)** not sure or certain □ *ragu-ragu; tdk pasti*: *I'm very dubious about whether we're doing the right thing.* **2** that may not be honest or safe □ *diragui; dicurigai*: *dubious financial dealings* ▸ **dubiously** *adv*

duchess /ˈdʌtʃəs/ *noun* [C] a woman who has the same position as a **duke** (= a man of high social position), or who is the wife of a **duke** □ *duchess*

duck¹ /dʌk/ *noun* (*pl* **ducks** or **duck**) **1** [C] a common bird that lives on or near water. Ducks

ducks

duck   drake

ducklings

have short legs, **webbed**, **feet** (= with pieces of skin between the toes) for swimming and a wide beak. □ *itik* **2** [C] a female **duck** □ *itik betina*

MORE **Duck** is often used for both males and females. A male duck is called a **drake** and a young duck is a **duckling**. The sound a duck makes is a **quack**.

3 [U] the meat of a **duck** □ *daging itik*: *roast duck with orange sauce*

duck² /dʌk/ *verb* **1** [I,T] to move your head down quickly so that you are not seen or hit by sb/ sth □ *menundukkan kepala cepat-cepat*: *The boys ducked out of sight behind a high hedge.* ◆ *I had to duck my head down to avoid the low doorway.* **2** [I,T] (*informal*) **duck (out of) sth** to try to avoid sth difficult or unpleasant □ *mengelak drpd*: *She tried to duck out of apologizing.* ◆ *The President is trying to duck responsibility for the crisis.* **3** [T] to push sb's head underwater for a short time, especially when playing □ *membenamkan kepala (sso) sekejap*: *The kids were ducking each other in the pool.*

He ducked.

duckling /ˈdʌklɪŋ/ *noun* [C, U] a young **duck**; the meat of a young **duck** □ *anak itik* ➲ note at **duck** ➲ picture at **duck**

duct /dʌkt/ *noun* [C] a tube that carries liquid, gas, etc. □ *salur; duktus*: *They got into the building through the air duct.* ◆ *tear ducts* (= in the eye)

dud /dʌd/ *noun* [C] (*informal*) a thing that cannot be used because it is not real or does not work properly □ *palsu; tipu*: *a dud note/coin/ firework*

dude /duːd/ *noun* [C] (*especially AmE slang*) a man □ *lelaki; mat*

due¹ /djuː/ *adj* [not before a noun]

due → duo

▶CAUSED BY **1** due to sb/sth caused by or because of sb/sth □ *disebabkan; kerana*: *His illness is probably due to stress.*
▶EXPECTED **2** expected or planned to happen or arrive □ *dijangka; dijadualkan; akan (tiba, dll)*: *The conference is due to start in four weeks' time.* ◆ *What time is the next train due (in)?* ◆ *The baby is due in May.*
▶OWED **3** having to be paid □ *perlu dibayar*: *The rent is due on the fifteenth of each month.* **4** due (to sb) that is owed to you because it is your right to have it □ *patut dibayar/diberi*: *Make sure you claim all the benefits that are due to you.* **5** due for sth expecting sth or having the right to sth □ *patut mendapat*: *I think that I'm due for a pay rise.*
IDM in due course at some time in the future, quite soon □ *apabila tiba masanya*: *All applicants will be informed of our decision in due course.*

due² /dju:/ *adv* [used before *north, south, east* and *west*] exactly □ *tepat ke*: *The plane was flying due east.*

due³ /dju:/ *noun*
IDM give sb his/her due to be fair to a person □ *utk berlaku adil (terhadap sso)*: *She doesn't work very quickly, but to give Sarah her due, she is very accurate.*

duel /'dju:əl/ *noun* [C] a formal type of fight with guns or other weapons which was used in the past to decide an argument between two men □ *perang tanding*

duet /dju'et/ (also **duo**) *noun* [C] a piece of music for two people to sing or play □ *duet* ⊃ look at **solo**

duffel coat (also **duffle coat**) /'dʌfl kəʊt/ *noun* [C] a coat made of thick wool cloth with a **hood** (= a part that covers your head). A duffel coat has **toggles** (= special long buttons). □ *kot dufel*

dug past tense, past participle of **dig¹**

duke (also **Duke**) /dju:k/ *noun* [C] a man of the highest social position □ *duke* ⊃ look at **duchess**

dull /dʌl/ *adj* (**duller**; **dullest**) **1** not interesting or exciting; boring □ *membosankan*: *Miss Potter's lessons are always so dull.* **2** not bright □ *suram; mendung; pudar*: *a dull and cloudy day* **3** not loud, sharp or strong □ *bunyi bengap; tdk kuat, nyaring, tajam, dll*: *Her head hit the floor with a dull thud.* ◆ *a dull pain* **OPP** **sharp** ▶ dullness *noun* [U] ▶ dully *adv*

duly /'dju:li/ *adv* (*formal*) in the correct or expected way □ *spt yg sepatutnya*: *We all duly assembled at 7.30 as agreed.*

dumb /dʌm/ *adj* (**dumber**; **dumbest**) **1** not able to speak □ *bisu*: *to be deaf and dumb* ◆ (*figurative*) *They were struck dumb with amazement.* **2** (*informal*) stupid □ *bodoh*: *What a dumb thing to do!*
PHR V dumb (sth) down to make sth less accurate and of worse quality, by trying to make it easier for people to understand □ *menurunkan aras sst*: *The BBC denies that its broadcasting has been dumbed down.*
▶ dumbly *adv*: *Ken did all the talking, and I just nodded dumbly.*

dumbfounded /dʌm'faʊndɪd/ *adj* very surprised □ *terpanjat*

dummy /'dʌmi/ *noun* [C] (*pl* **dummies**) **1** a model of a person, used especially when making clothes or for showing them in a shop window □ *patung*: *a tailor's dummy* **2** something that is made to look like sth else but that is not the real thing □ *olok-olok; palsu*: *The robbers used dummy handguns in the raid.* **3** (*informal*) a stupid person □ *orang bodoh*: *Don't just stand there like a dummy—help me!* **4** (*AmE* **pacifier**) a rubber object that you put in a baby's mouth to keep them quiet and happy □ *puting getah*

dummy

dump¹ /dʌmp/ *verb* [T] **1** to get rid of sth that you do not want, especially in a place which is not suitable □ *membuang*: *Nuclear waste should not be dumped in the sea.* ◆ (*figurative*) *I wish you wouldn't keep dumping all the extra work on me.* **2** to put sth down quickly or in a careless way □ *mencampakkan*: *The children dumped their coats and bags in the hall and ran off to play.* **3** (*informal*) to end a relationship with sb □ *meninggalkan*: *Did you hear that Laura dumped Chris last night?*

dump² /dʌmp/ *noun* [C] **1** a place where rubbish or waste material from factories, etc. is left □ *tempat buang sampah*: *a rubbish dump* **2** (*informal*) a place that is very dirty, untidy or unpleasant □ *tempat yg kotor, tdk kemas atau tdk menyenangkan*: *The flat is cheap but it's a real dump.* **SYN** for both meanings **tip**
IDM down in the dumps ⊃ **down¹**

dumpling /'dʌmplɪŋ/ *noun* [C] a small ball of **dough** (= a mixture of flour and water) that is cooked and usually eaten with meat □ *ladu*

dune /dju:n/ (also **'sand dune**) *noun* [C] a hill of sand by the sea or in the desert □ *gumuk* ⊃ picture on **page P10**

dung /dʌŋ/ *noun* [U] waste material from the bodies of large animals □ *tahi (lembu, dll)*: *cow dung*

dungarees /ˌdʌŋgə'ri:z/ (*AmE* **overalls**) *noun* [pl] a piece of clothing, similar to trousers, but covering your chest as well as your legs and with narrow pieces of cloth that go over the shoulders □ *seluar dungari*: *a pair of dungarees* ⊃ picture at **overall**

dungeon /'dʌndʒən/ *noun* [C] an old underground room used as a prison, especially in a castle □ *bilik penjara bawah tanah*

duo /'dju:əʊ/ *noun* [C] (*pl* **duos**) **1** two people playing music or singing together □ *pasangan* **2** = **duet**

dupe /djuːp/ *verb* [T] to lie to sb in order to make them believe sth or do sth □ *menipu; memperdaya*: *He was duped into giving them his credit card.*

duplicate¹ /ˈdjuːplɪkeɪt/ *verb* [T] **1** to make an exact copy of sth □ *membuat salinan; menduplikasi* **2** to do sth that has already been done □ *membuat apa-apa yg telah pun dibuat dahulu*: *We don't want to duplicate the work of other departments.* ▶ **duplication** /ˌdjuːplɪˈkeɪʃn/ *noun* [U]

duplicate² /ˈdjuːplɪkət/ *noun* [C] something that is exactly the same as sth else □ *salinan; (kunci, dll) pendua*
IDM **in duplicate** with two copies (for example of an official piece of paper) that are exactly the same □ *dlm dua salinan*: *The contract must be in duplicate.*
▶ **duplicate** *adj* [only *before* a noun]: *a duplicate key*

durable /ˈdjʊərəbl/ *adj* that can last a long time □ *tahan lama*: *a durable fabric* ▶ **durability** /ˌdjʊərəˈbɪləti/ *noun* [U]

duration /djuˈreɪʃn/ *noun* [U] (*formal*) the time that sth lasts □ *tempoh; sepanjang*: *Please remain seated for the duration of the flight.*

duress /djuˈres/ *noun* [U] (*formal*) threats or force that are used to make sb do sth □ *paksaan; keadaan dipaksa*: *He signed the confession under duress.*

during /ˈdjʊərɪŋ/ *prep* within the period of time mentioned □ *semasa; pd waktu*: *During the summer holidays we went swimming every day.* ◆ *Grandpa was taken ill during the night.*

> **HELP** **During** or **for**? Notice that you use **during** to refer to the period of time in which something happens and **for** to say how long something lasts: *I went shopping during my lunch break. I was out for about 25 minutes.*

dusk /dʌsk/ *noun* [U] the time in the evening when the sun has already gone down and it is nearly dark □ *senja* ➔ look at **dawn, twilight**

dust¹ /dʌst/ *noun* [U] very small pieces of dry dirt, sand, etc. in the form of a powder □ *habuk; debu*: *a thick layer of dust* ◆ *chalk/coal dust* ◆ *The tractor came up the track in a cloud of dust.* ◆ *a speck* (= a small piece) *of dust*
▶ **dusty** *adj* (**dustier; dustiest**): *This shelf has got very dusty.*

dust² /dʌst/ *verb* [I,T] to clean a room, furniture, etc. by removing dust with a cloth □ *membersihkan habuk*: *Let me dust those shelves before you put the books on them.* ➔ note at **clean²**

dustbin /ˈdʌstbɪn/ (*AmE* ˈgarbage can; ˈtrash can) *noun* [C] a large container for rubbish that you keep outside your house □ *tong sampah* ➔ picture at **bin**

duster /ˈdʌstə(r)/ *noun* [C] a soft dry cloth that you use for cleaning furniture, etc. □ *kain pengesat* ➔ picture at **bucket**

dustman /ˈdʌstmən/ *noun* [C] (*pl* -men /-mən/) a person whose job is to take away the rubbish that people put in **dustbins** □ *tukang angkat sampah*

dustpan /ˈdʌstpæn/ *noun* [C] a flat container with a handle into which you brush dirt from the floor □ *pengaup sampah*: *Where do you keep your dustpan and brush?* ➔ picture at **brush**

Dutch /dʌtʃ/ *adj* from the Netherlands □ *Belanda* ❶ For more information, look at the section on geographical names at the back of this dictionary.

dutiful /ˈdjuːtɪfl/ *adj* happy to respect and obey sb □ *taat; patuh*: *a dutiful son* ▶ **dutifully** /-fəli/ *adv*

duty /ˈdjuːti/ *noun* (*pl* **duties**) **1** [C,U] something that you have to do because people expect you to do it or because you think it is right □ *kewajipan*: *A soldier must do his duty.* ◆ *a sense of moral duty* **2** [C,U] the tasks that you do when you are at work □ *tugas*: *the duties of a policeman* ◆ *Which nurses are on night duty this week?* **3** [C,U] a tax that you pay, especially on goods that you bring into a country □ *duti*: *import duty*
IDM **on/off duty** (used about doctors, nurses, police officers, etc.) to be working/not working □ *bertugas/habis bertugas*: *The porter's on duty from 8 till 4.* ◆ *What time does she go off duty?*

duty-ˈfree *adj* (used about goods) that you can bring into a country without paying tax □ *bebas cukai*: *an airport duty-free shop*
▶ **duty-ˈfree** *adv*: *I bought this wine duty-free.* ➔ look at **tax-free**

duvet /ˈduːveɪ/ *noun* [C] a thick cover filled with feathers or another soft material that you sleep under to keep warm in bed □ *duvet* ➔ look at **eiderdown, quilt** ➔ picture at **bed**

DVD /ˌdiː viː ˈdiː/ *noun* [C] **d**igital **v**ideo**d**isc or **d**igital **v**ersatile **d**isc; a disk on which large amounts of information, especially photographs and video, can be stored, for use in a computer or **DVD player** □ *cakera video digital*: *Is it available on DVD yet?* ◆ *a DVD-ROM drive* ➔ picture at **computer**

ˈDVD burner (also ˌDVD ˈwriter) *noun* [C] a piece of equipment used for copying sound or information from a computer onto a **DVD** □ *pembakar DVD*

ˈDVD player *noun* [C] a piece of equipment that you use for playing **DVDs** □ *pemain DVD*

DVT /ˌdiː viː ˈtiː/ *abbr* = **deep vein thrombosis** □ *trombosis vena dlm*

dwarf¹ /dwɔːf/ *noun* [C] (*pl* **dwarfs** or **dwarves** /dwɔːvz/) **1** (in children's stories) a very small person with magic powers □ *orang kenit* **2** a person, animal or plant that is much smaller than the usual size □ *(orang, haiwan atau tumbuhan yg) kerdil; katik*

dwarf² /dwɔːf/ *verb* [T] (used about a large object) to make sth seem very small in comparison □ *menyebabkan (sst) kelihatan kerdil*: *The skyscraper dwarfs all the other buildings around.*

dwell /dwel/ verb [I] (pt, pp **dwelt** /dwelt/ or **dwelled**) (old-fashioned, formal) to live or stay in a place □ *tinggal*

PHR V dwell on/upon sth to think or talk a lot about sth that it would be better to forget □ *kerap memikirkan ttg sst*: *I don't want to dwell on the past. Let's think about the future.*

dweller /'dwelə(r)/ noun [C] (in compounds) a person or an animal that lives in the place mentioned □ *penghuni*: *city dwellers*

dwelling /'dwelɪŋ/ noun [C] (formal) the place where a person lives; a house or flat □ *tempat tinggal*

dwelt past tense, past participle of **dwell**

dwindle /'dwɪndl/ verb [I] **dwindle (away)** to become smaller or weaker □ *semakin berkurangan*: *Their savings dwindled away to nothing.*

dye¹ /daɪ/ verb [T] (**dyeing**; **dyes**; pt, pp **dyed**) to make sth a different colour □ *mencelup; mewarnakan*: *Does she dye her hair?* ♦ *I'm going to dye this blouse black.*

dye² /daɪ/ noun [C,U] a substance that is used to change the colour of sth □ *bahan pencelup/pewarna*

dyke (also **dike**) /daɪk/ noun [C] **1** a long thick wall that is built to prevent the sea or a river from covering low land with water □ *daik; tanggul* **2** (BrE) a long narrow space dug in the ground and used for taking water away from land □ *parit*

dynamic /daɪ'næmɪk/ adj **1** (used about a person) full of energy and ideas; active □ *dinamik* **2** (used about a force or power) that causes movement □ *dinamik* ▶ **dynamism** /'daɪnəmɪzəm/ noun [U]

dynamics /daɪ'næmɪks/ noun **1** [pl] the way in which people or things behave and react to each other in a particular situation □ *dinamik* **2** [U] the scientific study of the forces involved in movement □ *ilmu dinamik*: *fluid dynamics*

dynamite /'daɪnəmaɪt/ noun [U] **1** a powerful substance which can explode □ *dinamit; bahan letupan* **2** a thing or person that causes great excitement, shock, etc □ *orang/sst yg mengagumkan atau menggemparkan*: *His news was dynamite.*

dynamo /'daɪnəməʊ/ noun [C] (pl **dynamos**) a device that changes energy from the movement of sth such as wind or water into electricity □ *dinamo*

dynasty /'dɪnəsti/ noun [C] (pl **dynasties**) a series of rulers who are from the same family □ *dinasti*: *the Ming dynasty in China*

dysentery /'dɪsəntri/ noun [U] a serious disease which causes you to have **diarrhoea** (= the need to get rid of waste material from your body very often) and to lose blood □ *disenteri*

dyslexia /dɪs'leksiə/ noun [U] a difficulty that some people have with reading and spelling □ *disleksia* ▶ **dyslexic** noun [C], adj

E e

E, e /iː/ noun [C,U] (pl **Es**; **E's**; **e's** /iːz/) **1** the fifth letter of the English alphabet □ *E, e (huruf)*: *'Egg' begins with (an) 'E'.* **2 E** (used about music) the third note in the scale of C major □ *not ketiga dlm skala C major*: *E major/minor* ♦ *E flat*

E abbr = **east¹, eastern** (1) □ *Timur*: *E Asia*

e- /iː/ (in compounds) connected with the use of electronic communication, especially the Internet, for sending information, doing business, etc. □ *e-*: *e-commerce* ♦ *e-business* ♦ *an e-ticket*

each other

He's looking at himself.

They're looking at each other.

each /iːtʃ/ determiner, pron every individual person or thing □ *setiap; tiap-tiap*: *Each lesson lasts an hour.* ♦ *Each of the lessons lasts an hour.* ♦ *The lessons each last an hour.* ♦ *These T-shirts are £5 each.*

each 'other pron used for saying that A does the same thing to B as B does to A □ *satu sama lain*: *Emma and Dave love each other very much* (= Emma loves Dave and Dave loves Emma). ♦ *We looked at each other.*

eager /'iːgə(r)/ adj **eager (to do sth)**; **eager (for sth)** full of desire or interest □ *ingin sangat; amat berminat*: *We're all eager to start work on the new project.* ♦ *eager for success* **SYN keen** ▶ **eagerly** adv ▶ **eagerness** noun [U]

eagle /'iːgl/ noun [C] a very large bird that can see very well. It eats small birds and animals. □ *burung helang*

ear /ɪə(r)/ noun **1** [C] one of the two parts of the body of a person or an animal that are used for hearing □ *telinga*: *He pulled his hat down over his ears.* ⊃ picture at **body** ⊃ picture on page P12 **2** [sing] **an ear (for sth)** an ability to recognize and repeat sounds, especially in music or language □ *berkepandaian ttg muzik atau* *bahasa*: *Kimiko has a good ear for languages.* **3** [C] the top part of a plant that produces grain □ *bulir; tongkol*: *an ear of corn*

IDM **sb's ears are burning** used when a person thinks that other people are talking about them, especially in an unkind way □ *panas telinga (kerana menyangka dikata orang)*

go in one ear and out the other (*informal*) (used about information, etc.) to be forgotten quickly □ *masuk telinga kanan, keluar telinga kiri*: *Everything I tell him seems to go in one ear and out the other.*

play (sth) by ear to play a piece of music that you have heard without using written notes □ *memainkan muzik ikut dengar (tanpa nota)*: *She can read music, but she can also play by ear.*

play it by ear (*informal*) to decide what to do as things happen, instead of planning in advance □ *(bertindak) mengikut keadaan*: *We don't know what Alan's reaction will be, so we'll just have to play it by ear.*

prick up your ears ➔ **prick¹**

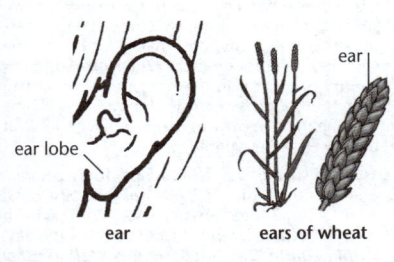

ear lobe

ear

ear

ears of wheat

earache /'ɪəreɪk/ *noun* [C,U] a pain in your ear □ *sakit telinga*: *I've got earache.* ➔ note at **ache**

eardrum /'ɪədrʌm/ *noun* [C] a thin piece of skin inside the ear that is tightly stretched and that allows you to hear sound □ *gegendang telinga*

earl /ɜːl/ *noun* [C] a British man of a high social position □ *earl*

'ear lobe *noun* [C] the round soft part at the bottom of your ear □ *cuping telinga*

early /'ɜːli/ *adj, adv* (**earlier**; **earliest**) **1** near the beginning of a period of time, a piece of work, a series, etc. □ *awal; peringkat permulaan*: *I have to get up early on weekday mornings.* ♦ *I think John's in his early twenties.* ♦ *The project is still only in its early stages.* **2** before the usual or expected time □ *awal*: *She arrived five minutes early for her interview.* **OPP** for both meanings **late**

IDM **at the earliest** not before the date or time mentioned □ *paling awal sekali*: *I can repair it by Friday at the earliest.*

the early hours very early in the morning, in the hours after midnight □ *awal pagi*

an early/a late night ➔ **night**

early on soon after the beginning □ *sejak awal-awal lagi; pd peringkat permulaan lagi*: *He achieved fame early on in his career.*

an early riser a person who usually gets up early in the morning □ *orang yg selalu bangun awal*

275   **earache → earth**

it's early days (yet) (*BrE*) used to say that it is too soon to know how a situation will develop □ *masih terlalu awal*

earmark /'ɪəmɑːk/ *verb* [T] **earmark sb/sth (for sth/sb)** to choose sb/sth to do sth in the future □ *memilih (sso); menguntukkan (sst)*: *The shop has been earmarked for closure.*

earn /ɜːn/ *verb* **1** [I,T] to get money by working □ *mendapat (gaji, upah, dsb)*: *How much does a dentist earn?* ♦ *I earn £20 000 a year.* ♦ *It's hard to earn a living as an artist.* **2** [T] to get money as profit or interest on money you lend, have in a bank, etc. □ *menghasilkan*: *Your money would earn more in a high-interest account.* **3** [T] to win the right to sth, for example by working hard □ *sepatutnya; sewajarnya*: *The team's victory today has earned them a place in the final.*

earnest /'ɜːnɪst/ *adj* serious or determined □ *serius dan tekun*: *He's such an earnest young man—he never makes a joke.* ♦ *They were having a very earnest discussion.*

IDM **in earnest** **1** happening more seriously or with more force than before □ *dgn bersungguh-sungguh*: *After two weeks work began in earnest on the project.* **2** serious and sincere about what you are going to do □ *bersungguh-sungguh*: *He was in earnest about wanting to leave university.*
▶ **earnestly** *adv*

earnings /'ɜːnɪŋz/ *noun* [pl] the money that a person earns by working □ *pendapatan*: *Average earnings have increased by 5%.*

earphones /'ɪəfəʊnz/ = **headphones**

earring /'ɪərɪŋ/ *noun* [C] a piece of jewellery that is worn in or on the lower part of the ear □ *anting-anting; subang*: *Are these clip-on earrings or are they for pierced ears?* ➔ picture at **jewellery**

earshot /'ɪəʃɒt/ *noun*

IDM **(be) out of/within earshot** (be) where a person cannot/can hear □ *di tempat yg jauh dr/ dlm pendengaran sso*: *Wait until he's out of earshot before you say anything about him.*

earth¹ /ɜːθ/ *noun* **1** **the earth**; **the Earth** [sing] the world; the planet on which we live □ *bumi; dunia*: *life on earth* ♦ *The earth goes round the sun.* ➔ note at **space** ➔ picture at **eclipse** **2** [U, sing] the surface of the world; land □ *permukaan bumi; tanah*: *The spaceship fell towards earth.* ♦ *I could feel the earth shake when the earthquake started.* **3** [U] the substance that plants grow in; soil □ *tanah*: *The earth around here is very fertile.* ➔ note at **ground** **4** [C, usually sing] (*AmE* **ground**) a wire that makes a piece of electrical equipment safer by connecting it to the ground □ *litar bumi*: *The green and yellow wire is the earth.*

IDM **charge/pay the earth** (*BrE informal*) to charge/pay a very large amount of money □ *mengenakan/membayar harga yg sangat mahal*: *Dan must have paid the earth for that new car.*

cost the earth/a fortune ➔ **cost²**

[C] **countable**, a noun with a plural form: *one book, two books* [U] **uncountable**, a noun with no plural form: *some sugar*

how/why/where/who etc. on earth (*informal*) used for emphasizing sth or expressing surprise □ *digunakan utk menegaskan sst atau menyatakan rasa hairan*: *Where on earth have you been?*

the earth

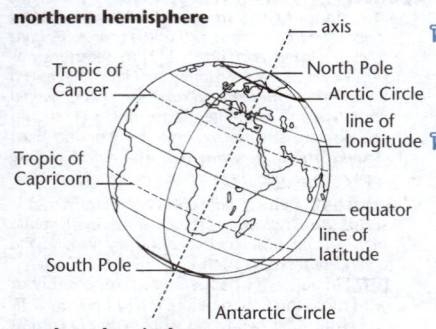

northern hemisphere
axis
Tropic of Cancer
North Pole
Arctic Circle
line of longitude
Tropic of Capricorn
equator
line of latitude
South Pole
Antarctic Circle
southern hemisphere

earth² /ɜːθ/ (*AmE* **ground**) *verb* [T] to make a piece of electrical equipment safer by connecting it to the ground with a wire □ *membumikan*: *Make sure the plug is earthed.*

earthenware /ˈɜːθnweə(r)/ *adj* made of very hard baked **clay** (= a type of earth) □ *barangan tembikar (diperbuat drpd tanah liat)*: *an earthenware bowl* ▶ **earthenware** *noun* [U]

earthly /ˈɜːθli/ *adj* (often in questions or negatives) possible □ *mungkin; munasabah*: *What earthly use is a gardening book to me? I haven't got a garden!* ◆ *There's no earthly reason why you shouldn't go.*

earthquake /ˈɜːθkweɪk/ (also *informal* **quake**) *noun* [C] sudden, violent movement of the earth's surface □ *gempa bumi*

earthworm /ˈɜːθwɜːm/ *noun* [C] a small, long, thin animal with no legs or eyes that lives in the soil □ *cacing*

ease¹ /iːz/ *noun* [U] a lack of difficulty □ *kesenangan; mudah; senang*: *She answered the questions with ease.* ⊃ *adjective* **easy**
IDM **(be/feel) at (your) ease** to be/feel comfortable, relaxed, etc. □ *berasa senang/selesa*: *They were all so kind and friendly that I felt completely at ease.*

ease² /iːz/ *verb* **1** [T] to move sth slowly and gently □ *menggerakkan sst perlahan-lahan*: *He eased the key into the lock.* **2** [I,T] to become or make sth less painful or serious □ *mengurangkan; berkurang; meringankan*: *The pain should ease by this evening.* ◆ *This money will ease their financial problems a little.* ⊃ *adjective* **easy**

IDM **ease sb's mind** to make sb feel less worried □ *menenangkan fikiran sso*: *The doctor tried to ease her mind about her son's illness.*
PHR V **ease off** to become less strong or unpleasant □ *berkurang; reda*: *Let's wait until the rain eases off.*
ease up to work less hard □ *kurangkan sedikit kerja keras*: *Ease up a bit or you'll make yourself ill!*

easel /ˈiːzl/ *noun* [C] a wooden frame that holds a picture while it is being painted □ *kuda-kuda*

easily /ˈiːzəli/ *adv* **1** without difficulty □ *dgn mudah/senang*: *I can easily ring up and check the time.* **2 easily the best, worst, nicest, etc.** without doubt □ *tdk disangsikan/diragu lagi*: *It's easily his best novel.*

east¹ /iːst/ *noun* [U, sing] (*abbr* E) **1** (also **the east**) the direction you look towards in order to see the sun rise; one of the **points of the compass** (= the main directions that we give names to) □ *timur*: *Which way is east?* ◆ *a cold wind from the east* ◆ *Which county is to the east of Oxfordshire?* ⊃ picture at **compass 2** (also **East**) the part of any country, city, etc. that is further to the east than the other parts □ *kawasan/bahagian timur*: *Norwich is in the east of England.* **3 the East** the countries of Asia, for example China and Japan □ *negara-negara timur* ⊃ look at **the Far East, the Middle East**

east² /iːst/ *adj, adv* **1** (also **East**) [only before a noun] in the east □ *di/ke timur*: *the east coast* ◆ *East Africa* **2** (used about a wind) coming from the east □ *di/ke timur* **3** to or towards the east □ *di/ke timur*: *They headed east.* ◆ *We live east of the city.*

eastbound /ˈiːstbaʊnd/ *adj* travelling or leading towards the east □ *menuju ke timur*: *The eastbound carriageway of the motorway is blocked.*

Easter /ˈiːstə(r)/ *noun* [U] a festival on a Sunday in March or April when Christians celebrate Christ's return to life; the time before and after **Easter Sunday** □ *Hari Easter*: *the Easter holidays* ◆ *Are you going away at Easter?*

'Easter egg *noun* [C] an egg, usually made of chocolate, that you give as a present at **Easter** □ *telur Easter*

easterly /ˈiːstəli/ *adj* **1** [only *before* a noun] towards or in the east □ *ke arah timur; di timur*: *They travelled in an easterly direction.* **2** (used about winds) coming from the east □ *timuran*: *cold easterly winds*

eastern (also **Eastern**) /ˈiːstən/ *adj* **1** [only *before* a noun] (*abbr* E) of, in or from the east of a place □ *(ttg/arah/dr) timur*: *Eastern Scotland* ◆ *the eastern shore of the lake* **2** from or connected with the countries of the East □ *(dr/berkenaan dgn) negara-negara di Timur*: *Eastern cookery* (= that comes from Asia)

eastwards /ˈiːstwədz/ (also **eastward**) *adv* towards the east □ *ke arah timur*: *The Amazon flows eastwards.* ▶ **eastward** *adj*: *to travel in an eastward direction*

easy¹ /ˈiːzi/ adj (easier; easiest) **1** not difficult □ *mudah; senang*: *an easy question* ◆ *It isn't easy to explain the system.* ◆ *The system isn't easy to explain.* **OPP hard 2** comfortable, relaxed and not worried □ *senang; lapang*: *an easy life* ◆ *My mind's easier now.* **OPP uneasy** ➔ noun, verb **ease**
IDM free and easy ➔ **free¹**
I'm easy (*informal*) used to say that you do not have a strong opinion when sb offers you a choice □ *saya tak kisah*: *'Do you want to watch this or the news?' 'I'm easy. It's up to you.'*

easy² /ˈiːzi/ adv (easier; easiest)
IDM easier said than done (*spoken*) more difficult to do than to talk about □ *kalau cakap memang senang*: *'You should get her to help you.' 'That's easier said than done.'*
go easy on sb/on/with sth (*informal*) **1** to be gentle or less strict with sb □ *jangan berkeras*: *Go easy on him; he's just a child.* **2** to avoid using too much of sth □ *kurangkan*: *Go easy on the salt; it's bad for your heart.*
take it/things easy to relax and not work too hard or worry too much □ *bersenang-senang*

easy 'chair noun [C] a large comfortable chair with arms □ *kerusi malas*

easy-'going adj (used about a person) calm, relaxed and not easily worried or upset by what other people do □ *jenis tak kisah sangat orangnya*: *Her parents are very easy-going. They let her do what she wants.* **SYN laid-back**

eat /iːt/ verb (pt **ate** /et/ (*especially AmE*) /eɪt/; pp **eaten** /ˈiːtn/) **1** [I,T] to put food into your mouth, then chew and swallow it □ *makan*: *Who ate all the biscuits?* ◆ *Eat your dinner up, Joe* (= finish it all). ◆ *She doesn't eat properly. No wonder she's so thin.* ◆ *Do you want something to eat?* **2** [I] to have a meal □ *makan*: *What time shall we eat?* ◆ *We ate at a pizzeria near our hotel.*
IDM have sb eating out of your hand to have control and power over sb □ *menjinakkan sso; membuat sso menurut apa yg disuruh, dsb*
have your cake and eat it ➔ **cake¹**
PHR V eat sth away/eat away at sth to damage or destroy sth slowly over a period of time □ *menghakis*: *The sea had eaten away at the cliff.*
eat out to have a meal in a restaurant □ *makan di luar*: *Would you like to eat out tonight?*

eater /ˈiːtə(r)/ noun [C] a person who eats in a particular way □ *pemakan*: *My uncle's a big eater* (= he eats a lot). ◆ *We're not great meat eaters in our family.*

eau de cologne /ˌəʊ də kəˈləʊn/ (also **cologne**) noun [U] a type of **perfume** (= a pleasant-smelling liquid) that is not very strong □ *air kolon*

eaves /iːvz/ noun [pl] the edges of a roof that stick out over the walls □ *cucur atap*: *There's a bird's nest under the eaves.*

eavesdrop /ˈiːvzdrɒp/ verb [I] (**eavesdropping**; **eavesdropped**) **eavesdrop (on sb/sth)** to listen secretly to other people talking □ *memasang telinga*: *They caught her eavesdropping on their conversation.*

the ebb /eb/ noun [sing] the time when sea water flows away from the land □ *air surut*

MORE The movement of sea water twice a day is called the **tide**. The opposite of **ebb tide** is **high tide**.

IDM the ebb and flow (of sth) (used about a situation, noise, feeling, etc.) a regular increase and decrease in the progress or strength of sth □ *turun naiknya sst*

eBay™ /ˈiːbeɪ/ noun [U] a website on the Internet where people can **auction** goods (= sell them to the person who offers the most money for them): *He buys rare baseball cards on eBay.*

TOPIC
eBay™
You can buy or sell things on an **auction website**. You **bid** (= say how much you want to pay) for the item you want. The person who offers the most money **wins the auction** and gets the item.

ebb /eb/ verb [I] **1** (used about sea water) to flow away from the land, as happens twice a day □ *beransur surut* **SYN go out 2 ebb (away)** (used about a feeling, etc.) to become weaker □ *semakin kurang/merosot/pudar*: *The crowd's enthusiasm began to ebb.*

ebony /ˈebəni/ noun [U] a hard black wood □ *kayu hitam*

'e-book noun [C] a book that you can read on a computer screen or on an electronic device that you hold in your hand □ *e-buku*: *You can download unlimited e-books for free.* ➔ look at **e-reader**

TOPIC
E-books
You can buy an e-book **over the Internet** and read it on an **e-reader/e-book reader** (= a small electronic device that you carry with you). You can keep many books on one e-reader. It is also possible to buy an **app** (= computer application) that will allow you to **download** e-books **onto** your computer, smartphone, iPod™, etc.

'e-book reader = **'e-reader**

eccentric /ɪkˈsentrɪk/ adj (used about people or their behaviour) strange or unusual □ *eksentrik; aneh; pelik*: *People said he was mad but I think he was just slightly eccentric.* ▶ **eccentric** noun [C]: *She's just an old eccentric.* ▶ **eccentricity** /ˌeksenˈtrɪsəti/ noun [C,U] (pl **eccentricities**)

ecclesiastical /ɪˌkliːziˈæstɪkl/ adj connected with or belonging to the Christian Church □ *berkaitan dgn gereja ataupun kepaderian*: *ecclesiastical law*

echo¹ /ˈekəʊ/ noun [C] (pl **echoes**) a sound that is repeated as it is sent back off a surface such as the wall of a tunnel □ *gema; gaung*: *I could hear the echo of footsteps somewhere in the distance.*

echo² /ˈekəʊ/ *verb* **1** [I] (used about a sound) to be repeated; to come back as an **echo** □ *bergema; bergaung*: *Their footsteps echoed in the empty church.* **2** [I,T] **echo sth (back); echo (with/to sth)** to repeat or send back a sound; to be full of a particular sound □ *menggemakan; bergema*: *The tunnel echoed back their calls.* ♦ *The hall echoed with their laughter.* **3** [T] to repeat what sb has said, done or thought □ *meniru; mengulangi; membeo*: *The child echoed everything his mother said.* ♦ *The newspaper article echoed my views completely.*

eclair /ɪˈkleə(r)/ *noun* [C] a type of long thin cake, usually filled with cream and covered with chocolate □ *eklair* ⊃ picture at **cake**

eclipse

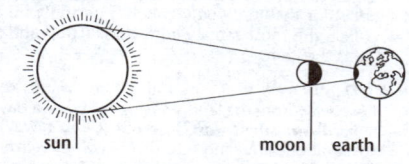

sun | moon | earth

eclipse¹ /ɪˈklɪps/ *noun* [C] an occasion when the moon or the sun seems to completely or partly disappear, because one of them is passing between the other and the earth □ *gerhana*: *a total/partial eclipse of the sun*

eclipse² /ɪˈklɪps/ *verb* [T] (used about the moon, etc.) to cause an **eclipse** of the sun, etc. □ *menyebabkan gerhana*

eco-friendly /ˌiːkəʊ ˈfrendli/ *adj* not harmful to the environment □ *mesra ekologi*: *eco-friendly products/fuel*

ecologist /iˈkɒlədʒɪst/ *noun* [C] a person who studies or is an expert in **ecology** □ *ahli ekologi*

ecology /iˈkɒlədʒi/ *noun* [U] the relationship between living things and their surroundings; the study of this subject □ *ekologi* ▶ **ecological** /ˌiːkəˈlɒdʒɪkl/ *adj*: *The oil spill caused an ecological disaster.* ▶ **ecologically** /-kli/ *adv*

economic /ˌiːkəˈnɒmɪk; ˌekə-/ *adj* **1** [only before a noun] connected with the supply of money, business, industry, etc. □ *(berkenaan dgn) ekonomi*: *The country faces growing economic problems.* **2** producing a profit □ *menguntungkan*: *The mine was closed because it was not economic.* **OPP** **uneconomic**

HELP Be careful. **Economical** has a different meaning.

economical /ˌiːkəˈnɒmɪkl; ˌekə-/ *adj* that costs or uses less time, money, fuel, etc. than usual □ *(yg) menjimatkan; jimat*: *The new model is a very economical car to run.* **OPP** **uneconomical** ▶ **economically** /-kli/ *adv*: *The train service could be run more economically.*

economic migrant *noun* [C] a person who moves from their own country to a new country in order to find work or have a better standard of living □ *penghijrah ekonomi*

economics /ˌiːkəˈnɒmɪks; ˌekə-/ *noun* [U] the study or principles of the way money, business and industry are organized □ *(ilmu) ekonomi*: *a degree in economics* ♦ *the economics of a company*

economist /ɪˈkɒnəmɪst/ *noun* [C] a person who studies or is an expert in **economics** □ *ahli ekonomi*

economize (also **-ise**) /ɪˈkɒnəmaɪz/ *verb* [I] **economize (on sth)** to save money, time, fuel, etc.; to use less of sth □ *menjimatkan*

economy /ɪˈkɒnəmi/ *noun* (*pl* **economies**) **1** **the economy** [C] the operation of a country's money supply, commercial activities and industry □ *ekonomi*: *There are signs of improvement in the economy.* ♦ *the economies of America and Japan* **2** [C,U] careful spending of money, time, fuel, etc.; trying to save, not waste sth □ *berjimat cermat, ekonomi*: *Our department is making economies in the amount of paper it uses.* ♦ *economy class* (= the cheapest class of air travel)

ecosystem /ˈiːkəʊsɪstəm/ *noun* [C] all the plants and living creatures in a particular area considered in relation to their physical environment □ *ekosistem*

ecotourism /ˈiːkəʊtʊərɪzəm (*BrE also*) -tɔːr-/ *noun* [U] holidays that are organized so that tourists can visit beautiful areas without harming the natural environment □ *ekopelancongan* ▶ **ecotourist** /-ɪst/ *noun* [C]

ecstasy /ˈekstəsi/ *noun* [C,U] (*pl* **ecstasies**) a feeling or state of great happiness □ *(perasaan) tersangat gembira*: *to be in ecstasy* ♦ *She went into ecstasies about the ring he had bought her.*

ecstatic /ɪkˈstætɪk/ *adj* extremely happy □ *tersangat gembira*

eczema /ˈeksɪmə/ *noun* [U] a disease which makes your skin red and dry so that you want to scratch it □ *ekzema*

ed. (also **Ed.**) *abbr* = **edition**(1), **editor**

eddy /ˈedi/ *noun* [C] (*pl* **eddies**) a movement of air, water or dust in a circle □ *olakan; pusaran*

edge¹ /edʒ/ *noun* [C] **1** the place where sth, especially a surface, ends □ *tepi; pinggir*: *the edge of a table* ♦ *The leaves were brown and curling at the edges.* ♦ *I stood at the water's edge.* **2** the sharp cutting part of a knife, etc. □ *mata (pisau, dsb)*

IDM **an/the edge on/over sb/sth** a small advantage over sb/sth □ *kelebihan*: *She knew she had the edge over the other candidates.*
(be) on edge to be nervous, worried or quick to become upset or angry □ *berasa gelisah/risau; cepat marah*: *I'm a bit on edge because I get my exam results today.*

edge² /edʒ/ *verb* **1** [I,T] **edge (your way/sth) across, along, away, back, etc.** to move yourself/

sth somewhere slowly and carefully □ *bergerak perlahan-lahan; mengengsot*: *We edged closer to get a better view.* ♦ *She edged her chair up to the window.* **2** [T, usually passive] edge sth (with sth) to put sth along the edge of sth else □ *bertepikan*: *The cloth was edged with lace.*

edgeways /ˈedʒweɪz/ (also **edgewise** /-waɪz/) adv
IDM not get a word in edgeways ➔ **word¹**

edgy /ˈedʒi/ adj (edgier; edgiest) (informal) nervous, worried or quick to become upset or angry □ *gelisah; risau; cepat marah*: *You seem very edgy. What's bothering you?*

edible /ˈedəbl/ adj good or safe to eat □ *boleh dimakan*: *Are these mushrooms edible?* **OPP** inedible

edifice /ˈedɪfɪs/ noun [C] (formal) a large impressive building □ *bangunan yg tersergam*

edit /ˈedɪt/ verb [T] **1** to prepare a piece of writing to be published, making sure that it is correct, the right length, etc. □ *mengedit; menyunting* **2** to make changes to text or data on screen on a computer □ *mengedit* **3** to prepare a film, TV or radio programme by cutting and arranging recorded material in a particular order □ *mengedit* **4** to be the editor of a newspaper, magazine, etc. □ *mengurus penerbitan sst akhbar, majalah, dsb*

edition /ɪˈdɪʃn/ noun [C] **1** (abbr **ed.**) the form in which a book is published; all the books, newspapers, etc. published in the same form at the same time □ *edisi*: *a paperback/hardback edition* ♦ *the online edition of 'Il Pais'* **2** one of a series of newspapers, magazines, TV or radio programmes □ *edisi*: *And now for this week's edition of 'Panorama'…*

editor /ˈedɪtə(r)/ noun [C] (abbr **ed.**) also (abbr **Ed.**) **1** the person who is in charge of all or part of a newspaper, magazine, etc. and who decides what should be included □ *editor; pengarang*: *the financial editor* ♦ *Who is the editor of 'The Times'?* **2** a person whose job is to prepare a book or other material to be published by checking for mistakes and correcting the text □ *editor; penyunting*: *an online/web editor* **3** a person whose job is to prepare a film, TV programme, etc. for showing to the public by cutting and putting the recorded material in the correct order □ *penyunting*

editorial /ˌedɪˈtɔːriəl/ adj connected with the task of preparing sth such as a newspaper, magazine or TV or radio programme to be published or broadcast □ *lidah pengarang*: *the magazine's editorial staff* ♦ *an editorial decision* ▶ **editorial** noun [C] an article in a newspaper, usually written by the editor, giving an opinion on an important subject

educate /ˈedʒukeɪt/ verb [T] to teach or train sb, especially in school □ *mendidik; memberi pelajaran*: *Young people should be educated to care for their environment.* ♦ *All their children were educated at private schools.*

educated /ˈedʒukeɪtɪd/ adj having studied and learnt a lot of things to a high standard □ *berpelajaran; berpendidikan*: *a highly educated woman* ♦ *He spoke in an educated voice.*

education /ˌedʒuˈkeɪʃn/ noun [U, sing] **1** the teaching or training of people, especially in schools □ *pendidikan*: *primary/secondary/higher/adult education* ♦ *She received an excellent education.* ➔ note at **school, study 2** [U] **Education** the subject of study that deals with how to teach; the institutions or people involved in this □ *subjek Pendidikan*: *a Bachelor of Education degree* ♦ *the Education Department* ▶ **educational** /-ʃənl/ adj: *an educational toy/visit/experience*

eel /iːl/ noun [C] a long fish that looks like a snake □ *belut*

eerie (also **eery**) /ˈɪəri/ adj strange and frightening □ *menyeramkan*: *an eerie noise* ▶ **eerily** /ˈɪərəli/ adv ▶ **eeriness** noun [U]

effect /ɪˈfekt/ noun **1** [C,U] (an) effect (on sb/sth) a change that is caused by sth; a result □ *kesan; akibat*: *the effects of acid rain on the lakes and forests* ♦ *Her shouting had little or no effect on him.* ♦ *Despite her terrible experience, she seems to have suffered no ill effects.* ➔ note at **affect** ➔ look at **after-effect, side effect 2** [C,U] a particular look, sound or impression that an artist, writer, etc. wants to create □ *kesan; tanggapan*: *How does the artist create the effect of moonlight?* ♦ *He likes to say things just for effect* (= to impress people). **3** effects [pl] (formal) your personal possessions □ *barang-barang peribadi*: *The insurance policy covers all baggage and personal effects.*
IDM bring/put sth into effect to cause sth to come into use □ *mula digunakan*: *The recommendations will soon be put into effect.*
come into effect (used especially about laws or rules) to begin to be used □ *mula berkuat kuasa*
in effect **1** in fact; for all practical purposes □ *sebenarnya*: *Though they haven't made an official announcement, she is, in effect, the new director.* **2** (used about a rule, a law, etc.) in operation; in use □ *berkuat kuasa; digunakan*: *The new rules will be in effect from next month.*
take effect **1** (used about a drug, etc.) to begin to work; to produce the result you want □ *mula berkesan*: *The anaesthetic took effect immediately.* **2** (used about a law, etc.) to come into operation □ *berkuat kuasa*: *The ceasefire takes effect from midnight.*
to this/that effect with this/that meaning □ *yg lebih kurang begitu maksudnya*: *I told him to leave her alone, or words to that effect.*

effective /ɪˈfektɪv/ adj **1** successfully producing the result that you want □ *berkesan; efektif; mujarab*: *a medicine that is effective against the common cold* ♦ *That picture would look more effective on a dark background.* **OPP**

effectively → eiderdown 280

ineffective 2 [only *before* a noun] real or actual, although perhaps not official □ *sebenar; hakiki*: *The soldiers gained effective control of the town.* ▶ **effectiveness** *noun* [U]

effectively /ɪˈfektɪvli/ *adv* **1** in a way that successfully produces the result you wanted □ *dgn berkesan*: *She dealt with the situation effectively.* **2** in fact; in reality □ *pd hakikatnya*: *It meant that, effectively, they had lost.*

effeminate /ɪˈfemɪnət/ *adj* (used about a man or his behaviour) like a woman □ *spt perempuan; pondan*

effervescent /ˌefəˈvesnt/ *adj* **1** (used about people and their behaviour) excited, enthusiastic and full of energy □ *ghairah; bersemangat; teruja* **SYN bubbly 2** (used about a liquid) having or producing small bubbles of gas □ *berbuih* **SYN** fizzy ▶ **effervescence** *noun* [U]

efficient /ɪˈfɪʃnt/ *adj* able to work well without making mistakes or wasting time and energy □ *cekap; efisien*: *Our secretary is very efficient.* ♦ *You must find a more efficient way of organizing your time.* **OPP** inefficient ▶ **efficiency** /ɪˈfɪʃnsi/ *noun* [U] ▶ **efficiently** *adv*

effigy /ˈefɪdʒi/ *noun* (*pl* effigies) **1** a statue of a famous or religious person, often shown lying down □ *patung yg menyerupai sso*: *stone effigies in the church* **2** a model of a person that makes them look ugly □ *model hodoh sso*: *The demonstrators burned a crude effigy of the president.*

effluent /ˈefluənt/ *noun* [U] (*formal*) liquid waste, especially chemicals produced by factories □ *cairan buangan; efluen; kumbahan*

effort /ˈefət/ *noun* **1** [C,U] the physical or mental strength or energy that you need to do sth; something takes a lot of energy □ *usaha; ikhtiar; tenaga*: *They have put a lot of effort into their studies this year.* ♦ *It's a long climb to the top, but well worth the effort.* **2 an effort (to do sth)** [C] an attempt to do sth, especially when it is difficult to do □ *sst yg sukar*: *I didn't feel like going out, but I'm glad I made the effort.* ♦ *He made no effort to contact his parents.* ♦ *It was a real effort to stay awake in the lecture.* ♦ *The project was a joint effort.*

effortless /ˈefətləs/ *adj* needing little or no effort so that sth seems easy □ *dgn mudah* ▶ **effortlessly** *adv*

EFL /ˌiː ef ˈel/ *abbr* English as a Foreign Language □ *EFL (Bahasa Inggeris Sebagai Bahasa Asing)*

e.g. /ˌiː ˈdʒiː/ *abbr* for example □ *misalnya*: *popular sports, e.g. football, tennis, swimming*

egalitarian /iˌɡælɪˈteəriən/ *adj* (used about a person, system, society, etc.) following the principle that everyone should have equal rights □ *egalitarian*

egg¹ /eɡ/ *noun* **1** [C] an almost round object with a hard shell that contains a young bird, insect or **reptile** (= an animal that has skin covered in scales) □ *telur*: *crocodile eggs*

MORE A female bird **lays** her eggs, often in a **nest**, and then **sits** on them until they **hatch**.

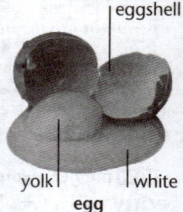

egg — eggshell, yolk, white

2 [C,U] a bird's egg, especially one from a chicken, etc., that we eat □ *telur (ayam, burung, dsb yg boleh dimakan)*: *egg yolks/whites* ➲ picture on **page P16**

MORE Eggs may be **boiled**, **fried**, **poached** or **scrambled**.

3 [C] (in women and female animals) the small cell that can join with a **sperm** (= a male seed) to make a baby □ *ovum; sel telur*: *an egg donor*
IDM put all your eggs in one basket to risk everything by depending completely on one thing, plan, etc. instead of giving yourself several possibilities □ *mempertaruhkan segala-galanya dlm satu usaha atau rancangan*

egg² /eɡ/ *verb*
PHR V egg sb on (to do sth) to encourage sb to do sth, especially sth that they should not do □ *menggesa; mendesak*

ˈegg cup *noun* [C] a small cup for holding a boiled egg □ *mangkuk telur*

eggplant /ˈeɡplɑːnt/ (*AmE*) = aubergine

eggshell /ˈeɡʃel/ *noun* [C,U] the hard outside part of an egg □ *kulit telur* ➲ picture at **egg**

ego /ˈiːɡəʊ/ (*BrE also*) /ˈeɡəʊ/ *noun* [C] (*pl* egos) the (good) opinion that you have of yourself □ *ego*: *It was a blow to her ego when she lost her job.*

egocentric /ˌeɡəʊˈsentrɪk; ˌiːɡ-/ *adj* thinking only about yourself and not what other people need or want □ *egosentrik; mementingkan diri sendiri sahaja* **SYN** selfish

egoism /ˈeɡəʊɪzəm; ˈiːɡ-/ (*also* egotism /ˈeɡətɪzəm; ˈiːɡ-/) *noun* [U] the fact of thinking that you are better or more important than anyone else □ *keegoan; egoisme* ▶ **egoist** /ˈeɡəʊɪst; ˈiːɡ-/ (*also* egotist /ˈeɡətɪst; ˈiːɡə-/) *noun* [C]: *I hate people who are egoists.* ▶ **egoistic** /ˌeɡəʊˈɪstɪk; ˌiːɡ-/ (*also* egotistical /ˌeɡəˈtɪstɪkl; ˌiːɡə-/) *adj*

eh /eɪ/ *exclam* (*BrE informal*) **1** used for asking sb to repeat sth □ *ha; apa*: *'Did you like the film?' 'Eh?' 'I asked if you liked the film!'* **2** used for asking sb to agree with you □ *ya; 'kan*: *'Good party, eh?'*

Eid (*also* Id) /iːd/ *noun* [sing] one of the two main Muslim festivals, especially one that celebrates the end of Ramadan (= a month when people do not eat during the day) □ *Aidil (fitri/adha)*

eiderdown /ˈaɪdədaʊn/ *noun* [C] (*BrE*) a covering for a bed filled with soft feathers, usually used on top of other coverings for the bed □ *cadar tebal gebu* ➲ look at **duvet**

eight /eɪt/ number **1** 8 □ 8 ⊃ note at **six** **2 eight-** [in compounds] having eight of sth □ *lapan*: *an eight-sided shape*

eighteen /ˌeɪˈtiːn/ number 18 □ *lapan belas* ⊃ note at **six** ▶ **eighteenth** /ˌeɪˈtiːnθ/ *ordinal number, noun* ⊃ note at **sixth**

eighth¹ /eɪtθ/ *ordinal number* 8th □ *kelapan; ke-8* ⊃ note at **sixth**

eighth² /eɪtθ/ *noun* [C] ⅛; one of eight equal parts of sth □ *satu per lapan*; ⅛

eighty /ˈeɪti/ *number* 80 □ *lapan puluh; 80* ⊃ note at **sixty** ▶ **eightieth** /ˈeɪtiəθ/ *ordinal number, noun* ⊃ note at **sixth**

either¹ /ˈaɪðə(r); ˈiːðə(r)/ *determiner, pron* **1** one or the other of two; it does not matter which □ *salah satu; mana-mana satu*: *You can choose either soup or salad, but not both.* ◆ *You can ask either of us for advice.* ◆ *Either of us is willing to help.* **2** both □ *kedua-dua*: *It is a pleasant road, with trees on either side.*

either² /ˈaɪðə(r); ˈiːðə(r)/ *adv* **1** [used after two negative statements] also □ *pun; juga*: *I don't like Pat and I don't like Nick much either.* ◆ *'I can't remember his name.' 'I can't either.'*

> **MORE** We can also say **neither can I**. Look at **too** for agreement with positive statements.

2 used for emphasizing a negative statement □ *lagipun*: *The restaurant is quite good. And it's not expensive, either.* **3 either … or …** used when you are giving a choice, usually of two things □ *sama ada… atau…*: *I can meet you either Thursday or Friday.* ◆ *Either you leave or I do.* ◆ *You can either write or phone.* ⊃ note at **neither, too**

ejaculate /iˈdʒækjuleɪt/ *verb* **1** [I] to send out **semen** (= liquid) from the **penis** (= the male sexual organ) **2** [I,T] (*old-fashioned*) to say sth suddenly □ *menyeru* ▶ **ejaculation** /iˌdʒækjuˈleɪʃn/ *noun* [C,U]

eject /iˈdʒekt/ *verb* **1** [T, often passive] (*formal*) **eject sb (from sth)** to push or send sb/sth out of a place (usually with force) □ *mengusir; menghalau*: *The protesters were ejected from the building.* **2** [I] to escape from an aircraft that is going to crash □ *melentingkan diri* **3** [I,T] to remove a disk from a machine, usually by pressing a button □ *mengeluarkan*: *To eject the CD, press this button.* ◆ *After recording for three hours, the DVD will eject automatically.*

eke /iːk/ *verb*
PHR V eke sth out to make a small amount of sth last a long time □ *menjimatkan*

elaborate¹ /ɪˈlæbərət/ *adj* very complicated; done or made very carefully □ *rumit; terperinci*: *an elaborate pattern* ◆ *elaborate plans* ▶ **elaborately** *adv*: *an elaborately decorated room*

elaborate² /ɪˈlæbəreɪt/ *verb* [I] (*formal*) **elaborate (on sth)** to give more details about sth □ *menjelaskan dgn lebih terperinci*: *Could you elaborate on that idea?*

---

281 **eight → elderly**

elapse /ɪˈlæps/ *verb* [I] (*formal*) (used about time) to pass □ *berlalu*

elastic¹ /ɪˈlæstɪk/ *noun* [U] material with rubber in it which can stretch □ *(bahan) elastik/ getah*

elastic² /ɪˈlæstɪk/ *adj* **1** (used about material, etc.) that returns to its original size and shape after being stretched □ *elastik; anjal; ada getah* **2** that can be changed; not fixed □ *anjal; boleh diubah*: *Our rules are quite elastic.*

eˌlastic ˈband = **rubber band**

elasticity /ˌiːlæˈstɪsəti; ˌelæ-; ɪˌlæ-/ *noun* [U] the quality that sth has of being able to stretch and return to its original size and shape □ *keanjalan; kekenyalan*

elated /iˈleɪtɪd/ *adj* very happy and excited □ *amat gembira* ▶ **elation** /iˈleɪʃn/ *noun* [U]

elbow

He elbowed past.   She nudged her.

elbow¹ /ˈelbəʊ/ *noun* [C] **1** the place where the bones of your arm join and your arm bends □ *siku*: *She jabbed him with her elbow.* ⊃ picture at **body 2** the part of the sleeve of a coat, jacket, etc. that covers the elbow □ *bahagian siku (baju, dsb)*: *His old jacket was worn at the elbows.*

elbow² /ˈelbəʊ/ *verb* [T] to push sb with your elbow □ *menyiku*: *He elbowed her out of the way.* ⊃ look at **nudge**

ˈelbow room *noun* [U] (*informal*) enough space to move freely □ *ruang*

elder¹ /ˈeldə(r)/ *adj* **1** [only *before* a noun] older (of two members of a family) □ *lebih tua; abang; kakak*: *My elder daughter is at university now but the other one is still at school.* ◆ *an elder brother/sister* **2** **the elder** [sing] the older of two people □ *(orang) yg lebih tua antara dua; abang; kakak*: *Who is the elder of the two?*

elder² /ˈeldə(r)/ *noun* **1 my, etc. elder** [sing] a person who is older than me, etc. □ *orang yg lebih tua*: *He is her elder by several years.* **2 elders** [pl] older people □ *orang tua-tua*: *Do children still respect the opinions of their elders?*

elderly /ˈeldəli/ *adj* (used about a person) old □ *agak tua; berumur*: *elderly relatives*

[C] **countable**, a noun with a plural form: *one book, two books*   [U] **uncountable**, a noun with no plural form: *some sugar*

eldest → element 282

> **HELP** This is a polite way of saying 'old'.

2 the elderly noun [pl] old people in general □ *orang-orang tua*: *The elderly need special care in winter.* ⊃ look at **old**

eldest /ˈeldɪst/ adj, noun [C] (the) oldest (of three or more members of a family) □ *paling tua; (anak) sulung*: *Their eldest child is a boy.* ♦ *John's got 4 boys. The eldest has just gone to university.*

elect /ɪˈlekt/ verb [T] **1 elect sb (to sth); elect sb (as sth)** to choose sb to have a particular job or position by voting for them □ *memilih; mengundi*: *He was elected to Parliament in 2010.* ♦ *The committee elected her as their representative.* **2** (formal) **elect to do sth** to decide to do sth □ *memilih*: *Many people elect to work from home.*

election /ɪˈlekʃn/ noun [C,U] (the time of) choosing a Member of Parliament, President, etc. by voting □ *pilihan raya*: *In America, presidential elections are held every four years.* ♦ *If you're interested in politics why not stand for election yourself?* ⊃ note at **politics**

> **CULTURE**
>
> In Britain **general elections** are held about every five years. Sometimes **by-elections** are held at other times. In each region (**constituency**) voters must choose one person from a list of **candidates**.

elector /ɪˈlektə(r)/ noun [C] a person who has the right to vote in an election □ *pengundi* ⊃ A more common word is **voter**. ▶ **electoral** /ɪˈlektərəl/ adj: *the electoral register/roll* (= the list of electors in an area)

electorate /ɪˈlektərət/ noun [C, with sing or pl verb] all the people who can vote in a region, country, etc. □ *para pengundi*

electric /ɪˈlektrɪk/ adj **1** producing or using electricity □ *elektrik*: *an electric current* ♦ *an electric kettle* **2** very exciting □ *amat menguja/menarik; penuh keghairahan*: *The atmosphere was electric.*

electrical /ɪˈlektrɪkl/ adj of or about electricity □ *(berkenaan dgn) elektrik*: *an electrical appliance* (= a machine that uses electricity) ♦ *an electrical engineer* (= a person who designs electrical systems and equipment)

the eˌlectric ˈchair noun [sing] a chair used in some countries for killing criminals with a very strong electric current □ *kerusi elektrik*

electrician /ɪˌlekˈtrɪʃn/ noun [C] a person whose job is to connect and repair electrical systems and equipment □ *juruelektrik* ⊃ note at **house**

electricity /ɪˌlekˈtrɪsəti/ noun [U] a type of energy that we use to make heat, light and power to work machines, etc. □ *tenaga elektrik*: *Turn that light off. We don't want to waste electricity.*

> **MORE** Electricity is usually **generated** in **power stations**. It may also be produced by **generators** or **batteries**.

eˌlectric ˈrazor = **shaver**

eˌlectric ˈshock (also **shock**) noun [C] a sudden painful feeling that you get if electricity goes through your body □ *kejutan elektrik*

electrify /ɪˈlektrɪfaɪ/ verb [T] (**electrifying**; **electrifies**; pt, pp **electrified**) **1** to supply sth with electricity □ *mengelektrikkan*: *The railways are being electrified.* **2** to make sb very excited □ *merangsangkan; menaikkan semangat*: *Ronaldo electrified the crowd with his pace and skill.*

electrocute /ɪˈlektrəkjuːt/ verb [T] to kill sb with electricity that goes through the body □ *membunuh dgn kejutan elektrik* ▶ **electrocution** /ɪˌlektrəˈkjuːʃn/ noun [U]

electrode /ɪˈlektrəʊd/ noun [C] one of two points where an electric current enters or leaves a battery, etc. □ *elektrod*

electron /ɪˈlektrɒn/ noun [C] part of an atom, that carries a negative electric charge □ *elektron* ⊃ look at **neutron**, **proton**

electronic /ɪˌlekˈtrɒnɪk/ adj **1** using electronics □ *elektronik*: *electronic equipment* ♦ *This dictionary is available in electronic form* (= on a computer disk). **2** done using a computer □ *elektronik; dgn menggunakan komputer*: *electronic banking/shopping* ▶ **electronically** /-kli/ adv

electronics /ɪˌlekˈtrɒnɪks/ noun [U] the technology used to produce computers, radios, etc.; the study of this technology □ *(ilmu) elektronik*: *the electronics industry*

elegant /ˈelɪgənt/ adj attractive and of good style or design □ *anggun*: *She looked very elegant in her new dress.* ♦ *an elegant coat* **SYN** *stylish* ▶ **elegance** noun [U] ▶ **elegantly** adv

element /ˈelɪmənt/ noun
▶ PART/AMOUNT **1** [C] one important part of sth □ *unsur; bahagian*: *Cost is an important element when we're thinking about holidays.* **2** [C, usually sing] **an element of sth** a small amount of sth □ *unsur; sedikit*: *There was an element of truth in what he said.*
▶ GROUP OF PEOPLE **3** [C] people of a certain type □ *anasir; elemen*: *The criminal element at football matches causes a lot of trouble.*
▶ CHEMISTRY **4** [C] one of the simple chemical substances, for example iron, gold, etc. □ *unsur*
▶ ELECTRICAL PART **5** [C] the metal part of a piece of electrical equipment that produces heat □ *elemen*: *The kettle needs a new element.*
▶ WEATHER **6 the elements** [pl] (bad) weather □ *cuaca; unsur-unsur alam*: *to be exposed to the elements*
▶ BASIC PRINCIPLES **7 elements** [pl] the basic principles of a subject that you have to learn first □ *prinsip asas* **SYN** *basics*: *He taught me the elements of map-reading.*
IDM **in/out of your element** in a situation where you feel comfortable/uncomfortable □ *bera-*

[I] **intransitive**, a verb which has no object: *He laughed.* | [T] **transitive**, a verb which has an object: *He ate an apple.*

sa selesa/canggung, kekok: Bill's in his element speaking to a large group of people, but I hate it.

elementary /ˌelɪˈmentri/ *adj* **1** connected with the first stages of learning sth □ *permulaan; asas: an elementary course in English* ♦ *a book for elementary students* **2** basic; not difficult □ *asas; mudah: elementary physics*

ˌeleˈmentary school *noun* [C] (*AmE*) a school for children aged 5 to 12 □ *sekolah rendah*

elephant

elephant /ˈelɪfənt/ *noun* [C] a very large grey animal with big ears, two **tusks** (= long curved teeth) and a **trunk** (= a very long nose) □ *gajah* ➲ picture on **page P12**

elevate /ˈelɪveɪt/ *verb* [T] (*formal*) to move sb/sth to a higher place or more important position □ *mengangkat; menaikkan; meninggikan; tinggi: an elevated platform* ♦ *He was elevated to the Board of Directors.* **SYN** raise

elevation /ˌelɪˈveɪʃn/ *noun* **1** [C,U] (*formal*) the process of moving to a higher place or more important position □ *pengangkatan; penaikan; peninggian: his elevation to the presidency* **2** [C] the height of a place above sea level □ *ketinggian: The city is at an elevation of 2 000 metres.*

elevator /ˈelɪveɪtə(r)/ (*AmE*) = **lift**²(1): *It's on the fifth floor, so we'd better take the elevator.*

eleven /ɪˈlevn/ *number* 11 □ *sebelas; 11* ➲ note at **six** ▸ **eleventh** /ɪˈlevnθ/ *ordinal number, noun* ➲ note at **sixth**

elf /elf/ *noun* [C] (*pl* **elves** /elvz/) (in stories) a small creature with pointed ears who has magic powers □ *orang bunian*

elicit /ɪˈlɪsɪt/ *verb* [T] (*formal*) **elicit sth (from sb)** to manage to get information, facts, a reaction, etc. from sb □ *mencungkil; mendapatkan*

eligible /ˈelɪdʒəbl/ *adj* **eligible (for sth/to do sth)** having the right to do or have sth □ *berhak; layak: In Britain, you are eligible to vote when you are eighteen.* **OPP** ineligible

eliminate /ɪˈlɪmɪneɪt/ *verb* [T] **1** to remove sb/sth that is not wanted or needed □ *membuang; mengeluarkan; menyingkirkan; menghapuskan: We must try and eliminate the problem.* **2** [often passive] to stop sb going further in a competition, etc. □ *menyingkirkan; terkeluar: The school team was eliminated in the first round of the competition.* ▸ **elimination** /ɪˌlɪmɪˈneɪʃn/ *noun* [C,U]

elite /eɪˈliːt/ *noun* [C, with sing or pl verb] a social group that is thought to be the best or most important because of its power, money, intelligence, etc. □ *elit: an intellectual elite* ▸ **elite** *adj: an elite group of artists*

elitism /eɪˈliːtɪzəm/ *noun* [U] the belief that some people should be treated in a special way □ *elitisme: Many people believe that private education encourages elitism.* ▸ **elitist** /-ɪst/ *noun* [C], *adj*

elk /elk/ (*AmE* **moose**) *noun* [C] a very large **deer** (= a large wild animal that eats grass) with large flat **antlers** (= horns shaped liked branches) on its head □ *elk; sejenis rusa besar*

ellipse /ɪˈlɪps/ *noun* [C] (*technical*) a regular oval (= shaped like an egg) shape □ *elips; bujur; bulat telur*

elk

elliptical /ɪˈlɪptɪkl/ *adj* **1** with a word or words left out of a sentence deliberately □ *menggugurkan kata-kata dgn sengaja: He made an elliptical remark* (= one that suggests more than is actually said). **2** (also **elliptic** /ɪˈlɪptɪk/) connected with or in the form of an **ellipse** □ *berbentuk elips atau bulat bujur* ▸ **elliptically** /-kli/ *adv: to speak/write elliptically*

elm /elm/ (also ˈ**elm tree**) *noun* [C] a tall tree with large leaves □ *pokok elm*

elocution /ˌeləˈkjuːʃn/ *noun* [U] the ability to speak clearly and pronounce words correctly, especially in public □ *seni pidato; gaya pengucapan*

elongated /ˈiːlɒŋgeɪtɪd/ *adj* long and thin in a way that is not normal □ *panjang tirus*

elope /ɪˈləʊp/ *verb* [I] **elope (with sb)** to run away secretly to get married □ *kahwin lari*

eloquent /ˈeləkwənt/ *adj* (*formal*) able to use language and express your opinions well, especially when you speak in public □ *petah; pandai berucap* ▸ **eloquence** *noun* [U] ▸ **eloquently** *adv*

else /els/ *adv* [used after words formed with *any-, every-, no-, some-* and after question words] another, different person, thing or place □ *lain; lagi: This isn't mine. It must be someone else's.* ♦ *Was it you who phoned me, or somebody else?* ♦ *Everybody else is allowed to stay up late.* ♦ *You'll have to pay. Nobody else will.* ♦ *What else would you like?* ♦ *I'm tired of that cafe—shall we go somewhere else for a change?*

elsewhere → embezzle 284

IDM **or else** otherwise; if not □ *kalau tdk; ataupun*: *You'd better go to bed now or else you'll be tired in the morning.* ◆ *He either forgot or else decided not to come.*

elsewhere /ˌelsˈweə(r)/ *adv* in or to another place □ *di/ke tempat lain*: *He's travelled a lot—in Europe and elsewhere.*

ELT /ˌiː el ˈtiː/ *abbr* English Language Teaching □ *ELT (Pengajaran Bahasa Inggeris)*

elude /iˈluːd/ *verb* [T] (*formal*) **1** to manage to avoid being caught by sb □ *mengelak; mengelakkan diri*: *The escaped prisoner eluded the police for three days.* **2** to be difficult or impossible for sb to remember □ *tdk ingat*: *I remember his face but his name eludes me.*

elusive /iˈluːsɪv/ *adj* not easy to catch, find or remember □ *sukar ditangkap, ditemui atau diingat*

elves plural of **elf**

emaciated /ɪˈmeɪʃieɪtɪd; ɪˈmeɪs-/ *adj* extremely thin and weak because of illness, lack of food, etc. □ *kurus kering dan lemah* ▶ emaciation /ɪˌmeɪsiˈeɪʃn/ *noun* [U]

email (also **e-mail**) /ˈiːmeɪl/ *noun* **1** [U] a way of sending electronic messages and data from one computer to another □ *e-mel*: *to send a message by email* **2** [C,U] a message or messages sent by email □ *e-mel*: *I'll send you an email tomorrow.* ◆ *to receive/get/open an email* ▶ email *verb* [T]: *I'll email the information to you.* ◆ *I'll email her the documents.*

TOPIC

Email

Enter your **username** (= the name you use on your computer) and **password** (= a secret word) to **access** your **email account**. First, you might want to **check your inbox** to see if anyone has **sent** you **an email**. When you **receive an email**, you can **open** it, read it, and then **reply** to it. You can also **forward** (= send) it to someone else, or **delete** (= remove) it. If you want to send someone a file, for example a photo or other document, you can **add it as an attachment**.

---

emanate /ˈeməneɪt/ *verb* [T] (*formal*) to produce or show sth □ *menunjukkan*: *He emanates confidence.*
PHRV **emanate from sth** to come from sth or somewhere □ *datang dr sst*: *The sound of loud music emanated from the building.*

emancipate /iˈmænsɪpeɪt/ *verb* [T] (*formal*) to give sb the same legal, social and political rights as other people □ *membebaskan* ▶ emancipated *adj*: *Are women now fully emancipated (= with the same rights and opportunities as men)?* ▶ emancipation /ɪˌmænsɪˈpeɪʃn/ *noun* [U]

embalm /ɪmˈbɑːm/ *verb* [T] to prevent a dead body from decaying by treating it with special substances □ *mengawet* ▶ embalmer *noun* [C]

embankment /ɪmˈbæŋkmənt/ *noun* [C] a wall of stone or earth that is built to stop a river from spreading into an area that should be dry, or to carry a road or railway □ *tambak; benteng*

embargo /ɪmˈbɑːɡəʊ/ *noun* [C] (*pl* embargoes) an official order to stop doing business with another country □ *sekatan*: *to impose an embargo on arms sales* ◆ *to lift/remove an embargo*

embark /ɪmˈbɑːk/ *verb* [I] to get on a ship □ *menaiki kapal*: *Passengers with cars and caravans must embark first.* **OPP** disembark
PHRV **embark on sth** (*formal*) to start sth (new) □ *memulakan sst*: *I'm embarking on a new career.* ▶ embarkation /ˌembɑːˈkeɪʃn/ *noun* [C,U]

embarrass /ɪmˈbærəs/ *verb* [T] **1** to make sb feel uncomfortable or shy □ *memalukan*: *Don't ever embarrass me in front of my friends again!* **2** to cause problems or difficulties for sb □ *memalukan*: *The Minister's mistake embarrassed the government.*

embarrassed /ɪmˈbærəst/ *adj* embarrassed (about/at sth); embarrassed (to do sth) feeling uncomfortable or shy because of sth silly you have done, because people are looking at you, etc. □ *berasa malu*: *He's embarrassed about his height.* ◆ *Some women are too embarrassed to consult their doctor about the problem.*

embarrassing /ɪmˈbærəsɪŋ/ *adj* making you feel uncomfortable or shy □ *(yg) memalukan*: *an embarrassing question/mistake* ▶ embarrassingly *adv*

embarrassment /ɪmˈbærəsmənt/ *noun* **1** [U] the feeling you have when you are embarrassed □ *rasa malu*: *I nearly died of embarrassment when he said that.* **2** [C] a person or thing that makes you embarrassed □ *orang atau sst yg memalukan*

embassy /ˈembəsi/ *noun* [C] (*pl* embassies) (the official building of) a group of **diplomats** (= officials who represent their country) and the **ambassador** (= the official with the highest position), who represent their government in a foreign country □ *kedutaan* ⊃ look at **consulate**

embed /ɪmˈbed/ *verb* [T] (embedding; embedded) [usually passive] to fix sth firmly and deeply (in sth else) □ *membenamkan; terbenam; tertanam*: *The axe was embedded in the piece of wood.*

embellish /ɪmˈbelɪʃ/ *verb* [T] (*formal*) **1** to make sth more beautiful by adding decoration to it □ *menghias* **SYN** decorate **2** to make a story more interesting by adding details that are not always true □ *menokok* ▶ embellishment *noun* [U,C]

ember /ˈembə(r)/ *noun* [C, usually pl] a piece of wood or coal that is not burning, but is still red and hot after a fire has died □ *bara*

embezzle /ɪmˈbezl/ *verb* [T] to steal money that you are responsible for or that belongs to your employer □ *menggelapkan wang* ▶ embezzlement *noun* [U]

ð **th**en   s **s**o   z **z**oo   ʃ **sh**e   ʒ vi**s**ion   h **h**ow   m **m**an   n **n**o   ŋ si**ng**   l **l**eg   r **r**ed   j **y**es   w **w**et

emblem /ˈembləm/ noun [C] an object or symbol that represents sth □ *lambang*: *The dove is the emblem of peace.*

embody /ɪmˈbɒdi/ verb [T] (embodying; embodies; pt, pp embodied) (formal) **1** to be a very good example of sth □ *terjelma; wujud; melambangkan*: *To me she embodies all the best qualities of a teacher.* **2** to include or contain sth □ *merangkumi; mengandungi*: *This latest model embodies many new features.* ▶ embodiment noun [C]: *She is the embodiment of a caring mother.*

embrace /ɪmˈbreɪs/ verb **1** [I,T] to put your arms around sb as a sign of love, happiness, etc. □ *memeluk; mendakap* **2** [T] (formal) to accept sth with enthusiasm □ *memeluk; menerima*: *She embraced Christianity in her later years.* **3** [T] (formal) to include □ *merangkum; meliputi*: *His report embraced all the main points.* ▶ embrace noun [C]: *He held her in a warm embrace.*

embroider /ɪmˈbrɔɪdə(r)/ verb **1** [I,T] to decorate cloth by sewing a pattern or picture on it □ *menyulam*: *an embroidered blouse* **2** [T] to add details that are not true to a story to make it more interesting □ *menokok tambah* ▶ embroidery /ɪmˈbrɔɪdəri/ noun [U]

embryo /ˈembriəʊ/ noun [C] (pl embryos /-əʊz/) a baby, an animal or a plant in the early stages of development before birth □ *embrio* ⊃ look at **foetus** ▶ embryonic /ˌembriˈɒnɪk/ adj

emerald /ˈemərəld/ noun [C] a bright green **precious stone** (= one that is rare and valuable) □ *(batu) zamrud*: *a ring studded with diamonds and emeralds* ▶ emerald (also ˌemerald ˈgreen) adj: *an emerald green dress*

emerge /iˈmɜːdʒ/ verb [I] emerge (from sth) **1** to appear or come out from somewhere □ *muncul; keluar*: *A man emerged from the shadows.* ♦ (figurative) *The country emerged from the war in ruins.* **2** to become known □ *muncul; timbul; keluar*: *It emerged that she was lying about her age.* ▶ emergence noun [U]: *the emergence of new technologies*

emergency /iˈmɜːdʒənsi/ noun [C,U] (pl emergencies) a serious event that needs immediate action □ *kecemasan*: *In an emergency phone 999 for help.* ♦ *The government has declared a state of emergency* (= a time when special plans or actions can be put into effect) *following the earthquake.* ♦ *an emergency exit*

eˈmergency brake (AmE) = **handbrake**

eˈmergency room noun [C] (abbr ER) (AmE) = **accident and emergency**

emigrant /ˈemɪɡrənt/ noun [C] a person who has gone to live in another country □ *emigran; penghijrah* ⊃ look at **immigrant**

emigrate /ˈemɪɡreɪt/ verb [I] emigrate (from …) (to …) to leave your own country to go and live in another □ *berhijrah*: *They emigrated from Ireland to Australia twenty years ago.* ▶ emigration /ˌemɪˈɡreɪʃn/ noun [C,U] ⊃ look at **immigrant, immigration, migrate**

eminent /ˈemɪnənt/ adj (formal) (used about a person) famous and important □ *terkemuka; terbilang*: *an eminent scientist*

eminently /ˈemɪnəntli/ adv (formal) very; extremely □ *amat; sangat*: *She is eminently suitable for the job.*

emit /iˈmɪt/ verb [T] (emitting; emitted) (formal) to send out sth, for example a smell, a sound, smoke, heat or light □ *mengeluarkan; memancarkan*: *The animal emits a powerful smell when scared.* ▶ emission /iˈmɪʃn/ noun [C,U]: *sulphur dioxide emissions from power stations*

emoticon /iˈməʊtɪkɒn/ noun [C] a symbol that shows your feelings when you send an email or text message. For example :-) represents a smiling face. □ *emotikon*

emotion /iˈməʊʃn/ noun [C,U] a strong feeling such as love, anger, fear, etc. □ *emosi*: *to control/express your emotions* ♦ *His voice was filled with emotion.* ♦ *Brown showed no emotion as the police took him away.*

emotional /iˈməʊʃənl/ adj **1** connected with people's feelings □ *(berkenaan dgn) emosi*: *emotional problems* **2** causing strong feelings □ *penuh emosi*: *an emotional issue* **3** having strong emotions and showing them in front of people □ *emosional; terlalu mengikut perasaan*: *Kelly gave an emotional speech.* ♦ *He always gets very emotional when I leave.* ▶ emotionally /-ʃənəli/ adv: *She felt physically and emotionally drained after giving birth.*

emotive /iˈməʊtɪv/ adj causing strong feelings □ *emotif*: *emotive language* ♦ *an emotive issue*

empathy /ˈempəθi/ noun [C,U] empathy (with/for sb/sth); empathy (between A and B) the ability to imagine how another person is feeling and so understand their mood □ *empati*: *Some adults have (a) great empathy with children.* ▶ empathize (also -ise) /ˈempəθaɪz/ verb [I] empathize (with sb/sth): *He's a popular teacher because he empathizes with his students.*

emperor /ˈempərə(r)/ noun [C] the ruler of an empire □ *maharaja*

emphasis /ˈemfəsɪs/ noun [C,U] (pl emphases /-siːz/) **1** emphasis (on sth) (giving) special importance or attention (to sth) □ *penekanan; penegasan; keutamaan*: *There's a lot of emphasis on science at our school.* ♦ *You should put a greater emphasis on quality rather than quantity when you write.* **2** the force that you give to a word or phrase when you are speaking; a way of writing a word to show that it is important □ *tekanan*: *In the word 'photographer' the emphasis is on the second syllable.* ♦ *I underlined the key phrases of my letter for emphasis.* **SYN** for both meanings **stress**

emphasize (also -ise) /ˈemfəsaɪz/ verb [T] emphasize (that …) to put emphasis on sth □ *menekankan; menegaskan; menitikberatkan*:

They emphasized that healthy eating is important. ◆ *They emphasized the importance of healthy eating.* **SYN** stress

emphatic /ɪmˈfætɪk/ *adj* said or expressed in a strong way □ *tegas*: *an emphatic refusal/denial* ▶ **emphatically** /-kli/ *adv*

empire /ˈempaɪə(r)/ *noun* [C] **1** a group of countries that is governed by one country □ *empayar*: *the Roman Empire* ⊃ look at **emperor**, **empress 2** a very large company or group of companies □ *empayar*: *a business empire*

empirical /ɪmˈpɪrɪkl/ *adj* (*formal*) based on experiments and practical experience, not on ideas □ *empirik*: *empirical evidence*

employ /ɪmˈplɔɪ/ *verb* [T] **1 employ sb (in/on sth); employ sb (as sth)** to pay sb to work for you □ *mengambil bekerja*; *menggaji*: *They employ 600 workers.* ◆ *Three people are employed on the task of designing a new computer system.* ◆ *He is employed as a lorry driver.* ⊃ look at **unemployed 2** (*formal*) **employ sth (as sth)** to use □ *menggunakan*: *In an emergency, an umbrella can be employed as a weapon.*

employee /ɪmˈplɔɪiː/ *noun* [C] a person who is paid to work for sb □ *pekerja*: *The factory has 500 employees.* ⊃ note at **job**

employer /ɪmˈplɔɪə(r)/ *noun* [C] a person or company that employs other people □ *majikan*: *The car factory is the largest employer in this town.*

employment /ɪmˈplɔɪmənt/ *noun* [U] **1** the state of having a paid job □ *pekerjaan*: *to be in/out of employment* ◆ *This bank can give employment to ten extra staff.* ◆ *It is difficult to find employment in the north of the country.* ⊃ note at **work** ⊃ look at **unemployment 2** (*formal*) the use of sth □ *penggunaan*: *the employment of force*

emˈployment agency *noun* [C] a company that helps people to find work and other companies to find workers □ *agensi pekerjaan*

empower /ɪmˈpaʊə(r)/ *verb* [T, usually passive] (*formal*) to give sb power or authority (to do sth) □ *memberikan kuasa* ▶ **empowerment** *noun* [U]: *the empowerment of the individual*

empress /ˈemprəs/ *noun* [C] **1** a woman who rules an empire □ *maharani* **2** the wife of an **emperor** (= a man who rules an empire) □ *maharani*

empty¹ /ˈempti/ *adj* (**emptier**; **emptiest**) **1** having nothing or nobody inside it □ *kosong*: *an empty box* ◆ *The bus was half empty.* **2** without meaning or value □ *kosong; tdk bermakna*: *It was an empty threat* (= it was not meant seriously). ◆ *My life feels empty now the children have left home.* **SYN** hollow ▶ **emptiness** *noun* [U]

empty² /ˈempti/ *verb* (**emptying**; **empties**; *pt, pp* **emptied**) **1** [T] **empty sth (out/out of sth)** to remove everything that is inside a container, etc. □ *mengosongkan*: *I've emptied a wardrobe for you to use.* ◆ *Luke emptied everything out of his desk and left.* **2** [I] to become empty □ *menjadi kosong*: *The cinema emptied very quickly once the film was finished.*

ˌempty-ˈhanded *adj* without getting what you wanted; without taking sth to sb □ *hampa; tdk mendapat apa-apa*: *The robbers fled empty-handed.*

EMU /ˌiː em ˈjuː/ *abbr* **Economic and Monetary Union** (of the countries of the European Union) □ *EMU (Kesatuan Kewangan Eropah)* ⊃ look at **euro**

emulate /ˈemjuleɪt/ *verb* [T] (*formal*) to try to do sth as well as, or better than, sb □ *mencontohi; meniru* ⊃ A less formal word is **copy**.

emulsion /ɪˈmʌlʃn/ *noun* [C,U] **1** a mixture of liquids that do not normally mix together, such as oil and water □ *emulsi* **2** (*also* **eˈmulsion paint**) (*BrE*) a type of paint used on walls and ceilings that dries without leaving a shiny surface □ *cat emulsi*

enable /ɪˈneɪbl/ *verb* [T] **enable sb/sth to do sth** to make it possible for sb/sth to do sth □ *membolehkan*: *The software enables you to access the Internet in seconds.* **SYN** allow

enamel /ɪˈnæml/ *noun* [U] **1** a hard shiny substance used for protecting or decorating metal, etc. □ *enamel*: *enamel paint* **2** the hard white outer covering of a tooth □ *enamel*

enchanted /ɪnˈtʃɑːntɪd/ *adj* **1** (in stories) affected by magic powers □ *kena sihir* **2** (*formal*) pleased or very interested □ *terpesona*: *The audience was enchanted by her singing.*

enchanting /ɪnˈtʃɑːntɪŋ/ *adj* very nice or pleasant; attractive □ *mempesonakan; sangat menarik* **SYN** delightful

encircle /ɪnˈsɜːkl/ *verb* [T] (*formal*) to make a circle round sth; to surround □ *mengelilingi; dikelilingi*: *London is encircled by the M25 motorway.*

encl. (*also* **enc.**) *abbr* **enclosed**; used on business letters to show that another document is being sent in the same envelope □ *singkatan utk 'disertakan' atau 'dilampirkan'*

enclose /ɪnˈkləʊz/ *verb* [T] **1** [usually passive] **enclose sth (in sth)** to surround sth with a wall, fence, etc.; to put one thing inside another □ *memagari; memasukkan; terkepung*: *The garden is enclosed by a high hedge.* ◆ *The jewels were enclosed in a strong box.* **2** to put sth in an envelope, package, etc. with sth else □ *menyertakan; melampirkan*: *Can I enclose a letter with this parcel?*

enclosed /ɪnˈkləʊzd/ *adj* **1** with walls, etc. all around □ *tertutup*: *He gets very nervous in enclosed spaces.* **2** sent with a letter, etc. □ *tertutup*: *Please complete the enclosed application form* ◆ *Please find enclosed my completed form.*

enclosure /ɪnˈkləʊʒə(r)/ *noun* [C] **1** a piece of land inside a wall, fence, etc. that is used for a particular purpose □ *kurungan*: *a wildlife enclosure* **2** something that is placed inside an envelope together with the letter □ *lampiran*

encode /ɪnˈkəʊd/ = **code²**(2)

encore¹ /ˈɒŋkɔː(r)/ noun [C] a short, extra performance at the end of a concert, etc. □ *persembahan tambahan/ulangan (pd akhir pementasan)*

encore² /ˈɒŋkɔː(r)/ exclam called out by an audience that wants the people who perform in a concert, etc. to sing or play sth extra □ *sorak pinta; lagi; ulang*

encounter¹ /ɪnˈkaʊntə(r)/ verb [T] **1** to experience sth (a danger, difficulty, etc.) □ *menghadapi; menemui*: *I've never encountered any discrimination at work.* **SYN** meet with sth **2** (formal) to meet sb unexpectedly; to experience or find sth unusual or new □ *terserempak/bertemu dgn*: *She was the most remarkable woman he had ever encountered.* ➲ look at **come across**

encounter² /ɪnˈkaʊntə(r)/ noun [C] **an encounter (with sb/sth); an encounter (between A and B)** an unexpected (often unpleasant) meeting or event □ *pertemuan; pertembungan*: *I've had a number of close encounters* (= situations which could have been dangerous) *with bad drivers.*

encourage /ɪnˈkʌrɪdʒ/ verb [T] **1 encourage sb/sth (in sth/to do sth)** to give hope, support or confidence to sb □ *menggalakkan*: *The teacher encouraged her students to ask questions.* ♦ *They will encourage students in their pursuit of higher education.* **2** to make sth happen more easily □ *menggalakkan*: *The government wants to encourage new businesses to start up in the area.* **OPP** for both meanings **discourage** ▶ **encouragement** noun [C,U] ▶ **encouraging** adj

encroach /ɪnˈkrəʊtʃ/ verb [I] (formal) **encroach (on/upon sth)** to use more of sth than you should □ *masuk ke; makan; mencerobohi; mengganggu*: *I do hope that I am not encroaching too much upon your free time.*

encyclopedia (also **encyclopaedia**) /ɪnˌsaɪkləˈpiːdiə/ noun [C] (pl **encyclopedias**) a book or set of books that gives information about very many subjects, arranged in the order of the alphabet (= from A to Z) □ *ensiklopedia* ➲ note at **book**

end¹ /end/ noun [C] **1** the furthest or final part of sth; the place or time where sth stops □ *hujung; akhir; tamat*: *My house is at the end of the street.* ♦ *I live in the end house.* ♦ *There are some seats at the far end of the room.* ♦ *I'm going on holiday at the end of October.* ♦ *He promised to give me an answer by the end of the week.* ♦ *She couldn't wait to hear the end of the story.*

> **HELP** In the end or at the end? The idiom **in the end** refers to time and means 'finally': *We were too tired to cook, so in the end we decided to eat out.* **At the end of sth** refers to the last part of a book, film, class, etc., at the point where it is about to finish: *At the end of the meal we had an argument about who should pay for it.*

2 (formal) an aim or purpose □ *matlamat; tujuan*: *They were prepared to do anything to achieve their ends.* **3** a little piece of sth that is left after the rest has been used □ *hujung; puntung*: *a cigarette end*

IDM **at an end** (formal) finished or used up □ *berakhir; tamat*: *Her career is at an end.*

at the end of the day (BrE informal) used to say the most important fact in a situation □ *pd akhirnya*: *At the end of the day, you have to make the decision yourself.*

at the end of your tether feeling that you cannot deal with a difficult situation any more, because you are too tired, worried, etc. □ *sudah tdk tahan lagi*

at a loose end ➲ **loose¹**

at your wits' end ➲ **wit**

bring/come/draw to an end (to cause sth) to finish □ *menamatkan; berakhir*: *His stay in England was coming to an end.*

a dead end ➲ **dead¹**

end to end in a line with the ends touching □ *hujung ke hujung*: *They put the tables end to end.*

in the end at last; finally □ *akhirnya*: *He wanted to get home early but in the end it was midnight before he left.*

make ends meet to have enough money for your needs □ *mencukupkan belanja*: *It's hard for us to make ends meet.*

make sb's hair stand on end ➲ **hair**

a means to an end ➲ **means**

no end of sth (informal) too many or much; a lot of sth □ *banyak; tdk habis-habis*: *She has given us no end of trouble.*

odds and ends ➲ **odds**

on end (used about time) continuously □ *lama; berjam-jam, dsb*: *He sits and reads for hours on end.*

put an end to sth to stop sth from happening any more □ *menghentikan*

end² /end/ verb [I,T] **end (in/with sth)** (to cause sth) to finish □ *habis; tamat; berakhir; menamatkan; mengakhiri*: *The road ends here.* ♦ *How does this story end?* ♦ *The match ended in a draw.* ♦ *I think we'd better end this conversation now.*

PHR V **end up (as sth); end up (doing sth)** to find yourself in a place/situation that you did not plan or expect □ *sudahnya; akhirnya*: *We got lost and ended up in the centre of town.* ♦ *She had always wanted to be a writer but ended up as a teacher.* ♦ *There was nothing to eat at home so we ended up getting a takeaway.*

endanger /ɪnˈdeɪndʒə(r)/ verb [T] to cause danger to sb/sth □ *membahayakan*: *Smoking seriously endangers your health.* ♦ *Pollution from the factory endangers public safety.*

endangered /ɪnˈdeɪndʒəd/ adj (used about animals, plants, etc.) in danger of becoming **extinct** (= no longer alive in the world) □ *terancam*: *The giant panda is an endangered species.* ➲ note at **environment**

[C] **countable**, a noun with a plural form: *one book, two books* [U] **uncountable**, a noun with no plural form: *some sugar*

endear /ɪnˈdɪə(r)/ verb [T] (formal) **endear sb/yourself to sb** to make sb/yourself liked by sb □ *membuat sso/diri sendiri disayangi atau disukai orang*: *She managed to endear herself to everybody by her kindness.* ▶ **endearing** adj: *an endearing habit* ▶ **endearingly** adv

endeavour (AmE **endeavor**) /ɪnˈdevə(r)/ verb [I] (formal) **endeavour to do sth** to try hard to do sth □ *mencuba; berusaha*: *She endeavoured to finish her work on time.* ▶ **endeavour** (AmE **endeavor**) noun [C,U]

endemic /enˈdemɪk/ adj **endemic (in/to …)** regularly found in a particular place or among a particular group of people and difficult to get rid of □ *endemik*: *Malaria is endemic in many hot countries.* ♦ *the endemic problem of racism*

ending /ˈendɪŋ/ noun [C] **1** the end (of a story, play, film, etc.) □ *akhir; berakhir; penghabisan*: *That film made me cry but I was pleased that it had a happy ending.* **2** the last part of a word, which can change □ *akhiran*: *When nouns end in -ch or -sh or -x, the plural ending is -es not -s.*

endive /ˈendaɪv/ (AmE) = **chicory**

endless /ˈendləs/ adj **1** very large in size or amount and seeming to have no end □ *tdk berhujung*: *The possibilities are endless.* **2** lasting for a long time and seeming to have no end □ *sangat lama; berjam-jam, dsb; tdk habis-habis*: *Our plane was delayed for hours and the wait seemed endless.* **SYN** **interminable** ▶ **endlessly** adv

endorse /ɪnˈdɔːs/ verb [T] **1** to say publicly that you give official support or agreement to a plan, statement, decision, etc. □ *menyokong*: *Members of all parties endorsed a ban on firearms.* **2** [usually passive] (BrE) to add a note to sb's **driving licence** (= the document which allows sb to drive a vehicle) to say that the driver has broken the law □ *mengendors* ▶ **endorsement** noun [C,U]

endow /ɪnˈdaʊ/ verb [T] to give a large sum of money to an institution such as a school or college □ *membiayai; dikurniai; dianugerahi*
PHR V **be endowed with sth** to naturally have a particular characteristic, quality, etc. □ *dikurniai*: *She was endowed with intelligence and wit.*

endowment /ɪnˈdaʊmənt/ noun [C,U] money that is given to a school, college, etc.; the act of giving this money □ *kurniaan; pembiayaan*

ˈend product noun [C] something that is produced by a particular process or activity □ *keluaran akhir; hasil*

endurance /ɪnˈdjʊərəns/ noun [U] the ability to continue doing sth painful or difficult for a long period of time without complaining □ *daya ketahanan*

endure /ɪnˈdjʊə(r)/ verb (formal) **1** [T] to suffer sth painful or uncomfortable, usually without complaining □ *menanggung; menahan*: *She endured ten years of loneliness.* **SYN** **bear** **2** [I] to continue □ *berkekalan* **SYN** **last** ▶ **enduring** adj

ˌend-ˈuser noun [C] a person who actually uses a product rather than one who makes or sells it, especially sb who uses a product connected with computers □ *pengguna akhir*

enemy /ˈenəmi/ noun (pl **enemies**) **1** [C] a person who hates and tries to harm you □ *musuh; seteru*: *They used to be friends but became* ***bitter enemies****.* ♦ *He has* ***made*** *several* ***enemies*** *during his career.* ⊃ noun **enmity**. **2** **the enemy** [sing, with sing or pl verb] the army or country that your country is fighting against □ *pihak musuh; musuh*: *The enemy is/are approaching.* ♦ *enemy forces*

energetic /ˌenəˈdʒetɪk/ adj full of or needing energy and enthusiasm □ *bertenaga; memerlukan banyak tenaga*: *Jogging is a very energetic form of exercise.* ▶ **energetically** /-kli/ adv

energy /ˈenədʒi/ noun (pl **energies**) **1** [U] the ability to be very active or do a lot of work without getting tired □ *tenaga; daya*: *Children are usually* ***full of energy****.* **2** **energies** [pl] the effort and attention that you give to doing sth □ *tenaga*: *She devoted all her energies to helping the blind.* **3** [U] the power that comes from coal, electricity, gas, etc. that is used for producing heat, driving machines, etc. □ *tenaga*: *nuclear energy*

enforce /ɪnˈfɔːs/ verb [T] to make people obey a law or rule or do sth that they do not want to □ *menguatkuasakan; memaksa*: *How will they enforce the new law?* ▶ **enforced** adj: *enforced redundancies* ▶ **enforcement** noun [U]

engage /ɪnˈɡeɪdʒ/ verb [T] (formal) **1** to interest or attract sb □ *menarik perhatian/minat*: *You need to engage the students' attention right from the start.* **2** **engage sb (as sth)** to give work to sb □ *mengambil (kerja); mengupah*: *They engaged him as a cook.* **3** **engage (with sth)** to make parts of a machine fit together □ *masukkan; masuk*: *Engage the clutch before selecting a gear.*
PHR V **engage in sth** to take part in sth □ *melibatkan diri; ikut serta*: *I don't engage in that kind of gossip!*

engaged /ɪnˈɡeɪdʒd/ adj **1** (formal) **engaged (in/on sth)** (used about a person) busy doing sth □ *sibuk*: *They are engaged in talks with the Irish government.* **2** **engaged (to sb)** having agreed to get married □ *bertunang*: *We've just* ***got engaged****.* ♦ *Susan is engaged to Jim.* **3** (especially AmE **busy**) (used about a telephone) in use □ *sedang digunakan*: *I can't get through—the line is engaged.* **4** (BrE) (used about a public toilet) in use □ *sedang digunakan; ada orang* **OPP** **vacant**

engagement /ɪnˈɡeɪdʒmənt/ noun [C] **1** an agreement to get married; the time when you are engaged □ *pertunangan*: *He broke off their engagement.* **2** (formal) an arrangement to go somewhere or do sth at a fixed time □ *janji* *temu; urusan*: *I can't come on Tuesday as I have a prior engagement.* **SYN** **appointment**

en·gagement ring *noun* [C] a ring, usually with **precious stones** (= ones that are rare and valuable) in it, that a man gives to a woman when they agree to get married □ *cincin pertunangan*: *a diamond engagement ring*

engine /ˈendʒɪn/ *noun* [C] **1** the part of a vehicle that produces power to make the vehicle move □ *enjin*: *This engine runs on diesel.* ♦ *a car/jet engine* ⊃ note at **motor 2** (also **locomotive**) a vehicle that pulls a railway train □ *kepala kereta api; lokomotif*

'engine driver (also **'train driver**; *AmE* **engineer**) *noun* [C] a person whose job is to drive a railway engine □ *pemandu kereta api*

engineer¹ /ˌendʒɪˈnɪə(r)/ *noun* [C] **1** a person whose job is to design, build or repair engines, machines, etc. □ *jurutera*: *a civil/chemical/electrical/mechanical engineer* **2** (*AmE*) = **engine driver**

engineer² /ˌendʒɪˈnɪə(r)/ *verb* [T] (*formal*) to arrange for sth to happen by careful secret planning □ *mengatur (secara rahsia)*: *Her promotion was engineered by her father.*

engineering /ˌendʒɪˈnɪərɪŋ/ *noun* [U] (the study of) the work that is done by an engineer □ *kejuruteraan*: *mechanical/civil/chemical engineering*

English¹ /ˈɪŋɡlɪʃ/ *noun* **1** [U] the language that is spoken in Britain, the US, Australia, etc. □ *bahasa Inggeris*: *Do you speak English?* ♦ *I've been learning English for 5 years.* **2 the English** [pl] the people of England □ *orang Inggeris*

English² /ˈɪŋɡlɪʃ/ *adj* belonging to England, the English people, the English language, etc. □ *keinggerisan*: *English history* ♦ *the English countryside* ⊃ note at **United Kingdom**

CULTURE

Be careful. The people of Scotland (the Scots) and of Wales (the Welsh) are **British**, not English.

the ˌEnglish ˈChannel = **channel¹(6)**

Englishman /ˈɪŋɡlɪʃmən/, **Englishwoman** /ˈɪŋɡlɪʃwʊmən/ *noun* [C] (*pl* **-men** /-mən/, **-women** /-wɪmɪn/) a person who comes from England or whose parents are English □ *lelaki Inggeris*

HELP We normally say: *I'm English* not *I'm an Englishman*.

ˌEnglish ˈmuffin (*AmE*) = **muffin(1)**

engrave /ɪnˈɡreɪv/ *verb* [T] **engrave A with B; engrave B on A** to cut words or designs on metal, stone, etc. □ *mengukirkan; menggores*: *The cup is engraved with his name.* ♦ *His name is engraved on the cup.*

engraving /ɪnˈɡreɪvɪŋ/ *noun* **1** [C] a design that is cut into a piece of metal or stone; a picture made from this □ *ukiran; turisan* **2** [U] the art

289 **engagement ring → enormity**

or process of cutting designs into wood, metal, etc. □ *pengukiran*

engrossed /ɪnˈɡrəʊst/ *adj* **engrossed (in/with sth)** so interested in sth that you give it all your attention □ *asyik; leka*: *She was completely engrossed in her book.*

enhance /ɪnˈhɑːns/ *verb* [T] (*formal*) to improve sth or to make sth look better □ *meningkatkan; menjadikan lebih menarik* ▶ **enhanced** *adj*: *enhanced efficiency* ▶ **enhancement** *noun* [C,U]: *the enhancement of sound quality*

enigma /ɪˈnɪɡmə/ *noun* [C] (*pl* **enigmas**) a person, thing or situation that is difficult to understand □ *sso/sst yg membingungkan* ▶ **enigmatic** /ˌenɪɡˈmætɪk/ *adj*

enjoy /ɪnˈdʒɔɪ/ *verb* [T] **1 enjoy sth/enjoy doing sth** to get pleasure from sth □ *suka; seronok; seronok menikmati*: *I really enjoyed that meal.* ♦ *He enjoys listening to music while he's driving.* ⊃ note at **like² enjoy yourself** to be happy; to have a good time □ *gembira; bersuka ria; betul-betul*: *I enjoyed myself at the party last night.*

enjoyable /ɪnˈdʒɔɪəbl/ *adj* giving pleasure □ *menyeronokkan*: *We spent an enjoyable few days in Scotland.* ▶ **enjoyably** /-əbli/ *adv*: *The evening passed enjoyably.*

enjoyment /ɪnˈdʒɔɪmənt/ *noun* [U,C] pleasure or a thing which gives pleasure □ *keseronokan*: *She gets a lot of enjoyment from teaching.* ♦ *One of her main enjoyments is foreign travel.*

enlarge /ɪnˈlɑːdʒ/ *verb* [I,T] to make sth bigger or to become bigger □ *memperbesar; membesarkan*: *I'm going to have this photo enlarged.*

PHR V **enlarge on sth** (*formal*) to say or write more about sth □ *memperkembang*

enlargement /ɪnˈlɑːdʒmənt/ *noun* [U,C] making sth bigger or sth that has been made bigger □ *pembesaran; sst yg telah dibesarkan*: *an enlargement of a photo* **OPP** **reduction**

enlighten /ɪnˈlaɪtn/ *verb* [T] (*formal*) to give sb information so that they understand sth better □ *menerangkan; menjelaskan*

enlightened /ɪnˈlaɪtnd/ *adj* having an understanding of people's needs, a situation, etc. that is not based on old-fashioned ideas □ *berkesedaran ttg sst yg berbeza drpd pemikiran lama*

enlist /ɪnˈlɪst/ *verb* **1** [T] to get help, support, etc. □ *mendapatkan (bantuan, sokongan, dsb)*: *We need to enlist your support.* **2** [I,T] to join the army, navy or air force; to make sb a member of the army, etc. □ *masuk tentera*: *They enlisted as soon as war was declared.*

enmity /ˈenməti/ *noun* [U] the feeling of hatred towards an enemy □ *permusuhan*

enormity /ɪˈnɔːməti/ *noun* [sing] (*formal*) the very great size, effect, etc. of sth; the fact that sth is very serious □ *besarnya; seriusnya; dahsyatnya: the enormity of a task/decision/problem*

enormous /ɪˈnɔːməs/ *adj* very big or very great □ *sangat besar; sangat: an enormous building* ◆ *enormous pleasure* SYN **huge** ▶ **enormously** *adv*

enough¹ /ɪˈnʌf/ *determiner, pron* **1** as much or as many of sth as necessary □ *cukup: We've saved enough money to buy a house.* ◆ *Not everybody can have a book—there aren't enough.* ◆ *If enough of you are interested, we'll arrange a trip to the theatre.* **2** as much or as many as you want □ *sudah cukup: I've had enough of living in a city (= I don't want to live in a city any more).* ◆ *Don't give me any more books. I've got quite enough already.*

enough² /ɪˈnʌf/ *adv* [used after verbs, adjectives and adverbs] **1** to the necessary amount or degree □ *cukup: You don't practise enough.* ◆ *He's old enough to travel alone.* ◆ *Does she speak Italian well enough to get the job?* SYN **sufficiently** ⊃ picture at **too 2** quite, but not very □ *agak: She plays well enough, for a beginner.*
IDM **fair enough** ⊃ **fair¹**
funnily, strangely, etc. enough it is funny, etc. that ... □ *yg anehnya/pelikanya: Funnily enough, I thought exactly the same myself.*
sure enough ⊃ **sure**

enquire (also **inquire**) /ɪnˈkwaɪə(r)/ *verb* [I,T] (*formal*) **enquire (about sb/sth)** to ask for information about sth □ *bertanya; menanyakan: Could you enquire when the trains to Cork leave?* ◆ *We need to enquire about hotels in Vienna.*
PHR V **enquire after sb** to ask about sb's health □ *bertanya khabar ttg sso*
enquire into sth to study sth in order to find out all the facts □ *menyiasat: The journalist enquired into the politician's financial affairs.*

enquirer (also **inquirer**) /ɪnˈkwaɪərə(r)/ *noun* [C] (*formal*) a person who asks for information □ *penanya*

enquiring (also **inquiring**) /ɪnˈkwaɪərɪŋ/ *adj* **1** interested in learning new things □ *ingin tahu: We should encourage children to have enquiring minds.* **2** asking for information □ *dgn tanda tanya: He gave me an enquiring look.* ▶ **enquiringly** (also **inquiringly**) *adv*

enquiry (also **inquiry**) /ɪnˈkwaɪəri/ *noun* (*pl* **enquiries**) **1** [C] (*formal*) **an enquiry (about/concerning/into sb/sth)** a request for information about sth; a question that you ask about sth □ *pertanyaan: a telephone enquiry* ◆ *I'll make some enquiries into English language courses in Oxford.* **2** [U] the act of asking about sth □ *bertanya: After weeks of enquiry he finally found what he was looking for.* **3** [C] **an enquiry (into sth)** an official process to find out the cause of sth □ *siasatan: After the accident there was an enquiry into safety procedures.*

enrage /ɪnˈreɪdʒ/ *verb* [T] (*formal*) [usually passive] to make sb very angry □ *membuat sso sangat marah*

enrich /ɪnˈrɪtʃ/ *verb* [T] **1** to improve the quality, flavour, etc. of sth □ *memperkaya; diperkaya: These cornflakes are enriched with vitamins.* **2** to make sb/sth rich or richer □ *mengayakan* OPP **impoverish** ▶ **enrichment** *noun* [U]

enrol (*AmE* **enroll**) /ɪnˈrəʊl/ *verb* [I,T] (**enrolling; enrolled**) to become or to make sb a member of a club, school, etc. □ *mendaftar (masuk): I've enrolled on an Italian course.* ◆ *They enrolled 100 new students last year.* ▶ **enrolment** (*AmE* **enrollment**) *noun* [C,U]: *Enrolment for the course will take place next week.*

en route /ˌɒ̃ ˈruːt/ *adv* **en route (from ...) (to ...); en route (for ...)** on the way; while travelling from/to a place □ *dlm perjalanan: The car broke down when we were en route for Dover.*

ensemble /ɒnˈsɒmbl/ *noun* **1** [C, with sing or pl verb] a small group of musicians, dancers or actors who perform together □ *kumpulan; ensembel; sekumpulan kecil ahli muzik, penari atau pelakon: a brass/wind/string ensemble* ◆ *The ensemble is/are based in Lyon.* **2** [C, usually sing] a set of clothes that are worn together □ *pakaian sedondon*

ensue /ɪnˈsjuː/ *verb* [I] (*formal*) to happen after (and often as a result of) sth else □ *berikutan*

en suite /ˌɒ̃ ˈswiːt/ *adj, adv* (used about a bedroom and bathroom) forming one unit □ *sebahagian drpd sst set: The bedroom has a bathroom en suite.*

ensure (*AmE* **insure**) /ɪnˈʃʊə(r)/ (*BrE also*) -ˈʃɔː(r)/ *verb* [T] to make sure that sth happens or is definite □ *memastikan; pastikan: Please ensure that the door is locked before you leave.*

entail /ɪnˈteɪl/ *verb* [T] (*formal*) to make sth necessary; to involve sth □ *memerlukan; melibatkan: The job sounds interesting but I'm not sure what it entails.*

entangled /ɪnˈtæŋɡld/ *adj* caught in sth else □ *terperangkap; tersangkut: The bird was entangled in the net.* ◆ (*figurative*) *She didn't want to get emotionally entangled (= involved) with him.*

enter /ˈentə(r)/ *verb*
▶COME/GO IN **1** [I,T] (*formal*) to come or go into a place □ *masuk: Don't enter without knocking.* ◆ *They all stood up when he entered the room.* ⊃ Much more common expressions are **come into** and **go into.** ⊃ *nouns* **entrance, entry**
▶BECOME MEMBER **2** [T] to become a member of sth, especially a profession or an institution □ *masuk; memasuki: She entered the legal profession in 2008.* ◆ *to enter school/college/university* ⊃ *noun* **entrant**
▶BEGIN ACTIVITY **3** [T] to begin or become involved in an activity, a situation, etc. □ *memulakan; melibatkan diri: When she entered the relationship, she had no idea he was already married.* ◆ *We have just entered a new phase in international relations.*

enterprise → entrance

▶EXAM/COMPETITION 4 [I,T] **enter (for) sth; enter sb (in/for sth)** to put your name or sb's name on the list for an exam, race, competition, etc. □ *memasuki; menyertai*: *I entered a competition in the Sunday paper and I won £200!*
▶WRITE INFORMATION 5 [T] **enter sth (in/into/on/ onto sth)** to put names, numbers, details, etc. in a list, book, computer, etc. □ *memasukkan*: *Enter your password and press return.* ◆ *I've entered all the data onto the computer.*

PHR V enter into sth 1 to start to think or talk about sth □ *memikirkan/memperkatakan ttg sst*: *I don't want to enter into details now.* **2** to be part of sth; to be involved in sth □ *termasuk; ada kena-mengena*: *This is a business matter. Friendship doesn't enter into it.*
enter into sth (with sb) to begin sth □ *memulakan sst*: *The government has entered into negotiations with the unions.*

enterprise /ˈentəpraɪz/ *noun* **1** [C] a company or business □ *perusahaan*: *a new industrial enterprise* **2** [C] a large project, especially one that is difficult □ *usaha; projek*: *It's a very exciting new enterprise.* ◆ *a joint enterprise* **SYN** venture **3** [U] the ability to think of new projects or create new businesses and make them successful □ *daya usaha*: *We need men and women of enterprise and energy.*

enterprising /ˈentəpraɪzɪŋ/ *adj* having or showing the ability to think of new projects or new ways of doing things and make them successful □ *berdaya usaha; pandai berusaha*: *One enterprising farmer opened up his field as a car park and charged people to park there.*

entertain /ˌentəˈteɪn/ *verb* **1** [I,T] to welcome sb as a guest, especially to your home; to give sb food and drink □ *meraikan tamu; menjamu*: *They entertain a lot.* ◆ *Barbeques are a favourite way of entertaining friends.* **2** [T] **entertain (sb) (with sth)** to interest and amuse sb in order to please them □ *menghiburkan; mengekalkan minat*: *I find it very hard to keep my class entertained on a Friday afternoon.*

entertainer /ˌentəˈteɪnə(r)/ *noun* [C] a person whose job is to amuse people, for example by singing, dancing or telling jokes □ *penghibur*: *a street entertainer*

entertaining /ˌentəˈteɪnɪŋ/ *adj* interesting and amusing □ *(yg) menghiburkan*: *an entertaining speech* ◆ *She was always so funny and entertaining.*

entertainment /ˌentəˈteɪnmənt/ *noun* [U,C] film, music, etc. used to interest and amuse people □ *hiburan*: *There isn't much entertainment for young people in this town.* ◆ *There's a full programme of entertainments every evening.*

enthral (*AmE* **enthrall**) /ɪnˈθrɔːl/ *verb* [T] (**enthralling; enthralled**) [usually passive] to hold sb's interest and attention completely □ *mempesonakan; terpesona*: *He was enthralled by her story.* ▶ **enthralling** *adj*

enthusiasm /ɪnˈθjuːziæzəm/ *noun* [U] **enthusiasm (for/about sth/doing sth)** a strong feeling of excitement or interest in sth and a desire to become involved in it □ *keghairahan; semangat; minat*: *Jan showed great enthusiasm for the new project.*

enthusiast /ɪnˈθjuːziæst/ *noun* [C] a person who is very interested in an activity or subject □ *penggemar; peminat*

enthusiastic /ɪnˌθjuːziˈæstɪk/ *adj* **enthusiastic (about sth/doing sth)** full of excitement and interest in sth □ *penuh minat; berminat*: *The kids are very enthusiastic about sport.* ▶ **enthusiastically** /-kli/ *adv*: *The film was received enthusiastically by the critics.*

entice /ɪnˈtaɪs/ *verb* [T] **entice sb (into sth/doing sth)** to persuade sb to do sth or to go somewhere by offering them sth nice □ *menarik; menggoda*: *Advertisements try to entice people into buying more things than they need.* ▶ **enticement** *noun* [C,U]

enticing /ɪnˈtaɪsɪŋ/ *adj* attractive and interesting □ *(yg) menarik/menggoda*

entire /ɪnˈtaɪə(r)/ *adj* [only before a noun] whole or complete □ *seluruh*: *He managed to read the entire book in two days.* **SYN** whole ▶ **entirely** *adv*: *I entirely agree with Michael.* ▶ **entirety** /ɪnˈtaɪərəti/ *noun* [U] (*formal*): *We must consider the problem in its entirety* (= as a whole).

entitle /ɪnˈtaɪtl/ *verb* [T, usually passive] **entitle sb (to sth)** to give sb the right to have or do sth □ *berhak*: *I think I'm entitled to a day's holiday—I've worked hard enough.*

entitled /ɪnˈtaɪtld/ *adj* (used about books, plays, etc.) with the title □ *bertajuk*: *Gloria read a poem entitled 'Salt'.*

entitlement /ɪnˈtaɪtlmənt/ *noun* (*formal*) **1** [U] **entitlement (to sth)** the official right to have or do sth □ *hak*: *This may affect your entitlement to compensation.* **2** [C] something that you have an official right to; the amount that you have the right to receive □ *kelayakan*: *Your contributions will affect your pension entitlements.*

entity /ˈentəti/ *noun* [C] (*pl* **entities**) something that exists separately from sth else and has its own identity □ *entiti*: *The kindergarten and the school are in the same building but they're really separate entities.*

entrance /ˈentrəns/ *noun* **1** [C] **the entrance (to/of sth)** the door, gate or opening where you go into a place □ *pintu masuk*: *I'll meet you at the entrance to the theatre.* **OPP** exit **2** [C] **entrance (into/onto sth)** the act of coming or going into a place, especially in a way that attracts attention □ *masuk; ketibaan*: *He made a dramatic entrance onto the stage.* **SYN** entry **OPP** exit **3** [U] **entrance (to sth)** the right to enter a place □ *masuk*: *They were refused entrance to the club because they were wearing trainers.* ◆ *an entrance fee* **SYN** entry ⊃ look at **admission, admittance 4** [U] **entrance (into/to sth)** permission to join a club, society, university, etc. □ *kemasukan*: *You*

VOWELS iː see i any ɪ sit e ten æ hat ɑː father ɒ got ɔː saw ʊ put uː too u usual

entrant → enzyme 292

don't need to take an entrance exam to get into university. ⊃ look at **admission**

entrant /ˈentrənt/ noun [C] a person who enters a profession, competition, exam, university, etc. □ *orang yg masuk; peserta*

entreat /ɪnˈtriːt/ verb [T] (formal) to ask sb to do sth, often in an emotional way □ *merayu* **SYN** beg

entrepreneur /ˌɒntrəprəˈnɜː(r)/ noun [C] a person who makes money by starting or running businesses, especially when this involves taking financial risks □ *usahawan* ▶ **entrepreneurial** /ˌɒntrəprəˈnɜːriəl/ adj: *entrepreneurial skills*

entrust /ɪnˈtrʌst/ verb [T] (formal) **entrust A with B/entrust B to A** to make sb responsible for sth □ *mengamanahkan; mempertanggungjawabkan*: *I entrusted Rachel with the arrangements for the party.* ♦ *I entrusted the arrangements for the party to Rachel.*

entry /ˈentri/ noun (pl **entries**)
▶ GOING IN **1** [C] the act of coming or going into a place □ *masuk*: *The thieves forced an entry into the building.* **SYN** **entrance** **2** [U] **entry (to/into sth)** the right to enter a place □ *masuk*: *The immigrants were refused entry at the airport.* ♦ *The sign says 'No Entry'.* ♦ *an entry visa* **SYN** **entrance** ⊃ look at **admission, admittance**
▶ JOINING GROUP **3** [U] the right to take part in sth or become a member of a group □ *kemasukan; masuk*: *countries seeking entry into the European Union*
▶ IN COMPETITION **4** [C] a person or thing that is entered for a competition, etc. □ *peserta*: *There were fifty entries for the Eurovision song contest.* ♦ *The winning entry is number 45!*
▶ WRITTEN INFORMATION **5** [C] one item that is written down in a list, account book, dictionary, etc. □ *catatan; masukan*: *an entry in a diary* ♦ *You'll find 'ice-skate' after the entry for 'ice'.* **6** [U] an act of recording information in a computer, book, etc. □ *pemasukan*: *More keyboarding staff are required for data entry.*
▶ DOOR **7** [C] (*AmE*) a door, gate, passage, etc. where you enter a building, etc. □ *pintu/jalan masuk* **SYN** **entrance**

envelop /ɪnˈveləp/ verb [T] (formal) to cover or surround sb/sth completely (in sth) □ *menyelubungi; meliputi*: *The hills were enveloped in mist.*

envelope /ˈenvələʊp; ˈɒn-/ noun [C] the paper cover for a letter □ *sampul surat*: *Have you written his address on the envelope?* ⊃ look at **stamped addressed envelope** ⊃ picture at **letter**

enviable /ˈenviəbl/ adj something that is **enviable** is the sort of thing that is good and that other people want to have too □ *sangat baik*: *He is in the enviable position of having two job offers to choose from.* ⊃ *verb and noun* **envy**

envious /ˈenviəs/ adj **envious (of sb/sth)** wanting sth that sb else has □ *iri hati*: *She was envious of her sister's success.* **SYN** **jealous** ⊃ *verb and noun* **envy** ▶ **enviously** adv

environment /ɪnˈvaɪrənmənt/ noun **1** [C,U] the conditions in which you live, work, etc. □ *persekitaran*: *a pleasant working environment* **2 the environment** [sing] the natural world, for example the land, air and water, in which people, animals and plants live □ *alam sekitar*: *We need stronger laws to protect the environment.* ⊃ look at **surroundings** ▶ **environmental** /ɪnˌvaɪrənˈmentl/ adj: *environmental science* ▶ **environmentally** /-təli/ adv: *environmentally damaging*

TOPIC

The environment

The environment is being damaged by air and water **pollution**. Many **species** of wildlife are **endangered**, partly as a result of **deforestation**, and trees and rivers are damaged by **acid rain**. **Environmentalists** are also concerned about **global warming** and the hole in the **ozone layer**. We can **conserve** the Earth's **resources** (= coal, oil, etc.) by **recycling** more **waste**, and by using **renewable energy** such as **solar power** (= from the sun) and **hydroelectric power** (= from water).

---

environmentalist /ɪnˌvaɪrənˈmentəlɪst/ noun [C] a person who wants to protect the environment □ *pencinta alam sekitar*

en vironmentally 'friendly (also **en-vironment-'friendly**) adj (used about products) not harming the environment □ *mesra alam*: *environmentally-friendly packaging*

envisage /ɪnˈvɪzɪdʒ/ verb [T] (formal) to think of sth as being possible in the future; to imagine □ *membayangkan; menjangka*: *I don't envisage any problems with this.*

envoy /ˈenvɔɪ/ noun [C] a person who is sent by a government with a message to another country □ *utusan*

envy¹ /ˈenvi/ noun [U] **envy (of sb)**; **envy (at/of sth)** the feeling that you have when sb else has sth that you want □ *rasa iri hati*: *It was difficult for her to hide her envy of her friend's success.* ⊃ look at **enviable, envious**
IDM **be the envy of sb** to be the person or thing that causes sb to feel **envy** □ *menimbulkan rasa iri hati; menjadi idaman*: *The city's transport system is the envy of many of its European neighbours.*

envy² /ˈenvi/ verb [T] (**envying**; **envies**; pt, pp **envied**) **envy (sb) (sth)** to want sth that sb else has; to feel envy □ *berasa iri hati*: *I've always envied your good luck.* ♦ *I don't envy you that job* (= I wouldn't like to have it).

enzyme /ˈenzaɪm/ noun [C] (*technical*) a substance, produced by all living things, that helps a chemical change happen or happen more quickly, without being changed itself □ *enzim*

ʌ **cup**   ɜː **bird**   ə **ago**   eɪ **pay**   əʊ **go**   aɪ **my**   aʊ **now**   ɔɪ **boy**   ɪə **near**   eə **hair**   ʊə **pure**

ephemeral /ɪˈfemərəl/ adj (formal) lasting or used for only a short time □ *fana; efemeral; tdk tahan lama* **SYN** short-lived

epic /ˈepɪk/ adj very long and exciting □ *hebat; agung: an epic struggle/journey* ▶ **epic** noun [C]: *The film 'Glory' is an American Civil War epic.*

epidemic /ˌepɪˈdemɪk/ noun [C] a large number of cases of people or animals suffering from the same disease at the same time □ *wabak*

epilepsy /ˈepɪlepsi/ noun [U] a disease of the brain that can cause a person to become unconscious (sometimes with violent movements that they cannot control) □ *gila babi; epilepsi*

epileptic /ˌepɪˈleptɪk/ noun [C] a person who suffers from **epilepsy** □ *penghidap gila babi/ epilepsi* ▶ **epileptic** adj: *an epileptic fit*

epilogue /ˈepɪlɒɡ/ (AmE also) / noun [C] a short piece that is added at the end of a book, play, etc. and that comments on what has gone before □ *epilog* ➲ look at **prologue**

episode /ˈepɪsəʊd/ noun [C] **1** one separate event in sb's life, a novel, etc □ *peristiwa: That's an episode in my life I'd rather forget.* **2** one part of a TV or radio story that is shown or told in several parts □ *episod*

epitaph /ˈepɪtɑːf/ noun [C] words that are written or said about a dead person, especially words written on a stone where they are buried □ *epitaf*

epitome /ɪˈpɪtəmi/ noun [sing] **the epitome (of sth)** a perfect example of sth □ *contoh unggul: Her clothes are the epitome of good taste.*

epitomize (also **-ise**) /ɪˈpɪtəmaɪz/ verb [T] to be typical of sth □ *merupakan contoh unggul: This building epitomizes modern trends in architecture.*

epoch /ˈiːpɒk/ noun [C] a period of time in history (that is important because of special events, characteristics, etc.) □ *zaman; epok*

equal¹ /ˈiːkwəl/ adj **1 equal (to sb/sth)** the same in size, amount, value, number or level □ *sama: This animal is equal in weight to a small car.* ◆ *They are equal in weight.* ◆ *They are of equal weight.* ◆ *Divide it into two equal parts.* **OPP** unequal **2** having the same rights or being treated the same as other people □ *sama; setaraf: This company has an equal opportunities policy* (= does not consider age, race, sex, etc. when employing sb). **3** (formal) **equal to sth** having the strength, ability, etc. to do sth □ *dpt; berupaya: I'm afraid Bob just isn't equal to the job.*
IDM **be on equal terms (with sb)** to have the same advantages and disadvantages as sb else □ *setaraf (dgn sso)*

equal² /ˈiːkwəl/ noun [C] a person who has the same ability, rights, etc. as you do □ *orang yg setanding, sama taraf, dsb: to treat somebody as an equal*

equal³ /ˈiːkwəl/ verb [T] (**equalling; equalled**, (AmE) **equaling; equaled**) **1** (used about numbers, etc.) to be the same as sth □ *sama dgn: 44 plus 17 equals 61 is written: 44 + 17 = 61.* **2** to be as good as sb/sth □ *menyamai: He ran an excellent race, equalling the world record.*

equality /ɪˈkwɒləti/ noun [U] the situation in which everyone has the same rights and advantages □ *kesamaan; persamaan: racial equality* (= between people of different races) **OPP** inequality

equalize (also **-ise**) /ˈiːkwəlaɪz/ verb [I] (in sport) to reach the same number of points as your opponent □ *menyamakan kedudukan: Wales equalized in the 87th minute to make the score two all.* ▶ **equalizer** (also **-iser**) noun [C]: *Rooney scored the equalizer.*

equally /ˈiːkwəli/ adv **1** to the same degree or amount □ *sama-sama: They both worked equally hard.* **2** in equal parts □ *sama rata/banyak: His money was divided equally between his children.* **3** (formal) (used when you are comparing two ideas or commenting on what you have just said) at the same time; but/and also □ *pd masa yg sama; tetapi; namun: I do not think what he did was right. Equally, I can understand why he did it.*

equate /ɪˈkweɪt/ verb [T] **equate sth (with sth)** to consider one thing as being the same as sth else □ *menyamakan: Some parents equate education with exam success.*

equation /ɪˈkweɪʒn/ noun [C] (in mathematics) a statement that two quantities are equal □ *persamaan: 2x + 5 = 11 is an equation.*

the equator (also **the Equator**) /ɪˈkweɪtə(r)/ noun [sing] the imagined line around the earth at an equal distance from the North and South Poles □ *khatulistiwa: north/south of the Equator* ◆ *The island is on the equator.* ➲ picture at **earth** ▶ **equatorial** /ˌekwəˈtɔːriəl/ adj: *equatorial rainforests* ◆ *an equatorial climate*

equestrian /ɪˈkwestriən/ adj (formal) connected with horse riding □ *(berkenaan dgn) menunggang kuda*

equilibrium /ˌiːkwɪˈlɪbriəm; ˌek-/ noun [U, sing] **1** a state of balance, especially between opposite forces or influences □ *keseimbangan: The point at which the solid and the liquid are in equilibrium is called the freezing point.* ◆ *We have achieved economic equilibrium.* **2** a calm state of mind and a balance of emotions □ *keseimbangan jiwa*

equip /ɪˈkwɪp/ verb [T] (**equipping; equipped**) **equip sb/sth (with sth) 1** [usually passive] to supply sb/sth with what is needed for a particular purpose □ *melengkapi; dilengkapi: We shall equip all schools with new computers over the next year.* ◆ *The flat has a fully-equipped kitchen.* **2** to prepare sb for a particular task □ *melengkapkan; menyediakan: The course equips students with all the skills necessary to become a chef.*

equipment → escalator

equipment /ɪˈkwɪpmənt/ noun [U] the things that are needed to do a particular activity □ *alat; kelengkapan*: *office/sports/computer equipment*

GRAMMAR Equipment is uncountable. We say **a piece of equipment** if we are talking about one item: *a very useful piece of kitchen equipment*.

equivalent /ɪˈkwɪvələnt/ adj **equivalent (to sth)** equal in value, amount, meaning, importance, etc. □ *sama*: *The British House of Commons is roughly equivalent to the American House of Representatives.* ▶ **equivalent** noun [C]: *There is no English equivalent to the French 'bon appétit'.*

ER /ˌiː ˈɑː(r)/ abbr (AmE) **emergency room**

er /ɜː(r)/ exclam used in writing to show the sound that sb makes when they cannot decide what to say next □ *a...; em...*

era /ˈɪərə (AmE also) / noun [C] a period of time in history (that is special for some reason) □ *zaman*: *The composer's death marked the end of an era.*

eradicate /ɪˈrædɪkeɪt/ verb [T] (formal) to destroy or get rid of sth completely □ *membasmi*: *Some diseases, such as smallpox, have been completely eradicated.* ▶ **eradication** /ɪˌrædɪˈkeɪʃn/ noun [U]

erase /ɪˈreɪz/ verb [T] (formal) to remove sth completely (a pencil mark, a computer file, etc.) □ *memadamkan*: (figurative) *He tried to erase the memory of those terrible years from his mind.* ⊃ We usually say **rub out** a pencil mark. ▶ **eraser** (especially AmE) = **rubber** (2)

e-reader (also **e-book reader**) noun [C] a device on which you can read electronic books, newspapers, etc. □ *e-pembaca* ⊃ note at **e-book**

erect¹ /ɪˈrekt/ adj **1** standing straight up □ *tegak*: *He stood with his head erect.* **2** (used about the male sexual organ) hard and standing up because of sexual excitement □ *tegak*

erect² /ɪˈrekt/ verb [T] (formal) to build sth or to stand sth straight up □ *mendirikan; membina*: *Huge TV screens were erected above the stage.* ♦ *to erect a statue*

erection /ɪˈrekʃn/ noun **1** [C] if a man has an **erection**, his **penis** (= his sexual organ) becomes hard and stands up because he is sexually excited □ *ereksi*: *to get/have an erection* **2** [U] (formal) the act of building sth or standing sth straight up □ *pembinaan*

erode /ɪˈrəʊd/ verb [T, usually passive] (used about the sea, the weather, etc.) to destroy sth slowly □ *menghakis*: *The cliff has been eroded by the sea.* ▶ **erosion** /ɪˈrəʊʒn/ noun [U]: *the erosion of rocks by the sea*

erotic /ɪˈrɒtɪk/ adj causing sexual excitement □ *erotik; memberahikan*: *an erotic film/poem/dream*

[I] **intransitive**, a verb which has no object: *He laughed.*

err /ɜː(r)/ verb [I] (formal) to be or do wrong; to make mistakes □ *membuat kesilapan; tersilap*

IDM err on the side of sth to do more of sth than is necessary in order to avoid the opposite happening □ *terlalu/lebih (berhati-hati, belas, bertoleransi, dll)*: *It is better to err on the side of caution* (= it is better to be too careful rather than not careful enough).

errand /ˈerənd/ noun [C] (old-fashioned) a short journey to take or get sth for sb, for example to buy sth from a shop □ *(perbuatan) pergi utk mengambil atau membuat sst; (kerja) suruhan*

erratic /ɪˈrætɪk/ adj (used about sb's behaviour, or about the quality of sth) changing without reason; that you can never be sure of □ *tdk menentu*: *Marc Jones is a talented player but he's very erratic* (= sometimes he plays well, sometimes badly). ▶ **erratically** /-kli/ adv

erroneous /ɪˈrəʊniəs/ adj (formal) not correct; based on wrong information □ *salah*: *erroneous conclusions/assumptions* ▶ **erroneously** adv

error /ˈerə(r)/ noun **1** [C] (formal) a mistake □ *kesilapan*: *The telephone bill was too high because of a computer error.* ♦ *an error of judgement* ♦ *to make an error* ⊃ note at **mistake**

HELP Error or **mistake**? **Error** is more formal than **mistake**. There are some expressions such as *error of judgement, human error* where only **error** can be used.

2 [U] the state of being wrong □ *kesilapan; tersilap*: *The letter was sent to you in error.* ♦ *The accident was the result of human error.*
IDM trial and error ⊃ **trial**

'error message noun [C] a message that appears on a computer screen which tells you that you have done sth wrong or that the program cannot do what you want it to do □ *pesan ralat*

erupt /ɪˈrʌpt/ verb [I] **1** (used about a **volcano**) to explode and throw out fire, burning rocks, smoke, etc. □ *meletus; meletup* **2** (used about violence, shouting, etc.) to start suddenly □ *meletup*: *The demonstration erupted into violence.* **3** (used about a person) to suddenly become very angry □ *meletup; naik berang*: *George erupted when he heard the news.* ▶ **eruption** noun [C,U]: *a volcanic eruption*

escalate /ˈeskəleɪt/ verb [I,T] **1 escalate (sth) (into sth)** (to cause sth) to become stronger or more serious □ *menjadi bertambah buruk; meningkatkan*: *The demonstrations are escalating into violent protest in all the major cities.* ♦ *The terrorist attacks escalated tension in the capital.* **2** (to cause sth) to become greater or higher; to increase □ *meningkatkan*: *The cost of housing in the south has escalated in recent years.* ▶ **escalation** /ˌeskəˈleɪʃn/ noun [C,U]

escalator /ˈeskəleɪtə(r)/ noun [C] moving stairs that carry people between different floors of a shop, etc. □ *eskalator; tangga gerak*

[T] **transitive**, a verb which has an object: *He ate an apple.*

escapade /ˌeskəˈpeɪd/ noun [C] an exciting experience that may be dangerous □ *perbuatan/ pengalaman yg mendebarkan*

escape[1] /ɪˈskeɪp/ verb 1 [I] escape (from sb/sth) to manage to get away from a place where you do not want to be; to get free □ *melarikan diri*: *They managed to escape from the burning building.* ♦ *Two prisoners have escaped.* 2 [I,T] to manage to avoid sth dangerous or unpleasant □ *terselamat*: *The two men in the other car escaped unhurt in the accident.* ♦ *David Smith escaped injury when his car skidded off the road.* ♦ *to escape criticism/punishment* 3 [T] to be forgotten or not noticed by sb □ *terlupa; terlepas drpd*: *His name escapes me.* ♦ *to escape somebody's notice* 4 [I] (used about gases or liquids) to come or get out of a container, etc. □ *keluar*: *There's gas escaping somewhere.* ▶ **escaped** adj: *The police have caught the escaped prisoner.*

escape[2] /ɪˈskeɪp/ noun 1 [C,U] escape (from sth) the act of escaping □ *(perbuatan) melarikan/melepaskan diri*: *There have been twelve escapes from the prison this year.* ♦ *She had a narrow/lucky escape when a lorry crashed into her car.* ♦ *When the guard fell asleep they were able to make their escape.* ⊃ look at **fire escape** 2 [U, sing] something that helps you forget your normal life □ *sst yg membantu (sso) melupakan realiti*: *For him, listening to music is a means of escape.* ♦ *an escape from reality*

escapism /ɪˈskeɪpɪzəm/ noun [U] an activity, a form of entertainment, etc. that helps you avoid or forget unpleasant or boring things □ *eskapisme*: *For John, reading is a form of escapism.* ▶ **escapist** /-ɪst/ adj

escort[1] /ˈeskɔːt/ noun 1 [C,U, with sing or pl verb] one or more people or vehicles that go with and protect sb/sth, or that go with sb/sth as an honour □ *pengiring*: *an armed escort* ♦ *He arrived under police escort.* 2 [C] (formal) a person who takes sb to a social event □ *teman* 3 [C] a person, especially a woman, who is paid to go out socially with sb □ *teman sosial*: *an escort agency*

escort[2] /ɪˈskɔːt/ verb [T] to go with sb to protect them or to show them the way □ *mengiringi; diiringi*: *The President's car was escorted by several police cars.* ♦ *Philip escorted her to the door.*

Eskimo /ˈeskɪməʊ/ noun [C] (pl Eskimo or Eskimos) a member of a race of people from northern Canada, and parts of Alaska, Greenland and Siberia. □ *Eskimo*

HELP Be careful. Some of these people prefer to be called **Inuit**.

ESL /ˌiː es ˈel/ abbr English as a Second Language □ *ESL (Bahasa Inggeris sebagai Bahasa Kedua)*

ESOL /ˈiːsɒl/ abbr English for speakers of other languages; the teaching of English as a foreign language to people who are living in the UK or Ireland □ *Bahasa Inggeris utk penutur bahasa lain*

ESP abbr /ˌiː es ˈpiː/ English for Specific/Special Purposes; the teaching of English to people who need it for a special reason, such as scientific study, a technical job, etc. □ *ESP (Bahasa Inggeris utk Tujuan Khas)*

esp. abbr = **especially**(1)

especial /ɪˈspeʃl/ adj [only before a noun] (formal) not usual; special □ *luar biasa; istimewa*: *This will be of especial interest to you.*

especially /ɪˈspeʃəli/ adv 1 (abbr esp.) more than other things, people, situations, etc.; particularly □ *terutamanya*: *She loves animals, especially dogs.* ♦ *Teenage boys, especially, can be very competitive.* ♦ *He was very disappointed with his mark in the exam, especially as he had worked so hard for it.* **SYN particularly** 2 for a particular purpose or person □ *khusus; istimewa*: *I made this especially for you.* ⊃ A less formal word is **specially**. 3 very (much) □ *sangat*: *It's not an especially difficult exam.* ♦ *'Do you like jazz?' 'Not especially.'* **SYN particularly**

espionage /ˈespiənɑːʒ/ noun [U] the act of finding out secret information about another country or organization □ *pengintipan* ⊃ verb **spy**

Esq. abbr (especially BrE formal) Esquire; used when you are writing a man's name on an envelope □ *Esq (Tuan)*: *Edward Hales, Esq.*

HELP This is old-fashioned and many people now prefer to write: *Mr Edward Hales.*

essay /ˈeseɪ/ noun [C] an essay (on/about sth) a short piece of writing on one subject □ *esei; karangan*: *a 1 000-word essay on tourism* ♦ *write an essay* ♦ *hand in an essay*

essence /ˈesns/ noun 1 [U] the basic or most important quality of sth □ *inti pati; inti sari*: *The essence of the problem is that there is not enough money available.* ♦ *Although both parties agree in essence, some minor differences remain.* 2 [C,U] a substance (usually a liquid) that is taken from a plant or food and that has a strong smell or taste of that plant or food □ *pati; esen*: *coffee/vanilla essence*

essential /ɪˈsenʃl/ adj completely necessary; that you must have or do □ *penting; sangat perlu*: *essential services* ♦ *essential medical supplies* ♦ *Maths is essential for a career in computers.* ♦ *It is essential that all school-leavers should have a qualification.* ⊃ note at **important** ▶ **essential** noun [C, usually pl]: *food, and other essentials such as clothing and heating*

essentially /ɪˈsenʃəli/ adv when you consider the basic or most important part of sth □ *pd asasnya*: *The problem is essentially one of money.* **SYN basically**

establish /ɪˈstæblɪʃ/ verb [T] 1 to start or create an organization, a system, etc. □ *menubuhkan; mendirikan; menentukan*: *The school was established in 1875.* ♦ *Before we start on the*

establishment → euphemism 296

project, we should establish some rules. **2** to make sth exist (especially a formal relationship with sb/sth) □ *mewujudkan; menjalin*: *The government is trying to establish closer links between the two countries.* **3** establish sb/sth (as sth) to cause sb/sth to be accepted □ *memantapkan kedudukan*: *She has been trying to establish herself as a novelist for years.* **4** to discover or find proof of the facts of a situation □ *membuktikan; memastikan*: *The police have not been able to establish the cause of the crash.*

establishment /ɪˈstæblɪʃmənt/ *noun* **1** [C] (*formal*) an organization, a large institution or a hotel □ *organisasi, institusi atau hotel*: *an educational establishment* **2 the Establishment** [sing] the people in positions of power in a country, who usually do not support change □ *golongan yg berkuasa* **3** [U] the act of creating or starting a new organization, system, etc. □ *penubuhan; pembentukan*: *the establishment of new laws on taxes*

ꜝestate /ɪˈsteɪt/ *noun* [C] **1** a large area of land in the countryside that is owned by one person or family □ *estet; tanah*: *He owns a large estate in Scotland.* **2** (*BrE*) an area of land that has a lot of houses or factories of the same type on it □ *kawasan*: *an industrial estate* (= where there are a lot of factories) ◆ *a housing estate* **3** all the money and property that sb leaves when they die □ *harta pusaka*: *Her estate was left to her daughter.*

eˈstate agent (*AmE* realtor™, ˈreal estate agent) *noun* [C] a person whose job is to buy and sell houses and land for other people □ *ejen hartanah* ⊃ note at **house**

eˈstate car (*AmE* station wagon) *noun* [C] a car with a door at the back and a long area for luggage behind the back seat □ *station wagon*

esteem /ɪˈstiːm/ *noun* [U] (*formal*) great respect; a good opinion of sb □ *rasa hormat*

esthetic (*AmE*) = aesthetic

esthetics (*AmE*) = aesthetics

ꜝestimate¹ /ˈestɪmət/ *noun* [C] **1** an estimate (of sth) a guess or judgement about the size, cost, etc. of sth, before you have all the facts and figures □ *anggaran*: *Can you give me a rough estimate of how many people will be at the meeting?* ◆ *At a conservative estimate* (= the real figure will probably be higher), *the job will take six months to complete.* **2** an estimate (for sth/doing sth) a written statement from a person who is going to do a job for you, for example a builder, telling you how much it will probably cost □ *anggaran*: *They gave me an estimate for repairing the roof.* ⊃ look at **quotation**
IDM a ballpark figure/estimate ⊃ **ballpark**

ꜝestimate² /ˈestɪmeɪt/ *verb* [T] estimate sth (at sth); estimate that … to calculate the size, cost, etc. of sth approximately, before you have all the facts and figures □ *menganggar*: *The police estimated the crowd at 10 000.* ◆ *She estimated that the work would take three months.*

estimation /ˌestɪˈmeɪʃn/ *noun* [U] (*formal*) opinion or judgement □ *pandangan; pendapat; penilaian*: *Who is to blame, in your estimation?*

estranged /ɪˈstreɪndʒd/ *adj* **1** no longer living with your husband/wife □ *sudah berpisah*: *her estranged husband* **2** estranged (from sb) no longer friendly or in contact with sb who was close to you □ *renggang*: *He became estranged from his family following an argument.*

estuary /ˈestʃuəri/ *noun* [C] (*pl* estuaries) the wide part of a river where it joins the sea □ *muara* ⊃ picture on page P10

ꜝetc. *abbr* et cetera; and so on, and other things of a similar kind □ *dsb; dll*: *sandwiches, biscuits, cakes, etc.*

eternal /ɪˈtɜːnl/ *adj* **1** without beginning or end; existing or continuing for ever □ *abadi*: *Some people believe in eternal life* (= after death). **2** [only *before* a noun] happening too often; seeming to last for ever □ *tdk henti-henti/habis-habis*: *I'm tired of these eternal arguments!* ▶ eternally /-nəli/ *adv*: *I'll be eternally grateful if you could help.*

eternity /ɪˈtɜːnəti/ *noun* **1** [U] time that has no end; the state or time after death □ *keabadian; alam baqa* **2** an eternity [sing] (*informal*) a period of time that never seems to end □ *lama sangat; menahun*: *It seemed like an eternity before the ambulance arrived.*

ethical /ˈeθɪkl/ *adj* **1** connected with beliefs about what is right or wrong □ *(berkenaan dgn) etika*: *That is an ethical problem.* **2** morally correct □ *mengikut etika; berakhlak*: *Although she didn't break the law, her behaviour was certainly not ethical.* ▶ ethically /-kli/ *adv*

ethics /ˈeθɪks/ *noun* **1** [pl] beliefs about what is morally correct or acceptable □ *etika; tatasusila*: *The medical profession has its own code of ethics.* **2** [U] the study of what is right and wrong in human behaviour □ *(ilmu) etika*

ethnic /ˈeθnɪk/ *adj* connected with or typical of a particular race or people that share a cultural tradition □ *etnik*: *ethnic minorities* ◆ *ethnic food/music/clothes*

ˌethnic ˈcleansing *noun* [U] the policy of forcing people of a certain race or religion to leave an area or country □ *pembersihan etnik*

etiquette /ˈetɪket/ *noun* [U] the rules of polite and correct behaviour □ *etiket; kesantunan*: *professional etiquette* ⊃ look at **netiquette**

etymology /ˌetɪˈmɒlədʒi/ *noun* (*pl* etymologies) **1** [U] the study of the origins and history of words and their meanings □ *etimologi* **2** [C] an explanation of the origin and history of a particular word □ *etimologi; asal usul kata*

EU /ˌiː ˈjuː/ *abbr* = European Union

euphemism /ˈjuːfəmɪzəm/ *noun* [C,U] using a polite word or expression instead of a more direct one when you are talking about sth that is unpleasant or embarrassing; a word used in this way □ *eufemisme; kiasan halus*: 'Pass away' is a euphemism for 'die'. ▶ **euphemistic** /ˌjuːfəˈmɪstɪk/ *adj*

euphoria /juːˈfɔːriə/ *noun* [U] (*formal*) a feeling of great happiness □ *kegembiraan yg amat sangat* ▶ **euphoric** /juːˈfɒrɪk (*AmE* also) / *adj*: My euphoric mood could not last.

euro /ˈjʊərəʊ/ *noun* [C] (*symbol* €) (*pl* **euros** or **euro**) (since 1999) a unit of money used in some countries of the European Union □ *euro*: The price is given in dollars or euros. ⊃ look at **EMU**

European¹ /ˌjʊərəˈpiːən/ *adj* of or from Europe □ (*berkenaan dgn/dari*) *Eropah*: European languages

European² /ˌjʊərəˈpiːən/ *noun* [C] a person from a European country □ *orang Eropah*

the ˌEuropean ˈUnion *noun* [sing] (*abbr* **EU**) an economic and political association of certain European countries □ *Kesatuan Eropah*

euthanasia /ˌjuːθəˈneɪziə/ *noun* [U] the practice (illegal in most countries) of killing without pain sb who wants to die because they are suffering from a disease that cannot be cured □ *eutanasia*

evacuate /ɪˈvækjueɪt/ *verb* [I,T] to move people from a dangerous place to somewhere safer; to leave a place because it is dangerous □ *mengungsikan*: Thousands of people were evacuated from the war zone. ♦ The village had to be evacuated when the river burst its banks. ♦ Locals were told to evacuate. ▶ **evacuation** /ɪˌvækjuˈeɪʃn/ *noun* [C,U]

evade /ɪˈveɪd/ *verb* [T] **1** to manage to escape from or to avoid meeting sb/sth □ *mengelak; mengelakkan diri*: They managed to evade capture and escaped to France. **2** to avoid dealing with or doing sth □ *mengelak drpd*: to evade responsibility ♦ I asked her directly, but she evaded the question. ⊃ *noun* **evasion**

evaluate /ɪˈvæljueɪt/ *verb* [T] (*formal*) to study the facts and then form an opinion about sth □ *menilai*: We evaluated the situation very carefully before we made our decision. ▶ **evaluation** /ɪˌvæljuˈeɪʃn/ *noun* [C,U]

evangelical /ˌiːvænˈdʒelɪkl/ *adj* of or belonging to a Christian group that emphasizes the authority of the Bible and the importance of people being saved through faith □ *berkenaan dgn agama Kristian; evangelika; evangelis*

evaporate /ɪˈvæpəreɪt/ *verb* **1** [I,T] (used about a liquid) to change into steam or gas and disappear □ *menyejat*: The water evaporated in the sunshine. ⊃ look at **condense 2** [I] to disappear completely □ *(menjadi) lenyap/hilang*: All her confidence evaporated when she saw the exam paper. ▶ **evaporation** /ɪˌvæpəˈreɪʃn/ *noun* [U]

evasion /ɪˈveɪʒn/ *noun* [C,U] **1** the act of avoiding sth that you should do □ *pengelakan*: He has been sentenced to two years' imprisonment for tax evasion. ♦ an evasion of responsibility **2** a statement that avoids dealing with a question or subject in a direct way □ *pengelakan; berdalih*: The President's reply was full of evasions. ⊃ *verb* **evade**

evasive /ɪˈveɪsɪv/ *adj* trying to avoid sth; not direct □ *bersifat mengelak*: Ann gave an evasive answer.

eve /iːv/ *noun* [C] the day or evening before a religious festival, important event, etc. □ *hari atau malam sebelum sst perayaan atau peristiwa penting*: New Year's Eve ♦ He injured himself on the eve of the final.

even¹ /ˈiːvn/ *adj* **1** flat, level or smooth □ *rata; datar*: The game must be played on an even surface. **OPP** **uneven 2** not changing; regular □ *tetap; tenang*: He's very even-tempered—in fact I've never seen him angry. **3** (used about a competition, etc.) equal, with one side being as good as the other □ *sama seimbang*: The contest was very even until the last few minutes of the game. **OPP** **uneven 4** (used about numbers) that can be divided by two □ *genap*: 2, 4, 6, 8, 10, etc. are even numbers. **OPP** **odd**

IDM **be/get even (with sb)** (*informal*) to hurt or harm sb who has hurt or harmed you □ *membalas dendam*

break even to make neither a loss nor a profit □ *pulang modal*

even² /ˈiːvn/ *adv* **1** used for emphasizing sth that is surprising □ *pun; langsung*: It isn't very warm here even in summer. ♦ He didn't even open the letter. **2** **even more, less, bigger, nicer, etc.** used when you are comparing things, to make the comparison stronger □ *lebih; bahkan*: You know even less about it than I do. ♦ It is even more difficult than I expected. ♦ We are even busier than yesterday.

IDM **even if** used for saying that what follows 'if' makes no difference □ *walaupun; sekalipun*: I wouldn't ride a horse, even if you paid me.

even so (used for introducing a new idea, fact, etc. that is surprising) in spite of that □ *namun demikian; walau bagaimanapun*: There are a lot of spelling mistakes; even so it's quite a good essay. **SYN** **nevertheless**

even though although □ *sungguhpun; walaupun*: I like her very much even though she can be very annoying. ⊃ note at **although**

evening /ˈiːvnɪŋ/ *noun* [C,U] the part of the day between the afternoon and the time that you go to bed □ *lewat petang; awal malam*: What are you doing this evening? ♦ We were out yesterday evening. ♦ I went to the cinema on Saturday evening. ♦ Tom usually goes swimming on Wednesday evenings. ♦ Most people watch TV in the evening. ♦ an evening class (= a course of lessons for adults that takes place in the evening) ⊃ note at **morning**

IDM **good evening** (*formal*) used when you see sb for the first time in the evening □ *selamat petang/malam*

HELP Often we just say **Evening**: 'Good evening, Mrs Wilson.' 'Evening, Mr Mills.'

evenly /ˈiːvnli/ *adv* in a smooth, regular or equal way □ *seimbang; sama rata*: *The match was very evenly balanced.* ◆ *Spread the cake mixture evenly in the tin.*

event /ɪˈvent/ *noun* [C] **1** something that happens, especially sth important or unusual □ *peristiwa*: *a historic event* ◆ *The events of the past few days have made things very difficult for the Government.* **2** a planned public or social occasion □ *acara; upacara*: *a fund-raising event* **3** one of the races, competitions, etc. in a sports programme □ *acara*: *The next event is the 800 metres.*

IDM **at all events/in any event** whatever happens □ *bagaimanapun*: *I hope to see you soon, but in any event I'll phone you on Sunday.*

in the event of sth (*formal*) if sth happens □ *sekiranya/jika berlaku*: *In the event of fire, leave the building as quickly as possible.*

eventful /ɪˈventfl/ *adj* full of important, dangerous or exciting things happening □ *penuh dgn peristiwa/kejadian*

eventual /ɪˈventʃuəl/ *adj* [only before a noun] happening at the end of a period of time or a process □ *berikutannya; akhirnya*: *It is impossible to say what the eventual cost will be.*

eventually /ɪˈventʃuəli/ *adv* in the end; finally □ *akhirnya*: *He eventually managed to persuade his parents to let him buy a motorbike.* **SYN** **finally**

ever /ˈevə(r)/ *adv* **1** (used in questions and negative sentences, and in sentences with *if*) at any time □ *pernah; jarang-jarang sekali; pd bila-bila masa*: *Do you ever wish you were famous?* ◆ *Nobody ever comes to see me.* ◆ *She* **hardly ever** (= almost never) *goes out.* ◆ *If you ever visit England, you must come and stay with us.* ◆ *Have you ever been to Spain?* **2** when you are comparing things □ *pernah*: *Today is hotter than ever.* ◆ *This is the best meal I have ever had.* **3** used with a question that begins with 'when', 'where', 'who', 'how', etc. to show that you are surprised or shocked □ *pula*: *How ever did he get back so quickly?* ◆ *What ever were you thinking about when you wrote this?* ⊃ look at **whatever, whenever, however**

IDM **(as) bad, good, etc. as ever** (as) bad, good, etc. as usual or as always □ *(sama) teruk, baik, dll spt biasa*: *In spite of his problems, Andrew is as cheerful as ever.*

ever after (used especially at the end of stories) from that moment on for always □ *selama-lamanya*: *The prince married the princess and they lived happily ever after.*

ever since ... all the time from ... until now □ *sejak*: *She has had a car ever since she was at university.*

ever so/ever such (a) (*BrE informal*) very □ *sangat; betul*: *He's ever so kind.* ◆ *He's ever such a kind man.*

for ever ⊃ **forever**

ever- /ˈevə(r)/ [in compounds] always; continuously □ *sentiasa*: *the ever-growing problem of pollution*

evergreen /ˈevəɡriːn/ *noun* [C], *adj* (a tree or bush) with green leaves all through the year □ *malar hijau* ⊃ look at **deciduous**

everlasting /ˌevəˈlɑːstɪŋ/ *adj* (*formal*) continuing for ever; never changing □ *abadi*: *everlasting life/love*

every /ˈevri/ *determiner* **1** [used with singular nouns] all of the people or things in a group of three or more □ *setiap; tiap-tiap*: *She knows every student in the school.* ◆ *There are 200 students in the school, and she knows every one of them.* ◆ *I've read every book in this house.* ◆ *You were out every time I phoned.* ⊃ note at **everybody 2** all that is possible □ *semua; segala*: *You have every chance of success.* ◆ *She had every reason to be angry.* **3** used for saying how often sth happens □ *setiap*: *We see each other every day.* ◆ *Take the medicine every four hours* (= at 8, 12, 4 o'clock, etc.). ◆ *I work every other day* (= on Monday, Wednesday, Friday, etc.). ◆ *One in every three marriages ends in divorce.*

everybody /ˈevribɒdi/ (*AmE* also) / (also **everyone** /ˈevriwʌn/) *pron* [with sing verb] every person; all people □ *semua/setiap orang*: *Is everybody here?* ◆ *The police questioned everyone who was at the party.* ◆ *I'm sure everybody else* (= all the other people) *will agree with me.* ⊃ note at **somebody**

HELP **Everyone** is only used about people and is not followed by 'of'. **Every one** means 'each individual person or thing' and is often followed by 'of': *Every one of his records has been successful.*

everyday /ˈevrideɪ/ *adj* [only before a noun] normal or usual □ *sehari-hari; harian; biasa*: *The Internet is now part of everyday life.*

everyone = **everybody**

everyplace (*AmE*) = **everywhere**

everything /ˈevriθɪŋ/ *pron* [with sing verb] **1** each thing; all things □ *semuanya; segala-galanya*: *Sam lost everything in the fire.* ◆ *Everything is very expensive in this shop.* ◆ *We can leave everything else* (= all the other things) *until tomorrow.* **2** the most important thing □ *segala-galanya*: *Money isn't everything.*

everywhere /ˈevriweə(r)/ (*AmE* also **everyplace** /ˈevripleɪs/) *adv* in or to every place □ *merata-rata; di mana-mana*: *I've looked everywhere.*

evict /ɪˈvɪkt/ *verb* [T] to force sb (officially) to leave the house or land which they are renting □ *mengusir*: *They were evicted for not paying the rent.* ▶ **eviction** *noun* [C,U]

evidence /ˈevɪdəns/ *noun* [U] **evidence (of/for sth); evidence that ...** the facts, signs, etc. that make you believe that sth is true □ *bukti; tanda(-tanda); keterangan*: *There was no evidence of a struggle in the room.* ◆ *You have abso-*

lutely no evidence for what you're saying! ◆ There was not enough evidence to prove him guilty. ◆ Her statement to the police was **used in evidence** against him. ◆ The witnesses to the accident will be asked to **give evidence** in court. ⊃ note at **court** ⊃ look at **proof**

> **GRAMMAR** Evidence is uncountable, so you cannot say 'an evidence', you must say 'a piece of evidence': *One **piece of evidence** is not enough to prove somebody guilty.*

IDM **(to be) in evidence** that you can see; present in a place □ *kelihatan*: *When we arrived, there was no ambulance in evidence.*

evident /ˈevɪdənt/ adj clear (to the eye or mind); obvious □ *nyata; jelas*: *It was evident that the damage was very serious.*

evidently /ˈevɪdəntli/ adv 1 clearly; in a way that can be easily seen or understood □ *nyata/jelas sekali*: *She was evidently extremely shocked at the news.* 2 according to what people say □ *nampaknya*: *Evidently he has decided to leave.*

evil¹ /ˈiːvl/ adj morally bad; causing trouble or harming people □ *jahat; buruk; durjana*: *In the play, Richard is portrayed as an evil king.* **OPP** good

evil² /ˈiːvl/ noun [U,C] a force that causes bad or harmful things to happen □ *kejahatan; kecelakaan; keburukan*: *The play is about the good and evil in all of us.* ◆ *Drugs and alcohol are two of the evils of modern society.* **OPP** good
IDM **the lesser of two evils** ⊃ **lesser**

evocative /ɪˈvɒkətɪv/ adj **evocative (of sth)** making you think of or remember a strong image or feeling, in a pleasant way □ *membangkitkan atau menimbulkan sst*: *evocative smells/sounds/music* ◆ *Her new book is wonderfully evocative of village life.*

evoke /ɪˈvəʊk/ verb [T] (formal) to produce a memory, feeling, etc. in sb in a pleasant way □ *membangkitkan*: *For me, that music always evokes hot summer evenings.* ◆ *Her novel evoked a lot of interest.*

evolution /ˌiːvəˈluːʃn; ˌev-/ noun [U] **1** the gradual development of plants, animals, etc. over many years as they adapt to changes in their environment □ *evolusi*: *Darwin's theory of evolution* **2** the process of change and development of sth that happens gradually □ *evolusi; perkembangan*: *Political evolution is a slow process.*

evolve /ɪˈvɒlv/ verb **1** [I,T] (formal) to develop or to make sth develop gradually, from a simple to a more advanced form □ *berkembang*: *His style of painting has evolved gradually over the past 20 years.* **2** [I] **evolve (from sth)** (used about plants, animals, etc.) to develop over many thousands of years from simple forms to more advanced ones □ *berevolusi*

ewe /juː/ noun [C] a female sheep □ *biri-biri betina* ⊃ note at **sheep** ⊃ picture at **goat**

ex- /eks/ [prefix] [in nouns] former □ *bekas*: *ex-wife* ◆ *ex-president*

---

evident → examination

exacerbate /ɪɡˈzæsəbeɪt/ verb [T] (formal) to make sth worse, especially a disease or problem □ *memburukkan lagi; membuat sst menjadi lebih buruk*: *The symptoms may be exacerbated by stress.* **SYN** aggravate ▸ **exacerbation** /ɪɡˌzæsəˈbeɪʃn/ noun [C,U]

exact¹ /ɪɡˈzækt/ adj **1** (completely) correct; accurate □ *tepat; sebenar; betul-betul*: *He's in his mid-fifties. Well, 56 to be exact.* ◆ *I can't tell you the exact number of people who are coming.* ◆ *She's the exact opposite of her sister.* **2** able to work in a way that is completely accurate □ *tepat; persis; jitu*: *You need to be very exact when you calculate the costs.* ▸ **exactness** noun [U]

exact² /ɪɡˈzækt/ verb [T] (formal) **exact sth (from sb)** to demand and get sth from sb □ *menuntut; menagih*

exacting /ɪɡˈzæktɪŋ/ adj needing a lot of care and attention; difficult □ *cerewet; rumit; sukar; berat*: *exacting work*

exactly /ɪɡˈzæktli/ adv **1** (used to emphasize that sth is correct in every way) just □ *tepat; betul-betul*: *You've arrived at exactly the right moment.* ◆ *I found exactly what I wanted.* **2** used to ask for, or give, completely correct information □ *tepat; betul; sebenarnya*: *He took exactly one hour to finish.* **3** (spoken) (used for agreeing with a statement) yes; you are right □ *betul*: *'I don't think she's old enough to travel on her own.' 'Exactly.'* **SYN** for all meanings **precisely**
IDM **not exactly** (spoken) **1** (used when you are saying the opposite of what you really mean) not really; not at all □ *bukan sebenarnya*: *He's not exactly the most careful driver I know.* **2** used as an answer to say that sth is almost true □ *tdk juga*: *'So you think I'm wrong?' 'No, not exactly, but …'*

exaggerate /ɪɡˈzædʒəreɪt/ verb [I,T] to make sth seem larger, better, worse, etc. than it really is □ *membesar-besarkan; menokok tambah; melebih-lebih*: *Don't exaggerate. I was only two minutes late, not twenty.* ◆ *The problems have been greatly exaggerated.* ▸ **exaggerated** adj: *exaggerated claims* ▸ **exaggeration** /ɪɡˌzædʒəˈreɪʃn/ noun [C,U]: *It's rather an exaggeration to say that all the students are lazy.*

exam /ɪɡˈzæm/ (also formal **examination**) noun [C] a written, spoken or practical test of what you know or can do □ *peperiksaan*: *an English exam* ◆ *the exam results* ◆ *to do/take/sit an exam* ◆ *to pass/fail an exam* ◆ *to revise for an exam* ⊃ note at **pass, study**

> **HELP** Exam or test? A **test** is usually shorter and less important than an exam.

ⓘ There are many notes in this dictionary to help you to prepare for exams. A list at the back of the dictionary shows you where to find them.

examination /ɪɡˌzæmɪˈneɪʃn/ noun **1** [C] (formal) = **exam** **2** [C,U] the act of looking at sb/sth carefully, especially to see if there is anything

---

[C] **countable**, a noun with a plural form: *one book, two books* [U] **uncountable**, a noun with no plural form: *some sugar*

examine → exception

wrong or to find the cause of a problem □ *pemeriksaan*: *a medical examination* ♦ *On close examination, it was found that the passport was false.*

examine /ɪgˈzæmɪn/ *verb* [T] **1** to consider or study an idea, a subject, etc. very carefully □ *meneliti; memeriksa; menyelidik*: *These theories will be examined in more detail later on in the lecture.* **2 examine sb/sth (for sth)** to look at sb/sth carefully in order to find out sth □ *memeriksa*: *The doctor examined me, but she couldn't find anything wrong* ♦ *The detective examined the room for clues.* **3** (*formal*) **examine sb (in/on sth)** to test what sb knows or can do □ *menguji*: *You will be examined on everything that has been taught in the course.*

examiner /ɪgˈzæmɪnə(r)/ *noun* [C] a person who tests sb in an exam □ *pemeriksa*

example /ɪgˈzɑːmpl/ *noun* [C] **1 an example (of sth)** something such as an object, a fact or a situation which shows, explains or supports what you say □ *contoh; misalan*: *I don't quite understand you. Can you give me an example of what you mean?* ♦ *This is a typical example of a Victorian house.* **2 an example (to sb)** a person or thing or a type of behaviour that is good and should be copied □ *contoh; teladan*: *Joe's bravery should be an example to us all.*
IDM **follow sb's example/lead** ⊃ **follow**
for example [The abbreviation for this is **e.g.**] used for giving a fact, situation, etc. which explains or supports what you are talking about □ *misalnya*: *In many countries, for example Spain, family life is much more important than here.* ♦ *popular pets, e.g. cats and dogs*

> **WRITING TIP**
>
> **Giving examples**
> When you are writing, giving examples helps to support your argument. You can use any of these phrases: *There is a similar word in many languages,* **for example** *in French and Italian.* ♦ *The report is incomplete; it does not include sales in France,* **for instance.** ♦ *It is possible to combine Computer Science with other subjects* **such as** *Physics.*

ℹ For more help with writing, look at **Wordpower Writing Tutor** at the back of this dictionary.
set a(n) (good/bad) example (to sb) to behave in a way that should/should not be copied □ *menjadi teladan/contoh (yg baik/buruk) (bagi sso)*: *Parents should always take care when crossing roads in order to set a good example to their children.*

exasperate /ɪgˈzæspəreɪt/ *verb* [T] to make sb angry; to annoy sb very much □ *berasa marah/geram; menggeramkan*: *This lack of progress exasperates me.* ▶ **exasperated** *adj*: *She was becoming exasperated with all their questions.* ▶ **exasperating** *adj*: *an exasperating problem* ▶ **exasperation** /ɪgˌzæspəˈreɪʃn/ *noun*

[U]: *He finally threw the book across the room in exasperation.*

excavate /ˈekskəveɪt/ *verb* [I,T] to dig in the ground to look for old objects or buildings that have been buried for a long time; to find sth by digging in this way □ *menggali*: *A Roman villa has been excavated in a valley near the village.* ▶ **excavation** /ˌekskəˈveɪʃn/ *noun* [C,U]: *Excavations on the site have revealed Saxon objects.*

exceed /ɪkˈsiːd/ *verb* [T] **1** to be more than a particular number or amount □ *melebihi*: *The weight should not exceed 20 kilos.* **2** to do more than the law, a rule, an order, etc. allows you to do □ *melampaui; melebihi*: *He was stopped by the police for exceeding the speed limit* (= driving faster than is allowed). ⊃ look at **excess, excessive**

exceedingly /ɪkˈsiːdɪŋli/ *adv* (*formal*) very □ *sangat; amat*: *an exceedingly difficult problem*

excel /ɪkˈsel/ *verb* (**excelling; excelled**) (*formal*) **1** [I] **excel (in/at sth/doing sth)** to be very good at doing sth □ *sangat baik/pandai*: *Regina excels at sports.* **2** [T] (*BrE*) **excel yourself** to do sth even better than you usually do □ *lebih baik drpd biasa*: *Rick's cooking is always good but this time he really excelled himself.*

excellence /ˈeksələns/ *noun* [U] the quality of being very good □ *kecemerlangan*: *The head teacher said that she wanted the school to be a centre of academic excellence.*

excellent /ˈeksələnt/ *adj* very good; of high quality □ *cemerlang*: *He speaks excellent French.* ⊃ note at **good** ▶ **excellently** *adv*

except¹ /ɪkˈsept/ *prep* **except (for) sb/sth; except that ...** not including sb/sth; apart from the fact that □ *melainkan; kecuali*: *The museum is open every day except Mondays.* ♦ *I can answer all of the questions except for the last one.* ♦ *It was a good hotel except that it was rather noisy.*

except² /ɪkˈsept/ *verb* [T, often passive] (*formal*) **except sb/sth (from sth)** to leave sb/sth out; to not include sb/sth □ *mengecualikan; dikecualikan*: *Nobody is excepted from helping with the housework.* ▶ **excepting** *prep*: *I swim every day excepting Sundays.*

exception /ɪkˈsepʃn/ *noun* [C] a person or thing that is not included in a general statement □ *kekecualian; kecuali*: *Most of his songs are awful but this one is an exception.* ♦ *Everybody was poor as a student and I was no exception.*
IDM **make an exception (of sb/sth)** to treat sb/sth differently □ *membuat pengecualian*: *We don't usually allow children under 14 but we'll make an exception in your case.*
with the exception of except for; apart from □ *kecuali; melainkan*: *He has won every major tennis championship with the exception of Wimbledon.*
without exception in every case; including everyone/everything □ *tanpa kekecualian*: *Everybody without exception must take the test.*

[I] **intransitive**, a verb which has no object: *He laughed.*   [T] **transitive**, a verb which has an object: *He ate an apple.*

exceptional /ɪkˈsepʃənl/ *adj* **1** very unusual □ *luar biasa*: *You will only be allowed to leave early in exceptional circumstances.* **2** unusually good □ *istimewa*: *We have had a really exceptional summer.* **SYN** **outstanding** ▶ **exceptionally** /-ʃənəli/ *adv*: *The past year has been exceptionally difficult for us.*

excerpt /ˈeksɜːpt/ *noun* [C] a short piece taken from a book, film, piece of music, etc. □ *petikan*

excess¹ /ɪkˈses/ *noun* [sing] **an excess (of sth)** more of sth than is necessary or usual; too much of sth □ *berlebihan; lebih*: *An excess of fat in your diet can lead to heart disease.*
IDM **in excess of** more than □ *lebih drpd*: *Her debts are in excess of £1 000.* ⊃ *verb* **exceed**

excess² /ˈekses/ *adj* [only before a noun] more than is usual or allowed; extra □ *(yg) berlebihan*: *Cut any excess fat off the meat.* ⊃ *verb* **exceed**

excess baggage *noun* [U] bags, cases, etc. taken on to a plane that weigh more than the amount each passenger is allowed to carry without paying extra □ *bagasi berlebihan*: *Her luggage was over 23 kilos, and she had to pay excess baggage charges.*

excessive /ɪkˈsesɪv/ *adj* too much; too great or extreme □ *berlebih-lebihan; terlampau*: *He was driving at excessive speed when he crashed.* ▶ **excessively** *adv*

exchange¹ /ɪksˈtʃeɪndʒ/ *noun* **1** [C,U] giving or receiving sth in return for sth else □ *bertukar-tukar; (sebagai) tukaran*: *a useful exchange of information* ◆ *We can offer free accommodation in exchange for some help in the house.* **2** [U] the relation in value between kinds of money used in different countries □ *pertukaran (wang)*: *What's the exchange rate/rate of exchange for dollars?* ⊃ look at **foreign exchange, stock exchange 3** [C] a visit by a group of students or teachers to another country and a return visit by a similar group from that country □ *pertukaran*: *She went on an exchange to Germany when she was sixteen.* **4** [C] an angry conversation or argument □ *pertengkaran*: *She had a **heated exchange** with her neighbours about the noise the night before.* **5** [C] = **telephone exchange**

exchange² /ɪksˈtʃeɪndʒ/ *verb* [T] **exchange sth for sth; exchange sth (with sb)** to give or receive sth in return for sth else □ *menukar; bertukar-tukar*: *I would like to exchange this skirt for a bigger size.* ◆ *Claire and Molly exchanged phone numbers with the boys.* ◆ *They exchanged glances* (= they looked at each other). ⊃ note at **shopping**

excise /ˈeksaɪz/ *noun* [U] a government tax on certain goods that are produced or sold inside a country, for example cigarettes, alcohol, etc. □ *eksais* ⊃ look at **customs**

excitable /ɪkˈsaɪtəbl/ *adj* easily excited □ *mudah teruja/terangsang*

excite /ɪkˈsaɪt/ *verb* [T] **1** to make sb feel happy and enthusiastic or nervous □ *menimbulkan rasa (seronok, ghairah, gembira, dll); merangsangkan; menguja*: *Don't excite the baby too much or we'll never get him off to sleep.* **2** to make sb react in a particular way □ *membangkitkan (minat, dll)*: *The programme excited great interest.*

excited /ɪkˈsaɪtɪd/ *adj* **excited (about/at/by sth)** feeling or showing happiness and enthusiasm; not calm □ *berasa seronok, gembira, teruja, dsb*: *Are you getting excited about your holiday?* ◆ *We're all very excited at the thought of moving house.* ▶ **excitedly** *adv*

excitement /ɪkˈsaɪtmənt/ *noun* [U] the state of being excited, especially because sth interesting is happening or will happen □ *keseronokan; kegembiraan; keadaan teruja/terangsang*: *There was **great excitement** as the winner's name was announced.* ◆ *The match was **full of excitement** until the very last minute.*

exciting /ɪkˈsaɪtɪŋ/ *adj* causing strong feelings of pleasure and interest □ *(yg) menyeronokkan/menguja/merangsangkan*: *That's very exciting news.* ◆ *Berlin is one of the most exciting cities in Europe.*

exclaim /ɪkˈskleɪm/ *verb* [I,T] to say sth suddenly and loudly because you are surprised, angry, etc. □ *berteriak; berseru*: *'I just don't believe it!' he exclaimed.*

exclamation /ˌekskləˈmeɪʃn/ *noun* [C] a short sound, word or phrase that you say suddenly because of a strong emotion, pain, etc. □ *teriakan; seruan*: *'Ouch!' is an exclamation.* **SYN** **interjection**

excla'mation mark (*AmE* **excla'mation point**) *noun* [C] a mark (!) that is written after an exclamation □ *tanda seruan*

exclude /ɪkˈskluːd/ *verb* [T] [not used in the continuous tenses] **1** to leave out; not include □ *tdk termasuk*: *The price excludes all extras such as drinks or excursions.* **OPP** **include 2 exclude sb/sth (from sth)** to prevent sb/sth from entering a place or taking part in sth □ *tdk membenarkan*: *Women are excluded from the temple.* ◆ *Jake was excluded from the game for cheating.* **OPP** **include 3** to decide that sth is not possible □ *menidakkan; menolak kemungkinan*: *The police had **excluded the possibility** that the child had run away.*

excluding /ɪkˈskluːdɪŋ/ *prep* leaving out; without □ *tdk termasuk*: *Lunch costs £10 per person excluding drinks.* **OPP** **including**

exclusion /ɪkˈskluːʒn/ *noun* [U] keeping or leaving sb/sth out □ *(perbuatan) tdk memasukkan atau membenarkan (sso/sst)*

exclusive¹ /ɪkˈskluːsɪv/ *adj* **1** [only before a noun] only to be used by or given to one person, group, etc.; not to be shared □ *khas; khusus*: *This car is for the Director's exclusive use.* ◆ *Tonight we are showing an exclusive interview with the new leader of the Labour Party* (= on only one TV or radio station). **2** expensive and not welcoming people who are thought to be of a lower social class □ *eksklusif*: *an exclusive restaurant* ◆ *a flat in an exclusive part of the city* **3 exclusive of sb/sth** not including sb/sth; without □ *tdk termasuk*: *Lunch costs £10 per person exclusive of drinks.*

exclusive² /ɪkˈskluːsɪv/ *noun* [C] a newspaper story that is given to and published by only one newspaper □ *berita, cerita, dsb eksklusif*

exclusively /ɪkˈskluːsɪvli/ *adv* only; not involving anyone/anything else □ *khas; khusus*: *The swimming pool is reserved exclusively for members of the club.*

excrement /ˈekskrɪmənt/ *noun* [U] (*formal*) the solid waste material that you get rid of from your body when you go to the toilet □ *tahi; najis* **SYN faeces**

excrete /ɪkˈskriːt/ *verb* [T] (*formal*) to get rid of solid waste material from the body □ *buang air besar; berak*

excruciating /ɪkˈskruːʃieɪtɪŋ/ *adj* extremely painful □ *sangat sakit; mengazabkan*

excursion /ɪkˈskɜːʃn/ *noun* [C] a short journey or trip that a group of people make for pleasure □ *lawatan; darmawisata*: *to go on an excursion to the seaside* ⊃ note at **travel**

excusable /ɪkˈskjuːzəbl/ *adj* that you can forgive □ *boleh dimaafkan*: *an excusable mistake* **OPP inexcusable**

excuse¹ /ɪkˈskjuːs/ *noun* [C] **an excuse (for sth/doing sth)** a reason (that may or may not be true) that you give in order to explain your behaviour □ *alasan*: *There's no excuse for rudeness.* ◆ *He always finds an excuse for not helping with the housework.* ◆ *to make an excuse*

excuse² /ɪkˈskjuːz/ *verb* [T] **1 excuse sb/sth (for sth/for doing sth)** to forgive sb for sth they have done wrong that is not very serious □ *memaafkan*: *Please excuse the interruption but I need to talk to you.* **2** to explain sb's bad behaviour and make it seem less bad □ *memberikan alasan; boleh memaafkan*: *Nothing can excuse such behaviour.* **3 excuse sb (from sth)** to free sb from a duty, responsibility, etc. □ *mengecualikan; meminta diri*: *She excused herself* (= asked if she could leave) *and left the meeting early.*

> **HELP** The expression **excuse me** is used when you interrupt somebody or when you want to start talking to somebody that you don't know: *Excuse me, can you tell me the way to the station?* In American English, and occasionally in British English, **excuse me** is used when you apologize for something: *Did I tread on your toe? Excuse me.*

execute /ˈeksɪkjuːt/ *verb* [T] **1** [usually passive] **execute sb (for sth)** to kill sb as an official punishment □ *dihukum mati*: *He was executed for murder.* **2** (*formal*) to perform a task, etc. or to put a plan into action □ *menjalankan;*

melaksanakan ▶ **execution** /ˌeksɪˈkjuːʃn/ *noun* [C,U]

executioner /ˌeksɪˈkjuːʃənə(r)/ *noun* [C] a person whose job is to **execute** criminals □ *pertanda; algojo; pelebaya*

executive¹ /ɪɡˈzekjətɪv/ *noun* **1** [C] a person who has an important position as a manager of a business or an organization □ *eksekutif*: *She's a senior executive in a computer company.* **2** [C, with sing or pl verb] the group of people who are in charge of an organization or a company □ *eksekutif; pegawai; pelaksana*: *The executive has/have yet to reach a decision.* **3 the executive** [sing, with sing or pl verb] the part of a government responsible for putting new laws into effect □ *kuasa eksekutif* ⊃ look at **judiciary, legislature**

executive² /ɪɡˈzekjətɪv/ *adj* [only before a noun] **1** (used in connection with people in business, government, etc.) concerned with managing, making plans, decisions, etc. □ *eksekutif*: *an executive director of the company* ◆ *executive decisions/jobs/duties* **2** (used about goods, buildings, etc.) designed to be used by important business people □ *eksekutif*: *an executive briefcase*

exemplary /ɪɡˈzempləri/ *adj* very good; that can be an example to other people □ *sangat baik; patut diteladani*: *exemplary behaviour*

exemplify /ɪɡˈzemplɪfaɪ/ *verb* [T] (**exemplifying; exemplifies;** *pt, pp* **exemplified**) to be a typical example of sth □ *merupakan contoh*

exempt¹ /ɪɡˈzempt/ *adj* [not before a noun] **exempt (from sth)** free from having to do sth or pay for sth □ *dikecualikan*: *Children under 16 are exempt from dental charges.*

exempt² /ɪɡˈzempt/ *verb* [T] (*formal*) **exempt sb/sth (from sth)** to say officially that sb does not have to do sth or pay for sth □ *mendapat pengecualian; dikecualikan* ▶ **exemption** *noun* [C,U]

exercise¹ /ˈeksəsaɪz/ *noun*
▶ACTIVITY **1** [U] physical or mental activity that keeps you healthy and strong □ *senaman; riadah; latihan*: *The doctor advised Sebastian to take regular exercise.* ◆ *Swimming is a good form of exercise.* **2** [C, often plural] a movement or activity that you do in order to stay healthy or to become skilled at sth □ *latihan*: *I do keep-fit exercises every morning.* ◆ *breathing/stretching/ relaxation exercises*
▶STUDY **3** [C] a piece of work that is intended to help you learn or practise sth □ *latihan*: *an exercise on phrasal verbs*
▶USE OF POWER, ETC. **4** [U] (*formal*) **exercise of sth** the use of sth, for example a power, right, etc. □ *penggunaan*: *the exercise of patience/judgement/ discretion* ◆ *the exercise of power by the government*
▶FOR PARTICULAR RESULT **5** [C] **an exercise in sth** an activity or a series of actions that have a particular aim □ *usaha*: *The project is an exercise in getting the best results at a low cost.*

exercise

She's doing sit-ups. She's stretching.

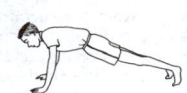

He's doing press-ups (AmE push-ups). She's touching her toes.

▶ FOR SOLDIERS **6** [C, usually pl] a series of activities by soldiers to practise fighting □ *latihan: military exercises*

exercise[2] /'eksəsaɪz/ *verb* **1** [T] to make use of sth, for example a power, right, etc. □ *menggunakan: You should exercise your right to vote.* **2** [I] to do some form of physical activity in order to stay fit and healthy □ *bersenam: It is important to exercise regularly.*

'exercise book (*AmE* notebook) *noun* [C] a small book for students to write their work in □ *buku latihan*

exert /ɪg'zɜːt/ *verb* [T] **1** to make use of sth, for example influence, strength, etc., to affect sb/sth □ *menggunakan; mengenakan: Parents exert a powerful influence on their children's opinions.* **2 exert yourself** to make a big effort □ *berusaha: You won't make any progress if you don't exert yourself a bit more.*

exertion /ɪg'zɜːʃn/ *noun* [U,C] using your body in a way that takes a lot of effort; something that you do that makes you tired □ *penggunaan tenaga; kerja berat: At his age physical exertion was dangerous.* ◆ *I'm tired after the exertions of the past few days.*

exhale /eks'heɪl/ *verb* [I,T] (*formal*) to breathe out so that air leaves your lungs □ *menghembuskan nafas* **OPP** inhale ▶ **exhalation** /ˌekshə'leɪʃn/ *noun* [C,U]

exhaust[1] /ɪg'zɔːst/ *noun* **1** [U] the waste gas that comes out of a vehicle, an engine or a machine □ *asap ekzos: car exhaust fumes/emissions* **2** [C] (also **ex'haust pipe**, (*AmE*) **tailpipe**) a pipe (particularly at the back of a car) through which waste gas escapes from an engine or machine □ *ekzos* ⟳ picture on **page P7**

exhaust[2] /ɪg'zɔːst/ *verb* [T] **1** to make sb very tired □ *amat meletihkan: The long journey to work every morning exhausted him.* **2** to use sth up completely; to finish sth □ *menghabiskan; habis: All the supplies of food have been exhausted.* **3** to say everything you can about a subject □ *membicarakan habis-habis; menuntaskan: Well, I think we've exhausted that topic.*

exhausted /ɪg'zɔːstɪd/ *adj* very tired □ *sangat letih; keletihan*

exhausting /ɪg'zɔːstɪŋ/ *adj* making sb very tired □ *(yg) meletihkan: Teaching young children is exhausting work.*

exhaustion /ɪg'zɔːstʃən/ *noun* [U] the state of being very tired □ *keletihan; kelesuan*

exhaustive /ɪg'zɔːstɪv/ *adj* including everything possible □ *lengkap; tuntas; menyeluruh: This list is certainly not intended to be exhaustive.*

ex'haust pipe = exhaust[1] (2)

exhibit[1] /ɪg'zɪbɪt/ *verb* [T] **1** to show sth in a public place for people to enjoy or to give them information □ *mempamerkan: His paintings have been exhibited in the local art gallery.* **2** (*formal*) to show clearly that you have a particular quality, feeling. etc. □ *menunjukkan: The refugees are exhibiting signs of exhaustion and stress.*

exhibit[2] /ɪg'zɪbɪt/ *noun* [C] an object that is shown in a museum, etc. or as a piece of evidence in a court of law □ *barang pameran; barang kes*

exhibition /ˌeksɪ'bɪʃn/ *noun* **1** [C] a collection of objects, for example works of art, that are shown to the public □ *pameran: an exhibition of photographs at the Mall Gallery* **2** [C] an occasion when a particular skill is shown to the public □ *pertunjukan: We saw an exhibition of Scottish dancing last night.* **3** [sing] (*formal*) the act of showing a quality, feeling, etc. □ *(perbuatan) memperlihatkan: The game was a superb exhibition of football at its best.*

exhibitor /ɪg'zɪbɪtə(r)/ *noun* [C] a person or a company that shows their work or products to the public □ *pempamer*

exhilarate /ɪg'zɪləreɪt/ *verb* [T, usually passive] to make sb feel very excited and happy □ *berasa girang: We felt exhilarated by our walk along the beach.* ▶ **exhilarating** *adj* ▶ **exhilaration** /ɪɡˌzɪlə'reɪʃn/ *noun* [U]

exile /'eksaɪl/ *noun* **1** [U] the state of being forced to live outside your own country (especially for political reasons) □ *buangan: The leader was deposed and driven into exile in 2009.* ◆ *They lived in exile in London for many years.* **2** [C] a person who is forced to live outside their own country (especially for political reasons) □ *orang buangan; pelarian* ⟳ look at **refugee** ▶ **exile** *verb* [T, usually passive]: *After the revolution the king was exiled.*

exist /ɪg'zɪst/ *verb* [I] **1** [not used in the continuous tenses] to be real; to be found in the real world; to live □ *wujud; hidup: Dreams only exist in our imagination.* ◆ *Fish cannot exist out of water.* **2 exist (on sth)** to manage to live □ *dpt hidup: I don't know how she exists on the wage she earns.*

existence /ɪɡˈzɪstəns/ noun 1 [U] the state of existing □ *kewujudan; wujud(nya); ada(nya)*: This is the oldest human skeleton *in existence*. ♦ How did the universe *come into existence*? 2 [sing] a way of living, especially when it is difficult □ *kehidupan; hidup*: The family endured a miserable existence living in one small room together.

existing /ɪɡˈzɪstɪŋ/ adj [only before a noun] that is already there or being used; present □ *yg ada*: Under the existing law you are not allowed to work in this country.

exit¹ /ˈeksɪt; ˈeɡzɪt/ noun [C] 1 a door or way out of a public building or vehicle □ *pintu; jalan keluar*: The emergency exit is at the back of the bus. OPP **entrance** 2 the act of leaving sth □ *(perbuatan) pergi/keluar*: If I see her coming I'll make a quick exit. ♦ an exit visa (= one that allows you to leave a country) 3 a place where traffic can leave a road or a **motorway** (= a wide road for fast traffic) to join another road □ *jalan keluar*: At the roundabout take the third exit.

exit² /ˈeksɪt; ˈeɡzɪt/ verb [I,T] (formal) 1 to leave a place □ *keluar*: He exited through the back door. 2 to finish using a computer program □ *keluar*: I exited the database and switched off the computer.

exodus /ˈeksədəs/ noun [sing] ~ (from …) (to …) (formal) a situation in which many people leave a place at the same time □ *perhijrahan besar-besaran*: the mass exodus from Paris to the country in the summer

exonerate /ɪɡˈzɒnəreɪt/ verb [T, often passive] (formal) to say officially that sb was not responsible for sth bad that happened □ *melepaskan; dilepaskan; membebaskan; dibebaskan*

exorbitant /ɪɡˈzɔːbɪtənt/ adj (formal) (used about the cost of sth) much more expensive than it should be □ *terlalu tinggi/mahal*

exotic /ɪɡˈzɒtɪk/ adj unusual or interesting because it comes from a different country or culture □ *eksotik*: exotic plants/animals/fruits

expand /ɪkˈspænd/ verb [I,T] to become or to make sth bigger □ *mengembang; mengembangkan*: Metals expand when they are heated. ♦ We hope to expand our business this year. OPP **contract**

PHR V **expand on sth** to give more details of a story, plan, idea, etc. □ *menjelaskan*

expanse /ɪkˈspæns/ noun [C] a large open area (of land, sea, sky, etc.) □ *(kawasan yg) luas terbentang*: I lay on my back and stared up at the vast expanse of blue sky.

expansion /ɪkˈspænʃn/ noun [U] the act of becoming bigger or of making sth become bigger □ *pengembangan*: The rapid expansion of the university has caused a lot of problems.

expansive /ɪkˈspænsɪv/ adj (formal) (used about a person) talking a lot in an interesting way; friendly □ *ramah*

expatriate /ˌeksˈpætriət/ (also *informal* **expat** /ˌeksˈpæt/) noun [C] a person who lives outside their own country □ *ekspatriat*: American expatriates in London

expect /ɪkˈspekt/ verb [T] 1 to think or believe that sb/sth will come or that sth will happen □ *menjangka; mengharapkan; mengandung*: She was expecting a letter from the bank this morning but it didn't come. ♦ I expect that it will rain this afternoon. ♦ I know the food's not so good, but what did you expect from such a cheap restaurant? (= it's not surprising) ♦ She's expecting a baby in the spring (= she's pregnant). ➲ note at **wait¹** 2 **expect sth (from sb); expect sb to do sth** to feel confident that you will get sth from sb or that they will do what you want □ *mengharapkan; dikehendaki*: He expects a high standard of work from everyone. ♦ Factory workers are often expected to work at nights. 3 [not used in the continuous tenses] (BrE) to think that sth is true or correct; to suppose □ *agaknya; rasanya*: 'Whose is this suitcase?' 'Oh it's Angela's, I expect.' ♦ 'Will you be able to help me later?' 'I expect so.'

expectancy /ɪkˈspektənsi/ noun [U] the state of expecting sth, especially sth good, to happen; hope □ *harapan*: a look/feeling of expectancy ➲ look at **life expectancy**

expectant /ɪkˈspektənt/ adj 1 hoping for sth good and exciting □ *penuh harapan*: an expectant audience ♦ expectant faces 2 having a baby soon □ *mengandung*: an expectant mother/father ▶ **expectantly** adv

expectation /ˌekspekˈteɪʃn/ noun (formal) 1 [C,U] **expectation (of sth)** the belief that sth will happen or come □ *jangkaan; harapan*: The dog was sitting under the table *in expectation* of food. 2 [C, usually pl] hope for the future □ *harapan*: They had great expectations for their son, but he didn't really live up to them.

IDM **against/contrary to (all) expectation(s)** very different to what was expected □ *bertentang drpd apa yg dijangka/diharapkan*: Contrary to all expectations, Val won first prize.

not come up to (sb's) expectations to not be as good as expected □ *tdk sebaik yg diharapkan*

expected /ɪkˈspektɪd/ adj that you think will happen □ *dijangka*: Double the expected number of people came to the meeting. OPP **unexpected**

expedient /ɪkˈspiːdiənt/ adj (formal) (used about an action) convenient or helpful for a purpose, but possibly not completely honest or moral □ *elok; wajar; bermanfaat*: The government decided that it was expedient not to increase taxes until after the election. ▶ **expediency** /ɪkˈspiːdiənsi/ noun [U]

expedition /ˌekspəˈdɪʃn/ noun [C] 1 a long journey for a special purpose □ *ekspedisi; pengembaraan*: a scientific expedition to Antarctica 2 a short journey that you make for pleasure □ *berjalan-jalan utk pergi (memancing, dll)*: a fishing expedition

expel /ɪkˈspel/ verb [T] (**expelling; expelled**) 1 to force sb to leave a country, school, club, etc. □ *mengusir; diusir; dibuang; diperintah keluar*: *The government has expelled all foreign journalists.* ◆ *The boy was expelled from school for smoking.* ◆ *The boy was expelled from school for fighting.* **2** (*technical*) to send sth out by force □ *mengeluarkan; menghembuskan*: *to expel air from the lungs* ⊃ noun **expulsion**

expend /ɪkˈspend/ *verb* [T] (*formal*) **expend sth (on sth)** to spend or use money, time, care, etc. in doing sth □ *menggunakan; menghabiskan; membelanjakan*: *I have expended a lot of time and energy on that project.*

expendable /ɪkˈspendəbl/ *adj* (*formal*) not considered important enough to be saved □ *boleh dikorbankan/dimusnahkan; tdk penting*: *In a war human life is expendable.*

expenditure /ɪkˈspendɪtʃə(r)/ *noun* [U, sing] (*formal*) the act of spending money; the amount of money that is spent □ *perbelanjaan*: *Government expenditure on education has been cut.*

expense /ɪkˈspens/ *noun* **1** [C,U] the cost of sth in time or money □ *belanja; kos*: *Running a car is a great expense.* ◆ *The movie was filmed in Tahiti at great expense.* **2 expenses** [pl] money that is spent for a particular purpose □ *perbelanjaan*: *You can claim back your travelling expenses.* **IDM at sb's expense 1** with sb paying; at sb's cost □ *atas perbelanjaan sso*: *My trip is at the company's expense.* **2** against sb, so that they look silly □ *mempersendakan sso*: *They were always making jokes at Paul's expense.*
at the expense of sth harming or damaging sth □ *dgn mengorbankan*: *He was a successful businessman, but it was at the expense of his family life.*

expensive /ɪkˈspensɪv/ *adj* costing a lot of money □ *mahal*: *Houses are very expensive in this area.* **OPP inexpensive, cheap** ▸ **expensively** *adv*

experience¹ /ɪkˈspɪəriəns/ *noun* **1** [U] the things that you have done in your life; the knowledge or skill that you get from seeing or doing sth □ *pengalaman*: *We all learn by experience.* ◆ *She has five years' teaching experience.* ◆ *I know from experience what will happen.* **2** [C] something that has happened to you (often sth unusual or exciting) □ *pengalaman*: *She wrote a book about her experiences in Africa.*

experience² /ɪkˈspɪəriəns/ *verb* [T] to have sth happen to you; to feel □ *mengalami*: *It was the first time I'd ever experienced failure.* ◆ *to experience pleasure/pain/difficulty*

experienced /ɪkˈspɪəriənst/ *adj* having the knowledge or skill that is necessary for sth □ *berpengalaman*: *He's an experienced diver.* **OPP inexperienced**

experiment¹ /ɪkˈsperɪmənt/ *noun* [C,U] a scientific test that is done in order to get proof of sth or to get new knowledge □ *uji kaji; eksperimen*: *to carry out/perform/conduct/do an experiment* ◆ *We need to prove this theory by experiment.*

expend → explanation

experiment² /ɪkˈsperɪmənt/ *verb* [I] **experiment (on/with sth)** to do tests to see if sth works or to try to improve it □ *membuat uji kaji/eksperimen; mencuba*: *Is it really necessary to experiment on animals?* ◆ *We're experimenting with a new timetable this month.*

experimental /ɪkˌsperɪˈmentl/ *adj* connected with experiments or trying new ideas □ *percubaan; eksperimental*: *We're still at the experimental stage with the new product.* ◆ *experimental drama* ▸ **experimentally** /-təli/ *adv*

expert /ˈekspɜːt/ *noun* [C] **an expert (at/in/on sth)** a person who has a lot of special knowledge or skill □ *pakar; orang yg mahir*: *a computer expert* ◆ *Let me try—I'm an expert at parking cars in small spaces.* ◆ *She's a leading expert in the field of genetics.* ▸ **expert** *adj*: *He's an expert cook.* ◆ *I think we should get expert advice on the problem.* ▸ **expertly** *adv*

expertise /ˌekspɜːˈtiːz/ *noun* [U] a high level of special knowledge or skill □ *kepakaran; kemahiran*: *Mr Dixon has many years of expertise in employment matters.*

expire /ɪkˈspaɪə(r)/ *verb* [I] (used about an official document, agreement, etc.) to come to the end of the time when you can use it or in which it has effect □ *tamat tempohnya; mati*: *My passport's expired. I'll have to renew it.* **SYN run out**

expiry /ɪkˈspaɪəri/ *noun* [U] the end of a period when you can use sth □ *tamatnya tempoh; (tarikh) luput*: *What's the expiry date on your credit card?*

explain /ɪkˈspleɪn/ *verb* [I,T] **explain (sth) (to sb)** **1** to make sth clear or easy to understand □ *menjelaskan; menerangkan*: *She explained how I should fill in the form.* ◆ *I don't understand. Can you explain it to me?*

HELP Note that you have to say 'Explain **it** to me' NOT 'Explain me it'.

2 to give a reason for sth □ *menjelaskan/menerangkan sebabnya*: *'This work isn't very good.' 'I wasn't feeling very well.' 'Oh, that explains it then.'* ◆ *The manager explained to the customers why the goods were late.*
IDM explain yourself 1 to give reasons for your behaviour, especially when it has upset sb □ *beritahu mengapa* **2** to say what you mean in a clear way □ *terangkan; jelaskan*
PHR V explain sth away to give reasons why sth is not your fault or is not important □ *menjelaskan sebab; memberi alasan*

explanation /ˌekspləˈneɪʃn/ *noun* **1** [C,U] **an explanation (for sth)** a statement, fact or situation that gives a reason for sth □ *keterangan; penjelasan*: *He could not give an explanation for his behaviour.* **2** [C] a statement or a piece of writing that makes sth easier to understand □ *penjelasan; penerangan; huraian*: *For a full* *explanation of how the machine works, turn to page 5.*

explanatory /ɪkˈsplænətri/ *adj* giving an explanation □ *(merupakan) penjelasan*: *There are some explanatory notes at the back of the book.* ♦ *Those instructions are self-explanatory (= they don't need explaining).*

explicable /ɪkˈsplɪkəbl; ˈeksplɪkəbl/ *adj* that can be explained □ *dpt dijelaskan*: *Barry's strange behaviour is only explicable in terms of the stress he is under.* OPP **inexplicable**

explicit /ɪkˈsplɪsɪt/ *adj* 1 clear, making sth easy to understand □ *jelas; eksplisit*: *I gave you explicit instructions not to touch anything.* ♦ *She was quite explicit about her feelings on the subject.* ⊃ look at **implicit** 2 not hiding anything □ *terang-terangan; eksplisit*: *Some of the sex scenes in that play were very explicit.* ▶ **explicitly** *adv*: *He was explicitly forbidden to stay out later than midnight.*

explode /ɪkˈspləʊd/ *verb* [I,T] to burst or to make sth burst with a loud noise □ *meletup; meledak*: *The bomb exploded without warning.* ♦ *The army exploded the bomb at a safe distance from the houses.* ♦ *(figurative) My father exploded (= became very angry) when I told him how much the car would cost to repair.* ⊃ *noun* **explosion**

exploit¹ /ɪkˈsplɔɪt/ *verb* [T] 1 to use sth or to treat sb unfairly for your own advantage □ *memperguna; mengeksploitasi; mengambil kesempatan*: *Some employers exploit foreign workers, making them work long hours for low pay.* 2 to develop sth or make the best use of sth □ *mengeksploitasi; menggunakan; mengusahakan*: *This region has been exploited for oil for fifty years.* ♦ *Solar energy is a source of power that needs to be exploited more fully.* ▶ **exploitation** /ˌeksplɔɪˈteɪʃn/ *noun* [U]: *They're making you work 80 hours a week? That's exploitation!*

exploit² /ˈeksplɔɪt/ *noun* [C] something exciting or interesting that sb has done □ *perbuatan handal atau menarik*

exploration /ˌekspləˈreɪʃn/ *noun* [C,U] the act of travelling around a place in order to learn about it □ *penjelajahan*: *space exploration*

exploratory /ɪkˈsplɒrətri/ *adj* done in order to find sth out □ *(bersifat) meninjau/menyiasat*: *The doctors are doing some exploratory tests to try and find out what's wrong.*

explore /ɪkˈsplɔː(r)/ *verb* [I,T] to travel around a place, etc. in order to learn about it □ *menjelajah; keluar melihat-lihat; meneliti*: *I've never been to Paris before—I'm going out to explore.* ♦ *They went on an expedition to explore the River Amazon.* ♦ *(figurative) We need to explore (= look carefully at) all the possibilities before we decide.*

explorer /ɪkˈsplɔːrə(r)/ *noun* [C] a person who travels round a place in order to learn about it □ *penjelajah*

[I] **intransitive**, a verb which has no object: *He laughed.*

explosion /ɪkˈspləʊʒn/ *noun* [C] 1 the sudden loud noise when sth like a bomb bursts violently □ *letupan; ledakan*: *Two people were killed in the explosion.* 2 a sudden and often surprising increase in sth □ *letusan; ledakan*: *the population explosion* ⊃ *verb* **explode**

explosive¹ /ɪkˈspləʊsɪv/ *adj* 1 capable of exploding and therefore dangerous □ *mudah meletup*: *Hydrogen is highly explosive.* 2 causing strong feelings or having dangerous effects □ *mudah meletus; sensitif*: *The situation is explosive. We must do all we can to calm people down.*

explosive² /ɪkˈspləʊsɪv/ *noun* [C,U] a substance that is used for causing explosions □ *bahan letupan*

exponent /ɪkˈspəʊnənt/ *noun* [C] 1 a person who supports an idea, a belief, etc. and persuades others that it is good □ *pendukung; pelopor; penganjur*: *She was a leading exponent of free trade during her political career.* 2 a person who is able to perform a particular activity with skill □ *orang yg ahli/mahir*: *the most famous exponent of the art of mime*

export¹ /ɪkˈspɔːt/ *verb* [I,T] 1 to send goods, etc. to another country, usually for sale □ *mengeksport*: *India exports tea and cotton.* 2 to move information from one computer program to another □ *mengeksport* OPP for both meanings **import**

export² /ˈekspɔːt/ *noun* 1 [U] sending goods to another country for sale □ *eksport*: *Most of our goods are produced for export.* ♦ *the export trade* 2 [C, usually pl] a product or service that is sent to another country for sale □ *(barang) eksport*: *What are Brazil's main exports?* OPP for both meanings **import** ▶ **exporter** *noun* [C]: *the world's largest exporter of cars* OPP **importer**

expose /ɪkˈspəʊz/ *verb* [T] 1 expose sth (to sb); expose sb/sth (as sth) to show sth that is usually hidden; to tell sth that has been kept secret □ *mendedahkan; memperlihatkan*: *She didn't want to expose her true feelings to her family.* ♦ *The politician was exposed as a liar on TV.* 2 expose sb/sth to sth to put sb/sth or yourself in a situation that could be difficult or dangerous □ *mendedahkan*: *to be exposed to radiation/ danger* 3 expose sb to sth to give sb the chance to experience sth □ *mendedahkan; berpeluang mengalami*: *I like jazz because I was exposed to it as a child.*

exposed /ɪkˈspəʊzd/ *adj* (used about a place) not protected from the wind and bad weather □ *terdedah*

exposure /ɪkˈspəʊʒə(r)/ *noun* 1 [U] being allowed or forced to experience sth □ *pendedahan*: *TV can give children exposure to other cultures from an early age.* ♦ *Exposure to radiation is almost always harmful.* 2 [U,C] the act of making sth public; the thing that is made public □ *pendedahan*: *The new movie has been given a lot of exposure in the media.* ♦ *The politician resigned because of the exposures about his private life.* 3 [U] a harmful condition when

[T] **transitive**, a verb which has an object: *He ate an apple.*

a person becomes very cold because they have been outside in very bad weather □ *(keadaan) terdedah kpd cuaca sejuk*: The climbers all died of exposure.

express¹ /ɪkˈspres/ *verb* [T] **1** to show sth such as a feeling or an opinion by words or actions □ *menyatakan; melahirkan rasa*: I found it very hard to express what I felt about her. ◆ to express fears/concern about something **2 express yourself** to say or write your feelings, opinions, etc. □ *menyatakan/melahirkan (pendapat, perasaan, dll)*: I don't think she expresses herself very well in that article.

express² /ɪkˈspres/ *adj* [only before a noun] **1** going or sent quickly □ *ekspres; segera*: an express coach **2** (used about a command, wish, etc.) clearly and definitely stated □ *(yg dinyatakan dgn) jelas*: It was her express wish that he should have the picture after her death. ▶ **express** *adv*: We'd better send the parcel express if we want it to get there on time.

express³ /ɪkˈspres/ (also exˈpress train) *noun* [C] a fast train that does not stop at all stations □ *kereta api ekspres*

expression /ɪkˈspreʃn/ *noun* **1** [U,C] something that you say that shows your opinions or feelings □ *penyataan; pengucapan; ucapan*: Freedom of expression is a basic human right. ◆ an expression of gratitude/sympathy/anger **2** [C] the look on sb's face that shows what they are thinking or feeling □ *air muka*: He had a puzzled expression on his face. **3** [C] a word or phrase with a particular meaning □ *ungkapan*: 'I'm starving' is an expression meaning 'I'm very hungry'. ◆ a slang/an idiomatic expression

expressive /ɪkˈspresɪv/ *adj* showing feelings or thoughts □ *penuh perasaan*: That is a very expressive piece of music. ◆ Philippa has a very expressive face. ▶ **expressively** *adv*

expressly /ɪkˈspresli/ *adv* **1** clearly; definitely □ *dgn jelas*: I expressly told you not to do that. **2** for a special purpose; specially □ *khusus*: These scissors are expressly designed for left-handed people.

expressway /ɪkˈspresweɪ/ (*AmE*) = **motorway**

expulsion /ɪkˈspʌlʃn/ *noun* [C,U] the act of making sb leave a place or an institution □ *pemecatan; tindakan buang sekolah, dsb*: There have been three expulsions from school this year. ⊃ *verb* **expel**

exquisite /ˈekskwɪzɪt; ɪkˈskwɪzɪt/ *adj* extremely beautiful and pleasing □ *sangat elok*: an exquisite piece of craftsmanship ◆ I think that ring is exquisite. ▶ **exquisitely** *adv*

ext. *abbr* = **extension** (3) □ *sambungan*: ext. 3492

extend /ɪkˈstend/ *verb* **1** [T] to make sth longer or larger (in space or time) □ *melanjutkan; memanjangkan; membesarkan; menjulurkan*: We're planning to extend the back of the house to give us more space. ◆ Since my injury I can't extend this leg fully (= make it completely straight).

express → extinct

◆ Could you extend your visit for a few days? **2** [I,T] to cover the area or period of time mentioned □ *menganjur; meluaskan*: The desert extends over a huge area of the country. ◆ The company is planning to extend its operations into Asia. **3** [T] (*formal*) to offer sth to sb □ *menghulurkan; menyampaikan*: to extend hospitality/a warm welcome/an invitation to somebody

extension /ɪkˈstenʃn/ *noun* [C] **1** a part that is added to a building □ *binaan tambahan*: They're building an extension on the hospital. **2** an extra period of time that you are allowed for sth □ *(masa) tambahan; tempoh lanjutan*: I've applied for an extension to my work permit. **3** (*abbr* **ext.**) a telephone that is connected to a central telephone in a house or to a **switchboard** (= a central point where all telephone calls are answered) in a large office building □ *sambungan*: What's your extension number? ◆ Can I have extension 4342, please?

extensive /ɪkˈstensɪv/ *adj* large in area or amount □ *luas; meluas*: The house has extensive grounds. ◆ Most of the buildings suffered extensive damage. ▶ **extensively** *adv*

extent /ɪkˈstent/ *noun* [sing, U] **the extent of sth** the length, area, size or importance of sth □ *takat; luasnya; sebanyak mana*: I was amazed at the extent of his knowledge. ◆ The **full extent** of the damage is not yet known.

IDM to a certain/to some extent used to show that sth is only partly true □ *setakat tertentu*: I agree with you to a certain extent but there are still a lot of points I disagree with.

to what extent how far; how much □ *setakat mana*: I'm not sure to what extent I believe her.

exterior¹ /ɪkˈstɪəriə(r)/ *noun* [C] the outside of sth; the appearance of sb/sth □ *bahagian luar; pd lahirnya*: The exterior of the house is fine but inside it isn't in very good condition. ◆ Despite his calm exterior, Steve suffers badly from stress.

exterior² /ɪkˈstɪəriə(r)/ *adj* on the outside □ *luar*: the exterior walls of a house **OPP interior**

exterminate /ɪkˈstɜːmɪneɪt/ *verb* [T] to kill a large group of people or animals □ *menghapuskan*: Once rats infest a building, they are very hard to exterminate. ▶ **extermination** /ɪk.stɜːmɪˈneɪʃn/ *noun* [U]

external /ɪkˈstɜːnl/ *adj* **1** connected with the outside of sth □ *luar(an)*: The cream is for external use only (= to be used on the skin). **2** coming from another place □ *luar*: You will be tested by an external examiner. **OPP** for both meanings **internal** ▶ **externally** /-nəli/ *adv*: The building has been restored externally and internally. ◆ The university has many externally-funded research projects. **OPP internally**

extinct /ɪkˈstɪŋkt/ *adj* **1** (used about a type of animal, plant, etc.) no longer existing □ *pupus*: Tigers are nearly extinct in the wild. **2** (used about a **volcano**) no longer active □ *mati* ▶ **extinction**

noun [U] □ *kepupusan*: *The giant panda is in danger of extinction.*

extinguish /ɪkˈstɪŋgwɪʃ/ *verb* [T] (*formal*) to cause sth to stop burning □ *memadamkan*: *The fire was extinguished very quickly.* ⊃ A less formal expression is **put out**. ▶ **extinguisher** = **fire extinguisher**

extort /ɪkˈstɔːt/ *verb* [T] (*formal*) **extort sth (from sb)** to get sth by using threats or violence □ *memeras ugut*: *The gang were found guilty of extorting money from small businesses.* ▶ **extortion** *noun* [U]

extortionate /ɪkˈstɔːʃənət/ *adj* (used especially about prices) much too high □ *terlampau tinggi; melampau-lampau*

extra[1] /ˈekstrə/ *adj, adv* more than is usual, expected, or than exists already □ *tambahan; lebih; lebih drpd biasa*: *I'll need some extra money for the holidays.* ♦ *'What size is this sweater?' 'Extra large.'* ♦ *Is wine included in the price of the meal or is it extra?* ♦ *I tried to be extra nice to him yesterday because it was his birthday.* ⊃ look at **additional**

extra[2] /ˈekstrə/ *noun* [C] **1** something that costs more, or that is not normally included □ *tambahan*: *The price of the holiday is all-inclusive, with no hidden extras.* **2** a person in a film, etc. who has a small unimportant part, for example in a crowd □ *pelakon tambahan*

extract[1] /ˈekstrækt/ *noun* [C] a part of a book, piece of music, etc., that has often been specially chosen to show sth □ *petikan; cabutan*: *The newspaper published extracts from the controversial novel.*

extract[2] /ɪkˈstrækt/ *verb* [T] (*formal*) to take sth out, especially with difficulty □ *mencabut; dicabut; mendapatkan*: *I think this tooth will have to be extracted.* ♦ *I wasn't able to extract an apology from her.*

extraction /ɪkˈstrækʃn/ *noun* (*formal*) **1** [U,C] the act of taking sth out □ *pencabutan; (perbuatan) mencabut; pengekstrakan*: *extraction of salt from the sea* ♦ *Dentists report that children are requiring fewer extractions* (= of teeth). **2** [U] family origin □ *keturunan*: *He's an American but he's of Italian extraction.*

extra-curricular /ˌekstrə kəˈrɪkjələ(r)/ *adj* not part of the **curriculum** (= the normal course of studies in a school or college) □ *luar kurikulum*: *The school offers many extra-curricular activities such as sport, music, drama, etc.*

extradite /ˈekstrədaɪt/ *verb* [T] to send a person who may be guilty of a crime from the country in which they are living to the country which wants to put them on trial for the crime □ *menyerah balik*: *The suspected terrorists were captured in Spain and extradited to France.* ▶ **extradition** /ˌekstrəˈdɪʃn/ *noun* [C,U]

extraordinary /ɪkˈstrɔːdnri/ *adj* not what you would expect in a particular situation; very strange or unusual □ *ganjil; pelik; luar biasa*: *That was extraordinary behaviour for a teacher!* ♦ *She has an extraordinary ability to whistle and sing at the same time.* **SYN** **incredible** ▶ **extraordinarily** /ɪkˈstrɔːdnrəli/ *adv*: *He was an extraordinarily talented musician.*

extrapolate /ɪkˈstræpəleɪt/ *verb* [I,T] (*formal*) **extrapolate (sth) (from/to sth)** to form an opinion or make a judgement about a new situation by using facts that you know from a different situation □ *membuat tentu luar; menentuluarkan (menganggar berdasarkan fakta)*: *The figures were obtained by extrapolating from past trends.* ♦ *We have extrapolated these results from research in other countries.* ▶ **extrapolation** /ɪkˌstræpəˈleɪʃn/ *noun* [U,C]

extraterrestrial /ˌekstrətəˈrestriəl/ *noun* [C] (in stories) a creature that comes from another planet; a creature that may exist on another planet □ *makhluk luar bumi; makhluk asing* ▶ **extraterrestrial** *adj*: *extraterrestrial beings/life*

extravagant /ɪkˈstrævəgənt/ *adj* **1** spending or costing too much money □ *boros; mahal*: *He's terribly extravagant—he travels everywhere by taxi.* ♦ *an extravagant present* **2** exaggerated; more than is usual, true or necessary □ *berlebih-lebihan; keterlaluan*: *the extravagant claims of advertisers* ▶ **extravagance** *noun* [C,U] ▶ **extravagantly** *adv*

extreme /ɪkˈstriːm/ *adj* **1** [only before a noun] the greatest or strongest possible □ *amat; amat sangat*: *You must take extreme care when driving at night.* ♦ *extreme heat/difficulty/poverty* **2** much stronger than is considered usual, acceptable, etc. □ *terlalu; keterlaluan*: *Her extreme views on immigration are shocking to most people.* **3** [only before a noun] as far away as possible from the centre in the direction mentioned □ *paling jauh; melampau; ekstrem*: *There could be snow in the extreme north of the country.* ♦ *politicians on the extreme left of the party* ⊃ look at **moderate, radical** ▶ **extreme** *noun* [C]: *Alex used to be very shy but now she's gone to the opposite extreme.*

extremely /ɪkˈstriːmli/ *adv* very □ *sangat; amat; sungguh*: *Listen carefully because this is extremely important.*

extreme ˈsport *noun* [C] a very dangerous sport or activity which some people do for fun □ *sukan ekstrem*: *He enjoys extreme sports, such as bungee jumping and hang-gliding.* ⊃ picture on **page P5**

extremist /ɪkˈstriːmɪst/ *noun* [C] a person who has extreme political opinions □ *pelampau* ⊃ look at **moderate, radical** ▶ **extremism** /ɪkˈstriːmɪzəm/ *noun* [U]

extremity /ɪkˈstreməti/ *noun* [C] (*pl* **extremities**) the part of sth that is furthest from the centre □ *bahagian paling hujung*

extricate /ˈekstrɪkeɪt/ *verb* [T] to manage to free sb/sth from a difficult situation or position □ *membebaskan; melepaskan*: *I finally managed to extricate myself from the meeting by saying that I had a train to catch.*

extrovert /ˈekstrəvɜːt/ noun [C] a person who is confident and full of life and who prefers being with other people to being alone □ *ekstrovert* OPP **introvert**

exuberant /ɪgˈzjuːbərənt/ adj (used about a person or their behaviour) full of energy and excitement □ *penuh semangat dan riang* ▶ **exuberance** noun [U]

eye[1] /aɪ/ noun [C] **1** one of the two organs of your body that you use to see with □ *mata*: *She opened/closed her eyes.* ♦ *He's got blue eyes.* ⊃ look at **black eye** ⊃ picture at **body**

> MORE When you close both eyes and open them again quickly, you **blink**. If you do this with only one eye, you **wink**. People with poor **eyesight** (= who cannot see well) usually wear **glasses** or use **contact lenses**. ⊃ picture at **blink, glasses**

2 the ability to see sth □ *mata; penglihatan*: *He has sharp eyes* (= he can see very well). ♦ *She has an eye for detail* (= she notices small details). **3** the hole at one end of a needle that the thread goes through □ *lubang jarum*
IDM **as far as the eye can see** ⊃ **far**[2]
be up to your eyes in sth (*informal*) to have more of sth than you can easily do or manage □ *sangat sibuk*: *I can't come out with you tonight—I'm up to my eyes in work.*
before sb's very eyes in front of sb so that they can clearly see what is happening □ *betul-betul di depan mata sso*
cast an eye/your eye(s) over sb/sth ⊃ **cast**[1]
catch sb's attention/eye ⊃ **catch**[1]
cry your eyes out ⊃ **cry**[1]
an eye for an eye used to say that you should punish sb by doing to them what they have done to sb else □ *hutang darah dibayar darah*
have (got) your eye on sb to watch sb carefully to make sure that they do nothing wrong □ *memerhatikan sso*
have (got) your eye on sth to be thinking about buying sth □ *ingin membeli sst*: *I've got my eye on a suit that I saw in the sales.*
in the eyes of sb/in sb's eyes in the opinion of sb □ *pd pandangan sso*: *She was still a child in her mother's eyes.*
in the public eye ⊃ **public**[1]
keep an eye on sb/sth to make sure that sb/sth is safe; to look after sb/sth □ *mengawasi; menengok-nengokkan*: *Please could you keep an eye on the house while we're away?*
keep an eye open/out (for sb/sth) to watch or look out for sb/sth □ *tolong tengok-tengokkan*: *I've lost my ring—could you keep an eye out for it?*
keep your eyes peeled/skinned (for sb/sth) (*informal*) to watch carefully for sb/sth □ *memasang mata* (*supaya segera nampak sso/sst*): *Keep your eyes peeled for the turning to the village.*
look sb in the eye ⊃ **look**[1]
the naked eye ⊃ **naked**
not bat an eye ⊃ **bat**[2]
see eye to eye (with sb) ⊃ **see**

set eyes on sb/sth to see sb/sth □ *melihat sst*: *He loved the house the moment he set eyes on it.*
there is more to sb/sth than meets the eye ⊃ **meet**
turn a blind eye ⊃ **blind**[1]
with your eyes open knowing what you are doing □ *dgn mata terbuka; dgn penuh kesedaran*: *You went into the new job with your eyes open, so you can't complain now.*

eye[2] /aɪ/ verb [T] (**eyeing** or **eying**; *pt, pp* **eyed**) to look at sb/sth closely □ *memerhatikan*: *She eyed the stranger with suspicion.*

eyeball /ˈaɪbɔːl/ noun [C] the whole of your eye (including the part which is hidden inside the head) □ *biji/bola mata*

eyebrow /ˈaɪbraʊ/ (also **brow**) noun [C] the line of hair that is above your eye □ *(bulu) kening* ⊃ picture at **body**
IDM **raise your eyebrows** ⊃ **raise**

ˈeye-catching adj (used about a thing) attracting your attention immediately because it is interesting, bright or pretty □ *menarik perhatian*

eyeglasses /ˈaɪɡlɑːsɪz/ (*AmE*) = **glasses**

eyelash /ˈaɪlæʃ/ (also **lash**) noun [C] one of the hairs that grow on the edges of your **eyelids** □ *bulu mata* ⊃ picture at **body**

ˈeye level noun at the same height as sb's eyes when they are standing up □ *paras mata*: *Computer screens should be at eye level.* ♦ *an eye-level grill*

eyelid /ˈaɪlɪd/ (also **lid**) noun [C] the piece of skin that can move to cover your eye □ *kelopak mata* ⊃ picture at **body**
IDM **not bat an eyelid** ⊃ **bat**[2]

eyeliner /ˈaɪlaɪnə(r)/ noun [U] a substance that you use to draw a dark line around your eyes to make them look more attractive □ *celak; penggaris mata*

ˈeye-opener noun [C] something that makes you realize the truth about sth □ *pembuka mata*: *That TV programme about the inner cities was a real eye-opener.*

eyeshadow /ˈaɪʃædəʊ/ noun [U] colour that is put on the skin above the eyes to make them look more attractive □ *pembayang mata*

eyesight /ˈaɪsaɪt/ noun [U] the ability to see □ *penglihatan*: *good/poor eyesight*

eyesore /ˈaɪsɔː(r)/ noun [C] something that is ugly and unpleasant to look at □ *sst yg menyakitkan/mencolok mata*: *All this litter in the streets is a real eyesore.*

eyewitness /ˈaɪwɪtnəs/ = **witness**[1] (1)

F → facilitate

F, f /ef/ noun [C,U] (pl **Fs**; **F's** /efs/) **1** the 6th letter of the English alphabet □ *F, f (huruf)*: 'Five' begins with (an) 'F'. **2 F** (used about music) the fourth note in the scale of C major □ *not keempat dlm skala C major*: F major/minor ◆ F sharp

F abbr = Fahrenheit □ *Fahrenheit*: Water freezes at 32°F

f abbr **1** = female **2** = feminine

FA /ˌef ˈeɪ/ abbr (BrE) **the Football Association** □ *FA (Persatuan Bola Sepak)*: the FA Cup

fable /ˈfeɪbl/ noun [C] a short story that teaches a moral lesson and that often has animals as the main characters □ *fabel; dongeng*: Aesop's fables

fabric /ˈfæbrɪk/ noun **1** [C,U] (a type of) cloth or soft material that is used for making clothes, curtains, etc. □ *fabrik*: cotton fabrics **2** [sing] the basic structure of a building or system □ *rangka; struktur; susunan*: The Industrial Revolution changed the fabric of society.

fabulous /ˈfæbjələs/ adj **1** very good; excellent □ *sangat bagus; hebat*: It was a fabulous concert. **2** very great □ *tersangat*: fabulous wealth/riches/beauty

facade /fəˈsɑːd/ noun [C] **1** the front wall of a large building that you see from the outside □ *muka depan* **2** [usually sing] the way sb/sth appears to be, which is different from the way sb/sth really is □ *pd zahirnya*: His good humour was just a facade.

face¹ /feɪs/ noun [C] **1** the front part of your head; the expression that is shown on it □ *muka; paras*: Go and wash your face. ◆ She has a very pretty face. ◆ Her face lit up (= showed happiness) when John came into the room. ➲ picture at **body 2 -faced** [in compounds] having the type of face or expression mentioned □ *bermuka*: a red-faced man ◆ round-faced/pale-faced **3** the front or one side of sth □ *bahagian muka/depan; sisi*: the north face of the mountain ◆ He put the cards face **up/down** on the table. ◆ a clock face ➲ picture at **clock**

IDM face to face (with sb/sth) close to and looking at sb/sth □ *bersua; bertemu muka*
keep a straight face ➲ **straight²**
lose face ➲ **lose**
make/pull faces/a face (at sb/sth) to make an expression that shows that you do not like sb/sth □ *membuat muka (monyok, dll); mencemik*: When she saw what was for dinner she pulled a face.
make/pull faces to make rude expressions with your face □ *membuat muka mengejek*: The children made faces behind the teacher's back.
save face ➲ **save¹**
to sb's face if you say sth to sb's face, you do it when that person is with you □ *di hadapan (muka) sso*: I wanted to say that I was sorry to her face, not on the phone. **OPP** behind sb's back

face² /feɪs/ verb **1** [I,T] to have your face or front pointing towards sb/sth or in a particular direction □ *menghadap*: The garden faces south. ◆ Can you all face the front, please? **2** [T] to need attention or action from sb □ *menghadapi*: There are several problems facing the government. ◆ We are faced with a difficult decision. **3** [T] to have to deal with sth unpleasant or difficult □ *sanggup; sanggup menghadapi*: I can't face another argument. ◆ He couldn't face going to work yesterday—he felt too ill.
IDM let's face it (informal) we must accept it as true □ *terpaksa menerima hakikat*: Let's face it, we can't afford a holiday this year.
PHR V face up to sth to accept a difficult or unpleasant situation and do sth about it □ *menerima*: She had to face up to the fact that she was wrong.

Facebook™ /ˈfeɪsbʊk/ noun [sing] a **social networking, site** (= a website for people who share your interests) ➲ note at **social networking**

facecloth /ˈfeɪsklɒθ/ (also **flannel**) noun [C] a small square piece of cloth that is used for washing the face, hands, etc. □ *tuala basuh muka (tangan, dsb)*

faceless /ˈfeɪsləs/ adj without individual character or identity □ *tanpa identiti; tdk dikenali*: faceless civil servants

facelift /ˈfeɪslɪft/ noun [C] a medical operation that makes your face look younger □ *pembedahan utk membuat muka kelihatan lebih muda* ➲ look at **plastic surgery**

facet /ˈfæsɪt/ noun [C] **1** one part or particular aspect of sth □ *segi; aspek*: There are many facets to this argument (= points that must be considered). **2** one side of a **precious** (= rare and valuable) stone □ *segi*

facetious /fəˈsiːʃəs/ adj trying to be amusing about a subject at a time that is not appropriate so that other people become annoyed □ *berseloroh (tdk kena pd tempatnya)*: He kept making facetious remarks during the lecture. ▸**facetiously** adv

face ˈvalue noun [U, sing] the cost or value that is shown on the front of stamps, coins, etc. □ *nilai muka*
IDM take sb/sth at (his, her, its) face value to accept sb/sth as he/she/it appears to be □ *menerima begitu sahaja*: Don't take his story at face value. There's something he hasn't told us yet.

facial /ˈfeɪʃl/ adj connected with a person's face □ *(berkenaan dgn) muka*: a facial expression ◆ facial hair

facile /ˈfæsaɪl/ adj (used about a comment, argument, etc.) not carefully thought out □ *cetek; lincir*

facilitate /fəˈsɪlɪteɪt/ verb [T] (formal) to make sth possible or easier □ *memudahkan*

facility /fəˈsɪləti/ noun (pl **facilities**) **1 facilities** [pl] services, buildings, equipment, etc. that make it possible to do sth □ *kemudahan*: *Our town has excellent sports facilities* (= a swimming pool, football ground, etc.). **2** [C] an extra function or ability that a machine, etc. may have □ *kemudahan tambahan; fungsi*: *a facility for checking spelling*

facsimile /fækˈsɪməli/ noun [C,U] an exact copy of a picture, piece of writing, etc. □ *salinan tepat; faksimile*

fact /fækt/ noun **1** [C] something that you know has happened or is true □ *fakta; kenyataan; hakikat*: *It is a scientific fact that light travels faster than sound.* ♦ *We need to know all the facts before we can decide.* ♦ *I know for a fact that Peter wasn't ill yesterday.* ♦ *The fact that I am older than you makes no difference at all.* ♦ *You must face facts and accept that he has gone.* **2** [U] true things; reality □ *kenyataan; hal/cerita sebenar*: *The film is based on fact.* **OPP** **fiction**
IDM as a matter of fact ➔ **matter**[1]
the fact (of the matter) is (that)… the truth is that … □ *sebenarnya*: *I would love a car, but the fact is that I just can't afford one.*
a fact of life something unpleasant that you must accept because you cannot change it □ *kenyataan hidup*: *Most people now see unemployment as just another fact of life.*
facts and figures detailed information □ *maklumat terperinci*: *Before we make a decision, we need some more facts and figures.*
the facts of life the details of sexual behaviour and how babies are born □ *hal-hal kelamin*
hard facts ➔ **hard**[1]
in (actual) fact **1** used for introducing more detailed information □ *malahan*: *It was cold. In fact it was freezing.* **2** used for emphasizing that sth is true) really; actually □ *sebenarnya; pd hakikatnya*: *I thought the lecture would be boring but in actual fact it was rather interesting.*

faction /ˈfækʃn/ noun [C] a small group of people within a larger one, whose members have some different aims and beliefs to those of the larger group □ *puak; kaum*: *rival factions within the administration*

factor /ˈfæktə(r)/ noun [C] **1** one of the things that influences a decision, situation, etc. □ *faktor*: *His unhappiness at home was a major factor in his decision to go abroad.* **2** (*technical*) (in mathematics) a whole number (except 1) by which a larger number can be divided □ *faktor*: *2, 3, 4 and 6 are factors of 12.*

factory /ˈfæktri, -təri/ noun [C] (pl **factories**) a building or group of buildings where goods are made in large quantities by machine □ *kilang*

factory farm noun [C] a type of farm where animals live inside in small spaces and eat special food so that they produce a large amount of meat, milk, etc. as quickly and cheaply as possible □ *ladang kilang* ▶ **factory farming** noun [U]

factual /ˈfæktʃuəl/ adj based on or containing things that are true or real □ *berdasarkan fakta; faktual*: *a factual account of the events* ➔ look at **fictional**

faculty /ˈfæklti/ noun [C] (pl **faculties**) **1** one of the natural abilities of a person's body or mind □ *kebolehan*: *the faculty of hearing/sight/speech* **2** (also **Faculty**) one department in a university, college, etc □ *fakulti; kakitangan akademik*: *the Faculty of Law/Arts* **3** [with sing or pl verb] all the teachers in a **faculty** of a university, college, etc. □ *fakulti*: *The Faculty has/have been invited to the meeting.*

fad /fæd/ noun [C] (*informal*) a fashion, interest, etc. that will probably not last long □ *fesyen, minat, dsb sementara*

fade /feɪd/ verb **1** [I,T] to become or make sth become lighter in colour or less strong or fresh □ *menjadi pudar/luntur; memudarkan*: *Jeans fade when you wash them.* ♦ *Look how the sunlight has faded these curtains.* **2** [I] **fade (away)** to disappear slowly (from sight, hearing, memory, etc.) □ *lenyap; hilang perlahan-lahan*: *The cheering of the crowd faded away.* ♦ *The smile faded from his face.*

faeces (AmE **feces**) /ˈfiːsiːz/ noun [pl] (*technical*) the solid waste material that you get rid of from your body when you go to the toilet □ *tahi; najis*

fag /fæg/ noun [C] (BrE slang) a cigarette □ *rokok*

Fahrenheit /ˈfærənhaɪt/ noun [U] (abbr **F**) the name of a scale which measures temperatures □ *Fahrenheit*: *Water freezes at 32° Fahrenheit (32°F).* ➔ look at **Celsius**

fail[1] /feɪl/ verb **1** [I,T] to not be successful in sth □ *gagal; tdk lulus; tdk berjaya*: *She failed her driving test.* ♦ *I feel that I've failed—I'm 25 and I still haven't got a steady job.* ➔ look at **pass**, **succeed 2** [I] **fail to do sth** to not do sth □ *tdk (membuat sst); lupa; cuai; gagal*: *She never fails to do her homework.* **3** [T] to decide that sb is not successful in a test, exam, etc □ *menggagalkan*: *The examiners failed half of the candidates.* **OPP** **pass 4** [I] to stop working □ *rosak; mati; tdk berfungsi*: *My brakes failed on the hill but I managed to stop the car.* **5** [I] (used about health, etc.) to become weak □ *menjadi lemah, kabur, dll; merosot*: *His eyesight is failing.* **6** [I,T] to not be enough or not do what people are expecting or wanting □ *tdk menjadi; mengecewakan*: *If the crops fail, people will starve.* ♦ *I think the government has failed us.*

fail[2] /feɪl/ noun [C] the result of an exam in which sb is not successful □ *gagal; tdk lulus* **OPP** **pass**
IDM without fail always, even if there are difficulties □ *tetap; mesti; tdk boleh tdk*: *She spends an hour in the gym each day without fail.*

failing[1] /ˈfeɪlɪŋ/ noun [C] a weakness or fault □ *kelemahan*: *She's not very patient—that's her only failing.*

failing² /ˈfeɪlɪŋ/ *prep* if sth is not possible □ *kalau tdk*: *Ask Jackie to go with you, or failing that, try Anne.*

failure /ˈfeɪljə(r)/ *noun* **1** [U] lack of success □ *kegagalan*: *All my efforts ended in failure.* **OPP** **success 2** [C] a person or thing that is not successful □ *gagal; tdk berjaya*: *His first attempt at skating was a miserable failure.* **OPP** **success 3** [C,U] **failure to do sth** not doing sth that people expect you to do □ *kegagalan; (perihal) tdk membuat sst*: *I was very disappointed at his failure to come to the meeting.* **4** [C,U] an example of sth not working properly □ *kerosakan; sakit; terputusnya (bekalan)*: *She died of heart failure.* ♦ *There's been a failure in the power supply.*

faint¹ /feɪnt/ *adj* (**fainter; faintest**) **1** (used about things that you can see, hear, feel, etc.) not strong or clear □ *kelam; kabur; samar-samar; sayup; sedikit*: *a faint light/sound* ♦ *There is still a faint hope that they will find more people alive.* **2** (used about actions, etc.) done without much effort □ *tdk bersungguh-sungguh*: *He made a faint protest.* **3** [not before a noun] (used about people) likely to become unconscious; very weak □ *rasa pitam; lemah; lesu*: *I feel faint—I'd better sit down.*
IDM **not have the faintest/foggiest (idea)** (*informal*) to not know at all □ *sedikit pun tdk tahu*: *I haven't the faintest idea where they've gone.*
▶**faintly** *adv*: *She smiled faintly.* ♦ *He looked faintly embarrassed.*

faint² /feɪnt/ *verb* [I] to become unconscious for a short time □ *pitam; pengsan* **SYN** **pass out** **OPP** **come round/to**

fair¹ /feə(r)/ *adj* (**fairer; fairest**) **1** appropriate and acceptable in a particular situation □ *wajar; patut; berpatutan*: *That's a fair price for that house.* ♦ *I think it's fair to say that the number of homeless people is increasing.* **OPP** **unfair 2** **fair (to/on sb)** treating each person or side equally, according to the law, the rules, etc. □ *adil*: *That's not fair—he got the same number of mistakes as I did and he's got a better mark.* ♦ *It wasn't fair on her to ask her to stay so late.* ♦ *a fair trial* **OPP** **unfair 3** quite good, large, etc. □ *agak (baik, besar, dll)*: *They have a fair chance of success.* **4** (used about the skin or hair) light in colour □ *cerah; putih*: *Chloe has fair hair and blue eyes.* **OPP** **dark** ⊃ look at **skin**(2) **5** (used about the weather) good, without rain □ *baik*: *a fair and breezy autumn day*
IDM **fair enough** (*spoken*) used to show that you agree with what sb has suggested □ *baiklah* **fair play** equal treatment of both/all sides according to the rules □ *keadilan; sikap adil*: *The referee is there to ensure fair play during the match.* **(more than) your fair share of sth** (more than) the usual or expected amount of sth □ *lebih drpd biasa*: *We've had more than our fair share of trouble this year.*

fair² /feə(r)/ *noun* [C] **1** (*BrE also* **funfair**) a type of entertainment in a field or park. At a **fair** you can ride on machines or try and win prizes at games. **Fairs** usually travel from town to town. □ *pesta ria* **2** a large event where people, businesses, etc. show and sell their goods □ *pesta; pameran; pasar ria*: *a trade fair* ♦ *the Frankfurt book fair*

fairground /ˈfeəɡraʊnd/ *noun* [C] a large outdoor area where **fairs** are held □ *tapak pesta*

fair-ˈhaired *adj* with light-coloured hair □ *berambut perang muda* **SYN** **blonde**

fairly /ˈfeəli/ *adv* **1** quite, not very □ *agak*: *He is fairly tall.* ⊃ note at **rather 2** in an acceptable way; in a way that treats people equally or according to the law, rules, etc. □ *dgn adil*: *I felt that the teacher didn't treat us fairly.* **OPP** **unfairly**

fairness /ˈfeənəs/ *noun* [U] treating people equally or according to the law, rules, etc. □ *keadilan*

fair-ˈtrade *adj* involving trade which helps to pay fair prices to workers in poor countries □ *perdagangan adil*: *We buy 10% of our bananas from fair-trade sources.*

fairy /ˈfeəri/ *noun* [C] (*pl* **fairies**) (in stories) a small creature with wings and magic powers □ *pari-pari*

ˈfairy tale (*also* **ˈfairy story**) *noun* [C] a story that is about **fairies**, magic, etc. □ *cerita dongeng*

faith /feɪθ/ *noun* **1** [U] **faith (in sb/sth)** strong belief (in sb/sth); trust □ *kepercayaan; keyakinan*: *I've got great/little faith in her ability to do the job.* ♦ *I have lost faith in him.* **2** [U] strong religious belief □ *iman*: *a man of great faith* **3** [C] a particular religion □ *agama*: *the Jewish faith*
IDM **in good faith** with honest reasons for doing sth □ *secara jujur*: *I bought the car in good faith. I didn't know it was stolen.*

faithful /ˈfeɪθfl/ *adj* **1** **faithful (to sb/sth)** always staying with and supporting a person, an organization or a belief; loyal □ *setia*: *He was always faithful to his wife* (= he didn't have sexual relations with anyone else). ♦ *Peter has been a faithful friend.* **OPP** **unfaithful 2** true to the facts; accurate □ *akur; tepat*: *a faithful description*
▶**faithfully** /-fəli/ *adv*

MORE **Yours faithfully** is used to end formal letters that you have started *Dear Sir or Madam.*

⊃ note at **sincere** ▶**faithfulness** *noun* [U] ⊃ look at **fidelity**

fake¹ /feɪk/ *noun* [C] **1** a work of art, etc. that seems to be real or genuine but is not □ *(sst yg) palsu* **2** a person who is not really what they appear to be □ *penipu* ▶**fake** *adj*: *a fake passport*

fake² /feɪk/ *verb* [T] **1** to copy sth and try to make people believe it is the real thing □ *memalsukan; menipu*: *He faked his father's signature.* **2** to make people believe that you are feeling sth that you are not □ *buat-buat; berpura-pura*: *I faked surprise when he told me the news.*

falcon /ˈfɔːlkən/ noun [C] a bird with long pointed wings that kills and eats other animals. Falcons can be trained to hunt. □ *burung falkon*

fall¹ /fɔːl/ verb [I] (pt **fell** /fel/; pp **fallen** /ˈfɔːlən/)
▶ DROP DOWN **1** to drop down towards the ground □ *jatuh; turun; gugur*: He **fell** off the ladder onto the grass. ♦ The rain was falling steadily. **2 fall (down/over)** to suddenly stop standing and drop to the ground □ *jatuh; tergelincir; tumbang*: She slipped on the ice and fell. ♦ The little boy fell over and hurt his knee.
▶ OF HAIR/CLOTH **3** to hang down □ *mengurai; terjurai*: Her hair fell down over her shoulders.
▶ DECREASE **4** to become lower or less □ *jatuh; turun*: The temperature is falling. ♦ The price of coffee has fallen again. **OPP** rise
▶ BE DEFEATED **5** to be defeated or captured □ *jatuh drpd kuasa; ditawan*: The Government fell because of the scandal.
▶ DIE IN WAR **6** (written) to be killed (in battle) □ *gugur; terkorban*: Millions of soldiers fell in the war.
▶ BECOME **7** to change into a different state; to become □ *jatuh (cinta, sakit, dll); tertidur; menjadi (buruk, dsb)*: He **fell asleep** on the sofa. ♦ They **fell in love** with each other in Spain. ♦ I must get some new shoes—these ones are **falling to pieces**.
▶ HAPPEN **8** (formal) to come or happen □ *jatuh; bersemayam dgn*: My birthday falls on a Sunday this year.
▶ BELONG TO GROUP **9** to belong to a particular group, type, etc. □ *terbahagi kpd*: Animals fall into two groups, those with backbones and those without.
IDM **fall flat** ➔ **flat¹**
fall foul of sb/sth to get in trouble with sb/sth because you have done sth wrong □ *bertelingkah*: At sixteen she fell foul of the law for the first time.
fall/get into arrears ➔ **arrears**
fall/slot into place ➔ **place¹**
fall/land on your feet ➔ **foot¹**
fall short (of sth) to not be enough; to not reach sth □ *kurang drpd (sst); tdk mencapai (sst)*: The pay rise fell short of what they had asked for.
PHR V **fall apart** to break (into pieces) □ *pecah; berkecai; terburai*: My car is falling apart.
fall back on sb/sth to use sb/sth when you are in difficulty □ *bergantung pd atau mengharapkan sso/sst*: When the electricity was cut off we fell back on candles.
fall for sb (informal) to be strongly attracted to sb; to fall in love with sb □ *jatuh hati*
fall for sth (informal) to be tricked into believing sth that is not true □ *terpedaya dgn*: He makes excuses and she falls for them every time.
fall out (with sb) (BrE) to argue and stop being friendly (with sb) □ *bergaduh; berkelahi*
fall through to fail or not happen □ *gagal; tdk jadi*: Our trip to Japan has fallen through.

fall² /fɔːl/ noun
▶ DOWN/OFF STH **1** [C] an act of falling down or off sth □ *jatuh; jatuhnya*: She had a nasty **fall** from her horse.

▶ AMOUNT/DISTANCE **2** [C] **a fall (of sth)** the amount of sth that has fallen or the distance that sth has fallen □ *turunnya; jatuhan; kejatuhan*: We have had a heavy fall of snow. ♦ a fall of four metres
▶ WATER **3 falls** [pl] a large amount of water falling down from a height □ *air terjun*: Niagara Falls **SYN** waterfall
▶ AUTUMN **4** [C] (AmE) = **autumn**
▶ DECREASE **5** [C] **a fall (in sth)** a decrease (in value, quantity, etc.) □ *kejatuhan; turunnya*: There has been a sharp fall in interest rates. **SYN** drop **OPP** rise
▶ DEFEAT **6** [sing] **the fall of sth** a (political) defeat; a failure □ *kejatuhan; kekalahan*: the fall of the Roman Empire
IDM **sb's fall from grace** a situation in which sb loses the respect that people had for them by doing sth wrong or immoral □ *kehilangan rasa hormat orang lain*

fallacy /ˈfæləsi/ noun [C,U] (pl **fallacies**) (formal) a false belief or a wrong idea □ *falasi; salah anggapan/tanggapan*: It's a fallacy that money brings happiness (= it's not true).

fallen past participle of **fall¹**

fallible /ˈfæləbl/ adj able or likely to make mistakes □ *boleh silap*: Even our new computerized system is fallible. **OPP** **infallible**

fallout /ˈfɔːlaʊt/ noun [U] dangerous waste that is carried in the air after a nuclear explosion □ *luruhan; gguran*

false /fɔːls/ adj **1** not true; not correct □ *tdk benar; salah*: I think the information you have been given is false. ♦ I got a completely false impression of him from our first meeting. **OPP** **true 2** not real; artificial □ *palsu*: false hair/eyelashes **OPP** **real, natural 3** not genuine, but made to look real in order to trick people □ *palsu*: This suitcase has a false bottom. ♦ a false name/passport **4** (used about sb's behaviour or expression) not sincere or honest □ *palsu; dibuat-buat*: a false smile ♦ false modesty
IDM **a false alarm** a warning about a danger that does not happen □ *gempar/amaran bahaya palsu*
a false friend a word in another language that looks similar to a word in your own but has a different meaning □ *kata bahasa asing yg kelihatan sama dgn kata bahasa sendiri tetapi maknanya lain*
on/under false pretences pretending to be or to have sth in order to trick people □ *dgn cara menipu*: She got into the club under false pretences—she isn't a member at all!
▶ **falsely** adv: He was falsely accused of theft. ♦ She smiled falsely at his joke.

false ˈteeth (also **dentures**) noun [pl] artificial teeth that are worn by sb who has lost their natural teeth □ *gigi palsu*

falsify /ˈfɔːlsɪfaɪ/ verb [T] (**falsifying**; **falsifies**; pt, pp **falsified**) (formal) to change a document, information, etc. so that it is no longer true in

falter → fan 314

order to trick sb □ *memalsukan*: *to falsify data/records/accounts*

falter /ˈfɔːltə(r)/ *verb* [I] **1** to become weak or move in a way that is not steady □ *terhuyung-hayang; terhenti-henti*: *The engine faltered and stopped.* **2** to lose confidence and determination □ *teragak-agak*: *Murray faltered and missed the ball.*

fame /feɪm/ *noun* [U] being known or talked about by many people because of what you have achieved □ *kemasyhuran*: *Pop stars achieve fame at a young age.* ♦ *The town's only **claim to fame** is that George Eliot was born there.*

famed /feɪmd/ *adj* famed (for sth) very well known (for sth) □ *masyhur; terkenal*: *Welsh people are famed for their singing.* ⊃ A more common word is **famous**.

familiar /fəˈmɪliə(r)/ *adj* **1** familiar (to sb) known to you; often seen or heard and therefore easy to recognize □ *biasa; dikenali*: *to look/sound familiar* ♦ *Chinese music isn't very familiar to people in Europe.* ♦ *It was a relief to see a familiar face in the crowd.* **OPP** unfamiliar **2** familiar with sth having a good knowledge of sth □ *tahu*: *People in Europe aren't very familiar with Chinese music.* **OPP** unfamiliar **3** familiar (with sb) (used about sb's behaviour) too friendly and informal □ *terlalu ramah dan tdk formal*: *I was annoyed by the waiter's familiar behaviour.*

familiarity /fəˌmɪliˈærəti/ *noun* [U] **1** familiarity (with sth) having a good knowledge of sth □ *kebiasaan; pengetahuan*: *His familiarity with the area was an advantage.* **2** being too friendly and informal □ *sikap terlalu ramah dan tdk formal*

familiarize (also -ise) /fəˈmɪliəraɪz/ *verb* [T] familiarize sb/yourself (with sth) to teach sb about sth or learn about sth until you know it well □ *membiasakan diri*: *I want to familiarize myself with the plans before the meeting.*

family /ˈfæməli/ *noun* (*pl* families) **1** [C, with sing or pl verb] a group of people who are related to each other □ *keluarga*: *I have quite a large family.* ♦ *a family of four* ♦ *the Dawson family*

> **MORE** Sometimes we use **family** to mean 'parents and their children' (a **nuclear family**); sometimes we use it to include other relatives, for example grandparents, aunts, uncles, etc. (an **extended family**).

> **GRAMMAR Family** is used with a singular verb when we are thinking of it as a unit: *Almost every family in the country owns a TV.* A plural verb is used when we are thinking of the members of the family as individuals: *My family are all very tall.*

2 [C,U] children □ *anak*: *We are planning to **start a family** next year* (= to have our first baby). ♦ *to bring up/raise a family* ♦ *Do you have any family?* **3** [C] a group of animals, plants, etc. that are of a similar type; a group of related things, especially languages □ *famili; rumpun*: *Lions belong to the cat family.*

IDM run in the family to be found very often in a family □ *ciri keluarga/keturunan*: *Red hair runs in the family.*

▶ **family** *adj*: *a family car* (= suitable for a family with children)

> **EXAM TIP**
>
> **Word families**
>
> When you learn a word, make a note of other words in the same family. For example, if you learn the word **rely**, you will see a note in the dictionary that points you to the noun **reliance** and the adjectives **reliable** and **reliant**. Learn word families to help you with exam questions where you have to rewrite a sentence changing the part of speech, but not the meaning.

family name *noun* [C] the name that is shared by members of a family □ *nama keluarga* **SYN** surname ⊃ note at **name**

family planning *noun* [U] controlling the number of children you have by using birth control □ *perancangan keluarga* ⊃ look at **contraception**

family tree *noun* [C] a diagram that shows the relationships between different members of a family over a long period of time □ *salasilah; susur galur (keturunan)*: *How far back can you trace your family tree?*

famine /ˈfæmɪn/ *noun* [C,U] a lack of food over a long period of time in a large area that can cause the death of many people □ *kebuluran*: *There is a severe famine in many parts of Africa.* ♦ *The long drought* (= a lack of rain or water) *was followed by famine.*

famished /ˈfæmɪʃt/ *adj* [not before a noun] (*informal*) very hungry □ *sangat lapar*: *When's lunch? I'm famished!*

famous /ˈfeɪməs/ *adj* famous (for sth) known about by many people □ *masyhur; terkenal*: *a famous singer* ♦ *Glasgow is famous for its museums and art galleries.* ♦ *One day, I'll be rich and famous.*

> **MORE Infamous** and **notorious** mean 'famous for being bad'.

famously /ˈfeɪməsli/ *adv* in a way that is famous □ *secara masyhur*: *the words Nelson famously uttered just before he died*

IDM get on/along famously to have a very good relationship with sb, especially from the first meeting □ *berkawan dgn baik sekali*: *My girlfriend and my father got on famously.*

fan¹ /fæn/ *noun* [C] **1** a person who admires and is very enthusiastic about a sport, a film star, a singer, etc. □ *peminat*: *football fans* ♦ *She's a Madonna fan.* ♦ *fan mail* (= letters from fans to the person they admire) **2** a machine with parts that turn around very quickly to create a current of cool or warm air □ *kipas*: *an electric fan* ♦ *a* *fan heater* 3 an object in the shape of half a circle made of paper, feathers, etc. that you wave in your hand to create a current of cool air □ *kipas*

fans

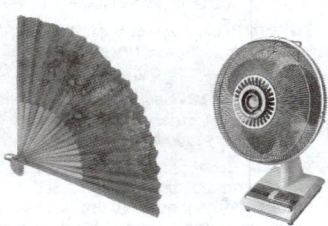

fan² /fæn/ *verb* [T] (**fanning**; **fanned**) **1** to make air blow on sb/sth by waving a fan, your hand, etc. in the air □ *mengipas*: *She used a newspaper to fan her face.* **2** to make a fire burn more strongly by blowing on it □ *menyemarakkan*: *The strong wind really fanned the flames.*
PHR V **fan out** to spread out □ *bertebar*: *The police fanned out across the field.*

fanatic /fəˈnætɪk/ *noun* [C] a person who is very enthusiastic about sth and may have extreme or dangerous opinions (especially about religion or politics) □ *fanatik*: *a health-food fanatic* ⊃ look at **freak** ▶**fanatical** /-kl/ (also **fanatic**) *adj*: *He's fanatical about keeping things tidy.* ▶**fanatically** /-kli/ *adv* ▶**fanaticism** /fəˈnætɪsɪzəm/ *noun* [C,U]

ˈfan belt *noun* [C] the belt that operates the machinery that cools a car engine □ *tali sawat kipas (kereta)*

fancy¹ /ˈfænsi/ *verb* [T] (**fancying**; **fancies**; *pt, pp* **fancied**) **1** (*BrE informal*) to like the idea of having or doing sth; to want sth or to want to do sth □ *hendak; ingin; sanggup*: *What do you fancy to eat?* ♦ *I don't fancy going out in this rain.* **2** (*BrE informal*) to be sexually attracted to sb □ *suka; tertarik pd*: *Jack keeps looking at you. I think he fancies you.* **3 fancy yourself (as) sth** to think that you would be good at sth; to think that you are sth (although this may not be true) □ *ingat; berangan*: *He fancied himself (as) a poet.*

fancy² /ˈfænsi/ *noun*
IDM **take sb's fancy** (*informal*) to attract or please sb □ *menarik minat sso; tertarik pd*: *If you see something that takes your fancy I'll buy it for you.*
take a fancy to sb/sth (*informal*) to start liking sb/sth □ *tertarik/jatuh hati pd sso/sst*: *I think that Laura's really taken a fancy to you.*

fancy³ /ˈfænsi/ *adj* (**fancier**; **fanciest**) not simple or ordinary □ *istimewa*; *bukan biasa*: *My father doesn't like fancy food.* ♦ *I just want a pair of black shoes—nothing fancy.* **OPP** **plain**

ˌfancy ˈdress *noun* [U] special clothes that you wear to a party at which people dress up to look like a different person (for example from history or a story) □ *pakaian beragam*: *We've been invited to a fancy dress party—I'm going as Napoleon.* ♦ *It was a Halloween party and everyone went in fancy dress.*

fan → far

fanfare /ˈfænfeə(r)/ *noun* [C] a short loud piece of music that is used for introducing sb important, for example a king or queen □ *muzik pengenalan*

fang /fæŋ/ *noun* [C] a long sharp tooth of a dog, snake, etc. □ *taring* ⊃ picture on **page P12**

ˈfanny pack /ˈfæni pæk/ (*AmE*) = **bumbag**

fantasize (also **-ise**) /ˈfæntəsaɪz/ *verb* [I,T] to imagine sth that you would like to happen □ *berkhayal; mengkhayalkan*: *He liked to fantasize that he had won a gold medal at the Olympics.*

fantastic /fænˈtæstɪk/ *adj* **1** (*informal*) very good; excellent □ *amat bagus; hebat*: *She's a fantastic swimmer.* ⊃ note at **good 2** (*informal*) very large or great □ *sangat (banyak, besar, dll)*: *A Rolls Royce costs a fantastic amount of money.* **3** strange and difficult to believe □ *pelik; yg bukan-bukan*: *a story full of fantastic creatures from other worlds* ▶**fantastically** /-kli/ *adv*

fantasy /ˈfæntəsi/ *noun* [C,U] (*pl* **fantasies**) a situation that you imagine but that is not true □ *khayalan*: *I have a fantasy about going to live in the Bahamas.* ♦ *They live in a world of fantasy.*
⊃ note at **imagination**

fanzine /ˈfænziːn/ *noun* [C] a magazine that is written by and for people who like a particular sports team, singer, etc. □ *majalah peminat*

FAQ /ˌef eɪ ˈkjuː/ *abbr* used in writing to mean **frequently asked questions** □ *FAQ (soalan yg paling kerap ditanya)*

far¹ /fɑː(r)/ *adj* (**farther** /ˈfɑːðə(r)/ or **further** /ˈfɜːðə(r)/, **farthest** /ˈfɑːðɪst/ or **furthest** /ˈfɜːðɪst/) **1** a long distance away □ *jauh*: *Let's walk—it's not far.* **2** [only *before* a noun] more distant (of two or more things) □ *(sebelah) sana*: *the far side of the river* **3** [only *before* a noun] a long way from the centre in the direction mentioned □ *paling (jauh dari tengah)*: *politicians from the far left of the party*
IDM **a far cry from sth/from doing sth** an experience that is very different from sth/doing sth □ *jauh berbeza*

far² /fɑː(r)/ *adv* (**farther** /ˈfɑːðə(r)/ or **further** /ˈfɜːðə(r)/, **farthest** /ˈfɑːðɪst/ or **furthest** /ˈfɜːðɪst/) **1** (at) a distance □ *jauh*: *London's not far from here.* ♦ *How far did we walk yesterday?* ♦ *If we sit too far away from the screen, I won't be able to see the film.* ♦ *I can't swim as far as you.* ♦ *How much further is it?*

> **HELP** **Far** or **a long way? Far** in this sense is usually used in negative sentences and questions. In positive sentences we say **a long way**: *It's a long way from here to the sea.* **Far** can also be used in sentences that have a negative meaning although they are positive in form: *Let's get a bus. It's much too far to walk.*

2 very much □ *jauh lebih; terlalu*: *She's far more intelligent than I thought.* ♦ *There's far too much salt in this soup.* **3** (to) a certain degree

---
VOWELS iː **see**   i **any**   ɪ **sit**   e **ten**   æ **hat**   ɑː **father**   ɒ **got**   ɔː **saw**   ʊ **put**   uː **too**   u **usual**

faraway → fashion

□ *setakat mana*: *How far have you got with your homework?* ♦ *The company employs local people as far as possible.* **4** a long time □ *jauh; larut*: *We danced far into the night.*

IDM **as far as** to the place mentioned but not further □ *sejauh*: *We walked as far as the river and then turned back.*

as/so far as used for giving your opinion or judgement of a situation □ *setakat; bagi*: *As far as I know, she's not coming, but I may be wrong.* ♦ *As far as school work is concerned, he's hopeless.* ♦ *As far as I'm concerned, this is the most important point.* ♦ *As far as I can see, the accident was John's fault, not Ann's.*

as far as the eye can see to the furthest place you can see □ *sepenjulat mata*

by far (used for emphasizing comparative or superlative words) by a large amount □ *jauh (lebih baik, dll); yg terbaik*: *Carmen is by far the best student in the class.*

far afield ⇒ **afield**

far from sth almost the opposite of sth; not at all □ *bukannya*: *He's far from happy* (= he's very sad or angry).

far from doing sth instead of doing sth □ *bukannya...malah*: *Far from enjoying the film, he fell asleep in the middle.*

far from it (*informal*) certainly not; just the opposite □ *tdk sekali-kali; malahan*: *'Did you enjoy your holiday?' 'No, far from it. It was awful.'*

few and far between ⇒ **few**

go far **1** to be enough □ *cukup*: *This food won't go very far between three of us.* **2** to be successful in life □ *berjaya*: *Dan is very talented and should go far.*

go too far to behave in a way that causes trouble or upsets other people □ *keterlaluan*: *He's always been naughty but this time he's gone too far.*

so far until now □ *setakat ini*: *So far the weather has been good but it might change.*

so far so good (*spoken*) everything has gone well until now □ *setakat ini semuanya beres*

faraway /ˈfɑːrəweɪ/ *adj* [only before a noun] **1** (*written*) a great distance away □ *jauh-jauh*: *He told us stories of faraway countries.* **2** (used about a look in sb's eyes) as if you are thinking of sth else □ *melayang jauh*: *She stared out of the window with a faraway look in her eyes.*

farce /fɑːs/ *noun* **1** [C,U] something important or serious that is not organized well or treated with respect □ *sst yg kucar-kacir; (seperti) sandiwara*: *The meeting was a farce—everyone was shouting at the same time.* **2** [C] a funny play for the theatre full of ridiculous situations □ *farsa; lelucon* ▶ **farcical** /ˈfɑːsɪkl/ *adj*

fare¹ /feə(r)/ *noun* [C] the amount of money you pay to travel by bus, train, taxi, etc. □ *tambang*: *What's the fare to Birmingham?* ♦ *Adults pay full fare, children pay half fare.* ⇒ look at **airfare**

fare² /feə(r)/ *verb* [I] (*formal*) to be successful or not successful in a particular situation □ *berjaya atau tdk dlm sst*: *How did you fare in your examination* (= did you do well or badly)?

the Far East *noun* [sing] China, Japan and other countries in East and South East Asia □ *Asia Timur dan Asia Tenggara; Timur Jauh* ⇒ look at **the Middle East**

farewell /ˌfeəˈwel/ *exclam* (*old-fashioned*) goodbye □ *selamat tinggal* ▶ **farewell** *noun* [C]: *He said his farewells and left.*

far-ˈfetched *adj* not easy to believe □ *tdk masuk akal; sukar dipercayai*: *It's a good book but the story's too far-fetched.*

farm¹ /fɑːm/ *noun* [C] an area of land with fields and buildings that is used for growing crops and keeping animals □ *kebun; ladang*: *to work on a farm* ♦ *farm buildings/workers/animals* ⇒ picture on **page P9, page P11**

farm² /fɑːm/ *verb* [I,T] to use land for growing crops or keeping animals □ *berladang*: *She farms 200 acres.*

farmer /ˈfɑːmə(r)/ *noun* [C] a person who owns or manages a farm □ *pekebun; peladang; penternak* ⇒ picture on **page P2**

farmhouse /ˈfɑːmhaʊs/ *noun* [C] the house on a farm where the farmer lives □ *rumah ladang* ⇒ picture on **page P11**

farming /ˈfɑːmɪŋ/ *noun* [U] managing a farm or working on it □ *berladang; perladangan; penternakan*: *farming methods/areas*

farmyard /ˈfɑːmjɑːd/ *noun* [C] an outside area near a **farmhouse** surrounded by buildings or walls □ *pekarangan bangunan-bangunan ladang* ⇒ picture on **page P11**

far-ˈreaching *adj* having a great influence on a lot of other things □ *meluas*: *far-reaching changes*

far-ˈsighted *adj* **1** being able to see what will be necessary in the future and making plans for it □ *berpandangan jauh* **2** (*AmE*) = **long-sighted**

fart /fɑːt/ *verb* [I] (*informal*) to suddenly let gas from the stomach escape from your bottom □ *kentut*

HELP Be careful. Some people find this word offensive. A more polite way of saying this is 'to break wind'.

▶ **fart** *noun* [C]

farther /ˈfɑːðə(r)/ ⇒ **far** ⇒ note at **further**

farthest /ˈfɑːðɪst/ ⇒ **far**

fascinate /ˈfæsɪneɪt/ *verb* [T] to attract or interest sb very much □ *menarik minat*: *Chinese culture has always fascinated me.* ▶ **fascinating** *adj* ▶ **fascination** /ˌfæsɪˈneɪʃn/ *noun* [C,U]

fascism (also **Fascism**) /ˈfæʃɪzəm/ *noun* [U] an extreme **right-wing** political system which is in favour of strong central government and does not allow anyone to speak against it □ *fahaman Fasis* ▶ **fascist** (also **Fascist**) /-ɪst/ *noun* [C], *adj*

fashion /ˈfæʃn/ *noun* **1** [C,U] the style of dressing or behaving that is the most popular at a particular time □ *fesyen*: *What is the latest fashion in hairstyles?* ♦ *a fashion show/model/magazine*

♦ *Jeans are always* **in fashion**. ♦ *I think hats will* **come back into fashion**. ♦ *That colour is* **out of fashion** *this year*. ➲ note at **clothes** 2 [sing] the way you do sth □ *cara*: *Watch him. He's been behaving* **in a very strange fashion**.

fashionable /ˈfæʃnəbl/ *adj* 1 popular or in a popular style at the time □ *bergaya*: *fashionable clothes* ♦ *a fashionable area/opinion* **OPP** **unfashionable** ➲ look at **old-fashioned** 2 considering fashion to be important □ *mementingkan fesyen*: *fashionable society* ▶**fashionably** /-əbli/ *adv*

fast¹ /fɑːst/ *adj* (**faster**; **fastest**) 1 able to move or act at great speed □ *pantas*; *cepat*; *laju*; *deras*: *a fast car/worker/runner/reader* ➲ note at **quick** 2 [not before a noun] (used about a clock or watch) showing a time that is later than the real time □ *cepat*: *The clock is five minutes fast*. **OPP** **slow** 3 [only *after* a noun] firmly fixed □ *(memasang, menambat, dll) dgn kukuh/teguh*; *mengejapkan*; *tdk luntur*: *He made the boat fast* (= he tied it to sth) *before he got out*. ♦ *Do you think the colour in this T-shirt is fast* (= will not come out when washed)?
IDM **fast and furious** very fast and exciting □ *rancak dan menarik*
hard and fast ➲ **hard¹**

fast² /fɑːst/ *adv* (**faster**; **fastest**) 1 quickly □ *dgn cepat/laju/pantas*: *The dog ran very fast*. 2 firmly or deeply □ *dgn kukuh*; *dgn nyenyak*: *Sam was* **fast asleep** *by 10 o'clock*. ♦ *Our car was stuck fast in the mud*.

fast³ /fɑːst/ *verb* [I] to eat no food for a certain time, usually for religious reasons □ *berpuasa*: *Muslims fast during Ramadan*. ▶**fast** *noun* [C]

fasten /ˈfɑːsn/ *verb* 1 [I,T] **fasten sth (up)** to close or join the two parts of sth; to become closed or joined □ *menutup*; *merapatkan*; *memasang*; *mengancing*; *dikancing*: *Please fasten your seat belts*. ♦ *Fasten your coat up—it's cold outside*. ♦ *My dress fastens at the back*. **OPP** **unfasten** 2 [T] to close or lock sth firmly so that it will not open □ *menutup*; *mengunci*: *Close the window and fasten it securely*. **OPP** **unfasten** 3 [T] **fasten sth (on/to sth); fasten A and B (together)** to fix or tie sth to sth, or two things together □ *memasang*; *mengenakan*; *mengikat*: *Fasten this badge on your jacket*. ♦ *How can I fasten these pieces of wood together?*

fastener /ˈfɑːsnə(r)/ (also **fastening** /ˈfɑːsnɪŋ/) *noun* [C] something that fastens things together □ *kancing*

fast food *noun* [U] food that can be served very quickly in special restaurants and is often taken away to be eaten in the street □ *makanan segera*: *a fast food restaurant*

fast-forward *verb* [T] to make a tape or video go forward quickly without playing it □ *maju*; *laju* ▶**fast forward** *noun* [U]: *Press fast forward to advance the video*. ♦ *the fast-forward button* ➲ look at **rewind**

fastidious /fæˈstɪdiəs/ *adj* difficult to please; wanting everything to be perfect □ *cerewet*

317 **fashionable → fatherhood**

fat¹ /fæt/ *adj* (**fatter**; **fattest**) 1 (used about people's or animal's bodies) weighing too much; covered with too much fat □ *gemuk*: *You'll get fat if you eat too much*. ♦ *fat legs, arms, etc*. **OPP** **thin** 2 (used about a thing) thick or full □ *tebal*; *kembung*: *a fat wallet/book*

OTHER WORDS FOR

fat

It is not polite to describe sb as **fat**. **Large** and **overweight** are sometimes used instead: *She's a rather large lady.* ♦ *I'm a bit overweight.* Generally it is not polite to refer to sb's weight when you talk to him/her. **Chubby** is mainly used to describe babies and children who are slightly fat in a pleasant way: *a baby with chubby cheeks.* Doctors use the word **obese** to describe people who are very fat in a way that is not healthy.

---

fat² /fæt/ *noun* 1 [U] the soft white substance under the skins of animals and people □ *lemak*: *I don't like meat with lots of fat on it*. ➲ *adjective* **fatty** 2 [C,U] the substance containing oil that we obtain from animals, plants or seeds and use for cooking □ *lemak*: *Cook the onions in a little fat*.

fatal /ˈfeɪtl/ *adj* 1 causing or ending in death □ *membawa maut*: *a fatal accident/disease/crash* ➲ look at **mortal** 2 causing trouble or a bad result □ *membawa padah*: *She made the fatal mistake of trusting him*. ▶**fatally** /-təli/ *adv*: *fatally injured*

fatality /fəˈtæləti/ *noun* [C] (*pl* **fatalities**) sb's death caused by an accident, in war, etc. □ *kematian*: *There were no fatalities in the fire*.

fate /feɪt/ *noun* 1 [C] your future; something that happens to you □ *nasib*: *Both men suffered the same fate—they both lost their jobs*. 2 [U] the power that some people believe controls everything that happens □ *takdir*: *It was fate that brought them together again after twenty years*.

fateful /ˈfeɪtfl/ *adj* having an important effect on the future □ *yg membawa kesan penting*; *bersejarah*: *a fateful decision*

father¹ /ˈfɑːðə(r)/ *noun* [C] 1 sb's male parent □ *bapa*: *John looks exactly like his father*. 2 **Father** the title of certain priests □ *Father (paderi)*: *Father O'Reilly*

father² /ˈfɑːðə(r)/ *verb* [T] to become a father by making a woman pregnant □ *menjadi bapa*: *to father a child*

Father Christmas (*especially AmE* **Santa Claus**) *noun* [C] (*BrE*) an imaginary old man with a red coat and a long white beard who, children believe, brings presents at Christmas □ *Santa Klaus*

fatherhood /ˈfɑːðəhʊd/ *noun* [U] the state of being a father □ *(keadaan sebagai) bapa*

[C] **countable**, a noun with a plural form: *one book, two books*   [U] **uncountable**, a noun with no plural form: *some sugar*

father-in-law noun [C] (pl **fathers-in-law**) the father of your husband or wife □ *bapa mentua*

fatherly /ˈfɑːðəli/ adj like or typical of a father □ *kebapaan; spt seorang bapa*: Would you like a piece of fatherly advice?

Father's Day noun [C] a day when fathers receive cards and gifts from their children, usually the third Sunday in June □ *Hari Bapa*

fathom /ˈfæðəm/ verb [T] [usually in the negative] to understand sth □ *memahami*: I can't fathom what he means.

fatigue /fəˈtiːɡ/ noun [U] 1 the feeling of being extremely tired □ *keletihan*: He was suffering from mental and physical fatigue. **SYN** **exhaustion** 2 weakness in metals caused by a lot of use □ *kelesuan*: The plane crash was caused by metal fatigue in a wing.

fatten /ˈfætn/ verb [T] **fatten sb/sth (up)** to make sb/sth fatter □ *menggemukkan*: He's fattening the pigs up for market.

fattening /ˈfætnɪŋ/ adj (used about food) that makes people fat □ *(yg) menggemukkan*: Chocolate is very fattening.

fatty /ˈfæti/ adj (**fattier; fattiest**) (used about food) having a lot of fat in or on it □ *berlemak*

faucet /ˈfɔːsɪt/ (AmE) = **tap²**(1)

fault¹ /fɔːlt/ noun [C] 1 something wrong or not perfect in sb's character or in a thing □ *kelemahan; kekurangan; kecacatan; kerosakan; kesilapan*: One of my faults is that I'm always late. ⊃ note at **mistake 2** 2 [U] responsibility for a mistake □ *kesalahan*: It will be your own fault if you don't pass your exams. ♦ It wasn't my fault!
IDM **be at fault** to be wrong or responsible for a mistake □ *bersalah*: The other driver was at fault—he didn't stop at the traffic lights.
find fault (with sb/sth) ⊃ **find¹**

fault² /fɔːlt/ verb [T] to find sth wrong with sb/sth □ *mencari kesalahan*: It was impossible to fault her English.

faultless /ˈfɔːltləs/ adj without any mistakes □ *tdk ada cacat celanya; sangat baik*: The pianist gave a faultless performance. **SYN** **perfect**

faulty /ˈfɔːlti/ adj (used especially about electricity or machinery) not working properly □ *rosak*: a faulty switch ♦ faulty goods

fauna /ˈfɔːnə/ noun [U] all the animals of an area or a period of time □ *fauna; haiwan*: the flora and fauna of South America ⊃ look at **flora**

faux pas /ˌfəʊ ˈpɑː/ noun [C] (pl **faux pas** /ˌfəʊ ˈpɑːz/) something you say or do that is embarrassing or offends people □ *sst yg memalukan atau menyinggung*: to make a faux pas

favorite (AmE) = **favourite**

favoritism (AmE) = **favouritism**

favour¹ (AmE **favor**) /ˈfeɪvə(r)/ noun 1 something that helps sb □ *pertolongan; tolong*: Would you do me a favour and post this letter for me? ♦ Could I ask you a favour? ♦ Are they paying you for the work, or are you doing it as a favour? 2 [U] **favour (with sb)** liking or approval □ *(perihal) disukai*: I'm afraid I'm out of favour with my neighbour since our last argument. ♦ The new boss's methods didn't find favour with the staff.
IDM **in favour of sb/sth** in agreement with □ *menyokong*: Are you in favour of private education?
in sb's favour to the advantage of sb □ *memihak kpd/memanfaati sso*: The committee decided in their favour.

favour² (AmE **favor**) /ˈfeɪvə(r)/ verb [T] 1 to support sb/sth; to prefer □ *sokong; suka; pilih*: Which suggestion do you favour? 2 to treat one person very well and so be unfair to others □ *lebih menyukai/menyayangi*: Parents must try not to favour one of their children.

favourable (AmE **favorable**) /ˈfeɪvərəbl/ adj 1 showing liking or approval □ *baik; menyenangkan*: He made a favourable impression on the interviewers. 2 (often used about the weather) suitable or helpful □ *baik; sesuai*: Conditions are favourable for skiing today. **OPP** for both meanings **unfavourable** ▶ **favourably** (AmE **favorably**) /-əbli/ adv

favourite¹ (AmE **favorite**) /ˈfeɪvərɪt/ adj liked more than any other □ *paling disukai/digemari*: What is your favourite colour? ♦ Who is your favourite singer?

favourite² (AmE **favorite**) /ˈfeɪvərɪt/ noun [C] 1 a person or thing that you like more than any others □ *kesukaan; kesayangan*: The other kids were jealous of Rose because she was the teacher's favourite. 2 **favourite (for sth/to do sth)** the horse, team, person, etc. that is expected to win □ *pilihan ramai (yg dijangka menang)*: Mimms is the hot favourite for the leadership of the party. **OPP** **outsider** 3 favorite = **bookmark**

favouritism (AmE **favoritism**) /ˈfeɪvərɪtɪzəm/ noun [U] giving unfair advantages to the person or people that you like best □ *pilih kasih*: The referee was accused of showing favouritism to the home side.

fawn¹ /fɔːn/ adj, noun [U] (of) a light yellowish-brown colour □ *warna perang kekuning-kuningan*

fawn² /fɔːn/ noun [C] a young **deer** (= a large wild animal that eats grass) □ *anak rusa* ⊃ note at **deer** ⊃ picture at **deer**

fax¹ /fæks/ noun 1 [C,U] a copy of a letter, etc. that you can send by telephone lines using a special machine □ *faks*: They need an answer today so I'll send a fax. ♦ The company contacted us by fax. 2 [C] (also **fax machine**) the machine that you use for sending faxes □ *mesin faks*: Have you got a fax? ♦ What's your fax number?

fax² /fæks/ verb [T] **fax sth (to sb); fax sb (sth)** to send sb a fax □ *menghantar dgn faks*: We will

faze /feɪz/ *verb* [T] (*informal*) to make sb worried or nervous □ *menggelabah*: *He doesn't get fazed by things going wrong.*

FBI /ˌef biː ˈaɪ/ *abbr* (*AmE*) **Federal Bureau of Investigation**; a section of the US government which deals with crimes that affect more than one state of the US, such as **terrorism** (= violent acts for political purposes) □ *FBI (Biro Siasatan Persekutuan)*

FC /ˌef ˈsiː/ *abbr* (*BrE*) **Football Club** □ *FC (Kelab Bola Sepak)*: *Everton FC*

FCO /ˌef siː ˈəʊ/ *abbr* = **Foreign and Commonwealth Office** □ *FCO (Pejabat Luar Negeri dan Komanwel)*

FE /ˌef ˈiː/ *abbr* = **further education**

fear¹ /fɪə(r)/ *noun* [C,U] the feeling that you have when sth dangerous, painful or frightening might happen □ *ketakutan; rasa takut; kebimbangan*: *He was shaking with fear after the accident.* ◆ *People in this area live in constant fear of crime.* ◆ *She showed no fear.* ◆ *This book helped me overcome my fear of dogs.* ◆ *My fears for his safety were unnecessary.*

IDM **no fear** (*spoken*) (used when answering a suggestion) certainly not □ *tentu tdk*

fear² /fɪə(r)/ *verb* [T] **1** to be afraid of sb/sth or of doing sth □ *takut; gentar*: *We all fear illness and death.* **2** to feel that sth bad might happen or might have happened □ *bimbang; khuatir; dikhuatiri*: *The government fears that it will lose the next election.* ◆ *Thousands of people are feared dead in the earthquake.*

PHR V **fear for sb/sth** to be worried about sb/sth □ *bimbang akan*: *Parents often fear for the safety of their children.*

fearful /ˈfɪəfl/ *adj* (*formal*) **1** fearful (of sth/doing sth); fearful that … afraid or worried about sth □ *takut; bimbang*: *You should never be fearful of starting something new.* ◆ *They were fearful that they would miss the plane.* ◆ Much more common words are **frightened**, **scared** and **afraid**. **2** [only before a noun] terrible □ *teruk; menggerunkan; dahsyat*: *the fearful consequences of war* ▸ **fearfully** /-fəli/ *adv* ▸ **fearfulness** *noun* [U]

fearless /ˈfɪələs/ *adj* never afraid □ *tdk mengenal takut; berani* ▸ **fearlessly** *adv* ▸ **fearlessness** *noun* [U]

feasible /ˈfiːzəbl/ *adj* possible to do □ *boleh laksana*: *a feasible plan* ▸ **feasibility** /ˌfiːzəˈbɪləti/ *noun* [U]

feast /fiːst/ *noun* [C] a large, special meal, especially to celebrate sth □ *kenduri; jamuan* ▸ **feast** *verb* [I] **feast (on sth)**: *They feasted on exotic dishes.*

feat /fiːt/ *noun* [C] something you do that shows great strength, skill or courage □ *perbuatan yg mengagumkan (kerana sukar dilakukan, dsb)*: *That new bridge is a remarkable feat of engineering.* ◆ *Persuading Helen to give you a pay rise was no mean feat* (= difficult to do).

feather /ˈfeðə(r)/ *noun* [C] one of the light, soft things that grow in a bird's skin and cover its body □ *bulu burung; bulu pelepah* ⇨ picture on **page P12**

feature¹ /ˈfiːtʃə(r)/ *noun* [C] **1** an important or noticeable part of sth □ *ciri; sifat*: *Mountains and lakes are the main features of the landscape of Wales.* ◆ *Noise is a feature of city life.* **2** a part of the face □ *bahagian muka*: *Her eyes are her best feature.* **3** **a feature (on sth)** a special article or programme about sth in a newspaper, on TV, etc. □ *rencana*: *There's a feature on kangaroos in this magazine.* **4** (*old-fashioned*) (also **feature film**) a long film that tells a story □ *filem cetera*

feature² /ˈfiːtʃə(r)/ *verb* **1** [T] to include sb/sth as an important part □ *memaparkan; menonjolkan*: *The film features many well-known actors.* **2** [I] **feature in sth** to have a part in sth □ *merupakan sebahagian drpd*: *Does marriage feature in your future plans?* **SYN** **figure**

featureless /ˈfiːtʃələs/ *adj* without any qualities or noticeable characteristics □ *tanpa ciri atau sifat yg jelas*: *a dull, featureless landscape*

Feb. *abbr* = **February** □ *Februari*: *18 Feb. 2012*

February /ˈfebruəri/ *noun* [U,C] (*abbr* **Feb.**) the 2nd month of the year, coming after January □ *Februari* ⇨ note at **January**

feces (*AmE*) = **faeces**

fed past tense, past participle of **feed¹**

federal /ˈfedərəl/ *adj* **1** organized as a **federation** □ *(berbentuk) persekutuan*: *a federal system of rule* **2** connected with the central government of a **federation** □ *(berkaitan dgn) persekutuan*: *That is a federal not a state law.*

federation /ˌfedəˈreɪʃn/ *noun* [C] a group of states, etc. that have joined together to form a single group □ *persekutuan*

fed ˈup *adj* [not before a noun] (*informal*) **fed up (with/of sb/sth/doing sth)** bored or unhappy; tired of sth □ *bosan*: *What's the matter? You look really fed up.* ◆ *I'm fed up with waiting for the phone to ring.*

fee /fiː/ *noun* [C] **1** [usually plural] the money you pay for professional advice or service from private doctors, lawyers, schools, universities, etc. □ *bayaran; yuran*: *We can't afford private school fees.* ◆ *Does the bank charge a fee?* **2** the cost of an exam, the cost of becoming a member of a club, the amount you pay to go into certain buildings, etc. □ *yuran*: *How much is the entrance fee?* ⇨ note at **pay²**

feeble /ˈfiːbl/ *adj* (**feebler; feeblest**) **1** with no energy or power; weak □ *lemah; tdk berdaya*: *a feeble old man* ◆ *a feeble cry* **2** not able to make sb believe sth □ *lemah*: *a feeble argument/excuse* ▸ **feebly** /ˈfiːbli/ *adv*

feed¹ /fiːd/ *verb* (*pt, pp* **fed** /fed/) **1** [T] **feed sb/sth (on) (sth)** to give food to a person or an

feed → fell

animal □ *memberi makan*: *Don't forget to feed the cat.* ◆ *I can't come yet. I haven't fed the baby.* ◆ *Some of the snakes in the zoo are fed (on) rats.* **2** [I] **feed (on sth)** (used about animals or babies) to eat □ *makan*: *What do horses feed on in the winter?* ◆ *Bats feed at night.* **3** [T] **feed A (with B); feed B into/to/through A** to supply sb/sth with sth; to put sth into sth else □ *membekalkan; memasukkan; menyuapkan*: *This channel feeds us with news and information 24 hours a day.* ◆ *Metal sheets are fed through the machine one at a time.*

feed² /fiːd/ noun **1** [C] a meal for an animal or a baby □ *waktu makan*: *When's the baby's next feed due?* **2** [U] food for animals □ *makanan (utk binatang)*: *cattle feed*

feedback /ˈfiːdbæk/ noun [U] information or comments about sth that sb has done which tells them how good or bad it is □ *maklum balas*: *The teacher spent five minutes with each of us to give us feedback on our homework.* ◆ *We like to get feedback from our customers.*

feel¹ /fiːl/ verb (pt, pp **felt** /felt/) **1** [I] (usually with an adjective) to be in the state that is mentioned □ *berasa; rasa*: *to feel cold/sick/tired/happy* ◆ *How are you feeling today?* ◆ *You'll feel better in the morning.* **2** [T] to notice or experience sth physical or emotional □ *rasa; terasa; merasa; merasakan*: *It was so cold that she could not feel her toes.* ◆ *I felt something crawling up my back.* ◆ *I don't feel any sympathy for Matt at all.* ◆ *You could feel the tension in the courtroom.* **3** [I] used to say how sth seems to you when you touch, see, smell, experience, etc. it □ *berasa; rasa; terasa*: *My new coat feels like leather but it's not.* ◆ *He felt as if he had been there before.* ◆ *My head feels as though it will burst.* ◆ *I felt (that) it was a mistake not to ask her advice.*

> **MORE** 'It' is often used as the subject of **feel** in this sense: *It feels as if it is going to snow soon.*

4 [T] to touch sth in order to find out what it is like □ *merasa; rasa*: *Feel this material. Is it cotton or silk?* ◆ *I felt her forehead to see if she had got a temperature.* **5** [T] to be affected by sth □ *rasa; berasa*: *Do you feel the cold in winter?* ◆ *She felt it badly when her mother died.* **6** [I] **feel (about) (for sb/sth)** to try to find sth with your hands instead of your eyes □ *meraba-raba*: *She felt about in the dark for the light switch.*

IDM **be/feel like jelly** ⊃ **jelly**
be/feel out of it ⊃ **out of**
be/feel sorry for sb ⊃ **sorry¹**
feel free (to do sth) (*informal*) used to tell sb they are allowed to do sth □ *silakanlah; jangan malu-malu utk*: *Feel free to use the phone.*
feel like sth/doing sth to want sth or to want to do sth □ *rasa hendak sst/membuat sst*: *Do you feel like going out?*
feel your age to realize that you are getting old, especially compared to other younger people around you □ *berasa diri sso tua*

have/feel a lump in your throat ⊃ **lump¹**
not feel yourself to not feel healthy or well □ *rasa lain; rasa tdk sihat*
PHR V **feel for sb** to understand sb's feelings and situation and feel sorry for them □ *bersimpati dgn sso*: *I really felt for him when his wife died.*
feel up to sth/to doing sth to have the strength and the energy to do or deal with sth □ *terdaya utk/hendak membuat sst*: *I really don't feel up to eating a huge meal.*

feel² /fiːl/ noun [sing] **1** an act of touching sth in order to learn about it □ *rasa; (perbuatan) menyentuh*: *Let me have a feel of that material.* **2** the impression sth gives you when you touch it; the impression that a place or situation gives you □ *rasa; suasana*: *You can tell it's wool by the feel.* ◆ *The town has a friendly feel.*

feeler /ˈfiːlə(r)/ noun [C, usually pl] either of the two thin parts on the heads of some insects and of some animals that live in shells that they use to feel and touch things with □ *sesungut* **SYN** **antenna**
IDM **put out feelers** (*informal*) to try to find out what people think about sth before you do it □ *merisik-risik*

feeling /ˈfiːlɪŋ/ noun **1** [C] **a feeling (of sth)** something that you feel in your mind or body □ *rasa; perasaan*: *a feeling of hunger/happiness/fear/helplessness* ◆ *I've got a funny feeling in my leg.* **2** [sing] a belief or idea that sth is true or is likely to happen □ *rasa*: *I get the feeling that Ian doesn't like me much.* ◆ *I have a nasty feeling that Jan didn't get our message.* **3** [C,U] **feeling(s) (about/on sth)** an attitude or opinion about sth □ *pendapat*: *What are your feelings on this matter?* ◆ *My own feeling is that we should postpone the meeting.* ◆ *Public feeling seems to be against the new road.* **4** [U,C, usually pl] strong emotion; sb's emotions □ *perasaan; (dgn penuh) perasaan*: *Let's practise that song again, this time with feeling.* ◆ *I have to tell Jeff his work's not good enough but I don't want to hurt his feelings.* **5** [C,U] **(a) feeling/feelings (for sb/sth)** love or understanding for sb/sth □ *rasa kasih terhadap sso; kebolehan memahami/menghayati sst*: *She doesn't have much (of a) feeling for music.* ◆ *He still has feelings for his ex-wife.* **6** [U] the ability to feel in your body □ *deria rasa*: *After the accident he lost all feeling in his legs.*
IDM **bad/ill feeling** unhappy relations between people □ *rasa tdk senang; sakit hati*: *The decision caused a lot of bad feeling at the factory.*
no hard feelings ⊃ **hard¹**

feet plural of **foot¹**

feisty /ˈfaɪsti/ adj (**feistier**; **feistiest**) (*informal*) (used about people) strong, determined and not afraid to argue □ *bertenaga; bersemangat; kuat; girang*

feline /ˈfiːlaɪn/ adj connected with an animal of the cat family; like a cat □ *(berkenaan dgn binatang) keluarga kucing; seperti kucing*

fell¹ past tense of **fall¹**

fell² /fel/ verb [T] to cut down a tree □ *menebang*

fellow¹ /'feləʊ/ noun [C] **1** (old-fashioned) a man □ *orang lelaki*: What's that fellow over there doing? **2** a person who is paid to study a particular thing at a university □ *fellow (universiti)*: Lisa Jones is a research fellow in the biology department. **3** a member of an academic or professional organization, or of certain universities □ *fellow (badan profesional)*: a fellow of New College, Oxford

fellow² /'feləʊ/ adj [only before a noun] another or others like yourself in the same situation □ *rakan*: Her fellow students were all older than her. ♦ fellow workers/passengers/citizens

fellowship /'feləʊʃɪp/ noun **1** [U] a feeling of friendship between people who share an interest □ *rasa persahabatan* **2** [C] a group or society of people who share the same interest or belief □ *perkumpulan* **3** [C] the position of a college or university fellow □ *jawatan 'fellow' di kolej/universiti*

felon /'felən/ noun [C] (especially AmE) a person who has committed a **felony** □ *penjenayah besar*

felony /'feləni/ noun [C,U] (pl felonies) (especially AmE) the act of committing a serious crime, such as murder; a crime of this type □ *jenayah; feloni* ➜ look at **misdemeanour**

felt¹ past tense, past participle of **feel¹**

felt² /felt/ noun [U] a type of soft cloth made from wool, etc. which has been pressed tightly together □ *sakhlat*: a felt hat

felt-tip 'pen (also **felt 'tip**) noun [C] a type of pen with a point made of felt □ *pena mata sakhlat* ➜ picture at **stationery**

female¹ /'fi:meɪl/ adj **1** being a woman or a girl □ *wanita; perempuan*: a female artist/employer/student ➜ look at **feminine 2** being of the sex that can produce eggs or give birth to babies □ *betina*: a female cat **3** (used about plants and flowers) that can produce fruit □ *betina* OPP for all meanings **male**

female² /'fi:meɪl/ noun [C] **1** an animal that can produce eggs or give birth to babies; a plant that can produce fruit □ *betina*: Is your mouse a male or a female? **2** a woman or a girl □ *wanita; perempuan*: More females than males become teachers. ➜ look at **male**

feminine /'femənɪn/ adj **1** typical of or looking like a woman; connected with women □ *(berkenaan dgn) wanita; spt wanita/perempuan*: My daughter always dresses like a boy. She hates looking feminine. ➜ note at **masculine** ➜ look at **female 2** (in English) of the forms of words used to describe females □ *feminin*: 'Lioness' is the feminine form of 'lion'. **3** (in the grammar of some languages) belonging to a certain class of nouns, adjectives or pronouns □ *feminin*: The German word for a flower is feminine. ➜ look at **masculine, neuter** ▶**femininity** /ˌfemə'nɪnəti/ noun [U]

321

fell → ferment

feminism /'femənɪzəm/ noun [U] the belief that women should have the same rights and opportunities as men □ *feminisme* ▶**feminist** /-ɪst/ noun [C], adj

gate

fence   wall

fence¹ /fens/ noun [C] a line of wooden or metal posts joined by wood, wire, metal, etc. to divide land or to keep animals in, or to keep people and animals out □ *pagar*

IDM sit on the fence ➜ **sit** ➜ picture on page P11

fence² /fens/ verb **1** [T] to surround land with a fence □ *memagar* **2** [I] to fight with a **foil** (= a long thin pointed weapon) as a sport □ *bermain pedang*

PHR V fence sth/sb in **1** to surround sth with a fence □ *memagari*: They fenced in their garden to make it more private. **2** to limit sb's freedom □ *dikurung; terikat; menyekat; tersekat*: She felt fenced in by so many responsibilities.

fence sth off to separate one area from another with a fence □ *memagari sst*

fencing /'fensɪŋ/ noun [U] the sport of fighting with **foils** (= long thin pointed weapons) □ *sukan pedang* ➜ picture on **page P5**

fend /fend/ verb

PHR V fend for yourself to look after yourself without help from anyone else □ *menjaga diri sendiri*: It's time Ben left home and learnt to fend for himself.

fend sb/sth off to defend yourself from sb/sth that is attacking you □ *menangkis sst; menangkis (serangan, kecaman, dsb) sso*: Politicians usually manage to fend off awkward questions.

fender /'fendə(r)/ noun [C] **1** (AmE) = **wing**(4) **2** a low metal frame in front of an open fire that stops coal or wood falling out □ *pengadang (api)*

feng shui /ˌfeŋ 'ʃu:i; ˌfʊŋ 'ʃweɪ/ noun [U] a Chinese system for deciding the right position for a building and for placing objects inside a building in order to make people feel comfortable and happy □ *feng syui*

fennel /'fenl/ noun [U] a vegetable that has a thick round part at the base of the leaves with a strong taste. The seeds and leaves are also used in cooking. □ *adas; fenel; jintan manis*

ferment¹ /fə'ment/ verb [I,T] to change or make the chemistry of sth change, especially sugar changing to alcohol □ *menapai; meragi*: The wine is starting to ferment. ▶**fermentation** /ˌfɜ:men'teɪʃn/ noun [U]

VOWELS   i: see   i any   ɪ sit   e ten   æ hat   ɑ: father   ɒ got   ɔ: saw   ʊ put   u: too   u usual

ferment² /ˈfɜːment/ noun [U] a state of political or social excitement and change □ *(dlm) keadaan bergolak; kekecohan*: *The country is in ferment and nobody's sure what will happen next.*

fern /fɜːn/ noun [C] a green plant with no flowers and a lot of long thin leaves □ *paku pakis*

ferocious /fəˈrəʊʃəs/ adj very aggressive and violent □ *ganas; bengis*: *a ferocious beast/attack/storm/war* ▶**ferociously** adv

ferocity /fəˈrɒsəti/ noun [U] violence; cruel and aggressive behaviour □ *keganasan; kebengisan* ⊃ adjective **fierce**

ferret¹ /ˈferɪt/ noun [C] a small animal with a long thin body, kept as a pet or for hunting other animals □ *feret; sejenis haiwan kecil*

ferret² /ˈferɪt/ verb [I] (*informal*) **ferret (about/around) (for sth)** to search for sth that is lost or hidden among a lot of things □ *mencari-cari; menggeledah*: *She opened the drawer and ferreted around for her keys.*
PHR V **ferret sb/sth out** (*informal*) to discover information or to find sb/sth by searching thoroughly, asking a lot of questions, etc. □ *mencungkil; mengorek*

ferry¹ /ˈferi/ noun [C] (pl **ferries**) a boat that carries people, vehicles or goods across a river or across a narrow part of the sea □ *feri*: *a car ferry* ⊃ note at **boat** ⊃ picture on **page P6**

ferry² /ˈferi/ verb [T] (**ferrying**; **ferries**; pt, pp **ferried**) to carry people or goods in a boat or other vehicle from one place to another, usually for a short distance □ *membawa; mengangkut*: *Could you ferry us across to the island?* ♦ *We share the job of ferrying the children to school.*

fertile /ˈfɜːtaɪl/ adj 1 (used about land or soil) that plants grow well in □ *subur* **OPP** **infertile** 2 (used about people, animals or plants) that can produce babies, fruit or new plants □ *subur; mudah membiak* **OPP** **infertile** ⊃ look at **sterile** 3 (used about sb's mind) full of ideas □ *subur; berdaya cipta*: *She has a fertile imagination.* ▶**fertility** /fəˈtɪləti/ noun [U]: *Nowadays women can take drugs to increase their fertility (= their chances of having a child).* **OPP** **infertility**

fertilize (also **-ise**) /ˈfɜːtəlaɪz/ verb [T] 1 (*technical*) to put a male seed into an egg, a plant or a female animal so that a baby, fruit or a young animal starts to develop □ *mensenyawakan* 2 to put natural or artificial substances on soil in order to make plants grow better □ *menyuburkan; membajai* ▶**fertilization** (also **-isation**) /ˌfɜːtəlaɪˈzeɪʃn/ noun [U]

fertilizer (also **-iser**) /ˈfɜːtəlaɪzə(r)/ noun [C,U] a natural or chemical substance that is put on land or soil to make plants grow better □ *baja* ⊃ look at **manure**

fervent /ˈfɜːvənt/ adj having or showing very strong feelings about sth □ *bersungguh-sungguh; bersemangat; (yg) membara; penuh ghairah*: *She's a fervent believer in women's rights.* ♦ *a fervent belief/hope/desire* ▶**fervently** adv

fervour (*AmE* **fervor**) /ˈfɜːvə(r)/ noun [U] very strong feelings about sth □ *keghairahan; semangat* **SYN** enthusiasm

fester /ˈfestə(r)/ verb [I] 1 (used about a cut or an injury) to become infected □ *bernanah; menanah*: *a festering sore/wound* 2 (used about an unpleasant situation, feeling or thought) to become more unpleasant because you do not deal with it successfully □ *membarah; melarat*

festival /ˈfestɪvl/ noun [C] 1 a series of plays, films, musical performances, etc. often held regularly in one place □ *pesta*: *the Cannes Film Festival* ♦ *a jazz festival* 2 a day or time when people celebrate sth (especially a religious event) □ *perayaan*: *Christmas is an important Christian festival.*

festive /ˈfestɪv/ adj happy, because people are enjoying themselves celebrating sth □ *suasana perayaan/berpesta; meriah*: *the festive season (= Christmas)*

festivity /feˈstɪvəti/ noun (pl **festivities**) 1 [pl] happy events when people celebrate sth □ *pesta; temasya*: *The festivities went on until dawn.* 2 [U] being happy and celebrating sth □ *keraian; keramaian*: *The wedding was followed by three days of festivity.*

fetch /fetʃ/ verb [T] 1 (*especially BrE*) to go to a place and bring back sb/sth □ *mengambil; menjemput*: *Shall I fetch you your coat?* ⊃ picture at **bring** 2 (used about goods) to be sold for the price mentioned □ *dijual (dgn harga)*: *'How much will your car fetch?' 'It should fetch about £2 000.'*

fete (also **fête**) /feɪt/ noun [C] (*BrE*) an outdoor event with competitions, entertainment and things to buy, often organized to make money for a particular purpose □ *pesta ria*: *the school/village/church fete*

fetus (*AmE*) = **foetus**

feud /fjuːd/ noun [C] **a feud (between A and B)**; **a feud (with sb) (over sb/sth)** an angry and serious argument between two people or groups that continues over a long period of time □ *permusuhan; persengketaan*: *a family feud (= within a family or between two families)* ▶**feud** verb [I]

feudal /ˈfjuːdl/ adj connected with the system of **feudalism** □ *feudal*: *the feudal system*

feudalism /ˈfjuːdəlɪzəm/ noun [U] the social system which existed in the Middle Ages in Europe, in which people worked and fought for a person who owned land and received land and protection from them in return □ *sistem feudal; feudalisme*

fever /ˈfiːvə(r)/ noun 1 [C,U] a condition of the body when it is too hot because of illness □ *demam*: *He has a high fever.* ⊃ note at **ill** ⊃ look at **temperature** 2 [sing] **a fever (of sth)** a state of nervous excitement □ *keadaan gelisah dan teruja*: *a fever of impatience*

feverish /ˈfiːvərɪʃ/ adj **1** suffering from or caused by a fever □ *demam*: *a feverish cold/dream* **2** showing great excitement □ *dlm keadaan tdk sabar-sabar/sangat teruja* ▶**feverishly** adv

few /fjuː/ determiner (**fewer**; **fewest**) adj, pron [used with a plural countable noun and a plural verb] **1** not many □ *tdk banyak*: *Few people live to be 100.* ♦ *There are fewer cars here today than yesterday.* ♦ *Few of the players played really well.* **2 a few** a small number of; some □ *beberapa*: *a few people* ♦ *a few hours/days/years* ♦ *I'll meet you later. I've got a few things to do first.* ♦ *I knew a few of the people there.* ➔ note at **less**

IDM **few and far between** not happening very often; not common □ *jarang-jarang; tdk banyak*: *Pubs are a bit few and far between in this area.*

a good few; quite a few a fairly large amount or number □ *agak banyak; banyak juga*: *It's been a good few years since I saw him last.*

fiancé (fem **fiancée**) /fiˈɒnseɪ/ noun [C] a person who has promised to marry sb □ *tunang*: *This is my fiancée Liz. We got engaged a few weeks ago.*

fiasco /fiˈæskəʊ/ noun [C] (pl **fiascos**, AmE also **fiascoes**) an event that does not succeed, often in a way that causes embarrassment □ *kegagalan; gagal sama sekali*: *Our last party was a complete fiasco.* **SYN** **disaster**

fib /fɪb/ noun [C] (informal) something you say that is not true □ *bohong*: *Please don't tell fibs.* **SYN** **lie** ▶**fib** verb [I] (**fibbing**; **fibbed**) **HELP** Fib is used when the lie does not seem very important.

fibre (AmE **fiber**) /ˈfaɪbə(r)/ noun **1** [U] parts of plants that you eat which are good for you because they help to move food quickly through your body □ *serat; serabut*: *Wholemeal bread is high in fibre.* **2** [C,U] a material or a substance that is made from natural or artificial threads □ *serat; gentian*

MORE **Natural** fibres are, for example, cotton and wool. **Man-made** or **synthetic** fibres are **nylon**, **polyester**, etc.

3 [C] one of the thin threads which form a natural or artificial substance □ *serat*: *cotton/wood/nerve/muscle fibres*

fibreglass (AmE **fiberglass**) /ˈfaɪbəɡlɑːs/ (also **glass ˈfibre**) noun [U] a material made from small threads of plastic or glass, used for making small boats, parts of cars, etc. □ *kaca gentian*

fickle /ˈfɪkl/ adj always changing your mind or your feelings so you cannot be trusted □ *kerap berubah; tdk tetap*: *a fickle friend*

fiction /ˈfɪkʃn/ noun [U] stories, novels, etc. which describe events and people that are not real □ *fiksyen; cereka*: *I don't read much fiction.* **OPP** **non-fiction** ➔ note at **literature** ➔ look at **fact**

fictional /ˈfɪkʃənl/ adj not real or true; only existing in stories, novels, etc. □ *(bersifat) fiksyen/cereka*: *fictional characters* ➔ look at **factual**

323 **feverish → field**

fictitious /fɪkˈtɪʃəs/ adj invented; not real □ *rekaan; palsu*: *The novel is set in a fictitious town called Eden.*

fiddle¹ /ˈfɪdl/ verb **1** [I] **fiddle (about/around) (with sth)** to play with sth carelessly, because you are nervous or not thinking □ *bermain-main sst kerana tdk tenang*: *Tristram sat nervously, fiddling with a pencil.* **2** [T] (informal) to change the details or facts of sth (business accounts, etc.) in order to get money dishonestly □ *memalsukan*: *She fiddled her expenses form.*

fiddle² /ˈfɪdl/ noun [C] (informal) **1** = **violin 2** (BrE) a dishonest action, especially one connected with money □ *penipuan; perlakuan tdk jujur*: *a tax fiddle*

fiddler /ˈfɪdlə(r)/ noun [C] a person who plays the **violin** (= a musical instrument with strings), especially to play **folk**, **music** (= traditional music) □ *penggesek; pemain biola*

fiddly /ˈfɪdli/ adj (**fiddlier**; **fiddliest**) (informal) difficult to do or manage with your hands (because small or complicated parts are involved) □ *renyah*

fidelity /fɪˈdeləti/ noun [U] **1** (formal) **fidelity (to sb/sth)** the quality of being faithful, especially to a wife or husband by not having a sexual relationship with anyone else □ *kesetiaan* ➔ A less formal word is **faithfulness**. **OPP** **infidelity** **2** the quality of being accurate or close to the original □ *ketepatan*: *the fidelity of the translation to the original text* ➔ look at **hi-fi**

fidget /ˈfɪdʒɪt/ verb [I] **fidget (with sth)** to keep moving your body, hands or feet because you are nervous, bored, excited, etc. □ *meresah; memain-mainkan*: *She fidgeted nervously with her keys.* ▶**fidgety** adj

field¹ /fiːld/ noun [C] **1** an area of land on a farm, usually surrounded by fences or walls, used for growing crops or keeping animals in □ *ladang; padang* ➔ picture on page P11 **2** an area of land used for sports, games or some other activity □ *padang; medan*: *a football field* ♦ *an airfield* (= where planes land and take off) ♦ *a battlefield* ➔ look at **pitch 3** an area of land where oil, coal or other minerals are found □ *medan*: *a North Sea oilfield* ♦ *a coalfield* **4** an area of study or knowledge □ *bidang; lapangan*: *He's an expert in the field of economics.* ♦ *That question is outside my field* (= not one of the subjects that I know about). **5** an area affected by or included in sth □ *medan; julat*: *a magnetic field* ♦ *It's outside my field of vision* (= I can't see it).

field² /fiːld/ verb **1** [T] to choose a team for games such as football, **cricket**, etc. □ *menurunkan*: *New Zealand is fielding an excellent team for the next match.* **2** [I,T] (in sports such as **cricket**, **baseball**, etc.) to (be ready to) catch and throw back the ball after sb has hit it □ *menjadi pemadang*

[C] **countable**, a noun with a plural form: *one book, two books* [U] **uncountable**, a noun with no plural form: *some sugar*

field day → figure 324

> **MORE** When one team is **fielding**, the other is **batting**.

'field day noun
IDM **have a field day** to get the opportunity to do sth you enjoy, especially sth other people do not approve of □ *seronok betul; beraya*: *The newspapers always have a field day when there's a political scandal.*

fielder /'fi:ldə(r)/ noun [C] (in sports such as **cricket** and **baseball**) a player who is trying to catch the ball rather than hit it □ *pemadang*

'field event noun [C] a sport, such as jumping and throwing, that is not a race and does not involve running □ *acara padang* ⊃ look at **track event**

'field hockey (*AmE*) = **hockey**(1)

'field trip noun [C] a journey made to study sth in its natural environment □ *lawatan lapangan*: *We went on a geography field trip.*

fieldwork /'fi:ldwɜːk/ noun [U] practical research work done outside school, college, etc. □ *kerja lapangan/luar*

fiend /fi:nd/ noun [C] 1 a very cruel person □ *setan; orang yg kejam/jahat* 2 (*informal*) a person who is very interested in one particular thing □ *orang yg sangat sukakan sst; gila (menjaga kesihatan, dll)*: *My dad's a real crossword fiend.*

fiendish /'fi:ndɪʃ/ adj 1 very unpleasant or cruel □ *spt setan; kejam* 2 (*informal*) clever and complicated □ *sangat bijak/licik*: *a fiendish plan* ▶**fiendishly** adv

fierce /fɪəs/ adj (**fiercer**; **fiercest**) 1 angry, aggressive and frightening □ *garang*: *The house was guarded by fierce dogs.* 2 very strong; violent □ *hebat; sengit; ganas*: *fierce competition for jobs* ♦ *a fierce attack* ⊃ noun **ferocity** ▶**fiercely** adv

fiery /'faɪəri/ adj (**fierier**; **fieriest**) 1 looking like fire □ *spt api; merah menyala*: *She has fiery red hair.* 2 quick to become angry □ *panas baran*: *a fiery temper* **SYN** **passionate**

fifteen /ˌfɪf'tiːn/ number 15 □ *lima belas; 15* ⊃ note at **six** ▶**fifteenth** /ˌfɪf'tiːnθ/ ordinal number, noun [C] □ *kelima belas; ke-15* ⊃ note at **sixth**

fifth¹ /fɪfθ/ ordinal number 5th □ *kelima; ke-5* ⊃ note at **sixth**

fifth² /fɪfθ/ noun [C] ⅕; one of five equal parts of sth □ *satu per lima;* ⅕

fifty /'fɪfti/ number 50 □ *lima puluh; 50* ⊃ note at **sixty** ▶**fiftieth** /'fɪftiəθ/ ordinal number, noun [C] □ *kelima puluh; ke-50* ⊃ note at **sixth**

fifty-'fifty adj, adv equal or equally (between two people, groups, etc.) □ *sama banyak; lima puluh lima puluh*: *You've got a fifty-fifty chance of winning.* ♦ *We'll divide the money fifty-fifty.*

fig /fɪg/ noun [C] (a type of tree with) a soft sweet fruit full of seeds that grows in warm countries and is often eaten dried □ *buah ara/tin* ⊃ picture on **page P14**

fig. abbr = **figure**¹(7): *See diagram at fig. 2.*

fight¹ /faɪt/ verb (pt, pp **fought** /fɔːt/) 1 [I,T] **fight (against sb/sth)** to use physical strength, guns, weapons, etc. against sb/sth □ *berperang; menentang; bergaduh; berkelahi*: *My younger brothers were always fighting.* ♦ *They gathered soldiers to fight the invading army.* 2 [I,T] **fight (against sth)** to try very hard to stop or prevent sth □ *berjuang menentang/melawan; berusaha menghapuskan*: *to fight a fire/a decision/prejudice* ♦ *to fight against crime/disease* 3 [I] **fight (for sth/to do sth)** to try very hard to get or keep sth □ *berjuang (utk mendapatkan/mempertahankan sst)*: *to fight for your rights* 4 [I] **fight (with sb) (about/over sth)** to argue □ *bertengkar*: *It's not worth fighting about money.* ⊃ look at **argue**, **quarrel**

PHR V **fight back** to attack sb who has attacked you □ *melawan balik*: *If he hits you again, fight back!*

▶**fighting** noun [U]: *Fighting broke out in the city last night.*

fight² /faɪt/ noun 1 [C] **a fight (with sb/sth); a fight (between A and B)** the act of using physical force against sb/sth □ *pergaduhan; bergaduh*: *Don't get into a fight at school, will you?* ♦ *Fights broke out between rival groups of fans.* 2 [sing] **a fight (against/for sth) (to do sth)** the work done trying to destroy, prevent or achieve sth □ *perjuangan*: *Protesters won their fight against the airport expansion.* 3 [C] (especially *AmE*) **a fight (with sb/sth) (about/over sth)** an argument about sth □ *pertengkaran*: *I had a fight with my mum over what time I had to be home.* 4 [U] the desire to continue trying or fighting □ *keazaman; semangat*: *I've had some bad luck but I've still got plenty of fight in me.*

IDM **pick a fight** ⊃ **pick¹**

fighter /'faɪtə(r)/ noun [C] 1 (also **'fighter plane**) a small fast military aircraft used for attacking enemy aircraft □ *kapal terbang pejuang*: *a fighter pilot* ♦ *a jet fighter* 2 a person who fights in a war or a **boxer** (= sb who fights with their hands in sport) □ *pejuang; peninju*

figurative /'fɪgərətɪv/ adj (used about a word or an expression) not used with its exact meaning but in a way that is different to give a special effect □ *kiasan*: *'He exploded with rage' is a figurative use of the verb 'to explode'.* ⊃ look at **literal**, **metaphor** ▶**figuratively** adv

figure¹ /'fɪgə(r)/ noun
▶NUMBER 1 [C] an amount (in numbers) or a price □ *jumlah; bilangan; angka; harga*: *The unemployment figures are lower this month.* ♦ *What sort of figure are you thinking of for your house?* 2 [C] a written sign for a number (0 to 9) □ *angka*: *Write the numbers in figures, not words.* ♦ *He has a six-figure income/an income in six figures (= £100 000 or more).* ♦ *Interest rates are now down to single figures (= less than 10%).* ♦ *double fig-*

[I] **intransitive**, a verb which has no object: *He laughed.*   [T] **transitive**, a verb which has an object: *He ate an apple.*

ures (= 10 to 99) **3 figures** [pl] (*informal*) mathematics □ *kira-kira*: *I don't have a head for figures* (= I'm not very good with numbers).

▶PERSON **4** [C] an important person □ *tokoh*: *an important political figure* **5** [C] the shape of the human body, especially a woman's body that is attractive □ *potongan badan; susuk tubuh*: *She's got a beautiful slim figure.* ➲ note at **build²** **6** [C] a person that you cannot see very clearly or do not know □ *lembaga; orang*: *Two figures were coming towards us in the dark.* ♦ *There were two figures on the right of the photo that I didn't recognize.*

▶PICTURE **7** [C] (*abbr* **fig.**) a diagram or picture used in a book to explain sth □ *rajah*: *Figure 3 shows the major cities of Peru.*

IDM **a ballpark figure/estimate** ➲ **ballpark** **facts and figures** ➲ **fact** **in round figures/numbers** ➲ **round¹**

figure² /ˈfɪɡə(r)/ *verb* **1** [I] **figure (as sth) (in/among sth)** to be included in sth; to be an important part of sth □ *muncul; disebut; terlibat*: *Women don't figure much in his novels.* **SYN** **feature 2** [T] (*especially AmE*) **figure (that)** to think or decide that sth is true □ *ingat; fikir*: *I figured he was here because I saw his car outside.*

IDM **it/that figures** (*informal*) that is what I expected; that makes sense □ *patut pun*

PHR V **figure on sth/on doing sth** (*especially AmE*) to include sth in your plans □ *bercadang; rancangnya*: *I figure on arriving in New York on Wednesday.*

figure sb/sth out to find an answer to sth or to understand sb □ *faham sso/sst*: *I can't figure out why she married him in the first place.*

figure of ˈeight (*AmE* **figure ˈeight**) *noun* [C] (*pl* **figures of ˈeight**) (*AmE* **figure ˈeights**) something in the shape of the number 8 □ *sst yg berbentuk angka lapan*

figure of ˈspeech *noun* [C] (*pl* **figures of ˈspeech**) a word or expression used in a different way from its usual meaning in order to make a special effect □ *kiasan*

file¹ /faɪl/ *noun* [C] **1** a box or a cover that is used for keeping papers together □ *fail*: *a box file* ➲ picture at **stationery 2** a collection of information that is stored together in a computer, with a particular name □ *fail*: *to open/close a file* ♦ *to create/delete/save/copy a file* **3** **a file (on sb/sth)** a collection of papers or information about sb/sth kept inside a file □ *fail*: *The police are now keeping a file on all known football hooligans.* **4** a metal tool with a rough surface used for shaping hard substances or for making surfaces smooth □ *kikir*: *a nail file* ➲ picture at **tool**

IDM **in single file** ➲ **single¹**
on file kept in a file □ *dlm fail*: *We have all the information you need on file.*
the rank and file ➲ **rank¹**

file² /faɪl/ *verb* **1** [T] **file sth (away)** to put and keep documents, etc. in a particular place so that you can find them easily; to put sth into a file □ *memfailkan*: *I filed the letters away in a drawer.*

325   **figure → film**

2 [I] **file in, out, past, etc.** to walk or march in a line □ *berbaris satu per satu*: *The children filed out of the classroom at the end of the lesson.* **3** [T] **file sth (away, down, etc.)** to shape sth hard or make sth smooth with a file □ *mengikir*: *to file your nails*

ˈfile sharing *noun* [U] the practice of sharing computer files with other people over the Internet or another computer network □ *perkongsian fail*: *illegal file sharing of music*

ˈfiling cabinet (*AmE* **ˈfile cabinet**) *noun* [C] a piece of office furniture with deep drawers for storing files □ *kabinet fail*

fill /fɪl/ *verb* **1** [I,T] **fill (sth/sb) (with sth)** to make sth full or to become full □ *mengisi; memenuhi; menjadi penuh*: *Can you fill the kettle for me?* ♦ *The news filled him with excitement.* ♦ *The room filled with smoke within minutes.* **2** [T] to do a job □ *mengisi jawatan*: *I'm afraid that teaching post has just been filled* (= sb has got the job). **3** [T] to use up your time doing sth □ *mengisi masa*: *How do you fill your day now that you're retired?*

PHR V **fill sth in 1** (*AmE* also **fill sth out**) to complete a form, etc. by writing information on it □ *mengisi*: *Could you fill in the application form, please?* **2** to fill a hole or space completely to make a surface flat □ *menampal*: *You had better fill in the cracks in the wall before you paint it.*
fill (sth) up to become or to make sth completely full □ *menjadi penuh*: *The room soon filled up.*

fillet (*AmE* **filet**) /ˈfɪlɪt/ *noun* [C,U] a piece of meat or fish with the bones taken out □ *filet*

filling¹ /ˈfɪlɪŋ/ *noun* **1** [C] the material that a dentist uses to fill a hole in a tooth □ *tampalan*: *a gold filling* ➲ note at **tooth 2** [C,U] the food inside a **sandwich** (= two slices of bread with food between them), cake, **pie** (= a type of baked food), etc. □ *inti* ➲ picture on **page P16**

filling² /ˈfɪlɪŋ/ *adj* (used about food) that makes you feel full □ *mengenyangkan*: *Pasta is very filling.*

film¹ /fɪlm/ *noun*

▶MOVING PICTURES **1** (*AmE* **movie**) [C] a story, play, etc. shown in moving pictures at the cinema or on TV □ *filem; wayang*: *Let's go to the cinema— there's a good film on this week.* ♦ *to watch a film on TV* ♦ *to see a film at the cinema* ♦ *a horror/ documentary/feature film* ♦ *a film director/producer/critic* **2** [U] the art or business of making films □ *perfileman*: *She's studying film and theatre.* ♦ *the film industry* **3** [U] moving pictures of real events □ *filem*: *The programme included film of the town one hundred years ago.*

▶IN CAMERA **4** [C,U] a roll of thin plastic that you use in some types of camera to take photographs □ *filem*: *to have a film developed* ➲ note at **camera**

▶THIN LAYER **5** [C, usually sing] a thin layer of a substance or material □ *lapisan; selaput*: *The oil forms a film on the surface of the water.*

CONSONANTS   p **p**en   b **b**ad   t **t**ea   d **d**id   k **c**at   g **g**ot   tʃ **ch**in   dʒ **J**une   f **f**all   v **v**an   θ **th**in

TOPIC
Films

My favourite **film** is **set** in Rome. It is **based on** a book and it **stars** several famous **actors**. The **dialogue** is in Italian, but there are English **subtitles**. **Critics** gave the film good **reviews** and praised the director (= the person who tells the actors what to do). The person who wrote the **script** won an award for the best **screenplay**. There is a **sequel** coming out next year. I saw the film at the **cinema** but it is also available on **DVD**. You can buy the **soundtrack** (= the music) on CD or as a **download** (= computer file).

film² /fɪlm/ verb [I,T] to record moving pictures of an event, story, etc. with a camera □ *memfilemkan; difilemkan*: They're filming in Oxford today. ◆ The man was filmed stealing from the shop.

'**film star** noun [C] a person who is a famous actor in films □ *bintang filem*

filter¹ /ˈfɪltə(r)/ noun [C] **1** a device for holding back substances from a liquid or gas that passes through it □ *turas; penapis*: a coffee filter ◆ an oil filter **2** a piece of coloured glass used with a camera to hold back some types of light □ *turas; penyaring*

filter² /ˈfɪltə(r)/ verb **1** [T] to pass a liquid through a filter □ *menuras; menapis*: Do you normally filter your water? **2** [I] filter in, out, through, etc. to move slowly and/or in small amounts □ *menembus masuk; beransur-ansur diketahui*: Sunlight filtered into the room through the curtains. ◆ (figurative) News of her illness filtered through to her friends.
PHR V filter sb/sth out (of sth) to remove sth that you do not want from a liquid, light, etc. using a special device or substance □ *menapis atau mengasingkan sso/sst (drpd sst)*: This chemical filters impurities out of the water. ◆ (figurative) This test is designed to filter out weaker candidates before the interview stage.

filth /fɪlθ/ noun [U] **1** unpleasant dirt □ *kotoran*: The room was covered in filth. **2** sexual words or pictures that cause offence □ *kata-kata, gambar, dll lucah*

filthy /ˈfɪlθi/ adj (filthier; filthiest) **1** very dirty □ *kotor* **2** (used about language, books, films, etc.) connected with sex in a way that causes offence □ *lucah*

fin /fɪn/ noun [C] **1** one of the parts of a fish that it uses for swimming □ *sirip* ⊃ picture on page P13 **2** a flat, thin part that sticks out of an aircraft, a vehicle, etc. to improve its balance and movement through the air or water □ *sirip*

final¹ /ˈfaɪnl/ adj **1** [only before a noun] last (in a series) □ *akhir*: This will be the final lesson of our course. ◆ I don't want to miss the final episode of that series. **2** not to be changed □ *muktamad*: The judge's decision is always final. ◆ I'm not lending you the money, and that's final!
IDM the last/final straw ⊃ straw

final² /ˈfaɪnl/ noun **1** [C] the last game or match in a series of competitions or sports events □ *perlawanan akhir*: The first two runners in this race go through to the final. ◆ the 2010 World Cup Finals (= the last few games in the competition) ⊃ look at semi-final **2** finals [pl] the exams you take in your last year at university □ *peperiksaan akhir*: I'm taking my finals in June.

finale /fɪˈnɑːli/ noun [C] the last part of a piece of music, a show, etc. □ *finale; bahagian terakhir*

finalist /ˈfaɪnəlɪst/ noun [C] a person who is in the final of a competition □ *peserta peringkat akhir* ⊃ look at semi-finalist

finalize (also **-ise**) /ˈfaɪnəlaɪz/ verb [T] to make firm decisions about plans, dates, etc. □ *memutuskan; menentukan dgn muktamad*: Have you finalized your holiday arrangements yet?

finally /ˈfaɪnəli/ adv **1** after a long time or delay □ *akhirnya*: It was getting dark when the plane finally took off. **SYN** eventually **2** used to introduce the last in a list of things □ *akhir sekali*: Finally, I would like to say how much we have all enjoyed this evening. **SYN** lastly **3** in a definite way so that sth will not be changed □ *dgn muktamad*: We haven't decided finally who will get the job yet.

finance¹ /ˈfaɪnæns; fəˈnæns/ noun **1** [U] the money you need to start or support a business, etc. □ *wang; biaya*: How will you raise the finance to start the project? **2** [U] the activity of managing money □ *kewangan*: Who is the new Minister of Finance? ◆ an expert in finance **3** finances [pl] the money a person, company, country, etc. has to spend □ *keadaan kewangan*: What are our finances like at the moment (= how much money have we got)?

finance² /ˈfaɪnæns; fəˈnæns/ verb [T] to provide the money to pay for sth □ *membiayai*: Your trip will be financed by the company.

financial /faɪˈnænʃl; fəˈnæ-/ adj connected with money □ *ttg kewangan*: The business got into financial difficulties. ▶**financially** adv /-ʃəli/

finch /fɪntʃ/ noun [C] a small bird with a short strong beak □ *burung cakar*

find¹ /faɪnd/ verb [T] (pt, pp found /faʊnd/)
▶BY CHANCE **1** to discover sth by chance □ *terjumpa; menemui; ditemui*: I've found a piece of glass in this milk. ◆ We went into the house and found her lying on the floor. ◆ This particular species can be found (= exists) all over the world.
▶BY SEARCHING **2** to discover sth that you want or that you have lost after searching for it □ *jumpa; menjumpai; mendapat; menemui; dpt mencari*: After six months she finally found a job. ◆ Scientists haven't yet found a cure for colds. ◆ I hope you find an answer to your problem. ◆ Did you find the pen you lost?

find → fingertip

MORE Notice the expressions **find the time**, **find the money**: *I never seem to find the time to read the newspaper these days.* ◆ *We'd like to go on holiday but we can't find the money.*

▶FROM EXPERIENCE **3** to have an opinion about sth because of your own experience □ *mendapati*: *I find that book very difficult to understand.* ◆ *We didn't find the film at all funny.* ◆ *How are you finding life as a student?*

▶REALIZE **4** to suddenly realize or discover sth □ *mendapati*: *I got home to find that I'd left the tap on all day.* ◆ *Ben turned a corner and suddenly found himself in the port.*

▶REACH **5** to arrive somewhere naturally □ *sampai*: *These birds find their way to Africa every year.*

IDM **find fault (with sb/sth)** to look for things that are wrong with sb/sth and complain about them □ *(asyik) mencari kesalahan (sso/sst)*: *Monica wouldn't make a good teacher because she's always finding fault with people.*

find your feet to become confident and independent in a new situation □ *dpt berdikari/bertapak*: *Don't worry if the job seems difficult at first—you'll soon find your feet.*

get/find your bearings ⊃ **bearing**

PHR V **find (sth) out** to get some information; to discover a fact □ *mendapat tahu (ttg sst)*: *Have you found out how much the tickets cost?* ◆ *I later found out that Will had been lying to me.*

find sb out to discover that sb has done sth wrong □ *mendapat tahu (sst ttg sso)*: *He had used a false name for years before they found him out.*

find² /faɪnd/ noun [C] a thing or a person that has been found, especially one that is valuable or useful □ *penemuan; jumpaan*: *Archaeologists made some interesting finds when they dug up the field.* ◆ *This new young player is quite a find!*

finder /ˈfaɪndə(r)/ noun [C] a person or thing that finds sth □ *orang yg menjumpai*

finding /ˈfaɪndɪŋ/ noun [C, usually pl] information that is discovered as a result of research into sth □ *dapatan*: *the findings of a survey/report/committee*

fine¹ /faɪn/ adj (**finer**; **finest**)
▶GOOD QUALITY **1** [usually before a noun] of very good quality, with great beauty or detail □ *indah; bagus; halus*: *a fine piece of work* ◆ *fine detail/carving/china*
▶IN GOOD HEALTH **2** in good health, or happy and comfortable □ *sihat; baik; bagus; selesa*: *'How are you?' 'Fine, thanks.'* ◆ *'Do you want to change places?' 'No, I'm fine here, thanks.'*
▶ACCEPTABLE **3** good enough; acceptable □ *elok; cukup bagus; bagus*: *'Do you want some more milk in your coffee?' 'No, that's fine, thanks.'* ◆ *Don't cook anything special—a sandwich will be fine.* ◆ *The hotel rooms were fine but the food was awful.*

HELP We do not use meanings **2** and **3** in questions or in the negative form, so you CANNOT say 'Are you fine?' or 'This isn't fine'.

▶WEATHER **4** bright with sun; not raining □ *baik; bagus*: *Let's hope it stays fine for the match tomorrow.*
▶VERY THIN **5** very thin or narrow □ *halus*: *That hairstyle's no good for me—my hair's too fine.* ◆ *You must use a fine pencil for the diagrams.* **OPP** thick
▶DETAIL **6** difficult to notice or understand □ *halus*: *I couldn't understand the finer points of his argument.* ◆ *There's a fine line between being reserved and being unfriendly.*
▶WITH SMALL GRAINS **7** made of very small pieces, grains, etc. □ *halus*: *Salt is finer than sugar.* **OPP** coarse ▶**fine** adv in a way that is good enough: *Keep going like that—you're doing fine.*

fine² /faɪn/ noun [C] a sum of money that you have to pay for breaking a law or rule □ *denda*: *a parking fine* ◆ *You'll get a fine if you park your car there.* ▶**fine** verb [T] **fine sb (for sth/doing sth)**: *He was fined £100 for driving without lights.* ⊃ note at **court**

finely /ˈfaɪnli/ adv **1** into small pieces □ *halus-halus*: *The onions must be finely chopped for this recipe.* **2** very accurately □ *dgn tepat/halus*: *a finely tuned instrument*

the fine ˈprint (*AmE*) = **the small print**

finger¹ /ˈfɪŋɡə(r)/ noun [C] one of the five parts at the end of each hand □ *jari*: *little finger, ring finger, middle finger, forefinger (or index finger), thumb* ⊃ picture at **body**

MORE Sometimes we think of the **thumb** as one of the fingers, sometimes we contrast it: *Hold the pen between your finger and thumb.* The five parts at the end of each foot are called **toes**.

IDM **cross your fingers**; **keep your fingers crossed** to hope that sb/sth will be successful or lucky □ *berharap; berdoa*: *There's nothing more we can do now—just cross our fingers and hope for the best.* ◆ *I'll keep my fingers crossed for you in your exams.*
have green fingers ⊃ **green¹**
snap your fingers ⊃ **snap¹**

finger² /ˈfɪŋɡə(r)/ verb [T] to touch or feel sth with your fingers □ *meraba; merasa (dgn jari)*

fingermark /ˈfɪŋɡəmɑːk/ noun [C] a mark on sth made by a dirty finger □ *bekas jari*

fingernail /ˈfɪŋɡəneɪl/ (also **nail**) noun [C] the thin hard layer that covers the outer end of each finger □ *kuku (jari tangan)* ⊃ picture at **body**

fingerprint /ˈfɪŋɡəprɪnt/ noun [C] the mark that is made by the pattern of lines on the tip of sb's finger □ *cap jari*: *The burglar left his fingerprints all over the house.*

fingertip /ˈfɪŋɡətɪp/ noun [C] the end of your finger □ *hujung jari*
IDM **have sth at your fingertips** to have sth ready for quick and easy use □ *ada sst (mak-*

finish → fireplace

lumat, dsb) di hujung jari: They asked some difficult questions but luckily I had all the facts at my fingertips.

finish¹ /ˈfɪnɪʃ/ *verb* **1** [I,T] **finish (sth/doing sth)** to complete sth or reach the end of sth □ *habis; tamat; mendapat tempat; menyiapkan*: What time does the film finish? ♦ Haven't you finished yet? You've taken ages! ♦ The Ethiopian runner won and the Kenyans finished second and third. ♦ Finish your work quickly! ♦ Have you finished writing that report? **2** [T] **finish sth (off/up)** to eat, drink or use the last part of sth □ *menghabiskan*: Finish up your milk, Tony! ♦ Who finished off all the bread? **3** [T] **finish sth (off)** to complete the last details of sth or make sth perfect □ *menyiapkan; menyelesaikan; menyempurnakan*: She stayed up all night to finish off the article she was writing. ♦ He's just **putting the finishing touches** to his painting.

PHR V **finish sb/sth off** (*informal*) to kill sb/sth; to be the thing that makes sb unable to continue □ *membunuh sso/sst; mengandaskan sso*: The cat played with the mouse before finishing it off. ♦ I was very tired towards the end of the race, and the last hill finished me off.

finish with sth to stop needing or using sth □ *tdk memerlukan lagi atau sudah selesai dgn sst*: I'll borrow that book when you've finished with it.

finish with sb (*informal*) to end a relationship with sb □ *memutuskan hubungan*: Sally's not going out with David any more—she finished with him last week.

finish² /ˈfɪnɪʃ/ *noun* [C] **1** the last part or end of sth □ *bahagian akhir; berakhir; akhir*: There was a dramatic finish to the race when two runners fell. ♦ I enjoyed the film **from start to finish**. **2** the last covering of paint, polish, etc. that is put on a surface to make it look good □ *kemasan*: a gloss/matt finish

finished /ˈfɪnɪʃt/ *adj* **1** [not before a noun] **finished (with sb/sth)** having stopped doing sth, using sth or dealing with sb/sth □ *selesai; habis*: 'Are you using the computer?' 'Yes, I won't be finished with it for another hour or so.' **2** [not before a noun] not able to continue □ *tamat; habis; lingkup*: The business is finished—there's no more money. **3** made; completed □ *selesai; siap*: the finished product/article

finite /ˈfaɪnaɪt/ *adj* having a definite limit or a fixed size □ *terhad; terbatas*: The world's resources are finite. **OPP** infinite

fir /fɜː(r)/ (also **ˈfir tree**) *noun* [C] a tree with leaves like needles, that do not fall off in winter □ *pokok fir*

ˈfir cone *noun* [C] the fruit of the **fir** tree □ *buah fir*

fire¹ /ˈfaɪə(r)/ *noun* **1** [C,U] burning and flames, especially when it destroys and is out of control □ *kebakaran; terbakar; membakar*: Firemen struggled for three hours to **put out the fire**. ♦ It had been a dry summer so there were many forest fires. ♦ In very hot weather, dry grass can **catch fire** (= start burning). ♦ Did someone **set fire to** that pile of wood? ♦ Help! The frying pan's **on fire**! **2** [C] burning wood or coal used for warming people or cooking food □ *api*: They tried to **light a fire** to keep warm. ♦ It's cold—don't let the fire go out! **3** [C] a machine for heating a room, etc. □ *alat pemanas*: a gas/an electric fire **4** [U] shooting from guns □ *tembakan*: The soldiers came **under fire** from all sides. ♦ I heard machine-gun fire in the distance.

IDM **come/be under fire** be strongly criticized □ *dikecam; dibidas*: The government has come under fire from all sides for its foreign policy.

get on/along like a house on fire ➜ **house¹**
open fire ➜ **open²**

fire² /ˈfaɪə(r)/ *verb* **1** [I,T] **fire (sth) (at/on/into sb/sth)** to shoot bullets, etc. from a gun or other weapon □ *menembak; membedil; memanah; melepaskan tembakan, anak panah, dsb; menyoal (dsb) bertalu-talu*: Can you hear the guns firing? ♦ She fired an arrow at the target. ♦ (*figurative*) If you stop firing questions at me, I might be able to answer! ♦ The soldiers fired on the crowd, killing twenty people. **2** [T] = **sack²** □ *memecat; membuang*: He was fired for always being late. **3** [T] **fire sb with sth** to produce a strong feeling in sb □ *membangkitkan*: Her speech fired me with determination.

ˈfire alarm *noun* [C] a bell or other signal to warn people that there is a fire □ *penggera kebakaran*

firearm /ˈfaɪərɑːm/ *noun* [C] a gun that you can carry □ *senjata api*

ˈfire brigade (*AmE* **ˈfire department**) *noun* [C, with sing or pl verb] an organization of people trained to deal with fires □ *pasukan bomba*

-fired /ˈfaɪəd/ [in compounds] using the fuel mentioned □ *dgn menggunakan bahan api yg disebutkan*: gas-fired central heating

ˈfire department (*AmE*) = **fire brigade**

ˈfire engine *noun* [C] a special vehicle that carries equipment for dealing with large fires □ *kereta bomba*

ˈfire escape *noun* [C] a special set of stairs on the outside of a building that people can go down if there is a fire □ *tangga kecemasan*

ˈfire extinguisher (also **extinguisher**) *noun* [C] a metal container with water or chemicals inside that you use for stopping small fires □ *alat pemadam api*

firefighter /ˈfaɪəfaɪtə(r)/ *noun* [C] a person whose job is to stop fires □ *pemadam kebakaran; ahli bomba*

firelight /ˈfaɪəlaɪt/ *noun* [U] the light that comes from a fire □ *cahaya api*

fireman /ˈfaɪəmən/ *noun* [C] (*pl* -**men** /-mən/) a man whose job is to stop fires □ *ahli bomba*

fireplace /ˈfaɪəpleɪs/ *noun* [C] the open place in a room where you light a fire □ *pendiangan*

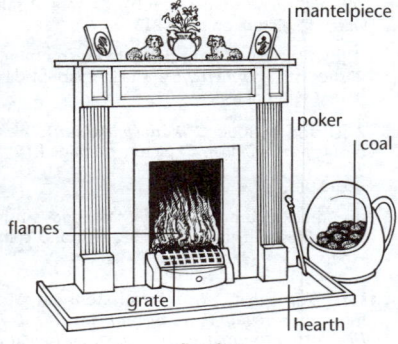

fireside → first aid

fireplace (labels: mantelpiece, poker, coal, flames, grate, hearth)

fireside /ˈfaɪəsaɪd/ noun [sing] the part of a room beside the fire □ *tepi/sisi perdiangan*: Come and sit by the fireside.

'fire station noun [C] a building where **firefighters** (= people who stop fires) wait to be called, and where the vehicles that they use are kept □ *balai bomba*

firewall /ˈfaɪəwɔːl/ noun [C] a part of a computer system that prevents people from getting at information without permission, but still allows them to receive information that is sent to them □ *tembok api* ⊃ note at **cybercrime**

firewood /ˈfaɪəwʊd/ noun [U] wood used for burning on fires □ *kayu api*

firework /ˈfaɪəwɜːk/ noun [C] a small object that burns or explodes with coloured lights and loud sounds, used for entertainment □ *bunga api*

firework

'firing squad noun [C] a group of soldiers who have been ordered to shoot and kill a prisoner □ *skuad penembak utk membunuh banduan*

firm¹ /fɜːm/ noun [C] a business company □ *firma; syarikat*: Which firm do you work for? ♦ a firm of solicitors

firm² /fɜːm/ adj (firmer; firmest) 1 able to stay the same shape when pressed; quite hard □ *pejal*: a firm mattress ♦ firm muscles 2 strong and steady or not likely to change □ *teguh; erat; tegas; pasti*: She kept a firm grip on her mother's hand. ♦ a firm commitment/decision/offer 3 firm (with sb) strong and in control □ *tegas; betul-betul (faham)*: He's very firm with his children. ♦ You have to show the examiner that you have a firm grasp (= good knowledge) of grammar.
IDM a firm hand strong control or discipline □ *yg tegas*: Those children need a teacher with a firm hand.
▶**firmly** adv ▶**firmness** noun [U]

first¹ /fɜːst/ determiner, ordinal number coming before all others; that has not happened before □ *(yg) pertama; sulung; mula-mula*: the first half of the game ♦ You've won first prize! ♦ King Charles I (= King Charles the First) ♦ What were your first impressions of this country when you arrived? ♦ She's expecting her first baby. ⊃ note at **sixth** ⊃ look at **one**
IDM at first glance/sight when first seen or examined □ *mula-mula nampak/kelihatan*: The task seemed impossible at first glance, but it turned out to be quite easy.
first/last thing ⊃ **thing**

first² /fɜːst/ adv 1 before any others □ *mula-mula; pertama*: Sue arrived first at the party. ♦ Mike's very competitive—he gets upset if he doesn't come first in every game. ♦ Do you want to go first or second? 2 before doing anything else □ *dulu; lebih dahulu*: I'll come out later. I've got to finish my homework first. 3 the time before all the other times; for the first time □ *pertama kali*: Where did you first meet your husband? 4 used for introducing the first thing in a list □ *yg pertama*: There are several people I would like to thank: First, my mother. **SYN** firstly 5 at the beginning □ *mula-mula*: When I first started my job I hated it.
IDM at first at the beginning □ *pd mulanya*: At first I thought he was joking, but then I realized he was serious.
come first to be more important to sb than anything else □ *yg diutamakan*: Although she enjoys her job, her family has always come first.
first and foremost more than anything else; most importantly □ *pertama sekali; yg utama*: He worked in TV but he was a stage actor first and foremost.
first come, first served (informal) people will be dealt with, served, seen, etc. strictly in the order in which they arrive □ *siapa dulu, dia dpt*: Tickets can be bought here on a first come, first served basis.
first of all as the first thing (to be done or said) □ *pertama sekali; terlebih dahulu*: In a moment I'll introduce our guest speaker, but first of all, let me thank you all for coming.
first off (informal) before anything else □ *mula-mula*: First off, let's decide who does what.
head first ⊃ **head¹**

first³ /fɜːst/ noun 1 the first [C] (pl the first) the first person or thing, people or things □ *yg pertama*: Are we the first to arrive? ♦ They enjoyed the holiday—their first for ten years. 2 a first [sing] an important event that is happening for the first time □ *yg pertama*: This operation is a first in medical history. 3 [C] a first (in sth) the highest level of degree given by a university in the UK □ *ijazah kelas pertama*: He got a first in History at Liverpool.
IDM from the (very) first from the beginning □ *dr mula lagi*: They hated each other from the first.

first 'aid noun [U] medical help that you give to sb who is hurt or ill before the doctor arrives □ *pertolongan cemas*: a first-aid kit/course ♦ to give somebody first aid

[C] **countable**, a noun with a plural form: *one book, two books*   [U] **uncountable**, a noun with no plural form: *some sugar*

first 'class noun [U] **1** the best and most expensive seats on a train, ship or plane □ *kelas pertama*: *There is more room in first class.* **2** (*BrE*) the way of sending letters, etc. that is faster but more expensive than **second class** □ *kelas satu* ▶ **first 'class** *adv*: *to travel first class* ♦ *to send a letter first class*

first-'class *adj* **1** of the best quality; of the highest standard □ *terbaik*: *a first-class player* ♦ *This book is really first-class.* SYN **excellent 2** [only *before* a noun] used about the best and most expensive seats on a train, ship or plane □ *kelas satu*: *a first-class cabin/seat/ticket* **3** [only *before* a noun] (*BrE*) used about the way of sending letters, etc. that is faster but more expensive than **second-class** □ *kelas pertama*: *first-class mail/letters/stamps* **4** [only *before* a noun] (used about a university degree in the UK) of the highest level □ *kelas pertama/satu*: *a first-class honours degree in geography*

first 'cousin = **cousin**

the ,first 'floor *noun* [C] **1** (*BrE*) the floor of a building above the **ground floor** (= the one on street level) □ *tingkat satu*: *I live in a flat on the first floor.* ♦ *a first-floor flat* **2** (*AmE*) = **ground floor**

first 'gear *noun* [C] the lowest gear on a car, bicycle, etc. □ *gear satu*: *To move off, put the car into first gear and slowly release the clutch.*

first-'hand *adj* (used about information, experience, a story, etc.) heard, seen or learnt by yourself, not from other people □ *langsung; secara langsung*: *He gave me a first-hand account of the accident* (= he had seen it).
▶ **first-'hand** *adv*: *I've experienced the problem first-hand, so I know how you feel.*

firstly /ˈfɜːstli/ *adv* used to introduce the first point in a list □ *pertamanya*: *They were angry firstly because they had to pay extra, and secondly because no one had told them about it.* SYN **first**

'first name *noun* [C] the first of your names that come before your family name □ *nama pertama*: *'What's Mr Vilimek's first name?' 'Petr, I think.'* ⊃ *note at* **name¹**

the ,first 'person *noun* [sing] **1** the words such as 'I', 'me', 'we', and the verb forms that go with them □ *orang pertama*: *'I am' is the first person singular of the verb 'to be'.* **2** the style of telling a story as if it happened to you □ *orang pertama*: *The author writes in the first person.*

first-'rate *adj* excellent; of the best quality □ *sangat baik*

'fir tree = **fir**

fish¹ /fɪʃ/ *noun* (*pl* **fish** *or* **fishes**) **1** [C] an animal that lives and breathes in water and swims □ *ikan*: *How many fish have you caught?* ♦ *I went diving on holiday—it was fantastic to see so many different fishes* (= types of fish). ⊃ *note at* **saltwater** ⊃ *picture on* **page P13**

HELP The plural form **fish** is more common. **Fishes** is used when we are talking about different types of fish.

2 [U] fish as food □ *ikan (makanan)*: *We're having fish for dinner.* ⊃ *picture on* **page P16**

CULTURE

In Britain a common type of fast food is **fish and chips**, which we buy at a **fish and chip shop**.

fish² /fɪʃ/ *verb* [I] **1 fish (for sth)** to try to catch fish □ *menangkap ikan; memancing; mengail*: *He's fishing for trout.* ♦ *They often* **go fishing** *at weekends.* **2 fish (around) (in sth) (for sth)** to search for sth in water or in a deep or hidden place □ *mencari-cari*: *She fished (around) for her keys in the bottom of her bag.*
PHR V **fish for sth** to try to get sth you want in an indirect way □ *memancing sst*: *to fish for an invitation*
fish sth out (of sth) to take or pull sth out (of sth) especially after searching for it □ *mengeluarkan sst (dr sst)*: *After the accident they fished the car out of the canal.*

fishcake /ˈfɪʃkeɪk/ *noun* [C] (especially *BrE*) pieces of fish mixed with potato that are made into a flat round shape, covered with **breadcrumbs** (= very small pieces of bread) and fried □ *kek ikan*

fisherman /ˈfɪʃəmən/ *noun* [C] (*pl* **-men** /-mən/) a person who catches fish either as a job or as a sport □ *nelayan* ⊃ *look at* **angler**

'fish ,finger (*AmE* **fish 'stick**) *noun* [C] a narrow piece of fish covered with **breadcrumbs** (= very small pieces of bread) or **batter** (= a mixture of flour, eggs and milk), usually frozen and sold in packs □ *jejari ikan*

fishing /ˈfɪʃɪŋ/ *noun* [U] catching fish as a job, sport or hobby □ *menangkap ikan*: *Fishing is a major industry in Iceland.* ⊃ *look at* **angling**

'fishing rod *noun* [C] a long thin stick with a line and a hook on it for catching fish □ *joran; batang kail*

fishmonger /ˈfɪʃmʌŋɡə(r)/ *noun* (*BrE*) **1** [C] a person whose job is to sell fish □ *penjual ikan* **2 the fishmonger's** [sing] a shop that sells fish □ *kedai ikan*

fishy /ˈfɪʃi/ *adj* (**fishier**; **fishiest**) **1** (*informal*) seeming wrong, dishonest or illegal □ *mencurigakan*: *The police thought the man's story sounded extremely fishy.* SYN **suspicious 2** tasting or smelling like a fish □ *hanyir*: *a fishy smell*

fist /fɪst/ *noun* [C] a hand with the fingers closed together tightly □ *penumbuk*: *She clenched her fists in anger.*

fist

fit → fixed

fit¹ /fɪt/ verb (**fitting**; **fitted**) **1** [I,T] to be the right size or shape for sb/sth □ *padan*: *These jeans fit very well.* ♦ *This dress doesn't fit me any more.* ♦ *This key doesn't fit in the lock.* **2** [T] **fit (sb/sth) in/into/on/onto sth** to find or have enough space for sb/sth □ *muat; memuatkan; menyelitkan*: *I can't fit into these trousers any more.* ♦ *Can you fit one more person in the car?* ♦ *I can't fit all these books onto the shelf.* **3** [T] to put or fix sth in the right place □ *memasang*: *The builders are fitting new windows today.* ♦ *I can't fit these pieces of the model together.* **4** [T] to be or make sb/sth right or suitable □ *(menjadikan sso/sst) sesuai*: *I don't think Tom's fitted for such a demanding job.* ♦ *The description fits Jo perfectly.* **PHR V** **fit sb/sth in**; **fit sb/sth in/into sth** to find time to see sb or to do sth □ *menyelitkan*: *The doctor managed to fit me in this morning.* ♦ *You're tired because you're trying to fit too much into one day.*

fit in (with sb/sth) to be able to live, work, etc. in an easy and natural way (with sb/sth) □ *menyesuaikan*: *The new girl found it difficult to fit in (with the other children) at school.* ♦ *I will happily change my plans to fit in with yours.*

fit² /fɪt/ adj (**fitter; fittest**) **1 fit (for sth/to do sth)** strong and in good physical health (especially because of exercise) □ *sihat; cergas*: *Swimming is a good way to keep fit.* ♦ *My dad's almost recovered from his illness, but he's still not fit enough for work.* ♦ *She goes to keep-fit classes.* **OPP** **unfit** **2 fit (for sb/sth); fit to do sth** good enough; suitable □ *sesuai; wajar*: *Do you think she is fit for the job?* ♦ *These houses are not fit (for people) to live in.* **3** (BrE informal) sexually attractive □ *mengghairahkan*

fit³ /fɪt/ noun **1** [C] a sudden attack of an illness, in which sb becomes unconscious and their body may make violent movements □ *sawan*: *to have fits* **2** [C] a sudden short period of coughing, laughing, etc. that you cannot control □ *batuk, ketawa, dll secara tiba-tiba yg tdk dpt dikawal*: *a fit of laughter/anger* **3** [sing] [usually after an adjective] the way in which sth (for example a piece of clothing) fits □ *padan; muat; longgar*: *a good/bad/tight/loose fit*

fitness /ˈfɪtnəs/ noun [U] **1** the condition of being strong and healthy □ *kesihatan dan kekuatan; ketegapan*: *Fitness is important in most sports.* **2 fitness for sth/to do sth** the quality of being suitable □ *kesesuaian*: *The directors were not sure about his fitness for the job.*

fitted /ˈfɪtɪd/ adj [only before a noun] made or cut to fit a particular space and fixed there □ *terpasang*: *a fitted carpet* ♦ *a fitted kitchen* (= one with fitted cupboards)

fitting¹ /ˈfɪtɪŋ/ adj **1** (formal) right; suitable □ *sesuai; wajar sekali*: *It is only fitting that this great team should play on one of the finest pitches in the world.* **2 -fitting** used in compounds to describe how clothes, etc. fit □ *digunakan dlm kata majmuk yg bermaksud ketat, longgar, dsb*: *a tight-fitting dress* ♦ *loose-fitting trousers*

fitting² /ˈfɪtɪŋ/ noun [C, usually pl] the things that are fixed in a building or on a piece of furniture but that can be changed or moved if necessary □ *perkakas; aksesori* ⊃ look at **fixture**

ˈfitting room noun [C] a room in a shop where you can put on clothes to see how they look □ *bilik acu* ⊃ look at **changing room**

five /faɪv/ number **1** 5 □ *lima*; 5 ⊃ note at **six** ⊃ look at **fifth 2 five-** [in compounds] having five of the thing mentioned □ *lima*: *a five-day week* **IDM** **nine to five** ⊃ **nine**

fiver /ˈfaɪvə(r)/ noun [C] (BrE informal) £5 or a five-pound note □ *wang kertas £5*: *Can you lend me a fiver?*

fix¹ /fɪks/ verb [T]
▸FASTEN **1** to put sth firmly in place so that it will not move □ *memasang; pasangkan; menumpukan; tertumpu*: *Can you fix this new handle to the door?* ♦ (figurative) *I found it difficult to keep my mind fixed on my work.*
▸ARRANGE **2 fix sth (up)** to decide or arrange sth □ *menentukan; menetapkan*: *We need to fix the price.* ♦ *Have you fixed (up) a date for the party?*
▸FOOD/DRINK **3** (especially AmE) **fix sth (for sb)** to prepare sth (especially food or drink) □ *menyediakan; membuat*: *Can I fix you a drink/a drink for you?*
▸REPAIR **4** to repair sth □ *membetulkan; membaiki*: *The electrician's coming to fix the cooker.*
▸RESULT **5** [usually passive] (informal) to arrange the result of sth in a way that is not honest or fair □ *diatur*: *Fans of the losing team suspected that the match had been fixed.*
PHR V **fix sb up (with sth)** (informal) to arrange for sb to have sth □ *mengaturkan; mendapatkan*: *I can fix you up with a place to stay.*

fix sth (up) to get sth ready □ *menyediakan*: *They're fixing up their spare room for the new baby.*

fix² /fɪks/ noun [C] **1** a solution to a problem, especially one that is easy or temporary □ *penyelesaian*: *There's no quick fix to this problem.* **2** [usually sing] (informal) a difficult situation □ *kesukaran*: *I was in a real fix—I'd forgotten my keys.* **3** [usually sing] (informal) a result that is dishonestly arranged □ *keputusan yg telah diatur*

fixation /fɪkˈseɪʃn/ noun [C] a fixation (with sth) an interest in sth that is too strong and not normal □ *kegilaan; keasyikan*: *I'm tired of James's fixation with football.*

fixed /fɪkst/ adj **1** staying the same □ *tetap*: *a fixed date/price/rent* **OPP** **movable** **2** (of ideas, etc.) not changing □ *tetap; sudah bertapak*: *He has such fixed ideas that you can't discuss anything with him.*
IDM **(of) no fixed abode/address** (formal) (with) no permanent place to live □ *tanpa tempat tinggal/alamat tetap*: *Daniel Stephens, of no fixed abode, was found guilty of robbery.*

how are you, etc. fixed (for sth)? (informal) used to ask how much of sth a person has, or to ask about arrangements □ *bertanyakan jumlah sst yg dimiliki sso atau rancangan sso*: *How are you fixed for cash?* ♦ *How are you fixed for Sunday* (= have you arranged anything to do)?

fixture /ˈfɪkstʃə(r)/ *noun* [C] **1** a sports event arranged for a particular day □ *perlawanan; perlumbaan*: *to arrange/cancel/play a fixture* **2** [usually pl] a piece of furniture or equipment that is fixed in a house or building and sold with it □ *perlengkapan tetap*: *Does the price of the house include fixtures and fittings?* ⊃ look at **fitting**

fizz /fɪz/ *noun* [U] the bubbles in a liquid and the sound they make □ *gas; buih*: *This lemonade's lost its fizz.* ▶ fizz *verb* [I]

fizzle /ˈfɪzl/ *verb*
PHR V **fizzle out** to end in a weak or disappointing way □ *menjadi hambar; berakhir begitu sahaja*: *The game started well but it fizzled out in the second half.*

fizzy /ˈfɪzi/ *adj* (**fizzier**; **fizziest**) (used about a drink) containing many small bubbles of gas □ *berbusa* ⊃ look at **still**

HELP Wine or mineral water that contains bubbles is usually described as **sparkling**, not **fizzy**.

fizzy ˈdrink (*AmE* **soda**) *noun* [C] a sweet drink without alcohol that contains many small bubbles □ *minuman berbusa*: *The only fizzy drinks I've got are cola and lemonade.*

fjord /fjɔːd/ *noun* [C] a long narrow piece of sea between **cliffs** (= high steep areas of rock), especially in Norway □ *fiord*

flabbergasted /ˈflæbəɡɑːstɪd/ *adj* (*informal*) extremely surprised and/or shocked □ *terperanjat; terkejut*

flabby /ˈflæbi/ *adj* (**flabbier**; **flabbiest**) having too much soft fat instead of muscle □ *menggeleber*: *a flabby stomach*

flag¹ /flæɡ/ *noun* [C] a piece of cloth with a special design on it that may be the symbol of a country, club, etc. or may have a particular meaning. A flag can be tied to a pole or held in the hand □ *bendera*: *the French flag* ♦ *the flag of France* ♦ *The flag is flying for the Queen's birthday.* ♦ *The train will leave when the guard waves his flag.* ⊃ picture on **page P11**

flag² /flæɡ/ *verb* [I] (**flagging**; **flagged**) to become tired or less strong □ *menjadi letih*
PHR V **flag sb/sth down** to wave to sb in a car to make them stop □ *menahan sso/sst supaya berhenti*: *to flag down a taxi*

flagrant /ˈfleɪɡrənt/ *adj* [only *before* a noun] (used about an action) shocking because it is done in a very obvious way and shows no respect for people, laws, etc. □ *terang-terangan (ttg perlakuan)*

flail /fleɪl/ *verb* [I,T] to wave or move about without control □ *terkapai-kapai; menggapai-gapai*: *The insect's legs were flailing in the air.* ♦ *Don't flail your arms about like that—you might hurt someone.*

flair /fleə(r)/ *noun* **1** [sing] **(a) flair for sth** a natural ability to do sth well □ *bakat*: *She has a flair for languages.* **2** [U] the quality of being interesting or having style □ *gaya*: *That poster is designed with her usual flair.*

flak /flæk/ *noun* [U] (*informal*) criticism □ *kritikan; bidasan*: *He'll get some flak for missing that goal.*

flake¹ /fleɪk/ *noun* [C] a small thin piece of sth □ *emping; serpihan*: *snowflakes* ♦ *flakes of paint*

flake² /fleɪk/ *verb* [I] **flake (off)** to come off in **flakes** □ *mengelupas*: *This paint is very old—it's beginning to flake (off).*

flaky /ˈfleɪki/ *adj* **1** tending to break into small, thin pieces □ *berkelupas*: *dry flaky skin* **2** (*especially BrE informal*) that does not work well □ *tdk berfungsi dgn baik*: *I found the software a bit flaky.* **3** (*AmE informal*) (of a person) behaving in a strange way □ *berperangai aneh*

flamboyant /flæmˈbɔɪənt/ *adj* **1** (used about a person) acting in a loud, confident way that attracts attention □ *menunjuk-nunjuk; melaram; ranggi*: *a flamboyant gesture/style/personality* **2** bright and easily noticed □ *garang (warna)*: *flamboyant colours* ▶ **flamboyance** *noun* [U] ▶ **flamboyantly** *adv*

flame /fleɪm/ *noun* [C,U] an area of bright burning gas that comes from sth that is on fire □ *api; lidah api; terbakar*: *The flame of the candle flickered by the open window.* ♦ *The house was in flames when the fire engine arrived.* ♦ *The piece of paper burst into flames in the fire* (= suddenly began to burn strongly). ♦ *a sheet of flame* ⊃ picture at **fireplace**

flaming /ˈfleɪmɪŋ/ *adj* [only *before* a noun] **1** (used about anger, an argument, etc.) violent □ *berapi-api; hebat*: *We had a flaming argument over the bills.* **2** burning brightly □ *menyala* **3** (*slang*) used as a mild swear word □ *sial; celaka*: *I can't get in—I've lost the flaming key.* **4** (used about colours, especially red) very bright □ *merah menyala*: *flaming red hair* ♦ *a flaming sunset*

flamingo /fləˈmɪŋɡəʊ/ *noun* [C] a large pink bird that has long legs and stands in water □ *flamingo*

flammable /ˈflæməbl/ *adj* able to burn easily □ *mudah terbakar*

HELP Be careful. **Inflammable** has the same meaning and is more common.

flan /flæn/ *noun* [C,U] (*BrE*) a round open **pie** (= a type of baked food) that is filled with eggs and cheese, fruit, etc. □ *flan*

flank¹ /flæŋk/ *noun* [C] **1** the left or right side of an army during a battle, or a sports team during a game □ *rusuk* **2** the side of an animal's body □ *rusuk; sisi*

flank² /flæŋk/ verb [T, usually passive] to be placed at the side or sides of □ *diapit; dipagari*: *The road was flanked by trees.*

flannel /ˈflænl/ noun 1 [U] a type of soft cloth made of wool □ *flanel* 2 [C] = **facecloth**

flap¹ /flæp/ noun [C] a piece of cloth, paper, etc. that is fixed to sth at one side only, often covering an opening □ *penutup; kelepai*: *the flap of an envelope*
IDM **be in/get into a flap** (*informal*) to be in/get into a state of worry or excitement □ *jadi menggelabah*

flap² /flæp/ verb (**flapping**; **flapped**) 1 [I,T] to move (sth) up and down or from side to side, especially in the wind □ *berkibar-kibar; mengepak-ngepak*: *The sails were flapping in the wind.* ♦ *The bird flapped its wings and flew away.* 2 [I] (*informal*) to become worried or excited □ *menggelabah*: *Stop flapping—it's all organized!*

flare¹ /fleə(r)/ verb [I] to burn for a short time with a sudden bright flame □ *menyala*
PHR V **flare up** 1 (used about a fire) to suddenly burn more strongly □ *memarak* 2 (used about violence, anger, etc.) to start suddenly or to become suddenly worse □ *tercetus*

flare² /fleə(r)/ noun 1 [sing] a sudden bright light or flame □ *nyalaan; pancaran* 2 [C] a thing that produces a bright light or flame, used especially as a signal □ *suar*

flared /fleəd/ adj (used about trousers and skirts) becoming wider towards the bottom edge □ *kembang*

flash¹ /flæʃ/ verb 1 [I,T] to produce or make sth produce a sudden bright light for a short time □ *memancar*: *The neon sign above the door flashed on and off all night.* ♦ *That lorry driver's flashing his lights at us* (= in order to tell us sth). 2 [T] to show sth quickly □ *menunjukkan sst sekilas*: *The detective flashed his card and went straight in.* 3 [I] to move very fast □ *(bergerak) secepat kilat; silih berganti dgn cepat*: *I saw something flash past the window.* ♦ *Thoughts kept flashing through my mind and I couldn't sleep.* 4 [T] to send sth by radio, TV, etc. □ *memancarkan; dipancar*: *The news of the disaster was flashed across the world.*
PHR V **flash back** (used about sb's thoughts) to return suddenly to a time in the past □ *terkenang kembali*: *Something he said made my mind flash back to my childhood.*

flash² /flæʃ/ noun 1 [C] a sudden bright light that comes and goes quickly □ *pancaran*: *a flash of lightning* 2 [C] **a flash (of sth)** a sudden strong feeling or idea □ *sekilas; kilasan*: *a flash of inspiration* ♦ *The idea came to me in a flash.* 3 [C,U] a bright light that you use with a camera for taking photographs when it is dark; the device for producing this light □ *lampu denyar*: *a camera with a built-in flash* ⊃ picture at **camera**
IDM **in/like a flash** very quickly □ *dlm sekelip mata; secepat kilat*
(as) quick as a flash ⊃ **quick¹**

flashback /ˈflæʃbæk/ noun [C] 1 a part of a film, play, etc. that shows sth that happened before the main story □ *imbas kembali* 2 a sudden, clear memory of sth that happened in the past □ *imbas kembali*: *a flashback to childhood*

flash drive (also **memory stick**; **pen drive**; *US* **B drive**) noun [C] a small memory device that can be used to store data from a computer and to move it from one computer to another □ *pemacu kilat* ⊃ picture at **computer**

flashlight /ˈflæʃlaɪt/ (*AmE*) = **torch** (1)

flashy /ˈflæʃi/ adj (**flashier**; **flashiest**) attracting attention by being very big, bright and expensive □ *menjolok mata*: *a flashy sports car*

flask /flɑːsk/ noun [C] 1 a bottle with a narrow neck that is used for storing and mixing chemicals in scientific work □ *kelalang* 2 (*BrE*) = **Thermos**™

flat¹ /flæt/ adj, adv (**flatter**; **flattest**)
▶LEVEL 1 smooth and level, with no parts that are higher than the rest □ *rata; datar; telentang; tersembam*: *The countryside in Essex is quite flat* (= there are not many hills). ♦ *I need a flat surface to write this letter on.* ♦ *a flat roof* ♦ *She lay flat on her back in the sunshine.*
▶NOT HIGH 2 not high or deep □ *rendah; leper*: *You need flat shoes for walking.* ♦ *a flat dish*
▶NOT EXCITING 3 without much interest or energy □ *hambar*: *Things have been a bit flat since Alex left.*
▶REFUSAL 4 [only before a noun] (used about sth that you say or decide) that will not change; firm □ *tegas; bulat-bulat*: *He answered our request with a flat 'No!'*
▶IN MUSIC 5 half a note lower than the stated note □ *flet* **OPP** **sharp** 6 lower than the correct note □ *flet; mendatar*: *That last note was flat. Can you sing it again?* ♦ *You're singing flat.* **OPP** **sharp**
▶DRINK 7 not fresh because it has lost its bubbles □ *hambar; tdk bergas lagi*: *Open a new bottle. That lemonade has gone flat.*
▶BATTERY 8 (*BrE*) no longer producing electricity; not working □ *mati; habis kuasa*: *We couldn't start the car because the battery was completely flat.*
▶TYRE 9 without enough air in it □ *kempis*: *This tyre looks flat—has it got a puncture?*
▶PRICE 10 that is the same for everyone; that is fixed □ *sama rata*: *We charge a flat fee of £20, however long you stay.*
▶TIME 11 (used for emphasizing how quickly sth is done) in exactly the time mentioned and no longer □ *tepat*: *She can get up and out of the house in ten minutes flat.*
IDM **fall flat** (used about a joke, a story, an event, etc.) to fail to produce the effect that you wanted □ *hambar; gagal*
fall flat on your face to fall so that you are lying on your front □ *jatuh tertiarap*: *He fell flat on his face in the mud.*
flat out as fast as possible; without stopping □ *bertungkus-lumus*: *He's been working flat out for two weeks and he needs a break.*

flat → flee 334

flat² /flæt/ noun 1 [C] (especially AmE **apartment**) a set of rooms that is used as a home (usually in a large building) □ *rumah pangsa*: Do you rent your flat or have you bought it? ◆ That old house has been divided into luxury flats. ⊃ note at **house** ⊃ picture on **page P9**

> **HELP** **Apartment** is the normal word in American English. In British English we say **apartment** when talking about a flat we are renting for a holiday, etc. rather than to live in: *We're renting an apartment in the South of France.*

2 [sing] **the flat (of sth)** the flat part or side of sth □ *bahagian rata; tapak (tangan)*: *the flat of your hand* 3 [C] (*symbol* ♭) a note which is half a note lower than the note with the same letter □ *not flet* ⊃ look at **sharp** 4 [C] (especially AmE) a tyre on a vehicle that has no air in it □ *tayar pancit/kempis*: *We had to stop to fix a flat.*

> **TOPIC**
> **Living in a flat**
>
> A tall building that contains many **flats** is called a **block of flats**. Blocks of flats are divided into **floors** (= levels): *I live in a second-floor flat.* If you **rent** a flat, you are the **tenant** and you pay money to the **landlord/landlady** (= the owner). The money that you pay every month is the **rent**. A **deposit** is money that you pay before you move in, but get back when you move out, if you have not damaged anything. Your flat may be **furnished** or **unfurnished**. People who share a flat with you but are not your family are called your **flatmates**.

flatly /ˈflætli/ adv 1 in a direct way; absolutely □ *bulat-bulat; sama sekali*: *He flatly denied the allegations.* 2 in a way that shows no interest or emotion □ *dgn nada hambar*

flatmate /ˈflætmeɪt/ noun [C] (BrE) a person who shares a flat with one or more other people □ *orang yg berkongsi rumah pangsa*

flat-ˈscreen (also ˌflat-ˈpanel) adj [only before a noun] (used about a television or computer monitor) very thin when compared with the traditional type □ *skrin rata* ⊃ picture at **computer**

flatten /ˈflætn/ verb [I,T] **flatten (sth) (out)** to become or make sth flat □ *menjadi rata; meratakan; meranapkan*: *The countryside flattens out as you get nearer the sea.* ◆ *The storms have flattened crops all over the country.*

flatter /ˈflætə(r)/ verb [T] 1 to say nice things to sb, often in a way that is not sincere, because you want to please them or because you want to get an advantage for yourself □ *mengampu; mengangkat* 2 **flatter yourself (that)** to choose to believe sth good about yourself although other people may not think the same □ *perasan*: *He flatters himself that he speaks fluent French.*

3 [usually passive] to give pleasure or honour to sb □ *berbesar hati; berasa bangga*: *I felt very flattered when they gave me the job.*

flattering /ˈflætərɪŋ/ adj making sb look or sound more attractive or important than they really are □ *membuat sso kelihatan/kedengaran lebih menarik*

flattery /ˈflætəri/ noun [U] saying good things about sb/sth that you do not really mean □ *kata-kata mengampu*

flaunt /flɔːnt/ verb [T] to show sth that you are proud of so that other people will admire it □ *menayang-nayangkan*

flautist /ˈflɔːtɪst/ (AmE **flutist**) noun [C] a person who plays the **flute** (= a musical instrument that you hold sideways and blow into) □ *pemain flut*

flavour¹ (AmE **flavor**) /ˈfleɪvə(r)/ noun [C,U] 1 the taste (of food) □ *rasa; perisa*: *ten different flavours of yogurt* ◆ *yogurt in ten different flavours* ◆ *Do you think a little salt would improve the flavour?* 2 [sing] an idea of the particular quality or character of sth □ *rasa*: *The website will give you a flavour of what the city is like.*

flavour² (AmE **flavor**) /ˈfleɪvə(r)/ verb [T] to give flavour to sth □ *memberi rasa/perisa; berperasa*: *Add a little nutmeg to flavour the sauce.* ◆ *strawberry-flavoured milkshake*

flavouring (AmE **flavoring**) /ˈfleɪvərɪŋ/ noun [C,U] something that you add to food or drink to give it a particular taste □ *bahan perasa*: *This orange juice contains no artificial flavourings.*

flaw /flɔː/ noun [C] 1 **a flaw (in sth)** a mistake in sth that makes it not good enough or causes it not to function as it should □ *kesilapan; kelemahan*: *There are some flaws in her argument.* 2 a mark or crack in an object that means that it is not perfect □ *kecacatan* 3 **a flaw (in sb/sth)** a bad quality in sb's character □ *kelemahan*: *His only real flaw is impatience.* ▸ **flawed** adj: *I think your plan is flawed.*

flawless /ˈflɔːləs/ adj with no faults or mistakes □ *tanpa cacat cela*: *a flawless diamond* **SYN** perfect

flea /fliː/ noun [C] a very small jumping insect without wings that lives on animals, for example cats and dogs. Fleas bite people and animals and make them scratch. □ *pinjal; kutu* ⊃ picture on **page P13**

ˈflea market noun [C] a market, often in a street, that sells old and used goods □ *pasar lambak*

fleck /flek/ noun [C, usually pl] a very small mark on sth; a very small piece of sth □ *bintik*: *After painting the ceiling, her hair was covered with flecks of blue paint.*

flee /fliː/ verb [I,T] (pt, pp **fled** /fled/) **flee (to …/ into …); flee (from) sb/sth** to run away or escape from sth □ *lari*: *The robbers fled the country with £100 000.*

fleece¹ /fliːs/ noun **1** [C] the wool coat of a sheep □ *bulu biri-biri* ◆ picture at **goat** **2** [U,C] a type of soft warm cloth that feels like sheep's wool; a warm piece of clothing made from this cloth, which you wear on the top half of your body □ *kain atau baju yg gebu*: *a fleece lining* ◆ *a bright red fleece* ◆ note at **sweater**

fleece² /fliːs/ verb [T] (*informal*) to take a lot of money from sb by charging them too much □ *memotong leher; menipu*: *Some local shops have been fleecing tourists.* **SYN** **rip sb off**

fleet /fliːt/ noun [C, with sing or pl verb] **1** a group of ships or boats that sail together □ *angkatan*: *a fishing fleet* **2** a fleet (of sth) a group of vehicles (especially taxis, buses or aircraft) that are travelling together or owned by one person or organization □ *kumpulan*

flesh /fleʃ/ noun [U] **1** the soft part of a human or animal body (between the bones and the skin) □ *daging; isi*: *Tigers are flesh-eating animals.*

> **MORE** The flesh of animals that we eat is called **meat**.

2 the part of a fruit or vegetable that is soft and can be eaten □ *isi* ◆ picture on **page P14** **IDM** **your (own) flesh and blood** a member of your family □ *darah daging*
in the flesh in person, not on TV, in a photograph, etc. □ *(orangnya) sendiri*
make your flesh creep to make you feel disgusted and/or nervous □ *menimbulkan rasa geli; menyeramkan*: *The way he smiled made her flesh creep.*

flew past tense of **fly¹**

flex¹ /fleks/ verb [T] to bend or move a leg, arm, muscle, etc. in order to exercise it □ *membengkokkan*

flex² /fleks/ (*BrE*) (*especially AmE* **cord**) noun [C,U] (a piece of) wire inside a plastic tube, used for carrying electricity to electrical equipment □ *wayar* ◆ picture at **rope**

> **MORE** At the end of a flex there is a **plug** which you fit into a **socket/power point**.

flexible /ˈfleksəbl/ adj **1** that can be changed easily □ *mudah diubah suai; fleksibel*: *flexible working hours* **2** able to bend or move easily without breaking □ *mudah lentur* **OPP** for both meanings **inflexible** ▶ **flexibility** /ˌfleksəˈbɪləti/ noun [U]

flick /flɪk/ verb **1** [T] **flick sth (away, off, onto, etc.)** to hit sth lightly and quickly with your finger or hand in order to move it □ *menjentik; menyapu-nyapu*: *She flicked the dust off her jacket.* ◆ *Please don't flick ash on the carpet.* **2** [I,T] **flick (sth) (away, off, out, etc.)** to move, or to make sth move, with a quick sudden movement □ *memetik*: *She flicked the switch and the light came on.*
PHR V **flick/flip through sth** to turn over the pages of a book, magazine, etc. quickly without reading everything □ *menyelak-nyelak*
▶ **flick** noun [C]

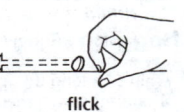

flicker¹ /ˈflɪkə(r)/ verb [I] **1** (used about a light or a flame) to keep going on and off as it burns or shines □ *berkelip-kelip*: *The candle flickered and went out.* **2** (used about a feeling, thought, etc.) to appear for a short time □ *terlintas sebentar*: *A smile flickered across her face.* **3** to move lightly and quickly up and down □ *berkelip*: *His eyelids flickered for a second and then he lay still.*

flicker² /ˈflɪkə(r)/ noun [C, usually sing] **1** a light that shines on and off quickly □ *kelipan*: *the flicker of the TV/flames* **2** a feeling of sth that only lasts for a short time □ *sekilas*: *a flicker of hope/interest/doubt* **3** a small, sudden movement of part of the body □ *kelipan*

flier = **flyer**

flies ◆ **fly**

flight /flaɪt/ noun **1** [C] a journey by air □ *penerbangan*: *to book a flight* ◆ *a direct/scheduled/ charter flight* ◆ *They met on a flight to Australia.* ◆ *a manned space flight to Mars* ◆ note at **journey, plane** **2** [C] an aircraft that takes you on a particular journey □ *penerbangan*: *Flight BA4351 from London to New York is boarding now* (= is ready for passengers to get on it). **3** [U] the act of flying □ *(perbuatan) terbang*: *It's unusual to see swans in flight* (= when they are flying). **4** [C] a number of stairs or steps going up or down □ *tingkat tangga*: *a flight of stairs* **5** [C,U] the act of running away or escaping from a dangerous or difficult situation □ *pelarian*: *the refugees' flight from the war zone*

ˈflight attendant noun [C] a person whose job is to serve and take care of passengers on an aircraft □ *atendan penerbangan; pramugara/pramugari*

flimsy /ˈflɪmzi/ adj (**flimsier, flimsiest**) **1** not strong; easily broken or torn □ *tdk kukuh/kuat; nipis*: *a flimsy bookcase* ◆ *a flimsy blouse* **2** weak; not making you believe that sth is true □ *lemah*: *He gave a flimsy excuse for his absence.*

flinch /flɪntʃ/ verb [I] **flinch (at sth); flinch (away)** to make a sudden movement backwards because of sth painful or frightening □ *tersentak; mengelak*: *She couldn't help flinching away as the dentist came towards her with the drill.*
PHR V **flinch from sth/doing sth** to avoid doing sth because it is unpleasant □ *mengelak; gentar*: *She didn't flinch from telling him the whole truth.*

fling¹ /flɪŋ/ verb [T] (*pt, pp* **flung** /flʌŋ/) to throw sb/sth suddenly and carelessly or with great force □ *mencampakkan; melemparkan*: *He flung his coat on the floor.*

fling² /flɪŋ/ noun [C] a short period of fun and pleasure □ *tempoh berseronok-seronok yg singkat*

flint /flɪnt/ noun **1** [U] very hard grey stone that produces **sparks** (= small flames) when you hit it against steel □ *flin* **2** [C] a small piece of **flint** or metal that is used to produce **sparks** (for example in a cigarette lighter) □ *batu api*

flip /flɪp/ *verb* (**flipping**; **flipped**) **1** [I,T] to turn (sth) over with a quick movement □ *membalikkan; membuka*: *She flipped the book open and started to read.* **2** [T] to throw sth into the air and make it turn over □ *membaling; melambung*: *Let's flip a coin to see who starts.* **3** [I] (*spoken*) **flip (out)** to become very angry or excited □ *marah*: *When his father saw the damage to the car he flipped.*

PHR V flick/flip through sth ➔ flick

'flip chart *noun* [C] large sheets of paper that can be turned over, used to give information at meetings □ *carta selak*

'flip-flop (*AmE* **thong**) *noun* [C, usually pl] a simple open shoe with a narrow piece of material that goes between your big toe and the toe next to it □ *selipar jepun* ➔ picture at **shoe**

flippant /ˈflɪpənt/ (also *informal* **flip**) *adj* not serious enough about things that are important □ *sambil lewa; semberono*

flipper /ˈflɪpə(r)/ *noun* [C] **1** a flat arm that is part of the body of some sea animals and that they use for swimming □ *kaki sirip*: *Seals have flippers.* ➔ picture at **seal** ➔ picture on **page P13** **2** a rubber shoe shaped like an animal's **flipper** that people wear so that they can swim better, especially underwater □ *kaki sirip getah*: *a pair of flippers* ➔ picture at **snorkel**

flipping /ˈflɪpɪŋ/ *adj, adv* (*slang*) used as a mild way of swearing □ *tak guna*: *When's the flipping bus coming?*

flirt¹ /flɜːt/ *verb* [I] **flirt (with sb)** to behave in a way that suggests you find sb attractive and are trying to attract them □ *mengurat; main cinta; bermain; menempah (maut, bahaya, dsb)*: *Who was that boy Irene was flirting with at the party?* ◆ (*figurative*) *to flirt with death/danger/disaster*

PHR V flirt with sth to think about doing sth (but not very seriously) □ *bermain-main/memikir-mikir ttg sst*: *She had flirted with the idea of becoming a teacher for a while.*

flirt² /flɜːt/ *noun* [C] a person who often **flirts** with people □ *kaki mengurat*

flirtatious /flɜːˈteɪʃəs/ *adj* behaving in a way that shows a sexual attraction to sb that is not serious □ *perangai menggoda; main cinta*: *a flirtatious smile* ▶ **flirtatiously** *adv*

flit /flɪt/ *verb* [I] (**flitting**; **flitted**) **flit (from A to B)**; **flit (between A and B)** to fly or move quickly from one place to another without staying anywhere for long □ *terbang; melompat; bertukar-tukar*: *She flits from one job to another.*

float¹ /fləʊt/ *verb* **1** [I] to move slowly through air or on water □ *mengapung; terapung-apung; melayang-layang; semerbak*: *Boats were floating* gently down the river. ◆ *The smell of freshly baked bread floated in through the window.* **2** [I] **float (in/on sth)** to stay on the surface of a liquid and not sink □ *timbul; terapung*: *Wood floats in water.* **3** [T] to sell shares in a company or business for the first time □ *mengapungkan*: *The company was floated on the stock market in 2009.* **4** [I,T] (used in **economics**) if a government **floats** its country's money or allows it to **float**, it allows its value to change freely according to the value of the money of other countries □ *mengapungkan; terapung*

float

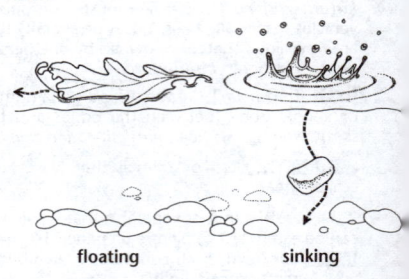

floating   sinking

float² /fləʊt/ *noun* [C] **1** a lorry or other vehicle that is decorated and used in a celebration that travels through the streets □ *kereta berhias*: *a carnival float* **2** a light object used in fishing that moves on the water when a fish has been caught □ *pelampung* **3** a light object used for helping people to learn to swim □ *pelampung; boya*

floating /ˈfləʊtɪŋ/ *adj* not fixed; not living permanently in one place □ *terapung*: *a floating population*

flock¹ /flɒk/ *noun* [C] **1** a group of sheep or birds □ *kawanan* ➔ look at **herd** **2** a large number of people □ *kumpulan*: *Flocks of tourists visit Barcelona every summer.*

flock² /flɒk/ *verb* [I] (used about people) to go or meet somewhere in large numbers □ *datang; pergi berduyun-duyun*: *People are flocking to her latest exhibition.*

flog /flɒg/ (*AmE* also /) *verb* [T] (**flogging**; **flogged**) **1** [usually passive] to hit sb hard several times with a stick or a **whip** (= a long thin piece of rope or leather) as a punishment □ *menyebat; membelasah* **2** (*BrE informal*) to sell sth □ *menjual*

flogging /ˈflɒgɪŋ/ (*AmE* also) *noun* [C,U] the act of hitting sb several times with a stick or a **whip** (= a long thin piece of rope or leather) as a punishment □ *(perbuatan) menyebat/membelasah*

flood¹ /flʌd/ *verb* **1** [I,T] to fill a place with water; to be filled or covered with water □ *membanjiri; melimpah; banjir*: *I left the taps on and flooded the bathroom.* ◆ *The River Trent floods almost every year.* **2** [I] **flood in/into/out of sth** to go somewhere in large numbers □ *membanjiri*: *Since the TV programme was shown, phone calls* *have been flooding into the studio.* **3** [I,T] (used about a thought, feeling, etc.) to fill sb's mind suddenly □ *melanda: At the end of the day all his worries came flooding back.*

flood² /flʌd/ *noun* [C] **1** a large amount of water that has spread from a river, the sea, etc. and that covers an area which should be dry □ *banjir; air bah: Many people have been forced to leave their homes because of the floods.* **2 a flood (of sth)** a large number or amount □ *banjiran; amat sangat: She received a flood of letters after the accident.*

floodlight /'flʌdlaɪt/ *noun* [C] a powerful light that is used for lighting places where sports are played, the outside of public buildings, etc. □ *lampu tebar cahaya*

floodlit /'flʌdlɪt/ *adj* lit by **floodlights** □ *diterangi cahaya limpah: a floodlit hockey match*

floor¹ /flɔː(r)/ *noun* **1** [C, usually sing] the flat surface that you walk on inside a building □ *lantai: Don't come in—there's broken glass on the floor!* ♦ *a wooden/concrete/marble floor* ◘ note at **ground 2** [C] all the rooms that are on the same level of a building □ *tingkat: My office is on the second floor.*

> **HELP** In Britain, the **ground floor** is the floor at street level, and the floor above is the **first floor**. In American English the **first floor** is the floor at street level.

3 [C, usually sing] the ground or surface at the bottom of the sea, a forest, etc. □ *dasar: the ocean/valley/cave/forest floor*

floor² /flɔː(r)/ *verb* [T] (*informal*) to surprise or confuse sb completely with a question or a problem □ *membingungkan: Some of the questions I was asked in the interview completely floored me.*

floorboard /'flɔːbɔːd/ *noun* [C] one of the long wooden boards used to make a floor □ *papan lantai* ◘ picture on **page P8**

flop¹ /flɒp/ *verb* [I] (**flopping; flopped**) **1 flop into/onto sth; flop (down/back)** to sit or lie down in a sudden and careless way because you are very tired □ *merebahkan badan/diri: I was so tired that all I could do was flop onto the sofa and watch TV.* **2 flop around, back, over, etc.** to move, hang or fall in an awkward way without control □ *menggelepar: Her hair flopped over her eyes.* **3** (used about a book, film, album, etc.) to be a complete failure with the public □ *gagal*

flop² /flɒp/ *noun* [C] (used about a film, play, party, etc.) something that is not a success; a failure □ *kegagalan; gagal: Her first novel was very successful but her second was a flop.* ♦ *a box-office flop*

floppy /'flɒpi/ *adj* (**floppier; floppiest**) soft and hanging downwards; not hard or stiff □ *terkelepai: a floppy hat*

floppy disk (also **floppy** (*pl* **floppies**) or **diskette**) *noun* [C] a square piece of plastic that can store information from a computer □ *cakera liut* ◘ look at **hard disk**

---

flood → flow

flora /'flɔːrə/ *noun* [pl] all the plants growing in a particular area □ *flora: He's studying the flora and fauna* (= the plants and animals) *of South America.* ◘ look at **fauna**

floral /'flɔːrəl/ *adj* decorated with a pattern of flowers, or made with flowers □ *berbunga-bunga; bunga: wallpaper with a floral design*

florist /'flɒrɪst/ *noun* **1** [C] a person who has a shop that sells flowers □ *penjual bunga* **2 a florist's** [sing] a shop that sells flowers □ *kedai bunga*

floss /flɒs/ = **dental floss**

flotation /fləʊ'teɪʃn/ *noun* **1** [C,U] the process of selling shares in a company to the public for the first time in order to make money □ *pengapungan (perihal perniagaan): plans for (a) flotation on the stock exchange* ♦ *a stock-market flotation* **2** [U] the act of floating on or in water □ *keapungan (tdk tenggelam)*

flounder /'flaʊndə(r)/ *verb* [I] **1** to find it difficult to speak or act (usually in a difficult or embarrassing situation) □ *gelabah; termangu-mangu: The questions they asked her at the interview had her floundering helplessly.* **2** to have a lot of problems and be in danger of failing completely □ *jatuh bangun; terkapai-kapai: By the end of the year, the business was floundering.* **3** to struggle to move or get somewhere in water, mud, etc. □ *terkial-kial*

flour /'flaʊə(r)/ *noun* [U] a very thin powder made from a type of grain such as **wheat** and used for making bread, cakes, biscuits, etc. □ *tepung*

flourish¹ /'flʌrɪʃ/ *verb* **1** [I] to be strong and healthy; to develop in a successful way □ *segar-bugar; berkembang maju: a flourishing business* **2** [T] to wave sth in the air so that people will notice it □ *melambai-lambaikan: He proudly flourished two tickets for the concert.*

flourish² /'flʌrɪʃ/ *noun* [C] an exaggerated movement □ *gerakan yg berlagak: He opened the door for her with a flourish.*

flout /flaʊt/ *verb* [T] to refuse to obey or accept sth □ *melanggar; mengingkari: to flout the rules of the organization* ♦ *to flout somebody's advice*

flow¹ /fləʊ/ *noun* [C, usually sing, U] **a flow (of sth/sb)** a steady, continuous movement of sth/sb □ *aliran: Press hard on the wound to stop the flow of blood.* **2** a supply of sth □ *pengaliran; aliran: the flow of information between the school and the parents* **3** the way in which words, ideas, etc. are joined together smoothly □ *luahan; (ketika sedang) bercakap dgn rancak: Once Charlie's in full flow, it's hard to stop him talking.*
IDM the ebb and flow (of sth) ◘ the **ebb**

flow² /fləʊ/ *verb* [I] **1** to move in a smooth and continuous way (like water) □ *mengalir: This river flows south into the English Channel.* ♦ *a fast-flowing stream* ♦ *Traffic began to flow* normally again after the accident. **2** (used about words, ideas, actions, etc.) to be joined together smoothly □ *berjalan lancar*: *As soon as we sat down at the table, the conversation began to flow.* **3** (used about hair and clothes) to hang down in a loose way □ *mengurai; berjurai*: *a long flowing dress*

'flow chart (also **'flow diagram**) *noun* [C] a diagram that shows the connections between different stages of a process or parts of a system □ *carta aliran*

flower¹ /ˈflaʊə(r)/ *noun* [C] **1** the coloured part of a plant or tree from which seeds or fruit grow □ *bunga*: *The plant has a beautiful red flower.* ♦ *The roses are in flower early this year.* ➲ picture at **plant** **2** a plant that is grown for its flowers □ *pokok bunga*: *to grow flowers* ♦ *a bunch of flowers*

> **MORE** A flower has thin soft coloured **petals**. It grows from a **bud** on the end of a **stem**. We **pick** flowers or buy them at the **florist's** (= flower shop), then **arrange** them in a **vase**. Flowers that are given or carried on a special occasion are called a **bouquet**.

flower² /ˈflaʊə(r)/ *verb* [I] to produce flowers □ *berbunga*: *This plant flowers in late summer.*

'flower bed (also **bed**) *noun* [C] a piece of ground in a garden or park where flowers are grown □ *batas bunga* ➲ picture on **page P8**

flowerpot /ˈflaʊəpɒt/ *noun* [C] a pot in which a plant can be grown □ *pasu bunga*

flowery /ˈflaʊəri/ *adj* **1** covered or decorated with flowers □ *berbunga-bunga*: *a flowery dress/hat/pattern* ➲ picture on **page P1** **2** (used about a style of speaking or writing) using long, difficult words when they are not necessary □ *berbunga*

flown *past participle of* **fly¹**

fl oz *abbr* = **fluid ounce**

flu /fluː/ (also *formal* **influenza**) *noun* [U] an illness that is like a bad cold but more serious. You usually feel very hot and your arms and legs hurt. □ *flu; selesema*

fluctuate /ˈflʌktʃueɪt/ *verb* [I] **fluctuate (between A and B)** (used about prices and numbers, or people's feelings) to change many times from one thing to another □ *turun naik; berubah-ubah*: *The number of students fluctuates between 100 and 150.* ▶ **fluctuation** /ˌflʌktʃuˈeɪʃn/ *noun* [C,U]

fluent /ˈfluːənt/ *adj* **1 fluent (in sth)** able to speak or write a foreign language easily and accurately □ *fasih*: *After a year in France she was fluent in French.* **2** (used about speaking, reading or writing) expressed in a smooth and accurate way □ *fasih; lancar*: *He speaks fluent German.* ▶ **fluency** /ˈfluːənsi/ *noun* [U]: *My knowledge of Japanese grammar is good but I need to work on my fluency.* ▶ **fluently** *adv*

fluff /flʌf/ *noun* [U] **1** very small pieces of wool, cotton, etc. that form into balls and collect on clothes and other surfaces □ *bulu-bulu* **2** the soft new fur on young animals or birds □ *bulu halus*

fluffy /ˈflʌfi/ *adj* (**fluffier; fluffiest**) **1** covered in soft fur □ *gebu*: *a fluffy kitten* **2** that looks or feels very soft and light □ *gebu*: *fluffy clouds/towels*

fluid¹ /ˈfluːɪd/ *noun* [C,U] a substance that can flow; a liquid □ *bendalir; air*: *The doctor told her to drink plenty of fluids.* ♦ *cleaning fluid* ♦ *correction fluid*

fluid² /ˈfluːɪd/ *adj* **1** able to flow smoothly like a liquid □ *mudah mengalir; (spt) bendalir; lemah gemalai*: (*figurative*) *I like her fluid style of dancing.* **2** (used about plans, etc.) able to change or likely to be changed □ *boleh diubah*

'fluid 'ounce *noun* [C] (*abbr* **fl oz**) a measure of liquid; in the UK, 0.0284 of a litre; in the US, 0.0295 of a litre. □ *auns bendalir* ❶ For more information about measurements, look at the section on using numbers at the back of this dictionary.

fluke /fluːk/ *noun* [C, usually sing] (*informal*) a surprising and lucky result that happens by accident, not because you have been clever or skilful □ *(secara) kebetulan*: *The result was no fluke. The better team won.*

flung *past tense, past participle of* **fling¹**

fluorescent /ˌflɔːˈresnt; ˌfluəˈr-/ *adj* **1** producing a bright white light □ *pendarfluor*: *fluorescent lighting* **2** very bright; seeming to shine □ *terang*: *fluorescent pink paint*

fluoride /ˈflɔːraɪd/ *noun* [U] a chemical that can be added to water or **toothpaste** (= a substance you use to clean your teeth) to help prevent bad teeth □ *fluorida*

flurry /ˈflʌri/ *noun* [C] (*pl* **flurries**) **1** a short time in which there is suddenly a lot of activity □ *tiba-tiba sibuk; kesibukan*: *a flurry of excitement/activity* **2** a sudden short fall of snow or rain □ *hujan/salji lari*

flush¹ /flʌʃ/ *verb* **1** [I] (used about a person or their face) to go red □ *menjadi merah (muka atau kulit)*: *Susan flushed and could not hide her embarrassment.* ➲ A more common word is **blush**. **2** [I,T] when a toilet **flushes** or you **flush**, water passes through it to clean it, after a handle, etc. has been pressed □ *mengepam; dipam*: *Please remember to flush the toilet after use.* ♦ *The toilet won't flush.* **3** [T] **flush sth away, down,** etc. to get rid of sth in a flow of water □ *menyimbah; mencurah*

flush² /flʌʃ/ *noun* [C, usually sing] **1** a hot feeling or red colour that you have in your face when you are embarrassed, excited, angry, etc. □ *(keadaan) merah muka*: *The cold wind brought a flush to our cheeks.* ♦ *a flush of anger* **2** the act of cleaning a toilet with a quick flow of water; the system for doing this □ *(perbuatan) mengepam; pam (tandas)*

flushed /flʌʃt/ *adj* with a hot red face □ *(muka sso) merah*: *You look very flushed. Are you sure you're all right?*

fluster /ˈflʌstə(r)/ verb [T, usually passive] to make sb feel nervous and confused (because there is too much to do or not enough time) □ *gelabah*: *Don't get flustered—there's plenty of time.* ▶**fluster** noun [sing]: *I always get in a fluster before exams.*

flute /fluːt/ noun [C] a musical instrument like a pipe that you hold sideways and play by blowing over a hole at one side □ *flut; seruling* ⊃ note at **music** ⊃ picture at **music** ▶**flutist** /ˈfluːtɪst/ (*AmE*) = **flautist**

flutter¹ /ˈflʌtə(r)/ verb 1 [I,T] to move or make sth move quickly and lightly, especially through the air □ *berkibar-kibar; mengepak-ngepak*: *The flags were fluttering in the wind.* • *The bird fluttered its wings and tried to fly.* 2 [I] your heart or stomach **flutters** when you feel nervous and excited □ *berdebar-debar*

flutter² /ˈflʌtə(r)/ noun [C, usually sing] a quick, light movement □ *(gerakan) mengepak-ngepak; kibaran; kerdipan*: *the flutter of wings/eyelids*

flux /flʌks/ noun [U] continuous movement and change □ *keadaan sentiasa berubah; perubahan berterusan*: *Our society is in a state of flux.*

ʔ fly¹ /flaɪ/ verb (flying; flies; *pt* flew /fluː/; *pp* flown /fləʊn/)
▶OF BIRD, AIRCRAFT, ETC. 1 [I,T] to move through the air □ *terbang*: *This bird has a broken wing and can't fly.* • *How long does it take to fly the Atlantic?*
▶PLANE 2 [I,T] to travel or carry sb/sth in an aircraft, etc. □ *terbang; menerbangkan*: *My daughter is flying (out) to Singapore next week.* • *Supplies of food were flown (in) to the starving people.* 3 [I,T] (used about a pilot) to control an aircraft □ *memandu*: *You have to have special training to fly a jumbo jet.*
▶MOVE QUICKLY 4 [I] to move quickly or suddenly, especially through the air □ *melayang; terbuka (dgn tiba-tiba); berlalu dgn cepat*: *A large stone came flying through the window.* • *I slipped and my shopping went flying everywhere.* • *Suddenly the door flew open and Mark came running in.* • *(figurative) The weekend has just flown by and now it's Monday again.*
▶MOVE IN AIR 5 [I] to move about or to make sth move about in the air □ *berkibar-kibar; melayang-layang*: *The flags are flying.* • *to fly a flag/kite* ⊃ noun **flight**
IDM **as the crow flies** ⊃ **crow¹**
fly off the handle (*informal*) to become very angry in an unreasonable way □ *naik berang*
let fly (at sb/sth) 1 to shout angrily at sb □ *memarahi*: *My parents really let fly at me when I got home late.* 2 to hit sb in anger □ *menyerang*: *She let fly at him with her fists.*

ʔ fly² /flaɪ/ noun [C] 1 (*pl* flies) a small insect with two wings □ *lalat*: *Flies buzzed round the dead cow.* ⊃ picture on **page P13** 2 (also **flies** [pl]) an opening down the front of a pair of trousers that fastens with buttons or a **zip** (= a device for fastening clothes, with two rows of metal or plastic teeth) and is covered with a narrow piece of cloth □ *bukaan seluar*: *Henry, your flies are undone.* ⊃ picture on **page P1**
IDM **a fly on the wall** a person who watches others without being noticed □ *menjadi pemerhati*: *I'd love to be a fly on the wall when he tells her the news.*
not harm/hurt a fly to be kind and gentle and unwilling to cause unhappiness □ *berhati lembut*

flyer (also **flier**) /ˈflaɪə(r)/ noun [C] 1 a person who travels in a plane as a pilot or a passenger □ *penerbang; juruterbang*: *frequent flyers* • *I'm a nervous flyer.* 2 a small sheet of paper that advertises a product or an event and is given to a large number of people □ *lembar iklan; risalah*

ʔ flying /ˈflaɪɪŋ/ adj [only before a noun] able to fly □ *terbang*: *flying insects*
IDM **get off to a flying start** to begin sth well; to make a good start □ *bermula dgn baik*
with flying colours with great success; very well □ *dgn cemerlang*: *Martin passed the exam with flying colours.*
▶**flying** noun [U]: *I'm scared of flying.*

flying ˈsaucer noun [C] a round **spacecraft** (= a vehicle that travels in space) that some people say they have seen and believe comes from another planet □ *piring terbang* ⊃ look at **UFO**

flying ˈvisit noun [C] a very quick visit □ *lawatan singkat*: *I can't stop. This is just a flying visit.*

flyover /ˈflaɪəʊvə(r)/ (*AmE* **overpass**) noun [C] a type of bridge that carries a road over another road □ *jejambat*

FM /ˌef ˈem/ abbr **frequency modulation**; one of the systems of sending out radio signals □ *FM*

foal /fəʊl/ noun [C] a young horse □ *anak kuda* ⊃ note at **horse**

foam¹ /fəʊm/ noun [U] 1 (also ˌfoam ˈrubber) a light rubber material that is used inside seats, etc. to make them comfortable □ *busa*: *a foam mattress* 2 a mass of small air bubbles that form on the surface of a liquid □ *busa; buih*: *white foam on the tops of the waves* 3 an artificial substance that is between a solid and a liquid and is made from very small bubbles □ *busa*: *shaving foam*

foam² /fəʊm/ verb [I] to produce **foam** □ *berbusa*: *We watched the foaming river below.*

fob /fɒb/ verb (fobbing; fobbed)
PHR V **fob sb off (with sth)** 1 to try to stop sb asking questions or complaining by telling them sth that is not true □ *mengelentong*: *Don't let them fob you off with any more excuses.* 2 to try to give sb sth that they do not want □ *menipu; memperkena*: *Don't try to fob me off with that old car—I want a new one.*

focal point /ˈfəʊkl pɔɪnt/ noun [sing] the centre of interest or activity □ *titik fokus*

ʔ focus¹ /ˈfəʊkəs/ verb [I,T] (focusing; focused or focussing; focussed) focus (sth) (on sth)

focus → follow

1 to give all your attention to sth □ *menumpukan (fikiran/perhatian)*: *to focus on a problem* 2 (used about your eyes or a camera) to change or be changed so that things can be seen clearly □ *memfokus(kan)*: *Gradually his eyes focused.* ♦ *I focussed (the camera) on the person in the middle of the group.*

focus² /ˈfəʊkəs/ *noun* [C, usually sing] the centre of interest or attention; special attention that is given to sb/sth □ *fokus; tumpuan*: *The school used to be the focus of village life.*

IDM **in focus/out of focus** (used about a photograph or sth in a photograph) clear/not clear □ *tepat/tdk tepat fokusnya*: *This picture is so badly out of focus that I can't recognize anyone.*

'focus group *noun* [C] a small group of people who are asked to discuss a particular subject. The information obtained is used for research into people's choices and preferences □ *kumpulan fokus*: *A focus group of 100 teachers considered new methods were an improvement.*

fodder /ˈfɒdə(r)/ *noun* [U] food that is given to farm animals □ *makanan binatang*

foe /fəʊ/ *noun* [C] (written) an enemy □ *musuh*

foetus (*AmE* **fetus**) /ˈfiːtəs/ *noun* [C] a young human or animal that is still developing in its mother's body □ *fetus; janin*

> **MORE** An **embryo** is at an earlier stage of development.

fog /fɒg/ (*AmE* usually) / *noun* [U,C] thick white cloud that forms close to the land or sea and is difficult to see through □ *kabut*: *Patches of dense fog are making driving dangerous.* ♦ *Bad fogs are common in November.* ⊃ note at **weather**

> **MORE** **Fog** is thicker than **mist**. **Haze** is caused by heat. **Smog** is caused by pollution.

foggy /ˈfɒgi/ (*AmE* also) / *adj* (**foggier**; **foggiest**) used to describe the weather when there is **fog** □ *berkabut*

IDM **not have the faintest/foggiest (idea)** ⊃ **faint¹**

foil¹ /fɔɪl/ *noun* 1 (also **tinfoil**) [U] metal that has been made into very thin sheets, used for putting around food □ *kerajang*: *aluminium foil* 2 [C] a long, thin, pointed weapon used in the sport of **fencing** □ *pedang anggar* ⊃ picture on **page P5**

foil² /fɔɪl/ *verb* [T] to prevent sb from succeeding, especially with a plan; to prevent a plan from succeeding □ *menggagalkan*: *The prisoners were foiled in their attempt to escape.*

foist /fɔɪst/ *verb*

PHR V **foist sth on/upon sb** to force sb to accept sth that they do not want □ *memaksa menerima*: *Jeff had a lot of extra work foisted on him when his boss was away.*

fold¹ /fəʊld/ *verb* 1 [T] **fold sth (up)** to bend one part of sth over another part in order to make it smaller, tidier, etc. □ *melipat*: *He folded the letter into three before putting it into the envelope.* ♦ *Fold up your clothes neatly and put them away please.* **OPP** **unfold** ⊃ picture at **crinkle** 2 [I] **fold (up)** to be able to be made smaller in order to be carried or stored more easily □ *(boleh) lipat*: *This table folds up flat.* ♦ *a folding bed* 3 [T] **fold A in B; fold B round/over A** to put sth around sth else □ *membalut*: *I folded the photos in a sheet of paper and put them away.* 4 [I] (used about a business, a play in the theatre, etc.) to close because it is a failure □ *gulung tikar; tutup*

IDM **cross/fold your arms** ⊃ **arm¹** ⊃ picture at **arm**

▶ **folding** *adj* [only *before* a noun]: *a folding chair*

fold² /fəʊld/ *noun* [C] 1 a curved shape that is made when there is more material, etc. than is necessary to cover sth □ *lipatan; bahagian yg beralun-alun*: *the folds of a curtain/dress* 2 the mark or line where sth has been folded □ *lipatan* 3 a small area inside a fence where sheep are kept together in a field □ *kandang*

folder /ˈfəʊldə(r)/ *noun* [C] 1 a cardboard or plastic cover that is used for holding papers, etc. □ *fail* ⊃ picture at **stationery** 2 a collection of files on one subject that is stored in a computer or on a disk □ *folder*

foliage /ˈfəʊliɪdʒ/ *noun* [U] (formal) all the leaves of a tree or plant □ *dedaun*

folk¹ /fəʊk/ *noun* 1 (*AmE* **folks**) [pl] (*informal*) people in general □ *orang*: *Some folk are never satisfied.* 2 [pl] a particular type of people □ *orang*: *Old folk often don't like change.* ♦ *country/city folk* 3 **folks** [pl] (*informal*) used as a friendly way of addressing more than one person □ *kawan-kawan*: *What shall we do today, folks?* 4 **folks** [pl] (*informal*) your parents or close relatives □ *orang tua (ibu bapa); keluarga*: *How are your folks?* 5 [U] music in the traditional style of a country or community □ *muzik rakyat*: *Do you like Irish folk?*

folk² /fəʊk/ *adj* [only *before* a noun] traditional in a community; of a traditional style □ *rakyat; tradisional*: *Robin Hood is an English folk hero.* ♦ *folk music* ♦ *a folk song*

folklore /ˈfəʊklɔː(r)/ *noun* [U] traditional stories and beliefs □ *cerita rakyat*

follow /ˈfɒləʊ/ *verb*

▶ GO AFTER 1 [I,T] to come, go or happen after sb/sth □ *mengikut; mengekori; menyusul*: *You go first and I'll follow (on) later.* ♦ *The dog followed her (around) wherever she went.* ♦ *I'll have soup followed by spaghetti.*

▶ BE RESULT 2 [I] **follow (on) (from sth)** to be the logical result of sth; to be the next logical step after sth □ *bermakna; mengikuti; menyusuli*: *It doesn't follow that old people can't lead active lives.* ♦ *Intermediate Book One follows on from Elementary Book Two.*

▶ ROAD/PATH 3 [T] to go along a road, etc.; to go in the same direction as sth □ *mengikut; ikut*: *Follow this road for a mile and then turn right at the station.* ♦ *The road follows the river for a few miles.*

follower → foodstuff

➤INSTRUCTIONS **4** [T] to do sth or to happen according to instructions, an example, what is usual, etc. ◻ *mengikut*: *When lighting fireworks, it is important to **follow the instructions** carefully.* ◆ *The day's events followed the usual pattern.*

➤UNDERSTAND **5** [I,T] to understand the meaning of sth ◻ *memahami*: *The children couldn't follow the plot of that film.*

➤KEEP WATCHING **6** [T] to keep watching or listening to sth as it happens or develops ◻ *menyorot; mengikuti*: *The film follows the career of a young dancer.* ◆ *Have you been following the tennis championships?*

➤INTERNET SITE **7** [T] to regularly read the messages that sb writes on an Internet site ◻ *mengikuti*: *Follow us at @OUPELTGlobal on Twitter.*

IDM **a hard act to follow** ➲ **hard**¹

as follows used for introducing a list ◻ *spt berikut*: *The names of the successful candidates are as follows …*

follow in sb's footsteps to do the same job as sb else who did it before you ◻ *mengikut jejak langkah sso*: *He followed in his father's footsteps and joined the army.*

follow sb's example/lead to do what sb else has done or decided to do ◻ *meneladani; mengikut teladan*

follow suit to do the same thing that sb else has just done ◻ *mengikut; berbuat demikian juga*

follow your nose to go straight forward ◻ *ikut terus*: *Turn right at the lights and after that just follow your nose until you get to the village.*

PHR V **follow sth through** to continue doing sth until it is finished ◻ *meneruskan sst hingga selesai*

follow sth up 1 to take further action about sth ◻ *menyusuli; susuli*: *You should follow up your email with a phone call.* **2** to find out more about sth ◻ *menyiasat selanjutnya*: *We need to follow up the story about the school.*

follower /ˈfɒləʊə(r)/ noun [C] **1** a person who follows or supports a person, belief, etc. ◻ *pengikut* **2** a person who regularly reads the messages that sb writes on an Internet site ◻ *peminat*: *a celebrity with thousands of followers on Facebook*

following¹ /ˈfɒləʊɪŋ/ adj **1** next (in time) ◻ *berikutnya*: *He became ill on Sunday and died the following day.* **2** that are going to be mentioned next ◻ *yg berikut*: *Please could you bring the following items to the next meeting …*

following² /ˈfɒləʊɪŋ/ noun **1** [sing] a group of people who support or admire sth ◻ *penyokong; pengikut*: *The Brazilian team has a large following in all parts of the world.* **2** **the following** [sing, pl] the person or thing (or people or things) that you will mention next ◻ *(orang, dll) yg berikut*: *The following is a summary of events.* ◆ *The following are the winners of the competition …*

following³ /ˈfɒləʊɪŋ/ prep after; as a result of ◻ *setelah; sesudah*: *Following the riots, many students have been arrested.*

follow-up noun [C] something that is done as a second stage to continue or develop sth ◻ *susulan*: *As a follow-up to the TV series, the BBC is publishing a book.*

folly /ˈfɒli/ noun [C,U] (pl **follies**) (formal) an act that is not sensible and may have a bad result ◻ *perlakuan yg bodoh*: *It would be folly to ignore their warnings.*

fond /fɒnd/ adj (**fonder**; **fondest**) **1** [not before a noun] **fond of sb/sth**; **fond of doing sth** liking a person or thing, or liking doing sth ◻ *suka; menyayangi*: *Teachers often **grow fond** of their students.* ◆ *Elephants are very fond of bananas.* ◆ *I'm not fond of getting up early.* **2** [only before a noun] kind and loving ◻ *penuh kasih sayang*: *I have **fond memories** of my grandmother.*

fondle /ˈfɒndl/ verb [T] to touch sb/sth gently in a loving or sexual way ◻ *mengusap; membelai-belai*

fondly /ˈfɒndli/ adv in a loving way ◻ *penuh kasih sayang/kemesraan*: *Miss Murphy will be fondly remembered by all her former students.*

fondness /ˈfɒndnəs/ noun [U, sing] (a) **fondness (for sb/sth)** a liking for sb/sth ◻ *suka akan; kesukaan; penuh rasa suka*: *I've always had a fondness for cats.* ◆ *My grandmother talks about her schooldays **with fondness**.*

font /fɒnt/ noun [C] **1** a large stone bowl in a church that holds water for a **baptism** (= a ceremony in which a person becomes a member of the Christian Church) ◻ *mangkuk air baptis* **2** the particular size and style of a set of letters that are used in printing, on a computer screen, etc. ◻ *huruf cetak/fon (komputer)*

food /fuːd/ noun **1** [U] the things that people or animals eat ◻ *makanan*: *Food and drink will be provided after the meeting.* ◆ *There is a shortage of food in some areas.* **2** [C,U] a particular type of food that you eat ◻ *makanan*: *My favourite food is pasta.* ◆ *Have you ever had Japanese food?* ◆ *baby food* ◆ *dog food* ◆ *health foods* ➲ note at **restaurant** ➲ picture on **page P16**

foodie /ˈfuːdi/ noun [C] (informal) a person who is very interested in cooking and eating different kinds of food ◻ *sso yg amat suka memasak dan merasa pelbagai jenis makanan yg berbeza; peminat makanan*

food mile noun [C] a measurement of the distance that food travels from the producer to the consumer and the fuel that this uses ◻ *ukuran jarak pergerakan makanan drpd pengeluar kpd pengguna dan bahan api yg digunakan*

food poisoning noun [U] an illness that is caused by eating food that is bad for you ◻ *keracunan makanan*

food processor noun [C] an electric machine that can mix food and also cut food into small pieces ◻ *pemproses makanan* ➲ picture at **mixer**

foodstuff /ˈfuːdstʌf/ noun [C, usually pl] a substance that is used as food ◻ *barang*

[C] **countable**, a noun with a plural form: *one book, two books*   [U] **uncountable**, a noun with no plural form: *some sugar*

fool → football

makanan: There has been a sharp rise in the cost of basic foodstuffs.

fool¹ /fuːl/ noun [C] a person who is silly or who acts in a silly way □ *bodoh; tolol*: I felt such a fool when I realized my stupid mistake. **SYN** idiot ⊃ look at **April Fool's Day**

IDM **make a fool of sb/yourself** to make sb/yourself look **foolish** or silly □ *memperbodohkan sso; berkelakuan bodoh*: Sheila got drunk and made a complete fool of herself.

fool² /fuːl/ verb 1 [T] **fool sb (into doing sth)** to trick sb □ *menipu; tertipu*: Don't be fooled into believing everything that the salesman says. 2 [I] to speak without being serious □ *bergurau; main-main*: You didn't really believe me when I said I was going to America, did you? I was only fooling.

PHR V **fool about/around** to behave in a silly way □ *bermain-main*: Stop fooling around with that knife or someone will get hurt!

foolhardy /ˈfuːlhɑːdi/ adj taking unnecessary risks □ *tunjuk berani*

foolish /ˈfuːlɪʃ/ adj 1 not sensible □ *bodoh*: I was foolish enough to trust him. 2 looking silly or feeling embarrassed □ *tolol; dungu*: I felt a bit foolish when I couldn't remember the man's name. **SYN** for both meanings **silly, stupid** ▶**foolishly** adv: I foolishly agreed to lend him money. ▶**foolishness** noun [U]

foolproof /ˈfuːlpruːf/ adj not capable of going wrong or being wrongly used □ *tdk mungkin gagal; terjamin*: Our security system is absolutely foolproof.

ẗ foot¹ /fʊt/ noun (pl **feet** /fiːt/)
▶PART OF BODY **1** [C] the lowest part of the leg, at the end of the leg, on which a person or an animal stands □ *kaki; berdiri; berjalan; (berjalan) kaki ayam*: People usually **get to** their **feet** (= stand up) for the national anthem. ◆ I usually go to school **on foot** (= walking). ◆ I need to sit down—I've been **on my feet** all day. ◆ There's broken glass on the floor, so don't walk around in **bare feet** (= without shoes and socks). ◆ She sat by the fire and the dog sat at her feet. ◆ a foot brake/pedal/pump (= one that is operated by your foot) ⊃ picture at **body**
▶-FOOTED **2** [in compounds] having or using the type of foot or number of feet mentioned □ *berkaki*: There are no left-footed players in the team. ◆ a four-footed creature
▶PART OF SOCK **3** [C] the part of a sock, etc. that covers the foot □ *bahagian kaki*
▶BOTTOM **4** [sing] **the foot of sth** the bottom of sth □ *kaki; bahagian bawah sst*: There's a note at the foot of the page. ◆ the foot of the stairs ◆ the foot of the bed **OPP** top
▶MEASUREMENT **5** [C] (abbr **ft**) a measure of length; 30.48 centimetres. There are 3 feet in a yard □ *kaki*: 'How tall are you?' 'Five foot six (inches).' ◆ a six-foot high wall ❶ For more information about measurements, look at the section on using numbers at the back of this dictionary.

IDM **be rushed/run off your feet** to be extremely busy; to have too many things to do □ *sangat sibuk*: Over Christmas we were rushed off our feet at work.

fall/land on your feet to be lucky in finding yourself in a good situation, or in getting out of a difficult situation □ *bernasib baik*: I really landed on my feet getting such a good job with so little experience.

find your feet ⊃ **find¹**

get/have cold feet ⊃ **cold¹**

get/start off on the right/wrong foot (with sb) (informal) to start a relationship well/badly □ *memulakan hubungan, dll dgn cara yg betul/salah*: I seem to have got off on the wrong foot with the new boss.

have one foot in the grave (informal) to be so old or ill that you are not likely to live much longer □ *hampir mati kerana sangat tua atau sakit tenat*

(back) on your feet completely healthy again after an illness or a time of difficulty □ *pulih/sihat kembali*

put your feet up to sit down and relax, especially with your feet off the floor and supported □ *berehat dgn kaki diampu*: I'm so tired that I just want to go home and put my feet up.

put your foot down (informal) to say firmly that sth must (not) happen □ *bertegas*: I put my foot down and told Andy he couldn't use our car any more.

put your foot in it (informal) to say or do sth that makes sb embarrassed or upset □ *membuat kesilapan yg bodoh*

set foot in/on sth to visit, enter or arrive at/in a place □ *menjejakkan kaki di sst tempat; masuk ke sst tempat*: No woman has ever set foot in the temple.

stand on your own (two) feet to take care of yourself without help; to be independent □ *berdikari*

under your feet in the way; stopping you from working, etc. □ *mengacau/mengganggu sso*: Would somebody get these children out from under my feet and take them to the park?

foot² /fʊt/ verb
IDM **foot the bill (for sth)** (informal) to pay (for sth) □ *membayar sst*

footage /ˈfʊtɪdʒ/ noun [U] part of a film showing a particular event □ *sedutan filem*: The documentary included footage of the assassination of Kennedy.

ẗ football /ˈfʊtbɔːl/ noun **1** (especially AmE **soccer**) [U] a game that is played by two teams of eleven players who try to kick a round ball into a goal □ *bola sepak*: a football pitch/match ◆ Tom plays football every Saturday. ⊃ note at **sport 2** [C] the large round ball that is used in this game □ *bola (sepak)*

HELP In the US **soccer** is the usual word for the game, since Americans use the word **football** to refer to **American Football**.

[I] **intransitive**, a verb which has no object: *He laughed.*   [T] **transitive**, a verb which has an object: *He ate an apple.*

football

football
footballers
(*AmE* soccer players)

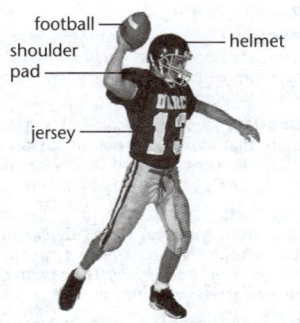

football
shoulder pad
helmet
jersey

American football player
(*AmE* football player)

footballer /ˈfʊtbɔːlə(r)/ (especially *AmE* **soccer player**) *noun* [C] a person who plays football □ *pemain bola sepak*: *a talented footballer*

foothold /ˈfʊthəʊld/ *noun* [C] (*figurative*) **1** a place where you can safely put your foot when you are climbing □ *tempat berpijak* **2** a strong position in a business or profession from which sb can progress □ *tapak*: *We need to get a foothold in the European market.*

footing /ˈfʊtɪŋ/ *noun* [sing] **1** being able to stand firmly on a surface □ *keseimbangan; kedudukan*: *Climbers usually attach themselves to a rope in case they* **lose their footing**. **2** the basis on which sth is established or organized □ *asas; tapak*: *The company is now* **on a firm footing** *and should soon show a profit.* **3** The level or position of sb/sth (in relation to sb/sth else) □ *kedudukan*: *to be* **on an equal footing** *with somebody*

footnote /ˈfʊtnəʊt/ *noun* [C] an extra piece of information that is added at the bottom of a page in a book □ *nota kaki*

footpath /ˈfʊtpɑːθ/ *noun* [C] a path for people to walk on, especially in the country □ *lorong pejalan kaki*: *a footpath through the woods* ➔ picture on **page P11**

footprint /ˈfʊtprɪnt/ *noun* [C] a mark that is left on the ground by a foot or a shoe □ *bekas tapak kaki* ➔ look at **track**

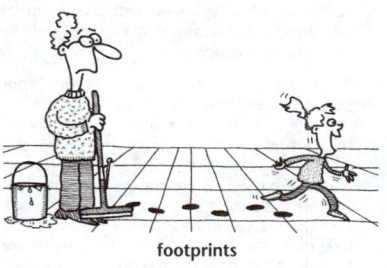

footprints

footstep /ˈfʊtstep/ *noun* [C] the sound of sb walking □ *bunyi tapak kaki; bunyi orang berjalan*: *I heard his footsteps in the hall.*
IDM **follow in sb's footsteps** ➔ **follow**

footwear /ˈfʊtweə(r)/ *noun* [U] boots or shoes □ *kasut, but, dsb*

for[1] /fə(r); *strong form* fɔː(r)/ *prep* **1** showing the person that will use or have sth □ *utk*: *Here is a letter for you.* ♦ *He made lunch for them.* ♦ *It's a book for children.* **2** in order to help sb/sth □ *utk*: *What can I do for you?* ♦ *You should take some medicine for your cold.* ♦ *Doctors are fighting for his life.* ♦ *shampoo for dry hair* **3** meaning sth or representing sb/sth □ *makna; bagi; utk*: *What's the 'C' for in 'BBC'?* ♦ *What's the Russian for 'window'?* ♦ *She plays hockey for England.* **4** in support of (sb/sth) □ *menyokong*: *Are you for or against shops opening on Sundays?* **5** in order to do, have or get sth □ *utk; mengapa*: *What's this gadget for?* ♦ *What did you do that for?* (= Why did you do that?) ♦ *Are you learning English for your job or for fun?* ♦ *She asked me for help.* ♦ *Phone now for information.* ♦ *to go for a walk/swim/drink* **6** (showing a reason) as a result of □ *kerana*: *Ben didn't want to come for some reason.* ♦ *He was sent to prison for robbery.* ♦ *I couldn't speak for laughing.* **7** (showing the price or value of sth) in exchange for □ *dgn harga; bagi; utk*: *I bought this car for £2 000.* ♦ *You get one point for each correct answer.* ♦ *I want to exchange this sweater for a larger one.* ♦ *The officer was accused of giving secret information for cash.* **8** [after an adjective] showing how usual, suitable, difficult, etc. sb/sth is in relation to sb/sth else □ *bagi; utk*: *She's tall for her age.* ♦ *It's quite warm for January.* ♦ *It's unusual for Alex to be late.* ♦ *I think Sandra is perfect for this job.* **9** showing the place that sb/sth will go to □ *ke*: *Is this the train for Glasgow?* ♦ *They set off for the shops.* **10** showing a length of time □ *selama; buat; utk*: *I'm going away for a few days.* ♦ *for a while/a long time/ages* ♦ *They have left the town* **for good** (= they will not return). ♦ *He was in prison for 20 years* (= he is not in prison now). ♦ *He has been in prison for 20 years* (= he is still in prison). ➔ note at **during, since**

CONSONANTS p **p**en b **b**ad t **t**ea d **d**id k **c**at g **g**ot tʃ **ch**in dʒ **J**une f **f**all v **v**an θ **th**in

for → forefinger

> **GRAMMAR** **Since** is used with a point in time and usually a perfect tense for showing when something began: *He has been in prison since 2008.* **Ago** is usually used with a past tense for showing when something began: *He went to prison 20 years ago.*

11 at a particular, fixed time □ *utk; pd*: *What did they give you for your birthday?* ♦ *Shall we have eggs for breakfast?* ♦ *I'm going to my parents' for Christmas.* ♦ *The appointment is for 10.30.* **12** showing how many times sth has happened □ *utk*: *I'm warning you for the last time.* ♦ *I met him for the second time yesterday.* **13** showing a distance □ *sejauh*: *He walked for ten miles.*
IDM **be (in) for it** (BrE informal) to be going to get into trouble or be punished □ *habislah; kena engkau*: *If you arrive late again you'll be in for it.*
for all in spite of □ *walaupun; sungguhpun*: *For all his money, he's a very lonely man.*
for ever ➲ **forever**

for² /fə(r); strong form fɔː(r)/ conj (formal) because □ *kerana*: *The children soon lost their way, for they had never been in the forest alone before.*

forage /ˈfɒrɪdʒ/ verb [I] **forage (for sth)** (used especially about animals) to search for food □ *mencari makanan*

forbid /fəˈbɪd/ verb [T] (**forbidding**; pt **forbade** /fəˈbeɪd/ or **forbad** /fəˈbæd/; pp **forbidden** /fəˈbɪdn/) **1 forbid sb to do sth** to order sb not to do sth □ *melarang*: *My parents forbade me to see Tim again.* **OPP** **allow** **2** [usually passive] to not allow sth □ *dilarang*: *Smoking is forbidden anywhere in the building.* ♦ *Photography is forbidden anywhere in the building.* **SYN** **prohibit** **OPP** for both meanings **allow**

forbidding /fəˈbɪdɪŋ/ adj looking unfriendly or frightening □ *menggerunkan*: *The coast near the village is rather grey and forbidding.*

ɡforce¹ /fɔːs/ noun **1** [U] physical strength or power □ *kekuatan; kekerasan*: *The force of the explosion knocked them to the ground.* ♦ *The police used force to break up the demonstration.* **2** [U] power and influence □ *kuasa; pengaruh*: *the force of public opinion* **3** [C] a person or thing that has power or influence □ *kuasa; daya*: *Britain is no longer a major force in international affairs.* ♦ *Julia has been the driving force behind the company's success.* **4** [C] a group of people who are trained for a particular purpose □ *tenaga kerja; pasukan*: *a highly trained workforce* ♦ *the police force* **5** [usually plural] the soldiers and weapons that an army, etc. has □ *angkatan bersenjata*: *the armed forces* **6** [C,U] (technical) a power that can cause change or movement □ *daya*: *the force of gravity*
IDM **bring sth/come into force** to start using a new law, etc.; to start being used □ *mula dikuatkuasakan*: *The government want to bring new anti-pollution legislation into force next year.*
force of habit if you do sth from or out of **force of habit**, you do it in a particular way because you have always done it that way in the past □ *sudah menjadi kebiasaan*
in force 1 (used about people) in large numbers □ *dlm bilangan yg banyak*: *The police were present in force at the football match.* **2** (used about a law, rule, etc.) being used □ *berkuat kuasa*: *The new speed limit is now in force.*
join forces (with sb) ➲ **join¹**

ɡforce² /fɔːs/ verb [T] **1 force sb (to do sth); force sb (into sth/doing sth)** to make sb do sth that they do not want to do □ *memaksa*: *She forced herself to speak to him.* ♦ *The President was forced into resigning.* **2** to use physical strength to do sth or to move sth □ *mengopak; merempuh*: *The window had been forced (open).* ♦ *We had to force our way through the crowd.* **3** to make sth happen when it will not happen naturally □ *memaksa*: *to force a smile/laugh* ♦ *To force the issue, I gave him until midday to decide.*

forceful /ˈfɔːsfl/ adj having the power to persuade people □ *hebat; penuh tenaga; bersemangat*: *He has a very forceful personality.* ♦ *a forceful speech*

forceps /ˈfɔːseps/ noun [pl] a special instrument that looks like a pair of scissors but is not sharp. **Forceps** are used by doctors for holding things firmly □ *forsep*: *a pair of forceps*

forcible /ˈfɔːsəbl/ adj [only before a noun] done using (physical) force □ *dgn menggunakan kekerasan*: *The police made a forcible entry into the building.* /-əbli/ adv: *The squatters were forcibly removed by the police.*

ford /fɔːd/ noun [C] a place in a river where you can walk or drive across because the water is not deep □ *harung-harungan*

fore /fɔː(r)/ noun
IDM **be/come to the fore** to be in or get into an important position so that you are noticed by people; to play an important part □ *tampil ke muka; berada di depan*

forearm /ˈfɔːrɑːm/ noun [C] the part of your arm between your elbow and your wrist □ *lengan bawah* ➲ picture at **body**

foreboding /fɔːˈbəʊdɪŋ/ noun [U, sing] a strong feeling that danger or trouble is coming □ *petanda buruk; rasa tdk sedap hati*: *She was filled with a sense of foreboding.*

ɡforecast /ˈfɔːkɑːst/ verb [T] (pt, pp **forecast** or **forecasted**) to say (with the help of information) what will probably happen in the future □ *meramal*: *The Chancellor did not forecast the sudden rise in inflation.* ♦ *Rain has been forecast for tomorrow.* ▶**forecast** noun [C]: *a sales forecast for the coming year* ➲ look at **weather forecast**

forecourt /ˈfɔːkɔːt/ noun [C] a large open area in front of a building such as a hotel or petrol station □ *pekarangan*

forefinger /ˈfɔːfɪŋɡə(r)/ (also ˈ**index finger**) noun [C] the finger next to the thumb □ *jari telunjuk*

forefront /ˈfɔːfrʌnt/ noun [sing] the leading position; the position at the front □ *barisan depan*: Our department is right **at the forefront of** scientific research.

forego = forgo

foregone[1] past participle of **forgo**

foregone[2] /ˈfɔːgɒn (AmE also) / adj
IDM **a foregone conclusion** a result that is or was certain to happen □ *sudah menjadi kepastian*: Her promotion was a foregone conclusion.

foreground /ˈfɔːgraʊnd/ noun [sing] **1** the part of a view, picture, photograph, etc. that appears closest to the person looking at it □ *latar depan*: Notice the artist's use of colour **in the foreground** of the picture. **2** a position where you will be noticed most □ *menonjolkan diri*: He likes to be in the foreground at meetings. **OPP** for both meanings **background**

forehand /ˈfɔːhænd/ noun [C] a way of hitting the ball in sports such as **tennis**, that is made with the inside of your hand facing forward □ *pukul sangga depan* **OPP** **backhand**

forehead /ˈfɔːhed (BrE also) /ˈfɒrɪd (AmE also) / (also **brow**) noun [C] the part of sb's face above the eyes and below the hair □ *dahi* ➔ picture at **body**

foreign /ˈfɒrən (AmE also) / adj **1** belonging to or connected with a country that is not your own □ *asing*: a foreign country/coin/accent ◆ to learn a foreign language **2** [only before a noun] dealing with or involving other countries □ *luar negeri*: foreign policy (= government decisions concerning other countries) ◆ foreign affairs/news/trade ◆ the French Foreign Minister **3** (used about an object or a substance) not being where it should be □ *luar negeri*: The X-ray showed up a **foreign body** (= object) in her stomach.

the Foreign and Commonwealth Office noun [sing, with sing or pl verb] (abbr **FCO**) the British government department that deals with relations with other countries □ *Pejabat Luar Negeri dan Komanwel*

CULTURE

Many people still refer to this department by its old name **the Foreign Office**.

foreigner /ˈfɒrənə(r) (AmE also) / noun [C] a person who belongs to a country that is not your own □ *orang asing*

foreign exchange noun [U,C] the system of buying and selling money from a different country; the place where it is bought and sold □ *pertukaran wang asing; pasaran wang asing*

the Foreign Secretary noun [C] the person in the government who is responsible for dealing with foreign countries □ *Menteri Luar Negeri* ➔ look at **Home Secretary**

foreleg /ˈfɔːleg/ noun [C] either of the two front legs of an animal that has four legs □ *kaki hadapan binatang* ➔ note at **hind** ➔ picture on page P12

foreman /ˈfɔːmən/, **forewoman** /ˈfɔːwʊmən/ noun [C] (pl -men /-mən/, -women /-wɪmɪn/) a worker who is in charge of a group of other factory or building workers □ *mandur, fomen*

foremost /ˈfɔːməʊst/ adj most famous or important; best □ *terkemuka; paling utama*: Laurence Olivier was among the foremost actors of the last century.
IDM **first and foremost** ➔ **first**[2]

forename /ˈfɔːneɪm/ noun [C] (formal) your first name, that is given to you when you are born □ *nama pertama* ➔ note at **name**

forensic /fəˈrensɪk; -ˈrenzɪk/ adj [only before a noun] using scientific methods to find out about a crime □ *forensik*: The police are carrying out forensic tests to try and find out the cause of death.

forerunner /ˈfɔːrʌnə(r)/ noun [C] **a forerunner (of sb/sth)** a person or thing that is an early example or a sign of sth that appears or develops later □ *pelopor; perintis*: Country music was undoubtedly one of the forerunners of rock and roll.

foresee /fɔːˈsiː/ verb [T] (pt foresaw /fɔːˈsɔː/; pp foreseen /fɔːˈsiːn/) to know or guess that sth is going to happen in the future □ *nampak; meramal(kan)*: Nobody could have foreseen the result of the election. ➔ look at **unforeseen**

foreseeable /fɔːˈsiːəbl/ adj that can be expected; that you can guess will happen □ *sejauh yg dpt dijangka/diramal/ternampak*: These problems were foreseeable. ◆ The weather won't change **in the foreseeable future** (= as far into the future as we can see).

foreseen past participle of **foresee**

foresight /ˈfɔːsaɪt/ noun [U] the ability to see what will probably happen in the future and to use this knowledge to make careful plans □ *pandangan jauh*: My neighbour had the foresight to move house before the new motorway was built. ➔ look at **hindsight**

foreskin /ˈfɔːskɪn/ noun [C] the piece of skin that covers the end of the male sexual organ □ *kulup; kulit khatan*

forest /ˈfɒrɪst (AmE also) / noun [C,U] a large area of land covered with trees □ *hutan*: a tropical forest ◆ a forest fire ➔ picture on page P10

MORE A **forest** is larger than a **wood**. A **jungle** is a forest in a tropical part of the world.

forestall /fɔːˈstɔːl/ verb [T] to take action to prevent sb from doing sth or sth from happening □ *menghalang; mengelakkan*

forestry /ˈfɒrɪstri (AmE also) / noun [U] the science of planting and taking care of trees in forests □ *perhutanan*

forethought /ˈfɔːθɔːt/ noun [U] careful thought about, or preparation for, the future □ *perancangan (masa depan)*: With forethought, most accidents can be avoided. ◆ With

---

VOWELS iː **see** i **any** ɪ **sit** e **ten** æ **hat** ɑː **father** ɒ **got** ɔː **saw** ʊ **put** uː **too** u **usual**

a little forethought, healthy eating at work can be quite easy.

forever /fərˈevə(r)/ *adv* **1** (also **for ever**) for all time; permanently □ *selama-lamanya*: *I wish the holidays would last forever!* ◆ *I realized that our relationship had finished forever.* **2** [only used with continuous tenses] very often; in a way which is annoying □ *sentiasa*; *kerap sangat*: *Our neighbours are forever having noisy parties.*

forewent *past tense* of **forgo**

foreword /ˈfɔːwɜːd/ *noun* [C] a piece of writing at the beginning of a book that introduces the book and/or its author □ *prakata*

forfeit /ˈfɔːfɪt/ *verb* [T] to lose sth or have sth taken away from you, usually because you have done sth wrong □ *kehilangan sst*: *Because of his violent behaviour he forfeited the right to visit his children.* ▶ **forfeit** *noun* [C]

forgave *past tense* of **forgive**

forge¹ /fɔːdʒ/ *verb* [T] **1** to put a lot of effort into making sth strong and successful □ *menempa; membina*: *Our school has forged links with a school in Romania.* **2** to make an illegal copy of sth □ *memalsukan*: *to forge a signature/banknote/passport* ⊃ look at **counterfeit**

PHR V forge ahead to go forward or make progress quickly □ *maju ke hadapan*: *I think it's now time to forge ahead with our plans to open a new shop.*

forge² /fɔːdʒ/ *noun* [C] a place where objects are made by heating and shaping metal □ *bengkel tempa*

forgery /ˈfɔːdʒəri/ *noun* (*pl* **forgeries**) **1** [U] the crime of illegally copying a document, painting, etc. □ *pemalsuan* **2** [C] a document, picture, etc. that is a copy of the real one □ *tiruan; karya palsu*

forget /fəˈɡet/ *verb* (*pt* **forgot** /fəˈɡɒt/; *pp* **forgotten** /fəˈɡɒtn/) **1** [T] **forget (doing) sth** to not be able to remember sth □ *terlupa; lupa*: *I've forgotten what I was going to say.* ◆ *I've forgotten her telephone number.* ◆ *He forgot that he had invited her to the party.* ◆ *I'll never forget meeting my husband for the first time.* **2** [I,T] **forget (about) sth**; **forget to do sth** to fail to remember to do sth that you ought to have done □ *lupa*: *'Why didn't you come to the party?' 'Oh dear! I completely forgot about it!'* ◆ *'Did you feed the cat?' 'Sorry, I forgot.'* ◆ *Don't forget to do your homework!* **3** [T] to fail to bring sth with you □ *tertinggal; terlupa membawa*: *When my father got to the airport he realized he'd forgotten his passport.*

HELP Forget or **leave**? When you are talking about something you have forgotten, and you want to say **where** it is, use the word **leave**. You CANNOT say: '*He forgot his passport at home.*' You have to say: '*He left his passport at home.*'

4 [I,T] **forget (about) sb/sth**; **forget about doing sth** to make an effort to stop thinking about sb/sth; to stop thinking that sth is possible □ *melupakan*; *lupakan*: *Forget about your work and enjoy yourself!* ◆ *'I'm sorry! I shouted at you.' 'Forget it* (= don't worry about it).*'* ◆ *Let's forget about cooking tonight and get a takeaway instead.*

forgetful /fəˈɡetfl/ *adj* often forgetting things □ *pelupa*: *My mother's nearly 80 and she's starting to get a bit forgetful.* **SYN** **absent-minded**

forgivable /fəˈɡɪvəbl/ *adj* that can be forgiven □ *dpt dimaafkan*

forgive /fəˈɡɪv/ *verb* [T] (*pt* **forgave** /fəˈɡeɪv/; *pp* **forgiven** /fəˈɡɪvn/) **1 forgive sb/yourself (for sth/for doing sth)** to stop being angry towards sb for sth that they have done wrong □ *memaafkan*: *I can't forgive his behaviour last night.* ◆ *I can't forgive him for his behaviour last night.* ◆ *I will never forgive him for behaving like that last night.* **2 forgive me (for doing sth)** used for politely saying sorry □ *maaf*: *Forgive me for asking, but where did you get that dress?* ▶ **forgiveness** *noun* [U]: *He begged for forgiveness for what he had done.*

forgiving /fəˈɡɪvɪŋ/ *adj* **forgiving (of sth)** ready and able to forgive □ *bersedia memaafkan; pemaaf*

forgo (also **forego**) /fɔːˈɡəʊ/ *verb* [T] (**forgoes** /-ˈɡəʊz/; *pt* **forwent** /-ˈwent/; *pp* **forgone** /-ˈɡɒn/) (*formal*) to decide not to have or do sth that you want □ *melepaskan; mengorbankan*

forgot *past tense* of **forget**

forgotten *past participle* of **forget**

fork¹ /fɔːk/ *noun* [C] **1** a small metal object with a handle and two or more **prongs** (= long pointed parts) that you use for lifting food to your mouth when eating □ *garpu*: *a knife and fork* ⊃ picture at **cutlery** **2** a large tool with a handle and three or more **prongs** (= long pointed parts) that you use for digging the ground □ *penggembur*: *a garden fork* ⊃ picture at **garden** **3** a place where a road, river, etc. divides into two parts; one of these parts □ *cabang*: *After about two miles you'll come to a fork in the road.*

fork² /fɔːk/ *verb* [I] **1** (used about a road, river, etc.) to divide into two parts □ *bercabang*: *Bear right where the road forks.* **2** to go along the left or right fork of a road □ *belok*: *Fork right up the hill.*

PHR V fork out (for sth) (*informal*) to pay for sth when you do not want to □ *terpaksa membayar*: *I forked out over £20 for that book.*

forked /fɔːkt/ *adj* with one end divided into two parts, like the shape of the letter 'Y' □ *bercabang*: *a bird with a forked tail* ◆ *the forked tongue of a snake*

forklift truck /ˌfɔːklɪft ˈtrʌk/ (also **ˈforklift**) *noun* [C] a vehicle with special equipment on the front for moving and lifting heavy objects □ *trak angkat susun*

forklift truck

forlorn /fəˈlɔːn/ *adj* lonely and unhappy; not cared for □ *sunyi dan sayu; terbiar*

form¹ /fɔːm/ *noun*

▶TYPE **1** [C] a particular type or variety of sth or a way of doing sth □ *bentuk; jenis*: *Swimming is a good form of exercise.* ◆ *We never eat meat in any form.*

▶SHAPE **2** [C,U] the shape of sb/sth; the way sth is presented □ *bentuk*: *He could just make out a shadowy form.* ◆ *The articles were published in book form.*

▶DOCUMENT **3** [C] an official document with questions on it and spaces where you give answers and personal information □ *borang*: *an entry form for a competition* ◆ *Please fill in an application form.* ◆ *an order form* (= a form that is filled in by sb ordering goods from a factory, shop, etc.)

▶BEING FIT **4** [U] (of a sports player, team, etc.) the state of being fit and strong □ *berkeadaan cukup baik/(tdk berapa baik)*: *to be in/out of form*

▶PERFORMANCE **5** [U] how well sb/sth is performing at a particular time, for example in sport or business □ *prestasi*: *to be on/off form* ◆ *On present form the Italian team should win easily.*

▶IN SCHOOL **6** [C] (*BrE old-fashioned*) a class in a school □ *tingkatan*: *Who's your form teacher?*

> **CULTURE**
>
> In Britain, the years at secondary school used to be called **first/second/third**, etc. **form**, but now they are usually called **Year 7** to **Year 11**. However the last two years of school (for pupils aged between 16 and 18) are still referred to as **the sixth form**.

▶OF WORD **7** [C] a way of spelling or changing a word in a sentence □ *bentuk*: *the irregular forms of the verbs* ◆ *The plural form of 'mouse' is 'mice'.*

IDM **true to form** ⊃ **true**

form² /fɔːm/ *verb*

▶START TO EXIST **1** [I,T] to begin to exist or to make sth exist □ *membentuk; dibentuk; terbentuk*: *A pattern was beginning to form in the monthly sales figures.* ◆ *These tracks were formed by rabbits.* **2** [T] to begin to have or think sth □ *membentuk; menjalin*: *I haven't formed an opinion about the new boss yet.* ◆ *to form a friendship*

▶MAKE **3** [T] to make or organize sth □ *membentuk*: *to form a government* ◆ *In English we usually form the past tense by adding '-ed'.*

▶MAKE SHAPE **4** [T] to become or make a particular shape □ *membuat; membentuk*: *The police formed a circle around the house.* ◆ *to form a line/queue*

▶HAVE FUNCTION **5** [T] to be the thing mentioned □ *merupakan*: *Seminars form the main part of the course.* ◆ *The survey formed part of a larger programme of market research.*

formal /ˈfɔːml/ *adj* **1** (used about language or behaviour) used when you want to appear serious or official and in situations in which you do not know the other people very well □ *formal*: *'Yours faithfully' is a formal way of ending a letter.* ◆ *She has a very formal manner—she doesn't seem to be able to relax.* ◆ *a formal occasion* (= one where you must behave politely and wear the clothes that people think are suitable) **OPP** **informal**

> **HELP** In this dictionary some words and phrases are marked *(formal)* or *(informal)*. This will help you to choose the right word for a particular situation. Often there is an informal or neutral (= neither formal nor informal) word with a similar meaning to a more formal one.

2 official □ *rasmi*: *I shall make a formal complaint to the hospital about the way I was treated.* ▶**formally** /-məli/ *adv*

formality /fɔːˈmæləti/ *noun* (*pl* **formalities**) **1** [C] an action that is necessary according to custom or law □ *formaliti; peraturan; adat*: *There are certain formalities to attend to before we can give you a visa.* **2** [C] a thing that you must do as part of an official process, but which has little meaning and will not affect what happens □ *formaliti; adat*: *Michael already knows he has the job so the interview is just a formality.* **3** [U] careful attention to rules of language and behaviour □ *keformalan; kerasmian*

format¹ /ˈfɔːmæt/ *noun* [C] the shape of sth or the way it is arranged or produced □ *format*: *It's the same book but in a different format.*

> **EXAM TIP**
>
> **Exam format**
>
> Find out what the exam will be like. How many parts are there? What are the different question types? What are the **time limits** and **word limits**? Find out how much time you will have to read the questions before a listening test begins. If your answers need to be written on an answer sheet, practise using one and check how much time, if any, you will have at the end of the exam to transfer your answers onto it. ⊃ note at **limit**

format² /ˈfɔːmæt/ *verb* [T] (**formatting**; **formatted**) **1** to prepare a computer disk so that data can be recorded on it □ *memformat*: *to format a disk* **2** to arrange text on a page or a screen □ *menyusun atur; memformat*: *to format a document*

formation /fɔːˈmeɪʃn/ *noun* **1** [U] the act of making or developing sth □ *pembentukan*: *the formation of a new government* **2** [C,U] an arrangement or pattern (especially of soldiers, ships, etc.) □ *formasi; bentukan*: *A number of planes flew over in formation.* **3** [C] a thing that is formed; the particular way in which it is formed □ *formasi; bertukan*: *cloud/rock formations*

formative /ˈfɔːmətɪv/ *adj* [only before a noun] having an important and lasting influence (on sb's character and opinions) □ *formatif; pengaruh yg penting dan berkesan*: *A child's early years are thought to be the most formative ones.*

former /ˈfɔːmə(r)/ adj [only before a noun] of an earlier time; belonging to the past □ *dahulu; bekas*: Bill Clinton, the former American president ◆ In former times people often had larger families.

the former /ˈfɔːmə(r)/ noun [sing] the first (of two people or things just mentioned) □ *yg pertama*: Of the two hospitals in the town—the General and the Royal—the former (= the General) has the better reputation. ᗒ look at **the latter**

formerly /ˈfɔːməli/ adv in the past; before now □ *dahulunya*: Namibia, formerly known as South-West Africa ◆ The hotel was formerly a castle.

> **HELP** Used to be is a more common way of saying **was formerly**: *The hotel used to be a castle.*

formidable /ˈfɔːmɪdəbl/ adj 1 causing you to be quite frightened □ *menggerunkan; menakutkan*: His mother is a rather formidable lady. 2 difficult to deal with; needing a lot of effort □ *sukar*: Reforming the education system will be a formidable task.

formula /ˈfɔːmjələ/ noun [C] (pl **formulas** or **formulae** /-liː/) 1 (*technical*) a group of signs, letters or numbers used in science or mathematics to express a general law or fact □ *formula; rumus*: What is the formula for converting miles to kilometres? 2 a list of (often chemical) substances used for making sth; the instructions for making sth □ *formula*: The formula for the new vaccine has not yet been made public. 3 **a formula for (doing) sth** a plan of how to get or do sth □ *formula; kaedah*: What is her formula for success? ◆ Unfortunately, there's no **magic formula** for a perfect marriage.

formulate /ˈfɔːmjʊleɪt/ verb [T] 1 to prepare and organize a plan or ideas for doing sth □ *membentuk; mengatur*: to formulate a plan 2 to express sth (clearly and exactly) □ *mengungkapkan*: She struggled to formulate a simple answer to his question.

forsake /fəˈseɪk/ verb [T] (pt **forsook** /fəˈsʊk/; pp **forsaken** /fəˈseɪkən/) **forsake sb/sth (for sb/sth)** (*formal*) 1 to leave sb/sth, especially when you have a responsibility to stay □ *meninggalkan; mengabaikan*: He had made it clear to his wife that he would never forsake her. **SYN** abandon 2 to stop doing sth, or leave sth, especially sth that you enjoy □ *meninggalkan*: She forsook the glamour of the city and went to live in the wilds of Scotland. **SYN** renounce

fort /fɔːt/ noun [C] a strong building that is used for military defence □ *kubu*

forth /fɔːθ/ adv
IDM and so forth and other things like those just mentioned □ *dan sebagainya*: The sort of job that you'll be doing is taking messages, making tea and so forth.
back and forth ᗒ **back³**

forthcoming /ˌfɔːθˈkʌmɪŋ/ adj 1 that will happen or appear in the near future □ *akan datang*: Look at our website for a list of **forthcoming events**. 2 [not before a noun] offered or given □ *diberikan*: If no money is forthcoming, we shall not be able to continue the project. 3 [not before a noun] (used about a person) ready to be helpful, give information, etc. □ *sedia menolong, memberikan maklumat, dll*: Kate isn't very forthcoming about her job, so I don't know what she does exactly.

forthright /ˈfɔːθraɪt/ adj saying exactly what you think in a clear and direct way □ *berterus terang*

fortieth ᗒ **forty**

fortification /ˌfɔːtɪfɪˈkeɪʃn/ noun [C, usually pl] walls, towers, etc., built especially in the past to protect a place against attack □ *pengubuan*

fortify /ˈfɔːtɪfaɪ/ verb [T] (**fortifying**; **fortifies**; pt, pp **fortified**) 1 to make a place ready to defend itself in an attack □ *mengubukan*: to fortify a city 2 to make sb/yourself feel stronger, braver, etc. □ *mempersiapkan diri*: He fortified himself against the cold with a hot drink.

fortnight /ˈfɔːtnaɪt/ noun [C, usually sing] (BrE) two weeks □ *dua minggu*: We're going on holiday for a fortnight. ◆ School finishes in a fortnight/in a fortnight's time (= two weeks from now).

fortnightly /ˈfɔːtnaɪtli/ adj, adv (happening or appearing) once every two weeks □ *dua minggu sekali*: This magazine is published fortnightly.

fortress /ˈfɔːtrəs/ noun [C] a castle or other large strong building that it is not easy to attack □ *kubu; kota*

fortunate /ˈfɔːtʃənət/ adj lucky □ *bernasib baik*: It was fortunate that he was at home when you phoned. **OPP** unfortunate

fortunately /ˈfɔːtʃənətli/ adv by good luck □ *nasib baik; mujurlah*: Fortunately the traffic wasn't too bad so I managed to get to the meeting on time. **SYN** luckily

fortune /ˈfɔːtʃuːn/ noun 1 [U] chance or the power that affects what happens in sb's life; luck □ *nasib; tuah*: Fortune was not on our side that day (= we were not lucky). **SYN** fate 2 [C,U] a very large amount of money □ *kekayaan; wang yg banyak*: I always **spend a fortune** on presents at Christmas. ◆ She went to Hollywood in search of **fame and fortune**. ᗒ note at **money** 3 [C, usually pl] the things (both good and bad) that happen to a person, family, country, etc. □ *untung nasib*: The country's fortunes depend on its industry being successful. 4 [C] what is going to happen to a person in the future □ *nasib*: Show me your hand and I'll try to **tell your fortune**. **SYN** fate, destiny
IDM cost the earth/a fortune ᗒ **cost²**

fortune-teller noun [C] a person who tells people what will happen to them in the future □ *tukang tilik*

forty /ˈfɔːti/ number 40 □ *empat puluh; 40* ◇ note at **sixty**

IDM forty winks (*informal*) a short sleep, especially during the day □ *tidur sebentar* ▶**fortieth** /ˈfɔːtiəθ/ *ordinal number, noun* ◇ note at **sixth**

forum /ˈfɔːrəm/ *noun* [C] a forum (for sth) a place or meeting where people can exchange and discuss ideas □ *forum*: *TV is now an important forum for political debate.*

forward¹ /ˈfɔːwəd/ *adv* 1 (also **forwards**) in the direction that is in front of you; towards the front, end or future □ *ke depan*: *Keep going forward and try not to look back.* 2 in the direction of progress □ *ke hadapan; maju*: *The discovery of a new form of treatment is a big step forward in the fight against cancer.* **SYN** for both meanings **ahead OPP** for both meanings **back, backward(s)** ❶ **Forward** is used after many verbs, for example **bring, come, look, put**. For the meaning of the expressions, look at the verb entries.

IDM backward(s) and forward(s) ◇ **backwards**

forward² /ˈfɔːwəd/ *adj* 1 [only *before* a noun] towards the front or future □ *ke hadapan*: *forward planning* 2 having developed earlier than is normal or expected; advanced □ *lebih cepat berkembang drpd biasa*: *Children who read before they are five are considered very forward.* **OPP backward** 3 behaving towards sb in a way that is too confident or too informal □ *keterlaluan; agak lancang*: *I hope you don't think I'm being too forward, asking you so many questions.*

forward³ /ˈfɔːwəd/ *verb* [T] 1 to send a letter, etc. received at one address to a new address □ *menghantarkan semula*: *The post office is forwarding all our mail.* ♦ *I'm forwarding this email to my manager.* 2 to help to improve sth or to make sth progress □ *memajukan*: *I'm trying to forward my career in publishing.*

forward⁴ /ˈfɔːwəd/ *noun* [C] an attacking player in a sport such as football □ *pemain barisan depan*

ˈforwarding address *noun* [C] a new address to which letters, etc. should be sent □ *alamat penghantaran semula*: *The previous owners didn't leave a forwarding address.*

ˈforward-looking *adj* thinking about or planning for the future; having modern ideas □ *memandang ke hadapan; berfikiran moden*

ˈforwards *adv* = **forward¹**(1)

ˈforward slash *noun* [C] a mark (/) used in computer commands and in Internet addresses □ *garis miring depan* ◇ look at **backslash**

forwent *past tense* of **forgo**

fossil /ˈfɒsl/ *noun* [C] (part of) an animal or plant that lived thousands of years ago and which has turned into rock □ *fosil*

ˈfossil fuel *noun* [C,U] fuel such as coal or oil, that was formed over millions of years from the remains of animals or plants □ *bahan api atau bahan bakar fosil*

fossilize (also **-ise**) /ˈfɒsəlaɪz/ *verb* [I,T] 1 (usually passive) to become or make sth become a fossil □ *menjadi fosil; memfosil; memfosilkan*: *fossilized bones* 2 to become or make sb/sth become fixed and unable to change or develop □ *menetapkan, menjadi muktamad*

foster /ˈfɒstə(r)/ (*AmE* also) / *verb* [T] 1 to help or encourage the development of sth (especially feelings or ideas) □ *menggalakkan*: *to foster somebody's friendship/trust* 2 (*especially BrE*) to take a child who needs a home into your family and to take care of them without becoming the legal parent □ *mengambil sebagai anak angkat sementara*: *to foster a child*

MORE The people who do this are **foster parents**. The child is a **foster child**.

◇ note at **child** ◇ look at **adopt**

fought *past tense, past participle* of **fight¹**

foul¹ /faʊl/ *adj* (**fouler; foulest**) 1 that smells or tastes disgusting □ *busuk; teruk*: *a foul-smelling cigar* ♦ *This coffee tastes foul!* 2 (*especially BrE*) very bad or unpleasant □ *teruk; buruk; sedang naik angin*: *Careful what you say—he's in a foul temper/mood.* ♦ *The foul weather prevented our plane from taking off.* 3 (used about language) very rude; full of swearing □ *(bahasa) kesat*: *foul language*

IDM fall foul of sb/sth ◇ **fall¹**

foul² /faʊl/ *verb* 1 [I,T] (used in sports) to do sth, or to do sth to sb, that is against the rules of the game □ *membuat faul; diserang*: *Rooney was fouled inside the box and the referee awarded his team a penalty.* 2 [T] to make sth dirty (with rubbish, waste, etc.) □ *mengotorkan*: *Do not allow your dog to foul the pavement.*

foul³ /faʊl/ *noun* [C] (used in sports) an action that is against the rules □ *faul*: *He was sent off for a foul on the goalkeeper.*

ˌfoul ˈplay *noun* [U] 1 violence or crime that causes sb's death □ *perbuatan khianat*: *The police suspect foul play.* 2 action that is against the rules of a sport □ *main faul/curang*

found¹ *past tense, past participle* of **find¹**

found² /faʊnd/ *verb* [T] 1 to start an organization, institution, etc. □ *menubuhkan; ditubuhkan*: *This museum was founded in 1683.* 2 to be the first to start building and living in a town or country □ *mengasaskan; mendirikan*: *Liberia was founded by freed American slaves.* 3 [usually passive] **be founded on (sth)** to base sth on sth □ *diasaskan*: *The book was founded on real life.*

foundation /faʊnˈdeɪʃn/ *noun* 1 **foundations** [pl] a layer of bricks, etc. under the surface of the ground that forms the solid base of a building □ *asas*: *The builders have only just started to lay the foundations of the new school.* 2 [C,U] the idea, principle, or fact on which sth is based □ *asas; berasas*: *This coursebook aims to give students a solid foundation in grammar.* ♦ *That rumour is completely without foundation* (= it is not true). 3 [C] an organization that provides money for a special purpose □ *yayasan*: *The British Heart Foundation* **4** [U] the act of starting a new institution or organization □ *penubuhan; pengasasan*: *The organization has grown enormously since its foundation in 1995.*

foun'dation course *noun* [C] a general course at a college that prepares students for longer or more difficult courses □ *kursus asas*

founder /ˈfaʊndə(r)/ *noun* [C] a person who starts a new institution or organization □ *pengasas*: *a portrait of the founder of our school*

founder 'member *noun* [C] one of the original members of a club, an organization, etc. □ *ahli pengasas*

foundry /ˈfaʊndri/ *noun* [C] (*pl* **foundries**) a place where metal or glass is melted and shaped into objects □ *faundri*

fountain /ˈfaʊntən/ *noun* [C] **1** a decoration (in a garden or in a square in a town) that sends a flow of water into the air; the water that comes out of a fountain □ *air pancut* ➔ picture on **page P11 2** a strong flow of liquid or another substance that is forced into the air □ *pancutan*: *a fountain of blood/sparks* **3** a person or thing that provides a large amount of sth □ *sumber*: *Ed's a fountain of information on football.*

'fountain pen *noun* [C] a type of pen that you fill with ink □ *pen (dakwat basah)* ➔ picture at **stationery**

four /fɔː(r)/ *number* **1** 4 □ *empat*; *4* ➔ note at **six 2 four-** [in compounds] having four of the thing mentioned □ *empat*: *four-legged animals*
IDM **on all fours** bent over with your hands and knees on the ground □ *merangkak*: *The children went through the tunnel on all fours.*

four-letter 'word *noun* [C] a swear word that shocks or offends people (often with four letters) □ *kata carut/lucah*

fourteen /ˌfɔːˈtiːn/ *number* 14 □ *empat belas*; *14* ➔ note at **six** ▶**fourteenth** /ˌfɔːˈtiːnθ/ *ordinal number, noun* ➔ note at **sixth** □ *keempat belas; ke-14*

fourth /fɔːθ/ *ordinal number* 4th □ *keempat; ke-4* ➔ note at **sixth**

MORE For ¼ we use the word **quarter**: *a quarter of an hour* (= 15 minutes)

four-wheel 'drive *noun* [U,C] an engine that turns all four wheels of a vehicle; a vehicle with this type of engine □ *(kenderaan) pacuan empat roda*

four-'wheeler (*AmE*) = **quad bike**

fowl /faʊl/ *noun* [C] (*pl* **fowl** or **fowls**) a bird, especially a chicken, that is kept on a farm □ *ayam*

fox /fɒks/ *noun* [C] a wild animal like a small dog with reddish-brown fur, a pointed nose and a thick tail □ *rubah*

fox

MORE A fox is often described as **sly** or **cunning**. A female fox is a **vixen**, a young fox is a **cub**.

foyer /ˈfɔɪeɪ/ *noun* [C] an entrance hall in a cinema, theatre, hotel, etc. where people can meet or wait □ *ruang legar; lobi*

fracking /ˈfrækɪŋ/ *noun* [U] the process or industry of getting gas out of the ground by using high pressure and fluid □ *proses atau industri pengeluaran gas dr tanah*

fraction /ˈfrækʃn/ *noun* [C] **1** a small part or amount □ *sedikit; seketika*: *For a fraction of a second I thought the car was going to crash.* **2** a division of a number □ *pecahan*: *½ and ¼ are fractions.*

fractionally /ˈfrækʃnəli/ *adv* to a very small degree; slightly □ *sedikit*: *fractionally faster/taller/heavier*

fracture /ˈfræktʃə(r)/ *noun* [C,U] a break in a bone or other hard material □ *patah; retak* ▶**fracture** *verb* [I,T]: *She fell and fractured her ankle.* ◆ *A water pipe fractured and flooded the bathroom.*

fragile /ˈfrædʒaɪl/ *adj* easily damaged or broken □ *mudah pecah*: *This bowl is very fragile. Please handle it carefully.*

fragment¹ /ˈfrægmənt/ *noun* [C] a small piece that has broken off or that comes from sth larger □ *serpihan; cebisan*: *The builders found fragments of Roman pottery on the site.* ◆ *I heard only a fragment of their conversation.*

fragment² /frægˈment/ *verb* [I,T] (*formal*) to break (sth) into small pieces □ *berpecah-pecah*: *The country is becoming increasingly fragmented by civil war.*

fragrance /ˈfreɪgrəns/ *noun* [C,U] a pleasant smell □ *bau wangi; keharuman* ➔ note at **smell²**

fragrant /ˈfreɪgrənt/ *adj* having a pleasant smell □ *harum*

frail /freɪl/ *adj* (**frailer**; **frailest**) weak or not healthy □ *lemah*: *My aunt is still very frail after her accident.*

frailty /ˈfreɪlti/ *noun* [C,U] (*pl* **frailties**) weakness of sb's body or character □ *kelemahan; lemahnya*

frame¹ /freɪm/ *noun* [C] **1** a border of wood or metal that goes around the outside of a door, picture, window, etc. □ *bingkai*: *a picture frame*

2 the basic strong structure of a piece of furniture, building, vehicle, etc. which gives it its shape □ *rangka*: *the frame of a bicycle/an aircraft* ⊃ picture at **bike** **3** [usually pl] a structure made of plastic or metal that holds the two **lenses** (= pieces of glass) in a pair of glasses □ *bingkai*: *gold-rimmed frames* ⊃ picture at **glasses** **4** [usually sing] the basic shape of a human or animal body □ *susuk badan; tubuh*: *He has a large frame but he's not fat.*

IDM **frame of mind** a particular state or condition of your feelings; the mood you are in □ *keadaan fikiran*: *I'm not in the right frame of mind for a party. I'd prefer to be on my own.*

frame² /freɪm/ *verb* [T] **1** to put a border around sth (especially a picture or photograph) □ *memasang bingkai*: *Let's have this photograph framed.* **2** [usually passive] to give false evidence against sb in order to make them seem guilty of a crime □ *menganiaya; kena aniaya*: *The man claimed that he had been framed by the police.* **3** (*formal*) to express sth in a particular way □ *mengungkapkan; diungkap*: *The question was very carefully framed.*

framework /'freɪmwɜːk/ *noun* [C] **1** the basic structure of sth that gives it shape and strength □ *rangka*: *A greenhouse is made of glass panels fixed in a metal framework.* ♦ (*figurative*) *the basic framework of society* **2** a system of rules or ideas which help you decide what to do □ *rangka*: *The plan may be changed but it will provide a framework on which we can build.*

franc /fræŋk/ *noun* [C] the unit of money that is used in Switzerland and several other countries (replaced in 2002 in France, Belgium and Luxembourg by the euro) □ *franc*

franchise /'fræntʃaɪz/ *noun* **1** [C,U] official permission to sell a company's goods or services in a particular area; a business or a service that is run in this way □ *francais*: *They have the franchise to sell this product in Cyprus.* ♦ *Most fast-food restaurants are operated under franchise.* ♦ *Most fast-food restaurants are franchises.* **2** [U] (*formal*) the right to vote in elections □ *hak mengundi*

frank /fræŋk/ *adj* (**franker**; **frankest**) [**More frank** is also common.] showing your thoughts and feelings clearly; saying what you mean □ *terus terang*: *To be perfectly frank with you, I don't think you'll pass your driving test.* ▶**frankly** *adv*: *Please tell me frankly what you think about my idea.* ▶**frankness** *noun* [U]

frankfurter /'fræŋkfɜːtə(r)/ *noun* (*AmE* also **wiener**) [C] a type of small smoked **sausage** (= meat formed in a long thin shape) □ *frankfurter*

frantic /'fræntɪk/ *adj* **1** very busy or done in a hurry □ *sibuk; kelam-kabut*: *Things are frantic in the office at this time of year.* ♦ *a frantic search for the keys* **SYN** **hectic** **2** extremely worried or frightened □ *kalut; sangat cemas*: *She went frantic when she couldn't find her child.* ♦ *frantic cries for help* ▶**frantically** /-kli/ *adv*

fraternal /frə'tɜːnl/ *adj* (*formal*) connected with the relationship that exists between brothers; like a brother □ *ttg hubungan antara saudara lelaki*: *fraternal love/rivalry*

fraternity /frə'tɜːnəti/ *noun* (*pl* **fraternities**) **1** [C] a group of people who share the same work or interests □ *golongan; ikatan*: *the medical fraternity* **2** [U] the feeling of friendship and support between people in the same group □ *persaudaraan; ukhuwah*

fraud /frɔːd/ *noun* **1** [U,C] (an act of) cheating sb in order to get money, etc. illegally □ *penipuan; (perbuatan) menipu*: *The accountant was sent to prison for fraud.* ♦ *Massive amounts of money are lost every year in credit card frauds.* **2** [C] a person who tricks sb by pretending to be sb else □ *penipu*

fraudulent /'frɔːdjələnt/ *adj* (*formal*) done in order to cheat sb; dishonest □ *palsu; secara menipu*: *the fraudulent use of stolen cheques*

fraught /frɔːt/ *adj* **1** **fraught with sth** filled with sth unpleasant □ *penuh dgn*: *a situation fraught with danger/difficulty* **2** (used about people) worried and nervous; (used about a situation) very busy so that people become nervous □ *tegang; agak kalut*: *Things are usually fraught at work on Mondays.*

fray /freɪ/ *verb* [I,T] **1** if cloth, etc. **frays** or becomes **frayed**, some of the threads at the end start to come apart □ *berbulu; berjumbai*: *This shirt is beginning to fray at the cuffs.* ♦ *She frayed the bottom of her jeans.* **2** if sb's nerves, etc. **fray** or become **frayed**, they start to get annoyed □ *menjadi tegang*: *Tempers began to fray towards the end of the match.*

freak¹ /friːk/ *noun* [C] **1** (*informal*) a person who has a very strong interest in sth □ *peminat; orang yg gila sst*: *a fitness/computer freak* **SYN** **fanatic** **2** a very unusual and strange event, person, animal, etc. □ *sso/sst yg aneh*: *The other kids think Ally's a freak because she doesn't watch TV.* ▶**freak** *adj*: *a freak accident/storm/result*

freak² /friːk/ *verb* [I,T] (*informal*) **freak (sb) (out)** if sb **freaks** or sth **freaks** them, they react very strongly to sth that makes them suddenly feel shocked, surprised, frightened, etc. □ *terkejut, marah, dsb*: *She freaked out when she heard the news.* ♦ *The film 'Snakes on a Plane' really freaked me out.*

freckle /'frekl/ *noun* [C, usually pl] a small brown spot on your skin □ *jagat; tetua*: *A lot of people with red hair have got freckles.* ⊃ look at **mole** ▶**freckled** *adj*

free¹ /friː/ *adj* (**freer**; **freest**) *adv*
▶NOT CONTROLLED **1** **free (to do sth)** not controlled by the government, rules, etc. □ *bebas; kebebasan*: *There is free movement of people across the border.* ♦ *free speech/a free press*
▶NOT IN PRISON **2** not in prison or in a **cage** (= a box made of bars), etc.; not held or controlled □ *bebas; membebaskan*: *The government set 6*

free → freeze

political prisoners **free** last year. ♦ There is nowhere around here where dogs can run free.
▶NO PAYMENT **3** costing nothing □ *percuma*: Admission to the museum is free of charge. ♦ Children under five usually travel free on trains.
▶WITHOUT STH **4 free from/of sth** not having sth dangerous, unpleasant, etc. □ *bebas; tdk (risau, terikat, sakit, dll)*: free of worries/responsibility ♦ free from pain
▶AVAILABLE **5** not busy or being used □ *tdk sibuk; lapang; kosong*: I'm afraid Mr Spencer is not free this afternoon. ♦ I don't get much **free time**. ♦ Is this seat free?
IDM feel free ⇒ feel¹
free and easy informal or relaxed □ *tdk formal; bersahaja*: The atmosphere in our office is very free and easy.
get, have, etc. a free hand to get, have, etc. permission to make your own decisions about sth □ *mendapat, mempunyai, dsb kebebasan*: I had a free hand in designing the course.
of your own free will because you want to, not because sb forces you □ *dgn kemahuan sendiri*

free² /friː/ verb [T] **1 free sb/sth (from sth)** to let a person or an animal leave or escape from a place where he/she/it is held □ *membebaskan*: to free a prisoner ♦ The protesters freed the animals from their cages. **SYN release 2 free sb/sth of/from sth** to take away sth that is unpleasant from sb □ *melegakan; menghilangkan*: The medicine freed her from pain for a few hours. **3 free sb/sth (up) for sth; free sb/sth (up) to do sth** to make sth available so that it can be used; to put sb in a position in which they can do sth □ *melepaskan; membolehkan*: If I cancel my trip, that will free me to see you on Friday.

free 'agent noun [C] a person who can do what they want because nobody else has the right to tell them what to do □ *(orang yg) bebas*

freedom /'friːdəm/ noun **1** [C,U] the right or ability to do or say what you want □ *kebebasan*: You have the freedom to come and go as you please. ♦ freedom of speech ♦ the rights and freedoms of the individual ⇒ look at **liberty 2** [U] the state of not being held prisoner or controlled by sb else □ *kebebasan; kemerdekaan*: The opposition leader was given his freedom after 25 years. **3** [U] **freedom from sth** the state of not being affected by sth unpleasant □ *kebebasan; tdk merasa*: freedom from fear/hunger/pain **4** [U] **the freedom of sth** the right to use sth without restriction □ *bebas (menggunakan sst)*: You can have the freedom of the ground floor, but please don't go upstairs.

'freedom fighter noun [C] a name to describe a person who uses violence to try to remove a government from power, by people who support this □ *pejuang kebebasan*

free 'enterprise noun [U] the operation of business without government control □ *perusahaan bebas*

freehand /'friːhænd/ adj [only before a noun]

adv (used about a drawing) (done) by hand, without the help of any instruments □ *dgn tangan*: a freehand sketch ♦ to draw freehand

free 'kick noun [C] (in the sports of football or rugby) a situation in which a player of one team is allowed to kick the ball because a member of the other team has broken a rule □ *tendangan percuma*

freelance /'friːlɑːns/ adj, adv earning money by selling your services or work to different organizations rather than being employed by a single company □ *bebas*: a freelance journalist ♦ She works freelance. ▶**freelance** (also **freelancer** /'friːlɑːnsə(r)/) noun [C] ▶**freelance** verb [I]: I left my full-time job because I can earn more by freelancing.

freely /'friːli/ adv **1** in a way that is not controlled or limited □ *dgn bebas; tanpa sekatan*: He is the country's first freely elected president for 40 years. **2** without trying to avoid the truth even though it might be embarrassing; in an honest way □ *dgn terus terang*: I freely admit that I made a mistake.

Freemason /'friːmeɪsn/ (also **mason**) noun [C] a man who belongs to an international secret society whose members help each other and who recognize each other by secret signs □ *Freemason*

free-'range adj (used about a system of farming) kept or produced in a place where animals can move around freely □ *ternak lepas; (telur, ayam, dsb) kampung*: free-range hens/turkeys ♦ We always buy free-range eggs. ⇒ look at **battery**

free 'speech noun [U] the right to express any opinion in public □ *kebebasan bersuara*

freeway /'friːweɪ/ (AmE) = **motorway**

freeze¹ /friːz/ verb (pt **froze** /frəʊz/; pp **frozen** /'frəʊzn/)
▶BECOME ICE **1** [I,T] to become hard (and often change into ice) because of extreme cold; to make sth do this □ *menjadi beku; membeku; beku*: Water freezes at 0° Celsius. ♦ The ground was frozen solid for most of the winter. ♦ frozen peas/fish/food
▶WEATHER **2** [I] used with 'it' to describe extremely cold weather when water turns into ice □ *tersangat sejuk (hingga membeku)*: I think it's going to freeze tonight.
▶BE VERY COLD **3** [I,T] to be very cold or to die from cold □ *kesejukan; mati kesejukan*: It was so cold on the mountain that we thought we would **freeze to death**. ♦ Turn the heater up a bit—I'm frozen stiff.
▶STOP MOVING **4** [I] to stop moving suddenly and completely because you are frightened or in danger □ *tertegun; tdk/jangan bergerak*: The terrible scream made her freeze with terror. ♦ Suddenly the man pulled out a gun and shouted 'Freeze!' **5** [I] when a computer screen **freezes** you cannot move any of the images, etc. on it, because there is a problem with the system □ *menjadi beku*

▶PRICES **6** [T] to keep the money people earn, prices, etc. at a fixed level for a certain period of time □ *membekukan; dibekukan*: *Spending on defence has been frozen for one year.*

freeze² /fri:z/ *noun* [C] **1** the fixing of the money people earn, prices, etc. at one level for a certain period of time □ *pembekuan* **2** a period of weather when the temperature stays below freezing point (0° Celsius) □ *tempoh cuaca sejuk membeku*

freezer /ˈfri:zə(r)/ (*also* deep ˈfreeze) *noun* [C] a large box or cupboard in which you can store food for a long time at a temperature below freezing point (0° Celsius) so that it stays frozen □ *peti sejuk beku* ⇒ look at **fridge** ⇒ picture on **page P8**

freezing¹ /ˈfri:zɪŋ/ *adj* (*informal*) very cold □ *sangat sejuk*: *I'm freezing!* ♦ *It's absolutely freezing outside.* ⇒ note at **cold**

freezing² /ˈfri:zɪŋ/ (*also* ˈfreezing point) *noun* [U] the temperature at which water freezes □ *takat beku*: *Last night the temperature fell to six degrees below freezing.*

freight /freɪt/ *noun* [U] goods that are carried from one place to another by ship, lorry, etc.; the system for carrying goods in this way □ *muatan; angkutan; pengangkutan*: *a freight train* ♦ *Your order will be sent by air freight.*

ˈfreight car (*AmE*) = **wagon**

freighter /ˈfreɪtə(r)/ *noun* [C] a ship or an aircraft that carries only goods and not passengers □ *kapal/kapal terbang pengangkut* ⇒ note at **boat**

French ˈbread *noun* [U] white bread in the shape of a long thick stick □ *roti Perancis*

French ˈfry (*especially AmE*) = **chip¹**(3)

French ˈwindow (*AmE* ˌFrench ˈdoor) *noun* [C] one of a pair of glass doors that open onto a garden □ *pintu tetingkap*

frenzied /ˈfrenzid/ *adj* that is wild and out of control □ *kegila-gilaan; tdk tentu arah; kelam-kabut*: *a frenzied attack* ♦ *frenzied activity*

frenzy /ˈfrenzi/ *noun* [sing, U] a state of great emotion or activity that is not under control □ *kekalutan; kesibukan*: *The crowd was in a frenzy at the speaker's words.* ♦ *I could hear a frenzy of activity in the kitchen.*

frequency /ˈfri:kwənsi/ *noun* (*pl* **frequencies**) **1** [U] the number of times sth happens in a particular period □ *kekerapan*: *Fatal accidents have decreased in frequency in recent years.* **2** [U] the fact that sth happens often □ *kekerapan*: *The frequency of child deaths from cancer near the nuclear power station is being investigated.* **3** [C,U] the rate at which a sound wave or radio wave **vibrates** (= moves up and down) □ *frekuensi*: *a high/low frequency*

frequent¹ /ˈfri:kwənt/ *adj* happening often □ *kerap*: *His visits became less frequent.* **OPP** **infrequent** ▶**frequently** *adv*

frequent² /friˈkwent/ *verb* [T] (*formal*) to go

freeze → friction

to a place often □ *selalu pergi*: *He spent most of his evenings in Paris frequenting bars and clubs.*

fresh /freʃ/ *adj* (**fresher**; **freshest**)
▶FOOD **1** (used especially about food) produced or picked very recently; not frozen or in a tin □ *segar; baharu*: *fresh bread/fruit/flowers* ⇒ look at **stale**
▶NEW **2** left somewhere or experienced recently □ *baharu; segar*: *fresh blood/footprints* ♦ *Write a few notes while the lecture is still fresh in your mind.* **3** new and different □ *baharu*: *They have decided to make a fresh start in a different town.* ♦ *I'm sure he'll have some fresh ideas on the subject.*
▶CLEAN **4** pleasantly clean or bright □ *segar; nyaman*: *Open the window and let some fresh air in.*
▶WATER **5** without salt; not sea water □ *tawar*: *a shortage of fresh water*
▶NOT TIRED **6** full of energy □ *segar*: *I'll think about the problem again in the morning when I'm fresh.*
▶JUST FINISHED **7** fresh from/out of sth having just finished sth □ *baru saja*: *Life isn't easy for a young teacher fresh from university.*
IDM break fresh/new ground ⇒ **ground¹**
▶**freshly** *adv*: *freshly baked bread* ▶**freshness** *noun* [U]

freshen /ˈfreʃn/ *verb* [T] freshen sth (up) to make sth cleaner or brighter □ *menyegarkan; menjadikan lebih ceria*: *Some new curtains and wallpaper would freshen up this room.*
PHR V freshen up to wash and make yourself clean and tidy □ *membersihkan diri*

fresher /ˈfreʃə(r)/ *noun* [C] (*BrE*) a student who has just started his or her first term at university □ *penuntut tahun pertama*

ˈfresh-faced *adj* having a young, healthy-looking face □ *bermuka muda*: *fresh-faced kids*

freshman /ˈfreʃmən/ *noun* [C] (*pl* -men /-mən/) (*AmE*) a student who is in their first year at college, high school, university, etc. □ *penuntut tahun pertama*

freshwater /ˈfreʃwɔ:tə(r)/ *adj* [only before a noun] living in water or having water that is not salty □ *air tawar*: *freshwater fish* ♦ *a freshwater lake*

fret¹ /fret/ *verb* [I] (**fretting**; **fretted**) fret (about/at/over sth) to be worried and unhappy about sth □ *risau*: *I was awake for hours fretting about my exams.*

fret² /fret/ *noun* [C] one of the bars across the long thin part of a **guitar** (= a musical instrument with strings), etc. that show you where to put your fingers to produce a particular sound □ *fret* ⇒ picture at **music**

Fri. *abbr* = **Friday**: *Fri. 27 May*

friction /ˈfrɪkʃn/ *noun* [U] **1** the rubbing of one surface or thing against another □ *geseran*: *You have to put oil in the engine to reduce friction between the moving parts.* **2** friction (between A and B) disagreement between people or groups

---

[C] **countable**, a noun with a plural form: *one book, two books*   [U] **uncountable**, a noun with no plural form: *some sugar*

Friday → fringe

□ *perselisihan*: There is a lot of friction between the older and younger members of staff.

Friday /ˈfraɪdeɪ; -di/ noun [C,U] (abbr **Fri.**) the day of the week after Thursday □ *Jumaat* ⊃ note at **Monday**

fridge /frɪdʒ/ (also formal **refrigerator**; AmE **icebox**) noun [C] a metal container with a door in which food, etc. is kept cold (but not frozen) so that it stays fresh □ *peti sejuk* ⊃ look at **freezer** ⊃ picture on page P8

friend /frend/ noun [C] **1** a person that you know and like (not a member of your family), and who likes you □ *kawan; sahabat*: Dalibor and I are old friends. We were at school together. ♦ We're only inviting close friends and relatives to the wedding. ♦ Carol's my best friend. ♦ A friend of mine told me about this restaurant. ♦ One of my friends told me about this restaurant. ⊃ look at **boyfriend, girlfriend, penfriend 2** a friend of/to sth a person who supports an organization, a charity, etc., especially by giving money; a person who supports a particular idea, etc. □ *sahabat; penyokong*: the Friends of the Churchill Hospital **3** a person you communicate with using a social networking, site (= a website for people who share your interests) □ *rakan sembang dlm laman sosial*: She's got 150 friends on Facebook. ⊃ note at **social networking**

IDM be/make friends (with sb) to be/become a friend (of sb) □ *berkawan (dgn sso)*: Tony is rather shy and finds it hard to make friends.
a false friend ⊃ **false**

TOPIC
Friends

People often **get to know** each other through work or school, and then **become friends**. A common informal word for friend is **mate**: *I'm going out with my mates.* **Friendly** people **get on well** (= have a good relationship) with lots of people. They usually find it easy to **make friends**. If you and a friend are very **close**, you can **chat** (= talk) about anything. Even if you don't see each other very often, you can **keep in touch** (for example by phone or email). When you **meet up/get together** again, you can **catch up on** (= find out about) each other's news.

friendly¹ /ˈfrendli/ adj (friendlier; friendliest) **1** friendly (to/towards(s) sb) behaving in a kind and open way □ *mesra*: Everyone here has been very friendly towards us. **OPP** unfriendly ⊃ note at **nice 2** showing kindness in a way that makes people feel happy and relaxed □ *ramah mesra*: a friendly smile/atmosphere **OPP** unfriendly **3** friendly with sb treating sb as a friend □ *baik dgn (sso)*: Nick's become quite friendly with the boy next door. ♦ Are you on friendly terms with your neighbours? **4** [in compounds] helpful to sb/sth; not harmful to sth □ *mesra; tdk menjejaskan*: This software is extremely user-friendly.

♦ ozone-friendly sprays **5** in which the people, teams, etc. taking part are not competing seriously □ *persahabatan*: a friendly argument ♦ I've organized a friendly match against my brother's team. ▶ **friendliness** noun [U]

friendly² /ˈfrendli/ noun [C] (pl friendlies) a sports match that is not part of an important competition □ *perlawanan persahabatan*

friendship /ˈfrendʃɪp/ noun **1** [C] a friendship (with sb); a friendship (between A and B) a relationship between people who are friends □ *persahabatan*: a close/lasting/lifelong friendship **2** [U] the state of being friends □ *persahabatan*: Our relationship is based on friendship, not love.

fright /fraɪt/ noun [C,U] a sudden feeling of fear or shock □ *ketakutan; rasa takut*: I hope I didn't give you a fright when I shouted. ♦ The child cried out in fright when she saw a dark shadow at the window.

frighten /ˈfraɪtn/ verb [T] to make sb/sth afraid or shocked □ *menakutkan*: That programme about the rise in the crime rate really frightened me.

PHR V frighten sb/sth away/off to cause a person or an animal to go away by frightening them or it □ *membuat sso/sst lari (kerana takut)*: Walk quietly so that you don't frighten the birds away.

frightened /ˈfraɪtnd/ adj **1** full of fear or worry □ *ketakutan; takut*: Frightened children were calling for their mothers. ♦ I was frightened that they would think that I was rude. **2** frightened of sb/sth afraid of a particular person, thing or situation □ *takut akan*: When I was young I was frightened of spiders. ⊃ note at **afraid**

frightening /ˈfraɪtnɪŋ/ adj making you feel afraid or shocked □ *(yg) menakutkan*: a frightening experience ♦ It's frightening that time passes so quickly.

frightful /ˈfraɪtfl/ adj (old-fashioned) **1** (used for emphasizing sth) very bad or great □ *sangat; betul-betul*: We're in a frightful rush. **2** very bad or unpleasant □ *teruk*: The weather this summer has been frightful. **SYN** for both meanings **awful, terrible**

frightfully /ˈfraɪtfəli/ adv (old-fashioned) very □ *sangat*: I'm frightfully sorry.

frigid /ˈfrɪdʒɪd/ adj **1** (usually used about a woman) unable to enjoy sex □ *tdk dpt menikmati seks* **2** not showing any emotion □ *dingin; tdk mesra*

frill /frɪl/ noun [C] **1** a decoration for the edge of a dress, shirt, etc. which is made by forming many folds in a narrow piece of cloth □ *ropol* **2** [usually pl] something that is added that you feel is not necessary □ *ciri-ciri istimewa/tambahan*: We just want a plain simple meal—no frills. ▶ **frilly** adj: a frilly dress

fringe¹ /frɪndʒ/ noun [C] **1** (AmE bangs [pl]) the part of your hair that is cut so that it hangs over your **forehead** (= the part of your face above

[I] **intransitive**, a verb which has no object: He laughed.   [T] **transitive**, a verb which has an object: He ate an apple.

your eyes) □ *rambut yg berjuntai di dahi*: *Your hair looks better with a fringe.* ⊃ picture at **hair** **2** a border for decoration on a piece of clothing, etc. that is made of a lot of hanging threads □ *jumbai; rumbai* **3** (BrE) the outer edge of an area or a group that is a long way from the centre or from what is usual □ *pinggir*: *Some people on the fringes of the socialist party are opposed to the policy on Europe.*

fringe² /frɪndʒ/ *verb*
IDM be fringed with sth to have sth as a border or around the edge □ *dipinggiri sst*: *The lake was fringed with pine trees.*

'fringe benefit *noun* [C, usually pl] an extra thing that is given to an employee in addition to the money he or she earns □ *faedah sampingan selain gaji*: *The fringe benefits of this job include a car and free health insurance.* ⊃ A more informal word is **perk**.

frisk /frɪsk/ *verb* **1** [T] to pass your hands over sb's body in order to search for hidden weapons, drugs, etc. □ *meraba periksa* **2** [I] (used about an animal or child) to play and jump about happily and with a lot of energy □ *terlompat-lompat gembira*

frisky /'frɪski/ *adj* (**friskier**; **friskiest**) full of life and wanting to play □ *bersemangat*

fritter /'frɪtə(r)/ *verb*
PHR V fritter sth away (on sth) to waste time or money on things that are not important □ *membuang-buang (masa atau wang dgn sst)*

frivolity /frɪ'vɒləti/ *noun* [U] silly behaviour (especially when you should be serious) □ *sikap tdk serius; sifat dangkal*

frivolous /'frɪvələs/ *adj* not serious; silly □ *tdk serius; dangkal*

frizzy /'frɪzi/ *adj* (**frizzier**; **frizziest**) (used about hair) very curly □ *berkeriting halus (rambut)*

fro /frəʊ/ *adv*
IDM to and fro ⊃ **to**

frog /frɒg (AmE also) / *noun* [C] a small animal with smooth skin and long back legs that it uses for jumping. Frogs live in or near water □ *katak*: *Our pond is full of frogs in the spring.* ⊃ picture on page P13

frogman /'frɒgmən (AmE also) / *noun* [C] (pl **-men** /-mən/) a person whose job is to work under the surface of water wearing special rubber clothes and using breathing equipment □ *juruselam*: *Police frogmen searched the river.*

frogspawn /'frɒgspɔːn (AmE also) / *noun* [U] a clear substance that looks like jelly and contains the eggs of a frog □ *telur katak (jernih dan lembut seakan jeli)* ⊃ picture on page P13

from /frəm; *strong form* frɒm (AmE also) / *prep* **1** showing the place, direction or time that sb/sth starts or started □ *dari*: *She comes home from work at 7 o'clock.* ◆ *a cold wind from the east* ◆ *Water was dripping from the tap.* ◆ *Peter's on holiday from next Friday.* ◆ *The supermarket is open from 8 a.m. till 8 p.m. every day.* **2** showing the person who sent or gave sth □ *drpd*: *I borrowed this jacket from my sister.* ◆ *a phone call from my father* **3** showing the origin of sb/sth □ *dr; drpd*: *'Where do you come from?' 'I'm from Australia.'* ◆ *cheeses from France and Italy* ◆ *quotations from Shakespeare* **4** showing the material which is used to make sth □ *drpd*: *Paper is made from wood.* ◆ *This sauce is made from cream and wine.*

HELP Made of tells us the material the object actually consists of: *a table made of wood* ◆ *a house made of bricks*

5 showing the distance between two places □ *dr*: *The house is five miles from the town centre.* ◆ *I work not far from here.* **6** showing the point at which a series of prices, figures, etc. starts □ *dr*: *Tickets cost from £3 to £11.* **7** showing the state of sb/sth before a change □ *dr; drpd*: *The time of the meeting has been changed from 7 to 8 o'clock.* ◆ *The article was translated from Russian into English.* ◆ *Things have gone from bad to worse.* **8** showing that sb/sth is taken away, removed or separated from sb/sth else □ *drpd*: *Children don't like being separated from their parents for a long period.* ◆ *(in mathematics) 8 from 12 leaves 4.* **9** showing sth that you want to avoid □ *drpd*: *There was no shelter from the wind.* ◆ *This game will stop you from getting bored.* **10** showing the cause of sth □ *kerana; akibat*: *People in the camps are suffering from hunger and cold.* **11** showing the reason for making a judgement or forming an opinion □ *drpd*: *You can tell quite a lot from somebody's handwriting.* **12** showing the difference between two people, places or things □ *antara; drpd*: *Can you tell margarine from butter?* ◆ *Is Portuguese very different from Spanish?*
IDM from ... on starting at a particular time and continuing for ever □ *sejak dr; mulai*: *She never spoke to him again from that day on.* ◆ *From now on you must earn your own living.*

front¹ /frʌnt/ *noun*
▶FORWARD PART/POSITION **1 the front** [C, usually sing] the side or surface of sth/sb that faces forward □ *bahagian depan*: *a dress with buttons down the front* ◆ *The front of a building was covered with ivy.* ◆ *a card with flowers on the front* ◆ *She slipped on the stairs and spilt coffee all down her front.* **2 the front** [sing] the most forward part of sth; the area that is just outside of or before sb/sth □ *bahagian depan; di depan*: *Young children should not travel in the front of the car.* ◆ *There is a small garden at the front of the house.*

HELP On the front, in front or **at the front? On the front of** means 'on the front surface of sth': *The number is shown on the front of the bus.*

In front (of sth) means 'further forward than another person or thing'; before sb/sth else: *A car has stopped in front of the bus.* ◆ *There were three people in front of me in the queue.*

front → frugal

At/In the front (of sth) means 'in the most forward part inside sth': *The driver sits at the front of the bus.* Look at these sentences too: *The teacher usually stands in front of the class.* ◆ *The noisy children were asked to sit at the front of the class* (= in the front seats).

▸IN WAR **3 the front** [C, usually sing] the line or area where fighting takes place in a war □ *barisan depan; medan pertempuran*: *to be sent to the front*

▸AREA OF ACTIVITY **4** [C] a particular area of activity □ *bahagian; bidang*: *Things are difficult on the political/economic front at the moment.* ◆ *Progress has been made on all fronts.*

▸HIDING FEELINGS **5** [sing] a way of behaving that hides your true feelings □ *selindungan*: *His brave words were just a front. He was really feeling very nervous.*

▸WEATHER **6** [C] a line or area where warm air and cold air meet □ *perenggan*: *A cold front is moving in from the north.*

IDM back to front ⊃ back¹

in front further forward than sb/sth □ *di hadapan*: *Some of the children ran on in front.* ◆ *After three laps the Kenyan runner was in front.* **SYN** ahead

in front of sb/sth **1** in a position further forward than but close to sb/sth □ *di hadapan/depan*: *The bus stops right in front of our house.* ◆ *Don't stand in front of the TV.* ◆ *The book was open in front of her on the desk.* ⊃ picture at **opposite**

HELP Be careful. **In front of** does not mean the same as **opposite**.

2 if you do sth in front of sb, you do it when that person is there in the same room or place as you □ *di hadapan/depan*: *Don't do that in front of the children.*

up front (informal) as payment before sth is done □ *dibayar dahulu*: *I want half the money up front and half when the job is finished.*

front² /frʌnt/ *adj* [only before a noun] on or at the front □ *depan*: *the front garden/room* ◆ *Open the front door.* ◆ *sit in the front row* ◆ *front teeth* ◆ *Have you seen the front page of today's paper?*

frontal /ˈfrʌntl/ *adj* [only before a noun] from the front □ *dr depan*: *a frontal attack*

frontier /ˈfrʌntɪə(r)/ *noun* **1** [C] **the frontier (between A and B)** the line where one country joins another; border □ *sempadan*: *the end of frontier controls in Europe* ⊃ note at **border 2 the frontiers** [pl] the limit between what we do and do not know □ *batas*: *Scientific research is constantly pushing back the frontiers of our knowledge about the world.*

front-page *adj* [only before a noun] interesting or important enough to appear on the front page of a newspaper □ *muka depan*: *front-page news/headlines*

frost¹ /frɒst/ *noun* [C,U] the weather condition when the temperature falls below freezing point (0° Celsius) and a thin layer of ice forms on the ground and other surfaces, especially at night □ *ibun; fros*: *a hard frost* ◆ *a chilly night with some ground frost*

frost² /frɒst/ *verb* [T] (*especially AmE*) = **ice²**
PHR V frost over/up to become covered with a thin layer of ice □ *berfros*: *The window has frosted over/up.* ⊃ look at **defrost**

frostbite /ˈfrɒstbaɪt/ *noun* [U] a serious medical condition of the fingers, toes, etc. that is caused by very low temperatures □ *luka beku*: *All the climbers were suffering from frostbite.*

frosted /ˈfrɒstɪd/ *adj* [only before a noun] (used about glass or a window) with a special surface so you cannot see through it □ *berkabut*

frosting /ˈfrɒstɪŋ/ (*especially AmE*) = **icing**

frosty /ˈfrɒsti/ *adj* (**frostier**; **frostiest**) **1** very cold, with frost (= ice on the ground) □ *berfros*: *a cold and frosty morning* **2** cold and unfriendly □ *dingin*: *a frosty welcome*

froth¹ /frɒθ/ *noun* [U] a mass of small white bubbles on the top of a liquid, etc. □ *buih; busa* ▸**frothy** *adj*: *frothy beer* ◆ *a frothy cappuccino*

froth² /frɒθ/ *verb* [I,T] to have or produce a mass of white bubbles □ *berbuih; berbusa*: *The mad dog was frothing at the mouth.*

frown /fraʊn/ *verb* [I] to show you are angry, serious, etc. by making lines appear on your forehead (= the part of your face above your eyes) □ *mengerutkan dahi*

PHR V frown on/upon sth to think that sth is not good or suitable □ *tdk menyukai/disukai*: *Smoking is very much frowned upon these days.* ◆ *Performing experiments on animals is very much frowned upon these days.* ◆ *Her parents frowned on her plans to go backpacking alone.* **SYN** disapprove
▸**frown** *noun* [C]

frown

froze past tense of **freeze¹**

frozen¹ past participle of **freeze¹**

frozen² /ˈfrəʊzn/ *adj* **1** (used about food) stored at a low temperature in order to keep it for a long time □ *sejuk beku*: *frozen meat/vegetables* **2** (*informal*) (used about people and parts of the body) very cold □ *sangat sejuk; kesejukan*: *My feet are frozen!* ◆ *I was frozen stiff.* **SYN** freezing **3** (used about water) with a layer of ice on the surface □ *beku; dilitupi ais*: *The pond is frozen. Let's go skating.*

frugal /ˈfruːgl/ *adj* **1** using only as much money or food as is necessary □ *berjimat cermat; berhemat*: *a frugal existence/life* **OPP** extravagant **2** (used about meals) small, simple and not costing very much □ *tdk mahal; secukup keperluan*: *a frugal lunch of bread and cheese* **SYN** meagre ▸**frugality** /fruˈgæləti/ *noun* [U] ▸**frugally** /ˈfruːgəli/ *adv*: *to live/eat frugally*

fruit /fruːt/ *noun* **1** [C,U] the part of a plant or tree that contains seeds and that we eat ☐ *buah*: *Try and eat more fresh fruit and vegetables.* ◆ *Marmalade is made with citrus fruit* (= oranges, lemons, etc.). ◆ *Is a tomato a fruit or a vegetable?* ◆ *fruit juice* ◆ *fruit salad* ⮕ picture on page P14

> **HELP** We can use the countable form of 'fruit' to talk about types of fruit: *The papaya is a tropical fruit.* ◆ *Most big supermarkets sell all sorts of tropical fruits.* When talking about an individual piece of fruit we usually use the name of the fruit: *Would you like an apple?* or we use the uncountable form: *Would you like some fruit?*

2 [C] the part of any plant in which the seed is formed ☐ *buah* **3** [pl] **the fruits (of sth)** a good result or success from work that you have done ☐ *hasil*: *It will be years before we see the fruits of this research.*

IDM bear fruit ⮕ bear¹

fruitful /'fruːtfl/ *adj* producing good results; useful ☐ *berhasil*: *fruitful discussions*

fruition /fru'ɪʃn/ *noun* [U] (*formal*) the time when a plan, etc. starts to be successful ☐ *berhasil*: *After months of hard work, our efforts were coming to fruition.*

fruitless /'fruːtləs/ *adj* producing poor or no results; not successful ☐ *tdk berhasil; sia-sia*: *a fruitless search* ◆ *It's fruitless to keep trying—she'll never agree to it.*

frustrate /frʌ'streɪt/ *verb* [T] **1** to cause a person to feel annoyed or impatient because they cannot do or achieve what they want ☐ *mengecewakan; menghampakan*: *It's the lack of money that really frustrates him.* **2** (*formal*) to prevent sb from doing sth or sth from happening ☐ *menghalang; mematahkan*: *The rescue work has been frustrated by bad weather conditions.* ▶**frustrated** *adj*: *He felt very frustrated at his lack of progress in learning Chinese.* ▶**frustrating** *adj*

frustration /frʌ'streɪʃn/ *noun* [C,U] a feeling of anger because you cannot get what you want; something that causes you to feel like this ☐ *rasa kecewa; kekecewaan*: *He felt anger and frustration at no longer being able to see very well.* ◆ *Every job has its frustrations.*

fry¹ /fraɪ/ *verb* [I,T] (**frying**; **fries**; *pt, pp* **fried**) to cook sth or to be cooked in hot fat or oil ☐ *menggoreng*: *to fry an egg* ◆ *a fried egg* ◆ *I could smell bacon frying in the kitchen.* ⮕ note at **cook, recipe**

fry² /fraɪ/ *noun* [C] (*pl* **fries**) (*especially AmE*) = **chip¹**(3) ☐ *kentang goreng*

'frying pan (*AmE* **frypan** /'fraɪpæn/) *noun* [C] a flat pan with a long handle that is used for frying food ☐ *kuali*

ft *abbr* = **foot¹**(5) ☐ *kaki*: *a room 10 ft by 6 ft*

fudge /fʌdʒ/ *noun* [U] a type of soft brown sweet made from sugar, butter and milk ☐ *sejenis manisan lembut*

fuel¹ /'fjuːəl/ *noun* **1** [U] material that is burned to produce heat or power ☐ *bahan api*: *What's the car's fuel consumption?* **2** [C] a type of fuel ☐ *bahan api*: *I think gas is the best fuel for central heating.*

fuel² /'fjuːəl/ *verb* [T] (**fuelling**; **fuelled**, (*AmE*) **fueling**; **fueled**) **1** to put petrol into a vehicle ☐ *mengisi petrol* **2** to make sb feel an emotion more strongly ☐ *memarakkan*: *Her interest in the Spanish language was fuelled by a visit to Spain.*

fugitive /'fjuːdʒətɪv/ *noun* [C] a person who is running away or escaping (for example from the police) ☐ *orang pelarian* ⮕ look at **refugee**

fulfil (*AmE* **fulfill**) /fʊl'fɪl/ *verb* [T] (**fulfilling**; **fulfilled**) **1** to make sth that you wish for happen; to achieve a goal ☐ *mencapai*: *He finally fulfilled his childhood dream of becoming a doctor.* ◆ *to fulfil your ambition/potential* **2** to do or have everything that you should or that is necessary ☐ *menunaikan; menepati; memenuhi*: *to fulfil a duty/obligation/promise/need* ◆ *The conditions of entry to university in this country are quite difficult to fulfil.* **3** to have a particular role or purpose ☐ *memainkan (peranan)*: *Italy fulfils a very important role within the European Union.* **4** to make sb feel completely happy and satisfied ☐ *memuaskan; memenuhi*: *I need a job that really fulfils me.* ▶**fulfilled** *adj*: *When I had my baby I felt totally fulfilled.* ▶**fulfilling** *adj*: *I found working abroad a very fulfilling experience.*

fulfilment (*AmE* **fulfillment**) /fʊl'fɪlmənt/ *noun* [U] the act of achieving a goal; the feeling of satisfaction that you have when you have done sth ☐ *pencapaian; kepuasan*: *the fulfilment of your dreams/hopes/ambitions* ◆ *to find personal/emotional fulfilment*

full¹ /fʊl/ *adj* (**fuller**; **fullest**)

▶WITH NO SPACE **1** holding or containing as much or as many as possible ☐ *penuh; sibuk*: *The bin needs emptying. It's full up* (= completely full). ◆ *a full bottle* ◆ *The bus was full so we had to wait for the next one.* ◆ (*figurative*) *We need a good night's sleep because we've got a full* (= busy) *day tomorrow.*

▶HAVING A LOT **2 full of sb/sth** containing a lot of sb/sth ☐ *penuh; banyak*: *The room was full of people.* ◆ *His work was full of mistakes.* ◆ *The children are full of energy.*

▶WITH FOOD **3 full (up)** having had enough to eat and drink ☐ *kenyang*: *No more, thank you. I'm full (up).*

▶COMPLETE **4** [only *before* a noun] complete; not leaving anything out ☐ *lengkap; sepenuhnya; penuh*: *I should like a full report on the accident, please.* ◆ *Full details of today's TV programmes are on page 20.* ◆ *He took full responsibility for what had happened.* ◆ *Please give your full name and address.*

▶MAXIMUM **5** [only *before* a noun] the highest or greatest possible ☐ *penuh; sepenuhnya; maksi-*

full → function

mum: *She got full marks in her French exam.* ♦ *The train was travelling at full speed.*

▶TALKING A LOT **6 full of sb/sth/yourself** pleased about or proud of sb/sth/yourself □ *asyik bercakap ttg (sst/diri sendiri)*: *When she got back from holiday she was full of everything they had seen.* ♦ *He's full of himself* (= thinks that he is very important) *since he got that new job.*

▶FAT **7** round or rather fat in shape □ *montok; bulat*: *She's got quite a full figure.* ♦ *He's quite full in the face.*

▶CLOTHES **8** (used about clothes) made with plenty of cloth □ *kembang*: *a full skirt*

IDM at full strength (used about a group) having all the people it needs or usually has □ *kuat*: *Nobody is injured, so the team will be at full strength for the game.*

at full stretch working as hard as possible □ *sepenuh tenaga*: *When the factory is operating at full stretch, it employs 800 people.*

full of beans/life with a lot of energy and enthusiasm □ *banyak kekuatan/tenaga; cukup segar*: *They came back from their holiday full of beans.*

have your hands full ⊃ **hand¹**

in full with nothing missing; completely □ *sepenuhnya*: *Your money will be refunded in full* (= you will get all your money back). ♦ *Please write your name in full.*

in full swing at the stage when there is the most activity □ *sedang rancak/meriah betul*: *When we arrived the party was already in full swing.*

in full view (of sb/sth) in a place where you can easily be seen □ *di depan (sso/sst)*: *In full view of the guards, he tried to escape over the prison wall.*

to the full as much as possible □ *sepenuhnya*: *to enjoy life to the full*

full² /fʊl/ *adv* **full in/on (sth)** straight; directly □ *betul-betul; tepat*: *John hit him full in the face.* ♦ *The two cars crashed full on.*

full-ˈblown *adj* [only *before* a noun] fully developed □ *sebenarnya; sudah betul-betul (melarat, dll)*: *Her anger turned into a full-blown tantrum.*

full ˈboard *noun* [U] (in a hotel, etc.) including all meals □ *penginapan termasuk makan* ⊃ note at **hotel** ⊃ look at **half board**, **bed and breakfast**

full-ˈfledged (*AmE*) = **fully fledged**

full-ˈlength *adj* [only *before* a noun] **1** (used about a picture, mirror, etc.) showing a person from head to foot □ *penuh; panjang* **2** not made shorter □ *penuh; lengkap*: *a full-length film* **3** (used about a dress, skirt, etc.) reaching the feet □ *labuh*

full ˈmoon *noun* [sing] the moon when it appears as a complete circle □ *bulan purnama*

full-ˈscale *adj* [only *before* a noun] **1** using every thing or person that is available □ *(yg) sepenuhnya*: *The police have started a full-scale murder investigation.* **2** (used about a plan, drawing, etc.) of the same size as the original object □ *sebesar saiz asal*: *a full-scale plan/model*

full ˈstop (*especially AmE* **period**) *noun* [C] a mark (.) that is used in writing to show the end of a sentence □ *titik; noktah*

full-ˈtime *adj*, *adv* (done or working) for all the normal period of work □ *penuh masa*: *He has a full-time job.* ♦ *He works full-time.* ♦ *We employ 800 full-time staff.* ⊃ look at **part-time**

fully /'fʊli/ *adv* completely; to the highest possible degree □ *benar-benar; cukup; sepenuhnya*: *I'm fully aware of the problem.* ♦ *All our engineers are fully trained.*

fully ˈfledged (*AmE also* **full-ˈfledged**) *adj* completely trained or completely developed □ *(yg) sepenuhnya/mantap*: *My sister is now a fully fledged solicitor.*

fumble /'fʌmbl/ *verb* [I] to try to find or take hold of sth with your hands in a nervous or careless way □ *terkial-kial; meraba-raba*: '*It must be here somewhere,*' *she said, fumbling in her pocket for her key.*

fume /fjuːm/ *verb* [I] to be very angry about sth □ *meradang*

fumes /fjuːmz/ *noun* [pl] smoke or gases that smell unpleasant and that can be dangerous to breathe in □ *wasap*: *diesel/petrol/exhaust fumes*

fun¹ /fʌn/ *noun* [U] pleasure and enjoyment; an activity or a person that gives you pleasure and enjoyment □ *keseronokan; seronok*: *We had a lot of fun at the party last night.* ♦ *The party was great fun.* ♦ *Have fun* (= enjoy yourself)*!* ♦ *It's no fun having to get up at 4 o'clock every day.*

IDM (just) for fun/for the fun of it (just) for entertainment or pleasure; not seriously □ *(hanya) utk suka-suka*: *I don't need English for my work. I'm learning it for fun.*

in fun as a joke □ *melawak*: *It was said in fun. They didn't mean to upset you.*

make fun of sb/sth to laugh at sb/sth in an unkind way; to make other people do this □ *mentertawakan atau mengejek sso/sst*: *The older children are always making fun of him because of his accent.*

poke fun at sb/sth ⊃ **poke**

fun² /fʌn/ *adj* amusing or enjoyable □ *seronok*: *to have a fun time/day out* ♦ *Brett's a fun guy.*

> **HELP Fun** or **funny**? **Fun** is not the same as **funny**: *The party was fun* (= it was enjoyable). ♦ *The film was funny* (= it made me laugh). **Funny** can also mean 'strange'.

function¹ /'fʌŋkʃn/ *noun* [C] **1** the purpose or special duty of a person or thing □ *fungsi; tugas*: *The function of the heart is to pump blood through the body.* ♦ *to perform/fulfil a function* **2** an important social event, ceremony, etc. □ *acara; upacara*: *The princess attends hundreds of official functions every year.*

function² /'fʌŋkʃn/ *verb* [I] to work correctly; to be in action □ *berfungsi, berjalan*: *Only one engine was still functioning.* **SYN operate**

functional /ˈfʌŋkʃənl/ *adj* **1** practical and useful rather than attractive □ *praktikal; fungsian*: *cheap functional furniture* **2** working; being used □ *berfungsi; berjalan*: *The system is now fully functional.*

functionality /ˌfʌŋkʃəˈnæləti/ *noun* (*pl* **functionalities**) **1** [U] the quality in sth of being very suitable for the purpose it was designed for □ *kefungsian* **SYN practicality 2** [U] the purpose that sth is designed for □ *fungsi*: *Manufacturing processes may be affected by the functionality of the product.* **3** [C,U] the functions that a computer or other electronic system can perform □ *fungsi*: *new software with additional functionality*

ˈfunction key *noun* [C] one of several keys on a computer, each marked with 'F' and a number, that can be used to perform a particular operation □ *kekunci fungsi*

fund¹ /fʌnd/ *noun* **1** [C] a sum of money that is collected for a particular purpose □ *dana; tabung*: *They contributed £100 to the disaster relief fund.* **2** **funds** [pl] money that is available and can be spent □ *wang*: *The hospital is trying to raise funds for a new kidney machine.*

fund² /fʌnd/ *verb* [T] to provide a project, school, charity, etc. with money □ *membiayai; dibiayai*: *education programmes funded by the UN*

fundamental /ˌfʌndəˈmentl/ *adj* basic and important; from which everything else develops □ *asas; dasar; utama*: *There will be fundamental changes in the way the school is run.* ◆ *There is a fundamental difference between your opinion and mine.* ➔ look at **essential** ▶**fundamentally** /-təli/ *adv*: *The government's policy on this issue has changed fundamentally.*

fundamentalist /ˌfʌndəˈmentəlɪst/ *noun* [C] a person who follows the basic rules and teachings of any religion very strictly □ *fundamentalis* ▶**fundamentalist** *adj*: *Christian fundamentalist teaching* ▶**fundamentalism** /-ɪzəm/ *noun* [U]

fundamentals /ˌfʌndəˈmentlz/ *noun* [pl] basic facts or principles □ *asas-asas*

ˈfund-raiser *noun* [C] a person whose job is to find ways of collecting money for a charity or an organization □ *penganjur kutipan derma* ▶**ˈfund-raising** *noun* [U]: *fund-raising events*

funeral /ˈfjuːnərəl/ *noun* [C] a ceremony (often a religious one) for burying or burning a dead person □ *pengebumian*: *The funeral will be held next week.*

> **MORE** The body of the dead person is carried in a **coffin**, on which there are often **wreaths** of flowers. The coffin is buried in a **grave** or is **cremated** (= burned).

ˈfuneral director = **undertaker**

funfair /ˈfʌnfeə(r)/ = **fair²**(1)

fungus /ˈfʌŋɡəs/ *noun* [C,U] (*pl* **fungi** /ˈfʌŋɡiː; -ɡaɪ/ *or* **funguses**) **1** a type of plant without leaves, flowers or green colouring, such as a **mushroom**. Some **fungi** can be harmful. □ *kulat* ➔ note at **mushroom** ➔ look at **toadstool** **2** a substance like a wet powder that grows on old wood or food, walls, etc. □ *kulat* ➔ look at **mould** ▶**fungal** /ˈfʌŋɡl/ *adj*: *a fungal disease/infection/growth*

funnel /ˈfʌnl/ *noun* [C] **1** an object that is wide at the top and narrow at the bottom, used for pouring liquid, powder, etc. into a small opening □ *corong* **2** the metal pipe which takes smoke or steam out of a ship, an engine, etc. □ *serombong*

funnily /ˈfʌnəli/ *adv* in a strange or unusual way □ *dgn cara yg ganjil/luar biasa*: *She's walking very funnily.*

IDM funnily enough used for expressing surprise at sth strange that has happened □ *(yg) hairannya*: *Funnily enough, my parents weren't at all cross about it.*

funny /ˈfʌni/ *adj* (**funnier**; **funniest**) **1** that makes you smile or laugh □ *lucu*: *a funny story* ◆ *He's an extremely funny person.* ◆ *That's the funniest thing I've heard in ages!* **2** strange or unusual; difficult to explain or understand □ *aneh; pelik; (rasa) tak sedap*: *Oh dear, the engine is making a funny noise.* ◆ *It's funny that they didn't phone to let us know they couldn't come.* ◆ *That's funny—he was here a moment ago and now he's gone.* **SYN peculiar** ➔ note at **fun²**, **humour** **3** (*informal*) slightly ill □ *rasa tak sedap badan*: *Can I sit down for a minute? I feel a bit funny.*

fur /fɜː(r)/ *noun* **1** [U] the soft thick hair that covers the bodies of some animals □ *bulu binatang* ➔ picture on **page P12 2** [C,U] the skin and hair of an animal that is used for making clothes, etc.; a piece of clothing that is made from this □ *bulu*: *a fur coat*

furious /ˈfjʊəriəs/ *adj* **1 furious (with sb); furious (at sth)** very angry □ *meradang; sangat marah*: *He was furious with her for losing the car keys.* ◆ *She was furious at having to walk home.* ➔ *noun* **fury** **2** very strong; violent □ *hebat; teruk*: *They had a furious argument.*

IDM fast and furious ➔ **fast¹**
▶**furiously** *adv*

furnace /ˈfɜːnɪs/ *noun* [C] a large, very hot fire, surrounded on all sides by walls, that is used for melting metal, burning rubbish, etc. □ *relau*

furnish /ˈfɜːnɪʃ/ *verb* [T] to put furniture in a room, house, etc. □ *melengkapi dgn perabot*: *The room was comfortably furnished.* ▶**furnished** *adj*: *She's renting a furnished room in Birmingham.*

furnishings /ˈfɜːnɪʃɪŋz/ *noun* [pl] the furniture, carpets, curtains, etc. in a room, house, etc. □ *perabot dan aksesori*

furniture /ˈfɜːnɪtʃə(r)/ *noun* [U] the things that can be moved, for example tables, chairs, beds, etc. in a room, house or office □ *perabot*: *modern/antique/second-hand furniture* ◆ *garden/office furniture*

furrow → future

> **GRAMMAR** **Furniture** is uncountable: *They only got married recently and they haven't got much furniture.* We say **a piece of furniture** if we are talking about one item: *The only nice piece of furniture in the room was an old-fashioned desk.*

furrow /ˈfʌrəʊ/ *noun* [C] **1** a line in a field that is made by a **plough** (= a farming machine that turns the earth) for planting seeds in □ *alur* **2** a deep line in the skin on sb's face □ *kerut* ⊃ look at **wrinkle**

furry /ˈfɜːri/ *adj* (**furrier**; **furriest**) having fur □ *berbulu*: *a small furry animal*

further[1] /ˈfɜːðə(r)/ *adj, adv* **1** (also **farther**) [the comparative of *far*] at or to a greater distance in time or space □ *lebih jauh; lebih dahulu*: *It's not safe to go any further.* ♦ *I can't remember any further back than 1970.* **2** more; to a greater degree □ *selanjutnya; kelak*: *Are there any further questions?* ♦ *Please let us know if you require any further information.* ♦ *I have nothing further to say on the subject.* ♦ *The museum is closed until further notice* (= until we say that it is open again). ♦ *Can I have time to consider the matter further?*

> **HELP** **Further** or **farther**? **Further** and **farther** can both be used when you are talking about distance: *Bristol is further/farther from London than Oxford is.* ♦ *I jumped further/farther than you did.* In other senses only **further** can be used: *We need a further week to finish the job.*

IDM **further afield** ⊃ **afield**

further[2] /ˈfɜːðə(r)/ *verb* [T] (formal) to help sth to develop or be successful □ *mempertingkatkan; membantu kemajuan*: *to further the cause of peace*

further eduˈcation *noun* [U] (abbr **FE**) (BrE) education that is provided for people after leaving school, but not at a university □ *pendidikan lanjutan* ⊃ look at **higher education**

furthermore /ˌfɜːðəˈmɔː(r)/ *adv* also; in addition □ *lagipun; tambahan pula*

furthest /ˈfɜːðɪst/ ⊃ **far**

furtive /ˈfɜːtɪv/ *adj* secret, acting as though you are trying to hide sth because you feel guilty □ *secara diam-diam/curi-curi*: *a furtive glance at the letter* ▶ **furtively** *adv*

fury /ˈfjʊəri/ *noun* [U] very great anger □ *kemarahan yg meluap-luap*: *She was speechless with fury.* ⊃ adjective **furious**

fuse[1] /fjuːz/ *noun* [C] **1** a small piece of wire in an electrical system, machine, etc. that melts and breaks if there is too much power. This stops the flow of electricity and prevents fire or damage □ *fius*: *A fuse has blown—that's why the house is in darkness.* ♦ *That plug needs a 15 amp fuse.* **2** a piece of rope, string, etc. or a device that is used to make a bomb, etc. explode at a particular time □ *sumbu*

fuse[2] /fjuːz/ *verb* [I,T] **1** (used about two things) to join together to become one; to make two things do this □ *melakur; bersatu; bercantum*: *As they heal, the bones will fuse together.* ♦ *The two companies have been fused into one large organization.* **2** to stop working because a **fuse**[1] (1) has melted; to make a piece of electrical equipment do this □ *terbakar*: *The lights have fused.* ♦ *I've fused the lights.*

fuselage /ˈfjuːzəlɑːʒ/ *noun* [C] the main part of a plane (not the engines, wings or tail) □ *fiuslaj*

fusion /ˈfjuːʒn/ *noun* [U, sing] the process or the result of joining different things together to form one □ *pergabungan; perpaduan*: *the fusion of two political systems*

fuss[1] /fʌs/ *noun* [sing, U] a time when people behave in an excited, a nervous or an angry way, especially about sth unimportant □ *kecoh; heboh*: *Mum always makes a fuss about my untidy bedroom.* ♦ *What's all the fuss about?* ♦ *It was all a fuss about nothing.*

IDM **make/kick up a fuss (about/over sth)** to complain strongly □ *mengomel/ bersungut (ttg sst)*

make a fuss of/over sb/sth to pay a lot of attention to sb/sth □ *bersusah payah melayan sso/ ttg sst*: *My grandmother used to make a big fuss of me when she visited.*

fuss[2] /fʌs/ *verb* [I] **1 fuss (over sb/sth)** to pay too much attention to sb/sth □ *bersusah payah*: *Stop fussing over all the details.* **2** to be worried or excited about small things □ *risau; cerewet*: *Stop fussing. We're not going to be late.*

IDM **not be fussed (about sb/sth)** (BrE informal) to not care very much □ *tdk peduli sangat*: '*Where do you want to go for lunch?*' '*I'm not fussed.*'

fussy /ˈfʌsi/ *adj* (**fussier**; **fussiest**) **1 fussy (about sth)** (used about people) giving too much attention to small details and therefore difficult to please □ *cerewet*: *He is very fussy about food* (= there are many things which he does not eat). ⊃ look at **particular, picky** **2** having too much detail or decoration □ *terlalu banyak hiasan*: *I don't like that pattern. It's too fussy.*

futile /ˈfjuːtaɪl/ *adj* (used about an action) having no success; useless □ *sia-sia*: *They made a last futile attempt to make him change his mind.* ▶ **futility** /fjuːˈtɪləti/ *noun* [U]

futon /ˈfuːtɒn/ *noun* [C] a Japanese **mattress** (= the soft part of a bed), often on a wooden frame, that can be used for sitting on or rolled out to make a bed □ *futon; sejenis tilam Jepun* ⊃ note at **bed**

future /ˈfjuːtʃə(r)/ *noun* **1 the future** [sing] the time that will come after the present □ *masa depan*: *Who knows what will happen in the future?* ♦ *in the near/distant future* (= soon/not soon) **2** [C] what will happen to sb/sth in the time after the present □ *masa depan*: *Our children's futures depend on a good education.* ♦ *The company's future does not look very hopeful.* **3** [U] the possi-

---

[I] **intransitive**, a verb which has no object: *He laughed.*   [T] **transitive**, a verb which has an object: *He ate an apple.*

bility of being successful □ *masa depan*: *I could see no future in this country so I left to work abroad.* **4 the future (tense)** [sing] the form of a verb that expresses what will happen after the present □ *kala depan* ❶ For more information about the future tense, look at the **Reference Section** at the back of this dictionary.

IDM **in future** from now on □ *lain kali*: *Please try to be more careful in future.*

▶ **future** *adj* [only *before* a noun]: *She met her future husband when she was still at school.* ♦ *You can keep that book for future reference* (= to look at again later).

fuzzy /ˈfʌzi/ *adj* (**fuzzier; fuzziest**) not clear □ *kabur; kelam*: *The photo was a bit fuzzy but I could just make out my mother in it.*

FYI /ˌef waɪ ˈaɪ/ *abbr* (*written*) **for your information** □ *utk makluman/pengetahuan anda*

G, g

G, g /dʒiː/ *noun* [C,U] (*pl* **Gs; G's; g's** /dʒiːz/) **1** the 7th letter of the English alphabet □ *G, g (huruf)*: *'Gentleman' begins with (a) 'G'.* **2 G** (used about music) the fifth note in the scale of C major □ *not kelima dlm skala C major*: *G major/minor* ♦ *G sharp*

g *abbr* = **gram**

gable /ˈɡeɪbl/ *noun* [C] the pointed part at the top of an outside wall of a house between two parts of the roof □ *tebar layar; gabel*

gadget /ˈɡædʒɪt/ *noun* [C] (*informal*) a small device, tool or machine that has a particular but usually unimportant purpose □ *alat*: *This car has all the latest gadgets.*

Gaelic /ˈɡeɪlɪk/ *adj, noun* [U] (of) the Celtic language and the culture of Ireland or Scotland □ *Gaelik*

gag¹ /ɡæɡ/ *noun* [C] **1** a piece of cloth, etc. that is put in or over sb's mouth in order to stop them from talking □ *sumbat mulut* **2** a joke □ *jenaka*

gag² /ɡæɡ/ *verb* [T] (**gagging; gagged**) to put a **gag** in or over sb's mouth □ *menyumbat mulut*

gage /ɡeɪdʒ/ (*AmE*) = **gauge¹**

gaily /ˈɡeɪli/ *adv* **1** in a bright and attractive way □ *berwarna-warni; penuh seri*: *a gaily decorated room* **2** happily □ *dgn riang atau girang*: *She waved gaily to the crowd.* **3** without thinking or caring about the effect of your actions on other people □ *dgn senang*: *She gaily announced that she was leaving.*

gain¹ /ɡeɪn/ *verb* **1** [T] to gradually get more of sth □ *memperoleh; bertambah*: *The train was gaining speed.* ♦ *to gain weight/confidence* **OPP** **lose 2** [T] to obtain or win sth, especially sth that you need or want □ *mendapat; memenangi*: *They managed to gain access to secret information.* ♦ *The country gained its independence ten years ago.* **3** [I,T] **gain (sth) (by/from sth/doing sth)** to get an advantage □ *mendapat manfaat/faedah; beruntung*: *I've got nothing to gain by staying in this job.* **OPP** **lose**

IDM **gain ground** to make progress; to become stronger or more popular □ *semakin maju/diterima*

PHR V **gain in sth** to gradually get more of sth □ *menjadi lebih (yakin, dll)*: *He's gained in confidence in the past year.*

gain on sb/sth to get closer to sb/sth that you are trying to catch □ *semakin dekat*: *I saw the other runners were gaining on me so I increased my pace.*

gain² /ɡeɪn/ *noun* [C,U] an increase, improvement or advantage in sth □ *keuntungan; pertambahan*: *We hope to make a gain* (= get more money than we paid) *when we sell our house.* ♦ *a gain in weight of one kilo* ♦ *He will do anything for personal gain, even if it means treating people badly.* **OPP** **loss**

gait /ɡeɪt/ *noun* [sing] the way that sb/sth walks □ *gaya jalan*

gal. *abbr* = **gallon**

gala /ˈɡɑːlə/ *noun* [C] a special social occasion or sports event □ *pesta; gala*: *a swimming gala*

galaxy /ˈɡæləksi/ *noun* **1** [C] (*pl* **galaxies**) a large group of stars and planets in space □ *galaksi* **2 the Galaxy; the Milky Way** [sing] the system of stars that contains our sun and its planets, seen as a bright band in the night sky □ *Bima Sakti*

gale /ɡeɪl/ *noun* [C] a very strong wind □ *angin kencang*: *Several trees blew down in the gale.* ⊃ look at **storm**

gallant /ˈɡælənt/ *adj* (*formal*) **1** showing courage in a difficult situation □ *berani*: *gallant men/soldiers/heroes* ♦ *He made a gallant attempt to speak French, but nobody could understand him.* **SYN** **brave 2** (used about men) polite to and showing respect for women □ *bersopan terhadap wanita*

gallantry /ˈɡæləntri/ *noun* [U] **1** courage, especially in battle □ *keberanian* **2** polite behaviour towards women by men □ *sikap bersopan terhadap wanita*

gallery /ˈɡæləri/ *noun* [C] (*pl* **galleries**) **1** a building or room where works of art are shown to the public □ *balai; galeri*: *an art gallery* ⊃ picture on **page P11 2** an upstairs area at the back or sides of a large hall or theatre where people can sit □ *galeri*

galley /ˈɡæli/ *noun* [C] **1** a long flat ship with sails, especially one used by the ancient Greeks or Romans in war □ *ghali; sejenis kapal zaman dahulu* **2** the kitchen on a ship or plane □ *dapur; galei*

gallon /ˈɡælən/ *noun* [C] (*abbr* **gal.**) a measure of liquid; 4.5 litres □ *gelen*

gallop → gap 362

> **MORE** There are **8 pints** in a gallon. An American gallon is the same as 3.8 litres.

ℹ For more information about measurements, look at the section on using numbers at the back of this dictionary.

gallop /ˈɡæləp/ verb [I] (used about a horse or a rider) to go at the fastest speed □ *menderap* ⊃ look at **canter**, **trot** ▶ **gallop** noun [sing]

gallows /ˈɡæləʊz/ noun [C] (pl **gallows**) a wooden frame used in the past on which people were killed by hanging □ *tempat hukum gantung*

galore /ɡəˈlɔː(r)/ adv [only *after* a noun] in large numbers or amounts □ *berlambak-lambak*: There will be prizes galore at our children's party on Saturday.

galvanize (also **-ise**) /ˈɡælvənaɪz/ verb [T] **1** galvanize sb (into sth/into doing sth) to make sb take action by shocking them or by making them excited □ *merangsangkan*: The urgency of his voice *galvanized them into action*. **2** (technical) to cover metal with **zinc** (= a silver-grey metal) in order to protect it from being damaged by water □ *menggalvani; menyadur atau menyalut*: a galvanized bucket ♦ galvanized steel

gamble¹ /ˈɡæmbl/ verb [I,T] gamble (sth) (on sth) to bet money on the result of a card game, horse race, etc. □ *berjudi; mempertaruhkan wang*: to gamble on horses ♦ She gambled all her money on the last race. **SYN** bet

PHR V gamble on sth/on doing sth to act in the hope that sth will happen although it may not □ *berharapkan atau mengharapkan sst (dgn membuat sst)*: I wouldn't gamble on the weather staying fine.

▶ **gambler** noun [C]: He's a compulsive gambler.
▶ **gambling** noun [U]: Some people want to ban Internet gambling.

gamble² /ˈɡæmbl/ noun [C] something you do that is a risk □ *pertaruhan; risiko*: Setting up this business was a bit of a gamble.

game¹ /ɡeɪm/ noun **1** [C] a game (of sth) a form of play or sport with rules; a time when you play it □ *permainan; perlawanan*: Shall we play a game? ♦ Let's have a game of chess. ♦ a game of football/rugby/tennis ♦ 'Monopoly' is a very popular **board game**. ♦ a new computer game ♦ Tonight's game is between Holland and Italy. ♦ The game ended in a draw. **2 games** [pl] an important sports competition □ *sukan*: Where were the last Olympic Games held? **3** [C] (in sports such as **tennis**) a section of a match that forms a unit in scoring □ *perlawanan*: two games all (= both players have won two games) **4** [C] how well sb plays a sport □ *permainan*: My new racket has really improved my game. **5** [C] an activity that you do to have fun □ *main-main*: Some children were playing a game of hide-and-seek. **6** [C] (informal) a secret plan or trick □ *muslihat*: Stop playing games with me and tell me where you've hidden my bag. **7** [U] wild animals or birds that are killed for sport or food □ *binatang buruan*: big game (= lions, tigers, etc.)

IDM give the game away to tell a person sth that you are trying to keep secret □ *pecah tembelang; membuka rahsia*: It was the expression on her face that gave the game away.

game² /ɡeɪm/ adj (used about a person) ready to try sth new, unusual, difficult, etc. □ *sanggup; bersedia*: I've never been sailing before but I'm game to try.

gamekeeper /ˈɡeɪmkiːpə(r)/ noun [C] a person who is responsible for the birds and animals that are kept on private land for people to hunt □ *penjaga mergastua*

ˈgame show noun [C] a television programme in which people play games or answer questions to win prizes □ *sejenis rancangan permainan di televisyen* ⊃ look at **quiz**

gammon /ˈɡæmən/ noun [U] (BrE) meat from the back leg or side of a pig that has been **cured** (= treated with salt or smoke to keep it fresh), usually served in thick slices □ *daging babi yg diawet atau disalai* ⊃ look at **bacon**, **ham**, **pork**

gander /ˈɡændə(r)/ noun [C] a male **goose** (= a bird like a large duck with a long neck) □ *angsa jantan*

gang¹ /ɡæŋ/ noun [C, with sing or pl verb] **1** an organized group of criminals □ *geng* **2** a group of young people who cause trouble, fight other groups, etc. □ *geng*: The woman was robbed by a gang of youths. ♦ gang warfare/violence **3** (informal) a group of friends who meet regularly □ *geng*

gang² /ɡæŋ/ verb

PHR V gang up on sb (informal) to join together with other people in order to act against sb □ *berpakat menentang sso*: She's upset because she says the other kids are ganging up on her.

gangrene /ˈɡæŋɡriːn/ noun [U] the death of a part of the body because the blood supply to it has been stopped as a result of disease or injury □ *gangren; kelemayuh* ▶ **gangrenous** /ˈɡæŋɡrɪnəs/ adj

gangster /ˈɡæŋstə(r)/ noun [C] a member of a group of criminals □ *gengster*

gangway /ˈɡæŋweɪ/ noun [C] **1** (BrE) a passage between rows of seats in a cinema, an aircraft, etc. □ *laluan* **2** a bridge that people use for getting on or off a ship □ *lawa; titi kapal*

gaol, gaoler (BrE) = **jail**, **jailer**

gap /ɡæp/ noun [C] **1** a gap (in/between sth) an empty space in sth or between two things □ *celah; luang*: The sheep got out through a gap in the fence. **2** a period of time when sth stops, or between two events □ *sela; terhentinya (sst)*: I returned to tennis after a gap of about two years. ♦ a gap in the conversation **3** a difference between people or their ideas □ *jurang*: The gap between the rich and the poor is getting wider. **4** a part of sth that is missing □ *tempat kosong; ke-*

ð **then**   s **so**   z **zoo**   ʃ **she**   ʒ **vi**sion   h **how**   m **man**   n **no**   ŋ **sing**   l **leg**   r **red**   j **yes**   w **wet**

kosongan: In this exercise you have to fill (in) the gaps in the sentences. ♦ *I think our new product should fill* ***a gap in the market***.
IDM **bridge a/the gap** ➔ **bridge²**

gape /geɪp/ *verb* [I] **1** gape (at sb/sth) to look at sb/sth for a long time with your mouth open because you are surprised, shocked, etc. □ *melopong; tercengang; ternganga*: *We gaped in astonishment when we saw what Amy was wearing.* **2** gape (open) to be or become wide open □ *terbuka; ternganga*: *a gaping hole/wound*

'**gap year** *noun* [C] (*BrE*) a year that a young person spends working and/or travelling, often between leaving school and starting university □ *tahun sela (utk bekerja/mengembara) sebelum memasuki universiti*: *I'm planning to take a gap year and go backpacking in India.*

garage /'gærɑːʒ; -rɪdʒ/ *noun* [C] **1** a small building where a car, etc. is kept □ *garaj*: *The house has a double garage* (= with space for two cars). **2** a place where vehicles are repaired and/or petrol is sold □ *bengkel kereta; stesen minyak*: *a garage mechanic* ➔ look at **petrol station**

garbage /'gɑːbɪdʒ/ (*especially AmE*) = **rubbish**

'**garbage can** (*AmE*) = **dustbin**

garbled /'gɑːbld/ *adj* (used about a message, story, etc.) difficult to understand because it is not clear □ *tak tentu biji butirnya*

garden¹ /'gɑːdn/ *noun* [C] **1** (*AmE* **yard**) a piece of land next to a house where flowers and vegetables can be grown, usually with a **lawn** (= an area of grass) □ *laman; pekarangan (rumah)*: *Let's have lunch in the garden.* ♦ *the back/front garden* ♦ *garden flowers* ♦ *garden chairs* (= for using in the garden) ➔ note at **yard** ➔ picture on page P8 **2** gardens [pl] a public park □ *taman*: *the Botanical Gardens*

garden² /'gɑːdn/ *verb* [I] to work in a garden □ *berkebun*: *She's been gardening all afternoon.*

'**garden centre** *noun* [C] a place where plants, seeds, garden equipment, etc. are sold □ *pusat jualan barang perkebunan*

gardener /'gɑːdnə(r)/ *noun* [C] a person who works in a garden as a job or for pleasure □ *tukang kebun; orang yg suka berkebun*

gardening /'gɑːdnɪŋ/ *noun* [U] looking after a garden □ *perkebunan*: *I'm going to do some gardening this afternoon.* ♦ *gardening tools/gloves*

'**garden party** *noun* [C] a formal social event that takes place outside usually in a large garden in summer □ *jamuan laman*

gargle /'gɑːgl/ *verb* [I] to wash your throat with a liquid (which you do not swallow) □ *berkumur*

garish /'geərɪʃ/ *adj* too bright or decorated and therefore unpleasant □ *menyilaukan; terlalu berhias* **SYN** **gaudy**

garlic /'gɑːlɪk/ *noun* [U] a plant of the onion family with a strong taste and smell that is used in cooking □ *bawang putih*: *Chop two cloves of garlic and fry in oil.* ➔ picture on page P15

363 **gape** ➔ **garrison**

garden equipment

- trowel
- hand fork
- rakes
- hoe
- watering can
- wheelbarrow
- lawnmower
- fork
- spade
- shovel
- blade
- handle
- reel
- shears
- hose

garment /'gɑːmənt/ *noun* [C] (*formal*) one piece of clothing □ *pakaian* ➔ look at **clothes**

garnish /'gɑːnɪʃ/ *verb* [T] to decorate a dish of food with a small amount of another food □ *menghias*: *Garnish the soup with a little parsley before serving.* ▸ **garnish** *noun* [U,C]

garrison /'gærɪsn/ *noun* [C] a group of soldiers who are living in and guarding a town or building □ *garison*

VOWELS iː see i any ɪ sit e ten æ hat ɑː father ɒ got ɔː saw ʊ put uː too u usual

gas → gay

gas¹ /gæs/ noun (pl gases; gasses) 1 [C,U] a substance like air that is not a solid or a liquid □ *gas*: Hydrogen and oxygen are gases. 2 [U] a particular type of gas or mixture of gases that is used for heating or cooking □ *gas*: a gas cooker 3 [U] (AmE) = **petrol**

gas² /gæs/ verb [T] (gassing; gassed) to poison or kill sb with gas □ *membunuh/meracuni dgn gas*

'gas chamber noun [C] a room that can be filled with poisonous gas in order to kill animals or people □ *bilik gas*

gash /gæʃ/ noun [C] a long deep cut or wound □ *luka dlm*: He had a nasty gash in his arm. ▶ **gash** verb [T]

'gas mask noun [C] an piece of equipment that is worn over the face to protect against poisonous gas □ *topeng gas*

'gas meter noun [C] an instrument that measures the amount of gas that you use in your home □ *meter gas*

gasoline /'gæsəliːn/ (AmE) = **petrol**

gasp /ɡɑːsp/ verb [I,T] 1 gasp (at sth) to take a sudden loud breath with your mouth open, usually because you are surprised or in pain □ *menghela nafas panjang*: She gasped in surprise at the news. 2 to have difficulty breathing: I pulled the boy out of the pool and he lay there **gasping for breath**. □ *tercungap-cungap* ▶ **gasp** noun [C]: to give a gasp of surprise/pain/horror

'gas station (AmE) = **petrol station**

gastric /'gæstrɪk/ adj [only before a noun] (technical) connected with the stomach □ *gaster; berkaitan dgn kawasan perut*: a gastric ulcer ♦ gastric juices (= the liquid in your stomach)

gastronomic /ˌgæstrə'nɒmɪk/ adj [only before a noun] connected with good food □ *(berkenaan dgn) makanan lazat*

gate /geɪt/ noun [C] 1 the part of a fence, wall, etc. like a door that can be opened to let people or vehicles through □ *pintu (pagar, dll)*: Please keep the garden gate closed. ⊃ picture at **fence** 2 (also **gateway**) the space in a wall, fence, etc. where the gate is □ *pintu (pagar, dll)*: Drive through the gates and you'll find the car park on the right. 3 the place at an airport where you get on or off a plane □ *pintu*: Lufthansa Flight 139 to Geneva is now boarding at gate 16.

gateau /'gætəʊ/ noun [C] (pl gateaux /'gætəʊz/) a large cake that is usually decorated with cream, fruit, etc. □ *kek gateau*: a strawberry gateau

gatecrash /'geɪtkræʃ/ verb [I,T] to go to a private party without being invited □ *pergi (ke sst majlis) tanpa undangan* ▶ **gatecrasher** noun [C]

gateway /'geɪtweɪ/ noun [C] 1 = **gate** (2) 2 [sing] the gateway to sth the place which you must go through in order to get to somewhere else □ *pintu masuk*: The port of Dover is England's gateway to Europe. ♦ (figurative) A good education can be the gateway to success.

gather /'gæðə(r)/ verb
▶COME/BRING TOGETHER 1 [I,T] gather (round) (sb/sth); gather sb/sth (round) (sb/sth) (used about people) to come or be brought together in a group □ *berkumpul; berkerumun*: A crowd soon gathered at the scene of the accident. ♦ We all gathered round and listened to what the guide was saying. ♦ The children were gathered around the teacher's desk. 2 [T] gather sth (together/up) to bring many things together □ *mengumpulkan*: He gathered up all his papers and put them away. ♦ They have gathered together a lot of information on the subject.
▶COLLECT 3 [T] (formal) to pick wild flowers, fruit, etc. from a wide area □ *memungut; memetik*: to gather mushrooms
▶UNDERSTAND 4 [I,T] to understand or find out sth (from sb/sth) □ *difahamkan; mendapat tahu*: I gather from your letter that you have several years' experience of this kind of work. ♦ 'She's been very ill recently.' 'So I gather.'
▶INCREASE 5 [I,T] to gradually become greater; to increase □ *bertambah; semakin*: I gathered speed as I cycled down the hill.

gathering /'gæðərɪŋ/ noun [C] a time when people come together; a meeting □ *perjumpaan*: a social/family gathering

gaudy /'gɔːdi/ adj (gaudier; gaudiest) too bright or decorated and therefore unpleasant □ *menyilaukan; terlalu berhias* **SYN** garish

gauge¹ (AmE also **gage**) /geɪdʒ/ noun [C] 1 an instrument for measuring the amount of sth □ *tolok; meter*: a fuel/temperature/pressure gauge 2 (technical) a measurement of the width of sth or of the distance between two things □ *tolok*: a narrow-gauge railway 3 a gauge (of sth) a fact that you can use to judge a situation, sb's feelings, etc. □ *ukuran*

gauge² /geɪdʒ/ verb [T] 1 to make a judgement or to calculate sth by guessing □ *menganggarkan; mengagak*: It was difficult to gauge the mood of the audience. 2 to measure sth accurately using a special instrument □ *mengukur*

gaunt /gɔːnt/ adj (used about a person) very thin because of illness, worry or not having enough food □ *kurus kering*

gauze /gɔːz/ noun [U] a thin material like a net, that is used for covering an area of skin that you have hurt or cut □ *kasa*

gave past tense of **give¹**

gawp /gɔːp/ verb [I] (informal) gawp (at sb/sth) to look for a long time in a stupid way because you are surprised, shocked, etc. □ *melongo; menengok*: Lots of drivers slowed down to gawp at the accident.

gay¹ /geɪ/ adj 1 sexually attracted to people of the same sex □ *homoseksual*: the gay community of New York ♦ a gay bar/club (= for gay people) ♦ *Is she gay?* ➔ noun **gayness** SYN **homosexual** OPP **straight 2** (**gayer**; **gayest**) (*old-fashioned*) happy and full of fun □ *riang; girang* ➔ noun **gaiety**

gay² /geɪ/ noun [C] a person, especially a man, who is sexually attracted to people of the same sex □ *homoseksual*: *lesbians and gays* SYN **homosexual** OPP **straight**

gaze /geɪz/ verb [I] to look steadily for a long time □ *merenung*: *She sat at the window gazing dreamily into space.* ▸**gaze** noun [sing]

GB abbr **1** /ˌdʒiː ˈbiː/ = **Great Britain 2** = **gigabyte**

Gb (also **Gbit**) abbr (*written*) = **gigabit**

GCSE /ˌdʒiː siː es ˈiː/ abbr **General Certificate of Secondary Education**; an examination that students in England, Wales and Northern Ireland take when they are about 16. They often take GCSEs in five or more subjects. For Scottish examinations, look at **SCE**. □ *peperiksaan GCSE* ➔ look at **A level**

GDP /ˌdʒiː diː ˈpiː/ abbr **gross domestic product**; the total value of all goods and services produced by a country in one year □ *KDNK (Keluaran Dlm Negara Kasar)* ➔ look at **GNP**

gear¹ /ɡɪə(r)/ noun **1** [C] the machinery in a vehicle that turns engine power into a movement forwards or backwards □ *gear*: *Most cars have four or five forward gears and a reverse.* ➔ picture at **bicycle 2** [U] a particular position of the gears in a vehicle □ *first/second/top/reverse gear* ♦ *to change gear* **3** [U] equipment or clothing that you need for a particular activity, etc. □ *pakaian; peralatan*: *camping/fishing/sports gear* **4** [U] (*informal*) clothes □ *pakaian*: *wearing the latest gear* **5** [U] a piece of machinery that is used for a particular purpose □ *peralatan*: *the landing gear of an aeroplane* ♦ *lifting gear*

gear² /ɡɪə(r)/ verb
PHR V **gear sth to/towards sb/sth** [often passive] to make sth suitable for a particular purpose or person □ *menyesuaikan sst utk sso/sst*: *There is a special course geared towards the older learner.*
gear up (for sb/sth); gear sb/sth up (for sb/sth) to get ready or to make sb/sth ready □ *bersiap sedia; menjadikan sso/sst bersiap sedia*

gearbox /ˈɡɪəbɒks/ noun [C] the metal case that contains the gears of a car, etc. □ *kotak gear*

'gear lever (also **'gearstick** /ˈɡɪəstɪk/ (*AmE*) **'gear shift**) noun [C] a stick that is used for changing gear in a car, etc. □ *batang gear* ➔ picture at **car**

gee /dʒiː/ exclam (*AmE*) used for expressing surprise, pleasure, etc. □ *wah; wau*

geek /ɡiːk/ noun [C] (*informal*) a person who is not popular or fashionable □ *sso yg tdk berfesyen atau popular*: *a computer geek* SYN **nerd** ▸**geeky** adj

geese plural of **goose**

gel /dʒel/ noun [C,U] [in compounds] a thick substance that is between a liquid and a solid

365 **gay → generalization**

□ *gel*: *hair gel* ♦ *shower gel*

gelatin /ˈdʒelətɪn/ (also **gelatine** /ˈdʒeləti:n/) noun [U] a clear substance that is made by boiling animal bones and is used in many products, especially in cooking, to make liquid thick or firm □ *gelatin*

gelignite /ˈdʒelɪɡnaɪt/ noun [U] a substance that is used for making explosions □ *gelignit*

gem /dʒem/ noun [C] **1** a rare and valuable stone that is used in jewellery □ *(batu) permata* **2** a person or thing that is especially good □ *sso/sst yg sangat baik*

Gemini /ˈdʒemɪnaɪ/ noun [C,U] the 3rd sign of the **zodiac** (= 12 signs which represent the positions of the sun, moon and planets), the Twins; a person born under this sign □ *Gemini*: *I'm a Gemini.* ➔ picture at **zodiac**

Gen. abbr = **General²**

gender /ˈdʒendə(r)/ noun [C,U] **1** (*formal*) the fact of being male or female □ *jantina* SYN **sex 2** (in some languages) the division of nouns, pronouns, etc. into classes (**masculine**, **feminine**, **neuter**); one of these classes □ *genus*

gene /dʒiːn/ noun [C] a unit of information inside a cell which controls what a living thing will be like. Genes are passed from parents to children. □ *gen* ➔ look at **genetics**

genera plural of **genus**

general¹ /ˈdʒenrəl/ adj **1** affecting all or most people, places, things, etc □ *umum; ramai*: *Dishwashers were once a luxury, but now they are in general use.* ♦ *a matter of general interest* ♦ *the general public* (= most ordinary people) **2** [only before a noun] referring to or describing the main part of sth, not the details □ *am*: *Your general health is very good.* ♦ *The introduction gives you a general idea of what the book is about.* ♦ *As a general rule, the most common verbs in English tend to be irregular.* **3** not limited to one subject, use or activity □ *am; (hospital, dll) besar*: *Children need a good general education.* ♦ *The quiz tests your general knowledge.* **4** [in compounds] with responsibility for the whole of an organization □ *ketua; (pengurus) besar*: *a general manager*
IDM **in general 1** in most cases; usually □ *pd umumnya*: *In general, standards of hygiene are good.* **2** as a whole □ *secara umum*: *I'm interested in Spanish history in general, and the civil war in particular.*

general² /ˈdʒenrəl/ noun [C] (*abbr* **Gen.**) an army officer in a very high position □ *jeneral*

general e'lection noun [C] an election in which all the people of a country vote to choose a government □ *pilihan raya umum* ➔ note at **election**

generalization (also **-isation**) /ˌdʒenrəlaɪˈzeɪʃn/ noun [C,U] a general statement that is based on only a few facts or examples; the act

[C] **countable**, a noun with a plural form: *one book, two books*   [U] **uncountable**, a noun with no plural form: *some sugar*

of making such a statement □ *anggapan umum; generalisasi*: *You can't make sweeping generalizations about French people if you've only been to France for a day!*

generalize (also -ise) /ˈdʒenrəlaɪz/ *verb* [I] **generalize (about sth)** to form an opinion or make a statement using only a small amount of information instead of looking at the details □ *membuat anggapan umum*: *You can't generalize about English food after only two days.* ◆ *You're generalizing. Every case is different.*

generally /ˈdʒenrəli/ *adv* **1** by or to most people □ *pd umumnya*: *He is generally considered to be a good doctor.* **2** usually □ *biasanya*: *She generally cycles to work.* **3** without discussing the details of sth □ *secara umum*: *Generally speaking, houses in America are bigger than houses in this country.*

generate /ˈdʒenəreɪt/ *verb* [T] to produce or create sth □ *menghasilkan; menjana*: *to generate heat/power/electricity*

generation /ˌdʒenəˈreɪʃn/ *noun* **1** [C, with sing or pl verb] all the people in a family, group or country who were born at about the same time □ *generasi*: *We should look after the planet for future generations.* ◆ *This photograph shows three generations of my family* (= children, parents and grandparents).

> **GRAMMAR** In the singular, **generation** is used with a singular or plural verb: *The younger generation only seem/seems to be interested in money.*

2 [C] the average time that children take to grow up and have children of their own, usually considered to be about 25-30 years □ *generasi*: *A generation ago foreign travel was still only possible for a few people.* **3** [U] the production of sth, especially heat, power, etc. □ *penghasilan; penjanaan*: *the generation of electricity by water power*

the geneˈ**ration gap** *noun* [sing] the difference in behaviour, and the lack of understanding, between young people and older people □ *jurang generasi*

generator /ˈdʒenəreɪtə(r)/ *noun* [C] a machine that produces electricity □ *penjana*

generic /dʒəˈnerɪk/ *adj* **1** shared by, including or typical of a whole group of things □ *panggilan umum*: *'Vine fruit' is the generic term for currants and raisins.* **2** (used about a product, especially a drug) not using the name of the company that made it □ *generik* ▸**generically** /-kli/ *adv*

generosity /ˌdʒenəˈrɒsəti/ *noun* [U] the quality of being generous □ *kemurahan hati*

generous /ˈdʒenərəs/ *adj* **1** happy to give more money, help, etc. than is usual or expected □ *murah hati*: *It was very generous of your parents to lend us all that money.* **2** larger than usual □ *banyak*: *a generous helping of pasta* ▸**generously** *adv*: *People gave very generously to our appeal for the homeless.*

genetic /dʒəˈnetɪk/ *adj* connected with **genes** (= the units in the cells of a living thing that control what it is like), or with **genetics** □ *genetik*: *The disease is caused by a genetic defect.* ▸**genetically** /-kli/ *adv*

geˌ**netically ˈmodified** *adj* (*abbr* **GM**) (used about food, plants, etc.) that has been grown from cells whose **genes** (= the units in the cells of a living thing that control what it is like) have been changed in an artificial way □ *diubah suai secara genetik*

geˌ**netic engi**ˈ**neering** *noun* [U] the science of changing the way a human, animal or plant develops by changing the information in its **genes** (= the units in the cells of a living thing that control what it is like) □ *kejuruteraan genetik*

genetics /dʒəˈnetɪks/ *noun* [U] the scientific study of the ways in which different characteristics are passed from each generation of living things to the next □ *(ilmu) genetik* ➔ look at **gene**

genial /ˈdʒiːniəl/ *adj* (used about a person) pleasant and friendly □ *ramah; baik*

genie /ˈdʒiːni/ *noun* [C] (in stories) a spirit with magic powers, especially one that lives in a bottle or a lamp □ *jin*

genitals /ˈdʒenɪtlz/ (also *formal* **genitalia** /ˌdʒenɪˈteɪliə/) *noun* [pl] the parts of sb's sex organs that are outside the body □ *kemaluan* ▸**genital** *adj*

genius /ˈdʒiːniəs/ *noun* **1** [U] very great and unusual intelligence or ability □ *kepintaran*: *Her idea was a stroke of genius.* **2** [C] a person who has very great and unusual ability, especially in a particular subject □ *genius*: *Einstein was a mathematical genius.* ➔ look at **prodigy** **3** [sing] **a genius for (doing) sth** a very good natural skill or ability □ *bakat; kebolehan*

genocide /ˈdʒenəsaɪd/ *noun* [U] the murder of all the people of a particular race, religion, etc. □ *pembunuhan kaum*

genome /ˈdʒiːnəʊm/ *noun* [C] the complete set of **genes** (= units of information) in a cell or living thing □ *genom*: *the human genome*

genre /ˈʒɒnrə; ˈʒɒnrə/ *noun* [C] (*formal*) a particular type or style of literature, art, film or music □ *genre*

gent (*informal*) = **gentleman**

genteel /dʒenˈtiːl/ *adj* behaving in a very polite and quiet way, often in order to make people think that you are from a high social class □ *halus budi pekerti* ▸**gentility** /dʒenˈtɪləti/ *noun* [U]

gentle /ˈdʒentl/ *adj* (**gentler**; **gentlest**) **1** (used about people) kind and calm; touching or treating people or things in a careful way so that they are not hurt □ *lemah lembut*: *'I'll try and be as* gentle as I can,' said the dentist. **2** not strong, violent or extreme □ *lembut; perlahan; landai*: *gentle exercise* ♦ *a gentle slope/curve* ▶**gentleness** *noun* [U] ▶**gently** /'dʒentli/ *adv*

gentleman /'dʒentlmən/ *noun* [C] (*pl* -**men** /-mən/) (also *informal* **gent** /dʒent/) **1** a man who is polite and who behaves well towards other people □ *lelaki yg bersopan santun*: *Everyone likes and respects Joe because he's a real gentleman.* **2** (*formal*) used when speaking to or about a man or men in a polite way □ *tuan-tuan; orang lelaki*: *Ladies and gentlemen* (= at the beginning of a speech) ♦ *Mrs Flinn, there is a gentleman here to see you.* **3** (*old-fashioned*) a rich man with a high social position □ *lelaki kaya dan berketurunan baik*: *a country gentleman*

the gents (also **the Gents**) // *noun* [sing] (*BrE informal*) a public toilet for men □ *tandas lelaki* ⊃ note at **toilet**

genuine /'dʒenjuɪn/ *adj* **1** real; true □ *tulen; sebenar*: *He thought that he had bought a genuine Rolex watch but it was a cheap fake.* ⊃ look at **imitation** **2** sincere and honest; that can be trusted □ *jujur; ikhlas*: *a very genuine person* ▶**genuinely** *adv*

genus /'dʒiːnəs/ *noun* [C] (*pl* **genera** /'dʒenərə/) (*technical*) a group into which animals, plants, etc. that have similar characteristics are divided □ *genus; jenis; kumpulan* ⊃ look at **class**, **family**, **species**

geographer /dʒi'ɒɡrəfə(r)/ *noun* [C] an expert in, or a student of, geography □ *ahli/pengkaji geografi*

geography /dʒi'ɒɡrəfi/ *noun* [U] **1** the study of the world's surface, physical qualities, climate, countries, products, population, etc. □ *(ilmu) geografi*: *human/physical/economic geography* **2** the physical arrangement of a place □ *rupa bumi; kedudukan tempat*: *We're studying the geography of Asia.* ▶**geographical** /,dʒiːə'ɡræfɪkl/ *adj* ▶**geographically** /-kli/ *adv*

geologist /dʒi'ɒlədʒɪst/ *noun* [C] a student of or an expert in **geology** □ *ahli geologi*

geology /dʒi'ɒlədʒi/ *noun* [U] the study of rocks, and of the way they are formed □ *(ilmu) geologi* ▶**geological** /,dʒiːə'lɒdʒɪkl/ *adj*

geometric /,dʒiːə'metrɪk/ (also **geometrical** /-ɪkl/) *adj* **1** connected with **geometry** □ *(berkenaan dgn) geometri* **2** consisting of regular shapes and lines □ *(berbentuk) geometri*: *a geometric design/pattern* ▶**geometrically** /-kli/ *adv*

geometry /dʒi'ɒmətri/ *noun* [U] the study in mathematics of lines, shapes, curves, etc. □ *geometri*

geothermal /,dʒiːəʊ'θɜːml/ *adj* connected with the natural heat of rock deep in the ground □ *geohaba*: *geothermal energy*

geriatrics /,dʒeri'ætrɪks/ *noun* [U] the medical care of old people □ *geriatrik* ▶**geriatric** *adj*

germ /dʒɜːm/ *noun* **1** [C, usually pl] a very small living thing that causes disease □ *kuman* ⊃ look

367   **gentleman → get**

at **bacteria**, **virus** **2** [sing] **the germ of sth** the beginning of sth that may develop □ *bibit*: *the germ of an idea*

German measles /,dʒɜːmən 'miːzlz/ (also **rubella**) *noun* [U] a mild disease that causes red spots all over the body. If a woman catches it when she is pregnant, it may harm the baby. □ *penyakit rubela*

germinate /'dʒɜːmɪneɪt/ *verb* [I,T] (used about a seed) to start growing; to cause a seed to do this □ *bercambah* ▶**germination** /,dʒɜːmɪ'neɪʃn/ *noun* [U]

gerund /'dʒerənd/ *noun* [C] a noun, ending in -ing, that has been made from a verb □ *gerund*: *In the sentence 'His hobby is collecting stamps', 'collecting' is a gerund.*

gestation /dʒe'steɪʃn/ *noun* [U, sing] the period of time that a baby human or animal develops inside its mother's body; the process of developing inside the mother's body □ *gestasi; kehamilan; kebuntingan*: *The gestation period of a horse is about eleven months.*

gesticulate /dʒe'stɪkjuleɪt/ *verb* [I] to make movements with your hands and arms in order to express sth □ *menggerak-gerakkan tangan (utk menyatakan sst)*

gesture[1] /'dʒestʃə(r)/ *noun* [C] **1** a movement of the hand, head, etc. that expresses sth □ *gerakan isyarat*: *I saw the boy make a rude gesture at the policeman before running off.* **2** something that you do that shows other people what you think or feel □ *tanda*

gesture[2] /'dʒestʃə(r)/ *verb* [I,T] to point at sth, to make a sign to sb □ *mengutau*: *She asked them to leave and gestured towards the door.*

get /get/ *verb* (**getting**; *pt* **got** /ɡɒt/; *pp* **got**, *AmE* **gotten** /'ɡɒtn/) **1** [T] [no passive] to receive, obtain or buy sth □ *mendapat; mendapatkan; dpt*: *I got a letter from my sister.* ♦ *Did you get a present for your mother?* ♦ *Did you get your mother a present?* ♦ *She got a job in a travel agency.* ♦ *Louise got 75% in the maths exam.* ♦ *I'll come if I can get time off work.* ♦ *How much did you get for your old car* (= when you sold it)? ♦ *to get a shock/surprise* **2** [T] **have got sth** to have sth □ *ada; mempunyai*: *I've got a lot to do today.* ♦ *Lee's got blond hair.* ♦ *Have you got a spare pen?* **3** [T] [no passive] to go to a place and bring sth back □ *mengambil; menjemput*: *Go and get me a pen, please.* ♦ *Sam's gone to get his mother from the station.* **SYN** **fetch** **4** [T] to catch or have an illness, pain, etc □ *kena*: *I think I'm getting a cold.* ♦ *He gets really bad headaches.* ♦ *Teenagers often get acne.* **5** [I,T] to become; to reach a particular state or condition; to make sb/sth be in a particular state or condition □ *menjadi; semakin; berada dlm sst keadaan/kedudukan*: *It's getting dark.* ♦ *to get angry/bored/annoyed* ♦ *to get fat* ♦ *I can't get used to my new bed.* ♦ *to get dressed* ♦ *When did you get married?*

CONSONANTS   p **p**en   b **b**ad   t **t**ea   d **d**id   k **c**at   ɡ **g**ot   tʃ **ch**in   dʒ **J**une   f **f**all   v **v**an   θ **th**in

get → get

♦ to **get** (sb) **pregnant** ♦ Just give me five minutes to **get ready**. ♦ He's always **getting into trouble** with the police. ♦ Don't **get** your dress dirty! ♦ She's shy, but she's great fun once you **get to know** her. **6** [I] used instead of 'be' in the passive □ *di-(gigit, curi, dll)*: She got bitten by a dog. ♦ Don't leave your wallet on the table or it'll get stolen. **7** [T] **get sb/sth to do sth** to make or persuade sb/sth to do sth □ *dpt; (berjaya) membuat*: I got him to agree to the plan. ♦ I can't get the TV to work. **8** [T] **get sth done** to cause sth to be done □ *bermaksud membuat sst*: Let's get this work done, then we can go out. ♦ I'm going to **get my hair cut**. ♦ I had to get the car repaired. **9** [T] [used with verbs in the -ing form] to start doing sth □ *mula (membuat sst)*: We don't have much time so we'd better get working. ♦ I got talking to a woman on the bus. ♦ We'd better **get going** if we don't want to be late. **10** [I] **get to do sth** to have the chance to do sth □ *berpeluang*: Did you get to try the new smartphone? **11** [I] to arrive at or reach a place □ *sampai; tiba; pergi*: We should get to London at about ten. ♦ Can you tell me how to get to the hospital? ♦ What time do you usually **get home**? ♦ I got half way up the mountain then gave up. ♦ How far have you got with your book? ➔ look at **get in 12** [I,T] to move or go somewhere; to move or put sth somewhere □ *membuat sst*: I can't swim so I couldn't get across the river. ♦ My grandmother's 92 and she doesn't get out of the house much. ♦ We couldn't get the piano upstairs. ♦ My foot was swollen and I couldn't get my shoe off. **13** [T] to use a form of transport □ *menaiki (kenderaan)*: Shall we walk or get the bus? **14** [T] **get (sb) sth; get sth (for sb)** to prepare food □ *menyediakan (makanan)*: Can I get you anything to eat? ♦ Joe's in the kitchen getting breakfast for everyone. **15** [T] to hit, hold or catch sb/sth □ *kena; memegang*: He got me by the throat and threatened to kill me. ♦ A boy threw a stone at me but he didn't get me. **16** [T] to hear or understand sth □ *dengar atau faham*: I'm sorry, I didn't get that. Could you repeat it? ♦ Did you **get that joke** that Karen told?

IDM **get somewhere/nowhere (with sb/sth)** to make/not make progress □ *mencapai/tdk mencapai kemajuan*: I'm getting nowhere with my research.

be getting at sth (*informal*) to try to say sth without saying it in a direct way; to suggest □ *maksud*: I'm not quite sure what you're getting at—am I doing something wrong?

be getting on (for) 1 to be getting old or late □ *semakin; lewat; berlalu*: He's getting on—he's over 70, I'm sure. **2** to be nearly a particular time, age or number □ *hampir*: Time's getting on—we don't want to be late. ♦ I'm not sure how old she is, but she must be getting on for 50. ❶ For other idioms containing **get**, look at the entries for the nouns, adjectives, etc. For example, **get rid of** is at **rid**.

PHR V **get about/around/round** (used about news, a story, etc.) to become known by many people □ *tersebar*: The rumour got around that Freddie wore a wig.

get sth across (to sb) to succeed in making people understand sth □ *menyampaikan*: The party failed to get its policies across to the voters.

get ahead to progress and be successful in sth, especially a career □ *maju dan berjaya*

get along 1 [usually used in the continuous tenses] (*informal*) to leave a place □ *pergi*: I'd love to stay, but I should be getting along now. **2 = get on**

get around 1 (*BrE also* **get about**) to move or travel from place to place □ *ke sana ke mari; berjalan*: My grandmother needs a stick to get around these days. **2 = get about/around/round**

get around sb/sth = get round sb/sth

get around to sth/doing sth = get round to sth/doing sth

get at sb to criticize sb a lot □ *mengkritik/mengecam sso*: The teacher's always getting at me about my spelling.

get at sb/sth to be able to reach sb/sth; to have sb/sth available for immediate use □ *dpt menghubungi sso; dpt mencapai/mengambil sst*: The files are locked away and I can't get at them.

get away (from …) to succeed in leaving or escaping from sb or a place □ *lepas; melarikan diri*: He kept talking to me and I couldn't get away from him. ♦ The thieves got away in a stolen car.

get away with sth/doing sth to do sth bad and not be punished for it □ *terlepas; tdk kena (hukum, dsb)*: He lied, but he got away with it.

get back to return to the place where you live or work □ *pulang*: When did you get back from Italy?

get sth back to be given sth that you had lost or lent □ *dpt balik; dipulangkan*: Can I borrow this book? You'll get it back next week, I promise.

get back to sb to speak to, write to, email or phone sb later, especially in order to give an answer □ *menghubungi sso kembali*: I'll get back to you on prices when I've got some more information.

get back to sth to return to doing sth or talking about sth □ *(tidur, kerja, dll) balik; kembali kpd*: I woke up early and couldn't get back to sleep. ♦ Let's get back to the point you raised earlier.

get behind (with sth) to fail to do, pay sth, etc. on time, and so have more to do, pay, etc. the next time □ *ketinggalan; terlambat*: to get behind with your work/rent

get by (on/in/with sth) to manage to live or do sth with difficulty □ *dpt (hidup atau membuat sst dgn susah payah)*: It's very hard to get by on such a low income. ♦ My Italian is good and I can get by in Spanish.

get sb down to make sb unhappy □ *membuat sso kecewa/muram*

get down to sth/doing sth to start working on sth □ *mulai membuat sst*: We'd better stop chatting and get down to work. ♦ I must get down to answering these letters.

get in to reach a place □ *tiba; sampai*: What time does your train get in?

get in; get into sth 1 to climb into a car □ *masuk (ke dlm kereta)*: We all got in and Tim drove off. **2** to be elected to a political position □ *menang* *(pilihan raya)*: Who do you think will get in at the next election?

get sb in to call sb to your house to do a job □ *memanggil (tukang paip, dll)*: We had to get a plumber in to fix the pipes.

get sth in 1 to collect or bring sth inside; to buy a supply of sth □ *mengumpul; membawa masuk*: It's going to rain—I'd better get the washing in from outside. **2** to manage to find an opportunity to say or do sth □ *berpeluang menyatakan/membuat sst*: He talked all the time and I couldn't get a word in.

get in on sth to become involved in an activity □ *mengambil bahagian; terlibat dlm sst*

get into sb (*informal*) (used about a feeling or attitude) to start affecting sb strongly, causing them to behave in an unusual way □ *kena*: I wonder what's got into him—he isn't usually unfriendly.

get into sth 1 to put on a piece of clothing with difficulty □ *memakai; muat*: I've put on so much weight I can't get into my trousers. **2** to start a particular activity; to become involved in sth □ *menceburi; mula; terlibat*: How did you first get into the music business? ♦ She has got into the habit of turning up late. ♦ We got into an argument about politics. **3** to become more interested in or familiar with sth □ *semakin menggemari; menjadi biasa*: I've been getting into yoga recently. ♦ It's taking me a while to get into my new job.

get off (sb/sth) used especially to tell sb to stop touching sb/sth □ *lepaskan; jangan sentuh*: Get off (me) or I'll call the police! ♦ Get off that money, it's mine!

get off (sth) 1 to leave a bus, train, etc.; to climb down from a bicycle, horse, etc. □ *turun* **2** to leave work with permission at a particular time □ *keluar*: I might be able to get off early today.

get off (with sth) to be lucky to receive no serious injuries or punishment □ *lepas; melepaskan; dilepaskan*: to get off with just a warning

get on to progress or become successful in life, in a career, etc. □ *maju; berjaya*: After leaving university she was determined to get on.

get on/along to have a particular amount of success □ *kemajuan; prestasi*: 'How did you get on at your interview?' 'I got the job!' ♦ How are you getting along on your course?

get on/onto sth to climb onto a bus, train, bicycle, horse, etc. □ *menaiki sst*: I got on just as the train was about to leave.

get on to sb (about sth) to speak or write to sb about a particular matter □ *menghubungi sso (ttg sst)*

get on/along with sb; get on/along (together) to have a friendly relationship with sb □ *mesra; baik dgn sso*: Do you get on well with your colleagues? ♦ We're not close friends but we get on together quite well.

get on/along with sth to make progress with sth that you are doing □ *kemajuan; maju*: How are you getting on with that essay?

get on with sth to continue doing sth, especially after an interruption □ *maju; kemajuan*: Stop talking and get on with your work!

get out (used about a piece of information) to become known, after being secret until now □ *terbongkar; diketahui orang*

get sth out (of sth) to take sth from its container □ *mengeluarkan sst (drpd sst)*: I got my keys out of my bag.

get out of sth/doing sth to avoid a duty or doing sth that you have said you will do □ *mengelak drpd sst/membuat sst*

get sth out of sb to persuade or force sb to give you sth □ *memujuk/memaksa sso memberikan sst*: His parents finally got the truth out of him.

get sth out of sb/sth to gain sth from sb/sth □ *mendapat sst drpd sso/sst*: I get a lot of pleasure out of music.

get over sth 1 to deal with a problem successfully □ *mengatasi; menyelesaikan*: We'll have to get over the problem of finding somewhere to live first. **2** to feel normal again after being ill or having an unpleasant experience □ *pulih; mengatasi*: He still hasn't got over his wife's death.

get sth over with (*informal*) to do and complete sth unpleasant that has to be done □ *menyelesaikan; selesai*: I'll be glad to get my visit to the dentist's over with.

get round = **get about/around/round**

get round/around sb (*informal*) to persuade sb to do sth or agree with sth □ *memujuk sso*: My father says he won't lend me the money but I think I can get round him.

get round/around sth to find a way of avoiding or dealing with a problem □ *mengelak drpd sst*

get round/around to sth/doing sth to find the time to do sth, after a delay □ *meluangkan masa utk membuat sst/melakukan sst*: I've been meaning to read that book for ages but I haven't got round to it yet.

get through sth to use or complete a certain amount or number of sth □ *menghabiskan/menyiapkan sst*: I got through a lot of money at the weekend. ♦ I got through an enormous amount of work today.

get (sb) through (sth) to manage to complete sth difficult or unpleasant; to help sb to do this □ *lulus; menyiapkan sst; membantu sso lulus/menyiapkan sst*: She got through her final exams easily.

get through (to sb) 1 to succeed in making sb understand sth □ *membuat sso faham*: They couldn't get through to him that he was completely wrong. **2** to succeed in speaking to sb on the phone □ *dpt menghubungi sso*: I couldn't get through to them because their phone was engaged all day.

get to sb (*informal*) to affect sb in a bad way □ *menggusarkan sso*: Public criticism is beginning to get to the team manager.

get sb/sth together to collect people or things in one place □ *mengumpulkan sst*: I'll just get my things together and then we'll go.

get together (with sb) to meet socially or in order to discuss or do sth □ *bertemu; berjumpa*:

Let's get together and talk about it. ⮕ look at **meet up**

get up to stand up □ *bangun; berdiri*: *He got up to let an elderly woman sit down.*

get (sb) up to get out of bed or make sb get out of bed □ *bangun tidur; mengejutkan (sso)*: *What time do you have to get up in the morning?* ◆ *Could you get me up at 6 tomorrow?* ⮕ note at **routine**

get up to sth 1 to reach a particular point or stage in sth □ *sampai*: *We've got up to the last section of our grammar book.* **2** to be busy with sth, especially sth secret or bad □ *membuat; dibuat*: *I wonder what the children are getting up to?*

getaway /ˈgetəweɪ/ *noun* [C] an escape (after a crime) □ *perihal melarikan diri*: *to make a getaway* ◆ *a getaway car/driver*

ˈget-together *noun* [C] (*informal*) an informal social meeting or party □ *perjumpaan*: *We're going to have a get-together on Saturday evening.*

ghastly /ˈgɑːstli/ *adj* (**ghastlier**; **ghastliest**) extremely unpleasant or bad □ *dahsyat*: *a ghastly accident* **SYN** terrible

ghetto /ˈgetəʊ/ *noun* [C] (*pl* **ghettoes**) a part of a town where many people of the same race, religion, etc. live in poor conditions □ *kawasan perumahan yg serba kekurangan*

ghost /gəʊst/ *noun* [C] the spirit of a dead person that a living person believes they can see or hear □ *hantu*: *I don't believe in ghosts.* ◆ *a ghost story* ⮕ look at **apparition**, **spectre**

ghostly /ˈgəʊstli/ *adj* (**ghostlier**; **ghostliest**) looking or sounding like a **ghost**; full of **ghosts** □ *spt hantu; menyeramkan*: *ghostly noises*

ˈghost town *noun* [C] a town that used to be busy and have people living in it, but is now empty □ *bandar tinggal (tiada penghuni)*

ghostwriter /ˈgəʊstraɪtə(r)/ *noun* [C] a person who writes a book, etc. for a famous person (whose name appears as the author) □ *penulis siluman*

giant /ˈdʒaɪənt/ *noun* [C] **1** an extremely large, strong person □ *raksasa; gergasi*: *a giant of a man* **2** something that is very large □ *raksasa*: *the multinational oil giants* (= very large companies) ▶ **giant** *adj* [only before a noun]: *a giant new shopping centre*

gibberish /ˈdʒɪbərɪʃ/ *noun* [U] words that have no meaning or that are impossible to understand □ *(cakap) meraban*: *I was so nervous in my interview I just spoke gibberish.*

giddy /ˈgɪdi/ *adj* (**giddier**; **giddiest**) having the feeling that everything is going round and that you are going to fall □ *pening; pusing kepala*: *I feel giddy. I must sit down.* **SYN** dizzy

gift /gɪft/ *noun* [C] **1** something that you give to sb; a present □ *hadiah*: *This watch was a gift from my mother.* ◆ *This week's magazine contains a free gift of some make-up.* ◆ *The company made a gift of a computer to a local school.* **SYN** present **2** a gift (for sth/doing sth) natural ability □ *bakat*: *I'd love to have a gift for languages like Mike has.* **SYN** talent

gifted /ˈgɪftɪd/ *adj* having natural ability or great intelligence □ *berbakat; bergeliga*

gig /gɪg/ *noun* [C] (*informal*) an event where a musician or band is paid to perform □ *persembahan*: *The band are doing gigs all around the country.*

gigabit /ˈgɪgəbɪt/ (*abbr* **Gb**; **Gbit**) *noun* [C] a unit of computer memory, equal to 2^{30} **bits** (= small units of information) □ *gigabait*

gigabyte /ˈgɪgəbaɪt/ (*abbr* **GB**) *noun* [C] a unit of computer memory, equal to 2^{30} **bytes** (= small units of information) □ *gigabait*

gigantic /dʒaɪˈgæntɪk/ *adj* extremely big □ *amat besar* **SYN** enormous, huge

giggle /ˈgɪgl/ *verb* [I] to laugh in a silly way that you can't control, because you are amused or nervous □ *mengekek* ▶ **giggle** *noun* [C]: *I've got the giggles* (= I can't stop laughing).

gill /gɪl/ *noun* [C, usually *pl*] one of the parts on the side of a fish's head that it breathes through □ *insang* ⮕ picture on **page P13**

gilt /gɪlt/ *noun* [U] a thin covering of gold □ *sepuhan emas*

gimmick /ˈgɪmɪk/ *noun* [C] an unusual idea to attract attention or to persuade people to buy sth □ *gimik*: *New magazines often use free gifts or other gimmicks to get people to buy them.*

gin /dʒɪn/ *noun* [C,U] a strong, alcoholic drink with no colour □ *(arak) gin*

ginger /ˈdʒɪndʒə(r)/ *noun* [U], *adj* **1** a root that tastes hot and is used as a spice in cooking □ *halia*: *ground ginger* ◆ *ginger biscuits* ⮕ picture on **page P14 2** (of) a light brownish-orange colour □ *perang kejingga-jinggaan*: *ginger hair*

ˌginger ˈale *noun* [U] a drink that does not contain alcohol and is flavoured with **ginger**. It does not contain alcohol but is often mixed with alcoholic drinks. □ *air halia*

ˌginger ˈbeer *noun* [U] a drink that is flavoured with **ginger**. Some types of ginger beer contain a small amount of alcohol. □ *bir halia*

gingerbread /ˈdʒɪndʒəbred/ *noun* [U] a sweet cake or soft biscuit flavoured with **ginger** □ *roti halia*: *a gingerbread man* (= a gingerbread biscuit in the shape of a person)

gingerly /ˈdʒɪndʒəli/ *adv* very slowly and carefully so as not to cause harm, make a noise, etc. □ *dgn berhati-hati*: *I removed the bandage very gingerly and looked at the cut.*

Gipsy = Gypsy

giraffe /dʒəˈrɑːf/ *noun* [C] (*pl* **giraffe** or **giraffes**) a large African animal with a very long neck, long legs, and big dark spots on its skin □ *zirafah*

girder /'gɜːdə(r)/ *noun* [C] a long, heavy piece of iron or steel that is used in the building of bridges, large buildings, etc. □ *galang*

girl /gɜːl/ *noun* [C] **1** a female child □ *budak perempuan: Is the baby a boy or a girl?* ♦ *There are more boys than girls in the class.* **2** a daughter □ *anak perempuan: They have two boys and a girl.* **3** (sometimes offensive) a young woman □ *gadis: The girl at the cash desk was very helpful.* **4 girls** [pl] a woman's female friends of any age □ *kawan-kawan perempuan: a night out with the girls*

girlfriend /'gɜːlfrend/ *noun* [C] **1** a girl or woman with whom sb has a romantic and/or sexual relationship □ *teman wanita: Has Frank got a girlfriend?* **2** (especially AmE) a girl or woman's female friend □ *kawan perempuan: I had lunch with a girlfriend.*

Girl 'Guide (old-fashioned) = guide¹(5)

girlhood /'gɜːlhʊd/ *noun* [U] the time when sb is a girl □ *zaman gadis*

girlish /'gɜːlɪʃ/ *adj* looking, sounding or behaving like a girl □ *macam (budak) perempuan: a girlish figure/giggle*

giro /'dʒaɪrəʊ/ *noun* (pl **giros**) (BrE) [U] a system for moving money from one bank, etc. to another □ *giro*

girth /gɜːθ/ *noun* [U,C] the measurement around sth, especially sb's waist □ *ukur lilit; lilitan: a man of enormous girth* ♦ *a tree one metre in girth/with a girth of one metre*

gist /dʒɪst/ *noun* [sing] **the gist (of sth)** the general meaning of sth rather than all the details □ *inti sari: I know a little Spanish so I was able to get the gist of what he said.*

give¹ /gɪv/ *verb* (pt **gave** /geɪv/; pp **given** /'gɪvn/) **1** [T] **give sb sth; give sth to sb** to let sb have sth, especially sth that they want or need □ *memberi; menghadiahkan: I gave Jackie a book for her birthday.* ♦ *Give me that book a minute—I just want to check something.* ♦ *I gave my bag to my friend to look after.* ♦ *I'll give you my phone number.* ♦ *The doctor gave me this cream for my skin.* ♦ *He was thirsty so I gave him a drink.* ♦ *Just phone and I'll give you all the help you need.* **2** [T] **give sb sth; give sth to sb** to make sb have sth, especially sth they do not want □ *memberikan: Mr Johns gives us too much homework.* ♦ *If you go to school with the flu, you'll give it to everyone.* **3** [T] to make sb have a particular feeling, idea, etc. □ *memberi: Swimming always gives me a good appetite.* ♦ *to give somebody a surprise/shock/fright* ♦ *What gives you the idea that he was lying?* **4** [T] **give (sb) sth; give sth to sb** to let sb have your opinion, decision, judgement, etc. □ *memberikan: Can you give me some advice?* ♦ *My boss has given me permission to leave early.* ♦ *The judge gave him five years in prison.* **5** [T] **give (sb) sth; give sth (to sb)** to speak to people in a formal situation □ *memberi: to give a speech/talk/lecture* ♦ *The officer was called to give evidence in court.* ♦ *Sarah's going to give me a cooking lesson.* **6** [T] **give (sb) sth for sth; give (sb) sth (to do sth)** to pay in order to have sth □ *membayar: How much did you give him for fixing the car?* ♦ (figurative) *I'd give anything (= I would love) to be able to sing like that.* **7** [T] to spend time dealing with sb/sth □ *menumpukan (perhatian, dsb); memikirkan: We need to give some thought to this matter urgently.* **8** [T] **give (sb/sth) sth** to do sth to sb/sth; to make a particular sound or movement □ *bermaksud membuat sst kpd sso/sst; membuat sst gerakan atau bunyi: to give somebody a kiss/push/hug/bite* ♦ *to give something a clean/wash/polish* ♦ *Give me a call when you get home.* ♦ *She opened the door and gave a shout of horror.* **9** [T] to perform or organize sth for people □ *mengadakan: The company gave a party to celebrate its 50th anniversary.* **10** [I] to bend or stretch under pressure □ *melentur; meregang: The branch began to give under my weight.*

IDM **give or take** more or less the number mentioned □ *lebih kurang: It took us two hours to get here, give or take five minutes.* **ⓘ** For other idioms containing **give**, look at the entries for the nouns, adjectives, etc. For example, **give way** is at **way**.

PHR V **give sth away** to give sth to sb without wanting money in return □ *memberikan: When she got older she gave all her toys away.* ♦ *We are giving away a free DVD with this month's issue.*

give sth/sb away to show or tell the truth about sth/sb which was secret □ *mendedahkan rahsia, dll; menunjukkan: He smiled politely and didn't give away his real feelings.*

give sth back to return sth to the person that you took or borrowed it from □ *memulangkan: I lent him some books months ago and he still hasn't given them back to me.*

give sth in to give sth to the person who is collecting it □ *menyerahkan/menghantar sst: I've got to give this essay in to my teacher by Friday.*

give in (to sb/sth) to stop fighting against sb/sth; to accept that you have been defeated □ *mengalah*

give off sth to send sth (for example smoke, a smell, heat, etc.) out into the air □ *mengeluarkan: Cars give off poisonous fumes.*

give out (used about a machine, etc.) to stop working □ *rosak; berhenti: His heart gave out and he died.*

give sth out to give one of sth to each person □ *mengedarkan: Please give out these books to the class.*

give up to stop trying to do sth; to accept that you cannot do sth □ *berputus asa; mengaku kalah: They gave up once the other team had scored their third goal.* ♦ *I give up. What's the answer?*

give sb up; give up on sb to stop expecting sb to arrive, succeed, improve, etc. □ *tdk berharap sso akan tiba, berjaya, maju, dll: I'd almost given him up, when he arrived, full of apologies.*

give → glaring

• Her work was so poor that all her teachers gave up on her.
give sth up; give up doing sth to stop doing or having sth that you did or had regularly before □ *berhenti (membuat) sst: Don't give up hope. Things are bound to improve.* • *I've tried many times to give up smoking.*
give yourself/sb up (to sb) to go to the police when they are trying to catch you; to tell the police where sb is □ *menyerah diri/menyerahkan sso (kpd sso)*
give up (to sb) to give sth to sb who needs or asks for it □ *memberikan sst (kpd sso): He gave up his seat on the bus to an elderly woman.*

give² /gɪv/ *noun* [U] the quality of being able to bend or stretch a little □ *memberi*
IDM give and take a situation in which two people, groups, etc., respect each other's rights and needs □ *tolak ansur: There has to be some give and take for a marriage to succeed.*

giveaway /ˈgɪvəweɪ/ *noun* [C] (*informal*) **1** a thing that is included free when you buy sth □ *hadiah percuma: There's usually some giveaway with that magazine.* **2** something that makes you guess the truth about sb/sth □ *(sst yg) mendedahkan rahsia: She said she didn't know about the money but her face was a dead (= complete) giveaway.*

given¹ *past participle of* **give¹**

given² /ˈgɪvn/ *adj* [only *before* a noun] already stated or decided □ *tertentu; ditentukan; bila-bila (masa): At any given time, up to 200 people are using the library.*

given³ /ˈgɪvn/ *prep* considering sth □ *memandangkan: Given that you had very little help, I think you did very well.*

'given name (especially *AmE*) = **first name**

glacial /ˈgleɪʃl; ˈgleɪsɪəl/ *adj* **1** (*technical*) connected with, or caused by, glaciers □ *berkaitan dgn atau disebabkan glasier: a glacial landscape* • *glacial deposits/erosion* **2** very cold □ *amat dingin; sejuk: glacial winds/temperatures* **SYN icy**

glacier /ˈglæsɪə(r)/ *noun* [C] a large mass of ice that moves slowly down a valley □ *glasier* ⊃ picture on **page P10**

glad /glæd/ *adj* **1** [not before a noun] **glad (about sth); glad to do sth/that ...** happy; pleased □ *gembira; lega: Are you glad about your new job?* • *I'm glad to hear he's feeling better.* • *I'm glad (that) he's feeling better.* • *I'll be glad when these exams are over.* ⊃ note at **happy 2 glad (of sth); glad (if ...)** grateful for sth □ *bersyukur; besar hati: If you are free, I'd be glad of some help.* • *I'd be glad if you could help me.* ▸**gladness** *noun* [U]

glade /gleɪd/ *noun* [C] a small open area of grass in a wood or forest □ *cerang; kawasan lapang dlm hutan*

gladiator /ˈglædieɪtə(r)/ *noun* [C] (in ancient Rome) a man who fought against another man or a wild animal in a public show □ *gladiator*

gladly /ˈglædli/ *adv* used for politely agreeing to a request or accepting an invitation □ *dgn senang hati/sukacita; tentu sekali: 'Could you help me carry these bags?' 'Gladly.'* • *She gladly accepted the invitation to stay the night.*

glamorize (*also* -**ise**) /ˈglæməraɪz/ *verb* [T] to make sth appear more attractive or exciting than it really is □ *membuat sst kelihatan sungguh menarik: TV tends to glamorize violence.*

glamour (*AmE also* **glamor**) /ˈglæmə(r)/ *noun* [U] the quality of seeming to be more exciting or attractive than ordinary things or people □ *daya tarikan; glamor: Young people are often attracted by the glamour of city life.* ▸**glamorous** /ˈglæmərəs/ *adj: the glamorous world of opera* ▸**glamorously** *adv*

glance¹ /glɑːns/ *verb* [I] to look quickly at sb/sth □ *memandang sekali lalu: She glanced round the room to see if they were there.* • *He glanced at her and smiled.* • *The receptionist glanced down the list of names.*
PHR V glance off (sth) to hit sth at an angle and move off again in another direction □ *menyipi: The ball glanced off his knee and into the net.*

glance² /glɑːns/ *noun* [C] a quick look □ *(perbuatan) memandang sekali lalu: to take/have a glance at the newspaper headlines*
IDM at a (single) glance with one look □ *dgn sekali imbas: I could tell at a glance that something was wrong.*
at first glance/sight ⊃ **first¹**

gland /glænd/ *noun* [C] any of the organs inside your body that produce chemical substances for your body to use □ *kelenjar: sweat glands* ▸**glandular** /ˈglændjʊlə(r)/ *adj: glandular fever* (= an infectious disease)

glare¹ /gleə(r)/ *verb* [I] **1 glare (at sb/sth)** to look at sb in a very angry way □ *menjegil* **2** to shine with strong light that hurts your eyes □ *menyilau*

glare² /gleə(r)/ *noun* **1** [C] a very angry look □ *jegilan* **2** [U] strong light that hurts your eyes □ *silauan: the glare of the sun/a car's headlights*

glaring /ˈgleərɪŋ/ *adj* **1** very easy to see; shocking □ *amat nyata/ketara: a glaring mistake/injustice* **2** (used about a light) too strong and bright □ *menyilaukan* **3** angry □ *(yg) marah: glaring eyes* ▸**glaringly** *adv: a glaringly obvious mistake*

glasses

wine glass tumbler beer mug

[I] **intransitive**, a verb which has no object: *He laughed.* [T] **transitive**, a verb which has an object: *He ate an apple.*

glass /glɑːs/ noun **1** [U] a hard substance that you can usually see through that is used for making windows, bottles, etc. □ *kaca*: He cut himself on broken glass. ♦ *a sheet/pane of glass* ♦ *a glass jar/dish/vase* **2** [C] a drinking container made of glass; the amount of liquid it contains □ *gelas*: *a wine glass* ♦ *a brandy glass* ♦ *Could I have a glass of water, please?*

glasses /ˈglɑːsɪz/ (also **spectacles** (informal **specs**; *AmE* also **eyeglasses**) noun [pl] two **lenses** (= pieces of glass or plastic) in a frame that a person wears in front of their eyes in order to be able to see better □ *cermin mata*: *My sister has to wear glasses.* ♦ *I need a new pair of glasses.* ♦ *I need some new glasses.* ♦ *reading glasses* ♦ *dark glasses*

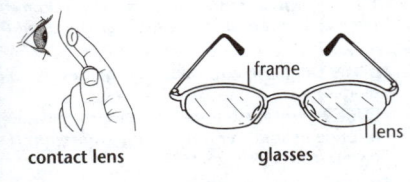

contact lens

frame
lens
glasses

glass ˈfibre = fibreglass

glasshouse /ˈglɑːshaʊs/ noun [C] a building with glass sides and a glass roof, for growing plants in □ *rumah hijau/tanaman* ⊃ look at **greenhouse**

glassy /ˈglɑːsi/ adj (**glassier**; **glassiest**) **1** looking like glass □ *spt kaca; licin* **2** (used about the eyes) showing no interest or expression □ *kosong*

glaze¹ /gleɪz/ verb [T] **1** to fit a sheet of glass into a window, etc. □ *memasang kaca pd (tingkap, dsb)* ⊃ look at **double glazing 2 glaze sth (with sth)** to cover a pot, brick, **pie** (= a type of baked food), etc. with a shiny transparent substance (before it is put into an oven) □ *menyepuh; mengglis; menyapu (putih/kuning telur, dll)*

PHR V glaze over (used about the eyes) to show no interest or expression □ *memandang kosong*

glaze² /gleɪz/ noun [C,U] (a substance that gives) a shiny transparent surface on a pot, brick, **pie** (= a type of baked food), etc. □ *glis; sepuh; bahan yg mengilatkan*

glazed /gleɪzd/ adj (used about the eyes, etc.) showing no interest or expression □ *(pandangan) kosong*

glazier /ˈgleɪziə(r)/ noun [C] a person whose job is to fit glass into windows, etc. □ *tukang kaca*

gleam /gliːm/ noun [C, usually sing] **1** a soft light that shines for a short time □ *cahaya; sinar malap*: *The gleam of moonlight on the water* **2** a small amount of sth □ *sedikit*: *a faint gleam of hope* **3** a sudden expression of an emotion in sb's eyes □ *sinaran mata*: *I saw a gleam of amusement in his eyes.* ▶ **gleam** verb [I]: *gleaming white teeth* ♦ *The children's eyes gleamed with enthusiasm.*

glean /gliːn/ verb [T] **glean sth (from sb/sth)** to obtain information, knowledge etc., sometimes with difficulty and often from various different places □ *dikutip; diambil; dikumpul*: *These figures have been gleaned from a number of studies.*

glee /gliː/ noun [U] a feeling of happiness, usually because sth good has happened to you or sth bad has happened to sb else □ *kegembiraan; keseronokan*: *She couldn't hide her glee when her rival came last in the race.* ▶ **gleeful** /ˈgliːfl/ adj ▶ **gleefully** /-fəli/ adv

glen /glen/ noun [C] a deep, narrow valley, especially in Scotland or Ireland □ *lembah sempit*

glib /glɪb/ adj using words in a way that is clever and quick, but not sincere □ *petah; lincir*: *a glib salesman/politician* ♦ *a glib answer/excuse* ▶ **glibly** adv ▶ **glibness** noun [U]

glide /glaɪd/ verb [I] **1** to move smoothly without noise or effort □ *meluncur*: *The dancers glided across the floor.* **2** to fly in a **glider** □ *melayang; meluncur*

glider /ˈglaɪdə(r)/ noun [C] a light aircraft without an engine that flies using air currents □ *pesawat peluncur* ⊃ look at **hang-glider** ⊃ picture on **page P6**

gliding /ˈglaɪdɪŋ/ noun [U] the sport of flying in a **glider** □ *sukan luncur udara*: *I've always wanted to go gliding.*

glimmer /ˈglɪmə(r)/ noun [C] **1** a weak light that is not steady □ *kelipan*: *I could see a faint glimmer of light in one of the windows.* **2** a small sign of sth □ *sedikit*: *a glimmer of hope* ▶ **glimmer** verb [I]

glimpse /glɪmps/ noun [C] **1 a glimpse (at/of sth)** a very quick and not complete view of sb/sth □ *imbasan*: *I just managed to catch a glimpse of the fox's tail as it ran down a hole.* **2 a glimpse (into/of sth)** a short experience of sth that helps you understand it □ *pandangan sepintas lalu*: *The programme gives us an interesting glimpse into the life of the cheetah.* ▶ **glimpse** verb [T]

glint /glɪnt/ verb [I] to shine with small bright flashes of light □ *kilauan; sinar*: *His eyes glinted at the thought of all that money.* ▶ **glint** noun [C]

glisten /ˈglɪsn/ verb [I] (used about wet surfaces) to shine □ *berkilat; berkilau*: *Her eyes glistened with tears.* ♦ *Tears glistened in her eyes.*

glitter /ˈglɪtə(r)/ noun [U] **1** a shiny appearance consisting of many small flashes of light □ *gemerlapan; kilauan*: *the glitter of jewellery* **2** the exciting quality that sth appears to have □ *daya tarikan*: *the glitter of a career in show business* **3** very small, shiny pieces of thin metal or paper, used as a decoration □ *perada*: *The children decorated their pictures with glitter.* ▶ **glitter** verb [I]

glittering /ˈglɪtərɪŋ/ adj **1** very impressive or successful □ *gilang-gemilang*: *a glittering event/*

glitz → glow

career/performance **2** shining brightly with many small flashes of light □ *bergemerlapan*

glitz /glɪts/ *noun* [U] the quality of appearing very attractive, exciting and impressive, in a way that is not always genuine □ *kegilangan* ▶ **glitzy**: *a glitzy, Hollywood-style occasion*

gloat /gləʊt/ *verb* [I] **gloat (about/over sth)** to show that you are happy about your own success or sb else's failure, in an unpleasant way □ *bermegah-megah*

global /ˈgləʊbl/ *adj* **1** affecting the whole world □ *sedunia; sejagat*: *the global effects of pollution* **2** considering or including all parts □ *menyeluruh*: *We must take a global view of the problem.* ▶ **globally** /-bəli/ *adv*

globalization (also **-isation**) /ˌgləʊbəlaɪˈzeɪʃn/ *noun* [U] the fact that different cultures and economic systems around the world are becoming connected and similar to each other because of the influence of large companies and of improved communication □ *globalisasi*

globalize (also **-ise**) /ˈgləʊbəlaɪz/ *verb* [I,T] if sth, for example a company, **globalizes** or is **globalized**, it operates all around the world □ *mengglobalisasikan*

the ˌglobal ˈvillage *noun* [sing] the world considered as a single community connected by computers, phones, the Internet, etc. □ *perkampungan global*

ˌglobal ˈwarming *noun* [sing] the increase in the temperature of the earth's atmosphere, caused by the increase of certain gases □ *pemanasan global* ⊃ note at **environment** ⊃ look at **greenhouse effect**

globe /gləʊb/ *noun* **1** [C] a round object with a map of the world on it □ *glob* **2 the globe** [sing] the earth □ *dunia*: *to travel all over the globe* **3** [C] any object shaped like a ball □ *(sst yg berbentuk) bulat*

ˌglobe ˈartichoke = **artichoke**

globetrotter /ˈgləʊbtrɒtə(r)/ *noun* [C] (*informal*) a person who travels to many countries □ *orang yg sering pergi ke serata dunia*

globule /ˈglɒbjuːl/ *noun* [C] a very small drop of a liquid □ *titisan*: *There were globules of fat in the soup.*

gloom /gluːm/ *noun* [U] **1** a feeling of being sad and without hope □ *kemuraman; kesuraman*: *The news brought deep gloom to the village.* **2** the state of being almost totally dark □ *kemalapan; kekelaman*

gloomy /ˈgluːmi/ *adj* (**gloomier**; **gloomiest**) **1** dark in a way that makes you feel sad □ *gelap; suram*: *This dark paint makes the room very gloomy.* **2** sad and without much hope □ *muram/suram*: *Don't be so gloomy—cheer up!* ▶ **gloomily** *adv*: *He stared gloomily at the phone.* ▶ **gloominess** *noun* [U]

glorified /ˈglɔːrɪfaɪd/ *adj* [only before a noun] described in a way that makes sb/sth seem better, bigger, more important, etc. than he/she/it really is □ *dibesar-besarkan*

glorify /ˈglɔːrɪfaɪ/ *verb* [T] (**glorifying**; **glorifies**; *pt, pp* **glorified**) to make sb/sth appear better or more important than he/she/it really is □ *membesar-besarkan*: *His biography does not attempt to glorify his early career.*

glorious /ˈglɔːriəs/ *adj* **1** having or deserving fame or success □ *cemerlang; gemilang*: *a glorious victory* **2** very beautiful or impressive □ *hebat; indah*: *a glorious day/view* ▶ **gloriously** *adv*

glory¹ /ˈglɔːri/ *noun* [U] **1** fame or honour that you get for achieving sth □ *kecemerlangan; kebanggaan*: *The winning team was welcomed home in a blaze of glory.* **2** great beauty □ *keindahan*

glory² /ˈglɔːri/ *verb* (**glorying**; **glories**; *pt, pp* **gloried**)

PHR V **glory in sth** to take (too much) pleasure or pride in sth □ *terlalu berbangga/megah*: *He gloried in his sporting successes.*

gloss¹ /glɒs/ (*AmE* also /) *noun* [U, sing] (a substance that gives sth) a smooth, shiny surface □ *kilauan; berkilat*: *gloss paint* ♦ *gloss photographs* ⊃ look at **matt**

gloss² /glɒs/ (*AmE* also /) *verb*

PHR V **gloss over sth** to avoid talking about a problem, mistake, etc. in detail □ *menutup; melindungi*

glossary /ˈglɒsəri/ (*AmE* also /) *noun* [C] (*pl* **glossaries**) a list of special or unusual words and their meanings, usually at the end of a text or book □ *glosari*

glossy /ˈglɒsi/ (*AmE* also /) *adj* (**glossier**; **glossiest**) smooth and shiny □ *licin berkilat*: *glossy hair* ♦ *a glossy magazine* (= printed on shiny paper)

glove /glʌv/ *noun* [C] a piece of clothing that covers your hand and has five separate parts for the fingers □ *sarung tangan*: *I need a new pair of gloves for the winter.* ♦ *leather/suede/woollen gloves* ♦ *rubber gloves* ⊃ look at **mitten** ⊃ picture at **bucket**

glove   mitten

glow /gləʊ/ *verb* [I] **1** to produce light and/or heat without smoke or flames □ *bercahaya; ber-*

nyala: *The cat's eyes glowed in the dark.* **2 glow (with sth)** to be warm or red because of excitement, exercise, etc. □ *menjadi merah; berseri: to glow with health/enthusiasm/pride/pleasure* ▶**glow** *noun* [sing]: *the glow of the sky at sunset*

glower /ˈɡlaʊə(r)/ *verb* [I] **glower (at sb/sth)** to look angrily (at sb/sth) □ *memandang dgn marah*

glowing /ˈɡləʊɪŋ/ *adj* saying that sb/sth is very good □ *memuji*: *His teacher wrote a glowing report about his work.* ▶**glowingly** *adv*

glucose /ˈɡluːkəʊs/ *noun* [U] a type of sugar that is found in fruit □ *glukosa*

glue¹ /ɡluː/ *noun* [U] a thick sticky liquid that is used for joining things together □ *perekat*: *You can make glue from flour and water.* ◆ *Stick the picture to the card with glue.*

glue² /ɡluː/ *verb* [T] **(gluing) glue A (to/onto B); glue A and B (together)** to join a thing or things together with glue □ *melekatkan*: *Do you think you can glue the handle back onto the teapot?* **IDM glued to sth** (*informal*) giving all your attention to sth and not wanting to leave it □ *melekap; terpaku*: *He just sits there every evening glued to the TV.*

glum /ɡlʌm/ *adj* sad and quiet □ *muram; sedih* ▶**glumly** *adv*

glut /ɡlʌt/ *noun* [C, usually sing] more of sth than is needed □ *banjiran; lebihan*: *The glut of coffee has forced down the price.*

glutton /ˈɡlʌtn/ *noun* [C] **1** a person who eats too much □ *pelahap* **2** (*informal*) **a glutton for sth** a person who enjoys having or doing sth difficult, unpleasant, etc. □ *orang yg suka sst yg sukar*: *She's a glutton for punishment—she never stops working.*

gluttony /ˈɡlʌtəni/ *noun* [U] the habit of eating and drinking too much □ *kelahapan*

GM /ˌdʒiː ˈem/ *abbr* = **genetically modified**

gm *abbr* = **gram**

GMT /ˌdʒiː em ˈtiː/ *abbr* **Greenwich Mean Time**; the exact time at Greenwich in England, used in the past for calculating time everywhere in the world □ *GMT (Waktu Min Greenwich—WMG)* ⊃ look at **Coordinated Universal Time**

gnarled /nɑːld/ *adj* rough and having grown into a strange shape, because of old age or hard work □ *kasar; berkerutu*: *a gnarled oak tree* ◆ *The old man had gnarled fingers.*

gnash /næʃ/ *verb* **IDM gnash your teeth** to feel very angry and upset about sth □ *mengeritkan gigi*

gnat /næt/ *noun* [C] a type of very small fly that bites □ *agas* **SYN midge**

gnaw /nɔː/ *verb* **1** [I,T] **gnaw (away) (at/on) sth** to bite sth many times □ *menggigit-gigit*: *The dog lay on the carpet gnawing away on its bone.* **2** [I] **gnaw (away) at sb** to make sb feel worried or frightened over a long period of time □ *mengerkah*: *Fear of the future gnawed away at her all the time.*

375

glower → go

gnome /nəʊm/ *noun* [C] (in children's stories, etc.) a little old man with a beard and a pointed hat who lives under the ground □ *gnom*

GNP /ˌdʒiː en ˈpiː/ *abbr* **gross national product**; the total value of all the goods and services produced by a country in one year, including money received from foreign countries □ *KNK (Keluaran Negara Kasar)* ⊃ look at **GDP**

go¹ /ɡəʊ/ *verb* [I] **(going; goes** /ɡəʊz/; *pt* **went** /went/; *pp* **gone** /ɡɒn/ (*AmE* also) /) **1** to move or travel from one place to another □ *bermaksud pergi atau bergerak*: *She always goes home by bus.* ◆ *We're going to London tomorrow.* ◆ *We've still got 50 miles to go.* ◆ *How fast does this car go?* ◆ *Caroline threw the ball and the dog went running after it.*

GRAMMAR **Been** is used as the past participle of **go** when somebody has travelled to a place and has returned. **Gone** means that somebody has travelled to a place but has not yet returned: *I've just been to Berlin. I got back this morning.* ◆ *John's gone to Peru. He'll be back in two weeks.*

2 to travel to a place to take part in an activity or do sth □ *pergi; menghadiri*: *Are you going to Dave's party?* ◆ *Shall we go swimming this afternoon?* ◆ *to go for a swim/drive/drink/walk/meal* ◆ *We went on a school trip to a museum.* ◆ *They've gone on holiday.* ◆ *We went to watch the match.* ◆ *I'll go and make the tea.* ◆ *He went to the cinema yesterday.* **3** to leave a place □ *pergi; berlepas*: *I have to go now. It's nearly 4 o'clock.* ◆ *What time does the train go?* **4** to belong to or stay in an institution □ *masuk*: *Which school does Ralph go to?* ◆ *to go to hospital/prison/college/university* **5** to lead to or reach a place or time □ *menuju; menghala*: *Where does this road go to?* **6** to be put or to fit in a particular place □ *masuk; muat*: *Where does this vase go?* ◆ *My clothes won't all go in one suitcase.* **7** to happen in a particular way; to develop □ *digunakan dgn maksud berlaku dgn cara tertentu; maju; berkembang*: *How's the new job going?* **8** to become; to reach a particular state □ *menjadi; sudah*: *Her hair is going grey.* ◆ *to go blind/deaf/bald/senile/mad* ◆ *The baby has gone to sleep.* **9** to stay in the state mentioned □ *kekal; terus*: *Many mistakes go unnoticed.* **10** to have certain words or a certain tune □ *bunyinya*: *How does that song go?* **11** to make a sound □ *berbunyi*: *The bell went early today.* ◆ *Cats go 'miaow'.* **12** (*spoken, informal*) used for saying what a person said □ *katanya*: *I said, 'How are you, Jim?' and he goes, 'It's none of your business!'* **13** to start an activity □ *mula*: *Everybody ready to sing? Let's go!* **14** to work correctly □ *berfungsi/berjalan dgn baik*: *This clock doesn't go.* ◆ *Is your car going at the moment?* **15** to be removed, lost, used, etc.; to disappear □ *dibuang, hilang, digunakan, dsb*: *I like the furniture, but that carpet will have to go.* ◆ *About half my salary goes on rent.* ◆ *Has your headache gone yet?* ◆ *Jeans will never go out of fashion.*

VOWELS iː **see** i **any** ɪ **sit** e **ten** æ **hat** ɑː **father** ɒ **got** ɔː **saw** ʊ **put** uː **too** u **usual**

16 to become worse or stop working correctly □ *rosak*: *The brakes on the car have gone.* ◆ *His sight/voice/mind has gone.* **17** [only used in the continuous tenses] (*informal*) to be available □ *terdapat; ada*: *Are there any jobs going in your department?* **18** (used about time) to pass □ *berlalu*: *The last hour went very slowly.* **19** (*informal*) used for saying that you do not want sb to do sth bad or stupid □ *digunakan utk menyatakan yg anda tdk mahu sso itu melakukan sst yg tdk anda ingini*: *You can borrow my bike again, but don't go breaking it this time!* ◆ *I hope John doesn't go and tell everyone about our plan.*

IDM **as people, things, etc. go** compared to the average person or thing □ *jika dibandingkan dgn orang, benda lain yg biasa*: *As Chinese restaurants go, it wasn't bad.*

be going to do sth 1 used for showing what you plan to do in the future □ *akan (membuat sst)*: *We're going to sell our car.* **2** used for saying that you think sth will happen □ *akan (berlaku)*: *It's going to rain soon.* ◆ *Oh no! He's going to fall!*

go all out for sth; go all out to do sth to make a great effort to do sth □ *berusaha sedaya upaya*

go for it (*informal*) to do sth after not being sure about it □ *buatlah (apa yg diingini itu); belilah, dsb*: *'Do you think we should buy it?' 'Yeah, let's go for it!'*

have a lot going for you to have many advantages □ *mempunyai banyak kelebihan*

Here goes! said just before you start to do sth difficult or exciting □ *Hah (diucapkan apabila memulakan sst yg sukar, dsb)*

to go 1 that is/are left before sth ends □ *lagi*: *How long (is there) to go before the end of the lesson?* **2** (*spoken*) that you can take away to eat or drink □ *beri*: *Two coffees to go, please.* ⓘ For other idioms containing **go**, look at the entries for the nouns, adjectives, etc. For example, **go astray** is at **astray**.

PHR V **go about** = **go round/around/about**

go about sth/doing sth to start trying to do sth difficult □ *(bagaimana utk) menjalankan/ membuat sst*: *I wouldn't have any idea how to go about building a house.*

go about with sb = **go round/around/about with sb**

go after sb/sth to try to catch or get sb/sth □ *mengejar sso/sst*: *I went after the boy who stole my wallet but he was too fast for me.*

go against sb to not be in sb's favour or not be to sb's advantage □ *tdk dimenangi oleh sso; tdk memihak kpd sso*: *The referee's decision went against him.*

go against sb/sth to do sth that sb/sth says you should not do □ *menentang atau mengingkari sso/sst*: *She went against her parents' wishes and married him.*

go ahead 1 to travel in front of other people in your group and arrive before them □ *pergi dahulu*: *I'll go ahead and tell them you're coming.* **2** to take place after being delayed or in doubt □ *dijalankan; diteruskan*: *Although several members were missing, the meeting went ahead without them.*

go ahead (with sth) to do sth after not being sure that it was possible □ *meneruskan; teruskan*: *We decided to go ahead with the match in spite of the heavy rain.* ◆ *'Can I take this chair?' 'Sure, go ahead.'*

go along to continue; to progress □ *semakin lama; lama-kelamaan*: *The course gets more difficult as you go along.*

go along with sb/sth to agree with sb/sth; to do what sb else has decided □ *bersetuju dgn sso/sst*: *I'm happy to go along with whatever you suggest.*

go around = **go round/around/about**

go around with sb = **go round/around/about with sb**

go away 1 to disappear or leave □ *lenyap; hilang*: *I've got a headache that just won't go away.* ◆ *Just go away and leave me alone!* **2** to leave home for a period of time, especially for a holiday □ *pergi*: *We're going away to the coast this weekend.*

go back (to sth) 1 to return to a place □ *kembali semula ke*: *It's a wonderful city and I'd like to go back there one day.* **2** to return to an earlier matter or situation □ *kembali kpd*: *Let's go back to the subject we were discussing a few minutes ago.* **3** to have its origins in an earlier period of time □ *boleh disusuli kembali ke*: *A lot of the buildings in the village go back to the 15th century.*

go back on sth to break a promise, an agreement, etc. □ *memungkiri*: *I promised to help them and I can't go back on my word.*

go back to sth/doing sth to start doing again sth that you had stopped doing □ *kembali kpd sst/ membuat sst*: *When the children got a bit older she went back to full-time work.*

go by 1 (used about time) to pass □ *berlalu*: *As time went by, her confidence grew.* **2** to pass a place □ *lalu*: *He stood at the window watching people go by.*

go by sth to use particular information, rules, etc. to help you decide your actions or opinions □ *mengikut; berpandukan*: *She'll be late if past experience is anything to go by.*

go down 1 (used about a ship, etc.) to sink □ *tenggelam* **2** (used about the sun) to disappear from the sky □ *terbenam* **3** to become lower in price, level, etc.; to fall □ *turun*: *The number of people out of work went down last month.*

go down (with sb) [used with adverbs, especially 'well' or 'badly' or in questions beginning with 'how'] to be received in a particular way by sb □ *diterima (baik atau sebaliknya)*: *The film went down well with the critics.*

go down with sth to catch an illness; to become ill with sth □ *diserang; kena*

go for sb to attack sb □ *menyerang sso*

go for sb/sth 1 to be true for a particular person or thing □ *benar bagi sso/sst*: *We've got financial problems but I suppose the same goes for a great many people.* **2** to choose sb/sth □ *memilih*: *I think I'll go for the roast chicken.*

go in (used about the sun) to disappear behind a cloud □ *hilang di sebalik awan*

go in for sth to enter or take part in an exam or competition □ *mengambil peperiksaan; masuk pertandingan*

go in for sth/doing sth to do or have sth as a hobby or interest □ *berminat dlm sst/membuat sst*

go into sth 1 to hit sth while travelling in/on a vehicle □ *melanggar; terlanggar*: *I couldn't stop in time and went into the back of the car in front.* **2** to start working in a certain type of job □ *memasuki (sst bidang); bekerja sebagai*: *When she left school she went into nursing.* **3** to look at or describe sth in detail □ *meneliti/menerangkan (secara terperinci)*: *I haven't got time to go into all the details now.*

go off 1 to explode □ *meletup*: *A bomb has gone off in the city centre.* **2** to make a sudden loud noise □ *berbunyi*: *I woke up when my alarm clock went off.* **3** (used about lights, heating, etc.) to stop working □ *padam; mati; tdk berfungsi*: *There was a power cut and all the lights went off.* **4** (used about food and drink) to become too old to eat or drink; to go bad □ *basi; busuk* **5** (BrE) to become worse in quality □ *merosot; (menjadi) teruk*: *I used to like that band but they've gone off recently.*

go off sb/sth to stop liking or being interested in sb/sth □ *tdk lagi berminat atau suka sso/sst*: *I went off spicy food after I was ill last year.*

go off (with sb) to leave (with sb) □ *lari/pergi (dgn sso)*: *I don't know where Sid is—he went off with John an hour ago.*

go off with sth to take sth that belongs to sb else □ *melarikan (sst)*

go on 1 (used about lights, heating, etc.) to start working □ *menyala*: *I saw the lights go on in the house opposite.* **2** (used about time) to pass □ *berlalu*: *As time went on, she became more and more successful.* **3** [used especially in the continuous tenses] to happen or take place □ *berlaku; berlangsung*: *Can anybody tell me what's going on here?* **4** (used about a situation) to continue without changing □ *berterusan*: *This is a difficult period but it won't go on forever.* **5** to continue speaking after stopping for a moment □ *terus; teruskan*: *Go on. What happened next?* **6** used for encouraging sb to do sth □ *seruan utk menggalakkan sso membuat sst*: *Oh go on, let me borrow your car. Just for tonight.*

go on sth to use sth as information so that you can understand a situation □ *menggunakan maklumat, dsb utk bertindak, dll*: *There were no witnesses to the crime, so the police had very little to go on.*

go on (about sb/sth) to talk about sb/sth for a long time in a boring or annoying way □ *tdk habis-habis bercakap ttg sso/sst*: *He went on and on about the people he works with.*

go/be on (at sb) (about sth) to keep complaining about sth □ *tdk habis-habis membebel/merungut*: *She's always (going) on at me to mend the roof.*

go on (doing sth) to continue doing sth without stopping or changing □ *terus (membuat sst)*: *We don't want to go on living here for the rest of our lives.*

go on (with sth) to continue doing sth, perhaps after a pause or break □ *meneruskan (apa yg sedang dibuat)*: *He ignored her and went on with his meal.*

go on to do sth to do sth after completing sth else □ *terus (membuat sst)*

go out 1 to leave the place where you live or work for a short time, especially in order to do sth enjoyable □ *keluar*: *Let's go out for a meal tonight* (= to a restaurant). ◆ *I'm just going out for a walk, I won't be long.* ◆ *He goes out with his friends a lot.* ⊃ look at **socialize 2** to stop being fashionable or in use □ *tdk lagi menjadi fesyen/popular*: *That kind of music went out in the seventies.* **3** (used about the sea) to move away from the land □ *surut*: *Is the tide coming in or going out?* **SYN** **ebb 4** to stop shining or burning □ *padam*: *Suddenly all the lights went out.*

go out (with sb); go out (together) to spend time with sb and have a romantic and/or sexual relationship with them □ *sering keluar bersama/ada hubungan asmara dgn sso*: *Is Fiona going out with anyone?* ◆ *They went out together for five years before they got married.*

go over sth to look at, think about or discuss sth carefully from beginning to end □ *menyemak; memikirkan; membincangkan*: *Go over your work before you hand it in.*

go over to sth to change to a different side, system, habit, etc. □ *beralih; bertukar*

go round [used especially after 'enough'] to be shared among all the people □ *cukup (utk semua orang)*: *In this area, there aren't enough jobs to go round.*

go round/around/about (used about a story, an illness, etc.) to pass from person to person □ *tersebar*: *There's a rumour going round that he's going to resign.* ◆ *There's a virus going round at work.*

go round (to ...) to visit sb's home, usually a short distance away □ *mengunjungi; pergi*: *I'm going round to Jo's for dinner tonight.*

go round/around/about with sb to spend time and go to places regularly with sb □ *mendampingi/bergaul dgn sso*: *Her parents don't like the people she has started going round with.*

go through to be completed successfully □ *berhasil; berjaya; diluluskan*: *The deal went through as agreed.*

go through sth 1 to look in or at sth carefully, especially in order to find sth □ *memeriksa/meneliti sst*: *I always start the day by going through my email.* ◆ *I went through all my pockets but I couldn't find my wallet.* **2** to look at, think about or discuss sth carefully from beginning to end □ *meneliti/memikirkan/membincangkan sst*: *We'll start the lesson by going through your*

homework. **3** to have an unpleasant experience □ *melalui; mengalami*: *I'd hate to go through such a terrible ordeal again.*
go through with sth to do sth unpleasant or difficult that you have decided, agreed or threatened to do □ *meneruskan (sst hal)*: *Do you think she'll go through with her threat to leave him?*
go together [used about two or more things] **1** to belong to the same set or group □ *seiring; bersama* **2** to look or taste good together □ *sesuai/padan dgn*
go towards sth to be used as part of the payment for sth □ *digunakan sebagai sebahagian drpd bayaran sst*: *The money I was given for my birthday went towards my new bike.*
go under 1 to sink below the surface of some water □ *tenggelam* **2** (*informal*) (used about a company) to fail and close □ *menjadi bankrap; lingkup*: *A lot of firms are going under in the recession.*
go up 1 to become higher in price, level, amount, etc □ *naik; meningkat*: *The birth rate has gone up by 10%.* SYN **rise 2** to start burning suddenly and strongly □ *terbakar*: *The car crashed into a wall and went up in flames.* **3** to be built □ *dibina*: *New buildings are going up all over town.*
go with sth 1 to be included with sth; to happen as a result of sth □ *merupakan sebahagian drpd*: *Pressure goes with the job.* **2** to look or taste good with sth else □ *sesuai/padan dgn sst*: *What colour carpet would go with the walls?* SYN **match**
go without (sth) to choose or be forced to not have sth □ *tdk; tanpa (sst)*: *They went without sleep night after night while the baby was ill.*

go² /gəʊ/ *noun* [C] (*pl* **goes** /gəʊz/) **1** a turn to play in a game, etc. □ *giliran*: *Whose go is it?* ♦ *Hurry up—it's your go.* SYN **turn 2** (*informal*) **a go (at sth/doing sth)** an occasion when you try to do sth □ *percubaan; (perbuatan) mencuba*: *Shall I have a go at fixing it for you?* ♦ *I've never played this game before, but I'll give it a go.* ♦ *Andrew passed his driving test first go.* SYN **attempt**
IDM **be on the go** (*informal*) to be very active or busy □ *sangat sibuk*: *I've been on the go all day and now I'm exhausted.*
have a go at sb (*informal*) to criticize sb/sth □ *mengkritik sso*: *Dad's always having a go at me about my hair.*
make a go of sth (*informal*) to be successful at sth □ *berjaya*: *The work is hard, but I'm determined to make a go of it.*

goad /gəʊd/ *verb* [T] **goad sb/sth (into sth/doing sth)** to cause sb to do sth by making them angry □ *mengacum*

'go-ahead¹ *noun* [sing] **the go-ahead (for sth)** permission to do sth □ *kebenaran*: *It looks like the council will give us the go-ahead for the new building.*

'go-ahead² *adj* enthusiastic to try new ways of doing things □ *maju; moden*

goal /gəʊl/ *noun* [C] **1** (in sports such as football, **hockey**, **rugby**) the area between two posts into which the ball must be kicked, hit, etc. for a point or points to be scored □ *gol*: *He crossed the ball in front of the goal.* ⊃ picture on **page P4** **2** the act of kicking or hitting the ball into the goal □ *gol*: *Everton won by three goals to two.* ♦ *to score a goal* **3** your purpose or aim □ *matlamat*: *This year I should achieve my goal of visiting all the capital cities of Europe.*

goalkeeper /'gəʊlkiːpə(r)/ (also *informal* **goalie** /'gəʊli/ or **keeper**) *noun* [C] (in sports such as football, etc.) the player who stands in front of the goal and tries to stop the other team from scoring □ *penjaga gol*: *The goalkeeper made a magnificent save.*

goalless /'gəʊlləs/ *adj* with no goals scored □ *tanpa gol*: *a goalless draw* ♦ *The match finished goalless.*

goalpost /'gəʊlpəʊst/ *noun* [C] (in sports such as football, etc.) one of the two posts that form the sides of a goal. □ *tiang gol*

goats

horn — bell

goat   kid

sheep

horn — fleece

ram   lamb   ewe

goat /gəʊt/ *noun* [C] a small animal with horns which lives in mountain areas or is kept on farms for its milk and meat □ *kambing*

goatee /gəʊˈtiː/ *noun* [C] a small pointed beard on a man's chin □ *janggut sejemput*

gobble /'gɒbl/ *verb* [I,T] (*informal*) **gobble sth (up/down)** to eat quickly and noisily □ *makan dgn gelojoh*

gobbledegook (also **gobbledygook**) /'gɒbldiguːk/ *noun* [U] (*informal*) complicated language that is hard to understand □ *bahasa yg berbelit-belit*

'go-between *noun* [C] a person who takes messages between two people or groups □ *orang tengah*

goblin /'gɒblɪn/ *noun* [C] (in stories) a small ugly creature who tricks people □ *goblin*

gobsmacked /ˈɡɒbsmækt/ *adj* (*informal*) so surprised that you are unable to speak □ *terbungkam*

god /ɡɒd/ *noun* **1 God** [sing] [not used with *the*] the being or spirit in Christianity, Islam and Judaism who people say prayers to and who people believe created the universe □ *Tuhan: Do you believe in God?* ♦ *Muslims worship God in a mosque.* **2** (*fem* **goddess** /ˈɡɒdes/) [C] a being or spirit that people believe has power over a particular part of nature or that represents a particular quality □ *dewa; Tuhan: Mars was the Roman god of war and Venus was the goddess of love.*

> **HELP** **God** is used in a number of expressions. Be careful. Some people think that it is wrong to use God's name in this way. **Oh my God!** expresses surprise or shock: *Oh my God! I've won the lottery!* We use **thank God** when we are happy and relieved about something: *Thank God you've arrived—I was beginning to think you'd had an accident.* We use **for God's sake** when we are asking somebody to do something and want to sound more urgent, or when we are angry with somebody: *For God's sake, shut up!* **Heaven** or **goodness** are used in some of these expressions in order to avoid using the word **God**.

godchild /ˈɡɒdtʃaɪld/ (also **god-daughter** /ˈɡɒdˌdɔːtə(r)/, **godson** /ˈɡɒdsʌn/) *noun* [C] a child who has a **godparent** □ *anak pembaptisan*

goddess /ˈɡɒdes/ *noun* [C] a female god □ *dewi; tuhan*

godforsaken /ˈɡɒdfəseɪkən/ *adj* [only before a noun] (used about a place) not interesting or attractive in any way □ *teruk; jelik*

godparent /ˈɡɒdpeərənt/ (also **godfather** /ˈɡɒdfɑːðə(r)/, **godmother** /ˈɡɒdmʌðə(r)/) *noun* [C] a person chosen by a child's family who promises to help the child and to make sure they are educated as a Christian □ *bapa pembaptisan*

godsend /ˈɡɒdsend/ *noun* [sing] something unexpected that is very useful because it comes just when it is needed □ *rahmat*

goggles /ˈɡɒɡlz/ *noun* [pl] special glasses that you wear to protect your eyes from water, wind, dust, etc. □ *gogal* ⊃ look at **mask**

going[1] /ˈɡəʊɪŋ/ *noun* **1** [sing] (*formal*) the act of leaving a place □ *pemergian: We were all saddened by his going.* **SYN** **departure** **2** [U] the rate or speed of travel, progress, etc. □ *(kadar) pencapaian; kemajuan: Three children in four years? That's not bad going!* **3** [U] how difficult it is to make progress □ *keadaan (sukar): The path up the mountain was rough going.* ♦ *It'll be hard going if we need to finish this by Friday!*
IDM **get out, go, leave, etc. while the going is good** to leave a place or stop doing sth while it is still easy to do so □ *pergi/berhenti sementara keadaan masih membenarkan*

going[2] /ˈɡəʊɪŋ/ *adj*
IDM **a going concern** a successful business □ *perniagaan yg maju*
the going rate (for sth) the usual cost (of sth) □ *kos; kadar bayaran: What's the going rate for an office cleaner?*

going-'over *noun* [sing] (*informal*) **1** a very careful examination of sth □ *periksa dgn teliti: Give the car a good going-over before deciding to buy it.* **2** a serious physical attack on sb □ *membelasah teruk*

goings-'on *noun* [pl] (*informal*) unusual things that are happening □ *kejadian luar biasa*

go-kart /ˈɡəʊ kɑːt/ *noun* [C] a vehicle like a very small car with no roof or doors, used for racing □ *go-kart* ▶ **go-karting** *noun* [U] the sport or activity of riding a **go-kart**: *We went go-karting yesterday.*

gold /ɡəʊld/ *noun* **1** [U] (*symbol* Au) a rare and valuable yellow metal that is used for making coins, jewellery, etc. □ *emas: Is your bracelet made of solid gold?* ♦ *22 carat gold* ♦ *a gold chain/watch* **2** [C] = **gold medal**
IDM **(as) good as gold** very well behaved □ *berkelakuan sangat baik*
have a heart of gold ⊃ **heart**
▶ **gold** *adj*: *The invitation was written in gold letters.*

golden /ˈɡəʊldən/ *adj* **1** made of gold or having a bright yellow colour like gold □ *emas; keemasan: a golden crown* ♦ *golden hair/sand* **2** best, most important, most liked, etc. □ *keemasan; paling penting: a golden opportunity* **3** celebrating the 50th anniversary of sth □ *ulang tahun ke-50: The couple celebrated their golden wedding last year.* ⊃ look at **silver**, **diamond**
IDM **the golden rule (of sth)** the most important principle to follow when doing sth in order to be successful □ *petua: When you run a marathon, the golden rule is: don't start too fast.*

goldfish /ˈɡəʊldfɪʃ/ *noun* [C] (*pl* **goldfish**) a small orange fish, often kept as a pet in a bowl □ *ikan emas* ⊃ note at **pet**

gold 'medal (also **gold**) *noun* [C] the prize for first place in a sports competition □ *pingat emas: How many gold medals did we win in the 2012 Olympics?* ⊃ look at **silver medal**, **bronze medal**

gold 'medallist *noun* [C] the winner of a **gold medal** □ *pemenang pingat emas*

gold mine *noun* [C] **1** a place where gold is taken from the ground □ *lombong emas* **2 a gold mine (of sth)** a place, person or thing that provides a lot of sth □ *sumber (maklumat, bahan, dsb): This website is a gold mine of information.*

golf /ɡɒlf/ (*AmE* also /) *noun* [U] a game that is played outdoors on a **golf course** and in which you use a **golf club** to hit a small hard ball into a series of holes (usually 18) □ *golf: to play a round of golf* ⊃ picture on **page P5**

golf club noun [C] a long metal stick that is specially shaped at one end and used for hitting a ball when playing **golf** □ *kayu golf* ⊃ look at **bat, racket, stick** ⊃ picture on **page P5**

golf course noun [C] a large area of land that is designed for playing **golf** on □ *padang golf*

golfer /'gɒlfə(r)/ (AmE also) / noun [C] a person who plays **golf** □ *pemain golf* ⊃ picture on **page P5**

golly /'gɒli/ exclam (old-fashioned, informal) used for expressing surprise □ *alamak*

gone¹ past participle of **go¹**

gone² /gɒn/ (AmE also) / adj [not before a noun] not present any longer; completely used or finished □ *habis; tiada; pergi*: He stood at the door for a moment, and then he was gone. ♦ Can I have some more ice cream, please, or is it all gone?

> **GRAMMAR** Gone meaning 'disappeared' or 'finished' is used with the verb **be**, as in the examples above. When we are thinking about where somebody has disappeared to, we use **have**: *Nobody knows where John has gone.*

gone³ /gɒn/ (AmE also) / prep later than □ *sudah lewat*: Hurry up! It's gone six already!

gonna /'gənə/ (informal) a way of writing 'going to' to show that sb is speaking in an informal way □ *akan*: 'What's he gonna do now?' she asked. ⊃ note at **contraction**

> **EXAM TIP**
> Do not write 'gonna' yourself (unless you are copying somebody's accent) because it might be marked as a mistake.

goo /guː/ noun [U] (informal) a sticky wet substance □ *benda lekit* **SYN** slime

good¹ /gʊd/ adj (**better**; **best**) **1** of a high quality or standard □ *baik; bagus*: a good book/film/actor ♦ That's a really good idea! ♦ The hotel was quite good, but not fantastic. **2** pleasant or enjoyable □ *seronok; baik*: It's good to be home again. ♦ good news/weather ♦ Have a good time at the party! **3** (used about a reason, etc.) acceptable and easy to understand □ *baik; bagus*: a good excuse/explanation/reason ♦ She has good reason to be pleased—she's just been promoted. **4** good at sth; good with sb/sth able to do sth or deal with sb/sth well □ *pandai*: Jane's really good at science subjects but she's no good at languages. ♦ He's very good with children. ♦ Are you any good at drawing? **5** morally right or well behaved □ *baik*: She was a very good person—she spent her whole life trying to help other people. ♦ Were the children good while we were out? **6** good (to sb); good of sb (to do sth) kind; helpful □ *baik hati*: They were good to me when I was ill. ♦ It was good of you to come. **7** good (for sb/sth) having a positive effect on sb/sth's health or condition □ *baik; bagus*: Green vegetables are very good for you. ♦ This cream is good for burns. **8** good (for sb/sth) suitable or convenient □ *baik; bagus; sesuai*: This beach is very good for surfing. ♦ I think Paul would be a good person for the job. ♦ 'When shall we meet?' 'Thursday would be a good day for me.' **9** used when you are pleased about sth □ *bagus(lah)*: 'Lisa's invited us to dinner next week.' 'Oh, good!' **10** a good ... great in number, amount, etc □ *(lebih) banyak, besar, jauh, dll; betul-betul*: a good many/a good few people (= a lot of people) ♦ a good distance (= a long way) ♦ a good (= at least) ten minutes/three miles ♦ Take a good (= long and careful) look at this photograph. ♦ What you need is a good rest. ♦ Give the fruit a good wash before you eat it. **11** good (for sth) that can be used or can provide sth □ *baik; masih boleh digunakan*: I've only got one good pair of shoes. ♦ This ticket's good for another three days.

IDM as good as almost □ *hampir; secara tdk langsung*: The project is as good as finished. **SYN** virtually

good for you, him, her, etc. (informal) used to show that you are pleased that sb has done sth clever □ *bagus(lah)*: 'I passed my driving test!' 'Well done! Good for you!' ❶ For other idioms containing **good**, look at the entries for the nouns, adjectives, etc. For example, **in good faith** is at **faith**.

> **OTHER WORDS FOR**
> **good**
> In informal English you can say **brilliant**, **fantastic** or **great** instead of 'very good'. **Excellent** and **wonderful** are more formal words: *an excellent example/opportunity*. We use particular words to describe particular things that are good: *delicious/tasty food* ♦ *a talented artist/player/writer* ♦ *an outstanding achievement/performance/piece of work*.

good² /gʊd/ noun [U] **1** behaviour that is morally right or acceptable □ *kebaikan*: the difference between good and evil ♦ I'm sure there's some good in everybody. **2** something that will help sb/sth; advantage □ *kebaikan; baiknya*: She did it for the good of her country. ♦ I know you don't want to go into hospital, but it's for your own good. ♦ What's the good of learning French if you have no chance of using it? ⊃ look at **goods**

IDM be no good (doing sth) to be of no use or value □ *tdk guna*: It's no good standing here in the cold. Let's go home. ♦ This sweater isn't any good. It's too small.

do you good to help or be useful to you □ *baik/bermanfaat utkmu*: It'll do you good to meet some new people.

for good for ever □ *buat selama-lamanya*: I hope they've gone for good this time!

not much good (informal) bad or not useful □ *teruk; tdk guna*: 'How was the party?' 'Not much good.'

do sb a/the world of good ⊃ **world**

goodbye /ˌɡʊdˈbaɪ/ exclam said when sb goes or you go □ *selamat tinggal/jalan*: Goodbye!

See you tomorrow! ♦ *We said goodbye to Steven at the airport.*

> **MORE** Other informal ways to say 'goodbye' are **bye** and **see you**.

▶**goodbye** *noun* [C]: *We said our goodbyes and left.*

Good Friday *noun* [C] the Friday before Easter when Christians remember the death of Christ □ *Good Friday*

good-humoured *adj* pleasant and friendly □ *baik serta ramah*

goodie (*informal*) = **goody**

goodies /ˈgʊdiz/ *noun* [pl] (*informal*) exciting things that are provided or given □ *benda-benda menarik*: *There were lots of cakes and other goodies on the table.*

good-looking *adj* (usually used about a person) attractive □ *lawa; kacak; jelita* **OPP** **ugly** ⊃ note at **beautiful**

good-natured *adj* friendly or kind □ *ramah mesra; baik hati*

goodness /ˈgʊdnəs/ *noun* [U] **1** the quality of being good □ *kebaikan akhlak* **SYN** **virtue** **2** the part of sth that has a good effect, especially on sb/sth's health □ *khasiat*: *Wholemeal bread has more goodness in it than white bread.*

> **HELP** Goodness is used in a number of expressions. We say *Goodness (me)!* to show that we are surprised. *Thank goodness* expresses happiness and relief: *Thank goodness it's stopped raining!* We say *For goodness' sake* when we are asking somebody to do something and want to sound more urgent or when we are angry with somebody: *For goodness' sake, hurry up!*

goodnight /ˌgʊdˈnaɪt/ *exclam* said late in the evening, before you go home or before you go to sleep □ *selamat malam*: *Goodnight! See you in the morning!*

goods /gʊdz/ *noun* [pl] **1** things that are for sale □ *barang-barang*: *a wide range of consumer goods* ♦ *electrical goods* ♦ *stolen goods* **2** (*BrE*) things that are carried by train or lorry □ *barang-barang*: *a goods train* ♦ *a heavy goods vehicle* (= HGV) ⊃ look at **freight**
IDM **come up with/deliver the goods** (*informal*) to do what you have promised to do □ *memenuhi janji*

good sense *noun* [U] good judgement or intelligence □ *akal; kebijaksanaan*: *He had the good sense to refuse the offer.*

goodwill /ˌgʊdˈwɪl/ *noun* [U] friendly, helpful feelings towards other people □ *(sikap) muhibah*: *The visit was designed to promote friendship and goodwill.*

goody (also **goodie**) /ˈgʊdi/ *noun* [C] (*pl* **goodies**) (*informal*) a good person in a film, book, etc. □ *orang baik* **OPP** **baddy**

goody-goody *noun* [C] (usually used in a critical way) a person who always behaves well to please people such as parents or teachers □ *(orang yg) menunjuk-nunjuk baik*

gooey /ˈguːi/ *adj* (*informal*) soft and sticky □ *melekit*: *gooey cakes*

goof /guːf/ *verb* [I] (*especially AmE informal*) to make a silly mistake □ *membuat kesilapan yg bodoh*

google /ˈguːgl/ *verb* [T,I] to type words into the **search engine** Google® in order to find information about sb/sth □ *mencari maklumat dlm Google*: *'Do you know who directed the last Harry Potter film?' 'No, I don't. Have you tried googling it?'*

goose /guːs/ *noun* [C] (*pl* **geese** /giːs/) a large bird with a long neck that lives on or near water. **Geese** are kept on farms for their meat and eggs. □ *angsa* ⊃ picture at **swan**

> **MORE** **Goose** is the general word for the bird and its meat. A male goose is called a **gander** and a young goose is a **gosling**.

gooseberry /ˈgʊzbəri/ *noun* [C] (*pl* **gooseberries**) a small green fruit that is covered in small hairs and has a sour taste □ *gusberi* ⊃ picture on **page P14**
IDM **play gooseberry** (*BrE*) to be with two people who have a romantic relationship and who want to be alone together □ *kacau daun*

goose pimples (also **goosebumps** /ˈguːsbʌmps/) *noun* [pl] small points or lumps which appear on your skin because you are cold or frightened □ *bulu roma meremang*

gore¹ /gɔː(r)/ *noun* [U] thick blood that comes from a wound □ *darah (luka)* ⊃ adjective **gory**

gore² /gɔː(r)/ *verb* [T] (used about an animal) to wound a person or another animal with a horn, etc. □ *menanduk*: *She was gored to death by a bull.*

gorge¹ /gɔːdʒ/ *noun* [C] a narrow valley with steep sides and a river running through it □ *gaung*

gorge² /gɔːdʒ/ *verb* [I,T] **gorge (yourself) (on/with sth)** to eat a lot of food □ *melahap*

gorgeous /ˈgɔːdʒəs/ *adj* (*informal*) extremely pleasant or attractive □ *sangat bagus/cantik*: *What gorgeous weather!* ♦ *You look gorgeous in that dress.* ⊃ note at **beautiful** ▶**gorgeously** *adv*

gorilla /gəˈrɪlə/ *noun* [C] a large black African **ape** (= an animal like a monkey without a tail) □ *gorila* ⊃ picture at **monkey**

gory /ˈgɔːri/ *adj* (**gorier; goriest**) full of violence and blood □ *banyak pertumpahan darah dan keganasan; mengerikan*: *a gory film*

gosh /gɒʃ/ *exclam* (*old-fashioned, informal*) used for expressing surprise, shock, etc. □ *wah; amboi; alamak; aduh*

gosling /ˈgɒzlɪŋ/ *noun* [C] a young **goose** (= a bird like a large duck with a long neck) □ *anak angsa*

gospel /ˈgɒspl/ noun 1 Gospel [C] one of the four books in the Bible that describe the life of Jesus Christ and the ideas which he taught □ *Gospel*: *St Matthew's/Mark's/Luke's/John's Gospel* 2 (also ˌgospel ˈtruth) [U] the truth □ *(sst yg) benar*: *You can't take what he says as gospel.* 3 (also ˈgospel music) [U] a style of religious music developed by African Americans □ *gospel*

gossip /ˈgɒsɪp/ noun 1 [U] informal talk about other people and their private lives, that is often unkind or not true □ *gosip; umpatan*: *Matt phoned me up to tell me the latest gossip.* 2 [C] an informal conversation about other people's private lives □ *bersembang-sembang*: *The two neighbours were having a good gossip over the fence.* 3 [C] a person who enjoys talking about other people's private lives □ *tukang gosip; kaki umpat* ▶ gossip verb [I]

ˈ**gossip column** noun [C] a part of a newspaper or magazine where you can read about the private lives of famous people □ *ruangan gosip/desas-desus* ➔ note at **newspaper**

got past tense, past participle of **get**

gotta /ˈgɒtə/ (*AmE informal*) a way of writing 'got to' or 'got a' to show that sb is speaking in an informal way □ *perlu; terpaksa; ada*: *I gotta go* (= I have got to go). ◆ *Gotta* (= have you got a) *minute?*

HELP Do not write 'gotta' yourself (unless you are copying somebody's accent) because it might be marked as a mistake.

gotten (*AmE*) past participle of **get**

gouge /gaʊdʒ/ verb [T] to make a hole in a surface using a sharp object in a rough way □ *menebuk; mengorek*

PHR V **gouge sth out** to remove or form sth by digging into a surface □ *mencungkil; mengorek*

gourmet /ˈgʊəmeɪ/ noun [C] a person who enjoys food and wine and knows a lot about it □ *gourmet; pakar makan minum*

ˈ**govern** /ˈgʌvn/ verb 1 [I,T] to rule or control the public affairs of a country, city, etc. □ *memerintah*: *The UK is governed by the Prime Minister and the Cabinet.* 2 [T, often passive] to influence or control sb/sth □ *ditentukan*: *Our decision will be governed by the amount of money we have to spend.*

ˈ**government** /ˈgʌvənmənt/ noun 1 often the Government [C, with sing or pl verb] the group of people who rule or control a country □ *kerajaan; pemerintah*: *He has resigned from the Government.* ◆ *The foreign governments involved are meeting in Geneva.* ◆ *government policies/money/ministers/officials* ➔ note at **politics** ➔ look at **opposition**

GRAMMAR Government is used with a singular verb when we are thinking of it as a unit: *The Government welcomes the proposal.* A plural verb is used when we are thinking about all the individual members of the government: *The Government are still discussing the problem.*

2 [U] the activity or method of controlling a country, city, etc. □ *pemerintahan*: *weak/strong/corrupt government* ◆ *communist/democratic/totalitarian government* ◆ *Which party is in government?* ▶ governmental /ˌgʌvnˈmentl/ adj

ˈ**governor** /ˈgʌvənə(r)/ noun [C] 1 a person who rules or controls a region or state (especially in the US) □ *gabenor*: *the Governor of New York State* 2 the leader or a member of a group of people who control an organization □ *gabenor*: *the governor of the Bank of England* ◆ *school governors*

gown /gaʊn/ noun [C] 1 a woman's long formal dress for a special occasion □ *gaun*: *a ball gown* 2 a long loose piece of clothing that is worn by judges, doctors performing operations, etc. □ *jubah*

GP /ˌdʒiː ˈpiː/ abbr general practitioner; a doctor who treats all types of illnesses and works in the community, not in a hospital □ *doktor*

GPS /ˌdʒiː piː ˈes/ abbr global positioning system; a system by which signals are sent from satellites (= electronic devices that move round the earth) to a special device, used to show the position of a person or thing on the surface of the earth very accurately □ *sistem kedudukan sejagat*: *The drivers all have GPS in their vans.* ◆ *I got a GPS for my birthday.* ➔ look at **satnav**

ˈ**grab** /græb/ verb (**grabbing**; **grabbed**) 1 [I,T] grab sth (from sb) to take sth with a sudden movement □ *merebut; merampas; menyambar*: *Helen grabbed the toy car from her little brother.* ◆ *Grab hold of his arm in case he tries to run!* ◆ *Someone had arrived before us and grabbed all the seats.* ◆ *Don't grab—there's plenty for everybody.* ◆ (*figurative*) *He grabbed the opportunity of a free trip to America.* ◆ (*figurative*) *I'll try to grab the waitress's attention.* ➔ look at **snatch** 2 [I] grab at/for sth to try to get or catch sb/sth □ *menyambar; menangkap*: *Jonathan grabbed at the ball but missed.* 3 [T] to get sth quickly because you are in a hurry □ *mengambil cepat-cepat*: *I'll just grab something to eat and then we'll go.* ▶ grab /græb/ noun [C]: *She made a grab for the boy but she couldn't stop him falling.*

grace /greɪs/ noun [U] 1 the ability to move in a smooth and controlled way □ *lemah gemalai* 2 extra time that is allowed for sth □ *tempoh* 3 a short prayer of thanks to God before or after a meal □ *doa kesyukuran*: *to say grace*

IDM **sb's fall from grace** ➔ **fall²**

have the grace to do sth to be polite enough to do sth □ *ada budi bahasa*

with good grace in a pleasant and reasonable way, without complaining □ *dgn rela/baik*: *He accepted the refusal with good grace.*

graceful /ˈgreɪsfl/ adj 1 moving in a smooth, attractive way or having a smooth, attractive form □ *lemah gemalai; anggun*: *a graceful dan-*

cer ◆ graceful curves **2** polite and kind in a difficult situation □ *bersopan*

> **HELP** Graceful has a different meaning.

▶**gracefully** /-fəli/ *adv*: *The goalkeeper rose gracefully to catch the ball.* ◆ *She accepted the decision gracefully* (= without showing her disappointment). ▶**gracefulness** *noun* [U]

graceless /ˈɡreɪsləs/ *adj* **1** not knowing how to be polite to people □ *kasar; kurang sopan* **2** (used about a movement or a shape) ugly and not elegant □ *kekok; canggung* ▶**gracelessly** *adv*

gracious /ˈɡreɪʃəs/ *adj* **1** (used about a person or their behaviour) kind, polite and generous □ *baik budi; berbudi bahasa; murah hati*: *a gracious smile* **2** [only before a noun] showing the easy comfortable way of life that rich people can have □ *mewah*: *gracious living*

> **HELP** Gracious has a different meaning.

IDM **Good gracious!** used for expressing surprise □ *masya-Allah; alamak*: *Good gracious! Is that the time?*
▶**graciously** *adv* ▶**graciousness** *noun* [U]

grade¹ /ɡreɪd/ *noun* [C] **1** the quality or the level of ability, importance, etc. that sb/sth has □ *gred*: *We need to use high-grade materials for this job.* **2** a mark that is given for school work, etc. or in an exam □ *gred; markah*: *He got good/poor grades this term.* ◆ *Very few students pass the exam with a grade A.* **3** (*AmE*) a class or classes in a school in which all the children are of a similar age □ *darjah; tingkatan*: *My daughter is in the third grade.*
IDM **make the grade** (*informal*) to reach the expected standard; to succeed □ *mencapai taraf yg diperlukan; berjaya*: *She wanted to be a professional tennis player, but she didn't make the grade.*

grade² /ɡreɪd/ *verb* [T, often passive] to put things or people into groups according to their quality, ability, size, etc. □ *menggredkan*: *I've graded their work from 1 to 10.* ◆ *Eggs are graded by size.*

gradient /ˈɡreɪdiənt/ *noun* [C] the degree at which a road, etc. goes up or down □ *kecerunan*: *The hill has a gradient of 1 in 4* (= 25%). ◆ *a steep gradient*

gradual /ˈɡrædʒuəl/ *adj* happening slowly or over a long period of time; not sudden □ *berangsur-ansur*: *There has been a gradual increase in the number of people without jobs.* **OPP sudden**
▶**gradually** /-dʒuəli/ *adv*: *After the war life gradually got back to normal.*

graduate¹ /ˈɡrædʒuət/ *noun* [C] **1 a graduate (in sth)** a person who has a first degree from a university, etc. □ *siswazah*: *a law graduate/a graduate in law* ◆ *a graduate of London University/a London University graduate* ➲ look at **postgraduate, undergraduate, bachelor, student 2** (*AmE*) a person who has completed a course at a school, college, etc. □ *lulusan; lepasan*: *a high-school graduate*

383

graceless → **grammar**

graduate² /ˈɡrædʒueɪt/ *verb* [I] **1 graduate (in sth) (from sth)** to get a (first) degree from a university, etc. □ *mendapat ijazah*: *She graduated in History from Cambridge University.* **2** (*AmE*) **graduate (from sth)** to complete a course at a school, college, etc. □ *tamat kursus* **3 graduate (from sth) to sth** to change (from sth) to sth more difficult, important, expensive, etc. □ *meningkat; beralih kpd*: *She's graduated from being a classroom assistant to becoming a teacher.*

graduation /ˌɡrædʒuˈeɪʃn/ *noun* **1** [U] the act of successfully completing a university degree or (in the US) studies at a high school □ *mendapat ijazah, diploma, dsb* **2** [sing] a ceremony in which certificates are given to people who have **graduated** □ *penyampaian ijazah, diploma, sijil, dsb; konvokesyen*

graffiti /ɡrəˈfiːti/ *noun* [U, pl] pictures or writing on a wall, etc. in a public place □ *grafiti*: *The wall was covered in graffiti.*

graffiti

graft /ɡrɑːft/ *noun* [C] **1** a piece of a living plant that is fixed onto another plant so that it will grow □ *cantuman* **2** a piece of living skin, bone, etc. that is fixed onto a damaged part of a body in an operation □ *graf*: *a skin graft* ▶**graft** *verb* [T] **graft sth onto sth**: *Skin from his leg was grafted onto the burnt area of his face.* ➲ look at **transplant**

grain /ɡreɪn/ *noun* **1** [U,C] the seeds of food plants such as rice, etc.; a single seed of such a plant □ *biji-bijian; biji; butir*: *The US is a major producer of grain.* ◆ *grain exports* ◆ *a few grains of rice* **2** [C] **a grain of sth** a very small piece of sth □ *butir; sekelumit*: *a grain of sand/salt/sugar* ◆ (*figurative*) *There isn't a grain of truth in the rumour.* **3** [U] the natural pattern of lines that can be seen or felt in wood, rock, stone, etc. □ *ira*: *to cut a piece of wood along/across the grain*
IDM **(be/go) against the grain** to be different from what is usual or natural □ *bertentangan dgn*

gram (also **gramme**) /ɡræm/ *noun* [C] (*abbr* **g, gm**) a measure of weight. There are 1 000 grams in a kilogram. □ *gram* ❶ For more information about weights, look at the section on using numbers at the back of this dictionary.

grammar /ˈɡræmə(r)/ *noun* **1** [U] the rules of a language, for example for forming words

[C] **countable**, a noun with a plural form: *one book, two books* [U] **uncountable**, a noun with no plural form: *some sugar*

grammar school → granted

or joining words together in sentences ▫ *tatabahasa; nahu*: *Russian grammar can be difficult for foreign learners.* **2** [U] the way in which sb uses the rules of a language ▫ *tatabahasa*: *You have a good vocabulary, but your grammar needs improvement.* **3** [C] a book that describes and explains the rules of a language ▫ *buku tatabahasa/nahu*: *a French grammar*

'grammar school *noun* [C] (in Britain, especially in the past) a type of secondary school for children from 11–18 who are good at academic subjects ▫ *sekolah menengah (akademik)*

grammatical /grəˈmætɪkl/ *adj* **1** connected with grammar ▫ *(berkenaan dgn) tatabahasa/ nahu*: *the grammatical rules for forming plurals* **2** following the rules of a language ▫ *gramatis*: *The sentence is not grammatical.* ▶ **grammatically** /-kli/ *adv*

gramme = gram

gran /græn/ (BrE *informal*) = grandmother

grand¹ /grænd/ *adj* (**grander**; **grandest**) **1** impressive and large or important (also used in names) ▫ *besar; tersergam; penting*: *Our house isn't very grand, but it has a big garden.* ◆ *She thinks she's very grand because she drives a Porsche.* ◆ *the Grand Canyon* ◆ *the Grand Hotel* ▶ *noun* **grandeur** **2** (*informal*) very good or pleasant ▫ *sangat bagus; seronok*: *You've done a grand job!* ▶ **grandly** *adv* ▶ **grandness** *noun* [U]

grand² /grænd/ *noun* [C] (*pl* **grand**) (*slang*) 1 000 pounds or dollars ▫ *ribu*

grandad (also **granddad**) /ˈgrændæd/ (BrE *informal*) = grandfather

grandchild /ˈgræntʃaɪld/ *noun* [C] the daughter or son of your child ▫ *cucu*

granddaughter /ˈgrændɔːtə(r)/ *noun* [C] a daughter of your child ▫ *cucu perempuan* ➔ look at **grandson**

grandeur /ˈgrændʒə(r)/ *noun* [U] (*formal*) **1** the quality of being large and impressive ▫ *kehebatan; keindahan*: *the grandeur of the Swiss Alps* **2** the feeling of being important ▫ *kebesaran; keagungan*

grandfather /ˈgrænfɑːðə(r)/ *noun* [C] the father of your father or mother ▫ *datuk* ➔ look at **grandmother**

> **MORE** In spoken or informal English more common words are **grandad** or **grandpa**.

'grandfather clock *noun* [C] a clock that stands on the floor in a tall wooden case ▫ *jam besar berdiri*

grandiose /ˈgrændiəʊs/ *adj* bigger or more complicated than necessary ▫ *hebat; besar-besaran*

grandma /ˈgrænmɑː/ (*informal*) = grandmother

grandmother /ˈgrænmʌðə(r)/ *noun* [C] the mother of your father or mother ▫ *nenek* ➔ look at **grandfather**

> **MORE** In spoken or informal English more common words are **gran**, **granny**, **grandma** or **nan**.

grandpa /ˈgrænpɑː/ (*informal*) = grandfather

grandparent /ˈgrænpeərənt/ *noun* [C] the mother or father of one of your parents ▫ *datuk; nenek*: *This is a picture of two of my great-grandparents (= the parents of one of my grandparents).*

> **MORE** If you need to make it clear which grandfather or grandmother you are talking about, you can say: *My maternal/paternal grandfather/grandmother* or *my mother's/ father's father/mother*.

grand piˈano *noun* [C] a large flat piano (with horizontal strings) ▫ *granpiano* ➔ picture at **piano**

grand 'slam *noun* [C] winning all of a set of important matches or competitions in a particular sport, for example **tennis** or **rugby** ▫ *grand slam*

grandson /ˈgrænsʌn/ *noun* [C] a son of your child ▫ *cucu lelaki* ➔ look at **granddaughter**

grandstand /ˈgrænstænd/ *noun* [C] rows of seats, usually covered by a roof, from which you get a good view of a sports competition, etc. ▫ *astaka besar; granstan*

grand 'total *noun* [C] the amount that you get when you add several totals together ▫ *jumlah besar*

granite /ˈgrænɪt/ *noun* [U] a hard grey rock ▫ *granit*

granny /ˈgræni/ *noun* (*pl* **grannies**) (*informal*) = grandmother

grant¹ /grɑːnt/ *verb* [T] **1** (*formal*) to (officially) give sb what they have asked for ▫ *memberi; mengabulkan*: *He was granted permission to leave early.* **2** to agree (that sth is true) ▫ *mengakui*: *I grant you that New York is an interesting place but I still wouldn't want to live there.*

> **IDM** **take sb/sth for granted** to be so used to sb/sth that you forget their true value and are not grateful ▫ *tdk menghargai sso/sst*: *In developed countries we take running water for granted.*
> **take it for granted** to accept sth as being true ▫ *menganggap; beranggapan*: *She takes it for granted that I'll help her with her homework.*

grant² /grɑːnt/ *noun* [C] money that is given by the government, etc. for a particular purpose ▫ *bantuan*: *a student grant (= to help pay for university education)* ◆ *to apply for/be awarded a grant*

granted /ˈgrɑːntɪd/ *adv* used for saying that sth is true, before you make a comment about it ▫ *benar*: *'You could have done more to help.' 'Granted, but you didn't ask me until yesterday.'*

granulated sugar /ˈgrænjuleɪtɪd ˈʃʊgə(r)/ noun [U] white sugar in the form of small grains □ *gula pasir*

granule /ˈgrænjuːl/ noun [C] a small hard piece of sth □ *butir*: *instant coffee granules*

grape /greɪp/ noun [C] a small soft green or purple fruit that grows in bunches on a **vine** (= a climbing plant) and that is used for making wine □ *anggur*: *a bunch of grapes* ⊃ picture on **page P14**

> **MORE** Green grapes are usually called 'white' and purple grapes are usually called 'black'. Grapes that have been dried are called **raisins**, **currants** or **sultanas**.

IDM sour grapes ⊃ sour

grapefruit /ˈgreɪpfruːt/ noun [C] (*pl* grapefruit *or* grapefruits) a large round yellow fruit with a thick skin and a sour taste □ *limau gedang* ⊃ picture on **page P14**

the grapevine /ˈgreɪpvaɪn/ noun [sing] the way that news is passed from one person to another □ *khabar angin; cakap-cakap orang*: *I heard on/through the grapevine that you're moving.*

graphs

graph /grɑːf/ noun [C] a diagram in which a line or a curve shows the relationship between two quantities, measurements, etc. □ *graf*: *a graph showing/to show the number of cars sold each month*

graphic /ˈgræfɪk/ adj 1 [only *before* a noun] connected with drawings, diagrams, etc. □ *grafik*: *graphic design* ♦ *a graphic artist* 2 (used about descriptions) clear and giving a lot of detail, especially about sth unpleasant □ *amat jelas*: *She described the accident in graphic detail.*
▶ **graphically** /-kli/ adv

graphics /ˈgræfɪks/ noun [pl] designs, diagrams, etc. that are used especially in the production of books, magazines, etc. □ *grafik*: *computer graphics*

graphite /ˈgræfaɪt/ noun [U] a soft black mineral that is used in pencils □ *grafit; sejenis karbon*

grapple /ˈgræpl/ verb [I] 1 grapple (with sb) to get hold of sb and fight with or try to control them □ *bergelut* 2 grapple (with sth/to do sth) to try to find a solution to a problem □ *menangani*

grasp¹ /grɑːsp/ verb [T] 1 to take hold of sb/sth suddenly and firmly □ *menyambar; memegang; menggenggam; merebut*: *Lisa grasped the child firmly by the hand before crossing the road.* ♦ (*figurative*) *to grasp an opportunity/a chance* 2 to understand sth completely □ *memahami*: *I don't think you've grasped how serious the situation is.*

PHR V grasp at sth to try to take hold of sth □ *cuba menyambar/mencekau*

grasp² /grɑːsp/ noun [sing, U] 1 a firm hold of sb/sth □ *genggaman*: *Get a good grasp on the rope before pulling yourself up.* ♦ *I grabbed the boy, but he slipped from my grasp.* 2 sb's understanding of a subject or of difficult facts □ *pemahaman*: *He has a good grasp of English grammar.* 3 the ability to get or achieve sth □ *jangkauan*: *Finally their dream was within their grasp.*

grasping /ˈgrɑːspɪŋ/ adj wanting very much to have a lot more money, power, etc. □ *tamak*

grass /grɑːs/ noun 1 [U] the common green plant with thin leaves which covers fields and parts of gardens. Cows, sheep, horses, etc. eat grass □ *rumput*: *Don't walk on the grass.* ♦ *I must cut the grass at the weekend.* ♦ *a blade* (= one leaf) *of grass*

> **MORE** An area of grass in a garden is called a **lawn**.

2 [C] one type of grass □ *rumput*: *an arrangement of dried flowers and grasses*

grasshopper /ˈgrɑːshɒpə(r)/ noun [C] an insect that lives in long grass or trees and that can jump high in the air. Grasshoppers make sounds with their legs. □ *belalang* ⊃ picture on **page P13**

grass roots noun [pl] the ordinary people in an organization, not those who make decisions □ *akar umbi*: *the grass roots of the party*

grassy /ˈgrɑːsi/ adj (grassier; grassiest) covered with grass □ *berumput*

grate¹ /greɪt/ noun [C] the metal frame that holds the wood, coal, etc. in a **fireplace** (= the open place in a room where you light a fire) □ *besi pendagang* ⊃ picture at **fireplace**

grate² /greɪt/ verb 1 [T] to rub food into small pieces using a **grater** □ *memarut*: *grated cheese/carrot* 2 [I] grate (on sb) to annoy sb □ *menjengkelkan* **SYN** irritate 3 [I] grate (against/on

grateful → great

sth) to make a sharp unpleasant sound (when two metal surfaces rub against each other) □ *berkeriut*

grateful /ˈgreɪtfl/ *adj* **grateful (to sb) (for sth); grateful (that …)** feeling or showing thanks (to sb) □ *berterima kasih*: *We are very grateful to you for all the help you have given us.* ♦ *He was very grateful that you did as he asked.* **OPP ungrateful** ⇨ *noun* **gratitude** ▸**gratefully** /-fəli/ *adv*

grater /ˈgreɪtə(r)/ *noun* [C] a kitchen tool that is used for cutting food (for example cheese) into small pieces by rubbing it across its rough surface □ *parut; pemarut* ⇨ picture at **kitchen**

gratify /ˈgrætɪfaɪ/ *verb* [T] (**gratifying; gratifies**; *pt, pp* **gratified**) [usually passive] (*formal*) to give sb pleasure and satisfaction □ *memuaskan hati* ▸**gratifying** *adj*

grating /ˈgreɪtɪŋ/ *noun* [C] a frame made of metal bars that is fixed over a hole in the road, a window, etc. □ *jeriji*

gratitude /ˈgrætɪtjuːd/ *noun* [U] **gratitude (to sb) (for sth)** the feeling of being grateful or of wanting to give your thanks □ *rasa terima kasih*: *We should like to express our gratitude to David for all his help.* **OPP ingratitude**

gratuity /grəˈtjuːəti/ *noun* [C] (*pl* **gratuities**) (*formal*) money that you give to sb who has provided a service for you □ *ganjaran; upah* **SYN tip**

grave¹ /greɪv/ *noun* [C] the place where a dead body is buried □ *kubur*: *I put some flowers on my grandmother's grave.* ⇨ note at **funeral** ⇨ look at **tomb**

IDM have one foot in the grave ⇨ **foot¹**

grave² /greɪv/ *adj* (*formal*) **1** bad or serious □ *serius; genting; buruk*: *These events could have grave consequences for us all.* ♦ *The children were in grave danger.* **2** (used about people) sad or serious □ *serius*: *He was looking extremely grave.* ⇨ *noun* **gravity**. ⇨ A much more common word for both senses is **serious**. ▸**gravely** *adv*: *gravely ill*

gravel /ˈgrævl/ *noun* [U] very small stones that are used for making roads, paths, etc. □ *batu kelikir*

gravestone /ˈgreɪvstəʊn/ *noun* [C] a stone in the ground that shows the name, dates, etc. of the dead person who is buried there □ *batu nisan* **SYN headstone, tombstone**

graveyard /ˈgreɪvjɑːd/ *noun* [C] an area of land, often next to a church, where dead people are buried □ *kawasan perkuburan* ⇨ look at **cemetery, churchyard**

gravity /ˈgrævəti/ *noun* [U] **1** the natural force that makes things fall to the ground when you drop them □ *graviti*: *the force of gravity* **2** (*formal*) importance □ *seriusnya; keseriusan* ⇨ A more common word is **seriousness**. ⇨ *adjective* **grave**

gravy /ˈgreɪvi/ *noun* [U] a thin sauce that is made from the juices that come out of meat while it is cooking □ *kuah* ⇨ look at **sauce**

gray (*especially AmE*) = **grey**

grayish (*especially AmE*) = **greyish**

graze¹ /greɪz/ *verb* **1** [I] (used about cows, sheep, etc.) to eat grass (that is growing in a field) □ *meragut*: *There were cows grazing by the river.* **2** [T] to break the surface of your skin by rubbing it against sth rough □ *melecet*: *The child fell and grazed her knee.* **3** [T] to pass sth and touch it lightly □ *tergesel; tergeser*: *The bullet grazed his shoulder.*

graze² /greɪz/ *noun* [C] a slight injury where the surface of the skin has been broken by being rubbed against sth rough □ *luka melecet*

grease¹ /griːs/ *noun* [U] **1** any thick substance containing oil, especially one that is used to make machines run smoothly □ *gris*: *Her hands were covered with oil and grease.* **2** the fat that comes from cooking meat □ *minyak; lemak*: *You'll need very hot water to get all the grease off those pans.*

grease² /griːs/ *verb* [T] to rub **grease** or fat on or in sth □ *menyapu minyak*: *Grease the tin thoroughly to stop the cake from sticking.*

greasy /ˈgriːsi/ *adj* (**greasier; greasiest**) covered with or containing a lot of **grease** □ *berminyak*: *greasy skin/hair* ♦ *greasy food*

great¹ /greɪt/ *adj* (**greater; greatest**)

▸LARGE **1** large in amount, degree, size, etc.; a lot of □ *sangat (banyak, besar, sukar, dll)*: *We had great difficulty in solving the problem.* ♦ *The party was a great success.*

▸PLEASANT **2** (*informal*) good; wonderful □ *bagus; seronok*: *We had a great time in Paris.* ♦ *It's great to see you again.* ⇨ note at **good, nice**

▸IMPORTANT **3** particularly important; of unusually high quality □ *(paling) ulung*: *Einstein was perhaps the greatest scientist of the century.* ⇨ note at **big**

▸VERY **4** [only *before* a noun] (*informal*) (used to emphasize adjectives of size, quantity, etc.) very; very good □ *amat*: *There was a great big dog in the garden.* ♦ *They were great friends.*

▸FAMILY **5** **great-** used before a noun to show a family relationship □ *digunakan di depan kn utk menunjukkan hubungan keluarga*

HELP Great- can be added to words for family members to show another generation: *your great-aunt* (= the aunt of your mother or father) ♦ *your great-grandchild* (= the son or daughter of one of your grandchildren) ♦ *your great-grandparents* (= the parents of your grandparents) ♦ *your great-great-grandfather* (= the grandfather of one of your grandparents).

IDM go to great lengths to make more effort than usual in order to achieve sth □ *bersusah payah*: *I went to great lengths to find this book for you.*

a good/great deal ⇨ **deal²**

make great strides to make very quick progress □ *membuat kemajuan dgn cepat*
▶ **greatness** *noun* [U]

great² /greɪt/ *noun* [C, usually pl] (*informal*) a person or thing of special ability or importance □ *ulung; agung*: *That film is one of the all-time greats.*

Great Britain (also **Britain**) *noun* [U] (*abbr* **GB**) England, Wales and Scotland □ *Great Britain* ➔ note at **United Kingdom**

greatly /ˈgreɪtli/ *adv* very much □ *amat; sangat*

greed /griːd/ *noun* [U] **greed (for sth)** a strong desire for more food, money, power, etc. than you really need □ *ketamakan*

greedy /ˈgriːdi/ *adj* (**greedier**; **greediest**) **greedy (for sth)** wanting more food, money, power, etc. than you really need □ *tamak*: *Don't be so greedy—you've had three pieces of cake already.* ▶ **greedily** *adv* ▶ **greediness** *noun* [U]

green¹ /griːn/ *adj* (**greener**; **greenest**) **1** having the colour of grass or leaves □ *(warna) hijau*: *dark/light/pale green* **2** connected with protecting the environment or the natural world □ *hijau; tdk membahayakan alam sekitar*: *the Green party* ♦ *green products* (= that do not damage the environment) **3** (*informal*) with little experience of life or a particular job □ *mentah; belum berpengalaman*: *I'm not so green as to believe that!* **4** a strange, pale colour (because you feel sick) □ *pucat*: *At the sight of all the blood he turned green and fainted.*
IDM **give sb/get the green light** (*informal*) to give sb/get permission to do sth □ *memberi sso/mendapat kebenaran*
green with envy wanting to have what sb else has got □ *iri hati*: *He was green with envy when he saw his neighbour's new car.* **SYN** **jealous**
have green fingers; (*AmE* **have a green thumb**) (*informal*) to have the ability to make plants grow well □ *tangan sejuk; handal berkebun*

green² /griːn/ *noun*
▶ COLOUR **1** [C,U] the colour of grass or leaves □ *warna hijau*: *They were dressed in green.* ♦ *The room was decorated in greens and blues.*
▶ VEGETABLES **2 greens** [pl] green vegetables that are usually eaten cooked □ *sayur-sayuran hijau*: *For a healthy diet you should eat more cabbage, spinach, broccoli and other greens.*
▶ AREA OF GRASS **3** [C] (*BrE*) an area of grass in the centre of a village □ *padang*: *the village green* ➔ picture on **page P11 4** [C] a flat area of very short grass used in games such as **golf** □ *kawasan hijau/leret*: *the 18th hole*
▶ POLITICS **5 Green** [C] a member of a green political party □ *ahli parti politik yg memperjuangkan alam sekitar*

green belt *noun* [C,U] (*BrE*) an area of open land around a city where building is not allowed □ *kawasan hijau*

green card *noun* [C] a document that allows sb from another country to live and work legally in the US □ *kad hijau*

greenery /ˈgriːnəri/ *noun* [U] attractive green leaves and plants □ *tumbuh-tumbuhan hijau; dedaunan*

greengrocer /ˈgriːnɡrəʊsə(r)/ *noun* (*BrE*) **1** [C] a person who has a shop that sells fruit and vegetables □ *kedai buah dan sayur* ➔ look at **grocer 2 the greengrocer's** [sing] a shop that sells fruit and vegetables □ *penjual buah dan sayur*

greenhouse /ˈgriːnhaʊs/ *noun* [C] a small building made of glass in which plants are grown □ *rumah hijau/tanaman* ➔ look at **glasshouse**, **hothouse**

the greenhouse effect *noun* [sing] the warming of the earth's atmosphere as a result of harmful gases, etc. in the air □ *kesan rumah hijau* ➔ look at **global warming**

greenish /ˈɡriːnɪʃ/ *adj* slightly green □ *kehijau-hijauan*

greet /ɡriːt/ *verb* [T] **1 greet sb (with sth)** to welcome sb when you meet them; to say hello to sb □ *menyapa; menegur; menyambut*: *He greeted me with a friendly smile.* ♦ (*figurative*) *As we entered the house we were greeted by the smell of cooking.* **2** [usually passive] **greet sb/sth (as/with sth)** to react to sb or receive sth in a particular way □ *disambut*: *The news was greeted with a loud cheer.*

greeting /ˈɡriːtɪŋ/ *noun* [C] the first words you say when you meet sb or write to them □ *sapaan; tegur sapa*: *'Hello' and 'Hi' are informal greetings.*

gregarious /ɡrɪˈɡeəriəs/ *adj* liking to be with other people □ *suka berkawan* **SYN** **sociable**

grenade /ɡrəˈneɪd/ *noun* [C] a small bomb that is thrown by hand or fired from a gun □ *grenad*

grew past tense of **grow**

grey¹ (especially *AmE* **gray**) /ɡreɪ/ *adj* (**greyer**; **greyest**) **1** having the colour between black and white □ *kelabu*: *dark/light/pale grey* ♦ *He was wearing a grey suit.* **2** having grey hair □ *beruban*: *He's going grey.* **3** (used about the weather) full of cloud; not bright □ *mendung*: *grey skies* ♦ *a grey day* **4** boring and sad; without interest or variety □ *membosankan; muram*: *Life seems grey and pointless without him.*

grey² (especially *AmE* **gray**) /ɡreɪ/ *noun* [C,U] the colour between black and white □ *warna kelabu*: *dressed in grey*

greyhound /ˈɡreɪhaʊnd/ *noun* [C] a large thin dog that can run very fast and that is used for racing □ *anjing greyhound*: *greyhound racing*

greyish (especially *AmE* **grayish**) /ˈɡreɪɪʃ/ *adj* slightly grey □ *kekelabu-kelabuan*

grid /ɡrɪd/ *noun* [C] **1** a pattern of straight lines that cross each other to form squares □ *grid*: *She drew a grid to show how the students had scored in each part of the test.* **2** a frame of parallel metal

gridlock → grit

or wooden bars, usually covering a hole in sth □ *kekisi* **3** a system of squares that are drawn on a map so that the position of any point can be described or found □ *grid: a grid reference* **4** the system of electricity wires, etc. taking power to all parts of a country □ *jaringan: the National Grid*

gridlock /'grɪdlɒk/ noun [U,C] a situation in which there are so many cars in the streets of a town that the traffic cannot move at all □ *kesesakan jalan raya* ▶ gridlocked *adj*

grief /gri:f/ noun [U] great sadness (especially because of the death of sb you love) □ *kesedihan* **IDM** **Good grief!** (*spoken*) used for expressing surprise or shock □ *masya-Allah; kata seru apabila terkejut: Good grief! Whatever happened to you?*

grievance /'gri:vəns/ noun [C] a grievance (against sb) something that you think is unfair and that you want to complain or protest about □ *rungutan; rasa tdk puas hati*

grieve /gri:v/ verb **1** [I,T] grieve (for sb) to feel great sadness (especially about the death of sb you love) □ *bersedih; sedih* **2** [T] (*formal*) to cause unhappiness □ *menyedihkan*

grill¹ /grɪl/ noun [C] **1** (*BrE*) a part of a cooker where the food is cooked by heat from above □ *gril* **2** a metal frame that you put food on to cook over an open fire □ *pemanggang* **3** = grille

grill² /grɪl/ verb [T] **1** (*especially AmE* broil) to cook under or on a grill □ *menggril; memanggang: grilled steak/chicken/fish* ⊃ note at **cook** **2** (*informal*) grill sb (about sth) to question sb for a long time □ *memisit*

grille (*also* grill) /grɪl/ noun [C] a metal frame that is placed over a window, a piece of machinery, etc. □ *jerjak*

grim /grɪm/ *adj* (grimmer; grimmest) **1** (used about a person) very serious; not smiling □ *serius; masam* **2** (used about a situation, news, etc.) unpleasant or worrying □ *muram; tdk menyenangkan; buruk: The news is grim, I'm afraid.* **3** (used about a place) unpleasant to look at; not attractive □ *muram; suram: a grim block of flats* **4** [not before a noun] (*BrE informal*) ill □ *tdk sihat: I was feeling grim yesterday, but I managed to get to work.* ▶ grimly *adv*

grimace /'grɪməs; grɪ'meɪs/ noun [C] an ugly expression on your face that shows that you are angry, disgusted or that sth is hurting you □ *seringai; kerut muka: a grimace of pain* ▶ grimace *verb* [I]: *She grimaced with pain.*

grime /graɪm/ noun [U] a thick layer of dirt □ *kotoran; daki*

grimy /'graɪmi/ *adj* (grimier; grimiest) very dirty □ *kotor; berdaki* ⊃ look at **filthy**

grin /grɪn/ verb [I] (grinning; grinned) grin (at sb) to give a wide smile (so that you show your teeth) □ *tersengih: She grinned at me as she came into the room.* ▶ grin *noun* [C]

grind¹ /graɪnd/ verb [T] (*pt, pp* ground /graʊnd/) **1** grind sth (down/up); grind sth (to/into sth) to press and break sth into very small pieces or into a powder between two hard surfaces or in a special machine □ *mengisar: Wheat is ground into flour.* ♦ *ground pepper* **2** to make sth sharp or smooth by rubbing it on a rough hard surface □ *mengasah; mencanai: to grind a knife on a stone* **3** grind sth in/into sth to press or rub sth into a surface □ *menenyeh-nenyeh: He ground his cigarette into the ashtray.* **4** to rub sth together or make sth rub together, often producing an unpleasant noise □ *mengeritkan; berkeriut: Some people grind their teeth while they're asleep.*
IDM **grind to a halt/standstill** to go slower and then stop □ *berhenti perlahan-lahan*

grind² /graɪnd/ noun [sing] (*informal*) an activity that is tiring and boring and that takes a lot of time □ *kerja yg membosankan: the daily grind of working life*

grinder /'graɪndə(r)/ noun [C] a machine for grinding □ *pengisar: a coffee grinder*

grip¹ /grɪp/ noun **1** [sing] a grip (on sb/sth) a firm hold (on sb/sth) □ *genggaman; pegangan; kawalan: I relaxed my grip and he ran away.* ♦ *The climber slipped and lost her grip.* ♦ (*figurative*) *The teacher kept a firm grip on the class.* **2** [sing] a grip (on sth) an understanding of sth □ *pemahaman* **3** [C] the person whose job it is to move the cameras while a film is being made □ *pengalih kamera*
IDM **come/get to grips with sth** to start to understand and deal with a problem □ *memahami dan menangani sst (masalah)*
get/keep/take a grip/hold (on yourself) (*informal*) to try to behave in a calmer or more sensible way; to control yourself □ *mengawal diri*
in the grip of sth experiencing sth unpleasant that cannot be stopped □ *yg sedang dilanda: a country in the grip of recession*

grip² /grɪp/ verb (gripping; gripped) **1** [I,T] to hold sb/sth tightly □ *menggenggam; memegang kuat-kuat: She gripped my arm in fear.* **2** [T] to interest sb very much; to hold sb's attention □ *mengasyikkan: The book grips you from start to finish.* ⊃ adjective **gripping**

gripe /graɪp/ noun [C] (*informal*) a statement complaining about sth □ *sungutan* **SYN** complaint ▶ gripe *verb* [I]

gripping /'grɪpɪŋ/ *adj* exciting; holding your attention □ *menarik; menguja: a gripping film/book*

grisly /'grɪzli/ *adj* (grislier; grisliest) extremely unpleasant and frightening and usually connected with death and violence □ *mengerikan: a grisly crime/death/murder* ⊃ look at **gruesome**

gristle /'grɪsl/ noun [U] a hard substance in a piece of meat that is unpleasant to eat □ *rawan: a lump of gristle* ▶ gristly /'grɪstli/ *adj*

grit¹ /grɪt/ noun [U] **1** small pieces of stone or sand □ *kersik; batu halus: I've got a piece of grit in my shoe.* **2** (*informal*) courage; determination that makes it possible for sb to continue doing sth difficult or unpleasant □ *kecekalan*

grit² /grɪt/ *verb* [T] (**gritting**; **gritted**) to spread **grit** or salt on a road that is covered with ice □ *menabur kersik*

IDM **grit your teeth 1** to bite your teeth tightly together □ *mengetapkan gigi*: *She gritted her teeth against the pain as the doctor examined her injured foot.* **2** to use your courage or determination in a difficult situation □ *mencekalkan hati*

groan /grəʊn/ *verb* [I] **groan (at/with sth)** to make a deep sad sound because you are in pain, or to show that you are unhappy about sth □ *mengerang; mengeluh*: *He groaned with pain.* ♦ *They were all moaning and groaning* (= complaining) *about the amount of work they had to do.* ▶ **groan** *noun* [C]

grocer /ˈɡrəʊsə(r)/ *noun* **1** [C] a person who has a shop that sells food and other things for the home □ *pekedai runcit* ⊃ look at **greengrocer 2** the **grocer's** [sing] a shop that sells food and other things for the home □ *kedai runcit*

groceries /ˈɡrəʊsəriz/ *noun* [pl] food and other things for the home that you buy regularly □ *barang-barang runcit*: *Can you help me unload the groceries from the car, please?*

groggy /ˈɡrɒɡi/ *adj* (**groggier**; **groggiest**) (*informal*) weak and unable to walk steadily because you feel ill, have not had enough sleep, etc. □ *lemah dan pening*: *She felt a bit groggy when she came round from the operation.*

groin /ɡrɔɪn/ *noun* [C] the front part of your body where it joins your legs □ *kelangkang*

groom¹ /ɡruːm/ *verb* [T] **1** to clean or look after an animal by brushing, etc. □ *membersihkan dan menjaga haiwan*: *to groom a horse/dog/cat* **2** [usually passive] **groom sb (for/as sth)** to choose and prepare sb for a particular career or job □ *melatih; mendidik*

groom² /ɡruːm/ *noun* [C] **1** a person who looks after horses, especially by cleaning and brushing them □ *penjaga kuda* **2** = **bridegroom**

groove /ɡruːv/ *noun* [C] a long deep line that is cut in the surface of sth □ *alur*

grope /ɡrəʊp/ *verb* **1** [I] **grope (about/around) (for sth)** to search for sth or find your way using your hands because you cannot see □ *menggagau; tergagau-gagau*: *He groped around for the light switch.* **2** [T] (*informal*) to touch sb sexually, especially when they do not want you to □ *meraba-raba*

gross /ɡrəʊs/ *adj* **1** [only *before* a noun] being the total amount before anything is taken away □ *kasar*: *gross income* (= before tax, etc. is taken away) ⊃ look at **net 2** [only *before* a noun] (*formal*) very great or serious □ *melampau; teruk*: *gross indecency/negligence/misconduct* **3** very rude and unpleasant □ *kasar* **4** very fat and ugly □ *gemuk gedempol serta hodoh*: *She's not just fat, she's positively gross!* **5** (*informal*) very unpleasant □ *hodoh* **SYN** *disgusting*

grossly /ˈɡrəʊsli/ *adv* very □ *sangat*: *grossly unfair*

389 **grit → ground**

grotesque /ɡrəʊˈtesk/ *adj* strange or ugly in a way that is not natural □ *aneh; hodoh*

grotty /ˈɡrɒti/ *adj* (**grottier**; **grottiest**) (*BrE informal*) unpleasant; of poor quality □ *kotor dan jelik*: *She lives in a grotty flat.*

ground¹ /ɡraʊnd/ *noun*
▶SURFACE OF EARTH **1 the ground** [sing] the solid surface of the earth □ *tanah*: *We sat on the ground to eat our picnic.* ♦ *He slipped off the ladder and fell to the ground.*
▶SOIL **2** [U] an area or type of soil □ *tanah*: *solid/marshy/stony ground*
▶AREA OF LAND **3** [C] a piece of land that is used for a particular purpose □ *kawasan*: *a sports ground* ♦ *a playground* ❶ An area of land that is not being used is called *waste ground*.
▶GARDENS **4 grounds** [pl] land or gardens surrounding a large building □ *pekarangan*: *the grounds of the palace*
▶AREA OF INTEREST **5** [U] an area of interest, study, discussion, etc. □ *perkara*: *The lecture went over the same old ground/covered a lot of new ground.* ♦ *to be on dangerous ground* (= saying sth likely to cause anger)
▶REASON **6** [C, usually pl] **grounds (for sth/doing sth)** a reason for sth □ *sebab-sebab; alasan*: *She retired on medical grounds.* ♦ *grounds for divorce*
▶ELECTRICAL WIRE **7** (*AmE*) = **earth¹**(4)

IDM **above/below ground** above/below the surface of the earth □ *atas/bawah tanah*
break fresh/new ground to make a discovery or introduce a new method or activity □ *membuat penemuan baharu; membawa pembaharuan*
gain ground ⊃ **gain¹**
get (sth) off the ground (used about a business, project, etc.) to make a successful start □ *mula bergerak/berjalan dgn jayanya*
give/lose ground (to sb/sth) to allow sb to have an advantage; to lose an advantage for yourself □ *ketinggalan; hilang pengaruh; berundur*: *They are not prepared to give ground on tax cuts.* ♦ *The Conservatives lost a lot of ground to the Liberal Democrats at the election.*
hold/keep/stand your ground to refuse to change your opinion or to be influenced by pressure from other people □ *tdk berganjak; kekal mempertahankan*
thin on the ground ⊃ **thin¹**

OTHER WORDS FOR

ground

The **Earth** is the name of the planet where we live. **Land** is the opposite of sea: *The sailors sighted land.* ♦ *The astronauts returned to Earth.* **Land** is also something that you can buy or sell: *The price of land in Tokyo is extremely high.* When you are outside, the surface under your feet is called **the ground**. When you are inside it is called **the floor**: *Don't sit on the ground. You'll get wet.* ♦ *Don't sit on the floor. I'll get another chair.* Plants grow in **earth** or **soil**.

ground² /graʊnd/ verb [T] **1** [usually passive] to force an aircraft, etc. to stay on the ground □ *tdk dibenarkan terbang; tdk dpt terbang*: *to be grounded by fog* **2** [usually passive] to punish a child by not allowing them to go out with friends for a period of time □ *tdk dibenarkan keluar*: *Emma was grounded for a whole week after she stayed out late without asking permission.* **3** (AmE) = **earth²**

ground³ past tense, past participle of **grind¹**

ˌground ˈbeef (AmE) = **mince**

ˈground crew (also **ˈground staff**) noun [C,U] the people in an airport whose job it is to look after an aircraft while it is on the ground □ *kakitangan di lapangan terbang*

ˌground ˈfloor (AmE ˌfirst ˈfloor) noun [C] the floor of a building that is at ground level □ *tingkat bawah*: *a ground-floor flat* ➷ note at **floor**

grounding /ˈgraʊndɪŋ/ noun [sing] **a grounding (in sth)** the teaching of the basic facts or principles of a subject □ *pengajaran asas*: *This book provides a good grounding in grammar.*

groundless /ˈgraʊndləs/ adj having no reason or cause □ *tdk berasas*: *Our fears were groundless.*

groundnut /ˈgraʊndnʌt/ = **peanut**

ˈground staff = **ground crew**

groundwork /ˈgraʊndwɜːk/ noun [U] work that is done in preparation for further work or study □ *persediaan asas*

ˈgroup¹ /gruːp/ noun [C] **1** [with sing or pl verb] a number of people or things that are together in the same place or that are connected in some way □ *kumpulan; lingkungan*: *a group of girls/trees/houses* ♦ *Students were standing in groups waiting for their exam results.* ♦ *He is in the 40—50 age group.* ♦ *Many young people dress as they do because of pressure from their peer group* (= the people of the same age). ♦ *people of many different social groups* ♦ *a pressure group* (= a political group that tries to influence the government) ♦ *Which blood group* (for example A, O, etc.) *do you belong to?* ♦ *Divide the class into groups.*

> **GRAMMAR** In the singular, **group** can be used with a singular or plural verb: *Our discussion group is/are meeting this week.* But if you are thinking of the members of the group as individuals who have come together, a plural verb is more common: *A group of us are planning to meet for lunch.*

2 (used in business) a number of companies that are owned by the same person or organization □ *kumpulan*: *a newspaper group* **3** (old-fashioned) a number of people who play music together □ *kumpulan*: *a pop group* **SYN** band ➷ note at **pop**

group² /gruːp/ verb [I,T] **group (sb/sth) (around/round sb/sth); group (sb/sth) (together)** to put sb/sth or to form into one or more groups □ *mengumpulkan; kumpulkan*: *Group these words according to their meaning.*

grove /grəʊv/ noun [C] a small group of trees, especially of one particular type □ *dusun*: *an olive grove*

grovel /ˈgrɒvl/ verb [I] (grovelling; grovelled, (AmE) groveling; groveled) **1** grovel (to sb) (for sth) to try too hard to please sb who is more important than you or who can give you sth that you want □ *menyembah-nyembah*: *to grovel for forgiveness* **2** grovel (around/about) (for sth) to move around on your hands and knees (usually when you are looking for sth) □ *merangkak-rangkak* ▸ grovelling adj: *I wrote a grovelling letter of apology.*

grow /grəʊ/ verb (pt grew /gruː/; pp grown /grəʊn/) **1** [I] grow (in sth) to increase in size or number; to develop into an adult form □ *tumbuh membesar; bertambah; meningkat*: *a growing child* ♦ *She's growing in confidence all the time.* ♦ *You must invest if you want your business to grow.* ♦ *Plants grow from seeds.* ♦ *Kittens soon grow into cats.* **2** [I,T] (used about plants) to exist and develop in a particular place; to make plants grow by giving them water, etc. □ *tumbuh; hidup; tanam*: *Palm trees don't grow in cold climates.* ♦ *We grow vegetables in our garden.* **3** [T] to allow your hair or nails to grow □ *(menjadi) panjang*: *Claire's growing her hair long.* ♦ *to grow a beard/moustache* **4** [I] to gradually change from one state to another; to become □ *menjadi semakin*: *It began to grow dark.* ♦ *to grow older/wiser/taller/bigger* ♦ *The teacher was growing more and more impatient.* ➷ A less formal word is **get**.

PHR V **grow into sth 1** to gradually develop into a particular type of person □ *menjadi*: *She has grown into a very elegant woman.* **2** to become big enough to fit into clothes, etc. □ *akan padan*: *The coat is too big for him, but he will soon grow into it.*

grow on sb to become more pleasing □ *lama-kelamaan mula menyukai*: *I didn't like ginger at first, but it's a taste that grows on you.*

grow out of sth to become too big or too old for sth □ *tdk muat lagi*: *She's grown out of that dress I made her last year.*

grow (sth) out (used about the style in which you have your hair cut) to disappear gradually as your hair grows; to allow your hair to grow in order to change the style □ *membiarkan rambut panjang semula (supaya hilang fesyen rambut yg ada)*

grow up 1 to develop into an adult □ *membesar; menjadi matang*: *What do you want to be when you grow up?* (= what job do you want to do later?) ♦ *She grew up* (= lived when she was a child) *in Spain.* **2** (used about a feeling, etc.) to develop or become strong □ *berkembang*: *A close friendship has grown up between them.*

grower /ˈgrəʊə(r)/ noun [C] a person or company that grows plants, fruit or vegetables to sell □ *penanam*: *a tobacco grower*

growing /ˈɡrəʊɪŋ/ adj [only before a noun] increasing □ *semakin bertambah*: *A growing number of people are becoming vegetarian these days.*

growl /ɡraʊl/ verb [I] growl (at sb/sth) (used about dogs and other animals) to make a low noise in the throat to show anger or to give a warning □ *menderam; menggeram* ▶growl noun [C]

grown[1] past participle of **grow**

grown[2] /ɡrəʊn/ adj [only before a noun] physically an adult □ *dewasa*: *a fully-grown elephant*

grown-up[1] adj physically or mentally adult □ *dewasa; matang*: *She's very grown-up for her age.* SYN **mature**

grown-up[2] noun [C] (used by children) an adult person □ *orang dewasa* SYN **adult**

growth /ɡrəʊθ/ noun 1 [U] the process of growing and developing □ *tumbesaran; pertumbuhan*: *A good diet is very important for children's growth.* ♦ *a growth industry* (= one that is growing) 2 [U, sing] an increase (in sth) □ *pertumbuhan*: *population growth* 3 [C] a lump caused by a disease that grows in a person's or an animal's body □ *ketumbuhan*: *a cancerous growth* 4 [U] something that has grown □ *tumbuh*: *several days' growth of beard*

grub /ɡrʌb/ noun 1 [C] the first form that an insect takes when it comes out of the egg. **Grubs** are short, fat and white. □ *ulat; lundi* 2 [U] (informal) food □ *makanan*

grubby /ˈɡrʌbi/ adj (grubbier; grubbiest) (informal) dirty after being used and not washed □ *comot; kotor*

grudge[1] /ɡrʌdʒ/ noun [C] a grudge (against sb) unfriendly feelings towards sb, because you are angry about what has happened in the past □ *dendam; rasa sakit hati*: *to bear a grudge against somebody*

grudge[2] /ɡrʌdʒ/ verb [T] grudge sb sth; grudge doing sth to be unhappy that sb has sth or that you have to do sth □ *berasa iri hati; tdk rela*: *I don't grudge him his success—he deserves it.* ♦ *I grudge having to pay so much tax.* ➲ look at **begrudge**

grudging /ˈɡrʌdʒɪŋ/ adj given or done although you do not want to □ *dgn berat hati*: *grudging thanks* ▶grudgingly adv

gruelling (AmE grueling) /ˈɡruːəlɪŋ/ adj very tiring and long □ *menjerihkan; melesukan*: *a gruelling nine-hour march*

gruesome /ˈɡruːsəm/ adj very unpleasant or shocking, and usually connected with death or injury □ *mengerikan* ➲ look at **grisly**

gruff /ɡrʌf/ adj (used about a person or a voice) rough and unfriendly □ *kasar; tdk mesra* ▶gruffly adv

grumble /ˈɡrʌmbl/ verb [I] to complain in a bad-tempered way; to keep saying that you do not like sth □ *merungut; bersungut*: *The students were always grumbling about the standard of the food.* ➲ look at **complain, moan** ▶grumble noun [C]

grumpy /ˈɡrʌmpi/ adj (grumpier; grumpiest) (informal) bad-tempered □ *perengus* ▶grumpily adv

grunt /ɡrʌnt/ verb [I,T] to make a short low sound in the throat. People **grunt** when they do not like sth or are not interested and do not want to talk □ *mendengus*: *I tried to find out her opinion but she just grunted.* ▶grunt noun [C]

guarantee[1] /ˌɡærənˈtiː/ noun [C] 1 a firm promise that sth will be done or that sth will happen □ *jaminan*: *The refugees are demanding guarantees about their safety before they return home.* 2 a written promise by a company that it will repair or replace a product if it breaks in a certain period of time □ *jaminan*: *The watch comes with a year's guarantee.* ♦ *Is the computer still under guarantee?* ➲ look at **warranty** 3 something that makes sth else certain to happen □ *jaminan*: *If you don't have a reservation there's no guarantee that you'll get a seat on the train.*

guarantee[2] /ˌɡærənˈtiː/ verb [T] 1 to promise that sth will be done or will happen □ *menjamin; memberi jaminan*: *They have guaranteed delivery within one week.* 2 to give a written promise to repair or replace a product if anything is wrong with it □ *dijamin*: *This washing machine is guaranteed for three years.* 3 to make sth certain to happen □ *menjamin*: *Tonight's win guarantees the team a place in the final.*

guard[1] /ɡɑːd/ noun
▶PROTECTING 1 [C] a person who protects a place or people, or who stops prisoners from escaping □ *pengawal*: *a security guard* ➲ look at **warder, bodyguard** 2 [U] the state of being ready to prevent attack or danger □ *kawalan; (keadaan) berkawal*: *Soldiers keep guard at the gate.* ♦ *Who is on guard?* ♦ *The prisoner arrived under armed guard.* ♦ *a guard dog*
▶SOLDIERS 3 [sing, with sing or pl verb] a group of soldiers, police officers, etc. who protect sb/sth □ *pengawal*: *The president always travels with an armed guard.*
▶COVER 4 [C] [in compounds] something that covers sth dangerous or protects sth □ *pengadang*: *a fireguard* ♦ *a mudguard* (= over the wheel of a bicycle)
▶ON TRAIN 5 (AmE conductor) [C] a person who is in charge of a train but does not drive it □ *pengawal*
▶IN SPORT 6 [U] a position that you take to defend yourself, especially in sports such as **boxing** □ *(keadaan) berjaga-jaga*: *(figurative) She doesn't trust journalists, and never lets her guard drop during interviews.*

IDM **on/off (your) guard** ready/not ready for an attack, surprise, mistake, etc. □ *tdk bersedia/bersedia*: *The question caught me off (my) guard and I didn't know what to say.*

guard² /gɑːd/ verb [T] **1** to keep sb/sth safe from other people; protect □ *menjaga; mengawal*: *The building was guarded by men with dogs.* ◆ (figurative) *a closely guarded secret* **2** to be ready to stop prisoners from escaping □ *mengawal*: *The prisoner was closely guarded on the way to court.*

PHR V **guard against sth** to try to prevent sth or stop sth happening □ *berjaga-jaga utk mengelakkan sst*

guarded /'gɑːdɪd/ adj (used about an answer, statement, etc.) careful; not giving much information or showing what you feel □ *berhati-hati*: *a guarded reply* **OPP** **unguarded** ▸ **guardedly** adv

guardian /'gɑːdiən/ noun [C] **1** a person or institution that guards or protects sth □ *penjaga; pelindung*: *The police are the guardians of law and order.* **2** a person who is legally responsible for the care of another person, especially of a child whose parents are dead □ *penjaga*

guerrilla (also **guerilla**) /gə'rɪlə/ noun [C] a member of a small military group which is not part of an official army and which makes surprise attacks on the enemy □ *gerila*

guess¹ /ges/ verb **1** [I,T] **guess (at sth)** to try and give an answer or make a judgement about sth without being sure of all the facts □ *meneka; mengagak*: *I'd guess that he's about 45.* ◆ *I tried to guess how much his new phone cost.* ◆ *If you're not sure of an answer, guess.* ◆ *We can only guess at her reasons for leaving.* **2** [I,T] to guess correctly; to give the correct answer when you are not sure about it □ *meneka*: *I guessed the answer straightaway.* ◆ *You'll never guess what Adam just told me!* ◆ *Did I guess right?* **3** [T] (especially AmE informal) to imagine that sth is probably true or likely; to suppose □ *agaknya; kira*: *I guess you're tired after your long trip.* **4** [T] used to show that you are going to say sth surprising or exciting □ *digunakan ketika hendak mengatakan sst yg memeranjatkan atau menarik*: *Guess what! I'm getting married!*

guess² /ges/ noun [C] an effort you make to imagine a possible answer or give an opinion when you cannot be sure if you are right □ *teka; tekaan*: *If you don't know the answer, then have a guess!* ◆ *I don't know how far it is, but at a guess I'd say about 50 miles.* ◆ *I'd say it'll take about four hours, but that's just a rough guess.*

IDM **anybody's/anyone's guess** something that nobody can be certain about □ *tiada siapa yg tahu*: *What's going to happen next is anybody's guess.*

your guess is as good as mine I do not know □ *entah; saya pun tdk tahu*: *'Where's Ron?' 'Your guess is as good as mine.'*

guesswork /'geswɜːk/ noun [U] the process of guessing □ *tekaan*: *I arrived at the answer by pure guesswork.*

guest /gest/ noun [C] **1** a person who is invited to a place or to a special event □ *tetamu*: *We've got guests this weekend.* ◆ *wedding guests* ◆ *Who is the guest speaker at the conference?* **2** a person who is staying at a hotel, etc. □ *tamu*: *This hotel has accommodation for 500 guests.*

IDM **be my guest** (informal) used to give sb permission to do sth that they have asked to do □ *silakan*: *'Could I have a look at your newspaper?' 'Be my guest!'*

'guest house noun [C] a small hotel, sometimes in a private house □ *rumah tumpangan*

guidance /'gaɪdns/ noun [U] **guidance (on sth)** help or advice □ *bimbingan; panduan*: *The centre offers guidance for unemployed people on how to find work.*

guide¹ /gaɪd/ noun [C]
▸BOOK/MAGAZINE **1** a book, magazine, etc. that gives information or help on a subject □ *(buku, dsb) panduan*: *Your Guide to Using the Internet* ◆ *Have we got a TV guide for this week?* **2** also **guidebook** /'gaɪdbʊk/) a book that gives information about a place to tourists or people who are travelling □ *buku panduan*: *The guide says that it was built 500 years ago.*
▸PERSON **3** a person who shows tourists or people who are travelling where to go □ *pemandu*: *She works as a tour guide in Venice.*
▸STH THAT HELPS **4** something that helps you to judge or plan sth □ *panduan*: *As a rough guide, use twice as much water as rice.*
▸GIRL **5 Girl Guide** a member of an organization called **the Guides** that teaches girls practical skills and organizes activities such as camping □ *Pandu Puteri* ➲ look at **Scout**

guide² /gaɪd/ verb [T] **1** to help a person or a group of people to find the way to a place; to show sb a place that you know well □ *menunjukkan jalan; memandu; berpandukan*: *He guided us through the busy streets to our hotel.* ◆ *We were guided around the museum by a young student.* ➲ note at **lead 2** to have an influence on sb/sth □ *mempengaruhi*: *I was guided by your advice.* **3** to help sb deal with sth difficult or complicated □ *membimbing; mengajar*: *The manual will guide you through every step of the procedure.* **4** to carefully move sb/sth or to help sb/sth to move in a particular direction □ *memandu; menuntun*: *A crane lifted the piano and two men carefully guided it through the window.*

guided /'gaɪdɪd/ adj led by a guide □ *berpandu*: *a guided tour/walk*

'guide dog noun [C] a dog trained to guide a person who is unable to see □ *anjing pemandu*

guideline /'gaɪdlaɪn/ noun **1** [C usually pl] official advice or rules on how to do sth □ *garis panduan* **2** something that can be used to help you make a decision or form an opinion □ *panduan*: *These figures are a useful guideline when buying a house.*

guild /gɪld/ noun [C, with sing or pl verb] an organization of people who do the same job or who have the same interests or aims □ *persatuan; perseikatan*: *the Screen Actors' Guild*

guillotine /'gɪləti:n/ noun [C] **1** a machine that was used in France in the past for cutting people's heads off □ *gilotin* **2** a machine used for cutting paper □ *pemotong kertas* ▶ guillotine verb [T]

guilt /gɪlt/ noun [U] **1** guilt (about/at sth) the unpleasant feelings that you have when you know or think that you have done sth bad □ *rasa bersalah*: *I sometimes feel guilt about not spending more time with my children.* **2** the fact of having broken a law □ *kesalahan; (perihal) bersalah*: *We took his refusal to answer questions as an admission of guilt.* **OPP** innocence **3** the responsibility for doing sth wrong or for sth bad that has happened □ *kesalahan*: *It's difficult to say whether the guilt lies with the parents or the children.* **SYN** blame

guilty /'gɪlti/ adj (guiltier; guiltiest) **1** guilty (about sth) having an unpleasant feeling because you have done sth bad □ *(rasa) bersalah*: *I feel really guilty about lying to Sam.* ♦ *It's hard to sleep with a guilty conscience.* **2** guilty (of sth) having broken a law; being responsible for doing sth wrong □ *bersalah*: *She pleaded guilty/not guilty to the crime.* ♦ *to be guilty of murder* ♦ *The jury found him guilty of fraud.* **OPP** innocent ▶ guiltily adv

guinea pig /'gɪni pɪg/ noun [C] **1** a small animal with no tail that is often kept as a pet □ *tikus belanda; marmut* ⊃ note at **pet 2** a person who is used in an experiment □ *orang yg menjadi bahan uji kaji*: *I volunteered to act as a guinea pig in their research into dreams.*

guise /gaɪz/ noun [C] a way in which sb/sth appears, which is often different from usual or hides the truth □ *samaran; dlm tugas sso (yg lain drpd tugasnya yg biasa)*: *The President was at the meeting in his guise as chairman of the charity.* ♦ *His speech presented racist ideas under the guise of nationalism.*

guitar /gɪ'tɑ:(r)/ noun [C] a type of musical instrument with strings that you play with your fingers or with a **plectrum** (= a small piece of plastic) □ *gitar* ⊃ note at **music** ⊃ picture at **music**

guitarist /gɪ'tɑ:rɪst/ noun [C] a person who plays the **guitar** □ *pemain gitar*

gulf /gʌlf/ noun **1** [C] a part of the sea that is almost surrounded by land □ *teluk*: *the Gulf of Mexico* **2** the Gulf [sing] the Persian Gulf, the area of sea between Arabia and Iran □ *Teluk Parsi* **3** [C] an important or serious difference between people in the way they live, think or feel □ *jurang*: *the gulf between rich and poor*

gull /gʌl/ (also seagull) noun [C] a white or grey bird that makes a loud noise and lives near the sea □ *burung camar*

gullible /'gʌləbl/ adj (used about a person) believing and trusting people too easily, and therefore easily tricked □ *mudah diperdaya*

gulp¹ /gʌlp/ verb **1** [I,T] gulp sth (down); gulp (for) sth to swallow large amounts of food, drink, etc. quickly □ *memolok; menggogok*: *He gulped down his breakfast and went out.* **2** [I] to make a swallowing movement because you are afraid, surprised, etc. □ *menelan (air liur)* **3** to breathe quickly and deeply, because you need more air □ *tercungap-cungap*: *She finally came to the surface, desperately gulping (for) air.*

gulp² /gʌlp/ noun [C] **1** a gulp (of sth) the amount that you swallow when you **gulp** □ *satu teguk/gogok* **2** the act of breathing in or swallowing sth □ *teguk; gogok*: *I drank my coffee in one gulp and ran out of the door.*

gum /gʌm/ noun **1** [C] either of the firm pink parts of your mouth that hold your teeth □ *gusi* ⊃ picture at **body 2** [U] a substance that you use to stick things together (especially pieces of paper) □ *perekat* **3** = **chewing gum**

gun¹ /gʌn/ noun [C] **1** a weapon that is used for shooting □ *senapang*: *The robber held a gun to the bank clerk's head.*

> **MORE** Verbs often used with 'gun' are **load, unload, point, aim, fire**. Different types of gun include **machine gun, pistol, revolver, rifle, shotgun.**

2 a tool that uses pressure to send out a substance or an object □ *(alat) penembak*: *a grease gun* ♦ *a staple gun*
IDM jump the gun ⊃ **jump¹**

gun² /gʌn/ verb [T] (gunning; gunned)
PHR V gun sb down (*informal*) to shoot and kill or seriously injure sb □ *menembak sso*

gunboat /'gʌnbəʊt/ noun [C] a small ship used in war that carries heavy guns □ *bot pembedil*

gunfight /'gʌnfaɪt/ noun [C] a fight between people using guns □ *tembak-menembak*

gunfire /'gʌnfaɪə(r)/ noun [U] the repeated firing of guns; the sound of guns firing □ *tembak-menembak*: *We could hear gunfire.*

gunman /'gʌnmən/ noun [C] (pl -men /-mən/) a man who uses a gun to steal from or kill people □ *penjenayah yg bersenjata api*

gunpoint /'gʌnpɔɪnt/ noun
IDM at gunpoint threatening to shoot sb □ *dgn mengacukan senapang, dsb*: *He held the hostages at gunpoint.*

gunpowder /'gʌnpaʊdə(r)/ noun [U] a powder that can explode and is used in guns, etc. □ *serbuk letupan*

gunshot /'gʌnʃɒt/ noun [C] the firing of a gun or the sound that it makes □ *tembakan; bunyi tembakan*

gurgle /'gɜ:gl/ verb [I] **1** to make a sound like water flowing quickly through a narrow space □ *membobok*: *a gurgling stream* **2** if a baby **gurgles**, it makes a noise in its throat because it is happy □ *mengagah-agah* ▶ gurgle noun [C]

guru → habit

guru /ˈguruː/ noun [C] **1** a spiritual leader or teacher in the Hindu or Sikh religion □ *guru* **2** a person whose opinions you admire and respect, and whose ideas you follow □ *mahaguru*: *a management/fashion guru*

gush /gʌʃ/ verb **1** [I] **gush (out of/from/into sth); gush out/in** (used about a liquid) to flow out suddenly and in great quantities □ *memancut; menyembur (keluar)*: *Blood gushed from the wound.* ♦ *I turned the tap on and water gushed out.* **2** [T] (used about a container/vehicle, etc.) to produce large amounts of a liquid □ *memancutkan; menyemburkan*: *The broken pipe was gushing water all over the road.* **3** [I,T] to express pleasure or admiration so much that it does not sound sincere □ *memuji, dsb keterlaluan* ▶ **gush** noun [C]: *a sudden gush of water*

gust /gʌst/ noun [C] a sudden strong wind □ *tiupan angin kencang yg tiba-tiba* ▶ **gust** verb [I]

gusto /ˈgʌstəʊ/ noun
IDM **with gusto** with great enthusiasm □ *dgn penuh semangat*: *They sang with great gusto.*

gut¹ /gʌt/ noun **1** [C] the tube in the body that food passes through when it leaves the stomach □ *usus*

> **MORE** A more technical word is **intestine**.

2 guts [pl] the organs in and around the stomach, especially of an animal □ *isi perut* **3** [C] a person's fat stomach □ *perut buncit* **4 guts** [pl] (*informal*) courage and determination □ *berani; cekal*: *It takes guts to admit that you are wrong.* ♦ *I don't have the guts to tell my boss what he's doing wrong.*

gut² /gʌt/ verb [T] (**gutting; gutted**) **1** to destroy the inside of a building □ *memusnahkan bahagian dlm bangunan*: *The warehouse was gutted by fire.* **2** to remove the organs from inside an animal, fish, etc. □ *membuang isi perut*

gut³ /gʌt/ adj [only before a noun] based on feelings and emotions rather than thought and reason □ *gerak hati*: *a gut feeling/reaction* ♦ *My gut instinct is to say no.*

gutter /ˈgʌtə(r)/ noun **1** [C] a long piece of metal or plastic with a curved bottom that is fixed to the edge of a roof to carry away the water when it rains □ *talang* ⊃ picture on **page P8** **2** [C] a lower part at the edge of a road along which the water flows away when it rains □ *longkang* **3** [sing] the very lowest level of society □ *golongan yg hidup melarat*: *She rose from the gutter to become a great star.*

guy /gaɪ/ noun **1** [C] (*informal*) a man or a boy □ *(orang) lelaki; pemuda*: *He's a nice guy.* **2 guys** [pl] (*informal*) used when speaking to a group of people of either sex □ *kalian*: *What do you guys want to eat tonight?* **3** [sing] (*BrE*) a model of a man that is burned on 5 November in memory of Guy Fawkes □ *patung* ⊃ look at **Bonfire Night**

guzzle /ˈgʌzl/ verb [I,T] (*informal*) to eat or drink too fast and too much □ *memolok; menggogok*

gym /dʒɪm/ noun **1** (also *formal* **gymnasium** /dʒɪmˈneɪziəm/; pl **gymnasiums** or **gymnasia** /-zɪə/) [C] a room or hall with equipment for doing physical exercise □ *gimnasium; gim*: *The school has built a new gym.* **2** [C] = **health club** □ *kelab kesihatan*: *I work out at the gym twice a week.* **3** [U] physical exercises done in a **gym** □ *latihan fizikal*: *Do you like gym?* ♦ *gym shoes* ⊃ picture on **page P3**

gymnast /ˈdʒɪmnæst/ noun [C] a person who does **gymnastics** □ *ahli gimnastik* ⊃ picture on **page P4**

gymnastics /dʒɪmˈnæstɪks/ noun [U] physical exercises that are done inside a building, often using special equipment such as bars and ropes □ *gimnastik*: *She won a gold medal in gymnastics.* ⊃ picture on **page P4**

gynaecology (*AmE* **gynecology**) /ˌgaɪnəˈkɒlədʒi/ noun [U] the study and treatment of the diseases and medical problems of women □ *ginekologi; sakit puan* ▶ **gynaecological** (*AmE* **gynecological**) /ˌgaɪnəkəˈlɒdʒɪkl/ adj ▶ **gynaecologist** (*AmE* **gynecologist**) /ˌgaɪnəˈkɒlədʒɪst/ noun [C]

Gypsy (also **Gipsy**) /ˈdʒɪpsi/ noun [C] (pl **Gypsies**) a member of a race of people who traditionally spend their lives travelling around from place to place, living in **caravans** (= homes with wheels that can be pulled by a car or by a horse) □ *orang gipsi* ⊃ look at **traveller**

> **MORE** Some people find the word **Gypsy** offensive and prefer **Romani**.

H h

H, h /eɪtʃ/ noun [C,U] (pl **Hs; H's; h's** /ˈeɪtʃɪz/) the 8th letter of the English alphabet □ *H, h (huruf)*: *'Hat' begins with (an) 'H'.*

ha¹ /hɑː/ exclam **1** used for showing that you are surprised or pleased □ *ha*: *Ha! I knew he was hiding something!* **2 ha! ha!** used in written language to show that sb is laughing □ *ha! ha!*

ha² abbr = **hectare**

habit /ˈhæbɪt/ noun **1** [C] **a/the habit (of doing sth)** something that you do often and almost without thinking, especially sth that is hard to stop doing □ *tabiat*: *I'm trying to get into the habit of hanging up my clothes every night.* ♦ *I'm trying to break the habit of staying up too late.* ⊃ adjective **habitual**

> **HELP** **Habit** or **custom**? A **habit** is usually something that is done by one person. A **custom** is something that is done by a group, community or nation: *the custom of giving presents at Christmas*

2 [U] usual behaviour □ *kebiasaan*: *I sometimes think I only drink coffee out of habit now—I don't really enjoy it.*
IDM force of habit ⇒ force¹
kick the habit ⇒ kick¹

habitable /ˈhæbɪtəbl/ *adj* (used about buildings) suitable to be lived in □ *sesuai didiami*
OPP uninhabitable

habitat /ˈhæbɪtæt/ *noun* [C] the natural home of a plant or an animal □ *habitat*: *I've seen wolves in the zoo, but not in their natural habitat.*

habitation /ˌhæbɪˈteɪʃn/ *noun* [U] (*formal*) the act of living in a place □ *(perihal) mendiami*

habitual /həˈbɪtʃuəl/ *adj* **1** which you always have or do; usual □ *biasa; lazim*: *He had his habitual nap after lunch.* **2** [only before a noun] doing sth very often □ *kaki (bohong, pukul, curi, minum dll)*: *a habitual criminal/drinker/liar*
▶ **habitually** /-tʃuəli/ *adv*

hack /hæk/ *verb* [I,T] **1** hack (away) (at) sth to cut sth in a rough way with a tool such as a large knife □ *menetak*: *He hacked away at the bushes.* **2** (*informal*) hack (into) (sth) to use a computer to look at and/or change information that is stored on another computer without permission □ *menggodam* ⇒ look at **phone hacking**

hacker /ˈhækə(r)/ *noun* [C] (*informal*) a person who secretly looks at and/or changes information on sb else's computer system without permission □ *penggodam*

had¹ /hæd/ *past tense, past participle* of **have**

had² /hæd/ *adj*
IDM be had (*informal*) to be tricked □ *tertipu*: *I've been had. This watch I bought doesn't work.*

hadn't /ˈhædnt/ *short for* had not

haemophilia (*AmE* hemophilia) /ˌhiːməˈfɪliə/ *noun* [U] a disease that causes a person to lose a lot of blood even from very small injuries because the blood does not **clot** (= stop flowing) □ *hemofilia*

haemophiliac (*AmE* hemophiliac) /ˌhiːməˈfɪliæk/ *noun* [C] a person who suffers from **haemophilia** □ *penghidap hemofilia*

haemorrhage (*AmE* hemorrhage) /ˈhemərɪdʒ/ *noun* [C,U] the loss of a lot of blood from inside the body □ *pendarahan* ▶ **haemorrhage** (*AmE* hemorrhage) *verb* [I]

haemorrhoids (especially *AmE* hemorrhoids) /ˈhemərɔɪdz/ (also **piles**) *noun* [pl] a medical condition in which the **veins** (= tubes that carry blood) near the **anus** (= the opening where waste food leaves the body) swell and become painful □ *hemoroid; buasir*

haggard /ˈhægəd/ *adj* (used about a person) looking tired or worried □ *lesu; cengkung*

haggle /ˈhægl/ *verb* [I] haggle (with sb) (over/about sth) to argue with sb until you reach an agreement, especially about the price of sth □ *berbalah; tawar-menawar*: *In the market,*

395 **habitable → hair**

some tourists were haggling over the price of a carpet.

hail¹ /heɪl/ *verb* **1** [T] hail sb/sth as sth to say in public that sb/sth is very good or very special □ *menyanjung; mengalu-alukan*: *The book was hailed as a masterpiece.* **2** [T] to call or wave to sb/sth □ *memanggil*: *to hail a taxi* **3** [I] when it **hails**, small balls of ice fall from the sky like rain □ *hujan batu (turun)* ⇒ note at **weather**

hail² /heɪl/ *noun* **1** [U] small balls of ice, called **hailstones**, that fall from the sky like rain □ *hujan batu* **2** [sing] a hail of sth a large amount of sth that is aimed at sb in order to harm them □ *hujan*: *a hail of bullets/stones/abuse*

hair /heə(r)/ *noun* **1** [U,C] the mass of long thin things that grow on the head and body of people and animals; one of these things □ *rambut; bulu roma; bulu*: *He has got short black hair.* ♦ *Dave's losing his hair (= going bald).* ♦ *The dog left hairs all over the furniture.* ⇒ picture at **body 2** -haired *adj* [in compounds] having the type of hair mentioned □ *berambut*: *a dark-haired woman* ♦ *a long-haired dog* **3** a thing that looks like a very thin thread that grows on the surface of some plants □ *bulu*: *The leaves and stem are covered in fine hairs.*
IDM keep your hair on (*spoken*) (used to tell sb to stop shouting and become less angry) calm down □ *jangan marah; bertenanglah*
let your hair down (*informal*) to relax and enjoy yourself after being formal □ *relaks dan berseronok-seronok*
make sb's hair stand on end to frighten or shock sb □ *meremang bulu roma*
not turn a hair to not show any reaction to sth that many people would find surprising or shocking □ *tdk menunjukkan rasa terkejut, dsb langsung*
split hairs ⇒ split¹

TOPIC

Hair

Light-coloured hair is called **blonde/blond** or **fair**, and reddish-brown hair is called **ginger**, **auburn** or **red**. As people get older they might **go grey**. In order to make your hair tidy or to **style** it, you **brush** or **comb** it. You wash it with **shampoo** and use a **hairdryer** to **blow-dry** it. You can **part** it/have a **parting** in the middle or on one side, and you might have a **fringe** (= a short piece of hair at the front). When you **go to the hairdresser's** you can have **your hair cut** or **trimmed** (= a small amount cut off). You might also **have it permed** (= made curly) or **straightened** (= made straight). You can also have your hair **coloured**, or ask the hairdresser for **highlights** (= areas of hair that are lighter than the rest). People who want to have longer hair sometimes **get extensions** (= artificial hair that is attached to a person's real hair). A **barber** is a hairdresser who only cuts men's hair.

hairbrush /ˈheəbrʌʃ/ noun [C] a brush that you use on your hair □ *berus rambut* ➲ picture at **brush**

haircut /ˈheəkʌt/ noun [C] **1** the act of sb cutting your hair □ *gunting rambut*: *You need (to have) a haircut.* **2** the style in which your hair has been cut □ *potongan rambut*: *That haircut really suits you.*

hairdo /ˈheəduː/ (*informal*) = **hairstyle**

hairdresser /ˈheədresə(r)/ noun **1** [C] a person whose job is to cut, shape, colour, etc. hair □ *pendandan rambut* ➲ look at **barber** **2 the hairdresser's** [sing] the place where you go to have your hair cut □ *kedai rambut*: *I've made an appointment at the hairdresser's for 10 o'clock.*

hairdryer (also **hairdrier**) /ˈheədraɪə(r)/ noun [C] a machine that dries hair by blowing hot air through it □ *pengering rambut*

hairgrip /ˈheəɡrɪp/ (*AmE* ˈbobby pin) noun [C] a piece of wire that is folded in the middle and used for holding hair in place □ *sepit rambut* ➲ look at **hairpin**

hairless /ˈheələs/ adj without hair □ *tdk berambut/berbulu; gondol* ➲ look at **bald**

hairline¹ /ˈheəlaɪn/ noun [C] the edge of sb's hair, especially at the front □ *garis rambut*

hairline² /ˈheəlaɪn/ adj (used about a crack in sth) very thin □ *halus*: *a hairline fracture of the leg*

hairpin /ˈheəpɪn/ noun [C] a piece of wire, shaped like a U, used for holding hair in place □ *pin rambut; klip rambut* ➲ look at **hairgrip**

ˌhairpin ˈbend (*AmE* ˌhairpin ˈcurve, ˌhairpin ˈturn) noun [C] a very sharp bend in a road, especially a mountain road □ *selekoh tajam*

ˈhair-raising adj that makes you very frightened □ *menakutkan; menyeramkan*: *a hair-raising experience*

hairslide /ˈheəslaɪd/ (also **slide**; *AmE* **barrette**) noun [C] a small decorative piece of metal or plastic used for holding hair in place □ *klip rambut*

hairspray /ˈheəspreɪ/ noun [U,C] a substance you spray onto your hair to hold it in place □ *penyembur rambut* SYN **lacquer**

hairstyle /ˈheəstaɪl/ (also *informal* **hairdo**) noun [C] the style in which your hair has been cut or arranged □ *potongan/fesyen rambut*

hairstylist /ˈheəstaɪlɪst/ (also **stylist**) noun [C] a person whose job it is to cut and shape sb's hair □ *pendandan rambut*

hairy /ˈheəri/ adj (**hairier**; **hairiest**) **1** having a lot of hair □ *berbulu* **2** (*slang*) dangerous or worrying □ *mendebarkan*

hajj (also **haj**) /hædʒ/ noun [sing] the **pilgrimage** (= religious journey) to Mecca that many Muslims make □ *(fardu) haji*

halal /ˈhælæl/ adj [only *before* a noun] (used about meat) from an animal that has been killed according to Muslim law □ *halal*

half¹ /hɑːf/ determiner, pron, noun [C] (pl **halves** /hɑːvz/) one of two equal parts of sth □ *setengah; separuh*: *three and a half kilos of potatoes* ◆ *Two halves make a whole.* ◆ *half an hour* ◆ *an hour and a half* ◆ *The second half of the book is more exciting.* ◆ *Giggs scored in the first half* (= of a match). ◆ *Half of this money is yours.* ◆ *Half the people in the office leave at 5.* ➲ verb **halve**

IDM **break, cut, etc. sth in half** to break, etc. sth into two parts □ *pecah; dibelah (dipotong, dikerat, dll) dua*

hair

bun	ponytail	parting (*AmE* part) — bunches	fringe (*AmE* bangs) — pigtails (*AmE* **braids**) — plait
long straight hair	short curly hair	beard — wavy hair	moustache (*AmE* mustache) — bald

[I] **intransitive**, a verb which has no object: *He laughed.*   [T] **transitive**, a verb which has an object: *He ate an apple.*

go half and half/go halves with sb (*BrE*) to share the cost of sth with sb □ *berkongsi; bahagi dua*
do nothing/not do anything by halves to do whatever you do completely and properly □ *membuat sst dgn bersungguh-sungguh dan sempurna*

half² /hɑːf/ *adv* not completely □ *separuh*: *half full* ♦ *The hotel was only half finished.* ♦ *He's half German* (= one of his parents is German).
IDM half past ... (in time) 30 minutes past an hour □ *setengah*: *half past six* (= 6.30)

> **HELP** In spoken British English people also say **half six** to mean 6.30.

not half as much, many, good, bad, etc. much less □ *tdk sebanyak, baik, teruk, dll*: *This episode wasn't half as good as the last.*

half-baked *adj* (*informal*) not thought about or planned well □ *tdk dirancang dgn baik*: *a half-baked idea/scheme*

half board *noun* [U] (*BrE*) a price for a room in a hotel, etc. which includes breakfast and an evening meal □ *inapan termasuk sarapan dan makan malam* ⊃ note at **hotel** ⊃ look at **full board, bed and breakfast**

half-brother *noun* [C] a brother with whom you share one parent □ *abang/adik (lelaki) tiri seibu atau sebapa* ⊃ look at **stepbrother**

half-hearted *adj* without interest or enthusiasm □ *separuh hati* ▶ **half-heartedly** *adv*

half-price *adj* costing half the usual price □ *separuh harga*: *a half-price ticket* ▶ **half-price** *adv*: *Children aged under four go half-price.*

half-sister *noun* [C] a sister with whom you share one parent □ *kakak/adik (perempuan) tiri seibu atau sebapa* ⊃ look at **stepsister**

half-term *noun* [C] (*BrE*) a short holiday in the middle of one of the periods into which a school year is divided □ *separuh penggal*

half-time *noun* [U] (in sport) the period of time between the two halves of a match □ *separuh masa*

halfway /ˌhɑːfˈweɪ/ *adj, adv* at an equal distance between two places; in the middle of a period of time □ *separuh jalan; pd pertengahan*: *They have a break halfway through the morning.* **SYN midway**

hall /hɔːl/ *noun* [C] 1 (also **hallway**) a room or passage that is just inside the front entrance of a house or public building □ *ruang depan*: *There is a public telephone in the entrance hall of this building.* ⊃ picture on **page P8** 2 a building or large room in which meetings, concerts, dances, etc. can be held □ *dewan*: *a concert hall* ⊃ look at **town hall**

hallmark /ˈhɔːlmɑːk/ *noun* [C] 1 a characteristic that is typical of sb □ *ciri tersendiri*: *The ability to motivate students is the hallmark of a good teacher.* 2 a mark that is put on objects made of valuable metals, giving information about the quality of the metal and when and where the object was made □ *cap kempa*

hallo = **hello**

hall of residence *noun* [C] (*pl* **halls of residence**) (*AmE* **dormitory**) (in colleges, universities, etc.) a building where students live □ *asrama*

Halloween (also **Hallowe'en**) /ˌhæləʊˈiːn/ *noun* [sing] the night of October 31st (before All Saints' Day) □ *'Halloween'*

> **CULTURE**
> People say that witches and ghosts appear on Halloween. Children dress up as witches, etc., and they go to people's houses and say **'trick or treat'**, threatening to do sth bad or play a trick if the people do not give them sweets, etc.

hallucination /həˌluːsɪˈneɪʃn/ *noun* [C,U] seeing or hearing sth that is not really there (because you are ill or have taken a drug) □ *halusinasi; rayan*: *Was the figure real or just a hallucination?* ♦ *to suffer from/have hallucinations*

hallway /ˈhɔːlweɪ/ = **hall**(1)

halo /ˈheɪləʊ/ *noun* [C] (*pl* **halos** or **haloes**) the circle of light that is drawn around the head of a holy person in a painting □ *halo*

halt /hɔːlt/ *noun* [sing] a stop (that does not last very long) □ *berhenti; terhenti*: *Work came to a halt when the machine broke down.*
IDM grind to a halt/standstill ⊃ **grind¹**
▶ **halt** *verb* [I,T] (*formal*): *An accident halted the traffic in the town centre for half an hour.*

halve /hɑːv/ *verb* 1 [I,T] to reduce by a half; to make sth reduce by a half □ *mengurangkan separuh*: *Shares in the company have halved in value.* ♦ *We aim to halve the number of people on our waiting list in the next six months.* 2 [T] to divide sth into two equal parts □ *membahagi dua*: *First halve the peach and then remove the stone.*

halves *plural of* **half**

ham /hæm/ *noun* [U] meat from a pig's back leg that has been **cured** (= treated with salt or smoke to keep it fresh) □ *ham* ⊃ note at **meat** ⊃ look at **bacon, gammon, pork**

hamburger /ˈhæmbɜːɡə(r)/ 1 (*especially AmE*) = **burger** 2 (*AmE*) = **mince**

hamlet /ˈhæmlət/ *noun* [C] a very small village □ *kampung kecil*

hammer¹ /ˈhæmə(r)/ *noun* [C] a tool with a heavy metal head that is used for hitting nails, etc. □ *tukul* ⊃ picture at **tool**

hammer² /ˈhæmə(r)/ *verb* 1 [I,T] **hammer sth (in/into/onto sth)** to hit with a hammer □ *menukul; mengetuk*: *She hammered the nail into the wall.* 2 [I,T] to hit sth several times, making a loud noise □ *mengetuk*: *He hammered on the door until somebody opened it.*

IDM **hammer sth into sb** to force sb to remember sth by repeating it many times ◻ *melatih tubi sst (supaya dpt dihafal oleh sso)*
hammer sth out to succeed in making a plan or agreement after a lot of discussion ◻ *mencapai persetujuan, dsb setelah berbincang panjang lebar*

hammering /ˈhæmərɪŋ/ *noun* **1** [U] the noise that is made by sb using a hammer or by sb hitting sth many times ◻ *(bunyi) ketukan* **2** [C] (*BrE informal*) a very bad defeat ◻ *kalah teruk*

hammock /ˈhæmək/ *noun* [C] a bed, made of rope or strong cloth, which is hung up between two trees or poles ◻ *buai rajut* ⊃ picture at **bed**

hamper¹ /ˈhæmpə(r)/ *verb* [T, usually passive] to make sth difficult ◻ *dihalang; terhalang*: *The building work was hampered by bad weather.*

hamper² /ˈhæmpə(r)/ *noun* [C] a large **basket** (= a container) with a lid that is used for carrying food ◻ *bakul bertutup*

hamster /ˈhæmstə(r)/ *noun* [C] a small animal that is kept as a pet. Hamsters are like mice but are fatter and do not have a tail. They store food in the sides of their mouths. ◻ *hamster* ⊃ note at **pet**

ɫhand¹ /hænd/ *noun*
▶PART OF BODY **1** [C] the part of your body at the end of your arm which has five fingers ◻ *tangan*: *He took the child by the hand.* ♦ *She was on her hands and knees* (= crawling on the floor) *looking for an earring.* ⊃ picture at **body**
▶-HANDED **2** -**handed** *adj* [in compounds] having, using or made for the type of hand(s) mentioned ◻ *bertangan; (digunakan dlm kata majmuk dgn maksud mempunyai, menggunakan atau utk jenis tangan yg disebutkan)*: *heavy-handed* (= clumsy and careless) ♦ *right-handed/left-handed*
▶HELP **3 a hand** [sing] (*informal*) some help ◻ *pertolongan; bantuan*: *I'll give you a hand with the washing up.* ♦ *Do you want/need a hand?*
▶ON CLOCK **4** [C] the part of a clock or watch that points to the numbers ◻ *jarum (jam)*: *the hour/minute/second hand* ⊃ picture at **clock**
▶WORKER **5** [C] a person who does physical work on a farm, in a factory, etc. ◻ *buruh*: *farmhands*
▶CARDS **6** [C] the set of playing cards that sb has been given in a game of cards ◻ *daun (terup)*: *to be dealt a good/bad hand*
IDM **(close/near) at hand** (*formal*) near in space or time ◻ *dekat; berhampiran; sudah hampir*: *Help is close at hand.*
be an old hand (at sth) ⊃ **old**
by hand 1 done by a person and not by machine ◻ *dgn tangan; buatan tangan*: *I had to do all the sewing by hand.* **2** not by post ◻ *hantar tangan*: *The letter was delivered by hand.*
catch sb red-handed ⊃ **catch¹**
change hands ⊃ **change¹**
a firm hand ⊃ **firm²**
(at) first hand (used about information that you have received) from sb who was closely involved ◻ *(didapati secara) langsung dr sumber asal*: *Did you get this information first hand?* ⊃ look at **second-hand**
get, have, etc. a free hand ⊃ **free¹**
get, have, etc. the upper hand ⊃ **upper**
get/lay your hands on sb/sth (*informal*) to catch sb ◻ *menangkap sso*: *Just wait till I get my hands on that boy!*
get/lay your hands on sth to find or obtain sth ◻ *mendapatkan sst*: *I need to get my hands on a good dictionary.*
give sb a big hand ⊃ **big**
hand in hand 1 holding each other's hands ◻ *berpimpin tangan*: *The couple walked hand in hand along the beach.* **2** usually happening together; closely connected ◻ *seiring; kait-mengait*: *Drought and famine usually go hand in hand.*
your hands are tied to not be in a position to do as you would like because of rules, promises, etc ◻ *terikat (kerana peraturan, janji, dll)*: *I'd like to help but my hands are tied.*
hands off (sb/sth) (*informal*) used for ordering sb not to touch sb/sth ◻ *jangan sentuh/usik*
hands up 1 used in a school, etc. for asking people to lift one hand and give an answer ◻ *angkat tangan*: *Hands up who'd like to go on the trip this afternoon?* **2** used by a person with a gun to tell other people to put their hands in the air ◻ *angkat tangan*
have sb eating out of your hand ⊃ **eat**
have a hand in sth to take part in or share sth ◻ *turut sama membuat sst; turut terlibat*: *Even members of staff had a hand in painting and decorating the new office.*
have your hands full to be very busy or too busy to do sth else ◻ *sangat sibuk*
a helping hand ⊃ **help¹**
hold sb's hand to give sb support in a difficult situation ◻ *memberi sokongan (moral) kpd sso*: *I'll come to the dentist's with you to hold your hand.*
hold hands (with sb) (used about two or more people) to hold each other's hands ◻ *berpimpin tangan*
in hand 1 (used about money, etc.) not yet used ◻ *dlm tangan; ada lagi (masa, dll)*: *If you have time in hand at the end of the exam, check what you have written.* **2** being dealt with at the moment; under control ◻ *sedang dibuat; dlm kawalan*: *The situation is in hand.* **OPP** **out of hand**
in your hands; in the hands of sb in your possession, control or care ◻ *dlm tangan (sso)*: *The document is no longer in my hands.* ♦ *The matter is in the hands of a solicitor.*
in safe hands ⊃ **safe¹**
keep your hand in to do an activity from time to time so that you do not forget how to do it or lose the skill ◻ *kekal mahir*: *I play tennis from time to time just to keep my hand in.*
know sth like the back of your hand ⊃ **know¹**
lend (sb) a hand/lend a hand (to sb) ⊃ **lend**
off your hands not your responsibility any more ◻ *lepas drpd tanggungjawab (sso)*
on hand available to help or to be used ◻ *(sentiasa) ada*: *There is always an adult on hand to*

help when the children are playing outside.
on your hands being your responsibility □ *dlm tangan (utk diurus, dll)*: *We seem to have a problem on our hands.*
on the one hand ... on the other (hand) used for showing opposite points of view □ *dr satu segi...sebaliknya pula...*: *On the one hand, of course, cars are very useful. On the other hand, they cause a huge amount of pollution.* ⊃ note at **contrast**
(get) out of hand not under control □ *tdk dpt dikawal lagi*: *Violence at football matches is getting out of hand.* **OPP in hand**
out of your hands not in your control; not your responsibility □ *tdk lagi dlm tangan (sso)*: *I can't help you, I'm afraid. The matter is out of my hands.*
shake sb's hand/shake hands (with sb)/shake sb by the hand ⊃ **shake**¹
to hand near or close to you □ *dekat; mudah dicapai/didapati*: *I'm afraid I haven't got a pen to hand.*
try your hand at sth ⊃ **try**¹
turn your hand to sth to have the ability to do sth □ *boleh membuat sst*: *She can turn her hand to all sorts of jobs.*
wash your hands of sb/sth ⊃ **wash**¹
with your bare hands ⊃ **bare**

hand² /hænd/ *verb* [T] **hand sb sth; hand sth to sb** to give or pass sth to sb □ *menghulurkan sst kpd sso*
IDM have (got) to hand it to sb used to show admiration and approval of sb's work or efforts □ *(sso itu) patut dipuji*: *You've got to hand it to Rita—she's a great cook.*
PHR V hand sth back (to sb) to give or return sth to the person who owns it or to where it belongs □ *memulangkan*
hand sth down (to sb) 1 to pass customs, etc. from older people to younger ones □ *menurunkan (adat, tradisi, dsb) (kpd sso)*: *These stories have been handed down from generation to generation.* **2** to pass clothes, toys, etc. from older children to younger ones in the family □ *menurunkan pakaian, mainan, dll (kpd adik)*
hand sth in (to sb) to give sth to sb in authority, especially a piece of work or sth that is lost □ *menyerahkan sst (kpd sso)*: *I found a wallet and handed it in to the police.*
hand sth on (to sb) to send or give sth to another person □ *memberi/mengedarkan sst (kpd sso)*: *When you have read the article, please hand it on to another student.*
hand sth out (to sb) to give sth to many people in a group □ *mengedarkan/membahagi-bahagikan sst (kpd sso)*: *Food was handed out to the starving people.*
hand (sth) over (to sb) to give sb else your position of power or the responsibility for sth □ *menyerahkan (jawatan, tanggungjawab, dsb) kpd (sso)*: *She resigned as chairperson and handed over to one of her younger colleagues.*
hand (sb) over to sb (used at a meeting or on the TV, radio, telephone, etc.) to let sb speak or listen to another person □ *menyerahkan A kpd B (supaya A dpt bercakap atau mende-ngar B)*: *I'm handing you over now to our foreign correspondent.*
hand sb/sth over (to sb) to give sb/sth (to sb) □ *memberi sso/sst (kpd sso)*: *People were tricked into handing over large sums of money.*
hand sth round to pass sth, especially food and drinks, to all the people in a group □ *mengedar-kan sst*

handbag /'hændbæg/ (*AmE* **purse**) *noun* [C] a small bag in which women carry money, keys, etc. □ *beg tangan* **SYN shoulder bag** ⊃ picture at **bag**

handbook /'hændbʊk/ *noun* [C] a small book that gives instructions on how to use sth or advice and information about a particular subject □ *buku panduan* ⊃ look at **manual²**

handbrake /'hændbreɪk/ (*AmE* **e'mergency brake**; **'parking brake**) *noun* [C] a device that is operated by hand to stop a car from moving when it is parked □ *brek tangan* ⊃ picture at **car**

handcuffs /'hændkʌfs/ (also **cuffs**) *noun* [pl] a pair of metal rings that are joined together by a chain and put around the wrists of prisoners □ *gari*

handful /'hændfʊl/ *noun* **1** [C] **a handful (of sth)** as much or as many of sth as you can hold in one hand □ *segenggam*: *a handful of sand* **2** [sing] **a handful (of sth)** a small number (of sb/sth) □ *beberapa; sebilangan kecil*: *Only a handful of people came to the meeting.* **3 a handful** [sing] (*informal*) a person or an animal that is difficult to control □ *liar; sukar dikawal*: *The little girl is quite a handful.*

handgun /'hændgʌn/ *noun* [C] a small gun that you can hold and fire with one hand □ *pistol*

,hand-'held *adj* [usually before a noun] small enough to be held in the hand while being used □ *dpt dipegang dlm tangan*: *a hand-held camera/computer/device*

handicap¹ /'hændikæp/ *noun* **1** (*old-fashioned*) = **disability**

> **HELP** Be careful. Many people now find this word offensive.

2 [C] something that makes doing sth more difficult; a disadvantage □ *kelemahan; kekurangan*: *Not speaking French is going to be a bit of a handicap in my new job.* **3** a disadvantage that is given to the strongest people competing in a sports event, etc. so that the weaker people have more chance □ *handikap*

handicap² /'hændikæp/ *verb* [T] (**handicap-ping**; **handicapped**) [usually passive] to give or be a disadvantage to sb □ *memberi handikap; merupakan kelemahan kekurangan*: *They were handicapped by their lack of education.*

handicapped /ˈhændikæpt/ *adj* (old-fashioned) = **disabled**

> **HELP** Be careful. Many people now find this word offensive.

handicraft /ˈhændikrɑːft/ *noun* **1** [C] an activity that needs skill with the hands as well as artistic ability, for example sewing □ *kraf tangan* **2 handicrafts** [pl] the objects that are produced by this activity □ *hasil kraf tangan*

handiwork /ˈhændiwɜːk/ *noun* [U] **1** a thing that you have made or done, especially using your artistic skill □ *kerja tangan*: *We admired her exquisite handiwork.* **2** something done by a particular person or group, especially sth bad □ *perbuatan*: *This looks like the handiwork of criminals.*

handkerchief /ˈhæŋkətʃɪf; -tʃiːf/ *noun* [C] (*pl* **handkerchiefs** or **handkerchieves** /-tʃiːvz/) a square piece of cloth or soft thin paper that you use for clearing your nose □ *sapu tangan*

> **HELP** A more informal word is **hanky** or **hankie**. A handkerchief that is made of soft thin paper is also called a **paper handkerchief** or a **tissue**.

handles

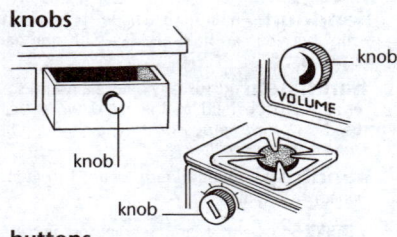

handle
door handle

knobs

knob
knob
knob

buttons

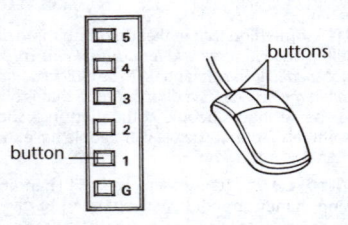

buttons
button

handle¹ /ˈhændl/ *verb* [T] **1** to deal with or to control sb/sth □ *mengendalikan; mengawal;*

menangani: *This port handles 100 million tons of cargo each year.* ♦ *I have a problem at work and I don't really know how to handle it.* **2** to touch or hold sth with your hand(s) □ *memegang*: *Wash your hands before you handle food.* ▶ **handler** *noun* [C]: *baggage/dog/food handlers*

handle² /ˈhændl/ *noun* [C] a part of sth that is used for holding or opening it □ *pemegang; tangkai; batang; hulu*: *She turned the handle and opened the door.* ⊃ picture at **garden, bag, cup**

IDM fly off the handle ⊃ **fly¹**

handlebar /ˈhændlbɑː(r)/ *noun* [C, usually pl] the metal bar at the front of a bicycle that you hold when you are riding it □ *hendal (basikal)* ⊃ picture at **bicycle**

hand luggage *noun* [U] (*AmE* **ˈcarry-on bag**) small bags, etc. that you can keep with you on a plane □ *bagasi tangan*: *You can only take one piece of hand luggage on this flight.*

handmade /ˌhændˈmeɪd/ *adj* made by hand and of very good quality, not by machine □ *buatan tangan*

handout /ˈhændaʊt/ *noun* [C] **1** food, money, etc. given to people who need it badly □ *pemberian (kebajikan)* **2** a document that is given to a lot of people, to advertise sth or explain sth, for example in a class □ *bahan sebaran*

ˌhand-ˈpicked *adj* carefully or personally chosen for a special purpose □ *dipilih dgn teliti; dipilih sendiri*

handrail /ˈhændreɪl/ *noun* [C] a bar which you can hold to stop you from falling (on stairs, from a building, etc.) □ *selusur*: *Hold on to the handrail—these steps are very slippery.*

handset /ˈhændset/ *noun* [C] **1** a mobile phone, especially the main part of the phone not including the battery or **SIM card** (= a plastic card that stores phone numbers, etc.) □ *telefon bimbit*: *handset manufacturers* **2** a device that you hold in your hand to operate a television, etc. □ *alat kawalan tangan* ⊃ look at **remote control 3** = **receiver**

ˈhands-free *adj* if a telephone, etc. is **hands-free**, you can use it without needing to hold it in your hand □ *bebas tangan*: *Are hands-free mobile phones really safe to use when driving?*

handshake /ˈhændʃeɪk/ *noun* [C] the act of shaking sb's right hand with your own when you meet them □ *jabat tangan*

handsome /ˈhænsəm/ *adj* (**handsomer**; **handsomest**) [More **handsome** and most **handsome** are more common.] **1** (used about a man) attractive □ *kacak* ⊃ note at **beautiful 2** (used about money, an offer, etc.) large or generous □ *banyak; besar*: *a handsome profit* ▶ **handsomely** *adv*: *Her efforts were handsomely rewarded.*

ˌhands-ˈon *adj* involving doing sth yourself, rather than watching sb else do it; practical □ *secara praktikal*: *She needs some hands-on computer experience.*

ʌ **c**up ɜː **b**ir**d** ə **a**go eɪ **p**ay əʊ **g**o aɪ **m**y aʊ **n**ow ɔɪ **b**oy ɪə **n**ear eə **h**air ʊə **p**ure

handwriting /ˈhændraɪtɪŋ/ noun [U] a person's style of writing by hand ◻ *tulisan tangan*

handwritten /ˌhændˈrɪtn/ adj written by hand, not typed or printed ◻ *(yg) ditulis tangan*

handy /ˈhændi/ adj (**handier**; **handiest**) **1** easy to use ◻ *berguna*: *a handy tip* ♦ *a handy gadget* **SYN useful 2 handy (for sth/doing sth)** within easy reach of sth; in a convenient place ◻ *dekat; di tempat yg mudah dicapai*: *Always keep a first-aid kit handy for emergencies.* **3** (*informal*) skilful in using your hands or tools to make or repair things ◻ *mahir/pandai (membuat atau membaiki sst)*: *Jane is very handy around the house.*
IDM come in handy to be useful at some time ◻ *berguna nanti*: *Don't throw that box away. It may come in handy.*

handyman /ˈhændimæn/ noun [sing] a man who is good at doing practical jobs inside and outside the house, either as a hobby or as a job ◻ *orang yg pandai membuat atau membaiki sst*

hang[1] /hæŋ/ verb (pt, pp **hung** /hʌŋ/) **1** [I,T] to fasten sth or be fastened at the top so that the lower part is free or loose ◻ *menggantung; menyangkut; menyidai*: *Hang your coat on the hook.* ♦ *I left the washing hanging on the line all day.* ♦ *She hung the picture over the fireplace.* **2** [I,T] to bend or let sth bend downwards ◻ *terkulai; terlentok*: *The dog's tongue was hanging out.* ♦ *He hung his head in shame.* **3** [I,T] (pt, pp **hanged**) to kill sb/yourself by putting a rope around the neck and allowing the body to drop downwards ◻ *menggantung*: *He was hanged for murder.* **4** [I] **hang (above/over sb/sth)** to stay in the air in a way that is unpleasant or threatening ◻ *menyelubungi*: *Smog hung in the air over the city.*
IDM be/get hung up (about/on sb/sth) to think about sb/sth all the time in a way that is not healthy or good ◻ *asyik memikirkan (ttg sso/sst)*: *She's really hung up about her parents' divorce.*
hang (on) in there (*spoken*) to have courage and keep trying, even though a situation is difficult ◻ *bertahan; jangan putus asa*: *The worst part is over now. Just hang on in there and be patient.*
PHR V hang about/around (*informal*) to stay in or near a place not doing very much ◻ *melepak*
hang back 1 to not want to do or say sth, often because you are shy or not sure of yourself ◻ *teragak-agak/tdk mahu (membuat atau menyatakan sst)* **2** to stay in a place after other people have left it ◻ *masih tinggal di sst tempat*
hang on 1 to hold sth tightly ◻ *pegang kuat-kuat*: *Hang on, don't let go!* **2** (*informal*) to wait for a short time ◻ *tunggu sekejap*: *Hang on a minute. I'm nearly ready.*
hang on sth to depend on sth ◻ *bergantung pd sst*: *A lot hangs on this decision.*
hang on to sth 1 to hold sth tightly ◻ *memegang sst kuat-kuat*: *He hung on to the child's hand as they crossed the street.* **2** (*informal*) to keep sth ◻ *menyimpan; tdk melepaskan*: *Let's hang on to the car for another year.*
hang out (*informal*) to spend a lot of time in a place ◻ *melepak*: *The local kids hang out at the park.*
hang sth out to put washing, etc. on a clothes line so that it can dry ◻ *menyidai/menjemur sst*
hang over sb to be present or about to happen in a way which is unpleasant or threatening ◻ *mengganggu fikiran/menghantui/merundung sso*: *This essay has been hanging over me for days.*
hang sth up to put sth on a nail, hook, etc. ◻ *menyangkut*: *Hang your coat up over there.*
hang up to end a telephone conversation and put the telephone down ◻ *meletakkan gagang telefon*
hang up on sb (*informal*) to end a telephone conversation without saying goodbye because you are angry ◻ *meletakkan gagang telefon (sebelum tamat perbualan kerana marah)*

hang[2] /hæŋ/ noun
IDM get the hang of (doing) sth (*informal*) to learn how to use or do sth ◻ *belajar menggunakan sst*: *It took me a long time to get the hang of the new system.*

hangar /ˈhæŋə(r)/ noun [C] a big building where planes are kept ◻ *hangar*

hanged past tense, past participle of **hang**[1] (3)

hanger /ˈhæŋə(r)/ (also ˈ**coat hanger**, ˈ**clothes hanger**) noun [C] a metal, plastic or wooden object with a hook that is used for hanging up clothes in a cupboard ◻ *penyangkut baju* ⊃ picture at **hook**

ˌhanger-ˈon noun [C] (pl ˌhangers-ˈon) a person who tries to be friendly with sb who is rich or important ◻ *konco*

ˈhang-glider noun [C] a type of frame covered with cloth, which a person holds and flies through the air with as a sport ◻ *peluncur angin (sukan)* ⊃ look at **glider** ⊃ picture at **parachute** ▶ ˈ**hang-gliding** noun [U]: *to go hang-gliding*

hanging /ˈhæŋɪŋ/ noun [C,U] death as a form of punishment for a crime, caused by putting a rope around a person's neck and letting the body drop downwards ◻ *hukuman gantung*

hangman /ˈhæŋmən/ noun **1** [C] a person whose job is to kill criminals as a form of punishment by hanging them with a rope ◻ *tukang gantung* **2** [U] a word game where the aim is to guess all the letters of a word before a picture of a person hanging is completed ◻ *permainan teka kata 'hangman'*

hangover /ˈhæŋəʊvə(r)/ noun [C] the headache and sick feeling that you have if you have drunk too much alcohol the night before ◻ *pening dan mual akibat terlalu banyak minum arak pd malam sebelumnya*

ˈhang-up noun [C] (*informal*) **a hang-up (about sb/sth)** an emotional problem about sth

hanker → hard

that makes you embarrassed or worried □ *(masalah emosi) betul-betul risau/malu ttg sst*: *He has a real hang-up about his height.*

hanker /ˈhæŋkə(r)/ *verb* [I] **hanker (after/for/to do sth)** to want sth very much (often sth that you cannot easily have) □ *teringin sangat; mengidamkan*

hanky (also **hankie**) /ˈhæŋki/ *noun* [C] (*pl* **hankies**) (*informal*) = **handkerchief**

Hanukkah /ˈhænʊkə/ *noun* [U] an eight-day Jewish festival and holiday in November or December □ *Hanukah (perayaan Yahudi)*

haphazard /hæpˈhæzəd/ *adj* with no particular order or plan; badly organized □ *sembarangan; lintang-pukang* ▶ **haphazardly** *adv*

happen /ˈhæpən/ *verb* [I] **1** (of an event or situation) to take place, usually without being planned first □ *berlaku; terjadi*: *Can you describe to the police what happened after you left the party?* ◆ *How did the accident happen?* **2 happen to sb/sth** to be what sb/sth experiences □ *terjadi*: *What do you think has happened to Julie? She should have been here an hour ago.* ◆ *What will happen to the business when your father retires?* **3 happen to do sth** to do sth by chance □ *kebetulan*: *I happened to meet him in London yesterday.*
IDM **as it happens/happened** (used when you are adding to what you have said) actually □ *secara kebetulan; sebenarnya*: *As it happens, I did remember to bring the book you wanted.*
it (just) so happens ⊃ **so¹**

OTHER WORDS FOR

happen

Happen and **occur** are usually used with events that are not planned. **Occur** is more formal than **happen**. **Take place** suggests that an event is planned: *The wedding took place on Saturday July 20th.*

happening /ˈhæpənɪŋ/ *noun* [C, usually pl] a thing that happens; an event (that is usually strange or difficult to explain) □ *kejadian*: *Strange happenings have been reported in that old hotel.*

happily /ˈhæpɪli/ *adv* **1** in a happy way □ *dgn senang hati/gembira*: *children playing happily on the beach* **2** it is lucky that □ *mujurlah*: *The police found my handbag and, happily, nothing had been stolen.* **SYN** **fortunately** **3** willingly □ *dgn rela*: *I would happily give up my job if I didn't need the money.*

happy /ˈhæpi/ *adj* (**happier**; **happiest**)
▶ FEELING/GIVING PLEASURE **1 happy (to do sth); happy for sb; happy that …** feeling or showing pleasure; pleased □ *gembira*: *I was really happy to see Mark again yesterday.* ◆ *You look very happy today.* ◆ *Congratulations! I'm very happy for you.* **OPP** **unhappy, sad 2** giving or causing pleasure □ *bahagia; gembira*: *a happy marriage/mem-*

ory/childhood ◆ *The film is sad but it has* **a happy ending.**
▶ GREETING **3 Happy** used to wish sb an enjoyable time □ *selamat*: *Happy Birthday!*: *Happy Birthday!*
▶ SATISFIED **4 happy (with/about sb/sth)** satisfied that sth is good and right; not worried □ *puas hati*: *I'm not very happy with what you've done.* ◆ *I'm not too happy about her living alone.*
▶ WILLING **5** [not before a noun] **happy to do sth** ready to do sth; pleased □ *bersedia; tdk keberatan*: *I'll be happy to see you any day next week.*
▶ LUCKY **6** [only before a noun] lucky □ *beruntung; bagus*: *a happy coincidence.* **SYN** **fortunate**
▶ **happiness** *noun* [U]

OTHER WORDS FOR

happy

You are usually **glad** or **pleased** about a particular event or situation. **Happy** is used for describing a state, condition of mind, etc. and it can also be used before the noun it describes: *This kind of music always makes me feel happy.* ◆ *She's such a happy child—she's always laughing.* **Delighted** means very happy about something: *I was delighted to meet her.* A **cheerful** person is happy and shows it in their behaviour or expression: *a cheerful, hard-working employee*

happy-go-lucky *adj* not caring or worried about life and the future □ *periang; sentiasa senang hati*

happy hour *noun* [C, usually sing] a time, usually in the evening, when a pub or bar sells alcoholic drinks at lower prices than usual □ *waktu minuman keras di pub atau bar dijual murah sedikit*

harass /ˈhærəs; həˈræs/ *verb* [T] to annoy or worry sb by doing unpleasant things to them, especially over a long time □ *(kerap) mengganggu*: *The court ordered him to stop harassing his ex-wife.* ▶ **harassment** *noun* [U]: *sexual harassment*

harassed /ˈhærəst; həˈræst/ *adj* tired and worried because you have too much to do □ *letih dan risau*

harbour¹ (*AmE* **harbor**) /ˈhɑːbə(r)/ *noun* [C,U] a place on the coast where ships can be tied up and protected from the sea and bad weather □ *pelabuhan* ⊃ picture on **page P10**

harbour² (*AmE* **harbor**) /ˈhɑːbə(r)/ *verb* [T] **1** to hide or protect sb/sth that is bad □ *menyembunyikan; memberi perlindungan*: *They were accused of harbouring terrorists.* **2** to keep feelings or thoughts secret in your mind for a long time □ *menyimpan; memendam*: *She began to harbour doubts about the decision.*

hard¹ /hɑːd/ *adj* (**harder**; **hardest**)
▶ NOT SOFT **1** not soft to touch; not easy to break or bend □ *keras*: *The bed was so hard that I couldn't sleep.* ◆ *Diamonds are the hardest known mineral.*
OPP **soft**
▶ NOT EASY **2 hard (for sb) (to do sth)** difficult to do or understand; not easy □ *sukar; susah*: *The*

[I] **intransitive**, a verb which has no object: *He laughed.*   [T] **transitive**, a verb which has an object: *He ate an apple.*

first question in the exam was very hard. ♦ This book is hard to understand./It is a hard book to understand. ♦ It's hard for young people to find good jobs nowadays. ♦ I find her attitude very **hard to take** (= difficult to accept). **SYN tough** **OPP easy 3** needing or using a lot of physical strength or mental effort □ *sukar; berat; keras; kuat*: It's a hard climb to the top of the hill. ♦ **Hard work** is said to be good for you. ♦ He's a hard worker. **4** (used about conditions) full of difficulty □ *sukar; susah*: She had a hard time when her parents died. ♦ *to have a hard day/life/ childhood*
▸NOT KIND **5** not feeling or showing kindness or pity; not gentle □ *keras; kasar*: You have to be hard to succeed in business. **OPP soft, lenient**
▸WEATHER **6** very cold □ *sangat sejuk*: The forecast is for a hard winter/frost. **OPP mild**
▸WATER **7** containing particular minerals so that soap does not make many bubbles □ *keras*: a **hard water** area **OPP soft**
IDM a hard act to follow a person or a thing that it is difficult to do better than □ *sukar ditandingi*
be hard at it to be working very hard doing sth □ *bekerja keras*
be hard on sb/sth 1 to treat sb/sth in a very strict or unkind way □ *bersikap keras terhadap sso*: Don't be too hard on her—she's only a child. **2** to be difficult for or unfair to sb/sth □ *sukar bagi sso*: Managing with very little money can be hard on students.
give sb a hard time (*informal*) to make a situation unpleasant, embarrassing or difficult for sb □ *membuat sst keadaan tdk senang, memalukan atau menyusahkan sso*
hard and fast (used about rules, etc.) that cannot be changed □ *tegas dan ketat*: There are no hard and fast rules about this.
hard facts information that is true, not just people's opinions □ *maklumat sebenar*
hard luck! ➔ **luck**
hard of hearing unable to hear well □ *pekak labang; agak pekak*
have a hard job doing/to do sth; have a hard time doing sth to do sth with great difficulty □ *sukar membuat sst*
learn the hard way ➔ **learn**
no hard feelings (*spoken*) used to tell sb you do not feel angry after an argument, etc. □ *tiada rasa dendam atau marah; jangan simpan di hati*: 'No hard feelings, I hope,' he said, offering me his hand.
take a hard line (on sth) to deal with sth in a very serious way that you will not allow anyone to change □ *bersikap tegas tanpa tolak ansur (ttg sst)*: The government has taken a hard line on people who drink and drive.
▸**hardness** *noun* [U]

hard² /hɑːd/ *adv* **1** with great effort, energy or attention □ *dgn bersungguh-sungguh; dgn sepenuh tenaga; (bekerja) keras*: He worked hard all his life. ♦ You'll have to try a bit harder than that. **2** with great force; heavily □ *dgn kuat; lebat (hujan, dsb)*: It was raining/snowing hard. ♦ He hit her hard across the face.

hard → harden

HELP Hard or **hardly?** Do not confuse **hard** with **hardly**. **Hardly** is an adverb meaning 'almost not': *I hardly ever go to concerts.* ♦ *I can hardly wait for my birthday.*

IDM be hard pressed/pushed/put to do sth to find sth very difficult to do □ *sukar membuat sst*: He was hard pressed to explain her sudden disappearance.
be hard up (for sth) to have too few or too little of sth, especially money □ *sangat kekurangan/ memerlukan*
die hard ➔ **die**
hard done by (*BrE*) not fairly treated □ *diperlakukan dgn tdk adil*: He felt very hard done by when he wasn't chosen for the team.

hardback /ˈhɑːdbæk/ *noun* [C] a book that has a hard cover □ *kulit keras*: This book is only available in hardback. ➔ look at **paperback**

hard-ˈboiled *adj* (used about an egg) boiled until it is solid inside □ *rebus keras*

ˌhard ˈcore *noun* [sing, with sing or pl verb] the members of a group who are the most active □ *kumpulan tegar*

ˌhard ˈcurrency *noun* [U] money belonging to a particular country that is easy to exchange and not likely to fall in value □ *mata wang kukuh*

ˌhard ˈdisk *noun* [C] a piece of hard plastic that is fixed inside a computer and is used for storing data and programs permanently □ *cakera keras* ➔ look at **floppy disk**

ˈhard drive *noun* [C, usually sing] a part of a computer that reads data on a **hard disk** □ *pemacu cakera keras*

TOPIC

Hard drive

Sometimes your computer may **crash** and you have to **reboot** it (= switch it off and on again). If your **hard drive fails**, you may lose all the data that you had **stored on** it, so it's a good idea to **back up your files** (= make copies of them), possibly on an **external hard drive** (= one that is not part of your computer).

ˌhard ˈdrug *noun* [C, usually pl] a powerful and illegal drug that some people take for pleasure and can become **addicted** to (= unable to stop taking or using it) □ *dadah kuat/keras*: Heroin and cocaine are hard drugs. ➔ look at **soft**

harden /ˈhɑːdn/ *verb* **1** [I,T] to become or to make sth hard or less likely to change □ *mengeras; bersikap keras*: The concrete will harden in 24 hours. ♦ The firm has hardened its attitude on this question. **2** [I] (used about sb's face, voice, etc.) to become serious and unfriendly □ *menjadi keras; tdk mesra* **3** [T, usually passive] **harden sb/sth/yourself** to make sb less kind or less easily shocked □ *menjadi lali; mangli;*

tdk berhati perut: *a hardened criminal* ♦ *War reporters get hardened to seeing suffering.*

hard-ˈheaded *adj* determined and not allowing yourself to be influenced by emotions □ *berpendirian tetap; tdk dipengaruhi oleh perasaan*: *a hard-headed businessman*

hard-ˈhearted *adj* not kind to other people and not considering their feelings □ *berhati batu* OPP soft-hearted

hard-ˈhitting *adj* that talks about or criticizes sb/sth in an honest and very direct way □ *dgn cara yg benar-benar terus terang*: *a hard-hitting campaign/speech/report*

hardly /ˈhɑːdli/ *adv* **1** almost no; almost not; almost none □ *hampir tiada/tdk langsung*: *There's hardly any coffee left.* ♦ *We hardly ever go out nowadays.* ♦ *I hardly spoke any English when I first came here.* ⊃ look at **almost 2** used especially after 'can' and 'could' and before the main verb to emphasize that sth is difficult to do □ *susah utk dilakukan*: *Speak up—I can hardly hear you.* **3** (used to say that sth has just begun, happened, etc.) only just □ *baru saja*: *She'd hardly gone to sleep before/when it was time to get up again.*

HELP Note that if 'hardly' is at the beginning of a sentence, the verb follows immediately. This use is found in formal writing: *Hardly had she gone to sleep when it was time to get up again.*

4 (used to suggest that sth is unlikely or unreasonable) not really □ *tdk mungkin*: *You can hardly expect me to believe that excuse!* ⊃ note at **hard** ⊃ look at **barely, scarcely**

hard-ˈnosed *adj* not affected by feelings or emotions when trying to get what you want □ *tegas; tdk dipengaruhi oleh perasaan*: *hard-nosed journalists/politicians*

hardship /ˈhɑːdʃɪp/ *noun* [C,U] a situation that is difficult or unpleasant because you do not have enough money, food, etc. □ *kesukaran; kesusahan*: *This new tax is going to cause a lot of hardship.*

hard ˈshoulder (*AmE* **shoulder**) *noun* [C] a narrow section of road at the side of a **motorway** (= a wide road for fast traffic) where cars are allowed to stop in an emergency □ *bahu jalan yg keras*

hardware /ˈhɑːdweə(r)/ *noun* [U] **1** the machinery and electronic parts of a computer system □ *perkakasan* ⊃ look at **software 2** tools and equipment that are used in the house and garden □ *perkakasan*: *a hardware shop*

hard-ˈwearing *adj* (*BrE*) (used about materials, clothes, etc.) strong and able to last for a long time □ *tahan lasak*

hard-ˈworking *adj* working with effort and energy □ *rajin*: *a hard-working man*

hardy /ˈhɑːdi/ *adj* (**hardier**; **hardiest**) strong and able to survive difficult conditions and bad weather □ *tahan lasak; lasak*: *a hardy plant*

hare /heə(r)/ *noun* [C] an animal like a **rabbit** (= a small animal with long ears) but bigger and with longer ears and legs □ *sejenis arnab* ⊃ picture at **rabbit**

harem /ˈhɑːriːm/ *noun* [C] a number of women living with one man, especially in Muslim societies. The part of the building the women live in is also called a harem. □ *harem*

harm¹ /hɑːm/ *noun* [U] damage or injury □ *kerosakan; kecederaan; mudarat*: *Peter ate some of those berries but they didn't do him any harm.* ♦ *Experienced staff watch over the children to make sure they don't come to any harm.*

IDM **no harm done** (*informal*) used to tell sb that they have not upset anyone or caused any damage or injury □ *tdk apa-apa*: *'Sorry about what I said to you last night.' 'That's all right, Jack, no harm done!'*

out of harm's way in a safe place □ *jauh drpd bahaya; di tempat yg selamat*: *Put the medicine out of harm's way where the children can't reach it.* **there is no harm in doing sth**; **it does no harm (for sb) to do sth** there's nothing wrong in doing sth (and sth good may result) □ *apa/tdk ada salahnya kalau (membuat sst)*: *I'm sure he'll say no, but there's no harm in asking.*

harm² /hɑːm/ *verb* [T] to cause injury or damage; hurt □ *mencederakan; merosakkan; menjejaskan*: *Too much sun can harm your skin.*

harmful /ˈhɑːmfl/ *adj* **harmful (to sb/sth)** causing harm □ *berbahaya; memudaratkan*: *Traffic fumes are harmful to the environment.*

harmless /ˈhɑːmləs/ *adj* **1** not able or not likely to cause damage or injury; safe □ *tdk berbahaya; tdk memudaratkan*: *You needn't be frightened—these insects are totally harmless.* **2** not likely to upset people □ *tdk menimbulkan rasa kurang senang*: *The children can watch that film—it's quite harmless.* ▶ **harmlessly** *adv*

harmonica /hɑːˈmɒnɪkə/ (also **ˈmouth organ**) *noun* [C] a small musical instrument that you play by moving it across your lips while you are blowing □ *harmonika*

harmonica

harmonious /hɑːˈməʊniəs/ *adj* **1** friendly, peaceful and without disagreement □ *harmoni* **2** (used about musical notes, colours, etc.) producing a pleasant effect when heard or seen together □ *harmoni* ▶ **harmoniously** *adv*

harmonize (also **-ise**) /ˈhɑːmənaɪz/ *verb* [I] **1 harmonize (with sth)** (used about two or more things) to produce a pleasant effect when seen, heard, etc. together □ *berharmoni* **2 harmonize (with sb/sth)** to sing or play music that sounds good combined with the main tune □ *mengharmonikan* ▶ **harmonization** (also **-isation**) /ˌhɑːmənaɪˈzeɪʃn/ *noun* [U]

harmony /ˈhɑːməni/ noun (pl **harmonies**) **1** [U] a state of agreement or of living together in peace ▫ *harmoni*: *We need to live more in harmony with our environment.* **2** [C,U] a pleasing combination of musical notes, colours, etc. ▫ *harmoni*: *There are some beautiful harmonies in that music.*

harness¹ /ˈhɑːnɪs/ noun [C] **1** a set of narrow pieces of leather that is put around a horse's neck and body so that it can pull sth ▫ *abah-abah* **2** a set of narrow pieces of material for fastening sth to sb's body or for stopping sb from moving around, falling, etc. ▫ *tali pengikat (utk keselamatan)*: *a safety harness*

harness² /ˈhɑːnɪs/ verb [T] **1** harness sth (to sth) to put a **harness** on a horse, etc. or to tie a horse, etc. to sth using a **harness** ▫ *memasangkan abah-abah*: *Two ponies were harnessed to the cart.* **2** to control the energy of sth in order to produce power or to achieve sth ▫ *memanfaatkan*: *to harness the sun's rays as a source of energy*

harp /hɑːp/ noun [C] a large musical instrument which has many strings stretching from the top to the bottom of a frame. You play the **harp** with your fingers. ▫ *hap* ⊃ picture at **music** ▶**harpist** /-pɪst/ noun [C]

harpoon /hɑːˈpuːn/ noun [C] a long thin weapon with a sharp pointed end and a rope tied to it that is used to catch **whales** (= very large sea animals) and large fish ▫ *tempuling* ▶**harpoon** verb [T]

harrowing /ˈhærəʊɪŋ/ adj making people feel very sad or upset ▫ *(yg) mengganggu perasaan*: *The programme showed harrowing scenes of the victims of the war.*

harsh /hɑːʃ/ adj (**harsher**; **harshest**) **1** very strict and unkind ▫ *keras*: *a harsh punishment/criticism* ♦ *The judge had some harsh words for the journalist's behaviour.* ⊃ look at **severe 2** unpleasant and difficult to live in, look at, listen to, etc. ▫ *teruk; (cahaya) menyilaukan; (suara) keras*: *She grew up in the harsh environment of London's East End.* ♦ *a harsh light/voice* **3** too strong or rough and likely to damage sth ▫ *kasar*: *This soap is too harsh for a baby's skin.* ▶**harshly** adv ▶**harshness** noun [U]

harvest /ˈhɑːvɪst/ noun **1** [C,U] the time of year when the grain, fruit, etc. is collected on a farm; the act of collecting the grain, fruit, etc. ▫ *musim menuai; penuaian*: *Farmers always need extra help with the harvest.* **2** [C] the amount of grain, fruit, etc. that is collected ▫ *tuaian, petikan, dsb*: *This year's wheat harvest was very poor.* ▶**harvest** verb [I,T]: *to harvest crops* ⊃ look at **combine harvester**

has /həz; strong form hæz/ ⊃ **have**

ˈhas-been noun [C] (*informal*) a person or thing that is no longer as famous, successful or important as before ▫ *orang yg tdk lagi terkenal, popular atau penting spt dahulu*

hash /hæʃ/ noun **1** [U] a hot dish of meat mixed together with potato and fried ▫ *sejenis makanan yg diperbuat drpd daging dan kentang* **2** [U] (*informal*) = **hashish 3** (also ˈ**hash sign**) (*BrE*) [C] the symbol (#), especially one on a telephone ▫ *lambang palang dua (pd telefon)*
IDM **make a hash of sth** (*informal*) to do sth badly ▫ *merosakkan*

hashish /ˈhæʃiːʃ/ (also informal **hash**) noun [U] a drug made from **hemp** (= a type of plant) that some people smoke for pleasure and which is illegal in many countries ▫ *hasyis* **SYN** **cannabis**

ˈhash sign = **hash** (3)

ˈhashtag /ˈhæʃtæg/ noun [C] a word or phrase with the symbol # in front of it, that is used in messages sent on the Internet to help people find the subjects that interest them ▫ *perkataan atau frasa yg disertai lambang palang dua*: *I searched for the hashtags '#jobs' and '#teaching' on Twitter.*

hasn't /ˈhæznt/ short for **has not**

hassle¹ /ˈhæsl/ noun (*informal*) **1** [C,U] a thing or situation that is annoying because it is complicated or involves a lot of effort ▫ *(keadaan yg) sukar*: *It's going to be a hassle having to change trains with all this luggage.* **2** [U] disagreeing or arguing ▫ *bertengkar; kecoh*: *I've decided what to do—please don't give me any hassle about it.*

hassle² /ˈhæsl/ verb [T] (*informal*) to annoy sb, especially by asking them to do sth many times ▫ *mengganggu*: *I wish he'd stop hassling me about decorating the house.* **SYN** **bother**

haste /heɪst/ noun [U] speed in doing sth, especially because you do not have enough time ▫ *kecepatan; tergesa-gesa*: *The letter had clearly been written in haste.*

hasten /ˈheɪsn/ verb (*formal*) **1** [I] hasten to do sth to be quick to do or say sth ▫ *segera; cepat-cepat*: *She hastened to apologize.* **2** [T] to make sth happen or be done earlier or more quickly ▫ *mempercepat*

hasty /ˈheɪsti/ adj (**hastier**; **hastiest**) **1** said or done too quickly ▫ *segera; cepat*: *He said a hasty 'goodbye' and left.* **2** hasty (in doing sth/to do sth) (used about a person) acting or deciding too quickly or without enough thought ▫ *terburu-buru; tergesa-gesa*: *Maybe I was too hasty in rejecting her for the job.* ▶**hastily** adv

hat /hæt/ noun [C] a covering that you wear on your head, usually when you are outside ▫ *topi*: *to wear a hat* ♦ *a sun hat* ⊃ picture on **page 406**
IDM **at the drop of a hat** ⊃ **drop²**

hatch¹ /hætʃ/ verb **1** [I] hatch (out) (used about a baby bird, insect, fish, etc.) to come out of an egg ▫ *menetas*: *Ten chicks hatched out this morning.* **2** [T] to make a baby bird, etc. come out of an egg ▫ *menetaskan* **3** [T] hatch sth (up) to think of a plan (usually to do sth bad) ▫ *merancang*: *He hatched a plan to avoid paying any income tax.*

hatch² /hætʃ/ noun [C] **1** an opening in the **deck** (= the floor) of a ship or the bottom of an aircraft through which goods are passed □ *hac* **2** an opening in the wall between a kitchen and another room that is used for passing food through □ *lubang (pd dinding di antara bilik dapur dan bilik makan)* **3** the door in a plane or **spacecraft** (= a vehicle that travels in space) □ *pintu pesawat*

hatchback /'hætʃbæk/ noun [C] a car with a large door at the back that opens upwards □ *kereta (dgn pintu belakang yg besar)* ➲ picture on **page P7**

hatchet /'hætʃɪt/ noun [C] a small **axe** (= a tool with a short handle and a metal head with a sharp edge used for cutting wood) □ *kapak kecil*

hate¹ /heɪt/ verb [T] **1** hate (sb/sth); hate (doing/to do sth) to have a very strong feeling of not liking sb/sth at all □ *benci; sangat tdk suka*: *I hate grapefruit.* ♦ *I hate it when it's raining like this.* ♦ *I hate to see the countryside spoilt.* ♦ *He hates driving at night.* ➲ note at **dislike**

> **MORE** Detest and loathe express a stronger feeling than **hate**.

2 used when saying sth you would prefer not to have to say or as a polite way of saying sorry for sth □ *tdk suka; maaf kerana terpaksa (mengganggu, bertanya, dsb)*: *I hate to say it, but I think she's failed the exam.* ♦ *I hate to bother you, but did you pick up my keys by mistake?*

hate² /heɪt/ noun **1** [U] a very strong feeling of not liking sb/sth at all □ *benci; sangat tdk suka*: *Jan gave her a look of pure hate.* **SYN** hatred **2** [C] a thing that you do not like at all □ *sst yg paling tdk disukai*: *Plastic flowers are one of my pet hates* (= the things that I particularly do not like).

hateful /'heɪtfl/ adj hateful (to sb) extremely unpleasant □ *(yg) menimbulkan rasa benci atau meluat; teruk*: *It was a hateful thing to say.*

hatred /'heɪtrɪd/ noun [U] hatred (for/of sb/sth) a very strong feeling of not liking sb/sth; hate □ *kebencian*

'hat-trick noun [C] three points, goals, etc. scored by one player in the same game; three successes achieved by one person □ *hatrik*: *to score a hat-trick*

haughty /'hɔːti/ adj (haughtier; haughtiest) proud, and thinking that you are better than other people □ *sombong; angkuh*: *She gave me a haughty look.* ▶ haughtily adv

haul¹ /hɔːl/ verb [T] to pull sth with a lot of effort or difficulty □ *menarik (dgn kuat atau susah payah)*: *A lorry hauled the car out of the mud.*

haul² /hɔːl/ noun **1** [C, usually sing] a haul (of sth) a large amount of sth that has been stolen, caught, collected, etc. □ *tangkapan; habuan*: *The fishermen came back with a good haul of fish.* **2** [sing] a distance to be travelled □ *jarak perjalanan*: *It seemed a long haul back home.*

haulage /'hɔːlɪdʒ/ noun [U] (BrE) the transport of goods by road, rail, etc.; the money charged for this □ *pengangkutan; bayaran pengangkutan*

haunt¹ /hɔːnt/ verb [T] **1** [often passive] if a **ghost** (= the spirit of a dead person) haunts a place, people say that they have seen it there □ *ditunggui (hantu); berhantu*: *The house is said to be haunted.* **2** (used about sth unpleasant or sad) to be always in your mind □ *sentiasa menghantui fikiran sso*: *His unhappy face has haunted me for years.*

haunt² /hɔːnt/ noun [C] a place that you visit regularly □ *tempat yg sering dikunjungi; tempat tumpuan*: *This cafe has always been a favourite haunt of mine.*

haunting /'hɔːntɪŋ/ adj having a quality that stays in your mind □ *sering bermain dlm fikiran*: *a haunting song*

have¹ /hæv/ verb [T] ❶ For the forms of 'have', look at the irregular verbs section at the back of this dictionary.

hats

cowboy hat

bowler (AmE derby)

top hat

sun hat — crown, brim

hood

hard hat

crash helmet — visor

baseball cap — peak

woolly hat

beret

cap

ʌ **c**u**p** ɜː **b**ir**d** ə **a**go eɪ **p**ay əʊ **g**o aɪ **m**y aʊ **n**ow ɔɪ **b**oy ɪə **n**ear eə **h**air ʊə **p**ure

▶OWN/HOLD **1** (*BrE also* **have got**) [not used in the continuous tenses] to own or to hold sth □ *mempunyai; ada*: *I've got a new camera.* ◆ *The flat has two bedrooms.* ◆ *He's got short dark hair.* ◆ *to have patience/enthusiasm/skill* ◆ *Have you got any brothers and sisters?* ◆ *Do you have time to check my work?* ⊃ look at **possess**

▶DUTY **2** (*also* **have got**) [not used in the continuous tenses] to have a particular duty or plan □ *ada (tugas atau rancangan tertentu)*: *Do you have any homework tonight?* ◆ *I've got a few things to do this morning, but I'm free later.*

▶HOLD/KEEP IN POSITION **3** (*also* **have got**) [not used in the continuous tenses] to hold sb/sth; to keep sth in a particular place □ *memegang; menahan; meletakkan*: *The dog had me by the leg.* ◆ *We've got our TV up on a shelf.*

▶ILLNESS **4** (*also* **have got**) [not used in the continuous tenses] to be ill with sth □ *menghidap*: *She's got a bad cold.* ◆ *to have flu/a headache/cancer/AIDS*

▶EXPERIENCE **5** to experience sth □ *mengalami*: *to have fun* ◆ *to have problems/difficulties* ◆ *to have an idea/an impression/a feeling* ◆ *to have an accident* **6** to suffer the effect of what sb else does to you □ *melalui*: *She had her bag stolen on the underground.*

▶DO STH **7** used with many nouns to talk about doing sth □ *bermaksud membuat sst*: *What time do you have breakfast?* ◆ *to have a drink/something to eat* ◆ *I'll just have a shower then we'll go.* ◆ *to have an argument/talk/chat*

▶CAUSE **8** to cause sb/sth to do sth or to be in a particular state □ *menyebabkan sso/sst membuat sst atau berada dlm sst keadaan*: *The music soon had everyone dancing.* ◆ *I'll have dinner ready when you get home.*

▶HAVE STH DONE **9** to arrange for sb to do sth □ *mengaturkan bagi sso utk membuat sst*: *I have my hair cut every six weeks.* ◆ *You should have your eyes tested.*

▶ENTERTAIN **10** to look after or entertain sb □ *menjaga; meraikan*: *We're having some people to dinner tomorrow.*

IDM **have had it** (*informal*) used about things that are completely broken, or dead □ *sudah rosak; sudah mati*: *This TV has had it. We'll have to buy a new one.* ❶ For other idioms containing **have**, look at the entries for the nouns, adjectives, etc. For example, **not have a clue** is at **clue**.

PHR V **have sb on** to trick sb as a joke □ *memperolokkan sso*: *Don't listen to what Jim says—he's only having you on.*

have (got) sth on 1 to be wearing sth □ *memakai*: *She's got a green jumper on.* **2** (*informal*) to have an arrangement to do sth □ *ada hal*: *I've got a lot on this week* (= I'm very busy).

have sth out to have part of your body removed □ *mencabut; memotong buang*: *to have a tooth/your appendix out*

have² /həv; *strong form* hæv/ *auxiliary verb* used for forming the perfect tenses □ *kk bantu yg digunakan utk membentuk kala sempurna* ❶ For more information, look at the **Reference Section** at the back of this dictionary.

haven /'heɪvn/ *noun* [C] **a haven (of sth); a haven (for sb/sth)** a place where people or animals can be safe and rest □ *tempat perlindungan*: *a haven of peace* ◆ *The lake is a haven for water birds.* ◆ *a tax haven* (= a country where income tax is low)

haven't /'hævnt/ *short for* **have not**

have to /'hæv tə; 'hæf tə; *strong form and before vowels* 'hæv tuː; 'hæf tuː/ (*also* **have got to**) *modal verb* used for saying that sb must do sth or that sth must happen □ *perlu; terpaksa; dikehendaki*: *He usually has to work on Saturday mornings.* ◆ *Do you have to have a visa to go to America?* ◆ *We don't have to* (= it's not necessary to) *go to the party if you don't want to* ◆ *We had to do lots of boring exercises.* ◆ *She's got to go to the bank this afternoon.* ◆ *There has to be a reason for his strange behaviour.* ⊃ A more common, less formal expression in British English is **have got to**. ⊃ note at **must** ❶ For more information about modal verbs, look at the **Reference Section** at the back of this dictionary.

havoc /'hævək/ *noun* [U] a situation in which there is a lot of damage or confusion □ *kemusnahan; kacau-bilau; keadaan kucar-kacir*: *The rail strikes will cause havoc all over the country.* ⊃ look at **wreak**

hawk /hɔːk/ *noun* [C] a type of large bird that catches and eats small animals and birds. **Hawks** can see very well. □ *burung lang*

MORE Hawks are a type of **bird of prey**.

hay /heɪ/ *noun* [U] grass that has been cut and dried for use as animal food □ *rumput kering*

hay fever *noun* [U] an illness that affects the eyes, nose and throat and is caused by breathing in **pollen** (= the powder produced by some plants) □ *demam alergi; rinitis alergi* ⊃ look at **allergy**

haywire /'heɪwaɪə(r)/ *adj*
IDM **be/go haywire** (*informal*) to be or become out of control □ *jadi kucar-kacir*: *I can't do any work because the computer's gone haywire.*

hazard¹ /'hæzəd/ *noun* [C] a danger or risk □ *bahaya; risiko*: *Smoking is a serious health hazard.* ◆ *Pollution is a serious health hazard.*

hazard² /'hæzəd/ *verb* [T] to make a guess or to suggest sth even though you know it may be wrong □ *cuba meneka*: *I don't know what he paid for the house but I could hazard a guess.*

hazardous /'hæzədəs/ *adj* involving risk or danger □ *berbahaya; ada risiko; berisiko*

haze /heɪz/ *noun* **1** [C,U] air that is difficult to see through because of heat, dust or smoke □ *jerebu* ⊃ note at **fog 2** [sing] a mental state in which you cannot think clearly □ *kabur fikiran*

hazel¹ /'heɪzl/ *noun* [C] a small tree or bush that produces nuts □ *pokok hazel*

hazel² /ˈheɪzl/ adj (used especially about eyes) light brown in colour □ *(warna) coklat muda*

hazelnut /ˈheɪzlnʌt/ noun [C] a small brown nut that we eat □ *kacang hazel* ⊃ picture at **nut**

hazy /ˈheɪzi/ adj (hazier; haziest) **1** not clear, especially because of heat □ *berjerebu; berkabut*: *The fields were hazy in the early morning sun.* **2** difficult to remember or understand clearly □ *kabur; samar-samar*: *a hazy memory* **3** (used about a person) uncertain, not expressing things clearly □ *kabur*: *She's a bit hazy about the details of the trip.*

HD /ˌeɪtʃ ˈdiː/ abbr = **high-definition**

he¹ /hiː/ pron (the subject of a verb) the male person mentioned earlier □ *dia (lelaki)*: *I spoke to John before he left.* ♦ *Look at that boy—he's going to fall in!*

> **GRAMMAR** If you want to refer to a person who could be either male or female, there are several ways to do this: **He or she, him or her, his or her,** and in writing **he/she** or **s/he** can be used: *If you are not sure, ask your doctor. He/She can give you further information.* It is now common to use **they, them** or **their**: *Everybody knows what they want.* ♦ *When somebody asks me a question I always try to give them a quick answer.* **They, them** and **their** are used in this way in this dictionary. However, it is also possible to make the sentence plural: *A baby cries when s/he is tired* ♦ *Babies cry when they are tired.*

he² /hiː/ noun [sing] a male animal □ *jantan*: *Is your cat a he or a she?*

head¹ /hed/ noun

▸PART OF BODY **1** [C] the part of your body above your neck □ *kepala*: *She turned her head to look at him.* ⊃ picture at **body**

▸-HEADED **2** [in compounds] having the type of head mentioned □ *berkepala*: *a bald-headed man*

▸MIND **3** [C] a person's mind, brain or mental ability □ *kepala; otak*: *Use your head!* (= Think!) ♦ *A horrible thought entered my head.*

▸IN CHARGE **4** [C,U] the person in charge of a group of people □ *ketua*: *the head of the family* ♦ *Several heads of state* (= official leaders of countries) *attended the funeral.* ♦ *the head waiter* **5** (also ˌhead ˈteacher) [C] the teacher in charge of a school □ *guru besar*: *Who is going to be the new head?*

▸SIDE OF COIN **6 heads** [U] the side of a coin with the head of a person on it □ *kepala*: *Heads or tails? Heads I go first, tails you do.*

▸TOP PART **7** [C, sing] the top, front or most important part □ *kepala; pangkal*: *to sit at the head of the table* ♦ *the head of a nail* ♦ *the head of the queue*

IDM bite sb's head off ⊃ **bite¹**
come to a head; bring sth to a head if a situation comes to a head or if you bring it to a head, it suddenly becomes very bad and you have to deal with it immediately □ *meruncing*

do sb's head in (BrE informal) to make sb upset and confused □ *membuat sso geram atau bingung*

get sth into your head; put sth into sb's head to start or to make sb start believing or thinking sth □ *percaya bahawa; ingat*: *Barry's got it into his head that glasses would make him more attractive.*

go to sb's head **1** to make sb drunk □ *membuat sso mabuk*: *Wine always goes straight to my head.* **2** to make sb too proud □ *membuat sso besar kepala*: *If you keep telling him how clever he is, it will go to his head!*

have a head for sth **1** to be good at sth □ *mempunyai kebolehan utk sst*: *to have a head for business/figures* **2** if sb does not **have a head for heights**, they feel nervous and think they are going to fall when they look down from a high place □ *tdk gayat*: *You need a good head for heights if you live on the top floor!*

a/per head for each person □ *seorang*: *How much will the meal cost a head?*

head first **1** with your head before the rest of your body □ *kepala dulu*: *Don't go down the slide head first.* **2** too quickly or suddenly □ *terburu-buru*: *Don't rush head first into a decision.*

head over heels (in love) loving sb very much □ *betul-betul jatuh cinta*: *Jane's fallen head over heels in love with Andy.*

hit the nail on the head ⊃ **hit¹**
keep your head to stay calm □ *bertenang*
keep your head above water to just manage to survive in a difficult situation, especially one in which you do not have enough money □ *hanya cukup makan saja*

keep your head down to try not to be noticed □ *cuba mengelak supaya orang tdk nampak*

laugh, scream, etc. your head off to laugh, shout, etc. very loudly and for a long time □ *ketawa, menjerit, dll dgn sekuat hati*

lose your head ⊃ **lose**
make head or tail of sth to understand sth □ *memahami sst*: *I can't make head or tail of this exercise.*

off the top of your head ⊃ **top¹**
out of/off your head (informal) crazy, often because of the effects of drugs or alcohol □ *tdk siuman*

put/get your heads together to make a plan with sb □ *sama-sama berbincang*

a roof over your head ⊃ **roof**
shake your head ⊃ **shake¹**
take it into your head to do sth to suddenly decide to do sth that other people consider strange □ *tiba-tiba hendak membuat sst*: *I don't know why Kevin took it into his head to enter that marathon!*

head² /hed/ verb
▸MOVE TOWARDS **1** [I] to move in the direction mentioned □ *menuju ke*: *The ship headed towards the harbour.* ♦ *Where are you heading?*
▸BE IN CHARGE **2** [T] to be in charge of or to lead sth □ *mengetuai*: *Do you think that he has the experience necessary to head a government?*

[I] **intransitive**, a verb which has no object: *He laughed.*   [T] **transitive**, a verb which has an object: *He ate an apple.*

> BE FIRST **3** [T] to be at the front of a line, top of a list, etc. □ *di hadapan sekali; di atas sekali*: *to head a procession*

> WRITE TITLE **4** [T, often passive] to give a title at the top of a piece of writing □ *bertajuk*: *The report was headed 'The State of the Market'.*

> FOOTBALL **5** [T] to hit the ball with your head □ *menanduk*: *He headed the ball into the net.*

PHR V **head for** to move towards a place □ *menuju ke arah*: *It's getting late—I think it's time to head for home.*

headache /'hedeɪk/ *noun* [C] **1** a pain in your head □ *sakit kepala*: *I've got a splitting* (= very bad) *headache.* ⊃ note at **ache 2** a person or thing that causes worry or difficulty □ *sst/sso yg memeningkan kepala*: *Paying the bills is a constant headache.*

heading /'hedɪŋ/ *noun* [C] the words written as a title at the top of a page or a piece of writing □ *tajuk*: *The company's aims can be grouped under three main headings.*

headlamp = **headlight**

headland /'hedlənd; -lænd/ *noun* [C] a narrow piece of land that sticks out into the sea □ *tanjung tinggi* ⊃ picture on **page P10**

headlight /'hedlaɪt/ (also **headlamp** /'hedlæmp/) *noun* [C] one of the two large bright lights at the front of a vehicle □ *lampu besar* ⊃ picture on **page P7**

headline /'hedlaɪn/ *noun* **1** the title of a newspaper article printed in large letters above the story □ *tajuk berita* **2 the headlines** [pl] the main items of news read on TV or radio □ *berita utama*

headlong /'hedlɒŋ/ *adv, adj* **1** with your head before the rest of your body □ *kepala dulu; tersungkur*: *I tripped and fell headlong into the road.* **2** too quickly; without enough thought □ *tergesa-gesa*: *He rushed headlong into buying the business.*

headmaster /ˌhedˈmɑːstə(r)/ (*fem* **headmistress** /ˌhedˈmɪstrəs/) *noun* [C] (*BrE old-fashioned*) (*AmE usually* **principal**) a teacher who is in charge of a school, especially a private school □ *guru besar*

head-'on *adj* [only *before* a noun] *adv* with the front of one car, etc. hitting the front of another □ *bertembung depan sama depan*: *a head-on crash*

headphones /'hedfəʊnz/ (also **earphones**) *noun* [pl] a piece of equipment worn over or in the ears that makes it possible to listen to music, the radio, etc. without other people hearing it □ *fon kepala* ⊃ note at **listen**

headquarters /ˌhedˈkwɔːtəz/ *noun* [U, with sing or pl verb] (*abbr* **HQ**) the place from where an organization is controlled; the people who work there □ *ibu pejabat*: *Where is/are the firm's headquarters?*

headrest /'hedrest/ *noun* [C] the part of a seat or chair that supports a person's head, especially on the front seat of a car □ *penyandar kepala*

409 headache → the health service

headscarf /'hedskɑːf/ *noun* [C] (*pl* **headscarves**) a square piece of cloth worn by women to cover the head □ *skarf kepala*

headset /'hedset/ *noun* [C] a pair of **headphones** (= a piece of equipment for listening that you wear over or in your ears), especially one with a **microphone** (= a device for speaking into) fixed to it □ *set/fon kepala*: *The pilot was talking into his headset.*

headstand /'hedstænd/ *noun* [C] a position in which a person has their head on the ground and their feet straight up in the air □ *dirian kepala*

head 'start *noun* [sing] an advantage that you have from the beginning □ *kelebihan pd permulaan (perlumbaan, dsb)*: *Being able to speak English gave her a head start at school.*

headstone /'hedstəʊn/ *noun* [C] a large stone with writing on, used to mark where a dead person is buried □ *batu nisan* **SYN** **gravestone, tombstone**

headstrong /'hedstrɒŋ/ *adj* doing what you want, without listening to advice from other people □ *degil; keras kepala*

head 'teacher = **head¹**(5)

headway /'hedweɪ/ *noun*

IDM **make headway** to go forward or make progress in a difficult situation □ *bergerak ke depan; mencatat kemajuan*

heal /hiːl/ *verb* [I,T] **heal (over/up)** to become healthy again; to make sth healthy again □ *sembuh; pulih; memulihkan*: *The cut will heal up in a few days.* ♦ (*figurative*) *Nothing he said could heal the damage done to their relationship.*

health /helθ/ *noun* [U] **1** the condition of sb's body or mind □ *kesihatan*: *Fresh fruit is good for your health.* ♦ *in good/poor health* ♦ (*figurative*) *the health of your marriage/finances* **2** the state of being well and free from illness □ *sihat*: *As long as you have your health, nothing else matters.* **3** the work of providing medical care □ *kesihatan*: *health insurance* ♦ *health and safety regulations* ♦ *the rising costs of health care*

'health centre *noun* [C] a building where a group of doctors see their patients □ *pusat kesihatan*

'health club (also **gym**) *noun* [C] a private club where people go to do physical exercise in order to stay or become healthy and fit □ *kelab kesihatan*

'health food *noun* [C,U] food that does not contain any artificial substances and is therefore thought to be good for your health □ *makanan kesihatan*

the 'health service *noun* [C] the organization of the medical services of a country □ *perkhidmatan kesihatan* ⊃ look at **the National Health Service**

CONSONANTS p **p**en b **b**ad t **t**ea d **d**id k **c**at g **g**ot tʃ **ch**in dʒ **J**une f **f**all v **v**an θ **th**in

healthy /ˈhelθi/ adj (**healthier**; **healthiest**) **1** not often ill; strong and well □ *sihat*: *a healthy child/animal/plant* **2** helping to produce good health □ *yg menyihatkan*; *sihat*: *a healthy climate/diet/lifestyle* **3** showing good health (of body or mind) □ *sihat*: *healthy skin and hair* **4** normal and sensible □ *sihat*; *wajar*: *There was plenty of healthy competition between the brothers.* **OPP** for all meanings **unhealthy** ▶ **healthily** adv

heap[1] /hiːp/ noun [C] **1 a heap (of sth)** an untidy pile of sth □ *timbunan*; *longgokan*: *a heap of books/papers* ◆ *All his clothes are in a heap on the floor!* ⊃ note at **pile** ⊃ look at **scrapheap 2** (*informal*) **a heap (of sth)**; **heaps (of sth)** a large number or amount; plenty □ *bertimbun-timbun*; *banyak*: *I've got a heap of work to do.* ◆ *There's heaps of time before the train leaves.* **IDM heaps better, more, older, etc.** (*informal*) much better, etc. □ *lebih baik, banyak, tua, dll*

heap[2] /hiːp/ verb [T] **1 heap sth (up)** to put things in a pile □ *menimbunkan*; *melonggokkan*; *memumbung*: *I'm going to heap all the leaves up over there.* ◆ *Add six heaped tablespoons of flour* (= in a recipe). **2 heap A on/onto B**; **heap B with A** to put a large amount of sth on sth/sb □ *melonggokkan*; *mencurahkan*: *He heaped food onto his plate.* ◆ *The press heaped the team with praise.*

hear /hɪə(r)/ verb (pt, pp **heard** /hɜːd/) **1** [I,T] [not used in the continuous tenses] to receive sounds with your ears □ *dengar*; *mendengar*: *Can you speak a little louder—I can't hear very well.* ◆ *I didn't hear you go out this morning.* ◆ *Did you hear what I said?* ⊃ note at **smell**[1]

> **HELP Hear** or **listen**? Often, **hear** means to receive a sound without necessarily trying to; to **listen** is to make a conscious or active effort to hear something: *I always wake up when I hear the birds singing.* ◆ *I love listening to music in the evening.* ◆ *Listen—I've got something to tell you.* Sometimes, **hear** can have a similar meaning to 'listen to': *We'd better hear what they have to say.*

2 [T] [not used in the continuous tenses] to be told about sth □ *dengar*; *menerima (berita, dsb)*: *I hear that you've been offered a job in Canada.* ◆ *'I passed my test!' 'So I've heard—well done!'* ◆ *I was sorry to hear about your mum's illness.*

> **HELP** Although this verb is not used in the continuous tenses, it is common to see the present participle (= *-ing* form): *Not hearing what he'd said over the noise of the machines, she just nodded and smiled.*

3 [T] (used about a judge, a court, etc.) to listen to the evidence in a trial in order to make a decision about it □ *mendengar*; *didengar*: *Your case will be heard this afternoon.*
IDM Hear! Hear! used for showing that you agree with what sb has just said, especially in a meeting □ *digunakan utk menyatakan persetujuan*
won't/wouldn't hear of sth to refuse to allow sth □ *tdk langsung membenarkan*: *I wanted to go to art school but my parents wouldn't hear of it.*
PHR V hear from sb to receive a letter, email, telephone call, etc. from sb □ *mendapat berita drpd sso*
hear of sb/sth to know about sb/sth because you have already been told about them/it □ *pernah dengar ttg sso/sst*: *Have you heard of the Bermuda Triangle?*

hearing /ˈhɪərɪŋ/ noun **1** [U] the ability to hear □ *pendengaran*: *Her hearing isn't very good so you need to speak louder.* **2** [C] a time when evidence is given to a judge in a court of law □ *pembicaraan*: *a court/disciplinary hearing* **3** [sing] a chance to give your opinion or explain your position □ *peluang utk menyatakan pendapat atau memberi penjelasan*: *to get/give somebody a fair hearing*
IDM hard of hearing ⊃ **hard**[1]
in/within sb's hearing near enough to sb that they can hear what is being said □ *dekat hingga dpt didengar oleh sso*

ˈhearing aid noun [C] a small device for people who cannot hear well that fits inside the ear and makes sounds louder □ *alat pendengar*

hearsay /ˈhɪəseɪ/ noun [U] things you have heard another person or other people say, which may or may not be true □ *khabar angin*; *cakap-cakap orang*

hearse /hɜːs/ noun [C] a large car used for carrying a dead person to their funeral □ *kereta mayat/jenazah*

heart /hɑːt/ noun
▸ **PART OF BODY 1** [C] the organ inside your chest that sends blood round your body □ *jantung*: *When you exercise your heart beats faster.* ◆ *heart disease/failure* ⊃ picture at **body**
▸ **FEELINGS/EMOTIONS 2** [C] the centre of sb's feelings and emotions □ *hati*: *She has a kind heart* (= she is kind and gentle). ◆ *They say he died of a broken heart* (= unhappiness caused by sb he loved).
▸ **-HEARTED 3** [in compounds] having the type of feelings or character mentioned □ *berhati (baik/jahat)*: *kind-hearted* ◆ *cold-hearted*
▸ **CENTRE 4** [sing] **the heart (of sth)** the most central or important part of sth; the middle □ *di tengah-tengah*; *pokok*; *inti*: *Rare plants can be found in the heart of the forest.* ◆ *Let's get straight to the heart of the matter.*
▸ **SHAPE 5** [C] a symbol that is shaped like a heart, often red or pink and used to show love □ *bentuk hati*: *He sent her a card with a big red heart on it.*
▸ **IN CARD GAMES 6 hearts** [pl] in a pack of playing cards, the **suit** (= one of the four sets) with red shapes like hearts on them □ *set daun terup lekuk*: *the queen of hearts* ⊃ note at **card** ⊃ picture at **card** **7** [C] one of the cards from this **suit** □ *daun lekuk*: *Play a heart, if you've got one.*

IDM **after your own heart** (used about people) similar to yourself or of the type you like best □ *sama spt diri sendiri atau yg disukai*
at heart really; in fact □ *sebenarnya*: *My father seems strict but he's a very kind man at heart.*
break sb's heart to make sb very sad □ *menghancurkan hati sso*
(off) by heart by remembering exactly; from memory □ *menghafal*: *Learning lists of words off by heart isn't a good way to increase your vocabulary.*
a change of heart ➔ **change²**
close/dear/near to sb's heart having a lot of importance and interest for sb □ *penting dan menjadi tumpuan minat sso*: *a subject that is very dear to my heart*
cross my heart ➔ **cross²**
from the (bottom of your) heart in a way that is true and sincere □ *drpd lubuk hati (sso)*: *I mean what I said from the bottom of my heart.*
have a heart of gold to be a very kind person □ *berhati emas*
have/with sb's (best) interests at heart ➔ **interest¹**
heart and soul with a lot of energy and enthusiasm □ *dgn seluruh jiwa raga*
your heart is not in sth used to say that you are not very interested in or enthusiastic about sth □ *tdk berminat sangat*: *It's hard to do a job if your heart isn't in it.*
your heart sinks to suddenly feel disappointed or sad □ *tawar hati; kecewa; sedih*: *When I saw the queues of people in front of me, my heart sank.*
in your heart (of hearts) used to say that you know that sth is true although you do not want to admit or believe it □ *dlm lubuk hati*: *She knew in her heart of hearts that she was making the wrong decision.*
lose heart ➔ **lose**
not have the heart (to do sth) to be unable to do sth unkind □ *tdk tergamak (utk melakukan sst)*: *I don't really have the time to help her, but I didn't have the heart to say no.*
pour your heart out (to sb) ➔ **pour**
set your heart on sth; have your heart set on sth to decide you want sth very much; to be determined to do or have sth □ *sangat menginingi sst; benar-benar berhasrat utk membuat atau memiliki sst*
take heart (from sth) to begin to feel more positive (because of sth) □ *berasa sedap hati atau mula menaruh harapan*
take sth to heart to be deeply affected or upset by sth □ *tersinggung*
to your heart's content as much as you want □ *sepuas-puasnya*
with all your heart; with your whole heart completely □ *dgn sepenuh hati*: *I hope with all my heart that things work out for you.*
young at heart ➔ **young¹**

heartache /'hɑːteɪk/ *noun* [U] great sadness or worry □ *kepiluan; seksaan jiwa*

'heart attack *noun* [C] a sudden serious illness when the heart stops working correctly, sometimes causing death □ *serangan jantung*: *She's had a heart attack.*

411   **heartache → heat**

heartbeat /'hɑːtbiːt/ *noun* [C] the regular movement or sound of the heart as it sends blood round the body □ *degupan jantung*

heartbreak /'hɑːtbreɪk/ *noun* [U] very great sadness □ *kesedihan; patah hati*

heartbreaking /'hɑːtbreɪkɪŋ/ *adj* making you feel very sad □ *amat menyedihkan*

heartbroken /'hɑːtbrəʊkən/ (also ˌbroken-ˈhearted) *adj* extremely sad because of sth that has happened □ *patah hati; amat sedih*: *Mary was heartbroken when John left her.*

hearten /'hɑːtn/ *verb* [T, usually passive] to encourage sb; to make sb feel happier □ *memberangsangkan; menggembirakan* **OPP** **dishearten**

heartening /'hɑːtnɪŋ/ *adj* encouraging; making you believe that sth good will happen □ *yg memberangsangkan/menggembirakan* **OPP** **disheartening**

heartfelt /'hɑːtfelt/ *adj* deeply felt; sincere □ *yg mendalam; tulus ikhlas*: *a heartfelt apology*

hearth /hɑːθ/ *noun* [C] the place where you have an open fire in the house; the area in front of an open fire □ *perdiangan; (tempat) di depan perdiangan* ➔ picture at **fireplace**

heartily /'hɑːtɪli/ *adv* **1** with obvious enthusiasm and enjoyment □ *dgn penuh semangat*: *He joined in heartily with the singing.* **2** very much; completely □ *benar-benar*

heartland /'hɑːtlænd/ *noun* [C] the most central or important part of a country, area, etc. □ *kawasan tengah*

heartless /'hɑːtləs/ *adj* unkind; cruel □ *tdk berhati perut* ▶ **heartlessly** *adv* ▶ **heartlessness** *noun* [U]

'heart-rending *adj* making you feel very sad □ *menyayat hati*: *The mother of the missing boy made a heart-rending appeal on TV.*

ˌheart-to-ˈheart *noun* [C] a conversation in which you say exactly what you really feel or think □ *dr hati ke hati*: *John's teacher had a heart-to-heart with him to find out what was worrying him.*

hearty /'hɑːti/ *adj* (**heartier**; **heartiest**) **1** showing warm and friendly feelings □ *mesra; bersungguh*: *a hearty welcome* **2** loud, happy and full of energy □ *kuat; bersemangat*: *a hearty laugh* **3** [only *before* a noun] (used about a meal) large; making you feel full □ *besar*: *a hearty breakfast* **4** showing that you feel strongly about sth □ *sungguh-sungguh*: *He nodded his head in hearty agreement.* ♦ *Hearty congratulations to everyone involved.*

heat¹ /hiːt/ *noun*
▶FEELING HOT **1** [U, sing] the feeling of sth hot □ *haba; panas; bahang*: *This fire doesn't give out much heat.* ♦ *The fire gave out a fierce heat.* **2** [sing] [often with *the*] hot weather □ *cuaca panas*: *I like the English climate because I can't*

VOWELS iː **see**   i **any**   ɪ **sit**   e **ten**   æ **hat**   ɑː **father**   ɒ **got**   ɔː **saw**   ʊ **put**   uː **too**   u **usual**

stand the heat. **3** [sing] a thing that produces heat □ *api; sumber haba*: *Remove the pan from the heat* (= the hot part of the cooker).
▶ STRONG FEELINGS **4** [U] a state or time of anger or excitement □ *keadaan marah atau teruja*: *In the heat of the moment, she threatened to resign.*
▶ RACE **5** [C] one of the first parts of a race or competition. The winners of the heats compete against other winners until the final result is decided □ *saringan*: *He won his heat and went through to the final.*
IDM **be on heat** (used about some female animals) to be ready to have mate □ *dlm keadaan mahu mengawan*

heat² /hiːt/ *verb* [I,T] **heat (sth) (up)** to become or to make sth hot or warm □ *menjadi panas; memanaskan*: *Wait for the oven to heat up before you put the pie in.* ♦ *The meal is already cooked but it will need heating up.*

heated /ˈhiːtɪd/ *adj* (used about a person or discussion) angry or excited □ *hangat; panas*: *a heated argument/debate* ▶ **heatedly** *adv*

heater /ˈhiːtə(r)/ *noun* [C] a machine used for making water or the air in a room, car, etc. hotter □ *alat pemanas*: *an electric/gas heater* ♦ *a water heater*

heath /hiːθ/ *noun* [C] an area of open land that is not used for farming and that is often covered with rough grass and other wild plants □ *kawasan rawa/semak*

heather /ˈheðə(r)/ *noun* [U] a low wild plant that grows especially on hills and land that is not farmed and has small purple, pink or white flowers □ *'heather' (bunga liar)*

heating /ˈhiːtɪŋ/ *noun* [U] a system for making rooms and buildings warm □ *sistem pemanasan*: *Our heating goes off at 10 p.m. and comes on again in the morning.* ⊃ look at **central heating**

heatwave /ˈhiːtweɪv/ *noun* [C] a period of unusually hot weather □ *masa cuaca lebih panas drpd biasa*

heave¹ /hiːv/ *verb* **1** [I,T] to lift, pull or throw sb/sth heavy with one big effort □ *mengangkat, menghela atau menghumbankan (sso/sst yg berat)*: *Take hold of this rope and heave!* ♦ *We heaved the cupboard up the stairs.* **2** [I] **heave (with sth)** to move up and down or in and out in a heavy but regular way □ *turun naik*: *His chest was heaving with the effort of carrying the cooker.* **3** [I] to experience the tight feeling you get in your stomach when you are just about to vomit (= bring up food from the stomach) □ *(berasa) mual*: *The sight of all that blood made her stomach heave.*
IDM **heave a sigh** to breathe out slowly and loudly □ *menarik nafas lega*: *He heaved a sigh of relief when he heard the good news.*

heave² /hiːv/ *noun* [C] a strong pull, push, throw, etc. □ *(perbuatan) mengangkat, menghela atau menghumban*

heaven /ˈhevn/ *noun* **1** [U] (also Heaven) the place where, in some religions, it is believed that God lives and where good people go when they die □ *syurga*: *to go to/be in heaven* **OPP** **hell** ⊃ note at **God 2** [U, sing] a place or a situation in which you are very happy □ *seronok sungguh*: *It was heaven on earth spending all winter skiing.* **3** **the heavens** [pl] (used in poetry and literature) the sky □ *langit*: *The stars shone brightly in the heavens that night.*

heavenly /ˈhevnli/ *adj* **1** [only *before* a noun] connected with heaven or the sky □ *langitan*: *heavenly bodies* (= the sun, moon, stars, etc.) **2** (*informal*) very pleasant; wonderful □ *sungguh (bagus, seronok, dll)*

heavy /ˈhevi/ *adj* (**heavier**; **heaviest**) **1** weighing a lot; difficult to lift or move □ *berat*: *This box is too heavy for me to carry.* **2** used when asking or stating how much sb/sth weighs □ *berat*: *How heavy is your suitcase?* **3** larger, stronger or more than usual □ *(digunakan dgn maksud lebih besar, kuat atau banyak drpd biasa); lebat; sesak; sibuk; kuat; berat*: *heavy rain* ♦ *heavy traffic* ♦ *a heavy smoker/drinker* (= sb who smokes/drinks a lot) ♦ *The sound of his heavy* (= loud and deep) *breathing told her that he was asleep.* ♦ *a heavy sleeper* (= sb who is difficult to wake) ♦ *a heavy meal* **4** (used about a material or substance) solid or thick □ *berat; tebal*: *heavy soil* ♦ *a heavy coat* **OPP** **light 5** full of hard work; (too) busy □ *sibuk; teruk*: *a heavy day/schedule/timetable* **6** serious, difficult or boring □ *serius; sukar; membosankan*: *His latest novel makes heavy reading.* ♦ *Things got a bit heavy when she started talking about her failed marriage.*
IDM **make heavy weather of sth** to make sth seem more difficult than it really is □ *menjadikan sst kelihatan lebih susah drpd sebenarnya*
take a heavy toll/take its toll (on sth) ⊃ **toll**
▶ **heavily** *adv* ▶ **heaviness** *noun* [U]

heavy-'duty *adj* [only *before* a noun] not easily damaged and therefore suitable for regular use or for hard physical work □ *tahan lasak*: *a heavy-duty tyre/carpet*

heavy-'handed *adj* **1** not showing much understanding of other people's feelings □ *cemerkap; kasar*: *a heavy-handed approach* **2** using unnecessary force □ *menindas*: *heavy-handed police methods*

heavy 'industry *noun* [C,U] industry that uses large machinery to produce metal, coal, vehicles, etc. □ *industri berat*

heavy 'metal *noun* [U] a style of very loud rock music that is played on electric instruments □ *muzik rock 'heavy metal'*

heavyweight /ˈheviweɪt/ *noun* [C] a person who is in the heaviest weight group in certain fighting sports □ *kelas berat*: *the world heavyweight boxing champion*

heckle /ˈhekl/ *verb* [I,T] to interrupt a speaker at a public meeting with difficult questions or rude comments □ *mengganggu penceramah* ▶ **heckler** /ˈheklə(r)/ *noun* [C]

hectare /ˈhekteə(r)/ noun [C] (abbr **ha**) a measure of land; 10 000 square metres ▫ *hektar*

hectic /ˈhektɪk/ adj very busy with of a lot of things that you have to do quickly ▫ *sangat sibuk* ▶ **hectically** /-kli/ adv

he'd /hiːd/ short for **he had**; **he would**

hedge¹ /hedʒ/ noun [C] a row of bushes or trees planted close together at the edge of a garden or field to separate one piece of land from another ▫ *pagar hidup (pokok renek atau pokok)* ⊃ picture on **page P11**

hedge² /hedʒ/ verb [I] to avoid giving a direct answer to a question ▫ *mengelak; berdolak-dalik*
IDM **hedge your bets** to protect yourself against losing or making a mistake by supporting more than one person or opinion ▫ *melindungi diri drpd kerugian atau kesilapan*

hedgehog /ˈhedʒhɒg/ (AmE usually) / noun [C] a small brown animal covered with **spines** (= sharp needles) ▫ *sejenis landak kecil*

spine
hedgehog

hedgerow /ˈhedʒrəʊ/ noun [C] a row of bushes, etc. especially at the side of a country road or around a field ▫ *pokok pagar renek*

heed¹ /hiːd/ verb [T] (formal) to pay attention to advice, a warning, etc. ▫ *ambil perhatian; menghiraukan*

heed² /hiːd/ noun
IDM **take heed (of sb/sth); pay heed (to sb/sth)** (formal) to pay careful attention to what sb says ▫ *mengambil berat; dengar baik-baik*: *You should take heed of your doctor's advice.*

heel¹ /hiːl/ noun [C] **1** the back part of your foot below your ankle ▫ *tumit*: *These shoes rub against my heels.* ⊃ picture at **body 2** the part of a sock, etc. that covers your heel ▫ *bahagian tumit* **3** the higher part of a shoe under the heel of your foot ▫ *tumit (kasut)*: *High heels* (= shoes with high heels) *are not practical for long walks.* ⊃ picture at **shoe 4 -heeled** having the type of heel mentioned ▫ *bertumit*: *high-heeled/low-heeled shoes*
IDM **dig your heels in** ⊃ **dig¹**
head over heels ⊃ **head¹**

heel² /hiːl/ verb [T] to repair the heel of a shoe ▫ *membaiki tumit kasut*

hefty /ˈhefti/ adj (**heftier**; **heftiest**) (informal) big and strong or heavy ▫ *tegap; sendo; berat*: *a hefty young man*

height /haɪt/ noun **1** [C,U] the measurement from the bottom to the top of a person or thing ▫ *tinggi*: *The nurse is going to check your height and weight.* ◆ *We need a fence that's about two metres in height.* ⊃ note at **tall** ⊃ picture at **length** ⊃ adjective **high 2** [U] the fact that sb is tall or sth is high ▫ *tinggi*: *He looks older than he is because of his height.* **3** [C,U] the distance that sth is above the ground ▫ *ketinggian*: *We are now flying at a height of 10 000 metres.* ◆ *The plane lost/gained height steadily.* ⊃ When talking about aeroplanes a more formal word for height is **altitude**. **4** [C, usually pl] a high place or area ▫ *tempat tinggi*: *I can't go up there. I'm afraid of heights.* **5** [sing] the strongest or most important part of sth ▫ *kemuncak*: *the height of summer*

heighten /ˈhaɪtn/ verb [I,T] to become or to make sth greater or stronger ▫ *meningkatkan; menambah; menyerlahkan*: *I'm using yellow paint to heighten the sunny effect of the room.*

heir /eə(r)/ noun [C] **heir (to sth)** the person with the legal right to **inherit** (= receive) money, property or a title when the owner dies ▫ *waris*: *He's the heir to a large fortune.*
MORE A female heir is often called an **heiress**.

heirloom /ˈeəluːm/ noun [C] something valuable that has belonged to the same family for many years ▫ *pusaka berharga*

held past tense, past participle of **hold¹**

helicopter /ˈhelɪkɒptə(r)/ (also informal **chopper**) noun [C] a small aircraft that can go straight up into the air. **Helicopters** have **blades** (= long thin metal parts that go round very fast) on top. ▫ *helikopter* ⊃ picture on **page P6**

helium /ˈhiːliəm/ noun [U] (symbol **He**) a gas which is lighter than air and which does not burn ▫ *helium*

hell /hel/ noun **1** [sing] (also **Hell**) the place where, in some religions, it is believed that bad people go to when they die ▫ *neraka*: *to go to/be in hell* ⊃ look at **heaven 2** [U, sing] (informal) a situation or place that is very unpleasant or painful ▫ *spt dlm neraka; benar-benar terseksa*: *He went through hell when his wife left him.* **3** [U] (slang) used as a swear word to show anger ▫ *sial; celaka*: *Oh hell, I've left my phone at home!*

HELP Be careful. Some people find this sense of hell offensive.

4 the hell (slang) used as a swear word in questions to show anger or surprise ▫ *digunakan sebagai kata makian dlm soalan utk menunjukkan rasa marah atau terkejut*: *Why the hell didn't you tell me this before?*
IDM **all hell broke loose** (informal) there was suddenly a lot of noise and confusion ▫ *keadaan menjadi kacau-bilau*
(just) for the hell of it (informal) for fun ▫ *(utk) suka-suka saja*
give sb hell (informal) to speak to sb very angrily or to be very strict with sb ▫ *teruk dimarahi atau dibuat oleh sso*
a/one hell of a … (informal) used to make an expression stronger or to mean 'very' ▫ *sangat (bagus, teruk, dll)*: *He got into a hell of a fight* (= a terrible fight).
like hell ⊃ **like¹**

he'll /hi:l/ short for **he will**

hellish /ˈhelɪʃ/ adj terrible; very unpleasant □ *teruk; dahsyat*: *a hellish experience*

hello (BrE also **hallo**) /həˈləʊ/ exclam, noun used when you meet sb, for attracting sb's attention or when you are using the telephone □ *helo* ➔ note at **introduce**

> **MORE** Other informal ways to say 'hello' are **hi** and **hiya**.

helm /helm/ noun [C] a handle or a wheel used for steering a boat or ship □ *kemudi*
IDM **at the helm** in charge of an organization, group of people, etc. □ *teraju/pimpinan*

helmet /ˈhelmɪt/ noun [C] a type of hard hat that you wear to protect your head □ *topi keledar*: *a crash helmet* ➔ picture at **bicycle**

help¹ /help/ verb **1** [I,T] **help (sb) (with sth); help (sb) (to) do sth; help sb (across, over, out of, into, etc.)** to do sth for sb in order to be useful or to make sth easier for them □ *bantu; membantu*: *Can I help?* ◆ *Could you help me with the cooking?* ◆ *I helped her to organize the day.* ◆ *My son's helping in our shop at the moment.* ◆ *She helped her grandmother up the stairs* (= supported her as she climbed the stairs). **2** [I] (*spoken*) to get sb's attention when you are in danger or difficulty □ *tolong*: *Help! I'm going to fall!* **3** [I,T] to make sth better or easier □ *dpt menolong*: *If you apologize to him it might help.* ◆ *This medicine should help your headache.* **4** [T] **help yourself (to sth)** to take sth (especially food and drink) that is offered to you □ *ambil sendiri; silakan*: *Help yourself to a drink!* ◆ *'Can I borrow your pen?' 'Yes, help yourself.'* **5** [T] **help yourself to sth** to take sth without asking permission; to steal □ *mengambil sst tanpa kebenaran*: *Don't just help yourself to my money!*
IDM **can/can't/could(n't) help (doing) sth/yourself** be able/not be able to stop or avoid doing sth □ *dpt/tdk dpt tahan drpd membuat sst*: *It was so funny I couldn't help laughing.* ◆ *I just couldn't help myself—I had to laugh.*
a helping hand some help □ *bantuan*: *My neighbour is always ready to give me a helping hand.*
PHRV **help (sb) out** to help sb in a difficult situation; to give money to help sb □ *menolong sso*

help² /help/ noun **1** [U] **help (with sth)** the act of helping □ *bantuan; pertolongan*: *Do you need any help with that?* ◆ *This map isn't much help.* ◆ *She stopped smoking with the help of her family and friends.* ◆ *He repaired his car with the help of his father.* ◆ *Run and get help—my son's fallen in the river!* **2** [sing] **a help (to sb)** a person or thing that helps □ *pembantu; sst yg membantu*: *Your directions were a great help—we found the place easily.*

helper /ˈhelpə(r)/ noun [C] a person who helps (especially with work) □ *pembantu*

helpful /ˈhelpfl/ adj giving help □ *yg membantu*: *helpful advice* ▶ **helpfully** /-fəli/ adv ▶ **helpfulness** noun [U]

helping /ˈhelpɪŋ/ noun [C] the amount of food that is put on a plate at one time □ *hidangan; jumlah makanan yg dimuatkan dlm sebuah pinggan*: *After two helpings of pasta, I couldn't eat any more.* ➔ look at **portion**

helpless /ˈhelpləs/ adj unable to take care of yourself or do things without the help of other people □ *tdk berdaya/berupaya*: *a helpless baby* ▶ **helplessly** adv: *They watched helplessly as their house went up in flames.* ▶ **helplessness** noun [U]

hem¹ /hem/ noun [C] the edge at the bottom of a piece of cloth (especially on a skirt, dress or trousers) that has been turned up and sewn □ *kelim*

hem² /hem/ verb [T] (**hemming; hemmed**) to turn up and sew the bottom of a piece of clothing or cloth □ *mengelim*
PHRV **hem sb in** to surround sb and prevent them from moving away □ *mengepung; terkepung*: *We were hemmed in by the crowd and could not leave.*

hemisphere /ˈhemɪsfɪə(r)/ noun [C] **1** one half of the earth □ *hemisfera*: *the northern/southern/eastern/western hemisphere* ➔ picture at **earth** **2** the shape of half a ball □ *separuh sfera*

hemophilia, hemophiliac (AmE) = **haemophilia, haemophiliac**

hemorrhage (AmE) = **haemorrhage**

hemorrhoids (AmE) = **haemorrhoids**

hemp /hemp/ noun [U] a plant that is used for making rope and rough cloth and for producing **cannabis** (= a drug which is illegal in many countries) □ *hem*

hen /hen/ noun [C] **1** a female bird that is kept for its eggs or its meat □ *ayam betina* ➔ note at **chicken** ➔ picture at **chicken 2** the female of any type of bird □ *burung betina*: *a hen pheasant* ➔ look at **cock**

hence /hens/ adv (*formal*) for this reason □ *oleh sebab itu*: *I've got some news to tell you—hence the letter.*

henceforth /ˌhensˈfɔːθ/ (also **henceforward** /ˌhensˈfɔːwəd/) adv (*formal*) from now on; in future □ *dr sekarang; selanjutnya*

henchman /ˈhentʃmən/ noun [C] (pl **-men** /-mən/) a person who is employed by sb to protect them and who may do things that are illegal or violent □ *orang yg diupah sebagai pengawal peribadi dan juga sebagai orang suruhan*

'hen party (also **'hen night**) noun [C] (*BrE*) a party that a woman who will soon be getting married has with her female friends □ *majlis keraian utk wanita sahaja* ➔ look at **stag night**

henpecked /ˈhenpekt/ adj used to describe a husband who always does what his wife tells him to do □ *takut bini*

hepatitis /ˌhepəˈtaɪtɪs/ noun [U] a serious disease of the liver (= one of the body's main organs) □ *hepatitis*

her¹ /hɜː(r)/ pron (the object of a verb or preposition) the woman or girl that was mentioned earlier □ *dia/nya (perempuan)*: He told Sue that he loved her. ♦ I've got a letter for your mother. Could you give it to her, please? ➲ note at **he** ➲ look at **she**

her² /hɜː(r)/ determiner of or belonging to the woman or girl mentioned earlier □ *nya (perempuan)*: That's her book. She left it there this morning. ♦ Fiona has broken her leg. ➲ look at **hers**

herald /ˈherəld/ verb [T] (written) to be a sign that sb/sth is going to happen soon □ *menandakan*: The minister's speech heralded a change of policy.

herb /hɜːb (AmE also) / noun [C] a plant whose leaves, seeds, etc. are used in medicine or in cooking □ *herba*: Add some herbs, such as rosemary and thyme. ➲ look at **spice** ➲ picture on page **P14**

herbal /ˈhɜːbl (AmE usually) / adj made of or using herbs □ *(diperbuat/menggunakan) herba*: herbal medicine/remedies

herd¹ /hɜːd/ noun [C] a large number of animals that live and feed together □ *kawanan; kumpulan*: a herd of cattle/deer/elephants ➲ note at **cow** ➲ look at **flock**

herd² /hɜːd/ verb [T] to move people or animals somewhere together in a group □ *menggiring*: The prisoners were herded onto the train.

here¹ /hɪə(r)/ adv **1** [after a verb or a preposition] in, at or to the place where you are or which you are pointing to □ *(di/ke) sini*: Come (over) here. ♦ The school is a mile from here. ♦ Please sign here. **2** at this point in a discussion or a piece of writing □ *di sini*: Here the speaker stopped and looked around the room. **3** used at the beginning of a sentence to introduce or draw attention to sb/sth □ *ini; sudah sampai*: Here is the 10 o'clock news. ♦ Here comes the bus. ♦ Here we are (= we've arrived).

> **HELP** Note the word order in the last example. We say *Here are the children.* but with a pronoun we say *Here they are.*

4 used for emphasizing a noun □ *ini*: I think you'll find this book here very useful.
IDM **here and there** in various places □ *di sana sini*
here goes (informal) used to say that you are about to do sth exciting, dangerous, etc. □ *hah (diucapkan apabila memulakan sst yg mengujakan, sukar, dsb)*: I've never done a backward dive before, but here goes!
here's to sb/sth used for wishing for the health, success, etc. of sb/sth while holding a drink □ *digunakan sebagai ucap selamat (sambil minum wain, dsb)*: Here's to a great holiday!
here you are; here you go (informal) used when you are giving sth to sb □ *nah (digunakan apabila memberikan sst kpd sso)*: Here you are—this is that book I was talking about.
neither here nor there not important □ *tdk penting*: My opinion is neither here nor there. If you like the dress then buy it.

here² /hɪə(r)/ exclam used for attracting sb's attention, when offering help or when giving sth to sb □ *mari; nah*: Here, let me help!

hereabouts /ˌhɪərəˈbaʊts/ (AmE **hereabout**) adv near this place □ *dekat-dekat sini*

hereafter /ˌhɪərˈɑːftə(r)/ adv (written) (used in legal documents, etc.) from now on □ *kemudian dr ini; selanjutnya*

hereditary /həˈredɪtri/ adj passed on from parent to child □ *turun-temurun*: a hereditary disease

heredity /həˈredəti/ noun [U] the process by which physical or mental qualities pass from parent to child □ *keturunan*

heresy /ˈherəsi/ noun [C,U] (pl **heresies**) a (religious) opinion or belief that is different from what is generally accepted to be true □ *bidaah*

heretic /ˈherətɪk/ noun [C] a person whose religious beliefs do not agree with what is generally accepted □ *pembidaah* ▶ **heretical** /həˈretɪkl/ adj

heritage /ˈherɪtɪdʒ/ noun [C, usually sing] the customs, qualities and culture of a country that have existed for a long time and that have great importance for the country □ *warisan*

hermit /ˈhɜːmɪt/ noun [C] a person who prefers to live alone, without contact with other people, often for religious reasons □ *pertapa*

hernia /ˈhɜːniə/ (also **rupture**) noun [C,U] the medical condition in which an organ inside the body, for example the stomach, pushes through the wall of muscle which surrounds it □ *hernia; burut*

hero /ˈhɪərəʊ (AmE also) / noun [C] (pl **heroes**) **1** a person who is admired, especially for having done sth difficult or good □ *wira; tokoh*: The team were given a hero's welcome on their return home. **2** the most important male character in a book, play, film, etc. □ *hero*: The hero of the film is a little boy. ➲ look at **heroine**, **villain**

heroic /həˈrəʊɪk/ adj (used about people or their actions) having a lot of courage □ *sangat berani*: a heroic effort ▶ **heroically** /-kli/ adv

heroin /ˈherəʊɪn/ noun [U] a powerful illegal drug that some people take for pleasure and then cannot stop taking □ *heroin (dadah)*

heroine /ˈherəʊɪn/ noun [C] **1** a woman who is admired, especially for having done sth difficult or good □ *srikandi; wirawati* **2** the most important female character in a book, play, film, etc. □ *heroin* ➲ look at **hero**

heroism /ˈherəʊɪzəm/ noun [U] great courage □ *keberanian; keperwiraan*

herring /ˈherɪŋ/ noun [C,U] (pl herring or herrings) a fish that swims in shoals (= large groups) in cold seas and is used for food □ *(ikan) hering* **IDM** a red herring ➔ red

hers /hɜːz/ pron of or belonging to her □ *kepunyaannya (perempuan)*: I didn't have a pen, but Helen lent me hers.

herself /hɜːˈself; weak form həˈs-/ pron 1 used when the female who does an action is also affected by it □ *dirinya (sendiri)*: She hurt herself quite badly when she fell downstairs. ♦ Irene looked at herself in the mirror. 2 used to emphasize the female who does the action □ *(dia) sendiri*: She told me the news herself. ♦ Has Rosy done this herself? (= or did sb else do it for her?)
IDM (all) by herself 1 alone □ *seorang diri*: She lives by herself. ➔ note at alone 2 without help □ *sendiri*: I don't think she needs any help—she can change a tyre by herself.
(all) to herself without having to share □ *tdk payah berkongsi lagi*: Julie has the bedroom to herself now her sister's left home.

he's /hiːz/ short for he is; he has

hesitant /ˈhezɪtənt/ adj hesitant (to do/about doing sth) slow to speak or act because you are not sure if you should or not □ *teragak-agak; berasa berat*: I'm very hesitant about criticizing him too much. ▶ hesitancy /ˈhezɪtənsi/ noun [U] ▶ hesitantly adv

hesitate /ˈhezɪteɪt/ verb [I] 1 hesitate (about/over sth) to pause before you do sth or before you take a decision, usually because you are uncertain or worried □ *ragu-ragu; teragak-agak*: He hesitated before going into her office. ♦ She's still hesitating about whether to accept the job or not. 2 hesitate (to do sth) to not want to do sth because you are not sure that it is right □ *berasa berat; segan*: Don't hesitate to phone if you have any problems. ▶ hesitation /ˌhezɪˈteɪʃn/ noun [C,U]: She agreed without a moment's hesitation.

heterosexual /ˌhetərəˈsekʃuəl/ adj sexually attracted to people of the opposite sex □ *heteroseksual* ➔ look at bisexual, homosexual ▶ heterosexual noun [C]

het up /ˌhet ˈʌp/ adj [not before a noun] (informal) het up (about/over sth) worried or excited about sth □ *risau; teruja*

hexagon /ˈheksəɡən/ noun [C] a shape with six sides □ *heksagon* ▶ hexagonal /heksˈæɡənl/ adj

hey /heɪ/ exclam (informal) used to attract sb's attention or to show that you are surprised or interested □ *hei*: Hey, what are you doing?
IDM hey presto people sometimes say 'hey presto' when they have done sth so quickly that it seems like magic □ *ungkapan yg kadangkala digunakan apabila sso telah berjaya membuat sst dgn pantas seolah-olah spt dgn silap mata*

heyday /ˈheɪdeɪ/ noun [sing] the period when sb/sth was most powerful, successful, rich, etc. □ *zaman gemilang*

HGV /ˌeɪtʃ dʒiː ˈviː/ abbr (BrE) heavy goods vehicle; a large vehicle such as a lorry □ *kenderaan barang berat*

hi /haɪ/ exclam (informal) used to say hello □ *hai*: Hi guys!

hibernate /ˈhaɪbəneɪt/ verb [I] (used about animals) to spend the winter in a state like deep sleep □ *berhibernat* ▶ hibernation /ˌhaɪbəˈneɪʃn/ noun [U]

hiccup (also **hiccough**) /ˈhɪkʌp/ noun 1 [C] a sudden, usually repeated sound that is made in the throat and that you cannot control □ *sedu* 2 (the) hiccups [pl] a series of hiccups □ *tersedu-sedu*: Don't eat so fast or you'll get hiccups! ♦ If you have the hiccups, try holding your breath. 3 [C] a small problem or difficulty □ *gendala*: There's been a slight hiccup in our holiday arrangements but I've got it sorted out now. ▶ hiccup (also hiccough) verb [I]

hide¹ /haɪd/ verb (pt hid /hɪd/; pp hidden /ˈhɪdn/) 1 [T] to put or keep sb/sth in a place where they or it cannot be seen; to cover sth so that it cannot be seen □ *menyembunyikan; menyorokkan; terselindung*: Where shall I hide the money? ♦ You couldn't see Bill in the photo —he was hidden behind John. 2 [I] to be or go in a place where you cannot be seen or found □ *sembunyi; menyorok*: Quick, run and hide! ♦ The child was hiding under the bed. 3 [T] hide sth (from sb) to keep sth secret, especially your feelings □ *menyembunyikan; merahsiakan*: She tried to hide her disappointment from them.

hide² /haɪd/ noun 1 [C] a place from which people can watch wild animals, birds, etc. without being seen □ *tempat menghendap (haiwan, burung)* 2 [C,U] the skin of a large animal, especially when it is used for leather □ *kulit; belulang*

hide-and-ˈseek noun [U] a children's game in which one person hides and the others try to find them □ *main sembunyi-sembunyi*

hideous /ˈhɪdiəs/ adj very ugly or unpleasant □ *sangat hodoh; teruk; dahsyat; terkutuk*: a hideous sight ♦ a hideous crime ♦ That new dress she's got is hideous. ▶ hideously adv

hiding /ˈhaɪdɪŋ/ noun 1 [U] the state of being hidden □ *bersembunyi*: The escaped prisoners are believed to be in hiding somewhere in London. ♦ to go into hiding 2 [C, usually sing] (informal) a punishment involving being hit hard many times □ *membelasah; dibelasah*: You deserve a good hiding for what you've done.

hierarchy /ˈhaɪərɑːki/ noun [C] (pl hierarchies) a system or an organization that has many levels from the lowest to the highest □ *hierarki; tatatingkat* ▶ hierarchical /ˌhaɪəˈrɑːkɪkl/ adj

hieroglyphics /ˌhaɪərəˈɡlɪfɪks/ noun [pl] the system of writing that was used in ancient

Egypt in which a small picture represents a word or sound □ *hiroglif; sistem tulisan lambang*

hi-fi /ˈhaɪ faɪ/ *noun* [C,U] equipment for playing recorded music that produces high quality sound □ *hi-fi* ►**hi-fi** *adj*: *a hi-fi system*

higgledy-piggledy /ˌhɪɡldi ˈpɪɡldi/ *adv, adj* (*informal*) not in any order; mixed up together □ *lintang-pukang*

high¹ /haɪ/ *adj* (**higher; highest**)
▶FROM BOTTOM TO TOP **1** (used about things) having a large distance between the bottom and the top □ *tinggi*: *high cliffs* ♦ *What's the highest mountain in the world?* ♦ *high heels* (on shoes) ♦ *The garden wall was so high that we couldn't see over it.* **OPP** **low** ⊃ note at **tall** ⊃ *noun* **height** **2** having a particular height □ *tingginya; setinggi; paras*: *The hedge is one metre high.* ♦ *knee-high boots*
▶FAR FROM GROUND **3** at a level which is a long way from the ground, or from sea level □ *tinggi*: *a high shelf* ♦ *The castle was built on high ground.* **OPP** **low**
▶MORE THAN USUAL **4** above the usual or normal level or amount □ *tinggi (pd paras atau jumlah yg lebih drpd biasa)*: *high prices* ♦ *at high speed* ♦ *a high level of unemployment* ♦ *He's got a high temperature.* ♦ *Oranges are high in vitamin C.* **OPP** **low**
▶BETTER THAN USUAL **5** better than what is usual □ *tinggi (lebih baik drpd biasa)*: *high-quality goods* ♦ *Her work is of a very high standard.* ♦ *He has a high opinion of you.* **OPP** **poor**
▶IMPORTANT **6** having an important position □ *tinggi (jawatan/kedudukan)*: *Sam only joined the company three years ago, but she's already quite high up.*
▶GOOD **7** morally good □ *tinggi; mulia; luhur*: *high ideals*
▶SOUND **8** not deep or lowv □ *tinggi; nyaring*: *Dogs can hear very high sounds.* ♦ *Women usually have higher voices than men.* **OPP** **low**
▶ON DRUGS **9** [not before a noun] (*informal*) high (on sth) under the influence of drugs, alcohol, etc. □ *khayal; mabuk*
▶IN CAR **10** (used about a gear in a car) that allows a faster speed □ *tinggi; lebih laju* **OPP** **low**
IDM **be left high and dry** ⊃ **leave**¹
a high/low profile ⊃ **profile**
It's about/high time ⊃ **time**¹

high² /haɪ/ *noun* [C] **1** a high level or point □ *tahap tinggi*: *Profits reached an all-time high last year.* **OPP** **low** **2** an area of high air pressure □ *kawasan tekanan tinggi* **OPP** **low** **3** (*informal*) a feeling of great pleasure or happiness that sb gets from doing sth exciting or being successful □ *keadaan suka atau gembira*: *He was on a high after passing all his exams.* ♦ *She talked about the highs and lows of her career.* **OPP** **low** **4** (*informal*) a feeling of great pleasure or happiness that may be caused by a drug, alcohol, etc. □ *khayal; mabuk*
IDM **on high** (*formal*) (in) a high place, the sky or heaven □ *(di) tempat tinggi, langit atau syurga; (pihak) atasan*: *The order came from on high.*

high³ /haɪ/ *adv* **1** at or to a high position or level □ *tinggi*: *The sun was high in the sky.* ♦ *I can't jump any higher.* ♦ *The plane flew high overhead.* ⊃ *noun* **height** **2** at a high level □ *tinggi*: *How high can you sing?* **OPP** for both meanings **low**
IDM **high and low** everywhere □ *di mana-mana*: *We've searched high and low for the keys.*
run high (used about the feelings of a group of people) to be especially strong □ *semakin tegang/memuncak*: *Emotions are running high in the neighbourhood where the murders took place.*

highbrow /ˈhaɪbraʊ/ *adj* interested in or concerned with matters that many people would find too serious to be interesting □ *utk orang yg terpelajar*: *highbrow newspapers/TV programmes*

high chair *noun* [C] a special chair with long legs and a table, for a small child to sit in when eating □ *kerusi tinggi kanak-kanak* ⊃ picture at **chair**

high-ˈclass *adj* of especially good quality □ *bermutu tinggi*: *a high-class restaurant*

High ˈCourt *noun* [C] the most important court of law in some countries □ *Mahkamah Tinggi*

high-defiˈnition *adj* (*abbr* **HD**) [only before a noun] using or produced by a system that gives very clear detailed images □ *berdefinisi tinggi*: *high-definition television*

higher eduˈcation *noun* [U] education and training at a college or university, especially to degree level □ *pendidikan tinggi* ⊃ look at **further education**

the ˈhigh jump *noun* [sing] the sport in which people try to jump over a bar in order to find out who can jump the highest □ *lompat tinggi* ⊃ look at **long jump**

highland /ˈhaɪlənd/ *adj* [only before a noun] **1** in or connected with an area of land that has mountains □ *kawasan pergunungan*: *highland streams* ⊃ look at **lowland** **2** [pl] in or connected with the Highlands (= the part of Scotland where there are mountains) □ *kawasan Pergunungan Scotland*

high-ˈlevel *adj* involving important people □ *peringkat tinggi*: *high-level talks*

highlight¹ /ˈhaɪlaɪt/ *verb* [T] **1** to emphasize sth so that people give it special attention □ *menekankan; menegaskan*: *The report highlighted the need for improved safety at football grounds.* **2** to mark part of a text with a different colour or to mark an area on a computer screen so that people give it more attention □ *menanda (teks) dgn penyerlah/warna lain*: *I've highlighted the important passages in yellow.*

highlight² /ˈhaɪlaɪt/ *noun* **1** [C] the best or most interesting part of sth □ *kemuncak sst; sorotan penting*: *The highlights of the match will be shown on TV tonight.* **2** **highlights** [pl] areas of

highlighter → hinder

lighter colour that are put in sb's hair □ *penyerlah; seri warna*

highlighter /ˈhaɪlaɪtə(r)/ (also **ˈhighlighter pen**) *noun* [C] a special pen used for marking words in a text in bright colours □ *pen penyerlah* ⊃ picture at **stationery**

highly /ˈhaɪli/ *adv* **1** to a high degree; very □ *sangat; amat*: *highly trained/educated/developed* ♦ *a highly paid job* ♦ *It's highly unlikely that anyone will complain.* **2** with admiration □ *mengagumi; (memandang) tinggi*: *I think very highly of your work.*

highly ˈstrung *adj* nervous and easily upset □ *mudah gugup*

Highness /ˈhaɪnəs/ *noun* **your/his/her Highness** [C] a title used when speaking about or to a member of a royal family □ *Yg Amat Mulia (Raja)*

high-ˈpowered *adj* **1** (used about people) important and successful □ *berwibawa*: *high-powered executives* **2** (used about things) having great power □ *berkuasa tinggi*: *a high-powered engine*

ˈhigh-rise *adj* [only before a noun] (used about a building) very tall and having a lot of floors □ *bertingkat tinggi*

ˈhigh school *noun* [C,U] a school for students between the ages of 11 and 18 in Britain, or 14 and 18 in some other countries □ *sekolah tinggi/menengah*

ˈhigh street *noun* [C] (*BrE*) (often used in names) the main street of a town □ *jalan besar/utama*: *The Post Office is in the High Street.*

high-tech (also **hi-tech**) /ˌhaɪ ˈtek/ *adj* using the most modern methods and machines, especially electronic ones □ *berteknologi tinggi*: *high-tech industries/hospitals* **OPP** **low-tech**

ˌhigh ˈtide *noun* [U] the time when the sea comes furthest onto the land □ *air pasang* **OPP** **low tide** ⊃ look at the **ebb**

highway /ˈhaɪweɪ/ *noun* [C] (especially *AmE*) a main road (between towns) □ *lebuh raya* ⊃ look at **motorway**

hijab /hɪˈdʒɑːb/ *noun* [C] a head covering worn in public by some Muslim women □ *hijab*

hijack /ˈhaɪdʒæk/ *verb* [T] **1** to take control of a plane, etc. by force, usually for political reasons □ *merampas*: *The plane was hijacked on its flight to Sydney.* ⊃ note at **crime** ⊃ look at **kidnap** **2** to take control of a meeting, an event, etc. in order to force people to pay attention to sth □ *mengambil alih (secara paksa); merampas*: *The rally was hijacked by right-wing extremists.* ▶ **hijack** *noun* [C]: *The hijack was ended by armed police.* ▶ **hijacker** *noun* [C] ▶ **hijacking** *noun* [C,U]

hike /haɪk/ *noun* [C] a long walk in the country □ *mengembara berjalan kaki*: *We went on a ten-mile hike at the weekend.* ▶ **hike** *verb* [I] ▶ **hiker** *noun* [C]

hiking /ˈhaɪkɪŋ/ *noun* [U] the activity of going for long walks in the country for pleasure □ *aktiviti jalan kaki*

> **HELP** **Go hiking** is used when you are talking about spending time hiking: *They went hiking in Wales for their holiday.*

hilarious /hɪˈleəriəs/ *adj* extremely funny □ *sangat lucu* ⊃ note at **humour** ▶ **hilariously** *adv*

hilarity /hɪˈlærəti/ *noun* [U] the state of finding sth very funny, which causes people to laugh loudly □ *kelucuan; keriuhan bunyi ketawa*

hill /hɪl/ *noun* [C] **1** a high area of land that is not as high as a mountain □ *bukit*: *There was a wonderful view from the top of the hill.* ⊃ picture on page P11 **2** a slope on a road □ *cerun*: *Take care when driving down steep hills.* ⊃ look at **uphill, downhill**

hillside /ˈhɪlsaɪd/ *noun* [C] the side of a hill □ *lereng bukit*

hilltop /ˈhɪltɒp/ *noun* [C] the top of a hill □ *puncak bukit*

hilly /ˈhɪli/ *adj* (**hillier; hilliest**) having a lot of hills □ *berbukit-bukau*: *The country's very hilly around here.*

hilt /hɪlt/ *noun* [C] the handle of a knife or a sword (= a long metal weapon) □ *hulu* **IDM** **to the hilt** to a high degree; completely □ *sepenuhnya; habis-habisan*: *I'll defend you to the hilt.*

him /hɪm/ *pron* (the object of a verb or preposition) the man or boy who was mentioned earlier □ *dia/nya (lelaki)*: *Helen told Ian that she loved him.* ♦ *I've got a letter for your father—can you give it to him, please?* ⊃ note at **he**

himself /hɪmˈself/ *pron* **1** used when the male who does an action is also affected by it □ *dirinya (sendiri)*: *He cut himself when he was shaving.* ♦ *John looked at himself in the mirror.* ⊃ picture at **each other 2** used to emphasize the male who does the action □ *(dia) sendiri*: *He told me the news himself.* ♦ *Did he write this himself?* (= or did sb else do it for him?)

IDM **(all) by himself 1** alone □ *seorang diri*: *He lives by himself.* ⊃ note at **alone 2** without help □ *sendiri*: *He should be able to cook a meal by himself.*

(all) to himself without having to share □ *tdk payah berkongsi lagi*: *Charlie has the bedroom to himself now his brother's left home.*

hind /haɪnd/ *adj* [only before a noun] (used about an animal's legs, etc.) at the back □ *(kaki, dsb) belakang* ⊃ picture on page P12

> **MORE** We also say **back legs**. The legs at the front are the **front legs** or **forelegs**.

hinder /ˈhɪndə(r)/ *verb* [T] to make it more difficult for sb/sth to do sth □ *menghalang; terhalang; melambatkan*: *A lot of scientific work is hindered by lack of money.*

hindrance /'hɪndrəns/ noun [C] a person or thing that makes it difficult for you to do sth ▫ *penghalang; halangan*

hindsight /'haɪndsaɪt/ noun [U] the understanding that you have of a situation only after it has happened ▫ *pengetahuan drpd apa yg sudah berlaku*: *With hindsight, I wouldn't have lent him the money.* ⊃ look at **foresight**

Hindu /'hɪnduː; ˌhɪn'duː/ noun [C] a person whose religion is Hinduism ▫ *Hindu* ▶ **Hindu** adj: *Hindu beliefs*

Hinduism /'hɪnduːɪzəm/ noun [U] the main religion of India that includes the worship of one or more gods and the belief that, after death, people will return to life in a different form. ▫ *agama Hindu*

hinge¹ /hɪndʒ/ noun [C] a piece of metal that joins two sides of a box, door, etc. together and allows it to be opened or closed ▫ *engsel*

hinge² /hɪndʒ/ verb
PHR V **hinge on sth** to depend on sth ▫ *bergantung pd sst*: *The future of the project hinges on the meeting today.*

hinge

hint¹ /hɪnt/ noun **1** [C] something that you suggest in an indirect way ▫ *sst yg disebut secara tdk langsung; kiasan*: *If you keep mentioning parties, maybe they'll **take the hint** and invite you.* **2** [C] something that suggests what will happen in the future ▫ *tanda-tanda*: *The first half of the match gave no hint of the excitement to come.* **SYN** **sign 3** [usually sing] a small amount of sth ▫ *sedikit*: *There was a hint of sadness in his voice.* **SYN** **suggestion 4** [C] a piece of advice or information ▫ *petua*: *helpful hints* **SYN** **tip**

hint² /hɪnt/ verb [I,T] **hint (at sth); hint that …** to suggest sth in an indirect way ▫ *membayangkan*: *They only hinted at their great disappointment.* ♦ *He hinted that he might be moving to Greece.*

hip¹ /hɪp/ noun [C] the part of the side of your body above your legs and below your waist ▫ *pinggul*: *He stood there angrily with his hands on his hips.* ⊃ picture at **body**

hip² /hɪp/ exclam
IDM **hip, hip, hurray/hurrah** shouted three times when a group wants to show that it is pleased with sb or with sth that has happened ▫ *hep hep hore*

hip hop noun [U] a type of dance music with spoken words and a steady beat played on electronic instruments ▫ *hip hop (muzik)*

hippie (also **hippy**) /'hɪpi/ noun [C] (pl **hippies**) a person who rejects the usual values and way of life of western society. Especially in the 1960s, **hippies** showed that they were different by wearing brightly coloured clothes, having long hair and taking drugs. ▫ *hipi*

hippopotamus /ˌhɪpə'pɒtəməs/ noun [C] (pl **hippopotamuses** /-məsɪz/ or **hippopotami** /-maɪ/) (also informal **hippo**) a large African animal with a large head and short legs that lives in or near rivers ▫ *badak air*

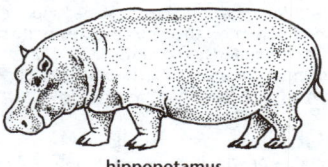

hippopotamus
(also hippo)

rhinoceros
(also rhino)

hire¹ /'haɪə(r)/ verb [T] **1** (AmE **rent**) **hire sth (from sb)** to have the use of sth for a short time by paying for it ▫ *menyewa*

HELP **Hire** or **rent**? In British English, you **hire** something for a short time: *We hired a car for the day.* You **rent** something if the period of time is longer: *to rent a house/flat/TV.* In American English **rent** is used in both situations.

2 to give sb a job for a short time ▫ *mengupah*: *We'll have to hire somebody to mend the roof.*

HELP In American English **hire** is also used for talking about permanent jobs: *We just hired a new secretary.*

PHR V **hire sth (out) (to sb)** (AmE **rent**) to allow sb to use sth for a short fixed period in exchange for money ▫ *menyewakan*: *We hire (out) our vans by the day.*

HELP In British English, **rent** or **let** is used if the period of time is longer: *Mrs Higgs rents out rooms to students.* ♦ *We let our house while we were in France for a year.*

hire² /'haɪə(r)/ noun [U] the act of paying to use sth for a short time ▫ *penyewaan*: *Car hire is expensive in this country.* ♦ *Do you have bicycles for hire?*

hire purchase noun [U] (BrE) (abbr **h.p.**) a way of buying goods. You do not pay the full price immediately but by **instalments** (= small regular payments) until the full amount is paid ▫ *sewa beli*: *a hire purchase agreement for a car*

his¹ /hɪz/ determiner of or belonging to the man or boy who was mentioned earlier □ *-nya (lelaki)*: Peter has sold his car. ◆ He hurt his shoulder skiing.

his² /hɪz/ pron of or belonging to him □ *nya (lelaki)*: This is my book so that one must be his. ⊃ note at **he**

hiss /hɪs/ verb 1 [I,T] to make a sound like a very long 's' to show that you are angry or do not like sth □ *mendesis; mendesis-desis*: The cat hissed at me. ◆ The speech was hissed and booed. 2 [T] to say sth in a quiet angry voice □ *desis; mendesis*: 'Stay away from me!' she hissed. ▶ hiss noun [C]

historian /hɪˈstɔːriən/ noun [C] a person who studies or who is an expert in history □ *ahli sejarah; sejarawan*

historic /hɪˈstɒrɪk/ (*AmE* also)/ adj famous or important in history □ *bersejarah*: The ending of apartheid was a historic event. ⊃ note at **important**

historical /hɪˈstɒrɪkl/ (*AmE* also) / adj that really lived or happened; connected with real people or events in the past □ *(berkaitan dgn) sejarah*: historical events/records/research ▶ historically /-kli/ adv

history /ˈhɪstri/ noun (*pl* histories) 1 [U] all the events of the past □ *sejarah*: an important moment in history ⊃ look at **natural history** 2 [C, usually sing] the series of events or facts that is connected with sb/sth □ *sejarah; rekod (perubatan, jenayah, dll) masa lalu*: He has a history of violence. ◆ a patient's medical history 3 [U] the study of past events □ *sejarah*: a degree in history ◆ History was my favourite subject at school. 4 [C] a written description of past events □ *sejarah*: She's writing a new history of Europe.

> **HELP History** or **story**? **History** is something true that really happened. A **story** is a description of a series of events that may or may not have happened.

IDM **go down in/make history** to be or do sth so important that it will be recorded in history □ *menempa sejarah*: She made history by becoming the first woman President.
the rest is history ⊃ **rest²**

hit¹ /hɪt/ verb [T] (**hitting**; *pt, pp* **hit**) 1 to make sudden, violent contact with sb/sth □ *melanggar; menghentam; memukul*: The bus left the road and hit a tree. ◆ to hit somebody in the eye/across the face/on the nose 2 **hit sth (on/against sth)** to knock a part of your body, etc. against sth □ *terlanggar; terhantuk*: Peter hit his head on the low beam. 3 to have a bad or unpleasant effect on sb/sth □ *menjejaskan; mengganggu (fikiran, dsb)*: Inner city areas have been badly hit by unemployment. ◆ Her father's death has hit her very hard. 4 to reach a place or a level □ *sampai ke; menemui; mencapai*: If you follow this road you should hit the motorway in about ten minutes.

[I] **intransitive**, a verb which has no object: *He laughed.*

◆ The price of oil hit a new high yesterday. 5 to experience sth unpleasant or difficult □ *menemui; menghadapi*: Things were going really well until we hit this problem. 6 to suddenly come into sb's mind; to make sb realize or understand sth □ *tiba-tiba perasan/teringat/menyedari*: I thought I recognized the man's face and then it hit me—he was my old maths teacher!

IDM **hit it off (with sb)** (*informal*) to like sb when you first meet them □ *secocok/lekas mesra (dgn sso)*: When I first met Tony's parents, we didn't really hit it off.
hit the nail on the head to say sth that is exactly right □ *tepat sekali*
hit the jackpot to win a lot of money or have a big success □ *mendapat untung besar*
hit the roof (*informal*) to become very angry □ *sangat marah; naik angin*

PHR V **hit back (at sb/sth)** to attack (with words) sb who has attacked you □ *mengecam balik*: The Prime Minister hit back at his critics.
hit on sth to suddenly find sth by chance □ *tiba-tiba mendapat idea, dsb ttg sst*: I finally hit on a solution to the problem.
hit out (at sb/sth) to attack sb/sth □ *memukul, menyerang atau mengecam (sso/sst)*: The man hit out at the policeman.

> **OTHER WORDS FOR**
> **hit**
> **Strike** is a more formal word than **hit**. **Beat** means to hit many times: *He was badly beaten in the attack.* **Punch** means to hit somebody or something hard with your hand closed, for example when two people are fighting: *She punched him in the face.* **Smack** means to hit somebody with your hand flat, especially as a punishment: *I think it's wrong to smack children.*

hit² /hɪt/ noun [C] 1 the act of hitting sth □ *pukulan*: The ship took a **direct hit** and sank. ◆ She gave her brother a hard hit on the head. 2 a person or thing that is very popular or successful □ *sso/sst yg sangat popular*: The album was a big hit. 3 a result of a search on a computer, especially on the Internet □ *hasil carian di komputer, terutamanya di Internet; kemungkinan*

IDM **make a hit (with sb)** (*informal*) to make a good impression on sb □ *dikagumi/disukai (sso)*: The new teacher seems to have made a hit with the students.

ˌhit-and-ˈmiss (also ˌhit-or-ˈmiss) adj (*informal*) not well organized; careless □ *(secara) rambang*: This method is a bit hit-or-miss, but it usually works.

ˌhit-and-ˈrun adj [only *before* a noun] (used about a road accident) caused by a driver who does not stop to help □ *langgar lari*

hitch¹ /hɪtʃ/ verb 1 [I,T] (*informal*) to get a free ride in a person's car; to travel around in this way by waiting by the side of a road and trying to get passing cars to stop □ *menumpang*: I managed to hitch to Paris in just six hours. ◆ We missed the

[T] **transitive**, a verb which has an object: *He ate an apple.*

bus so we had to *hitch a lift*. ⊃ look at **hitchhike 2** [T] to fasten sth to sth else □ *menambat; mengikat*: *to hitch a trailer to the back of a car*

hitch² /hɪtʃ/ *noun* [C] a small problem or difficulty □ *gendala; gangguan*: *a technical hitch*

hitchhike /ˈhɪtʃhaɪk/ (also *informal* **hitch**) *verb* [I] to travel by waiting by the side of a road and holding out your hand or a sign until a driver stops and takes you in the direction you want to go □ *mengembara tumpang*: *He hitchhiked across Europe.*

> **MORE** **Hitchhike** is usually used to talk about travelling long distances in this way for pleasure. **Hitch** can be used to mean the same, but it is also used to talk about travelling short distances in this way, for example because your car has broken down or you have missed a bus. **Hitch** can also be used transitively: *I hitched a lift/ride to the nearest petrol station.* **Thumb a lift** means the same.

▶**hitchhiker** *noun* [C]

hi-tech = **high-tech**

hitherto /ˌhɪðəˈtuː/ *adv* (*formal*) until now □ *sehingga kini*

hit-or-ˈmiss = **hit-and-miss**

HIV /ˌeɪtʃ aɪ ˈviː/ *noun* [U] **human immunodeficiency virus**; a virus which destroys the body's ability to fight infection and which causes the illness **AIDS** □ *HIV*

hive /haɪv/ = **beehive**

hiya /ˈhaɪjə/ *exclam* (*informal*) used to say hello to sb in an informal way □ *hai*

HM *abbr* **His/Her Majesty's** □ *DYMM (Duli Yg Maha Mulia); Diraja (dlm nama kapal tentera laut)*: *HMS (= Her Majesty's Ship) Invincible*

hmm (also **hm**) /m; hm/ *exclam* used when you are not sure of sth or when you are thinking about sth □ *em... menggumam*

HM ˈRevenue and ˈCustoms *noun* [sing] the government department in the UK that collects taxes □ *Jabatan Hasil dan Kastam*

hoard¹ /hɔːd/ *noun* [C] a store (often secret) of money, food, etc. □ *sorokan*

hoard² /hɔːd/ *verb* [I,T] **hoard (sth) (up)** to collect and store large quantities of sth (often secretly) □ *menyimpan dgn sorok-sorok*

hoarding /ˈhɔːdɪŋ/ (*BrE*) = **billboard**

hoarse /hɔːs/ *adj* (used about a person or their voice) sounding rough and quiet, especially because of a sore throat □ *serak*: *a hoarse whisper*
▶**hoarsely** *adv*

hoax /həʊks/ *noun* [C] a trick to make people believe sth that is not true, especially sth unpleasant □ *main-main; olok-olok*: *The fire brigade answered the call, but found that it was a hoax.*

hob /hɒb/ (*AmE* **stovetop**) *noun* [C] the surface on the top of a cooker that is used for boiling, frying, etc. □ *hob*

421　　　　　　　　　　　　　　　　**hitch → hold**

hobble /ˈhɒbl/ *verb* [I] to walk with difficulty because your foot or leg is hurt □ *berjalan terincut-incut*: *He hobbled home on his twisted ankle.*

hobby /ˈhɒbi/ *noun* [C] (*pl* **hobbies**) something that you do regularly for pleasure in your free time □ *hobi*: *Danesh's hobbies are flower arranging and mountain biking.* **SYN** **pastime** ⊃ picture on **page P3**

hockey /ˈhɒki/ *noun* [U] **1** (*BrE*) a game that is played on a field by two teams of eleven players who try to hit a small hard ball into a goal with a curved wooden stick □ *hoki* ⊃ picture on **page P4**

> **HELP** In the US **hockey** is usually called **field hockey** to show that it is not **ice hockey**.

2 (*AmE*) = **ice hockey**

hoe /həʊ/ *noun* [C] a garden tool with a long handle that is used for turning the soil and for removing plants that you do not want □ *cangkul; tajak* ⊃ picture at **garden**

hog¹ /hɒɡ/ (*AmE* also) / *noun* [C] a male pig that is kept for its meat □ *babi jantan*
IDM **go the whole hog** (*informal*) to do sth as completely as possible □ *membuat sst habis-habisan atau sepenuhnya*: *Instead of getting a taxi, why not go the whole hog and hire a limousine for the evening?*

hog² /hɒɡ/ (*AmE* also) / *verb* [T] (**hogging; hogged**) (*informal*) to take or keep too much or all of sth for yourself □ *memonopoli*: *The red car was hogging the middle of the road so no one could overtake.*

Hogmanay /ˈhɒɡməneɪ/ *noun* [U] the Scottish name for New Year's Eve (31 December) and the celebrations that take place then □ *perayaan hari akhir tahun di Scotland*

hoist /hɔɪst/ *verb* [T] to lift or pull sth up, often by using ropes, etc. □ *mengangkat; menaikkan*: *to hoist a flag/sail*

hold¹ /həʊld/ *verb* (*pt, pp* **held** /held/)
▶IN HANDS **1** [T] to take sb/sth and keep them or it in your hand, etc. □ *memegang*: *He held a book in his hand.* ◆ *The woman was holding a baby in her arms.* ◆ *Hold my hand. This is a busy road.* ◆ *They are holding hands* (= holding each other's hands).

They held hands.

▶IN POSITION **2** [T] to keep sth in a certain position □ *mengekalkan sst dlm kedudukan tertentu*: *Hold your head up straight.* ◆ *Hold the camera still or you'll spoil the picture.* ◆ *These two screws hold the shelf in place.*

▶SUPPORT **3** [T] to take the weight of sb/sth □ *menampung*: *Are you sure that branch will be strong enough to hold you?*

hold → hold-up

▶ CONTAIN **4** [T] to contain or have space for a particular amount □ *muat; dpt mengandungi; berisi*: *The car holds five people.* ♦ *How much does this bottle hold?*

▶ SB PRISONER **5** [T] to keep a person in a position or place by force □ *menahan*: *The terrorists are holding three men hostage.* ♦ *A man is being held at the police station.*

▶ STAY SAME **6** [I] to remain the same □ *bertahan; berterusan; tdk berubah*: *I hope this weather holds till the weekend.* ♦ *What I said still holds—nothing has changed.*

▶ OWN **7** [T] to have sth, usually in an official way □ *memegang; memiliki*: *Does he hold a British passport?* ♦ *She holds the world record in the 100 metres.*

▶ OPINION **8** [T] to have an opinion, etc. □ *mempunyai (pendapat); berpendapat*: *They hold the view that we shouldn't spend any more money.* **9** [T] to believe that sth is true about a person □ *mempercayai sst ttg sso*: *I hold the parents responsible for the child's behaviour.*

▶ EVENT, MEETING, ETC. **10** [T] to organize an event; to have a meeting, an election, a concert, etc. □ *mengadakan*: *They're holding a party for his fortieth birthday.* ♦ *The Olympic Games are held every four years.*

▶ CONVERSATION **11** [T] to have a conversation □ *berbual*: *It's impossible to hold a conversation with all this noise.*

▶ ON TELEPHONE **12** [I,T] to wait until the person you are calling is ready □ *tunggu*: *I'm afraid his phone is engaged. Will you hold the line?*

IDM **Hold it!** (*spoken*) Stop! Do not move! □ *Berhenti!; Jangan bergerak!* ❶ For other idioms containing **hold**, look at the entries for the nouns, adjectives, etc. For example, **hold your own** is at **own**.

PHR V **hold sth against sb** to not forgive sb because of sth they have done □ *menyimpan dendam atau anggapan buruk terhadap sso*

hold sb/sth back 1 to prevent sb from making progress □ *menghalang kemajuan/perkembangan sso* **2** to prevent sb/sth from moving forward □ *membendung atau menahan sso/sst*: *The police tried to hold the crowd back.*

hold sth back 1 to refuse to give some of the information that you have □ *merahsiakan sst*: *The police are sure that she is holding something back. She knows much more than she is saying.* **2** to control an emotion and stop yourself from showing what you really feel □ *menahan (perasaan, dsb)*: *He fought to hold back tears of anger and frustration.*

hold off (sth/doing sth) to delay sth □ *menangguhkan (sst/membuat sst)*

hold on 1 to wait or stop for a moment □ *tunggu sebentar*: *Hold on. I'll be with you in a minute.* **2** to manage in a difficult or dangerous situation □ *bertahan*: *They managed to hold on until a rescue party arrived.*

hold onto sb/sth to hold sb/sth tightly □ *memegang sso/sst kuat-kuat*: *The boy held onto his mother because he didn't want her to go.*

hold onto sth to keep sth; to not give or sell sth □ *terus menyimpan/tdk menjual sst*: *They've offered me a lot of money for this painting, but I'm going to hold onto it.*

hold out to last (in a difficult situation) □ *bertahan; boleh tahan lagi*: *How long will our supply of water hold out?*

hold sth out to offer sth by moving it towards a person or animal in your hand □ *menghulurkan*: *He held out a carrot to the horse.*

hold out for sth (*informal*) to cause a delay while you continue to ask for sth □ *melewat-lewatkan utk mendapatkan sst*: *Union members are holding out for a better pay offer.*

hold sb/sth up to make sb/sth late; to cause a delay □ *menjadikan sso/sst terlambat; melambatkan*: *We were held up by the traffic.*

hold up sth to steal from a bank, shop, vehicle, etc. using a gun □ *merompak (bank, kedai, dll)*

hold² /həʊld/ *noun* **1** [C] the act or manner of having sb/sth in your hand(s) □ *pegangan*: *to have a firm hold on the rope* ♦ *judo/wrestling holds* **2** [sing] **a hold (on/over sb/sth)** influence or control □ *pengaruh*: *The new government has strengthened its hold on the country.* **3** [C] the part of a ship or an aircraft where goods are stored □ *palka; peraka*: *Five men were found hiding in the ship's hold.*

IDM **catch, get, grab, take, etc. hold (of sb/sth) 1** to take sb/sth in your hands □ *menyambar (sso/sst)*: *I managed to catch hold of the dog before it ran out into the road.* **2** to take control of sb/sth; to start to have an effect on sb/sth □ *menguasai atau mempengaruhi sso/sst*: *Mass hysteria seemed to have taken hold of the crowd.*

get/keep/take a grip/hold (on yourself) ➔ **grip¹**

get hold of sb to find sb or make contact with sb □ *menghubungi sso*: *I've been trying to get hold of the complaints department all morning.*

get hold of sth to find sth that will be useful □ *mendapatkan sst*: *I must try and get hold of a good second-hand bicycle.*

on hold 1 delayed until a later time or date □ *menangguhkan*: *We'll have to put our holiday plans on hold until we've saved enough money.* **2** if a person on the telephone is put **on hold**, they have to wait until the person that they want to talk to is free □ *menunggu*: *I'll just pop you on hold.*

holdall /ˈhəʊldɔːl/ *noun* [C] a large bag that is used for carrying clothes, etc. when you are travelling □ *beg besar (utk pakaian, dll)* ➔ picture at **bag**

holder /ˈhəʊldə(r)/ *noun* [C] [in compounds] **1** a person who has or holds sth □ *pemegang; penyandang*: *a season-ticket holder* ♦ *the world record holder in the 100 metres* ♦ *holders of European passports* **2** something that contains or holds sth □ *pemegang*: *a toothbrush holder*

'hold-up *noun* [C] **1** a delay □ *gendala; sst yg menyebabkan kelambatan*: *'What's the hold-up?' 'There's been an accident ahead of us.'* **2** the act of stealing from a bank, etc. using a gun □ *rompakan*: *The gang have carried out three hold-ups of high street banks.*

hole /həʊl/ *noun* [C] **1** an opening; an empty space in sth solid □ *lubang*: *The pavement is full of holes.* ◆ *There are holes in my socks.* ◆ *I've got a hole in my tooth.* **2** the place where an animal lives in the ground or in a tree □ *lubang; korok*: *a mouse hole* **3** (in the sport of **golf**) the hole in the ground that you must hit the ball into. Each section of the **golf course** (= the large area of grass where you play) is also called a hole □ *lubang*: *an eighteen-hole golf course*

holiday /ˈhɒlədeɪ/ *noun* **1** (*AmE* **vacation**) [C,U] a period of rest from work or school (often when you go and stay away from home) □ *cuti; percutian; bercuti*: *We're going to Italy for our summer holidays this year.* ◆ *How much holiday do you get a year in your new job?* ◆ *Mr Phillips isn't here this week. He's away on holiday.* ◆ *I'm going to take a week's holiday in May and spend it at home.* ◆ *the school/Christmas/Easter/summer holidays* **2** [C] a day of rest when many people do not go to work, school, etc. often for religious or national celebrations □ *hari cuti/kelepasan*: *Next Monday is a holiday.* ◆ *New Year's Day is a bank/public holiday in Britain.*

> **MORE** **Holiday** in this sense is used in both British and American English. A day when you choose not go to work is also called a **day off**: *I'm having two days off next week when we move house.* **Leave** is time when you do not go to work for a special reason: *sick leave* ◆ *maternity leave* (= for a mother with a new baby) ◆ *unpaid leave*.

TOPIC

Holidays

You can choose your holiday from a **brochure** and book it at a **travel agent's** or you can do it yourself online. Some people do a lot of **sightseeing** when they **go on holiday**. They **look round** historical buildings and **take photographs**. Others prefer to **sunbathe** on a **beach** and **go swimming** or **snorkelling**. Many people go on a **package holiday** which is organized by a company, and they pay a fixed price that includes their travel, accommodation, etc. They might stay in a large hotel in a holiday **resort**. Other people **go backpacking** (= travel cheaply, carrying their clothes in a backpack), **go on safari** (= take a trip to see wild animals, especially in East Africa), or go on a **cruise** (= a holiday on a large ship). Most people like to buy some **souvenirs** before they go home.

'holiday camp *noun* [C] (*BrE*) a place that provides a place to stay and organized entertainment for people on holiday □ *kawasan percutian*

holidaymaker /ˈhɒlədeɪmeɪkə(r); -dɪmeɪ-/ *noun* [C] (*BrE*) a person who is away from home on holiday □ *orang yg bercuti*

hole → home

hollow¹ /ˈhɒləʊ/ *adj* **1** with a hole or empty space inside □ *gerongang; lompang*: *a hollow tree* **2** (used about parts of the face) sinking deep into the face □ *cengkung*: *hollow cheeks* ◆ *hollow-eyed* **3** (used about a sound) seeming to come from a **hollow** place □ *lompong*: *hollow footsteps* **4** not sincere □ *kosong; palsu*: *a hollow laugh/voice* ◆ *hollow promises/threats*

hollow² /ˈhɒləʊ/ *noun* [C] an area that is lower than the land around it □ *lekuk*

hollow³ /ˈhɒləʊ/ *verb*

PHR V **hollow sth out** to take out the inside part of sth □ *mengorek isi sst*

holly /ˈhɒli/ *noun* [U] a plant that has shiny dark green leaves with sharp points and red **berries** (= small round fruit) in the winter. It is often used as a Christmas decoration. □ *pokok holi*

holocaust /ˈhɒləkɔːst (*AmE* also) / *noun* [C] a situation where a great many things are destroyed and a great many people die □ *malapetaka; kemusnahan*: *a nuclear holocaust*

hologram /ˈhɒləɡræm (*AmE* also) / *noun* [C] an image or picture which appears to stand out from the flat surface it is on when light falls on it □ *hologram*

holster /ˈhəʊlstə(r)/ *noun* [C] a leather case used for carrying a gun that is fixed to a belt or worn under the arm □ *sarung pistol*

holy /ˈhəʊli/ *adj* (**holier**; **holiest**) **1** connected with God or with religion and therefore very special or important □ *suci*: *the Holy Bible* ◆ *holy water* ◆ *The Koran is the holy book of Islam.* **2** (used about a person) good in a moral and religious way □ *warak; soleh*: *a holy life/man* ▶**holiness** *noun* [U]

homage /ˈhɒmɪdʒ/ *noun* [U,C, usually sing] (*formal*) **homage** (**to sb/sth**) something that is said or done to show respect publicly for sb □ *penghormatan*: *to pay/do homage to the dead leader*

home¹ /həʊm/ *noun* **1** [C,U] the place where you live or where you feel that you belong □ *rumah; tempat tinggal*: *She left home* (= left her parents' house and began an independent life) *at the age of 21.* ◆ *Children from broken homes* (= whose parents are divorced) *sometimes have learning difficulties.* ◆ *That old house would make an ideal family home.* ⊃ note at **house** ⊃ picture on **page P9**

> **HELP** Be careful. The preposition *to* is not used before 'home': *It's time to go home.* ◆ *She's usually tired when she gets/arrives home.* If you want to talk about somebody else's home you have to say: *at Jane and Andy's* or: *at Jane and Andy's place/house.*

2 [C] a place that provides care for a particular type of person or for animals □ *rumah*: *a children's home* (= for children who have no parents to look after them) ◆ *an old people's home*

VOWELS iː see i any ɪ sit e ten æ hat ɑː father ɒ got ɔː saw ʊ put uː too u usual

3 [sing] **the home of sth** the place where sth began □ *tempat bermulanya*: *Greece is said to be the home of democracy.*

IDM at home 1 in your house, flat, etc. □ *di rumah*: *Is anybody at home?* ◆ *Tomorrow we're staying at home all day.*

> **HELP** In American English **home** is often used without the preposition **at**: *Is anybody home?*

2 comfortable, as if you were in your own home □ *selesa; spt (di) rumah sendiri*: *Please make yourself at home.* ◆ *I felt quite at home on the ship.* **3** (used in sport) played in the town to which the team belongs □ *di tempat sendiri*: *Liverpool are playing at home on Saturday.* **OPP away**

romp home/to victory ⊃ **romp**

home² /həʊm/ *adj* [only *before* a noun] **1** connected with home □ *rumah; di rumah; kampung halaman; keluarga*: *home cooking* ◆ *your home address/town* ◆ *a happy home life* (= with your family) **2** (*especially BrE*) connected with your own country, not with a foreign country □ *dlm negeri; tempatan*: *The Home Secretary is responsible for home affairs.* **3** (used in sport) connected with a team's own sports ground □ *di tempat sendiri; tuan rumah*: *The home team has a lot of support.* ◆ *a home game* **OPP away**

home³ /həʊm/ *adv* at, in or to your home or home country □ *di/ke rumah atau negara sendiri*: *We must be getting home soon.* ◆ *She'll be flying home for New Year.*

IDM bring sth home to sb to make sb understand sth fully □ *menyedarkan sso ttg sst*

drive sth home (to sb) ⊃ **drive¹**

home⁴ /həʊm/ *verb*

PHR V home in on sb/sth to move towards sb/sth □ *menuju ke sso/sst*: *The police homed in on the house where the thieves were hiding.*

homecoming /ˈhəʊmkʌmɪŋ/ *noun* [C,U] the act of returning home, especially when you have been away for a long time □ *kepulangan*

home-grown *adj* (used about fruit and vegetables) grown in your own garden □ *ditanam sendiri*

homeland /ˈhəʊmlænd/ *noun* [sing] the country where you were born or that your parents came from, or to which you feel you belong □ *tanah air; tanah tumpah darah*: *Many refugees have been forced to leave their homeland.*

homeless /ˈhəʊmləs/ *adj* **1** having no home □ *tdk ada rumah/tempat tinggal* **2 the homeless** *noun* [pl] people who have no home □ *orang yg tdk ada rumah/tempat tinggal* ▶ **homelessness** *noun* [U]

homely /ˈhəʊmli/ *adj* (**homelier**; **homeliest**) (*BrE*) (used about a place) simple but also pleasant or welcoming □ *sederhana*

home-made *adj* made at home; not bought in a shop □ *buatan sendiri*: *home-made cakes*

the Home Office *noun* [sing] the department of the UK government that is responsible for the law, the police and prisons within the UK and for decisions about who can enter the country □ *Kementerian Dlm Negeri*

homeopath (*BrE* also **homoeopath**) /ˈhəʊmiəpæθ/ (*AmE* also) / *noun* [C] a person who treats sick people using **homeopathy** □ *ahli homeopati*

homeopathy (*BrE* also **homoeopathy**) /ˌhəʊmiˈɒpəθi/ (*AmE* also) / *noun* [U] the treatment of a disease by giving very small amounts of a drug that would cause the disease if given in large amounts □ *homeopati* ▶ **homeopathic** (*BrE* also **homoeopathic**) /ˌhəʊmiəˈpæθɪk/ (*AmE* also) / *adj*: *homeopathic medicine*

home page *noun* [C] the first of a number of pages of information on the Internet that belongs to a person or an organization. A **home page** contains connections to other pages of information. □ *laman utama*

the Home Secretary *noun* [C] (*BrE*) the minister who is in charge of the Home Office □ *Menteri Dlm Negeri* ⊃ look at **the Foreign Secretary**

homesick /ˈhəʊmsɪk/ *adj* **homesick (for sb/sth)** sad because you are away from home and you miss it □ *merindui kampung halaman*: *She was very homesick for Canada.* ▶ **homesickness** *noun* [U]

hometown /ˈhəʊmtaʊn/ *noun* [C] the place where you were born or lived as a child □ *kampung halaman*

homeward /ˈhəʊmwəd/ *adj*, *adv* (also **homewards**) going towards home □ *pulang*: *the homeward journey* ◆ *to travel homewards*

homework /ˈhəʊmwɜːk/ *noun* [U] work that is given by teachers for students to do at home □ *kerja rumah*: *Have we got any homework?* ◆ *We've got a translation to do for homework.* ◆ *I haven't done my homework yet.* ⊃ note at **study** ⊃ look at **housework**

> **GRAMMAR Homework** is uncountable, so we have to say **a piece of homework** (not 'a homework') and **a lot of homework** (not 'homeworks').

homicidal /ˌhɒmɪˈsaɪdl/ *adj* likely to murder sb □ *cenderung membunuh*: *a homicidal maniac*

homicide /ˈhɒmɪsaɪd/ *noun* [C,U] (*especially AmE*) the illegal killing of one person by another; murder □ *pembunuhan; homisid*

homoeopath, homoeopathy (*BrE*) = **homeopath, homeopathy**

homonym /ˈhɒmənɪm/ (*AmE* also) / *noun* [C] a word that is spelt or pronounced like another word but that has a different meaning □ *homonim*

homophobia /ˌhɒməˈfəʊbiə; ˌhəʊm-/ noun [U] a strong dislike and fear of **homosexual** people □ *homofobia* ▶**homophobic** *adj*

homophone /ˈhɒməfəʊn/ *noun* [C] a word that is pronounced the same as another word but that has a different spelling and meaning □ *homofon*: *'Flower' and 'flour' are homophones.*

homosexual /ˌhəʊməˈsekʃuəl/ (*BrE also* ˌhɒm-/ *adj* sexually attracted to people of the same sex □ *homoseksual* ⊃ look at **bisexual**, **gay**, **heterosexual**, **lesbian** ▶**homosexual** noun [C] ▶**homosexuality** /ˌhəʊməˌsekʃuˈæləti/ (*BrE also* ˌhɒm-/ *noun* [U]

Hon *abbr* 1 = **Honorary**(2): *Hon President* 2 = **Honourable**(2)

honest /ˈɒnɪst/ *adj* 1 (used about a person) telling the truth and never stealing or cheating □ *jujur; terus terang*: *Just be honest—do you like this skirt or not?* ◆ *To be honest, I don't think that's a very good idea.* 2 showing honest qualities □ *jujur; ikhlas*: *an honest face* ◆ *I'd like your honest opinion, please.* **OPP** for both meanings **dishonest** ▶**honesty** *noun* [U] **OPP** **dishonesty**

honestly /ˈɒnɪstli/ *adv* 1 in an honest way □ *secara jujur; dgn terus terang*: *He tried to answer the lawyer's questions honestly.* 2 used for emphasizing that what you are saying is true □ *betul*: *I honestly don't know where she has gone.* 3 used for expressing disapproval □ *alamak; betullah*: *Honestly! What a mess!*

honey /ˈhʌni/ *noun* 1 [U] the sweet sticky substance that is made by **bees** (= black and yellow insects) and that people eat □ *madu* ⊃ picture on **page P16** 2 [C] (*informal*) a person that you like or love; a way of addressing sb that you like or love □ *sayang*: *He's a real honey—always ready to help.* ◆ *Honey, I'm home.*

honeycomb /ˈhʌnikəʊm/ *noun* [C,U] a structure of shapes with six sides, in which bees keep their eggs and **honey** □ *sarang lebah (madu); indung madu*

honeymoon /ˈhʌnimuːn/ *noun* [C] a holiday that is taken by two people who have just got married □ *bulan madu*: *We had our first argument while we were on our honeymoon.*

honk /hɒŋk/ (*AmE also*) / *verb* [I,T] to sound the horn of a car; to make this sound □ *membunyikan hon kereta*

honorable (*AmE*) = **honourable**

honorary /ˈɒnərəri/ *adj* 1 given as an honour (without the person needing the usual certificates, etc.) □ *kehormat*: *to be awarded an honorary degree* 2 often **Honorary** (*abbr* **Hon**) not paid □ *kehormat*: *He is the Honorary President.*

honour[1] (*AmE* **honor**) /ˈɒnə(r)/ *noun* 1 [U] the respect from other people that a person, country, etc. gets because of high standards of behaviour and moral character □ *penghormatan; terhormat*: *the guest of honour* (= the most important one) ⊃ look at **dishonour** 2 [sing] (*formal*) something that gives pride or pleasure □ *penghormatan; kebanggaan*: *It was a great honour to be asked to speak at the conference.* 3 [U] the quality of doing what is morally right □ *kehormatan; maruah; nama baik*: *I give you my word of honour.* 4 **Honours** [pl] (*abbr* **Hons**) a university course that is of a higher level than a basic course □ *kepujian*: *a First Class Honours degree* 5 (*also* **honours**) [pl] if you pass an exam **with honours**, you receive a special mark for having achieved a very high standard □ *kepujian*
IDM **in honour of sb/sth; in sb/sth's honour** out of respect for sb/sth □ *sempena atau sebagai penghormatan bagi sso/sst*: *A party was given in honour of the guests from Bonn.*

honour[2] (*AmE* **honor**) /ˈɒnə(r)/ *verb* [T] 1 **honour sb/sth (with sth)** to show great (public) respect for sb/sth or to give sb pride or pleasure □ *menghormati; berbesar hati*: *I am very honoured by the confidence you have shown in me.* 2 to do what you have agreed or promised □ *menunaikan (janji, dll)*

honourable (*AmE* **honorable**) /ˈɒnərəbl/ *adj* 1 acting in a way that makes people respect you; having or showing honour □ *mulia; berhormat* **OPP** **dishonourable** 2 [only before a noun] **the Honourable** (*abbr* **the Hon**) a title that is given to some high officials and to Members of Parliament when they are speaking to each other □ *Yg Berhormat* ▶**honourably** /-əbli/ *adv*

Hons /ɒnz/ *abbr* = **Honours**[1](4): *John North BSc (Hons)*

hood /hʊd/ *noun* [C] 1 the part of a coat, etc. that you pull up to cover your head and neck in bad weather □ *hud; tudung (yg dilekatkan pd baju, kot, dsb)* ⊃ picture at **hat** 2 a piece of cloth that covers sb's head so that they cannot be recognized or so that they cannot see □ *tudung* 3 (*especially BrE*) a folding cover for a car, etc. □ *hud; bumbung*: *We drove all the way with the hood down.* 4 (*AmE*) = **bonnet**(2)

hoody (*also* **hoodie**) /ˈhʊdi/ *noun* [C] (*pl* **hoodies**) (*BrE informal*) a jacket or **sweatshirt** (= a warm piece of clothing with long sleeves) with a **hood** □ *baju sejuk hud* ⊃ picture on **page P1**

hoof /huːf/ *noun* [C] (*pl* **hoofs** *or* **hooves** /huːvz/) the hard part of the foot of horses and some other animals □ *kuku; telapuk; huf* ⊃ look at **paw** ⊃ picture at **horse** ⊃ picture on **page P12**

hook[1] /hʊk/ *noun* [C] 1 a curved piece of metal, plastic, etc. that is used for hanging things on, catching fish with, etc. □ *cangkuk; mata kail*: *Put your coat on the hook over there.* ◆ *a fish hook* 2 (used in boxing) a way of hitting sb that is done with the arm bent □ *tumbukan sauk*: *a right hook* (= with the right arm)
IDM **off the hook** (used about the top part of a telephone) not in position, so that telephone calls cannot be received □ *(gagang telefon) tdk diletakkan dgn betul*
get/let sb off the hook (*informal*) to free yourself or sb else from a difficult situation or punishment

□ *melepaskan sso (drpd kesusahan atau hukuman)*: *My father paid the money I owed and got me off the hook.*

hook² /hʊk/ *verb* 1 [I,T] to fasten or catch sth with a hook or in the shape of a hook; to be fastened in this way □ *mencangkukkan; menyangkutkan*: *We hooked the trailer to the back of our car.* ◆ *The curtain simply hooks onto the rail.* 2 [T] to put sth around sth else so that you can hold on to it or move it □ *menyangkutkan*: *Hook the rope through your belt.*
PHR V **hook (sth) up (to sth)** to connect sb/sth to a piece of electronic equipment or to a power supply □ *menyambungkan (sso/sst) dgn (sst)*

hooks

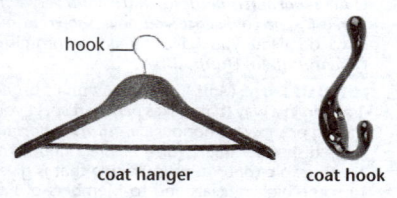

coat hanger   coat hook

ˌhook and ˈeye *noun* [C] a thing that is used for fastening clothes □ *kancing cangkuk dan mata* ➲ picture at **button**

hooked /hʊkt/ *adj* 1 shaped like a hook □ *bengkok*: *a hooked nose* 2 [not before a noun] (*informal*) **hooked (on sth)** needing sth that is bad for you, especially drugs □ *ketagih*: *to be hooked on gambling* **SYN** **addicted** 3 [not before a noun] (*informal*) **hooked (on sth)** enjoying sth very much, so that you want to do it, see it, etc. as much as possible □ *sangat meminati sst*: *Suzi is hooked on computer games.*

hooky /ˈhʊki/ (*AmE*)
IDM **play hooky** (*old-fashioned, informal*) = **play truant**

hooligan /ˈhuːlɪɡən/ *noun* [C] a person who behaves in a violent and aggressive way in public places □ *samseng*: *football hooligans* ➲ look at **lout, yob** ▶ **hooliganism** /ˈhuːlɪɡənɪzəm/ *noun* [U]

hoop /huːp/ *noun* [C] a large metal or plastic ring □ *relang; gelung*

hooray = **hurray**

hoot¹ /huːt/ *verb* [I,T] (*BrE*) to sound the horn of a car or to make a loud noise □ *membunyikan hon; berbuat bising dgn kuat*: *The driver hooted (his horn) at the dog but it wouldn't move.* ◆ *They hooted with laughter at the suggestion.*

hoot² /huːt/ *noun* 1 [C] (*especially BrE*) a short loud laugh or shout □ *teriakan atau ketawa yg kuat*: *hoots of laughter* 2 [sing] (*spoken*) a situation or a person that is very funny □ *(sso/sst yg) lucu*: *Bob is a real hoot!* 3 [C] (*BrE*) the loud sound that is made by the horn of a vehicle □ *bunyi hon; pon-pon* 4 [C] the cry of an **owl** (= a bird with large round eyes that hunts animals at night) □ *bunyi burung hantu*

hoover /ˈhuːvə(r)/ *verb* [I,T] (*BrE*) to clean a carpet, etc. with a machine that sucks up the dirt □ *membersihkan dgn pembersih vakum*: *The bedroom carpet needs hoovering.* **SYN** **vacuum**
▶ **Hoover™** *noun* [C] **SYN** **vacuum cleaner**

hooves *plural* of **hoof**

hop¹ /hɒp/ *verb* [I] (**hopping**; **hopped**) 1 (used about a person) to jump on one leg □ *meloncat (-loncat) dgn sebelah kaki*: *I twisted my ankle so badly I had to hop all the way back to the car.* 2 (used about an animal or a bird) to jump with both or all feet together □ *meloncat; melompat* 3 **hop (from sth to sth)** to change quickly from one activity or subject to another □ *melompat (drpd satu perkara ke satu perkara lain, dsb)*
IDM **Hop it!** (*slang*) Go away! □ *Pergi!*
PHR V **hop in/into sth**; **hop out/out of sth** (*informal*) to get in or out of a car, etc. (quickly) □ *masuk/naik sst; melompat keluar sst*
hop on/onto sth; **hop off sth** (*informal*) to get onto/off a bus, etc. (quickly) □ *melompat naik sst; melompat keluar*

hop² /hɒp/ *noun* 1 [C] a short jump by a person on one leg or by a bird or an animal with its feet together □ *loncatan; lompatan* 2 [C] a tall climbing plant with flowers □ *bunga hop* 3 **hops** [pl] the flowers of this plant that are used in making beer □ *bunga hop*

hop

He's hopping.   She's jumping.

The ball is bouncing.

hope¹ /həʊp/ *verb* [I,T] **hope that …**; **hope to do sth**; **hope (for sth)** to want sth to happen or be true □ *harap; berharap*: *I hope that you feel better soon.* ◆ *Hoping to hear from you soon* (= at the end of a letter or email). ◆ *'Is it raining?' 'I hope not. I haven't got a coat with me.'* ◆ *'Are you coming to London with us?' 'I'm not sure yet but I hope so.'*

hope² /həʊp/ noun 1 [C,U] (a) hope (of/for sth); (a) hope of doing sth; (a) hope that ... the feeling of wanting sth to happen and thinking that it will □ *harapan*: *What hope is there for the future?* ♦ *There is no hope of finding anybody else alive.* ♦ *David has high hopes of becoming a jockey* (= is very confident about it). ♦ *She never gave up hope that a cure for the disease would be found.* 2 [sing] a person, a thing or a situation that will help you get what you want □ *harapan*: *Please can you help me? You're my last hope.*
IDM dash sb's hopes (of sth/of doing sth) ⊃ dash¹
in the hope of sth/that ... because you want sth to happen □ ... *dgn harapan (agar)*: *I came here in the hope that we could talk privately.*
pin (all) your hopes on sb/sth ⊃ pin²
a ray of hope ⊃ ray

hopeful /'həʊpfl/ adj 1 hopeful (about sth); hopeful that ... believing that sth that you want will happen □ *berasa ada harapan*: *He's very hopeful about the success of the business.* ♦ *The ministers seem hopeful that an agreement will be reached.* **SYN** optimistic 2 making you think that sth good will happen □ *memberi harapan*: *a hopeful sign* **SYN** promising

hopefully /'həʊpfəli/ adv 1 (*informal*) used to say what you hope will happen □ *harap-harap; semoga*: *Hopefully, we'll be finished by 6 o'clock.* 2 showing hope □ *dgn penuh harapan*: *She smiled hopefully at me, waiting for my answer.*

hopeless /'həʊpləs/ adj 1 giving no hope that sth/sb will be successful or get better □ *tdk ada harapan/tdk ada gunanya*: *It's hopeless. There is nothing we can do.* 2 (*informal*) hopeless (at sth) (used about a person) often doing things wrong; very bad at doing sth □ *tdk guna langsung; tdk pandai langsung*: *I'm absolutely hopeless at tennis.* ▶hopelessly adv: *They were hopelessly lost.* ▶hopelessness noun [U]

horde /hɔːd/ noun [C] a very large number of people □ *berduyun-duyun orang*

horizon /həˈraɪzn/ noun 1 [sing] the line where the earth and sky appear to meet □ *kaki langit; ufuk*: *The ship appeared and disappeared over the horizon.* ⊃ picture on **page P10** 2 horizons [pl] the limits of your knowledge or experience □ *batas pengetahuan/pengalaman*: *Foreign travel is a good way of expanding your horizons.*
IDM on the horizon likely to happen soon □ *nampaknya akan berlaku tdk lama lagi*: *There are further job cuts on the horizon.*

horizontal /ˌhɒrɪˈzɒntl/ adj going from side to side, not up and down; flat or level □ *mendatar; mengufuk; (palang) lintang*: *horizontal lines* ♦ *The gymnasts were exercising on the horizontal bars.* ⊃ look at **vertical, perpendicular** ⊃ picture at **line** ▶horizontally /-təli/ adv

hormone /'hɔːməʊn/ noun [C] a substance in your body that influences how you grow and develop □ *hormon*

horn /hɔːn/ noun [C] 1 one of the hard pointed things that some animals have on their heads □ *tanduk; cula; sumbu* ⊃ picture at **goat** ⊃ picture on **page P12** 2 one of the group of metal musical instruments that you play by blowing into them □ *hon*: *the French horn* ⊃ picture at **music** 3 the thing in a car, etc. that gives a loud warning sound □ *hon kereta, dsb*: *Don't sound your horn late at night.* ⊃ picture at **car**

horoscope /'hɒrəskəʊp/ (*AmE* also) / noun [C] (also stars [pl]) a statement about what is going to happen to a person in the future, based on the position of the stars and planets when they were born □ *horoskop*: *What does my horoscope for next week say?* ⊃ note at **zodiac** ⊃ look at **astrology**

horrendous /hɒˈrendəs/ (*AmE usually*) / adj (*informal*) very bad or unpleasant □ *teruk; dahsyat*: *The queues here are absolutely horrendous.* ▶horrendously adv

horrible /'hɒrəbl/ (*AmE* also) / adj 1 (*informal*) bad or unpleasant □ *teruk; dahsyat*: *This coffee tastes horrible!* ♦ *Don't be so horrible* (= unkind)! ♦ *I've got a horrible feeling that I've forgotten something.* ⊃ note at **bad** 2 shocking and/or frightening □ *(yg) mengerikan/menakutkan*: *a horrible murder/death/nightmare* **SYN** for both meanings **terrible** ▶horribly /-əbli/ adv

horrid /'hɒrɪd/ (*AmE* also) / adj (*informal*) very unpleasant or unkind □ *teruk; bersikap kasar, dsb*: *horrid weather* ♦ *I'm sorry that I was so horrid last night.* **SYN** horrible

horrific /həˈrɪfɪk/ adj 1 extremely bad and shocking or frightening □ *yg amat mengerikan/menakutkan*: *a horrific murder/accident/attack* 2 (*informal*) very bad or unpleasant □ *sangat teruk*: ▶horrifically /-kli/ adv: *horrifically expensive*

horrify /'hɒrɪfaɪ/ (*AmE usually*) / verb [T] (horrifying; horrifies; pt, pp horrified) to make sb feel extremely shocked, disgusted or frightened □ *amat memeranjatkan/menjijikkan/menakutkan* ▶horrified adj: *He was horrified when he discovered the truth.* ▶horrifying adj

horror /'hɒrə(r)/ (*AmE usually*) / noun 1 [U, sing] a feeling of great fear or shock □ *perasaan takut/gerun yg amat sangat*: *They watched in horror as the building collapsed.* 2 [C,U] something that makes you feel frightened or shocked □ *(sst yg) menakutkan/memeranjatkan; (filem, cerita, dsb) seram*: *a horror film/story* ♦ *the horrors of war*

horse /hɔːs/ noun 1 [C] a large animal that is used for riding on or for pulling or carrying heavy loads □ *kuda*: *a horse and cart*

MORE Horse is often used for both males and females. A male horse is a **stallion**, a female horse is a **mare** and a young horse is a **foal**.

2 the horses [pl] (*informal*) horse racing □ *lumba kuda*: *He won some money on the horses.*
IDM on horseback sitting on a horse □ *menunggang kuda; berkuda*

horseback riding → hostage

horse

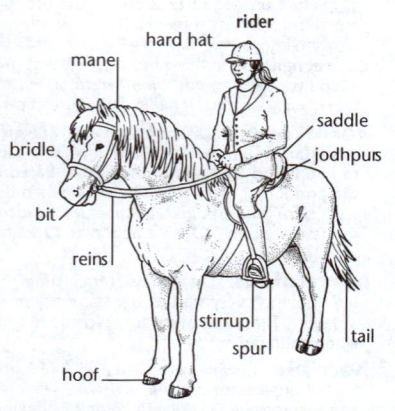

labelled diagram: rider, hard hat, mane, saddle, bridle, jodhpurs, bit, reins, stirrup, spur, tail, hoof

> **MORE** Police officers who ride horses are called **mounted police**.

horseback riding (*AmE*) = **riding**

horse chestnut *noun* [C] **1** a large tall tree with pink or white flowers, and nuts that grow inside cases that are covered with sharp points □ *pokok berangan kuda* **2** (also *informal* **conker**) the smooth brown nut from this tree □ *berangan kuda*

horseman /'hɔːsmən/ *noun* [C] (*pl* -**men** /-mən/) a man who rides a horse □ *penunggang kuda (lelaki): an experienced horseman*

horsepower /'hɔːspaʊə(r)/ *noun* [C] (*pl* **horsepower**) (*abbr* **h.p.**) a measure of the power of an engine □ *kuasa kuda*

horse racing (also **racing**) *noun* [U] the sport in which a **jockey** rides a horse in a race to win money □ *lumba kuda*

> **MORE** Horse racing takes place at a **racecourse**. People often **bet** on the results of horse races.

⊃ picture on **page P5**

horseshoe /'hɔːsʃuː; 'hɔːʃʃuː/ (also **shoe**) *noun* [C] a piece of metal in the shape of a U that is fixed to the bottom of a horse's foot. □ *ladam* ❶ Some people believe that horseshoes bring good luck.

horsewoman /'hɔːswʊmən/ *noun* [C] (*pl* -**women** /-wɪmɪn/) a woman who rides a horse □ *penunggang kuda (wanita)*

horticulture /'hɔːtɪkʌltʃə(r)/ *noun* [U] the study or practice of growing flowers, fruit and vegetables □ *hortikultur: a college of agriculture and horticulture* ▶ **horticultural** /ˌhɔːtɪ'kʌltʃərəl/ *adj*

hose /həʊz/ (also **hosepipe** /'həʊzpaɪp/) *noun* [C,U] a long rubber or plastic tube that water can flow through □ *hos; paip getah* ⊃ picture at **garden**

hospice /'hɒspɪs/ *noun* [C] a special hospital where people who are dying are cared for □ *hospis*

hospitable /hɒ'spɪtəbl; 'hɒspɪtəbl/ *adj* (used about a person) friendly and kind to visitors □ *ramah mesra serta suka menerima tetamu* **OPP** **inhospitable**

hospital /'hɒspɪtl/ *noun* [C] a place where ill or injured people are treated □ *hospital: He was rushed to hospital in an ambulance.* ◆ *to be admitted to/discharged from hospital* ◆ *a psychiatric/mental hospital* ⊃ note at **disease, doctor, hurt**

> **HELP** If a person goes **to hospital** or is **in hospital** (without 'the' in British English), he/she is a patient receiving treatment there: *His mother's in hospital.* ◆ *She cut her hand and had to go to hospital.* 'The hospital' refers to one particular hospital, or indicates that the person is only visiting the building temporarily: *He went to the hospital to visit Jana.*

> **TOPIC**
> ### Hospitals
> If somebody has an **accident**, they may need to go to **hospital** (**the hospital** in American English) for medical **treatment**. Dial *999* and call an **ambulance**. They will be taken first to **A & E** (= the accident and emergency department). If you **cut** yourself very badly, you might need **stitches** (= small lines of thread used to sew your skin together). If your arm, ankle, etc. is **painful** and **swollen**, a doctor might take an **X-ray** to see if it is **broken**. A person who is being treated in a hospital by **doctors** and **nurses** is a **patient**. If people **have an operation/have surgery**, it is performed by a **surgeon** in an **operating theatre**. Patients sleep in a **ward** (= a room shared with other patients). The fixed times during the day when you are allowed to visit somebody in hospital are called **visiting hours**.

hospitality /ˌhɒspɪ'tæləti/ *noun* [U] looking after guests and being friendly and welcoming towards them □ *layanan baik; ketamuan; keraian*

host /həʊst/ *noun* [C] **1** a person who invites guests to their house, etc. and provides them with food, drink, etc. □ *tuan rumah: It's polite to write a thank-you letter to your host.* ◆ *I'll be staying with a host family while I study English in the UK.* ⊃ look at **hostess 2** a person who introduces a TV or radio show and talks to the guests □ *pengacara; hos: a game show host* **3 a host of sth** a large number of people or things □ *sangat banyak: I've got a whole host of things I want to discuss with him.* ▶ **host** *verb* [T]: *The city is aiming to host the Olympic Games in ten years' time.*

hostage /'hɒstɪdʒ/ *noun* [C] a person who is caught and kept prisoner by a person or group. He or she may be killed or injured if the person or group who is holding them does not get what they are asking for □ *tawanan*: *The gunmen tried to take the staff hostage.* ◆ *The hijackers say they will hold the passengers hostage until their demands are met.* ➲ look at **ransom**

hostel /'hɒstl/ *noun* [C] **1** a place like a cheap hotel where people can stay when they are living away from home □ *asrama; hostel*: *a youth hostel* ◆ *a student hostel* **2** (*BrE*) a building where people who have no home can stay for a short time □ *asrama*

hostess /'həʊstəs (*BrE also*) -stes/ *noun* [C] **1** a woman who invites guests to her house, etc. and provides them with food, drink, etc. □ *tuan rumah (wanita)* ➲ look at **host 2** a woman who introduces a TV or radio show and talks to the guests □ *pengacara*

hostile /'hɒstaɪl (*AmE also*) / *adj* hostile (to/towards sb/sth) having very strong feelings against sb/sth □ *(yg) menunjukkan sikap permusuhan atau menentang*: *a hostile crowd* ◆ *They are very hostile to any change.*

hostility /hɒ'stɪləti/ *noun* **1** [U] hostility (to/towards sth) very strong feelings against sth □ *permusuhan; sikap bermusuh; penentangan*: *She didn't say anything but I could sense her hostility.* **2** hostilities [pl] fighting in a war □ *pertempuran*

hot¹ /hɒt/ *adj* (hotter; hottest) **1** having a high temperature □ *panas*: *Can I open the window? I'm really hot.* ◆ *It's hot today, isn't it?* ◆ *It was boiling hot (= very hot) on the beach.* ◆ *Be careful—the plates are hot.* ◆ *a hot meal (= one that has been cooked)* ➲ note at **cold** ➲ look at **humid 2** (used about food) causing a burning feeling in your mouth □ *pedas*: *hot curry* SYN **spicy** **3** (*informal*) difficult or dangerous to deal with □ *susah hendak diurus atau ditangani*: *The defenders found the Italian strikers too hot to handle.* **4** (*informal*) exciting and popular □ *hebat*: *This band is hot stuff!*

IDM in hot pursuit following sb who is moving fast □ *mengejar kuat-kuat*

hot² /hɒt/ *verb* (hotting; hotted)

PHR V hot up (*BrE informal*) to become more exciting □ *semakin hangat/hebat*: *The election campaign has really hotted up in the past few days.*

hot-'air balloon = **balloon**(2)

'hot dog *noun* [C] a hot **sausage** (= meat formed in a long thin shape) in a soft bread roll □ *hot dog* ➲ picture on page P16

hotel /həʊ'tel/ *noun* [C] a place where you pay to stay when you are on holiday or travelling □ *hotel*: *to stay in/at a hotel* ◆ *I've booked a double room at the Grand Hotel.* ◆ *a two-star hotel*

TOPIC

Hotels

You make a **reservation** for a **double**, **single** or **twin-bedded/twin** (= with two single beds) room at a hotel. When you arrive you **check in** or **register** at **reception** and when you leave you **check out**. If your accommodation is **full board**, all your meals are included, and **half board** includes breakfast and an evening meal. If you stay in a **motel**, you can park your car near your room. A **bed and breakfast (B and B)** is a private house which provides a room for the night and breakfast.

hotelier /həʊ'teliə(r); -lieɪ/ *noun* [C] a person who owns or manages a hotel □ *pemilik/pengurus hotel*

hothouse /'hɒthaʊs/ *noun* [C] a heated glass building where plants are grown □ *rumah tanaman* ➲ look at **greenhouse**

hotline /'hɒtlaɪn/ *noun* [C] a special telephone line to a business or an organization □ *talian penting*

hotlink /'hɒtlɪŋk/ = **hyperlink**

hotly /'hɒtli/ *adv* **1** in an angry or excited way □ *dgn marah/hangat*: *They have hotly denied the newspaper reports.* **2** closely and with determination □ *(mengejar/dikejar) dgn dekat*: *The dog ran off, hotly pursued by its owner.*

hot-'water bottle *noun* [C] a rubber container that is filled with hot water and put in a bed to warm it □ *botol air panas (diperbuat drpd getah)*

hound¹ /haʊnd/ *noun* [C] a type of dog that is used for hunting or racing □ *anjing pemburu*

hound² /haʊnd/ *verb* [T] to follow and disturb sb □ *memburu (dan mengganggu)*: *Many famous people complain of being hounded by the press.*

hour /'aʊə(r)/ *noun* **1** [C] (*abbr* hr) a period of 60 minutes □ *jam*: *He studies for three hours most evenings.* ◆ *The programme lasts about half an hour.* ◆ *I'm going shopping now. I'll be back in about an hour.* ◆ *In two hours' time I'll be having lunch.* ◆ *a four-hour journey* ◆ *Japan is eight hours ahead of the UK.* ◆ *I get paid by the hour.* ◆ *How much do you get paid per/an hour?* **2** [C] the distance that you can travel in about 60 minutes □ *(jarak perjalanan dlm masa satu) jam*: *London is only two hours away.* **3** [C] a period of about an hour when sth particular happens □ *waktu*: *I'm going shopping in my lunch hour.* ◆ *The traffic is very bad in the rush hour.* **4** hours [pl] the period of time when sb is working or a shop, etc. is open □ *waktu kerja/buka*: *Employees are demanding shorter working hours.* **5** hours [pl] a long time □ *berjam-jam*: *He went on speaking for hours and hours.* **6** the hour [sing] the time when a new hour starts (= 1 o'clock, 2 o'clock, etc.) □ *tepat pukul (1, 2, dsb)*: *Buses are on the hour and at twenty past the hour.*

IDM at/till all hours at/until any time □ *pd/hingga bila-bila masa; lewat*: *She stays out till all hours (= very late).*

at an unearthly hour ➲ **unearthly**
the early hours ➲ **early**

hourly /ˈaʊəli/ *adj* [only before a noun] *adv* **1** (done, happening, etc.) every hour □ *setiap jam; sejam sekali*: *an hourly news bulletin* ◆ *Trains run hourly.* **2** for one hour □ *sejam*: *What is your hourly rate of pay?*

house¹ /haʊs/ *noun* [C] (*pl* **houses** /ˈhaʊzɪz/)
▶BUILDING **1** a building that is made for people to live in □ *rumah*: *We live in a three-bedroom/three-bedroomed house* ⊃ look at **bungalow**, **cottage**, **flat** ⊃ picture on page P8, page P9

> **HELP** **House** or **home**? Your **home** is the place where you live, even if it is not a house: *Let's go home to my flat.* Your home is also the place where you feel that you belong. A **house** is just a building: *We've only just moved into our new house and it doesn't feel like home yet.*

2 [usually sing] all the people who live in one house □ *seisi rumah*: *Don't shout. You'll wake the whole house up.* **3** a building that is used for a particular purpose □ *bangunan (utk tujuan tertentu)*: *a warehouse*
▶COMPANY **4** a large firm involved in a particular kind of business □ *syarikat; gedung*: *a fashion/publishing house*
▶RESTAURANT **5** a restaurant, usually that sells one particular type of food □ *restoran*: *a curry/spaghetti house* ◆ *house wine* (= the cheapest wine in a restaurant)
▶PARLIAMENT **6 House** a group of people who meet to make a country's laws □ *Dewan*: *the House of Commons* ◆ *the Houses of Parliament* ⊃ note at **Parliament**
▶IN THEATRE, ETC. **7** [usually sing] the audience at a theatre or cinema, or the area where they sit □ *penonton; panggung*: *There was a full house for the play this evening.*

IDM **get on/along like a house on fire** (*informal*) to immediately become good friends with sb □ *dgn cepat menjadi mesra dan rapat*
on the house paid for by the pub, restaurant, etc. that you are visiting; free □ *percuma*: *Your first drink is on the house.*

TOPIC

Houses

If you want to **move house** (= leave your home and go to live in a different one) you go to an **estate agent**, who is a person whose job is to sell **property** (= houses, land, etc.). The money that you borrow in order to buy a house is called a **mortgage**. A party given by somebody who has just **moved into** (= started living in) a house is called a **house-warming**.

You can **extend** your house to make it bigger. You **do up/renovate** your house by repairing and decorating it. If you do the work yourself it is called **DIY** (= do it yourself): *They're spending the weekend doing DIY.* Otherwise you may need a **plumber** (to fit or repair water pipes, bathrooms, etc.), an **electrician** (to connect or repair the electrical system) or a **carpenter** (to make or repair wooden structures).

---

house² /haʊs/ *verb* [T] **1** to provide sb with a place to live □ *memberi tempat tinggal*: *The Council must house homeless families.* **2** to contain or keep sth □ *menempatkan; terletak*: *Her office is housed in a separate building.*

houseboat /ˈhaʊsbəʊt/ *noun* [C] a boat on a river, etc. where sb lives and which usually stays in one place □ *bot kediaman*

housebound /ˈhaʊsbaʊnd/ *adj* unable to leave your house because you are old or ill □ *terpaksa duduk di rumah sahaja*

household /ˈhaʊshəʊld/ *noun* [C] all the people who live in one house and the work, money, organization, etc. that is needed to look after them □ *(isi) rumah/keluarga; rumah tangga*: *Most households now own at least one car.* ▶ **household** *adj* [only before a noun]: *household expenses*

householder /ˈhaʊshəʊldə(r)/ *noun* [C] a person who rents or owns the house that they live in □ *penyewa/pemilik rumah*

ˈhouse husband *noun* [C] a man who stays at home to cook, clean, take care of the children, etc. while his wife or partner goes out to work □ *lelaki yg mengurus rumah tangga* ⊃ look at **housewife**

housekeeper /ˈhaʊskiːpə(r)/ *noun* [C] a person who is paid to look after sb else's house and organize the work in it □ *pengurus rumah*

housekeeping /ˈhaʊskiːpɪŋ/ *noun* [U] **1** the work involved in looking after a house □ *pengurusan rumah* **2** the money that you need to manage a house □ *belanja rumah*

the ˌHouse of ˈCommons (also **the Commons**) *noun* [with sing or pl verb] (in the UK and Canada) the part of Parliament whose members are elected by the people of the country □ *Dewan Rakyat* ⊃ note at **Parliament**

the ˌHouse of ˈLords (also **the Lords**) *noun* [with sing or pl verb] the group of people (who are not elected) who meet to discuss the laws that have been suggested by the House of Commons □ *Dewan Pertuanan* ⊃ note at **Parliament**

the ˌHouse of ˌRepreˈsentatives *noun* [sing] the group of people who are elected to make new laws in the US □ *Dewan Perwakilan/Rakyat* ⊃ look at **Congress**, **the Senate**

ˈhouse-proud *adj* paying great attention to the care, cleaning, etc. of your house □ *suka mengemas dan merapikan rumah*

ˌhouse-to-ˈhouse *adj* [only before a noun] going to each house □ *dr rumah ke rumah*: *The police are making house-to-house enquiries.*

ˈhouse-warming *noun* [C] a party that you have when you have just moved into a new home □ *jamuan masuk rumah baharu*

housewife /ˈhaʊswaɪf/ noun [C] (pl **housewives**) a woman who does not have a job outside the home and who spends her time cleaning the house, cooking, looking after her family, etc. □ *suri rumah* ➪ look at **house husband**

housework /ˈhaʊswɜːk/ noun [U] the work that is needed to take care of a home and family, for example cleaning and cooking □ *kerja rumah*: *to do the housework* ➪ note at **clean**

> **HELP** Be careful. **Homework** (not **housework**) is work that is given by teachers for students to do at home.

housing /ˈhaʊzɪŋ/ noun [U] houses, flats, etc. for people to live in □ *perumahan*: *poor housing conditions* ♦ *a housing shortage*

housing estate noun [C] (BrE) an area where there are a large number of similar houses that were built at the same time □ *kawasan perumahan*

hover /ˈhɒvə(r)/ verb [I] **1** (used about a bird, etc.) to stay in the air in one place □ *terkatung-katung; mengambang* **2** (used about a person) to wait near sb/sth □ *tercegat-cegat*: *He hovered nervously outside the office.*

hovercraft /ˈhɒvəkrɑːft/ noun [C] (pl **hovercraft**) a type of boat that can move over land or water, held up by air being forced downwards □ *hoverkraf* ➪ picture on **page P6**

how /haʊ/ adv, conj **1** (often used in questions) in what way □ *bagaimana(kah); cara*: *How do you spell your name?* ♦ *Can you show me how to use this machine?* ♦ *I can't remember how to get there.* ♦ *How ever did you manage to find me here?* ➪ look at **however** **2** used when you are asking about sb's health or feelings □ *bagaimanakah (keadaan); apa khabar*: *'How is your mother?' 'She's much better, thank you.'* ♦ *How are you feeling today?* ♦ *How do you feel about your son joining the army?*

> **HELP** You use 'how' only when you are asking about a person's health. When you are asking about a person's character or appearance you say **what** ... **like**?: *'What are your new neighbours like?' 'They seem very friendly and quiet.'*

3 used when you are asking about sb's opinion of a thing or a situation □ *bagaimanakah; macam manakah*: *How was the weather?* ♦ *How is your meal?* ♦ *How did the interview go?* **4** used in questions when you are asking about the degree, amount, age, etc. of sb/sth □ *berapa*: *How old are you?* ♦ *How much is that?* **5** used for expressing surprise, pleasure, etc. □ *alangkah; betapa; sungguh*: *She's gone. How strange!* ♦ *I can't believe how expensive it is!*
IDM how/what about ...? ➪ **about²**
How come? ➪ **come**
How do you do? (formal) used when meeting sb for the first time □ *sapaan ketika pertama kali bertemu sso* ➪ note at **introduce**

> **HELP** Be careful. **How are you?** and **How do you do?** are answered differently: *'How do you do?'* is answered with the same words: *'How do you do?'* The answer to *'How are you?'* depends on how you are feeling: *'I'm fine.'/'Very well.'/'Much better.'*

however /haʊˈevə(r)/ adv, conj **1** (formal) (used for adding a comment to what you have just said) although sth is true □ *(walau) bagaimanapun; namun demikian*: *Sales are poor this month. There may, however, be an increase before Christmas.*

> **HELP** When **ever** is used to emphasize **how**, meaning 'in what way' it is written as a separate word: *How ever could he afford a car like that?*

➪ note at **contrast 2** in whatever way □ *apa cara sekalipun*: *However I sat I couldn't get comfortable.* ♦ *You can dress however you like.* **3** [before an adjective or adverb] to whatever degree □ *walau bagaimana ... sekalipun*: *He won't wear a hat however cold it is.* ♦ *You can't catch her however fast you run.*

howl /haʊl/ verb [I] to make a long loud sound □ *meraung; melolong; menderu*: *I couldn't sleep because there was a dog howling all night.* ♦ *The wind howled around the house.* ▶**howl** noun [C]

h.p. /ˌeɪtʃ ˈpiː/ (also **HP**) abbr **1** = **horsepower 2** (BrE) = **hire purchase**

HQ /ˌeɪtʃ ˈkjuː/ abbr = **headquarters**

HR /ˌeɪtʃ ˈɑː(r)/ abbr = **human resources**

hr abbr (pl **hrs**) = **hour** (1): *3 hrs 15 mins*

HRH /ˌeɪtʃ ɑːr ˈeɪtʃ/ abbr **His/Her Royal Highness** □ *Duli Yg Maha Mulia*: *HRH Prince Harry*

hub /hʌb/ noun [C, usually sing] **1 the hub (of sth)** the central and most important part of a place or an activity □ *pusat*: *the commercial hub of the city* **2** the central part of a wheel □ *hab*

hubbub /ˈhʌbʌb/ noun [sing, U] **1** the noise made by a lot of people talking at the same time □ *riuh-rendah*: *I couldn't hear the announcement over the hubbub.* **2** a situation in which there is a lot of noise, excitement and activity □ *keriuhan*: *the hubbub of city life*

huddle¹ /ˈhʌdl/ verb [I] **huddle (up) (together) 1** to get close to other people because you are cold or frightened □ *berhimpit-himpit*: *The campers huddled together around the fire.* **2** to make your body as small as possible because you are cold or frightened □ *mengerekot*: *She huddled up in her sleeping bag and tried to get some sleep.* ▶**huddled** adj: *We found the children lying huddled together on the ground.*

huddle² /ˈhʌdl/ noun [C] a small group of people or things that are close together □ *kumpulan; kelompok*: *They all stood in a huddle, laughing and chatting.*

hue /hjuː/ noun [C] (written) a colour; a particular shade of a colour □ *warna*
IDM **hue and cry** strong public protest about sth □ *bantahan awam yg kuat; bantahan keras*: There was a hue and cry about the new taxes.

huff /hʌf/ noun
IDM **in a huff** (informal) in a bad mood because sb has annoyed or upset you □ *dlm keadaan meradang*: Did you see Sam **go off in a huff** when he wasn't chosen for the team?

hug /hʌɡ/ verb [T] (**hugging**; **hugged**) 1 to put your arms around sb, especially to show that you love them □ *memeluk; mendakap*: He hugged his mother and sisters and got on the train. 2 to hold sth close to your body □ *memeluk*: She hugged the parcel to her chest as she ran. 3 (used about a ship, car, road, etc.) to stay close to sth □ *menyusuri*: to hug the coast ▶**hug** noun [C]: Noel's crying—I'll go and give him a hug.

huge /hjuːdʒ/ adj very big □ *sangat besar*: a huge amount/quantity/sum/number ◆ a huge building ◆ The film was a huge success. ◆ This is a huge problem for us. **SYN** **enormous** ▶**hugely** adv: hugely successful/popular/expensive

huh /hʌ/ exclam (informal) used for expressing anger, surprise, etc. or for asking a question □ *hah*: They've gone away, huh? They didn't tell me.

hull /hʌl/ noun [C] the main part of a ship □ *badan kapal*

hullabaloo /ˌhʌləbəˈluː/ noun [sing] a lot of loud noise, for example made by people shouting □ *kehebohan; kekecohan*

hum /hʌm/ verb (**humming**; **hummed**) 1 [I,T] to sing with your lips closed □ *menggumamkan (lagu); bersenandung*: You can hum the tune if you don't know the words. 2 [I] to make a continuous low noise □ *mendengung; berdengung*: The machine began to hum as I switched it on. ▶**hum** noun [sing]: the hum of machinery/distant traffic

human¹ /ˈhjuːmən/ adj connected with people, not with animals, machines or gods; typical of people □ *(berkenaan dgn) manusia*: the human body ◆ The disaster was caused by **human error**. ▶**humanly** adv: They did all that was humanly possible to rescue him (= everything that a human being could possibly do).

human² /ˈhjuːmən/ (also ˌhuman ˈbeing) noun [C] a person □ *manusia*: Dogs can hear much better than humans.

humane /hjuːˈmeɪn/ adj having or showing kindness or understanding, especially to a person or an animal that is suffering □ *berperikemanusiaan*: Animals must be kept in humane conditions. **OPP** **inhumane** ▶**humanely** adv

humanitarian /hjuːˌmænɪˈteəriən/ adj concerned with trying to make people's lives better and reduce suffering □ *(sikap) perikemanusiaan/belas kasihan*: Many countries have sent **humanitarian aid** to the earthquake victims.

humanity /hjuːˈmænəti/ noun 1 [U] all the people in the world, thought of as a group □ *manusia sejagat*: crimes **against humanity** **SYN** **the human race** 2 [U] the quality of being kind and understanding □ *perikemanusiaan*: The prisoners were treated with humanity. **OPP** **inhumanity** 3 **(the) humanities** [pl] the subjects of study that are concerned with the way people think and behave, for example literature, history, etc. □ *ilmu kemanusiaan* ⊃ look at **science**

ˌhuman ˈnature noun [U] feelings, behaviour, etc. that all people have in common □ *sifat/tabii manusia*

the ˌhuman ˈrace noun [sing] all the people in the world, when thought of as a group □ *bangsa manusia* **SYN** **humanity**

ˌhuman reˈsources noun [U, with sing or pl verb] (abbr **HR**) the department in a company that deals with employing and training people □ *sumber manusia* **SYN** **personnel**

ˌhuman ˈrights noun [pl] the basic freedoms that all people should have, for example the right to say what you think, to travel freely, etc. □ *hak asasi manusia*

humble¹ /ˈhʌmbl/ adj (**humbler**; **humblest**) 1 not thinking that you are better or more important than other people; not proud □ *rendah diri; tdk sombong*: He became very rich and famous but he always remained a very humble man. ⊃ look at **modest** ⊃ noun **humility** 2 not special or important □ *tdk penting; tdk berpangkat; (keturunan) rendah*: She comes from a humble background. ▶**humbly** /ˈhʌmbli/ adv: He apologized very humbly for his behaviour.

humble² /ˈhʌmbl/ verb [T] to make sb feel that they are not as good or important as they thought □ *merendahkan diri (sso); menundukkan*

humid /ˈhjuːmɪd/ adj (used about the air or climate) warm and feeling slightly wet □ *lembap*: Hong Kong is hot and humid in summer. ▶**humidity** /hjuːˈmɪdəti/ noun [U]

humiliate /hjuːˈmɪlieɪt/ verb [T] to make sb feel ashamed or stupid □ *memalukan; malu*: I felt humiliated when the teacher laughed at my work. ▶**humiliating** adj: a humiliating defeat ▶**humiliation** /hjuːˌmɪliˈeɪʃn/ noun [C,U]

humility /hjuːˈmɪləti/ noun [U] the quality of not thinking that you are better than other people □ *sifat rendah hati* ⊃ adjective **humble**

hummus (also **houmous**) /ˈhʊməs; ˈhuːməs/ noun [U] a type of food originally from the Middle East that is a soft mixture of **chickpeas**, **sesame** seeds, oil, lemon juice and **garlic** □ *sejenis makanan*

humorless (AmE) = **humourless**

humorous /ˈhjuːmərəs/ adj amusing or funny □ *lucu*: He gave a humorous account of their trip to Spain. ▶**humorously** adv

humour¹ (*AmE* humor) /ˈhjuːmə(r)/ *noun* [U] **1** the funny or amusing qualities of sb/sth □ *kelucuan; jenaka*: *It is sometimes hard to understand the humour* (= the jokes) *of another country.* **2** being able to see when sth is funny and to laugh at things □ *rasa lucu*: *I can't stand people with no sense of humour.* **3** -humoured (*AmE* -humored) [in compounds] having or showing a particular mood □ *angin*: *good-humoured*

> **TOPIC**
>
> **Humour**
>
> Do you have a **good sense of humour**? What do you find **funny/amusing**? When something is **hilarious**, do you **burst out laughing**? Some people are **witty** (= use words in a clever way). **Clowns** do **slapstick** (= for example, falling over or covering people with water). A **practical joke** is something you do to make a person look silly. **Comedians** tell **jokes** and may use **satire** to **make fun of** people such as politicians.

humour² (*AmE* humor) /ˈhjuːmə(r)/ *verb* [T] to keep sb happy by doing what they want □ *melayan kerenah (sso)*

humourless (*AmE* humorless) /ˈhjuːmələs/ *adj* having no sense of fun; serious □ *tdk mempunyai rasa lucu*

hump /hʌmp/ *noun* [C] a large lump that sticks out above the surface of sth, for example on the back of a **camel** (= an animal that lives in the desert) □ *bonggol; ponok* ⊃ picture at **camel**

hunch¹ /hʌntʃ/ *verb* [I,T] to bend your back and shoulders forward into a round shape □ *membongkok; membongkokkan*

hunch² /hʌntʃ/ *noun* [C] (*informal*) a thought or an idea that is based on a feeling rather than on facts or information □ *gerak hati; rasa-rasa*: *I've got a hunch that she'll be back soon.*

hunchback /ˈhʌntʃbæk/ *noun* [C] a person with a back that has a lump on it □ *si bongkok*

hundred /ˈhʌndrəd/ *number* **1** (*pl* hundred) 100 □ *seratus*; 100: *two hundred* ♦ *one hundred people in the room.* ♦ *She's a hundred today.*

> **HELP** Note that when we are saying a number, for example 1 420, we put 'and' after the word **hundred**: *one thousand four hundred and twenty*

2 hundreds (*informal*) a lot; a large amount □ *sangat banyak*: *I've got hundreds of things to do today.* ❶ For more information about numbers, look at the section on using numbers at the back of this dictionary.

hundredth¹ /ˈhʌndrədθ/ *ordinal number* 100th □ *satu per seratus* ⊃ note at **sixth**

hundredth² /ˈhʌndrədθ/ *noun* [C] ¹⁄₁₀₀; one of a hundred equal parts of sth □ *keseratus; ke-100*

hundredweight /ˈhʌndrədweɪt/ *noun* [C] (*abbr* cwt.) a measure of weight, about 50.8 kilograms □ *ratus berat* ❶ For more information about weights, look at the section on using numbers at the back of this dictionary.

hung past tense, past participle of **hang¹**

hunger¹ /ˈhʌŋɡə(r)/ *noun* **1** [U] the state of not having enough food to eat, especially when this causes illness or death □ *kelaparan*: *Many people die of hunger every day in the camp.* **2** [U] the feeling caused by a need to eat □ *rasa lapar*: *Hunger is one reason why babies cry.*

> **HELP** Be careful. You cannot say *I have hunger* in English. You must say *I am hungry.*

3 [sing] hunger (for sth) a strong desire for sth □ *keinginan besar/dahaga (akan sst)*: *a hunger for knowledge/fame/success* ⊃ look at **thirst**

hunger² /ˈhʌŋɡə(r)/ *verb*

PHR V hunger for/after sth (*formal*) to have a strong desire for sth □ *sangat mengingini sst; dahaga akan sst*

hunger strike *noun* [C,U] a time when sb (especially a prisoner) refuses to eat because they are protesting about sth □ *mogok lapar*: *to be/go on hunger strike*

hungry /ˈhʌŋɡri/ *adj* (hungrier; hungriest) **1** wanting to eat □ *lapar*: *I'm hungry. Let's eat soon.* ♦ *There were hungry children begging for food in the streets.* ⊃ look at **thirsty 2** hungry for sth wanting sth very much □ *sangat menginginkan/dahaga akan (sst)*: *People were hungry for change.*

IDM go hungry to not have any food □ *berlapar; kelaparan*
▶ hungrily *adv*

hunk /hʌŋk/ *noun* [C] **1** a large piece of sth □ *ketul besar*: *a hunk of bread/cheese/meat* **2** (*informal*) a man who is big, strong and attractive □ *lelaki kacak (berbadan besar dan kuat)*

hunt¹ /hʌnt/ *verb* [I,T] **1** hunt (for) (sb/sth) to try to find sb/sth □ *memburu; mencari*: *The police are still hunting the murderer.* **2** to run after wild animals, etc. in order to catch or kill them either for sport or for food □ *berburu; memburu; diburu*: *Owls hunt at night.* ♦ *Are tigers still being hunted in India?*

> **HELP** We often use the expression **go hunting** when we are talking about people spending time hunting.

hunt² /hʌnt/ *noun* [C] **1** the act of hunting wild animals, etc. □ *perburuan; berburu*: *a fox hunt* **2** [usually sing] a hunt (for sb/sth) the act of looking for sb/sth that is difficult to find □ *pencarian; (perbuatan) mencari*: *The police have launched a hunt for the missing child.*

hunter /ˈhʌntə(r)/ *noun* [C] a person that hunts wild animals for sport or food; an animal that hunts its food □ *pemburu*

hunting /'hʌntɪŋ/ noun [U] the act of following and killing wild animals or birds as a sport or for food □ *berburu* ⊃ look at **shoot**

hurdle¹ /'hɜːdl/ noun 1 [C] a type of light fence that a person or a horse jumps over in a race □ *pagar lompat*: *to clear a hurdle* (= to jump over it successfully) 2 **the hurdles** [pl] a race in which runners or horses have to jump over **hurdles** □ *acara lompat pagar*: *the 200 metres hurdles* 3 [C] a problem or difficulty that you must solve or deal with before you can achieve sth □ *halangan; rintangan*

hurdle² /'hɜːdl/ verb [I,T] **hurdle (over sth)** to jump over sth while you are running □ *berlari sambil melompati (sst)*

hurl /hɜːl/ verb [T] to throw sth with great force □ *menghumbankan; membalingkan; mencampakkan*

hurray (also **hooray**) /həˈreɪ/ (also **hurrah** /həˈrɑː/) exclam used for expressing great pleasure, approval, etc. □ *hore*: *Hurray! We've won!*
IDM hip, hip, hurray/hurrah ⊃ **hip²**

hurricane /'hʌrɪkən/ noun [C] a violent storm with very strong winds □ *hurikan; ribut taufan* ⊃ note at **storm**

hurried /'hʌrid/ adj done (too) quickly □ *dgn tergesa-gesa/gopoh*: *a hurried meal* ▶ **hurriedly** adv

hurry¹ /'hʌri/ verb (**hurrying**; **hurries**; pt, pp **hurried**) 1 [I] to move or do sth quickly because there is not much time □ *bergegas; tergesa-gesa; cepat*: *Don't hurry. There's plenty of time.* ◆ *They hurried back home after school.* ◆ *Several people hurried to help.* 2 [T] **hurry sb (into sth/doing sth)** to cause sb/sth to do sth, or sth to happen, more quickly □ *menggesa; digesa*: *Don't hurry me. I'm going as fast as I can.* ◆ *He was hurried into a decision.* 3 [T, usually passive] to do sth too quickly □ *tergesa-gesa*: *Good food should never be hurried.* **SYN** for all meanings **rush**
PHR V **hurry up (with sth)** (informal) to move or do sth more quickly □ *cepat(lah); lekas(lah)*: *Hurry up or we'll miss the train.*

hurry² /'hʌri/ noun [U] the need or wish to do sth quickly □ *(keadaan) tergesa-gesa; terburu-buru*: *Take your time. There's no hurry.* **SYN** **rush**
IDM in a hurry quickly □ *dgn tergesa-gesa; cepat-cepat*: *She got up late and left in a hurry.*
in a hurry (to do sth) wanting to do sth soon; impatient □ *cepat/lekas (hendak membuat sst)*: *They are in a hurry to get the job done before the winter.*
in no hurry (to do sth); not in any hurry (to do sth) 1 not needing or wishing to do sth quickly □ *(keadaan) tergesa-gesa; terburu-buru*: *We weren't in any hurry so we stopped to admire the view.* 2 not wanting to do sth □ *tdk mahu (membuat sst)*: *I am in no hurry to repeat that experience.*

hurt¹ /hɜːt/ verb (pt, pp **hurt**) 1 [T,I] to cause sb/ yourself physical pain or injury □ *mencederakan; (ter)cedera; menyakitkan*: *Did he hurt himself?* ◆ *I fell and hurt my arm.* ◆ *No one was seriously hurt in the accident.* ◆ *These shoes hurt; they're too tight.* 2 [I] to feel painful □ *berasa sakit*: *My leg hurts.* ◆ *It hurts when I lift my leg.* ◆ *Where exactly does it hurt?* 3 [T] to make sb unhappy; to upset sb □ *melukai perasaan; menyakitkan hati*: *His unkind remarks hurt her deeply.* ◆ *I didn't want to hurt his feelings.*
IDM it won't/wouldn't hurt (sb/sth) (to do sth) (informal) used to say that sb should do sth □ *apa salahnya (kalau sso/sst) (membuat sst)*: *It wouldn't hurt you to help with the housework occasionally.*

> **OTHER WORDS FOR**
> **hurt**
> A person may be **wounded** by a knife, sword, gun, etc., usually as a result of fighting: *a wounded soldier.* People are usually **injured** in an accident: *Five people were killed in the crash and twelve others were injured.* **Hurt** and **injured** are similar in meaning but **hurt** is more often used when the damage is not very great: *I hurt my leg when I fell off my bike.*

hurt² /hɜːt/ adj 1 injured physically □ *cedera*: *None of the passengers were badly/seriously hurt.* 2 upset and offended by sth that sb has said or done □ *luka (hati); tersinggung*: *She was deeply hurt that she had not been invited to the party.*

hurt³ /hɜːt/ noun [U] a feeling of unhappiness because sb has been unkind or unfair to you □ *perasaan luka hati/tersinggung*: *There was hurt and real anger in her voice.*

hurtful /'hɜːtfl/ adj **hurtful (to sb)** making sb feel upset and offended □ *melukakan hati* **SYN** **unkind**

hurtle /'hɜːtl/ verb [I] to move with great speed, perhaps causing danger □ *meluru*: *The lorry came hurtling towards us.*

husband /'hʌzbənd/ noun [C] a man that a woman is married to □ *suami*: *Her ex-husband sees the children once a month.*

hush¹ /hʌʃ/ verb [I] (spoken) used to tell sb to be quiet, to stop talking or crying □ *diam; syh*: *Hush now and try to sleep.*
PHR V **hush sth up** to hide information to stop people knowing about sth; to keep sth secret □ *menyembunyikan/merahsiakan sst*

hush² /hʌʃ/ noun [sing] no noise or sound at all □ *senyap/kesenyapan*

hush-ˈhush adj (informal) very secret □ *rahsia*

husk /hʌsk/ noun [C] the dry outer covering of nuts, fruits and seeds, especially of grain □ *sekam; kulit*: *Brown rice has not had the husks removed.*

husky¹ /'hʌski/ adj (**huskier**; **huskiest**) (used about a person or their voice) sounding rough and quiet □ *serak; parau*

husky² /ˈhʌski/ noun [C] (pl **huskies**) a strong dog with thick fur that is used in teams for pulling heavy loads over snow ◻ *anjing huski*

hustle /ˈhʌsl/ verb [T] to push or move sb in a way that is not gentle ◻ *mengasak; menolak*

hut /hʌt/ noun [C] a small building with one room, usually made of wood or metal ◻ *pondok*: *a beach hut* ♦ *a wooden/mud hut*

hutch /hʌtʃ/ noun [C] a wooden box with a front made of wire, that is used for keeping **rabbits** (= small animals with long ears) or other animals in ◻ *sangkar*

hybrid /ˈhaɪbrɪd/ noun [C] **1** an animal or a plant that has parents of different types ◻ *kacukan (binatang, tanaman)*: *A mule is a hybrid of a male donkey and a female horse.* **2 hybrid (between/of A and B)** something that is the product of mixing two or more different things ◻ *hibrid; campuran*: *The music was a hybrid of Western pop and traditional folk song.* **SYN mixture**

hydrant /ˈhaɪdrənt/ noun [C] a pipe in a street from which water can be taken for stopping fires, cleaning the streets, etc. ◻ *pili/paip bomba*

hydraulic /haɪˈdrɔːlɪk/ (BrE also) -ˈdrɒl-/ adj operated by water or another liquid moving through pipes, etc. under pressure ◻ *hidraulik*: *hydraulic brakes*

hydroelectric /ˌhaɪdrəʊɪˈlektrɪk/ adj using the power of water to produce electricity; produced by the power of water ◻ *hidroelektrik*: *a hydroelectric dam/plant* ♦ *hydroelectric power* ⊃ note at **environment**

hydrogen /ˈhaɪdrədʒən/ noun [U] (symbol H) a light gas with no colour. **Hydrogen** and **oxygen** (= another gas) form water (H_2O). ◻ *hidrogen*

hygiene /ˈhaɪdʒiːn/ noun [U] (the rules of) keeping yourself and things around you clean, in order to prevent disease ◻ *kebersihan*: *High standards of hygiene are essential when you are preparing food.* ♦ *personal hygiene*

hygienic /haɪˈdʒiːnɪk/ adj clean, without the bacteria that cause disease ◻ *bersih*: *hygienic conditions* **OPP unhygienic** ▸**hygienically** /-kli/ adv

hymn /hɪm/ noun [C] a religious song that Christians sing together in church, etc. ◻ *him; mazmur*

hype¹ /haɪp/ noun [U] (informal) advertisements that tell you how good and important a new product, film, etc. is ◻ *gembar-gembur*: *Don't believe all the hype—the book is rubbish!*

hype² /haɪp/ verb [T] **hype sth (up)** to exaggerate how good or important sth is ◻ *menggembar-gemburkan; digembar-gemburkan*: *His much-hyped new movie is released next week.*

hyperactive /ˌhaɪpərˈæktɪv/ adj (used especially about children and their behaviour) too active and only able to keep quiet and still for short periods ◻ *hiperaktif; terlampau aktif* ▸**hyperactivity** /ˌhaɪpəræk'tɪvəti/ noun [U]

hyperlink /ˈhaɪpəlɪŋk/ (also **hotlink**) noun [C] a place in an electronic document on a computer that is connected to another electronic document ◻ *hiperpautan*: *Click on the hyperlink.*

hypermarket /ˈhaɪpəmɑːkɪt/ noun [C] (BrE) a very large shop outside a town that sells a wide variety of goods ◻ *pasar raya besar*

hyphen /ˈhaɪfn/ noun [C] the mark (-) used for joining two words together (for example *left-handed, red-hot*) or to show that a word has been divided and continues on the next line ◻ *sempang* ⊃ look at **dash**

hyphenate /ˈhaɪfəneɪt/ verb [T] to join two words together with a **hyphen** ◻ *membubuh sempang* ▸**hyphenation** /ˌhaɪfəˈneɪʃn/ noun [U]

hypnosis /hɪpˈnəʊsɪs/ noun [U] (the producing of) an unconscious state where sb's mind and actions can be controlled by another person ◻ *hipnosis*: *She was questioned under hypnosis.*

hypnotize (also **-ise**) /ˈhɪpnətaɪz/ verb [T] to put sb into an unconscious state where the person's mind and actions can be controlled ◻ *menghipnosis* ▸**hypnotic** /hɪpˈnɒtɪk/ adj ▸**hypnotism** /ˈhɪpnətɪzəm/ noun [U] ▸**hypnotist** /-tɪst/ noun [C]

hypochondriac /ˌhaɪpəˈkɒndriæk/ noun [C] a person who is always worried about their health and believes they are ill, even when there is nothing wrong ◻ *hipokondriak*

hypocrisy /hɪˈpɒkrəsi/ noun [U] behaviour in which sb does not act according to the moral standards that they claim to have ◻ *kepurapuraan*

hypocrite /ˈhɪpəkrɪt/ noun [C] a person who pretends to have moral standards or opinions which they do not really have. **Hypocrites** say one thing and do another ◻ *hipokrit; orang yg berpura-pura*: *What a hypocrite! She says she's against the hunting of animals but she's wearing a fur coat.* ▸**hypocritical** /ˌhɪpəˈkrɪtɪkl/ adj ▸**hypocritically** /-kli/ adv

hypodermic /ˌhaɪpəˈdɜːmɪk/ noun [C] a medical instrument with a long needle that is used for giving sb an **injection** (= putting a drug under the skin) ◻ *hipodermik (alat utk menyuntik ubat)* ▸**hypodermic** adj: *a hypodermic needle/syringe*

hypothesis /haɪˈpɒθəsɪs/ noun [C] (pl **hypotheses** /-siːz/) an idea that is suggested as the possible explanation for sth but has not yet been found to be true or correct ◻ *hipotesis*

hypothetical /ˌhaɪpəˈθetɪkl/ adj based on situations that have not yet happened, not on facts ◻ *(berdasarkan) andaian/hipotesis*: *That's a hypothetical question because we don't know what the situation will be next year.* ▸**hypothetically** /-kli/ adv

hysteria /hɪˈstɪəriə/ noun [U] a state in which a person or a group of people cannot control their emotions, for example cannot stop laughing, crying, shouting, etc. □ *histeria*: *mass hysteria*

hysterical /hɪˈsterɪkl/ *adj* **1** very excited and unable to control your emotions □ *emosi tdk terkawal; spt diserang histeria*: *hysterical laughter* ♦ *She was hysterical with grief.* **2** (*informal*) very funny □ *sangat lucu* ▶**hysterically** /-kli/ *adv*

hysterics /hɪˈsterɪks/ *noun* [pl] **1** an expression of extreme fear, excitement or anger that makes sb lose control of their emotions □ *keadaan amat takut, suka atau marah yg tdk terkawal*: *She went into hysterics when they told her the news.* ♦ (*informal*) *My father would have hysterics* (= be very angry) *if he knew I was with you.* **2** (*informal*) a state of being unable to stop laughing □ *ketawa sampai nak pecah perut*: *The comedian had the audience in hysterics.*

Hz /hɜːts/ *abbr* **hertz**; (used in radio) a measure of **frequency** (= the rate at which a sound wave moves up and down) □ *Hz*

I i

I, i /aɪ/ *noun* [C,U] (*pl* **Is**; **I's**; **i's** /aɪz/) the 9th letter of the English alphabet □ *I, i (huruf)*: *'Ice' begins with (an) 'I'.*

I /aɪ/ *pron* (the subject of a verb) the person who is speaking or writing □ *saya; aku*: *I phoned and said that I was busy.* ♦ *I'm not going to fall, am I?*

ice¹ /aɪs/ *noun* [U] water that has frozen and become solid □ *ais; air batu*: *Do you want ice in your orange juice?* ♦ *I slipped on a patch of ice.* ♦ *black ice* (= ice on roads, that cannot be seen easily) ⊃ picture on **page P10**

IDM **break the ice** to say or do sth that makes people feel more relaxed, especially at the beginning of a party or meeting □ *menghilangkan rasa tdk selesa*: *She smiled to break the ice.*

cut no ice (with sb) to have no influence or effect on sb □ *tdk ada kesan; tdk termakan*: *His excuses cut no ice with me.*

on ice 1 (used about wine, etc.) kept cold by being surrounded by ice □ *disejukkan dlm ais*: *The table is set, the candles are lit and the champagne is on ice.* **2** (used about a plan, etc.) waiting to be dealt with later; delayed □ *diketepikan/ditangguhkan dahulu*: *We've had to put our plans to go to Australia on ice for the time being.*

ice² /aɪs/ (*especially AmE* **frost**) *verb* [T] to decorate a cake by covering it with a mixture of sugar, butter, chocolate, etc. □ *mengaising* ⊃ look at **icing**

PHR V **ice (sth) over/up** to cover sth or become covered with ice □ *dilitupi ais*: *The windscreen of the car had iced over in the night.*

iceberg /ˈaɪsbɜːg/ *noun* [C] a very large block of ice that floats in the sea □ *aisberg*
IDM **the tip of the iceberg** ⊃ **tip¹**

icebox /ˈaɪsbɒks/ (*AmE*) = **fridge**

ˈice cap *noun* [C] a layer of ice that permanently covers parts of the earth □ *litupan ais*: *Are the polar ice caps* (= at the North and South Poles) *in danger of melting?*

ˌice-ˈcold *adj* very cold □ *sangat sejuk*: *ice-cold beer* ♦ *Your hands are ice-cold.*

ˌice ˈcream *noun* **1** [U] a frozen sweet food that is made from cream □ *aiskrim*: *Desserts are served with cream or ice cream.* ⊃ picture on **page P16** **2** [C] an amount of **ice cream** that is served to sb, often in a **cone** (= a special container that you can eat) □ *sepotong, dsb aiskrim*: *a strawberry ice cream*

ˈice cube *noun* [C] a small block of ice that you put in a drink to make it cold □ *ketulan ais/air batu*

iced /aɪst/ *adj* (used about drinks) very cold □ *berais*: *iced tea*

ˈice hockey (*AmE* **hockey**) *noun* [U] a game that is played on ice by two teams who try to hit a **puck** (= small flat rubber object) into a goal with long wooden sticks □ *hoki ais* ⊃ note at **hockey** ⊃ picture on **page P4**

ˈice ˌlolly *noun* [C] (*AmE* **Popsicle™**) a piece of flavoured ice on a stick □ *aiskrim batang* ⊃ look at **lollipop**

ˈice rink (*also* **rink**, **ˈskating rink**) *noun* [C] a large area of ice, or a building containing a large area of ice, which is used for **skating** (= moving on the ice wearing special boots) □ *gelanggang luncur*

ˈice skate = **skate²**(1)

ˈice-skate = **skate¹**

ˈice skating = **skating**(1)

icicle /ˈaɪsɪkl/ *noun* [C] a pointed piece of ice that is formed by water freezing as it falls or runs down from sth □ *isikel*

icing /ˈaɪsɪŋ/ (*AmE* **frosting**) *noun* [U] a mixture of sugar, butter, chocolate, etc. that is used to decorate cakes □ *aising* ⊃ picture at **cake**

icon /ˈaɪkɒn/ *noun* [C] **1** a small picture or symbol on a computer screen that represents a program □ *ikon*: *Click on the printer icon with the mouse.* **2** a person or thing that is considered to be a symbol of sth □ *lambang; simbol*: *Madonna and other pop icons of the 1980s* **3** (*also* **ikon**) a painting or statue of a holy person that is also thought of as a holy object □ *gambar/patung suci*

iconic /aɪˈkɒnɪk/ *adj* acting as a sign or symbol of sth □ *yg menjadi lambang*: *iconic images of New York, such as the Empire State Building*

ICT /ˌaɪ siː ˈtiː/ *noun* [U] (*BrE*) **information and communications technology**; the study of the use of computer, the Internet, video and other technology as a subject in British schools □ *teknologi maklumat dan komunikasi (TMK)*

icy /ˈaɪsi/ *adj* (**icier; iciest**) **1** very cold □ *sangat sejuk*: *icy winds/water/weather* **SYN** **freezing** **2** covered with ice □ *dilitupi ais*: *icy roads*

ID /ˌaɪ ˈdiː/ *abbr* (*informal*) = **identification**(2), **identity** □ *(kad, dsb) pengenalan*: *You must carry ID at all times.*

Id = **Eid**

I'd /aɪd/ short for **I had**; **I would**

I'D card = **identity card**

idea /aɪˈdɪə/ *noun* **1** [C] **an idea (for sth); an idea (of sth/of doing sth)** a plan, thought or suggestion, especially about what to do in a particular situation □ *idea; cadangan; rancangan*: *That's a good idea!* ♦ *He's got an idea for a new play.* ♦ *I had the bright idea of getting Jane to help me with my homework.* ♦ *Has anyone got any ideas of how to tackle this problem?* ♦ *It was your idea to invite so many people to the party.* **2** [sing] **an idea (of sth)** a picture or impression in your mind □ *gambaran; tanggapan; (perbuatan) membayangkan*: *You have no idea* (= you can't imagine) *how difficult it was to find a time that suited everybody.* ♦ *The programme gave a good idea of what life was like before the war.* ♦ *Staying in to watch the football on TV is not my idea of a good time.* **3** [C] **an idea (about sth)** an opinion or belief □ *pendapat; fikiran*: *She has her own ideas about how to bring up children.* **4** [the idea [sing] **the idea (of sth/of doing sth)** the aim or purpose of sth □ *tujuan; maksud*: *The idea of the course is to teach the basics of car maintenance.*
IDM **get the idea** to understand the aim or purpose of sth □ *faham (tujuan sst)*: *Right! I think I've got the idea.*
get the idea that ... to get the feeling or impression that ... □ *mendapat tanggapan bahawa; ingat*: *Where did you get the idea that I was paying for this meal?*
have an idea that ... to feel or think that ... □ *rasa-rasanya*: *I'm not sure but I have an idea that they've gone on holiday.*
not have the faintest/foggiest (idea) ⊃ **faint¹**

ideal¹ /aɪˈdiːəl/ *adj* **ideal (for sb/sth)** the best possible; perfect □ *ideal; unggul; paling baik*: *She's the ideal candidate for the job.* ♦ *In an ideal world there would be no poverty.* ♦ *It would be an ideal opportunity for you to practise your Spanish.*

ideal² /aɪˈdiːəl/ *noun* [C] **1** an idea or principle that seems perfect to you and that you want to achieve □ *prinsip*: *She finds it hard to live up to her parents' high ideals.* ♦ *political/moral/social ideals* **2** [usually sing] **an ideal (of sth)** a perfect example of a person or thing □ *ideal; impian; idaman*: *It's my ideal of what a family home should be.*

idealism /aɪˈdiːəlɪzəm/ *noun* [U] the belief that a perfect life, situation, etc. can be achieved, even when this is not very likely □ *idealisme*: *Young people are usually full of idealism.* ⊃ look at **realism** ▶ **idealist** /-ɪst/ *noun* [C]: *Most people are idealists when they are young.* ▶ **idealistic** /ˌaɪdɪəˈlɪstɪk/ *adj*

idealize (also **-ise**) /aɪˈdiːəlaɪz/ *verb* [T] to imagine or show sb/sth as being better than he/she/it really is □ *menganggap sebagai ideal*: *Old people often idealize the past.*

ideally /aɪˈdiːəli/ *adv* **1** perfectly □ *paling sesuai; benar-benar*: *They are ideally suited to each other.* **2** in an ideal situation □ *secara ideal; seelok-eloknya*: *Ideally, no class should be larger than 25.*

identical /aɪˈdentɪkl/ *adj* **1** **identical (to/with sb/sth)** exactly the same as; similar in every detail □ *serupa; sama*: *I can't see any difference between these two pens—they look identical to me.* ♦ *That watch is identical to the one I lost yesterday.* **2** **the identical** [only before a noun] the same □ *yg sama*: *This is the identical room we stayed in last year.* ▶ **identically** /-kli/ *adv*

i‚dentical ˈtwin *noun* [C] either of two children born at the same time from the same mother who have developed from a single egg. **Identical twins** are of the same sex and look very similar. □ *kembar seiras*

identification /aɪˌdentɪfɪˈkeɪʃn/ *noun* **1** [U,C] the process of showing, recognizing or giving proof of who or what sb/sth is □ *pengenalpastian; pengecaman*: *The identification of the bodies of those killed in the explosion was very difficult.* **2** (*abbr* **ID**) [U] an official paper, document, etc. that is proof of who you are □ *(kad, dokumen, dsb) pengenalan*: *Do you have any identification?* **3** [U,C] **identification (with sb/sth)** a strong feeling of understanding or sharing the same feelings as sb/sth □ *identifikasi*: *children's identification with TV heroes*

identify /aɪˈdentɪfaɪ/ *verb* [T] (**identifying; identifies**; *pt, pp* **identified**) **identify sb/sth (as sb/sth)** to recognize or be able to say who or what sb/sth is □ *mengenal pasti; mengecamkan*: *The police need someone to identify the body.* ♦ *We must identify the cause of the problem before we look for solutions.*
PHR V **identify sth with sth** to think or say that sth is the same as sth else □ *menganggap sama; menyamakan*: *You can't identify nationalism with fascism.*
identify with sb to feel that you understand and share what sb else is feeling □ *memahami atau bersimpati dgn sso*: *I found it hard to identify with the woman in the film.*
identify (yourself) with sb/sth to support or be closely connected with sb/sth □ *mengaitkan diri dgn sso/sst*: *She became identified with the new political party.*

identity /aɪˈdentəti/ *noun* [C,U] (*pl* **identities**) (*abbr* **ID**) who or what a person or thing is □ *identiti; siapa*: *There are few clues to the identity of the killer.* ♦ *The region has its own cultural identity.* ♦ *The arrest was a case of mistaken identity* (= the wrong person was arrested).

identity card (also **ID card**) noun [C] a card with your name, photograph, etc. that is proof of who you are ▫ *kad pengenalan*

ideology /ˌaɪdiˈɒlədʒi/ noun [C,U] (pl **ideologies**) a set of ideas that a political or economic system is based on ▫ *ideologi*: *Marxist ideology* ▶**ideological** /ˌaɪdiəˈlɒdʒɪkl/ adj

idiom /ˈɪdiəm/ noun [C] an expression whose meaning is different from the meanings of the individual words in it ▫ *idiom; ungkapan; simpulan bahasa*: *The idiom 'bring something home to somebody' means 'make somebody understand something'.*

idiomatic /ˌɪdiəˈmætɪk/ adj **1** using language that contains expressions that are natural to sb who has spoken that language from birth ▫ *idiomatik*: *He speaks good idiomatic English.* **2** containing an idiom ▫ *beridiom; berbunga-bunga*: *an idiomatic expression*

idiosyncrasy /ˌɪdiəˈsɪŋkrəsi/ noun [C,U] (pl **idiosyncrasies**) a person's particular way of behaving, thinking, etc., especially when it is unusual ▫ *kelakuan tersendiri; keanehan sso; perilaku khusus sso*: *Wearing a raincoat, even on a hot day, is one of her idiosyncrasies.* ▶**idiosyncratic** /ˌɪdiəsɪŋˈkrætɪk/ adj: *His teaching methods are idiosyncratic but successful.*

idiot /ˈɪdiət/ noun [C] (*informal*) a very stupid person ▫ *(orang) bodoh/tolol*: *I was an idiot to forget my passport.* ▶**idiotic** /ˌɪdiˈɒtɪk/ adj ▶**idiotically** /-kli/ adv

idle /ˈaɪdl/ adj **1** not wanting to work hard ▫ *malas*: *He has the ability to succeed but he is just bone idle* (= very lazy). **SYN** **lazy 2** not doing anything; not being used ▫ *tdk berbuat apa-apa*: *She can't bear to be idle.* ◆ *The factory stood idle while the machines were being repaired.* **3** [only before a noun] not to be taken seriously because it will not have any result ▫ *kosong*: *an idle promise/threat* ◆ *idle chatter/curiosity* ▶**idleness** noun [U] ▶**idly** /ˈaɪdli/ adv

idol /ˈaɪdl/ noun [C] **1** a person (such as a film star) who is admired or loved ▫ *pujaan*: *a pop/football/teen/screen idol* **2** a statue that people treat as a god ▫ *berhala*

idolize (also **-ise**) /ˈaɪdəlaɪz/ verb [T] to love or admire sb very much or too much ▫ *memuja; mendewa-dewakan*: *He is an only child and his parents idolize him.*

idyllic /ɪˈdɪlɪk/ adj very pleasant and peaceful; perfect ▫ *aman damai; sempurna; cukup bagus*: *an idyllic holiday*

i.e. /ˌaɪ ˈiː/ abbr that is; in other words ▫ *iaitu*: *deciduous trees, i.e. those which lose their leaves in autumn*

if /ɪf/ conj **1** used in sentences in which one thing only happens or is true when another thing happens or is true ▫ *jika; kalau*: *If you see him, give him this letter.* ◆ *We won't go to the beach if it rains.* ◆ *If I had more time, I would learn another language.* ◆ *I might see her tomorrow. If not, I'll see her at the weekend.* ➔ note at **case, when 2** when; every time ▫ *jika; apabila*: *If I try to phone her she just hangs up.* ◆ *If metal gets hot it expands.* **3** used after verbs such as 'ask', 'know', 'remember' ▫ *sama ada*: *They asked if we would like to go too.* ◆ *I can't remember if I posted the letter or not.* ➔ note at **whether 4** used when you are asking sb to do sth or suggesting sth politely ▫ *kalau/sekiranya boleh*: *If you could just come this way, sir.* ◆ *If I might suggest something …*
IDM **as if** ➔ **as**
even if ➔ **even²**
if I were you used when you are giving sb advice ▫ *jika sayalah*: *If I were you, I'd leave now.*
if it wasn't/weren't for sb/sth if a particular person or situation did not exist or was not there; without sb/sth ▫ *kalau tdk kerana sso/sst*: *If it wasn't for him, I wouldn't stay in this country.*
if only used for expressing a strong wish ▫ *kalaulah*: *If only I could drive.* ◆ *If only he'd write.*

igloo /ˈɪɡluː/ noun [C] (pl **igloos**) a small house that is built from blocks of hard snow ▫ *iglu*

ignite /ɪɡˈnaɪt/ verb [I,T] (*formal*) to start burning or to make sth start burning ▫ *bernyala; menyalakan*: *A spark from the engine ignited the petrol.*

ignition /ɪɡˈnɪʃn/ noun **1** [C, usually sing] the electrical system that starts the engine of a car ▫ *(sistem) pencucuh*: *to turn the ignition on/off* ◆ *First of all, put the key in the ignition.* ➔ picture at **car 2** [U] the act of starting to burn or making sth start to burn ▫ *pencucuhan*

ignominious /ˌɪɡnəˈmɪniəs/ adj (*formal*) making you feel embarrassed ▫ *(yg) memalukan*: *The team suffered an ignominious defeat.* ▶**ignominiously** adv

ignorance /ˈɪɡnərəns/ noun [U] **ignorance (of/about sth)** a lack of information or knowledge ▫ *kejahilan; tdk tahu*: *The workers were in complete ignorance of the management's plans.*

ignorant /ˈɪɡnərənt/ adj **1 ignorant (of/about sth)** not knowing about sth ▫ *jahil; tdk tahu*: *Many people are ignorant of their rights.* **2** (*informal*) having or showing bad manners ▫ *tdk tahu adat/adab*: *an ignorant person/remark* ➔ look at **ignore**

ignore /ɪɡˈnɔː(r)/ verb [T] to pay no attention to sb/sth ▫ *tdk mempedulikan/menghiraukan*: *I said hello to Debbie but she totally ignored me* (= acted as though she hadn't seen me). ◆ *Alison ignored her doctor's advice about getting more exercise.*

HELP Be careful. **Ignore** and **be ignorant** are different in meaning.

ikon = **icon** (3)

I'll /aɪl/ short for **I will; I shall**

ill¹ /ɪl/ adj **1** [not before a noun] (*AmE* **sick**) not in good health; not well ▫ *sakit; tdk sihat*: *I can't drink milk because it makes me feel ill.* ◆ *My mother* was **taken ill** suddenly last week. ♦ My grandfather is **seriously ill** in hospital. ➲ note at **doctor 2** [only before a noun] bad or harmful □ *buruk; tdk baik; tdk sihat*: He resigned because of **ill health**. ♦ I'm glad to say I suffered no **ill effects** from all that rich food. ➲ noun **illness**

TOPIC

Feeling ill

If you are **suffering from** an **illness**, you feel **ill**. If you have a **fever**, for example when you have **flu**, you have a high **temperature**. If you catch a **cold**, you will start **sneezing**. You might also have a **cough** and a **sore throat**. If you **come down with chickenpox** or **measles**, your skin is covered in red **spots**. If you become ill when you eat, touch or breathe in something that does not normally make other people ill, you have an **allergy**, for example **hay fever**. You might come out in a **rash** (= an area of small red spots). A disease that moves easily from one person to another is **infectious** or **contagious** (= passed by touch). If your illness is not serious, you will quickly **get better**. When somebody is ill, we usually wish them '**Get well soon!**'

ill² /ɪl/ *adv* **1** [in compounds] badly or wrongly □ *digunakan dgn maksud tdk baik, teruk, dll*: You would be **ill-advised** to drive until you have fully recovered. **2** (*formal*) only with difficulty; not easily □ *dgn susah payah; tdk (mampu, dll)*: They could ill afford the extra money for better heating. **IDM** augur well/ill for sb/sth ➲ **augur** bode well/ill (for sb/sth) ➲ **bode** bad/ill feeling ➲ **feeling**

illegal /ɪˈliːɡl/ *adj* not allowed by the law □ *menyalahi undang-undang; haram*: It is illegal to drive a car without insurance. ♦ illegal drugs/immigrants/activities **OPP** legal ▶**illegally** /-ɡəli/ *adv*

illegality /ˌɪliˈɡæləti/ *noun* (*pl* illegalities) **1** [U] the state of being illegal □ *keharaman* **2** [C] an illegal act □ *tindakan yg menyalahi undang-undang* ➲ look at **legality**

illegible /ɪˈledʒəbl/ *adj* difficult or impossible to read □ *tdk dapat dibaca*: Your handwriting is quite illegible. **OPP** legible ▶**illegibly** /-əbli/ *adv*

illegitimate /ˌɪləˈdʒɪtəmət/ *adj* **1** (*old-fashioned*) (used about a child) born to parents who are not married to each other □ *(ttg anak) luar nikah; haram* **2** not allowed by law; against the rules □ *(yg) menyalahi undang-undang atau peraturan; secara haram*: the illegitimate use of company money **OPP** for both meanings legitimate ▶**illegitimacy** /ˌɪləˈdʒɪtəməsi/ *noun* [U] ▶**illegitimately** *adv*

ill-ˈfated *adj* not lucky □ *malang*: the ill-fated ship, the Titanic

illicit /ɪˈlɪsɪt/ *adj* (used about an activity or substance) not allowed by law or by the rules of society □ *(secara) haram/sulit*: the illicit trade in ivory ♦ They were having an illicit affair.

illiterate /ɪˈlɪtərət/ *adj* **1** not able to read or write □ *buta huruf* **OPP** literate **2** (used about a piece of writing) very badly written □ *teruk; banyak salah* **3** [usually after a noun or adverb] not knowing much about a particular subject □ *jahil; tdk pandai*: computer illiterate ▶**illiteracy** /ɪˈlɪtərəsi/ *noun* [U]: adult illiteracy **OPP** literacy

illness /ˈɪlnəs/ *noun* **1** [U] the state of being physically or mentally ill □ *sakit*: He's missed a lot of school through illness. ♦ There is a history of mental illness in the family. **2** [C] a type or period of physical or mental ill health □ *penyakit*: a minor/serious illness ♦ He died after a short illness. ➲ note at **disease** ➲ adjective **ill**

illogical /ɪˈlɒdʒɪkl/ *adj* not sensible or reasonable □ *tdk munasabah/masuk akal*: It seems illogical to me to pay somebody to do work that you could do yourself. **OPP** logical ▶**illogicality** /ɪˌlɒdʒɪˈkæləti/ *noun* [C,U] (*pl* illogicalities) ▶**illogically** /ɪˈlɒdʒɪkli/ *adv*

ill-ˈtreat *verb* [T] to treat sb/sth badly or in an unkind way □ *menganiaya*: This cat has been ill-treated. ▶**ill-ˈtreatment** *noun* [U]

illuminate /ɪˈluːmɪneɪt/ *verb* [T] (*formal*) **1** to shine light on sth or to decorate sth with lights □ *menerangi; menghias dgn lampu*: The palace was illuminated by spotlights. **2** to explain sth or make sth clear □ *menerangkan; menjelaskan*

illuminating /ɪˈluːmɪneɪtɪŋ/ *adj* helping to explain sth or make sth clear □ *(yg) memperjelas; (yg) memberi gambaran jelas*: an illuminating discussion

illumination /ɪˌluːmɪˈneɪʃn/ *noun* **1** [U,C] light or the place where a light comes from □ *(sumber) cahaya; penerangan*: The only illumination in the room came from the fire. **2** illuminations [pl] (*BrE*) brightly coloured lights that are used for decorating a street, town, etc. □ *lampu hiasan jalan, dsb*: Christmas illuminations

illusion /ɪˈluːʒn/ *noun* **1** [C,U] a false idea, belief or impression □ *khayalan; tanggapan palsu; ilusi*: I have no illusions about the situation—I know it's serious. ♦ I think Peter's **under the illusion** that he'll be the new director. **2** [C] something that your eyes tell you is there or is true but in fact is not □ *ilusi; maya*: That line looks longer, but in fact the lines are the same length. It's an **optical illusion**. ➲ picture at **optical illusion**

illusory /ɪˈluːsəri/ *adj* (*formal*) not real, although seeming to be □ *khayalan*: The profits they had hoped for proved to be illusory.

illustrate /ˈɪləstreɪt/ *verb* [T] **1** to add pictures, diagrams, etc. to a book or magazine □ *mengilustrasi; memberi gambar, gambar rajah, dsb*: Most cookery books are illustrated. **2** to explain or make sth clear by using examples, pictures or diagrams □ *menerangkan/menjelaskan dgn contoh, gambar, dll*: These statistics illustrate the point that I was making very well.

illustration /ˌɪləˈstreɪʃn/ *noun* **1** [C] a drawing, diagram or picture in a book or magazine □ *ilustrasi; gambar; gambar rajah, dsb:* colour illustrations **2** [U] the activity or art of illustrating □ *mengilustrasi; melukis gambar, gambar rajah, dsb* **3** [C] an example that makes a point or an idea clear □ *contoh:* Can you give me an illustration of what you mean?

illustrator /ˈɪləstreɪtə(r)/ *noun* [C] a person who draws or paints pictures for books, etc. □ *ilustrator; pelukis ilustrasi*

illustrious /ɪˈlʌstriəs/ *adj* (*formal*) famous and successful □ *terkenal; terbilang*

I'm /aɪm/ short for **I am**

image /ˈɪmɪdʒ/ *noun* [C] **1** the general impression that a person or an organization gives to the public □ *imej:* When you meet him, he's very different from his public image. **2** a mental picture or idea of sb/sth □ *bayangan; gambaran:* I have an image of my childhood as always sunny and happy. **3** a picture or description that appears in a book, film or painting □ *gambar; gambaran:* horrific images of war **4** a copy or picture of sb/sth seen in a mirror, through a camera, on TV, computer, etc. □ *gambar; imej; bayang-bayang:* A perfect image of the building was reflected in the lake. ♦ (figurative) He's **the (spitting) image of** his father (= he looks exactly like him).

imagery /ˈɪmɪdʒəri/ *noun* [U] language that produces pictures in the minds of the people reading or listening □ *imejan; gambaran:* poetic imagery

imaginable /ɪˈmædʒɪnəbl/ *adj* that you can imagine □ *dpt dibayangkan:* Sophie made all the excuses imaginable when she was caught stealing. ♦ His house was equipped with every imaginable luxury.

imaginary /ɪˈmædʒɪnəri/ *adj* existing only in the mind; not real □ *rekaan; khayalan:* Many children have imaginary friends.

imagination /ɪˌmædʒɪˈneɪʃn/ *noun* [U,C] the ability to create mental pictures or new ideas □ *(daya) imaginasi; daya citra; fikiran kreatif:* He has a lively imagination. ♦ She's very clever but she doesn't **have** much **imagination**.

HELP Imagination or fantasy? **Imagination** is a creative quality that a person has. **Fantasy** refers to thoughts, stories, etc. that are not related to reality.

2 [C] the part of the mind that uses this ability □ *imaginasi; fikiran:* If you **use** your **imagination**, you should be able to guess the answer.

imaginative /ɪˈmædʒɪnətɪv/ *adj* having or showing imagination □ *berimaginasi; imaginatif:* She's always full of imaginative ideas. ▸ **imaginatively** *adv*

imagine /ɪˈmædʒɪn/ *verb* [T] **1 imagine that ...; imagine sb/sth (doing/as sth)** to form a picture or idea in your mind of what sth/sb might be like □ *membayangkan; bayangkan:* Imagine that you're lying on a beach. ♦ It's not easy to imagine your brother as a doctor. ♦ I can't imagine myself cycling 20 miles a day. **2** to see, hear or think sth that is not true or does not exist □ *berkhayal; (mempunyai) khayalan:* She's always imagining that she's ill but she's fine really. ♦ I thought I heard someone downstairs, but I must have been **imagining things**. **3** to think that sth is probably true □ *rasa; ingat; fikir* **SYN** suppose: I imagine he'll be coming by car.

imam /ɪˈmɑːm/ *noun* [C] (in Islam) a religious man who leads the prayers in a **mosque** (= a building where Muslims meet and worship) □ *imam*

imbalance /ɪmˈbæləns/ *noun* [C] **an imbalance (between A and B); an imbalance (in/of sth)** a difference; not being equal □ *ketidakseimbangan:* an imbalance in the numbers of men and women teachers

imbecile /ˈɪmbəsiːl/ *noun* [C] a stupid person □ *(si) bodoh/tongong/tolol* **SYN** **idiot**

IMF /ˌaɪ em ˈef/ *abbr* the **International Monetary Fund**; the organization within the United Nations which is concerned with trade and economic development □ *IMF (Tabung Kewangan Antarabangsa)*

imitate /ˈɪmɪteɪt/ *verb* [T] **1** to copy sb/sth □ *meniru:* Small children learn by imitating their parents. **2** to copy the speech or actions of sb/sth, often in order to make people laugh □ *mengajuk:* She could imitate her mother perfectly.

imitation /ˌɪmɪˈteɪʃn/ *noun* **1** [C] a copy of sth real □ *tiruan:* Some artificial flowers are good imitations of real ones. ➔ look at **genuine** **2** [U] the act of copying sb/sth □ *peniruan; (perbuatan) meniru:* Good pronunciation of a language is best learnt **by imitation**. **3** [C] the act of copying the way sb talks and behaves, especially in order to make people laugh □ *ajukan; (perbuatan) mengajuk:* Can you do any imitations of politicians?

immaculate /ɪˈmækjələt/ *adj* **1** perfectly clean and tidy □ *bersih dan rapi:* immaculate white shirts **2** without any mistakes □ *sempurna; tiada cela langsung* **SYN** perfect: an immaculate performance ▸ **immaculately** *adv*

immaterial /ˌɪməˈtɪəriəl/ *adj* **immaterial (to sb/sth)** not important □ *tdk penting:* It's immaterial to me whether we go today or tomorrow.

immature /ˌɪməˈtjʊə(r)/ (*AmE* also) / *adj* **1** (used about a person) behaving in a way that is not sensible and is typical of people who are much younger □ *kurang matang; tdk matang:* He's too immature to take his work seriously. **2** not fully grown or developed □ *belum matang; masih muda; mentah:* an immature body **OPP** for both meanings **mature**

immeasurable /ɪˈmeʒərəbl/ *adj* (*formal*) too large, great, etc. to be measured □ *tdk terukur:* to cause immeasurable harm ▸ **immeasurably** /-əbli/ *adv:* Housing standards improved immeasurably after the war.

immediacy /ɪˈmiːdiəsi/ noun [U] (formal) the quality of being available or seeming to happen close to you and without delay □ *kesegeraan*: *Letters do not have the same immediacy as email.*

immediate /ɪˈmiːdiət/ adj **1** happening or done without delay □ *segera; serta-merta*: *I'd like an immediate answer to my proposal.* ◆ *The government responded with immediate action.* **2** [only before a noun] existing now and needing urgent attention □ *paling penting*: *Tell me what your immediate needs are.* **3** [only before a noun] nearest in time, position or relationship □ *terdekat*: *They won't make any changes in the immediate future.* ◆ *He has left most of his money to his immediate family* (= wife, parents, children, brothers and sisters).

immediately /ɪˈmiːdiətli/ adv, conj **1** at once; without delay □ *dgn segera*: *Can you come home immediately after work?* ◆ *I couldn't immediately see what he meant.* **2** nearest in time or position □ *sebaik-baik sahaja*: *Who's the girl immediately in front of Simon?* ◆ *What did you do immediately after you left school?* **3** very closely; directly □ *secara langsung*: *He wasn't immediately involved in the crime.* **4** (BrE) as soon as □ *sebaik sahaja*: *I opened the letter immediately I got home.*

immense /ɪˈmens/ adj very big or great □ *sangat besar; amat; sungguh*: *immense difficulties/importance/power* ◆ *She gets immense pleasure from her garden.*

immensely /ɪˈmensli/ adv extremely; very much □ *amat; sangat*: *immensely enjoyable* ◆ *'Did you enjoy the party?' 'Yes, immensely.'*

immensity /ɪˈmensəti/ noun [U] an extremely large size □ *besarnya; luasnya*: *the immensity of the universe*

immerse /ɪˈmɜːs/ verb [T] **1** immerse sth (in sth) to put sth into a liquid so that it is covered □ *merendamkan; direndam*: *Make sure the spaghetti is fully immersed in the boiling water.* **2** immerse yourself (in sth) to involve yourself completely in sth so that you give it all your attention □ *asyik/leka (membuat sst)*: *Rachel's usually immersed in a book.* ▶ **immersion** /ɪˈmɜːʃn/ noun [U]: *Immersion in cold water resulted in rapid loss of heat.* ◆ *a two-week immersion course in French* (= in which the student will hear and use only French).

immigrant /ˈɪmɪɡrənt/ noun [C] a person who has come into a foreign country to live there permanently □ *pendatang; imigran*: *The government plans to tighten controls to prevent illegal immigrants.* ◆ *London has a high immigrant population.*

MORE A society with many immigrant communities is a **multicultural society**. Groups of immigrants or children of immigrants who share a common cultural tradition are an **ethnic minority**.

immigrate /ˈɪmɪɡreɪt/ verb [I] (especially AmE) to come and live permanently in a country after leaving your own country □ *berimigrasi*

HELP In British English it is more common to use the verb **emigrate**, which is used in connection with the place that somebody has come from: *My parents emigrated to this country from Jamaica.*

immigration /ˌɪmɪˈɡreɪʃn/ noun [U] **1** the process of coming to live permanently in a country that is not your own; the number of people who do this □ *imigresen; kemasukan pendatang*: *There are greater controls on immigration than there used to be.* **2** (also immiˈgration control) the control point at an airport, port, etc. where the official documents of people who want to come into a country are checked □ *imigresen*: *When you leave the plane you have to go through customs and immigration.* ⊃ look at **emigrate, emigrant, emigration**

imminent /ˈɪmɪnənt/ adj (usually used about sth unpleasant) almost certain to happen very soon □ *mungkin akan berlaku*: *Heavy rainfall means that flooding is imminent.* ▶ **imminently** adv

immobile /ɪˈməʊbaɪl/ adj not moving or not able to move □ *tdk bergerak; tdk dpt bergerak; kaku*: *The hunter stood immobile until the lion had passed.* **OPP** mobile ▶ **immobility** /ˌɪməˈbɪləti/ noun [U]

immobilize (also -ise) /ɪˈməʊbəlaɪz/ verb [T] to prevent sb/sth from moving or working normally □ *menyebabkan tdk dpt bergerak atau tdk boleh berfungsi; melumpuhkan*: *The railways have been completely immobilized by the strike.* ◆ *This device immobilizes the car to prevent it being stolen.*

immobilizer (also -iser) /ɪˈməʊbəlaɪzə(r)/ noun [C] a device in a vehicle that prevents thieves from starting the engine when the vehicle is parked □ *peranti pelumpuh (kenderaan)*

immoral /ɪˈmɒrəl/ (AmE also) / adj (used about people or their behaviour) considered wrong or not honest by most people □ *tdk bermoral; tdk berakhlak*: *It's immoral to steal.* **OPP** moral

HELP Be careful. **Amoral** has a different meaning.

▶ **immorality** /ˌɪməˈræləti/ noun [U] **OPP** morality ▶ **immorally** /ɪˈmɒrəli/ (AmE also) / adv

immortal /ɪˈmɔːtl/ adj living or lasting for ever □ *abadi; kekal*: *Nobody is immortal—we all have to die some time.* **OPP** mortal ▶ **immortality** /ˌɪmɔːˈtæləti/ noun [U]

immortalize (also -ise) /ɪˈmɔːtəlaɪz/ verb [T] to give lasting fame to sb/sth □ *mengabadikan*: *He immortalized their relationship in a poem.*

immune /ɪˈmjuːn/ adj **1** immune (to sth) having natural protection against a certain disease or illness □ *imun; lali*: *You should be immune to measles if you've had it already.* ◆ *These vitamins* help to strengthen your **immune system**. 2 **immune (to sth)** not affected by sth □ *lali*: *You can say what you like—I'm immune to criticism!* 3 **immune (from sth)** protected from a danger or punishment □ *terlindung; kebal; terkecuali*: *Young children are immune from prosecution.*

immunity /ɪˈmjuːnəti/ *noun* [U] the ability to avoid or not be affected by disease, criticism, punishment by law, etc. □ *keimunan; kelalian; kekebalan*: *In many countries people have no immunity to diseases like measles.* ♦ *Ambassadors to other countries receive* **diplomatic immunity** (= protection from being arrested, etc.)

immunize (also **-ise**) /ˈɪmjunaɪz/ *verb* [T] to protect sb from a disease, usually by putting a **vaccine** (= a substance that protects the body) into their blood □ *mengimunkan; diimunkan; melalikan*: *Before visiting certain countries you will need to be immunized against cholera.* ⊃ look at **inoculate**, **vaccinate** ▶ **immunization** (also **-isation**) /ˌɪmjunaɪˈzeɪʃn/ *noun* [C,U]

imp /ɪmp/ *noun* [C] (in stories) a small creature like a little man, who has magic powers and behaves badly □ *anak syaitan*

impact /ˈɪmpækt/ *noun* 1 [C, usually sing] **an impact (on/upon sb/sth)** a powerful effect or impression □ *kesan*: *I hope this anti-smoking campaign will make/have an impact on young people.* ♦ *I hope this road safety campaign will make/have an impact on drivers.* 2 [C,U] the action or force of one object hitting another □ *impak; hentaman; hantukan*: *The impact of the crash threw the passengers out of their seats.* ♦ *The bomb exploded on impact.*

impair /ɪmˈpeə(r)/ *verb* [T] (*formal*) to damage sth or make it weaker □ *merosakkan; menjejaskan*: *Ear infections can result in impaired hearing.*

impale /ɪmˈpeɪl/ *verb* [T] **impale sb/sth (on sth)** to push a sharp pointed object through sb/sth □ *menikam; tertikam*: *The boy fell out of the tree and impaled his leg on some railings.*

impart /ɪmˈpɑːt/ *verb* [T] (*formal*) 1 **impart sth (to sb)** to pass information, knowledge, etc. to other people □ *menyampaikan; memberitahu*: *He rushed home eager to impart the good news.* 2 **impart sth (to sth)** to give a certain quality to sth □ *memberi*: *The low lighting imparted a romantic atmosphere to the room.*

impartial /ɪmˈpɑːʃl/ *adj* not supporting one person or group more than another; fair □ *adil; saksama; tdk berat sebelah*: *The referee must be impartial.* ▶ **impartiality** /ˌɪmˌpɑːʃiˈæləti/ *noun* [U] **OPP** **partiality** ▶ **impartially** /ɪmˈpɑːʃəli/ *adv*

impassable /ɪmˈpɑːsəbl/ *adj* (used about a road, etc.) impossible to travel on because it is blocked □ *tdk dpt dilalui*: *Flooding and fallen trees have made many roads impassable.* **OPP** **passable**

impassioned /ɪmˈpæʃnd/ *adj* (used especially about a speech) showing strong feelings about sth □ *penuh dgn perasaan; yg meluap-luap*: *an impassioned plea/speech/defence*

impassive /ɪmˈpæsɪv/ *adj* (used about a person) showing no emotion or reaction □ *tdk menunjukkan sebarang perasaan* ▶ **impassively** *adv*

impatient /ɪmˈpeɪʃnt/ *adj* 1 **impatient (at sth/with sb)** not able to stay calm and wait for sb/sth; easily annoyed by sb/sth that seems slow □ *tdk sabar*: *The passengers are getting impatient at the delay.* ♦ *It's no good being impatient with small children.* **OPP** **patient** 2 **impatient for/to do sth** wanting sth to happen soon □ *tdk sabar-sabar lagi*: *By the time they are sixteen many young people are impatient to leave school.* ▶ **impatience** *noun* [U]: *He began to explain for the third time with growing impatience.* **OPP** **patience** ▶ **impatiently** *adv* **OPP** **patiently**

impeccable /ɪmˈpekəbl/ *adj* without any mistakes or faults; perfect □ *baik sekali; sempurna*: *impeccable behaviour* ♦ *His accent is impeccable.* ▶ **impeccably** /-əbli/ *adv*

impede /ɪmˈpiːd/ *verb* [T] (*formal*) to make it difficult for sb/sth to move or go forward □ *menghalang; terhalang*: *The completion of the new motorway has been impeded by bad weather conditions.*

impediment /ɪmˈpedɪmənt/ *noun* [C] (*formal*) 1 **an impediment (to sth)** something that makes it difficult for a person or thing to move or progress □ *halangan; penghalang*: *The high rate of tax is a major impediment to new businesses.* 2 something that makes speaking difficult □ *kecacatan*: *Jane had a speech impediment*

impending /ɪmˈpendɪŋ/ *adj* [only before a noun] (usually used about sth bad) that will happen soon □ *(yg) akan berlaku/terjadi; tdk lama lagi*: *There was a feeling of impending disaster in the air.*

impenetrable /ɪmˈpenɪtrəbl/ *adj* 1 impossible to enter or go through □ *tdk dpt diterobosi/dilalui*: *The jungle was impenetrable.* 2 impossible to understand □ *sukar difahami*: *an impenetrable mystery*

imperative /ɪmˈperətɪv/ *adj* (*formal*) very important or urgent □ *sangat mustahak; penting sekali*: *It's imperative that you see a doctor immediately.*

the imperative /ɪmˈperətɪv/ *noun* [sing] the form of the verb that is used for giving orders □ *imperatif; bentuk perintah*: *In 'Shut the door!' the verb is in the imperative.*

imperceptible /ˌɪmpəˈseptəbl/ *adj* too small to be seen or noticed □ *tdk dpt dilihat atau dikesan*: *The difference between the original painting and the copy was almost imperceptible.* **OPP** **perceptible** ▶ **imperceptibly** /-əbli/ *adv*: *Almost imperceptibly winter was turning into spring.*

imperfect /ɪmˈpɜːfɪkt/ *adj* with mistakes or faults □ *tdk sempurna*: *an imperfect system* **OPP** **perfect** ▶ **imperfectly** *adv*

imperfection /ɪmpəˈfekʃn/ noun [C,U] a fault or weakness in sb/sth □ *ketidaksempurnaan; tdk sempurna; kekurangan; cacat*: They learned to live with each other's imperfections.

imperial /ɪmˈpɪəriəl/ adj [only before a noun] **1** connected with an empire or its ruler □ *berkenaan dgn empayar atau pemerintahnya*: the imperial palace **2** connected with the system for measuring length, weight and volume that, in the past, was used for all goods in the UK and is still used for some □ *imperial (ttg sistem ukuran)* ⇨ look at **inch, foot, yard, ounce, pound, pint, gallon, metric**

imperialism /ɪmˈpɪəriəlɪzəm/ noun [U] a political system in which a rich and powerful country has **colonies** (= countries that it controls) □ *imperialisme* ▶**imperialist** /-ɪst/ adj, noun [C]

impersonal /ɪmˈpɜːsənl/ adj **1** not showing friendly human feelings; cold in feeling or atmosphere □ *tdk bersifat peribadi; tdk mesra*: My hotel room was very impersonal. **2** not referring to any particular person □ *tdk merujuk kpd sesiapa tertentu*: Can we try to keep the discussion as impersonal as possible, please?

impersonate /ɪmˈpɜːsəneɪt/ verb [T] to copy the behaviour and way of speaking of a person or to pretend to be a different person □ *menyamar; mengajuk*: a comedian who impersonates politicians ▶**impersonation** /ɪmˌpɜːsəˈneɪʃn/ noun [C,U] ▶**impersonator** /ɪmˈpɜːsəneɪtə(r)/ noun [C]

impertinent /ɪmˈpɜːtɪnənt/ adj (formal) not showing respect; rude □ *biadab; kurang ajar*: I do apologize. It was impertinent of my son to speak to you like that.

> **HELP** The opposite is NOT **pertinent**. It is **polite** or **respectful**.

▶**impertinence** noun [U]: He had the impertinence to ask my age. ▶**impertinently** adv

imperturbable /ˌɪmpəˈtɜːbəbl/ adj (formal) not easily worried by a difficult situation □ *tenang*

impervious /ɪmˈpɜːviəs/ adj impervious (to sth) **1** not affected or influenced by sth □ *lali*: She was impervious to criticism. **2** (technical) not allowing water, etc. to pass through □ *kedap; tdk telus*

impetuous /ɪmˈpetʃuəs/ adj acting or done quickly and without thinking □ *terburu-buru; gopoh*: an impetuous decision ⇨ A more common word is **impulsive**. ▶**impetuously** adv

impetus /ˈɪmpɪtəs/ noun [U, sing] (an) impetus (for sth); (an) impetus (to do sth) something that encourages sth else to happen □ *dorongan; rangsangan*: This scandal provided the main impetus for changes in the rules. ♦ I need fresh impetus to start working on this essay again.

impinge /ɪmˈpɪndʒ/ verb [I] (formal) impinge on/upon sth to have a noticeable effect on sth, especially a bad one □ *mendatangkan kesan; menjejaskan*: I'm not going to let my job impinge on my home life.

[C] **countable**, a noun with a plural form: one book, two books

443   **imperfection → import**

implant /ˈɪmplɑːnt/ noun [C] something that is put into a person's body in a medical operation □ *(bahan) implan*: dental implants ⇨ look at **transplant**

implausible /ɪmˈplɔːzəbl/ adj not easy to believe □ *sukar dipercayai*: an implausible excuse OPP **plausible**

implement¹ /ˈɪmplɪment/ verb [T] to start using a plan, system, etc. □ *melaksanakan*: Some teachers are finding it difficult to implement the government's educational reforms. ▶**implementation** /ˌɪmplɪmenˈteɪʃn/ noun [U]

implement² /ˈɪmplɪmənt/ noun [C] a tool or instrument (especially for work outdoors) □ *alat; perkakas*: farm implements ⇨ note at **tool**

implicated /ˈɪmplɪkeɪtɪd/
IDM be implicated in sth to be involved in sth unpleasant, especially a crime □ *terbabit; terlibat*: A well-known politician was implicated in the scandal.

implication /ˌɪmplɪˈkeɪʃn/ noun **1** [C, usually pl] implications (for/of sth) the effect that sth might have on sth else in the future □ *implikasi; kesan*: The new law will have serious implications for our work. **2** [C,U] something that is suggested or said in a way that is not direct □ *maksud tdk langsung*: The implication of what she said was that we had made a bad mistake. ⇨ verb **imply 3** [U] implication (in sth) the fact of being involved, or of involving sb, in sth unpleasant, especially a crime □ *pembabitan; terbabitnya*: The player's implication in this scandal could affect his career. ⇨ verb **implicate**

implicit /ɪmˈplɪsɪt/ adj **1** not expressed in a direct way but understood by the people involved □ *tersirat; secara tak langsung*: We had an implicit agreement that we would support each other. ⇨ look at **explicit 2** complete; total □ *mutlak; penuh*: I have implicit faith in your ability to do the job. ▶**implicitly** adv

implore /ɪmˈplɔː(r)/ verb [T] (formal) to ask sb with great emotion to do sth, because you are in a very serious situation □ *merayu*: She implored him not to leave her alone. **SYN** beg

imply /ɪmˈplaɪ/ verb [T] (implying; implies; pt, pp implied) to suggest sth in an indirect way or without actually saying it □ *membayangkan; menandakan (secara tdk langsung)*: He didn't say so—but he implied that I was lying. ⇨ noun **implication**

impolite /ˌɪmpəˈlaɪt/ adj rude □ *kurang sopan*: I think it was impolite of him to ask you to leave. **SYN** rude, discourteous OPP polite ▶**impolitely** adv

import¹ /ˈɪmpɔːt/ noun **1** [C, usually pl] a product or service that is brought into one country from another □ *(barangan) import*: What are your country's major imports? OPP **export 2** [U] (also **importation**) the act of bringing goods or services into a country □ *pengimportan*:

[U] **uncountable**, a noun with no plural form: some sugar

new controls on the import of certain goods from abroad

import² /ɪmˈpɔːt/ *verb* [T] **1** **import sth (from ...)** to buy goods, etc. from a foreign country and bring them into your own country □ *mengimport*: *imported goods* ◆ *Britain imports wine from France/Italy/Spain.* ◆ *(figurative) We need to import some extra help from somewhere fast.* OPP **export 2** to move information into a computer program from another program □ *mengimport* ▶**importer** *noun* [C] OPP **exporter**

importance /ɪmˈpɔːtns/ *noun* [U] the quality of being important □ *(perihal) penting; pentingnya*: *The decision was of great importance to the future of the business.*

important /ɪmˈpɔːtnt/ *adj* **1** **important (to sb); important (for sb/sth) (to do sth); important that ...** having great value or influence; very necessary □ *penting; mustahak*: *an important meeting/decision/factor* ◆ *This job is very important to me.* ◆ *It's important not to be late.* ◆ *It's important for people to see the results of what they do.* ◆ *It was important to me that you were there.* **2** (used about a person) having great influence or authority □ *penting; berwibawa*: *Milton was one of the most important writers of his time.* ▶**importantly** *adv*

OTHER WORDS FOR

important

Essential and **vital** both mean 'very important or completely necessary': *It is essential/vital that our children get the best possible education.* ◆ *Fresh fruit and vegetables are an essential/a vital part of a healthy diet.* We also say **play a vital/key role in ...** *The police play a key role in our society.* Something that is important in history is **historic**: *a historic decision/event/occasion.*

---

importation /ˌɪmpɔːˈteɪʃn/ = **import¹** (2)

impose /ɪmˈpəʊz/ *verb* **1** [T] **impose sth (on/upon sb/sth)** to make a law, rule, opinion, etc. be accepted by using your power or authority □ *mengenakan*: *A new tax will be imposed on wine and spirits.* ◆ *Parents should try not to impose their own ideas on their children.* **2** [I] **impose (on/upon sb/sth)** to ask or expect sb to do sth that may cause extra work or trouble □ *menyusahkan; membebankan*: *I hate to impose on you but can you lend me some money?* ▶**imposition** /ˌɪmpəˈzɪʃn/ *noun* [U,C]: *the imposition of military rule*

imposing /ɪmˈpəʊzɪŋ/ *adj* big and important; impressive □ *mengagumkan; tersergam*: *They lived in a large, imposing house near the park.*

impossible /ɪmˈpɒsəbl/ *adj* **1** not able to be done or to happen □ *mustahil; tdk mungkin*: *It's impossible for me to be there before 12.* ◆ *I find it almost impossible to get up in the morning!* ◆ *That's impossible! (= I don't believe it!)* OPP **possible 2** very difficult to deal with □ *sukar ditangani/dikawal*: *This is an impossible situation!* ◆ *He's always been an impossible child.* ▶**the impossible** *noun* [sing]: *Don't attempt the impossible!* ▶**impossibility** /ɪmˌpɒsəˈbɪləti/ *noun* [C,U] (*pl* **impossibilities**): *What you are suggesting is a complete impossibility!*

impossibly /ɪmˈpɒsəbli/ *adv* extremely □ *amat; sangat*: *impossibly complicated*

impostor /ɪmˈpɒstə(r)/ *noun* [C] a person who pretends to be sb else in order to trick other people □ *penyamar*

impotent /ˈɪmpətənt/ *adj* **1** without enough power to influence a situation or to change things □ *tdk mempunyai kuasa; lemah* SYN **powerless 2** (used about a man) not capable of having sex □ *mati pucuk* ▶**impotence** *noun* [U]

impoverish /ɪmˈpɒvərɪʃ/ *verb* [T] (*formal*) to make sb/sth poor or lower in quality □ *memiskinkan; mengurangkan mutu* OPP **enrich**

impractical /ɪmˈpræktɪkl/ *adj* **1** not sensible or realistic □ *tdk praktikal; tdk sesuai*: *It would be impractical to take our bikes on the train.* **2** (used about a person) not good at doing ordinary things that involve using your hands; not good at organizing or planning things □ *tdk tahu membuat kerja-kerja yg menggunakan tangan; tdk pandai dr segi pengurusan atau perancangan*: *He's clever but completely impractical.* OPP *for both meanings* **practical**

imprecise /ˌɪmprɪˈsaɪs/ *adj* not clear or exact □ *tdk tepat*: *imprecise instructions* OPP **precise**

impress /ɪmˈpres/ *verb* [T] **1** **impress sb (with sth); impress sb that ...** to make sb feel admiration and respect □ *menimbulkan rasa kagum; mengagumkan*: *She's always trying to impress people with her new clothes.* ◆ *It impressed me that he understood immediately what I meant.* **2** (*formal*) **impress sth on/upon sb** to make the importance of sth very clear to sb □ *menekankan; menyedarkan*: *You should impress on John that he must pass these exams.*

impressed /ɪmˈprest/ *adj* **impressed (by/with sb/sth)** feeling admiration for sb/sth because you think they are particularly good, interesting, etc. □ *kagum; memandang tinggi*: *I must admit I am impressed.* ◆ *We were all impressed by her enthusiasm.*

impression /ɪmˈpreʃn/ *noun* [C] **1** an idea, a feeling or an opinion that you get about sb/sth □ *tanggapan*: *What's your first impression of the new director?* ◆ *I'm not sure but I have/get the impression that Jane's rather unhappy.* ◆ *I was under the impression (= I believed, but I was wrong) that you were married.* **2** the effect that a person or thing produces on sb else □ *tanggapan*: *She gives the impression of being older than she really is.* ◆ *Do you think I made a good impression on your parents?* **3** an amusing copy of the way sb acts or speaks □ *ajukan*: *My brother can do a good impression of the Prime Minister.* SYN **impersonation 4** a mark that is left when an object has been pressed hard into a surface □ *kesan; bekas*

impressionable /ɪmˈpreʃənəbl/ adj easy to influence □ *mudah terpengaruh*: *Sixteen is a very impressionable age.*

impressive /ɪmˈpresɪv/ adj causing a feeling of admiration and respect because of the importance, size, quality, etc. of sth □ *hebat; mengagumkan*: *an impressive building/speech* ♦ *The way he handled the situation was most impressive.*

imprint /ˈɪmprɪnt/ noun [C] a mark made by pressing an object on a surface □ *kesan; teraan*: *the imprint of a foot in the sand*

imprison /ɪmˈprɪzn/ verb [T, often passive] to put or keep sb in prison □ *memenjarakan; dipenjarakan*: *He was imprisoned for armed robbery.* ▶**imprisonment** noun [U]: *She was sentenced to five years' imprisonment.*

improbable /ɪmˈprɒbəbl/ adj not likely to be true or to happen □ *tdk mungkin*: *an improbable explanation* ♦ *It is highly improbable that Alexandra will arrive tonight.* **SYN** unlikely **OPP** probable ▶**improbability** /ɪmˌprɒbəˈbɪləti/ noun [U] ▶**improbably** /ɪmˈprɒbəbli/ adv

impromptu /ɪmˈprɒmptjuː/ adj (done) without being prepared or organized □ *tanpa persediaan*: *an impromptu party*

improper /ɪmˈprɒpə(r)/ adj (formal) 1 illegal or dishonest □ *salah; tdk jujur*: *It seems that she had been involved in improper business deals.* 2 not suitable for the situation; rude in a sexual way □ *tdk wajar; tdk senonoh; tdk sopan*: *It would be improper to say anything else at this stage.* ♦ *He lost his job for making improper suggestions to several of the women.* **OPP** for both meanings proper ▶**improperly** adv **OPP** properly

impropriety /ˌɪmprəˈpraɪəti/ noun [U,C] (pl **improprieties**) (formal) behaviour or actions that are morally wrong or not appropriate □ *kelakuan/tindakan yg tdk wajar, tdk senonoh atau tdk sopan*: *She was unaware of the impropriety of her remark.*

improve /ɪmˈpruːv/ verb [I,T] to become or to make sth better □ *bertambah baik; memperbaiki; mempertingkat*: *Your work has greatly improved.* ♦ *I hope the weather will improve later on.* ♦ *Your vocabulary is excellent but you could improve your pronunciation.*
PHR V **improve on/upon sth** to produce sth that is better than sth else □ *memperbaik; mempertingkat*: *Nobody will be able to improve on that score* (= nobody will be able to make a higher score).

improvement /ɪmˈpruːvmənt/ noun [C,U] **(an) improvement (on/in sth)** (a) change which makes the quality or condition of sb/sth better □ *perbaikan; (perbuatan) mempertingkat atau membaiki*: *Your written work is in need of some improvement.* ♦ *There's been (a) considerable improvement in your mother's condition.* ♦ *These marks are an improvement on your previous ones.*

improvise /ˈɪmprəvaɪz/ verb [I,T] 1 to make, do, or manage sth without preparation, using what you have □ *mengimprovisasi (menggunakan apa-apa yg ada sahaja)*: *If you can't find the equipment you need, you'll have to improvise.* 2 to play music, speak or act using your imagination instead of written or remembered material □ *mengimprovisasi; mereka-reka*: *It was obvious that the actor had forgotten his lines and was trying to improvise.* ▶**improvisation** /ˌɪmprəvaɪˈzeɪʃn/ noun [C,U]

impudent /ˈɪmpjədənt/ adj (formal) very rude; lacking respect and not polite □ *biadab; kurang ajar* ⊃ A more informal word is **cheeky**. ▶**impudently** adv ▶**impudence** noun [U]

impulse /ˈɪmpʌls/ noun [C] 1 [usually sing] **an impulse (to do sth)** a sudden desire to do sth without thinking about the results □ *desakan; gerak hati*: *Her first impulse was to run away.* 2 (technical) a force or movement of energy that causes a reaction □ *impuls*: *nerve/electrical impulses*
IDM **on (an) impulse** without thinking or planning and not considering the results □ *mengikut gerak hati; tanpa berfikir*: *When I saw the child fall in the water, I just acted on impulse and jumped in after her.*

impulsive /ɪmˈpʌlsɪv/ adj likely to act suddenly and without thinking; done without careful thought □ *suka mengikut gerak hati*: *He is an impulsive character.* ▶**impulsively** adv ▶**impulsiveness** noun [U]

impure /ɪmˈpjʊə(r)/ adj 1 not pure or clean; consisting of more than one substance mixed together (and therefore not of good quality) □ *tdk tulen; tdk murni*: *impure metals* 2 (old-fashioned) (used about thoughts and actions connected with sex) not moral; bad □ *kotor; keji* **OPP** for both meanings pure

impurity /ɪmˈpjʊərəti/ noun (pl **impurities**) 1 [C, usually pl] a substance that is present in small amounts in another substance, making it dirty or of poor quality □ *kekotoran; bendasing*: *People are being advised to filter their water to remove impurities.* 2 [U] (old-fashioned) the state of being morally bad □ *ketidaksucian* ⊃ look at **purity**

in¹ /ɪn/ adv, prep 1 (used to show place) inside or to a position inside a particular area or object □ *di; di/ke dlm; dlm; sampai*: *a country in Africa* ♦ *islands in the Pacific* ♦ *in a box* ♦ *I read about it in the newspaper.* ♦ *He lay in bed.* ♦ *She put the keys in her pocket.* ♦ *His wife's in hospital.* ♦ *She opened the door and went in.* ♦ *My suitcase is full. I can't get any more in.* ♦ *When does the train get in* (= to the station)*?* 2 at home or at work □ *ada (di rumah/tempat kerja)*: *I knocked at the door, but he wasn't in.* ♦ *She won't be in till late today.* **OPP** out 3 contained in; forming the whole or part of sth □ *dlm; di dlm*: *What's in this casserole?* ♦ *There are 31 days in January.* 4 (showing time) during a period of time □ *pd; dlm*: *My birthday is in August.* ♦ *in spring/summer/autumn/winter*

• He was born in 1980. • You could walk there in about an hour (= it would take that long to walk there). **5** (showing time) after a period of time □ *dlm masa*: I'll be finished in ten minutes. **6** wearing sth □ *memakai*: They were all dressed in black for the funeral. • I've never seen you in a suit before. • a woman in a yellow dress **7** showing the condition or state of sb/sth □ *digunakan utk menunjukkan keadaan atau kedudukan sso/sst*: My father is in poor health. • This room is in a mess! • Richard's in love. • He's in his mid-thirties. **8** used with feelings □ *digunakan utk menyatakan perasaan*: I watched in horror as the plane crashed to the ground. • He was in such a rage I didn't dare to go near him. **9** showing sb's job or the activity sb is involved in □ *dlm (bidang)*: He's got a good job in advertising. • All her family are in politics (= they are politicians). • He's in the army. **10** used for saying how things are arranged □ *dlm; (digunakan utk menyatakan cara sst diatur)*: We sat in a circle. • She had her hair in plaits. **11** used for saying how sth is written or expressed □ *dgn menggunakan; dlm*: Please write in pen. • They were talking in Italian/French/Polish. • to work in groups/teams **12** used for giving the rate of sth and for talking about numbers □ *dlm*: One family in four in the UK owns a cat. **13** received by sb official □ *diterima*: All applications must be in by 20 March. **14** (used about the sea) at the highest point, when the water is closest to the land □ *(air) pasang*: The tide's coming in. ❶ For special uses with many verbs and nouns, for example **in time**, **give in**, look at the verb and noun entries.

IDM **be in for it/sth** (informal) to be going to experience sth unpleasant □ *akan terkejut, kena marah, dll; habislah*: He'll be in for a shock when he gets the bill. • You'll be in for it when Mum sees what you've done.

be/get in on sth (informal) to be included or involved in sth □ *bersama-sama dlm; turut serta*: I'd like to be in on the new project.

have (got) it in for sb (informal) to be unpleasant to sb because they have done sth to upset you □ *menaruh dendam terhadap sso*: John's had it in for me ever since I missed his party.

in² /ɪn/ *adj* (informal) fashionable at the moment □ *disukai ramai; menjadi fesyen*: the in place to go • The colour grey is very in this season.

in³ /ɪn/ *noun*

IDM **the ins and outs (of sth)** the details and difficulties (involved in sth) □ *selok-belok (sst)*: Will somebody explain the ins and outs of the situation to me?

in. *abbr* = **inch¹**

inability /ˌɪnəˈbɪləti/ *noun* [sing] **inability (to do sth)** lack of ability, power or skill □ *ketidakmampuan; ketidakupayaan*: He has a complete inability to listen to other people's opinions. **OPP** **ability** ⊃ *adjective* **unable**

inaccessible /ˌɪnækˈsesəbl/ *adj* very difficult or impossible to reach or contact □ *tdk dapat didatangi/dihampiri/dihubungi*: That beach is inaccessible by car. **OPP** **accessible** ▶ **inaccessibility** /ˌɪnækˌsesəˈbɪləti/ *noun* [U]

inaccurate /ɪnˈækjərət/ *adj* not correct or accurate; with mistakes □ *tdk tepat*: an inaccurate report/description/statement **OPP** **accurate** ▶ **inaccuracy** /ɪnˈækjərəsi/ *noun* [C,U] (*pl* **inaccuracies**): There are always some inaccuracies in newspaper reports. ▶ **inaccurately** *adv*

inaction /ɪnˈækʃn/ *noun* [U] doing nothing; lack of action □ *ketiadaan tindakan; tdk bertindak*: The crisis was blamed on the government's earlier inaction. **OPP** **action**

inactive /ɪnˈæktɪv/ *adj* doing nothing; not active □ *tdk aktif; tdk berbuat apa-apa*: The virus remains inactive in the body. **OPP** **active** ▶ **inactivity** /ˌɪnækˈtɪvəti/ *noun* [U] **OPP** **activity**

inadequate /ɪnˈædɪkwət/ *adj* **1** **inadequate (for sth/to do sth)** not enough; not good enough □ *tdk cukup; tdk memadai*: the problem of inadequate housing **OPP** **adequate** **2** (used about a person) not able to deal with a problem or situation; not confident □ *kekurangan*: There was so much to learn in the new job that for a while I felt totally inadequate. ▶ **inadequately** *adv* ▶ **inadequacy** /ɪnˈædɪkwəsi/ *noun* [C,U] (*pl* **inadequacies**): his inadequacy as a parent

inadmissible /ˌɪnədˈmɪsəbl/ *adj* (formal) that cannot be allowed or accepted, especially in a court of law □ *tdk boleh diterima; tdk dibenarkan*: inadmissible evidence **OPP** **admissible**

inadvertently /ˌɪnədˈvɜːtəntli/ *adv* without thinking, not on purpose □ *dgn tdk sengaja*: She had inadvertently left the letter where he could find it. **SYN** **unintentionally** ▶ **inadvertent** *adj*

inadvisable /ˌɪnədˈvaɪzəbl/ *adj* (formal) not sensible; not showing good judgement □ *tdk bijak; sebaik-baiknya jangan*: It is inadvisable to go swimming after a meal. **OPP** **advisable**

inane /ɪˈneɪn/ *adj* without any meaning; silly □ *kosong; bodoh*: an inane remark ▶ **inanely** *adv*

inanimate /ɪnˈænɪmət/ *adj* not alive □ *tak bernyawa; jamadat*: A rock is an inanimate object. **OPP** **animate**

inappropriate /ˌɪnəˈprəʊpriət/ *adj* not suitable □ *tdk sesuai*: Isn't that dress rather inappropriate for the occasion? **OPP** **appropriate**

inarticulate /ˌɪnɑːˈtɪkjələt/ *adj* **1** (used about a person) not able to express ideas and feelings clearly □ *tdk dpt meluahkan idea/perasaan dgn jelas* **2** (used about speech) not clear or well expressed □ *kabur; tdk jelas* **OPP** for both meanings **articulate** ▶ **inarticulately** *adv*

inasmuch as /ˌɪnəzˈmʌtʃ əz/ *conj* (formal) because of the fact that □ *oleh sebab*: We felt sorry for the boys inasmuch as they had not realized that what they were doing was wrong.

inattention /ˌɪnəˈtenʃn/ *noun* [U] lack of attention □ *kurang perhatian*: The tragic accident was the result of a moment's inattention. **OPP** **attention**

inattentive /ˌɪnəˈtentɪv/ *adj* not paying attention □ *tdk memberikan perhatian penuh*: *One inattentive student can disturb the whole class.* **OPP** **attentive**

inaudible /ɪnˈɔːdəbl/ *adj* not loud enough to be heard □ *tdk dpt didengar* **OPP** **audible** ▶ **inaudibly** /-əbli/ *adv*

inaugurate /ɪˈnɔːɡjəreɪt/ *verb* [T] **1** to introduce a new official, leader, etc. at a special formal ceremony □ *merasmikan perlantikan; mengisytiharkan*: *He will be inaugurated as President next month.* **2** to start, introduce or open sth new, often at a special formal ceremony □ *memulakan; merasmikan* ▶ **inaugural** /ɪˈnɔːɡjərəl/ *adj* [only before a noun]: *the President's inaugural speech* ▶ **inauguration** /ɪˌnɔːɡjəˈreɪʃn/ *noun* [C,U]

inauspicious /ˌɪnɔːˈspɪʃəs/ *adj* (*formal*) showing signs that the future will not be good or successful □ *(ada tanda-tanda) tdk baik*: *He made an inauspicious start.* **OPP** **auspicious**

inbox /ˈɪnbɒks/ *noun* [C] the place on a computer where you can see new email messages □ *peti masuk*: *I have a stack of emails in my inbox.*

Inc. (also **inc**) /ɪŋk/ *abbr* (*AmE*) = **incorporated** □ *Inc (Perbadanan)*: *Manhattan Drugstores Inc.*

incalculable /ɪnˈkælkjələbl/ *adj* (*formal*) very great; too great to calculate □ *tdk terkira; tdk terhingga*: *an incalculable risk*

incapable /ɪnˈkeɪpəbl/ *adj* **1** incapable of sth/doing sth not able to do sth □ *tdk berupaya; tdk dpt (berbuat sst)*: *She is incapable of hard work/working hard.* ♦ *He's quite incapable of unkindness* (= too nice to be unkind). **2** not able to do, manage or organize anything well □ *tdk mampu (menjalankan tugas, dsb)*: *As a doctor, she's totally incapable.* **OPP** for both meanings **capable**

incapacitate /ˌɪnkəˈpæsɪteɪt/ *verb* [T] (*formal*) to make sb/sth unable to live or work normally □ *menjadi tdk berupaya*: *They were completely incapacitated by the heat in Spain.*

incarcerate /ɪnˈkɑːsəreɪt/ *verb* [T] (*formal*) incarcerate sb (in sth) to put sb in prison or in another place from which they cannot escape □ *mengurung; memenjarakan* **SYN** **imprison** ▶ **incarceration** /ɪnˌkɑːsəˈreɪʃn/ *noun* [U]

incarnation /ˌɪnkɑːˈneɪʃn/ *noun* [C] **1** (in some religions) one of a series of lives in a particular form □ *penjelmaan semula*: *He believed he was a prince in a previous incarnation.* ⊃ look at **reincarnation 2** the incarnation of sth (a person that is) a perfect example of a particular quality □ *lambang*: *She is the incarnation of goodness.*

incendiary /ɪnˈsendiəri/ *adj* [only before a noun] that causes a fire □ *yg menyebabkan kebakaran*: *an incendiary bomb/device*

incense /ˈɪnsens/ *noun* [U] a substance that produces a sweet smell when burnt, used especially in religious ceremonies □ *setanggi; dupa*

incensed /ɪnˈsenst/ *adj* incensed (by/at sth)

---

inattentive → incinerator

very angry □ *sangat marah; naik berang* **SYN** **furious**

incentive /ɪnˈsentɪv/ *noun* [C,U] (an) incentive (for/to sb/sth) (to do sth) something that encourages you (to do sth) □ *galakan; insentif*: *There's no incentive for young people to do well at school because there aren't any jobs when they leave.*

incessant /ɪnˈsesnt/ *adj* never stopping (and usually annoying) □ *tdk henti-henti; terus-menerus*: *incessant rain/noise/chatter* **SYN** **constant** ⊃ look at **continual** ▶ **incessantly** *adv*

incest /ˈɪnsest/ *noun* [U] illegal sex between members of the same family, for example brother and sister □ *(perbuatan) sumbang mahram*

incestuous /ɪnˈsestjuəs/ *adj* **1** involving illegal sex between members of the same family □ *(yg) sumbang mahram*: *an incestuous relationship* **2** (used about a group of people and their relationships with each other) too close; not open to anyone outside the group □ *terlalu rapat; tertutup*: *Life in a small community can be very incestuous.*

inch¹ /ɪntʃ/ *noun* [C] (*abbr* in.) a measure of length; 2.54 centimetres. There are 12 **inches** in a foot □ *inci*: *He's 5 foot 10 inches tall.* ♦ *Three inches of rain fell last night.* ❶ For more information about measurements, look at the section on using numbers at the back of this dictionary.

inch² /ɪntʃ/ *verb* [I,T] inch forward, past, through, etc. to move slowly and carefully in the direction mentioned □ *bergerak perlahan-lahan; mengengsot*: *He inched (his way) forward along the cliff edge.*

incidence /ˈɪnsɪdəns/ *noun* [sing] (*formal*) incidence of sth the number of times sth (usually unpleasant) happens; the rate of sth □ *kekerapan berlakunya sst; kadar*: *a high incidence of crime/disease/unemployment*

incident /ˈɪnsɪdənt/ *noun* [C] (*formal*) something that happens (especially sth unusual or unpleasant) □ *kejadian; peristiwa*: *There were a number of incidents after the football match.* ♦ *a diplomatic incident* (= a dangerous or unpleasant situation between countries)

incidental /ˌɪnsɪˈdentl/ *adj* incidental (to sth) happening as part of sth more important □ *sampingan; tambahan*: *The book contains various themes that are incidental to the main plot.*

incidentally /ˌɪnsɪˈdentli/ *adv* used to introduce extra news, information, etc. that the speaker has just thought of □ *oh ya*: *Incidentally, that new restaurant you told me about is excellent.* ⊃ A less formal expression is **by the way**.

incinerate /ɪnˈsɪnəreɪt/ *verb* [T] (*formal*) to destroy sth completely by burning □ *membakar*

incinerator /ɪnˈsɪnəreɪtə(r)/ *noun* [C] a container or machine for burning rubbish, etc. □ *pembakar*

incision /ɪnˈsɪʒn/ noun [C] (formal) a cut carefully made into sth (especially into a person's body as part of a medical operation) □ *bedahan; pemotongan*

incisive /ɪnˈsaɪsɪv/ adj **1** showing clear thought and good understanding of what is important, and having the ability to express this □ *jelas dan tepat*: *an incisive mind* ◆ *incisive comments* **2** showing sb's ability to take decisions and act quickly and directly □ *tajam*: *an incisive move*

incite /ɪnˈsaɪt/ verb [T] **incite sb (to sth); incite sth** to encourage sb to do sth by making them very angry or excited □ *menghasut; mengapi-apikan; menggalakkan*: *He was accused of inciting the crowd to violence.* ▶ **incitement** noun [C,U]: *He was guilty of incitement to violence.*

incl. abbr = including, inclusive □ *termasuk*: *total £59.00 incl. tax*

inclination /ˌɪnklɪˈneɪʃn/ noun [C,U] **inclination (to do sth); inclination (towards/for sth)** a feeling that makes sb want to behave in a particular way □ *kecenderungan; (perihal) hendak/ingin*: *He did not show the slightest inclination to help.* ◆ *She had no inclination for a career in teaching.*

incline¹ /ɪnˈklaɪn/ verb **1** [I] (formal) **incline to/towards sth** to tend to behave in a particular way or make a particular choice □ *cenderung*: *I don't know what to choose, but I'm inclining towards the fish.* **2** [T] to bend (your head) forward □ *membongkok*: *He inclined his head in agreement.* **3** [I] **incline towards sth** to be at an angle in a particular direction □ *condong*: *The land inclines towards the shore.*

incline² /ˈɪnklaɪn/ noun [C] (formal) a slight hill □ *lerengan; landaian*: *a steep/slight incline* **SYN** slope

inclined /ɪnˈklaɪnd/ adj **1** [not before a noun] **inclined (to do sth)** tending to do sth □ *cenderung*: *I know Amir well, so I'm inclined to believe what he says.* **2 inclined to do sth** likely to do sth □ *cenderung; mungkin*: *She's inclined to change her mind very easily.* **3** having a natural ability in the subject mentioned □ *berbakat*: *to be musically inclined*

include /ɪnˈkluːd/ verb [T] [not used in the continuous tenses] **1** to have as one part; to contain (among other things) □ *termasuk*: *The price of the holiday includes the flight, the hotel and car hire.* ◆ *The crew included one woman.* ⊃ note at **contain 2 include sb/sth (as/in/on sth)** to make sb/sth part of (another group, etc.) □ *memasukkan; menyertakan; termasuk*: *The children immediately included the new girl in their games.* ◆ *Everyone was disappointed, myself included.* **OPP** for both meanings **exclude** ▶ **inclusion** /ɪnˈkluːʒn/ noun [U]: *The inclusion of all that violence in the film was unnecessary.*

including /ɪnˈkluːdɪŋ/ prep (abbr **incl.**) having as a part □ *termasuk*: *It costs £17.99, including postage and packing.* **OPP** excluding

inclusive /ɪnˈkluːsɪv/ adj (abbr **incl.**) **1 inclusive (of sth)** (used about a price, etc.) including or containing everything; including the thing mentioned □ *termasuk*: *Is that an inclusive price or are there some extras?* ◆ *The rent is inclusive of electricity.* **2** [only after a noun] including the dates, numbers, etc. mentioned □ *termasuk*: *You are booked at the hotel from Monday to Friday inclusive* (= including Monday and Friday).

HELP When talking about time, **through** is often used in American English instead of **inclusive**: *We'll be away (from) Friday through Sunday.*

incognito /ˌɪnkɒɡˈniːtəʊ/ adv hiding your real name and identity (especially if you are famous and do not want to be recognized) □ *dgn menyembunyikan identiti sendiri (orang terkenal)*: *to travel incognito*

incoherent /ˌɪnkəʊˈhɪərənt/ adj not clear or easy to understand; not saying sth clearly □ *tdk keruan*: *incoherent mumbling* **OPP** coherent ▶ **incoherence** noun [U] ▶ **incoherently** adv

income /ˈɪnkʌm; -kəm/ noun [C,U] the money you receive regularly as payment for your work or as interest on money you have saved, etc. □ *pendapatan*: *It's often difficult for a family to live on one income.* ⊃ note at **pay**

MORE We talk about a **monthly** or an **annual** income. An income may be **high** or **low**. Your **gross** income is the amount you earn before paying tax. Your **net** income is your income after tax.

income tax noun [U] the amount of money you pay to the government according to how much you earn □ *cukai pendapatan*

incoming /ˈɪnkʌmɪŋ/ adj [only before a noun] **1** arriving or being received □ *baru tiba/diterima*: *incoming flights/passengers* ◆ *incoming phone calls* **2** new; recently elected □ *baharu*: *the incoming government*

incomparable /ɪnˈkɒmprəbl/ adj so good or great that it does not have an equal □ *tdk ada tolok bandingnya*: *incomparable beauty* ⊃ verb **compare**

incompatible /ˌɪnkəmˈpætəbl/ adj **incompatible with sb/sth** very different and therefore not able to live or work happily with sb or exist with sth □ *tdk bersesuaian; tdk serasi*: *The hours of the job are incompatible with family life.* **OPP** compatible ▶ **incompatibility** /ˌɪnkəmˌpætəˈbɪləti/ noun [C,U] (pl **incompatibilities**)

incompetent /ɪnˈkɒmpɪtənt/ adj lacking the necessary skill to do sth well □ *tdk cekap*: *He is completely incompetent at his job.* ◆ *an incompetent teacher/manager* **OPP** competent ▶ **incompetent** noun [C]: *She's a total incompetent at basketball.* ▶ **incompetence** noun [U] ▶ **incompetently** adv: *The business was run incompetently.*

incomplete /ˌɪnkəmˈpliːt/ adj having a part or parts missing; not total □ *tdk lengkap; tdk* *sempurna*: *Unfortunately the jigsaw puzzle was incomplete.* **OPP complete** ▶ **incompletely** *adv*

incomprehensible /ˌɪnˌkɒmprɪˈhensəbl/ *adj* impossible to understand □ *tdk dpt difahami*: *an incomprehensible explanation* ♦ *Her attitude is totally incomprehensible to the rest of us.* **OPP comprehensible, understandable** ▶ **incomprehension** /ˌɪnˌkɒmprɪˈhenʃn/ *noun* [U]

inconceivable /ˌɪnkənˈsiːvəbl/ *adj* impossible or very difficult to believe or imagine □ *sukar utk mempercayai; tdk dpt dibayangkan*: *It's inconceivable that he would have stolen anything.* **OPP conceivable**

inconclusive /ˌɪnkənˈkluːsɪv/ *adj* not leading to a definite decision or result □ *tdk berkesimpulan; tiada kepastian*: *an inconclusive discussion* ♦ *inconclusive evidence* (= that doesn't prove anything) **OPP conclusive** ▶ **inconclusively** *adv*

incongruous /ɪnˈkɒŋɡruəs/ *adj* strange and out of place; not suitable in a particular situation □ *tdk kena pd tempatnya; tdk sesuai*: *That huge table looks rather incongruous in such a small room.* ▶ **incongruously** *adv* ▶ **incongruity** /ˌɪnkɒnˈɡruːəti/ *noun* [U]

inconsiderate /ˌɪnkənˈsɪdərət/ *adj* (used about a person) not thinking or caring about the feelings, or needs of other people □ *tdk bertimbang rasa*: *It was inconsiderate of you not to offer her a lift.* **SYN thoughtless OPP considerate** ▶ **inconsiderately** *adv* ▶ **inconsiderateness** *noun* [U]

inconsistent /ˌɪnkənˈsɪstənt/ *adj* **1** inconsistent (with sth) (used about statements, facts, etc.) not the same as sth else; not matching, so that one thing must be wrong or not true □ *tdk konsisten; tdk selaras*: *The witnesses' accounts of the event are inconsistent.* ♦ *These new facts are inconsistent with the earlier information.* **2** (used about a person) likely to change (in attitude, behaviour, etc.) so that you cannot depend on them □ *tdk tekal; tdk tetap*: *She's so inconsistent—sometimes her work is good and sometimes it's really awful.* **OPP** for both meanings **consistent** ▶ **inconsistency** /ˌɪnkənˈsɪstənsi/ *noun* [C,U] (*pl* **inconsistencies**): *There were far too many inconsistencies in her argument.* **OPP consistency** ▶ **inconsistently** *adv*

inconspicuous /ˌɪnkənˈspɪkjuəs/ *adv* not easily noticed □ *tdk ketara; tdk mudah dilihat*: *I tried to make myself as inconspicuous as possible so that no one would ask me a question.* **OPP conspicuous** ▶ **inconspicuously** *adv*

incontinent /ɪnˈkɒntɪnənt/ *adj* unable to control the passing of **urine** (= liquid waste) and **faeces** (= solid waste) from the body □ *tdk dpt mengawal buang air kecil atau air besar* ▶ **incontinence** *noun* [U]

inconvenience /ˌɪnkənˈviːniəns/ *noun* [U,C] trouble or difficulty, especially when it affects sth that you need to do; a person or thing that causes this □ *kesulitan*: *We apologize for any inconvenience caused by the delays.* ▶ **inconvenience** *verb* [T] **SYN put sb out**

449 **incomprehensible → increment**

inconvenient /ˌɪnkənˈviːniənt/ *adj* causing trouble or difficulty, especially when it affects sth that you need to do □ *menyusahkan*: *It's a bit inconvenient at the moment—could you phone again later?* **OPP convenient** ▶ **inconveniently** *adv*

incorporate /ɪnˈkɔːpəreɪt/ *verb* [T] incorporate sth (in/into/within sth) to make sth a part of sth else; to have sth as a part □ *memasukkan; menyertakan*: *I'd like you to incorporate this information into your report.* **SYN include** ▶ **incorporation** /ɪnˌkɔːpəˈreɪʃn/ *noun* [U]

incorporated /ɪnˈkɔːpəreɪtɪd/ *adj* (*abbr* **Inc.**) (following the name of a company) formed into a **corporation** (= an organization that is recognized by law) □ *diperbadankan*

incorrect /ˌɪnkəˈrekt/ *adj* not right or true □ *tdk betul; salah*: *Incorrect answers should be marked with a cross.* **OPP correct** ▶ **incorrectly** *adv*

incorrigible /ɪnˈkɒrɪdʒəbl/ *adj* (used about a person or their behaviour) very bad; too bad to be corrected or improved □ *teruk; tdk dpt diperbaiki/dibetulkan lagi*: *an incorrigible liar*

increase¹ /ɪnˈkriːs/ *verb* [I,T] increase (sth) (from A) (to B); increase (sth) (by sth) to become or to make sth larger in number or amount □ *bertambah; menambah; meningkatkan*: *She increased her speed to overtake the lorry.* ♦ *My employer would like me to increase my hours of work from 25 to 30.* ♦ *The rate of inflation has increased by 1% to 7%.* **OPP decrease, reduce**

increase² /ˈɪnkriːs/ *noun* [C,U] (an) increase (in sth) a rise in the number, amount or level of sth □ *peningkatan; pertambahan; bertambahnya; kenaikan*: *There has been a sharp increase of nearly 50% on last year's figures.* ♦ *Doctors expect some further increase in the spread of the disease.* ♦ *They are demanding a large wage increase.* **OPP decrease, reduction**

IDM on the increase becoming greater or more common; increasing □ *kian meningkat; semakin bertambah*: *Attacks by dogs on children are on the increase.*

increasingly /ɪnˈkriːsɪŋli/ *adv* more and more □ *semakin; kian bertambah*: *increasingly difficult/important/dangerous* ♦ *It's becoming increasingly clear that Sam is doing no work in this subject.*

incredible /ɪnˈkredəbl/ *adj* **1** impossible or very difficult to believe □ *mustahil/sukar dipercayai*: *I found Jacqueline's account of the event incredible.* **SYN unbelievable OPP credible 2** (*informal*) extremely good or big □ *sungguh/sangat (bagus, besar, banyak, dll)*: *He earns an incredible salary.* ▶ **incredibly** /-əbli/ *adv*: *We have had some incredibly strong winds recently.*

increment /ˈɪŋkrəmənt/ *noun* [C] (*formal*) an increase in a number or an amount, especially a regular pay increase □ *kenaikan; tambahan*:

[C] **countable**, a noun with a plural form: *one book, two books*   [U] **uncountable**, a noun with no plural form: *some sugar*

a salary of £25 000 with annual increments ▶**incremental** /ˌɪŋkrəˈmentl/ adj: incremental costs ▶**incrementally** /-təli/ adv

incriminate /ɪnˈkrɪmɪneɪt/ verb [T] to provide evidence that sb is guilty of a crime □ *membabitkan; menunjukkan sso bersalah*: The police searched the house but found nothing to incriminate the man.

incubate /ˈɪŋkjubeɪt/ verb **1** [T] to keep an egg at the right temperature so that it can develop and break open □ *mengeram* **2** [I,T] (used about a disease) to develop without showing signs; (used about a person or an animal) to carry a disease without showing signs □ *mengeramkan; dieramkan*: Some viruses incubate for weeks.

incubation /ˌɪŋkjuˈbeɪʃn/ noun **1** [U] the process of **incubating** eggs □ *pengeraman* **2** [C] (also incu'bation period) the period between catching a disease and the time when signs of it appear □ *tempoh pengeraman*

incubator /ˈɪŋkjubeɪtə(r)/ noun [C] **1** a heated machine used in hospitals for keeping small or weak babies alive □ *inkubator* **2** a heated machine for keeping eggs warm until the young birds are born □ *alat pengeram*

incur /ɪnˈkɜː(r)/ verb [T] (incurred; incurring) (formal) to suffer the unpleasant results of a situation that you have caused □ *menanggung (hutang, dll); membangkitkan (kemarahan, dll)*: to incur debts/somebody's anger

incurable /ɪnˈkjʊərəbl/ adj that cannot be cured or made better □ *tdk dpt diubati*: an incurable disease OPP curable ▶**incurably** /-əbli/ adv: incurably ill/romantic

indebted /ɪnˈdetɪd/ adj indebted (to sb) (for sth) very grateful to sb □ *terhutang budi*: I am deeply indebted to my family and friends for all their help.

indecent /ɪnˈdiːsnt/ adj shocking to many people in society, especially because sth involves sex or the body □ *lucah; cabul; tdk sopan*: indecent photos/behaviour/language ◆ Those tiny swimming trunks are indecent! OPP decent ▶**indecency** /ɪnˈdiːsnsi/ noun [U, sing] ▶**indecently** adv

indecision /ˌɪndɪˈsɪʒn/ noun (also indecisiveness) [U] the state of being unable to decide □ *keadaan tdk dpt membuat keputusan*: This indecision about the future is really worrying.

indecisive /ˌɪndɪˈsaɪsɪv/ adj not able to make decisions easily □ *tdk dpt membuat keputusan; tdk tegas* OPP decisive ▶**indecisively** adv: He stood at the crossroads indecisively, wondering which way to go. ▶**indecisiveness** noun = **indecision**

ʔ**indeed** /ɪnˈdiːd/ adv **1** (used for emphasizing a positive statement or answer) really; certainly □ *tentu sekali; sungguh*: 'Have you had a good holiday?' 'We have indeed.' **2** used after 'very' with an adjective or adverb to emphasize the quality mentioned □ *sungguh*: Thank you very much indeed. ◆ She's very happy indeed. **3** (used for adding information to a statement) in fact □ *malah; bahkan*: It's important that you come at once. Indeed, it's essential. **4** used for showing interest, surprise, anger, etc. □ *ya; betul*: 'They were talking about you last night.' 'Were they indeed!'

indefensible /ˌɪndɪˈfensəbl/ adj (used about behaviour, etc.) completely wrong; that cannot be defended or excused □ *tdk dpt dipertahankan/dimaafkan*

indefinable /ˌɪndɪˈfaɪnəbl/ adj difficult or impossible to describe □ *sukar diterangkan*: She has that indefinable quality that makes an actress a star. ▶**indefinably** /-əbli/ adv

indefinite /ɪnˈdefɪnət/ adj not fixed or clear □ *tdk pasti; tdk tentu*: She will be away for the indefinite future. OPP definite

the inˌdefinite ˈarticle noun [C] the name used for the words *a* and *an* □ *kata sandang tak pasti/tentu* ⊃ look at **the definite article** ⓘ For more information about the indefinite article, look at the Reference Section at the back of this dictionary.

indefinitely /ɪnˈdefɪnətli/ adv for a period of time that has no fixed end □ *utk tempoh yg tdk dpt ditentukan*: The meeting was postponed indefinitely.

indelible /ɪnˈdeləbl/ adj that cannot be removed or washed out □ *tdk dpt dipadamkan; dihapuskan/dilupakan*: indelible ink ◆ (figurative) The experience made an indelible impression on me. ▶**indelibly** /-əbli/ adv

indent /ɪnˈdent/ verb [T] to start a line of writing further away from the edge of the page than the other lines □ *menginden; memulakan baris sejarak dr jidar kiri*

ʔ**independence** /ˌɪndɪˈpendəns/ noun [U] independence (from sb/sth) (used about a person, country, etc.) the state of being free and not controlled by another person, country, etc. □ *kebebasan; kemerdekaan*: In 1947 India achieved independence from Britain. ◆ financial independence

CULTURE

On **Independence Day** (4 July) Americans celebrate the day in 1776 when America declared itself independent from Britain.

ʔ**independent** /ˌɪndɪˈpendənt/ adj **1** independent (of/from sb/sth) free from and not controlled by another person, country, etc □ *bebas; merdeka*: Most former colonies are now independent nations. ◆ independent schools/TV (= not supported by government money) **2** not influenced by or connected with sb/sth □ *tersendiri; bebas*: Complaints against the police should be investigated by an independent body. ◆ Two independent opinion polls have obtained similar results. **3** independent (of sb/sth) not needing or wanting help ▫ *berkdikari; tdk mahu bergantung kpd orang lain*: *I got a part-time job because I wanted to be financially independent of my parents.* **OPP** dependent ▶independently *adv* independently (of sb/sth): *Scientists working independently of each other have had very similar results.*

indescribable /ˌɪndɪˈskraɪbəbl/ *adj* too good or bad to be described ▫ *tdk terperikan*: *indescribable poverty/luxury/noise* ▶indescribably /-əbli/ *adv*

indestructible /ˌɪndɪˈstrʌktəbl/ *adj* that cannot be easily damaged or destroyed ▫ *tdk dpt dimusnahkan*

index /ˈɪndeks/ *noun* [C] (*pl* indexes) **1** a list in order from A to Z, usually at the end of a book, of the names or subjects that are referred to in the book ▫ *indeks*: *If you want to find all the references to London, look it up in the index.* **2** (*BrE*) = card index **3** (*pl* indexes *or* indices /ˈɪndɪsiːz/) a way of showing how the price, value, rate, etc. of sth has changed ▫ *indeks*: *the cost-of-living index* ▶index *verb* [T]: *The books in the library are indexed by subject and title.*

¹index finger = forefinger

Indian /ˈɪndiən/ *noun* [C], *adj* **1** (a person) from the Republic of India ▫ *orang India*: *Indian food is hot and spicy.* **2** (*old-fashioned*) = **Native American**: *The Sioux were a famous Indian tribe.* ➔ look at **West Indian**

indicate /ˈɪndɪkeɪt/ *verb* **1** [T] to show that sth is probably true or exists ▫ *menunjukkan*: *Recent research indicates that children are getting too little exercise.* **2** [T] to say sth in an indirect way ▫ *membayangkan*: *The spokesman indicated that an agreement was likely soon.* **3** [T] to make sb notice sth, especially by pointing to it ▫ *menunjukkan*: *The receptionist indicated where I should sign.* ◆ *The boy seemed to be indicating that I should follow him.* **4** [I,T] (*BrE*) to signal that your car, etc. is going to turn ▫ *memberikan isyarat*: *The lorry indicated left but turned right.*

indication /ˌɪndɪˈkeɪʃn/ *noun* [C,U] an indication (of sth/doing sth); an indication that ... something that shows sth; a sign ▫ *tanda; petunjuk*: *There was no indication of a struggle.* ◆ *There is every indication that he will make a full recovery.*

indicative /ɪnˈdɪkətɪv/ *adj* (*formal*) being or giving a sign of sth ▫ *menunjukkan*: *Is the unusual weather indicative of climatic changes?*

indicator /ˈɪndɪkeɪtə(r)/ *noun* [C] **1** something that gives information or shows sth; a sign ▫ *petunjuk; tanda*: *The indicator showed that we had plenty of petrol.* ◆ *The unemployment rate is a reliable indicator of economic health.* **2** (*AmE* ˈturn signal, *informal* blinker) the flashing light on a car, etc. that shows that it is going to turn right or left ▫ *lampu penunjuk; lampu signal* ➔ picture on page P7

indices *plural of* **index** (3)

indictment /ɪnˈdaɪtmənt/ *noun* [C] **1** an indictment (of sth) something that shows how bad sth is ▫ *penunjuk keburukan*: *The fact that many children leave school with no qualifications is an indictment of our education system.* **2** a written paper that officially accuses sb of a crime ▫ *indikmen*

indie /ˈɪndi/ *adj* [only *before* a noun] (used about a company, person or product) not part of a large organization; independent ▫ *bebas; tersendiri*: *an indie publisher* ◆ *indie music*

indifference /ɪnˈdɪfrəns/ *noun* [U] indifference (to sb/sth) a lack of interest or feeling towards sb/sth ▫ *sikap acuh tak acuh/tdk ambil peduli*: *He has always shown indifference to the needs of others.*

indifferent /ɪnˈdɪfrənt/ *adj* **1** indifferent (to sb/sth) not interested in or caring about sb/sth ▫ *tdk ambil peduli*: *The manager of the shop seemed indifferent to our complaints.* **2** not very good ▫ *tdk begitu baik; kurang bermutu*: *The standard of football in the World Cup was rather indifferent.* ▶indifferently *adv*

indigenous /ɪnˈdɪdʒənəs/ *adj* (used about people, animals or plants) living or growing in the place where they are from originally ▫ *asli; yg asal*

indigestible /ˌɪndɪˈdʒestəbl/ *adj* (used about food) difficult or impossible for the stomach to deal with ▫ *sukar atau tdk dpt dihadam*

indigestion /ˌɪndɪˈdʒestʃən/ *noun* [U] pain in the stomach that is caused by difficulty in dealing with food ▫ *ketakcernaan*: *Peppers give me indigestion.*

indignant /ɪnˈdɪɡnənt/ *adj* indignant (with sb) (about/at sth); indignant (that) ... shocked or angry because sb has said or done sth that you do not like and do not agree with ▫ *marah; berang; meradang*: *They were indignant that they had to pay more for worse services.* ▶indignantly *adv*

indignation /ˌɪndɪɡˈneɪʃn/ *noun* [U] indignation (at/about sth); indignation that ... shock and anger because sth is unfair or unreasonable ▫ *kemarahan; keberangan*: *commuters' indignation at the rise in fares*

indignity /ɪnˈdɪɡnəti/ *noun* [U,C] (*pl* indignities) indignity (of sth/of doing sth) a situation that makes you feel embarrassed because you are not treated with respect; an act that causes this feeling ▫ *penghinaan; yg menjatuhkan maruah*: *the daily indignities of imprisonment* **SYN** humiliation

indigo /ˈɪndɪɡəʊ/ *adj* very dark blue in colour ▫ *biru nila* ▶indigo *noun* [U]

indirect /ˌɪndəˈrekt; -daɪˈr-/ *adj* **1** not being the direct cause of sth; not having a direct connection with sth ▫ *tak langsung*: *an indirect result* **2** that avoids saying sth in an obvious way ▫ *tak langsung*: *an indirect answer to a question*

indirect object → indulgence 452

3 not going in a straight line or using the shortest route □ *tdk terus*: *We came the indirect route to avoid driving through London.* **OPP** for all meanings direct ▶**indirectly** *adv* **OPP** directly ▶**indirectness** *noun* [U]

indirect object *noun* [C] a person or thing that an action is done to or for □ *objek tak langsung*: *In the sentence, 'I sent him an email', 'him' is the indirect object.* ⊃ look at direct object ❶ For more information about indirect objects, look at the **Reference Section** at the back of this dictionary.

indirect speech = reported speech

indiscreet /ˌɪndɪˈskriːt/ *adj* not careful or polite in what you say or do □ *kurang berhemat; kurang berhati-hati* **OPP** discreet ▶**indiscreetly** *adv*

indiscretion /ˌɪndɪˈskreʃn/ *noun* [C,U] behaviour that is not careful or polite, and that might cause embarrassment or offence □ *tingkah laku kurang hemat*

indiscriminate /ˌɪndɪˈskrɪmɪnət/ *adj* done or acting without making sensible judgement or caring about the possible harmful effects □ *secara sembarangan; tdk teliti*: *Martin is indiscriminate in his choice of friends.* ▶**indiscriminately** *adv*

indispensable /ˌɪndɪˈspensəbl/ *adj* very important, so that it is not possible to be without it □ *amat diperlukan; tdk boleh tdk*: *A car is indispensable nowadays if you live in the country.* **SYN** essential **OPP** dispensable

indisputable /ˌɪndɪˈspjuːtəbl/ *adj* definitely true; that cannot be shown to be wrong □ *tdk dpt dinafikan; tdk boleh dipertikai lagi*

indistinct /ˌɪndɪˈstɪŋkt/ *adj* not clear □ *kurang jelas; samar-samar*: *indistinct figures/sounds/memories* **OPP** distinct ▶**indistinctly** *adv*

indistinguishable /ˌɪndɪˈstɪŋgwɪʃəbl/ *adj* indistinguishable (from sth) appearing to be the same □ *tdk dpt dibezakan*: *From a distance the two colours are indistinguishable.* **OPP** distinguishable

individual¹ /ˌɪndɪˈvɪdʒuəl/ *adj* **1** [only before a noun] considered separately rather than as part of a group □ *satu-satu; berasingan*: *Each individual animal is weighed and measured before being set free.* **2** for or from one person □ *utk satu-satu orang; perseorangan; khusus*: *an individual portion of butter* ◆ *Children need individual attention when they are learning to read.* **3** typical of one person in a way that is different from other people □ *tersendiri*: *I like her individual style of dressing.*

individual² /ˌɪndɪˈvɪdʒuəl/ *noun* [C] **1** one person, considered separately from others or a group □ *individu; orang perseorangan; orang*: *Are the needs of society more important than the rights of the individual?* **2** (*informal*) a person of the type that is mentioned □ *orang*: *She's a strange individual.*

individuality /ˌɪndɪˌvɪdʒuˈæləti/ *noun* [U] the qualities that make sb/sth different from other people or things □ *keindividuan; identiti/ciri tersendiri*: *People often try to express their individuality by the way they dress.*

individually /ˌɪndɪˈvɪdʒuəli/ *adv* separately; one by one □ *secara perseorangan; seorang demi seorang*: *The teacher talked to each member of the class individually.*

indivisible /ˌɪndɪˈvɪzəbl/ *adj* that cannot be divided or split into smaller pieces □ *tdk boleh dibahagikan; tdk terbahagikan*

indoctrinate /ɪnˈdɒktrɪneɪt/ *verb* [T] to force sb to accept particular beliefs without allowing them to consider others □ *mengindoktrinasikan; menanam fahaman tertentu dlm fikiran sso*: *For 20 years the people have been indoctrinated by the government.* ▶**indoctrination** /ɪnˌdɒktrɪˈneɪʃn/ *noun* [U]

indoor /ˈɪndɔː(r)/ *adj* [only before a noun] done or used inside a building □ *dlm rumah/bangunan*: *indoor games* ◆ *an indoor swimming pool* **OPP** outdoor

indoors /ˌɪnˈdɔːz/ *adv* in or into a building □ *di dlm rumah/bangunan*: *Oh dear! I've left my sunglasses indoors.* ◆ *Let's go indoors.* **OPP** outdoors, out of doors

induce /ɪnˈdjuːs/ *verb* [T] (*formal*) **1** to make or persuade sb to do sth □ *memujuk; membuat; mendorong*: *Nothing could induce him to change his mind.* **2** to cause or produce sth □ *menyebabkan*: *herbal tea that induces sleep*

inducement /ɪnˈdjuːsmənt/ *noun* [C,U] something that is offered to sb to make them do sth □ *pendorong; galakan; umpan*: *financial inducements to mothers to stay at home*

induction /ɪnˈdʌkʃn/ *noun* [U,C] the process of introducing sb to a new job, skill, organization, etc.; an event at which this takes place □ *aruhan; induksi*: *an induction day for new students*

indulge /ɪnˈdʌldʒ/ *verb* **1** [I,T] indulge (yourself) (in sth) to allow yourself to have or do sth for pleasure □ *menurut kehendak hati; memuaskan keinginan*: *I'm going to indulge myself and go shopping for some new clothes.* ◆ *Maria never indulges in gossip.* ◆ *At the weekends he indulges his passion for fishing.* **2** [T] to give sb/sth what he/she/it wants or needs □ *menurutkan kemahuan; memanjakan*: *You shouldn't indulge that child. It will make him very selfish.*

indulgence /ɪnˈdʌldʒəns/ *noun* **1** [U] the state of having or doing whatever you want □ *(keadaan) mengikut nafsu/kemahuan*: *to lead a life of indulgence* ◆ *Over-indulgence in chocolate makes you fat.* **2** [C] something that you have or do because it gives you pleasure □ *kesukaan; kegemaran*: *The holiday was an extravagant indulgence.*

ð **then** s **so** z **zoo** ʃ **she** ʒ **vi**sion h **how** m **man** n **no** ŋ **si**ng l **leg** r **red** j **yes** w **wet**

indulgent /ɪnˈdʌldʒənt/ adj allowing sb to have or do whatever they want □ *memanjakan; mengikutkan kemahuan*: indulgent parents ▶**indulgently** adv

industrial /ɪnˈdʌstriəl/ adj 1 [only before a noun] connected with industry □ *perindustrian*: industrial development ♦ industrial workers 2 having a lot of factories, etc. □ *perindustrian; perusahaan*: an industrial region/country/town

in‚dustrial ˈaction noun [U] action that workers take, especially stopping work, in order to protest about sth to their employers □ *tindakan perindustrian; mogok*: to threaten (to take) industrial action SYN **strike**

industrialist /ɪnˈdʌstriəlɪst/ noun [C] a person who owns or manages a large **industrial** company □ *usahawan*

industrialize (also -ise) /ɪnˈdʌstriəlaɪz/ verb [I,T] to develop industries in a country □ *menjadi negara perindustrian; mengindustrikan*: Japan industrialized rapidly at the end of the 19th century. ▶**industrialization** (also -isation) /ɪnˌdʌstriəlaɪˈzeɪʃn/ noun [U]

industrious /ɪnˈdʌstriəs/ adj always working hard □ *rajin; tekun* SYN **hard-working**

industry /ˈɪndəstri/ noun (pl industries) 1 [U] the production of goods in factories □ *industri; perusahaan*: Is British industry being threatened by foreign imports? ♦ heavy/light industry 2 [C] the people and activities involved in producing sth, providing a service, etc. □ *industri*: the tourist/catering/entertainment industry ♦ the steel industry

inedible /ɪnˈedəbl/ adj (formal) not suitable to be eaten □ *tdk boleh dimakan*: an inedible plant OPP **edible**

ineffective /ˌɪnɪˈfektɪv/ adj not producing the effect or result that you want □ *tdk berkesan; tdk efektif* OPP **effective**

inefficient /ˌɪnɪˈfɪʃnt/ adj not working or producing results in the best way, so that time or money is wasted □ *tdk cekap; tdk efisien*: Our heating system is very old and extremely inefficient. ♦ an inefficient secretary OPP **efficient** ▶**inefficiency** /ˌɪnɪˈfɪʃənsi/ noun [U] ▶**inefficiently** adv

ineligible /ɪnˈelɪdʒəbl/ adj ineligible (for/to do sth) without the necessary certificates, etc. to do or get sth □ *tdk layak*: ineligible to vote OPP **eligible** ▶**ineligibility** /ˌɪnelɪdʒəˈbɪləti/ noun [U]

inept /ɪˈnept/ adj inept (at sth) not able to do sth well □ *tdk cekap; tdk pandai*: She is totally inept at dealing with people. OPP **adept**

inequality /ˌɪnɪˈkwɒləti/ noun [C,U] (pl inequalities) (a) difference between groups in society because one has more money, opportunities, etc. than the other □ *ketidaksamarataan; ketaksamaan*: There will be problems as long as inequality between the races exists. OPP **equality**

inert /ɪˈnɜːt/ adj (formal) not able to move or act □ *tdk bergerak-gerak; lengai*

inertia /ɪˈnɜːʃə/ noun [U] 1 a lack of energy; not being able to move or change □ *tdk bermaya, inersia* 2 the physical force that keeps things where they are or keeps them moving in the direction they are travelling □ *inersia*

inescapable /ˌɪnɪˈskeɪpəbl/ adj (formal) that cannot be avoided □ *tdk dpt dielak; pasti berlaku*: an inescapable conclusion

inevitable /ɪnˈevɪtəbl/ adj that cannot be avoided or prevented from happening □ *tdk dpt dielak atau dihalang*: With more cars on the road, traffic jams are inevitable. ▶**the inevitable** noun [sing]: They fought to save the firm from closure, but eventually had to accept the inevitable. ▶**inevitability** /ɪnˌevɪtəˈbɪləti/ noun [U] ▶**inevitably** /ɪnˈevɪtəbli/ adv

inexcusable /ˌɪnɪkˈskjuːzəbl/ adj that cannot be allowed or forgiven □ *tdk dpt dimaafkan*: Their behaviour was quite inexcusable. OPP **excusable**

inexhaustible /ˌɪnɪɡˈzɔːstəbl/ adj that cannot be finished or used up completely □ *tdk akan habis*: Our energy supplies are not inexhaustible.

inexpensive /ˌɪnɪkˈspensɪv/ adj low in price □ *tdk mahal; murah*: an inexpensive camping holiday SYN **cheap** OPP **expensive** ▶**inexpensively** adv

inexperience /ˌɪnɪkˈspɪəriəns/ noun [U] not knowing how to do sth because you have not done it before □ *kurang/tdk berpengalaman*: The mistakes were all due to inexperience. OPP **experience** ▶**inexperienced** adj: He's too young and inexperienced to be given such responsibility.

inexplicable /ˌɪnɪkˈsplɪkəbl/ adj that cannot be explained □ *tdk dpt diterangkan*: Her sudden disappearance is quite inexplicable. OPP **explicable** ▶**inexplicably** /-əbli/ adv

infallible /ɪnˈfæləbl/ adj 1 (used about a person) never making mistakes or being wrong □ *tdk pernah silap*: Even the most careful editor is not infallible. 2 always doing what you want it to do; never failing □ *tdk pernah gagal; pasti berkesan*: No computer is infallible. OPP for both meanings **fallible** ▶**infallibility** /ɪnˌfæləˈbɪləti/ noun [U]

infamous /ˈɪnfəməs/ adj (formal) infamous (for sth) famous for being bad □ *terkenal kerana jahat*: The area is infamous for crime. SYN **notorious** ⊃ look at **famous**

infancy /ˈɪnfənsi/ noun [U] the time when you are a baby or young child □ *zaman bayi*: (figurative) Research in this field is still in its infancy.

infant /ˈɪnfənt/ noun [C] (formal) 1 a baby or very young child □ *bayi*: There is a high rate of infant mortality (= many children die when they are still babies). ⊃ In spoken or informal English more common words are **baby, toddler** and **child**. 2 (in Britain and Australia) a child at school between the ages of 4 and 7 □ *anak kecil*: Mrs Davies teaches infants.

VOWELS iː see i any ɪ sit e ten æ hat ɑː father ɒ got ɔː saw ʊ put uː too u usual

infantile → inflammation 454

infantile /'ɪnfəntaɪl/ *adj* (used about behaviour) typical of, or connected with, a baby or very young child and therefore not appropriate for adults or older children □ *kebudak-budakan*: *infantile jokes*

infantry /'ɪnfəntri/ *noun* [U, with sing or pl verb] soldiers who fight on foot □ *infantri; pasukan (tentera) berjalan kaki*: *The infantry was/were supported by heavy gunfire.*

'infant school *noun* [C] (in Britain and Australia) a school for children between the ages of 4 and 7 □ *tadika* ⊃ look at **primary school**

infatuated /ɪn'fætʃueɪtɪd/ *adj* **infatuated (with sb/sth)** having a very strong feeling of love or attraction for sb/sth that usually does not last long and makes you unable to think about anything else □ *tergila-gila akan*: *The young girl was infatuated with one of her teachers.* ▶ **infatuation** /ɪn,fætʃu'eɪʃn/ *noun* [C,U]

infect /ɪn'fekt/ *verb* [T] **1** [usually passive] **infect sb/sth (with sth)** to cause sb/sth to have a disease or illness □ *menjangkiti*: *We must clean the wound before it becomes infected.* ◆ *Many thousands of people have been infected with the virus.* **2** to make people share a particular feeling or emotion □ *menjangkit; dijangkiti; berjangkit-jangkit kpd*: *Paul's happiness infected the whole family.*

infected /ɪn'fektɪd/ *adj* containing harmful bacteria □ *dijangkiti kuman; terjangkit*: *The wound from the dog bite had become infected.* ◆ *an infected water supply*

infection /ɪn'fekʃn/ *noun* **1** [U] the act of becoming or making sb ill □ *jangkitan; infeksi*: *A dirty water supply can be a source of infection.* ◆ *There is a danger of infection.* **2** [C] a disease or illness that is caused by harmful bacteria, etc. and affects one part of your body □ *penyakit; jangkitan*: *She is suffering from a chest infection.* ◆ *an ear infection*

> **MORE** Infections can be caused by **bacteria** or **viruses**. An informal word for these is **germs**.

infectious /ɪn'fekʃəs/ *adj* (used about a disease, illness, etc.) that can be easily passed on to another person □ *mudah berjangkit*: *Flu is a highly infectious disease.* ◆ (figurative) *infectious laughter* ⊃ look at **contagious**

infer /ɪn'fɜː(r)/ *verb* [T] (*formal*) (**inferring; inferred**) **infer sth (from sth)** to form an opinion or decide that sth is true from the information you have □ *membuat kesimpulan*: *I inferred from our conversation that he was unhappy with his job.* ▶ **inference** /'ɪnfərəns/ *noun* [C,U]

inferior /ɪn'fɪəriə(r)/ *adj* **inferior (to sb/sth)** low or lower in social position, importance, quality, etc □ *rendah darjat, kedudukan, mutu, dsb*: *This material is obviously inferior to that one.* ◆ *Don't let people make you feel inferior.* **OPP** **superior** ▶ **inferior** *noun* [C]: *She always treats me as* her intellectual inferior. ▶ **inferiority** /ɪn,fɪəri'ɒrəti/ (*AmE* also) / *noun* [U]

in,feri'ority complex *noun* [C] the state of feeling less important, clever, successful, etc. than other people □ *perasaan rendah diri*

infertile /ɪn'fɜːtaɪl/ *adj* **1** (used about a person or an animal) not able to have babies or produce young □ *mandul; tdk subur* **2** (used about land) not able to grow strong healthy plants □ *tdk subur* **OPP** for both meanings **fertile** ▶ **infertility** /,ɪnfɜː'tɪləti/ *noun* [U]: *infertility treatment* **OPP** **fertility**

infested /ɪn'festɪd/ *adj* **infested (with sth)** (used about a place) with large numbers of unpleasant animals or insects in it □ *penuh dgn; meremut*: *The warehouse was infested with rats.*

infidelity /,ɪnfɪ'deləti/ *noun* [U,C] (*pl* **infidelities**) the act of not being faithful to your wife, husband or partner, by having a sexual relationship with sb else □ *kecurangan* ⊃ A less formal word is **unfaithfulness**.

infiltrate /'ɪnfɪltreɪt/ *verb* [I,T] to enter an organization, etc. secretly so that you can find out what it is doing □ *menerobos; menyusup; menyeludup masuk*: *The police managed to infiltrate the gang of terrorists.* ▶ **infiltration** /,ɪnfɪl'treɪʃn/ *noun* [C,U] ▶ **infiltrator** /'ɪnfɪltreɪtə(r)/ *noun* [C]

infinite /'ɪnfɪnət/ *adj* **1** very great □ *sangat; amat*: *You need infinite patience for this job.* **2** without limits; that never ends □ *tdk terbatas; tdk terhingga*: *Supplies of oil are not infinite.* **OPP** for both meanings **finite**

infinitely /'ɪnfɪnətli/ *adv* very much □ *sangat; amat*: *Your English is infinitely better than my German.*

infinitive /ɪn'fɪnətɪv/ *noun* [C] the basic form of a verb □ *infinitif*

> **GRAMMAR** The infinitive is sometimes used with *to* and sometimes without *to*, depending on what comes before it: *He can sing.* ◆ *He wants to sing.*

infinity /ɪn'fɪnəti/ *noun* **1** [U] space or time without end □ *infiniti; ketakterhinggaan*: *The ocean seemed to stretch over the horizon into infinity.* **2** [U,C] (*symbol* ∞) (in mathematics) the number that is larger than any other □ *infiniti*

infirmary /ɪn'fɜːməri/ *noun* [C] (*pl* **infirmaries**) (used mainly in names) a hospital □ *hospital; rumah sakit*: *The Manchester Royal Infirmary*

inflamed /ɪn'fleɪmd/ *adj* (used about a part of the body) red and swollen or painful because of an infection or injury □ *bengkak; radang*

inflammable /ɪn'flæməbl/ *adj* that burns easily □ *mudah terbakar*: *Petrol is highly inflammable.*

> **HELP** Be careful. **Flammable** has the same meaning but is less common.

inflammation /,ɪnflə'meɪʃn/ *noun* [C,U] a condition in which a part of the body becomes

ʌ **c**u**p**   ɜː **b**i**rd**   ə **a**go   eɪ **p**ay   əʊ **g**o   aɪ **m**y   aʊ **n**ow   ɔɪ **b**oy   ɪə **n**ear   eə **h**air   ʊə **p**ure

red, sore and swollen because of infection or injury □ *radang; keradangan*

inflatable /ɪnˈfleɪtəbl/ *adj* that can or must be filled with air □ *boleh kembung; boleh diisi angin/udara*: *an inflatable dinghy/mattress*

inflate /ɪnˈfleɪt/ *verb* [I,T] to fill sth with air; to become filled with air □ *mengembung; menggelembung* ➔ A less formal word is **blow up**: *Can you help me blow up some balloons for the party?* **OPP** **deflate**

inflation /ɪnˈfleɪʃn/ *noun* [U] a general rise in prices; the rate at which prices rise □ *inflasi; kadar inflasi*: *the inflation rate/rate of inflation* ♦ *Inflation now stands at 3%.*

inflection (also **inflexion**) /ɪnˈflekʃn/ *noun* [C,U] **1** a change in the form of a word, especially its ending, that changes its function in the grammar of the language, for example *-ed, -est* □ *tasrif; fleksi; infleksi* **2** the rise and fall of your voice when you are talking □ *turun naik nada suara; intonasi* **SYN** **intonation**

inflexible /ɪnˈfleksəbl/ *adj* **1** that cannot be changed or made more suitable for a particular situation □ *tdk boleh diubah; keras; ketat; tdk fleksibel* **2** (of people or organizations) unwilling to change their opinions, decisions or the way in which they do things □ *tdk mudah berubah (sikap)*: *He has a very inflexible attitude to change.* **3** (used about a material) difficult or impossible to bend □ *tegar; keras; tdk boleh dilentur* **SYN** for all meanings **rigid** **OPP** for all meanings **flexible** ▸**inflexibility** /ɪnˌfleksəˈbɪləti/ *noun* [U] ▸**inflexibly** /ɪnˈfleksəbli/ *adv*

inflict /ɪnˈflɪkt/ *verb* [T] **inflict sth (on sb)** to force sb to have sth unpleasant or that they do not want □ *membebani; mengenakan*: *Don't inflict your problems on me—I've got enough of my own.*

ˈin-flight *adj* [only *before* a noun] happening or provided during a journey in a plane □ *berlaku dlm penerbangan*: *in-flight entertainment*

influence¹ /ˈɪnfluəns/ *noun* **1** [U,C] **(an) influence (on/upon sb/sth)** the power to affect, change or control sb/sth □ *pengaruh*: *TV can have a strong influence on children.* ♦ *Nobody should drive while they are under the influence of alcohol.* **2** [C] **an influence (on sb/sth)** a person or thing that affects or changes sb/sth □ *pengaruh*: *His new girlfriend has been a good influence on him.* ♦ *cultural/environmental influences*

influence² /ˈɪnfluəns/ *verb* [T] to have an effect on or power over sb/sth so that he/she/it changes □ *mempengaruhi*: *You must decide for yourself. Don't let anyone else influence you.* ♦ *Her style of painting has been influenced by Japanese art.*

HELP **Influence** or **affect**? **Affect** and **influence** are often very similar in meaning. **Affect** is usually used when the change is physical and **influence** is more often used to describe a change of opinion or attitude: *Drinking alcohol can affect your ability to drive.* ♦ *TV advertise-*

---

455 **inflatable → information technology**

ments have influenced my attitude towards the homeless.

influential /ˌɪnfluˈenʃl/ *adj* **influential (in sth/in doing sth)** having power or influence □ *berpengaruh*: *an influential politician* ♦ *He was influential in getting the hostages set free.*

influenza /ˌɪnfluˈenzə/ (*formal*) = **flu**

influx /ˈɪnflʌks/ *noun* [C, usually sing] **an influx (of sb/sth) (into …)** large numbers of people or things arriving suddenly □ *banjiran; berduyun-duyun*: *the summer influx of visitors from abroad*

inform /ɪnˈfɔːm/ *verb* [T] **inform sb (of/about sth)** to give sb information (about sth), especially in an official way □ *memberitahu*: *You should inform the police of the accident.* ♦ *I have not been informed when the ceremony will take place.*
PHR V **inform on sb** to give information to the police, etc. about what sb has done wrong □ *memberi maklumat ttg sso*: *The wife of the killer informed on her husband.* ➔ look at **informed**

informal /ɪnˈfɔːml/ *adj* relaxed and friendly or suitable for a relaxed occasion □ *tdk formal; tdk rasmi*: *Don't get dressed up for the party—it'll be very informal.* ♦ *The two leaders had informal discussions before the conference began.* **OPP** **formal**

HELP Some words and expressions in this dictionary are described as (*informal*). This means that you can use them when you are speaking to friends or people that you know well but that you should not use them in written work, official letters, etc.

▸**informality** /ˌɪnfɔːˈmæləti/ *noun* [U]: *an atmosphere of informality* ▸**informally** /-məli/ *adv*: *I was told informally* (= not officially) *that our plans had been accepted.*

informant /ɪnˈfɔːmənt/ *noun* [C] a person who gives secret knowledge or information about sb/sth to the police or a newspaper □ *pemberi maklumat; informan*: *The journalist refused to name his informant.* ➔ look at **informer**

information /ˌɪnfəˈmeɪʃn/ *noun* [U] **information (on/about sb/sth)** knowledge or facts □ *maklumat; keterangan; pengetahuan*: *For further information please see our website.* ♦ *Can you give me some information about evening classes in Italian, please?* ♦ *a tourist information centre* ➔ look at **FYI**

GRAMMAR The word **information** is uncountable. When we are talking about a single item, we say a **bit/piece of information** (not 'an information').

inforˌmation techˈnology *noun* [U] (*abbr* **IT**) the study or use of electronic equipment, especially computers, for collecting, storing and sending out information □ *teknologi maklumat*

informative → inhibit 456

informative /ɪnˈfɔːmətɪv/ *adj* giving useful knowledge or information □ *bermaklumat*

informed /ɪnˈfɔːmd/ *adj* having knowledge or information about sth □ *berpengetahuan; yg maklum; berdasarkan maklumat*: *Consumers cannot make informed choices unless they are told all the facts.* ◆ *Do keep me informed of any changes.* ◆ *They are not fully informed about the situation yet.*

informer /ɪnˈfɔːmə(r)/ *noun* [C] a criminal who gives the police information about other criminals □ *pemberi maklumat* ➲ look at **informant**

infrared /ˌɪnfrəˈred/ *adj* (used about light) that produces heat but that you cannot see □ *inframerah*: *infrared radiation* ◆ *an infrared lamp* ➲ look at **ultraviolet**

infrastructure /ˈɪnfrəstrʌktʃə(r)/ *noun* [C,U] the basic systems and services that are necessary for a country or an organization to run smoothly, for example transport, and water and power supplies □ *infrastruktur*

infrequent /ɪnˈfriːkwənt/ *adj* not happening often □ *jarang-jarang; tdk kerap* **OPP** **frequent** ▶ **infrequently** *adv*

infringe /ɪnˈfrɪndʒ/ *verb* (*formal*) **1** [T] to break a rule, law, agreement, etc. □ *melanggar (undang-undang, dsb)*: *The material can be copied without infringing copyright.* **2** [I] **infringe on/upon sth** to reduce or limit sb's rights, freedom, etc. □ *mencerobohi*: *She refused to answer questions that infringed on her private affairs.* ▶ **infringement** *noun* [C,U]

infuriate /ɪnˈfjʊərieɪt/ *verb* [T] to make sb very angry □ *membuat sso marah* ▶ **infuriating** *adj*: *an infuriating habit* ▶ **infuriatingly** *adv*

infuse /ɪnˈfjuːz/ *verb* **1** [T] (*formal*) to have an effect on all parts of sth □ *memberikan kesan*: *Politics infuses all aspects of our lives.* ◆ *Her novels are infused with sadness.* **2** [I,T] if you infuse **herbs** (= certain types of plant), etc. or they **infuse**, you put them in hot water until their flavour has passed into the water □ *menyeduh; merendam*

ingenious /ɪnˈdʒiːniəs/ *adj* **1** (used about a thing or an idea) made or planned in a clever way □ *bijak*: *an ingenious plan for making lots of money* ◆ *an ingenious device/experiment/invention* **2** (used about a person) full of new ideas and clever at finding solutions to problems or at inventing things □ *pintar; bijak* ▶ **ingeniously** *adv* ▶ **ingenuity** /ˌɪndʒəˈnjuːəti/ *noun* [U]

ingrained /ɪnˈɡreɪnd/ *adj* **ingrained (in sb/sth)** (used about a habit, an attitude, etc.) that has existed for a long time and is therefore difficult to change □ *berakar umbi; tertanam; sebati*: *ingrained prejudices/beliefs*

ingratiate /ɪnˈɡreɪʃieɪt/ *verb* [T] (*formal*) **ingratiate yourself (with sb)** to make yourself liked by doing or saying things that will please people, especially people who might be useful to you □ *mengampu (sso); mengangkat (sso)*: *He was always trying to ingratiate himself with his teachers.* ▶ **ingratiating** *adj*: *an ingratiating smile* ▶ **ingratiatingly** *adv*

ingratitude /ɪnˈɡrætɪtjuːd/ *noun* [U] (*formal*) the state of not showing or feeling thanks for sth that has been done for you; not being grateful □ *sikap tdk mengenang budi* **OPP** **gratitude**

ingredient /ɪnˈɡriːdiənt/ *noun* [C] **1** one of the items of food you need to make sth to eat □ *bahan; ramuan*: *Mix all the ingredients together in a bowl.* **2** one of the qualities necessary to make sth successful □ *ciri; unsur*: *The film has all the ingredients of success.*

inhabit /ɪnˈhæbɪt/ *verb* [T] to live in a place □ *mendiami; didiami; tinggal*: *Are the Aran Islands inhabited* (= do people live there)?

inhabitant /ɪnˈhæbɪtənt/ *noun* [C, usually pl] a person or an animal that lives in a place □ *penduduk; penghuni*: *The local inhabitants protested at the plans for a new motorway.*

> **HELP** When you want to know how many people live in a particular place, you say: *What is the population of …?* NOT: *How many inhabitants are there in …?* However, when you answer this question you can say: *The population is 10 000.* OR: *It has 10 000 inhabitants.*

inhale /ɪnˈheɪl/ *verb* [I,T] to breathe in □ *menyedut/menarik nafas*: *Be careful not to inhale the fumes from the paint.* **OPP** **exhale**

inherent /ɪnˈhɪərənt/ *adj* **inherent (in sb/sth)** that is a basic or permanent part of sb/sth and that cannot be removed □ *terdpt; wujud; ada pd*: *The risk of collapse is inherent in any business.* ▶ **inherently** *adv*: *No matter how safe we make them, cars are inherently dangerous.*

inherit /ɪnˈherɪt/ *verb* [T] **inherit sth (from sb)** **1** to receive property, money, etc. from sb who has died □ *mewarisi harta*: *I inherited quite a lot of money from my mother. She left me $12 000 when she died.*

> **MORE** The person who inherits from sb is that person's **heir**.

2 to receive a quality, characteristic, etc. from your parents or family □ *mewarisi sifat*: *She has inherited her father's gift for languages.*

inheritance /ɪnˈherɪtəns/ *noun* [C,U] the act of **inheriting**; the money, property, etc. that you **inherit** □ *harta pusaka/warisan*: *inheritance tax*

inhibit /ɪnˈhɪbɪt/ *verb* [T] **1** to prevent sth or make sth happen more slowly □ *menyekat; menghindar; menghalang*: *a drug to inhibit the growth of tumours* **2** **inhibit sb (from sth/from doing sth)** to make sb nervous and embarrassed so that they are unable to do sth □ *menghindar; menghalang*: *The fact that her boss was there inhibited her from saying what she really felt.*

[I] **intransitive**, a verb which has no object: *He laughed.*   [T] **transitive**, a verb which has an object: *He ate an apple.*

▶**inhibited** *adj*: *The young man felt shy and inhibited in the roomful of women.* **OPP uninhibited**

inhibition /ˌɪnhɪˈbɪʃn; ˌɪnɪˈb-/ *noun* [C,U] a shy or nervous feeling that stops you from saying or doing what you really want □ *rasa segan atau malu-malu*: *After the first morning of the course, people started to lose their inhibitions.*

inhospitable /ˌɪnhɒˈspɪtəbl/ *adj* 1 (used about a place) not pleasant to live in, especially because of the weather □ *tdk sesuai didiami*: *the inhospitable Arctic regions* 2 (used about a person) not friendly or welcoming to guests □ *tdk mesra; dingin* **OPP** for both meanings **hospitable**

ˌin-ˈhouse *adj* [only *before* a noun] existing or happening within a company or an organization □ *dalaman*: *an in-house magazine*

inhuman /ɪnˈhjuːmən/ *adj* 1 very cruel and without pity □ *kejam; tdk berperikemanusiaan*: *inhuman treatment/conditions* 2 not seeming to be human and therefore frightening □ *bkn spt manusia*: *an inhuman noise*

inhumane /ˌɪnhjuːˈmeɪn/ *adj* very cruel; not caring if people or animals suffer □ *kejam; tdk berperikemanusiaan*: *the inhumane conditions in which animals are kept on some large farms* **OPP humane**

inhumanity /ˌɪnhjuːˈmænəti/ *noun* [U] very cruel behaviour □ *kekejaman; sikap tdk berperikemanusiaan*: *The 20th century was full of examples of man's inhumanity to man.* **OPP humanity**

⚡**initial¹** /ɪˈnɪʃl/ *adj* [only *before* a noun] happening at the beginning; first □ *awal; permulaan*: *My initial reaction was to refuse, but I later changed my mind.* ♦ *the initial stages of our survey*

⚡**initial²** /ɪˈnɪʃl/ *noun* [C, usually pl] the first letter of a name □ *parap; huruf pertama pd nama*: *Alison Elizabeth Wilson's initials are A.E.W.*

initial³ /ɪˈnɪʃl/ *verb* [T] (**initialling; initialled**, (*AmE*) **initialing; initialed**) to mark or sign sth with your initials □ *memarapi; menandatangani dgn tandatangan singkat*: *Any changes made on the document should be initialled by you.*

⚡**initially** /ɪˈnɪʃəli/ *adv* at the beginning; at first □ *pada mulanya*: *I liked the job initially, but it soon got quite boring.*

initiate /ɪˈnɪʃieɪt/ *verb* [T] 1 (*formal*) to start sth □ *memulakan*: *to initiate peace talks* 2 **initiate sb (into sth)** to explain sth to sb or make them experience sth for the first time □ *memperkenalkan*: *I wasn't initiated into the joys of skiing until I was 30.* 3 **initiate sb (into sth)** to bring sb into a group by means of a special ceremony □ *menginisiasi; membawa masuk/menerima ke dlm sst kumpulan*: *to initiate somebody into a secret society* ▶ **initiation** /ɪˌnɪʃiˈeɪʃn/ *noun* [U]: *All the new students had to go through a strange initiation ceremony.*

⚡**initiative** /ɪˈnɪʃətɪv/ *noun* 1 [C] a new plan for solving a problem or improving a situation □ *tindakan rasmi*: *a new government initiative to help people start small businesses* 2 [U] the ability to see and do what is necessary without waiting for sb to tell you □ *daya usaha; inisiatif*: *Don't keep asking me how to do it. Use your initiative.* 3 **the initiative** [sing] the power or opportunity to act and gain an advantage before other people do □ *kelebihan; kuasa bertindak*: *to take/lose the initiative*

IDM on your own initiative without being told by sb else what to do □ *atas daya usaha sendiri* **take the initiative** to be first to act to influence a situation □ *mengambil inisiatif; berusaha memulakan sst*: *Let's take the initiative and start organizing things now.*

inject /ɪnˈdʒekt/ *verb* [T] 1 to put a drug under the skin of a person's or an animal's body with a **syringe** (= a needle) □ *menyuntik* 2 **inject sth (into sth)** to add sth □ *menyuntikkan; menambahkan*: *They injected a lot of money into the business.*

injection /ɪnˈdʒekʃn/ *noun* 1 [C,U] **(an) injection (of sth) (into sb/sth)** the act of **injecting** a drug or other substance □ *penyuntikan; suntikan; (perbuatan) menyuntik*: *to give somebody an injection of penicillin* ♦ *a tetanus injection* ♦ *An anaesthetic was administered by injection.* **SYN jab** 2 [C] a large amount of sth that is added to sth to help it □ *suntikan*: *The theatre needs a huge cash injection if it is to stay open.* 3 [U,C] the act of forcing liquid into sth □ *pancitan; suntikan*: *fuel injection*

injunction /ɪnˈdʒʌŋkʃn/ *noun* [C] **an injunction (against sb)** an official order from a court of law to do/not do sth □ *injunksi; perintah*: *An injunction prevented the programme from being shown on TV.*

⚡**injure** /ˈɪndʒə(r)/ *verb* [T] to harm or hurt yourself or sb else physically, especially in an accident □ *mencederakan; cedera*: *The goalkeeper seriously injured himself when he hit the goalpost.* ♦ *She fell and injured her back.* ⊃ note at **hurt**

⚡**injured** /ˈɪndʒəd/ *adj* 1 physically or mentally hurt □ *tercedera; terluka*: *an injured arm/leg* ♦ *injured pride* 2 **the injured** *noun* [pl] people who have been hurt □ *mereka yg tercedera; mangsa yg cedera*: *The injured were rushed to hospital.*

⚡**injury** /ˈɪndʒəri/ *noun* [C,U] (*pl* **injuries**) **(an) injury (to sb/sth)** harm done to a person's or an animal's body, especially in an accident □ *kecederaan; luka*: *They escaped from the accident with only minor injuries.* ♦ *serious injury/injuries*

ˈinjury time *noun* [U] (*BrE*) time that is added to the end of a football, etc. match when there has been time lost because of injuries to players □ *masa kecederaan*

injustice /ɪnˈdʒʌstɪs/ *noun* [U,C] the fact of a situation being unfair; an unfair act □ *ketidakadilan; hal yg tdk adil*: *racial/social injustice* ♦ *People are protesting about the injustice of the new tax.*

IDM do sb an injustice to judge sb unfairly □ *berlaku tdk adil terhadap sso*: *I'm afraid I've done you both an injustice.*

ink /ɪŋk/ *noun* [U,C] coloured liquid that is used for writing, drawing, etc. □ *dakwat*: *Please write in ink, not pencil.*

inkling /ˈɪŋklɪŋ/ *noun* [C, usually sing] **an inkling (of sth/that ...)** a slight feeling (about sth) □ *bayangan ttg sst; syak*: *I had an inkling that something was wrong.*

ˈink-pad *noun* [C] a thick piece of soft material full of ink, used with a rubber stamp □ *pad dakwat* ⊃ picture at **stationery**

inky /ˈɪŋki/ *adj* covered in ink; very dark □ *berlumuran dakwat; gelap-gelita*: *inky fingers* ◆ *an inky night sky*

inland /ˈɪnlænd/ *adj*, /ˌɪnˈlænd/ *adv* away from the coast or borders of a country □ *pedalaman*: *inland areas* ◆ *The village lies twenty miles inland.* ◆ *Goods are carried inland along narrow mountain roads.*

ˈin-laws *noun* [pl] (*informal*) your husband's or wife's mother and father or other relatives □ *mentua; ipar*: *My in-laws are coming to lunch on Sunday.*

inlet /ˈɪnlet/ *noun* [C] **1** a narrow area of water that stretches into the land from the sea or a lake, or between islands □ *serokan; teluk kecil* **2** an opening through which liquid, air or gas can enter a machine □ *salur masuk*: *a fuel inlet* OPP **outlet**

inmate /ˈɪnmeɪt/ *noun* [C] one of the people living in an institution such as a prison □ *penghuni; banduan (dlm penjara)*

inn /ɪn/ *noun* [C] (*BrE*) a small hotel or old pub usually in the country □ *rumah penginapan*

innate /ɪˈneɪt/ *adj* (used about an ability or quality) that you have when you are born □ *semula jadi*: *the innate ability to learn*

inner /ˈɪnə(r)/ *adj* [only *before* a noun] **1** (of the) inside; towards or close to the centre of a place □ *sebelah dlm; dlm*: *The inner ear is very delicate.* ◆ *an inner courtyard* OPP **outer** **2** (used about a feeling, etc.) that you do not express or show to other people; private □ *dlm hati; jiwa; batin*: *Everyone has inner doubts.*

ˌinner ˈcity *noun* [C] the poor parts of a large city, near the centre, that often have a lot of social problems □ *kawasan sesak dan miskin dlm sst bandar*: *There are huge problems in our inner cities.* ◆ *Inner-city schools often have difficulty in attracting good teachers.*

innermost /ˈɪnəməʊst/ *adj* [only *before* a noun] **1** (used about a feeling or thought) most secret or private □ *yg terpendam; di lubuk hati*: *She never told anyone her innermost thoughts.* **2** nearest to the centre or inside of sth □ *paling jauh ke dlm*: *the innermost shrine of the temple*

innings /ˈɪnɪŋz/ *noun* [C] (*pl* **innings**) a period of time in a game of **cricket** when it is the turn of one player or team to **bat** (= hit the ball) □ *inning; pusingan*

innocence /ˈɪnəsns/ *noun* [U] **1** the fact of not being guilty of a crime, etc. □ *(keadaan) tdk bersalah, tdk berdosa, dsb*: *The accused man protested his innocence throughout his trial.* OPP **guilt** **2** lack of knowledge and experience of the world, especially of bad things □ *kesucian; tdk tahu apa-apa*: *the innocence of childhood*

innocent /ˈɪnəsnt/ *adj* **1 innocent (of sth)** not having done wrong □ *tdk bersalah*: *An innocent man was arrested by mistake.* ◆ *to be innocent of a crime* SYN **blameless** OPP **guilty** **2** [only *before* a noun] being hurt or killed in a crime, war, etc. although not directly involved in it □ *tdk berdosa; tdk bersalah*: *innocent victims of a bomb blast* ◆ *He was an innocent bystander.* **3** not wanting to cause harm or upset sb □ *tdk berniat apa-apa*: *He got very aggressive when I asked an innocent question about his past life.* **4** not knowing the bad things in life; believing everything you are told □ *tdk tahu apa-apa*: *She was so innocent as to believe that politicians never lie.* SYN **naive**
▶ **innocently** *adv*: *'What are you doing here?' she asked innocently* (= pretending she did not know the answer).

innocuous /ɪˈnɒkjuəs/ *adj* (*formal*) not meant to cause harm or upset sb □ *tdk bermaksud utk menyakitkan hati*: *I made an innocuous remark about teachers and she got really angry.* SYN **harmless**

innovate /ˈɪnəveɪt/ *verb* [I] to create new things or ways of doing sth □ *memperkenalkan sst yg baharu* ▶ **innovation** /ˌɪnəˈveɪʃn/ *noun* [C,U] **(an) innovation (in sth)** [C]: *technological innovations in industry* ▶ **innovative** /ˈɪnəvətɪv, ˈɪnəveɪtɪv/ *adj*: *innovative methods/designs/products* ▶ **innovator** /ˈɪnəveɪtə(r)/ *noun* [C]

innuendo /ˌɪnjuˈendəʊ/ *noun* [C,U] (*pl* **innuendoes** or **innuendos**) an indirect way of talking about sb/sth, usually suggesting sth bad or rude □ *sindiran*: *His speech was full of sexual innuendo.*

innumerable /ɪˈnjuːmərəbl/ *adj* too many to be counted □ *tdk terkira banyaknya*

inoculate /ɪˈnɒkjuleɪt/ *verb* [T] **inoculate sb (against sth)** to protect a person or an animal from a disease by giving them a mild form of the disease with an **injection** (= putting a substance under their skin with a needle) □ *menginokulasi*: *The children have been inoculated against tetanus.*
⊃ look at **immunize, vaccinate** ▶ **inoculation** /ɪˌnɒkjuˈleɪʃn/ *noun* [C,U]

inoffensive /ˌɪnəˈfensɪv/ *adj* not likely to offend or upset sb □ *tdk menyakitkan hati; tdk menyinggung*: *a gentle and inoffensive man* SYN **harmless** OPP **offensive**

inopportune /ɪnˈɒpətjuːn/ *adj* (*formal*) happening at a bad time □ *tdk sesuai pd waktunya; salah waktu* SYN **inappropriate, inconvenient** OPP **opportune**

inordinate /ɪnˈɔːdɪnət/ adj (formal) much greater than usual or expected □ *terlalu; terlampau*: They spent an **inordinate** amount of time and money on the production. ▶ **inordinately** adv

inorganic /ˌɪnɔːˈɡænɪk/ adj not made of or coming from living things □ *tak organik*: Rocks and metals are inorganic substances. **OPP** organic

input¹ /ˈɪnpʊt/ noun 1 [C,U] input (of sth) (into/to sth) what you put into sth to make it successful □ *masukan (idea, dll); input*: We need some input from teachers into this book. 2 [U] the act of putting information into a computer □ *pemasukan; input*: The computer breakdown means we have lost the whole day's input. ⊃ look at output

input² /ˈɪnpʊt/ verb [T] (inputting; pt, pp input or inputted) to put information into a computer □ *memasukkan; menginput*: to input text/data/figures

inquest /ˈɪŋkwest/ noun [C] an official investigation to find out how sb died □ *inkues; siasatan rasmi*: to hold an inquest

inquire, inquirer, inquiring, inquiry = enquire, enquirer, enquiring, enquiry

inquisitive /ɪnˈkwɪzətɪv/ adj 1 too interested in finding out about what other people are doing □ *suka ambil tahu (hal orang lain)*: Don't be so inquisitive. It's none of your business. **SYN** nosy 2 interested in finding out about many different things □ *suka ingin tahu*: You need an inquisitive mind to be a scientist. **SYN** curious ▶ **inquisitively** adv ▶ **inquisitiveness** noun [U]

insane /ɪnˈseɪn/ adj 1 seriously mentally ill □ *gila; tdk siuman* 2 not showing sensible judgement □ *gila; sasau; kurang siuman*: You must be insane to leave such a great job. ⊃ look at mad ▶ **insanely** adv: insanely jealous ▶ **insanity** /ɪnˈsænəti/ noun [U]

insanitary /ɪnˈsænətri/ adj (formal) dirty and likely to cause disease □ *tdk bersih; kotor*: The restaurant was closed because of the insanitary condition of the kitchen. ⊃ look at sanitary

insatiable /ɪnˈseɪʃəbl/ adj that cannot be satisfied; very great □ *tdk pernah puas; tersangat besar*: an insatiable desire for knowledge ◆ an insatiable appetite

inscribe /ɪnˈskraɪb/ verb [T] (formal) inscribe A (on/in B); inscribe B (with A) to write sth on sth or cut words into the surface of sth □ *menulis; mengukir*: The names of all the previous champions are inscribed on the cup. ◆ The book was inscribed with the author's name.

inscription /ɪnˈskrɪpʃn/ noun [C] words that are written or cut on sth □ *inskripsi; tulisan*: There was a Latin inscription on the tombstone.

insect /ˈɪnsekt/ noun [C] a small animal with six legs, two pairs of wings and a body which is divided into three parts □ *serangga*: Ants, flies, beetles, butterflies and mosquitoes are all insects. ◆ an insect bite/sting ⊃ picture on page P13

HELP Some other small animals, for example spiders, are often also called insects although this is not strictly correct.

insecticide /ɪnˈsektɪsaɪd/ noun [C,U] a substance that is used for killing insects □ *racun serangga* ⊃ look at pesticide

insecure /ˌɪnsɪˈkjʊə(r)/ adj 1 insecure (about sb/sth) not confident about yourself or your relationships with other people □ *tdk yakin pd diri sendiri*: Many teenagers are insecure about their appearance. 2 not safe or protected □ *tdk selamat; tdk kukuh; goyah*: This ladder feels a bit insecure. ◆ The future of the company looks very insecure. **OPP** for both meanings secure ▶ **insecurely** adv ▶ **insecurity** /ˌɪnsɪˈkjʊərəti/ noun [U]: Their aggressive behaviour is a sign of insecurity. **OPP** security

insensitive /ɪnˈsensətɪv/ adj insensitive (to sth) 1 not knowing or caring how another person feels and therefore likely to hurt or upset them □ *tdk sensitif; tdk menghiraukan perasaan orang lain*: Some insensitive reporters tried to interview the families of the accident victims. ◆ an insensitive remark 2 not able to feel or react to sth □ *tdk peka; tdk sensitif*: insensitive to pain/cold/criticism **OPP** for both meanings sensitive ▶ **insensitively** adv ▶ **insensitivity** /ɪnˌsensəˈtɪvəti/ noun [U]

inseparable /ɪnˈseprəbl/ adj that cannot be separated from sb/sth □ *tdk boleh dipisahkan; tdk boleh berenggang*: inseparable friends **OPP** separable

insert /ɪnˈsɜːt/ verb [T] (formal) to put sth into sth or between two things □ *memasukkan; menyelitkan; menyisipkan*: I decided to insert a paragraph in the text. ◆ Position the cursor where you want to insert a word. ▶ **insertion** noun [C,U]

inshore adj /ˈɪnʃɔː(r)/ adv /ˌɪnˈʃɔː(r)/ in or towards the part of the sea that is close to the land □ *pesisir; ke tepi pantai*: inshore fishermen ◆ Sharks don't often come inshore.

inside¹ /ˌɪnˈsaɪd/ prep, adj [only before a noun] adv 1 in, on or to the inner part or surface of sth □ *di/ke dlm; bahagian dlm*: Is there anything inside the box? ◆ It's safer to be inside the house in a thunderstorm. ◆ We'd better stay inside until the rain stops. ◆ It's getting cold. Let's go inside. ◆ the inside pages of a newspaper **OPP** outside 2 (formal) (used about time) in less than; within □ *dlm masa; kurang drpd*: Your prescription will be ready inside an hour. 3 known or done by sb in a group or an organization □ *drpd orang dlm*: The robbers seemed to have had some inside information about the bank's security system. 4 (slang) in prison □ *dlm penjara*: He was sentenced to three years inside.

inside² /ˌɪnˈsaɪd/ noun 1 [C] the inner part or surface of sth □ *bahagian dlm*: The door was locked from the inside. ◆ There's a label somewhere on the inside. **OPP** outside 2 insides [pl] (infor-

insider → inspire

mal) the organs inside the body □ *bahagian dlm tubuh; perut*: *The coffee warmed his insides.* **IDM** **inside out** with the inner surface on the outside □ *terbalik*: *You've got your jumper on inside out.* ⊃ picture at **back**
know sth inside out ⊃ **know¹**

insider /ɪnˈsaɪdə(r)/ *noun* [C] a person who knows a lot about a group or an organization because they are a part of it □ *orang dlm*: *The book gives us an insider's view of how government works.*

insidious /ɪnˈsɪdiəs/ *adj* (*formal*) spreading gradually or without being noticed, but causing serious harm □ *tersembunyi tetapi berbahaya; terpendam dan berbahaya*: *the insidious effects of polluted water supplies* ▶ **insidiously** *adv*

insight /ˈɪnsaɪt/ *noun* [C,U] **(an) insight (into sth)** an understanding of what sb/sth is like □ *wawasan; pemahaman; gambaran*: *The book gives a good insight into the lives of the poor.*

insignia /ɪnˈsɪɡniə/ *noun* [C] (*pl* **insignia**) the symbol or sign that shows sb's position, or that they are a member of a group or an organization □ *tanda kebesaran; lambang kuasa/kedaulatan; lambang pangkat*: *the royal insignia* ♦ *His uniform bore the insignia of a captain.*

insignificant /ˌɪnsɪɡˈnɪfɪkənt/ *adj* of little value or importance □ *tdk penting*: *an insignificant detail* ♦ *Working in such a big company made her feel insignificant.* **OPP** **significant** ▶ **insignificance** *noun* [U] ▶ **insignificantly** *adv*

insincere /ˌɪnsɪnˈsɪə(r)/ *adj* saying or doing sth that you do not really believe □ *tdk ikhlas*: *His apology sounded insincere.* ♦ *Dan gave an insincere smile.* **OPP** **sincere** ▶ **insincerely** *adv* ▶ **insincerity** /ˌɪnsɪnˈserəti/ *noun* [U] **OPP** **sincerity**

insinuate /ɪnˈsɪnjueɪt/ *verb* [T] to suggest sth unpleasant in an indirect way □ *menyindir; memerli*: *She seemed to be insinuating that our work was below standard.* ▶ **insinuation** /ɪnˌsɪnjuˈeɪʃn/ *noun* [C,U]: *to make insinuations about somebody's honesty*

insipid /ɪnˈsɪpɪd/ *adj* having almost no taste or flavour; not interesting or exciting □ *hambar; tawar; tdk ada rasa*

insist /ɪnˈsɪst/ *verb* [I] **1 insist (on sth/doing sth); insist that ...** to say strongly that you must have or do sth, or that sb else must do sth □ *mendesak; memaksa; seboleh-boleh hendakkan/mahukan*: *He always insists on the best.* ♦ *Dan insisted on coming too.* ♦ *My parents insist that I come home by taxi.* ♦ *'Have another drink.' 'Oh all right, if you insist.'* **2 insist (on sth); insist that ...** to say firmly that sth is true (when sb does not believe you) □ *berkeras mengatakan; menegaskan*: *She insisted on her innocence.* ♦ *Benjamin insisted that the accident wasn't his fault.* ▶ **insistence** *noun* [U]

insistent /ɪnˈsɪstənt/ *adj* **1 insistent (on sth/doing sth); insistent that ...** saying strongly that you must have or do sth, or that sb else must do sth □ *mendesak; berkeras menyuruh*: *Doctors are insistent on the need to do more exercise.* ♦ *She was most insistent that we should all be there.* **2** continuing for a long time in a way that cannot be ignored □ *tdk henti-henti*: *the insistent ringing of the telephone* ▶ **insistently** *adv*

insolent /ˈɪnsələnt/ *adj* (*formal*) lacking respect; rude □ *biadab; kurang ajar*: *insolent behaviour* ▶ **insolence** *noun* [U] ▶ **insolently** *adv*

insoluble /ɪnˈsɒljəbl/ *adj* **1** that cannot be explained or solved □ *tdk dpt diselesaikan*: *We faced almost insoluble problems.* **2** that cannot be dissolved in a liquid □ *tdk terlarut* **OPP** for both meanings **soluble**

insomnia /ɪnˈsɒmniə/ *noun* [U] the condition of being unable to sleep □ *insomnia; tdk dpt tidur*: *Do you ever suffer from insomnia?* ⊃ look at **sleepless**

insomniac /ɪnˈsɒmniæk/ *noun* [C] a person who cannot sleep □ *penghidap insomnia*

inspect /ɪnˈspekt/ *verb* [T] **1 inspect sb/sth (for sth)** to look at sth closely or in great detail □ *memeriksa; meneliti*: *The detective inspected the room for fingerprints.* **SYN** **examine** **2** to make an official visit to make sure that rules are being obeyed, work is being done properly, etc. □ *memeriksa*: *All food shops should be inspected regularly.* ▶ **inspection** *noun* [C,U]: *The fire prevention service will carry out an inspection of the building next week.* ♦ *On inspection, the passport turned out to be false.*

inspector /ɪnˈspektə(r)/ *noun* [C] **1** an official who visits schools, factories, etc. to make sure that rules are being obeyed, work is being done properly, etc. □ *pegawai pemeriksa; nazir; merinyu*: *a health and safety inspector* **2** (*BrE*) a police officer with quite an important position □ *inspektor* **3** a person whose job is to check passengers' tickets on buses or trains □ *pemeriksa* **4** (*AmE*) = **surveyor**(2)

inspiration /ˌɪnspəˈreɪʃn/ *noun* **1** [C,U] **an inspiration (to/for sb); inspiration (to do/for sth)** a feeling, person or thing that makes you want to do sth or gives you exciting new ideas □ *(sumber) ilham/inspirasi*: *The beauty of the mountains was a great source of inspiration to the writer.* ♦ *What gave you the inspiration to become a dancer?* **2** [C,U, usually sing] (*informal*) a sudden good idea □ *ilham; inspirasi*: *I've had an inspiration—why don't we go to that new club?* ♦ *The answer came to me in a flash of inspiration.*

inspire /ɪnˈspaɪə(r)/ *verb* [T] **1 inspire sth; inspire sb (to do sth)** to make sb want to do or create sth □ *mengilhamkan; memberikan inspirasi kpd; mendorong*: *Nelson Mandela's autobiography inspired her to go into politics.* ♦ *The attack was inspired by racial hatred.* **2 inspire sb (with sth); inspire sth (in sb)** to make sb feel, think, etc. sth □ *membangkitkan; menimbulkan*: *to be inspired with enthusiasm* ♦ *The guide's nervous manner did not inspire much confidence in us.* ▶ **inspiring** *adj*: *an inspiring speech.*

inspired /ɪnˈspaɪəd/ adj **1** having excellent qualities or abilities □ *cemerlang*: *The pianist gave an inspired performance.* **2** (in compounds) used to form adjectives to show how sth has been influenced □ *terdorong*: *a politically-inspired killing*

instability /ˌɪnstəˈbɪləti/ noun [U] the state of being likely to change □ *ketidakstabilan*: *There are growing signs of political instability.* **OPP** **stability** ⊃ adjective **unstable**

install (AmE also **instal**) /ɪnˈstɔːl/ verb [T] **1** to put a piece of equipment, etc. in place so that it is ready to be used □ *memasang*: *We are waiting to have our new washing machine installed.* ♦ *to install a computer system* **SYN** **put sth in 2** *install sb (as sth)* to put sb or yourself in a position or place □ *melantik secara rasmi*: *He was installed as President yesterday.* ▶**installation** /ˌɪnstəˈleɪʃn/ noun [C,U]: *a military/nuclear installation* ♦ *the installation of a new chairman*

instalment (AmE **installment**) /ɪnˈstɔːlmənt/ noun [C] **1** one of the regular payments that you make for sth until you have paid the full amount □ *ansuran; bayaran ansuran*: *to pay for something in instalments* **2** one part of a story that is shown or published as a series □ *bahagian; episod*: *Don't miss next week's exciting instalment of this new drama.*

instance /ˈɪnstəns/ noun [C] *an instance (of sth)* an example or case (of sth) □ *kejadian*: *There have been several instances of racial attacks in the area.* ♦ *In most instances the drug has no side effects.*
IDM *for instance* for example □ *misalnya*: *There are several interesting places to visit around here—Warwick, for instance.* ⊃ note at **example**

instant¹ /ˈɪnstənt/ adj **1** happening immediately □ *serta-merta; segera*: *The film was an instant success.* ♦ *She took an instant dislike to me.* ♦ *A new government cannot bring about instant change.* **SYN** **immediate 2** [only before a noun] (used about food) that can be prepared quickly and easily, usually by adding hot water □ *segera*: *instant coffee*

instant² /ˈɪnstənt/ noun [C, usually sing] **1** a very short period of time □ *seketika; sebentar*: *Alex thought for an instant and then agreed.* **2** a particular point in time □ *ketika; sekarang juga*: *At that instant I realized I had been tricked.* ♦ *Stop doing that this instant* (= now)! **SYN** for both meanings **moment**

instantaneous /ˌɪnstənˈteɪniəs/ adj happening immediately or extremely quickly □ *dgn serta-merta; dgn segera* ▶**instantaneously** adv

instantly /ˈɪnstəntli/ adv without delay; immediately □ *dgn segera*: *I asked him a question and he replied instantly.*

instant messaging noun [U] a system on the Internet that allows people to exchange written messages with each other very quickly □ *pemesejan segera*

TOPIC

Instant messaging

If you want to **chat with** someone on the Internet you can use **instant messaging** to exchange short written messages. When you **log on**, you can show that you are **online** and available to chat.

---

instead /ɪnˈsted/ adv, prep *instead (of sb/sth/doing sth)* in the place of sb/sth □ *sebagai ganti; dan bukannya; sebaliknya*: *I couldn't go so my husband went instead.* ♦ *Instead of 7.30 could I come at 8.00?* ♦ *You should play football instead of just watching it on TV.*

instigate /ˈɪnstɪɡeɪt/ verb [T] (formal) to make sth start to happen □ *memulakan; menghasut* ▶**instigation** /ˌɪnstɪˈɡeɪʃn/ noun [U]

instil (AmE **instill**) /ɪnˈstɪl/ verb [T] (instilling; instilled) *instil sth (in/into sb)* to make sb think or feel sth □ *menanamkan; menyemaikan*: *Parents should try to instil a sense of responsibility into their children.*

instinct /ˈɪnstɪŋkt/ noun [C,U] the natural tendency that causes a person or an animal to behave in a particular way without thinking or learning about it □ *naluri; rasa hati*: *Birds learn to fly by instinct.* ♦ *In a situation like that you don't have time to think—you just act on instinct.* ▶**instinctive** /ɪnˈstɪŋktɪv/ adj: *Your instinctive reaction is to run from danger.* ▶**instinctively** adv

institute¹ /ˈɪnstɪtjuːt/ noun [C] an organization that has a particular purpose; the building used by this organization □ *institut*: *the Institute of Science and Technology* ♦ *institutes of higher education*

institute² /ˈɪnstɪtjuːt/ verb [T] (formal) to introduce a system, policy, etc., or start a process □ *memulakan; memperkenalkan*: *The government has instituted a new scheme for youth training.*

institution /ˌɪnstɪˈtjuːʃn/ noun **1** [C] a large, important organization that has a particular purpose, such as a bank, a university, etc. □ *institusi; perbadanan*: *the financial institutions in the City of London* **2** [C] a building where certain people with special needs live and are looked after □ *rumah kebajikan; hospital (pesakit jiwa)*: *a mental institution* (= a hospital for the mentally ill) ♦ *She's been in institutions all her life.* **3** [C] a social custom or habit that has existed for a long time □ *institusi; kebiasaan; adat*: *the institution of marriage* **4** [U] the act of introducing a system, policy, etc., or of starting a process □ *bermulanya; (perbuatan) memulakan; memperkenalkan*: *the institution of new safety procedures*

institutional /ˌɪnstɪˈtjuːʃənl/ adj connected with an institution □ *(berkenaan dgn) institusi*: *The old lady is in need of institutional care.*

instruct /ɪnˈstrʌkt/ verb [T] 1 instruct sb (to do sth) to give an order to sb; to tell sb to do sth □ *menyuruh; memerintah*: The soldiers were instructed to shoot above the heads of the crowd. 2 (formal) instruct sb (in sth) to teach sb sth □ *mengajar*: Children must be instructed in road safety before they are allowed to ride a bike on the road.

instruction /ɪnˈstrʌkʃn/ noun 1 instructions [pl] detailed information on how you should use sth, do sth, etc. □ *arahan*: Read the instructions on the back of the packet carefully. ◆ You should always follow the instructions. 2 [C] an instruction (to do sth) an order that tells you what to do or how to do sth □ *arahan; perintah*: The guard was under strict instructions not to let anyone in or out. 3 [U] (formal) instruction (in sth) the act of teaching sth to sb □ *pengajaran; ajaran*: The staff need instruction in the use of the new booking system.

instructive /ɪnˈstrʌktɪv/ adj giving useful information □ *banyak maklumat berguna* ▶ instructively adv

instructor /ɪnˈstrʌktə(r)/ noun [C] a person whose job is to teach a practical skill or sport □ *pengajar pelatih*: a driving/fitness/golf instructor

instrument /ˈɪnstrəmənt/ noun [C] 1 a tool that is used for doing a particular job or task □ *alat; peralatan*: surgical/optical/precision instruments ⊃ note at **tool** 2 something that is used for playing music □ *alat muzik*: Do you play an instrument? ⊃ note at **music** 3 something that is used for measuring speed, distance, temperature, etc. in a car, plane or ship □ *alatan*: the instrument panel of a plane 4 (formal) something that sb uses in order to achieve sth □ *alat*: The press should be more than an instrument of the government.

TOPIC

Musical instruments

Musical instruments may be **stringed** (*violins, guitars, etc.*), **brass** (*horns, trumpets, etc.*), **woodwind** (*flutes, clarinets, etc.*) or **keyboard** (*piano, organ, synthesizer, etc.*). **Percussion** instruments include *drums* and *cymbals*.

instrumental /ˌɪnstrəˈmentl/ adj 1 instrumental in doing sth helping to make sth happen □ *memainkan peranan penting*: She was instrumental in getting him the job. 2 for musical instruments without voices □ *instrumental*: instrumental music

insubordinate /ˌɪnsəˈbɔːdɪnət/ adj (formal) (used about a person or behaviour) not obeying rules or orders □ *ingkar; tdk menurut arahan atau perintah* ▶ insubordination /ˌɪnsəˌbɔːdɪˈneɪʃn/ noun [U]: He was dismissed from the army for insubordination.

[I] **intransitive**, a verb which has no object: *He laughed.*

insubstantial /ˌɪnsəbˈstænʃl/ adj (formal) not large, solid or strong □ *tdk besar, kukuh, kuat, cukup, dll*: a hut built of insubstantial materials **OPP** substantial

insufferable /ɪnˈsʌfrəbl/ adj (formal) (used about a person or behaviour) extremely unpleasant or annoying □ *menyakitkan hati; keterlaluan*

insufficient /ˌɪnsəˈfɪʃnt/ adj insufficient (for sth/to do sth) not enough □ *tdk cukup*: The students complained that they were given insufficient time for the test. **OPP** sufficient ▶ insufficiently adv

insular /ˈɪnsjələ(r)/ adj only interested in your own country, ideas, etc. and not in those from outside □ *berfikiran sempit* ▶ insularity /ˌɪnsjuˈlærəti/ noun [U]

insulate /ˈɪnsjuleɪt/ verb [T] insulate sth (against/from sth) to protect sth with a material that prevents electricity, heat or sound from passing through □ *menebat; melindungi*: The walls are insulated against noise. ▶ insulation /ˌɪnsjuˈleɪʃn/ noun [U]

insult¹ /ɪnˈsʌlt/ verb [T] to speak or act rudely to sb □ *menghina; terhina*: I felt very insulted when I didn't even get an answer to my letter. ◆ He was thrown out of the hotel for insulting the manager.

insult² /ˈɪnsʌlt/ noun [C] a rude comment or action □ *hinaan; penghinaan; cacian; maki-memaki*: The drivers were standing in the road yelling insults at each other.

insulting /ɪnˈsʌltɪŋ/ adj insulting (to sb/sth) making sb feel offended □ *menghina*: insulting behaviour/remarks ◆ That poster is insulting to women.

insuperable /ɪnˈsuːpərəbl/ adj (formal) (used about a problem, etc.) impossible to solve □ *tdk dpt diatasi*

insurance /ɪnˈʃʊərəns (BrE also) -ˈʃɔːr-/ noun 1 [U] insurance (against sth) an arrangement with a company in which you pay them regular amounts of money and they agree to pay the costs if, for example, you die or are ill, or if you lose or damage sth □ *insurans*: life/car/travel/household insurance ◆ an insurance policy ◆ to take out insurance against fire and theft 2 [U] the business of providing insurance □ *(perniagaan) insurans*: He works in insurance. 3 [U, sing] (an) insurance (against sth) something you do to protect yourself (against sth unpleasant) □ *jaminan; perlindungan*: Many people take vitamin pills as an insurance against illness.

insure /ɪnˈʃʊə(r) (BrE also) -ˈʃɔː(r)/ verb [T] 1 insure sb/sth (against/for sth) to buy or to provide insurance □ *menginsuranskan*: They insured the painting for £10 000 against damage or theft. 2 (AmE) = ensure

insurgent /ɪnˈsɜːdʒənt/ noun [C, usually pl] (formal) a person fighting against the government or armed forces of their own country □ *pemberontak* **SYN** rebel ▶ insurgent adj **SYN** rebellious

[T] **transitive**, a verb which has an object: *He ate an apple.*

insurmountable /ˌɪnsəˈmaʊntəbl/ adj (formal) (used about a problem, etc.) impossible to solve □ tdk dpt diatasi

insurrection /ˌɪnsəˈrekʃn/ noun [C,U] (formal) violent action against the rulers of a country or the government □ pemberontakan (bersenjata)

intact /ɪnˈtækt/ adj [not before a noun] complete; not damaged □ dlm keadaan baik; tdk rosak/terjejas: Very few of the buildings remain intact following the earthquake.

intake /ˈɪnteɪk/ noun [C, usually sing] 1 the amount of food, drink, etc. that you take into your body □ pengambilan; makan; minum: My doctor told me to reduce my salt intake. 2 the (number of) people who enter an organization or institution during a certain period □ pengambilan (pelajar, dll); bilangan (orang) yg diambil masuk: This year's intake of students is down 10%. 3 the act of taking sth into your body, especially breath □ pengambilan

intangible /ɪnˈtændʒəbl/ adj difficult to describe, understand or measure □ sukar diperikan, dimengerti atau diukur: The benefits of good customer relations are intangible. **OPP** tangible

integral /ˈɪntɪɡrəl/ adj 1 integral (to sth) necessary in order to make sth complete □ penting; perlu: Spending a year in France is **an integral part of** the university course. 2 included as part of sth □ (yg) merupakan sebahagian drpd: The car has an integral solar panel.

integrate /ˈɪntɪɡreɪt/ verb 1 [T] integrate sth (into sth); integrate A and B/integrate A with B to join things so that they become one thing or work together □ menggabungkan; menyatukan; menyepadukan: The two small schools were integrated into one large one. ♦ These programs can be integrated with your existing software. 2 [I,T] integrate (sb) (into/with sth) to join in and become part of a group or community, or to make sb do this □ mengintegrasikan; berintegrasi: It took Amir a while to integrate into his new school. ⊃ look at segregate ▶**integration** /ˌɪntɪˈɡreɪʃn/ noun [U]: racial integration ⊃ look at segregation

integrity /ɪnˈteɡrəti/ noun [U] the quality of being honest and having strong moral principles □ integriti; kejujuran: He's a person **of great integrity** who will say exactly what he thinks.

intellect /ˈɪntəlekt/ noun 1 [U] the power of the mind to think and to learn □ daya fikir; intelek: a woman of considerable intellect 2 [C] an extremely intelligent person □ intelektual; intelek: He was one of the most brilliant intellects of his time.

intellectual¹ /ˌɪntəˈlektʃuəl/ adj 1 [only before a noun] connected with sb's ability to think, reason and understand things □ intelektual; daya fikir: The boy's intellectual development was very advanced for his age. 2 (used about a person) well educated and enjoying activities in which you have to think seriously about things □ intelektual ▶**intellectually** /-tʃuəli/ adv

intellectual² /ˌɪntəˈlektʃuəl/ noun [C] a person who is well educated and enjoys thinking seriously about things □ cendekiawan; intelek; intelektual

intelligence /ɪnˈtelɪdʒəns/ noun [U] 1 the ability to understand, learn and think □ kecerdasan; kepintaran: a person of normal intelligence ♦ an intelligence test 2 important information about a person or country □ maklumat risikan: to receive intelligence about somebody ♦ enemy intelligence

intelligent /ɪnˈtelɪdʒənt/ adj having or showing the ability to understand, learn and think; clever □ cerdas; cerdik; pintar; bijak: All their children are very intelligent. ♦ an intelligent question ▶**intelligently** adv

---
OTHER WORDS FOR

intelligent

Bright, clever and (especially in US English) smart all mean 'intelligent'. Bright is used especially to talk about young people: She's the brightest girl in the class. People who are clever or smart are able to understand and learn things quickly: He's smarter than his brother. Clever and smart can also describe actions or ideas that show intelligence: What a clever idea! ♦ a smart career move (= an action that will help your career).

---

intelligible /ɪnˈtelɪdʒəbl/ adj (used especially about speech or writing) possible or easy to understand □ boleh/mudah difahami **SYN** understandable **OPP** unintelligible

intend /ɪnˈtend/ verb [T] 1 intend to do sth/ doing sth to plan or mean to do sth □ berniat; bercadang; mahu; hendak: I'm afraid I spent more money than I had intended. ♦ I certainly don't intend to wait here all day! ♦ They had intended staying in Wales for two weeks but the weather was so bad that they left after one. ⊃ noun intention 2 intend sth for sb/sth; intend sb to do sth to plan, mean or make sth for a particular person or purpose □ dimaksudkan (utk sso); bermaksud: You shouldn't have read that letter—it wasn't intended for you. ♦ I didn't intend you to have all the work.

intended /ɪnˈtendɪd/ adj 1 [only before a noun] that you are trying to achieve or reach □ dirancang, diharapkan, disasarkan: the intended purpose ♦ The bullet missed its intended target. 2 intended for sb/sth; intended as sth; intended to be/do sth planned or designed for sb/sth □ bertujuan utk; utk sso/sst: The book is intended for children. ♦ The notes are intended as an introduction to the course. ♦ The lights are intended to be used in the garden.

intense /ɪnˈtens/ adj very great, strong or serious □ terlalu/amat sangat (besar, kuat, serius, dll): intense heat/cold/pressure ♦ intense anger/

interest/desire ▶**intensely** *adv*: *They dislike each other intensely.* ▶**intensity** /ɪnˈtensəti/ *noun* [U]: *I wasn't prepared for the intensity of his reaction to the news.*

intensify /ɪnˈtensɪfaɪ/ *verb* [I,T] (**intensifying**; **intensifies**; *pt, pp* **intensified**) to become or to make sth greater or stronger □ *meningkatkan; menjadi bertambah hebat/buruk*: *The government has intensified its campaign against obesity.* ♦ *Fighting in the region has intensified.* ▶**intensification** /ɪnˌtensɪfɪˈkeɪʃn/ *noun* [U]

intensive /ɪnˈtensɪv/ *adj* **1** involving a lot of work or care in a short period of time □ *intensif*: *an intensive investigation/course* **2** (used about methods of farming) aimed at producing as much food as possible from the land or money available □ *intensif*: *intensive agriculture* ▶**intensively** *adv*

in‚tensive ˈcare *noun* [U] special care in hospital for patients who are very seriously ill or injured; the department that gives this care □ *rawatan rapi*: *She was in intensive care for a week after the crash.*

intent¹ /ɪnˈtent/ *adj* **1 intent (on/upon sth)** showing great attention □ *asyik; khusyuk*: *She was so intent upon her work that she didn't hear me come in.* **2 intent on/upon sth/doing sth** determined to do sth □ *bersungguh-sungguh; berazam*: *He's always been intent on making a lot of money.* ▶**intently** *adv*

intent² /ɪnˈtent/ *noun* [U] (*formal*) what sb intends to do; intention □ *niat; maksud; tujuan*: *He was charged with possession of a gun with intent to commit a robbery.* ♦ *to do something with evil/good intent*
IDM **to/for all intents and purposes** in effect, even if not completely true □ *boleh dikatakan*: *When they scored their fourth goal the match was, to all intents and purposes, over.*

intention /ɪnˈtenʃn/ *noun* [C,U] **(an) intention (of doing sth/to do sth)** what sb intends or means to do; a plan or purpose □ *hajat; niat; maksud*: *Our intention was to leave early in the morning.* ♦ *I have no intention of staying indoors on a nice sunny day like this.* ♦ *I borrowed the money with the intention of paying it back the next day.*

intentional /ɪnˈtenʃənl/ *adj* done on purpose, not by chance □ *sengaja; disengajakan*: *I'm sorry I took your jacket—it wasn't intentional!* **SYN** **deliberate** **OPP** **unintentional** ▶**intentionally** /-ʃənəli/ *adv*: *I can't believe the boys broke the window intentionally.*

interact /ˌɪntərˈækt/ *verb* [I] **1 interact (with sb)** (used about people) to communicate or mix with sb, especially while you work, play or spend time together □ *berinteraksi; bergaul*: *He is studying the way children interact with each other at different ages.* **2** (used about two things) to have an effect on each other □ *saling bertindak* ▶**interaction** *noun* [U,C] **interaction (between/with sb/sth)** [U]: *interaction between the two departments*

interactive /ˌɪntərˈæktɪv/ *adj* **1** that involves people working together and having an influence on each other □ *interaktif; berinteraksi*: *The college uses interactive language-learning techniques.* **2** involving direct communication both ways, between a computer, etc. and the person using it □ *interaktif*: *interactive TV/computer games* ➲ picture on **page P3**

ˌinteractive ˈwhiteboard (*abbr* **IWB**) *noun* [C] a piece of classroom equipment using a computer connected to a large screen that you can write on or use to control the computer by touching it with your finger or a pen □ *papan putih interaktif*: *Nearly every classroom has an interactive whiteboard.*

intercept /ˌɪntəˈsept/ *verb* [T] to stop or catch sb/sth that is moving from one place to another □ *memintas; menyekat*: *Detectives intercepted him at the airport.* ▶**interception** *noun* [U,C]

interchangeable /ˌɪntəˈtʃeɪndʒəbl/ *adj* **interchangeable (with sth)** able to be used in place of each other without making any difference to the way sth works □ *boleh ditukar ganti*: *Are these two words interchangeable* (= do they have the same meaning)? ▶**interchangeably** /-əbli/ *adv*

intercom /ˈɪntəkɒm/ *noun* [C] a system of communication by radio or telephone inside an office, plane, etc.; the device you press or switch on to start using this system □ *interkom*

interconnect /ˌɪntəkəˈnekt/ *verb* [I,T] **interconnect (A) (with B)**; **interconnect A and B** to connect similar things; to be connected to similar things □ *saling bersambung; saling berhubung*: *electronic networks which interconnect thousands of computers around the world*

intercontinental /ˌɪntəˌkɒntɪˈnentl/ *adj* between continents □ *antara benua*: *intercontinental flights*

intercourse /ˈɪntəkɔːs/ *noun* (*formal*) = **sex**(3)

interdependent /ˌɪntədɪˈpendənt/ *adj* depending on each other □ *saling bergantung*: *Exercise and good health are generally interdependent.* ♦ *interdependent economies/organizations* ▶**interdependence** *noun* [U]

interest¹ /ˈɪntrəst; -trest/ *noun* **1** [U, sing] **an interest (in sb/sth)** a desire to learn or hear more about sb/sth or to be involved with sb/sth □ *minat*: *She's begun to show a great interest in politics.* ♦ *I wish he'd take more interest in his children.* ♦ *Don't lose interest now!* **2** [U] the quality that makes sth interesting □ *(menarik) minat; tarikan*: *I thought this article might be of interest to you.* ♦ *Computers hold no interest for me.* ♦ *places of historical interest* **3** [C, usually pl] something that you enjoy doing or learning about □ *kegemaran; kesukaan*: *What are your interests and hobbies?* **4** [U] **interest (on sth)** the money that you pay for borrowing money from a bank, etc. or the money that you earn when you keep money in a bank, etc. □ *faedah; bunga*: *We pay 6% interest* on our mortgage at the moment. ♦ The **interest rate** has never been so high/low. ♦ Some companies offer **interest-free** loans. ⊃ note at **loan**

IDM **have/with sb's (best) interests at heart** to want sb to be happy and successful, even though your actions may not show it □ *utk kebaikan/manfaat sso*: Don't be angry with your father—you know he has your best interests at heart.

in sb's interest(s) to sb's advantage □ *demi kebaikan/kepentingan sso*: Using less water is in the public interest.

in the interest(s) of sth in order to achieve or protect sth □ *utk kepentingan sst*: In the interest(s) of safety, please fasten your seat belts.

interest² /ˈɪntrəst, -trest/ *verb* [T] to make sb want to learn or hear more about sth or to become involved in sth □ *menarik minat/perhatian*: It might interest you to know that I didn't accept the job. ♦ The subject of the talk was one that interests me greatly.

PHR V **interest sb in sth** to persuade sb to buy, have, do sth □ *membangkitkan minat sso (ttg sst); menarik perhatian sso (kpd sst)*: Can I interest you in our new brochure?

interested /ˈɪntrəstɪd/ *adj* **1** [not before a noun] **interested (in sth/sb); interested in doing sth; interested to do sth** wanting to know or hear more about sth/sb; enjoying or liking sth/sb □ *berminat; ingin tahu; tertarik*: They weren't interested in my news at all! ♦ I'm really not interested in going to university. ♦ I was interested to hear that you've got a new job. Where is it? **OPP** **uninterested** ⊃ note at **like**

HELP If you like what you are doing, and want to know or hear more, then you are **interested** in it. The person or thing that makes you feel like this is **interesting**.

2 [only *before* a noun] involved in or affected by sth; in a position to gain from sth □ *berkepentingan*: As an interested party (= sb who is directly involved), I was not allowed to vote. **OPP** **disinterested**

interesting /ˈɪntrəstɪŋ, -trest-/ *adj* **interesting (to do sth); interesting that ...** enjoyable and entertaining; holding your attention □ *menarik*: an interesting person/book/idea/job ♦ It's always interesting to hear about the customs of other societies. ♦ It's interesting that Luisa chose Peru for a holiday. ▶**interestingly** *adv*

interface /ˈɪntəfeɪs/ *noun* [C] **1** the way a computer program gives information to a user or receives information from a user, in particular the appearance of the screen □ *antara muka*: the user interface **2** a connection or computer program that joins one device or system to another □ *alat pengantara muka alat penyambung*: the interface between computer and printer **3** **the interface (between A and B)** the point where two people, things, systems, etc. meet and affect each other □ *ruang hubung kait atau persemukaan*: the interface between manufacturing and sales

465   **interest → intermarry**

interfere /ˌɪntəˈfɪə(r)/ *verb* [I] **1** **interfere (in sth)** to get involved in a situation which does not involve you and where you are not wanted □ *tangan; masuk campur*: You shouldn't interfere in your children's lives—let them make their own decisions. **2** **interfere (with sth)** to prevent sth from succeeding or being done or happening as planned □ *mengganggu*: Every time the telephone rings it interferes with my work. ♦ She never lets her private life interfere with her career. **3** **interfere (with sth)** to touch or change sth without permission □ *mengusik*: Many people feel that scientists shouldn't interfere with nature. ▶**interfering** *adj*

interference /ˌɪntəˈfɪərəns/ *noun* [U] **1** **interference (in sth)** the act of getting involved in a situation that does not involve you and where you are not wanted □ *campur tangan; masuk campur*: I resented my mother's interference in my affairs. **2** extra noise (because of other signals or bad weather) that prevents you from receiving radio, TV or telephone signals clearly □ *gangguan*

interim¹ /ˈɪntərɪm/ *adj* [only *before* a noun] not final or lasting; temporary until sb/sth more permanent is found □ *interim; sementara*: an interim arrangement ♦ The deputy head teacher took over in **the interim period** until a replacement could be found.

interim² /ˈɪntərɪm/ *noun*
IDM **in the interim** in the time between two things happening; until a particular event happens □ *sementara itu*

interior /ɪnˈtɪəriə(r)/ *noun* **1** [C, usually sing] the inside part of sth □ *bahagian dlm*: I'd love to see the interior of the castle. ♦ the earth's interior **OPP** **exterior** **2** **the interior** [sing] the central part of a country or continent that is a long way from the coast □ *pedalaman*: an expedition into the interior of Australia **3** **the Interior** [sing] a country's own news and affairs that do not involve other countries □ *dlm negeri*: the Department of the Interior ▶**interior** *adj* [only *before* a noun]: *interior walls*

inˌterior deˈsign *noun* [U] the art or job of choosing colours, furniture, carpets, etc. to decorate the inside of a house □ *rekaan dalaman* ▶**inˌterior deˈsigner** *noun* [C]

interjection /ˌɪntəˈdʒekʃn/ *noun* [C] a word or phrase that is used to express surprise, pain, pleasure, etc. (for example Oh!, Hurray! or Wow!) □ *kata seru; seruan* **SYN** **exclamation**

interlude /ˈɪntəluːd/ *noun* [C] a period of time between two events or activities □ *(waktu) selang*: They finally met again after an interlude of several years. ♦ Their stay in Karnak was a pleasant interlude in their busy lives. ⊃ note at **interval**

intermarry /ˌɪntəˈmæri/ *verb* [I] (**intermarrying; intermarries;** *pt, pp* **intermarried**) to marry sb from a different religion, culture, coun-

intermediary → interrogate

try, etc. ☐ *berkahwin campur* ▶**intermarriage** /ˌɪntəˈmærɪdʒ/ *noun* [U]

intermediary /ˌɪntəˈmiːdiəri/ *noun* [C] (*pl* **intermediaries**) **an intermediary (between A and B)** a person or an organization that helps two people or groups to reach an agreement, by being a means of communication between them ☐ *orang tengah; perantara*

intermediate /ˌɪntəˈmiːdiət/ *adj* **1** in between two things in position, level, etc. ☐ *pertengahan*: *an intermediate step/stage in a process* **2** having more than a basic knowledge of sth but not yet advanced; suitable for sb who is at this level ☐ *pertengahan*: *an intermediate student/book/level*

interminable /ɪnˈtɜːmɪnəbl/ *adj* lasting for a very long time and therefore boring or annoying ☐ *lama sangat; tak habis-habis; berjela; meleret*: *an interminable delay/speech* ♦ *The wait seemed interminable.* **SYN endless** ▶**interminably** /-əbli/ *adv*

intermission /ˌɪntəˈmɪʃn/ *noun* [C] (*especially AmE*) a short period of time separating the parts of a film, play, etc. ☐ *selingan; waktu/masa rehat* ⮕ note at **interval**

intermittent /ˌɪntəˈmɪtənt/ *adj* stopping for a short time and then starting again several times ☐ *sekejap-sekejap; sekejap ada, sekejap tak ada*: *There will be intermittent showers.* ▶**intermittently** *adv*

intern /ɪnˈtɜːn/ *verb* [T, usually passive] (*formal*) **intern sb (in sth)** to keep sb in prison for political reasons, especially during a war ☐ *menahan; memenjarakan* ▶**internment** *noun* [U]

⚑**internal** /ɪnˈtɜːnl/ *adj* **1** [only *before* a noun] of or on the inside (of a place, person or object) ☐ *dalaman*: *internal injuries/organs* **2** happening or existing inside a particular organization ☐ *dalaman*: *an internal exam* (= one arranged and marked inside a particular school or college) ♦ *an internal police inquiry* **3** (used especially about political or economic affairs) inside a country ☐ *dlm negeri*: *a country's internal affairs/trade/markets* ♦ *an internal flight* **OPP** for all meanings **external** ▶**internally** /-nəli/ *adv*: *This medicine is not to be taken internally* (= not swallowed). **OPP externally**

⚑**international** /ˌɪntəˈnæʃnəl/ *adj* involving two or more countries ☐ *antarabangsa*: *an international agreement/flight/football match* ♦ *international trade/law/sport* ⮕ look at **local, national, regional** ▶**internationally** /-ʃənəli/ *adv*

⚑**Internet** /ˈɪntənet/ *usually* **the Internet** (also *informal* **the Net**) *noun* [sing] the international system of computers that makes it possible for you to see information from all around the world on your computer and to send information to other computers ☐ *Internet*: *I read about it on the Internet.* ♦ *Do you have Internet access?* ⮕ look at **intranet, ISP, Wi-Fi**™

TOPIC
The Internet

If you want to **use the Internet**, you need a computer. If you don't have **Internet access** at home, you can go to an **Internet cafe** to **surf the Net**. In order to visit a **website**, you need to type in a **URL/web address** (for example, www.oup.com/elt, which we say as 'double-U double-U double-U dot o-u-p dot com slash e-l-t'). If you want to find information about something **on the Internet**, but you don't know where to **look it up**, you can **do a search** using a **search engine**. You can buy things **online**, join a discussion in a **chat room**, post questions on a **message board**, or **download** music (but be careful you don't get a **virus**!)

internship /ˈɪntɜːnʃɪp/ *noun* [C] (*AmE*) **1** a period of time during which sb, especially a student, gets practical experience in a job, for example during the summer holiday ☐ *tempoh latihan*: *a 6-week internship at a television station* ⮕ look at **work experience 2** a job that an advanced student of medicine, whose training is nearly finished, does in a hospital to get further practical experience ☐ *latihan amali*

⚑**interpret** /ɪnˈtɜːprɪt/ *verb* **1** [T] **interpret sth (as sth)** to explain or understand the meaning of sth ☐ *mentafsir*: *Your silence could be interpreted as rudeness.* ♦ *How would you interpret this part of the poem?* **OPP misinterpret 2** [I] **interpret (for sb)** to translate what sb is saying into another language as you hear it ☐ *menterjemah*: *He can't speak English so he'll need somebody to interpret for him.*

⚑**interpretation** /ɪnˌtɜːprɪˈteɪʃn/ *noun* [C,U] **1** an explanation or understanding of sth ☐ *tafsiran; interpretasi*: *What's your interpretation of these statistics?* ♦ *What he meant by that remark is* **open to interpretation** (= it can be explained in different ways). **2** the way an actor or musician chooses to perform or understand a character or piece of music ☐ *cara sso pelakon membawa sst watak atau pemuzik mempersembahkan muzik*: *a modern interpretation of 'Hamlet'*

interpreter /ɪnˈtɜːprɪtə(r)/ *noun* [C] a person whose job is to translate what sb is saying immediately into another language ☐ *jurubahasa*: *The President spoke to the crowd through an interpreter.* ⮕ look at **translator**

interrelate /ˌɪntərɪˈleɪt/ *verb* [I,T] [usually passive] (*formal*) (used about two or more things) to connect or be connected very closely so that each has an effect on the other ☐ *saling berkaitan/berhubungan* ▶**interrelated** *adj*

interrogate /ɪnˈterəgeɪt/ *verb* [T] **interrogate sb (about sth)** to ask sb a lot of questions over a long period of time, especially in an aggressive way ☐ *menyoal siasat; memisit*: *The prisoner was interrogated for six hours.* ▶**interrogator** /ɪnˈterəgeɪtə(r)/ *noun* [C] ▶**interrogation** /ɪnˌterəˈgeɪʃn/ *noun* [C,U]: *The prisoner broke down* **under interrogation** *and confessed.*

interrogative¹ /ˌɪntəˈrɒɡətɪv/ *adj* **1** (*formal*) asking a question; having the form of a question □ *mengandungi pertanyaan*: *an interrogative tone/gesture/remark* **2** (in grammar) used in questions □ *tanya*: *an interrogative sentence/pronoun/determiner/adverb*

interrogative² /ˌɪntəˈrɒɡətɪv/ *noun* [C] a question word □ *kata tanya*: *'Who', 'what' and 'where' are interrogatives.*

interrupt /ˌɪntəˈrʌpt/ *verb* **1** [I,T] **interrupt (sb/sth) (with sth)** to say or do sth that makes sb stop what they are saying or doing □ *menyampuk; mencelah; mengganggu*: *He kept interrupting (me) with silly questions.* **2** [T] to stop the progress of sth for a short time □ *menghentikan seketika*: *The programme was interrupted by an important news flash.*

interruption /ˌɪntəˈrʌpʃn/ *noun* [U,C] the act of interrupting sb/sth; the thing that interrupts sb/sth □ *gangguan*: *I need to work for a few hours without interruption.* ♦ *I've had so many interruptions this morning that I've done nothing!*

intersect /ˌɪntəˈsekt/ *verb* [I,T] (used about roads, lines, etc.) to meet or cross each other □ *bersilang*: *The lines intersect at right angles.*

intersection /ˌɪntəˈsekʃn/ *noun* [C] the place where two or more roads, lines, etc. meet or cross each other □ *persimpangan*

intersperse /ˌɪntəˈspɜːs/ *verb* [T, usually passive] to put things at various points in sth □ *menyisipkan; menyelangi*: *His speech was interspersed with jokes.*

intertwine /ˌɪntəˈtwaɪn/ *verb* [I,T] if two things **intertwine** or if you **intertwine** them, they become very closely connected and difficult to separate □ *berjalin; saling berkait; berkait rapat*: *His interests in business and politics were closely intertwined.*

interval /ˈɪntəvl/ *noun* [C] **1** a period of time between two events □ *tempoh; selang; jarak waktu*: *There was a long interval between sending the letter and getting a reply.* **2** a short break separating the different parts of a play, film, concert, etc. □ *selingan; waktu rehat*: *There will be two 15-minute intervals, when the bar will be open.* **3** [usually pl] a short period during which sth different happens from what is happening for the rest of the time □ *tempoh*: *There'll be a few sunny intervals between the showers today.*
IDM **at intervals** with time or spaces between □ *sering; selang*: *I visit my grandparents at regular intervals.* ♦ *Plant the trees at two-metre intervals.*

OTHER WORDS FOR

interval

Some words that have a similar meaning to interval are **intermission**, **break**, **recess**, **interlude** and **pause**. In British English we use **interval** for a break in a performance. The US word is **intermission**. A **break** is especially in connection with periods of work or study, for example a **lunch/tea break** in an office, factory or school: *The children play outside in the breaks at school.* ♦ *You've worked so hard you've earned a break.* In American English a break at school is called **(a) recess**. In British English **recess** is a longer period of time when work or business stops, especially in Parliament or the law courts: *Parliament is in recess.* ♦ *the summer recess.* An **interlude** is a short period of time that passes between two events, during which something different happens: *a peaceful interlude in the fighting*, and a **pause** is a short temporary stop in action or speech: *After a moment's pause, she answered.*

---

intervene /ˌɪntəˈviːn/ *verb* [I] **1 intervene (in sth)** to become involved in a situation in order to improve it □ *campur tangan*: *She would have died if the neighbours hadn't intervened.* ♦ *to intervene in a dispute* **2** to interrupt sb who is speaking in order to say sth □ *mencelah; menyela* **3** (used about events, etc.) to happen in a way that delays sth or stops it from happening □ *mengganggu; menghalang; menggendalakan*: *If no further problems intervene, we should be able to finish in time.* ▶ **intervention** /ˌɪntəˈvenʃn/ *noun* [U,C] **intervention (in sth)**: *military intervention in the crisis*

intervening /ˌɪntəˈviːnɪŋ/ *adj* [only before a noun] coming or existing between two events, dates, objects, etc. □ *berselang*: *the intervening years/days/months*

interview¹ /ˈɪntəvjuː/ *noun* [C] **1 an interview (for sth)** a meeting at which sb is asked questions to find out if they are suitable for a job, course of study, etc. □ *temu duga*: *to attend an interview* ⊃ note at **job 2 an interview (with sb)** a meeting at which a journalist asks sb questions in order to find out their opinion, etc. □ *temu bual; wawancara*: *There was an interview with the Prime Minister on TV last night.* ♦ *The actress refused to give an interview* (= answer questions).

interview² /ˈɪntəvjuː/ *verb* [T] **1 interview sb (for sth)** to ask sb questions to find out if they are suitable for a job, course of study, etc. □ *menemu duga*: *How many applicants did you interview for the job?* **2 interview sb (about sth)** to ask sb questions about their opinions, private life, etc. especially on the radio or TV or for a newspaper, magazine, etc. □ *menemu bual; mewawancara*: *Next week, I will be interviewing Spielberg about his latest movie.* **3 interview sb (about sth)** to ask sb questions at a private meeting □ *menyoal siasat*: *The police are waiting to interview the injured girl.*

interviewee /ˌɪntəvjuːˈiː/ *noun* [C] a person who is questioned in an interview □ *orang yg ditemu duga/diwawancara*

interviewer /ˈɪntəvjuːə(r)/ *noun* [C] a person who asks the questions in an interview □ *orang yg menemu duga; pewawancara*

intestine /ɪnˈtestɪn/ *noun* [C, usually pl] the tube in your body that carries food away from

intimacy → introduce

your stomach to the place where it leaves your body ☐ *usus* ⇒ A less formal word is **gut**. ⇒ picture at **body** ▶**intestinal** /ɪnˈtestɪnl/ ˌɪnteˈstaɪnl/ *adj*

intimacy /ˈɪntɪməsi/ *noun* [U] the state of having a close personal relationship with sb ☐ *hubungan mesra; kemesraan*: *Their intimacy grew over the years.*

intimate /ˈɪntɪmət/ *adj* **1** (used about people) having a very close relationship ☐ *rapat; akrab; intim*: *They're intimate friends.* **2** very private and personal ☐ *peribadi; sulit*: *They told each other their most intimate secrets.* **3** (used about a place, an atmosphere, etc.) quiet and friendly ☐ *suasana intim; selesa*: *I know an intimate little restaurant we could go to.* **4** very detailed ☐ *mendlm; terperinci*: *He's lived here all his life and has an intimate knowledge of the area.* ▶**intimately** *adv*

intimidate /ɪnˈtɪmɪdeɪt/ *verb* [T] **intimidate sb (into sth/doing sth)** to frighten or threaten sb, often in order to make them do sth ☐ *menakut-nakutkan; menggertak; mengancam*: *She refused to be intimidated by their threats.* ▶**intimidating** *adj*: *The teacher had rather an intimidating manner.* ▶**intimidation** /ɪnˌtɪmɪˈdeɪʃn/ *noun* [U]: *The rebel troops controlled the area by intimidation.*

⚑ **into** /ˈɪntə; *before vowels* ˈɪntʊ; *strong form* ˈɪntuː/ *prep* **1** moving to a position inside or in sth ☐ *masuk/pergi ke; (masuk) ke dlm*: *Come into the house.* ◆ *I'm going into town.* **OPP out of** **2** in the direction of sth ☐ *ke (dlm/arah)*: *Please speak into the microphone.* ◆ *At this point we were driving into the sun and had to shade our eyes.* **3** to a point at which you hit sth ☐ *bermaksud melanggar*: *I backed the car into a wall.* ◆ *She walked into a glass door.* **4** showing a change from one thing to another ☐ *menjadi; menyalin (pakaian); ke dlm*: *We're turning the spare room into a study.* ◆ *She changed into her jeans.* ◆ *Translate the passage into German.* **5** concerning or involving sth ☐ *berkenaan dgn*: *an inquiry into safety procedures* **6** used when you are talking about dividing numbers ☐ *dibahagikan dgn*: *7 into 28 goes 4 times.*

IDM be into sth (*spoken, informal*) to be very interested in sth, for example as a hobby ☐ *sangat meminati sst; gila-gilakan sst*: *I'm really into canoeing.* ⇒ note at **like**

intolerable /ɪnˈtɒlərəbl/ *adj* too bad, unpleasant or difficult to bear or accept ☐ *sangat teruk; tdk tertahan*: *The living conditions were intolerable.* ◆ *intolerable pain* **SYN unbearable** **OPP tolerable** ⇒ *verb* **tolerate** ▶**intolerably** /-əbli/ *adv*

intolerant /ɪnˈtɒlərənt/ *adj* **intolerant (of sb/sth)** not able to accept behaviour or opinions that are different from your own; finding sb/sth too unpleasant to bear ☐ *tdk bertoleransi; tdk sabar/sanggup*: *She's very intolerant of young children.* **OPP tolerant** ▶**intolerance** *noun* [U] **OPP tolerance** ▶**intolerantly** *adv*

intonation /ˌɪntəˈneɪʃn/ *noun* [C,U] the rise and fall of your voice while you are speaking ☐ *intonasi; turun naik nada suara* **SYN inflection**

intoxicated /ɪnˈtɒksɪkeɪtɪd/ *adj* (*formal*) **1** having had too much alcohol to drink; drunk ☐ *mabuk* **2** very excited and happy ☐ *terlalu seronok; mabuk*: *She was intoxicated by her success.* ▶**intoxication** /ɪnˌtɒksɪˈkeɪʃn/ *noun* [U]

intranet /ˈɪntrənet/ *noun* [C] a system of computers inside an organization that makes it possible for people who work there to look at the same information and to send information to each other ☐ *intranet* ⇒ look at **the Internet**

intransitive /ɪnˈtrænsətɪv/ *adj* (used about a verb) used without an object. **Intransitive** verbs are marked '[I]' in this dictionary. ☐ *tak transitif* **OPP transitive** ❶ For more information about intransitive verbs, look at the **Reference Section** at the back of this dictionary. ▶**intransitively** *adv*: *The verb is being used intransitively.*

intrepid /ɪnˈtrepɪd/ *adj* (*formal*) without any fear of danger ☐ *berani*: *an intrepid climber*

intricacy /ˈɪntrɪkəsi/ *noun* **1 intricacies** [pl] **the intricacies of sth** the complicated parts or details of sth ☐ *selok-belok yg rumit*: *It's difficult to understand all the intricacies of the situation.* **2** [U] the quality of having complicated parts, details or patterns ☐ *kerumitan; rumitnya*

intricate /ˈɪntrɪkət/ *adj* having many small parts or details put together in a complicated way ☐ *rumit; kompleks*: *an intricate pattern* ◆ *The story has an intricate plot.* ▶**intricately** *adv*

intrigue¹ /ɪnˈtriːɡ/ *verb* [T] to make sb very interested and wanting to know more ☐ *tertarik*: *I was intrigued by the way he seemed to know all about us already.* ▶**intriguing** *adj*: *an intriguing story*

intrigue² /ˈɪntriːɡ/ *noun* [C,U] secret plans to do sth, especially sth bad ☐ *rancangan jahat; komplot*: *The film is about political intrigues against the government.* ◆ *His new novel is full of intrigue and suspense.*

intrinsic /ɪnˈtrɪnsɪk; -zɪk/ *adj* [only *before* a noun] belonging to sth as part of its nature; basic ☐ *intrinsik; pd asasnya*: *The object is of no intrinsic value* (= the material it is made of is not worth anything). ▶**intrinsically** /-kli/ *adv*

⚑ **introduce** /ˌɪntrəˈdjuːs/ *verb* [T]
▶PEOPLE **1 introduce sb (to sb)** to tell two or more people who have not met before what each other's names are ☐ *memperkenalkan*: *'Who's that girl over there?' 'Come with me and I'll introduce you to her.'* **2 introduce yourself (to sb)** to tell sb you have met for the first time what your name is ☐ *memperkenalkan diri*: *He came over and introduced himself to me.*
▶RADIO/TV PROGRAMME **3** to be the first or main speaker on a radio or TV programme telling the audience who is going to speak, perform, etc.

[I] **intransitive**, a verb which has no object: *He laughed.*   [T] **transitive**, a verb which has an object: *He ate an apple.*

□ ***memperkenalkan***: *May I introduce my first guest on the show tonight …*
▶NEW EXPERIENCE **4 introduce sb to sth** to make sb begin to learn about sth or do sth for the first time □ ***memperkenalkan; memberi pendedahan awal***: *This page will introduce you to the basic aims of our society.*
▶NEW PRODUCT/LAW **5 introduce sth (in/into sth)** to bring in sth new, use sth, or take sth to a place for the first time □ ***memperkenalkan; mula (dilaksanakan, dibawa masuk, dll)***: *The new law was introduced in 2010.* ◆ *The company is introducing a new range of cars this summer.* ◆ *a newly-introduced ban on mobile phones in schools* ◆ *Goats were first introduced to the island in the 17th century.*

TOPIC

Introducing people

In Britain there are a number of different ways of introducing one person to another, depending on the occasion. In a formal introduction, we use a person's title followed by the surname. In an informal situation, or when introducing children, we use first names. In both formal and informal introductions we say **this is**, when referring to the people we are introducing, NOT 'he/she is' and NOT 'here is' (*formal*) '*May I introduce you. Dr Waters*, **this is** *Mr Jones. Mr Jones, Dr Waters.*' ◆ (*informal*) '*Mrs Smith*, **this is** *my daughter, Jane.*' ◆ (*informal*) '*John, meet Mary.*' An informal response to an introduction is **Hello** or **Nice to meet you**. A formal response is **How do you do?** The other person also replies: '*How do you do?*' When people are introduced, they often **shake hands**.

ɪ introduction /ˌɪntrəˈdʌkʃn/ *noun*
▶STH NEW **1** [U] **introduction of sth (into sth)** the act of bringing in sth new; using sth or taking sth to a place for the first time □ ***pengenalan; (perbuatan) memperkenalkan***: *the introduction of new teaching methods*
▶PEOPLE **2** [C, usually pl] the act of telling two or more people each other's names for the first time □ ***(perbuatan) memperkenalkan sso kpd sso***: *I think I'll get my father to **make/do the introductions**—he's better at remembering names!*
▶FIRST EXPERIENCE **3** [sing] **an introduction to sth** the first experience of sth □ ***permulaan; pengenalan***: *My first job—in a factory—was not a pleasant introduction to work.*
▶OF BOOK/SPEECH **4** [C] the first part of a book, a piece of written work or a talk which gives a general idea of what is going to follow □ ***pendahuluan; pengenalan***: *a brief introduction*
▶TO SUBJECT **5** [C] **an introduction (to sth)** a book for people who are beginning to study a subject □ ***buku pengantar***: '*An Introduction to English Grammar*'

introductory /ˌɪntrəˈdʌktəri/ *adj* **1** happening or said at the beginning in order to give a general idea of what will follow □ ***pengenalan; pendahuluan***: *an introductory speech/chapter/*

---

469 **introduction → invalid**

remark SYN **opening 2** intended as an introduction to a subject or an activity □ ***pengenalan; permulaan***: *introductory courses* **3** offered for a short time only, when a product is first on sale □ ***tawaran pengenalan***: *an **introductory price/offer***

introvert /ˈɪntrəvɜːt/ *noun* [C] a quiet, shy person who prefers to be alone than with other people □ ***orang yg introvert/pendiam/pemalu*** OPP **extrovert** ▶**introverted** *adj*

intrude /ɪnˈtruːd/ *verb* [I] **intrude (on/upon sb/sth)** to enter a place or situation without permission or when you are not wanted □ ***menceroboh; mengganggu***: *I'm sorry to intrude on your Sunday lunch but …*

intruder /ɪnˈtruːdə(r)/ *noun* [C] a person who enters a place without permission and often secretly □ ***penceroboh***

intrusion /ɪnˈtruːʒn/ *noun* [C,U] **(an) intrusion (on/upon/into sth)** something that disturbs you or your life when you want to be private □ ***gangguan; pencerobohan***: *This was another example of press intrusion into the affairs of the royals.* ▶**intrusive** /ɪnˈtruːsɪv/ *adj*

intuition /ˌɪntjuˈɪʃn/ *noun* [C,U] the feeling or understanding that makes you believe or know sth is true without being able to explain why □ ***gerak hati; intuisi***: *She knew, by intuition, about his illness although he never mentioned it.* ▶**intuitive** /ɪnˈtjuːɪtɪv/ *adj* ▶**intuitively** *adv*: *Intuitively, she knew that he was lying.*

Inuit /ˈɪnjuɪt; ˈɪnuɪt/ *noun* [pl] a race of people from northern Canada and parts of Greenland and Alaska □ ***kaum Inuit*** ▶**Inuit** *adj* ⊃ look at **Eskimo**

inundate /ˈɪnʌndeɪt/ *verb* [T, usually passive] **1 inundate sb (with sth)** to give or send sb so many things that they cannot deal with them all □ ***membanjiri; dibanjiri***: *We were inundated with applications for the job.* SYN **swamp 2** (*formal*) to cover an area of land with water □ ***melimpah; membanjiri; dilanda banjir***: *After the heavy rains the fields were inundated.* ⊃ A less formal word is **flood**.

invade /ɪnˈveɪd/ *verb* **1** [I,T] to enter a country with an army in order to attack and take control of it □ ***menyerang; melanggar***: *When did the Romans invade Britain?* ⊃ note at **war 2** [T] to enter in large numbers, often where sb/sth is not wanted □ ***datang beramai-ramai; diserbu***: *The whole area has been invaded by tourists.* ⊃ *noun* ▶**invader** *noun* [C]

invalid[1] /ɪnˈvælɪd/ *adj* **1** not legally or officially acceptable □ ***tdk sah***: *I'm afraid your passport is invalid.* **2** not correct according to reason; not based on all the facts □ ***tdk logik; tdk munasabah***: *an invalid argument* **3** (used about an instruction, etc.) of a type that the computer cannot recognize □ ***tdk sah; tdk diterima***: *an invalid command* OPP for all meanings **valid**

invalid² /ˈɪnvəlɪd/ *noun* [C] a person who has been very ill for a long time and needs other people to take care of them □ *orang yg sakit/uzur*

invalidate /ɪnˈvælɪdeɪt/ *verb* [T] (*formal*) **1** to prove that an idea, a story, an argument, etc. is wrong □ *membuktikan tdk benar*: *This new piece of evidence invalidates his version of events.* **2** to make a document, contract, election, etc. no longer legally or officially valid or acceptable □ *menjadikan tdk sah; membatalkan* OPP for both meanings **validate** ▶**invalidation** /ɪnˌvælɪˈdeɪʃn/ *noun* [U]

invaluable /ɪnˈvæljuəbl/ *adj* invaluable (to/ for sb/sth) extremely useful □ *amat berguna/ berharga*: *invaluable help/information/support*

> HELP Be careful. **Invaluable** is not the opposite of valuable. The opposite of valuable is **valueless** or **worthless**.

invariable /ɪnˈveəriəbl/ *adj* not changing □ *tetap; tdk berubah-ubah*

invariably /ɪnˈveəriəbli/ *adv* always □ *selalunya; setiap kali*: *She invariably arrives late.*

invasion /ɪnˈveɪʒn/ *noun* [C,U] **1** the act of entering another country with your army in order to take control of it □ *penyerangan; serangan; pelanggaran*: *the threat of invasion* **2** the act of entering a place where you are not wanted and disturbing sb □ *pencerobohan; gangguan*: *Such questions are an invasion of privacy.* ⊃ *verb* **invade**

invent /ɪnˈvent/ *verb* [T] **1** to think of or make sth for the first time □ *mencipta; mereka*: *When was the camera invented?* **2** to say or describe sth that is not true □ *mereka-reka; membuat-buat*: *I realized that he had invented the whole story.* ▶**inventor** *noun* [C]

invention /ɪnˈvenʃn/ *noun* **1** [C] a thing that has been made or designed by sb for the first time □ *ciptaan; rekaan*: *The electric car is a useful invention.* **2** [U] the action or process of making or designing sth for the first time □ *penciptaan; terciptanya*: *Books had to be written by hand before the invention of printing.* **3** [C,U] telling a story or giving an excuse that is not true □ *rekaan*: *It was obvious that his story about being robbed was (an) invention.*

inventive /ɪnˈventɪv/ *adj* having clever and original ideas □ *berdaya cipta* ▶**inventiveness** *noun* [U]

inventory /ˈɪnvəntri/ *noun* [C] (*pl* **inventories**) a detailed list, for example of all the furniture in a house, goods in a shop, etc. □ *inventori; senarai barang-barang*: *The landlord is coming to make an inventory of the contents of the flat.*

invert /ɪnˈvɜːt/ *verb* [T] (*formal*) to put sth in the opposite order or position to the way it usually is □ *menterbalikkan; diterbalikkan*: *What you see in a mirror is an inverted image of yourself.*

inˌverted ˈcommas (*BrE*) = quotation marks: *to put something in inverted commas*

invest /ɪnˈvest/ *verb* [I,T] invest (sth) (in sth) **1** to put money into a bank, business, property, etc. in the hope that you will make a profit □ *melaburkan*: *Many firms have invested heavily in this project.* ♦ *I've invested all my money in the company.* ⊃ note at **money 2** to spend money, time or energy on sth that you think is good or useful □ *membeli; membelanjakan; menggunakan (masa atau tenaga)*: *I'm thinking of investing in a new guitar.* ♦ *You have to invest a lot of time if you really want to learn a language well.* ▶**investor** *noun* [C]

investigate /ɪnˈvestɪɡeɪt/ *verb* [I,T] to try to find out all the facts about sth □ *menyiasat*: *A murder was reported and the police were sent to investigate.* ♦ *A group of experts are investigating the cause of the crash.* ▶**investigator** *noun* [C]

investigation /ɪnˌvestɪˈɡeɪʃn/ *noun* [C,U] (an) investigation (into sth) an official examination of the facts about a subject, situation, problem, etc. □ *siasatan; penyiasatan*: *The airlines are going to carry out an investigation into security procedures at airports.* ♦ *The matter is still under investigation by the police.*

investigative /ɪnˈvestɪɡətɪv/ *adj* trying to find out all the facts about sb/sth □ *siasatan*: *investigative journalism*

investment /ɪnˈvestmənt/ *noun* **1** [U,C] (an) investment (in sth) the act of putting money in a bank, business, property, etc.; the amount of money that you put in □ *pelaburan*: *investment in local industry* ♦ *The company will have to make an enormous investment to update their computer systems.* **2** [C] a thing that is worth buying □ *belian; pelaburan*: *This coat has been a good investment—I've worn it for three years.*

invigilate /ɪnˈvɪdʒɪleɪt/ *verb* [I,T] (*BrE*) to watch the people taking an exam to make sure that nobody is cheating □ *mengawasi peperiksaan* ▶**invigilator** *noun* [C]

invigorate /ɪnˈvɪɡəreɪt/ *verb* [T, often passive] to make sb feel healthy, fresh and full of energy □ *menyegarkan; berasa segar/cergas*: *I felt invigorated after my run.* ▶**invigorating** *adj*

invincible /ɪnˈvɪnsəbl/ *adj* too strong or powerful to be defeated □ *tdk dpt dikalahkan/ ditundukkan; kebal*

invisible /ɪnˈvɪzəbl/ *adj* invisible (to sb/sth) that cannot be seen □ *tdk dpt dilihat*: *Bacteria are invisible to the naked eye.* OPP **visible** ▶**invisibility** /ɪnˌvɪzəˈbɪləti/ *noun* [U] ▶**invisibly** /ɪnˈvɪzəbli/ *adv*

invitation /ˌɪnvɪˈteɪʃn/ *noun* **1** [C] an invitation to sb/sth (to sth/to do sth) a written or spoken request to go somewhere or do sth □ *undangan; jemputan*: *Did you get an invitation to the conference?* ♦ *a wedding invitation*

MORE You may **accept** an invitation, or you may **turn it down** or **decline** it.

2 [U] the act of inviting sb or being invited □ *(perbuatan) menjemput/dijemput; jemputan; undangan*: Entry is by invitation only. ♦ *a letter of invitation*

invite /ɪnˈvaɪt/ *verb* [T] **1 invite sb (to/for sth)** to ask sb to come somewhere or to do sth □ *menjemput; mengundang; mengajak*: We invited all the family to the wedding. ♦ *Successful applicants will be invited for interview next week.* **2** to make sth unpleasant likely to happen □ *mengundang; mencari; menempah*: You're inviting trouble if you carry so much money around.

PHR V **invite sb back 1** to ask sb to return with you to your home □ *mengajak; menjemput*: Shall we invite the others back for coffee after the meeting? **2** to ask sb to come to your home a second time, or after you have been a guest at their home □ *mengajak datang lagi; membalas jemputan*

invite sb in to ask sb to come into your home □ *menjemput masuk*

invite sb out to ask sb to go out somewhere with you □ *mengajak sso keluar bersama*: We've been invited out to the theatre by my aunt and uncle.

invite sb over/round (*informal*) to ask sb to come to your home □ *mempelawa/mengajak sso datang ke rumah*: I've invited Marco and his family round for lunch on Sunday.

MORE Note that **ask** can be used instead of **invite** in all senses.

inviting /ɪnˈvaɪtɪŋ/ *adj* attractive and pleasant □ *menarik; menggoda; enak*: The smell of cooking was very inviting.

invoice /ˈɪnvɔɪs/ *noun* [C] an official paper that lists goods or services that you have received and says how much you have to pay for them □ *invois*

involuntary /ɪnˈvɒləntri/ *adj* done without wanting or meaning to □ *dgn tdk sengaja; tiba-tiba*: She gave an involuntary gasp of pain as the doctor inserted the needle. **OPP** **voluntary**, **deliberate** ▶ **involuntarily** /ɪnˈvɒləntrəli/ *adv*

involve /ɪnˈvɒlv/ *verb* [T] **1** [not used in the continuous tenses] to make sth necessary □ *melibatkan*: The job involves a lot of travelling. **2** [not used in the continuous tenses] if a situation, an event or an activity involves sb, they take part in it □ *melibatkan; terlibat; mengenai*: The story involves a woman who cycled to India with her child. ♦ *More than 100 people were involved in the project.* **3 involve sb/sth in (doing) sth** to cause sb/sth to take part in or be concerned with sth □ *membabitkan; melibatkan*: Please don't involve me in your family arguments.

involved /ɪnˈvɒlvd/ *adj* **1** [not before a noun] **involved (in sth)** closely connected with sth; taking an active part in sth □ *terlibat*: I'm very involved in local politics. **2** [not before a noun] **involved (with sb)** having a sexual relationship with sb □ *mempunyai hubungan*: She is involved with an older man. **3** difficult to understand; complicated □ *rumit; sukar difahami*: The book has a very involved plot.

involvement /ɪnˈvɒlvmənt/ *noun* [C,U] the act of taking part in sth □ *penglibatan*: They deny any involvement in the robbery.

inward /ˈɪnwəd/ *adv, adj* **1** (also **inwards**) towards the inside or centre □ *ke dlm*: Stand in a circle facing inwards. **2** [only before a noun] inside your mind, not shown to other people □ *batin; jiwa*: my inward feelings **OPP** for both meanings **outward**

inwardly /ˈɪnwədli/ *adv* in your mind; secretly □ *di dlm hati*: He was inwardly relieved that they could not come to the party.

iodine /ˈaɪədiːn/ *noun* [U] (*symbol* I) a substance that is found in sea water. A liquid containing **iodine** is sometimes used to clean cuts in your skin. □ *iodin*

IOU /ˌaɪ əʊ ˈjuː/ *abbr* **I owe you**; a piece of paper that you sign showing that you owe sb some money □ *surat mengaku berhutang; resit hutang*

IPA /ˌaɪ piː ˈeɪ/ *abbr* the **International Phonetic Alphabet**; an alphabet that is used to show the pronunciation of words in any language □ *IPA (Abjad Fonetik Antarabangsa)*

iPod™ /ˈaɪpɒd/ *noun* [C] a type of **MP3 player** (= a small piece of equipment that can store information taken from the Internet and that you carry with you): Gary listens to his iPod when he's training. ⊃ note at **podcast**

TOPIC

iPods

You can listen to music on your **iPod™** wherever you are, using **headphones**. You can **download** music from the Internet or copy it from a CD, **flash drive**, etc. to your computer's **hard drive**, and then **load tracks** (= put songs) onto your iPod™. There are also **podcasts** (= recordings of radio broadcasts or videos, taken from the Internet) that you can load onto your iPod™. At home you can plug it into a **docking station** (= a device with speakers) to hear the music aloud.

IQ /ˌaɪ ˈkjuː/ *abbr* **intelligence quotient**; a measure of how intelligent sb is □ *IQ (Darjah Kecerdasan)*: have a high/low IQ ♦ *an IQ of 120*

IRA /ˌaɪ ɑːr ˈeɪ/ *abbr* the **Irish Republican Army**; an illegal organization which has fought for Northern Ireland to be united with the Republic of Ireland □ *IRA (Tentera Republikan Ireland)*

irate /aɪˈreɪt/ *adj* (*formal*) very angry □ *berang; sangat marah*

iris /ˈaɪrɪs/ *noun* [C] the coloured part of your eye □ *iris* ⊃ look at **pupil**

Irish /ˈaɪrɪʃ/ adj from Ireland □ *dr Ireland* ❶ For more information, look at the section on geographical names at the back of this dictionary.

iron¹ /ˈaɪən/ noun 1 [U] (symbol **Fe**) a hard strong metal that is used for making steel and is found in small quantities in food and in blood □ *besi; waja*: *an iron bar* ◆ *iron ore* ◆ *The doctor gave me iron tablets.* ◆ (figurative) *The general has an iron* (= very strong) *will.* ➲ picture at **corrugated** 2 [C] an electrical instrument with a flat bottom that is heated and used to smooth clothes after you have washed and dried them □ *seterika*: *a steam iron*

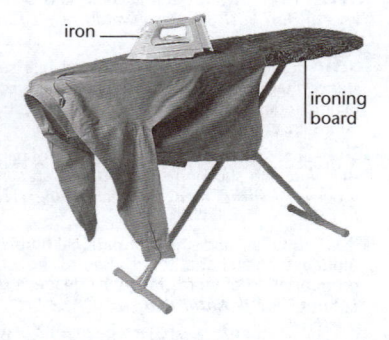

iron ——
ironing board

iron² /ˈaɪən/ verb [I,T] to use an iron to make clothes, etc. smooth □ *menggosok; menyeterika*: *Could you iron this dress for me?*

HELP **Do the ironing** is often used instead of iron: *I usually do the ironing on Sunday.*

PHR V **iron sth out** to get rid of any problems or difficulties that are affecting sth □ *menyelesaikan (masalah, dsb)*

ironic /aɪˈrɒnɪk/ (also **ironical** /aɪˈrɒnɪkl/) adj 1 meaning the opposite of what you say □ *ironik*: *Jeff sometimes offends people with his ironic sense of humour.* ➲ look at **sarcastic** 2 (used about a situation) strange or amusing because it is unusual or unexpected □ *pelik; aneh*: *It is ironic that the busiest people are often the most willing to help.* ▶ **ironically** /-kli/ adv

ironing /ˈaɪənɪŋ/ noun [U] clothes, etc. that you have just ironed or that you need to iron □ *pakaian, dsb yg hendak atau baru digosok*: *a large pile of ironing*

ˈironing board noun [C] a special narrow table covered with cloth that you iron clothes on □ *papan seterika* ➲ picture at **iron**

irony /ˈaɪrəni/ noun (pl **ironies**) 1 [C,U] an unusual or unexpected part of a situation, etc. that seems strange or amusing □ *sst yg pelik atau bertentangan dgn apa yg dijangka atau diharapkan*: *The irony was that when he finally got the job, he discovered that he didn't like it.* 2 [U] a way of speaking that shows you are joking or that you mean the opposite of what you say □ *ironi; sindiran halus*: *'The English are such good cooks,' he said with heavy irony.*

irrational /ɪˈræʃənl/ adj not based on reason or clear thought □ *tdk waras; tdk rasional*: *an irrational fear of spiders* ▶ **irrationality** /ɪˌræʃəˈnæləti/ noun [U] ▶ **irrationally** /ɪˈræʃənəli/ adv

irreconcilable /ɪˌrekənˈsaɪləbl/ adj (formal) (used about people or their ideas and beliefs) so different that they cannot be made to agree □ *sangat bertentangan; tdk dpt diselesaikan/ didamaikan* ▶ **irreconcilably** /-əbli/ adv

irregular /ɪˈreɡjələ(r)/ adj 1 not having an even, smooth shape or pattern □ *tdk sekata*: *an irregular outline* **OPP** **regular** 2 happening at times that you cannot predict □ *tdk tetap*: *His visits became more and more irregular.* **OPP** **regular** 3 not allowed according to the rules or social customs □ *tdk mengikut peraturan*: *It is highly irregular for a doctor to give information about patients without their permission.* 4 not following the usual rules of grammar □ *tdk sekata*: *'Caught' is an irregular past tense form.* **OPP** **regular** ▶ **irregularity** /ɪˌreɡjəˈlærəti/ noun [C,U] (pl **irregularities**) ▶ **irregularly** adv

irrelevant /ɪˈreləvənt/ adj not connected with sth or important to it □ *tdk berkaitan*: *That evidence is irrelevant to the case.* **OPP** **relevant** ▶ **irrelevance** (also **irrelevancy**; pl **irrelevancies**) noun [U,C] ▶ **irrelevantly** adv

irreparable /ɪˈrepərəbl/ adj that cannot be repaired □ *tdk dpt dibaiki/dipulih*: *Irreparable damage has been done to the ancient forests of Eastern Europe.* ▶ **irreparably** /-əbli/ adv

irreplaceable /ˌɪrɪˈpleɪsəbl/ adj (used about sth very valuable or special) that cannot be replaced □ *tdk dpt diganti* **OPP** **replaceable**

irrepressible /ˌɪrɪˈpresəbl/ adj full of life and energy □ *periang; riang; tdk dpt ditahan*: *young people full of irrepressible good humour* ▶ **irrepressibly** /-əbli/ adv

irresistible /ˌɪrɪˈzɪstəbl/ adj 1 so strong that it cannot be stopped or prevented □ *tdk dpt ditahan*: *an irresistible urge to laugh* 2 **irresistible (to sb)** very attractive □ *sungguh menawan; sangat menarik*: *He seems to think he's irresistible to women.* ➲ verb **resist** ▶ **irresistibly** /-əbli/ adv

irrespective of /ˌɪrɪˈspektɪv əv/ prep not affected by □ *tdk kira; tanpa mengambil kira*: *Anybody can take part in the competition, irrespective of age.*

irresponsible /ˌɪrɪˈspɒnsəbl/ adj not thinking about the effect your actions will have; not sensible □ *tdk bertanggungjawab*: *It is irresponsible to let small children go out alone.* **OPP** **responsible** ▶ **irresponsibility** /ˌɪrɪˌspɒnsəˈbɪləti/ noun [U] ▶ **irresponsibly** /ˌɪrɪˈspɒnsəbli/ adv

irreverent /ɪˈrevərənt/ adj not feeling or showing respect □ *sikap tdk hormat*: *This comedy has an irreverent look at the world of politics.* ▶ **irreverence** noun [U] ▶ **irreverently** adv

irreversible /ˌɪrɪˈvɜːsəbl/ adj that cannot be stopped or changed ◻ *tdk dpt dihentikan atau dipulihkan spt sediakala*: *an irreversible decision* ♦ *The disease can do irreversible damage to the body.* ▶**irreversibly** /-əbli/ adv

irrigate /ˈɪrɪgeɪt/ verb [T] to supply water to an area of land so that crops will grow ◻ *mengairi; membekalkan air*: *irrigated land/crops* ▶**irrigation** /ˌɪrɪˈgeɪʃn/ noun [U]: *irrigation channels*

irritable /ˈɪrɪtəbl/ adj becoming angry easily ◻ *cepat/lekas marah*: *to be/feel/get irritable* **SYN** bad-tempered ▶**irritability** /ˌɪrɪtəˈbɪləti/ noun [U] ▶**irritably** /ˈɪrɪtəbli/ adv

irritate /ˈɪrɪteɪt/ verb [T] 1 to make sb angry ◻ *membuat sso marah; menyakitkan hati*: *It really irritates me the way he keeps repeating himself.* **SYN** annoy 2 to cause a part of the body to be painful or sore ◻ *merengsakan*: *I don't use soap because it irritates my skin.* ▶**irritating** adj: *I found her extremely irritating* ▶**irritation** /ˌɪrɪˈteɪʃn/ noun [C,U]

irritated /ˈɪrɪteɪtɪd/ adj irritated (at/by/with sth) annoyed or angry ◻ *(berasa) jengkel*: *She was getting more and more irritated at his comments.*

is /ɪz/ ⊃ be

-ish [in compounds] 1 from the country mentioned ◻ *bahasa atau orang dr negara tertentu*: *Turkish* ♦ *Irish* 2 having the nature of; like ◻ *mempunyai tabii sst; menyerupai*: *childish* 3 fairly; approximately ◻ *kira-kira; agak-agak*: *reddish* ♦ *thirtyish*

Islam /ˈɪzlɑːm; ɪzˈlɑːm/ noun [U] the religion of Muslim people. Islam teaches that there is only one God and that Muhammad is His Prophet. ◻ *(agama) Islam* ▶**Islamic** /ɪzˈlæmɪk; -ˈlɑːm-/ adj: *Islamic law*

island /ˈaɪlənd/ noun [C] 1 a piece of land that is surrounded by water ◻ *pulau*: *the islands of the Caribbean* ♦ *the Greek islands* ♦ *life on a small island* ⊃ picture on **page P10** 2 (BrE) = **traffic island**

islander /ˈaɪləndə(r)/ noun [C] a person who lives on a small island ◻ *penduduk pulau*

isle /aɪl/ noun [C] an island ◻ *pulau*: *the Isle of Wight* ♦ *the British Isles*

HELP Isle is most commonly used in names.

isn't /ˈɪznt/ short for **is not**

isolate /ˈaɪsəleɪt/ verb [T] isolate sb/sth (from sb/sth) to put or keep sb/sth separate from other people or things ◻ *mengasingkan; memencilkan; menyebabkan perhubungan terputus*: *Some farms were isolated by the heavy snowfalls.* ♦ *We need to isolate all the animals with the disease so that the others don't catch it.*

isolated /ˈaɪsəleɪtɪd/ adj 1 isolated (from sb/sth) alone or apart from other people or things ◻ *terpencil; diasingkan*: *an isolated village deep in the countryside* ♦ *I was kept isolated from the other patients.* 2 not connected with others; happening once ◻ *tdk berkaitan; terpencil; satu-satunya*: *an isolated case of food poisoning*

isolation /ˌaɪsəˈleɪʃn/ noun [U] isolation (from sb/sth) the state of being separate and alone; the act of separating sb/sth ◻ *pemencilan; pengasingan; (perihal) terpencil/berasingan*: *He lived in complete isolation from the outside world.* ♦ *In isolation each problem does not seem bad, but together they are quite worrying.* ⊃ look at **loneliness**, **solitude**

ISP /ˌaɪ es ˈpiː/ abbr **Internet Service Provider**; a company that provides you with an Internet connection and services such as email, etc. ◻ *Pembekal Khidmat Internet*

issue¹ /ˈɪʃuː/ (BrE also) /ˈɪsjuː/ noun 1 [C] a problem or subject for discussion ◻ *isu; hal; perkara; persoalan*: *I want to raise the issue of overtime pay at the meeting.* ♦ *The government cannot avoid the issue of homelessness any longer.* ♦ *If you have any issues with the new timetable, ring our helpline.* 2 [C] one in a series of things that are published or produced ◻ *keluaran; terbitan*: *Do you have last week's issue of this magazine?* 3 [U] the act of publishing or giving sth to people ◻ *pengeluaran; pemberian*: *the issue of blankets to the refugees*

IDM **make an issue (out) of sth** to give too much importance to a small problem ◻ *menjadikan sst sebagai isu*: *OK, we disagree on this but let's not make an issue of it.*

issue² /ˈɪʃuː/ (BrE also) /ˈɪsjuː/ verb 1 [T] to give or say sth to sb officially ◻ *mengeluarkan; diberikan*: *The new employees were issued with uniforms.* ♦ *to issue a visa* ♦ *The police will issue a statement later today.* 2 [T] to produce sth such as a magazine or article ◻ *menerbitkan; mengeluarkan*: *We issue a monthly newsletter for students.*

PHR V **issue from sth** (formal) to come or go out ◻ *keluar; datang*: *An angry voice issued from the loudspeaker.*

IT /ˌaɪ ˈtiː/ abbr = **information technology**

it /ɪt/ pron 1 [used as the subject or object of a verb, or after a preposition] the animal or thing mentioned earlier ◻ *ia; -nya; digunakan utk merujuk kpd apa-apa yg disebut sebelumnya*: *Look at that car. It's going much too fast.* ♦ *The children went up to the dog and patted it.*

HELP It can also refer to a baby whose sex you do not know: *Is it a boy or a girl?*

2 used for identifying a person ◻ *digunakan utk merujuk kpd sso*: *It's your Mum on the phone.* ♦ *'Who's that?' 'It's the postman.'* ♦ *It's me!* ♦ *It's him!* 3 used in the position of the subject or object of a verb when the real subject or object is at the end of the sentence ◻ *digunakan utk merujuk kpd subjek atau objek di hujung ayat*: *It's hard for them to talk about their problems.* ♦ *I think it doesn't really matter what time we arrive.* 4 used in the position of the subject of a verb when you are talking about time, the date,

italics → jacket potato

distance, the weather, etc. □ *digunakan sebagai subjek kk apabila merujuk kpd masa, tarikh dsb*: *It's nearly half past eight.* ◆ *It's Tuesday today.* ◆ *It's about 100 kilometres from London.* ◆ *It was very cold at the weekend.* ◆ *It's raining.* **5** used when you are talking about a situation □ *digunakan utk merujuk kpd sst keadaan*: *It gets very crowded here in the summer.* ◆ *I'll come at 7 o'clock if it's convenient.* ◆ *It's a pity they can't come to the party.* **6** used for emphasizing a part of a sentence □ *digunakan utk memberi penekanan kpd sebahagian drpd ayat*: *It was Jerry who said it, not me.* ◆ *It's your health I'm worried about, not the cost.*
IDM **that/this is it 1** that/this is the answer or the main point □ *betul*: *That's it! You've solved the puzzle!* **2** that/this is the end □ *setakat ini saja; cukuplah*: *That's it, I've had enough! I'm going home!*

italics /ɪˈtælɪks/ *noun* [pl] a type of writing or printing in which the letters do not stand straight up □ *huruf condong; italik*: *All the example sentences in the dictionary are printed in italics.* ▶ **italic** *adj*

itch /ɪtʃ/ *noun* [C] the feeling on your skin that makes you want to rub or scratch it □ *rasa gatal*: *I've got an itch on my back.* ▶ **itch** *verb* [I]: *My whole body is itching.* ▶ **itchy** *adj*: *This shirt is itchy.* ◆ *My skin is all itchy.*

it'd /ˈɪtəd/ *short for* **it had; it would**

item /ˈaɪtəm/ *noun* [C] **1** one single thing on a list or in a collection □ *benda; perkara*: *Some items arrived too late to be included in the catalogue.* ◆ *What is the first item on the agenda?* **2** one single article or object □ *benda; barang*: *Can I pay for each item separately?* ◆ *an item of clothing* **3** a single piece of news □ *berita*: *There was an interesting item about Spain in yesterday's news.*

itemize (also **-ise**) /ˈaɪtəmaɪz/ *verb* [T] to make a list of all the separate items in sth □ *menyenaraikan*: *an itemized telephone bill*

itinerant /aɪˈtɪnərənt/ *adj* (*formal*) [only before a noun] travelling from place to place □ *pergi dr satu tempat ke satu tempat*: *an itinerant circus family*

itinerary /aɪˈtɪnərəri/ *noun* [C] (*pl* **itineraries**) a plan of a journey, including the route and the places that you will visit □ *jadual perjalanan*

it'll /ˈɪtl/ *short for* **it will**

its /ɪts/ *determiner* of or belonging to a thing □ *-nya*: *The club held its Annual General Meeting last night.* ➜ note at **it's**

it's /ɪts/ *short for* **it is; it has**

> **HELP** Be careful. **It's** is a short way of saying *it is* or *it has*. **Its** means 'belonging to it' and does not have an apostrophe: *The bird has broken its wing.*

itself /ɪtˈself/ *pron* **1** used when the animal or thing that does an action is also affected by it

[I] **intransitive**, a verb which has no object: *He laughed.*

□ *dirinya*: *The cat was washing itself.* ◆ *The company has got itself into financial difficulties.* **2** used to emphasize sth □ *sendiri*: *The building itself is beautiful, but it's in a very ugly part of town.*
IDM **(all) by itself 1** without being controlled by a person; automatically □ *dgn sendirinya; secara automatik*: *The central heating comes on by itself before we get up.* **2** alone □ *sendiri*: *The house stood all by itself on the hillside.* ➜ note at **alone**

ITV /ˌaɪ tiː ˈviː/ *abbr* (*BrE*) Independent Television; a group of TV companies in the UK that are paid for by advertising □ *ITV (Televisyen Persendirian)*: *to watch a film on ITV*

I've /aɪv/ *short for* **I have**

ivory /ˈaɪvəri/ *noun* [U] the hard white substance that the **tusks** (= long teeth) of an elephant are made of □ *gading*

ivy /ˈaɪvi/ *noun* [U] a climbing plant that has dark leaves with three or five points □ *pokok ivy*

J j

J, j /dʒeɪ/ *noun* [C,U] (*pl* **Js**; **J's**; **j's** /dʒeɪz/) the 10th letter of the English alphabet □ *J, j (huruf)*: *'Jam' begins with (a) 'J'.*

jab¹ /dʒæb/ *verb* [I,T] **jab sb/sth (with sth); jab sth into sb/sth** to push at sb/sth with a sudden, rough movement, usually with sth sharp □ *menusuk; mencucuk; menyigung*: *She jabbed me in the ribs with her elbow.* ◆ *The robber jabbed a gun into my back and ordered me to move.*

jab² /dʒæb/ *noun* [C] **1** a sudden rough push with sth sharp □ *tusukan; cucukan*: *He gave me a jab in the ribs with the stick.* **2** (*BrE informal*) the act of putting a drug, etc. under sb's skin with a needle □ *suntikan*: *I'm going to the doctor's to have a flu jab today.* **SYN** **injection**

jack¹ /dʒæk/ *noun* [C] **1** a piece of equipment for lifting a car, etc. off the ground, for example in order to change its wheel □ *bicu; jek* **2** the card between the ten and the queen in a pack of cards □ *(daun terup) pekak* ➜ note at **card** ➜ picture at **card**

jack² /dʒæk/ *verb*
PHR V **jack sth in** (*slang*) to stop doing sth □ *berhenti membuat sst*: *Jerry got fed up with his job and jacked it in.*
jack sth up to lift a car, etc. using a **jack** □ *membicu/menaikkan/mengejek sst*: *We jacked the car up to change the wheel.*

jacket /ˈdʒækɪt/ *noun* [C] a short coat with sleeves □ *jaket*: *a denim/leather jacket* ◆ *Do you have to wear a jacket and tie to work?* ➜ look at **life jacket** ➜ picture on **page P1**

jacket po'tato (also **baked po'tato**) *noun* [C] a potato that is cooked in the oven in its skin □ *kentang bakar berkulit* ➜ picture on **page P16**

[T] **transitive**, a verb which has an object: *He ate an apple.*

jackknife /ˈdʒæknaɪf/ verb [I] (used about a lorry that is in two parts) to go out of control and bend suddenly in a dangerous way □ *hilang kawalan dan melipat*

the jackpot /ˈdʒækpɒt/ noun [C] the largest money prize that you can win in a game □ *cepumas*
IDM hit the jackpot ⊃ hit¹

Jacuzzi™ /dʒəˈkuːzi/ noun [C] a large bath in which the water moves around, giving you a pleasant feeling □ *Jacuzzi™ (jakuzi)*

jade /dʒeɪd/ noun [U] **1** a hard stone that is usually green and is used in making jewellery □ *(batu) jed* **2** a bright green colour □ *warna jed; hijau batu lumut* ▶ jade adj

jaded /ˈdʒeɪdɪd/ adj tired and bored after doing the same thing for a long time without a break □ *letih dan bosan*

jagged /ˈdʒægɪd/ adj rough with sharp points □ *bercerancang: jagged rocks*

jaguar /ˈdʒægjuə(r)/ noun [C] a large wild cat with black spots that comes from Central and South America □ *jaguar*

jail¹ /dʒeɪl/ = **prison** □ *penjara: She was sent to jail for ten years.*

jail² /dʒeɪl/ verb [T] to put sb in prison □ *memenjarakan; dipenjarakan: She was jailed for ten years.*

jailer /ˈdʒeɪlə(r)/ noun [C] (old-fashioned) a person whose job is to guard prisoners □ *pengawal penjara*

ᵢ jam¹ /dʒæm/ noun **1** [U] a sweet substance that you spread on bread, made by boiling fruit and sugar together □ *jem: a jar of raspberry jam* ⊃ look at **jelly** ⊃ picture on **page P16**

> **MORE** Jam made from oranges or lemons is called **marmalade**.

2 [C] a situation in which you cannot move because there are too many people or vehicles □ *kesesakan lalu lintas: a traffic jam* **3** [C, sing] (*informal*) a difficult situation □ *kesulitan: We're in a bit of a jam without our passports or travel documents.*

jam² /dʒæm/ verb (**jamming**; **jammed**) **1** [T] jam sb/sth in, under, between, etc. sth to push or force sb/sth into a place where there is not much room □ *menyumbatkan; mengasak: She managed to jam everything into her suitcase.* **2** [I,T] jam (sth) (up) to become or to make sth unable to move so that it does not work □ *tersekat; tersangkut; rosak: Something is jamming (up) the machine.* ◆ *The paper keeps jamming in the photocopier.* ◆ *I can't open the door. The lock's jammed.* **3** [T, usually passive] jam sth (up) (with sb/sth) to fill sth with too many people or things □ *penuh sesak; padat; dihujani: The cupboard was jammed full of old newspapers and magazines.* ◆ *The suitcase was jam-packed with* (= completely full of) *designer clothes.* ◆ *The switchboard was jammed with hundreds of calls from unhappy customers.* **4** [T] to send out signals in order to stop radio programmes, etc. from being received or heard clearly □ *mengganggu siaran radio, dsb*

PHR V jam on the brakes/jam the brakes on to stop a car suddenly by pushing hard on the **brake** (= the device for making a vehicle stop) with your foot □ *menekan brek dgn segera*

Jan. abbr = **January** □ *Januari: 1 Jan. 2013*

jangle /ˈdʒæŋgl/ verb [I,T] to make a noise like metal hitting against metal; to move sth so that it makes this noise □ *menggemerencingkan; menggoyang-goyangkan (kunci, dsb) supaya bergemerencing: The baby smiles if you jangle your keys.* ▶ jangle noun [U]

janitor /ˈdʒænɪtə(r)/ (*AmE*) = **caretaker**

ᵢ January /ˈdʒænjuəri/ noun [U,C] (*abbr* **Jan.**) the 1st month of the year, coming after December □ *Januari*

> **HELP** Note how the names of the months are used in sentences: *We're going skiing in January.* ◆ *last/next January* ◆ *We first met on January 31st, 2009.* ◆ *Our wedding anniversary is at the end of January.* ◆ *January mornings can be very dark in Britain.* ◆ *Michael's birthday is (on) January 17.* We say 'on January the seventeenth' or 'on the seventeenth of January' or, in American English, 'January seventeenth'. In both British and American English, the months of the year are always written with a capital letter.

jar¹ /dʒɑː(r)/ noun [C] **1** a container with a lid, usually made of glass and used for keeping food, etc. in □ *botol; balang: a jam jar* ◆ *a large storage jar for flour* ⊃ picture at **container 2** the food that a **jar** contains □ *sebotol; sebalang: a jar of honey/jam/coffee*

jar² /dʒɑː(r)/ verb (**jarring**; **jarred**) **1** [T] to hurt or damage sth as a result of a sharp knock □ *terhantuk; tersentak: He fell and jarred his back.* **2** [I] jar (on sb/sth) to have an unpleasant or annoying effect □ *tdk menyenangkan; menyakitkan hati: The dripping tap jarred on my nerves.*

jargon /ˈdʒɑːgən/ noun [U] special or technical words that are used by a particular group of people in a particular profession and that other people do not understand □ *jargon: medical/scientific/legal/computer jargon*

jaundice /ˈdʒɔːndɪs/ noun [U] a disease that makes your skin and eyes yellow □ *penyakit kuning; jaundis*

jaundiced /ˈdʒɔːndɪst/ adj **1** not expecting sb/sth to be good or useful, especially because of experiences that you have had in the past □ *(pandangan) yg diracuni; tdk sihat: He had a jaundiced view of life.* ◆ *She looked on politicians with a jaundiced eye.* **2** suffering from **jaundice** □ *mengalami penyakit jaundis*

javelin → jetty

javelin /ˈdʒævlɪn/ noun **1** [C] a long stick with a pointed end that is thrown in sports competitions □ *lembing* **2 the javelin** [sing] the event or sport of throwing the **javelin** as far as possible □ *acara rejam lembing*

jaw /dʒɔː/ noun **1** [C] either of the two bones in your face that contain your teeth □ *rahang*: *the lower/upper jaw* ➪ picture at **body 2 jaws** [pl] the mouth (especially of a wild animal) □ *mulut*: *The lion came towards him with its jaws open.*

jazz¹ /dʒæz/ noun [U] a style of music with a strong rhythm, originally of African-American origin □ *(muzik) jaz*: *modern/traditional jazz* ➪ look at **classical, pop, rock**

jazz² /dʒæz/ verb
PHR V jazz sth up (*informal*) to make sth brighter, more interesting or exciting □ *memeriahkan/menceriakan sst*

jealous /ˈdʒeləs/ adj **1** feeling upset or angry because you think that sb you like or love is showing interest in sb else □ *cemburu*: *Tim seems to get jealous whenever Sue speaks to another boy!* **2 jealous (of sb/sth)** feeling angry or sad because you want to be like sb else or because you want what sb else has □ *iri hati*: *He's always been jealous of his older brother.* ♦ *I'm very jealous of your new car—how much did it cost?* **SYN** envious ▸**jealously** adv ▸**jealousy** noun [C,U] (pl **jealousies**)

jeans /dʒiːnz/ noun [pl] trousers made of denim (= strong, usually blue, cotton cloth) □ *(seluar) jean*: *These jeans are a bit too tight.* ♦ *a pair of jeans* ➪ picture on **page P1**

Jeep™ /dʒiːp/ noun [C] a small, strong vehicle suitable for travelling over rough ground □ *Jeep™ (jip)*

jeer /dʒɪə(r)/ verb [I,T] **jeer (at) sb/sth** to laugh or shout rude comments at sb/sth to show your lack of respect for him or it □ *mengejek-ejek; mencemuh*: *The spectators booed and jeered at the losing team.* ▸**jeer** noun [C, usually pl]: *The Prime Minister was greeted with jeers in the House of Commons today.*

jelly /ˈdʒeli/ noun (pl **jellies**) (*AmE* **Jell-O™** /ˈdʒeləʊ/) **1** [C,U] a soft, solid brightly coloured food that shakes when it is moved. **Jelly** is made from sugar and fruit juice and is eaten cold at the end of a meal, especially by children □ *jeli*: *raspberry jelly and ice cream* **2** [U] a type of jam that does not contain any solid pieces of fruit □ *jeli; jem*: *blackcurrant jelly*
IDM be/feel like jelly (used especially about the legs or knees) to feel weak because you are nervous, afraid, etc. □ *berasa lemah*: *My legs felt like jelly before the exam.*
turn to jelly (used about the legs and knees) to suddenly become weak because of fear □ *lemah lutut*

jellyfish /ˈdʒelifɪʃ/ noun [C] (pl **jellyfish**) a sea animal with a soft transparent body and long thin parts that can sting you □ *ampai-ampai; ubur-ubur*

jeopardize (also **-ise**) /ˈdʒepədaɪz/ verb [T] to risk harming or destroying sth □ *membahayakan; menyebabkan terancam*: *He would never do anything to jeopardize his career.*

jeopardy /ˈdʒepədi/ noun
IDM in jeopardy in a dangerous position and likely to be lost or harmed □ *tergugat; terancam*: *The future of the factory and 15 000 jobs are in jeopardy.*

jellyfish

jerk¹ /dʒɜːk/ verb [I,T] to move or make sb/sth move with a sudden sharp movement □ *menyentap; tersentap*: *She jerked the door open.* ♦ *His head jerked back as the car set off.* ▸**jerky** adj ▸**jerkily** /-kɪli/ adv

jerk² /dʒɜːk/ noun [C] **1** a sudden sharp movement □ *sentakan* **2** (*especially AmE slang*) a stupid or annoying person □ *(si) bodoh/tolol*

jersey /ˈdʒɜːzi/ noun **1** [C] a piece of clothing made of wool that you wear over a shirt □ *(baju) jersi* **SYN** jumper, pullover ➪ note at **sweater** **2** [C] a shirt worn by sb playing a sports game □ *jersi* ➪ picture at **football 3** [U] soft thin cloth made of cotton or wool that is used for making clothes □ *kain jersi*

Jesus /ˈdʒiːzəs/ (also **Jesus ˈChrist**) = **Christ**

jet¹ /dʒet/ noun [C] **1** a fast plane □ *pesawat jet* **2** a fast, thin current of water, gas, etc. coming out of a small hole □ *pancutan; pancitan*

jet² /dʒet/ (**jetting; jetted**) verb [I] (*informal*) **jet off** to fly somewhere in a plane □ *menaiki jet*

jet ˈblack adj very dark black in colour □ *hitam pekat*

jet ˈengine noun [C] a powerful engine that makes planes fly by pushing out a current of hot air and gases at the back □ *enjin jet*

jet lag noun [U] the tired feeling that people often have after a long journey in a plane to a place where the local time is different □ *letih lesu kerana penerbangan antara tempat yg berbeza zon waktunya* ▸**ˈjet-lagged** adj

the ˈjet set noun [sing] the group of rich, successful and fashionable people (especially those who travel around the world a lot) □ *'jet set'; golongan yg hidup mewah*

Jet Ski™ noun [C] a vehicle with an engine, like a motorbike, for riding across water □ *Jet Ski* ▸**ˈjet-skiing** noun [U]

jetty /ˈdʒeti/ noun [C] (pl **jetties**) (also **ˈlanding stage**; *AmE* **dock**) a stone wall or wooden platform built out into the sea or a river where boats are tied and where people can get on and off them □ *jeti*

Jew /dʒuː/ noun [C] a person whose family originally came from the ancient Hebrew people of Israel and/or whose religion is Judaism □ *orang Yahudi* ▶ Jewish adj

jewel /ˈdʒuːəl/ noun 1 [C] a valuable stone (for example a diamond) □ *batu permata* SYN **gem** 2 [pl] pieces of jewellery or objects that contain **precious** (= rare and valuable) stones □ *barang kemas*

jeweller (*AmE* **jeweler**) /ˈdʒuːələ(r)/ noun 1 [C] a person whose job is to buy, sell, make or repair jewellery and watches □ *jauhari; tukang emas* 2 **the jeweller's** [sing] a shop where jewellery and watches are made, sold and repaired □ *kedai emas*

jewellery (*AmE* **jewelry**) /ˈdʒuːəlri/ noun [U] objects such as rings, etc. that are worn as personal decoration □ *barang kemas*: *a piece of jewellery*

jewellery

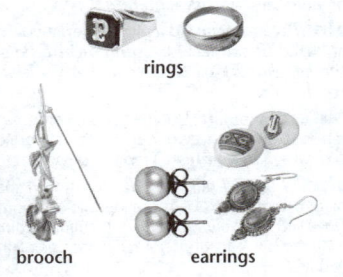

clasp
chain
bead
locket
beads
necklaces
charm
bangle
charm bracelet
bracelets
rings
brooch
earrings

jig¹ /dʒɪɡ/ noun [C] a type of quick dance with jumping movements; the music for this dance □ *tarian jig*

jig² /dʒɪɡ/ verb [I] (**jigging**; **jigged**) **jig about/ around** to move about in an excited or impatient way □ *melonjak-lonjak; terlonjak-lonjak*

jiggle /ˈdʒɪɡl/ verb [T] (*informal*) to move sth quickly from side to side □ *menggoyang-goyangkan*: *She jiggled her car keys to try to distract the baby.*

jigsaw /ˈdʒɪɡsɔː/ (also **ˈjigsaw puzzle**) noun [C] a picture on cardboard or wood that is cut into small pieces and has to be fitted together again □ *susun suai gambar; jigsaw*

jingle¹ /ˈdʒɪŋɡl/ noun 1 [sing] a ringing sound like small bells, made by metal objects gently hitting each other □ *dentingan*: *the jingle of coins* 2 [C] a short simple tune or song that is easy to remember and is used in advertising on TV or radio □ *dendang iklan*

jingle² /ˈdʒɪŋɡl/ verb [I,T] to make or cause sth to make a pleasant gentle sound like small bells ringing □ *mendentingkan; berdenting*: *She jingled the coins in her pocket.*

jinx /dʒɪŋks/ noun [C, sing] (*informal*) bad luck; a person or thing that people believe brings bad luck to sb/sth □ *pembawa sial* ▶ jinx verb [T] ▶ jinxed adj: *After my third accident in a month, I began to think I was jinxed.*

the jitters /ˈdʒɪtəz/ noun [pl] (*informal*) feelings of fear or worry, especially before an important event or before having to do sth difficult □ *perasaan gugup*: *Just thinking about the exam gives me the jitters!*

jittery /ˈdʒɪtəri/ adj (*informal*) nervous or worried □ *berasa gugup/risau*: *She felt jittery and tense.*

job /dʒɒb/ noun [C] 1 the work that you do regularly to earn money □ *pekerjaan*: *She took/ got a job as a waitress.* ◆ *A lot of people will lose their jobs if the factory closes.* ⊃ note at **office**, **pay**, **retire**, **work** ⊃ picture on **page P2**

> **HELP** **Post** and **position** are formal words for job: *I would like to apply for the post/position of Marketing Manager.*

2 a task or a piece of work □ *kerja*: *I always have a lot of jobs to do in the house at weekends.* ◆ *The garage has done a good/bad job on our car.* 3 [usually sing] a duty or responsibility □ *tugas*: *It's not his job to tell us what we can and can't do.*

IDM **do the job/trick** (*informal*) to get the result that is wanted □ *sesuai/bagus (utk kerja yg perlu dibuat itu)*: *This extra strong glue should do the job.*

have a hard job doing/to do sth ⊃ **hard¹**

it's a good job (*BrE spoken*) it is a good or lucky thing □ *mujurlah; nasib baiklah*: *It's a good job you reminded me—I had completely forgotten!*

jobless → joint

just the job/ticket (*informal*) exactly what is needed in a particular situation □ *memang sesuai (utk sst)*: *This dress will be just the job for Helen's party.*
make a bad, good, etc. job of sth to do sth badly, well, etc. □ *membuat sst dgn teruk, baik, dsb*
make the best of sth/a bad job ⊃ **best³**
out of a job without paid work □ *menganggur* ⊃ A more formal word is **unemployed**.

TOPIC

Jobs

When you **apply for a job**, you usually **fill in an application form** or send your **CV** with a **covering letter** (= a letter containing extra information about yourself). Then you **have an interview**. If it goes well and the employer is satisfied with your **references** (= letters that describe your character and abilities, often from a former employer), you will **get the job**. You **sign the contract** and become an **employee**. A job can be **well paid/highly paid** or **badly paid/low-paid**. A job can be **full-time** or **part-time**, **permanent** or **temporary**. If your **working conditions** are good and you have the chance to **be promoted** (= be given a more important job), then you will probably get a lot of **job satisfaction**.

TOPIC

Leaving a job

If you want to **leave your job**, you **resign** or **hand in** your **resignation/notice**. If a company no longer needs an employee, it will **make** him/her **redundant**. If an employee's work is not good enough, the company may **dismiss** him/her. In less formal English we use the verbs **fire** or **sack**, or the noun **the sack**: *Her boss fired/sacked her.* ◆ *Her boss gave her the sack.* ◆ *She got the sack.* When you stop working because you have reached a certain age (usually 60 or 65), you **retire**.

jobless /ˈdʒɒbləs/ *adj* **1** (usually used about large numbers of people) without paid work □ *menganggur* **SYN** **unemployed 2 the jobless** *noun* [pl] people without paid work □ *(golongan) pengangguran* ▸**joblessness** *noun* [U] **SYN** **unemployment**

jockey /ˈdʒɒki/ *noun* [C] a person who rides horses in races, especially as a profession □ *joki* ⊃ look at **DJ** ⊃ picture on page P5

jodhpurs /ˈdʒɒdpəz/ *noun* [pl] special trousers that you wear for riding a horse □ *seluar penunggang kuda* ⊃ picture at **horse**

jog¹ /dʒɒɡ/ *verb* (**jogging**; **jogged**) **1** [I] to run slowly, especially as a form of exercise □ *berjoging*

HELP When we talk about jogging for pleasure or exercise, it is more usual to say **go jogging**: *I go jogging most evenings.*

2 [T] to push or knock sb/sth slightly □ *menolak; menyigung*: *He jogged my arm and I spilled the milk.* **SYN** **nudge**
IDM **jog sb's memory** to say or do sth that makes sb remember sth □ *membuat sso mengingat kembali akan sst*

jog² /dʒɒɡ/ *noun* [sing] **1** a slow run as a form of exercise □ *joging*: *She goes for a jog before breakfast.* **2** a slight push or knock □ *(perbuatan) menolak atau menyigung* **SYN** **nudge**

jogger /ˈdʒɒɡə(r)/ *noun* [C] a person who goes **jogging** for exercise □ *orang yg berjoging*

join¹ /dʒɔɪn/ *verb*
▸ CONNECT **1** [T] **join A to B**; **join A and B (together)** to fasten or connect one thing to another □ *menyambungkan; mencantumkan; menghubungkan*: *The Channel Tunnel joins Britain to France.* ◆ *The two pieces of wood had been carefully joined together.* ◆ *We've knocked down the wall and joined the two rooms into one.*
▸ BECOME ONE **2** [I,T] **join (up) (with sb/sth)** to meet or unite (with sb/sth) to form one thing or group □ *bertemu; bersambung; bercantum*: *Do the two rivers join (up) at any point?* ◆ *Where does this road join the motorway?* ◆ *Would you like to join us for a drink?* ◆ *We'll join up with the other class later.*
▸ CLUB **3** [I,T] to become a member of a club or an organization □ *masuk; menyertai*: *I've joined an aerobics class.* ◆ *He joined the company three months ago.*
▸ TAKE PART **4** [T] to take your place in sth or to take part in sth □ *menyertai; ikut sama*: *We'd better go and join the queue if we want to see the film.* ◆ *Come downstairs and join the party.*
5 [I,T] **join (with) sb in sth/in doing sth/to do sth**; **join together in doing sth/to do sth** to take part with sb (often in doing sth for sb else) □ *bersama; bersama-sama*: *Everybody here joins me in wishing you the best of luck in your new job.* ◆ *The whole school joined together to sing the school song.*
IDM **join forces (with sb)** to work together in order to achieve a shared goal □ *bergabung; berpadu tenaga*: *The two companies joined forces to win the contract.*
PHR V **join in (sth/doing sth)** to take part in an activity □ *ikut sama (membuat sst)*: *Everyone started singing but Frank refused to join in.*
join up to become a member of the army, navy or air force □ *masuk tentera*

join² /dʒɔɪn/ *noun* [C] a place where two things are fixed or connected □ *sambungan*: *He glued the handle back on so cleverly that you couldn't see the join.*

joiner /ˈdʒɔɪnə(r)/ *noun* [C] a person whose job is to make the wooden parts of a building □ *tukang kayu halus* ⊃ look at **carpenter**

joint¹ /dʒɔɪnt/ *adj* [only *before* a noun] shared or owned by two or more people □ *bersama*: *Have you and your husband got a joint account* (= a shared bank account)? ◆ *a joint decision* ▸**jointly** *adv*

joint² /dʒɔɪnt/ noun [C] **1** a part of the body where two bones fit together and are able to bend □ *sendi*: *the knee joint* **2** the place where two or more things are fastened or connected together, especially to form a corner □ *sambungan* **3** (BrE) a large piece of meat that you cook whole in the oven □ *ketul daging yg besar*: *a joint of lamb*

joke¹ /dʒəʊk/ noun **1** [C] something said or done to make people laugh, especially a funny story □ *jenaka; kelakar*: *to tell/crack jokes* ♦ *a dirty joke* (= about sex) ♦ *I'm sorry, I didn't get the joke* (= understand it). ➔ note at **humour 2** [sing] a ridiculous person, thing or situation □ *bahan ketawa*: *The salary he was offered was a joke!*
IDM make a joke of sth to laugh about sth that is serious or should be taken seriously □ *mempersendakan*: *It's unkind to make jokes about people.*
play a joke/trick on sb to trick sb in order to amuse yourself or other people □ *mempermain-mainkan sso*
see the joke ➔ see
take a joke to be able to laugh at a joke against yourself □ *boleh bergurau*: *The trouble with Pete is he can't take a joke.*

joke² /dʒəʊk/ verb [I] **1 joke (with sb) (about sth)** to say sth to make people laugh; to tell a funny story □ *melawak; bergurau senda*: *She spent the evening laughing and joking with her old friends.* **2** to say sth that is not true because you think it is funny □ *bergurau; berseloroh*: *I never joke about religion.* ♦ *Don't get upset. I was only joking!*
IDM you must be joking; you're joking (spoken) (used to express great surprise) you cannot be serious □ *takkanlah; mustahillah*

joker /ˈdʒəʊkə(r)/ noun [C] **1** a person who likes to tell jokes or play tricks □ *orang yg suka melawak* **2** an extra card which can be used instead of any other one in some card games □ *(daun terup) joker* ➔ picture at **card**

jolly /ˈdʒɒli/ adj (**jollier**; **jolliest**) happy □ *periang; girang*

jolt¹ /dʒəʊlt/ verb [I,T] to move or make sb/sth move in a sudden rough way □ *menyentak; tersentak; terhinggut-hinggut*: *The lorry jolted along the bumpy track.* ♦ *The crash jolted all the passengers forward.*

jolt² /dʒəʊlt/ noun [usually sing] **1** a sudden movement □ *sentakan*: *The train stopped with a jolt.* **2** a sudden surprise or shock □ *kejutan*: *His sudden anger gave her quite a jolt.*

jostle /ˈdʒɒsl/ verb [I,T] to push hard against sb in a crowd □ *mengasak-asak*

jot /dʒɒt/ verb (**jotting**; **jotted**)
PHR V jot sth down to make a quick short note of sth □ *mencatat*: *Let me jot down your address.*

journal /ˈdʒɜːnl/ noun [C] **1** a newspaper or a magazine, especially one in which all the articles are about a particular subject or profession □ *jurnal; akhbar*: *a medical/scientific journal* **2** a written record of the things you do, see, etc. each day □ *jurnal; catatan harian*: *Have you read his journal of the years he spent in India?* ➔ look at **diary**

journalism /ˈdʒɜːnəlɪzəm/ noun [U] the profession of collecting and writing about news in newspapers and magazines or talking about it on the TV or radio □ *kewartawanan*

journalist /ˈdʒɜːnəlɪst/ noun [C] a person whose job is to collect and write about news in newspapers and magazines or to talk about it on the TV or radio □ *wartawan* ➔ note at **newspaper** ➔ look at **reporter**

journey /ˈdʒɜːni/ noun [C] an act of travelling from one place to another, usually on land □ *perjalanan*: *Did you have a good journey?* ♦ *a two-hour journey* ♦ *The journey to work takes me 45 minutes.* ♦ *We'll have to break the journey* (= stop for a rest). ➔ note at **travel**

MORE A **journey** can include both air and sea travel. To refer specifically to a journey by air we say a **flight** and by sea we say a **voyage** or, if it is for pleasure, a **cruise**.

jovial /ˈdʒəʊviəl/ adj (used about a person) happy and friendly □ *riang gembira*

joy /dʒɔɪ/ noun **1** [U] a feeling of great happiness □ *kegembiraan*: *We'd like to wish you joy and success in your life together.* **2** [C] a person or thing that gives you great pleasure □ *sst yg menggembirakan; kegembiraan*: *the joys of fatherhood* ♦ *That class is a joy to teach.* **3** [U] [used in questions and negative sentences] (BrE informal) success or satisfaction □ *kepuasan; kejayaan; berjaya*: *'I asked again if we could have seats with more legroom but got no joy from the check-in clerk.'*
IDM jump for joy ➔ **jump¹**
sb's pride and joy ➔ **pride¹**

joyful /ˈdʒɔɪfl/ adj very happy □ *gembira*: *a joyful occasion* ▸ **joyfully** /-fəli/ adv ▸ **joyfulness** noun [U]

joyless /ˈdʒɔɪləs/ adj unhappy □ *tdk bahagia*: *The couple had a joyless marriage.*

joyriding /ˈdʒɔɪraɪdɪŋ/ noun [U] the crime of stealing a car and driving it for pleasure, usually in a fast and dangerous way □ *(perbuatan jenayah) bersiar-siar dgn kereta yg dicuri* ▸ **joyride** noun [C] ▸ **joyrider** noun [C]

joystick /ˈdʒɔɪstɪk/ noun [C] a stick with a handle that is used to control movement on a computer, aircraft, machine, etc. □ *kayu bedik*

JP /ˌdʒeɪ ˈpiː/ abbr = **Justice of the Peace**

Jr /ˈdʒuːniə(r)/ abbr (AmE) = **Junior¹**(3): *Samuel P Carson, Jr*

Jr = **Junior¹**(3)

jubilant /ˈdʒuːbɪlənt/ adj (formal) extremely happy, especially because of a success □ *sangat gembira*: *The football fans were jubilant at their team's victory in the cup.*

jubilation /ˌdʒuːbɪˈleɪʃn/ noun [U] (formal) great happiness because of a success □ *kegembiraan*

jubilee /ˈdʒuːbɪliː/ noun [C] a special anniversary of an event that took place a certain number of years ago, and the celebrations that go with it □ *jubli*: *It's the company's golden jubilee this year* (= it is 50 years since it was started).

> **MORE** An anniversary or jubilee can be **silver** (25 years), **golden** (50 years) or **diamond** (60 years).

Judaism /ˈdʒuːdeɪɪzəm/ noun [U] the religion of the Jewish people □ *agama Yahudi*

judge¹ /dʒʌdʒ/ noun [C] **1** a person in a court of law whose job is to decide how criminals should be punished and to make legal decisions □ *hakim*: *The judge sentenced the man to seventeen years in prison.* ➲ note at **court 2** a person who decides who has won a competition □ *hakim; pengadil*: *a panel of judges* **3** [usually sing] a judge of sth a person who has the ability or knowledge to give an opinion about sth □ *penilai; orang yg pandai menilai*: *You're a good judge of character—what do you think of him?*

judge² /dʒʌdʒ/ verb **1** [I,T] to form or give an opinion about sb/sth based on the information you have □ *membuat penilaian; menjangka; menganggap; berdasarkan*: *Judging by/from what he said, his work is going well.* ♦ *It's difficult to judge how long the project will take.* ♦ *The party was judged a great success by everybody.* **2** [I,T] to decide the result or winner of a competition □ *mengadili*: *The head teacher will judge the competition.* **3** [I,T] to form an opinion about sb/sth, especially when you do not approve of them or it □ *menilai; menganggap; membuat kesimpulan ttg sso*: *Don't judge him too harshly—he's had a difficult time.* **4** [T] to decide if sb is guilty or innocent in a court of law □ *membicarakan; menghakimi*: *It was the hardest case he had ever had to judge.*

judgement (also judgment) /ˈdʒʌdʒmənt/ noun **1** [U] the ability to form opinions or to make sensible decisions □ *pertimbangan; penilaian*: *He always shows excellent judgement in his choice of staff.* ♦ *to have good/poor/sound judgement* **2** [C,U] an opinion that you form after carefully considering the information you have □ *pendapat*: *What, in your judgement, would be the best course of action?* **3** judgment [C,U] an official decision made by a judge or a court of law □ *keputusan hakim/mahkamah*: *The man collapsed when the judgment was read out in court.*

judicial /dʒuˈdɪʃl/ adj connected with a court of law, a judge or a legal judgment □ *kehakiman*: *the judicial system*

judiciary /dʒuˈdɪʃəri/ noun the judiciary [C, with sing or pl verb] (pl judiciaries) the judges of a country or a state, when they are considered as a group □ *badan kehakiman*: *an independent judiciary* ➲ look at **executive, legislature**

judicious /dʒuˈdɪʃəs/ adj (formal) (used about a decision or an action) sensible and carefully considered; showing good judgement □ *bijak* ▶**judiciously** adv

judo /ˈdʒuːdəʊ/ noun [U] a sport from Asia in which two people fight and try to throw each other to the ground □ *judo* ➲ look at **martial arts**

carafe | jug (AmE pitcher) | pitcher (AmE jug)

lip

jug /dʒʌg/ (AmE pitcher) noun [C] a container with a handle used for holding or pouring liquids □ *jag*: *a milk jug* ♦ *a jug of water*

juggle /ˈdʒʌgl/ verb [I,T] **1** juggle (with sth) to keep three or more objects such as balls in the air at the same time by throwing them one at a time and catching them quickly □ *menjugel; main lambung-lambung* **2** juggle sth (with sth) to try to deal with two or more important jobs or activities at the same time □ *cuba menguruskan beberapa kerja atau kegiatan pd waktu yg sama*

juggler /ˈdʒʌglə(r)/ noun [C] a person who juggles to entertain people □ *penjugel*

juice /dʒuːs/ noun [C,U] **1** the liquid that comes from fruit and vegetables □ *jus*: *carrot/grapefruit/lemon juice* ♦ *I'll have an orange juice, please.* **2** the liquid that comes from a piece of meat when it is cooked □ *air rebusan daging*: *You can use the juices of the meat to make gravy.* **3** the liquid in your stomach that helps you break down the food you eat □ *jus*: *gastric/digestive juices*

skittle

juggler

juicy /ˈdʒuːsi/ adj (juicier; juiciest) **1** containing a lot of juice □ *berjus*: *juicy oranges* **2** (informal) (used about information) interesting because it is shocking □ *menarik; syok-syok*: *juicy gossip*

jukebox /ˈdʒuːkbɒks/ noun [C] a machine in a bar, etc. that plays music when money is put in □ *peti muzik*

Jul. abbr = July □ *Julai*: *4 Jul. 2012*

July /dʒuˈlaɪ/ noun [U,C] (abbr Jul.) the 7th month of the year, coming after June □ *Julai* ⊃ note at **January**

jumble¹ /ˈdʒʌmbl/ verb [T, usually passive] **jumble sth (up/together)** to mix things together in a confused and untidy way □ *mencampuradukkan; bercampur aduk*: *I must sort my clothes out—they're all jumbled up in the drawer.*

jumble² /ˈdʒʌmbl/ noun 1 [sing] an untidy group of things □ *himpunan/timbunan pelbagai benda yg bercampur aduk*: *a jumble of papers/ideas* **SYN mess** 2 [U] (BrE) a collection of old things for a **jumble sale** □ *himpunan benda-benda lama atau buruk*: *Have you got any jumble you don't want?*

'jumble sale (AmE **'rummage sale**) noun [C] a sale of old things that people do not want any more. Clubs, churches, schools and other organizations hold **jumble sales** to get money. □ *jualan lambak*

jumbo¹ /ˈdʒʌmbəʊ/ noun [C] (pl **jumbos**) (also **jumbo 'jet**) a very large aircraft that can carry several hundred passengers □ *jet jumbo*

jumbo² /ˈdʒʌmbəʊ/ adj [only before a noun] (informal) very large □ *raksasa; sangat besar*

jump¹ /dʒʌmp/ verb
▶MOVE OFF GROUND 1 [I] to move quickly into the air by pushing yourself up with your legs and feet, or by stepping off a high place □ *melompat*: *to jump into the air/off a bridge/onto a chair* ♦ *How high can you jump?* ♦ *Jump up and down to keep warm.* ⊃ picture at **hop**
▶GO OVER 2 [T] to get over sth by jumping □ *melompati*: *The dog jumped the fence and ran off down the road.*
▶MOVE QUICKLY 3 [I] to move quickly and suddenly □ *bergegas (bangun, dll)*: *The phone rang and she jumped up to answer it.* ♦ *A taxi stopped and we jumped in.*
▶FROM SURPRISE/FEAR 4 [I] to make a sudden movement because of surprise or fear □ *tersentak*: *'Oh, it's only you—you made me jump,' he said.*
▶INCREASE 5 [I] **jump (from sth) to sth; jump (by) (sth)** to increase suddenly by a very large amount □ *meningkat dgn mendadak; melambung naik*: *His salary jumped from £20 000 to £28 000 last year.* ♦ *Prices jumped (by) 50% in the summer.*
▶CHANGE SUDDENLY 6 [I] **jump (from sth) to sth** to go suddenly from one point in a series, a story, etc. to another □ *melompat*: *The book kept jumping from the present to the past.*
IDM climb/jump on the bandwagon ⊃ **bandwagon**
jump for joy to be extremely happy about sth □ *melonjak gembira; sangat gembira*
jump the gun to do sth too soon, before the proper time □ *membuat sst sebelum tiba masanya*
jump the queue (BrE) to go to the front of a line of people without waiting for your turn □ *memotong baris*
jump to conclusions to decide that sth is true without thinking about it carefully enough □ *membuat kesimpulan dgn terburu-buru*
PHR V jump at sth to accept an opportunity, offer, etc. with enthusiasm □ *terus menerima*: *Of course I jumped at the chance to work in New York for a year.*

jump² /dʒʌmp/ noun [C] 1 an act of jumping □ *lompatan; loncatan; terjun*: *With a huge jump the horse cleared the hedge.* ♦ *to do a parachute jump* ⊃ look at **high jump, long jump** 2 a thing to be jumped over □ *lompatan; sst yg hendak dilompati*: *The third jump consisted of a five-bar gate.* ♦ *a ski jump* 3 **a jump (in sth)** a sudden increase in amount, price or value □ *melambung naik*: *a 20% jump in profits*

jumper /ˈdʒʌmpə(r)/ noun [C] 1 (BrE) a piece of clothing with long sleeves, usually made of wool, that you wear on the top part of your body □ *(baju) jumper* **SYN jersey, pullover** ⊃ note at **sweater** ⊃ picture on **page P1** 2 a person or an animal that jumps □ *pelompat*

jumpy /ˈdʒʌmpi/ adj (informal) nervous or worried □ *gugup; risau*: *I always get a bit jumpy if I'm travelling by plane.*

Jun. abbr = **June** □ *Jun*: *10 Jun. 2012*

junction /ˈdʒʌŋkʃn/ noun [C] a place where roads, railway lines, etc. meet □ *simpang; persimpangan*

June /dʒuːn/ noun [U,C] (abbr **Jun.**) the 6th month of the year, coming after May □ *Jun* ⊃ note at **January**

jungle /ˈdʒʌŋgl/ noun [C,U] a thick forest in a hot tropical country □ *hutan*: *the jungles of Africa and South America* ⊃ note at **forest**

junior¹ /ˈdʒuːniə(r)/ adj 1 **junior (to sb)** having a low or lower position (than sb) in an organization, etc. □ *rendah*: *a junior officer/doctor/employee* ♦ *A lieutenant is junior to a captain in the army.* 2 [only before a noun] (BrE) of or for children below a particular age □ *rendah; junior; remaja*: *the junior athletics championships* 3 **Junior** (abbr **Jr**) (especially AmE) used after the name of a son who has the same first name as his father □ *Junior (anak)*: *Sammy Davis, Junior* ⊃ look at **senior**

junior² /ˈdʒuːniə(r)/ noun 1 [C] a person who has a low position in an organization, etc. □ *orang yg pangkatnya rendah dlm sst organisasi, dsb*: *office juniors* 2 [sing] [with **his, her, your**, etc.] a person who is younger than sb else by the number of years mentioned □ *orang yg lebih muda*: *She's two years his junior/his junior by two years.* 3 [C] (in Britain) a child who goes to **junior school** □ *murid sekolah rendah*: *The juniors are having an outing to a museum today.* ⊃ look at **senior**

junior 'high school (also **junior 'high**) noun [C,U] (in the US) a school for young people between the ages of 12 and 14 □ *Sekolah Menengah (Tahap Rendah)* ⊃ look at **senior high school**

junior school → juvenile 482

'junior school noun [C,U] (in Britain) a school for children between the ages of 7 and 11 □ *sekolah rendah* ➔ look at **primary school**

junk /dʒʌŋk/ noun [U] (informal) things that are old or useless or do not have much value □ *barang-barang, buruk atau tdk berguna*: *There's an awful lot of junk up in the attic.*

'junk food noun [U] (informal) food that is not very good for you but that is ready to eat or quick to prepare □ *makanan ringan*

junkie /'dʒʌŋki/ noun [C] (informal) a person who is unable to stop taking dangerous drugs □ *penagih dadah* **SYN** **addict**

'junk mail noun [U] advertising material that is sent to people who have not asked for it □ *mel remeh* ➔ look at **spam**

junta /'dʒʌntə/ noun [C, with sing or pl verb] a group, especially of military officers, who rule a country by force □ *junta*

Jupiter /'dʒuːpɪtə(r)/ noun [sing] the planet that is fifth in order from the sun □ *Musytari; Jupiter*

jurisdiction /ˌdʒʊərɪs'dɪkʃn/ noun [U] legal power or authority; the area in which this power can be used □ *kuasa; bidang kuasa*: *That question is outside the jurisdiction of this council.*

juror /'dʒʊərə(r)/ noun [C] a member of a **jury** □ *ahli juri*

jury /'dʒʊəri/ noun [C, with sing or pl verb] (pl **juries**) **1** a group of members of the public in a court of law who listen to the facts about a crime and decide if sb is guilty or not guilty □ *juri*: *Has/Have the jury reached a verdict?* ➔ note at **court 2** a group of people who decide who is the winner in a competition □ *jemaah pengadil/hakim*: *The jury is/are about to announce the winners.*

just¹ /dʒʌst/ adv **1** exactly □ *tepat; betul-betul*: *It's just 8 o'clock.* ♦ *That's just what I meant.* ♦ *You're just as clever as he is.* ♦ *The room was too hot before, but now it's just right.* ♦ *He looks just like his father.* ♦ *My arm hurts just here.* **2** almost not □ *hampir tdk*: *I could only just hear what she was saying.* ♦ *We got to the station just in time.* **3** a very short time before □ *baru saja; tdk lama*: *She's just been to the shops.* ♦ *He'd just returned from France when I saw him.* ♦ *They came here just before Easter.* **4** at exactly this/that moment, or immediately after □ *baru saja hendak; ketika itu*: *He was just about to break the window when he noticed a policeman.* ♦ *I was just going to phone my mother when she arrived.* ♦ *Just as I was beginning to enjoy myself, John said it was time to go.* ♦ *Just then the door opened.* **5** really; absolutely □ *sungguh*: *The whole day was just fantastic!* **6** only □ *hanya; sahaja*: *She's just a child.* ♦ *Just a minute! I'm nearly ready.* **7** [often with the imperative] used for getting attention or to emphasize what you are saying □ *digunakan utk mendapatkan perhatian atau utk menekankan apa yg sedang dikatakan*: *Just let me speak for a moment, will you?* ♦ *I just don't want to go to the party.* **8** used with *might, may* or *could* to express a slight possibility □ *mungkin*: *This might just/just might be the most important decision of your life.*

IDM **all/just the same** ➔ **same**

it is just as well (that ...) it is a good thing □ *nasib baiklah; mujurlah*: *It's just as well you remembered to bring your umbrella!*

just about almost or approximately □ *hampir-hampir; kira-kira*: *I've just about finished.* ♦ *Karen's plane should be taking off just about now.*

just now 1 at this exact moment or during this exact period □ *sekarang*: *I can't come with you just now—can you wait 20 minutes?* **2** a very short time ago □ *baru tadi*: *I saw Tony just now.*

just so exactly right □ *betul; betul-betul begitu*

not just yet not now, but probably quite soon □ *belum lagi; sekejap lagi*

just² /dʒʌst/ adj fair and right; reasonable □ *adil; saksama*: *I don't think that was a very just decision.* ▶ **justly** adv

justice /'dʒʌstɪs/ noun **1** [U] the fair treatment of people □ *keadilan*: *a struggle for justice* **2** [U] the quality of being fair or reasonable □ *kemunasabahan; adilnya; berasas*: *Everybody realized the justice of what he was saying.* **3** [U] the law and the way it is used □ *keadilan*: *the criminal justice system* **4** (also **Justice**) [C] (*AmE*) a judge in a court of law □ *hakim*

IDM **do justice to sb/sth; do sb/sth justice** to treat sb/sth fairly or to show the real quality of sb/sth □ *berlaku adil terhadap sso/sst; menunjukkan kelebihan sebenar sso/sst*: *The review doesn't do justice to her talents.* ♦ *I don't like him, but to do him justice, he's a very clever man.*

a miscarriage of justice ➔ **miscarriage**

Justice of the 'Peace noun [C] (*abbr* **JP**) a person who judges less serious cases in a court of law □ *Jaksa Pendamai*

justifiable /'dʒʌstɪfaɪəbl, ˌdʒʌstɪ'faɪəbl/ adj that you can accept because there is a good reason for it □ *patut; wajar; dpt dipertahankan; berjustifikasi*: *His action was entirely justifiable.* ▶ **justifiably** /-əbli/ adv

justification /ˌdʒʌstɪfɪ'keɪʃn/ noun [C,U] **(a) justification (for sth/doing sth)** (a) good reason □ *alasan yg kuat/kukuh; justifikasi*: *I can't see any justification for tax rises.*

justify /'dʒʌstɪfaɪ/ verb [T] (**justifying**; **justifies**; *pt, pp* **justified**) to give or be a good reason for sth □ *memberikan alasan yg kuat/kukuh; memberikan justifikasi*: *Can you justify your decision?*

jut /dʒʌt/ verb [I] (**jutting**; **jutted**) **jut (out) (from/into/over sth)** to stick out further than the surrounding surface, objects, etc. □ *menganjur; menjulur*: *rocks that jut out into the sea*

juvenile /'dʒuːvənaɪl/ adj **1** [only before a noun] (*formal*) of, for or involving young people who are not yet adults □ *budak-budak; juvenil*: *juvenile crime* **2** silly and more typical of a child

than an adult □ *kebudak-budakan*: *Patrick's twenty but he is still quite juvenile.* **SYN** childish
▶**juvenile** *noun* [C]

juvenile de'linquent *noun* [C] a young person who is guilty of committing a crime □ *delinkuen juvenil; pesalah budak-budak*

juxtapose /ˌdʒʌkstəˈpəʊz/ *verb* [T] (*formal*) to put two people, things, etc. very close together, especially in order to show how they are different □ *mengatur seiring*: *The artist achieves a special effect by juxtaposing light and dark.*
▶**juxtaposition** /ˌdʒʌkstəpəˈzɪʃn/ *noun* [C,U]

K k

K, k /keɪ/ *noun* [C,U] (*pl* Ks; K's; k's /keɪz/) the 11th letter of the English alphabet □ *K, k* (*huruf*): *'Kate' begins with (a) 'K'.*

K /keɪ/ *abbr* **1** (*informal*) one thousand □ *K* (*seribu*): *She earns 22K* (= £22 000) *a year.* **2** = kilometre(s) **3** = kilobyte

kaleidoscope /kəˈlaɪdəskəʊp/ *noun* **1** [C] a toy that consists of a tube containing mirrors and small pieces of coloured glass. When you look into one end of the tube and turn it, you see changing patterns of colours. □ *kaleidoskop* **2** [sing] a situation, pattern, etc. containing a lot of different parts that are always changing □ *silih berganti*

kangaroo /ˌkæŋgəˈruː/ *noun* [C] (*pl* kangaroos) an Australian animal that moves by jumping on its strong back legs and that carries its young in a **pouch** (= a pocket of skin) on its stomach □ *kanggaru*

karaoke /ˌkæriˈəʊki/ *noun* [U] a type of entertainment in which a machine plays only the music of popular songs so that people can sing the words themselves □ *karaoke*

karat (*AmE*) = carat

karate /kəˈrɑːti/ *noun* [U] a style of fighting originally from Japan in which the hands and feet are used as weapons □ *karate* ➔ look at martial arts ➔ picture on page P5

kart /kɑːt/ = go-kart

kayak /ˈkaɪæk/ *noun* [C] a light narrow boat for one person in which the part where you sit is covered over □ *kayak* ➔ look at canoe ▶**kayaking** *noun* [U]: *I'm going to go kayaking in Wales.*

KB (*also* **K**) *abbr* = kilobyte

Kb (*also* **Kbit**) *abbr* = kilobit

kebab /kɪˈbæb/ *noun* [C] small pieces of meat, vegetables, etc. that are cooked on a **skewer** (= a stick) □ *kebab* ➔ picture on page P16

483 **juvenile delinquent → keep**

paddle

kayak

canoe

keel¹ /kiːl/ *noun* [C] a long piece of wood or metal on the bottom of a boat that stops it falling over sideways in the water □ *lunas*

keel² /kiːl/ *verb*
PHR V **keel over** to fall over □ *terbalik; rebah; tersungkur*

keen /kiːn/ *adj* (keener; keenest) **1** keen (to do sth/on doing sth/that …) very interested in sth; wanting to do sth □ *sangat berminat; giat; ingin*: *They are both keen gardeners.* ♦ *I failed the first time but I'm keen to try again.* ♦ *I wasn't too keen on going camping.* ♦ *She was keen that we should all be there.* ➔ note at like **2** (used about one of the senses, a feeling, etc.) good or strong □ *tajam*: *Foxes have a keen sense of smell.*
IDM **keen on sb/sth** very interested in or having a strong desire for sb/sth □ *menaruh hati terhadap sso; sangat berminat akan sst*: *He's very keen on jazz.*
▶**keenly** *adv*
▶**keenness** *noun* [U]

keep¹ /kiːp/ *verb* (*pt, pp* kept /kept/)
▶STAY **1** [I] to continue to be in a particular state or position □ *digunakan dgn maksud terus berada dlm sst keadaan atau kedudukan*: *You must keep warm.* ♦ *That child can't keep still.* ♦ *I still keep in touch with my old school friends.* **2** [T] to make sb/sth stay in a particular state, place or condition □ *membuat sso/sst berada dlm sst keadaan, tempat atau kedudukan*: *Please keep this door closed.* ♦ *He kept his hands in his pockets.* ♦ *I'm sorry to keep you waiting.*
▶CONTINUE **3** [I] keep doing sth to continue doing sth or to repeat an action many times □ *terus; terus-menerus; asyik*: *Keep going until you get to the church and then turn left.* ♦ *She keeps asking me silly questions.*
▶DELAY **4** [T] to delay sb/sth; to prevent sb from leaving □ *menyebabkan sso/sst lewat; menahan*: *Where's the doctor? What's keeping him?*
▶NOT GIVE BACK/SAVE **5** [T] to continue to have sth; to save sth for sb □ *menyimpan; tdk perlu memulangkan balik; menjaga*: *You can keep that book—I don't need it any more.* ♦ *Can I keep the car until next week?* ♦ *Can you keep my seat for me till I get back?*

VOWELS iː see i any ɪ sit e ten æ hat ɑː father ɒ got ɔː saw ʊ put uː too u usual

keep → kerosene

▶PUT/STORE **6** [T] to have sth in a particular place □ *menyimpan*: *Where do you keep the matches?* ◆ *Keep your passport in a safe place.*

▶ANIMALS **7** [T] to have and look after animals □ *memelihara; menternak*: *They keep ducks on their farm.*

▶FOOD **8** [I] to stay fresh □ *tahan; kekal segar*: *Drink up all the milk—it won't keep in this weather.*

▶PROMISE/ARRANGEMENT **9** [T] to do what you promised or arranged □ *menepati*: *Can you keep a promise?* ◆ *She didn't keep her appointment at the dentist's.* ◆ *to keep a secret* (= not tell it to anyone)

▶DIARY/RECORD **10** [T] to write down sth that you want to remember □ *mencatat; menulis*: *Keep a record of how much you spend.* ◆ *to keep a diary*

▶SUPPORT **11** [T] to support sb with your money □ *menyara; menanggung*: *You can't keep a family on the money I earn.*

IDM **keep going** to make an effort, especially when you are in a difficult situation □ *terus berusaha*: *You just have to keep yourself busy and keep going.* ◆ *Keep going, Sarah, you're nearly there.*

keep it up to continue doing sth as well as you are doing it now □ *teruskan* ❶ For other idioms containing **keep**, look at the entries for the nouns, adjectives, etc. For example, **keep count** is at **count**.

PHR V **keep at it/sth** to continue to work on/at sth □ *terus membuat sst; teruskanlah*: *Keep at it—we should be finished soon.*

keep away from sb/sth to not go near sb/sth □ *jauhkan dr sso/sst; jangan mendekati sso/sst; jangan pergi ke*: *Keep away from the town centre this weekend.*

keep sb/sth back to prevent sb/sth from moving forwards □ *menahan atau membendung sso/sst*: *The police tried to keep the crowd back.*

keep sth back (from sb) to refuse to tell sb sth □ *menyembunyikan atau merahsiakan sst (drpd sso)*: *I know he's keeping something back; he knows much more than he says.*

keep sth down to make sth stay at a low level, to stop sth increasing □ *membuat kekal rendah; tdk meningkatkan; (suara) jangan kuat*: *Keep your voice down.*

keep sb from sth/from doing sth to prevent sb from doing sth □ *menghalang sso membuat sst*

keep sth from sb to refuse to tell sb sth □ *tdk memberitahu atau merahsiakan sst drpd sso*

keep off sth to not go near or on sth □ *jangan mendekati sst; jangan pijak (rumput)*: *Keep off the grass!*

keep sth off (sb/sth) to stop sth touching or going on sb/sth □ *menjauhkan sst drpd (sso/sst); tdk kena, tdk menyentuh, dll (sso/sst)*: *I'm trying to keep the flies off the food.*

keep on (doing sth) to continue doing sth or to repeat an action many times, especially in an annoying way □ *terus; terus-menerus; asyik*: *He keeps on interrupting me.*

keep on (at sb) (about sb/sth) to continue talking to sb in an annoying or complaining way □ *asyik mengomel, berleter, dsb kpd sso (ttg sso/sst)*: *She kept on at me about my homework until I did it.*

keep (sb/sth) out (of sth) to not enter sth; to stop sb/sth entering sth □ *menghalang sso/sst drpd masuk ke sst tempat, dsb*: *They put up a fence to keep people out of their garden.*

keep to sth to not leave sth; to do sth in the usual, agreed or expected way □ *ikut (jalan, lorong, dsb); tdk terkeluar drpd, menepati atau mematuhi sst*: *Keep to the path!* ◆ *He didn't keep to our agreement.*

keep sth to/at sth to not allow sth to rise above a particular level □ *mengekalkan sst pd sst tahap*: *We're trying to keep costs to a minimum.*

keep sth up 1 to prevent sth from falling down □ *tdk jatuh* **2** to make sth stay at a high level □ *tetap pd tahap yg tinggi*: *We want to keep up standards of education.* **3** to continue doing sth □ *terus membuat sst*: *How long can the baby keep up that crying?*

keep up (with sb) to do sth at the same speed as sb □ *menyaingi atau bersaing dgn sso*: *Can't you walk a bit slower? I can't keep up with you.* ◆ *Some students struggle to keep up when they move to a new school.*

keep up (with sb/sth) to know about what is happening □ *mengikuti perkembangan, dsb (sst)*: *You have to read the latest magazines if you want to keep up.*

keep² /kiːp/ *noun* [U] food, clothes and all the other things that you need to live □ *sara hidup* **IDM** **for keeps** (*informal*) for always □ *utk selama-lamanya*: *Take it. It's yours for keeps.*

keeper /ˈkiːpə(r)/ *noun* [C] **1** a person who guards or looks after sth □ *penjaga*: *a zookeeper* **2** (*informal*) = **goalkeeper**

keeping /ˈkiːpɪŋ/ *noun*
IDM **in/out of keeping (with sth) 1** that does/does not look good with sth □ *sesuai*: *That modern table is out of keeping with the style of the room.* **2** in/not in agreement with a rule, belief, etc. □ *selaras; sesuai; (tdk selaras atau tdk sesuai)*: *The Council's decision is in keeping with government policy.*

keg /keg/ *noun* [C] a round metal or wooden container, used especially for storing beer □ *tong kecil*

kennel /ˈkenl/ *noun* [C] a small house for a dog □ *rumah anjing*

kept past tense, past participle of **keep¹**

kerb (*AmE* **curb**) /kɜːb/ *noun* [C] the edge of the raised path at the side of a road, usually made of long pieces of stone □ *bebendul jalan; tepi jalan*: *They stood on the kerb waiting to cross the road.* ⊃ picture at **roundabout**

kernel /ˈkɜːnl/ *noun* [C] **1** the inner part of a nut or seed □ *isirung; isi* **2** the most important part of an idea or a subject □ *inti sari, inti pati*

kerosene /ˈkerəsiːn/ (*AmE*) = **paraffin**

ketchup /ˈketʃəp/ noun [U] a thick cold sauce made from tomatoes that is eaten with hot or cold food ◻ *sos tomato*

kettle /ˈketl/ noun [C] a container with a lid, used for boiling water ◻ *cerek*: *an electric kettle*

kettles

kettle — electric kettle

kettledrum /ˈketldrʌm/ noun [C] a large metal drum with a round bottom and a thin plastic top that can be made looser or tighter to produce different musical notes. A set of **kettledrums** is usually called **timpani**. ◻ *gendang belanga; gendang kawah; nagara* ⊃ picture at music

key¹ /kiː/ noun [C]
▶TOOL FOR LOCKING
1 a metal object that is used for locking a door, starting a car, etc. ◻ *anak kunci*: *Have you seen my car keys anywhere?* ♦ *We need a spare key to the front door.* ♦ *a bunch of keys*
▶MOST IMPORTANT PART
2 [usually sing] **the key (to sth)** something that helps you achieve or understand sth ◻ *kunci*: *A good education is the key to success.*
▶ON PIANO/COMPUTER **3** one of the parts of a piano, computer, etc. that you press with your fingers to make it work ◻ *kekunci; mata*: *Press the return key to enter the information.* ⊃ picture at computer, music
▶IN MUSIC **4** a set of musical notes that is based on one particular note ◻ *nada*: *The concerto is in the key of A minor.*
▶ANSWERS **5** a set of answers to exercises or problems ◻ *senarai jawapan*: *an answer key*
▶ON MAP **6** a list of the symbols and signs used in a map or book, showing what they mean ◻ *petunjuk*
IDM under lock and key ⊃ lock²

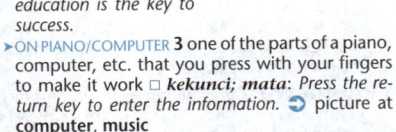

key² /kiː/ verb [T] **key sth (in)** to put information into a computer or give it an instruction by typing ◻ *menaip masuk*: *Have you keyed that report yet?* ♦ *First, key in your password.*

key³ /kiː/ adj [usually before a noun] very important ◻ *utama*: *Tourism is a key industry in Spain.* ♦ *a key issue/factor/point* ⊃ note at important

keyboard /ˈkiːbɔːd/ noun [C] **1** the set of keys on a piano, computer, etc. ◻ *papan kekunci*: *Arianne was tapping away at her keyboard.* ⊃ picture at computer, piano **2** an electrical musical instrument like a small piano ◻ *papan nada*: *The recording features Herbie Hancock on keyboard.* ⊃ picture at music

keyhole /ˈkiːhəʊl/ noun [C] the hole in a lock where you put the key ◻ *lubang kunci*

keyhole ˈsurgery noun [U] (especially *BrE*) medical operations which involve only a very small cut being made in the patient's body ◻ *pembedahan yg melibatkan belahan yg kecil pd badan*

keypad /ˈkiːpæd/ noun [C] a small set of buttons with numbers on that you press when you use a telephone, computer, etc. ◻ *pad kekunci*

ˈkey ring noun [C] a ring on which you keep keys ◻ *gelang kunci*

keyword /ˈkiːwɜːd/ noun [C] **1** a word that tells you about the main idea or subject of sth ◻ *kunci; perkara utama*: *When you're studying a language, the keyword is patience.* **2** a word or phrase that is used to give an instruction to a computer ◻ *kata kunci*

kg abbr = kilo ◻ *kg (kilogram): weight 10kg*

khaki /ˈkɑːki/ adj, noun [U] (of) a pale brownish-yellow or brownish-green colour ◻ *(warna) khaki*: *the khaki uniforms of the desert soldiers*

kHz /ˈkɪləhɜːts/ abbr kilohertz; (used in radio) a measure of **frequency** (= the rate at which a sound wave moves up and down) ◻ *kHz (kilohertz)*

kibibit /ˈkɪbɪbɪt/ (abbr Kib; Kibit) = kilobit (2)

kibibyte /ˈkɪbɪbaɪt/ = kilobyte (2)

kick¹ /kɪk/ verb **1** [I,T] to hit or move sb/sth with your foot ◻ *menendang; menyepak; menerajang*: *He kicked the ball wide of the net.* ♦ *The police kicked the door down.* **2** [I,T] to move your foot or feet ◻ *menghayunkan (kaki)*: *You must kick harder if you want to swim faster.*
IDM **kick the habit** to stop doing sth harmful that you have done for a long time ◻ *membuang sst tabiat*
kick yourself to be annoyed with yourself because you have done sth stupid, missed an opportunity, etc. ◻ *berasa geram pd diri sendiri*
PHR V **kick off** to start sth, especially a game of football ◻ *memulakan perlawanan*
kick sb out (of sth) (*informal*) to force sb to leave a place ◻ *menendang/ditendang keluar*: *to be kicked out of university*

kick² /kɪk/ noun [C] **1** an act of kicking ◻ *tendangan; sepakan*: *She gave the door a kick and it closed.* **2** (*informal*) a feeling of great pleasure, excitement, etc. ◻ *keseronokan*: *He seems to get a real kick out of driving fast.*

[C] **countable**, a noun with a plural form: *one book, two books*
[U] **uncountable**, a noun with no plural form: *some sugar*

kick-off noun [C] the start of a game of football □ *permulaan perlawanan*: *Kick-off is at 2.30.*

kid¹ /kɪd/ noun 1 [C] (*informal*) a child or young person □ *budak*: *How are your kids?* 2 **kid brother/sister** [C] (*especially AmE informal*) younger brother/sister □ *adik* 3 [C,U] a young goat (= a small animal with horns that lives in mountain areas) or its skin □ *anak kambing*: *a kid jacket* ⊃ picture at **goat**

kid² /kɪd/ verb [I,T] (**kidding**; **kidded**) (*informal*) to trick sb/yourself by saying sth that is not true; to make a joke about sth □ *menipu diri sendiri*; *memperolok-olokkan sso*: *I didn't mean it. I was only kidding.*

kiddie (also **kiddy**) /ˈkɪdi/ noun [C] (*pl* **kiddies**) (*informal*) a child □ *budak-budak*

kidnap /ˈkɪdnæp/ verb [T] (**kidnapping**; **kidnapped**) to take sb away by force and demand money for their safe return □ *menculik*: *The child was kidnapped and £50 000 ransom was demanded for her release.* ⊃ look at **hijack** ▶ **kidnapper** noun [C]: *The kidnappers demanded £50 000.* ▶ **kidnapping** noun [C,U] ⊃ note at **crime**

kidney /ˈkɪdni/ noun 1 [C] one of the two parts of your body that separate waste liquid from your blood □ *buah pinggang*; *ginjal* ⊃ picture at **body** 2 [U,C] the kidneys of an animal when they are cooked and eaten as food □ *ginjal*: *steak and kidney pie*

kill¹ /kɪl/ verb 1 [I,T] to make sb/sth die □ *membunuh*; *terbunuh*; *terkorban*: *Smoking kills.* ♦ *She was killed instantly in the crash.* 2 [T] (*spoken*) to be very angry with sb □ *sangat marah*: *My mum will kill me when she sees this mess.* 3 [T] to cause sth to end or fail □ *menggagalkan*; *menghapuskan*: *The minister's opposition killed the idea stone dead.* 4 [T] (*informal*) to cause sb pain; to hurt □ *berasa sakit*; *menyakitkan*: *My feet are killing me.* 5 [T] (*informal*) **kill yourself/sb** to make yourself/sb laugh a lot □ *ketawa macam nak mati*: *We were killing ourselves laughing.*

IDM **kill time, an hour, etc.** to spend time doing sth that is not interesting or important while you are waiting for sth else to happen □ *menghabiskan masa, sejam, dsb*

kill two birds with one stone to do one thing which will achieve two results □ *sambil menyelam minum air*

PHR V **kill sth off** to cause sth to die or to not exist any more □ *membunuh*; *menghapuskan*; *menamatkan sst*

OTHER WORDS FOR

kill

Murder means to kill a person on purpose: *This was no accident. The old lady was murdered.* **Assassinate** means to kill for political reasons: *President Kennedy was assassinated.*

Slaughter and **massacre** mean to kill a large number of people: *Hundreds of people were massacred when the army opened fire on the crowd.* **Slaughter** is also used of killing an animal for food.

kill² /kɪl/ noun [usually sing] 1 the act of killing □ (*perbuatan*) *membunuh*: *Lions often make a kill in the evening.* 2 an animal or animals that have been killed □ *binatang yg dibunuh*; *buruan*; *mangsa*: *The eagle took the kill back to its young.*

killer /ˈkɪlə(r)/ noun [C] a person, animal or thing that kills □ *pembunuh*: *a killer disease* ♦ *He's a dangerous killer who may strike again.*

killing /ˈkɪlɪŋ/ noun [C] act of killing a person on purpose; a murder □ *pembunuhan*: *There have been a number of brutal killings in the area recently.*

IDM **make a killing** (*informal*) to make a large profit quickly □ *mendapat keuntungan besar*

kiln /kɪln/ noun [C] a type of large oven for baking pots, bricks, etc. that are made of clay (= a type of earth) to make them hard □ *tanur*; *ketuhar utk membakar tembikar atau batu bata, dsb.*

kilo /ˈkiːləʊ/ noun [C] (*pl* **kilos**) = **kilogram**

kilobit /ˈkɪləbɪt/ noun [C] (*abbr* **Kb**; **Kbit**) 1 a unit of computer memory, equal to 1 000 **bits** (= the smallest units of information) □ *kilobait* 2 (also **kibibit**) a unit of computer memory, equal to 1 024 **bits** (= the smallest units of information) □ *kilobait*

kilobyte /ˈkɪləbaɪt/ noun [C] (*abbr* **K**; **KB**) 1 a unit of computer memory, equal to 1 000 **bytes** (= small units of information) □ *kilobait* 2 (also **kibibyte**) a unit of computer memory, equal to 1 024 **bytes** (= small units of information) □ *kilobait*

kilogram (also **kilogramme** /ˈkɪləɡræm/ **kilo**) noun [C] (*abbr* **kg**) a measure of weight; 1 000 grams □ *kilo*: *a kilogram of rice* ♦ *I bought two kilos of potatoes.* ⓘ For more information about weights, look at the section on using numbers at the back of this dictionary.

kilometre (*AmE* **kilometer**) /ˈkɪləmiːtə(r); kɪˈlɒmɪtə(r)/ noun [C] (*abbr* **k**, **km**) a measure of length; 1 000 metres □ *kilometer*: *They live 100 km from Paris.*

kilowatt /ˈkɪləwɒt/ noun [C] (*abbr* **kW**; **kw**) a measure of electric power; 1 000 **watts** □ *kilowatt*

kilt /kɪlt/ noun [C] a skirt that is worn by men as part of the national dress of Scotland; a similar skirt worn by women □ *kilt*

kin /kɪn/ ⊃ **next of kin**

kind¹ /kaɪnd/ noun [C] a type of person or thing □ *jenis*: *The concert attracted people of all kinds.* ♦ *The concert attracted all kinds of people.* ♦ *What kind of car have you got?* ♦ *Many kinds of plant and animal are being lost every year.* ♦ *In the evenings I listen to music, write letters, that kind of thing.* **SYN** **sort, type**

GRAMMAR Remember that **kind** is countable, so you CANNOT say: *I like all kind of music.* You should say: *I like all kinds of music. Kinds of* may be followed by a singular or plural noun: *There are so many kinds of camera/cameras on the market that it's hard to know which is best.*

IDM **a kind of** (*informal*) used for describing sth in a way that is not very clear □ *semacam*: *I had a kind of feeling that something would go wrong.* ◆ *There's a funny kind of smell in here.*
kind of (*spoken*) slightly; a little □ *agak*: *I'm kind of worried about the interview.*
of a kind 1 of poor quality □ *tdk berapa baik*: *The village has a bus service of a kind—two buses a week!* **2** the same □ *serupa; sama saja*: *The friends were two of a kind—very similar in so many ways.*

kind² /kaɪnd/ *adj* (**kinder**; **kindest**) **kind (to sb); kind (of sb) (to do sth)** caring about others; friendly and generous □ *baik hati; baik*: *Everyone's been so kind to us since we came here!* ◆ *It was kind of you to offer, but I don't need any help.* **OPP** **unkind**

kindergarten /ˈkɪndəɡɑːtn/ *noun* [C] a school for children aged from about 2 to 5 □ *tadika* **SYN** **nursery school**

kind-ˈhearted *adj* kind and generous □ *berhati baik*

kindly /ˈkaɪndli/ *adv* **1** in a kind way □ *dgn baik; mesra; lembut*: *The nurse smiled kindly.* **2** (*old-fashioned, informal*) (used for asking sb to do sth) please □ *tolong*: *Would you kindly wait a moment?* ▶ **kindly** *adj* [only *before* a noun]: *a kindly face*

kindness /ˈkaɪndnəs/ *noun* [C,U] the quality of being kind; a kind act. □ *kebaikan hati; budi baik*: *Thank you very much for all your kindness.*

king /kɪŋ/ *noun* [C] **1** (the title of) a man who rules a country. A king is usually the son or close relative of the former ruler □ *raja*: *The new king was crowned in Westminster Abbey.* ◆ *King Edward VII* (= the seventh) ◆ (*figurative*) *The lion is the king of the jungle.* ➔ look at **queen**, **prince**, **princess 2** the most important piece used in the game of **chess**, that can move one square in any direction □ *raja (dlm permainan catur)* **3** one of the four playing cards in a pack with a picture of a king □ *(daun terup) raja*: *the king of spades* ➔ note at **card** ➔ picture at **card**

kingdom /ˈkɪŋdəm/ *noun* [C] **1** a country that is ruled by a king or queen □ *kerajaan*: *the United Kingdom* **2** one of the parts of the natural world □ *alam*: *the animal kingdom*

ˈking-size (also **ˈking-sized**) *adj* bigger than usual □ *saiz ekstra besar, panjang, dsb*: *a king-size bed*

kink /kɪŋk/ *noun* [C] a turn or bend in sth that should be straight □ *pintalan*

kiosk /ˈkiːɒsk/ *noun* [C] a very small building in the street where newspapers, sweets, cigarettes, etc. are sold □ *gerai; warung*

kip /kɪp/ *verb* [I] (**kipping**; **kipped**) (*BrE informal*) to sleep □ *tidur*: *You could kip on the sofa if you like.* ▶ **kip** *noun* [sing, U]: *I'm going to have a kip.* ◆ *I didn't get much kip last night.*

kipper /ˈkɪpə(r)/ *noun* [C] a type of fish that has been kept for a long time in salt, and then smoked □ *ikan salai*

kiss /kɪs/ *verb* [I,T] to touch sb with your lips to show love or friendship, or when saying hello or goodbye □ *mencium; mengucup*: *They sat in the back row of the cinema, kissing and cuddling.* ◆ *He kissed her on the cheek.* ◆ *They kissed each other goodbye.* ▶ **kiss** *noun* [C]: *a kiss on the lips/cheek*

kit¹ /kɪt/ *noun* **1** [C] a set of parts that you buy and put together in order to make sth □ *kit*: *a kit for a model aeroplane* **2** [C,U] a set of tools, equipment or clothes that you need for a particular purpose, sport or activity □ *alat; perkakas;*

kitchen utensils

- ladle
- spatula
- peeler
- rolling pin
- bread knife
- wooden spoon
- chopping board
- whisk
- grater
- colander
- sieve
- tin opener (*esp AmE* **can opener**)
- corkscrew

CONSONANTS   p **p**en   b **b**ad   t **t**ea   d **d**id   k **c**at   ɡ **g**ot   tʃ **ch**in   dʒ **J**une   f **f**all   v **v**an   θ **th**in

perlengkapan: *a tool kit* ♦ *a drum kit* ♦ *football/gym kit*

kit² /kɪt/ *verb* (**kitting**; **kitted**)
PHR V **kit sb/yourself out/up (in/with sth)** to give sb all the necessary clothes, equipment, tools, etc. for sth □ *memperlengkapi sso/diri (dgn sst)*

kitchen /ˈkɪtʃɪn/ *noun* [C] a room where food is prepared and cooked □ *(bilik) dapur*: *We usually eat in the kitchen.* ⮕ picture on **page P8, 487**

kite /kaɪt/ *noun* [C] a toy which consists of a light frame covered with paper or cloth. **Kites** are flown in the wind on the end of a long piece of string □ *layang-layang*: *to fly a kite*

kitesurfing /ˈkaɪtsɜːfɪŋ/ (also **kiteboarding** /ˈkaɪtbɔːdɪŋ/) *noun* [U] the sport of riding on water while standing on a short wide board and being pulled along by wind power, using a large **kite** □ *luncur angin*

kitten /ˈkɪtn/ *noun* [C] a young cat □ *anak kucing* ⮕ note at **cat**

kitty /ˈkɪti/ *noun* [C] (*pl* **kitties**) **1** a sum of money that is collected from a group of people and used for a particular purpose □ *tabung*: *All the students in the flat put £20 a week into the kitty.* **2** (*spoken*) a way of calling or referring to a cat □ *(panggilan utk) kucing*

kiwi /ˈkiːwiː/ *noun* [C] (*pl* **kiwis**) **1** a New Zealand bird with a long beak and short wings that cannot fly □ *burung kiwi* **2** (also **ˈkiwi fruit**) a fruit with brown skin that is green inside with black seeds □ *buah kiwi* ⮕ picture on **page P14**

km *abbr* = **kilometre**

knack /næk/ *noun* [sing] (*informal*) **knack (of/for doing sth)** skill or ability to do sth (difficult) that you have naturally or you can learn □ *bakat, kebolehan*: *Knitting isn't difficult once you've got the knack of it.*

knead /niːd/ *verb* [T] to press and squeeze **dough** (= a mixture of flour and water) with your hands in order to make bread, etc. □ *menguli*

knee /niː/ *noun* [C] **1** the place where your leg bends in the middle □ *lutut*: *Angie fell and grazed her knee.* ♦ *She was on her hands and knees on the floor looking for her earrings.* ♦ *Come and sit on my knee.* ⮕ picture at **body** **2** the part of a pair of trousers, etc. that covers the knee □ *bahagian lutut*: *There's a hole in the knee of those jeans.*

kneecap /ˈniːkæp/ *noun* [C] the bone that covers the front of the knee □ *tempurung lutut* ⮕ picture at **body**

ˌknee-ˈdeep *adj, adv* up to your knees □ *separas lutut*: *The water was knee-deep in places.*

kneel /niːl/ *verb* [I] (*pt, pp* **knelt** /nelt/; *AmE* also **kneeled**) **kneel (down)** to rest on one or both knees □ *melutut*: *She knelt down to talk to the child.*

knew past tense of **know¹**

kneel

She's kneeling.   He's squatting.

He's crouching.

knickers /ˈnɪkəz/ (*AmE* **panties**) *noun* [pl] a piece of underwear for women that covers the area between the waist and the top of the legs □ *seluar dlm perempuan*: *a pair of knickers*

knife¹ /naɪf/ *noun* [C] (*pl* **knives** /naɪvz/) a sharp blade with a handle. A knife is used for cutting things or as a weapon □ *pisau*: *The carving knife is very blunt/sharp.* ♦ *a knife and fork* ♦ *a penknife/pocket knife/bread knife* ⮕ picture at **cutlery, kitchen**

knife² /naɪf/ *verb* [T] to deliberately injure sb with a knife □ *menikam* **SYN** **stab**

knight /naɪt/ *noun* [C] **1** a soldier who fought on a horse in the Middle Ages □ *kesateria* **2** a man who has been given a title of honour by a king or queen and who can use **Sir** in front of his name □ *orang yg dikurniakan suatu darjah kehormatan oleh raja/ratu* **3** a piece used in the game of **chess** that is shaped like a horse's head □ *kuda (dlm permainan catur)* ▶ **knighthood** /ˈnaɪthʊd/ *noun* [C]: *He received a knighthood.*

knit /nɪt/ *verb* [I,T] (**knitting**; *pt, pp* **knitted** or *AmE* **knit**) **1** to make sth (for example an article of clothing) with wool using two long needles or a special machine □ *mengait*: *I'm knitting a sweater for my nephew.* ⮕ look at **crochet** ⮕ picture at **sew** **2 knit** [only used in this form] joined closely together □ *rapat; bersatu padu*: *a closely/tightly knit village community* ▶ **knitting** *noun* [U]: *I usually do some knitting while I'm watching TV.* ♦ *Where's my knitting?*

ˈknitting needle = **needle** (2)

knitwear /ˈnɪtweə(r)/ *noun* [U] articles of clothing that have been knitted □ *pakaian yg dikait*: *the knitwear department*

knives plural of **knife**

knob /nɒb/ noun [C] **1** a round switch on a machine (for example a TV) that you press or turn □ *tombol*: *the volume control knob* **2** a round handle on a door, drawer, etc. □ *tombol; cembul* ⊃ picture at **drawer** ⊃ picture at **handle**

knock¹ /nɒk/ verb **1** [I] **knock (at/on sth)** to make a noise by hitting sth firmly with your hand □ *mengetuk*: *Is that someone knocking at the door?* ♦ *I knocked on the window but she didn't hear me.* **2** [T] **knock sth (on/against sth)** to hit sb/sth hard, often by accident □ *terlanggar; terhantuk; memukul; menumbuk*: *He knocked the vase onto the floor.* ♦ *Be careful not to knock your head on the shelf when you get up.* ♦ *to knock somebody unconscious* **3** [T] (*informal*) to say bad things about sb/sth; to criticize sb/sth □ *mengkritik; mencela*: *'I hate this town.' 'Don't knock it—there are far worse places to live.'*

IDM **knock on wood** ⊃ **wood**

PHRV **knock about/around** (*informal*) to be in a place; to travel and live in various places □ *ada/ berada (di sst tempat); mengembara*: *Is last week's newspaper still knocking about?*

knock sb down to hit sb causing them to fall to the ground □ *melanggar sso*: *The old lady was knocked down by a cyclist.*

knock sth down to destroy a building, etc. □ *merobohkan sst*: *They knocked down the old factory because it was unsafe.*

knock off (sth) (*spoken*) to stop working □ *habis kerja, dsb*: *What time do you knock off?*

knock sth off 1 (*informal*) to reduce a price by a certain amount □ *mengurangkan harga*: *He agreed to knock £10 off the price.* **2** (*slang*) to steal sth □ *mencuri sst*

knock sb out 1 to hit sb so that they become unconscious or cannot get up again for a while □ *memukul; menumbuk sso hingga pengsan atau hingga tdk dpt bangun*: *The punch on the nose knocked him out.* **2** (used about a drug, alcohol, etc.) to cause sb to sleep or become unconscious □ *menyebabkan sso tertidur*: *Those three glasses of vodka really knocked her out.*

knock sb out (of sth) to beat a person or team in a competition so that they do not play any more games in it □ *mengalahkan; menyingkirkan*: *Belgium was knocked out of the European Cup by France.*

knock sb/sth over to cause sb/sth to fall over □ *melanggar sst hingga terjatuh, terbalik, tertumpah, dll*: *Be careful not to knock over the drinks.*

knock² /nɒk/ noun [C] a sharp hit from sth hard or the sound it makes □ *ketukan; hantukan*: *a nasty knock on the head* ♦ *I thought I heard a knock at the door.* ♦ (*figurative*) *She has suffered some hard knocks* (= bad experiences) *in her life.*

knocker /ˈnɒkə(r)/ noun [C] a piece of metal fixed to the outside of a door that you hit against the door to attract attention □ *pengetuk pintu*

⊃ picture on **page P8**

knock-on adj (especially *BrE*) causing other events to happen one after the other □ *menye- babkan perkara lain turut berlaku satu lepas satu*: *An increase in the price of oil has a knock-on effect on other goods.*

knockout /ˈnɒkaʊt/ noun [C] **1** a hard hit that causes sb to become unconscious or to be unable to get up again for a while □ *pukulan yg merebahkan sso atau menyebabkannya pengsan* **2** a competition in which the winner of each game goes on to the next part but the person who loses plays no more games □ *kalah mati*

knot¹ /nɒt/ noun [C] **1** a place where two ends or pieces of rope, string, etc. have been tied to- gether □ *simpul; simpulan*: *to tie/untie a knot* ⊃ picture at **loop** **2** a measure of the speed of a ship; approximately 1.8 kilometres per hour □ *knot*

knot² /nɒt/ verb [T] (**knotting; knotted**) to fas- ten sth together with a knot □ *menyimpulkan*

know¹ /nəʊ/ verb (pt **knew** /njuː/; pp **known** /nəʊn/) [not used in the continuous tenses]
▸HAVE INFORMATION **1** [I,T] **know (about sth); know (that)...** to have knowledge or informa- tion in your mind □ *tahu; mengetahui*: *I don't know much about sport.* ♦ *Did you know that she was coming?* ♦ *Do you know where this bus stops?* ♦ *Do you know their telephone number?* ♦ *'You've got a flat tyre.' 'I know.'* ♦ *Do you know the way to the restaurant?*
▸FEEL SURE **2** [T,I] to feel certain; to be sure of sth □ *tahu*: *I just know you'll pass the exam!* ♦ *As far as I know* (= I think it is true but I am not absolutely sure), *the meeting is next Monday afternoon.*
▸BE FAMILIAR **3** [T] to be familiar with a person or a place; to have met sb or been somewhere before □ *kenal; mengenali; tahu*: *We've known each other for years.* ♦ *I don't know this part of London well.*

MORE You can use **meet** to talk about the first time you see and talk to someone, or are introduced to someone: *Rahul and I met at uni- versity in 2008.* After you meet someone and gradually become friends, you **get to know** him/her: *Kevin's wife seems very interesting. I'd like to get to know her better.*

▸GIVE NAME **4** [T, often passive] **know sb/sth as sth** to give sth a particular name; to recognize sb/sth as sth □ *dikenali sebagai*: *Istanbul was previously known as Constantinople.*
▸SKILL **5** [T] **know how to do sth** to have learnt sth and be able to do it □ *tahu; pandai*: *Do you know how to make pancakes?*

HELP Be careful. In front of a verb you must use **how to**. You CANNOT say: *I know make pancakes.*

know → kW

▶EXPERIENCE **6** [T] to have personal experience of sth ◻ *tahu; mengalami; merasai*: Many people in western countries don't know what it's like to be hungry. **7** [T] [only in the past and perfect tenses] to have seen, heard, or experienced sth ◻ *pernah mendengar, melihat atau mengalami sst*: I've known him go a whole day without eating. ◆ It's been known to snow in June.

> **HELP** Although this verb is not used in the continuous tenses, it is common to see the present participle (= -ing form): *Knowing how he'd react if he ever found out about it, she kept quiet.*

IDM **God, goodness, Heaven, etc. knows 1** I do not know ◻ *Tuhan saja yg tahu; entah*: They've ordered a new car but goodness knows how they're going to pay for it. **2** used for emphasizing sth ◻ *memang*: I hope I get an answer soon. Goodness knows, I've waited long enough. ⇨ note at **God**

I might have known ⇨ **might¹**

know better (than that/than to do sth) to have enough sense to realize that you should not do sth ◻ *sepatutnya lebih tahu (ttg mudarat sst dan oleh itu tdk melakukannya)*: I thought you knew better than to go out in the rain with no coat on.

know sth inside out/like the back of your hand (*informal*) to be very familiar with sth ◻ *betul-betul tahu; biasa ttg sst*

know what you are talking about (*informal*) to have knowledge of sth from your own experience ◻ *tahu ttg sst (kerana ada pengalaman ttgnya)*: I've lived in London so I know what I'm talking about.

know what's what (*informal*) to have all the important information about sth; to fully understand sth ◻ *tahu apa yg penting, mana yg baik atau sebaliknya, dsb*

let sb know to tell sb about sth ◻ *memberitahu sso*: Could you let me know what time you're arriving?

show sb/know/learn the ropes ⇨ **rope¹**

you know used when the speaker is thinking of what to say next, or to remind sb of sth ◻ *awak tahu; er…*: Well, you know, it's rather difficult to explain. ◆ I've just met Marta. You know—Jim's ex-wife.

you never know (*spoken*) you cannot be certain ◻ *manalah tahu; kalau-kalau*: Keep those empty boxes. You never know, they might come in handy one day.

PHR V **know of sb/sth** to have information about or experience of sb/sth ◻ *tahu (akan sso/sst)*: Do you know of any pubs around here that serve food?

know² /nəʊ/ *noun*

IDM **in the know** (*informal*) having information that other people do not ◻ *tahu*

'**know-all** (also '**know-it-all**) *noun* [C] an annoying person who behaves as if they know everything ◻ *orang yg (kononnya) serba tahu*

'**know-how** *noun* [U] (*informal*) practical knowledge of or skill in sth ◻ *kepandaian*

knowing /ˈnəʊɪŋ/ *adj* showing that you know about sth that is thought to be secret ◻ *penuh erti; bermakna*: a knowing look

knowingly /ˈnəʊɪŋli/ *adv* **1** on purpose; deliberately ◻ *dgn sengaja*: I've never knowingly lied to you. **2** in a way that shows that you know about sth that is thought to be secret ◻ *dgn penuh erti*: He smiled knowingly at her.

'**know-it-all** = **know-all**

knowledge /ˈnɒlɪdʒ/ *noun* **1** [U, sing] **knowledge (of/about sth)** information, understanding and skills that you have gained through learning or experience ◻ *pengetahuan*: I have a working knowledge of French (= enough to be able to make myself understood). **2** [U] the state of knowing about a particular fact or situation ◻ *pengetahuan*: He denied all knowledge of the affair. ◆ She did it **without my knowledge** (= I did not know about it).

IDM **be common/public knowledge** to be sth that everyone knows ◻ *semua orang sudah tahu*

to (the best of) your knowledge from the information you have, although you may not know everything ◻ *berdasarkan pengetahuan saya*: To the best of my knowledge they are still living there.

knowledgeable /ˈnɒlɪdʒəbl/ *adj* having a lot of knowledge ◻ *berpengetahuan luas*: She's very knowledgeable about history. ▶ **knowledgeably** /-əbli/ *adv*

known *past participle* of **know¹**

knuckle /ˈnʌkl/ *noun* [C] the bones where your fingers join the rest of your hand ◻ *buku jari* ⇨ picture at **body**

koala /kəʊˈɑːlə/ *noun* [C] an Australian animal with thick grey fur that lives in trees and looks like a small bear ◻ *beruang koala*

the Koran (also **Qur'an**) /kəˈrɑːn/ *noun* [sing] the most important book in the Islamic religion ◻ *al-Quran*

koala

kosher /ˈkəʊʃə(r)/ *adj* (used about food) prepared according to the rules of Jewish law ◻ *kosher (makanan halal dr segi agama Yahudi)*

kph /ˌkeɪ piː ˈeɪtʃ/ *abbr* kilometres per hour ◻ *km/j (kilometer sejam)*

kung fu /ˌkʌŋ ˈfuː/ *noun* [U] a Chinese style of fighting using the feet and hands as weapons ◻ *kung fu* ⇨ look at **martial arts**

kW (also **kw**) *abbr* = kilowatt ◻ *kW (kilowatt)*: a 2kW electric heater

L → lacking

L

L, l /el/ noun [C,U] (pl **Ls; L's; l's** /elz/) the 12th letter of the English alphabet □ *L, l (huruf)*: 'Language' begins with (an) 'L'.

l abbr **1** [in writing] **l** = litre **2 L** (BrE) used on a sign on a car to show that the driver is learning to drive □ *L (pemandu yg sedang belajar memandu)* **3 L** large (size) □ *L (saiz besar)*: *S, M and L* (= small, medium and large)

Lab abbr (in British politics) Labour □ *Parti Buruh (di UK)*

lab /læb/ (informal) = laboratory

price tag   label   ticket

label¹ /'leɪbl/ noun [C] **1** a piece of paper, etc. that is fixed to sth and which gives information about it □ *label*: *There is a list of all the ingredients on the label.* **2** a company that produces and sells music, CDs, etc □ *label (syarikat rakaman)*: *It's his first release for a major label.*

label² /'leɪbl/ verb [T] (**labelling; labelled**, (AmE) **labeling; labeled**) **1** [usually passive] to fix a label or write information on sth □ *melabelkan* **2 label sb/sth (as) sth** to describe sb/sth in a particular way, especially unfairly □ *mengecap; melabel*

laboratory /ləˈbɒrətri/ noun [C] (pl **laboratories**) (also informal **lab**) a room or building that is used for scientific research, testing, experiments, etc. or for teaching about science □ *makmal*: *The blood samples were sent to the laboratory for analysis.* ♦ *a physics laboratory* ➔ look at **language laboratory**

laborious /ləˈbɔːriəs/ adj needing a lot of time and effort □ *berat; menjerihkan; sukar dibuat*: *a laborious task/process/job* ▸**laboriously** adv

labour¹ (AmE **labor**) /'leɪbə(r)/ noun **1** [U] work, usually of a hard, physical kind □ *kerja; kerja buruh*: *manual labour* (= work using your hands) **2** [U] workers, when thought of as a group □ *buruh*: *There is a shortage of skilled labour.* **3** [U,C, usually sing] the process of giving birth to a baby □ *(proses) bersalin; sakit bersalin*: *She went into labour in the early hours of this morning.* ♦ *She was in labour for ten hours.* ♦ *She had a difficult labour.* **4** = **the Labour Party**

labour² (AmE **labor**) /'leɪbə(r)/ verb [I] **1 labour (away)** to work hard at sth □ *bekerja keras*: *She laboured on her book for two years.* **2** to move or do sth with difficulty and effort □ *bersusah payah*

laboured (AmE **labored**) /'leɪbəd/ adj done slowly or with difficulty □ *sukar*: *laboured breathing*

labourer (AmE **laborer**) /'leɪbərə(r)/ noun [C] a person whose job involves hard physical work □ *buruh*: *unskilled/farm labourers*

the 'Labour Party (also **Labour**) noun [sing, with sing or pl verb] one of the main political parties in Britain. The **Labour Party** supports the interests of working people □ *Parti Buruh (politik British)*: *He has always voted Labour.* ♦ *a Labour MP* ➔ note at **party** ➔ look at **the Conservative Party, the Liberal Democrats**

'labour-saving adj reducing the amount of work needed to do sth □ *yg menjimatkan tenaga*: *labour-saving devices such as washing machines and dishwashers*

labyrinth /ˈlæbərɪnθ/ noun [C] a complicated set of paths and passages, which is difficult to find your way through □ *jalan, lorong, dsb yg berselirat*: *a labyrinth of corridors* **SYN maze**

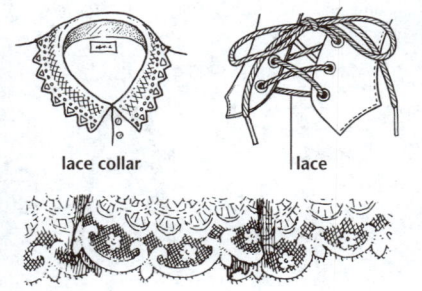

lace collar   lace

lace

lace¹ /leɪs/ noun **1** [U] cloth that is made of very thin threads sewn in patterns with small holes in between □ *renda*: *lace curtains* ♦ *a collar made of lace* ➔ adjective **lacy 2** = **shoelace**: *Do up your laces or you'll trip over them.*

lace² /leɪs/ verb [I,T] **lace (sth) (up)** to tie or fasten sth with a **lace¹**(2) □ *mengikat*: *She was sitting on the end of the bed lacing up her boots.* ▸**lace-up** adj, noun [C]: *lace-up shoes* ♦ *a pair of lace-ups*

lack¹ /læk/ noun [U, sing] **a lack (of sth)** the state of not having sth or not having enough of sth □ *kekurangan*: *A lack of food forced many people to leave their homes.* ♦ *The trip was cancelled through lack of interest.*

lack² /læk/ verb [T] to have none or not enough of sth □ *tdk ada; tdk mempunyai; kurang*: *She seems to lack the will to succeed.*

lacking /ˈlækɪŋ/ adj [not before a noun] **1 lacking in sth** not having enough of sth □ *tdk mempunyai; kurang*: *He's certainly not lacking in intelligence.* **2** not present or available

[C] **countable**, a noun with a plural form: *one book, two books*   [U] **uncountable**, a noun with no plural form: *some sugar*

□ *kekurangan*: *I feel there is something lacking in my life.*

lacklustre /ˈlæklʌstə(r)/ *adj* not interesting or exciting □ *tdk menarik; hambar*: *a lacklustre performance* **SYN** **dull**

laconic /ləˈkɒnɪk/ *adj* (*formal*) using only a few words to say sth □ *ringkas; pendek* ▶ **laconically** /-kli/ *adv*

lacquer /ˈlækə(r)/ *noun* [U] **1** a type of transparent paint that is put on wood, metal, etc. to give it a hard, shiny surface □ *lakuer; sampang; pengilat* **2** (*old-fashioned*) a liquid that you put on your hair to keep it in place □ *lakuer; penyembur rambut* **SYN** **hairspray**

lacy /ˈleɪsi/ *adj* made of or looking like **lace** (= material made of thin threads with small holes that form a pattern) □ *berenda; dibuat drpd kain renda*

lad /læd/ *noun* (*BrE informal*) **1** [C] (*old-fashioned*) a boy or young man □ *budak lelaki; anak muda*: *School has changed since I was a lad.* **2 the lads** [pl] a group of friends that a man spends time with □ *teman*: *a night out with the lads*

rung

step

ladder   stepladder

ladder /ˈlædə(r)/ *noun* [C] **1** a piece of equipment that is used for climbing up sth. A **ladder** consists of two long pieces of metal, wood or rope with steps fixed between them □ *tangga*: (*figurative*) *to climb the ladder of success* ⊃ look at **stepladder 2** (*AmE* **run**) a long hole in **tights** or **stockings** (= the thin pieces of clothing that women wear to cover their legs), where the threads have broken □ *carik pd stoking*: *Oh no! I've got a ladder in my tights.* ▶ **ladder** *verb* [T]

laden /ˈleɪdn/ *adj* [not before a noun] **laden (with sth)** having or carrying a lot of sth □ *sarat; lebat dgn buah*: *The travellers were laden down with luggage.* ◆ *The orange trees were laden with fruit.*

the ˈLadies *noun* [sing] (*BrE informal*) a public toilet for women □ *tandas wanita* ⊃ note at **toilet**

ladle¹ /ˈleɪdl/ *noun* [C] a large deep spoon with a long handle, used especially for serving soup

□ *senduk* ⊃ picture at **kitchen**

ladle² /ˈleɪdl/ *verb* [T] to serve food with a **ladle** □ *menyenduk*

lady /ˈleɪdi/ *noun* [C] (*pl* **ladies**) **1** a polite way of saying 'woman', especially when you are referring to an older woman □ *wanita*: *The old lady next door lives alone.* **2** (*formal*) used when speaking to or about a woman or women in a polite way □ *puan; wanita*: *Ladies and gentlemen* (= at the beginning of a speech) ◆ *Mrs Flinn, there's a lady here to see you.* **3** a title used before the name of a woman who has a high social position □ *gelaran 'Lady' (UK)*: *Lady Elizabeth Groves* ⊃ look at **Lord**

ladybird /ˈleɪdibɜːd/ (*AmE* **ladybug** /ˈleɪdibʌg/) *noun* [C] a small insect that is red or yellow with black spots □ *kumbang kura-kura* ⊃ picture on **page P13**

lag¹ /læɡ/ *verb* [I] (**lagging**; **lagged**) **lag (behind)**; **lag (behind sb/sth)** to move or develop more slowly than sb/sth □ *ketinggalan; tertinggal*: *James has missed a lot of classes and is lagging behind the others at school.*

lag² /læɡ/ (also **ˈtime lag**) *noun* [C] a period of time between two events; a delay □ *jeda/sela (masa)* ⊃ look at **jet lag**

lager /ˈlɑːɡə(r)/ *noun* [C,U] (*BrE*) a type of light beer that is a gold colour □ *lager (bir)*: *Three pints of lager, please.* ⊃ note at **beer**

lagoon /ləˈɡuːn/ *noun* [C] a lake of salt water that is separated from the sea by sand or rock □ *lagun*

laid *past tense, past participle* of **lay¹**

laid-back /ˌleɪd ˈbæk/ *adj* (*informal*) calm and relaxed; seeming not to worry about anything □ *tenang dan santai* **SYN** **easy-going**

lain *past participle* of **lie²**

lake /leɪk/ *noun* [C] a large area of water that is surrounded by land □ *tasik*: *They've gone sailing on the lake.* ◆ *We all swam in the lake.* ◆ *Lake Constance* ⊃ picture on **page P10**

OTHER WORDS FOR

lake

A **lake** is usually big enough to sail on: *Lake Como*. A **pond** may be big enough for animals to drink from or may be a very small area of water in a garden: *We have a fish pond in our garden*. A **pool** is a much smaller area of water: *When the tide went out, pools of water were left among the rocks*. An artificial pool, however, can be larger: *a swimming pool*. A **puddle** is a small pool of water made by the rain.

---

lamb /læm/ *noun* **1** [C] a young sheep □ *anak biri-biri* ⊃ note at **sheep** ⊃ picture at **goat 2** [U] the meat of a young sheep □ *daging biri-biri muda*: *lamb chops* ⊃ note at **meat**

lame /leɪm/ *adj* **1** (used mainly about animals) not able to walk properly because of an injury to the leg or foot □ *tempang*: *The horse is lame* and cannot work. **2** (used about an excuse, argument, etc.) not easily believed; weak □ *tdk munasabah; lemah*

lament /ləˈment/ *noun* [C] (*formal*) a song, poem or other expression of sadness for sb who has died or for sth that has ended □ *lagu/puisi sedih* ▶ **lament** *verb* [T]

laminated /ˈlæmɪneɪtɪd/ *adj* **1** (used about wood, plastic, etc.) made by sticking several thin layers together □ *berlamina*: *laminated glass* **2** covered with thin transparent plastic for protection □ *bersalut plastik*

lamp /læmp/ *noun* [C] a device that uses electricity, gas or oil to produce light □ *lampu*: *a street lamp* ◆ *a table/desk/bicycle lamp* ◆ *a sunlamp*

lamps

lampshade

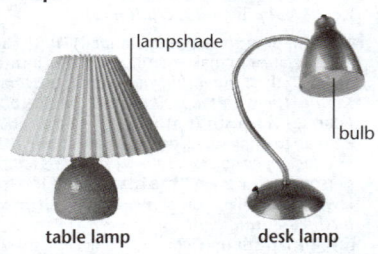

bulb

table lamp   desk lamp

ˈlamp post *noun* [C] a tall pole at the side of the road with a light on the top □ *tiang lampu* ⊃ look at **street light** ⊃ picture on **page P11**

lampshade /ˈlæmpʃeɪd/ *noun* [C] a cover for a lamp that makes it look more attractive and makes the light softer □ *terendak lampu* ⊃ picture at **lamp**

LAN /læn/ *abbr* **local area network**; a system that connects computers inside a single building or buildings in the same area □ *Rangkaian Kawasan Setempat* ⊃ look at **WAN**

land¹ /lænd/ *noun* **1** [U] the solid part of the surface of the earth (= not sea) □ *daratan*: *Penguins can't move very fast* **on land**. **OPP** **sea** ⊃ note at **ground 2** [U] an area of ground □ *tanah*: *The land rose to the east.* ◆ *She owns 500 acres of land in Scotland.* **3** [U] ground, soil or earth of a particular kind □ *tanah*: *The land is rich and fertile.* ◆ *arid/barren land* ◆ *arable/agricultural/industrial land* **4** [C] (*written*) a country or region □ *tanah air; negeri; negara*: *She died far from her native land.* ◆ *to travel to distant lands* ⊃ note at **country**

land² /lænd/ *verb* **1** [I,T] to come down from the air or to bring sth down to the ground □ *hinggap; jatuh; mendarat*: *The bird landed on the roof.* ◆ *He fell off the ladder and landed on his back.* ◆ *The pilot landed the aeroplane safely.* ◆ *His flight is due to land at 3 o'clock.* **OPP** **take off** **2** [I,T] to go onto land or put sth onto land from a ship □ *mendaratkan*: *to land cargo* **3** [T] to succeed in getting sth, especially sth that a lot of people want □ *berjaya mendapat*: *The company has just landed a million-dollar contract.*

IDM **fall/land on your feet** ⊃ **foot¹**

PHR V **land up (in …)** (*BrE informal*) to finish in a certain position or situation □ *akhirnya*: *He landed up in a prison cell for the night.*

land sb with sb/sth (*informal*) to give sb sth unpleasant to do, especially because nobody else wants to do it □ *membosankan atau menyusahkan sso dgn sso/sst*

landfill /ˈlændfɪl/ *noun* **1** [C,U] an area of land where large amounts of waste material are buried □ *tempat pelupusan sampah* **2** [U] waste material that will be buried; the burying of waste material □ *sampah yg akan dilupus; pelupusan sampah*

landing /ˈlændɪŋ/ *noun* [C] **1** the area at the top of a set of stairs in a house, or between one set of stairs and another in a large building □ *pelantar tangga* **2** the act of coming down onto the ground (in an aircraft) □ *pendaratan; (perbuatan) mendarat*: *The plane made an emergency landing in a field.* ◆ *a crash landing* ◆ *a safe landing* **OPP** **take-off** ⊃ picture at **take-off**

ˈlanding card *noun* [C] a form on which you have to write details about yourself when flying to a foreign country □ *kad pendaratan*

ˈlanding gear = **undercarriage**

ˈlanding stage = **jetty**

ˈlanding strip = **airstrip**

landline /ˈlændlaɪn/ *noun* [C] a telephone connection that uses wires carried on poles or under the ground □ *talian tetap* ⊃ look at **mobile phone**

landlord /ˈlændlɔːd/ (*fem* **landlady** /ˈlændleɪdi/; *pl* **landladies**) *noun* [C] **1** a person who rents a house or room to people for money □ *tuan rumah* **2** (*BrE*) a person who owns or manages a pub, small hotel, etc. □ *tuan punya/pengurus pub, hotel kecil, dsb*

landmark /ˈlændmɑːk/ *noun* [C] **1** an object (often a building) that can be seen easily from a distance and will help you to recognize where you are □ *mercu tanda; (bangunan, dsb) tanda tempat*: *Big Ben is one of the landmarks on London's skyline.* **2** **a landmark (in sth)** an important stage or change in the development of sth □ *peristiwa penting*

landmine /ˈlændmaɪn/ *noun* [C] a bomb placed on or under the ground, which explodes when sb moves or drives over it □ *periuk api; ranjau darat*

landscape¹ /ˈlændskeɪp/ *noun* **1** [C, usually sing] everything you can see when you look across a large area of land □ *landskap; pemandangan darat*: *an urban/industrial landscape* ⊃ note at **scenery** ⊃ picture on **page P10 2** [C,U] a picture or a painting that shows a view of the countryside; this style of painting □ *lukisan*

landscape → laptop

pemandangan darat: *one of Constable's landscapes* **3** [U] (*technical*) the way of printing a document in which the top of the page is one of the longer sides □ *landskap*: *Select the landscape option when printing the file.* ➲ look at **portrait** ➲ picture at **computer**

landscape² /ˈlændskeɪp/ *verb* [T] to improve the appearance of an area of land by changing its design and planting trees, flowers, etc. □ *membuat seni taman*

landslide /ˈlændslaɪd/ *noun* [C] **1** the sudden fall of a mass of earth, rocks, etc. down the side of a mountain □ *tanah runtuh*: *Part of the railway line was buried beneath a landslide.* **2** a great victory for one person or one political party in an election □ *kemenangan besar*

lane /leɪn/ *noun* [C] **1** a narrow road in the country □ *lorong*: *We found a route through country lanes to avoid the traffic jam on the main road.* ➲ picture on **page P11 2** used in the names of roads □ *Lorong*: *Crossley Lane* **3** a section of a wide road that is marked by painted white lines to keep lines of traffic separate □ *lorong*: *a four-lane motorway* ◆ *the inside/middle/fast/outside lane* **4** a section of a sports track, swimming pool, etc. for one person to go along □ *lorong*: *The British athlete is in lane two.* ➲ picture on **page P4 5** a route or path that is regularly used by ships or aircraft □ *laluan kapal/kapal terbang*: *the busy shipping lanes of the English Channel*

language /ˈlæŋɡwɪdʒ/ *noun*
▸OF A COUNTRY **1** [C] the system of communication in speech and writing that is used by people of a particular country □ *bahasa*: *How many languages can you speak?* ◆ *What is your first language* (= your mother tongue)? ◆ *They fell in love in spite of the language barrier* (= having different first languages).
▸COMMUNICATION **2** [U] the system of sounds and writing that people use to express their thoughts, ideas and feelings □ *bahasa*: *written/spoken language*
▸STYLE OF SPEAKING/WRITING **3** [U] words of a particular type or words that are used by a particular person or group □ *bahasa*: *bad* (= rude) *language* ◆ *legal language* ◆ *the language of Shakespeare*
▸SIGNS/SYMBOLS **4** [U] any system of signs, symbols, movements, etc. that is used to express sth □ *bahasa*: *sign language* (= using your hands, not speaking) ➲ look at **body language**
▸COMPUTING **5** [C,U] a system of symbols and rules that is used to operate a computer □ *bahasa*: *BASIC is a common computer language.*

language laboratory *noun* [C] (*pl* **language laboratories**) a room in a school or college that contains special equipment to help students to learn foreign languages by listening to CDs or tapes, watching DVDs or videos, recording themselves, etc. □ *makmal bahasa*

lanky /ˈlæŋki/ *adj* (**lankier**; **lankiest**) (used about a person) very tall and thin □ *tinggi lampai*

lantern /ˈlæntən/ *noun* [C] a type of light that can be carried, with a metal frame, glass sides and a light or **candle** (= a tall stick that you burn) inside □ *tanglung*

lanyard /ˈlænjɑːd; -jəd/ *noun* [C] a string or wire that you wear around your neck or wrist for holding sth □ *tali yg digantung di leher atau pergelangan tangan utk mengikat sesuatu; lanyard*: *I carry my ID card on a lanyard round my neck.* ◆ *The lanyard keeps your iPod around your neck so your music is always available.*

lap¹ /læp/ *noun* [C] **1** the flat area that is formed by the upper part of your legs when you are sitting down □ *riba; pangkuan*: *The child sat quietly on his mother's lap.* **2** one journey around a running track, etc. □ *pusingan*: *There are three more laps to go in the race.* **3** one part of a long journey □ *bahagian (perjalanan)*

lap² /læp/ *verb* (**lapping**; **lapped**) **1** [I] (used about water) to make gentle sounds as it moves against sth □ *memukul/menampar perlahan-lahan*: *The waves lapped against the side of the boat.* **2** [T] **lap sth (up)** (usually used about an animal) to drink sth using the tongue □ *menjilat*: *The cat lapped up the cream.* **3** [T] to pass another person in a race who has been round the track fewer times than you □ *mendahului dgn satu pusingan atau lebih*
PHR V **lap sth up** (*informal*) to accept sth with great enjoyment without stopping to think if it is good, true, etc. □ *menerima bulat-bulat*

lapel /ləˈpel/ *noun* [C] one of the two parts of the front of a coat or jacket that are folded back □ *lapel; kelepet kolar*

lapse¹ /læps/ *noun* [C] **1** a short time when you cannot remember sth or you are not thinking about what you are doing □ *terlupa; kehilangan tumpuan*: *a lapse of memory* ◆ *The crash was the result of a temporary lapse in concentration.* **2** a period of time between two things that happen □ *selang; tempoh*: *She returned to work after a lapse of ten years bringing up her family.* ➲ look at **elapse 3** a piece of bad behaviour from sb who usually behaves well □ *kesilapan oleh sso yg berkelakuan baik*

lapse² /læps/ *verb* [I] **1** (used about a contract, an agreement, etc.) to finish or stop, often by accident □ *luput*: *My membership has lapsed because I forgot to renew it.* **2** to become weaker or stop for a short time □ *berkurang; merosot*: *My concentration lapsed during the last part of the exam.*
PHR V **lapse into sth** to gradually pass into a worse or less active state or condition; to start speaking or behaving in a less acceptable way □ *semakin merosot; menjadi*: *to lapse into silence/a coma*

laptop /ˈlæptɒp/ *noun* [C] a small computer that is easy to carry and that can use batteries for power □ *komputer riba*: *Moira took her laptop to Korea.* ➲ note at **computer** ➲ picture at **computer**

lard /lɑːd/ noun [U] hard white fat that is used in cooking □ *lemak babi*

larder /'lɑːdə(r)/ noun [C] a large cupboard or small room that is used for storing food □ *almari makanan* **SYN** pantry

large /lɑːdʒ/ adj (**larger**; **largest**) greater in size, amount, etc. than usual; big □ *besar*: *a large area/house/family/appetite* ◆ *a large number of people* ◆ *I'd like a large coffee, please.* ◆ *We have this shirt in small, medium or large.* ⊃ note at **big, fat**

IDM at large 1 as a whole; in general □ *pd keseluruhannya; pd amnya*: *He is well known to scientists but not to the public at large.* **2** (used about a criminal, animal, etc.) not caught; free □ *tdk ditangkap; bebas*: *One of the escaped prisoners is still at large.*

by and large mostly; in general □ *pd umumnya*: *By and large the school is very efficient.*

largely /'lɑːdʒli/ adv mostly □ *sebahagian besarnya*: *His success was largely due to hard work.*

large-scale adj happening over a large area or affecting a lot of people □ *secara besar-besaran*: *large-scale production/unemployment*

lark /lɑːk/ noun [C] a small brown bird with a pleasant song □ *burung lark*

larva /'lɑːvə/ noun [C] (pl **larvae** /'lɑːviː/) an insect that has just come out of its egg and has a short fat soft body with no legs □ *larva* ⊃ picture on **page P13**

laryngitis /ˌlærɪn'dʒaɪtɪs/ noun [U] a mild illness of the throat that makes it difficult to speak □ *laringitis*

laser /'leɪzə(r)/ noun [C] a device that produces a controlled line of very powerful light □ *laser*

lash¹ /læʃ/ verb **1** [I,T] (used especially about wind, rain and storms) to hit sth with great force □ *memukul-mukul*: *The rain lashed against the windows.* **2** [T] to hit sb with a piece of rope, leather, etc.; to move sth like a piece of rope, leather, etc. violently □ *menyebat* **3** [T] **lash A to B; lash A and B together** to tie two things together firmly with rope, etc. □ *mengikat*: *The two boats were lashed together.*

PHR V lash out (at/against sb/sth) to suddenly attack sb/sth (with words or by hitting them or it) □ *menyerang atau mengecam (sso/sst)*: *The actor lashed out at a photographer outside his house.*

lash² /læʃ/ noun [C] **1** = **eyelash 2** a hit with a **whip** (= a long thin piece of rope or leather) □ *sebat; sebatan*

lass /læs/ (also **lassie** /'læsi/) noun [C] (*informal*) a girl or young woman □ *gadis*

HELP Lass is most commonly used in Scotland and the North of England.

lasso /læ'suː/ noun [C] (pl **lassos** or **lassoes**) a long rope that is tied in a circle at one end and is used for catching cows and horses □ *laso; tanjul* ▶ **lasso** verb [T]

495 **lard → last**

last¹ /lɑːst/ determiner, adj, adv, noun [C] (pl **the last**) **1** at the end; after all the others □ *akhir; penghabisan; hujung sekali*: *December is the last month of the year.* ◆ *Would the last person to leave please turn off the lights?* ◆ *Our house is the last one on the left.* ◆ *She lived alone for the last years of her life.* ◆ *The British athlete came in last.* ◆ *Her name is last on the list.* ◆ *Alex was the last to finish.* ◆ *They were the last to arrive.* **2** used about a time, period, event, etc. in the past that is nearest to the present □ *tadi; lalu; lepas; terakhir*: *last night/week/Saturday/summer* ◆ *We have been working on the book for the last six months.* ◆ **The last time** *I saw her was in London.* ◆ *We'll win this time, because they beat us* **last time**. ◆ *When did you last have your eyes checked?* ◆ *When I saw her last she seemed very happy.*

HELP Last or **latest**? **The latest** means 'most recent' or 'newest'. **The last** means the one before the present one: *His last novel was a huge success, but the latest one is much less popular.*

3 final □ *terakhir*: *This is my last chance to take the exam.* ◆ *Alison's retiring—tomorrow is her last day at work.* ◆ *We finished* **the last of the** *bread at breakfast so we'd better get some more.* **4** [only before a noun] not expected or not suitable □ *paling tdk dijangka; paling tdk sesuai*: *He's the last person I thought would get the job.*

IDM at (long) last in the end; finally □ *akhirnya*: *After months of separation they were together at last.*

first/last thing ⊃ **thing**

have the last laugh to be the person, team, etc. who is successful in the end □ *yg akhirnya menang atau berjaya*

have, etc. the last word to be the person who makes the final decision or the final comment □ *yg membuat kata pemutus; yg hendak menang*

in the last resort; (as) a last resort when everything else has failed; the person or thing that helps when everything else has failed □ *sebagai jalan terakhir*: *In the last resort my grandad could play in the match.*

last but not least (used before the final item in a list) just as important as all the other items □ *yg terakhir tetapi tdk kurang pentingnya*

last/next but one, two, etc. one, two, etc. away from the last/next □ *satu, dua, dsb dr hujung, akhir atau dr yg di sebelah*: *I live in the next house but one on the right.* ◆ *X is the last letter but two of the alphabet* (= the third letter from the end).

a last-ditch attempt a final effort to avoid sth unpleasant or dangerous □ *usaha terakhir*

the last minute/moment the final minute/moment before sth happens □ *pd saat terakhir*: *We arrived at the last minute to catch the train.* ◆ *a last-minute change of plan*

VOWELS iː see i any ɪ sit e ten æ hat ɑː father ɒ got ɔː saw ʊ put uː too u usual

last → latter

the last/final straw ➔ straw
▶ lastly adv: Lastly, I would like to thank the band who played this evening. SYN finally

last² /lɑːst/ verb [not used in the continuous tenses] **1** [T] to continue for a period of time □ *berlangsung; berterusan*: The exam lasts three hours. ◆ How long does a cricket match last? ◆ The flight seemed to last forever. **2** [I,T] to continue to be good or to function □ *bertahan; tahan*: Do you think this weather will last till the weekend? ◆ It's only a cheap radio but it'll probably last a year or so. **3** [I,T] to be enough for what sb needs □ *cukup; tahan*: This money won't last me till the end of the month.

> **HELP** Although this verb is not used in the continuous tenses, it is common to see the present participle (= -ing form): *An earthquake lasting approximately 20 seconds struck the city last night.*

lasting /'lɑːstɪŋ/ adj continuing for a long time □ *berpanjangan; kekal*: The book left a lasting impression on me.

last-minute adj done, decided or organized just before sth happens or before it is too late □ *pd saat-saat terakhir*: a last-minute holiday

> **EXAM TIP**
>
> **Last-minute learning**
>
> In the weeks before your exam, keep a note of any points that are particularly difficult and make a list of things to check over the evening before your exam. These might be notes in the dictionary about words that you often get confused, or verb tenses (look at the note at **tense**), or groups of words about a particular topic. Keep your last-minute list short!

last name = surname

latch¹ /lætʃ/ noun [C] **1** a small metal bar that is used for fastening a door or a gate. You have to lift the **latch** in order to open the door. □ *selak* **2** (*especially BrE*) a type of lock for a door that you open with a key from the outside □ *selak kunci*

latch² /lætʃ/ verb
PHR V latch on (to sth) (*informal*) to understand sth □ *faham (sst)*: It took them a while to latch on to what she was talking about.

late /leɪt/ adj (later; latest) adv **1** near the end of a period of time □ *lewat*: in the late afternoon/summer/20th century ◆ in the late morning ◆ His mother's in her late fifties (= between 55 and 60). ◆ in late May/late in May ◆ We got back home late in the evening. **OPP** early **2** after the usual or expected time □ *lambat; lewat*: I'm sorry I'm late. ◆ She was ten minutes late for school. ◆ The ambulance arrived too late to save him. ◆ to be late with the rent ◆ The buses are running late today. ◆ to stay up late **OPP** early **3** near the end of the day □ *lewat; larut (malam)*: It's getting late—let's go home. **OPP** early **4** [only before a noun] no longer alive; dead □ *mendiang; arwah*: his late wife

IDM an early/a late night ➔ **night**
later on at a later time □ *kemudian; kemudian hari*: Later on you'll probably wish that you'd worked harder at school. ◆ Bye—I'll see you a bit later on.
sooner or later ➔ **soon**

latecomer /'leɪtkʌmə(r)/ noun [C] a person who arrives or starts sth late □ *orang yg datang atau memulakan sst lewat*

lately /'leɪtli/ adv in the period of time up until now; recently □ *akhir-akhir ini*: What have you been doing lately? ◆ Hasn't the weather been dreadful lately? ➔ note at **recently**

latent /'leɪtnt/ adj existing, but not yet very noticeable, active or well developed □ *terpendam*: latent defects/disease ◆ latent talent

later¹ /'leɪtə(r)/ adv at a time in the future; after the time you are talking about □ *kelak; nanti*: See you later. ◆ I met her again three years later. ➔ note at **then**

later² /'leɪtə(r)/ adj coming after sth else or at a time in the future □ *kemudian*: The game has been postponed to a later date.

lateral /'lætərəl/ adj connected with the side of sth or with movement to the side □ *sisian; lateral*: the lateral branches of a tree ◆ lateral eye movements ▶ laterally /-rəli/ adv

latest /'leɪtɪst/ adj [only before a noun] very recent or new □ *terbaharu; mutakhir*: the latest fashions ◆ the latest news ◆ the terrorists' latest attack on the town ➔ note at **last¹**

the latest noun [sing] (*informal*) the most recent or the newest thing or piece of news □ *benda atau berita yg terbaharu*: This is the very latest in computer technology. ◆ This is the latest in a series of attacks by this terrorist group.
IDM at the latest no later than the time or the date mentioned □ *paling lewat; selewat-lewatnya*: You need to hand your projects in by Friday at the latest.

lather /'lɑːðə(r)/ noun [U] a white mass of bubbles that are produced when you mix soap with water □ *buih sabun*

Latin /'lætɪn/ noun [U] the language that was used in ancient Rome □ *Latin* ▶ **Latin** adj: Latin poetry ◆ Spanish, Italian and other Latin languages (= that developed from Latin)

Latin American noun [C], adj (a person who comes) from Latin America (the parts of Central and South America where Spanish or Portuguese is spoken) □ *Amerika Latin*: Latin American music

latitude /'lætɪtjuːd/ noun [U] the distance of a place north or south of the **equator** (= the line around the middle of the earth) □ *latitud* ➔ look at **longitude** ➔ picture at **earth**

> **MORE** Latitude is measured in **degrees**.

latter /'lætə(r)/ adj [only before a noun] (*formal*) nearer to the end of a period of time; later

□ *(yg) terkemudian; (bahagian) akhir*: *Interest rates should fall in the latter half of the year.* ▶ **latterly** *adv*

the latter /'lætə(r)/ *noun* [sing], *pron* the second (of two people or things that are mentioned) □ *yg kedua*: *The options were History and Geography. I chose the latter.*

> **MORE** The first of two people or things that are mentioned is **the former**.

laugh¹ /lɑːf/ *verb* [I] to make the sounds that show you are happy or amused □ *ketawa; gelak*: *His jokes always make me laugh.* ♦ *to laugh out loud* ⊃ note at **humour**
IDM **die laughing** ⊃ **die**
PHR V **laugh at sb/sth** **1** to show, by laughing, that you think sb/sth is funny □ *ketawa/geli hati melihat (sso/sst)*: *The children laughed at the clown.* **2** to show that you think sb is ridiculous □ *mentertawakan*: *Don't laugh at him. He can't help the way he speaks.*

laugh² /lɑːf/ *noun* [C] **1** the sound or act of laughing □ *ketawa*: *Her jokes got a lot of laughs.* ♦ *We all had a good laugh at what he'd written.* **2 a laugh** [sing] (*informal*) an occasion or a person that is very funny □ *sso/sst yg menggelikan hati*: *The party was a good laugh.*
IDM **for a laugh** as a joke □ *utk bergurau/bersuka-suka; sebagai jenaka*
have the last laugh ⊃ **last¹**

laughable /'lɑːfəbl/ *adj* deserving to be laughed at; of very poor quality; ridiculous □ *yg menggelikan hati; tdk masuk akal*

laughing stock *noun* [C] a person or thing that other people laugh at (in an unpleasant way) □ *bahan ketawa*

laughter /'lɑːftə(r)/ *noun* [U] the sound or act of laughing □ *gelak ketawa; ketawa*: *Everyone roared with laughter.*

launch¹ /lɔːntʃ/ *verb* [T] **1** to start sth new or to show sth for the first time □ *melancarkan*: *to launch a new product onto the market* **2** to send sth such as a **spacecraft** (= a vehicle that travels in space), weapon, etc. into space, into the sky or through the water □ *melancarkan*: *to launch a missile* ♦ *The lifeboat was launched immediately.*

launch² /lɔːntʃ/ *noun* [C] **1** [usually sing] the act of **launching** a ship, **spacecraft** (= a vehicle that travels in space), new product, etc. □ *pelancaran*: *The official launch date for our newest product is 10 May.* **2** a large motorboat □ *motobot besar*

launder /'lɔːndə(r)/ *verb* [T] **1** (*formal*) to wash, dry and iron clothes, etc. □ *mendobi; membasuh dan menyeterika*: *freshly laundered sheets* **2** to move money that has been obtained illegally into foreign bank accounts or legal businesses so that it is difficult for other people to know where the money came from □ *melaburkan wang haram*

launderette (also **laundrette**) /lɔːn'dret/ (*AmE* **Laundromat**™ /'lɔːndrəmæt/) *noun* [C] a type of shop where you pay to wash and dry your clothes in machines □ *kedai dobi layan diri*

laundry /'lɔːndri/ *noun* (*pl* **laundries**) **1** [U] clothes, etc. that need washing or that are being washed □ *kain baju kotor*: *dirty laundry* ⊃ A more common expression is **the washing**. **2** [C] a business where you send sheets, clothes, etc. to be washed and dried □ *kedai dobi*

lava /'lɑːvə/ *noun* [U] hot liquid rock that comes out of a **volcano** (= a mountain that explodes) □ *lava; lahar* ⊃ picture at **volcano**

lavatory /'lævətri/ *noun* [C] (*pl* **lavatories**) (*formal*) **1** a toilet □ *tandas* **2** a room that contains a toilet, a place to wash your hands, etc. □ *bilik air*: *Where's the ladies' lavatory, please?* ⊃ note at **toilet**

lavender /'lævəndə(r)/ *noun* [U] a garden plant with purple flowers that smells very pleasant □ *lavender*

lavish¹ /'lævɪʃ/ *adj* **1** large in amount or number □ *mewah; berlebih-lebihan*: *a lavish meal* **2** giving or spending a large amount of money □ *sungguh banyak*: *She was always very lavish with her presents.*

lavish² /'lævɪʃ/ *verb*
PHR V **lavish sth on sb/sth** to give a lot of sth, often too much, to sb/sth □ *memberi (sst) dgn banyak atau berlebih-lebihan kpd sso; melimpahi*

law /lɔː/ *noun* **1 the law** [U] all the laws in a country or state □ *undang-undang*: *Stealing is against the law.* ♦ *to break the law* ♦ *to obey the law* ⊃ look at **legal 2** [C] an official rule of a country or state that says what people may or may not do □ *undang-undang*: *There's a new law about the use of mobile phones while driving.* ⊃ note at **rule 3** [U] the law as a subject of study or as a profession □ *undang-undang*: *She is studying law.* ♦ *My brother works for a law firm in Brighton.* ⊃ look at **legal 4** [C] (in science) a statement of what always happens in certain situations or conditions □ *hukum*: *the laws of mathematics/gravity*
IDM **law and order** a situation in which the law is obeyed □ *undang-undang dan ketenteraman* ⊃ note at **court**, **crime**

law-abiding *adj* (used about a person) obeying the law □ *patuh kpd undang-undang*: *law-abiding citizens*

lawbreaker /'lɔːbreɪkə(r)/ *noun* [C] a person who does not obey the law; a criminal □ *orang yg melanggar undang-undang; penjenayah*

law court *noun* [C] (*BrE*) = **court¹** (1)

lawful /'lɔːfl/ *adj* allowed or recognized by law □ *sah; menurut undang-undang*: *We shall use all lawful means to obtain our demands.* ⊃ look at **legal**, **legitimate**

lawless /'lɔːləs/ *adj* (used about a person or their actions) breaking the law □ *tdk berun-*

lawn → lead

dang-undang; tdk mematuhi undang-undang ▶**lawlessness** *noun* [U]

lawn /lɔːn/ *noun* [C,U] an area of grass in a garden or park that is regularly cut □ *halaman berumput* ➜ picture on **page P9**

lawnmower /ˈlɔːnməʊə(r)/ *noun* [C] a machine that is used for cutting the grass in a garden □ *mesin rumput* ➜ picture at **garden**

lawsuit /ˈlɔːsuːt/ *noun* [C] a legal argument in a court of law that is between two people or groups and not between the police and a criminal □ *tuntutan mahkamah*: *to file a lawsuit*

lawyer /ˈlɔːjə(r)/ *noun* [C] a person who is trained and qualified to advise people about the law □ *peguam*: *to consult a lawyer*

> **MORE** A **solicitor** is a lawyer who gives legal advice, prepares legal documents, arranges the buying or selling of land, etc. A **barrister** is a lawyer who speaks for you in a court of law. The American term is **attorney**.

lax /læks/ *adj* not having high standards; not strict □ *tdk ketat; cuai*: *Their security checks are rather lax.* **SYN** careless

laxative /ˈlæksətɪv/ *noun* [C] a medicine, food or drink that makes the body get rid of solid waste material easily □ *laksatif; julap* ▶**laxative** *adj*

lay¹ /leɪ/ *verb* [T] (*pt, pp* laid /leɪd/)
▶PUT DOWN **1** to put sb/sth carefully in a particular position or on a surface □ *meletakkan; membentangkan*: *Before they started, they laid newspaper on the floor.* ♦ *He laid the child gently down on her bed.* ♦ *'Don't worry,' she said, laying her hand on my shoulder.* ➜ note at **lie²** **2** to put sth in the correct position for a particular purpose □ *memasang*: *They're laying new electricity cables in our street.*
▶EGGS **3** to produce eggs □ *bertelur*: *Hens lay eggs.*
▶PREPARE **4** to prepare sth for use □ *memasang; menyediakan*: *The police have laid a trap for him and I think they'll catch him this time.* ♦ *Can you lay the table please* (= put the knives, forks, plates, etc. on it)?
▶WITH NOUN **5** (used with some nouns to give a similar meaning to a verb) to put □ *meletakkan*: *They laid all the blame on him* (= they said he was responsible). ♦ *to lay emphasis on something* (= emphasize it)
IDM get/lay your hands on sb/sth ➜ **hand¹**
PHR V lay sth down to give sth as a rule □ *menetapkan; ditetapkan*: *It's all laid down in the rules of the club.*
lay off (sb) (*informal*) to stop annoying sb □ *berhenti mengganggu sso*: *Can't you lay off me for a bit?*
lay sb off to stop giving work to sb □ *memberhentikan kerja (sso)*: *They've laid off 500 workers at the car factory.*

lay sth on (*informal*) to provide sth □ *menyediakan/memberi sst*: *They're laying on a trip to London for everybody.*
lay sth out **1** to spread out a number of things so that you can see them easily or so that they look nice □ *mempamerkan; meletakkan*: *All the food was laid out on a table in the garden.* **2** to arrange sth in a planned way □ *menyusun atur*: *The new shopping centre is very attractively laid out.*

lay² /leɪ/ *adj* [only *before* a noun] **1** without special training in or knowledge of a particular subject □ *orang biasa (bukan profesional)* **2** (used about a religious teacher) who has not been officially trained as a priest □ *bukan paderi*: *a lay preacher*

lay³ *past tense of* **lie²**

layabout /ˈleɪəbaʊt/ *noun* [C] (*BrE informal*) a person who is lazy and does not do much work □ *pemalas; berat tulang*

'lay-by (*pl* lay-bys) (*AmE* ˈrest area; ˈrest stop) *noun* [C] an area at the side of a road where vehicles can stop for a short time □ *hentian sebelah jalan*

layer /ˈleɪə(r)/ *noun* [C] a piece or quantity of sth that is on sth else or between other things □ *lapisan; lapis*: *A thin layer of dust covered everything in the room.* ♦ *It's very cold. You'll need several layers of clothing.* ♦ *the top/bottom layer* ♦ *the inner/outer layer*

layman /ˈleɪmən/ *noun* [C] (*pl* -men /-mən/) (also **layperson**) a person who does not have special training in or knowledge of a particular subject □ *orang biasa/awam*: *a medical reference book for the layman*

layout /ˈleɪaʊt/ *noun* [C, usually sing] the way in which the parts of sth are arranged □ *susun atur, reka letak*: *The magazine has a new page layout.*

laze /leɪz/ *verb* [I] **laze (about/around)** to do very little; to rest or relax □ *bermalas-malas; bersantai*

lazy /ˈleɪzi/ *adj* (lazier; laziest) **1** (used about a person) not wanting to work □ *malas*: *Don't be lazy. Come and give me a hand.* **2** making you feel that you do not want to do very much □ *bermalas-malas*: *a lazy summer's afternoon* **3** moving slowly or without much energy □ *malas*: *a lazy smile* ▶**lazily** *adv* ▶**laziness** *noun* [U]

lb *abbr* **pound(s)**; a measure of weight □ *lb (paun)*

lead¹ /liːd/ *verb* (*pt, pp* led /led/)
▶SHOW THE WAY **1** [T] to go with or in front of a person or an animal to show the way or to make them or it go in the right direction □ *membawa; menuntun; memimpin*: *The teacher led the children out of the hall and back to the classroom.* ♦ *She led the horse into its stable.* ♦ *The receptionist led the way to the boardroom.* ♦ *to lead somebody by the hand*

> **HELP** Lead, guide or direct? You usually **guide** a tourist or somebody who needs special help,

[I] **intransitive**, a verb which has no object: *He laughed.*   [T] **transitive**, a verb which has an object: *He ate an apple.*

by going with them: *to guide visitors around Oxford* ♦ *He guided the blind woman to her seat.* If you **direct** somebody, you explain with words how to get somewhere: *Could you direct me to the nearest Post Office, please?*

▶ROAD/PATH **2** [I] to go to a place □ *menuju/menghala ke*: *I don't think this path leads anywhere.*
▶CAUSE **3** [I] **lead to sth** to have sth as a result □ *membawa kpd; mengakibatkan*: *Eating too much sugar can lead to all sorts of health problems.* **4** [T] **lead sb to do sth** to influence what sb does or thinks □ *menyebabkan; mendorong; mempengaruhi*: *He led me to believe he really meant what he said.*
▶LIFE **5** [T] to have a particular type of life □ *menjalani*: *They lead a very busy life.* ♦ *to lead a life of crime*
▶BE BEST/FIRST **6** [I,T] to be winning or in first place in front of sb □ *mendahului*: *The champion is leading (her rival) by 18 seconds.* ♦ *The department led the world in cancer research.*
▶BE IN CONTROL **7** [I,T] to be in control or the leader of sth □ *mengetuai*: *to lead a discussion*
IDM **lead sb astray** to make sb start behaving or thinking in the wrong way □ *menyebabkan sso terpesong/tersesat*
PHR V **lead up to sth** to be an introduction to or cause of sth □ *membawa kpd*

lead² /liːd/ *noun*
▶FIRST PLACE **1 the lead** [sing] the first place or position in front of other people or organizations □ *tempat pertama; berada di hadapan*: *The French athlete has gone into the lead.* ♦ *Who is in the lead?* ♦ *Britain has taken the lead in developing computer software for that market.* **2** [sing] the distance or amount by which sb/sth is in front of another person or thing □ *mendahului*: *The company has a lead of several years in the development of the new technology.*
▶INFORMATION **3** [C] a piece of information that may help to give the answer to a problem □ *petunjuk*: *The police are following all possible leads to track down the killer.*
▶ACTOR **4** [C] the main part in a play, show or other situation □ *peranan/watak utama*: *Who's playing the lead in the new film?* ♦ *Jill played a lead role in getting the company back into profit.*
▶FOR DOG **5** [C] a long piece of leather, chain or rope that is used for controlling a dog. The **lead** is connected to a **collar** (= a band that is put around the neck) □ *tali cawak; rantai anjing*: *All dogs must be kept on a lead.*
▶FOR ELECTRICITY **6** [C] a piece of wire that carries electricity to a piece of equipment □ *wayar*: *The lead on this stereo isn't long enough.*
IDM **follow sb's example/lead** ⊃ **follow**

lead³ /led/ *noun* **1** [U] (*symbol* Pb) a soft heavy grey metal. Lead is used in pipes, roofs, etc. □ *plumbum* **2** [C,U] the black substance inside a pencil that makes a mark when you write □ *grafit* ⊃ picture at **stationery**

leader /ˈliːdə(r)/ *noun* [C] **1** a person who is a manager or in charge of sth □ *ketua*: *a strong leader* ♦ *She is a natural leader* (= she knows how

to tell other people what to do). **2** the person or thing that is best or in first place □ *sso/sst yg terbaik atau mendahului yg lain*: *The leader has just finished the third lap.* ♦ *The new shampoo soon became a market leader.*

leadership /ˈliːdəʃɪp/ *noun* **1** [U] the state or position of being a manager or the person in charge □ *pucuk pimpinan*: *Who will take over the leadership of the party?* **2** [U] the qualities that a leader should have □ *daya kepimpinan*: *She's got good leadership skills.* **3** [C, with sing or pl verb] the people who are in charge of a country, an organization, etc. □ *pemimpin; pucuk pimpinan*

leading /ˈliːdɪŋ/ *adj* [only *before* a noun] **1** best or most important □ *utama; terkemuka*: *He's one of the leading experts in this field.* ♦ *She played a leading role in getting the business started.* **2** that tries to make sb give a particular answer □ *soalan pimpin*: *The lawyer was warned not to ask the witness leading questions.*

lead story /ˈliːd stɔːri/ *noun* [C] (*pl* **lead stories**) the most important piece of news in a newspaper or on a news programme □ *berita utama*

leaf¹ /liːf/ *noun* [C] (*pl* **leaves** /liːvz/) one of the thin, flat, usually green parts of a plant or tree □ *daun*: *The trees lose their leaves in autumn.* ⊃ picture at **plant**, **tree**

leaf² /liːf/ *verb*
PHR V **leaf through sth** to turn the pages of a book, etc. quickly and without looking at them carefully □ *menyelak-nyelak (buku, dsb)*

leaflet /ˈliːflət/ *noun* [C] a printed piece of paper that gives information about sth. **Leaflets** are usually given free of charge □ *risalah*: *I picked up a leaflet advertising a new club.*

leafy /ˈliːfi/ *adj* (**leafier**; **leafiest**) **1** having many leaves □ *berdaun lebat; rimbun*: *leafy green vegetables* **2** (used about a place) with many trees □ *banyak pokok*

league /liːɡ/ *noun* [C] **1** a group of sports clubs that compete with each other for a prize □ *liga*: *the football league* ♦ *Which team is top of the league at the moment?* ⊃ look at **rugby** **2** a level of quality, ability, etc. □ *taraf*: *He is so much better than the others. They're just not in the same league.* **3** a group of people, countries, etc. that join together for a particular purpose □ *liga*: *the Women's League for Peace*
IDM **in league (with sb)** having a secret agreement (with sb) □ *berpakat (dgn sso)*

leak¹ /liːk/ *verb* **1** [I,T] to allow liquid or gas to get through a hole or crack □ *bocor*: *The boat was leaking badly.* **2** [I] (used about liquid or gas) to get out through a hole or crack □ *bocor; tiris*: *Water is leaking in through the roof.* **3** [T] **leak sth (to sb)** to give secret information to sb □ *membocorkan*: *The committee's findings were leaked to the press before the report was published.*

leak → learnt

PHR V **leak out** (used about secret information) to become known □ *diketahui orang*

leak² /liːk/ *noun* [C] **1** a small hole or crack which liquid or gas can get through □ *bocor; bocoran*: *There's a leak in the pipe.* ♦ *The roof has sprung a leak.* **2** the liquid or gas that gets through a hole □ *bocoran*: *a gas leak* **3** the act of giving away information that should be kept secret □ *kebocoran* ▶ **leaky** *adj*

leakage /ˈliːkɪdʒ/ *noun* [C,U] the act of coming out of a hole or crack; the liquid or gas that comes out □ *kebocoran*: *a leakage of dangerous chemicals*

lean

She is leaning against a tree.   He is leaning out of a window.

lean¹ /liːn/ *verb* (*pt, pp* **leant** /lent/ *or* **leaned** /liːnd/) **1** [I] to move the top part of your body and head forwards, backwards or to the side □ *bersandar; membongkok; menjengah; menjenguk*: *He leaned across the table to pick up the phone.* ♦ *She leaned out of the window and waved.* ♦ *Just lean back and relax.* **2** [I] to be in a position that is not straight or vertical □ *senget; condong*: *That wardrobe leans to the right.* **3** [I,T] **lean (sth) against/on sth** to rest against sth so that it gives support; to put sth in this position □ *menyandarkan; bersandar*: *She stopped and leant on the gate.* ♦ *Please don't lean bicycles against this window.*

lean² /liːn/ *adj* **1** (used about a person or an animal) thin and in good health □ *kurus* **2** (used about meat) having little or no fat □ *tdk berlemak* **3** not producing much □ *sedikit; tdk berhasil sangat*: *a lean harvest*

leap¹ /liːp/ *verb* [I] (*pt, pp* **leapt** /lept/ *or* **leaped** /liːpt/) **1** to jump high or a long way □ *melompat; melonjak*: *The horse leapt over the wall.* ♦ *A fish suddenly leapt out of the water.* ♦ *We all leapt into the air when they scored the goal.* ♦ (figurative) *Share prices leapt to a record high yesterday.* **2** to move quickly □ *bergerak cepat-cepat (bingkas, melenting, menerpa, dsb)*: *I looked at the clock and leapt out of bed.* ♦ *She leapt back when the pan caught fire.*

PHR V **leap at sth** to accept a chance or offer with enthusiasm □ *cepat-cepat menerima*: *She leapt at the chance to work in TV.*

leap² /liːp/ *noun* [C] **1** a big jump □ *lompatan; lonjakan*: *He took a flying leap at the wall but didn't get over it.* ♦ (figurative) *My heart gave a leap when I heard the news.* **2** a sudden large change or increase in sth □ *kemajuan besar; peningkatan yg mendadak*: *The development of penicillin was a great leap forward in the field of medicine.*

leapfrog /ˈliːpfrɒɡ/ (*AmE* also) / *noun* [U] a children's game in which one person bends over and another person jumps over their back □ *main lompat katak*

leapt *past tense, past participle* of **leap¹**

leapfrog

'leap year *noun* [C] one year in every four, in which February has 29 days instead of 28 □ *tahun lompat*

learn /lɜːn/ *verb* (*pt, pp* **learnt** /lɜːnt/ *or* **learned** /lɜːnd/) **1** [I,T] **learn (sth) (from sb/sth)** to get knowledge, a skill, etc. (from sb/sth) □ *belajar*: *I'm not very good at driving yet—I'm still learning.* ♦ *We're learning about China at school.* ♦ *Debbie is learning to play the piano.* ♦ *to learn a foreign language/a musical instrument* ♦ *Where did you learn how to swim?* ⊃ note at **study 2** [I] **learn (of/about) sth** to get some information about sth; to find out □ *mengetahui; mendapat tahu*: *I was sorry to learn about your father's death.* **3** [T] to study sth so that you can repeat it from memory □ *menghafal*: *The teacher said we have to learn the poem for tomorrow.* **4** [I] to understand or realize □ *faham; menyedari*: *We should have learned by now that we can't rely on her.* ♦ *It's important to learn from your mistakes.*

IDM **learn the hard way** to understand or realize sth by having an unpleasant experience rather than by being told □ *belajar drpd pengalaman pahit*

learn your lesson to understand what you must do/not do in the future because you have had an unpleasant experience □ *mengambil iktibar; belajar; serik*

show sb/know/learn the ropes ⊃ **rope¹**

learned /ˈlɜːnɪd/ *adj* having a lot of knowledge from studying; for people who have a lot of knowledge □ *berilmu; ilmiah*: *a learned scholar* ♦ *a learned journal*

learner /ˈlɜːnə(r)/ *noun* [C] a person who is learning □ *orang yg baru/sedang belajar*: *a learner driver* ♦ *textbooks for young learners*

learning /ˈlɜːnɪŋ/ *noun* [U] **1** the process of learning sth □ *pembelajaran*: *new methods of language learning* **2** knowledge that you get from studying □ *ilmu*

learnt *past tense, past participle* of **learn**

lease /liːs/ noun [C] a legal agreement that allows you to use a building or land for a fixed period of time in return for rent □ *perjanjian sewa; pajakan*: The lease on the flat runs out/expires next year. ▶**lease** verb [T]: They lease the land from a local farmer. ◆ Part of the building is leased out to tenants.

least /liːst/ determiner, pron, adv **1** [used as the superlative of *little*] smallest in size, amount, degree, etc. □ *paling kecil, sedikit, kurang, dsb*: He's got the least experience of all of us. ◆ You've done the most work, and I'm afraid John has done the least. **2** less than anyone/anything else; less than at any other time □ *paling (tdk perlu, kurang mahal, tdk dijangka, dll)*: He's the person who needs help least. ◆ I bought the least expensive tickets. ◆ My uncle always appears when we're least expecting him. **OPP** for both meanings **most**

IDM at least 1 not less than, and probably more □ *sekurang-kurangnya*: It'll take us at least two hours to get there. **2** even if nothing else is true or you do nothing else □ *sekurang-kurangnya; setidak-tidaknya*: It may not be beautiful but at least it's cheap. ◆ You could at least say you're sorry! **3** used for correcting sth that you have just said □ *kalau tdk silaplah*: I saw him—at least I think I saw him.

at the (very) least not less and probably much more □ *paling kurang pun; paling tdk pun*: It'll take six months to build, at the very least.

last but not least ⊃ last¹

least of all especially not □ *lebih-lebih lagi*: Nobody should be worried, least of all you.

not in the least (bit) not at all □ *sama sekali tdk; tdk langsung pun*: It doesn't matter in the least. ◆ I'm not in the least bit worried.

to say the least ⊃ say¹

leather /ˈleðə(r)/ noun [U] the skin of animals which has been specially treated. Leather is used to make shoes, bags, coats, etc. □ *kulit*: a leather jacket

leave¹ /liːv/ verb (pt, pp **left** /left/)
▸GO AWAY **1** [I,T] to go away from sb/sth □ *meninggalkan; pergi; bertolak; berhenti*: We should leave now if we're going to get there by 8 o'clock. ◆ I felt sick in class so I left the room. ◆ At what age do most people leave school in your country? ◆ Hal left his wife for another woman.

HELP Leave or **depart?** If you **leave** sb/sth it may be permanently or just for a short time: He leaves the house at 8.00 every morning. ◆ He left New York and went to live in Canada. **Depart** is a more formal word and is used about boats, trains, aeroplanes, etc: The 6.15 train for Bath departs from Platform 3.

▸LET STH STAY **2** [T] to cause or allow sb/sth to stay in a particular place or condition; to not deal with sth □ *membiarkan; biarkan*: Leave the door open, please. ◆ Don't leave the iron on when you are not using it. ◆ Why do you always leave your homework till the last minute?
▸PUT **3** [T] to put sth somewhere □ *meninggalkan*: Val left a message on her answerphone. ◆ I left him a note.
▸CAUSE **4** [T] to make sth happen or stay as a result □ *meninggalkan*: Don't put that cup on the table. It'll leave a mark.
▸REMAIN **5** [T] to not use sth □ *tinggalkan; meninggalkan*: Leave some milk for me, please.
▸FORGET **6** [T] **leave sth (behind)** to forget to bring sth with you □ *tertinggal*: I'm afraid I've left my homework at home. Can I give it to you tomorrow? ◆ I can't find my glasses. Maybe I left them behind at work. ⊃ note at **forget**
▸AFTER DEATH **7** [T] to give sth to sb when you die □ *meninggalkan; mewariskan*: In his will he left everything to his three sons.
▸RESPONSIBILITY **8** [T] to give the care of or responsibility for sb/sth to another person □ *menyerahkan*: I'll leave it to you to organize all the food.

IDM be left high and dry to be left without help in a difficult situation □ *terbiar; terlantar; ditinggalkan terkapai-kapai*

leave sb/sth alone to not touch, annoy or speak to sb/sth □ *biarkan atau jangan ganggu sso/sst*

leave go (of sth) to stop touching or holding sth □ *lepaskan sst*: Leave go of my arm—you're hurting me!

leave sb in the lurch to leave sb without help in a difficult situation □ *meninggalkan sso dlm keadaan susah*

leave sth on one side ⊃ side¹

PHR V leave sb/sth out (of sth) to not include sb/sth □ *tdk memasukkan (sso/sst), meninggalkan/tertinggal (sso/sst)*: This doesn't make sense. I think you've left out a word.

leave² /liːv/ noun [U] a period of time when you do not go to work □ *cuti*: Diplomats working abroad usually get a month's home leave each year. ◆ annual leave ◆ sick leave ◆ Molly's not working—she's **on maternity leave**. ⊃ note at **holiday**

leaves plural of **leaf¹**

lecture /ˈlektʃə(r)/ noun [C] **1** a lecture (on/about sth) a talk that is given to a group of people to teach them about a particular subject, especially as part of a university course □ *kuliah; syarahan*: The college has asked a journalist to come and **give a lecture** on the media. ◆ a course of lectures ⊃ note at **university 2** a serious talk to sb that explains what they have done wrong or how they should behave □ *teguran; khutbah*: We got a lecture from a policeman about playing near the railway. ▶**lecture** verb [I,T]: Alex lectures in European Studies at London University. ◆ The policeman lectured the boys about playing ball games in the road.

lecturer /ˈlektʃərə(r)/ noun [C] a person who gives talks to teach people about a subject, especially as a job in a university □ *pensyarah*

led past tense, past participle of **lead¹**

ledge /ledʒ/ noun [C] a narrow shelf underneath a window, or a narrow piece of rock that sticks out on the side of a **cliff** (= a high steep area of rock) or mountain □ *belebas*

leech → legitimate 502

leech /li:tʃ/ noun [C] a small creature with a soft body and no legs that usually lives in water and that fastens itself to other creatures and sucks their blood □ *lintah*

leek /li:k/ noun [C] a long thin vegetable that is white at one end with thin green leaves □ *lik (sayur)* ⊃ picture on **page P15**

left¹ past tense, past participle of **leave**¹

left² /left/ adj 1 [only before a noun] on the side where your heart is in the body □ *kiri*: *I've broken my left arm.* **OPP right** 2 still available after everything else has been taken or used □ *tinggal; masih ada lagi*: *Is there any bread left?* ♦ *How much time do we have left?* ♦ *If there's any money left over, we'll have a cup of coffee.*

left³ /left/ adv to or towards the left □ *ke kiri; ke arah kiri*: *Turn left just past the Post Office.* **OPP right**

left⁴ /left/ noun [sing] 1 the left side □ *sebelah kiri*: *In Britain we drive on the left.* ♦ *Our house is just to/on the left of that tall building.* ♦ *If you look to your left you'll see one of the city's most famous landmarks.* **OPP right** 2 **the Left** [with sing or pl verb] political parties or groups that support **socialism** (= the political idea that everyone is equal and that money should be equally divided) □ *puak/sayap kiri*: *The Left is/are losing popularity.* ⊃ look at **left wing**

left-hand adj [only before a noun] of or on the left □ *sebelah kiri*: *the left-hand side of the road* ♦ *a left-hand drive car* **OPP right-hand**

left-'handed adj, adv 1 using the left hand rather than the right hand □ *kidal*: *Are you left-handed?* ♦ *I write left-handed.* 2 made for left-handed people to use □ *utk orang kidal*: *left-handed scissors* **OPP right-handed**

left-'luggage office (*AmE* **'baggage room**) noun [C] the place at a railway station, etc. where you can leave your luggage for a short time □ *pejabat bagasi*

leftovers /ˈleftəʊvəz/ noun [pl] food that has not been eaten when a meal has finished □ *baki makanan*

left 'wing noun [sing] 1 [with sing or pl verb] the members of a political party, group, etc. that want more social change than the others in their party □ *golongan sayap kiri*: *the left wing of the Labour Party* 2 the left side of the field in some team sports □ *bahagian kiri; sayap kiri*: *He plays on the left wing for Manchester United.* ▸**left-wing** adj **OPP right wing**

leg /leg/ noun [C] 1 one of the parts of the body on which a person or an animal stands or walks □ *kaki*: *A spider has eight legs.* ♦ *She sat down and crossed her legs.* ⊃ picture at **body** 2 the part of a pair of trousers, etc. that covers the leg □ *bahagian kaki*: *There's a hole in the leg of my trousers/ my trouser leg.* 3 one of the parts of a chair, table etc. on which it stands □ *kaki*: *the leg of a chair/ table* ♦ *a chair/table leg* 4 one part or section of a journey, competition, etc. □ *bahagian; peringkat*: *The band are in Germany on the first leg of their world tour.*
IDM pull sb's leg ⊃ **pull**¹
stretch your legs ⊃ **stretch**¹

legacy /ˈlegəsi/ noun [C] (pl **legacies**) money or property that is given to you after sb dies, because they wanted you to have it □ *harta pusaka; warisan*: *He received a large legacy from his grandmother.*

legal /ˈli:gl/ adj 1 [only before a noun] using or connected with the law □ *(berkaitan dgn) undang-undang*: *legal advice* ♦ *to take legal action against somebody* ♦ *the legal profession* 2 allowed by law □ *sah; dibenarkan oleh undang-undang*: *It is not legal to drive a car without insurance.* **OPP illegal** ⊃ look at **lawful**, **legitimate** ▸**legally** /ˈli:gəli/ adv: *Schools are legally responsible for the safety of their pupils.*

legality /li:ˈgæləti/ noun [U] the state of being legal □ *kesahan; sahnya* **OPP illegality**

legalize (also **-ise**) /ˈli:gəlaɪz/ verb [T] to make sth legal □ *membenarkan di sisi undang-undang; mengesahkan*

legend /ˈledʒənd/ noun 1 [C,U] an old story or group of stories that may or may not be true; this type of story □ *legenda*: *the legend of Robin Hood* ♦ *According to legend, Robin Hood lived in Sherwood Forest.* **SYN myth** 2 [C] a famous person or event □ *legenda*: *a movie/jazz/baseball legend* ⊃ look at **star** ▸**legendary** /ˈledʒəndri/ adj: *the legendary heroes of Greek myths* ♦ *Michael Jordan, the legendary basketball star*

leggings /ˈleɡɪŋz/ noun [pl] a piece of women's clothing that fits tightly over both legs from the waist to the feet, like a very thin pair of trousers □ *seluar leging*

legible /ˈledʒəbl/ adj that is clear enough to be read easily □ *mudah dibaca*: *His writing is so small that it's barely legible.* ♦ *legible handwriting* **OPP illegible** ⊃ look at **readable** ▸**legibility** /ˌledʒəˈbɪləti/ noun [U] ▸**legibly** /ˈledʒəbli/ adv

legislate /ˈledʒɪsleɪt/ verb [I] **legislate (for/ against sth)** to make a law or laws □ *menggubal*

legislation /ˌledʒɪsˈleɪʃn/ noun [U] 1 a group of laws □ *undang-undang; perundangan*: *The government is introducing new legislation to help small businesses.* 2 the process of making laws □ *penggubalan*

legislative /ˈledʒɪslətɪv/ adj [only before a noun] (*formal*) connected with the act of making and passing laws □ *perundangan*: *a legislative assembly/body/council*

legislature /ˈledʒɪsleɪtʃə(r)/ noun [C] (*formal*) a group of people who have the power to make and change laws □ *badan perundangan*: *the national/state legislature* ⊃ look at **executive**, **judiciary**

legitimate /lɪˈdʒɪtɪmət/ adj 1 reasonable or acceptable □ *wajar; munasabah*: *a legitimate*

ʌ **c**u**p**   ɜː **b**i**rd**   ə **a**go   eɪ **p**ay   əʊ **g**o   aɪ **m**y   aʊ **n**ow   ɔɪ **b**oy   ɪə **n**ear   eə **h**air   ʊə **p**ure

excuse/question/concern **2** allowed by law □ *sah: Could he earn so much from legitimate business activities?* **OPP illegitimate** ➔ look at **lawful**, **legal** **3** (*old-fashioned*) (used about a child) having parents who are married to each other □ *sah* **OPP illegitimate** ▶**legitimacy** /lɪˈdʒɪtɪməsi/ *noun* [U] ▶**legitimately** *adv*

leisure /ˈleʒə(r)/ *noun* [U] the time when you do not have to work; free time □ *masa lapang: Shorter working hours mean that people have more leisure.* ♦ *leisure activities* ➔ picture on **page P3**

IDM **at your leisure** (*formal*) when you have free time □ *bila lapang/senang: Take this document home and read it at your leisure.*

ˈleisure centre *noun* [C] a public building where you can do sports and other activities in your free time □ *pusat kegiatan masa lapang*

leisurely /ˈleʒəli/ *adj* without hurry □ *tanpa gopoh-gapah: a leisurely Sunday breakfast* ♦ *I always cycle at a leisurely pace.*

lemon /ˈlemən/ *noun* [C,U] a yellow fruit with sour juice that is used for giving flavour to food and drink □ *lemon: a slice of lemon* ♦ *Add the juice of 2 lemons.* ➔ note at **rind** ➔ picture on **page P14**

lemonade /ˌleməˈneɪd/ *noun* [C,U] **1** (*BrE*) a sweet lemon drink with a lot of bubbles in it □ *lemonad* **2** a drink that is made from fresh lemon juice, sugar and water □ *minuman/air lemon*

lend /lend/ *verb* [T] (*pt, pp* **lent** /lent/) **1** **lend sb sth**; **lend sth to sb** to allow sb to use sth for a short time or to give sb money that must be paid back after a certain period of time □ *meminjamkan: Could you lend me £10 until Friday?* ♦ *He lent me his bicycle.* ♦ *He lent his bicycle to me.* ➔ picture at **borrow**

HELP Be careful not to confuse **lend** with its opposite **borrow**.

2 (*formal*) **lend sth (to sth)** to give or add sth □ *memberi/menambah (sst): to lend advice/support* ♦ *This evidence lends weight to our theory.*

IDM **lend (sb) a hand/lend a hand (to sb)** to help sb □ *menolong (sso)*

PHR V **lend itself to sth** to be suitable for sth □ *sesuai utk sst*

lender /ˈlendə(r)/ *noun* [C] a person or an organization that lends sth, especially money □ *pemberi pinjaman*

length /leŋθ/ *noun*
▶SIZE/MEASUREMENT **1** [U,C] how long sth is; the size of sth from one end to the other □ *panjang; panjangnya: to measure the length of a room* ♦ *It took an hour to walk the length of Oxford Street.* ♦ *The tiny insect is only one millimetre in length.* ♦ *This snake can grow to a length of two metres.* ➔ look at **width**, **breadth**
▶TIME **2** [U] the amount of time that sth lasts □ *lamanya: Many people complained about the length of time they had to wait.* ♦ *the length of a class/speech/film*

503

leisure → lens

length

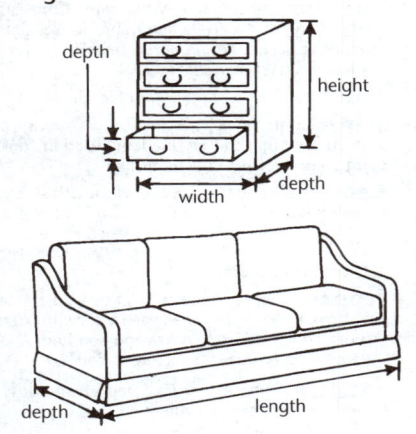

▶OF BOOK, ETC. **3** [U] the number of pages in a book, a letter, etc. □ *panjang: Her novels vary in length.*
▶OF SWIMMING POOL **4** [C] the distance from one end of a swimming pool to the other □ *jarak (panjang) kolam renang: I can swim a length in thirty seconds.*
▶LONG THIN PIECE **5** [C] a piece of sth long and thin □ *keping; batang; utas: a length of material/rope/string*

IDM **at length** for a long time or in great detail □ *dgn lama sekali; dgn panjang lebar: We discussed the matter at great length.*
go to great lengths ➔ **great¹**
the length and breadth of sth to or in all parts of sth □ *serata pelosok/ceruk rantau: They travelled the length and breadth of India.*

lengthen /ˈleŋθən/ *verb* [I,T] to become longer or to make sth longer □ *memanjang; memanjangkan; melabuhkan (pakaian)*

lengthways /ˈleŋθweɪz/ (also **lengthwise** /ˈleŋθwaɪz/) *adv* in a direction from one end to the other of sth □ *secara memanjang: Fold the paper lengthwise.*

lengthy /ˈleŋθi/ *adj* (**lengthier**; **lengthiest**) very long □ *panjang lebar; lama*

lenient /ˈliːniənt/ *adj* (used about a punishment or person who punishes) not as strict as expected □ *tdk keras; ringan; bersikap lembut* ▶**leniency** /ˈliːniənsi/ (also **lenience**) *noun* [U] ▶**leniently** *adv*

lens /lenz/ *noun* [C] **1** a curved piece of glass that makes things look bigger, clearer, etc. when you look through it □ *kanta* ➔ picture at **camera**

MORE Some people wear **contact lenses** to help them see better. You may use a **zoom** or **telephoto lens** on your camera.

2 = **contact lens** ➔ picture at **glasses**

Lent /lent/ noun [U] a period of 40 days starting in February or March, when some Christians stop doing or eating certain things for religious reasons □ *Lent: I'm giving up smoking for Lent.* ◆ *I'm giving up chocolate for Lent.*

lent past tense, past participle of **lend**

lentil /'lentl/ noun [C] a small brown, orange or green seed that can be dried and used in cooking □ *kacang dal: lentil soup/stew*

Leo /'li:əʊ/ noun [C,U] (pl **Leos**) the 5th sign of the **zodiac** (= 12 signs which represent the positions of the sun, moon and planets), the Lion; a person born under this sign □ *Leo: I'm a Leo.* ⊃ picture at **zodiac**

leopard /'lepəd/ noun [C] a large wild animal of the cat family that has yellow fur with dark spots. Leopards live in Africa and Southern Asia. □ *harimau bintang* ⊃ picture at **lion**

> **MORE** A female leopard is called a **leopardess** and a baby is called a **cub**.

leotard /'li:ətɑ:d/ noun [C] a piece of clothing that fits the body tightly from the neck down to the tops of the legs. Leotards are worn by dancers or women doing certain sports □ *leotad.* ⊃ picture at **ballet**

leper /'lepə(r)/ noun [C] a person who suffers from **leprosy** □ *pesakit kusta*

leprosy /'leprəsi/ noun [U] a serious infectious disease that affects the skin, nerves, etc. and can cause parts of the body to fall off □ *penyakit kusta*

lesbian /'lezbiən/ noun [C] a woman who is sexually attracted to other women □ *lesbian* ▶**lesbian** adj: *a lesbian relationship* ◆ *the lesbian and gay community* ▶**lesbianism** /'lezbiənɪzəm/ noun [U] ⊃ look at **gay**, **homosexual**

less¹ /les/ determiner, pron, adv 1 [used with uncountable nouns] a smaller amount (of) □ *sedikit; kurang: It took less time than I thought.* ◆ *I'm too fat—I must try to eat less.* ◆ *It's not far—it'll take less than an hour to get there.* **OPP** more

> **GRAMMAR** Some people use **less** with plural nouns: *less cars*, but **fewer** is the form which is still considered to be correct: *fewer cars*.

2 not so much (as) □ *kurang: He's less intelligent than his brother.* ◆ *It rains less in London than in Manchester.* ◆ *People work less well when they're tired.*
IDM **I, etc. couldn't care less** ⊃ **care²**
less and less becoming smaller and smaller in amount or degree □ *semakin tdk/kurang*
more or less ⊃ **more²**

less² /les/ prep taking a certain number or amount away □ *kurang: You'll earn £10 an hour, less tax.* **SYN** minus

lessen /'lesn/ verb [I,T] to become less; to make sth less □ *berkurangan; mengurangkan*

lesser /'lesə(r)/ adj, adv [only before a noun] not as great/much as □ *kurang; tdk begitu: He is guilty and so,* **to a lesser extent,** *is his wife.* ◆ *a lesser-known artist*
IDM **the lesser of two evils** the better of two bad things □ *yg kurang teruk antara dua perkara yg teruk, buruk, dsb*

lesson /'lesn/ noun [C] 1 a period of time when you learn or teach sth □ *pelajaran: She gives piano lessons.* ◆ *I want to have/take extra lessons in English conversation.* ◆ *a driving lesson*
2 something that is intended to be or should be learnt □ *pengajaran; iktibar: I'm sure we can all learn some lessons from this disaster.*
IDM **learn your lesson** ⊃ **learn**

let /let/ verb [T] (**letting**; pt, pp **let**)
▶ALLOW 1 to allow sth to happen □ *membiarkan: He's let the dinner burn again!* ◆ *Don't let the fire go out.* 2 **let sb/sth do sth** to allow sb/sth to do sth; to make sb/sth able to do sth □ *membenarkan: My parents let me stay out till 11 o'clock.* ◆ *I wanted to borrow Dave's bike but he wouldn't let me.* ◆ *This ticket lets you travel anywhere in the city for a day.* ⊃ note at **allow**

> **HELP** You cannot use **let** in the passive here. You must use **allow** or **permit** and **to**: *They let him take the exam again.* ◆ *He was allowed to take the exam again.*

3 to allow sb/sth to go somewhere □ *membenarkan atau membiarkan sso/sst pergi, keluar, masuk, dsb; membebaskan: Open the windows and let some fresh air in.* ◆ *She was let out of prison yesterday.*
▶MAKING SUGGESTIONS 4 used for making suggestions about what you and other people can do □ *mari; ayuh: 'Let's go to the cinema tonight.' 'Yes, let's.'*

> **HELP** The negative is **let's not** or (in British English only) **don't let's**: *Let's not/Don't let's go to that awful restaurant again.*

▶OFFERING HELP 5 used for offering help to sb □ *biar: Let me help you carry your bags.*
▶HOUSE/ROOM 6 **let sth (out) (to sb)** to allow sb to use a building, room, etc. in return for rent □ *menyewakan: They let out two rooms to students.* ◆ *There's a flat to let in our block.* ⊃ note at **hire**
IDM **let sb/sth go; let go of sb/sth** to stop holding sb/sth □ *melepaskan sso/sst: Let me go. You're hurting me!* ◆ *Hold the rope and don't let go of it.*
let yourself go 1 to relax without worrying what other people think □ *berseronok-seronok sesuka hati: After work I like to go out with friends and let myself go.* **2** to allow yourself to become untidy, dirty, etc. □ *tdk menghiraukan lagi ttg rupa, kebersihan diri, dsb: He used to be so smart but after he got married he just let himself go.* ❶ For other idioms containing **let**, look at the entries for the nouns, adjectives, etc. For example, **let sth slip** is at **slip**.
PHR V **let sb down** to not do sth that you promised to do for sb; to disappoint sb □ *mengece-*

wakan sso: *Bob really let me down when he didn't finish the work on time.*

let on (about sth) (to sb) to tell sb a secret □ *memberitahu (sst rahsia, dsb) (kpd sso)*: *He didn't let on how much he'd paid for the vase.*

let sb off to not punish sb, or to give sb less of a punishment than expected □ *melepaskan*: *He expected to go to prison but they let him off with a fine.*

let sth out to make a sound with your voice □ *menjerit, mengeluh, meraung, memekik, dsb*: *to let out a scream/sigh/groan/yell*

lethal /ˈliːθl/ *adj* that can cause death or great damage □ *boleh membawa maut; amat berbahaya*: *a lethal weapon/drug* ▶ **lethally** /ˈliːθəli/ *adv*

lethargy /ˈleθədʒi/ *noun* [U] the feeling of being very tired and not having any energy □ *kelesuan; (keadaan) tdk bermaya* ▶ **lethargic** /ləˈθɑːdʒɪk/ *adj*

letters and cards

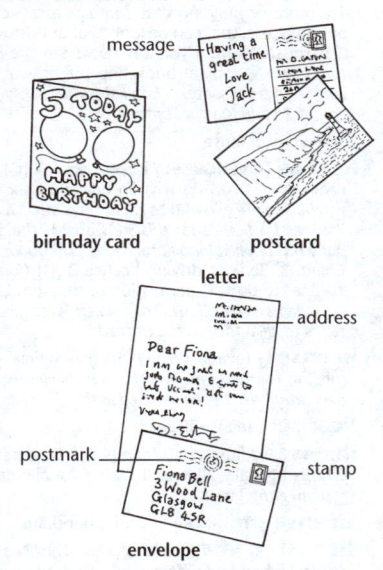

message — *Having a great time Love Jack*

birthday card   postcard

letter

address

postmark   stamp

envelope

letter /ˈletə(r)/ *noun* [C] **1** a written or printed message that you send to sb □ *surat*: *I got a letter from Matthew this morning.* ◆ *I'm writing a thank-you letter to my uncle for the flowers he sent.* ⊃ note at **post** **2** a written or printed sign that represents a sound in a language □ *huruf*: *'Z' is the last letter of the English alphabet.*

> **MORE** Letters may be written or printed as **capitals** or **small** letters: *Is 'east' written with a capital or a small 'e'?*

letter box *noun* [C] **1** a hole in a door or wall for putting letters, etc. through □ *tempat surat* ⊃ picture on **page P8 2** (*AmE* **mailbox**) a small box near the main door of a building or by the road in which letters are left for the owner to collect □ *peti surat* **3** = **postbox**

lettuce /ˈletɪs/ *noun* [C,U] a plant with large green leaves which are eaten cold in salads □ *daun salad*: *a lettuce leaf* ⊃ picture on **page P15**

leukaemia (*AmE* **leukemia**) /luːˈkiːmɪə/ *noun* [U] a serious disease of the blood which often results in death □ *leukemia*

level¹ /ˈlevl/ *noun* [C] **1** the amount, size or number of sth (compared to sth else) □ *aras; paras*: *a low level of unemployment* ◆ *high stress/pollution levels* **2** the height, position, standard, etc. of sth □ *peringkat*: *He used to play tennis at a high level.* ◆ *intermediate-level students* ◆ *top-level discussions* **3** a way of considering sth □ *segi*: *on a spiritual/personal/professional level* **4** a flat surface or layer □ *tingkat; lapis*: *a multi-level shopping centre*

level² /ˈlevl/ *adj* **1** with no part higher than any other; flat □ *rata; datar*: *Make sure the shelves are level before you fix them in position.* ◆ *Put the tent up on level ground.* ◆ *a level teaspoon of sugar* **2 level (with sb/sth)** at the same height, standard or position □ *sama (paras, tinggi, kedudukan, dsb)*: *The boy's head was level with his father's shoulder.* ◆ *The teams are level on 34 points.*

IDM **a level playing field** a situation in which everyone has an equal chance of success □ *keadaan yg sama rata*

level³ /ˈlevl/ *verb* [T] (**levelling; levelled**, *AmE* **leveling; leveled**) to make sth flat, equal or level □ *meratakan; menyamakan; menyamaratakan; meranapkan*: *The ground needs levelling before we lay the patio.* ◆ *Juventus levelled the score with a late goal.* ◆ *Many buildings were levelled (= destroyed) in the earthquake.*

PHR V **level sth at sb/sth** to aim sth at sb/sth □ *mengacukan atau melemparkan sst kpd sso/sst*: *They levelled serious criticisms at the standard of teaching.*

level off/out to become flat, equal or level □ *mendatar; menjadi rata*

ˌlevel ˈcrossing (*AmE* **ˈrailroad crossing**) *noun* [C] a place where a railway crosses the surface of a road □ *lintasan kereta api*

ˌlevel-ˈheaded *adj* calm and sensible; able to make good decisions in a difficult situation □ *waras; tenang*

lever /ˈliːvə(r)/ *noun* [C] **1** a handle that you pull or push in order to make a machine, etc. work □ *tuil*: *Pull the lever towards you.* ◆ *the gear lever in a car* **2** a bar or tool that is used to lift or open sth when you put pressure or force on one end □ *tuil; tuas; pengumpil*: *You need to get the tyre off with a lever.* ▶ **lever** *verb* [T]: *The police had to lever the door open.*

leverage /ˈliːvərɪdʒ/ *noun* [U] **1** the act of using a **lever** (= a bar or tool) to lift or open sth;

levy → lick 506

the force needed to do this □ *penuilan; daya tuil* **2** (*formal*) the ability to influence what people do □ *pengaruh; kuasa*: *diplomatic leverage*

levy /ˈlevi/ *verb* [T] (**levying**; **levies**; *pt*, *pp* **levied**) (*written*) **levy sth (on sb)** to officially demand and collect money, etc. □ *mengenakan*: *to levy a tax*

liability /ˌlaɪəˈbɪləti/ *noun* (*pl* **liabilities**) **1** [U] **liability (for sth)** the state of being responsible for sth □ *tanggungjawab*: *The company cannot accept liability for damage to cars in this car park.* **2** [C] (*informal*) a person or thing that can cause a lot of problems, cost a lot of money, etc. □ *sso/sst yg menyusahkan*

liable /ˈlaɪəbl/ *adj* [not before a noun] **1 liable (for sth)** (in law) responsible for sth □ *bertanggungjawab* **2 liable to do sth** likely to do sth □ *boleh melakukan/mendapat sst*: *We're all liable to have accidents when we are very tired.* **3 liable to sth** likely to have or suffer from sth □ *mudah kena*: *The area is liable to floods.*

liaise /liˈeɪz/ *verb* [I] **liaise (with sb/sth)** to work closely with a person, group, etc. and give them or it regular information about what you are doing □ *berhubung; menjadi pengantara*

liaison /liˈeɪzn/ *noun* **1** [U, sing] **liaison (between A and B)** communication between two or more people or groups that work together □ *hubungan; perhubungan* **2** [C] a secret sexual relationship □ *hubungan sulit*

liar /ˈlaɪə(r)/ *noun* [C] a person who does not tell the truth □ *pembohong*: *She called me a liar.* ➲ look at **lie¹**

Lib Dem /ˌlɪb ˈdem/ *abbr* = **Liberal Democrat**

libel /ˈlaɪbl/ *noun* [C,U] the act of printing a statement about sb that is not true and would give people a bad opinion of them □ *libel; fitnah bertulis*: *The singer is suing the newspaper for libel.* ▶ **libel** *verb* [T] (**libelling**; **libelled**, (*AmE*) **libeling**; **libeled**): *He claims he was libelled in the magazine article.*

liberal /ˈlɪbərəl/ *adj* **1** accepting different opinions or kinds of behaviour □ *bersikap terbuka*: *He has very liberal parents.* **SYN tolerant** **2** (in politics) believing in or based on principles of commercial freedom, freedom of choice, and avoiding extreme social and political change □ *liberal*: *liberal policies/politicians* **3** not strictly limited in amount or variety □ *banyak* ▶ **liberal** *noun* [C]: *Charles has always considered himself a liberal.* ▶ **liberalism** /ˈlɪbərəlɪzəm/ *noun* [U]

the Liberal Democrats *noun* [pl] (*abbr* **Lib Dems**) a political party in Britain that represents views that are not extreme □ *Parti Demokrat Liberal (politik British)*

liberally /ˈlɪbərəli/ *adv* freely or in large amounts □ *dgn banyak; secara bebas; tanpa terhad*

liberate /ˈlɪbəreɪt/ *verb* [T] **liberate sb/sth (from sth)** to allow sb/sth to be free □ *membebaskan; dibebaskan*: *France was liberated in 1945.* ▶ **liberation** /ˌlɪbəˈreɪʃn/ *noun* [U]

liberated /ˈlɪbəreɪtɪd/ *adj* free from the restrictions of traditional opinions or ways of behaving □ *bebas drpd kongkongan tradisi*

liberty /ˈlɪbəti/ *noun* [C,U] (*pl* **liberties**) the freedom to go where you want, do what you want, etc. □ *kebebasan*: *We must defend our civil liberties at all costs.* ➲ look at **freedom**
IDM at liberty (to do sth) free or allowed to do sth □ *bebas/dibenarkan (membuat sst)*: *You are at liberty to leave when you wish.*

Libra /ˈliːbrə/ *noun* [C,U] the 7th sign of the **zodiac** (= 12 signs which represent the positions of the sun, moon and planets), the Scales; a person born under this sign □ *Libra*: *I'm a Libra.* ➲ picture at **zodiac**

librarian /laɪˈbreəriən/ *noun* [C] a person who works in or is in charge of a library □ *pustakawan*

library /ˈlaɪbrəri; ˈlaɪbri/ *noun* [C] (*pl* **libraries**) **1** a room or building that contains a collection of books, etc. that can be looked at or borrowed □ *perpustakaan*: *My library books are due back tomorrow.* ➲ look at **bookshop** **2** a private collection of books, etc. □ *koleksi buku, dll*: *a new edition to add to your library*

lice plural of **louse**

licence (*AmE* **license**) /ˈlaɪsns/ *noun* **1** [C] **a licence (for sth/to do sth)** an official paper that shows you are allowed to do or have sth □ *lesen*: *You need a licence for this software.* ♦ *The company has applied for a licence to import goods into China.* ➲ look at **driving licence** **2** [U] (*formal*) **licence (to do sth)** permission or freedom to do sth □ *kebenaran; izin*: *The soldiers were given licence to kill if they were attacked.*

license¹ /ˈlaɪsns/ *verb* [T] to give official permission for sth □ *memberi lesen; berlesen*: *The new drug hasn't been licensed in the US.*

license² (*AmE*) = **licence**

licensee /ˌlaɪsənˈsiː/ *noun* [C] (*BrE*) a person who is officially allowed to sell alcoholic drinks □ *pemegang lesen*

ˈlicense plate (*AmE*) = **number plate**

ˈlicensing laws *noun* [pl] (*BrE*) the laws that control when and where alcoholic drinks can be sold □ *undang-undang pelesenan*

lick

licking   biting   swallowing

lick /lɪk/ *verb* [T] to move your tongue across sth □ *menjilat*: *The child licked the spoon clean.* ♦ *I licked the envelope and stuck it down.* ▶ **lick** *noun* [C]

ð **then**   s **so**   z **zoo**   ʃ **she**   ʒ **vi**sion   h **how**   m **man**   n **no**   ŋ **si**ng   l **leg**   r **red**   j **yes**   w **wet**

licorice (especially AmE) = **liquorice**

lid /lɪd/ noun [C] **1** the top part of a box, pot, etc. that can be lifted up or taken off □ *tudung; tutup*: I can't get the lid off this jar. ➲ picture at **container, piano, teapot 2** = **eyelid**

lie¹ /laɪ/ verb [I] (**lying**; *pt, pp* **lied**) **lie (to sb) (about sth)** to say or write sth that you know is not true □ *berbohong; membohong*: He lied about his age in order to join the army. ◆ How could you lie to me? ▸**lie** noun [C]: to tell a lie ◆ That story about his mother being ill was just a **pack of lies**. ➲ look at **fib, liar**

> **MORE** You tell a **white lie** in order not to hurt sb's feelings.

lie² /laɪ/ verb [I] (**lying**; *pt* **lay** /leɪ/; *pp* **lain** /leɪn/) **1** to be in or move into a flat or horizontal position (so that you are not standing or sitting) □ *berbaring; terletak*: He lay on the sofa and went to sleep. ◆ to lie on your back/side/front ◆ The book lay open in front of her.

> **HELP** **Lie** or **lay**? Do not confuse **lie²** and **lay**. **Lie** does not have an object: *He is lying on the beach*. The past simple is: **lay**: *She was tired so she lay on the bed*. **Lay** has an object: *He is laying a carpet in our new house*. The past simple is **laid**: *She laid her child on the bed*.

2 to be or stay in a certain state or position □ *berada; terletak; terbentang*: Snow lay thick on the ground. ◆ The hills lie to the north of the town. ◆ They are young and their whole lives lie ahead of them. **3 lie (in sth)** to exist or to be found somewhere □ *terdapat; terletak*: The problem lies in deciding when to stop.

IDM lie in wait (for sb) to hide somewhere waiting to attack, surprise or catch sb □ *menunggu utk menyerang hendap, memeranjatkan atau menangkap sso*

lie low to try not to attract attention to yourself □ *cuba bersembunyi; tdk menonjolkan diri*

PHR V **lie about/around** to relax and do nothing □ *duduk-duduk; bersantai*

lie back to relax and do nothing while sb else works, etc. □ *duduk berehat*

lie behind sth to be the real hidden reason for sth □ *sebab sebenar di sebalik sst*: We may never know what lay behind his decision to resign.

lie down (used about a person) to be in or move into a flat or horizontal position so that you can rest □ *berbaring*

> **MORE** We also say **have a lie-down**.

lie in (*informal*) to stay in bed later than usual because you do not have to get up □ *bangun lambat*

> **MORE** We also say **have a lie-in**.

➲ look at **oversleep**

lie with sb (to do sth) (*formal*) to be sb's responsibility to do sth □ *terletak di tangan sso*

ˈlie detector noun [C] a piece of equipment that can show if a person is telling the truth or not □ *pengesan bohong*

Lieut. abbr = **Lieutenant**

lieutenant /lefˈtenənt/ noun [C] (abbr **Lieut.**; **Lt**) an officer at a middle level in the army, navy or air force □ *leftenan*

life /laɪf/ noun (*pl* **lives** /laɪvz/)
▸BEING ALIVE **1** [U] the quality that people, animals or plants have when they are not dead □ *hidup; kehidupan*: Do you believe in life after death? ◆ to bring somebody/come back to life **2** [C,U] the state of being alive as a human being □ *nyawa; jiwa*: Would you **risk your life** to protect your property? ◆ Doctors fought all night to **save her life**.
▸LIVING THINGS **3** [U] living things □ *hidupan*: Life on earth began in a very simple form. ◆ No life was found on the moon. ◆ There was no sign of life in the deserted house. ◆ plant life
▸PERIOD OF TIME **4** [C,U] the period during which sb/sth is alive or exists □ *hayat; hidup; kehidupan; umur*: I've lived in this town **all my life**. ◆ I spent my early life in London. ◆ to have a short/long/exciting life
▸EXPERIENCE/ACTIVITIES **5** [U] the things that you may experience while you are alive □ *kehidupan*: Life can be hard for a single parent. ◆ I'm not happy with the situation, but I suppose **that's life**. **6** [C,U] a way of living □ *kehidupan*: They went to America to **start a new life**. ◆ They **lead a busy life**. ◆ married life
▸ENERGY **7** [U] energy; activity □ *tenaga; kegiatan*: Young children are **full of life**. ◆ These streets **come to life** in the evenings.
▸REALITY **8** [U] something that really exists and is not just a story, a picture, etc. □ *hidup; kehidupan (sebenar)*: I wonder what that actor's like **in real life**. ◆ Do you draw people from life or from photographs?

IDM **a fact of life** ➲ **fact**
the facts of life ➲ **fact**
full of beans/life ➲ **full¹**
get a life (*spoken*) used to say to sb to stop being boring and do sth more interesting □ *berserononoklah sedikit*
have the time of your life ➲ **time¹**
lose your life ➲ **lose**
a matter of life and/or death ➲ **matter¹**
take your (own) life to kill yourself □ *membunuh diri*
a walk of life ➲ **walk²**
a/sb's way of life ➲ **way¹**

life-and-ˈdeath (*also* ˌlife-or-ˈdeath) adj [only *before* a noun] very serious or dangerous □ *antara hidup dan mati*: a life-and-death struggle/matter/decision

lifebelt /ˈlaɪfbelt/ (*also* **lifebuoy**) noun [C] (*BrE*) a ring that is made from light material which will float. A lifebelt is thrown to a person who has fallen into water to stop them from sinking. □ *boya/pelampung keselamatan*

lifeboat /ˈlaɪfbəʊt/ noun [C] **1** a special boat that is used for rescuing people who are in dan-

lifebuoy → light

ger at sea □ *bot penyelamat* ⊃ picture on page P6 **2** a small boat that is carried on a large ship and that is used to escape from the ship if it is in danger of sinking □ *bot penyelamat/keselamatan* ⊃ note at **boat**

lifebuoy /ˈlaɪfbɔɪ/ = **lifebelt**

ˈlife coach *noun* [C] a person who is employed by sb to give them advice about how to achieve the things they want in their life and work □ *pembimbing hidup*

ˈlife cycle *noun* [C] the series of forms into which a living thing changes as it develops □ *kitaran hidup*

ˈlife expectancy *noun* [C,U] (*pl* **life expectancies**) the number of years that a person is likely to live □ *jangka hayat*

lifeguard /ˈlaɪfgɑːd/ *noun* [C] a person at a beach or swimming pool whose job is to rescue people who are in difficulty in the water □ *anggota penyelamat*

ˈlife jacket (*especially AmE* **ˈlife vest**) *noun* [C] a plastic or rubber jacket without sleeves that can be filled with air. A life jacket is used to make sb float if they fall into water. □ *jaket keselamatan; baju pelampung* ⊃ picture at **boat**

lifeless /ˈlaɪfləs/ *adj* **1** dead or appearing to be dead □ *tdk bernyawa; mati; spt tdk bernyawa* **2** without energy or interest □ *tdk bermaya* **SYN** **dull**

lifelike /ˈlaɪflaɪk/ *adj* looking like a real person or thing □ *spt betul; tampak hidup*: *The flowers are made of silk but they are very lifelike.*

lifeline /ˈlaɪflaɪn/ *noun* [C] something that is very important for sb and that they depend on □ *tali keselamatan; sst yg amat penting*: *For many old people their telephone is a lifeline.*

lifelong /ˈlaɪflɒŋ/ *adj* [only *before* a noun] for all of your life □ *sepanjang hayat; seumur hidup*: *a lifelong friend*

ˌlife-or-ˈdeath = **life-and-death**

ˈlife-size (*also* **ˈlife-sized**) *adj* of the same size as the real person or thing □ *sebesar saiz sebenar*: *a life-sized statue*

lifespan /ˈlaɪfspæn/ *noun* [C] the length of time that sth is likely to live, work, last, etc. □ *jangka hayat; tempoh hidup*: *A mosquito has a lifespan of only a few days.*

ˈlife story *noun* [C] (*pl* **life stories**) the story of sb's life □ *riwayat hidup*

lifestyle /ˈlaɪfstaɪl/ *noun* [C] the way that you live □ *gaya hidup*

lifetime /ˈlaɪftaɪm/ *noun* [C] the period of time that sb is alive □ *masa hayat; selama hayat; sepanjang hidup*

ˈlife vest (*especially AmE*) = **life jacket**

lift¹ /lɪft/ *verb*
▸RAISE **1** [T] **lift sb/sth (up)** to move sb/sth to a higher level or position □ *mengangkat*: *He lifted the child up onto his shoulders.* ♦ *Lift your arm very gently and see if it hurts.* ♦ *It took two men to lift the piano.*
▸MOVE SB/STH **2** [T] to move sb/sth from one place or position to another □ *mengalihkan; mengambil; menurunkan*: *She lifted the suitcase down from the rack.*
▸REMOVE LAW **3** [T] to end or remove a rule, law, etc □ *menarik balik; memansuhkan; membatalkan*: *The ban on public meetings has been lifted.*
▸MAKE SB HAPPY **4** [I,T] to become or make sb happier □ *meriangkan; menceriakan*: *The news lifted our spirits.*
▸CLOUDS, FOG, ETC. **5** [I] to rise up and disappear □ *menyingsing; lenyap; hilang*: *The mist lifted towards the end of the morning.*
▸COPY **6** [T] (*informal*) **lift sth (from sb/sth)** to steal or copy sth □ *mencuri; menjiplak; mencedok*: *Most of his essay was lifted straight from the textbook.* ⊃ look at **shoplifting**
PHR V **lift off** (used about a **spacecraft**) to rise straight up from the ground □ *melancar naik* ⊃ look at **lift-off**

lift² /lɪft/ *noun* **1** (*AmE* **elevator**) [C] a machine in a large building that is used for carrying people or goods from one floor to another □ *lif*: *It's on the third floor so we'd better take the lift.* **2** [C] a free ride in a car, etc. □ *tumpang naik kereta, dsb*: *Can you give me a lift to the station, please?* ♦ *I got a lift from a passing car.* **3** [sing] (*informal*) a feeling of being happier or more confident than before □ *(sst yg) menaikkan semangat/ meriangkan*: *Passing the exam gave him a real lift.* **4** [sing] the act of moving or being moved to a higher position □ *angkat*: *Her only reaction was a slight lift of one eyebrow.*
IDM **thumb a lift/ride** ⊃ **thumb²**

ˈlift-off *noun* [C] the start of the flight of a **spacecraft** (= a vehicle that travels in space) when it leaves the ground □ *pelancaran*

ligament /ˈlɪgəmənt/ *noun* [C] a short, strong part inside the body that joins a bone to another bone □ *ligamen; urat rawan* ⊃ look at **tendon**

light¹ /laɪt/ *noun* **1** [U,C] the energy from the sun, a lamp, etc. that allows you to see things □ *cahaya*: *a beam/ray of light* ♦ *The light was too dim for us to read by.* ♦ *Strong light is bad for the eyes.* ♦ *We could see strange lights in the sky.*

> **MORE** You may see things by **sunlight**, **moonlight**, **firelight**, **candlelight** or **lamplight**.

2 [C] something that produces light, for example an electric lamp □ *lampu*: *Suddenly all the lights went out/came on.* ♦ *the lights of the city in the distance* ♦ *If the lights (= traffic lights) are red, stop!* ♦ *That car hasn't got its lights on.*

> **MORE** A light may be **on** or **off**. You **put**, **switch** or **turn** a light **on**, **off** or **out**: *Shall I put the light on? It's getting dark in here.* ♦ *Please turn the lights out before you leave.*

3 [C] something, for example a match, that can be used to light a cigarette, start a fire, etc. □ *api (mancis, pemetik api, dsb)*: *Have you got a light?*

IDM **bring sth/come to light** to make sth known or to become known □ *mendedahkan; (menjadi) diketahui*

cast light on sth ⊃ **cast¹**

give sb/get the green light ⊃ **green¹**

in a good, bad, etc. light (used about the way that sth is seen or described by other people) well, badly, etc. □ *kelihatan baik/buruk, dsb*: *The newspapers often portray his behaviour in a bad light.*

in the light of because of; considering □ *berdasarkan; memandangkan*

set light to sth to cause sth to start burning □ *membakar*

shed light on sth ⊃ **shed²**

light² /laɪt/ *adj* (**lighter**; **lightest**)
▶FULL OF LIGHT **1** having a lot of light □ *terang; bercahaya*: *In summer it's still light at 10 o'clock.* ◆ *a light room* **OPP** **dark**
▶COLOUR **2** pale □ *muda; pucat*: *a light-blue sweater* **OPP** **dark**
▶NOT HEAVY **3** not of great weight □ *ringan; nipis; tdk tebal*: *Carry this bag—it's the lightest.* ◆ *I've lost weight—I'm five kilos lighter than I used to be.* ◆ *light clothes* (= for summer) **OPP** **heavy**
▶GENTLE **4** not using much force □ *perlahan; lembut*: *a light touch on the shoulder*
▶EASY **5** not tiring or difficult □ *ringan*: *light exercise* ◆ *light entertainment/reading*
▶SMALL AMOUNT **6** not great in amount, degree, etc. □ *tdk banyak; kurang; ringan; lembut*: *Traffic in London is light on a Sunday.* ◆ *a light prison sentence* ◆ *a light wind* ◆ *a light breakfast*
▶SLEEP **7** [only *before* a noun] (used about sleep) not deep □ *tdk nyenyak*: *I'm a light sleeper, so the slightest noise wakes me.* ▶ **lightness** *noun* [U]

light³ /laɪt/ *verb* (*pt, pp* **lit**) **HELP** Lighted is also used as the past tense and past participle, especially before nouns: *The church was full of lighted candles.* **1** [I,T] to begin or to make sth begin to burn □ *menyala; menyalakan; menghidupkan*: *The gas cooker won't light.* ◆ *to light a fire* ◆ *Candles were lit in memory of the dead.* **2** [T] to give light to sth □ *menerangi; diterangi*: *The street is well/badly lit at night.* ◆ *We only had a small torch to light our way through the forest.*

PHR V **light (sth) up 1** to start smoking a cigarette □ *mula menghisap rokok*: *Several people got off the train and lit up immediately.* **2** to make sth bright with light □ *menerangi*: *The fireworks lit up the whole sky.* **3** (used about sb's face, eyes, etc.) to become bright with happiness or excitement □ *menyerikan; menceriakan*

light⁴ /laɪt/ *adv* without much luggage □ *tdk membawa banyak barang/bagasi*: *I always travel light.*

'light bulb = **bulb**(1)

lighted past tense, past participle of **light³**

lighten /'laɪtn/ *verb* [I,T] **1** to become or to make sth brighter □ *cerah; terang; mencerahkan; menerangkan* **2** to become lighter in weight or to make sth lighter □ *menjadi ringan; meringankan*

lighter /'laɪtə(r)/ = **cigarette lighter**

light-'headed *adj* not in complete control of your thoughts and movements □ *pening-pening lalat*

light-'hearted *adj* **1** intended to be funny and enjoyable □ *tdk serius; lucu dan menghiburkan* **2** happy and without problems □ *riang; gembira*

lighthouse /'laɪthaʊs/ *noun* [C] a tall building with a light at the top to warn ships of danger near the coast □ *rumah api*

lighting /'laɪtɪŋ/ *noun* [U] the quality or type of lights used in a room, building, etc. □ *pencahayaan; cahaya; lampu*

lighthouse

lightly /'laɪtli/ *adv* **1** gently; with very little force □ *dgn perlahan*: *He touched her lightly on the arm.* **2** only a little; not much □ *sedikit; tdk banyak; separuh (masak)*: *lightly cooked/spiced/whisked* **3** not seriously; without serious thought □ *tdk bersungguh-sungguh; memandang ringan*: *We do not take our customers' complaints lightly.*

IDM **get off/be let off lightly** to avoid serious punishment or trouble □ *terlepas dgn hukuman ringan sahaja; terlepas drpd kesusahan teruk, dsb*

lightning¹ /'laɪtnɪŋ/ *noun* [U] a bright flash of light that appears in the sky during a storm □ *kilat*: *The tree was struck by lightning and burst into flames.* ◆ *a flash of lightning* ⊃ note at **storm** ⊃ look at **thunder**

lightning² /'laɪtnɪŋ/ *adj* [only *before* a noun] very quick or sudden □ *spt kilat; pantas*: *a lightning attack*

lightweight /'laɪtweɪt/ *noun* [C], *adj* **1** a person who is in one of the lightest weight groups in certain fighting sports □ *kelas ringan; 'lightweight'*: *a lightweight boxing champion* **2** (a thing) weighing less than usual □ *(sst yg) ringan atau nipis*: *a lightweight suit for the summer*

likable = **likeable**

like¹ /laɪk/ *prep, conj*
▶SIMILAR TO **1** similar to sb/sth □ *serupa; sama; spt*: *You look very/just/exactly like your father.* ◆ *Those two singers sound like cats!* ◆ *Your house is nothing like how I imagined it.* ⊃ note at **how**

HELP If you want a description of sb/sth, you ask, **'What is he/she/it like?'**: *Tell me about your town. What's* (= what is) *it like?* ♦ *What was it like being interviewed on TV?* Notice that we do NOT use **like** in the answer to these questions: *'What's your brother like?' 'He's tall and fair, and rather serious.'* If you only want to ask about the appearance of sb/sth, you can say, **'What does he/she/it look like?'**: *'What does your brother look like?' 'He's tall and fair, with blue eyes.'*

2 [in compounds] in the manner of; similar to □ *spt; macam; seakan-akan*: *childlike innocence/simplicity* ♦ *a very lifelike statue*

▶TYPICAL **3** typical of a particular person □ *memang macam itu*: *It was just like Maria to be late.*

▶SAME AS **4** in the same way as sb/sth □ *spt; macam*: *Stop behaving like children.* ♦ *That's not right. Do it like this.* ♦ *She can't draw like her sister can.* ♦ *She behaves like she owns the place.* ⊃ note at **as**

▶FOR EXAMPLE **5** for example; such as □ *spt; misalnya*: *They enjoy most team games, like football and rugby.* ⊃ note at **as**

▶SAY **6** (*slang*) (used before saying what sb said, how sb felt, etc.) □ *slanga yg digunakan sebelum menyatakan apa-apa yg dikatakan oleh sso, perasaan sso, dsb*: *When I saw the colour of my hair I was like 'Wow, I can't believe it!'*

IDM **like anything** (*spoken*) very much, fast, hard, etc. □ *sangat cepat*: *We had to pedal like anything to get up the hill.*
like hell (*informal*) very much; with a lot of effort □ *bagai nak gila*: *I'm working like hell at the moment.*
nothing like ⊃ **nothing**
that's more like it used to say that sth is better than before □ *macam itulah*: *The sun's coming out now—that's more like it!*

like² /laɪk/ *verb* [T] **1 like sb/sth; like doing sth; like to do sth; like sth about sb/sth** to find sb/sth pleasant; to enjoy sth □ *suka akan; gemar; menyukai*: *He's nice. I like him a lot.* ♦ *Do you like their new flat?* ♦ *How do you like John's new girlfriend?* ♦ *I like my coffee strong.* ♦ *I like playing tennis.* ♦ *I like to go to the cinema on Thursdays.* ♦ *What is it you like about Sarah so much?* ♦ *She didn't like it when I shouted at her.* ♦ *I don't like him borrowing my things without asking.* ♦ *The job seems strange at first, but you'll **get to like** it.* ♦ *I don't like **the look/sound/idea/thought of** that.* **OPP** **dislike** ⊃ note at **dislike**

GRAMMAR If you **like doing sth**, you enjoy it: *I like listening to music.* If you **like to do sth**, you might not enjoy it, but you do it because it is a habit, or because you think it is a good idea: *I like to go to the dentist every six months.*

2 to want □ *suka; hendak; mahu*: *Do what you like. I don't care.* ♦ *We can go whenever you like.* ♦ *I didn't like to disturb you while you were eating.*

HELP **Would like** is a more polite way to say 'want': *Would you like something to eat?* ♦ *I'd like to speak to the manager.* ♦ *We'd like you to come to dinner on Sunday.* ♦ *How would you like to come to Scotland with us?* **Would like** is followed by the infinitive with *to*, not by the *-ing* form.

IDM **I like that!** (*BrE old-fashioned informal*) used for saying that sth is not true or not fair □ *Baguslah tu!*
if you like used for agreeing with sb or suggesting sth in a polite way □ *jika awak suka/mahu*: *'Shall we stop for a rest?' 'Yes, if you like.'*
like the look/sound of sb/sth to have a good impression of sb/sth after seeing or hearing about them or it □ *suka akan sso/sst*

OTHER WORDS FOR

like

If you **like** doing sth very much, you can say 'I **enjoy/spend a lot of time** doing …': *She enjoys playing tennis.* You can also say 'I **love** (playing) tennis', 'I'm really **keen on** (playing) tennis', or 'I'm really **into** tennis'. If you like studying sth or finding out about sth, use **interested in**: *He's very interested in the history of tennis.*

like³ /laɪk/ *noun* **1 likes** [pl] things that you like □ *kesukaan*: *Tell me about some of your **likes and dislikes**.* **2** [sing] a person or thing that is similar to sb/sth else □ *sso/sst yg serupa, sama atau spt itu*: *I enjoy going round castles, old churches **and the like**.* ♦ *She was a great singer, and we may never see her like/the like of her again.* ▶**like** *adj* (*formal*)

likeable (also **likable**) /ˈlaɪkəbl/ *adj* (used about a person) easy to like; pleasant □ *disukai; disenangi*

likelihood /ˈlaɪklihʊd/ *noun* [U] the chance of sth happening; how likely sth is to happen □ *kemungkinan*: *There seems very little likelihood of success.* **SYN** **probability**

likely /ˈlaɪkli/ *adj, adv* (**likelier**; **likeliest**) **1 likely (to do sth)** probable or expected □ *mungkin; agaknya*: *Do you think it's likely to rain?* ♦ *The boss is not likely to agree.* ♦ *It's not likely that the boss will agree.* ⊃ note at **probable 2** probably suitable □ *mungkin sesuai*: *a likely candidate for the job* **OPP** for both meanings **unlikely**
IDM **not likely!** (*informal*) certainly not □ *tak mungkin*

liken /ˈlaɪkən/ *verb* [T] (*formal*) **liken sb/sth to sb/sth** to compare one person or thing with another □ *menyamakan; mengumpamakan*: *This young artist has been likened to Picasso.*

likeness /ˈlaɪknəs/ *noun* [C,U] the fact of being similar in appearance; an example of this □ *persamaan; (perihal) serupa*: *The witness's drawing turned out to be **a good likeness of** the attacker.*

likewise /ˈlaɪkwaɪz/ *adv* (*formal*) the same; in a similar way □ *begitu juga; spt itu*: *I intend to* send a letter of apology and suggest that you do likewise.

liking /ˈlaɪkɪŋ/ noun [sing] **a liking (for sb/sth)** the feeling that you like sb/sth □ *kesukaan; kegemaran; suka; gemar*: I have a liking for spicy food.
IDM too ... for your liking that you do not like because he/she/it has too much of a particular quality □ *terlalu... utk saya*: The music was a bit too loud for my liking.

lilac /ˈlaɪlək/ noun **1** [C,U] a tree or large bush that has large purple or white flowers in spring □ *pokok lilak* **2** [U] a pale purple colour □ *warna ungu muda* ▶ lilac adj

lilo (also **Li-lo™**) /ˈlaɪləʊ/ noun [C] (pl **lilos**) (BrE) a plastic or rubber bed that you fill with air when you want to use it. A **lilo** is used on the beach or for camping. □ *Li-lo™ (tilam angin)*

lily /ˈlɪli/ noun [C] (pl **lilies**) a type of plant that has large white or coloured flowers in the shape of a bell □ *bunga lili/bakung*

limb /lɪm/ noun [C] **1** a leg or an arm of a person □ *anggota badan; tangan atau kaki* **2** one of the main branches of a tree □ *dahan*
IDM out on a limb without the support of other people □ *dlm keadaan terasing atau berisiko (tanpa bantuan, sokongan, dsb)*

lime /laɪm/ noun **1** [U] a white substance that is used in traditional building methods and also to help plants grow □ *kapur* **2** [C] a fruit that looks like a small green lemon □ *buah limau nipis* ⇒ picture on **page P14** **3** [U] (also **lime ˈgreen**) a yellowish-green colour □ *warna hijau pucuk pisang*

the limelight /ˈlaɪmlaɪt/ noun [U] the centre of public attention □ *perhatian ramai*: to be in/out of the limelight

limit¹ /ˈlɪmɪt/ noun [C] **1** the greatest or smallest amount of sth that is allowed or possible □ *had; batas*: a speed/age/time limit ◆ He was fined for exceeding the speed limit. ◆ There's a limit to the amount of time I'm prepared to spend on this. **2** the outside edge of a place or area □ *batas; sempadan*: the city limits ◆ Lorries are not allowed within a two-mile limit of the town centre.
IDM off limits (used about a place) where people are not allowed to go □ *kawasan larangan*
within limits only up to a reasonable point or amount □ *ada hadnya/batasnya*

EXAM TIP

Word limit

In a **writing exam** you are told how many words you must write for each task. Practise writing the correct number before the exam. Knowing how many words you usually write on a line will help you to count as you write. You will lose marks if you are **over** or **under the word limit** (= write too many or too few words).

---

limit² /ˈlɪmɪt/ verb [T] **limit sb/sth (to sth)** to keep sb/sth within or below a certain amount, size, degree or area □ *mengehadkan; dihadkan*: I'm limiting myself to one cup of coffee a day.

limitation /ˌlɪmɪˈteɪʃn/ noun **1** [C,U] **(a) limitation (on sth)** the act of limiting or controlling sth; a condition that puts a limit on sth □ *pembatasan; pengehadan*: There are no limitations on what we can do. **2 limitations** [pl] things that you cannot do □ *batas kemampuan/keupayaan*: It is important to know your own limitations.

limited /ˈlɪmɪtɪd/ adj small in number, amount, etc. □ *terhad; terbatas*: Book early for the show because there are only a limited number of seats available. **OPP unlimited**

ˌlimited ˈcompany noun [C] (abbr **Ltd**) a company whose owners only have to pay a limited amount of the money that they owe if the company fails □ *syarikat berhad*

limousine /ˈlɪməziːn, ˌlɪməˈziːn/ (also informal **limo** /ˈlɪməʊ/) noun [C] a large expensive car that usually has a sheet of glass between the driver and the passengers in the back □ *limousin; kereta besar mewah*

limp¹ /lɪmp/ adj not firm or strong □ *lembik; tdk keras; layu; tdk bermaya*: You should put those flowers in water before they go limp.

limp² /lɪmp/ verb [I] to walk with difficulty because you have hurt your leg or foot □ *(berjalan) terdengkot-dengkot*: The goalkeeper limped off the field with a twisted ankle. ▶ limp noun [sing]: to walk with a limp

lines

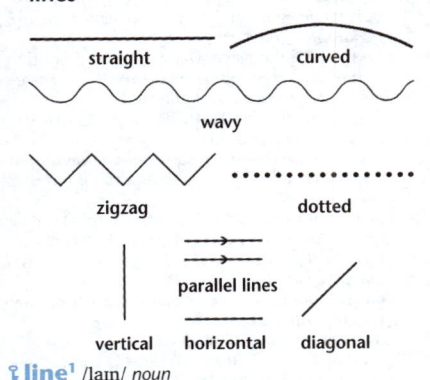

straight
curved
wavy
zigzag
dotted
parallel lines
vertical   horizontal   diagonal

line¹ /laɪn/ noun
▶LONG THIN MARK **1** [C] a long thin mark on the surface of sth or on the ground □ *garis; garisan; kedut-kedut*: to draw a line ◆ a straight/wiggly/dotted line ◆ The old lady had lines on her forehead. ◆ The ball was definitely over the line. ◆ the finishing line of a race
▶DIVISION **2** [C] a border or limit between one place or thing and another □ *sempadan; garisan; batas*: to cross state lines ◆ There's a thin line between showing interest and being nosy.

line → link

▶ROW **3** [C] a row of people, things, words on a page, etc. □ *barisan; deretan*: *There was a long line of people waiting at the Post Office.* ♦ *a five-line poem* ♦ *Start each paragraph on a new line.*

▶SERIES **4** [C] a series of people in a family, or of things or events that follow each other in time □ *keturunan; deretan; barisan*: *He comes from a long line of musicians.*

▶WORDS **5 lines** [pl] the words that are spoken by an actor in a play, etc. □ *dialog; baris*: *to learn your lines*

▶STRING **6** [C] a piece of rope or string □ *tali (ampaian, kail, dsb)*: *Hang out the clothes on the (washing) line, please.* ♦ *a fishing line*

▶TELEPHONE **7** [C] a telephone or electricity wire or connection □ *talian; sambungan*: *I'm sorry—the line is engaged. Can you try again later?* ♦ *I'll just check for you. Can you hold the line* (= wait)?

▶RAILWAY **8** [C] a section of railway track □ *jalan (landasan) kereta api*: *The accident was caused by a cow on the line.*

▶DIRECTION **9** [C, usually sing] a direction or course of movement, thought or action □ *arah; cara; pendirian*: *He was so drunk he couldn't walk in a straight line.* ♦ *The answer's not quite correct, but you're on the right lines.* ♦ *The two countries' economies are developing along similar lines.*

▶ACTIVITY **10** [C] something that you do as a job, do well, or enjoy doing □ *bidang*: *What line of business/work are you in?*

▶PRODUCT **11** [sing] one type of goods in a shop, etc. □ *keluaran; barang keluaran*: *a new line in environment-friendly detergents*

▶TRANSPORT **12** [C] a company that provides transport by air, ship, etc. □ *syarikat penerbangan, perkapalan, bas, dsb*: *an airline*

▶ARMY **13** [C] the place where an army is fighting □ *barisan pertempuran/pertahanan*: *There's renewed fighting on the front line.*

IDM draw the line at sth/doing sth ⮕ **draw¹**
drop sb a line ⮕ **drop¹**
in line for sth likely to get sth □ *bakal mendapat sst*: *You could be in line for promotion if you keep working like this.*
in line with sth; out of line with sth (not) similar to sth; (not) in agreement with sth □ *(tdk) selaras/(tdk) sejajar dgn sst*: *These changes will bring the industry in line with the new laws.*
on line connected to or available on a computer system □ *dlm talian*
overstep the mark/line ⮕ **overstep**
somewhere along/down the line ⮕ **somewhere**
take a hard line (on sth) ⮕ **hard¹**
toe the line ⮕ **toe²**

line² /laɪn/ *verb* [T] **1** [often passive] to cover the inside surface of sth with a different material □ *melapik; dilapik* **2** to form lines or rows along sth □ *membarisi; menjajari*: *Crowds lined the streets to watch the race.*
PHR V line up (for sth) (*AmE*) to form a line of people □ *berbaris (utk sst)* **SYN** queue
line sth up to arrange or organize sth □ *mem-*

bariskan/mengatur sst: *She lined the bottles up on the shelf.*

lined /laɪnd/ *adj* **1** covered in lines □ *berkedut; bergaris*: *a face lined with age* ♦ *lined paper* **2** -**lined** [in compounds] having the object mentioned all along the side(s); having the inside surface covered with the material mentioned □ *dijajari; dilapik*: *a tree-lined avenue* ♦ *fur-lined boots*

linen /ˈlɪnɪn/ *noun* [U] **1** a type of strong cloth that is made from a natural substance from a plant □ *kain linen* **2** sheets and other types of cloth used in the house to cover beds, tables, etc. □ *kain cadar, alas meja, dsb*: *bedlinen*

liner /ˈlaɪnə(r)/ *noun* [C] **1** a large ship that carries people, etc. long distances □ *kapal besar (yg membawa penumpang, dsb)* ⮕ note at **boat** ⮕ picture on **page P6 2** something that is put inside sth else to keep it clean or protect it. A **liner** is usually thrown away after it has been used □ *pelapik; alas*: *a dustbin liner*

linger /ˈlɪŋɡə(r)/ *verb* [I] **linger (on)** to stay somewhere or do sth for longer than usual □ *berlambat-lambat; memandang, dsb lama-lama*: *His eyes lingered on the money in her bag.*

lingerie /ˈlænʒəri/ *noun* [U] (used in shops, etc.) women's underwear □ *pakaian dlm wanita*

linguist /ˈlɪŋɡwɪst/ *noun* [C] a person who is good at learning foreign languages; a person who studies or teaches language(s) □ *ahli bahasa*

linguistic /lɪŋˈɡwɪstɪk/ *adj* connected with language or the study of language □ *linguistik; berkenaan dgn bahasa atau kajian bahasa*

linguistics /lɪŋˈɡwɪstɪks/ *noun* [U] the scientific study of language □ *ilmu linguistik/bahasa*

lining /ˈlaɪnɪŋ/ *noun* [C,U] material that covers the inside surface of sth □ *lapik; pelapik*: *I've torn the lining of my coat.*
IDM every cloud has a silver lining ⮕ **cloud¹**

link¹ /lɪŋk/ *noun* [C] **1 a link (between A and B); a link (with sb/sth)** a connection or relationship between two or more people or things □ *hubungan; kaitan*: *There is a strong link between smoking and heart disease.* ♦ *There is a strong link between obesity and heart disease.* **2** a means of travelling or communicating between two places □ *penghubung*: *To visit similar websites to this one, click on the links at the bottom of the page.* **3** one ring of a chain □ *mata rantai* ⮕ picture at **padlock**

link² /lɪŋk/ *verb* [T] **link A to/with B; link A and B (together)** to make a connection between two or more people or things □ *menghubungkan; mengaitkan; dihubungkan*: *The new bridge will link the island to the mainland.* ♦ *The computers are linked together in a network.*
PHR V link up (with sb/sth) to join together (with sb/sth) □ *dihubungkan (dgn sso/sst)*: *The bands have linked up for a charity concert.*

link-up noun [C] the joining together or connection of two or more things □ *penghubungan; perangkaian; asosiasi*

linoleum /lɪˈnəʊliəm/ (also informal **lino** /ˈlaɪnəʊ/) noun [U] a type of strong material with a hard shiny surface, used for covering floors □ *linoleum; tikar getah*

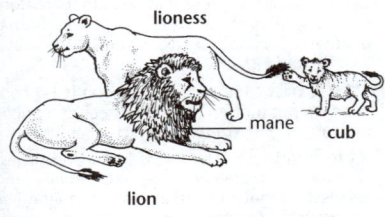

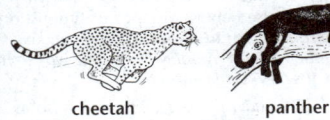

lioness

mane cub

lion

leopard tiger

cheetah panther

lion /ˈlaɪən/ noun [C] a large animal of the cat family that lives in Africa and parts of southern Asia. Male **lions** have a **mane** (= hair around their head and neck). □ *singa*

MORE A female lion is called a **lioness** and a young lion is called a **cub**. The noise a lion makes is a **roar**.

IDM **the lion's share (of sth)** (BrE) the largest or best part of sth when it is divided □ *bahagian terbesar*

lip /lɪp/ noun [C] **1** either of the two soft edges at the opening of your mouth □ *bibir*: *to kiss somebody on the lips* ⮕ picture at **body**

MORE You have a **top/upper** lip and a **bottom/lower** lip.

2 -lipped [in compounds] having the type of lips mentioned □ *mempunyai bibir*: *thin-lipped* **3** the edge of a cup or sth that is shaped like a cup □ *bibir; tepi* ⮕ picture at **jug**
IDM **purse your lips** ⮕ **purse²**

lip gloss noun [U,C] a substance that is put on your lips to make them look shiny □ *pengilat bibir*

lip-read verb [I,T] (pt, pp **lip-read**) to understand what sb is saying by looking at the movements of their lips □ *membaca gerak bibir*

lipstick /ˈlɪpstɪk/ noun [U,C] a substance that is used for giving colour to your lips □ *gincu bi-*

513 **link-up → listen**

bir; lipstik: *to put on some lipstick* ◆ *a new lipstick*

liqueur /lɪˈkjʊə(r)/ noun [C,U] a strong sweet alcoholic drink that is often drunk in small quantities after a meal □ *likur; sopi manis*

liquid /ˈlɪkwɪd/ noun [C,U] a substance, for example water, that is not solid or a gas and that can flow or be poured □ *cecair* ▶ **liquid** adj

liquidate /ˈlɪkwɪdeɪt/ verb [T] **1** to close a business because it has no money left □ *membubarkan* **2** to destroy or remove sb/sth that causes problems □ *menghapuskan* ▶ **liquidation** /ˌlɪkwɪˈdeɪʃn/ noun [U]: *If the company doesn't receive a big order soon, it will have to go into liquidation.*

liquidize (also **-ise**) /ˈlɪkwɪdaɪz/ verb [T] to cause sth to become liquid □ *menjadikan cecair; mengisar cair* ▶ **liquidizer** (also **-iser**) (BrE) = blender

liquor /ˈlɪkə(r)/ noun [U] (AmE) strong alcoholic drinks; spirits □ *arak; minuman keras*

liquorice (AmE **licorice**) /ˈlɪkərɪʃ/ noun [U] a black substance, made from a plant, that is used in some sweets □ *likuoris*

liquor store (AmE) = off-licence

lisp /lɪsp/ noun [C] a speech fault in which 's' is pronounced as 'th' □ *pelat menyebut huruf 's'*: *He speaks with a slight lisp.* ▶ **lisp** verb [I,T]

list /lɪst/ noun [C] a series of names, figures, items, etc. that are written, printed or said one after another □ *senarai*: *a checklist of everything that needs to be done* ◆ *a waiting list* ◆ *Your name is third on the list.* ⮕ note at **last-minute** ▶ **list** verb [T]: *to list items in alphabetical order*

listen /ˈlɪsn/ verb [I] **1 listen (to sb/sth)** to pay attention to sb/sth in order to hear them or it □ *mendengar*: *Now please listen carefully to what I have to say.* ◆ *to listen to music/the radio* ⮕ note at **hear 2 listen to sb/sth** to take notice of or believe what sb says □ *mendengar; mengendahkan*: *You should listen to your parents' advice.*
PHR V **listen (out) for sth** to wait to hear sth □ *mendengar-dengarkan*: *to listen (out) for a knock on the door*
listen in (on/to sth) to listen to sb else's private conversation □ *memasang telinga; mencuri dengar*: *Have you been listening in on my phone calls?*

TOPIC

Listening to music

A **hi-fi** or **stereo** is a machine used for listening to CDs, etc. When you want to listen to music, you **put a CD on** (= make it start playing). If you want to make the music louder, you **turn the volume up**. If you want to make it quieter, you **turn** it **down**. A small music player that you carry around with you is called an **MP3 player** or **iPod™**.

⮕ note at **iPod™**

VOWELS iː see i any ɪ sit e ten æ hat ɑː father ɒ got ɔː saw ʊ put uː too u usual

▶**listen** noun (informal): *Have a listen and see if you can hear anything.*

listener /ˈlɪsənə(r)/ noun [C] a person who listens □ *pendengar*: *When I'm unhappy I always phone Charlie—he's such a good listener.* ♦ *The new radio show has attracted a record number of listeners.*

listless /ˈlɪstləs/ adj tired and without energy □ *lesu; tdk bermaya* ▶**listlessly** adv

lit past tense, past participle of **light**³

liter (AmE) = **litre**

literacy /ˈlɪtərəsi/ noun [U] the ability to read and write □ *kenal/celik huruf* OPP **illiteracy** ↻ look at **numeracy**

literal /ˈlɪtərəl/ adj 1 (used about the meaning of a word or phrase) original or basic □ *literal; sebenar*: *The adjective 'big-headed' is hardly ever used in its literal sense.* ↻ look at **figurative**, **metaphor** 2 (used when translating, etc.) dealing with each word separately without looking at the general meaning □ *harfiah*: *A literal translation is not always accurate.*

literally /ˈlɪtərəli/ adv 1 according to the basic or original meaning of the word, etc □ *mengikut makna sebenar; secara harfiah; bulat-bulat*: *You can't translate these idioms literally.* 2 (informal) used for emphasizing sth □ *betul-betul; benar-benar*: *We were literally frozen to death (= we were very cold).*

literary /ˈlɪtərəri/ adj of or concerned with literature □ *(berkenaan dgn) sastera atau kesusasteraan*: *literary criticism* ♦ *a literary journal*

literate /ˈlɪtərət/ adj 1 able to read and write □ *kenal/celik huruf* OPP **illiterate** ↻ look at **numerate** ↻ noun **literacy** 2 having education or knowledge in a particular area □ *terpelajar*: *computer-literate (= able to use a computer)*

literature /ˈlɪtrətʃə(r)/ noun [U] 1 writing that is considered to be a work of art □ *kesusasteraan; sastera*: *French literature* ♦ *a great work of literature* 2 **literature (on sth)** printed material about a particular subject □ *risalah; bahan bercetak*: *promotional literature*

> **TOPIC**
>
> **Literature**
>
> If you study **literature** at school or university, you study **poetry** (= collections of poems), **drama** (= plays) and **fiction** (= novels). A person who writes plays is a **playwright** and someone who writes poetry is a **poet**. A great work of literature is called a **classic**: *'Alice in Wonderland' is a childhood classic.* The study of Greek and Latin literature is called **classics**.

litigation /ˌlɪtɪˈɡeɪʃn/ noun [U] the process of taking legal action in a court of law □ *litigasi; tindakan undang-undang*: *The company has been in litigation with its previous auditors for a year.*

litre (AmE **liter**) /ˈliːtə(r)/ noun [C] (abbr **l**) a measure of liquid □ *liter*: *ten litres of petrol* ♦ *a litre bottle of wine* ❶ For more information about measurements, look at the section on using numbers at the back of this dictionary.

litter /ˈlɪtə(r)/ noun 1 [U] pieces of paper, rubbish, etc. that are left in a public place □ *sampah sarap* 2 [C] all the young animals that are born to one mother at the same time □ *seperinduk*: *a litter of six puppies* ▶**litter** verb [T]: *The streets were littered with rubbish.*

ˈlitter bin (AmE **ˈtrash can**) noun [C] a container to put rubbish in, in the street or a public building □ *tong sampah* ↻ picture at **bin**

little¹ /ˈlɪtl/ adj [The forms **littler** and **littlest** are rare. It is more common to use **smaller** and **smallest**.] 1 not big; small □ *kecil*: *a little bag of sweets* ♦ *Do you want the big one or the little one?* ♦ *a little mistake/problem* ↻ note at **small**

> **HELP** **Little** is often used with another adjective: *a little old lady* ♦ *a cute little kitten* ♦ *What a funny little shop!*

2 young □ *kecil*: *a little girl/boy* ♦ *my little (= younger) brother* ♦ *I was very naughty when I was little.* 3 (used about distance or time) short □ *sedikit; sekejap; tdk jauh*: *Do you mind waiting a little while?* ♦ *We only live a little way from here.* ♦ *It's only a little further.*

little² /ˈlɪtl/ adv, pron, determiner 1 [also as a noun after *the*] not much or not enough □ *sedikit; tdk banyak; tdk cukup*: *I slept very little last night.* ♦ *a little-known author* ♦ *They have very little money.* ♦ *There is little hope that she will recover.* ↻ look at **less**, **least** 2 **a little** a small amount; to a small degree □ *sedikit*: *I like a little sugar in my tea.* ♦ *Could I have a little help, please?* ♦ *'Is there any butter left?' 'Yes, just a little.'* ♦ *This skirt is a little too tight.*

> **MORE** **A little bit** or **a bit** is often used instead of 'a little': *I was feeling a little bit tired so I decided not to go out.*

IDM **little by little** slowly □ *sedikit demi sedikit*: *After the accident her strength returned little by little.*

live¹ /lɪv/ verb 1 [I] to have your home in a particular place □ *tinggal; duduk*: *Where do you live?* ♦ *He still lives with his parents.* 2 [I] to be or stay alive □ *hidup*: *She hasn't got long to live.* ♦ *to live to a great age* 3 [I,T] to pass or spend your life in a certain way □ *hidup*: *to live a quiet life* ♦ *to live in comfort/poverty* 4 [I] to enjoy all the opportunities of life fully □ *menikmati hidup*: *I want to live a bit before settling down.*
IDM **live/sleep rough** ↻ **rough**⁴
PHR V **live by sth** to follow a particular belief or set of principles □ *hidup berpandukan sst*

live by doing sth to get the money, food, etc. you need by doing a particular activity □ *menyara hidup/mencari rezeki dgn membuat sst*: *They live by hunting and fishing.*

not live sth down to be unable to make people forget sth bad or embarrassing that you have done □ *tdk dapat membuat orang melupakan sst*

live for sb/sth to consider sb/sth to be the most important thing in your life □ *hidup hanya utk sso/sst*: He felt he had nothing to live for after his wife died.

live off sb/sth to depend on sb/sth in order to live □ *hidup dgn bergantung pd sso/sst*: Barry lives off tinned food. ◆ She could easily get a job but she still lives off her parents.

live on to continue to live or exist □ *terus hidup; tetap dikenang*: Mozart is dead but his music lives on.

live on sth 1 to have sth as your only food □ *hidup dgn makan sst sahaja*: to live on bread and water **2** to manage to buy what you need to live □ *menyara hidup dgn (wang yg ada)*: I don't know how they live on so little money!

live out sth 1 to actually do sth that you only imagined doing before □ *mengalami apa yg diimpikan*: to live out your dreams/fantasies **2** to spend the rest of your life in a particular way □ *hidup sepanjang hayat (dgn cara tertentu)*: They lived out their last few years in Peru.

live through sth to survive an unpleasant experience □ *hidup melalui/menempuh sst pengalaman*: She lived through two wars.

live together to live in the same house, etc. as sb and have a sexual relationship with them □ *hidup bersama; bersekedudukan*

live it up to enjoy yourself in an exciting way, usually spending a lot of money □ *hidup dgn mewah; berjoli*

live up to sth to be as good as expected □ *spt yg dijangkakan/diharapkan*: Children sometimes find it hard to live up to their parents' expectations.

live with sb = **live together**

live with sth to accept sth unpleasant that you cannot change □ *hidup dgn terpaksa menghadapi/menerima sst*: It can be hard to live with the fact that you are getting older.

live² /laɪv/ adj, adv
▶NOT DEAD **1** having life; not dead □ *hidup; bernyawa*: Have you ever touched a **real live** snake?
▶RADIO/TV PROGRAMME **2** seen or heard as it is happening □ *secara langsung*: live coverage of the Olympic Games ◆ This programme is coming live from the Millennium Stadium. ◆ to go out live on TV
▶PERFORMANCE **3** given or made when people are watching or listening; not recorded □ *di depan penonton*: The cafe has live music on Saturdays.
▶ELECTRICITY **4** (used about a wire, etc.) carrying electricity □ *hidup (elektrik)*: That cable is live.
▶BOMB, ETC. **5** (used about a bomb, bullet, etc.) that has not yet exploded □ *hidup; belum meletup*: live ammunition

livelihood /'laɪvlihʊd/ noun [C, usually sing] the way that you earn money □ *mata pencarian; punca pendapatan*: When the factory closed he lost his livelihood.

515   **live → load**

lively /'laɪvli/ adj (livelier; liveliest) full of energy, interest, excitement, etc. □ *cergas dan bersemangat; rancak; meriah*: lively children ◆ The town is quite lively at night.

liven /'laɪvn/ verb
PHR V **liven (sb/sth) up** to become or make sb/sth become more interesting and exciting □ *menjadi lebih cergas, bersemangat, rancak, meriah, dsb*: Once the band began to play the party livened up.

liver /'lɪvə(r)/ noun **1** [C] the part of your body that cleans your blood □ *hati* ⊃ picture at **body 2** [U] the liver of an animal when it is cooked and eaten as food □ *hati*: fried liver and onions

lives plural of **life**

livestock /'laɪvstɒk/ noun [U] animals that are kept on a farm, such as cows, pigs, sheep, etc. □ *binatang ternakan*

living¹ /'lɪvɪŋ/ adj **1** alive now □ *masih hidup*: He has no living relatives. ⊃ note at **alive 2** [only before a noun] still used or practised now □ *masih digunakan/diamalkan*: living languages/traditions OPP for both meanings **dead**

living² /'lɪvɪŋ/ noun **1** [C, usually sing] money to buy things that you need in life □ *nafkah hidup; wang utk berbelanja; mata pencarian*: What do you do **for a living**? **2** [U] your way or quality of life □ *cara hidup; kos hidup; taraf hidup*: The cost of living has risen in recent years. ◆ The **standard of living** is very high in that country.

living room (BrE also **sitting room**) noun [C] the room in a house where people sit, relax, watch TV, etc. together □ *ruang/bilik tamu* ⊃ picture on **page P8**

lizard /'lɪzəd/ noun [C] a small animal with four legs, dry skin and a long tail □ *cicak*

load¹ /ləʊd/ noun [C] **1** something (heavy) that is being or is waiting to be carried □ *beban; muatan*: a truck carrying a load of sand ⊃ picture at **pulley 2** [in compounds] the quantity of sth that can be carried □ *jumlah yg muat dibawa; penuh*: bus loads of tourists **3 loads (of sth)** [pl] (informal) a lot (of sth) □ *banyak; bertimbun-timbun*: There are loads of things to do in Dublin in the evenings.
IDM **a load of rubbish, etc.** (informal) nonsense □ *karut belaka/semata-mata*

load² /ləʊd/ verb **1** [I,T] **load (sth/sb) (up) (with sth); load (sth/sb) (into/onto sth)** to put a large quantity of sth into or onto sb/sth □ *memuatkan; memasukkan*: Have you finished loading yet? ◆ They loaded the plane (up) with supplies. ◆ Load the washing into the machine. **2** [I] to receive a load □ *dimuatkan barang-barang*: The ship is still loading. **3** [T] to put sth into a machine,

[C] **countable**, a noun with a plural form: *one book, two books*   [U] **uncountable**, a noun with no plural form: *some sugar*

loaded → location 516

a weapon, etc. so that it can be used □ *mengisi; memasukkan: to load film into a camera* ♦ *to load a gun* **4** [T] to put data or a program into a computer □ *memasukkan: Have you loaded the software?* **OPP** for all meanings **unload**

loaded /ˈləʊdɪd/ adj **1** loaded (with sth) carrying a load; full and heavy □ *bermuatan; sarat* **2** [not before a noun] (*informal*) having a lot of money; rich □ *banyak duit; kaya raya* **3** giving an advantage □ *berat sebelah; memihak kpd sso/sst: The system is loaded in their favour.* **4** (used especially about a gun or a camera) containing a bullet, a film, etc. □ *berisi peluru, filem, dsb*

loaf /ləʊf/ noun [C] (pl **loaves** /ləʊvz/) bread baked in one piece □ *buku/bantal roti; lof: a loaf of bread* ⊃ picture at **bread**

loan /ləʊn/ noun **1** [C] money, etc. that sb/sth lends you □ *pinjaman: to take out a bank loan* ♦ *to pay off a loan* ⊃ note at **money** ⊃ look at **borrow 2** [U] the act of lending sth or the state of being lent □ *(perbuatan) meminjamkan/dipinjamkan: The books are on loan from the library.* ▸ **loan** verb [T] (*formal*) loan sth (to sb)

HELP In American English **loan** as a verb is less formal and more common.

TOPIC
Loans

If you **can't afford** (= don't have enough money for) sth, you can **take out** a **loan**, for example from a bank. You can say: *I'm going to borrow some money from the bank* or: *The bank is going to lend me some money*. You will then **owe** the money and you will have to **pay it back**: *I'm paying back the £1000 that I owe in instalments—£50 every month*. The money you owe is called a **debt** (/det/): *I've got lots of debts*. When you borrow from a bank you also have to pay extra money called **interest**. The money that you borrow in order to buy a house, etc. is a **mortgage** (/ˈmɔːɡɪdʒ/).

loath (also **loth**) /ləʊθ/ adj (*formal*) loath to do sth □ *not willing to do sth* □ *tdk mahu; tdk suka; enggan: He was loath to admit his mistake.*

loathe /ləʊð/ verb [T] [not used in the continuous tenses] to hate sb/sth □ *berasa benci/meluat* **SYN** detest

HELP Although this verb is not used in the continuous tenses, it is common to see the present participle (= -ing form): *Loathing the thought of having to apologize, she knocked on his door.*

▸ **loathing** noun [U] ▸ **loathsome** /ˈləʊðsəm/ adj: *a loathsome place*

loaves plural of **loaf**

lob /lɒb/ verb [I,T] (**lobbing**; **lobbed**) (in sport) to hit, kick or throw a ball high into the air, so that it lands behind your opponent □ *lob; memukul, menendang atau membaling tinggi* ▸ **lob** noun [C]

lobby¹ /ˈlɒbi/ noun [C] (pl **lobbies**) **1** the area that is just inside a large building, where people can meet and wait □ *ruang legar; lobi: a hotel lobby* **2** [with sing or pl verb] a group of people who try to influence politicians to do or not do sth □ *(kumpulan) lobi: the anti-gun lobby*

lobby² /ˈlɒbi/ verb [I,T] (**lobbying**; **lobbies**; pt, pp **lobbied**) to try to influence a politician or the government to do or not do sth □ *melobi; cuba mempengaruhi*

lobe /ləʊb/ noun [C] **1** = **ear lobe** ⊃ picture at **ear 2** one part of an organ of the body, especially the brain or lungs □ *lobus*

lobster /ˈlɒbstə(r)/ noun **1** [C] a large sea creature with eight legs. A **lobster** is bluish-black but it turns red when it is cooked. □ *udang karang* ⊃ picture at **shellfish 2** [U] meat from a **lobster** eaten as food □ *masakan; udang karang*

local¹ /ˈləʊkl/ adj of a particular place (near you) □ *tempatan; setempat: local newspapers/radio* ♦ *the local doctor/policeman/plumber* ⊃ look at **international, national, regional** ▸ **locally** /ˈləʊkəli/ adv: *I do most of my shopping locally.*

local² /ˈləʊkl/ noun [C] **1** [usually pl] a person who lives in a particular place □ *penduduk atau orang tempatan: The locals seem very friendly.* **2** (*BrE informal*) a pub that is near your home where you often go to drink □ *pub berdekatan dgn rumah*

localize (also **-ise**) /ˈləʊkəlaɪz/ verb [T] to limit sth to a particular place or area □ *menyetempatkan*

local time noun [U] the time at a particular place in the world □ *waktu tempatan: We arrive in Singapore at 2 o'clock in the afternoon, local time.*

locate /ləʊˈkeɪt/ verb [T] **1** to find the exact position of sb/sth □ *mencari; mengesan; menentukan tempat: The damaged ship has been located two miles off the coast.* **2** to put or build sth in a particular place □ *meletakkan; menempatkan: They located their headquarters in Swindon.* ▸ **located** adj: *Where exactly is your office located?*

location /ləʊˈkeɪʃn/ noun **1** [C] a place or position □ *lokasi; tempat: Several locations have been suggested for the new office block.* **2** [U] the act of finding where sb/sth is □ *pencarian; (perbuatan) mencari: Police enquiries led to the location of the terrorists' hideout.*

IDM **on location** (used about a film, TV programme, etc.) made in a suitable place away from the building where films, etc. are usually made □ *di lokasi: The series was filmed on location in Thailand.*

[I] **intransitive**, a verb which has no object: *He laughed.*
[T] **transitive**, a verb which has an object: *He ate an apple.*

loch /lɒk/ noun [C] the Scottish word for a lake □ *tasik*: *the Loch Ness monster*

lock¹ /lɒk/ verb 1 [I,T] to close or fasten (sth) so that it can only be opened with a key □ *mengunci; dikunci*: *The door won't lock.* ♦ *Have you locked the car?* OPP **unlock** 2 [T] to put sb/sth in a safe place and lock it □ *mengunci*: *Lock your passport in a safe place.* 3 [T] be locked in sth to be involved in an angry argument, etc. with sth, or to be holding sb very tightly □ *bertegang leher; berpeluk rapat*: *The two sides were locked in a bitter dispute.* ♦ *They were locked in a passionate embrace.*
PHR V **lock sth away** to keep sth in a safe or secret place that is locked □ *mengunci sst (di tempat selamat atau rahsia)*
lock sb in/out to lock a door so that a person cannot get in/out □ *mengunci pintu supaya sso tdk dpt keluar atau masuk*: *I locked myself out of the house and had to climb in through the window.*
lock (sth) up to lock all the doors, windows, etc. of a building □ *mengunci (pintu, tingkap, dsb)*: *Make sure that you lock up before you leave.*
lock sb up to put sb in prison □ *memenjarakan*

lock² /lɒk/ noun [C] 1 something that is used for fastening a door, lid, etc. so that you need a key to open it again □ *kunci*: *to turn the key in the lock* ➔ look at **padlock** ➔ picture at **key** 2 a device with a key that prevents a vehicle or machine from being used □ *mangga*: *a bicycle lock* ♦ *a steering lock* ➔ picture at **bicycle** 3 a part of a river or a **canal** (= an artificial river) where the level of water changes. Locks have gates at each end and are used to allow boats to move to a higher or lower level. □ *pintu air*
IDM **pick a lock** ➔ **pick¹**
under lock and key in a locked place □ *di tempat yg berkunci*

locker /'lɒkə(r)/ noun [C] a small cupboard that can be locked in a school or sports centre, where you can leave your clothes, books, etc. □ *lokar; gerobok kecil*

locket /'lɒkɪt/ noun [C] a piece of jewellery that you wear on a chain around your neck and which opens so that you can put a picture, etc. inside □ *loket* ➔ picture at **jewellery**

locksmith /'lɒksmɪθ/ noun [C] a person who makes and repairs locks □ *tukang kunci*

locomotive /ˌləʊkə'məʊtɪv/ = **engine**(2)

locust /'ləʊkəst/ noun [C] a flying insect from Africa and Asia that moves in very large groups, eating and destroying large quantities of plants □ *belalang juta*

lodge¹ /lɒdʒ/ noun [C] 1 a small house in the country □ *pondok persinggahan* 2 a room at the entrance to a large building such as a college or factory □ *bilik (pengawal, porter, dsb)*

lodge² /lɒdʒ/ verb 1 [T] (*formal*) **lodge sth (with sb) (against sb/sth)** to make a statement complaining about sth to a public organization or authority □ *membuat aduan*: *They lodged a compensation claim against the factory.* 2 [I] to pay to live in sb's house with them □ *menumpang; menyewa bilik*: *He lodged with a family for his first term at university.* 3 [I,T] to become firmly fixed or to make sth do this □ *tersangkut; terbenam*

lodger /'lɒdʒə(r)/ noun [C] a person who pays rent to live in a house as a member of the family □ *penyewa* ➔ look at **boarder**

lodging /'lɒdʒɪŋ/ noun 1 [C,U] a place where you can stay □ *tempat penginapan*: *The family offered full board and lodging* (= a room and all meals) *in exchange for English lessons.* 2 **lodgings** [pl] (*old-fashioned*) a room or rooms in sb's house where you can pay to stay □ *bilik sewa*

loft /lɒft/ noun [C] the room or space under the roof of a house or other building □ *loteng; pagu* ➔ look at **attic** ➔ picture on **page P8**

log¹ /lɒg/ (*AmE also*) / noun [C] 1 a thick piece of wood that has fallen or been cut from a tree □ *kayu balak* ➔ picture at **tree** ➔ picture on **page P10** 2 (*also* **logbook**) the official written record of a ship's or an aircraft's journey □ *buku log*: *to keep a log*

log² /lɒg/ (*AmE also*) / verb [T] (**logging**; **logged**) to keep an official written record of sth □ *membuat catatan dlm buku log*
PHR V **log in/on** to perform the actions that allow you to start using a computer system □ *log masuk*: *You need to key in your password to log on.* ➔ note at **computer**
log off/out to perform the actions that allow you to finish using a computer system □ *log keluar (komputer)*

logarithm /'lɒgərɪðəm/ (*AmE also*) / (*also informal* **log**) noun [C] one of a series of numbers arranged in lists that allow you to solve problems in mathematics by adding or taking away numbers instead of multiplying or dividing □ *logaritma*

logbook /'lɒgbʊk/ (*AmE also*) / = **log¹**(2)

loggerheads /'lɒgəhedz/ (*AmE also*) / noun
IDM **at loggerheads (with sb)** strongly disagreeing (with sb) □ *bertelagah (dgn sso)*

logic /'lɒdʒɪk/ noun [U] 1 a sensible reason or way of thinking □ *logik*: *There is no logic in your argument.* 2 the science of using reason □ *ilmu logik/mantik*: *the rules of logic*

logical /'lɒdʒɪkl/ adj 1 seeming natural, reasonable or sensible □ *logik; wajar; munasabah*: *There is only one logical conclusion.* OPP **illogical** 2 thinking in a sensible way □ *logik*: *a logical mind* ▶ **logically** /-kli/ adv

login /'lɒgɪn/ (*AmE also*) / (*also* **log-on** /'lɒgɒn/) noun 1 [U] the act of starting to use a computer system, usually by typing a name or word that you choose to use □ *log masuk*: *If you've forgotten your login ID, click this link.* 2 [C] the name that you use to enter a computer system □ *nama log masuk*: *Enter your login and password and press 'go'.*

logo /ˈləʊgəʊ/ noun [C] (pl logos) a printed symbol or design that a company or an organization uses as its special sign □ *logo; lambang*: *the company/brand logo*

loiter /ˈlɔɪtə(r)/ verb [I] to stand or walk around somewhere for no obvious reason □ *melepak; berpelesiran*

lollipop /ˈlɒlipɒp/ (also **lolly** /ˈlɒli/ pl lollies) noun [C] a sweet on a stick □ *gula-gula batang; lolipop* ⇨ look at **ice lolly**

lone /ləʊn/ adj [only before a noun] **1** without any other people; alone □ *bersendirian; seorang diri*: *a lone swimmer* SYN **solitary 2** (used about a parent) single; without a partner □ *tunggal*

lonely /ˈləʊnli/ adj (**lonelier**; **loneliest**) **1** unhappy because you are not with other people □ *kesepian; kesunyian*: *to feel sad and lonely* **2** (used about a situation or a period of time) sad and spent alone □ *sepi; sunyi*: *lonely nights in front of the TV* **3** [only before a noun] far from other people and places where people live □ *terpencil; sunyi sepi*: *a lonely house in the hills* ⇨ note at **alone** ▸**loneliness** noun [U] ⇨ look at **solitude**, **isolation**

loner /ˈləʊnə(r)/ noun [C] (informal) a person who prefers being alone to being with other people □ *penyendiri*

lonesome /ˈləʊnsəm/ adj (AmE) lonely or making you feel lonely □ *kesunyian; terpencil* ⇨ note at **alone**

long¹ /lɒŋ/ adj (**longer** /ˈlɒŋgə(r)/, **longest** /ˈlɒŋgɪst/) measuring a large amount in distance or time □ *panjang; lama; jauh*: *She has lovely long hair.* ♦ *We had to wait a long time.* ♦ *a very long journey/book/corridor* ♦ *Nurses work very long hours.* ♦ *I walked a long way today.* OPP **short** ⇨ note at **far** ⇨ picture at **hair** ⇨ noun **length**

HELP **Long** is also used when you are asking for or giving information about how much something measures in length, distance or time: *How long is the film?* ♦ *The insect was only 2 millimetres long.* ♦ *a five-mile-long traffic jam*

IDM **a long shot** a person or thing that probably will not succeed, win, etc. □ *cubaan, tekaan, dsb liar (yakni tdk mungkin berjaya)*
at the longest not longer than the stated time □ *paling lama*: *It will take a week at the longest.*
go a long way (used about money, food, etc.) to be used for buying a lot of things, feeding a lot of people, etc. □ *(wang, makanan, dsb) akan dpt membeli banyak benda, memberi makan banyak orang, dll*
have a long way to go to need to make a lot more progress before sth can be achieved □ *masih jauh lagi; masih belum cukup bersedia*
in the long run after a long time; in the end □ *dlm jangka panjang*

in the long/short term ⇨ **term¹**
▸**long** noun [U]: *I'm sorry I haven't written to you for so long.* ♦ *This shouldn't take long.*

long² /lɒŋ/ adv (**longer** /ˈlɒŋgə(r)/, **longest** /ˈlɒŋgɪst/) **1** for a long time □ *lama*: *She didn't stay long.* ♦ *You shouldn't have to wait long.* ♦ *I hope we don't have to wait much longer.* ♦ *They won't be gone for long.* ♦ *Just wait here—I won't be long.* ♦ *'How long will it take to get there?' 'Not long.'*

HELP **Long** or **a long time**? **Long** and **a long time** are both used as expressions of time. In positive sentences **a long time** is usually used: *They stood there for a long time.* **Long** is only used in positive sentences with another adverb, for example 'too', 'enough', 'ago', etc: *We lived here long ago.* ♦ *I've put up with this noise long enough. I'm going to make a complaint.* Both **long** and **a long time** can be used in questions: *Were you away long/a long time?* In negative sentences there is sometimes a difference in meaning between **long** and **a long time**: *I haven't been here long* (= I arrived only a short time ago). ♦ *I haven't been here for a long time* (= it is a long time since I was last here).

2 a long time before or after a particular time or event □ *lama*: *We got married long before we moved here.* ♦ *Don't worry—they'll be here before long.* ♦ *All that happened long ago.* **3** for the whole of the time that is mentioned □ *sepanjang*: *The baby cried all night long.*
IDM **as/so long as** on condition that □ *asalkan*: *As long as no problems arise we should get the job finished by Friday.* SYN **provided (that)**
no/not any longer not any more □ *tdk lagi*: *They no longer live here.* ♦ *They don't live here any longer.*

long³ /lɒŋ/ verb [I] **long for sth; long (for sb) to do sth** to want sth very much, especially sth that is not likely □ *ingin sekali*: *She longed to return to Greece.* SYN **yearn** ▸**longing** noun [C,U]: *a longing for peace* ▸**longingly** adv

long-distance adj [only before a noun] (used about travel or communication) between places that are far from each other □ *jarak jauh*: *a long-distance lorry driver* ▸**long distance** adv

long-haul adj [only before a noun] connected with the transport of people or goods over long distances □ *perjalanan jarak jauh*: *a long-haul flight*

longitude /ˈlɒŋgɪtjuːd/ noun [U] the distance of a place east or west of a line from the North Pole to the South Pole that passes through Greenwich in London. **Longitude** is measured in degrees. □ *longitud* ⇨ look at **latitude** ⇨ picture at **earth**

the long jump noun [sing] the sport in which people try to jump as far as possible □ *(acara) lompat jauh* ⇨ look at **high jump**

long-life adj designed to last for a long time □ *tahan lama*: *a long-life battery* ♦ *long-life milk*

long-lived *adj* that has lived or lasted for a long time □ *hidup lama; bertahan lama; berlarutan*: *a long-lived dispute*

long-range *adj* [only *before* a noun] **1** that can go or be sent over long distances □ *jarak jauh*: *long-range nuclear missiles* **2** of or for a long period of time starting from the present □ *jangka panjang*: *the long-range weather forecast*

long-sighted (*AmE* **far-sighted**) *adj* able to see things clearly only when they are quite far away □ *rabun dekat* OPP **short-sighted, nearsighted**

long-standing *adj* that has lasted for a long time □ *telah lama*: *a long-standing arrangement*

long-suffering *adj* (used about a person) having a lot of troubles but not complaining □ *lama menderita*

long-term *adj* of or for a long period of time □ *jangka panjang*: *long-term planning*

long-winded *adj* (used about sth that is written or spoken) boring because it is too long □ *meleret-leret; terlalu panjang lebar*

loo /luː/ *noun* [C] (*pl* **loos**) (*BrE informal*) toilet □ *tandas* ⊃ note at **toilet**

look¹ /lʊk/ *verb*
▸USE EYES **1** [I,T] **look (at sth)** to turn your eyes in a particular direction (in order to pay attention to sb/sth) □ *tengok; menengok; melihat; memandang*: *Sorry, I wasn't looking. Can you show me again?* ◆ *Look carefully at this picture.* ◆ *to look out of the window* ◆ *She blushed and looked away.* ◆ *Look who's come to see us.* ◆ *Look where you're going!*
▸SEARCH **2** [I] **look (for sb/sth)** to try to find (sb/sth) □ *mencari*: *We've been looking for you everywhere. Where have you been?* ◆ *to look for work* ◆ *'I can't find my shoes.' 'Have you looked under the bed?'*
▸SEEM/APPEAR **3** [I] **look (like sb/sth) (to sb); look (to sb) as if /as though ...** to seem or appear □ *nampaknya; kelihatan*: *You look very smart in that shirt.* ◆ *to look tired/ill/sad/well/happy* ◆ *The boy looks like his father.* ◆ *That film looks good—I might go and see it.* ◆ *You look (to me) as if/as though you need some sleep.*
▸LISTEN **4** [I] used for asking sb to listen to what you are saying □ *digunakan utk meminta sso mendengar apa yg anda katakan*: *Look, Will, I know you are busy but could you give me a hand?*
▸FACE DIRECTION **5** [I] to face a particular direction □ *menghadap; menghala*: *This room looks south so it gets the sun all day.*
▸INTEND **6** [I] **look to do sth** to aim to do sth □ *mengharapkan*: *We are looking to double our profits over the next five years.*

HELP **Look, watch** or **see**? If you **look** at sth, you pay attention to it: *Look carefully. Can you see anything strange?* When you look at sth for a time, paying attention to what happens, you **watch** it: *Watch what I do, then you try.* If you become conscious of sth, you **see** it: *I saw a girl riding past on a bicycle.* **See** can also mean 'to watch a film, play, TV programme': *We went to see a movie last night.*

IDM **look bad; not look good** to be considered bad manners □ *nampak tak baik*: *It'll look bad if we get there an hour late.*
look your best to look as beautiful or attractive as possible □ *kelihatan*
look down your nose at sb/sth (*especially BrE informal*) to think that you are better than sb else; to think that sth is not good enough for you □ *memandang rendah pd sso*
look good to seem to be encouraging □ *nampaknya baik*: *This year's sales figures are looking good.*
look sb in the eye to look straight at sb without feeling embarrassed or afraid □ *berani memandang sso*
(not) look yourself to (not) look as well or healthy as usual □ *nampak macam tak sihat*
look on the bright side (of sth) to be positive about a bad situation, thinking of the advantages and not the disadvantages □ *memikirkan yg positif (di sebalik sst kesusahan, dsb)*
never/not look back to become and continue being successful □ *terus maju, berjaya, dsb*

PHR V **look after sb/sth/yourself** to be responsible for or take care of sb/sth/yourself □ *menjaga sso/sst/diri sendiri*: *I want to go back to work if I can find somebody to look after the children.* ◆ *The old lady's son looked after all her financial affairs.* ⊃ note at **care²**
look ahead to think about or plan for the future □ *memikirkan ttg masa depan*
look at sth 1 to examine or study sth □ *melihat, memeriksa, meneliti, dsb sst*: *My tooth aches. I think a dentist should look at it.* ◆ *The government is looking at ways of reducing unemployment.* ◆ *Could I look at (= read) the newspaper when you've finished with it?* **2** to consider sth □ *melihat (sst)*: *Different races and nationalities look at life differently.*
look back (on sth) to think about sth in your past □ *mengenang kembali (sst)*
look down on sb/sth to think that you are better than sb/sth □ *memandang rendah pd sso*
look forward to sth/doing sth to wait with pleasure for sth to happen □ *menanti-nanti akan sst atau utk membuat sst*: *I'm really looking forward to the weekend.*
look into sth to study or try to find out sth □ *mengkaji/menyiasat sst*: *A committee was set up to look into the causes of the accident.*
look on to watch sth happening without taking any action □ *memandang; memerhatikan*: *All we could do was look on as the house burned.*
look on sb/sth as sth; look on sb/sth with sth to think of sb/sth in a particular way □ *memandang atau menganggap sso/sst sebagai sst*: *They seem to look on me as someone who can advise them.*

look out to be careful or to pay attention to sth dangerous □ *awas; jaga-jaga*: *Look out! There's a bike coming.*
look out (for sb/sth) to pay attention in order to see, find or avoid sb/sth □ *mencari (sso/sst); berjaga-jaga ttg (sso/sst)*: *Look out for thieves!*
look round 1 to turn your head in order to see sb/sth □ *menoleh ke belakang* **2** to look at many things (before buying sth) □ *melihat-lihat*: *She looked round but couldn't find anything she liked.*
look round sth to walk around a place looking at things □ *melihat-lihat sst tempat*: *to look round a town/shop/museum*
look through sth to read sth quickly □ *membaca sst cepat-cepat*
look to sb for sth; look to sb to do sth to expect sb to do or to provide sth □ *mengharapkan sso utk pertolongan atau sst pemberian*: *He always looked to his father for advice.*
look up 1 to move your eyes upwards to look at sb/sth □ *memandang*: *She looked up and smiled.* **2** (informal) to improve □ *semakin baik*: *Business is looking up.*
look sth up to search for information in a book □ *mencari sst*: *to look up a word in a dictionary*
look up to sb to respect and admire sb □ *menghormati sso*

look² /lʊk/ *noun*
▸USING EYES **1** [C] the act of looking □ *(perbuatan) melihat; lihat; tengok*: *Have a look at this article.* ♦ *Take a close look at the contract before you sign it.*
▸SEARCH **2** [C, usually sing] **a look (for sb/sth)** a search □ *(perbuatan) mencari*: *I'll have a good look for that book later.*
▸EXPRESSION **3** [C] the expression on sb's face □ *air muka; kelihatan*: *He had a worried look on his face.*
▸APPEARANCE **4 looks** [pl] sb's appearance □ *rupa; paras*: *He's lucky—he's got good looks and intelligence.*
▸FASHION **5** [C] a fashion or style □ *gaya; fesyen*: *The shop has a new look to appeal to younger customers.*
IDM **by/from the look of sb/sth** judging by the appearance of sb/sth □ *nampaknya; memandangkan keadaan sso/sst*: *It's going to be a fine day by the look of it.*
like the look/sound of sb/sth ➪ **like²**

'look-in *noun*
IDM **(not) give sb a look-in; (not) get/have a look-in** (informal) to (not) give sb, or to (not) have a chance to do sth □ *(tdk) memberi peluang kpd sso, atau (tdk) mendapat peluang utk membuat sst*: *Tina doesn't get a look-in when Ben's playing on the computer.*

-looking /'lʊkɪŋ/ [in compounds] having the appearance mentioned □ *rupanya*: *an odd-looking building* ♦ *He's very good-looking.*

lookout /'lʊkaʊt/ *noun* [C] (a person who has) the responsibility of watching to see if danger is coming; the place this person watches from □ *pengawal; peninjau; tempat berkawal/meninjau*: *One of the gang acted as lookout.*
IDM **be on the lookout for sb/sth; keep a lookout for sb/sth** to pay attention in order to see, find or avoid sb/sth □ *mencari (sso/sst); berjaga-jaga ttg (sso/sst)*

loom¹ /luːm/ *verb* [I] **loom (up)** to appear as a shape that is not clear and in a way that seems frightening □ *muncul; menjelma*: *The mountain loomed (up) in the distance.*

loom² /luːm/ *noun* [C] a piece of equipment that is used for **weaving** (= making cloth by passing pieces of thread over and under other pieces) □ *alat tenun*

loony /'luːni/ *noun* [C] (pl **loonies**) (slang) a person who is crazy □ *orang yg gila/tdk siuman*
▶**loony** *adj*: *I'm tired of his loony ideas.*

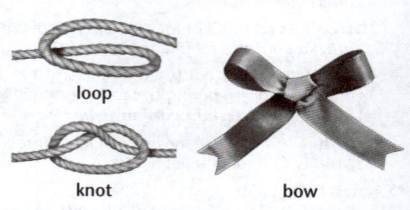

loop

knot   bow

loop /luːp/ *noun* [C] a curved or round shape made by a line curving round and joining or crossing itself □ *gelung*: *a loop in a rope* ♦ *The road goes around the lake in a loop.*
IDM **in the loop/out of the loop** (informal) part of a group of people that is dealing with sth important/not part of this group □ *termasuk dlm kumpulan yg membuat keputusan penting/tdk termasuk dlm kumpulan ini*
▶**loop** *verb* [I,T]: *He was trying to loop a rope over the horse's head.*

loophole /'luːphəʊl/ *noun* [C] a way of avoiding sth because the words of a rule or law are badly chosen □ *jalan keluar*

loose¹ /luːs/ *adj*
▸NOT TIED/FIXED **1** not tied up or shut in sth; free □ *lepas; terlepas; membiarkan lepas*: *The horse managed to get loose and escape.* ♦ *I take the dog to the woods and let him loose.* ♦ *She wore her long hair loose.* **2** not firmly fixed □ *goyang; goyah*: *I've got a loose tooth* ♦ *The saucepan handle is a bit loose so be careful.* **3** not contained in sth or joined together □ *tercerai-cerai; satu-satu (duit syiling, helaian kertas, dll)*: *loose change (= coins)* ♦ *some loose sheets of paper*
▸CLOTHES **4** not fitting closely; not tight □ *longgar*: *These trousers don't fit. They're much too loose round the waist.* **OPP** **tight**
▸NOT EXACT **5** not completely accurate or the same as sth □ *tdk berapa tepat*: *a loose translation*
IDM **all hell broke loose** ➪ **hell**
at a loose end having nothing to do and feeling bored □ *tdk ada apa-apa yg hendak dibuat*
▶**loosely** *adv*: *The film is loosely based on the life of Beethoven.*

loose² /luːs/ *noun*
IDM **on the loose** escaped and dangerous □ *(ter)lepas; bebas*: *a lion on the loose from a zoo*

loose 'cannon *noun* [C] a person, usually a public figure, who often behaves in a way that nobody can predict □ *org yg tdk dapat diramal tingkah lakunya*

loose-'leaf *adj* (used about a book, file, etc.) with pages that can be removed or added separately □ *helai cerai*: *a loose-leaf binder*

loosen /'luːsn/ *verb* [I,T] to become or make sth less tight □ *menjadi longgar; melonggarkan*: *The rope holding the boat loosened.* ◆ *to loosen your tie/belt* ◆ *Don't loosen your grip on the rope or you'll fall.*
PHR V **loosen (sb/sth) up** to relax or move more easily □ *melonggarkan; menjadi relaks*: *These exercises will help you to loosen up.*

loot /luːt/ *verb* [I,T] to steal things during a war or period of fighting □ *menjarah; merampas barang*

lop /lɒp/ *verb* [T] (**lopping**; **lopped**) to cut branches off a tree □ *memotong; mencantas*
PHR V **lop sth off/away** to cut sth off/away □ *memotong, mencantas atau memenggal sst*

lopsided /ˌlɒpˈsaɪdɪd/ *adj* with one side lower or smaller than the other □ *senget*: *a lopsided smile*

lord /lɔːd/ *noun* [C] **1** a man with a very high position in society □ *pembesar*: *the Lord Mayor of London* ◆ *Lord and Lady Derby* **2 the Lord** [sing] God; Christ □ *Tuhan* **3 the Lords** [with sing or pl verb] (*BrE*) (members of) the House of Lords □ *(ahli) Dewan Pertuanan*: *The Lords has/have voted against the bill.*

lorry /'lɒri/ *noun* [C] (*pl* **lorries**) (*BrE*) (*especially AmE* **truck**) a large strong motor vehicle that is used for carrying goods by road □ *lori* ⮕ note at **van** ⮕ picture on **page P7**

lose /luːz/ *verb* (*pt, pp* **lost** /lɒst (*AmE* also)/) **1** [T] to become unable to find sth □ *hilang; kehilangan*: *I've lost my purse. I can't find it anywhere.* **2** [T] to no longer have sb/sth □ *kehilangan*: *She lost a leg in the accident.* ◆ *He lost his wife last year* (= she died). ◆ *to lose your job* **3** [T] to have less of sth □ *hilang; kehilangan; menyusut; rugi*: *to lose weight/interest/patience* ◆ *The company is losing money all the time.* **OPP** **gain** **4** [T] (*informal*) to cause sb not to understand sth □ *membuat sso tdk faham*: *You've totally lost me! Please explain again.* **5** [I,T] to not win; to be defeated □ *kalah*: *We played well but we lost 2-1.* ◆ *to lose a court case/an argument* ◆ *Parma lost to Milan in the final.* **6** [I,T] to become poorer (as a result of sth) □ *rugi*: *The company lost on the deal.* **7** [T] to waste time, a chance, etc. □ *membuang masa, peluang, dll*: *Hurry up! There's no time to lose.*
IDM **give/lose ground (to sb/sth)** ⮕ **ground¹**
keep/lose your cool ⮕ **cool³**
keep/lose count (of sth) ⮕ **count²**
keep/lose your temper ⮕ **temper**
keep/lose track of sb/sth ⮕ **track¹**
lose your bearings to become confused about where you are □ *sesat; keliru*
lose face to lose the respect of other people □ *terhina; jatuh air muka*
lose your head to become confused or very excited □ *hilang pertimbangan*
lose heart to stop believing that you will be successful in sth you are trying to do □ *menjadi tawar hati*
lose it (*spoken*) to go crazy or suddenly become unable to control your emotions □ *hilang akal; tdk dpt mengawal perasaan*
lose your life to be killed □ *terbunuh*
lose sight of sb/sth to no longer be able to see sb/sth □ *tdk nampak sso/sst; lupa akan (sst)*: *We eventually lost sight of the animal in some trees.* ◆ (*figurative*) *We mustn't lose sight of our original aim.*
lose your touch to lose a special skill or ability □ *hilang sst kemahiran atau kepandaian*
lose touch (with sb/sth) to no longer have contact (with sb/sth) □ *terputus hubungan (dgn sso/sst)*: *I've lost touch with a lot of my old school friends.*
a losing battle a competition, fight, etc. in which it seems that you will fail to be successful □ *perjuangan yg sia-sia*
win/lose the toss ⮕ **toss**
PHR V **lose out (on sth/to sb)** (*informal*) to be at a disadvantage □ *rugi; ketinggalan*: *If a teacher pays too much attention to the brightest students in the class, the others lose out.*

loser /'luːzə(r)/ *noun* [C] **1** a person who is defeated □ *orang yg kalah*: *He is a bad loser. He always gets angry if I beat him.* **2** a person who is never successful □ *orang yg tdk pernah berjaya* **3** a person who suffers because of a particular situation, decision, etc. □ *orang yg kerugian*

loss /lɒs/ *noun* **1** [C,U] **(a) loss (of sth)** the state of no longer having sth or not having as much as before; the act of losing sth □ *kehilangan*: *loss of blood/sleep* ◆ *weight/hair loss* ◆ *Have you reported the loss of your wallet?* ◆ *The plane crashed with great loss of life.* **2** [C] **a loss (of sth)** the amount of money which is lost by a business □ *kerugian*: *The firm made a loss of £5 million.* ⮕ look at **profit** **3** [C] **a loss (to sb)** the disadvantage that is caused when sb/sth leaves or is taken away; the person or thing that causes this disadvantage □ *kehilangan*: *If she leaves, it/she will be a big loss to the school.*
IDM **at a loss** not knowing what to do or say □ *bingung; tdk tahu apa yg hendak dibuat*
cut your losses to stop wasting time or money on sth that is not successful □ *berhenti membuat sst (supaya tdk terus kerugian wang, masa, dsb)*

lost¹ *past tense, past participle of* **lose**

lost² /lɒst (*AmE* also) / *adj* **1** unable to find your way; not knowing where you are □ *sesat*: *This isn't the right road—we're completely lost!*

lost property → love

• If you **get lost**, stop and ask someone the way. **2** that cannot be found or that no longer exists □ *hilang; lenyap*: *The letter must have got lost in the post.* **3** unable to deal with a situation or to understand sth □ *bingung*: *Sorry, I'm lost. Could you explain the last part again?* **4 lost on sb** not noticed or understood by sb □ *tdk berkesan; tdk difahami oleh sso*: *The humour of the situation was completely lost on Joe.*

IDM get lost (*slang*) used to rudely tell sb to go away □ *berambuslah*

a lost cause a goal or an aim that cannot be achieved □ *usaha yg memang tdk akan berjaya*

lost for words not knowing what to say □ *tdk terkata apa-apa*

lost 'property *noun* [U] things that people have lost or left in a public place and that are kept in a special office for the owners to collect □ *barang hilang*

lot¹ /lɒt/ *pron, determiner* **a lot (of); lots (of)** a large amount or number (of things or people) □ *banyak; ramai*: '*How many do you need?*' '*A lot.*' ♦ *I've got a lot to do today.* ♦ *Have some more cake. There's lots left.* ♦ **An awful lot** of (= very many) *people will be disappointed if the concert is cancelled.* ♦ *There seem to be **quite a lot** of new shops opening.* ♦ *Sit here—there's lots of room.* ♦ *Lots of love, Billy* (= an informal ending for a letter).

> **GRAMMAR** In negative statements and questions, **much** and **many** are more usual: *A lot of girls go to dancing classes, but not many boys.* ♦ '*How much would a car like that cost?*' '*A lot!*'

lot² /lɒt/ *adv* (*informal*) **1 a lot; lots** [before an adjective or adverb] very much □ *lebih*: *a lot bigger/better/faster* ♦ *They see lots more of each other than before.* **2 a lot** very much or often □ *banyak; sering*: *Thanks a lot—that's very kind.* ♦ *It generally rains a lot at this time of year.*

lot³ /lɒt/ *noun* [sing, with sing or pl verb] (*informal*) all of sth; the whole of a group of things or people □ *semuanya; sekumpulan*: *When we opened the bag of potatoes the whole lot was/were bad.* ♦ *The manager has just sacked **the lot of them!*** ♦ *Just one more suitcase and **that's the lot!*** ♦ '*How many of these books shall we take?*' '*The lot.*' ♦ *You count those kids and I'll count **this lot**.*

IDM draw lots ⊃ **draw¹**

lo-tech = low-tech

loth = loath

lotion /ˈləʊʃn/ *noun* [C,U] liquid that you use on your hair or skin □ *losen*: *suntan lotion*

lottery /ˈlɒtəri/ *noun* [C] (*pl* lotteries) a way of making money for the government, for charity, etc. by selling tickets with numbers on them and giving prizes to the people who have bought certain numbers which are chosen by chance □ *loteri*

[I] **intransitive**, a verb which has no object: *He laughed.*

loud /laʊd/ *adj* (louder; loudest) *adv* **1** making a lot of noise; not quiet □ *kuat; lantang*: *Can you turn the TV down? It's too loud.* ♦ *You'll have to speak louder—the people at the back can't hear.* **OPP** quiet, soft

> **HELP Loud** or **noisy**? **Loud** is usually used to describe the sound itself or the thing producing the sound: *a loud noise/bang* ♦ *loud music.* **Noisy** is used to describe a person, animal, place, event, etc. that is very loud or too loud: *a noisy road/party/engine/child*

2 (used about clothes or colours) too bright □ *(warna) garang; menyilau; (pakaian) mencolok mata*: *a loud shirt*

IDM out loud so that people can hear it □ *kuat-kuat*: *Shall I read this bit out loud to you?*
▶ **loudly** *adv* ▶ **loudness** *noun* [U]

loudspeaker /ˌlaʊdˈspiːkə(r)/ *noun* [C] **1** a piece of electrical equipment for speaking, playing music, etc. to a lot of people □ *pembesar suara* **2** = speaker(3) □ *pembesar suara*

lounge¹ /laʊndʒ/ *noun* [C] **1** the part of an airport where passengers wait □ *ruang menunggu*: *the departure lounge* **2** (*BrE*) a comfortable room in a house or hotel where you can sit and relax □ *bilik rehat* **SYN** living room

lounge² /laʊndʒ/ *verb* [I] **lounge (about/around)** to sit, stand or lie in a lazy way □ *melepak-lepak*

louse /laʊs/ *noun* [C] (*pl* lice /laɪs/) a small insect that lives on the bodies of animals and people □ *kutu*

lousy /ˈlaʊzi/ *adj* (lousier; lousiest) (*informal*) very bad □ *teruk*: *We had lousy weather on holiday.*

lout /laʊt/ *noun* [C] a young man who behaves in a rude, rough or stupid way □ *pemuda yg kurang ajar; samseng* ⊃ look at **hooligan, yob**

lovable (also **loveable**) /ˈlʌvəbl/ *adj* having a character or appearance that is easy to love □ *mudah disayangi*: *a lovable little boy*

love¹ /lʌv/ *noun*
▶ AFFECTION **1** [U] a strong feeling that you have when you like sb/sth very much □ *cinta; kasih*: *a mother's love for her children* ♦ *to **fall in love** with somebody* ♦ *It was **love at first sight**. They got married two months after they met!* ♦ *He's **madly in love** with her.* ♦ *a love song/story*
▶ ENJOYMENT **2** [U, sing] a strong feeling of interest in or enjoyment of sth □ *minat*: *a love of adventure/nature/sport*
▶ SB/STH YOU LIKE **3** [C] a person, a thing or an activity that you like very much □ *kesukaan; kegemaran; kekasih*: *His great love was always music.* ♦ *Who was your first love?*
▶ FRIENDLY NAME **4** [C] (*BrE informal*) used as a friendly way of speaking to sb, often sb you do not know □ *sayang (sapaan)*: '*Hello, love. What can I do for you?*'
▶ IN TENNIS **5** [U] a score of zero □ *kosong*: *The score is forty-love.*

[T] **transitive**, a verb which has an object: *He ate an apple.*

IDM **give/send sb your love** to give/send sb a friendly message □ *sampaikan/kirim salam sayang*: *Give Maria my love when you next see her.*
(lots of) love (from) used at the end of a letter to a friend or a member of your family □ *salam kasih mesra (drpd)*: *See you soon. Love, Jim*
make love (to sb) to have sex □ *meniduri/ menyetubuhi (sso)*

love² /lʌv/ *verb* [T] **1** [not used in the continuous tenses] to like sb/sth in the strongest possible way □ *sayang; menyayangi; mengasihi*: *I split up from my girlfriend last year, but I still love her.* ◆ *She loves her children.* **2** to like or enjoy sth very much □ *suka; gemar*: *I love the summer!* ◆ *I really love swimming in the sea.* ◆ *'What do you think of this music?' 'I love it!'* **3 would love sth/to do sth** used to say that you would very much like sth/ to do sth □ *suka; ingin sekali*: *'Would you like to come?' 'I'd love to.'* ◆ *'What about a drink?' 'I'd love one.'* ◆ *We'd love you to come and stay with us.*

'love affair *noun* [C] **1** a romantic and/or sexual relationship between two people who are in love and not married to each other □ *hubungan asmara; cinta*: *She had a love affair with her tennis coach.* **2** a great enthusiasm for sth □ *kegemaran*

lovely /'lʌvli/ *adj* (**lovelier**; **loveliest**) **1** beautiful or attractive □ *cantik; indah; merdu*: *a lovely room/voice/expression* ◆ *You look lovely with your hair short.* **2** enjoyable or pleasant; very nice □ *seronok; menyeronokkan*: *We had a lovely holiday.* ⊃ note at **nice**
IDM **lovely and warm, peaceful, fresh, etc.** used for emphasizing how good sth is because of the quality mentioned □ *sangat bagus dan panas, aman damai, segar, dll*: *These blankets are lovely and soft.* ▶ **loveliness** *noun* [U]

lover /'lʌvə(r)/ *noun* [C] **1** a partner in a sexual relationship with sb who they are not married to □ *kendak; kekasih*: *He discovered that his wife had a lover.* ◆ *The park was full of young lovers holding hands.* **2** a person who likes or enjoys the thing mentioned □ *pencinta; penggemar*: *a music lover* ◆ *an animal lover*

loving /'lʌvɪŋ/ *adj* **1** feeling or showing love or care □ *penyayang; penuh kasih sayang*: *She's very loving towards her brother.* ◆ *a loving family* **SYN** **affectionate 2** [in compounds] **-loving** loving the thing or activity mentioned □ *suka*: *a fun-loving girl* ▶ **lovingly** *adv*

low¹ /ləʊ/ *adj* (**lower**; **lowest**) *adv*
▶ NOT HIGH/TALL **1** close to the ground or to the bottom of sth □ *bawah; rendah*: *Hang that picture a bit higher, it's much too low!* ◆ *That plane is flying very low.*
▶ LEVEL/VALUE **2** below the usual or normal level or amount □ *rendah*: *Temperatures were very low last winter.* ◆ *The price of fruit is lower in the summer.* ◆ *low wages* ◆ *low-fat yogurt* **3** below what is normal or acceptable in quality, importance or development □ *rendah*: *a low standard of living* ◆ *low status*
▶ SOUND/VOICE **4** deep or quiet □ *rendah; perlahan*: *His voice is already lower than his father's.* ◆ *A group of people in the library were speaking in low voices.*
▶ UNHAPPY **5** not happy and lacking energy □ *muram; lemah*: *He's been feeling a bit low since his illness.*
▶ LIGHT/HEAT **6** (used about a light, an oven, etc.) made to produce only a little light or heat □ *kecil; malap*: *Cook the rice on a low heat for 20 minutes.* ◆ *The low lighting adds to the restaurant's atmosphere.*
▶ IN CAR **7** (used about a gear in a car) that allows a slower speed □ *rendah* **OPP** **high**
IDM **high and low** ⊃ **high³**
a high/low profile ⊃ **profile**
lie low ⊃ **lie²**
run low (on sth) to start to have less of sth than you need; to start to be less than is needed □ *hampir kehabisan (sst)*: *We're running low on coffee—shall I go and buy some?*

low² /ləʊ/ *noun* [C] a low point, level, figure, etc □ *paras rendah*: *Unemployment has fallen to a new low.* **OPP** **high**

'low-down *noun*
IDM **give sb/get the low-down (on sb/sth)** (*informal*) to tell sb/be told the true facts or secret information (about sb/sth) □ *memberi sso (atau mendapatkan) maklumat sebenar atau rahsia (ttg sso/sst)*

lower¹ /'ləʊə(r)/ *adj* [only before a noun] below sth or at the bottom of sth □ *bawah*: *She bit her lower lip.* ◆ *the lower deck of a ship* **OPP** **upper**

lower² /'ləʊə(r)/ *verb* [T] **1** to make or let sb/ sth go down □ *menurunkan*: *They lowered the boat into the water.* ◆ *to lower your head/eyes* **2** to make sth less in amount, quality, etc. □ *mengurangkan; merendahkan*: *The virus lowers resistance to other diseases.* ◆ *Could you lower your voice slightly? I'm trying to sleep.* **OPP** for both meanings **raise**

,lower 'case *noun* [U] letters that are written or printed in their small form; not in capital letters □ *huruf kecil*: *The text is all in lower case.* ◆ *lower-case letters* **OPP** **upper case**

,low-'key *adj* quiet and not wanting to attract a lot of attention □ *tdk menonjol; sederhana*: *The wedding will be very low-key. We're only inviting ten people.*

lowland /'ləʊlənd/ *noun* [C, usually pl] a flat area of land at about sea level □ *tanah rendah; tanah pamah*: *the lowlands near the coast* ◆ *lowland areas*

,low-'lying *adj* (used about land) near to sea level; not high □ *(kawasan) rendah*

low-tech (also **lo-tech**) /ˌləʊ 'tek/ *adj* (*informal*) not using the most modern technology or methods □ *teknologi kurang canggih; teknologi rendah* **OPP** **high-tech**

low tide noun [U] the time when the sea is at its lowest level □ *air surut*: At low tide you can walk out to the island. **OPP** high tide

loyal /ˈlɔɪəl/ adj (used about a person) not changing in your friendship or beliefs □ *setia*: a loyal friend/supporter **SYN** faithful **OPP** disloyal ▶loyally adv ▶loyalty /ˈlɔɪəlti/ noun [C,U] (pl loyalties)

lozenge /ˈlɒzɪndʒ/ noun [C] **1** = diamond(2) **2** a sweet that you suck if you have a cough or a sore throat □ *lozeng*

L-plate /ˈel pleɪt/ noun [C] a sign with a large red letter L (for 'learner') on it, that you fix to a car to show that the driver is learning to drive □ *plat L*

Lt abbr = Lieutenant

Ltd /ˈlɪmɪtɪd/ abbr (BrE) = limited company □ *Bhd (Berhad)*: Pierce and Co. Ltd

lubricant /ˈluːbrɪkənt/ noun [C,U] a substance, for example oil, that makes the parts of a machine work easily and smoothly □ *pelincir*

lubricate /ˈluːbrɪkeɪt/ verb [T] to put oil, etc. onto or into sth so that it works smoothly □ *membubuh pelincir; melincirkan* ▶lubrication /ˌluːbrɪˈkeɪʃn/ noun [U]

lucid /ˈluːsɪd/ adj (formal) **1** (used about sth that is said or written) clear and easy to understand □ *jelas*: a lucid style/description **2** (used about sb's mind) not confused; clear and normal □ *waras* ▶lucidity /luːˈsɪdəti/ noun [U] ▶lucidly adv

luck /lʌk/ noun [U] **1** success or good things that happen by chance □ *tuah; nasib baik*: We'd like to wish you lots of luck in your new career. ♦ He says this necklace will bring you luck. ♦ I could hardly believe my luck when they offered me the job. ♦ With a bit of luck, we'll finish this job today. **2** chance; the force that people believe makes things happen □ *untung nasib*: There's no skill in this game—it's all luck. ♦ to have good/bad luck ⊃ look at fortune
IDM Bad luck!; Hard luck! used to show pity for sb □ *kasihan*: 'Bad luck! Maybe you'll win next time.'
be in/out of luck to be lucky/to not be lucky □ *bernasib baik/malang*: I was in luck—they had one ticket left!
Good luck (to sb)! used to wish that sb is successful □ *selamat/semoga berjaya*: Good luck! I'm sure you'll get the job.
push your luck ⊃ push¹
worse luck ⊃ worse

lucky /ˈlʌki/ adj (luckier; luckiest) **1** (used about a person) having good luck □ *bernasib baik; beruntung*: He's lucky to be alive after an accident like that. ♦ With so much unemployment, I count myself lucky that I've got a job. ♦ 'I'm off on holiday next week.' 'Lucky you!' **2** (used about a situation, event, etc.) having a good result □ *mujur; nasib baik*: It's lucky I got here before the rain started. ♦ a lucky escape **3** (used about a thing) bringing success or good luck □ *bertuah*: a lucky number ♦ It was not my lucky day. **OPP** unlucky
IDM you'll be lucky used to tell sb that sth they are expecting will probably not happen □ *jangan haraplah*: You're hoping for a ticket for Sunday's match? You'll be lucky!
▶luckily /ˈlʌkɪli/ adv: Luckily, I remembered to bring some money. ⊃ note at sudden

lucrative /ˈluːkrətɪv/ adj (formal) allowing sb to earn a lot of money □ *menguntungkan*: a lucrative contract/business/market

ludicrous /ˈluːdɪkrəs/ adj very silly □ *lucu; tdk munasabah*: What a ludicrous idea! **SYN** ridiculous ▶ludicrously adv: a ludicrously expensive project

lug /lʌɡ/ verb [T] (lugging; lugged) (informal) to carry or pull sth very heavy with great difficulty □ *mengheret*

luggage /ˈlʌɡɪdʒ/ noun [U] bags, suitcases, etc. used for carrying sb's clothes and things on a journey □ *bagasi*: 'How much luggage are you taking with you?' 'Only one suitcase.' ♦ You're only allowed one piece of hand luggage (= a bag that you carry with you on the plane). **SYN** baggage

luggage rack noun [C] a shelf above the seats in a train or bus for putting your bags, etc. on □ *rak bagasi* ⊃ picture at rack

lukewarm /ˌluːkˈwɔːm/ adj **1** (used about liquids) only slightly warm □ *suam-suam kuku* **2** lukewarm (about sb/sth) not showing much interest or desire □ *tdk berminat sangat; agak dingin*

lull¹ /lʌl/ noun [C, usually sing] a lull (in sth) a short period of quiet between times of activity □ *(waktu) tenang/reda*

lull² /lʌl/ verb [T] **1** to make sb relaxed and calm □ *menenangkan; menyebabkan (sso) terlelan*: She sang a song to lull the children to sleep. **2** lull sb into sth to make sb feel safe, and not expecting anything bad to happen □ *melalaikan; meredakan*: Our success lulled us into a false sense of security.

lullaby /ˈlʌləbaɪ/ noun [C] (pl lullabies) a gentle song that you sing to help a child to go to sleep □ *dodoi*

lumber¹ /ˈlʌmbə(r)/ (especially AmE) = timber(1)

lumber² /ˈlʌmbə(r)/ verb **1** [I] to move in a slow, heavy way □ *berjalan dgn perlahan dan berat*: A family of elephants lumbered past. **2** [T, usually passive] (informal) lumber sb (with sb/sth) to give sb a responsibility or job that they do not want □ *membebani*

luminous /ˈluːmɪnəs/ adj that shines in the dark □ *berkilau*: a luminous watch

lump¹ /lʌmp/ noun [C] **1** a piece of sth solid of any size or shape □ *ketul*: The sauce was full of lumps. ♦ a lump of coal/cheese/wood **2** a swelling under the skin □ *benjol*: You'll have a bit of a lump on your head where you banged it.

IDM **have/feel a lump in your throat** to feel pressure in your throat because you are about to cry □ *termengkelan*

lump² /lʌmp/ *verb* [T] **lump A and B together; lump A (in) with B** to put or consider different people or things together in the same group □ *melonggokkan; mengelompokkan*
IDM **lump it** (*informal*) to accept sth unpleasant because you have no choice □ *terpaksa menerima juga*: *That's the deal—like it or lump it.*

ˈlump sum *noun* [C] an amount of money paid all at once rather than in several smaller amounts □ *bayaran sekali gus*

lumpy /ˈlʌmpi/ *adj* full of or covered with lumps □ *berketul-ketul; berbonjol-bonjol*: *This bed is very lumpy.* **OPP** *smooth*

lunacy /ˈluːnəsi/ *noun* [U] behaviour that is very stupid □ *perbuatan gila; kegilaan*: *It was lunacy to drive so fast in that terrible weather.* **SYN** *madness*

lunar /ˈluːnə(r)/ *adj* connected with the moon □ *(berkenaan dgn) bulan*: *a lunar spacecraft/eclipse/landscape*

lunatic¹ /ˈluːnətɪk/ *noun* [C] (*informal*) a person who behaves in a stupid way doing crazy and often dangerous things □ *orang yg gila* **SYN** *madman, maniac*

lunatic² /ˈluːnətɪk/ *adj* stupid; crazy □ *gila-gila*: *a lunatic idea*

lunch /lʌntʃ/ *noun* [C,U] a meal that you have in the middle of the day □ *makan tengah hari*: *Hot and cold lunches are served between 12 and 2.*
◆ *What would you like for lunch?* ⊃ note at **meal**
▶ **lunch** *verb* [I] (*formal*)

MORE A **packed lunch** is food that you prepare at home and take to school or work. People at a **business lunch/working lunch** eat lunch together while continuing to discuss business. In Britain lunches served to children at school are called **school dinners**.

ˈlunch hour *noun* [C, usually sing] the time around the middle of the day when you stop work or school to have **lunch** □ *waktu rehat makan tengah hari*: *I went to the shops in my lunch hour.*

lunchtime /ˈlʌntʃtaɪm/ *noun* [C,U] the time around the middle of the day when **lunch** is eaten □ *waktu makan tengah hari*: *I'll meet you at lunchtime.*

lung /lʌŋ/ *noun* [C] one of the two organs of your body that are inside your chest and are used for breathing □ *paru-paru* ⊃ picture at **body**

lunge /lʌndʒ/ *noun* [C, usually sing] **a lunge (at sb); a lunge (for sb/sth)** a sudden powerful forward movement of the body, especially when trying to attack sb/sth □ *terpaan; terkaman*: *She made a lunge for the ball.* ▶ **lunge** *verb* [I]: *He lunged towards me with a knife.*

lurch¹ /lɜːtʃ/ *noun* [C, usually sing] a sudden movement forward or to one side □ *tersenggut*

IDM **leave sb in the lurch** ⊃ **leave¹**
▶ **lurch** *verb* [I]: *Suddenly the horse lurched to one side and the child fell off.*

lure¹ /lʊə(r)/ *verb* [T] to persuade or trick sb to go somewhere or do sth, usually by offering them sth nice □ *menarik sso utk pergi ke sst tempat atau melakukan sst*: *Young people are lured to the city by the prospect of a job and money.*

lure² /lʊə(r)/ *noun* [C] the attractive qualities of sth □ *godaan; daya tarikan*: *the lure of money/fame/adventure*

lurid /ˈlʊərɪd/ (*BrE also*) /ˈljʊər-/ *adj* **1** having colours that are too bright, in a way that is not attractive □ *berwarna yg menyilaukan*: *a lurid purple and orange dress* **2** (used about a story or a piece of writing) deliberately shocking, especially because of violent or unpleasant detail □ *mengejutkan; penuh sensasi* ▶ **luridly** *adv*

lurk /lɜːk/ *verb* [I] to wait somewhere secretly especially in order to do sth bad or illegal □ *menghendap; terhendap-hendap*: *I thought I saw somebody lurking among the trees.*

luscious /ˈlʌʃəs/ *adj* (used about food) tasting very good □ *lazat*: *luscious fruit*

lush /lʌʃ/ *adj* (used about plants or gardens) growing well, with a lot of healthy grass and plants close together □ *subur*

lust¹ /lʌst/ *noun* **1** [U] **lust (for sb)** strong sexual desire □ *nafsu berahi* **2** [C,U] **(a) lust (for sth)** (a) very strong desire to have or get sth □ *keinginan yg kuat; keghairahan*: *a lust for power* ◆ *(a) lust for life* (= enjoyment of life)

lust² /lʌst/ *verb* [I] **lust (after sb); lust (after/for sth)** to feel a very strong desire for sb/sth □ *berahi akan (sso); amat mengingini (sst)*: *to lust for power/success/fame*

lustful /ˈlʌstfl/ *adj* full of sexual desire □ *penuh berahi*: *lustful thoughts* ▶ **lustfully** /-fəli/ *adv*

luxurious /lʌgˈʒʊəriəs/ *adj* very comfortable; full of expensive and beautiful things □ *mewah*: *a luxurious hotel* ▶ **luxuriously** *adv*

luxury /ˈlʌkʃəri/ *noun* (*pl* **luxuries**) **1** [U] the enjoyment of expensive and beautiful things; great comfort and pleasure □ *kemewahan*: *They are said to be living in luxury in Barbados.*
◆ *to lead a life of luxury* ◆ *a luxury hotel/car/yacht* **2** [C] something that is enjoyable and expensive that you do not really need □ *(sst yg) mewah*: *She bought flowers, chocolates and other luxuries.* **3** [U, sing] a pleasure which you do not often have □ *kenikmatan*: *It was (an) absolute luxury to do nothing all weekend.*

LW *abbr* (*especially BrE*) **long wave**; a band of radio waves with a length of more than 1000 metres □ *gelombang panjang*: *1 500m LW*

lynch /lɪntʃ/ *verb* [T] (used about a crowd of people) to kill, usually by hanging, sb who is thought to be guilty of a crime without a legal trial in a court of law □ *membunuh atau menggantung sso tanpa perbicaraan*

lyric /ˈlɪrɪk/ *adj* (used about poetry) expressing personal feelings and thoughts □ *lirik*: *lyric poems*

lyrical /ˈlɪrɪkl/ *adj* like a song or a poem, expressing strong personal feelings □ *(bersifat) lirik*

lyrics /ˈlɪrɪks/ *noun* [pl] the words of a song □ *seni kata; lirik*

M m

M, m /em/ *noun* [C,U] (*pl* Ms; M's; m's /emz/) the 13th letter of the English alphabet □ *M, m (huruf)*: *'Mark' begins with an) 'M'*.

M *abbr* **1** (also **med**) = **medium¹** □ *M (saiz sedang)* **2** /em/ (*BrE*) = **motorway** □ *lebuh raya*: *heavy traffic on the M25*

m *abbr* **1 m** = **metre** □ *m (meter)*: *a 500m race* **2 m** = **million** □ *juta*: *population 10m*

MA /ˌem ˈeɪ/ *abbr* **Master of Arts**; a second degree that you receive when you complete a more advanced course or piece of research in an arts subject at university or college □ *MA (Sarjana Sastera)* ➲ look at **BA, MSc**

mac /mæk/ (also **mackintosh**) *noun* [C] (*especially BrE*) a coat that is made to keep out the rain □ *baju hujan*

macabre /məˈkɑːbrə/ *adj* unpleasant and frightening because it is connected with death □ *menyeramkan*: *a macabre tale/joke/ritual*

macaroni /ˌmækəˈrəʊni/ *noun* [U] a type of **pasta** (= Italian food made from flour and water) in the shape of short tubes □ *makaroni*

machete /məˈʃeti/ *noun* [C] a wide heavy knife used as a cutting tool and as a weapon □ *sejenis parang*

machine /məˈʃiːn/ *noun* [C] [often in compounds] a piece of equipment with moving parts that is designed to do a particular job. A machine usually needs electricity, gas, steam, etc. in order to work □ *mesin*: *a washing/sewing/knitting machine* ♦ *a machine for making pasta* ➲ note at **tool**

maˈchine gun *noun* [C] a gun that fires bullets very quickly and continuously □ *mesingan* ➲ note at **gun**

machinery /məˈʃiːnəri/ *noun* [U] machines in general, especially large ones; the moving parts of a machine □ *jentera*: *farm/agricultural/industrial machinery*

macho /ˈmætʃəʊ/ *adj* (*informal*) (used about a man or his behaviour) having qualities typical of men, like strength and courage, but using them in an aggressive way □ *'macho'; jantan sejati*: *He's too macho to ever admit he was wrong and apologize.*

mackintosh /ˈmækɪntɒʃ/ = **mac**

mad /mæd/ *adj* (**madder**; **maddest**)
➤ILL **1** having a mind that does not work normally; mentally ill □ *gila; tdk siuman*: *They realized that he had gone mad.*

> **HELP** Mentally ill is the polite way of describing a person who is not mentally normal.

➤STUPID **2** (*BrE*) not at all sensible; stupid □ *gila; kurang waras*: *You must be mad to drive in this weather.*
➤ANGRY **3** [not before a noun] **mad (at/with sb) (about sth)** very angry □ *sangat marah*: *His laziness drives me mad!* ♦ (*especially AmE*) *Don't get/go mad at him. He didn't mean to do it.*
➤VERY INTERESTED **4** (*informal*) **mad about/on sb/sth** liking sb/sth very much □ *gila; sangat suka*: *He's mad on computer games at the moment.* ♦ *Steve's mad about Jane.*
➤WILD **5** not controlled; wild or very excited □ *tdk terkawal; liar*: *The audience was cheering and clapping like mad* (= very hard). ♦ *When Brad Pitt appeared on the hotel balcony his fans went mad.*

madam /ˈmædəm/ *noun* [sing] **1** (*formal*) used as a polite way of speaking to a woman, especially to a customer in a shop or restaurant □ *puan*: *Can I help you, madam?* ➲ look at **sir 2 Madam** used for beginning a formal letter to a woman when you do not know her name □ *Puan*: *Dear Madam, I am writing in reply ...*

ˌmad ˈcow disease (*informal*) = **BSE**

maddening /ˈmædnɪŋ/ *adj* that makes you very angry or annoyed □ *memanaskan hati; menyakitkan hati*: *She has some really maddening habits.* ➤**maddeningly** *adv*

made *past tense, past participle of* **make¹**

madly /ˈmædli/ *adv* **1** in a wild or crazy way □ *gila-gila; tdk tentu arah*: *They were rushing about madly.* **2** (*informal*) very; extremely □ *sangat; terlalu*: *They're madly in love.*

madman /ˈmædmən/ *noun* [C] (*pl* -men /-mən/) a person who behaves in a wild or crazy way □ *orang gila* SYN **lunatic**

madness /ˈmædnəs/ *noun* [U] crazy or stupid behaviour that could be dangerous □ *(kelakuan) spt orang gila; kegilaan*: *It would be madness to take a boat out on the sea in such rough weather.*

magazine /ˌmæɡəˈziːn/ (also *informal* **mag** /mæɡ/) *noun* [C] a type of large thin book with a paper cover that you can buy every week or month containing articles, photographs, etc. often on a particular topic □ *majalah*: *a fashion/computer/gardening magazine* ➲ note at **newspaper**

magenta /məˈdʒentə/ *adj* reddish-purple in colour □ *merah lembayung; magenta* ➤**magenta** *noun* [U]

maggot /ˈmægət/ noun [C] a young insect before it grows wings and legs and becomes a fly □ *ulat; berenga* ➔ picture at **worm**

magic¹ /ˈmædʒɪk/ noun [U] **1** a secret power that some people believe can make strange or impossible things happen by saying special words or doing special things □ *kuasa ajaib; kesaktian; sihir*: The witch had used her magic to turn the children into frogs. ➔ look at **black magic** **2** the art of doing tricks that seem impossible, in order to entertain people □ *silap mata* **3** a special quality that makes sth seem wonderful □ *keajaiban; keistimewaan*: I'll never forget the magic of that moment.

magic² /ˈmædʒɪk/ adj **1** used in or using magic □ *ajaib; sakti*: a magic spell/potion/charm/trick ◆ There is no magic formula for passing exams—just hard work. **2** having a special quality that makes sth seem wonderful □ *menakjubkan; istimewa*: Respect is the magic ingredient in our relationship.

magical /ˈmædʒɪkl/ adj **1** that seems to use magic □ *ajaib*: a herb with magical powers to heal **2** wonderful and exciting □ *penuh keajaiban; istimewa*: Our holiday was absolutely magical. ▶ **magically** /-kli/ adv

magician /məˈdʒɪʃn/ noun [C] **1** a person who performs magic tricks to entertain people □ *ahli silap mata* ➔ look at **conjuror** **2** (in stories) a man who has magic powers □ *tukang sihir* ➔ look at **wizard**

ˌmagic ˈwand = **wand**

magistrate /ˈmædʒɪstreɪt/ noun [C] an official who acts as a judge in cases involving less serious crimes □ *majistret*

magnanimous /mæɡˈnænɪməs/ adj kind, generous and forgiving (especially towards an enemy or opponent) □ *baik hati; murah hati*

magnate /ˈmæɡneɪt/ noun [C] a person who is rich, powerful and successful, especially in business □ *usahawan yg unggul; sso tokoh yg kaya, berkuasa dan berjaya, khususnya dlm bidang perniagaan*: a media/property/shipping magnate

magnesium /mæɡˈniːziəm/ noun [U] (symbol Mg) a light, silver-white metal that burns with a bright white flame □ *magnesium*

magnet /ˈmæɡnət/ noun [C] a piece of iron, steel, etc. that can attract and pick up other metal objects □ *magnet; besi berani*

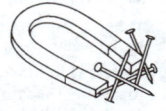

magnetic /mæɡˈnetɪk/ adj **1** having the ability to attract metal objects □ *bermagnet*: magnetic fields ◆ a magnetic tape/disk (= containing electronic information that can be read by a computer or other machine) **2** having a quality that strongly attracts people □ *berdaya tarikan*: a magnetic personality ▶ **magnetism** /ˈmæɡnətɪzəm/ noun [U]: Nobody could resist his magnetism.

[C] **countable**, a noun with a plural form: *one book, two books*

magnificent /mæɡˈnɪfɪsnt/ adj extremely impressive and attractive □ *hebat; menakjubkan; mengagumkan*: What a magnificent castle! **SYN** splendid ▶ **magnificence** noun [U] ▶ **magnificently** adv

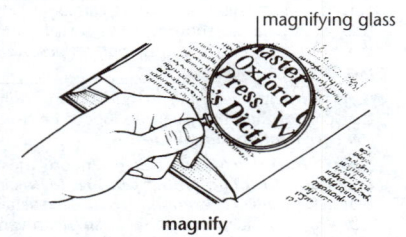

magnifying glass

magnify

magnify /ˈmæɡnɪfaɪ/ verb [T] (magnifying; magnifies; pt, pp magnified) **1** to make sth look bigger than it is, usually using a special piece of equipment □ *membesar-besarkan*: to magnify something under a microscope **SYN** enlarge **2** to make sth seem more important than it really is □ *membesar-besarkan*: to magnify a problem **SYN** exaggerate ▶ **magnification** /ˌmæɡnɪfɪˈkeɪʃn/ noun [U]

ˈmagnifying glass noun [C] a round piece of glass, usually with a handle, that is used for making things look bigger than they are □ *kanta pembesar* ➔ picture at **magnify**

magnitude /ˈmæɡnɪtjuːd/ noun [U] the great size or importance of sth □ *besarnya; pentingnya*

mahogany /məˈhɒɡəni/ noun [U] the hard dark reddish-brown wood from a tropical tree that is used especially for making furniture □ *mahogani*

maid /meɪd/ noun [C] a woman whose job is to clean in a hotel or large house □ *pembantu (rumah)* ➔ look at **chambermaid**

maiden name /ˈmeɪdn neɪm/ noun [C] a woman's family name before marriage □ *nama keluarga (sso wanita) sebelum berkahwin* ➔ note at **name** ➔ look at **née**

ˌmaiden ˈvoyage /ˌmeɪdn ˈvɔɪdʒ/ noun [C] the first journey of a new ship □ *pelayaran sulung*

mail /meɪl/ (BrE also post) noun [U] **1** the system for collecting and sending letters and packages □ *mel; sistem pos*: to send a parcel by airmail/surface mail ➔ note at **post** **2** the letters, etc. that you receive □ *mel; surat, bungkusan, dsb pos*: There isn't much mail today. **3** = email ▶ **mail** verb [T] (especially AmE)

mailbox /ˈmeɪlbɒks/ noun [C] **1** (AmE) = **letter box**(2) **2** (AmE) = **postbox** **3** a computer program that receives and stores email □ *peti mel*

ˈmailing list noun [C] a list of the names and addresses of people to whom advertising ma-

[U] **uncountable**, a noun with no plural form: *some sugar*

mailman → majority

terial or information is regularly sent by a business or an organization □ *senarai mel*

mailman /ˈmeɪlmæn/ *noun* (*pl* -men /-men/) (*AmE*) = **postman**

mail ˈorder *noun* [U] a method of shopping. You choose what you want from a **catalogue** (= a book or Internet site showing goods for sale) and the goods are sent to you by post. □ *pesanan pos* ➔ note at **online**

maim /meɪm/ *verb* [T] to hurt sb so badly that part of their body can no longer be used □ *mencederakan hingga cacat*

main¹ /meɪn/ *adj* [only *before* a noun] most important □ *utama; paling penting*: *My main reason for wanting to learn English is to get a better job.* ◆ *a busy main road* ◆ *He doesn't earn very much but he's happy, and that's* **the main thing**. **SYN chief**
IDM in the main (*formal*) generally; mostly □ *pd keseluruhannya; kebanyakannya*: *We found English people very friendly in the main.*

main² /meɪn/ *noun* **1** [C] a large pipe or wire that carries water, gas or electricity between buildings □ *salur utama*: *The water main has burst.* **2 the mains** [pl] (*BrE*) the place where the supply of gas, water or electricity to a building starts; the system of providing these services to a building □ *sumber bekalan*: *Turn the water off at the mains.* ◆ *mains gas/water/electricity*

mainframe /ˈmeɪnfreɪm/ (also **mainframe comˈputer**) *noun* [C] a large powerful computer, usually the centre of a system that is shared by many users □ *kerangka utama* ➔ look at **PC**

mainland /ˈmeɪnlænd/ *noun* [sing] the main part of a country or continent, not including the islands around it □ *tanah besar*: *mainland Greece*

mainly /ˈmeɪnli/ *adv* mostly □ *kebanyakannya*: *The students here are mainly from Japan.*

mainstay /ˈmeɪnsteɪ/ *noun* [C] a person or thing that is the most important part of sth, which makes it possible for it to exist or to be successful □ *tulang belakang*: *Cocoa is the mainstay of the country's economy.*

mainstream /ˈmeɪnstriːm/ *noun* [sing] the ideas and opinions that are considered normal because they are shared by most people; the people who hold these opinions and beliefs □ *aliran utama*: *The Green Party is not* **in the mainstream** *of British politics.*

maintain /meɪnˈteɪn/ *verb* [T] **1** to make sth continue at the same level, standard, etc. □ *mengekalkan*: *We need to maintain the quality of our goods but not increase the price.* ◆ *to maintain law and order* **2** to keep sth in good condition by checking and repairing it regularly □ *menyenggara*: *to maintain a road/building/machine* ◆ *The house is large and expensive to maintain.* **3** to keep saying that sth is true even when others disagree or do not believe it □ *mempertahankan*: *I still maintain that I was right to*

sack him. ◆ *She has always maintained her innocence.* **4** to support sb with your own money □ *menanggung; menyara*: *He has to maintain a child from his previous marriage.*

maintenance /ˈmeɪntənəns/ *noun* [U] **1** keeping sth in good condition □ *penyenggaraan*: *This house needs a lot of maintenance.* ◆ *car maintenance* **2** (*BrE*) money that sb must pay regularly to a former wife, husband or partner especially when they have had children together □ *nafkah*: *He has to pay maintenance to his ex-wife.*

maisonette /ˌmeɪzəˈnet/ *noun* [C] (*BrE*) a flat on two floors that is part of a larger building □ *maisonet (apartmen)*

maize /meɪz/ (*AmE* **corn**) *noun* [U] a tall plant which produces yellow grains in a large mass that are cooked and eaten □ *jagung* ➔ look at **sweetcorn**

Maj. *abbr* = **major²**(1) □ *singkatan utk pangkat 'mejar'*

majestic /məˈdʒestɪk/ *adj* impressive because of its size or beauty □ *hebat; agung*: *a majestic mountain landscape* ▸ **majestically** /-kli/ *adv*

majesty /ˈmædʒəsti/ *noun* (*pl* **majesties**) **1** [U] the impressive and attractive quality that sth has □ *kehebatan; keagungan*: *the splendour and majesty of the palace and its gardens* **2 His/Her/Your Majesty** [C] (*formal*) used when speaking to or about a royal person □ *Duli Yg Maha Mulia*: *Her Majesty the Queen*

major¹ /ˈmeɪdʒə(r)/ *adj* **1** [only *before* a noun] very large, important or serious □ *utama; besar*: *The patient needs major heart surgery.* ◆ *There haven't been any major problems.* **OPP minor 2** of one of the two types of **key¹**(4) in which music is usually written □ *major*: *the key of D major* ➔ look at **minor**

major² /ˈmeɪdʒə(r)/ *noun* **1** (*abbr* **Maj.**) [C] an officer of a middle level in the army or the US air force □ *mejar* **2** [C] (*AmE*) the main subject or course of a student at college or university; the student who studies it □ *mata pelajaran utama*: *Her major is French.*

major³ /ˈmeɪdʒə(r)/ *verb*
PHR V major in sth (*AmE*) to study sth as your main subject at college or university □ *mengkhusus dlm (sst) mata pelajaran*

ˌmajor ˈgeneral *noun* [C] an officer of a high level in the army □ *mejar jeneral*

majority /məˈdʒɒrəti/ (*AmE* also /-ˈdʒɔːr-/) *noun* (*pl* **majorities**) **1** [sing, with sing or pl verb] **majority (of sb/sth)** the largest number or part of a group of people or things □ *kebanyakan*: *The majority of students in the class come/comes from Japan.* ◆ *This treatment is not available in* **the vast majority** *of hospitals.* **OPP minority 2** [C, usually sing] **majority (over sb)** (in an election) the difference in the number of votes for the person/party who came first and the person/party who came second □ *majoriti; kelebihan undi*: *He was elected by/with a majority of almost 5 000 votes.*

[I] **intransitive**, a verb which has no object: *He laughed.*   [T] **transitive**, a verb which has an object: *He ate an apple.*

MORE If you have an **overall majority**, you got more votes than all the other people/parties added together.

IDM **be in the/a majority** to form the largest number or part of sth □ *sebahagian besar*: *Women are in the majority in the teaching profession.*

make¹ /meɪk/ *verb* [T] (*pt, pp* **made** /meɪd/)
▶CREATE **1** to produce or create sth □ *membuat; menghasilkan; diperbuat*: *to make bread* ◆ *This model is made of steel, and that one is made out of used matches.* ◆ *Cheese is made from milk.* ◆ *Those cars are made in Slovakia.* ◆ *Shall I make you a sandwich/make a sandwich for you?* ◆ *to make breakfast* ◆ *to make a hole in something* ◆ *to make a law/rule* ◆ *to make a movie*
▶PERFORM ACTION **2** [used with nouns] to perform a certain action □ *membuat*: *to make a mistake/noise* ◆ *to make a guess/comment/statement/suggestion* ◆ *to make progress* ◆ *I've made an appointment to see the doctor.*

HELP **Make** can be used like this with a number of different nouns. Often there is a verb with a similar form, for example **make a decision = decide**. But if you use 'make' + noun, you can use an adjective with it: *He made the right decision.* ◆ *They made a generous offer.*

▶CAUSE **3** to cause a particular effect, feeling, situation, etc. □ *membuat*: *The film made me cry.* ◆ *Flying makes him nervous.* ◆ *Her remarks made the situation worse.* ◆ *I'll make it clear to him that we won't pay.* ◆ *Make sure you lock the car.* ◆ *You don't need to know much of a language to make yourself understood.* ◆ *to make trouble/a mess/a noise*
▶BECOME **4** to make sb/sth become sth; to have the right qualities to become sth □ *menjadi-(kan); melantik; dilantik*: *She was made (= given the job of) President.* ◆ *You can borrow some money this time, but don't make a habit of it.* ◆ *Karen explains things very clearly—she'd make a good teacher.* **5** to become sth; to achieve sth □ *menjadi; mencapai*: *I'm hoping to make head of the department by the time I'm thirty.*
▶FORCE **6** **make sb do sth** to force sb/sth to do sth □ *memaksa; menyuruh*: *You can't make her come with us if she doesn't want to.* ◆ *They made me repeat the whole story.*

GRAMMAR In the passive we must use **to**: *He was made to wait at the police station.*

▶MONEY/NUMBERS/TIME **7** used with money, numbers and time □ *digunakan utk bercakap ttg wang, bilangan dan masa*: *How much do you think he makes (= earns) a month?* ◆ *to make a lot of money* ◆ *5 and 7 make 12.* ◆ *'What's the time?' 'I make it 6.45.'*
▶GET TO **8** to manage to reach a place or go somewhere □ *sampai; tiba*: *We should make Bristol by about 10.* ◆ *I can't make the meeting next week.*

IDM **make do with sth** to use sth that is not good enough because nothing better is available □ *terpaksa menggunakan apa yg ada*: *If we can't get limes, we'll have to make do with lemons.*
make it to manage to do sth; to succeed □ *berjaya; selamat*: *She'll never make it as an actress.* ◆ *He's badly injured—it looks like he might not make it (= survive).* ❶ For other idioms containing **make**, look at the entries for the nouns, adjectives, etc. For example, **make amends** is at **amends**.

PHR V **be made for sb/each other** to be well matched to sb/each other □ *sesuai; sama padan*: *Jim and Alice seem made for each other.*
make for sb/sth to move towards sb/sth □ *pergi ke sso/sst*
make for sth to help or allow sth to happen □ *membuat; menghasilkan*: *Arguing all the time doesn't make for a happy marriage.*
make sb/sth into sb/sth to change sb/sth into sb/sth □ *membuat atau mengubah sso/sst menjadi sso/sst (yg lain)*: *She made her spare room into an office.*
make of sb/sth to understand the meaning or nature of sb/sth □ *faham akan atau dpt difahamkan ttg sso/sst*: *What do you make of Colin's letter?*
make off (with sth) (*informal*) to leave or escape in a hurry, for example after stealing sth □ *cabut lari (dgn sst)*: *Someone's made off with my wallet!*
make sb/sth out 1 to understand sb/sth □ *memahami sso/sst*: *I just can't make him out.* **2** to be able to see or hear sb/sth; to manage to read sth □ *dpt melihat atau mendengar sso/sst; dpt membaca sst*: *I could just make out her signature.*
make out that …; make yourself out to be sth to say that sth is true and try to make people believe it □ *mengatakan; berpura-pura*: *He made out that he was a millionaire.* ◆ *She's not as clever as she makes herself out to be.*
make (yourself/sb) up to put powder, colour, etc. on your/sb's face to make it look attractive □ *mengenakan mekap; bersolek*
make sth up 1 to form sth □ *membentuk*: *the different groups that make up our society* **2** to invent sth, often sth that is not true □ *mereka-reka*: *to make up an excuse* **3** to make a number or an amount complete; to replace sth that has been lost □ *mencukupkan; menggenapkan*: *We need one more person to make up our team.*
make up for sth to do sth that corrects a bad situation □ *menggantikan*: *Her enthusiasm makes up for her lack of experience.*
make it up to sb (*informal*) to do sth that shows that you are sorry for what you have done to sb or that you are grateful for what they have done for you □ *mengganti rugi; menebus*: *You've done me a big favour. How can I make it up to you?*
make (it) up (with sb) to become friends again after an argument □ *berbaik semula*: *Has she made it up with him yet?*

make² /meɪk/ *noun* [C] the name of the company that produces sth □ *buatan; jenama*: *'What make of car does he drive?' 'A Ford, I think.'*
IDM **on the make** always trying to make money

make-believe → manage

make-believe noun [U] things that sb imagines or invents that are not real □ *pepura; khayalan*

makeover /'meɪkəʊvə(r)/ noun [C,U] the process of improving the appearance of a person or a place, or of changing the impression that sth gives □ *pemindaan atau pembaikan rupa paras, penampilan atau tanggapan sso atau sst*

maker /'meɪkə(r)/ noun [C] a person, company or machine that makes sth □ *pembuat: a film-maker* ♦ *If it doesn't work, send it back to the maker.* ♦ *an ice cream maker*

makeshift /'meɪkʃɪft/ adj made to be used for a short time until there is sth better □ *sementara: They slept in makeshift shelters made from old cardboard boxes.*

make-up noun **1** [U] powder, cream, etc. that you put on your face to make yourself more attractive. Actors use **make-up** to change their appearance when they are acting □ *mekap; alat solek: to put on/take off make-up* ⊃ look at **cosmetic** ⊃ verb **make (yourself/sb) up 2** [sing] sb's character □ *sifat: He can't help his temper. It's part of his make-up.*

making /'meɪkɪŋ/ noun [sing] the act of doing or producing sth; the process of being made □ *pembuatan: breadmaking* ♦ *This movie has been three years in the making.*
IDM be the making of sb to be the reason that sb is successful □ *membuat sso berjaya: University was the making of Gina.*
have the makings of sth to have the necessary qualities for sth □ *berpotensi utk (menjadi) sst: The book has the makings of a good film.*

maladjusted /ˌmæləˈdʒʌstɪd/ adj (used about a person) not able to behave well with other people □ *salah suai*

malaria /məˈleəriə/ noun [U] a serious disease in hot countries that you get from the bite of a **mosquito** (= a small flying insect) □ *malaria*

male[1] /meɪl/ adj belonging to the sex that does not give birth to babies or produce eggs □ *lelaki; jantan: a male goat* ♦ *a male model/nurse/colleague* ⊃ look at **masculine, female**

male[2] /meɪl/ noun [C] a male person or animal □ *lelaki; jantan* ⊃ look at **female**: *the body of a white male aged about 40*

male ˈchauvinism = **chauvinism** (2)

malice /'mælɪs/ noun [U] a wish to hurt other people □ *niat jahat* ▸**malicious** /məˈlɪʃəs/ adj ▸**maliciously** adv

malignant /məˈlɪɡnənt/ adj (used about a disease) likely to cause death if not controlled □ *malignan; membahayakan: He has a malignant brain tumour.* ♦ *malignant cells* **OPP** benign

mall /mæl; mɔːl/ (also **shopping mall**) (*especially AmE*) a large building or covered area that has many shops, restaurants, etc. inside it □ *pusat beli-belah: Some teenagers were hanging out at the mall.* ⊃ look at **shopping centre**

malleable /'mæliəbl/ adj **1** (used about metal or plastic) that can be hit or pressed into different shapes easily without breaking □ *boleh ditempakan, mudah dibentuk* **2** (used about people or ideas) easily influenced or changed □ *mudah dibentuk/dipengaruhi/diubah* ▸**malleability** /ˌmæliəˈbɪləti/ noun [U]

mallet /'mælɪt/ noun [C] a heavy wooden hammer □ *tukul kayu* ⊃ picture at **tool**

malnutrition /ˌmælnjuːˈtrɪʃn/ noun [U] bad health that is the result of not having enough food or enough of the right kind of food □ *kekurangan zat makanan* ▸**malnourished** /ˌmælˈnʌrɪʃt/ adj: *The children were badly malnourished.*

malt /mɔːlt/ noun [U] grain that is used for making beer and **whisky** (= a strong alcoholic drink) □ *malt*

maltreat /ˌmælˈtriːt/ verb [T] (*formal*) to treat a person or an animal in a cruel or unkind way □ *menganiaya* ▸**maltreatment** noun [U]

mammal /'mæml/ noun [C] an animal of the type that gives birth to live babies, not eggs, and feeds its young on milk from its own body □ *mamalia: Whales, dogs and humans are mammals.* ⊃ picture on **page P12**

mammoth /'mæməθ/ adj very big □ *raksasa; sangat besar*

man[1] /mæn/ noun (pl **men** /men/) **1** [C] an adult male person □ *lelaki: men, women and children* **2** [U] humans as a group; the human race □ *manusia: Early man lived by hunting.* ♦ *the damage man has caused to the environment* **3** [C] a person of either sex, male or female □ *orang: All men are equal.* ♦ *No man could survive long in such conditions.* **4** [C] [in compounds] a man who comes from a particular place; a man who has a particular job or interest □ *orang; ahli (perniagaan, sukan, dll): a Frenchman* ♦ *a businessman* ♦ *sportsmen and women*
IDM the man in the street an ordinary man or woman □ *orang biasa*
the odd man/one out ⊃ **odd**

man[2] /mæn/ verb [T] (**manning**; **manned**) to operate sth or to provide people to operate sth □ *mengendalikan: The telephones are manned 24 hours a day.*

manage /'mænɪdʒ/ verb **1** [I,T] [often with *can* or *could*] to succeed in doing or dealing with sth difficult; to be able to do sth □ *dpt (membuat atau menguruskan sst): However did you manage to find us here?* ♦ *I can't manage this suitcase. It's too heavy.* ♦ *Paula can't manage next Tuesday* (= she can't come then) *so we'll meet another day.* ⊃ note at **could 2** [I] **manage (without/with sb/sth); manage (on sth)** to deal with a difficult situation; to continue in spite of difficulties □ *dpt* *(mengatasi sst keadaan yg sukar, terus hidup, dll)*: My grandmother couldn't manage without her neighbours. ◆ Can you manage with just one assistant? ◆ It's hard for a family to manage on just one income. **3** [T] to be in charge or control of sth □ *mengurus; mengendalikan*: She manages a small advertising business. ◆ You need to manage your time more efficiently.

manageable /ˈmænɪdʒəbl/ *adj* not too big or too difficult to deal with □ *dpt dibuat; mudah diurus*

management /ˈmænɪdʒmənt/ *noun* **1** [U] the control or organization of sth □ *pengurusan*: Good classroom management is vital with large groups of children. **2** [C,U, with sing or pl verb] the people who control a business or company □ *pihak pengurusan*: The hotel is now **under new management**.

GRAMMAR In the singular, **management** is used with a singular or plural verb: *The management is/are considering making some workers redundant.*

manager /ˈmænɪdʒə(r)/ *noun* [C] **1** a man or woman who controls an organization or part of an organization □ *pengurus*: a bank manager **2** a person who looks after the business affairs of a singer, actor, etc. □ *pengurus* **3** a person who is in charge of a sports team □ *pengurus*: the England manager

manageress /ˌmænɪdʒəˈres/ *noun* [C] *(old-fashioned)* a woman who is in charge of a shop or restaurant □ *pengurus (wanita)*

managerial /ˌmænəˈdʒɪəriəl/ *adj* connected with the work of a manager □ *pengurusan*: Do you have any managerial experience?

managing diˈrector *noun* [C] a person who controls a business or company □ *pengarah urusan*

mandarin /ˈmændərɪn/ *noun* [C] a type of small orange □ *limau mandarin*

mandate /ˈmændeɪt/ *noun* [usually sing] the power that is officially given to a group of people to do sth, especially after they have won an election □ *mandat*: The union leaders had a clear mandate from their members to call a strike.

mandatory /ˈmændətəri/ (*BrE* also) mænˈdeɪtəri/ *adj* (*formal*) that you must do, have, obey, etc. □ *mandatori*: a mandatory life sentence **SYN** compulsory

mane /meɪn/ *noun* [C] the long hair on the neck of some animals □ *surai* ⊃ picture at horse, lion ⊃ picture on **page P12**

maneuver (*AmE*) = **manoeuvre**

mangle /ˈmæŋɡl/ *verb* [T, usually passive] to damage sth so badly that it is difficult to see what it looked like originally □ *(menjadi) remuk*: The motorway was covered with the mangled wreckage of cars.

mango /ˈmæŋɡəʊ/ *noun* [C] (*pl* **mangoes** or **mangos**) a tropical fruit that has a yellow and red skin and is yellow inside □ *(buah) mangga/*

manageable → mankind

mempelam ⊃ picture on **page P14**

manhole /ˈmænhəʊl/ *noun* [C] a hole in the street with a lid over it through which sb can go to look at the pipes, etc. that are underground □ *lurang*

manhood /ˈmænhʊd/ *noun* [U] the state of being a man rather than a boy □ *peringkat dewasa (lelaki); kedewasaan*

mania /ˈmeɪniə/ *noun* **1** [C] (*informal*) a great enthusiasm for sth □ *gila*: World Cup mania is sweeping the country. **2** [U] a serious mental illness that may cause sb to be very excited or violent □ *mania*

maniac /ˈmeɪniæk/ *noun* [C] **1** a person who behaves in a wild and stupid way □ *orang gila*: to drive like a maniac **SYN** lunatic, madman **2** a person who has a stronger love of sth than is normal □ *orang yg gila (sst)*: a football/sex maniac

manic /ˈmænɪk/ *adj* **1** full of nervous energy or excited activity □ *tdk tenteram; bagai nak gila*: His behaviour became more manic as he began to feel stressed. **2** connected with **mania** (2) □ *manik*

manicure /ˈmænɪkjʊə(r)/ *noun* [C,U] treatment to make your hands and nails look attractive □ *rias tangan dan kuku*: to have a manicure

manifest /ˈmænɪfest/ *verb* [I,T] (*formal*) manifest (sth/itself) (in/as sth) to show sth or to be shown clearly □ *menunjukkan/diperlihatkan dgn jelas*: Mental illness can manifest itself in many forms. ▶ manifest *adj*: manifest failure/anger ▶ manifestly *adv*: manifestly unfair

manifestation /ˌmænɪfeˈsteɪʃn/ *noun* [C,U] (*formal*) a sign that sth is happening □ *manifestasi; pernyataan*

manifesto /ˌmænɪˈfestəʊ/ *noun* [C] (*pl* manifestos) a written statement by a political party that explains what it hopes to do if it becomes the government in the future □ *manifesto*

manioc /ˈmæniɒk/ = **cassava**

manipulate /məˈnɪpjuleɪt/ *verb* [T] **1** to influence sb so that they do or think what you want □ *memanipulasikan*: Clever politicians know how to manipulate public opinion. **2** to use, move or control sth with skill □ *memanipulasikan; mengendalikan* ▶ manipulation /məˌnɪpjuˈleɪʃn/ *noun* [C,U]

manipulative /məˈnɪpjələtɪv/ *adj* **1** able to influence sb or force sb to do what you want, often in an unfair way □ *manipulatif*: manipulative behaviour **2** (*formal*) connected with the ability to handle objects with skill □ *kebolehan mengendalikan sst dgn mahir; kemahiran mengendalikan sst*

mankind /mænˈkaɪnd/ *noun* [U] all the people in the world □ *manusia*: A nuclear war would be a threat to all mankind.

VOWELS iː see i any ɪ sit e ten æ hat ɑː father ɒ got ɔː saw ʊ put uː too u usual

manly /ˈmænli/ adj (**manlier**; **manliest**) typical of or suitable for a man □ *bersifat lelaki*: *a deep manly voice* ▸ **manliness** noun [U]

man-ˈmade adj made by people, not formed in a natural way; artificial □ *buatan manusia*: *man-made fabrics such as nylon and polyester*

manner /ˈmænə(r)/ noun **1** [sing] the way that you do sth or that sth happens □ *cara*: *Stop arguing! Let's try to act in a civilized manner.* **2** [sing] the way that sb behaves towards other people □ *sikap; gaya*: *to have an aggressive/a relaxed/a professional manner* **3** **manners** [pl] a way of behaving that is considered acceptable in your country or culture □ *tingkah laku*: *Their children have no manners* (= behave very badly). ◆ *In some countries it is bad manners to show the soles of your feet.*

IDM **all manner of ...** every kind of ... □ *pelbagai*: *You meet all manner of people in my job.*

mannerism /ˈmænərɪzəm/ noun [C] sb's particular way of speaking or a particular movement they often do □ *gaya; tabiat*

manoeuvre¹ (AmE **maneuver**) /məˈnuːvə(r)/ noun **1** [C] a movement that needs care or skill □ *pengendalian; gerakan yg memerlukan banyak kemahiran*: *Parking the car in such a small space would be a tricky manoeuvre.* **2** [C,U] something clever that you do in order to win sth, trick sb, etc. □ *muslihat; taktik*: *political manoeuvre(s)* **SYN** **move** **3** **manoeuvres** [pl] a way of training soldiers when large numbers of them practise fighting in battles □ *latihan ketenteraan*

manoeuvre² (AmE **maneuver**) /məˈnuːvə(r)/ verb [I,T] to move (sth) to a different position using skill □ *mengalihkan dgn susah payah kedudukan sst*: *The driver was manoeuvring his lorry into a narrow gateway.*

manor /ˈmænə(r)/ (also **ˈmanor house**) noun [C] a large house in the country that has land around it □ *manor; rumah besar di desa*

manpower /ˈmænpaʊə(r)/ noun [U] the people that you need to do a particular job □ *tenaga manusia*: *There is a shortage of skilled manpower in the computer industry.*

mansion /ˈmænʃn/ noun [C] a very large house □ *rumah agam*

manslaughter /ˈmænslɔːtə(r)/ noun [U] the crime of killing sb without intending to do so □ *pembunuhan tanpa niat* ➲ look at **murder**

mantelpiece /ˈmæntlpiːs/ noun [C] a narrow shelf above the space in a room where a fire goes □ *pepara perapian* ➲ picture at **fireplace**

manual¹ /ˈmænjuəl/ adj using your hands; operated by hand □ *dgn menggunakan tangan; kerja kasar; buruh kasar; manual*: *Office work can sometimes be more tiring than manual work.* ◆ *a skilled manual worker* ◆ *Does your car have a manual or an automatic gearbox?* ▸ **manually** /-juəli/ adv

manual² /ˈmænjuəl/ noun [C] a book that explains how to do or operate sth □ *buku panduan; manual*: *a training manual* ◆ *a car manual*

manufacture /ˌmænjuˈfæktʃə(r)/ verb [T] to make sth in large quantities using machines □ *mengilang; mengeluarkan*: *a local factory that manufactures furniture* **SYN** **produce** ▸ **manufacture** noun [U]: *The manufacture of chemical weapons should be illegal.*

manufacturer /ˌmænjuˈfæktʃərə(r)/ noun [C] a person or company that makes sth □ *pengilang*: *a car manufacturer* ◆ *Always follow the manufacturer's instructions.*

manufacturing /ˌmænjuˈfæktʃərɪŋ/ noun [U] the business or industry of producing goods in large quantities in factories, etc. □ *perkilangan; pembuatan*: *Many jobs in manufacturing were lost during the recession.*

manure /məˈnjʊə(r)/ noun [U] the waste matter from animals that is put on the ground in order to make plants grow better □ *baja*: *horse manure* ➲ look at **fertilizer**

manuscript /ˈmænjuskrɪpt/ noun [C] **1** a copy of a book, piece of music, etc. before it has been printed □ *manuskrip* **2** a very old book or document that was written by hand □ *manuskrip*

many /ˈmeni/ determiner, pron [used with plural nouns or verbs] **1** a large number of people or things □ *banyak*: *Have you made many friends at school yet?* ◆ *Not many of my friends smoke.* ◆ *Not many of my friends drive.* ◆ *Many of the mistakes were just careless.* ◆ *There are too many mistakes in this essay.* ◆ *I've known her for a good/great many* (= very many) *years.*

HELP **Many** or **a lot of**? **Many** in positive sentences sounds quite formal: *Many people have smartphones nowadays.* When speaking or writing informally we usually use **a lot of**: *A lot of people have smartphones nowadays.* In negative sentences and questions, however, **many** can always be used without sounding formal: *I don't know many cheap places to eat.* ◆ *Are there many hotels in this town?*

2 used to ask about the number of people or things, or to refer to a known number □ *banyak; ramai*: *How many children have you got?* ◆ *How many came to the meeting?* ◆ *I don't work as many hours as you.* ◆ *There are half/twice as many boys as girls in the class.* **3** [in compounds] having a lot of the thing mentioned □ *banyak*: *a many-sided shape* **4** **many a** [used with a singular noun and verb] a large number of □ *banyak; ramai*: *I've heard him say that many a time.*

Maori /ˈmaʊri/ noun [C] (pl **Maori** or **Maoris**) a member of the race of people who were the original people to live in New Zealand □ *orang Maori* ▸ **Maori** adj

map /mæp/ *noun* [C] a drawing or plan of (part of) the surface of the earth that shows countries, rivers, mountains, roads, etc. □ *peta: a map of the world* ◆ *a road/street map* ◆ *I can't find Cambridge on the map.* ◆ *to read a map* ➔ look at **atlas**
▶ **map** *verb* [T] (**mapping**; **mapped**): *The region is so remote it has not yet been mapped.*

maple /ˈmeɪpl/ *noun* [C] a tree that has leaves with five points and that produces a very sweet liquid that you can eat □ *mapel: maple syrup*

Mar. *abbr* = **March** □ *Mac: 17 Mar. 1956*

marathon /ˈmærəθən/ *noun* [C] **1** a long running race, in which people run about 42 kilometres □ *maraton: Have you ever run a marathon?* **2** an activity that lasts much longer than expected □ *sst yg mengambil masa lebih lama drpd dijangkakan: The interview was a real marathon.*

marble /ˈmɑːbl/ *noun* **1** [U] a hard attractive stone that is used to make statues and parts of buildings □ *marmar: a marble statue* **2** [C] a small ball of coloured glass that children play with □ *guli* **3 marbles** [pl] the children's game that you play by rolling **marbles** along the ground trying to hit other **marbles** □ *main guli*

March /mɑːtʃ/ *noun* [U,C] (*abbr* **Mar.**) the 3rd month of the year, coming after February □ *Mac* ➔ note at **January**

march¹ /mɑːtʃ/ *verb* **1** [I] to walk with regular steps (like a soldier) □ *berkawad: The President saluted as the troops marched past.* **2** [I] to walk in a determined way □ *berjalan dgn tegas: She marched up to the manager and demanded an apology.* **3** [T] to make sb walk or march somewhere □ *memaksa sso berjalan ke sst tempat: The prisoner was marched away.* **4** [I] to walk in a large group to protest about sth □ *berarak: The demonstrators marched through the centre of town.*

march² /mɑːtʃ/ *noun* [C] **1** an organized walk by a large group of people who are protesting about sth □ *perarakan: a peace march* ➔ look at **demonstration 2** a journey made by marching □ *berkawad: The soldiers were tired after their long march.*

mare /meə(r)/ *noun* [C] a female horse □ *kuda betina* ➔ note at **horse**

margarine /ˌmɑːdʒəˈriːn/ *noun* [U] a food that is similar to butter, made of animal or vegetable fats □ *marjerin*

margin /ˈmɑːdʒɪn/ *noun* [C] **1** the empty space at the side of a page in a book, etc. □ *margin; jidar; tepi muka surat* **2** [usually sing] the amount of space, time, votes, etc. by which you win sth □ *beza; perbezaan: He won by a wide/narrow/comfortable margin.* **3** the amount of profit that a company makes on sth □ *keuntungan* **4** [usually sing] an amount of space, time, etc. that is more than you need □ *margin; (kelebihan) ruang, masa, dsb: It is a complex operation with little **margin for error**.* **5** the area around the edge of sth □ *pinggir; tepi:*

533   map → mark

the margins of the Pacific Ocean

marginal /ˈmɑːdʒɪnl/ *adj* small in size or importance □ *kecil; tdk penting: The differences are marginal.* ▶ **marginally** /-nəli/ *adv:* In most cases costs will increase only marginally.

marijuana /ˌmærəˈwɑːnə/ *noun* [U] a drug that is smoked and is illegal in many countries □ *ganja*

marina /məˈriːnə/ *noun* [C] a place where pleasure boats can be tied up and protected from the sea and bad weather □ *marina; pangkalan kapal persiaran*

marinade /ˌmærɪˈneɪd/ *noun* [C,U] a mixture of oil, wine, spices, etc. in which meat or fish is left before it is cooked in order to make it softer or to give it a particular flavour □ *pemerap*

marinate /ˈmærɪneɪt/ (also **marinade**) *verb* [I,T] if you **marinate** food or it **marinates**, you leave it in a **marinade** before cooking it □ *perap*

marine¹ /məˈriːn/ *adj* [only *before* a noun] **1** connected with the sea □ *laut: marine life* **2** connected with ships or sailing □ *marin; laut: marine insurance*

marine² /məˈriːn/ *noun* [C] a soldier who has been trained to fight on land or at sea □ *tentera laut*

marital /ˈmærɪtl/ *adj* [only *before* a noun] connected with marriage □ *(berkenaan dgn) perkahwinan: marital problems*

marital status *noun* [U] (*written*) (used on official documents) if you are married, single, divorced, etc. □ *status perkahwinan*

maritime /ˈmærɪtaɪm/ *adj* connected with the sea or ships □ *maritim; kelautan; laut: a maritime museum*

mark¹ /mɑːk/ *verb* [T]
▶ WRITE **1** to put a sign on sth □ *menandakan; membubuh (tanda, harga, dll): We marked the price on all items in the sale.* ◆ *I'll mark all the boxes I want you to move.*
▶ SPOIL **2** to spoil the appearance of sth by making a mark on it □ *bertanda; meninggalkan kesan: The white walls were dirty and marked.*
▶ SHOW POSITION **3** to show where sth is or where sth happened □ *menandakan; ditandakan: The route is marked in red.* ◆ *Flowers mark the spot where he died.*
▶ CELEBRATE **4** to celebrate or officially remember an important event □ *memperingati: The ceremony marked the fiftieth anniversary of the opening of the school.*
▶ SHOW CHANGE **5** to be a sign that sth new is going to happen □ *menandakan: This decision marks a change in government policy.*
▶ GIVE GRADE **6** to look at sb's schoolwork, etc., show where there are mistakes and give it a number or letter to show how good it is □ *menanda; memeriksa: Why did you mark that answer wrong?* ◆ *He has 100 exam papers to mark.*

[C] **countable**, a noun with a plural form: *one book, two books*   [U] **uncountable**, a noun with no plural form: *some sugar*

mark → marooned 534

▶IN SPORT **7** to stay close to a player of the opposite team so that they cannot play easily □ *mengawal rapi*: *Hughes was marking Taylor.*

PHR V **mark sb/sth down as/for sth** to decide that sb/sth is of a particular type or suitable for a particular use □ *mengenal pasti sso/sst sebagai sst atau utk sst*: *From the first day of school, the teachers marked Fred down as a troublemaker.*

mark sth out to draw lines to show the position of sth □ *menandakan dgn garis*: *Spaces for each car were marked out in the car park.*

mark sth up/down to increase/decrease the price of sth that you are selling □ *menaikkan/mengurangkan harga*: *All goods have been marked down by 15%.*

mark² /maːk/ *noun* [C]
▶SPOT/DIRT **1** a spot or line that spoils the appearance of sth □ *tanda; kesan; bekas*: *There's a dirty mark on the front of your shirt.* ♦ *If you put a hot cup down on the table it will leave a mark.* ⊃ look at **birthmark 2** something that shows who or what sb/sth is, especially by making them or it different from others □ *tanda*: *My horse is the one with the white mark on its face.*
▶SYMBOL **3** a written or printed symbol that is a sign of sth □ *tanda*: *a question/punctuation/exclamation mark*
▶SIGN **4** a sign of a quality or feeling □ *tanda*: *They stood in silence for two minutes as a mark of respect.*
▶GRADE **5** a number or letter you get for school work that tells you how good your work was □ *markah*: *She got very good marks in the exam.* ♦ *The pass mark is 60 out of 100.* ♦ *to get full marks* (= everything correct)
▶LEVEL **6** the level or point that sth/sb has reached □ *tahap; paras*: *The race is almost at the halfway mark.*
▶EFFECT **7** an effect that people notice and will remember □ *kesan*: *The time he spent in prison left its mark on him.* ♦ *He was only eighteen when he first made his mark in politics.*
▶MODEL/TYPE **8** a particular model or type of sth □ *model; jenis*: *the new SL 53 Mark III*

HELP Be careful. You cannot use **mark** to talk about the product itself, or the company that makes it. Instead, use **brand** or, especially for cars and electrical goods, **make**: *What brand of coffee do you buy?* ♦ *What make is your car?*

▶TARGET **9** (*formal*) a person or an object towards which sth is directed □ *sasaran*: *The arrow hit/missed its mark.* ♦ *His judgement of the situation is wide of the mark* (= wrong). **SYN** target
▶MONEY **10** the former unit of money in Germany (replaced in 2002 by the euro) □ *mark (mata wang Jerman)*
IDM **on your marks, get set, go!** used at the start of a sports race □ *ke garisan, sedia, mula!*
overstep the mark/line ⊃ **overstep**
quick, slow, etc. off the mark quick, slow, etc. in reacting to a situation □ *cepat, lambat, dll bertindak balas dlm sst keadaan*

marked /maːkt/ *adj* clear; noticeable □ *jelas; ketara*: *There has been a marked increase in vandalism in recent years.* ▶**markedly** /ˈmaːkɪdli/ *adv*: *Her background is markedly different from mine.*

marker /ˈmaːkə(r)/ *noun* [C] something that shows the position of sth □ *penanda*: *I've highlighted the important sentences with a marker pen.*

market¹ /ˈmaːkɪt/ *noun* **1** [C] a place where people go to buy and sell things □ *pasar*: *a market stall/trader/town* ♦ *a cattle/fish/meat market* ⊃ note at **shop** ⊃ look at **flea market, hypermarket, supermarket** ⊃ picture on **page P11 2** [C] business or commercial activity; the amount of buying and selling of a particular type of goods □ *pasaran*: *The company currently has a 10% share of the market.* ♦ *the property/job market* **3** [C,U] a country, an area or a group of people that buys sth; the number of people who buy sth □ *pasaran*: *The company is hoping to expand into the European Market.* ♦ *There's no market for very large cars when petrol is so expensive.* ⊃ look at **black market, stock market**
IDM **on the market** available to buy □ *di pasaran*: *This is one of the best cameras on the market.*

market² /ˈmaːkɪt/ *verb* [T] to sell sth with the help of advertising □ *memasarkan*: *It is marketed as a healthy snack.*

marketable /ˈmaːkɪtəbl/ *adj* that can be sold easily because people want it □ *boleh dipasarkan*

marketing /ˈmaːkɪtɪŋ/ *noun* [U] the activity of showing and advertising a company's products in the best possible way □ *pemasaran*: *Effective marketing will lead to increased sales.* ♦ *the international marketing department*

marketplace /ˈmaːkɪtpleɪs/ *noun* **1 the marketplace** [sing] the activity of competing with other companies to buy and sell goods, services, etc. □ *pasaran* **2** [C] the place in a town where a market is held □ *pasar*

market research (also **market research**) *noun* [U] the study of what people want to buy and why □ *penyelidikan pasaran*: *to carry out/do market research*

marking /ˈmaːkɪŋ/ *noun* [C, usually pl] shapes, lines and patterns of colour on an animal or a bird, or painted on a road, vehicle, etc. □ *tanda; tompok, garis, corak, dsb*

marksman /ˈmaːksmən/ *noun* [C] (*pl* -men /-mən/) a person who can shoot very well with a gun □ *jaguh tembak; penembak jitu*

marmalade /ˈmaːməleɪd/ *noun* [U] a type of jam that is made from oranges or lemons □ *marmalad; jem oren*

maroon /məˈruːn/ *adj, noun* [U] (of) a dark brownish-red colour □ *merah pulasan*

marooned /məˈruːnd/ *adj* in a place that you cannot leave □ *terkandas; terdampar*: *The sailors were marooned on a desert island.*

[I] **intransitive**, a verb which has no object: *He laughed.* [T] **transitive**, a verb which has an object: *He ate an apple.*

marquee /maːˈkiː/ noun [C] a very large tent that is used for parties, shows, etc. □ *khemah besar*

marriage /ˈmærɪdʒ/ noun **1** [C,U] the state of being husband and wife □ *perkahwinan*: *They are getting divorced after five years of marriage.* ◆ *a happy marriage* **2** [C] a wedding ceremony □ *majlis perkahwinan*: *The marriage took place at a registry office.* ⊃ note at **wedding** ⊃ verb **get married (to sb)** or **marry (sb)**

married /ˈmærɪd/ adj **1 married (to sb)** having a husband or wife □ *(sudah) berkahwin*: *a married man/woman/couple* ◆ *Sasha's married to Mark.* ◆ *They're planning to get married in summer.* OPP **unmarried, single 2** [only before a noun] connected with marriage □ *berumah tangga; berkenaan dgn perkahwinan*: *How do you like married life?*

marrow /ˈmærəʊ/ noun **1** = **bone marrow 2** [C,U] (BrE) a large vegetable with green skin that is white inside □ *labu bulu* ⊃ picture on page P15

marry /ˈmæri/ verb (marrying; marries; pt, pp married) **1** [I,T] to take sb as your husband or wife □ *berkahwin; mengahwini*: *They married when they were very young.* ◆ *When did he ask you to marry him?* ⊃ note at **wedding** ⊃ look at **divorce**

> **HELP** **Get married** is more commonly used than **marry**: *When are Jo and Mark getting married?* ◆ *We got married in 2003.* Note that we say 'get married **to** sb', NOT 'with' sb.

2 [T] to join two people together as husband and wife □ *menikahkan; mengahwinkan*: *We asked the local vicar to marry us.* ⊃ noun **marriage**

Mars /maːz/ noun [sing] the red planet, that is fourth in order from the sun □ *Marikh* ⊃ look at **Martian**

marsh /maːʃ/ noun [C,U] an area of soft wet land □ *tanah paya* ▶ **marshy** adj

marshal /ˈmaːʃl/ noun [C] **1** a person who helps to organize or control a large public event □ *pengawas*: *Marshals are directing traffic in the car park.* **2** (AmE) an officer of a high level in the police or fire department or in a court of law □ *marsyal*

marsupial /maːˈsuːpiəl/ noun [C] any animal that carries its young in a **pouch** (= a pocket of skin) on the mother's stomach □ *(haiwan) marsupial*: *Kangaroos and koalas are marsupials.*

martial /ˈmaːʃl/ adj [only before a noun] (formal) connected with war □ *(berkenaan dgn) perang*

martial 'arts noun [pl] fighting sports such as **karate** or **judo**, in which you use your hands and feet as weapons □ *seni mempertahankan diri*

Martian /ˈmaːʃn/ noun [C] (in stories) a creature that comes from the planet Mars □ *makhluk dr Marikh*

martyr /ˈmaːtə(r)/ noun [C] **1** a person who is killed because of what they believe □ *orang yg dibunuh kerana kepercayaannya* **2** a person who tries to make people feel sorry for them □ *orang yg suka menagih simpati*: *Don't be such a martyr! You don't have to do all the housework.* ▶ **martyrdom** /ˈmaːtədəm/ noun [U]

marvel /ˈmaːvl/ noun [C] a person or thing that is wonderful or that surprises you □ *sso/sst yg menakjubkan; keajaiban; ajaib*: *The new building is a marvel of modern technology.* ▶ **marvel** verb [I] (**marvelling**; **marvelled**, (AmE) **marveling**; **marveled**) (formal) **marvel (at sth)**: *We marvelled at how much they had managed to do.*

marvellous (AmE **marvelous**) /ˈmaːvələs/ adj very good; wonderful □ *sangat baik; mengagumkan*: *a marvellous opportunity* SYN **fantastic** ▶ **marvellously** (AmE **marvelously**) adv

Marxism /ˈmaːksɪzəm/ noun [U] the political and economic thought of Karl Marx □ *Marxisme* ⊃ look at **communism, socialism, capitalism** ▶ **Marxist** /-ɪst/ noun [C], adj: *Marxist ideology*

marzipan /ˈmaːzɪpæn/ (AmE usually) / noun [U] a food that is made of sugar, egg and **almonds** (= a type of nut). Marzipan is used to make sweets or to put on cakes. □ *marzipan*

masc abbr = **masculine**

mascara /mæˈskaːrə/ noun [U] a beauty product that is used to make your **eyelashes** (= the hairs around your eyes) dark and attractive □ *maskara*

mascot /ˈmæskət/ noun [C] a person, animal or thing that is thought to bring good luck □ *maskot*

masculine /ˈmæskjəlɪn/ adj **1** with the qualities that people think are typical of men □ *maskulin; kelelakian*: *a deep, masculine voice* ◆ *Her short hair makes her look quite masculine.* ⊃ look at **feminine, male, manly 2** (in English) of the forms of words used to describe males □ *maskulin; ttg kata yg ada ciri kelelakian* **3** (in the grammar of some languages) belonging to a certain class of nouns, adjectives or pronouns □ *tergolong dlm kn, kata ganti nama atau adjektif (dlm sesetengah bahasa)*: *The French word for 'sun' is masculine.*

> **MORE** In English grammar **masculine** words refer to male people or animals: *'He' is a masculine pronoun.* **Feminine** words refer to female people or animals: *'She' is a feminine pronoun.* In some languages all nouns are given a **gender**; usually **masculine, feminine** or **neuter**.

▶ **masculinity** /ˌmæskjuˈlɪnəti/ noun [U]

mash /mæʃ/ verb [T] to mix or crush sth until it is soft □ *melecek; melenyek*: *mashed potatoes*

mask[1] /maːsk/ noun [C] something that you wear that covers your face or part of your face. People wear **masks** in order to hide or protect their faces or to make themselves look different □ *topeng*: *a surgical/Halloween mask* ⊃ look at

mask → match 536

gas mask, goggles ➲ picture at snorkel ➲ picture on page P5

mask² /mɑːsk/ verb [T] to hide a feeling, smell, fact, etc. □ *menyelindung; menyembunyikan; menghilangkan*: He masked his anger with a smile.

masked /mɑːskt/ adj wearing a mask □ *bertopeng*: a masked gunman

masochism /ˈmæsəkɪzəm/ noun [U] the enjoyment of pain, or of what most people would find unpleasant □ *masokisme; keseronokan drpd kesakitan atau seksa*: He swims in the sea even in winter—that's sheer masochism! ➲ look at sadism ▶ **masochist** /-ɪst/ noun [C] ▶ **masochistic** /ˌmæsəˈkɪstɪk/ adj

mason /ˈmeɪsn/ noun [C] **1** a person who makes things from stone □ *tukang batu* **2** = Freemason

masonry /ˈmeɪsnri/ noun [U] the parts of a building that are made of stone □ *binaan batu*

masquerade /ˌmæskəˈreɪd; ˌmɑːsk-/ noun [C] a way of behaving that hides the truth or sb's true feelings □ *penyamaran; kepura-puraan* ▶ **masquerade** verb [I] **masquerade as sth**: Two people, masquerading as doctors, knocked at the door and asked to see the child.

mass¹ /mæs/ noun **1** [C] a mass (of sth) a large amount or number of sth □ *banyak; timbunan; kepulan*: a dense mass of smoke ◆ (informal) There were masses of people at the market today. **2 the masses** [pl] ordinary people when considered as a political group □ *rakyat; orang ramai*: a TV programme that brings science to the masses **3** [U] (in physics) the quantity of material that sth contains □ *jisim*: the mass of a planet **4 Mass** [C,U] the ceremony in some Christian churches when people eat bread and drink wine in order to remember the last meal that Christ had before he died □ *Mass*: to go to Mass

mass² /mæs/ adj [only before a noun] involving a large number of people or things □ *banyak; beramai-ramai*: a mass murderer ◆ mass unemployment

mass³ /mæs/ verb [I,T] to come together or bring people or things together in large numbers □ *berkumpul*: The students massed in the square.

massacre /ˈmæsəkə(r)/ noun [C] the killing of a large number of people or animals □ *pembunuhan beramai-ramai/banyak* ➲ note at kill ▶ **massacre** verb [T]

massage /ˈmæsɑːʒ/ noun [C,U] the act of rubbing and pressing sb's body in order to reduce pain or to help them relax □ *urut; (perbuatan) mengurut*: to give somebody a massage ▶ **massage** verb [T]

massive /ˈmæsɪv/ adj very big □ *sangat besar; banyak*: the massive walls of the castle ◆ He suffered a massive heart attack. ◆ a massive increase in prices SYN huge ▶ **massively** adv

mass-market adj [only before a noun] (used about goods, etc.) produced for very large numbers of people □ *pasaran luas*

mass media noun [pl] newspapers, TV and radio that reach a large number of people □ *media massa; sebaran am*

mass-produce verb [T] to make large numbers of similar things by machine in a factory □ *mengeluarkan secara besar-besaran*: mass-produced goods ▶ **mass production** noun [U]

mast /mɑːst/ noun [C] **1** a tall wooden or metal pole for holding a ship's sails or a flag □ *tiang* ➲ picture on page P6 **2** a tall pole that is used for sending out radio or TV signals □ *menara*

master¹ /ˈmɑːstə(r)/ noun [C] **1** a person who has great skill at doing sth □ *tukang yg mahir; orang yg ahli atau pakar*: a master builder ◆ an exhibition of work by French masters (= artists) **2** (BrE old-fashioned) a male teacher (usually in a private school) □ *guru (lelaki)*: the chemistry master **3** a film or tape from which copies can be made □ *salinan asal*: the master copy

master² /ˈmɑːstə(r)/ verb [T] **1** to learn how to do sth well □ *menguasai; memperoleh kemahiran*: It takes years of study to master a foreign language. **2** to control sth □ *mengawal; menguasai*: to master a situation

mastermind /ˈmɑːstəmaɪnd/ noun [C] a very clever person who has planned or organized sth □ *perancang; dalang*: The mastermind behind the robbery was never caught. ▶ **mastermind** verb [T]: The police failed to catch the man who masterminded the robbery.

masterpiece /ˈmɑːstəpiːs/ noun [C] a work of art, music, literature, etc. that is of the highest quality □ *karya agung*

master's degree (also master's) noun [C] a second or higher university degree. You usually get a **master's degree** by studying for one or two years after your first degree □ *Ijazah Sarjana*: Master of Arts (MA) ◆ Master of Science (MSc)

mastery /ˈmɑːstəri/ noun [U] **1** mastery (of sth) great skill at doing sth □ *penguasaan; kemahiran*: His mastery of the violin was quite exceptional for a child. **2** mastery (of/over sb/sth) control over sb/sth □ *penguasaan; kuasa; menguasai*: The battle was fought for mastery of the seas.

masturbate /ˈmæstəbeɪt/ verb [I,T] to make yourself or sb else feel sexually excited by touching and rubbing the sex organs □ *melancap* ▶ **masturbation** /ˌmæstəˈbeɪʃn/ noun [U]

mat /mæt/ noun [C] **1** a piece of carpet or other thick material that you put on the floor □ *tikar; alas*: a doormat ➲ look at rug **2** a small piece of material that you put under sth on a table □ *alas*: a table mat ◆ a beer mat ◆ a mouse mat

match¹ /mætʃ/ noun **1** [C] a small stick of wood, cardboard, etc. that you use for starting

ð **then**   s **so**   z **zoo**   ʃ **she**   ʒ vi**s**ion   h **h**ow   m **m**an   n **n**o   ŋ si**ng**   l **l**eg   r **r**ed   j **y**es   w **w**et

a fire, lighting a cigarette, etc. □ *mancis; gores api*: *to light/strike a match* ◆ *a box of matches* **2** [C] an organized game or sports event □ *perlawanan*: *a tennis/football match* **3** [sing] a match for sb; sb's match a person or thing that is as good as or better than sb/sth else □ *(sso/sst yg) setanding*: *Charo is no match for her mother when it comes to cooking* (= she doesn't cook as well as her mother). ◆ *I think you've met your match in Dave—you won't beat him.* **4** [sing] a match (for sb/sth) something that looks good with sth else □ *(sst yg) sesuai/padan*: *Those shoes aren't a very good match with your dress.*

match² /mætʃ/ *verb* **1** [I,T] to have the same colour or pattern as sth else; to look good with sth else □ *sepadan; sesuai*: *Your shirt and jacket don't match.* ◆ *That shirt doesn't match your jacket.* **2** [T] to find sb/sth that is like or suitable for sb/sth else □ *memadankan*: *The agency tries to match single people with suitable partners.* ◆ *In this exercise, match the words with the pictures.* **3** [T] to be as good as or better than sb/sth else □ *setanding; menandingi*: *The two teams are very evenly matched.* ◆ *Taiwan produces the goods at a price that Europe cannot match.*

PHR V match up to be the same □ *selaras*: *The statements of the two witnesses don't match up.*
match sth up (with sth) to fit or put sth together (with sth else) □ *memadankan sst (dgn sst)*: *What you have to do is match up each star with his or her pet.*
match up to sb/sth to be as good as sb/sth □ *sebaik spt sso/sst*: *The film didn't match up to my expectations.*

matchbox /'mætʃbɒks/ *noun* [C] a small box for matches □ *kotak mancis* ⮕ picture at **container**

matching /'mætʃɪŋ/ *adj* [only *before* a noun] (used about clothes, objects, etc.) having the same colour, pattern, style, etc. and therefore looking attractive together □ *sepadan; bersesuaian*: *a pine table with four matching chairs*

matchstick /'mætʃstɪk/ *noun* [C] the thin wooden part of a match □ *batang mancis*

mate¹ /meɪt/ *noun* [C] **1** (*informal*) a friend or sb you live, work or do an activity with □ *kawan; teman*: *He's an old mate of mine.* ◆ *a flatmate/classmate/team-mate/playmate* ⮕ note at **friend** **2** (*BrE slang*) used when speaking to a man □ *kawan; beb*: *Can you give me a hand, mate?* **3** one of a male and female pair of animals, birds, etc. □ *pasangan*: *The female sits on the eggs while her mate hunts for food.* **4** an officer on a ship □ *pegawai kapal* **5** = **checkmate**

mate² /meɪt/ *verb* **1** [I] (used about animals and birds) to have sex and produce young □ *mengawan*: *Pandas rarely mate in zoos.* **2** [T] to bring two animals together so that they can mate □ *mengawankan* **SYN** for both meanings **breed**

material¹ /mə'tɪəriəl/ *noun* **1** [C,U] cloth (for making clothes, etc.) □ *kain*: *Is there enough material for a dress?* **2** [C,U] a substance that can be used for making or doing sth □ *bahan*: *raw materials* ◆ *writing/teaching/building materials* ◆ *This new material is strong but it is also very light.* **3** [U] facts or information that you collect before you write a book, article, etc. □ *bahan; maklumat*: *She's collecting material for her latest novel.*

material² /mə'tɪəriəl/ *adj* **1** [only *before* a noun] connected with real or physical things rather than the spirit or emotions □ *kebendaan*: *We should not value material comforts too highly.* ⮕ look at **spiritual 2** important and needing to be considered □ *penting*: *material evidence*

HELP This meaning of the word is not common. Look at **immaterial**.

▶ materially /-riəli/ *adv*

materialism /mə'tɪəriəlɪzəm/ *noun* [U] the belief that money and possessions are the most important things in life □ *sikap kebendaan; materialisme* ▶ materialist /-ɪst/ *noun* [C] ▶ materialistic /mə,tɪəriə'lɪstɪk/ *adj*

materialize (also -ise) /mə'tɪəriəlaɪz/ *verb* [I] to become real; to happen □ *menjadi kenyataan; muncul*: *The pay rise that they had promised never materialized.*

maternal /mə'tɜ:nl/ *adj* **1** behaving as a mother would behave; connected with being a mother □ *keibuan*: *maternal love/instincts* **2** [only *before* a noun] related through your mother's side of the family □ *sebelah ibu*: *your maternal grandfather* ⮕ look at **paternal**

maternity /mə'tɜ:nəti/ *adj* connected with women who are going to have or have just had a baby □ *berkaitan dgn mengandung atau bersalin*: *maternity clothes* ◆ *the hospital's maternity ward* ⮕ look at **paternity**

mathematician /,mæθəmə'tɪʃn/ *noun* [C] a person who studies or is an expert in mathematics □ *ahli matematik*

mathematics /,mæθə'mætɪks/ *noun* [U] (*formal*) the science or study of numbers, quantities or shapes □ *matematik*: *the school mathematics curriculum* ⮕ look at **algebra, arithmetic, geometry**

HELP The British abbreviation is **maths**, in American English it is **math**: *Maths is my favourite subject.*

▶ mathematical /-ɪkl/ *adj*: *mathematical calculations/problems* ▶ mathematically /-kli/ *adv*

matinee (also **matinée**) /'mætɪneɪ/ *noun* [C] an afternoon performance of a play, film, etc. □ *pertunjukan siang*

matrimony /'mætrɪməni/ *noun* [U] (*formal*) the state of being married □ *perkahwinan* ▶ matrimonial /,mætrɪ'məʊniəl/ *adj*

matron /'meɪtrən/ *noun* [C] **1** a woman who works as a nurse in a school □ *matron* **2** (*old-fashioned*) a nurse who is in charge of the other nurses in a hospital (now usually called a **senior nursing officer**) □ *ketua jururawat; matron*

matt (*AmE* also **matte**) /mæt/ *adj* not shiny □ *pusam*: *This paint gives a matt finish.* ➲ look at **gloss**

matted /'mætɪd/ *adj* (used especially about hair) forming a thick mass, especially because it is wet and/or dirty □ *kusut-masai*

matter¹ /'mætə(r)/ *noun* **1** [C] a subject or situation that you must think about and give your attention to □ *hal; perkara*: *It's a personal matter and I don't want to discuss it with you.* ♦ *Finding a job will be no easy matter.* ♦ *To simplify/complicate matters* **2** [sing] **the matter (with sb/sth)** the reason sb/sth has a problem or is not good □ *hal; kena*: *She looks sad. What's the matter with her?* ♦ *There seems to be something the matter with the car.* ♦ *Eat that food! There's nothing the matter with it.* **3** [U] all physical substances; a substance of a particular kind □ *jirim; bahan*: *reading matter* ♦ *waste matter* ♦ *organic matter*
IDM **another/a different matter** something much more serious, difficult, etc. □ *lain pula halnya*: *I can speak a little Japanese, but reading it is quite another matter.*
as a matter of fact to tell the truth; in reality □ *sebenarnya*: *I like him very much, as a matter of fact.*
for that matter in addition; now that I think about it □ *pun begitu juga*: *Mick is really fed up with his course. I am too, for that matter.*
(be) a matter of sth/doing sth a situation in which sth is needed □ *merupakan soal (sst)/membuat sst*: *Learning a language is largely a matter of practice.*
a matter of course something that you always do; the usual thing to do □ *sebagai biasa*: *Goods leaving the factory are checked as a matter of course.*
a matter of hours, minutes, etc.; a matter of inches, metres, etc. only a few hours, minutes, etc. □ *beberapa jam, minit, dll*: *The fight lasted a matter of seconds.*
a matter of life and/or death extremely urgent and important □ *soal hidup mati*
a matter of opinion a subject on which people do not agree □ *soal pendapat*: *'I think the government is doing a good job.' 'That's a matter of opinion.'*
no matter who, what, where, etc. it is not important who, what, where, etc. □ *tdk kira siapa, apa, di mana, dsb*: *They never listen, no matter what you say.*
to make matters/things worse ➲ **worse**

matter² /'mætə(r)/ *verb* [I] [not used in the continuous tenses] **matter (to sb)** to be important □ *penting*: *It doesn't really matter how much it costs.* ♦ *Nobody's hurt, and that's all that matters.* ♦ *Some things matter more than others.* ♦ *It doesn't matter to me what he does in his free time.*

HELP Compare **it doesn't matter** and **I don't mind**: *'I've broken a cup!' 'It was an old one. It doesn't matter* (= it is not important).' ♦ *'What shall we have for dinner?' 'I don't mind* (= I will be happy with any type of dinner).'

matter-of-fact *adj* said or done without showing any emotion, especially when it would seem more normal to express your feelings □ *bersahaja*: *He was very matter-of-fact about his illness.*

mattress /'mætrəs/ *noun* [C] the soft part of a bed that you lie on □ *tilam* ➲ picture at **bed**

mature /mə'tʃʊə(r)/ (*AmE* also) / *adj* **1** behaving in a sensible adult way □ *dewasa*: *Is she mature enough for such responsibility?* **2** fully grown or fully developed □ *matang*: *a mature tree/bird/animal* **OPP** for both meanings **immature** ▶**mature** *verb* [I]: *He matured a lot during his two years at college.* ▶**maturity** /mə'tʃʊərəti/ (*AmE* also) / *noun* [U]

maul /mɔ:l/ *verb* [T] (usually used about a wild animal) to attack and injure sb □ *mencederakan*

mauve /məʊv/ *adj, noun* [U] (of) a pale purple colour □ *(berwarna) ungu muda/merah senduduk*

max /mæks/ *abbr* = **maximum** □ *maksimum*: *max temp 21°C* **OPP** **min.**

maxim /'mæksɪm/ *noun* [C] a few words that express a rule for good or sensible behaviour □ *maksim; moto; pepatah*: *Our maxim is: 'If a job's worth doing, it's worth doing well.'*

maximize (also **-ise**) /'mæksɪmaɪz/ *verb* [T] to increase sth as much as possible □ *memaksimumkan*: *to maximize profits* **OPP** **minimize**

maximum /'mæksɪməm/ *noun* [sing] (*abbr* **max**) the greatest amount or level of sth that is possible, allowed, etc. □ *maksimum*: *The bus can carry a maximum of 40 people.* ♦ *That is the maximum we can afford.* **OPP** **minimum** ▶**maximum** *adj* [only before a noun]: *a maximum speed of 120 miles per hour*

May /meɪ/ *noun* [U,C] the 5th month of the year, coming after April □ *Mei* ➲ note at **January**

may /meɪ/ *modal verb* (*negative* **may not**; *pt* **might** /maɪt/; *negative* **might not**) **1** used for saying that sth is possible □ *mungkin*: *'Where's Sue?' 'She may be in the garden.'* ♦ *You may be right.* ♦ *I may be going to China next year.* ♦ *They may have forgotten the meeting.* **2** used for contrasting two facts □ *sungguhpun*: *He may be very clever but he can't do anything practical.* **3** used as a polite way of asking for and giving permission □ *boleh(kah); boleh*: *May I use your phone?* ♦ *You may not take photographs in the museum.* **4** (*formal*) used for expressing wishes and hopes □ *semoga*: *May you both be very happy.* ❶ For more information about modal verbs, look at the **Reference Section** at the back of this dictionary.
IDM **may/might as well (do sth)** ➲ **well¹**

maybe /'meɪbi/ *adv* perhaps; possibly □ *mungkin; barangkali*: *'Are you going to come?'*

'Maybe.' ◆ There were three, maybe four armed men. ◆ Maybe I'll accept the invitation and maybe I won't. ➲ note at **perhaps**

May Day noun [C] 1st May □ *1 Mei; Hari Pekerja*

> **CULTURE**
>
> **May Day** is traditionally celebrated as a spring festival, and in some countries as a holiday in honour of working people.

mayonnaise /ˌmeɪəˈneɪz/ noun [U] a thick cold white sauce made with eggs and oil □ *mayones*

mayor /meə(r)/ noun [C] a person who is elected to be the leader of a group of people who manage the affairs of a town or city □ *datuk bandar*: *the Lord Mayor of London*

mayoress /meəˈres/ noun [C] a woman **mayor**, or a woman who is married to or helps a **mayor** □ *datuk bandar (wanita)*

maze /meɪz/ noun [C] a system of paths which is designed to confuse you so that it is difficult to find your way out □ *lorong berselirat*: (figurative) *a maze of winding streets* SYN **labyrinth**

MB abbr = megabyte: *512MB of memory*

Mb (also **Mbit**) abbr = megabit

MBA /ˌem biː ˈeɪ/ abbr **Master of Business Administration**; an advanced university degree in business □ *MBA (Sarjana Pengurusan Perniagaan)*

MD /ˌem ˈdiː/ abbr **Doctor of Medicine** □ *MD (Doktor Perubatan)*

me /miː/ pron (used as an object) the person who is speaking or writing □ *saya*: *He telephoned me yesterday.* ◆ *She wrote to me last week.* ◆ *Hello, is that Frank? It's me, Sadiq.*

meadow /ˈmedəʊ/ noun [C] a field of grass □ *padang rumput* ➲ picture on **page P10**

meagre (AmE **meager**) /ˈmiːɡə(r)/ adj too small in amount □ *sedikit; tdk seberapa*: *a meagre salary*

meal /miːl/ noun [C] the time when you eat or the food that is eaten at that time □ *waktu makan; hidangan*: *Shall we go out for a meal on Friday?* ◆ *a heavy/light meal* ◆ *What time do you have your evening meal?* ➲ note at **lunch**, **restaurant**

IDM **a square meal** ➲ **square¹**

> **TOPIC**
>
> **Meals**
>
> The main **meals** of the day are **breakfast**, **lunch** and **dinner**. **Tea** and **supper** are usually smaller meals, but some people use these words to talk about the main evening meal. The midday meal can be called **dinner**. Before a meal you **lay the table** by putting a **tablecloth**, **cutlery** (= knives, forks and spoons), etc. on it. After the meal you **clear the table** and **wash up/wash the dishes**. If you don't want to cook, you can **go out for a meal/eat out** (= go to a restaurant) or you can get a **takeaway** (= a meal that you collect and take home). A **picnic** is a meal that you prepare at home and take to eat outdoors. Something small that you eat between meals is a **snack**.

mealtime /ˈmiːltaɪm/ noun [C] the time at which a meal is usually eaten □ *waktu makan*

mean¹ /miːn/ verb [T] (pt, pp **meant** /ment/)
➤HAVE AS MEANING **1** [not used in the continuous tenses] to express, show or have as a meaning □ *bermakna; makna; bererti; erti*: *What does this word mean?* ◆ *The bell means that the lesson has ended.* ◆ *Does the name 'Kate Wallace' mean anything to you* (= do you know who she is)*?*

> **HELP** Although this verb is not used in the continuous tenses, it is common to see the present participle (= *-ing* form): *The weather during filming was terrible, meaning that several scenes had to be shot again later.*

➤WANT TO SAY **2** to want or intend to say sth; to refer to sb/sth □ *bermaksud; maksud*: *Well, she said 'yes' but I think she really meant 'no'.* ◆ *What do you mean by 'a lot of money'?* ◆ *I only meant that I couldn't come tomorrow—any other day would be fine.* ◆ *I see what you mean, but I'm afraid it's not possible.* ➲ note at **think**

> **HELP** Note that **mean** cannot be used when we want to say 'to have the opinion that'. We say: *I think that …* or *In my opinion …* : *I think that she'd be silly to buy that car.* **I mean** is often used in conversation when you want to explain something you have just said or to add more information: *What a terrible summer—I mean it's rained almost all the time.* **I mean** is also used to correct something you have just said: *We went there on Tuesday, I mean Thursday.*

➤INTEND TO DO **3** [often passive] **mean (sb) to do sth; mean sth (as/for sth/sb); mean sb/sth to be sth** to intend sth; to be supposed to be/do sth □ *bermaksud*: *I'm sure she didn't mean to upset you.* ◆ *She meant the present to be for both of us.* ◆ *I didn't mean you to cook the whole meal!* ◆ *It was only meant as a joke.* ◆ *What's this picture meant to be?*

➤BE SERIOUS **4** to be serious or sincere about sth □ *benar-benar serius*: *He said he loved me but I don't think he meant it!*

➤CAUSE **5** to make sth likely; to cause □ *bermakna*: *The shortage of teachers means that classes are larger.*

➤BE IMPORTANT **6 mean sth (to sb)** to be important to sb □ *penting; bermakna*: *This job means a lot to me.* ◆ *Money means nothing to her.*

IDM **be meant to be sth** to be considered or said to be sth □ *dianggap/dikatakan sst*: *That restaurant is meant to be excellent.*

mean well to want to be kind and helpful but usually without success □ *berniat baik*: *My*

[C] **countable**, a noun with a plural form: *one book, two books*   [U] **uncountable**, a noun with no plural form: *some sugar*

mother means well but I wish she'd stop treating me like a child.

mean² /miːn/ adj (meaner; meanest) **1** mean (with sth) wanting to keep money, etc. for yourself rather than let other people have it □ *lokek; bakhil*: It's no good asking him for any money—he's much too mean. ♦ They're mean with the food in the canteen. **OPP** generous **2** mean (to sb) (used about people or their behaviour) unkind □ *busuk hati*: It was mean of him not to invite you too. **3** [only before a noun] average □ *min; purata*: the mean temperature ▶meanness noun [U]

meander /miˈændə(r)/ verb [I] **1** (used about a river, road, etc.) to have a lot of curves and bends □ *berliku-liku* ➲ picture on **page P10** **2** to walk or travel slowly or without any definite direction □ *merayau-rayau* ▶meander noun [C]: The town is situated on a meander of the river.

meaning /ˈmiːnɪŋ/ noun **1** [C,U] the thing or idea that sth represents; what sb is trying to communicate □ *makna; erti*: This word has two different meanings in English. ♦ What do you think the meaning is of the last line of the poem? **2** [U] the purpose or importance of an experience □ *makna; tujuan*: Having a child gave new meaning to their lives.

meaningful /ˈmiːnɪŋfl/ adj **1** useful, important or interesting □ *bermakna*: Most people need a meaningful relationship with another person. **2** (used about a look, expression, etc.) trying to express a certain feeling or idea □ *penuh bermakna*: They kept giving each other meaningful glances across the table. ▶meaningfully /-fəli/ adv

meaningless /ˈmiːnɪŋləs/ adj without meaning, reason or sense □ *tdk bermakna*: The figures are meaningless if we have nothing to compare them with.

means /miːnz/ noun **1** [C] (pl means) a means (of doing sth) a method of doing sth □ *cara; kaedah; jalan*: Do you have any means of transport (= a car, bicycle, etc.)? ♦ Is there any means of contacting your husband? **2** [pl] (formal) all the money that sb has □ *kemampuan; wang; kekayaan*: This car is beyond the means of most people.
IDM by all means used to say that you are happy for sb to have or do sth □ *silakan; tentu sekali*: 'Can I borrow your newspaper?' 'By all means.'
by means of by using □ *dgn menggunakan; melalui*: We got out of the hotel by means of the fire escape.
by no means; not by any means (used to emphasize sth) not at all □ *sebenarnya bukan/tdk*: I'm by no means sure that this is the right thing to do.
a means to an end an action or thing that is not important in itself but is a way of achieving sth else □ *semata-mata utk (mencapai sst tujuan)*: I don't enjoy my job, but it's a means to an end.

meant past tense, past participle of **mean¹**

[I] **intransitive**, a verb which has no object: *He laughed.*

meantime /ˈmiːntaɪm/ noun
IDM in the meantime in the time between two things happening □ *sementara itu*: Our house isn't finished so in the meantime we're living with my mother.

meanwhile /ˈmiːnwaɪl/ adv during the same time or during the time between two things happening □ *sementara itu*: Peter was at home studying. Omar, meanwhile, was out with his friends.

measles /ˈmiːzlz/ noun [U] a common infectious disease, especially among children, in which your body feels hot and your skin is covered in small red spots □ *(penyakit) campak*

> **GRAMMAR** Measles looks like a plural noun but is used with a singular verb: *Measles is a very dangerous disease.*

measly /ˈmiːzli/ adj (informal) much too small in size, amount or value □ *sedikit sangat; sangat kecil; tdk berpada*: All that work for this measly amount of money!

measure¹ /ˈmeʒə(r)/ verb **1** [I,T] to find the size, weight, quantity, etc. of sb/sth in standard units by using an instrument □ *mengukur; menyukat*: to measure the height/width/length/depth of something ♦ Could you measure how wide the table is to see if it will fit into our room? **2** [T] to be a certain height, width, length, etc. □ *berukuran*: The room measures five metres across. **3** [T] measure sth (against sth) to judge the value or effect of sth □ *membandingkan; dibandingkan*: Our sales do not look good when measured against those of our competitors.
PHR V measure up (sb/sth) to measure sb/sth □ *mengukur sso/sst*
measure up (to sth) to be as good as you need to be or as sb expects you to be □ *memenuhi jangkaan/harapan*: Did the holiday measure up to your expectations?

measure² /ˈmeʒə(r)/ noun **1** [C, usually pl] an official action that is done for a special reason □ *langkah*: The government is to take new measures to reduce inflation. ♦ As a temporary measure, the road will have to be closed. **2** [sing] (formal) a/some measure of sth a certain amount of sth; some □ *sedikit*: The play achieved a measure of success. **3** [sing] a way of understanding or judging sth □ *menunjukkan*: The school's popularity is a measure of the teachers' success. **4** [C] a way of describing the size, amount, etc. of sth □ *ukuran*: A metre is a measure of length. ➲ look at **tape measure**
IDM for good measure in addition to sth, especially to make sure that there is enough □ *sebagai tambahan*: He made a few extra sandwiches for good measure.
made to measure specially made or perfectly suitable for a particular person, use, etc. □ *yg dibuat khas; tempah*: I'm getting a suit made to measure for the wedding.

measurement /ˈmeʒəmənt/ noun **1** [U] the act or process of measuring sth □ *pengukuran*:

[T] **transitive**, a verb which has an object: *He ate an apple.*

the metric system of measurement **2** [C] a size, amount, etc. that is found by measuring □ *ukuran; sukatan*: *What are the exact measurements of the room?* (= how wide, long, etc. is it?)

'measuring tape = **tape measure**

meat /miːt/ *noun* [U] the parts of animals or birds that people eat □ *daging*: *meat and two vegetables* ♦ *meat-eating animals* ♦ *a piece/slice of meat*

> **TOPIC**
>
> **Meat**
>
> We get **pork**, **ham** or **bacon** from a pig, **beef** from a cow and **veal** from a calf (= a young cow). **Mutton** comes from a sheep, but we get **lamb** from a lamb (= a young sheep). We often call beef, mutton and lamb **red meat**. Pale-coloured meat such as chicken is called **white meat**. We can **fry**, **grill**, **roast** or **stew** meat. We **carve** a **joint** of meat. Meat can be described as **tough** or **tender**, **lean** or **fatty**. Uncooked meat is **raw**. You buy meat at **the butcher's**. A person who does not eat meat is a **vegetarian**.

meaty /'miːti/ *adj* (**meatier**; **meatiest**) **1** like meat, or containing a lot of meat □ *banyak daging*: *meaty sausages* **2** containing a lot of important or good ideas □ *isi*: *a meaty topic for discussion* **3** large and fat □ *berisi*: *meaty tomatoes*

mebibit /'mebɪbɪt/ (*abbr* **Mib**; **Mibit**) = **megabit**(2)

mebibyte /'mebɪbaɪt/ (*abbr* **MiB**) = **megabyte**(2)

Mecca /'mekə/ *noun* **1** [sing] the city in Saudi Arabia where the Prophet Muhammad was born, which is the centre of Islam □ *Makkah* **2 mecca** [C, usually sing] a place that many people wish to visit because of a particular interest □ *tempat tumpuan*: *Italy is a mecca for art lovers.*

mechanic /mə'kænɪk/ *noun* **1** [C] a person whose job is to repair and work with machines □ *mekanik*: *a car mechanic* **2 mechanics** [U] the science of how machines work □ *ilmu mekanik* **3 the mechanics** [pl] the way in which sth works or is done □ *selok-belok*: *Don't ask me—I don't understand the mechanics of the legal system.*

mechanical /mə'kænɪkl/ *adj* **1** connected with or produced by machines □ *mekanikal*: *a mechanical pump* ♦ *mechanical engineering* **2** (used about sb's behaviour) done like a machine as if you are not thinking about what you are doing □ *macam mesin; secara automatik; tanpa berfikir*: *He played the piano in a dull and mechanical way.* ▶ **mechanically** /-kli/ *adv*

mechanism /'mekənɪzəm/ *noun* [C] **1** a set of moving parts in a machine that does a certain task □ *mekanisme*: *Our car has an automatic locking mechanism.* **2** the way in which sth works or is done □ *cara; prosedur*: *I'm afraid there is no mechanism for dealing with your complaint.*

541 **measuring tape → mediaeval**

mechanize (also **-ise**) /'mekənaɪz/ *verb* [T] to use machines instead of people to do work □ *menggunakan mesin; menjenterakan*: *We have mechanized the entire production process.* ▶ **mechanization** (also **-isation**) /ˌmekənaɪ'zeɪʃn/ *noun* [U]

the Med /med/ (*informal*) = **the Mediterranean**

med *abbr* = **medium²**(2)

medal — medals — shield

trophy — rosette — cup

medal /'medl/ *noun* [C] a small flat piece of metal, usually with a design and words on it, which is given to sb who has shown courage or as a prize in a sport □ *pingat*: *to win a gold/silver/bronze medal in the Olympics*

medallion /mə'dæliən/ *noun* [C] a small round piece of metal on a chain which is worn as jewellery around the neck □ *medalion*

medallist (*AmE* **medalist**) /'medəlɪst/ *noun* [C] a person who has won a **medal**, especially in sport □ *pemenang pingat*: *an Olympic gold medallist*

meddle /'medl/ *verb* [I] **meddle (in/with sth)** to take too much interest in sb's private affairs or to touch sth that does not belong to you □ *campur tangan*: *She hated her mother meddling in her private life.*

media /'miːdiə/ *noun* [U, with sing or pl verb] TV, radio, newspapers and the Internet used as a means of communication □ *media*: *The reports in the media have been greatly exaggerated.* ➲ note at **newspaper** ➲ look at **mass media**

> **GRAMMAR** Media is used with a singular or plural verb: *The media always take/takes a great interest in the royal family.*

mediaeval = **medieval**

CONSONANTS p **p**en b **b**ad t **t**ea d **d**id k **c**at g **g**ot tʃ **ch**in dʒ **J**une f **f**all v **v**an θ **th**in

mediate /ˈmiːdieɪt/ verb [I,T] **mediate (in sth) (between A and B)** to try to end a disagreement between two or more people or groups □ *menjadi orang tengah*: *As a supervisor she had to mediate between her colleagues and the management.* ▶ **mediation** /ˌmiːdiˈeɪʃn/ noun [U] ▶ **mediator** /ˈmiːdieɪtə(r)/ noun [C]

medical[1] /ˈmedɪkl/ adj connected with medicine and the treatment of illness □ *(berkenaan dgn) perubatan*: *medical treatment/care* ♦ *the medical profession* ▶ **medically** /-kli/ adv: *medically fit/unfit for work*

medical[2] /ˈmedɪkl/ noun [C] an examination of your body by a doctor to check your state of health □ *pemeriksaan doktor/kesihatan*: *to have a medical*

medication /ˌmedɪˈkeɪʃn/ noun [C,U] medicine that a doctor has given to you □ *ubat*: *Are you on any medication?*

medicinal /məˈdɪsɪnl/ adj useful for curing illness or infection □ *ubat*: *medicinal plants*

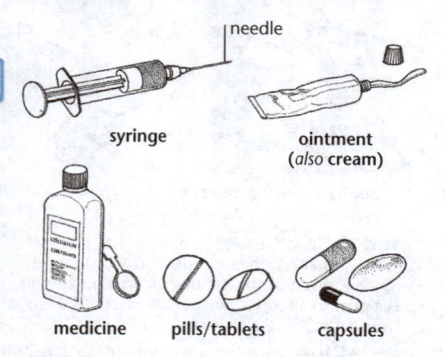

needle
syringe
ointment (also cream)
medicine
pills/tablets
capsules

medicine /ˈmedsn; ˈmedɪsn/ noun 1 [U] the science of preventing and treating illness □ *ilmu perubatan*: *to study medicine* 2 [C,U] a substance, especially a liquid, that you take in order to cure an illness □ *ubat*: *Take this medicine three times a day.* ♦ *cough medicine* ➔ note at **doctor**

medieval (also **mediaeval**) /ˌmediˈiːvl/ adj connected with **the Middle Ages** (= the period in history between about 1000 AD and 1450 AD) □ *(berkenaan dgn) zaman pertengahan*

mediocre /ˌmiːdiˈəʊkə(r)/ adj of not very high quality □ *tdk begitu baik*: *He gave a mediocre performance* ▶ **mediocrity** /ˌmiːdiˈɒkrəti/ noun [U]

meditate /ˈmedɪteɪt/ verb [I] **meditate (on/upon sth)** to think carefully and deeply, especially for religious reasons or to make your mind calm □ *bermeditasi; bertafakur*: *I've been meditating on what you said last week.* ▶ **meditation** /ˌmedɪˈteɪʃn/ noun [U]

the Mediterranean /ˌmedɪtəˈreɪniən/ (also informal **the Med**) noun [sing], adj [only before a noun] (of) the Mediterranean Sea or the countries around it □ *Laut Mediterranean*: *Mediterranean cookery*

medium[1] /ˈmiːdiəm/ adj 1 in the middle between two sizes, lengths, temperatures, etc.; average □ *pertengahan; sederhana*: *She was of medium height.* ♦ *Would you like the small, medium or large packet?* ♦ *a medium-sized car/town/dog* 2 (used about meat) cooked until it is brown all the way through □ *sederhana masak* ➔ look at **rare, well done**

medium[2] /ˈmiːdiəm/ noun 1 [C] (pl **media** or **mediums**) a means you can use to express or communicate sth □ *perantara*: *The Internet is the modern medium of communication.* ♦ *English is the medium of instruction in the school.* ♦ *the medium of radio/television* ➔ look at **media, mass media** 2 [C,U] (abbr **med**) medium size □ *(saiz) sedang/sederhana*: *Have you got this shirt in (a) medium?* 3 [C] (pl **mediums**) a person who says that they can speak to the spirits of dead people □ *medium; perantara*

medley /ˈmedli/ noun [C] 1 a piece of music consisting of several tunes or songs played one after the other without a break □ *aneka lagu* 2 a mixture of different things □ *aneka; pelbagai; cacamarba*: *a medley of styles/flavours*

meek /miːk/ adj (**meeker**; **meekest**) (used about people) quiet, and doing what other people say without asking questions □ *ikut kata* ▶ **meekly** adv ▶ **meekness** noun [U]

meet /miːt/ verb (pt, pp **met** /met/)
▶ COME TOGETHER 1 [I,T] to come together by chance or because you have arranged it □ *berjumpa*: *What time shall we meet for lunch?* ♦ *I just met Kareem on the train.* 2 [T] to go to a place and wait for sb/sth to arrive □ *menunggu*: *I'll come and meet you at the station.*
▶ FOR THE FIRST TIME 3 [I,T] to see and know sb for the first time □ *bertemu; berkenalan*: *Have you two met before?* ♦ *Where did you first meet your husband?* ➔ note at **know**
▶ IN COMPETITION 4 [I,T] to play, fight, etc. together as opponents in a sports competition □ *bertemu dgn*: *These two teams met in last year's final.* ♦ *Yamada will meet Suzuki in the second round.*
▶ EXPERIENCE STH 5 [T] to experience sth, often sth unpleasant □ *menemui*: *We will never know how he met his death.*
▶ JOIN 6 [I,T] to touch, join or make contact with □ *bertemu*: *The two roads meet not far from here.* ♦ *His eyes met hers.*
▶ BE ENOUGH 7 [T] to be enough for sth; to be able to deal with sth □ *memenuhi; menerima; menyahut*: *The money that I earn is enough to meet our basic needs.* ♦ *to meet a challenge*
IDM **make ends meet** ➔ **end**[1]
there is more to sb/sth than meets the eye sb/sth is more interesting or complicated than he/she/it seems □ *lebih drpd yg disangka*: *Do you think there's more to their relationship than meets the eye?*

PHR V **meet up (with sb)** (*informal*) to meet sb, especially after a period of being apart □ *berjumpa (dgn sso)*: *I have a few things I need to do now, but let's meet up later.* ⊃ look at **get together**

meet with sb (*especially AmE*) to meet sb, especially for discussion □ *bertemu dgn sso*: *The President met with his advisers early this morning.*

meet with sth to get a particular answer, reaction or result □ *mendapat; menemui*: *to meet with success/failure/opposition*

meeting /ˈmiːtɪŋ/ *noun* **1** [C] an organized occasion when a number of people come together in order to discuss or decide sth □ *mesyuarat*: *The group hold regular meetings all year.* ♦ *We need to have a meeting to discuss these matters.*

> **MORE** We **call**, **arrange** or **organize** a meeting. We can also **cancel** or **postpone** a meeting.

2 [sing] the people at a meeting □ *mesyuarat*: *The meeting was in favour of the new proposals.* **3** [C] the coming together of two or more people □ *perjumpaan; pertemuan*: *Christmas is a time of family meetings and reunions.*

meg /meg/ (*informal*) = **megabyte**: *more than 512 megs of memory* ♦ *a 24-meg broadband*

megabit /ˈmegəbɪt/ *noun* [C] (*abbr* Mb; Mbit) **1** a unit of computer memory, equal to 10^6 (= 1 000 000) **bits** (= the smallest units of information) □ *megabit* **2** (also **mebibit**) a unit of computer memory, equal to 2^{20} (= 1 048 576) **bits** (= the smallest units of information) □ *megabit*

megabyte /ˈmegəbaɪt/ *noun* [C] (*abbr* MB) (also *informal* **meg**) **1** a unit of computer memory, equal to 10^6 (= 1 000 000) **bytes** (= small units of information) □ *megabait*: *a 512-megabyte flash drive* **2** (also **mebibyte**) a unit of computer memory, equal to 2^{20} (= 1 048 576) **bytes** (= small units of information) □ *megabait*: *a 40-megabyte hard disk*

megaphone /ˈmegəfəʊn/ *noun* [C] a piece of equipment that you speak through to make your voice sound louder when speaking to a crowd □ *megafon*

melancholy /ˈmelənkəli; -kɒli/ *noun* [U] (*formal*) a feeling of sadness which lasts for a long time □ *kemurungan; kesedihan* ▶ **melancholy** *adj*

mellow /ˈmeləʊ/ *adj* (**mellower**; **mellowest**) **1** (used about colours or sounds) soft and pleasant □ *lembut*: *mellow autumn colours* **2** (used about people) calm and relaxed □ *lunak; tenang dan penyabar*: *My dad's grown mellower as he's got older.* ▶ **mellow** *verb* [I,T]: *Experience had mellowed her views about many things.*

melodic /məˈlɒdɪk/ *adj* **1** [only *before* a noun] connected with the main tune in a piece of music □ *berkenaan dgn melodi*: *The melodic line is carried by the clarinets.* **2** = **melodious**

melodious /məˈləʊdiəs/ (also **melodic**) *adj* pleasant to listen to, like music □ *merdu*: *a rich melodious voice* ▶ **melodiously** *adv*

meeting → membrane

melodrama /ˈmelədrɑːmə/ *noun* [C,U] a story, play or film in which a lot of exciting things happen and in which people's emotions are stronger than in real life □ *melodrama*

melodramatic /ˌmelədrəˈmætɪk/ *adj* (often disapproving) making things seem more exciting or serious than they really are □ *melodramatik*: *Don't be so melodramatic, Simon—of course you're not going to die!* ♦ *a melodramatic plot full of deceit and murder*

melody /ˈmelədi/ *noun* [C] (*pl* melodies) a song or tune; the main tune of a piece of music □ *melodi*

melon /ˈmelən/ *noun* [C,U] a large round fruit with a thick yellow or green skin and a lot of seeds □ *tembikai* ⊃ picture on **page P14**

melt /melt/ *verb* **1** [I,T] to change or make sth change from a solid to a liquid by means of heat □ *menjadi cair; mencair*: *When we got up in the morning the snow had melted.* ♦ *First melt the butter in a saucepan.* ⊃ look at **thaw 2** [I] (used about sb's feelings, etc.) to become softer or less strong □ *(menjadi) lembut hati*: *My heart melted when I saw the baby.*

PHR V **melt away** to disappear □ *melenyap; beransur-ansur pergi*: *The crowd slowly melted away when the speaker had finished.*

melt sth down to heat a metal or glass object until it becomes liquid □ *meleburkan sst*

meltdown /ˈmeltdaʊn/ *noun* [U,C] a serious accident in which the central part of a nuclear **reactor** (= a very large machine that produces nuclear energy) melts, causing harmful substances to escape □ *peleburan bahagian pusat reaktor nuklear*: (*figurative*) *The country is in economic meltdown.*

melting pot *noun* [C] a place where a lot of different cultures, ideas, etc. come together □ *tempat pertembungan; wadah tumpuan*: *New York is a melting pot of different cultures.*

member /ˈmembə(r)/ *noun* [C] a person, animal or thing that belongs to a group, a club, an organization, etc. □ *ahli*: *All the members of the family were there.* ♦ *to become a member of a club* ♦ *a member of staff*

Member of Parliament *noun* [C] (*abbr* MP) a person who has been elected to represent people from a particular area in Parliament □ *Ahli Parlimen*: *the MP for Oxford East*

membership /ˈmembəʃɪp/ *noun* **1** [U] the state of being a member of a group, an organization, etc. □ *keahlian; keanggotaan*: *To apply for membership, please fill in the enclosed form.* ♦ *a membership card/fee* **2** [C,U] the people who belong to a group, an organization, etc. □ *(jumlah) ahli*: *Membership has fallen in the past year* (= the number of members has decreased).

membrane /ˈmembreɪn/ *noun* [C] a thin skin which covers certain parts of a person's or an animal's body □ *membran*

memento /məˈmentəʊ/ noun [C] (pl mementoes; mementos) something that you keep to remind you of sb/sth □ *cenderamata; cenderahati* **SYN** souvenir

memo /ˈmeməʊ/ noun [C] (pl memos) (also formal **memorandum**) a note sent from one person or office to another within an organization □ *memo*

memoirs /ˈmemwɑːz/ noun [pl] sb's written account of their own life and experiences □ *memoir; kisah kenangan* **SYN** autobiography

memorabilia /ˌmeməˈrəˈbɪliə/ noun [U] things that people buy because they are connected with a famous person, event, etc. □ *memorabilia: Beatles/Titanic/war memorabilia*

memorable /ˈmemərəbl/ adj worth remembering or easy to remember □ *sukar dilupai: The concert was a memorable experience.* **SYN** unforgettable ▶ **memorably** /-əbli/ adv

memorandum /ˌmeməˈrændəm/ noun (pl memoranda /-də/) (formal) = memo

memorial /məˈmɔːriəl/ noun [C] a memorial (to sb/sth) something that is built or done to remind people of an event or a person □ *peringatan: a memorial to the victims of the bombing* ♦ *a war memorial* ♦ *a memorial service*

memorize (also -ise) /ˈmeməraɪz/ verb [T] to learn sth so that you can remember it exactly □ *menghafal: Actors have to memorize their lines.*

memory /ˈmeməri/ noun (pl memories) **1** [C] sb's ability to remember things □ *daya ingat; ingatan: to have a good/bad memory* ♦ *The drug can affect your short-term memory.* **2** [C,U] the part of your mind in which you store things that you remember □ *ingatan: That day remained firmly in my memory for the rest of my life.* ♦ *Are you going to do your speech from memory, or are you going to use notes?* **3** [C] something that you remember □ *kenangan: That is one of my happiest memories.* ♦ *childhood memories* **4** [C,U] the part of a computer where information is stored □ *ingatan: This computer has a 640k memory/640k of memory.*
IDM **in memory of sb** in order to remind people of sb who has died □ *utk memperingati sso: A service was held in memory of the dead.*
jog sb's memory ⊃ **jog¹**
refresh your memory ⊃ **refresh**

ˈmemory card noun [C] an electronic device that can be used to store data, used especially with cameras, mobile phones, music players, etc. □ *kad memori*

ˈmemory stick = flash drive

men plural of **man¹**

menace /ˈmenəs/ noun **1** [C] a menace (to sb/sth) a danger or threat □ *ancaman; bahaya: The new road is a menace to everyone's safety.* **2** [U] a quality, feeling, etc. that is threatening or frightening □ *ancaman: He spoke with menace in his voice.* **3** [C] a person or thing that causes trouble □ *pengacau; pengganggu* ▶ **menace** verb [T] ▶ **menacing** adj

mend¹ /mend/ verb [T] to repair sth that is damaged or broken □ *membaiki, menjerumat, menampal, dsb: Can you mend the hole in this jumper for me?* ♦ (figurative) *They tried to mend their differences.* **SYN** repair

mend² /mend/ noun
IDM **be on the mend** (informal) to be getting better after an illness or injury □ *beransur sembuh: She's been in bed for a week but she's on the mend now.*

menial /ˈmiːniəl/ adj (used about work) not skilled or important □ *(kerja) kasar: a menial job*

meningitis /ˌmenɪnˈdʒaɪtɪs/ noun [U] a dangerous illness which affects the brain and the **spinal, cord** (= the inside of the bones in your back) □ *meningitis*

the menopause /ˈmenəpɔːz/ noun [sing] the time when a woman stops **menstruating** and can no longer have children. This usually happens around the age of 50. □ *putus haid*

menstrual /ˈmenstruəl/ adj connected with the time when a woman **menstruates** each month □ *berkenaan dgn haid: The average length of a woman's menstrual cycle is 28 days.*

menstruate /ˈmenstrueɪt/ verb [I] (formal) (used about women) to lose blood once a month from the **womb** (= the part of the body where a baby grows) □ *datang haid* ⊃ A more common way of saying this is **have a period.** ▶ **menstruation** /ˌmenstruˈeɪʃn/ noun [U]

mental /ˈmentl/ adj [only before a noun] **1** of or in the mind; involving the process of thinking □ *mental; akal: It's fascinating to watch a child's mental development.* ♦ *mental arithmetic* (= counting with numbers done in your head) **2** connected with illness of the mind □ *mental: a mental illness/hospital* ♦ *mental health*

mentality /menˈtæləti/ noun [C] (pl mentalities) a type of mind or way of thinking □ *mentaliti; pemikiran: I just can't understand his mentality!* ♦ *the criminal mentality*

mentally /-təli/ adv connected with or happening in the mind □ *secara mental: She's mentally ill.* ♦ *The baby is very mentally alert.*

mention /ˈmenʃn/ verb [T] to say or write sth about sb/sth without giving much information □ *menyebut: He mentioned (to me) that he might be late.* ♦ *Did she mention what time the film starts?*
IDM **don't mention it** used as a polite reply when sb thanks you for sth □ *(ungkapan balas ucapan sso mengucapkan terima kasih); sama-sama: 'Thank you for all your help.' 'Don't mention it.'*
not to mention (used to emphasize sth) and also; as well as □ *dan juga; di samping: This is a great habitat for birds, not to mention other wildlife.*
▶ **mention** noun [C,U]: *It was odd that there wasn't even a mention of the riots in the newspaper.*

menu /'menjuː/ noun [C] **1** a list of the food that you can choose at a restaurant □ *menu; senarai hidangan*: Could we have/see the menu, please? ◆ I hope there's soup **on the menu**. ◆ They do a special lunchtime menu here. ⊃ note at **restaurant** **2** a list of choices in a computer program which is shown on the screen □ *menu: a pull-down menu*

'menu bar noun [C] a horizontal bar at the top of a computer screen that contains **drop-down menus** (= lists of possible choices) such as 'File', 'Edit' and 'Help' □ *bar menu*

MEP /ˌem iː 'piː/ abbr **Member of the European Parliament** □ *MEP (Ahli Parlimen Eropah)*

mercenary¹ /'mɜːsənəri/ noun [C] (pl **mercenaries**) a soldier who fights for any group or country that will pay them □ *askar upahan*

mercenary² /'mɜːsənəri/ adj interested only in making money □ *mata duitan*: I know his motives are entirely mercenary.

merchandise /'mɜːtʃəndaɪs, -daɪz/ noun [U] (*formal*) goods that are for sale □ *barang jualan*

merchant /'mɜːtʃənt/ noun [C] a person whose job is to buy and sell goods, usually of one particular type, in large amounts □ *pedagang*

the ˌmerchant 'navy noun [C, with sing or pl verb] a country's commercial ships and the people who work on them □ *angkatan kapal perdagangan*

merciful /'mɜːsɪfl/ adj feeling or showing mercy □ *penuh belas kasihan/rahmat*: His death was a merciful release from pain. ▶ **mercifully** /-fəli/ adv

merciless /'mɜːsɪləs/ adj showing no mercy □ *tanpa belas kasihan* ▶ **mercilessly** adv

Mercury /'mɜːkjəri/ noun [sing] the planet that is nearest to the sun □ *Utarid*

mercury /'mɜːkjəri/ noun [U] (*symbol* Hg) a heavy silver-coloured metal that is usually in liquid form. **Mercury** is used in **thermometers** (= instruments that measure temperature). □ *merkuri; raksa*

mercy /'mɜːsi/ noun [U] kindness shown by sb/sth who has the power to make sb suffer □ *belas kasihan*: The prisoners begged for mercy from the king. ◆ The rebels were **shown no mercy**. They were taken out and shot.

IDM **at the mercy of sb/sth** having no power against sb/sth that is strong □ *nasib (sso/sst) semata-mata di tangan sso/sst (yg lain)*: The climbers spent the night on the mountain at the mercy of the wind and rain.

mere /mɪə(r)/ adj (**merest**) [no comparative] [only *before* a noun] **1** (used for emphasizing how small or unimportant sth is) nothing more than □ *hanya; cuma; semata-mata*: 90% of the country's land is owned by a mere 2% of the population. **2** used to say that just the fact that sb/sth is present in a situation is enough to have an influence □ *sahaja*: The mere thought of giving a speech in public makes me feel sick.

IDM **the merest** even a very small amount of sth □ *sedikit sahaja pun*: The merest smell of the fish market made her feel ill.

merely /'mɪəli/ adv (*formal*) only; just □ *hanya; cuma; semata-mata*: I don't want to place an order. I am merely making an enquiry.

merge /mɜːdʒ/ verb **1** [I] **merge (with/into sth); merge (together)** to become part of sth larger □ *bergabung; bercantum*: This stream merges with the river a few miles downstream. ◆ Three small companies merged into one large one. ◆ Fact and fiction merge together in his latest book. **2** [T] to join things together so that they become one □ *menggabungkan; menyatukan*: We have merged the two classes into one. **SYN** amalgamate

merger /'mɜːdʒə(r)/ noun [C,U] **a merger (with sb/sth); a merger (between/of A and B)** the act of joining two or more companies together □ *penggabungan; penyatuan*

meridian /məˈrɪdiən/ noun [C] a line that we imagine on the surface of the earth that joins the North Pole to the South Pole and passes through a particular place □ *meridian: the prime meridian* ⊃ look at **longitude**

meringue /məˈræŋ/ noun [C,U] a mixture of sugar and egg white that is cooked in the oven; a cake made from this □ *'meringue'*

merit¹ /'merɪt/ noun **1** [U] the quality of being good □ *kebaikan; kecemerlangan*: There is a lot of merit in her ideas. ◆ He got the job **on merit**, not because he's the manager's son. **2** [C, usually pl] an advantage or a good quality of sb/sth □ *merit; kebaikan; kelebihan*: Each case must be judged separately on its own merits (= not according to general principles).

merit² /'merɪt/ verb [T] (*formal*) to be good enough for sth; to deserve □ *patut; wajar*: This suggestion merits further discussion.

mermaid /'mɜːmeɪd/ noun [C] (in stories) a woman who has the tail of a fish instead of legs and who lives in the sea □ *ikan duyung*

merriment /'merɪmənt/ noun [U] happiness, fun and the sound of people laughing □ *kegembiraan; gelak ketawa* **SYN** mirth

merry /'meri/ adj (**merrier**; **merriest**) **1** happy □ *gembira: merry laughter* ◆ **Merry Christmas** (= used to say you hope sb has a happy holiday) **2** (*especially BrE informal*) slightly drunk □ *agak mabuk* ▶ **merrily** adv: She was singing merrily.

'merry-go-round noun [C] (*BrE also* **roundabout**; *AmE also* **carousel**) a big round platform that turns round and round and has model animals, etc. on it for children to ride on □ *kuda pusing*

mesh /meʃ/ noun [C,U] material made of threads that are twisted together like a net □ *jaringan*: *a fence made of wire mesh*

mesmerize (also -ise) /ˈmezməraɪz/ verb [T] to hold sb's attention completely □ *terpukau*: *The audience seemed to be mesmerized by the speaker's voice.*

mess¹ /mes/ noun **1** [C, usually sing] the state of being dirty or untidy; a person or thing that is dirty or untidy □ *(keadaan) kotor/tdk kemas/ berkecah*: *The kitchen's in a terrible mess!* ♦ *My hair is a mess.* ♦ *You can paint the door, but don't make a mess!* **2** [sing] the state of having problems or trouble □ *(keadaan) bermasalah/ kucar-kacir*: *The company is in a financial mess.* ♦ *to make a mess of your life*

mess² /mes/ verb [T] (AmE informal) to make sth dirty or untidy □ *mengotorkan*: *Don't mess your hands.*

PHR V **mess about/around 1** to behave in a silly and annoying way □ *bermain-main* **2** to spend your time in a relaxed way without any real purpose □ *merepes-repes*: *We spent Sunday just messing around at home.*
mess sb about/around to treat sb in a way that is not fair or reasonable, for example by changing your plans without telling them □ *bersikap tdk patut terhadap sso*
mess about/around with sth to touch or use sth in a careless way □ *mengusik sst; menggunakan sst tanpa hemat; bermain-main*: *It is dangerous to mess about with fireworks.*
mess sth up 1 to make sth dirty or untidy □ *mengotorkan; menyelerakkan* **2** to do sth badly or spoil sth □ *mencelarukan sst*: *I really messed up the last question in the exam.*
mess with sb/sth to deal or behave with sb/sth in a way that you should not □ *memperlakukan sso/sst dgn cara yg tdk patut*: *You shouldn't mess with people's feelings.*

message /ˈmesɪdʒ/ noun **1** [C] a written or spoken piece of information that you send to or leave for a person when you cannot speak to them □ *pesanan*: *Mr Vos is not here at the moment. Can I take a message?* ♦ *Could you give a message to Kate, please?* ♦ *If he's not in I'll leave a message on his answering machine.* **2** [C] a piece of information that is sent in electronic form □ *mesej*: *an email message* ♦ *There were six messages in my inbox.* **3** [sing] an important idea that a book, speech, etc. is trying to communicate □ *mesej*: *It was a funny film but it also had a serious message.* ♦ *The advertising campaign is trying to get the message across that smoking kills.* ♦ *The advertising campaign is trying to get the message across that recycling is important.*
IDM **get the message** (informal) to understand what sb means even if it is not clearly stated □ *faham (apa yg cuba disampaikan)*: *He finally got the message and went home.*

'message board noun [C] a place on a website where a user can write or read messages □ *papan mesej*: *I posted a question on the message board.* ⊃ note at **Internet**

messenger /ˈmesɪndʒə(r)/ noun [C] a person who carries a message □ *utusan; pembawa pesanan, maklumat, dsb*

Messiah (also **messiah**) /məˈsaɪə/ noun [C] a person, for example Jesus Christ, who is expected to come and save the world □ *Al-Masih*

messy /ˈmesi/ adj (**messier**; **messiest**) **1** dirty or untidy □ *kotor; tdk kemas; berserak*: *a messy room* **2** that makes sb/sth dirty □ *(yg) kotor dan leceh*: *Painting the ceiling is a messy job.* **3** having or causing problems or trouble □ *bercelaru; kucar-kacir*: *a messy divorce*

met past tense of **meet**

metabolism /məˈtæbəlɪzəm/ noun [U, sing] the chemical processes in the body that change food, etc. into energy □ *metabolisme*: *The body's metabolism is slowed down by extreme cold.* ▶**metabolic** /ˌmetəˈbɒlɪk/ adj: *a high/low metabolic rate*

metal /ˈmetl/ noun [C,U] a type of solid substance that is usually hard and shiny and that heat and electricity can travel through □ *logam*: *metals such as tin, iron, gold and steel* ♦ *to recycle scrap metal* ♦ *a metal bar/pipe*

metallic /məˈtælɪk/ adj looking like metal or making a noise like one piece of metal hitting another □ *spt logam*: *a metallic blue car* ♦ *harsh metallic sounds*

metamorphosis /ˌmetəˈmɔːfəsɪs/ noun [C] (pl **metamorphoses** /-əsiːz/) (formal) a complete change of form (as part of natural development) □ *metamorfosis; perubahan bentuk*: *the metamorphosis of a tadpole into a frog*

metaphor /ˈmetəfə(r); -fɔː(r)/ noun [C,U] a word or phrase that is used to show that one thing has the same qualities as another; a way of making a comparison □ *metafora*: *'Her words were a knife in his heart' is a metaphor.* ⊃ look at **simile** ▶**metaphorical** /ˌmetəˈfɒrɪkl/ (AmE also)/ adj ▶**metaphorically** /-kli/ adv

mete /miːt/ verb
PHR V **mete sth out (to sb)** (formal) to give sb a punishment; to make sb suffer bad treatment □ *(hukuman) mengenakan; menjatuhkan*: *Severe penalties were meted out by the court.*

meteor /ˈmiːtiə(r); -ɔː(r)/ noun [C] a small piece of rock, etc. in space. When a meteor enters the earth's atmosphere it makes a bright line in the night sky. □ *meteor; tahi bintang*

meteoric /ˌmiːtiˈɒrɪk (AmE also) / adj very fast or successful □ *(naik atau berjaya) dgn begitu cepat*: *a meteoric rise to fame*

meteorite /ˈmiːtiəraɪt/ noun [C] a piece of rock from space that hits the earth's surface □ *meteorit*

meteorologist /ˌmiːtiəˈrɒlədʒɪst/ noun [C] a person who studies the weather □ *ahli meteorologi; ahli kaji cuaca*

meteorology /ˌmiːtiəˈrɒlədʒi/ noun [U] the study of the weather and climate ▫ *meteorologi; kaji cuaca* ▶ meteorological /ˌmiːtiərəˈlɒdʒɪkl/ adj

meter /ˈmiːtə(r)/ noun [C] **1** a piece of equipment that measures the amount of gas, water, electricity, etc. you have used ▫ *meter; jangka*: *a parking meter* **2** (AmE) = **metre** ▶ meter verb [T]: *Is your water metered?*

method /ˈmeθəd/ noun [C] a way of doing sth ▫ *cara; kaedah*: *What method of payment do you prefer? Cash, credit or debit card?* ◆ *modern teaching methods*

methodical /məˈθɒdɪkl/ adj having or using a well organized and careful way of doing sth ▫ *teratur; sistematik*: *Paul is a very methodical worker.* ▶ methodically /-kli/ adv

methodology /ˌmeθəˈdɒlədʒi/ noun [C,U] (*pl* methodologies) (*formal*) a way of doing sth based on particular principles and methods ▫ *metodologi; perkaedahan*: *language teaching methodologies* ▶ methodological /ˌmeθədəˈlɒdʒɪkl/ adj

meticulous /məˈtɪkjələs/ adj giving or showing great attention to detail; very careful ▫ *sangat teliti*: *meticulous checking* ▶ meticulously adv

metre (AmE meter) /ˈmiːtə(r)/ noun [C] (*abbr* m) a measure of length; 100 centimetres ▫ *meter*: *a two-metre high wall* ◆ *Who won the 100 metres?*

metric /ˈmetrɪk/ adj using the system of measurement that is based on metres, grams, litres, etc. ▫ *meter*: *the metric system* ➜ look at **imperial**

metropolis /məˈtrɒpəlɪs/ noun [C] a very large city ▫ *metropolis; kota* ▶ metropolitan /ˌmetrəˈpɒlɪtən/ adj

mg *abbr* = **milligram**

MHz /ˈmegəhɜːts/ *abbr* **megahertz**; (used in radio) a measure of **frequency** (= the rate at which a sound wave moves up and down) ▫ *MHz (megahertz)*

miaow /miˈaʊ/ noun [C] the sound that a cat makes ▫ *ngiau* ▶ miaow verb [I] ➜ look at **purr**

MiB *abbr* = **mebibyte**

Mib (also Mibit) *abbr* = **mebibit**

mice plural of **mouse**

microbe /ˈmaɪkrəʊb/ noun [C] an extremely small living thing that you can only see under a **microscope** (= a piece of equipment that makes small objects look bigger) and that may cause disease ▫ *mikrob*

microblogging /ˈmaɪkrəʊblɒɡɪŋ/ noun [U] the activity of sending regular short messages over the Internet to tell people what you are doing or what interests you ▫ *penghantaran pesanan ringkas secara kerap melalui Internet* ➜ note at **blog**

microchip /ˈmaɪkrəʊtʃɪp/ (also chip) noun [C] a very small piece of **silicon** (= a chemical element) that is used inside a computer, etc. to make it work ▫ *mikrocip*

microcosm /ˈmaɪkrəʊkɒzəm/ noun [C] **a microcosm (of sth)** something that is a small example of sth larger ▫ *mikrokosma; dunia kecil*: *Our little village is a microcosm of society as a whole.*

microphone /ˈmaɪkrəfəʊn/ (also *informal* mike) noun [C] a piece of electrical equipment that is used for making sounds louder or for recording them ▫ *mikrofon*

microprocessor /ˌmaɪkrəʊˈprəʊsesə(r)/ noun [C] a small unit of a computer that controls all the other parts of the system ▫ *mikropemproses*

microscope /ˈmaɪkrəskəʊp/ noun [C] a piece of equipment that makes very small objects look big enough for you to be able to see them ▫ *mikroskop*: *to examine something under a microscope*

microscopic /ˌmaɪkrəˈskɒpɪk/ adj too small to be seen without a **microscope** ▫ *mikroskopik*

microwave /ˈmaɪkrəweɪv/ noun [C] **1** (also microwave 'oven) a type of oven that cooks or heats food very quickly using **microwaves** ▫ *ketuhar gelombang mikro* **2** a short electric wave that is used for sending radio messages and for cooking food ▫ *gelombang mikro* ▶ microwave verb [T] ➜ note at **cook**

mid- /mɪd/ [in compounds] in the middle of ▫ *tengah*: *mid-morning coffee* ◆ *a mid-air collision* ◆ *She's in her mid-thirties.*

midday /ˌmɪdˈdeɪ/ noun [U] at or around 12 o'clock in the middle of the day ▫ *tengah hari*: *We arranged to meet at midday.* ◆ *the heat of the midday sun* **SYN** noon ➜ look at **midnight**

middle¹ /ˈmɪdl/ noun **1** [sing] **the middle (of sth)** the part, point or position that is at about the same distance from the two ends or sides of sth ▫ *tengah; tengah-tengah*: *the white line in the middle of the road* ◆ *Here's a photo of me with my two brothers. I'm the one in the middle.*

> **HELP** **Middle** or **centre**? **Centre** and **middle** are often very similar in meaning, but **centre** is used when you mean the exact middle of something: *How do you find the centre of a circle?* ◆ *There was a large table in the middle of the room.* ◆ *The bee stung me right in the middle of my back.* When you are talking about a period of time only **middle** may be used: *in the middle of the night* ◆ *the middle of July*

2 [C] (*informal*) your waist ▫ *bahagian pinggang*: *I want to lose weight around my middle.*
IDM **be in the middle of sth/doing sth** to be busy doing sth ▫ *tengah sibuk (membuat sst)*: *Can you call back in five minutes—I'm in the middle of feeding the baby.*
in the middle of nowhere a long way from any town ▫ *ceruk mana*

middle² /ˈmɪdl/ adj [only before a noun] in the middle □ *tengah*: I wear my ring on my **middle finger** (= the longest finger). ◆ Pens are in the middle drawer.

ˌmiddle ˈage noun [U] the time when you are about 40 to 60 years old □ *zaman umur pertengahan*: in early/late middle age ▶ **ˌmiddle-ˈaged** adj: a middle-aged man

the ˌMiddle ˈAges noun [pl] the period of European history from about 1100 to 1450 AD □ *Zaman Pertengahan*

ˌmiddle ˈclass noun [sing, with sing or pl verb] (also **the ˌmiddle ˈclasses** [pl]) the group of people in society whose members are neither very rich nor very poor and that includes professional and business people □ *kelas pertengahan*: the upper/lower middle class ◆ the growth of the middle classes ⇒ look at **upper class, working class** ▶ **ˌmiddle-ˈclass** adj: a middle-class background ◆ a middle-class attitude (= traditional views, typical of the middle class)

the ˌMiddle ˈEast noun [sing] an area that covers SW Asia and NE Africa □ *Timur Tengah* ▶ **ˌMiddle ˈEastern** adj

middleman /ˈmɪdlmæn/ noun [C] (pl **-men** /-men/) **1** a person or company who buys goods from the company that makes them and then sells them to sb else □ *orang tengah* **2** a person who helps to arrange things between two people who do not want to talk directly to each other □ *perantara*

ˈmiddle school noun [C] (in Britain) a school for children aged between 9 and 13 □ *sekolah rendah atas*

midge /mɪdʒ/ noun [C] a very small flying insect that can bite people □ *sera* **SYN** **gnat**

midget /ˈmɪdʒɪt/ noun [C] a very small person □ *orang kerdil*

> **HELP** Be careful. This word is considered offensive.

the Midlands /ˈmɪdləndz/ noun [sing, with sing or pl verb] the central part of England around Birmingham and Nottingham □ *kawasan Midlands*

midnight /ˈmɪdnaɪt/ noun [U] 12 o'clock at night □ *tengah malam*: They left the party **at midnight**. ◆ The clock struck midnight. ⇒ look at **midday**

midriff /ˈmɪdrɪf/ noun [C] the part of your body between your chest and your waist □ *bahagian tengah badan (di antara dada dgn pinggang)*

midst /mɪdst/ noun [U] the middle of sth; among a group of people or things □ *sedang; tengah; (di) tengah-tengah*: The country is **in the midst of** a recession. ◆ They realized with a shock that there was an enemy **in their midst**.

midway /ˌmɪdˈweɪ/ adj, adv in the middle of a period of time or between two places □ *pertengahan; pertengahan jalan*: The village lies midway between two large towns. **SYN** **halfway**

midweek /ˌmɪdˈwiːk/ noun [U] the middle of the week (= Tuesday, Wednesday and Thursday) □ *pertengahan minggu* ▶ **midweek** adv: If you travel midweek it will be less crowded.

the Midwest /ˌmɪdˈwest/ noun [sing] the northern central part of the US □ *bahagian tengah utara AS*

midwife /ˈmɪdwaɪf/ noun [C] (pl **midwives** /-waɪvz/) a person who is trained to help women give birth to babies □ *bidan*

might¹ /maɪt/ modal verb (negative **might not**; short form **mightn't** /ˈmaɪtnt/) **1** used as the form of 'may' when you report what sb has said □ *mungkin*: He said he might be late (= his words were, 'I may be late'). **2** used for saying that sth is possible □ *mungkin*: 'Where's Vinay?' 'He might be upstairs.' ◆ I think I might have forgotten the tickets. ◆ She might not come if she's very busy. **3** (BrE formal) used to ask for sth or suggest sth very politely □ *boleh*: I wonder if I might go home half an hour early today? ⓘ For more information about modal verbs, look at the **Reference Section** at the back of this dictionary.

IDM **I might have known** used for saying that you are not surprised that sth has happened □ *memang sudah dijangka*: I might have known he wouldn't help.
may/might as well (do sth) ⇒ **well¹**
you, etc. might do sth used when you are angry to say what sb could or should have done □ *anda, dsb sepatutnya (membuat sst)*: They might at least have phoned if they're not coming.

might² /maɪt/ noun [U] (formal) great strength or power □ *kekuatan*: I pushed **with all my might**, but the rock did not move.

mighty¹ /ˈmaɪti/ adj (**mightier**; **mightiest**) very strong or powerful □ *sangat kuat; amat berkuasa*

mighty² /ˈmaɪti/ adv (AmE informal) very □ *sangat; amat*: That's mighty kind of you.

migraine /ˈmiːgreɪn/ noun [C,U] a terrible pain in your head that makes you feel sick □ *migrain*

migrant /ˈmaɪgrənt/ noun [C] a person who goes from one place to another, especially in order to find work □ *penghijrah; orang yg berpindah-randah*

migrate /maɪˈgreɪt/ verb [I] **1** (used about animals and birds) to travel from one part of the world to another at the same time every year □ *berpindah* **2** (used about a large number of people) to go and live and work in another place □ *berpindah; berhijrah*: Country people were forced to migrate to the cities to find work. ⇒ look at **emigrate** ▶ **migration** /maɪˈgreɪʃn/ noun [C,U] ▶ **migratory** /ˈmaɪgrətri; maɪˈgreɪtəri/ adj: migratory flights/birds

mike /maɪk/ noun [C] (informal) = **microphone**

milage = mileage

mild /maɪld/ adj (**milder**; **mildest**) **1** not strong; not very bad □ *lembut; sederhana; ringan; tdk (keras, teruk, dll)*: a mild soap ◆ a mild winter ◆ a mild punishment **2** kind and gentle □ *lembut dan baik hati*: He's a very mild man—you never see him get angry. **3** (used about food) not having a strong taste □ *tdk kuat rasanya; tdk begitu pedas, masin, dsb*: mild cheese ▶ **mildness** noun [U]

mildly /ˈmaɪldli/ adv **1** not very; slightly □ *agak; sedikit*: mildly surprised **2** in a gentle way □ *dgn lembut*: He spoke mildly to the child.

mile /maɪl/ noun **1** [C] a measure of length; 1.6 kilometres. There are 1 760 yards in a **mile** □ *batu*: The nearest beach is seven miles away. ◆ It's a seven-mile drive to the beach. ❶ For more information about measurements, look at the section on using numbers at the back of this dictionary. **2 miles** [pl] a long way □ *jauh*: How much further is it? We've walked miles already. ◆ From the top of the hill you can see for miles. **3** [C] a lot □ *jauh*: He missed the target by a mile. ◆ I'm feeling miles better this morning.
IDM see, hear, tell, spot, etc. sb/sth a mile off (*informal*) used to say that sb/sth is very obvious □ *nampak ketara*: He's lying—you can tell that a mile off.

mileage (also **milage**) /ˈmaɪlɪdʒ/ noun **1** [C,U] the distance that has been travelled, measured in miles □ *perbatuan*: The car is five years old but it has a low mileage. **2** [U] (*informal*) the amount of use that you get from sth □ *faedah*: The newspapers got a lot of mileage out of the scandal.

mileometer = milometer

milestone /ˈmaɪlstəʊn/ noun [C] a very important event □ *peristiwa penting*: The concert was a milestone in the band's history.

militant /ˈmɪlɪtənt/ adj ready to use force or strong pressure to get what you want □ *militan; bersedia menggunakan kekerasan atau tekanan*: The workers were in a very militant mood. ▶ **militant** noun [C] ▶ **militancy** /-ənsi/ noun [U]

military /ˈmɪlətri/ adj [only before a noun] connected with soldiers or the army, navy, etc □ *(berkenaan dgn) tentera*: All men in that country have to do two years' military service. ◆ to take military action

militia /məˈlɪʃə/ noun [C, with sing or pl verb] a group of people who are not professional soldiers but who have had military training □ *militia; tentera awam*

milk¹ /mɪlk/ noun [U] **1** a white liquid that is produced by some animals as food for their young. People drink milk and use it to make butter and cheese □ *susu*: skimmed/long-life/low-fat milk ◆ a carton of milk **2** a white liquid that is produced by women and female animals to feed their babies □ *susu* **3** the juice of some plants or trees that looks like milk □ *jus; susu; santan*: coconut milk ➲ picture on **page P14**

milk² /mɪlk/ verb [T] **1** to take milk from an animal such as a cow □ *memerah susu* **2** to get as much money, advantage, etc. for yourself from sb/sth as you can, without caring about others □ *memerah; memeras*: He milked the company of a small fortune.

milkman /ˈmɪlkmən/ noun [C] (pl **-men** /-mən/) a person who takes milk to people's houses every day □ *penjual susu*

milkshake /ˈmɪlkʃeɪk/ noun [C,U] a drink made of milk with an added flavour of fruit or chocolate □ *susu kocak* ➲ picture on **page P16**

milky /ˈmɪlki/ adj like milk, or made with milk □ *spt susu; bersusu*: milky white skin ◆ milky coffee

the Milky ˈWay = the Galaxy (2)

mill¹ /mɪl/ noun [C] **1** a building that contains a large machine that was used in the past for making grain into flour □ *kilang; kincir (angin)* ➲ look at **windmill 2** a factory that is used for making certain kinds of material □ *kilang*: a cotton/paper/steel mill **3** a kitchen tool that is used for making sth into powder □ *pengisar*: a pepper mill

mill² /mɪl/ verb [T] to produce sth in a **mill** □ *mengilang*
PHR V mill about/around (*informal*) (used about a large number of people or animals) to move around in a place with no real purpose □ *berlegar-legar*

millennium /mɪˈleniəm/ noun [C] (pl **millennia** /-niə/ or **millenniums**) a period of 1 000 years □ *alaf; milenium*: How did you celebrate the millennium?

millet /ˈmɪlɪt/ noun [U] a plant with a lot of small seeds that are used as food for people and birds □ *sekoi*

milli- /ˈmɪli/ [in compounds] (used in units of measurement) one thousandth □ *mili-*: a millisecond

milligram (also **milligramme**) /ˈmɪlɪɡræm/ noun [C] (abbr **mg**) a measure of weight. There are 1 000 **milligrams** in a gram. □ *milligram*

millilitre (*AmE* **milliliter**) /ˈmɪlɪliːtə(r)/ noun [C] (abbr **ml**) a measure of liquid. There are 1 000 **millilitres** in a litre. □ *mililiter*

millimetre (*AmE* **millimeter**) /ˈmɪlɪmiːtə(r)/ noun [C] (abbr **mm**) a measure of length. There are 1 000 **millimetres** in a metre. □ *milimeter*

millinery /ˈmɪlɪnəri/ noun [U] the business of making or selling women's hats □ *perniagaan membuat topi wanita*

million /ˈmɪljən/ number (abbr **m**) **1** 1 000 000 □ *juta*: Nearly 60 million people live in Britain. ◆ Millions of people are at risk from the disease.

HELP Notice that you use **million** without 's' when talking about more than one million: *six million people*

2 a million; millions (of) (*informal*) a very large amount □ *berjuta-juta; sangat banyak*: *I still have a million things to do.* ♦ *There are millions of reasons why you shouldn't go.* ⓘ For more information about numbers, look at the section on using numbers at the back of this dictionary.

millionaire /ˌmɪljəˈneə(r)/ *noun* [C] a person who has a million pounds, dollars, etc.; a very rich person □ *jutawan*

millionth¹ /ˈmɪljənθ/ *ordinal number* 1 000 000th □ *kesejuta*

millionth² /ˈmɪljənθ/ *noun* [C] one of a million equal parts of sth □ *satu per sejuta*: *a millionth of a second*

milometer (also **mileometer**) /maɪˈlɒmɪtə(r)/ (*AmE* **odometer**, *informal* **clock**) *noun* [C] an instrument in a vehicle that measures the distance it has travelled □ *meter batu*

mime /maɪm/ (also **pantomime**) *noun* [U,C] the use of movements of your hands and body and the expression on your face to tell a story or to act sth without speaking; a performance using this method of acting □ *lakonan bisu*: *The performance consisted of dance, music and mime.* ▶ **mime** *verb* [I,T]

mimic¹ /ˈmɪmɪk/ *verb* [T] (**mimicking; mimicked**) to copy sb's behaviour, movements, voice, etc. in an amusing way □ *meniru; mengajuk; memimik*: *She's always mimicking the teachers.*

mimic² /ˈmɪmɪk/ *noun* [C] a person who can copy sb's behaviour, movements, voice, etc. in an amusing way □ *ahli mimik*: *He is a gifted mimic.* ▶ **mimicry** /ˈmɪmɪkri/ *noun* [U]

min. *abbr* **1** = **minute¹**(1) □ *minit*: *fastest time: 6 min.* **2** = **minimum²** □ *minimum*: *min. temp tomorrow 2°* OPP **max**

minaret /ˌmɪnəˈret/ *noun* [C] a tall thin tower, usually part of a **mosque** (= a religious building), from which Muslims are called to come and say prayers □ *menara*

mince /mɪns/ (*AmE* **ground 'beef**; **hamburger**) *noun* [U] meat that has been cut into very small pieces with a special machine □ *daging kisar* ▶ **mince** *verb* [T]

ˌmince ˈpie *noun* [C] a small round **pastry** (= a mixture of flour, fat and water) filled with **mincemeat** (= a mixture of dried fruit, sugar, etc.), traditionally eaten in Britain at Christmas time □ *pai buah-buahan kering*

mind¹ /maɪnd/ *noun* [C,U] the part of your brain that thinks and remembers; your thoughts, feelings and intelligence □ *minda; fikiran*: *There were all sorts of thoughts running through my mind.* ♦ *My mind wandered as the teacher went on talking.* ♦ *He has a brilliant mind.* ♦ *Not everybody has the right sort of mind for this work.* ♦ *the conscious/unconscious mind*
IDM **at/in the back of your mind** ➜ **back¹**

be in two minds (about sth/ doing sth) ➜ **two**
be/go out of your mind (*informal*) to be or become crazy or very worried □ *menjadi gila atau amat risau*: *I was going out of my mind when Tina didn't come home on time.*
bear in mind (that); bear/keep sb/sth in mind to remember or consider (that); to remember sb/sth □ *ingat; ingat akan sso/sst*: *We'll bear/keep your suggestion in mind for the future.*
bring/call sb/sth to mind to be reminded of sb/sth; to remember sb/sth □ *terkenang atau teringat akan sso/sst*
cast your mind back ➜ **cast¹**
change your mind ➜ **change¹**
come/spring to mind if sth comes/springs to mind, you suddenly remember or think of it □ *timbul dlm fikiran*
cross your mind ➜ **cross²**
ease sb's mind ➜ **ease²**
frame of mind ➜ **frame¹**
give sb a piece of your mind ➜ **piece¹**
go clean out of your mind ➜ **clean³**
have sb/sth in mind (for sth) to be considering sb/sth as suitable for sth; to have a plan □ *menganggap sso/sst sesuai (utk sst); ingat hendak (membuat sst, dsb)*: *Who do you have in mind for the job?*
have/keep an open mind ➜ **open¹**
keep your mind on sth to continue to pay attention to sth □ *menumpukan perhatian pd sst*: *Keep your mind on the road while you're driving!*
make up your mind to decide □ *membuat keputusan*: *I can't make up my mind which sweater to buy.*
on your mind worrying you □ *risau (memikirkan sst)*: *Don't bother her with that. She's got enough on her mind already.*
prey on sb's mind ➜ **prey²**
put/set your/sb's mind at rest to make sb stop worrying □ *melegakan fikiran sso*: *The results of the blood test set his mind at rest.*
slip your mind ➜ **slip¹**
speak your mind ➜ **speak**
state of mind ➜ **state¹**
take sb's mind off sth to help sb not to think or worry about sth □ *menolong sso melupakan atau tdk risau ttg sst*
to my mind in my opinion □ *pd pendapat saya*: *To my mind, this is a complete waste of time!*

mind² /maɪnd/ *verb* **1** [I,T] [usually in questions, answers, and negative sentences] to feel annoyed, upset or uncomfortable about sth/sb □ *tdk selesa ttg sst/sso*: *I'm sure Simon won't mind if you don't invite him.* ♦ *I don't mind what you do—it's your decision.* ♦ *Do you mind having to travel so far to work every day?* ♦ *Are you sure your parents won't mind me coming?* ♦ *'Would you like tea or coffee?' 'I don't mind.'* (= I'm happy to have either) ♦ *I wouldn't mind a break right now* (= I would like one). ➜ note at **matter²** **2** [T] (used in a question as a polite way of asking sb to do sth or for permission to do sth) could you …?; may I …? □ *bolehkah*: *Would you mind closing the window for me?* ♦ *Do you mind driving? I'm feeling rather tired.* **3** [T] used to tell sb to be careful of sth or to pay attention to sb/sth □ *jaga-jaga*;

kisah; pedulikan: *It's a very low doorway so mind your head.* ◆ *Mind that step!* ◆ *Don't mind me! I won't disturb you.* **4** [T] (*especially BrE*) to look after or watch sb/sth for a short time □ *menjaga; jagakan*: *Could you mind my bag while I go and get us some drinks?*

IDM **mind you** used for attracting attention to a point you are making or for giving more information □ *lagipun; memang pun; tetapi*: *Paul seems very tired. Mind you, he has been working very hard recently.*

mind your own business to pay attention to your own affairs, not other people's □ *jagalah urusan sendiri; jangan masuk campur hal orang*: *Stop asking me personal questions and mind your own business!*

never mind do not worry; it does not matter □ *tak mengapa; tak apalah*: *'I forgot to post your letter.' 'Never mind, I'll do it later.'*

PHR V **mind out** (*informal*) Get out of the way! □ *lalu; beralih*: *Mind out! There's a car coming.*

'mind-boggling *adj* (*informal*) difficult to imagine, understand or believe □ *sukar hendak dibayangkan, difahami atau dipercayai*: *Mind-boggling amounts of money were being discussed.*

minded /'maɪndɪd/ *adj* [in compounds] **1** having the type of mind mentioned □ *berfikiran*: *a strong-minded/open-minded/narrow-minded person* **2** interested in the thing mentioned □ *berminat dlm bidang; mementingkan*: *money-minded*

minder /'maɪndə(r)/ *noun* [C] a person whose job is to look after and protect sb/sth □ *penjaga*: *a star surrounded by her minders*

mindful /'maɪndfl/ *adj* (*formal*) **mindful of sb/sth**; **mindful that …** remembering sb/sth and considering them or it when you do sth □ *sedar; yg mengambil berat ttg sst; prihatin terhadap sst*: *Mindful of the danger of tropical storms, I decided not to go out.*

mindless /'maɪndləs/ *adj* **1** done or acting without thought and for no particular reason □ *tanpa berfikir panjang; tdk berhati perut*: *mindless violence* **2** not needing thought or intelligence □ *tdk perlu memerah otak*: *a mindless and repetitive task*

'mind map (also **spidergram**) *noun* [C] a diagram that you make in order to plan a project, an essay, etc. You write down as many words and ideas as you can think of that are linked to the main topic. □ *peta minda*

WRITING TIP

Preparing to write

Making a mind map is a good way to **brainstorm** (= think of as many ideas as you can in a short time) your ideas before you start to write. You can then use this diagram as the basis of a plan for your writing.

❶ For more help with writing, look at **Wordpower Writing Tutor** at the back of this dictionary.

---

551 **mind-boggling → minibeast**

mine¹ /maɪn/ *pron* of or belonging to me □ *milik saya*: *'Whose is this jacket?' 'It's mine.'* ◆ *She wanted one like mine.* ◆ *May I introduce a friend of mine* (= one of my friends)*?* ⇨ look at **my**

mine² /maɪn/ *noun* [C] **1** a deep hole, or a system of passages under the ground where minerals such as coal, tin, gold, etc. are dug □ *lombong*: *a coal/salt/gold mine* ⇨ look at **quarry** **2** a bomb that is hidden under the ground or underwater and explodes when sb/sth touches it □ *periuk api*: *The car went over a mine and blew up.*

mine³ /maɪn/ *verb* **1** [I,T] to dig in the ground for minerals such as coal, tin, gold, etc. □ *melombong*: *Diamonds are mined in South Africa.* ⇨ look at **mining** **2** [T] to put **mines²**(2) in an area of land or sea □ *memasang periuk api*

minefield /'maɪnfiːld/ *noun* [C] **1** an area of land or sea where **mines²**(2) have been hidden □ *kawasan periuk api* **2** a situation that is full of hidden dangers or difficulties □ *kancah*: *a political minefield*

miner /'maɪnə(r)/ *noun* [C] a person whose job is to work in a **mine²**(1) to get coal, salt, tin, etc. □ *pelombong*

mineral /'mɪnərəl/ *noun* [C] a natural substance such as coal, salt, oil, etc., especially one that is found in the ground. Some minerals are also present in food and drink and are very important for good health □ *mineral; (bahan) galian*: *a country rich in minerals* ◆ *the recommended daily intake of vitamins and minerals*

'mineral water *noun* [U] water from a spring in the ground that contains minerals or gases and is thought to be good for your health □ *air mineral*

mingle /'mɪŋgl/ *verb* [I,T] **mingle A and B (together)**; **mingle (A) (with B)** to mix with other things or people □ *mencampurkan; bercampur; bergaul*: *The colours slowly mingled together to make a muddy brown.* ◆ *His excitement was mingled with fear.* ◆ *to mingle with the rich and famous*

mini- /'mɪni/ [in compounds] very small □ *mini*: *a miniskirt* ◆ *minigolf*

miniature /'mɪnətʃə(r)/ *noun* [C] a small copy of sth which is much larger □ *miniatur; kecil*: *a miniature camera*

IDM **in miniature** exactly the same as sb/sth else but in a very small form □ *tak ubah spt; dlm bentuk kecil*

minibeast /'mɪnibiːst/ *noun* [C] (*BrE*) (used especially in schools) any small animal that does not have a **backbone** (= the row of bones in the middle of your back) □ *haiwan kecil yg tdk ada tulang belakang*: *minibeasts such as worms, snails, centipedes, ants and spiders*

[C] **countable**, a noun with a plural form: *one book, two books* [U] **uncountable**, a noun with no plural form: *some sugar*

minibus /ˈmɪnɪbʌs/ noun [C] (especially BrE) a small bus with seats for about twelve people □ *bas mini*

minimal /ˈmɪnɪməl/ adj very small in amount, size or level; as little as possible □ *minimum; paling sedikit*: *The project must be carried out at minimal cost.*

minimize (also **-ise**) /ˈmɪnɪmaɪz/ verb [T] **1** to make sth as small as possible (in amount or level) □ *mengurangkan*: *We shall try to minimize the risks to the public.* **2** to try to make sth seem less important than it really is □ *memperkecil* **3** to make sth small on a computer screen □ *mengecilkan* **OPP** maximize

minimum¹ /ˈmɪnɪməm/ adj [only before a noun] the smallest possible or allowed; extremely small □ *minimum*: *to introduce a national minimum wage* (= the lowest amount of money that an employer is legally allowed to pay workers) **OPP** maximum ►**minimum** adv: *We'll need £200 minimum for expenses.*

minimum² /ˈmɪnɪməm/ noun [sing] (abbr **min.**) the smallest amount or level that is possible or allowed □ *minimum; sekurang-kurangnya*: *I need a minimum of seven hours' sleep.* ◆ *We will try and keep the cost of the tickets to a minimum.* **OPP** maximum

mining /ˈmaɪnɪŋ/ noun [U] [in compounds] the process or industry of getting minerals, metals, etc. out of the ground by digging □ *perlombongan*: *coal/tin/gold mining*

minister /ˈmɪnɪstə(r)/ noun [C] **1** (BrE) **Minister** a member of the government, often the head of a government department □ *menteri*: *the Minister for Transport* ➔ look at **cabinet**, **prime minister**, **secretary 2** a priest in some Protestant churches □ *paderi* ➔ look at **vicar**

ministerial /ˌmɪnɪˈstɪəriəl/ adj connected with a government minister or department □ *(berkenaan dgn) menteri*

ministry /ˈmɪnɪstri/ noun [C] (pl **ministries**) (BrE) (also **department**) a government department that has a particular area of responsibility □ *kementerian*: *the Ministry of Defence*

HELP **Department** is the only word used in American English.

mink /mɪŋk/ noun [C] a small wild animal that is kept for its thick brown fur which is used to make expensive coats □ *mink*

minor¹ /ˈmaɪnə(r)/ adj **1** not very big, serious or important (when compared with others) □ *kecil; kurang (penting, serius, dll)*: *It's only a minor problem. Don't worry.* ◆ *She's gone into hospital for a minor operation.* **OPP** major **2** of one of the two types of **key¹**(4) in which music is usually written □ *minor*: *a symphony in F minor* ➔ look at **major**

minor² /ˈmaɪnə(r)/ noun [C] (used in law) a person who is not legally an adult □ *orang yg di bawah umur*

MORE In Britain you are a minor until you are eighteen, which is when you **come of age**.

minority /maɪˈnɒrəti (AmE also) / noun [C] (pl **minorities**) **1** [usually sing, with sing or pl verb] the smaller number or part of a group; less than half □ *sebilangan kecil; minoriti*: *Only a minority of students become/becomes involved in politics.* **OPP** majority **2** a small group of people who are of a different race or religion to most of the people in the community or country where they live □ *kelompok minoriti*: *Schools in Britain need to do more to help children of ethnic minorities.*
IDM **be in a/the minority** to be the smaller of two groups □ *kumpulan minoriti; bilangan yg kecil*: *Men are in the minority in the teaching profession.* ➔ look at **in a/the majority**

mint /mɪnt/ noun **1** [U] a **herb** (= a type of plant) whose leaves are used to give flavour to food, drinks, etc. □ *pudina*: *lamb with mint sauce* ➔ picture on **page P14 2** [C] a type of sweet with a strong fresh flavour □ *gula-gula berperasa pudina* **3** [sing] the place where money in the form of coins and notes is made by the government □ *kilang wang* ►**mint** verb [T]: *freshly minted coins*

minus¹ /ˈmaɪnəs/ prep **1** (used in sums) less; take away □ *tolak*: *Six minus two is four (6 −2 = 4).* **OPP** plus ➔ look at **subtract 2** (used about a number) below zero □ *minus*: *The temperature will fall to minus 10.* **3** (informal) without sth that was there before □ *kurang; tanpa*: *We're going to be minus a car for a while.*

minus² /ˈmaɪnəs/ noun [C] **1** (also ˈminus sign) the symbol (−) used in mathematics □ *anda tolak/minus* **2** (also ˈminus point) (informal) a negative quality; a disadvantage □ *kekurangan*: *Let's consider the pluses and minuses of moving out of the city.* **OPP** for both meanings **plus**

minus³ /ˈmaɪnəs/ adj **1** (used in mathematics) lower than zero □ *minus*: *a minus figure* **2** [not before a noun] (used in a system of grades given for school work) slightly lower than □ *minus*: *I got A minus (A−) for my essay.* **OPP** for both meanings **plus**

minuscule /ˈmɪnəskjuːl/ adj extremely small □ *sangat kecil*

ˈminus point = minus²(2)

ˈminus sign = minus²(1)

minute¹ /ˈmɪnɪt/ noun **1** [C] (abbr **min.**) one of the 60 parts that make up one hour; 60 seconds □ *minit*: *It's twelve minutes to nine.* ◆ *He telephoned ten minutes ago.* ◆ *The programme lasts for about fifty minutes.* **2** [sing] (spoken) a very short time; a moment □ *sebentar*: *Just/Wait a minute* (= wait)! *You've forgotten your notes.* ◆ *Have you got a minute?*—*I'd like to talk to you.* **3** **the minutes** [pl] a written record of what is said and decided at a meeting □ *minit (mesyuarat)*: *to take the minutes* (= to write them down)
IDM **(at) any minute/moment (now)** (informal)

very soon □ *pd bila-bila masa sahaja*: *The plane should be landing any minute now.*
in a minute very soon □ *sebentar lagi*: *I'll be with you in a minute.*
the last minute/moment ➪ **last¹**(1)
the minute/moment (that) as soon as □ *sebaik sahaja*: *I'll tell him you rang the minute (that) he gets here.*
this minute immediately; now □ *sekarang juga; baru sahaja*: *I don't know what I'm going to do yet—I've just this minute found out.*
up to the minute (*informal*) having the most recent information □ *terbaharu; terkini*: *For up to the minute information on flight times, phone this number …*

minute² /maɪˈnjuːt/ *adj* (**minutest**) [no comparative] **1** very small □ *sangat kecil*: *I couldn't read his writing. It was minute!* **SYN tiny 2** very exact or accurate □ *tepat; terperinci*: *She was able to describe the man in minute/the minutest detail.*

miracle /ˈmɪrəkl/ *noun* **1** [C] a wonderful event that seems impossible and that is believed to be caused by God or a god □ *mukjizat; keajaiban* **2** [sing] a lucky thing that happens that you did not expect or think was possible □ *kejadian yg ghaib; mujur*: *It's a miracle (that) nobody was killed in the crash.*
IDM work/perform miracles to achieve very good results □ *menghasilkan kejayaan*: *The new diet and exercise programme has worked miracles for her.*

miraculous /mɪˈrækjələs/ *adj* completely unexpected and very lucky □ *sungguh menakjubkan*: *She's made a miraculous recovery.* ▶ **miraculously** *adv*

mirage /ˈmɪrɑːʒ, mɪˈrɑːʒ/ *noun* [C] something that you think you see in very hot weather, for example water in a desert, but which does not really exist □ *logamaya*

mirror /ˈmɪrə(r)/ *noun* [C] a piece of special flat glass that you can look into in order to see yourself or what is behind you □ *cermin*: *to look in the mirror* ♦ *a rear-view mirror* (= in a car, so that the driver can see what is behind) ➪ picture at **car** ➪ picture on **page P8**

MORE A mirror **reflects** images. What you see in a mirror is a **reflection**.

▶ **mirror** *verb* [T]: *The trees were mirrored in the lake.*

mirth /mɜːθ/ *noun* [U] (*written*) happiness, fun and the sound of people laughing □ *gelak ketawa*: *There was much mirth in the audience.* **SYN merriment**

misapprehension /ˌmɪsæprɪˈhenʃn/ *noun* [U,C] (*formal*) to have the wrong idea about sth or to believe sth is true when it is not □ *salah faham*: *I was under the misapprehension that this course was for beginners.*

misbehave /ˌmɪsbɪˈheɪv/ *verb* [I] to behave badly □ *berkelakuan tdk baik* **OPP behave** ▶ **misbehaviour** (*AmE* **misbehavior**) /ˌmɪsbɪˈheɪvjə(r)/ *noun* [U]

553 **minute → miserable**

miscalculate /ˌmɪsˈkælkjuleɪt/ *verb* [I,T] to make a mistake in calculating or judging a situation, an amount, etc. □ *salah kira/anggar/agak*: *The driver totally miscalculated the speed at which the other car was travelling.* ▶ **miscalculation** /ˌmɪskælkjuˈleɪʃn/ *noun* [C,U]

miscarriage /ˈmɪskærɪdʒ/ *noun* [C,U] giving birth to a baby a long time before it is ready to be born, with the result that it cannot live □ *keguguran* ➪ look at **abortion**
IDM a miscarriage of justice an occasion when sb is punished for a crime that they did not do □ *salah laksana keadilan*

miscarry /ˌmɪsˈkæri/ *verb* [I] (**miscarrying**; **miscarries**; *pt*, *pp* **miscarried**) to give birth to a baby before it is ready to be born, with the result that it cannot live □ *mengalami keguguran; gugur*

miscellaneous /ˌmɪsəˈleɪniəs/ *adj* consisting of many different types or things □ *pelbagai*: *a box of miscellaneous items for sale*

mischief /ˈmɪstʃɪf/ *noun* [U] bad behaviour (usually of children) that is not very serious □ *kenakalan; nakal*: *The children are always getting into mischief.*

mischievous /ˈmɪstʃɪvəs/ *adj* (usually used about children) liking to behave badly and embarrassing or annoying people □ *nakal* ▶ **mischievously** *adv*

misconception /ˌmɪskənˈsepʃn/ *noun* [C] a wrong idea or understanding of sth □ *tanggapan salah*: *It is a popular misconception* (= many people wrongly believe) *that people need meat to be healthy.*

misconduct /ˌmɪsˈkɒndʌkt/ *noun* [U] (*formal*) unacceptable behaviour, especially by a professional person □ *salah laku*: *The doctor was dismissed for gross* (= very serious) *misconduct.*

misconstrue /ˌmɪskənˈstruː/ *verb* [T] (*formal*) **misconstrue sth (as sth)** to understand sb's words or actions wrongly □ *menyalahtafsirkan* ➪ look at **construe**

misdemeanour (*AmE* **misdemeanor**) /ˌmɪsdɪˈmiːnə(r)/ *noun* [C] something slightly bad or wrong that a person does; a crime that is not very serious □ *kesalahan kecil* ➪ look at **felony**

miser /ˈmaɪzə(r)/ *noun* [C] a person who loves having a lot of money but hates spending it □ *si bakhil; pelokek* ▶ **miserly** *adj*

miserable /ˈmɪzrəbl/ *adj* **1** very unhappy □ *sedih; muram*: *Oh dear, you look miserable. What's wrong?* **2** unpleasant; making you feel unhappy □ *tdk menyenangkan; teruk*: *What miserable weather!* (= grey, cold and wet) **SYN dismal 3** too small or of bad quality □ *sangat sedikit*: *I was offered a miserable salary so I didn't take the job.* ▶ **miserably** /-əbli/ *adv*: *I stared miserably out of the window.* ♦ *He failed miserably as an actor.*

misery → miss 554

misery /ˈmɪzəri/ noun [U,C] (pl miseries) great unhappiness or suffering □ *kesengsaraan; (perihal) menderita*: I couldn't bear to see him in such misery. ♦ the miseries of war

IDM **put sb out of their misery** (informal) to stop sb worrying about sth by telling the person what they want to know □ *melegakan hati sso (dgn memberitahu apa yg ingin diketahuinya)*: Put me out of my misery—did I pass or not?

put sth out of its misery to kill an animal because it has an illness or injury that cannot be treated □ *membunuh binatang (kerana kasihan)*

misfire /ˌmɪsˈfaɪə(r)/ verb [I] to fail to have the intended result or effect □ *gagal; tdk jadi*: The plan misfired.

misfit /ˈmɪsfɪt/ noun [C] a person who is not accepted by other people, especially because their behaviour or ideas are very different □ *orang yg canggung atau tdk dpt menyesuaikan diri*

misfortune /ˌmɪsˈfɔːtʃuːn/ noun [C,U] (formal) (an event, accident, etc. that brings) bad luck or disaster □ *nasib malang; musibah*: I hope I don't ever have the misfortune to meet him again.

misgiving /ˌmɪsˈɡɪvɪŋ/ noun [C,U] a feeling of doubt or worry □ *keraguan; perasaan ragu-ragu*: I had serious misgivings about leaving him on his own.

misguided /ˌmɪsˈɡaɪdɪd/ adj wrong because you have understood or judged a situation badly □ *salah (kerana kurang faham atau tdk pandai menilai sst keadaan)*: She only moved the victim in a misguided effort to help.

mishap /ˈmɪshæp/ noun [C,U] a small accident or piece of bad luck that does not have serious results □ *kemalangan kecil*: to have a slight mishap

misinform /ˌmɪsɪnˈfɔːm/ verb [T] (formal) to give sb the wrong information □ *memberikan maklumat yg salah*: I think you've been misinformed—no one is going to lose their job in the near future.

misinterpret /ˌmɪsɪnˈtɜːprɪt/ verb [T] misinterpret sth (as sth) to understand sth wrongly □ *menyalahtafsirkan; salah tafsir*: His comments were misinterpreted as a criticism of the project. **OPP** interpret ▶misinterpretation /ˌmɪsɪntɜːprɪˈteɪʃn/ noun [C,U]: Parts of the speech were open to misinterpretation (= easy to understand wrongly).

misjudge /ˌmɪsˈdʒʌdʒ/ verb [T] **1** to form a wrong opinion of sb/sth, usually in a way which is unfair to them or it □ *salah anggap* **2** to guess time, distance, etc. wrongly □ *salah agak*: He misjudged the speed of the other car and almost crashed. ▶misjudgement (also misjudgment) noun [C,U]

mislay /ˌmɪsˈleɪ/ verb [T] (mislaying; mislays; pt, pp mislaid /-ˈleɪd/) to lose sth, usually for a short time, because you cannot remember where you put it □ *lupa di mana sst telah diletakkan*

mislead /ˌmɪsˈliːd/ verb [T] (pt, pp misled /-ˈled/) to make sb have the wrong idea or opinion about sb/sth □ *memperdaya; mengelirukan* ▶misleading adj: a misleading advertisement

mismanage /ˌmɪsˈmænɪdʒ/ verb [T] to manage or organize sth badly □ *salah mengurus* ▶mismanagement noun [U]

misplaced /ˌmɪsˈpleɪst/ adj given to sb/sth that is not suitable or good enough to have it □ *tdk kena pd tempatnya*: misplaced loyalty

misprint /ˈmɪsprɪnt/ noun [C] a mistake in printing or typing □ *salah cetak/taip*

mispronounce /ˌmɪsprəˈnaʊns/ verb [T] to say a word or letter wrongly □ *salah menyebut*: People always mispronounce my surname. ▶mispronunciation /ˌmɪsprəˌnʌnsiˈeɪʃn/ noun [C,U]

misread /ˌmɪsˈriːd/ verb [T] (pt, pp misread /-ˈred/) misread sth (as sth) to read or understand sth wrongly □ *salah membaca; silap mentafsir*: He misread my silence as a refusal.

misrepresent /ˌmɪsˌreprɪˈzent/ verb [T, usually passive] to give a wrong description of sb/sth □ *memberi gambaran yg salah*: In the newspaper article they were misrepresented as uncaring parents. ▶misrepresentation /ˌmɪsˌreprɪzenˈteɪʃn/ noun [C,U]

Miss /mɪs/ used as a title before the family name of a young woman or a woman who is not married □ *Cik*: Dear Miss Holland, … ♦ That's all, thank you, Miss Dawson.

HELP Miss, Mrs, Ms and Mr are all titles that we use in front of sb's family name, NOT his/her first name, unless it is included with the family name: Is there a Miss (Emma) Hudson here? NOT: Miss Emma

miss¹ /mɪs/ verb
▶NOT HIT/CATCH **1** [I,T] to fail to hit, catch, etc. sth □ *tdk kena; terlepas*: She tried to catch the ball but she missed. ♦ The bullet narrowly missed his heart.
▶NOT SEE/HEAR **2** [T] to not see, hear, understand, etc. sb/sth □ *tdk nampak, dengar, faham, dll*: The house is on the corner, so you can't miss it. ♦ They completely missed the point of what I was saying. ♦ My Mum will know there's something wrong. She doesn't miss much.
▶NOT GO **3** [T] to fail to go to or do sth □ *ketinggalan*: Of course I'm coming to your wedding. I wouldn't miss it for the world (= used to emphasize that you really want to do sth). ♦ You can't afford to miss meals (= not eat meals) now you're pregnant.
▶BE LATE **4** [T] to arrive too late for sb/sth □ *ketinggalan*: Hurry up or you'll miss the train!
▶FEEL SAD **5** [T] to feel sad because sb is not with you any more, or because you have not got or cannot do sth that you once had or did □ *merindui; terasa kehilangan*: I'll miss you terribly when you go away. ♦ What did you miss most when you lived abroad?

ð **then** s **so** z **zoo** ʃ **she** ʒ vi**sion** h **how** m **man** n **no** ŋ si**ng** l **leg** r **red** j **yes** w **wet**

▶NOTICE STH NOT THERE **6** [T] to notice that sb/sth is not where they or it should be □ *sedar akan ketiadaan atau kehilangan sso/sst*: *When did you first miss your handbag?*
▶AVOID STH BAD **7** [T] to avoid sth unpleasant □ *dpt mengelak*: *If we leave now, we'll miss the rush-hour traffic.*

PHR V **miss sb/sth out** to not include sb/sth □ *meninggalkan (atau tertinggal)*: *You've missed out several important points in your report.* **miss out (on sth)** to not have a chance to have or do sth □ *terlepas; rugi*: *You'll miss out on all the fun if you stay at home.*

miss² /mɪs/ *noun* [C] a failure to hit, catch or reach sth □ *(perihal) terlepas atau tdk kena*: *After several misses he finally managed to hit the target.*

IDM **give sth a miss** (especially BrE informal) to decide not to do or have sth □ *tdk membuat, mengambil, dsb sst*: *I think I'll give aerobics a miss tonight.*
a near miss ⊃ **near¹**

missile /'mɪsaɪl/ *noun* [C] **1** a powerful exploding weapon that can be sent long distances through the air □ *peluru berpandu; misil*: *nuclear missiles* **2** an object that is thrown at sb in order to hurt them □ *peluru; benda-benda yg dibaling utk mencederakan sso atau sst*: *The rioters threw missiles such as bottles and stones.*

missing /'mɪsɪŋ/ *adj* **1** lost, or not in the right or usual place □ *hilang; tdk ada*: *a missing person* ◆ *Two files have gone missing from my office.* **2** (used about a person) not present after a battle, an accident, etc. but not known to have been killed □ *hilang*: *Many soldiers were listed as missing in action.* **3** not included, often when it should have been □ *tertinggal*: *Fill in the missing words in the text.*

mission /'mɪʃn/ *noun* [C]
▶OFFICIAL JOB/GROUP **1** an important official job that sb is sent somewhere to do, especially to another country □ *tugas khas; misi*: *Your mission is to send back information about the enemy's movements.* **2** a group of people who are sent to a foreign country to perform a special task □ *perwakilan; misi*: *a British trade mission to China*
▶PLACE **3** a place where people are taught about the Christian religion, given medical help, etc. by missionaries □ *pusat kegiatan mubaligh; misi*
▶YOUR DUTY **4** a particular task which you feel it is your duty to do □ *misi; kewajipan*: *Her work with the poor was more than just a job—it was her mission in life.*
▶JOURNEY **5** a special journey made by a **spacecraft** (= a vehicle that travels in space) or military aircraft □ *misi; pengembaraan*: *a mission to the moon*

missionary /'mɪʃənri/ *noun* [C] (*pl* **missionaries**) a person who is sent to a foreign country to teach about the Christian religion □ *mubaligh*

misspell /ˌmɪs'spel/ *verb* [T] (*pt, pp* misspelled or misspelt /ˌmɪs'spelt/) to spell sth wrongly □ *salah mengeja*

mist¹ /mɪst/ *noun* [C,U] a cloud made of very small drops of water in the air just above the ground, that makes it difficult to see □ *kabus; kabut*: *The fields were covered in mist.* ⊃ note at **fog, weather** ▶**misty** *adj*: *a misty morning* ⊃ look at **foggy**

mist² /mɪst/ *verb*
PHR V **mist (sth) up/over** to cover or be covered with very small drops of water that make it difficult to see □ *mengabuskan; berkabut*: *My glasses misted up when I came in from the cold.*

mistake¹ /mɪ'steɪk/ *noun* [C] something that you think or do that is wrong □ *kesilapan*: *Try not to make any mistakes in your essays.* ◆ *a spelling mistake* ◆ *It was a big mistake to trust her.* ◆ *I made the mistake of giving him my address.*

IDM **by mistake** as a result of being careless □ *tersilap; tdk sengaja*: *The terrorists shot the wrong man by mistake.*

OTHER WORDS FOR

mistake

Error is more formal than **mistake**: *a computing error*. When you **make a mistake** you **do** sth **wrong**: *I got the answer wrong.* ◆ *You must have the wrong number* (= on the phone). **Fault** indicates who is responsible for sth bad: *The accident wasn't my fault. The other driver pulled out in front of me.* **Fault** is also used to describe a problem or weakness that sb/sth has: *a technical fault.*

mistake² /mɪ'steɪk/ *verb* [T] (*pt* mistook /mɪ'stʊk/; *pp* mistaken /mɪ'steɪkən/) to be wrong about sth □ *tersilap; tersalah (faham, dsb)*: *I think you've mistaken my meaning.* ◆ *There was no mistaking* (= it was impossible to mistake) *his anger.*

PHR V **mistake sb/sth for sb/sth** to think wrongly that sb/sth is sb/sth else □ *tersilap menyangka*: *I'm sorry, I mistook you for a friend of mine.*

mistaken /mɪ'steɪkən/ *adj* wrong; not correct □ *tersilap; silap; salah*: *I thought the film was a comedy but I must have been mistaken.* ◆ *a case of mistaken identity* ◆ *a mistaken belief/idea* ▶**mistakenly** *adv*

mistletoe /'mɪsltəʊ/ *noun* [U] a plant with white **berries** (= small round fruit) and green leaves. Mistletoe grows on trees. □ *'mistletoe'*

CULTURE

Mistletoe is used as a decoration inside houses in Britain at Christmas time. There is a tradition of kissing people 'under the mistletoe'.

mistook *past tense* of **mistake²**

mistreat /ˌmɪs'triːt/ *verb* [T] to be cruel to a person or an animal □ *menganiayai*: *The owner* of the zoo was accused of mistreating the animals. ►**mistreatment** noun [U]

mistress /ˈmɪstrəs/ noun [C] **1** a woman who is having a secret sexual relationship with a married man □ *perempuan simpanan* **2** (*formal*) a woman who is in authority or control □ *wanita yg berkuasa*: *She is the mistress of plain speech.*

mistrust /ˌmɪsˈtrʌst/ verb [T] to have no confidence in sb/sth because you think they or it may be harmful □ *tdk percaya akan (sso/sst); mencurigai*: *I always mistrust politicians who smile too much.* ⊃ look at **distrust** ►**mistrust** noun [U, sing]: *She has a deep mistrust of strangers.*

misty /ˈmɪsti/ ⊃ **mist**[1]

misunderstand /ˌmɪsʌndəˈstænd/ verb [I,T] (*pt, pp* misunderstood /-ˈstʊd/) to understand sb/sth wrongly □ *salah faham*: *I misunderstood the instructions and answered too many questions.*

misunderstanding /ˌmɪsʌndəˈstændɪŋ/ noun **1** [C,U] a situation in which sb/sth is not understood correctly □ *salah faham; kekeliruan*: *The contract is written in both languages to avoid any misunderstanding.* **2** [C] a disagreement or an argument □ *perselisihan faham*

misuse /ˌmɪsˈjuːz/ verb [T] to use sth in the wrong way or for the wrong purpose □ *menyalahgunakan*: *These chemicals can be dangerous if misused.* ►**misuse** /ˌmɪsˈjuːs/ noun [C,U]

mitigate /ˈmɪtɪɡeɪt/ verb [T] (*formal*) to make sth less serious, painful, unpleasant, etc. □ *mengurangkan; meringankan* ►**mitigating** adj: *Because of the mitigating circumstances (= that made the crime seem less bad) the judge gave her a lighter sentence.*

mitten /ˈmɪtn/ (also **mitt** /mɪt/) noun [C] a type of glove that has one part for the thumb and another part for all four fingers □ *miten* ⊃ look at **glove** ⊃ picture at **glove**

mix[1] /mɪks/ verb **1** [I,T] **mix (A) with (B); mix (A and B) (together)** if two or more substances mix or if you mix them, they combine to form a new substance □ *bercampur; mencampurkan; membancuh*: *Oil and water don't mix.* ♦ *Mix all the ingredients together in a bowl.* ♦ *to mix a cocktail (= by mixing various drinks)* **2** [I] **mix (with sb)** to be with and talk to other people □ *bergaul*: *He mixes with all types of people at work.* **3** [T] to combine different recordings of voices and/or instruments to produce a single piece of music □ *menggabungkan*

IDM **be/get mixed up in sth** (*informal*) to be/ become involved in sth bad or unpleasant □ *terlibat dgn sst*

PHR V **mix sth up** to put sth in the wrong order □ *mencampuradukkan; bercampur aduk*: *He was so nervous that he dropped his speech and got the pages all mixed up.*

mix sb/sth up (with sb/sth) to confuse sb/sth with sb/sth else □ *terkeliru antara sso/sst (dgn sso/sst yg lain)*: *I always get him mixed up with his brother.*

mix[2] /mɪks/ noun **1** [C, usually sing] a group of different types of people or things □ *campuran*: *We need a good racial mix in the police force.* **2** [C,U] a special powder that contains all the substances needed to make sth. You add water or another liquid to this powder □ *campuran; adunan*: *cake mix*

mixed /mɪkst/ adj **1** being both good and bad □ *bercampur-baur; bercampur-campur*: *I have mixed feelings about leaving my job.* **2** made or consisting of different types of person or thing □ *campur*: *Was your school mixed or single-sex?* ♦ *a mixed salad*

mixed ˈmarriage noun [C] a marriage between people of different races or religions □ *kahwin campur*

mixed-ˈup adj (*informal*) confused because of emotional problems □ *kacau fikiran; fikiran terganggu*: *He has been very mixed-up since his parents' divorce.*

mixers

food processor

hand-held blender

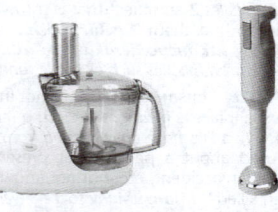

blender
(*BrE also* **liquidizer**)

electric whisk

mixer /ˈmɪksə(r)/ noun [C] a machine that is used for mixing sth □ *pengadun; pembancuh*: *a food/cement mixer*

mixture /ˈmɪkstʃə(r)/ noun **1** [sing] a combination of different things □ *campuran*: *Monkeys eat a mixture of leaves and fruit.* ♦ *I stood and stared with a mixture of amazement and horror.* **2** [C,U] a substance that is made by mixing other substances together □ *campuran; adunan*: *cake mixture* ♦ *a mixture of eggs, flour and milk*

ˈmix-up noun [C] (*informal*) a mistake in the planning or organization of sth □ *kekeliruan*:

There was a mix-up and we were given the wrong ticket.

ml *abbr* = **millilitre** □ *ml (mililiter)*: *contents 75ml*

mm *abbr* = **millimetre** □ *mm (milimeter)*: *a 35mm camera*

mo *abbr* (*AmE*) (*pl* **mos**) = **month**

moan /məʊn/ *verb* [I] **1** to make a low sound because you are in pain, very sad, etc. □ *mengerang*: *to moan with pain* **2** (*informal*) to keep saying what is wrong about sth; to complain □ *merungut-rungut*: *The English are always moaning about the weather.* ▶ **moan** *noun* [C]

moat /məʊt/ *noun* [C] a hole that was dug around a castle and filled with water to make it difficult for enemies to attack □ *mot; parit yg dikorek dlm dan lebar serta berair di sekeliling istana*

mob¹ /mɒb/ *noun* [C, with sing or pl verb] a large crowd of people that may become violent or cause trouble □ *kumpulan perusuh*

mob² /mɒb/ *verb* [T] (**mobbing**; **mobbed**) to form a large crowd around sb, for example in order to see or touch them □ *mengerumuni*: *The band was mobbed by fans as they left the hotel.*

mobile¹ /ˈməʊbaɪl/ *adj* able to move or be moved easily □ *mudah bergerak; mudah dialih*: *My daughter is much more mobile now she has her own car.* ♦ *a mobile shop/library* ▶ **mobility** /məʊˈbɪləti/ *noun* [U]

mobile² /ˈməʊbaɪl/ *noun* [C] **1** = **mobile phone 2** a decoration that you hang from the ceiling and that moves when the air around it moves □ *perhiasan gantungan*

mobile phone (*BrE* **mobile**; *AmE* **cellphone**) *noun* [C] a small telephone that you can carry around with you □ *telefon bimbit* ➲ note at **telephone**: *In most countries it's illegal to drive while using a mobile phone.* ♦ *Please switch off your mobile before the performance begins.*

TOPIC

Mobile phones

Calling from a **mobile phone/cellphone** can be more convenient than from a **landline** (= a normal telephone), because **mobiles** can be used anywhere where there is a **signal**. You can also use a mobile to **text** somebody/**send** somebody an **SMS** or a **text message** (= a short written message). If you call somebody, but you cannot **get through** (= make contact), you can leave a message on their **voicemail**. To use a **pay-as-you-go** phone you first have to buy **credit** (= pay money so you can make calls and send text messages), and then **top up** your phone (= pay more money) when the credit **runs out**. You also need to **recharge** your phone when its **battery** is **flat** (= not producing electricity).

mobilize (also **-ise**) /ˈməʊbəlaɪz/ *verb* **1** [T] to organize people or things to do sth □ *menge-*

557

ml → model

rahkan; mendapatkan (sokongan, dsb); menggemblengkan: *They mobilized the local residents to oppose the new development.* **2** [I,T] (used about the army, navy, etc.) to get ready for war □ *bersiap sedia utk berperang*

mock¹ /mɒk/ *verb* [I,T] (*formal*) to laugh at sb/sth in an unkind way or to make other people laugh at them or it □ *memperolok-olokkan; mengejek* ➲ Less formal and more common expressions are **laugh at** and **make fun of**.

mock² /mɒk/ *adj* [only before a noun] not real or genuine □ *tiruan; olok-olok; dibuat-buat*: *He held up his hands in mock surprise.* ♦ *a mock interview/examination*

mock³ /mɒk/ *noun* [usually pl] (in Britain) a practice exam that you do before the official one □ *peperiksaan percubaan*

EXAM TIP

Mock exams

A mock exam gives you the chance to work under exam conditions, to discover your strengths and weaknesses and whether you can complete the exam in the time allowed. When you get the results of your mock exam, pay special attention to what you got wrong, so that you can practise and improve for the real exam.

mockery /ˈmɒkəri/ *noun* [U] comments or actions that make sb/sth look silly or stupid □ *perbuatan mengejek; ejekan*: *She couldn't stand any more of their mockery.* **SYN** ridicule **IDM** **make a mockery of sth** to make sth seem silly or useless □ *memperolok-olokkan*: *The trial made a mockery of justice* (= the trial was not fair).

ˈmock-up *noun* [C] a model of sth that shows what it will look like or how it will work □ *contoh; model terperinci*

modal /ˈməʊdl/ (also **modal ˈverb**) *noun* [C] a verb, for example 'might', 'can' or 'must' that is used with another verb for expressing possibility, permission, intention, etc. □ *kk modus* **ⓘ** For more information about modal verbs, look at the **Reference Section** at the back of this dictionary.

mode /məʊd/ *noun* [C] **1** a type of sth or way of doing sth □ *cara; gaya*: *a mode of transport/life* **2** one of the ways in which a machine can work □ *mod*: *Switch the camera to automatic mode.*

model¹ /ˈmɒdl/ *noun* [C]
▶COPY **1** a copy of sth that is usually smaller than the real thing □ *model*: *a model aeroplane* ♦ *a working model* (= one in which the parts move) ➲ picture on **page P3**
▶MACHINE **2** one of the machines, vehicles, etc. that is made by a particular company □ *model; keluaran*: *The latest models are on display at the show.*
▶GOOD EXAMPLE **3** a person or thing that is a good example to copy □ *contoh; misali*: *a model student* ♦ *Children often use older brothers or sisters as role models* (= copy the way they behave).

►FASHION **4** a person who is employed to wear clothes at a fashion show or for magazine photographs □ *peragawati; peragawan; model*: *a fashion/male model*

►FOR ARTIST **5** a person who is painted, drawn or photographed by an artist □ *model*: *Gwen John was Rodin's model.*

model² /ˈmɒdl/ *verb* (**modelling; modelled,** (*AmE*) **modeling; modeled**) **1** [I,T] to wear and show clothes at a fashion show or for photographs □ *memperagakan*: *to model swimsuits* **2** [I,T] to make a model of sth □ *membentuk*: *This clay is difficult to model.*

PHR V **model sth/yourself on sb/sth** to make sth/yourself similar to sth/sb else □ *menconto-hi; meniru*: *The house is modelled on a Roman villa.*

modelling (*AmE* **modeling**) /ˈmɒdəlɪŋ/ *noun* [U] the work of a fashion model □ *kerja sebagai model*

modem /ˈməʊdem/ *noun* [C] a piece of equipment that connects two or more computers together by means of a telephone line so that information can go from one to the other □ *modem* ➔ note at **Internet**

moderate¹ /ˈmɒdərət/ *adj* **1** being, having, using, etc. neither too much nor too little of sth □ *sederhana*: *a moderate amount of success.* **2** having or showing opinions, especially about politics, that are not extreme □ *sederhana; tdk melampau*: *moderate policies/views* ➔ look at **extreme, radical** ►**moderately** *adv*: *His career has been moderately successful.*

moderate² /ˈmɒdəreɪt/ *verb* [I,T] to become or to make sth less strong or extreme □ *menyederhanakan; mengurangkan*: *The union moderated its original demands.* ►**moderator** *noun* [C] a person who prevents offensive material from being published on a website: *A moderator had removed the message.* ➔ note at **chat room**

moderate³ /ˈmɒdərət/ *noun* [C] a person whose opinions, especially about politics, are not extreme □ *(orang yg) sederhana* ➔ look at **extremist**

moderation /ˌmɒdəˈreɪʃn/ *noun* [U] the quality of being reasonable and not being extreme □ *kesederhanaan; secara sederhana*: *Alcohol can harm unborn babies even if it's taken in moderation.*

⚡ modern /ˈmɒdn/ *adj* **1** of the present or recent times □ *masa ini; moden*: *Pollution is one of the major problems in the modern world.* **2** [only *before* a noun] (used about styles of art, music, etc.) new and different from traditional styles □ *moden*: *modern jazz/architecture/art* **3** having all the newest methods, equipment, designs, etc. □ *moden; terkini*: *It is one of the most modern hospitals in the country.* **SYN** **up to date** ➔ look at **old-fashioned**

modernize (also **-ise**) /ˈmɒdənaɪz/ *verb* [T] to make sth suitable for use today using new methods, styles, etc. □ *memodenkan* ►**modernization** (also **-isation**) /ˌmɒdənaɪˈzeɪʃn/ *noun* [U]: *The house is large but is in need of modernization.*

ˌmodern ˈlanguage *noun* [usually pl] a language that is spoken now and that you study at school or college □ *bahasa moden*

modest /ˈmɒdɪst/ *adj* **1** not very large □ *sederhana*: *a modest pay increase* **2** not talking too much about your own abilities, good qualities, etc. □ *tdk menunjuk-nunjuk*: *She got the best results in the exam but she was too modest to tell anyone.* ➔ look at **humble, proud 3** (used about a woman's clothes) not showing much of the body □ *sopan; tdk mencolok mata* ►**modesty** *noun* [U] ►**modestly** *adv*

modify /ˈmɒdɪfaɪ/ *verb* [T] (**modifying; modifies;** *pt, pp* **modified**) to change sth slightly □ *mengubah suai*: *We shall need to modify the existing plan.* ►**modification** /ˌmɒdɪfɪˈkeɪʃn/ *noun* [C,U]

modular /ˈmɒdjələ(r)/ *adj* **1** (used about a course of study, especially at a British university or college) consisting of separate units from which students may choose several □ *bermodul*: *a modular course* **2** (used about machines, buildings, etc.) consisting of separate parts or units that can be joined together □ *bermodul*

module /ˈmɒdjuːl/ *noun* [C] a unit that forms part of sth bigger □ *modul*: *You must complete three modules* (= courses that you study) *in your first year.*

mohair /ˈməʊheə(r)/ *noun* [U] very soft wool that comes from a **goat** (= a small animal with horns that lives in mountain areas) □ *mohair*: *a mohair jumper*

Mohammed = **Muhammad**

moist /mɔɪst/ *adj* slightly wet □ *lembap*: *Her eyes were moist with tears.* ♦ *Keep the soil moist or the plant will die.* ➔ note at **wet** ►**moisten** /ˈmɔɪsn/ *verb* [I,T]

moisture /ˈmɔɪstʃə(r)/ *noun* [U] water in small drops on a surface, in the air, etc. □ *kelembapan*

moisturize (*BrE also* **-ise**) /ˈmɔɪstʃəraɪz/ *verb* [I,T] to put a special cream on your skin to make it less dry □ *melembapkan* ►**moisturizer** (*BrE also* **-iser** /-raɪzə(r)/) *noun* [C,U]

molar /ˈməʊlə(r)/ *noun* [C] one of the large teeth at the back of your mouth □ *geraham; molar*

molasses /məˈlæsɪz/ (*AmE*) = **treacle**

mold, moldy (*AmE*) = **mould, mouldy**

mole /məʊl/ *noun* [C] **1** a small animal with dark fur that lives underground and is almost unable to see □ *mole* **2** a small dark spot on sb's skin that never goes away □ *tahi lalat* ➔ look at **freckle 3** (*informal*) a person who works in one organization and gives secret information to another organization ◻ *musuh dlm selimut; pengintip* ➔ look at **spy**

molecule /ˈmɒlɪkjuːl/ noun [C] the smallest unit into which a substance can be divided without changing its chemical nature ◻ *molekul* ➔ look at **atom**

molest /məˈlest/ verb [T] to attack sb, especially a child, in a sexual way ◻ *menyerang; memperkosa*

mollusc (AmE mollusk) /ˈmɒləsk/ noun [C] any creature with a soft body that is not divided into different sections, and usually a hard outer shell. **Snails** and **slugs** are molluscs. ◻ *moluska* ➔ look at **shellfish**

molt (AmE) = **moult**

molten /ˈməʊltən/ adj (used about metal or rock) made liquid by very great heat ◻ *lebur*

mom /mɒm/ (AmE) = **mum**

moment /ˈməʊmənt/ noun 1 [C] a very short period of time ◻ *sebentar*: One moment, please (= please wait). ◆ Joe left just a few moments ago. 2 [sing] a particular point in time ◻ *ketika; detik*: Just at that moment my mother arrived. ◆ the moment of birth/death ◆ I'm waiting for **the right moment** to give him the news.
IDM (at) any minute/moment (now) ➔ **minute**[1]
at the moment now ◻ *ketika ini*: I'm afraid she's busy at the moment. Can I take a message? ➔ note at **actually**
for the moment/present for a short time; for now ◻ *buat masa ini*: This coat is fine for the moment, but I'll need a new one next winter.
in a moment very soon ◻ *sekejap lagi*: Just wait here. I'll be back in a moment.
the last minute/moment ➔ **last**[1]
the minute/moment (that) ➔ **minute**[1]
on the spur of the moment ➔ **spur**[1]

momentary /ˈməʊməntri/ adj lasting for a very short time ◻ *seketika*: a momentary lack of concentration ▸ momentarily /-trəli/ adv

momentous /məˈmentəs/ adj very important ◻ *penting; bersejarah*: a momentous decision/event/change

momentum /məˈmentəm/ noun [U] the ability to keep increasing or developing; the force that makes sth move faster and faster ◻ *kebolehan/kuasa utk bertambah, berkembang, dsb; momentum*: The environmental movement is gathering momentum.

mommy /ˈmɒmi/ (AmE) = **mummy**(1)

Mon. abbr = **Monday** ◻ *Isnin*: Mon. 6 June

monarch /ˈmɒnək/ (AmE also) / noun [C] a king or queen ◻ *raja; ratu*

monarchy /ˈmɒnəki/ noun (pl monarchies) 1 [sing, U] the system of government or rule by a king or queen ◻ *pemerintahan beraja* 2 [C] a country that is governed by a king or queen ◻ *negara beraja* ➔ look at **republic**

monastery /ˈmɒnəstri/ noun [C] (pl monasteries) a place where **monks** (= religious men) live together in a religious community ◻ *biara*

559 **molecule → money**

➔ look at **convent**

Monday /ˈmʌndeɪ; -di/ noun [C,U] (abbr Mon.) the day of the week after Sunday ◻ *Isnin*: I visit my grandparents every Monday after school.

HELP Days of the week are always written with a capital letter. Note how we use them in sentences: I'm going to see her **on Monday**. ◆ (informal) I'll see you Monday. ◆ I finish work a bit later **on Mondays/on a Monday**. ◆ Monday morning/afternoon/evening/night ◆ last/next Monday ◆ a week on Monday/Monday week (= not next Monday, but the Monday after that) ◆ The museum is open Monday to Friday, 10 till 4.30. ◆ Did you see that article about Italy in Monday's paper?

monetary /ˈmʌnɪtri/ adj [only before a noun] connected with money ◻ *kewangan*: the government's monetary policy

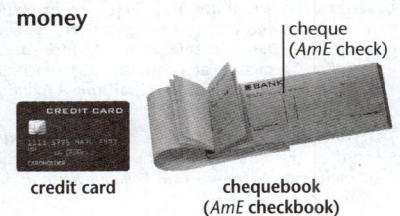

money

cheque (AmE check)

credit card

chequebook (AmE checkbook)

cash

coin

note (AmE bill)

money /ˈmʌni/ noun [U] the means of paying for sth or buying sth (= coins or notes) ◻ *wang; duit*: Will you **earn** more money in your new job? ◆ The new road will **cost** a lot of money. ◆ If we do the work ourselves we will **save** money. ◆ The government **make** a huge amount of money out of tobacco tax. ➔ note at **pay** ➔ look at **pocket money**
IDM be rolling in money/in it ➔ **roll**[2]
get your money's worth to get full value for the money you have spent ◻ *berbaloi*
to put money on sth to bet money on sth ◻ *mempertaruh*: He put all his money on a horse.
SYN bet ➔ note at **loan**

TOPIC

Money

You can **save** money in a bank **account**, and this money is called your **savings**. You can spend **cash** (= notes and coins) to buy things,

money order → monster 560

or you can write a **cheque**. If you use a **debit card**, the money comes straight out of your bank account. If you use a **credit card**, you pay later. If you have a **cash card**, you can **withdraw** (= take out) money from your bank account at a **cash machine**. If you spend more money than is in your account you are **overdrawn**.

Some people **invest** money, for example in the **stock exchange**, and make a **fortune** (= a large amount of money). People who have a lot of money are **rich/wealthy**, and someone who often **gives** money **away**, for example to **charity**, is **generous**.

money order (AmE) = postal order

mongrel /ˈmʌŋgrəl/ noun [C] a dog that has parents of different breeds □ *anjing kacukan* ⊃ look at **pedigree**

monitor¹ /ˈmɒnɪtə(r)/ noun [C] **1** a machine that shows information or pictures on a screen like a TV □ *monitor*: *a PC with a 17-inch colour monitor* ⊃ picture at **computer 2** a machine that records or checks sth □ *monitor*: *A monitor checks the baby's heartbeat.*

monitor² /ˈmɒnɪtə(r)/ verb [T] to check, record or test sth regularly for a period of time □ *mengawasi; memantau*: *Pollution levels in the lake are closely monitored.*

monk /mʌŋk/ noun [C] a member of a religious group of men who live in a **monastery** (= a special building) and do not get married or have possessions □ *rahib; biarawan* ⊃ look at **nun**

monkey   gorilla

monkey /ˈmʌŋki/ noun [C] an animal with a long tail that lives in hot countries and can climb trees □ *monyet* ⊃ look at **ape**

MORE Chimpanzees and gorillas are apes, although people sometimes call them monkeys.

IDM **monkey business** silly or dishonest behaviour □ *kenakalan; tipu muslihat*

mono /ˈmɒnəʊ/ adj (used about recorded music or a system for playing it) having the sound coming from one direction only □ *mono* ⊃ look at **stereo**

mono- /ˈmɒnəʊ/ [combining form] (in nouns and adjectives) one; single □ *satu*; *mono-*: *monorail* ♦ *monogamy*

monochrome /ˈmɒnəkrəʊm/ adj (used about a photograph or picture) using only black, white and shades of grey □ *monokrom; hitam putih*

monoculture /ˈmɒnəkʌltʃə(r)/ noun [U] the practice of growing only one type of crop on a certain area of land □ *monokultur*

monogamy /məˈnɒgəmi/ noun [U] the fact or custom of being married to, or having a sexual relationship with, only one person at a particular time □ *monogami* ⊃ look at **bigamy, polygamy** ▶ **monogamous** /məˈnɒgəməs/ adj: *a monogamous relationship* ♦ *Most birds are monogamous.*

monolingual /ˌmɒnəˈlɪŋgwəl/ adj using only one language □ *ekabahasa*: *This is a monolingual dictionary.* ⊃ look at **bilingual**

monologue (AmE also **monolog**) /ˈmɒnəlɒg/ (AmE also) / noun [C] a long speech by one person, for example in a play □ *monolog*

monopolize (also **-ise**) /məˈnɒpəlaɪz/ verb [T] to control sth so that other people cannot share it □ *memonopoli*: *She completely monopolized the conversation. I couldn't get a word in.*

monopoly /məˈnɒpəli/ noun [C] (pl **monopolies**) **a monopoly (on/in sth) 1** the control of an industry or service by only one company; a type of goods or a service that is controlled in this way □ *monopoli*: *The company has a monopoly on broadcasting international football.* **2** the complete control, possession or use of sth; something that belongs to only one person or group and is not shared □ *monopoli*

monorail /ˈmɒnəʊreɪl/ noun [C] a railway in which the train runs on a single track, usually high above the ground □ *monorel*

monosyllabic /ˌmɒnəsɪˈlæbɪk/ adj **1** having only one syllable □ *(bersifat) ekasukuan; mempunyai hanya satu suku kata; ekasuku*: *a monosyllabic word* **2** saying very little, in a way that seems rude to other people □ *berkata atau bercakap terlalu sedikit (hingga kelihatan kurang sopan)*

monosyllable /ˈmɒnəsɪləbl/ noun [C] a short word, such as 'leg', that has only one syllable □ *kata ekasuku*

monotonous /məˈnɒtənəs/ adj never changing and therefore boring □ *sama; tdk berubah-ubah; membosankan*: *monotonous work* ♦ *a monotonous voice* ▶ **monotonously** adv

monotony /məˈnɒtəni/ noun [U] the state of being always the same and therefore boring □ *keadaan yg sentiasa sama dan membosankan; kebosanan*: *the monotony of working on a production line*

monsoon /ˌmɒnˈsuːn/ noun [C] the season when it rains a lot in Southern Asia; the rain that falls during this period □ *monsun*

monster /ˈmɒnstə(r)/ noun [C] (in stories) a creature that is large, ugly and frightening

ð **then**   s **so**   z **zoo**   ʃ **she**   ʒ **vi**s**ion**   h **how**   m **man**   n **no**   ŋ **si**ng   l **leg**   r **red**   j **yes**   w **wet**

□ *raksasa; orang yg sangat kejam*: *a monster with three heads* ♦ (*figurative*) *The murderer was described as a dangerous monster.*

monstrosity /mɒnˈstrɒsəti/ *noun* [C] (*pl* monstrosities) something that is very large and ugly, especially a building □ *sst yg besar dan hodoh*

monstrous /ˈmɒnstrəs/ *adj* **1** that people think is shocking and unacceptable because it is morally wrong or unfair □ *mengejutkan; teruk betul; tdk adil betul*: *It's monstrous that she earns less than he does for the same job!* **2** very large (and often ugly or frightening) □ *sangat besar*: *a monstrous creature*

month /mʌnθ/ *noun* [C] (*abbr* mth) **1** one of the twelve periods of time into which the year is divided □ *bulan*: *They are starting work next month.* ♦ *Have you seen this month's 'Vogue'?* **2** the period of about 30 days from a certain date in one month to the same date in the next, for example 13 May to 13 June □ *bulan*: *'How long will you be away?' 'For about a month.'* ♦ *a six-month course*

monthly¹ /ˈmʌnθli/ *adj, adv* (happening or produced) once every month □ *bulanan*: *a monthly meeting/magazine/visit* ♦ *Are you paid weekly or monthly?*

monthly² /ˈmʌnθli/ *noun* [C] (*pl* monthlies) a magazine that is published once a month □ *terbitan bulanan*

monument /ˈmɒnjumənt/ *noun* [C] a monument (to sb/sth) **1** a building or statue that is built to remind people of a famous person or event □ *tugu peringatan; monumen* **2** an old building or other place that is of historical importance □ *bangunan bersejarah*

monumental /ˌmɒnjuˈmentl/ *adj* [only before a noun] very great, large or important □ *amat (hebat, besar atau penting)*: *a monumental success/task/achievement*

moo /muː/ *noun* [C] the sound that a cow makes □ *lenguh; bunyi lembu* ➲ note at **cow** ▶**moo** *verb* [I]

mood /muːd/ *noun* **1** [C,U] the way that you are feeling at a particular time □ *keadaan perasaan; angin*: *to be in a bad/good mood* (= to feel angry/happy) ♦ *Turn that music down a bit—I'm not in the mood for it.* ♦ *Are you in the mood to go and see a film tonight?* **2** [C] a time when you are angry or bad-tempered □ *angin tak baik*: *Becky's in one of her moods again.* **SYN** **temper** **3** [sing] the way that a group of people feel about sth □ *suasana*: *The mood of the crowd suddenly changed and violence broke out.*

moody /ˈmuːdi/ *adj* (moodier; moodiest) **1** often changing moods in a way that people cannot predict □ *ada angin; kepala angin*: *You never know where you are with Andy because he's so moody.* **2** bad-tempered or unhappy, often for no particular reason □ *angin tak baik; muram* ▶**moodily** *adv* ▶**moodiness** *noun* [U]

moon /muːn/ *noun* **1** the moon [sing] the object that shines in the sky at night and that moves round the earth once every 28 days □ *bulan*: *The moon's very bright tonight.* ➲ picture at **eclipse**

MORE The moon as it appears at its different stages, can be called a **new moon**, a **full moon**, a **half-moon** or a **crescent moon**.

➲ *adjective* **lunar** **2** [C] an object like the moon that moves around another planet □ *bulan*: *How many moons does Neptune have?*
IDM **once in a blue moon** ➲ **once**
over the moon (*informal*) (*especially BrE*) extremely happy and excited about sth □ *sungguh gembira; seronok sangat*

moonlight /ˈmuːnlaɪt/ *noun* [U] light that comes from the moon □ *cahaya bulan*: *The lake looked beautiful in the moonlight.*

moonlit /ˈmuːnlɪt/ *adj* lit by the moon □ *diterangi cahaya bulan*

moor¹ /mɔː(r); mʊə(r)/ (also moorland) *noun* [C,U] a wild open area of high land that is covered with grass and **heather** (= a low plant that has small purple, pink or white flowers) □ *mur*: *We walked across the moors.* ➲ look at **heath**

moor² /mɔː(r); mʊə(r)/ *verb* [I,T] moor (sth to sth) to fasten a boat to the land or to an object in the water with a rope or chain □ *menambat/ mengikat perahu, dsb*

mooring /ˈmɔːrɪŋ/ *noun* [C, usually pl] a place where a boat is tied; the ropes, chains, etc. used to fasten a boat □ *tambatan; tali, rantai, dsb tambatan*

moorland /ˈmɔːlənd/ = **moor¹**

moose /muːs/ (*AmE*) = **elk**

mop¹ /mɒp/ *noun* [C] a tool for washing floors that has a long handle with a bunch of thick strings or soft material at the end □ *mop; pengelap lantai* ➲ picture at **bucket**

mop² /mɒp/ *verb* [T] (mopping; mopped) **1** to clean a floor with water and a **mop** □ *mengelap lantai* **2** to remove liquid from sth using a dry cloth □ *mengesat; mengelap*: *to mop your forehead with a handkerchief*
PHR V **mop sth up** to get rid of liquid from a surface with a **mop** or dry cloth □ *mengelap sst*: *Mop up that tea you've spilt or it'll leave a stain!*

mope /məʊp/ *verb* [I] mope (about/around) to spend your time doing nothing and feeling sorry for yourself because you are unhappy □ *bermuram*: *Moping around the house all day won't make the situation any better.*

moped /ˈməʊped/ *noun* [C] a type of small, not very powerful motorbike □ *motosikal ringan*

moral¹ /ˈmɒrəl/ (*AmE* also) / *adj* **1** [only before a noun] concerned with what is right and wrong □ *(prinsip) moral*: *Some people refuse to eat meat*

moral → morsel 562

on moral grounds (= because they believe it to be wrong). ♦ a moral dilemma/issue/question **2** having a high standard of behaviour that is considered good and right by most people □ *bermoral*: *She has always led a very moral life.* **OPP** immoral ⇒ look at amoral

IDM moral support help or confidence that you give to sb who is nervous or worried □ *sokongan moral*: *I went to the dentist's with him just to give him some moral support.*

moral² /ˈmɒrəl (AmE also)/ noun **1** morals [pl] standards of good behaviour □ *akhlak*: *These people appear to have no morals.* **2** [C] a lesson in the right way to behave that can be learnt from a story or an experience □ *pengajaran; iktibar*: *The moral of the play is that friendship is more important than money.*

morale /məˈrɑːl/ noun [U] how happy, sad, confident, etc. a group of people feels at a particular time □ *semangat*: *The team's morale was low/high before the match* (= they felt worried/confident). ♦ *to boost/raise/improve morale*

morality /məˈræləti/ noun [U] principles concerning what is good and bad or right and wrong behaviour □ *prinsip moral; moraliti*: *a debate about the morality of abortion* **SYN** ethics **OPP** immorality

moralize (also -ise) /ˈmɒrəlaɪz (AmE also)/ verb [I] moralize (about/on sth) to tell other people what the right or wrong way to behave is □ *berhujah ttg moral*

morally /ˈmɒrəli (AmE also)/ adv connected with standards of what is right or wrong □ *dr segi moral; bermoral*: *Parents should be morally responsible for their children.* ♦ *morally right/wrong*

morbid /ˈmɔːbɪd/ adj showing interest in unpleasant things, for example disease and death □ *suka akan perkara-perkara yg tdk menyenangkan atau yg mengerikan*

more¹ /mɔː(r)/ determiner, pron a larger number or amount of people or things; something extra as well as what you have □ *lebih banyak; lebih; lagi*: *There were more people than I expected.* ♦ *We had more time than we thought.* ♦ *There's room for three more people.* ♦ *I couldn't eat any more.* ♦ *I can't stand much more of this.* ♦ *Tell me more about your job.* **OPP** less, fewer

IDM more and more an increasing amount or number □ *semakin bertambah/banyak*: *There are more and more cars on the road.*

what's more (used for adding another fact) also; in addition □ *tambahan pula; lebih (teruk, dsb) lagi*: *The hotel was awful and what's more it was miles from the beach.*

more² /mɔː(r)/ adv **1** used to form the comparative of many adjectives and adverbs □ *lebih*: *She was far/much more intelligent than her sister.* ♦ *a course for more advanced students* ♦ *Please write more carefully.* **OPP** less **2** to a greater degree than usual or than sth else □ *lebih*: *I like him far/*much more *than his wife.* **OPP** for both meanings less

IDM more or less approximately; almost □ *lebih kurang*: *We are more or less the same age.*

the more, less, etc.... the more, less, etc.... used to show that two things change to the same degree □ *semakin ... semakin*: *The more she thought about it, the more depressed she became.*

not any more not any longer □ *tdk lagi*: *She doesn't live here any more.*

moreover /mɔːrˈəʊvə(r)/ adv (written) (used for adding another fact) also; in addition □ *lagipun*: *This firm did the work very well. Moreover, the cost was not too high.*

morgue /mɔːɡ/ noun [C] a building where dead bodies are kept until they are buried or burned □ *rumah mayat* ⇒ look at mortuary

morning /ˈmɔːnɪŋ/ noun [C,U] **1** the early part of the day between the time when the sun rises and midday □ *pagi*: *Pat's going to London tomorrow morning.* ♦ *Bye, see you in the morning* (= tomorrow morning). ♦ *I've been studying hard all morning.* ♦ *Dave makes breakfast every morning.* ♦ *She only works in the mornings.* **2** the part of the night that is after midnight □ *dinihari*: *I was woken by a noise in the early hours of the morning.* ♦ *He didn't come home until three in the morning.*

HELP Note that when we are talking about a particular morning, we say **on Monday, Tuesday, Wednesday, etc. morning**, but when we are talking generally about doing sth at the time of day we say **in the morning**. 'Afternoon' and 'evening' are used in the same way.
When you use the adjectives **early** or **late** before 'morning', 'afternoon' or 'evening' you must use the preposition **in**: *The accident happened in the early morning.* ♦ *We arrived in the late afternoon.* With other adjectives, use **on**: *They set out on a cold, windy afternoon.* ♦ *School starts on Monday morning.* No preposition is used before **this, tomorrow, yesterday**: *Let's go swimming this morning.* ♦ *I'll phone Liz tomorrow evening.* ♦ *What did you do yesterday afternoon?*

IDM Good morning (formal) used when you see sb for the first time in the morning □ *Selamat pagi*

HELP Often we just say **Morning**: *Morning Kay, how are you today?*

moron /ˈmɔːrɒn/ noun [C] (informal) a rude way of referring to sb who you think is very stupid □ *si tolol; orang dungu*: *Stop treating me like a moron!* ▸ moronic /məˈrɒnɪk/ adj

morose /məˈrəʊs/ adj bad-tempered, and not saying much to other people □ *bengkeng; muram* ▸ morosely adv

morphine /ˈmɔːfiːn/ noun [U] a powerful drug that is used for reducing pain □ *morfin*

morsel /ˈmɔːsl/ noun [C] a very small piece of sth, usually food □ *kepingan; cebisan*

mortal¹ /ˈmɔːtl/ adj **1** that cannot live for ever and must die □ *fana*: *We are all mortal.* **OPP** **immortal 2** (*written*) that will result in death □ *membawa maut*: *a mortal wound/blow* ♦ *to be in mortal danger* ➔ look at **fatal 3** very great or extreme □ *amat; sangat*: *They were in mortal fear of the enemy.* ▶ **mortally** /-təli/ adv

mortal² /ˈmɔːtl/ noun [C] (*formal*) a human being □ *manusia*

mortality /mɔːˈtæləti/ noun [U] **1** the fact that you will die □ *kefanaan; (hakikat) akan mati*: *He didn't like to think about his own mortality.* **2** the number of deaths in one period of time or in one place □ *kadar kematian*: *Infant mortality is high in the region.*

mortar /ˈmɔːtə(r)/ noun **1** [U] a mixture of cement (= a grey powder), sand and water used in building for holding bricks and stones together □ *lepa; mortar* **2** [C] a type of heavy gun that fires a type of bomb high into the air □ *mortar* **3** [C] a small hard bowl in which you can crush some foods or substances into powder with a **pestle** (= a heavy tool with a round end) □ *lesung* ➔ picture at **squeeze**

mortgage /ˈmɔːɡɪdʒ/ noun [C] money that you borrow in order to buy a house or flat □ *pinjaman gadai janji*: *We took out a £100 000 mortgage.* ➔ note at **loan**

mortician /mɔːˈtɪʃn/ (*AmE*) = **undertaker**

mortify /ˈmɔːtɪfaɪ/ verb [I,T] (**mortifying; mortifies**; *pt, pp* **mortified**) [usually passive] to feel or to make sb feel very embarrassed □ *berasa tersangat malu*: *She was mortified to realize he had heard every word she said.* ▶ **mortification** /ˌmɔːtɪfɪˈkeɪʃn/ noun [U] ▶ **mortifying** adj: *How mortifying to have to apologize to him!*

mortuary /ˈmɔːtʃəri/ noun [C] (*pl* **mortuaries**) a room, usually in a hospital, where dead bodies are kept before they are buried or burned □ *bilik mayat* ➔ look at **morgue**

mosaic /məʊˈzeɪɪk/ noun [C,U] a picture or pattern that is made by placing together small coloured stones, pieces of glass, etc. □ *mozek*

Moslem /ˈmɒzləm/ = **Muslim**

mosque /mɒsk/ noun [C] a building where Muslims meet and worship □ *masjid*

mosquito /məˈskiːtəʊ; mɒˈs-/ noun [C] (*pl* **mosquitoes**) a small flying insect that lives in hot countries and bites people or animals to drink their blood. Some types of **mosquito** spread **malaria** (= a very serious disease). □ *nyamuk* ➔ picture on **page P13**

moss /mɒs/ noun [C,U] a small soft green plant, with no flowers, that grows in wet places, especially on rocks or trees □ *lumut* ▶ **mossy** adj

most¹ /məʊst/ determiner, pron **1** [used as the superlative of *many* and *much*] greatest in number or amount □ *paling banyak*: *Who got the most points?* ♦ *The children had the most fun.* ♦ *We all worked hard but I did the most.* **OPP** **least, fewest 2** nearly all of a group of people or things □ *kebanyakan*: *Most people in this country have a TV.* ♦ *I like most Italian food.*

> **HELP** When **most** is followed by a noun which has **the, this, my**, etc. before it, we must use **most of**: *Most of my friends were able to come to the wedding.* ♦ *It rained most of the time we were in England.*

IDM **at (the) most** not more than a certain number, and probably less □ *paling (banyak, dll)*: *There were 20 people there, at the most.* **for the most part** usually or mostly □ *biasanya* **make the most of sth** to get as much pleasure, profit, etc. as possible from sth □ *menggunakan (peluang, dll) dgn sebaik-baiknya*: *You won't get another chance—make the most of it!*

most² /məʊst/ adv **1** used to form the superlative of many adjectives and adverbs □ *paling*: *It's the most beautiful house I've ever seen.* ♦ *I work most efficiently in the morning.* **OPP** **least 2** more than anyone/anything else □ *paling*: *What do you miss most when you're abroad?* **OPP** **least 3** (*formal*) very □ *sangat; sungguh*: *We heard a most interesting talk about Japan.*

mostly /ˈməʊstli/ adv in almost every case; almost all the time □ *selalunya; kebanyakannya*: *Our students come mostly from Japan.*

MOT /ˌem əʊ ˈtiː/ abbr (also **MO'T test**) a test in the UK to make sure that vehicles over a certain age are safe to drive □ *ujian Kementerian Pengangkutan (UK)*: *My car failed its MOT.*

motel /məʊˈtel/ noun [C] a hotel near a main road for people who are travelling by car □ *motel* ➔ note at **hotel**

moth /mɒθ/ noun [C] an insect with wings that usually flies at night. Some **moths** eat cloth and leave small holes in your clothes. □ *rama-rama* ➔ picture on **page P13**

mothball /ˈmɒθbɔːl/ noun [C] a small ball made of a chemical substance that protects clothes in cupboards from **moths** □ *ubat gegat*

mother¹ /ˈmʌðə(r)/ noun [C] the female parent of a person or an animal □ *ibu; emak*: *a mother and baby group* ♦ *a mother-to-be* (= a woman who is pregnant) ♦ *a mother of two* (= a woman with two children) ♦ *I saw your mother in town yesterday.* ➔ look at **mum, mummy, stepmother**

mother² /ˈmʌðə(r)/ verb [T] to look after sb as a mother does □ *memelihara; menjaga*: *Stop mothering me—I can look after myself!*

motherhood /ˈmʌðəhʊd/ noun [U] the state of being a mother □ *menjadi ibu*

ˈmother-in-law noun [C] (*pl* **mothers-in-law**) the mother of your husband or wife □ *ibu mentua*

motherland /ˈmʌðəlænd/ noun [C] (*formal*) the country where you or your family were born and which you feel a strong emotional connection with □ *tanah air; ibu pertiwi*

motherly /ˈmʌðəli/ *adj* having the qualities of a good mother □ *(bersifat) keibuan; seperti seorang ibu*: *motherly love/instincts/advice*

'Mother's Day *noun* [C] a day when mothers receive cards and gifts from their children, celebrated in Britain on the fourth Sunday in Lent and in the US on the 2nd Sunday in May □ *Hari Ibu*

'mother tongue *noun* [C] the first language that you learnt to speak as a child □ *bahasa ibunda*

motif /məʊˈtiːf/ *noun* [C] a picture or pattern on sth □ *motif; corak*: *a flower motif*

motion¹ /ˈməʊʃn/ *noun* 1 [U] movement or a way of moving □ *gerakan; pergerakan; bergerak*: *The motion of the ship made us all feel sick.* ♦ *Pull the lever to set the machine in motion* (= make it start moving). ⊃ look at **slow motion** 2 [C] a formal suggestion at a meeting that you discuss and vote on □ *usul; cadangan*: *The motion was carried/rejected by a majority of eight votes.*

motion² /ˈməʊʃn/ *verb* [I,T] **motion to sb (to do sth); motion (for) sb (to do sth)** to make a movement, usually with your hand, that tells sb what to do □ *memberi isyarat; mengisyaratkan*: *I motioned to the waiter.* ♦ *The manager motioned for me to sit down.*

motionless /ˈməʊʃnləs/ *adj* not moving □ *tdk bergerak*

motivate /ˈməʊtɪveɪt/ *verb* [T] **1** [usually passive] to cause sb to act in a particular way □ *mendorong; didorong*: *Her reaction was motivated by fear.* **2** to make sb want to do sth, especially sth that involves hard work and effort □ *merangsang; memotivasikan*: *Our new teacher certainly knows how to motivate his classes.* ♦ *I just can't motivate myself to do anything this morning.* ▶ **motivated** *adj*: *highly motivated students* ▶ **motivation** /ˌməʊtɪˈveɪʃn/ *noun* [C,U]: *He's clever enough, but he lacks motivation.*

motive /ˈməʊtɪv/ *noun* [C,U] **(a) motive (for sth/doing sth)** a reason for doing sth, often sth bad □ *motif; tujuan*: *The police couldn't discover a motive for the murder.*

motor¹ /ˈməʊtə(r)/ *noun* [C] a device that uses petrol, gas, electricity, etc. to produce movement and makes a machine, etc. work □ *motor*: *The washing machine doesn't work. I think something is wrong with the motor.*

> **MORE** **Engine**, not **motor**, is usually used in connection with cars and motorbikes.

motor² /ˈməʊtə(r)/ *adj* [only before a noun] **1** having or using the power of an engine or a motor □ *bermotor*: *a motor vehicle* **2** (*especially BrE*) connected with vehicles that have engines, especially cars □ *(berkaitan dgn) kereta/kenderaan bermotor*: *the motor industry* ♦ *motor racing*

motorbike /ˈməʊtəbaɪk/ (*also formal* **motorcycle**) *noun* [C] a vehicle that has two wheels and an engine □ *motosikal; motor*: *He rides a classic Harley Davidson motorbike.* ♦ *Simon comes to work on a motorbike.* ⊃ picture on **page P7**

motorboat /ˈməʊtəbəʊt/ *noun* [C] a small fast boat that has a motor □ *motobot*

'motor car (*BrE formal*) = **car**(1)

motorcycle /ˈməʊtəsaɪkl/ (*formal*) = **motorbike**

motorcyclist /ˈməʊtəsaɪklɪst/ *noun* [C] a person who rides a motorbike □ *penunggang motosikal*

motoring /ˈməʊtərɪŋ/ *noun* [U] driving in a car □ *memandu; berkereta*: *a motoring holiday*

motorist /ˈməʊtərɪst/ *noun* [C] a person who drives a car □ *pemandu kereta* ⊃ note at **driving** ⊃ look at **pedestrian**

motorized (*also* -**ised**) /ˈməʊtəraɪzd/ *adj* [only before a noun] that has an engine □ *dilengkapi motor; bermotor*: *a motorized wheelchair*

motorway /ˈməʊtəweɪ/ (*AmE* **expressway, freeway**) *noun* [C] (*abbr* M) a wide road where traffic can travel fast for long distances between large towns □ *lebuh raya* ⊃ note at **road**

motto /ˈmɒtəʊ/ *noun* [C] (*pl* **mottoes** *or* **mottos**) a short sentence or phrase that expresses the aims and beliefs of a person, a group, an organization, etc □ *cogan kata*: *'Live and let live.' That's my motto.*

mould¹ (*AmE* **mold**) /məʊld/ *noun* **1** [C] a container that you pour a liquid or substance into. The liquid then becomes solid in the same shape as the container, for example after it has cooled or cooked □ *acuan*: *Pour the chocolate into the heart-shaped mould.* **2** [C, usually sing] a particular type □ *jenis; perwatakan*: *She doesn't fit into the usual mould of sales directors.* **3** [U] a soft green or black substance like fur that grows in wet places or on old food □ *kulapuk; cendawan* ⊃ look at **fungus** ▶ **mouldy** (*AmE* **moldy**) *adj*: *The cheese had gone mouldy.*

mould² (*AmE* **mold**) /məʊld/ *verb* [T] **mould A (into B); mould B (from/out of A)** to make sth into a particular shape or form by pressing it or by putting it into a **mould¹**(1) □ *membentuk; dibentuk*: *First mould the dough into a ball.* ♦ *a bowl moulded from clay*

moult (*AmE* **molt**) /məʊlt/ *verb* [I] (used about an animal or a bird) to lose hairs or feathers before growing new ones □ *bersalin bulu*

mound /maʊnd/ *noun* [C] **1** a large pile of earth or stones; a small hill □ *timbunan (tanah atau batu); busut; anak bukit* **2** (*spoken*) **a mound (of sth)** a pile or a large amount of sth □ *setimbun*: *I've got a mound of work to do.* **SYN** for both meanings **heap**

mount¹ /maʊnt/ *verb* **1** [T] to organize sth □ *mengadakan; menganjurkan; melancarkan*: *to mount a protest/a campaign/an exhibition/an attack* **2** [I] to increase gradually in level or amount □ *meningkat; bertambah*: *The tension mounted as the end of the match approached.* **3** [T] (*written*) to go up sth or up on to sth □ *naik ke; menaiki; memanjat*: *He mounted the platform and began to speak.* **4** [I,T] to get on a horse or bicycle □ *naik (ke atas)*: *He mounted his horse and rode away.* **OPP** dismount **5** [T] mount sth (on/onto/in sth) to fix sth firmly on sth else □ *memasang; melekapkan*: *The gas boiler was mounted on the wall.*

PHR V mount up to increase (often more than you want) □ *bertambah; meningkat*: *When you're buying food for six people the cost soon mounts up.*

mount² /maʊnt/ *noun* [C] Mount (*abbr* Mt) (used in names) a mountain □ *gunung*: *Mt Everest/Vesuvius/Fuji*

mountain /ˈmaʊntən/ *noun* [C] **1** a very high hill □ *gunung*: *Which is the highest mountain in the world?* ♦ *mountain roads/scenery/villages* ♦ *a mountain range* ⊃ picture on **page P10 2** a mountain (of sth) a large amount of sth □ *bertimbun*: *I've got a mountain of work to do.*

'mountain bike *noun* [C] a bicycle with a strong frame, wide tyres and many different gears (= speeds) designed for riding on rough ground □ *basikal bukit*

HELP We usually use **go mountain biking** to talk about riding a mountain bike for pleasure.

mountaineering /ˌmaʊntəˈnɪərɪŋ/ *noun* [U] the sport of climbing mountains □ *(kegiatan) mendaki gunung* ▶ mountaineer *noun* [C]

mountainous /ˈmaʊntənəs/ *adj* **1** having many mountains □ *bergunung-ganang*: *a mountainous region* **2** very large in size or amount □ *menggunung*: *The mountainous waves made sailing impossible.* **SYN** huge

mountainside /ˈmaʊntənsaɪd/ *noun* [C] the land on the side of a mountain □ *lereng gunung*

mounted /ˈmaʊntɪd/ *adj* [only before a noun] riding a horse □ *berkuda*: *mounted police*

mounting /ˈmaʊntɪŋ/ *adj* [only before a noun] increasing □ *(yg semakin meningkat/bertambah*: *mounting unemployment/tension/concern*

mourn /mɔːn/ *verb* [I,T] mourn (for/over) sb/sth to feel and show great sadness, especially because sb has died □ *bersedih; berkabung*: *He is still mourning (for) his wife.* ▶ mourning *noun* [U]: *He wore a black armband to show he was in mourning.*

mourner /ˈmɔːnə(r)/ *noun* [C] a person who goes to a funeral as a friend or relative of the person who has died □ *orang yg menghadiri upacara pengebumian yg berkabung*

mournful /ˈmɔːnfl/ *adj* (*written*) very sad □ *sedih; sayu*: *a mournful song* ▶ mournfully /-fəli/ *adv*

mouse /maʊs/ *noun* [C] (*pl* mice /maɪs/) **1** a very small animal with fur and a long thin tail □ *tikus*: *Mice, rats and hamsters are members of the rodent family.* **2** a piece of equipment, connected to a computer, for moving around the screen and entering commands without touching the keys □ *tetikus*: *Use the mouse to drag the icon to a new position.* ⊃ picture at **computer**

'mouse mat (*AmE* 'mouse pad) *noun* [C] a small piece of material that is the best kind of surface on which to use a computer mouse □ *pad tetikus; pelapik tetikus*

mousse /muːs/ *noun* [C,U] **1** a cold dessert (= a sweet food) made with cream and egg whites and flavoured with fruit, chocolate, etc.; a similar dish flavoured with fish, vegetables, etc. □ *mus (pencuci mulut)*: *a chocolate/strawberry mousse* ♦ *salmon mousse* **2** a substance that is used on hair to make it stay in a particular style □ *mus perapi (utk rambut)*

moustache (*AmE* mustache) /məˈstɑːʃ/ *noun* [C] hair that grows on a man's top lip, between the mouth and nose □ *misai* ⊃ picture at **hair**

mouth¹ /maʊθ/ *noun* [C] (*pl* mouths /maʊðz/) **1** the part of your face that you use for eating and speaking □ *mulut*: *to open/close your mouth* ⊃ picture at **body 2** the place where a river enters the sea □ *kuala; muara* **3** -mouthed /-maʊðd/ [in compounds] having a particular type of mouth or a particular way of speaking □ *dgn mulut (terlopong, dll); bermulut (bising, dll)*: *We stared open-mouthed in surprise.* ♦ *He's a loud-mouthed bully.*

IDM keep your mouth shut (*informal*) to not say sth to sb because it is a secret or because it will upset or annoy them □ *tdk buka mulut; tutup mulut*

mouth² /maʊð/ *verb* [I,T] to move your mouth as if you were speaking but without making any sound □ *menggerak-gerakkan mulut seolah-olah bercakap tanpa suara*: *Vinay was outside the window, mouthing something to us.*

mouthful /ˈmaʊθfʊl/ *noun* **1** [C] the amount of food or drink that you can put in your mouth at one time □ *sesuap; seteguk* **2** [sing] a word or phrase that is long or difficult to say □ *(sst) yg susah disebut*: *Her name is a bit of a mouthful.*

'mouth organ = harmonica

mouthpiece /ˈmaʊθpiːs/ *noun* [C] **1** the part of a telephone, musical instrument, etc. that you put in or near your mouth □ *corong cakap; pemipit* ⊃ picture at **music 2** a person, newspaper, etc. that a particular group uses to express its opinions □ *jurucakap*: *Pravda was the mouthpiece of the Soviet government.*

'mouth-watering *adj* (used about food) that looks or smells very good □ *mengecurkan air liur*

movable /ˈmuːvəbl/ *adj* that can be moved □ *boleh dialih* **OPP** fixed ⊃ look at **portable, mobile**

move¹ /muːv/ *verb*

move → MPV

➤ CHANGE POSITION **1** [I,T] to change position or to put sth in a different position □ *mengalihkan; bergerak*: The station is so crowded you **can hardly move**. ◆ Please move your car. It's blocking the road. ◆ The meeting has been moved to Thursday. **2** [I,T] **move along, down, over, up,** etc. to move (sth) further in a particular direction in order to make space for sb/sth else □ *beralih; alihkan*: If we move up a bit, Rob can sit here too. ◆ Move your head down—I can't see the screen.

➤ MAKE PROGRESS **3** [I] **move (on/ahead)** to make progress □ *bergerak maju; ada kemajuan*: When the new team of builders arrived, things started moving very quickly.

➤ TAKE ACTION **4** [I] to take action □ *bertindak*: Unless we move quickly lives will be lost.

➤ CHANGE HOUSE, JOB, ETC. **5** [I,T] to change the place where you live, work, study, etc. □ *berpindah; beralih*: Our neighbours are moving to Exeter next week. ◆ to **move house** ◆ Yuka's moved down to the beginners' class.

➤ CAUSE STRONG FEELINGS **6** [T] to cause sb to have strong feelings, especially of sadness □ *mengharukan; berasa terharu*: Many people were **moved to tears** by reports of the massacre.

IDM **get moving** to go, leave or do sth quickly □ *cepatlah (pergi, buat sst, dll)*
get sth moving to cause sth to make progress □ *mula membuat sst berjalan lancar, mencapai kemajuan, dsb*

PHR V **move in (with sb)** to start living in a new home (with sb) □ *pindah utk tinggal (bersama sso)*
move·off (used about a vehicle) to start a journey; to leave □ *pergi; mula bergerak*
move on (to sth) to start doing or discussing sth new □ *beralih kpd (sst yg lain)*
move out to leave your old home □ *berpindah*

move² /muːv/ noun [C] **1** a change of place or position □ *gerakan; langkah; gerak-geri*: She was watching every move I made. **2** a change in the place where you live or work □ *perpindahan; berpindah*: a move to a bigger house **3** action that you take because you want to achieve a particular result □ *langkah*: Both sides want to negotiate but neither is prepared to **make the first move**. ◆ Asking him to help me was **a good move**. **4** (in chess and other games) a change in the position of a piece □ *gerak; giliran (utk menggerakkan buah catur, dsb)*: It's your move.

IDM **be on the move** to be going somewhere □ *bergerak; berjalan; membuat perjalanan*: We've been on the move for four hours so we should stop for a rest.
get a move on (*informal*) to hurry □ *pergi cepat*: I'm late. I'll have to get a move on.
make a move to start to go somewhere □ *pergi; bertolak*: It's time to go home. Let's make a move.

movement /ˈmuːvmənt/ noun

➤ CHANGING POSITION **1** [C,U] an act of moving □ *pergerakan; gerakan; bergerak*: The dancer's movements were smooth and controlled. ◆ The seat belt doesn't allow much freedom of movement. ◆ I could see some movement (= sb/sth moving) in the trees. **2** [C,U] an act of moving or being moved from one place to another □ *pergerakan; bergerak*: the slow movement of the clouds across the sky

➤ GROUP OF PEOPLE **3** [C] a group of people who have the same aims or ideas □ *pergerakan; gerakan*: I support the peace movement.

➤ SB'S ACTIVITIES **4** **movements** [pl] sb's actions or plans during a period of time □ *gerak-geri*: Detectives have been watching the man's movements for several weeks.

➤ CHANGE OF IDEAS/BEHAVIOUR **5** [C, usually sing] **a movement (away from/towards sth)** a general change in the way people think or behave □ *pergerakan; arah aliran*: There's been a movement away from the materialism of the 1980s.

➤ MUSIC **6** [C] one of the main parts of a long piece of music □ *babak*: a symphony in four movements

movie /ˈmuːvi/ noun (*especially AmE*) **1** = film¹(1) □ *wayang*: Shall we go and see a movie? ◆ a science fiction/horror movie ◆ a movie director/star ◆ a movie theater (= a cinema) **2** **the movies** [pl] = **cinema**(1) □ *wayang*: Let's go to the movies.

moving /ˈmuːvɪŋ/ adj **1** causing strong feelings, especially of sadness □ *mengharukan; menyentuh perasaan*: a deeply moving speech/story **2** [only before a noun] that moves □ *bergerak*: It's a computerized machine with few moving parts.

mow /məʊ/ verb [I,T] (*pt* **mowed**; *pp* **mown** /məʊn/ or **mowed**) to cut grass using a **mower** □ *memesin rumput*: to mow the lawn

PHR V **mow sb down** to kill sb with a gun or a car □ *membunuh sso*

mower /ˈməʊə(r)/ noun [C] a machine for cutting grass □ *mesin potong rumput*: a lawnmower ◆ an electric mower

mown past participle of **mow**

MP /ˌem ˈpiː/ abbr (*especially BrE*) = **Member of Parliament**

MP3 /ˌem piː ˈθriː/ noun [C,U] a method of reducing the size of a computer file containing sound, or a file that is reduced in size in this way □ *mp3*

MP'3 player noun [C] a small piece of equipment that can store information taken from the Internet and that you carry with you, for example so that you can listen to music. An MP3 player can open and play MP3 files. □ *pemain mp3* ➔ note at **iPod™, listen, podcast**

mpg /ˌem piː ˈdʒiː/ abbr **miles per gallon** □ *bsg (batu segelen)*: This car does 40 mpg (= you can drive 40 miles on one gallon of petrol).

mph /ˌem piː ˈeɪtʃ/ abbr **miles per hour** □ *bsj (batu sejam)*: a 70 mph speed limit

MPV /ˌem piː ˈviː/ noun [C] **multi-purpose vehicle**; a large car that can carry a number of people □ *kenderaan serba guna*

Mr /ˈmɪstə(r)/ abbr used as a title before the name of a man □ *Encik: Mr (Matthew) Wallace* ♦ *I'd like to speak to Mr Wallace.* ➲ note at **Miss**

Mrs /ˈmɪsɪz/ abbr used as a title before the name of a married woman □ *Puan: Mrs (Belinda) Allan* ♦ *Good morning, Mrs Allan.* ➲ note at **Miss**

MS /ˌem ˈes/ abbr = **multiple sclerosis**

Ms /mɪz; məz/ used as a title before the family name of a woman who may or may not be married □ *gelaran sebelum nama sso wanita yg mungkin berkahwin atau tdk berkahwin: Ms (Keiko) Harada* ♦ *Dear Ms Harada, ...* ➲ note at **Miss**

> **MORE** Some women prefer the title **Ms** to **Mrs** or **Miss**. We can also use it if we do not know whether or not a woman is married.

MSc /ˌem es ˈsiː/ abbr Master of Science; a second degree that you receive when you complete a more advanced course or piece of research in a science subject at university or college □ *MSc (Sarjana Sains)* ➲ look at **BSc, MA**

Mt abbr = **Mount²** □ *G (Gunung): Mt Everest*

mth abbr (pl **mths**) = **month**

much /mʌtʃ/ determiner, pron, adv **1** [used with uncountable nouns, mainly in negative sentences and questions, or after *as, how, so, too*] a large amount of sth □ *banyak: I haven't got much money.* ♦ *Did she say much?* ♦ *You've given me too much food.* ♦ *How much time have you got?* ♦ *I can't carry that much!* ♦ *Eat as much as you can.* ♦ *How much is it* (= what does it cost)?

> **HELP** In positive statements we usually use **a lot of** NOT **much**: *I've got a lot of experience.*

2 to a great degree □ *sangat; kerap; lebih: I don't like her very much.* ♦ *Do you see Sashi much?* (= very often) ♦ *Do you see much of Sashi?* ♦ *much taller/prettier/harder* ♦ *much more interesting/unusual* ♦ *much more quickly/happily* ♦ *You ate much more than me.* **3** [with past participles used as adjectives] very □ *sangat; amat: a much-needed rest*

IDM **much the same** very similar □ *kira-kira sama: Softball is much the same as baseball.*
not much good (at sth) not skilled (at sth) □ *tdk berapa pandai: I'm not much good at singing.*
not much of a ... not a good ... □ *bukannya (misalnya, seorang tukang masak) yg pandai: She's not much of a cook.*
not up to much ➲ **up**
nothing much ➲ **nothing**

muck¹ /mʌk/ noun [U] **1** the waste from farm animals, used to make plants grow better □ *baja kandang/asli* ➲ A more common word is **manure**. **2** (*BrE informal*) dirt or mud □ *kotoran; lumpur*

muck² /mʌk/ verb (*informal*)
PHR V **muck about/around** to behave in a silly way or to waste time □ *main-main (membuang masa): Stop mucking around and come and help me!*
muck sth up to do sth badly; to spoil sth □ *membuat sst dgn teruk; merosakkan: I was so nervous that I completely mucked up my interview.*

mucus /ˈmjuːkəs/ noun [U] (*formal*) a sticky substance that is produced in some parts of the body, especially the nose □ *lendir; hingus*

mud /mʌd/ noun [U] soft, wet earth □ *lumpur: He came home from the football match covered in mud.*

muddle /ˈmʌdl/ verb [T] **1** muddle sth (up) to put things in the wrong place or order or to make them untidy □ *mencampuradukkan: Try not to get those papers muddled up.* **2** muddle sb (up) to confuse sb □ *mengelirukan; terkeliru: I do my homework and schoolwork in separate books so that I don't get muddled up.* ▶ muddle noun [C,U]: *If you get in a muddle, I'll help you.* ▶ muddled adj

muddy /ˈmʌdi/ adj (**muddier; muddiest**) full of or covered in mud □ *berlumpur: muddy boots* ♦ *It's very muddy down by the river.*

mudguard /ˈmʌdɡɑːd/ noun [C] a curved cover over the wheel of a bicycle or motorbike □ *madgad*

muesli /ˈmjuːzli/ noun [U] food made of grains, nuts, dried fruit, etc. that you eat with milk for breakfast □ *muesli*

muezzin /muˈezɪn; mjuː-/ noun [C] a man who calls Muslims to come to a **mosque** (= a religious building) to pray □ *muazin*

muffin /ˈmʌfɪn/ noun [C] **1** (*AmE* ˌEnglish ˈmuffin) a type of bread roll often eaten hot with butter □ *mufin* **2** a type of small cake □ *mufin; baulu* ➲ picture at **cake**

muffle /ˈmʌfl/ verb [T] to make a sound quieter and more difficult to hear □ *meredamkan: He put his hand over his mouth to muffle his laughter.* ▶ muffled adj: *I heard muffled voices outside.*

muffler /ˈmʌflə(r)/ (*AmE*) = **silencer**

mug¹ /mʌɡ/ noun [C] **1** a large cup with straight sides and a handle □ *kole: a coffee mug* ♦ *a mug of tea* ♦ *a beer mug* (= a large glass with a handle) ➲ picture at **cup, glass 2** (*informal*) a person who seems stupid □ *(orang yg) dungu*

mug² /mʌɡ/ verb [T] (**mugging; mugged**) to attack and steal from sb in the street □ *menyerang; menyamun: Keep your wallet out of sight or you'll get mugged.* ▶ mugger noun [C] ➲ note at **thief** ▶ mugging noun [C,U]: *The mugging took place around midnight.*

muggy /ˈmʌɡi/ adj (used about the weather) warm and slightly wet in an unpleasant way □ *panas dan lembap*

Muhammad (also Mohammed) /məˈhæmɪd/ noun [sing] the **prophet** (= a person who is chosen by God to give his message to

VOWELS iː see i any ɪ sit e ten æ hat ɑː father ɒ got ɔː saw ʊ put uː too u usual

mule → mundane

people) who started the religion of Islam □ *Nabi Muhammad s.a.w.*

mule /mjuːl/ *noun* [C] an animal that is used for carrying heavy loads and whose parents are a horse and a **donkey** (= an animal like a small horse with long ears) □ *baghal*

mull /mʌl/ *verb*
PHR V **mull sth over** to think about sth carefully and for a long time □ *memikir-mikirkan ttg sst*: *Don't ask me for a decision right now. I'll have to mull it over.*

multi- /'mʌlti/ [in compounds] more than one; many □ *multi-; berbilang; pelbagai*: *multi-coloured* ♦ *a multimillionaire* ♦ *a multi-ethnic society*

multicultural /ˌmʌlti'kʌltʃərəl/ *adj* for including people of many different races, languages, religions and customs □ *pelbagai budaya*: *a multicultural society*

multiculturalism /ˌmʌlti'kʌltʃərəlɪzəm/ *noun* [U] the practice of giving importance to all cultures in a society □ *fahaman pelbagai budaya*

multilateral /ˌmʌlti'lætərəl/ *adj* involving more than two groups of people, countries, etc. □ *berbilang hala*: *They signed a multilateral agreement.* ⊃ look at **bilateral, unilateral**

multimedia /ˌmʌlti'miːdiə/ *adj* [only before a noun] using sound, pictures and film on a computer in addition to text on the screen □ *multimedia*: *multimedia systems/products*

multinational[1] /ˌmʌlti'næʃnəl/ *adj* existing in or involving many countries □ *multinasional; berbilang negara*: *multinational companies*

multinational[2] /ˌmʌlti'næʃnəl/ *noun* [C] a large and powerful company that operates in several different countries □ *multinational*: *The company is owned by Ford, the US multinational.*

multiple[1] /'mʌltɪpl/ *adj* [only before a noun] involving many people or things or having many parts □ *berbagai-bagai; berbilang; banyak*: *a multiple pile-up* (= a crash involving many vehicles)

multiple[2] /'mʌltɪpl/ *noun* [C] a number that contains another number an exact number of times □ *angka kandungan*: *12, 18 and 24 are multiples of 6.*

multiple-choice *adj* (used about exam questions) showing several different answers from which you have to choose the right one □ *pelbagai pilihan*

EXAM TIP

Multiple-choice

Part of your exam might be a multiple-choice paper. Each question has three or four possible answers. You need to select the correct one by putting a mark in the box next to the answer you have chosen. Don't spend too long on any one question, and always give an answer. Even if you don't know the answer you can guess, and, who knows, you might be right!

---

multiple sclerosis /ˌmʌltɪpl sklə'rəʊsɪs/ *noun* [U] (*abbr* MS) a serious disease which causes you to slowly lose control of your body and become less able to move □ *sklerosis berbilang*

multiplex /'mʌltɪpleks/ *noun* [C] a large cinema with several separate rooms with screens □ *multipleks*

multiply /'mʌltɪplaɪ/ *verb* (multiplying; multiplies; *pt, pp* multiplied) **1** [I,T] multiply A by B to increase a number by the number of times mentioned □ *mendarab*: *2 multiplied by 4 makes 8 (2 x 4 = 8)* **OPP** divide **2** [I,T] to increase or make sth increase by a very large amount □ *menggandakan; berganda-ganda; bertambah*: *We've multiplied our profits over the last two years.* ▸ **multiplication** /ˌmʌltɪplɪ'keɪʃn/ *noun* [U] ⊃ look at **division, addition, subtraction**

multi-purpose /ˌmʌlti 'pɜːpəs/ *adj* that can be used for several different purposes □ *serba guna*: *a multi-purpose tool/machine*

multi-storey 'car park (also ˌmulti-'storey; *AmE* ˈparking garage) *noun* [C] a large building with several floors for parking cars in □ *tempat letak kereta bertingkat-tingkat*

multitasking /ˌmʌlti'tɑːskɪŋ/ *noun* [U] **1** the ability of a computer to operate several programs at the same time □ *(pengendalian) berbilang tugas; multitugas* **2** the activity of doing several things at the same time □ *membuat pelbagai kerja secara serentak; multitugas*

multitude /'mʌltɪtjuːd/ *noun* [C] (*formal*) a very large number of people or things □ *sangat ramai/banyak*

mum /mʌm/ (*AmE* mom) *noun* [C] (*informal*) mother □ *mak*: *Is that your mum?* ♦ *Can I have a drink, Mum?* ⊃ look at **mummy**

mumble /'mʌmbl/ *verb* [I,T] to speak quietly without opening your mouth properly, so that people cannot hear the words □ *menggumam*: *I can't hear if you mumble.* ⊃ look at **mutter**

mummy /'mʌmi/ *noun* [C] (*pl* mummies) **1** (*AmE* mommy) (*informal*) a child's word for mother □ *mak*: *Here comes your mummy now.* **2** the dead body of a person or an animal which has been kept by rubbing it with special oils and covering it in cloth □ *mumia*

mumps /mʌmps/ *noun* [U] an infectious disease, especially of children, that causes the neck to swell □ *beguk*: *to have/catch (the) mumps*

munch /mʌntʃ/ *verb* [I,T] munch (on sth) to bite and eat sth noisily □ *mengunyah*: *He sat there munching (on) an apple.*

mundane /mʌn'deɪn/ *adj* ordinary; not interesting or exciting □ *biasa; tdk menarik*: *a mundane job*

municipal /mjuːˈnɪsɪpl/ adj connected with a town or city that has its own local government □ *perbandaran*: municipal buildings (= the town hall, public library, etc.)

munitions /mjuːˈnɪʃnz/ noun [pl] military supplies, especially bombs and guns □ *senjata*

mural /ˈmjʊərəl/ noun [C] a large picture painted on a wall □ *mural; lukisan dinding*

murder /ˈmɜːdə(r)/ noun **1** [C,U] the crime of killing a person illegally and on purpose □ *pembunuhan*: to commit murder ◆ *a vicious murder* ◆ *the murder victim/weapon* ➪ note at **crime** ➪ look at **manslaughter 2** [U] (*informal*) a very difficult or unpleasant experience □ *(pengalaman yg sukar sekali atau memang teruk)*: It's murder trying to work when it's so hot.

IDM get away with murder to do whatever you want without being stopped or punished □ *berbuat sesuka hati*: He lets his students get away with murder.
▶**murder** verb [I,T] ➪ note at **kill** ▶**murderer** noun [C]

murderous /ˈmɜːdərəs/ adj intending or likely to murder □ *hendak atau mungkin membunuh*

murky /ˈmɜːki/ adj (murkier; murkiest) dark and unpleasant or dirty □ *suram; keruh; tdk bersih*: The water in the river looked very murky. ◆ (*figurative*) According to rumours, the new boss had a murky past.

murmur /ˈmɜːmə(r)/ verb [I,T] to say sth in a low quiet voice □ *membisikkan*: He murmured a name in his sleep. ▶**murmur** noun [C]

muscle /ˈmʌsl/ noun [C,U] one of the parts inside your body that you can make tight or relax in order to produce movement □ *otot*: Riding a bicycle is good for developing the leg muscles. ◆ Lifting weights builds muscle.

muscular /ˈmʌskjələ(r)/ adj **1** connected with the muscles □ *(berkenaan dgn) otot*: muscular pain/tissue **2** having large strong muscles □ *tegap dan berotot-otot*: a muscular body

museum /mjuˈziːəm/ noun [C] a building where collections of valuable and interesting objects are kept and shown to the public □ *muzium*: Have you been to the Science Museum in London? ➪ look at **gallery** ➪ picture on **page P11**

mushroom /ˈmʌʃrʊm; -ruːm/ noun [C] a type of plant which grows very quickly, has a flat or round top and can be eaten as a vegetable □ *cendawan* ➪ picture on **page P15**

MORE A mushroom is a type of **fungus**. Some, but not all, **fungi** can be eaten. **Toadstool** is a name for some types of poisonous fungi.

music /ˈmjuːzɪk/ noun [U] **1** an arrangement of sounds in patterns to be sung or played on instruments □ *muzik*: What sort of music do you like? ◆ classical/pop/rock music ◆ to write/compose music ◆ a music lesson/teacher ➪ note at **instrument, pop 2** the written signs that represent the sounds of music □ *skor muzik*: Can you read music?

TOPIC

Music

A large group of **musicians** playing **classical music** together on different **instruments** is an **orchestra**. They are directed by a **conductor**. Music is **composed** (= written) by a **composer** and musicians learn to **read music** in order to play it. There are different types of classical **composition**, for example a **symphony** (= a long piece of music for an orchestra) or an **opera** (= a piece for the theatre where the words are sung). Note that we usually say 'play **the** violin, the piano, etc.': *I've been learning the flute for four years*. When talking about modern music such as pop, rock, etc. it is possible to say 'play drums, guitar, etc.', without the: *He plays bass in a band*.

musical¹ /ˈmjuːzɪkl/ adj **1** [only before a noun] connected with music □ *(berkaitan dgn) muzik*: Can you play a musical instrument (= the piano, the violin, the trumpet, etc.)? **2** interested in or good at music □ *berbakat atau berminat dlm bidang muzik*: He's very musical. **3** having a pleasant sound like music □ *merdu*: a musical voice ▶**musically** /-kli/ adv: She is musically gifted.

musical² /ˈmjuːzɪkl/ noun [C] a play or film which has singing and dancing in it □ *muzikal* ➪ look at **opera**

musician /mjuˈzɪʃn/ noun [C] a person who plays a musical instrument or writes music, especially as a job □ *ahli muzik* ➪ note at **music**

Muslim (also **Moslem**) /ˈmʊzlɪm/ noun [C] a person whose religion is Islam □ *Muslim; orang Islam* ▶**Muslim** (also **Moslem**) adj: Muslim traditions/beliefs

muslin /ˈmʌzlɪn/ noun [U] a type of thin cotton cloth □ *muslin; kain kasa*

mussel /ˈmʌsl/ noun [C] a shellfish (= a creature with a shell that lives in water) that you can eat, with a black shell in two parts □ *kupang; siput sudu* ➪ picture at **shellfish**

must¹ /məst; strong form mʌst/ modal verb (negative **must not**; short form **mustn't** /ˈmʌsnt/) **1** used for saying that it is necessary that sth happens □ *mesti*: I must remember to go to the bank today. ◆ You mustn't take photographs in here. It's forbidden.

GRAMMAR Compare **must** and **have to**. **Must** expresses the speaker's personal opinion: *I must wash my hair tonight*. **Have to** expresses what is necessary according to a law or rule, or the opinion of a person in authority: *Children have to go to school*. ◆ *My doctor says I have to give up smoking*. ◆ *My doctor says I have to get more exercise*. In formal, written language **must** is also used to express laws or rules: Mo-

[C] **countable**, a noun with a plural form: *one book, two books*   [U] **uncountable**, a noun with no plural form: *some sugar*

Musical Instruments

strings

violin — bow — viola — cello — double bass — harp (string)

brass

French horn, tuba, trumpet, trombone, saxophone

woodwind

oboe (reed) — clarinet (key) — bassoon — recorder — piccolo — flute (mouthpiece)

percussion

bass drum, triangle, xylophone, tambourine, cymbals, kettledrum

keyboard, electric guitar (fret, amplifier), guitar, banjo

[I] **intransitive**, a verb which has no object: *He laughed.*   [T] **transitive**, a verb which has an object: *He ate an apple.*

bile phones must be switched off in the library. Be careful: **mustn't** means 'it is not allowed': *You mustn't use a dictionary in the exam.* **Don't have to** means 'it is not necessary': *This book is easy to understand, so you don't have to use a dictionary.*

2 used for saying that you feel sure that sth is true □ *tentu*: *Have something to eat. You must be hungry.* ♦ *I can't find my watch. I must have left it at home.*

GRAMMAR When you feel sure that sth is true *now*, use **must** with an infinitive: *I can smell smoke. There must be a fire somewhere.* When you feel sure that sth was true *in the past*, use **must have** with a past participle: *It's wet outside. It must have rained last night.* In sentences like this, **must have** is pronounced /mʌstəv/.

3 used for giving sb advice □ *harus; mesti*: *You really must see that film. It's wonderful.* ❶ For more information about modal verbs, look at the Reference Section at the back of this dictionary.

must[2] /mʌst/ *noun* [C] a thing that you strongly recommend □ *kemestian*: *This book is a must for all science fiction fans.*

mustache (*AmE*) = **moustache**

mustard /'mʌstəd/ *noun* [U] a cold yellow or brown sauce that tastes hot and is eaten in small amounts with meat □ *mustard*

musty /'mʌsti/ *adj* (**mustier**; **mustiest**) having an unpleasant old or wet smell because of a lack of fresh air □ *hapak*: *The rooms in the old house were dark and musty.*

mutant /'mju:tənt/ *noun* [C] a living thing that is different from other living things of the same type because of a change in its **genetic** (= basic) structure □ *mutan*

mutation /mju:'teɪʃn/ *noun* [C,U] a change in the **genetic** (= basic) structure of a living or developing thing; an example of such a change □ *mutasi*: *mutations caused by radiation*

mute /mju:t/ *adj* **1** not speaking □ *senyap; tdk berkata-kata; membisu*: *a look of mute appeal* ♦ *The child sat mute in the corner of the room.* **SYN** silent **2** (*old-fashioned*) (used about a person) unable to speak □ *bisu* **SYN** dumb

muted /'mju:tɪd/ *adj* **1** (used about colours or sounds) not bright or loud; soft □ *lembut* **2** (used about a feeling or reaction) not strongly expressed □ *tdk kuat; tdk secara lantang*: *muted criticism* ♦ *a muted response*

mutilate /'mju:tɪleɪt/ *verb* [T, usually passive] to damage sb's body very badly, often by cutting off parts □ *mencacatkan* ▶ **mutilation** /ˌmju:tɪ'leɪʃn/ *noun* [C,U]

mutiny /'mju:təni/ *noun* [C,U] (*pl* **mutinies**) an act of a group of people, especially sailors or soldiers, refusing to obey the person who is in command □ *pemberontakan*: *There'll be a mutiny if conditions don't improve.* ▶ **mutiny** *verb* [I]

mutter /'mʌtə(r)/ *verb* [I,T] to speak in a low,

571 **must → mystery**

quiet and often angry voice that is difficult to hear □ *menggumam; bersungut dgn suara yg perlahan*: *He muttered something about being late and left the room.* ➪ look at **mumble**

mutton /'mʌtn/ *noun* [U] the meat from an adult sheep □ *daging biri-biri* ➪ note at **meat**

mutual /'mju:tʃuəl/ *adj* **1** (used about a feeling or an action) felt or done equally by both people involved □ *saling; bersama*: *We have a mutual agreement* (= we both agree) *to help each other out when necessary.* ♦ *I just can't stand her and I'm sure the feeling is mutual* (= she doesn't like me either). **2** [only *before* a noun] shared by two or more people □ *bersama; sama-sama*: *mutual interests* ♦ *It seems that Jane is a mutual friend of ours.* ▶ **mutually** /-tʃuəli/ *adv*

muzzle /'mʌzl/ *noun* [C] **1** the nose and mouth of an animal, especially a dog or a horse □ *muncung* ➪ picture on **page P12 2** a cover made of leather or wire that is put over an animal's nose and mouth so that it cannot bite □ *berongsong* **3** the open end of a gun where the bullets come out □ *muncung* ▶ **muzzle** *verb* [T, usually passive]: *Dogs must be kept muzzled.*

MW *abbr* **1 medium wave**; a band of radio waves with a length of between 100 and 1000 metres □ *singkatan utk 'gelombang sederhana'* **2** (*pl* **MW**) **megawatt(s)** □ *megawatt*

my /maɪ/ *determiner* of or belonging to me □ *(milik) saya*: *This is my husband, Giles.* ♦ *My favourite colour is blue.* ➪ look at **mine**[1]

myself /maɪ'self/ *pron* **1** used when the person who does an action is also affected by it □ *diri saya (sendiri)*: *I looked at myself in the mirror.* ♦ *I felt rather pleased with myself.* **2** used to emphasize the person who does the action □ *saya sendiri*: *I'll speak to her myself.* ♦ *I'll do it myself* (= if you don't want to do it for me). **IDM** (**all**) **by myself 1** alone □ *seorang diri*: *I live by myself.* ➪ note at **alone 2** without help □ *sendiri*: *I painted the house all by myself.*

mysterious /mɪ'stɪəriəs/ *adj* **1** that you do not understand or cannot explain; strange □ *penuh misteri; aneh*: *Several people reported seeing mysterious lights in the sky.* **2** (used about a person) keeping sth secret or refusing to explain sth □ *berahsia-rahsia; merahsiakan*: *They're being very mysterious about where they're going this evening.* ▶ **mysteriously** *adv*

mystery /'mɪstri/ *noun* (*pl* **mysteries**) **1** [C] a thing that you cannot understand or explain □ *misteri; tanda tanya*: *The cause of the accident is a complete mystery.* ♦ *It's a mystery to me what my sister sees in her boyfriend.* **2** [U] the quality of being strange and secret and full of things that are difficult to explain □ *misteri; rahsia*: *There's a lot of mystery surrounding this case.* **3** [C] a story, film or play in which crimes or strange events are only explained at the end □ *cerita, filem, dsb misteri*: *Agatha Christie was a prolific writer of (murder) mysteries.*

mystic /ˈmɪstɪk/ noun [C] a person who spends their life developing their spirit and communicating with God or a god □ *ahli mistik; ahli sufi (Islam)*

mystical /ˈmɪstɪkl/ (also **mystic**) adj connected with the spirit; strange and wonderful □ *mistik; kebatinan; menakjubkan*: Watching the sun set over the island was an almost mystical experience.

mysticism /ˈmɪstɪsɪzəm/ noun [U] the belief that you can reach complete truth and knowledge of God or gods by prayer, thought and development of the spirit □ *(faham) mistik; kebatinan; tasawuf*: Eastern mysticism

mystify /ˈmɪstɪfaɪ/ verb [T] (**mystifying**; **mystifies**; pt, pp **mystified**) to make sb confused because they cannot understand sth □ *membingungkan; menghairankan*: I was mystified by the strange note he'd left behind.

mystique /mɪˈstiːk/ noun [U, sing] the quality of being mysterious or secret that makes sb/sth seem interesting or attractive □ *keanehan; kepelikan; perihal mistik*

myth /mɪθ/ noun [C] **1** a story from past times, especially one about gods and men of courage. **Myths** often explain natural or historical events. □ *mitos* **SYN** legend **2** an idea or story which many people believe but that does not exist or is false □ *dongeng; cerita karut*: The idea that money makes you happy is a myth.

mythical /ˈmɪθɪkl/ adj **1** existing only in **myths** (1) □ *mitos; dongengan*: mythical beasts/heroes **2** not real or true; existing only in the imagination □ *khayalan; khayali*

mythology /mɪˈθɒlədʒi/ noun [U] very old stories and the beliefs contained in them □ *mitologi; kumpulan mitos*: Greek and Roman mythology ▶ **mythological** /ˌmɪθəˈlɒdʒɪkl/ adj: mythological figures/stories

---

N, n /en/ noun [C,U] (pl **Ns**; **N's**; **n's** /enz/) the 14th letter of the English alphabet □ *N, n (huruf)*: 'Nicholas' begins with (an) 'N'.

N (AmE No.) abbr = **north¹**, **northern** □ *Utara*: N Yorkshire

naff /næf/ adj (BrE informal) lacking style, taste or quality □ *tiada gaya; cita rasa atau kualiti*: There was a naff band playing.

nag /næɡ/ verb (**nagging**; **nagged**) **1** [I,T] **nag (at) sb** to continuously complain to sb about their behaviour or to ask them to do sth many times □ *meleteri; berleter*: My parents are always nagging (at) me to work harder. **2** [I,T] to worry or trouble sb continuously □ *terus-menerus mengganggu*: a nagging doubt/headache

nail¹ /neɪl/ noun [C] **1** the thin hard layer that covers the ends of your fingers and toes □ *kuku*: Don't bite your nails! ♦ fingernails/toenails ➲ picture at **body 2** a small thin piece of metal that is used for holding pieces of wood together, hanging pictures on, etc. □ *paku*: to hammer in a nail ➲ picture at **bolt**
IDM hit the nail on the head ➲ **hit¹**

nail² /neɪl/ verb [T] to fasten sth to sth with a nail or nails □ *memakukan*
PHR V nail sb down (to sth) to make a person say clearly what they want or intend to do □ *menyuruh sso menentukan/menetapkan sst dgn pasti*: She says she'll visit us in the summer but I can't nail her down to a definite date.

ˈnail-biting adj [usually before a noun] making you feel very excited or anxious because you do not know what is going to happen □ *mencemaskan*: It's been a nail-biting couple of weeks waiting for my results.

ˈnail brush noun [C] a small brush for cleaning your nails □ *berus kuku* ➲ picture at **brush**

ˈnail file noun [C] a small metal tool with a rough surface that you use for shaping your nails □ *kikir kuku*

ˈnail polish (BrE also **ˈnail varnish**) noun [U] a liquid that people paint on their nails to give them colour □ *pengilat kuku*

naive (also **naïve**) /naɪˈiːv/ adj without enough experience of life and too ready to believe or trust other people □ *naif; masih mentah; betul bendul*: I was too naive to realize what was happening. ♦ a naive remark/question/view **SYN** innocent ▶ **naively** (also **naïvely**) adv: She naively accepted the first price he offered. ▶ **naivety** (also **naïvety** /naɪˈiːvəti/) noun [U]

naked /ˈneɪkɪd/ adj **1** not wearing any clothes □ *telanjang; tdk berpakaian; terdedah*: He came to the door naked except for a towel. ♦ naked shoulders/arms ➲ look at **bare**, **nude 2** [only before a noun] (used about sth that is usually covered) not covered □ *tdk bertutup/ bertudung; terbuka; terdedah*: a naked flame/ bulb/light **3** [only before a noun] (used about emotions, etc.) clearly shown or expressed in a way that is often shocking □ *terang-terangan, terbuka*: naked aggression/ambition/fear
IDM the naked eye the normal power of your eyes without the help of glasses, a machine, etc. □ *mata kasar*: Bacteria are too small to be seen with the naked eye.

name¹ /neɪm/ noun **1** [C] a word or words by which sb/sth is known □ *nama*: What's your name, please? ♦ Do you know the name of this flower? **2** [sing] an opinion that people have of a person or thing □ *nama*: That area of London has rather a bad name. **SYN** reputation **3** [C] a famous person □ *orang ternama*: All the big names in show business were invited to the party.
IDM by name using the name of sb/sth □ *(tahu)*

nama sso/sst: It's a big school but the head teacher knows all the children by name.

call sb names ⊃ **call**[1]

in the name of sb; **in sb's name** for sb/sth; officially belonging to sb □ *atas nama sso: The contract is in my name.*

in the name of sth used to give a reason or excuse for an action, even when what you are doing might be wrong □ *atas nama sst: They acted in the name of democracy.*

make a name for yourself; **make your name** to become well known and respected □ *mencipta nama: She made a name for herself as a journalist.*

TOPIC

Names

Your **first name** is the name your parents choose for you when you are born. In Christian countries this is sometimes called your **Christian name**. Your parents may give you one or more other names after your first name, called your **middle name**, which you rarely use except on formal, official documents, where all names are referred to as your **forenames**. **Surname** is the word usually used for your **family name** which you are born with. When a woman marries, she may change her surname to be the same as her husband's. Her surname before marriage is then called her **maiden name**.

name[2] /neɪm/ verb [T] **1 name sb/sth (after sb)** to give sb/sth a name □ *menamai: Columbia was named after Christopher Columbus.*

> **HELP** When you are saying what someone's name is, you can use **be called**: *Their youngest son is called Mark.*

2 to say what the name of sb/sth is □ *menamakan: The journalist refused to name the person who had given her the information.* ♦ *Can you name all the planets?* **3** to state sth exactly □ *menyebutkan: Name your price—we'll pay it!*

nameless /ˈneɪmləs/ adj **1** without a name or with a name that you do not know □ *tdk bernama; tdk diketahui namanya* **2** whose name is kept a secret □ *tdk disebutkan namanya: a well-known public figure who shall remain nameless* SYN **anonymous**

namely /ˈneɪmli/ adv (used for giving more detail about what you are saying) that is to say □ *iaitu: There is only one person who can overrule the death sentence, namely the President.*

namesake /ˈneɪmseɪk/ noun [C] a person who has the same name as another □ *(orang yg) senama*

nan /næn/ (also **nana**, **nanna**) noun [C] (informal) (used by children) grandmother □ *nenek: my nan and grandad*

nanny /ˈnæni/ noun [C] (pl **nannies**) a woman whose job is to look after a family's children and who usually lives in the family home □ *pengasuh kanak-kanak*

573 **name → narrow**

nanometre (AmE **nanometer**) /ˈnænəʊmiːtə(r)/ noun [C] (abbr **nm**) one thousand millionth of a metre □ *nanometer*

nanotechnology /ˌnænəʊtekˈnɒlədʒi/ noun [U] the branch of technology that deals with structures that are less than 100 **nanometres** long. Scientists often build these structures using individual **molecules** (= the smallest units into which a substance can be divided without changing its chemical nature) of substances. □ *nanoteknologi*

nap /næp/ noun [C] a short sleep that you have during the day □ *tidur sekejap* ⊃ look at **snooze** ▶ **nap** verb [I] (**napping**; **napped**)

nape /neɪp/ noun [sing] the back part of your neck □ *tengkuk*

napkin /ˈnæpkɪn/ noun [C] a piece of cloth or paper that you use when you are eating to protect your clothes or for cleaning your hands and mouth □ *napkin; kertas kesat tangan: a paper napkin* SYN **serviette**

nappy /ˈnæpi/ noun [C] (pl **nappies**) (AmE **diaper**) a piece of soft thick cloth or paper that a baby or very young child wears around its bottom and between its legs □ *lampin: Does his nappy need changing?* ♦ *disposable nappies* (= that you throw away when they have been used)

narcotic /nɑːˈkɒtɪk/ noun [C] **1** a powerful illegal drug that affects your mind in a harmful way □ *narkotik; dadah* **2** a substance or drug that relaxes you, stops pain, or makes you sleep □ *narkotik; ubat pelali, tidur, dsb* ▶ **narcotic** adj

narrate /nəˈreɪt/ verb [T] (formal) to tell a story □ *menceritakan* ▶ **narration** /nəˈreɪʃn/ noun [C,U]

narrative /ˈnærətɪv/ noun (formal) **1** [C] the description of events in a story □ *cerita; naratif* **2** [U] the process or skill of telling a story □ *penceritaan; kepandaian bercerita*

narrator /nəˈreɪtə(r)/ noun [C] the person who tells a story or explains what is happening in a play, film, etc. □ *pencerita; tukang cerita*

narrow[1] /ˈnærəʊ/ adj (**narrower**; **narrowest**) **1** having only a short distance from side to side □ *sempit; tdk lebar: The bridge is too narrow for two cars to pass.* OPP **wide, broad 2** by a small amount □ *sedikit; kecil; nyaris-nyaris: That was a very narrow escape. You were lucky.* ♦ *a narrow defeat/victory* **3** not large □ *terhad; terbatas; kecil: a narrow circle of friends* ▶ **narrowness** noun [U]

narrow[2] /ˈnærəʊ/ verb [I,T] to become or make sth narrower □ *dikecilkan; mengecilkan: The road narrows in 50 metres.* ♦ *He narrowed his eyes at her.*

PHR V **narrow sth down** to make a list of things smaller □ *mengehadkan/membataskan sst: The police have narrowed down their list of suspects to three.*

VOWELS iː **see** i **any** ɪ **sit** e **ten** æ **hat** ɑː **father** ɒ **got** ɔː **saw** ʊ **put** uː **too** u **usual**

narrowly /ˈnærəuli/ adv only by a small amount □ *nyaris-nyaris*

narrow-ˈminded adj not willing to listen to new ideas or to the opinions of other people □ *berfikiran sempit* OPP broad-minded, open-minded

nasal /ˈneɪzl/ adj **1** connected with the nose □ *(berkenaan dgn) hidung*: *a nasal spray* **2** (used about sb's voice) produced partly through the nose □ *sengau*

nasty /ˈnɑːsti/ adj (nastier; nastiest) very bad or unpleasant □ *teruk; tdk menyenangkan; marah*: *a nasty accident* ♦ *I had a nasty feeling he would love me.* ♦ *When she was asked to leave she got/turned nasty.* ♦ *a nasty bend in the road* ♦ *What's that nasty smell in this cupboard?* ▶ **nastily** adv ▶ **nastiness** noun [U]

nation /ˈneɪʃn/ noun [C] a country or all the people in a country □ *negara*: *a summit of the leaders of seven nations* ⊃ note at **country**

national¹ /ˈnæʃnəl/ adj connected with all of a country; typical of a particular country □ *nasional; kebangsaan; negara*: *Here is today's national and international news.* ♦ *a national newspaper* ♦ *national costume* ⊃ look at **international, regional, local** ▶ **nationally** /-nəli/ adv

national² /ˈnæʃnəl/ noun [C] (formal) a citizen of a particular country □ *rakyat; warganegara*

ˌnational ˈanthem noun [C] the official song of a country that is played at public events □ *lagu kebangsaan*

the ˌNational ˈHealth Service noun [sing] (abbr NHS) the system that provides free or cheap medical care for everyone in Britain and that is paid for by taxes □ *Perkhidmatan Kesihatan Negara (UK)* ⊃ look at **health service**

ˌNational Inˈsurance noun [U] (abbr NI) (in Britain) the system of payments that have to be made by employers and employees to the government to help people who are ill, unemployed, old, etc. □ *Insurans Nasional (UK)*: *to pay National Insurance contributions*

nationalise = nationalize

nationalism /ˈnæʃnəlɪzəm/ noun [U] **1** the desire of a group of people who share the same race, culture, language, etc. to form an independent country □ *nasionalisme* **2** a feeling of love or pride for your own country; a feeling that your country is better than any other □ *nasionalisme; semangat kebangsaan*

nationalist /ˈnæʃnəlɪst/ noun [C] a person who wants their country or region to become independent □ *nasionalis; pejuang kebangsaan*: *a Welsh nationalist*

nationalistic /ˌnæʃnəˈlɪstɪk/ adj having strong feelings of love for or pride in your own country so that you think it is better than any other □ *nasionalistik; bersemangat kebangsaan*

HELP Nationalistic is usually used in a critical way, meaning that a person's feelings of pride are too strong.

nationality /ˌnæʃəˈnæləti/ noun [C,U] (pl nationalities) the state of being legally a citizen of a particular country □ *kerakyatan; kewarganegaraan*: *to have French nationality* ♦ *students of many nationalities* ♦ *to have dual nationality* (= of two countries)

nationalize (also -ise) /ˈnæʃnəlaɪz/ verb [T] to put a company or an organization under the control of the government □ *memiliknegarakan* OPP privatize ▶ **nationalization** (also -isation) /ˌnæʃnəlaɪˈzeɪʃn/ noun [U]

ˌnational ˈpark noun [C] a large area of beautiful land that is protected by the government so that the public can enjoy it □ *taman negara*

nationwide /ˌneɪʃnˈwaɪd/ adj, adv over the whole of a country □ *seluruh negara*: *The police launched a nationwide hunt for the killer.*

native¹ /ˈneɪtɪv/ adj **1** [only before a noun] connected with the place where you were born or where you have always lived □ *asal; ibunda*: *your native language/country/city* ♦ *native Londoners* **2** [only before a noun] connected with the people who originally lived in a country before other people, especially white people, came to live there □ *asli; peribumi*: *native art/dance*

HELP Be careful. This sense of **native** is sometimes considered offensive

3 native (to ...) (used about an animal or plant) living or growing naturally in a particular place □ *asli; berasal drpd*: *This plant is native to South America.* ♦ *a native species/habitat*

native² /ˈneɪtɪv/ noun [C] **1** a person who was born in a particular place □ *anak watan*: *a native of New York* **2** [usually pl] (old-fashioned) the people who were living in Africa, America, etc. originally, before the Europeans arrived there □ *peribumi*

HELP Be careful. This sense of **native** is now considered offensive.

ˌNative Aˈmerican (also Aˌmerican ˈIndian) adj, noun [C] (of) a member of the race of people who were the original people to live in America □ *peribumi Amerika*

ˌnative ˈspeaker noun [C] a person who speaks a language as their first language and has not learnt it as a foreign language □ *penutur asli*: *All our Spanish teachers are native speakers.*

NATO (also Nato) /ˈneɪtəu/ abbr North Atlantic Treaty Organization; a group of European countries, Canada and the US, who agree to give each other military help if necessary □ *NATO (Pertubuhan Perjanjian Atlantik Utara)*

natural /ˈnætʃrəl/ adj **1** [only before a noun] existing in nature; not made or caused by humans □ *semula jadi*: *I prefer to see animals in their natural habitat rather than in zoos.* ♦ *Britain's* *natural resources* include coal, oil and gas. ◆ She died of *natural causes* (= of old age or illness). **2** usual or normal □ *biasa; memang wajar*: It's natural to feel nervous before an interview. **OPP** **unnatural** **3** that you had from birth or that was easy for you to learn □ *semula jadi*: a natural gift for languages **4** [only *before* a noun] (used about parents or their children) related by blood □ *(anak) kandung/sebenar*: She's his stepmother, not his natural mother.

natural history noun [U] the study of plants and animals □ *kajian alam semula jadi*

naturalist /ˈnætʃrəlɪst/ noun [C] a person who studies plants and animals □ *ahli alamiah*

naturalize (also **-ise**) /ˈnætʃrəlaɪz/ verb [T, usually passive] to make sb a citizen of a country where they were not born □ *mewarganegarakan* ▶**naturalization** (also **-isation**) /ˌnætʃrəlaɪˈzeɪʃn/ noun [U]

naturally /ˈnætʃrəli/ adv **1** of course; as you would expect □ *sudah tentu*: The team was naturally upset about its defeat. **2** in a natural way; not forced or artificial □ *secara semula jadi*: naturally wavy hair ◆ He is naturally a very cheerful person. **3** in a way that is relaxed and normal □ *bersahaja*: Don't try and impress people. Just act naturally.

nature /ˈneɪtʃə(r)/ noun **1** [U] all the plants, animals, etc. in the universe and all the things that happen in it that are not made or caused by people □ *alam semula jadi*: the forces of nature (for example volcanoes, hurricanes, etc.) ◆ the wonders/beauties of nature ⬆ note at **scenery**

HELP You cannot say 'the nature' with this meaning. Use another word: I love walking in **the countryside**. ◆ We have to protect **the environment**.

2 [C,U] the qualities or character of a person or thing □ *sifat (semula jadi)*: It's not in his nature to be unkind. ◆ It's human nature never to be completely satisfied. ◆ She's basically honest by nature. **3** [sing] a type of sth □ *jenis*: I'm not very interested in things of that nature. ◆ books of a scientific nature **4 -natured** [in compounds] having a particular quality or type of character □ *bersifat*: a kind-natured man
IDM second nature ⬆ **second¹**

naughty /ˈnɔːti/ adj (**naughtier; naughtiest**) (especially *BrE*) (when you are talking to or about a child) not obeying □ *nakal*: It was very naughty of you to wander off on your own. **SYN** **badly behaved** ▶**naughtily** adv ▶**naughtiness** noun [U]

nausea /ˈnɔːziə/ noun [U] the feeling that you are going to **vomit** (= bring up food from the stomach) □ *rasa loya* ⬆ look at **sick**

nauseate /ˈnɔːzieɪt/ verb [T] to cause sb to feel sick or disgusted □ *meloyakan; menjijikkan* ▶**nauseating** adj

nautical /ˈnɔːtɪkl/ adj connected with ships, sailors or sailing □ *nautika*

---

575 **natural history → near**

naval /ˈneɪvl/ adj connected with the navy □ *(berkenaan dgn) tentera laut*: a naval base/officer/battle

navel /ˈneɪvl/ (also informal **belly button**) noun [C] the small hole or lump in the middle of your stomach □ *pusat*

navigable /ˈnævɪɡəbl/ adj (used about a river or narrow area of sea) that boats can sail along □ *boleh dilalui/dilayari*

navigate /ˈnævɪɡeɪt/ verb **1** [I] to use a map, etc. to find your way to somewhere □ *memandu arah*: If you drive, I'll navigate. ⬆ look at **satnav** **2** [T] to sail a boat along a river or across a sea □ *melayari* **3** [I,T] to find your way around on the Internet or on a website □ *melayari* ▶**navigator** /ˈnævɪɡeɪtə(r)/ noun [C] ▶**navigation** /ˌnævɪˈɡeɪʃn/ noun [U]

navy /ˈneɪvi/ noun [C, with sing or pl verb] (*pl* **navies**) the part of a country's armed forces that fights at sea in times of war □ *tentera laut*: to join the navy/the Navy ◆ Their son is in **the navy**/the Navy. ⬆ note at **war** ⬆ look at **air force, army, merchant navy** ⬆ *adjective* **naval**

GRAMMAR In the singular, **navy** is used with a singular or plural verb: The Navy is/are introducing a new warship this year.

navy blue (also **navy**) adj, noun [U] (of) a very dark blue colour □ *biru tua*

NB (also **nb**) /ˌen ˈbiː/ abbr (from Latin **nota bene**; used before a written note) take special notice of □ *Perhatian*: NB There is a charge for reservations.

NE abbr = **north-east¹** □ *Timur Laut*: NE Scotland

near¹ /nɪə(r)/ adj (**nearer; nearest**) adv, prep **1** not far away in time or distance; close □ *dekat; terdekat*: Let's walk to the library. It's quite near. ◆ We're hoping to move to Wales in the near future (= very soon). ◆ Where's the nearest Post Office? ◆ The day of the interview was getting nearer. ◆ It's a little village near Cardiff. ⬆ note at **nearby, next**

HELP Near or **close? Close** and **near** are often the same in meaning but in some phrases, such as the following, only one of them may be used: a close friend/relative ◆ the near future ◆ a close contest

2 near- [in compounds] almost □ *hampir*: a near-perfect performance **3** [usually **nearest**] similar; most similar □ *paling sama dgn*: He was the nearest thing to (= the person most like) a father she had ever had. ⬆ look at **o.n.o.**
IDM close/dear/near to sb's heart ⬆ **heart** a near miss a situation where sth nearly hits you or where sth bad nearly happens □ *hampir-hampir kena; sipi-sipi; nyaris-nyaris*: The bullet flew past his ear. It was a very near miss. a near thing a situation in which you are successful, but which could also have ended badly □ *sst*

[C] **countable**, a noun with a plural form: *one book, two books* | [U] **uncountable**, a noun with no plural form: *some sugar*

near → need 576

yg mujur: *Phew! That was a near thing! It could have been a disaster.*
nowhere near ⊃ nowhere
to the nearest ... followed by a number when you are calculating or measuring approximately □ *paling hampir*: *We worked out the cost to the nearest 50 dollars.*

near² /nɪə(r)/ *verb* [T,I] to get closer to sth in time or distance □ *semakin dekat; mendekati*: *At last we were nearing the end of the project.*

nearby /ˌnɪəˈbaɪ/ *adj, adv* not far away in distance □ *berdekatan*: *A new restaurant has opened nearby.* ♦ *We went out to a nearby restaurant.*

> **HELP** **Nearby** or **near**? Notice that **nearby** as an adjective is only used before the noun. **Near** cannot be used before a noun in this way: *We went out to a nearby restaurant.* ♦ *The restaurant we went to is quite near.*

nearly /ˈnɪəli/ *adv* almost; not completely or exactly □ *hampir; hampir-hampir*: *It's nearly five years since I've seen him.* ♦ *Linda was so badly hurt she very nearly died.* ♦ *It's not far now. We're nearly there.*
IDM **not nearly** much less than; not at all □ *tdk*: *It's not nearly as warm as it was yesterday.*

nearsighted /ˌnɪəˈsaɪtɪd/ (*especially AmE*) = **short-sighted**

neat /niːt/ *adj* (**neater**; **neatest**) **1** arranged or done carefully; tidy and in order □ *kemas; rapi*: *Please keep your room neat and tidy.* ♦ *neat rows of figures* **2** (used about a person) liking to keep things tidy and in order □ *kemas; rapi*: *The new secretary was very neat and efficient.* **3** simple but clever □ *bijak*: *a neat solution/explanation/idea/trick* **4** (*AmE informal*) good; nice □ *bagus; baik*: *That's a really neat car!* **5** (*AmE straight*) (used about an alcoholic drink) on its own, without ice, water or any other liquid □ *keras; tdk bercampur ais, air, dsb*: *a neat whisky* ▶ **neatly** *adv*: *neatly folded clothes* ▶ **neatness** *noun* [U]

necessarily /ˈnesəsərəli; ˌnesəˈserəli/ *adv* used to say that sth cannot be avoided or has to happen □ *semestinya; memanglah*: *The number of tickets available is necessarily limited.*
IDM **not necessarily** used to say that sth might be true but is not definitely or always true □ *tdk semestinya*

necessary /ˈnesəsəri/ *adj* **necessary (for sb/sth) (to do sth)** that is needed for a purpose or a reason □ *perlu*: *A good diet is necessary for a healthy life.* ♦ *It's not necessary for you all to come.* ♦ *If necessary, I can pick you up after work that day.*
SYN **essential** **OPP** **unnecessary**

necessitate /nəˈsesɪteɪt/ *verb* [T] (*formal*) to make sth necessary □ *memerlukan*

necessity /nəˈsesəti/ *noun* (*pl* **necessities**) **1** [U] **necessity (for sth/to do sth)** the need for sth; the fact that sth must be done or must happen □ *perlu; perlunya; terpaksa*: *Is there any necessity for change?* ♦ *There's no necessity to write every single name down.* ♦ *They sold the car out of necessity* (= because they had to). **2** [C] something that you must have □ *keperluan*: *Clean water is an absolute necessity.*

neck /nek/ *noun* [C] **1** the part of your body that joins your head to your shoulders □ *leher*: *She wrapped a scarf around her neck.* ♦ *Giraffes have long necks.* ⊃ picture at **body** **2** the part of a piece of clothing that goes round your neck □ *leher baju*: *a polo-neck/V-neck sweater* ♦ *The neck on this shirt is too tight.* ⊃ picture on page **P1** **3** **-necked** [in compounds] having the type of neck mentioned □ *berleher*: *a round-necked sweater* **4** [C] the long narrow part of sth □ *leher*: *the neck of a bottle*
IDM **by the scruff (of the/sb's neck) ⊃ scruff**
neck and neck (with sb/sth) equal or level with sb in a race or competition □ *sama-sama di hadapan*
up to your neck in sth having a lot of sth to deal with □ *sangat sibuk*: *We're up to our necks in work at the moment.*

necklace /ˈnekləs/ *noun* [C] a piece of jewellery that you wear around your neck □ *kalung* ⊃ picture at **jewellery**

necktie /ˈnektaɪ/ (*AmE*) = **tie²**(1)

nectar /ˈnektə(r)/ *noun* [U] a sweet liquid that is produced by flowers and collected by **bees** (= black and yellow insects) to make **honey** (= a sweet substance that we eat) □ *nektar; manisan bunga*

née /neɪ/ *adj* used in front of the family name that a woman had before she got married □ *nee (merujuk kpd nama keluarga sso wanita sebelum berkahwin)*: *Louise Mitchell, née Greenan* ⊃ look at **maiden name**

need¹ /niːd/ *verb* [T] [not usually used in the continuous tenses] **1** **need sb/sth (for sth/to do sth)** if you need sb/sth, you want or must have them or it □ *memerlukan; perlu*: *All living things need water.* ♦ *I need a new bag. The strap's broken on this one.* ♦ *Does Roshni need any help?* ♦ *I need to find a doctor.* ♦ *I need you to go to the shop for me.* **2** to have to □ *perlu*: *Do we need to buy the tickets in advance?* ♦ *I need to ask some advice.* ♦ *You didn't need to bring any food but it was very kind of you.*

> **GRAMMAR** Note that the question form of the main verb **need** is **do I need?**, etc. and the past tense is **needed** (question form **did you need?**, etc.; negative **didn't need**).

3 **need (sth) doing** if sth needs doing, it is necessary or must be done □ *perlu*: *This jumper needs washing.* ♦ *He needed his eyes testing.*

need² /niːd/ *modal verb*

> **GRAMMAR** The forms of **need** as a modal verb are: present tense **need** in all persons; negative **need not** (needn't /ˈniːdnt/), question form **need I?**, etc.

[I] **intransitive**, a verb which has no object: *He laughed.*   [T] **transitive**, a verb which has an object: *He ate an apple.*

[not used in the continuous tenses; used mainly in questions or negative sentences after *if* and *whether*, or with words like *hardly, only, never*] to have to □ *perlu*: *Need we pay the whole amount now?* ◆ *You needn't come to the meeting if you're too busy.* ◆ *I **hardly** need remind you* (= you already know) *that this is very serious.*

> **GRAMMAR** When talking about the past, **needn't have** with a past participle shows that you *did* something but discovered after doing it that it was *not* necessary: *I needn't have gone to the hospital* (= I went but it wasn't necessary). **Didn't need to** with an infinitive usually means that you did *not* do something because you *already* knew that it was not necessary: *I didn't need to go to the hospital* (= I didn't go because it wasn't necessary).

ℹ For more information about modal verbs, look at the **Reference Section** at the back of this dictionary.

need³ /niːd/ *noun* **1** [U, sing] **need (for sth); need (for sb/sth) to do sth** a situation in which you must have or do sth □ *keperluan; perlu*: *We are all in need of a rest.* ◆ *There is a growing need for new books in schools.* ◆ *There's no need for you to come if you don't want to.* ◆ *Do phone me if you feel the need to talk to someone.* **2** [C, usually pl] the things that you must have □ *keperluan*: *He doesn't earn enough to pay for his basic needs.* ◆ *Parents must consider their children's emotional as well as their physical needs.* **3** [U] the state of not having enough food, money or support □ *kesusahan*: *a campaign to help families in need*

needle /ˈniːdl/ *noun* [C]
▶FOR SEWING **1** a small thin piece of metal with a point at one end and an **eye** (= a hole) at the other that is used for sewing □ *jarum*: *to thread a needle with cotton* ➔ look at **pins and needles** ➔ picture at **sew**
▶FOR KNITTING **2** (also ˈknitting needle) one of two long thin pieces of metal or plastic with a point at one end that are used for knitting □ *jarum kait*: *knitting needles* ➔ picture at **sew**
▶FOR DRUGS **3** the sharp metal part of a **syringe** (= an instrument that is used for putting drugs into sb's body or for taking blood out) □ *jarum suntikan*: *a hypodermic needle* ➔ picture at **medicine**
▶ON INSTRUMENT **4** a thin metal part on a scientific instrument that moves to point to the correct measurement or direction □ *jarum*: *The needle on the petrol gauge showed 'empty'.*
▶ON TREE **5** the thin, hard pointed leaf of certain trees that stay green all year □ *jejarum*: *pine needles* ➔ picture at **tree**

needless /ˈniːdləs/ *adj* that is not necessary and that you can easily avoid □ *tdk perlu*: *We had gone through a lot of needless worry. He was safe at home.* ▶**needlessly** *adv*

needlework /ˈniːdlwɜːk/ *noun* [U] something that you sew by hand, especially for decoration □ *jahit-menjahit*

needy /ˈniːdi/ *adj* (**needier; neediest**) **1** not having enough money, food, clothes, etc. □ *serba kekurangan; susah; miskin* **2 the needy** *noun* [pl] people who do not have enough money, food, clothes, etc. □ *orang yg serba kekurangan/susah/miskin*

negative¹ /ˈneɡətɪv/ *adj* **1** bad or harmful □ *negatif; tdk baik*: *The effects of the new rule have been rather negative.* **OPP** **positive 2** only thinking about the bad qualities of sb/sth □ *negatif*: *I'm feeling very negative about my job—in fact I'm thinking about leaving.* ◆ *If you go into the match with a negative attitude, you'll never win.* **OPP** **positive 3** (used about a word, phrase or sentence) meaning 'no' or 'not' □ *negatif; tdk; bukan*: *a negative sentence* ◆ *His reply was negative/He gave a negative reply* (= he said 'no'). **OPP** **affirmative 4** (*abbr* **neg.**) (used about a medical or scientific test) showing that sth has not happened or has not been found □ *negatif*: *The results of the pregnancy test were negative.* **OPP** **positive 5** (used about a number) less than zero □ *negatif; kurang drpd sifar* **OPP** **positive** ▶**negatively** *adv*

negative² /ˈneɡətɪv/ *noun* [C] **1** a word, phrase or sentence that says or means 'no' or 'not' □ *negatif; (kata ungkapan, dsb) nafi*: *Roger answered in the negative* (= he said no). ◆ *'Never', 'neither' and 'nobody' are all negatives.* **OPP** **affirmative 2** a piece of film from which we can make a photograph. The light areas of a negative are dark on the final photograph and the dark areas are light. □ *negatif*

neglect /nɪˈɡlekt/ *verb* [T] **1** to give too little or no attention or care to sb/sth □ *mengabaikan; terbiar*: *Don't neglect your health.* ◆ *The old house had stood neglected for years.* **2** (*formal*) **neglect to do sth** to fail or forget to do sth □ *cuai; gagal; terlupa*: *He neglected to mention that he had spent time in prison.* ▶**neglect** *noun* [U]: *The garden was like a jungle after years of neglect.* ▶**neglected** *adj*: *neglected children*

negligence /ˈneɡlɪdʒəns/ *noun* [U] not being careful enough; lack of care □ *kecuaian*: *The accident was a result of negligence.* ▶**negligent** /ˈneɡlɪdʒənt/ *adj* ▶**negligently** *adv*

negligible /ˈneɡlɪdʒəbl/ *adj* very small and therefore not important □ *sedikit sahaja*

negotiable /nɪˈɡəʊʃiəbl/ *adj* that can be decided or changed by discussion □ *boleh dirunding*: *The price is not negotiable/non-negotiable.*

negotiate /nɪˈɡəʊʃieɪt/ *verb* **1** [I] **negotiate (with sb) (for/about sth)** to talk to sb in order to decide or agree about sth □ *berunding*: *The unions are still negotiating with management about this year's pay claim.* **2** [T] to decide or agree sth by talking about it □ *merundingkan*: *to negotiate an agreement/a deal/a settlement* **3** [T] to get over, past or through sth difficult □ *melalui; melepasi*: *To escape, prisoners would have to negotiate a five-metre wall.* ▶**negotiator** *noun* [C]

negotiation /nɪˌɡəʊʃiˈeɪʃn/ noun [pl, U] discussions at which people try to decide or agree sth □ *rundingan; perundingan*: *to enter into/break off negotiations* ♦ *The pay rise is still* **under negotiation**.

neigh /neɪ/ noun [C] the long high sound that a horse makes □ *ringkik (bunyi kuda)* ▶ **neigh** verb [I]

neighbour (AmE **neighbor**) /ˈneɪbə(r)/ noun [C] **1** a person who lives near you □ *jiran*: *My neighbours are very friendly.* ♦ *our* **next-door neighbours 2** a person or thing that is near or next to another □ *(orang atau sst yg) dekat/sebelah-menyebelah; jiran*: *Britain's nearest neighbour is France.* ♦ *Discuss the answers with your neighbour.*

neighbourhood (AmE **neighborhood**) /ˈneɪbəhʊd/ noun [C] a particular part of a town and the people who live there □ *kawasan (kejiranan)*: *a friendly neighbourhood*

neighbouring (AmE **neighboring**) /ˈneɪbərɪŋ/ adj [only before a noun] near or next to □ *berdekatan; berjiran*: *Farmers from neighbouring villages come into town each week for the market.*

neighbourly (AmE **neighborly**) /ˈneɪbəli/ adj friendly and helpful □ *ramah mesra dan suka membantu jiran*

neither /ˈnaɪðə(r); ˈniːðə(r)/ determiner, pron, adv **1** (used about two people or things) not one and not the other □ *kedua-dua... (misalnya, pasukan) tdk...*: *Neither team played very well.* ♦ *Neither of the teams played very well.* ♦ *'Would you like tea or juice?' 'Neither, thank you. I'm not thirsty.'*

> **GRAMMAR** Notice that **neither** is followed by a singular noun and verb: *Neither day was suitable.* The noun or pronoun that follows **neither of** is in the plural but the verb may be singular or plural: *Neither of the days is/are suitable.*

2 also not; not either □ *juga tdk*: *I don't eat meat and neither does Carlos.* ♦ *'I don't like fish.' 'Neither do I.'* ♦ *(informal) 'I don't like fish.' 'Me neither.'*

> **GRAMMAR** In this sense **nor** can be used in the same way: *'I don't like fish.' 'Nor do I.'* Notice that when you use **not ... either** the order of words is different: *I don't eat meat and Carlos doesn't either.* ♦ *'I haven't seen that film.' 'I haven't either.'*

3 neither ... nor not ... and not □ *baik... mahupun... tdk*: *Neither Carlos nor I eat meat.* ➪ look at **either**

> **GRAMMAR Neither ... nor** can be used with a singular or a plural verb: *Neither Stella nor Meena was/were at the meeting.*

neon /ˈniːɒn/ noun [U] (symbol **Ne**) a type of gas that is used for making bright lights and signs □ *neon*

nephew /ˈnefjuː; ˈnevjuː/ noun [C] the son of your brother or sister; the son of your husband's or wife's brother or sister □ *anak saudara lelaki* ➪ look at **niece**

nepotism /ˈnepətɪzəm/ noun [U] giving unfair advantages to your own family if you are in a position of power, especially by giving them jobs □ *nepotisme*

Neptune /ˈneptjuːn/ noun [sing] the planet that is 8th in order from the sun □ *Neptun*

nerd /nɜːd/ noun [C] (informal) a person who spends a lot of time on a particular interest and who is not always popular or fashionable □ *orang yg tdk bergaya dan membosankan*: *a computer nerd* **SYN geek** ▶ **nerdy** adj

nerve /nɜːv/ noun **1** [C] one of the long thin threads in your body that carry feelings or other messages to and from your brain □ *saraf*: *nerve endings* **2 nerves** [pl] worried, nervous feelings □ *rasa gemuruh*: *Breathing deeply should help to* **calm/steady your nerves**. ♦ *I was a* **bag of nerves** *before my interview.* **3** [U] the courage that you need to do sth difficult or dangerous □ *keberanian*: *Racing drivers need a lot of nerve.* ♦ *He didn't* **have the nerve** *to ask Maria to go out with him.* ♦ *Some pilots* **lose their nerve** *and can't fly any more.* **4** [sing, U] (informal) a way of behaving that people think is not acceptable □ *berani betul*: *You've got a nerve, calling me lazy!*
IDM get on sb's nerves (informal) to annoy sb or make sb angry □ *menyebabkan sso marah*

ˈnerve-racking adj making you very nervous or worried □ *amat membingungkan/mencemaskan; penuh ketegangan*

nervous /ˈnɜːvəs/ adj **1 nervous (about/of sth/doing sth)** worried or afraid □ *berasa gugup/risau; takut*: *I'm a bit nervous about travelling on my own.* ♦ *I always* **get nervous** *just before a match.* ♦ *a nervous laugh/smile/voice* ♦ *She was nervous of giving the wrong answer.* **OPP confident 2** connected with the nerves of the body □ *(berkaitan dgn) saraf*: *a nervous disorder* ▶ **nervously** adv ▶ **nervousness** noun [U]

ˌnervous ˈbreakdown (also **breakdown**) noun [C] a time when sb suddenly becomes so unhappy that they cannot continue living and working normally □ *patah jiwa*: *to have a nervous breakdown*

the ˈnervous system noun [C] your brain and all the nerves in your body □ *sistem saraf*

nest /nest/ noun [C] **1** a structure that a bird builds to keep its eggs and babies in □ *sarang* ➪ picture on **page P12 2** the home of certain animals or insects □ *sarang*: *a wasps' nest* ▶ **nest** verb [I]

ˈnest egg noun [C] (informal) an amount of money that you save to use in the future □ *wang simpanan*

nestle /ˈnesl/ verb [I,T] to be or go into a position where you are comfortable, protected or hidden □ *duduk, dsb dlm keadaan selesa, terlindung atau tersembunyi*: *The baby nestled her head on her mother's shoulder.*

net¹ /net/ noun **1** [U] material that has large, often square, spaces between the threads □ *jaring*: *net curtains* **2** [C] a piece of net that is used for a particular purpose □ *jaring; jala; kelambu*: *a tennis/fishing/mosquito net* ⊃ look at **safety net** ⊃ picture on **page P4 3 the Net** (*informal*) = **the Internet**

net² (also nett) /net/ adj net (of sth) (used about a number or amount) from which nothing more needs to be taken away □ *bersih*: *I earn about £15 000 net* (= after tax, etc. has been paid). ♦ *The net weight of the biscuits is 350g* (= not including the box). ♦ *a net profit* ⊃ look at **gross**

net³ /net/ verb [T] (netting; netted) **1** to gain sth as a profit □ *mendapat untung* **2** to catch sth with a net; to kick a ball into a net □ *menjaring; menjala; menangguk; menjaringkan*

netball /ˈnetbɔːl/ noun [U] a game that is played by two teams of seven players, usually women. Players score by throwing the ball through a high net hanging from a ring. □ *bola jaring*

netbook /ˈnetbʊk/ noun [C] a laptop (= a small computer) designed especially for using the Internet and email □ *komputer riba kecil* ⊃ note at **computer**

netiquette /ˈnetɪket/ noun [U] (*informal*) the rules of correct or polite behaviour among people using the Internet □ *etika dlm Internet; netika*

TOPIC

Netiquette

When you take part in an **online discussion** on a **message board/bulletin board** (= a place where you can read or write messages on the Internet), it is important to follow the rules of **netiquette**. When you **post a message** or **follow a thread** (= add your comments), you should not **go off-topic** (= talk about things that are not connected to the topic of the discussion), or write everything in capital letters. As in real life, you should be polite and show respect to the other people taking part.

Net surfer = **surfer**(2)

netting /ˈnetɪŋ/ noun [U] material that is made of long pieces of string, thread, wire, etc. that are tied together with spaces between them □ *jaring; kain net*

nettle /ˈnetl/ noun [C] a wild plant with large leaves. Some **nettles** make your skin red and painful if you touch them. □ *netel*

network¹ /ˈnetwɜːk/ noun [C] **1** a system of roads, railway lines, nerves, etc. that are connected to each other □ *rangkaian; jaringan*: *an underground railway network* **2** a group of people or companies that work closely together □ *rangkaian*: *We have a network of agents who sell our goods all over the country.* **3** a number of computers that are connected together so that information can be shared □ *rangkaian*: *The network allows users to share files.* **4** a group of TV or radio companies that are connected and that send out the same programmes at the same time in different parts of a country □ *rangkaian*: *the four big US television networks*

network² /ˈnetwɜːk/ verb **1** [T] to connect a number of computers together in order to share information □ *merangkaikan komputer* **2** [I] to talk to people who may be useful to you in your work □ *berhubung*: *Conferences are a great place to network.* ▸ **networking** noun [U] ⊃ look at **social networking**

neurologist /ˌnjʊəˈrɒlədʒɪst/ noun [C] a doctor who studies and treats diseases of the nerves □ *doktor pakar neurologi*

neurology /ˌnjʊəˈrɒlədʒi/ noun [U] the scientific study of nerves and their diseases □ *neurologi* ▸ **neurological** /ˌnjʊərəˈlɒdʒɪkl/ adj: *He suffered severe neurological damage.*

neuron /ˈnjʊərɒn/ (*especially BrE* **neurone** /ˈnjʊərəʊn/) noun [C] a cell that carries information within the brain and between the brain and other parts of the body; a nerve cell □ *neuron*

neurosis /njʊəˈrəʊsɪs/ noun [C] (*pl* **neuroses** /-əʊsiːz/) a mental illness that causes strong feelings of fear and worry □ *neurosis; sejenis penyakit mental*

neurotic /njʊəˈrɒtɪk/ adj **1** suffering from a neurosis □ *mengalami neurosis* **2** worried about things in a way that is not normal □ *selalu bimbang tak tentu pasal*

neuter¹ /ˈnjuːtə(r)/ adj (used about a word in some languages) not **masculine** or **feminine** according to the rules of grammar □ *neutral; neuter* ⊃ note at **masculine**

neuter² /ˈnjuːtə(r)/ verb [T] to remove the sexual parts of an animal □ *mengembiri* ⊃ look at **castrate**

neutral¹ /ˈnjuːtrəl/ adj **1** not supporting or belonging to either side in an argument, war, etc. □ *berkecuali*: *I don't take sides when my brothers argue—I remain neutral.* ♦ *The two sides agreed to meet on neutral ground.* ♦ *They escaped to Switzerland, which was a neutral country during the Second World War.* **2** having or showing no strong qualities, emotions or colour □ *neutral*: *neutral colours* ♦ *a neutral tone of voice*

neutral² /ˈnjuːtrəl/ noun [U] the position of the gears (= a part of the machinery in a vehicle) when no power is sent from the engine to the wheels □ *neutral*

neutrality /njuːˈtræləti/ noun [U] the state of not supporting either side in an argument, war, etc. □ *keberkecualian*

neutralize (also -ise) /ˈnjuːtrəlaɪz/ verb [T] to take away the effect of sth □ *menjadikan tdk berkesan; meneutralkan*: *to neutralize a threat*

neutron /ˈnjuːtrɒn/ noun [C] part of the **nucleus** (= the central part) of an atom that carries no electric charge □ *neutron* ⊃ look at **electron, proton**

never /ˈnevə(r)/ adv 1 at no time; not ever □ *belum/tdk pernah; tdk langsung; tdk akan; jangan*: *I've never been to Portugal.* ♦ *He never ever eats meat.* ♦ (*formal*) *Never before has such a high standard been achieved.* 2 used for emphasizing a negative statement □ *tdk sekali-kali; tdk langsung pun; yakah*: *I never realized she was so unhappy.* ♦ *Roy never so much as looked at us* (= he didn't even look at us). ♦ *'I got the job!' 'Never!'* (= expressing surprise)
IDM never mind ⊃ **mind²**
you never know ⊃ **know¹**

nevertheless /ˌnevəðəˈles/ adv (*formal*) in spite of that □ *walau bagaimanapun*: *It was a cold, rainy day. Nevertheless, more people came than we had expected.* **SYN** nonetheless ⊃ note at **contrast**

new /njuː/ adj (newer; newest) 1 that has recently been built, made, discovered, etc. □ *baharu*: *a new design/film/hospital* ♦ *a new method of treating mental illness* ♦ *new evidence* **OPP** old 2 different or changed from what was before □ *baharu*: *I've just started reading a new book.* ♦ *to make new friends* **OPP** old 3 new (to sb) that you have not seen, learnt, etc. before □ *baharu; belum pernah dilihat, dipelajari, dll*: *This type of machine is new to me.* ♦ *to learn a new language* 4 new (to sth) having just started being or doing sth □ *baharu*: *a new parent* ♦ *She's new to the job and needs a lot of help.* ♦ *a new member of the club*
IDM a (whole) new/different ball game ⊃ **ball game**
break fresh/new ground ⊃ **ground¹**
▶ newness noun [U]

New Age adj connected with a way of life that rejects modern Western values and is based on spiritual ideas and beliefs □ *'New Age': a New Age festival* ♦ *New Age travellers* (= people in Britain who reject the values of modern society and travel from place to place living in their vehicles)

newborn /ˈnjuːbɔːn/ adj [only before a noun] (used about a baby) that has been born very recently □ *bayi yg baru lahir*

newcomer /ˈnjuːkʌmə(r)/ noun [C] a person who has just arrived in a place □ *pendatang baharu; orang baharu*

newfangled /ˌnjuːˈfæŋɡld/ adj new or modern in a way that the speaker does not like □ *baharu (tetapi tdk berapa disukai)*

newly /ˈnjuːli/ adv [usually before a past participle] recently □ *(yg) baru*: *the newly appointed Minister of Health*

newly-wed noun [C, usually pl] a person who has recently got married □ *pengantin baharu*

news /njuːz/ noun 1 [U] information about sth that has happened recently □ *berita*: *Write and tell me all your news.* ♦ *Have you had any news from Susie recently?* ♦ *That's news to me* (= I didn't know that). ♦ *I've got some good news: you've passed the exam!*

GRAMMAR News is uncountable. When we are talking about a single item we say **a piece of news** (not 'a news'). News is followed by a singular verb: *The news is very depressing.*

2 the news [sing] a regular programme giving the most recent news on the radio or TV □ *(siaran) berita*: *We always watch the 10 o'clock news on TV.* ♦ *I heard about the accident on the news.*
IDM break the news (to sb) to be the first to tell sb about sth important that has happened □ *memberitahu sst berita (kpd sso)*

newsagent /ˈnjuːzeɪdʒənt/ (*AmE* newsdealer /ˈnjuːzdiːlə(r)/) noun 1 [C] a person who owns or works in a shop that sells newspapers and magazines, etc. □ *wakil penjual akhbar* 2 the newsagent's [sing] a shop that sells newspapers, magazines, etc. □ *kedai surat khabar, majalah, dsb*

newscaster /ˈnjuːzkɑːstə(r)/ = **newsreader**

newsgroup /ˈnjuːzɡruːp/ noun [C] a place in a computer network, especially the Internet, where people can discuss a particular subject and exchange information about it □ *kumpulan berita*

newsletter /ˈnjuːzletə(r)/ noun [C] a report about an organization that is sent regularly to members and other people who may be interested □ *surat berita*

newspaper /ˈnjuːzpeɪpə(r)/ noun 1 (also **paper**) [C] large folded pieces of paper printed with news, advertisements and articles on various subjects. Newspapers are printed and sold either every day or every week and some also appear online □ *surat khabar; akhbar*: *a daily/weekly/Sunday newspaper* ♦ *an online newspaper* ♦ *a newspaper article* ♦ *I read about it in the newspaper.* ♦ *She works for the local newspaper* (= the company that produces it) 2 [U] the paper on which newspapers are printed □ *(kertas) surat khabar*: *We wrapped the plates in newspaper.* ⊃ look at **media**

TOPIC

Newspapers

Newspapers and the **journalists/reporters** who write **articles** for them are called **the press**. The **editor** decides what is printed. **Quality** newspapers deal with the news in a serious way. **Tabloids** have small pages, and some of them have **sensational** (= shocking) stories and **gossip columns** (= reports about famous people's private lives). Photographers who follow famous people in order to take photographs of them are called **paparazzi**. You can buy **newspapers** and **magazines** at **the newsagent's** or you might have them delivered to your house by a **paper boy** or **paper girl**. Many **newspapers** are also available online.

newsreader /ˈnjuːzriːdə(r)/ (also **newscaster**) noun [C] a person who reads the news on the radio or TV □ *pembaca berita*

'news-stand (AmE) = **bookstall**

the New Testament noun [sing] the second part of the Bible that describes the life and teachings of Jesus Christ □ *Wasiat Baharu* ⊃ look at **the Old Testament**

new 'year (also **New Year**) noun [U, sing] the first few days of January □ *tahun baharu*: *Happy New Year!* ◆ *We will get in touch in the new year.* ◆ **New Year's Eve** (= 31 December) ◆ **New Year's Day** (= 1 January)

next /nekst/ adj, adv **1** [usually with *the*] coming immediately after sth in order, space or time; closest □ *berikutnya; seterusnya; di sebelah*: *The next bus leaves in twenty minutes.* ◆ *The next name on the list is Paulo.* ◆ *Who is next?*

> **HELP** **Next** or **nearest**? **The next** means 'the following' in a series of events or places: *When is your next appointment?* ◆ *Turn left at the next traffic lights.* **The nearest** means 'the closest' in time or place: *Where's the nearest supermarket?*

2 [used without *the* before days of the week, months, seasons, years, etc.] the one immediately following the present one □ *depan*: *See you again next Monday.* ◆ *Let's go camping next weekend.* ◆ *next summer/next year/next Christmas* **3** after this or after that; then □ *selepas itu; kemudian; kali berikutnya*: *I wonder what will happen next.* ◆ *I know Joe arrived first, but who came next?* ◆ *It was ten years until I next saw her.* ⊃ note at **then** **4** **the next** noun [sing] the person or thing that is next □ *(orang/sst) yg berikutnya*: *If we miss this train, we'll have to wait two hours for the next.*
IDM **last/next but one, two,** etc. ⊃ **last¹**

,next 'door adj, adv in or into the next house or building □ *sebelah rumah; di sebelah*: *our next-door neighbours* ◆ *Who lives next door?* ◆ *The school is next door to an old people's home.*

next of 'kin noun [C] (pl **next of kin**) your closest living relative or relatives □ *waris kadim/terdekat*: *My husband is my next of kin.*

next to prep **1** at the side of sb/sth; beside □ *di sebelah*: *He sat down next to Gita.* ◆ *There's a cafe next to the cinema.* **2** in a position after sth □ *selain; selepas*: *Next to English my favourite subject is Maths.*
IDM **next to nothing** almost nothing □ *hampir tiada langsung; sedikit sekali*: *We took plenty of money but we've got next to nothing left.*

NGO /ˌen dʒiː ˈəʊ/ noun [C] (pl **NGOs**) non-governmental organization; a charity, association,

581 **newsreader → nick**

etc. that is independent of government and business □ *NGO (Badan Bukan Kerajaan)*

NHS /ˌen eɪtʃ ˈes/ abbr (BrE) = **National Health Service**

NI abbr = **National Insurance**

nib /nɪb/ noun [C] the metal point of a pen, where the ink comes out □ *mata pen, mata pena* ⊃ picture at **stationery**

nibble /ˈnɪbl/ verb [I,T] to eat sth by taking small bites □ *menggigis; mengutil*: *The bread had been nibbled by mice.* ▶**nibble** noun [C]

nice /naɪs/ adj (**nicer**; **nicest**) **1** pleasant, enjoyable or attractive □ *bagus; baik; sedap; menarik*: *a nice place/feeling/smile* ◆ *I'm not eating this—it doesn't taste very nice.* ◆ *Did you have a nice time?* ◆ *You look very nice.* ◆ *It would be nice to spend more time at home.* ◆ *'Hi, I'm Kate.' 'I'm Fergus—**nice to meet you.*' ◆ *Have a nice day!* (a friendly way of saying goodbye, especially to customers) **2** (informal) used before adjectives and adverbs to emphasize how pleasant or suitable sth is □ *baik; seronok*: *It's nice and warm by the fire.* ◆ *a nice long chat* **3** **nice (to sb); nice (of sb) (to do sth); nice (about sth)** kind; friendly □ *baik; mesra*: *What a nice girl!* ◆ *Everyone was very nice to me when I felt ill.* ◆ *It was really nice of Donna to help us.* ◆ *The neighbours were very nice about it when I hit their car.* **OPP** **nasty** ▶**nicely** adv ▶**niceness** noun [U]

> **OTHER WORDS FOR**
> **nice**
>
> In informal English you can say **great**, **lovely** or **wonderful** instead of 'nice' or 'very nice': *The party was great.* ◆ *We had a lovely weekend.* When you want to talk about a person, you can say 'He/She is **lovely**' or 'He/She is very **friendly**'. We also say: *a cosy /an attractive room* ◆ *beautiful/lovely weather* ◆ *expensive/fashionable/smart clothes.*

niche /niːʃ; nɪtʃ/ noun [C] **1** a job, position, etc. that is suitable for you □ *pekerjaan/kedudukan yg sesuai*: *to find your niche in life* **2** (in business) an opportunity to sell a particular product to a particular group of people □ *'niche'; pasaran khusus* **3** a place in a wall that is further back, where a statue, etc. can be put □ *keluk dinding*

nick¹ /nɪk/ noun [C] a small cut in sth □ *luka kecil; calar*
IDM **in good/bad nick** (BrE slang) in a good/bad state or condition □ *dlm keadaan baik/teruk, buruk, dsb*
in the nick of time only just in time □ *mujurlah sempat*

nick² /nɪk/ verb [T] **1** to make a very small cut in sb/sth □ *melukai, terluka, tercalar* **2** (BrE slang) to steal sth □ *mengebas; mencuri* **3** (BrE slang) to arrest sb □ *menangkap*

nickel /'nɪkl/ noun **1** [U] (symbol Ni) a hard silver-white metal that is often mixed with other metals □ *nikel* **2** [C] an American or Canadian coin that is worth five cents □ *syiling 5 sen (AS/Kanada)*

nickname /'nɪkneɪm/ noun [C] an informal name that is used instead of your real name, usually by your family or friends □ *nama timangan; gelaran* ▶ **nickname** verb [T]

nicotine /'nɪkəti:n/ noun [U] the poisonous substance in **tobacco** (= the dried leaves used for making cigarettes) □ *nikotina*

niece /ni:s/ noun [C] the daughter of your brother or sister; the daughter of your husband's or wife's brother or sister □ *anak saudara perempuan*: *My niece Jenny will be two next month.* ⊃ look at **nephew**

niggle /'nɪgl/ verb **1** [I,T] niggle (at) sb to annoy or worry sb □ *menimbulkan kemarahan; merisaukan*: *His untidy habits really niggled her.* **2** [I] niggle (about/over sth) to complain or argue about things that are not important □ *cerewet (ttg perkara yg remeh-temeh)* ▶ **niggle** noun: *There were no major problems, just a few niggles*

niggling /'nɪglɪŋ/ adj not very serious (but that does not go away) □ *bermain-main dlm fikiran; mengganggu; terus-menerus*: *niggling doubts* ♦ *a niggling injury*

night /naɪt/ noun [C,U] **1** the part of the day when it is dark and when most people sleep □ *malam*: *I had a strange dream last night.* ♦ *The baby cried all night.* ♦ *It's a long way home. Why don't you stay the night?* ♦ *We will be away for a few nights.* **2** the time between late afternoon and when you go to bed □ *malam; lewat petang atau awal malam*: *Let's go out on Saturday night.* ♦ *He doesn't get home until 8 o'clock at night.* ♦ *I went out with Kate the other night* (= a few nights ago).

> **HELP** Note the use of different prepositions with **night**. **At** is most common: *I'm not allowed out after 11 o'clock at night.* **By** is used about something that you usually do in the night-time: *These animals sleep by day and hunt by night.* **In/during** the night is usually used for the night that has just passed: *I woke up twice in the night.* **On** is used when you are talking about one particular night: *On the night of Saturday 30 June.* **Tonight** means the night or evening of today: *Where are you staying tonight?*

IDM **an early/a late night** an evening when you go to bed earlier/later than usual □ *tidur awal/lambat*: *Try to have an early night before the exam.*

in/at the dead of night ⊃ **dead²**

a night out an evening that you spend out of the house enjoying yourself □ *keluar bersuka-suka pd waktu malam*

nightclub /'naɪtklʌb/ noun [C] = **club¹**(2)

nightdress /'naɪtdres/ (also informal **nightie** /'naɪti/) noun [C] a loose dress that a girl or woman wears in bed □ *gaun/baju tidur*

nightingale /'naɪtɪŋgeɪl/ noun [C] a small brown bird that has a beautiful song □ *burung bulbul*

nightlife /'naɪtlaɪf/ noun [U] the entertainment that is available in the evenings in a particular place □ *hiburan malam*: *It's a small town with very little nightlife.*

nightly /'naɪtli/ adj, adv happening every night □ *setiap malam*: *a nightly news bulletin*

nightmare /'naɪtmeə(r)/ noun [C] **1** a frightening or unpleasant dream □ *mimpi buruk*: *I had a terrible nightmare about being stuck in a lift last night.* **2** (informal) an experience that is very unpleasant or frightening □ *pengalaman yg teruk atau menakutkan*: *Travelling in the rush hour can be a real nightmare.*

'night-time noun [U] the time when it is dark □ *waktu malam*

nightwatchman /naɪt'wɒtʃmən (AmE also)/ noun [C] (pl **-men** /-mən/) a man who guards a building at night □ *jaga/pengawal malam*

nil /nɪl/ noun [U] the number 0 (especially as the score in some games) □ *kosong*: *We won two-nil/by two goals to nil.* ⊃ note at **zero**

nimble /'nɪmbl/ adj (**nimbler**; **nimblest**) able to move quickly and lightly □ *lincah* ▶ **nimbly** /'nɪmbli/ adv

nine /naɪn/ number 9 □ *sembilan; 9* ⊃ note at **six**

IDM **nine to five** the hours that you work in most offices □ *sembilan hingga lima*: *a nine-to-five job*

nineteen /ˌnaɪn'ti:n/ number 19 □ *sembilan belas; 19* ⊃ note at **six** ▶ **nineteenth** /ˌnaɪn'ti:nθ/ ordinal number, noun ⊃ note at **sixth**

ninety /'naɪnti/ number 90 □ *sembilan puluh* ⊃ note at **sixty** ▶ **ninetieth** /'naɪntiəθ/ ordinal number, noun ⊃ note at **sixth**

ninth¹ /naɪnθ/ ordinal number 9th □ *kesembilan; ke-9* ⊃ note at **sixth**

ninth² /naɪnθ/ noun [C] 1/9; one of nine equal parts of sth □ *satu per sembilan*; $\frac{1}{9}$

nip /nɪp/ verb (**nipping**; **nipped**) **1** [I,T] to give sb/sth a quick bite or to quickly squeeze a piece of sb's skin between your thumb and finger □ *menggigit; mencubit*: *She nipped him on the arm.* **2** [I] (BrE spoken) to go somewhere quickly and/or for a short time □ *pergi sekejap*

IDM **nip sth in the bud** to stop sth bad before it develops or gets worse □ *menghentikan/menghalang sst dr awal lagi*
▶ **nip** noun [C]

nipple /'nɪpl/ noun [C] **1** either of the two small dark circles on either side of your chest. A baby can suck milk from his or her mother's breast through the **nipples**. □ *puting* **2** (AmE) = **teat**(1)

niqab /nɪˈkɑːb/ noun [C] a piece of cloth that covers the face but not usually the eyes, worn in public by some Muslim women ◻ *hijab*

nit /nɪt/ noun [C] the egg of a small insect that lives in the hair of people or animals ◻ *telur kutu*

'nit-picking noun [U] the habit of finding small mistakes in sb's work or paying too much attention to small, unimportant details ◻ *asyik mencari kesalahan yg remeh-temeh; tumpuan kpd perkara yg remeh-temeh* ▶ **'nit-picking** adj

nitrogen /ˈnaɪtrədʒən/ noun [U] (symbol N) a gas that has no colour, taste or smell. Nitrogen forms about 80% of the air around the earth. ◻ *nitrogen*

the nitty-gritty /ˌnɪti ˈɡrɪti/ noun [sing] (*informal*) the most important facts, not the small or unimportant details ◻ *butir-butir asas; perkara-perkara yg pokok*

nm abbr = **nanometre**

No. (also **no.**) abbr 1 (pl **Nos**; **nos**) (AmE **#**) = **number**[1](2) ◻ *nombor*: *No. 10 Downing Street* ◆ *tel no. 512364* 2 (AmE) = **North, Northern**

no[1] /nəʊ/ exclam 1 used for giving a negative reply ◻ *tdk; belum*: '*Are you ready?*' '*No, I'm not.*' ◆ '*Would you like something to eat?*' '*No, thank you.*' ◆ '*Can I borrow the car?*' '*No, you can't.*' **OPP yes**

> **HELP** You can also use **no** when you want to agree with a negative statement: '*This programme's not very good.*' '*No, you're right. It isn't.*'

2 used for expressing surprise or shock ◻ *seruan utk menyatakan rasa terperanjat atau terkejut*: '*Mike's had an accident.*' '*Oh, no!*'

no[2] /nəʊ/ determiner, adv 1 not any; not a ◻ *tdk ada; tdk; bukan*: *I have no time to talk now.* ◆ *No visitors may enter without a ticket.* ◆ *He's no friend of mine.* ◆ *Alice is feeling no better this morning.* 2 used for saying that sth is not allowed ◻ *tdk dibenarkan; jangan*: *No smoking.* ◆ *No flash photography.* ◆ *No parking.*

nobility /nəʊˈbɪləti/ noun 1 **the nobility** [sing, with sing or pl verb] people of high social position who have titles such as that of Duke or Duchess ◻ *golongan bangsawan* **SYN** aristocracy 2 [U] (*formal*) the quality of having courage and honour ◻ *kemuliaan*

noble[1] /ˈnəʊbl/ adj (**nobler**; **noblest**) 1 honest; full of courage and care for others ◻ *mulia; berhati mulia*: *a noble leader* ◆ *noble ideas/actions* 2 belonging to the highest social class ◻ *bangsawan*: *a man of noble birth* ▶ **nobly** /ˈnəʊbli/ adv: *He nobly sacrificed his own happiness for that of his family.*

noble[2] /ˈnəʊbl/ noun [C] (in past times) a person who belonged to the highest social class and had a special title ◻ *orang bangsawan* ⊃ A more common word nowadays is **peer**.

nobody[1] /ˈnəʊbədi/ (also **'no one**) pron no person; not anyone ◻ *tdk sesiapa pun*: *He screamed but nobody came to help him.* ◆ *No one else was around.* ◆ *There was nobody at home.*

> **HELP** **None of**, not **nobody**, must be used before words like *the, his, her, those*, etc. or before a pronoun: *None of my friends remembered my birthday.* ◆ *I've asked all my classmates but none of them are free.*

nobody[2] /ˈnəʊbədi/ noun [C] (pl **nobodies**) a person who is not important or famous ◻ *orang yg tdk penting/terkenal*: *She rose from being a nobody to being a superstar.*

nocturnal /nɒkˈtɜːnl/ adj 1 (used about animals and birds) awake and active at night and asleep during the day ◻ *nokturnal; aktif pd waktu malam*: *Owls are nocturnal birds.* 2 (*formal*) happening in the night ◻ *pd waktu malam*: *a nocturnal adventure*

nod

He nodded his head.

nod /nɒd/ verb [I,T] (**nodding**; **nodded**) to move your head up and down as a way of saying 'yes' or as a sign to sb to do sth ◻ *mengangguk*: *Everybody at the meeting nodded in agreement.* ◆ *Nod your head if you understand what I'm saying and shake it if you don't.*

PHR V **nod off** (*informal*) to go to sleep for a short time ◻ *tertidur/terlelap*
▶ **nod** noun [C]

no-'frills adj [only before a noun] (used especially about a service or product) including only the basic features, without anything that is unnecessary, especially things added to make sth more attractive or comfortable ◻ *tanpa ciri tambahan*: *a no-frills airline*

no-'go area noun [sing] a place, especially part of a city, where it is very dangerous to go because there is a lot of violence or crime ◻ *tempat berbahaya*

noise /nɔɪz/ noun [C,U] a sound, especially one that is loud or unpleasant ◻ *bunyi; bunyi bising; hingar*: *Did you hear a noise downstairs?* ◆ *Try not to make a noise if you come home late.* ◆ *What an awful noise!* ◆ *Why is the engine making so much noise?*

noiseless /ˈnɔɪzləs/ adj making no sound ◻ *tdk berbunyi* ▶ **noiselessly** adv

noisy /ˈnɔɪzi/ adj (**noisier**; **noisiest**) making a lot of or too much noise; full of noise ◻ *bising*: *The*

nomad → nonsensical 584

clock was so noisy that it kept me awake. ◆ noisy children/traffic/crowds ◆ The classroom was very noisy. ⊃ note at **loud** ▸**noisily** adv

nomad /ˈnəʊmæd/ noun [C] a member of a community that moves with its animals from place to place □ *orang nomad* ▸**nomadic** /nəʊˈmædɪk/ adj

ˈno-manˈs-land noun [U, sing] an area of land between the borders of two countries or between two armies during a war and which is not controlled by either □ *kawasan bebas*

nominal /ˈnɒmɪnl/ adj 1 being sth in name only but not in reality □ *pd nama sahaja*: *the nominal leader of the country* (= sb else is really in control) 2 (used about a price, sum of money, etc.) very small; much less than normal □ *sedikit; nominal*: *Because we are friends he only charges me a nominal rent.* ▸**nominally** /-nəli/ adv: *He was nominally in charge of the company.*

nominate /ˈnɒmɪneɪt/ verb [T] nominate sb/sth (for/as sth) to formally suggest that sb/sth should be given a job, role, prize, etc. □ *mencalonkan*: *I would like to nominate Bob Fry as chairman.* ◆ *The film has been nominated for three Oscars.* ◆ *You may nominate a representative to speak for you.* ▸**nomination** /ˌnɒmɪˈneɪʃn/ noun [C,U]

nominee /ˌnɒmɪˈniː/ noun [C] a person who is suggested for an important job, role, prize, etc. □ *calon*

non- /nɒn/ [in compounds] not □ *bukan; tdk; tak; tanpa*: *non-biodegradable* ◆ *non-flammable*

ˌnon-acaˈdemic adj connected with technical or practical subjects rather than subjects of interest to the mind □ *bukan akademik/ilmiah*

ˌnon-alcoˈholic adj (used about drinks) not containing any alcohol □ *tanpa alkohol*: *non-alcoholic drinks*

nonchalant /ˈnɒnʃələnt/ adj behaving in a calm and relaxed way and not appearing to be worried or excited □ *acuh tak acuh; selamba* ▸**nonchalance** /-ləns/ noun [U] ▸**nonchalantly** adv

ˌnon-comˈmittal adj not saying or showing exactly what your opinion is or which side of an argument you agree with □ *tdk menyatakan (pendapat, dsb) dgn pasti*

nonconformist /ˌnɒnkənˈfɔːmɪst/ noun [C] a person who behaves or thinks differently from most other people in society □ *orang yg bukan konformis/pengakur* **OPP** conformist ▸**nonconformist** adj

ˈnon-count = uncountable

ˌnon-deˈfining adj (used about clauses) giving extra information about a noun phrase, inside commas in writing or in a particular **intonation** (= the rise and fall of your voice) in speech □ *(utk klausa) memberikan maklumat tambahan ttg sst frasa nama* ❶ For more information, look at the **Reference Section** at the back of this dictionary.

nondescript /ˈnɒndɪskrɪpt/ adj not having any interesting or unusual qualities □ *tdk menarik/menonjol*

none¹ /nʌn/ pron none (of sb/sth) not any, not one (of a group of three or more) □ *tdk ada; tdk satu/seorang pun*: *They gave me a lot of information but none of it was very helpful.* ◆ *I've got four brothers but none of them live/lives nearby.* ◆ *'Have you brought any books to read?' 'No, none.'* ◆ *I went to several shops but none had what I was looking for.*

GRAMMAR With uncountable nouns **none of** means 'not any of' and we use a singular verb: *None of our money goes towards illegal activities*. With countable nouns **none of** means 'not one of' and can be used with a singular verb (less formal) or a plural verb (more formal): *None of the children likes/like spinach.*

When we are talking about two people or things we use **neither**, not **none**: *Neither of my brothers lives nearby.* Note the difference between **none** and **no**. **No** must go in front of a noun, but **none** replaces the noun: *I told him that I had no money left.* ◆ *When he asked me how much money I had left, I told him that I had none.*

none² /nʌn/ adv
IDM none the wiser/worse knowing no more than before; no worse than before □ *masih tdk faham/tahu; tdk apa-apa*: *We talked for a long time but I'm still none the wiser.*
none too happy, clean, pleased, etc. (*informal*) not very happy, clean, pleased, etc. □ *tdk begitu gembira, bersih, suka, dll*

nonetheless /ˌnʌnðəˈles/ adv (*formal*) in spite of this fact □ *walau bagaimanapun*: *It won't be easy but they're going to try nonetheless.* **SYN** nevertheless ⊃ note at **contrast**

ˌnon-exˈistent adj not existing or not available □ *tdk wujud/ada*

ˌnon-ˈfiction noun [U] writing that is about real people, events and facts □ *bukan fiksyen*: *You'll find biographies in the non-fiction section of the library.* **OPP** fiction

nonplussed /ˌnɒnˈplʌst/ adj confused; not able to understand □ *kebingungan*

ˌnon-reˈnewable adj (used about natural sources of energy such as gas or oil) that cannot be replaced after use □ *tdk boleh dibaharui*

nonsense /ˈnɒnsns/ (*AmE* also) / noun [U] 1 ideas, statements or beliefs that you think are ridiculous or not true □ *karut; bukan-bukan*: *Don't talk nonsense!* ◆ *It's nonsense to say you aren't good enough to go to university!* **SYN** rubbish 2 silly or unacceptable behaviour □ *kelakuan yg bukan-bukan*: *The head teacher won't stand for any nonsense.*

nonsensical /nɒnˈsensɪkl/ adj ridiculous; without meaning □ *yg karut/bukan-bukan*

ð **then**   s **so**   z **zoo**   ʃ **she**   ʒ **vision**   h **how**   m **man**   n **no**   ŋ **sing**   l **leg**   r **red**   j **yes**   w **wet**

non-'smoker *noun* [C] a person who does not smoke cigarettes, etc. ☐ *bukan perokok* **OPP** smoker ▶ **non-'smoking** *adj*: *You can request a non-smoking room at the hotel.*

non-'starter *noun* [C] (*informal*) a person, plan or idea that has no chance of success ☐ *(orang yg) tak mungkin berjaya; (idea, rancangan, dsb yg) tdk boleh pakai langsung*

non-'stick *adj* (used about a pan, etc.) covered with a substance that prevents food from sticking to it ☐ *tak melekat*

non-'stop *adj, adv* without a stop or a rest ☐ *tanpa berhenti-henti; terus*: *a non-stop flight to Mumbai* ♦ *He talked non-stop for two hours about his holiday.*

non-'violence *noun* [U] fighting for political or social change without using force, for example by not obeying laws ☐ *tanpa kekerasan* ▶ **non-'violent** *adj*: *a non-violent protest*

noodle /'nuːdl/ *noun* [C, usually pl] long thin pieces of food made of flour, egg and water that are cooked in boiling water or used in soups ☐ *mi* ⊃ picture on **page P16**

nook /nʊk/ *noun* [C] a small quiet place or corner (in a house, garden, etc.) ☐ *ceruk* **IDM** **every nook and cranny** (*informal*) every part of a place ☐ *semua ceruk*

noon /nuːn/ *noun* [U] 12 o'clock in the middle of the day; midday ☐ *tengah hari (tepat); pukul 12 tengah hari*: *At noon the sun is at its highest point in the sky.* **SYN** midday ⊃ look at **midnight**

no one = **nobody**[1]

noose /nuːs/ *noun* [C] a circle that is tied in the end of a rope and that gets smaller as one end of the rope is pulled ☐ *jerat; pencerut*: *a hangman's noose*

no place (especially *AmE*) = **nowhere**: *I have no place else to go*

nor /nɔː(r)/ *conj, adv* **1** neither ... nor ... and not ☐ *ataupun*: *I have neither the time nor the inclination to listen to his complaints again.* **2** [used before a positive verb to agree with sth negative that has just been said] also not; neither ☐ *pun tdk/belum*: *'I don't like golf.' 'Nor do I.'* ♦ *'We haven't been to America.' 'Nor have we.'*

> **MORE** In this sense **neither** can be used in the same way: *'I won't be here tomorrow.' 'Nor/ Neither will I.'*

3 [used after a negative statement to add some more information] also not ☐ *pun tdk; ataupun*: *Michael never forgot her birthday. Nor their wedding anniversary for that matter.*

norm /nɔːm/ *noun* [C] (often with *the*) a situation or way of behaving that is usual or expected ☐ *norma; kebiasaan*: *Storing photos on computers has become the norm.* ♦ *social/cultural norms*

normal[1] /'nɔːml/ *adj* typical, usual or ordinary; what you expect ☐ *biasa*: *I'll meet you at the normal time.* ♦ *It's quite normal to feel angry in a situation like this.* **OPP** abnormal

585 **non-smoker → north-eastern**

normal[2] /'nɔːml/ *noun* [U] the usual or average state, level or standard ☐ *normal; (keadaan) biasa*: *temperatures above/below normal* ♦ *Things are back to normal at work now.*

normality /nɔː'mæləti/ (*AmE* also **normalcy** /'nɔːmlsi/) *noun* [U] the state of being normal ☐ *keadaan yg biasa; kenormalan*

normalize (also **-ise**) /'nɔːməlaɪz/ *verb* [I,T] (*formal*) to become or make sth become normal again or return to how it was before ☐ *memulihkan (hubungan, dll) supaya kembali spt biasa*: *The two countries agreed to normalize relations* (= return to a normal, friendly relationship, for example after a disagreement or a war).

normally /'nɔːməli/ *adv* **1** usually ☐ *biasanya*: *I normally leave the house at 8 o'clock.* ♦ *Normally he takes the bus.* **2** in the usual or ordinary way ☐ *secara biasa/normal*: *The man wasn't behaving normally.*

north[1] /nɔːθ/ *noun* [U, sing] (*abbr* N; No.) **1** (also **the north**) the direction that is on your left when you watch the sun rise; one of the **points of the compass** (= the main directions that we give names to) ☐ *utara*: *cold winds from the north* ♦ *Which way is north?* ♦ *I live to the north of* (= further north than) *Chicago.* ⊃ picture at **compass 2 the north; the North** the northern part of a country, a city, a region or the world ☐ *bahagian utara*: *Houses are less expensive in the North of England than in the South.* ♦ *I live in the north of Athens.* ⊃ look at **south, east, west**

north[2] /nɔːθ/ *adj, adv* **1** [only *before* a noun] in the north ☐ *(di) utara; sebelah utara*: *The new offices will be in North London.* ♦ *The north wing of the hospital was destroyed in a fire.* **2** (used about a wind) coming from the north ☐ *dr utara* **3** to or towards the north ☐ *(ke) utara*: *We got onto the motorway going north instead of south.* ♦ *The house faces north.* ♦ *Is Rouen north of Paris?*

northbound /'nɔːθbaʊnd/ *adj* travelling or leading towards the north ☐ *ke utara*: *northbound traffic*

north-'east[1] (also **the north-east**) *noun* [sing] (*abbr* NE) the direction or a region that is an equal distance between north and east ☐ *(arah atau bahagian) timur laut* ⊃ picture at **compass**

north-'east[2] *adj, adv* in, from or to the **north-east** of a place or country ☐ *(di, dr atau ke) timur laut*: *the north-east coast of Australia* ♦ *If you look north-east you can see the mountains.*

north-'easterly *adj* **1** [only *before* a noun] towards the north-east ☐ *ke arah timur laut*: *in a north-easterly direction* **2** (used about a wind) coming from the north-east ☐ *dr timur laut*

north-'eastern *adj* (*abbr* NE) [only *before* a noun] connected with the north-east of a place or country ☐ *(berkaitan dgn bahagian) timur laut*

,north-'eastwards (also ,north-'eastward) adv towards the north-east □ *ke arah timur laut*: *Follow the A619 north-eastward.*

northerly /ˈnɔːðəli/ adj **1** [only before a noun] to, towards or in the north □ *(ke, ke arah atau di) utara*: *Keep going in a northerly direction.* **2** (used about a wind) coming from the north □ *dr utara*

northern (also Northern) /ˈnɔːðən/ adj (abbr N) of, in or from the north of a place □ *(berkaitan dgn, di atau dr) utara*: *She has a northern accent.* ♦ *in northern Australia*

northerner /ˈnɔːðənə(r)/ noun [C] a person who was born in or who lives in the northern part of a country □ *orang utara*

northernmost /ˈnɔːðənməʊst/ adj furthest north □ *paling utara*: *the northernmost island of Japan*

the ,North 'Pole noun [sing] the point on the Earth's surface which is furthest north □ *Kutub Utara* ⊃ picture at **earth**

northwards /ˈnɔːθwədz/ (also northward) adv towards the north □ *ke arah utara*: *Continue northwards out of the city for about five miles.* ▶ **northward** adj: *in a northward direction*

,north-'west¹ (also the north-west) noun [sing] (abbr NW) the direction or a region that is an equal distance between north and west □ *(arah atau bahagian) barat laut* ⊃ picture at **compass**

,north-'west² adj, adv in, from or to the north-west of a place or country □ *(di, dr atau ke) barat laut*: *the north-west coast of Scotland* ♦ *Our house faces north-west.*

,north-'westerly adj **1** [only before a noun] towards the north-west □ *ke arah barat laut*: *in a north-westerly direction* **2** (used about a wind) coming from the north-west □ *dr barat laut*

,north-'western adj (abbr NW) [only before a noun] connected with the north-west of a place or country □ *(berkaitan dgn bahagian) barat laut*

,north-'westwards (also ,north-'westward) adv towards the north-west □ *ke arah barat laut*: *Follow the A40 north-westward for ten miles.*

nose¹ /nəʊz/ noun [C] **1** the part of your face, above your mouth, that is used for breathing and smelling □ *hidung*: *Breathe in through your nose and out through your mouth.* ⊃ picture at **body** **2** -nosed [in compounds] having the type of nose mentioned □ *berhidung*: *red-nosed* ♦ *big-nosed* **3** the front part of a plane, etc. □ *muncung*: *The nose of the plane was badly damaged.*
> **IDM** blow your nose ⊃ **blow¹**
> follow your nose ⊃ **follow**
> look down your nose at sb/sth ⊃ **look¹**
> poke/stick your nose into sth (*informal*) to be interested in or try to become involved in sth which does not concern you □ *masuk campur dlm (sst)*
> turn your nose up at sth (*informal*) to refuse sth because you do not think it is good enough for you □ *tdk mahu menerima sst kerana dianggap tdk cukup bagus*

nose² /nəʊz/ verb [I] (used about a vehicle) to move forward slowly and carefully □ *bergerak perlahan-lahan*
> **PHR V** nose about/around (*informal*) to look for sth, especially private information about sb □ *mencari-cari sst*

nosebleed /ˈnəʊzbliːd/ noun [C] a sudden flow of blood that comes from your nose □ *hidung berdarah*

nosedive /ˈnəʊzdaɪv/ noun [C] a sudden sharp fall or drop □ *junaman; jatuh menjunam*: *Oil prices took a nosedive in the crisis.* ▶ **nosedive** verb [I]: *All of a sudden the plane nosedived.*

nostalgia /nɒˈstældʒə/ (AmE also /nə-/) noun [U] a feeling of pleasure, mixed with sadness, when you think of happy times in the past □ *nostalgia*: *She was suddenly filled with nostalgia for her university days.* ▶ **nostalgic** /nɒˈstældʒɪk/ (AmE also /nə-/) adj ▶ **nostalgically** /-kli/ adv

nostril /ˈnɒstrəl/ noun [C] one of the two openings at the end of your nose that you breathe through □ *lubang hidung* ⊃ picture at **body**

nosy (also nosey) /ˈnəʊzi/ adj (*informal*) too interested in other people's personal affairs □ *suka mengambil tahu hal orang*: *a nosy neighbour*

not /nɒt/ adv **1** used to form the negative with **auxiliary verbs** (= the verbs 'be', 'do' and 'have') and with **modal verbs** (= verbs such as 'can', 'must' and 'will'). Not is often pronounced or written *n't* in informal situations □ *tdk; bukan; belum*: *It's not/it isn't raining now.* ♦ *I cannot/can't see from here.* ♦ *He didn't invite me.* ♦ *Don't you like spaghetti?* ♦ *I hope she will not/won't be late.* ♦ *You're German, aren't you?* **2** used to give the following word or phrase a negative meaning □ *tdk; jangan*: *He told me not to phone.* ♦ *She accused me of not telling the truth.* ♦ *Not one person replied to my advertisement.* ♦ *It's not easy.* ♦ *He's not very tall.* **3** used to give a short negative reply □ *tdk; bukan*: '*Do you think they'll get divorced?*' '*I hope not.*' (= I hope they will not.) ♦ '*Can I borrow £20?*' '*Certainly not!*' ♦ '*Whose turn is it to do the shopping?*' '*Not mine.*' **4** used with *or* to give a negative possibility □ *tdk*: *Shall we tell her or not?* ♦ *I don't know if/whether he's telling the truth or not.*
> **IDM** not at all **1** used as a way of replying when sb has thanked you □ *(ungkapan balas bagi ucapan terima kasih); sama-sama*: '*Thanks for the present.*' '*Not at all, don't mention it.*' **2** used as a way of saying 'no' or 'definitely not' □ *sama sekali tdk*: '*Do you mind if I come too?*' '*Not at all.*' ♦ *The instructions are not at all clear.*
> not only ... (but) also used for emphasizing the fact that there is sth more to add □ *bukan sa-*

haja... malah: They not only have two houses in London, they also have one in France.

notable /ˈnəʊtəbl/ *adj* **notable (for sth)** interesting or important enough to receive attention □ *menarik; penting; terkenal*: The area is notable for its wildlife.

notably /ˈnəʊtəbli/ *adv* used for giving an especially important example of what you are talking about □ *terutama sekali*: Several politicians, most notably the Prime Minister and the Home Secretary, have given the proposal their full support.

notation /nəʊˈteɪʃn/ *noun* [U,C] a system of signs or symbols used to represent information, especially in mathematics, science and music □ *notasi; tatatanda*

notch¹ /nɒtʃ/ *noun* [C] **1** a level on a scale of quality □ *takuk; tahap*: This meal is certainly **a notch above** the one we had here. **2** a cut in an edge or surface, often in the shape of a V, sometimes used to help you count sth □ *takuk; takik*

notch² /nɒtʃ/ *verb*
PHR V **notch sth up** to score or achieve sth □ *meraih; mencapai*: Lewis notched up his best ever time in the 100 metres.

note¹ /nəʊt/ *noun*
▸TO REMIND YOU **1** [C] some words that you write down quickly to help you remember sth □ *catatan; nota*: I'd better **make a note of** your name and address. ◆ **Keep a note of** who has paid and who hasn't. ◆ The lecturer advised the students to **take notes** while he was speaking.

> **EXAM TIP**
>
> **Revision notes**
>
> Write down the key words and phrases that you want to learn on small pieces of paper. Stick them in places where you will see them every day, such as your mirror, computer or fridge.

▸SHORT LETTER **2** [C] a short letter □ *nota*: This is just a note to thank you for having us to dinner. ◆ If Mark's not at home we'll leave a note for him. ◆ a sick note from your doctor
▸IN BOOK **3** [C] a short explanation or extra piece of information that is given at the back of a book, etc. or at the bottom or side of a page □ *nota*: ➲ look at **footnote**
▸MONEY **4** [C] (also **banknote**; *AmE* **bill**) a piece of paper money □ *wang kertas*: I'd like the money in £10 notes, please. ➲ picture at **money**
▸IN MUSIC **5** [C] a single musical sound made by a voice or an instrument; a written sign that represents a musical sound □ *not*: I can only remember the first few notes of the song.
▸QUALITY **6** [sing] something that shows a certain quality or feeling □ *nada; suasana*: The meeting ended on a rather unpleasant note.
IDM **compare notes (with sb)** ➲ **compare**
take note (of sth) to pay attention to sth and be sure to remember it □ *mengambil perhatian (ttg sst)*

---

587 **notable → nothing**

note² /nəʊt/ *verb* [T] **1** to notice or pay careful attention to sth □ *memerhatikan; perasan*: He noted a slight change in her attitude towards him. ◆ Please note that this office is closed on Tuesdays. **2** to mention sth □ *menyebut*: I'd like to note that the project has so far been extremely successful.
PHR V **note sth down** to write sth down so that you remember it □ *mencatat*

notebook /ˈnəʊtbʊk/ *noun* [C] **1** a small book in which you write down things that you want to remember □ *buku nota/catatan* **2** (also **ˈnotebook comˌputer**) a **laptop** (= a small computer) that can work with a battery and be easily carried □ *komputer riba kecil* ➲ note at **computer** **3** (*AmE*) = **exercise book**

noted /ˈnəʊtɪd/ *adj* (*formal*) **noted (for/as sth)** well known; famous □ *terkenal*: The hotel is noted for its food.

notepad /ˈnəʊtpæd/ *noun* [C] sheets of paper in a block that are used for writing things on □ *pad catatan*

notepaper /ˈnəʊtpeɪpə(r)/ *noun* [U] paper that you write letters on □ *kertas catatan*

noteworthy /ˈnəʊtwɜːði/ *adj* interesting or important; that is worth noticing □ *patut diberi perhatian*

nothing /ˈnʌθɪŋ/ *pron* not anything; no thing □ *tdk ada apa-apa*: There's nothing in this suitcase. ◆ I'm bored—there's **nothing to do** here. ◆ There was **nothing else** to say. ◆ 'What's the matter?' 'Oh, nothing.' ◆ 'Thank you so much for all your help.' 'It was nothing.' ◆ The doctor said there's nothing wrong with me. ➲ note at **zero**
IDM **be/have nothing to do with sb/sth** to have no connection with sb/sth □ *tdk kena-mengena dgn sso/sst*: That question has nothing to do with what we're discussing. ◆ Keep out of this—it's nothing to do with you.
come to nothing ➲ **come**
do nothing/not do anything by halves ➲ **half¹**
for nothing 1 for no payment; free □ *tanpa bayaran; percuma*: Children under four are allowed in for nothing. **2** for no good reason or with no good result □ *tdk berguna; sia-sia*: His hard work was all for nothing.
next to nothing ➲ **next to**
nothing but only □ *hanya...*: We've had nothing but trouble with this car.
nothing like 1 not at all like □ *tdk langsung spt*: She looks nothing like either of her parents. **2** not at all; not nearly □ *sama sekali tdk*: There's nothing like enough food for all of us.
nothing much not a lot of sth; nothing of importance □ *tdk ada apa(-apa) sangat*: It's a nice town but there's nothing much to do in the evenings. ◆ 'What did you do at the weekend?' 'Nothing much.'
(there's) nothing to it (it's) very easy □ *senang sahaja*: You'll soon learn—there's nothing to it really.
stop at nothing ➲ **stop¹**

[C] **countable**, a noun with a plural form: *one book, two books*   [U] **uncountable**, a noun with no plural form: *some sugar*

there is/was nothing (else) for it (but to do sth) there is/was no other action possible □ *tdk ada jalan lain (kecuali...)*: There was nothing for it but to resign.

notice¹ /ˈnəʊtɪs/ noun **1** [U] the act of paying attention to sth or knowing about sth □ *perhatian; pengetahuan*: The protests are finally making the government **take notice**. ♦ **Take no notice** of what he said—he was just being silly. ♦ Some people don't **take** any **notice of** (= choose to ignore) speed limits. ♦ It has **come to** my **notice** that you have missed a lot of classes. **2** [C] a piece of paper or a sign giving information, a warning, etc. that is put where everyone can read it □ *notis; pemberitahuan; peringatan*: There's a notice on the board saying 'that the meeting has been cancelled.' ♦ The notice said 'No dogs allowed'. **3** [U] a warning that sth is going to happen □ *notis; memberitahu lebih awal*: I can't produce a meal **at** such **short notice**! ♦ I wish you'd **give** me more **notice** when you're going to be off work. ♦ The swimming pool is closed **until further notice** (= until we are told that it will open again). ♦ She's **handed in** her **notice** (written a letter to say that she is leaving her job).

notice² /ˈnəʊtɪs/ verb [I,T] [not usually used in the continuous tenses] to see and become conscious of sth □ *perasan; menyedari; nampak*: 'What kind of car was the man driving?' 'I'm afraid I didn't notice.' ♦ I noticed (that) he was carrying a black briefcase. ♦ Did you notice which direction she went in? ♦ We didn't notice him leave/him leaving.

noticeable /ˈnəʊtɪsəbl/ adj easy to see or notice □ *ketara*: The scar from the accident was hardly noticeable. ▶ **noticeably** /-əbli/ adv

noticeboard /ˈnəʊtɪsbɔːd/ (*AmE* **ˈbulletin board**) noun [C] a board on a wall for putting written information where everyone can read it □ *papan kenyataan*

notify /ˈnəʊtɪfaɪ/ verb [T] (notifying; notifies; pt, pp notified) notify sb (of sth) to tell sb about sth officially □ *memberitahu* ▶ **notification** /ˌnəʊtɪfɪˈkeɪʃn/ noun [C,U]

notion /ˈnəʊʃn/ noun [C] **a notion (that .../of sth)** something that you have in your mind; an idea □ *tanggapan; idea; rasa-rasa*: I had a vague notion that I had seen her before.

notional /ˈnəʊʃənl/ adj existing only in the mind; not based on facts or reality □ *hanya dlm fikiran*

notoriety /ˌnəʊtəˈraɪəti/ noun [U] the state of being well known for sth bad □ *nama buruk; (perihal) terkenal kerana kejahatan*

notorious /nəʊˈtɔːriəs/ adj **notorious (for/as sth)** well known for sth bad □ *terkenal kerana kejahatan*: a notorious criminal ♦ This road is notorious for the number of accidents on it. **SYN** infamous ▶ **notoriously** adv

notwithstanding /ˌnɒtwɪθˈstændɪŋ; -wɪð-/ prep, adv (formal) in spite of sth □ *walaupun*

nought /nɔːt/ (especially AmE **zero**) noun [C] the figure 0 □ *kosong; sifar*: A million is written with six noughts. ♦ We say 0.1 'nought point one'.

ˌnoughts and ˈcrosses (*AmE* tic-tac-toe) noun [U] a game for two players in which each player tries to win by writing three 0s or three Xs in a line. □ *main pangkah-pangkah; main kandang babi (lembu, dsb)*

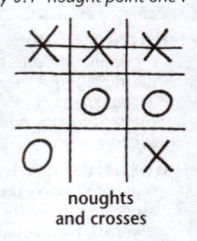

noughts and crosses

noun /naʊn/ noun [C] a word that is the name of a thing, an idea, a place or a person □ *kata nama*: 'Water', 'happiness', 'France' and 'James' are all nouns. ⊃ look at **countable, uncountable**

nourish /ˈnʌrɪʃ/ verb [T] **1** to give sb/sth the right kind of food so that they or it can grow and be healthy □ *menyuburkan; memberi makan* **2** (formal) to allow a feeling, an idea, etc. to grow stronger □ *memupuk; menaruh (perasaan, dll)* ▶ **nourishment** noun [U]

Nov. abbr = **November** □ *November*: 17 Nov. 2012

novel¹ /ˈnɒvl/ noun [C] a book that tells a story about people and events that are not real □ *novel*: a romantic/historical/detective novel ⊃ note at **book**

novel² /ˈnɒvl/ adj new and different □ *baharu; berlainan*: That's a novel idea! Let's try it.

novelist /ˈnɒvəlɪst/ noun [C] a person who writes novels □ *novelis; penulis novel*

novelty /ˈnɒvlti/ noun (pl novelties) **1** [U] the quality of being new and different □ *kebaharuan*: The novelty of the new job soon wore off. **2** [C] something new and unusual □ *sst yg baharu atau berlainan*: It was quite a novelty not to have to get up early. **3** [C] a small, cheap object that is sold as a toy or decoration □ *mainan/hiasan picisan*

November /nəʊˈvembə(r)/ noun [U,C] (abbr **Nov.**) the 11th month of the year, coming after October □ *November* ⊃ note at **January**

novice /ˈnɒvɪs/ noun [C] a person who is new and without experience in a certain job, situation, etc. □ *orang baharu* **SYN** beginner

now /naʊ/ adv, conj **1** (at) the present time □ *sekarang; kini*: We can't go for a walk now—it's raining. ♦ Where are you living now? ♦ **From now on** I'm going to work harder. ♦ **Up till now** we haven't been able to afford a house of our own. ♦ He will be on his way home **by now**. ♦ I can manage **for now** but I might need some help later. **2** immediately □ *sekarang juga*: Go now before anyone sees you. ♦ You must go to the doctor **right now**. **3** used to introduce or to emphasize what you are saying, or while pausing to think □ *(digunakan utk* *memulakan atau menekankan apa yg hendak dinyatakan); nah, sekarang, nanti, dll: Now listen to what he's saying.* ◆ *What does he want now?* ◆ *Now, let me think.*

MORE **Now then** is also used: *Now then, what was I saying?*

4 **now (that)**… *because of the fact that* □ *sekarang (ini)*: *Now (that) the children have left home we can move to a smaller house.*
IDM **any moment, day, minute, second, etc. (now)** ➲ **any**
just now ➲ **just¹**
(every) now and again/then *from time to time* □ *sekali-sekala*: *We see each other now and then, but not very often.* **SYN** **occasionally**
now what? 1 *used when you are annoyed because sb keeps interrupting you* □ *apalagi*: *'Dad?' 'Now what?'* **2** *used to say that you do not know what to do next in a particular situation* □ *seterusnya bagaimana?*
right now ➲ **right²**

nowadays /ˈnaʊədeɪz/ *adv* at the present time (when compared with the past) □ *sekarang ini*: *I don't go to London much nowadays* (= but I did in the past). **SYN** **today**

ɪ nowhere /ˈnəʊweə(r)/ *adv* not in or to any place; not anywhere □ *tdk ada tempat; tdk di/ ke mana-mana*: *I'm afraid there's nowhere to stay in this village.* ◆ *I don't like it here, but there's nowhere else for us to sit.*
IDM **get somewhere/nowhere (with sb/sth)** ➲ **get**
in the middle of nowhere ➲ **middle¹**
nowhere near *far from* □ *jauh dr; sama sekali tdk*: *We've sold nowhere near enough tickets to make a profit.*

noxious /ˈnɒkʃəs/ *adj* (*formal*) harmful or poisonous □ *berbahaya; beracun*: *noxious gases*

nozzle /ˈnɒzl/ *noun* [C] a narrow tube that is put on the end of a pipe to control the liquid or gas coming out □ *muncung*

nr *abbr* (*BrE*) = **near¹**(1) □ *dekat*: *Masham, nr Ripon*

nuance /ˈnjuːɑːns/ *noun* [C] a very small difference in meaning, feeling, sound, etc. □ *nuansa; perbezaan halus*

ɪ nuclear /ˈnjuːkliə(r)/ *adj* **1** using, producing or resulting from the energy that is produced when the **nucleus** of an atom is split □ *nuklear*: *nuclear energy* ◆ *a nuclear power station* ◆ *nuclear war/weapons* ➲ look at **atomic 2** connected with the **nucleus** of an atom □ *nuklear*: *nuclear physics*

ˌ**nuclear reˈactor** (also **reactor**) *noun* [C] a very large machine that produces nuclear energy □ *reaktor nuklear*

nucleus /ˈnjuːkliəs/ *noun* [C] (*pl* **nuclei** /-kliaɪ/) **1** the central part of an atom or of certain cells □ *nukleus* **2** the central or most important part of sth □ *teras*

nude¹ /njuːd/ *adj* not wearing any clothes □ *telanjang; bogel* ➲ look at **bare, naked** ▶ **nudity** /ˈnjuːdəti/ *noun* [U]: *This film contains scenes of nudity.*

589   nowadays → number plate

nude² /njuːd/ *noun* [C] a picture or photograph of a person who is not wearing any clothes □ *lukisan/gambar bogel*
IDM **in the nude** not wearing any clothes □ *telanjang; bogel*

nudge /nʌdʒ/ *verb* [T] to touch or push sb/sth gently, especially with your elbow □ *menyiku; menyigung* ➲ picture at **elbow** ▶ **nudge** *noun* [C]: *to give somebody a nudge*

nudist /ˈnjuːdɪst/ *noun* [C] a person who does not wear any clothes because they believe this is more natural and healthy □ *orang yg mengamalkan amalan bogel*: *a nudist beach/camp* ▶ **nudism** /ˈnjuːdɪzəm/ *noun* [U]

nuisance /ˈnjuːsns/ *noun* [C] a person, thing or situation that annoys you or causes you trouble □ *pengacau; pengganggu; sst yg menyusahkan; leceh betul*: *It's a nuisance having to queue for everything.*

numb /nʌm/ *adj* not able to feel anything; not able to move □ *kebas*: *My fingers were numb with cold.* ◆ *I'll give you an injection and the tooth will go numb.* ▶ **numb** *verb* [T]: *We were numbed by the dreadful news.* ▶ **numbness** *noun* [U]

ɪ number¹ /ˈnʌmbə(r)/ *noun*
▶WORD/SYMBOL **1** [C] a word or symbol that indicates a quantity □ *nombor; angka*: *Choose a number between ten and twenty.* ◆ *2, 4, 6, etc. are **even numbers** and 1, 3, 5, etc. are **odd numbers**.* ◆ *a three-figure number* (= from 100 to 999)
▶POSITION **2** [C] (*abbr* **No.**; **no.**) (*AmE abbr* **#**) used before a number to show the position of sth in a series □ *nombor*: *We live at number 32 Moorland Road.* ◆ *room No 347*
▶TELEPHONE, ETC. **3** [C] a group of numbers that is used to identify sb/sth □ *nombor*: *a telephone number* ◆ *a code number*
▶QUANTITY **4** [C,U] **a number (of sth)** a quantity of people or things □ *bilangan*: *a large number of visitors* ◆ *We must reduce the number of accidents on the roads.* ◆ *Pupils in the school have doubled in number in recent years.* ◆ *There are **a number of** (= several) things I don't understand.*
▶MAGAZINE **5** [C] (*BrE*) a copy of a magazine, newspaper, etc. □ *naskhah; keluaran*: *Back numbers of 'New Scientist' are available from the publishers.*
▶SONG **6** [C] (*informal*) a song or dance □ *lagu; tarian*: *They sang a slow romantic number.*
IDM **any number of** very many □ *banyak*: *There could be any number of reasons why she isn't here.*
in round figures/numbers ➲ **round¹**
your opposite number ➲ **opposite**

number² /ˈnʌmbə(r)/ *verb* [T] **1** to give a number to sth □ *memberi nombor; menombori*: *The houses are numbered from 1 to 52.* **2** used for saying how many people or things there are □ *berjumlah*: *Our forces number 40 000.*

ˈ**number plate** (*AmE* ˈ**license plate**) *noun* [C] the sign on the front and back of a vehicle that shows the **registration number** (= the particular combination of numbers and letters belonging to that vehicle) □ *plat nombor*

numeracy /ˈnjuːmərəsi/ *noun* [U] a good basic knowledge of mathematics; the ability to understand and work with numbers □ *kefahaman asas terhadap prinsip matematik; celik angka*: *standards of numeracy and literacy* ⊃ look at **literacy**

numeral /ˈnjuːmərəl/ *noun* [C] a sign or symbol that represents a quantity □ *angka*: *Roman numerals* (= I, II, III, IV, etc.)

numerate /ˈnjuːmərət/ *adj* having a good basic knowledge of mathematics □ *tahu mengira; kenal prinsip matematik* ⊃ look at **literate**

numerical /njuːˈmerɪkl/ *adj* of or shown by numbers □ *(berkenaan dgn) nombor/angka/bilangan*: *to put something in numerical order*

numerous /ˈnjuːmərəs/ *adj* (*formal*) existing in large numbers; many □ *banyak; ramai*

nun /nʌn/ *noun* [C] a member of a religious group of women who live together in a **convent** (= a special building) and do not marry or have possessions □ *biarawati; rahib wanita* ⊃ look at **monk**

nurse¹ /nɜːs/ *noun* [C] a person who is trained to look after sick or injured people □ *jururawat*: *a male nurse* ♦ *a psychiatric nurse* ♦ *a community/district nurse* (= who visits sick people in their homes to care for them) ⊃ note at **hospital** ⊃ picture on **page P2**

nurse² /nɜːs/ *verb* **1** [T] to take care of sb who is sick or injured; to take care of an injury □ *merawat; menjaga*: *She nursed her mother back to health.* ♦ *Ahmed is still nursing a back injury.* **2** [T] (*formal*) to have a strong feeling or idea in your mind for a long time □ *menaruh*: *Tim had long nursed the hope that Sharon would marry him.* **3** [T] to hold sb/sth in a loving way □ *membelai*: *He nursed the child in his arms.* **4** [I,T] to feed a baby or young animal with milk from the breast; to drink milk from the mother's breast □ *menyusui; menyusukan; menetek*

nursery /ˈnɜːsəri/ *noun* (*pl* **nurseries**) **1** [C,U] a place where small children and babies are looked after so that their parents can go to work □ *taman asuhan kanak-kanak* ⊃ look at **crèche** **2** [C] a place where young plants are grown and sold □ *tapak semaian*

ˈnursery ˈrhyme *noun* [C] a traditional poem or song for young children □ *lagu/puisi kanak-kanak tradisional*

ˈnursery ˈschool *noun* [C] a school for children aged from about 2 to 5 □ *tadika* **SYN** **kindergarten**

nursing /ˈnɜːsɪŋ/ *noun* [U] the job of being a nurse □ *kejururawatan; menjadi jururawat*

ˈnursing ˈhome *noun* [C] a small private hospital, often for old people □ *rumah penjagaan*

nurture /ˈnɜːtʃə(r)/ *verb* [T] (*formal*) **1** to take special care of sth/sb that is growing and developing □ *memelihara (sst yg sedang membesar dan berkembang); mengasuh; mendidik (kanak-kanak)*: *These delicate plants need careful nurturing.* ♦ *children nurtured by loving parents* **2** to help sth to develop and be successful □ *memupuk*: *It's important to nurture a good working relationship.* ▶ **nurture** *noun* [U] (*formal*)

nut /nʌt/ *noun* [C] **1** a dry fruit that consists of a hard shell with a seed inside. Many types of nut can be eaten □ *kekeras; kacang*: *to crack a nut* (= to open it) **2** a small piece of metal with a round hole in the middle through which you put a **bolt** (= long round piece of metal) to fasten things together □ *nat*: *to tighten a nut* ⊃ picture at **bolt**

nuts

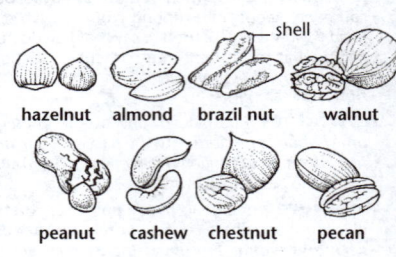

hazelnut almond brazil nut walnut
shell

peanut cashew chestnut pecan

nutcracker /ˈnʌtkrækə(r)/ [C] (*BrE also* **nutcrackers** [pl]) *noun* a tool that you use for breaking open the shell of a nut □ *kacip kekeras*

nutmeg /ˈnʌtmeg/ *noun* [C,U] a type of hard seed that is often made into powder and used as a spice in cooking □ *buah pala*

nutrient /ˈnjuːtriənt/ *noun* [C] a substance that is needed to keep a living thing alive and healthy □ *nutrien*: *Plants take minerals and other nutrients from the soil.*

nutcracker

nutrition /njuˈtrɪʃn/ *noun* [U] the food that you eat and the way that it affects your health □ *pemakanan*: *Good nutrition is essential for children's growth.* ▶ **nutritional** /-ʃənl/ *adj*

nutritious /njuˈtrɪʃəs/ *adj* (used about a food) very good for you □ *berkhasiat*

nuts /nʌts/ *adj* [not before a noun] (*informal*) crazy □ *gila*: *I'll go nuts if that phone doesn't stop ringing.* ♦ *She's driving me nuts with all her stupid questions.*

nutshell /ˈnʌtʃel/ *noun*
IDM **in a nutshell** using few words □ *ringkasnya; pendek kata*

nutty /ˈnʌti/ *adj* (**nuttier; nuttiest**) containing or tasting of nuts □ *mengandungi kacang; berasa kacang*

nuzzle /'nʌzl/ verb [I,T] to press or rub sb/sth gently with the nose □ *menggesel-geselkan hidung*

NW abbr = **north-west¹, north-western** □ *Barat Laut: NW Australia*

nylon /'naɪlɒn/ noun [U] a very strong artificial material that is used for making clothes, rope, brushes, etc. □ *nilon*

nymph /nɪmf/ noun [C] (in ancient Greek and Roman stories) a spirit of nature in the form of a young woman that lives in rivers, woods, etc. □ *pari-pari; bidadari*

O, o /əʊ/ noun [C,U] (pl Os; O's; o's /əʊz/) 1 the 15th letter of the English alphabet □ *O, o (huruf)*: 'Orange' begins with (an) 'O'. 2 (used when you are speaking) zero □ *kosong*: My number is five O nine double four (= 50944). ⊃ note at **zero**

O = **oh**

oak /əʊk/ noun 1 (also **'oak tree**) [C] a type of large tree with hard wood that is common in many northern parts of the world □ *pohon oak* 2 [U] the wood from the oak tree □ *kayu oak*: a solid oak table ⊃ look at **acorn**

OAP /,əʊ eɪ 'pi:/ abbr (BrE) = **old-age pensioner**

oar /ɔ:(r)/ noun [C] a long pole that is flat and wide at one end and that you use for rowing (= moving a small boat through water) □ *dayung; pengayuh* ⊃ look at **paddle** ⊃ picture at **boat**

oasis /əʊ'eɪsɪs/ noun [C] (pl oases /-si:z/) a place in the desert where there is water and where plants grow □ *oasis*

oath /əʊθ/ noun [C] 1 a formal promise □ *sumpah*: They have to swear/take an oath of loyalty. 2 (old-fashioned) = **swear word**

IDM be on/under oath to have made a formal promise to tell the truth in a court of law □ *telah bersumpah; mengangkat sumpah*

oats /əʊts/ noun [pl] a type of grain that is used as food for animals and for making flour, etc. □ *oat*

obedient /ə'bi:diənt/ adj obedient (to sb/sth) doing what you are told to do □ *mengikut kata; patuh; taat*: As a child he was always obedient to his parents. **OPP** disobedient ▶ obedience noun [U] ▶ obediently adv

obese /əʊ'bi:s/ adj (used about people) very fat, in a way that is not healthy □ *terlalu gemuk; boyak* ⊃ note at **fat** ▶ obesity /əʊ'bi:səti/ noun [U]

obey /ə'beɪ/ verb [I,T] to do what you are told to do □ *mematuhi; mentaati*: Soldiers are trained to obey orders. **OPP** disobey

obituary /ə'bɪtʃuəri/ noun [C] (pl obituaries) a piece of writing about sb's life that is printed in a newspaper soon after they have died □ *obituari; siaran takziah*

object¹ /'ɒbdʒɪkt/ (AmE usually) / noun [C] 1 a thing that can be seen and touched, but is not alive □ *benda; barang; objek*: The shelves were filled with objects of all shapes and sizes. ◆ everyday/household objects 2 the object of sth a person or thing that causes a feeling, interest, thought, etc. □ *(sso/sst yg menjadi) tumpuan*: the object of his desire/affections 3 the noun or phrase describing the person or thing that is affected by the act of a verb □ *objek* ⊃ look at **subject** 4 an aim or purpose □ *tujuan; matlamat*: Making money is his sole object in life.

GRAMMAR In the sentences: I sent a letter to Eva. ◆ I sent Eva a letter. 'a letter' is the **direct object** of the verb and 'Eva' is the **indirect object**.

IDM money, etc. is no object money, etc. is not important or is no problem □ *wang, dll tdk menjadi masalah*: They always want the best. Expense is no object.

object² /əb'dʒekt/ verb 1 [I] object (to sb/sth); object (to doing sth/to sb doing sth) to not like or to be against sb/sth □ *menentang; membangkang*: Many people object to the new tax. ◆ I object to companies trying to sell me things over the phone. 2 [T] to say a reason why you think sth is wrong □ *membantah*: 'I think that's unfair,' he objected. **SYN** for both meanings **protest** ▶ objector noun [C]

objection /əb'dʒekʃn/ noun [C] an objection (to sb/sth); an objection (to doing sth/to sb doing sth) a reason why you do not like or are against sb/sth □ *bantahan*: We listed our objections to the proposed new road. ◆ I have no objection to you using my desk while I'm away.

objectionable /əb'dʒekʃənəbl/ adj very unpleasant □ *amat tdk menyenangkan*

objective¹ /əb'dʒektɪv/ noun [C] something that you are trying to achieve; an aim □ *tujuan; matlamat*: Our objective is to finish by the end of the year. ◆ to achieve your objective **SYN** goal

objective² /əb'dʒektɪv/ adj not influenced by your own personal feelings; considering only facts □ *objektif; tdk dipengaruhi perasaan*: Please try and give an objective report of what happened. ◆ It's hard to be objective about your own family. **OPP** subjective ▶ objectively adv: He is too upset to see things objectively. ▶ objectivity /,ɒbdʒek'tɪvəti/ noun [U]

obligation /,ɒblɪ'ɡeɪʃn/ noun [C,U] (an) obligation (to sb) (to do sth) the state of having to do sth because it is a law or duty, or because you have promised □ *kewajipan; tanggungjawab*: Unfortunately the shop is under no obligation to give you your money back. ◆ We have an obliga-

obligatory → obsession 592

tion to help people who are in need. ♦ *By refusing to examine the animal, the vet failed to fulfil his professional obligations.*

obligatory /əˈblɪɡətri/ *adj* (*formal*) that you must do □ *wajib; perlu*: *It is obligatory to get insurance before you drive a car.* **OPP** optional

oblige /əˈblaɪdʒ/ *verb* 1 [T, usually passive] to force sb to do sth □ *terpaksa*: *Parents are obliged by law to send their children to school.* ♦ *Although I wasn't hungry, I felt obliged to eat something.* 2 [I,T] (*formal*) to do what sb asks; to be helpful □ *menolong; membantu*: *If you ever need any help, I'd be happy to oblige.* ▶**obliged** *adj* [not before a noun] (*formal*): *Thanks for your help. I'm much obliged to you.* ▶**obliging** *adj* (*formal*): *I asked my neighbour for advice and he was very obliging.*

oblique /əˈbliːk/ *adj* 1 not expressed or done in a direct way □ *(secara) tdk langsung*: *an oblique reference/approach/comment* **SYN** indirect 2 (used about a line) at an angle; sloping □ *miring, serong* ▶**obliquely** *adv*: *He referred only obliquely to their recent problems.* ♦ *Always cut stems obliquely to enable flowers to absorb more water.*

obliterate /əˈblɪtəreɪt/ *verb* [T, often passive] (*formal*) to remove all signs of sth by destroying or covering it completely □ *menghapuskan; memusnahkan; melindungi*

oblivion /əˈblɪviən/ *noun* [U] 1 a state in which you do not realize what is happening around you, usually because you are unconscious or asleep □ *keadaan tdk sedar*: *I was in a state of complete oblivion.* 2 the state in which sb/sth has been forgotten and is no longer famous or important □ *dilupakan*: *His work faded into oblivion after his death.*

oblivious /əˈblɪviəs/ *adj* **oblivious (to/of sb/sth)** not noticing or realizing what is happening around you □ *tdk sedar*: *She was completely oblivious of all the trouble she had caused.*

oblong /ˈɒblɒŋ/ (*AmE* also) /- *adj, noun* [C] (of) a shape with two long sides and two short sides and four **right angles** (= angles of 90°) □ *empat segi panjang; persegi bujur* **SYN** rectangle

obnoxious /əbˈnɒkʃəs/ *adj* extremely unpleasant, especially in a way that offends people □ *jelik; menimbulkan rasa meluat; menyakitkan hati*

oboe /ˈəʊbəʊ/ *noun* [C] a musical instrument made of wood that you play by blowing through it □ *obo* ➲ picture at **music**

obscene /əbˈsiːn/ *adj* 1 connected with sex in a way that most people find disgusting and which causes offence □ *lucah*: *obscene books/gestures/language* 2 very large in size or amount in a way that some people find unacceptable □ *sangat banyak, besar, dsb; keterlaluan*: *He earns an obscene amount of money.*

obscenity /əbˈsenəti/ *noun* (*pl* **obscenities**) 1 [U] sexual language or behaviour, especially in books, plays, etc. which shocks people and causes offence □ *kelucahan* 2 [C] sexual words or acts that shock people and cause offence □ *kata-kata, dsb lucah*: *He shouted a string of obscenities out of the car window.*

obscure¹ /əbˈskjʊə(r)/ *adj* 1 not well known □ *tdk terkenal; tdk diketahui ramai*: *an obscure Spanish poet* 2 not easy to see or understand □ *kabur; sukar difahami*: *For some obscure reason, he decided to give up his well-paid job, to become a writer.* ▶**obscurity** /əbˈskjʊərəti/ *noun* [U]

obscure² /əbˈskjʊə(r)/ *verb* [T] to make sth difficult to see or understand □ *melindungi; mengaburkan*: *A high fence obscured our view.*

observance /əbˈzɜːvəns/ *noun* [U, sing] **observance (of sth)** the practice of obeying or following a law, custom, etc. □ *amalan mematuhi undang-undang, adat, dsb*

observant /əbˈzɜːvənt/ *adj* good at noticing things around you □ *tajam pemerhatian*: *An observant passer-by gave the police a full description of the men.*

observation /ˌɒbzəˈveɪʃn/ *noun* 1 [U] the act of watching sb/sth carefully, especially to learn sth □ *pemerhatian; memerhati*: *My research involves the observation of animals in their natural surroundings.* ♦ *The patient is being kept under observation.* 2 [U] the ability to notice things □ *pencerapan; daya pemerhatian*: *Scientists need good powers of observation.* 3 [C] **an observation (about/on sth)** (*formal*) something that you say or write about sth □ *komen*: *He began by making a few general observations about the sales figures.* ➲ More common words are **remark** and **comment**.

observatory /əbˈzɜːvətri/ *noun* [C] (*pl* **observatories**) a building from which scientists can watch the stars, the weather, etc. □ *balai cerap*

observe /əbˈzɜːv/ *verb* [T] 1 (*formal*) to see or notice sb/sth □ *nampak; melihat; dilihat*: *A man and a woman were observed leaving by the back door.* 2 to watch sb/sth carefully, especially to learn more about them or it □ *memerhatikan*: *We observed the birds throughout the breeding season.* 3 (*formal*) to make a comment □ *mengatakan; kata(nya)*: *'We're late,' she observed.* 4 (*formal*) to obey a law, rule, etc. □ *mematuhi; mengikut*: *to observe the speed limit*

observer /əbˈzɜːvə(r)/ *noun* [C] 1 a person who watches sb/sth □ *orang yg memerhati; pemerhati*: *According to observers, the plane exploded shortly after take-off.* 2 a person who attends a meeting, lesson, etc. to watch and listen but who does not take part □ *pemerhati*

obsess /əbˈses/ *verb* [I,T] [usually passive] to completely fill your mind so that you cannot think of anything else □ *asyik memikirkan; menghantui fikiran*: *He became obsessed with getting his revenge.* ♦ *He's obsessed by computers.*

obsession /əbˈseʃn/ *noun* **obsession (with sb/sth)** 1 [U] the state in which you can only think

ʌ **c**up ɜː **b**ir**d** ə **a**g**o** eɪ p**ay** əʊ g**o** aɪ m**y** aʊ n**ow** ɔɪ b**oy** ɪə n**ear** eə h**air** ʊə p**ure**

obsessive → occupier

about one person or thing so that you cannot think of anything else □ *keadaan asyik memikirkan sso/sst*: *The media's obsession with the prince continues.* **2** [C] a person or thing that you think about too much □ *orang atau perkara yg menghantui fikiran*

obsessive /əbˈsesɪv/ *adj* thinking too much about one particular person or thing; behaving in a way that shows this □ *terlalu memikirkan ttg sso/sst; keterlaluan*: *He's obsessive about not being late.* ♦ *obsessive cleanliness*

obsolete /ˈɒbsəliːt/ *adj* no longer useful because sth better has been invented □ *usang*

obstacle /ˈɒbstəkl/ *noun* [C] **1 an obstacle (to sth/doing sth)** something that makes it difficult for you to do sth or go somewhere □ *halangan*: *Not speaking a foreign language was a major obstacle to her career.* **2** an object that is in your way and that makes it difficult for you to move forward □ *penghalang*

obstetrician /ˌɒbstəˈtrɪʃn/ *noun* [C] a hospital doctor who looks after women who are pregnant □ *pakar obstetrik*

obstinate /ˈɒbstɪnət/ *adj* refusing to change your opinions, way of behaving, etc. when other people try to persuade you to □ *degil; keras kepala*: *an obstinate refusal to apologize* **SYN stubborn** ▶ **obstinacy** /ˈɒbstɪnəsi/ *noun* [U] ▶ **obstinately** *adv*

obstruct /əbˈstrʌkt/ *verb* [T] to stop sb/sth from happening or moving either by accident or deliberately □ *menghalang; mengadang*: *Could you move on, please? You're obstructing the traffic if you park there.*

obstruction /əbˈstrʌkʃn/ *noun* **1** [U] the act of stopping sth from happening or moving □ *(perbuatan) menghalang* **2** [C] a thing that stops sb/sth from moving or doing sth □ *halangan*: *This car is causing an obstruction.*

obstructive /əbˈstrʌktɪv/ *adj* trying to stop sb/sth from moving or doing sth □ *(yg) menghalang*

ɡ obtain /əbˈteɪn/ *verb* [T] (*formal*) to get sth □ *mendapat(kan); memperoleh*: *to obtain advice/information/permission* ♦ *Where can I obtain tickets for the play?*

obtainable /əbˈteɪnəbl/ *adj* that you can get □ *dpt diperoleh*: *Full details are obtainable from our website.*

obtuse /əbˈtjuːs/ *adj* (*formal*) slow to understand sth □ *lembap; lambat memahami*: *Are you being deliberately obtuse?* ▶ **obtuseness** *noun* [U]

ob‚tuse ˈangle *noun* [C] an angle between 90° and 180° □ *sudut cakah* ➲ look at **acute angle, reflex angle, right angle**

ɡ obvious /ˈɒbviəs/ *adj* **obvious (to sb)** easily seen or understood □ *jelas; nyata; ketara*: *For obvious reasons, I'd prefer not to give my name.* ♦ *His disappointment was obvious to everyone.* **SYN clear** ▶ **obviously** *adv*: *There has obviously been a mistake.*

ɡ occasion /əˈkeɪʒn/ *noun* **1** [C] a particular time when sth happens □ *masa; kali*: *I have met Bill on two occasions.* **2** [C] a special event, ceremony, etc □ *peristiwa*: *Their wedding was a memorable occasion.* **3** [sing] the suitable or right time (for sth) □ *masa (yg sesuai); peluang; kesempatan*: *I shall tell her what I think if the occasion arises* (= if I get the chance).

HELP Occasion or opportunity? You use **occasion** when you mean the time is right or suitable for something: *I saw them at the funeral, but it was not a suitable occasion for discussing holiday plans.* You use **opportunity** or **chance** when you mean that it is possible to do something: *I was only in Paris for one day and I didn't get the opportunity/chance to visit the Louvre.*

IDM on occasion(s) sometimes but not often □ *kadang-kadang*

occasional /əˈkeɪʒənl/ *adj* [only before a noun] done or happening from time to time but not very often □ *sekali-sekala*: *We have the occasional argument but most of the time we get on.* ▶ **occasionally** /əˈkeɪʒnəli/ *adv*: *We see each other occasionally.*

occult /əˈkʌlt/ *adj* **1** [only before a noun] connected with magic powers and things that cannot be explained by reason or science □ *(berkenaan dgn) kuasa ghaib, sihir, dsb* **2 the occult** /əˈkʌlt/ *noun* [sing] magic powers, ceremonies, etc. □ *ilmu ghaib, sihir, dsb*

occupant /ˈɒkjəpənt/ *noun* [C] a person who is in a building, car, etc. at a particular time □ *orang yg berada dlm sst bangunan, kereta, dll; penginap; penghuni; penumpang*

occupation /ˌɒkjuˈpeɪʃn/ *noun* **1** [C] (*formal*) a job or profession; the way in which you spend your time □ *pekerjaan; kegemaran*: *Please state your occupation on the form.* ➲ note at **work²** **2** [U] the act of the army of one country taking control of another country; the period of time that this situation lasts □ *pendudukan; penaklukan*: *the Roman occupation of Britain* **3** [U] the act of living in or using a room, building, etc. □ *menghuni; tinggal di*

occupational /ˌɒkjuˈpeɪʃənl/ *adj* [only before a noun] connected with your work □ *(berkaitan dgn) pekerjaan*: *Accidents are an occupational hazard* (= a risk connected with a particular job) *on building sites.*

ɡ occupied /ˈɒkjupaɪd/ *adj* **1** [not before a noun] being used by sb □ *sedang digunakan; sudah ada orang*: *Is this seat occupied?* **2** busy doing sth □ *sibuk*: *Looking after the children keeps me fully occupied.* ➲ look at **preoccupied 3** (used about a country or a piece of land) under the control of another country □ *diduduki; ditakluki*: *His country had been occupied for many years.*

occupier /ˈɒkjupaɪə(r)/ *noun* [C] (*formal*) a person who owns, lives in or uses a house, piece of land, etc. □ *penghuni*

occupy /ˈɒkjupaɪ/ verb [T] (occupying; occupies; pt, pp occupied) **1** to fill a space or period of time □ *memenuhi*: *The large table occupied most of the room.* **SYN** take up **2** (formal) to live in or use a house, piece of land, etc. □ *menghuni; menduduki*: *The house next door has not been occupied for some months.* **3** to take control of a building, country, etc. by force □ *menguasai; menduduki*: *The rebel forces have occupied the TV station.* **4** occupy sb/yourself to keep sb/yourself busy □ *memenuhi/mengisi masa*: *How does he occupy himself now that he's retired?*

occur /əˈkɜː(r)/ verb [I] (occurring; occurred) **1** (formal) to happen, especially in a way that has not been planned □ *berlaku; terjadi*: *The accident occurred late last night.* ⇒ note at **happen** **2** to exist or be found somewhere □ *terdapat*: *The virus occurs more frequently in children.*

PHR V occur to sb (used about an idea or a thought) to come into your mind □ *terfikir; terlintas di fikiran*: *It never occurred to John that his wife might be unhappy.*

occurrence /əˈkʌrəns/ noun [C] something that happens or exists □ *kejadian; terjadinya*

ocean /ˈəʊʃn/ noun **1** [U] (especially AmE) the mass of salt water that covers most of the surface of the earth □ *laut; lautan*: *Two thirds of the earth's surface is covered by ocean.*

MORE Ocean is used in science and geography in British English, but the more general word is sea: *I swam in the sea.* In American English it is more usual to say ocean: *I swam in the ocean.*

2 Ocean [C] one of the five main areas into which the water is divided □ *Lautan*: *the Atlantic/Indian/Pacific Ocean* ⇒ look at **sea**
IDM a drop in the ocean ⇒ **drop²**
▸oceanic /ˌəʊʃiˈænɪk/ adj: *oceanic fish*

ochre (AmE also ocher) /ˈəʊkə(r)/ noun [U] a pale brownish-yellow colour □ *(warna) kuning tanah; oker* ▸ochre adj

o'clock /əˈklɒk/ adv used after the numbers one to twelve for saying what the time is □ *pukul*: *Lunch is at 12 o'clock.*

HELP Be careful. **o'clock** can only be used with full hours: *We arranged to meet at 5 o'clock.* *It's 5.30 already and he's still not here.*

Oct. abbr = October □ *Oktober*: *13 Oct. 2012*

octagon /ˈɒktəɡən/ noun [C] a shape that has eight straight and equal sides □ *oktagon; bentuk segi lapan* ▸octagonal /ɒkˈtæɡənl/ adj

octave /ˈɒktɪv/ noun [C] the set of eight musical notes that western music is based on □ *oktaf*

October /ɒkˈtəʊbə(r)/ noun [U,C] (abbr Oct.) the 10th month of the year, coming after September □ *Oktober* ⇒ note at **January**

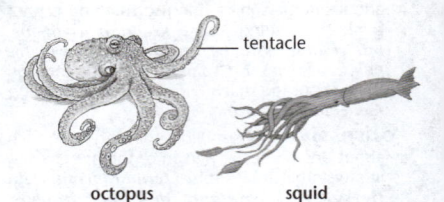

[I] **intransitive**, a verb which has no object: *He laughed.*

---

tentacle

octopus   squid

octopus /ˈɒktəpəs/ noun [C] a sea animal with a soft body and eight **tentacles** (= long thin parts like arms) □ *sotong kurita*

odd /ɒd/ adj (odder; oddest)
▸STRANGE **1** strange; unusual □ *pelik; aneh; ganjil*: *There's something odd about him.* • *It's a bit odd that she didn't phone to say she couldn't come.* **SYN** peculiar **2** odd- [in compounds] strange or unusual in the way mentioned □ *aneh; pelik*: *an odd-sounding name*
▸NOT REGULAR **3** [only before a noun] not regular or fixed; happening sometimes □ *sekali-sekala*: *He makes the odd mistake, but nothing very serious.*
▸VARIOUS **4** [only before a noun] that is left after other similar things have been used □ *saki-baki; reja-reja*: *He made the bookshelves out of a few odd bits of wood.*
▸NOT MATCHING **5** not with the pair or set it belongs to; not matching □ *tdk sepasang*: *You're wearing odd socks.*
▸NUMBER **6** (of a number) that cannot be divided by two □ *ganjil*: *One, three, five and seven are all odd numbers.* **OPP** even
▸APPROXIMATELY **7** (usually used after a number) a little more than □ *lebih sedikit drpd*: *'How old do you think he is?' 'Well, he must be thirty odd, I suppose.'*
IDM the odd man/one out one that is different from all the others in a group □ *sso/sst yg ganjil*: *Her brothers and sisters were much older than she was. She was always the odd one out.*
▸oddly adv: *Oddly enough, the most expensive tickets sold fastest.* ▸oddness noun [U]

oddity /ˈɒdəti/ noun [C] (pl oddities) a person or thing that is unusual □ *orang atau sst yg ganjil*

odd jobs noun [pl] small jobs or tasks of various types □ *kerja rencam*

oddments /ˈɒdmənts/ noun [pl] (especially BrE) **1** pieces of cloth, wood, etc. that is left after the rest has been used □ *reja; perca; lebihan* **2** small items that are not part of a set □ *benda kecil yg bukan sebahagian drpd suatu set*

odds /ɒdz/ noun [pl] the odds (on/against sth/sb) (used for saying how probable sth is) the degree to which sth is likely to happen □ *kemungkinan*: *The odds on him surviving are very slim* (= he will probably die). • *The odds are against you* (= you are not likely to succeed). • *The odds are in your favour* (= you are likely to succeed).
IDM against (all) the odds happening although it seemed impossible □ *walaupun nampaknya spt tdk mungkin*

[T] **transitive**, a verb which has an object: *He ate an apple.*

be at odds (with sb) (over sth) to disagree with sb about sth □ *berselisih faham (dgn sso) (ttg sst)*

be at odds (with sth) to be different from sth, when the two things should be the same □ *tdk sama (dgn sst)*

odds and ends (*informal*) small things of little value or importance □ *pelbagai barang kecil yg tdk berharga*

ode /əʊd/ *noun* [C] a poem that is written to or about a person or thing or to celebrate a special event □ *oda; sajak panjang*: *Keats's 'Ode to a Nightingale'*

odometer /əʊˈdɒmɪtə(r)/ (*AmE*) = **milometer**

odour (*AmE* **odor**) /ˈəʊdə(r)/ *noun* [C] (*formal*) a smell (often an unpleasant one) □ *bau; bau yg tdk enak* ➔ note at **smell²**

odourless (*AmE* **odorless**) /ˈəʊdələs/ *adj* without a smell □ *tdk berbau*

of /əv; *strong form* ɒv/ *prep* **1** belonging to, connected with, or part of sth/sb □ *bermaksud kepunyaan, berkaitan dgn, ttg atau sebahagian drpd sso/sst*: *the roof of the house* ◆ *the result of the exam* ◆ *the back of the book* ◆ *the leader of the party* ◆ *a friend of mine* (= one of my friends) **2** made, done or produced by sb □ *oleh*: *the poems of Milton* **3** showing sb/sth □ *menunjukkan sso/sst*: *a map of York* ◆ *a photograph of my parents* **4** used for saying what sb/sth is or what a thing contains or is made of □ *digunakan utk menyatakan apa sso/sst itu atau kandungan sst atau dibuat drpd apa*: *a woman of intelligence* ◆ *the city of Paris* ◆ *a glass of milk* ◆ *a crowd of people* ◆ *It's made of silver.* ◆ *a feeling of anger* **5** with measurements, directions and expressions of time and age □ *digunakan utk menyatakan ukuran, arah dan ungkapan ttg masa dan usia*: *a litre of milk* ◆ *the fourth of July* ◆ *a girl of 12* ◆ *an increase of 2.5%* ◆ *five miles north of Leeds* **6** showing that sb/sth is part of a larger group □ *drpd*: *some of the people* ◆ *three of the houses* **7** indicating the reason for or cause of sth □ *kerana; disebabkan oleh*: *He died of pneumonia.* **8** used after a noun describing an action to show either who did the action or who it happened to □ *digunakan selepas kn yg memerikan sst perbuatan utk menunjukkan siapa yg melakukannya atau berlaku kpd siapa*: *the arrival of the president* (= he arrives) ◆ *the murder of the president* (= he is murdered) **9** with some verbs □ *digunakan dgn kk tertentu*: *This perfume smells of roses.* ◆ *Think of a number.* ◆ *It reminds me of you.* **10** with some adjectives □ *digunakan dgn adjektif tertentu*: *I'm proud of you.* ◆ *She's jealous of her.*
IDM **of course** ➔ **course**

off¹ /ɒf/ (*AmE* also) / *adv, prep* **1** down or away from a place or a position on sth □ *dr; turun (dr); pergi*: *to fall off a ladder/motorbike/wall* ◆ *We got off the bus.* ◆ *I shouted to him but he just walked off.* ◆ *I must be off* (= I must leave here). *It's getting late.* ◆ *When are you off to Spain?* ◆ (*figurative*) *We've got off the subject.* **2** used with verbs that mean 'remove' or 'separate' □ *digunakan dgn kk yg bermaksud 'menanggalkan' atau 'mengasingkan'*: *She took her coat off.* ◆ *He shook the rain off his umbrella.* **OPP** **on** **3** joined to and leading away from □ *bercabang dr*: *My street is off the Cowley Road.* **4** at some distance from sth □ *jauh*: *The island of Elba is just off the west coast of Italy.* ◆ *Christmas is still a long way off* (= it is a long time until then). **5** (used about a plan or arrangement) not going to happen; cancelled □ *dibatalkan*: *The meeting/wedding/trip is off.* **OPP** **on** **6** (used about a machine, a light, etc.) not connected, working or being used □ *tdk dipasang atau digunakan; tutup; padamkan; matikan*: *Please make sure the TV/light/heating is off.* **7** not present at work, school, etc. □ *tdk hadir; tdk bekerja*: *She's off work/off sick with a cold.* ◆ *I'm having a day off* (= a day's holiday) *next week.* **8** cheaper; less by a certain amount □ *lebih murah; kurang*: *cars with £600 off* ◆ *£600 off the price of a car* **9** not eating or using sth □ *tdk mahu makan atau tdk mahu menggunakan sst*: *The baby's off his food.* **ⓘ** For special uses with many verbs, for example **go off**, look at the verb entries.
IDM **off and on; on and off** sometimes; starting and stopping □ *sekali-sekala; sekejap-sekejap*: *It has been raining on and off all day.*
well/badly off having/not having a lot of money □ *berada/tdk berada*: *They don't seem too badly off—they have smart clothes and a nice house.*

off² /ɒf/ (*AmE* also) / *adj* (*informal*) [not before a noun] **1** (used about food or drink) no longer fresh enough to eat or drink □ *sudah basi; busuk*: *The milk's off.* **2** (*spoken*) unfriendly □ *agak dingin*: *My neighbour was rather off with me today.*

offal /ˈɒfl/ (*AmE* also) / *noun* [U] the heart and other organs of an animal, used as food □ *organ/bahagian dlm binatang yg boleh dimakan*

ˈoff chance *noun* [sing] a slight possibility □ *sedikit kemungkinan; kalau-kalau*: *She popped round **on the off chance** of finding him at home.*

ˈoff day *noun* [C] (*informal*) a day when things go badly or you do not work well □ *hari serba tak kena; hari yg semua dibuat tdk jadi*: *Even the best players have off days occasionally.*

off-ˈduty *adj* not at work □ *luar waktu bertugas; tdk bekerja*: *an off-duty police officer*

offence (*AmE* **offense**) /əˈfens/ *noun* **1** [C] (*formal*) **an offence (against sth)** a crime; an illegal action □ *kesalahan*: *to commit an offence* ◆ *a criminal/minor/serious/sexual offence* **2** [U] **offence (to sb/sth)** the act of upsetting or insulting sb □ *menyinggung perasaan sso*: *I didn't mean to cause you any offence.*
IDM **take offence (at sth)** to feel upset or hurt by sb/sth □ *berasa tersinggung (kerana sst)*

offend /əˈfend/ *verb* **1** [T, often passive] to hurt sb's feelings; to upset sb □ *menyinggung* *perasaan sso; tersinggung*: I hope they won't be offended if I don't come. ◆ He felt offended that she hadn't written for so long. **2** [I] (*formal*) to do sth illegal; to commit a crime □ *melanggar undang-undang; melakukan kesalahan/jenayah*: The prisoner had offended again within days of his release from jail.

offender /əˈfendə(r)/ *noun* [C] **1** (*formal*) a person who breaks the law or commits a crime □ *pesalah*: Young offenders should not be sent to adult prisons. ◆ a first offender (= sb who has committed a crime for the first time) **2** a person or thing that does sth wrong □ *orang atau sst yg melakukan kesalahan*

offensive¹ /əˈfensɪv/ *adj* **1** offensive (to sb) unpleasant; insulting □ *menyakitkan hati; menghina*: offensive behaviour/language/remarks OPP **inoffensive 2** [only before a noun] (*formal*) used for or connected with attacking □ *utk menyerang*: offensive weapons OPP **defensive** ▶ **offensively** *adv*

offensive² /əˈfensɪv/ *noun* [C] a military attack □ *serangan (tentera)*
IDM **be on the offensive** to be the first to attack sb/sth, rather than waiting for them to attack you □ *menyerang dulu sebelum diserang*

offer¹ /ˈɒfə(r)/ (*AmE also*) / *verb* **1** [T] offer sth (to sb) (for sth); offer (sb) sth to ask if sb would like sth or to give sb the chance to have sth □ *menawarkan; memberi*: He offered his seat on the bus to an old lady. ◆ I've been offered a job in London. ◆ He offered (me) £2 000 for the car and I accepted. **2** [I] offer (to do sth) to say or show that you will do sth for sb if they want □ *menawarkan diri*: I don't want to do it but I suppose I'll have to offer. ◆ My brother's offered to help me paint the house. **3** [T] to make sth available or to provide the opportunity for sth □ *memberi; menawarkan*: The job offers plenty of opportunity for travel.

offer² /ˈɒfə(r)/ (*AmE also*) / *noun* [C] **1** an offer (of sth); an offer (to do sth) a statement offering to do sth or give sth to sb □ *tawaran*: She accepted my offer of help. ◆ Thank you for your kind offer to help.

MORE We can **make, accept, refuse, turn down** or **withdraw** an offer.

2 an offer (of sth) (for sth) an amount of money that you say you will give for sth □ *tawaran*: They've made an offer for the house. ◆ We've turned down (= refused) an offer of £150 000. ⊃ look at **o.n.o. 3** a low price for sth in a shop, usually for a short time □ *tawaran*: See below for details of our special holiday offer.
IDM **on offer 1** for sale or available □ *menawarkan*: The college has a wide range of courses on offer. **2** (*especially BrE*) for sale at a lower price than usual for a certain time □ *ditawarkan dgn harga murah*: This cheese is on offer until next week.

offering /ˈɒfərɪŋ/ (*AmE also*) / *noun* [C] something that is given or produced for other people to watch, enjoy, etc. □ *pemberian; hadiah; persembahan*

offhand¹ /ˌɒfˈhænd/ (*AmE also*) / *adj* (used about behaviour) not showing any interest in sb/sth in a way that seems rude □ *bersikap bersahaja*: an offhand manner/voice

offhand² /ˌɒfˈhænd/ (*AmE also*) / *adv* without having time to think; immediately □ *bersikap bersahaja (tanpa ada masa utk memikirkannya dahulu)*: I can't tell you what it's worth offhand.

office /ˈɒfɪs/ (*AmE usually*) / *noun* **1** [C] a room, set of rooms or a building where people work, usually sitting at desks □ *pejabat*: I usually get to the office at about 9 o'clock. ◆ The firm's **head office** (= the main branch of the company) is in Cairo. ◆ Please phone again during office hours.

HELP In the US doctors and dentists have **offices**. In Britain they have **surgeries**.

2 [C] [in compounds] a room or building that is used for a particular purpose, especially for providing a service □ *pejabat*: the tax/ticket/tourist office ⊃ look at **booking office, box office, post office 3 Office** [sing] a government department, including the people who work there and the work they do □ *jabatan; pejabat*: the Foreign/Home Office **4** [C,U] an official position, often as part of a government or other organization □ *jawatan; membentuk kerajaan*: The Labour party was in office from 1997 to 2010.

TOPIC

Office work

I work as a **secretary** for a large **firm** of lawyers. The **company** employs over 50 **members of staff**. I work in an **open-plan office** so I share a large room with my **colleagues** (= the people I work with). On my desk I have a **PC** (= personal computer) and a **printer**. My **duties** include **typing** letters and emails for my boss, **filing** (= putting documents into files), answering the phone and doing the **photocopying**. I go to **meetings** and take the **minutes** (= write down what is said). I am also responsible for **ordering stationery** (= pens, paper, envelopes, etc.) and making **travel arrangements** for my boss's business trips. I work **nine to five** and have twenty days' holiday a year.

office block *noun* [C] a large building that contains offices, usually belonging to more than one company □ *bangunan pejabat* ⊃ picture on **page P11**

officer /ˈɒfɪsə(r)/ (*AmE also*) / *noun* [C] **1** a person who is in a position of authority in the armed forces □ *pegawai (tentera)*: an army/air-force officer **2** a person who is in a position of authority in the government or a large organization □ *pegawai (kerajaan, dll)*: a prison/customs/welfare officer **3** = **police officer**

official¹ /əˈfɪʃl/ *adj* **1** [only before a noun] connected with the position of sb in authority

☐ *rasmi*: *official duties/responsibilities* **2** accepted and approved by the government or some other authority ☐ *rasmi*: *The scheme has not yet received official approval.* ◆ *The country's official language is Spanish.* **3** that is told to the public, but which may or may not be true ☐ *rasmi*: *The official reason for his resignation was that he wanted to spend more time with his family.* **OPP** for all meanings **unofficial**

official² /əˈfɪʃl/ *noun* [C] a person who has a position of authority ☐ *pegawai*: *The reception was attended by MPs and high-ranking officials.*

> **MORE** An **office worker** is a person who works in an office, at a desk. An **official** is a person who has a position of responsibility in an organization, often the government: *senior government officials.* An **officer** is either a person who gives orders to others in the armed forces or is a member of the police force. However the word is sometimes used like **official**: *She's a tax officer in the Civil Service.*

officialdom /əˈfɪʃldəm/ *noun* [U] groups of people in positions of authority in large organizations who seem more interested in following the rules than in being helpful ☐ *pegawai (atau mereka yg diberi kuasa) yg lebih mementingkan peraturan drpd membantu orang ramai*

officially /əˈfɪʃəli/ *adv* **1** publicly and by sb in a position of authority ☐ *secara rasmi*: *The new school was officially opened last week.* **2** according to a particular set of laws, rules, etc. ☐ *menurut undang-undang, peraturan, dsb*: *Officially we don't accept children under six, but we'll make an exception in this case.*

officious /əˈfɪʃəs/ *adj* too ready to tell other people what to do and use the power you have to give orders ☐ *suka mengarah dan megah kerana ada sedikit kuasa*

offing /ˈɒfɪŋ/ (*AmE* also) / *noun*
IDM **in the offing** (*informal*) likely to appear or happen soon ☐ *akan (muncul, berlaku, dsb) tdk lama lagi*

ˈoff-licence *noun* [C] (*AmE* ˈ**liquor store**) a shop which sells alcoholic drinks in bottles and cans ☐ *kedai yg menjual minuman keras utk dibawa pulang sahaja*

offline /ˌɒfˈlaɪn/ (*AmE* also) / *adj, adv* not directly controlled by or connected to a computer or the Internet ☐ *luar talian*: *For offline orders, call this number.* ◆ *Could you tell me how to write an email offline?* ⇒ look at **online**

offload /ˌɒfˈləʊd/ (*AmE* also) / *verb* [T] (*informal*) **offload sth (on/onto sb)** to give away sth that you do not want to sb else ☐ *melego; melepaskan beban*: *It's nice to have someone you can offload your problems onto.*

ˌoff-ˈpeak *adj, adv* [only *before* a noun] available, used or done at a less popular or busy time ☐ *luar puncak; tdk sibuk*: *an off-peak train ticket/bus pass/phone call* ◆ *It's cheaper to travel off-peak.* ⇒ look at **peak**

ˌoff-ˈputting *adj* unpleasant in a way that stops you from liking sb/sth ☐ *tdk menyenangkan*

offset /ˈɒfset (*AmE* also) / *verb* [T] (**offsetting**; *pt, pp* **offset**) to make the effect of sth less strong or noticeable ☐ *mengimbangi*: *The disadvantages of the scheme are more than offset by the advantages.*

offshoot /ˈɒfʃuːt (*AmE* also) / *noun* [C] a thing that develops from sth else, especially a small organization that develops from a larger one ☐ *cabang*

offshore /ˌɒfˈʃɔː(r) (*AmE* also) / *adj, adv* in the sea but not very far from the land ☐ *pesisir/luar pantai*: *an offshore oil rig* ◆ *a ship anchored offshore*

offside *adj* **1** /ˌɒfˈsaɪd (*AmE* also) / (used about a player in football and other sports) in a position that is not allowed by the rules of the game ☐ *ofsaid* **2** /ˈɒfsaɪd (*AmE* also) / (*BrE*) (used about a part of a vehicle) on the side that is furthest away from the edge of the road ☐ *sebelah kanan (kenderaan)*

offspring /ˈɒfsprɪŋ (*AmE* also) / *noun* [C] (*pl* **offspring**) (*formal*) a child or children; the young of an animal ☐ *anak*: *to produce/raise offspring*

ˌoff-ˈwhite *adj* not pure white ☐ *keputih-putihan*

often /ˈɒfn; ˈɒftən (*AmE* also) / *adv* **1** many times ☐ *kerap; sering; selalu*: *We often go swimming at the weekend.* ◆ *I'm sorry I didn't write very often.* ◆ *How often should you go to the dentist?* **SYN** **frequently 2** in many cases ☐ *selalunya; sering kali*: *Old houses are often damp.* **SYN** **commonly**
IDM **every so often** sometimes; from time to time ☐ *dr semasa ke semasa*
more often than not usually ☐ *selalunya*

ogre /ˈəʊɡə(r)/ *noun* [C] **1** (in children's stories) a very large, cruel and frightening creature that eats people ☐ *gergasi; raksasa* **2** a person who is unpleasant and frightening ☐ *orang yg jelik atau menggerunkan*

oh (also **O**) /əʊ/ *exclam* **1** used for reacting to sth that sb has said ☐ *Oh*: '*I'm a teacher.*' '*Oh? Where?*' **2** used to express surprise, fear, joy, etc. ☐ *oh*: '*Oh no!*' *she cried as she began to read the letter.*

ˈoh well = **well³**(2)

oil /ɔɪl/ *noun* [U] **1** a thick dark liquid that comes from under the ground and is used as a fuel or to make machines work smoothly ☐ *minyak (petrol, dsb)*: *Britain obtains oil from the North Sea.* **2** a thick liquid that comes from animals or plants and is used in cooking ☐ *minyak masak*: *cooking/vegetable/sunflower/olive oil* ▶ **oil** *verb* [T]

oilfield /ˈɔɪlfiːld/ *noun* [C] an area where there is oil under the ground or under the sea ☐ *kawasan/medan minyak*

VOWELS iː see i any ɪ sit e ten æ hat ɑː father ɒ got ɔː saw ʊ put uː too u usual

oil painting noun [C] a picture that has been painted using paint made with oil □ *lukisan cat minyak*

oil rig (also **rig**) noun [C] a large platform in the sea with equipment for getting oil out from under the sea □ *pelantar minyak*

oil slick (also **slick**) noun [C] an area of oil that floats on the sea, usually after a ship carrying oil has crashed □ *tumpahan minyak*

oil well (also **well**) noun [C] a hole that is made deep in the ground or under the sea in order to obtain oil □ *telaga minyak*

oily /ˈɔɪli/ adj (**oilier**; **oiliest**) covered with oil or like oil □ *berminyak*: *Mechanics always have oily hands.* ◆ *oily food*

ointment /ˈɔɪntmənt/ (also **cream**) noun [C,U] a smooth substance that you put on sore skin or on an injury to help it get better □ *salap* ➔ picture at **medicine**

OK[1] (also **okay**) /əʊˈkeɪ/ adj, adv, exclam (informal) **1** all right; good or well enough □ *OK; okey; baiklah*: 'Did you have a nice day?' 'Well, it was OK, I suppose.' ◆ *Is it okay if I come at about 7?* **2** yes; all right □ *ya*: 'Do you want to come with us?' 'OK.'

OK[2] (also **okay**) /əʊˈkeɪ/ noun [sing] agreement or permission □ *kebenaran*: *As soon as my parents give me the OK, I'll come and stay with you.*

old /əʊld/ adj (**older**; **oldest**)
▸AGE **1** [used with a period of time or with *how*] of a particular age □ *berusia; usia; berumur; umur*: *That building is 500 years old.* ◆ *The book is aimed at eight- to ten-year-olds.* ◆ *How old are you?* ➔ note at **age**[1]
▸NOT YOUNG **2** having lived a long time □ *tua; berumur*: *My mother wasn't very old when she died.* ◆ *He's only 50 but he looks older.* ◆ *to get/grow old* **OPP** **young** **3** **the old** noun [pl] old people □ *orang tua*: *The old feel the cold more than the young.* ➔ look at **the elderly, the aged**
▸NOT NEW **4** that has existed for a long time; connected with past times □ *lama; tua; dahulu*: *This house is quite old.* ◆ *old ideas/traditions* ◆ *In the old days, people generally had larger families than nowadays.* **OPP** **new, modern 5** having been used a lot □ *lama*: *I got rid of all my old clothes.* **OPP** **new** ➔ look at **second-hand 6** [only before a noun] former □ *lama*: *I earn any old rubbish in my diary.* **SYN** **previous 7** [only before a noun] known for a long time □ *lama*: *She's a very old friend of mine. We knew each other at school.*

GRAMMAR **Older** and **oldest** are the usual comparative and superlative forms of **old**: *My father's older than my mother.* ◆ *I'm the oldest in the class.* **Elder** and **eldest** can be used when comparing the ages of people, especially members of a family. However, it is only used in phrases like: *elder brother* and: *eldest daughter* It is not used with *than*, so it is not correct to say, 'My sister is elder than me.'

▸NOT IMPORTANT **8** [only before a noun] (informal) used for emphasizing that sth has little importance or value □ *apa-apa; mana-mana; (utk menyatakan sst yg tdk penting atau tdk bernilai)*: *I write any old rubbish in my diary.*
IDM **be an old hand (at sth)** to be good at sth because you have done it often before □ *orang lama (yakni berpengalaman)*: *She's an old hand at dealing with the press.*

old age noun [U] the part of your life when you are old □ *usia tua*: *He's enjoying life in his old age.* ➔ look at **youth**

old-age pension noun [U] (BrE) money paid by the state to people above a certain age □ *pesara*
▸**old-age pensioner** (also **pensioner**) noun [C] (abbr **OAP**) ➔ look at **pension**

HELP The expression **senior citizen** is more polite and is more common nowadays.

Old English = **Anglo-Saxon**(3)

old-fashioned adj **1** usual in the past but not now □ *fesyen lama*: *old-fashioned clothes/ideas* ◆ *That word sounds a bit old-fashioned.* **2** (used about people) believing in old ideas, customs, etc □ *kolot; ketinggalan zaman*: *My parents are quite old-fashioned about some things.* ➔ look at **modern, unfashionable**

the Old Testament noun [sing] the first part of the Bible that tells the history of the Jewish people before the birth of Christ □ *Wasiat Lama (Kitab Zabur)* ➔ look at **the New Testament**

oligarch /ˈɒlɪɡɑːk/ noun [C] **1** a member of a government in which only a small group of people hold all the power □ *oligarki* **2** an extremely rich and powerful person □ *hartawan*

olive /ˈɒlɪv/ noun **1** [C] a small green or black fruit with a bitter taste, used for food and oil □ *buah zaitun*: *Fry the onions in a little olive oil.* **2** (also **olive green**) [U] a colour between yellow and green □ *hijau kekuning-kuningan* ▸**olive** adj

the Olympic Games /əˌlɪmpɪk ˈɡeɪmz/ (also **the Olympics**) noun [pl] an international sports competition which is organized every four years in a different country □ *Sukan Olimpik*: *to win a medal at/in the Olympics* ◆ *the Winter/Summer Olympics* ▸**Olympic** adj [only before a noun]: *Who holds the Olympic record for the 1500 metres?*

ombudsman /ˈɒmbʊdzmən; -mæn/ noun [sing] an official whose job is to examine and report on complaints made by ordinary people about public organizations □ *ombudsman; pegawai penyiasat aduan orang ramai terhadap organisasi awam*

omelette (AmE **omelet**) /ˈɒmlət/ noun [C] a dish made of eggs that have been beaten and fried □ *telur dadar*

omen /ˈəʊmən/ noun [C] a sign of sth that will happen in the future □ *petanda; alamat*: *a good/bad omen for the future*

ominous /ˈɒmɪnəs/ *adj* suggesting that sth bad is going to happen □ *menandakan sst yg tdk baik akan berlaku; menandakan hari akan hujan*: *Those black clouds look ominous.*

omission /əˈmɪʃn/ *noun* [C,U] something that has not been included; the act of not including sb/sth □ *sst yg tdk dimasukkan/disertakan; (perbuatan) tdk memasukkan/menyertakan*: *There were several omissions on the list of names.*

omit /əˈmɪt/ *verb* [T] (**omitting**; **omitted**) **1** to not include sth; to leave sth out □ *tdk memasukkan/menyertakan*: *Several verses of the song can be omitted.* **2** (*formal*) **omit to do sth** to forget or choose not to do sth □ *terlupa/tdk membuat sst*

on /ɒn/ (*AmE also*) / *adv, prep* **1** (also *formal* **upon**) supported by, fixed to or touching sth, especially a surface □ *di; di atas*: *on the table/ceiling/wall* ◆ *We sat on the beach/grass/floor.* ◆ *She was carrying the baby on her back.* ◆ *Write it down on a piece of paper.* ◆ *The ball hit me on the head.* **2** in a place or position □ *di (sst tempat atau kedudukan)*: *on a farm/housing estate/campsite* ◆ *a house on the river/seafront/border* ◆ *I live on the other side of town.* **3** used with ways of travelling and types of travel □ *menaiki; (bermaksud utk menyatakan cara membuat perjalanan dan jenis perjalanan)*: *on the bus/train/plane* ◆ *We came on foot* (= we walked). ◆ *Eddie went past on his bike.* ◆ *to go on a trip/journey/excursion*

> **HELP** Note that we say **in the car**.

4 with expressions of time □ *pd*: *on August 19th* ◆ *on Monday* ◆ *on Christmas Day* ◆ *on your birthday* **5** showing that sth continues □ *terus; berterusan*: *The man shouted at us but we walked on.* ◆ *The speeches went on and on until everyone was bored.* **6** wearing sth; carrying sth in your pocket or bag □ *memakai; ada membawa*: *What did she have on?* ◆ *to put your shoes/coat/hat/make-up on* ◆ *I've got no money on me.* ◆ *You should carry ID on you at all times.* **7** working; being used □ *berjalan; terpasang; buka; hidupkan*: *All the lights were on.* ◆ *Switch the TV on.* **8** immediately or soon after □ *sebaik-baik sahaja*: *He telephoned her on his return from New York.* **9** about sth □ *ttg; berkenaan dgn*: *We've got a test on irregular verbs tomorrow.* ◆ *a talk/a book/an article on Japan* **10** happening or arranged to happen □ *bermaksud berlaku atau akan berlangsung; ada; jadi*: *What's on at the cinema?* ◆ *Is the meeting still on, or has it been cancelled?* **11** using drugs or medicine; using a particular kind of food or fuel □ *mengambil; memakan; menggunakan*: *to be on medication/antibiotics/heroin* ◆ *Gorillas live on leaves and fruit.* ◆ *Does this car run on petrol or diesel?* **12** showing direction □ *di (menunjukkan arah)*: *on the right/left* ◆ *on the way to school* **13** showing the reason for or starting point of sth □ *berdasarkan*: *She doesn't eat meat on principle.* ◆ *The film is based on a true story.* **14** receiving a certain amount of money □ *bermaksud mendapat jumlah wang tertentu*: *What will you be on* (= how much will you earn) *in your new job?* ◆ *He's been (living) on unemployment benefit since he lost his job.* **15** paid for by sb □ *dibayar oleh sso*: *The drinks are on me!* **16** using sth; by means of sth □ *di; pd*: *I was (talking)* **on the phone** *to Laura.* ◆ *I saw it on TV.* ◆ *I cut my hand on some glass.* ◆ *Dave spends most evenings* **on the Internet**. **17** showing the thing or person that is affected by an action or is the object of an action □ *pd*: *Divorce can have a bad effect on children.* ◆ *He spends a lot on clothes.* ◆ *Don't waste your time on that.* **18** compared to □ *berbanding dgn*: *Sales are up 10% on last year.* ❶ For special uses with many verbs and nouns, for example **get on**, **on holiday**, see the verb and noun entries.

IDM **from now/then on** starting from this/that time and continuing □ *mulai sekarang; sejak itu*: *From then on she never spoke to him again.*

not on (*informal*) not acceptable □ *tdk boleh (diterima)*: *No, you can't stay out that late. It's just not on.*

off and on; on and off ➔ **off¹**

PHR V **be/go on at sb** ➔ **go¹**

once /wʌns/ *adv, conj* **1** one time only; on one occasion □ *sekali (sahaja)*: *I've only been to France once.* ◆ *once a week/month/year* ◆ *I visit them about once every six months.* **2** at some time in the past □ *(pd) suatu ketika dahulu*: *This house was once the village school.* **SYN** **formerly** **3** as soon as; when □ *sebaik sahaja; apabila*: *Once you've practised a bit you'll find that it's quite easy.*

IDM **all at once** all at the same time or suddenly □ *semua sekali serentak; tiba-tiba*: *People began talking all at once.* ◆ *All at once she got up and left the room.*

at once 1 immediately; now □ *dgn segera*: *Come here at once!* **2** at the same time □ *serentak; sekali gus*: *I can't understand if you all speak at once.*

just this once; (just) for once on this occasion only □ *sekali ini sahaja*: *Just this once, I'll help you with your homework.*

once again/more again, as before □ *sekali lagi*: *Spring will soon be here once again.*

once and for all now and for the last time □ *sekali ini sahaja lagi; yg muktamad*: *You've got to make a decision once and for all.*

once in a blue moon (*informal*) almost never □ *jarang-jarang sekali; hampir tdk pernah*

once in a while sometimes but not often □ *sekali-sekala*

once more one more time □ *sekali lagi*: *Let's listen to that track once more, shall we?*

once upon a time (used at the beginning of a children's story) a long time ago; in the past □ *pd satu masa dahulu*: *Once upon a time there was a princess ...*

oncoming /ˈɒnkʌmɪŋ/ (*AmE also*) / *adj* [only before a noun] coming towards you □ *datang dr arah depan*: *oncoming traffic*

one¹ /wʌn/ *number, determiner* **1** the number 1 □ *satu; se*: *There's only one biscuit left.* ◆ *The*

[C] **countable**, a noun with a plural form: *one book, two books*   [U] **uncountable**, a noun with no plural form: *some sugar*

journey takes one hour. ◆ *If you take one from ten it leaves nine.* ⊃ note at **six** ⊃ look at **first** **2** used with *the other*, *another* or *other(s)* to make a contrast □ *satu (sama lain)*: *The twins are so alike that it's hard to tell one from the other.* **3 the one** used for emphasizing that there is only one of sth □ *satu-satunya*: *She's the one person I trust.* ◆ *We can't all get in the one car.* **4** (used when you are talking about a time in the past or future without actually saying when) a certain □ *satu (masa, hari, dsb)*: *He came to see me one evening last week.* ◆ *We must go and visit them one day.*

IDM **(all) in one** all together or combined □ *sekali; gabungan*: *It's a printer and scanner all in one.*

the odd man/one out ⊃ **odd**

one after another/the other first one, then the next, etc. □ *seorang demi seorang; satu satu; berturut-turut*: *One after another the winners went up to get their prizes.*

one at a time separately □ *satu-satu; satu per satu*: *I'll deal with the problems one at a time.* **SYN** **individually**

one by one separately □ *satu lepas/demi satu; seorang lepas/demi seorang*: *One by one, people began to arrive at the meeting.*

one or two a few □ *satu dua*: *I've borrowed one or two new books from the library.*

one² /wʌn/ *pron* [C] **1** used instead of repeating a noun □ *satu*: *I think I'll have an apple. Would you like one?* **2** used after *this*, *that*, *which* or after an adjective instead of a noun □ *yg (ini, itu, dll)*: *'Which dress do you like?' 'This one.'* ◆ *'Can I borrow some books of yours?' 'Yes. Which ones?'* ◆ *'This coat's a bit small. You need a bigger one.'* ◆ *That idea is a very good one.* **3 the one/the ones** used before a group of words that show which person or thing you are talking about □ *yg; satu*: *My house is the one after the post office.* ◆ *If you find some questions difficult, leave out the ones you don't understand.* **4 one of** a member (of a certain group) □ *salah seorang/satu*: *He's staying with one of his friends.* ◆ *One of the children is crying.*

> **GRAMMAR** **One of** is always followed by a plural noun. The verb is singular because the subject is **one**: *One of our assistants is ill.* ◆ *One of the buses was late.*

5 (*formal*) used for referring to people in general, including the speaker or writer □ *kita; sso itu*: *One must be sure of one's facts before criticizing other people.*

> **HELP** This use of **one** is very formal and now sounds old-fashioned. It is much more usual to say **you**.

one a'nother *pron* used when you are saying that each member of a group does sth to or for the other people in the group □ *satu sama lain*: *We exchanged news with one another.*

one-'off *adj* [only *before* a noun] something that is made or that happens only once □ *hanya sekali; satu kali sahaja*: *a one-off payment/opportunity* ▶ **one-off** *noun* [C]: *It was just a one-off; it won't happen again.*

one-on-'one (*AmE*) = **one-to-one**

onerous /'əʊnərəs (*AmE* also) / *adj* (*formal*) needing great effort; causing trouble or worry □ *membebankan*: *an onerous duty/task/responsibility* **SYN** **taxing**

oneself /wʌn'self/ *pron* (*formal*) **1** used when the person who does an action is also affected by it □ *diri sendiri*: *One can teach oneself to play the piano but it is easier to have lessons.* **2** used to emphasize the person who does the action □ *sendiri*: *One could easily arrange it all oneself.*

IDM **(all) by oneself** **1** alone □ *seorang diri; sendirian* ⊃ note at **alone** **2** without help □ *sendiri*

one-'sided *adj* **1** (used about an opinion, an argument, etc.) showing only one point of view; not balanced □ *satu pihak; satu segi; berat sebelah*: *Some newspapers give a very one-sided view of politics.* **2** (used about a relationship or a competition) not equal □ *berat sebelah*: *The match was very one-sided—we lost 12-1.*

one-to-'one (*AmE* usually **one-on-'one**) *adj, adv* between only two people □ *seorang ke seorang; satu lawan satu*: *one-to-one English lessons* (= one teacher to one student)

one-'way *adv, adj* **1** (used about roads) that you can only drive along in one direction □ *(jalan, dsb) sehala*: *a one-way street* **2** (*especially AmE*) (used about a ticket) that you can use to travel somewhere but not back again □ *(tiket) sehala*: *a one-way ticket* **SYN** **single**

ongoing /'ɒŋɡəʊɪŋ (*AmE* also) / *adj* [usually before a noun] continuing to exist now □ *berterusan; sedang berjalan*: *It's an ongoing problem.*

onion /'ʌnjən/ *noun* [C,U] a white or red vegetable with many layers. Onions are often used in cooking and have a strong smell □ *bawang*: *a kilo of onions* ◆ *onion soup* ⊃ picture on **page P15**

online /ˌɒn'laɪn (*AmE* also) / *adj, adv* controlled by or connected to a computer or to the Internet □ *dlm talian*: *an online ticket booking system* ◆ *I'm studying French online.* ⊃ note at **Internet** ⊃ look at **offline**

> **TOPIC**
>
> **Online**
>
> Many people like to **shop online**. You can **browse the website** or use the **search box** of a shop or **online retailer** (= a company that sells things on the Internet) to find what you want. When you want to buy something, you **add it to your basket** (= click a button by the item). When you have finished shopping, you **go to a checkout** (= click another button) to pay for your purchases, using a credit or debit card. You can also buy or sell things on **eBay™** (= a website where people can sell goods to the person who offers the most money for them).

onlooker /ˈɒnlʊkə(r)/ (AmE also) / noun [C] a person who watches sth happening without taking part in it □ *orang yg melihat (sst kejadian)*

only /ˈəʊnli/ adj [only before a noun] adv, conj **1** with no others existing or present □ *hanya... sahaja; sahaja*: *This is the only dress we have in your size.* ◆ *I was the only woman in the room.* **2** and nobody or nothing else; no more than □ *hanya*: *She only likes pop music.* ◆ *I've only asked a few friends to the party.* ◆ *It's only 1 o'clock.* **3** the most suitable or the best □ *hanya*: *She's the only person for the job.*

> **GRAMMAR** In written English **only** is usually placed *before* the word it refers to. In spoken English we can use stress to show which word it refers to and **only** does not have to change position: *I only kissed ˈJane* (= I kissed Jane and no one else). ◆ *I ˈonly kissed Jane* (= I kissed Jane but I didn't do anything else).

4 (informal) except that; but □ *cuma*: *The film was very good, only it was a bit too long.* **IDM** if only ⊃ if
not only ... but also ⊃ not
only just **1** not long ago □ *baru sahaja*: *I've only just started this job.* **2** almost not □ *hampir-hampir tdk; hanya cukup-cukup*: *We only just had enough money to pay for the meal.* **SYN** hardly

ˌonly ˈchild noun [C] a child who has no brothers or sisters □ *anak tunggal*

o.n.o. (also ono) abbr (BrE) or near/nearest offer (used in small advertisements to show that sth may be sold at a lower price than the price that has been asked) □ *dgn harga paling hampir*: *Motorbike for sale. £750 o.n.o.*

onset /ˈɒnset/ (AmE also) / noun [sing] the onset (of sth) the beginning (often of sth unpleasant) □ *bermulanya*: *the onset of winter/a headache*

onslaught /ˈɒnslɔːt/ (AmE also) / noun [C] an onslaught (on/against sb/sth) a violent or strong attack □ *serangan hebat*: *an onslaught on government policy*

onto (also on to) /ˈɒntə; before vowels ˈɒntu (AmE also) / prep to a position on sth □ *ke atas; ke*: *The cat jumped onto the sofa.* ◆ *The bottle fell off the table onto the floor.* ◆ *The crowd ran onto the pitch.*
IDM be onto sb (informal) to have found out about sth illegal that sb is doing □ *mengetahui kegiatan (haram) sso*: *The police were onto the car thieves.*
be onto sth to have some information, etc. that could lead to an important discovery □ *menemui sst*

onwards /ˈɒnwədz/ (AmE also) / (also onward /ˈɒnwəd/ (AmE also) /) adv **1** from ... onwards continuing from a particular time □ *berterusan (dr sst masa); seterusnya*: *From September onwards it usually begins to get colder.* **2** (formal) forward □ *ke depan*: *The road stretched onwards into the distance.*

ooze /uːz/ verb [I,T] ooze from/out of sth; ooze (with) sth to flow slowly out or to allow sth to

601

onlooker → open

flow slowly out □ *meleleh*: *Blood was oozing from a cut on his head.* ◆ *The fruit was oozing juice.*

op /ɒp/ (informal) = operation(1)

opaque /əʊˈpeɪk/ adj **1** that you cannot see through □ *legap*: *opaque glass in the door* **2** (formal) difficult to understand; not clear □ *kabur; tdk jelas* **OPP** for both meanings transparent

OPEC /ˈəʊpek/ abbr **Organization of Petroleum Exporting Countries** □ *OPEC (Pertubuhan Negara-negara Pengeksport Petroleum)*

the ˈopen noun [sing] outside; the countryside □ *di luar*: *After working in an office all week, I like to be out in the open at weekends.*
IDM bring sth out into the open; come out into the open to make sth known publicly; to be known publicly □ *diketahui umum*: *I'm glad our secret has come out into the open at last.*

open¹ /ˈəʊpən/ adj
▸NOT CLOSED **1** not closed or covered □ *terbuka; terdedah*: *Don't leave the door open.* ◆ *an open window* ◆ *I can't get this bottle of wine open.* ◆ *She stared at me with her eyes wide open.* ◆ *The diary was lying open on her desk.* ◆ *The curtains are open so that we could see into the room.* ◆ *His shirt was open at the neck.*
▸OF LAND/SEA **2** [only before a noun] away from towns and buildings; at a distance from the land □ *terbentang; membentang*: *open country* ◆ *on the open sea*
▸FOR VISITORS/CUSTOMERS **3** open (to sb/sth); open (for sth) available for people to enter, visit, use, etc.; not closed to the public □ *dibuka*: *The bank isn't open till 9.30.* ◆ *The new shopping centre will soon be open.* ◆ *The competition is open to everyone.* ◆ *The gardens are open to the public in the summer.* ◆ *The hotel damaged by the bomb is now open for business again.* **OPP** closed, shut
▸OF CHARACTER **4** not keeping feelings and thoughts hidden □ *terus terang; terang-terangan*: *Elena doesn't mind talking about her feelings—she's a very open person.* ◆ *He looked at him with open dislike.*
▸NOT DECIDED **5** [not before a noun] not finally decided; still being considered □ *terbuka; belum diputuskan*: *Let's leave the details open.*
IDM have/keep an open mind (about/on sth) to be ready to listen to or consider new ideas and suggestions □ *sedia mempertimbangkan sst*
in the open air outside □ *di luar (bangunan)*: *Somehow, food eaten in the open air tastes much better.*
keep an eye open/out (for sb/sth) ⊃ eye¹
open to sth willing to receive sth □ *sedia menerima sst*: *I'm always open to suggestions.*
with your eyes open ⊃ eye¹
with open arms in a friendly way that shows that you are pleased to see sb or have sth □ *dgn tangan terbuka*: *The Unions welcomed the government's decision with open arms.*

open² /ˈəʊpən/ verb **1** [I,T] to move sth or part of sth so that it is no longer closed; to move so as to be no longer closed □ *membuka; dibuka*;

CONSONANTS p **p**en b **b**ad t **t**ea d **d**id k **c**at g **g**ot tʃ **ch**in dʒ **J**une f **f**all v **v**an θ **th**in

open-air → operation 602

terbuka; selak: *This window won't open—it's stuck.* ♦ *The parachute failed to open and he was killed.* ♦ *The book opened at the very page I needed.* ♦ *Open the curtains, will you?* ♦ *to open your eyes/hand/mouth* ♦ *to open a bag/letter/box* **OPP** close, shut **2** [I,T] to make it possible for people to enter a place □ *membuka; dibuka*: *Does that shop open on Sundays?* ♦ *The museum opens at 10.* ♦ *The company is opening two new branches soon.* ♦ *Police finally opened the road six hours after the accident.* **OPP** close, shut **3** [I,T] to start (sth) □ *membuka; memulakan*: *The play opens in London next month.* ♦ *The chairman opened the meeting by welcoming everybody.* ♦ *I'd like to open a bank account.* **OPP** close **4** [T] to start a computer program or file so that you can use it on the screen □ *membuka*

IDM **open fire (at/on sb/sth)** to start shooting: *He ordered his men to open fire.* □ *mula menembak (sso/sst)*

PHR V **open into/onto sth** to lead to another room, area or place □ *terbuka terus (ke sst); membawa kpd (sst)*: *This door opens onto the garden.*

open out to become wider □ *melebar*

open up 1 to talk about what you feel and think □ *berterus terang* **2** to open a door □ *buka pintu*: *'Open up,' shouted the police to the man inside.*

open (sth) up 1 to become available or to make sth available □ *terbuka; boleh didapati*: *When I left school all sorts of opportunities opened up for me.* **2** to start business □ *dibuka; membuka*: *The restaurant opened up last year.*

open-'air *adj* [only *before* a noun] not inside a building □ *di luar (bangunan); di tempat terbuka*: *an open-air swimming pool*

'open day *noun* [C] a day when the public can visit a place that they cannot usually go into □ *hari terbuka*: *The school is having an open day next month.*

opener /'əʊpnə(r)/ *noun* [C] [in compounds] a thing that takes the lid, etc. off sth □ *pembuka*: *a tin opener* ♦ *a bottle opener*

opening /'əʊpnɪŋ/ *noun* [C]
▶ SPACE/HOLE **1** a space or hole that sb/sth can go through □ *lubang; bukaan*: *We were able to get through an opening in the hedge.*
▶ BEGINNING **2** the beginning or first part of sth □ *permulaan*: *The film is famous for its dramatic opening.*
▶ CEREMONY **3** a ceremony to celebrate the first time a public building, road, etc. is used □ *pembukaan*: *the opening of the new hospital*
▶ JOB **4** a job which is available □ *jawatan kosong; lowongan*: *We have an opening for a sales manager at the moment.*
▶ OPPORTUNITY **5** a good opportunity □ *peluang*: *I'm sure she'll be a great journalist—all she needs is an opening.* ▶ **opening** *adj* [only *before* a noun]: *the opening chapter of a book* ♦ *the opening ceremony of the Olympic Games*

openly /'əʊpənli/ *adv* honestly; not keeping anything secret □ *secara terus terang*: *I think you should discuss your feelings openly with each other.*

open-'minded *adj* ready to consider new ideas and opinions □ *berfikiran terbuka* **OPP** narrow-minded

openness /'əʊpənnəs/ *noun* [U] the quality of being honest and ready to talk about your feelings □ *kejujuran; sifat berterus terang*

open-'plan *adj* (used about a large area inside a building) not divided into separate rooms □ *sistem terbuka*: *an open-plan office*

the ˌOpen Uni'versity *noun* [sing] (in Britain) a university whose students study mainly at home. Their work is sent to them by post or email and there are special television, radio and online programmes for them. □ *Open University*

opera /'ɒprə/ *noun* [C,U] a play in which most of the words are sung to music; works of this kind performed as entertainment □ *opera*: *an opera by Mozart* ♦ *Do you like opera?* ♦ *a comic opera* ⊃ look at **musical, soap opera**

'opera house *noun* [C] a theatre where operas are performed □ *panggung opera*

operate /'ɒpəreɪt/ *verb* **1** [I,T] to work, or to make sth work □ *menjalankan; berjalan; mengendalikan; berfungsi*: *I don't understand how this machine operates.* ♦ *These switches here operate the central heating.* **SYN** function **2** [I] to act or to have an effect □ *bertindak*: *Several factors were operating to our advantage.* **3** [I,T] to do business; to manage sth □ *beroperasi; menjalankan perniagaan, dll*: *The firm operates from its central office in Delhi.* **4** [I] operate (on sb/sth) (for sth) to cut open sb's body in hospital in order to deal with a part that is damaged, infected, etc. □ *membedah*: *The surgeon is going to operate on her in the morning.* ♦ *He was operated on for appendicitis.*

operatic /ˌɒpəˈrætɪk/ *adj* connected with opera □ *(berkenaan dgn) opera*: *operatic music*

'operating system *noun* [C] a computer program that organizes a number of other programs at the same time □ *sistem pengendalian*

'operating theatre (also **theatre,** *AmE* **'operating room**) *noun* [C] a room in a hospital where medical operations are performed □ *bilik bedah*

operation /ˌɒpəˈreɪʃn/ *noun*
▶ MEDICAL **1** [C] (also *informal* **op**) the process of cutting open a patient's body in order to deal with a part inside □ *pembedahan*: *He had an operation to remove his appendix.* ⊃ note at **hospital**
▶ ACTIVITY **2** [C] an organized activity that involves many people doing different things □ *operasi; kerja; usaha*: *A rescue operation was mounted to find the missing children.*
▶ BUSINESS **3** [C] a business or company involving many parts □ *operasi; kegiatan perniagaan; perusahaan*: *a huge international operation*

ð **then** s **so** z **zoo** ʃ **she** ʒ **vision** h **how** m **man** n **no** ŋ **sing** l **leg** r **red** j **yes** w **wet**

➤COMPUTING **4** [C] an act performed by a machine, especially a computer □ *operasi*: *The computer can perform millions of operations per second.*

➤MACHINE/SYSTEM **5** [U] the way in which you make sth work □ *pengendalian*: *The operation of these machines is extremely simple.*

IDM **be in operation; come into operation** to be/start working or having an effect □ *berjalan; dijalankan; dilaksanakan*: *The new tax system will come into operation in the spring.*

operational /ˌɒpəˈreɪʃənl/ *adj* **1** connected with the way a business, machine, system, etc. works □ *operasional; (berkaitan dgn) operasi* **2** ready for use □ *boleh digunakan; mula beroperasi/berfungsi*: *The new factory is now fully operational.* **3** [only *before* a noun] connected with military operations □ *(berkaitan dgn) kegiatan tentera*

operative /ˈɒpərətɪv (*AmE* also) -/ *adj* (*formal*) **1** working, able to be used; in use □ *berkuat kuasa; dikuatkuasakan*: *The new law will be operative from 1 May.* **2** [only *before* a noun] connected with a medical operation □ *(berkaitan dgn) pembedahan*

operator /ˈɒpəreɪtə(r)/ *noun* [C] **1** a person whose job is to work a particular machine or piece of equipment □ *operator; jurumesin*: *a keyboard operator* **2** a person whose job is to connect telephone calls, for the public or in a particular building □ *telefonis; operator telefon*: *Dial 100 for the operator.* ◆ *a switchboard operator* **3** a person or company that does certain types of business □ *pengendali*: *a tour operator*

opinion /əˈpɪnjən/ *noun* [C] **an opinion (of sb/sth); an opinion (on/about sth)** what you think about sb/sth □ *pendapat; pandangan*: *She asked me for my opinion of her new hairstyle and I told her.* ◆ *He has very strong opinions on almost everything.* ◆ **In my opinion**, *you're making a terrible mistake.* ⊃ note at **point of view**, **think** **2** [U] what people in general think about sth □ *pendapat; pandangan*: *Public opinion is in favour of a change in the law.*

IDM **be of the opinion that ...** (*formal*) to think or believe that ... □ *berpendapat bahawa...*

have a good, high, etc. opinion of sb/sth; have a bad, low, poor, etc. opinion of sb/sth to think that sb/sth is good/bad □ *berpandangan baik/buruk ttg sso/sst*

a matter of opinion ⊃ **matter**[1]

oˈpinion poll = **poll**[1](1)

opium /ˈəʊpiəm/ *noun* [U] a powerful drug that is made from the juice of a type of **poppy** (= a type of flower) □ *candu; madat*

opp. *abbr* = **opposite**

opponent /əˈpəʊnənt/ *noun* [C] **1** (in sport or competitions) a person who plays against sb □ *lawan*: *They are the toughest opponents we've played against.* **2 an opponent (of sth)** a person who disagrees with sb's actions, plans or beliefs and tries to stop or change them □ *penentang*: *the President's political opponents*

opportune /ˈɒpətjuːn/ *adj* (*formal*) **1** (used about a time) suitable for doing a particular thing, so that it is likely to be successful □ *sesuai*: *The offer could not have come at a more opportune moment.* **SYN** **favourable** **2** (used about an action or event) done or happening at the right time to be successful □ *kena/sesuai/tepat pd masa/waktunya*: *an opportune remark* **OPP** for both meanings **inopportune**

opportunism /ˌɒpəˈtjuːnɪzəm/ *noun* [U] making use of a situation for your own good and not caring about other people □ *oportunisme; sikap oportunis*

opportunist /ˌɒpəˈtjuːnɪst/ (also **opportunistic** /ˌɒpətjuːˈnɪstɪk/) *adj* not done in a planned way; making use of an opportunity □ *oportunis; orang yg pandai mengambil kesempatan*: *an opportunist crime* ▶ **opportunist** *noun* [C]: *80% of burglaries are committed by casual opportunists.*

opportunity /ˌɒpəˈtjuːnəti/ *noun* [C,U] (*pl* **opportunities**) **an opportunity (for sth/to do sth)** a chance to do sth that you would like to do; a situation or a time in which it is possible to do sth that you would like to do □ *peluang*: *There will be plenty of opportunity for asking questions later.* ◆ *I have a* **golden opportunity** *to go to America now that my sister lives there.* ◆ *When we're finally alone, I'll* **take the opportunity** *to ask him a few personal questions.* ◆ *I'll give Steve your message if I* **get the opportunity**. **SYN** **chance** ⊃ note at **occasion**

oppose /əˈpəʊz/ *verb* [T] to disagree with sb's beliefs, actions or plans and to try to change or stop them □ *menentang*: *They opposed the plan to build a new road.*

opposed /əˈpəʊzd/ *adj* **opposed to sth** disagreeing with a plan, action, etc.; believing that sth is wrong □ *menentang*: *She has always been strongly opposed to experiments on animals.*

IDM **as opposed to** (used to emphasize the difference between two things) rather than; and not □ *bukan(nya)*: *Your work will be judged on quality, as opposed to quantity.*

opposing /əˈpəʊzɪŋ/ *adj* [only *before* a noun] **1** (used about teams, armies, etc.) playing, fighting, working, etc. against each other □ *penentang; lawan*: *a player from the opposing side* **2** (used about opinions, attitudes, etc.) very different from each other □ *bertentangan; berlawanan*: *They have opposing views.*

opposite /ˈɒpəzɪt; -sɪt/ *adj, adv, prep* (*abbr* **opp.**) **1** in a position on the other side of sb/sth; facing □ *bertentangan; berhadapan; di hadapan*: *The old town and the new town are on opposite sides of the river.* ◆ *You sit there and I'll sit opposite.*

HELP Sometimes **opposite** is used after a noun: *Write your answer in the space opposite.*

VOWELS i: see i any ɪ sit e ten æ hat ɑ: father ɒ got ɔ: saw ʊ put u: too u usual

2 completely different ☐ *bertentangan; sebaliknya*: *I can't walk with you because I'm going in the opposite direction.* ◆ *the opposite sex* (= the other sex)

IDM **your opposite number** a person who does the same job or has the same position as you in a different company, organization, team, etc. ☐ *rakan sejawat*: *The Prime Minister met his Italian opposite number.*

▶ **opposite** *noun* [C]: *'Hot' is the opposite of 'cold'.*

opposite

They're sitting opposite each other.

She's sitting in front of him.

opposition /ˌɒpəˈzɪʃn/ *noun* **1** [U] **opposition (to sb/sth)** the feeling of disagreeing with sth and the act of trying to change it ☐ *penentang; tentangan*: *He expressed strong opposition to the plan.* **2 the opposition** [sing, with sing or pl verb] the person or team who you compete against in sport, business, etc. ☐ *pihak lawan*: *We need to find out what the opposition is doing.* **3 the Opposition** [sing, with sing or pl verb] the politicians or the political parties that are in a parliament but not in the government ☐ *pihak Pembangkang*: *the leader of the Opposition* ◆ *Opposition MPs*

oppress /əˈpres/ *verb* [T, usually passive] to treat a group of people in a cruel and unfair way by not allowing them the same freedom and rights as others ☐ *menindas; menekan* ▶ **oppressed** *adj*: *an oppressed minority* ▶ **oppression** /əˈpreʃn/ *noun* [U]: *a struggle against oppression*

oppressive /əˈpresɪv/ *adj* **1** allowing no freedom; controlling by force ☐ *(yg) menindas* **2** (used especially about heat or the atmosphere) causing you to feel very uncomfortable ☐ *merimaskan; menyebabkan rasa rimas*

opt /ɒpt/ *verb* [I] **opt to do sth/for sth** to choose to do or have sth after thinking about it ☐ *memilih*: *She opted for a career in music.*

PHR V **opt out (of sth)** to choose not to take part in sth ☐ *memilih utk tdk menyertai; berhenti; keluar*: *Employees may opt out of the company's pension plan.*

optical /ˈɒptɪkl/ *adj* connected with the sense of sight ☐ *(berkenaan dgn) penglihatan*: *optical instruments*

optical illusion *noun* [C] an image that tricks the eye and makes you think you can see sth that you cannot ☐ *maya; ilusi penglihatan*

optical illusions

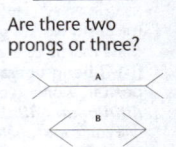

Are there two prongs or three?

Which line is longer, A or B?

optician /ɒpˈtɪʃn/ *noun* [C] a person whose job is to test eyes, sell glasses, etc ☐ *pakar optik*: *I have to go to the optician's* (= the shop) *for an eye test.*

optimal /ˈɒptɪməl/ = **optimum**

optimism /ˈɒptɪmɪzəm/ *noun* [U] the feeling that the future will be good or successful ☐ *optimisme; rasa optimis*: *There is considerable optimism that the economy will improve.* **OPP** pessimism ▶ **optimist** /-ɪst/ *noun* [C]

optimistic /ˌɒptɪˈmɪstɪk/ *adj* **optimistic (about sth/that ...)** expecting good things to happen or sth to be successful; showing this feeling ☐ *optimistik; tinggi harapan*: *I've applied for the job but I'm not very optimistic that I'll get it.* **SYN** positive **OPP** pessimistic ▶ **optimistically** /-kli/ *adv*

optimum /ˈɒptɪməm/ (also **optimal**) *adj* [only before a noun] the best possible; producing the best possible results ☐ *optimum*: *optimum growth* ◆ *the optimum conditions for effective learning*

option /ˈɒpʃn/ *noun* [U,C] something that you can choose to do; the freedom to choose ☐ *opsyen; pilihan*: *She looked carefully at all the options before deciding on a career.* ◆ *Students have the option of studying part-time or full-time.* ◆ *If you're late again, you will give us no option but to dismiss you.* **SYN** choice

optional /ˈɒpʃənl/ *adj* that you can choose or not choose ☐ *tdk diwajibkan; boleh memilih; pilihan*: *an optional subject at school* **OPP** compulsory, obligatory

or /ɔː(r)/ *conj* **1** used in a list of possibilities or choices ☐ *atau*: *Would you like to sit here or next to the window?* ◆ *Are you interested or not?* ◆ *For the main course, you can have lamb, beef or fish.* ⊃ look at **either 2** [after a negative] and neither; and not ☐ *atau; ataupun*: *Alexi hasn't phoned or emailed me for weeks.* ◆ *I've never been either to Italy or Spain.* ⊃ look at **neither 3** if not; otherwise ☐ *jika tdk*: *Don't drive so fast or you'll have an accident!* **SYN** or else **4** used between two numbers to show approximately how many ☐ *atau*: *I've been there five or six times.* **5** used before a word or phrase that explains or comments on what has been said before ☐ *atau*: *20% of the population, or one in five*

IDM **or something/somewhere**; **someone/something/somewhere or other** (*spoken*) used for showing that you are not sure, cannot remember or do not know which thing or place ☐ *atau lebih kurang begitu/di situ*: *She's a computer programmer or something.* ◆ *He muttered something or other about having no time and disappeared.*

oral¹ /ˈɔːrəl/ adj **1** spoken, not written □ *lisan: an oral test* **2** [only before a noun] concerning or using the mouth □ *(berkenaan dgn) mulut: oral hygiene* ⊃ look at **aural** ▶ **orally** /ˈɔːrəli/ adv: *You can ask the questions orally or in writing.* ◆ *This medicine is taken orally (= is swallowed).*

oral² /ˈɔːrəl/ noun [C] a spoken exam □ *ujian lisan: I've got my German oral next week.*

EXAM TIP

Oral/speaking exams

Check what the time limits are for the exam. Practise speaking for the necessary amount of time, to get used to how much you can say in that time. In the exam, never stop and say 'I've finished' or 'That's all'; continue speaking until you are told to stop.

orange¹ /ˈɒrɪndʒ/ (AmE also) / noun **1** [C,U] a round fruit with a thick skin that is divided into sections inside and is a colour between red and yellow □ *buah oren: orange juice/peel* ◆ *an orange tree* ⊃ picture on **page P14 2** [U,C] a drink made from oranges with the taste of oranges; a glass of this drink □ *minuman oren: freshly squeezed orange* **3** [C,U] the colour of this fruit, between red and yellow □ *warna oren/jingga*

orange² /ˈɒrɪndʒ/ (AmE also) / adj having the colour orange □ *(warna) oren/jingga: orange paint*

orange squash noun [C,U] (BrE) a drink made by adding water to a liquid that tastes of orange □ *minuman berperasa oren*

orang-utan /ɔːˌræŋ uːˈtæn; əˈræŋ uːtæn/ noun [C] a large animal that has long arms and reddish hair, like a **monkey** (= an animal that lives in hot countries and can climb trees) with no tail and that lives in South East Asia □ *orang utan* ⊃ look at **ape**

orator /ˈɒrətə(r)/ (AmE also) / noun [C] (formal) a person who is good at making public speeches □ *pemidato*

orbit /ˈɔːbɪt/ noun [C,U] a curved path taken by a planet or another object as it moves around another planet, star, moon, etc. □ *orbit: the earth's orbit around the sun* ▶ **orbit** verb [I,T]

orbital /ˈɔːbɪtl/ adj [only before a noun] **1** connected with the **orbit** of a planet or another object in space □ *(berkenaan dgn) orbit* **2** (BrE) (used about a road) built around the outside of a city or town to reduce the amount of traffic travelling through the centre □ *pekeliling (berkenaan dgn jalan)* ▶ **orbital** noun [C, usually sing]

orchard /ˈɔːtʃəd/ noun [C] a piece of land on which fruit trees are grown □ *dusun; kebun (buah): a cherry orchard* ⊃ picture on **page P11**

orchestra /ˈɔːkɪstrə/ noun [C] a large group of musicians who play various musical instruments together, led by a **conductor** □ *orkestra: a symphony orchestra* ⊃ note at **music** ▶ **orchestral** /ɔːˈkestrəl/ adj

orchid /ˈɔːkɪd/ noun [C] a beautiful and sometimes rare type of plant that has flowers of unusual shapes and bright colours □ *orkid*

ordain /ɔːˈdeɪn/ verb [T, usually passive] *ordain sb (as) (sth)* to make sb a priest or minister □ *mentahbiskan; melantik paderi (dlm agama Kristian): He was ordained (as) a priest last year.* ⊃ look at **ordination**

ordeal /ɔːˈdiːl/ (BrE also) ˈɔːdiːl/ noun [C, usually sing] a very unpleasant or difficult experience □ *pengalaman pahit/getir*

order¹ /ˈɔːdə(r)/ noun
▶ARRANGEMENT **1** [U, sing] the way in which people or things are arranged in relation to each other □ *susunan; urutan: a list of names in alphabetical order* ◆ *Try to put the things you have to do in order of importance.* ◆ *What's the order of events today?* **2** [U] an organized state, where everything is in its right place □ *teratur: I really must put my notes in order, because I can never find what I'm looking for.* **OPP** **disorder**
▶CONTROLLED STATE **3** [U] the situation in which laws, rules, authority, etc. are obeyed □ *keamanan; ketenteraman: Following last week's riots, order has now been restored.* ⊃ look at **disorder**
▶INSTRUCTION **4** [C] *an order (for sb) (to do sth)* something that you are told to do by sb in a position of authority □ *perintah; arahan: In the army, you have to obey orders at all times.* ◆ *She gave the order for the work to be started.*
▶GOODS **5** [C,U] *an order (for sth)* a request asking for sth to be made, supplied or sent □ *pesanan: The company has just received a major export order.* ◆ *The book I need is on order (= they are waiting for it to arrive).*
▶FOOD/DRINKS **6** [C] a request for food or drinks in a hotel, restaurant, etc.; the food or drinks you asked for □ *pesanan: Can I take your order now, sir?*
IDM **in order to do sth** with the purpose or intention of doing sth; so that sth can be done □ *utk/supaya (dpt membuat sst): We left early in order to avoid the traffic.*
in/into reverse order ⊃ **reverse³**
in working order ⊃ **working**
law and order ⊃ **law**
out of order 1 (used about a machine, etc.) not working properly or not working at all □ *rosak: I had to walk up to the tenth floor because the lift was out of order.* **2** (BrE informal) (used about sb's behaviour) unacceptable, because it is rude, etc. □ *tdk patut/wajar: That comment was completely out of order!*

order² /ˈɔːdə(r)/ verb **1** [T] *order sb (to do sth)* to use your position of authority to tell sb to do sth or to say that sth must happen □ *menyuruh; memerintah(kan): I'm not asking you to do your homework, I'm ordering you!* ◆ *The company was ordered to pay compensation to its former employees.* **2** [T] to ask for sth to be made, supplied or sent somewhere □ *memesan: The shop didn't have the book I wanted so I ordered it.* **3** [I,T] *order (sb) (sth); order (sth) (for sb)* to ask for food or drinks in a restaurant, hotel, etc. □ *memesan*: *Are you ready to order yet, madam?* ♦ *Can you order me a sandwich while I make a phone call?* ♦ *Could you order a sandwich for me?*

PHR V **order sb about/around** to keep telling sb what to do and how to do it □ *mengarahkan sso membuat itu dan ini*: *Stop ordering me about! You're not my father.*

orderly¹ /ˈɔːdəli/ *adj* **1** arranged or organized in a tidy way □ *teratur*: *an orderly office/desk* **2** peaceful; behaving well □ *teratur; aman* **OPP** for both meanings **disorderly**

orderly² /ˈɔːdəli/ *noun* [C] (*pl* **orderlies**) a worker in a hospital, usually doing jobs that do not need special training □ *atendan (hospital)*

ordinal /ˈɔːdɪnl/ (also ˌordinal ˈnumber) *noun* [C] a number that shows the order or position of sth in a series □ *ordinal*: *'First', 'second', and 'third' are ordinals.* ⇒ look at **cardinal**

ordinarily /ˈɔːdnrəli/ *adv* usually; generally □ *biasanya*: *Ordinarily, I don't work as late as this.* **SYN** **normally**

ordinary /ˈɔːdnri/ *adj* normal; not unusual or different from others □ *biasa*: *It's interesting to see how ordinary people live in other countries.* ♦ *Simon was wearing a suit, but I was in my ordinary clothes.*
IDM **out of the ordinary** unusual; different from normal □ *luar biasa*

ordination /ˌɔːdɪˈneɪʃn/ *noun* [U,C] the act or ceremony of making sb a priest, etc. □ *pentahbisan; upacara pelantikan paderi* ⇒ look at **ordain**

ore /ɔː(r)/ *noun* [C,U] rock or earth from which metal can be taken □ *bijih*: *iron ore*

organ /ˈɔːɡən/ *noun* [C] **1** one of the parts inside your body that have a particular function □ *organ*: *vital organs* (= those such as the heart and liver which help to keep you alive) ♦ *sexual/reproductive organs* ⇒ picture at **body** **2** a large musical instrument like a piano with pipes through which air is forced. Organs are often found in churches □ *organ*: *organ music* ▶**organist** /-nɪst/ *noun* [C]: *the church organist*

organic /ɔːˈɡænɪk/ *adj* **1** (used about food or farming methods) produced by or using natural materials, without artificial chemicals □ *organik*: *organic vegetables* ♦ *organic farming* **2** produced by or from living things □ *organik*: *organic compounds/molecules* **OPP** **inorganic** ▶**organically** /-kli/ *adv*: *organically grown/produced*

organism /ˈɔːɡənɪzəm/ *noun* [C] a living thing, especially one that is so small that you can only see it with a **microscope** (= a piece of equipment that makes small objects look bigger) □ *organisma*

organization (also -**isation**) /ˌɔːɡənaɪˈzeɪʃn/ *noun* **1** [C] a group of people who form a business, club, etc. together in order to achieve a particular aim □ *pertubuhan; organisasi*: *She works for a voluntary organization helping homeless people.* **2** [U] the activity of making preparations or arrangements for sth □ *pengelolaan; perancangan*: *An enormous amount of organization went into the festival.* **3** [U] the way in which sth is organized, arranged or prepared □ *penyusunan; susunan*: *Your written work lacks organization.* **OPP** **disorganization** ▶**organizational** (also -**isational**) /-ʃənl/ *adj*: *The job requires a high level of organizational ability.*

organize (also -**ise**) /ˈɔːɡənaɪz/ *verb* **1** [T] to plan or arrange an event, activity, etc. □ *mengatur; merancang*: *The school organizes trips to various places of interest.* **2** [I,T] to put or arrange things into a system or logical order □ *mengatur; menyusun*: *Can you decide what needs doing? I'm hopeless at organizing.* ♦ *You need to organize your work more carefully.* ▶**organizer** (also -**iser**) *noun* [C]: *The organizers of the concert said that it had been a great success.*

organized (also -**ised**) /ˈɔːɡənaɪzd/ *adj* **1** [only *before* a noun] involving a large number of people working together to do sth in a way that has been carefully planned □ *terancang*: *an organized campaign against cruelty to animals* ♦ *organized crime* (= done by a large group of professional criminals) **2** arranged or planned in the way mentioned □ *diatur*: *a carefully/badly/well-organized trip* **OPP** **disorganized 3** (used about a person) able to plan your work, life, etc. well □ *teratur*: *I wish I were as organized as you!* **OPP** **disorganized**

orgasm /ˈɔːɡæzəm/ *noun* [U,C] the point of greatest sexual pleasure □ *orgasma; puncak syahwat*: *to have an orgasm*

orgy /ˈɔːdʒi/ *noun* [C] (*pl* **orgies**) **1** a party, involving a lot of eating, drinking and sexual activity □ *pesta liar (seks)* **2 an orgy (of sth)** a period of doing sth in a wild way, without control □ *(tempoh melakukan sst) secara liar dan tdk terkawal*: *The gang went on an orgy of destruction.*

the Orient /ˈɔːriənt/ *noun* [sing] (*formal*) the eastern part of the world, especially China and Japan □ *Timur; Asia Timur (terutamanya China dan Jepun)*

orient /ˈɔːrient/ (*BrE also* **orientate**) *verb* [T] **orient yourself** to find out where you are; to become familiar with a place □ *mencari kedudukan; menyesuaikan diri (dgn sst tempat); mengorientasikan* ⇒ look at **disorientate**

oriental /ˌɔːriˈentl/ *adj* Oriental coming from or belonging to the East or Far East □ *(berkenaan dgn) Timur atau Asia Timur*: *oriental languages*

HELP Be careful. When it refers to a person, this word is offensive. It is better to say 'Asian'.

orientate /ˈɔːriənteɪt/ (*BrE*) = **orient**

orientation /ˌɔːriənˈteɪʃn/ *noun* [U] the feelings, beliefs or interests that a person or an organization has □ *kecenderungan*: *a person's religious/political/sexual orientation*

oriented /ˈɔːrientɪd/ (also **orientated** /ˈɔːriənteɪtɪd/) adj for or interested in a particular type of person or thing □ *berorientasikan; ditujukan; cenderung*: a company selling male-oriented products ♦ She's very career orientated.

orienteering /ˌɔːriənˈtɪərɪŋ/ noun [U] a sport in which you find your way across country on foot, as quickly as possible, using a map and a **compass** (= an instrument that shows direction) □ *sukan berjalan kaki merentas desa berpandukan peta dan kompas*

origami /ˌɒrɪˈɡɑːmi/ noun [U] the Japanese art of folding paper into attractive shapes □ *origami*

⚑ **origin** /ˈɒrɪdʒɪn/ (AmE also) / noun [C, usually pl, U] **1** the point from which sth starts; the cause of sth □ *asal; asal usul; permulaan; punca*: This particular tradition **has its origins in** Wales. ♦ Many English words are of Latin origin. **2** the country, race, culture, etc. that a person comes from □ *asal; berasal drpd; berketurunan*: people of African origin

⚑ **original¹** /əˈrɪdʒənl/ adj **1** [only before a noun] first; earliest (before any changes or developments) □ *asal*: The original meaning of this word is different from the meaning it has nowadays. **2** new and interesting; different from others of its type □ *baharu dan menarik; tersendiri; asli*: There are no original ideas in his work. **3** made or created first, before copies □ *asal; asli*: 'Is that the original painting?' 'No, it's a copy.'

⚑ **original²** /əˈrɪdʒənl/ noun [C] the first document, painting, etc. that was made; not a copy □ *asal*: Could you make a photocopy of my birth certificate and give the original back to me?

originality /əˌrɪdʒəˈnæləti/ noun [U] the quality of being new and interesting □ *keaslian; ciri tersendiri*

⚑ **originally** /əˈrɪdʒənəli/ adv in the beginning, before any changes or developments □ *asalnya; pd mulanya*: I'm from London originally, but I left when I was young.

originate /əˈrɪdʒɪneɪt/ verb [I] (formal) to happen or appear for the first time in a particular place or situation □ *berasal*

ornament /ˈɔːnəmənt/ noun [C] an object that you have because it is attractive, not because it is useful. Ornaments are used to decorate rooms, etc. □ *perhiasan; hiasan*

ornamental /ˌɔːnəˈmentl/ adj made or put somewhere in order to look attractive, not for any practical use □ *(sebagai) hiasan*

ornate /ɔːˈneɪt/ adj covered with a lot of small complicated designs as decoration □ *penuh hiasan; berkerawang*

ornithology /ˌɔːnɪˈθɒlədʒi/ noun [U] the study of birds □ *ornitologi* ▶ **ornithologist** /-dʒɪst/ noun [C]

orphan /ˈɔːfn/ noun [C] a child whose parents are dead □ *anak yatim piatu* ▶ **orphan** verb [T, usually passive]: She was orphaned when she was three and went to live with her grandparents.

➔ note at **child**

orphanage /ˈɔːfənɪdʒ/ noun [C] a home for children whose parents are dead □ *rumah anak yatim* ➔ A more common word is **children's home**.

orthodox /ˈɔːθədɒks/ adj **1** that most people believe, do or accept; usual □ *ortodoks; lazim*: orthodox opinions/methods **OPP** unorthodox **2** (in certain religions) closely following the old, traditional beliefs, ceremonies, etc. □ *ortodoks*: an orthodox Jew ♦ the Greek Orthodox Church

orthopaedics (AmE **orthopedics**) /ˌɔːθəˈpiːdɪks/ noun [U] the area of medicine connected with injuries and diseases of the bones or muscles □ *ortopedik* ▶ **orthopaedic** (AmE **orthopedic**) adj: an orthopaedic surgeon/hospital

ostentatious /ˌɒstenˈteɪʃəs/ adj **1** expensive or noticeable in a way that is intended to impress other people □ *menonjol*: ostentatious gold jewellery **2** behaving in a way that is intended to impress people with how rich or important you are □ *menunjuk-nunjuk* ▶ **ostentatiously** adv

osteopath /ˈɒstiəpæθ/ noun [C] a person whose job is treating some diseases and physical problems by pressing and moving the bones and muscles □ *osteopat; pakar osteopati* ▶ **osteopathy** /ˌɒstiˈɒpəθi/ noun [U]

ostracize (also **-ise**) /ˈɒstrəsaɪz/ verb [T] (formal) to refuse to allow sb to be a member of a social group; to refuse to meet or talk to sb □ *menyisihkan; memulaukan*

ostrich /ˈɒstrɪtʃ/ (AmE also) / noun [C] a very large African bird with a long neck and long legs, which can run very fast but which cannot fly □ *burung unta*

⚑ **other** /ˈʌðə(r)/ adj, pron **1** in addition to or different from the one or ones that have already been mentioned □ *(yg) lain*: I hadn't got any other plans that evening so I accepted their invitation. ♦ If you're busy now, I'll come back some other time. ♦ I like this jumper but not the colour. Have you got any others? ♦ Some of my friends went to university, others didn't. ♦ She doesn't care what other people think. ➔ look at **another**

HELP Other cannot be used after 'an'.

2 [after the, my, your, his, her, etc. with a singular noun] the second of two people or things, when the first has already been mentioned □ *yg satu, sebelah, dsb lagi*: I can only find one sock. Have you seen the other one? **3** [after the, my, your, his, her, etc. with a plural noun] the rest of a group or number of people or things □ *yg lain; yg lain-lain(nya)*: Their youngest son still lives with them but their other children have left home. ♦ I'll have to wear this shirt because all my others are dirty. ♦ Mick and I got a taxi there, the others walked.

otherwise → out

IDM **in other words** used for saying sth in a different way □ *dgn perkataan lain*: *My boss said she would have to let me go. In other words, she sacked me.*
one after another/the other ⊃ **one¹**
the other day, morning, week, etc. recently, not long ago □ *tempoh hari; hari itu; baru-baru ini*: *An old friend rang me the other day.*
other than [usually after a negative] apart from; except (for) □ *selain drpd*: *The plane was a little late, but other than that the journey was fine.*
the other way round in the opposite way or order □ *terbalik; sebaliknya*: *My appointment's at 3 and Lella's is at 3.15—or was it the other way round?*
somebody/something/somewhere or other ⊃ **or**

otherwise /ˈʌðəwaɪz/ *adv, conj* **1** (used for stating what would happen if you do not do sth or if sth does not happen) if not □ *kalau/jika tdk*: *You have to press the red button, otherwise it won't work.* **2** apart from that □ *selain itu*: *I'm a bit tired but otherwise I feel fine.* **3** in a different way to the way mentioned; differently □ *sebaliknya*: *I'm afraid I can't see you next weekend, I'm otherwise engaged* (= I will be busy doing sth else).

otter /ˈɒtə(r)/ *noun* [C] a river animal that has brown fur and eats fish □ *memerang*

ouch /aʊtʃ/ (also **ow**) *exclam* used when reacting to a sudden feeling of pain □ *adoi; aduh*

ought to /ˈɔːt tə; *before vowels and in final position* ˈɔːt tu/ *modal verb* (*negative* **ought not to**; *short form* **oughtn't to** /ˈɔːtnt tə/ *before vowels and in final position* /ˈɔːtnt tu/) **1** used to say what sb should do □ *mestilah; sepatutnya*: *You ought to visit your parents more often.* ◆ *She oughtn't to make private phone calls in work time.* ◆ *He oughtn't to have been driving so fast.* **2** used to say what should happen or what you expect □ *agaknya; pasti; sepatutnya*: *She ought to pass her test.* ◆ *They ought to be here by now. They left at six.* ◆ *There ought to be more buses in the rush hour.* **3** used for asking for and giving advice about what to do □ *harus; baik; elok*: *You ought to read this book. It's really interesting.* ❶ For more information about modal verbs, look at the **Reference Section** at the back of this dictionary.

ounce /aʊns/ *noun* **1** [C] (*abbr* **oz**) a measure of weight; 28.35 grams. There are 16 ounces in a pound □ *auns*: *For this recipe you need four ounces of flour.* ❶ For more information about weights, look at the section on using numbers at the back of this dictionary. **2** [sing] (usually in negative statements) **an ounce of sth** a very small amount of sth □ *sedikit (pun)*: *That boy hasn't got an ounce of imagination.*

our /ɑː(r); ˈaʊə(r)/ *determiner* of or belonging to us □ *(milik) kita; kami*: *Our house is at the bottom of the road.* ◆ *This is our first visit to Britain.*

ours /ɑːz; ˈaʊəz/ *pron* the one or ones belonging to us □ *kita; kami*: *Their garden is quite nice but I prefer ours.*

ourselves /ɑːˈselvz; ˌaʊə's-/ *pron* **1** used when the people who do an action are also affected by it □ *diri kita/kami (sendiri)*: *Let's forget all about work and just enjoy ourselves.* ◆ *They asked us to wait so we sat down and made ourselves comfortable.* ◆ *We built the house ourselves.* **2** used to emphasize the people who do the action □ *kita/kami sendiri*: *Do you think we should paint the flat ourselves* (= or should we ask sb else to do it for us)?

IDM **(all) by ourselves** **1** alone □ *sendirian*: *Now that we're by ourselves, could I ask you a personal question?* ⊃ note at **alone** **2** without help □ *sendiri*: *We managed to move all our furniture into the new flat by ourselves.*

oust /aʊst/ *verb* [T] **oust sb (from sth/as sth)** to force sb out of a job or position of power, especially in order to take their place □ *menyingkirkan; menggulingkan*: *The rebels finally managed to oust the government from power.* ◆ *He was ousted as chairman.*

out¹ /aʊt/ *adj, adv* **1** away from the inside of a place □ *keluar; ke luar*: *He opened the drawer and took a fork out.* ◆ *She opened the window and put her head out.* ◆ *Can you show me the way out?* **2** not at home or in your place of work □ *keluar; di luar*: *My manager was out when she called.* ◆ *I'd love a night out—I'm bored with staying at home.* **3** a long distance away from a place, for example from land or your country □ *jauh*: *The current is quite strong so don't swim too far out.* **4** (used about the sea) when the water is furthest away from the land □ *surut*: *Don't swim when the tide is on the way out.* **5** used for showing that sth is no longer hidden □ *keluar; muncul; kembang (bunga, dsb); bocor (rahsia)*: *I love the spring when all the flowers are out.* ◆ *The secret's out now. There's no point pretending any more.* **6** made available to the public; published □ *keluar; diterbitkan*: *There'll be a lot of controversy when her book comes out next year.* **7** in a loud voice; clearly □ *dgn suara yg kuat; dgn jelas*: *She cried out in pain.* **8** (used about a player in a game or sport) not allowed to continue playing □ *keluar*: *If you get three answers wrong, you're out.* **9** (used about a ball, etc. in a game or sport) not inside the playing area and therefore not allowed □ *ke luar*: *Although the player argued with the umpire, the ball was clearly out.* **10** (used when you are calculating sth) making or containing a mistake; wrong □ *salah; selisih; lari*: *My guess was only out by a few centimetres.* **11** (*informal*) not possible or acceptable □ *tdk boleh*: *I'm afraid Friday is out. I've got a meeting that day.* **12** not in fashion □ *bukan fesyen lagi*: *Short skirts are out this season.* **13** (used about a light or a fire) not on; not burning □ *padam*: *The lights are out. They must be in bed.* ◆ *Once the fire*

was completely out, experts were sent in to inspect the damage. ❶ For special uses with many verbs, for example **look out**, look at the verb entries.
IDM **be out for sth; be out to do sth** to try hard to get or do sth □ *hendak mendapat/membuat sst*: *I'm not out for revenge.*
down and out ⇒ **down¹**
out-and-out complete □ *betul-betul*: *It was out-and-out war between us.*
ˌout ˈloud = **aloud**

ˈout² /aʊt/ *prep* **1** (used with verbs expressing movement) away from the inside of sth □ *ke luar; keluar dr; mengeluarkan; bangun*: *She took her purse out of her bag.* ♦ *to get out of bed* **OPP** **into** **2** away from or no longer in a place or situation □ *tdk ada; tdk lagi (berada di sst tempat atau dlm sst keadaan)*: *He's out of the country on business.* ♦ *The doctors say she's out of danger.* **3** at a distance from a place □ *(jauh) dr*: *We live a long way out of London.* **4** used for saying which feeling causes you to do sth □ *kerana*: *We were only asking out of curiosity.* **5** used for saying what you use to make sth else □ *diperbuat drpd*: *What is this knife made out of?* ♦ *to be made out of wood/metal/plastic/gold* **6** from among a number or set □ *antara; drpd*: *Nine out of ten people prefer this model.* **7** from; having sth as its source □ *drpd*: *I copied the recipe out of a book.* ♦ *I paid for it out of the money I won on the lottery.* **8 out of sth** used for saying that you no longer have sth □ *kehabisan; tdk ada*: *to be out of milk/sugar/coffee* ♦ *He's been out of work for months.* **9** used for saying that sth is not as it should be □ *tdk (teratur, dll)*: *My notes are all out of order and I can't find the right page.*
IDM **be/feel out of it** to be/feel lonely and unhappy because you are not included in sth □ *terasing; tersisih*: *I don't speak French so I felt rather out of it at the meeting.*

out³ /aʊt/ *verb* [T] to say publicly that sb is homosexual (= sexually attracted to people of the same sex), especially when they would rather keep it a secret □ *memberitahu semua orang bahawa sso itu sebenarnya homoseksual*: *The politician was eventually outed by a tabloid newspaper.*

the outback /ˈaʊtbæk/ *noun* [sing] the part of a country (especially Australia) which is a long way from the coast and towns, and where few people live □ *daerah pedalaman*

outboard motor /ˌaʊtbɔːd ˈməʊtə(r)/ *noun* [C] an engine that can be fixed to a boat □ *motor sangkut*

outbox /ˈaʊtbɒks/ *noun* [C] the place on a computer where new email messages that you write are stored before you send them □ *peti keluar*

outbreak /ˈaʊtbreɪk/ *noun* [C] the sudden start of sth unpleasant (especially a disease or violence) □ *meletusnya; tercetusnya; merebaknya*: *an outbreak of cholera/fighting*

outburst /ˈaʊtbɜːst/ *noun* [C] a sudden expression of a strong feeling, especially anger □ *cetusan (perasaan); tiba-tiba naik angin*: *Afterwards, she apologized for her outburst.*

outcast /ˈaʊtkɑːst/ *noun* [C] a person who is no longer accepted by society or by a group of people □ *orang terbuang*: *a social outcast*

outclass /ˌaʊtˈklɑːs/ *verb* [T, often passive] to be much better than sb/sth, especially in a game or competition □ *jauh lebih baik; (bentuk pasif) tdk sebaik orang, dsb yg dibandingkan itu*

outcome /ˈaʊtkʌm/ *noun* [C] the result or effect of an action or an event □ *hasil; keputusan*

outcrop /ˈaʊtkrɒp/ *noun* [C] a large mass of rock that stands above the surface of the ground □ *singkapan; batuan yg menjulur ke permukaan tanah*

outcry /ˈaʊtkraɪ/ *noun* [C, usually sing] (*pl* **outcries**) a strong protest by a large number of people because they disagree with sth □ *bantahan kuat oleh ramai orang*: *The public outcry forced the government to change its mind about the new tax.*

outdated /ˌaʊtˈdeɪtɪd/ *adj* not useful or common any more; old-fashioned □ *kolot; ketinggalan zaman*: *A lot of the computer equipment is getting outdated.*

outdo /ˌaʊtˈduː/ *verb* [T] (**outdoing; outdoes** /-ˈdʌz/; *pt* **outdid** /-ˈdɪd/; *pp* **outdone** /-ˈdʌn/) to do sth better than another person; to be more successful than sb else □ *mengatasi; melebihi*: *Not to be outdone* (= not wanting anyone else to do better), *she tried again.*

outdoor /ˈaʊtdɔː(r)/ *adj* [only *before* a noun] happening, done, or used outside, not in a building □ *luar*: *an outdoor swimming pool* ♦ *outdoor clothing/activities* **OPP** **indoor**

outdoors /ˌaʊtˈdɔːz/ *adv* outside a building □ *di luar (bangunan)*: *It's a very warm evening so why don't we eat outdoors?* **SYN** **out of doors** **OPP** **indoors** ⇒ look at **outside**

outer /ˈaʊtə(r)/ *adj* [only *before* a noun] **1** on the outside of sth □ *luar*: *the outer layer of skin on an onion* **2** far from the inside or the centre of sth □ *bahagian luar; pinggir*: *the outer suburbs of a city* **OPP** for both meanings **inner**

outermost /ˈaʊtəməʊst/ *adj* [only *before* a noun] furthest from the inside or centre □ *paling luar/jauh* **OPP** **innermost**

ˌouter ˈspace = **space¹** (2)

outfit /ˈaʊtfɪt/ *noun* [C] a set of clothes that are worn together for a particular occasion or purpose □ *pakaian*: *I'm going to buy a whole new outfit for the party.*

outgoing /ˈaʊtɡəʊɪŋ/ *adj* **1** friendly and interested in other people and new experiences □ *ramah dan mesra* **SYN** **sociable** **2** [only *before* a noun] leaving a job or a place □ *yg akan keluar, berhenti, tamat perkhidmatan, dsb*: *the outgoing president/government* ♦ *Put all the outgoing mail in a pile on that table.* **OPP** **incoming**

outgoings → outside 610

outgoings /ˈaʊtɡɔɪŋz/ noun [pl] (BrE) an amount of money that you spend regularly, for example every week or month □ *wang keluar* **OPP** income

outgrow /ˌaʊtˈɡrəʊ/ verb [T] (pt outgrew /-ˈɡruː/; pp outgrown /-ˈɡrəʊn/) to become too old or too big for sth □ *tdk muat; tdk lagi meminati sst, mempunyai sst tabiat, dll*

outing /ˈaʊtɪŋ/ noun [C] a short trip for pleasure □ *bersiar-siar: to go on an outing to the zoo*

outlandish /aʊtˈlændɪʃ/ adj very strange or unusual □ *aneh; pelik: outlandish clothes*

outlast /ˌaʊtˈlɑːst/ verb [T] to continue to exist or to do sth for a longer time than sb/sth □ *bertahan; tahan/hidup lebih lama (drpd sst/sso)*

outlaw¹ /ˈaʊtlɔː/ verb [T] to make sth illegal □ *diharamkan*

outlaw² /ˈaʊtlɔː/ noun [C] (used in past times) a person who has done sth illegal and is hiding to avoid being caught □ *penjahat*

outlay /ˈaʊtleɪ/ noun [C, usually sing] outlay (on sth) money that is spent, especially in order to start a business or project □ *perbelanjaan*

outlet /ˈaʊtlet/ noun [C] **1** an outlet (for sth) a way of expressing and making good use of strong feelings, ideas or energy □ *jalan keluar; cara menyalurkan (perasaan, tenaga, dll): Gary found an outlet for his aggression in boxing.* **2** a shop, business, etc. that sells goods made by a particular company or of a particular type □ *kedai; peruncit: fast food/retail outlets* **3** a pipe through which a gas or liquid can escape □ *saluran keluar* **OPP** inlet

outline¹ /ˈaʊtlaɪn/ verb [T] outline sth (to sb) to tell sb or give the most important facts or ideas about sth □ *menggariskan; menerangkan secara ringkas*

outline² /ˈaʊtlaɪn/ noun [C] **1** a description of the most important facts or ideas about sth □ *garis kasar; ringkasan: a brief outline of Indian history* **2** a line that shows the shape or outside edge of sb/sth □ *garis bentuk: She could see the outline of a person through the mist.*

outlive /ˌaʊtˈlɪv/ verb [T] to live or exist longer than sb/sth □ *hidup lebih lama*

outlook /ˈaʊtlʊk/ noun [C] **1** an outlook (on sth) your attitude to or feeling about life and the world □ *pandangan: an optimistic outlook on life* **2** outlook (for sth) what will probably happen □ *harapan; jangkaan masa depan: The outlook for the economy is not good.*

outlying /ˈaʊtlaɪɪŋ/ adj [only before a noun] far away from the centre of a town or city □ *terpencil: The bus service to the outlying villages is very poor.*

outmoded /ˌaʊtˈməʊdɪd/ adj no longer common or fashionable □ *ketinggalan zaman*

outnumber /ˌaʊtˈnʌmbə(r)/ verb [T, often passive] to be greater in number than an enemy, another team, etc. □ *melebihi (bilangan); lebih banyak/ramai: The enemy troops outnumbered us by three to one.* ◆ *We were completely outnumbered.*

out of ˈdate adj **1** old-fashioned □ *ketinggalan zaman: Her ideas were out of date.* **2** no longer valid □ *tdk sah lagi* ⊃ look at up to date

out-of-ˈwork adj [only before a noun] unable to find a job; unemployed □ *tiada kerja; menganggur: an out-of-work actor*

outpatient /ˈaʊtpeɪʃnt/ noun [C] a person who goes to a hospital for treatment but who does not stay there during the night □ *pesakit luar*

outpost /ˈaʊtpəʊst/ noun [C] a small town or camp that is away from other places □ *pangkalan luar (pekan/kem); tempat terpencil: a remote outpost* ◆ *the last outpost of civilization*

output /ˈaʊtpʊt/ noun [U,C] **1** the amount that a person or machine produces □ *output; keluaran: Output has increased in the past year.* **2** the information that a computer produces □ *output; data output: data output* ⊃ look at input

outrage /ˈaʊtreɪdʒ/ noun **1** [U] great anger □ *kemarahan: a feeling of outrage* **2** [C] something that is very bad or wrong and that causes you to feel great anger □ *sst yg teruk atau tdk baik yg menimbulkan kemarahan: It's an outrage that such poverty should exist in the 21st century.* ▶ outrage verb [T]

outrageous /aʊtˈreɪdʒəs/ adj that makes you very angry or shocked □ *(yg) menimbulkan kemarahan; (yg) mengejutkan: outrageous behaviour/prices* ▶ outrageously adv

outright /ˈaʊtraɪt/ adj [only before a noun] adv **1** open and direct; in an open and direct way □ *terus terang: She told them outright what she thought about it.* **2** complete and clear; completely and clearly □ *nyata: an outright victory* ◆ *to win outright* **3** not gradually; immediately □ *terus; serta-merta; segera: They were able to buy the house outright.*

outset /ˈaʊtset/ noun [sing]
IDM at/from the outset (of sth) at/from the beginning (of sth) □ *pd/dr mula lagi*

outside¹ /ˌaʊtˈsaɪd/ noun **1** [C, usually sing] the outer side or surface of sth □ *bahagian luar: There is a list of all the ingredients on the outside of the packet.* **2** [sing] the area that is near or round a building, etc. □ *luar: We've only seen the church from the outside.* **3** [sing] the part of a road, a track, etc. that is away from the side that you usually drive on, run on, etc □ *lorong luar: The other runners all overtook him on the outside.* **OPP** for all meanings inside
IDM at the outside at the most □ *paling: It will take us 3 days at the outside.*

outside² /ˈaʊtsaɪd/ adj [only before a noun] **1** of or on the outer side or surface of sth □ *(bahagian) luar: the outside walls of a building* **SYN**

external 2 not part of the main building □ *luar: an outside toilet* SYN **external 3** not connected with or belonging to a particular group or organization □ *luar: We can't do all the work by ourselves. We'll need outside help.* **4** (used about a chance or possibility) very small □ *sangat kecil: an outside chance of winning*

IDM **the outside world** people, places, activities, etc. that are away from the area where you live and your own experience of life □ *dunia luar; di luar lingkungan persekitaran dan pengalaman sso*

outside³ /ˌaʊtˈsaɪd/ *adv, prep* **1** in, at or to a place that is not in a room or not in a building □ *di luar: Please wait outside for a few minutes.* ◆ *Leave your muddy boots outside the door.*

MORE When we mean 'outside a building', we can also say **outdoors** and **out of doors**.

2 not in □ *luar drpd; di luar: You may do as you wish outside office hours.* ◆ *a small village just outside Stratford*

outsider /ˌaʊtˈsaɪdə(r)/ *noun* [C] **1** a person who is not accepted as a member of a particular group □ *orang luar* **2** a person or an animal in a race or competition that is not expected to win □ *pelumba (orang atau binatang) yg dijangka tdk akan menang* OPP **favourite**

outsize /ˈaʊtsaɪz/ *adj* (often used about clothes) larger than usual □ *lebih besar drpd biasa*

outskirts /ˈaʊtskɜːts/ *noun* [pl] the parts of a town or city that are furthest from the centre □ *pinggir: They live on the outskirts of Athens.*

outspoken /aʊtˈspəʊkən/ *adj* saying exactly what you think or feel although you may shock or upset other people □ *celopar; lepas cakap; terus terang: Linda is very outspoken in her criticism.*

outstanding /aʊtˈstændɪŋ/ *adj* **1** extremely good; excellent □ *cemerlang: The results in the exams were outstanding.* **2** not yet paid, done or dealt with □ *belum dibayar; belum disiapkan/ diselesaikan: A large amount of the work is still outstanding.* ◆ *outstanding debts/issues*

outstandingly /aʊtˈstændɪŋli/ *adv* very well; extremely □ *sangat; amat: outstandingly good/successful*

outstretched /ˌaʊtˈstretʃt/ *adj* reaching as far as possible □ *terhulur; terkedang: He came towards her with his arms outstretched.*

outward /ˈaʊtwəd/ *adj* [only before a noun] **1** connected with the way things seem to be rather than what is actually true □ *luaran; pd zahirnya: Despite her cheerful outward appearance, she was in fact very unhappy.* **2** (used about a journey) going away from the place that you will return to later □ *keluar; (perjalanan) pergi* OPP **return 3** away from the centre or from a particular point □ *ke luar: outward movement/ pressure* OPP **inward** ▶ **outwardly** *adv: He remained outwardly calm so as not to frighten the children.*

outwards /ˈaʊtwədz/ (especially AmE **outward**) *adv* towards the outside or away from the place where you are □ *ke luar: This door opens outwards.*

outweigh /ˌaʊtˈweɪ/ *verb* [T] to be more in amount or importance than sth □ *lebih berat/ penting; melebihi: The advantages outweigh the disadvantages.*

outwit /ˌaʊtˈwɪt/ *verb* [T] (**outwitting**; **outwitted**) to gain an advantage over sb by doing sth clever □ *mengalahkan/memperdayakan (sso dgn bijak); mengakali*

oval /ˈəʊvl/ *adj, noun* [C] shaped like an egg; a shape like that of an egg □ *bujur; lonjong; jorong* ➲ picture at **shape**

ovary /ˈəʊvəri/ *noun* [C] (*pl* **ovaries**) one of the two parts of the female body that produce eggs □ *ovari*

ovation /əʊˈveɪʃn/ *noun* [C] an enthusiastic reaction given by an audience when they like sb/ sth very much □ *tepukan sanjungan: The dancers got a standing ovation* (= the audience stood up) *at the end of the performance.*

oven /ˈʌvn/ *noun* [C] the part of a cooker shaped like a box with a door on the front. You put food in the oven to cook or heat it □ *ketuhar: Cook in a hot oven for 50 minutes.* ◆ *a microwave oven*

over /ˈəʊvə(r)/ *adv, prep* **1** covering sth □ *di atas; menutupi: She put a blanket over the sleeping child.* ◆ *She hung her coat over the back of the chair.* **2** straight above sth, but not touching it □ *di atas: There's a painting over the bookcase.* ◆ *We watched the plane fly over.* ➲ look at **above 3** across to the other side of sth □ *melepasi; merentangi: The horse jumped over the fence.* ◆ *a bridge over the river* ➲ note at **across 4** on or to the other side □ *di sebalik; di sebelah sana: The student turned the paper over and read the first question.* **5** down or sideways from a vertical position □ *ke bawah; ke sisi: I fell over in the street this morning.* ◆ *He leaned over to speak to the woman next to him.* **6** above or more than a number, price, etc. □ *lebih; lebih drpd: She lived in Athens for over ten years.* ◆ *suitable for children aged 10 and over* **7** used for expressing distance □ *di: He's over in America at the moment.* ◆ *Sit down over there.* ◆ *Come over here, please.* **8** not used □ *lebih; tinggal; baki: There are a lot of cakes left over from the party.* **9** finished □ *tamat; selesai; habis: The exams are all over now.* **10** [used with *all*] everywhere □ *di merata-rata: There was blood all over the place.* ◆ *I can't find my glasses. I've looked all over for them.* **11** used for saying that sth is repeated □ *semula; lagi; lagi-lagi: You'll have to start all over again* (= from the beginning). ◆ *She kept saying the same thing over and over again.* **12** about; on the subject of □ *ttg; mengenai: We quarrelled over money.* **13** during □ *semasa: We met several times over the Christmas holiday.* ❶ For special uses with many verbs, for example **get over sth**, look at the verb entries.

over- /'əʊvə(r)/ [in compounds] **1** more than usual; too much □ *terlalu banyak; berlebihan; secara berlebihan; keterlaluan*: *to oversleep* ◆ *over-optimistic* ◆ *overactive* **2** completely □ *amat; sangat: overjoyed* **3** upper; outer; extra □ *lebih; luar; tambahan: overcoat* ◆ *overtime* **4** over; above □ *atas: overcast* ◆ *to overhang*

overall¹ /ˌəʊvərˈɔːl/ *adv, adj* [only before a noun] **1** including everything; total □ *keseluruhan*: *What will the overall cost of the work be?* **2** generally; when you consider everything □ *pd keseluruhannya*: *Overall, I can say that we are pleased with the year's work.*

overalls (AmE coveralls)   dungarees (AmE overalls)   apron

overall² /ˈəʊvərɔːl/ *noun* **1** [C] (BrE) a piece of clothing like a coat that you wear over your clothes to keep them clean when you are working □ *baju luar* **2 overalls** (AmE **coveralls**) [pl] a piece of clothing that covers your legs and body (and sometimes your arms) that you wear over your clothes to keep them clean when you are working □ *overal; baju monyet* **3** (AmE) **overalls** = **dungarees**

overawe /ˌəʊvərˈɔː/ *verb* [T, usually passive] to impress sb so much that they feel nervous or frightened □ *terlalu kagum*

overbalance /ˌəʊvəˈbæləns/ *verb* [I] to lose your balance and fall □ *kehilangan imbangan*

overbearing /ˌəʊvəˈbeərɪŋ/ *adj* trying to control other people in an unpleasant way □ *suka menguasai orang lain*: *an overbearing manner* **SYN** **domineering**

overboard /ˈəʊvəbɔːd/ *adv* over the side of a boat or ship into the water □ *jatuh, dsb ke dlm air (dr bot, kapal, dsb)*
IDM **go overboard (on/about/for sb/sth)** to be too excited or enthusiastic about sb/sth □ *terlampau ghairah (terhadap sso/akan sst)*

overcame past tense of **overcome**

overcast /ˌəʊvəˈkɑːst/ *adj* (used about the sky) covered with cloud □ *mendung*

overcharge /ˌəʊvəˈtʃɑːdʒ/ *verb* [I,T] to ask sb to pay too much money for sth □ *mengenakan harga berlebihan*: *The taxi driver overcharged me.* ↪ look at **charge**

overcoat /ˈəʊvəkəʊt/ *noun* [C] a long thick coat that you wear in cold weather □ *kot luar*

overcome /ˌəʊvəˈkʌm/ *verb* [T] (*pt* **overcame** /-ˈkeɪm/; *pp* **overcome**) **1** to manage to control or defeat sb/sth □ *mengalahkan; mengatasi*: *She tried hard to overcome her fear of flying.* **2** [usually passive] to be extremely strongly affected by sth □ *melanda; dilanda*: *He was overcome with emotion and had to leave the room.*

overcrowded /ˌəʊvəˈkraʊdɪd/ *adj* (used about a place) with too many people inside □ *penuh sesak*: *The trains are overcrowded on Friday evenings.*

overdo /ˌəʊvəˈduː/ *verb* [T] (**overdoing**; **overdoes** /-ˈdʌz/; *pt* **overdid** /-ˈdɪd/; *pp* **overdone** /-ˈdʌn/) **1** to use or do too much of sth □ *keterlaluan; berlebih-lebihan* **2** to cook sth too long □ *terlampau masak*: *The meat was overdone.*
IDM **overdo it/things** to work, etc. too hard □ *(bekerja, dsb) keterlaluan*: *Exercise is fine but don't overdo it.*

overdose /ˈəʊvədəʊs/ *noun* [C] an amount of a drug or medicine that is too large and so is not safe □ *dos berlebihan*: *to take an overdose* ↪ look at **dose**

overdraft /ˈəʊvədrɑːft/ *noun* [C] an amount of money that you have spent that is greater than the amount you have in your bank account; an arrangement that allows you to borrow this money □ *overdraf*

overdrawn /ˌəʊvəˈdrɔːn/ *adj* having spent more money than you have in your bank account □ *terlebih belanja (wang dlm akaun bank)*: *I checked my balance and discovered I was overdrawn.*

overdue /ˌəʊvəˈdjuː/ *adj* late in arriving, happening, being paid, returned, etc. □ *lewat; lambat*: *an overdue library book* ◆ *Her baby is a week overdue.*

overestimate /ˌəʊvərˈestɪmeɪt/ *verb* [T] to guess that sb/sth is bigger, better, more important, etc. than he/she/it really is □ *menganggar lebih*: *I overestimated how much we could manage to do in a weekend.* **OPP** **underestimate**

overflow

'Oh no! The bath's overflowing!'

overflow /ˌəʊvəˈfləʊ/ verb 1 [I,T] overflow (with sth) to be so full that the contents go over the sides □ *melimpah*: *The tap was left on and the bath overflowed.* ♦ *The roads are overflowing with cars.* 2 [I] overflow (into sth) to be forced out of a place or a container that is too full □ *melimpah*: *The crowd overflowed into the street.*

overgrown /ˌəʊvəˈɡrəʊn/ adj covered with plants that have grown too big and untidy □ *semak; penuh dgn tumbuhan yg menyemak*

overhang /ˌəʊvəˈhæŋ/ verb [I,T] (pt, pp overhung) to stick out, over and above sth else □ *menganjur di atas*: *The overhanging trees kept the sun off us.* ⇨ picture at **overlap**

overhaul /ˌəʊvəˈhɔːl/ verb [T] to look at sth carefully and change or repair it if necessary □ *membaik pulih*: *to overhaul an engine* ▸ overhaul /ˈəʊvəhɔːl/ noun [C]

overhead adj /ˈəʊvəhed/ , adv /ˌəʊvəˈhed/ above your head □ *atas; di atas*: *overhead electricity cables* ♦ *A helicopter flew overhead.*

overheads /ˈəʊvəhedz/ noun [pl] (AmE overhead [U]) money that a company must spend on things like heat, light, rent, etc. □ *overhed*

overhear /ˌəʊvəˈhɪə(r)/ verb [T] (pt, pp overheard /-ˈhɜːd/) to hear what sb is saying by accident, when they are speaking to sb else and not to you □ *terdengar*

overhung past tense, past participle of **overhang**

overjoyed /ˌəʊvəˈdʒɔɪd/ adj [not before a noun] overjoyed (at sth/to do sth) very happy □ *sangat gembira*

overland /ˈəʊvəlænd/ adj not by sea or by air □ *ikut jalan darat*: *an overland journey* ▸ overland adv

overlap

overlapping tiles   overlapping dates   overhanging branches

overlap /ˌəʊvəˈlæp/ verb [I,T] (overlapping; overlapped) 1 when two things overlap, part of one covers part of the other □ *bertindih; bertindan*: *Make sure that the two pieces of material overlap.* 2 to be partly the same as sth □ *bertindan*: *Our jobs overlap to some extent.* ▸ overlap /ˈəʊvəlæp/ noun [C,U]

overleaf /ˌəʊvəˈliːf/ adv on the other side of the page □ *di muka surat sebalik*: *Full details are given overleaf.*

overload /ˌəʊvəˈləʊd/ verb [T] 1 [often passive] to put too many people or things into or onto sth □ *menyaratkan; terlalu penuh; sesak*: *an overloaded vehicle* 2 overload sb (with sth) to give sb too much of sth □ *terlalu dibebani*: *to be overloaded with work/information* 3 to put too much electricity through sth □ *mempunyai beban lebih*: *If you use too many electrical appliances at one time you may overload the system.*

overlook /ˌəʊvəˈlʊk/ verb [T] 1 to fail to see or notice sth □ *tdk nampak; terlepas perhatian*: *to overlook a spelling mistake* ♦ *She felt that her opinion had been completely overlooked.* 2 to see sth wrong and decide to forget it □ *mengetepikan; memaafkan*: *I will overlook your behaviour this time but don't let it happen again.* 3 to have a view over sth □ *berpemandangan; menghala*: *My room overlooks the sea.*

overnight /ˌəʊvəˈnaɪt/ adj [only before a noun] adv 1 for one night □ *satu malam; semalam*: *an overnight bag* (= containing the things you need for one night away from home) ♦ *We stayed overnight in Hamburg.* 2 (happening) very suddenly □ *tiba-tiba*: *She became a star overnight.*

overpass /ˈəʊvəpɑːs/ (AmE) = **flyover**

overpay /ˌəʊvəˈpeɪ/ verb [T] (pt, pp overpaid) [usually passive] to pay sb too much; to pay sb more than their job is worth □ *membayar lebih* **OPP** underpay

overpower /ˌəʊvəˈpaʊə(r)/ verb [T] to be too strong for sb □ *terlalu kuat utk diatasi; (bentuk pasif) tdk dpt mengatasi; menjadi lemas, lemah, dll*: *The fireman was overpowered by the heat and smoke.* ▸ overpowering adj: *an overpowering smell*

overran past tense of **overrun**

overrate /ˌəʊvəˈreɪt/ verb [T, often passive] to think that sth/sb is better than he/she/it really is □ *menilai terlalu tinggi* **OPP** underrate

overreact /ˌəʊvəriˈækt/ verb [I] overreact (to sth) to react too strongly, especially to sth unpleasant □ *bertindak balas berlebihan atau keterlaluan* ▸ overreaction noun [sing, U]

override /ˌəʊvəˈraɪd/ verb [T] (pt overrode /-ˈrəʊd/; pp overridden /-ˈrɪdn/) 1 to use your authority to reject sb's decision, order, etc. □ *menolak*: *They overrode my protest and continued with the meeting.* 2 to be more important than sth □ *mengatasi; lebih penting*

overriding /ˌəʊvəˈraɪdɪŋ/ adj [only before a noun] more important than anything else □ *utama; lebih penting*: *Our overriding concern is safety.*

overrode past tense of **override**

overrule /ˌəʊvəˈruːl/ verb [T] to use your authority to change what sb else has already decided or done □ *menolak*: *The Appeal Court overruled the judge's decision.*

overrun /ˌəʊvəˈrʌn/ verb (pt overran /-ˈræn/; pp overrun) 1 [T, often passive] to spread all over an area in great numbers □ *dipenuhi; dilanda*: *The city was completely overrun by rats.* 2 [I,T]

oversaw → owe 614

to use more time or money than expected □ *melampaui/melebihi waktu*: The meeting overran by 30 minutes.

oversaw *past tense of* **oversee**

overseas /ˌəʊvəˈsiːz/ *adj* [only *before* a noun] *adv* in, to or from another country that you have to cross the sea to get to □ *luar negeri*: overseas students studying in Britain ♦ Frank has gone to live overseas.

oversee /ˌəʊvəˈsiː/ *verb* [T] (*pt* oversaw /-ˈsɔː/; *pp* overseen /-ˈsiːn/) to watch sth to make sure that it is done properly □ *menyelia*

overshadow /ˌəʊvəˈʃædəʊ/ *verb* [T] **1** to cause sb/sth to seem less important or successful □ *menyebabkan sso kelihatan kurang penting atau kurang berjaya; membayangi*: Connor always seemed to be overshadowed by his sister. **2** to cause sth to be less enjoyable □ *menyuramkan*

oversight /ˈəʊvəsaɪt/ *noun* [C,U] something that you do not notice or do (that you should have noticed or done) □ *kealpaan; kesilapan*

oversimplify /ˌəʊvəˈsɪmplɪfaɪ/ *verb* [I,T] (oversimplifying; oversimplifies; *pt, pp* oversimplified) to explain sth in such a simple way that its real meaning is lost □ *mempermudah*

oversleep /ˌəʊvəˈsliːp/ *verb* [I] (*pt, pp* overslept /-ˈslept/) to sleep longer than you should have done □ *bangun lambat*: I overslept and was late for school. ⊃ look at lie in, sleep in

overstate /ˌəʊvəˈsteɪt/ *verb* [T] to say sth in a way that makes it seem more important than it really is □ *memperbesar-besar* OPP understate

overstep /ˌəʊvəˈstep/ *verb* [T] (overstepping; overstepped) to go further than what is normal or allowed □ *melampaui; melanggar*: to overstep your authority ♦ He tends to overstep the boundaries of good taste.
IDM **overstep the mark/line** to behave in a way that people think is not acceptable □ *melampaui batas*

overt /əʊˈvɜːt; ˈəʊvɜːt/ *adj* (*formal*) done in an open way and not secretly □ *terang-terangan; nyata*: There was little overt support for the project. OPP covert ▶overtly *adv*: overtly political activities

overtake /ˌəʊvəˈteɪk/ *verb* [T] (*pt* overtook /-ˈtʊk/; *pp* overtaken /-ˈteɪkən/) **1** to go past another person, car, etc. because you are moving faster □ *memotong*: The lorry overtook me on the bend. **2** to become greater in number, amount or importance than sth else □ *mengatasi*: Nuclear energy may overtake oil as the main fuel.

overthrow /ˌəʊvəˈθrəʊ/ *verb* [T] (*pt* overthrew /-ˈθruː/; *pp* overthrown /-ˈθrəʊn/) to remove a leader or government from power, by using force □ *menggulingkan* ▶overthrow /ˈəʊvəθrəʊ/ *noun* [sing]

overtime /ˈəʊvətaɪm/ *noun* [U] time that you spend at work after your usual working hours; the money that you are paid for this □ *lebih masa*: Betty did ten hours' overtime last week. ▶overtime *adv*: I have been working overtime for weeks.

overtone /ˈəʊvətəʊn/ *noun* [C, usually pl] something that is suggested but not expressed in an obvious way □ *berbau; tersirat*: Some people claimed there were racist overtones in the advertisement.

overtook *past tense of* **overtake**

overture /ˈəʊvətʃʊə(r)/ (*AmE usually*) / *noun* **1** [C] a piece of music that is the introduction to a musical play such as an **opera** or a **ballet** □ *overtur* **2** [C, usually pl] (*formal*) an act of being friendly towards sb, especially because you want to be friends, to start a business relationship, etc. □ *percubaan utk berbaik-baik*

overturn /ˌəʊvəˈtɜːn/ *verb* **1** [I,T] to turn over or turn sth over so that the top is at the bottom □ *terbalik*: The car overturned but the driver escaped unhurt. **2** [T] to officially decide that a decision is wrong and change it □ *mengubah; menterbalikkan*

overview /ˈəʊvəvjuː/ *noun* [C] a general description that gives the most important facts about sth □ *gambaran keseluruhan; pemerian umum*

overweight /ˌəʊvəˈweɪt/ *adj* too heavy or fat □ *gemuk; berat badan berlebihan*: I'm a bit overweight—I think I might go on a diet. OPP underweight ⊃ note at fat

overwhelm /ˌəʊvəˈwelm/ *verb* [T, usually passive] **1** to cause sb to feel such a strong emotion that they do not know how to react □ *dilanda; ditenggelami; diselubungi*: The new world champion was overwhelmed by all the publicity. **2** to be so powerful, big, etc., that sb cannot deal with it □ *mengalahkan; dihujani*: He overwhelmed his opponent with his superb technique. ♦ The TV company was overwhelmed by complaints.

overwhelming /ˌəʊvəˈwelmɪŋ/ *adj* extremely great or strong □ *sangat banyak, kuat, dll*: Anne-Marie had an overwhelming desire to return home. ▶overwhelmingly *adv*

overwork /ˌəʊvəˈwɜːk/ *verb* [I,T] to work or make sb work too hard □ *bekerja teruk*: They are overworked and underpaid. ▶overwork *noun* [U]

ovulate /ˈɒvjuleɪt/ *verb* [I] (of a woman or female animal) to produce an egg from the **ovary** (= part of the female body) □ *mengovum; ovulat* ▶ovulation /ˌɒvjuˈleɪʃn/ *noun* [U]: when ovulation takes place

ow /aʊ/ = **ouch**

owe /əʊ/ *verb* [T] **1 owe sth (to sb); owe sb for sth** to have to pay money to sb for sth that they have done or given □ *berhutang*: I owe Katrina a lot of money. ♦ I owe a lot of money to Katrina. ♦ I still owe you for that bread you bought yesterday. ⊃ note at **loan** ⊃ look at **debt** **2 owe sb sth; owe sth to sb** to feel that you should do sth for sb or give sth to sb, especially because they have done sth for you □ *harus; patut: Claudia owes me an explanation.* ♦ *I owe you an apology.* **3 owe sth to sb/sth** to have sth (for the reason given) □ *kerana; berkat: She said she owes her success to hard work and determination.*

owing /'əʊɪŋ/ *adj* [not before a noun] **owing (to sb)** not yet paid □ *terhutang; belum dibayar: How much is still owing to you?*

'owing to *prep* because of □ *kerana: The match was cancelled owing to bad weather.*

owl /aʊl/ *noun* [C] a bird with large eyes that hunts small animals at night □ *burung hantu/pungguk*

own¹ /əʊn/ *adj, pron* **1** used to emphasize that sth belongs to a particular person □ *sendiri: I saw him do it with my own eyes.* ♦ *This is his own house.* ♦ *This house is his own.* ♦ *Rachel would like her own room/a room of her own.* **2** used to show that sth is done or made without help from another person □ *sendiri: The children are old enough to get their own breakfast.*

owl

IDM **come into your own** to have the opportunity to show your special qualities □ *menunjukkan kebolehan yg ada*

get/have your own back (on sb) (*informal*) to hurt sb who has hurt you □ *membalas dendam*

hold your own (against sb/sth) to be as strong, good, etc. as sb/sth else □ *dpt bertahan (terhadap sso/sst)*

(all) on your, etc. own 1 alone □ *seorang diri; sendirian: John lives all on his own.* ⊃ note at **alone 2** without help □ *sendiri: I managed to repair the car all on my own.*

own² /əʊn/ *verb* [T] to have sth belonging to you □ *mempunyai; memiliki; milik: We don't own the house. We just rent it.* ♦ *a privately owned company*

PHR V **own up (to sth)** (*informal*) to tell sb that you have done sth wrong □ *mengaku (membuat sst): None of the children owned up to breaking the window.* ⊃ A more formal word is **confess**.

owner /'əʊnə(r)/ *noun* [C] a person who owns sth □ *tuan punya; pemilik: a house/dog owner*

ownership /'əʊnəʃɪp/ *noun* [U] the state of owning sth □ *pemilikan: in private/public ownership*

ox /ɒks/ *noun* [C] (*pl* **oxen** /'ɒksn/) a **bull** (= male cow) that has been **castrated** (= had part of its sex organs removed) and is used for pulling or carrying heavy loads □ *lembu jantan* ⊃ note at **cow** ⊃ look at **bull**

oxygen /'ɒksɪdʒən/ *noun* [U] (*symbol* O) a gas that you cannot see, taste or smell. Plants and animals cannot live without **oxygen**. □ *(simbol O) oksigen*

oyster /'ɔɪstə(r)/ *noun* [C] a type of **shellfish** (= a creature with a shell that lives in water) that you can eat. Some **oysters** produce **pearls** (= small hard round white objects used to make jewellery). □ *tiram* ⊃ picture at **shellfish**

oz *abbr* = **ounce**(1) □ *oz (auns): Add 4oz flour.*

ozone /'əʊzəʊn/ *noun* [U] a poisonous gas which is a form of **oxygen** □ *ozon*

'ozone-friendly *adj* (used about cleaning products, etc.) not containing chemicals that could harm the **ozone layer** □ *endah ozon*

the 'ozone layer *noun* [sing] the layer of **ozone** high up in the atmosphere that helps to protect the earth from the harmful effects of the sun □ *lapisan ozon: a hole in the ozone layer* ⊃ note at **environment** ⊃ look at **CFC**

P p

P, p /piː/ *noun* [C,U] (*pl* **Ps**; **P's**; **p's** /piːz/) the 16th letter of the English alphabet □ *P, p (huruf): 'Pencil' begins with (a) 'P'.*

p *abbr* **1** (*pl* **pp**) = **page¹** □ *ms (muka surat); hal (halaman): See p.94 and pp.63-96.* **2** (*BrE informal*) = **penny**(1), **pence** □ *peni: a 46p stamp* **3** **P** (on a road sign) parking □ *tempat meletak kereta*

PA /ˌpiː 'eɪ/ *abbr, noun* [C] (*especially BrE*) **personal assistant**; a person who types letters, answers the telephone, arranges meetings, etc. for just one manager □ *PA (Pembantu Peribadi)*

p.a. *abbr* (from Latin) per annum; in or for a year □ *setahun; tahunan: salary: £25 000 p.a.*

pace¹ /peɪs/ *noun* **1** [U, sing] **pace (of sth)** the speed at which you walk, run, etc. or at which sth happens □ *langkah; kadar (kecepatan, kemajuan, kebolehan, dll.): to run at a steady/gentle pace* ♦ *I can't stand the pace of life in London.* ♦ *Students are encouraged to work at their own pace* (= as fast or as slowly as they like). **2** [C] the distance that you move when you take one step □ *langkah: Take two paces forward and then stop.* **SYN** step

IDM **keep pace (with sb/sth)** to move or do sth at the same speed as sb/sth else; to change as quickly as sth else is changing □ *bersaing/seiring (dgn sso/sst); mengikut: Wages are not keeping pace with inflation.*

set the pace to move or do sth at the speed that others must follow □ *menentukan kelajuan, kepesatan, dll: Pinto set the pace for the first three miles.*

pace² /peɪs/ verb [I,T] to walk up and down in the same area many times, especially because you are nervous or angry □ *berjalan mundar-mandir*

pacemaker /'peɪsmeɪkə(r)/ noun [C] **1** a machine that helps to make sb's heart beat regularly or more strongly □ *perentak jantung* **2** a person in a race who sets the speed that the others try to follow □ *penentu rentak/kadar kelajuan*

pacifier /'pæsɪfaɪə(r)/ (*AmE*) = **dummy** (4)

pacifism /'pæsɪfɪzəm/ noun [U] the belief that all wars are wrong and that you should not fight in them □ *pasifisme; antipeperangan* ▶ **pacifist** /-ɪst/ noun [C]

pacify /'pæsɪfaɪ/ verb [T] (**pacifying**; **pacifies**; *pt, pp* **pacified**) to make sb who is angry or upset be calm or quiet □ *menenangkan; meredakan*

pack¹ /pæk/ verb **1** [I,T] to put your things into a suitcase, etc. before you go away or go on holiday □ *mengemaskan beg pakaian*: *Have you packed yet?* ◆ *Have you packed your toothbrush?* ◆ *I'll have to pack my suitcase in the morning.*

HELP The expression **do your packing** means the same.

OPP **unpack 2** [T] to put things into containers so they can be stored, transported or sold □ *memasukkan ke dlm kotak, dsb*: *I packed all my books into boxes.* **OPP** **unpack 3** [T, often passive] (*informal*) to fill with people or things until crowded or full □ *penuh sesak; padat; penuh; sarat; memenuhi*: *The train was absolutely packed.* ◆ *The book is packed with useful information.* ◆ *People packed the pavements, waiting for the president to arrive.*

PHR V **pack sth in** (*informal*) to stop doing sth □ *meninggalkan; berhenti; sudahlah*: *I've packed in my job.* ◆ *I've had enough of you boys arguing—just pack it in, will you!*

pack sth in/into sth to do a lot in a short time □ *membuat banyak perkara dlm masa yg singkat*: *They packed a lot into their three days in Rome.*

pack sth out [usually passive] to fill with people □ *penuh sesak*: *The bars are packed out every night.*

pack up (*BrE informal*) **1** (used about a machine, engine, etc.) to stop working □ *rosak*: *My old car packed up last week so now I cycle to work.* **2** to finish working or doing sth □ *berhenti (membuat kerja, dsb)*: *There was nothing else to do so we packed up and went home.*

pack² /pæk/ noun [C]
▶ CONTAINER **1** (especially *AmE*) a small box, bag, etc. in which things are packed to be sold in a shop □ *bekas; bungkus pek; kotak*
▶ SET OF THINGS **2** a set of things that are supplied together for a particular purpose □ *pek; bungkus; kotak*: *an information pack* ◆ *These batteries are sold in packs of four.* ◆ (*figurative*) *Everything she told me was a pack of lies.* ➲ look at **package, packet, parcel**
▶ BAG **3** = **backpack¹**: *It was hard to walk fast with the heavy pack on my back.*
▶ OF ANIMALS **4** [with sing or pl verb] a group of wild animals that hunt together □ *kawanan; kumpulan*: *a pack of dogs/wolves*
▶ OF PEOPLE **5** a large group of similar people or things, especially one that you do not like or approve of □ *kumpulan; gerombolan*: *a pack of journalists*
▶ OF CARDS **6** (*AmE* **deck**) a complete set of playing cards □ *set (daun pakau)*: *a pack of cards* ➲ note at **card** ➲ picture at **card**

package /'pækɪdʒ/ noun [C] **1** (*AmE*) = **parcel, packet** (1) **2** (*BrE*) something, or a number of things, covered in paper or in a box □ *bungkusan*: *There's a large package on the table for you.* ➲ look at **pack, packet, parcel 3** a number of things that must be bought or accepted together □ *pakej*: *a software package* ◆ *a financial aid package* ▶ **package** verb [T]: *Goods that are attractively packaged sell more quickly.*

'package holiday (*AmE* **'package tour**) noun [C] a holiday that is organized by a company for a fixed price that includes the cost of travel, hotels, etc. □ *percutian berpakej* ➲ note at **holiday**

packaging /'pækɪdʒɪŋ/ noun [U] all the materials (boxes, bags, paper, etc.) that are used to cover or protect goods before they are sold □ *bahan pembungkus*: *Attractive packaging can help to sell a product.* ➲ picture at **container**

packed /pækt/ adj **1** extremely full of people □ *sesak*: *The restaurant was packed.* **SYN** **crowded 2** containing a lot of a particular thing □ *penuh dgn*: *a book packed with information*

packed 'lunch noun [C] (*BrE*) food that you prepare at home and take with you to eat at work or school □ *bekal makan tengah hari*

packer /'pækə(r)/ noun [C] a person, company or machine that puts goods, especially food, into boxes, plastic, paper, etc. to be sold □ *pembungkus*

packet /'pækɪt/ noun **1** (*abbr* **pkt**) (*AmE* **pack; package**) [C] a small box, bag, etc. in which things are packed to be sold in a shop □ *paket*: *a packet of sweets/biscuits/crisps* ◆ *a cigarette packet* ➲ look at **pack, package, parcel** ➲ picture at **container 2** [sing] (*informal*) a large amount of money □ *banyak duit*: *That new kitchen must have cost them a packet.*

packing /'pækɪŋ/ noun [U] **1** the act of putting your clothes, possessions, etc. into boxes or cases in order to take or send them somewhere □ *(perbuatan) membungkus, mengemaskan beg pakaian, dsb*: *We're going on holiday tomorrow so I'll do my packing tonight.* **2** soft material that you use to stop things from being damaged or broken when you are sending them somewhere □ *bahan pembungkus*: *The price includes postage and packing.*

pact /pækt/ noun [C] **(a) pact between A and B** a formal agreement between two or more people, groups or countries □ *pakatan*

pad¹ /pæd/ noun [C] **1** a thick piece of soft material, used for cleaning or protecting sth or to make sth a different shape □ *pad; lapik*: *Remove eye make-up with cleanser and a cotton-wool pad.* ◆ *a jacket with shoulder pads* ➲ picture at **football 2** a number of pieces of paper that are fastened together at one end □ *pad: a notepad* **3** the soft part on the bottom of the feet of some animals, for example dogs and cats □ *tapak kaki* **4** the place where a **spacecraft** (= a vehicle that travels in space) takes off □ *landas pelancaran: a launch pad*

pad² /pæd/ verb (**padding; padded**) **1** [T, usually passive] **pad sth (with sth)** to fill or cover sth with soft material in order to protect it, make it larger or more comfortable, etc. □ *melapik; berlapik*: *I sent the photograph frame in a padded envelope.* **2** [I] **pad about, along, around, etc.** to walk quietly, especially because you are not wearing shoes □ *melapik; berlapik*: *He got up and padded into the bathroom.*

PHR V pad sth out to make a book, speech, etc. longer by adding things that are not necessary □ *menokok tambah (buku, ucapan, dsb) supaya lebih panjang*

padding /ˈpædɪŋ/ noun [U] soft material that is put inside sth to protect it or to make it larger, more comfortable, etc. □ *bahan lapik; pad*

paddle¹ /ˈpædl/ noun [C] a short pole that is flat and wide at one or both ends and that you use for moving a small boat through water □ *dayung* ➲ look at **oar** ➲ picture at **kayak**

paddle² /ˈpædl/ verb **1** [I,T] to move a small boat through water using a short pole that is flat and wide at one or both ends □ *mendayung*: *We paddled down the river.* ➲ look at **row 2** [I] to walk in water that is not very deep □ *meranduk*: *We paddled in the stream.*

paddock /ˈpædək/ noun [C] a small field where horses are kept □ *padang kecil utk kuda; padok*

paddy /ˈpædi/ (also **ˈpaddy field**) noun [C] (pl **paddies**) a field in which rice is grown □ *sawah; bendang: a rice paddy*

padlock /ˈpædlɒk/ noun [C] a type of lock that you can use for fastening gates, bicycles, etc. □ *mangga; ibu kunci* ▶**padlock** verb [T] **padlock sth (to sth)**: *I padlocked my bicycle to a lamp post.*

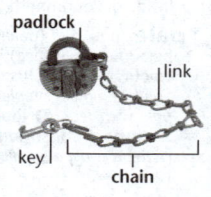

padlock
link
key
chain

paediatrician (*AmE* **pediatrician**) /ˌpiːdiəˈtrɪʃn/ noun [C] a doctor who deals with the diseases of children □ *pakar pediatrik*

paediatrics (*AmE* **pediatrics**) /ˌpiːdiˈætrɪks/ noun [U] the area of medicine connected with the diseases of children □ *(bidang) pediatrik* ▶**paediatric** (*AmE* **pediatric**) adj

paella /paɪˈelə/ noun [U,C] a Spanish dish made with rice, meat, fish and vegetables □ *paella (hidangan Sepanyol)*

pagan /ˈpeɪɡən/ adj having religious beliefs that do not belong to any of the main religions □ *pagan; jahiliah* ▶**pagan** noun [C]

page¹ /peɪdʒ/ noun [C] (abbr p) **1** one or both sides of a piece of paper in a book, magazine, etc □ *muka surat; halaman*: *The letter was three pages long.* ◆ *Turn over the page.* ◆ *Turn to page 12 of your book.* ◆ *the front page of a newspaper* **2** a section of data that can be shown on a computer screen at any one time □ *laman*: *Go to our home page* (= the main page of an organization).

page² /peɪdʒ/ verb [T] to call sb by sending a message to a **pager**, or by calling their name through a **loudspeaker** (= a piece of equipment fixed to a wall in a public place) □ *mengeloi; memanggil*

pageant /ˈpædʒənt/ noun [C] **1** a type of public entertainment at which people dress in clothes from past times and give outdoor performances of scenes from history □ *pertunjukan dramatik* **2** (*especially AmE*) a beauty competition for young women □ *pertandingan ratu cantik*

pageantry /ˈpædʒəntri/ noun [U] impressive public events or ceremonies with many people wearing special clothes □ *upacara atau majlis yg gilang-gemilang*: *the pageantry of royal occasions*

pager /ˈpeɪdʒə(r)/ noun [C] a small machine that you carry, that makes a sound when sb sends you a message □ *alat keloi* **SYN** **bleeper**

pagoda /pəˈɡəʊdə/ noun [C] a religious building in South or East Asia in the form of a tall tower with several levels, each with a roof □ *pagoda; bangunan keagamaan*

paid¹ past tense, past participle of **pay¹**

paid² /peɪd/ adj (of work, etc.) for which people receive money □ *yg ada bayarannya*: *Neither of them is currently in paid employment.*

ˈpaid-up adj [only before a noun] having paid all the money that you owe, for example to become a member of a club □ *berbayar; sudah membayar*: *He's a fully paid-up member of Friends of the Earth.*

pain¹ /peɪn/ noun **1** [C,U] the unpleasant feeling that you have when a part of your body has been hurt or when you are ill □ *sakit; kesakitan*: *to be in pain* ◆ *He screamed with pain.* ◆ *chest pains*

HELP **Pain** or **ache**? We use **ache** for a long, continuous pain and **pain** for sudden, short, sharp periods of pain. Therefore we usually say: *I've got earache/backache/toothache/a headache* but: *He was admitted to hospital with pains in his chest.* For the use of 'a' or 'an' with **ache**, look at the note at **ache**.

pain → pallid

2 [U] sadness that you feel because sth bad has happened □ *kesedihan; kepedihan*: *the pain of losing a parent*

IDM **a pain (in the neck)** (*informal*) a person, thing or situation that makes you angry or annoyed □ *sso/sst yg menyakitkan hati*

pain² /peɪn/ *verb* [T] (*formal*) to make sb feel sad or upset □ *membuat sso berasa sedih; menyedihkan*: *It pains me to think how much money we've wasted.* **SYN** **hurt**

pained /peɪnd/ *adj* showing that you are sad or upset □ *(yg) sedih*: *a pained expression*

painful /ˈpeɪnfl/ *adj* **painful (for sb) (to do sth)** **1** that causes pain □ *menyakitkan; sakit*: *A wasp sting can be very painful.* ♦ *painful joints* ♦ *My ankle is still too painful to walk on.* **2** making you feel upset or embarrassed □ *menyedihkan; menyeksakan*: *a painful experience/memory* ▶ **painfully** /-fəli/ *adv*

painkiller /ˈpeɪnkɪlə(r)/ *noun* [C] a drug that is used for reducing pain □ *ubat penahan sakit*

painless /ˈpeɪnləs/ *adj* that does not cause pain □ *tdk menyakitkan*: *The animals' death is quick and painless.* ▶ **painlessly** *adv*

pains /peɪnz/ *noun*
IDM **be at/take (great) pains to do sth; take (great) pains (with/over sth)** to make a special effort to do sth well □ *bersusah payah*: *He was at pains to hide his true feelings.*

painstaking /ˈpeɪnzteɪkɪŋ/ *adj* very careful and taking a long time □ *teliti; cermat*: *The painstaking search of the wreckage gave us clues as to the cause of the crash.* **SYN** **thorough** ▶ **painstakingly** *adv*

paint¹ /peɪnt/ *noun* **1** [U] coloured liquid that you put onto a surface to decorate or protect it □ *cat*: *green/orange/yellow paint* ♦ *The door will need another coat of paint.* **2** [U] coloured liquid that you can use to make a picture □ *cat minyak, cat air, dsb*: *oil paint* ♦ *watercolour paint* **3** **paints** [pl] a collection of tubes or blocks of paint that an artist uses for painting pictures □ *cat (lukisan)*: *oil paints*

paint² /peɪnt/ *verb* [I,T] **1** to put paint onto a surface or an object □ *mengecat*: *We painted the fence.* ♦ *The walls were painted pink.* **2** to make a picture of sb/sth using paints □ *melukis gambar*: *I'm painting a picture of some flowers.*

paintbox /ˈpeɪntbɒks/ *noun* [C] a box that contains blocks or tubes of paint of many colours □ *kotak warna*

paintbrush /ˈpeɪntbrʌʃ/ *noun* [C] a brush that you use for painting with □ *berus cat; berus lukis* ➲ picture at **brush**

painter /ˈpeɪntə(r)/ *noun* [C] **1** a person whose job is to paint buildings, walls, etc. □ *tukang cat*: *a painter and decorator* **2** a person who paints pictures □ *pelukis cat*: *a famous painter* ➲ note at **art**

painting /ˈpeɪntɪŋ/ *noun* **1** [C] a picture that sb has painted □ *lukisan*: *a famous painting by Van Gogh*

MORE A **drawing** is not done with paints, but with pencils, pens, etc.

2 [U] the act of painting pictures or buildings □ *seni lukis*: *painting and decorating* ➲ note at **art** ➲ picture on **page P3**

paintwork /ˈpeɪntwɜːk/ *noun* [U] a painted surface, especially on a vehicle □ *cat (pd sst permukaan – kereta, dinding, dsb)*

pair¹ /peə(r)/ *noun* [C] **1** two things of the same type that are used or worn together □ *pasang*: *a pair of shoes/gloves/earrings* **2** a thing that consists of two parts that are joined together □ *sst benda yg terdiri drpd dua bahagian (gunting, cermin mata, seluar, dll)*: *a pair of scissors/glasses/trousers* ➲ picture at **glasses** **3** [with sing or pl verb] two people or animals that are doing sth together □ *pasangan*: *These boxers have fought several times, and tonight the pair meet again.*

MORE We use **couple** to refer to two people who are married or in a relationship together.

IDM **in pairs** two at a time □ *berpasangan; sepasang*: *These earrings are only sold in pairs.* ♦ *The students were working in pairs.*

pair² /peə(r)/ *verb*
PHR V **pair (sb/sth) off (with sb)** to come together, especially to form a romantic relationship; to bring two people together for this purpose □ *memasangkan/menjodohkan sso (dgn sso)*: *She's always trying to pair me off with her brother.*

pair up (with sb) to join together with another person or group to work, play a game, etc. □ *berpasangan (dgn sso)*: *I paired up with another student and we did the project together.*

pajamas (*AmE*) = **pyjamas**

palace /ˈpæləs/ *noun* [C] a large house that is or was the home of a king or queen □ *mahligai; istana*: *Did you visit Buckingham Palace?* ♦ *a royal palace*

palate /ˈpælət/ *noun* [C] the top part of the inside of your mouth □ *lelangit*

pale /peɪl/ *adj* (**paler**; **palest**) **1** (used about a person or their face) having skin that is light in colour, often because of fear or illness □ *pucat*: *She has a pale complexion.* ♦ *I felt myself go/turn pale with fear.* ➲ look at **pallid** ➲ *noun* **pallor** **2** not bright or strong in colour □ *pucat; muda (warna)*: *a pale yellow dress* **OPP** **dark** ▶ **pale** *verb* [I]

pall /pɔːl/ *verb* [I] to become less interesting or important □ *menjemukan; membosankan*: *After a few months, the excitement of his new job began to pall.*

pallid /ˈpælɪd/ *adj* (used about a person or their face) light in colour, especially because of illness

□ *pucat*: *His pallid complexion made him look unhealthy.* ➲ look at **pale**

pallor /ˈpælə(r)/ *noun* [U] pale colouring of the face, especially because of illness or fear □ *kepucatan; pucat*

palm¹ /pɑːm/ *noun* [C] **1** the flat, inner surface of your hand □ *tapak tangan*: *She held the coins tightly in the palm of her hand.* ➲ picture at **body 2** (also ˈpalm tree) a tall straight type of tree that grows in hot countries. **Palms** have a lot of large leaves at the top but no branches. □ *pokok palma*

palm² /pɑːm/ *verb*
PHR V **palm sb off (with sth)** (*informal*) to persuade sb to believe sth that is not true in order to stop them asking questions or complaining □ *membohongi sso (dgn sst alasan, dsb yg tdk benar)*
palm sth off (on sb) (*informal*) to persuade sb to accept sth that they do not want □ *memberikan sst yg tdk dikehendaki/disukai (kpd orang lain)*: *She's always palming off the worst jobs on her assistant.*

palmtop /ˈpɑːmtɒp/ *noun* [C] a very small computer that can be held in one hand □ *komputer tatang/telapak*

paltry /ˈpɔːltri/ *adj* too small to be considered important or useful □ *tdk seberapa*: *a paltry sum of money*

pamper /ˈpæmpə(r)/ *verb* [T] to take care of sb very well and make them feel as comfortable as possible □ *memanjakan*

pamphlet /ˈpæmflət/ *noun* [C] a very thin book with a paper cover containing information about a particular subject □ *risalah*

pan /pæn/ *noun* [C] a metal container with a handle or handles that is used for cooking food in; the contents of a pan □ *periuk bertangkai*: *Cook the spaghetti in a pan of boiling water.*

pancake /ˈpænkeɪk/ *noun* [C] a type of very thin round cake that is made by frying a mixture of flour, milk and eggs □ *lempeng; kuih dadar* ➲ picture on **page P16**

ˈ**Pancake Day** *noun* [U,C] (*informal*) a Tuesday in February when people in Britain traditionally eat **pancakes**. Pancake Day is the day before the period of Lent begins. □ *Hari Pancake* ➲ look at **Shrove Tuesday**

panda /ˈpændə/ *noun* [C] a large black and white animal that comes from China □ *panda*

pandemic /pænˈdemɪk/ *noun* [C] a disease that spreads over a whole country or the whole world □ *pandemik*

pandemonium /ˌpændəˈməʊniəm/ *noun* [U] a state of great noise and confusion

□ *hiruk-pikuk* SYN **chaos**

pander /ˈpændə(r)/ *verb*
PHR V **pander to sb/sth** to do or say exactly what sb wants especially when this is not reasonable □ *mengikut kehendak sso/sst*: *He refuses to pander to his boss's demands.*

p. and p. (also p. & p.) *abbr* (*BrE*) **postage and packing** □ *setem dan bungkusan*: *price: £29 incl. p. and p.*

pane /peɪn/ *noun* [C] a piece of glass in a window, etc. □ *kaca tingkap*: *a windowpane*

panel /ˈpænl/ *noun* [C] **1** a square or long thin piece of wood, metal or glass that forms part of a door or wall □ *panel; kepingan papan, logam atau kaca*: *They smashed one of the glass panels in the front door.* **2** [with sing or pl verb] a group of people who give their advice or opinions about sth; a group of people who discuss topics of interest on TV or radio □ *ahli panel*: *a panel of judges* (= in a competition) ♦ *a panel game* (= a TV game show with two teams) **3** a flat surface that contains the equipment for controlling a vehicle, machine, etc. □ *panel*: *a control/display panel*

panelling (*AmE* paneling) /ˈpænəlɪŋ/ *noun* [U] large flat pieces of wood used to cover and decorate walls, ceilings, etc. □ *panel*

panellist (*AmE* panelist) /ˈpænəlɪst/ *noun* [C] a member of a **panel**(2) □ *ahli panel*

pang /pæŋ/ *noun* [C, usually pl] a sudden strong feeling of emotional or physical pain □ *tusukan rasa (cemburu, lapar, dll)*: *a pang of jealousy* ♦ *hunger pangs*

panic /ˈpænɪk/ *noun* [C,U] a sudden feeling of fear that cannot be controlled and stops you from thinking clearly □ *panik; cemas*: *There was a mad panic when the alarm went off.* ♦ *People fled in panic as the fire spread.* ▶ **panic** *verb* [I] (panicking; panicked): *Stay calm and don't panic.*

ˈ**panic-stricken** *adj* very frightened in a way that stops you from thinking clearly □ *sangat cemas*

panorama /ˌpænəˈrɑːmə/ *noun* [C] a view over a wide area of land □ *panorama* ▶ **panoramic** /ˌpænəˈræmɪk/ *adj*

pant /pænt/ *verb* [I] to breathe quickly, for example after running or because it is very hot □ *mencungap* ▶ **pant** *noun* [C]

panther /ˈpænθə(r)/ *noun* [C] a large wild animal of the cat family with black fur □ *harimau kumbang* ➲ picture at **lion**

panties /ˈpæntiz/ (*AmE*) = **knickers**

pantomime /ˈpæntəmaɪm/ *noun* [C,U] **1** (also *informal* panto /ˈpæntəʊ/) (in Britain) a type of play for children, with music, dancing and jokes □ *pantomim*

pantry → paradise

> **CULTURE**
> Pantomimes are usually performed at Christmas and are based on traditional children's stories.
>
> 2 = mime

pantry /'pæntri/ noun [C] (pl **pantries**) a small room where food is kept □ *bilik utk menyimpan makanan* **SYN** **larder**

pants /pænts/ 1 (*BrE*) = **underpants**: *a pair of pants* 2 (*AmE*) = **trousers**: *ski pants*

pantyhose /'pæntihəʊz/ (*AmE*) = **tights**

paparazzi /ˌpæpəˈrætsi/ noun [pl] photographers who follow famous people around in order to get pictures of them to sell to a newspaper or magazine □ *jurugambar curi yg memburu orang terkenal*

papaya /pəˈpaɪə/ (also **pawpaw**) noun [C] a large tropical fruit which is sweet and orange inside and has small black seeds □ *(buah) betik/ papaya* ➔ picture on **page P14**

paper /'peɪpə(r)/ noun
▶ FOR WRITING, ETC. 1 [U] material made in thin sheets that you use for writing or drawing on, covering things, etc. □ *kertas*: *a piece/sheet of paper* ♦ *a paper handkerchief*

> **MORE** Types of paper include **filter paper, tissue paper, toilet paper** and **writing paper**.

▶ NEWSPAPER 2 [C] a newspaper □ *surat khabar; akhbar*: *Where's today's paper?* ➔ note at **newspaper**
▶ DOCUMENTS 3 **papers** [pl] important letters or pieces of paper that have information written on them □ *surat-surat*: *The document you want is somewhere in the pile of papers on her desk.*
▶ EXAM 4 [C] a set of exam questions; the answers that people write to the questions □ *kertas peperiksaan*: *The history exam is divided into three papers.*
▶ PIECE OF WRITING 5 [C] a piece of writing on a particular subject that is written for people who know a lot about the subject □ *kertas*: *At the conference, the Professor presented a paper on Sri Lankan poetry.*
IDM **on paper 1** in writing □ *secara bertulis*: *I've had nothing on paper to say that I've been accepted.* **2** as an idea, but not in a real situation □ *dr segi teori*: *The scheme seems fine on paper, but would it work in practice?* **SYN** **in theory**

paperback /'peɪpəbæk/ noun [C,U] a book that has a paper cover □ *(buku) kulit lembut*: *The novel is available in paperback.* ➔ look at **hardback**

'paper boy, 'paper girl noun [C] a boy or girl who takes newspapers to people's houses □ *budak (lelaki) penghantar surat khabar*

'paper clip noun [C] a small piece of bent wire that is used for holding pieces of paper together □ *klip kertas* ➔ picture at **stationery**

paperwork /'peɪpəwɜːk/ noun [U] **1** the written work that is part of a job, such as writing letters and reports and filling in forms, etc. □ *kerja tulis-menulis*: *I hate doing paperwork.* **2** documents that need to be prepared, collected, etc. in order for a piece of business to be completed □ *dokumen*: *Some of the paperwork is missing from this file.*

papier mâché /ˌpæpieɪ ˈmæʃeɪ/ noun [U] paper mixed with glue or flour and water, that is used to make decorative objects □ *kertas khas utk membuat barang hiasan*

paprika /'pæprɪkə/ noun [U] a red powder that you can use in cooking as a mild spice □ *paprika*

papyrus /pəˈpaɪrəs/ noun (pl **papyri** /pəˈpaɪriː/) **1** [U] a tall plant that grows in water □ *papirus; sejenis tumbuhan air* **2** [C,U] paper made from the **stems** (= the central part) of the **papyrus** plant, used in ancient Egypt for writing and drawing on □ *kertas yg dibuat drpd batang papirus*

par /pɑː(r)/ noun [U] (in the sport of **golf**) the standard number of times a good player should hit the ball in order to complete a particular hole or series of holes □ *par*
IDM **below par** (*informal*) not as good or as well as usual □ *tdk sebaik/sihat spt biasa*
on a par with sb/sth of an equal level, standard, etc. to sb/sth else □ *setanding dgn sso/sst*: *Is a teacher's salary on a par with a doctor's?*

par. (also **para.**) *abbr* = **paragraph**

parable /'pærəbl/ noun [C] a short story that teaches a lesson, especially one told by Jesus in the Bible □ *cerita ibarat*

parabola /pəˈræbələ/ noun [C] a curve like the path of an object that is thrown through the air and falls back to earth □ *parabola*

parachute   hang-glider

parachute /'pærəʃuːt/ noun [C] a piece of equipment made of thin cloth, that opens and lets a person fall to the ground slowly when they jump from a plane □ *payung terjun* ▸ **parachute** *verb* [I]

parade /pəˈreɪd/ noun [C] **1** a celebration of a special day or event, usually with bands in the streets and decorated vehicles □ *perarakan*: *the Lord Mayor's parade* **2** an occasion when a group of people stand or walk in a line so that people can look at them □ *perbarisan; perarakan*: *a military parade* ♦ *a fashion parade*

paradise /'pærədaɪs/ noun **1 Paradise** [U] [without *a* or *the*] the place where some people think that good people go after they die □ *syurga* **SYN** **heaven** **2** [C] a perfect place □ *tempat* *yg sangat istimewa (indah, dsb)*: *This beach is a paradise for windsurfers.*

paradox /ˈpærədɒks/ *noun* [C] a situation or statement with two or more parts that seem strange or impossible together □ *paradoks*: *It's a paradox that some countries produce too much food while in many other countries people are starving.* ▸**paradoxical** /ˌpærəˈdɒksɪkl/ *adj* ▸**paradoxically** /-kli/ *adv*

paraffin /ˈpærəfɪn/ (*AmE* **kerosene**) *noun* [U] a type of oil that is burned to produce heat or light □ *parafin; minyak tanah*

paragliding /ˈpærəɡlaɪdɪŋ/ *noun* [U] a sport in which you wear a special piece of equipment like a **parachute** (a piece of thin cloth that opens when you jump from a plane), jump from a high place and are carried along by the wind before coming down to earth □ *sukan luncur udara*

paragraph /ˈpærəɡrɑːf/ *noun* [C] (*abbr* **par.**, **para.**) a part of a piece of writing that usually consists of several sentences. □ *paragraf*

EXAM TIP

Paragraphs

When you write an essay, it is important to organize your writing into paragraphs to show how your ideas develop. Each paragraph should contain a separate idea and include at least two sentences that relate to this idea. You start each paragraph on a new line.

parallel¹ /ˈpærəlel/ *adj, adv* **1 parallel (to sth)** (used about two lines, etc.) with the same distance between them for all their length □ *selari*: *parallel lines* ♦ *The railway runs parallel to the road.* ➲ picture at **line 2** similar and happening at the same time □ *sama; serupa*: *The two brothers followed parallel careers in different companies.*

parallel² /ˈpærəlel/ *noun* [C,U] a person, thing or situation that is similar to another one in a different situation, place or time □ *sst yg sama; tolok banding*: *The party's huge election victory is without parallel in its history.*

paralyse (*AmE* **paralyze**) /ˈpærəlaɪz/ *verb* [T] **1** to make a person unable to move their body or a part of it □ *menjadi lumpuh*: *She is paralysed from the waist down.* **2** to make sb/sth unable to work in a normal way □ *melumpuhkan* ▸**paralysis** /pəˈræləsɪs/ *noun* [U]: *The disease can cause paralysis or even death.* ♦ *There has been complete paralysis of the country's railway system.*

paramedic /ˌpærəˈmedɪk/ *noun* [C] a person who has had special training in treating people who are hurt or ill, but who is not a doctor or nurse □ *pekerja paramedik/separa perubatan*

paramilitary /ˌpærəˈmɪlətri/ *adj* organized in the same way as, but not belonging to, an official army □ *separa tentera*: *a paramilitary group* ▸**paramilitary** *noun* [C, usually pl] (*pl* **paramilitaries**)

621　　　　　　　　　　　　　　　　**paradox → pare**

paramount /ˈpærəmaʊnt/ *adj* (*formal*) most important □ *paling penting/utama*: *Safety is paramount in car design.*

paranoia /ˌpærəˈnɔɪə/ *noun* [U] **1** a type of mental illness in which you wrongly believe that other people want to harm you □ *paranoia* **2** (*informal*) a feeling that other people want to harm you or are saying bad things about you, when you have no evidence for this □ *perasaan curiga dan syak wasangka*

paranoid /ˈpærənɔɪd/ *adj* wrongly believing that other people are trying to harm you or are saying bad things about you □ *paranoid; rasa curiga yg tdk wajar*

paraphernalia /ˌpærəfəˈneɪliə/ *noun* [U] a large number of different objects that you need for a particular purpose □ *sejumlah barang berlainan utk aktiviti tertentu*

paraphrase /ˈpærəfreɪz/ *verb* [T] to express sth again using different words so that it is easier to understand □ *parafrasa; menjelaskan semula dgn kata-kata lain* ▸**paraphrase** *noun* [C]

parasite /ˈpærəsaɪt/ *noun* [C] a plant or an animal that lives in or on another plant or animal and gets its food from it □ *parasit*

parasol /ˈpærəsɒl/ (*AmE usually*) / *noun* [C] an object like an umbrella that is used to create shade and protect you from the sun □ *payung*

paratroops /ˈpærətruːps/ *noun* [pl] soldiers who are trained to jump from a plane with a **parachute** (= a piece of equipment on their backs that opens and allows them to fall slowly) □ *askar payung terjun*

parcel /ˈpɑːsl/ (*AmE also* **package**) *noun* [C] something that is covered in paper or put into a thick envelope and sent or given to sb □ *bungkusan* ➲ look at **pack, package, packet**

parched /pɑːtʃt/ *adj* very hot and dry, or very thirsty □ *kering kontang; amat dahaga*: *Nothing would grow in the parched soil.* ♦ *Can I have a drink? I'm parched!*

pardon¹ /ˈpɑːdn/ (*also* ˌpardon ˈme) *exclam* **1** used for asking sb to repeat what they have just said because you did not hear or understand it □ *tolong ulang sekali lagi* **2** used by some people to mean *sorry* or *excuse me* □ *maaf*

pardon² /ˈpɑːdn/ *noun* [C,U] an official decision not to punish sb for a crime □ *pengampunan* ▸**pardon** *verb* [T] **pardon sb (for sth/doing sth)**

> **MORE** **I beg your pardon** is a formal way of saying 'sorry': *Oh, I beg your pardon. I had no idea this was your seat.*

pare /peə(r)/ *verb* [T] **1 pare sth (off/away)** to remove the thin outer layer of sth □ *mengupas*: *First, pare the skin away.* ♦ *She pared the apple.* **2 pare sth (back/down)** to gradually reduce the size or amount of sth □ *mengurangkan secara*

VOWELS　iː **see**　i **any**　ɪ **sit**　e **ten**　æ **hat**　ɑː **father**　ɒ **got**　ɔː **saw**　ʊ **put**　uː **too**　u **usual**

parent → part

beransur-ansur (saiz/jumlah): *The training budget has been pared back to a minimum.*

parent /ˈpeərənt/ *noun* [C] **1** a person's mother or father □ *ibu atau bapa*: *He's still living with his parents.*

> **MORE** A **single parent** is a mother or father who is bringing up their child or children alone, without the other parent. A **foster parent** is a person who looks after a child who is not legally their own.

2 a company that owns smaller companies of the same type □ *syarikat induk*: *a parent company*

parental /pəˈrentl/ *adj* [only *before* a noun] of a parent or parents □ *(berkenaan dgn) ibu bapa*: *parental support/advice*

parenthesis /pəˈrenθəsɪs/ (*pl* **parentheses** /pəˈrenθəsiːz/) (*especially AmE*) = **bracket**[1] (1)

parenthood /ˈpeərənthʊd/ *noun* [U] the state of being a parent □ *(keadaan) menjadi ibu bapa*

parish /ˈpærɪʃ/ *noun* [C] an area or district which has its own church; the people who live in this area □ *kariah*: *the parish church* ▶ **parishioner** /pəˈrɪʃənə(r)/ *noun* [C]

park[1] /pɑːk/ *noun* [C] **1** an open area in a town, often with grass or trees, where people can go to walk, play, etc. □ *taman*: *Let's go for a walk in the park.* ⊃ picture on **page P11** **2** [in compounds] a large area of land that is used for a special purpose □ *taman*: *a national park* ♦ *a business park* ♦ *a theme park*

park[2] /pɑːk/ *verb* [I,T] to leave the vehicle that you are driving somewhere for a period of time □ *meletakkan kereta*: *It's very expensive to park in the centre of town.* ♦ *Somebody's parked their car in front of the exit.*

parking /ˈpɑːkɪŋ/ *noun* [U] **1** the act of leaving a car, lorry, etc. somewhere for a time □ *(perbuatan) meletakkan kereta, lori, dsb*: *The sign said 'No Parking'.* **2** a space or area for leaving cars, lorries, etc. □ *tempat letak kereta*: *There is ample free parking behind the hotel.*

> **MORE** A place where many cars can be parked and left is called a **car park**. A place where one car can be parked is called a **parking space**. If you **park** where you are not allowed to, a **traffic warden** might give you a **parking ticket**.

'parking brake (*AmE*) = **handbrake**

'parking garage (*AmE*) = **multi-storey car park**

'parking lot (*AmE*) = **car park**

'parking meter *noun* [C] a machine that you put coins into to pay for parking a car in the space beside it for a period of time □ *meter tempat letak kereta*

'parking ticket *noun* [C] a piece of paper that orders you to pay money as a punishment for parking your car where it is not allowed □ *saman letak kereta*

parliament /ˈpɑːləmənt/ *noun* **1** [C, with sing or pl verb] the group of people who are elected to make and change the laws of a country □ *parlimen*: *the German parliament* **2 Parliament** [U, with sing or pl verb] the parliament of the United Kingdom □ *Parlimen*: *a Member of Parliament (MP)*

> **CULTURE**
>
> The UK Parliament consists of **the House of Lords**, whose members have been appointed rather than elected, and **the House of Commons**, whose members have been elected by the people to represent areas of the country (called **constituencies**).

parliamentary /ˌpɑːləˈmentri/ *adj* [only *before* a noun] connected with a parliament □ *(berkaitan dgn) parlimen*

parody /ˈpærədi/ *noun* [C,U] (*pl* **parodies**) a piece of writing, speech or music that copies the style of sb/sth in a funny way □ *parodi; ajukan; sendaan*: *a parody of a spy novel* ▶ **parody** *verb* [T] (**parodying**; **parodies**; *pt*, *pp* **parodied**)

parole /pəˈrəʊl/ *noun* [U] permission that is given to a prisoner to leave prison early on the condition that he or she behaves well □ *parol*: *He's going to be released on parole.*

parrot /ˈpærət/ *noun* [C] a type of tropical bird with a curved beak and usually with very bright feathers. **Parrots** are kept as pets can be trained to copy what people say. □ *burung nuri*

'parrot-fashion *adv* (*BrE*) without understanding the meaning of something □ *menghafal sst tanpa mengetahui maknanya*: *to learn something parrot-fashion*

parsley /ˈpɑːsli/ *noun* [U] a **herb** (= a type of plant) with small curly leaves that are used in cooking or for decorating food □ *parsli* ⊃ picture on **page P14**

parsnip /ˈpɑːsnɪp/ *noun* [C] a long thin white vegetable, that grows under the ground □ *parsnip* ⊃ picture on **page P15**

part[1] /pɑːt/ *noun*

▶ SOME **1** [U] **part of sth** some, but not all of sth □ *bahagian*: *Part of the problem is lack of information.* ♦ *Part of the building was destroyed in the fire.*

▶ PIECE **2** [C] one of the pieces, areas, periods, things, etc. that together with others forms the whole of sth □ *bahagian*: *Which part of Spain do you come from?* ♦ *The film is good in parts.* ♦ *spare parts for a car* ♦ *a part of the body* ♦ *I enjoy being part of a team.*

▶ REGION **3 parts** [pl] (*old-fashioned*, *informal*) a region or area □ *kawasan; tempat*: *Are you from these parts?* ⊃ note at **area**

▶ OF BOOK/SERIES **4** [C] a section of a book, TV series, etc. □ *bahagian*: *You can see part two of this series at the same time next week.*

▶ IN FILM/PLAY **5** [C] a role or character in a play, film, etc. □ *peranan*: *He played the part of Macbeth.* ♦ *I had a small part in the school play.*

►EQUAL AMOUNT **6** [C] an amount or quantity (of a liquid or substance) ▫ *bahagian*: *Use one part cleaning fluid to ten parts water.*
►HAIR **7** (*AmE*) = **parting**

IDM **the best/better part of sth** most of sth; more than half of sth, especially a period of time ▫ *sebahagian besar; lebih setengah; hampir*: *They've lived here for the best part of forty years.*
for the most part ➔ **most¹**
for my, his, their, etc. part in my, his, their, etc. opinion; personally ▫ *bagi saya, dia, mereka, dsb*
have/play a part (in sth) to be involved in sth ▫ *memainkan peranan/terlibat (dlm sst)*
in part not completely ▫ *sebahagiannya*: *The accident was, in part, the fault of the driver.*
on the part of sb/on sb's part made, done or felt by sb ▫ *pd/bagi pihak sso*: *There is concern on the part of the teachers that class sizes will increase.* ♦ *I'm sorry. It was a mistake on my part.*
take part (in sth) to join with other people in an activity ▫ *mengambil bahagian dlm sst*: *We all took part in the discussion.*

part² /pɑːt/ *verb* **1** [I,T] (*formal*) **part (sb) (from sb)** to leave or go away from sb; to separate people or things ▫ *berpisah; memisahkan*: *We exchanged telephone numbers when we parted.* ♦ *He hates being parted from his children for long.* **2** [I,T] to move apart; to make things or people move apart ▫ *merenggangkan; meleraikan; merekah*: *Her lips were slightly parted.* **3** [T] to separate the hair on your head so as to make a clear line that goes from the back of your head to the front ▫ *membelah (rambut)*: *She parts her hair in the middle.* ➔ look at **parting**
IDM **part company (with sb/sth)** to go different ways or to separate after being together ▫ *berpisah (dgn sso/sst)*
PHR V **part with sth** to give or sell sth to sb ▫ *memberikan/menjual sst*: *When we went to live in Italy, we had to part with our horses.*

part³ /pɑːt/ *adv* not completely one thing and not completely another ▫ *sebahagiannya*: *She's part Russian and part Chinese.*

ˌpart exˈchange *noun* [U] (*BrE*) a way of buying sth, such as a car, in which you give your old one as some of the payment for a more expensive one ▫ *tukar beli*

partial /ˈpɑːʃl/ *adj* **1** not complete ▫ *separa; tdk sepenuhnya*: *The project was only a partial success.* **2** **partial to sth** (*old-fashioned*) liking sth very much ▫ *amat gemar/suka*: *He's very partial to ice cream.* ►**partially** /-ʃəli/ *adv*

partiality /ˌpɑːʃiˈæləti/ *noun* [U] (*formal*) the unfair support of one person, team, etc. above another ▫ *sikap berat sebelah*: *The referee was accused of partiality towards the home team.* **OPP** **impartiality** ➔ look at **impartial**

participant /pɑːˈtɪsɪpənt/ *noun* [C] a person who takes part in sth ▫ *peserta*

participate /pɑːˈtɪsɪpeɪt/ *verb* [I] **participate (in sth)** to take part or become involved in sth ▫ *menyertai*: *Students are encouraged to participate in the running of the college.* ►**participation** /pɑːˌtɪsɪˈpeɪʃn/ *noun* [U]

participle /pɑːˈtɪsɪpl/ *noun* [C] a word that is formed from a verb and that ends in *-ing* (present participle) or *-ed, -en*, etc. (past participle). Participles are used to form tenses of the verb, or as adjectives ▫ *partisipel*: *'Hurrying' and 'hurried' are the present and past participles of 'hurry'.*

particle /ˈpɑːtɪkl/ *noun* [C] **1** a very small piece ▫ *cebisan kecil; remah; sekelumit*: *dust particles* **2** a small word that is not as important as a noun, verb or adjective ▫ *partikel*: *In the phrasal verb 'break down', 'down' is an adverbial particle.*

particular /pəˈtɪkjələ(r)/ *adj* **1** [only before a noun] used to emphasize that you are talking about one person, thing, time, etc. and not about others ▫ *tertentu; khusus*: *Is there any particular dish you enjoy making?* **2** connected with one person or thing and not with others ▫ *tertentu; masing-masing*: *Everybody has their own particular problems.* **3** [only before a noun] greater than usual; special ▫ *lebih drpd biasa; khas*: *This article is of particular interest to me.* **4** [not before a noun] **particular (about/over sth)** difficult to please ▫ *cerewet*: *Some people are extremely particular about what they eat.* ➔ look at **fussy**
IDM **in particular** especially ▫ *yg tertentu*: *Is there anything in particular you'd like to do tomorrow?*

particularly /pəˈtɪkjələli/ *adv* especially; more than usual or more than others ▫ *terutamanya*: *I'm particularly interested in Indian history.* ♦ *The match was excellent, particularly the second half.*

particulars /pəˈtɪkjələz/ *noun* [pl] (*formal*) facts or details about sb/sth ▫ *butiran*: *The police took down all the particulars about the missing child.*

parting /ˈpɑːtɪŋ/ *noun* **1** [C,U] saying goodbye to, or being separated from, another person (usually for quite a long time) ▫ *perpisahan* **2** (*AmE* **part**) [C] the line in sb's hair where it is divided in two with a **comb** (= a flat piece of metal or plastic with teeth) ▫ *belahan*: *a side/centre parting* ➔ look at **part²** ➔ picture at **hair**

partisan¹ /ˌpɑːtɪˈzæn, ˈpɑːtɪzæn/ *adj* showing too much support for one person, group or idea, especially without considering it carefully ▫ *berat sebelah*: *Most newspapers are politically partisan.* **SYN** **one-sided**

partisan² /ˌpɑːtɪˈzæn, ˈpɑːtɪzæn/ *noun* [C] **1** a person who strongly supports a particular leader, group or idea ▫ *partisan; penyokong; pemihak (politik)* **SYN** **follower** **2** a member of an armed group that is fighting secretly against enemy soldiers who have taken control of its country ▫ *partisan; gerila*

partition /pɑːˈtɪʃn/ noun 1 [C] something that divides a room, office etc. into two or more parts, especially a thin or temporary wall ▫ *sekatan; pengadang* 2 [U] the division of a country into two or more countries ▫ *pemecahan* ▶ **partition** verb [T]

partly /ˈpɑːtli/ adv not completely ▫ *sebahagiannya*: *She was only partly responsible for the mistake.*

partner /ˈpɑːtnə(r)/ noun [C] 1 the person that you are married to or live with as if you are married ▫ *pasangan; suami; isteri*: *a marriage partner* ♦ *All members of staff and their partners are invited.* 2 one of the people who owns a business ▫ *rakan kongsi*: *business partners* 3 a person that you are doing an activity with as a team, for example dancing or playing a game ▫ *pasangan*: *a tennis partner* 4 a country or an organization that has an agreement with another ▫ *rakan; sekutu*: *Britain's EU partners* ▶ **partner** verb [T]: *Hales partnered his brother in the doubles, and they won the gold medal.*

partnership /ˈpɑːtnəʃɪp/ noun 1 [U] the state of being a partner in business ▫ *(keadaan) menjadi rakan kongsi; berkongsi*: *Simona went into partnership with her sister and opened a shop in Rome.* 2 [C,U] a relationship between two people, organizations, etc. ▫ *perkongsian*: *Marriage is a partnership for life.* ♦ *a civil partnership* (= between two people of the same sex) 3 [C] a business owned by two or more people ▫ *perkongsian perniagaan*: *a junior member of the partnership*

part of ˈspeech noun [C] one of the groups that words are divided into, for example noun, verb, adjective, etc. ▫ *jenis/golongan kata*

EXAM TIP

Parts of speech

When you do a **gap-fill exercise** (= where you choose the correct word to fill a gap in a sentence), it is important to know whether you need a noun, verb, adjective, etc. You also need to know whether to use a singular or plural noun, what tense a verb should be, whether to use the definite or indefinite article, etc.

part-ˈtime adj, adv for only a part of the working day or week ▫ *sambilan*: *She's got a part-time job.* ⊃ look at **full-time**

party /ˈpɑːti/ noun [C] (pl **parties**) 1 (also **Party**) a group of people who have the same political aims and ideas and who are trying to win elections to parliament, etc. ▫ *parti*: *Which party are you going to vote for in the next election?* ♦ *a political party* ⊃ note at **politics**

CULTURE

The two main political parties in Great Britain are the **Labour** Party (left-wing) and the **Conservative** (or **Tory**) Party (right-wing). There is also a centre party called the **Liberal Democrats** and some other smaller parties. In the United States the main political parties are the **Republican Party** and the **Democratic Party**.

2 a social occasion to which people are invited in order to eat, drink and enjoy themselves ▫ *parti; majlis keramaian*: *When we've moved into our new house we're going to* **have a party**. ♦ *a birthday/dinner party* 3 a group of people who are working, travelling, etc. together ▫ *kumpulan; pasukan*: *a party of tourists* 4 (formal) one of the people or groups of people involved in a legal case ▫ *pihak*: *the guilty/innocent party* ⊃ look at **third party**

pass¹ /pɑːs/ verb

▶MOVE 1 [I,T] to move past or to the other side of sb/sth ▫ *lalu; berselisih; melebihi*: *The street was crowded and the two buses couldn't pass.* ♦ *I passed him in the street but he didn't say hello.*

HELP Passed or past? Passed is a verb and past is an adjective or preposition: *The summer months passed slowly.* ♦ *The past week was very hot.* ♦ *Our house is just past the church.*

2 [I,T] pass (sth) along, down, through, etc. (sth) to go or move, or make sth move, in the direction mentioned ▫ *lalu; melalukan; melewati*: *A plane passed overhead.* ♦ *We'll have to pass the wire through the window.*
▶GIVE 3 [T] pass sth (to sb) to give sth to sb ▫ *menghulurkan; hulurkan*: *Could you pass (me) the salt, please?*
▶BALL 4 [I,T] pass (sth) (to sb) to kick, hit or throw the ball to sb on your own team ▫ *menghantar*: *He passed (the ball) to Walcott.*
▶TIME 5 [I] to go by ▫ *berlalu*: *At least a year had passed since she had last seen them.* ♦ *It was a long journey but the time passed very quickly.* 6 [T] to spend time, especially when you are bored or waiting for sth ▫ *menghabiskan masa*: *I'll have to think of something to do to* **pass the time** *in hospital.*
▶EXAM 7 [I,T] to achieve the necessary standard in an exam, test, etc. ▫ *lulus*: *Good luck in the exam! I'm sure you'll pass.* **OPP** fail

HELP Be careful. **Pass an exam** does NOT mean 'do an exam'. Use **take/sit an exam** to mean this.

8 [T] to test sb/sth and say that he/she/it is good enough ▫ *meluluskan*: *The examiner passed most of the students.*
▶LAW 9 [T] to officially approve a law, etc. by voting ▫ *meluluskan*: *One of the functions of Parliament is to pass new laws.*
▶BE ALLOWED 10 [I] to be allowed or accepted ▫ *membiarkan; tdk menghiraukan*: *I didn't like what he was saying but I* **let it pass**.
▶GIVE OPINION 11 [T] pass sth (on sb/sth) to give an opinion, judgement, etc. ▫ *menilai; menjatuhkan (hukuman) membiarkan; tdk menghiraukan*: *The judge* **passed sentence** *on the young man* (= said what his punishment would be).

IDM **pass the buck (to sb)** to make sb else responsible for a difficult situation □ *menyalahkan orang lain*

pass water (*formal*) to get rid of waste liquid from your body □ *buang air kecil*

PHR V **pass away** used as a polite way of saying 'die' □ *meninggal dunia*

pass by (sb/sth) to go past □ *lalu/melewati (sso/sst)*: *I pass by your house on the way to work.*

pass sth down to give or teach sth to people who will live after you have died □ *menurunkan (ilmu pengetahuan, kepandaian, dll)*

pass for sb/sth to be accepted as sb/sth that he/she/it is not □ *nampak seperti sso/sst*: *His mother looks so young she'd pass for his sister.*

pass sb/sth off (as sb/sth) to say that a person or a thing is sth that he/she/it is not □ *menyamar; menipu dgn mengatakan sso/sst itu (sebagai sso/sst yg lain)*: *He tried to pass the work off as his own.*

pass sth on (to sb) to give sth to sb else, especially after you have been given it or used it yourself □ *memberikan/menyampaikan sst (kpd sso)*: *Could you pass the message on to Mr Roberts?*

pass out to become unconscious □ *pengsan* **SYN** faint **OPP** come round/to

pass² /pɑːs/ *noun* [C] **1** a successful result in an exam □ *lulus*: *The pass mark is 50%.* ♦ *Grades A, B and C are passes.* **OPP** fail **2** an official piece of paper that gives you permission to enter or leave a building, travel on a bus or train, etc. □ *kebenaran; pas*: *Show your student pass when you buy a ticket.* ➔ look at **boarding pass** **3** the act of kicking, hitting or throwing the ball to sb on your own team in some sports □ *hantaran* **4** a road or way over or through mountains □ *genting*: *a mountain pass*

passable /ˈpɑːsəbl/ *adj* **1** good enough but not very good □ *boleh tahan*: *My French is not brilliant but it's passable.* **2** [not before a noun] (used about roads, rivers, etc.) possible to use or cross; not blocked □ *boleh dilalui* **OPP** impassable

passage /ˈpæsɪdʒ/ *noun* **1** [C] (also **passageway** /ˈpæsɪdʒweɪ/) a long, narrow way with walls on either side that connects one place with another □ *laluan; lorong*: *a secret underground passage* **2** [C] a tube in your body which air, liquid, etc. can pass through □ *saluran*: *the nasal passages* **3** [C] a short part of a book, a speech or a piece of music □ *petikan; rangkap*: *The students were given a passage from the novel to study.* **4** [sing] the process of passing □ *berlakunya*: *His painful memories faded with* **the passage of time**.

passenger /ˈpæsɪndʒə(r)/ *noun* [C] a person who is travelling in a car, bus, train, plane, etc. but who is not driving it or working on it □ *penumpang*: *The plane was carrying 200 passengers.*

passer-by *noun* [C] (*pl* **passers-by**) a person who is walking past sb/sth □ *orang yg lalu-lalang*

passing¹ /ˈpɑːsɪŋ/ *noun* [U] the process of going by □ *peredaran*: *the passing of time*

IDM **in passing** done or said quickly, while you are thinking or talking about sth else □ *sepintas lalu*: *He mentioned the house in passing but he didn't give any details.*

passing² /ˈpɑːsɪŋ/ *adj* [only before a noun] **1** lasting for only a short time □ *sementara; seketika*: *a passing phase/thought/interest* **SYN** brief **2** going past □ *(yg) lalu*: *I stopped a passing car and asked for help.*

passion /ˈpæʃn/ *noun* **1** [C,U] (a) very strong feeling, especially of love, hate or anger □ *perasaan yg meluap-luap*: *He was a very violent man, controlled by his passions.* **2** [sing] **a passion (for sb)** very strong sexual love or attraction □ *cinta berahi; keberahian*: *He longed to tell Sashi of his passion for her.* **3** [sing] **a passion for sth** a very strong liking for or interest in sth □ *ghairah; sangat gemar*: *She has a passion for history.*

passionate /ˈpæʃənət/ *adj* **1** showing or feeling very strong love or sexual attraction □ *penuh berahi; ghairah*: *a passionate kiss* **2** showing or caused by very strong feelings □ *penuh semangat; berkobar-kobar*: *The president gave a passionate speech about crime.* ▶ **passionately** *adv*: *He believes passionately in democracy.*

passive /ˈpæsɪv/ *adj* **1** showing no reaction, feeling or interest; not active □ *tdk giat; pasif*: *Some people prefer to play a passive role in meetings.* **2** used about the form of a verb or a sentence when the subject of the sentence is affected by the act of the verb □ *bentuk pasif*: *In the sentence 'He was bitten by a dog', the verb is passive.* ➔ look at **active**

HELP You can also say: 'The verb is in the passive'.

▶ **passively** *adv*

passive smoking *noun* [U] the act of breathing in smoke from other people's cigarettes □ *merokok secara pasif; menyedut asap rokok drpd perokok lain*

Passover /ˈpɑːsəʊvə(r)/ *noun* [sing] the most important Jewish festival, which takes place in spring and lasts seven or eight days □ *Passover*

passport /ˈpɑːspɔːt/ *noun* [C] **1** an official document that identifies you as a citizen of a particular country and that you have to show when you enter or leave a country □ *pasport*: *You have to go through* **passport control** (= where passports are checked) *at the airport.* ♦ *a passport photo*

MORE You **apply for** or **renew** your passport at the **passport office**. This office **issues** new passports.

2 a passport to sth a thing that makes it possible to achieve sth □ *kunci; pasport*: *a passport to success*

password /ˈpɑːswɜːd/ *noun* [C] **1** a secret word or phrase that you need to know in order to be allowed into a place □ *kata laluan; kata*

past → pat 626

rahsia **2** a series of letters and/or numbers that you must type into a computer or computer system in order to be able to use it □ *kata laluan*: *Please enter your password.*

past¹ /pɑːst/ *adj* **1** [only before a noun] just finished; last □ *lepas; lalu*: *He's had to work very hard during the past year.* **2** already gone; belonging to a time before the present □ *sudah; lalu; lepas; lampau; dahulu*: *in past centuries/times* ◆ *I'd rather forget some of my past mistakes.*

past² /pɑːst/ *noun* **1 the past** [sing] the time that has gone by; things that happened in an earlier time □ *masa lalu/lampau; dahulu*: *the recent/distant past* ◆ *Writing letters seems to be a thing of the past.* **2** [C] a person's life or career before now □ *sejarah; masa lampau silam*: *We don't know anything about his past.* **3 the past**; **the past 'tense** [sing] the form of a verb used to describe actions in the past □ *kata lampau*: *The past tense of 'take' is 'took'.* ❶ For more information about the past tenses, look at the **Reference Section** at the back of this dictionary.

past³ /pɑːst/ *prep, adv* **1** (used when telling the time) after; later than □ *lepas; lewat*: *It's ten (minutes) past three.* ◆ *It was past midnight when we got home.* ◆ *A week went past and nothing had happened.* **2** from one side to the other of sb/sth; further than or on the other side of sb/sth □ *melepasi*: *He walked straight past me.* ◆ *She looked right past me without realizing who I was.* **3** above or further than a certain point, limit or age □ *melebihi; tdk (peduli, berdaya, larat, dll)*: *Unemployment is now past the 2 million mark.* ◆ *I'm so tired that I'm past caring* (= I don't care any more) *what we eat.*

IDM **not put it past sb (to do sth)** [used with *would*] to think sb is capable of doing sth bad □ *tdk hairan jika sso itu tergamak membuat sst*: *I wouldn't put it past him to do a thing like that.*

past it (*BrE informal*) too old □ *sudah terlalu tua*

pasta /ˈpæstə/ *noun* [U] an Italian food made from flour, water and sometimes eggs, formed into different shapes, cooked, and usually served with a sauce □ *pasta* ⊃ picture on **page P16**

> **GRAMMAR** **Pasta** is uncountable. If we are talking about one piece, we say **a bit of pasta** (not 'a pasta').

paste¹ /peɪst/ *noun* **1** [C,U] a soft, wet mixture, usually made of a powder and a liquid and sometimes used for sticking things □ *perekat; gam; pes*: *wallpaper paste* ◆ *Mix the flour and milk into a paste.* **2** [U] [in compounds] a soft mixture of food that you can spread onto bread, etc. □ *pes*: *fish/chicken paste*

paste² /peɪst/ *verb* [T] **1** to stick sth to sth else using **paste** □ *menampal; melekatkan*: *He pasted the picture into his book.* **2** (in computing) to copy or move text into a document from somewhere else □ *menampal*: *This function allows you to cut and paste text.*

pastel /ˈpæstl/ *adj* (used about colours) pale; not strong □ *berwarna muda*

pasteurized (also **-ised**) /ˈpɑːstʃəraɪzd/ *adj* (used about milk or cream) free from bacteria because it has been heated and then cooled □ *dipasteurkan*

pastime /ˈpɑːstaɪm/ *noun* [C] something that you enjoy doing when you are not working □ *kegiatan masa lapang* **SYN** **hobby**

pastoral /ˈpɑːstərəl/ *adj* **1** (connected with the work of a priest or a teacher) giving help and advice on personal matters rather than on matters of religion or education □ *(berkaitan dgn kerja paderi atau guru) memberi nasihat* **2** connected with pleasant country life □ *(berkaitan dgn) kehidupan di desa*

past 'participle *noun* [C] the form of the verb that ends in *-ed*, *-en*, etc. □ *partisipel lampau (ttg kk)* ❶ For more information about the use of tenses, look at the **Reference Section** at the back of this dictionary.

past 'perfect (also **pluperfect**) *noun* [sing] the tense of a verb that describes an action that was finished before another event happened □ *kala lampau sempurna (ttg kk)* ❶ For more information about the past perfect, look at the **Reference Section** at the back of this dictionary.

pastry /ˈpeɪstri/ *noun* (*pl* **pastries**) **1** [U] a mixture of flour, fat and water that is rolled out flat and cooked as a base or covering for **pies** (= a type of baked food), etc. □ *pastri* **2** [C] a small cake made with **pastry** □ *kuih (pastri)*

past 'tense (also **the past**) *noun* [sing] the tense of a verb that describes an action that happened in the past □ *kala lampau (ttg kk)*: *The past tense of 'take' is 'took'.* ❶ For more information about the past perfect, look at the **Reference Section** at the back of this dictionary.

pasture /ˈpɑːstʃə(r)/ *noun* [C,U] a field or land covered with grass, where cows, etc. can feed □ *padang rumput*

pasty /ˈpæsti/ *noun* [C] (*pl* **pasties**) (*BrE*) a small **pie** (= a type of baked food) containing meat and/or vegetables □ *pai*

pat¹ /pæt/ *verb* [T] (**patting**; **patted**) to touch sb/sth gently with a flat hand, especially as a sign of friendship, care, etc. □ *menepuk* ⊃ picture at **stroke**

pat² /pæt/ *noun* [C] a gentle friendly touch with a flat hand □ *tepukan*: *He gave her knee an affectionate pat.*

IDM **a pat on the back (for sth/doing sth)** approval for sth good that a person has done □ *pujian (kerana sst/membuat sst)*: *She deserves a pat on the back for all her hard work.*

pat³ /pæt/ *adj* [only before a noun] *adv* (used about an answer, comment, etc.) said in a quick or simple way that does not sound natural or realistic □ *begitu mudah diucapkan (hingga dirasakan spt tdk betul-betul benar)*

| ð **then** | s **so** | z **zoo** | ʃ **she** | ʒ **vi**s**ion** | h **how** | m **man** | n **no** | ŋ **si**ng | l **leg** | r **red** | j **yes** | w **wet** |

patch¹ /pætʃ/ noun [C] **1** a patch (of sth) a part of a surface that is different in some way from the area around it □ *tompok*: *Drive carefully. There are patches of ice on the roads.* ◆ *a bald patch* **2** a piece of material that you use to cover a hole in clothes, etc. □ *tampalan; tampung*: *I sewed patches on the knees of my jeans.* **3** a small piece of cloth that you wear over one eye, usually because the eye is damaged □ *penutup mata* **4** a small piece of land, especially for growing vegetables or fruit □ *petak (tanah)*: *a vegetable patch* **IDM** **go through a bad patch** (*informal*) to experience a difficult or unhappy period of time □ *melalui detik-detik sukar*
not a patch on sb/sth (*especially BrE informal*) not nearly as good as sb/sth □ *tdk sebagus sso/sst*: *Her new book isn't a patch on her others.*

patch² /pætʃ/ verb [T] to cover a hole in clothes, etc. with a piece of cloth in order to repair it □ *menampal; menampung*: *patched jeans*
PHR V **patch sth up 1** to repair sth, especially in a temporary way by adding a new piece of material □ *membaiki sst* **2** to stop arguing with sb and to be friends again □ *berbaik-baik semula*: *Have you tried to patch things up with her?*

patchwork /'pætʃwɜːk/ noun [U] a type of sewing in which small pieces of cloth of different colours and patterns are sewn together □ *kerja tampal cantum*

patchy /'pætʃi/ adj **1** existing or happening in some places but not others □ *di sana sini; bertompok-tompok*: *patchy fog/clouds/rain* **2** not complete; good in some parts but not in others □ *tdk lengkap*: *My knowledge of German is rather patchy.*

pâté /'pæteɪ/ noun [U] food that is made by making meat, fish or vegetables into a smooth, thick mixture that is served cold and spread on bread, etc. □ *pate*: *liver pâté*

patent¹ /'pætnt; 'peɪtnt/ noun [C,U] the official right to be the only person to make, use or sell a new product; the document that proves this □ *paten* ▶**patent** verb [T]

patent² /'peɪtnt/ adj [only before a noun] (*formal*) clear; obvious □ *jelas; ketara*: *a patent lie* ▶**patently** adv

patent leather /ˌpeɪtnt 'leðə(r)/ noun [U] a type of leather with a hard, shiny surface, used especially for making shoes and bags □ *kulit kilat*

paternal /pə'tɜːnl/ adj **1** behaving as a father would behave; connected with being a father □ *(berkenaan dgn atau spt) bapa* **2** [only before a noun] related through the father's side of the family □ *sebelah bapa*: *my paternal grandparents* ⊃ look at **maternal**

paternity /pə'tɜːnəti/ noun [U] the fact of being the father of a child □ *(keadaan menjadi) bapa*: *paternity leave* (= time that the father of a new baby is allowed to have away from work) ⊃ look at **maternity**

path /pɑːθ/ noun [C] **1** a way across a piece of land that is made by or used by people walking □ *lorong; laluan*: *the garden path* ◆ *Keep to the path or you may get lost.* ⊃ picture on **page P8**

MORE **Pathway** is similar in meaning: *There was a narrow pathway leading down the cliff.*

2 the line along which sb/sth moves; the space in front of sb/sth as he/she/it moves □ *laluan; lintasan*: *the flight path of an aeroplane*

pathetic /pə'θetɪk/ adj **1** causing you to feel pity or sadness □ *menyedihkan*: *the pathetic cries of the hungry children* **2** (*informal*) very bad, weak or useless □ *teruk; lemah; tdk memuaskan*: *What a pathetic performance! The team deserved to lose.* ▶**pathetically** /-kli/ adv

pathological /ˌpæθə'lɒdʒɪkl/ adj **1** caused by feelings that you cannot control; not reasonable or sensible □ *disebabkan oleh perasaan yg tdk dpt dikawal; tdk munasabah*: *He's a pathological liar* (= he cannot stop lying). ◆ *pathological fear/hatred/violence* **2** caused by or connected with disease or illness □ *penyakit*: *pathological depression* **3** connected with **pathology** □ *(berkaitan dgn) patologi* ▶**pathologically** /-kli/ adv

pathologist /pə'θɒlədʒɪst/ noun [C] a doctor who is an expert in **pathology**, and examines dead bodies to find out why a person has died □ *ahli patologi*

pathology /pə'θɒlədʒi/ noun [U] the scientific study of diseases of the body □ *patologi*

pathos /'peɪθɒs/ noun [U] (in writing, speech and plays) a quality that produces feelings of sadness and pity □ *sifat dlm pertuturan atau penulisan yg menimbulkan rasa belas kasihan; kehibaan*

patience /'peɪʃns/ noun [U] **1** patience (with sb/sth) the quality of being able to stay calm and not get angry, especially when there is a difficulty or you have to wait a long time □ *kesabaran*: *I've got no patience with people who don't even try.* ◆ *to lose patience with somebody* **OPP** impatience **2** (*AmE* solitaire) a card game for only one player □ *permainan 'solitaire'*

patient¹ /'peɪʃnt/ noun [C] a person who is receiving medical treatment □ *pesakit*: *a hospital patient* ⊃ note at **hospital**

patient² /'peɪʃnt/ adj patient (with sb/sth) able to stay calm and not get angry, especially when there is a difficulty or you have to wait a long time □ *sabar*: *He's very patient with young children.* **OPP** impatient ▶**patiently** adv: *She sat patiently waiting for her turn.*

patio /'pætiəʊ/ noun [C] (*pl* patios /-əʊz/) a flat, hard area, usually behind a house, where people can sit, eat, etc. outside □ *patio; beranda* ⊃ look at **terrace, veranda**

patriot /'peɪtriət/ (*BrE also*) /'pæt-/ noun [C] a person who loves their country and is ready

patriotic → pay 628

to defend it against an enemy □ *patriot; setia negarawan* ▶**patriotism** /ˈpeɪtriətɪzəm/ (BrE also) ˈpæt-/ *noun* [U]

patriotic /ˌpeɪtriˈɒtɪk (BrE also) ˌpæt-/ *adj* having or showing great love for your country □ *patriotik; setia negara* ▶**patriotically** /-kli/ *adv*

patrol¹ /pəˈtrəʊl/ *verb* [I,T] (**patrolling; patrolled**) to go round an area, building, etc. at regular times to make sure that it is safe and that nothing is wrong □ *meronda*

patrol² /pəˈtrəʊl/ *noun* **1** [C,U] the act of going round an area, building, etc. at regular times to make sure that it is safe and that nothing is wrong □ *rondaan: a police car on patrol in the area* **2** [C] a group of soldiers, vehicles, etc. that patrol sth □ *pasukan peronda: a naval/police patrol* ♦ *a patrol car/boat*

patron /ˈpeɪtrən/ *noun* [C] **1** a person who gives money and support to artists, writers and musicians □ *penaung: a patron of the arts* **2** a famous person who supports an organization such as a charity and whose name is used in advertising it □ *penaung* ➲ look at **sponsor 3** (*formal*) a person who uses a particular shop, theatre, restaurant, etc. □ *pelanggan tetap; pelanggan: This car park is for patrons only.*

patronage /ˈpætrənɪdʒ; ˈpeɪt-/ *noun* [U] the support, especially financial, that is given to a person or an organization by a patron □ *naungan: Patronage of the arts comes from businesses and private individuals.*

patronize (also **-ise**) /ˈpætrənaɪz/ *verb* [T] **1** to treat sb in a way that shows that you think you are better, more intelligent, experienced, etc. than they are □ *merendah-rendahkan* **2** (*formal*) to be a regular customer of a shop, restaurant, etc. □ *menjadi pelanggan tetap* ▶**patronizing** (also **-ising**) *adj*: *I hate that patronizing smile of hers.* ▶**patronizingly** (also **-isingly**) *adv*

ˌpatron ˈsaint *noun* [C] a religious person who is believed by Christians to protect a particular place or people doing a particular activity □ *keramat pelindung: St David is the patron saint of Wales.*

patter /ˈpætə(r)/ *noun* [sing] the sound of many quick light steps or knocks on a surface □ *bunyi tapak kaki, ketukan ringan, dsb: the patter of the children's feet on the stairs* ▶**patter** *verb* [I]

pattern /ˈpætn/ *noun* [C] **1** the regular way in which sth happens, develops, or is done □ *corak; pola: Her days all seemed to follow the same pattern.* ♦ *changing patterns of behaviour/work/weather* **2** a regular arrangement of lines, shapes, colours, etc. as a design □ *corak: a shirt with a floral pattern on it* **SYN** design ➲ picture on page P1 **3** a design, a set of instructions or a shape to cut around that you use in order to make sth □ *pola: a dress/sewing pattern*

patterned /ˈpætənd/ *adj* decorated with a pattern(2) □ *bercorak* ➲ picture on page P1

pause¹ /pɔːz/ *verb* [I] **pause (for sth)** to stop talking or doing sth for a short time before continuing □ *berhenti sejenak: He paused for a moment before answering my question.*

pause² /pɔːz/ *noun* **1** [C] **a pause (in sth)** a short period of time during which sb stops talking or stops what they are doing □ *berhenti sejenak: He continued playing for twenty minutes without a pause.* ➲ note at **interval 2** (also ˈpause button) [C,U] a control that allows you to stop a CD, DVD, etc. for a short time □ *butang jeda: Can you press pause while I go and make a cup of tea?*

pave /peɪv/ *verb* [T, often passive] **pave sth (with sth)** to cover an area of ground with **paving stones** or bricks □ *menurap*

pavement /ˈpeɪvmənt/ (*AmE* **sidewalk**) *noun* [C] a hard flat area at the side of a road for people to walk on □ *laluan jalan kaki* ➲ picture at **roundabout** ➲ picture on **page P11**

pavilion /pəˈvɪliən/ *noun* [C] (BrE) **1** a building at a sports ground where players can change their clothes □ *pavilion* **2** a temporary building used at public events and exhibitions □ *astaka*

ˈpaving stone *noun* [C] a flat piece of stone that is used for covering the ground □ *batu turap*

paw¹ /pɔː/ *noun* [C] the foot of animals such as dogs, cats, bears, etc. □ *(tapak) kaki binatang* ➲ picture on **page P12**

paw² /pɔː/ *verb* [I,T] **paw (at) sth** (used about an animal) to touch or scratch sb/sth several times with a paw □ *(bagi binatang) menyentuh atau menguis dgn kaki: The dog pawed at my sleeve.*

pawn¹ /pɔːn/ *noun* [C] **1** (in the game of **chess**) one of the eight pieces that are of least value and importance □ *bidak* **2** a person who is used or controlled by other more powerful people □ *orang yg dijadikan alat*

pawn² /pɔːn/ *verb* [T] to leave a valuable object with a **pawnbroker**, in return for money. If you cannot pay back the money after a certain period, the object can be sold or kept. □ *menggadaikan*

pawnbroker /ˈpɔːnbrəʊkə(r)/ *noun* [C] a person who lends money to people when they leave sth of value with them □ *tuan punya pajak gadai*

pawpaw /ˈpɔːpɔː/ = **papaya**

pay¹ /peɪ/ *verb* (*pt, pp* **paid**) **1** [I,T] **pay (sb) (for sth); pay (sb) sth (for sth)** to give sb money for work, goods, services, etc. □ *membayar: She is very well paid.* ♦ *The work's finished but we haven't paid for it yet.* ♦ *We paid the dealer £3 000 for the car.* **2** [T] **pay sth (to sb)** to give the money that you owe for sth □ *membayar; menjelaskan: Have you paid her the rent yet?* ♦ *to pay a bill/fine* **3** [I,T] to be worth doing □ *berbaloi: It would pay you to get professional advice before making a decision.* **4** [I,T] to make a profit □ *bermanfaat:*

ʌ cup ɜː bird ə ago eɪ pay əʊ go aɪ my aʊ now ɔɪ boy ɪə near eə hair ʊə pure

It's hard to make farming pay. **5** [I] **pay (for sth)** to suffer or be punished because of your beliefs or actions ◻ *menanggung akibat; menerima padah*: *You'll pay for that remark!*
IDM **charge/pay the earth** ➪ **earth¹**
pay attention (to sb/sth) to listen carefully to or to take notice of sb/sth ◻ *memberikan perhatian (kpd sso/sst)*
pay sb a compliment; pay a compliment to sb to say that you like sb about sb ◻ *memuji sso; memberi pujian kpd sso*
pay your respects (to sb) (*formal*) to visit sb as a sign of respect ◻ *mengunjungi/menziarahi sso*: *Hundreds came to pay their last respects to her* (= went to her funeral).
pay tribute to sb/sth to say good things about sb/sth and show your respect for sb/sth ◻ *memberi penghormatan dgn kata-kata pujian*
put paid to sth to destroy or finish sth ◻ *memusnahkan/menggagalkan sst*: *The bad weather put paid to our picnic.*
PHR V **pay sb/sth back** to give money back to sb that you borrowed from them ◻ *membayar balik wang (kpd sso)*: *Can you lend me £5? I'll pay you back/I'll pay it back to you on Friday.*
pay sb back (for sth) to punish sb for making you or sb else suffer ◻ *membalas dendam (kerana sst)*: *What a mean trick! I'll pay you back one day.*
pay off (*informal*) to be successful ◻ *berjaya; berhasil*: *All her hard work has paid off! She passed her exam.*
pay sth off to pay all the money that you owe for sth ◻ *menjelaskan sepenuhnya hutang, dsb*: *to pay off a debt/mortgage*
pay up (*informal*) to pay the money that you owe ◻ *membayar hutang*: *If you don't pay up, we'll take you to court.*

pay² /peɪ/ *noun* [U] money that you get regularly for work that you have done ◻ *gaji*: *It's a boring job but the pay is good.* ◆ *a pay increase/rise*

TOPIC

Pay

Pay is the general word for money that you **earn** (= get regularly for work that you have done). **Wages** are paid weekly or daily in cash. A **salary** is paid monthly, directly into a bank account. When your wages or salary are increased, you get a **pay rise**. Your **income** is all the money you get regularly, both for work you have done, and as interest on money you have saved. **Payment** is money for work that you do once or not regularly. You pay a **fee** for professional services, for example to a doctor, lawyer, etc. The money that you have to pay to the government is called **tax**.

---

payable /ˈpeɪəbl/ *adj* [not before a noun] that should or must be paid ◻ *mesti dibayar; dibayar kpd*: *A 10% deposit is payable in advance.* ◆ *Please make the cheque payable to Helena Braun.*

pay-as-you-ˈgo *adj* connected with a system of paying for a service before you use it, rather than paying for it later ◻ *bayar sebelum guna*: *pay-as-you-go mobile phones* ➪ note at **mobile phone**

payee /ˌpeɪˈiː/ *noun* [C] a person that money, especially a cheque, is paid to ◻ *penerima (bayaran)*

payment /ˈpeɪmənt/ *noun* **payment (for sth)** **1** [U] the act of paying sb or of being paid ◻ *pembayaran; bayaran*: *payment of a bill* ◆ *I did the work last month but I haven't had any payment for it yet.* ➪ note at **pay²** **2** [C] an amount of money that you must pay ◻ *bayaran*: *They asked for a payment of £100 as a deposit.*

ˌpay-per-ˈview *noun* [U] a system of receiving television programmes in which you pay an extra sum of money to watch a particular programme, such as a film or a sports event ◻ *bayaran mengikut tontonan*

payslip /ˈpeɪslɪp/ *noun* [C] (*BrE*) a piece of paper that your employer gives you each month to show how much money you have been paid and how much tax, etc. has been taken off ◻ *slip gaji*: *There seems to be a mistake on my payslip.*

PC /ˌpiːˈsiː/ *abbr* **1** personal computer; a computer that is designed for one person to use at work or at home ◻ *PC; komputer peribadi* ➪ note at **computer** ➪ look at **mainframe** ➪ picture at **computer 2** (*BrE*) = **police constable 3** = politically correct

PE /ˌpiːˈiː/ *abbr* physical education; the school subject of sport and exercise ◻ *PJ (Pendidikan Jasmani)*: *a PE lesson*

pea /piː/ *noun* [C] a small round green seed that is eaten as a vegetable. A number of **peas** grow together in a **pod** (= a long thin case). ◻ *kacang pis* ➪ picture on **page P15**

peace /piːs/ *noun* [U] **1** a situation or a period of time in which there is no war or violence in a country or area ◻ *keamanan*: *The two communities now manage to live in peace together.* ◆ *A UN force has been sent in to keep the peace.* **2** the state of being calm or quiet ◻ *kedamaian; ketenteraman*: *He longed to escape from the city to the peace and quiet of the countryside.* ◆ *I'm tired—can't you just leave me in peace* (= stop disturbing me)*?*

peaceful /ˈpiːsfl/ *adj* **1** not wanting or involving war, violence or argument ◻ *aman; damai*: *a peaceful protest/demonstration* **2** calm and quiet ◻ *damai; tenang; tenteram*: *a peaceful village* ▶ **peacefully** /-fəli/ *adv*: *The siege ended peacefully and nobody was hurt.* ▶ **peacefulness** *noun* [U]

peacetime /ˈpiːstaɪm/ *noun* [U] a period when a country is not at war ◻ *masa aman*

peach /piːtʃ/ *noun* **1** [C] a soft round fruit with reddish-orange skin and a large stone in its centre ◻ *buah pic* ➪ picture on **page P14** **2** [U] a pinkish-orange colour ◻ *warna kuning kemerah-merahan* ▶ **peach** *adj*

peacock → pedigree 630

peacock /ˈpiːkɒk/ noun [C] a large bird with beautiful long blue and green tail feathers that it can lift up and spread out □ *burung merak (jantan)*

peak¹ /piːk/ noun [C] **1** the point at which sth is the highest, best, strongest, etc. □ *puncak; kemuncak*: *a man at the peak of his career* **2** the pointed top of a mountain □ *puncak; kemuncak*: *snow-covered peaks* ⊃ picture on page P10 **3** the stiff front part of a cap which sticks out above your eyes □ *birai topi* ⊃ picture at **hat**

peak² /piːk/ verb [I] to reach the highest point or value □ *mencapai kemuncak; memuncak*: *Sales peak just before Christmas.*

peak³ /piːk/ adj [only before a noun] used to describe the highest level of sth, or a time when the greatest number of people are doing or using sth □ *(peringkat/tahap) puncak; sesak*: *The athletes are all in peak condition.* ♦ *Summer is the peak period for most hotels.* ⊃ look at **off-peak**

peal /piːl/ noun [C] the loud ringing of a bell or bells □ *bunyi loceng yg bergema kuat; bunyi ketawa yg kuat*: (figurative) *peals of laughter* ▶ peal verb [I]

peanut /ˈpiːnʌt/ noun **1** (BrE also **groundnut**) [C] a nut that grows underground in a thin shell □ *kacang tanah* ⊃ picture at **nut 2 peanuts** [pl] (informal) a very small amount of money □ *(wang/bayaran) yg sangat sedikit*: *We get paid peanuts for doing this job.*

peanut butter noun [U] a thick soft substance made from very finely chopped peanuts, usually eaten spread on bread □ *mentega kacang*

pear /peə(r)/ noun [C] a fruit that has a yellow or green skin and is white inside. **Pears** are wider at the bottom than at the top. □ *buah pear* ⊃ picture on page P14

pearl /pɜːl/ noun [C] a small hard round white object that grows inside the shell of an **oyster** (= a type of creature that lives in water). Pearls are used to make jewellery □ *mutiara*: *pearl earrings*

peasant /ˈpeznt/ noun [C] (used especially in past times) a person who owns or rents a small piece of land on which they grow food and keeps animals in order to feed their family □ *petani*

HELP Be careful. This word is considered offensive nowadays.

peat /piːt/ noun [U] a soft black or brown natural substance that is formed from dead plants just under the surface of the ground in cool, wet places. It can be burned as a fuel or used in the garden to make plants grow better. □ *gambut*

pebble /ˈpebl/ noun [C] a smooth round stone that is found in or near water □ *batu kecil; kerakal* ⊃ picture on page P10

pecan /ˈpiːkən/ noun [C] a type of nut that you can eat, with a smooth pinkish-brown shell □ *kacang pekan* ⊃ picture at **nut**

peck /pek/ verb [I,T] **1 peck (at) sth** (used about a bird) to eat or bite sth with its beak □ *mematuk* **2** (informal) to kiss sb quickly and lightly □ *mencium sekilas*: *She pecked him on the cheek and then left.* ▶ peck noun [C]

peckish /ˈpekɪʃ/ adj (BrE informal) hungry □ *lapar*

peculiar /pɪˈkjuːliə(r)/ adj **1** unusual or strange □ *aneh; pelik*: *There's a very peculiar smell in here.* **SYN** odd **2 peculiar to sb/sth** only belonging to one person or found in one place □ *khusus terdapat; hanya ada*: *a species of bird peculiar to South East Asia*

peculiarity /pɪˌkjuːliˈærəti/ noun (pl peculiarities) **1** [C] a strange or unusual characteristic, quality or habit □ *sifat aneh*: *There are some peculiarities in her behaviour.* **2** [C] a characteristic or a quality that only belongs to one particular person, thing or place □ *ciri khusus*: *the cultural peculiarities of the English* **3** [U] the quality of being strange or unusual □ *keanehan*

peculiarly /pɪˈkjuːliəli/ adv **1** especially; very □ *sungguh; amat*: *Lilian's laugh can be peculiarly annoying.* **2** in a way that is especially typical of one person, thing or place □ *khusus; istimewa*: *a peculiarly Italian custom* **3** in a strange and unusual way □ *aneh; pelik*: *Luke is behaving very peculiarly.*

pedagogic /ˌpedəˈɡɒdʒɪk/ (also **pedagogical** /-ɪkl/) adj connected with ways of teaching □ *(berkaitan dgn) pedagogi/pengajaran*

pedal /ˈpedl/ noun [C] the part of a bicycle, car or other machine that you push with your foot in order to make it move or work □ *pedal; pengayuh; injak-injak* ⊃ picture at **bicycle, piano** ▶ pedal verb [I,T] (pedalling; pedalled, (AmE) pedaling; pedaled): *She had to pedal hard to get up the hill.*

pedantic /pɪˈdæntɪk/ adj too worried about small rules or details □ *terlalu mementingkan peraturan atau butir-butir remeh* ▶ pedantically /-kli/ adv

pedestal /ˈpedɪstl/ noun [C] the base on which a column, statue, etc. stands □ *kekaki*

pedestrian /pəˈdestriən/ noun [C] a person who is walking in the street (not travelling in a vehicle) □ *pejalan kaki* ⊃ look at **motorist**

pedestrian crossing (AmE **crosswalk**) noun [C] a place where vehicles must stop to allow **pedestrians** to cross the road □ *lintasan pejalan kaki* ⊃ look at **zebra crossing**

pediatrician, pediatrics (AmE) = **paediatrician, paediatrics**

pedigree¹ /ˈpedɪɡriː/ noun [C] **1** an official record of the animals from which a particular animal has been bred □ *pedigri* ⊃ look at **mongrel 2** a person's family history, especially when this is impressive □ *salasilah*

pedigree² /ˈpedɪɡriː/ adj [only before a noun] (used about an animal) of high quality because

[I] **intransitive**, a verb which has no object: *He laughed.*

[T] **transitive**, a verb which has an object: *He ate an apple.*

the family of animals that it comes from are all of the same breed and specially chosen □ *pedigri; baka sejati*

pee /pi:/ *verb* [I] (*informal*) to get rid of waste water from your body □ *kencing* **SYN** urinate ▶**pee** *noun* [U, sing]

peek /pi:k/ *verb* [I] (*informal*) **peek (at sth)** to look at sth quickly and secretly because you should not be looking at it □ *mengintai sepintas; mencuri tengok*: *No peeking at your presents before your birthday!* ▶**peek** *noun* [sing]: *to have a quick peek*

peel¹ /pi:l/ *verb* **1** [T] to take the skin off a fruit or vegetable □ *mengupas; mengopek*: *Could you peel the potatoes, please?* **2** [I,T] **peel (sth) (off/away/back)** to come off or to take sth off a surface in one piece or in small pieces □ *mengopek; menanggalkan*: *I peeled off the price label before handing her the book.*
IDM **keep your eyes peeled/skinned (for sb/sth)** ➲ **eye¹**

peel² /pi:l/ *noun* [U] the skin of a fruit or vegetable □ *kulit (buah atau sayuran)*: *apple/potato peel* ➲ look at **rind, skin** ➲ picture on page P14

peeler /ˈpi:lə(r)/ *noun* [C] a special knife for taking the skin off fruit and vegetables □ *pengupas*: *a potato peeler* ➲ picture at **kitchen**

peep¹ /pi:p/ *verb* [I] **1** **peep (at sth)** to look at sth quickly and secretly, especially through a small opening □ *mengintai; memandang sekilas* **2** to be just able to be seen □ *nampak sedikit; muncul*: *The moon is peeping out from behind the clouds.*

peep² /pi:p/ *noun* [sing] (*informal*) **1** a quick look □ *pandangan sekilas; menjenguk*: *Have a peep in the bedroom and see if the baby is asleep.* **2** a sound □ *bunyi*: *There hasn't been a peep out of the children for hours.*

peer¹ /pɪə(r)/ *noun* [C] **1** a person who is of the same age or position in society as you □ *rakan sebaya; orang yg sama taraf*: *Children hate to look stupid in front of their peers.* **2** (in Britain) a member of the **nobility** (= people of the highest social class, who have special titles) □ *orang bangsawan*

peer² /pɪə(r)/ *verb* [I] **peer (at sb/sth)** to look closely or carefully at sb/sth, for example because you cannot see very well □ *melihat (sso/sst) dgn teliti*: *He peered at the photo, but it was blurred.*

peerage /ˈpɪərɪdʒ/ *noun* **1** [sing] all the **peers¹**(2) as a group □ *golongan bangsawan* **2** [C] the position of a **peer¹**(2) □ *taraf/kedudukan bangsawan*

ˈpeer group *noun* [C] a group of people who are all of the same age and social position □ *kelompok sebaya/setara*

peeved /pi:vd/ *adj* (*informal*) quite angry or annoyed □ *agak marah*

peg¹ /peg/ *noun* [C] **1** a piece of wood, metal, etc. on a wall or door that you hang your coat on □ *pepaku; (pasak) penyangkut* **2** (also ˈtent

peg) a piece of metal that you push into the ground to keep one of the ropes of a tent in place □ *pancang; pasak* **3** (also ˈclothes peg; *AmE* ˈclothes pin) a type of small wooden or plastic object used for fastening wet clothes to a clothes line □ *sepit baju*

pegs

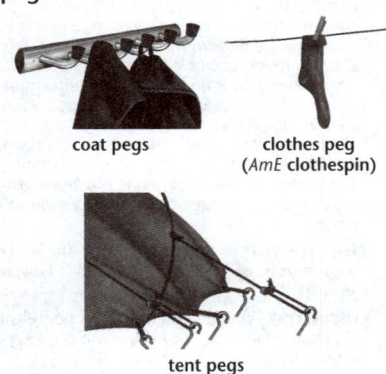

coat pegs

clothes peg
(*AmE* **clothespin**)

tent pegs

peg² /peg/ *verb* [T] (**pegging; pegged**) **1** **peg sth (out)** to fasten sth with a **peg** □ *memancang; memasak; menyepit* **2** **peg sth (at/to sth)** to fix or keep sth at a certain level □ *menetapkan*: *Wage increases were pegged at 5%.*

pelican /ˈpelɪkən/ *noun* [C] a large bird that lives near water in warm countries. A **pelican** has a large beak that it uses for catching and holding fish. □ *burung undan*

pellet /ˈpelɪt/ *noun* [C] **1** a small hard ball of any substance, often of soft material that has become hard □ *until; gentelan* **2** a very small metal ball that is fired from a gun □ *penabur; kacang-kacang*: *shotgun pellets*

pelt /pelt/ *verb* **1** [T] **pelt sb (with sth)** to attack sb/sth by throwing things □ *membaling; melempari* **2** [I] **pelt (down)** (used about rain) to fall very heavily □ *turun mencurah-curah*: *It's absolutely pelting down.* **3** [I] (*informal*) to run very fast □ *memecut; berlari pantas*: *Some kids pelted past us.*

pelvis /ˈpelvɪs/ *noun* [C] the set of wide bones at the bottom of your back, to which your leg bones are joined □ *pelvis* ➲ picture at **body** ▶**pelvic** /ˈpelvɪk/ *adj*

pen /pen/ *noun* [C] **1** an object that you use for writing in ink □ *pen*: *a ballpoint/felt-tip/marker/fountain pen* **2** a small piece of ground with a fence around it that is used for keeping animals in □ *kandang*: *a sheep pen*

penal /ˈpi:nl/ *adj* [only *before* a noun] connected with punishment by law □ *penal; (berkenaan dgn) hukuman*: *the penal system*

penalize (also **-ise**) /ˈpiːnəlaɪz/ verb [T] **1** to punish sb for breaking a law or rule ▫ *mendenda; menghukum* **2** to cause sb to have a disadvantage ▫ *menyebabkan sso berada dlm keadaan yg merugikan atau kekurangan*: *Children should not be penalized because their parents cannot afford to pay.*

penalty /ˈpenəlti/ noun [C] (pl **penalties**) **1** a punishment for breaking a law, rule or contract ▫ *hukuman; denda*: *the death penalty* ♦ *What's the maximum penalty for using your mobile phone while driving?* **2** a disadvantage or sth unpleasant that happens as the result of sth ▫ *padah; akibat*: *I didn't work hard enough and I paid the penalty. I failed all my exams.* **3** (in sport) a punishment for one team and an advantage for the other team because a rule has been broken ▫ *penalti*: *The referee awarded a penalty to the home team.*

the ˈpenalty area noun [C] the marked area in front of the goal in football ▫ *kawasan penalti*

penance /ˈpenəns/ noun [C,U] a punishment that you give yourself to show you are sorry for doing sth wrong ▫ *penebusan dosa*

pence plural of **penny**

pencil¹ /ˈpensl/ noun [C,U] an object that you use for writing or drawing. Pencils are usually made of wood and contain a thin stick of a black or coloured substance ▫ *pensel*: *Bring a pencil and paper with you.* ♦ *Write in pencil, not ink.* ⊃ picture at **stationery**

pencil² /ˈpensl/ verb [T] (**pencilling; pencilled**, (AmE) **penciling; penciled**) to write or draw with a pencil ▫ *menulis/melukis dgn pensel*
PHR V **pencil sth/sb in** to write down the details of an arrangement that might have to be changed later ▫ *mencatat (janji temu, dll) buat sementara waktu*: *Shall we pencil the next meeting in for the fourteenth?*

ˈpencil case noun [C] a small bag or box that you keep pens, pencils, etc. in ▫ *kotak pensel*

ˈpencil sharpener noun [C] a small device that you use for making pencils sharp ▫ *pengasah pensel* ⊃ picture at **stationery**

pendant /ˈpendənt/ noun [C] a small attractive object that you wear on a chain around your neck ▫ *loket*

pending /ˈpendɪŋ/ adj, prep (formal) **1** waiting to be done or decided ▫ *belum dibuat/diputuskan*: *The judge's decision is still pending.* **2** until sth happens ▫ *sementara menunggu*: *He took over the leadership pending the elections.*

ˈpen drive = **flash drive**

pendulum /ˈpendjələm/ noun [C] **1** a chain or stick with a heavy weight at the bottom that moves regularly from side to side to work a clock ▫ *bandul* **2** a way of describing a situation that changes from one thing to its opposite ▫ *sst* kedudukan atau keadaan yg berubah kpd sebaliknya: *Since last year's election, the pendulum of public opinion has swung against the government.*

penetrate /ˈpenɪtreɪt/ verb [I,T] **1** to go through or into sth, especially when this is difficult ▫ *menembusi; menusuk*: *The knife penetrated ten centimetres into his chest.* **2** to manage to understand sth difficult ▫ *memahami*: *Scientists have still not penetrated the workings of the brain.* **3** to be understood or realized ▫ *faham akan; menyedari*: *I was back at home when the meaning of her words finally penetrated.* ▶ **penetration** /ˌpenɪˈtreɪʃn/ noun [U]

penetrating /ˈpenɪtreɪtɪŋ/ adj **1** (used about sb's eyes or of a way of looking) making you feel uncomfortable because it seems sb knows what you are thinking ▫ *tajam*: *a penetrating look/stare/gaze* ♦ *penetrating blue eyes* **2** showing that you have understood sth completely and quickly ▫ *tajam; pintar*: *a penetrating question/comment* **3** loud and hard ▫ *nyaring* **4** spreading deeply or widely ▫ *menusuk; meresap*: *penetrating cold*

penfriend /ˈpenfrend/ (especially AmE **ˈpen pal**) noun [C] a person that you become friendly with by exchanging letters or emails, often a person who you have never met ▫ *sahabat pena*

penguin /ˈpeŋgwɪn/ noun [C] a black and white bird that cannot fly and that lives in the Antarctic ▫ *burung penguin*

penicillin /ˌpenɪˈsɪlɪn/ noun [U] a substance that is used as a drug for preventing and treating infections caused by bacteria ▫ *penisilin*

penguin

peninsula /pəˈnɪnsjələ/ noun [C] an area of land that is almost surrounded by water ▫ *semenanjung*

penis /ˈpiːnɪs/ noun [C] the male sex organ that is used for getting rid of waste liquid and for having sex ▫ *zakar*

penitent /ˈpenɪtənt/ adj (formal) sorry for having done sth wrong ▫ *kesal; insaf*

penitentiary /ˌpenɪˈtenʃəri/ noun [C] (pl **penitentiaries**) (AmE) a prison ▫ *penjara*

penknife /ˈpennaɪf/ noun [C] (pl **penknives** /ˈpennaɪvz/) a small knife with one or more blades that fold away when not being used ▫ *pisau lipat*

penniless /ˈpenɪləs/ adj having no money; poor ▫ *tdk berduit langsung; papa kedana*

penknife

penny /ˈpeni/ noun [C] (pl **pence** /pens/ or **pennies**) **1** (abbr **p**) a small brown British coin. There are a hundred pence in a pound ▫ *peni: a fifty-pence piece/coin* **2** (AmE) a cent ▫ *satu sen (AS)*

MORE In sense 1, **pennies** is used to refer to the coins, and **pence** to refer to an amount of money. In sense 2, the plural is **pennies**.

ˈpen pal (especially AmE) = **penfriend**

pension /ˈpenʃn/ noun [C] money that is paid regularly by a government or company to sb who has stopped working because of old age or who cannot work because they are ill ▫ *(duit) pencen: The state pension age for men and women is 65.* ♦ *She lives on her pension and her savings.* ♦ *a disability/widow's pension* ♦ *a retirement/old-age pension* ➲ note at **retire** ▸**pensioner** = **old-age pensioner**

pentagon /ˈpentəgən/ noun **1** [C] a shape that has five straight and equal sides ▫ *pentagon* **2 the Pentagon** [sing] a large government building near Washington DC in the US that contains the main offices of the US military forces; the military officials who work there ▫ *Pentagon*

pentathlon /penˈtæθlən/ noun [C] a sports competition in which you have to take part in five different events ▫ *pentatlon* ➲ look at **triathlon**

penthouse /ˈpenthaʊs/ noun [C] an expensive flat at the top of a tall building ▫ *megapuri*

pent-up /ˌpent ˈʌp/ adj [only before a noun] (used about feelings) that you hold inside and do not express ▫ *terpendam: pent-up anger*

penultimate /penˈʌltɪmət/ adj [only before a noun] (in a series) the one before the last one ▫ *yg kedua terakhir: 'Y' is the penultimate letter of the alphabet.*

people /ˈpiːpl/ noun **1** [pl] more than one person ▫ *orang: How many people are coming to the party?*

HELP People or persons? **People** is almost always used instead of the plural form **persons**. **Persons** is very formal and is usually used in legal language: *Persons under the age of eighteen are not permitted to buy cigarettes.*

2 [C] (pl **peoples**) (formal) all the men, women and children who belong to a particular place or race ▫ *orang; rakyat; bangsa: The President addressed the American people.* ♦ *the French-speaking peoples of the world* **3 the people** [pl] the ordinary citizens of a country ▫ *rakyat: The President is popular because he listens to the people.* **4** [pl] men and women who work in a particular activity ▫ *orang: business/sports people*

pepper[1] /ˈpepə(r)/ noun **1** [U] a black or white powder with a hot taste that is used for flavouring food ▫ *(serbuk) lada sulah atau lada hitam: salt and pepper* **2** [C] a green, red or yellow vegetable that is almost empty inside ▫ *lada benggala: stuffed green peppers* ➲ picture on page P15

pepper[2] /ˈpepə(r)/ verb [T, usually passive] **pepper sb/sth with sth** to hit sb/sth with a series of small objects, especially bullets ▫ *menghujani; menubi: The wall had been peppered with bullets.*

peppermint /ˈpepəmɪnt/ noun **1** [U] a natural substance with a strong fresh flavour that is used in sweets and medicines ▫ *(perasa) pudina* **2** [C] (also **mint**) a sweet with a **peppermint** flavour ▫ *pepermin; gula-gula berperasa pudina* ➲ look at **spearmint**

ˈpep talk /ˈpep tɔːk/ noun [C] (informal) a speech that is given to encourage people or to make them work harder ▫ *kata-kata perangsang*

per /pə(r); strong form pɜː(r)/ prep for each ▫ *per; se; setiap: The speed limit is 110 kilometres per hour.* ♦ *Rooms cost 60 dollars per person per night.*

perceive /pəˈsiːv/ verb [T] (formal) **1** to notice or realize sth ▫ *nampak; melihat; menyedari: Scientists failed to perceive how dangerous the level of pollution had become.* **2** to understand or think of sth in a particular way ▫ *menanggap; mengerti; merasakan: I perceived his comments as a criticism.* **SYN** see ➲ noun **perception**

per ˈcent (AmE **percent**) adj, adv, noun [C, with sing or pl verb] (pl **per cent**) (symbol %) in or of each hundred; one part in every hundred ▫ *peratus: There is a ten per cent service charge.* ♦ *You get 10% off if you pay cash.* ♦ *90% of the population owns a TV.* ♦ *The price of bread has gone up by 50 per cent in two years.*

percentage /pəˈsentɪdʒ/ noun [C, with sing or pl verb] the number, amount, rate, etc. of sth, expressed as if it is part of a total which is a hundred; a part or share of a whole ▫ *peratusan; peratus: What percentage of people voted in the last election?*

perceptible /pəˈseptəbl/ adj (formal) that can be seen or felt ▫ *dpt dilihat atau dirasakan: a barely perceptible change in colour* **OPP** **imperceptible** ▸**perceptibly** /-əbli/ adv

perception /pəˈsepʃn/ noun (formal) **1** [U] the ability to notice or understand sth ▫ *penanggapan; persepsi* **2** [C] a particular way of looking at or understanding sth; an opinion ▫ *tanggapan; persepsi: What is your perception of the situation?* ➲ verb **perceive**

perceptive /pəˈseptɪv/ adj (formal) quick to notice or understand things ▫ *cepat menyedari/memahami; persepitf: She is very perceptive.* ▸**perceptively** adv

perch[1] /pɜːtʃ/ verb **1** [I] (used about a bird) to sit on a branch, etc. ▫ *bertenggek* **2** [I,T] to sit or be put on the edge of sth ▫ *bertenggek; tertenggek: The house was perched on the edge of a cliff.*

perch → period 634

perch² /pɜːtʃ/ noun [C] a place where a bird sits, especially a branch or a bar for this purpose □ *tempat bertengger*

percussion /pəˈkʌʃn/ noun [U] drums and other instruments that you play by hitting them □ *genderang* ⊃ note at **instrument** ⊃ picture at **music**

perennial /pəˈreniəl/ adj that happens often or that lasts for a long time □ *berterusan; berlarutan*: *a perennial problem*

perfect¹ /ˈpɜːfɪkt/ adj 1 completely good; without faults or weaknesses □ *sangat baik; sempurna*: *The car is two years old but it is still in perfect condition.* **OPP** imperfect 2 perfect (for sb/sth) exactly suitable or right □ *paling sesuai*: *Ken would be perfect for the job.* 3 [only before a noun] complete; total □ *betul-betul*: *What she was saying made perfect sense to me.* ♦ *a perfect stranger* 4 used to describe the tense of a verb that is formed with *has/have/had* and the past participle □ *(kala) sempurna*: *the present perfect tense* ▶ **perfectly** adv: *Laura understood perfectly what I meant.* ♦ *He played the piece of music perfectly.*

perfect² /pəˈfekt/ verb [T] to make sth perfect □ *menjadikan betul-betul baik/bagus*: *Vinay is spending a year in France to perfect his French.*

the ˈperfect = the perfect tense

perfection /pəˈfekʃn/ noun [U] the state of being perfect or without fault □ *kesempurnaan; betul-betul (baik, masak, dll)*: *The steak was cooked to perfection.*

perfectionist /pəˈfekʃənɪst/ noun [C] a person who always does things as well as they possibly can and who expects others to do the same □ *orang yg mengutamakan kesempurnaan*

the ˈperfect tense (also the ˈperfect) noun [sing] the tense of a verb that is formed with *has/have/had* and the past participle □ *kala sempurna (ttg kk)*: *'I have finished' is in the present perfect tense.* ❶ For more information about the perfect tense, look at the **Reference Section** at the back of this dictionary.

perforate /ˈpɜːfəreɪt/ verb [T] to make a hole or holes in sth □ *melubangi; menebuk*

perforation /ˌpɜːfəˈreɪʃn/ noun 1 [C] a series of small holes in paper, etc. that make it easy for you to tear it □ *tebukan; lubang-lubang* 2 [U] the act of making a hole or holes in sth □ *penebukan*

perform /pəˈfɔːm/ verb 1 [T] (formal) to do a piece of work or sth that you have been ordered to do □ *membuat; melakukan; mengerjakan*: *to perform an operation/an experiment/a task* 2 [I,T] to take part in a play or to sing, dance, etc. in front of an audience □ *membuat persembahan*: *She is currently performing at the National Theatre.* 3 [I] perform (well/badly/poorly) to work or function well or badly □ *menunjukkan prestasi/pencapaian*: *The company has not been performing well recently.*

IDM work/perform miracles ⊃ **miracle**

performance /pəˈfɔːməns/ noun 1 [C] the act of performing sth in front of an audience; something that you perform □ *persembahan; pertunjukan*: *What time does the performance start?* 2 [C] the way a person performs in a play, concert, etc. □ *persembahan*: *His moving performance in the film won him an Oscar.* 3 [C,U] the way in which you do sth, especially how successful you are □ *prestasi; pencapaian*: *The company's performance was disappointing last year.* 4 [U] (used about a machine, etc.) how well or badly sth works □ *prestasi*: *a car with outstanding performance* 5 [U, sing] (formal) the act or process of doing a task, an action, etc □ *pelaksanaan; menjalankan*: *the performance of your duties*

performer /pəˈfɔːmə(r)/ noun [C] 1 a person who performs for an audience □ *orang yg membuat persembahan; penghibur, pelakon, penyanyi, dsb*: *a brilliant performer* 2 a person or thing that behaves or works in the way mentioned □ *sso/sst yg berkelakuan atau yg kerjanya spt yg disebutkan*: *Diana is a poor performer in exams.*

the perˈforming ˈarts noun [pl] arts such as music, dance and drama which are performed for an audience □ *seni yg dipersembahkan utk penonton*

perfume /ˈpɜːfjuːm/ noun [C,U] 1 (BrE also scent) a liquid with a sweet smell that you put on your body to make yourself smell nice □ *minyak/air wangi*: *Are you wearing perfume?* 2 a pleasant, often sweet, smell □ *bau harum/wangi*: *The flowers had a delicate perfume.* ⊃ note at **smell²**

perhaps /pəˈhæps (BrE also) præps/ adv (used when you are not sure about sth) possibly □ *mungkin; barangkali*: *Perhaps he's forgotten.* ♦ *She was, perhaps, one of the most famous writers of the time.* **SYN** maybe

> **HELP** Perhaps and maybe are often used to make something sound more polite: *Perhaps/Maybe it would be better if you came back tomorrow* (= Please come back tomorrow).

peril /ˈperəl/ noun (formal) 1 [U] great danger □ *bahaya besar*: *A lack of trained nurses is putting patients' lives in peril.* 2 [C] something that is very dangerous □ *bahaya*: *the perils of drug abuse* ▶ **perilous** /ˈperələs/ adj ⊃ More common words are **danger** and **dangerous**.

perimeter /pəˈrɪmɪtə(r)/ noun [C] the outside edge or limit of an area of land □ *sempadan; perimeter*: *the perimeter fence of the army camp*

period /ˈpɪəriəd/ noun [C] 1 a length of time □ *tempoh; masa; zaman*: *The scheme will be introduced for a six-month trial period.* ♦ *Her son is going through a difficult period at the moment.* ♦ *What period of history are you most interested in?* 2 a lesson in school □ *waktu*: *We have five*

ʌ **c**up ɜː **b**ird ə **a**go eɪ **p**ay əʊ **g**o aɪ **m**y aʊ **n**ow ɔɪ **b**oy ɪə **n**ear eə **h**air ʊə **p**ure

periods of English a week. **3** the time every month when a woman loses blood from her body □ *haid*: *When did you last have a period?* **4** (*especially AmE*) = **full stop**

periodic /ˌpɪəriˈɒdɪk/ (also **periodical**) *adj* happening regularly and fairly often □ *berkala*: *We have periodic meetings to check on progress.* ▶ **periodically** /-kli/ *adv*: *All machines need to be checked periodically.*

periodical /ˌpɪəriˈɒdɪkl/ *noun* [C] (*formal*) a magazine that is produced regularly □ *majalah, dsb*

peripheral¹ /pəˈrɪfərəl/ *adj* **1** (*formal*) **peripheral (to sth)** not as important as the main aim, part, etc. of sth □ *tdk berapa penting; kurang penting*: *peripheral information* ♦ *Fund-raising is peripheral to their main activities.* **2** (*technical*) connected with the edge of a particular area □ *pinggiran; sempadan*: *the peripheral nervous system* ♦ *peripheral vision*

peripheral² /pəˈrɪfərəl/ *noun* [C] a piece of equipment that is connected to a computer □ *peranti persisian; alat tambahan*: *monitors, printers and other peripherals*

periphery /pəˈrɪfəri/ *noun* [C, usually sing] (*pl* **peripheries**) (*formal*) **1** the outer edge of a particular area □ *pinggir; sempadan*: *industrial development on the periphery of the town* **2** the less important part of sth, for example of a particular activity or of a social or political group □ *tdk berapa penting; kurang penting*: *minor parties on the periphery of American politics*

periscope /ˈperɪskəʊp/ *noun* [C] a device like a long tube, containing mirrors, used especially in a **submarine** (= a type of ship that can travel underwater) to see above the surface of the sea □ *periskop*

perish /ˈperɪʃ/ *verb* [I] (*formal*) to die or be destroyed □ *mati; terkorban; musnah*: *Thousands perished in the war.*

perishable /ˈperɪʃəbl/ *adj* (used about food) that will go bad quickly □ *cepat busuk; tdk tahan lama*

perjury /ˈpɜːdʒəri/ *noun* [U] (*formal*) the act of telling a lie in a court of law □ *sumpah bohong* ▶ **perjure** /ˈpɜːdʒə(r)/ *verb* [T] **perjure yourself**: *She admitted that she had perjured herself while giving evidence.*

perk¹ /pɜːk/ *noun* [C] (*informal*) something extra that you get from your employer in addition to money □ *faedah istimewa*: *Travelling abroad is one of the perks of the job.*

perk² /pɜːk/ *verb*

PHR V perk (sb/sth) up (*informal*) to become happier; to make sb/sth become happier and have more energy □ *menjadi lebih ceria dan bertenaga*

perm /pɜːm/ *noun* [C] the treatment of hair with special chemicals in order to make it curly □ *keriting rambut* ⊃ look at **wave** ▶ **perm** *verb* [T]: *She has had her hair permed.*

periodic → perpetuate

permanent /ˈpɜːmənənt/ *adj* lasting for a long time or for ever; that will not change □ *kekal; tetap; sentiasa*: *The accident left him with a permanent scar.* ♦ *Are you looking for a permanent or a temporary job?* ▶ **permanence** *noun* [U] ▶ **permanently** *adv*: *Has she left permanently?*

permissible /pəˈmɪsəbl/ *adj* (*formal*) **permissible (for sb) (to do sth)** that is allowed by law or by a set of rules □ *dibenarkan*: *It is not permissible for banks to release their customers' personal details.*

permission /pəˈmɪʃn/ *noun* [U] **permission (for sth); permission (for sb) (to do sth)** the act of allowing sb to do sth, especially when this is done by sb in a position of authority □ *izin; kebenaran*: *I'm afraid you can't leave without permission.* ♦ *to ask/give permission for something*

> **HELP** Be careful. **Permission** is uncountable. A document which says that you are allowed to do something is a **permit**.

permissive /pəˈmɪsɪv/ *adj* having, allowing or showing a lot of freedom that many people do not approve of, especially in sexual matters □ *permisif; terlalu bebas*

permit¹ /pəˈmɪt/ *verb* (**permitting; permitted**) **1** [T] (*formal*) to allow sb to do sth or to allow sth to happen □ *membenarkan; mengizinkan*: *You are not permitted to smoke in the hospital.* ♦ *You are not permitted to use mobile phones in the hospital.* ♦ *His visa does not permit him to work.* ⊃ note at **allow 2** [I,T] to make sth possible □ *mengizinkan; membolehkan*: *Let's have a barbecue at the weekend, weather permitting.*

permit² /ˈpɜːmɪt/ *noun* [C] an official document that says you are allowed to do sth, especially for a limited period of time □ *permit; surat izin*: *Next month I'll have to apply for a new work permit.*

perpendicular /ˌpɜːpənˈdɪkjələ(r)/ *adj* **1** at an angle of 90° to sth □ *serenjang; tegak lurus*: *Are the lines perpendicular to each other?* ⊃ look at **horizontal, vertical 2** pointing straight up □ *tegak*: *The path was almost perpendicular* (= it was very steep).

perpetrate /ˈpɜːpətreɪt/ *verb* [T] (*formal*) **perpetrate sth (against/upon/on sb)** to commit a crime or do sth wrong or evil □ *melakukan (jenayah, keganasan, dsb)*: *to perpetrate a crime/fraud/massacre* ♦ *violence perpetrated against women and children*

perpetual /pəˈpetʃuəl/ *adj* **1** continuing for a long period of time without stopping □ *sentiasa; sepanjang masa*: *They lived in perpetual fear of losing their jobs.* **2** repeated many times in a way which is annoying □ *berterusan; tdk henti-henti*: *How can I work with these perpetual interruptions?* ▶ **perpetually** /-tʃuəli/ *adv*

perpetuate /pəˈpetʃueɪt/ *verb* [T] (*formal*) to cause sth to continue for a long time

[C] **countable**, a noun with a plural form: *one book, two books* [U] **uncountable**, a noun with no plural form: *some sugar*

☐ *mengekalkan; meneruskan*: to perpetuate an argument

perplexed /pəˈplekst/ *adj* not understanding sth; confused ☐ *bingung; keliru*

persecute /ˈpɜːsɪkjuːt/ *verb* [T] 1 [often passive] **persecute sb (for sth)** to treat sb in a cruel and unfair way, especially because of race, religion or political beliefs ☐ *menganiaya; menyeksa*: *persecuted minorities* 2 to deliberately annoy sb and make their life unpleasant ☐ *mengganggu* ▶ **persecution** /ˌpɜːsɪˈkjuːʃn/ *noun* [C,U]: *the persecution of minorities* ▶ **persecutor** /ˈpɜːsɪkjuːtə(r)/ *noun* [C]

persevere /ˌpɜːsɪˈvɪə(r)/ *verb* [I] **persevere (at/in/with sth)** to continue trying to do or achieve sth that is difficult ☐ *bertekun; tabah (meneruskan sst)*: *The treatment is painful but I'm going to persevere with it.* ▶ **perseverance** *noun* [U]

persist /pəˈsɪst/ *verb* [I] 1 **persist (in sth/doing sth)** to continue doing sth even though other people say that you are wrong or that you should not do it ☐ *terus; tetap*: *If you persist in making so much noise, I shall call the police.* 2 to continue to exist ☐ *berterusan*: *If your symptoms persist you should consult your doctor.* ▶ **persistence** *noun* [U]: *Finally her persistence was rewarded and she got exactly what she wanted.*

persistent /pəˈsɪstənt/ *adj* 1 determined to continue doing sth even though people say that you are wrong or that you should not do it ☐ *tabah; terus mendesak*: *Some salesmen can be very persistent.* 2 lasting for a long time or happening often ☐ *berterusan; berulang-ulang; tdk baik-baik*: *a persistent cough* ▶ **persistently** *adv*

person /ˈpɜːsn/ *noun* [C] (*pl* **people**) 1 a man or woman; a human being ☐ *orang*: *I would like to speak to the person in charge.* ♦ *He's just the person we need for the job.* ⊃ note at **people**

> **HELP** In very formal or official cases the plural of *person* can be **persons**.

2 **-person** [in compounds] a person doing the job mentioned ☐ *digunakan utk membentuk kata majmuk yg bermaksud orang yg melakukan pekerjaan yg disebutkan; juru*: *a salesperson/spokesperson* 3 one of the three types of pronoun in grammar. *I/we* are the first person, *you* is the second person and *he/she/it/they* are the third person. ☐ *diri*

IDM in person seeing or speaking to sb face to face (not speaking on the telephone or writing a letter, etc.) ☐ *sendiri*: *I went to apologize to her in person.*

personal /ˈpɜːsənl/ *adj*
▶YOUR OWN 1 [only *before* a noun] of or belonging to one particular person ☐ *persendirian; peribadi*: *personal belongings* ♦ *Judges should not let their personal feelings influence their decisions.*
▶FEELINGS, ETC. 2 connected with your feelings, health or relationships with other people

☐ *peribadi*: *I should like to speak to you in private. I have something personal to discuss.* ♦ *Do you mind if I ask you a personal question?*
▶NOT OFFICIAL 3 not connected with sb's job or official position ☐ *peribadi*: *Please keep personal phone calls to a minimum.* ♦ *I try not to let work interfere with my personal life.*
▶DONE BY PERSON 4 [only *before* a noun] done by a particular person rather than by sb who is acting for them ☐ *sendiri; peribadi*: *The Prime Minister made a personal visit to the victims in hospital.*
▶FOR EACH PERSON 5 [only *before* a noun] made or done for one particular person rather than for a large group of people or for people in general ☐ *peribadi*: *We offer a personal service to all our customers.*
▶APPEARANCE/CHARACTER 6 speaking about sb's appearance or character in an unpleasant or unfriendly way ☐ *menyentuh peribadi*: *It started as a general discussion but then people started to get personal and an argument began.* 7 [only *before* a noun] connected with the body ☐ *diri*: *personal hygiene* ♦ *She's always worrying about her personal appearance.*

ˌpersonal asˈsistant = PA
ˌpersonal comˈputer = PC (1)

personality /ˌpɜːsəˈnæləti/ *noun* (*pl* **personalities**) 1 [C,U] the different qualities of sb's character that make them different from other people ☐ *keperibadian; watak*: *The children all have very different personalities.* 2 [U] the quality of having a strong, interesting and attractive character ☐ *personaliti*: *A good entertainer needs a lot of personality.* 3 [C] a famous person (especially in sport, on TV, etc.) ☐ *tokoh; personaliti*: *a TV personality* **SYN** **celebrity**

personalize (also **-ise**) /ˈpɜːsənəlaɪz/ *verb* [T] to mark sth in some way to show that it belongs to you ☐ *memberi tanda nama*: *Their towels were personalized with their initials.*

personally /ˈpɜːsənəli/ *adv* 1 used to show that you are expressing your own opinion ☐ *bagi diri saya; bagi saya*: *Personally, I think that nurses deserve more money.* 2 done by you yourself, not by sb else acting for you ☐ *sendiri*: *I will deal with this matter personally.* 3 in a way that is connected with one particular person rather than a group of people ☐ *secara persendirian; seorang*: *I wasn't talking about you personally—I meant all teachers.* 4 in a way that is intended to offend ☐ *berniat menyinggung (perasaan sso); tersinggung*: *Please don't take it personally, but I would just rather be alone this evening.* 5 in a way that is connected with sb's private life, rather than their job ☐ *secara persendirian/peribadi*: *Have you had any dealings with any of the suspects, either personally or professionally?*

ˌpersonal ˈpronoun *noun* [C] any of the pronouns *I, me, she, her, he, him, we, us, you, they, them* ☐ *ganti nama diri*

ˌpersonal ˈstereo *noun* [C] a small piece of equipment with **headphones** (= a piece of equipment worn over or in the ears) that you can carry with you in order to listen to music □ *stereo bimbit*

personal trainer *noun* [C] a person who is paid by sb to help them exercise, especially by deciding what types of exercise are best for them □ *pelatih peribadi*

personify /pəˈsɒnɪfaɪ/ *verb* [T] (**personifying; personifies;** *pt, pp* **personified**) **1** to be an example in human form of a particular quality □ *menjadi lambang*: *She is kindness personified.* **2** to describe an object or a feeling as if it were a person □ *mempersonifikasikan*: *The river was personified as a goddess.* ▶**personification** /pəˌsɒnɪfɪˈkeɪʃn/ *noun* [C,U]

personnel /ˌpɜːsəˈnel/ *noun* **1** [pl] the people who work for a large organization or one of the armed forces □ *kakitangan; staf*: *sales/medical/technical personnel* **2** (also **personˈnel department**) [U, with sing or pl verb] the department of a large company or organization that deals with employing and training people □ *jabatan perjawatan/personel*: *Personnel is/are currently reviewing pay scales.* **SYN** **human resources**

perspective /pəˈspektɪv/ *noun* **1** [C] your opinion or attitude towards sth □ *perspektif; sudut pandangan*: *Try and look at this from my perspective.* **2** [U] the ability to think about problems and decisions in a reasonable way without exaggerating them □ *perspektif; secara lebih wajar*: *Hearing about others' experiences often helps to put your own problems into perspective* (= makes them seem less important than you thought). ♦ *Try to keep these issues in perspective* (= do not exaggerate them). **3** [U] the art of drawing on a flat surface so that some objects appear to be further away than others □ *perspektif*

perspire /pəˈspaɪə(r)/ *verb* [I] (*formal*) to lose liquid through your skin when you are hot □ *berpeluh* ▶**perspiration** /ˌpɜːspəˈreɪʃn/ *noun* [U] ⊃ A more common word is **sweat**.

⚑persuade /pəˈsweɪd/ *verb* [T] **1 persuade sb (to do sth); persuade sb (into sth/doing sth)** to make sb do sth by giving them good reasons □ *memujuk*: *It was difficult to persuade Louise to change her mind.* ♦ *We eventually persuaded Sanjay into coming with us.* **OPP** **dissuade** **2** (*formal*) **persuade sb that ...; persuade sb (of sth)** to make sb believe sth □ *meyakinkan; membuat sso percaya*: *She had persuaded herself that she was going to fail.* ♦ *The jury was not persuaded of her innocence.* ⊃ look at **convince**

persuasion /pəˈsweɪʒn/ *noun* **1** [U] the act of persuading sb to do sth or to believe sth □ *pujukan*: *It took a lot of persuasion to get Alan to agree.* **2** [C] (*formal*) a religious or political belief □ *kepercayaan; fahaman*: *politicians of all persuasions*

persuasive /pəˈsweɪsɪv/ *adj* able to persuade sb to do or believe sth □ *yg pandai memujuk/meyakinkan*: *the persuasive power of advertising* ▶**persuasively** *adv* ▶**persuasiveness** *noun* [U]

pertinent /ˈpɜːtɪnənt/ *adj* (*formal*) closely connected with the subject being discussed □ *berkaitan; jitu*: *to ask a pertinent question*

perturb /pəˈtɜːb/ *verb* [T] (*formal*) to make sb worried or upset □ *merisaukan; risau; mengganggu* ▶**perturbed** *adj*

pervade /pəˈveɪd/ *verb* [T] (*formal*) to spread through and be noticeable in every part of sth □ *merebak; meresap; menyelinap*: *A sadness pervades most of her novels.*

pervasive /pəˈveɪsɪv/ *adj* that is present in all parts of sth □ *(yg) merebak/meresap*: *a pervasive mood of pessimism*

perverse /pəˈvɜːs/ *adj* (*formal*) liking to behave in a way that is not acceptable or reasonable or that most people think is wrong □ *sengaja suka membuat sst yg menyakitkan hati atau yg tdk disukai orang*: *Derek gets perverse pleasure from shocking his parents.* ▶**perversely** *adv* ▶**perversity** /pəˈvɜːsəti/ *noun* [U]

perversion /pəˈvɜːʃn/ *noun* [U,C] **1** sexual behaviour that is not considered normal or acceptable by most people □ *sumbaleweng; perilaku seks yg luar tabii* **2** the act of changing sth from right to wrong or from good to bad □ *pemutarbalikan; pemutarbelitan*: *That statement is a perversion of the truth.*

pervert¹ /pəˈvɜːt/ *verb* [T] **1** to change a system, process, etc. in a bad way □ *memutarbelitkan*: *to pervert the course of justice* (= to deliberately prevent the police from finding out the truth about a crime) **2** to cause sb to think or behave in a way that is not moral or acceptable □ *memesongkan*

pervert² /ˈpɜːvɜːt/ *noun* [C] a person whose sexual behaviour is not thought to be natural or normal by most people □ *penyumbaleweng*

pessimism /ˈpesɪmɪzəm/ *noun* [U] **pessimism (about/over sth)** the state of expecting or believing that bad things will happen and that things will not be successful □ *sikap pesimis; pesimisme* **OPP** **optimism** ▶**pessimistic** /ˌpesɪˈmɪstɪk/ *adj* ▶**pessimistically** /-kli/ *adv*

pessimist /ˈpesɪmɪst/ *noun* [C] a person who always thinks that bad things will happen or that things will not be successful □ *orang yg pesimis* **OPP** **optimist**

pest /pest/ *noun* [C] **1** an insect or an animal that destroys plants, food, etc. □ *makhluk perosak* **2** (*informal*) a person or thing that annoys you □ *pengacau*: *That child is such a pest!*

pester /ˈpestə(r)/ *verb* [T] **pester sb (for sth); pester sb (to do sth)** to annoy sb, for example by asking them sth many times □ *mengganggu; mendesak*: *to pester somebody for money* ♦ *The kids kept pestering me to take them to the park.*

pesticide /ˈpestɪsaɪd/ *noun* [C,U] a chemical substance that is used for killing animals, especially insects, that eat food crops □ *racun perosak* ⊃ look at **insecticide**

pestle /'pesl/ *noun* [C] a small heavy tool with a round end used for crushing some foods or substances in a **mortar** (= a hard bowl) □ *antan; anak lesung; alu; penumbuk* ⊃ picture at **squeeze**

pet /pet/ *noun* [C] **1** an animal or bird that you keep in your home for pleasure rather than for food or work □ *binatang kesayangan: a pet dog/cat/hamster* ♦ *a pet shop* (= where pets are sold) **2** a person who is treated better than others because they are liked more than any others □ *kesayangan: She's the teacher's pet.*

TOPIC
Pets

Dogs, cats, rabbits, hamsters and guinea pigs are all popular pets. Goldfish are kept in tanks, and budgerigars (= a type of bird) in cages. Some people keep exotic pets, such as snakes. Some pets love being stroked, but they might scratch or bite if they are frightened. If you have a pet, you need to look after it. You should feed it, groom it and take it to the vet (= animal doctor). If an animal is very ill, the vet might have to put it down (= kill it) to stop it suffering.

petal /'petl/ *noun* [C] one of the thin soft coloured parts of a flower □ *kelopak bunga* ⊃ picture at **plant**

pet 'hate *noun* [C] something that you particularly do not like □ *kebencian:* Filling in forms is one of my pet hates.

petition /pə'tɪʃn/ *noun* [C] a written document, signed by many people, that asks a government, etc. to do or change sth □ *surat rayuan; petisyen:* More than 50 000 people signed the petition protesting about the new road. ♦ *I signed an online petition against changes to the health service.* ▶ petition *verb* [I,T]

petrified /'petrɪfaɪd/ *adj* very frightened □ *amat ketakutan*

petrol /'petrəl/ (*AmE* **gas; gasoline**) *noun* [U] the liquid that is used as fuel for vehicles such as cars and motorbikes □ *petrol* ⊃ note at **car** ⊃ look at **diesel**

petroleum /pə'trəʊliəm/ *noun* [U] mineral oil that is found under the ground or sea and is used to make petrol, plastic and other types of chemical substances □ *petroleum*

'petrol station (also **'service station;** *AmE* **gas station**) *noun* [C] a place where you can buy petrol and other things for your car □ *stesen minyak* ⊃ look at **garage**

petty /'peti/ *adj* **1** small and unimportant □ *remeh-temeh; tdk penting; kecil; ringan:* He didn't want to get involved with the petty details. ♦ *petty crime/theft* (= that is not very serious) **SYN minor 2** unkind or unpleasant to other people (for a reason that does not seem very important) □ *berperangai buruk: petty jealousy/revenge*

pew /pju:/ *noun* [C] a long wooden seat in a church □ *kerusi panjang gereja*

pewter /'pju:tə(r)/ *noun* [U] a grey metal made by mixing tin with **lead** (= a soft heavy metal), used especially in the past for making cups, dishes, etc.; objects made from this metal □ *piuter*

PG /,pi: 'dʒi:/ *abbr* (*BrE*) (used about films which are not suitable for children to watch without an adult) parental guidance □ *mengandungi adegan-adegan yg tdk sesuai utk kanak-kanak*

pH /,pi: 'eɪtʃ/ *noun* [sing] a measurement of the level of acid or **alkali** in a substance. In the pH range of 0 to 14 a reading of below 7 shows an acid and one of above 7 shows an **alkali**. □ *pH*

phantom /'fæntəm/ *noun* [C] **1** (*written*) the spirit of a dead person that is seen or heard by sb who is still living □ *hantu* ⊃ A more common word is **ghost**. **2** something that you think exists, but that is not real □ *bayang-bayangan; khayalan*

pharmaceutical /,fɑ:mə'su:tɪkl/ (*BrE also* -'sju:-/ *adj* [only *before* a noun] connected with the production of medicines and drugs □ *farmaseutikal: pharmaceutical companies*

pharmacist /'fɑ:məsɪst/ = **chemist**(1)

pharmacy /'fɑ:məsi/ *noun* (*pl* **pharmacies**) **1** [C] a shop or part of a shop where medicines and drugs are prepared and sold □ *farmasi*

> **MORE** A shop that sells medicine is also called **a chemist's (shop)** in British English or a **drugstore** in American English.

2 [U] the preparation of medicines and drugs □ *farmasi*

phase¹ /feɪz/ *noun* [C] a stage in the development of sb/sth □ *fasa; peringkat:* Julie went through a difficult phase when she started school.

phase² /feɪz/ *verb*

PHR V **phase sth in** to introduce or start using sth gradually in stages over a period of time □ *memperkenalkan sst secara berperingkat-peringkat:* The tax system was phased in over two years.

phase sth out to stop using sth gradually in stages over a period of time □ *menghentikan penggunaan sst secara berperingkat-peringkat:* The older machines are gradually being phased out and replaced by new ones.

PhD /,pi: eɪtʃ 'di:/ *abbr* Doctor of Philosophy; an advanced university degree that you receive when you complete a piece of research into a special subject □ *Ph.D (Doktor Falsafah): She has a PhD in History.*

pheasant /'feznt/ *noun* [C] (*pl* **pheasants** *or* **pheasant**) a type of bird with a long tail. The males have brightly coloured feathers. Pheasants are often shot for sport and eaten. □ *burung kuang bayas*

phenomenal /fəˈnɒmɪnl/ adj very great or impressive □ *luar biasa; sangat besar, mengagumkan, dsb*: *phenomenal success* ▶**phenomenally** /-nəli/ adv

phenomenon /fəˈnɒmɪnən/ noun [C] (pl **phenomena** /-mə/) a fact or an event in nature or society, especially one that is not fully understood □ *fenomena*: *Acid rain is not a natural phenomenon. It is caused by pollution.*

phew /fjuː/ exclam a sound which you make to show that you are hot, tired or happy that sth bad did not happen or has finished □ *hui*: *Phew, it's hot!* ◆ *Phew, I'm glad that interview's over!*

philanthropist /fɪˈlænθrəpɪst/ noun [C] a rich person who helps the poor and those in need, especially by giving money □ *dermawan*

philanthropy /fɪˈlænθrəpi/ noun [U] the practice of helping the poor and those in need, especially by giving money □ *sifat dermawan; kedermawanan; kemurahan hati* ▶**philanthropic** /ˌfɪlənˈθrɒpɪk/ adj: *philanthropic work*

philosopher /fəˈlɒsəfə(r)/ noun [C] a person who has developed a set of ideas and beliefs about the meaning of life □ *ahli falsafah*: *the Greek philosopher Aristotle*

philosophical /ˌfɪləˈsɒfɪkl/ (also **philosophic**) adj **1** connected with **philosophy** □ *(berkenaan dgn) falsafah*: *a philosophical debate* **2** philosophical (about sth) staying calm and not getting upset or worried about sth bad that happens □ *berfalsafah; tenang; tabah*: *He is quite philosophical about failing the exam and says he will try again next year.* ▶**philosophically** /-kli/ adv

philosophy /fəˈlɒsəfi/ noun (pl **philosophies**) **1** [U] the study of ideas and beliefs about the meaning of life □ *falsafah*: *a degree in philosophy* **2** [C] a set of beliefs that tries to explain the meaning of life or give rules about how to behave □ *falsafah; prinsip/pegangan hidup*: *Her philosophy is 'If a job's worth doing, it's worth doing well'.*

phishing /ˈfɪʃɪŋ/ noun [U] the activity of tricking people by getting them to give their identity, bank account numbers, etc. over the Internet or by email, and then using these to steal money from them □ *kegiatan memancing data* ⊃ note at **cybercrime**

phlegm /flem/ noun [U] the thick substance that is produced in your nose and throat when you have a cold □ *hingus; kahak*

phlegmatic /flegˈmætɪk/ adj (formal) not easily made angry or upset; calm □ *tenang*

phobia /ˈfəʊbiə/ noun [C] a very strong fear or hatred that you cannot explain □ *fobia; rasa takut/benci*: *She has a phobia about flying.* ◆ *arachnophobia* (= fear of spiders)

phone /fəʊn/ noun (informal) **1** [U] = **telephone**(1): *a phone conversation* ◆ *You can book the tickets by phone/over the phone.* **2** [C] = **telephone**(2): *The phone is ringing—could you answer it?* ◆ *Could everyone switch off their phones before we start?* ⊃ note at **telephone**, **mobile phone**, **smartphone**
IDM on the phone/telephone 1 using the telephone □ *sedang bercakap di telefon*: *He's been on the phone to Kate for more than an hour.* **2** having a phone in your home □ *ada telefon*: *They're not on the phone at their holiday cottage.*
▶**phone** verb [I,T]: *Did anybody phone while I was out?* ◆ *Could you phone the restaurant and book a table?* ◆ *I'm busy at the moment, so can I phone you back later?* **SYN** ring, call

ˈ**phone book** = telephone directory

ˈ**phone box** = telephone box

ˈ**phone call** = call²(1)

phonecard /ˈfəʊnkɑːd/ noun [C] a small plastic card that you can use in some telephones instead of money □ *kad telefon*

ˈ**phone hacking** noun [U] the practice of secretly looking at or listening to information on sb else's mobile phone □ *penggodam telefon*: *The journalist admitted five charges of phone hacking while working for the paper.* ◆ *the phone hacking scandal*

ˈ**phone-in** noun [C] a radio or TV programme during which you can ask a question or give your opinion by telephone □ *rancangan melalui telefon*

phonetic /fəˈnetɪk/ adj **1** (used about spelling) having a close relationship with the sounds represented □ *fonetik*: *Spanish spelling is phonetic, unlike English spelling.* **2** connected with the sounds of human speech; using special symbols to represent these sounds □ *fonetik*: *the phonetic alphabet* ▶**phonetically** /-kli/ adv

phonetics /fəˈnetɪks/ noun [U] the study of the sounds of human speech □ *(ilmu) fonetik*

phoney (AmE **phony**) /ˈfəʊni/ adj (informal) (**phonier; phoniest**) not real □ *palsu; dibuat-buat*: *She spoke with a phoney Russian accent.* **SYN** fake ▶**phoney** (AmE **phony**) noun [C]

photo /ˈfəʊtəʊ/ (pl **photos** /-təʊz/) = **photograph**: *Shall I take your photo?* ◆ *a photo album*

photocopier /ˈfəʊtəʊkɒpiə(r)/ (especially AmE **copier**) noun [C] a machine that makes copies of documents by photographing them □ *mesin fotokopi*

photocopy /ˈfəʊtəʊkɒpi/ noun [C] (pl **photocopies**) a copy of a document, a page in a book, etc. that is made by a **photocopier** □ *fotokopi* **SYN** Xerox™ ⊃ look at **copy** ▶**photocopy** verb (also **copy**) [I,T] (**photocopying; photocopies**; pt, pp **photocopied**)

photograph /ˈfəʊtəgrɑːf/ (also **photo**) noun [C] a picture that is taken with a camera □ *gambar foto; gambar*: *to take a photograph* ◆ *She looks younger in real life than she did in the photograph.* ⊃ note at **camera** ⊃ look at **negative**, **slide** ▶**photograph** verb [T]

photographer /fəˈtɒɡrəfə(r)/ noun [C] a person who takes photographs □ *jurugambar*: *a fashion/wildlife photographer* ➔ look at **cameraman**

photographic /ˌfəʊtəˈɡræfɪk/ adj connected with photographs or **photography** □ *(berkaitan dgn) gambar foto/fotografi*

photography /fəˈtɒɡrəfi/ noun [U] the skill or process of taking photographs □ *fotografi*: *wildlife photography* ➔ picture on **page P3**

photosynthesis /ˌfəʊtəʊˈsɪnθəsɪs/ noun [U] the process by which green plants turn **carbon dioxide** (= a gas) and water into food using energy obtained from light from the sun □ *fotosintesis*

phrasal verb /ˌfreɪzl ˈvɜːb/ noun [C] a verb that is combined with an adverb or a preposition to give a new meaning, such as 'look after' or 'put off' □ *frasa kk* ➔ look at **verb**

phrase¹ /freɪz/ noun [C] a group of words that are used together. A phrase does not contain a full verb □ *frasa*: *'First of all' and 'a bar of chocolate' are phrases.* ➔ look at **sentence**

phrase² /freɪz/ verb [T] to express sth in a particular way □ *mengungkapkan*: *The statement was phrased so that it would offend no one.*

ˈphrase book noun [C] a book that gives common words and useful phrases in a foreign language. People often use phrase books when they travel to another country whose language they do not know. □ *buku ungkapan*

physical /ˈfɪzɪkl/ adj 1 connected with your body rather than your mind □ *jasmani; fizikal*: *physical fitness/strength/disabilities* 2 [only before a noun] connected with real things that you can touch, or with the laws of nature □ *fizikal; alamiah*: *physical geography* (= the natural features on the face of the earth) 3 [only before a noun] connected with physics □ *(berkenaan dgn) fizik*: *physical chemistry/laws* ▸**physically** /-kli/ adv: *to be physically fit* ♦ *It will be physically impossible to get to London before ten.*

ˌphysical ˈtherapy (*AmE*) = **physiotherapy**

physician /fɪˈzɪʃn/ (*especially AmE formal*) = **doctor¹** (1)

physicist /ˈfɪzɪsɪst/ noun [C] a person who studies or is an expert in physics □ *ahli fizik*

physics /ˈfɪzɪks/ noun [U] the scientific study of natural forces such as light, sound, heat, electricity, pressure, etc. □ *fizik* ➔ note at **science**: *the laws of physics* ♦ *a school physics department*

physiology /ˌfɪziˈɒlədʒi/ noun [U] 1 the scientific study of the normal functions of living things □ *fisiologi*: *the department of anatomy and physiology* 2 the way in which a particular living thing functions □ *fisiologi*: *the physiology of the horse* ♦ *plant physiology* ▸**physiological** /ˌfɪziəˈlɒdʒɪkl/ adj: *the physiological effect of space travel* ▸**physiologically** /-kli/ adv

physiotherapist /ˌfɪziəʊˈθerəpɪst/ noun [C] a person who is trained to use **physiotherapy** □ *ahli fisioterapi*

physiotherapy /ˌfɪziəʊˈθerəpi/ (*AmE* ˌphysical ˈtherapy) noun [U] the treatment of disease or injury by exercise, light, heat, **massage** (= rubbing the muscles), etc. □ *fisioterapi*

physique /fɪˈziːk/ noun [C] the size and shape of sb's body □ *susuk tubuh*: *a strong muscular physique* SYN **build**

pianist /ˈpiənɪst/ noun [C] a person who plays the piano □ *pemain piano*

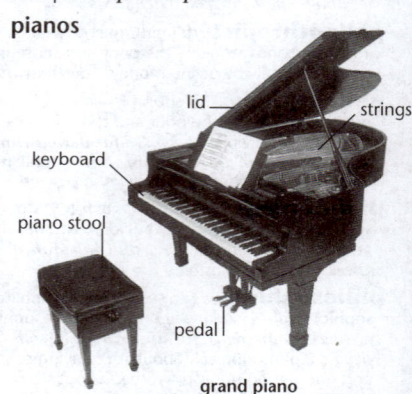

pianos

[illustration of grand piano with labels: lid, strings, keyboard, piano stool, pedal]

grand piano

[illustration of upright piano]

upright piano

piano /piˈænəʊ/ noun [C] (*pl* **pianos** /-nəʊz/) a large musical instrument that you play by pressing down black and white keys □ *piano*: *an upright piano* ♦ *a grand piano*

piccolo /ˈpɪkələʊ/ noun [C] (*pl* **piccolos**) a small **flute** (= a musical instrument that you hold sideways and blow into) that plays high notes □ *pikolo* ➔ picture at **music**

pick¹ /pɪk/ verb [T] 1 to choose sb/sth from a group of people or things □ *memilih; dipilih*: *They picked Giles as their captain.* ♦ *Have I picked a bad time to visit?* ➔ look at **select** 2 to take a flower, fruit or vegetable from the place where it is growing □ *memetik*: *to pick flowers/grapes/cotton* 3 to remove a small piece or pieces of sth with your fingers □ *membuang; mengorek; mengutip*: *Don't pick your nose!* ♦ *She picked a hair off her jacket.*

IDM **have a bone to pick with sb** ➔ **bone¹**
pick and choose to choose only the things that you like or want very much □ *memilih-milih*
pick a fight (with sb) to start a fight with sb deliberately □ *mencari pasal utk bergaduh (dgn sso)*
pick a lock to open a lock without using a key □ *mencungkil-cungkil kunci (utk membukanya tanpa anak kunci)*
pick sb's pocket to steal money, etc. from sb's pocket or bag □ *menyeluk saku sso*
pick your way across, over, through, etc. sth to walk carefully, choosing the best places to put your feet □ *melangkah dgn berhati-hati*: *She picked her way over the rough ground.*

PHR V **pick at sth** 1 to eat only small amounts of food because you are not hungry □ *makan hendak tak hendak saja* 2 to touch sth many times with your fingers □ *menarik-narik sst; mengutil*
pick on sb to behave unfairly or in a cruel way towards sb □ *berlaku tdk adil atau zalim terhadap sso*
pick sb/sth out to choose or recognize sb/sth from a number of people or things; identify □ *memilih atau mengecam sso/sst*: *I immediately picked Jean out in the photo.*
pick up to become better; to improve □ *bertambah baik*
pick up speed to get faster □ *bertambah laju*
pick sb up to collect sb, in a car, etc. □ *menjemput atau mengambil sso*: *We've ordered a taxi to pick us up at ten.*
pick sb/sth up to take hold of and lift sb/sth □ *mengangkat sso/sst*: *Lucy picked up the child and gave him a cuddle.*
pick sth up 1 to learn sth without formal lessons □ *belajar*: *Joe picked up a few words of Spanish on holiday.* 2 to go and get sth; to collect sth □ *mengambil sst*: *I have to pick up my jacket from the cleaner's.* 3 to get or find sth □ *menjumpai sst*: *I picked up this book at the market.* 4 to receive an electronic signal, sound or picture □ *dpt menerima siaran*: *We were able to pick up the BBC World Service in Delhi.*

pick² /pɪk/ *noun* 1 [sing] the one that you choose; your choice □ *pilihan*: *You can have whichever cake you like. Take your pick.* 2 [sing] the best of a group □ *terbaik*: *You can see the pick of the new films at this year's festival.* 3 = **pickaxe** 4 = **plectrum**

pickaxe /ˈpɪkæks/ (AmE **pickax**, **pick**) *noun* [C] a tool that consists of a curved iron bar with sharp points at both ends, fixed onto a wooden handle. Pickaxes are used for breaking stones or hard ground. □ *beliung*

picket /ˈpɪkɪt/ *noun* [C] a worker or group of workers who stand outside the entrance to a building to protest about sth, especially in order to stop people entering a factory, etc. during a strike □ *orang yg berpiket* ▶ **picket** *verb* [I,T]

pickle /ˈpɪkl/ *noun* 1 [C, usually pl] a vegetable that is cooked and put in salt water or **vinegar** (= a liquid with a strong sharp taste), served cold with meat, salads, etc. □ *jeruk; acar* 2 [U] (BrE) a cold thick sauce made from fruit and vegetables, that is served with meat, cheese, etc. □ *jeruk; acar*: *a cheese and pickle sandwich* ▶ **pickle** *verb* [T]: *pickled onions*

pickpocket /ˈpɪkpɒkɪt/ *noun* [C] a person who steals things from other people's pockets or bags in public places □ *penyeluk saku*

pickup /ˈpɪkʌp/ (also **ˈpickup truck**) *noun* [C] a type of vehicle that has an open part with low sides at the back □ *lori pikap*

picky /ˈpɪki/ *adj* (*informal*) (used about a person) liking only certain things and difficult to please □ *cerewet* ➔ look at **fussy**

picnic /ˈpɪknɪk/ *noun* [C] a meal that you take with you to eat outdoors □ *perkelahan; berkelah*: *We had a picnic on the beach.* ➔ note at **meal** ▶ **picnic** *verb* [I] (**picnicking**; **picnicked**)

pictorial /pɪkˈtɔːriəl/ *adj* expressed in pictures □ *dlm bentuk gambar*: *pictorial representations of objects*

picture¹ /ˈpɪktʃə(r)/ *noun* [C] 1 a painting, drawing or photograph □ *gambar; lukisan*: *Who painted the picture in the hall?* ◆ *The teacher asked us to* **draw a picture** *of our families.* ◆ *Have you got any pictures of your trip?* ➔ picture on **page P8** 2 an image on a TV screen □ *gambar*: *They showed pictures of the crash on the news.* 3 a description of sth that gives you a good idea of what it is like □ *gambaran*: *The police are trying to build up a picture of exactly what happened.*

picture² /ˈpɪktʃə(r)/ *verb* [T] 1 **picture sb/sth (as sth)** to imagine sb/sth in your mind □ *membayangkan*: *I can't picture Ivan as a father.* 2 [usually passive] to show sb/sth in a photograph or picture □ *digambarkan; dilukis; bergambar*: *She is pictured here with her parents.*

picturesque /ˌpɪktʃəˈresk/ *adj* (usually used about an old building or place) attractive □ *cantik; menarik*: *a picturesque fishing village*

pie /paɪ/ *noun* [C,U] meat, vegetables or fruit baked in a dish with **pastry** (= a mixture of flour, fat and water) on the bottom, sides and top □ *pai*: *apple pie* ◆ *meat pie* ➔ picture on **page P16**

piece¹ /piːs/ *noun* [C]
▶ SEPARATE AMOUNT 1 an amount or example of sth □ *helai; keping; buah; satu; (kadangkala tdk diterjemahkan)*: *a piece of paper* ◆ *a piece of furniture* ◆ *a good piece of work* ◆ *a piece of information/advice/news*
▶ PART OF STH 2 one of the parts that sth is made of □ *bahagian*: *We'll have to* **take** *the engine to* **pieces** *to find the problem.* 3 one of the parts into which sth breaks □ *serpihan*: *The plate fell to the floor and smashed* **to pieces**. ◆ *The vase lay in* **pieces** *on the floor.*
▶ ART, MUSIC ETC. 4 a single work of art, music, etc. □ *karya; lagu*: *He played a piece by Chopin.*
▶ NEWS ARTICLE 5 **a piece (on/about sb/sth)** an article in a newspaper or magazine □ *rencana*;

piece → pile

makalah: *There's a good piece on China in today's paper.*
▶ COIN **6** a coin of the value mentioned □ *duit syiling*: *a fifty-pence piece*
▶ IN GAMES **7** one of the small objects that you use when you are playing games such as **chess** □ *buah*

IDM **bits and pieces** ⊃ **bit¹**
give sb a piece of your mind to speak to sb angrily because of sth they have done □ *memarahi sso*
go to pieces to be no longer able to work or behave normally because of a difficult situation □ *patah hati hingga tdk bersemangat utk bekerja, dsb*: *When his wife died he seemed to go to pieces.*
in one piece not broken or injured □ *selamat; tdk cedera, dsb*: *I've only been on a motorbike once, and I was just glad to get home in one piece.*
a piece of cake (*informal*) something that is very easy □ *kacang uncit*

piece² /piːs/ *verb*
PHR V **piece sth together 1** to discover the truth about sth from different pieces of information □ *mengetahui hal sebenar drpd maklumat yg ada*: *Detectives are trying to piece together the last few days of the man's life.* **2** to sth together from several pieces □ *mencantumkan; memasang*

piecemeal /ˈpiːsmiːl/ *adj, adv* (done or happening) a little at a time □ *sedikit demi sedikit; secara uncit*

ˈpie chart *noun* [C] a diagram consisting of a circle divided into parts to show the size of particular parts in relation to the whole □ *carta pai* ⊃ picture at **graph**

pier

pier /pɪə(r)/ *noun* [C] **1** a large wooden or metal structure that is built out into the sea in holiday towns, where people can walk □ *jeti* **2** a large wooden or metal structure that is built out into the sea from the land. Boats can stop at **piers** so that people or goods can be taken on or off. □ *tambangan; jeti*

pierce /pɪəs/ *verb* **1** [T] to make a hole in sth with a sharp point □ *menebuk; menindik*: *I'm going to* **have my ears pierced**. **2** [I,T] **pierce (through/into) sth** to manage to go through or into sth □ *menembusi*: *A scream pierced the air.*

piercing¹ /ˈpɪəsɪŋ/ *adj* **1** (used about sb's eyes or a look) seeming to know what you are thinking □ *tajam* **2** (used about the wind, pain, a loud noise, etc.) strong and unpleasant □ *menusuk; nyaring*

piercing² /ˈpɪəsɪŋ/ *noun* [U,C] the act of making holes in parts of the body as a decoration; a hole that is made □ *bertindik; tindik*: *body piercing* ♦ *Her face is covered in piercings.*

piety /ˈpaɪəti/ *noun* [U] a way of behaving that shows a deep respect for God and religion □ *kewarakan; sifat warak* ⊃ *adjective* **pious**

pig¹ /pɪɡ/ *noun* [C] **1** an animal with pink, black or brown skin, short legs, a wide nose and a curly tail, and that is kept on farms for **pork** (= its meat) □ *babi; khinzir*: *a pig farmer* ⊃ note at **meat**

> **MORE** **Pig** is often used for both males and females. A male pig is a **boar**, a female pig is a **sow** and a young pig is a **piglet**. When they make a noise, piglets **squeal** and pigs **grunt**.

2 (*informal*) an unpleasant person or a person who eats too much □ *babi; pelahap*: *She* **made a pig of herself** *with the ice cream* (= ate too much).

pig² /pɪɡ/ *verb* [T] (**pigging**; **pigged**) (*informal*) **pig yourself** to eat too much □ *melahap*
PHR V **pig out (on sth)** (*informal*) to eat too much of sth □ *melahap (sst)*

pigeon /ˈpɪdʒɪn/ *noun* [C] a fat grey bird that often lives in towns □ *burung merpati*

pigeonhole /ˈpɪdʒɪnhəʊl/ *noun* [C] one of a set of small open boxes that are used for putting papers or letters in □ *petak surat*

piggyback /ˈpɪɡibæk/ *noun* [C] the way of carrying sb, especially a child, on your back □ *dukung atas belakang; kokka*: *to give somebody a piggyback*

ˈpiggy bank *noun* [C] a small box, often shaped like a pig, that children save money in □ *tabung duit*

ˌpig-ˈheaded *adj* (*informal*) not prepared to change your mind or say that you are wrong □ *kepala batu* ⊃ look at **stubborn, obstinate**

piglet /ˈpɪɡlət/ *noun* [C] a young pig □ *anak babi/khinzir*

pigment /ˈpɪɡmənt/ *noun* [C,U] a substance that gives colour to things □ *pigmen*: *The colour of your skin depends on the amount of pigment in it.*

pigsty /ˈpɪɡstaɪ/ (*also* **sty**; *AmE* **pigpen** /ˈpɪɡpen/) *noun* [C] (*pl* **pigsties**) a small building where pigs are kept □ *kandang babi/khinzir*

pigtail /ˈpɪɡteɪl/ (*AmE* **braid**) *noun* [C] hair that is tied together in one or two lengths made by **plaiting** (= crossing three pieces of hair over and under each other) □ *tocang* ⊃ picture at **hair**

pile¹ /paɪl/ *noun* [C] **1** a number of things lying on top of each other, or an amount of sth lying in a mass □ *timbunan*: *a pile of books/sand* ♦ *He put the coins in neat piles.* ♦ *She threw the clothes in a pile on the floor.*

[I] **intransitive**, a verb which has no object: *He laughed.*   [T] **transitive**, a verb which has an object: *He ate an apple.*

pile → pinafore

HELP **Pile** or **heap**? A **pile** may be tidy or untidy. A **heap** is always untidy.

2 [usually plural] (*informal*) **piles of sth** a lot of sth □ *bertimbun-timbun*: *I've got piles of work to do this evening.*

pile² /paɪl/ *verb* [T] **1 pile sth (up)** to put things one on top of the other to form a pile □ *menimbunkan; melonggokkan*: *We piled the boxes in the corner.* **2 pile A on(to) B; pile B with A** to put a lot of sth on top of sth □ *melonggokkan*: *She piled the papers on the desk.* ♦ *The desk was piled with papers.*

PHR V **pile into, out of, off, etc. sth** (*informal*) to go into, out of, off, etc. sth quickly and all at the same time □ *berasak-asak masuk, naik, keluar, turun, dsb sst*: *The children piled onto the train.*

pile up (used about sth bad) to increase in quantity □ *semakin menimbun*: *Our problems are really piling up.*

piles /paɪlz/ = **haemorrhoids**

'pile-up *noun* [C] a crash that involves several cars, etc. □ *perlanggaran bertindan-tindih*

pilgrim /'pɪlgrɪm/ *noun* [C] a person who travels a long way to visit a religious place □ *penziarah ke tempat suci; jemaah (haji)*

pilgrimage /'pɪlgrɪmɪdʒ/ *noun* [C,U] a long journey that a person makes to visit a religious place □ *ziarah ke tempat suci; naik haji*

pill /pɪl/ *noun* **1** [C] a small round piece of medicine that you swallow □ *pil*: *Take one pill, three times a day after meals.* ♦ *a sleeping pill* ➔ look at **tablet** ➔ picture at **medicine** **2 the pill; the Pill** [sing] a **pill** that some women take regularly so that they do not become pregnant □ *pil perancang keluarga*: *She is on the pill.*

pillar /'pɪlə(r)/ *noun* [C] **1** a column of stone, wood or metal that is used for supporting part of a building □ *tiang* **2** a person who has a strong character and is important to sb/sth □ *tonggak; penunjang*: *Dave was a pillar of strength to his sister when she was ill.*

'pillar box *noun* [C] (*old-fashioned*) (in Britain) a tall round red box in a public place into which you can post letters, which are then collected by sb from the post office □ *peti surat* ➔ look at **postbox, letter box**

pillion /'pɪliən/ *noun* [C] a seat for a passenger behind the driver on a motorbike □ *tempat duduk pembonceng* ▶ **pillion** *adv*: *to ride pillion on a motorbike*

pillow /'pɪləʊ/ *noun* [C] a large cloth bag filled with soft material that you put under your head when you are in bed □ *bantal* ➔ picture at **bed**

pillowcase /'pɪləʊkeɪs/ *noun* [C] a thin soft cover for a **pillow** □ *sarung bantal*

pilot¹ /'paɪlət/ *noun* [C] a person who flies an aircraft □ *juruterbang*: *an airline pilot* ➔ picture on **page P2**

pilot² /'paɪlət/ *verb* [T] **1** to fly an aircraft or guide a ship □ *memandu; mengemudi* **2** to lead sb/sth through a difficult situation □ *memandu; membimbing*: *The booklet pilots you through the process of starting your own business.* **3** to test a new product, idea, etc. that will be used by everyone □ *merintiskan; menguji*: *The new exam is being piloted in schools in Italy.*

pilot³ /'paɪlət/ *adj* [only before a noun] done as an experiment or to test sth that will be used by everyone □ *rintis*: *The pilot scheme will run for six months.*

pimple /'pɪmpl/ *noun* [C] a small spot on your skin □ *jerawat* ➔ look at **goose pimples**

PIN /pɪn/ (also **'PIN number**) *noun* [C, usually sing] **personal identification number**; a number given to you, for example by a bank, so that you can use a plastic card to take out money from a **cash machine** (= a special machine in or outside a bank) □ *nombor PIN*: *I've forgotten my PIN.*

pin¹ /pɪn/ *noun* [C] **1** a short thin piece of metal with a round head at one end and a sharp point at the other. Pins are used for fastening together pieces of cloth, paper, etc. □ *pin; jarum peniti; penyemat* **2** a thin piece of wood or metal that is used for a particular purpose □ *pin; cemat*: *a hairpin* ♦ *a two-pin plug* ➔ picture at **plug**

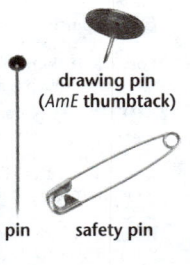

drawing pin (*AmE* thumbtack)

pin   safety pin

pin² /pɪn/ *verb* [T] (**pinning**; **pinned**) **1 pin sth to/ on sth; pin sth together** to fasten sth with a pin or pins □ *mengepin; menyemat; melekatkan*: *Could you pin this notice on the board, please?* **2 pin sb/sth against, to, under, etc. sth** to make sb/sth unable to move by holding or pressing down on them or it □ *memegang; menghimpit; menindih; tertindih; tersepit*: *They pinned him against a wall and stole his wallet.* ♦ *He was pinned under the fallen tree.*

IDM **pin (all) your hopes on sb/sth** to believe completely that sb/sth will help you or will succeed □ *meletakkan (sepenuh) harapan pd sso/sst*

PHR V **pin sb down** **1** to hold sb so they cannot move □ *memegang, menghimpit, menindih, dsb sso/sst* **2** to force sb to decide sth or to say exactly what they are going to do □ *mendesak, memaksa, dsb sso*: *Can you pin her down to what time she'll be coming?*

pin sth down to describe or explain exactly what sth is □ *menyatakan atau menjelaskan dgn pasti*

pinafore /'pɪnəfɔː(r)/ *noun* [C] (*especially BrE*) a loose dress with no sleeves, usually worn over other clothes □ *pinafor*

pincer /ˈpɪnsə(r)/ *noun* **1 pincers** [pl] a tool made of two crossed pieces of metal that is used for holding things, pulling nails out of wood, etc. □ *ragum; kakaktua* **2** [C] one of the two sharp, curved front legs of some **shellfish** (= creatures with shells that live in water) that are used for holding things □ *sepit* ➲ picture on **page P13**

pinch¹ /pɪntʃ/ *verb* **1** [T] to hold a piece of sb's skin tightly between your thumb and first finger, especially in order to hurt them □ *mencubit*: *Paul pinched his brother and made him cry.* **2** [I,T] to hold sth too tight, often causing pain □ *menyepit; menekan*: *I've got a pinched nerve in my neck.* **3** [T] (*informal*) to steal □ *mencuri*: *Who's pinched my pen?*

pinch

PHR V **pinch in** (on some small computer devices) to make the screen smaller using your finger and thumb □ *mengecilkan* OPP **zoom** ➲ note at **touch screen**

pinch² /pɪntʃ/ *noun* [C] **1** the holding of sb's skin tightly between your finger and thumb □ *cubitan*: *She gave him a little pinch on the arm.* **2** the amount of sth that you can pick up with your thumb and first finger □ *secubit*: *a pinch of salt*

IDM **at a pinch** used to say that sth can be done if it is really necessary □ *kalau terpaksa/terdesak*: *We can fit six people round this table at a pinch.*

take sth with a pinch of salt to think that sth is probably not true or accurate □ *mewahamkan; meragui*

pinched /pɪntʃt/ *adj* (used about sb's face) thin and pale because of illness or cold □ *cengkung*

pine¹ /paɪn/ *noun* **1** [C] (also ˈpine tree) a tall tree that has **needles** (= thin pointed leaves) □ *pohon pain*

MORE Trees, such as the **pine**, that do not lose their leaves in winter are called **evergreens**.

2 [U] the wood from **pine** trees, often used for making furniture □ *kayu pain*: *a pine table*

pine² /paɪn/ *verb* [I] **pine (for sb/sth)** to be very unhappy because sb has died or gone away □ *rindu; merindui*: *She pined for months after he'd gone.*

pineapple /ˈpaɪnæpl/ *noun* [C,U] a large sweet fruit that is yellow inside and has a thick brown skin with sharp points. **Pineapples** grow in hot countries. □ *nanas* ➲ picture on **page P14**

ˈ**pine tree** = **pine¹**(1)

ping /pɪŋ/ *noun* [C] a short high noise that is made by a small bell or by a metal object hitting against sth □ *bunyi denting*: *The lift went ping and the doors opened.* ▶ **ping** *verb* [I]

ˈ**ping-pong** (*informal*) = **table tennis**

pink /pɪŋk/ *adj, noun* [U] (of) a pale red colour □ *merah samar*: *She was dressed in pink.*

pinnacle /ˈpɪnəkl/ *noun* [C] **1** the most important or successful part of sth □ *puncak; mercu; kemuncak*: *Celia is at the pinnacle of her career.* **2** a high pointed rock on a mountain □ *puncak; mercu*

pinpoint /ˈpɪnpɔɪnt/ *verb* [T] **1** to find the exact position of sth □ *menunjukkan dgn tepat*: *to pinpoint a place on the map* **2** to describe or explain exactly what sth is □ *mengenal pasti; memastikan*: *First we have to pinpoint the cause of the failure.*

ˌ**pins and ˈneedles** *noun* [U] a strange, sometimes painful feeling that you get in a part of your body after it has been in one position for too long and when the blood is returning to it □ *(rasa) semut-semut*

pint /paɪnt/ *noun* [C] **1** (*abbr* **pt**) a measure of liquid; 0.57 of a litre □ *pain*: *a pint of milk*

MORE There are **8 pints** in a gallon. An American pint is 0.47 of a litre.

ⓘ For more information about measurements, look at the section on using numbers at the back of this dictionary. **2** (*BrE informal*) a pint of beer □ *satu pain bir*: *We had a pint and a sandwich at the local pub.*

ˈ**pin-up** *noun* [C] (*informal*) a picture of an attractive person, made to be put on a wall; a person who appears in these pictures □ *gambar tempel; model gambar tempel*

pioneer /ˌpaɪəˈnɪə(r)/ *noun* [C] **1 a pioneer (in/of sth)** a person who is one of the first to develop an area of human knowledge, culture, etc. □ *perintis; pelopor*: *Yuri Gagarin was one of the pioneers of space exploration.* **2** a person who is one of the first to go and live in a particular area □ *peneroka*: *the pioneers of the American West* ▶ **pioneer** *verb* [T]: *a technique pioneered in the US*

pious /ˈpaɪəs/ *adj* having or showing a deep belief in religion □ *warak* ▶ **piously** *adv* ➲ *noun* **piety**

pip /pɪp/ *noun* [C] (*BrE*) the small seed of an apple, a lemon, an orange, etc. □ *biji* ➲ picture on **page P14**

pipe¹ /paɪp/ *noun* [C] **1** a tube that carries gas or liquid □ *paip*: *a gas/water pipe* **2** a tube with a small bowl at one end that is used for smoking **tobacco** (= the dried leaves used for making cigarettes) □ *paip*: *to smoke a pipe* **3** a simple musical instrument that consists of a tube with holes in it. You blow into it to play it. □ *seruling; pipa*

pipe² /paɪp/ *verb* [T] to carry liquid or gas in pipes □ *menyalurkan melalui paip*: *Water is piped to all the houses in the town.*

PHR V **pipe up** (*informal*) to suddenly say sth □ *tiba-tiba bersuara*: *Suddenly Shirin piped up with a question.*

pipeline /ˈpaɪplaɪn/ *noun* [C] a line of pipes that are used for carrying liquid or gas over a long distance □ *talian paip*
IDM **in the pipeline** being planned or prepared □ *sedang dirancang atau disediakan*

piper /ˈpaɪpə(r)/ *noun* [C] a person who plays music on a pipe, or who plays the **bagpipes** (= a typically Scottish musical instrument) □ *pemain seruling; pemain begpaip*

piracy /ˈpaɪrəsi/ *noun* [U] **1** the crime of attacking ships in order to steal from them □ *kegiatan melanun* **2** the illegal copying of books, CDs, etc. □ *cetak rompak*

pirate¹ /ˈpaɪrət/ *noun* [C] **1** a criminal who attacks ships in order to steal from them □ *lanun* **2** a person who copies books, CDs, computer programs, etc. in order to sell them illegally □ *pencetak rompak*

pirate² /ˈpaɪrət/ *verb* [T] to make an illegal copy of a book, CD, etc. in order to sell it □ *mencetak rompak*

Pisces /ˈpaɪsiːz/ *noun* [C,U] the 12th sign of the **zodiac** (= 12 signs which represent the positions of the sun, moon and planets), the Fishes; a person born under this sign □ *Pisces*: *I'm a Pisces.* ⊃ picture at **zodiac**

pistachio /pɪˈstæʃiəʊ; -ˈstɑːʃiəʊ/ *noun* [C] (*pl* **pistachios**) (also **piˈstachio nut**) the small green nut of an Asian tree □ *kacang pistasio*

pistol /ˈpɪstl/ *noun* [C] a small gun that you hold in one hand □ *pistol* ⊃ note at **gun**

piston /ˈpɪstən/ *noun* [C] a piece of metal in an engine, etc. that fits tightly inside a metal tube. The piston is moved up and down inside the tube and causes other parts of the engine to move. □ *omboh*

pit¹ /pɪt/ *noun* **1** [C] a large hole that is made in the ground □ *lubang*: *They dug a large pit to bury the dead animals.* **2** [C] = **coal mine 3 the pits** [pl] the place on a motor racing track where cars stop for fuel, new tyres, etc. during a race □ *ruang perhentian* **4** [C] (*AmE*) = **stone**(4)
IDM **be the pits** (*informal*) to be very bad □ *teruk*: *The food in that restaurant is the pits!*

pit² /pɪt/ *verb* [T] (**pitting**; **pitted**) to make small holes in the surface of sth □ *melubang-lubangkan; berlubang-lubang*: *The front of the building was pitted with bullet marks.*
PHR V **pit A against B** to test one person or thing against another in a fight or competition □ *mengadukan; beradu; melawan*: *The two strongest teams were pitted against each other in the final.*

pitch¹ /pɪtʃ/ *noun* **1** [C] (*BrE*) a special area of ground where you play certain sports □ *padang*: *a football/hockey/cricket pitch* ⊃ look at **court**, **field 2** [sing] the strength or level of feelings, activity, etc. □ *tahap; aras*: *The children's excitement almost reached fever pitch.* **3** [U] how high or low a sound is, especially a musical note □ *nada; pic*: *I think somebody's singing off pitch.* **4** [C] talk or arguments used by sb who is trying to sell sth or persuade sb to do sth □ *kelentong*: *a sales pitch* ♦ *to make a pitch for something*

pitch² /pɪtʃ/ *verb* **1** [I,T] to throw; to be thrown □ *membaling; melempar*: *Doug pitched his empty can into the bushes.* **2** [T] to set sth at a particular level □ *melaraskan; menentukan tahap penyampaian (dsb) sesuai utk golongan tertentu; bernada*: *The talk was pitched at people with far more experience than me.* ♦ *a high-pitched voice* **3** [T] **pitch sth (at sb)** to try to sell a product to a particular group of people or in a particular way □ *menujukan; ditujukan; dilaraskan*: *This new breakfast cereal is being pitched at kids.* **4** [T] to put up a tent or tents □ *mendirikan khemah*: *We could pitch our tents in that field.*
PHR V **pitch in** (*informal*) to join in and work together with other people □ *turut sama*: *Everybody pitched in to clear up the flood damage.*

ˌpitch-ˈblack *adj* completely dark; with no light at all □ *gelap-gelita*

pitcher /ˈpɪtʃə(r)/ *noun* [C] **1** a large container for holding and pouring liquids □ *kendi; bekas utk mengisi cecair* ⊃ picture at **jug 2** (in the sport of **baseball**) the player who throws the ball to a player from the other team, who tries to hit it □ *pembaling* **3** (*AmE*) = **jug**

piteous /ˈpɪtiəs/ *adj* (*formal*) that makes you feel pity or sadness □ *menimbulkan rasa belas; sayu* ▶ **piteously** *adv*

pitfall /ˈpɪtfɔːl/ *noun* [C] a danger or difficulty, especially one that is hidden or not obvious □ *bahaya atau kesukaran yg tdk diduga*

pith /pɪθ/ *noun* [U] the white substance inside the skin of an orange, lemon, etc. □ *kulit dlm*

pithy /ˈpɪθi/ *adj* (**pithier**; **pithiest**) (used about a comment, piece of writing, etc.) short but expressed in a clear, direct way □ *bernas*: *a pithy comment*

pitiful /ˈpɪtɪfl/ *adj* causing you to feel pity or sadness □ *menyedihkan*: *the pitiful groans of the wounded soldiers* ▶ **pitifully** /-fəli/ *adv*

pitiless /ˈpɪtɪləs/ *adj* having or showing no pity for other people's suffering □ *tanpa belas kasihan* ▶ **pitilessly** *adv*

pitta (*AmE* **pita**) /ˈpiːtə/ (*BrE also*) /ˈpɪtə/ *noun* [U,C] a type of flat bread in the shape of an **oval** that can be split open and filled □ *sejenis roti leper yg berbentuk bulat*: *pitta bread with hummus*

pity¹ /ˈpɪti/ *noun* **1** [U] a feeling of sadness that you have for sb/sth that is suffering or in trouble □ *belas kasihan*: *The situation is his fault so I don't feel any pity for him.* **2** [sing] something that makes you feel a little sad or

pity → place 646

disappointed □ *sayang(nya); sayang sekali*: 'You're too late. Emily left five minutes ago.' 'Oh, what a pity!' ♦ *It's a pity that Bina couldn't come.*
SYN shame
IDM **take pity on sb** to help sb who is suffering or in trouble because you feel sorry for them □ *menolong sso kerana kasihan*

pity² /ˈpɪti/ *verb* [T] (**pitying**; **pities**; *pt, pp* **pitied**) to feel pity or sadness for sb who is suffering or in trouble □ *berasa belas kasihan*

pivot¹ /ˈpɪvət/ *noun* [C] **1** the central point on which sth turns or balances □ *paksi* **2** the central or most important person or thing □ *tunjang; pusat*: *West Africa was the pivot of the cocoa trade.*

pivot² /ˈpɪvət/ *verb* [I] to turn or balance on a central point □ *berputar*

pixel /ˈpɪksl/ *noun* [C] any of the very small individual areas on a computer, TV or camera screen, which together form the whole image □ *piksel*

pixelate (also **pixellate**) /ˈpɪksəleɪt/ *verb* [T] to divide an image into **pixels**, sometimes in order to hide sb's identity, especially on television □ *membahagikan sst imej kpd piksel*

pixie /ˈpɪksi/ *noun* [C] (in children's stories) a creature like a small person with pointed ears that has magic powers □ *pari-pari kecil*

pizza /ˈpiːtsə/ *noun* [C,U] an Italian dish consisting of a flat round bread base with vegetables, cheese, meat, etc. on top, which is cooked in an oven □ *piza* ⇨ picture on **page P16**

pkt *abbr* = **packet**(1)

pl. *abbr* = **plural**

placard /ˈplækɑːd/ *noun* [C] a large written or printed notice that is put in a public place or carried on a stick in a protest march □ *sepanduk*

placate /pləˈkeɪt/ *verb* [T] (*formal*) to make sb feel less angry about sth □ *menyejukkan/ melembutkan hati*

place¹ /pleɪs/ *noun* [C]
▶POSITION/AREA **1** [C] a particular position or area □ *tempat; bahagian; kedudukan*: *Show me the exact place where it happened.* ♦ *This would be a good place to sit down and have a rest.* ♦ *The wall was damaged in several places.*

▶TOWN/BUILDING **2** [C] a particular village, town, country, etc. □ *tempat*: *Which places did you go to in Italy?* ♦ *Vienna is a very beautiful place.* **3** [C] a building or area that is used for a particular purpose □ *tempat*: *The square is a popular meeting place for young people.* ♦ *The town is full of inexpensive eating places.*

▶SEAT **4** [C] a seat or position that can be used by sb/sth □ *tempat; tempat duduk*: *They went into the classroom and sat down in their places.* ♦ *Go on ahead and save me a place in the queue.*

HELP **Place**, **space** or **room**? A **place** is a seat or position for someone/something. A place where you can park your car is also called a **space**. You use **space** and **room** when you are talking about empty areas: *This piano takes up too much space.* ♦ *There is enough room for three people in the back of the car.*

▶ROLE **5** [sing] your position in society; your role □ *tempat; tugas; peranan*: *I feel it is not my place to criticize my boss.*

▶IN COLLEGE/TEAM **6** [C] an opportunity to study at a college, play for a team, etc. □ *tempat*: *Abina has got a place to study law at Oxford University.* ♦ *Laila is now sure of a place on the team.*

▶CORRECT POSITION **7** [C] the usual or correct position or occasion for sth □ *tempat; tempatnya; masanya*: *The room was tidy. Everything had been put away in its place.* ♦ *A funeral is not the place to discuss business.*

▶SB'S HOME **8** [sing] (*spoken*) sb's home □ *rumah*: *Her parents have got a place on the coast.*

▶IN COMPETITION **9** [C, usually sing] the position that you have at the end of a race, competition, etc. □ *tempat*: *Cara finished in second place.*

▶IN NUMBER **10** [C] the position of a number after the **decimal, point** (= a small round mark used to separate the parts of a number) □ *titik*: *Your answer should be correct to three decimal places.*

IDM **all over the place** everywhere □ *di merata-rata tempat*

change/swap places (with sb) to take sb's seat, position, etc. and let them have yours □ *bertukar tempat*: *Let's change places so that you can look out of the window.*

fall/slot into place (used about sth that is complicated or difficult to understand) to become organized or clear in your mind □ *mula menjadi jelas, difahami, dsb*: *After two weeks in my new job, everything suddenly started to fall into place.*

in the first, second, etc. place (*informal*) used when you are giving a list of reasons for sth or explaining sth □ *pertama sekali, yg keduanya, dsb* **SYN** **firstly**, **secondly**, *etc.*

in place 1 in the correct or usual position □ *pd tempatnya*: *Use tape to hold the picture in place.* **2** (used about plans or preparations) finished and ready to be used □ *siap; sedia*: *All the preparations for the trip are now in place.*

in sb's place/shoes in sb's situation or position □ *jika sayalah, awaklah, dll (di tempat sso itu)*: *If I were in your place I would wait a year before getting married.*

in place of sb/sth; **in sb/sth's place** instead of sb/ sth □ *sebagai ganti*

placard   banner

out of place 1 not in the correct or usual place □ *tdk di tempatnya* **2** not suitable for a particular situation □ *tdk kena pd tempatnya; canggung*: *I felt very out of place among all those clever people.*

put sb in his/her place to show that sb is not as clever, important, etc. as they believe □ *membuat sso sedar diri*: *It really put her in her place when she failed to qualify for the race.*

put yourself in sb's place to imagine that you are in the same situation as sb else □ *bayangkan jika anda yg menghadapi sst situasi itu*: *Put yourself in Steve's place and you will realize how worried he must be.*

take place (used about a meeting, an event, etc.) to happen □ *berlaku; berlangsung*: *The ceremony took place in glorious sunshine.* ⊃ note at **happen**

place² /pleɪs/ *verb* [T]

▶INTO POSITION **1** (*formal*) to put sth carefully or deliberately in a particular position □ *meletakkan*: *The chairs had all been placed in neat rows.* ♦ *The poster was placed where everyone could see it.* **2** to put sb in a particular position or situation □ *meletakkan; menempatkan*: *His behaviour placed me in a difficult situation.* ♦ *to place somebody in charge* ♦ *Rhoda was placed third in the competition.*

▶ATTITUDE **3** used to express the attitude that sb has to sb/sth □ *menaruh; menempatkan*: *We placed our trust in you and you failed us.* ♦ *The blame for the disaster was placed firmly on the company.*

▶RECOGNIZE **4** [usually in negative statements] to recognize sb/sth and be able to identify them or it □ *mengenal pasti*: *Her face is familiar but I just can't quite place her.*

▶ORDER/BET **5** to give instructions about sth or to ask for sth to happen □ *membuat (taruhan, pesanan, dll); menempah*: *to place a bet on something* ♦ *to place an order for something*

'place name *noun* [C] the name of a city, town, etc. □ *nama tempat*

placid /'plæsɪd/ *adj* (used about a person or an animal) calm and not easily excited □ *tenang*: *a placid baby/horse* ▶ **placidly** *adv*

plagiarize (also **-ise**) /'pleɪdʒəraɪz/ *verb* [T,I] to copy another person's ideas, words or work and pretend that they are your own □ *menjiplak; memplagiat*: *He was accused of plagiarizing his colleague's results.* ▶ **plagiarism** /'pleɪdʒərɪzəm/ *noun* [U,C]: *accusations of plagiarism* ♦ *The text was full of plagiarisms.*

plague¹ /pleɪɡ/ *noun* **1 the plague** [U] an infectious disease spread by **rats** (= animals like a large mice) that makes large spots form on the body, causes a very high temperature and often results in death □ *hawar; sampar hawar bubon* **2** [C,U] any infectious disease that spreads quickly and kills many people □ *wabak* **3** [C] **a plague of sth** a large number of unpleasant animals or insects that come into an area at one time □ *serbuan; serangan*: *a plague of ants/locusts*

plague² /pleɪɡ/ *verb* [T] to cause sb/sth a lot of

647

place → plan

trouble □ *menimpa; melanda; mengacau*: *The project was plagued by a series of disasters.*

plaice /pleɪs/ *noun* [C,U] (*pl* **plaice**) a type of flat sea fish that we eat □ *ikan plais/sebelah*

plain¹ /pleɪn/ *adj* (**plainer**; **plainest**) **1** easy to see, hear or understand; clear □ *jelas; nyata; terang-terang*: *It was plain that he didn't want to talk about it.* ♦ *She made it plain that she didn't want to see me again.* **2** (used about people, thoughts, actions, etc.) saying what you think; direct and honest □ *terus terang*: *I'll be plain with you. I don't like the idea.* **3** simple in style; not decorated or complicated □ *ringkas; mudah; biasa*: *My father likes plain English cooking.* **4** [only before a noun] all one colour; without a pattern on it □ *polos; tdk bercorak*: *a plain blue jumper* ⊃ picture on **page P1 5** (used especially about a woman or girl) not beautiful or attractive □ *tdk cantik/lawa*: *She's a rather plain child.*

plain² /pleɪn/ *noun* [C] (also **plains** [pl]) a large area of flat land with few trees □ *dataran*

plain³ /pleɪn/ *adv* (*informal*) completely □ *betul-betul*: *That's plain silly.*

plain-'clothes *adj* [only *before* a noun] (used about a police officer) in ordinary clothes, not uniform □ *berpakaian preman*: *a plain-clothes detective*

plain 'flour *noun* [U] flour that does not contain **baking powder** (= powder that makes cakes, etc. rise) □ *tepung biasa* ⊃ look at **self-raising flour**

plainly /'pleɪnli/ *adv* **1** clearly □ *jelas sekali*: *He was plainly very upset.* **2** using simple words to say sth in a direct and honest way □ *dgn terus terang*: *She told him plainly that he was not doing his job properly.* **3** in a simple way, without decoration □ *secara sederhana/ringkas*: *She was plainly dressed and wore no make-up.*

plaintiff /'pleɪntɪf/ *noun* [C] a person who starts a legal action against sb in a court of law □ *plaintif; pihak yg menuntut* ⊃ look at **defendant**

plaintive /'pleɪntɪv/ *adj* sounding sad, especially in a weak complaining way □ *sedih; sayu*: *a plaintive cry/voice* ▶ **plaintively** *adv*

plait /plæt/ (*AmE* **braid**) *verb* [T] to cross three or more long pieces of hair, rope, etc. over and under each other to make one thick piece □ *menocang; memintal* ▶ **plait** (*AmE* **braid**) *noun* [C] ⊃ picture at **plait**

plan¹ /plæn/ *noun* **1** [C] **a plan (for sth/to do sth)** an idea or arrangement for doing or achieving sth in the future □ *rancangan*: *We usually make our holiday plans in January.* ♦ *The firm has no plans to employ more people.* ♦ *There has been a change of plan—we're meeting at the restaurant.* ♦ *If everything goes according to plan* (= happens as we planned) *we should be home by midnight.* **2** [C] a detailed map of a building, town, etc.

[C] **countable**, a noun with a plural form: *one book, two books*   [U] **uncountable**, a noun with no plural form: *some sugar*

plan → plant

☐ *pelan*: *a street plan of Berlin* **3 plans** [pl] detailed drawings of a building, machine, road, etc. that show its size, shape and measurements ☐ *pelan*: *We're getting an architect to* **draw up** *some* **plans** *for a new kitchen.* **4** [C] a diagram that shows how sth is to be organized or arranged ☐ *pelan; rangka; gambar rajah*: *Before you start writing an essay, you should make a brief plan.*

EXAM TIP

Planning your answer

It is very important to plan your answers in a writing exam. Always make some notes about what you want to say before you start, and write down some key vocabulary. Look at the **Writing Tutor** for help with writing different types of essay.

plan² /plæn/ *verb* (**planning**; **planned**) **1** [I,T] **plan (sth) (for sth)** to decide, organize or prepare for sth you want to do in the future ☐ *merancang*: *to plan for the future* ♦ *You need to plan your work more carefully.* ♦ *We're planning a surprise for Gwen's 50th birthday.* **2** [I] **plan (on sth/doing sth)**; **plan (to do sth)** to intend or expect to do sth ☐ *merancang; menjangka*: *I'm planning on having a holiday in July.* ♦ *We plan to arrive at about 4 o'clock.* **3** [T] to make a diagram or a design of sth ☐ *membuat pelan; mereka bentuk*: *You need an expert to help you plan the garden.* ▶**planning** *noun* [U]: *The project requires careful planning.*

plane¹ /pleɪn/ (also **aeroplane**; *AmE* **airplane**) *noun* [C] **1** a vehicle with wings and one or more engines that can fly through the air ☐ *kapal terbang*: *Has her plane landed yet?* ♦ *a plane ticket* ♦ *a plane crash* ♦ *Have you ever been on a plane?* ⊃ picture on page P6 **2** (*technical*) a flat surface ☐ *satah*: *the horizontal/vertical plane* **3** a tool used for making the surface of wood smooth by taking very thin pieces off it ☐ *ketam* ⊃ picture at **tool**

TOPIC

Travelling by plane

A large **airport** may have more than one **terminal**. You go to the **check-in desk** and **check in** (= say that you have arrived). You might be able to choose an **aisle** seat or a **window** seat. There is often an **online check-in** so that you can do this before you go to the airport. You **check in** the **baggage** that will go into the **hold** (= the part of the plane where goods are stored) but you carry your **hand luggage** with you onto the plane. You wait in the **departure lounge**, and when your flight is called you go to the correct **gate**. You need to show your **boarding pass** in order to get on the plane. The plane **takes off** from the **runway**. The **flight attendants/cabin crew** look after you during the flight. If you are taking an international flight (= travelling to a different country), you will have to show your **passport** at **immigration** when you land. Then you collect your luggage from **baggage reclaim** and exit through **customs**.

plane² /pleɪn/ *verb* [T] to make the surface of a piece of wood flat and smooth using a **plane¹** (3) ☐ *mengetam*

planet /ˈplænɪt/ *noun* **1** [C] a very large round object in space that moves around the sun or another star ☐ *planet*: *the planets of our solar system* ⊃ note at **space 2 the planet** [sing] the world we live in; the Earth, especially when talking about the environment ☐ *Bumi*: *the battle to save the planet*

planetarium /ˌplænɪˈteəriəm/ *noun* [C] a building with a curved ceiling that represents the sky at night. It is used for showing the positions and movements of the planets and stars for education and entertainment. ☐ *planetarium*

plank /plæŋk/ *noun* [C] a long flat thin piece of wood that is used for building or making things ☐ *papan*

plankton /ˈplæŋktən/ *noun* [U, with sing or pl verb] very small forms of plant and animal life that live in water ☐ *plankton*

plant

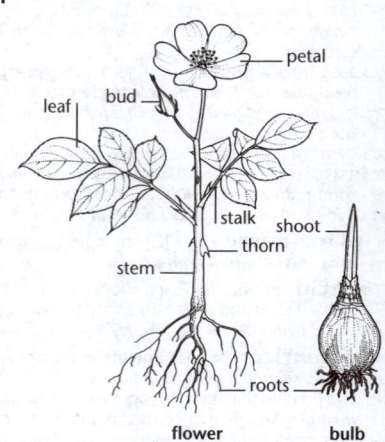

petal, bud, leaf, stalk, shoot, thorn, stem, roots

flower   bulb

plant¹ /plɑːnt/ *noun* [C] **1** a living thing that grows in the ground and usually has leaves, a **stem** (= the central part) and roots ☐ *tumbuh-tumbuhan; pokok*: *a tomato plant* ♦ *a plant pot* (= a container for plants) **2** a very large factory ☐ *kilang; loji*: *a car plant* ♦ *a nuclear reprocessing plant*

plant² /plɑːnt/ *verb* [T] **1** to put plants, seeds, etc. in the ground to grow ☐ *menanam; ditanam*: *Bulbs should be planted in the autumn.* **2 plant sth (with sth)** to cover or supply a garden, area of land, etc. with plants ☐ *menanami; ditanami*: *The field's been planted with wheat this*

[I] **intransitive**, a verb which has no object: *He laughed.*

[T] **transitive**, a verb which has an object: *He ate an apple.*

plantation → platoon

year. **3** to put yourself/sth firmly in a particular place or position □ *menempatkan; meletakkan*: *He planted himself in the best seat.* **4 plant sth (on sb)** to hide sth, especially sth illegal, in sb's clothing, property, etc. in order to make them seem guilty of a crime □ *meletakkan sst (yg haram) pd sso dgn tujuan utk memerangkapnya*: *The women claimed that the stolen money had been planted on them.* **5 plant sth** to hide sth such as a bomb in a place where it will not be found □ *meletakkan sst di tempat yg tersembunyi*: *The police think that terrorists may have planted the bomb.*

plantation /plɑːnˈteɪʃn/ *noun* [C] **1** a large area of land, especially in a hot country, where **tobacco** (= the plant used for making cigarettes), tea, cotton, etc. are grown □ *ladang*: *a coffee plantation* **2** an area of land where trees are grown to produce wood □ *ladang; hutan tanaman*

plaque /plɑːk/ *noun* **1** [C] a flat piece of stone or metal, usually with names and dates on it, that is fixed on a wall in memory of a famous person or event □ *plak; tanda peringatan* **2** [U] a harmful substance that forms on your teeth □ *plak*

plasma /ˈplæzmə/ (also **plasm** /ˈplæzəm/) *noun* [U] the clear liquid part of blood, in which the blood cells, etc., float □ *plasma*

plasma screen *noun* [C] a type of television or computer screen that is larger and thinner than most screens and produces a very clear image □ *skrin plasma*

plaster¹ /ˈplɑːstə(r)/ *noun* **1** [U] a mixture of a special powder and water that becomes hard when it is dry. **Plaster** is put on walls and ceilings to form a smooth surface. □ *lepa; plaster* **2** (also **plaster of ˈParis**) [U] a white powder that is mixed with water and becomes hard when dry. It is then used especially for making copies of statues or for holding broken bones in place □ *kapur Paris; bersimen*: *a plaster bust of Julius Caesar* ♦ *When Alan broke his leg it was in plaster for six weeks.* **3** (also **ˈsticking plaster**) [C] a small piece of sticky material that is used to cover a cut, etc. on the body □ *plaster*

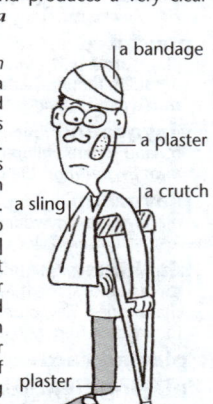

a bandage
a plaster
a sling
a crutch
plaster

His arm is in a sling.
His leg is in plaster.

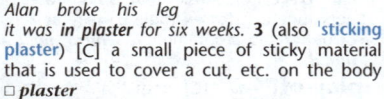

plaster² /ˈplɑːstə(r)/ *verb* [T] **1** to cover a wall, etc. with **plaster¹** (1) to make the surface smooth □ *melepa; memplaster* **2 plaster sb/sth (in/with sth)** to cover sb/sth with a large amount of sth □ *menampal*: *He plastered his walls with posters.*

plastic¹ /ˈplæstɪk/ *noun* [C,U] a light, strong material that is made with chemicals and is used for making many different kinds of objects □ *plastik*: *A lot of kitchen utensils are made of plastic.* ♦ *Plastics and other synthetic materials are commonly used today.*

plastic² /ˈplæstɪk/ *adj* made of plastic □ *(diperbuat drpd) plastik*: *plastic cups* ♦ *a plastic bag*

plastic ˈsurgery *noun* [U] a medical operation to repair or replace damaged skin or to improve the appearance of sb's face or body □ *pembedahan plastik* ⊃ look at **facelift**, **surgery**

plate /pleɪt/ *noun* **1** [C] a flat, usually round, dish for eating or serving food from □ *pinggan*: *a plastic/paper/china plate* ♦ *a plate of food*

> **MORE** You eat your main course from a **dinner plate**. You may put bread, etc. on a **side plate**. You eat cereal or a pudding from a **bowl**.

2 [C] a thin flat piece of metal or glass □ *plat; kepingan*: *a steel/metal plate* **3** [C] a flat piece of metal with sth written on it □ *plat*: *The brass plate beside the door said 'Dr Dawson'.* **4** [U] metal that has a thin covering of gold or silver □ *saduran*: *gold/silver plate*

plateau /ˈplætəʊ/ *noun* [C] (*pl* **plateaus** /-təʊz/ *or* **plateaux** /-təʊ/) **1** a large high area of flat land □ *penara; dataran tinggi* **2** a state where there is little development or change □ *tahap mendatar*: *House prices seem to have reached a plateau.*

plateful /ˈpleɪtfʊl/ *noun* [C] the amount of food that a plate can hold □ *sepinggan*

platform /ˈplætfɔːm/ *noun* [C] **1** the place where you get on or off trains at a railway station □ *platform*: *Which platform does the train to York leave from?* **2** a flat surface, higher than the level of the floor or ground, on which people stand when they are speaking or performing, so that the audience can see them □ *pentas*: *Coming onto the platform now is tonight's conductor, Jane Glover.* **3** [usually sing] the ideas and aims of a political party that wants to be elected □ *manifesto*: *They fought the election on a platform of low taxes.* **4** the type of computer system or the software that is used □ *jenis sistem atau perisian komputer*: *an IBM platform* ♦ *a multimedia platform*

platinum /ˈplætɪnəm/ *noun* [U] (*symbol* **Pt**) a silver-coloured metal that is often used for making expensive jewellery □ *platinum*: *a platinum wedding ring*

platonic /pləˈtɒnɪk/ *adj* (used about a relationship between two people) friendly but not sexual □ *platonik*

platoon /pləˈtuːn/ *noun* [C] a small group of soldiers □ *platun*

CONSONANTS   p **p**en   b **b**ad   t **t**ea   d **d**id   k **c**at   g **g**ot   tʃ **ch**in   dʒ **J**une   f **f**all   v **v**an   θ **th**in

plausible → playschool

plausible /ˈplɔːzəbl/ *adj* that you can believe; reasonable □ *munasabah*: *a plausible excuse* **OPP** implausible

play¹ /pleɪ/ *verb*
➤HAVE FUN **1** [I] **play (with sb/sth)** to do sth to enjoy yourself; to have fun □ *bermain*: *The children have been playing on the beach all day.* ♦ *Emma's found a new friend to play with.*
➤GAMES/SPORTS **2** [I,T] to take part in a game or sport □ *bermain*: *to play football/tennis/hockey* ♦ *I usually play against Bill.* ♦ *She played him at table tennis and won.* ♦ *Do you know how to play chess?* ♦ *Who's Brazil playing next in the World Cup?*
➤MUSICAL INSTRUMENT **3** [I,T] **play (sth) (on sth)** to make music with a musical instrument □ *bermain; memainkan*: *to play the piano/guitar/trumpet* ♦ *My son's learning the piano. He plays very well.* ♦ *She played a few notes on the violin.* ⊃ note at **music**
➤CDS, DVDS, ETC. **4** [I,T] to make a CD, DVD, etc. produce sound □ *main; mainkan; memasang*: *My favourite song was playing on the radio.* ♦ *Shall I play the DVD for you again?*
➤ACT/PERFORM **5** [I,T] to act in a play, film, TV programme, etc.; to act the role of sb □ *berlakon; memegang peranan*: *Richard is going to play Romeo.*

HELP Play a part, role, etc. is often used in a figurative way: *Britain has played an active part in the recent discussions.* ♦ *John played a key role in organizing the protest.*

➤OF LIGHT **6** [I] (*formal*) to move quickly and lightly □ *bermaksud bergerak dgn pantas dan ampung; (kiasan: cahaya yg menari-nari, dsb)*: *Sunlight played on the surface of the sea.* ❶ For idioms containing **play**, look at the entries for the nouns, adjectives, etc. For example **play it by ear** is at **ear**.
PHR V **play at sth/being sth** to do sth with little interest or effort □ *main-main (membuat sst)*: *He's only playing at studying. He'd prefer to get a job now.* ♦ *What is that driver playing at (= doing)?*
play sth back (to sb) to turn on and watch or listen to a film, music, etc. that you have recorded □ *memainkan balik sst yg telah dirakam*: *Play that last scene back to me again.*
play sth down to make sth seem less important than it really is □ *cuba mengecilkan/meremehkan sst yg sebenarnya adalah penting*: *to play down a crisis*
play A off against B to make people compete or argue with each other, especially for your own advantage □ *melaga-lagakan; mengadu-dombakan*: *I think she enjoys playing one friend off against another.*
play on sth to use and take advantage of sb's fears or weaknesses □ *mempergunakan (kelemahan sso) utk mencapai tujuan sendiri*: *This advertising campaign plays on people's fears of illness.*

play (sb) up (*informal*) to cause sb trouble or pain □ *meragam; menyusahkan*: *The car always plays up in wet weather.*

play² /pleɪ/ *noun* **1** [U] activity done for enjoyment only, especially by children □ *bermain*: *Young children learn through play.* ♦ *the happy sound of children at play* **2** [C] a piece of writing performed by actors in the theatre, or on TV or radio □ *drama*: *Would you like to see a play while you're in London?* ♦ *a radio/TV play* ⊃ note at **theatre** **3** [U] the playing of a game or sport □ *permainan*: *Bad weather stopped play yesterday.*

HELP We **play** tennis, football, etc. but we CANNOT say *a play* of tennis. We have **a game** of tennis.

4 [U] a control on a CD or DVD player, etc. that you press to start the tape, etc. running □ *main*: *Put the DVD into the machine then press play.*
IDM fair play ⊃ **fair¹**

playboy /ˈpleɪbɔɪ/ *noun* [C] a rich man who spends his time enjoying himself □ *lelaki kaya yg suka berfoya-foya*

player /ˈpleɪə(r)/ *noun* [C] **1** a person who plays a game or sport □ *pemain*: *a game for four players* ♦ *She's an excellent tennis player.* ⊃ picture at **football** **2** [in compounds] a machine on which you can watch pictures or listen to sound that has been recorded on CD, DVD, etc. □ *(alat) pemain*: *a CD/DVD player* **3** a person who plays a musical instrument □ *pemain muzik*: *a piano player*

playful /ˈpleɪfl/ *adj* **1** full of fun; wanting to play □ *suka main-main*: *a playful puppy* **2** done or said in fun; not serious □ *main-main; bergurau*: *a playful remark*

playground /ˈpleɪɡraʊnd/ *noun* [C] an area of land where children can play □ *padang/taman permainan*: *the school playground*

playgroup /ˈpleɪɡruːp/ (also **playschool**) a place where very young children go to play and learn □ *tadika* ⊃ look at **nursery school**

playhouse /ˈpleɪhaʊs/ *noun* **1** [sing] used in the name of some theatres □ *panggung; teater*: *the Liverpool Playhouse* **2** [C] a model of a house for children to play in □ *pondok mainan*

ˈplaying card = card (4)

ˈplaying field *noun* [C] a large field used for sports □ *padang bola*
IDM a level playing field ⊃ **level²**

playlist /ˈpleɪlɪst/ *noun* [C] a list of songs and pieces of music that sb chooses and puts together, for example to play at a party or on a radio programme □ *senarai lagu dan muzik*

ˈplay-off *noun* [C] a match between two teams or players who have equal scores to decide the winner □ *perlawanan semula*: *They lost to Chicago in the play-offs.*

playschool /ˈpleɪskuːl/ = playgroup

plaything /ˈpleɪθɪŋ/ noun [C] (old-fashioned) a toy □ *barang mainan*

playtime /ˈpleɪtaɪm/ noun [C,U] (BrE) a period of time between lessons when children at school can go outside to play □ *waktu main*

playwright /ˈpleɪraɪt/ noun [C] a person who writes plays for the theatre, TV or radio □ *penulis drama; dramatis* **SYN** dramatist ⇒ note at **literature**

plc (also **PLC**) /ˌpiː el ˈsiː/ abbr (BrE) **Public Limited Company**; used after the name of a company □ *Syarikat (Awam) Berhad*

plea /pliː/ noun [C] **1** (formal) a plea (for sth) an important and emotional request □ *rayuan*: *a plea for help* **2** a plea of sth a statement made by or for sb in a court of law □ *akuan*: *a plea of guilty/not guilty*

plead /pliːd/ verb **1** [I] plead (with sb) (to do/for sth) to ask sb for sth in a very strong and serious way □ *merayu*: *She pleaded with him not to leave her.* ♦ *He pleaded for mercy.* ⇒ look at **beg** **2** [I] to state in a court of law that you did or did not do a crime □ *mengaku*: *The defendant pleaded not guilty to the charge of theft.* **3** [T] plead sth (for sth) to give sth as an excuse or explanation for sth □ *memberikan alasan*: *He pleaded family problems for his lack of concentration.* **4** [I,T] plead (sth) (for sb/sth) (used especially about a lawyer in a court of law) to support sb's case □ *membela*: *He needs the very best lawyer to plead (his case) for him.*

pleasant /ˈpleznt/ adj (**pleasanter**; **pleasantest**) [**More pleasant** and **most pleasant** are more common.] nice, enjoyable or friendly □ *seronok; menyenangkan*: *a pleasant evening/climate/place/view* ♦ *a pleasant smile/voice/manner* **OPP** unpleasant ▸ **pleasantly** adv

please¹ /pliːz/ exclam used as a polite way of asking for sth or telling sb to do sth □ *sila; tolong*: *Come in, please.* ♦ *Please don't spend too much money.* ♦ *Sit down, please.* ♦ *Two cups of coffee, please.*

IDM **yes, please** used when you are accepting an offer of sth politely □ *ya (kalau boleh)*: *'Sugar?' 'Yes, please.'* **OPP** No, thank you

please² /pliːz/ verb [I,T] to make sb happy □ *menggembirakan; menyenangkan/memuaskan hati sso*: *There's just no pleasing some people* (= some people are impossible to please). **SYN** satisfy **2** [I] [not used as the main verb in a sentence; used after words like *as, what, whatever, anything,* etc.] to want; to choose □ *suka; sesuka hati*: *You can't always do as you please.* ♦ *She has so much money she can buy anything she pleases.*

IDM **please yourself** to be able to do whatever you want □ *(buat) ikut suka/sesuka hati*: *Without anyone else to cook for, I can please myself what I eat.*

pleased /pliːzd/ adj [not before a noun] pleased (with sb/sth); pleased to do sth; pleased that ... happy or satisfied about sth □ *gembira; puas hati*: *John seems very pleased with his new car.* ♦ *Aren't you pleased to see me?* ♦ *We're only too pleased* (= very happy) *to help.* ♦ *I'm so pleased that you've decided to stay another week.* ⇒ note at **happy**

pleasing /ˈpliːzɪŋ/ adj giving you pleasure and satisfaction □ *menyenangkan/memuaskan hati*: *The exam results are very pleasing this year.*

pleasurable /ˈpleʒərəbl/ adj (formal) enjoyable □ *menyeronokkan*: *a pleasurable experience*

pleasure /ˈpleʒə(r)/ noun **1** [U] the feeling of being happy or satisfied □ *kegembiraan; keseronokan*: *Parents get a lot of pleasure out of watching their children grow up.* ♦ *It gives me great pleasure to introduce our next speaker.* **2** [U] enjoyment (rather than work) □ *berseronok-seronok*: *What brings you to Paris—business or pleasure?* **3** [C] an event or activity that you enjoy or that makes you happy □ *nikmat; keseronokan; ungkapan balas bagi ucapan terima kasih*: *It's been a pleasure to work with you.* ♦ *'Thanks for your help.' 'It's a pleasure.'*

IDM **take (no) pleasure in sth/doing sth** to enjoy/not enjoy (doing) sth □ *suka (tdk suka) membuat sst*

with pleasure used as a polite way of saying that you are happy to do sth □ *tentu sekali*: *'Could you give me a lift into town?' 'Yes, with pleasure.'*

pleat /pliːt/ noun [C] a permanent fold that is sewn or pressed into a piece of cloth □ *lisu*: *a skirt with pleats at the front*

plectrum /ˈplektrəm/ (also informal **pick**) noun [C] a small piece of metal, plastic, etc. that you use to play a musical instrument such as a guitar □ *plektrum; pemetik tali gitar dsb*

pledge /pledʒ/ noun [C] a pledge (to do sth) a formal promise or agreement □ *ikrar; janji* ▸ **pledge** verb [T] pledge sth (to sb/sth): *The Government has pledged £5 million to help the victims of the disaster.*

plentiful /ˈplentɪfl/ adj available in large amounts or numbers □ *sangat banyak*: *Fruit is plentiful at this time of year.* **OPP** scarce

plenty /ˈplenti/ pron, adv **1** plenty (of sb/sth) as much or as many of sth as you need □ *cukup; banyak*: *'Shall I get some more coffee?' 'No, we've still got plenty.'* ♦ *There's still plenty of time to get there.* ♦ *Have you brought plenty to drink?* **2** [before *more*] a lot □ *banyak*: *There's plenty more ice cream.* **3** [with *big, long, tall,* etc. followed by *enough*] (informal) easily □ *cukup*: *'This shirt's too small.' 'Well, it looks plenty big enough to me.'*

pliable /ˈplaɪəbl/ (also **pliant** /ˈplaɪənt/) adj **1** easy to bend or shape □ *mudah dilenturkan/dibentuk* **2** (used about a person) easy to influence □ *mudah dipengaruhi*

pliers /ˈplaɪəz/ noun [pl] a metal tool with handles, that is used for holding things firmly and for cutting wire □ *playar*: *a pair of pliers* ⇒ picture at **tool**

plight /plaɪt/ noun [sing] (formal) a bad or difficult state or situation □ *keadaan yg sukar atau teruk*

plimsoll /ˈplɪmsəl/ noun [C] (BrE) a light shoe made of **canvas** (= strong cloth) that is especially used for sports, etc. □ *kasut kanvas; sniker: a pair of plimsolls* ⊃ look at **trainer**

plod /plɒd/ verb [I] (**plodding**; **plodded**) **plod (along/on)** to walk slowly and in a heavy or tired way □ *melangkah dgn berat atau lesu: We plodded on through the rain for nearly an hour.*

PHR V plod along/on to make slow progress, especially with difficult or boring work □ *merangkak-rangkak; membuat sst dgn lambat: I just plod on with my work and never seem to get anywhere.*

plonk /plɒŋk (AmE also) / verb [T] (informal) **1 plonk sth (down)** to put sth down on sth, especially noisily or carelessly □ *meletakkan (dgn sembarangan); mencampakkan: Just plonk your bag down anywhere.* **2 plonk (yourself) (down)** to sit down heavily and carelessly □ *menghenyakkan diri: He just plonked himself down in front of the TV.*

plop¹ /plɒp/ noun [C, usually sing] a sound like that of a small object dropping into water □ *bunyi kelepuk/celepuk*

plop² /plɒp/ verb [I] (**plopping**; **plopped**) to fall making a **plop** □ *jatuh berkelepuk: The frog plopped back into the water.*

plot¹ /plɒt/ noun [C] **1** the series of events which form the story of a novel, film, etc. □ *plot; jalan cerita: The play had a very weak plot.* ♦ *I can't follow the plot of this novel.* **2 a plot (to do sth)** a secret plan made by several people to do sth wrong or illegal □ *komplot; pakatan jahat: a plot to kill the president* **3** a small piece of land, used for a special purpose □ *petak: a plot of land*

plot² /plɒt/ verb (**plotting**; **plotted**) **1** [I,T] **plot (with sb) (against sb)** to make a secret plan to do sth wrong or illegal □ *berkomplot: They were accused of plotting against the government.* ♦ *The terrorists had been plotting this campaign for years.* **2** [T] to mark sth on a map, diagram, etc. □ *memplot: to plot the figures on a graph*

plough (AmE **plow**) /plaʊ/ noun [C] a large piece of equipment which is pulled by a **tractor** (= a large vehicle that is used on farms) or by an animal. A plough turns the soil over ready for seeds to be planted. □ *bajak; tenggala* ⊃ look at **snowplough** ▶ **plough** (AmE **plow**) verb [I,T] (figurative): *The book was long and boring but I managed to plough through it* (= read it with difficulty).

ploy /plɔɪ/ noun [C] **a ploy (to do sth)** something that you say or do in order to get what you want or to persuade sb to do sth □ *helah; rancangan*

pluck¹ /plʌk/ verb [T] **1 pluck sth/sb (from sth/out)** to remove or take sth/sb from a place □ *mengambil; memetik: He plucked the letter from my hands.* **2** to pull the feathers out of a bird in order to prepare it for cooking □ *mencabut bulu* **3** to play a musical instrument, especially a **guitar** by pulling the strings with your fingers □ *memetik*

IDM pluck up courage to try to get enough courage to do sth □ *memberanikan diri*

PHR V pluck at sth to pull sth gently several times □ *menarik-narik*

pluck² /plʌk/ noun [U] (informal) courage and determination □ *keberanian; kegigihan* ▶ **plucky** adj (**pluckier**; **pluckiest**)

plug¹ /plʌɡ/ noun [C] **1** a plastic or rubber object with two or three metal pins, which connects a piece of electrical equipment to the electricity supply □ *palam: I'll have to change the plug on the kettle.* **2** a round piece of rubber or plastic that you use to block the hole in a sink, bath, etc. □ *penyumbat: She pulled out the plug and let the water drain away.* **3** (informal) a mention that sb makes of a new book, film, etc. in order to encourage people to buy or see it □ *promosi: He managed to get in a plug for his new book.*

plug² /plʌɡ/ verb [T] (**plugging**; **plugged**) **1** to fill or block a hole with sth that fits tightly into it □ *menyumbat: He managed to plug the leak in the pipe.* **2** (informal) to say good things about a new book, film, etc. in order to make people buy or see it □ *mempromosikan: They're really plugging that song on the radio at the moment.*

PHR V plug sth in to connect a piece of electrical equipment to the electricity supply or to another piece of equipment □ *memasang palam: Is the microphone plugged in?* **OPP unplug**

plugs

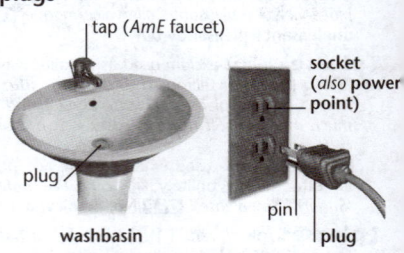

tap (AmE faucet)

socket (also power point)

plug

washbasin

pin

plug

plughole /ˈplʌɡhəʊl/ noun [C] (BrE) a hole in a bath, etc. where the water flows away □ *lubang salir*

plum /plʌm/ noun [C] a soft, round fruit with red or yellow skin and a stone in the middle □ *(buah) plum* ⊃ picture on **page P14**

plumage /ˈpluːmɪdʒ/ noun [U] a bird's feathers □ *buluan (burung)*

plumber /ˈplʌmə(r)/ noun [C] a person whose job is to put in or repair water pipes, baths, toilets, etc. □ *tukang paip* ⊃ note at **house** ⊃ picture on **page P2**

plumbing /ˈplʌmɪŋ/ noun [U] **1** all the pipes, taps, etc. in a building □ *sistem paip* **2** the work of a person who puts in and repairs water pipes, taps, etc. □ *kerja memasang paip, dsb*

plume /pluːm/ *noun* [C] **1** a narrow cloud of smoke that rises in the air □ *kepulan* **2** a large feather or group of feathers, often worn as a decoration □ *bulu burung (yg dipakai sebagai perhiasan)*

plummet /ˈplʌmɪt/ *verb* [I] to fall suddenly and quickly from a high level or position □ *jatuh menjunam; merosot teruk*: *Share prices have plummeted to an all-time low.* **SYN** plunge

plump¹ /plʌmp/ *adj* (**plumper**; **plumpest**) (used about a person or an animal) pleasantly fat □ *montok; tembam*: *the baby's plump cheeks*

plump² /plʌmp/ *verb*
PHR V **plump for sb/sth** (*informal*) to choose or decide to have sb/sth □ *memilih sso/sst*: *I think I'll plump for the roast chicken, after all.*

plunder /ˈplʌndə(r)/ *noun* [U] the act of stealing from people or places, especially during war or fighting; the goods that are stolen □ *menjarah; merampas* ▶ **plunder** *verb* [I,T]

plunge¹ /plʌndʒ/ *verb* **1** [I,T] to move or make sb/sth move suddenly forwards and/or downwards □ *terjun; menjunam; terjunam*: *She lost her balance and plunged 100 feet to her death.* ♦ *The earthquake plunged entire towns over the edge of the cliffs.* **2** [I] to decrease suddenly and quickly □ *menjunam*: *Share prices plunged overnight.*
PHR V **plunge into sth/in 1** to jump into sth, especially with force □ *terjun; menjunam; terjunam*: *He ran to the river and plunged in.* **2** to start doing sth with energy and enthusiasm □ *membuat sst (dgn ghairah)*: *Think carefully before you plunge into buying a house.*
plunge sth into sth/in to push sth suddenly and with force into sth □ *menusuk; membenamkan*: *She plunged the knife deep into his chest.*
plunge sb/sth into sth to cause sb/sth to suddenly be in the state mentioned □ *menjerumuskan; dilanda; diselubungi*: *The country has been plunged into chaos by the floods.*

plunge² /plʌndʒ/ *noun* [C] a sudden jump, drop or fall □ *jatuh; terjunam*: *the plunge in house prices*
IDM **take the plunge** (*informal*) to decide to do sth difficult after thinking about it for quite a long time □ *mengambil keputusan (utk melakukan sst)*: *After going out together for five years, they took the plunge and got married.*

pluperfect /ˌpluːˈpɜːfɪkt/ = **past perfect**

plural /ˈplʊərəl/ *noun* [C] (*abbr* pl.) the form of a noun, verb, etc. which refers to more than one person or thing □ *majmuk*: *The plural of 'boat' is 'boats'.* ♦ *The verb should be in the plural.* ▶ **plural** *adj* ➔ look at **singular**

plus¹ /plʌs/ *prep* **1** and; added to □ *tambah; campur*: *Two plus two is four (2 + 2 = 4).* **OPP** **minus** **2** in addition to; and also □ *serta; dan juga*: *You have to work five days a week plus every other weekend.*

plus² /plʌs/ *noun* [C] **1** an advantage of a situation □ *kelebihan*: *My work is five minutes from my house, which is a definite plus.* **2** the symbol (+) used in mathematics □ *tanda campur*: *He put a plus instead of a minus.* **OPP** **minus**

plus³ /plʌs/ *adj* [only *after* a noun] **1** or more □ *lebih*: *I'd say there were 30 000 plus at the match.* **2** [not before a noun] (used for marking work done by students) slightly above □ *campur*: *I got a B plus (= B+) for my homework.* **OPP** **minus**

plush /plʌʃ/ *adj* (*informal*) comfortable and expensive □ *mewah*: *a plush hotel*

Pluto /ˈpluːtəʊ/ *noun* [sing] the name of a large round object in space which **orbits** (= goes around) the sun □ *Pluto*

CULTURE

Pluto was known as the ninth planet in the **solar system** until 2006.

plutonium /pluːˈtəʊniəm/ *noun* [U] (*symbol* **Pu**) a chemical element that is used in nuclear weapons and in producing nuclear energy □ *plutonium*

ply /plaɪ/ *verb* [I,T] (**plying**; **plies**; *pt*, *pp* **plied**) to try to sell services or goods to people, especially on the street □ *berjaja*: *Boat owners were plying their trade to passing tourists.* ♦ *to ply for business*
PHR V **ply sb with sth** to keep giving sb food and drink, or asking sb questions □ *asyik menjamu sso; menghujani*: *They plied us with food from the moment we arrived.*

plywood /ˈplaɪwʊd/ *noun* [U] board made by sticking several thin layers of wood together □ *papan lapis*

PM *abbr* = **prime minister**

p.m. (*AmE also* **P.M.**) /ˌpiː ˈem/ *abbr* (from Latin) post meridiem; after midday □ *tengah hari; petang*: *The appointment is at 3 p.m.* ➔ look at **a.m.**

pneumatic /njuːˈmætɪk/ *adj* **1** filled with air □ *pneumatik (berisi udara)*: *a pneumatic tyre* **2** worked by air under pressure □ *pneumatik (dijalankan oleh udara mampat)*: *a pneumatic drill*

pneumonia /njuːˈməʊniə/ *noun* [U] a serious illness of the lungs which makes breathing difficult □ *pneumonia*

PO /ˌpiː ˈəʊ/ *abbr* [in compounds] = **post office** □ *Pejabat Pos*: *a PO box*

poach /pəʊtʃ/ *verb* [T] **1** to cook food gently in liquid □ *memasak makanan dgn sedikit air; merenih*: *poached eggs/fish* **2** to hunt animals illegally on sb else's land □ *memburu curi*: *The men were caught poaching elephants.* **3** to take an idea from sb else and use it as though it is your own □ *menciplak* **4** to take workers from another company in an unfair way □ *mencuri*

poacher /ˈpəʊtʃə(r)/ noun [C] a person who hunts animals illegally on sb else's land □ *pemburu curi*

PO box noun [C] a place in a post office where letters, packages, etc. are kept until they are collected by the person they were sent to □ *Peti Surat*: *The address is PO Box 4287, Nairobi, Kenya.*

pocket¹ /ˈpɒkɪt/ noun [C] **1** a piece of cloth like a small bag that is sewn inside or on a piece of clothing and is used for carrying things in □ *saku; poket*: *He always walks with his hands in his trouser pockets.* ◆ *a pocket dictionary/calculator* (= one small enough to fit in your pocket) ➲ picture on page P1 **2** a small bag or container that is fixed to the inside of a car door, suitcase, etc. and used for putting things in □ *poket*: *There are safety instructions in the pocket of the seat in front of you.* ➲ picture at **pool 3** used to talk about the amount of money that you have to spend □ *wang; kemampuan*: *They sell cars to suit every pocket.* ◆ *He had no intention of paying for the meal out of his own pocket.* **4** a small area or group that is different from its surroundings □ *kawasan; kelompok; tompok*: *a pocket of warm air*
IDM pick sb's pocket ➲ pick¹

pocket² /ˈpɒkɪt/ verb [T] **1** to put sth in your pocket □ *memasukkan ke dlm poket*: *He took the letter and pocketed it quickly.* **2** to steal or win money □ *mencuri/memenangi wang*

pocket money noun [U] (*especially AmE* **allowance**) an amount of money that parents give a child to spend, usually every week □ *wang saku*

pod /pɒd/ noun [C] the long, green part of some plants, such as peas and beans, that contains the seeds □ *lenggai* ➲ picture on page P15

podcast /ˈpɒdkɑːst/ noun [C] a recording of a radio broadcast or a video that can be taken from the Internet □ *rakaman siaran radio atau video yg terdapat dlm Internet*: *I download podcasts of radio shows and listen to them in the car.* ➲ note at iPod™

TOPIC
Podcasts
You can **download a podcast** to your computer or **portable MP3 player** and watch or listen to it whenever you want to. If you **subscribe to a podcast** (= say that you want to receive regular broadcasts), your computer will **download** each new **episode** (= part) in a series.

podiatrist /pəˈdaɪətrɪst/ = chiropodist
podiatry /pəˈdaɪətri/ = chiropody
podium /ˈpəʊdiəm/ noun [C] a small platform for people to stand on when they are speaking, performing, etc. in public □ *podium*

poem /ˈpəʊɪm/ noun [C] a piece of writing arranged in short lines. Poems try to express thoughts and feelings with the help of sound and rhythm □ *puisi; sajak*: *He wrote poems about the beauty of the countryside.* ◆ *She read the poem aloud.*

poet /ˈpəʊɪt/ noun [C] a person who writes poems □ *penyair; penyajak*

poetic /pəʊˈetɪk/ (also **poetical** /-ɪkl/) adj connected with poetry or like a poem □ *(berkaitan dgn) puisi atau spt puisi* ▶**poetically** /-kli/ adv

poetry /ˈpəʊətri/ noun [U] a collection of poems; poems in general □ *puisi*: *Shakespeare's poetry and plays* ◆ *Do you like poetry?* **SYN** **verse** ➲ note at literature ➲ look at prose

poignant /ˈpɔɪnjənt/ adj causing sadness or pity □ *(yg) memilukan*: *a poignant memory* ▶**poignancy** /-jənsi/ noun [U] ▶**poignantly** /-jəntli/ adv

point¹ /pɔɪnt/ noun
▶FACT/OPINION **1** [C] a particular fact, idea or opinion that sb expresses □ *poin; perkara; maksud*: *You make some interesting points in your essay.* ◆ *I see your point but I don't agree with you.*

MORE We can **bring up**, **raise**, **make**, **argue**, **emphasize** and **illustrate** a point.

▶IMPORTANT IDEA **2 the point** [sing] the most important part of what is being said; the main piece of information □ *perkara penting; pokok*: *It makes no difference how much it costs—the point is we don't have any money!* ◆ *She always talks and talks and takes ages to get to the point.* **3** [C] an important idea or thought that needs to be considered □ *perkara; hal*: *'Have you checked what time the last bus back is?' 'That's a point—no, I haven't.'*
▶PURPOSE **4** [sing] **the point (of/in sth/doing sth)** the meaning, reason or purpose of sth □ *gunanya; faedah; tujuan*: *She's said no, so what's the point of telephoning her again?* ◆ *There's no point in talking to my parents—they never listen.*
▶QUALITY **5** [C] a detail, characteristic or quality of sb/sth □ *sifat; ciri-ciri*: *Make a list of your strong points and your weak points* (= good and bad qualities).
▶PLACE/TIME **6** [C] a particular place, position or moment □ *tempat; kedudukan; masa; takat*: *The library is a good starting point for that sort of information.* ◆ *He has reached the high point of his career.* ◆ *the boiling/freezing point of water* ◆ *He waved to the crowd and it was at that point that the shot was fired.* ◆ *At one point I thought I was going to laugh.*
▶DIRECTION **7** [C] one of the marks of direction around a compass □ *arah kompas*: *the points of the compass* (= North, South, East, West, etc.)
▶IN COMPETITION **8** [C] (*abbr* **pt**) a single mark in some games, sports, etc. that you add to others to get the score □ *mata; poin*: *to score a point* ◆ *Rios needs two more points to win the match.*

➤ MEASUREMENT **9** [C] a unit of measurement for certain things □ *mata*: *The value of the dollar has fallen by a few points.*
➤ IN NUMBERS **10** [C] a small round mark used when writing parts of numbers □ *perpuluhan*: *She ran the race in 11.2 (eleven point two) seconds.*
➤ SHARP END **11** [C] the thin sharp end of sth □ *mata; hujung*: *the point of a pin/needle/pencil*
IDM **be on the point of doing sth** be just going to do sth □ *baru hendak membuat sst*: *I was on the point of going out when the phone rang.*
beside the point ➔ **beside**
have your, etc. (good) points to have some good qualities □ *ada baiknya/kelebihannya*: *Bill has his good points, but he's very unreliable.*
make a point of doing sth to make sure you do sth because it is important or necessary □ *memastikan (membuat sst)*: *He made a point of locking all the doors and windows before leaving the house.*
point of view a way of looking at a situation; an opinion □ *pandangan; pendapat*: *From my point of view, it would be better to wait a little longer.*
SYN viewpoint, standpoint ➔ note at **think**

> **HELP** **Point of view** or **opinion**? Do not confuse **from my point of view** with **in my opinion**. The first means 'from my position in life' (= as a student, business person, teacher, etc.). The second means 'I think': *From an advertiser's point of view, TV is a wonderful medium.* ◆ *In my opinion, people watch too much TV.*

a sore point ➔ **sore¹**
sb's strong point ➔ **strong**
take sb's point to understand and accept what sb is saying □ *menerima dan memahami pendapat sso*
to the point connected with what is being discussed □ *tepat; jitu*: *His speech was short and to the point.* **SYN** relevant
up to a point partly □ *sebahagiannya*: *I agree with you up to a point.*

point² /pɔɪnt/ *verb* **1** [I] **point (at/to sb/sth)** to show where sth is or to draw attention to sth using your finger, a stick, etc. □ *menuding; menunjuk*: *'I'll have that one,' she said, pointing to a chocolate cake.* **2** [I,T] **point (sth) (at/towards sb/sth)** to aim (sth) in the direction of sb/sth □ *menghalakan; mengarahkan*: *She pointed the gun at the target and fired.* **3** [I] to face in a particular direction or to show that sth is in a particular direction □ *menghala; menunjukkan*: *The sign pointed towards the motorway.* ◆ *Turn round until you're pointing north.* **4** [I] **point to sth** to show that sth is likely to exist, happen or be true □ *menunjukkan*: *Research points to a connection between diet and cancer.*
PHR V **point sth out (to sb)** to make sb look at sth; to make sth clear to sb □ *menunjukkan sst (kpd sso)*: *The guide pointed out all the places of interest to us on the way.* ◆ *I'd like to point out that we haven't got much time left.*

point-'blank *adj* [only *before* a noun], *adv* **1** (used about a shot) from a very close position □ *jarak dekat*: *He was shot in the leg at point-blank range.* **2** (used about sth that is said) very direct and not polite; not allowing any discussion □ *terus terang; bulat-bulat*: *He told her point-blank to get out of the house and never come back.*

pointed /'pɔɪntɪd/ *adj* **1** having a sharp end □ *tajam; runcing; mancung*: *a pointed stick/nose* **2** said in a critical way □ *membidas secara tdk langsung*: *She made a pointed comment about people who are always late.* ▶ **pointedly** *adv*

pointer /'pɔɪntə(r)/ *noun* [C] **1** a piece of helpful advice or information □ *petunjuk; nasihat*: *Could you give me some pointers on how best to tackle the problem?* **2** a stick that is used to point to things on a map, etc. □ *penunjuk* **3** a small arrow on a computer screen that you move by moving the mouse □ *penuding; penunjuk*

pointless /'pɔɪntləs/ *adj* without any use or purpose □ *tdk berguna*: *It's pointless to try and make him agree.* ▶ **pointlessly** *adv* ▶ **pointlessness** *noun* [U]

poise /pɔɪz/ *noun* [U] a calm, confident way of behaving □ *sikap tenang dan yakin*

poised /pɔɪzd/ *adj* [not before a noun] **1** not moving but ready to move □ *bersedia*: *'Shall I call the doctor or not?' he asked, his hand poised above the telephone.* **2** **poised (to do sth)** ready to act; about to do sth □ *bersedia*: *The government is poised to take action if the crisis continues.* **3** calm and confident □ *tenang dan yakin*

poison¹ /'pɔɪzn/ *noun* [C,U] a substance that kills or harms you if you eat or drink it □ *racun*: *rat poison* ◆ *poison gas* ◆ *a deadly poison*

poison² /'pɔɪzn/ *verb* [T] **1** to kill, harm or damage sb/sth with poison □ *meracun*: *The police confirmed that the murder victim had been poisoned.* **2** to put poison in sth □ *membubuh racun*: *The cup of coffee had been poisoned.* **3** to spoil or ruin sth □ *meracuni; menghancurkan*: *The quarrel had poisoned their relationship.* ▶ **poisoned** *adj*: *a poisoned drink*

poisoning /'pɔɪzənɪŋ/ *noun* [U] the giving or taking of poison or a dangerous substance □ *keracunan*: *He got food poisoning from eating fish that wasn't fresh.*

poisonous /'pɔɪzənəs/ *adj* **1** causing death or illness if you eat or drink it □ *beracun*: *a poisonous plant* **2** (used about animals, etc.) producing and using poison to attack its enemies □ *berbisa*: *He was bitten by a poisonous snake.* **3** very unpleasant and intended to upset sb □ *berniat jahat; menyakitkan hati*: *He wrote him a poisonous letter criticizing his behaviour.*

poke /pəʊk/ *verb* **1** [T] to push sb/sth with a finger, stick or other long, thin object □ *mencucuk*: *Be careful you don't poke yourself in the eye with that stick!* **2** [I,T] **poke (sth) into, through, out of, down, etc. sth** to push or move sth quickly into sth or in a certain direction □ *menjolok; memasukkan; menjenguk*: *He poked the stick down* the hole to see how deep it was. ♦ A child's head poked up from behind the wall. **3** to send a short message to a friend on a **social networking** site (= a service on the Internet for people who share your interests) ▫ *menghantar pesanan ringkas kpd kawan melalui laman sosial* ➔ note at **social networking**

poke

She poked the fire.

IDM **poke fun at sb/sth** to make jokes about sb/sth, often in an unkind way ▫ *memperolok-olokkan sso*

poke/stick your nose into sth ➔ **nose¹**
▶ **poke** *noun* [C]

poker /'pəʊkə(r)/ *noun* **1** [U] a type of card game usually played to win money ▫ *poker* **2** [C] a metal stick for moving the coal or wood in a fire ▫ *penggodek api* ➔ picture at **fireplace**

poky /'pəʊki/ *adj* (**pokier**; **pokiest**) (*BrE informal*) (used about a house, room, etc.) too small ▫ *sempit*: *a poky little office*

polar /'pəʊlə(r)/ *adj* [only *before* a noun] of or near the North or South Pole ▫ *(berkenaan atau dekat dgn) kutub*: *the polar regions*

'polar bear *noun* [C] a large white bear that lives in the area near the North Pole ▫ *beruang kutub*

polarize (also **-ise**) /'pəʊləraɪz/ *verb* [I,T] (*formal*) to separate or make people separate into two groups with completely opposite opinions ▫ *berpecah dua; menyebabkan berlakunya polarisasi*: *Public opinion has polarized on this issue.* ♦ *The issue has polarized public opinion.*

pole /pəʊl/ *noun* [C] **1** a long, thin piece of wood or metal, used especially to hold sth up ▫ *tiang; batang; galah*: *a flagpole* ♦ *a tent pole* **2** either of the two points at the exact top and bottom of the earth ▫ *kutub*: *the North/South Pole* ➔ picture at **earth**

the 'pole vault *noun* [sing] the sport of jumping over a high bar with the help of a long pole ▫ *lompat galah*

police¹ /pə'liːs/ *noun* [pl] the official organization whose job is to make sure that people obey the law, and to prevent and solve crime; the people who work for this organization ▫ *polis*: *Dial 999 if you need to call the police.* ♦ *a police car* ♦ *Kamal wants to join the police force when he finishes school.* ♦ *the local police station*

HELP You CANNOT say 'a police' meaning one man or woman. We usually refer to 'police officers'. When we are talking about the organization, we always use **the**: *There were over 100 police on duty.* ♦ *The police are investigating the murder.*

police² /pə'liːs/ *verb* [T] to keep control in a place by using the police or a similar official group ▫ *mengawal*: *The cost of policing football games is extremely high.*

po'lice 'constable (also **constable**) *noun* [C] (*abbr* **PC**) (in Britain) a police officer of the lowest level ▫ *konstabel polis*

policeman /pə'liːsmən/ *noun* [C] (*pl* **policemen**) a male police officer ▫ *pegawai polis lelaki*

po'lice officer (also **officer**) *noun* [C] a member of the police ▫ *pegawai polis* ➔ note at **official²** ➔ picture on **page P2**

policewoman /pə'liːswʊmən/ *noun* [C] (*pl* **policewomen**) a female police officer ▫ *pegawai polis wanita*

policy /'pɒləsi/ *noun* (*pl* **policies**) **1** [C,U] **policy (on sth)** a plan of action agreed or chosen by a government, a company, etc. ▫ *dasar*: *The Conservatives have a new set of policies on health.* ♦ *It is company policy not to allow children on the premises.* **2** [C,U] a way of behaving that you think is best in a particular situation ▫ *amalan*: *It's my policy only to do business with people I like.* **3** [C] a document that shows an agreement that you have made with an insurance company ▫ *polisi*: *an insurance policy*

polio /'pəʊliəʊ/ *noun* [U] a serious disease which can cause you to lose the power in certain muscles ▫ *polio*

polish¹ /'pɒlɪʃ/ *noun* **1** [U] a cream, liquid, etc. that you put on sth to clean it and make it shine ▫ *penggilap*: *a tin of shoe polish* ➔ picture at **bucket** **2** [sing] the act of polishing sth ▫ *(perbuatan) menggilap*: *I'll give the glasses a polish before the guests arrive.*

polish² /'pɒlɪʃ/ *verb* [T] to make sth shine by rubbing it and often by putting a special cream or liquid on it ▫ *menggilap*: *to polish your shoes/a table*
PHR V **polish sth off** (*informal*) to finish sth quickly ▫ *menghabiskan sst*: *The two of them polished off a whole chicken for dinner!*

polished /'pɒlɪʃt/ *adj* **1** shiny because of polishing ▫ *berkilat*: *polished wood floors* **2** (used about a performance, etc.) of a high standard ▫ *cemerlang*: *Most of the actors gave a polished performance.*

polite /pə'laɪt/ *adj* (**politer**; **politest**) [More **polite** and **most polite** are also common.] having good manners and showing respect for others ▫ *beradab; sopan*: *The assistants in that shop are always very helpful and polite.* ♦ *He gave me a polite smile.* **OPP** **impolite** ▶ **politely** *adv* ▶ **politeness** *noun* [U]

political /pə'lɪtɪkl/ *adj* **1** connected with politics and government ▫ *(berkenaan dgn) politik/kerajaan*: *a political leader/debate/party* ♦ *She has very strong political opinions.* **2** (used about people) interested in politics ▫ *berminat dlm politik*: *She became very political at university.* **3** concerned with competition for power inside an organization ▫ *politik*: *I suspect he was* *dismissed for political reasons.* ▶**politically** /-kli/ *adv*: *Politically he's fairly right wing.*

po¦litical a¦sylum *noun* [U] protection given by a state to a person who has left their own country for political reasons □ *suaka politik*

po¦litically cor¦rect *adj* (*abbr* **PC**) used to describe language or behaviour that carefully avoids offending particular groups of people □ *bahasa atau perilaku yg tdk menyinggung mana-mana pihak* ▶**po¦litical cor¦rectness** *noun* [U]

po¦litical 'science = **politics**(4)

politician /ˌpɒləˈtɪʃn/ *noun* [C] a person whose job is in politics, especially one who is a member of parliament or of the government □ *ahli politik*: *Politicians of all parties supported the war.*

politics /ˈpɒlətɪks/ *noun* **1** [U, with sing or pl verb] the work and ideas that are connected with governing a country, a town, etc. □ *politik*: *to go into politics* ♦ *Politics has/have never been of great interest to me.* **2** [pl] a person's political opinions and beliefs □ *pandangan/pegangan politik*: *His politics are extreme.* **3** [U, with sing or pl verb] matters concerned with competition for power between people in an organization □ *politik*: *office politics* **4** (*also* **Po¦litical 'Science**) [U] the scientific study of government □ *sains politik*: *a degree in Politics* ➲ note at **congress, election, parliament, party**

TOPIC

Politics

In **democratic** countries, **the government** (= the people who control the country) are chosen in **elections**. People **vote for** (= choose) a **candidate** (= a person who wants to be elected). Most **politicians** belong to a **political party**. **Left-wing** parties desire equality (= everyone having the same rights and advantages) and believe that the government should own the main industries. **Right-wing** parties support the system in which industries are owned by individual people and not the state. In the United Kingdom, the person who leads the government is called the **Prime Minister**, and the people who make and change laws are called **Parliament**. In the United States, this group of people is called **Congress** and the head of the government is the **President**.

---

poll¹ /pəʊl/ *noun* [C] **1** (*also* **opinion poll**) a way of finding out public opinion by asking a number of people their views on sth □ *tinjauan pendapat*: *This was voted best drama series in a viewers' poll.* **2** the process of voting in a political election; the number of votes given □ *pilihan raya*: *The country will go to the polls* (= vote) *in June.*

poll² /pəʊl/ *verb* [T] **1** to receive a certain number of votes in an election □ *mendapat undi*: *The Liberal Democrat candidate polled over 3 000 votes.* **2** to ask members of the public their opinion on a subject □ *meninjau pendapat*: *Of those polled, only 20 per cent were in favour of changing the law.*

pollen /ˈpɒlən/ *noun* [U] a fine, usually yellow, powder which is formed in flowers. It makes other flowers of the same type produce seeds when it is carried to them by the wind or by insects, etc. □ *debunga*

pollinate /ˈpɒləneɪt/ *verb* [T] to put **pollen** into a flower or plant so that it produces seeds □ *mendebungakan*: *flowers pollinated by bees/ the wind* ▶**pollination** /ˌpɒləˈneɪʃn/ *noun* [U]

polling /ˈpəʊlɪŋ/ *noun* [U] the process of voting in an election □ *pembuangan undi; pengundian*

pollutant /pəˈluːtənt/ *noun* [C] a substance that **pollutes** air, rivers, etc. □ *bahan cemar*

pollute /pəˈluːt/ *verb* [T] to make air, rivers, etc. dirty and dangerous □ *mencemar*: *Traffic fumes are polluting our cities.* ♦ *The beach has been polluted with oil.*

pollution /pəˈluːʃn/ *noun* [U] **1** the act of making the air, water, etc. dirty and dangerous □ *pencemaran*: *Major steps are being taken to control the pollution of beaches.* **2** substances that **pollute** □ *bahan cemar*: *The rivers are full of pollution.* ➲ note at **environment**

polo /ˈpəʊləʊ/ *noun* [U] a game for two teams of players riding horses. The players try to score goals by hitting a ball with **mallets** (= long wooden hammers). □ *polo*

'polo neck *noun* [C] a high round **collar** (= the part around the neck) on a piece of clothing that is rolled over and that covers most of your neck; a piece of clothing with a **polo neck** □ *kolar polo*

polyester /ˌpɒliˈestə(r)/ (*AmE also* /ˈ /) *noun* [U] an artificial cloth that is used for making clothes, etc. □ *poliester*

polygamy /pəˈlɪɡəmi/ *noun* [U] the custom of having more than one wife or husband at the same time □ *poligami* ➲ look at **bigamy, monogamy** ▶**polygamist** /-mɪst/ *noun* [C] ▶**polygamous** /pəˈlɪɡəməs/ *adj*: *a polygamous society*

polystyrene /ˌpɒliˈstaɪriːn/ *noun* [U] a light firm plastic substance that is used for packing things so that they do not get broken □ *polistirena*

polythene /ˈpɒliθiːn/ (*AmE* **polyethylene** /ˌpɒliˈeθəliːn/) *noun* [U] a type of very thin plastic material often used to make bags for food, etc. or to keep things dry □ *politena*

pomp /pɒmp/ *noun* [U] the impressive nature of a large official occasion or ceremony □ *gilang-gemilang*

pompous /ˈpɒmpəs/ *adj* showing that you think you are more important than other people, for example by using long words that sound impressive □ *angkuh; bongkak; menggunakan bahasa yg penuh gah*

pond /pɒnd/ *noun* [C] an small area of still water □ *kolam* ➲ note at **lake** ➲ picture on **page P11**

ponder /'pɒndə(r)/ *verb* [I,T] (*formal*) **ponder (on/over) sth** to think about sth carefully or for a long time □ *berfikir-fikir*: *The teacher gave us a question to ponder over before the next class.*

pong /pɒŋ/ *noun* [C] (*BrE informal*) a strong unpleasant smell □ *bau busuk*: *a terrible pong* ➲ note at **smell²** ▸ **pong** *verb* [I]

pony /'pəʊni/ *noun* [C] (*pl* **ponies**) a small horse □ *kuda padi*

ponytail /'pəʊniteɪl/ *noun* [C] long hair that is tied at the back of the head and that hangs down in one piece □ *(ikat rambut) ekor kuda* ➲ picture at **hair**

'pony-trekking *noun* [U] the activity of riding horses for pleasure in the country □ *menunggang kuda (utk bersiar-siar)*

poo /puː/ *noun* [C,U] a child's word for the solid waste material that you get rid of from your body when you go to the toilet □ *berak; tahi* ▸ **poo** *verb* [I]

poodle /'puːdl/ *noun* [C] a type of dog with thick curly fur that is sometimes cut into a special pattern □ *anjing poodle*

pooh /puː/ *exclam* (*BrE informal*) said when you smell sth unpleasant □ *ceh; isy*

pool

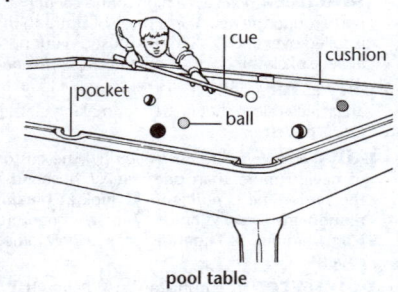

cue
cushion
pocket
ball

pool table

pool¹ /puːl/ *noun*
▸FOR SWIMMING **1** [C] = **swimming pool** □ *kolam renang*: *She swims ten lengths of the pool every morning.*
▸OF LIQUID **2** a small amount of water, especially one that has formed naturally □ *kolam*: *a rock pool* (= between rocks by the sea) ➲ picture on **page P10 3** [C] **a pool (of sth)** a small amount of liquid lying on a surface □ *lopak; tompokan; tumpahan*: *There's a huge pool of water on the kitchen floor.* ➲ note at **lake**
▸OF LIGHT **4** [C] a small area of light □ *sorotan; tompokan*: *a pool of light*
▸GROUP OF THINGS/PEOPLE **5** [C] a quantity of money, goods, etc. that is shared between a group of people □ *tabung; kumpulan*: *There is a pool of cars that anyone in the company can use.*
▸GAME **6** [U] a game for two people played with 16 balls on a table. Players use **cues** (= long sticks) to try to hit the balls into pockets at the edge of the table □ *permainan pool*: *a pool table* ➲ look at **billiards, snooker**

pool² /puːl/ *verb* [T] to collect money, ideas, etc. together from a number of people □ *mengumpulkan*: *If we pool our ideas we should come up with a good plan.*

poor /pɔː(r); pʊə(r)/ *adj* (**poorer; poorest**) **1** not having enough money to have a comfortable life □ *miskin*: *The family was too poor to buy new clothes.* ♦ *Richer countries could do more to help poorer countries.* OPP **rich 2 the poor** *noun* [pl] people who do not have enough money to have a comfortable life □ *orang miskin/susah*: *They provided food and shelter for the poor.* **3** [only before a noun] used when you are showing that you feel sorry for sb □ *kasihan*: *Poor Dan! He's very upset!* **4** of low quality or in a bad condition □ *kurang baik; tdk bermutu*: *Paul is in very poor health.* ♦ *The industry has a poor safety record.*

poorly¹ /'pɔːli/ *adv* not well; badly □ *kurang baik; teruk; rendah; sedikit*: *a poorly paid job*

poorly² /'pɔːli/ *adj* (*BrE informal*) not well; ill □ *tdk sihat*: *I'm feeling a bit poorly.*

pop¹ /pɒp/ *noun* **1** [U] (also **'pop music**) modern music that is most popular among young people □ *pop*: *a pop group* ➲ look at **jazz, rock, classical 2** [C] a short sudden sound like a small explosion □ *bunyi pop*: *There was a loud pop as the champagne cork came out of the bottle.*

> **TOPIC**
>
> **Pop music**
>
> I like most kinds of music, including **pop**, **rock**, **hip hop** and **reggae**. I love going to **gigs** (= concerts). My favourite **band/group** is 'Alphagarden'. I'm one of their biggest **fans**. I love the **singer** because he has such a great **voice**! The **drummer** and **guitarist** play well, too. All their **songs** have good **lyrics** (= words) and the **tunes/melodies** are very **catchy** (= easy to remember). Last year they released an **album** (= a collection of songs on one CD) which became a big **hit** (= was very successful). They don't often **play live** (= with people watching), but next year they are going **on tour** (= performing in various places). I already have tickets to **go to a concert**.

pop² /pɒp/ *verb* (**popping; popped**) **1** [I,T] to make a short sudden sound like a small explosion; to cause sth to do this □ *meletup*: *The balloon popped.* ♦ *He popped the balloon.* **2** [I] **pop across, down, out, etc.** to come or go somewhere quickly or suddenly □ *pergi/datang sebentar*: *I'm just popping out to the shops.* **3** [T] **pop sth in, into, etc. sth** to put or take sth some-

where quickly or suddenly □ *meletakkan sst dgn cepat-cepat*: *She popped the note into her bag.*
PHR V **pop in** to make a quick visit □ *singgah sebentar; menjenguk*: *Why don't you pop in for a cup of tea?*
pop out to come out (of sth) suddenly or quickly □ *keluar sebentar*: *A window opened and a man's head popped out.*
pop up (*informal*) to appear or happen when you are not expecting it □ *tiba-tiba muncul/ berlaku*

pop. abbr = **population** □ *penduduk*: *pop. 12m*

popcorn /'pɒpkɔːn/ noun [U] a type of food made from **maize** (= a tall plant with yellow grains) that is heated until it bursts and forms light white balls that are eaten with salt or sugar on them □ *bertih jagung*

pope /pəʊp/ noun [C] the head of the Roman Catholic Church □ *Paus*

poplar /'pɒplə(r)/ noun [C] a tall thin straight tree with soft wood □ *pokok poplar*

'pop music = **pop¹(1)**

'popper /'pɒpə(r)/ = **press stud**

poppy /'pɒpi/ noun [C] (*pl* **poppies**) a bright red wild flower that has small black seeds □ *bunga popi*

Popsicle™ /'pɒpsɪkl/ (*AmE*) = **ice lolly**

popular /'pɒpjələ(r)/ adj 1 **popular (with sb)** liked by many people or by most people in a group □ *disukai ramai*: *a popular holiday resort* ♦ *That teacher has always been very popular with his pupils.* **OPP** **unpopular** 2 made for the tastes and knowledge of ordinary people □ *umum*: *The popular newspapers seem more interested in scandal than news.* 3 [only before a noun] of or for a lot of people □ *umum; ramai*: *The programme is being repeated by popular demand.*

popularity /ˌpɒpjuˈlærəti/ noun [U] the quality or state of being liked by many people □ *kepopularan*: *The band's popularity is growing.*

popularize (also **-ise**) /'pɒpjələraɪz/ verb [T] to make a lot of or most people like sth □ *mempopularkan*: *The film did a lot to popularize her novels.*

popularly /'pɒpjələli/ adv by many people; generally □ *ramai; umum*: *The Conservatives are popularly known as the Tories.*

populate /'pɒpjuleɪt/ verb [T, usually passive] to fill a particular area with people □ *mendiami; menghuni*: *Hong Kong is very densely populated.*

population /ˌpɒpjuˈleɪʃn/ noun (*abbr* **pop.**) 1 [C,U] the number of people who live in a particular area, city or country □ *penduduk*: *What is the population of your country?* ♦ *an increase/a fall in population* 2 [C] all the people who live in a particular place or all the people or animals of a particular type that live somewhere □ *penduduk; penghuni*: *the local population* ♦ *the male/female population* ♦ *The prison population* has increased in recent years.

'pop-up adj [only before a noun] 1 (used about a computer menu, etc.) that can be brought to the screen quickly while you are working on another document □ *timbul (ttg menu komputer)*: *a pop-up menu/window* 2 (used about a book, etc.) containing a picture that stands up when the pages are opened □ *timbul (ttg gambar)*

porcelain /'pɔːsəlɪn/ noun [U] a hard white substance that is used for making expensive cups, plates, etc. □ *porselin*

porch /pɔːtʃ/ noun [C] 1 a small covered area at the entrance to a house or church □ *anjung* ⊃ picture on **page P8** 2 (*AmE*) = **veranda**

pore¹ /pɔː(r)/ noun [C] one of the small holes in your skin through which sweat can pass □ *liang; pori*

pore² /pɔː(r)/ verb
PHR V **pore over sth** to study or read sth very carefully □ *meneliti; menelaah*

pork /pɔːk/ noun [U] meat from a pig □ *daging babi/khinzir* ⊃ note at **meat** ⊃ look at **bacon, gammon, ham**

pornography /pɔːˈnɒɡrəfi/ (also *informal* **porn** /pɔːn/) noun [U] magazines, films, websites, etc. that describe or show sexual acts in order to cause sexual excitement □ *pornografi; bahan-bahan lucah* ▶ **pornographic** /ˌpɔːnəˈɡræfɪk/ adj

porous /'pɔːrəs/ adj having many small holes that allow water or air to pass through slowly □ *poros; berliang-liang kecil; berongga*: *porous material/rocks/surfaces*

porpoise /'pɔːpəs/ noun [C] a sea animal that looks like a large fish with a pointed nose and that lives in groups □ *sejenis ikan lumba-lumba* ⊃ look at **dolphin**

porridge /'pɒrɪdʒ/ (*AmE* also /) noun [U] a soft, thick, white food that is made from **oats** (= a type of grain) boiled with milk or water and eaten hot, especially for breakfast □ *bubur*

port /pɔːt/ noun 1 [C] a town or city that has a large area of water where ships load goods, etc □ *bandar pelabuhan*: *Hamburg is a major port.* 2 [C,U] an area where ships stop to let goods and passengers on and off □ *pelabuhan*: *a naval port* ♦ *The damaged ship reached port safely.* 3 [U] a strong sweet red wine □ *port (wain)* 4 [U] the side of a ship that is on your left when you are facing towards the front of the ship □ *sebelah kiri kapal*: *the port side* **OPP** **starboard** ⊃ note at **boat**

portable /'pɔːtəbl/ adj that can be moved or carried easily □ *mudah alih; bimbit*: *a portable TV* ⊃ look at **movable, mobile**

portal /'pɔːtl/ noun [C] a website which is used as a point to enter the Internet, giving links to information that will be useful to a person interested in particular kinds of things □ *portal: a business/news/shopping portal*

porter /'pɔːtə(r)/ *noun* [C] **1** a person whose job is to carry suitcases, etc. at a railway station, airport, etc. □ *porter* **2** a person whose job is to be in charge of the entrance of a hotel or other large building □ *porter; penjaga pintu*

portfolio /pɔːt'fəʊliəʊ/ *noun* [C] (*pl* portfolios) **1** a thin flat case used for carrying documents, drawings, etc. □ *portfolio; bekas leper utk membawa sst* **2** a collection of photographs, drawings, etc. that you use as an example of your work, especially when applying for a job □ *portfolio; kumpulan hasil kerja sso*

porthole /'pɔːthəʊl/ *noun* [C] a small round window in a ship □ *tingkap magun*

portion /'pɔːʃn/ *noun* [C] **a portion (of sth) 1** a part or share of sth □ *bahagian: What portion of your salary goes on tax?* ◆ *We must both accept a portion of the blame.* **2** an amount of food for one person (especially in a restaurant) □ *hidangan: Could we have two extra portions of chips, please?*
➪ look at **helping**

portrait /'pɔːtreɪt, -trət/ *noun* **1** [C] a picture, painting or photograph of a person □ *potret: to paint somebody's portrait* **2** [C] a description of sb/sth in words □ *gambaran* **3** [U] (*technical*) the way of printing a document in which the top of the page is one of the shorter sides □ *portrait (cetak secara menegak)* ➪ look at **landscape**
➪ picture at **computer**

portray /pɔː'treɪ/ *verb* [T] **1** to show sb/sth in a picture; to describe sb/sth in a piece of writing □ *menunjukkan dlm gambar; menggambarkan: Zola portrayed life in 19th-century France.* **2 portray sb/sth as sth** to describe sb/sth in a particular way □ *menggambarkan: In many of his novels life is portrayed as being hard.* **3** to act the part of sb in a play or film □ *melakonkan watak: In this film she portrays a very old woman.*
▸ **portrayal** /pɔː'treɪəl/ *noun* [C,U]

pose¹ /pəʊz/ *verb* [T] **1** to create or give sb sth that they have to deal with □ *menimbulkan; mengemukakan: to pose a problem/threat/challenge/risk* ◆ *to pose* (= ask) *a question* **2** [I] to sit or stand in a particular position for a painting, photograph, etc. □ *duduk atau berdiri (dgn gaya tertentu utk dilukis, diambil gambar, dsb); menggayakan: After the wedding we all posed for photographs.* **3** [I] **pose as sb/sth** to pretend to be sb/sth □ *menyamar sebagai: The robbers got into the house by posing as telephone engineers.* **4** [I] to behave in a way that is intended to impress people who see you □ *berlagak-lagak: They hardly swam at all. They just sat posing at the side of the pool.*

pose² /pəʊz/ *noun* [C] **1** a position in which sb stands, sits, etc. especially in order to be painted or photographed □ *gaya berdiri, duduk, dsb (utk bergambar, dilukis, dsb): He adopted a relaxed pose for the camera.* **2** a way of behaving that is intended to impress people who see you □ *lagak: His show of interest is just a pose.*

posh /pɒʃ/ *adj* (**posher**; **poshest**) (*informal*) **1** fashionable and expensive □ *mewah: We went for a meal in a really posh hotel.* **SYN** stylish **2** (*BrE*) (used about people) belonging to or typical of a high social class □ *spt golongan atasan*

position¹ /pə'zɪʃn/ *noun*
▸PLACE **1** [C,U] the place where sb/sth is or should be □ *kedudukan: Are you happy with the position of the chairs?* ◆ *All the dancers were in position waiting for the music to begin.*
▸OF BODY, ETC. **2** [C,U] the way in which sb/sth sits, sleeps or stands, or the direction that sth is pointing in □ *kedudukan: My leg hurts when I change position.* ◆ *Turn the switch to the off position.*
▸SITUATION **3** [C, usually sing] the state or situation that sb/sth is in □ *keadaan; kedudukan: I'm in a very difficult position.* ◆ *I'm sorry, I'm not in a position to help you financially.*
▸OPINION **4** [C] **a position (on sth)** what you think about sth; your opinion □ *pendirian: What is your position on school uniform?*
▸LEVEL OF IMPORTANCE **5** [C,U] the place or level of a person, company, team, etc. compared to others □ *kedudukan; taraf; tempat: the position of women in society* ◆ *Max finished the race in second position.* ◆ *Wealth and position are very important to some people.*
▸JOB **6** [C] (*formal*) a job □ *jawatan: There have been over a hundred applications for the position of Sales Manager.* **SYN** post
▸IN SPORT **7** [C] the part you play in a team game □ *kedudukan: Danny can play any position except goalkeeper.*

position² /pə'zɪʃn/ *verb* [T] to put sb/sth in a particular place or position □ *meletakkan; menempatkan: Mary positioned herself near the door so she could get out quickly.*

positive /'pɒzətɪv/ *adj*
▸CONFIDENT **1** thinking or talking mainly about the good things in a situation; feeling confident and sure that sth good will happen □ *positif; menggalakkan: Their reaction to my idea was generally positive.* ◆ *I feel very positive about our team's chances this season.* ◆ *Positive thinking will help you to succeed.* **OPP** negative
▸CERTAIN/DEFINITE **2 positive (about sth/that ...)** certain; sure □ *pasti: Are you positive that this is the woman you saw?* **3** clear; definite □ *positif; sah: There is no positive evidence that he is guilty.* ◆ *to take positive action*
▸SCIENTIFIC TEST **4** showing that sth has happened or is present □ *jelas; pasti; positif: The result of the pregnancy test was positive.* ◆ *Two athletes tested positive for steroids.* **OPP** negative
▸NUMBER **5** more than zero □ *nombor positif* **OPP** negative

positively /'pɒzətɪvli/ *adv* **1** (used for emphasizing sth) really; extremely □ *betul-betul: He wasn't just annoyed—he was positively furious!* **2** in a way that shows you are thinking about the good things in a situation, not the bad □ *secara positif: Thinking positively helps many people deal* with stress. **3** with no doubt; firmly □ *dgn pasti; betul-betul*: *I was positively convinced that I was doing the right thing.*

possess /pə'zez/ *verb* [T] [not used in the continuous tenses] **1** (*formal*) to have or own sth □ *memiliki; mempunyai*: *They lost everything they possessed in the fire.* ♦ *Paola possesses a natural ability to make people laugh.* **2** to influence sb or to make sb do sth □ *mempengaruhi; menyebabkan sso membuat sst*: *What possessed you to say a thing like that!*

> **HELP** Although this verb is not used in the continuous tenses, it is common to see the present participle (= *-ing* form): *Any student possessing the necessary qualifications will be considered for the course.*

possession /pə'zeʃn/ *noun* **1** [U] (*formal*) the state of having or owning sth □ *pemilikan; memiliki; menguasai*: *The gang were caught in possession of stolen goods.* ♦ *Enemy forces took possession of the town.* **2** [C, usually pl] something that you have or own □ *harta benda; barang-barang*: *Bud packed all his possessions and left.*

possessive /pə'zesɪv/ *adj* **1** possessive (of/about sb/sth) not wanting to share sb/sth □ *lokek; terlalu mengongkong*: *Dan is so possessive about his toys—he won't let other children play with them.* **2** used to describe words that show who or what a person or thing belongs to □ *(kata/bentuk) milik*: *'My', 'your' and 'his' are possessive adjectives.* ♦ *'Mine', 'yours' and 'his' are possessive pronouns.*

possessor /pə'zesə(r)/ *noun* [C] (*formal*) a person who has or owns sth □ *pemilik*

possibility /ˌpɒsə'bɪləti/ *noun* (*pl* possibilities) **1** [U,C] (a) possibility (of sth/doing sth); (a) possibility that … the fact that sth might exist or happen, but is not likely to □ *kemungkinan*: *There's not much possibility of the letter reaching you before Saturday.* ♦ *There is a strong possibility that the fire was started deliberately.* **2** [C] one of the different things that you can do in a particular situation or in order to achieve sth □ *kemungkinan; pilihan*: *There is a wide range of possibilities open to us.*

possible /'pɒsəbl/ *adj* **1** that can happen or be done □ *mungkin; dpt*: *I'll phone you back as soon as possible.* ♦ *Could you give me your answer today, if possible?* ♦ *The doctors did everything possible to save his life.* ♦ *You were warned of all the possible dangers.* **OPP** impossible **2** that might exist or happen but is not certain to □ *mungkin; boleh jadi*: *the possible side effects of the drug* **3** reasonable or acceptable in a particular situation □ *mungkin; berpotensi*: *There are several possible explanations.* ⮕ look at **probable 4** used after adjectives to emphasize that sth is the best, worst, etc. of its type □ *mungkin*: *Alone and with no job or money, I was in the worst possible situation.*

possibly /'pɒsəbli/ *adv* **1** perhaps □ *mungkin; boleh jadi*: *'Will you be free on Sunday?' 'Possibly.'* ♦ *Could you possibly give me some help tomorrow?*

SYN maybe **2** (used for emphasizing sth) according to what is possible □ *yg mungkin*: *I will leave as soon as I possibly can.* ♦ *I can't possibly finish this work today.*

post¹ /pəʊst/ *noun*
▶LETTERS **1** (*especially AmE* mail) [U] the system or organization for collecting and dealing with letters, packages, etc. □ *pos*: *The document is too valuable to send by post.* ♦ *If you hurry you might catch the post* (= post it before everything is collected). **2** (*AmE* mail) [U] letters, packages, etc. that are collected or brought to your house □ *(surat, bungkusan, dll) pos*: *Has the post come yet this morning?* ♦ *There wasn't any post for you.*
▶JOB **3** [C] (*formal*) a job □ *jawatan*: *The post was advertised in the local newspaper.* **SYN** position
▶SOLDIER/GUARD **4** [C] a place where sb is on duty or is guarding sth □ *pos; tempat bertugas*: *The soldiers had to remain at their posts all night.*
▶METAL/WOOD **5** [C] a vertical piece of metal or wood that is put in the ground to mark a position or to support sth □ *tiang*: *a goal post* ♦ *Can you see a signpost anywhere?* **6** (also posting) [C] a message sent to a discussion group on the Internet □ *mesej; pesanan*: *The forum doesn't allow posts from non-members.* ⮕ note at **chat room, netiquette**
IDM by return (of post) ⮕ return²

post² /pəʊst/ *verb* **1** (*especially AmE* mail) [T] to send a letter, package, etc. by post □ *mengepos*: *This letter was posted in Edinburgh yesterday.* **2** [T] to send sb to go and work somewhere □ *menugaskan/ditugaskan utk bekerja*: *After two years in London, Angela was posted to the Tokyo office.* **3** [T] to put sb on guard or on duty in a particular place □ *menempatkan (sso utk mengawal atau bekerja)*: *Policemen were posted outside the building.* **4** [T, often passive] to put a notice where everyone can see it □ *menampalkan; melekatkan*: *The exam results will be posted on the main noticeboard.* **5** [I,T] to put information or pictures on a website □ *memaparkan*: *The winners' names will be posted on our website.* ♦ *The photos have been provided by fans who post on the message board.*

> **TOPIC**
>
> **Posting letters**
>
> **Post** (noun and verb) is more commonly used in British English and **mail** in American English. However, the noun **mail** is often used in British English, for example in the official name of the Post Office organization, the **Royal Mail**. When you have written a **letter** you put it in an **envelope**, **address** it, **put/stick** a **stamp** on it and put it in a **postbox** (*US* **mailbox**). The address should include the **postcode** (*US* **zip code**). You can choose to send **parcels** and letters by **airmail** or **surface mail**. If it is urgent, you might send it by **courier**. You can order goods to be delivered by mail, using a **mail-order** service.

postage /'pəʊstɪdʒ/ noun [U] the amount that you must pay to send a letter, package etc. □ *bayaran pos*

'postage stamp = **stamp¹**(1)

postal /'pəʊstl/ adj [only before a noun] connected with the sending and collecting of letters, packages, etc. □ *(berkenaan dgn) perkhidmatan pos*

'postal order (AmE **'money order**) noun [C] a piece of paper that you can buy at a post office that represents a certain amount of money. A **postal order** is a safe way of sending money by post. □ *wang pos*

postbox (BrE)　　　mailbox (AmE)

postbox /'pəʊstbɒks/ (also **'letter box**; AmE **mailbox**) noun [C] a box in a public place where you put letters, etc. that you want to send □ *peti surat* ➲ look at **pillar box**

postcard /'pəʊstkɑːd/ noun [C] a card that you write a message on and send to sb. **Postcards** have a picture on one side and are usually sent without an envelope. □ *poskad* ➲ picture at **letter**

postcode /'pəʊstkəʊd/ (AmE **zip code**) noun [C] a group of letters and/or numbers that you put at the end of an address □ *poskod*

poster /'pəʊstə(r)/ noun [C] **1** a large printed picture or a notice in a public place, often used to advertise sth □ *poster* **2** a large picture printed on paper that is put on a wall for decoration □ *poster*

posterity /pɒ'sterəti/ noun [U] (formal) the future and the people who will be alive then □ *generasi akan datang*: *We should all look after our environment for the sake of posterity.*

postgraduate /ˌpəʊst'grædʒuət/ noun [C] a person who is doing further studies at a university after taking their first degree □ *lepas ijazah* ➲ look at **graduate, undergraduate**

posthumous /'pɒstjʊməs/ adj given or happening after sb has died □ *selepas mati; anumerta*: *a posthumous medal for bravery* ▶ **posthumously** adv

posting /'pəʊstɪŋ/ noun [C] **1** a job in another country that you are sent to do by your employer □ *tugas*: *an overseas posting* **2** = **post¹**(6)

'Post-it™ (also **'Post-it note**) noun [C] a small piece of coloured, sticky paper that you use for writing a note on, and that can be easily removed □ *nota lekap/tampal*

postman /'pəʊstmən/ (AmE **mailman**) noun [C] (pl **-men** /-mən/) a person whose job is to take letters, packages, etc. to people's houses □ *posmen*

postmark /'pəʊstmɑːk/ noun [C] an official mark over a stamp on a letter, package, etc. that says when and where it was posted □ *cap pos* ➲ picture at **letter**

post-mortem /ˌpəʊst 'mɔːtəm/ noun [C] a medical examination of a dead body to find out how the person died □ *post-mortem; bedah siasat mayat*

post-natal /ˌpəʊst 'neɪtl/ adj [only before a noun] connected with the period after the birth of a baby □ *lepas bersalin; postnatum* **OPP** **antenatal**

'post office noun [C] (abbr **PO**) **1** a place where you can buy stamps, post packages, etc. □ *pejabat pos*: *Where's the main post office?* **2** **the Post Office** [sing] the national organization that is responsible for collecting and dealing with letters, packages, etc. □ *Jabatan Perkhidmatan Pos*: *He works for the Post Office.*

postpone /pə'spəʊn/ verb [T] to arrange that sth will happen at a later time than the time you had planned; to delay □ *menangguhkan*: *The match was postponed because of water on the pitch.* ➲ look at **cancel** ▶ **postponement** noun [C,U]

postscript /'pəʊstskrɪpt/ = **PS**

posture /'pɒstʃə(r)/ noun [C,U] the way that a person sits, stands, walks, etc. □ *postur; cara duduk, berdiri, berjalan, dsb*: *Poor posture can lead to backache.*

post-'war adj existing or happening in the period after the end of a war, especially the Second World War □ *lepas perang*

pot¹ /pɒt/ noun [C] **1** a round container that is used for cooking food in □ *periuk; belanga*: *pots and pans* **2** a container that you use for a particular purpose □ *pasu, bekas, tin, botol, teko, dsb*: *a flowerpot* ♦ *a pot of paint* **3** the amount that a pot contains □ *seperiuk, setin, seteko, dsb*: *We drank two pots of tea.*

pot² /pɒt/ verb [T] (**potting; potted**) **1** to put a plant into a pot filled with soil □ *menanam dlm pasu* **2** to hit a ball into one of the pockets in the table in the game of **pool, billiards** or **snooker** (= games that are played on special tables) □ *memasukkan bola ke dlm poket (dlm permainan pool, biliard atau snuker)*: *He potted the black ball into the corner pocket.*

potassium /pə'tæsiəm/ noun [U] (symbol **K**) a chemical element that exists as a soft, silver-white metal and is used combined with other

potato → pour

potato /pəˈteɪtəʊ/ noun [C,U] (pl potatoes) a round vegetable that grows under the ground with a brown, yellow or red skin. Potatoes are white or yellow inside □ *ubi kentang*: *mashed potato* ♦ *to peel potatoes* ➾ note at **recipe** ➾ picture on page P15

po‚tato ˈcrisp (AmE poˈtato chip) = **crisp²**

potent /ˈpəʊtnt/ adj strong or powerful □ *kuat*: *a potent drug* ▸**potency** /ˈpəʊtnsi/ noun [U]

potential¹ /pəˈtenʃl/ adj [only before a noun] that may possibly become sth, happen, be used, etc. □ *mungkin; berpotensi*: *Wind power is a potential source of energy.* ♦ *potential customers* **SYN** possible ▸**potentially** /-ʃəli/ adv

potential² /pəˈtenʃl/ noun [U] the qualities or abilities that sb/sth has but that may not be fully developed yet □ *potensi*: *That boy has great potential as an athlete.*

pothole /ˈpɒthəʊl/ noun [C] 1 a hole in the surface of a road that is formed by traffic and bad weather □ *lubang; lopak* 2 a deep hole in rock that is formed by water over thousands of years □ *lubang gua*

potholing /ˈpɒthəʊlɪŋ/ noun [U] the sport of climbing down inside **potholes** (2) and walking through underground tunnels □ *kembara lubang gua*: *to go potholing*

potion /ˈpəʊʃn/ noun [C] 1 a drink of medicine or poison □ *posyen; minuman* 2 (in stories) a liquid with magic powers □ *posyen; cecair sakti*: *a magic/love potion*

ˈpot plant noun [C] (BrE) a plant that you grow in a pot and keep inside a building □ *pokok pasu*

potter¹ /ˈpɒtə(r)/ (AmE **putter** /ˈpʌtə(r)/) verb [I] **potter** (about/around) to spend your time doing small jobs or things that you enjoy without hurrying □ *menggeropes*: *Grandpa spends most of the day pottering about in the garden.*

potter² /ˈpɒtə(r)/ noun [C] a person who makes **pottery** from baked **clay** (= a type of earth) □ *tukang tembikar*

pottery /ˈpɒtəri/ noun (pl **potteries**) 1 [U] pots, dishes, etc. that are made from baked **clay** (= a type of earth) □ *barang-barang tembikar* 2 [U] the activity or skill of making dishes, etc. from clay □ *seni tembikar*: *a pottery class* 3 [C] a place where **clay** pots and dishes are made □ *kilang tembikar*

potty¹ /ˈpɒti/ adj (**pottier**; **pottiest**) (BrE old-fashioned informal) 1 crazy or silly □ *gila; sasar; bodoh* 2 **potty about sb/sth** liking sb/sth very much □ *tergila-gilakan; gila*: *Penny's potty about Mark.*

potty² /ˈpɒti/ noun [C] (pl **potties**) a plastic bowl that young children use when they are too small to use a toilet □ *ketur*

pouch /paʊtʃ/ noun [C] 1 a small bag □ *pau; dompet*: *a leather pouch* 2 a pocket of skin on the stomach of some female animals, for example **kangaroos**, in which they carry their babies □ *kantung* ➾ picture at **kangaroo**

poultry /ˈpəʊltri/ noun 1 [pl] birds, for example chickens, **ducks**, etc. that are kept for their eggs or their meat □ *ayam, itik dsb* 2 [U] the meat from these birds □ *daging ayam, itik, dsb*: *Eat plenty of fish and poultry.*

pounce /paʊns/ verb [I] **pounce (on sb/sth)** to attack sb/sth by jumping suddenly on them or it □ *menerkam; menyerkap*: *The cat sat motionless, waiting to pounce on the mouse.* ♦ (figurative) *He was quick to pounce on any mistakes I made.*

pound¹ /paʊnd/ noun 1 [C] (also ‚pound ˈsterling) (symbol £) the unit of money in the UK; one hundred pence (100p) □ *(simbol £) paun*: *Melissa earns £26 000 a year.* ♦ *Can you change a ten-pound note?* ♦ *a pound coin* **the pound** [sing] the value of the UK pound on international money markets □ *nilai mata wang paun*: *The pound has fallen against the dollar.* ♦ *How many yen are there to the pound?* 3 [C] (abbr **lb**) a measure of weight; equal to 0.454 of a kilogram □ *paun*: *The carrots cost 45p a pound.* ♦ *Half a pound of mushrooms, please.* ❶ For more information about weights, look at the section on using numbers at the back of this dictionary.

pound² /paʊnd/ verb 1 [I,T] **pound (at/ against/on) sth** to hit sth hard many times making a lot of noise □ *menumbuk/mengetuk bertalu-talu*: *Great waves pounded the rocks.* ♦ *She pounded on the door with her fists.* 2 [I] **pound along, down, up, etc.** to walk with heavy, noisy steps in a particular direction □ *(berjalan, dsb) gedebak-gedebuk*: *Jason went pounding up the stairs three at a time.* 3 [I] (used about your heart, blood, etc.) to beat quickly and loudly □ *berdegap-degup*: *Her heart was pounding with fear.* 4 [T] to hit sth many times to break it into smaller pieces □ *menumbuk, menghancurkan, melumatkan*

pour /pɔː(r)/ verb 1 [T] to make a liquid or other substance flow steadily out of or into a container □ *menuang; mencurah*: *Pour the sugar into a bowl.* 2 [I] (used about a liquid, smoke, light, etc.) to flow out of or into sth quickly and steadily, and in large quantities □ *mencurah; keluar (berkepul-kepul, dsb)*: *Tears were pouring down her cheeks.* ♦ *She opened the curtains and sunlight poured into the room.* 3 [T] **pour sth (out)** to serve a drink to sb by letting it flow from a container into a cup or glass □ *menuangkan*: *Have you poured out the tea?* 4 [I] **pour (down) (with rain)** to rain heavily □ *(hujan) turun mencurah-curah*: *The rain poured down all day long.* ♦ *I'm not going out. It's pouring with rain.* 5 [I] to come or go somewhere continuously in large numbers □ *membanjiri; keluar/masuk berduyun-duyun*: *People were pouring out of the station.*

| VOWELS | iː see | i any | ɪ sit | e ten | æ hat | ɑː father | ɒ got | ɔː saw | ʊ put | uː too | u usual |

pout → practicality

IDM **pour your heart out (to sb)** to tell sb all your personal problems, feelings, etc. □ *mencurahkan perasaan (kpd sso)*

PHR V **pour sth out** to speak freely about what you think or feel about sth that has happened to you □ *meluahkan pendapat atau perasaan*: *to pour out all your troubles*

pout /paʊt/ *verb* [I] to push your lips, or your bottom lip, forward to show that you are annoyed about sth or to look sexually attractive □ *memuncungkan* ▶**pout** *noun* [C]

poverty /ˈpɒvəti/ *noun* [U] the state of being poor □ *kemiskinan*: *There are millions of people in this country who are living in poverty.*

poverty-stricken /ˈpɒvəti strɪkən/ *adj* very poor □ *terlalu miskin; papa kedana*

powder /ˈpaʊdə(r)/ *noun* [U,C] a dry substance that is in the form of very small grains □ *serbuk*: *washing powder* ♦ *Grind the spices into a fine powder.* ▶**powder** *verb* [T]

powdered /ˈpaʊdəd/ *adj* (used about a substance that is usually liquid) dried and made into powder □ *(dlm bentuk) serbuk atau tepung*: *powdered milk/soup*

power¹ /ˈpaʊə(r)/ *noun*
▶CONTROL **1** [U] **power (over sb/sth)**; **power (to do sth)** the ability to control people or things or to do sth □ *kuasa*: *The aim is to give people more power over their own lives.* ♦ *to have somebody in your power* ♦ *It's not in my power* (= I am unable) *to help you.* **2** [U] political control of a country or area □ *kuasa; berkuasa*: *When did this government come to power?* ♦ *to take/seize power*
▶ABILITY **3** **powers** [pl] a particular ability of the body or mind □ *daya; kebolehan; keupayaan*: *He has great powers of observation.* ♦ *She had to use all her powers of persuasion on him.*
▶AUTHORITY **4** [C] **the power (to do sth)** the right or authority to do sth □ *kuasa*: *Do the police have the power to stop cars without good reason?*
▶COUNTRY **5** [C] a country with a lot of influence in world affairs or that has great military strength □ *kuasa*: *Britain is no longer a world power.* ♦ *a military/economic power*
▶ENERGY **6** [U] the energy or strength that sb/sth has □ *daya; tenaga; kekuatan*: *The ship was helpless against the power of the storm.* ♦ *He hit the ball with as much power as he could.*
▶ELECTRICITY **7** [U] energy that can be collected and used for operating machines, making electricity, etc. □ *tenaga kuasa*: *nuclear/wind/solar power*

power² /ˈpaʊə(r)/ *verb* [T] to supply energy to sth to make it work □ *membekalkan kuasa*: *What powers the motor in this machine?* ▶ **-powered** *adj*: *a solar-powered calculator* ♦ *a high-powered engine*

ˈpower cut *noun* [C] a time when the supply of electricity stops, for example during a storm □ *gangguan bekalan elektrik*

powerful /ˈpaʊəfl/ *adj* **1** having a lot of control or influence over other people □ *(sangat) berkuasa*: *a powerful nation* ♦ *a rich and powerful businessman* **2** having great strength or force □ *(sangat) kuat; berkuasa/berkeupayaan tinggi*: *a powerful car/engine/telescope* ♦ *a powerful swimmer* **3** having a strong effect on your mind or body □ *amat berkesan; kuat*: *The Prime Minister made a powerful speech.* ♦ *a powerful drug* ▶**powerfully** /-fəli/ *adv*

powerless /ˈpaʊələs/ *adj* **1** without strength, influence or control □ *tdk berdaya/berupaya; tanpa kuasa* **2** **powerless to do sth** completely unable to do sth □ *tdk berdaya; langsung tdk dpt berbuat apa-apa*: *I stood and watched him struggle, powerless to help.*

ˈpower plant (*AmE*) = **power station**

ˈpower point (*BrE*) = **socket**(1)

ˈpower station (*AmE* **ˈpower plant**) *noun* [C] a place where electricity is produced □ *stesen jana kuasa*

pp *abbr* **1 pp.** plural of **p.** (1) □ *muka surat; halaman* **2 p.p.** (before the name at the end of a letter) instead of □ *bagi pihak*: *pp Mark Dilks* (= from Mark Dilks, but signed by sb else because Mark Dilks is away)

PR /ˌpiː ˈɑː(r)/ *abbr* **1** = **public relations 2** = **proportional representation**

practicable /ˈpræktɪkəbl/ *adj* (*formal*) (used about an idea, a plan or a suggestion) able to be done successfully □ *boleh dilaksanakan/dipraktikkan/dibuat*: *The scheme is just not practicable.*

practical¹ /ˈpræktɪkl/ *adj*
▶ACTION NOT IDEAS **1** concerned with actually doing sth rather than with ideas or thought □ *amali; praktik*: *Have you got any practical experience of working on a farm?* ⊃ look at **theoretical**
▶LIKELY TO WORK **2** that is likely to succeed; right or sensible □ *praktikal*: *We need to find a practical solution to the problem.* **OPP** **impractical**
▶USEFUL **3** very suitable for a particular purpose; useful □ *praktis; sesuai; berguna*: *a practical little car, ideal for the city* **OPP** **impractical**
▶SENSIBLE **4** (used about people) making sensible decisions and good at dealing with problems □ *bersikap praktis; praktikal*: *We must be practical. It's no good buying a house we cannot afford.* **OPP** **impractical**
▶GOOD WITH HANDS **5** (used about a person) good at making and repairing things □ *praktikal*: *Brett's very practical and has made a lot of improvements to their new house.*

practical² /ˈpræktɪkl/ *noun* [C] (*BrE informal*) a lesson or exam where you do or make sth rather than just writing □ *amali; praktikal*: *He passed the theory paper but failed the practical.*

practicality /ˌpræktɪˈkæləti/ *noun* **1** [U] the quality of being suitable and realistic, or likely to succeed □ *kepraktisan; kesesuaian; kewajaran*: *I am not convinced of the practicality of the scheme.* **2 practicalities** [pl] the real facts rather than ideas or thoughts □ *hal-hal yg praktikal*: *Let's look at the practicalities of the situation.*

practical joke noun [C] a trick that you play on sb that makes them look silly and makes other people laugh □ *gurauan utk mempermainkan sso* ➲ note at **humour**

practically /ˈpræktɪkli/ adv 1 almost; very nearly □ *hampir; dekat*: *My essay is practically finished now.* 2 in a realistic or sensible way □ *secara praktis*: *Practically speaking, we can't afford it.*

practice /ˈpræktɪs/ noun
▸ACTION NOT IDEAS 1 [U] action rather than ideas or thought □ *praktik; amalan*: *Your suggestion sounds fine in theory, but would it work in practice?* ◆ *I can't wait to put what I've learnt into practice.* ➲ look at **theory**
▸WAY OF DOING STH 2 [C,U] (formal) the usual or expected way of doing sth in a particular organization or situation; a habit or custom □ *kebiasaan; amalan*: *It is standard practice not to pay bills until the end of the month.*
▸FOR IMPROVING SKILL 3 [C,U] (a period of) doing an activity many times or training regularly so that you become good at it □ *latihan*: *piano/football practice* ◆ *His accent should improve with practice.*
▸OF DOCTOR/LAWYER 4 [U] the work or the place of work of a doctor or lawyer □ *kerja doktor atau peguam*: *Dr Roberts doesn't work in a hospital. He's in general practice* (= he's a family doctor). 5 [C] the business of a doctor, dentist or lawyer □ *klinik (doktor/doktor gigi); firma guaman*: *a successful medical/dental practice*
IDM **be/get out of practice** to find it difficult to do sth because you have not done it for a long time □ *lama tdk berlatih atau membuat sst*: *I'm not playing very well at the moment. I'm really out of practice.*
in practice in reality □ *sebenarnya*

practise (AmE **practice**) /ˈpræktɪs/ verb [I,T] 1 **practise for sth**; **practise (sth) (on sb/sth)** to do an activity or train regularly so that you become very good at sth □ *berlatih*: *She's practising for her flute exam.* ◆ *If you want to play a musical instrument well, you must practise every day.* ◆ *He likes to practise his English on me.* 2 to do sth or take part in sth regularly or publicly □ *mengamalkan; (taat) mengikut ajaran agama, dsb*: *a practising Catholic/Jew/Muslim* 3 **practise (sth/as sth)** to work as a doctor or lawyer □ *bekerja sebagai doktor atau peguam*: *He was banned from practising medicine.* ◆ *She's practising as a barrister in Leeds.*

practised (AmE **practiced**) /ˈpræktɪst/ adj **practised (in sth)** very good at sth, because you have done it a lot or often □ *pandai; terlatih*: *He was practised in the art of inventing excuses.*

practitioner /prækˈtɪʃənə(r)/ noun [C] a person who works in a profession, especially medicine or law □ *pengamal (perubatan, undang-undang, dll)*: *a dental practitioner* ➲ look at **GP**

pragmatic /prægˈmætɪk/ adj dealing with problems in a practical way rather than by following ideas or principles □ *pragmatik*

prairie /ˈpreəri/ noun [C] a very large area of flat land covered in grass with few trees (especially in North America) □ *prairi*

praise¹ /preɪz/ noun [U] what you say when you are expressing admiration for sb/sth □ *pujian*: *The survivors were full of praise for the paramedics.*

praise² /preɪz/ verb [T] **praise sb/sth (for sth)** to say that sb/sth is good and should be admired □ *memuji; dipuji*: *The firefighters were praised for their courage.*

praiseworthy /ˈpreɪzwɜːði/ adj that should be admired and recognized as good □ *patut dipuji*

pushchair (AmE **stroller**)
pram (AmE **baby carriage**)

pram /præm/ (AmE **baby carriage**) noun [C] a small vehicle on four wheels for a young baby, pushed by a person on foot □ *kereta sorong bayi*

prance /prɑːns/ verb [I] to move about with quick, high steps, often because you feel proud or pleased with yourself □ *berjingkrak-jingkrak*

prank /præŋk/ noun [C] a trick that is played on sb as a joke □ *usikan; senda gurau*: *a childish prank*

prat /præt/ noun [C] (BrE slang) a stupid person □ *(si) bodoh; tongong betul*: *What a prat!*

prawn /prɔːn/ (AmE **shrimp**) noun [C] a small **shellfish** (= a creature with a shell that lives in water) that you can eat, which becomes pink when cooked □ *udang* ➲ picture on **page P13**

pray /preɪ/ verb [I,T] **pray (to sb) (for sb/sth)** 1 to speak to God or a god in order to give thanks or to ask for help □ *berdoa; bersembahyang*: *They knelt down and prayed for peace.* ◆ *They prayed that the war would end soon.* 2 to hope very much that sth will happen □ *berharap*: *We're praying for good weather on Saturday.*

prayer /preə(r)/ noun 1 [C] **a prayer (for sb/sth)** the words that you say when you speak to God or a god □ *doa*: *Let's say a prayer for all the people who are ill.* ◆ *a prayer book* 2 [U] the act of speaking to God or a god □ *sembahyang*: *to kneel in prayer*

preach → predatory

preach /priːtʃ/ verb 1 [I,T] to give a **sermon** (= a talk on a religious subject), especially in a church ▫ *memberi khutbah; berkhutbah* 2 [T] to say that sth is good and persuade other people to accept it ▫ *menganjurkan*: *I always preach caution in situations like this.* 3 [I] to give sb advice on moral behaviour, in a way which they find boring or annoying ▫ *berkhutbah; berleter*: *I'm sorry, I didn't mean to preach.*

preacher /ˈpriːtʃə(r)/ noun [C] a person who gives **sermons** (= talks on religious subjects), for example in a church ▫ *pengkhutbah*

precarious /prɪˈkeəriəs/ adj not safe or certain; dangerous ▫ *tdk selamat; berbahaya; tdk tentu*: *That ladder looks very precarious.* ▸ **precariously** adv

precaution /prɪˈkɔːʃn/ noun [C] **a precaution (against sth)** something that you do now in order to avoid danger or problems in the future ▫ *langkah beringat/mencegah*: *precautions against fire/theft* ◆ *You should always **take the precaution of** locking your valuables in the hotel safe.* ▸ **precautionary** /prɪˈkɔːʃənəri/ adj

precede /prɪˈsiːd/ verb [I,T] (formal) to happen, come or go before sb/sth ▫ *mendahului/sebelum*: *Look at the table on the preceding page.*

precedence /ˈpresɪdəns/ noun [U] **precedence (over sb/sth)** the right that sb/sth has to come before sb/sth else because he/she/it is more important ▫ *keutamaan; didahulukan*: *In business, making a profit seems to **take precedence** over everything else.*

precedent /ˈpresɪdənt/ noun [C,U] an official action or decision that has happened in the past and that is considered as an example or rule to follow in the same situation later ▫ *duluan; kebiasaan; sst yg pernah berlaku sebelumnya*: *We don't want to **set a precedent** by allowing one person to come in late or they'll all want to do it.* ◆ *Such protests are **without precedent** in recent history.* ⊃ look at **unprecedented**

precinct /ˈpriːsɪŋkt/ noun 1 [C] (BrE) a special area of shops in a town where cars are not allowed ▫ *kawasan khas (dilarang kenderaan masuk)*: *a shopping precinct* 2 [C] (AmE) one of the parts into which a town or city is divided ▫ *kawasan (di bawah pengawasan sst balai polis)* 3 **precincts** [pl] (formal) the area near or around a building ▫ *kawasan sekitar*: *the hospital and its precincts*

precious /ˈpreʃəs/ adj 1 of great value (usually because it is rare or difficult to find) ▫ *amat berharga*: *In overcrowded Hong Kong, every small piece of land is precious.* 2 loved very much ▫ *amat disayangi; kesayangan*: *The painting was very precious to her.*

precious metal noun [C] a metal which is very rare and valuable and often used in jewellery ▫ *logam berharga*: *Gold and silver are precious metals.*

precious stone (also **stone**) noun [C] a stone which is very rare and valuable and often used in jewellery ▫ *batu permata*: *diamonds and other precious stones*

precipice /ˈpresəpɪs/ noun [C] a very steep side of a high mountain or rock ▫ *cenuram*

precis /ˈpreɪsiː/ noun [C,U] (pl **precis** /-siːz/) a short version of a speech or a piece of writing that gives the main points or ideas ▫ *ringkasan*: *to write/give/make a precis of a report* **SYN** summary

precise /prɪˈsaɪs/ adj 1 clear and accurate ▫ *tepat*: *precise details/instructions/measurements* ◆ *He's in his forties—well, forty-four, to be precise.* ◆ *She couldn't be very precise about what her attacker was wearing.* **OPP** imprecise 2 [only before a noun] exact; particular ▫ *tepat; betul-betul*: *I'm sorry. I can't come just **at this precise moment**.* 3 (used about a person) taking care to get small details right ▫ *teliti; cerewet*: *He's very precise about his work.*

precisely /prɪˈsaɪsli/ adv 1 exactly ▫ *tepat*: *The time is 10.03 precisely.* 2 used to emphasize that sth is very true or obvious ▫ *sebenarnya*: *It's precisely because I care about you that I got so angry when you stayed out late.* 3 (spoken) (used for agreeing with a statement) yes, that is right ▫ *benar; betul*: *'So, if we don't book now, we probably won't get a flight?' 'Precisely.'*

precision /prɪˈsɪʒn/ noun [U] the quality of being clear or exact ▫ *ketepatan; kepersisan; tepat*: *The plans were drawn with great precision.*

preclude /prɪˈkluːd/ verb [T] (formal) **preclude sth; preclude sb from doing sth** to prevent sth from happening or sb from doing sth; to make sth impossible ▫ *menghalang*: *Lack of time precludes any further discussion.*

precocious /prɪˈkəʊʃəs/ adj (used about children, often in a critical way) having developed certain abilities and ways of behaving at a much younger age than usual ▫ *cepat matang; macam orang tua*: *a precocious child who started her acting career at the age of 5*

preconceived /ˌpriːkənˈsiːvd/ adj [only before a noun] (used about an idea or opinion) formed before you have enough information or experience ▫ *praanggap*

preconception /ˌpriːkənˈsepʃn/ noun [C] an idea or opinion that you have formed about sb/sth before you have enough information or experience ▫ *praanggapan*

predator /ˈpredətə(r)/ noun [C] an animal that kills and eats other animals ▫ *pemangsa*

predatory /ˈpredətri/ adj 1 (used about animals) living by killing and eating other animals ▫ *bersifat pemangsa* 2 (used about people) using weaker people for their own financial or sexual advantage ▫ *(ttg orang) mengeksploitasi orang lain utk kepentingan sendiri*: *a predatory insurance salesman* ◆ *a predatory look*

[I] **intransitive**, a verb which has no object: *He laughed.*   [T] **transitive**, a verb which has an object: *He ate an apple.*

predecessor /ˈpriːdɪsesə(r)/ noun [C] **1** the person who was in a job or position before the person who is in it now □ *orang yg terdahulu; bekas pemegang jawatan*: *The new head teacher is much better than her predecessor.* **2** a thing such as a machine, that has been followed or replaced by sth else □ *(sst yg) terdahulu*: *This computer is faster than its predecessors.* ⊃ look at **successor**

predicament /prɪˈdɪkəmənt/ noun [C] an unpleasant and difficult situation that is hard to get out of □ *keadaan susah; kesusahan*

predicative /prɪˈdɪkətɪv/ adj (used about an adjective) not used before a noun □ *predikatif*: *You cannot say 'an asleep child' because 'asleep' is a predicative adjective.*

> **MORE** An adjective that *can* be used before a noun is called **attributive**. Most adjectives, for example 'big', can be either predicative or attributive: *The house is big.* ♦ *It's a big house.*

▸predicatively *adv*

predict /prɪˈdɪkt/ verb [T] to say that sth will happen in the future □ *meramalkan*: *Scientists still cannot predict exactly when earthquakes will happen.*

> **EXAM TIP**
>
> **Predicting listening**
>
> In a **listening exam** you can often predict something about what the speakers may say about a topic, and some of the vocabulary that they will use, before you listen. Read the questions and see if you can predict what type of information you need to be listening for. Is the answer going to be a number, a date, a time, an occupation, a sport, a musical instrument, etc.? It will also help to think about what part of speech is needed to fill the gap.

predictable /prɪˈdɪktəbl/ adj **1** that was or could be expected to happen □ *boleh diramalkan*: *a predictable result* **2** (used about a person) always behaving in a way that you would expect and therefore boring □ *memang sudah dijangka*: *I knew you were going to say that—you're so predictable.* **OPP** for both meanings **unpredictable** ▸predictably /-əbli/ *adv*

prediction /prɪˈdɪkʃn/ noun [C,U] saying what will happen; what sb thinks will happen □ *ramalan*: *The exam results confirmed my predictions.*

predictive /prɪˈdɪktɪv/ adj [usually before a noun] **1** (*formal*) connected with the ability to show what will happen in the future □ *berupaya utk meramal* **2** (used about a computer program) allowing you to enter text on a computer or a mobile phone more quickly by using the first few letters of each word to predict what you want to say □ *(ttg program komputer) mempercepat kemasukan teks dlm komputer atau telefon bimbit dgn menggunakan huruf-huruf awal setiap perkataan utk menjangka perkara yg hendak dikatakan*: *predictive messaging*

predominance /prɪˈdɒmɪnəns/ noun [sing] the state of being more important or greater in number than other people or things □ *(keadaan) lebih penting, ramai atau banyak*: *There is a predominance of Japanese tourists in Hawaii.*

predominant /prɪˈdɒmɪnənt/ adj most noticeable, powerful or important □ *utama; paling ketara, berkuasa atau penting*: *The predominant colour was blue.*

predominantly /prɪˈdɒmɪnəntli/ adv mostly; mainly □ *kebanyakannya; lebih banyak*: *The population of the island is predominantly Spanish.*

predominate /prɪˈdɒmɪneɪt/ verb [I] (*formal*) **predominate (over sb/sth)** to be most important or greatest in number □ *melebihi; menguasai; mengatasi*

pre-empt /priˈempt/ verb [T] **1** to prevent sth from happening by taking action to stop it □ *menggagalkan; menghalang; membatalkan*: *Her departure pre-empted any further questions.* **2** to do or say sth before sb else does □ *mendahului*: *She was just about to apologize when he pre-empted her.*

pre-emptive /priˈemptɪv/ adj done to stop sb taking action, especially action that will be harmful to you □ *bertindak terlebih dahulu (utk menghalang)*: *a pre-emptive attack/strike on the military base*

preface /ˈprefəs/ noun [C] a written introduction to a book that explains what it is about or why it was written □ *prakata; kata pendahuluan/pengantar*

prefect /ˈpriːfekt/ noun [C] (in some British schools) a student who has special duties and responsibilities. **Prefects** often help to make sure that the younger students behave properly. □ *pengawas*

prefer /prɪˈfɜː(r)/ verb [T] (**preferring; preferred**) [not used in the continuous tenses] **prefer sb/sth (to sb/sth); prefer to do sth; prefer doing sth** to choose sth rather than sth else; to like sb/sth better □ *lebih suka*: *Would you prefer tea or coffee?* ♦ *Marianne prefers not to walk home on her own at night.* ♦ *My parents would prefer me to study law at university.*

> **GRAMMAR** Notice the different ways that **prefer** can be used: *Helen prefers going* by train to flying (= generally or usually). ♦ *Helen would prefer to go* by train rather than (to) fly (= on this occasion). Although this verb is not used in the continuous tenses, it is common to see the present participle (= *-ing* form): *Their elder son had gone to work in London, preferring not to join the family firm.*

> **HELP Prefer** is generally rather formal. Instead of: *I prefer skating to skiing* we can say: *I like skating better than skiing.*

preferable /ˈprefrəbl/ *adj* preferable (to sth/doing sth) better or more suitable □ *lebih baik*: *Going anywhere is preferable to staying at home for the weekend.*

preferably /ˈprefrəbli/ *adv* used to show which person or thing would be better or preferred, if you are given a choice □ *sebaik-baiknya; kalau boleh*: *Give me a ring tonight—preferably after 7 o'clock.*

preference /ˈprefrəns/ *noun* [C, U] (a) preference (for sth) an interest in or desire for one thing more than another □ *pilihan; lebih suka*: *What you wear is entirely a matter of personal preference.* ♦ *Please list your choices in order of preference* (= put the things you want most first on the list).
IDM give (a) preference to sb/sth to give special treatment to one person or group rather than to others □ *keutamaan*: *When allocating accommodation, we will give preference to families with young children.*

preferential /ˌprefəˈrenʃl/ *adj* [only before a noun] giving or showing special treatment to one person or group rather than to others □ *istimewa*: *I don't see why he should get preferential treatment—I've worked here just as long as he has!*

prefix /ˈpriːfɪks/ *noun* [C] a letter or group of letters that you put at the beginning of a word to change its meaning, such as **un-** in **unhappy** □ *awalan* ⊃ look at **suffix**

pregnancy /ˈpregnənsi/ *noun* [U,C] (*pl* pregnancies) the state of being pregnant □ *kehamilan; mengandung*

pregnant /ˈpregnənt/ *adj* (used about a woman or female animal) having a baby developing in her body □ *hamil; mengandung*: *Liz is five months pregnant.* ♦ *to get pregnant* ⊃ note at **baby**

> **MORE** It is also possible to say: *Liz is expecting a baby* or: *Liz is going to have a baby.*

prehistoric /ˌpriːhɪˈstɒrɪk (*AmE also*) / *adj* from the time in history before events were written down □ *prasejarah*

prejudice¹ /ˈpredʒudɪs/ *noun* [C,U] prejudice (against sb/sth) a strong unreasonable feeling of not liking or trusting sb/sth, especially when it is based on their race, religion or sex □ *prasangka; prejudis*: *a victim of racial prejudice*

prejudice² /ˈpredʒudɪs/ *verb* [T] **1** prejudice sb (against sb/sth) to influence sb so that they have an unreasonable or unfair opinion about sb/sth □ *berprasangka; menaruh prasangka*: *The newspaper stories had prejudiced the jury against him.* **2** to have a harmful effect on sb/sth □ *menjejaskan; merosakkan*: *Continuing to live with her violent father may prejudice the child's welfare.*

prejudiced /ˈpredʒədɪst/ *adj* not liking or trusting sb for no other reason than their race, religion or sex □ *berprasangka*

preliminary¹ /prɪˈlɪmɪnəri/ *adj* coming or happening before sth else that is more important □ *permulaan; awal*: *After a few preliminary remarks the discussions began.*

preliminary² /prɪˈlɪmɪnəri/ *noun* [C, usually pl] (*pl* preliminaries) an action or event that is done before and in preparation for another event □ *persiapan; persediaan; (acara, tindakan, dsb) permulaan*: *Once the preliminaries are over, we can get down to business.*

prelude /ˈpreljuːd/ *noun* [C] **1** a short piece of music, especially as an introduction to a longer piece □ *pendahuluan* **2** (*formal*) prelude (to sth) an action or event that happens before sth else or that forms an introduction to sth □ *permulaan*

premature /ˈpremətʃə(r); ˌpreməˈtʃʊə(r)/ *adj* **1** happening before the normal or expected time □ *pramatang; tdk cukup bulan*: *Her baby was premature* (= born before the expected time). **2** acting or happening too soon □ *terlalu awal/cepat*: *I think our decision was premature. We should have thought about it for longer.* ▶ **prematurely** *adv*

premeditated /priːˈmedɪteɪtɪd/ *adj* (used about a crime) planned in advance □ *dirancang terlebih dahulu*

premier¹ /ˈpremiə(r)/ *adj* [only before a noun] most important; best □ *paling utama, baik, penting, dsb*: *a premier chef* ♦ *the Premier League* (= in football)

premier² /ˈpremiə(r)/ *noun* [C] (used especially in newspapers) the leader of the government of a country □ *perdana menteri* **SYN** prime minister

premiere /ˈpremieə(r)/ *noun* [C] the first public performance of a film or play □ *tayangan/pertunjukan perdana*: *the world premiere of his new play* ♦ *The film will have its premiere in July.* ▶ **premiere** *verb* [I,T]: *His new movie premieres in New York this week.*

premises /ˈpremɪsɪz/ *noun* [pl] the building and the land around it that a business owns or uses □ *premis; bangunan dan pekarangannya*: *The health club is moving to larger premises.* ♦ *Children are not allowed on the premises.*

premium /ˈpriːmiəm/ *noun* [C] **1** an amount of money that you pay regularly to a company for insurance against accidents, damage, etc. □ *premium (insuran)*: *a monthly premium of £25* **2** an extra payment □ *bayaran tambahan*: *You must pay a premium for express delivery.*

premonition /ˌpriːməˈnɪʃn; ˌprem-/ *noun* [C] a premonition (of sth) a feeling that sth unpleasant is going to happen in the future □ *prarasa; alamat; petanda*: *a premonition of disaster*

preoccupation /priˌɒkjuˈpeɪʃn/ *noun* [U,C] preoccupation (with sth) the state of thinking and/or worrying continuously about sth □ *peri-*

hal terlalu memikirkan sst; keasyikan: She was irritated by his preoccupation with money.

preoccupied /priˈɒkjupaɪd/ *adj* **preoccupied (with sth)** not paying attention to sb/sth because you are thinking or worrying about sb/sth else □ *dlm keadaan asyik memikirkan sst: Sarah is very preoccupied with her work at present.* ⊃ look at **occupied**

preoccupy /priˈɒkjupaɪ/ *verb* [T] (**preoccupying**; **preoccupies**; *pt, pp* **preoccupied**) to fill sb's mind so that they do not think about anything else; to worry sb □ *asyik memikirkan sst*

preparation /ˌprepəˈreɪʃn/ *noun* **1** [U] getting sb/sth ready □ *penyediaan; persediaan: The team has been training hard in preparation for the big game.* ◆ *exam preparation* **2** [C, usually pl] **preparation (for sth/to do sth)** something that you do to get ready for sth □ *persediaan; persiapan: We started to make preparations for the wedding six months ago.*

preparatory /prɪˈpærətri/ *adj* (*formal*) done in order to get ready for sth □ *persediaan*

preˈparatory school (also ˈprep school) *noun* [C] **1** (in Britain) a private school for children aged between 7 and 13 □ *sekolah (rendah) persendirian* **2** (in the US) a private school that prepares students for college □ *sekolah (tinggi) persediaan*

prepare /prɪˈpeə(r)/ *verb* [I,T] **prepare (sb/sth) (for sb/sth)** to get ready or to make sb ready □ *bersedia; bersiap; menyediakan: Bo helped me prepare for the exam.* ◆ *The course prepares foreign students for studying at university.* ◆ *to prepare a meal*

IDM **be prepared for sth** to be ready for sth difficult or unpleasant □ *bersiap sedia utk menghadapi sst*

be prepared to do sth to be ready and happy to do sth □ *bersedia utk membuat sst: I am not prepared to stay here and be insulted.*

preposition /ˌprepəˈzɪʃn/ *noun* [C] a word or phrase that is used before a noun or pronoun to show place, time, direction, etc. □ *kata sendi nama; preposisi: 'In', 'for', 'to' and 'out of' are all prepositions.*

preposterous /prɪˈpɒstərəs/ *adj* (*formal*) silly; ridiculous; not to be taken seriously □ *tdk munasabah; tdk masuk akal*

ˈprep school = **preparatory school**

prerequisite /ˌpriːˈrekwəzɪt/ *noun* [C] (*formal*) **a prerequisite (for/of sth)** something that is necessary for sth to happen or exist □ *prasyarat; syarat: Is a good education a prerequisite of success?* ⊃ look at **requisite**

prerogative /prɪˈrɒɡətɪv/ *noun* [C] (*formal*) a special right that sb/sth has □ *hak istimewa: It is the Prime Minister's prerogative to fix the date of the election.*

prescribe /prɪˈskraɪb/ *verb* [T] **1** to say what medicine or treatment sb should have □ *mempreskripsikan; menentukan jenis ubat: Can you prescribe something for my cough please,* *doctor?* **2** (*formal*) (used about a person or an organization with authority) to say that sth must be done □ *menetapkan; menentukan: The law prescribes that the document must be signed in the presence of two witnesses.*

prescription /prɪˈskrɪpʃn/ *noun* [C,U] an official piece of paper on which a doctor has written the name of the medicine that you need; the medicine itself □ *preskripsi; arahan bertulis doktor ttg jenis ubat yg perlu diambil: a prescription for sleeping pills* ◆ *Some medicines are only available from the chemist on prescription* (= with a prescription from a doctor). ⊃ note at **doctor**

presence /ˈprezns/ *noun* **1** [U] the fact of being in a particular place □ *kehadiran; ada(nya); di hadapan: He apologized to her in the presence of the whole family.* ◆ *an experiment to test for the presence of oxygen* **OPP** **absence** **2** [sing] a number of soldiers or police officers who are in a place for a special reason □ *kehadiran: There was a huge police presence at the demonstration.*

present¹ /ˈpreznt/ *adj* **1** [only before a noun] existing or happening now □ *sekarang; kini: We hope to overcome our present difficulties very soon.* **2** [not before a noun] being in a particular place □ *hadir: There were 200 people present at the meeting.* **OPP** **absent**

IDM **the present day** modern times □ *masa ini: In some countries traditional methods of farming have survived to the present day.*

present² /ˈpreznt/ *noun* **1** [C] something that you give to sb or receive from sb □ *hadiah: a birthday/wedding/leaving/Christmas present* **SYN** **gift** **2** *usually* **the present** [sing] the time now □ *masa sekarang: We live in the present but we must learn from the past.* ◆ *I'm rather busy at present. Can I call you back later?* ⊃ note at **actually 3 the present** [sing] = **the present tense**

IDM **for the moment/present** ⊃ **moment**

present³ /prɪˈzent/ *verb* [T] **1 present sb with sth; present sth (to sb)** to give sth to sb, especially at a formal ceremony □ *menghadiahkan; menghadiahi; memberikan: All the dancers were presented with flowers.* ◆ *Flowers were presented to all the dancers.* **2 present sth (to sb)** to show sth that you have prepared to people □ *membentangkan; mengemukakan: Good teachers try to present their material in an interesting way.* **3 present sb with sth; present sth (to sb)** to give sb sth that has to be dealt with □ *menimbulkan: The manager presented us with a bill for the broken chair.* ◆ *Learning English presented no problem to him.* **4** to introduce a TV or radio programme □ *mengacarakan: She used to present a gardening programme on TV.* **5** to show a play, etc. to the public □ *mempersembahkan: The Theatre Royal is presenting a new production of 'Ghosts'.* **6 present sb (to sb)** to introduce sb to a person in a formal ceremony □ *memperkenalkan: The teams were presented to the President before the game.*

presentable /prɪˈzentəbl/ *adj* good enough to be seen by people you do not know well □ *elok; sesuai; kemas*

presentation /ˌpreznˈteɪʃn/ *noun* **1** [C,U] the act of giving or showing sth to sb □ *penyampaian*: *The head will now make a presentation to the winners of the competition.* **2** [U] the way in which sth is shown, explained, offered, etc. to people □ *penyampaian*: *Untidy presentation of your work may lose you marks.* **3** [C] a formal talk at which sth is shown or explained to a group of people □ *penyampaian; ceramah; pertunjukan*: *Each student has to give a short presentation on a subject of his/her choice.* **4** [C] a formal ceremony at which a prize, etc. is given to sb □ *majlis penyampaian*

presenter /prɪˈzentə(r)/ *noun* [C] (*BrE*) a person who introduces a TV or radio programme □ *juruacara; penyampai*

presently /ˈprezntli/ *adv* **1** (*especially AmE*) now □ *sekarang; kini*: *The management are presently discussing the matter.* **SYN** currently **2** (*written*) after a short time □ *selepas itu*: *Presently I heard the car door shut.* **3** soon □ *sebentar lagi; tdk lama lagi*: *I'll be finished presently.* **SYN** shortly

HELP Notice that when **presently** means 'soon' it usually comes at the end of the sentence. When it means 'after a short time' it usually comes at the beginning of the sentence. When it means 'now' it goes with the verb.

present participle *noun* [C] the form of the verb that ends in *-ing* □ *partisipel kini*
ⓘ For more information about the use of tenses, look at the **Reference Section** at the back of this dictionary.

the present perfect *noun* [sing] the form of a verb that expresses an action done in a time period from the past to the present, formed with the present tense of *have* and the past participle of the verb □ *kala kini sempurna*: *'I've finished', 'She hasn't arrived'* and *'I've been studying'* are all in the present perfect.

the present tense (also **the present**) *noun* [sing] the tense of the verb that you use when you are talking about what is happening or what exists now □ *kala kini*

preservative /prɪˈzɜːvətɪv/ *noun* [C,U] a substance that is used for keeping food, etc. in good condition □ *bahan awet*

preserve /prɪˈzɜːv/ *verb* [T] to keep sth safe or in good condition □ *mengekalkan; memelihara; mengawet*: *They've managed to preserve most of the wall paintings in the caves.* ▶ **preservation** /ˌprezəˈveɪʃn/ *noun* [U]

preside /prɪˈzaɪd/ *verb* [I] to be in charge of a discussion, meeting, etc. □ *mempengerusikan*
PHR V **preside over sth** to be in control of or responsible for sth □ *mengetuai*

presidency /ˈprezɪdənsi/ *noun* (*pl* presidencies) **1 the presidency** [sing] the position of being president □ *jawatan presiden* **2** [C] the period of time that sb is president □ *tempoh menjadi presiden*

president /ˈprezɪdənt/ *noun* [C] **1** (also President) the leader of a **republic** (= a country with an elected government and no king or queen) □ *presiden*: *the president of France* ♦ *President Obama* ♦ *the US president* **2** the person with the highest position in some organizations □ *presiden* ▶ **presidential** /ˌprezɪˈdenʃl/ *adj*: *presidential elections*

press¹ /pres/ *noun*
▶NEWSPAPERS **1** *usually* **the press** [sing, with sing or pl verb] newspapers and the journalists who work for them □ *pihak akhbar; pemberita*: *The story has been reported on TV and in the press.* ♦ *the local/national press* ♦ *The press support/supports government policy.* ⊃ note at **newspaper**
2 [sing, U] the type or amount of reports that newspapers write about sb/sth □ *liputan akhbar*: *This company has had a bad press recently.* ♦ *The strike got very little press.*
▶PRINTING MACHINE **3** [C,U] a machine for printing books, newspapers, etc.; the process of printing them □ *mesin cetak*: *All details were correct at the time of going to press.*
▶BUSINESS **4** [C] a business that prints books, etc □ *percetakan*: *Oxford University Press*
▶ACT OF PUSHING **5** [C, usually sing] an act of pushing sth firmly □ *(perbuatan) menekan atau memicit*: *Give that button a press and see what happens.*

press² /pres/ *verb*
▶PUSH/SQUEEZE **1** [I,T] to push sth firmly □ *menekan; memicit*: *Just press that button and the door will open.* ♦ *He pressed the lid firmly shut.* ♦ *Press here to open.* ⊃ picture at **squeeze 2** [T] to put weight onto sth, for example in order to get juice out of it □ *memerah*: *to press grapes* **3** [T] to hold sb/sth firmly in a loving way □ *memeluk; merangkul*: *She pressed the photo to her chest.* **4** [I] **press across, against, around, etc. (sth)** to move in a particular direction by pushing □ *mengasak-asak*: *The crowd pressed against the line of policemen.*
▶TRY TO PERSUADE **5** [T] **press (sb) (for sth/to do sth)** to try to persuade or force sb to do sth □ *memujuk; mendesak*: *to press somebody for an answer* ♦ *I pressed them to stay for dinner.*
▶SAY/REPEAT STH **6** [T] to express or repeat sth in an urgent way □ *menekankan; menegaskan*: *I don't want to press the point, but you still owe me money.*
▶MAKE SMOOTH **7** [T] to make a piece of clothing smooth by using an iron □ *menggosok; menyeterika*: *This shirt needs pressing.*
IDM **be hard pressed/pushed/put to do sth** ⊃ **hard²**
be pressed for sth to not have enough of sth □ *tdk cukup (sst); kesuntukan (sst)*: *I must hurry. I'm really pressed for time.*
bring/press charges (against sb) ⊃ **charge¹**

PHR V press ahead/forward/on (with sth) to continue doing sth even though it is difficult or hard work □ *meneruskan (sst)*: *They pressed on with the building work in spite of the bad weather.*

'press conference *noun* [C] a meeting when a famous or important person answers questions from newspaper and TV journalists □ *persidangan akhbar*: *to hold a press conference*

pressing /'presɪŋ/ *adj* that must be dealt with immediately □ *segera; mendesak* **SYN** urgent

'press stud (also **popper**; *AmE* **snap**) *noun* [C] two round pieces of metal or plastic that you press together in order to fasten a piece of clothing □ *butang ketap* ⊃ picture at **button**

'press-up (*AmE* **'push-up**) *noun* [C] a type of exercise in which you lie on your front on the floor and push your body up with your arms □ *tekan tubi*: *I do 50 press-ups every morning.* ⊃ picture at **exercise**

pressure /'preʃə(r)/ *noun* **1** [U] the force that is produced when you press on or against sth □ *tekanan*: *Apply pressure to the cut and it will stop bleeding.* ◆ *The pressure of the water caused the dam to crack.* **2** [C,U] the force that a gas or liquid has when it is contained inside sth □ *tekanan*: *high/low blood pressure* ◆ *You should check your tyre pressures regularly.* **3** [U] worries or difficulties that you have because you have too much to deal with □ *desakan; tekanan*: *financial pressures* ◆ *I find it difficult to cope with pressure at work.* **SYN** stress

IDM put pressure on sb (to do sth) to force sb to do sth □ *memaksa/mendesak sso (utk melakukan sst)*: *His boss is putting pressure on him to resign.*

under pressure 1 (used about liquid or gas) contained inside sth or sent somewhere using force □ *di bawah tekanan*: *Water is forced out through the hose under pressure.* **2** being forced to do sth □ *mendesak; memaksa*: *Anna was under pressure from her parents to leave school and get a job.* **3** worried or in difficulty because you have too much to deal with □ *ditekan*: *I perform poorly under pressure, so I hate exams.*

▶ **pressure** *verb* = **pressurize**

'pressure group *noun* [C, with sing or pl verb] a group of people who are trying to influence what a government or other organization does □ *kumpulan pendesak*

pressurize (also **-ise**) /'preʃəraɪz/ (also **pressure**) *verb* [T] **pressurize sb (into sth/doing sth)** to use force or influence to make sb do sth □ *memaksa; dipaksa*: *Some workers were pressurized into taking early retirement.*

pressurized (also **-ised**) /'preʃəraɪzd/ *adj* (used about air in an aircraft) kept at the pressure at which people can breathe □ *(yg) tekanan udaranya diimbangkan*

prestige /pre'stiːʒ/ *noun* [U] the respect and admiration that people feel for a person because they have a high social position or have been very successful □ *martabat; prestij*: *jobs in supermarkets with low prestige* ▶ **prestigious** /pre'stɪdʒəs/ *adj*: *a prestigious prize/school/job*

presumably /prɪ'zjuːməbli/ *adv* I imagine; I suppose □ *barangkali; mengandaikan*: *Presumably this rain means the match will be cancelled?*

presume /prɪ'zjuːm/ *verb* [T] to think that sth is true even if you do not know for sure; to suppose □ *menganggap; agaknya*: *The house looks empty so I presume they are away on holiday.* **SYN** assume ▶ **presumption** /prɪ'zʌmpʃn/ *noun* [C]

presumptuous /prɪ'zʌmptʃuəs/ *adj* confident that sth will happen or that sb will do sth without making sure first, in a way that annoys people □ *memandai-mandai*: *It was very presumptuous of him to say that I would help without asking me first.*

presuppose /ˌpriːsə'pəʊz/ *verb* [T] (*formal*) to accept sth as true or existing and act on that belief, before it has been proved to be true □ *suka membuat andaian ttg sst*: *Teachers sometimes presuppose a fairly high level of knowledge by the students.* **SYN** presume

pretence (*AmE* **pretense**) /prɪ'tens/ *noun* [U, sing] an action that makes people believe sth that is not true □ *kepura-puraan; pura-pura*: *She was unable to keep up the pretence that she loved him.*

IDM on/under false pretences ⊃ **false**

pretend /prɪ'tend/ *verb* [I,T] **1** to behave in a particular way in order to make other people believe sth that is not true □ *berpura-pura*: *You can't just pretend that the problem doesn't exist.* ◆ *Paul's not really asleep. He's just pretending.* **2** (used especially about children) to imagine that sth is true as part of a game □ *berpura-pura; berolok-olok*: *The kids were under the bed pretending to be snakes.*

pretentious /prɪ'tenʃəs/ *adj* trying to appear more serious or important than you really are □ *menunjuk-nunjuk; berlagak*: *I think it sounds pretentious to use a lot of foreign words.*

pretext /'priːtekst/ *noun* [C] a reason that you give for doing sth that is not the real reason □ *alasan; helah*: *Tariq left on the pretext of having an appointment at the dentist's.*

pretty¹ /'prɪti/ *adv* (*informal*) quite; fairly □ *agak*: *The film was pretty good but not fantastic.* ◆ *I'm pretty certain that Alex will agree.* ⊃ note at **rather**

IDM pretty much/nearly/well almost; very nearly □ *hampir*: *I won't be long. I've pretty well finished.*

pretty² /'prɪti/ *adj* (**prettier**; **prettiest**) attractive and pleasant to look at or hear □ *cantik; sedap; merdu*: *a pretty girl/smile/dress/garden/name* ⊃ note at **beautiful** ▶ **prettily** *adv*: *The room is prettily decorated.* ▶ **prettiness** *noun* [U]

prevail /prɪ'veɪl/ *verb* [I] (*formal*) **1** to exist or be common in a particular place or at a particu-

prevailing → prickly 672

lar time □ *wujud; diamalkan*: *In some areas traditional methods of farming still prevail.* **2 prevail (against/over sb/sth)** to win or be accepted, especially after a fight or discussion □ *mengatasi*: *In the end justice prevailed and the men were set free.*

prevailing /prɪˈveɪlɪŋ/ *adj* [only before a noun] **1** existing or most common at a particular time □ *lazim; wujud pd (sst) ketika itu*: *the prevailing climate of opinion* **2** (used about the wind) most common in a particular area □ *lazim*: *The prevailing wind is from the south-west.*

prevalent /ˈprevələnt/ *adj* (formal) most common in a particular place at a particular time □ *lazim; yg wujud pd (sst) ketika itu; tersebar luas*: *The prevalent atmosphere was one of fear.* ▶**prevalence** *noun* [U]: *an increase in the prevalence of heart disease*

prevent /prɪˈvent/ *verb* [T] **prevent sb/sth (from) (doing sth)** to stop sth happening or to stop sb doing sth □ *menghalang; mencegah*: *This accident could have been prevented.* ♦ *Her parents tried to prevent her from going to live with her boyfriend.* ⊃ **Prevent** is more formal than **stop**. ▶**prevention** *noun* [U]: *accident/crime prevention*

preventable /prɪˈventəbl/ *adj* that can be prevented □ *dpt dihalang/dicegah*: *Many accidents are preventable.*

preventive /prɪˈventɪv/ (also **preventative** /prɪˈventətɪv/) *adj* [only before a noun] intended to stop or prevent sth from happening □ *pencegahan; bersifat mencegah*: *preventative medicine*

preview /ˈpriːvjuː/ *noun* [C] a chance to see a play, film, etc. before it is shown to the general public □ *pratonton*

previous /ˈpriːviəs/ *adj* [only before a noun] coming or happening before or earlier □ *sebelumnya; terdahulu*: *Do you have previous experience of this type of work?* ♦ *Matt has two children from his previous marriage.* ♦ *the previous day* ▶**previously** *adv*: *Before I moved to Spain, I had previously worked in Italy.*

prey¹ /preɪ/ *noun* [U] an animal or bird that is killed and eaten by another animal or bird □ *pemangsa*: *The eagle is a bird of prey* (= it kills and eats other birds or small animals).

prey² /preɪ/ *verb* [I]
IDM prey on sb's mind to cause sb to worry or think about sth □ *menghantui/mengganggu fikiran*: *The thought that he was responsible for the accident preyed on the train driver's mind.*
PHR V prey on sth (used about an animal or bird) to kill and eat other animals or birds □ *memangsakan; menjadikan mangsa*: *Owls prey on mice and other small animals.*

price¹ /praɪs/ *noun* **1** [C] the amount of money that you must pay in order to buy sth □ *harga*: *What's the price of petrol now?* ♦ *We can't afford to buy the car at that price.* ♦ *There's no price on* (= written on) *this jar of coffee.*
MORE A shop may **raise/increase, reduce/bring down** or **freeze** its prices. The prices **rise/go up** or **fall/go down**.
2 [sing] unpleasant things that you have to experience in order to achieve sth or as a result of sth □ *pengorbanan*: *Sleepless nights are a small price to pay for having a baby.*
IDM at any price even if the cost is very high or if it will have unpleasant results □ *walau berapa pun harganya; dgn apa cara sekalipun*: *Richard was determined to succeed at any price.*
at a price costing a lot of money or involving sth unpleasant □ *dgn bayaran yg tinggi*: *He'll help you get a job—at a price.*
not at any price never; not for any reason □ *walau apa pun; tdk sekali-kali*

price² /praɪs/ *verb* [T] to fix the price of sth or to write the price on sth □ *berharga; membubuh harga*: *The books were all priced at between £5 and £10.*

OTHER WORDS FOR

price

A **charge** is the amount of money that you must pay for using something: *Is there a charge for parking here?* ♦ *admission charges.* You use **cost** when you are talking about paying for services or about prices in general without mentioning an actual sum of money: *The cost of electricity is going up.* ♦ *the cost of living.* The **price** of something is the amount of money that you must pay in order to buy it.

priceless /ˈpraɪsləs/ *adj* of very great value □ *tdk ternilai harganya*: *priceless jewels and antiques* ⊃ look at **worthless, valuable, invaluable**

'price list *noun* [C] a list of the prices of the goods that are on sale □ *senarai harga*

pricey /ˈpraɪsi/ *adj* (**pricier; priciest**) (*informal*) expensive □ *mahal*

prick¹ /prɪk/ *verb* [T] to make a small hole in sth or to cause sb pain with a sharp point □ *mencucuk*: *She pricked her finger on a needle.*
IDM prick up your ears (used about an animal) to hold up the ears in order to listen carefully to sth □ *menegakkan/mengangkat telinga*: (*figurative*) *Mike pricked up his ears when he heard Emma's name mentioned.*

prick² /prɪk/ *noun* [C] the sudden pain that you feel when sth sharp goes into your skin □ *rasa mencucuk*

prickle¹ /ˈprɪkl/ *noun* [C] one of the sharp points on some plants and animals □ *duri*: *Hedgehogs are covered in prickles.* ⊃ look at **spine**

prickle² /ˈprɪkl/ *verb* [I] to have or make sb/sth have an uncomfortable feeling on the skin □ *terasa mencucuk-cucuk*: *I don't like that shirt—it prickles.* ♦ *His skin prickled with fear.*

prickly /ˈprɪkli/ *adj* (**pricklier; prickliest**) **1** covered with sharp points □ *berduri*: *a prickly bush*

[I] **intransitive**, a verb which has no object: *He laughed.* [T] **transitive**, a verb which has an object: *He ate an apple.*

2 causing an uncomfortable feeling on the skin □ *berasa mencucuk-cucuk*: *That T-shirt makes my skin go all prickly.* 3 (*informal*) (used about a person) easily made angry □ *mudah naik marah*: *Don't mention his accident—he's a bit prickly about it.*

pride¹ /praɪd/ *noun* 1 [U, sing] pride (in sth/doing sth) the feeling of pleasure that you have when you or people who are close to you do sth good or own sth good □ *rasa bangga*: *I take a great pride in my work.* ♦ *Jane's parents watched with pride as she went up to collect her prize.* ♦ *You should feel pride in your achievement.* ♦ *We take great pride in offering the best service in town.* 2 [sing] the pride of sth/sb a person or thing that is very important or of great value to sth/sb □ *kebanggaan*: *The new stadium was the pride of the whole town.* 3 [U] the respect that you have for yourself □ *harga diri; maruah*: *You'll hurt his pride if you refuse to accept the present.* 4 [U] the feeling that you are better than other people □ *keangkuhan; angkuh; tinggi diri*: *Male pride forced him to suffer in silence.* ⊃ *adjective* **proud**
IDM sb's pride and joy a thing or person that gives sb great pleasure or satisfaction □ *(sst yg menjadi) kebanggaan sso*

pride² /praɪd/ *verb*
PHR V pride yourself on sth/doing sth to feel pleased about sth good or clever that you can do □ *berasa bangga (kerana sst/membuat sst)*: *Fabio prides himself on his ability to cook.*

priest /priːst/ *noun* [C] a person who performs religious ceremonies in some religions □ *paderi; pendeta; sami*: *The priest gave a blessing at the end of the service.* ♦ *the ordination of women priests*

MORE In some religions a female priest is called a **priestess**.

prim /prɪm/ *adj* (**primmer**; **primmest**) (used about a person) always behaving in a careful or formal way and easily shocked by anything that is rude □ *terlalu tertib atau bersopan* ▶ **primly** *adv*

primaeval = primeval

primarily /ˈpraɪmərəli; praɪˈmerəli/ *adv* more than anything else; mainly □ *terutamanya*: *The course is aimed primarily at beginners.*

primary¹ /ˈpraɪməri/ *adj* [only before a noun] 1 most important; main □ *utama*: *Smoking is one of the primary causes of lung cancer.* 2 connected with the education of children between about 4 and 11 years old □ *rendah*

primary² /ˈpraɪməri/ (also ˌprimary eˈlection) *noun* [C] (*pl* **primaries**) (in the US) an election in which a political party chooses the person who will represent the party for a later important election, such as for president □ *pilihan raya peringkat awal*

ˌprimary ˈcolour *noun* [C] any of the colours red, yellow or blue. You can make any other colour by mixing **primary colours** in different ways. □ *warna utama/primer*

673 **pride¹ → princess**

ˌprimary eˈlection = primary²

ˌprimary ˈschool *noun* [C,U] (in Britain) a school for children between the ages of 4 and 11 □ *sekolah rendah*: *a local primary school*

MORE **Primary school** consists of **infant school** and **junior school**. Children attend **infant school** from the age of four and **junior school** from the age of seven. When they leave **primary school** at the age of eleven, they go on to **secondary school**.

⊃ note at **school**

primate /ˈpraɪmeɪt/ *noun* [C] any animal that belongs to the group that includes humans, and animals such as **monkeys** and **apes** □ *primat*

prime¹ /praɪm/ *adj* [only before a noun] 1 main; the first example of sth that sb would think of or choose □ *utama*: *She is a prime candidate as the next team captain.* 2 of very good quality; best □ *terbaik*: *prime pieces of beef* 3 having all the typical qualities □ *paling jelas*: *That's a prime example of what I was talking about.*

prime² /praɪm/ *noun* [sing] the time when sb is strongest, most beautiful, most successful, etc. □ *masa terbaik; puncak*: *Several of the team are past their prime.* ♦ *In his prime, he was a fine actor.* ♦ *to be in the prime of life*

prime³ /praɪm/ *verb* [T] prime sb (for/with sth) to give sb information in order to prepare them for sth □ *menyogokkan maklumat (supaya menjawab, dsb spt apa yg dikehendaki)*: *The politician had been well primed with all the facts before the interview.*

ˌprime ˈminister *noun* [C] (*abbr* PM) the leader of the government in some countries, for example Britain □ *perdana menteri* ⊃ look at **minister**: *The games were opened by the prime minister of Thailand.*

primeval (also primaeval) /praɪˈmiːvl/ *adj* from the earliest period of the history of the world; very ancient □ *purbakala; zaman purba; dahulu kala*: *primeval forests*

primitive /ˈprɪmətɪv/ *adj* 1 very simple and not developed □ *primitif; ringkas dan tdk maju*: *The washing facilities in the camp were very primitive.* 2 [only before a noun] connected with a very early stage in the development of humans or animals □ *primitif*: *Primitive man lived in caves and hunted wild animals.*

primrose /ˈprɪmrəʊz/ *noun* [C] a yellow spring flower □ *bunga 'primrose'*

prince /prɪns/ *noun* [C] 1 a son or other close male relative of a king or queen □ *putera (raja)*: *the Prince of Wales* 2 the male ruler of a small country □ *raja*

princess /ˌprɪnˈses/ *noun* [C] 1 a daughter or other close female relative of a king or queen □ *puteri*: *Princess Anne* 2 the wife of a **prince** □ *isteri putera (raja)*

principal¹ /'prɪnsəpl/ adj [only before a noun] most important; main □ *utama*: *the principal characters in a play* ▶ **principally** /-pli/ adv: *Our products are designed principally for the European market.*

principal² /'prɪnsəpl/ (also **head, head teacher**) noun [C] the head of some schools, colleges, etc. □ *pengetua*

principle /'prɪnsəpl/ noun 1 [C,U] a rule for good behaviour, based on what a person believes is right □ *prinsip; pendirian*: *He doesn't eat meat **on principle**.* ♦ *She refuses to wear fur. It's **a matter of principle** with her.* ♦ *a person of high moral principles* 2 [C] a basic general law, rule or idea □ *prinsip; hukum*: *The system works **on the principle** that heat rises.* ♦ *The course teaches the basic principles of car maintenance.*
IDM **in principle** in general, but possibly not in detail □ *pd prinsipnya/dasarnya*: *His proposal sounds fine in principle, but there are a few points I'm not happy about.*

print¹ /prɪnt/ verb
▶LETTERS/PICTURES **1** [T] to put words, pictures, etc. onto paper by using a special machine □ *mencetak; mengecap*: *How much did it cost to print the posters?* ♦ *Print your work on both sides.*
▶BOOKS, ETC. **2** [T] to produce books, newspapers, etc. in this way □ *mencetak; menerbitkan*: *50 000 copies of the textbook were printed.*
▶PUBLISH **3** [T] to include sth in a book, newspaper, etc □ *menyiarkan; menerbitkan*: *The newspaper should not have printed the photographs of the crash.*
▶PHOTOGRAPH **4** [T] to make a photograph from a digital image or a piece of film □ *mencuci (filem)*: *She printed the children's portraits.*
▶WRITE **5** [I,T] to write with letters that are not joined together □ *menulis dgn huruf satu-satu (bukan tulisan sambung)*: *Please print your name clearly at the top of the paper.*
▶MAKE DESIGN **6** [T] to put a pattern onto cloth, paper, etc. □ *mengecap*: *printed cotton/wallpaper*
PHR V **print (sth) out** to print information from a computer onto paper □ *mencetak*: *I'll just print out this file.*
▶**printing** noun [U]

print² /prɪnt/ noun
▶LETTERS/WORDS **1** [U] the letters, words, etc. in a book, newspaper, etc. □ *cetakan*: *The print is too small for me to read without my glasses.*
▶NEWSPAPERS/BOOKS **2** [U] used to refer to the business of producing newspapers, books, etc. □ *percetakan*: *the print unions/workers*
▶MARK **3** [C] a mark that is by sth pressing onto sth else □ *kesan; bekas; cap (jari)*: *His prints were found at the scene of the crime.* ⊃ look at **fingerprint, footprint**
▶PICTURE **4** [C] a picture that was made by printing □ *gambar cetak*: *a framed set of prints*
▶PHOTOGRAPH **5** [C] a photograph (when it has been printed from a digital file) □ *gambar foto*: *I ordered an extra set of prints for my friends.*

IDM **in print 1** (used about a book) still available from the company that published it □ *masih boleh didapati* **2** (used about sb's work) published in a book, newspaper, etc. □ *diterbitkan*
out of print (used about a book) no longer available from the company that published it; not being printed any more □ *sudah tiada dlm cetakan (tdk dijual lagi)*

printer /'prɪntə(r)/ noun [C] **1** a machine that prints out information from a computer onto paper □ *mesin cetak*: *a laser printer* ⊃ picture at **computer 2** a person or company that prints books, newspapers, etc. □ *pencetak*

printing /'prɪntɪŋ/ noun [U] **1** the act of producing letters, pictures, patterns, etc. on sth by pressing a surface covered with ink against it □ *pencetakan*: *the invention of printing by Gutenberg* **2** the act of printing a number of copies of a book at one time □ *percetakan*: *The book is in its sixth printing.*

'printing press (also **press**) noun [C] a machine that is used for printing books, newspapers, etc. □ *mesin cetak*

printout /'prɪntaʊt/ noun [C,U] information from a computer that is printed onto paper □ *cetakan*

prior /'praɪə(r)/ adj [only before a noun] existing before or earlier □ *sebelumnya; terlebih dahulu*: *She was unable to attend because of a prior engagement.*

priority /praɪ'ɒrəti/ noun (pl **priorities**) **1** [C] something that is most important or that you must do before anything else □ *keutamaan; paling penting*: *Our **top priority** is to get food and water to the refugee camps.* ♦ *I'll **make it my priority** to sort out your problem.* **2** [U] **priority (over sb/sth)** the state of being more important than sb/sth or of coming before sb/sth else □ *keutamaan; prioriti*: *We give priority to families with small children.* ♦ *Emergency cases **take priority** over other patients in hospital.* ▶ **prioritize** (also **-ise**) /praɪ'ɒrətaɪz/ verb [I,T]: *You should make a list of all the jobs you have to do and prioritize them.*

'prior to prep (formal) before □ *sebelum*: *Prepare the surface prior to applying the first coat of paint.*

prise /praɪz/ (especially AmE **prize, pry**) verb [T] **prise sth off, apart, open, etc.** to use force to open sth, remove a lid, etc. □ *mengumpil*: *He prised the door open with an iron bar.*

prism /'prɪzəm/ noun [C] **1** a solid figure with ends that are parallel and of the same size and shape, and with sides whose opposite edges are equal and parallel □ *prisma* **2** a piece of glass or plastic in the shape of a triangle, which separates light that passes through it into seven colours □ *prisma*

prison /'prɪzn/ (also **jail**) noun [C,U] a building where criminals are kept as a punishment □ *penjara*: *The terrorists were **sent to prison** for twenty-five years.* ♦ *He will be **released from prison**

next month. **SYN** jail ⮕ note at **court** ⮕ look at **imprison**

HELP If a person goes **to prison** or is **in prison** (without 'the'), he/she has to stay there as a prisoner: *He was sent to prison for two years.* 'The prison' refers to a particular prison, or indicates that a person is only visiting the building temporarily: *The politician visited the prison and said that conditions were poor.*

prisoner /ˈprɪznə(r)/ *noun* [C] a person who is being kept in prison □ *banduan*: *a political prisoner*

IDM hold/take sb captive/prisoner ⮕ **captive¹**

prisoner of ˈwar *noun* [C] a soldier, etc. who is caught by the enemy during a war and who is kept in prison until the end of the war □ *tawanan perang*

privacy /ˈprɪvəsi/ *noun* [U] **1** the state of being alone and not watched or disturbed by other people □ *bersendirian*: *There is not much privacy in large hospital wards.* **2** the state of being free from the attention of the public □ *hak kebersendirian*: *The star claimed that the photographs were an invasion of privacy.*

private¹ /ˈpraɪvət/ *adj* **1** belonging to or intended for one particular person or group and not to be shared by others □ *persendirian; peribadi*: *This is private property. You may not park here.* ◆ *a private letter/conversation* **2** with nobody else present □ *bersendirian; sulit*: *I would like a private interview with the personnel manager.* **3** not wanting to share thoughts and feelings with other people □ *suka bersendiri*: *He's a very private person.* **4** owned, done or organized by a person or company, and not by the government □ *swasta; persendirian*: *a private hospital/school* (= you pay to go there) ◆ *a private detective* (= one who is not in the police) **OPP** **public** **5** not connected with work or business □ *peribadi*: *He never discusses his private life with his colleagues at work.* **6** (used about classes, lessons, etc.) given by a teacher to one student or a small group for payment □ *persendirian*: *Claire gives private English lessons at her house.*
▶ privately *adv*

private² /ˈpraɪvət/ *noun* [C] a soldier of the lowest level □ *prebet*

IDM **in private** with nobody else present □ *secara bersendirian/sulit*: *May I speak to you in private?*

privatize (also -ise) /ˈpraɪvətaɪz/ *verb* [T] to sell a business or an industry that was owned by the government to a private company □ *menswastakan*: *The electricity industry was privatized several years ago.* **OPP** **nationalize** ▶ privatization (also -isation) /ˌpraɪvətaɪˈzeɪʃn/ *noun* [U]

privilege /ˈprɪvəlɪdʒ/ *noun* **1** [C,U] a special right or advantage that only one person or group has □ *hak istimewa*: *Prisoners who behave well enjoy special privileges.* **2** [sing] a special advantage or opportunity that gives you great pleasure □ *keistimewaan; penghormatan*: *It was a great privilege to hear her sing.*

privileged /ˈprɪvəlɪdʒd/ *adj* having an advantage or opportunity that most people do not have □ *mempunyai hak istimewa*: *Only a privileged few are allowed to enter this room.* ◆ *I feel very privileged to be playing for the national team.*
⮕ look at **underprivileged**

prize¹ /praɪz/ *noun* [C] something of value that is given to sb who is successful in a race, competition, game, etc. □ *hadiah*: *She won first prize in the competition.* ◆ *a prize-winning novel*

prize² /praɪz/ *adj* [only *before* a noun] winning, or good enough to win, a prize □ *yg memenangi (atau layak) menerima hadiah*: *a prize flower display*

prize³ /praɪz/ *verb* [T] **1** to consider sth to be very valuable □ *menghargai; dihargai*: *This picture is one of my most prized possessions.* **2** (especially *AmE*) = **prise**

pro /prəʊ/ (*pl* pros) (*informal*) **1** = **professional²(2)** □ *profesional*: *a golf pro* **2** = **professional²(3)**

IDM **the pros and cons** the reasons for and against doing sth □ *baik buruknya*: *We should consider all the pros and cons before reaching a decision.* ⮕ look at **advantage**

pro- /prəʊ/ [in compounds] in favour of; supporting □ *pro-, yg menyokong*: *pro-democracy*
⮕ look at **anti-**

proactive /ˌprəʊˈæktɪv/ *adj* controlling a situation by making things happen, rather than waiting for things to happen and then reacting to them □ *proaktif*

probability /ˌprɒbəˈbɪləti/ *noun* (*pl* probabilities) **1** [U, sing] how likely sth is to happen □ *kebarangkalian; kemungkinan*: *At that time there seemed little probability of success.* **2** [C] something that is likely to happen □ *kemungkinan*: *Closure of the factory now seems a probability.*

probable /ˈprɒbəbl/ *adj* that you expect to happen or to be true; likely □ *mungkin; ada kemungkinan*: *I suppose it's possible that they might still come but it doesn't seem very probable.*
OPP **improbable** ⮕ look at **possible**

HELP **Probable** or **likely**? Notice that **probable** and **likely** mean the same but are used differently: *It's probable that he will be late.* ◆ *He is likely to be late.*

probably /ˈprɒbəbli/ *adv* almost certainly □ *barangkali; mungkin*: *I will phone next week, probably on Wednesday.*

probation /prəˈbeɪʃn/ *noun* [U] **1** a system that allows sb who has committed a crime not to go to prison if they go to see to a **probation officer** regularly for a fixed period of time □ *pemerhatian; pengawasan*: *Jamie is on probation for two years.* **2** a period of time at the start of a new job when you are tested to see if you are

probe → produce

suitable □ *tempoh percubaan*: *a three-month probation period*

probe¹ /prəʊb/ *verb* [I,T] **1 probe (into sth)** to ask questions in order to find out secret or hidden information □ *menyiasat*: *The newspapers are now probing into the President's past.* **2** to examine or look for sth, especially with a long thin instrument □ *memeriksa secara teliti*: *The doctor probed the cut for pieces of broken glass.* ▶ **probing** *adj*: *to ask probing questions*

probe² /prəʊb/ *noun* [C] **1** the process of asking questions, collecting facts, etc. in order to find out hidden information about sth □ *penyiasatan*: *a police probe into illegal financial dealing* **2** a long thin tool that you use for examining sth that is difficult to reach, especially a part of the body □ *(alat) kuar*

problem /ˈprɒbləm/ *noun* [C] **1** something that causes difficulty or trouble □ *masalah*: *social/family/financial/technical problems* ◆ *You won't solve the problem if you ignore it.* ◆ *The company will face problems from unions if it sacks workers.* ◆ *It's going to cause problems if Donna brings her husband.* ◆ *I can't play because I've got a problem with my knee.* ◆ *'Can you fix this for me?' 'No problem.'* ◆ *It's a great painting—the problem is I've got nowhere to put it.* **2** a question that you have to solve by thinking about it □ *masalah*: *a maths/logic problem*

problematic /ˌprɒbləˈmætɪk/ (also **problematical** /-ɪkl/) *adj* difficult to deal with; full of problems □ *bermasalah, menyusahkan*

procedure /prəˈsiːdʒə(r)/ *noun* [C,U] the usual or correct way for doing sth □ *prosedur; tatacara*: *What's the procedure for making a complaint?*

proceed /prəˈsiːd/ *verb* [I] **1 proceed (with sth)** to continue doing sth; to continue being done □ *meneruskan; berjalan*: *The building work was proceeding according to schedule.* **2 proceed to do sth** to do sth next, after having done sth else first □ *mula terus*: *Once he had calmed down he proceeded to tell us what had happened.*

proceedings /prəˈsiːdɪŋz/ *noun* [pl] (*formal*) **1 proceedings (against sb/for sth)** legal action □ *prosiding; tindakan undang-undang*: *to start divorce proceedings* **2** events that happen, especially at a formal meeting, ceremony, etc. □ *acara*: *The proceedings were interrupted by demonstrators.*

proceeds /ˈprəʊsiːdz/ *noun* [pl] **proceeds (of/from sth)** money that you get when you sell sth □ *hasil kutipan*: *The proceeds from the sale will go to charity.*

process¹ /ˈprəʊses (AmE also)/ *noun* [C] **1** a series of actions that you do for a particular purpose □ *proses*: *We've just begun the complicated process of selling the house.* **2** a series of changes that happen naturally □ *proses*: *Mistakes are a normal part of the learning process.*

IDM **in the process** while you are doing sth else □ *semasa*: *We washed the dog yesterday—and we all got very wet in the process.*
in the process of sth/doing sth in the middle of doing sth □ *dlm proses/sedang (membuat sst)*: *They are in the process of moving house.*

process² /ˈprəʊses (AmE also)/ *verb* [T] **1** to treat sth, for example with chemicals, in order to preserve it, change it, etc. □ *memproses; diproses*: *Cheese is processed so that it lasts longer.* **2** to deal with information, for example on a computer □ *memproses*: *It will take about ten days to process your application.*

procession /prəˈseʃn/ *noun* [C,U] a number of people, vehicles, etc. that move slowly in a line, especially as part of a ceremony □ *perarakan*: *to walk in procession* ◆ *a funeral procession*

processor /ˈprəʊsesə(r) (AmE usually)/ *noun* [C] a machine or person that **processes** sth □ *pemproses* ⊃ look at **food processor**, **word processor**

proclaim /prəˈkleɪm/ *verb* [T] (*formal*) to make sth known officially or publicly □ *mengisytiharkan; mengumumkan*: *The day has been proclaimed a national holiday.* ▶ **proclamation** /ˌprɒkləˈmeɪʃn/ *noun* [C,U]: *to make a proclamation of war*

procure /prəˈkjʊə(r)/ *verb* [T] (*formal*) **procure sth (for sb)** to obtain sth, especially with difficulty □ *mendapat(kan)*: *I managed to procure two tickets for the match.*

prod /prɒd/ *verb* [I,T] (**prodding**; **prodded**) to push or press sb/sth with your finger or a pointed object □ *mengejan; menggesa*: (*figurative*) *Ruth works quite hard but she does need prodding occasionally.* ▶ **prod** *noun* [C]: *to give the fire a prod with a stick* ▶ **prodding** *noun* [U]

prodigious /prəˈdɪdʒəs/ *adj* (*formal*) very large or powerful and surprising □ *amat banyak, kuat atau menakjubkan*: *He seemed to have a prodigious amount of energy.*

prodigy /ˈprɒdədʒi/ *noun* [C] (*pl* **prodigies**) a child who is unusually good at sth □ *orang (selalunya kanak-kanak) yg mempunyai bakat luar biasa*: *Mozart was a child prodigy.* ⊃ look at **genius**

produce¹ /prəˈdjuːs/ *verb* [T]
▶ GOODS **1** to make sth to be sold, especially in large quantities □ *mengeluarkan; menghasilkan*: *The factory produces 20 000 cars a year.* **SYN manufacture**
▶ MAKE NATURALLY **2** to grow or make sth by a natural process □ *menghasilkan*: *This region produces most of the country's wheat.* ◆ (*figurative*) *He's the greatest athlete this country has produced.*
▶ MAKE WITH SKILL **3** to create sth using skill □ *menghasilkan*: *The children have produced some beautiful pictures for the exhibition.*
▶ EFFECT/RESULT **4** to cause a particular effect or result □ *mengakibatkan; menimbulkan*: *Her remarks produced roars of laughter.*

produce → profile

➤ SHOW **5** to show sth so that sb else can look at or examine it ☐ *mengemukakan*: *to produce evidence in court*
➤ FILM/PLAY **6** to be in charge of preparing a film, play, etc. so that it can be shown to the public ☐ *menerbitkan*: *She is producing 'Romeo and Juliet' at the local theatre.*

produce² /ˈprɒdjuːs/ *noun* [U] food, etc. that is grown on a farm and sold ☐ *hasil*: *fresh farm produce*

producer /prəˈdjuːsə(r)/ *noun* [C] **1** a person, company or country that makes or grows sth ☐ *pengeluar*: *Brazil is a major producer of coffee.* **2** a person who deals with the business side of organizing a play, film, etc. ☐ *penerbit*: *Hollywood screenwriters, actors and producers* **3** a person who arranges for sb to make a programme for TV or radio, or a record, CD, etc. ☐ *penerbit*: *an independent television producer*

product /ˈprɒdʌkt/ *noun* [C] **1** something that is made in a factory or that is formed naturally ☐ *hasil; keluaran; produk*: *dairy/meat/pharmaceutical/software products* ♦ *The company has just launched a new product.* ♦ *Carbon dioxide is one of the waste products of this process.* **2 product of sth** the result of sth ☐ *hasil; akibat*: *The industry's problems are the product of government policy.*

production /prəˈdʌkʃn/ *noun* **1** [U] the making or growing of sth, especially in large quantities ☐ *pengeluaran; penghasilan*: *The latest model will be in production from April.* ♦ *This farm specializes in the production of organic vegetables.* ♦ *mass production* **2** [U] the amount of sth that is made or grown ☐ *pengeluaran*: *a rise/fall in production* ♦ *a high level of production* **3** [C] a play, film or programme that has been made for the public ☐ *penerbitan; pementasan*
IDM **on production of sth** when you show sth ☐ *dgn menunjukkan (sst)*: *You can get a ten per cent discount on production of your membership card.*

productive /prəˈdʌktɪv/ *adj* **1** that makes or grows sth, especially in large quantities ☐ *produktif; berdaya keluaran*: *The company wants to sell off its less productive factories.* **2** useful (because results come from it) ☐ *produktif; berhasil*: *a productive discussion* ▶ **productivity** /ˌprɒdʌkˈtɪvəti/ (*AmE* also) / *noun* [U]

Prof. /prɒf/ *abbr* = professor

profess /prəˈfes/ *verb* [T] (*formal*) **1** to say that sth is true or correct, even when it is not ☐ *mengatakan (kononnya)*: *Marianne professed to know nothing at all about it, but I did not believe her.* **2** to state openly that you have a particular belief, feeling, etc ☐ *menyatakan bahawa*: *He professed his hatred of war.*

profession /prəˈfeʃn/ *noun* [C] **1** a job that needs a high level of training and/or education ☐ *profesion; ikhtisas*: *the medical/legal/teaching profession* ♦ *She's thinking of entering the nursing profession.* ⊃ note at **work²** **2 the … profession** [with sing or pl verb] all the people who work in a particular profession ☐ *golongan*: *The legal profession is/are trying to resist the reforms.*
IDM **by profession** as your job ☐ *dr segi pekerjaan*: *George is an accountant by profession.*

professional¹ /prəˈfeʃənl/ *adj* **1** [only before a noun] connected with a job that needs a high level of training and/or education ☐ *profesional; pakar*: *Get professional advice from your lawyer before you take any action.* ♦ *professional qualifications* **2** doing sth in a way that shows skill, training or care ☐ *profesional; yg menunjukkan tahap kemahiran, latihan atau keprihatinan yg tinggi*: *The police are trained to deal with every situation in a calm and professional manner.* ♦ *Her application was neatly typed and looked very professional.* **3** (used about a sport, etc.) done by people who are paid; doing a sport, etc. as a job or for money ☐ *profesional*: *He's planning to* **turn professional** *after the Olympics.* ♦ *professional football* **OPP** **amateur**

professional² /prəˈfeʃənl/ *noun* [C] **1** a person who works in a job that needs a high level of training and/or education ☐ *profesional*: *doctors and other health professionals* **2** (also *informal* **pro**) a person who plays or teaches a sport, etc. for money ☐ *profesional*: *a top golf professional* **3** (also *informal* **pro**) a person who has a lot of skill and experience ☐ *profesional; orang yg betul-betul mahir dan berpengalaman*: *This was clearly a job for a professional.*

professionalism /prəˈfeʃənəlɪzəm/ *noun* [U] a way of doing a job that shows great skill and experience ☐ *keprofesionalan; profesionalisme*: *We were impressed by the professionalism of the staff.*

professionally /prəˈfeʃənəli/ *adv* **1** in a way that shows great skill and experience ☐ *secara profesional* **2** for money; by a professional person ☐ *sebagai… (pemuzik, pemain, dll) profesional*: *Rob plays the saxophone professionally.*

professor /prəˈfesə(r)/ *noun* [C] (*abbr* **Prof.**) **1** (*especially BrE*) a university teacher of the highest level ☐ *profesor*: *She's professor of English at Bristol University.* **2** (*AmE*) a teacher at a college or university ☐ *pensyarah*: *a chemistry professor*

proficient /prəˈfɪʃnt/ *adj* **proficient (in/at sth/doing sth)** able to do a particular thing well; skilled ☐ *cekap*: *We are looking for someone who is proficient in French.* ▶ **proficiency** /prəˈfɪʃnsi/ *noun* [U] **proficiency (in sth/doing sth)**: *a certificate of proficiency in English*

profile /ˈprəʊfaɪl/ *noun* [C] **1** a person's face or head seen from the side, not the front ☐ *pandangan sisi muka; profil*: *I did a sketch of him in profile.* **2** a short description of sb/sth that gives useful information ☐ *profil*: *We're building up a profile of our average customer.* ♦ *You should be careful what you put on your* **Facebook profile** *(= a description and photograph(s) of yourself on an Internet site), as it isn't always private.*

[C] **countable**, a noun with a plural form: *one book, two books*   [U] **uncountable**, a noun with no plural form: *some sugar*

profit → prohibition

IDM **a high/low profile** a way of behaving that does/does not attract other people's attention □ *menonjolkan/tdk menonjolkan diri*: *I don't know much about the subject—I'm going to keep a low profile at the meeting tomorrow.*

profit¹ /ˈprɒfɪt/ *noun* [C,U] the money that you make when you sell sth for more than it cost you □ *keuntungan*: *Did you make a profit on your house when you sold it?* ♦ *I'm hoping to sell my shares at a profit.* **OPP** loss

profit² /ˈprɒfɪt/ *verb* [I,T] (*formal*) profit (from/by sth) to get an advantage from sth; to give sb an advantage □ *mendapat untung, manfaat, faedah, dsb*: *Who will profit most from the tax reforms?*

profitable /ˈprɒfɪtəbl/ *adj* **1** that makes money □ *(yg) menguntungkan*: *a profitable business* **2** helpful or useful □ *berfaedah; berguna*: *We had a profitable discussion yesterday.* ▶ profitably /-əbli/ *adv*: *to spend your time profitably* ▶ profitability /ˌprɒfɪtəˈbɪləti/ *noun* [U]

profound /prəˈfaʊnd/ *adj* **1** very great; that you feel very strongly □ *amat; sangat*: *The experience had a profound influence on her.* **2** needing or showing a lot of knowledge or thought □ *mendalam*: *He's always making profound statements about the meaning of life.* **SYN** deep ▶ profoundly *adv*: *I was profoundly relieved to hear the news.*

profuse /prəˈfjuːs/ *adj* (*formal*) given or produced in great quantity □ *banyak; berlebih-lebih; berulang kali*: *profuse apologies* ▶ profusely *adv*: *She apologized profusely for being late.*

profusion /prəˈfjuːʒn/ *noun* [sing, with sing or pl verb, U] (*formal*) a very large quantity of sth □ *banyak; lebat; mencurah-curah; melimpah-limpah*: *a profusion of colours* ♦ *Roses grew in profusion against the old wall.* **SYN** abundance

program¹ /ˈprəʊɡræm/ *noun* [C] **1** a set of instructions that you give to a computer so that it will do a particular task □ *program*: *to write a program*

> **HELP** When we are talking about computers, both the American and the British spelling is **program**. For every other meaning the British spelling is **programme** and the American spelling is **program**.

2 (*AmE*) = **programme¹**

program² /ˈprəʊɡræm/ *verb* [I,T] (programming; programmed) to give a set of instructions to a computer □ *memprogram; mengatur cara*: *In this class, students will learn how to program.*

programme¹ (*AmE* program) /ˈprəʊɡræm/ *noun* [C] **1** a plan of things to do □ *rancangan*: *What's (on) your programme today?* (= what are you going to do today?) ♦ *The leaflet outlines the government's programme of educational reforms.* **2** a show or other item that is sent out on the radio or TV □ *rancangan*: *a TV/radio programme* ♦ *We've just missed an interesting programme on elephants.* ⊃ note at **television 3** a little book or piece of paper which you get at a concert, a sports event, etc. that gives you information about what you are going to see □ *buku cenderamata/atur cara*: *a theatre programme* ⊃ note at **program**

programme² (*AmE* program) /ˈprəʊɡræm/ *verb* [T] (programming; programmed, *AmE* also programing; programed) [usually passive] **1** to plan for sth to happen at a particular time □ *merancang*: *The road is programmed for completion next May.* **2** to make sb/sth work or act automatically in a particular way □ *memprogram; diprogram*: *The lights are programmed to come on as soon as it gets dark.*

programmer /ˈprəʊɡræmə(r)/ *noun* [C] a person whose job is to write programs for a computer □ *pengatur cara*

progress¹ /ˈprəʊɡres/ *noun* [U] **1** movement forwards or towards achieving sth □ *kemajuan*: *Anna's making progress at school.* ♦ *to make slow/steady/rapid/good progress* **2** change or improvement in society □ *perkembangan*: *scientific progress*

IDM **in progress** happening now □ *sedang dijalankan*: *Silence! Examination in progress.*

progress² /prəˈɡres/ *verb* [I] **1** to become better; to develop (well) □ *maju; berkembang*: *Medical knowledge has progressed rapidly in the last twenty years.* **SYN** advance **2** to move forward; to continue □ *berterusan; semakin (larut, dll)*: *I got more and more tired as the evening progressed.* **SYN** go on

progression /prəˈɡreʃn/ *noun* [C,U] (a) progression (from sth) (to sth) movement forward or a development from one stage to another □ *pergerakan; kemaraan; kemajuan*: *You've made the progression from beginner to intermediate level.*

progressive /prəˈɡresɪv/ *adj* **1** using modern methods and ideas □ *progresif*: *a progressive school* **2** happening or developing steadily □ *berperingkat-peringkat; beransur-ansur*: *a progressive reduction in the number of staff*

progressively /prəˈɡresɪvli/ *adv* steadily; a little at a time □ *semakin*: *The situation became progressively worse.*

the proˌ**gressive** ˈ**tense** = **the continuous tense**

prohibit /prəˈhɪbɪt (*AmE* also) / *verb* [T] (*formal*) prohibit sb/sth (from doing sth) to say that sth is not allowed by law □ *melarang*: *English law prohibits anyone under 18 from buying cigarettes.* **SYN** forbid, prevent

prohibition /ˌprəʊɪˈbɪʃn/ *noun* **1** [U] the act of stopping sth being done or used, especially by law □ *pelarangan; larangan*: *the prohibition of smoking in public places* **2** [C] (*formal*) a prohibition (on/against sth) a law or rule that stops sth being done or used □ *larangan*: *There is a prohibition on the carrying of knives.*

[I] **intransitive**, a verb which has no object: *He laughed.* [T] **transitive**, a verb which has an object: *He ate an apple.*

prohibitive /prəˈhɪbətɪv (AmE also) / adj (used about a price or cost) so high that it prevents people from buying sth or doing sth □ *terlalu mahal*: *The price of houses in the centre of town is prohibitive.* ▶ prohibitively adv

project¹ /ˈprɒdʒekt/ noun [C] **1** a piece of work, often involving many people, that is planned and organized carefully □ *projek*: *a major project to reduce pollution in our rivers* ♦ *a housing project* **2** a piece of school work in which the student has to collect information about a certain subject and then write about it □ *projek*: *Our group chose to do a project on rainforests.*

project² /prəˈdʒekt/ verb
▶ PLAN **1** [T, usually passive] to plan sth that will happen in the future □ *merancang(kan); dirancang(kan)*: *the band's projected world tour*
▶ GUESS **2** [T, usually passive] to guess or calculate the size, cost or amount of sth □ *menjangka; dijangka*: *a projected increase of 10%* **SYN** forecast
▶ LIGHT/IMAGE **3** [T] project sth (on/onto sth) to make light, a picture from a film, etc. appear on a flat surface or screen □ *memancarkan; menayangkan*: *Images are projected onto the retina of the eye.*
▶ SOUND **4** [T] to make a sound so that it can be heard at a distance □ *meluncurkan; melancarkan; melaungkan (suara)*: *Actors must learn to project their voices.*
▶ STICK OUT **5** [I] (*formal*) to stick out □ *menjulur; menganjur*: *The balcony projects one metre out from the wall.*
▶ PRESENT YOURSELF **6** [T] to show or represent sb/sth/yourself in a certain way □ *menonjolkan; menampilkan*: *The government is trying to project a more caring image.*

projection /prəˈdʒekʃn/ noun **1** [C] a guess about a future amount, situation, etc. based on the present situation □ *unjuran; pengunjuran*: *sales projections for the next five years* **2** [U] the act of making light, a picture from a film, a computer image, etc. appear on a surface □ *penayangan*

projector /prəˈdʒektə(r)/ noun [C] a piece of equipment that **projects** images, pictures or films onto a screen or wall □ *projektor*: *a film/data/overhead projector*

proliferate /prəˈlɪfəreɪt/ verb [I] (*formal*) to increase quickly in number □ *bertambah banyak dgn cepat; membiak* ▶ proliferation /prəˌlɪfəˈreɪʃn/ noun [U, sing]

prolific /prəˈlɪfɪk/ adj (used especially about a writer, artist, etc.) producing a lot □ *prolifik; banyak menghasilkan karya*: *a prolific goal scorer* ♦ *Picasso was extremely prolific all through his life.*

prologue /ˈprəʊlɒɡ (AmE also) / noun [C] a piece of writing or a speech that introduces a play, poem, etc. □ *prolog* ➔ look at **epilogue**

prolong /prəˈlɒŋ (AmE also) / verb [T] to make sth last longer □ *memanjangkan*

prolonged /prəˈlɒŋd (AmE also) / adj continuing for a long time □ *berpanjangan; berlarutan; lama*: *There was a prolonged silence before anybody spoke.*

prom /prɒm/ noun [C] **1** = **promenade 2** a dance that is held at the end of a school year □ *prom; majlis tari-menari pd akhir tahun*

promenade /ˌprɒməˈnɑːd/ (also **prom**) noun [C] a wide path where people walk beside the sea in a town on the coast □ *sesiaran*

prominent /ˈprɒmɪnənt/ adj **1** important or famous □ *penting; terkenal*: *a prominent political figure* **2** noticeable; easy to see □ *menonjol; ketara*: *The church is the most prominent feature of the village.* ▶ prominence noun [U, sing]: *The newspaper gave the affair great prominence.* ▶ prominently adv

promiscuous /prəˈmɪskjuəs/ adj having sexual relations with many people □ *mempunyai hubungan seks rambang* ▶ promiscuity /ˌprɒmɪˈskjuːəti/ noun [U]

promise¹ /ˈprɒmɪs/ verb **1** [I,T] promise (to do sth); promise (sb) that ... to say definitely that you will do or not do sth or that sth will happen □ *berjanji*: *She promised to phone every week.* ♦ *She promised (me) that she would write.* **2** [T] promise sth (to sb); promise sb sth to say definitely that you will give sth to sb □ *menjanjikan; berjanji utk memberikan*: *Can you promise your support?* ♦ *You have to give him the money if you promised it to him.* ♦ *My dad has promised me a bicycle.* **3** [T] to show signs of sth, so that you expect it to happen □ *menandakan; dijangka*: *It promises to be an exciting occasion.*

promise² /ˈprɒmɪs/ noun **1** [C] a promise (to do sth/that ...) a written or spoken statement or agreement that you will or will not do sth □ *janji*: *You should never break a promise.* ♦ *Make sure you keep your promise to always do your homework.* ♦ *I want you to make a promise that you won't do that again.* ♦ *I give you my promise that I won't tell anyone.* **2** [U] signs that you will be able to do sth well or be successful □ *(ada) harapan*: *He showed great promise as a musician.*

promising /ˈprɒmɪsɪŋ/ adj showing signs of being very good or successful □ *mempunyai harapan*: *a promising young writer*

promote /prəˈməʊt/ verb [T] **1** to encourage sth; to help sth to happen or develop □ *menggalakkan; memupuk*: *to promote good relations between countries* **2** promote sth (as sth) to advertise sth in order to increase its sales or make it popular □ *mempromosikan*: *The new face cream is being promoted as a miracle cure for wrinkles.* **3** [often passive] promote sb (from sth) (to sth) to give sb a higher position or more important job □ *menaikkan pangkat, kedudukan, dsb*: *He's been promoted from assistant manager to manager.* **OPP** demote ➔ note at **job**

promoter /prəˈməʊtə(r)/ noun [C] a person who organizes or provides the money for an event □ *promoter; penganjur*

promotion /prəˈməʊʃn/ noun 1 [C,U] promotion (to sth) a move to a higher position or more important job □ *kenaikan pangkat, kedudukan, dsb*: *The new job is a promotion for her.* OPP **demotion** 2 [C,U] things that you do in order to advertise a product and increase its sales □ *promosi*: *It's all part of a special promotion of the new book.* 3 [U] (*formal*) promotion (of sth) the activity of trying to make sth develop or become accepted by people □ *perihal menggalakkan/memupuk*: *We need to work on the promotion of health, not the treatment of disease.*

prompt¹ /prɒmpt/ adj 1 immediate; done without delay □ *segera*: *We need a prompt decision on this matter.* 2 [not before a noun] prompt (in doing sth/to do sth) (used about a person) quick; acting without delay □ *cepat*: *We are always prompt in paying our bills.* ♦ *She was prompt to point out my mistake.*

prompt² /prɒmpt/ verb 1 [T] to cause sth to happen; to make sb decide to do sth □ *menyebabkan; membuat sst berlaku*: *What prompted you to give up your job?* 2 [I,T] to encourage sb to speak by asking questions or to remind an actor of his or her words in a play □ *membantu sso utk meneruskan percakapannya; membantu pelakon mengingat dialog*: *The speaker had to be prompted several times.* ▸ **prompting** noun [U]: *He apologized without any prompting.*

prompt³ /prɒmpt/ noun [C] 1 a word or words said to an actor to remind them of what to say next □ *kata(-kata) utk membantu pelakon ingat semula dialog*: *When she forgot her lines I had to give her a prompt.* 2 a sign on a computer screen that shows that the computer has finished what it was doing and is ready for more instructions □ *penggesa*: *Wait for the prompt to come up, then type in your password.*

promptly /ˈprɒmptli/ adv 1 immediately; without delay □ *dgn segera*: *I invited her to dinner and she promptly accepted.* 2 (also prompt) at exactly the time that you have arranged □ *tepat pd masanya*: *We arrived promptly at 12 o'clock.* ♦ *I'll pick you up at 7 o'clock prompt.* SYN **punctually**

prone /prəʊn/ adj prone to sth/to do sth likely to suffer from sth or to do sth bad □ *cenderung (mendapat sakit atau membuat sst yg tdk baik)*: *prone to infection/injury/heart attacks* ♦ *Working without a break makes you more prone to error.* ♦ *to be* **accident-prone** (= to have a lot of accidents)

prong /prɒŋ/ (*AmE usually*) / noun [C] 1 each of the two or more long pointed parts of a fork □ *gigi garpu* 2 each of the separate parts of an attack, argument, etc. that sb uses to achieve sth □ *penjuru* 3 **-pronged** [in compounds] having the number or type of **prongs** mentioned □ *bergigi; penjuru*: *a three-pronged attack*

pronoun /ˈprəʊnaʊn/ noun [C] a word that is used in place of a noun or a phrase that contains a noun □ *kata ganti nama*: *'He', 'it', 'hers', 'me', 'them', etc. are all pronouns.* ➲ look at **personal pronoun**

pronounce /prəˈnaʊns/ verb 1 [T] to make the sound of a word or letter in a particular way □ *menyebut; membunyikan*: *You don't pronounce the 'b' at the end of 'comb'.* ♦ *How do you pronounce your surname?* ➲ noun **pronunciation** 2 [T] (*formal*) to say or give sth formally, officially or publicly □ *menyatakan secara rasmi; mengumumkan*: *The judge will pronounce sentence today.* 3 [I,T] (*formal*) pronounce (on sth) to give your opinion on sth, especially formally □ *mengatakan; memberikan pendapat*: *The play was pronounced 'brilliant' by all the critics.*

pronounced /prəˈnaʊnst/ adj very noticeable; obvious □ *ketara*: *His English is excellent although he speaks with a pronounced French accent.*

pronunciation /prəˌnʌnsiˈeɪʃn/ noun 1 [U,C] the way in which a language or a particular word or sound is said □ *sebutan*: *American pronunciation* ➲ verb **pronounce** 2 [U] sb's way of speaking a language □ *gaya sebutan*: *His grammar is good but his pronunciation is awful!*

> **EXAM TIP**
>
> **Pronunciation**
>
> Make sure you know how to pronounce important words for the topics you will have to talk about in your **oral/speaking exam**. Use the **phonetic transcription** (= the special symbols that show you how to say a word) to help you, or listen to the sound on the Wordpower CD-ROM to get the pronunciation right. You can practise your pronunciation using the 'Record your pronunciation' feature on the CD-ROM.

proof /pruːf/ noun 1 [U] proof (of sth); proof that ... information, documents, etc. which show that sth is true □ *bukti*: *'We need some* **proof of identity**,*' the shop assistant said.* ♦ *You've got no proof that John took the money.* ➲ look at **evidence** ➲ verb **prove** 2 [C, usually pl] (*technical*) a first copy of printed material that is produced so that mistakes can be corrected □ *pruf*: *She was checking the proofs of her latest novel.*

-proof /pruːf/ adj [in compounds] able to protect against the thing mentioned □ *kalis*: *a soundproof room* ♦ *a waterproof/windproof jacket*

prop¹ /prɒp/ noun [C] 1 a stick or other object that you use to support sth or to keep sth in position □ *sangga; topang*: *Rescuers used props to stop the roof of the tunnel collapsing.* 2 [usually pl] an object that is used in a play, film, etc. □ *alatan (utk pementasan, penggambaran, filem, dsb)*: *He's responsible for all the stage props, machinery and lighting.*

prop² /prɒp/ verb [T] (propping; propped) to support sb/sth or keep sb/sth in position by putting them or it against or on sth □ *menyandarkan; menyendal; menopang*: *I'll use this book to* *prop the window open.* ♦ *He propped his bicycle against the wall.*

PHR V **prop sth up** to support sth that would otherwise fall or fail □ *menopang/menyandarkan sst*

propaganda /ˌprɒpəˈɡændə/ *noun* [U] information and ideas that may be exaggerated or false, which are used to gain support for a political leader, party, etc. □ *propaganda; diayah: political propaganda*

propagate /ˈprɒpəɡeɪt/ *verb* 1 [T] (*formal*) to spread an idea, a belief or a piece of information among many people □ *mempropagandakan; menyebarkan: TV advertising propagates a false image of the ideal family.* 2 [I,T] to produce new plants from a parent plant □ *membiakkan; mengacukkan: Mum propagated many of her own plants every summer.* ▶ **propagation** /ˌprɒpəˈɡeɪʃn/ *noun* [U]

propel /prəˈpel/ *verb* [T] (**propelling; propelled**) to move, drive or push sb/sth forward or in a particular direction □ *menjalankan, menolak atau mendorong (sst ke depan)*

propeller /prəˈpelə(r)/ *noun* [C] a device with several blades that turn round very fast in order to make a ship or a plane move □ *propeler; kipas; baling-baling*

propensity /prəˈpensəti/ *noun* [C] (*pl* **propensities**) (*formal*) **propensity (for sth); propensity (for doing sth); propensity (to do sth)** a habit of or a liking for behaving in a particular way □ *kecenderungan; kecondongan: He showed a propensity for violence.* ♦ *She has a propensity to exaggerate.* **SYN inclination**

proper /ˈprɒpə(r)/ *adj* 1 [only *before* a noun] (*especially BrE*) right, suitable or correct □ *betul; sesuai: If you're going skiing you must have the proper clothes.* ♦ *I've got to get these pieces of paper in the proper order.* 2 [only *before* a noun] that you consider to be real or good enough □ *betul-betul: I didn't see much of the flat yesterday. I'm going to go today and have a proper look.* 3 (*formal*) socially and morally acceptable □ *sopan; wajar; patut: I think it would be only proper for you to apologize.* **OPP improper** 4 [only *after* a noun] real or main □ *sebenarnya; bahagian tengah-tengah/ utama: We travelled through miles of suburbs before we got to the city proper.*

properly /ˈprɒpəli/ *adv* 1 (*especially BrE*) correctly; in an acceptable way □ *dgn betul: The teacher said I hadn't done my homework properly.* ♦ *These shoes don't fit properly.* 2 in a way that is socially and morally acceptable; politely □ *dgn sopan/baik: If you two children can't behave properly, then we'll have to go home.* **OPP improperly**

ˌproper ˈnoun (also ˌproper ˈname) *noun* [C] a word which is the name of a particular person or place and begins with a capital letter □ *nama khas: 'Mary' and 'Rome' are proper nouns.*

property /ˈprɒpəti/ *noun* (*pl* **properties**) 1 [U] a thing or things that belong to sb □ *harta; barang: The sack contained stolen property.* ♦ *Is this bag your property?* ♦ *This file is government property.* ➔ look at **lost property** 2 [U] land and buildings □ *hartanah: Property prices vary enormously from area to area.* 3 [C] one building and the land around it □ *bangunan; tanah: There are a lot of empty properties in the area.* 4 [C, usually pl] (*formal*) a special quality or characteristic that a substance, etc. has □ *sifat; khasiat: Some plants have healing properties.*

ˈproperty developer = **developer**

prophecy /ˈprɒfəsi/ *noun* [C] (*pl* **prophecies**) a statement about what is going to happen in the future □ *ramalan: to fulfil a prophecy* (= to make it come true)

prophesy /ˈprɒfəsaɪ/ *verb* [T] (**prophesying; prophesies**; *pt, pp* **prophesied**) to say what you think will happen in the future □ *membuat ramalan: to prophesy disaster/war*

prophet /ˈprɒfɪt/ *noun* [C] 1 (also **Prophet**) (in the Christian, Jewish and Muslim religions) a person who is sent by God to teach the people and give them messages from God □ *nabi* 2 a person who tells what is going to happen in the future □ *tukang ramal* ▶ **prophetic** /prəˈfetɪk/ *adj*

proportion /prəˈpɔːʃn/ *noun* 1 [C] a part or share of a whole □ *bahagian: A large proportion of the earth's surface is covered by sea.* 2 [U] **proportion (of sth to sth)** the relationship between the size or amount of two things □ *kadar; nisbah: The proportion of men to women in the college has changed dramatically over the years.* 3 **proportions** [pl] the size or shape of sth □ *bentuk; saiz (besar, kecil, dsb): a room of fairly generous proportions* ♦ *Political unrest is reaching alarming proportions.*

IDM **in proportion** the right size in relation to other things □ *seimbang: to draw something in proportion* ♦ *She's so upset that it's hard for her to keep the problem in proportion* (= to her it seems more important or serious than it really is).

in proportion to sth by the same amount or number as sth else; relative to □ *setimpal atau mengikut kadar yg sama dgn sst: Salaries have not risen in proportion to inflation.* ♦ *The room is very long in proportion to its width.*

out of proportion (to sth) 1 too big, small, etc. in relation to other things □ *tdk seimbang* 2 too great, serious, important, etc. in relation to sth □ *tdk setimpal langsung; berlebih-lebih: His reaction was completely out of proportion to the situation.*

proportional /prəˈpɔːʃənl/ *adj* **proportional (to sth)** of the right size, amount or degree compared with sth else □ *seimbang; setimpal: Salary is proportional to years of experience.*

proˌportional ˌrepresenˈtation *noun* [U] (*abbr* **PR**) a system that gives each political party in an election a number of seats in a parliament in direct relation to the number of votes it receives □ *perwakilan berkadar* ➔ look at **representation**

proposal /prəˈpəʊzl/ noun [C] **1** a proposal (for/to do sth); a proposal that ... a plan that is formally suggested □ *cadangan; usul*: *a new proposal for raising money* ♦ *a proposal to build more student accommodation* ♦ *May I make a proposal that we all give an equal amount?* **2** an act of formally asking sb to marry you □ *lamaran; pinangan*

propose /prəˈpəʊz/ verb **1** [T] to formally suggest sth as a possible plan or action □ *mencadangkan; mengusulkan*: *At the meeting a new advertising campaign was proposed.* **2** [T] to intend to do sth; to have sth as a plan □ *bercadang*: *What do you propose to do now?* **3** [I,T] propose (to sb) to ask sb to marry you □ *melamar; meminang*: *to propose marriage* **4** [T] propose sb for/as sth to suggest sb for an official position □ *mencadangkan*: *I'd like to propose Anna Marsh as Chairperson.*

proposition /ˌprɒpəˈzɪʃn/ noun [C] **1** an idea, a plan or an offer, especially in business; a suggestion □ *usul; cadangan; tawaran*: *A month's holiday in Spain is a very attractive proposition.* **2** an idea or opinion that sb expresses about sth □ *saranan; kenyataan*: *That's a very interesting proposition. But can you prove it?*

proprietor /prəˈpraɪətə(r)/ (fem **proprietress** /prəˈpraɪətrəs/) noun [C] (formal) the owner of a business, a hotel, etc. □ *tuan punya*

prose /prəʊz/ noun [U] written language that is not poetry □ *prosa*: *to write in prose* ⊃ look at **poetry**

prosecute /ˈprɒsɪkjuːt/ verb [I,T] prosecute sb (for sth) to officially charge sb with a crime and try to show that they are guilty, in a court of law □ *mendakwa*: *the prosecuting counsel/lawyer/attorney* ♦ *He was prosecuted for theft.* ⊃ look at **defend**

prosecution /ˌprɒsɪˈkjuːʃn/ noun **1** [U,C] the process of officially charging sb with a crime and of trying to show that they are guilty, in a court of law □ *pendakwaan; didakwa*: *Failure to pay your parking fine will result in prosecution.* ♦ *to bring a prosecution against somebody* **2** the prosecution [sing, with sing or pl verb] the person or group of people who try to show that sb is guilty of a crime in a court of law □ *pihak pendakwa*: *The prosecution claim/claims that Lloyd was driving at 100 miles per hour.* ⊃ note at **court** ⊃ look at **the defence**

prosecutor /ˈprɒsɪkjuːtə(r)/ noun [C] **1** a public official who charges sb officially with a crime and **prosecutes** them in court □ *pendakwa*: *the public/state prosecutor* **2** a lawyer who leads the case against the person who is accused of a crime □ *pendakwa*

prospect /ˈprɒspekt/ noun **1** [U, sing] prospect (of sth/of doing sth) the possibility that sth will happen □ *kemungkinan; harapan*: *There's little prospect of better weather before next week.* **2** [sing] prospect (of sth/of doing sth) a thought about what may or will happen in the future □ *kemungkinan; memikirkan (ttg apa yg akan/mungkin berlaku)*: *The prospect of becoming a father filled James with horror.* **3** prospects [pl] chances of being successful in the future □ *prospek; peluang utk maju atau berjaya pd masa depan*: *good job/career/promotion prospects*

prospective /prəˈspektɪv/ adj likely to be or to happen; possible □ *bakal*: *They are worried about prospective changes in the law.*

prospectus /prəˈspektəs/ noun [C] a small book which gives information about a school or college in order to advertise it □ *prospektus; risalah*

prosper /ˈprɒspə(r)/ verb [I] to develop in a successful way; to be successful, especially with money □ *berjaya; menjadi maju/makmur*

prosperity /prɒˈsperəti/ noun [U] the state of being successful, and having a lot of money □ *kemakmuran; kesenangan; kejayaan*: *Tourism has brought prosperity to many parts of Spain.*

prosperous /ˈprɒspərəs/ adj rich and successful □ *makmur; kaya dan berjaya*

prostitute /ˈprɒstɪtjuːt/ noun [C] a person, especially a woman, who earns money by having sex with people □ *pelacur*

prostitution /ˌprɒstɪˈtjuːʃn/ noun [U] the work of a **prostitute** □ *pelacuran*

prostrate /ˈprɒstreɪt/ adj (formal) lying flat on the ground, facing downwards □ *meniarap; tertiarap*

protagonist /prəˈtæɡənɪst/ noun [C] (formal) the main character in a play, film or book □ *protagonis* ⊃ look at **hero**

protect /prəˈtekt/ verb [T] protect sb/sth (against/from sth) to keep sb/sth safe; to defend sb/sth □ *melindungi; dilindungi*: *Parents try to protect their children from danger as far as possible.* ♦ *Bats are a protected species* (= they must not be killed).

protection /prəˈtekʃn/ noun [U] protection (against/from sth) the act of keeping sb/sth safe so that he/she/it is not harmed or damaged □ *perlindungan*: *Vaccination gives protection against diseases.* ♦ *After the attack the man was put under police protection.*

protective /prəˈtektɪv/ adj **1** [only before a noun] that prevents sb/sth from being damaged or harmed □ *pelindung*: *In certain jobs workers need to wear protective clothing.* **2** protective (of/towards sb/sth) wanting to keep sb/sth safe □ *bersifat melindungi*: *Female animals are very protective of their young.*

protector /prəˈtektə(r)/ noun [C] a person who protects sb/sth □ *pelindung*

protein /ˈprəʊtiːn/ noun [C,U] a substance found in food such as meat, fish and eggs. It is important for helping people and animals to grow and be healthy. □ *protein*

protest¹ /ˈprəʊtest/ noun [U,C] protest (against sth) a statement or action that shows that you do not like or approve of sth □ *bantahan*: He resigned **in protest** against the decision. ◆ The trade union organized a protest against the redundancies.
IDM **under protest** not happily and after expressing disagreement □ *dgn bantahan*: Fiona agreed to pay in the end but only under protest.

protest² /prəˈtest/ verb 1 [I,T] protest (about/against/at sth) to say or show that you do not approve of or agree with sth, especially publicly □ *membantah*: Students have been protesting against the government's decision.

HELP In American English **protest** is used without a preposition: *They protested the government's handling of the situation.*

2 [T] to say sth firmly, especially when others do not believe you □ *menegaskan; mempertahankan*: She has always protested her innocence.

HELP **Protest** or **complain**? **Protest** is stronger and usually used about more serious things than **complain**. You **protest** about something that you feel is not right or fair, you **complain** about the quality of something or about a less serious action: *to protest about a new tax* ◆ *to complain about the poor weather*

▶**protester** noun [C]: *Protesters blocked the road outside the factory.*

Protestant /ˈprɒtɪstənt/ noun [C] a member of the Christian church that separated from the Catholic church in the 16th century □ *Protestan* ▶**Protestant** adj: *a Protestant church* ⊃ look at **Roman Catholic**

protocol /ˈprəʊtəkɒl (*AmE* also) / noun [U] a system of fixed rules and formal behaviour used in official meetings or other very formal situations □ *protokol; tatacara*: *a breach of protocol* (= *a failure to follow it*) ◆ *the protocol of diplomatic visits*

proton /ˈprəʊtɒn/ noun [C] part of the **nucleus** (= the central part) of an atom that carries a positive electric charge □ *proton* ⊃ look at **electron, neutron**

prototype /ˈprəʊtətaɪp/ noun [C] the first model or design of sth from which other forms will be developed □ *prototaip; contoh ulung*

protrude /prəˈtruːd/ verb [I] (*formal*) protrude (from sth) to stick out from a place or surface □ *menjulur; menonjol; terjojol, jongang, dll*: *protruding eyes/teeth*

protrusion /prəˈtruːʒn/ noun [C,U] (*formal*) a thing that sticks out from a place or surface; the fact of doing this □ *sst yg menonjol keluar; penonjolan*: *a protrusion on the rock face*

proud /praʊd/ adj (**prouder**; **proudest**)
1 proud (of sb/sth); proud to do sth/that … feeling pleased and satisfied about sth that you own or have done □ *bangga; megah*: They are very proud of their new house. ◆ I feel very proud to be part of such a successful organization. ◆ You should feel very proud that you have been chosen. 2 feeling that you are better and more important than other people □ *bermegah-megah; bongkak*: Now she's at university she'll be much too proud to talk to us! 3 having respect for yourself and not wanting to lose the respect of others □ *(ber)maruah; (ada) harga diri*: He was too proud to ask for help. ⊃ noun **pride** ▶**proudly** adv: *'I did all the work myself,' he said proudly.*

prove /pruːv/ verb (*pp* **proved**, *AmE* **proven**)
1 [T] prove sth (to sb) to use facts and evidence to show that sth is true □ *membuktikan*: It will be difficult to prove that she was lying. ◆ She tried to prove her innocence to the court. ◆ He felt he needed **to prove a point** (= show other people that he was right). ⊃ noun **proof** 2 [I] to show a particular quality over a period of time □ *terbukti; ternyata*: The job proved more difficult than we'd expected. 3 [T] prove yourself (to sb) to show other people how good you are at doing sth and/or that you are capable of doing sth □ *membuktikan kepandaian, kebolehan, dsb (diri sso itu)*: He constantly feels that he has to prove himself to others.

proven /ˈpruːvn (*BrE* also) ˈpruː-/ adj [only before a noun] that has been shown to be true □ *terbukti*: *a proven fact*

proverb /ˈprɒvɜːb/ noun [C] a short well-known sentence or phrase that gives advice or says that sth is generally true in life □ *peribahasa; bidalan*: *'All's fair in love and war' is a proverb.* ⊃ look at **saying**

proverbial /prəˈvɜːbiəl/ adj [only before a noun] used to show that you are referring to a particular **proverb** or well-known phrase □ *berkenaan dgn peribahasa/bidalan*: *He drinks like the proverbial fish.* ▶**proverbially** /-biəli/ adv

provide /prəˈvaɪd/ verb [T] provide sb (with sth); provide sth (for sb) to give sth to sb or make sth available for sb to use □ *memberikan; menyediakan; membekalkan*: This book will provide you with all the information you need. ◆ We are able to provide accommodation for two students. **SYN** supply ⊃ noun **provision**
PHR V **provide for sb** to give sb all that they need to live, for example food and clothing □ *menyara hidup*: Robin has four children to provide for.
provide for sth to make preparations to deal with sth that might happen in the future □ *bersedia utk sst kemungkinan; mengambil kira*: We did not provide for such a large increase in prices.

provided /prəˈvaɪdɪd/ (also **providing**) conj provided/providing (that) only if; on condition that □ *asalkan; dgn syarat*: She agreed to go and work abroad provided (that) her family could go with her.

province /ˈprɒvɪns/ noun 1 [C] one of the main parts into which some countries are

[C] **countable**, a noun with a plural form: *one book, two books* [U] **uncountable**, a noun with no plural form: *some sugar*

provincial → psychiatrist

divided, that has its own local government □ *wilayah*: *Canada has ten provinces.* ⇒ look at **county, state 2 the provinces** [pl] all the parts of a country except the capital city □ *daerah luar ibu kota*

provincial /prəˈvɪnʃl/ *adj* **1** [only *before* a noun] connected with one of the large areas that some countries are divided into □ *(berkenaan dgn) wilayah*: *provincial governments/elections* **2** connected with the parts of a country that do not include its most important city □ *(berkenaan dgn) daerah luar ibu kota*: *a provincial town/newspaper* **3** (used about a person or their ideas) not wanting to consider new or different ideas or fashions □ *bersifat kekampungan*: *provincial attitudes*

provision /prəˈvɪʒn/ *noun* (*formal*) **1** [U] the giving or supplying of sth to sb or making sth available for sb to use □ *peruntukan*: *The council is responsible for the provision of education and social services.* **2** [U] **provision for sb/sth** preparations that you make to deal with sth that might happen in the future □ *persediaan*: *She* **made provision for** (= planned for the financial future of) *the children in the event of her death.* **3 provisions** [pl] supplies of food and drink, especially for a long journey □ *bekalan makanan dan minuman* ⇒ *verb* **provide**

provisional /prəˈvɪʒənl/ *adj* only for the present time; that is likely to be changed in the future □ *sementara*: *The provisional date for the next meeting is 18 November.* ♦ *a provisional driving licence* (= that you use when you are learning to drive) **SYN temporary** ▸**provisionally** /-nəli/ *adv*: *I've only repaired the bike provisionally—we'll have to do it properly later.*

provocation /ˌprɒvəˈkeɪʃn/ *noun* [U,C] the act of doing or saying sth deliberately to try to make sb angry or upset; something that is said or done to cause this □ *perbuatan atau kata-kata yg membangkitkan kemarahan*: *You should never hit children, even* **under** *extreme provocation.* ⇒ *verb* **provoke**

provocative /prəˈvɒkətɪv/ *adj* **1** intended to make sb angry or upset or to cause an argument □ *yg membangkitkan kemarahan*: *He made a provocative remark about a woman's place being in the home.* **2** intended to cause sexual excitement □ *yg menggairahkan*: *a provocative look* ▸**provocatively** *adv*

provoke /prəˈvəʊk/ *verb* [T] **1** to cause a particular feeling or reaction □ *menimbulkan; membangkitkan*: *an article intended to provoke discussion* **2 provoke sb (into sth/into doing sth)** to say or do sth that you know will make a person angry or upset □ *membuat sso marah atau sakit hati*: *The lawyer claimed his client was provoked into acts of violence.* ⇒ *noun* **provocation**

prow /praʊ/ *noun* [C] (*formal*) the pointed front part of a ship or boat □ *haluan* **OPP stern**

prowess /ˈpraʊəs/ *noun* [U] (*formal*) great skill at doing sth □ *kehandalan*: *academic/sporting prowess*

prowl /praʊl/ *verb* [I,T] **prowl (about/around)** (used about an animal that is hunting or a person who is waiting for a chance to steal sth or do sth bad) to move around an area quietly so that you are not seen or heard □ *merayau-rayau*: *I could hear someone prowling around outside so I called the police.* ▸**prowl** *noun* [sing]: *an intruder* **on the prowl** ▸**prowler** *noun* [C]: *The police have arrested a prowler outside the hospital.*

proximity /prɒkˈsɪməti/ *noun* [U] (*formal*) **proximity (of sb/sth) (to sb/sth)** the state of being near to sb/sth in distance or time □ *kedekatan; dekatnya*: *The proximity of the new offices to the airport is a great advantage.*

proxy /ˈprɒksi/ *noun* [U] the authority that you give to sb to act for you if you cannot do sth yourself □ *proksi; wakil*: *to vote* **by proxy**

prude /pruːd/ *noun* [C] a person who is easily shocked by anything connected with sex □ *orang yg kolot (dlm hal seks)* ▸**prudish** *adj*

prudent /ˈpruːdnt/ *adj* (*formal*) sensible and careful when making judgements and decisions; avoiding unnecessary risks □ *bijak; berhati-hati*: *It would be prudent to get some more advice before you invest your money.* ▸**prudence** *noun* [U] ▸**prudently** *adv*

prune[1] /pruːn/ *noun* [C] a dried **plum** (= a soft round fruit with a stone inside) □ *(buah) prun*

prune[2] /pruːn/ *verb* [T] to cut branches or parts of branches off a tree or bush in order to give it a better shape □ *mencantas; memangkas*

pry /praɪ/ *verb* (**prying**; **pries**; *pt, pp* **pried**) **1** [I] **pry (into sth)** to try to find out about other people's private affairs □ *cuba mengambil tahu ttg hal orang lain*: *I'm sick of you prying into my personal life.* **2** [T] (*especially AmE*) = **prise**

PS (also **ps**) /ˌpiː ˈes/ *noun* [C], *abbr* **postscript** an extra message or extra information that is added at the end of an email, a note, etc. □ *Catatan Tambahan*: *Love Tessa. PS I'll bring the car.*

pseudonym /ˈsuːdənɪm; ˈsjuː-/ *noun* [C] a name used by sb, especially a writer, instead of their real name □ *nama samaran*

psych /saɪk/ *verb*
PHR V psych yourself up (*informal*) to prepare yourself in your mind for sth difficult □ *menyediakan diri; bersedia*: *I've got to psych myself up for this interview.*

psyche /ˈsaɪki/ *noun* [C] (*formal*) the mind; your deepest feelings and attitudes □ *jiwa*: *the human/female/national psyche*

psychedelic /ˌsaɪkəˈdelɪk/ *adj* (used about art, music, clothes, etc.) having bright colours or patterns or strange sounds □ *psikedelik; mempunyai warna atau corak yg menyilaukan mata atau bunyi yg aneh*

psychiatrist /saɪˈkaɪətrɪst/ *noun* [C] a doctor who is trained to treat people with mental illness □ *pakar psikiatri/sakit jiwa*

psychiatry /saɪˈkaɪətri/ noun [U] the study and treatment of mental illness ⊃ *psikiatri* ⊃ look at **psychology** ▶**psychiatric** /ˌsaɪkiˈætrɪk/ adj: *a psychiatric hospital/unit/nurse*

psychic /ˈsaɪkɪk/ adj (used about a person or their mind) seeming to have unusual powers that cannot be explained, for example knowing what sb else is thinking or being able to see into the future ⊐ *psikik; berkuasa ghaib*

psycho /ˈsaɪkəʊ/ (informal) = **psychopath**

psychoanalysis /ˌsaɪkəʊəˈnæləsɪs/ (also **analysis**) noun [U] a method of treating sb with mental illness by asking about their past experiences, feelings, dreams, etc. in order to find out what is making them unhappy ⊐ *psikoanalisis* ▶**psychoanalyse** (AmE **psychoanalyze**) /ˌsaɪkəʊˈænəlaɪz/ verb [T]

psychoanalyst /ˌsaɪkəʊˈænəlɪst/ noun [C] a person who treats sb with a mental illness by using **psychoanalysis** ⊐ *ahli psikoanalisis*

psychological /ˌsaɪkəˈlɒdʒɪkl/ adj 1 connected with the mind or the way that it works ⊐ *dr segi psikologi: Has her ordeal caused her long-term psychological damage?* 2 [only before a noun] connected with **psychology** ⊐ *(berkenaan dgn) psikologi* ▶**psychologically** /-kli/ adv: *Psychologically, it was a bad time to be starting a new job.*

psychologist /saɪˈkɒlədʒɪst/ noun [C] a scientist who studies the mind and the way that people behave ⊐ *ahli psikologi*

psychology /saɪˈkɒlədʒi/ noun 1 [U] the scientific study of the mind and the way that people behave ⊐ *psikologi; kajian ttg mental dan jiwa: child psychology* ⊃ look at **psychiatry** 2 [sing] the type of mind that a person or group of people has ⊐ *psikologi; cara pemikiran: If we understood the psychology of the killer we would have a better chance of catching him.*

psychopath /ˈsaɪkəpæθ/ (also informal **psycho**) noun [C] a person who has a serious mental illness that may cause them to hurt or kill other people ⊐ *psikopat; orang gila*

psychosis /saɪˈkəʊsɪs/ noun [C,U] (pl **psychoses**) a very serious mental illness that affects your whole character ⊐ *psikosis* ▶**psychotic** /saɪˈkɒtɪk/ adj, noun [C]: *a psychotic patient/individual*

psychotherapy /ˌsaɪkəʊˈθerəpi/ noun [U] the treatment of mental illness by discussing sb's feelings rather than by giving them drugs ⊐ *psikoterapi*

pt abbr (pl **pts**) 1 = **pint**(1) ⊐ *pain: 2 pts milk* 2 = **point**¹(7) ⊐ *mata: Laura 5pts, Arthur 4pts*

PTO (also **pto**) /ˌpiː tiː ˈəʊ/ abbr (at the bottom of a page) **please turn over** ⊐ *selak ke muka surat sebelah*

pub /pʌb/ (also formal **public house**) noun [C] a place where people go to buy and drink alcohol and that also often serves food ⊐ *pub; kedai arak: a pub lunch ◆ a quiz at the local pub ◆ Are you coming to the pub tonight?*

puberty /ˈpjuːbəti/ noun [U] the time when a child's body is changing and becoming physically like that of an adult ⊐ *baligh; cukup umur: to reach puberty* **SYN** **adolescence**

pubic /ˈpjuːbɪk/ adj [only before a noun] of the area around the sexual organs ⊐ *pubik: pubic hair*

public¹ /ˈpʌblɪk/ adj 1 [only before a noun] connected with ordinary people in general ⊐ *awam; orang ramai: Public opinion was in favour of the war. ◆ How much public support is there for the government's policy?* 2 provided for the use of people in general ⊐ *awam: a public library/telephone ◆ public spending* (= money that the government spends on education, health care, etc.) 3 known, seen or heard by many people ⊐ *diketahui umum: We're going to make the news public soon. ◆ It was the band's last public appearance.* **OPP** for all meanings **private**
IDM **be common/public knowledge** ⊃ **knowledge**
go public 1 to tell people about sth that is a secret ⊐ *mendedahkan kpd umum: The sacked employee went public with his stories of corruption inside the company.* 2 (used about a company) to start selling shares to the public ⊐ *menjual saham kpd orang ramai*
in the public eye often appearing on TV, in magazines, etc. ⊐ *di mata umum*
▶**publicly** /-kli/ adv: *The company refused to admit publicly that it had acted wrongly.*

public² /ˈpʌblɪk/ noun [sing, with sing or pl verb] 1 **the public** people in general ⊐ *orang ramai; umum: The university swimming pool is open to the public in the evenings. ◆ The police have asked for help from members of the public. ◆ The public is/are generally in favour of the new law.* 2 a group of people who are all interested in sth or who have sth in common ⊐ *kumpulan orang tertentu: the travelling public*
IDM **in public** when other people are present ⊐ *di depan umum; di khalayak ramai: This is the first time that Miss Potter has spoken about her experience in public.*

publican /ˈpʌblɪkən/ noun [C] (BrE) a person who owns or manages a pub ⊐ *tuan punya atau pengurus pub*

publication /ˌpʌblɪˈkeɪʃn/ noun 1 [U] the act of preparing a book, magazine, etc. and making it available to the public in print or on the Internet ⊐ *penerbitan: His latest book has just been accepted for publication.* 2 [C] a book, magazine, etc. that has been published ⊐ *penerbitan; terbitan: specialist publications* 3 [U] the act of making sth known to the public ⊐ *pengumuman: the publication of exam results*

public company (also **public limited company**) noun [C] (BrE) (abbr **plc**) a large company that sells its shares to the public ⊐ *syarikat awam*

public convenience noun [C] (BrE) a toilet in a public place that anyone can use □ *tandas awam*

public 'house (formal) = **pub**

publicity /pʌbˈlɪsəti/ noun [U] 1 notice or attention from newspapers, TV, etc. □ *publisiti*: *to seek/avoid publicity* 2 the business of attracting people's attention to sth/sb; advertising □ *publisiti; pengiklanan*: *There has been a lot of publicity for this film.*

publicize (also -ise) /ˈpʌblɪsaɪz/ verb [T] to attract people's attention to sth □ *membuat/diberi publisiti*: *The event has been well publicized and should attract a lot of people.*

public limited 'company = **public company**

public re'lations noun (abbr PR) 1 [U] the job of giving information to the public about an organization or person in order to create a good impression □ *perhubungan awam*: *a Public Relations Officer* 2 [pl] the state of the relationship between an organization and the public □ *perhubungan awam*: *Giving money to local charities is good for public relations.*

public 'school noun [C] 1 (in Britain, especially in England) a private school for children aged between 13 and 18 □ *sekolah swasta*

> **CULTURE**
> Parents have to pay to send their children to one of these schools. Many public schools are boarding schools (= schools where children can live while they are studying). Famous public schools are Eton and Rugby.

2 (in the US, Australia, Scotland and other countries) a local school that any child can go to that provides free education □ *sekolah kerajaan*

public-'spirited adj always ready to help other people and the public in general □ *berbakti utk orang ramai*

public 'transport noun [U] (the system of) buses, trains, etc. that run according to a series of planned times and that anyone can use □ *pengangkutan awam*: *to travel by/on public transport*

publish /ˈpʌblɪʃ/ verb 1 [I,T] to prepare a book, magazine, etc. and make it available to the public in print or on the Internet □ *menerbitkan*: *This dictionary was published by Oxford University Press.* 2 [T] (used about a writer, etc.) to have your work put in a book, magazine, etc. □ *menerbitkan*: *Dr Wreth has published several articles on the subject.* 3 [T] to make sth known to the public □ *mengumumkan*: *Large companies must publish their accounts every year.*

publisher /ˈpʌblɪʃə(r)/ noun [C] a person or company that publishes books, magazines, etc. □ *penerbit*

publishing /ˈpʌblɪʃɪŋ/ noun [U] the business of preparing books, magazines, etc. to be sold in print or on the Internet □ *penerbitan*: *a career in publishing* ◆ *digital publishing*

puck /pʌk/ noun [C] a small flat rubber object that is used as a ball in **ice hockey** (= a sport) □ *cakera getah keras* ⊃ note at **hockey**

pudding /ˈpʊdɪŋ/ noun [C,U] (BrE) 1 any sweet food that is eaten at the end of a meal □ *pencuci mulut*: *What's for pudding today?* ⊃ look at **sweet** ⊃ A more formal word is **dessert**. 2 a type of sweet food that is made from bread, flour or rice with eggs, milk, etc. □ *puding*: *rice pudding*

puddle /ˈpʌdl/ noun [C] a small pool of water or other liquid, especially rain, that has formed on the ground □ *lopak* ⊃ note at **lake**

puff¹ /pʌf/ verb 1 [I,T] to smoke a cigarette, pipe etc. □ *menghisap rokok, paip, dsb*: *to puff on a cigarette* 2 [I,T] (used about air, smoke, wind, etc.) to blow or come out in clouds □ *keluar berkepul-kepul*: *Smoke was puffing out of the chimney.* 3 [I] to breathe loudly or quickly, for example when you are running □ *tercungap-cungap*: *He was puffing hard as he ran up the hill.* 4 [I] **puff along, in, out, up, etc.** to move in a particular direction with loud breaths or small clouds of smoke □ *bergerak dgn tercungap-cungap atau dgn mengeluarkan asap berkepul-kepul*: *The train puffed into the station.*
PHR V puff sth out/up to cause sth to become larger by filling it with air □ *mengembangkan*: *The trumpet player was puffing out his cheeks.*
puff up (used about part of the body) to become swollen □ *bengkak*: *Her arm puffed up when she was stung by a wasp.*

puff² /pʌf/ noun [C] (BrE informal) 1 one breath that you take when you are smoking a cigarette or pipe □ (*perbuatan*) *menghisap rokok atau paip*: *to take/have a puff on a cigarette* 2 a small amount of air, smoke, wind, etc. that is blown or sent out □ *hembusan; tiupan*: *a puff of smoke*

puffed /pʌft/ (also **puffed 'out**) adj [not before a noun] finding it difficult to breathe, for example because you have been running □ *tercungap-cungap*

puffin /ˈpʌfɪn/ noun [C] a black and white bird with a large, brightly coloured beak that lives near the sea, common in the North Atlantic □ *burung pufin*

puffy /ˈpʌfi/ adj (**puffier**; **puffiest**) (used about a part of sb's body) looking soft and swollen □ *sembap; bengkak*: *Your eyes look a bit puffy. Have you been crying?*

puke /pjuːk/ verb [I,T] (informal) to be sick □ (*slang*) *muntah* SYN **vomit** ▸ **puke** noun [U]

pull¹ /pʊl/ verb 1 [I,T] to use force to move sb/sth towards yourself □ *menarik; menyentap*: *I pulled on the rope to make sure that it was secure.* ◆ *to pull the trigger of a gun* ◆ *I felt someone pull at my sleeve and turned round.* ◆ *They managed to pull the child out of the water just in time.* 2 [T]

pull sth on, out, up, down, etc. to move sth in the direction that is described □ *menarik; mencabut*: *She pulled her sweater on/She pulled on her sweater.* ◆ *He pulled up his trousers/He pulled his trousers up.* ◆ *I switched off the TV and pulled out the plug.* ◆ *It's dark—pull the curtains* (= close them). ◆ *He felt in his pocket and pulled out a pen.* **3** [T] to hold or be fastened to sth and move it along behind you in the direction that you are going □ *menarik; ditarik*: *That cart is too heavy for one horse to pull.* **4** [I,T] to move your body or a part of your body away with force □ *menarik; mengelak*: *She pulled away as he tried to kiss her.* ◆ *I pulled back my fingers just as the door slammed.* **5** [T] to damage a muscle, etc. by using too much force □ *tergeliat; salah urat*: *I've pulled a muscle in my thigh.*

pull/push

She's pulling the dog.

He's pushing the car.

IDM **make/pull faces/a face (at sb/sth)** ➔ **face¹**
pull sb's leg (*informal*) to play a joke on sb by trying to make them believe sth that is not true □ *mempermain-mainkan sso*
pull out all the stops (*informal*) to make the greatest possible effort to achieve sth □ *berusaha sedaya upaya*
pull (your) punches [usually used in negative sentences] (*informal*) to be careful about what you say or do in order not to shock or upset anyone □ *bercakap atau membuat sst baik-baik (supaya tdk memeranjatkan atau menyakitkan hati sesiapa)*: *The film pulls no punches in its portrayal of urban violence.*
pull your socks up (*BrE*) to start working harder or better than before □ *mencuba lebih kuat atau memperbaiki perilaku*
pull strings to use your influence to gain an advantage □ *menggunakan pengaruh (sso)*
pull your weight to do your fair share of the work □ *sama-sama bekerja*

PHR V **pull away (from sb/sth)** to start moving forward, leaving sb/sth behind □ *pergi/berlalu (dr sso/sst)*: *We waved as the bus pulled away.*

pull sth down to destroy a building □ *merobohkan sst*
pull in (to sth); pull into sth 1 (used about a train) to enter a station □ *masuk stesen* **2** (used about a car, etc.) to move to the side of the road and stop □ *menepi dan berhenti*
pull sth off (*informal*) to succeed in sth □ *berjaya membuat sst*: *to pull off a business deal*
pull out (used about a car, etc.) to move away from the side of the road □ *bergerak keluar*: *I braked as a car suddenly pulled out in front of me.*
pull out (of sth) (used about a train) to leave a station □ *keluar dr stesen*
pull (sb/sth) out (of sth) (to cause sb/sth) to leave sth □ *menarik/mengundurkan diri*: *The Americans have pulled their team out of the competition.* ◆ *We've pulled out of the deal.*
pull over (used about a vehicle or its driver) to slow down and move to the side of the road □ *menepi*: *I pulled over to let the ambulance past.*
pull through (sth) to survive a dangerous illness or a difficult time □ *selamat; sembuh*
pull together to do sth or work together with other people in an organized way and without fighting □ *berusaha/bekerja bersama-sama*
pull yourself together to control your feelings and behave in a calm way □ *menenangkan diri*: *Pull yourself together and stop crying!*
pull up (to cause a car, etc.) to stop □ *berhenti*

pull² /pʊl/ *noun* **1** [C] **a pull (at/on sth)** the act of moving sb/sth towards you using force □ *tarikan; sentapan*: *I gave a pull on the rope to check it was secure.* **2** [sing] a physical force or an attraction that makes sb/sth move in a particular direction □ *tarikan*: *the earth's gravitational pull* ◆ (*figurative*) *He couldn't resist the pull of the city.*

pulley /ˈpʊli/ *noun* [C] a piece of equipment, consisting of a wheel and a rope, that is used for lifting heavy things □ *kapi*

pullover

/ˈpʊləʊvə(r)/ *noun* [C] (*especially BrE*) a knitted piece of clothing for the upper part of the body, made of wool, with long sleeves and no buttons □ *baju sejuk sarung; 'pullover'* **SYN** jersey, jumper ➔ note at sweater

load

pulley

ˈpull tab (*AmE*) = **ring pull**

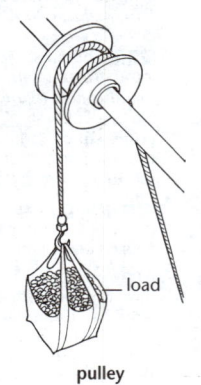

pulp /pʌlp/ *noun* **1** [sing,U] a soft substance that is made especially by crushing sth □ *makanan, dll yg dilenyek; pulpa*: *Mash the beans to a pulp.* **2** [U] the soft inner part of some fruits or vegetables □ *isi*

pulsate /pʌlˈseɪt/ verb [I] to move or shake with strong regular movements □ *berdenyut; bergetar*: *a pulsating rhythm*

pulse¹ /pʌls/ noun 1 [C, usually sing] the regular beating in your body as blood is pushed around it by your heart. You can feel your **pulse** at your wrist, neck, etc. □ *nadi*: *Your pulse rate increases after exercise.* ♦ *to feel/take somebody's pulse* (= to count how many times it beats in one minute) 2 **pulses** [pl] the seeds of some plants such as **beans** and **peas** that are cooked and eaten as food □ *kekacang*

pulse² /pʌls/ verb [I] to move with strong regular movements □ *berdenyut*

pulverize (also -ise) /ˈpʌlvəraɪz/ verb [T] 1 (*formal*) to crush sth into a fine powder □ *mengisar/menumbuk hingga lumat* 2 (*especially BrE informal*) to defeat or destroy sb/sth completely □ *menewaskan/mengalahkan sama sekali*: *We pulverized the opposition.* **SYN** for both meanings **crush**

pump¹ /pʌmp/ noun [C] 1 a machine that is used for forcing a gas or liquid in a particular direction □ *pam*: *Have you got a bicycle pump?* ♦ *a petrol pump* ➔ picture at **bicycle** 2 [usually pl] a flat woman's shoe with no fastening □ *kasut sarung*: *ballet pumps*

pump² /pʌmp/ verb 1 [T] to force a gas or liquid to go in a particular direction □ *mengepam; mengalir*: *Your heart pumps blood around your body.* 2 [I] (used about a liquid) to flow in a particular direction as if forced by a **pump** □ *keluar*: *Blood was pumping out of the wound.* 3 [I,T] to be moved or to move sth very quickly up and down or in and out □ *menggoncang-goncangkan; melocok-locok*: *He pumped his arms up and down to keep warm.*

PHR V pump sth into sth/sb to put a lot of sth into sth/sb □ *mengasakkan; memasukkan; melaburkan (wang)*: *He pumped all his savings into the business.*

pump sth up to fill sth with air, for example by using a **pump** □ *mengepam/mengembungkan sst*: *to pump up a car tyre*

pumpkin /ˈpʌmpkɪn/ noun [C,U] a very large round vegetable with thick orange skin that is cooked and eaten □ *labu* ➔ picture on **page P15**

pun /pʌn/ noun [C] an amusing use of a word that can have two meanings or of different words that sound the same □ *penggunaan lucu sst perkataan yg ada dua maksud atau perkataan yg berlainan tetapi sama bunyinya*: *We're banking on them lending us the money—no pun intended!*

ᵢpunch¹ /pʌntʃ/ verb [T] 1 **punch sb (in/on sth)** to hit sb/sth hard with your **fist** (= closed hand) □ *menumbuk*: *He punched Mike hard in the stomach and ran away.* ♦ *to punch somebody on the nose* ♦ *She punched the air when she heard the good news.* ➔ note at **hit** 2 to make a hole in sth with a **punch²**(2) □ *menebuk*: *He punched a hole in the ticket.*

ᵢpunch² /pʌntʃ/ noun 1 [C] a hard hit with your **fist** (= closed hand) □ *tumbukan*: *She gave him a hard punch on the arm.* 2 [C] a machine or tool that you use for making holes in sth □ *penebuk*: *a ticket punch* ♦ *a hole punch* ➔ picture at **stationery** 3 [U] a drink made from wine, fruit juice and sugar □ *minuman 'punch'*
IDM pull (your) punches ➔ **pull¹**

punchline /ˈpʌntʃlaɪn/ noun [C] the last and most important words of a joke or story □ *bahagian lucu dlm sst jenaka*

ˈpunch-up noun [C] (*BrE informal*) a fight in which people hit each other □ *bertumbuk*

punctual /ˈpʌŋktʃuəl/ adj doing sth or happening at the right time; not late □ *tepat pd masanya*: *It is important to be punctual for your classes.*

> **HELP** In spoken English we say that the train, bus, etc. was **on time**, not punctual.

▶ **punctuality** /ˌpʌŋktʃuˈæləti/ noun [U]: *Japanese trains are famous for their punctuality.*
▶ **punctually** /ˈpʌŋktʃuəli/ adv

punctuate /ˈpʌŋktʃueɪt/ verb 1 [T] **punctuate sth (with sth)** to interrupt sth many times □ *menyelangi; diselangi*: *Her speech was punctuated with bursts of applause.* 2 [I,T] to divide writing into sentences and phrases by adding full stops, question marks, etc. □ *membubuh tanda baca*

punctuation /ˌpʌŋktʃuˈeɪʃn/ noun [U] the marks used for dividing writing into sentences and phrases □ *tanda baca*: *Punctuation marks include full stops, commas and question marks.*

puncture /ˈpʌŋktʃə(r)/ noun [C] a small hole made by a sharp point, especially in a bicycle or car tyre □ *pancit* ▶ **puncture** verb [I,T]

pungent /ˈpʌndʒənt/ adj (used about a smell) very strong □ *bau tajam (yg menusuk hidung)*

ᵢpunish /ˈpʌnɪʃ/ verb [T] **punish sb (for sth/for doing sth)** to make sb suffer because they have done sth bad or wrong □ *menghukum; mendera*: *The children were severely punished for telling lies.*

punishable /ˈpʌnɪʃəbl/ adj **punishable (by sth)** (used about a crime, etc.) that you can be punished for doing □ *yg boleh dihukum*: *a punishable offence* ♦ *In some countries drug smuggling is punishable by death.* ♦ *In some countries murder is punishable by death.*

punishing /ˈpʌnɪʃɪŋ/ adj that makes you very tired or weak □ *sangat meletihkan*: *The Prime Minister had a punishing schedule, visiting five countries in five days.*

punishment /'pʌnɪʃmənt/ noun [C,U] the action or way of punishing sb □ *hukuman*: *He was excluded from school for a week as a punishment.* ♦ **capital punishment** (= punishment by death)

punitive /'pju:nətɪv/ adj (formal) **1** intended as a punishment □ *punitif; bersifat menghukum*: *to take punitive measures against somebody* **2** (used about taxes, etc.) very severe and that people find very difficult to pay □ *amat membebankan*: *punitive taxation*

punk /pʌŋk/ noun **1** [U] a type of loud music that was popular in Britain in the late 1970s and early 1980s. **Punk** musicians deliberately tried to offend people with traditional opinions. □ *muzik punk* **2** [C] a person who likes **punk** music and often has brightly coloured hair and unusual clothes □ *punk*

punt /pʌnt/ noun [C] a long boat with a flat bottom and square ends which you move by pushing the end of a long pole against the bottom of the river □ *perahu jalur* ▶**punt** verb [I]: *We spent the day punting on the river.* ♦ *to go punting*

puny /'pju:ni/ adj (**punier**; **puniest**) very small and weak □ *kecil dan lemah; kerdil*

pup /pʌp/ noun [C] **1** = **puppy 2** the young of some animals □ *anak beberapa jenis binatang (misalnya anjing laut)*: *a seal pup*

pupil /'pju:pl/ noun [C] **1** (*especially BrE*) a child in school □ *murid*: *There are 28 pupils in my class.* ⊃ note at **school**

HELP Pupil is starting to become old-fashioned, so now we often use **student**, especially when talking about older children.

2 a person who is taught art, music, etc. by an expert □ *anak murid*: *He was a pupil of Liszt.* **3** the round black hole in the middle of your eye □ *anak mata; pupil*

puppet /'pʌpɪt/ noun [C] **1** a model of a person or an animal that you can move by pulling the strings which are tied to it or by putting your hand inside it and moving your fingers □ *anak patung; boneka* **2** a person or an organization that is controlled by sb else □ *boneka*: *The occupying forces set up a puppet government.*

puppy /'pʌpi/ (also **pup**) noun [C] (*pl* **puppies**) a young dog □ *anak anjing* ⊃ note at **dog**

purchase /'pɜ:tʃəs/ noun (formal) **1** [U] the act of buying sth □ *pembelian; (perbuatan) membeli*: *to take out a loan for the purchase of a car* **2** [C] something that you buy □ *belian*: *These shoes were a poor purchase—they're falling apart already.* ♦ *to make a purchase* ▶**purchase** verb [T]: *Many employees have the opportunity to purchase shares in the company they work for.*

purchaser /'pɜ:tʃəsə(r)/ noun [C] (formal) a person who buys sth □ *pembeli*: *The purchaser of the house agrees to pay a deposit of 10%.* ⊃ look at **vendor**

pure /pjʊə(r)/ adj (**purer**; **purest**)

689   **punishment → purpose**

▶NOT MIXED **1** not mixed with anything else □ *tulen; murni; tdk bercampur apa-apa*: *pure orange juice* ♦ *pure silk*
▶CLEAN **2** clean and not containing any harmful substances □ *bersih*: *pure air/water* **OPP** **impure**
▶COMPLETE **3** [only *before* a noun] complete and total □ *semata-mata*: *We met by pure chance.*
▶MORALLY GOOD **4** not doing or knowing anything evil or anything that is connected with sex □ *suci; murni*: *a young girl still pure in mind and body* **OPP** **impure**
▶SOUND/COLOUR/LIGHT **5** very clear; perfect □ *jelas; terang; betul-betul*: *She was dressed in pure white.*
▶SUBJECT **6** [only *before* a noun] (used about an area of learning) concerned only with increasing knowledge rather than having practical uses □ *tulen*: *pure mathematics* **OPP** **applied**

purée /'pjʊəreɪ/ noun [C,U] a food that you make by cooking a fruit or vegetable and then pressing and mixing it until it is smooth and liquid □ *puri*: *apple/tomato purée* ▶**purée** verb [T]

purely /'pjʊəli/ adv only or completely □ *hanya; semata-mata*: *It's not purely a question of money.*

purge /pɜ:dʒ/ verb [T] **purge sth (of sb)**; **purge sb (from sth)** to remove people that you do not want from a political party or other organization □ *menyingkirkan* ▶**purge** noun [C]: *The General carried out a purge of his political enemies.*

purify /'pjʊərɪfaɪ/ verb [T] (**purifying**; **purifies**; pt, pp **purified**) to remove dirty or harmful substances from sth □ *membersihkan; menulenkan*: *purified water*

puritan /'pjʊərɪtən/ noun [C] a person who thinks that it is wrong to enjoy yourself □ *orang yg menganggap bersuka ria itu berdosa* ▶**puritan** (also **puritanical** /ˌpjʊərɪ'tænɪkl/) adj: *a puritan attitude to life*

purity /'pjʊərəti/ noun [U] the state of being pure □ *kebersihan; ketulenan; kemurnian*: *the purity of the water* ⊃ look at **impurity**

purple /'pɜ:pl/ adj, noun [U] (having) the colour of blue and red mixed together □ *warna ungu*: *His face was purple with rage.*

purpose /'pɜ:pəs/ noun **1** [C] the aim or intention of sth □ *tujuan; maksud*: *The main purpose of this meeting is to decide what we should do next.* ♦ *You may only use the telephone for business purposes.* **2** **purposes** [pl] what is needed in a particular situation □ *tujuan*: *For the purposes of this demonstration, I will use model cars.* **3** [U] a meaning or reason that is important to you □ *keazaman*: *A good leader inspires people with a sense of purpose.* **4** [U] the ability to plan sth and work hard to achieve it □ *azam; tekad*: *I was impressed by his strength of purpose.* ⊃ look at **cross purposes**

IDM on purpose not by accident; with a particular intention □ *dgn sengaja*: *'You've torn a*

[C] **countable**, a noun with a plural form: *one book, two books*   [U] **uncountable**, a noun with no plural form: *some sugar*

purposeful → pushover 690

page out of my book!' 'I'm sorry, I didn't do it on purpose.' **SYN** deliberately
to/for all intents and purposes ➾ intent²

purposeful /ˈpɜːpəsfl/ adj having a definite aim or plan ▫ *penuh azam*: *Greg strode off down the street looking purposeful.* ▸ **purposefully** /-fəli/ adv

purposely /ˈpɜːpəsli/ adv with a particular intention ▫ *sengaja*: *I purposely waited till everyone had gone so that I could speak to you in private.* **SYN** deliberately

purr /pɜː(r)/ verb [I] (used about a cat) to make a continuous low sound that shows pleasure ▫ *berbunyi mendengkur* ➾ look at **miaow**

purse¹ /pɜːs/ noun [C] **1** a small bag made of leather, etc., for carrying coins and often also paper money, used especially by women ▫ *beg duit; dompet* ➾ look at **wallet 2** (*AmE*) = **handbag** ➾ picture at **bag**

purse² /pɜːs/ verb
IDM **purse your lips** to press your lips together to show that you do not like sth ▫ *memuncungkan bibir*: *He frowned and pursed his lips.*

pursue /pəˈsjuː/ verb [T] (*formal*) **1** to try to achieve sth or to continue to do sth over a period of time ▫ *mengikut; meneruskan*: *to pursue a career in banking* ♦ *She didn't seem to want to pursue the discussion so I changed the subject.* **2** to follow sb/sth in order to catch them or it ▫ *mengejar; dikejar*: *The robber ran off pursued by two policemen.* ➾ A less formal word is **chase**.

pursuer /pəˈsjuːə(r)/ noun [C] a person who is following and trying to catch sb/sth ▫ *orang yg mengejar*

pursuit /pəˈsjuːt/ noun **1** [U] the act of trying to achieve or to get sth ▫ *usaha mencari; memburu*: *the pursuit of pleasure* **2** [C] an activity that you do either for work or for pleasure ▫ *kegiatan*: *outdoor/leisure pursuits* **3** the act of following or chasing sb ▫ *perbuatan mengejar*
IDM **in hot pursuit** ➾ **hot¹**
in pursuit (of sb/sth) trying to catch or get sb/sth ▫ *mengejar atau memburu (sso/sst)*: *He neglected his family in pursuit of his own personal ambitions.*

pus /pʌs/ noun [U] a thick yellowish liquid that may form in a part of your body that has been hurt ▫ *nanah*

push¹ /pʊʃ/ verb
▸MOVE STH **1** [I,T] to use force to move sb/sth forward or away from you ▫ *menolak; menyorong*: *She pushed him into the water.* ♦ *to push a pram* ♦ *She pushed the door shut with her foot.* ➾ picture at **pull 2** [I,T] to move forward by pushing sb/sth ▫ *mengasak; menolak ke tepi; mengasak-asak*: *John pushed his way through the crowd.* ♦ *to push past somebody* ♦ *People were pushing and shoving to try to get to the front.*
▸SWITCH/BUTTON **3** [I,T] to press a switch, button, etc., for example in order to start a machine ▫ *menekan*: *Push the red button if you want the bus to stop.*
▸PERSUADE/FORCE **4** [T] **push sb (to do sth /into doing sth); push sb (for sth)** to try to make sb do sth that they do not want to do ▫ *memaksa; mendesak*: *My friend pushed me into entering the competition.* ♦ *Ella will not work hard unless you push her.*
▸NEW PRODUCT **5** [T] (*informal*) to try to make sth seem attractive, for example so that people will buy it ▫ *mempromosikan*: *They are launching a major publicity campaign to push their new product.*
IDM **be hard pressed/pushed/put to do sth** ➾ **hard²**
be pushed for sth (*BrE informal*) to not have enough of sth ▫ *tdk cukup/kesuntukan sst*: *Hurry up. We're really pushed for time.*
push your luck; push it/things (*informal*) to take a risk because you have successfully avoided problems in the past ▫ *mengambil risiko*: *You didn't get caught last time, but don't push your luck!*
PHR V **push sb about/around** to give orders to sb in a rude and unpleasant way ▫ *memerintah-rintah sso*: *Don't let your boss push you around.*
push ahead/forward (with sth) to continue with sth ▫ *meneruskan (sst)*
push for sth to try hard to get sth ▫ *berusaha sedaya upaya; mendesak*: *Jim is pushing for a pay rise.*
push in to join a line of people waiting for sth by standing in front of others who were there before you ▫ *memotong barisan*
push on to continue a journey ▫ *meneruskan perjalanan*: *Although it was getting dark, we decided to push on.*
push sb/sth over to make sb/sth fall down by pushing them or it ▫ *menolak sso/sst hingga jatuh*

push² /pʊʃ/ noun [C] an act of pushing ▫ *tolakan; (perbuatan) menolak/menekan*: *Can you help me give the car a push to get it started?* ♦ *The car windows opened at the push of a button.*
IDM **at a push** (*BrE informal*) if it is really necessary (but only with difficulty) ▫ *jika terdesak*: *We can get ten people round the table at a push.*
give sb the push (*BrE informal*) to tell sb you no longer want them in a relationship, or in a job ▫ *memutuskan hubungan; memecat*

'push-button adj [only before a noun] (used about a machine, etc.) that you work by pressing a button ▫ *tekan butang*: *a radio with push-button controls*

pushchair /ˈpʊʃtʃeə(r)/ (*BrE also* **buggy**; *AmE* **stroller**) noun [C] a chair on wheels that you use for pushing a young child in ▫ *kereta sorong* ➾ picture at **pram**

pusher /ˈpʊʃə(r)/ noun [C] (*informal*) a person who sells illegal drugs ▫ *pengedar dadah*

pushover /ˈpʊʃəʊvə(r)/ noun [C] (*informal*) **1** something that is easy to do or win ▫ *perkara*

[I] **intransitive**, a verb which has no object: *He laughed.*   [T] **transitive**, a verb which has an object: *He ate an apple.*

mudah; **kacang 2** a person who is easy to persuade to do sth □ *orang yg senang dipengaruhi*

'push-up (*AmE*) = **press-up**

pushy /'puʃi/ *adj* (**pushier; pushiest**) (*informal*) (used about a person) trying hard to get what you want, in a way that seems rude □ *suka mendesak*: *You need to be pushy to be successful in show business.*

put /pʊt/ *verb* [T] (**putting;** *pt, pp* **put**)

▶IN PLACE/POSITION **1** to move sb/sth into a particular place or position □ *meletakkan; menaruh; menidurkan (anak)*: *She put the book on the table.* ♦ *Did you put sugar in my tea?* ♦ *When do you put the children to bed?*

▶FIX **2** to fix sth to or in sth else □ *membubuh; memasang; mengenakan*: *Can you put (= sew) a button on this shirt?* ♦ *We're going to put a picture on this wall.*

▶WRITE **3** to write sth □ *menulis; tulis*: *12.30 on Friday? I'll put it in my diary.* ♦ *What did you put for question 2?*

▶INTO STATE/CONDITION **4 put sb/sth in/into sth** to bring sb/sth into the state or condition mentioned □ *meletakkan; membuat*: *This sort of weather always puts me in a bad mood.* ♦ *I was put in charge of the project.* ♦ *It was time to put our ideas into practice.*

▶AFFECT SB/STH **5** to make sb/sth feel sth or be affected by sth □ *membuat sso/sst berasa sst; meletakkan*: *This will put pressure on them to finish the job quickly.* ♦ *Don't put the blame on me!* ♦ *The new teacher soon put a stop to cheating in tests.*

▶GIVE VALUE **6** to give or fix a particular value or importance to sb/sth □ *menentukan; meletakkan*: *We'll have to put a limit on how much we spend.* ♦ *I'd put him in my top five favourite writers.*

▶EXPRESS **7** to say or express sth □ *mengatakan; menyatakan*: *I don't know exactly how to put this, but …* ♦ *To put it another way, you're sacked.* ♦ *Put simply, he just wasn't good enough.*

IDM **put it to sb that …** (*formal*) to suggest to sb that sth is true □ *mencadangkan/mengemukakan kpd sso bahawa...*: *I put it to you that this man is innocent.* ❶ For other idioms containing **put**, look at the entries for the nouns, adjectives, etc. For example, **put an end to sth** is at **end**.

PHR V **put sth/yourself across/over** to say what you want to say clearly, so that people can understand it □ *menyampaikan (apa yg hendak dikatakan)*: *He didn't put his ideas across very well at the meeting.*

put sth aside 1 to save sth, especially money, to use later □ *menyimpan (wang, dll)* **2** to ignore or forget sth □ *mengetepikan; melupakan*: *We agreed to put aside our differences and work together.*

put sb away (*informal*) to send sb to prison □ *memasukkan ke dlm penjara*

put sth away 1 to put sth where you usually keep it because you have finished using it □ *menyimpan*: *Put the tools away if you've finished with them.* **2** to save money to spend later □ *mengum-*

691

push-up → put

pul wang: *She puts part of her wages away in the bank every week.*

put sth back 1 to return sth to its place □ *menyimpan balik*: *to put books back on the shelf* **2** to move sth to a later time □ *menangguhkan; menunda*: *The meeting's been put back until next week.* **OPP** **bring sth forward 3** to change the time shown on a clock to an earlier time □ *mengundurkan jarum jam*: *We have to put the clocks back tonight.* **OPP** **put sth forward**

put sb/sth before/above sb/sth to treat sb/sth as more important than sb/sth else □ *mengutamakan atau mementingkan sso/sst lebih drpd sso/sst yg lain*: *He puts his children before anything else.*

put sth by to save money to use later □ *menyimpan wang*: *Her grandparents had put some money by for her wedding.*

put sb down (*informal*) **1** to say things to make sb seem stupid or silly □ *merendah-rendahkan*: *He's always putting his wife down.* **2** to put a baby to bed □ *menidurkan*

put sth down 1 to stop holding sth and put it on the floor, a table, etc. □ *meletakkan*: *She put her book down to answer the phone.* **2** to write sth □ *mencatatkan; menulis*: *I'll put that down in my diary.* **3** to pay part of the cost of sth □ *membayar (sebahagian)*: *We put down a 10% deposit on a car.* **4** (used about a government, an army or the police) to stop sth by force □ *mengundurkan; menghapuskan*: *to put down a rebellion* **5** to kill an animal because it is old, sick or dangerous □ *mematikan/membunuh (binatang)*: *The dog was very sick and had to be put down.*

put sth down to sth to believe that sth is caused by sth □ *menganggap sst itu disebabkan oleh (sst perkara)*: *I put his bad exam results down to laziness rather than a lack of ability.*

put yourself/sb forward to suggest that you or another person should be considered for a job, etc. □ *mengemukakan atau mencadangkan diri sendiri/sso (utk sst)*: *His name was put forward for the position of chairman.*

put sth forward 1 to change the time shown on a clock to a later time □ *mengedepankan jam*: *We put the clocks forward in spring.* **OPP** **put sth back 2** to move sth to an earlier time or date □ *mendahulukan* **3** to suggest sth □ *mengemukakan*: *She put forward a plan to help the homeless.*

put sth in 1 to fix equipment or furniture in position so that it can be used □ *memasang sst*: *We're having a shower put in.* **SYN** **install 2** to include a piece of information, etc. in sth that you write □ *menyertakan; menyebut*: *In your letter, you forgot to put in the time your plane would arrive.* **3** to ask for sth officially □ *mengemukakan*: *to put in an invoice/request*

put sth in; put sth into sth/into doing sth to spend time, etc. on sth □ *menumpukan (masa, dll) utk sst/membuat sst*: *She puts all her time and energy into her business.*

putrid → puzzle

put sb off (sb/sth/doing sth) 1 to say to a person that you can no longer do what you had agreed □ *memberitahu sso bahawa sst itu dibatalkan (atau ditunda)*: They were coming to stay last weekend but I had to put them off at the last moment. **2** to make sb not like sb/sth or not want to do sth □ *membuat sso tdk suka (sso/sst) atau tdk mahu (membuat sst)*: The accident put me off driving for a long time. **3** to make sb unable to give their attention to sth □ *mengganggu; mengacau*: Don't stare at me—you're putting me off!

put sth off to turn or switch a light off □ *memadamkan*: She put off the light and went to sleep.

put sth off; put off doing sth to move sth to a later time □ *menangguhkan/menunda (sst/membuat sst)*: She put off writing her essay until the last minute. **SYN** delay

put sth on 1 to dress yourself in sth □ *memakai; pakai*: Put on your coat! ♦ I'll have to put my glasses on. **OPP** take sth off **2** to cover an area of your skin with sth □ *menyapu; memakai*: You'd better put some sun cream on. **3** to switch on a piece of electrical equipment □ *memasang (lampu, dll)*: It's too early to put the lights on yet. **4** to make a tape, a CD, etc. begin to play □ *memasang; memainkan*: Let's put some music on. **5** to become heavier □ *semakin berisi; bertambah gemuk*: I put on weight very easily. **OPP** lose **6** to organize or prepare sth for people to see or use □ *mempersembahkan; mengadakan; menyediakan*: The school is putting on 'Macbeth'. ♦ They put on extra trains in the summer. **7** to pretend to be feeling sth; to pretend to have sth □ *berpura-pura; buat-buat*: He's not angry with you really: he's just putting it on.

put sth on sth 1 to add an amount of money, etc. to the cost or value of sth □ *menambah/menaikkan (harga, cukai, dsb)*: The government want to put more tax on the price of a packet of cigarettes. **2** to bet money on sth □ *mempertaruhkan wang atas sst*: He put £10 on a horse. **SYN** bet

put sb out 1 to give sb trouble or extra work □ *menyusahkan sso*: He put his hosts out by arriving very late. **SYN** inconvenience **2** to make sb upset or angry □ *membuat sso marah atau sakit hati*: I was quite put out by their selfish behaviour.

put sth out 1 to take sth out of your house and leave it □ *membawa keluar (sampah, dll)*: to put the rubbish out **2** to make sth stop burning □ *memadamkan (api, dsb)*: to put out a fire **SYN** extinguish **3** to switch off a piece of electrical equipment □ *memadamkan (lampu, dll)*: They put out the lights and locked the door. **4** to give or tell the public sth, often on the TV or radio or in newspapers □ *mengumumkan*: The police put out a warning about the escaped prisoner.

put yourself out to do sth for sb, even though it brings you trouble or extra work □ *bersusah payah; menyusahkan (diri/sso)*: 'I'll give you a lift home.' 'I don't want you to put yourself out. I'll take a taxi.'

put sth/yourself over = **put sth/yourself across/over**

put sb through sth to make sb experience sth unpleasant □ *menyebabkan sso mengalami sst yg sukar, teruk, dsb*

put sb/sth through to make a telephone connection that allows sb to speak to sb □ *menyambungkan (panggilan telefon)*: Could you put me through to Jeanne, please?

put sth to sb to suggest sth to sb; to ask sb sth □ *mencadangkan/bertanyakan sst kpd sso*: I put the question to her.

put sth together to build or repair sth by joining its parts together □ *memasang/membaiki sst*: The furniture comes with instructions on how to put it together.

put sth towards sth to give money to pay part of the cost of sth □ *menyumbangkan wang utk sst*: We all put a pound towards a leaving present for Joe.

put sb up to give sb food and a place to stay □ *memberi penginapan kpd sso*: She had missed the last train home, so I offered to put her up for the night.

put sth up 1 to lift or hold sth up □ *mengangkat/menaikkan sst; angkat (tangan)*: Put your hand up if you know the answer. **2** to build sth □ *membina/mendirikan sst*: to put up a fence/tent **3** to fix sth to a wall, etc. so that everyone can see it □ *menampal/meletakkan sst (pd dinding, dsb)*; *mempamerkan*: to put up a notice **4** to increase sth □ *menaikkan (harga, dsb)*: Some shops put up their prices just before Christmas.

put up sth to try to stop sb attacking you □ *cuba menentang*: The old lady put up a struggle against her attacker.

put up with sb/sth to suffer sb/sth unpleasant and not complain about it □ *tahan atas sanggup (dgn sso/sst)*: I don't know how they put up with this noise.

putrid /ˈpjuːtrɪd/ *adj* (used about dead animals or plants) smelling very bad □ *sangat busuk (ttg bangkai atau tumbuhan reput)*: the putrid smell of rotten meat **SYN** foul

putt /pʌt/ *verb* [I,T] (in the sport of **golf**) to hit the ball gently when it is near the hole □ *memukul leret*

putter /ˈpʌtə(r)/ (*AmE*) = **potter¹**

putty /ˈpʌti/ *noun* [U] a soft substance that is used for fixing glass into windows that becomes hard when dry □ *dempul*

puzzle¹ /ˈpʌzl/ *noun* [C] **1** a game or toy that makes you think a lot □ *teka-teki*: a book of crossword puzzles ♦ a jigsaw puzzle ♦ I like to do puzzles. **2** [usually sing] something that is difficult to understand or explain □ *sst yg sukar dijelaskan atau difahami; misteri*: The reasons for his actions have remained a puzzle to historians. **SYN** mystery

puzzle² /ˈpʌzl/ verb [T] to make sb feel confused because they do not understand sth □ *membingungkan*: *Her strange illness puzzled all the experts.*
PHR V **puzzle over sth** to think hard about sth in order to understand or explain it □ *memikir-mikirkan*: *to puzzle over a mathematical problem*
puzzle sth out to find the answer to sth by thinking hard □ *cuba mendapatkan jawapan ttg sst dgn memikir-mikirkannya*: *The letter was in Italian and it took us an hour to puzzle out what it said.*

puzzled /ˈpʌzld/ adj not able to understand or explain sth □ *bingung; kebingungan*: *a puzzled expression*

PVC /ˌpiː viː ˈsiː/ noun [U] a strong plastic material used to make a wide variety of products, such as clothing, pipes, floor coverings, etc. □ *pvc (klorida polivinil)*

pyjamas (AmE **pajamas**) /pəˈdʒɑːməz/ noun [pl] loose trousers and a loose shirt that you wear in bed □ *pijama; baju tidur* ➲ picture on **page P1**

HELP Notice that you use **pyjama** (without an 's') before another noun: *pyjama trousers*

pylon /ˈpaɪlən/ noun [C] a tall metal tower that supports heavy electrical wires □ *pilon; menara wayar elektrik*

pyramid /ˈpɪrəmɪd/ noun [C] **1** a shape with a flat base and three or four sides in the shape of triangles □ *piramid* ➲ picture at **cube 2** a large building in the shape of a **pyramid**. The ancient Egyptians built stone **pyramids** as places to bury their kings and queens. □ *piramid*

python /ˈpaɪθən/ noun [C] a large snake that kills animals by squeezing them very hard □ *ular sawa*

Q, q /kjuː/ noun [C,U] (pl **Qs**; **Q's**; **q's** /kjuːz/) the 17th letter of the English alphabet □ *Q, q (huruf)*: *'Queen' begins with (a) 'Q'.*

Q abbr = **question¹**(1) □ *soalan*: *Qs 1-5 are compulsory.*

QR code /ˌkjuː ˈɑː kəʊd/ noun [C] **quick response code**; a pattern of black and white squares that contains information, such as timetables, links to websites, etc. You can read this information using the camera on your **smartphone** (= a mobile phone with some computer functions). □ *kod QR*

qt abbr = **quart**

quack /kwæk/ noun [C] the sound made by a **duck** (= a bird that lives on or near water) □ *kuek* ▶ **quack** verb [I] ➲ note at **duck**

quad bike /ˈkwɒd baɪk/ (AmE ˌfour-ˈwheeler) noun [C] a motorbike with four large wheels, used for riding over rough ground, often for fun □ *motosikal beroda empat*

quadrangle /ˈkwɒdræŋgl/ (also **quad**) noun [C] a square open area with buildings round it in a school, college, etc. □ *medan (empat persegi)*

quadruple /kwɒˈdruːpl/ verb [I,T] to multiply or be multiplied by four □ *bertambah empat kali ganda*

quaint /kweɪnt/ adj attractive or unusual because it seems to belong to the past □ *aneh dan menarik*

quake /kweɪk/ verb [I] (used about a person, the earth or a building) to shake □ *menggeletar*: *to quake with fear* ▶ **quake** noun [C] (informal) = **earthquake**

qualification /ˌkwɒlɪfɪˈkeɪʃn/ noun **1** [C] an exam that you have passed or a course of study that you have completed □ *kelulusan*: *to have a teaching/nursing qualification* ♦ *She left school at 16 with no formal qualifications.* ➲ note at **degree 2** [C] a skill or quality that you need to do a particular job □ *kelayakan; syarat; keperluan*: *Is there a height qualification for the police force?* **3** [C,U] something that limits the meaning of a general statement or makes it weaker □ *pembatasan; syarat*: *I can recommend him for the job without qualification.* ♦ *She accepted the proposal with only a few qualifications.* **4** [U] the fact of doing what is necessary in order to be able to do a job, play in a competition, etc. □ *(perihal) lulus atau melayakkan diri*: *Italy achieved qualification for the championships with their win over Wales.*

qualified /ˈkwɒlɪfaɪd/ adj **1 qualified (for sth/ to do sth)** having passed an exam or having the knowledge, experience, etc. in order to be able to do sth □ *berkelayakan*: *Duncan is well qualified for this job.* ♦ *a fully qualified doctor* ♦ *I don't feel qualified to comment—I know nothing about the subject.* **2** not complete; limited □ *bersyarat; terbatas*: *My boss gave only qualified approval to the plan.* **OPP** for both meanings **unqualified**

qualify /ˈkwɒlɪfaɪ/ verb (**qualifying**; **qualifies**; pt, pp **qualified**) **1** [I] **qualify (as sth)** to pass the examination that is necessary to do a particular job □ *lulus; bertauliah*: *It takes five years to qualify as a vet.* **2** to have the qualities that are necessary for sth □ *sesuai dianggap sebagai*: *A cup of coffee and a sandwich doesn't really qualify as a meal.* **3** [I,T] **qualify (sb) (for sth/to do sth)** to have or give sb the right to have or do sth □ *melayakkan; berhak; layak*: *How many years must you work to qualify for a pension?* ♦ *This exam will qualify me to teach music.* **4** [I] **qualify (for**

qualitative → quarter 694

sth) to win the right to enter a competition or continue to the next part □ *melayakkan; layak*: *Our team has qualified for the final.* **5** [T] to limit the meaning of a general statement or make it weaker □ *membataskan*: *I must qualify what I said earlier—it wasn't quite true.*

qualitative /ˈkwɒlɪtətɪv/ *adj* connected with how good sth is, rather than with how much of it there is □ *kualitatif*: *qualitative analysis/research* ➔ look at **quantitative**

quality /ˈkwɒləti/ *noun* (*pl* **qualities**) **1** [U, sing] how good or bad sth is □ *kualiti*: *This paper isn't very good quality.* ♦ *to be of good/poor/top quality* ♦ *goods of a high quality* ♦ *high-quality goods* ♦ *the quality of life in our cities* **2** [U] a high standard or level □ *mutu*: *Aim for quality rather than quantity in your writing.* **3** [C] something that is typical of a person or thing □ *sifat*: *Vicky has all the qualities of a good manager.*

qualm /kwɑːm/ *noun* [C, usually pl] a feeling of doubt or worry that what you are doing may not be morally right □ *keraguan; rasa ragu-ragu*: *I don't have any qualms about asking them to lend us some money.*

quandary /ˈkwɒndəri/ *noun* [C, usually sing] a state of not being able to decide what to do; a difficult situation □ *keadaan serba salah; kebingungan*: *I'm in a quandary—should I ask her or not?*

quantify /ˈkwɒntɪfaɪ/ *verb* [T] (**quantifying**; **quantifies**; *pt, pp* **quantified**) to describe or express sth as an amount or a number □ *mentaksirkan*: *The risks to health are impossible to quantify.*

quantitative /ˈkwɒntɪtətɪv/ *adj* connected with the amount or number of sth rather than with how good it is □ *kuantitatif*: *quantitative research* ➔ look at **qualitative**

quantity /ˈkwɒntəti/ *noun* [C,U] (*pl* **quantities**) **1** a number or an amount of sth □ *kuantiti; jumlah*: *Add a small quantity of salt.* ♦ *It's cheaper to buy goods in large quantities.* **2** a large number or amount of sth □ *banyak*: *It's usually cheaper to buy in quantity.*
IDM an unknown quantity ➔ **unknown**[1]

quarantine /ˈkwɒrəntiːn/ (*AmE* also) / *noun* [U] a period of time when a person or an animal that has or may have an infectious disease must be kept away from other people or animals □ *kuarantin*

quark /kwɑːk/ *noun* [C] a very small part of matter (= a substance). There are several types of **quark** and it is thought that **protons** (= parts of an atom that carry a positive electric charge), **neutrons** (= parts of an atom that carry no electric charge), etc. are formed from them. □ *kuark*

quarrel[1] /ˈkwɒrəl/ (*AmE* also) / *noun* **1** [C] a **quarrel (about/over sth)** an angry argument or disagreement □ *pergaduhan; pertengkaran*: *We sometimes have a quarrel about who should*

do the washing-up. ➔ note at **argument** ➔ look at **fight 2** [U] **quarrel with sb/sth** a reason for complaining about or disagreeing with sb/sth □ *masalah; sebab utk merungut atau tdk bersetuju dgn sso/sst*: *I have no quarrel with what has just been said.*

quarrel[2] /ˈkwɒrəl/ (*AmE* also) / *verb* [I] (**quarrelling**; **quarrelled**, (*AmE*) **quarreling**; **quarreled**) **1 quarrel (with sb) (about/over sth)** to have an angry argument or disagreement □ *bergaduh; bertengkar*: *The children are always quarrelling!* ♦ *I don't want to quarrel with you about it.* ➔ look at **argue**, **fight 2 quarrel with sth** to disagree with sth □ *tdk bersetuju dgn sso*

quarrelsome /ˈkwɒrəlsəm/ (*AmE* also) / *adj* (used about a person) liking to argue with other people □ *suka berkelahi atau bertengkar* **SYN** **argumentative**

quarry[1] /ˈkwɒri/ (*AmE* also) / *noun* (*pl* **quarries**) **1** [C] a place where large amounts of sand, stone, etc. are dug out of the ground □ *kuari* ➔ look at **mine 2** [sing] a person or an animal that is being hunted □ *buruan*

quarry[2] /ˈkwɒri/ (*AmE* also) / *verb* [I,T] (**quarrying**; **quarries**; *pt, pp* **quarried**) to dig, stone, sand, etc. out of the ground □ *menguari; menggali keluar*: *to quarry for marble*

quart /kwɔːt/ *noun* [C] (*abbr* **qt**) a measure of liquid; 1.14 litres. There are 2 pints in a **quart**. □ *kuart*

HELP An American quart is 0.94 of a litre.

quarter /ˈkwɔːtə(r)/ *noun*
➤ OF 4 PARTS **1** [C] one of four equal parts of sth □ *suku*: *The programme lasts for three quarters of an hour.* ♦ *a mile and a quarter* ♦ *to cut an apple into quarters*
➤ 15 MINUTES **2** [sing] 15 minutes before or after every hour □ *lima belas minit lagi pukul...; pukul... suku*: *I'll meet you at (a) quarter past six.* ♦ *It's (a) quarter to three.*

HELP In American English you say '(a) quarter after' and '(a) quarter of': *I'll meet you at (a) quarter after six.* ♦ *It's a quarter of three.*

➤ 3 MONTHS **3** [C] a period of three months □ *suku tahun*: *You get a gas bill every quarter.*
➤ PART OF TOWN **4** [C] a part of a town, especially a part where a particular group of people live □ *kawasan*: *the Chinese quarter of the city*
➤ PERSON/GROUP **5** [C] a person or group of people who may give help or information or who have certain opinions □ *pihak*: *Jim's parents haven't got much money so he can't expect any help from that quarter.*
➤ 25 CENTS **6** [C] (in the US or Canada) a coin that is worth 25 cents (¼ dollar) □ *syiling 25 sen*
➤ PLACE TO LIVE **7** **quarters** [pl] a place that is provided for people, especially soldiers, to live in □ *tempat tinggal*
➤ WEIGHT **8** [C] four **ounces** (= a measure of weight) of sth; ¼ of a pound □ *suku paun*: *a quarter of mushrooms*

at close quarters ➲ **close³**

quarter-final *noun* [C] one of the four matches between the eight players or teams left in a competition □ *suku akhir* ➲ look at **semi-final**

quarterly /ˈkwɔːtəli/ *adj, adv* (produced or happening) once every three months □ *suku tahunan; tiga bulan sekali*: *a quarterly magazine*

quartet /kwɔːˈtet/ *noun* [C] **1** four people who sing or play music together □ *kuartet; kumpulan empat penyanyi/pemuzik* **2** a piece of music for four people to sing or play together □ *(muzik) kuartet*

quartz /kwɔːts/ *noun* [U] a type of hard rock that is used in making very accurate clocks or watches □ *kuarza*

quash /kwɒʃ/ *verb* [T] (*formal*) **1** to say that an official decision is no longer true or legal □ *membatalkan* **2** to stop or defeat sth by force □ *menumpaskan; mematahkan*: *to quash a rebellion*

quaver /ˈkweɪvə(r)/ *verb* [I] if sb's voice quavers, it shakes, usually because the person is nervous or afraid □ *bergetar; becakap dgn nada menggeletar*: *'I'm not safe here, am I?' she asked in a quavering voice.*

quay /kiː/ *noun* [C] a platform where goods and passengers are loaded on and off boats □ *bagan*

quayside /ˈkiːsaɪd/ *noun* [sing] the area of land that is near a quay □ *tepi bagan*

queasy /ˈkwiːzi/ *adj* feeling sick; wanting to **vomit** (= bring up food from the stomach) □ *loya, mual*

queen /kwiːn/ *noun* [C] **1** (also **Queen**) the female ruler of a country □ *ratu*: *Queen Elizabeth II* (= the second) ➲ look at **king, prince, princess 2** (also **Queen**) the wife of a king □ *raja permaisuri* **3** (in the game of **chess**) the most powerful piece, that can move any distance and in all directions □ *menteri* **4** one of the four playing cards in a pack with a picture of a queen □ *ratu*: *the queen of hearts* ➲ note at **card** ➲ picture at **card 5** the largest and most important female in a group of insects □ *ratu (lebah)*: *the queen bee*

queer /kwɪə(r)/ *adj* (**queerer**; **queerest**) (*old-fashioned*) strange or unusual □ *aneh, pelik*: *She had a queer feeling that she was being watched.* **SYN** odd

quell /kwel/ *verb* [T] (*formal*) to end sth □ *menumpaskan; mematahkan; menghentikan*

quench /kwentʃ/ *verb* [T] **quench your thirst** to drink so that you no longer feel thirsty □ *menghilangkan (dahaga)*

query /ˈkwɪəri/ *noun* [C] (*pl* **queries**) a question, especially one asking for information or expressing a doubt about sth □ *pertanyaan; soalan*: *Does anyone have any queries?* ▶ **query** *verb* [T] (**querying**; **queries**; *pt, pp* **queried**): *We queried the bill but were told it was correct.*

695 **quarter-final → question tag**

quest /kwest/ *noun* [C] (*formal*) a long search for sth that is difficult to find □ *pencarian; usaha mencari*: *the quest for happiness/knowledge/truth*

question¹ /ˈkwestʃən/ *noun* **1** [C] (*abbr* Q) a question (about/on sth) a sentence or phrase that asks for an answer □ *soalan*: *Put up your hand if you want to **ask a question**.* ◆ *In the examination, you must **answer** five **questions** in one hour.* ◆ *What's the answer to Question 5?* ◆ *There will be a Q and A* (= question and answer) *session at the end of the talk.* **2** [C] a problem or difficulty that needs to be discussed or dealt with □ *soal; masalah*: *The resignations **raise the question** of who will take over.* ◆ ***The question is**, how are we going to raise the money?* **3** [U] doubt or confusion about sth □ *keraguan*: *There is no question about her enthusiasm for the job.* ◆ *His honesty is **beyond question**.* ◆ *The results of the report were accepted **without question**.*

IDM in question that is being considered or talked about □ *(yg) sedang dibincang; (yg) berkenaan*: *The lawyer asked where she was on the night in question.*

no question of no possibility of □ *tdk ada kemungkinan*: *There is no question of him leaving hospital yet.*

out of the question impossible □ *tdk mungkin*: *A new car is out of the question. It's just too expensive.*

(be) a question of sth/of doing sth a situation in which sth is needed □ *soal (ttg sst/membuat sst)*: *It's not difficult—it's just a question of finding the time to do it.*

question² /ˈkwestʃən/ *verb* [T] **1 question sb (about/on sth)** to ask sb a question or questions □ *menyoal*: *The police questioned him for several hours.* **2** to express or feel doubt about sth □ *mempersoalkan; meragui*: *She told me she was from the council so I didn't question her right to be there.* ◆ *to question somebody's sincerity/honesty*

questionable /ˈkwestʃənəbl/ *adj* **1** that you have doubts about; not certain □ *boleh dipersoalkan; agak diragui*: *It's questionable whether we'll finish in time.* **2** likely to be dishonest or morally wrong □ *boleh dipersoalkan*: *questionable motives* **OPP** for both meanings **unquestionable**

question mark *noun* [C] the sign (?) that you use when you write a question □ *tanda soal*

questionnaire /ˌkwestʃəˈneə(r)/ *noun* [C] a list of questions that are answered by many people. A **questionnaire** is used to collect information about a particular subject □ *borang soal selidik*: *to complete/fill in a questionnaire*

question tag (also **tag**) *noun* [C] a short phrase such as 'isn't it?' or 'did you?' at the end of a sentence that changes it into a question and is often used to ask sb to agree with you □ *soalan tempelan*

[C] **countable**, a noun with a plural form: *one book, two books*   [U] **uncountable**, a noun with no plural form: *some sugar*

queue /kjuː/ (*AmE* line) *noun* [C] a line of people, cars, etc. that are waiting for sth or to do sth ◻ *barisan (menunggu)*: We had to **wait in a queue** for hours to get tickets. ◆ *to **join the end of a queue*** ◆ *We were told to **form a queue** outside the doors.*
IDM jump the queue ⊃ jump¹
▶**queue** *verb* [I] **queue (up) (for sth)**: *to queue for a bus*

quiche /kiːʃ/ *noun* [C,U] a type of food made of **pastry** (= a mixture of flour, fat and water) filled with egg and milk with cheese, onion, etc. and cooked in the oven. You can eat **quiche** hot or cold. ◻ *'quiche'* ⊃ picture on **page P16**

quick¹ /kwɪk/ *adj* (**quicker**; **quickest**) **1** done with speed; taking or lasting a short time ◻ *cepat; pantas; sekejap*: *May I make a quick telephone call?* ◆ *This dish is quick and easy to make.* ◆ *His quick thinking saved her life.* ◆ *We need to make a quick decision.* **2 quick (to do sth)** doing sth at speed or in a short time ◻ *cepat; pantas; lekas*: *It's quicker to travel by train.* ◆ *She is a quick worker.* ◆ *She was quick to point out the mistakes I had made.*

> **HELP** **Quick** or **fast**? **Fast** is more often used for describing a person or thing that moves or can move at great speed: *a fast horse/car/runner.* **Quick** is more often used for describing something that is done in a short time: *a quick decision/visit*

3 used to form adjectives ◻ *cepat; lekas*: *quick-thinking* ◆ *quick-drying paint*
IDM quick/slow on the uptake ⊃ uptake

quick² /kwɪk/ *adv* (*informal*) quickly ◻ *cepat; cepat-cepat*: *Come over here quick!*
IDM (as) quick as a flash very quickly ◻ *secepat kilat*: *Quick as a flash, he grabbed my money and ran.*

quicken /ˈkwɪkən/ *verb* [I,T] (*formal*) to become quicker or make sth quicker ◻ *bertambah cepat, mempercepat*: *She felt her heartbeat quicken as he approached.* ◆ *He quickened his pace to catch up with them.*

quickly /ˈkwɪkli/ *adv* fast; in a short time ◻ *dgn cepat*: *He quickly undressed and got into bed.* ◆ *I'd like you to get here as quickly as possible.*

quicksand /ˈkwɪksænd/ *noun* [U] deep wet sand that you sink into if you walk on it ◻ *pasir jerlus*

quid /kwɪd/ *noun* [C] (*pl* **quid**) (*BrE informal*) a pound (in money); £1 ◻ *satu paun (wang)*: *Can you lend me a couple of quid until tomorrow?*

quiet¹ /ˈkwaɪət/ *adj* (**quieter**; **quietest**) **1** with very little or no noise ◻ *diam; senyap; perlahan*: *Be quiet!* ◆ *His voice was quiet but firm.* ◆ *Go into the library if you want to work. It's much quieter in there.* **OPP** loud **2** without much activity or many people ◻ *sepi; lengang; tdk giat*: *The streets are very quiet on Sundays.* ◆ *Business is quiet at this time of year.* ◆ *a quiet country village*

◆ *We lead a quiet life.* **3** (used about a person) not talking very much ◻ *diam; pendiam*: *You're very quiet today. Is anything wrong?* ◆ *He's very quiet and shy.*
IDM keep quiet about sth; keep sth quiet to say nothing about sth ◻ *tdk/jangan cakap apa-apa (ttg sst); merahsiakan sst*: *Would you keep quiet about me leaving until I've told the boss?* ▶**quietly** *adv*: *Try and shut the door quietly!*
▶**quietness** *noun* [U]

quiet² /ˈkwaɪət/ *noun* [U] the state of being calm and without much noise or activity ◻ *keheningan; ketenangan; kesunyian*: *the **peace and quiet** of the countryside*
IDM on the quiet secretly ◻ *secara senyap-senyap/diam-diam*: *She's given up chocolate but she still has an occasional piece on the quiet.*

quieten /ˈkwaɪətn/ *verb* [T] to make sb/sth quiet ◻ *menyenyapkan; mendiamkan; menenangkan*
PHR V quieten (sb/sth) down to become quiet or to make sb/sth quiet ◻ *menyenyapkan, mendiamkan atau menenangkan (sso/sst)*: *When you've quietened down, I'll tell you what happened.*

quilt /kwɪlt/ *noun* [C] a cover for a bed that has a thick warm material, for example feathers, inside it ◻ *kuilt; sejenis cadar tebal* ⊃ look at **duvet**

quintet /kwɪnˈtet/ *noun* [C] **1** a group of five people who sing or play music together ◻ *kuintet; kumpulan lima penyanyi/pemuzik* **2** a piece of music for five people to sing or play together ◻ *(muzik) kuintet*

quirk /kwɜːk/ *noun* [C] **1** an aspect of sb's character or behaviour that is strange ◻ *keanehan; sifat aneh*: *You'll soon get used to the boss's little quirks.* **2** a strange thing that happens by chance ◻ *kebetulan; takdir*: *By a strange **quirk of fate** they met again several years later.* ▶**quirky** *adj*: *Some people don't like his quirky sense of humour.*

quit /kwɪt/ *verb* (**quitting**; *pt, pp* **quit**) **1** [I,T] **quit (as sth)** to leave a job, etc. or to go away from a place ◻ *berhenti kerja, dsb; meninggalkan sst tempat*: *She quit as manager of the volleyball team.* **2** [T] (*especially AmE informal*) to stop doing sth ◻ *berhenti*: *to quit smoking* **3** [I,T] to close a computer program ◻ *keluar*

quite /kwaɪt/ *adv* **1** not very; to a certain degree; rather ◻ *agak; juga*: *The film's quite good.* ◆ *It's quite a good film.* ◆ *I quite enjoy cooking.* ◆ *They had to wait quite a long time.* ◆ *It's quite cold today.* ◆ *We still meet up quite often.* ⊃ note at **rather** **2** (used for emphasizing sth) completely; very ◻ *betul-betul; memang*: *Are you quite sure you don't mind?* ◆ *I quite agree—you're quite right.* ◆ *To my surprise, the room was quite empty.* **SYN** absolutely **3** (*BrE*) used for showing that you agree with or understand sth ◻ *memang; betul*: *'We didn't win, but at least we tried.' 'Yes, quite.'*
IDM not quite used for showing that there is almost enough of sth, or that it is almost suitable

□ *hampir-hampir; berapa; begitu*: *There's not quite enough bread for breakfast.* ◆ *These shoes don't quite fit.*

quite a used for showing that sth is unusual □ *agak hebat, luar biasa, teruk, dll*: *That's quite a problem.*

quite enough used for emphasizing that no more of sth is wanted or needed □ *sudah cukup*: *I've had quite enough of listening to you two arguing!* ◆ *That's quite enough wine, thanks.*

quite a few; quite a lot (of) a fairly large amount or number □ *agak banyak; banyak juga*: *We've received quite a few enquiries.*

quits /kwɪts/ *adj*

IDM **be quits (with sb)** (*informal*) if two people are **quits**, it means that neither of them owes the other anything □ *kira selesai*: *You buy me a drink and then we're quits.*

quiver /ˈkwɪvə(r)/ *verb* [I] to shake slightly □ *bergetar*: *to quiver with rage/excitement/fear* **SYN** tremble

quiz[1] /kwɪz/ *noun* [C] (*pl* quizzes) a game or competition in which you have to answer questions □ *kuiz*: *a general knowledge quiz* ◆ *a television quiz show*

quiz[2] /kwɪz/ *verb* [T] (quizzing; quizzes; *pt, pp* quizzed) to ask sb a lot of questions in order to get information □ *menyoal banyak-banyak*

quizzical /ˈkwɪzɪkl/ *adj* (used about a look, smile, etc.) seeming to ask a question □ *penuh tanda tanya atau agak hairan* ▶ quizzically /-kli/ *adv*

quorum /ˈkwɔːrəm/ *noun* [sing] the smallest number of people that must be at a meeting before it can make official decisions □ *kuorum*

quota /ˈkwəʊtə/ *noun* [C] the number or amount of sth that is allowed or that you must do □ *kuota*: *We have a fixed quota of work to get through each day.*

quotation /kwəʊˈteɪʃn/ (also **quote**) *noun* [C] **1** a phrase from a book, speech, play, etc. that sb repeats because it is interesting or useful □ *petikan*: *a quotation from Shakespeare* **2** a statement that says how much a piece of work will probably cost □ *sebut harga*: *You should get quotations from three different builders.* ➲ look at **estimate**

quoˈtation marks (also *informal* quotes, *BrE also* inverted commas) *noun* [pl] the signs ('…') or ("…") that you put around a word, a sentence, etc. to show that sb said or wrote, that it is a title or that you are using it in a special way □ *tanda petikan*

quote /kwəʊt/ *verb* **1** [I,T] quote (sth) (from sb/sth) to repeat exactly sth that sb else has said or written before □ *memetik; mengulang apa yg disebutkan oleh sso*: *The minister asked the newspaper not to quote him.* **2** [T] to give sth as an example to support what you are saying □ *menyebut*: *She quoted several reasons why she was unhappy about the decision.* **3** [T] to say what the cost of a piece of work, etc. will probably be □ *menyebut harga*: *How much did they quote you*

697

quits → race

for repairing the roof?

quotes /kwəʊts/ (*informal*) = quotation marks

the Qur'an = the Koran

R, r /ɑː(r)/ *noun* [C,U] (*pl* Rs; R's; r's /ɑː(r)z/) the 18th letter of the English alphabet □ *R, r (huruf)*: *'Rabbit' begins with an 'R'.*

R. *abbr* = river □ *sungai*: *R. Thames*

R & B /ˌɑːr ən ˈbiː/ *noun* [U] **rhythm and blues**; a type of music that is a mixture of **blues** (= slow sad music) and **jazz** (= music with a strong rhythm) □ *R & B; muzik gabungan Blues dan Jaz*

rabbi /ˈræbaɪ/ *noun* [C] (*pl* rabbis) a Jewish religious leader and teacher of Jewish law □ *rabai*

rabbit   hare

rabbit /ˈræbɪt/ *noun* [C] a small animal with long ears □ *arnab*: *a wild rabbit* ◆ *a rabbit hutch* (= a cage for rabbits) ➲ note at **pet**

MORE The children's word for a rabbit is **bunny**.

ˈrabbit warren (also warren) *noun* [C] **1** a system of holes and underground tunnels where wild **rabbits** live □ *sarang arnab; lubang arnab* **2** a building or part of a city with many narrow passages or streets □ *bangunan atau bahagian bandar yg mempunyai banyak laluan sempit atau lorong*: *The council offices were a real rabbit warren.*

rabble /ˈræbl/ *noun* [C] a noisy crowd of people who are or may become violent □ *gerombolan*

rabies /ˈreɪbiːz/ *noun* [U] a very dangerous disease that a person can get if they are bitten by an animal that has the disease □ *penyakit anjing gila*

race[1] /reɪs/ *noun* **1** [C] a race (against/with sb/sth); a race for sth/to do sth a competition between people, animals, cars, etc. to see which is the fastest or to see which can achieve sth first □ *perlumbaan*: *to run/win/lose a race* ◆ *to come first/second/last in a race* ◆ *Rescuing victims of the earthquake is now a race against time.* ◆ *the*

CONSONANTS   p **p**en   b **b**ad   t **t**ea   d **d**id   k **c**at   g **g**ot   tʃ **ch**in   dʒ **J**une   f **f**all   v **v**an   θ **th**in

race → radiator

race for the presidency ♦ *the race to find a cure for AIDS* **2 the races** [pl] (*BrE*) an occasion when a number of horse races are held in one place □ *lumba kuda*: *We're going to the races for the day.* **3** [C,U] one of the groups into which people can be divided according to the colour of their skin, their hair type, the shape of their face, etc. □ *ras*: *a child of mixed race* ⊃ look at **human race** **4** [C] a group of people who have the same language, customs, history, etc. □ *bangsa; kaum; keturunan*: *the Spanish race*
IDM the rat race ⊃ **rat**

race² /reɪs/ *verb* **1** [I,T] **race (against/with) (sb/sth)** to have a competition with sb/sth to find out who is the fastest or to see who can do sth first □ *berlumba*: *I'll race you home.* **2** [T] to make an animal or a vehicle take part in a race □ *memperlumbakan*: *He races pigeons as a hobby.* **3** [I,T] to go very fast or to move sb/sth very fast □ *berkejar; dikejarkan*: *We raced up the stairs.* ♦ *The child had to be raced to hospital.*

racecourse /ˈreɪskɔːs/ (*AmE* **racetrack**) *noun* [C] a place where horse races take place □ *padang lumba kuda*

racehorse /ˈreɪshɔːs/ *noun* [C] a horse that is trained to run in races □ *kuda lumba*

ˌrace reˈlations *noun* [pl] the relations between people of different races who live in the same town, area, etc. □ *hubungan antara kaum*

racetrack /ˈreɪstræk/ = **racecourse**

racial /ˈreɪʃl/ *adj* connected with people's race; happening between people of different races □ *(berkenaan dgn) bangsa atau kaum*: *racial tension/discrimination* ▶ **racially** /-ʃəli/ *adv*: *a racially mixed school*

racing /ˈreɪsɪŋ/ *noun* [U] **1** = **horse racing 2** the sport of taking part in races □ *lumba*: *motor racing* ♦ *a racing driver/car*

racism /ˈreɪsɪzəm/ *noun* [U] the belief that some races of people are better than others; unfair ways of treating people that show this belief □ *rasisme; faham perkauman*: *to take measures to combat racism* ▶ **racist** /-ɪst/ *noun* [C], *adj*: *He's a racist.* ♦ *racist beliefs/views/remarks*

rack¹ /ræk/ *noun* [C] [in compounds] a piece of equipment, usually made of bars, that you can put things in or on □ *rak; tetingkat*: *I got on the train and put my bags up in the luggage rack.* ♦ *We need a roof rack on the car for all this equipment.*

racks

luggage rack   plate rack

roof rack   wine rack

IDM go to rack and ruin to be in or get into a bad state because of a lack of care □ *menjadi semakin rosak atau binasa*

rack² /ræk/ *verb*
IDM rack your brains to try hard to think of sth or remember sth □ *memeras otak*

racket /ˈrækɪt/ *noun* **1** [sing] (*informal*) a loud noise □ *bunyi bising; riuh-rendah*: *Stop making that terrible racket!* **2** [C] an illegal way of making money □ *kegiatan haram*: *a drugs racket* **3** (also **racquet**) [C] a piece of sports equipment that you use to hit the ball in sports such as **tennis** and **badminton** □ *raket* ⊃ picture at **badminton** ⊃ picture on **page P4**

MORE Rackets have **strings**, but **bats** do not.

racy /ˈreɪsi/ *adj* (**racier**; **raciest**) (used especially about writing) having a style that is exciting and amusing, sometimes in a way that is connected with sex □ *agak tdk senonoh (ttg penulisan)*: *a racy novel*

radar /ˈreɪdɑː(r)/ *noun* [U] a system that uses radio waves for finding the position of moving objects, for example ships and planes □ *radar*: *This plane is hard to detect by radar.*

radiant /ˈreɪdiənt/ *adj* **1** showing great happiness □ *berseri-seri*: *a radiant smile* **2** sending out light or heat □ *bersinar; berbahang*: *the radiant heat/energy of the sun*

radiate /ˈreɪdieɪt/ *verb* **1** [T] (used about people) to clearly show a particular quality or emotion in your appearance or behaviour □ *memancarkan; terpancar*: *She radiated self-confidence in the interview.* **2** [T] to send out light or heat □ *menyinarkan; memancarkan* **3** [I] to go out in all directions from a central point □ *bercabang seperti jejari*: *Narrow streets radiate from the village square.*

radiation /ˌreɪdiˈeɪʃn/ *noun* [U] **1** powerful and very dangerous rays that are sent out from certain substances. You cannot see or feel **radiation** but it can cause serious illness or death. □ *sinaran* ⊃ look at **radioactive 2** heat, light or energy that is sent out from sth □ *sinaran*: *ultraviolet radiation*

radiator /ˈreɪdieɪtə(r)/ *noun* [C] **1** a piece of equipment that is usually fixed to the wall and is used for heating a room. **Radiators** are made of metal and filled with hot water. □ *penyinar* ⊃ picture on **page P8 2** a piece of equipment that is used for keeping a vehicle cool □ *radiator*

ð **then**   s **so**   z **zoo**   ʃ **she**   ʒ **vision**   h **how**   m **man**   n **no**   ŋ **sing**   l **leg**   r **red**   j **yes**   w **wet**

radical¹ /'rædɪkl/ adj **1** (used about changes in sth) very great; complete □ *radikal; menyeluruh*: *The tax system needs radical reform.* ♦ *radical change* **2** wanting great social or political change □ *radikal*: *to have radical views* ⇒ look at **moderate, extreme** ▶**radically** /-kli/ adv: *The First World War radically altered the political map of Europe.*

radical² /'rædɪkl/ noun [C] a person who wants great social or political change □ *radikal* ⇒ look at **moderate, extremist**

radii plural of **radius**

radio /'reɪdiəʊ/ noun (pl **radios**) **1** often **the radio** [U, sing] the activity of sending out programmes for people to listen to; the programmes that are sent out □ *(siaran) radio*: *I always listen to the radio in the car.* ♦ *I heard an interesting report on the radio this morning.* ♦ *a radio station/programme* ♦ *national/local radio* ⇒ look at **media** **2** [C] a piece of equipment that is used for receiving and/or sending radio messages or programmes (on a ship, plane, etc. or in your house) □ *radio*: *a car radio*

> **MORE** You **put**, **switch** or **turn** a radio **on** or **off**. You may also **turn** it **up** or **down** to make it louder or quieter. To choose a particular **station**, you **tune in to** it.

3 [U] the sending or receiving of messages through the air by electrical signals □ *radio*: *to keep in radio contact* ♦ *radio signals/waves* ▶**radio** verb [I,T] (pt, pp **radioed**)

radioactive /ˌreɪdiəʊˈæktɪv/ adj sending out powerful and very dangerous energy that is produced when atoms are broken up. This energy cannot be seen or felt but can cause serious illness or death □ *radioaktif*: *the problem of the disposal of radioactive waste from power stations* ⇒ look at **radiation** ▶**radioactivity** /ˌreɪdiəʊækˈtɪvəti/ noun [U]

radiographer /ˌreɪdiˈɒɡrəfə(r)/ noun [C] a person in a hospital who is trained to take X-rays (= pictures of your bones, etc.) or to use X-rays for the treatment of certain illnesses □ *jururadiografi*

radish /'rædɪʃ/ noun [C] a small red vegetable that is white inside with a strong taste. You eat radishes in salads. □ *sejenis lobak* ⇒ picture on page P15

radium /'reɪdiəm/ noun [U] (symbol **Ra**) a chemical element that is used in the treatment of diseases such as cancer □ *radium*

radius /'reɪdiəs/ noun (pl **radii** /-diaɪ/) **1** the distance from the centre of a circle to the outside edge □ *jejari* ⇒ look at **diameter, circumference** ⇒ picture at **circle** **2** a round area that is measured from a point in its centre □ *lingkungan*: *The wreckage of the plane was scattered over a radius of several miles.*

raffle /'ræfl/ noun [C] a way of making money for a charity or a project by selling tickets with numbers on them. Later some numbers are chosen and the tickets with these numbers on them win prizes. □ *rafel*

raft /rɑːft/ noun [C] **1** a flat structure made of pieces of wood tied together and used as a boat or a floating platform □ *rakit* **2** a small boat made of rubber or plastic that is filled with air □ *bot getah atau plastik yg berisi angin* ⇒ look at **white-water rafting**

rafter /'rɑːftə(r)/ noun [C] one of the long pieces of wood that support a roof □ *kasau*

rag /ræɡ/ noun **1** [C,U] a small piece of old cloth that you use for cleaning □ *kain buruk* **2 rags** [pl] clothes that are very old and torn □ *kain baju buruk*

rage¹ /reɪdʒ/ noun [C,U] a feeling of violent anger that is difficult to control □ *keberangan; berang*: *to fly into a rage* ♦ *He was trembling with rage.*

rage² /reɪdʒ/ verb [I] **1** **rage (at/against/ about sb/sth)** to show great anger about sth, especially by shouting □ *naik berang*: *He raged against the injustice of it all.* **2** (used about a battle, disease, storm, etc.) to continue with great force □ *semakin sengit/teruk; mengganas; membadai; menular*: *The battle raged for several days.* ▶**raging** adj [only before a noun]: *a raging headache*

ragged /'ræɡɪd/ adj **1** (used about clothes) old and torn □ *koyak rabak* **2** not straight; untidy □ *bergerigi*: *a ragged edge/coastline*

raid /reɪd/ noun [C] **a raid (on sth) 1** a short surprise attack on an enemy by soldiers, ships or aircraft □ *serangan*: *an air raid* **2** a surprise visit by the police looking for criminals or illegal goods □ *serbuan* **3** a surprise attack on a building in order to steal sth □ *serangan; rompakan*: *a bank raid* ▶**raid** verb [T]: *Police raided the club at dawn this morning.*

rail /reɪl/ noun **1** [C] a bar fixed to a wall, which you can hang things on □ *rel; gegalang*: *a towel/ curtain/picture rail* ⇒ picture at **curtain** ⇒ picture on page P8 **2** [C] a wooden or metal bar placed round sth to stop you falling □ *susur*: *She leaned on the ship's rail and gazed out to sea.* **3** [C, usually pl] each of the two metal bars that form the track that trains run on □ *rel/landasan kereta api* **4** [U] the railway system; trains as a means of transport □ *(perkhidmatan) kereta api*: *rail travel/services/fares*

railcard /'reɪlkɑːd/ noun [C] (BrE) a special card that allows you to buy train tickets at a lower price if you are an old person, a young person, student, etc. □ *kad yg membolehkan sso membeli tiket kereta api pd harga yg lebih rendah*

railing /'reɪlɪŋ/ noun [C, usually pl] a fence (around a park, garden, etc.) that is made of metal bars □ *pagar pancang* ⇒ picture on page P11

railroad crossing (AmE) = **level crossing**

railway /ˈreɪlweɪ/ (*AmE* **railroad** /ˈreɪlrəʊd/) *noun* [C] **1** (*BrE* **railway line**) the metal lines on which trains travel between one place and another □ *rel/landasan kereta api*: *In Canada there is a railway which goes right across the Rocky Mountains.* **2** the whole system of tracks, the trains and the organization and people needed to operate them □ *(perkhidmatan) kereta api*: *He works on the railways.* ♦ *a railway engine/company*

railway station = station¹ (1)

rain¹ /reɪn/ *noun* **1** [U] the water that falls from the sky □ *hujan*: *Take your umbrella, it looks like rain* (= as if it is going to rain). ♦ *It's pouring with rain* (= the rain is very heavy). ➪ note at **weather** ➪ look at **shower**, **acid rain 2 rains** [pl] (in tropical countries) the time of the year when there is a lot of rain □ *musim hujan*: *When the rains come in July, the people move to higher ground.*
IDM (as) right as rain ➪ **right¹**

rain² /reɪn/ *verb* **1** [I] [used with *it*] to fall as rain □ *hujan (turun)*: *Oh no! It's raining again!* ♦ *Is it raining hard?* ♦ *We'll go out when it stops raining.* **2** [I,T] **rain (sth) (down) (on sb/sth)** to fall or make rain fall on sb/sth in large quantities □ *menghujani*: *Bombs rained down on the city.*
PHR V be rained off to be cancelled or to have to stop because it is raining □ *dibatalkan kerana hujan*: *The tennis was rained off.*

rainbow /ˈreɪnbəʊ/ *noun* [C] a curved band of many colours that sometimes appears in the sky when the sun shines through rain □ *pelangi*

rain check *noun*
IDM take a rain check on sth (*spoken*) to refuse an invitation or offer but say that you might accept it later □ *menolak sst tawaran atau pelawaan tetapi mungkin akan menerimanya kemudian*

raincoat /ˈreɪnkəʊt/ *noun* [C] a long light coat which keeps you dry in the rain □ *baju hujan*

raindrop /ˈreɪndrɒp/ *noun* [C] a single drop of rain □ *titis hujan*

rainfall /ˈreɪnfɔːl/ *noun* [U, sing] the total amount of rain that falls in a particular place during a month, year, etc. □ *hujan; banyaknya hujan yg turun dlm sst tempoh tertentu (sebulan, setahun, dsb)*

rainforest /ˈreɪnfɒrɪst (*AmE* also /) *noun* [C] a thick forest in tropical parts of the world that have a lot of rain □ *hutan hujan*: *the Amazon rainforest*

rainy /ˈreɪni/ *adj* (**rainier**; **rainiest**) having or bringing a lot of rain □ *(selalu) hujan; membawa hujan*: *a rainy day* ♦ *floods during the rainy season*
IDM keep/save sth for a rainy day to save sth, especially money, for a time when you really need it □ *menyimpan sst (terutamanya wang) utk digunakan apabila perlu*

raise¹ /reɪz/ *verb* [T]
▶ MOVE UPWARDS **1** to lift sth/sb/yourself up □ *angkat; mengangkat*: *If you want to leave the room, raise your hand.* ♦ *He raised himself up on one elbow.* **OPP lower** ➪ note at **rise²**
▶ INCREASE **2 raise sth (to sth)** to increase the level of sth or to make sth better or stronger □ *menaikkan; meninggikan*: *to raise taxes/salaries/prices* ♦ *The hotel needs to raise its standards.* ♦ *There's no need to raise your voice* (= speak loudly or angrily). **OPP lower** ➪ note at **rise²**
▶ COLLECT MONEY **3** to get money from people for a particular purpose □ *mengutip; memungut*: *We are doing a sponsored walk to raise money for charity.* ♦ *a fund-raising event*
▶ INTRODUCE TOPIC **4** to introduce a subject that needs to be talked about or dealt with □ *membangkitkan; menimbulkan*: *I would like to raise the subject of money.* ♦ *This raises the question of why nothing was done before.*
▶ CAUSE **5** to cause a particular reaction or emotion □ *memberitahu; membangkitkan; menimbulkan*: *The neighbours raised the alarm* (= told everyone there was a fire/an emergency) *when they saw smoke coming out of the window.* ♦ *to raise hopes/fears/suspicions in people's minds*
▶ CHILD/ANIMAL **6** to look after a child or an animal until they are an adult □ *memelihara; menyara*: *You can't raise a family on what I earn.* ➪ look at **bring sb up**
▶ FARM ANIMALS/PLANTS **7** to breed animals or grow a type of plant for a particular purpose □ *menternak; menanam*: *Sheep are raised for meat and wool.*
IDM raise your eyebrows to show that you are surprised or that you do not approve of sth □ *mengangkat kening (utk menunjukkan rasa hairan atau tdk suka)*

raise² /reɪz/ *noun* [C] (*AmE*) = **rise¹** (2)

raisin /ˈreɪzn/ *noun* [C] a dried **grape** (= a small fruit that grows in bunches), used in cakes, etc. □ *kismis* ➪ look at **sultana**

rake /reɪk/ *noun* [C] a garden tool with a long handle and a row of metal teeth, used for collecting leaves or making the earth smooth □ *pencakar* ➪ picture at **garden**
PHR V rake sth in (*informal*) to earn a lot of money, especially when it is done easily □ *mengaut (keuntungan, dsb)*: *She's been raking it in since she got promoted.*
rake sth up (*informal*) to start talking about sth that it would be better to forget □ *mengungkitungkit*: *Don't rake up all those old stories again.*
▶ **rake** *verb* [T]: *to rake up the leaves*

rally¹ /ˈræli/ *noun* [C] (*pl* **rallies**) **1** a large public meeting, especially one held to support a political idea □ *perhimpunan*: *a peace rally* **2** a race for cars or motorbikes on public roads □ *rali* **3** (in **tennis** and similar sports) a series of hits of the ball before a point is won □ *rali*

rally² /ˈræli/ *verb* (**rallying**; **rallies**; *pt, pp* **rallied**) **1** [I,T] **rally (sb/sth) (around/behind/to sb)** to come together or to bring people together in order to help or support sb/sth □ *bersatu utk membantu atau menyokong (sso/sst)*: *The cabinet rallied behind the Prime Minister.* **2** [I] to get stronger, healthier, etc. after an illness or a period of weakness □ *pulih*: *He never really rallied after the operation.* **SYN recover**

PHR V rally round to come together to help sb □ *bersatu menyokong*: *When I was in trouble, my family all rallied round.*

RAM /ræm/ *noun* [U] **random-access memory**; computer memory in which data can be changed or removed and can be looked at in any order □ *Ingatan Capaian Rawak*: *32 megabytes of RAM* ➲ look at **ROM**

ram¹ /ræm/ *verb* [T] (**ramming**; **rammed**) to crash into sth or push sth with great force □ *menghentam; menyasak; menyumbat*

ram² /ræm/ *noun* [C] a male sheep □ *biri-biri jantan* ➲ note at **sheep** ➲ picture at **goat**

Ramadan /ˈræmədæn; ˌræməˈdæn/ *noun* [C,U] the 9th month of the Muslim year, when Muslims do not eat or drink anything from when the sun rises in the morning to when it goes down in the evening □ *Ramadan* ➲ look at **Eid**

ramble¹ /ˈræmbl/ *verb* [I] **1** to walk in the countryside for pleasure, especially as part of an organized group □ *berjalan utk bersiar-siar*: *to go rambling* **2** ramble (on) (about sth) to talk for a long time in a confused way □ *merepek; merapu*: *Halfway through his speech he began to ramble.*

ramble² /ˈræmbl/ *noun* [C] a long, organized walk in the country for pleasure □ *(pergi) berjalan utk bersiar-siar* ▶ **rambler** *noun* [C]

rambling /ˈræmblɪŋ/ *adj* **1** (used about a building) spreading in many directions □ *tdk sekata bentuknya; bersambung sana sini*: *a rambling old house in the country* **2** (used about a speech or piece of writing) very long and confused □ *meleret-leret dan merepek*

ramp /ræmp/ *noun* [C] **1** a slope that joins two parts of a road, path, building, etc. when one is higher than the other □ *tanjakan*: *There are ramps at both entrances for wheelchair access.* **2** (*AmE*) = **slip road**

rampage¹ /ˈræmpeɪdʒ/ *noun*
IDM be/go on the rampage to move through a place in a violent group, usually breaking things and attacking people □ *mengganas; mengamuk*

rampage² /ræmˈpeɪdʒ/ *verb* [I] to move through a place in a violent group, usually breaking things and attacking people □ *mengganas; mengamuk*: *The football fans rampaged through the town.*

rampant /ˈræmpənt/ *adj* (used about sth bad) existing or spreading everywhere in a way that is very difficult to control □ *menular; menjadi-jadi*: *Car theft is rampant in this town.*

ramshackle /ˈræmʃækl/ *adj* (usually used about a building) old and needing repair □ *kopak-kapik; cabuk; daif*

ran *past tense of* **run¹**

ranch /rɑːntʃ/ *noun* [C] a large farm, especially in the US or Australia, where cows, horses, sheep, etc. are kept □ *ladang ternak*

rancid /ˈrænsɪd/ *adj* if food containing fat is **rancid**, it tastes or smells unpleasant because it is no longer fresh □ *tengik; perat*: *rancid butter*

random /ˈrændəm/ *adj* **1** chosen by chance □ *rambang*: *For the survey they interviewed a random selection of people in the street.* **2** [only before a noun] (*informal*) (used especially about a person) not known or not identified □ *tdk dikenali*: *Some random guy gave me fifty pounds.* **3** (*informal*) a thing or a person that is **random** is strange and does not make sense, often in a way that amuses or interests you □ *aneh*: *Mum, you're so random!*
IDM at random without thinking or deciding in advance what is going to happen □ *secara rambang*: *The competitors were chosen at random from the audience.*
▶ **randomly** *adv*

ˌrandom-ˈaccess ˈmemory *noun* [U] = **RAM**

randy /ˈrændi/ *adj* (**randier**; **randiest**) (*BrE informal*) sexually excited □ *gasang; bernafsu syahwat*

rang *past tense of* **ring²**

range¹ /reɪndʒ/ *noun* **1** [C, usually sing] a range (of sth) a variety of things that belong to the same group □ *pelbagai; aneka jenis*: *The course will cover a whole range of topics.* ◆ *This shop has a very wide range of clothes.* **2** [C] the limits between which sth can vary □ *lingkungan; julat*: *That car is outside my price range.* ◆ *I don't think this game is suitable for all age ranges.* **3** [C,U] the distance that it is possible for sb/sth to travel, see, hear, etc. □ *jarak*: *Keep out of range of the cameras.* ◆ *The gunman shot the policeman at close range.* ◆ *They can pick up signals at a range of 400 metres.* **4** [C] a line of mountains or hills □ *banjaran*: *the great mountain range of the Alps* ➲ picture on **page P10**

range² /reɪndʒ/ *verb* [I] **1** range between A and B; range from A to B to vary between two amounts, sizes, etc., including all those between them □ *antara; berbeza-beza antara*: *The ages of the students range from 15 to 50.* **2** range (from A to B) to include a variety of things in addition to those mentioned □ *antara*: *She's had a number of different jobs, ranging from chef to swimming instructor.*

ranger /ˈreɪndʒə(r)/ *noun* [C] a person whose job is to take care of a park, a forest or an area of the countryside □ *renjer*

rank¹ /ræŋk/ *noun* **1** [C,U] the position, especially a high position, that sb has in an organization such as the army, or in society □ *pangkat; darjat; taraf*: *General is one of the highest ranks in the army.* ◆ *She's much higher in rank than I am.* **2** the ranks [pl] the ordinary soldiers in the army;

the members of any large group □ *askar biasa; barisan*: At the age of 43, he was forced to **join the ranks of** the unemployed. **3** [C] a group or line of things or people □ *barisan; perhentian teksi*: a taxi rank

IDM **the rank and file** the ordinary soldiers in the army; the ordinary members of an organization □ *askar biasa; pekerja biasa*

rank² /ræŋk/ verb [I,T] [not used in the continuous tenses] **rank (sb/sth) (as sth)** to give sb/sth a particular position on a scale according to importance, quality, success, etc.; to have a position of this kind □ *diletakkan; menempatkan; berpangkat*: She's ranked as one of the world's top players. ♦ a high-ranking police officer

ransack /ˈrænsæk/ verb [T] **ransack sth (for sth)** to make a place untidy, causing damage, because you are looking for sth □ *menyelongkar; menggeledah*: The house had been ransacked by burglars.

ransom /ˈrænsəm/ noun [C,U] the money that you must pay to free sb who has been captured illegally and who is being kept as a prisoner □ *wang tebusan*: The kidnappers demanded a ransom of $500 000 for the boy's release.

IDM **hold sb to ransom** to keep sb as a prisoner and say that you will not free them until you have received a certain amount of money □ *menahan sso sehingga mendapat wang tebusan* ➲ look at **hostage**
▶ **ransom** verb [I,T]

rant /rænt/ verb [I,T] **rant (on) (about sth); rant at sb** to speak or complain about sth in a loud and/or angry way □ *mengherdik; menghamun*
▶ **rant** noun [C]

rap¹ /ræp/ noun **1** [C] a quick, sharp hit or knock on a door, window, etc. □ *ketukan*: There was a sharp rap on the door. **2** [C,U] a style or a piece of music with a fast strong rhythm, in which the words are spoken fast, not sung □ *muzik rap* ➲ look at **rapper**

rap² /ræp/ verb (**rapping**; **rapped**) **1** [I,T] to hit a hard object or surface several times quickly and lightly, making a noise □ *mengetuk*: She rapped angrily on/at the door. **2** [T] (*informal*) (used mainly in newspapers) to criticize sb strongly □ *mengecam; membidas*: Minister raps police over rise in crime. **3** [I] to speak the words of a **rap¹**(2) □ *menyanyi lagu rap*

rape¹ /reɪp/ verb [T] to force a person to have sex when they do not want to, using threats or violence □ *merogol*

rape² /reɪp/ noun **1** [U,C] the crime of forcing sb to have sex when they do not want to □ *rogol; (perbuatan) merogol*: to commit rape **2** [sing] (*formal*) **the rape (of sth)** the act of destroying sth beautiful □ *pemusnahan; pencabulan*

rapid /ˈræpɪd/ adj happening very quickly or moving with great speed □ *pesat; pantas; cepat*: She made rapid progress and was soon the best in the class. ▶ **rapidity** /rəˈpɪdəti/ noun (*formal*): The rapidity of economic growth has astonished most people. ▶ **rapidly** adv

rapids /ˈræpɪdz/ noun [pl] a part of a river where the water flows very fast over rocks □ *jeram*

rapist /ˈreɪpɪst/ noun [C] a person who forces sb to have sex when they do not want to □ *perogol* ➲ look at **rape**

rappel /ræˈpel/ (AmE) = **abseil**

rapper /ˈræpə(r)/ noun [C] a person who performs a **rap¹**(2) (= a piece of music with a strong fast rhythm, in which the words are spoken, not sung) □ *penyanyi muzik rap*

rapport /ræˈpɔː(r)/ noun [sing, U] **rapport (with sb); rapport (between A and B)** a friendly relationship in which people understand each other very well □ *hubungan baik dan mesra*: She has established a close rapport with clients.

rapt /ræpt/ adj so interested in one particular thing that you are not conscious of anything else □ *asyik; ralit*: a rapt audience ♦ She listened with rapt attention.

rapture /ˈræptʃə(r)/ noun [U] a feeling of extreme happiness □ *kegembiraan yg amat sangat*
IDM **go into raptures (about/over sb/sth)** to feel and show that you think that sb/sth is very good □ *memperkatakan, dsb ttg sso/sst dgn penuh ghairah*: I didn't like the film much but my boyfriend went into raptures about it.

rare /reə(r)/ adj (**rarer**; **rarest**) **1 rare (for sb/sth to do sth); rare (to do sth)** not done, seen, happening, etc. very often □ *jarang dibuat, ditemui, berlaku, dsb*: a rare bird/flower/plant **2** (used about meat) not cooked for very long so that the inside is still red □ *kurang masak*: a rare steak ➲ look at **medium**, **well done** ▶ **rarely** adv: Human beings rarely live to be over 100 years old.

raring /ˈreərɪŋ/ adj **raring to do sth** wanting to start doing sth very much □ *tdk sabar-sabar*: They were raring to try out the new computer.

rarity /ˈreərəti/ noun (pl **rarities**) **1** [C] a thing or a person that is unusual and is therefore often valuable or interesting □ *(sst/sso yg) luar biasa*: Women in senior positions should not be a rarity. **2** [U] the quality of being rare □ *(perihal) jarang ditemui*: The rarity of this stamp increases its value a lot.

rascal /ˈrɑːskl/ noun [C] (*informal*) a person, especially a child or man, who shows little respect for other people and enjoys playing jokes on them □ *budak nakal; penipu; bangsat; tdk jujur*: Come here, you little rascal!

rash¹ /ræʃ/ noun **1** [C, usually sing] an area of small red spots that appear on your skin when you are ill or have a reaction to sth □ *ruam*: He came out in a rash where the plant had touched him. **2** [sing] **a rash (of sth)** a series of unpleasant events of the same kind happening over a short period of time □ *merebaknya (sst); (sst yg) menjadi-jadi*

rash² /ræʃ/ *adj* (used about people) doing things that might be dangerous or bad without thinking about the possible results first; (used about actions) done in this way □ *gopoh; terburu-buru: a rash decision/promise* ▶**rashly** *adv*

rasher /ˈræʃə(r)/ *noun* [C] (*BrE*) a slice of **bacon** (= meat from a pig) □ *hirisan daging babi/ khinzir*

raspberry /ˈrɑːzbəri/ *noun* [C] (*pl* **raspberries**) a small, soft, red fruit which grows on bushes □ *rasberi: raspberry jam* ⊃ picture on page P14

rat /ræt/ *noun* [C] an animal like a large mouse □ *tikus: Rats belong to the family of animals that are called rodents.*
IDM **the rat race** the way of life in which everyone is only interested in being better or more successful than everyone else □ *cara hidup yg berlumba-lumba mengejar kejayaan*

rate¹ /reɪt/ *noun* [C] **1** a measurement of the speed at which sth happens or the number of times sth happens or exists during a particular period □ *kadar: The birth rate* (= the number of children born each year) *is falling.* ◆ *The population is increasing at the rate of less than 0.5% a year.* ◆ *an exchange rate of one pound to 1.5 dollars* **2** a fixed amount of money that sth costs or that sb is paid □ *kadar: The basic rate of pay is £10 an hour.* ◆ *We offer special reduced rates for students.* ⊃ look at **first-rate, second-rate**
IDM **at any rate** (*spoken*) **1** whatever else might happen □ *apa sekalipun: Well, that's one good piece of news at any rate.* **2** used when you are giving more exact information about sth □ *setidak-tidaknya; walau bagaimanapun: He said that they would be here by ten. At any rate, I think that's what he said.*
the going rate (for sth) ⊃ **going²**

rate² /reɪt/ *verb* [not used in the continuous tenses] **1** [T, usually passive] to say how good you think sb/sth is □ *menilai; menganggap: She's rated among the best tennis players of all time.* **2** [I,T] to be good, important, etc. enough to be treated in a particular way □ *mendapat; cukup bagus, penting, dsb utk disebut, mendapat layanan tertentu, dll: The accident wasn't very serious—it didn't rate a mention in the local newspaper.* ◆ *The match rated as one of their worst defeats.*

rather /ˈrɑːðə(r)/ *adv* quite □ *agak: It was a rather nice day.* ◆ *It was rather a nice day.* ◆ *It cost rather a lot of money.* ◆ *I was rather hoping that you'd be free on Friday.*

HELP If you use **rather** with a positive word, it sounds as if you are very surprised and pleased: *My teacher doesn't look very friendly, but he is actually rather nice.* You can use **rather** with a negative word to criticize sth: *This room's rather untidy.* **Rather**, **quite** and **fairly** can all mean 'not very'. **Rather** is the strongest and **fairly** is the weakest. **Pretty** has the same meaning as **rather** but is informal.

IDM **or rather** used as a way of correcting sth you have said, or making it more exact □ *atau lebih tepat: She lives in London, or rather she lives in a suburb of London.*
rather than instead of; in place of □ *sebaliknya; bukan: I think I'll just have a sandwich rather than a full meal.*
would rather ... (than) would prefer to □ *lebih suka... (drpd): I'd rather go to the cinema than watch TV.*

ratify /ˈrætɪfaɪ/ *verb* [T] (**ratifying**; **ratifies**; *pt, pp* **ratified**) to make an agreement officially valid by voting for or signing it □ *mengesahkan: The treaty was ratified by all the member states.* ▶**ratification** /ˌrætɪfɪˈkeɪʃn/ *noun* [U]

rating /ˈreɪtɪŋ/ *noun* **1** [C] a measurement of how popular, important, good, etc. sth is □ *pentaksiran; penilaian* **2 the ratings** [pl] a set of figures showing the number of people who watch a particular TV programme, etc., used to show how popular the programme is □ *kadar kepopularan*

ratio /ˈreɪʃiəʊ/ *noun* [C] (*pl* **ratios**) **ratio (of A to B)** the relation between two numbers which shows how much bigger one quantity is than another □ *nisbah: The ratio of boys to girls in this class is three to one* (= there are three times as many boys as girls).

ration /ˈræʃn/ *noun* [C] a limited amount of food, petrol, etc. that you are allowed to have when there is not enough for everyone to have as much as they want □ *catuan* ▶**ration** *verb* [T]: *In the desert water is strictly rationed.* ▶**rationing** *noun* [U]

rational /ˈræʃnəl/ *adj* **1** based on reason; sensible or logical □ *waras: There must be a rational explanation for why he's behaving like this.* **2** (used about a person) able to use logical thought rather than emotions to make decisions □ *rasional* **SYN** **reasonable** **OPP** **irrational** ▶**rationally** /-nəli/ *adv*

rationale /ˌræʃəˈnɑːl/ *noun* [C] (*formal*) **rationale (behind/for/of sth)** the principles or reasons which explain a particular decision, plan, belief, etc. □ *rasional; taakulan asas; asas yg logik: What is the rationale behind these new exams?* **SYN** **reasoning**

rationalize (also **-ise**) /ˈræʃnəlaɪz/ *verb* **1** [I,T] to find reasons that explain why you have done sth (perhaps because you do not like the real reason) □ *merasionalkan* **2** [T] to make a business or a system better organized □ *merasionalisasikan* ▶**rationalization** (also **-isation**) /ˌræʃnəlaɪˈzeɪʃn/ *noun* [C,U]

rattle¹ /ˈrætl/ *verb* **1** [I,T] to make a noise like hard things hitting each other, or to shake sth so that it makes this noise □ *mendetar-detarkan; menggoncang: The windows were rattling all night in the wind.* ◆ *He rattled the money in the tin.* **2** [T] (*informal*) to make sb suddenly become worried □ *mencemaskan; menggemparkan: The news of his arrival really rattled her.*

rattle → reaction

PHR V **rattle sth off** to say a list of things you have learnt very quickly □ *mengatakan sst dgn cepat*: *She rattled off the names of every player in the team.*

rattle² /'rætl/ *noun* [C] **1** [usually sing] a noise made by hard things hitting each other □ *detaran* **2** a toy that a baby can shake to make a noise □ *kelentong*

raucous /'rɔːkəs/ *adj* (used about people's voices) loud and unpleasant □ *garau; parau*: *raucous laughter*

ravage /'rævɪdʒ/ *verb* [T] to damage sth very badly; to destroy sth □ *memusnahkan; membinasakan*: *The forests were ravaged by the winter storms.*

rave¹ /reɪv/ *verb* [I] **1** (*informal*) **rave (about sb/sth)** to say very good things about sb/sth □ *memuji-muji*: *Everyone's raving about her latest album!* **2** to speak angrily or in a wild way □ *menengking-nengking; meracau*

rave² /reɪv/ *noun* [C] a large party held outside or in an empty building, at which people dance to electronic music □ *majlis tarian rancak*

raven /'reɪvn/ *noun* [C] a large black bird that makes an unpleasant sound □ *burung raven*

ravenous /'rævənəs/ *adj* very hungry □ *sangat lapar* ▶ **ravenously** *adv*

ˌrave reˈview *noun* [C] an article in a newspaper, etc. that says very good things about a new book, film, play, etc. □ *ulasan memuji*

ravine /rə'viːn/ *noun* [C] a narrow deep valley with steep sides □ *gaung*

raving /'reɪvɪŋ/ *adj* [only before a noun] *adv* (*informal*) talking or behaving in a way that shows they are crazy □ *betul-betul*: *Have you gone raving mad?*

raw /rɔː/ *adj* **1** not cooked □ *mentah*: *Raw vegetables are good for your teeth.* **2** in the natural state; not yet made into anything □ *mentah*: *raw materials* (= that are used to make things in factories, etc.) **3** used about an injury where the skin has come off from being rubbed □ *melecet*: *There's a nasty raw place on my heel where my shoes have rubbed.*

ray /reɪ/ *noun* [C] a line of light, heat or energy □ *sinar*: *the sun's rays* ◆ *ultraviolet rays* ⮕ look at **X-ray**
IDM **a ray of hope** a small chance that things will get better □ *sinar harapan*

razor /'reɪzə(r)/ *noun* [C] a sharp instrument which people use to shave with □ *pisau cukur*: *an electric razor* ◆ *a disposable razor*

ˈrazor blade *noun* [C] the thin sharp piece of metal that you put in a **razor** □ *pisau cukur*

Rd *abbr* = **road** (2) □ *Jln (Jalan): 21 Hazel Rd*

RE /ˌɑːr 'iː/ *noun* [U] **religious education**; a school subject in which students learn about different religions □ *RE (pendidikan agama): an RE teacher*

re /riː/ *prep* about or concerning sth; used at the beginning of a business letter or an email to introduce the subject □ *berhubungan dgn; ttg; berkenaan dgn; mengenai*: *Re your letter of 1 September ...* ◆ *Re: travel expenses*

re- /riː/ [in compounds] again □ *semula; kembali; lagi*: *reapply* ◆ *reappearance* ◆ *reassuring*

reach¹ /riːtʃ/ *verb* **1** [T] to arrive at a place or condition that you have been going towards □ *sampai; mencapai*: *We won't reach Dover before 12.* ◆ *The two sides hope to reach an agreement sometime today.* ◆ *Sometimes the temperature reaches 45°C.* ◆ *The team reached the semi-final last year.* ◆ *to reach a decision/conclusion/compromise* **2** [I,T] **reach (out) (for sb/sth); reach (sth) (down)** to stretch out your arm to try and touch or get sth □ *menghulurkan tangan; mencapai; menyeluk*: *The child reached out for her mother.* ◆ *She reached into her bag for her purse.* **3** [I,T] to be able to touch sth □ *sampai*: *Can you get me that book off the top shelf? I can't reach.* ◆ *He couldn't reach the light switch.* ◆ *I need a longer ladder. This one won't reach.* **4** [T] to communicate with sb, especially by telephone; contact □ *menghubungi*: *You can reach me at this number.*

reach² /riːtʃ/ *noun* [sing] the distance that you can stretch your arm □ *huluran; jangkauan*
IDM **beyond/out of (sb's) reach 1** outside the distance that you can stretch your arm □ *di luar capaian/jangkauan (sso); jauh drpd (sso)*: *Keep this medicine out of the reach of children.* **2** not able to be got or done by sb □ *di luar keupayaan (sso); tdk tercapai (oleh sso)*: *A job like that is completely beyond his reach.*
within (sb's) reach 1 inside the distance that you can stretch your arm □ *tercapai; dpt dicapai/dijangkau (oleh sso)* **2** able to be achieved by sb □ *boleh dicapai*: *We were one goal ahead with ten minutes left and so could sense that victory was within our reach.*
within (easy) reach of sth not far from sth □ *tdk jauh dr sst*

react /ri'ækt/ *verb* [I] **1** **react (to sth) (by doing sth)** to do or say sth because of sth that has happened or been said □ *bereaksi; bertindak balas*: *He reacted to the news by jumping up and down and shouting.* ◆ *The players reacted angrily to the decision.* **2** **react (to sth)** to become ill after eating, breathing, etc. a particular substance □ *mendapat (tindak balas)*: *He reacted badly to the drug and had to go to hospital.* **3** **react (with sth/together)** (used about a chemical substance) to change after coming into contact with another substance □ *bertindak balas*: *Iron reacts with water and air to produce rust.*
PHR V **react against sb/sth** to behave or talk in a way that shows that you do not like the influence of sb/sth (for example authority, your family, etc.) □ *bertindak balas terhadap (atau menentang) sso/sst*

reaction /ri'ækʃn/ *noun*
▶ **TO EVENT 1** [C,U] **(a) reaction (to sb/sth)** something that you do or say because of sth that has

happened □ *tindak balas; reaksi: Could we have your reaction to the latest news, Prime Minister?* ◆ *I shook him to try and wake him up but there was no reaction.*

▶TO SB/SITUATION **2** [C,U] (**a) reaction (against sb/sth)** behaviour that shows that you do not like the influence of sb/sth (for example authority, your family, etc.) □ *tindak balas menentang (sso/sst): Her strange clothes are a reaction against the conservative way she was brought up.*

▶TO FOOD, DRUGS, ETC. **3** [C] **a reaction (to sth)** a bad effect that your body experiences because of sth that you have eaten, touched or breathed □ *tindak balas terhadap: She had an **allergic reaction** to something in the food.*

▶TO DANGER **4** [C, usually pl] the physical ability to act quickly when sth happens □ *tindak balas: If the other driver's reactions hadn't been so good, there would have been an accident.*

▶IN CHEMISTRY **5** [C,U] (*technical*) a chemical change produced by two or more substances coming into contact with each other □ *tindak balas: a nuclear reaction*

reactionary /ri'ækʃənri/ *noun* [C] (*pl* **reactionaries**) a person who tries to prevent political or social change □ *reaksioner* ▶**reactionary** *adj: reactionary views/politics/groups*

reactor /ri'æktə(r)/ = **nuclear reactor**

read[1] /riːd/ *verb* (*pt, pp* **read** /red/) **1** [I,T] to look at words or symbols and understand them □ *membaca: He never learnt to read and write.* ◆ *Have you read any good books lately?* ◆ *Can you read music?* **2** [I,T] **read (sb) (sth); read sth (to sb)** to say written words to sb □ *membaca: My father used to read me stories when I was a child.* ◆ *I hate reading out loud.* **3** to discover or find out about sb/sth by reading □ *mengetahui: I read about the accident in the local paper.* **4** [T] to be able to understand sth from what you can see □ *membaca; mengagak: A man came to read the gas meter.* ◆ *Profoundly deaf people often learn to read lips.* ◆ *I've no idea what he'll say—I can't read his mind!* **5** [T] to show words or a sign of sth □ *menunjukkan; menyatakan: The sign read 'Keep Left'.* **6** [T] (*formal*) to study a subject at university □ *mempelajari: She read Modern Languages at Cambridge.*

PHR V **read sth into sth** to think that there is a meaning in sth that may not really be there □ *mentafsirkan/mengesyaki ada maksud lain*

read on to continue reading; to read the next part of sth □ *terus membaca*

read sth out to read sth to other people □ *membacakan sst*

read sth through to read sth to check details or to look for mistakes □ *membaca sambil menyemak sst: I read my essay through a few times before handing it in.*

read up on sth to read a lot about a subject □ *membaca segala yg dpt ttg sst*

read[2] /riːd/ *noun* [sing] (*informal*) a period or the act of reading □ *pembacaan; bahan bacaan: I generally **have a quick read** of the newspaper over breakfast.* ◆ *Her detective novels are usually a good read.*

readable /'riːdəbl/ *adj* **1** easy or interesting to read □ *menarik utk dibaca* **2** able to be read □ *boleh dibaca: machine-readable data* ➲ look at **legible**

reader /'riːdə(r)/ *noun* [C] **1** a person who reads sth (a particular newspaper, magazine, type of book, etc.) □ *pembaca: She's an avid reader of science fiction.* **2** [with an adjective] a person who reads in a particular way □ *pembaca: a fast/slow reader* **3** a book for practising reading □ *buku bacaan: a series of English graded readers*

readership /'riːdəʃɪp/ *noun* [sing] the number of people who regularly read a particular newspaper, magazine, etc. □ *jumlah pembaca: The newspaper has a readership of 200 000.*

readily /'redɪli/ *adv* **1** easily, without difficulty □ *mudah; senang: Most vegetables are **readily available** at this time of year.* **2** without pausing; without being forced □ *dgn segera; tanpa dipaksa: He readily admitted that he was wrong.*

readiness /'redinəs/ *noun* [U] **1 readiness (for sth)** the state of being ready or prepared □ *kesediaan* **2 readiness (to do sth)** the state of being prepared to do sth without arguing or complaining □ *kesediaan; kesanggupan: The bank have indicated their readiness to lend him the money.*

reading /'riːdɪŋ/ *noun* **1** [U] what you do when you read □ *(perbuatan) membaca: I haven't had time to do much reading lately.* ◆ *Her hobbies include painting and reading.* **2** [U] books, articles, etc. that are intended to be read □ *bahan bacaan: The information office gave me a pile of **reading matter** to take away.* **3** [C] the particular way in which sb understands sth □ *tafsiran; tanggapan: What's your reading of the situation?* **4** [C] the number or measurement that is shown on an instrument □ *bacaan: a reading of 20°*

readjust /ˌriːə'dʒʌst/ *verb* **1** [I] **readjust (to sth)** to get used to a different or new situation □ *menyesuaikan diri semula: After her divorce, it took her a long time to readjust to being single again.* **2** [T] to change or move sth slightly □ *menyesuaikan/melaraskan semula* ▶**readjustment** *noun* [C,U]

ˌread-only 'memory *noun* [U] = **ROM**

ready /'redi/ *adj* (**readier; readiest**) **1 ready to do sth; ready (with/for sth)** prepared and happy to do sth □ *bersedia: You know me—I'm always ready to help.* ◆ *Charlie's always ready with advice.* ◆ *The men were angry and ready for a fight.* ◆ *I know it's early, but I'm ready for bed.* **2 ready (for sb/sth); ready (to do sth)** prepared and able to do sth or to be used □ *bersedia; menyediakan; sediakan; bersiap: The car will be ready for you to collect on Friday.* ◆ *He isn't ready to take his driving test—he hasn't had enough lessons.* ◆ *I'm meeting him at 7, so I don't have long to **get ready**.* ◆ *I'll go*

real → reappear

and get the dinner ready. ♦ *Have your money ready before you get on the bus.* **3** *adv* [in compounds] already made or done; not done especially for you □ *siap; tersedia*: *ready-cooked food* ♦ *There are no ready-made answers to this problem—we'll have to find our own solution.*

real¹ /riːl; rɪəl/ *adj*
▶ NOT IMAGINED **1** actually existing, not imagined □ *sebenar; nyata*: *The film is based on real life.* ♦ *This isn't a real word, I made it up.* ♦ *We have a real chance of winning.* ♦ *Closure of the factory is a very real danger.*
▶ NATURAL **2** natural, not artificial □ *asli; tulen*: *This shirt is real silk.*
▶ TRUE **3** actually true; not only what people think is true □ *benar; sebenar*: *The name he gave to the police wasn't his real name.*
▶ GENUINE **4** [only *before* a noun] having all, not just some, of the qualities necessary to really be sth □ *sejati; betul-betul*: *She was my first real girlfriend.*
▶ BIG **5** [only *before* a noun] (used to emphasize a state, feeling or quality) strong or big □ *betul-betul*: *Money is a real problem for us at the moment.* ♦ *He made a real effort to be polite.*
IDM **for real** genuine or serious □ *betul-betul*: *Her tears weren't for real.* ♦ *Was he for real when he offered you the job?*
the real thing (*informal*) something genuine, not a copy □ *sst yg tulen atau asli*: *This painting is just a copy. The real thing is in a gallery.* ♦ *She's had boyfriends before but this time she says it's the real thing* (= real love).

real² /riːl; rɪəl/ *adv* (*AmE informal*) very; really □ *sangat; betul-betul*

real estate *noun* [U] (especially *AmE*) property in the form of land and buildings □ *hartanah*

real estate agent (*AmE*) = **estate agent**

realise = **realize**

realism /ˈriːəlɪzəm/ *noun* [U] **1** behaviour that shows that you accept the facts of a situation and are not influenced by your feelings □ *realisme; sikap dsb yg berdasarkan kenyataan* ➔ look at **idealism 2** (in art, literature, etc.) showing things as they really are □ *realisme*

realist /ˈriːəlɪst/ *noun* [C] **1** a person who accepts the facts of a situation, and does not try to pretend that it is different □ *realis*: *I'm a realist—I don't expect the impossible.* **2** an artist or writer who shows things as they really are □ *realis*

realistic /ˌriːəˈlɪstɪk/ *adj* **1** sensible and understanding what it is possible to achieve in a particular situation □ *realistik; bersikap praktikal*: *We have to be realistic about our chances of winning.* **2** showing things as they really are □ *realistik; spt sebenar*: *a realistic drawing/description* **3** not real but appearing to be real □ *realistik; nampak spt benar*: *The monsters in the film were very realistic.* **OPP** for all meanings **unrealistic** ▶ **realistically** /-kli/ *adv*

reality /riˈæləti/ *noun* (*pl* **realities**) **1** [U] the way life really is, not the way it may appear to be or how you would like it to be □ *kenyataan; realiti*: *I enjoyed my holiday, but now it's back to reality.* ♦ *We have to face reality and accept that we've failed.* **2** [C] a thing that is actually experienced, not just imagined □ *kenyataan; hakikatnya*: *Films portray war as heroic and exciting, but the reality is very different.*
IDM **in reality** in fact, really (not the way sth appears or has been described) □ *sebenarnya*: *People say this is an exciting city but in reality it's rather boring.*

reality check *noun* [usually sing] (*informal*) an occasion when you are reminded of how things are in the real world, rather than how you would like things to be □ *sedar akan hal sebenarnya*: *It's time for a reality check—you're never going to finish that book!*

reality TV *noun* [U] television shows that are based on real people (not actors) in real situations, presented as entertainment □ *TV realiti*

realize (also **-ise**) /ˈriːəlaɪz/ *verb* [T] **1** to know and understand that sth is true or that sth has happened □ *sedar; menyedari; menduga; sangka*: *I'm sorry I mentioned it; I didn't realize how much it upset you.* ♦ *Didn't you realize (that) you needed to bring money?* **2** to become conscious of sth or that sth has happened, usually some time later □ *menyedari; perasan*: *When I got home, I realized that I had left my keys at the office.* **3** to make sth that you imagined become reality □ *menjadi kenyataan*: *His worst fears were realized when he saw the damage caused by the fire.*
▶ **realization** (also **-isation**) /ˌriːəlaɪˈzeɪʃn; ˌrɪəl-/ *noun* [U]

really /ˈriːəli/ *adv* **1** actually; in fact □ *sebenarnya*: *I couldn't believe it was really happening.* ♦ *He said he was sorry but I don't think he really meant it.* ♦ *She wasn't really angry, she was only pretending.* **2** *Is it really true?* **2** very; very much □ *benar-benar; betul-betul*: *I'm really tired.* ♦ *I really hope you enjoy yourself.* ♦ *I really tried but I couldn't do it.* **3** used in negative sentences to make what you are saying less strong □ *betul-betul*: *I don't really agree with that.* **4** used in questions when you are expecting sb to answer 'No' □ *takkanlah*: *You don't really expect me to believe that, do you?* **5** used as a question for expressing surprise, interest, doubt, etc. □ *betulkah; yakah*: *'She's left her husband.' 'Really? When did that happen?'*

Realtor™ /ˈriːəltə(r)/ (*AmE*) = **estate agent**

reap /riːp/ *verb* [T] **1** to obtain sth, especially sth good, as a direct result of sth that you have done □ *memperoleh; mendapat*: *If you work hard now, you'll reap the benefits later on.* **2** to cut and collect a crop, especially **corn, wheat** (= types of plant grown for their grain), etc., from a field □ *menuai; memotong; mendapat hasil*

reappear /ˌriːəˈpɪə(r)/ *verb* [I] to appear again or be seen again □ *muncul semula* ▶ **reappearance** *noun* [C,U]

reappraisal /ˌriːəˈpreɪzl/ noun [C,U] the new examination of a situation, way of doing sth, etc. in order to decide if any changes are necessary □ *penilaian semula*

rear¹ /rɪə(r)/ noun 1 [sing] **the rear** the back part □ *bahagian belakang*: *There are toilets at the rear of the plane.* 2 [C, usually sing] the part of your body that you sit on; your bottom □ *punggung; buntut*
IDM **bring up the rear** to be the last one in a race, a line of people, etc. □ *corot; berada di belakang sekali*
▶**rear** *adj* [only *before* a noun]: *the rear window/lights of a car* ⊃ picture on page P7

rear² /rɪə(r)/ verb 1 [T] to care for young children or animals until they are fully grown □ *memelihara; membela; membesarkan*: *She reared a family of five on her own.* 2 [T] to breed and look after animals on a farm, etc. □ *menternak; membela*: *to rear cattle/poultry* 3 [I] **rear (up)** (used about horses) to stand only on the back legs □ *mendompak*

rearrange /ˌriːəˈreɪndʒ/ verb [T] 1 to change the position or order of things □ *menyusun/mengatur semula*: *We've rearranged the living room to make more space.* 2 to change a plan, meeting, etc. that has been fixed □ *mengatur semula*

reason¹ /ˈriːzn/ noun 1 [C] **a reason (for sth/for doing sth); a reason why …/that …** a cause or an explanation for sth that has happened or for sth that sb has done □ *sebab; alasan*: *What's your reason for being so late?* ♦ *Is there any reason why you couldn't tell me this before?* ♦ *He said he couldn't come but he didn't give a reason.* ♦ *The reason (that) I'm phoning you is to ask a favour.* ♦ *For some reason they can't give us an answer until next week.* ♦ *She left the job for personal reasons.* 2 [C,U] **(a) reason (to do sth); (a) reason (for sth/for doing sth)** something that shows that it is right or fair to do sth □ *sebab; patut*: *I have reason to believe that you've been lying.* ♦ *I think we have reason for complaint.* ♦ *You have every reason* (= you are completely right) *to be angry, considering how badly you've been treated.* 3 [U] the ability to think and to make sensible decisions □ *kebolehan berfikir*: *Only human beings are capable of reason.* 4 [U] what is right or acceptable □ *sst yg wajar atau berpatutan*: *I tried to persuade him not to drive but he just wouldn't listen to reason.* ♦ *I'll pay anything within reason for a ticket.*
IDM **it stands to reason** (*informal*) it is obvious if you think about it □ *memang wajar/patut*

reason² /ˈriːzn/ verb [I,T] to form a judgement or opinion about sth, after thinking about it in a logical way □ *menaakul; membuat kesimpulan*
PHR V **reason with sb** to talk to sb in order to persuade them to behave or think in a more reasonable way □ *memujuk sso supaya berkelakuan atau berfikir dgn cara yg lebih waras*

reasonable /ˈriːznəbl/ *adj* 1 fair, practical and sensible □ *patut; wajar*: *I think it's rea-sonable to expect people to keep their promises.* ♦ *I tried to be reasonable even though I was very angry.* **OPP** **unreasonable** 2 acceptable and appropriate in a particular situation □ *berpatutan*: *It was a lovely meal and the bill was very reasonable!* 3 quite good, high, big, etc. but not very □ *agak (baik, tinggi, besar, dll); boleh tahan*: *His work is of a reasonable standard.*

reasonably /ˈriːznəbli/ *adv* 1 fairly or quite (but not very) □ *agak*: *The weather was reasonably good but not brilliant.* 2 in a sensible and fair way □ *secara wajar/berpatutan*: *If you think about my suggestion reasonably, you'll realize that I'm right.*

reasoning /ˈriːzənɪŋ/ noun [U] the process of thinking about sth and making a judgement or decision □ *pemikiran; taakulan*: *What's the reasoning behind his sudden decision to leave?*

reassurance /ˌriːəˈʃʊərəns/ (*BrE also*) -ˈʃɔːr-/ noun [U,C] advice or help that you give to sb to stop them worrying or being afraid □ *kata-kata yg menenangkan atau meyakinkan sso*: *I need some reassurance that I'm doing things the right way.*

reassure /ˌriːəˈʃʊə(r)/ (*BrE also*) -ˈʃɔː(r)/ verb [T] to say or do sth in order to stop sb worrying or being afraid □ *menenangkan hati; meyakinkan*: *The mechanic reassured her that the engine was fine.* ▶**reassuring** *adj* ▶**reassuringly** *adv*

rebate /ˈriːbeɪt/ noun [C] a sum of money that is given back to you because you have paid too much □ *rebat; potongan (harga, cukai, dll)*: *to get a tax rebate*

rebel¹ /ˈrebl/ noun [C] 1 a person who fights against their country's government because they want things to change □ *pemberontak*
SYN **insurgent** 2 a person who refuses to obey people in authority or to accept rules □ *orang yg suka memberontak/melawan*: *At school he had a reputation as a rebel.*

rebel² /rɪˈbel/ verb [I] (**rebelling**; **rebelled**) **rebel (against sb/sth)** to fight against authority, society, a law, etc. □ *memberontak; menentang*: *She rebelled against her parents by marrying a man she knew they didn't approve of.*

rebellion /rɪˈbeljən/ noun [C,U] 1 an occasion when some of the people in a country try to change the government, using violence □ *pemberontakan* 2 the act of fighting against authority or refusing to accept rules □ *penentangan*: *Voting against the leader of the party was an act of open rebellion.*

rebellious /rɪˈbeljəs/ *adj* not doing what authority, society, etc. wants you to do □ *suka memberontak/melawan*: *rebellious teenagers*

reboot /ˌriːˈbuːt/ verb [I,T] if you **reboot** a computer or if it **reboots**, you turn it off and then turn it on again immediately □ *menghidupkan semula (komputer)*

rebound /rɪˈbaʊnd/ verb [I] rebound (from/off sth) to hit sth/sb and then go in a different direction □ *melantun*: *The ball rebounded off Cole and went into the goal.* ▶ **rebound** /ˈriːbaʊnd/ noun [C]

rebuff /rɪˈbʌf/ noun [C] an unkind refusal of an offer or suggestion □ *(perbuatan) menolak* ▶ **rebuff** verb [T]

rebuild /ˌriːˈbɪld/ verb [T] (pt, pp rebuilt /ˌriːˈbɪlt/) to build sth again □ *membina semula*: *Following the storm, a great many houses will have to be rebuilt.*

rebuke /rɪˈbjuːk/ verb [T] (formal) to speak angrily to sb because they have done sth wrong □ *menegur; memarahi* ▶ **rebuke** noun [C]

recall /rɪˈkɔːl/ verb [T] (formal) 1 to remember sth (a fact, an event, an action, etc.) from the past □ *mengingat; ingat*: *I don't recall exactly when I first met her.* ♦ *She couldn't recall meeting him before.* 2 to order sb to return; to ask for sth to be returned □ *memanggil balik; meminta dipulangkan*: *The company has recalled all the faulty hairdryers.*

recap /ˈriːkæp/ (recapping; recapped) (informal) (also formal recapitulate /ˌriːkəˈpɪtʃʊleɪt/) verb [I,T] to repeat or look again at the main points of sth to make sure that they have been understood □ *mengulang/mengingat balik*: *Let's quickly recap what we've done in today's lesson, before we finish.*

recapture /ˌriːˈkæptʃə(r)/ verb [T] 1 to win back sth that was taken from you by an enemy □ *menawan semula*: *Government troops have recaptured the city.* 2 to catch a person or an animal that has escaped □ *menangkap semula* 3 to create or experience again sth from the past □ *mewujudkan/mengalami semula*: *The film brilliantly recaptures life in the 1930s.*

recede /rɪˈsiːd/ verb [I] 1 to move away and begin to disappear □ *semakin jauh/menghilang; susut; surut*: *The coast began to recede into the distance.* 2 (used about a hope, fear, chance, etc.) to become smaller or less strong □ *semakin tipis* 3 (used about a man's hair) to fall out and stop growing at the front of the head □ *semakin botak di depan*: *He's got a receding hairline.*

receipt /rɪˈsiːt/ noun 1 [C] a receipt (for sth) a piece of paper that is given to show that you have paid for sth □ *resit*: *Keep the receipt in case you want to exchange the shirt.* 2 [U] (formal) receipt (of sth) the receiving of sth □ *penerimaan*: *Payment must be made within seven days of receipt of the goods.*

receive /rɪˈsiːv/ verb [T] 1 receive sth (from sb/sth) to get or accept sth that sb sends or gives to you □ *mendapat; menerima*: *I received a letter from an old friend last week.* ♦ *to receive a phone call/a prize* 2 to experience a particular kind of treatment or injury □ *mendapat; mengalami*: *We received a warm welcome from our hosts.* ♦ *He received several cuts and bruises in the accident.* 3 [often passive] to react to sth new in a particular way □ *diterima*: *The film has been well received by the critics.*

receiver /rɪˈsiːvə(r)/ noun [C] 1 (also handset) the part of a telephone that is used for listening and speaking □ *gagang telefon* ➔ note at telephone 2 a piece of TV or radio equipment that changes electronic signals into sounds or pictures □ *(alat) penerima*

recent /ˈriːsnt/ adj that happened or began only a short time ago □ *baru-baru ini; baru*: *In recent years there have been many changes.* ♦ *This is a recent photograph of my daughter.*

recently /ˈriːsntli/ adv not long ago □ *baru-baru ini; tdk lama dahulu*: *She worked here until quite recently.* ♦ *Have you seen Paul recently?*

> **HELP** Recently or lately? Recently can refer to both a point in time and a period of time. If it refers to a point in time, use the past simple tense: *He got married recently.* If it refers to a period, use the present perfect or present perfect continuous tense: *I haven't done anything interesting recently.* ♦ *She's been working hard recently.* Lately can only refer to a period of time. It is used only with the present perfect or present perfect continuous tense: *I've seen a lot of films lately.* ♦ *I've been spending too much money lately.*

receptacle /rɪˈseptəkl/ noun [C] (formal) a container □ *bekas*

reception /rɪˈsepʃn/ noun 1 [U] the place inside the entrance of a hotel or office building where guests or visitors go when they first arrive □ *tempat menyambut tetamu*: *Leave your key at/in reception if you go out, please.* ♦ *the reception desk* 2 [C] a formal party to celebrate sth or to welcome an important person □ *majlis*: *Their wedding reception was held at a local hotel.* ♦ *There will be an official reception at the embassy for the visiting ambassador.* 3 [sing] the way people react to sth □ *sambutan*: *The play got a mixed reception* (= some people liked it, some people didn't). 4 [U] the quality of radio, TV or mobile phone signals □ *penerimaan*: *TV reception is very poor where we live.*

receptionist /rɪˈsepʃənɪst/ noun [C] a person who works in a hotel, a doctor's surgery, an office, etc. answering the telephone and dealing with visitors and guests when they arrive □ *penyambut tetamu*: *a hotel receptionist*

receptive /rɪˈseptɪv/ adj receptive (to sth) ready to listen to new ideas, suggestions, etc. □ *(bersikap) terbuka*

recess /rɪˈses; ˈriːses/ noun 1 [C,U] a period of time when parliament or other groups that meet for official discussions do not meet □ *waktu rehat; waktu tdk bersidang* 2 [U] (AmE) a short break during a trial in a court of law □ *berhenti rehat* ➔ note at interval 3 [C] part of a wall that is further back than the rest, forming a space □ *ceruk* 4 [C] a part of a room that receives very little light □ *ceruk*

recession /rɪˈseʃn/ noun [C,U] a period when the business and industry of a country is not successful ◻ *kemelesetan*: *The country is now in recession.* ♦ *How long will the recession last?*

recharge /ˌriːˈtʃɑːdʒ/ verb [I,T] to fill a battery with electrical power; to fill up with electrical power ◻ *mengecas*: *He plugged the drill in to recharge it.* ◑ look at **charge** ▶**rechargeable** *adj*: *rechargeable batteries*

recipe /ˈresəpi/ noun [C] **1** a recipe (for sth) the instructions for cooking or preparing sth to eat ◻ *resipi*: *a recipe for chocolate cake* **2** a recipe for sth the way to get or produce sth ◻ *cara*: *Putting Dave in charge of the project is a recipe for disaster.*

TOPIC

A recipe
Shepherd's pie

Peel four potatoes, then **cut** them in pieces and **boil** them in a **saucepan** of water. When they are cooked, **strain** them in a **colander** to remove the water, then **mash** them with some butter and milk. Next **slice** an onion, and **fry** it in a **frying pan**. Add some **minced** meat, some **chopped** tomatoes and herbs (= special leaves used in cooking), and put the mixture in a **casserole** dish, with the **mashed potato** on top. **Grate** some cheese on the potato, and then **bake** in the **oven** for half an hour.

---

recipient /rɪˈsɪpiənt/ noun [C] (*formal*) a person who receives sth ◻ *penerima*

reciprocal /rɪˈsɪprəkl/ adj involving two or more people or groups who agree to help each other or to behave in the same way towards each other ◻ *saling; dua hala*: *The arrangement is reciprocal. They help us and we help them.*

reciprocate /rɪˈsɪprəkeɪt/ verb [I,T] reciprocate (sth) (with sth) to behave or feel towards sb in the same way as they behave or feel towards you ◻ *membalas*: *Her love for him was not reciprocated.* ♦ *I wasn't sure whether to laugh or to reciprocate with a remark of my own.* ▶**reciprocation** /rɪˌsɪprəˈkeɪʃn/ noun [U]

recital /rɪˈsaɪtl/ noun [C] a formal public performance of music or poetry ◻ *resital*: *a piano recital* ◑ look at **concert**

recite /rɪˈsaɪt/ verb [I,T] to say a poem, piece of literature, etc. that you have learned, especially to an audience ◻ *melafazkan*: *Each child had to recite a poem to the class*

reckless /ˈrekləs/ adj not thinking about possible bad or dangerous results that could come from your actions ◻ *tdk hati-hati; tdk menghiraukan (keselamatan, akibat, dll)*: *reckless driving* ♦ *a reckless disregard for safety* ▶**recklessly** adv

reckon /ˈrekən/ verb [T] **1** (*informal*) to think; to have an opinion about sth ◻ *agak; rasa; kira*: *She's very late now. I reckon (that) she isn't coming.* ♦ *I think she's forgotten. What do you reckon?* **2** to calculate sth approximately ◻ *agak; menganggar*: *The journey was reckoned to take half an hour.*

PHR V **reckon on sth** to expect sth to happen and therefore to base a plan or action on it ◻ *menyangka (sst)*: *I didn't book in advance because I wasn't reckoning on tickets being so scarce.*
reckon (sth) up to calculate the total amount or number of sth ◻ *mengira/menjumlahkan sst*
reckon with sb/sth to think about sb/sth as a possible problem ◻ *mengambil kira sso/sst*: *They were a political force to be reckoned with.* ♦ *I didn't reckon with there being so much traffic.*

reckoning /ˈrekənɪŋ/ noun [U,C] the act of calculating sth, especially in a way that is not very exact ◻ *menurut perkiraan kasar*: *By my reckoning you still owe me £5.*

reclaim /rɪˈkleɪm/ verb [T] **1** reclaim sth (from sb/sth) to get back sth that has been lost or taken away ◻ *menuntut/mendapatkan balik*: *Reclaim your luggage after you have been through passport control.* **2** to make wet land suitable for use ◻ *menebus guna* **3** to get back useful materials from waste products ◻ *memulih guna* ▶**reclamation** /ˌrekləˈmeɪʃn/ noun [U]: *land reclamation*

recline /rɪˈklaɪn/ verb [I,T] to sit or lie back in a relaxed and comfortable way ◻ *bersandar* ▶**reclining** adj: *The car has reclining seats at the front.*

recluse /rɪˈkluːs/ noun [C] a person who lives alone and likes to avoid other people ◻ *penyendiri; orang yg bertapa* ▶**reclusive** /rɪˈkluːsɪv/ adj: *a reclusive millionaire*

recognition /ˌrekəɡˈnɪʃn/ noun **1** [U] the fact that you can identify sb/sth that you see ◻ *pengenalan; (perihal) kenal/mengenal*: *She looked at me with no sign of recognition on her face.* **2** [U, sing] the act of accepting that sth exists, is true or is official ◻ *pengiktirafan*: *There is a growing recognition that older people are important in the workplace.* **3** [U] a public show of respect for sb's work or actions ◻ *pengiktirafan; penghargaan*: *She has received public recognition for her services to charity.* ♦ *Please accept this gift in recognition of the work you have done.*

recognizable (also -isable) /ˈrekəɡnaɪzəbl; ˌrekəɡˈnaɪzəbl/ adj recognizable (as sb/sth) that can be identified as sb/sth ◻ *dpt dikenali*: *He was barely recognizable with his new short haircut.* ▶**recognizably** (also -isably) /-əbli/ adv

recognize (also -ise) /ˈrekəɡnaɪz/ verb [T] **1** to know again sb/sth that you have seen or heard before ◻ *kenal; mengenal; mengecam*: *I recognized him but I couldn't remember his name.* **2** to accept that sth exists or is true ◻ *menyedari; mengakui*: *I recognize that some of my ideas are unrealistic.* **3** to accept sth officially ◻ *mengiktiraf*: *My qualifications are not recognized in other countries.* **4** to show officially that you think sth that sb has done is good ◻ *menghargai*: *The company gave her a special present to recognize her long years of service.*

recoil /rɪˈkɔɪl/ verb [I] to quickly move away from sb/sth unpleasant □ *tersentak dan mengundur kerana ngeri, takut, dll*: *She recoiled in horror at the sight of the rat.*

recollect /ˌrekəˈlekt/ verb [I,T] to remember sth, especially by making an effort □ *ingat; mengingat*: *I don't recollect exactly when it happened.*

recollection /ˌrekəˈlekʃn/ noun 1 [U] **recollection (of sth/doing sth)** the ability to remember □ *ingatan; ingat*: *I have no recollection of promising to lend you money.* 2 [C, usually pl] something that you remember □ *kenangan*: *I have only vague recollections of the town where I spent my early years.* **SYN** for both meanings **memory**

recommend /ˌrekəˈmend/ verb [T] 1 **recommend sb/sth (to sb) (for/as sth)** to say that sb/sth is good and that sb should try or use them or it □ *mengesyorkan; mencadangkan*: *Which film would you recommend?* ♦ *Could you recommend me a good hotel?* ♦ *We hope that you'll recommend this restaurant to all your friends.* ♦ *Doctors don't always recommend drugs as the best treatment for every illness.* 2 to tell sb what you strongly believe they should do □ *menasihatkan*: *I recommend that you get some legal advice.* ♦ *I wouldn't recommend (your) travelling on your own. It could be dangerous.* ♦ *It is recommended that machines are checked every year.*

recommendation /ˌrekəmenˈdeɪʃn/ noun 1 [C] a statement about what should be done in a particular situation □ *syor; nasihat*: *In their report on the crash, the committee make several recommendations on how safety could be improved.* 2 [C,U] saying that sth is good and should be tried or used □ *syor; cadangan*: *I visited Seville on a friend's recommendation and I really enjoyed it.*

recompense /ˈrekəmpens/ verb [T] (formal) **recompense sb (for sth)** to give money, etc. to sb for special efforts or work or because you are responsible for a loss they have suffered □ *memberi ganti rugi*: *The airline has agreed to recompense us for the damage to our luggage.* ▶ **recompense** noun [sing, U]: *Please accept this cheque in recompense for our poor service.*

reconcile /ˈrekənsaɪl/ verb [T] 1 **reconcile sth (with sth)** to find a way of dealing with two ideas, situations, statements, etc. that seem to be opposite to each other □ *menyelaraskan; menyesuaikan*: *She finds it difficult to reconcile her career ambitions with her responsibilities to her children.* 2 [often passive] **reconcile sb (with sb)** to make people become friends again after an argument □ *berbaik-baik semula*: *After years of not speaking to each other, she and her parents were eventually reconciled.* 3 **reconcile yourself to sth** to accept an unpleasant situation because there is nothing you can do to change it □ *(terpaksa) menerima* ▶ **reconciliation** /ˌrekənsɪliˈeɪʃn/ noun [sing, U]: *The negotiators are hoping to bring about a reconciliation between the two sides.*

reconnaissance /rɪˈkɒnɪsns/ noun [C,U] the study of a place or area for military reasons □ *peninjauan; tinjauan*: *The plane was shot down while on a reconnaissance mission over enemy territory.*

reconsider /ˌriːkənˈsɪdə(r)/ verb [I,T] to think again about sth, especially because you may want to change your mind □ *mempertimbangkan semula*: *Public protests have forced the government to reconsider their policy.*

reconstruct /ˌriːkənˈstrʌkt/ verb [T] 1 to build again sth that has been destroyed or damaged □ *membina semula* 2 to get a full description or picture of sth using the facts that are known □ *membina semula*: *The police are trying to reconstruct the victim's movements on the day of the murder.*

reconstruction /ˌriːkənˈstrʌkʃn/ noun [C,U] 1 the activity of building again sth that has been damaged or destroyed □ *pembinaan semula* 2 a short film showing events that are known to have happened, made in order to try and get more information or better understanding □ *lakonan semula*: *a reconstruction of the crime using actors*

record¹ /ˈrekɔːd/ noun 1 [C] **a record (of sth)** a written account of what has happened, been done, etc. □ *rekod; catatan*: *The teachers keep records of the children's progress.* ♦ *medical records* ♦ *It's on record that he was out of the country at the time of the murder.* 2 [C] the best performance or the highest or lowest level, etc. ever reached in sth, especially in sport □ *rekod*: *Who holds the world record for high jump?* ♦ *She's hoping to break the record for the 100 metres.* ♦ *He did it in record time* (= very fast). 3 [C] the facts, events, etc. that are known (and sometimes written down) about sb/sth □ *rekod; piring hitam*: *The police said that the man had a criminal record* (= he had been found guilty of crimes in the past). ♦ *This airline has a bad safety record.* 4 [C] a thin, round piece of plastic on which music is recorded □ *rekod*: *a record collection*

IDM **off the record** (used about sth a person says) not to be treated as official; not intended to be made public □ *secara tdk rasmi*: *She told me off the record that she was going to resign.*
put/set the record straight to correct a mistake by telling sb the true facts □ *membetulkan salah faham*

record² /rɪˈkɔːd/ verb 1 [T] to write down or film facts or events so that they can be referred to later and will not be forgotten □ *mencatat; merekodkan*: *He recorded everything in his diary.* ♦ *At the inquest the coroner recorded a verdict of accidental death.* 2 [I,T] to put music, a film, a programme, etc. onto a CD or DVD so that it can be listened to or watched again later □ *merakam*: *Quiet, please! We're recording.* ♦ *The band has recently recorded a new album.* ♦ *There's a* concert I would like to record from the radio this evening.

record-breaker *noun* [C] a person or thing that achieves a better result or higher level than has ever been achieved before □ *(yg) memecah rekod* ▶**record-breaking** *adj* [only before a noun] the best, fastest, highest, etc. ever: *We did the journey in record-breaking time.*

recorder /rɪˈkɔːdə(r)/ *noun* [C] **1** a machine for recording sound and/or pictures □ *(alat) perakam: a tape/DVD/video recorder* **2** a type of musical instrument that is often played by children. You play it by blowing through it and covering the holes in it with your fingers. □ *rekorder* ⊃ picture at **music**

recording /rɪˈkɔːdɪŋ/ *noun* **1** [C] sound or pictures that have been put onto a CD, video, etc. □ *rakaman: the Berlin Philharmonic's recording of Mahler's Sixth symphony* **2** [U] the process of making a CD, film, etc. □ *perakaman: a recording session/studio*

record label = **label**¹(2)

record player *noun* [C] a machine that you use for playing records in order to listen to music, etc. on them □ *alat main rekod/piring hitam*

recount /rɪˈkaʊnt/ *verb* [T] (*formal*) to tell a story or describe an event □ *menceritakan*

recourse /rɪˈkɔːs/ *noun* [U] (*formal*) the fact of having to use sth or ask sb for help in a difficult situation □ *perlu melakukan sst utk mengatasi sst keadaan yg sukar: She made a complete recovery without recourse to surgery.*

recover /rɪˈkʌvə(r)/ *verb* **1** [I] recover (from sth) to become well again after you have been ill □ *sembuh; pulih: It took him two months to recover from the operation.* **2** [I] recover (from sth) to get back to normal again after a bad experience, etc □ *pulih: The old lady never really recovered from the shock of being mugged.* **3** [T] recover sth (from sb/sth) to find or get back sth that was lost or stolen □ *menjumpai/mendapat balik: Police recovered the stolen goods from a warehouse in South London.* **4** [T] to get back the use of your senses, control of your emotions, etc. □ *pulih; menenteramkan diri: He needs daily exercise if he's going to recover the use of his legs.*

recovery /rɪˈkʌvəri/ *noun* **1** [C, usually sing] recovery (from sth) a return to good health after an illness or to a normal state after a difficult period of time □ *pemulihan; penyembuhan; (perihal) pulih/sembuh: to make a good/ quick/speedy/slow recovery* ♦ *She's on the road to recovery* (= getting better all the time) *now.* ♦ *the prospects of economic recovery* **2** [U] recovery (of sth/sb) getting back sth that was lost, stolen or missing □ *penjumpaan semula; (perihal) menjumpai/mendapatkan semula*

recreation /ˌrekriˈeɪʃn/ *noun* [U, sing] the fact of enjoying yourself and relaxing when you are not working; a way of doing this □ *rekreasi: recreation activities such as swimming or reading* ▶**recreational** *adj*

recreational vehicle (*AmE*) = **camper**(2)

recrimination /rɪˌkrɪmɪˈneɪʃn/ *noun* [C, usually pl, U] an angry statement accusing sb of sth, especially in answer to a similar statement from them □ *(perbuatan) tuduh-menuduh: bitter recriminations*

recruit¹ /rɪˈkruːt/ *verb* [I,T] to find new people to join a company, an organization, the armed forces, etc. □ *merekrut; mengambil ahli/ kakitangan baharu: to recruit young people to the teaching profession* ▶**recruitment** *noun* [U]

recruit² /rɪˈkruːt/ *noun* [C] a person who has just joined the army or another organization □ *rekrut; ahli baharu*

rectangle /ˈrektæŋgl/ *noun* [C] a shape with four straight sides and four **right angles** (= angles of 90°). Two of the sides are longer than the other two. □ *segi empat tepat* **SYN** **oblong** ⊃ picture at **shape** ▶**rectangular** /rekˈtæŋɡjələ(r)/ *adj*

rectify /ˈrektɪfaɪ/ *verb* [T] (rectifying; rectifies; *pt, pp* rectified) (*formal*) to correct sth that is wrong □ *membetulkan*

rectum /ˈrektəm/ *noun* [C] the end section of the tube where solid food waste collects before leaving the body □ *rektum*

recuperate /rɪˈkuːpəreɪt/ *verb* [I] (*formal*) recuperate (from sth) to get well again after an illness or injury □ *sembuh; pulih* ▶**recuperation** /rɪˌkuːpəˈreɪʃn/ *noun* [U]

recur /rɪˈkɜː(r)/ *verb* [I] (recurring; recurred) to happen again or many times □ *berulang: a recurring problem/nightmare* ▶**recurrence** /rɪˈkʌrəns/ *noun* [C,U] ▶**recurrent** /rɪˈkʌrənt/ *adj*

recycle /ˌriːˈsaɪkl/ *verb* [T] **1** to put used objects and materials through a process so that they can be used again □ *mengitar semula: recycled paper* ♦ *Aluminium cans can be recycled.* ⊃ note at **environment** **2** to keep used objects and materials and use them again □ *mengguna semula: Don't throw away your plastic carrier bags—recycle them!* ▶**recyclable** *adj: Most plastics are recyclable.* ▶**recycling** *noun* [U]: *the recycling of glass* ♦ *a recycling bin*

red /red/ *adj, noun* [C,U] (redder; reddest) **1** (of the) colour of blood □ *(berwarna) merah: red wine* ♦ *She was dressed in red.* ⊃ look at **crimson, maroon, scarlet** **2** a colour that some people's faces become when they are embarrassed, angry, shy, etc. □ *merah padam: He went bright red when she spoke to him.* ♦ *to turn/be/go red in the face* **3** (used about sb's hair or an animal's fur) (of) a colour between red, orange and brown □ *perang kemerah-merahan: She's got red hair and freckles.*

IDM **be in the red** (*informal*) to have spent more money than you have in the bank, etc. □ *dlm keadaan debit (berhutang): I'm £500 in the red at the moment.* **OPP** **be in the black**
catch sb red-handed ⊃ **catch¹**

red card → refer

a red herring an idea or subject which takes people's attention away from what is really important □ *sst yg memesongkan perhatian drpd apa yg sebenarnya penting*
see red ⊃ **see**

red 'card noun [C] (in football) a card that is shown to a player who is being sent off the field for doing sth wrong □ *kad merah* ⊃ look at **yellow card**

the ˌred 'carpet noun [sing] a piece of red carpet that is put outside to receive an important visitor; a special welcome for an important visitor □ *permaidani merah*: *I didn't expect to be given the red carpet treatment!*

redcurrant /ˌredˈkʌrənt; ˈredkʌrənt/ noun [C] a small round red fruit that you can eat □ *'redcurrant'; sejenis beri merah*: *redcurrant jelly*

redden /ˈredn/ verb [I,T] to become red or to make sth red □ *menjadi merah; memerah(kan)* ⊃ **Go red** (or when talking about a person's face, **blush**) is more common.

reddish /ˈredɪʃ/ adj fairly red in colour □ *kemerah-merahan*

redeem /rɪˈdiːm/ verb [T] **1** to prevent sth from being completely bad □ *mengimbangi (perkara lain yg kurang baik)*: *The redeeming feature of the job is the good salary.* **2** **redeem yourself** to do sth to improve people's opinion of you, especially after you have done sth bad □ *menebus maruah*

redemption /rɪˈdempʃn/ noun [U] the act of being saved from evil □ *selamat drpd kejahatan*
IDM beyond redemption too bad to be saved or improved □ *tdk boleh diselamatkan atau dibaiki lagi*

redevelop /ˌriːdɪˈveləp/ verb [T] to build or arrange an area, a town, a building, etc. in a different and more modern way □ *membangunkan semula*: *They're redeveloping the city centre.*
▶ **redevelopment** noun [U]

redhead /ˈredhed/ noun [C] a person who has red hair □ *orang yg berambut merah*

ˌred-'hot adj (used about a metal) so hot that it turns red □ *pijar; merah menyala*

redial /ˌriːˈdaɪəl/ verb [I,T] to call the same telephone number again □ *mendail balik*

redistribute /ˌriːdɪˈstrɪbjuːt; ˌriːˈdɪs-/ verb [T] to share sth out among people in a different way from before □ *mengagihkan semula* ▶ **redistribution** /ˌriːdɪstrɪˈbjuːʃn/ noun [U]

ˌred 'pepper = **pepper¹** (2)

ˌred 'tape noun [U] official rules that must be followed which seem unnecessary and often cause delay and difficulty in achieving sth □ *pita merah; peraturan rasmi, dsb yg melengahkan sst*

reduce /rɪˈdjuːs/ verb [T] **reduce sth (from sth) (to sth); reduce sth (by sth)** to make sth less or smaller in quantity, price, size, etc. □ *mengurangkan*: *The sign said 'Reduce speed now'.* ♦ *I bought this shirt because the price was reduced from £50 to £25.* **OPP increase**
PHR V reduce sb/sth (from sth) to sth [often passive] to force sb/sth into a particular state or condition, usually a bad one □ *menyebabkan; membuat*: *One of the older boys reduced the small child to tears.*

reduction /rɪˈdʌkʃn/ noun **1** [C,U] **reduction (in sth)** the act of becoming or making sth less or smaller □ *pengurangan; berkurangnya*: *a sharp reduction in the number of students* **2** [C] the amount by which sth is made smaller, especially in price □ *potongan*: *There were massive reductions in the June sales.*

redundant /rɪˈdʌndənt/ adj **1** (BrE) (used about employees) no longer needed for a job and therefore out of work □ *diberhentikan kerja*: *When the factory closed 800 people were made redundant.* ⊃ note at **job 2** not necessary or wanted □ *tdk diperlukan atau dikehendaki*
▶ **redundancy** /rɪˈdʌndənsi/ noun [C,U] (pl **redundancies**): *redundancy pay*

reed /riːd/ noun [C] **1** a tall plant, like grass, that grows in or near water □ *mensiang* **2** a thin piece of wood, metal or plastic at the end of some musical instruments which produces a sound when you blow through it □ *rid* ⊃ picture at **music**

reef /riːf/ noun [C] a long line of rocks, plants, etc. just below or above the surface of the sea □ *terumbu*: *a coral reef*

reek /riːk/ verb [I] **reek (of sth)** to smell strongly of sth unpleasant □ *berbau busuk atau tdk menyenangkan*: *His breath reeked of tobacco.*
▶ **reek** noun [sing]

reel¹ /riːl/ noun [C] a round object that thread, wire, film for cameras, etc. is put around □ *gelendong*: *a cotton reel* ♦ *a reel of film* ⊃ look at **spool** ⊃ picture at **garden, sewing**

reel² /riːl/ verb [I] **1** to walk without being able to control your legs, for example because you are drunk or you have been hit □ *terhuyung-hayang* **2** to feel very shocked or upset about sth □ *menjadi bingung; pusing (fikiran, dsb)*: *His mind was still reeling from the shock of seeing her again.*
PHR V reel sth off to say or repeat sth from memory quickly and without having to think about it □ *menyebut atau mengulangi sst dgn cepat dan lancar*: *She reeled off a long list of names.*

ref /ref/ (informal) = **referee** (1)

ref. /ref/ abbr = **reference** (3): *ref. no. 3456*

refer /rɪˈfɜː(r)/ verb (**referring; referred**)
PHR V refer to sb/sth (as sth) to mention or talk about sb/sth □ *memaksudkan; merujuk kpd*: *When he said 'some students', do you think he was referring to us?* ♦ *She always referred to Ben as 'that nice man'.*

refer to sb/sth 1 to describe or be connected with sb/sth □ *bermaksud; merangkum*: *The term 'adolescent' refers to young people between the ages of 12 and 17.* **2** to find out information by asking sb or by looking in a book, etc. □ *merujuk kpd*: *If you don't understand a word you may refer to your dictionaries.*

refer sb/sth to sb/sth to send sb/sth to sb/sth else for help or to be dealt with □ *merujukkan*: *The doctor has referred me to a specialist.*

referee /ˌrefəˈriː/ *noun* [C] **1** (also *informal* **ref**) the official person in sports such as football who controls the match and prevents players from breaking the rules □ *pengadil* ➲ look at **umpire 2** (*BrE*) a person who gives information about your character and ability, usually in a letter, for example when you are hoping to be chosen for a job □ *orang yg dirujuk bagi mengetahui keperibadian dan kebolehan sso*: *Her teacher agreed to act as her referee.* ▶ **referee** *verb* [I,T]

reference /ˈrefrəns/ *noun*
▶ MENTIONING SB/STH **1** [C,U] (a) reference (to sb/sth) a written or spoken comment that mentions sb/sth □ *rujukan; (perihal) menyebut*: *The article made a direct reference to a certain member of the royal family.*
▶ LOOKING FOR INFORMATION **2** [U] looking at sth for information □ *rujukan*: *The guidebook might be useful for future reference.*
▶ IN BUSINESS **3** [C] (*abbr* **ref.**) a special number that identifies a letter, etc. □ *rujukan*: *Please quote our reference when replying.*
▶ FOR NEW JOB **4** [C] a statement or letter describing sb's character and ability that is given to a possible future employer □ *rujukan; surat sokongan*: *My boss gave me a good reference.* ➲ note at **job**

TOPIC

References

When you apply for a job you are usually asked to **give references**. These are the job titles, names and addresses of two or more people who know you well. The new employer can contact them to check that you are suitable for new job. You can ask a teacher or a previous employer to give you a reference, but not a friend or a member of your family.

▶ IN BOOK **5** [C] a note, especially in a book, that tells you where certain information came from or can be found □ *rujukan*: *There is a list of references at the end of each chapter.*
IDM **with reference to sb/sth** (*formal*) about or concerning sb/sth □ *merujuk kpd atau berkenaan dgn sso/sst*: *I am writing with reference to your letter of 10 April …*

'reference book *noun* [C] a book that you use to find a piece of information □ *buku rujukan*: *dictionaries, encyclopedias and other reference books*

referendum /ˌrefəˈrendəm/ *noun* [C,U] (*pl* **referendums** or **referenda** /-də/) an occasion when all the people of a country can vote on a particular political question □ *referendum;* *pungutan suara*: *The government will hold a referendum on the issue.*

refill /ˌriːˈfɪl/ *verb* [T] to fill sth again □ *mengisi semula; menambah*: *Can I refill your glass?* ▶ **refill** /ˈriːfɪl/ *noun* [C]: *I'd like to buy a refill for my pen.*

refine /rɪˈfaɪn/ *verb* [T] **1** to make a substance pure and free from other substances □ *menapis*: *to refine sugar/oil* **2** to improve sth by changing little details □ *memperhalus; memperbaiki*: *to refine a theory*

refined /rɪˈfaɪnd/ *adj* **1** (used about a substance) that has been made pure by having other substances taken out of it □ *bertapis*: *refined sugar/oil/flour* **OPP** **unrefined** **2** (used about a person) polite; having very good manners □ *halus budi pekertinya* **3** improved and therefore producing a better result □ *diperbaiki; diperhalus*

refinement /rɪˈfaɪnmənt/ *noun* **1** [C] a small change that improves sth □ *perbaikan*: *The new model has electric windows and other refinements.* **2** [U] good manners and polite behaviour □ *kehalusan budi pekerti*

refinery /rɪˈfaɪnəri/ *noun* [C] (*pl* **refineries**) a factory where a substance is made pure by having other substances taken out of it □ *kilang penapisan*: *an oil/sugar refinery*

reflect /rɪˈflekt/ *verb* **1** [T, usually passive] **reflect sb/sth (in sth)** to show an image of sb/sth on the surface of sth such as a mirror, water or glass □ *membayangkan; terbayang*: *She caught sight of herself reflected in the shop window.* **2** [T] to send back light, heat or sound from a surface □ *memantulkan*: *The windows reflected the bright morning sunlight.* **3** [T] to show or express sth □ *membayangkan; menggambarkan*: *His music reflects his interest in African culture.* **4** [I] **reflect (on/upon sth)** to think, especially deeply and carefully, about sth □ *memikirkan; merenungkan*: *I really need some time to reflect on what you've said.*
PHR V **reflect (well, badly, etc.) on sb/sth** to give a particular impression of sb/sth □ *membawa (nama baik/buruk) kpd sso/sst*: *It reflects badly on the whole school if some of its pupils misbehave in public.*

reflection /rɪˈflekʃn/ *noun* **1** [C] an image that you see in a mirror, in water or on a shiny surface □ *bayang*: *He admired his reflection in the mirror.* **2** [U] the sending back of light, heat or sound from a surface □ *pemantulan; pantulan* **3** [C] a thing that shows what sb/sth is like □ *gambaran; bayangan*: *Your clothes are a reflection of your personality.* **4** [sing] **a reflection on/upon sb/sth** something that causes people to form a good or bad opinion about sb/sth □ *gambaran; sst yg membawa nama baik atau buruk*: *Parents often feel that their children's behaviour is a reflection on themselves.* **5** [U,C] careful thought about sth □ *pemikiran; renungan*: *A week off would give her time for reflection.*

reflective → refusal 714

IDM **on reflection** after thinking again □ *setelah difikirkan semula*: I think, on reflection, that we were wrong.

reflective /rɪˈflektɪv/ *adj* **1** (*formal*) (used about a person, mood, etc.) thinking deeply about things □ *berfikir mendalam*: *a reflective expression* **2** (used about a surface) sending back light or heat □ *yg memantul (cahaya atau haba)*: *Wear reflective strips when you're cycling at night.* **3** reflective (of sth) showing what sth is like □ *mencerminkan; menggambarkan; membayangkan*

reflector /rɪˈflektə(r)/ *noun* [C] **1** a surface that **reflects** light, heat or sound that hits it □ *pemantul* **2** a small piece of glass or plastic on a bicycle or on clothing that can be seen at night when light shines on it □ *reflektor; pemantul*

reflex /ˈriːfleks/ *noun* **1** [C] (also **reflex action**) a sudden movement or action that you make without thinking □ *tindakan refleks*: *She put her hands out as a reflex to stop her fall.* **2** **reflexes** [pl] the ability to act or move quickly when necessary □ *kepekaan*: *A good tennis player needs to have excellent reflexes.*

ˌreflex ˈangle *noun* [C] an angle of more than 180° □ *sudut refleks* ➪ look at **acute angle, obtuse angle, right angle**

reflexion (*BrE*) = **reflection**

reflexive /rɪˈfleksɪv/ *adj* [C] (of a word or verb form) showing that the person who performs an action is also affected by it □ *refleksif*: *In 'He cut himself', 'cut' is a **reflexive verb** and 'himself' is a **reflexive pronoun**.*

reflexology /ˌriːfleksˈɒlədʒi/ *noun* [U] a type of treatment in which sb's feet are rubbed in a particular way in order to heal other parts of their body or to make them feel relaxed □ *refleksologi* ▶ **reflexologist** /ˌriːfleksˈɒlədʒɪst/ *noun* [C]

reform /rɪˈfɔːm/ *verb* **1** [T] to change a system, the law, etc. in order to make it better □ *membuat pembaharuan*: *to reform the examination system* **2** [I,T] to improve your behaviour; to make sb do this □ *berubah/mengubah (perangai); membuang tabiat buruk*: *Our prisons aim to reform criminals, not simply to punish them.* ▶ **reform** *noun* [C,U]: *a major reform to the system*

reformer /rɪˈfɔːmə(r)/ *noun* [C] a person who tries to change society and make it better □ *reformis*

refrain¹ /rɪˈfreɪn/ *verb* [I] (*formal*) refrain (from sth/doing sth) to stop yourself doing sth; to not do sth □ *menahan diri (drpd melakukan sst); tdk (melakukan sst)*: *Please refrain from eating in the classroom.*

refrain² /rɪˈfreɪn/ *noun* [C] the part of a song that is repeated, usually at the end of each **verse** (= a group of lines that is not repeated) □ *baris ulang* **SYN** **chorus**

refresh /rɪˈfreʃ/ *verb* **1** [T] to make sb/sth feel less tired or less hot and full of energy again □ *menyegarkan semula*: *He looked refreshed after a good night's sleep.* **2** [T,I] to get the most recent information, for example on an Internet page, usually by clicking on a button □ *segar semula*: *Click here to refresh this document.* ♦ *The page refreshes automatically.*

IDM **refresh your memory** to remind sb/yourself about sth □ *mengingatkan semula ttg (sso/sst)*: *Could you refresh my memory about what we said on this point last week?*

refreshing /rɪˈfreʃɪŋ/ *adj* **1** pleasantly new or different □ *menyenangkan atau memberangsangkan (kerana baharu atau lain drpd biasa)*: *It makes a refreshing change to meet somebody who is so enthusiastic.* **2** making you feel less tired or hot □ *menyegarkan*: *a refreshing swim/shower/drink*

refreshment /rɪˈfreʃmənt/ *noun* **1** **refreshments** [pl] light food and drinks that are available at a cinema, theatre or other public place □ *makanan atau minuman ringan; kudapan* **2** [U] (*formal*) the fact of making sb feel stronger and less tired or hot; food or drink that helps to do this □ *penyegaran; makanan atau minuman yg menyegarkan*

refrigerate /rɪˈfrɪdʒəreɪt/ *verb* [T] to make food, etc. cold in order to keep it fresh □ *menyejukkan* ▶ **refrigeration** /rɪˌfrɪdʒəˈreɪʃn/ *noun* [U]: *Keep all meat products under refrigeration.*

refrigerator /rɪˈfrɪdʒəreɪtə(r)/ *noun* (*formal*) = **fridge** □ *peti sejuk*: *This dessert can be served straight from the refrigerator.*

refuge /ˈrefjuːdʒ/ *noun* [U,C] refuge (from sb/sth) protection from danger, trouble, etc.; a place that is safe □ *perlindungan; tempat berlindung*: *We had to take refuge from the rain under a tree.* ♦ *a refuge for the homeless* **SYN** **shelter**

refugee /ˌrefjuˈdʒiː/ *noun* [C] a person who has been forced to leave their country for political or religious reasons, or because there is a war, not enough food, etc. □ *orang pelarian*: *a refugee camp* ➪ look at **fugitive, exile**

refund /ˈriːfʌnd/ *noun* [C] a sum of money that is paid back to you, especially because you have paid too much or you are not happy with sth you have bought □ *membayar balik*: *to claim/demand/get a refund* ➪ note at **shopping** ▶ **refund** /rɪˈfʌnd; ˈriːfʌnd/ *verb* [T] ▶ **refundable** /rɪˈfʌndəbl/ *adj*: *The deposit is not refundable.*

refurbish /ˌriːˈfɜːbɪʃ/ *verb* [T] to clean and decorate a room, building, etc. in order to make it more attractive, more useful, etc. □ *membersihkan; membaharui; menghias semula* ▶ **refurbishment** *noun* [U,C]: *The hotel is now closed for refurbishment.*

refusal /rɪˈfjuːzl/ *noun* [U,C] (a) refusal (of sth); (a) refusal (to do sth) the act of saying or showing that you will not do, give or accept sth □ *penolakan; keengganan*: *I can't understand her refusal to see me.*

refuse¹ /rɪˈfjuːz/ verb [I,T] to say or show that you do not want to do, give or accept sth □ *menolak; tdk mahu; enggan*: He refused to listen to what I was saying. ♦ My application for a grant has been refused.

refuse² /ˈrefjuːs/ noun [U] (formal) things that you throw away; rubbish □ *sampah sarap*: the refuse collection (= when dustbins are emptied)

regain /rɪˈɡeɪn/ verb [T] to get sth back that you had lost □ *mendapat balik; sedar semula, dsb*: to regain consciousness

regal /ˈriːɡl/ adj very impressive; typical of or suitable for a king or queen □ *mengagumkan; spt raja atau ratu*

regard¹ /rɪˈɡɑːd/ verb [T] 1 regard sb/sth as sth; regard sb/sth (with sth) to think of sb/sth (in the way mentioned) □ *menganggap; dianggap; memandang*: Do you regard this issue as important? ♦ Her work is highly regarded (= people have a high opinion of it). ♦ In some villages newcomers are regarded with suspicion. 2 (formal) to look at sb/sth for a while □ *memandang; memerhati*: She regarded us with interest. **IDM** as regards sb/sth (formal) in connection with sb/sth □ *berhubung atau berkenaan dgn sso/sst*: What are your views as regards this proposal?

regard² /rɪˈɡɑːd/ noun 1 [U] regard to/for sb/sth attention to or care for sb/sth □ *perhatian; sikap mengambil berat; mempedulikan*: He shows little regard for other people's feelings. 2 [U, sing] (a) regard (for sb/sth) a feeling of admiration for sb/sth; respect □ *rasa hormat; memandang tinggi*: She obviously **has** great **regard** for your ability. 3 regards [pl] (used especially to end a letter politely) kind thoughts; best wishes □ *salam (hormat, mesra, dsb)*: Please give my **regards** to your parents. ♦ Kind regards, Cecily **IDM** in/with regard to sb/sth; in this/that/one regard (formal) about sb/sth; connected with sb/sth □ *berhubung dgn atau mengenai sso/sst; dlm hal ini/itu*: With regard to the details—these will be finalized later.

regarding /rɪˈɡɑːdɪŋ/ prep (formal) about or in connection with □ *berkenaan dgn; mengenai; ttg*: Please write if you require further information regarding this matter.

regardless /rɪˈɡɑːdləs/ adv, prep regardless (of sb/sth) paying no attention to sb/sth; treating problems and difficulties as unimportant □ *tanpa menghiraukan; tdk kira*: I suggested she should stop but she **carried on regardless**. ♦ Everybody will receive the same, regardless of how long they've worked here.

regatta /rɪˈɡætə/ noun [C] an event at which there are boat races □ *perlumbaan perahu*

regenerate /rɪˈdʒenəreɪt/ verb [I,T] to grow again; to make sth grow or grow strong again □ *tumbuh semula; membentuk semula*: Once they have been destroyed, brain cells do not regenerate. ♦ The money will be used to regenerate the old part of the town. ▶ regeneration /rɪˌdʒenəˈreɪʃn/ noun [U]

reggae /ˈreɡeɪ/ noun [U] a type of West Indian music with a strong rhythm □ *(muzik) rege*

regime /reɪˈʒiːm/ noun [C] a method or system of government □ *rejim*: a military/fascist regime

regiment /ˈredʒɪmənt/ noun [C, with sing or pl verb] a group of soldiers in the army who are commanded by a **colonel** (= an officer of a high level) □ *rejimen* ▶ regimental /ˌredʒɪˈmentl/ adj

regimented /ˈredʒɪmentɪd/ adj (formal) (too) strictly controlled □ *dikawal/dikelolakan dgn terlalu ketat*

region /ˈriːdʒən/ noun [C] 1 a part of the country or the world; a large area of land □ *kawasan; rantau*: desert/tropical/polar regions ♦ This region of France is very mountainous. ⊃ note at **area** 2 an area of your body □ *bahagian*: He's been having pains in the region of his heart. **IDM** in the region of sth about or approximately □ *sekitar; kira-kira; dlm lingkungan*: There were somewhere in the region of 30 000 people at the rally.

regional /ˈriːdʒənl/ adj connected with a particular region □ *(berkenaan dgn) kawasan atau rantau*: regional accents ⊃ look at **local, international, national**

register¹ /ˈredʒɪstə(r)/ verb
▶PUT NAME ON LIST 1 [I,T] to put a name on an official list □ *mendaftar(kan); didaftar(kan)*: You should register with a doctor nearby. ♦ All births, deaths and marriages must be registered.
▶MEASUREMENT 2 [I,T] to show sth or to be shown on a measuring instrument □ *menunjukkan; mencatatkan; merakamkan*: The thermometer registered 32°C. ♦ The earthquake registered 6.4 on the Richter scale.
▶SHOW FEELING 3 [T] to show feelings, opinions, etc □ *menunjukkan; memperlihatkan*: Her face registered intense dislike.
▶NOTICE STH 4 [I,T] [often used in negative sentences] to notice sth and remember it; to be noticed and remembered □ *perasan; ingat*: He barely registered our presence. ♦ He told me his name but it didn't register.
▶LETTER 5 [T] to send a letter or package by **registered mail** □ *mengirim dgn pos berdaftar*: Parcels containing valuable goods should be registered.

register² /ˈredʒɪstə(r)/ noun 1 [C] an official list of names, etc. or a book that contains this kind of list □ *daftar*: The teacher calls the register first thing in the morning. ♦ the electoral register (= of people who are able to vote in an election) 2 [C,U] the type of language (formal or informal) that is used in a piece of writing □ *laras (bahasa)*: The essay suddenly switches from a formal to an informal register.

ˌregistered ˈmail (BrE also ˌregistered ˈpost) noun [U] a method of sending a letter

register office → rein

or package in which the person sending it can claim money if it arrives late or if it is lost or damaged □ *pos berdaftar*

register office = registry office

registrar /ˌredʒɪˈstrɑː(r); ˈredʒɪstrɑː(r)/ *noun* [C] **1** a person whose job is to keep official lists, especially of births, marriages and deaths □ *pendaftar* **2** a person who is responsible for keeping information about the students at a college or university □ *pendaftar*

registration /ˌredʒɪˈstreɪʃn/ *noun* [U] putting sb/sth's name on an official list □ *pendaftaran*: *Registration for evening classes will take place on 8 September.*

registration number *noun* [C] the numbers and letters on the front and back of a vehicle that are used to identify it □ *nombor pendaftaran*

registry /ˈredʒɪstri/ *noun* [C] (*pl* registries) a place where official lists are kept □ *pejabat pendaftaran*

registry office (also register office) *noun* [C] an office where a marriage can take place and where births, marriages and deaths are officially written down □ *pejabat pendaftaran (perkahwinan, kelahiran dan kematian)* ⊃ note at **wedding**

regret¹ /rɪˈɡret/ *verb* [T] (regretting; regretted) **1** to feel sorry that you did sth or that you did not do sth □ *menyesal*: *I hope you won't regret your decision later.* ♦ *Do you regret not taking the job?* **2** (*formal*) used as a way of saying that you are sorry for sth □ *kesal; meminta maaf*: *I regret to inform you that your application has been unsuccessful.*

regret² /rɪˈɡret/ *noun* [C,U] a feeling of sadness about sth that cannot now be changed □ *rasa sesal*: *Do you have any regrets about not going to university?* ▶ **regretful** /-fl/ *adj*: *a regretful look/smile* ▶ **regretfully** /-fəli/ *adv*

regrettable /rɪˈɡretəbl/ *adj* that you should feel sorry or sad about □ *patut disesali/dikesali*: *It is deeply regrettable that we were not informed sooner.* ▶ **regrettably** /-əbli/ *adv*

regular¹ /ˈreɡjələ(r)/ *adj*
▶AT SAME TIME **1** having the same amount of space or time between each thing or part □ *sekata; nalar; tetap*: *a regular heartbeat* ♦ *Nurses checked her blood pressure at regular intervals.* ♦ *The fire alarms are tested on a regular basis.* ♦ *We have regular meetings every Thursday.* **OPP** irregular
▶FREQUENT **2** done or happening often □ *selalu; kerap kali*: *The doctor advised me to take regular exercise.* ♦ *Accidents are a regular occurrence on this road.* **3** [only before a noun] going somewhere or doing sth often □ *biasa; kerap*: *a regular customer* ♦ *We're regular visitors to Britain.*
▶USUAL **4** [only before a noun] normal or usual □ *biasa*: *Who is your regular dentist?*
▶SAME SHAPE **5** not having any individual part that is different from the rest □ *sekata*: *regular teeth/features* ♦ *a regular pattern* **OPP** irregular
▶PERMANENT **6** fixed or permanent □ *tetap*: *a regular income/job* ♦ *a regular soldier/army*
▶ORDINARY **7** (*especially AmE*) standard, average or normal □ *biasa*: *Regular or large fries?*
▶GRAMMAR **8** (used about a noun, verb, etc.) having the usual or expected plural, verb form, etc. □ *malar*: *'Walk' is a regular verb.* **OPP** irregular
▶ **regularly** *adv*: *to have a car serviced regularly* ♦ *Ravi regularly takes part in competitions but this is the first one that he has won.* ▶ **regularity** /ˌreɡjuˈlærəti/ *noun* [U,C]: *My car breaks down with increasing regularity.*

regular² /ˈreɡjələ(r)/ *noun* [C] **1** (*informal*) a person who goes to a particular shop, bar, restaurant, etc. very often □ *pelanggan tetap* **2** a person who usually does a particular activity or sport □ *kaki (sst kegiatan atau sukan)* **3** a permanent member of the army, navy, etc. □ *askar tetap*

regulate /ˈreɡjuleɪt/ *verb* [T] **1** to control sth by using laws or rules □ *mengawal; mengatur* **2** to control a machine, piece of equipment, etc. □ *melaraskan*: *You can regulate the temperature in the car with this dial.*

regulation /ˌreɡjuˈleɪʃn/ *noun* **1** [C, usually pl] an official rule that controls how sth is done □ *peraturan*: *to observe/obey the safety regulations* ♦ *The plans must comply with EU regulations.* **2** [U] the control of sth by using rules □ *pengawalan*: *state regulation of imports and exports*

rehabilitate /ˌriːəˈbɪlɪteɪt/ *verb* [T] to help sb to live a normal life again after an illness, being in prison, etc. □ *memulihkan* ▶ **rehabilitation** /ˌriːəˌbɪlɪˈteɪʃn/ *noun* [U]: *a rehabilitation centre for drug addicts*

rehearsal /rɪˈhɜːsl/ *noun* [C,U] the time when you practise a play, dance, piece of music, etc. before you perform it to other people □ *latihan; raptai*: *a dress rehearsal* (= when all the actors wear their stage clothes) ▶ **rehearse** /rɪˈhɜːs/ *verb* [I,T]

reign /reɪn/ *verb* [I] **1** reign (over sb/sth) (used about a king or queen) to rule a country □ *memerintah* **2** reign (over sb/sth) to be the best or most important in a particular situation □ *menguasai; menerajui*: *the reigning world champion* **3** to be present as the most important quality of a particular situation □ *berleluasa; melanda*: *Chaos reigned after the first snow of winter.* ▶ **reign** *noun* [C]

reimburse /ˌriːɪmˈbɜːs/ *verb* [T] (*formal*) to pay money back to sb □ *membayar balik*: *The company will reimburse you in full for your travelling expenses.*

rein /reɪn/ *noun* [C, usually pl] a long narrow leather band that is attached to a metal bar in a horse's mouth and is held by the rider in order to control the horse □ *tali kekang* ⊃ picture at **horse**

reincarnation /ˌriːɪnkɑːˈneɪʃn/ noun 1 [U] the belief that people who have died can live again in a different body □ *penjelmaan semula*: *Do you believe in reincarnation?* 2 [C] a person or an animal whose body is believed to contain the spirit of a dead person □ *jelmaan semula*: *He believes he is the reincarnation of an Egyptian princess.* ⊃ look at **incarnation**

reindeer /ˈreɪndɪə(r)/ noun [C] (pl **reindeer**) a type of large brown wild animal with **antlers** (= horns shaped like branches), that lives in cold northern regions □ *rusa kutub*

antler

reindeer

reinforce /ˌriːɪnˈfɔːs/ verb [T] to make sth stronger □ *memperkuat; memperkukuh*: *Concrete can be reinforced with steel bars.* ♦ *She reinforced her argument with plenty of evidence.*

reinforcement /ˌriːɪnˈfɔːsmənt/ noun 1 **reinforcements** [pl] extra people who are sent to make an army, navy, etc. stronger □ *tenaga bantuan* 2 [U] the act of making sth stronger □ *pengukuhan; (perihal) memperteguh*: *The sea wall is weak in places and needs reinforcement.*

reinstate /ˌriːɪnˈsteɪt/ verb [T] 1 **reinstate sb (in/as sth)** to give back a job or position that was taken from sb □ *mengembalikan jawatan*: *He was cleared of the charge of theft and reinstated as Head of Security.* 2 to return sth to its former position or role □ *mengembalikan kedudukan; mendapat tempat* ▶ **reinstatement** noun [U]

reject¹ /rɪˈdʒekt/ verb [T] to refuse to accept sb/sth □ *menolak*: *The plan was rejected as being impractical.* ♦ *I've rejected all the candidates for the job except one.* ▶ **rejection** noun [C,U]: *Gargi got a rejection from Leeds University.* ♦ *There has been total rejection of the new policy.*

reject² /ˈriːdʒekt/ noun [C] a person or thing that is not accepted because he/she/it is not good enough □ *(sso/sst yg) ditolak*: *Rejects are sold at half price.*

rejoice /rɪˈdʒɔɪs/ verb [I] (formal) **rejoice (at/over sth)** to feel or show great happiness □ *berasa gembira; bergembira* ▶ **rejoicing** noun [U]: *There were scenes of rejoicing when the war ended.*

rejuvenate /rɪˈdʒuːvəneɪt/ verb [T, often passive] to make sb/sth feel or look younger □ *mempermuda* ▶ **rejuvenation** /rɪˌdʒuːvəˈneɪʃn/ noun [U]

relapse /rɪˈlæps/ verb [I] to become worse again after an improvement □ *berbalik (semula); kambuh*: *to relapse into bad habits* ▶ **relapse** /ˈriːlæps/ noun [C]: *The patient had a relapse and then died.*

relate /rɪˈleɪt/ verb [T] 1 **relate A to/with B** to show or make a connection between two or more things □ *mengaitkan*: *The report relates heart disease to high levels of stress.* 2 (formal) **relate sth (to sb)** to tell a story to sb □ *menceritakan*: *He related his side of the story to a journalist.*

PHR V relate to sb/sth 1 to be concerned or involved with sth □ *berkenaan dgn sso/sst*: *That question is very interesting but it doesn't really relate to the subject that we're discussing.* 2 to be able to understand how sb feels □ *memahami*: *Some teenagers find it hard to relate to their parents.*

related /rɪˈleɪtɪd/ adj **related (to sb/sth)** 1 connected with sb/sth □ *berkait; ada kaitan; berkaitan*: *The rise in the cost of living is directly related to the price of oil.* 2 of the same family □ *bersaudara*: *We are related by marriage.*

relation /rɪˈleɪʃn/ noun 1 **relations** [pl] **relations (with sb); relations (between A and B)** the way that people, groups, countries, etc. feel about or behave towards each other □ *hubungan*: *The police officer stressed that good relations with the community were essential.* 2 [C,U] **relation (between sth and sth); relation (to sth)** the connection between two or more things □ *perkaitan; kaitan*: *There seems to be little relation between the cost of the houses and their size.* ♦ *Their salaries bear no relation to the number of hours they work.* 3 [C] a member of your family □ *saudara; sanak saudara*: *a near/close/distant relation* **SYN** relative

HELP Note the expressions: *What relation are you to each other?* (= Are you sisters, cousins, etc.?) and *Are you any relation to each other?*

IDM in/with relation to sb/sth 1 concerning sb/sth □ *berkenaan dgn atau berkaitan dgn sso/sst*: *Many questions were asked, particularly in relation to the cost of the new buildings.* 2 compared with □ *berbanding dgn*: *Prices are low in relation to those in other parts of Europe.*

relationship /rɪˈleɪʃnʃɪp/ noun 1 [C] **a relationship (with sb/sth)** the way that people, groups, countries, etc. feel about or behave towards each other □ *hubungan*: *The relationship between the parents and the school has improved greatly.* 2 [C] **a relationship (with sb); a relationship (between A and B)** a friendly or loving connection between people □ *hubungan*: *to have a relationship with somebody* ♦ *He'd never been in a serious relationship before he got married.* ♦ *The film describes the relationship between a young man and an older woman.* ♦ *Do you have a close relationship with your brother?* 3 [C,U] **a relationship (to sb); a relationship (between A and B)** the way in which two or more things are connected □ *hubungan; kaitan*: *Is there a relationship between violence on TV and the increase in crime?* 4 [C,U] **a relationship (to sb); a relationship (between A and B)** a family connection □ *hubungan (persaudaraan)*: *'What is your relationship to Bruce?' 'He's married to my cousin.'*

relative¹ /ˈrelətɪv/ adj 1 **relative (to sth)** when compared to sb/sth else □ *relatif; berbanding* *dgn; agak*: *the position of the earth relative to the sun* ♦ *They live in relative luxury.* **2** referring to an earlier noun, phrase or sentence □ *relatif*: *In the phrase 'the lady who lives next door', 'who' is a relative pronoun.* ❶ For more information about relative pronouns and clauses, look at the **Reference Section** at the back of this dictionary.

relative² /ˈrelətɪv/ *noun* [C] a member of your family □ *(sanak) saudara*: *a close/distant relative* **SYN** relation

relatively /ˈrelətɪvli/ *adv* to quite a large degree, especially when compared to others □ *agak*: *Spanish is a relatively easy language to learn.*

relax /rɪˈlæks/ *verb* **1** [I] to rest while you are doing sth enjoyable, especially after work or effort □ *bersenang-senang; santai*: *This holiday will give you a chance to relax.* ♦ *They spent the evening relaxing in front of the TV.* **SYN** unwind **2** [I] to become calmer and less worried □ *bertenang; menenangkan*: *Relax—everything's going to be OK!*

> **MORE** In informal English **chill out** and **take it easy** can be used instead of **relax**.

3 [I,T] to become or make sb/sth become less hard or tight □ *mengurangkan ketegangan; mengendurkan*: *You should be able to feel all your muscles relaxing.* ♦ *A hot bath will relax you after a hard day's work.* ♦ *Don't relax your grip on the rope!* **4** [T] to make rules or laws less strict □ *melonggarkan; mengendurkan*: *The regulations on importing animals have been relaxed.*

relaxation /ˌriːlækˈseɪʃn/ *noun* **1** [C,U] a way or ways to rest and enjoy yourself, especially after work or effort □ *kegiatan utk bersantai atau berehat*: *Everyone needs time for rest and relaxation.* **2** [U] making sth less strict, tight or strong □ *pengenduran; pelonggaran*

relaxed /rɪˈlækst/ *adj* not worried or tense □ *tenang; tdk tegang; santai*: *I felt surprisingly relaxed before my interview.* ♦ *The relaxed atmosphere made everyone feel at ease.* **SYN** calm ➲ look at **stressed**

relaxing /rɪˈlæksɪŋ/ *adj* pleasant, helping you to rest and become less worried □ *menenangkan; merehatkan*: *a quiet relaxing holiday*

relay¹ /ˈriːleɪ; ˌriːˈleɪ/ *verb* [T] (*pt, pp* **relayed**) **1** to receive and then pass on a signal or message □ *menyampaikan*: *Instructions were relayed to us by phone.* **2** to put a programme on the radio or TV □ *menyiarkan*

relay² /ˈriːleɪ/ (also ˈrelay race) *noun* [C] a race in which each member of a team runs, swims, etc. one part of the race □ *lari berganti-ganti*

release¹ /rɪˈliːs/ *verb* [T]
▶SET FREE **1 release sb/sth (from sth)** to allow sb/sth to be free □ *membebaskan; melepaskan*: *He's been released from prison.* ♦ (*figurative*) *His firm released him for two days a week to go on a training course.*
▶STOP HOLDING STH **2** to stop holding sth so that it can move, fly, fall, etc. freely □ *melepaskan*: *1 000 balloons were released at the ceremony.* ♦ (*figurative*) *Crying is a good way to release pent-up emotions.*
▶MOVE STH **3** to move sth from a fixed position □ *melepaskan*: *He released the handbrake and drove off.*
▶MAKE PUBLIC **4** to allow sth to be known by the public □ *mengumumkan; diumumkan*: *The identity of the victim has not been released.* **5** to make a film, CD, etc. available so the public can see or hear it □ *mengeluarkan; menayangkan; menerbitkan*: *Their new album is due to be released next week.*

release² /rɪˈliːs/ *noun* [C,U] **1 (a) release (of sb/sth) (from sth)** the freeing of sb/sth or the state of being freed □ *pembebasan; kelegaan*: *The release of the hostages took place this morning.* ♦ *the release of carbon dioxide into the atmosphere* ♦ *I had a great feeling of release when my exams were finished.* **2** a book, film, CD, piece of news, etc. that has been made available to the public; the act of making sth available to the public □ *sst yg baru diterbitkan, dikeluarkan, disiarkan atau ditayangkan*: *a press release* ♦ *The band played their latest release.* ♦ *The film won't be/go on release until March.*

relegate /ˈrelɪɡeɪt/ *verb* [T] to put sb/sth into a lower level or position □ *menurunkan (kedudukan, dsb)*: *She was relegated to the role of assistant.* ♦ *The football team finished bottom and were relegated to the second division.* ▶**relegation** /ˌrelɪˈɡeɪʃn/ *noun* [U]

relent /rɪˈlent/ *verb* [I] **1** to finally agree to sth that you had refused □ *menjadi lembut hati atau kurang berkeras*: *Her parents finally relented and allowed her to go to the concert.* **2** to become less determined, strong, etc. □ *mereda*: *The heavy rain finally relented and we went out.*

relentless /rɪˈlentləs/ *adj* not stopping or changing □ *tdk henti-henti*: *the relentless fight against crime* ▶**relentlessly** *adv*: *The sun beat down relentlessly.*

relevant /ˈreləvənt/ *adj* **relevant (to sb/sth)** **1** connected with what is happening or being talked about □ *berkaitan; relevan*: *Much of what was said was not directly relevant to my case.* **2** important and useful □ *relevan; penting dan berguna*: *Many people feel that poetry is no longer relevant in today's world.* **OPP** for both meanings **irrelevant** ▶**relevance** *noun* [U]: *I honestly can't see the relevance of what he said.*

> **EXAM TIP**
>
> **Relevant information**
>
> When you are writing or speaking in an exam, it is important to only include relevant information in your answers. If you give information that is not relevant, you risk wasting time and losing marks.

reliable /rɪˈlaɪəbl/ adj that you can trust □ *boleh dipercayai/diharap*: *Japanese cars are usually very reliable.* ◆ *Is he a reliable witness?* ▸ **unreliable** ⊃ verb **rely** ▶**reliability** /rɪˌlaɪəˈbɪləti/ noun [U] ▶**reliably** /rɪˈlaɪəbli/ adv: *I have been reliably informed that there will be no trains tomorrow.*

reliance /rɪˈlaɪəns/ noun [U] **reliance on sb/sth 1** being able to trust sb/sth □ *(perihal) mempercayai*: *Don't place too much reliance on her promises.* **2** the fact of not being able to live or work without sb/sth □ *kebergantungan; pergantungan*: *the country's reliance on imported oil* ▸**SYN** **dependence** ⊃ verb **rely**

reliant /rɪˈlaɪənt/ adj **reliant on sb/sth** not able to live or work without sb/sth □ *bergantung pd*: *They are totally reliant on the state for financial support.* ▸**SYN** **dependent** ⊃ look at **self-reliant** ⊃ verb **rely**

relic /ˈrelɪk/ noun [C] an object, custom, etc. from the past that still survives today □ *peninggalan; relik*

relief /rɪˈliːf/ noun **1** [U, sing] **relief (from sth)** the feeling that you have when sth unpleasant stops or becomes less strong □ *lega*: *The drugs brought him some relief from the pain.* ◆ *What a relief! That awful noise has stopped.* ◆ *It was a great relief to know they were safe.* ◆ *to breathe a sigh of relief* ◆ *To my relief, he didn't argue with my suggestion at all.* **2** [U] the act of removing or reducing pain, worry, etc. □ *kelegaan*: *These tablets provide pain relief for up to four hours.* **3** [U] money or food that is given to help people who are in trouble or difficulty □ *bantuan*: *disaster relief for the flood victims* ▸**SYN** **aid 4** [U] a reduction in the amount of tax you have to pay □ *pelepasan cukai*

relieve /rɪˈliːv/ verb [T] to make an unpleasant feeling or situation stop or get better □ *melegakan; mengurangkan*: *This injection should relieve the pain.* ◆ *We played cards to relieve the boredom.* ▸**PHR V** **relieve sb of sth** (*formal*) to take sth away from sb □ *melepaskan sso drpd sst (tugas, tanggungjawab, dll)*: *General Scott was relieved of his command.*

relieved /rɪˈliːvd/ adj pleased because your fear or worry has been taken away □ *berasa lega*: *I was very relieved to hear that you weren't seriously hurt.*

religion /rɪˈlɪdʒən/ noun **1** [U] the belief in a god or gods and the activities connected with this □ *agama*: *I never discuss politics or religion.* **2** [C] one of the systems of beliefs that is based on a belief in a god or gods □ *agama*: *the Christian/Hindu/Muslim/Sikh religion*

religious /rɪˈlɪdʒəs/ adj **1** [only before a noun] connected with religion □ *(berkenaan dgn) agama*: *religious faith* **2** having a strong belief in a religion □ *warak*: *a deeply religious person*

religiously /rɪˈlɪdʒəsli/ adv **1** very carefully or regularly □ *dgn teliti/tekun*: *She stuck to the diet religiously.* **2** in a religious way □ *dgn warak*

relinquish /rɪˈlɪŋkwɪʃ/ verb [T] (*formal*) to stop having or doing sth □ *melepaskan; meninggalkan* ⊃ A more common expression is **give up**.

relish¹ /ˈrelɪʃ/ verb [T] to enjoy sth very much or wait with pleasure for sth to happen □ *menikmati; berasa seronok*: *I don't relish the prospect of getting up early tomorrow.*

relish² /ˈrelɪʃ/ noun **1** [U] (*written*) great enjoyment □ *keseronokan; penuh nikmat*: *She accepted the award with obvious relish.* **2** [U,C] a thick, cold sauce made from fruit and vegetables □ *sejenis acar*

relive /ˌriːˈlɪv/ verb [T] to remember sth and imagine that it is happening again □ *mengenang kembali; terbayang semula*

reload /ˌriːˈləʊd/ verb [I,T] to put sth into a machine again □ *mengisi semula*: *The shooting stopped while he reloaded.* ◆ *to reload a disk into a computer*

reluctant /rɪˈlʌktənt/ adj **reluctant (to do sth)** not wanting to do sth because you are not sure it is the right thing to do □ *agak enggan/ keberatan* ▶**reluctance** noun [U]: *Tony left with obvious reluctance.* ▶**reluctantly** adv

rely /rɪˈlaɪ/ verb [I] (**relying; relies;** *pt, pp* **relied**) ▸**PHR V** **rely on/upon sb/sth (to do sth) 1** to need sb/sth and not be able to live or work properly without them or it □ *berharap; bergantung*: *The old lady had to rely on other people to do her shopping for her.* **2** to trust sb/sth to work or behave well □ *percaya*: *Can I rely on you to keep a secret?* ⊃ look at **reliable, reliant** ⊃ noun **reliance**

remain /rɪˈmeɪn/ verb [I] **1** to stay or continue in the same place or condition □ *kekal; tetap; tinggal*: *to remain silent/standing/seated* ◆ *Josef went to live in America but his family remained behind in Europe.* ⊃ note at **stay 2** to be left after other people or things have gone □ *tinggal*: *Today only a few stones remain of the castle.* ◆ *to remain behind after class* **3** to still need to be done, said or dealt with □ *masih belum*: *It remains to be seen* (= we do not know yet) *whether we've made the right decision.* ◆ *Although he seems very pleasant, the fact remains that I don't trust him.*

remainder /rɪˈmeɪndə(r)/ noun [sing, with sing or pl verb] *usually* **the remainder** the people, things, etc. that are left after the others have gone away or been dealt with; the rest □ *baki; selebihnya; yg tinggal*

remaining /rɪˈmeɪnɪŋ/ adj [only before a noun] still needing to be done or dealt with □ *yg tinggal*: *The remaining twenty patients were transferred to another hospital.* ◆ *Any remaining tickets for the concert will be sold on the door.*

remains /rɪˈmeɪnz/ noun [pl] **1** what is left behind after other parts have been used or taken away □ *sisa; peninggalan*: *The builders found the remains of a Roman mosaic floor.* **2** (*formal*) a dead body (sometimes one that has been found somewhere a long time after death) □ *mayat*: *Human remains were discovered in the wood.*

remand /rɪˈmɑːnd/ *noun* [U] the time before a prisoner's trial takes place □ *tahanan*: *a remand prisoner*
IDM **on remand** (used about a prisoner) waiting for the trial to take place □ *dlm tahanan*
▶**remand** *verb* [T]: *The man was remanded in custody* (= kept in prison until the trial).

remark¹ /rɪˈmɑːk/ *verb* [I,T] **remark (on/upon sb/sth)** to say or write sth □ *berkata; mengatakan; membuat komen*: *A lot of people have remarked on the similarity between them.* **SYN** **comment** ⊃ look at **observation**

remark² /rɪˈmɑːk/ *noun* [C] something that you say or write about sb/sth □ *catatan*: *The teacher added a few personal remarks at the bottom of the page.* ◆ *He made a number of rude remarks about the food.*

remarkable /rɪˈmɑːkəbl/ *adj* unusual and surprising in a way that people notice □ *luar biasa*: *That is a remarkable achievement for someone so young.* **SYN** **astonishing** ▶**remarkably** /-əbli/ *adv*

remedial /rɪˈmiːdiəl/ *adj* [only *before* a noun] **1** aimed at improving or correcting a situation □ *pemulihan* **2** helping people who are slow at learning sth □ *pemulihan*: *remedial English classes*

remedy¹ /ˈremədi/ *noun* [C] (*pl* **remedies**) **a remedy (for sth)** **1** a way of solving a problem □ *cara menyelesaikan/mengatasi (sst)*: *There is no easy remedy for unemployment.* **SYN** **solution** **2** something that makes you better when you are ill or in pain □ *ubat; rawatan*: *Hot lemon with honey is a good remedy for colds.*

remedy² /ˈremədi/ *verb* [T] (**remedying**; **remedies**; *pt*, *pp* **remedied**) to change or improve sth that is wrong or bad □ *membetulkan; memperbaiki*: *to remedy an injustice*

remember /rɪˈmembə(r)/ *verb* [I,T] **1** **remember (sb/sth)**; **remember (doing sth)**; **remember that ...** to have sb/sth in your mind or to bring sb/sth back into your mind □ *ingat*: *We arranged to go out tonight—remember?* ◆ *As far as I can remember, I haven't seen him before.* ◆ *I'm sorry. I don't remember your name.* ◆ *Do you remember meeting him for the first time?* ◆ *Remember that we're having visitors tonight.* ◆ *Can you remember when we bought the stereo?* **2** **remember (sth/to do sth)** to not forget to do what you have to do □ *ingat; jangan lupa; tdk lupa*: *Did you remember your camera?* ◆ *Remember to turn the lights off before you leave.*

GRAMMAR If you **remember to do sth**, you don't forget to do it: *It's my mother's birthday. I must remember to phone her.* If you **remember doing sth**, you have a picture or memory in your mind of doing it: *Do you remember going to the cinema for the first time?*

IDM **remember me to sb** used when you want to send good wishes to a person you have not seen for a long time □ *sampaikan salam saya kpd (sso)*: *Please remember me to your parents.* ⊃ note at **remind**

remembrance /rɪˈmembrəns/ *noun* [U] (*formal*) thinking about and showing respect for sb who is dead □ *peringatan; memperingati*: *a service in remembrance of those killed in the war*

remind /rɪˈmaɪnd/ *verb* [T] **1** **remind sb (about/of sth)**; **remind sb (to do sth/that ...)** to help sb to remember sth, especially sth important that they have to do □ *mengingatkan; ingatkan*: *Can you remind me of your address?* ◆ *He reminded the children to wash their hands.* ◆ *Remind me what we're supposed to be doing tomorrow.* **2** **remind sb of sb/sth** to cause sb to remember sb/sth □ *mengingatkan; teringat*: *That smell reminds me of school.* ◆ *You remind me of your father.*

HELP You **remember** something by yourself. If somebody or something **reminds** you of something, he/she/it causes you to remember it: *Did you remember to phone Ali last night?* ◆ *Please remind me to phone Ali later.*

reminder /rɪˈmaɪndə(r)/ *noun* [C] something that makes you remember sth □ *peringatan*: *We received a reminder that we hadn't paid the electricity bill.*

reminisce /ˌremɪˈnɪs/ *verb* [I] **reminisce (about sb/sth)** to talk about pleasant things that happened in the past □ *mengenang kembali*

reminiscent /ˌremɪˈnɪsnt/ *adj* [not *before* a noun] that makes you remember sb/sth; similar to □ *mengingatkan (sso kpd sst yg serupa)*: *His suit was strongly reminiscent of an old army uniform.*

remnant /ˈremnənt/ *noun* [C] a piece of sth that is left after the rest has gone □ *saki-baki; reja; yg tinggal*: *These few trees are the remnants of a huge forest.*

remorse /rɪˈmɔːs/ *noun* [U] **remorse (for sth/doing sth)** a feeling of sadness because you have done sth wrong □ *sesal; penyesalan*: *She was filled with remorse for what she had done.* ⊃ look at **guilt** ▶**remorseful** /-fl/ *adj* ▶**remorsefully** /-fəli/ *adv*

remorseless /rɪˈmɔːsləs/ *adj* **1** not stopping or becoming less strong □ *tdk henti-henti; tanpa berkurang*: *a remorseless attack on somebody* **2** showing no pity □ *tanpa belas kasihan*: *a remorseless killer* ▶**remorselessly** *adv*

remote /rɪˈməʊt/ *adj* (**remoter**; **remotest**) **1** **remote (from sth)** far away from where other people live □ *terpencil*: *a remote island in the Pacific* **2** [only *before* a noun] far away in time □ *masa silam/depan yg jauh; dahulu kala*: *the remote past/future* **3** not very friendly or interested in other people □ *dingin; suka menyendiri*: *He seemed rather remote.* **4** not very great □ *sedikit; tipis; kecil*: *I haven't the remotest idea who* *could have done such a thing.* ◆ *a remote possibility* ▶**remoteness** *noun* [U]

re|mote con|trol *noun* 1 [U] a system for controlling sth from a distance □ *kawalan jauh*: *The doors can be opened by remote control.* 2 (also **remote**) [C] a piece of equipment for controlling sth from a distance □ *alat kawalan jauh*

remotely /rɪˈməʊtli/ *adv* (used in negative sentences) to a very small degree; at all □ *sedikit pun (tdk); langsung (tdk)*: *I'm not remotely interested in your problems.*

removal /rɪˈmuːvl/ *noun* 1 [U] the act of taking sb/sth away □ *penyingkiran; pembatalan*: *the removal of restrictions/regulations/rights* 2 [C,U] the activity of moving from one house to live in another □ *pemindahan; berpindah*: *a removal van*

remove /rɪˈmuːv/ *verb* [T] (*formal*) 1 **remove sb/sth (from sth)** to take sb/sth off or away □ *mengalihkan; menanggalkan; menghilangkan; mengeluarkan; membuang*: *Remove the saucepan from the heat.* ◆ *This washing powder will remove most stains.* ◆ *to remove doubts/fears/problems* ◆ *I would like you to remove my name from your mailing list.* ◆ *He had an operation to remove the tumour.* ⊃ Less formal expressions are **take off, out,** etc. 2 **remove sb (from sth)** to make sb leave their job or position □ *menyingkirkan*: *The person responsible for the error has been removed from his post.*

removed /rɪˈmuːvd/ *adj* [not before a noun] far or different from sth □ *jauh berbeza*: *Hospitals today are far removed from what they were fifty years ago.*

remover /rɪˈmuːvə(r)/ *noun* [C,U] a substance that cleans off paint, dirty marks, etc. □ *penanggal; penghilang*: *make-up remover*

the Renaissance /rɪˈneɪsns/ *noun* [sing] the period in Europe during the 14th, 15th and 16th centuries when people became interested in the ideas and culture of ancient Greece and Rome, and used these influences in their own art, literature, etc □ *Zaman Renaissance*: *Renaissance art*

render /ˈrendə(r)/ *verb* [T] (*formal*) 1 to cause sb/sth to be in a certain condition □ *memberi; menghulur*: *She was rendered speechless by the criticism.* 2 to give help, etc. to sb □ *menyebabkan; membuat*: *to render somebody a service/render a service to somebody*

rendezvous /ˈrɒndɪvuː; -deɪ-/ *noun* [C] (*pl* **rendezvous** /-vuːz/) 1 **a rendezvous (with sb)** a meeting that you have arranged with sb □ *janji temu; pertemuan*: *He had a secret rendezvous with Daniela.* 2 a place where people often meet □ *tempat pertemuan*: *The cafe is a popular rendezvous for students.*

rendition /renˈdɪʃn/ *noun* [C] the performance of sth, especially a song or piece of music; the particular way in which it is performed □ *persembahan; penyampaian*

721 remote control → renunciation

renegade /ˈrenɪɡeɪd/ *noun* [C] [often used as an adjective] (*formal*) (usually used in a critical way) a person who leaves one political, religious, etc. group to join another that has very different views or beliefs □ *orang yg keluar drpd agama, kumpulan politik dsb; yg murtad; pembelot; pengkhianat*

renew /rɪˈnjuː/ *verb* [T] 1 to start sth again □ *memulakan semula; tercetus kembali; menjalin semula*: *renewed outbreaks of violence* ◆ *to renew a friendship* 2 to do sth with new strength or energy □ *memulihkan; menyegarkan*: *After a break he set to work with renewed enthusiasm.* 3 to make sth valid for a further period of time □ *membaharui*: *to renew a contract/passport/library book* ▶**renewal** /rɪˈnjuːəl/ *noun* [C,U]: *When is your passport due for renewal?*

renewable /rɪˈnjuːəbl/ *adj* 1 (used about sources of energy) that can be replaced naturally □ *boleh dibaharui*: *renewable resources such as wind and solar power* **OPP** **non-renewable** ⊃ note at **environment** 2 that can be continued or replaced with a new one for another period of time □ *boleh dibaharui*: *The contract is for two years but it is renewable.*

renounce /rɪˈnaʊns/ *verb* [T] (*formal*) to say formally that you no longer want to have sth or to be connected with sb/sth □ *melepaskan; meninggalkan; menolak; tdk mengaku* ⊃ *noun* **renunciation**

renovate /ˈrenəveɪt/ *verb* [T] to repair an old building and put it back into good condition □ *memperbaiki; membaik pulih; mengubah suai* ⊃ note at **house** ▶**renovation** /ˌrenəˈveɪʃn/ *noun* [C,U]: *The house is in need of renovation.*

renown /rɪˈnaʊn/ *noun* [U] (*formal*) fame and respect that you get for doing sth especially well □ *terkenal; kemasyhuran; masyhur* ▶**renowned** *adj* **renowned (for/as sth)**: *The region is renowned for its food.*

rent¹ /rent/ *noun* [U,C] money that you pay regularly for the use of land, a house or a building □ *sewa*: *a high/low rent* ◆ *She was allowed to live there rent-free until she found a job.* ◆ *Is this house for rent* (= available to rent)?

rent² /rent/ *verb* [T] 1 **rent sth (from sb)** to pay money for the use of land, a building, a machine, etc. □ *menyewa; menyewakan*: *Do you own or rent your flat?* ◆ *to rent a car* ⊃ note at **flat, hire** 2 **rent sth (out) (to sb)** to allow sb to use land, a building, a machine, etc. for money □ *menyewakan*: *We could rent out the small bedroom to a student.* ⊃ look at **hire** 3 (*AmE*) = **hire¹** (1) ▶**rented** *adj*: *a rented house*

rental /ˈrentl/ *noun* [C,U] money that you pay when you rent a telephone, car, etc. □ *sewa*

renunciation /rɪˌnʌnsiˈeɪʃn/ *noun* [U] (*formal*) saying that you no longer want sth or believe in sth □ *pelepasan; penolakan; (perihal) meninggalkan/tdk mengaku* ⊃ *verb* **renounce**

reorganize → replace

reorganize (also **-ise**) /riˈɔːɡənaɪz/ verb [I,T] to organize sth again or in a new way □ *menyusun semula* ▶**reorganization** (also **-isation**) /ˌriːˌɔːɡənaɪˈzeɪʃn/ noun [C,U]: *reorganization of the school system*

Rep. abbr = **Republican**(2)

rep /rep/ (also formal **representative**) noun [C] a person whose job is to travel round a particular area and visit companies, etc., to sell the products of a particular firm □ *wakil*: *a sales rep for a drinks company*

repair¹ /rɪˈpeə(r)/ verb [T] to put sth old or damaged back into good condition □ *membaiki*: *These cars can be expensive to repair.* ◆ *How much will it cost to have the TV repaired?* **SYN** **fix, mend** ⊃ look at **irreparable**

repair² /rɪˈpeə(r)/ noun [C,U] something that you do to fix sth that is damaged □ *kerja membaiki*: *The school is closed for repairs to the roof.* ◆ *The road is in need of repair.* ◆ *The bridge is under repair.* ◆ *The bike was damaged beyond repair so I threw it away.*
IDM **in good, bad, etc. repair** in a good, bad, etc. condition □ *dlm keadaan baik, teruk, dll*

repatriate /ˌriːˈpætrieɪt/ verb [T] to send or bring sb back to their own country □ *menghantar pulang* ▶**repatriation** /ˌriːˌpætriˈeɪʃn/ noun [C,U]

repay /rɪˈpeɪ/ verb [T] (pt, pp **repaid** /rɪˈpeɪd/) **1** **repay sth (to sb); repay (sb) sth** to pay back money that you owe to sb □ *membayar balik*: *to repay a debt/loan* ◆ *When will you repay the money to them?* ◆ *When will you repay them the money?* **2** **repay sb (for sth)** to give sth to sb in return for help, kindness, etc. □ *membalas; membayar balik*: *How can I ever repay you for all you have done for me?*

repayable /rɪˈpeɪəbl/ adj that you can or must pay back □ *yg boleh atau mesti dibayar balik*: *The loan is repayable over three years.*

repayment /rɪˈpeɪmənt/ noun **1** [U] paying sth back □ *pembayaran balik*: *the repayment of a loan* **2** [C] money that you must pay back to sb/sth regularly □ *bayaran balik*: *I make monthly repayments on my loan.*

repeal /rɪˈpiːl/ verb [T] (formal) to officially make a law no longer valid □ *memansuhkan*

repeat¹ /rɪˈpiːt/ verb **1** [I,T] **repeat (sth/yourself)** to say, write or do sth again or more than once □ *mengulang*: *Don't repeat the same mistake again.* ◆ *Could you repeat what you just said?* ◆ *The essay is quite good, but you repeat yourself several times.* ◆ *Raise your left leg ten times, then repeat with the right.* **2** [T] **repeat sth (to sb)** to say or write sth that sb else has said or written or that you have learnt □ *mengulangi; ulang; menceritakan balik*: *Please don't repeat what you've heard here to anyone.* ◆ *Repeat each sentence after me.* ⊃ noun **repetition**

repeat² /rɪˈpiːt/ noun [C] something that is done, shown, given, etc. again □ *ulangan*: *I think I've seen this programme before—it must be a repeat.*

repeated /rɪˈpiːtɪd/ adj [only before a noun] done or happening many times □ *berulang kali*: *There have been repeated accidents on this stretch of road.* ▶**repeatedly** adv: *I've asked him repeatedly not to leave his bicycle there.*

repel /rɪˈpel/ verb [T] (**repelling; repelled**) **1** to send or push sb/sth back or away □ *menolak; menangkis* **2** to make sb feel disgusted □ *menimbulkan rasa jijik*: *The dirt and smell repelled her.* ⊃ adjective **repulsive**

repellent¹ /rɪˈpelənt/ adj (formal) causing a strong feeling of disgust □ *(yg) menjijikkan*: *a repellent smell*

repellent² /rɪˈpelənt/ noun [C,U] a chemical substance that is used to keep insects, etc. away □ *bahan pencegah/penghalau*: *a mosquito repellent*

repent /rɪˈpent/ verb [I,T] (formal) **repent (sth/of sth)** to feel and show that you are sorry about sth bad that you have done □ *bertaubat; menyesali*: *He later repented his hasty decision.* ◆ *to repent of your sins* ▶**repentance** noun [U] ▶**repentant** adj

repercussion /ˌriːpəˈkʌʃn/ noun [C, usually pl] an unpleasant effect or result of sth you do □ *akibat; kesan*: *His resignation will have serious repercussions.*

repertoire /ˈrepətwɑː(r)/ noun [C] **1** all the plays or music that an actor or a musician knows and can perform □ *repertoir*: *He must have sung every song in his repertoire last night.* **2** all the things that a person is able to do □ *himpunan*

repetition /ˌrepəˈtɪʃn/ noun [U,C] the action of doing sth again; something that you do or that happens again □ *pengulangan; berulang lagi*: *to learn by repetition* ◆ *Let's try to avoid a repetition of what happened last Friday.* ▶**repetitious** /ˌrepəˈtɪʃəs/ adj: *a long and repetitious speech* ⊃ verb **repeat**

repetitive /rɪˈpetətɪv/ adj not interesting because the same thing is repeated many times □ *diulang-ulang; balik-balik itu*

rephrase /ˌriːˈfreɪz/ verb [T] to say or write sth using different words in order to make the meaning clearer □ *menyusun semula; pemfrasaan semula menyatakan dlm perkataan lain*

replace /rɪˈpleɪs/ verb [T] **1** to take the place of sb/sth; to use sb/sth in place of another person or thing □ *menggantikan*: *Teachers will never be replaced by computers in the classroom.* **2** **replace sb/sth (with/by sb/sth)** to exchange sb/sth for sb/sth that is better or newer □ *mengganti balik*: *We will replace any goods that are damaged.* **3** to put sth back in the place where it was before □ *meletakkan balik*: *Please replace the books on the shelves when you have finished with them.* ⊃ A more common and less formal expression is **put back**.

ð **then**   s **so**   z **zoo**   ʃ **she**   ʒ **vi**s**ion**   h **how**   m **man**   n **no**   ŋ **si**ng   l **leg**   r **red**   j **yes**   w **wet**

replaceable /rɪˈpleɪsəbl/ adj that can be replaced □ *(yg) boleh diganti* **OPP** **irreplaceable**

replacement /rɪˈpleɪsmənt/ noun 1 [U] exchanging sb/sth for sb/sth that is better or newer □ *penggantian; (perihal) mengganti/diganti*: *The carpets are in need of replacement.* 2 [C] a person or thing that will take the place of sb/sth □ *pengganti*: *Mary is leaving next month so we must advertise for a replacement for her.*

replay¹ /ˈriːpleɪ/ noun [C] 1 a sports match that is played again because neither team won the first time □ *perlawanan semula* 2 something on TV, on a DVD, etc. that you watch or listen to again □ *ulangan; ulang tayang*: *Now let's see an action replay of that tremendous goal!*

replay² /ˌriːˈpleɪ/ verb [T] 1 to play a sports match, etc. again because neither team won the first time □ *mengadakan perlawanan semula* 2 to play again sth that you have recorded □ *memainkan/menayangkan semula*: *They kept replaying the goal over and over again.*

replenish /rɪˈplenɪʃ/ verb [T] **replenish sth (with sth)** (formal) to make sth full again by replacing what has been used □ *menambahkan lagi, mengisi lagi*: *to replenish food and water supplies*

replica /ˈreplɪkə/ noun [C] **a replica (of sth)** an exact copy of sth □ *replika; salinan tepat*

replicate /ˈreplɪkeɪt/ verb [T] (formal) to copy sth exactly □ *mereplikakan; menyalin dgn tepat* **SYN** **duplicate** ▶ **replication** /ˌreplɪˈkeɪʃn/ noun [U]

ⸯreply /rɪˈplaɪ/ verb [I,T] (replying; replies; pt, pp replied) **reply (to sb/sth) (with sth)** to say, write or do sth as an answer to sb/sth □ *menjawab; jawab*: *I wrote to Sue but she hasn't replied.* ♦ *'Yes, I will,' she replied.* ♦ *to reply to a question* ♦ *Brazil replied to Chile's early goal with a penalty.* ◯ note at **answer²** ▶ **reply** noun [C,U] (pl **replies**): *Al nodded in reply to my question.*

ⸯreport¹ /rɪˈpɔːt/ verb 1 [I,T] **report (to sb/sth) (on sb/sth); report (to sb)** to give people information about what you have seen, heard, done, etc. □ *melaporkan; mengatakan; memberitahu; menunjukkan*: *The research team will report to the committee on their findings next month.* ♦ *The company reported huge profits last year.* ♦ *Several people reported seeing/having seen the boy.* ♦ *Several people reported that they had seen the boy.* ♦ *Call me if you have anything new to report.* 2 [I,T] **report (on) sth** (in a newspaper or on the TV or radio) to write or speak about sth that has happened □ *melaporkan*: *The paper sent a journalist to report on the events.* 3 [T] (formal) **be reported to be/as sth** used to say that you have heard sth said, but you are not sure if it is true □ *mengatakan; dikatakan*: *The 70-year-old actor is reported to be/as being comfortable in hospital.* 4 [T] **report sb/sth (to sb) (for sth)** to tell a person in authority about an accident, a crime, etc. or about sth wrong that sb has done □ *melaporkan; mengadu*: *Someone reported her to the head teacher for cheating.* ♦ *The boy was reported missing early this morning.* ♦ *All accidents must be reported to the police.* 5 [I] **report (to sb/sth) (for sth)** to tell sb that you have arrived □ *melaporkan diri*: *On your arrival, please report to the reception desk.*

PHR V **report back (on sth) (to sb)** to give information to sb about sth they have asked you to find out about □ *melapor balik (ttg sst) (kpd sso)*: *One person in each group will then report back on what you've decided to the class.*

report to sb [not used in the continuous tenses] to have sb as your manager in the company or organization that you work for □ *melapor kpd sso*

ⸯreport² /rɪˈpɔːt/ noun [C] 1 **a report (on/of sth)** a written or spoken description of what you have seen, heard, done, studied, etc. □ *laporan*: *newspaper reports* ♦ *a report on the company's finances* ♦ *a first-hand report* (= from the person who saw what happened) 2 a written statement about the work of a student at school, college, etc. □ *laporan kemajuan*: *to get a good/bad report*

reˌported ˈspeech (also ˌindirect ˈspeech) noun [U] the fact of reporting what sb has said, not using the actual words. If sb says '*I'll phone again later*', this becomes *She said that she would phone again later* in reported speech. □ *cakap pindah* ◯ look at **direct speech** ❶ For more information about reported speech, look at the **Reference Section** at the back of this dictionary.

reporter /rɪˈpɔːtə(r)/ noun [C] a person who writes about the news in a newspaper or speaks about it on the TV or radio □ *pemberita* ◯ note at **newspaper** ◯ look at **journalist**

ⸯrepresent /ˌreprɪˈzent/ verb [T] 1 to act or speak in the place of sb else; to be the **representative** of a group or country □ *mewakili*: *You will need a lawyer to represent you in court.* ♦ *It's an honour for an athlete to represent his or her country.* 2 to be equal to sth; to be sth □ *merupakan*: *These results represent a major breakthrough in our understanding of cancer.* 3 to be a picture, sign, example, etc. of sb/sth □ *melambangkan*: *The yellow lines on the map represent minor roads.* 4 to describe sb/sth in a particular way □ *menggambarkan*: *In the book Billy is represented as a very cruel person.*

representation /ˌreprɪzenˈteɪʃn/ noun 1 [U,C] the way that sb/sth is shown or described; something that shows or describes sth □ *gambaran; representasi*: *The article complains about the representation of women in advertising.* ◯ look at **proportional representation** 2 [U] (formal) having sb to speak for you □ *perwakilan; representasi*

ⸯrepresentative¹ /ˌreprɪˈzentətɪv/ noun [C] 1 a person who has been chosen to act or speak for sb else or for a group □ *wakil*: *a union representative* 2 (formal) = **rep**

representative² /ˌreprɪˈzentətɪv/ *adj* **representative (of sb/sth)** typical of a larger group to which sb/sth belongs □ *mewakili; representatif*: *Tonight's audience is not representative of national opinion.*

repress /rɪˈpres/ *verb* [T] **1** to control an emotion or to try to prevent it from being shown or felt □ *menahan; memendam*: *She tried to repress her anger.* **2** to limit the freedom of a group of people □ *menindas* ▶ **repression** /rɪˈpreʃn/ *noun* [U]: *protests against government repression*

repressed /rɪˈprest/ *adj* **1** (used about a person) having emotions and desires that they do not show or express □ *tertekan* **2** (used about an emotion) that you do not show □ *tertahan; terpendam*: *repressed anger/desire*

repressive /rɪˈpresɪv/ *adj* that limits people's freedom □ *(yg) menindas*: *a repressive government*

reprieve /rɪˈpriːv/ *verb* [T] **1** to stop or delay the punishment of a prisoner who was going to be punished by death □ *membatalkan atau menangguhkan* **2** to officially cancel or delay plans to close sth or end sth □ *menangguhkan* ▶ **reprieve** *noun* [C]: *The judge granted him a last-minute reprieve.*

reprimand /ˈreprɪmɑːnd/ *verb* [T] (*formal*) **reprimand sb (for sth)** to tell sb officially that they have done sth wrong □ *menegur (kesalahan sso)* ▶ **reprimand** *noun* [C]: *a severe reprimand*

reprisal /rɪˈpraɪzl/ *noun* [C,U] a violent or aggressive act towards sb because of sth bad that they have done towards you □ *pembalasan; tindakan balas*

reproach /rɪˈprəʊtʃ/ *verb* [T] **reproach sb (for/with sth)** to tell sb that they are responsible for sth bad that has happened □ *menegur (kesalahan sso); menyalahkan; menyesali*: *You've nothing to reproach yourself for. It wasn't your fault.* **SYN** blame ▶ **reproach** *noun* [C,U]: *His behaviour is beyond reproach* (= cannot be criticized). ◆ *Alison felt her manager's reproaches were unfair.* ▶ **reproachful** /-fl/ *adj*: *a reproachful look* ▶ **reproachfully** /-fəli/ *adv*

reproduce /ˌriːprəˈdjuːs/ *verb* **1** [T] to produce a copy of sth □ *meniru; menghasilkan semula*: *It is very hard to reproduce a natural environment in the laboratory.* **2** [I,T] (used about people, animals and plants) to produce young □ *membiak*: *Fish reproduce by laying eggs.*

reproduction /ˌriːprəˈdʌkʃn/ *noun* **1** [U] the process of producing babies or young □ *pembiakan*: *sexual reproduction* **2** [U] the production of copies of sth □ *penyalinan; penghasilan semula*: *Digital recording gives excellent sound reproduction.* **3** [C] a copy of a painting, etc. □ *salinan*

reproductive /ˌriːprəˈdʌktɪv/ *adj* [only before a noun] connected with the production of young animals, plants, etc. □ *(berkaitan dgn) pembiakan*: *the male reproductive organs*

reproof /rɪˈpruːf/ *noun* [C,U] (*formal*) something that you say to sb when you do not approve of what they have done □ *teguran*

reptile /ˈreptaɪl/ *noun* [C] an animal that has cold blood and a skin covered in scales, and whose young come out of eggs □ *reptilia*: *Crocodiles, turtles and snakes are all reptiles.* ⊃ look at **amphibian** ⊃ picture on **page P13**

republic /rɪˈpʌblɪk/ *noun* [C] a country that has an elected government and a president □ *republik*: *the Republic of Ireland* ⊃ look at **monarchy**

republican /rɪˈpʌblɪkən/ *noun* [C] **1** a person who supports the system of an elected government with no king or queen □ *republikan; orang yg menyokong kerajaan republik* **2** **Republican** (*abbr* **Rep.**) a member of the Republican Party of the US □ *ahli Parti Republikan (AS)* ⊃ look at **Democrat** ▶ **republican** *adj*

the Republican Party *noun* [sing] one of the two main political parties of the US □ *Parti Republikan (AS)* ⊃ look at **the Democratic Party**

repudiate /rɪˈpjuːdieɪt/ *verb* [T] (*formal*) to say that you refuse to accept or believe sth □ *menolak; enggan (menerima, mempercayai, dsb)*: *to repudiate a suggestion/an accusation/responsibility*

repugnant /rɪˈpʌgnənt/ *adj* (*formal*) **repugnant (to sb)** making you feel disgust □ *menjijikkan*: *We found his suggestion absolutely repugnant.* ◆ *The idea of eating meat was totally repugnant to her.* **SYN** **repulsive**

repulsive /rɪˈpʌlsɪv/ *adj* that causes a strong feeling of disgust □ *menjijikkan* ⊃ *verb* **repel** ▶ **repulsion** /rɪˈpʌlʃn/ *noun* [U]

reputable /ˈrepjətəbl/ *adj* honest and providing a good service □ *mempunyai nama baik; boleh dipercayai* **OPP** **disreputable**

reputation /ˌrepjuˈteɪʃn/ *noun* [C] **a reputation (for/as sth)** the opinion that people in general have about what sb/sth is like □ *nama (baik/buruk); reputasi*: *to have a good/bad reputation* ◆ *Adam has a reputation for being late.* **SYN** **name**

repute /rɪˈpjuːt/ *noun* [U] (*formal*) the opinion that people in general have of sb/sth □ *reputasi (baik); nama baik*: *She's a writer of international repute* (= having a good reputation in many countries).

reputed /rɪˈpjuːtɪd/ *adj* generally said to be sth, although it is not certain □ *dikatakan*: *She's reputed to be the highest-paid sportswoman in the world.* ▶ **reputedly** *adv*

request¹ /rɪˈkwest/ *noun* [C,U] **request (for sth/that ...)** an act of asking for sth □ *permintaan*: *a request for help* ◆ *I'm going to make a request for a larger desk.* ◆ *to grant/turn down a request* ◆ *Single rooms are available on request.*

request² /rɪˈkwest/ verb [T] (formal) **request sth (from/of sb)** to ask for sth □ *meminta*: *Passengers are requested not to bring hot drinks onto the coach.* ♦ *to request a loan from the bank* ⊃ **Request** is more formal than **ask**.

require /rɪˈkwaɪə(r)/ verb [T] **1** to need sth □ *memerlukan*: *a situation that requires tact and diplomacy* ⊃ **Require** is more formal than **need**. **2** [often passive] to officially demand or order sth □ *menghendaki; dikehendaki*: *Passengers are required by law to wear seat belts.*

requirement /rɪˈkwaɪəmənt/ noun [C] something that you need or that you must do or have □ *keperluan; kemestian; syarat*: *university entrance requirements*

requisite /ˈrekwɪzɪt/ adj [only before a noun] (formal) necessary for a particular purpose □ *yang diperlukan*: *She lacks the requisite experience for this job.* ▶**requisite** noun [C]: *A university degree has become a requisite for entry into most professions.* ⊃ look at **prerequisite**

rescue /ˈreskju:/ verb [T] **rescue sb/sth (from sb/sth)** to save sb/sth from a situation that is dangerous or unpleasant □ *menyelamatkan*: *He rescued a child from drowning.* ▶**rescue** noun [C,U]: *Ten fishermen were saved in a daring sea rescue.* ♦ *Blow the whistle if you're in danger, and someone should* **come to your rescue**. ♦ *rescue workers/boats/helicopters* ▶**rescuer** noun [C]

research /rɪˈsɜ:tʃ; ˈri:sɜ:tʃ/ noun [U] **research (into/on sth)** detailed and careful study of sth to find out more information about it □ *penyelidikan*: *to do research into something* ♦ *scientific/medical/historical research* ♦ *We are carrying out market research to find out who our typical customer is.* ▶**research** verb [I,T] **research (into/in/on) (sth)**: *Scientists are researching into the possible causes of childhood diseases.* ♦ *They're researching ways of reducing traffic in the city centre.*

researcher /rɪˈsɜ:tʃə(r)/ noun [C] a person who does research □ *penyelidik*

resemble /rɪˈzembl/ verb [T] to be or look like sb/sth else □ *serupa; mirip*: *Laura closely resembles her brother.* ▶**resemblance** /rɪˈzemblens/ noun [C,U] **(a) resemblance (to sb/sth); (a) resemblance (between A and B)**: *a family resemblance* ♦ *The boys* **bear** *no resemblance to their father.*

resent /rɪˈzent/ verb [T] to feel angry about sth because you think it is unfair □ *berasa geram/sakit hati*: *I resent his criticism.* ♦ *Louise bitterly resented being treated differently from the men.* ▶**resentful** /-fl/ adj ▶**resentfully** /-fəli/ adv ▶**resentment** noun [sing, U]: *She felt deep resentment at the way she'd been treated.*

reservation /ˌrezəˈveɪʃn/ noun **1** [C] a seat, table, room, etc. that you have **reserved** □ *tempahan*: *We have reservations in the name of Dvorak.* ♦ *I'll phone the restaurant to* **make a reservation**. **2** [C,U] a feeling of doubt about sth (such as a plan or an idea) □ *keraguan*: *I have some reservations about letting Julie go out alone.* **3** (also **reserve**) [C] an area of land in the US that is kept separate for Native Americans to live in □ *tanah rizab*

reserve¹ /rɪˈzɜ:v/ verb [T] **reserve sth (for sb/sth)** **1** to keep sth for a special reason or to use at a later time □ *menyimpan; menguntukkan; mengekhaskan; dikhaskan*: *The car park is reserved for hotel guests only.* **2** to ask for a seat, table, room, etc. to be available at a future time □ *menempah*: *to reserve theatre tickets* **SYN book**

reserve² /rɪˈzɜ:v/ noun **1** [C, usually pl] something that you keep for a special reason or to use at a later date □ *simpanan*: *oil reserves* **2** [C] an area of land where the plants, animals, etc. are protected by law □ *simpanan; simpan*: *a nature reserve* ♦ *He works as a warden on a* **game reserve** *in Kenya.* **3** [U] the quality of being shy or keeping your feelings hidden □ *sifat pemalu/pendiam*: *It took a long time to break down her reserve and get her to relax.* **4** [C] (in sport) a person who will play in a game if one of the usual members of the team cannot play □ *pemain simpanan* **5** [C] = **reservation**(3)

IDM **in reserve** that you keep and use only if you need to □ *dlm simpanan*: *Keep some money in reserve for emergencies.*

reserved /rɪˈzɜ:vd/ adj shy and keeping your feelings hidden □ *pemalu; pendiam; berat mulut* **OPP** **unreserved**

reservoir /ˈrezəvwɑ:(r)/ noun [C] a large lake where water is stored to be used by a particular area, city, etc. □ *takungan; kolam air*

reside /rɪˈzaɪd/ verb [I] (formal) **reside (in/at ...)** to have your home in or at a particular place □ *tinggal; menetap*

residence /ˈrezɪdəns/ noun **1** [C] (formal) a house, especially an impressive or important one □ *kediaman* **2** [U] the state of having your home in a particular place □ *(perihal) tinggal atau menetap*: *The family applied for permanent residence in the United States.* ♦ *a* **hall of residence** *for college students* ♦ *Some birds have* **taken up residence** *in our roof.*

resident /ˈrezɪdənt/ noun [C] **1** a person who lives in a place □ *penduduk*: *local residents* **2** a person who is staying in a hotel □ *penghuni*: *The hotel bar is open only to residents.* ▶**resident** adj

residential /ˌrezɪˈdenʃl/ adj **1** (used about a place or an area) that has houses rather than offices, large shops or factories □ *kediaman*: *They live in a quiet residential area.* **2** that provides a place for sb to live □ *tempat tinggal*: *This home provides residential care for the elderly.*

residual /rɪˈzɪdjuəl/ adj [only before a noun] (formal) still present at the end of a process □ *sisa-sisa; baki*: *There are still a few residual problems with the computer program.*

residue /ˈrezɪdju:/ noun [C, usually sing] (formal) what is left after the main part of sth is taken or used □ *baki; sisa*: *The washing powder left a white residue on the clothes.*

resign /rɪˈzaɪn/ *verb* [I,T] **resign (as sth); resign (from sth)** to leave your job or position □ *meletak jawatan*: *He's resigned as chairman of the committee.* ➔ note at **job**
PHR V **resign yourself to sth/doing sth** to accept sth that is unpleasant but that you cannot change □ *terpaksa menerima*: *Jamie resigned himself to the fact that she was not coming back to him.*

resignation /ˌrezɪɡˈneɪʃn/ *noun* 1 [C,U] **resignation (from sth)** a letter or statement that says you want to leave your job or position □ *(surat, dsb) peletakan jawatan*: *to hand in your resignation* ♦ *a letter of resignation* ➔ note at **job** 2 [U] the state of accepting sth unpleasant that you cannot change □ *perihal terpaksa menerima sst (keadaan, dll)*: *They accepted their defeat with resignation.*

resigned /rɪˈzaɪnd/ *adj* **resigned (to sth/doing sth)** accepting sth that is unpleasant but that you cannot change □ *terpaksa menerima*: *Ben was resigned to the fact that he would never be an athlete.*

resilient /rɪˈzɪliənt/ *adj* strong enough to deal with illness, a shock, change, etc. □ *tahan; kuat; tdk mudah patah semangat* ▸**resilience** *noun* [U]

resin /ˈrezɪn/ *noun* [C,U] 1 a sticky substance that is produced by some trees and plants □ *resin; damar* 2 an artificial substance used in making plastics □ *resin*

resist /rɪˈzɪst/ *verb* [I,T] 1 to try to stop sth happening or to stop sb from doing sth; fight back against sth/sb □ *menentang; melawan*: *The government are resisting pressure to change the law.* ♦ *to resist arrest* **SYN** **oppose** 2 to stop yourself from having or doing sth that you want to have or do □ *menahan; tahan*: *I couldn't resist telling Nadia what we'd bought for her.*

resistance /rɪˈzɪstəns/ *noun* [U] 1 **resistance (to sb/sth)** trying to stop sth from happening or to stop sb from doing sth; fighting back against sb/sth □ *tentangan; rintangan*: *The government troops overcame the resistance of the rebel army.* 2 **resistance (to sth)** the power in sb's body not to be affected by disease □ *ketahanan; daya tahan*: *People with AIDS have very little resistance to infection.*

resistant /rɪˈzɪstənt/ *adj* **resistant (to sth)** 1 not harmed or affected by sth □ *tahan*: *plants that are resistant to disease* ♦ *This watch is water-resistant.* 2 not wanting sth and trying to prevent sth happening □ *menentang; enggan*: *resistant to change*

resolute /ˈrezəluːt/ *adj* having or showing great determination □ *tegas; teguh*: *resolute leadership* ♦ *a resolute refusal to change* ➔ A more common word is **determined**. ▸**resolutely** *adv*

resolution /ˌrezəˈluːʃn/ *noun* 1 [C] a formal decision that is taken after a vote by a group of people □ *ketetapan; resolusi*: *The UN resolution condemned the invasion.* 2 [U] solving or settling a problem, disagreement, etc. □ *penyelesaian* 3 [U] the quality of being firm and determined □ *ketegasan; tegas* 4 [C] a firm decision to do or not to do sth □ *azam; resolusi*: *Alison made a New Year's resolution to walk to school every day.*

resolve /rɪˈzɒlv/ *verb* (*formal*) 1 [T] to find an answer to a problem □ *menyelesaikan*: *Most of the difficulties have been resolved.* **SYN** **settle** 2 [I,T] to decide sth and be determined not to change your mind □ *berazam*: *He resolved never to repeat the experience.*

resonant /ˈrezənənt/ *adj* (*formal*) deep, clear and continuing for a long time □ *bergema; bertalun*: *a deep resonant voice* ▸**resonance** *noun* [U]: *Her voice had a thrilling resonance.*

resort[1] /rɪˈzɔːt/ *noun* [C] a place where a lot of people go to on holiday □ *tempat peranginan*: *a seaside/ski resort* ➔ note at **holiday**
IDM **in the last resort; (as) a last resort** ➔ **last**[1]

resort[2] /rɪˈzɔːt/ *verb* [I] **resort to sth/doing sth** to do or use sth bad or unpleasant because you feel you have no choice □ *terpaksa (membuat sst sebagai jalan keluar)*: *After not sleeping for three nights I finally resorted to sleeping pills.*

resounding /rɪˈzaʊndɪŋ/ *adj* [only before a noun] 1 very great □ *amat besar (hebat, teruk, dll)*: *a resounding victory/win/defeat/success* 2 very loud □ *berguna*: *resounding cheers*

resource /rɪˈsɔːs/ (*BrE also*) -ˈzɔːs (*AmE also*) / *noun* [C, usually pl] a supply of sth, a piece of equipment, etc. that is available for sb to use □ *sumber*: *Russia is rich in natural resources such as oil and minerals.*

resourceful /rɪˈsɔːsfl/ (*BrE also*) -ˈzɔːs-/ *adj* good at finding ways of doing things □ *pintar; pandai berikhtiar*

respect[1] /rɪˈspekt/ *noun* 1 [U] **respect (for sb/ sth)** the feeling that you have when you admire or have a high opinion of sb/sth □ *rasa hormat*: *I have little respect for people who are arrogant.* ♦ *to win/lose somebody's respect* ➔ look at **self-respect** 2 [U] **respect (for sb/sth)** polite behaviour or care towards sb/sth that you think is important □ *rasa hormat*: *We should all treat older people with respect.* ♦ *He has no respect for her feelings.* **OPP** **disrespect** 3 [C] a detail or point □ *segi; hal*: *In what respects do you think things have changed in the last ten years?* ♦ *Her performance was brilliant in every respect.*
IDM **pay your respects** ➔ **pay**[1]
with respect to sth (*formal*) about or concerning sth □ *berkenaan dgn sst*: *The groups differ with respect to age.*

respect[2] /rɪˈspekt/ *verb* [T] 1 **respect sb/ sth (for sth)** to admire or have a high opinion of sb/sth □ *menghormati*: *I respect him for his honesty.* 2 to show care for or pay attention to sb/sth □ *menghormati*: *We should respect other people's cultures and values.* ▸**respectful** /-fl/ *adj* **respectful (to/towards sb)**: *They are not always* respectful towards their teacher. **OPP** disrespectful ▶respectfully /-fəli/ adv

respectable /rɪˈspektəbl/ adj **1** considered by society to be good, proper or correct □ *dihormati; sopan*: *a respectable family* ♦ *He combed his hair and tried to look respectable for the interview.* **2** quite good or large □ *agak (baik, banyak, besar, dsb)*: *a respectable salary* ▶respectably /rɪˈspektəˈbɪləti/ noun [U]

respective /rɪˈspektɪv/ adj [only before a noun] belonging separately to each of the people who have been mentioned □ *masing-masing*: *Helen and Sue's respective start times are 8.15 and 9.00.*

respectively /rɪˈspektɪvli/ adv in the same order as sb/sth that was mentioned □ *masing-masing*

respiration /ˌrespəˈreɪʃn/ noun [U] (formal) breathing □ *pernafasan; respirasi*

respite /ˈrespaɪt/ noun [sing, U] respite (from sth) a short period of rest from sth that is difficult or unpleasant □ *rehat; lega; kelegaan*: *There was a brief respite from the fighting.*

respond /rɪˈspɒnd/ verb [I] **1** (formal) respond (to sb/sth) (with/by sth) to say or do sth as an answer or reaction to sth □ *menjawab; membalas*: *He responded to my question with a nod.* ♦ *Gerrard responded to the manager's criticism by scoring two goals.* ⊃ note at **answer** ⊃ **Respond** is more formal than **answer** or **reply**. **2** respond (to sb/sth) to have or show a good or quick reaction to sb/sth □ *bergerak balas; berkesan*: *The patient did not respond very well to the new treatment.*

response /rɪˈspɒns/ noun [C,U] (a) response (to sb/sth) an answer or reaction to sb/sth □ *jawapan; gerak balas; respons*: *I've sent out 20 letters of enquiry but I've had no responses yet.* ♦ *The government acted in response to economic pressure.*

responsibility /rɪˌspɒnsəˈbɪləti/ noun (pl responsibilities) **1** [U,C] responsibility (for sb/sth); responsibility (to do sth) a duty to deal with sth so that it is your fault if sth goes wrong □ *tanggungjawab*: *I refuse to take responsibility if anything goes wrong.* ♦ *Who has responsibility for the new students?* ♦ *It is John's responsibility to make sure the orders are sent out on time.* ♦ *I feel that I have a responsibility to help them—after all, they did help me.* **2** [U] the fact of sth being your fault □ *tanggungjawab*: *No group has yet admitted responsibility for planting the bomb.* **SYN** blame
IDM shift the blame/responsibility (for sth) (onto sb) ⊃ **shift¹**

responsible /rɪˈspɒnsəbl/ adj
▶HAVING DUTY **1** [not before a noun] responsible (for sb/sth); responsible (for doing sth) having the job or duty of dealing with sb/sth, so that it is your fault if sth goes wrong □ *bertanggungjawab*: *The school is responsible for the safety of the children in school hours.* ♦ *The manager is responsible for making sure the shop is run properly.*
▶CAUSING STH **2** [not before a noun] responsible (for sth) being the thing or person whose caused sth to happen □ *bertanggungjawab; menyebabkan*: *Who was responsible for the accident?*
▶REPORTING TO SB **3** [not before a noun] responsible (to sb/sth) having to report to sb/sth with authority, or to sb who you are working for, about what you are doing □ *bertanggungjawab kpd*: *Members of Parliament are responsible to the electors.*
▶RELIABLE **4** (used about a person) that you can trust to behave well and in a sensible way □ *bertanggungjawab*: *Mai is responsible enough to take her little sister to school.* **OPP** irresponsible
▶JOB **5** (used about a job) that is important and that should be done by a person who can be trusted □ *bertanggungjawab*

responsibly /rɪˈspɒnsəbli/ adv in a sensible way that shows you can be trusted □ *dgn penuh tanggungjawab*

responsive /rɪˈspɒnsɪv/ adj paying attention to sb/sth and reacting in a suitable or positive way □ *responsif; bertindak balas dgn cepat*: *By being responsive to changes in the market, the company has had great success.*

rest¹ /rest/ verb **1** [I] to relax, sleep or stop after a period of activity or because of illness □ *berehat*: *We've been walking for hours. Let's rest here for a while.* **2** [T] to not use a part of your body for a period of time because it is tired or painful □ *merehatkan; tdk menggunakan*: *Your knee will get better as long as you rest it as much as you can.* **3** [I,T] rest (sth) on/against sth to place sth in a position where it is supported by sth else; to be in such a position □ *menyandarkan; meletakkan*: *She rested her head on his shoulder and went to sleep.*
IDM let sth rest to not talk about sth any longer □ *cukuplah (jangan ungkit/cakap lagi)*
PHR V rest on sb/sth to depend on sb/sth or be based on sth □ *bergantung pd; berdasarkan*: *The whole theory rests on a very simple idea.*

rest² /rest/ noun **1** [sing, with sing or pl verb] the rest (of sb/sth) the part that is left; the ones that are left □ *selebihnya; yg lain*: *We had lunch and spent the rest of the day on the beach.* ♦ *She takes no interest in what happens in the rest of the world.* ♦ *They were the first people to arrive. The rest came later.* ♦ *The rest of our bags are still in the car.* **2** [C,U] a period of relaxing, sleeping or doing nothing □ *rehat; berehat*: *I can't walk any further! I need a rest.* ♦ *I'm going upstairs to have a rest before we go out.* ♦ *Try not to worry now. Get some rest and think about it tomorrow.* ♦ *I sat down to give my bad leg a rest.*
IDM at rest (formal) not moving □ *tdk bergerak*: *Do not open the door until the vehicle is at rest.*
come to rest to stop moving □ *berhenti*: *The car crashed through a wall and came to rest in a field.*
put/set your/sb's mind at rest ⊃ **mind¹**
the rest is history used when you are telling a story to say that you are not going to tell the end

of the story, because everyone knows it already □ *sudah diketahui umum*

'rest area (also **'rest stop**) (*AmE*) = **lay-by**

restart /ˌriːˈstɑːt/ *verb* [I,T] to start again or make sth start again after it has stopped □ *memulakan atau menghidupkan sst semula*: *Restart your computer to see if this solves the problem.*

restaurant /ˈrestrɒnt/ (*AmE* also /-rɑːnt/) *noun* [C] a place where you can buy and eat a meal □ *restoran; kedai makan*: *a fast food/hamburger restaurant* ♦ *a Chinese restaurant* ⊃ look at **cafe**, **takeaway**

TOPIC

Restaurants

A **cafe**, a **sandwich bar**, a **takeaway** or a **fast-food restaurant** is often a good place to **have a snack** or eat a meal cheaply, but for a special occasion you can go to a **restaurant**. If it is popular, you should **reserve/book a table** in advance. You choose from the **menu** and a **waiter** or **waitress** takes your **order**. A **set menu** gives a limited choice of **courses** or **dishes** at a **fixed price**. An **à la carte** menu lists all the separate dishes available. You can **order** a **starter** (= a light first course), a **main course** and a **pudding/dessert**. If you want alcoholic drinks, you can ask to see the **wine list**. At the end of the meal you must pay the **bill**. Friends often **split the bill** (= each pays for a share of the meal). If **service** is not included in the bill, people usually leave a **tip** (= a small amount of extra money).

---

restful /ˈrestfl/ *adj* giving a relaxed, peaceful feeling □ *tenang; menenangkan*: *I find this piece of music very restful.*

restless /ˈrestləs/ *adj* **1** unable to relax or be still because you are bored, nervous or impatient □ *gelisah; resah*: *The children always get restless on long journeys.* **2** (used about a period of time) without sleep or rest □ *resah; tanpa tidur atau rehat* ▸ **restlessly** *adv*

restoration /ˌrestəˈreɪʃn/ *noun* **1** [C,U] the return of sth to its original condition; the things that are done to achieve this □ *pemulihan; (perihal) membaik pulih*: *The house is in need of restoration.* **2** [U] the return of sth to its original owner □ *pengembalian; pemulangan*: *the restoration of stolen property to its owner*

restore /rɪˈstɔː(r)/ *verb* [T] **1 restore sb/sth (to sb/sth)** to put sb/sth back into their or its former condition or position □ *membaik pulih; memulihkan; mengembalikan*: *She restores old furniture as a hobby.* ♦ *In the recent elections, the former president was restored to power.* **2** (formal) **restore sth to sb** to give sth that was lost or stolen back to sb □ *mengembalikan; memulangkan*: *The police have now restored the painting to its rightful owner.*

restrain /rɪˈstreɪn/ *verb* [T] **restrain sb/sth (from/doing sth)** to keep sb or sth under control; to prevent sb or sth from doing sth □ *menahan; mengawal*: *I had to restrain myself from saying something rude.*

restrained /rɪˈstreɪnd/ *adj* not showing strong feelings □ *terkawal; tegang*

restraint /rɪˈstreɪnt/ *noun* **1** [C] **a restraint (on sb/sth)** a limit or control on sth □ *sekatan; kawalan*: *Are there any restraints on what the newspapers are allowed to publish?* **2** [U] the quality of behaving in a calm or controlled way □ *kesabaran; sifat mengawal perasaan*: *It took a lot of restraint on my part not to hit him.* ♦ *Soldiers have to exercise self-restraint even when provoked.* **SYN** **self-control**

restrict /rɪˈstrɪkt/ *verb* [T] **restrict sb/sth (to sth/doing sth)** to put a limit on sb/sth □ *mengehadkan; membatasi*: *There is a plan to restrict the use of cars in the city centre.*

restricted /rɪˈstrɪktɪd/ *adj* controlled or limited □ *terhad*: *There is only restricted parking available.*

restriction /rɪˈstrɪkʃn/ *noun* **restriction (on sth)** **1** [C] something (sometimes a rule or law) that limits the number, amount, size, freedom, etc. of sb/sth □ *pengehadan; sekatan*: *parking restrictions in the city centre* ♦ *The government is to impose tighter restrictions on the number of immigrants permitted to settle in this country.* **2** [U] the act of limiting the freedom of sb/sth □ *sekatan; had*: *This ticket permits you to travel anywhere, without restriction.*

restrictive /rɪˈstrɪktɪv/ *adj* limiting; preventing people from doing what they want □ *mengehad; terhad; terbatas*

restroom /ˈrestruːm; -rʊm/ *noun* [C] (*AmE*) a room with a toilet in a public place such as a hotel, shop, etc. □ *tandas* ⊃ note at **toilet**

'rest stop (*AmE*) = **lay-by**

result¹ /rɪˈzʌlt/ *noun*
▸ CAUSED BY STH **1** [C] something that happens because of sth else; the final situation at the end of a series of actions □ *akibat; hasil*: *The traffic was very heavy and as a result I arrived late.* ♦ *This wasn't really the result that I was expecting.*
▸ OF COMPETITION **2** [C] the score at the end of a game, competition or election □ *keputusan; skor*: *Do you know today's football results?* ♦ *The results of this week's competition will be published next week.* ♦ *The result of the by-election was a win for the Liberal Democrats.*
▸ OF EXAM **3** [C, usually pl] the mark given for an exam or test □ *keputusan*: *When do you get your exam results?*
▸ OF MEDICAL TEST **4** [C] something that is discovered by a medical test □ *keputusan*: *I'm still waiting for the result of my X-ray.* ♦ *The result of the test was negative.*
▸ SUCCESS **5** [C,U] a good effect of an action □ *kesan; hasil*: *He has tried very hard to find a job, until now without result.* ♦ *The treatment is beginning to show results.*

result² /rɪˈzʌlt/ verb [I] **result (from sth)** to happen or exist because of sth □ *akibat; disebabkan oleh*: *Ninety per cent of the deaths resulted from injuries to the head.*

PHR V **result in sth** to cause sth to happen; to produce as an effect □ *menyebabkan/mengakibatkan sst*: *There has been an accident on the motorway, resulting in long delays.*

resume /rɪˈzuːm; -ˈzjuːm/ verb [I,T] (formal) to begin again or continue after a pause or interruption □ *memulakan semula; menyambung balik*: *Normal service will resume as soon as possible.*

résumé /ˈrezjumeɪ/ (AmE) = **CV**

resumption /rɪˈzʌmpʃn/ noun [sing, U] (formal) beginning again or continuing after a pause or interruption □ *bermula semula; penyambungan semula*

resurrect /ˌrezəˈrekt/ verb [T] to bring back sth that has not been used or has not existed for a long time □ *menghidupkan (atau membangkitkan, menyiarkan, menggunakan, dsb) semula*: *From time to time they resurrect old programmes and show them again on TV.*

resurrection /ˌrezəˈrekʃn/ noun **1 the Resurrection** [sing] (in the Christian religion) the return to life of Jesus Christ □ *Kebangkitan Jesus Christ* **2** [U] the action of bringing back sth that has not existed or not been used for a long time □ *perihal menghidupkan (atau membangkitkan, menyiarkan, menggunakan, dsb) semula*

resuscitate /rɪˈsʌsɪteɪt/ verb [T] to make sb start breathing again after they have almost died □ *menyedarkan semula*: *Unfortunately, all efforts to resuscitate the patient failed.* ▶ **resuscitation** /rɪˌsʌsɪˈteɪʃn/ noun [U]: *mouth-to-mouth resuscitation*

retail /ˈriːteɪl/ noun [U] the selling of goods to the public in shops, etc. □ *runcit* ⊃ look at **wholesale**

retailer /ˈriːteɪlə(r)/ noun [C] a person or company that sells goods to the public □ *peruncit*: *local retailers* ◆ *an online retailer*

retain /rɪˈteɪn/ verb [T] (formal) to keep or continue to have sth; not to lose sth □ *mengekalkan; menyimpan*: *Despite all her problems, she has managed to retain a sense of humour.* ⊃ noun **retention**

retaliate /rɪˈtælieɪt/ verb [I] **retaliate (against sb/sth)** to react to sth unpleasant that sb does to you by doing sth unpleasant in return □ *membalas*: *They have announced that they will retaliate against anyone who attacks their country.* ▶ **retaliation** /rɪˌtæliˈeɪʃn/ noun [U] **retaliation (against sb/sth) (for sth)**: *The terrorist group said that the shooting was in retaliation for the killing of one of its members.*

retarded /rɪˈtɑːdɪd/ adj (old-fashioned) slower to develop than normal □ *terencat*

HELP Be careful. Many people find this word offensive.

729

result → retreat

retention /rɪˈtenʃn/ noun [U] the act of keeping sth or of being kept □ *pengekalan; mengekalkan* ⊃ verb **retain**

rethink /ˌriːˈθɪŋk/ verb [I,T] (pt, pp **rethought** /-ˈθɔːt/) to think about sth again because you probably need to change it □ *memikirkan semula*: *The government has been forced to rethink its economic policy.*

reticent /ˈretɪsnt/ adj (formal) **reticent (about sth)** not willing to tell people about things □ *segan bercakap; berat mulut; enggan bercakap*: *She was shy and reticent.* ◆ *He was extremely reticent about his personal life.* ▶ **reticence** noun [U]

retina /ˈretɪnə/ noun [C] the area at the back of your eye that is sensitive to light and sends signals to the brain about what is seen □ *retina*

retire /rɪˈtaɪə(r)/ verb [I] **1 retire (from sth)** to leave your job and stop working, usually because you have reached a certain age □ *bersara*: *She retired from the company at the age of 60.* ⊃ note at **job** ⊃ look at **old-age pension**

MORE After someone **retires**, we say that he/she **is retired**. A **pension** is the money that retired people receive regularly from their former employer and/or the government.

2 (formal) to leave and go to a quiet or private place □ *beredar; beredar (ke tempat yg senyap atau utk bersendirian)*: *to retire to bed*

retired /rɪˈtaɪəd/ adj having stopped work permanently □ *(yg) bersara*: *a retired teacher*

retirement /rɪˈtaɪəmənt/ noun **1** [C,U] the act of stopping working permanently □ *persaraan*: *She has decided to take early retirement.* ◆ *The former world champion has announced his retirement from the sport.* **2** [sing, U] the situation or period after **retiring** from work □ *bersara*: *We all wish you a long and happy retirement.* ⊃ look at **old-age pensioner**, **senior citizen**

retiring /rɪˈtaɪərɪŋ/ adj (used about a person) shy and quiet □ *pemalu; pendiam*

retort /rɪˈtɔːt/ verb [T] to reply quickly to what sb says, in an angry or amusing way □ *membalas (menjawab) pantas*: *'Who asked you for your opinion?' she retorted.* ▶ **retort** noun [C]: *an angry retort*

retrace /rɪˈtreɪs/ verb [T] to repeat a past journey, series of events, etc. □ *patah balik; menjejak semula; mengingat semula*: *If you retrace your steps, you might see where you dropped the ticket.*

retract /rɪˈtrækt/ verb [I,T] (formal) to say that sth you have said is not true □ *menarik balik*: *When he appeared in court, he retracted the confession he had made to the police.*

retreat¹ /rɪˈtriːt/ verb [I] **1** (used about an army, etc.) to move backwards in order to leave a battle or in order not to become involved in a

R

VOWELS   iː **see**   i **any**   ɪ **sit**   e **ten**   æ **hat**   ɑː **father**   ɒ **got**   ɔː **saw**   ʊ **put**   uː **too**   u **usual**

retreat → reunion 730

battle □ *berundur*: *The order was given to retreat.* **OPP** **advance** **2** to move backwards; to go to a safe or private place □ *mengundur; mengasingkan diri*: (figurative) *She seems to retreat into a world of her own sometimes.*

retreat² /rɪˈtriːt/ *noun* **1** [C,U] the act of moving backwards, away from a difficult or dangerous situation □ *pengunduran; berundur*: *The invading forces are now in retreat.* **OPP** **advance** **2** [C] a private place where you can go when you want to be quiet or to rest □ *tempat sunyi (utk berehat atau mencari ketenangan)*: *a religious retreat*

retribution /ˌretrɪˈbjuːʃn/ *noun* [U] (*formal*) **retribution (for sth)** punishment for a crime □ *hukuman; balasan*

retrieve /rɪˈtriːv/ *verb* [T] **1 retrieve sth (from sb/sth)** to get sth back from the place where it was left or lost □ *mendapatkan balik; mengambil balik*: *Police divers retrieved the body from the canal.* **2** to find information that has been stored on a computer □ *mendapatkan semula*: *The computer can retrieve all the data about a particular customer.* **3** to make a bad situation or a mistake better; to put sth right □ *memulihkan (atau membetulkan, menyelamatkan, dsb) keadaan*: *The team was losing two-nil at half-time but they managed to retrieve the situation in the second half.* ▶ **retrieval** /rɪˈtriːvl/ *noun* [U]

retro /ˈretrəʊ/ *adj* using styles or fashions from the recent past □ *berdasarkan sst yg silam*: *She dresses in a 1980s retro style.*

retrospect /ˈretrəspekt/ *noun*
IDM **in retrospect** thinking about sth that happened in the past, often seeing it differently from the way you saw it at the time □ *apabila ditinjau kembali*: *In retrospect, I can see what a stupid mistake it was.*

retrospective /ˌretrəˈspektɪv/ *adj* **1** looking again at the past □ *meninjau kembali; retrospektif*: *a retrospective analysis of historical events* **2** (used about laws, decisions, payments, etc.) intended to take effect from a date in the past □ *kebelakangan; retrospektif*: *Is this new tax law retrospective?* ▶ **retrospectively** *adv*

return¹ /rɪˈtɜːn/ *verb*
▶GO/COME BACK **1** [I] **return (to/from ...)** to come or go back to a place □ *kembali; pulang*: *I leave on the 10th July and return on the 25th.* ♦ *I shall be returning to this country in six months.* ♦ *When did you return from Italy?* ♦ *He left his home town when he was 18 and never returned.*
▶TO EARLIER STATE **2** [I] **return (to sth/doing sth)** to go back to the former or usual activity, situation, condition, etc. □ *kembali; menyambung semula*: *The strike is over and they will return to work on Monday.* ♦ *It is hoped that train services will return to normal soon.*
▶HAPPEN AGAIN **3** [I] to come back; to happen again □ *berbalik; datang balik*: *If the pain returns, make another appointment to see me.*
▶GIVE BACK **4** [T] **return sth (to sb/sth)** to give, send, put or take sth back □ *memulangkan; mengembalikan*: *I've stopped lending him things because he never returns them.* ♦ *Application forms must be returned by 14 March.*
▶DO THE SAME **5** [T] to react to sth that sb does, says or feels by doing, saying, or feeling sth similar □ *membalas*: *I've phoned them several times and left messages but they haven't returned any of my calls.* ♦ *We'll be happy to return your hospitality if you ever come to our country.*
▶IN TENNIS **6** [T] to hit or throw the ball back □ *membalas*: *to return a service/shot*

return² /rɪˈtɜːn/ *noun*
▶COMING BACK **1** [sing] **a return (to/from ...)** coming or going back to a place or to a former activity, situation or condition □ *kepulangan; pulang; sekembalinya; kembali*: *I'll contact you on my return from holiday.* ♦ *He has recently made a return to form* (= started playing well again).
▶GIVING BACK **2** [U] giving, sending, putting or taking sth back □ *pengembalian; pemulangan*: *I demand the immediate return of my passport.*
▶TICKET **3** [C] (*BrE also* **reˌturn ˈticket**; *AmE* **ˌround ˈtrip**; **ˌround-trip ˈticket**) a ticket to travel to a place and back again □ *tiket pergi balik*: *A day return to Oxford, please.* ♦ *Is the return fare cheaper than two singles?* **OPP** **single, one-way**
▶ON COMPUTER **4** [sing] (*also* **the reˈturn key**) the button on a computer that you press when you reach the end of a line or of an instruction □ *kekunci kembali*: *To exit this option, press return.*
▶PROFIT **5** [C,U] **(a) return (on sth)** the profit from a business, etc. □ *pulangan*: *This account offers high returns on all investments.*
▶IN TENNIS **6** [C] the act of hitting or throwing the ball back □ *hantaran balas*: *She hit a brilliant return.*
IDM **by return (of post)** (*BrE*) immediately; by the next post □ *segera (dgn pos yg berikutnya)*
in return (for sth) as payment or in exchange (for sth); as a reaction to sth □ *sebagai balasan (terhadap sst)*: *Please accept this present in return for all your help.*

returnable /rɪˈtɜːnəbl/ *adj* that can or must be given or taken back □ *boleh dipulangkan*: *a non-returnable deposit*

the reˈturn key = **return²(5)**

reˌturn ˈticket = **return²(4)**

retweet /ˌriːˈtwiːt/ *verb* [I,T] to send a message that someone has sent you on the Twitter™ **social networking service** (= short communications using the Internet) to other people □ *menghantar semula mesej yg diterima melalui laman sosial Twitter kpd orang lain*: *People love to retweet job ads.*

reunion /riːˈjuːniən/ *noun* **1** [C] a social occasion or party attended by a group of people who have not seen each other for a long time □ *majlis perjumpaan*: *The college holds an annual reunion for former students.* **2** [C,U] **a reunion (with sb/between A and B)** coming together again after being apart □ *pertemuan semula*:

The released hostages had an emotional reunion with their families at the airport.

reunite /ˌriːjuːˈnaɪt/ verb [I,T] **reunite (A with/ and B)** to join two or more people, groups, etc. together again; to come together again □ *menyatukan semula; mempertemukan semula*: *The missing child was found by the police and reunited with his parents.*

reuse /ˌriːˈjuːz/ verb [T] to use sth that has been used before □ *guna semula*: *Save money by reusing envelopes.*

Rev. abbr = reverend: *Rev. Jesse Jackson*

rev¹ /rev/ verb [I,T] (**revving; revved**) **rev (sth) (up)** when an engine **revs** or when you **rev** it, it runs quickly and noisily □ *meligatkan*

rev² /rev/ noun [C] (*informal*) (used when talking about an engine's speed) one complete turn □ *putaran*: *4 000 revs per minute* ⊃ look at **revolution**

reveal /rɪˈviːl/ verb [T] **1 reveal sth (to sb)** to make sth known that was secret or unknown before □ *mendedahkan; memberitahu*: *He refused to reveal any names to the police.* **2** To show sth that was hidden before □ *menunjukkan; menampakkan*: *The X-ray revealed a tiny fracture in her right hand.*

revealing /rɪˈviːlɪŋ/ adj **1** allowing sth to be known that was secret or unknown before □ *(yg) mendedahkan*: *This book provides a revealing insight into the world of politics.* **2** allowing sth to be seen that is usually hidden, especially sb's body □ *(yg) mendedahkan; terdedah*: *a very revealing swimsuit*

revel /ˈrevl/ verb (**revelling; revelled**, (AmE) **reveling; reveled**)
PHR V revel in sth/doing sth to enjoy sth very much □ *amat seronok (akan sst/membuat sst)*: *He likes being famous and revels in the attention he gets.*

revelation /ˌrevəˈleɪʃn/ noun **1** [C] something that is made known that was secret or unknown before, especially sth surprising □ *pendedahan*: *This magazine is full of revelations about the private lives of the stars.* **2** [sing] a thing or a person that surprises you and makes you change your opinion about sb/sth □ *sst yg meranjatkan/tdk diduga*

revenge /rɪˈvendʒ/ noun [U] **revenge (on sb) (for sth)** something that you do to punish sb who has hurt you, made you suffer, etc. □ *dendam; membalas dendam*: *He made a fool of me and now I want to get my revenge.* ◆ *He wants to take revenge on the judge who sent him to prison.* ◆ *The shooting was in revenge for an attack by the nationalists.* ⊃ look at **vengeance** ▶ **revenge** verb [T] **revenge yourself on sb**: *She revenged herself on her enemy.* ⊃ look at **avenge**

revenue /ˈrevənjuː/ noun [U] (also [pl] **revenues**) money regularly received by a government, company, etc. □ *hasil*: *Revenue from income tax rose last year.*

reverberate /rɪˈvɜːbəreɪt/ verb [I] (used about a sound) to be repeated several times as it hits and is sent back from different surfaces □ *bergema; bertalun*: *Her voice reverberated around the hall.* ▶ **reverberation** /rɪˌvɜːbəˈreɪʃn/ noun [C,U]

reverence /ˈrevərəns/ noun [U] (*formal*) **reverence (for sb/sth)** a feeling of great respect □ *rasa hormat; takzim*

reverend /ˈrevərənd/ adj [only *before* a noun] (*abbr* **Rev.**) the title of a Christian priest □ *Reverend (gelaran paderi)*

reverent /ˈrevərənt/ adj (*formal*) showing great respect □ *penuh hormat*

reversal /rɪˈvɜːsl/ noun [U,C] the act of changing sth to the opposite of what it was before; an occasion when this happens □ *kebalikan; pembalikan*: *The government insists that there will be no reversal of policy.* ◆ *The decision taken yesterday was a complete reversal of last week's decision.*

reverse¹ /rɪˈvɜːs/ verb **1** [T] to put sth in the opposite position to normal or to how it was before □ *menterbalikkan*: *Today's results have reversed the order of the top two teams.* **2** [T] to exchange the positions or functions of two things or people □ *menterbalikkan; bertukar ganti*: *Jane and her husband have reversed roles—he stays at home now and she goes to work.* **3** [I,T] to go backwards in a vehicle, etc.; to make a vehicle go backwards □ *mengundur(kan)*: *It will probably be easier to reverse into that parking space.* ◆ *He reversed his brand new car into a wall.*
IDM **reverse (the) charges** (*BrE*) to make a telephone call that will be paid for by the person who receives it □ *(panggilan telefon) caj balikan*: *Phone us when you get there, and reverse the charges.*

HELP The American expression is to **call collect**.

reverse² /rɪˈvɜːs/ noun **1** [sing] **the reverse (of sth)** the complete opposite of what was said just before, or of what is expected □ *sebaliknya; kebalikan; bertentangan*: *Of course I don't dislike you—quite the reverse* (= I like you very much). ◆ *This course is the exact reverse of what I was expecting.* **2** (also **reˌverse ˈgear**) [U] the control in a car, etc. that allows it to move backwards □ *gear undur*: *Leave the car in reverse while it's parked on this hill.* ◆ *Where's reverse in this car?*
IDM **in reverse** in the opposite order, starting at the end and going back to the beginning □ *terbalik; menyongsang* **SYN** **backwards**

reverse³ /rɪˈvɜːs/ adj [only *before* a noun] opposite to what is expected or has just been described □ *sebaliknya; bertentangan; berlawanan*
IDM **in/into reverse order** starting with the last one and going backwards to the first one □ *secara terbalik; dlm urutan terbalik*: *The results will be announced in reverse order.*

[C] **countable**, a noun with a plural form: *one book, two books*   [U] **uncountable**, a noun with no plural form: *some sugar*

reversible /rɪˈvɜːsəbl/ *adj* (used about clothes) that can be worn with either side on the outside □ *boleh diterbalikkan; dua-dua belah boleh dipakai*: *a reversible coat*

revert /rɪˈvɜːt/ *verb* [I] **revert (to sth)** to return to a former state or activity □ *kembali; berbalik*: *The land will soon revert to jungle if it is not farmed.* ♦ *If this is unsuccessful we will revert to the old system.*

review¹ /rɪˈvjuː/ *noun* **1** [C,U] the examining or considering again of sth in order to decide if changes are necessary □ *kajian semula; tinjauan semula*: *There will be a review of your contract after the first six months.* ♦ *The system is in need of review.* **2** [C] a newspaper or magazine article, or an item on TV or radio, in which sb gives an opinion on a new book, film, play, etc. □ *ulasan*: *The film got bad reviews.* **3** [C] a look back at sth in order to check, remember, or be clear about sth □ *tinjauan semula; ulang kaji*: *a review of the major events of the year*

review² /rɪˈvjuː/ *verb* [T] **1** to examine or consider sth again in order to decide if changes are necessary □ *mengkaji semula; meninjau semula*: *Your salary will be reviewed after one year.* **2** to look at or think about sth again to make sure that you understand it □ *meneliti semula*: *Let's review what we've done in class this week.* **3** to write an article or to talk on TV or radio, giving an opinion on a new book, film, play, etc. □ *mengulas*: *In this week's edition our film critic reviews the latest films.*

reviewer /rɪˈvjuːə(r)/ *noun* [C] a person who writes about new books, films, etc. □ *pengulas*

revise /rɪˈvaɪz/ *verb* **1** [T] to make changes to sth in order to correct or improve it □ *menyemak semula; mengubah*: *The book has been revised for this new edition.* ♦ *I revised my opinion of him when I found out that he had lied.* **2** [I,T] (*BrE*) **revise (sth/for sth)** to read or study again sth that you have learnt, especially when preparing for an exam □ *mengulang kaji*: *I can't come out tonight. I'm revising for my exam.* ♦ *Let's revise the past perfect.* ♦ *None of the things I had revised came up in the exam.*

revision /rɪˈvɪʒn/ *noun* **1** [C,U] the changing of sth in order to correct or improve it □ *penyemakan; semakan*: *It has been suggested that the whole system is in need of revision.* **2** [U] (*BrE*) the work of reading or studying again sth you have learnt, especially when preparing for an exam □ *ulang kaji*: *I'm going to have to do a lot of revision for History.*

EXAM TIP

Revision

It is very important to prepare for exams by revising. Do not leave all your revision until the night before the exam, but try to revise little and often. That way you can build up your knowledge gradually, making sure that you have learnt everything that you need to know for the exam.

revival /rɪˈvaɪvl/ *noun* **1** [C,U] the act of becoming or making sth strong or popular again □ *pemulihan; kebangkitan semula*: *economic revival* ♦ *a revival of interest in traditional farming methods* **2** [C] a new performance of a play that has not been performed for some time □ *pementasan semula*: *a revival of the musical 'The Sound of Music'*

revive /rɪˈvaɪv/ *verb* [I,T] **1** to become, or to make sb/sth become, conscious or strong and healthy again □ *pulih; memulihkan; hidup kembali; kembali segar; menyedarkan*: *Hopes have revived for an early end to the fighting.* ♦ *I'm very tired but I'm sure a cup of coffee will revive me.* ♦ *Attempts were made to revive him but he was already dead.* **2** to become or to make sth popular again; to begin to do or use sth again □ *menghidupkan semula*: *Public interest in athletics has revived now that the national team is doing well.* ♦ *to revive an old custom*

revoke /rɪˈvəʊk/ *verb* [T] (*formal*) to officially cancel sth so that it is no longer valid □ *membatalkan*

revolt /rɪˈvəʊlt/ *verb* **1** [I] **revolt (against sb/sth)** to protest in a group, often violently, against the person or people in power □ *memberontak; membantah*: *A group of generals revolted against the government.* **2** to behave in a way that is the opposite of what sb expects of you □ *memberontak*: *Teenagers often revolt against parental discipline.* **3** [T] to make sb feel disgusted or ill □ *berasa jijik/mual*: *The sight and smell of the meat revolted him.* ⇨ *noun* **revulsion** ▶ **revolt** *noun* [C,U]: *The people rose in revolt against the corrupt government.*

revolting /rɪˈvəʊltɪŋ/ *adj* extremely unpleasant □ *menjijikkan; teruk; dahsyat*: *What a revolting smell!* SYN **disgusting**

revolution /ˌrevəˈluːʃn/ *noun* **1** [C,U] action taken by a large group of people to try to change the government of a country, especially by violent action □ *revolusi; pemberontakan*: *the French Revolution of 1789* ♦ *a country on the brink of revolution* **2** [C] **a revolution (in sth)** a complete change in methods, opinions, etc., often as a result of progress □ *revolusi; perubahan*: *the Industrial Revolution* **3** [C,U] a movement around sth; one complete turn around a central point (for example in a car engine) □ *peredaran; putaran*: *400 revolutions per minute* ⇨ look at **rev**

revolutionary¹ /ˌrevəˈluːʃənəri/ *adj* **1** connected with or supporting political **revolution** □ *(berkaitan dgn atau menyokong) revolusi*: *the revolutionary leaders* **2** producing great changes; very new and different □ *revolusioner; mengakibatkan perubahan besar; betul-betul baharu dan berlainan*: *revolutionary advances in medicine*

revolutionary² /ˌrevəˈluːʃənəri/ *noun* [C] (*pl* **revolutionaries**) a person who starts or supports action to try to change the government of a country, especially by using violence □ *revolusioner; orang yg mencetus atau menyokong revolusi*

revolutionize (also **-ise**) /ˌrevəˈluːʃənaɪz/ verb [T] to change sth completely, usually improving it □ *merevolusikan; mengubah sepenuhnya*: *a discovery that could revolutionize the treatment of mental illness*

revolve /rɪˈvɒlv/ verb [I] to move in a circle around a central point □ *beredar; berputar*: *The earth revolves around the sun.*

PHR V **revolve around sb/sth** to have sb/sth as the most important part □ *berkisar di sekitar sso/sst*: *Her life revolves around the family.*

revolver /rɪˈvɒlvə(r)/ noun [C] a type of small gun with a container for bullets that turns round □ *revolver; sejenis pistol* ⊃ note at **gun**

revolving /rɪˈvɒlvɪŋ/ adj that goes round in a circle □ *putar; pusingan*: *revolving doors*

revulsion /rɪˈvʌlʃn/ noun [U] a feeling of disgust (because sth is extremely unpleasant) □ *rasa jijik* ⊃ verb **revolt**

reward[1] /rɪˈwɔːd/ noun **reward (for sth/for doing sth) 1** [C,U] something that you achieve or are given because you have done sth good, worked hard, etc. □ *ganjaran; anugerah*: *Winning the match was just reward for all the effort.* **2** [C] an amount of money that is given in exchange for helping the police, returning sth that was lost, etc. □ *ganjaran; hadiah*: *Police are offering a reward for information leading to a conviction.*

reward[2] /rɪˈwɔːd/ verb [T, often passive] **reward sb (for sth/for doing sth)** to give sth to sb because they have done sth good, worked hard, etc. □ *memberi ganjaran; mendatangkan hasil*: *Victoria was rewarded for all her hard work with a rise in salary.*

rewarding /rɪˈwɔːdɪŋ/ adj (used about an activity, a job, etc.) giving satisfaction; making you happy because you think it is important, useful, etc. □ *memuaskan*

rewind /ˌriːˈwaɪnd/ verb [T] (pt, pp **rewound**) to make a video or tape go backwards □ *putar semula* ▸ **rewind** noun [U] ⊃ look at **fast forward**

rewrite /ˌriːˈraɪt/ verb [T] (pt **rewrote** /-ˈrəʊt/; pp **rewritten** /-ˈrɪtn/) to write sth again in a different or better way □ *menulis semula*

rhetoric /ˈretərɪk/ noun [U] (formal) a way of speaking or writing that is intended to impress or influence people but is not always sincere □ *retorik* ▸ **rhetorical** /rɪˈtɒrɪkl/ (AmE also) /-/ adj ▸ **rhetorically** /-kli/ adv

rheˈtorical ˈquestion noun [C] a question that does not expect an answer □ *soalan retorik*

rheumatism /ˈruːmətɪzəm/ noun [U] an illness that causes pain in your muscles and where your bones are connected □ *reumatisme*

rhinoceros /raɪˈnɒsərəs/ noun [C] (pl **rhinoceros** or **rhinoceroses**) (also informal **rhino**) a large animal from Africa or Asia, with thick skin and with either one or two horns on its nose □ *badak sumbu* ⊃ picture at **hippopotamus**

rhubarb /ˈruːbɑːb/ noun [U] a plant with red stalks (= the long thin parts) that can be cooked and eaten as fruit □ *pokok rubarb*

rhyme[1] /raɪm/ noun **1** [C] a word that has the same sound as another □ *kata berima* **2** [C] a short piece of writing, or sth spoken, in which the word at the end of each line sounds the same as the word at the end of the line before it □ *rima; puisi berima* ⊃ look at **nursery rhyme 3** [U] the use of words in a poem or song that have the same sound, especially at the ends of lines □ *bentuk berima*: *All of his poetry was written in rhyme.*

rhyme[2] /raɪm/ verb **1** [I] **rhyme (with sth)** to have the same sound as another word; to contain lines that end with words that sound the same □ *berima; bersajak*: *'Tough' rhymes with 'stuff'.* **2** [T] **rhyme sth (with sth)** to put together words that have the same sound □ *menggubah rima; menyajakkan*

rhythm /ˈrɪðəm/ noun [C,U] a regular repeated pattern of sound or movement □ *irama; ritma; rentak*: *I'm not keen on the tune but I love the rhythm.* ◆ *He's a terrible dancer because he has no sense of rhythm.* ◆ *He tapped his foot in rhythm with the music.* ▸ **rhythmic** /ˈrɪðmɪk/ (also **rhythmical** /ˈrɪðmɪkl/) adj: *the rhythmic qualities of African music* ▸ **rhythmically** /-kli/ adv

rib /rɪb/ noun [C] **1** one of the curved bones that go round your chest □ *tulang rusuk*: *He's so thin that you can see his ribs.* ⊃ picture at **body 2** a piece of meat with one or more bones from the ribs of an animal □ *daging rusuk*

ribbon /ˈrɪbən/ noun [C,U] a long, thin piece of cloth that is used for tying or decorating sth □ *reben*: *a present wrapped in a blue ribbon* ⊃ picture at **medal**, **wrap**

rice /raɪs/ noun [U] short, thin, white or brown grain from a plant that grows on wet land in hot countries. *We cook and eat rice* □ *beras; nasi; padi*: *boiled/fried/steamed rice*

rich /rɪtʃ/ adj (**richer**; **richest**)
▸WITH A LOT OF MONEY **1** having a lot of money or property; not poor □ *kaya*: *a rich family/country* ◆ *one of the richest women in the world* **SYN** wealthy, well-to-do **OPP** poor **2** **the rich** noun [pl] people with a lot of money or property □ *orang kaya*: *the rich and famous*
▸FULL OF STH **3** **rich in sth** containing a lot of sth □ *kaya*: *Oranges are rich in vitamin C.* **4** very interesting and full of variety □ *beraneka ragam*: *the region's rich history and culture*
▸FOOD **5** containing a lot of fat, oil, sugar or cream and making you feel full quickly □ *sangat lemak/manis*: *a rich chocolate cake*
▸SOIL **6** containing the substances that make it good for growing plants in □ *subur*: *a rich well-drained soil*

riches → rift

▶COLOUR/SOUND/SMELL **7** strong and deep □ *hebat; pekat; kuat; semerbak*: *a rich purple* ▶**richness** *noun* [U]

riches /'rɪtʃɪz/ *noun* [pl] (*formal*) a lot of money or property □ *kekayaan* **SYN** **wealth**

richly /'rɪtʃli/ *adv* **1** in a generous way □ *banyak; dgn mewah*: *She was richly rewarded for her hard work.* **2** in a way that people think is right □ *betul; sangat patut*: *His promotion was richly deserved.*

rickety /'rɪkəti/ *adj* likely to break; not strongly made □ *goyah*: *a rickety old fence* ♦ *rickety furniture*

rickshaw /'rɪkʃɔː/ *noun* [C] a small light vehicle with two wheels, used especially in some Asian countries to carry passengers. It is pulled by sb walking or riding a bicycle. □ *beca; lanca*

ricochet /'rɪkəʃeɪ/ *verb* [I] (*pt, pp* **ricocheted** /'rɪkəʃeɪd/) **ricochet (off sth)** (used about a moving object) to fly away from a surface after hitting it □ *melantun*: *The bullet ricocheted off the wall and grazed his shoulder.*

rid /rɪd/ *verb* [T] (**ridding**; *pt, pp* **rid**)
IDM **get rid of sb/sth** to make yourself free of sb/sth that is annoying you or that you do not want; to throw sth away □ *lepas atau bebas drpd sso/sst; membuang sst*: *Let's get rid of that old chair and buy a new one.*
be rid of sb/sth (*formal*) to be free of sb/sth that is annoying you or that you do not want □ *bebas drpd*: *He was a nuisance and we're well rid of him* (= it will be much better without him).
PHR V **rid yourself/sb/sth of sb/sth** (*formal*) to make yourself/sb/sth free from sb/sth that is unpleasant or not wanted □ *melepaskan; membuang; menghapuskan; menghilangkan; menyingkirkan*: *He was unable to rid himself of his fears and suspicions.*

riddance /'rɪdns/ *noun*
IDM **good riddance (to sb/sth)** used for expressing pleasure or satisfaction that sb/sth that you do not like has gone □ *baguslah dah berambus (atau jahanam, dibuang, dll)*

ridden¹ past participle of **ride¹**

ridden² /'rɪdn/ *adj* [often in compounds] (*formal*) full of □ *penuh dgn*: *She was guilt-ridden.* ♦ *She was ridden with guilt.*

riddle /'rɪdl/ *noun* [C] **1** a difficult question that you ask people for fun that has a clever or amusing answer □ *teka-teki* **2** a person, a thing or an event that you cannot understand or explain □ *sso/sst yg membingungkan atau menimbulkan tanda tanya; misteri*

riddled /'rɪdld/ *adj* **riddled with sth** full of sth, especially sth unpleasant □ *penuh dgn*: *This essay is riddled with mistakes.*

ride¹ /raɪd/ *verb* (*pt* **rode** /rəʊd/; *pp* **ridden** /'rɪdn/) **1** [I,T] to sit on a horse and control it as it moves □ *menunggang kuda*: *We rode through the woods and over the moor.* ♦ *Which horse is Dettori riding in the next race?*

HELP **Go riding** is a common way of talking about riding a horse for pleasure in British English: *She goes riding every weekend.* In American English **go horseback riding** is used.

2 [I,T] to sit on a bicycle, motorbike, etc. and control it as it moves □ *menunggang (basikal, motosikal, dll)*: *She jumped onto her motorbike and rode off* (= went away). ♦ *Can John ride a bicycle yet?* **3** [I,T] (*especially AmE*) to travel as a passenger in a bus, car, etc. □ *menaiki bas, kereta, dll sebagai penumpang*: *She rode the bus to school every day.* ▶**rider** *noun* [C]: *She's an experienced rider.* ♦ *three horses and their riders*

ride² /raɪd/ *noun* [C] **1** a short journey on a horse or bicycle, or in a car, bus, etc. □ *perjalanan*: *We went for a bike ride on Saturday.* ♦ *It's only a short bus/train ride into town.* **2** used to describe what a journey or trip is like □ *perjalanan*: *a smooth/bumpy/comfortable ride* **3** a large moving machine which you pay to go on for fun or excitement; an occasion when you go on one of these □ *mainan yg ditunggang*: *My favourite fairground ride is the roller coaster.*
IDM **take sb for a ride** (*informal*) to cheat or trick sb □ *menipu sso*

ridge /rɪdʒ/ *noun* [C] **1** a long, narrow piece of high land along the top of a line of hills or mountains □ *rabung* **2** a line where two surfaces meet at an angle □ *rabung*: *the ridge of the roof*

ridicule /'rɪdɪkjuːl/ *noun* [U] unkind behaviour or comments that make sb/sth look silly □ *cemuhan; ejekan*: *He had become an object of ridicule.* ▶**ridicule** *verb* [T]: *The idea was ridiculed by everybody.*

ridiculous /rɪ'dɪkjələs/ *adj* very silly or unreasonable □ *pelik; tdk munasabah*: *They're asking a ridiculous* (= very high) *price for that house.* **SYN** **absurd** ▶**ridiculously** *adv*

riding /'raɪdɪŋ/ (also **horse riding**; *AmE* **'horseback riding**) *noun* [U] the sport or hobby of riding a horse □ *(sukan atau hobi) menunggang kuda*: *Kate goes riding every weekend.* ♦ *riding boots* ♦ *a riding school* ➔ picture at **horse**

rife /raɪf/ *adj* [not before a noun] (*formal*) (used especially about bad things) very common □ *merebak*: *Rumours are rife that his wife has left him.*

rifle¹ /'raɪfl/ *noun* [C] a long gun that you hold against your shoulder to shoot with □ *senapang*: *She fired the rifle.* ➔ note at **gun**

rifle² /'raɪfl/ *verb* [I,T] **rifle (through) sth** to search sth, usually in order to steal sth from it □ *menggeledah; menyelongkar*: *I caught him rifling through the papers on my desk.*

rift /rɪft/ *noun* [C] **1** a serious disagreement between friends, groups, etc. that stops their relationship from continuing □ *perselisihan; perbalahan*: *a growing rift between the brothers* **2** a very large crack or opening in the ground, a rock, etc. □ *rekahan*

rig¹ /rɪg/ verb [T] (rigging; rigged) to arrange or control an event, etc. in an unfair way, in order to get the result you want □ *memanipulasikan; dikendalikan dgn tdk jujur*: They claimed that the competition had been rigged.

PHR V **rig sth up** to make sth quickly, using any materials you can find □ *membuat; mendirikan*: We tried to rig up a shelter using our coats.

rig² /rɪg/ = oil rig

rigging /'rɪgɪŋ/ noun [U] the ropes, etc. that support a ship's sails □ *tali-temali*

right¹ /raɪt/ adj
▶ MORALLY GOOD **1** (used about behaviour, actions, etc.) fair; morally and socially correct □ *baik; elok; betul; wajar*: It's not right to pay people so badly. ◆ What do you think is **the right thing** to do? **OPP** wrong
▶ CORRECT **2** correct; true □ *betul; benar*: I'm afraid that's not the right answer. ◆ Have you got **the right time**? ◆ You're quite right—the film does start at 7 o'clock. ◆ You were right about the weather—it did rain. ◆ 'You're Chinese, aren't you?' 'Yes, that's right.' **OPP** wrong
▶ MOST SUITABLE **3** right (for sb/sth) best; most suitable □ *betul; sesuai*: I hope I've made **the right decision**. ◆ I'm sure we've chosen **the right person** for the job. ◆ I would help you to wash the car, but I'm not wearing the right clothes. **OPP** wrong
▶ NORMAL **4** healthy or normal; as it should be □ *sihat; betul; kena*: The car exhaust doesn't sound right—it's making a funny noise. ◆ I don't know what it is, but something's just not right. **OPP** wrong
▶ NOT LEFT **5** [only *before* a noun] on or of the side of the body that faces east when a person is facing north □ *kanan*: Most people write with their right hand. ◆ He's blind in his right eye. **OPP** left
▶ COMPLETE **6** [only *before* a noun] (BrE spoken) (used for emphasizing sth bad) real or complete □ *betul-betul*: I'll look a right idiot in that hat!
IDM **get/start off on the right/wrong foot (with sb)** ⊃ foot¹
get on the right/wrong side of sb ⊃ side¹
on the right/wrong track ⊃ track¹
put sth right to correct sth or deal with a problem □ *membetulkan sst*: There's something wrong with the lawnmower. Do you think you'll be able to put it right?
right (you are)! (spoken) 'yes, I will' or 'yes, I agree' □ *baiklah*: 'See you later.' 'Right you are!' **SYN** OK
(as) right as rain completely healthy and normal □ *sihat walafiat*
▶ **rightness** noun [U]

right² /raɪt/ adv, exclam
▶ EXACTLY **1** directly □ *betul-betul*: The train was right on time. ◆ He was sitting right beside me.
▶ COMPLETELY **2** all the way □ *terus*: Did you watch the film right to the end? ◆ There's a high wall that goes right round the house.
▶ IMMEDIATELY **3** immediately □ *segera*: Wait here a minute—I'll be right back.
▶ CORRECTLY **4** in the way that it should happen or should be done □ *dgn betul*: Have I spelt your name right? ◆ Nothing seems to be going right for me at the moment. **OPP** wrong
▶ NOT LEFT **5** to the right side □ *ke kanan*: Turn right at the traffic lights. **OPP** left
▶ TO GET ATTENTION **6** (spoken) (used for preparing sb for sth that is about to happen) get ready; listen □ *baiklah*: Have you got your seat belts on? Right, off we go!
IDM **right/straight away** ⊃ away
right now at this moment; exactly now □ *ketika ini; sekarang juga*: We can't discuss this right now.
serve sb right ⊃ serve

right³ /raɪt/ noun **1** [U] what is morally good and fair □ *betul*: Does a child of ten really understand the difference between right and wrong? ◆ You **did right** to tell me what happened. **OPP** wrong **2** [U,C] the right (to sth/to do sth) a thing that you are allowed to do according to the law; a moral authority to do sth □ *hak*: Freedom of speech is one of the basic **human rights**. ◆ **civil rights** (= the rights each person has to political and religious freedom, etc.) ◆ *animal rights campaigners* ◆ Everyone has the right to a fair trial. ◆ You **have no right** to tell me what to do. **3** [sing] the right side or direction □ *(sebelah) kanan*: We live in the first house **on the right**. ◆ Take the first right and then the second left. **OPP** left **4 the Right** [sing, with sing or pl verb] the people or political parties who believe in individual responsibility, rather than state support □ *Sayap atau Puak (berhaluan) Kanan*: The Right in British politics is represented by the Conservative Party. ⊃ look at **right wing**
IDM **be in the right** to be correct and fair □ *di pihak benar; betul*: You don't need to apologize. You were in the right and he was in the wrong.
by rights according to what is fair or correct □ *sepatutnya*: By rights, half the profit should be mine.
in your own right because of what you are yourself and not because of other people □ *sendiri*
within your rights (to do sth) acting in a reasonable or legal way □ *berhak (utk membuat sst)*: You are quite within your rights to demand to see your lawyer.

right⁴ /raɪt/ verb [T] to put sb/sth/yourself back into a normal position □ *membetulkan (kedudukan, dll)*: The boat tipped over and then righted itself again.
IDM **right a wrong** to do sth to correct an unfair situation or sth bad that you have done □ *membetulkan (apa yg salah atau tdk adil)*

right angle noun [C] an angle of 90° □ *sudut tegak*: A square has four right angles. ⊃ look at **acute angle, obtuse angle, reflex angle** ⊃ picture at **angle**

right-angled adj having or consisting of a right angle □ *bersudut tegak*: a right-angled triangle

right-click verb [I,T] right-click (on) sth to press the button on a mouse that is on the right

righteous → ring 736

side, in order to choose a particular function on a computer screen □ *klik kanan*

righteous /ˈraɪtʃəs/ adj (formal) that you think is morally good or fair □ *wajar; patut: righteous anger/indignation* ⊃ look at **self-righteous**

rightful /ˈraɪtfl/ adj [only before a noun] (formal) legally or morally correct; fair □ *(yg) berhak/benar* ▶ **rightfully** /-fəli/ adv

right-hand adj [only before a noun] of or on the right of sb/sth □ *sebelah kanan: The postbox is on the right-hand side of the road.* ♦ *in the top right-hand corner of the screen* OPP **left-hand**

right-handed adj using the right hand for writing, etc. and not the left □ *menggunakan tangan kanan* OPP **left-handed**

right-hand 'man noun [sing] the person you depend on most to help and support you in your work □ *orang kanan: the President's right-hand man*

rightly /ˈraɪtli/ adv correctly or fairly □ *dgn betul; sepatutnya; memang wajar: He's been sacked and quite rightly, I believe.*

right of 'way noun (pl **rights of way**) **1** [C,U] (especially BrE) a path across private land that the public may use; legal permission to go into or through another person's land □ *jalan; laluan; hak utk lalu-lalang: Walkers have right of way through the farmer's field.* **2** [U] (used in road traffic) the fact that a vehicle in a particular position is allowed to drive into or across a road before another vehicle in a different position □ *hak laluan: He should have stopped—I had the right of way.*

right 'wing noun [sing, with sing or pl verb] the people or political parties who believe in individual responsibility, rather than state support □ *(golongan) sayap kanan* ▶ **right-wing** adj: *a right-wing government* OPP **left wing**

rigid /ˈrɪdʒɪd/ adj **1** not able or not wanting to change or be changed □ *tegar* SYN **inflexible 2** difficult to bend; stiff □ *tegar; keras; kaku; kejang: a rucksack with a rigid frame* ♦ *She was rigid with fear.* ▶ **rigidity** /rɪˈdʒɪdəti/ noun [U] ▶ **rigidly** adv: *The speed limit must be rigidly enforced.*

rigorous /ˈrɪɡərəs/ adj done very carefully and with great attention to detail □ *rapi; terperinci: Rigorous tests are carried out on drinking water.* ▶ **rigorously** adv: *The country's press is rigorously controlled.*

rigour (AmE **rigor**) /ˈrɪɡə(r)/ noun (formal) **1** [U] doing sth carefully with great attention to detail □ *kerapian; terperinci: The tests were carried out with rigour.* **2** [U] the quality of being strict □ *keketatan; ketatnya: the full rigour of the law* **3** [C, usually pl] difficult conditions □ *kejerihan; keadaan teruk*

rim /rɪm/ noun [C] an edge at the top or outside of sth that is round □ *bibir; tepi; bingkai: the rim of a cup* ♦ *She wore spectacles with gold rims.*

rind /raɪnd/ noun [C,U] the thick hard skin on the outside of some fruits, some types of cheese, meat, etc. □ *kulit*

> **MORE** We say the **rind** or **peel** of a lemon or an orange. The soft covering on a fruit like a banana can be called a **peel** or a **skin**.

ring¹ /rɪŋ/ noun
▶ JEWELLERY **1** [C] a piece of jewellery that you wear on your finger □ *cincin: a gold/wedding ring* ♦ *an engagement ring* ♦ *A diamond ring glittered on her finger.* ⊃ picture at **jewellery**
▶ CIRCLE **2** [C] [in compounds] a round object of any material with a hole in the middle □ *cecincin; simpai: curtain rings* ♦ *a key ring* (= for holding keys) **3** [C] a round mark or shape □ *lingkaran; bulatan: The coffee cup left a ring on the table top.* ♦ *Stand in a ring and hold hands.*
▶ FOR PERFORMANCE **4** [C] the space with seats all around it where a performance, etc. takes place □ *gelanggang: a boxing ring*
▶ FOR COOKING **5** [C] (AmE **burner**) [C] one of the round parts on the top of an electric or gas cooker on which you can put pans □ *penunu: an electric cooker with an oven, a grill and four rings*
▶ GROUP OF PEOPLE **6** [C] a number of people who are involved in sth that is secret or not legal □ *sindiket; kumpulan sulit/haram: a spy/drugs ring*
▶ OF BELL **7** [C] the sound made by a bell; the act of ringing a bell □ *dentingan; (perbuatan) membunyikan loceng: There was a ring at the door.*
▶ QUALITY **8** [sing] **a ring of sth** a particular quality that words or sounds have □ *nada: What the man said had a ring of truth about it* (= sounded true).

IDM **give sb a ring** (BrE informal) to telephone sb □ *menelefon sso: I'll give you a ring in the morning.*

ring² /rɪŋ/ verb (pt **rang** /ræŋ/; pp **rung** /rʌŋ/)
▶ TELEPHONE **1** [I,T] (especially AmE **call**) **ring (sb/sth) (up)** to telephone sb/sth □ *menelefon: What time will you ring tomorrow?* ♦ *I rang up yesterday and booked the hotel.* ♦ *Ring the station and ask what time the next train leaves.* SYN **phone** ⊃ note at **telephone**
▶ BELL **2** [I,T] to make a sound like a bell or to cause sth to make this sound □ *berdering; membunyikan loceng: Is that the phone ringing?* ♦ *We rang the door bell but nobody answered.* **3** [I] **ring (for sb/sth)** to ring a bell in order to call sb, ask for sth, etc. □ *memanggil (dgn membunyikan loceng): 'Did you ring, sir?' asked the stewardess.* ♦ *Ring for the nurse if you need help.*
▶ WITH SOUND **4** [I] **ring (with sth)** to be filled with loud sounds □ *riuh; berkumandang; berdengung: The music was so loud it made my ears ring.*
▶ WITH QUALITY **5** [I] (used about words or sounds) to have a certain effect when you hear them □ *berbunyi: Her words didn't ring true* (= you felt that you could not believe what she said).
▶ SURROUND **6** [T] (pt, pp **ringed**) [often passive] to surround sb/sth □ *mengepung; melingkari; dilingkari: The whole area was ringed with police.*
▶ DRAW CIRCLE **7** [T] (pt, pp **ringed**) (especially BrE)

to draw a circle around sth □ *membuat bulatan*: *Ring the correct answer in pencil.* **SYN** circle

IDM **ring a bell** to sound familiar or to remind you, not very clearly, of sb/sth □ *rasa-rasa macam pernah dengar*: '*Do you know Josef Vos?*' '*Well, the name rings a bell.*'

PHR V **ring (sb) back** (*BrE*) to telephone sb again or to telephone sb who has telephoned you □ *menelefon (sso) balik*: *I can't talk now—can I ring you back?*

ring in (*BrE*) to telephone a TV or radio show, or the place where you work □ *menelefon*: *Mandy rang in sick this morning.*

ring off to put down the telephone, because you have finished speaking □ *menamatkan panggilan telefon*

ring out to sound loudly and clearly □ *kedengaran kuat dan jelas*

ringleader /ˈrɪŋliːdə(r)/ *noun* [C] a person who leads others in crime or in causing trouble □ *ketua geng*: *The ringleaders were jailed for 15 years.*

ˈring pull (*AmE* ˈpull tab) *noun* [C] a small piece of metal with a ring which you pull to open cans of food, drink, etc. □ *relang tarik*

ˈring road *noun* [C] (*BrE*) a road that is built all around a town so that traffic does not have to go into the town centre □ *jalan keliling* ⊃ look at **bypass**

ringtone /ˈrɪŋtəʊn/ *noun* [C] the sound that your phone makes when sb is calling you. *Ringtones are often short tunes.* □ *nada dering*

rink /rɪŋk/ = **skating rink**

rinse /rɪns/ *verb* [T] to wash sth in water in order to remove soap or dirt □ *membilas*: *Rinse your hair thoroughly after each shampoo.* ▶**rinse** *noun* [C]

riot /ˈraɪət/ *noun* [C] a situation in which a group of people behave in a violent way in a public place, often as a protest □ *rusuhan*: *Further riots have broken out in the city.*

IDM **run riot 1** to behave in a wild way without any control □ *bertindak liar*: *At the end of the match, the crowd ran riot.* **2** if your imagination, a feeling, etc. **runs riot** you allow it to develop and continue without trying to control it □ *membiarkan (fikiran, perasaan, dll) meliar*

▶**riot** *verb* [I]: *There is a danger that the prisoners will riot if conditions do not improve.* ▶**rioter** *noun* [C]

riotous /ˈraɪətəs/ *adj* **1** wild or violent; lacking in control □ *liar; tdk terkawal* **2** wild and full of fun □ *liar dan seronok*: *a riotous party* ♦ *riotous laughter*

ˈriot shield = **shield¹** (2)

RIP /ˌɑːr aɪ ˈpiː/ *abbr* (written on the stones where dead people are buried) **rest in peace** □ *semoga bersemadi dgn sejahtera*

rip¹ /rɪp/ *verb* (**ripping**; **ripped**) **1** [I,T] to tear or be torn quickly and suddenly □ *mengoyakkan; terkoyak; koyak; rabak*: *Oh no! My dress has ripped!* ♦ *He ripped the letter in half/two and threw it in the bin.* ♦ *The blast of the bomb ripped*

737 **ringleader → rise**

the house apart. **2** [T] to remove sth quickly and violently, often by pulling it □ *mengoyakkan*: *He ripped the poster from the wall.* **3** [T] to copy sound or video files from a website or CD onto a computer □ *menyalin*

PHR V **rip sb off** (*informal*) to cheat sb by charging too much money for sth □ *menipu*

rip through sth to move very quickly and violently through sth □ *melanda; (api) menjilat*: *The house was badly damaged when fire ripped through the first floor.*

rip sth up to tear sth into small pieces □ *mengoyak-ngoyakkan*

rip² /rɪp/ *noun* [C] a long tear (in cloth, etc.) □ *rabak; koyak*

ripe /raɪp/ *adj* (**riper**; **ripest**) **1** (used about fruit, grain, etc.) ready to be picked and eaten □ *masak* **2 ripe (for sth)** ready for sth or in a suitable state for sth □ *sedia utk* ▶**ripen** /ˈraɪpən/ *verb* [I,T]

ˈrip-off *noun* [C] (*informal*) something that costs a lot more than it should □ *penipuan; (sst yg) mencekik darah*: *The food in that restaurant is a complete rip-off!*

ripple

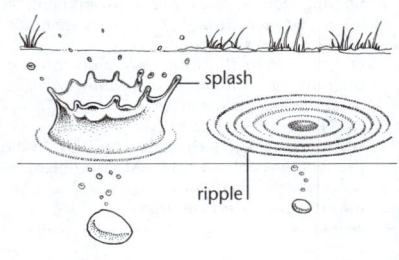

splash

ripple

ripple /ˈrɪpl/ *noun* [C] **1** a very small wave or movement on the surface of water □ *riak* **2** [usually sing] **a ripple (of sth)** a sound that gradually becomes louder and then quieter again; a feeling that gradually spreads through a person or a group of people □ *alunan; perasaan yg melanda*: *a ripple of laughter* ▶**ripple** *verb* [I,T]

rise¹ /raɪz/ *noun* **1** [C] **a rise (in sth)** an increase in an amount, a number or a level □ *kenaikan; naiknya; peningkatan; meningkatnya*: *There has been a sharp rise in the number of people out of work.* **OPP drop, fall 2** [C] (*AmE* **raise**) an increase in the money you are paid for the work you do □ *kenaikan gaji*: *I'm hoping to get a rise next April.* ♦ *a 10% pay rise* **3** [sing] **the rise (of sth)** the process of becoming more powerful or important □ *kebangkitan*: *the rise of fascism in Europe* ♦ *her rapid rise to fame/power*

IDM **give rise to sth** (*formal*) to cause sth to happen or exist □ *menimbulkan; membangkitkan*

rise² /raɪz/ *verb* [I] (*pt* **rose** /rəʊz/; *pp* **risen** /ˈrɪzn/)

risk → road 738

▶MOVE UPWARDS **1** to move upwards; to become higher, stronger or to increase □ *naik*: *Smoke was rising from the chimney.* ♦ *The temperature has risen to nearly forty degrees.* **OPP** fall

HELP Rise or raise? **Rise** does not have an object. When people or things **rise**, they move upwards: *The helicopter rose into the air.* ♦ *The river has risen (by) several metres.* **Rise** can also mean 'increase': *Prices are always rising.* **Raise** must have an object. When you **raise** something, you lift it up or increase it: *He raised his head from the pillow.* ♦ *Shops are always raising prices.*

▶GET UP **2** (*formal*) to get up from a chair, bed, etc. □ *bangun*: *The audience rose and applauded the singers.*

▶SUN/MOON **3** to appear above the **horizon** (= the line where the earth meets the sky) □ *terbit*: *The sun rises in the east and sets in the west.* **OPP** set

▶BECOME POWERFUL **4** to become more successful, powerful, important, etc. □ *meningkat; naik*: *He rose through the ranks to become the company director.* ♦ *She rose to power in the 90s.*

▶COME FROM **5** to come from □ *timbul*: *Shouts of protest rose from the crowd.*

▶FIGHT **6** (*formal*) **rise (up) (against sb/sth)** to start fighting against your ruler, government, etc. □ *bangkit menentang*: *The people were afraid to rise up against the dictator.*

▶BE SEEN **7** (*formal*) to be seen above or higher than sth else □ *meninggi; menjulang*: *A range of mountains rose in the distance.*
IDM an early riser ⇨ early
rise to the occasion, challenge, task, etc. to show that you are able to deal with a problem, etc. successfully □ *berjaya menghadapi keadaan; mampu menyahut cabaran, dsb*
▶**rising** *adj*: *the rising cost of living* ♦ *a rising young rock star*

risk¹ /rɪsk/ *noun* **1** [C,U] **(a) risk (of sth/that …);** **(a) risk (to sb/sth)** a possibility of sth dangerous or unpleasant happening; a situation that could be dangerous or have a bad result □ *risiko*: *Don't take any risks when you're driving.* ♦ *You could drive a car without insurance, but it's **not worth the risk**.* ♦ *Scientists say these pesticides **pose a risk** to wildlife.* ♦ *If we don't leave early enough, we **run the risk** of missing the plane.* ♦ *Small children are most **at risk** from the disease.* **2** [sing] a person or thing that might cause danger □ *yg berbahaya*: *If he knows your real name, he's a security risk.*
IDM at your own risk having the responsibility for whatever may happen □ *atas tanggungan sendiri*: *This building is in a dangerous condition—enter at your own risk.*
at the risk of sth/doing sth even though there could be a bad effect □ *sekalipun ada risiko*: *He rescued the girl at the risk of his own life.*

risk² /rɪsk/ *verb* [T] **1** to put sth or yourself in a dangerous position □ *mengambil risiko; membahayakan*: *The man risked his life to save the little boy.* **2** to do sth that may mean that you get into a situation which is unpleasant for you □ *menerima kemungkinan*: *If you don't work hard now, you risk failing your exams.*

risky /ˈrɪski/ *adj* (**riskier; riskiest**) involving the possibility of sth bad happening □ *berisiko; berbahaya* **SYN** dangerous: *a risky investment*

rite /raɪt/ *noun* [C] a ceremony performed by a particular group of people, often for religious purposes □ *upacara (keagamaan)*: *funeral rites*

ritual /ˈrɪtʃuəl/ *noun* [C,U] a series of actions that is always done in the same way □ *upacara amal; ritual*: *(a) religious ritual* ▶**ritual** *adj* [only before a noun] ▶**ritually** /-tʃuəli/ *adv*

rival¹ /ˈraɪvl/ *noun* [C] a person or thing that is competing with you □ *saingan; tandingan*: *It seems that we're rivals for the sales manager's job.* ▶**rival** *adj*: *rival companies*

rival² /ˈraɪvl/ *verb* [T] (**rivalling; rivalled**, (*AmE*) **rivaling; rivaled**) **rival sb/sth (for/in sth)** to be as good as sb/sth □ *menyaingi; menandingi*: *Nothing rivals skiing for sheer excitement.*

rivalry /ˈraɪvlri/ *noun* [C,U] (*pl* **rivalries**) **rivalry (between A and B); rivalry (with sb)** competition between people, groups, etc. □ *persaingan; pertandingan*: *There was a lot of rivalry between the sisters.*

river /ˈrɪvə(r)/ *noun* [C] (*abbr* R.) a large, natural flow of water that goes across land and into the sea □ *sungai*: *the River Nile* ♦ *He sat down on the bank of the river to fish.* ⇨ picture on page P10

MORE A river **flows** into the sea. The place where it joins the sea is the river **mouth**. A boat sails **on** the river. We sail **up** or **down** river and walk **along** the river (= by the side of it). The ground by the side of a river is the **bank**.

riverside /ˈrɪvəsaɪd/ *noun* [sing] the land next to a river □ *tepi sungai*: *a riverside hotel*

rivet¹ /ˈrɪvɪt/ *noun* [C] a metal pin for fastening two pieces of metal together □ *rivet*

rivet² /ˈrɪvɪt/ *verb* [T, usually passive] to keep sb very interested □ *terpegun; terpukau; tertarik*: *I was riveted by her story.* ▶**riveting** *adj*

roach /rəʊtʃ/ (*AmE*) = cockroach

road /rəʊd/ *noun* [C] **1** a hard surface built for vehicles to travel on □ *jalan*: *Turn left off the main* (= important) *road.* ♦ *road signs* **2 Road** (*abbr* **Rd**) used in names of roads, especially in towns □ *Jalan*: *60 Marylebone Road, London*
IDM by road in a car, bus, etc. □ *menaiki kereta, bas, dll*: *It's going to be a terrible journey by road—let's take the train.*
on the road travelling □ *dlm perjalanan*: *We were on the road for 14 hours.*

OTHER WORDS FOR

road

Roads connect towns and cities. A **street** is a road that is in a town or city and has buildings at the side: *a street map of York.* Streets

---

[I] **intransitive**, a verb which has no object: *He laughed.*   [T] **transitive**, a verb which has an object: *He ate an apple.*

often have the word **Road** in their name: *Abbey Road*. **Motorways** (*AmE* **freeways/expressways**) are large roads for traffic travelling fast over long distances, avoiding towns. A **lane** is a narrow road in the country. It can also be one section of a motorway: *He passed me in the fast lane.*

roadblock /ˈrəʊdblɒk/ noun [C] a barrier put across a road by the police or army to stop traffic □ *sekatan jalan*

ˈroad rage noun [U] a situation in which a driver becomes extremely angry or violent with the driver of another car because of the way they are driving □ *kemarahan pemandu terhadap pemandu lain ketika di jalan raya*

roadside /ˈrəʊdsaɪd/ noun [C, usually sing] the edge of a road □ *tepi jalan*: *a roadside cafe*

ˈroad tax noun [C,U] (*BrE*) a tax which the owner of a vehicle has to pay to be allowed to drive it on public roads □ *cukai jalan*

the roadway /ˈrəʊdweɪ/ noun [sing] a road or the part of a road used by vehicles □ *jalan*

roadworks /ˈrəʊdwɜːks/ noun [pl] work that involves repairing or building roads □ *kerja membina/membaiki jalan raya*

roadworthy /ˈrəʊdwɜːði/ adj in good enough condition to be driven on the road □ *layak utk dipandu di jalan raya*

roam /rəʊm/ verb [I,T] to walk or travel with no particular plan or aim □ *merayau*: *Gangs of youths were roaming the streets looking for trouble.*

roaming /ˈrəʊmɪŋ/ noun [U] using a mobile phone by connecting to a different company's network, for example when you are in a different country □ *perayauan*

roar /rɔː(r)/ verb 1 [I] to make a loud, deep sound □ *mengaum; ketawa berdekah-dekah*: *She roared with laughter at the joke.* ◆ *The lion opened its huge mouth and roared.* 2 [I,T] to shout sth very loudly □ *menempikkan; bertempik* 3 [I] **roar along, down, past, etc.** to move in the direction mentioned, making a loud, deep sound □ *berderum*: *A motorbike roared past us.* ▶ **roar** noun [C]: *the roar of heavy traffic on the motorway* ◆ *roars of laughter*

roaring /ˈrɔːrɪŋ/ adj [only before a noun] 1 making a very loud noise □ *berderam-derum* 2 (used about a fire) burning very well □ *bergelojak; menggelojak; bertempik* 3 very great □ *sangat; begitu; amat*: *a roaring success*

roast¹ /rəʊst/ verb 1 [I,T] to cook or be cooked in an oven or over a fire □ *memanggang*: *a smell of roasting meat* ◆ *to roast a chicken* 2 [T] to heat and dry sth □ *merendang; menggoreng (tanpa minyak)*: *roasted peanuts* ⊃ note at **cook** ▶ **roast** adj [only before a noun]: *roast beef/potatoes/chestnuts*

roast² /rəʊst/ noun 1 [C,U] a piece of meat that has been cooked in an oven □ *daging panggang* 2 [C] (*especially AmE*) an outdoor meal at which food is cooked over a fire □ *majlis barbeku* ⊃ look at **barbecue**

rob /rɒb/ verb [T] (robbing; robbed) **rob sb/sth (of sth)** to take money, property, etc. from a person or place illegally □ *merompak*: *to rob a bank* ⊃ note at **steal**

PHR V **rob sb/sth (of sth)** to take sth away from sb/sth that they or it should have □ *menyebabkan sso tdk dpt sst atau tdk dpt membuat sst*: *His illness robbed him of the chance to play for his country.*

robber /ˈrɒbə(r)/ noun [C] a person who steals from a place or a person, especially using violence or threats □ *perompak* ⊃ note at **thief**

robbery /ˈrɒbəri/ noun [C,U] (pl robberies) the crime of stealing from a place or a person, especially using violence or threats □ *rompakan*: *They were found guilty of armed robbery* (= using a weapon).

robe /rəʊb/ noun [C] 1 a long, loose piece of clothing, especially one that is worn at ceremonies □ *jubah* 2 (*AmE*) = **dressing gown**

robin /ˈrɒbɪn/ noun [C] a small brown bird with a bright red chest □ *burung robin*

robot /ˈrəʊbɒt/ noun [C] a machine that works automatically and can do some tasks that a human can do □ *robot*: *These cars are built by robots.*

robust /rəʊˈbʌst/ adj (robuster; robustest) strong and healthy □ *tegap; sihat dan kuat*

rock¹ /rɒk/ noun
▶HARD MATERIAL 1 [U] the hard, solid material that forms part of the surface of the earth □ *batuan*: *layers of rock formed over millions of years* 2 [C, usually pl] a large mass of rock that sticks out of the sea or the ground □ *batuan; batu besar*: *The ship hit the rocks and started to sink.* 3 [C] a single large piece of rock □ *batu*: *The beach was covered with rocks that had broken away from the cliffs.*
▶STONE 4 [C] (*AmE*) a small piece of rock that can be picked up □ *batu kecil*: *The boy threw a rock at the dog.* ⊃ picture on page P10
▶MUSIC 5 (also ˈrock music) [U] a type of music with a very strong beat, played on musical instruments like electric guitars, drums, etc. □ *muzik rok*: *I prefer jazz to rock.* ◆ *a rock singer/band* ⊃ look at **classical, jazz, pop**
▶SWEET 6 [U] (*BrE*) a type of hard sweet made in long, round sticks □ *gula-gula keras*: *a stick of rock*

IDM **on the rocks** 1 (used about a marriage, business, etc.) having problems and likely to fail □ *retak* 2 (used about drinks) served with ice but no water □ *(minuman) dgn ais*: *whisky on the rocks*

rock² /rɒk/ verb 1 [I,T] to move backwards and forwards or from side to side; to make sb/sth do this □ *berayun; berbuai-buai; mengayunkan; membuaikan*: *boats rocking gently on the waves*

• He rocked the baby in his arms to get her to sleep. **2** [T] to shake sth violently □ *menggegarkan; digegarkan*: *The city was rocked by a bomb blast*. **3** [T] to shock sb □ *menggoncang; amat memeranjatkan*
IDM **rock the boat** (*informal*) to do sth that causes problems or upsets people □ *mengganggu; membuat kacau*: *They employ mainly quiet people who won't complain and rock the boat*.

,**rock and 'roll** (also **rock 'n' roll**) *noun* [U] a type of music with a strong beat that was most popular in the 1950s □ *muzik 'rock-and-roll'*

,**rock 'bottom** *noun* [U] (*informal*) the lowest point □ *takat paling rendah; dlm keadaan paling teruk*: *He hit rock bottom when he lost his job and his wife left him.* • *rock-bottom prices*

'**rock climbing** *noun* [U] the sport of climbing rocks and mountains with ropes, etc. □ *mendaki gunung atau batuan tinggi*

rocket¹ /'rɒkɪt/ *noun* [C] **1** a vehicle that is used for travel into space □ *roket*: *a space rocket* • *to launch a rocket* **2** a weapon that travels through the air and that carries a bomb □ *peluru berpandu* **SYN** missile **3** a type of firework (= an object that explodes in a beautiful way when you light it with a match) that shoots high into the air □ *bunga api roket*

rocket² /'rɒkɪt/ *verb* [I] to increase or rise very quickly □ *naik menjulang/mendadak*: *Prices have rocketed recently.*

'**rock music** = **rock¹**(5)

,**rock 'n' 'roll** = **rock and roll**

rocky /'rɒki/ *adj* (**rockier**; **rockiest**) covered with or made of rocks □ *berbatu-batan*: *a rocky coastline*

rod /rɒd/ *noun* [C] [often in compounds] a thin straight piece of wood, metal, etc. □ *batang; rod*: *a fishing rod*

rode past tense of **ride¹**

rodent /'rəʊdnt/ *noun* [C] a type of small animal, such as a **rat**, a **rabbit**, a mouse, etc. which has strong sharp front teeth □ *rodensia*

rodeo /'rəʊdiəʊ; rəʊ'deɪəʊ/ *noun* [C] (*pl* **rodeos**) (especially in the US) a competition or performance in which people show their skill in riding wild horses, catching cows, etc. □ *rodeo*

roe /rəʊ/ *noun* [U] the eggs of a fish, that can be eaten □ *telur ikan*

rogue /rəʊɡ/ *adj* [only *before* a noun] behaving differently from other similar people or things, often causing damage □ *meta*: *a rogue gene/ program*

role /rəʊl/ *noun* [C] **1** the position or function of sb/sth in a particular situation □ *peranan; tugas*: *Parents play a vital role in their children's education.* • *a role model* (= a person that you admire and try to copy) **2** a person's part in a play, film, etc. □ *peranan*: *She was chosen to play the role of Cleopatra.* • *a leading role in the film*

'**role-play** *noun* [C,U] an activity used especially in teaching in which a person acts a part □ *lakon peranan*

rolls

toilet roll

bread rolls

roll of tape

roll¹ /rəʊl/ *noun*
▶OF PAPER, ETC. **1** [C] something made into the shape of a tube by turning it round and round itself □ *gulung*: *a roll of film/wallpaper*
▶BREAD **2** [C] bread baked in a round shape for one person to eat □ *(roti) rol*: *a cheese roll* (= filled with cheese) ➔ picture at **bread**
▶MOVEMENT **3** [C] an act of moving or making sth move by turning over and over □ *golekan; gulingan*: *Everything depended on one roll of the dice.* **4** a movement from side to side □ *olengan*: *the roll of a ship*
▶LIST OF NAMES **5** [C] an official list of names □ *daftar*: *the electoral roll* (= the list of people who can vote in an election)
▶SOUND **6** [C] a long, low sound □ *bunyi deram-derum*: *a roll of drums*

roll² /rəʊl/ *verb*
▶TURN OVER **1** [I,T] to move by turning over and over; to make sth move in this way □ *bergolek; berguling; menggolekkan; menggulingkan*: *The apples fell out of the bag and rolled everywhere.* • *He tried to roll the rock up the hill.* **2** [I,T] **roll (sth) (over)** to turn over and over; to make sth do this □ *bergolek-golek; menggolekkan*: *The horse was rolling in the dirt.* • *The car rolled over in the crash.* • *We rolled the log over to see what was underneath.*
▶MOVE SMOOTHLY **3** [I] to move smoothly, often on wheels □ *meluncur; bercucuran*: *The car began to roll back down the hill.* • *Tears were rolling down her cheeks.*
▶MAKE BALL/TUBE **4** [I,T] **roll (sth) (up)** to make sth into the shape of a ball or tube □ *menggulung; menggentel-gentel*: *I rolled the string into a ball.* • *The insect rolled up when I touched it.*
OPP unroll
▶MAKE FLAT **5** [T] **roll sth (out)** to make sth become flat by moving sth heavy over it □ *menggelek; mencanai*: *Roll out the pastry thinly.*
▶OF SHIP, ETC. **6** [I] to move from side to side □ *beroleng-oleng*: *The ship began to roll in the storm.*
IDM **be rolling in money/in it** (*informal*) to have a lot of money □ *banyak duit; berkepuk-kepuk duit*

ð **then**   s **so**   z **zoo**   ʃ **she**   ʒ **vision**   h **how**   m **man**   n **no**   ŋ **sing**   l **leg**   r **red**   j **yes**   w **wet**

roller → roof

PHR V **roll in** (*informal*) to arrive in large numbers or amounts □ *datang melimpah-limpah*: *Offers of help have been rolling in.*
roll up (*informal*) (used about a person or a vehicle) to arrive, especially late □ *tiba*

roller /'rəʊlə(r)/ *noun* [C] **1** a piece of equipment or part of a machine that is shaped like a tube and used, for example, to make sth flat or to help sth move □ *penggelek; penggolek*: *a roller blind on a window* ⊃ picture at **curtain** **2** [usually pl] a small plastic tube that hair is rolled around to give it curls □ *penggulung*

Rollerblade™ /'rəʊləbleɪd/ *noun* [C] a boot with one row of narrow wheels on the bottom □ *Rollerblade™; sejenis sepatu roda*: *a pair of Rollerblades* ⊃ picture at **skate** ▶ **rollerblade** *verb* [I] ▶ **rollerblading** *noun* [U]

HELP Go rollerblading is a common way of talking about rollerblading for pleasure: *We go rollerblading every weekend.*

'roller coaster *noun* [C] a narrow metal track that goes up and down and round tight bends, and that people ride on in a small train for fun and excitement □ *'roller coaster'*

'roller skate (also **skate**) *noun* [C] a type of shoe with two pairs of small wheels on the bottom □ *sepatu roda*: *a pair of roller skates* ⊃ picture at **skate** ▶ **roller skate** *verb* [I] ▶ **'roller skating** *noun* [U]

'rolling pin *noun* [C] a piece of wood, etc. in the shape of a tube, that you use for making **pastry** (= a mixture of flour, fat and water) flat and thin before cooking it □ *pencanai; torak* ⊃ picture at **kitchen**

ROM /rɒm/ *abbr* **read-only memory**; computer memory that contains instructions or data that cannot be changed or removed □ *Ingatan Baca Sahaja* ⊃ look at **CD-ROM, RAM**

the Roma /'rəʊmə/ *noun* [pl] the **Romani** people □ *orang Romani*

Roman /'rəʊmən/ *adj* **1** connected with ancient Rome or the Roman Empire □ *(berkenaan dgn) Rom kuno atau Empayar Rom*: *Roman coins* ♦ *the Roman invasion of Britain* **2** connected with the modern city of Rome □ *(berkenaan dgn) kota Rom* ▶ **Roman** *noun* [C]

the ˌRoman ˈalphabet *noun* [sing] the letters A to Z, used in most western European languages □ *abjad Rumi*

ˌRoman ˈCatholic (also **Catholic**) *noun* [C], *adj* (a member) of the Christian Church which has the Pope as its head □ *Roman Katolik*: *She's (a) Roman Catholic.* ⊃ look at **Protestant**

ˌRoman Caˈtholicism (also **Catholicism**) *noun* [U] the beliefs of the Roman Catholic Church □ *kepercayaan mazhab Roman Katolik*

romance /rəʊ'mæns; 'rəʊmæns/ *noun* **1** [C] a relationship between two people who are in love with each other □ *percintaan; asmara*: *The film was about a teenage romance.* **2** [U] a feeling or atmosphere of love or of sth new, special and exciting □ *perasaan/suasana romantik; suasana yg menarik, indah, istimewa, dsb* **3** [C] a novel about a love affair □ *kisah cinta*: *historical romances*

Romani (also **Romany**) /'rɒməni; 'rəʊm-/ *noun* (*pl* -**ies**) **1** [C] a member of a race of people who traditionally spend their lives travelling around from place to place, living in **caravans** (= homes with wheels that can be pulled by a car or by a horse) □ *ahli kaum Romani* ⊃ look at **Gypsy, traveller** **2** [U] the language of the Romani people □ *bahasa orang Romani*

ˌRoman ˈnumeral *noun* [pl] one of the letters used by the ancient Romans as numbers □ *angka Roman*

HELP Roman numerals, for example IV (= 4) and X (= 10), are still used sometimes. For example, they may be found numbering the pages and chapters of books, or on some clocks.

romantic¹ /rəʊ'mæntɪk/ *adj* **1** having a quality that strongly affects your emotions or makes you think about love; showing feelings of love □ *romantik; romantis*: *a romantic candlelit dinner* ♦ *She isn't very romantic—she never says she loves me.* **2** involving a relationship between two people who are in love with each other □ *percintaan; asmara*: *Reports of a romantic relationship between the two film stars have been strongly denied.* **3** having or showing ideas about life that are emotional rather than real or practical □ *romantis; tdk praktikal*: *He has a romantic idea that he'd like to live on a farm in Scotland.* ▶ **romantically** /-kli/ *adv*

romantic² /rəʊ'mæntɪk/ *noun* [C] a person who has ideas that are not based on real life or that are not very practical □ *orang yg romantik/ romantis*

romanticize (also -**ise**) /rəʊ'mæntɪsaɪz/ *verb* [I,T] to make sth seem more interesting, exciting, etc. than it really is □ *membuat sst kelihatan lebih menarik drpd sebenarnya*

romp /rɒmp/ *verb* [I] (used about children and animals) to play in a happy and noisy way □ *bermain-main*
IDM **romp home/to victory** to win easily □ *menang dgn mudah*: *United romped to a 4-0 victory over Juventus.*
▶ **romp** *noun* [C]

roof /ruːf/ *noun* [C] (*pl* **roofs**) **1** the part of a building, vehicle, etc. which covers the top of it □ *bumbung; atap*: *sloping/tiled roof* ♦ *the roof of a car* ♦ *The library and the sports hall are under one roof* (= in the same building). ⊃ picture on **page P9** **2** the highest part of the inside of sth □ *bumbung; langit-langit*: *The roof of the cave had collapsed.* ♦ *The soup burned the roof of my mouth.*
IDM **hit the roof** ⊃ **hit¹**
a roof over your head somewhere to live □ *tempat tinggal*: *I might not have any money, but at least I've got a roof over my head.*

'roof rack *noun* [C] a structure that you fix to the roof of a car and use for carrying luggage or other large objects □ *rak di bumbung kereta* ➔ picture at **rack**

rooftop /'ru:ftɒp/ *noun* [C, usually pl] the outside of the roof of a building □ *(bahagian) atas bumbung*: *From the tower we looked down over the rooftops of the city.*

room /ru:m; rʊm/ *noun* **1** [C] a part of a house or building that has its own walls, floor and ceiling □ *bilik*: *a sitting/dining/living room* ♦ *I sat down in the waiting room until the doctor called me.* ♦ *I'd like to book a double room for two nights next month.* **2** [U] **room (for sb/sth); room (to do sth)** space; enough space □ *ruang*: *These chairs take up too much room.* ♦ *I threw away my old clothes to make room in the wardrobe for some new ones.* ♦ *There were so many people that there wasn't any room to move.* ➔ note at **place¹** ➔ look at **space** **3** [U] **room for sth** the opportunity or need for sth □ *peluang; kesempatan; ruang*: *There's room for improvement in your work* (= it could be much better). ♦ *The lack of time gives us very little room for manoeuvre.*

roomful /'ru:mfʊl; 'rʊm-/ *noun* [C] a large number of people or things in a room □ *(orang/barang) sebilik penuh*

'roommate // *noun* [C] a person that you share a room with in a flat, etc. □ *teman sebilik*

roomy /'ru:mi/ *adj* (**roomier**; **roomiest**) having plenty of space □ *lapang*: *a roomy house/car* **SYN** **spacious**

roost /ru:st/ *noun* [C] a place where birds rest or sleep □ *reban; tempat bertenggek* ▶ **roost** *verb* [I]

rooster /'ru:stə(r)/ (*AmE*) = **cock¹** (1)

root¹ /ru:t/ *noun* **1** [C] the part of a plant that grows under the ground and takes in water and food from the soil □ *akar*: *The deep roots of these trees can cause damage to buildings.* ♦ *root vegetables such as carrots and parsnips* ➔ picture at **plant**, **tree 2** [C] the part of a hair or tooth that is under the skin and that fixes it to the rest of the body □ *akar* **3 roots** [pl] the feelings or connections that you have with a place because you or your family have lived there □ *asal usul* **4** [C] the basic cause or origin of sth □ *punca*: *Let's try and get to the root of the problem.* ➔ look at **square root**

root² /ru:t/ *verb*
PHR V **root about/around (for sth)** to search for sth by moving things □ *menyelongkar/mencari-cari (sst)*: *What are you rooting around in my bag for?*
root for sb (*informal*) to give support to sb who is in a competition, etc. □ *menyokong sso yg sedang bertanding*
root sth out to find and destroy sth bad completely □ *membanteras/membasmi sst*

rope¹ /rəʊp/ *noun* [C,U] very thick, strong string that is used for tying or lifting heavy things, climbing up, etc. □ *tali*: *The rope broke and she fell.* ♦ *We need some rope to tie up the boat with.*
IDM **show sb/know/learn the ropes** to show sb/know/learn how a job should be done □ *menunjukkan sso/tahu/belajar selok-belok sst*

rope² /rəʊp/ *verb* [T] **rope A to B/A and B together** to tie sb/sth with a rope □ *mengikat*
PHR V **rope sb in (to do sth)** (*informal*) to persuade sb to help in an activity, especially when they do not want to □ *memujuk/menarik sso (utk membuat sst)*: *I've been roped in to help with the school play.*
rope sth off to put ropes round or across an area in order to keep people out of it □ *mengepung sst dgn tali*

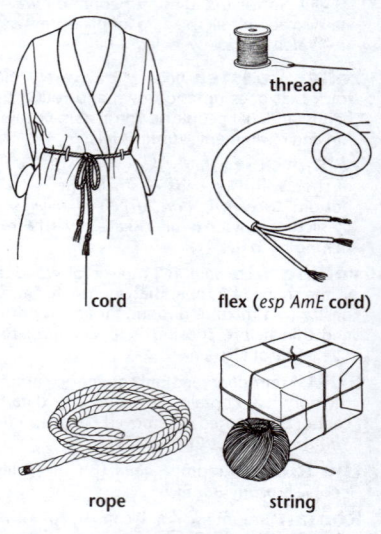

rosary /'rəʊzəri/ *noun* [C] (*pl* **rosaries**) a string of small round pieces of wood, etc. used for counting prayers □ *tasbih*

rose¹ past tense of **rise²**

rose² /rəʊz/ *noun* [C] a flower with a sweet smell, that grows on a bush that usually has **thorns** (= sharp points) growing on it □ *bunga ros/mawar*

rosé /'rəʊzeɪ/ *noun* [U] pink wine □ *'rose'*

rosemary /'rəʊzməri/ *noun* [U] a **herb** (= a type of plant) with small narrow leaves that smell sweet and are used in cooking □ *rosmeri; sejenis herba berdaun wangi*

rosette /rəʊ'zet/ *noun* [C] a round decoration made from **ribbons** (= long pieces of coloured cloth) that you wear on your clothes. Rosettes are given as prizes or worn to show that sb supports a particular political party. □ *roset* ➔ picture at **medal**

roster /ˈrɒstə(r)/ (AmE) = rota

rostrum /ˈrɒstrəm/ noun [C] a platform that sb stands on to make a public speech, etc. ▢ *pentas pidato; rostrum*

rosy /ˈrəʊzi/ adj (**rosier**; **rosiest**) **1** pink and pleasant in appearance ▢ *kemerah-merahan: rosy cheeks* **2** likely to be good or successful ▢ *cerah: The future was looking rosy.*

rot /rɒt/ verb [I,T] (**rotting**; **rotted**) to go bad or make sth go bad as part of a natural process ▢ *reput; merepukan: Too many sweets will rot your teeth!* **SYN** **decay** ▶**rot** noun [U]

rota /ˈrəʊtə/ (AmE **roster**) noun [C] a list of people who share a certain job or task and the times that they are each going to do it ▢ *jadual: We organize the cleaning on a rota.*

rotary /ˈrəʊtəri/ adj [only before a noun] moving in circles round a central point ▢ *putar*

rotate /rəʊˈteɪt/ verb [I,T] **1** to turn in circles round a central point; to make sth do this ▢ *berputar; memutarkan: The earth rotates on its axis.* **2** to happen in turn or in a particular order; to make sth do this ▢ *mengikut giliran: We rotate the duties so that nobody is stuck with a job they don't like.*

rotation /rəʊˈteɪʃn/ noun [C,U] **1** movement in a circle round a central point ▢ *putaran: one rotation every 24 hours* **2** happening or making things happen in a particular order ▢ *silih berganti: The company is chaired by all the members in rotation.*

rotor /ˈrəʊtə(r)/ noun [C] a part of a machine that turns round, for example the blades that go round on top of a **helicopter** (= a small aircraft that can go straight up in the air) ▢ *rotor*

rotten /ˈrɒtn/ adj **1** (used about food and other substances) old and not fresh enough or good enough to use ▢ *reput; busuk: rotten vegetables* **2** (*informal*) very unpleasant ▢ *teruk; tdk baik: That was a rotten thing to say!* **3** [only before a noun] (*spoken*) used to emphasize that you are angry ▢ *teruk: You can keep your rotten job!*

rouge /ruːʒ/ noun [U] (*old-fashioned*) a red powder or cream used for giving more colour to the cheeks ▢ *pemerah pipi*

ʔ rough¹ /rʌf/ adj (**rougher**; **roughest**) **1** not smooth or level ▢ *kasar; kesat; lekak-lekuk: rough ground* **OPP** **smooth 2** made or done quickly or without much care ▢ *kasar: a rough estimate* ◆ *Can you give me a rough idea of what time you'll be arriving?* **SYN** **approximate 3** violent; not calm or gentle ▢ *kasar; (laut, dsb) bergelora; (angin) bertiup kencang: You can hold the baby, but don't be rough with him.* ◆ *The sea was rough and half the people on the boat were seasick.* **4** (*BrE informal*) looking or feeling ill ▢ *tdk sihat: You look a bit rough—are you feeling all right?* **5** difficult and unpleasant ▢ *menyukarkan/malang (bagi sso)* **SYN** **tough**: *He's had a really rough time recently* (= he's had a lot of problems) ▶**roughness** noun [U]

rough² /rʌf/ noun

IDM **in rough** (*BrE*) done quickly without worrying about mistakes, as a preparation for the finished piece of work or drawing ▢ *secara kasar*
take the rough with the smooth to accept difficult or unpleasant things in addition to pleasant things ▢ *menerima baik buruk*

rough³ /rʌf/ verb
IDM **rough it** (*informal*) to live without all the comfortable things that you usually have ▢ *hidup bersusah payah (sedikit): You have to rough it a bit when you go camping.*

rough⁴ /rʌf/ adv using force or violence ▢ *kasar: Does the team always play this rough?*
IDM **live/sleep rough** (*BrE*) to live or sleep outdoors, usually because you have no home or money ▢ *tinggal/tidur di luar (kerana tiada rumah atau wang)*

roughage /ˈrʌfɪdʒ/ noun [U] the part of food that helps food and waste products to pass through the body ▢ *makanan pelawas* **SYN** **fibre**

roughen /ˈrʌfn/ verb [T] to make sth less smooth or soft ▢ *mengasarkan; mengesatkan; menjadi kasar/kesat*

ʔ roughly /ˈrʌfli/ adv **1** not exactly; approximately ▢ *kira-kira; secara kasar: It took roughly three hours, I suppose.* **2** in a violent way; not gently ▢ *dgn kasar: He grabbed her roughly by her arm.*

roulette /ruːˈlet/ noun [U] a gambling game in which a ball is dropped onto a moving wheel that has holes with numbers on them. The players bet on which number hole the ball will be in when the wheel stops. ▢ *rolet*

ʔ round¹ /raʊnd/ (**rounder**; **roundest**) adj having the shape of a circle or a ball ▢ *bulat: a round table*
IDM **in round figures/numbers** given to the nearest 10, 100, 1 000, etc.; not given in exact numbers ▢ *angka/jumlah yg dibundarkan kpd*

ʔ round² /raʊnd/ adv, prep **1** in a full circle ▢ *berputar-putar; berpusing-pusing: The wheels spun round and round but the car wouldn't move.* ◆ *How long would it take to walk round the world?* **2** on, to or from the other side of sth ▢ *keliling: We were just talking about Ravi and he came round the corner.* ◆ (*figurative*) *It wasn't easy to see a way round the problem* (= a way of solving it). **3** on all sides of sb/sth; surrounding sb/sth ▢ *sebalik: He had a bandage right round his head.* ◆ *We sat round the table, talking late into the night.* **4** from one place, person, etc. to another ▢ *mengedarkan: Pass the photographs round for everyone to see.* ◆ *I've been rushing round all day.* **5** in or to a particular area or place ▢ *di/ke kawasan atau tempat tertentu: Do you live round here?* ◆ *I'll come round to see you at about 8 o'clock.* **6** turning to look or go in the opposite direction ▢ *menoleh ke belakang; memusingkan balik: Don't look round but the teacher's just come in.* ◆ *She turned the car round and drove off.* **7** in or to many parts of sth □ *di/ke sekeliling (tempat)*: *Let me* **show** *you* **round** *the house.* ♦ *He spent six months travelling round Europe.*

HELP Around has the same meaning as **round** and is more common in American English.

❶ For special uses with many verbs, for example **come round**, **get round**, **go round**, etc. see the verb entries.

IDM the other way round ⊃ **other**
round about (sth) 1 approximately □ *kira-kira*: *We hope to arrive round about 6.00.* **2** in the area near a place □ *di sekitar (sst tempat)*: *I know all the good places to eat round about here.*
round the bend (*BrE informal*) crazy □ *jadi gila*: *His behaviour is driving me round the bend* (= annoying me very much). **SYN mad**

round³ /raʊnd/ *noun* [C]
▶EVENTS **1** a number or series of events, etc. □ *siri; beberapa*: *a further round of talks with other European countries*
▶IN SPORT **2** one part of a game or competition □ *pusingan*: *Parma will play Real Madrid in the next round.* **3** (in the sport of **golf**) one game, usually of 18 holes □ *pusingan*: *to play a round of golf*
▶REGULAR ACTIVITIES **4** a regular series of visits, etc., often as part of a job □ *siri lawatan yg biasa semasa menjalankan tugas (bagi posmen, dll)*: *The postman's round takes him about three hours.* ♦ *Dr Adamou is on his daily round of the wards.*
▶DRINKS **5** a number of drinks (one for all the people in a group) □ *satu minuman utk setiap satu orang dlm sst kumpulan; giliran (belanja minum)*: *It's my round* (= it's my turn to buy the drinks).
▶APPLAUSE **6** a short, sudden period of loud noise □ *bunyi kuat yg tiba-tiba dan sebentar; tepukan*: *The last speaker got the biggest round of applause.*
▶SHOT **7** a bullet or a number of bullets, fired from a gun □ *tembakan*: *He fired several rounds at us.*

round⁴ /raʊnd/ *verb* [T] to go round sth □ *mengelilingi; menyusuri*: *The police car rounded the corner at high speed.*

PHR V round sth off to do sth that completes a job or an activity □ *mengakhiri sst (dgn membuat sst)*: *We rounded off the meal with coffee and chocolates.*
round sb/sth up to bring sb/sth together in one place □ *menghimpunkan; mengumpulkan*: *The teacher rounded up the children.*
round sth up/down to increase/decrease a number, price, etc. to the next highest/lowest whole number □ *menaikkan/mengurangkan (bilangan, harga, dll) ke nombor bulat yg terdekat*

roundabout¹ /'raʊndəbaʊt/ *noun* [C] **1** a circle where several roads meet, that all the traffic has to go round in the same direction □ *bulatan* **2** (*AmE* **merry-go-round**) a round platform made for children to play on. They sit or stand on it and sb pushes it round. □ *mainan pentas pusing* ⊃ picture at **swing 3** (*BrE*) = **merry-go-round**

roundabout² /'raʊndəbaʊt/ *adj* longer than is necessary or usual; not direct □ *berpusing-pusing; berbelit-belit; tdk langsung*: *We got lost and came by rather a roundabout route.*

rounded /'raʊndɪd/ *adj* **1** having a round shape □ *berbentuk bulat atau bundar*: *a surface with rounded edges* ♦ *rounded shoulders* **2** having a wide variety of qualities that combine to produce sth pleasant, complete and balanced □ *lengkap; seimbang; sempurna*: *a fully rounded education*

rounders /'raʊndəz/ *noun* [U] a British game played especially in schools by two teams using a **bat** and ball. Each player tries to hit the ball and then run around the four sides of a square before the other team can return the ball. □ *raunders*

round 'trip *noun* [C] **1** a journey to a place and back again □ *perjalanan pergi balik*: *It's a four-mile round trip to the centre of town.* **2** (also ˌround-trip 'ticket) (*AmE*) = **return²(4)**

rouse /raʊz/ *verb* [T] (*formal*) **1** to make sb wake up □ *mengejutkan; menjagakan; membangunkan*: *She was sleeping so soundly that I couldn't rouse her.* **2** to make sb/sth very angry, excited, interested, etc. □ *membangkitkan (kemarahan, minat, dll); merangsangkan*

rousing /'raʊzɪŋ/ *adj* exciting and powerful □ *bersemangat; merangsangkan; memberangsangkan*: *a rousing speech*

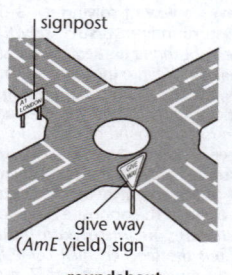

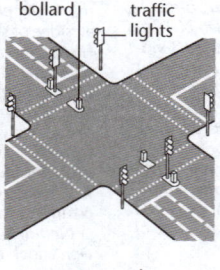

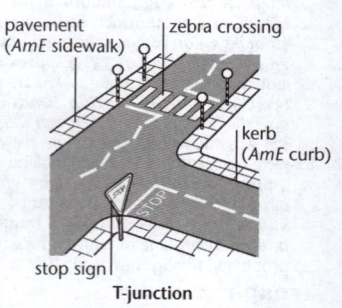

signpost
give way (*AmE* yield) sign
roundabout

bollard
traffic lights
crossroads

pavement (*AmE* sidewalk)
zebra crossing
kerb (*AmE* curb)
stop sign
T-junction

[I] **intransitive**, a verb which has no object: *He laughed.* [T] **transitive**, a verb which has an object: *He ate an apple.*

rout /raʊt/ verb [T] to defeat sb completely □ *menumpaskan* ▶**rout** noun [C]

route /ruːt/ noun [C] **1** a route (from A) (to B) a way from one place to another □ *jalan; laluan*: *What is the most direct route from Bordeaux to Lyon?* ♦ *I got a leaflet about the bus routes from the information office.* **2** a route to sth a way of achieving sth □ *jalan; cara*: *Hard work is the only route to success.* **3** used before the number of a main road in the US □ *jalan; laluan*

router /ˈruːtə(r)/ (*AmE* also) / noun [C] a device which sends data to the parts of a computer network. You can use a router to connect your computer or laptop to the Internet. □ *penghala*

routine¹ /ruːˈtiːn/ noun **1** [C,U] the usual order and way in which you regularly do things □ *rutin; kelaziman*: *Make exercise part of your daily routine.* **2** [U] tasks that have to be done again and again and so are boring □ *rutin; tugas biasa yg perlu dibuat sentiasa*: *I gave up the job because I couldn't stand the routine.* **3** [C] a series of movements, jokes, etc. that are part of a performance □ *rutin*: *a dance/comedy routine*

TOPIC

Daily routine

On **weekdays** (= Monday to Friday), I **wake up** when the alarm goes off and **get up** at 7.30. If I **oversleep** (= sleep too long), I know that I will be late for work. I **have a shower** and wash my hair. I **blow-dry** my hair with a hairdryer and **get dressed**. I have breakfast at about 8.00, while listening to the radio. I **brush my teeth** and then at 8.30 I leave the house to walk to the station. The train is very crowded with other commuters because it is rush hour. I work from **nine to five**, with a **lunch hour** from one until two. After work I like spending time with friends. We go to the cinema, or to a bar or cafe for a drink. **Twice a week** I go to the gym because I like to keep fit. I **get home** some time after 7.00 and have dinner. In the evening I **relax** and watch TV or read the paper. I **go to bed** at 11.00 and **fall asleep** straight away.

---

routine² /ruːˈtiːn/ adj **1** normal and regular; not unusual or special □ *rutin; biasa*: *The police would like to ask you some routine questions.* **2** boring; not exciting □ *rutin; membosankan*: *It's a very routine job, really.*

routinely /ruːˈtiːnli/ adv regularly; as part of a routine □ *secara rutin/berkala*: *The machines are routinely checked every two months.*

row¹ /rəʊ/ noun [C] **1** a line of people or things □ *baris; deret*: *a row of books* ♦ *The children were all standing in a row at the front of the class.* **2** a line of seats in a theatre, cinema, etc. □ *baris*: *Our seats were in the back row.* ♦ *a front-row seat* **IDM** **in a row** one after another; without a break □ *sebaris; berderet*: *It rained solidly for four days in a row.*

row² /rəʊ/ verb **1** [I,T] to move a boat through the water using **oars** (= long thin pieces of wood with flat parts at the end) □ *mendayung; mengayuh*: *We often go rowing on the lake.* **2** [T] to carry sb/sth in a boat that you row □ *membawa dgn perahu*: *Could you row us over to the island?* ⊃ look at **paddle** ▶**row** noun [sing]

row³ /raʊ/ noun (especially *BrE*) **1** [C] a row (about/over sth) a noisy argument or a serious disagreement between two or more people, groups, etc. □ *perkelahian; bertekak; bergaduh*: *When I have a row with my girlfriend, I always try to make up as soon as possible.* ♦ *A row has broken out between the main parties over education.* ⊃ note at **argument** **2** [sing] a loud noise □ *bunyi bising; keriuhan*: *What a row! Could you be a bit quieter?* ▶**row** verb [I] row (with sb) (about/over sth): *Pete and I are always rowing about money.*

HELP Be careful when you use the word **row** that you use the correct pronunciation, as **row** /rəʊ/ and **row** /raʊ/ have different meanings.

rowboat /ˈrəʊbəʊt/ (*AmE*) = **rowing boat**

rowdy /ˈraʊdi/ adj (**rowdier**; **rowdiest**) noisy and likely to cause trouble □ *riuh-rendah dan mungkin berbuat kacau*: *The football fans soon got rowdy.* ▶**rowdily** adv ▶**rowdiness** noun [U]

rowing boat (*AmE* **rowboat**) noun [C] a small boat that you move through the water using **oars** (= long thin pieces of wood with flat parts at the end) □ *perahu dayung* ⊃ note at **boat** ⊃ picture at **boat**

royal /ˈrɔɪəl/ adj [only before a noun] **1** connected with a king or queen or a member of their family □ *diraja*: *the royal family* **2** (used in the names of organizations) supported by a member of the royal family □ *diraja*: *the Royal Society for the Protection of Birds* ▶**royal** noun (*informal*): *the Queen, the Princes and other royals*

Royal 'Highness noun [C] used when you are speaking to or about a member of the royal family □ *Duli Yg Teramat Mulia; Duli Yg Maha Mulia*

royalty /ˈrɔɪəlti/ noun (*pl* **royalties**) **1** [U] members of the royal family □ *kerabat diraja* **2** [C, usually pl] an amount of money that is paid to the person who wrote a book, piece of music, etc. every time their work is sold or performed □ *royalti*: *The author earns a 2% royalty on each copy sold.*

rpm /ˌɑː piː ˈem/ abbr revolutions per minute □ *psm (putaran seminit)*: *engine speed 2 500 rpm*

RSI /ˌɑːr es ˈaɪ/ noun [U] repetitive strain injury; pain and swelling, especially in the wrists and hands, caused by doing the same movement many times in a job or an activity □ *RSI (rasa sakit terutamanya pd pergelangan tangan dan tangan akibat membuat sst gerakan berulang kali)*

CONSONANTS   p **p**en   b **b**ad   t **t**ea   d **d**id   k **c**at   g **g**ot   tʃ **ch**in   dʒ **J**une   f **f**all   v **v**an   θ **th**in

RSVP /ˌɑːr es viː ˈpiː/ abbr (from French) **répondez s'il vous plaît**; (used on invitations) please reply □ *sila jawab*

Rt Hon abbr **Right Honourable**; a title used in Britain about people of high social rank and the most important ministers in the government □ *YB (Yg Berhormat)*

rub /rʌb/ verb (**rubbing**; **rubbed**) **1** [I,T] to move your hand, a cloth, etc. backwards and forwards on the surface of sth while pressing firmly □ *menggosok-gosok; menggesel-gesel: Ralph rubbed his hands together to keep them warm.* ♦ *The cat rubbed against my leg.* **2** [T] **rub sth in (to sth)** to put a cream, liquid, etc. onto a surface by rubbing □ *menyapu: Apply a little of the lotion and rub it into the skin.* **3** [I,T] **rub (on/against sth)** to press on/against sth, often causing pain or damage □ *menggesel: These new shoes are rubbing against my heels.*

IDM **rub salt into the wound/sb's wounds** to make sb who feels bad feel even worse □ *membuat sso yg menghadapi sst keadaan yg buruk berasa lebih teruk lagi*

rub shoulders with sb to meet and spend time with famous people □ *bergaul dgn orang ternama: As a journalist you rub shoulders with the rich and famous.*

PHR V **rub it/sth in** to keep reminding sb of sth embarrassing that they want to forget □ *mengungkit-ungkit sst: I know it was a stupid mistake, but there's no need to rub it in!*

rub off (on/onto sb) (used about a good quality) to be passed from one person to another □ *(ttg sst sifat yg baik) menjangkit pd atau diikuti oleh sso: Let's hope some of her enthusiasm rubs off onto her brother.*

rub sth off (sth) to remove sth from a surface by rubbing □ *menanggalkan/membuang sst (drpd sst): He rubbed the dirt off his boots.*

rub sth out (BrE) to remove the marks made by a pencil, etc. using a rubber, etc. □ *memadam sst: That answer is wrong. Rub it out.*

▶**rub** noun [C, usually sing]

rubber /ˈrʌbə(r)/ noun **1** [U] a strong substance that can be stretched and does not allow water to pass through it, used for making tyres, boots, etc. Rubber is made from the juice of a tropical tree or is produced using chemicals □ *getah: a rubber ball* ♦ *rubber gloves* ♦ *foam rubber* **2** [C] (especially AmE **eraser**) a small piece of rubber that you use for removing pencil marks from paper; a piece of soft material used for removing **chalk** (= soft stone that you use for writing or drawing) marks from a board □ *pemadam* ⊃ picture at **stationery** **3** (informal) (especially AmE) = **condom**

rubber band (also eˌlastic ˈband) noun [C] a thin round piece of rubber that is used for holding things together □ *gelang getah: a pile of envelopes with a rubber band round them* ⊃ picture at **stationery**

rubber stamp noun [C] **1** a small tool that you use for printing a name, date, etc. on a document □ *cap getah* ⊃ picture at **stationery** **2** a person or group who gives official approval to sth without thinking about it first □ *orang atau kumpulan yg memberi kelulusan rasmi tanpa berfikir langsung* ▶**rubber-stamp** verb [T]: *The committee have no real power—they just rubber-stamp the chairman's ideas.*

rubbery /ˈrʌbəri/ adj like rubber □ *liat: This meat is rubbery.*

rubbish /ˈrʌbɪʃ/ (especially AmE **garbage**; AmE **trash**) noun [U] **1** things that you do not want any more; waste material □ *sampah: The dustmen collect the rubbish every Monday.* ♦ *a rubbish bin* ♦ *It's only rubbish—throw it away.* ⊃ look at **waste** **2** something that you think is bad, silly or wrong □ *sst yg tdk berguna atau bermutu; bukan-bukan: I thought that film was absolute rubbish.* ♦ *Don't talk such rubbish.* **SYN** **nonsense**

rubbish tip = **tip**¹ (4)

rubble /ˈrʌbl/ noun [U] pieces of broken brick, stone, etc., especially from a damaged building □ *runtuhan; puing*

rubella /ruːˈbelə/ = **German measles**

ruby /ˈruːbi/ noun [C] (pl **rubies**) a red **precious stone** (= one that is rare and valuable) □ *batu delima*

rucksack /ˈrʌksæk/ noun [C] (BrE) = **backpack**¹

rudder /ˈrʌdə(r)/ noun [C] a piece of wood or metal that is used for controlling the direction of a boat or plane □ *kemudi*

rude /ruːd/ adj (**ruder**; **rudest**) **1 rude (to sb) (about sb/sth)** not polite □ *biadab: She was very rude to me about my new jacket.* ♦ *It's rude to interrupt when people are speaking.* ♦ *I think it was rude of them not to phone and say that they weren't coming.* **SYN** **impolite 2** connected with sex, using the toilet, etc. in a way that might offend people □ *cabul; lucah: a rude joke/word/gesture* **SYN** **offensive 3** [only before a noun] sudden and unpleasant □ *mengejutkan: If you're expecting any help from him, you're in for a rude shock.* ▶**rudely** adv ▶**rudeness** noun [U]

rudimentary /ˌruːdɪˈmentri/ adj (formal) very basic or simple □ *asas*

rudiments /ˈruːdɪmənts/ noun [pl] (formal) **the rudiments (of sth)** the most basic facts of a particular subject, skill, etc. □ *asas-asas*

ruffle /ˈrʌfl/ verb [T] **1 ruffle sth (up)** to make sth untidy or no longer smooth □ *meronyokkan; mengusik-usik: to ruffle somebody's hair* **2** [often passive] to make sb annoyed or confused □ *membuat sso marah atau gelabah*

rug /rʌɡ/ noun [C] **1** a piece of thick material that covers a small part of a floor □ *ambal; hamparan* ⊃ look at **carpet**, **mat** ⊃ picture on page **P8 2** (BrE) a large piece of thick cloth that you put over your legs to keep warm □ *kain tebal (utk menyelimutkan kaki atau bahu)*

rugby /ˈrʌgbi/ *noun* [U] a game that is played by two teams of 13 or 15 players with a ball shaped like an egg that can be carried, kicked or thrown □ *ragbi* ➲ look at **league** ➲ picture on page P4

> **MORE** **Rugby League** is played with 13 players in a team, **Rugby Union** with 15 players.

rugged /ˈrʌgɪd/ *adj* **1** (used about land) rough, with a lot of rocks and not many plants □ *berbatu-batan* **2** (used about a man) strong and attractive □ *tegap dan menarik* **3** strong and made for difficult conditions □ *tahan lasak*

ruin¹ /ˈruːɪn/ *verb* [T] **1** to damage sth so badly that it loses all its value, pleasure, etc. □ *memusnahkan; merosakkan*: *The bad news ruined my week.* ♦ *That one mistake ruined my chances of getting the job.* **2** to cause sb to lose all their money, hope of being successful, etc. □ *memusnahkan; menghancurkan; jatuh papa*: *The cost of the court case nearly ruined them.*

ruin² /ˈruːɪn/ *noun* **1** [U] the state of being destroyed or very badly damaged □ *kehancuran*: *The city was in a state of ruin.* **2** [U] the fact of having no money, of having lost your job, position, etc. □ *punca kepapaan, kehancuran, dll*: *Many small companies are facing financial ruin.* **3** [U] something that causes a person, company, etc. to lose all their money, job, position, etc. □ *keruntuhan* **4** [C] (also **ruins**) the parts of a building that are left standing after it has been destroyed or badly damaged □ *puing*: *the ruins of the ancient city of Pompeii*
IDM **go to rack and ruin** ➲ **rack¹**
in ruin(s) badly damaged or destroyed □ *hancur binasa; musnah*: *After the accident her life seemed to be in ruins.*

ruined /ˈruːɪnd/ *adj* [only before a noun] destroyed or severely damaged so that only parts remain □ *termusnah*: *a ruined building*

ruinous /ˈruːɪnəs/ *adj* (*formal*) causing serious problems, especially with money □ *menyebabkan masalah besar, terutamanya dr segi kewangan*

rule¹ /ruːl/ *noun*
➤OF ACTIVITY/GAME **1** [C] an official statement that tells you what you must or must not do in a particular situation or when playing a game □ *peraturan*: *to obey/break a rule* ♦ *Do you know the rules of chess?* ♦ *It's against the rules to talk during the exam.* ♦ *The company have strict rules and regulations governing employees' dress.*

> **HELP** **Rule** or **law**? A **law** is stronger. You can be punished by the legal system if you break it.

➤ADVICE **2** [C] a piece of advice about what you should do in a particular situation □ *petua*: *There are no hard and fast rules for planning healthy meals.*
➤NORMAL SITUATION **3** [sing] what is usual □ *kebiasaan; kelaziman*: *Large families are the exception rather than the rule nowadays.* ♦ *As a general rule, women live longer than men.* ♦ *I don't read much as a rule.*

747 **rugby → rumour**

➤OF LANGUAGE **4** [C] a description of what is usual or correct in a language □ *peraturan*: *What is the rule for forming the past tense?*
➤GOVERNMENT **5** [U] government; control □ *pemerintahan; kuasa*: *The country is under military rule.*
IDM **bend the rules** ➲ **bend¹**
the golden rule (of sth) ➲ **golden**
a rule of thumb a simple piece of practical advice, not involving exact details or figures □ *mengikut kebiasaan*
work to rule ➲ **work¹**

rule² /ruːl/ *verb* [I,T] **1 rule (over sb/sth)** to have power over a country, group of people, etc. □ *memerintah; menguasai; dikuasai*: *Julius Caesar ruled over a vast empire.* ♦ (*figurative*) *His whole life was ruled by his ambition to become President.* **2 rule (on sth); rule (in favour of/against sb/sth)** to make an official decision □ *memutuskan*: *The judge will rule on whether or not the case can go ahead.*
PHR V **rule sb/sth out** to say that sb/sth is not possible, cannot do sth, etc.; to prevent sth □ *menolak (mengetepikan, dsb) sso/sst*: *The government has ruled out further increases in train fares next year.*

ruler /ˈruːlə(r)/ *noun* [C] **1** a person who rules a country, etc. □ *pemerintah*: *The country was finally united under one ruler.* **2** a straight piece of wood, plastic, etc. marked with centimetres, that you use for measuring sth or for drawing straight lines □ *pembaris* ➲ picture at **stationery**

ruling¹ /ˈruːlɪŋ/ *adj* [only before a noun] with the most power in an organization, a country, etc. □ *yg memerintah/berkuasa*: *the ruling political party*

ruling² /ˈruːlɪŋ/ *noun* [C] an official decision □ *keputusan*

rum /rʌm/ *noun* [U,C] a strong alcoholic drink that is made from the juice of **sugar cane** (= a plant from which sugar is made) □ *rum*

rumble /ˈrʌmbl/ *verb* [I] to make a long deep sound □ *menderam; bergemuruh; (perut) berkeroncong*: *I was so hungry that my stomach was rumbling.* ▶**rumble** *noun* [sing]: *a rumble of thunder*

rummage /ˈrʌmɪdʒ/ *verb* [I] to move things and make them untidy while you are looking for sth □ *membongkar; menyelongkar*: *Nina rummaged through the drawer looking for the tin opener.*

ˈrummage sale (*AmE*) = **jumble sale**

rumour (*AmE* **rumor**) /ˈruːmə(r)/ *noun* [C,U] **(a) rumour (about/of sb/sth)** (a piece of) news or information that many people are talking about but that is possibly not true □ *khabar angin*: *I didn't start the rumour about Barry's operation.* ♦ **Rumour has it** (= people are saying) *that Lena has resigned.* ♦ *to confirm/deny a rumour* (= to say that it is true/not true)

VOWELS iː **see** i **any** ɪ **sit** e **ten** æ **hat** ɑː **father** ɒ **got** ɔː **saw** ʊ **put** uː **too** u **usual**

rumoured (AmE **rumored**) /ˈruːməd/ adj reported or said, but perhaps not true □ *mengikut khabar angin*: *They are rumoured to be getting divorced.*

rump /rʌmp/ noun [C] the back end of an animal □ *(bahagian) pinggul*: *rump steak* (= meat from the rump)

run¹ /rʌn/ verb (**running**; pt **ran** /ræn/; pp **run**)
▶ ON FOOT **1** [I,T] to move using your legs, going faster than a walk □ *berlari*: *I had to run to catch the bus.* ♦ *I often go running in the evenings* (= as a hobby). ♦ *I ran nearly ten kilometres this morning.* ♦ *to run a marathon*
▶ MANAGE **2** [T] to organize or be in charge of sth; to provide a service □ *menguruskan; mengelolakan*: *She runs a restaurant.* ♦ *They run English courses all the year round.*
▶ VEHICLE **3** [T] to use and pay for a vehicle □ *menggunakan; memakai*: *It costs a lot to run a car.*
▶ OF MACHINE **4** [I,T] to operate or function; to make sth do this □ *berjalan; menjalankan; berfungsi*: *The engine is running very smoothly now.* ♦ *We're running a new computer program today.*
▶ MOVE SOMEWHERE **5** [I,T] to move, or move sth, quickly in a particular direction □ *bermaksud bergerak atau menggerakkan sst dgn cepat dlm arah tertentu*: *I've been running around after the kids all day.* ♦ *The car ran off the road and hit a tree.* ♦ *She ran her finger down the list of passengers.*
▶ LEAD **6** [I] to lead from one place to another; to be in a particular position □ *menuju; menghala*: *The road runs along the side of a lake.*
▶ CONTINUE **7** [I] to continue for a time □ *berlangsung*: *My contract has two months left to run.* ♦ *The play ran for nearly two years in a London theatre.*
▶ HAPPEN **8** [I] to operate at a particular time □ *berjalan (mengikut jadual, dll)*: *All the trains are running late this morning.* ♦ *We'd better hurry up—we're running behind schedule.*
▶ LIQUID **9** [I,T] to flow; to make water flow □ *mengalir; berair*: *When it's really cold, my nose runs.* ♦ *I can hear a tap running somewhere.* ♦ *to run a bath/a tap* **10** [I] **run with sth** to be covered with flowing water □ *dibasahi (air, peluh, dsb)*: *My face was running with sweat.*
▶ COLOUR **11** [I] to spread, for example when clothes are washed □ *turun*: *Don't put that red shirt in the washing machine. It might run.*
▶ IN NEWSPAPER **12** [T] to publish sth in a newspaper or magazine □ *menyiarkan*: *'The Independent' is running a series of articles on pollution.*
▶ TEST **13** [T] **run a test/check (on sth)** to do a test or check on sth □ *memeriksa; menguji*: *They're running checks on the power supply to see what the problem is.*
▶ IN ELECTION **14** [I] **run (for sth)** to be one of the people who hopes to be chosen in an election □ *bertanding*: *He's running for president.*
IDM **be running at sth** to be at or near a certain level □ *berada pada tahap*: *Inflation was running at 26%.*
run for it to run in order to escape □ *lari; melarikan diri* ❶ For other idioms containing **run**, look at the entries for the nouns, adjectives, etc. For example, **run in the family** is at **family**.
PHR V **run across sb/sth** to meet or find sb/sth by chance □ *terserempak dgn sso; terjumpa sst*
run after sb/sth to try to catch sb/sth □ *mengejar sso/sst*
run away to escape from somewhere □ *lari; cabut lari*: *He's run away from home.*
run (sth) down to stop functioning gradually; to make sth do this □ *menjadi semakin perlahan, berkurang, dsb; menjadi lemah, merosot dsb*: *Turn the lights off or you'll run the battery down.*
run sb/sth down 1 to hit a person or an animal with your vehicle □ *melanggar; dilanggar*: *She was run down by a bus.* **2** to criticize sb/sth □ *mengutuk; menghina*: *He's always running her down in front of other people.*
run into sb (informal) to meet sb by chance □ *terserempak dgn sso*
run into sth to have difficulties or a problem □ *menghadapi; menemui*: *If you run into any problems, just let me know.*
run (sth) into sb/sth to hit sb/sth with a car, etc. □ *melanggar atau merempuh sso/sst*: *He ran his car into a brick wall.*
run sth off to copy sth, using a machine □ *membuat salinan sst*
run off with sth to take or steal sth □ *melarikan/membawa lari sst*
run out (of sth) to finish your supply of sth; to come to an end □ *kehabisan (sst); tamat (tempoh, dsb sst)*: *We've run out of coffee.* ♦ *Time is running out.* ♦ *My passport runs out next month.*
run sb/sth over to hit a person or an animal with your vehicle □ *melanggar (atau menggelek) sso/sst*: *The child was run over as he was crossing the road.*
run through sth to discuss or read sth quickly □ *membincangkan/membaca sst dgn cepat*: *She ran through the names on the list.*

run² /rʌn/ noun
▶ ON FOOT **1** [C] an act of running on foot □ *(perbuatan) berlari*: *I go for a three-mile run every morning.* ♦ *The prisoner tried to make a run for it* (= to escape on foot).
▶ IN CAR, ETC. **2** [C] a journey by car, train, etc. □ *perjalanan*: *The bus was picking up kids on the school run.*
▶ OF SUCCESS/FAILURE **3** [sing] a series of similar events or sth that continues for a very long time □ *rentetan; berturut-turut*: *We've had a run of bad luck recently.*
▶ SUDDEN DEMAND **4** [sing] **a run on sth** a sudden great demand for sth □ *laris; permintaan yg tiba-tiba banyak*: *There's always a run on sunglasses in hot weather.*
▶ IN SPORTS **5** [C] a point in the sports of **baseball** and **cricket** □ *larian*: *Our team won by two runs.*
6 (AmE) = **ladder**(2)
IDM **in the long run** ➔ **long¹**

on the run hiding or trying to escape from sb/sth □ *melarikan diri*: *The escaped prisoner is still on the run.*

runaway¹ /ˈrʌnəweɪ/ *adj* [only *before* a noun] **1** out of control □ *terlepas; tdk terkawal*: *a runaway horse/car/train* **2** happening very easily □ *(berlaku dgn) mudah*: *a runaway victory*

runaway² /ˈrʌnəweɪ/ *noun* [C] a person, especially a child, who has left or escaped from somewhere □ *orang (terutamanya kanak-kanak) yg lari dr sst tempat*

run-ˈdown *adj* **1** (used about a building or place) in bad condition □ *terbiar*: *a run-down block of flats* **2** [not before a noun] very tired and not healthy □ *lesu; tdk berapa sihat*

rung¹ /rʌŋ/ *noun* [C] one of the bars that form the steps of a **ladder** (= a piece of equipment that is used for climbing up sth) □ *anak tangga* ⊃ picture at **ladder**

rung² past participle of **ring²**

runner /ˈrʌnə(r)/ *noun* [C] **1** a person or an animal that runs, especially in a race □ *pelari*: *a cross-country/long-distance runner* **2** a person who takes guns, drugs, etc. illegally from one country to another □ *penyeludup*: *a drug runner*

ˌrunner-ˈup *noun* [C] (*pl* **runners-up**) the person or team that finished second in a race or competition □ *naib johan; pemenang kedua*

running¹ /ˈrʌnɪŋ/ *noun* [U] **1** the action or sport of running □ *berlari; lari*: *How often do you go running?* ◆ *running shoes* **2** the process of managing a business or other organization □ *pengurusan; penyenggaraan*: *She's not involved in the day-to-day running of the office.* ◆ *the running costs of a car* (= petrol, insurance, repairs, etc.)

IDM **in/out of the running (for sth)** (*informal*) having/not having a good chance of getting or winning sth □ *ada/tdk ada peluang (utk memenangi, mendapatkan, dsb sst)*

running² /ˈrʌnɪŋ/ *adj* **1** used after a number and a noun to say that sth has happened a number of times in the same way without a change □ *berturut-turut*: *Our school has won the competition for four years running.* **2** [only *before* a noun] (used about water) flowing or available from a tap □ *mengalir; air paip*: *There is no running water in the cottage.* **3** [only *before* a noun] not stopping; continuous □ *berterusan*: *a running battle between two rival gangs*

ˌrunning ˈcommentary *noun* [C] a spoken description of sth while it is happening □ *ulasan selari*

runny /ˈrʌni/ *adj* (**runnier**; **runniest**) **1** (used about your eyes or nose) producing too much liquid □ *berair; berhingus*: *Their children always seem to have runny noses.* **2** containing more liquid than is usual or than you expected □ *cair*: *runny jam*

ˈrun-up *noun* [sing] **1** the period of time before a certain event □ *masa (hari, saat, dsb) menjelang (sst peristiwa)*: *the run-up to the election* **2** (in sport) a run that people do in order to be going fast enough to do an action, such as jumping or throwing □ *lari landas*

runway /ˈrʌnweɪ/ *noun* [C] a long piece of ground with a hard surface where aircraft take off and land at an airport □ *landasan*

rupture /ˈrʌptʃə(r)/ *noun* [C,U] **1** a sudden bursting or breaking □ *pecah* **2** (*formal*) the sudden ending of good relations between two people or groups □ *putusnya hubungan* **3** = **hernia** ▶ **rupture** *verb* [I,T]: *Her appendix ruptured and she had to have emergency surgery.*

rural /ˈrʊərəl/ *adj* connected with the country, not the town □ *luar bandar*: *This part of France is very rural.* ⊃ look at **urban**, **rustic**

ruse /ruːz/ *noun* [C] a trick or clever plan □ *tipu helah/muslihat*

rush¹ /rʌʃ/ *verb* **1** [I,T] to move or do sth with great speed, often too fast □ *meluru; bergegas; berkejar; berebut-rebut; pergi (dgn cepat)*: *I rushed back home when I got the news.* ◆ *Don't rush off—I want to talk to you.* ◆ *The public rushed to buy shares in the company.* ◆ *She rushed her lunch, so that she could get back to work as soon as possible.* **2** [T] to take sb/sth to a place very quickly □ *membawa dgn segera; dikejarkan*: *He suffered a heart attack and was rushed to hospital.* **3** [I,T] **rush (sb) (into sth/into doing sth)** to do sth or make sb do sth without thinking about it first □ *menggesa; digesa*: *Don't let yourself be rushed into marriage.* ◆ *Please don't rush me—I'm thinking!*

IDM **be rushed/run off your feet** ⊃ **foot¹**

rush² /rʌʃ/ *noun*

▶HURRY **1** [sing] a sudden quick movement □ *(perbuatan) menyerbu atau meluru; tergesa-gesa*: *At the end of the match there was a rush for the exits.* ◆ *I was so nervous, all my words came out in a rush.* **2** [sing, U] a situation in which you are in a hurry and need to do things quickly □ *tergesa-gesa; terburu-buru*: *I can't stop now. I'm in a terrible rush.* ◆ *Don't hurry your meal. There's no rush.*

▶BUSY SITUATION **3** [sing] a time when there is a lot of activity and people are very busy □ *masa sibuk; kesibukan*: *We'll leave early to avoid the rush.*

▶SUDDEN DEMAND **4** [sing] **a rush (on sth)** a time when many people try to get sth □ *(masa orang) bergegas atau berebut-rebut (utk mendapatkan sst)*: *There's always a rush on umbrellas when it rains.*

▶PLANT **5** [C] a type of tall grass that grows near water □ *menerung*

ˈrush hour *noun* [C] the time each day when there is a lot of traffic because people are travelling to or from work □ *waktu sibuk (jalan raya)*: *rush-hour traffic*

rust /rʌst/ *noun* [U] a reddish-brown substance that forms on the surface of iron, etc., caused by the action of air and water □ *karat* ▶ **rust** *verb* [I,T]: *Some parts of the car had rusted.*

rustic /ˈrʌstɪk/ adj typical of the country or of country people; simple ◻ *spt di desa; kedesaan*: *The whole area is full of rustic charm.* ➲ look at **rural, urban**

rustle /ˈrʌsl/ verb [I,T] to make a sound like dry leaves or paper moving ◻ *berkersik; mengersik*: *There was a rustling noise in the bushes.*

PHR V **rustle sth up (for sb)** (*informal*) to make or find sth quickly for sb and without planning it ◻ *mencari sso atau membuat sst cepat-cepat*: *to rustle up a quick snack*
▶ **rustle** noun [sing]

rusty /ˈrʌsti/ adj (**rustier**; **rustiest**) **1** (used about metal objects) covered with **rust** as a result of being in contact with water and air ◻ *berkarat*: *rusty tins* **2** (used about a skill) not as good as it was because you have not used it for a long time ◻ *berkarat; tdk berapa pandai lagi*: *My French is rather rusty.*

rut /rʌt/ noun [C] **1** a deep track that a wheel makes in soft ground ◻ *bekas roda (di tanah lembut)* **2** a boring way of life that is difficult to change ◻ *kebosanan cara hidup*: *I felt I was stuck in a rut in my old job.*

ruthless /ˈruːθləs/ adj (used about people and their behaviour) hard and cruel; determined to get what you want and showing no pity to others ◻ *tdk ada belas kasihan; tdk berhati perut*: *a ruthless dictator* ▶ **ruthlessly** adv ▶ **ruthlessness** noun [U]

RV /ˌɑː ˈviː/ (*AmE*) **recreational vehicle** = **camper**(2)

rye /raɪ/ noun [U] a plant that is grown in colder countries for its grain, which is used to make flour and also **whisky** (= a strong alcoholic drink) ◻ *rai*

S s

S, s /es/ noun [C,U] (*pl* **Ss; S's; s's** /ˈesɪz/) the 19th letter of the English alphabet ◻ *S, s (huruf)*: *'School' begins with (an) 'S'.*

S abbr **1** = **small**(1) ◻ *kecil (kependekan)* **2** = **south**[1], **southern** ◻ *selatan*: *S Yorkshire* **3** = **saint** ◻ *keramat*

sabbath /ˈsæbəθ/ often **the Sabbath** noun [sing] the day of the week for rest and prayer in certain religions (Sunday for Christians, Saturday for Jews) ◻ *(hari) Sabat*

sabotage /ˈsæbətɑːʒ/ noun [U] damage that is done on purpose and secretly in order to prevent an enemy being successful, for example by destroying machinery, roads, bridges, etc. ◻ *sabotaj; (perbuatan) merosakkan*: *industrial/economic/military sabotage* ▶ **sabotage** verb [T]

saccharin /ˈsækərɪn/ noun [U] a very sweet substance that can be used instead of sugar ◻ *sakarin*

sachet /ˈsæʃeɪ/ noun [C] a closed plastic or paper package that contains a very small amount of liquid or powder ◻ *uncang; paket*: *a sachet of shampoo/sugar/coffee* ➲ picture at **container**

sack[1] /sæk/ noun [C] a large bag made from a rough heavy material, paper or plastic, used for carrying or storing things ◻ *karung; guni*: *sacks of flour/potatoes*

IDM **get the sack** (*BrE*) to be told by your employer that you can no longer continue working for them (usually because you have done sth wrong) ◻ *dipecat; dibuang kerja*: *Tony got the sack for poor work.*

give sb the sack (*BrE*) to tell an employee that they can no longer continue working for you (because of bad work, behaviour, etc.) ◻ *memecat sso*: *Tony's work wasn't good enough and he was given the sack.* ➲ note at **job**

sack[2] /sæk/ (*especially AmE* **fire**) verb [T] to tell an employee that they can no longer work for you (because of bad work, bad behaviour, etc.) ◻ *memecat*: *Her boss has threatened to sack her if she's late again.*

sacred /ˈseɪkrɪd/ adj **1** connected with God, a god or religion ◻ *suci*: *The Koran is the sacred book of Muslims.* **2** too important and special to be changed or harmed ◻ *suci; murni; kudus; penting*: *a sacred tradition*

sacrifice[1] /ˈsækrɪfaɪs/ noun [U,C] **1** the act of giving up sth that is important or valuable to you in order to get or do sth that seems more important; something that you give up in this way ◻ *pengorbanan*: *If we're going to have a holiday this year, we'll have to make some sacrifices.* **2** **sacrifice (to sb)** the act of offering sth to a god, especially an animal that has been killed in a special way; an animal, etc. that is offered in this way ◻ *korban*

sacrifice[2] /ˈsækrɪfaɪs/ verb **1** [T] **sacrifice sth (for sb/sth)** to give up sth that is important or valuable to you in order to get or do sth that seems more important ◻ *mengorbankan*: *She is not willing to sacrifice her career in order to have children.* **2** [I,T] to kill an animal and offer it to a god, in order to please the god ◻ *membuat korban*

sacrilege /ˈsækrəlɪdʒ/ noun [U, sing] treating a religious object or place without the respect that it deserves ◻ *pencabulan*

sad /sæd/ adj (**sadder**; **saddest**) **1** **sad (to do sth); sad (that …)** unhappy or causing sb to feel unhappy ◻ *sedih*: *We are very sad to hear that you are leaving.* ◆ *I'm very sad that you don't trust me.* ◆ *That's one of the saddest stories I've ever heard!* ◆ *a sad poem/song/film* **2** bad or unacceptable ◻ *menyedihkan*: *It's a sad state of affairs when your best friend doesn't trust you.* ▶ **sadden** /ˈsædn/ verb [T] (*formal*): *The news of your father's death saddened me greatly.* ▶ **sadness** noun [C,U]

[I] **intransitive**, a verb which has no object: *He laughed.*
[T] **transitive**, a verb which has an object: *He ate an apple.*

OTHER WORDS FOR

sad

If something **upsets** you, you feel **unhappy** about it: *This will upset a lot of people.* **Upset** is also an adjective: *I felt upset about what they had said.* If you feel **miserable**, you are very sad. If you feel **depressed**, you feel very sad and without hope. This feeling often lasts for a long period of time: *He's been very depressed since he lost his job.* You can describe sad things that happen as **depressing**: *depressing news.*

saddle[1] /'sædl/ *noun* [C] **1** a seat, usually made of leather, that you put on a horse so that you can ride it □ *pelana* ⊃ picture at **horse 2** a seat on a bicycle or motorbike □ *tempat duduk* ⊃ picture at **bicycle**

saddle[2] /'sædl/ *verb* [T] to put a **saddle** on a horse □ *memasang/dipasang pelana*: *Their horses were saddled and waiting.*
PHR V **saddle sb with sth** to give sb a responsibility or task that they do not want □ *membebani sso dgn sst*

sadism /'seɪdɪzəm/ *noun* [U] getting pleasure, especially sexual pleasure, from hurting other people □ *sadisme; mendapat kepuasan nafsu drpd perbuatan menyeksa orang lain* ⊃ look at **masochism**

sadist /'seɪdɪst/ *noun* [C] a person who gets pleasure, especially sexual pleasure, from hurting other people □ *(orang yg) sadis; orang yg mendapat nikmat drpd perbuatan menyeksa orang lain* ▶ **sadistic** /sə'dɪstɪk/ *adj* ▶ **sadistically** /-kli/ *adv*

sadly /'sædli/ *adv* **1** unfortunately □ *malangnya; sayang sekali*: *Sadly, after eight years of marriage they had grown apart.* **2** in a way that shows unhappiness □ *dgn sedih*: *She shook her head sadly.* **3** in a way that is wrong □ *(dgn cara yg) silap/salah*: *If you think that I've forgotten what you did, you're sadly mistaken.*

sae /ˌes eɪ 'iː/ *abbr* (*BrE*) = **stamped addressed envelope** □ *sampul surat bersetem dan beralamat*: *Please enclose an sae.*

safari /sə'fɑːri/ *noun* [C,U] (*pl* **safaris**) a trip to see or hunt wild animals, especially in East Africa □ *safari*: *to be/go on safari* ⊃ note at **holiday**

safe[1] /seɪf/ *adj* (**safer**, **safest**) **1** [not before a noun] **safe (from sb/sth)** free from danger; not able to be hurt □ *selamat*: *She didn't feel safe in the house on her own.* ♦ *Do you think my car will be safe in this street?* ♦ *Keep the papers where they will be safe from fire.* **2 safe (to do sth); safe (for sb)** not likely to cause danger, harm or risk □ *selamat*: *Don't sit on that chair, it isn't safe.* ♦ *I left my suitcase in a safe place and went for a cup of coffee.* ♦ *She's a very safe driver.* ♦ *It's not safe to walk alone in the streets at night here.* ♦ *Is it safe to drink the water here?* ♦ *Is this drug safe for children?* ♦ *I think it's safe to say that the situation is unlikely to change for some time.* **3** [not before a noun] not hurt, damaged or lost □ *selamat;*

751   **saddle → sail**

terselamat: *After the accident he checked that all the passengers were safe.* ♦ *After five days the child was found, safe and sound.*
IDM **in safe hands** with sb who will take good care of you □ *dlm keadaan selamat*
on the safe side not taking risks; being very careful □ *supaya lebih selamat* ▶ **safely** *adv*: *I rang my parents to tell them I had arrived safely.*

safe[2] /seɪf/ *noun* [C] a strong metal box or cupboard with a special lock that is used for keeping money, jewellery, documents, etc. in □ *peti besi keselamatan*

safeguard /'seɪfɡɑːd/ *noun* [C] **a safeguard (against sb/sth)** something that protects against possible dangers □ *pelindung* ▶ **safeguard** *verb* [T]: *to safeguard somebody's interests/rights/privacy*

safety /'seɪfti/ *noun* [U] the state of being safe; the state of not being dangerous or in danger □ *keselamatan*: *In the interests of safety, smoking is forbidden.* ♦ *In the interests of safety, please stay behind the yellow line.* ♦ *road safety* (= preventing road accidents) ♦ *New safety measures have been introduced on trains.*

'safety belt = **seat belt**

'safety net *noun* [C] **1** a net that is placed underneath sb who is high above the ground to catch them if they fall □ *jaring keselamatan* **2** an arrangement that helps to prevent disaster (usually with money) if sth goes wrong □ *jaring keselamatan; sst yg dpt menyelamatkan jika berlaku kegagalan, dsb*

'safety pin *noun* [C] a metal pin with a point that is bent back towards the head, which is covered so that it cannot be dangerous □ *pin baju* ⊃ picture at **pin**

'safety valve *noun* [C] a device in a machine that allows steam, gas, etc. to escape if the pressure becomes too great □ *injap keselamatan*

sag /sæɡ/ *verb* [I] (**sagging**; **sagged**) to hang or to bend down, especially in the middle □ *melendut; menggeleber*

saga /'sɑːɡə/ *noun* [C] a very long story; a long series of events □ *saga; kisah panjang*

sage /seɪdʒ/ *noun* [U] a **herb** (= a type of plant) with flat, light green leaves that have a strong smell and are used in cooking □ *sej (tumbuhan herba)*

Sagittarius /ˌsædʒɪ'teəriəs/ *noun* [C,U] the 9th sign of the **zodiac** (= 12 signs which represent the positions of the sun, moon and planets) the Archer; a person born under this sign □ *Sagitarius*: *I'm (a) Sagittarius.* ⊃ picture at **zodiac**

said past tense, past participle of **say**[1]

sail[1] /seɪl/ *verb* **1** [I,T] (used about a boat or ship and the people on it) to travel on water in a ship or boat of any type □ *belayar*: *I stood at the window and watched the ships sailing by.* ♦ *to sail round the world* ♦ *to sail the seas* **2** [I,T] to travel in

sail → salmonella 752

and control a boat with sails, especially as a sport ▫ *melayarkan; mengemudi; belayar*: *My father is teaching me to sail.* ◆ *I've never sailed this kind of yacht before.*

HELP When we are talking about spending time sailing a boat for pleasure, we say **go sailing**: *We often go sailing at weekends.*

3 [I] to begin a journey on water ▫ *belayar; bertolak*: *When does the ship sail?* ◆ *We sail for Santander at 6 o'clock tomorrow morning.* 4 [I] to move somewhere quickly in a smooth or proud way ▫ *bergerak pantas dgn lancar atau megah; melayang*: *The ball sailed over the fence and into the neighbour's garden.* ◆ *Mary sailed into the room, completely ignoring all of us.*

IDM **sail through (sth)** to pass a test or exam easily ▫ *lulus dgn mudah*

sail² /seɪl/ *noun* 1 [C] a large piece of strong cloth that is fixed onto a ship or boat. The wind blows against the sail and moves the ship along. ▫ *layar* ⊃ picture on **page P6** 2 [sing] a trip on water in a ship or boat with a sail ▫ *pelayaran; (perihal) belayar*: *Would you like to go for a sail in my boat?* 3 [C] a set of boards that the wind moves round that are fixed to a **windmill** (= a building used for making flour from grain) or **wind turbine** (= a building used to make electricity) ▫ *baling-baling* ⊃ picture at **windmill**

IDM **set sail** (*formal*) to begin a journey by sea ▫ *belayar*: *Columbus set sail for India.*

sailboard /'seɪlbɔːd/ = **windsurfer** (1)

sailboat /'seɪlbəʊt/ (*AmE*) = **sailing boat**

sailing /'seɪlɪŋ/ *noun* [U] the sport of being in, and controlling, small boats with sails ▫ *belayar*: *They do a lot of sailing.* ⊃ picture on **page P3**

'sailing boat (*AmE* **sailboat**) *noun* [C] a boat with a sail or sails ▫ *perahu layar*

sailor /'seɪlə(r)/ *noun* [C] a person who works on a ship or a person who sails a boat ▫ *kelasi*: *a ship with four sailors on board*

saint /seɪnt; snt/ *noun* [C] 1 (*abbr* S; St) a very good or religious person who is given special respect after death by the Christian Church ▫ *saint; keramat* ⊃ look at **patron saint**

HELP When it is used as a title, **saint** is written with a capital letter: *Saint Patrick*. In the names of places, churches, etc. the short form **St** is usually used: *St Andrew's Church*. Before names **saint** is pronounced /snt/.

2 a very good, kind person ▫ *keramat hidup; orang yg sangat baik*

sake /seɪk/ *noun* [C]

IDM **for Christ's/God's/goodness'/Heaven's/pity's sake** (*spoken*) used to emphasize that it is important to do sth, or to show that you are annoyed ▫ *demi Tuhan, ya Tuhan, dsb*: *For goodness' sake, hurry up!* ◆ *Why have you taken so long, for God's sake?*

HELP Be careful. **For God's sake** and especially **for Christ's sake** may offend some people.

for the sake of sb/sth; for sb's/sth's sake in order to help sb/sth ▫ *kerana sso/sst*: *Don't go to any trouble for my sake.* ◆ *They only stayed together for the sake of their children/for their children's sake.*
for the sake of sth/of doing sth in order to get or keep sth; for the purpose of sth ▫ *demi/kerana sst*: *She gave up her job for the sake of her health.*

salad /'sæləd/ *noun* [C,U] a mixture of vegetables, usually not cooked, that you often eat together with other foods ▫ *salad*: *All main courses are served with salad.* ⊃ picture on **page P16**

salami /sə'lɑːmi/ *noun* [U,C] (*pl* **salamis**) a type of large spicy **sausage** (= meat that is made into a long thin shape) served cold in thin slices ▫ *salami (sosej)*

salary /'sæləri/ *noun* [C,U] (*pl* **salaries**) the money that a person receives (usually every month) for the work they have done ▫ *gaji*: *My salary is paid directly into my bank account.* ◆ *a high/low salary* ⊃ note at **pay²**

sale /seɪl/ *noun* 1 [C,U] the act of selling or being sold; the occasion when sth is sold ▫ *penjualan*: *She raised the money through the sale of her house..* ◆ *a sale of used toys* 2 **sales** [pl] the number of items sold ▫ *jualan*: *Sales of smartphones have increased rapidly.* ◆ *The company reported excellent sales figures.* 3 **sales** [U] (also **'sales department**) the part of a company that deals with selling its products ▫ *jualan*: *Jodie works in sales/in the sales department.* ◆ *a sales representative/sales rep* 4 [C] a time when shops sell things at prices that are lower than usual ▫ *jualan murah*: *The sale starts on December 28th.* ◆ *I got several bargains in the sales.* ⊃ look at **car boot sale, jumble sale**

IDM **for sale** offered for sb to buy ▫ *utk dijual*: *This painting is not for sale.* ◆ *I see our neighbours have put their house up for sale.*
on sale 1 available for sb to buy, especially in shops ▫ *dijual*: *This week's edition is on sale now at your local newsagents.* 2 (*AmE*) offered at a lower price than usual ▫ *dijual murah*

'sales clerk (*AmE*) = **shop assistant**

'sales department = **sale** (3)

salesman /'seɪlzmən/, **saleswoman** /'seɪlzwʊmən/, **salesperson** /'seɪlzpɜːsn/ *noun* [C] (*pl* **-men** /-mən/, **-women** /-wɪmɪn/, **-persons** or **-people** /-piːpl/) a person whose job is selling things to people ▫ *jurujual*

salient /'seɪliənt/ *adj* [only *before* a noun] most important or noticeable ▫ *paling penting; ketara; menonjol*

saliva /sə'laɪvə/ *noun* [U] the liquid that is produced in the mouth ▫ *air liur* ⊃ look at **spit**

salmon /'sæmən/ *noun* [C,U] (*pl* **salmon**) a large fish with silver skin and pink meat that we eat ▫ *ikan salmon*: *smoked salmon*

salmonella /ˌsælmə'nelə/ *noun* [U] a type of bacteria that makes people sick if they eat infected food; an illness caused by this bacteria ☐ *salmonela (bakteria)*

salon /'sælɒn/ noun [C] **1** a shop where you can have beauty or hair treatment or where you can buy expensive clothes ☐ *salun* **2** (old-fashioned) a room in a large house that is used for receiving guests ☐ *bilik tamu* **3** (in the past) a regular meeting of writers, artists and other guests at the house of a famous or important person ☐ *perjumpaan ahli seni*

saloon /sə'luːn/ (AmE **sedan**) noun [C] a car with a fixed roof and a **boot** (= a space in the back for luggage) ☐ *kereta salun*

salt¹ /sɔːlt/ (BrE also /sɒlt/) noun [U] a common white substance that is found in sea water and the earth. Salt is used in cooking for flavouring food ☐ *garam*: *Season with* **salt and pepper**. ♦ *Add a pinch* (= a small amount) *of salt*.
IDM **rub salt into the wound/sb's wounds** ➔ **rub**
take sth with a pinch of salt ➔ **pinch²**
▶ **salt** adj [only before a noun]: *salt water*

salt² /sɔːlt/ verb [T, usually passive] to put salt on or in sth ☐ *menggarami; bergaram*: *salted peanuts*

saltwater /'sɔːltwɔːtə(r)/ adj living in the sea ☐ *air masin; (hidup di) laut*: *a saltwater fish*
MORE Fish that live in rivers are **freshwater** fish.

salty /'sɔːlti/ adj (**saltier; saltiest**) having the taste of or containing salt ☐ *masin*: *I didn't like the soup; it was too salty*.

salute /sə'luːt/ noun [C] **1** an action that a soldier, etc. does to show respect, by touching the side of his or her head with the right hand ☐ *tabik hormat*: *to give a salute* **2** something that shows respect for sb ☐ *penghormatan*: *The next programme is a salute to a great film star.*
▶ **salute** verb [I,T]: *The soldiers saluted as they marched past the general.*

salvage¹ /'sælvɪdʒ/ noun [U] the action of saving things that have been or are likely to be lost or damaged, especially in an accident or a disaster; the things that are saved ☐ *penyelamatan; (operasi, syarikat, dsb) penyelamat; barang-barang yg diselamatkan*: *a salvage operation/company/team*

salvage² /'sælvɪdʒ/ verb [T] **salvage sth (from sth)** to manage to rescue sth from being lost or damaged; to rescue sth or a situation from disaster ☐ *menyelamatkan*: *They salvaged as much as they could from the house after the fire.*

salvation /sæl'veɪʃn/ noun **1** [U] (in the Christian religion) being saved from the power of evil ☐ *(perihal) diselamatkan* **2** [U, sing] a thing or person that rescues sb/sth from danger, disaster, etc. ☐ *penyelamat*

same /seɪm/ adj, adv, pron **1 the same ... (as sb/sth); the same ... that ...** not different, not another or other; exactly the one or ones that you have mentioned before ☐ *sama*: *My brother and I had the same teacher at school.* ♦ *They both said the same thing.* ♦ *I'm going to wear the same clothes as/that I wore yesterday.* ♦ *This one looks exactly the same as that one.* **2 the same ... (as sb/sth); the same ... that ...** exactly like the one already mentioned ☐ *sama; serupa*: *I wouldn't buy the same car again* (= the same model of car). ♦ *We treat all the children in the class the same.* ♦ *I had the same experience as you some time ago.* ♦ *All small babies look the same.* ♦ *Is there another word that means the same as this?*

HELP We cannot say 'a same ...' To express this idea we use **the same sort of**: *I'd like the same sort of job as my father.*

IDM **all/just the same** used when saying or writing sth which contrasts in some way with what has gone before ☐ *walau bagaimanapun*: *I understand what you're saying. All the same, I don't agree with you.* ♦ *I don't need to borrow any money, but thanks all the same for offering.*
at the same time 1 together; at one time ☐ *sekali gus; serentak*: *I can't think about more than one thing at the same time.* **2** on the other hand; however ☐ *namun begitu*: *It's a very good idea but at the same time it's rather risky.*
much the same ➔ **much**
on the same wavelength ➔ **wavelength**
(the) same again (spoken) a request to be served or given the same drink as before ☐ *yg sama juga lagi*
same here (spoken) the same thing is also true for me ☐ *saya pun/juga*: *'I'm bored.' 'Same here.'*
(the) same to you (spoken) used as an answer when sb says sth rude to you or wishes you sth ☐ *(bagi cacian) engkau pun sama; utk membalas ucap selamat, selalunya ucapan yg sama diulang kembali*: *'You idiot!' 'Same to you!'* ♦ *'Have a good weekend.' 'The same to you.'*

sample /'sɑːmpl/ noun [C] **1** a small number or amount of sb/sth that is looked at, tested, examined, etc. to find out what the rest is like ☐ *contoh; sampel*: *The interviews were given to a random sample of shoppers.* ♦ *to take a blood sample* ♦ *a free sample of shampoo* ➔ look at **specimen** **2** a piece of recorded music or sound that is used in a new piece of music ☐ *sampel; contoh*: *'Candy' includes a sample from a Walker Brothers song.* ▶ **sample** verb [T]: *You are welcome to sample any of our wines before making a purchase.*

sanatorium /ˌsænə'tɔːriəm/ (especially AmE **sanitarium**) noun [C] a type of hospital where patients who need a long period of treatment for an illness can stay ☐ *sanatorium*

sanction¹ /'sæŋkʃn/ noun **1** [C, usually pl] **sanctions (against sb)** an official order that limits business, contact, etc. with a particular country, in order to make it do sth, such as obey international law ☐ *sekatan*: *The sanctions against those countries have now been lifted.* **2** [U] (formal) official permission to do or change sth ☐ *kebenaran*

3 [C] a punishment for breaking a rule or law □ *hukuman; sanksi*

sanction² /ˈsæŋkʃn/ *verb* [T] to give official permission for sth □ *membenarkan*

sanctuary /ˈsæŋktʃuəri/ *noun* (*pl* **sanctuaries**) **1** [C] a place where birds or animals are protected from being hunted □ *kawasan perlindungan* **2** [C,U] a place or area where sb can be safe from enemies, the police, etc. □ *tempat perlindungan; suaka*

sand /sænd/ *noun* **1** [U] a powder consisting of very small grains of rock, found in deserts and on beaches □ *pasir*: *a grain of sand* ➔ picture on **page P10 2** [U,C, usually pl] a large area of sand □ *(kawasan) pasir*: *miles of golden sands*

sandal /ˈsændl/ *noun* [C] a type of light, open shoe that people wear when the weather is warm □ *sandal* ➔ picture at **shoe**

sandcastle /ˈsændkɑːsl/ *noun* [C] a pile of sand that looks like a castle, made by children playing on a beach □ *istana pasir*

ˈsand dune = **dune**

sandpaper /ˈsændpeɪpə(r)/ *noun* [U] strong paper with a rough surface on it that is used for rubbing surfaces in order to make them smooth □ *kertas pasir*

sandwich¹ /ˈsænwɪtʃ; -wɪdʒ/ *noun* [C] two slices of bread with food between them □ *sandwic*: *a ham/cheese sandwich* ➔ picture on **page P16**

sandwich² /ˈsænwɪtʃ; -wɪdʒ/

PHR V **sandwich sb/sth (between sb/sth)** to place sb/sth in a very narrow space between two other things or people □ *mengapitkan; menghimpit; terhimpit*

sandy /ˈsændi/ *adj* (**sandier**; **sandiest**) covered with or full of sand □ *berpasir*

sane /seɪn/ *adj* (**saner**; **sanest**) **1** (used about a person) mentally normal; not crazy □ *siuman*: *No sane person would do anything like that.* **2** (used about a person or an idea, a decision, etc.) sensible; showing good judgement □ *waras; munasabah* **OPP** for both meanings **insane** ➔ *noun* **sanity**

sang past tense of **sing**

sanitarium /ˌsænəˈteəriəm/ (*AmE*) = **sanatorium**

sanitary /ˈsænətri/ *adj* [only *before* a noun] connected with the protection of health, for example how human waste is removed □ *kebersihan*: *Sanitary conditions in the refugee camps were terrible.* ➔ look at **insanitary**

ˈsanitary towel (*AmE* **ˈsanitary napkin**) *noun* [C] a thick piece of soft material that women use to absorb blood lost during their period (3) □ *tuala wanita* ➔ look at **tampon**

sanitation /ˌsænɪˈteɪʃn/ *noun* [U] the equipment and systems that keep places clean, especially by removing human waste □ *sanitasi*

sanity /ˈsænəti/ *noun* [U] **1** the state of having a normal healthy mind □ *kesiuman* **2** the state of being sensible and reasonable □ *kewarasan* **OPP** for both meanings **insanity** ➔ *adjective* **sane**

sank past tense of **sink¹**

Santa Claus /ˈsæntə klɔːz/ **Santa** = **Father Christmas**

sap¹ /sæp/ *noun* [U] the liquid in a plant or tree □ *sap; getah*

sap² /sæp/ *verb* [T] (**sapping**; **sapped**) **sap (sb of) sth** to make sb/sth weaker; to destroy sth gradually □ *melemahkan; menghilangkan*: *Years of failure have sapped (him of) his confidence.*

sapling /ˈsæplɪŋ/ *noun* [C] a young tree □ *anak pokok*

sapphire /ˈsæfaɪə(r)/ *noun* [C,U] a bright blue **precious** (= rare and valuable) stone □ *batu nilam*

sarcasm /ˈsɑːkæzəm/ *noun* [U] the use of words or expressions to mean the opposite of what they actually say. People use sarcasm in order to criticize other people or to make them look silly. □ *sindiran; perli* ➔ look at **ironic** ▶ **sarcastic** /sɑːˈkæstɪk/ *adj*: *He's always making sarcastic comments.* ▶ **sarcastically** /-kli/ *adv*

sardine /ˌsɑːˈdiːn/ *noun* [C] a type of very small silver fish that we cook and eat □ *sardin*: *a tin of sardines*

sari /ˈsɑːri/ *noun* [C] a dress that consists of a long piece of silk or cotton that women, particularly Indian women, wear around their bodies □ *sari*

sash /sæʃ/ *noun* [C] a long piece of cloth that is worn round the waist or over the shoulder, often as part of a uniform □ *selempang; bengkung*

Sat. *abbr* = **Saturday** □ *Sabtu*: *Sat 2 May*

sat past tense, past participle of **sit**

Satan /ˈseɪtn/ *noun* a name for the Devil □ *Iblis* ➔ look at **devil**

sari

satchel /ˈsætʃəl/ *noun* [C] a bag, often carried over the shoulder, used by children for taking books to and from school □ *beg galas*

satellite /ˈsætəlaɪt/ *noun* [C] **1** an electronic device that is sent into space and moves round the earth or another planet for a particular purpose □ *satelit*: *a weather/communications satellite* **2** a natural object that moves round a bigger object in space □ *satelit*

ˈsatellite dish (also **dish**) *noun* [C] a large round piece of equipment on the outside of houses that receives signals from a **satellite**(1), so that people can watch **satellite TV** □ *ceper satelit* ⊃ picture on **page P8**

'satellite television (also **'satellite TV**) *noun* [U] TV programmes that are sent out using a **satellite**(1) □ *televisyen satelit*

satin /'sætɪn/ *noun* [U] a type of cloth that is smooth and shiny □ *satin: a satin dress/ribbon*

satire /'sætaɪə(r)/ *noun* **1** [U] the use of humour to attack a person, an organization, an idea, etc. that you think is bad or silly □ *satira* ⊃ note at **humour 2** [C] a satire (on sb/sth) a piece of writing or a play, film, etc. that uses satire □ *satira: a satire on political life* ▶ **satirical** /sə'tɪrɪkl/ *adj: a satirical magazine* ▶ **satirically** /-kli/ *adv*

satirize (also **-ise**) /'sætəraɪz/ *verb* [T] to use **satire** to show the faults in a person, an organization, an idea, etc. □ *menyindir/ mempersenda/menegur kelemahan sso atau sst melalui satira*

ˇsatisfaction /ˌsætɪs'fækʃn/ *noun* [U] the feeling of pleasure that you have when you have done, got or achieved what you wanted; something that gives you this feeling □ *rasa puas (hati); kepuasan (hati): Roshni stood back and looked at her work with a sense of satisfaction.* ◆ *We finally found a solution that was to everyone's satisfaction.* ◆ *She was about to have the satisfaction of seeing her book in print.* **OPP** **dissatisfaction**

satisfactory /ˌsætɪs'fæktəri/ *adj* good enough for a particular purpose; acceptable □ *memuaskan: This piece of work is not satisfactory. Please do it again.* **OPP** **unsatisfactory** ▶ **satisfactorily** /ˌsætɪs'fæktərəli/ *adv: Work is progressing satisfactorily.*

ˇsatisfied /'sætɪsfaɪd/ *adj* satisfied (with sb/ sth) pleased because you have had or done what you wanted □ *puas hati; puas: a satisfied customer* ◆ *a satisfied smile* **OPP** **dissatisfied**

ˇsatisfy /'sætɪsfaɪ/ *verb* [T] (**satisfying; satisfies;** *pt, pp* **satisfied**) **1** to make sb pleased by doing or giving them what they want □ *memuaskan hati; puas hati: No matter how hard I try, my piano teacher is never satisfied.* **2** to have or do what is necessary for sth □ *memenuhi; memuaskan: Make sure you satisfy the entry requirements before you apply to the university.* ◆ *I had a quick look inside the parcel just to satisfy my curiosity.* **3** satisfy sb (that …) (*formal*) to show or give proof to sb that sth is true or has been done □ *meyakinkan: Once the police were satisfied that they were telling the truth, they were allowed to go.*

ˇsatisfying /'sætɪsfaɪɪŋ/ *adj* pleasing, giving satisfaction □ *memuaskan: I find it satisfying to see people enjoying something I've cooked.*

satnav /'sætnæv/ *noun* [C,U] (*BrE*) **satellite navigation**; a computer system that uses information obtained from **satellites** (= electronic devices that move round the earth) to guide the driver of a vehicle □ *pengemudian satelit: All our company's drivers have satnav.* ◆ *Have you got a satnav?* ⊃ look at **GPS** ⊃ picture at **car**

satsuma /sæt'suːmə/ *noun* [C] a type of small orange □ *oren satsuma*

saturate /'sætʃəreɪt/ *verb* [T] **1** to make sth extremely wet □ *menyebabkan (sst) basah; lencun: The continuous rain had saturated the soil.* **2** [often passive] to fill sth so completely that it is impossible to add any more □ *memenuhi; dipenuhi; tepu: The market is saturated with cheap imports.* ▶ **saturated** *adj: Her clothes were saturated.* ▶ **saturation** /ˌsætʃə'reɪʃn/ *noun* [U]

ˇSaturday /'sætədeɪ; -di/ *noun* [C,U] (*abbr* **Sat.**) the day of the week after Friday □ *Sabtu* ⊃ note at **Monday**

Saturn /'sætɜːn; -tən/ *noun* [sing] the planet that is 6th in order from the sun and that has rings around it □ *Zuhal*

ˇsauce /sɔːs/ *noun* [C,U] a thick hot or cold liquid that you eat on or with food □ *sos: The chicken was served in a delicious sauce.* ◆ *spaghetti with tomato sauce* ⊃ look at **gravy** ⊃ picture on **page P16**

saucepan /'sɔːspən/ *noun* [C] a round metal pot with a handle that is used for cooking things on top of a cooker □ *periuk bertangkai*

saucer /'sɔːsə(r)/ *noun* [C] a small round plate that a cup stands on □ *piring* ⊃ picture at **cup**

sauna /'sɔːnə/ *noun* [C] **1** a type of bath where you sit in a room that is very hot □ *mandi sauna: to have a sauna* **2** the room that you sit in to have a sauna □ *bilik mandi sauna*

saunter /'sɔːntə(r)/ *verb* [I] to walk without hurrying □ *berjalan lengah-lengah*

sausage /'sɒsɪdʒ/ *noun* [C,U] a mixture of meat cut into very small pieces and spices, etc. that is made into a long thin shape. Some sausage is eaten cold in slices; other types are cooked and then served whole □ *sosej: liver sausage* ◆ *We had sausages and chips for lunch.*

savage /'sævɪdʒ/ *adj* very cruel or violent □ *kejam; ganas; sangat teruk: He was the victim of a savage attack.* ◆ *The book received savage criticism.* ▶ **savage** *verb* [T] to attack sb violently: *The boy died after being savaged by a dog.* ▶ **savagely** *adv* ▶ **savagery** /'sævɪdʒri/ *noun* [U]

ˇsave¹ /seɪv/ *verb*

▶ KEEP SAFE **1** [T] save sb/sth (from sth/from doing sth) to keep sb/sth safe from death, harm, loss, etc. □ *menyelamatkan: to save somebody's life* ◆ *to save somebody from drowning* ◆ *We are trying to save the school from closure.*

▶ MONEY **2** [I,T] save (sth) (up) (for sth) to keep or not spend money so that you can use it later □ *menyimpan (wang); menabung: I'm saving up for a new bike.* ◆ *Do you manage to save any of your wages?* ⊃ note at **money**

▶ FOR FUTURE **3** [T] to keep sth for future use □ *menyimpan; simpankan: I'll be home late, so please save me some dinner.* ◆ *Save that box. It*

save → say

might come in useful. ♦ *If you get there first, please save me a seat.*
▸NOT WASTE **4** [I,T] **save (sb) (sth) (on) sth** to avoid wasting time, money, etc. □ *menjimatkan: It will save you twenty minutes on the journey if you take the express train.* ♦ *You can save on petrol by getting a smaller car.* ♦ *This car will save you a lot on petrol.*
▸AVOID STH BAD **5** [T] **save (sb) sth/doing sth** to avoid, or make sb able to avoid, doing sth unpleasant or difficult □ *mengelakkan: If you make an appointment, it will save you waiting.*
▸IN SPORT **6** [I,T] (in games such as football, hockey, etc.) to stop a goal being scored □ *menyelamatkan: to save a penalty*
▸COMPUTING **7** [I,T] to store information in a computer by giving a special instruction □ *menyimpan: Don't forget to save the file before you close it.*
IDM keep/save sth for a rainy day ⊃ **rainy**
save face to prevent yourself losing the respect of other people □ *menjaga maruah diri*

save² /seɪv/ *noun* [C] (in football, etc.) the act of preventing a goal from being scored □ *(perbuatan) menghalang jaringan gol: The goalkeeper made a great save.*

saver /ˈseɪvə(r)/ *noun* [C] **1** a person who saves money for future use □ *penyimpan; penabung: The rise in interest rates is good news for savers.* **2** [in compounds] a thing that helps you save time, money, or the thing mentioned □ *penjimat: a great time-saver*

saving /ˈseɪvɪŋ/ *noun* **1** [C] **a saving (of sth) (on sth)** an amount of time, money, etc. that you do not have to use or spend □ *penjimatan: The sale price represents a saving of 25% on the usual price.* **2 savings** [pl] money that you have saved for future use □ *wang simpanan: All our savings are in the bank.* ♦ *I opened a savings account at my local bank.*

saviour (*AmE* **savior**) /ˈseɪvjə(r)/ *noun* [C] a person who rescues or saves sb/sth from danger, loss, death, etc. □ *penyelamat*

savoury (*AmE* **savory**) /ˈseɪvəri/ *adj* (used about food) having a taste that is not sweet □ *tdk manis (berempah, dsb)* ⊃ look at **sweet**

saw¹ *past tense* of **see**

saw² /sɔː/ *noun* [C] a tool that is used for cutting wood, etc. A saw has a blade with sharp teeth on it, and a handle at one or both ends. □ *gergaji* ⊃ picture at **tool** ▸**saw** *verb* [I,T] (*pt* **sawed**; *pp* **sawn** /sɔːn/ (*AmE*) **sawed**): *to saw through the trunk of a tree* ♦ *He sawed the log up into small pieces.*

sawdust /ˈsɔːdʌst/ *noun* [U] very small pieces of wood that fall like powder when you are cutting a large piece of wood □ *habuk kayu; tahi gergaji*

sawn *past participle* of **saw**

saxophone /ˈsæksəfəʊn/ (also *informal* **sax** /sæks/) *noun* [C] a metal musical instrument that you play by blowing into it. Saxophones are especially used for playing modern music, for example jazz □ *saksofon: This track features Dexter Gordon on sax.* ⊃ picture at **music**

say¹ /seɪ/ *verb* [T] (**says** /sez/; *pt*, *pp* **said** /sed/)
▸SPEAK **1 say sth (to sb); say that ...; say sth (about sb)** to speak or tell sb sth, using words □ *mengatakan; kata; cakap: 'Please come back,' she said.* ♦ *I said goodbye to her at the station.* ♦ *We can ask him, but I'm sure he'll say no.* ♦ *The teacher said we should hand in our essays on Friday.* ♦ *He said to his mother that he would phone back later.* ♦ *They just sat there without saying anything.* ♦ *'This isn't going to be easy,' she said to herself* (= she thought). ♦ *'What time is she coming?' 'I don't know—she didn't say.'* ♦ ***It is said that*** *cats can sense the presence of ghosts.*

> **HELP Say** or **tell? Say** is often used with the actual words that were spoken or before **that** in reported speech: *'I'll catch the 9 o'clock train,' he said.* ♦ *He said that he would catch the 9 o'clock train.* Notice that you say something **to** somebody: *He said to me that he would catch the 9 o'clock train.* **Tell** is always followed by a noun or pronoun, showing who you were speaking to: *He told me that he would catch the 9 o'clock train.* **Tell**, not **say**, can also be used when you are talking about giving orders or advice: *I told them to hurry up.* ♦ *She's always telling me what I ought to do.*

▸EXPRESS OPINION **2** to express an opinion on sth □ *kata; dikatakan; dinyatakan: I wouldn't say she's unfriendly—just shy.* ♦ *What is the artist trying to say in this painting?* ♦ *Well, what do you say? Do you think it's a good idea?* ♦ *It's hard to say what I like about the book.* ♦ *'When will it be finished?' 'I couldn't say* (= I don't know)*.'*
▸IMAGINE **3** to imagine or guess sth about a situation; to suppose □ *katalah; katakanlah: We will need, say, £5 000 for a new car.* ♦ *Say you don't get a place at university, what will you do then?*
▸SHOW FEELINGS **4 say sth (to sb)** to show a feeling, a situation, etc. without using words □ *menunjukkan; membayangkan: His angry look said everything about the way he felt.*
▸WRITTEN INFORMATION **5** to give written information □ *menunjukkan; mengatakan: What time does it say on that clock?* ♦ *The map says the hotel is just past the railway bridge.* ♦ *The sign clearly says 'No dogs'.*
IDM easier said than done ⊃ **easy**
go without saying to be clear, so that you do not need to say it □ *sudah pasti; tentu sekali: It goes without saying that the children will be well looked after at all times.*
have a lot, nothing, etc. to say for yourself to have a lot, nothing, etc. to say in a particular situation □ *ada banyak, tdk ada apa-apa, dsb yg dpt dikatakan atau alasan yg dpt diberikan (oleh sso) ttg sst keadaan: Late again! What have you got to say for yourself?*
I dare say ⊃ **dare¹**

[I] **intransitive**, a verb which has no object: *He laughed.*   [T] **transitive**, a verb which has an object: *He ate an apple.*

I must say (*spoken*) used to emphasize your opinion □ *digunakan utk menegaskan pendapat, dsb*: *I must say, I didn't believe him at first.*
let's say for example □ *katakan(lah)*: *You could work two mornings a week, let's say Tuesday and Friday.*
say no (to sth) to refuse an offer, a suggestion, etc. □ *menolak*: *If you don't go to Madrid, you're saying no to a great opportunity.*
say when (*spoken*) used to tell sb to say when you have poured enough drink in their glass or put enough food on their plate □ *Cakap bila dah cukup*
that is to say ... which means ... □ *iaitu...*: *We're leaving on Friday, that's to say in a week's time.*
to say the least used to say that sth is in fact much worse, more serious, etc. than you are saying □ *kalau hendak dikatakan, (sst) paling tdk*: *Adam's going to be annoyed, to say the least, when he sees his car.*

say² /seɪ/ *noun* [sing, U] **(a) say (in sth)** the authority or right to decide sth □ *hak bersuara*: *I'd like to have some say in the arrangements for the party.*
IDM **have your say** to express your opinion □ *menyuarakan pendapat*: *Thank you for your comments. Now let somebody else have their say.*

saying /'seɪɪŋ/ *noun* [C] a well-known phrase that gives advice about sth or says sth that many people believe is true □ *pepatah*: *'Love is blind' is an old saying.* ⊃ look at **proverb**

scab /skæb/ *noun* [C,U] a mass of dried blood that forms over a part of the body where the skin has been cut or broken □ *kuping* ⊃ look at **scar**

scaffold /'skæfəʊld/ *noun* [C] a platform on which criminals were killed in past times by hanging □ *pelantar tempat hukum gantung*

scaffolding /'skæfəldɪŋ/ *noun* [U] long metal poles and wooden boards that form a structure which is put next to a building so that people who are building, painting, etc. can stand and work on it □ *perancah; aram*

scald /skɔːld/ *verb* [T] to burn sb/sth with very hot liquid □ *melecur; melepuh*: *I scalded my arm badly when I was cooking.* ▶ **scald** *noun* [C]
▶ **scalding** *adj*: *scalding hot water*

scale¹ /skeɪl/ *noun*
▷ SIZE **1** [C,U] the size of sth, especially when compared to other things □ *saiz (besar, kecil, dsb)*: *We shall be making the product on a large scale next year.* ♦ *At this stage it is impossible to estimate the full scale of the disaster.*
▷ FOR MEASURING **2** [C] a series of numbers, amounts, etc. that are used for measuring or fixing the level of sth □ *skala; tangga (gaji, dsb)*: *The earthquake measured 6.5 on the Richter scale.* ♦ *the new pay scale for nurses*
▷ FOR MEASURING **3** [C] a series of marks on a tool or piece of equipment that you use for measuring sth □ *skala; ukuran*: *The ruler has one scale in centimetres and one scale in inches.*

scales

bathroom scales

scale

kitchen scales

fish scales

the scale of C

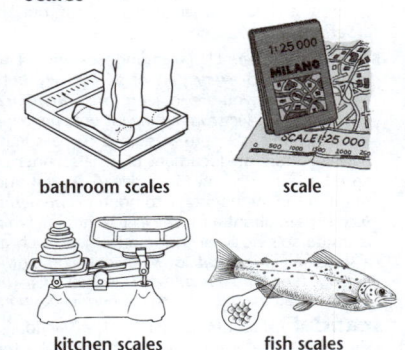

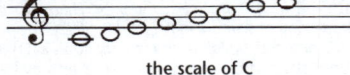

▷ OF MAP/DRAWING **4** [C] the relationship between the actual size of sth and its size on a map or plan □ *skala*: *The map has a scale of one centimetre to a kilometre.* ♦ *a scale of 1:50 000* (= one to fifty thousand) ♦ *We need a map with a larger scale.* ♦ *a scale model*
▷ FOR WEIGHING **5 scales** [pl] a piece of equipment that is used for weighing sb/sth □ *alat timbang; penimbang*: *I weighed it on the kitchen scales.*
▷ IN MUSIC **6** [C] a series of musical notes which go up or down in a fixed order. People play or sing scales to improve their technical ability □ *skala; skel/tangga nada*: *the scale of C major*
▷ ON FISH **7** [C] one of the small flat pieces of hard material that cover the body of fish and some animals □ *sisik*: *the scales of a snake*

scale² /skeɪl/ *verb* [T] (*formal*) to climb to the top of sth very high and steep □ *memanjat; mendaki*
PHR V **scale sth up/down** to increase/decrease the size, number, importance, etc. of sth □ *meningkatkan/mengurangkan sst*: *Police have scaled up their search for the missing boy.*

scallop /'skɒləp/ *noun* [C] a **shellfish** (= a creature with a shell that lives in water) that you can eat, with two flat round shells that fit together □ *kapis; kekapis*

scalp /skælp/ *noun* [C] the skin on the top of your head that is under your hair □ *kulit kepala*

scalpel /'skælpəl/ *noun* [C] a small knife that is used by **surgeons** (= doctors who perform medical operations) when they are doing operations □ *pisau bedah*

scam /skæm/ *noun* [C] (*informal*) a clever and dishonest plan for making money □ *penipuan (wang)*

scamper /ˈskæmpə(r)/ verb [I] (used especially about a child or small animal) to run quickly □ *berlari cepat*

scan /skæn/ verb [T] (scanning; scanned) 1 to look at or read every part of sth quickly until you find what you are looking for □ *membaca sepintas lalu*: Vic scanned the list until he found his own name. ➔ note at **skim** 2 to pass light over a picture or document using a **scanner** (= an electronic machine) in order to copy it and put it in the memory of a computer □ *mengimbas* 3 (used about a machine) to examine what is inside sb's body or inside an object such as a suitcase □ *mengimbas*: Machines scan all the luggage for bombs and guns. ▶ scan noun [C]: The scan showed the baby was in the normal position.

scandal /ˈskændl/ noun 1 [C,U] an action, a situation or behaviour that shocks people; the public feeling that is caused by such behaviour □ *skandal*: The chairman resigned after being involved in a financial scandal. ♦ There was no suggestion of scandal in his private life. ♦ The poor state of school buildings is a real scandal. 2 [U] talk about sth bad or wrong that sb has or may have done □ *fitnah; mengata*: to spread scandal about somebody

scandalize (also -ise) /ˈskændəlaɪz/ verb [T] to cause sb to feel shocked by doing sth that they think is bad or wrong □ *memeranjatkan*

scandalous /ˈskændələs/ adj very shocking or wrong □ *yg memeranjatkan*: It is scandalous that so much money is wasted.

Scandinavia /ˌskændɪˈneɪviə/ noun [sing] the group of countries in northern Europe that consists of Denmark, Norway and Sweden. Sometimes Finland and Iceland are also said to be part of Scandinavia. □ *Skandinavia* ▶ Scandinavian adj, noun [C]

scanner /ˈskænə(r)/ noun [C] 1 a machine used for looking at or recording images □ *pengimbas*: The scanner can detect cancer at an early stage. 2 a device which copies pictures and documents so that they can be stored on a computer □ *pengimbas*: I used the scanner to send the document by email.

scant /skænt/ adj [only before a noun] not very much; not as much as necessary □ *kurang; sedikit*

scanty /ˈskænti/ adj (scantier; scantiest) too small in size or amount □ *sangat sedikit*: We didn't learn much from the scanty information they gave us. ▶ scantily adv: I realized I was too scantily dressed for the cold weather.

scapegoat /ˈskeɪpɡəʊt/ noun [C] a person who is punished for things that are not their fault □ *kambing hitam*: When Alison was sacked she felt she had been **made a scapegoat** for all of the company's problems.

scar /skɑː(r)/ noun [C] a mark on the skin that is caused by a wound that has healed □ *parut*: The operation didn't leave a very big scar. ➔ look at **scab** ▶ scar verb [I,T] (scarring; scarred): William's face was scarred for life in the accident.

scarce /skeəs/ adj not existing in large quantities; hard to find □ *tdk banyak; sukar didapati*: Food for birds and animals is scarce in the winter. **OPP** plentiful ▶ scarcity /ˈskeəsəti/ noun [C,U] (pl scarcities): (a) scarcity of food/jobs/resources

scarcely /ˈskeəsli/ adv 1 only just; almost not □ *baru sahaja; hampir tiada; tdk berapa (kenal, dll)*: There was scarcely a car in sight. ♦ She's not a friend of mine. I scarcely know her. ➔ look at **hardly** 2 used to suggest that sth is not reasonable or likely □ *tdk mungkin; takkanlah*: You can scarcely expect me to believe that after all you said before.

scare¹ /skeə(r)/ verb 1 [T] to make a person or an animal frightened □ *menakutkan*: The sudden noise scared us all. ♦ It scares me to think what might happen. 2 [I] to become frightened □ *berasa takut*: I don't scare easily, but when I saw the snake I was terrified.
PHR V **scare sb/sth away/off** to make a person or an animal leave or stay away by frightening them or it □ *menyebabkan sso/sst lari kerana ditakutkan*: Don't make any noise or you'll scare the birds away.

scare² /skeə(r)/ noun [C] 1 a situation where many people are afraid or worried about sth □ *keadaan yg menimbulkan ketakutan atau kebimbangan ramai*: Last night there was a **bomb scare** in the city centre. 2 a feeling of being frightened □ *rasa takut*: It wasn't a serious heart attack but it gave him a scare.

scarecrow /ˈskeəkrəʊ/ noun [C] a very simple model of a person that is put in a field in order to frighten away the birds □ *orang-orangan*

scared /skeəd/ adj scared (of sb/sth); scared (of doing sth/to do sth) frightened □ *takut*: Are you scared of the dark? ♦ She's scared of walking home alone. ♦ Everyone was too scared to move.

scarf /skɑːf/ noun [C] (pl scarves /skɑːvz/ or scarfs /skɑːfs/) 1 a long thin piece of cloth, usually made of wool, that you wear around your neck to keep warm □ *skarf* 2 a piece of cloth that women wear around their neck or over their head or shoulders to keep warm or for decoration □ *skarf; kain tudung*

scarlet /ˈskɑːlət/ adj, noun [U] (of) a bright red colour □ *(warna) merah menyala*

scary /ˈskeəri/ adj (scarier; scariest) (informal) frightening □ *menakutkan*: a scary ghost story ♦ It was a bit scary driving in the mountains at night.

scathing /ˈskeɪðɪŋ/ adj scathing (about sb/sth) expressing a very strong negative opinion about sb/sth; very critical □ *(kecaman, dsb) keras, tajam, pedas, dll*: a scathing attack on the new leader ♦ scathing criticism

scatter /ˈskætə(r)/ verb 1 [T] to drop or throw things in different directions over a wide area □ *menaburkan; menyerakkan*: The wind scat-

tered the papers all over the room. **2** [I] (used about a group of people or animals) to move away quickly in different directions □ *bertempiaran*

scattered /ˈskætəd/ *adj* spread over a large area or happening several times during a period of time □ *berselerak; (di) sana sini: There will be sunny intervals with scattered showers today.*

scavenge /ˈskævɪndʒ/ *verb* [I,T] to look for food, etc. among waste and rubbish □ *menyelongkar mencari makan* ▶**scavenger** *noun* [C]: *Scavengers steal the food that the lion has killed.*

SCE /ˌes siː ˈiː/ *abbr* **Scottish Certificate of Education.** Students in Scotland take the **SCE** at Standard grade at the age of about 16 and at Higher grade at about 17. □ *SCE (Sijil Pelajaran Scotland)*

scenario /səˈnɑːriəʊ/ *noun* [C] (*pl* **scenarios**) **1** one way that things may happen in the future □ *senario; satu kemungkinan (apa yg akan berlaku): A likely scenario is that the company will get rid of some staff.* **2** a description of what happens in a play or film □ *senario; rangka lakon*

scene /siːn/ *noun*
▶PLACE **1** [C] the place where sth happened □ *tempat kejadian: the scene of a crime/an accident* ◆ *An ambulance was on the scene in minutes.*
▶IN PLAY, FILM, ETC. **2** [C] one part of a book, play, film, etc. in which the events happen in one place □ *adegan; babak: The first scene of 'Hamlet' takes place on the castle walls.*
▶AREA OF ACTIVITY **3 the scene** [sing] the way of life or the present situation in a particular area of activity □ *keadaan; dunia: The political scene in that part of the world is very confused.* ◆ *the fashion scene*
▶VIEW **4** [C,U] what you see around you in a particular place □ *persekitaran: Her new job was no better, but at least it would be a change of scene.*
▶ARGUMENT **5** [C] an occasion when sb expresses great anger or another strong emotion in public □ *buat gaduh/kecoh: There was quite a scene when she refused to pay the bill.*
IDM **set the scene (for sth) 1** to create a situation in which sth can easily happen or develop □ *membawa kpd: His arrival set the scene for another argument.* **2** to give sb the information and details they need in order to understand what comes next □ *mempersiapkan: The first part of the programme was just setting the scene.*

scenery /ˈsiːnəri/ *noun* [U] **1** the natural beauty that you see around you in the country □ *pemandangan: The scenery is superb in the mountains.* ⊃ note at **nature** **2** the furniture, painted cloth, boards, etc. that are used on the stage in a theatre □ *latar: The scenery is changed during the interval.*

OTHER WORDS FOR

scenery

Country and **countryside** both mean land away from towns and cities. We use the word **countryside** if we want to emphasize the natural features such as hills, rivers, trees, etc. that are found there: *beautiful countryside* ◆ *the destruction of the countryside by new roads.* We say that an area of the country has beautiful **scenery** when it is attractive to look at. The **landscape** of a particular area is the way the features of it are arranged: *Trees and hedges are a typical feature of the British landscape.* ◆ *an urban landscape* (= in a city or town). You have a **view** of something when you look out of a window or down from a high place: *There was a marvellous view of the sea from our hotel room.*

---

scenic /ˈsiːnɪk/ *adj* having beautiful **scenery** □ *berpemandangan indah*

scent /sent/ *noun* **1** [C,U] a pleasant smell □ *bau (wangi): This flower has no scent.* ⊃ note at **smell**² **2** [C,U] the smell that an animal leaves behind and that some other animals can follow □ *bau* **3** [U] (*BrE old-fashioned*) = **perfume**(1) **4** [sing] the feeling that sth is going to happen □ *bau: The scent of victory was in the air.* ▶**scent** *verb* [T]: *The dog scented a rabbit and ran off.* ▶**scented** *adj*

sceptic (*AmE* **skeptic**) /ˈskeptɪk/ *noun* [C] a person who doubts that sth is true, right, etc. □ *skeptik* ▶**sceptical** (*AmE* **skeptical**) /-kl/ *adj* **sceptical (of/about sth)**: *Many doctors are sceptical about the value of alternative medicine.*

scepticism (*AmE* **skepticism**) /ˈskeptɪsɪzəm/ *noun* [U] a general feeling of doubt about sth; a feeling that you are not likely to believe sth □ *skeptisisme*

schedule¹ /ˈʃedjuːl/ *noun* **1** [C,U] a plan of things that will happen or of work that must be done □ *jadual: Max has a busy schedule for the next few days.* ◆ *to be ahead of/behind schedule* (= to have done more/less than was planned) **2** (*AmE*) = **timetable**

schedule² /ˈʃedjuːl/ *verb* [T] **schedule sth (for sth)** to arrange for sth to happen or be done at a particular time □ *menjadualkan; dijadualkan: We've scheduled the meeting for Monday morning.* ◆ *The train was scheduled to arrive at 10.07.* ◆ *Is it a scheduled flight?* (= one that leaves at a regular time each day or week)

scheme¹ /skiːm/ *noun* [C] (*BrE*) **1 a scheme (to do sth/for doing sth)** an official plan or system for doing or organizing sth □ *skim; rancangan: a new scheme to provide houses in the area* ◆ *a local scheme for recycling newspapers* **2** a clever plan to do sth □ *rancangan (licik, dsb): He's thought of a new scheme for making money fast.* ⊃ look at **colour scheme**

scheme² /skiːm/ *verb* [I,T] to make a secret or dishonest plan □ *membuat rancangan sulit atau jahat: She felt that everyone was scheming to get rid of her.*

schizophrenia /ˌskɪtsəˈfriːniə/ *noun* [U] a serious mental illness in which a person confuses the real world and the world of the imagination and often behaves in strange and unexpected ways □ *skizofrenia* ►**schizophrenic** /ˌskɪtsə-ˈfrenɪk/ *adj, noun* [C]

scholar /ˈskɒlə(r)/ *noun* [C] **1** a person who studies and has a lot of knowledge about a particular subject □ *sarjana; ilmuwan* **2** a person who has passed an exam or won a competition and has been given a **scholarship**(1) to help pay for their studies □ *pemegang biasiswa*: *He has come here as a British Council scholar.* ⊃ look at **student**

scholarly /ˈskɒləli/ *adj* **1** (used about a person) spending a lot of time studying and having a lot of knowledge about an academic subject □ *terpelajar; berilmu* ⊃ look at **studious** **2** connected with academic study □ *ilmiah; akademik*: *a scholarly journal* SYN **academic**

scholarship /ˈskɒləʃɪp/ *noun* **1** [C] an amount of money that is given to a person who has passed an exam or won a competition, in order to help pay for their studies □ *biasiswa*: *to win a scholarship to Yale* **2** [U] serious study of an academic subject □ *kesarjanaan*

school /skuːl/ *noun*
►EDUCATION **1** [C] the place where children go to be educated □ *sekolah*: *Where did you go to school?* ◆ *They're building a new school in our area.* ◆ *Do you have to wear a school uniform?* ◆ *Was your school co-educational* (= for boys and girls) *or single-sex?* **2** [U] the time you spend at a school; the process of being educated in a school □ *sekolah; bersekolah*: *Their children are still at school.* ◆ *Children start school at 5 years old in Britain and can leave school at 17.* ◆ *School starts at 9 o'clock and finishes at about 3.30.* ◆ *After school we usually have homework to do.*

HELP You say **school** (without 'the') when you are talking about going there for the usual reasons (that is, as a student or teacher): *Where do your children go to school?* ◆ *I enjoyed being at school.* ◆ *Do you walk to school?* You say **the school** if you are talking about going there for a different reason (for example, as a parent): *I have to go to the school on Thursday to talk to John's teacher.* You must also use **a** or **the** when more information about the school is given: *Rahul goes to the school in the next village.* ◆ *She teaches at a special school for children with learning difficulties.*

3 [sing, with sing or pl verb] all the students and teachers in a school □ *sekolah (semua murid dan guru)*: *The whole school is/are going on a trip tomorrow.* **4** [in compounds] connected with school □ *sekolah*: *children of school age* ◆ *The bus was full of schoolchildren.* ◆ *It is getting increasingly difficult for school-leavers to find jobs.* ◆ *Schoolteachers have been awarded a 2% pay rise.* ◆ *I don't have many good memories of my schooldays.* ◆ *I went skating with some of my school friends.*
►FOR PARTICULAR SKILL **5** [C] a place where you go to learn a particular subject □ *sekolah*: *a language/driving/drama/business school*
►COLLEGE/UNIVERSITY **6** [C,U] (*AmE*) a college or university □ *kolej; universiti*: *famous schools like Yale and Harvard* ◆ *He's still in school.* **7** [C] a department of a university that teaches a particular subject □ *pusat pengajian; fakulti*: *the school of geography at Leeds University*
►ARTISTS **8** [C] a group of writers, artists, etc. who have the same ideas or style □ *aliran; angkatan*: *the Flemish school of painting*
►FISH **9** [C] a large group of fish, etc., swimming together □ *kawan; kumpulan ikan*: *a school of dolphins*

IDM **a school of thought** the ideas or opinions that one group of people share □ *aliran fikiran; mazhab*: *There are various schools of thought on this matter.*

TOPIC

Schools

Children go to **primary** and **secondary** schools. These can be **private** or **state** schools (= paid for by the government), and sometimes they are also **boarding** schools (= where students live and sleep). A school for very young children is a **nursery school**. Schools have **classrooms** and every **pupil/student** is a member of a **class**. During **lessons** pupils study **subjects**, and after school they can do **extra-curricular** activities, such as sport or drama. Some **teachers** are **strict** while others are **lenient**, and sometimes they give pupils a lot of **homework**. It is important to get good **marks**, especially in **exams** at the end of **term**. Students who **bully** their **classmates** or **skip school/play truant** (= do not go to school when they should) usually **get into trouble** with the **head teacher**.

schoolchild /ˈskuːltʃaɪld/ *noun* [C] (*pl* **schoolchildren** /-tʃɪldrən/) a child who goes to school □ *murid; pelajar*

schooling /ˈskuːlɪŋ/ *noun* [U] the time that you spend at school; your education □ *persekolahan*

science /ˈsaɪəns/ *noun* **1** [U] the study of and knowledge about the physical world and natural laws □ *(ilmu) sains*: *Modern science has discovered a lot about the origin of life.* ◆ *Fewer young people are studying science at university.* **2** [C] one of the subjects into which science can be divided □ *sains (cabang atau bidang tertentu dlm ilmu sains)* ⊃ look at **art**

MORE **Chemistry**, **physics** and **biology** are all **sciences**. **Scientists** do **research** and **experiments** in a **laboratory** to see what happens and to try to discover new information. The study of people and society is called **social science**.

science fiction *noun* [U] books, films, etc. about imaginary events that take place in the future, often involving travel in space □ *cereka sains*

scientific /ˌsaɪənˈtɪfɪk/ adj **1** connected with or involving science □ *(berkaitan dgn) sains*: *We need more funding for scientific research.* ◆ *scientific instruments* **2** (used about a way of thinking or of doing sth) careful and logical □ *saintifik*: *a scientific study of the way people use language* ▶**scientifically** /-kli/ adv: *Sorting out the files won't take long if we do it scientifically.*

scientist /ˈsaɪəntɪst/ noun [C] a person who studies or teaches science, especially biology, chemistry or physics □ *ahli sains; saintis*: *a research scientist* ◆ *nuclear scientists*

scintillating /ˈsɪntɪleɪtɪŋ/ adj very clever, amusing and interesting □ *pintar, menarik dan menghiburkan*: *The lead actor gave a scintillating performance.*

blade

scissors   **nail clippers**

scissors /ˈsɪzəz/ noun [pl] a tool for cutting paper or cloth, that has two sharp blades with handles, joined together in the middle □ *gunting*

> **GRAMMAR** Scissors are plural: *These scissors are blunt.* We say **a pair of scissors**, NOT 'a scissors'.

scoff /skɒf/ (*AmE* also) / verb **1** [I] scoff (at sb/sth) to speak about sb/sth in a way that shows you think that he/she/it is stupid or ridiculous □ *mengejek; mentertawakan* **2** [T] (*BrE informal*) to eat a lot of sth quickly □ *melahap*

scold /skəʊld/ verb [I,T] scold sb (for sth/for doing sth) to speak angrily to sb because they have done sth bad or wrong □ *memarahi* ⊃ A more common expression is **tell sb off**.

scone /skɒn; skəʊn/ noun [C] a small round cake that you eat in your hand and eat with butter, cream and jam on it □ *skon*

scoop¹ /skuːp/ noun [C] **1** a tool like a spoon used for picking up flour, grain, etc. □ *pencedok; senduk; skup* **2** the amount that one scoop contains □ *sepencedok; sesenduk; seskup*: *a scoop of ice cream* **3** an exciting piece of news that is reported by one newspaper, TV or radio station before it is reported anywhere else □ *skup (berita)*

scoop² /skuːp/ verb [T] **1** scoop sth (out/up) to make a hole in sth or to take sth out by using a **scoop** or sth similar □ *mengorek*: *Scoop out the middle of the pineapple.* **2** scoop sb/sth (up) to move or lift sb/sth using a continuous action □ *mencedok; mengaut; menyauk*: *He scooped up the child and ran.* **3** to get a story before all other newspapers, TV stations, etc. □ *mendapat skup* **4** to win money or a big or important prize □ *menggondol*: *The film has scooped all the awards this year.*

scooter /ˈskuːtə(r)/ noun [C] **1** a light motor-bike with a small engine □ *skuter* ⊃ picture on **page P7 2** a child's toy with two wheels that you stand on and move by pushing one foot against the ground □ *skuter mainan*

scope /skəʊp/ noun **1** [U] scope (for sth/to do sth) the chance or opportunity to do sth □ *peluang; kesempatan*: *The job offers plenty of scope for creativity.* **2** [sing] the variety of subjects that are being discussed or considered □ *skop; cakupan*: *The government was unwilling to extend the scope of the inquiry.*

scorch /skɔːtʃ/ verb [T] to burn sth so that its colour changes but it is not destroyed □ *terbakar; hangus*: *I scorched my blouse when I was ironing it.*

scorching /ˈskɔːtʃɪŋ/ adj (*informal*) very hot □ *panas terik*: *It was absolutely scorching on Tuesday.*

score¹ /skɔː(r)/ noun **1** [C] the number of points, goals, etc. that sb/sth gets in a game, a competition, an exam, etc. □ *bilangan mata, markah, gol, dsb; skor*: *What was the final score?* ◆ *The score is 3-2 to Liverpool.* ◆ *The top score in the test was 80%.* **2** [C] the written form of a piece of music □ *skor; susunan muzik*: *an orchestral score* **3** scores [pl] very many □ *amat banyak*: *Scores of people have written to offer their support.*

IDM on that score as far as that is concerned □ *ttg (hal) itu*: *Lan will be well looked after. Don't worry on that score.*

score² /skɔː(r)/ verb [I,T] to get points, goals, etc. in a game, a competition, an exam, etc. □ *mendapat mata, markah, gol, dsb*: *The team still hadn't scored by half-time.* ◆ *Louise scored the highest marks in the exam.*

scoreboard /ˈskɔːbɔːd/ noun [C] a large board that shows the score during a game, competition, etc. □ *papan mata/skor*

scorn¹ /skɔːn/ noun [U] scorn (for sb/sth) the strong feeling that you have when you do not respect sb/sth □ *penghinaan; cemuhan*

scorn² /skɔːn/ verb [T] **1** to feel or show a complete lack of respect for sb/sth □ *menghina; mencemuh*: *The President scorned his critics.* **2** to refuse to accept help or advice, especially because you are too proud □ *menolak; enggan menerima*: *The old lady scorned all offers of help.* ▶**scornful** /ˈskɔːnfl/ adj: *a scornful look/smile/remark* ▶**scornfully** /-fəli/ adv

Scorpio /ˈskɔːpiəʊ/ noun [C,U] (pl Scorpios) the 8th sign of the **zodiac** (= 12 signs which represent the positions of the sun, moon and planets), the **Scorpion**; a person born under this sign □ *Skorpio*: *I'm a Scorpio.* ⊃ picture at **zodiac**

scorpion /ˈskɔːpiən/ noun [C] a creature

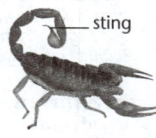

sting

scorpion

Scot → scratch 762

which looks like a large insect and lives in hot countries. A **scorpion** has a long curved tail with a poisonous sting in it. □ *kala jengking*

Scot /skɒt/ *noun* [C] a person who comes from Scotland □ *orang Scotland*

Scotch /skɒtʃ/ *noun* [U,C] a type of **whisky** (= a strong alcoholic drink) that is made in Scotland; a glass of this □ *Scotch (wiski)*

Scotch tape™ (*AmE*) = **Sellotape™**

Scots /skɒts/ *adj* of or connected with people from Scotland □ *(berkenaan dgn) orang Scotland*

Scottish /ˈskɒtɪʃ/ *adj* of or connected with Scotland, its people, culture, etc. □ *(berkenaan dgn) Scotland*

scoundrel /ˈskaʊndrəl/ *noun* [C] (*old-fashioned*) a man who behaves very badly towards other people, especially by being dishonest □ *penyangak; penipu*

scour /ˈskaʊə(r)/ *verb* [T] **1** to search a place very carefully when you are looking for sb/sth □ *menggeledah* **2** to clean sth by rubbing it hard with sth rough □ *menyental*: *to scour a dirty pan*

scourge /skɜːdʒ/ *noun* [C] a person or thing that causes a lot of trouble or suffering □ *punca kesusahan/kesengsaraan*: *Inflation was the scourge of the 1970s.*

scout /skaʊt/ *noun* [C] **1 Scout** a member of the **Scouts** (= an organization that teaches young people how to look after themselves and encourages them to help others). Scouts do sport, learn useful skills, go camping, etc. □ *pengakap* ⊃ look at **Guide** **2** a soldier who is sent on in front of the rest of the group to find out where the enemy is or which is the best route to take □ *peninjau*

scowl /skaʊl/ *noun* [C] a look on your face that shows you are angry or in a bad mood □ *muka merah/masam* ⊃ look at **frown** ▶ **scowl** *verb* [I]

scrabble /ˈskræbl/ *verb* [I] (*especially BrE*) to move your fingers or feet around quickly, trying to find sth or get hold of sth □ *meraba-raba (utk mencari sst)*: *She scrabbled about in her purse for some coins.*

scramble /ˈskræmbl/ *verb* [I] **1** to climb quickly up or over sth using your hands to help you; to move somewhere quickly □ *bergegas-gegas*: *He scrambled up the hill and over the wall.* ◆ *He scrambled to his feet* (= off the ground) *and ran off into the trees.* ◆ *The children scrambled into the car.* **2** scramble (for sth/to do sth) to fight or move quickly to get sth which a lot of people want □ *berebut-rebut*: *People stood up and began scrambling for the exits.* ◆ *Everyone was scrambling to get the best bargains.* ▶ **scramble** *noun* [sing]

scrambled ˈeggs *noun* [U,C] eggs mixed together with milk and then cooked in a pan □ *telur goreng hancur*

[I] **intransitive**, a verb which has no object: *He laughed.*

scrap¹ /skræp/ *noun* **1** [C] a small piece of sth □ *cebisan; perca; reja*: *a scrap of paper/cloth* ◆ *scraps of food* SYN **bit** **2** [U] something that you do not want any more but that is made of material that can be used again □ *sekerap*: *The car was sold for scrap.* ◆ *scrap paper* **3** [C] (*informal*) a short fight or argument □ *pergaduhan; pertengkaran*

scrap² /skræp/ *verb* [T] (**scrapping; scrapped**) to get rid of sth that you do not want any more □ *membuang; membatalkan*: *I think we should scrap that idea.*

scrapbook /ˈskræpbʊk/ *noun* [C] a large book with empty pages that you can stick pictures, newspaper articles, etc. in □ *buku skrap*

scrape¹ /skreɪp/ *verb* **1** [T] scrape sth (down/out/off) to remove sth from a surface by moving a sharp edge across it firmly □ *mengikis*: *Scrape all the mud off your boots before you come in.* **2** [T] scrape sth (against/along/on sth) to damage or hurt sth by rubbing it against sth rough or hard □ *tergesel; melecet*: *Mark fell and scraped his knee.* ◆ *Sunita scraped the car against the wall.* **3** [I,T] scrape (sth) against/along/on sth to rub (sth) against sth and make a sharp unpleasant noise □ *menggeser*: *The branches scraped against the window.* **4** [T] (*BrE*) to manage to get or win sth with difficulty □ *mendapat sst dgn susah payah; lulus cukup makan*: *I just scraped a pass in the maths exam.*

PHR V **scrape by (on sth)** to manage to live on the money you have, but with difficulty □ *hidup dgn (gaji, rezeki, dsb yg) ala kadar*: *We can just scrape by on my salary.*

scrape through (sth) to succeed in doing sth with difficulty □ *berjaya (membuat sst) dgn susah payah*: *to scrape through an exam* (= just manage to pass it)

scrape sth together/up to get or collect sth together with difficulty □ *dgn susah payah mengumpul sst*

scrape² /skreɪp/ *noun* [C] **1** the action or unpleasant sound of one thing rubbing hard against another □ *bunyi geseran* **2** damage or an injury caused by rubbing against sth rough □ *geseran; tergesel; melecet*: *I got a nasty scrape on my knee.* **3** (*informal*) a difficult situation that was caused by your own stupid behaviour □ *masalah; kesusahan*

ˈscrapheap *noun* [C] a large pile of objects, especially metal, that are no longer wanted □ *timbunan besi buruk, dsb*

IDM **on the scrapheap** (*informal*) not wanted any more □ *tdk diperlukan lagi; spt sampah*: *Many of the unemployed feel that they are on the scrapheap.*

scrappy /ˈskræpi/ *adj* (*informal*) (**scrappier; scrappiest**) not organized or tidy and so not pleasant to see □ *tdk teratur; culang-caling*: *a scrappy essay/football match*

scratch¹ /skrætʃ/ *verb* **1** [I,T] scratch (at sth) to rub your skin with your nails □ *menggaru; menggaruk*: *Don't scratch at your insect bites*

[T] **transitive**, a verb which has an object: *He ate an apple.*

or they'll get worse. ♦ *Could you scratch my back for me?* ♦ *She sat and scratched her head as she thought about the problem.* **2** [I,T] to make a mark on a surface or a slight cut on sb's skin with sth sharp □ *mencakar*: *The cat will scratch if you annoy it.* ♦ *The table was badly scratched.* **3** [T] to use sth sharp to make or remove a mark □ *mencalarkan; menggores; mengikis*: *He scratched his name on the top of his desk.* ♦ *I tried to scratch the paint off the table.* **4** [I] to make a sound by rubbing a surface with sth sharp □ *berkerik; mengerik-ngerik*: *The dog was scratching at the door to go outside.*

scratch² /skrætʃ/ noun **1** [C] a cut, mark or sound that was made by sth sharp rubbing a surface □ *calar*: *There's a scratch on the car door.* **2** [sing] an act of scratching part of the body □ *(perbuatan) menggaru-garu*: *The dog had a good scratch.*
IDM **from scratch** from the very beginning □ *dr permulaan*: *I'm learning Spanish from scratch.*
(be/come) up to scratch (*informal*) (to be/become) good enough □ *mencapai tahap yg dikehendaki; memuaskan*

scrawl /skrɔːl/ verb [I,T] to write sth quickly in an untidy and careless way □ *menulis dgn tulisan cakar ayam*: *He scrawled his name across the top of the paper.* ▶ **scrawl** noun [sing]: *Her signature was just a scrawl.* ⊃ look at **scribble**

scrawny /ˈskrɔːni/ adj (*informal*) (**scrawnier; scrawniest**) very thin in a way that is not attractive □ *kurus kering*

scream¹ /skriːm/ verb [I,T] **scream (sth) (out) (at sb)** to cry out loudly in a high voice because you are afraid, excited, angry, in pain, etc. □ *menjerit*: *She saw a rat and screamed out.* ♦ *'Don't touch that,' he screamed.* ♦ *She screamed at the children to stop.* ♦ *He screamed with pain.* ♦ *He clung to the edge of the cliff, screaming for help.* ♦ *Cathy screamed his name.* ⊃ look at **shout**

scream² /skriːm/ noun **1** [C] a loud cry in a high voice □ *jeritan*: *a scream of pain* **2** [sing] (*informal, old-fashioned*) a person or thing that is very funny □ *sso/sst yg sangat lucu*: *Mel's a real scream.*

screech /skriːtʃ/ verb [I,T] to make an unpleasant loud, high sound □ *berkerik; memekik*: *'Get out of here,' she screeched at him.* ⊃ look at **shriek** ▶ **screech** noun [sing]: *the screech of brakes*

screen¹ /skriːn/ noun **1** [C] the glass surface of a TV or computer where the picture or information appears □ *skrin*: *They were staring at the television screen.* ♦ *Move your cursor to the top of the screen.* ⊃ picture at **camera, computer** **2** [C] the large flat surface on which films are shown □ *skrin; layar perak* **3** [sing, U] films and TV □ *filem; televisyen*: *Some actors look better in real life than on screen.* **4** [C] a flat vertical surface that is used for dividing a room or keeping sb/sth out of sight □ *skrin; adang-adang; tabir*: *The nurse pulled the screen round the bed.*

screen² /skriːn/ verb [T] **1 screen sb/sth (off) (from sb/sth)** to hide or protect sb/sth from sb/sth else □ *menghadang*: *The bed was screened off while the doctor examined him.* ♦ *to screen your eyes from the sun* **2 screen sb (for sth)** to examine or test sb to find out if they have a particular disease or if they are suitable for a particular job □ *memeriksa; menapis*: *All women over 50 should be screened for breast cancer.* ♦ *The Ministry of Defence screens all job applicants.* **3** to show sth on TV or in a cinema □ *menayangkan*

screenplay /ˈskriːnpleɪ/ noun [C] the words that are written for a film, together with instructions for how it is to be acted and made into a film □ *lakon layar; skrip filem* ⊃ note at **film**

'screen saver noun [C] a computer program that replaces what is on the screen with a moving image if the computer is not used for a certain amount of time □ *penyelamat skrin*

screenshot /ˈskriːnʃɒt/ noun [C] an image of the display on a screen, used when showing how a program works □ *syot layar; tangkap layar*

screenwriter /ˈskriːnraɪtə(r)/ noun [C] a person who writes instructions about what happens in a film and the words the actors say □ *penulis skrip lakon layar*

screw¹ /skruː/ noun [C] a thin pointed piece of metal used for fixing two things, for example pieces of wood, together. You turn a screw with a **screwdriver** □ *skru*: *One of the screws is loose.* ⊃ picture at **bolt**

screw² /skruː/ verb **1** [T] **screw sth (on, down, etc.)** to fasten sth with a screw or screws □ *menskru*: *The bookcase is screwed to the wall.* ♦ *The lid is screwed down so you can't remove it.* **2** [I,T] to fasten sth, or to be fastened, by turning □ *memulas; memutar*: *The legs screw into holes in the underside of the seat.* ♦ *Make sure that you screw the top of the jar on tightly.* **3** [T] **screw sth (up) (into sth)** to squeeze sth, especially a piece of paper, into a tight ball □ *menggumpalkan*: *He screwed the letter up into a ball and threw it away.*
PHR V **screw (sth) up** (*slang*) to make a mistake and cause sth to fail □ *merosakkan sst*: *You'd better not screw up this deal.*
screw your eyes, face, etc. up to change the expression on your face by nearly closing your eyes, in pain or because the light is strong □ *mengernyitkan mata, muka, dsb*

screwdriver /ˈskruːdraɪvə(r)/ noun [C] a tool that you use for turning **screws** □ *pemutar skru* ⊃ picture at **tool**

scribble /ˈskrɪbl/ verb [I,T] **1** to write sth quickly and carelessly □ *mencoret; menulis cepat-cepat dgn tulisan yg teruk*: *to scribble a note down on a pad* ⊃ look at **scrawl** **2** to make marks with a pen or pencil that are not letters or pictures □ *menconteng*: *The children had scribbled all over the walls.* ▶ **scribble** noun [C,U]

script /skrɪpt/ noun **1** [C] the written form of a play, film, speech, etc. □ *skrip*: *Who wrote the* script for the movie? **2** [C,U] a system of writing □ *sistem tulisan*: *Arabic/Cyrillic/Roman script*

scripture /ˈskrɪptʃə(r)/ (also **the scriptures**) *noun* [U, pl] the books of a religion, such as the Bible □ *kitab suci*

scroll¹ /skrəʊl/ *noun* [C] a long roll of paper with writing on it □ *skrol; gulungan kertas*

scroll² /skrəʊl/ *verb* [I] **scroll (up/down/across)** to move text up and down or left and right on a computer screen □ *menatal*: *Scroll down to the bottom of the page.*

ˈscroll bar *noun* [C] a strip at the edge of a computer screen that you use to move the text up and down or left and right □ *bar tatal*

scrounge /skraʊndʒ/ *verb* [I,T] (*informal*) **scrounge (sth) (from/off sb)** to get sth by asking another person to give it to you instead of making an effort to get it for yourself □ *mengecek; meminta*: *Lucy is always scrounging money off her friends.*

scrub¹ /skrʌb/ *verb* [I,T] (**scrubbing**; **scrubbed**) **1 scrub (sth) (down/out)** to clean sth with soap and water by rubbing it hard, often with a brush □ *menggosok; menyental*: *to scrub (down) the floor/walls* **2 scrub (sth) (off/out); scrub (sth) (off sth/out of sth)** to remove sth or be removed by scrubbing □ *menanggalkan (tanda, dll) dgn menyental, mengikis, dsb*: *to scrub the dirt off the walls* ♦ *I hope these coffee stains will scrub out.*

scrub² /skrʌb/ *noun* **1** [sing] an act of cleaning sth by rubbing it hard, often with a brush □ *(perbuatan) menyental*: *This floor needs a good scrub.* **2** [U] small trees and bushes that grow in an area that has very little rain □ *belukar; semak*

scruff /skrʌf/ *noun*
IDM by the scruff (of the/sb's neck) by the back of an animal's or person's neck □ *dgn memegang (tengkuk baju sso)*: *She picked up the puppy by the scruff of the neck.*

scruffy /ˈskrʌfi/ *adj* (**scruffier**; **scruffiest**) dirty and untidy □ *comot dan selekeh*: *He always looks so scruffy.* ♦ *scruffy jeans*

scrum /skrʌm/ *noun* [C] (in the sport of **rugby**) when several players put their heads down in a circle and push against each other to try to get the ball □ *skrum*

scruples /ˈskruːplz/ *noun* [pl] a feeling that stops you from doing sth that you think is morally wrong □ *rasa bersalah (yg menyebabkan kita tdk mahu melakukan sst yg tdk baik)*: *I've got no scruples about asking them for money (= I don't think it's wrong).*

scrupulous /ˈskruːpjələs/ *adj* **1** very careful or paying great attention to detail □ *teliti*: *a scrupulous investigation into the causes of the disaster* **2** careful to be honest and do what is right □ *prihatin* **OPP** **unscrupulous** ▶ **scrupulously** *adv*: *scrupulously clean/honest/tidy*

scrutinize (also **-ise**) /ˈskruːtənaɪz/ *verb* [T] to look at or examine sth carefully □ *meneliti*: *The immigration official scrutinized every page of my passport.* ▶ **scrutiny** /ˈskruːtəni/ *noun* [U]: *The police kept all the suspects under close scrutiny.*

scuba-diving /ˈskuːbə daɪvɪŋ/ *noun* [U] the activity of swimming underwater using special equipment for breathing □ *selam skuba*: *to go scuba-diving* ⊃ picture at **snorkel**

scuff /skʌf/ *verb* [T] to make a mark on your shoes or with your shoes, for example by kicking sth or by rubbing your feet along the ground □ *mencalarkan; menggoreskan*

scuffle /ˈskʌfl/ *noun* [C] a short, not very violent, fight □ *pergelutan*

sculptor /ˈskʌlptə(r)/ *noun* [C] a person who makes **sculptures** from stone, wood, etc. □ *pengukir; pengarca* ⊃ note at **art**

sculpture /ˈskʌlptʃə(r)/ *noun* **1** [C,U] a work of art that is a figure or an object made from stone, wood, metal, etc. □ *ukiran; arca* **2** [U] the art of making **sculptures** □ *seni ukir; seni arca* ⊃ note at **art**

scum /skʌm/ *noun* [U] **1** a dirty or unpleasant substance on the surface of a liquid □ *kekam* **2** (*slang*) an insulting word for people that you have no respect for □ *sampah (masyarakat)*: *Drug dealers are scum.*

scurry /ˈskʌri/ *verb* [I] (**scurrying**; **scurries**; *pt, pp* **scurried**) to run quickly with short steps; to hurry □ *berlari tergesa-gesa; mencalai*

scuttle /ˈskʌtl/ *verb* [I] to run quickly with short steps □ *lari cepat-cepat*: *The spider scuttled away when I tried to catch it.*

scythe /saɪð/ *noun* [C] a tool with a long handle and a long, curved blade. You use a **scythe** to cut long grass, etc. □ *sabit*

SE *abbr* = **south-east¹**, **south-eastern**: *SE Asia*

sea /siː/ *noun* **1** *often* **the sea** [U] the salt water that covers large parts of the surface of the earth □ *laut*: *The sea is quite calm/rough today.* ♦ *Do you live by the sea?* ♦ *to travel by sea* ♦ *There were several people swimming in the sea.* ⊃ picture on page P10 ⊃ note at **ocean 2** *often* **Sea** [C] a particular large area of salt water. A sea may be part of a larger area of water or may be surrounded by land □ *Laut*: *the Mediterranean Sea* ♦ *the Black Sea* ⊃ look at **ocean 3** [C] (*also* **seas** [pl]) the state or movement of the waves of the sea □ *laut bergelora; gelombang*: *The boat sank in heavy (= rough) seas off the Scottish coast.* **4** [sing] a large amount of sb/sth close together □ *lautan*: *The pavement was just a sea of people.*
IDM at sea 1 sailing in a ship □ *belayar*: *They spent about three weeks at sea.* **2** not understanding or not knowing what to do □ *bingung*: *When I first started this job, I was completely at sea.*

the ˈseabed *noun* [sing] the floor of the sea □ *dasar laut*

seafood /ˈsiːfuːd/ *noun* [U] fish and sea creatures that we eat, especially **shellfish** (= creatures with shells that live in water) □ *makanan laut*

the seafront /'si:frʌnt/ noun [sing] the part of a town facing the sea □ *tepi laut*: *The hotel is right **on the seafront**.* ♦ *to walk **along the seafront***

seagull /'si:gʌl/ = **gull**

seal¹ /si:l/ verb [T] **1 seal sth (up/down)** to close or fasten a package, an envelope, etc. □ *melekatkan*: *The parcel was sealed with tape.* ♦ *to seal (down) an envelope* **2 seal sth (up)** to fill a hole or cover sth so that air or liquid does not get in or out □ *mengedap; menampal*: *The food is packed in sealed bags to keep it fresh.* **3** (formal) to make sth sure, so that it cannot be changed or argued about □ *memutuskan; menyelesaikan; memeterai*: *to seal an agreement*

PHR V seal sth off to stop any person or thing from entering or leaving an area or building □ *menutup sst (supaya tdk ada yg dpt keluar atau masuk)*: *The building was sealed off by the police.*

seal² /si:l/ noun [C]
1 an official design or mark that is put on a document, an envelope, etc. to show that it is genuine or that it has not been opened □ *cap; mohor*: *The letter bore the President's seal.* **2** something that stops air or liquid from getting in or out of sth □ *pengedap*: *The seal has worn and oil is escaping.* **3** a small piece of paper, metal, plastic, etc. on a bottle, box, etc. that you must break before you can open it □ *meterai; tanda*: *Check the seal isn't broken.* **4** a grey animal with short fur that lives in and near the sea and that eats fish. Seals have no legs and swim with the help of **flippers** (= short flat arms) □ *anjing laut*: *a colony of seals*

flipper

seal

'sea level noun [U] the average level of the sea, used for measuring the height of places on land □ *aras laut*: *The town is 500 metres above sea level.*

'sea lion noun [C] a large **seal** that lives by the Pacific Ocean □ *singa laut*

seam /si:m/ noun [C] **1** the line where two pieces of cloth are sewn together □ *kelim* **2** a layer of coal under the ground □ *lipit*

seaman /'si:mən/ noun [C] (pl **-men** /-mən/) a sailor □ *kelasi; pelaut*

seamless /'si:mləs/ adj with no spaces or pauses between one part and the next □ *berterusan; tanpa sambungan yg jelas*: *a seamless flow of talk* ▶ **seamlessly** adv

seance /'seıɒ̃s/ noun [C] a meeting at which people try to talk to the spirits of dead people □ *upacara pemujaan roh (orang mati)*

search¹ /sɜ:tʃ/ verb [I,T] **search (sb/sth) (for sb/sth); search (through sth) (for sth)** to examine sth carefully because you are looking for sth; to look for sth that is missing □ *memeriksa; mencari*: *The men were arrested and searched for drugs.* ♦ *Were your bags searched at the airport?* ♦ *They are still searching for the missing child.*

765 **the seafront → season**

♦ *She searched through the papers on the desk, looking for the letter.*

search² /sɜ:tʃ/ noun [C,U] the act of looking for sth □ *pencarian*: *the search for the missing boy* ♦ *She walked round for hours **in search of** her missing dog.* ♦ *to do a search on the Internet*

'search engine noun [C] a computer program that searches the Internet for information □ *enjin gelintar; enjin carian* ➔ note at **Internet**

searcher /'sɜ:tʃə(r)/ noun [C] **1** a person who is looking for sb/sth □ *pencari* **2** a program that allows you to look for particular information on a computer □ *pencari; penggelintar*

searching /'sɜ:tʃɪŋ/ adj (used about a look, question, etc.) trying to find out the truth □ *tajam; teliti*: *The customs officers asked a lot of searching questions about our trip.*

'search party noun [C] an organized group of people who are looking for sb/sth that is lost or missing □ *pasukan pencari*

'search warrant noun [C] an official piece of paper that gives the police the right to search a building, etc. □ *waran geledah*

seashell /'si:ʃel/ noun [C] the empty shell of a small animal that lives in the sea □ *kulit siput; cangkerang*

seashells

seashore /'si:ʃɔ:(r)/ noun [U] usually **the seashore** the part of the land that is next to the sea □ *(tepi) pantai*: *We were looking for shells **on the seashore**.*

seasick /'si:sɪk/ adj feeling sick or **vomiting** (= bringing up food from the stomach) because of the movement of a boat or ship □ *mabuk laut*: *to feel/get/be seasick* ➔ look at **airsick, carsick, travel-sick**

seaside /'si:saɪd/ noun [sing] often **the seaside** an area on the coast, especially one where people go on holiday □ *tepi laut*: *to go to the seaside* ♦ *a seaside town*

season¹ /'si:zn/ noun [C] **1** one of the four main periods of the year □ *musim*: *In cool countries, the four seasons are spring, summer, autumn and winter.* ♦ *the dry/rainy season* **2** the period of the year when sth is common or popular or when sth usually happens or is done □ *musim*: *the football season*

IDM in season 1 (used about fresh foods) available in large quantities because it is the right time of the year □ *sedang musim*: *Tomatoes are cheapest when they are in season.* **2** (used about a female animal) ready to have sex □ *sedang berahi*

out of season 1 (used about fresh foods) not available in large quantities because it is the wrong time of the year □ *bukan musim* **2** (used about a place where people go on holiday) at the time of year when it is least popular with

VOWELS i: **see** i **any** ɪ **sit** e **ten** æ **hat** ɑ: **father** ɒ **got** ɔ: **saw** ʊ **put** u: **too** u **usual**

tourists □ *luar musim*: *This hotel is much cheaper out of season.*

season² /ˈsiːzn/ *verb* [T] to add salt, spices, etc. to food in order to make it taste better □ *membubuh perasa* ▶ **seasoning** *noun* [C,U]: *Add seasoning to the soup and serve with bread.*

seasonal /ˈsiːzənl/ *adj* happening or existing at a particular time of the year □ *bermusim*: *There are a lot of seasonal jobs in the summer.*

seasoned /ˈsiːznd/ *adj* having a lot of experience of sth □ *sudah biasa; berpengalaman*: *a seasoned traveller*

ˈseason ticket *noun* [C] a ticket that allows you to make a particular journey by bus, train, etc. or to go to a theatre or watch a sports team as often as you like for a fixed period of time □ *tiket langganan*

seat¹ /siːt/ *noun* [C] **1** something that you sit on □ *tempat duduk*: *Please take a seat* (= sit down). ♦ *the back/driving/passenger seat of a car* ➔ picture at **bicycle**, **car 2** the part of a chair, etc. that you sit on □ *tempat duduk*: *a steel chair with a plastic seat* **3** a place in a theatre, on a plane, etc. where you pay to sit □ *tempat duduk*: *There are no seats left on that flight.* **4** an official position as a member of a parliament, etc. □ *kerusi*: *to win/lose a seat*
IDM **be in the driving seat** ➔ **driving¹**
take a back seat ➔ **back²**

seat² /siːt/ *verb* [T] **1** [often passive] (*formal*) to give sb a place to sit; to sit down □ *duduk*: *Please be seated.* **2** to have seats or chairs for a particular number of people □ *dpt menampung*

ˈseat belt (also **ˈsafety belt**) *noun* [C] a long narrow piece of cloth that is fixed to the seat in a car or plane and that you wear around your body, so that you are not thrown forward if there is an accident □ *tali pinggang keledar*: *to fasten/unfasten your seat belt* ➔ look at **belt** ➔ picture at **car**

seating /ˈsiːtɪŋ/ *noun* [U] the seats or chairs in a place or the way that they are arranged □ *tempat duduk*: *The conference hall has seating for 500 people.*

seaweed /ˈsiːwiːd/ *noun* [U] a plant that grows in the sea. There are many different types of seaweed. □ *rumpai laut* ➔ picture on page **P10**

sec /sek/ (*informal*) = **second²**(2)

secluded /sɪˈkluːdɪd/ *adj* far away from other people, roads, etc.; very quiet □ *terpencil*: *a secluded beach/garden* ▶ **seclusion** /sɪˈkluːʒn/ *noun* [U]

second¹ /ˈsekənd/ *determiner, ordinal number, adv* 2nd □ *kedua*: *We are going on holiday in the second week in July.* ♦ *Birmingham is the second largest city in Britain after London.* ♦ *She poured herself a second cup of coffee.* ♦ *Our team finished second.* ♦ *I came second in the competition.* ♦ *Queen Elizabeth the Second* ♦ *the second of* January ♦ *January the second* ➔ note at **sixth**
IDM **second nature (to sb)** something that has become a habit or that you can do easily because you have done it so many times □ *kebiasaan*: *With practice, driving becomes second nature.*
second thoughts a change of mind or opinion about sth; doubts that you have when you are not sure if you have made the right decision □ *setelah difikirkan balik; keraguan*: *On second thoughts, let's go today, not tomorrow.* ♦ *I'm starting to have second thoughts about accepting their offer.*

second² /ˈsekənd/ *noun*
▶ SHORT TIME **1** [C] (*abbr* **sec**) one of the 60 parts into which a minute is divided □ *saat*: *She can run 100 metres in just over 11 seconds.* **2** (also *informal* **sec**) [C] a short time □ *sekejap*: *Wait a second, please.* **SYN** **moment**
▶ PRODUCT **3** [C, usually pl] something that has a small fault and that is sold at a lower price □ *barang-barang yg ada cacat atau rosak sedikit*: *The clothes are all seconds.*
▶ IN CAR **4** [U] the second of the **gears** (= speeds) that a vehicle can move forward in □ *gear dua*: *Once the car's moving, put it in second.*
▶ UNIVERSITY **5** [C] **a second (in sth)** the second highest level of degree given by a British university □ *ijazah kelas dua*: *to get an upper/a lower second in physics*

second³ /ˈsekənd/ *verb* [T] to support sb's suggestion or idea at a meeting so that it can then be discussed and voted on □ *menyokong*

second⁴ /sɪˈkɒnd/ *verb* [T, usually passive] (*especially BrE*) **second sb (from sth) (to sth)** to send an employee to another department, office, etc. in order to do a different job for a short period of time □ *dipinjam atau ditukar ke jabatan lain utk sementara* ▶ **secondment** *noun* [U,C]: *They met while she was on secondment from the Foreign Office.*

secondary /ˈsekəndri/ *adj* **1** less important than sth else □ *tdk begitu penting*: *Other people's opinions are secondary—it's my opinion that counts.* **2** caused by or developing from sth else □ *sekunder; sampingan*: *She developed a secondary infection following a bad cold.*

ˈsecondary school *noun* [C] a school for children aged from 11 to 18 □ *sekolah menengah* ➔ note at **primary school**

ˌsecond ˈbest¹ *adj* not quite the best but the next one after the best □ *yg kedua terbaik*: *the second-best time in the 100 metres race* ➔ look at **best**

ˌsecond ˈbest² *noun* [U] something that is not as good as the best, or not as good as you would like □ *sst yg bukan paling baik*: *I'm not prepared to accept second best.*

ˌsecond ˈclass *noun* [U] **1** (also **ˈstandard class**) the ordinary, less expensive seats on a train, ship, etc □ *kelas dua*: *You can never get a seat in second class.* **2** (in Britain) the way of sending letters, etc. that costs less but takes longer to arrive than **first class** □ *kelas dua*

second-'class adj **1** of little importance □ *tdk berapa penting*: *Old people should not be treated as second-class citizens.* **2** [only before a noun] used about the ordinary, less expensive seats on a train, ship, etc. □ *kelas dua* **3** [only before a noun] (in Britain) used about the way of sending letters, etc. that costs less but takes longer to arrive than **first class** □ *kelas dua* **4** [only before a noun] (used about a British university degree) of the level that is next after **first-class** □ *ijazah kelas dua* ▸ second-'class adv

,second 'cousin noun [C] the child of your mother's or father's cousin □ *dua pupu*

,second 'floor noun [C] the floor in a building that is two floors above the lowest floor □ *tingkat dua*: *I live on the second floor.* ♦ *a second-floor flat*

> **HELP** In American English the second floor is next above the lowest.

the ,second 'hand noun [C] the hand on some clocks and watches that shows seconds □ *jarum saat*

,second-'hand adj **1** already used or owned by sb else □ *terpakai*: *a second-hand car* ⊃ look at **old 2** (used about news or information) that you heard from sb else, and did not see or experience yourself □ *drpd orang lain* ⊃ look at **first-hand** ▸ second-hand adv: *I bought this bike second-hand.*

,second 'language noun [C] a language that sb learns to speak well and that they use for work or at school, but that is not the language they learned first □ *bahasa kedua*: *ESL is short for English as a Second Language.*

secondly /'sekəndli/ adv (used when you are giving your second reason or opinion) also □ *kedua*: *Firstly, I think it's too expensive and secondly, we don't really need it.*

,second 'name noun [C] (especially BrE) **1** = surname □ *nama keluarga* **2** a second personal name □ *nama kedua*: *His second name is Prabhakar, after his father.*

,second-'rate adj of poor quality □ *kurang bermutu; tdk begitu baik*: *a second-rate poet*

secrecy /'si:krəsi/ noun [U] the fact of being secret or keeping sth secret □ *kerahsiaan; berahsia*: *I must stress the importance of secrecy in this matter.*

⚑ **secret**[1] /'si:krət/ adj **1 secret (from sb)** that is not or must not be known by other people □ *rahsia; sulit*: *We have to keep the party secret from Carmen.* ♦ *a secret address* ♦ *a secret love affair* **2** [only before a noun] used to describe actions that you do not tell anyone about □ *rahsia; secara sorok-sorok/diam-diam*: *a secret drinker* ♦ *She's got a secret admirer.* ▸ secretly adv: *The government secretly agreed to pay the kidnappers.*

⚑ **secret**[2] /'si:krət/ noun **1** [C] something that is not or must not be known by other people □ *rahsia; sulit*: *to keep a secret* ♦ *to let somebody in on/tell somebody a secret* ♦ *I can't tell you where we're going—it's a secret.* ♦ *It's no secret that they don't like each other* (= everyone knows). **2** [sing] **the secret (of/to sth/doing sth)** the only way or the best way of doing or achieving sth □ *rahsia*: *What is the secret of your success* (= how did you become so successful)*?*

IDM **in secret** without other people knowing □ *secara rahsia*: *to meet in secret*

,secret 'agent (also agent) noun [C] a person who tries to find out secret information, especially about the government of another country □ *perisik* ⊃ look at **spy**

secretarial /,sekrə'teəriəl/ adj involving or connected with the work that a **secretary** does □ *kesetiausahaan*: *secretarial skills/work*

⚑ **secretary** /'sekrətri/ noun [C] (pl **secretaries**) **1** a person who works in an office. A **secretary** types letters, answers the telephone, keeps records, etc. □ *setiausaha*: *the director's personal secretary* ⊃ note at **office 2** an official of a club or society who is responsible for keeping records, writing letters, etc. □ *setiausaha*: *the membership secretary* **3 Secretary** (in the US) the head of a government department, chosen by the President □ *setiausaha*: *Secretary of the Treasury* ⊃ look at **minister 4 Secretary** (BrE) = **Secretary of State**(1)

,Secretary of 'State noun [C] **1** (also **Secretary**) (in Britain) the head of one of the main government departments □ *Menteri*: *the Secretary of State for Defence* **2** (in the US) the head of the government department that deals with foreign affairs □ *Setiausaha Negara*

secrete /sɪ'kri:t/ verb [T] **1** (used about a part of a plant, animal or person) to produce a liquid □ *merembeskan* **2** (formal) to hide sth in a secret place □ *menyorokkan; menyembunyikan*

secretion /sɪ'kri:ʃn/ noun [C,U] (formal) a liquid that is produced by a plant or an animal; the process by which the liquid is produced □ *rembesan; perembesan*: *The frog covers its skin in a poisonous secretion for protection.*

secretive /'si:krətɪv/ adj liking to keep things secret from other people □ *berahsia*: *Wendy is very secretive about her private life.* ▸ secretively adv ▸ secretiveness noun [U]

the ,secret 'service noun [sing] the government department that tries to find out secret information about other countries and governments □ *jabatan perisik*

sect /sekt/ noun [C] a group of people who have a particular set of religious or political beliefs. A **sect** has often broken away from a larger group. □ *mazhab; puak*

sectarian /sek'teəriən/ adj connected with the differences that exist between groups of people who have different religious views □ *sektarian; mazhab atau puak*: *sectarian attacks/violence*

section /'sekʃn/ noun [C] **1** one of the parts into which sth is divided □ *bahagian*: *the string section of an orchestra* ◆ *the financial section of a newspaper* ◆ *The library has an excellent reference section.* **2** a view or drawing of sth as if it was cut from the top to the bottom so that you can see the inside □ *keratan*: *The illustration shows a section through a leaf.*

sector /'sektə(r)/ noun [C] **1** a part of the business activity of a country □ *sektor*: *The manufacturing sector has declined in recent years.* ◆ *the public/private sector* **2** a part of a particular area, especially an area under military control □ *sektor; bahagian*: *the occupied sector of the city*

secular /'sekjələ(r)/ adj not concerned with religion or the church □ *sekular; duniawi*

secure[1] /sɪ'kjʊə(r)/ adj **1** free from worry or doubt; confident □ *terjamin; selamat; yakin*: *Children need to feel secure.* ◆ *to be financially secure* **OPP** insecure **2** not likely to be lost □ *selamat*: *Business is good so his job is secure.* ◆ *a secure investment* **SYN** safe **3** not likely to fall or be broken; firmly fixed □ *kukuh*: *That ladder doesn't look very secure.* **SYN** stable **4** secure (against/from sb/sth) well locked or protected □ *dikunci, ditutup, dsb dgn selamat*: *Make sure the house is secure before you go to bed.* ▶ securely adv: *All doors and windows must be securely fastened.*

secure[2] /sɪ'kjʊə(r)/ verb [T] **1** secure sth (to sth) to fix or lock sth firmly □ *memasang, mengunci, mengikat, dsb dgn kukuh*: *The load was secured with ropes.* ◆ *Secure the rope to a tree or a rock.* **2** secure sth (against/from sth) to make sth safe □ *melindungi*: *The sea wall needs strengthening to secure the town against flooding.* **3** to obtain or achieve sth, especially by having to make a big effort □ *mendapat*: *The company has secured a contract to build ten planes.*

security /sɪ'kjʊərəti/ noun (pl securities) **1** [U] things that you do to protect sb/sth from attack, danger, thieves, etc. □ *keselamatan*: *Security was tightened at the airport before the President arrived.* ◆ *The robbers were caught on the bank's security cameras.* **2** [U] the section of a large company or organization that deals with the protection of buildings, equipment and workers □ *bahagian keselamatan/sekuriti*: *If you see a suspicious bag, contact airport security immediately.* **3** [U] the state of feeling safe and being free from worry; protection against the difficulties of life □ *rasa selamat; perlindungan*: *Children need the security of a stable home environment.* ◆ *financial/job security* **OPP** insecurity **4** [C,U] something of value that you use when you borrow money. If you cannot pay the money back then you lose the thing you gave as **security** □ *cagaran*: *You may need to use your house as security for the loan.*

sedan /sɪ'dæn/ (*AmE*) = saloon

sedate[1] /sɪ'deɪt/ adj quiet, calm and well behaved □ *tenang*

sedate[2] /sɪ'deɪt/ verb [T] to give a person or animal a drug to make them feel calm or want to sleep □ *memberi ubat penenang/sedatif*: *The lion was sedated and treated by a vet.* ▶ sedation /sɪ'deɪʃn/ noun [U]: *The doctor put her under sedation.*

sedative /'sedətɪv/ noun [C] a drug that makes you feel calm or want to sleep □ *ubat penenang/sedatif* ⮕ look at **tranquilliser**

sedentary /'sedntri/ adj involving a lot of sitting down; not active □ *banyak duduk; tdk aktif*: *a sedentary lifestyle/job*

sediment /'sedɪmənt/ noun [U] a thick substance that forms at the bottom of a liquid □ *mendapan; keladak*

seduce /sɪ'dju:s/ verb [T] **1** to persuade sb to have sex with you □ *menggoda* **2** seduce sb (into sth/doing sth) to persuade sb to do sth they would not usually agree to do □ *menggoda*: *Special offers seduce customers into spending their money.* ▶ seduction /sɪ'dʌkʃn/ noun [C,U]

seductive /sɪ'dʌktɪv/ adj **1** sexually attractive □ *(yg) menggoda/memberahikan*: *a seductive smile* **2** attractive in a way that makes you want to have or do sth □ *(yg) menggoda/menarik*: *The idea of retiring to the coast is highly seductive.*

see /si:/ verb (*pt* saw /sɔ:/; *pp* seen /si:n/)
▶ USE EYES **1** [I,T] to become conscious of sth, using your eyes; to use the power of sight □ *melihat; nampak*: *It was so dark that we couldn't see.* ◆ *On a clear day you can see for miles.* ◆ *Have you seen my wallet anywhere?* ◆ *I've just seen a mouse run under the cooker.* ◆ *He looked for her but couldn't see her in the crowd.* ⮕ note at **look[1]**, **smell[1]**
▶ FILM, TV, ETC. **2** [T] to look at or watch a film, play, TV programme, etc. □ *menonton; tengok*: *Did you see that programme on sharks last night?* ◆ *Have you seen Spielberg's latest film?*
▶ VISIT **3** [T] to spend time with sb; to visit sb □ *berjumpa; mengunjungi*: *I saw Alan at the weekend; we had dinner together.* ◆ *You should see a doctor about that cough.*
▶ UNDERSTAND **4** [I,T] to understand sth; to realize sth □ *nampak; faham*: *Do you see what I mean?* ◆ *She doesn't see the point in spending so much money on a car.* ◆ *'You have to key in your password first.' 'Oh, I see.'*
▶ HAVE OPINION **5** [T] to have an opinion about sth □ *pandangan*: *How do you see the situation developing?*
▶ IMAGINE **6** [T] to imagine sth as a future possibility □ *dpt melihat; nampak*: *I can't see her changing her mind.*
▶ FIND OUT **7** [T] to find out sth by looking, asking or waiting □ *tengok*: *Go and see if the postman has been yet.* ◆ *We'll wait and see what happens before making any decisions.* ◆ *'Can we go swimming today, Dad?' 'I'll see.'* ◆ *I saw in the paper that they're building a new theatre.*

► MAKE SURE **8** [T] to do what is necessary in a situation; to make sure that sb does sth □ *memastikan*: *I'll see that he gets the letter.*

► HAPPEN **9** [T] to be the time when an event happens □ *berlaku*: *Last year saw huge changes in the education system.*

► HELP **10** [T] to go with sb, for example to help or protect them □ *menemani; mengiringi*: *He asked me if he could see me home, but I said no.* ♦ *I'll see you to the door.*

IDM as far as the eye can see ⇒ far²

let me see; let's see (*informal*) used when you are thinking or trying to remember sth □ *nanti kejap*: *Where did I put the car keys? Let's see. I think I left them by the telephone.*

see eye to eye (with sb) to agree with sb; to have the same opinion as sb □ *bersependapat; bersetuju (dgn sso)*: *We don't always see eye to eye on political matters.*

see if ... to try to do sth □ *cuba tengok*: *I'll see if I can find time to do it.* ♦ *See if you can undo this knot.*

see the joke to understand what is funny about a joke or trick □ *memahami jenaka*

see red (*informal*) to become very angry □ *naik berang*

see you (later) (*informal*) used for saying goodbye to sb you expect to see soon or later that day □ *jumpa lagi (nanti)*

see you around (*informal*) used for saying goodbye to sb you have made no arrangement to see again □ *selamat tinggal/jalan*

you see (*formal*) used for giving a reason □ *kau/awak tahulah (selalunya tdk diterjemahkan)*: *She's very unhappy. He was her first real boyfriend, you see.*

PHR V see about sth/doing sth to deal with sth □ *menguruskan/menyediakan sst*: *I've got to go to the station to see about changing my ticket.*

see sb off to go with sb to the railway station, the airport, etc. in order to say goodbye to them □ *menghantar sso*

see through sb/sth to be able to see that sb/sth is not what he/she/it appears □ *tahu muslihat sso/sst*: *The police immediately saw through his story.*

see to sb/sth to do what is necessary in a situation; to deal with sb/sth □ *membuat apa yg perlu (bagi sso/sst keadaan); menguruskan sst*: *I'll see to the travel arrangements and you book the hotel.*

seed /siːd/ *noun* **1** [C,U] the small hard part of a plant from which a new plant of the same kind can grow □ *biji; biji benih*: *a packet of sunflower seeds* ♦ *Grass seed should be sown in the spring.* ⇒ picture on **page P14 2** [C] the start of a feeling or an event that continues to grow □ *bibit; benih*: *Her answer planted the seeds of doubt in my mind.* **3** [C] a player in a sports competition, especially tennis, who is expected to finish in a high position □ *pemain pilihan*: *the number one seed*

seeded /ˈsiːdɪd/ *adj* (used about a player or a team in a sports competition) expected to finish in a high position □ *pilihan*

769 **seed → segment**

seedless /ˈsiːdləs/ *adj* having no seeds □ *tdk berbiji; tanpa biji*: *seedless grapes*

seedling /ˈsiːdlɪŋ/ *noun* [C] a very young plant or tree that has grown from a seed □ *anak benih*

seedy /ˈsiːdi/ *adj* (**seedier**; **seediest**) dirty and unpleasant; possibly connected with illegal or immoral activities □ *kotor dan tdk menyenangkan; mungkin ada kaitan dgn kegiatan haram atau tdk bermoral*: *a seedy hotel/neighbourhood*

seeing /ˈsiːɪŋ/ (also **seeing that, seeing as**) *conj* (*informal*) because; as □ *memandangkan*: *Seeing as we're going the same way, I'll give you a lift.*

seek /siːk/ *verb* [T] (*pt, pp* **sought** /sɔːt/) (*formal*) **1** to try to find or get sth □ *mencari*: *Politicians are still seeking a peaceful solution.* **2 seek sth (from sb)** to ask sb for sth □ *mendapatkan; meminta*: *You should seek advice from a solicitor about what to do next.* **3 seek (to do sth)** to try to do sth □ *mencari*: *They are still seeking to find a peaceful solution to the conflict.* **SYN** attempt **4 -seeking** [in compounds] looking for or trying to get the thing mentioned □ *mencari; mencuba mendapatkan*: *attention-seeking behaviour* ♦ *a heat-seeking missile*

seeker /ˈsiːkə(r)/ *noun* [C] [often in compounds] a person who is trying to find or get sth □ *pencari*: *an attention seeker* ♦ *asylum seekers*

seem /siːm/ *verb* [I] [not used in the continuous tenses] **seem (to sb) (to be) sth; seem (like) sth** to give the impression of being or doing sth □ *nampaknya*: *Emma seems (like) a very nice girl.* ♦ *Emma seems to be a very nice girl.* ♦ *It seems to me that we have no choice.* ♦ *You seem happy today.* ♦ *This machine doesn't seem to work.* **SYN** appear

seeming /ˈsiːmɪŋ/ *adj* (*formal*) [only before a noun] appearing to be sth □ *pd zahirnya kelihatan*: *Despite her seeming enthusiasm, Sandra didn't really help very much.* **SYN** apparent
► **seemingly** *adv*: *a seemingly endless list of complaints*

seen *past participle* of **see**

seep /siːp/ *verb* [I] (used about a liquid) to flow very slowly through sth □ *meresap*: *Water started seeping in through small cracks.*

ˈsee-saw *noun* [C] an outdoor toy for children that consists of a long piece of wood that is balanced in the middle. One child sits on each end of the see-saw and one goes up while the other is down. □ *jongkang-jongket*

seethe /siːð/ *verb* [I] **1** to be very angry but to try not to show it □ *sangat marah*: *I was seething with frustration.* **2** (*formal*) **seethe (with sth)** to be very crowded □ *penuh sesak*: *The streets were seething with people.*

segment /ˈsɛɡmənt/ *noun* [C] **1** a section or part of sth □ *bahagian; segmen*: *I've divided the sheet of paper into three segments.* ♦ *a segment of the population* **2** one of the parts into which

| CONSONANTS | p **p**en | b **b**ad | t **t**ea | d **d**id | k **c**at | g **g**ot | tʃ **ch**in | dʒ **J**une | f **f**all | v **v**an | θ **th**in |

an orange can be divided □ *ulas* ⊃ picture on page P14

segregate /ˈsegrɪgeɪt/ *verb* [T] **segregate sb/sth (from sb/sth)** to separate one group of people or things from the rest □ *mengasingkan: The two groups of football fans were segregated to avoid trouble.* ⊃ look at **integrate** ▶ **segregation** /ˌsegrɪˈgeɪʃn/ *noun* [U]: *racial segregation* (= separating people of different races)

seismic /ˈsaɪzmɪk/ *adj* [only *before* a noun] connected with or caused by **earthquakes** (= violent movements of the earth's surface) □ *seismos*

seize /siːz/ *verb* [T] **1** to take hold of sb/sth suddenly and firmly □ *menyambar; merampas: The thief seized her handbag and ran off with it.* ◆ (*figurative*) *to seize a chance/an opportunity* SYN **grab 2** to take control or possession of sb/sth □ *merampas: The police seized 50 kilos of illegal drugs.* **3** [usually passive] (used about an emotion) to affect sb suddenly and very strongly □ *dilanda; dikuasai; dicengkam: I felt myself seized by panic.*
PHR V **seize (on/upon) sth** to make use of a good and unexpected chance □ *terus menerima; mengambil kesempatan: He seized on a mistake by the goalkeeper and scored.*
seize up (used about a machine) to stop working because it is too hot, does not have enough oil, etc. □ *terhenti*

seizure /ˈsiːʒə(r)/ *noun* **1** [U] using force or legal authority to take control or possession of sth □ *perampasan: the seizure of 30 kilos of heroin by police* **2** [C] a sudden strong attack of an illness, especially one affecting the brain □ *serangan (penyakit)*

seldom /ˈseldəm/ *adv* not often □ *jarang sekali; jarang-jarang: There is seldom snow in Athens.* ◆ *I very seldom go to the theatre.* SYN **rarely**

select¹ /sɪˈlekt/ *verb* [T] to choose sb/sth from a number of similar things □ *memilih: The best candidates will be selected for interview.*

> HELP **Select** or **choose**? **Select** is more formal than **choose** and suggests that a lot of care is taken when making the decision.

select² /sɪˈlekt/ *adj* (*formal*) **1** [only *before* a noun] carefully chosen as the best of a group □ *terpilih; pilihan: A university education is no longer the privilege of a select few.* **2** used or owned by rich people □ *eksklusif*

selection /sɪˈlekʃn/ *noun* **1** [U] the process of choosing or being chosen □ *pemilihan: The manager is responsible for team selection.* **2** [C] a number of people or things that have been chosen □ *pilihan: a selection of hits from the fifties and sixties* **3** [C] a number of things from which you can choose □ *pilihan: This shop has a very good selection of toys.* SYN **choice, range**

selective /sɪˈlektɪv/ *adj* **1** concerning only some people or things; not general □ *terpilih: a selective school* (= one that chooses which students to admit, often according to ability) **2** careful when choosing □ *memilih: She's very selective about who she invites to her parties.* ▶ **selectively** *adv*

self /self/ *noun* [C] (*pl* **selves** /selvz/) a person's own nature or qualities □ *diri (sendiri); sifat (sso): It's good to see you back to your old self again* (= feeling well or happy again). ◆ *Her spiteful remark revealed her true self* (= what she was really like).

self- /self/ [in compounds] of, to or by yourself or itself □ *diri; kendiri; berkenaan dgn, kpd atau oleh diri sendiri: self-assessment* ◆ *self-taught*

self-addressed envelope = **stamped addressed envelope**

self-assurance = **assurance**(2)

self-assured = **assured**

self-catering *adj* (*BrE*) (used about a holiday or a place to stay) where meals are not provided for you so you cook them yourself □ *makan sendiri*

self-centred (*AmE* **self-centered**) *adj* thinking only about yourself and not about other people □ *penting diri* ⊃ look at **selfish**

self-confessed *adj* [only *before* a noun] admitting that you are sth or do sth that most people consider to be bad □ *mengaku dirinya*

self-confident *adj* feeling sure about your own value and abilities □ *yakin diri* ⊃ look at **confident** ▶ **self-confidence** *noun* [U]: *Many women lack the self-confidence to apply for senior jobs.*

self-conscious *adj* too worried about what other people think about you □ *malu; berasa canggung: He's self-conscious about being short.* ▶ **self-consciously** *adv* ▶ **self-consciousness** *noun* [U]

self-contained *adj* **1** not needing or depending on other people □ *berdikari* **2** (*BrE*) (used about a flat, etc.) having its own private entrance, kitchen and bathroom □ *serba lengkap: self-contained accommodation*

self-control *noun* [U] the ability to control your emotions and appear calm even when you are angry, afraid, excited, etc □ *kebolehan mengawal perasaan; ketabahan: to lose/keep your self-control*

self-defence (*AmE* **self-defense**) *noun* [U] the use of force to protect yourself or your property □ *pertahanan diri; mempertahankan diri: Lee is learning karate for self-defence.* ◆ *to shoot somebody in self-defence* (= because they are going to attack you)

self-destruct *verb* [I] (used about a machine, etc.) to destroy itself □ *binasa diri* ▶ **self-destructive** *adj*

self-discipline *noun* [U] the ability to make yourself do sth difficult or unpleasant □ *disiplin* *diri*: *It takes a lot of self-discipline to give up smoking.* ◆ *It takes a lot of self-discipline to train for a marathon.*

self-em'ployed *adj* working for yourself and earning money from your own business □ *bekerja sendiri*

self-es'teem *noun* [U] a good opinion of your own character and abilities □ *harga diri*: *a man with high/low self-esteem*

self-'evident *adj* that does not need any proof or explanation; clear □ *jelas; nyata*

self-ex'planatory *adj* clear and easy to understand; not needing to be explained □ *jelas dgn sendirinya*: *The book's title is self-explanatory.*

self-im'portant *adj* thinking that you are more important than other people □ *bongkak; sombong* **SYN** **arrogant** ▸ self-im'portance *noun* [U] ▸ self-im'portantly *adv*

self-in'dulgent *adj* allowing yourself to have or do things you enjoy (sometimes when it would be better to stop yourself) □ *(suka) menurut nafsu* ▸ self-in'dulgence *noun* [U]

self-'interest *noun* [U] thinking about what is best for yourself rather than for other people □ *kepentingan sendiri*

selfish /'selfɪʃ/ *adj* thinking only about your own needs or wishes and not about other people's □ *mementingkan diri sendiri*: *a selfish attitude* ◆ *I'm sick of your selfish behaviour!* **OPP** **unselfish, selfless** ⊃ look at **self-centred** ▸ selfishly *adv* ▸ selfishness *noun* [U]

selfless /'selfləs/ *adj* thinking more about other people's needs or wishes than your own □ *tdk mementingkan diri sendiri* **OPP** **selfish** ⊃ look at **unselfish**

self-'made *adj* having become rich or successful by your own efforts □ *berjaya atas usaha sendiri*: *a self-made millionaire*

self-'pity *noun* [U] the state of thinking too much about your own problems or troubles and feeling sorry for yourself □ *perasaan kasihan terhadap diri sendiri*

self-'portrait *noun* [C] a picture that you draw or paint of yourself □ *potret diri*

self-'raising 'flour (*AmE* self-rising 'flour) *noun* [U] flour that contains **baking powder** (= a substance that makes cakes, etc. rise during cooking) □ *tepung naik sendiri* ⊃ look at **plain flour**

self-re'liant *adj* not depending on help from anyone else □ *berdikari* ⊃ look at **reliant**

self-re'spect *noun* [U] a feeling of confidence and pride in yourself □ *harga diri; maruah*: *Old people need to keep their dignity and self-respect.* ⊃ look at **respect** ▸ self-re'specting *adj* [often in negative sentences]: *No self-respecting language student* (= nobody who is serious about learning a language) *should be without this book.*

self-'righteous *adj* believing that you are

771   self-employed → sell-by date

always right and other people are wrong, so that you are better than other people □ *menganggap diri sendiri saja yg betul* ⊃ look at **righteous** ▸ self-'righteously *adv* ▸ self-'righteousness *noun* [U]

self-rising 'flour (*AmE*) = **self-raising flour**

self-'sacrifice *noun* [U] giving up what you need or want in order to help others □ *pengorbanan diri*

self-'service *adj* (used about a shop, petrol station, restaurant, etc.) where you serve yourself and then pay for the goods □ *layan diri*

self-suf'ficient *adj* able to produce or provide everything that you need without help from other people or having to buy from other people □ *mampu diri; cukup utk keperluan sendiri*

sell /sel/ *verb* (*pt, pp* **sold** /səʊld/)
▸ EXCHANGE FOR MONEY **1** [I,T] **sell (sb) (sth) (at/ for sth); sell (sth) (to sb) (at/for sth)** to give sth to sb who pays for it and is then the owner of it □ *menjual*: *We are going to sell our car.* ◆ *I sold my guitar to my neighbour for £200.* ◆ *Would you sell me your ticket?* ◆ *I offered them a lot of money but they wouldn't sell.* **2** [T] to offer sth for people to buy □ *menjual; jual*: *Excuse me, do you sell stamps?* ◆ *to sell insurance/advertising space*
▸ BE BOUGHT **3** [I,T] to be bought by people in the way or in the numbers mentioned; to be offered at the price mentioned □ *dijual*: *Her books sell well abroad.* ◆ *These watches sell at £1 000 each in the shops but you can have this one for £500.* ◆ *This paper sells over a million copies a day.*
▸ PERSUADE **4** [T] to make people want to buy sth □ *melariskan*: *They rely on advertising to sell their products.* **5** [T] **sell sth/yourself to sb** to persuade sb to accept sth; to persuade sb that you are the right person for a job, position, etc. □ *meyakinkan*: *Now we have to try and sell the idea to the management.* ⊃ *noun for senses 1 to 4 is* **sale**
IDM **be sold on sth** (*informal*) to be very enthusiastic about sth □ *suka/ghairah akan sst*
PHR V **sell sth off** to sell sth in order to get rid of it, often at a low price □ *menjual (murah)*: *The shops sell their remaining winter clothes off in the spring sales.*
sell out; be sold out (used about tickets for a concert, football game, etc.) to be all sold □ *habis dijual*: *All the tickets sold out within two hours.* ◆ *The concert was sold out weeks ago.*
sell out (of sth); be sold out (of sth) to sell all of sth so that no more is/are available to be bought □ *habis dijual*: *I'm afraid we've sold out of bread.*
sell up to sell everything you own, especially your house, your business, etc. (in order to start a new life, move to another country, etc.) □ *menjual semua harta benda*

'sell-by date *noun* [C] (*BrE*) the date printed on food packages after which the food should not be sold □ *tarikh habis tempoh*: *This milk is past its sell-by date.*

VOWELS   iː see   i any   ɪ sit   e ten   æ hat   ɑː father   ɒ got   ɔː saw   ʊ put   uː too   u usual

seller /ˈselə(r)/ noun [C] **1** [in compounds] a person or business that sells □ *penjual*: *a bookseller* ♦ *a flower seller* **OPP** **buyer** **2** something that is sold, especially in the amount or way mentioned □ *jualan*: *This magazine is a big seller in the 25-40 age group.* ➔ look at **bestseller**

Sellotape™ /ˈseləteɪp/ (*BrE* ˈsticky tape, *AmE* ˈScotch tape™) noun [U] a type of clear sticky tape that is sold in rolls and used for sticking things □ *Sellotape™; pita perekat* ➔ look at **tape** ➔ picture at **stationery** ▶ **sellotape** verb [T]

ˈsell-out noun [C, usually sing] a play, concert, etc. for which all the tickets have been sold □ *berjaya betul*: *Next week's final is likely to be a sell-out.* ♦ *The band are on a sell-out tour.*

selves plural of **self**

semantic /sɪˈmæntɪk/ adj connected with the meaning of words and sentences □ *semantik* ▶ **semantically** /-kli/ adv

semblance /ˈsembləns/ noun [sing, U] (*formal*) (a) semblance of sth the appearance of being sth or of having a certain quality □ *memperlihatkan; kelihatan spt (sst)*

semen /ˈsiːmen/ noun [U] the liquid that is produced by the male sex organs containing **sperm** (= the seed necessary for making babies) □ *mani; semen*

semester /sɪˈmestə(r)/ noun [C] one of the two periods of time that the school or college year is divided into □ *semester*: *the spring/fall semester* ➔ look at **term**

semi /ˈsemi/ noun [C] (*pl* semis /ˈsemiz/) (*BrE informal*) a house that is joined to another one with a shared wall between them, forming a pair of houses □ *rumah berkembar*

semi- /ˈsemi/ [in compounds] half; partly □ *semi; separa; separuh; setengah*: *semicircular* ♦ *semi-final*

semicircle /ˈsemisɜːkl/ noun [C] one half of a circle; something that is arranged in this shape □ *separuh bulatan*: *Please sit in a semicircle.* ➔ picture at **circle** ▶ **semicircular** /ˌsemiˈsɜːkjələ(r)/ adj: *a semicircular driveway*

semicolon /ˌsemiˈkəʊlən/ noun [C] the mark (;) used in writing for separating parts of a sentence or items in a list □ *koma bertitik*

ˌsemi-deˈtached adj (used about a house) joined to another house with a shared wall on one side forming a pair of houses □ *(rumah) berkembar* ➔ picture on **page P9**

ˌsemi-ˈfinal noun [C] one of the two games in a sports competition that decide which players or teams will play each other in the final □ *separuh akhir*: *He's through to the semi-finals.* ➔ look at **quarter-final**, **final** ▶ **ˌsemi-ˈfinalist** noun [C]

seminar /ˈsemɪnɑː(r)/ noun [C] **1** a class at a university, college, etc. in which a small group of students discuss or study a subject with a teacher □ *seminar*: *I've got a seminar on Goethe this morning.* **2** a meeting for business people in which working methods, etc. are taught or discussed □ *seminar*: *a one-day management seminar*

Sen. abbr = **Senator**

senate /ˈsenət/ noun [C, with sing or pl verb] often the Senate one of the two groups of elected politicians who make laws in the government in some countries, for example the US □ *senat* ➔ look at **Congress**, **the House of Representatives**

senator /ˈsenətə(r)/ noun [C] often Senator (*abbr* Sen.) a member of the Senate □ *senator*: *Senator McCarthy*

send /send/ verb [T] (*pt, pp* sent /sent/) **1** send sth (to sb/sth); send (sb) sth to make sth go or be taken somewhere, especially by post, radio, etc. □ *menghantar; mengirim*: *to send a letter/parcel/message/email to somebody* ♦ *Don't forget to send me a postcard.* **2** to tell sb to go somewhere or to do sth; to arrange for sb to go somewhere □ *menyuruh; menghantar*: *My company is sending me on a training course next month.* ♦ *She sent the children to bed early.* ♦ *to send somebody to prison* ♦ *I'll send someone round to collect you at ten o'clock.* **3** to cause sb/sth to move in a particular direction, often quickly or as a reaction that cannot be prevented □ *menyebabkan*: *I accidentally pushed the table and sent all the drinks flying.* **4** send sb (to/into sth) to make sb have a particular feeling or enter a particular state □ *membuat*: *The movement of the train sent me to sleep.*

IDM give/send sb your love ➔ **love¹**

PHR V **send for sb/sth** to ask for sb to come to you; to ask for sth to be brought or sent to you □ *memanggil atau panggil sso/sst*: *Quick! Send for an ambulance!*

send sth in to send sth to a place where it will be officially dealt with □ *menghantar sst*: *I sent my application in three weeks ago but I still haven't had a reply.*

send away (to sb) (for sth); send off (for sth) to write to sb and ask for sth to be sent to you □ *menulis (surat) kpd sso utk meminta sst*: *Let's send off for some holiday brochures.*

send sb off (*BrE*) (used in a sports match) to order a player who has broken a rule to leave the field and not to return □ *menyuruh pemain keluar padang*: *Jones was sent off for a foul in the first half.*

send sth off to post sth □ *mengirim/mengeposkan sst*: *I'll send the information off today.*

send sth out 1 to send sth to a lot of different people or places □ *menghantar sst*: *We sent out the invitations two months before the wedding.* **2** to produce sth, for example light, heat, sound, etc. □ *menghasilkan sst*: *The sun sends out light and heat.*

send sb/sth up (*informal*) to make sb/sth look ridiculous or silly, especially by copying them or it in a way that is intended to be amusing □ *mengajuk atau mengejek sso/sst*

senile /ˈsiːnaɪl/ *adj* behaving in a confused and strange way, and unable to remember things because of old age □ *nyanyuk*: *I think she's going senile.* ▶ **senility** /səˈnɪləti/ *noun* [U]

senior[1] /ˈsiːniə(r)/ *adj* **1** senior (to sb) having a high or higher position in a company, an organization, etc. □ *kanan; lebih tinggi pangkatnya*: *a senior lecturer/officer/manager* ♦ *He's senior to me.* **OPP** junior **2** often **Senior** (*abbr* **Snr**; **Sr**) (*especially AmE*) used after the name of a man who has the same name as his son, to avoid confusion □ *Bapa* **OPP** junior **3** (*BrE*) (used in schools) older □ *kelas/tingkatan atas*: *This common room is for the use of senior pupils only.* **4** (*AmE*) connected with the final year at high school or college □ *tahun akhir*: *the senior prom*

senior[2] /ˈsiːniə(r)/ *noun* [C] **1** a person who is older or or of a higher position (than one or more other people) □ *sso yg lebih tua atau lebih kanan*: *My oldest sister is ten years my senior.* ♦ *She felt undervalued, both by her colleagues and her seniors.* **OPP** junior **2** (*BrE*) one of the older students at a school □ *pelajar kelas/tingkatan atas* **3** (*AmE*) a student in the final year of school, college or university □ *penuntut tahun akhir*: *high school seniors*

,senior ˈcitizen *noun* [C] an older person, especially sb who has retired from work □ *warga tua* ➲ look at **old-age pensioner**

,senior ˈhigh school (also ,senior ˈhigh) *noun* [C,U] (in the US) a school for young people between the ages of 14 and 18 □ *Sekolah Tinggi Senior* ➲ look at **junior high school**

seniority /ˌsiːniˈɒrəti (*AmE* also) / *noun* [U] the position or importance that a person has in a company, an organization, etc. in relation to others □ *kekananan*: *The names are listed below in order of seniority.*

sensation /senˈseɪʃn/ *noun* **1** [C] a feeling that is caused by sth affecting your body or part of your body □ *rasa; perasaan*: *a pleasant/an unpleasant/a tingling sensation* **SYN** feeling **2** [U] the ability to feel when touching or being touched □ *deria rasa*: *For some time after the accident he had no sensation in his legs.* **SYN** feeling **3** [C, usually sing] a general feeling or impression that is difficult to explain □ *rasa; perasaan*: *I had the peculiar sensation that I was floating in the air.* **SYN** feeling **4** [C, usually sing] great excitement, surprise or interest among a group of people; sb/sth that causes this excitement □ *sensasi; kegemparan*: *The young American caused a sensation by beating the top player.*

sensational /senˈseɪʃənl/ *adj* **1** causing, or trying to cause, a feeling of great excitement, surprise or interest among people □ *menimbulkan sensasi*: *This magazine specializes in sensational stories about the rich and famous.* ➲ note at **newspaper 2** (*informal*) extremely good or beautiful; very exciting □ *hebat sekali* **SYN** fantastic ▶ **sensationally** /-ʃənəli/ *adv*

sense[1] /sens/ *noun*
▶ SIGHT, HEARING, ETC. **1** [C] one of the five natural physical powers of sight, hearing, smell, taste and touch, that people and animals have □ *deria*: *I've got a cold and I've lost my sense of smell.* ♦ *Dogs have an acute sense of hearing.*
▶ FEELING **2** [sing] a feeling of sth □ *rasa*: *I felt a tremendous sense of relief when the exams were finally over.* ♦ *She only visits her family out of a sense of duty.*
▶ NATURAL ABILITY **3** [U, sing] the ability to understand sth; the ability to recognize what sth is or what its value is □ *(daya) memahami atau menyedari sst*: *She seems to have lost all sense of reality.* ♦ *I like him—he's got a great sense of humour.* ♦ *I'm always getting lost. I've got absolutely no sense of direction.* **4** [U, sing] a natural ability to do or produce sth well □ *kepandaian*: *Good business sense made her a millionaire.* ♦ *He's got absolutely no dress sense (= he dresses very badly).*
▶ JUDGEMENT **5** [U] the ability to think or act in a reasonable or sensible way; good judgement □ *ada otak; masuk akal; pertimbangan yg waras*: *At least he had the sense to stop when he realized he was making a mistake.* ♦ *I think there's a lot of sense in what you're saying.* ➲ look at **common sense**
▶ REASON **6** [U] **sense (in doing sth)** the reason for doing sth; purpose □ *tujuan; alasan*: *What's the sense in making the situation more difficult for yourself?* ♦ *There's no sense in going any further—we're obviously lost.*
▶ MEANING **7** [C] (used about a word, phrase, etc.) a meaning □ *maksud; erti*: *This word has two senses.*
IDM **come to your senses** to finally realize that you should do sth because it is the most sensible thing to do □ *sedar (akan sst); insaf*
in a sense in one particular way but not in other ways; partly □ *dr satu segi; sebahagiannya*: *In a sense you're right, but there's more to the matter than that.*
make sense 1 to be possible to understand; to have a clear meaning □ *dpt difahami; masuk akal*: *What does this sentence mean? It doesn't make sense to me.* **2** (used about an action) to be sensible or logical □ *baik; wajar*: *I think it would make sense to wait for a while before making a decision.*
make sense of sth to manage to understand sth that is not clear or is difficult to understand □ *memahami sst*: *I can't make sense of these instructions.*
talk sense ➲ **talk**[1]

sense[2] /sens/ *verb* [T] [not used in the continuous tenses] to realize or become conscious of sth; to get a feeling about sth even though you cannot see it, hear it, etc. □ *merasakan; rasa*: *I sensed that something was wrong as soon as I went in.*

senseless → separate

HELP Although this verb is not used in the continuous tenses, it is common to see the present participle (= *-ing* form): *Sensing a scandal, the tabloid photographers rushed to the star's hotel.*

senseless /ˈsensləs/ *adj* **1** having no meaning or purpose □ *tdk bermakna/berguna* **2** [not before a noun] unconscious □ *tdk sedarkan diri*: *He was beaten senseless.*

sensibility /ˌsensəˈbɪləti/ *noun* (*pl* sensibilities) **1** [U,C] the ability to understand and experience deep feelings, for example in art, literature, etc. □ *kepekaan* **2** sensibilities [pl] sb's feelings, especially when they are easily offended □ *perasaan*

⚑ **sensible** /ˈsensəbl/ *adj* (used about people and their behaviour) able to make good judgements based on reason and experience; practical □ *berakal; waras; bijak*: *a sensible person/decision/precaution* ♦ *Stop joking and give me a sensible answer.* ♦ *I think it would be sensible to leave early, in case there is a lot of traffic.* **OPP** silly, foolish ▶sensibly /-əbli/ *adv*: *Let's sit down and discuss the matter sensibly.*

HELP Sensible or sensitive? Sensible is connected with common sense, reasonable action and good judgement. Sensitive is connected with feelings and emotions and with the five senses of sight, hearing, touch, smell and taste.

⚑ **sensitive** /ˈsensətɪv/ *adj*
▶THINKING OF FEELINGS **1** sensitive (to sth) showing that you are conscious of and able to understand people's feelings, problems, etc. □ *sensitif; peka*: *It wasn't very sensitive of you to mention her boyfriend. You know they've just split up.* ♦ *She always tries to be sensitive to other people's feelings.* **OPP** insensitive ⇨ note at sensible
▶EASILY UPSET **2** sensitive (about/to sth) easily upset, offended or annoyed, especially about a particular subject □ *sensitif; mudah tersinggung*: *She's still a bit sensitive about her divorce.* ♦ *He's very sensitive to criticism.* **OPP** insensitive
▶SUBJECT/SITUATION **3** needing to be dealt with carefully because it is likely to cause anger or trouble □ *sensitif*: *This is a sensitive period in the negotiations between the two countries.*
▶TO PAIN, COLD, ETC. **4** sensitive (to sth) easily hurt or damaged; painful, especially if touched □ *sensitif*: *a new cream for sensitive skin* ♦ *My teeth are very sensitive to hot or cold food.*
▶SCIENTIFIC INSTRUMENT **5** able to measure very small changes □ *sensitif; peka*: *a sensitive instrument*
▶sensitively *adv*: *The investigation will need to be handled sensitively.* ▶sensitivity /ˌsensəˈtɪvəti/ *noun* [U]: *I think your comments showed a complete lack of sensitivity.*

sensual /ˈsenʃuəl/ *adj* connected with physical or sexual pleasure □ *sensual; mengghairahkan*: *the sensual rhythms of Latin music* ▶sensuality /ˌsenʃuˈæləti/ *noun* [U]

sensuous /ˈsenʃuəs/ *adj* giving pleasure to the mind or body through the senses □ *membelai rasa; mengghairahkan*: *the sensuous feel of pure silk* ▶sensuously *adv* ▶sensuousness *noun* [U]

sent *past tense, past participle of* **send**

⚑ **sentence**¹ /ˈsentəns/ *noun* [C] **1** a group of words containing a subject and a verb, that expresses a statement, a question, etc. When a sentence is written, it begins with a capital letter and ends with a full stop □ *ayat*: *You don't need to write a long letter. A couple of sentences will be enough.* ⇨ note at paragraph ⇨ look at phrase **2** the punishment given by a judge to sb who has been found guilty of a crime □ *hukuman*: *20 years in prison was a very harsh sentence.* ⇨ note at court

sentence² /ˈsentəns/ *verb* [T] sentence sb (to sth) (used about a judge) to tell sb who has been found guilty of a crime what the punishment will be □ *menjatuhkan hukuman*: *The judge sentenced her to three months in prison for shoplifting.*

sentiment /ˈsentɪmənt/ *noun* **1** [C,U] (*formal*) an attitude or opinion that is often caused or influenced by emotion □ *sentimen; pendapat*: *His comments expressed my sentiments exactly.* **2** [U] feelings such as pity, romantic love, sadness, etc. that influence sb's actions or behaviour (sometimes in situations where this is not appropriate) □ *sentimen perasaan*: *There's no room for sentiment in business.*

sentimental /ˌsentɪˈmentl/ *adj* **1** producing or connected with emotions such as romantic love, pity, sadness, etc. which may be too strong or not appropriate □ *sentimental; penuh perasaan*: *How can you be sentimental about an old car!* ♦ *a sentimental love song* **2** connected with happy memories or feelings of love rather than having any financial value □ *sentimental; penuh kenangan manis*: *The jewellery wasn't worth much but it had great sentimental value to me.* ▶sentimentality /ˌsentɪmenˈtæləti/ *noun* [U] [disapproving] ▶sentimentally /ˌsentɪˈmentəli/ *adv*

sentry /ˈsentri/ *noun* [C] (*pl* sentries) a soldier who stands outside a building and guards it □ *sentri; (askar) pengawal*

separable /ˈsepərəbl/ *adj* able to be separated □ *boleh dipisahkan/diasing-asingkan* **OPP** inseparable

⚑ **separate**¹ /ˈseprət/ *adj* **1** different; not connected □ *berlainan; berbeza*: *We stayed in separate rooms in the same hotel.* **2** separate (from sth/sb) apart; not together □ *berasingan*: *You should always keep your cash and credit cards separate.*

⚑ **separate**² /ˈsepəreɪt/ *verb* **1** [T] separate sb/sth (from sb/sth) to keep people or things apart; to be between people or things with the result that they are apart □ *memisahkan; dipisahkan*: *The two sides of the city are separated by the river.* **SYN** divide **2** [I,T] separate (sb/sth) (from sb/

sth) to stop being together; to cause people or things to stop being together □ *memisahkan; berpisah; terpisah*: *I think we should separate into two groups.* ♦ *The friends separated at the airport.* ♦ *I got separated from my friends in the crowd.* ♦ *The police were called to separate the two men.* **3** [I] to stop living together as a couple with your wife, husband or partner □ *berpisah*: *His parents separated when he was still a baby.*

separated /ˈsepəreɪtɪd/ *adj* not living together as a couple any more □ *berpisah*: *My wife and I are separated.*

separately /ˈseprətli/ *adv* apart; not together □ *secara berasingan*: *Shall we pay separately or all together?*

separation /ˌsepəˈreɪʃn/ *noun* **1** [C,U] the act of separating or being separated; a situation or period of being apart □ *pemisahan; perpisahan*: *Separation from family and friends made me very lonely.* **2** [C] an agreement where a couple decide not to live together any more □ *berpisah*: *a trial separation*

Sept. *abbr* = **September**: *2 Sept. 1920*

September /sepˈtembə(r)/ *noun* [U,C] (*abbr* **Sept.**) the 9th month of the year, coming after August □ *September* ➔ note at **January**

septic /ˈseptɪk/ *adj* infected with poisonous bacteria □ *septik*: *The wound went septic.*

sequel /ˈsiːkwəl/ *noun* [C] a **sequel (to sth) 1** a book, film, etc. that continues the story of the one before □ *buku, filem, dsb susulan* **2** something that happens after, or is the result of, an earlier event □ *ekoran; akibat*

sequence /ˈsiːkwəns/ *noun* **1** [C] a number of things (actions, events, etc.) that happen or come one after another □ *turutan; urutan*: *Complete the following sequence: 1, 4, 8, 13, …* **2** [C,U] the order in which a number of things happen or are arranged □ *urutan; susunan*: *The photographs are in sequence.*

sequin /ˈsiːkwɪn/ *noun* [C] a small flat shiny circle that is sewn onto clothing as decoration □ *labuci* ▶ **sequinned** *adj*

serene /səˈriːn/ *adj* calm and peaceful □ *tenang*: *Her smile was serene.* ▶ **serenely** *adv* ▶ **serenity** /səˈrenəti/ *noun* [U]

sergeant /ˈsɑːdʒənt/ *noun* [C] (*abbr* **Sgt**) **1** a member of one of the middle ranks in the army or air force □ *sarjan* **2** an officer with a middle position in the police force □ *sarjan*

serial /ˈsɪəriəl/ *noun* [C] a story in a magazine or on TV or radio that is told in a number of parts over a period of time □ *bersiri*: *the first part of a sixteen-part drama serial* ➔ note at **series** ▶ **serialize** (also **-ise**) /ˈsɪəriəlaɪz/ *verb* [T]: *The novel was serialized on TV in six parts.*

'serial number *noun* [C] the number put on sth in order to identify it □ *nombor bersiri*

series /ˈsɪəriːz/ *noun* [C] (*pl* **series**) **1** a number of things that happen one after another and are of the same type or connected □ *rentetan; ber-turut-turut; siri*: *a series of events* ♦ *There has been a series of burglaries in this district recently.* **2** a number of programmes on radio or TV which have the same main characters and each tell a complete story □ *siri*

HELP **Series** or **serial**? In a **series** each part is a different, complete story involving the same main characters. In a **serial** the same story continues in each part.

serious /ˈsɪəriəs/ *adj* **1** bad or dangerous □ *teruk; berat; serius*: *a serious accident/illness/offence* ♦ *Pollution is a very serious problem.* ♦ *Her condition is serious and she's likely to be in hospital for some time.* **2** needing to be treated as important, not just for fun □ *serius*: *Don't laugh, it's a serious matter.* ♦ *a serious discussion* **3** **serious (about sth/about doing sth)** (used about a person) not joking; thinking deeply □ *sungguh-sungguh; serius*: *Are you serious about starting your own business* (= are you really going to do it)? ♦ *He's terribly serious. I don't think I've ever seen him laugh.* ♦ *You're looking very serious. Was it bad news?* ▶ **seriousness** *noun* [U]

seriously /ˈsɪəriəsli/ *adv* **1** in a serious way □ *dgn serius; teruk; parah; tenat*: *Three people were seriously injured in the accident.* ♦ *My mother is seriously ill.* ♦ *It's time you started to think seriously about the future.* **2** used at the beginning of a sentence to show that you are not joking or that you really mean what you are saying □ *sebenarnya*: *Seriously, I do appreciate all your help.* ♦ *Seriously, you've got nothing to worry about.* **3** used for expressing surprise at what sb has said and asking if it is really true □ *Betulkah?*: *'I'm 40 today.' 'Seriously? You look a lot younger.'*

IDM **take sb/sth seriously** to treat sb or sth as important □ *menganggap sso/sst dgn serius*: *You take everything too seriously! Relax and enjoy yourself.*

sermon /ˈsɜːmən/ *noun* [C] a speech on a religious or moral subject that is usually given by a religious leader as part of a service in church □ *khutbah*

serpent /ˈsɜːpənt/ *noun* [C] (in literature) a snake, especially a large one □ *ular*

serrated /səˈreɪtɪd/ *adj* having a row of points in V-shapes along the edge □ *bergerigi*: *a knife with a serrated edge*

servant /ˈsɜːvənt/ *noun* [C] a person who is paid to work in sb's house, doing work such as cooking, cleaning, etc. □ *orang gaji; pembantu rumah*: *They treat their mother like a servant.* ➔ look at **civil servant**

serve¹ /sɜːv/ *verb*
▶ FOOD/DRINK **1** [T] to give food or drink to sb during a meal; to take an order and then bring food or drink to sb in a restaurant, bar, etc. □ *menghidangkan*: *Breakfast is served from 7.30 to 9.00 a.m.* **2** [T] (used about an amount) to be enough for a certain number of people □ *cukup*

serve → set 776

utk: *According to the recipe, this dish serves four.*
▶IN SHOP **3** [I,T] to take a customer's order; to give help, sell goods, etc. □ *melayan; dilayan*: *There was a long queue of people waiting to be served.*
▶BE USEFUL **4** [I,T] to be useful or suitable for a particular purpose □ *digunakan; dijadikan*: *The judge said the punishment would serve as a warning to others.* ♦ *It's an old car but it will serve our purpose for a few months.*
▶PERFORM DUTY **5** [I,T] to perform a duty or provide a service for the public or for an organization □ *memberi khidmat; berkhidmat*: *During the war, he served in the army.* ♦ *She became a nurse because she wanted to serve the community.*
▶IN PRISON **6** [T] to spend a period of time in prison as a punishment □ *menjalani hukuman*: *He is currently serving a ten-year sentence for fraud.*
▶IN TENNIS, ETC. **7** [I,T] to start play by hitting the ball □ *membuat servis*: *She served an ace.*
IDM **first come, first served** ➔ **first²**
serve sb right used when sth unpleasant happens to sb and you do not feel sorry for them because you think it is their own fault □ *padan muka sso*: *'I feel sick.' 'It serves you right for eating so much.'*

serve² /sɜːv/ *noun* [C] = **service¹** (8)

server /ˈsɜːvə(r)/ *noun* [C] a computer that stores information that a number of computers can share □ *pelayan* ➔ look at **client**

service¹ /ˈsɜːvɪs/ *noun*
▶PROVIDING STH **1** [C] a system or an organization that provides the public with sth that it needs; the job that an organization does □ *perkhidmatan*: *There is a regular bus service to the airport.* ♦ *the postal service* ♦ *the National Health Service* ♦ *We offer a number of financial services.* ➔ look at **civil service**
▶IN RESTAURANT, HOTEL, ETC. **2** [U] the work or the quality of work done by sb when serving a customer □ *layanan; perkhidmatan*: *I enjoyed the meal but the service was terrible.* ♦ *Is service included in the bill?*
▶WORK/HELP **3** [U,C] work done for sb; help given to sb □ *khidmat; berkhidmat*: *He left the police force after thirty years' service.*
▶OF VEHICLE/MACHINE **4** [C,U] the checks, repairs, etc. that are necessary to make sure that a machine is working properly □ *servis; penyenggaraan*: *We take our car for a service every six months.*
▶ARMY, NAVY, ETC. **5** [U] (also **the services** [pl]) the armed forces; the army, navy or air force; the work done by the people in them □ *angkatan tentera*: *They both joined the services when they left school.* ♦ *Do you have to do military service in your country?*
▶RELIGIOUS CEREMONY **6** [C] a religious ceremony, usually including prayers, singing, etc. □ *upacara (agama)*: *a funeral service*
▶AT SIDE OF ROAD **7 services** [pl] (also ˈ**service station**) a place at the side of a **motorway** (= a wide road for fast traffic) where there is a petrol station, a shop, toilets, a restaurant, etc. □ *kawasan rehat; hentian*: *It's five miles to the next services.*
▶IN TENNIS, ETC. **8** (also **serve**) [C] the first hit of the ball at the start of play; a player's turn to serve (7) □ *servis*: *She's not a bad player but her service is weak.*

service² /ˈsɜːvɪs/ *verb* [T] to examine and, if necessary, repair a car, machine, etc. □ *menservis; menyenggara*: *All cars should be serviced at regular intervals.*

serviceman /ˈsɜːvɪsmən/, **servicewoman** /ˈsɜːvɪswʊmən/ *noun* [C] (*pl* **-men** /-mən/, **-women** /-wɪmɪn/) a person who is a member of the armed forces □ *anggota tentera (lelaki)*

ˈ**service station 1** = **petrol station 2** = **service¹** (7)

serviette /ˌsɜːviˈet/ *noun* [C] a square of cloth or paper that you use when you are eating to keep your clothes clean and to clean your mouth or hands on □ *kain/kertas kesat mulut atau tangan* SYN **napkin**

sesame /ˈsesəmi/ *noun* [U] a tropical plant grown for its seeds and their oil, which are used in cooking □ *bijan; lenga*

session /ˈseʃn/ *noun* **1** [C] a period of doing a particular activity □ *sesi*: *The whole album was recorded in one session.* ♦ *She has a session at the gym every week.* **2** [C,U] a formal meeting or series of meetings of a court of law, parliament, etc. □ *sidang; sesi*: *This court is now in session.*

set¹ /set/ *verb* (**setting**; *pt, pp* **set**)
▶PUT IN PLACE **1** [T] to put sb/sth in a particular place or position □ *meletakkan*: *I set the box down carefully on the floor.*
▶CAUSE/START **2** [T] to cause sb/sth to be in a particular state; to start sth happening □ *bermaksud menyebabkan atau memulakan sst*: *The new government set the prisoners free.* ♦ *The rioters set a number of cars on fire.*
▶PLAY/BOOK/FILM **3** [T, often passive] to make the action of a book, play, film, etc. take place in a particular time, situation, etc. □ *berlatarbelakangkan*: *The film is set in 16th-century Spain.*
▶PREPARE/ARRANGE **4** [T] to prepare or arrange sth for a particular purpose □ *menyediakan; mengatur; mengunci (jam)*: *I set my alarm for 6.30.* ♦ *to set the table* (= to put the plates, knives, forks, etc. on it) **5** [T] to decide or arrange sth □ *menentukan; menetapkan*: *Can we set a limit of two hours for the meeting?* ♦ *They haven't set the date for their wedding yet.*
▶JEWELLERY **6** [T] to fix a **precious stone** (= one that is rare and valuable), etc. in a piece of jewellery □ *mengikat; memasang*: *The brooch had three diamonds set in gold.*
▶EXAMPLE/STANDARD **7** [T] to do sth good that people have to try to copy or achieve □ *menunjukkan (teladan yg baik); menempa; menentukan*: *Try to set a good example to the younger children.* ♦ *He has set a new world record.* ♦ *They set high standards of customer service.*
▶WORK/TASK **8** [T] to give sb a piece of work or a task □ *menugaskan; memberi tugas*: *We've been set a lot of homework this weekend.* ♦ *I've set*

myself *a target* of four hours' study every evening.
▶BECOME HARD **9** [I] to become firm or hard □ *mengeras*: *The concrete will set solid/hard in just a few hours.*
▶BONE **10** [T] to fix a broken bone in the correct position so that it can get better □ *membetulkan*: *The doctor set her broken leg.*
▶SUN/MOON **11** [I] to go down below the **horizon** = the line where the earth meets the sky) in the evening □ *terbenam; jatuh*: *We sat and watched the sun setting.* **OPP** rise ❶ For idioms containing **set**, look at the entries for the nouns, adjectives, etc. For example, **set sail** is at **sail**. □ *(mula) belayar*

PHR V **set about doing sth** to start doing sth, especially dealing with a problem or task □ *mula membuat sst*: *How would you set about tackling this problem?*
set sth aside to keep sth to use later □ *menyimpan sst*: *I try to set aside part of my wages every week.*
set sb/sth back to delay sb/sth □ *melambatkan sso/sst*: *The bad weather has set our plans back six weeks.*
set forth (*formal*) to start a journey □ *berangkat; memulakan perjalanan*
set in to arrive and remain for a period of time □ *tiba dan (berlaku) berterusan utk beberapa jangka waktu*: *I'm afraid that the bad weather has set in.*
set off to leave on a journey □ *bertolak*: *We set off at 3 o'clock this morning.*
set sth off to do sth which starts a reaction □ *menyebabkan (sst berlaku)*: *When this door is opened, it sets off an alarm.*
set on/upon sb [usually passive] to attack sb suddenly □ *diserang*: *I opened the gate, and was immediately set on by a large dog.*
set out to leave on a journey □ *bertolak; pergi*
set out to do sth to decide to achieve sth □ *mula membuat sst (utk mencapai sst tujuan)*: *He set out to prove that his theory was right.*
set (sth) up to start a business, an organization, a system, etc. □ *memulakan sst (perniagaan, pertubuhan, dll)*: *The company has set up a new branch in Wales.*

set² /set/ *noun* [C] **1** a number of things that belong together □ *set; peranggu*: *a set of kitchen knives* ◆ *In the first set of questions, you have to fill in the gaps.* ◆ *a set of instructions* ◆ *a spare set of keys* ◆ *a chess set* **2** a piece of equipment for receiving TV or radio signals □ *set; alat*: *a TV set* **3** the furniture, painted cloth, boards, etc. that are made to be used in a play or film □ *set; latar*: *a musical with spectacular sets* **4** (in sports such as tennis) a group of games forming part of a match □ *set*: *She won in straight sets* (= without losing a set).

set³ /set/ *adj* **1** placed in a particular position □ *terletak*: *deep-set eyes* ◆ *Our house is quite set back from the road.* **2** fixed and not changing; firm □ *tetap*: *There are no set hours in my job.* ◆ *I'll have the set menu* (= with a fixed price and limited choice of dishes). **3** that everyone must study for an exam □ *ditentukan; ditetapkan*:

set → settle

We have to study three set texts for French. **4** **set (for sth); set (to do sth)** ready, prepared or likely to do sth □ *bersedia; sedia*: *Okay, I'm set—let's go!* ◆ *I was all set to leave when the phone rang.* ◆ *The Swiss team look set for victory.*
IDM **be set against sth/doing sth** to be determined that sth will not happen or that you will not do sth □ *menentang sst; tdk mahu melakukan sst*
be set on sth/doing sth to be determined to do or have sth □ *berazam membuat sst*: *She's set on a career in acting.*

setback /'setbæk/ *noun* [C] a difficulty or problem that stops you progressing as fast as you would like □ *halangan; rintangan; gendala*: *She suffered a major setback when she missed the exams through illness.*

'set square (*AmE* **triangle**) *noun* [C] an instrument for drawing straight lines and angles, made from a flat piece of plastic or metal in the shape of a triangle with one angle of 90° □ *sesiku*

settee /se'tiː/ *noun* [C] a long soft seat with a back and arms that more than one person can sit on □ *kerusi panjang; sofa* **SYN** **sofa**

setting /'setɪŋ/ *noun* [C] **1** the position sth is in; the place and time in which sth happens □ *persekitaran; seting*: *The hotel is in a beautiful setting, close to the sea.* **2** one of the positions of the controls of a machine □ *seting*: *Cook it in the oven on a low setting.*

settle /'setl/ *verb*
▶END ARGUMENT **1** [I,T] to put an end to an argument or a disagreement □ *menyelesaikan*: *They settled the dispute without going to court.* ◆ *They settled out of court.* ◆ *We didn't speak to each other for years, but we've settled our differences now.*
▶DECIDE/ARRANGE **2** [T] to decide or arrange sth finally □ *menetapkan; ditetapkan; diatur*: *Everything's settled. We leave on the 9 o'clock flight on Friday.*
▶PERMANENT HOME **3** [I] to go and live permanently in a new country, area, town, etc. □ *menetap; bermastautin*: *A great many immigrants have settled in this country.*
▶BECOME COMFORTABLE **4** [I,T] to put yourself or sb else into a comfortable position □ *duduk, baring, dsb dgn selesa*: *I settled in front of the TV for the evening.* ◆ *She settled herself beside him on the sofa.* **5** [I,T] to become or to make sb/sth calm or relaxed □ *menenangkan; diam*: *The baby wouldn't settle.*
▶COME TO REST **6** [I] to land on a surface and stop moving □ *hinggap*: *A flock of birds settled on the roof.*
▶PAY MONEY **7** [I,T] to pay money that you owe □ *menyelesaikan; melangsaikan*: *to settle a bill/a debt*
PHR V **settle down** **1** to get into a comfortable position, sitting or lying □ *duduk, baring, dsb*

settled → sewing 778

dgn selesa: I made a cup of tea and settled down with the newspapers. **2** to start having a quieter way of life, especially by staying in the same place or getting married □ *memulakan cara hidup yg lebih tenang; berumah tangga*: She had a number of jobs abroad before she eventually settled down. **3** to become calm and quiet □ *reda; tenang; diam*: Settle down! It's time to start the lesson.

settle down to sth to start doing sth which involves all your attention □ *menumpukan perhatian (membuat sst)*: Before you settle down to your work, could I ask you something?

settle for sth to accept sth that is not as good as what you wanted □ *(terpaksa) menerima*: We're going to have to settle for the second prize.

settle in/into sth to start feeling comfortable in a new home, job, etc. □ *menyesuaikan diri; mula selesa (di rumah baharu, dsb)*: How are the children settling in at their new school?

settle on sth to choose or decide sth after considering many different things □ *memilih (sst)*

settle up (with sb) to pay money that you owe to sb □ *membayar hutang (pd sso)*

settled /'setld/ *adj* **1** not changing or not likely to change □ *tetap; mantap*: More settled weather is forecast for the next few days. **2** comfortable; feeling that you belong (in a home, a job, a way of life, etc.) □ *selesa*: We feel very settled here.

settlement /'setlmənt/ *noun* [C,U] **1** an official agreement that ends an argument; the act of reaching an agreement □ *penyelesaian*: a divorce settlement ◆ the settlement of a dispute **2** a place that a group of people have built and live in, where few or no people lived before; the process of people starting to live in a place □ *petempatan; penempatan; pendudukan*: There is believed to have been a prehistoric settlement on this site. ◆ the settlement of the American West

settler /'setlə(r)/ *noun* [C] a person who goes to live permanently in a place where not many people live □ *peneroka*: the first white settlers in Australia

ˌset-ˈtop ˈbox *noun* [C] a device that changes a **digital** (= using a particular electronic system) television signal into a form which can be seen on an ordinary television □ *kotak set-top*

ˈset-up *noun* [usually sing] (*informal*) a way of organizing sth; a system □ *struktur; sistem*: I've only been here a couple of weeks and I don't really know the set-up.

seven /'sevn/ *number* **1** 7 □ *tujuh* ◆ note at **six** **2** [in compounds] having seven of the thing mentioned □ *tujuh*: a seven-sided coin

seventeen /ˌsevn'ti:n/ *number* 17 □ *tujuh belas; 17* ◆ note at **six** ▶ **seventeenth** /ˌsevn'ti:nθ/ *ordinal number, noun* ◆ note at **sixth**

seventh¹ /'sevnθ/ *ordinal number* 7th □ *ketujuh; ke-7* ◆ note at **sixth**

seventh² /'sevnθ/ *noun* [C] ½; one of seven equal parts of sth □ *satu per tujuh*; $1/7$

seventy /'sevnti/ *number* 70 □ *tujuh puluh; 70* ◆ note at **sixty** ▶ **seventieth** /'sevntiəθ/ *ordinal number, noun* ◆ note at **sixth**

sever /'sevə(r)/ *verb* [T] (*formal*) **1** to cut sth into two pieces; to cut sth off □ *memotong; memutuskan; terputus*: The builders accidentally severed a water pipe. ◆ His hand was almost severed in the accident. **2** to end a relationship or communication with sb □ *memutuskan*: He has severed all links with his former friends.

several /'sevrəl/ *pron, determiner* more than two but not very many; a few □ *beberapa*: It took her several days to recover from the shock. ◆ There were lots of applications for the job—several of them from very well-qualified people. ◆ I don't think it's a good idea for several reasons.

severe /sɪ'vɪə(r)/ *adj* (**severer**; **severest**) **1** extremely bad or serious □ *teruk*: The company is in severe financial difficulty. ◆ He suffered severe injuries in the fall. ◆ severe weather conditions **2** causing sb to suffer, be upset or have difficulties □ *keras; tanpa belas kasihan*: Such terrible crimes deserve the severest punishment. ◆ I think your criticism of her work was too severe. ◆ look at **harsh** ▶ **severely** *adv*: The roof was severely damaged in the storm. ◆ The report severely criticizes the Health Service. ▶ **severity** /sɪ'verəti/ *noun* [U]: I don't think you realize the severity of the problem.

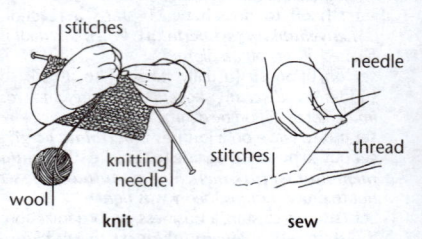

stitches | needle
knitting needle | stitches | thread
wool
knit | **sew**

sew /səʊ/ *verb* [I,T] (*pt* **sewed**; *pp* **sewn** /səʊn/ or **sewed**) **sew (sth) (on)** to join pieces of cloth, or to join sth to cloth, using a needle and thread and forming **stitches** (= lines of thread) □ *menjahit*: I can't sew. ◆ A button's come off my shirt—I'll have to sew it back on.
PHR V **sew sth up 1** to join two things by sewing; to repair sth by sewing two things together □ *menjahit*: to sew up a hole **2** (*informal*) to arrange sth so that it is certain to happen or be successful □ *mengatur/menyelesaikan sst*: I think we've got the deal sewn up.

sewage /'su:ɪdʒ/ *noun* [U] the waste material from people's bodies that is carried away from their homes through special pipes □ *kumbahan*

sewed *past tense of* **sew**

sewer /'su:ə(r)/ *noun* [C] an underground pipe that carries human waste to a place where it can be treated □ *pembetung*

sewing /'səʊɪŋ/ *noun* [U] **1** using a needle and thread to make or repair things □ *jahit; jahitan*:

ʌ cup ɜː bird ə ago eɪ pay əʊ go aɪ my aʊ now ɪɔ boy ɪə near eə hair ʊə pure

I always take a sewing kit when I travel. ♦ *a sewing machine* ⊃ picture on page P3 **2** something that is being sewn □ *jahitan*: *Have you seen my sewing?*

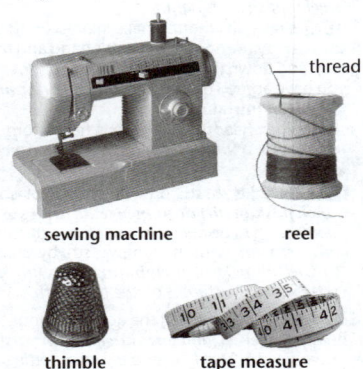

sewing machine

reel

thread

thimble

tape measure

sewn *past participle of* **sew**

sex /seks/ *noun* **1** [U] the state of being either male or female □ *jantina*: *Applications are welcome from anyone, regardless of sex or race.* ♦ *Do you mind what sex your baby is?* SYN **gender** **2** [C] one of the two groups consisting of all male people or all female people □ *kaum lelaki/ perempuan: the male/female sex* ♦ *He's always found it difficult to get on with* **the opposite sex** (= women). **3** (*also formal* **intercourse**, ˌsexual ˈintercourse) [U] the physical act in which the sexual organs of two people touch and which can result in a woman having a baby □ *hubungan jenis; seks*: *to have sex with somebody* ♦ *sex education in schools*

sexism /ˈseksɪzəm/ *noun* [U] the unfair treatment of people, especially women, because of their sex; the attitude that causes this □ *seksisme; sikap berat sebelah berdasarkan jantina* ▶ **sexist** /ˈseksɪst/ *adj*: *a sexist attitude to women* ♦ *sexist jokes* ▶ **sexist** *noun* [C]

sexual /ˈsekʃuəl/ *adj* connected with sex □ *(berkaitan dgn) jantina atau seks; seksual*: *sexual problems* ♦ *the sexual organs* ♦ *a campaign for sexual equality* (= to get fair and equal treatment for both men and women) ⊃ look at **sexy** ▶ **sexually** /ˈsekʃəli/ *adv*: *to be sexually attracted to somebody*

ˌsexual ˈintercourse (*formal*) = **sex** (3)

sexuality /ˌsekʃuˈæləti/ *noun* [U] the nature of sb's sexual activities or desires □ *keseksualan; tabii atau dorongan seks*

sexy /ˈseksi/ *adj* (**sexier**; **sexiest**) (*informal*) sexually attractive or exciting □ *seksi; menggiurkan*: *Do you find the lead singer sexy?* ♦ *a sexy dress*

Sgt *abbr* = **sergeant**

sh (*also* **shh**) /ʃ/ *exclam* used to tell sb to stop making noise □ *sy*: *Sh! People are trying to sleep in here.*

shabby /ˈʃæbi/ *adj* (**shabbier**; **shabbiest**) **1** in bad condition because of having been used or worn too much □ *buruk*: *a shabby suit* **2** (used about people) dressed in an untidy way; wearing clothes that are in bad condition □ *selekeh* **3** (used about the way that sb is treated) unfair; not generous □ *tdk patut; buruk; teruk* ▶ **shabbily** *adv*: *a shabbily dressed man* ♦ *She felt she'd been treated shabbily by her employers.*

shack /ʃæk/ *noun* [C] a small building, usually made of wood or metal, that has not been built well □ *pondok; gubuk*

ʔ shade¹ /ʃeɪd/ *noun*
▶OUT OF SUN **1** [U] an area that is not in direct light from the sun and is darker and cooler than areas in the sun □ *tempat redup/teduh*: *It was so hot that I had to go and sit in the shade.* ⊃ picture at **shadow**
▶ON LAMP, ETC. **2** [C] something that keeps out light or makes it less bright □ *pelindung cahaya – terendak lampu, bidai, dsb*: *a lampshade*
▶COLOUR **3** [C] **a shade (of sth)** a type of a particular colour □ *corak warna*: *a shade of green*
▶IN PICTURE **4** [C] the dark areas in a picture, especially the use of these to produce variety □ *bahagian gelap*: *Your painting needs more light and shade.*
▶OF OPINION/FEELING **5** [C, usually pl] a small difference in the form or nature of sth □ *perbezaan; nuansa*: *a word with various shades of meaning*
▶SLIGHTLY **6** [sing] **a shade** a little; slightly □ *sedikit*: *I feel a shade more optimistic now.*
▶GLASSES **7** **shades** [pl] (*informal*) = **sunglasses**

shade² /ʃeɪd/ *verb* [T] **1** to protect sth from direct light; to give shade to sth □ *melindungi; meneduhi*: *The sun was so bright that I had to shade my eyes.* **2** **shade sth (in)** to make an area of a drawing darker, for example with a pencil □ *menggelapkan*: *The trees will look more realistic once you've shaded them in.*

shadow **shade**

ʔ shadow¹ /ˈʃædəʊ/ *noun* **1** [C] a dark shape on a surface that is caused by sth being between the light and that surface □ *bayang-bayang*: *The dog was chasing its own shadow.* ♦ *The shadows lengthened as the sun went down.* **2** [U] an area that is dark because sth prevents direct light from reaching it □ *tempat gelap*: *His face was*

shadow → shallow

in shadow. **3** [sing] a very small amount of sth □ *sedikit (pun)*: *I know without **a shadow of doubt** that he's lying.*
IDM **cast a shadow (across/over sth)** ⊃ **cast¹**

shadow² /ˈʃædəʊ/ *verb* [T] to follow sb and watch their actions □ *mengekori*: *The police shadowed the suspect for three days.*

shadow³ /ˈʃædəʊ/ *adj* [only *before* a noun] (in British politics) belonging to the biggest political party that is not in power, with special responsibility for a particular subject, for example education or defence. **Shadow** ministers would probably become government ministers if their party won the next election □ *bayangan*: *the shadow Cabinet*

shadowy /ˈʃædəʊi/ *adj* **1** dark and full of shadows □ *gelap; teduh*: *a shadowy forest* **2** difficult to see because there is not much light □ *samar-samar; tdk jelas; spt bayang-bayang*: *A shadowy figure was coming towards me.* **3** that not much is known about □ *kabur; bermisteri* SYN **mysterious**

shady /ˈʃeɪdi/ *adj* (**shadier; shadiest**) **1** giving shade; giving protection from the sun □ *teduh; redup*: *I found a shady spot under the trees and sat down.* **2** (*informal*) not completely honest or legal □ *tdk betul-betul jujur; (mungkin) menyalahi undang-undang*

shaft /ʃɑːft/ *noun* [C] **1** a long, narrow hole in which sth can go up and down or enter or leave □ *syaf; lubang*: *a lift shaft* • *a mine shaft* **2** a bar that connects parts of a machine so that power can pass between them □ *aci; batang*

shaggy /ˈʃægi/ *adj* (**shaggier; shaggiest**) **1** (used about hair, material, etc.) long, thick and untidy □ *lebat dan berjumbai-jumbai* **2** covered with long, thick, untidy hair □ *berbulu panjang; berjumbai-jumbai*: *a shaggy dog*

shake

They shook hands.   He shook his head.

shake¹ /ʃeɪk/ *verb* (*pt* **shook** /ʃʊk/; *pp* **shaken** /ˈʃeɪkən/) **1** [I,T] to move or move sb/sth from side to side or up and down with short, quick movements □ *menggerakkan; bergegar; menggoncang; bergoncang; menggeletar; terketar-ketar*: *I was so nervous that I was shaking.* • *The whole building shakes when big trucks go past.* • (*figurative*) *His voice shook with emotion as he described the accident.* • *Shake the bottle before taking the medicine.* • *She shook him to wake him up.* **2** [T] to disturb or upset sb/sth □ *memeranjatkan; menggemparkan*: *The scandal has shaken the whole country.* **3** [T] to cause sth to be less certain; to cause doubt about sth □ *menggoncangkan*: *Nothing seems to shake her belief that she was right.*
IDM **shake sb's hand/shake hands (with sb)/ shake sb by the hand** to take sb's hand and move it up and down (when you meet sb, to show that you have agreed on sth, etc.) □ *berjabat tangan* ⊃ note at **introduce**
shake your head to move your head from side to side, as a way of saying no □ *menggeleng kepala*
PHR V **shake sb/sth off** to get rid of sb/sth □ *melepaskan diri atau mengelak drpd sso/sst*: *I don't seem to be able to shake off this cold.*
shake sth off (sth) to remove sth by shaking □ *menghilangkan, membuang, sembuh drpd (sst)*: *Shake the crumbs off the tablecloth.*

ⁱ **shake²** /ʃeɪk/ *noun* [C] the act of shaking sth or being shaken □ *goncangan; gelengan*: *a shake of the head* • *You'll have to give the bottle a few shakes.*

ˈ**shake-up** *noun* [C] a complete change in the structure or organization of sth □ *rombakan*

shaky /ˈʃeɪki/ *adj* (**shakier; shakiest**) **1** shaking or feeling weak because you are frightened or ill □ *menggeletar; goyang* **2** not firm; weak or not very good □ *goyah; goyang; tdk berapa baik*: *The table's a bit shaky so don't put anything heavy on it.* • *They've had a shaky start to the season, losing most of their games.* ▶ **shakily** *adv*

ⁱ **shall** /ʃəl; *strong form* ʃæl/ *modal verb* (*negative* **shall not**; *short form* **shan't** /ʃɑːnt/; *pt* **should** /ʃʊd/; *negative* **should not**; *short form* **shouldn't** /ˈʃʊdnt/) **1** (*formal*) used with 'I' and 'we' in future tenses, instead of 'will' □ *akan*: *I shall be very happy to see him again.* • *We shan't be arriving until 10 o'clock.* • *At the end of this year, I shall have been working here for five years.* **2** used for asking for information or advice ⊃ (*digunakan utk meminta maklumat atau nasihat*) *harus; hendak*: *What time shall I come?* • *Where shall we go for our holiday?* **3** used for offering to do sth □ *mahu(kah); hendak(kah)*: *Shall I help you carry that box?* • *Shall we drive you home?* **4** **shall we** used for suggesting that you do sth with the person or people that you are talking to □ *mahukah; bagaimana kalau*: *Shall we go out for a meal this evening?* **5** (*formal*) used for saying that sth must happen or will definitely happen □ *akan*: *In the rules it says that a player shall be sent off for using bad language.* ❶ For more information about modal verbs, look at the **Reference Section** at the back of this dictionary.

shallot /ʃəˈlɒt/ *noun* [C] a vegetable like a small onion □ *bawang merah*

ⁱ **shallow** /ˈʃæləʊ/ *adj* (**shallower; shallowest**) **1** not deep; with not much distance between top and bottom □ *cetek; dangkal; tohor*: *The sea is very shallow here.* • *a shallow dish* **2** not having or showing serious or deep thought □ *berfikiran cetek/dangkal*: *a shallow person/book* OPP **deep** ▶ **shallowness** *noun* [U]

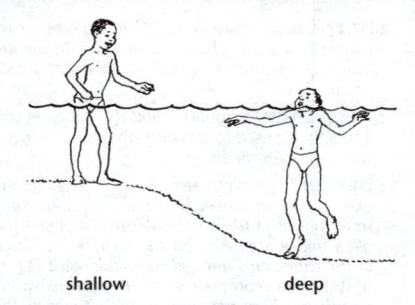

shallow   deep

shame¹ /ʃeɪm/ noun 1 [U] the unpleasant feelings such as embarrassment and sadness that you get when you have done sth stupid or wrong; the ability to have these feelings □ *rasa malu*: She was **filled with shame** at the thought of how she had lied to her mother. ♦ His actions have **brought shame on** his whole family. ♦ He doesn't care how he behaves in public. He's got **no shame**! ⊃ adjective **ashamed** 2 **a shame** [sing] a fact or situation that makes you feel disappointed □ *sayang sekali; sayangnya*: It's **a shame** about Adam failing his exams, isn't it? ♦ **What a shame** you have to leave so soon. ♦ It would be a shame to miss an opportunity like this.

shame² /ʃeɪm/ verb [T] to make sb feel shame for sth bad that they have done □ *membuat sso berasa malu*

shameful /ˈʃeɪmfl/ adj that sb should feel bad about; shocking □ *(yg) memalukan*: a shameful waste of public money ▶ shamefully /-fəli/ adv

shameless /ˈʃeɪmləs/ adj not feeling embarrassed about doing sth bad; having no shame □ *tdk malu*: a shameless display of greed and bad manners ▶ shamelessly adv

shampoo /ʃæmˈpuː/ noun (pl shampoos) 1 [C,U] a liquid that you use for washing your hair; a similar liquid for cleaning carpets, cars, etc. □ *syampu*: shampoo for greasy/dry/normal hair 2 [C, usually sing] the act of washing sth with **shampoo** □ *(perbuatan) mensyampu* ▶ shampoo verb [T] (shampooing; shampoos; pt, pp shampooed)

shamrock /ˈʃæmrɒk/ noun [C,U] a plant with three leaves, which is the national symbol of Ireland □ *syamrok (sejenis tumbuhan)*

shandy /ˈʃændi/ noun [C,U] (especially BrE) (pl shandies) a drink that is a mixture of beer and lemonade (= a sweet lemon drink with bubbles) □ *syandi* ⊃ note at **beer**

shan't /ʃɑːnt/ short for **shall not**

shanty town /ˈʃænti taʊn/ noun [C] an area, usually on the edge of a big city, where poor people live in bad conditions in buildings that they have made themselves □ *kawasan melarat*

shape¹ /ʃeɪp/ noun 1 [C,U] the form of the outer edges or surfaces of sth; an example of sth that has a particular form □ *bentuk*: a round/ square/rectangular shape ♦ a cake **in the shape of** a heart ♦ clothes to fit people of **all shapes and sizes** ♦ Squares, circles and triangles are all different shapes. ♦ I could just **make out** a dark shape in the distance. ♦ The country is roughly square **in shape**. 2 [U] the physical condition of sb/sth; the good or bad state of sb/sth □ *keadaan (fizikal sso/sst)*: She was **in** such bad **shape** (= so ill) that she had to be taken to hospital. ♦ I go swimming regularly to keep **in shape**. 3 [sing] **the shape (of sth)** the organization, form or structure of sth □ *bentuk*: Recent developments have changed the shape of the company.

IDM **out of shape** 1 not in the usual or correct shape □ *rosak bentuknya*: My sweater's gone out of shape now that I've washed it. 2 not physically fit □ *tdk cukup sihat*: You're out of shape. You should get more exercise.

take shape to start to develop well □ *terbentuk*: Plans to expand the company are beginning to take shape.

shapes

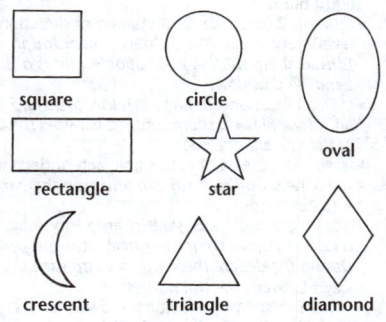

square   circle   oval
rectangle   star
crescent   triangle   diamond

shape² /ʃeɪp/ verb [T] 1 **shape sth (into sth)** to make sth into a particular form □ *membentuk*: Shape the mixture into small balls. 2 to influence the way in which sth develops; to cause sth to have a particular form or nature □ *membentuk*: His political ideas were shaped by his upbringing.

shaped /ʃeɪpt/ adj [in compounds] having the shape mentioned □ *berbentuk*: an L-shaped room

shapeless /ˈʃeɪpləs/ adj not having a clear shape □ *tdk berbentuk*: a shapeless dress

share¹ /ʃeə(r)/ verb 1 [T] **share sth (out)** to divide sth between two or more people □ *membahagi-bahagikan*: We shared the pizza out between the four of us. 2 [I,T] **share (sth) (with sb)** to have, use, do or pay sth together with another person or other people □ *berkongsi; turut serta*: I share a flat with four other people. ♦ I shared my sandwiches with Jim. ♦ We share the same interests. 3 [T] **share sth (with sb)** to tell sb about sth; to allow sb to know sth □ *berkongsi; menceritakan*: Sometimes it helps to share your problems.

CONSONANTS   p **p**en   b **b**ad   t **t**ea   d **d**id   k **c**at   g **g**ot   tʃ **ch**in   dʒ **J**une   f **f**all   v **v**an   θ **th**in

share → shed 782

share² /ʃeə(r)/ noun **1** [sing] share (of sth) a part or an amount of sth that has been divided between several people □ *bahagian*: *We each pay a share of the household bills.* ◆ *I'm willing to take my share of the blame.* **2** [C, usually pl] shares (in sth) one of many equal parts into which the value of a company is divided, that can be sold to people who want to own part of the company □ *saham*: *a fall in share prices*
IDM (more than) your fair share of sth ⇒ **fair¹** the lion's share (of sth) ⇒ **lion**

shareholder /ˈʃeəhəʊldə(r)/ noun [C] an owner of shares in a company □ *pemegang saham*

shark /ʃɑːk/ noun [C] (pl sharks or shark) a large, often dangerous, sea fish that has a lot of sharp teeth □ *ikan yu/jerung* ⇒ picture at **dolphin**

sharp¹ /ʃɑːp/ adj (sharper; sharpest)
▸EDGE/POINT **1** having a very thin but strong edge or point; that can cut or make a hole in sth easily □ *tajam*: *a sharp knife* ◆ *sharp teeth* **OPP** blunt
▸CHANGE **2** (used about a change of direction or level) very great and sudden □ *mendadak; tajam*: *a sharp rise/fall in inflation* ◆ *This is a sharp bend, so slow down.*
▸CLEAR **3** clear and definite □ *jelas*: *the sharp outline of the hills* ◆ *a sharp contrast between the lives of the rich and the poor*
▸MIND, EYES, EARS **4** able to think, act, understand, see or hear quickly □ *tajam; pintar*: *a sharp mind* ◆ *to have sharp eyes*
▸WORDS/COMMENTS **5** said in an angry way; intended to upset sb or be critical □ *tajam; pedas*: *During the debate there was a sharp exchange of views between the two parties.*
▸ACTIONS/MOVEMENTS **6** quick and sudden □ *cepat dan tiba-tiba*: *One short sharp blow was enough to end the fight.*
▸PAIN **7** very strong and sudden □ *mencucuk-cucuk*: *a sharp pain in the chest* **OPP** dull
▸TASTE/FEELING **8** (used about sth that affects the senses) strong; not mild or gentle, often causing an unpleasant feeling □ *kuat; pedar; menusuk*: *a sharp taste* ◆ *a sharp wind*
▸IN MUSIC **9** (symbol #) half a note higher than the stated note □ *syap*: *in the key of C sharp minor* **OPP** flat **10** slightly higher that the correct note □ *(sumbang) tinggi*: *That last note was sharp. Can you sing it again?* **OPP** flat ▸**sharply** adv: *The road bends sharply to the left.* ◆ *Share prices fell sharply this morning.* ▸**sharpness** noun [U]

sharp² /ʃɑːp/ adv **1** exactly on time □ *tepat*: *Be here at 3 o'clock sharp.* **2** turning suddenly □ *dgn tiba-tiba; terus*: *Go to the traffic lights and turn sharp right.* **3** slightly higher than the correct note □ *(sumbang) tinggi* ⇒ look at **flat**

sharp³ /ʃɑːp/ noun [C] (symbol #) (in music) a note that is half a note higher than the note with the same letter □ *syap* ⇒ look at **flat**

sharpen /ˈʃɑːpən/ verb [I,T] to become or to make sth sharp or sharper □ *mengasah; menajamkan*: *to sharpen a knife* ◆ *This knife won't sharpen.*

sharpener /ˈʃɑːpnə(r)/ noun [C] an object or a tool that is used for making sth sharp □ *pengasah*: *a pencil/knife sharpener*

shatter /ˈʃætə(r)/ verb **1** [I,T] (used about glass, etc.) to break or break sth into very small pieces □ *hancur berderai*: *I dropped the glass and it shattered on the floor.* ◆ *The force of the explosion shattered the windows.* **2** [T] to destroy sth completely □ *menghancurkan; memusnahkan*: *Her hopes were shattered by the news.*

shattered /ˈʃætəd/ adj **1** very shocked and upset □ *terkejut besar* **2** (informal) very tired □ *sangat letih*: *I'm absolutely shattered.*

shave¹ /ʃeɪv/ verb [I,T] shave (sth) (off) to remove hair from the face or another part of the body with a razor (= a very sharp piece of metal) □ *bercukur; mencukur*: *I cut myself shaving this morning.* ◆ *When did you shave off your moustache?* ◆ *to shave your legs*
PHR V shave sth off (sth) to cut a very small amount from sth □ *mengetam*: *We'll have to shave a bit off the door to make it close properly.*

shave² /ʃeɪv/ noun [C, usually sing] the act of shaving □ *bercukur*: *to have a shave* ◆ *I need a shave.*
IDM a close shave/thing ⇒ **close³**

shaven /ˈʃeɪvn/ adj having been shaved □ *dicukur/bercukur licin*: *clean-shaven* (= not having a beard or moustache)

shaver /ˈʃeɪvə(r)/ (also eˌlectric ˈrazor) noun [C] an electric tool that is used for removing hair from the face or another part of the body □ *pencukur*

shawl /ʃɔːl/ noun [C] a large piece of cloth that is worn by a woman round her shoulders or head, or that is put round a baby □ *sebai; selendang*

she /ʃiː/ pron (the subject of a verb) the female person who has already been mentioned □ *dia (perempuan)*: *'What does your sister do?' 'She's a dentist.'* ◆ *I asked her a question but she didn't answer.* ⇒ note at **he**

shear /ʃɪə(r)/ verb [T] (pt sheared; pp sheared or shorn) to cut the wool off a sheep □ *memotong/mengetam bulu biri-biri*

shears /ʃɪəz/ noun [pl] a tool that is like a very large pair of scissors and that is used for cutting things in the garden □ *gunting; kekacip*: *a pair of shears* ⇒ picture at **garden**

sheath /ʃiːθ/ noun [C] (pl sheaths /ʃiːðz/) a cover for a knife or other sharp weapon □ *sarung* ⇒ picture at **sword**

she'd /ʃiːd/ short for **she had**; **she would**

shed¹ /ʃed/ noun [C] a small building that is used for keeping things in □ *bangsal*: *a garden shed* ◆ *a bicycle shed*

shed² /ʃed/ verb [T] (shedding; pt, pp shed) **1** to get rid of or remove sth that is not wanted □ *membuang; melepaskan; menyingkirkan* **2** to lose sth because it falls off □ *gugur; menanggalkan; bersalin (kulit)*: *This snake sheds its skin every year.* ♦ *Autumn is coming and the trees are beginning to shed their leaves.*

IDM **shed blood** (*formal*) to kill or injure people □ *menumpahkan darah*

shed light on sth to make sth clear and easy to understand □ *menjelaskan; menerangkan*

shed tears to cry □ *menangis*

sheep /ʃiːp/ noun [C] (pl sheep) an animal that is kept on farms and used for its wool or meat □ *biri-biri* ⊃ note at **meat** ⊃ picture at **goat**

> **MORE** A male sheep is a **ram**; a female sheep is a **ewe** and a young sheep is a **lamb**. When sheep make a noise they **bleat**. This is written as **baa**. The meat from sheep is called **lamb** or **mutton**.

sheepdog /'ʃiːpdɒg/ noun [C] a dog that has been trained to control sheep □ *anjing gembala biri-biri*

sheepish /'ʃiːpɪʃ/ adj feeling or showing embarrassment because you have done sth silly □ *tersipu-sipu*: *a sheepish grin* ▶ **sheepishly** adv

sheepskin /'ʃiːpskɪn/ noun [U] the skin of a sheep, including the wool, from which coats, etc. are made □ *kulit biri-biri*: *a sheepskin rug/jacket*

sheer /ʃɪə(r)/ adj **1** [only before a noun] used to emphasize the size, degree or amount of sth □ *betul-betul*: *It's sheer stupidity to drink and drive.* ♦ *It was sheer luck that I happened to be in the right place at the right time.* ♦ *Her success is due to sheer hard work.* ♦ *I only agreed out of sheer desperation.* **2** very steep; almost vertical □ *sangat curam*: *Don't walk near the edge. It's a sheer drop to the sea.*

sheet /ʃiːt/ noun [C] **1** a large piece of cloth used on a bed □ *cadar*: *I've just changed the sheets on the bed.* ⊃ picture at **bed 2** a piece of paper that is used for writing, printing, etc. on □ *helai kertas*: *a sheet of notepaper* ♦ *Write each answer on a separate sheet.* ⊃ look at **balance sheet 3** a flat, thin piece of any material □ *keping*: *a sheet of metal/glass* **4** a wide, flat area of sth □ *lapisan*: *The road was covered with a sheet of ice.*

sheikh (also **sheik**) /ʃeɪk/ noun [C] an Arab prince or leader □ *syeikh*

shelf /ʃelf/ noun [C] (pl shelves /ʃelvz/) a long flat piece of wood, glass, etc. that is fixed to a wall or in a cupboard, used for putting things on □ *rak; tingkat-tingkat*: *I put up a shelf in the kitchen.* ♦ *I reached up and took down the book from the top shelf.* ♦ *a bookshelf* ⊃ picture on page P8

she'll /ʃiːl/ short for **she will**

shell¹ /ʃel/ noun **1** [C,U] a hard covering that protects eggs, nuts and some animals □ *kulit;* *cangkerang*: *Some children were collecting shells on the beach.* ♦ *a piece of eggshell* ♦ *Tortoises have a hard shell.* ⊃ picture at **nut, shellfish, snail** ⊃ picture on **page P10, page P13, page P14** **2** [C] a metal container that explodes when it is fired from a large gun □ *peluru meriam* **3** [C] the walls or hard outer structure of sth □ *kerangka*: *The body shell of the car is made in another factory.*

IDM **come out of your shell** to become less shy and more confident when talking to other people □ *kurang sedikit malu dan lebih berkeyakinan*

go, retreat, etc. into your shell to suddenly become shy and stop talking □ *(tiba-tiba) menjadi malu*

shell² /ʃel/ verb [T] **1** to fire shells¹(2) from a large gun □ *menembak dgn meriam* **2** to take the shell¹(1) off a nut or another kind of food □ *mengupas; mengopek*: *to shell peas*

shellfish

lobster
claw
mussel
shell
oyster
clam

shellfish /'ʃelfɪʃ/ noun (pl shellfish) **1** [C] a type of animal that lives in water and has a shell □ *kerang-kerangan* ⊃ picture on **page P13 2** [U] these animals eaten as food □ *kerang-kerangan*

shelter¹ /'ʃeltə(r)/ noun **1** the fact of having a place to live or stay □ *tempat tinggal*: *to give somebody food and shelter* **2** [U] shelter (from sth) protection from danger or bad weather □ *perlindungan*: *We looked around for somewhere to take shelter from the storm.* **3** [C] a small building that gives protection, for example from bad weather or attack □ *tempat perlindungan/ berteduh*: *a bus shelter* ♦ *an air-raid shelter* **4** [C] a building, usually owned by a charity, where people or animals can stay if they do not have a home, or have been badly treated □ *rumah perlindungan*: *an animal shelter* **SYN** **refuge**

shelter² /'ʃeltə(r)/ verb **1** [T] shelter sb/sth (from sb/sth) to protect sb/sth; to provide a safe place away from harm or danger □ *melindungi*: *The trees shelter the house from the wind.* **2** [I] shelter (from sth) to find protection or a safe place □ *berlindung*: *Let's shelter from the rain under that tree.*

sheltered /ˈʃeltəd/ adj **1** (used about a place) protected from bad weather □ *terlindung* **2** protected from unpleasant things in your life □ *terlindung*: *We had a sheltered childhood, living in the country.*

shelve /ʃelv/ verb [T] to decide not to continue with a plan, etc., either for a short time or permanently □ *menangguhkan*: *Plans for a new motorway have been shelved.*

shelves plural of **shelf**

shelving /ˈʃelvɪŋ/ noun [U] a set of shelves □ *rak; tingkat-tingkat*

shepherd¹ /ˈʃepəd/ noun [C] a person whose job is to look after sheep □ *gembala (biri-biri)*

shepherd² /ˈʃepəd/ verb [T] to lead and look after people so that they do not get lost □ *menggiring; memandu*

sheriff /ˈʃerɪf/ noun [C] (in the US) an officer of the law who is responsible for a particular town or part of a state □ *syerif*

sherry /ˈʃeri/ noun [C,U] (pl **sherries**) a type of strong Spanish wine; a glass of this wine □ *syeri (wain)*

she's /ʃiːz; ʃiz/ short for **she is**; **she has**

shield¹ /ʃiːld/ noun [C] **1** (in past times) a large piece of metal or wood that soldiers carried to protect themselves □ *perisai* **2** (also ˈriot shield) a piece of equipment made of strong plastic, that the police use to protect themselves from angry crowds □ *perisai* **3** a person or thing that is used to protect sb/sth, especially by forming a barrier □ *pelindung; pengadang*: *The metal door acted as a shield against the explosion.* **4** an object or a drawing in the shape of a **shield**, sometimes used as a prize in a sports competition □ *perisai* ⊃ picture at **medal**

shield² /ʃiːld/ verb [T] **shield sb/sth (against/ from sb/sth)** to protect sb/sth from danger or damage □ *melindungi*: *I shielded my eyes from the bright light with my hand.*

shift¹ /ʃɪft/ verb [I,T] **1** to move or be moved from one position or place to another □ *beralih; berganjak; mengalihkan*: *She shifted uncomfortably in her chair.* ♦ *He shifted his desk closer to the window.* **2** to change your opinion of or attitude towards sb/sth □ *berakhir; bertukar*: *Public attitudes towards marriage have shifted over the years.*
IDM **shift the blame/responsibility (for sth) (onto sb)** to make sb else responsible for sth you should do or for sth bad you have done □ *menyalahkan (sso) (kerana sst)*

shift² /ʃɪft/ noun **1** [C] **a shift (in sth)** a change in your opinion of or attitude towards sth □ *peralihan; perubahan*: *There has been a shift in public opinion away from supporting the strikes.* **2** [C, with sing or pl verb] (in a factory, etc.) one of the periods that the working day is divided into; the group who work during this period □ *syif*: *The night shift has/have just gone off duty.* ♦ *to work in shifts* ♦ *shift work/workers* ♦ *to be on the day/night shift* **3** [sing] one of the keys that you use for writing on a computer, etc., that allows you to write a capital letter □ *kekunci anjak*: *the shift key*

shifty /ˈʃɪfti/ adj (informal) (**shiftier**; **shiftiest**) seeming to be dishonest; looking guilty about sth □ *licik; mencurigakan*: *shifty eyes*

shilling /ˈʃɪlɪŋ/ noun [C] **1** a British coin worth five pence that was used in past times □ *syiling (unit mata wang British)* **2** the basic unit of money in some countries, for example Kenya □ *syiling (unit mata wang asas sesetengah negara)*

shimmer /ˈʃɪmə(r)/ verb [I] to shine with a soft light that seems to be moving □ *berkilau-kilau*: *Moonlight shimmered on the sea.*

shin /ʃɪn/ noun [C] the bone down the front part of your leg from your knee to your ankle □ *tulang kering* ⊃ picture at **body**

shine¹ /ʃaɪn/ verb (pt, pp **shone** /ʃɒn/) **1** [I] to send out or send back light; to be bright □ *bersinar; memancar*: *I could see a light shining in the distance.* ♦ *The sea shone in the light of the moon.* **2** [T] to direct a light at sb/sth □ *menyuluh*: *The policeman shone a torch on the stranger's face.*

shine² /ʃaɪn/ noun [sing] **1** a bright effect caused by light hitting a polished surface □ *sinaran; kilauan; kilat* **2** the act of polishing sth so that it shines □ *(perbuatan) menggilap/ mengilatkan*

shingle /ˈʃɪŋgl/ noun [U] small pieces of stone lying in a mass on a beach □ *batu kerikil*

ˈshin guard (BrE also ˈshin pad) noun [C] a thick piece of material used to protect the **shin** when playing some sports □ *pad tulang kering*

shiny /ˈʃaɪni/ adj (**shinier**; **shiniest**) causing a bright effect when in the sun or in light □ *berkilat*: *The shampoo leaves your hair soft and shiny.* ♦ *a shiny new car*

ship¹ /ʃɪp/ noun [C] a large boat used for carrying passengers or goods by sea □ *kapal*: *to travel by ship* ♦ *to launch a ship* ⊃ note at **boat**

ship² /ʃɪp/ verb [T] (**shipping**; **shipped**) to send or carry sth by ship or by another type of transport □ *menghantar atau mengangkut (dgn kapal atau kenderaan lain)*

shipbuilder /ˈʃɪpbɪldə(r)/ noun [C] a person or company who makes or builds ships □ *pembina kapal* ▶ **shipbuilding** noun [U]

shipment /ˈʃɪpmənt/ noun **1** [U] the carrying of goods from one place to another □ *pengiriman; penghantaran* **2** [C] a quantity of goods that are sent from one place to another □ *kiriman; hantaran*

shipping /ˈʃɪpɪŋ/ noun [U] **1** ships in general or considered as a group □ *kapal-kapal* **2** the carrying of goods from one place to another □ *penghantaran; pengiriman*: *a shipping company*

shipwreck /'ʃɪprek/ *noun* [C,U] an accident at sea in which a ship is destroyed by a storm, rocks, etc. and sinks; a ship which is destroyed in this way □ *nahas kapal* ▶**shipwrecked** *adj*: *a shipwrecked sailor* ♦ *a shipwrecked vessel*

shipyard /'ʃɪpjɑːd/ *noun* [C] a place where ships are repaired or built □ *limbungan kapal*

shirk /ʃɜːk/ *verb* [I,T] to avoid doing sth that is difficult or unpleasant, especially because you are too lazy □ *mengelak (membuat sst)*: *to shirk your responsibilities*

shirt /ʃɜːt/ *noun* [C] a piece of clothing made of cotton, etc. worn on the upper part of the body □ *kemeja*: *to wear a shirt and tie* ♦ *Nigel wears a crisp white shirt to the office every day.* ➲ picture on page P1

> **MORE** A shirt usually has a **collar** at the neck, long or short **sleeves**, and **buttons** down the front.

shiver /'ʃɪvə(r)/ *verb* [I] to shake slightly, especially because you are cold or frightened □ *menggigil*: *shivering with cold/fright* ▶**shiver** *noun* [C]: *The thought sent a shiver down my spine.*

shoal /ʃəʊl/ *noun* [C] a large group of fish that feed and swim together □ *kawan/kumpulan (ikan)*

shock¹ /ʃɒk/ *noun* 1 [C,U] the feeling that you get when sth unpleasant happens suddenly; the situation that causes this feeling □ *terperanjat; terkejut*: *The sudden noise gave him a shock.* ♦ *The bad news came as a shock to her.* ♦ *I'm still suffering from shock at the news.* ♦ *His mother is in a state of shock.* 2 [U] a serious medical condition of extreme weakness caused by damage to the body □ *kejutan; renjatan*: *He was in/went into shock after the accident.* 3 [C] a violent shaking movement (caused by a crash, an explosion, etc.) □ *gegaran*: *the shock of the earthquake* 4 [C] = electric shock

shock² /ʃɒk/ *verb* 1 [T] to cause an unpleasant feeling of surprise in sb □ *memeranjatkan; terperanjat*: *We were shocked by his death.* ♦ *I'm sorry, I didn't mean to shock you when I came in.* 2 [I,T] to make sb feel disgusted or offended □ *mengejutkan; memeranjatkan*: *These films deliberately set out to shock.* ▶**shocked** *adj*: *a shocked expression/look*

shocking /'ʃɒkɪŋ/ *adj* 1 that offends or upsets people; that is morally wrong □ *(yg) mengejutkan*: *a shocking accident* ♦ *shocking behaviour/news* 2 (*BrE informal*) very bad □ *teruk*: *The weather has been absolutely shocking.*

shod past tense, past participle of **shoe²**

shoddy /'ʃɒdi/ *adj* (**shoddier**; **shoddiest**) 1 made carelessly or with poor quality materials □ *tdk bermutu*: *shoddy goods* 2 dishonest or unfair □ *tdk jujur/adil* ▶**shoddily** *adv*

shoes

shoelace

shoes — toe, heel

wellingtons (*AmE* rubber boots) — boot

sandal — flip-flops (*AmE* thongs)

trainers (*AmE* sneakers) — sole — slippers

shoe¹ /ʃuː/ *noun* [C] 1 a type of covering for the foot, usually made of leather or plastic □ *kasut*: *a pair of shoes* ♦ *running shoes* ♦ *What size are your shoes/What is your shoe size?* ♦ *I tried on a nice pair of shoes but they didn't fit.* ➲ picture on page P1 2 = horseshoe
IDM in sb's place/shoes ➲ **place¹**

shoe² /ʃuː/ *verb* [T] (*pt, pp* **shod** /ʃɒd/) to fit a **horseshoe** (= a piece of metal in the shape of a U) on a horse □ *memasang ladam*

shoelace /'ʃuːleɪs/ (also **lace**, *AmE* also **shoestring** /'ʃuːstrɪŋ/) *noun* [C] a long thin piece of material like string used to fasten a shoe □ *tali kasut*: *to tie/untie a shoelace* ➲ picture at **shoe**

shone past tense, past participle of **shine¹**

shoo¹ /ʃuː/ *exclam* used to tell a child or animal to go away □ *syuh (menghalau)*

shoo² /ʃuː/ *verb* [T] (*pt, pp* **shooed**) **shoo sb/sth away, off, out, etc.** to make sb/sth go away by saying 'shoo' and waving your hands □ *syuh (menghalau)*

shook past tense of **shake**¹

shoot¹ /ʃuːt/ verb (pt, pp **shot** /ʃɒt/)
▸GUN **1** [I,T] **shoot (sth) (at sb/sth)** to fire a gun or another weapon □ *menembak; memanah*: *Don't shoot!* ♦ *She shot an arrow at the target, but missed it.* **2** [T] to injure or kill a person or animal with a gun □ *menembak*: *The policeman was shot in the arm.* ♦ *The soldier was shot dead.*
▸ANIMALS **3** [I,T] to hunt and kill birds and animals with a gun as a sport □ *berburu*: *He goes shooting at the weekends.* ➜ look at **hunting**
▸MOVE FAST **4** [I,T] to move somewhere quickly and suddenly; to make sth move in this way □ *meluru; meluncur*: *The car shot past me at 100 miles per hour.*
▸PAIN **5** [I] to go very suddenly along part of your body □ *mencucuk*: *The pain shot up my leg.* ♦ *shooting pains in the chest*
▸FILM/PHOTOGRAPH **6** [I,T] to make a film or photograph of sth □ *membuat penggambaran*: *They shot the scene ten times.*
▸IN SPORTS **7** [I,T] **shoot (at sth)** (in football, etc.) to try to kick, hit or throw the ball into the goal □ *menjaringkan gol*: *He should have shot instead of passing.* ➜ noun **shot**

PHR V **shoot sb/sth down** to make sb/sth fall to the ground by shooting them or it □ *menembak sso/sst jatuh*: *The helicopter was shot down by a missile.*
shoot up to increase by a large amount; to grow very quickly □ *meningkat (naik); membesar dgn cepat*: *Prices have shot up in the past year.*

shoot² /ʃuːt/ noun [C] a new part of a plant or tree □ *tunas* ➜ picture at **plant**

shooting noun [C] a situation in which a person is shot with a gun □ *tembakan*: *Terrorist groups claimed responsibility for the shootings.* **2** [U] the sport of shooting animals and birds with guns □ *perburuan*: *pheasant shooting* **3** [U] the process of filming a film □ *penggambaran; perfileman*: *Shooting began early this year.*

shooting ˈstar noun [C] a piece of rock that burns with a bright light as it travels through space □ *tahi bintang* ➜ look at **comet**

shop¹ /ʃɒp/ (AmE **store**) noun [C] a building or part of a building where things are bought and sold □ *kedai*: *a cake/shoe/sports/toy shop* ♦ *a corner shop* (= a local shop, usually at the corner of a street) ♦ *When do the shops open?*

MORE The **butcher**, the **baker**, etc. is the person who sells a particular thing. We usually call their shop **the butcher's**, **the baker's** etc. instead of 'the butcher's shop', etc.

IDM **talk shop** ➜ **talk**¹

TOPIC
Shops

Before I **go shopping**, I make a **shopping list**. I buy bread and cakes **at the baker's**, where a shop assistant serves me. I buy meat at the **butcher's**, fish at the **fishmonger's**, fruit and vegetables at the **greengrocer's** and flowers at the **florist's**. If I want to buy everything in one shop, I go to the **supermarket**. There's a **market** in town on Fridays, and once a month there's a **farmer's market**, where you can buy local and **organic produce** (= food grown without chemicals).

shop² /ʃɒp/ verb [I] (**shopping**; **shopped**) **shop (for sth)** to go to a shop or shops in order to buy things □ *membeli-belah*: *He's shopping for some new clothes.*

HELP **Go shopping** is more common than **shop**: *We go shopping every Saturday.*

PHR V **shop around (for sth)** to look at the price and quality of an item in different shops before you decide where to buy it □ *menengok-nengok harga (sst)*
▸**shopper** noun [C]

shopaholic /ˌʃɒpəˈhɒlɪk/ noun [C] (*informal*) a person who enjoys shopping very much and spends too much time or money doing it □ *kaki membeli-belah*

ˈshop assistant (AmE ˈ**sales clerk**, **clerk**) noun [C] a person who works in a shop □ *pembantu kedai* ➜ picture on **page P2**

ˌshop ˈfloor noun [sing] (BrE) an area of a factory where things are made; the people who make things in a factory □ *bahagian pengeluaran; pekerja kilang*

shopkeeper /ˈʃɒpkiːpə(r)/ (AmE **storekeeper**) noun [C] a person who owns or manages a small shop □ *pekedai; tuan punya kedai*

shoplifter /ˈʃɒplɪftə(r)/ noun [C] a person who steals sth from a shop while pretending to be a customer □ *pencuri barang kedai* ➜ note at **thief**

shoplifting /ˈʃɒplɪftɪŋ/ noun [U] the crime of stealing goods from a shop while pretending to be a customer □ *(perbuatan) mencuri barang kedai*: *He was arrested for shoplifting.*

shopping /ˈʃɒpɪŋ/ noun [U] **1** the activity of going to the shops and buying things □ *membeli-belah*: *We always do the shopping on a Friday night.* ♦ *a shopping basket/bag/trolley* ➜ note at **supermarket** **2** (*especially BrE*) the things that you have bought in a shop □ *barang-barang belian*: *Can you help me to put the shopping in the car?*

TOPIC
Shopping

If you **go shopping** in the **sales**, you can often get good **bargains** (= things at a cheaper **price** than usual). You might spend time **browsing** (= looking at lots of things), or **window-shopping** (= looking in shop windows without intending to **buy** anything). If you are buying clothes, you **try** them **on** in the **fitting room**.

[I] **intransitive**, a verb which has no object: *He laughed.* [T] **transitive**, a verb which has an object: *He ate an apple.*

You pay at the **cash desk**, where the **shop assistant** will give you a **receipt** (= a piece of paper). If you are not satisfied with a **product** you have bought, **take** it **back** to the shop. There you can **exchange** it or ask for a **refund** (= your money back).

'shopping centre (*AmE* **'shopping center**) *noun* [C] a place where there are many shops, either outside or in a covered building □ *pusat beli-belah* ➔ look at **mall** ➔ picture on **page P11**

shore¹ /ʃɔː(r)/ *noun* [C,U] the land at the edge of a sea or lake □ *pantai; pesisir* ➔ look at **ashore** ➔ picture on **page P10**

shore² /ʃɔː(r)/ *verb*
PHR V **shore sth up 1** to support part of a building or other large structure by placing large pieces of wood or metal against or under it so that it does not fall down □ *menopang; memasang jernang; menunjang* **2** to help to support sth that is weak or going to fail □ *menyokong*: *The measures were aimed at shoring up the economy.*

shorn *past participle* of **shear**

ʰ short¹ /ʃɔːt/ *adj* (**shorter**; **shortest**) *adv*
▶LENGTH/DISTANCE **1** not measuring much from one end to the other □ *pendek; singkat*: *a short line/distance/dress* ◆ *This essay is rather short.* ◆ *short hair* **OPP** **long** ➔ picture at **hair** ➔ *verb* **shorten**
▶HEIGHT **2** less than the average height □ *pendek*: *a short, fat man* **OPP** **tall**
▶TIME **3** not lasting a long time □ *singkat; pendek; sekejap*: *a short visit/film* ◆ *She left a short time ago.* ◆ *to have a short memory* (= to only remember things that have happened recently) **OPP** **long** ➔ *verb* **shorten**
▶NOT ENOUGH **4 short (of/on sth)** not having enough of what is needed □ *kurang; kekurangan*: *Because of illness, the team is two players short.* ◆ *Good secretaries are in short supply* (= there are not enough of them). ◆ *We're a bit short of money at the moment.* ◆ *Your essay is a bit short on detail.* ➔ *noun* **shortage**
▶NAME/WORD **5 short for sth** used as a shorter way of saying sth □ *singkatan; kependekan*: *'Bill' is short for 'William'.*
▶IMPATIENT **6 short (with sb)** (used about a person) speaking in an impatient and angry way to sb □ *bengkeng*: *What's the matter with Michael? He was really short with me just now.* ➔ *adverb* **shortly**
▶SUDDENLY **7** suddenly □ *tiba-tiba*: *She stopped short when she saw the accident.*
IDM **cut sb short** to not allow sb to finish speaking; to interrupt sb □ *memotong cakap sso*
fall short (of sth) ➔ **fall¹**
for short as a short form □ *singkatannya*: *She's called 'Diana', or 'Di' for short.*
go short (of sth) to be without enough (of sth) □ *kekurangan; tdk cukup sst*: *He made sure his family never went short of food.*
in the long/short term ➔ **term¹**

in short in a few words □ *ringkasnya; pendeknya*
run short (of sth) to have used up most of sth so there is not much left □ *kehabisan (sst)*: *We're running short of coffee.*
short of sth/doing sth apart from; except for □ *selain; melainkan; kecuali*: *Nothing short of a miracle will save us now.*
stop short of sth/doing sth ➔ **stop¹**

short² /ʃɔːt/ *noun* [C] **1** (*BrE*) a small strong alcoholic drink □ *(sedikit) arak*: *I prefer wine to shorts.* **2** (*informal*) = **short circuit**

shortage /'ʃɔːtɪdʒ/ *noun* [C] a situation where there is not enough of sth □ *kekurangan*: *a food/housing/water shortage* ◆ *a shortage of trained teachers*

ˌshort 'circuit (also *informal* **short**) *noun* [C] a bad electrical connection that causes a machine to stop working □ *litar pintas* ▶ **ˌshort-ˈcircuit** (also *informal* **short**) *verb* [I,T]: *The lights short-circuited.*

shortcoming /'ʃɔːtkʌmɪŋ/ *noun* [C, usually pl] a fault or weakness □ *kekurangan; kelemahan*

ˌshort 'cut *noun* [C] a quicker, easier or more direct way to get somewhere or to do sth □ *jalan pintas; cara mudah*: *He took a short cut to school through the park.*

shorten /'ʃɔːtn/ *verb* [I,T] to become shorter or to make sth shorter □ *memendekkan* **OPP** **lengthen**

shortfall /'ʃɔːtfɔːl/ *noun* [C] **shortfall (in sth)** the amount by which sth is less than you need or expect □ *kurangan; jumlah yg kurang*

shorthand /'ʃɔːthænd/ *noun* [U] a method of writing quickly that uses signs or short forms of words □ *trengkas*: *to write in shorthand* ◆ *a shorthand typist*

shortlist /'ʃɔːtlɪst/ *noun* [C, usually sing] a list of the best people for a job, etc. who have been chosen from all the people who want the job □ *senarai terpilih*: *She's one of the four people on the shortlist.* ▶ **shortlist** *verb* [T]: *Six candidates were shortlisted for the post.*

ˌshort-ˈlived *adj* lasting only for a short time □ *sebentar; tdk kekal lama*

ʰ shortly /'ʃɔːtli/ *adv* **1** soon; not long □ *sebentar lagi; tdk lama lagi*: *The manager will see you shortly.* **2** in an impatient, angry way □ *dgn bengkeng*: *She spoke rather shortly to the customer.*

shorts /ʃɔːts/ *noun* [pl] **1** a type of short trousers ending above the knee that you wear in hot weather, while playing sports, etc. □ *seluar pendek* **2** (*AmE*) = **boxer shorts**

> **GRAMMAR** **Shorts** are plural, so we cannot say, for example, 'a new short'. The following are possible: *I need some shorts/a pair of shorts.* ◆ *These shorts are too small.*

short-sighted → shout

,short-'sighted *adj* **1** (*AmE* usually **near-sighted**) able to see things clearly only when they are very close to you □ *rabun jauh*: *I have to wear glasses because I'm short-sighted.* **OPP long-sighted 2** not considering what will probably happen in the future □ *tdk berpandangan jauh*: *a short-sighted attitude/policy*

,short-'staffed *adj* (used about an office, a shop, etc.) not having enough people to do the work □ *kekurangan kakitangan*

,short 'story *noun* [C] a piece of writing that is shorter than a novel □ *cerpen*

,short 'temper *noun* [sing] a tendency to become angry very quickly and easily □ *panas baran*: *He has a short temper.* ▶ **short-'tempered** *adj*: *She's rather short-tempered when she's tired.*

,short-'term *adj* lasting for a short period of time from the present □ *jangka pendek*: *short-term plans/memory*

shot¹ /ʃɒt/ *noun*
▶WITH GUN **1** [C] **a shot (at sb/sth)** an act of firing a gun, etc., or the noise that this makes □ *tembakan*: *to take a shot at the target* ◆ *The policeman fired a warning shot into the air.*
▶TRY **2** [C, usually sing] (*informal*) **a shot (at sth/at doing sth)** an attempt at doing sth □ *percubaan*: *Let me have a shot at it* (= let me try to do it). ◆ *Just give it your best shot* (= try as hard as you can). **SYN** attempt
▶IN SPORT **3** [C] the act of kicking, throwing or hitting a ball in order to score a point or a goal □ *tendangan, lontaran, pukulan, dsb bola*: *Giggs scored with a low shot into the corner of the net.* ◆ *Good shot!* **4** *often* **the shot** [sing] the heavy ball that is used in the sports competition called the **shot-put** □ *lontar peluru*
▶PHOTOGRAPH **5** [C] a photograph or a picture in a film □ *gambar foto*: *I got some good shots of the runners as they crossed the line.*
▶DRUG **6** [C] a small amount of a drug that is put into your body using a needle □ *suntikan*: *a shot of penicillin/morphine*
IDM **call the shots/tune** ⊃ **call¹**
like a shot (*informal*) very quickly; without stopping to think about it □ *dgn cepat; tanpa teragak-agak*: *If someone invited me on a free holiday, I'd go like a shot.*
a long shot ⊃ **long¹**

shot² past tense, past participle of **shoot¹**

shotgun /'ʃɒtɡʌn/ *noun* [C] a long gun that is used for shooting small animals and birds □ *senapang patah* ⊃ note at **gun**

the 'shot-put *noun* [sing] the event or sport of throwing a heavy metal ball as far as possible □ *lontar peluru*

should /ʃəd/ *strong form* /ʃʊd/ *modal verb* (*negative* **should not**; *short form* **shouldn't** /'ʃʊdnt/) **1** (used for saying that it is right or appropriate for sb to do sth, or for sth to happen) ought to □ *sepatutnya; seharusnya*: *The police should do* something about street crime in this area. ◆ *Children shouldn't be left on their own.* ◆ *I'm tired. I shouldn't have gone to bed so late/I should have gone to bed earlier.* **2** used for giving or asking for advice □ *harus*: *You should try that new restaurant.* ◆ *Do you think I should phone him?* ◆ *What should I do?* **3** used for saying that you expect sth is true or will happen □ *seharusnya*: *It's 4.30. They should be in New York by now.* ◆ *It should stop raining soon.* **4** (*BrE formal*) used with 'I/we' instead of 'would' in 'if' sentences □ *digunakan dgn 'I/we' dlm ayat bersyarat*: *I should be most grateful if you could send me …* **5** (*formal*) used after 'if' and 'in case' to refer to a possible event or situation □ *sekiranya; jika*: *If you should decide to accept, please phone us.* ◆ *Should you decide to accept …* **6** used as the past tense of 'shall' when we report what sb says □ *digunakan sebagai kk kala lampau bagi 'shall'*: *He asked me if he should come today* (= he asked 'Shall I come today?'). **7** **I should imagine, say, think, etc.** used to give opinions that you are not certain about □ *mungkin; rasanya*: *This picture is worth a lot of money, I should think.* ❶ For more information about modal verbs, look at the **Reference Section** at the back of this dictionary.

shoulder¹ /'ʃəʊldə(r)/ *noun* [C] **1** the part of your body between your neck and the top of your arm □ *bahu*: *I asked him why he'd done it but he just shrugged his shoulders* (= raised his shoulders to show that he did not know or care). ◆ *She fell asleep with her head on his shoulder.* ⊃ picture at **body 2** **-shouldered** [in compounds] having the type of shoulders mentioned □ *berbahu (spt yg disebutkan)*: *a broad-shouldered man* **3** a part of a dress, coat, etc. that covers the shoulders □ *bahagian bahu*: *a jacket with padded shoulders* **4** (*AmE*) = **hard shoulder**
IDM **have a chip on your shoulder** ⊃ **chip¹**
rub shoulders with sb ⊃ **rub**
a shoulder to cry on used to describe a person who listens to your problems and understands how you feel □ *tempat utk mengadu*

shoulder² /'ʃəʊldə(r)/ *verb* [T] **1** to accept the responsibility for sth □ *memikul*: *to shoulder the blame/responsibility* for something **2** to push sb/sth with your shoulder □ *menolak dgn bahu*

'shoulder bag *noun* [C] a type of bag that you carry over one shoulder with a long narrow piece of cloth, leather, etc. □ *beg galas* ⊃ picture on **page P1**

'shoulder blade *noun* [C] either of the two large flat bones on each side of your back, below your shoulders □ *tulang belikat* ⊃ picture at **body**

shout /ʃaʊt/ *verb* **1** [I,T] **shout sth (at/to sb); shout sth out** to say sth in a loud voice □ *menjeritkan; meneriakkan*: *'Careful,' she shouted.* ◆ *The captain shouted instructions to his team.* **2** [I] **shout (at/to sb); shout out** to speak or cry out in a very loud voice □ *menjerit; memekik*: *There's no need to shout—I can hear you.* ◆ *The teacher shouted angrily at the boys.* ◆ *to shout out in pain/excitement* ⊃ look at **scream**

PHR V **shout sb down** to shout so that sb who is speaking cannot be heard □ *menjerit-jerit utk menenggelamkan suara sso*: *The speaker was shouted down by a group of protesters.*
shout sth out to say sth in a loud voice □ *meneriakkan*: *The students kept shouting out the answers, so we stopped playing in the end.*
▶ **shout** *noun* [C]

shove /ʃʌv/ *verb* [I,T] (*informal*) to push with a sudden, rough movement □ *menolak*: *Everybody in the crowd was pushing and shoving.* ◆ *The policeman shoved the thief into the back of the police car.* ▶ **shove** *noun* [C, usually sing]: *to give somebody/something a shove*

shovel /ˈʃʌvl/ *noun* [C] a tool used for picking up and moving earth, snow, sand, etc. □ *penyodok* ᗧ look at **spade** ᗧ picture at **garden**
▶ **shovel** *verb* [I,T] (**shovelling**; **shovelled**; (*AmE*) **shoveling**; **shoveled**): *to shovel snow*

show¹ /ʃəʊ/ *verb* (*pt* **showed**; *pp* **shown** /ʃəʊn/ or **showed**)
▶ MAKE CLEAR **1** [T] to make sth clear; to give information about sth □ *menunjukkan; menerangkan*: *Research shows that most people get too little exercise.* ◆ *This graph shows how prices have gone up in the last few years.*
▶ LET SB SEE **2** [T] **show sb/sth (to sb); show sb (sth)** to let sb see sth/sb □ *menunjukkan*: *I showed the letter to him.* ◆ *I showed him the letter.* ◆ *She showed me what she had bought.* ◆ *They're showing his latest film at our local cinema.* ◆ *She was showing signs of nerves.* ◆ *This white T-shirt really shows the dirt.* ◆ *The picture showed him arguing with a photographer.*
▶ TEACH **3** [T] to help sb to do sth by doing it yourself; to explain sth □ *menunjukkan; mengajar; menerangkan*: *Can you show me how to make pancakes?*
▶ GUIDE **4** [T] to lead sb to or round a place; to explain how to go to a place □ *menunjukkan; membawa; mengiringi*: *I'll come with you and show you the way.* ◆ *Shall I show you to your room?* ◆ *A guide showed us round the museum.*
▶ BE SEEN **5** [I] to be able to be seen; to appear □ *menunjukkan; menampakkan*: *I tried not to let my disappointment show.*
IDM **show sb/know/learn the ropes** ᗧ **rope¹**
PHR V **show off** (*informal*) to try to impress people by showing them how clever you are □ *menunjuk-nunjuk*: *John was showing off in front of his sister's friends.*
show sth off to show people sth that you are proud of □ *mempertunjukkan*
show up (*informal*) to arrive, especially when sb is expecting you □ *datang*: *Where have you been? I thought you'd never show up.*
show (sth) up to allow sth to be seen □ *menampakkan (sst) dgn jelas*: *The sunlight shows up those dirty marks on the window.*
show sb up (*informal*) to make sb embarrassed about their behaviour or appearance □ *memalukan sso*: *He showed her up by shouting at the waiter.*

show² /ʃəʊ/ *noun* **1** [C] a type of entertainment performed for an audience □ *pertunjukan; persembahan*: *a TV comedy show* ◆ *a quiz show* **2** [C,U] an occasion when a collection of things are brought together for people to look at □ *pertunjukan; pameran*: *a dog show* ◆ *a fashion show* ◆ *Paintings by local children will be on show at the town hall next week.* **3** [sing] an occasion when you let sb see sth □ *menunjukkan*: *a show of emotion/gratitude/temper* **4** [C,U] something that a person does or has in order to make people believe sth that is not true □ *kepurapuraan; berpura-pura*: *Although she hated him, she put on a show of politeness.* ◆ *His self-confidence is all show* (= he is not as confident as he pretends to be).

ˈshow business (also *informal* **showbiz** /ˈʃəʊbɪz/) *noun* [U] the business of entertaining people in the theatre, in films, on TV, etc. □ *dunia hiburan*: *He's been in show business since he was five years old.*

showdown /ˈʃəʊdaʊn/ *noun* [C, usually sing] a final argument, meeting or fight at the end of a long disagreement □ *perdebatan, pertemuan atau perlawanan akhir utk mencari penyelesaian*: *The management are preparing for a showdown with the union.*

shower¹ /ˈʃaʊə(r)/ *noun* [C] **1** a piece of equipment that produces a spray of water that you stand under to wash; the small room or part of a room that contains a shower □ *paip hujan; pancuran; bilik mandi berpaip hujan*: *The shower doesn't work.* ◆ *She's in the shower.* ◆ *I'd like a room with a shower, please.* ᗧ picture on **page P8** **2** an act of washing yourself by standing under a shower □ *mandi (paip hujan)*: *I'll just have a quick shower then we can go out.* **3** a short period of rain □ *hujan (sebentar)*: *a heavy shower* ᗧ look at **rain**, **acid rain** **4** a lot of very small objects that fall or fly through the air together □ *hujan*: *a shower of sparks/broken glass*

shower² /ˈʃaʊə(r)/ *verb* **1** [I] to wash yourself under a shower □ *mandi dgn paip hujan*: *I came back from my run, showered and got changed.* **2** [I,T] **shower (down) on sb/sth; shower sb with sth** to cover sb/sth with a lot of small falling objects □ *menghujani*: *Ash from the volcano showered down on the town.* ◆ *People suffered cuts after being showered with broken glass.*

showing /ˈʃəʊɪŋ/ *noun* **1** [C] an act of showing a film, etc. □ *pertunjukan*: *The second showing of the film begins at 8 o'clock.* **2** [sing] how sb/sth behaves; how successful sb/sth is □ *perilaku; prestasi*: *On its present showing, the party should win the election.*

showjumping /ˈʃəʊdʒʌmpɪŋ/ *noun* [U] a competition in which a person rides a horse over a series of jumps □ *pertandingan lompat kuda*

shown *past participle of* **show¹**

ˈshow-off *noun* [C] (*informal*) a person who tries to impress others by showing them how clever he/she is, or by showing them sth he/she is proud of □ *orang yg suka menunjuk-nunjuk*: *She's such a show-off, always boasting about how good she is at this and that.*

showroom /'ʃəʊruːm; -rʊm/ *noun* [C] a type of large shop where customers can look at goods such as cars, furniture and electrical items that are on sale □ *bilik pameran*

shrank *past tense* of **shrink**

shrapnel /'ʃræpnəl/ *noun* [U] small pieces of metal that fly around when a bomb explodes □ *serpihan bom*

shred¹ /ʃred/ *verb* [T] (**shredding**; **shredded**) to tear or cut sth into **shreds** □ *mencarik; meracik*: *shredded cabbage*

shred² /ʃred/ *noun* 1 [C] a small thin piece of material that has been cut or torn off □ *carik; cebis*: *His clothes were torn to shreds by the rose bushes.* 2 [sing] [in negative sentences] **not a shred of sth** a very small amount of sth □ *sedikit*: *There wasn't a shred of truth in her story.*

shrewd /ʃruːd/ *adj* (**shrewder**; **shrewdest**) able to make good decisions because you understand a situation well □ *pintar; bijak*: *a shrewd thinker/decision* ▶ **shrewdly** *adv*

shriek /ʃriːk/ *verb* 1 [I] to make a short, loud, noise in a high voice □ *menjerit; memekik*: *She shrieked in fright.* ♦ *The children were shrieking with laughter.* 2 [T] to say sth loudly in a high voice □ *menjerit; memekik*: *'Stop it!' she shrieked.* ⊃ look at **screech** ▶ **shriek** *noun* [C]

shrill /ʃrɪl/ *adj* (**shriller**; **shrillest**) (used about a sound) high and unpleasant □ *nyaring*: *a shrill cry*

shrimp /ʃrɪmp/ *noun* [C] 1 a small sea creature with a shell and a lot of legs that turns pink when you cook it. **Shrimps** are smaller than **prawns**. □ *udang* 2 (*AmE*) = **prawn**

shrine /ʃraɪn/ *noun* [C] a place that is important to a particular person or group of people for religious reasons or because it is connected with a special person □ *tempat suci; makam*

shrink

'Oh no! My T-shirt has shrunk!'

shrink /ʃrɪŋk/ *verb* (*pt* **shrank** /ʃræŋk/ *or* **shrunk** /ʃrʌŋk/; *pp* **shrunk**) 1 [I,T] to become smaller or make sth smaller □ *mengecut; kecut; susut*: *My T-shirt shrank in the wash.* ♦ (*figurative*) *TV has shrunk the world.* ♦ *The rate of inflation has shrunk to 4%.* 2 [I] to move back because you are frightened or shocked □ *berundur*: *We shrank back against the wall when the dog appeared.*

PHR V shrink from sth/doing sth to not want to do sth because you find it unpleasant □ *enggan membuat sst*

shrivel /'ʃrɪvl/ *verb* [I,T] (**shrivelling**; **shrivelled**, (*AmE*) **shriveling**; **shriveled**) **shrivel (sth) (up)** to become or make sth become smaller, especially because of dry conditions □ *mengecut; menjadi kering dan kerepot*: *The plants shrivelled up and died in the hot weather.*

shroud¹ /ʃraʊd/ *noun* [C] a cloth or sheet that is put round a dead body before it is buried □ *kain kapan*

shroud² /ʃraʊd/ *verb* [T, usually passive] **shroud sth (in sth)** to cover or hide sth □ *menyelubungi*

Shrove Tuesday /,ʃrəʊv 'tjuːzdeɪ; -di/ *noun* [C] the day before **Lent** (= a period of 40 days during which some Christians do not eat certain foods) □ *'Shrove Tuesday'* ⊃ look at **Pancake Day**

CULTURE

In some countries people celebrate the period before Shrove Tuesday as **carnival**. In Britain many people eat **pancakes** (= very thin round cakes made of flour, milk and eggs) on this day.

shrub /ʃrʌb/ *noun* [C] a small bush □ *pokok renek*

shrubbery /'ʃrʌbəri/ *noun* [C] (*pl* **shrubberies**) an area where a lot of small bushes have been planted □ *rumpun pokok renek*

shrug /ʃrʌg/ *verb* [I,T] (**shrugging**; **shrugged**) to lift your shoulders as a way of showing that you do not know sth or are not interested □ *mengangkat bahu*: *'Who knows?' she said and shrugged.* ♦ *'It doesn't matter to me,' he said, shrugging his shoulders.*

shrug

PHR V shrug sth off to not allow sth to affect you in a bad way □ *tdk menghiraukan*

mempedulikan: *An actor has to learn to shrug off criticism.*
▶**shrug** *noun* [C, usually sing]: *I asked him if he was sorry and he just answered with a shrug.*

shrunk *past tense, past participle of* **shrink**

shrunken /ˈʃrʌŋkən/ *adj* that has become smaller (and less attractive) □ *mengecut*

shudder /ˈʃʌdə(r)/ *verb* [I] to suddenly shake hard, especially because of an unpleasant feeling or thought □ *menggeletar; bergegar*: *Just thinking about the accident makes me shudder.* ♦ *The engine shuddered violently and then stopped.*
▶**shudder** *noun* [C]

shuffle¹ /ˈʃʌfl/ *verb* **1** [I] to walk by sliding your feet along instead of lifting them off the ground □ *berjalan menyeret kaki*: *The child shuffled past, wearing her mother's shoes.* **2** [I,T] to move your body or feet around because you are uncomfortable or nervous □ *mengubah kedudukan (kerana resah, dsb)*: *The audience were so bored that they began to shuffle in their seats.* **3** [I,T] to mix a pack of playing cards before a game □ *mengocok*: *It's your turn to shuffle.* ♦ *She shuffled the cards carefully.*

shuffle² /ˈʃʌfl/ *noun* [C, usually sing] **1** a way of walking without lifting your feet off the ground □ *(cara berjalan) menyeret kaki* **2** an act of **shuffling** cards □ *(perbuatan) mengocok*

shun /ʃʌn/ *verb* [T] (**shunning**; **shunned**) to avoid sth/sb; to keep away from sth/sb □ *menjauhi; memulaukan*: *She was shunned by her family when she married him.*

shunt /ʃʌnt/ *verb* [T] **1** to push a train from one track to another □ *memiraukan* **2** to move sb/sth to a different place, especially a less important one □ *memindahkan; mengalih*: *John was shunted sideways to a job in sales.*

shut¹ /ʃʌt/ *verb* (**shutting**; *pt, pp* **shut**) **1** [I,T] to make sth close; to become closed □ *menutup; tertutup*: *Could you shut the door, please?* ♦ *I can't shut my suitcase.* ♦ *Shut your books, please.* ♦ *He shut his eyes and tried to go to sleep.* ♦ *This window won't shut properly.* ♦ *The doors open and shut automatically.* **2** [I,T] (BrE) (used about a shop, restaurant, etc.) to stop doing business for the day; to close □ *ditutup*: *What time do the shops shut on Saturday?*

PHR V **shut sb/sth away** to keep sb/sth in a place where people cannot find or see them or it □ *mengurung sso/menyimpan sst*

shut (sth) down (used about a factory, etc.) to close, or close sth, for a long time or for ever □ *menutup (sst); ditutup*: *Financial problems forced the business to shut down.*

shut sb/yourself in (sth) to put sb in a room and keep them there; to go to a room and stay there □ *mengurung*: *She shut herself in her room and refused to come out.*

shut sth in sth to trap sth by closing a door, lid, etc. on it □ *mengurung; menyepit; tersepit*: *Tony shut his fingers in the door of the car.*

shut sb/sth/yourself off (from sth) to keep sb/ sth/yourself apart from sth □ *mengasingkan diri/sst (drpd sst)*: *He shuts himself off from the rest of the world.*

shut sb/sth out to stop yourself from having particular feelings □ *tdk membenarkan sso/sst masuk; menghalang; menyingkirkan*: *He tried to shut out all thoughts of the accident.*

shut (sb) up (*informal*) to stop or make sb stop talking □ *sso diam/berhenti bercakap*: *I wish you'd shut up!* ♦ *Nothing can shut him up once he's started.*

shut sb/sth up (in sth) to put sb/sth somewhere and stop them leaving □ *mengurung sso/sst (dlm sst); dipenjarakan*: *He was shut up in prison for nearly ten years.*

shut² /ʃʌt/ *adj* [not before a noun] **1** in a closed position □ *ditutup; tertutup*: *Make sure the door is shut properly before you leave.*

HELP **Shut** or **closed**? We can use **closed** before a noun: *a closed door*, but not **shut**.

2 (BrE) not open to the public □ *ditutup; tutup*: *The restaurant was shut so we went to one round the corner.*

IDM **keep your mouth shut** ➔ **mouth¹**

shutter /ˈʃʌtə(r)/ *noun* [C] **1** a wooden or metal cover that is fixed outside a window and that can be opened or shut. A shop's **shutter** usually slides down from the top of the shop window. □ *penutup; bidai* ➔ picture at **curtain** **2** the part at the front of a camera that opens for a very short time to let light in so that a photograph can be taken □ *pengatup*

shuttle /ˈʃʌtl/ *noun* [C] a plane, bus or train that travels regularly between two places □ *perkhidmatan (kapal terbang, bas atau kereta api) ulang-alik*

shuttlecock /ˈʃʌtlkɒk/ *noun* [C] (in the sport of **badminton**) the small, light object that is hit over the net □ *bulu tangkis* ➔ picture at **badminton**

shy¹ /ʃaɪ/ *adj* (**shyer**; **shyest**) **1** nervous and uncomfortable about meeting and speaking to people; showing that sb feels like this □ *malu; malu-malu*: *She's very shy with strangers.* ♦ *a shy smile* **2** [not before a noun] **shy (of/about sth/ doing sth)** frightened to do sth or to become involved in sth □ *segan; takut*: *She's not shy of telling people what she thinks.* ▶**shyly** *adv* ▶**shyness** *noun* [U]: *He didn't overcome his shyness till he had left school.*

shy² /ʃaɪ/ *verb* [I] (**shying**; **shies**; *pt, pp* **shied**) (used about a horse) to suddenly move back or sideways in fear □ *mengundur atau mengelak ke tepi kerana takut*

PHR V **shy away from sth/from doing sth** to avoid doing sth because you are afraid □ *mengelak drpd melakukan sst*

sibling /ˈsɪblɪŋ/ *noun* [C] (*formal*) a brother or a sister □ *adik-beradik*

sick → side 792

> **HELP** In everyday language we use **brother(s) and sister(s)**: *Have you got any brothers and sisters?*

sick¹ /sɪk/ *adj*
▶ILL **1** not well □ *sakit: a sick child* ◆ *Do you get paid for days when you're **off sick** (= away from work)?* ◆ *You're too ill to work today—you should **phone in sick**.*

> **HELP** Note that **be sick** in British English usually means 'to bring up food from the stomach; vomit'.

2 the sick *noun* [pl] people who are ill □ *orang sakit: All the sick and wounded were evacuated.*
▶WANTING TO VOMIT **3** feeling ill in your stomach so that you may **vomit** (= bring up food from the stomach) □ *berasa loya/hendak muntah: I feel sick—I think it was that fish I ate.* ◆ *Don't eat any more or you'll make yourself sick.* ⊃ look at **airsick, carsick, nausea, seasick, travel-sick**.
▶BORED/ANGRY **4 sick of sb/sth** (*informal*) feeling bored or annoyed because you have had too much of sb/sth □ *jemu; bosan: I'm sick of my job.* ◆ *I'm sick of tidying up your mess!* **5 sick (at/about sth)** very annoyed or disgusted by sth □ *berasa benci/meluat: He felt sick at the sight of so much waste.*
▶CRUEL **6** (*informal*) mentioning disease, suffering, death, etc. in a cruel or disgusting way □ *menjelikkan: He offended everyone with a sick joke about blind people.*
IDM **be sick** (*BrE*) to bring up food from the stomach □ *muntah: It's common for women to be sick in the first months of pregnancy.* **SYN vomit**
make sb sick to make sb very angry □ *membuat sso marah/meluat: Oh, stop complaining. You make me sick!*
sick to death of sb/sth feeling tired of or annoyed by sb/sth □ *bosan/menyampah (akan sso/sst): I'm sick to death of his grumbling.*

sick² /sɪk/ *noun* [U] (*BrE informal*) food that sb has brought up from their stomach □ *muntah: There was sick all over the car seat.* **SYN vomit**

sicken /'sɪkən/ *verb* [T] to make sb feel disgusted □ *membuat sso berasa meluat, benci, dsb: The level of violence in the film sickens me.*
▶**sickening** *adj*: *His head made a sickening sound as it hit the road.*

sickle /'sɪkl/ *noun* [C] a tool with a curved blade and a short handle, used for cutting grass, etc. □ *sabit*.

'sick leave *noun* [U] a period spent away from work, etc. because of illness □ *cuti sakit: Mike's been off on sick leave since March.*

sickly /'sɪkli/ *adj* (**sicklier; sickliest**) **1** (used about a person) weak and often ill □ *selalu sakit: a sickly child* **2** unpleasant; causing you to feel ill □ *memualkan; meloyakan: the sickly smell of rotten fruit*

sickness /'sɪknəs/ *noun* **1** [U] the state of being ill □ *sakit: A lot of workers are absent because of sickness.* **2** [C,U] a particular type of illness □ *penyakit: pills for seasickness* ◆ *Sleeping sickness is carried by the tsetse fly.* **3** [U] (*BrE*) a feeling in your stomach that may make you bring up food through your mouth □ *rasa loya; muntah: Symptoms of the disease include sickness and diarrhoea.*

side¹ /saɪd/ *noun* [C]
▶LEFT/RIGHT **1** the area to the left or right of sth; the area in front of or behind sth □ *sebelah: We live (on) **the other side** of the main road.* ◆ *It's more expensive to live on the north side of town.* ◆ *In Japan they drive on **the left-hand side** of the road.* ◆ *She sat at the side of his bed/at his bedside.*
▶NOT TOP OR BOTTOM **2** one of the surfaces of sth except the top, bottom, front or back □ *tepi; sisi: I went round to the side of the building.* ◆ *The side of the car was damaged.*
▶EDGE **3** the edge of sth, away from the middle □ *tepi: Make sure you stay **at the side** of the road when you're cycling.* ◆ *We moved **to one side** to let the doctor get past.*
▶OF BODY **4** the right or the left part of your body, especially from under your arm to the top of your leg □ *sisi; sebelah (kanan/kiri): She lay on her side.* ◆ *The soldier stood with his hands by his sides.*
▶NEAR TO SB/STH **5** a place or position very near to sb/sth □ *samping: Her mother stood at her side.*
▶OF STH FLAT/THIN **6** either of the two flat surfaces of sth thin □ *belah; permukaan: Write on both sides of the paper.*
▶SURFACE **7** one of the flat outer surfaces of sth □ *sisi: A cube has six sides.*
▶-SIDED **8** -sided [in compounds] having the number of sides mentioned □ *bersisi: a six-sided coin*
▶IN FIGHT/COMPETITION **9** either of two or more people or groups who are fighting, playing, arguing, etc. against each other □ *pihak; pasukan: The two sides agreed to stop fighting.* ◆ *the winning/losing side* ◆ *Whose side are you on?* (= Who do you want to win?)
▶OF STORY **10** what is said by one person or group that is different from what is said by another □ *belah; pihak: I don't know whose side of the story to believe.*
▶OF FAMILY **11** your mother's or your father's family □ *sebelah (bapa/ibu): There is no history of illness on his mother's side.*
IDM **err on the side of sth** ⊃ **err**
get on the right/wrong side of sb to please/annoy sb □ *menyukakan hati sso/membuat sso marah: He tried to get on the right side of his new boss.*
look on the bright side ⊃ **look¹**
on/from all sides; on/from every side in/from all directions □ *di/dlm semua arah; di sekeliling*
on the big, small, high, etc. side (*informal*) slightly too big, small, high, etc. □ *agak besar, kecil, tinggi, dsb*
on the safe side ⊃ **safe¹**
put sth on/to one side; leave sth on one side to leave or keep sth so that you can use it or deal with it later □ *mengetepikan sst dahulu: You should put some money to one side for the future.*

[I] **intransitive**, a verb which has no object: *He laughed.* [T] **transitive**, a verb which has an object: *He ate an apple.*

side by side next to each other; close together □ *sebelah-menyebelah; berdampingan*: *They walked side by side along the road.*
take sides (with sb) to show that you support one person rather than another in an argument □ *memihak kpd sso*: *Parents should never take sides when their children are quarrelling.*

side[2] /saɪd/ *verb*
PHR V side with sb (against sb) to support sb in an argument □ *memihak kpd sso*

sideboard /'saɪdbɔːd/ *noun* [C] a type of low cupboard about as high as a table, that is used for storing plates, etc. in a **dining room** (= a room that is used for eating in) □ *almari rendah utk pinggan mangkuk* ⊃ picture on page P8

sideburns /'saɪdbɜːnz/ *noun* [pl] hair that grows down a man's face in front of his ears □ *bauk; jambang*

'side dish *noun* [C] a small amount of food, for example a salad, served with the main course of a meal □ *hidangan sampingan*: *a side dish of vegetables*

'side effect *noun* [C] **1** an unpleasant effect that a drug may have in addition to its useful effects □ *kesan sampingan*: *Side effects of the drug include nausea and dizziness.* **2** an unexpected effect of sth that happens in addition to the intended effect □ *kesan sampingan*: *One of the side effects when the chemical factory closed was that fish returned to the river.*

sideline /'saɪdlaɪn/ *noun* **1** [C] something that you do in addition to your regular job, especially to earn extra money □ *kerja sampingan*: *He's an engineer, but he repairs cars as a sideline.* **2 sidelines** [pl] the lines that mark the two long sides of the area used for playing sports such as football, tennis, etc.; the area behind this □ *garisan tepi*
IDM on the sidelines not involved in an activity; not taking part in sth □ *hanya memerhatikan; menjadi pemerhati*

sidelong /'saɪdlɒŋ/ *adj* [only before a noun] directed from the side; sideways □ *dr tepi; kerlingan; jelingan*: *a sidelong glance*

'side order *noun* [C] a small amount of food ordered in a restaurant to go with the main dish, but served separately □ *hidangan tambahan*: *a side order of chips* ⊃ look at **side dish**

'side road *noun* [C] a small road which joins a bigger main road □ *jalan samping*

'side street *noun* [C] a narrow or less important street near a main street □ *jalan samping*

sidetrack /'saɪdtræk/ *verb* [T] **sidetrack sb (into doing sth)** [usually passive] to make sb forget what they are doing or talking about and start doing or talking about sth less important □ *memesongkan*

sidewalk /'saɪdwɔːk/ (*AmE*) = **pavement**

sideways /'saɪdweɪz/ *adv, adj* **1** to, towards or from one side □ *ke atau dari sisi/tepi*: *He jumped sideways to avoid being hit.* ♦ *She gave him a sideways look.* **2** with one of the sides at the top □ *ke sisi*: *We'll have to turn the sofa sideways to get it through the door.*

siding /'saɪdɪŋ/ *noun* [C] **1** a short track beside a main railway line, where trains can stand when they are not being used □ *landasan sisi* **2** (*AmE*) material used to cover and protect the outside walls of buildings □ *bahan pelindung dinding di luar bangunan*

sidle /'saɪdl/ *verb* [I] **sidle up/over (to sb/sth)** to move towards sb/sth in a nervous way, as if you do not want anyone to notice you □ *berjalan dgn diam-diam (ke arah sso/sst)*

siege /siːdʒ/ *noun* [C,U] a situation in which an army surrounds a town for a long time or the police surround a building so that nobody can get in or out □ *pengepungan*

siesta /si'estə/ *noun* [C] a short sleep or rest that people take in the afternoon, especially in hot countries □ *tidur (petang) sebentar*: *to have/take a siesta*

sieve /sɪv/ *noun* [C] a type of kitchen tool that has a metal or plastic net, used for separating solids from liquids or very small pieces of food from large pieces □ *tapis; ayak*: *Pour the soup through a sieve to get rid of any lumps.* ⊃ picture at **kitchen** ▶ **sieve** *verb* [T]: *to sieve flour*

sift /sɪft/ *verb* **1** [T] to pass flour, sugar or a similar substance through a **sieve** in order to remove any lumps □ *mengayak*: *to sift flour/sugar* **2** [I,T] **sift (through) sth** to examine sth very carefully □ *meneliti; menyemak dgn teliti*: *It took weeks to sift through all the evidence.*

sigh /saɪ/ *verb* **1** [I] to let out a long, deep breath that shows you are tired, sad, disappointed, etc. □ *mengeluh*: *She sighed with disappointment at the news.* **2** [T] to say sth with a **sigh** □ *mengeluh; keluh*: *'I'm so tired,' he sighed.* **3** [I] to make a long sound like a **sigh** □ *berdesir* ▶ **sigh** *noun* [C]
IDM heave a sigh ⊃ **heave**[1]

sight[1] /saɪt/ *noun*
▶ABILITY TO SEE **1** [U] the ability to see □ *penglihatan*: *He lost his sight in the war* (= he became blind). ♦ *My grandmother has very poor sight.*
▶ACT OF SEEING **2** [sing] **the sight of sb/sth** the act of seeing sb/sth □ *(apabila) melihat/terlihat*: *I feel ill at the sight of blood.*
▶HOW FAR YOU CAN SEE **3** [U] a position where sb/sth can be seen □ *kelihatan; pandangan*: *They waited until the plane was in/within sight and then fired.* ♦ *When we get over this hill the town should come into sight.* ♦ *She didn't let the child out of her sight.*
▶WHAT YOU CAN SEE **4** [C] something that you see □ *pemandangan; pandangan*: *The burned-out building was a terrible sight.*
▶INTERESTING PLACES **5 sights** [pl] places of interest that are often visited by tourists □ *tempat-tempat menarik*: *When you come to New York I'll show you the sights.*
▶PERSON/THING **6 a sight** [sing] (*informal*) a person or thing that looks strange or amusing □ *sso/sst*

sight → Sikh 794

yg kelihatan aneh/lucu: *You should have seen Anna in my jacket—she did look a sight!*
▸ ON GUN **7** [C, usually pl] the part of a gun that you look through in order to aim it □ *pembidik*: *He had the deer in his sights now.*
▸ -SIGHTED **8** [in compounds] having eyes that are weak in a particular way □ *rabun (jauh/dekat)* ➲ look at **long-sighted, short-sighted**
IDM at first glance/sight ➲ **first¹**
catch sight of sb/sth ➲ **catch¹**
in sight likely to happen or come soon □ *mungkin berlaku (tercapai, dll)*: *A peace settlement is in sight.*
lose sight of sb/sth ➲ **lose**
on sight as soon as you see sb/sth □ *sebaik sahaja nampak*: *The soldiers were ordered to shoot the enemy on sight.*

sight² /saɪt/ verb [T] (formal) to see sb/sth, especially after looking out for them or it □ *melihat; nampak*

sighting /ˈsaɪtɪŋ/ noun [C] an occasion when sb/sth is seen □ *(sso/sst) dilihat*: *the first sighting of a new star*

sightseeing /ˈsaɪtsiːɪŋ/ noun [U] visiting the sights of a city, etc. as a tourist □ *melawat tempat-tempat menarik*: *We did some sightseeing in Rome.* ➲ note at **holiday**

sightseer /ˈsaɪtsiːə(r)/ noun [C] a person who visits the sights of a city, etc. as a tourist □ *pelancong/pelawat (ke tempat-tempat menarik)* ➲ look at **tourist**

§ sign¹ /saɪn/ noun [C]
▸ SHOWING STH **1** sign (of sth) something that shows that sb/sth is present, exists or may happen □ *tanda*: *The patient was showing some signs of improvement.* ♦ *As we drove into the village there wasn't a sign of life anywhere* (= we couldn't see anyone).
▸ FOR INFORMATION/WARNING **2** a piece of wood, paper, metal, etc. that has writing or a picture on it that gives you a piece of information, an instruction or a warning □ *papan tanda, dsb*: *What does that sign say?* ♦ *a road sign* ♦ *Follow the signs to Banbury.* ➲ picture at **roundabout**
▸ MOVEMENT **3** a movement that you make with your head, hands or arms that has a particular meaning □ *tanda; isyarat*: *I made a sign for him to follow me.* ♦ *I'll give you a sign when it's time for you to speak.*
▸ SYMBOL **4** a type of shape, mark or symbol that has a particular meaning □ *tanda; lambang*: *In mathematics, a cross is a plus sign.*
▸ STAR SIGN **5** = **star sign**

§ sign² /saɪn/ verb **1** [I,T] to write your name on a letter, document, etc. to show that you have written it or that you agree with what it says □ *menyain; menandatangani*: *'Could you sign here, please?'* ♦ *I forgot to sign the cheque.* ♦ *The two presidents signed the treaty.* ➲ noun **signature 2** [I,T] sign (sb) (up) to get sb to sign a contract to work for you □ *mengambil (pekerja, pemain, dll)*: *Real Madrid have signed two new players.* **3** [I] to communicate using sign language □ *berhubung dlm bahasa isyarat*: *Dave's deaf friend taught him to sign.*
PHR V sign in/out to write your name to show you have arrived at or left a hotel, club, etc. □ *mendaftar masuk/keluar*
sign up (for sth) to agree formally to do sth □ *mendaftar (utk sst)*: *I've signed up for evening classes.*

§ signal /ˈsɪɡnəl/ noun [C] **1** a sign, an action or a sound that sends a particular message □ *isyarat*: *When I give (you) the signal, run!* **2** an event, an action or a fact that shows that sth exists or is likely to happen □ *tanda*: *The fall in unemployment is a clear signal that the economy is improving.* **3** a set of lights used to give information to drivers □ *lampu isyarat*: *a stop signal* **4** a series of radio waves, etc. that are sent out or received □ *isyarat*: *a signal from a satellite* ♦ *I can't get a signal on my mobile phone here.* ▸ signal verb [I,T] (signalling; signalled, (AmE) signaling; signaled): *She was signalling wildly that something was wrong.*

signatory /ˈsɪɡnətri/ noun [C] (pl signatories) signatory (to sth) one of the people or countries that sign an agreement, etc. □ *penandatangan*

§ signature /ˈsɪɡnətʃə(r)/ noun [C] a person's name, written by that person and always written in the same way □ *tandatangan*: *I couldn't read his signature.* ➲ verb **sign**

significance /sɪɡˈnɪfɪkəns/ noun [U] the importance or meaning of sth □ *signifikan; pentingnya; makna*: *Few people realized the significance of the discovery.*

§ significant /sɪɡˈnɪfɪkənt/ adj **1** important or large enough to be noticed or to have an effect □ *penting; ketara; nyata*: *There has been a significant improvement in your work.* **2** having a particular meaning □ *ada makna*: *It could be significant that he took out life insurance shortly before he died.* ♦ *Police said that the time of the murder was extremely significant.* ▸ significantly adv: *Attitudes have changed significantly since the 1980s.*

signify /ˈsɪɡnɪfaɪ/ verb [T] (signifying; signifies; pt, pp signified) (formal) **1** to be a sign of sth □ *(merupakan) tanda/makna*: *What do those lights signify?* **SYN** mean **2** to express or indicate sth □ *menunjukkan*: *They signified their agreement by raising their hands.*

'sign language noun [U] a language used especially by people who cannot hear or speak, using their hands to make signs instead of using spoken words □ *bahasa isyarat*

signpost /ˈsaɪnpəʊst/ noun [C] a sign at the side of a road that gives information about directions and distances to towns □ *tiang tanda* ➲ picture at **roundabout** ➲ picture on **page P11**

Sikh /siːk/ noun [C] a member of a religion called **Sikhism** (= a religion that developed from Hinduism in India, but that teaches that there is only one god) □ *Sikh*

silence /ˈsaɪləns/ noun **1** [U] no noise or sound at all □ *kesenyapan; (perihal) senyap*: *There must be silence during examinations.* **SYN** quiet **2** [C,U] a period when nobody speaks or makes a noise □ *kesenyapan; (keadaan) senyap*: *My question was met with an awkward silence.* ◆ *We ate in silence.* **3** [U] not making any comments about sth □ *diam; senyap; tdk berkata apa-apa*: *I can't understand his silence on the matter.* ▶ silence verb [T]

silencer /ˈsaɪlənsə(r)/ noun [C] **1** (*AmE* **muffler**) a device which is fixed to the **exhaust pipe** (= the long tube zunder a vehicle) to reduce the noise made by the engine □ *alat penyenyap* **2** a device which is fixed to a gun to reduce the noise that it makes when it is fired □ *alat penyenyap; peredam bunyi*

silent /ˈsaɪlənt/ adj **1** where there is no noise; making no noise □ *senyap; sunyi; sepi*: *The house was empty and silent.* **SYN** quiet **2** [only before a noun] not using spoken words □ *senyap-senyap; dlm hati*: *a silent prayer/protest* **3** silent (on/about sth) refusing to speak about sth □ *diam; tdk berkata apa-apa*: *The policeman told her she had the right to remain silent.* **4** (used about a letter) not pronounced □ *tdk dibunyikan*: *The 'b' in 'comb' is silent.* ▶ silently adv: *She crept silently away.*

silhouette /ˌsɪluˈet/ noun [C] the dark solid shape of sb/sth seen against a light background □ *bayang; siluet* ▶ silhouetted adj

silicon /ˈsɪlɪkən/ noun [U] (*symbol* **Si**) a chemical element that exists as a grey solid or a brown powder, and is found in rocks and sand. It is used in making glass and electronic equipment. □ *silikon*

ˌsilicon ˈchip noun [C] a piece of **silicon** that is used in computers, etc. □ *cip silikon*

silk /sɪlk/ noun [U] the soft smooth cloth that is made from threads produced by a **silkworm** (= a very small creature) □ *sutera*: *a silk shirt/dress*

silky /ˈsɪlki/ adj (**silkier**; **silkiest**) smooth, soft and shiny; like silk □ *licin dan lembut; spt sutera*: *silky hair*

sill /sɪl/ noun [C] a shelf that is at the bottom of a window, either inside or outside □ *ambang*: *a windowsill* ⊃ picture on **page P8**

silly /ˈsɪli/ adj (**sillier**; **silliest**) **1** not showing thought or understanding; stupid □ *bodoh*: *a silly mistake* ◆ *Don't be so silly!* **SYN** foolish **OPP** sensible **2** appearing ridiculous, so that people will laugh □ *lucu; pandir*: *I'm not wearing that hat—I'd look silly in it.* ▶ silliness noun [U]

silt /sɪlt/ noun [U] sand, soil or mud that collects at the sides or on the bottom of a river □ *kelodak; lanar*

silver¹ /ˈsɪlvə(r)/ noun [U] **1** (*symbol* **Ag**) a valuable greyish-white metal that is used for making jewellery, coins, etc. □ *perak*: *a silver spoon/necklace* ◆ *That's a nice ring. Is it silver?* **2** [U] coins made from silver or sth that looks like silver □ *duit syiling (perak atau spt perak)*: *I need £2 in silver for the parking meter.* **3** [U] objects that are made of silver, for example knives, forks, spoons and dishes □ *barang-barang perak*: *The thieves stole some jewellery and some valuable silver.* **4** [C] = silver medal
IDM every cloud has a silver lining ⊃ cloud¹

silver² /ˈsɪlvə(r)/ adj **1** having the colour of silver □ *berwarna perak*: *a silver sports car* **2** celebrating the 25th anniversary of sth □ *ulang tahun ke-25*: *the silver jubilee of the Queen's accession in 1977* ⊃ look at **diamond, golden**

ˌsilver ˈmedal (also **silver**) noun [C] a small flat round piece of silver that is given to the person or team that comes second in a sports competition □ *pingat perak*: *to win a silver medal at the Olympic Games* ⊃ look at **bronze medal, gold medal** ▶ ˌsilver ˈmedallist noun [C]

silverware /ˈsɪlvəweə(r)/ noun [U] **1** objects that are made of or covered with silver, especially knives, forks, dishes, etc. that are used for eating and serving food □ *barangan perak*: *a piece of silverware* **2** (*AmE*) = **cutlery**

silvery /ˈsɪlvəri/ adj having the appearance or colour of silver □ *keperak-perakan*: *an old lady with silvery hair*

SIM card /ˈsɪm kɑːd/ noun [C] a plastic card inside a mobile phone that stores phone numbers, etc. □ *kad sim*

similar /ˈsɪmələ(r)/ adj similar (to sb/sth); similar (in sth) like sb/sth but not exactly the same □ *seakan-akan; serupa*: *Our houses are very similar in size.* ◆ *My teaching style is similar to that of many other teachers.* **OPP** different, dissimilar ▶ similarly adv: *The plural of 'shelf' is 'shelves'. Similarly, the plural of 'wolf' is 'wolves'.*

similarity /ˌsɪməˈlærəti/ noun (pl **similarities**) **1** [U, sing] similarity (to sb/sth); similarity (in sth) the state of being like sb/sth but not exactly the same □ *keserupaan; serupa*: *She bears a remarkable/striking similarity to her mother.* **2** [C] a similarity (between A and B); a similarity (in/of sth) a characteristic that people or things have which makes them similar □ *persamaan*: *Although there are some similarities between the two towns, there are a lot of differences too.* ◆ *similarities in/of style* **OPP** difference

---

WRITING TIP

How to compare similar things

To say that two people, things, etc. are equal or identical in some way, use **as** + adjective/adverb + **as**: *John is as tall as Sarah* or: *Sarah is as tall as John* (= they are both the same height): *Jim ran as fast as Frank* or: *Frank ran as fast as Jim* (= they both ran at the same speed).

You can also compare two people or things using **Both X and Y ...**, **Like X, Y ...** or **X, like Y, ...**: *Both Jane and Fred play football for the school team.* ◆ *Like his father, Joe is very intelligent.*

simile → sinful

• Oxford, like Bologna, is an ancient university town. ⊃ note at **difference**

ⓘ For more help with writing, look at **Wordpower Writing Tutor** at the back of this dictionary.

simile /ˈsɪməli/ noun [C,U] a word or phrase that compares sth to sth else, using the words 'like' or 'as'; the use of such words and phrases. For example, 'a face like a mask' and 'as white as snow' are similes. □ *perumpamaan; perbandingan* ⊃ look at **metaphor**

simmer /ˈsɪmə(r)/ verb [I,T] to cook sth gently in a liquid that is almost boiling □ *mereneh*

simple /ˈsɪmpl/ adj (simpler; simplest) [You can also use **more simple** and **most simple**.] **1** easy to understand, do or use; not difficult or complicated □ *mudah; senang*: This dictionary is written in simple English. • *a simple task/method/ solution* • *I can't just leave the job. It's not as simple as that.* SYN **easy 2** without decoration or unnecessary extra things □ *ringkas; sederhana*: *a simple black dress* • *The food is simple but perfectly cooked.* SYN **basic** OPP **fancy 3** used for saying that the thing you are talking about is the only thing that is important or true □ *semata-mata*: *I'm not going to buy it for the simple reason that (= only because) I haven't got enough money.* **4** (used about a person or a way of life) natural and not complicated □ *sederhana*: *a simple life in the country* **5** (old-fashioned) not intelligent; slow to understand □ *lembap; tumpul*

simplicity /sɪmˈplɪsəti/ noun [U] **1** the quality of being easy to understand, do or use □ (*perihal*) *mudahnya*: *We all admired the simplicity of the plan.* **2** the quality of having no decoration or unnecessary extra things; being natural and not complicated □ *kesederhanaan*: *I like the simplicity of her paintings.*

simplify /ˈsɪmplɪfaɪ/ verb [T] (simplifying; simplifies; pt, pp simplified) to make sth easier to do or understand; to make sth less complicated □ *memudahkan; meringkaskan*: *The process of applying for visas has been simplified.* ▶ **simplification** /ˌsɪmplɪfɪˈkeɪʃn/ noun [C,U]

simplistic /sɪmˈplɪstɪk/ adj (disapproving) making a problem, situation, etc. seem less difficult and complicated than it really is □ *terlalu mudah; mempermudah*

simply /ˈsɪmpli/ adv **1** used to emphasize how easy or basic sth is □ *mudah sahaja; hanya*: *Simply add hot water and stir.* **2** (used to emphasize an adjective) completely □ *betul-betul; memang*: *That meal was simply excellent.* SYN **absolutely 3** in a way that makes sth easy to understand □ *dgn cara yg mudah*: *Could you explain it more simply?* **4** in a simple, basic way; without decoration or unnecessary extra things □ *secara sederhana*: *They live simply, with very few luxuries.* **5** only □ *hanya; semata-mata*: *There's no need to get angry. The whole problem is simply a misunderstanding.* SYN **just**

simulate /ˈsɪmjuleɪt/ verb [T] to create certain conditions that exist in real life using computers, models, etc., usually for study or training purposes □ *mensimulasi*: *The astronauts trained in a machine that simulates conditions in space.* ▶ **simulation** /ˌsɪmjuˈleɪʃn/ noun [C,U]: *a computer simulation of a nuclear attack*

simultaneous /ˌsɪmlˈteɪniəs/ adj happening or done at exactly the same time as sth else □ *serentak* ▶ **simultaneously** adv

sin /sɪn/ noun [C,U] an action or way of behaving that is not allowed by a religion □ *dosa*: *He believes it is a sin for two people to live together without being married.* ▶ **sin** verb [I] (sinning; sinned) ▶ **sinner** noun [C]

since /sɪns/ adv, conj, prep **1** from a particular time in the past until a later time in the past or until now □ *sejak*: *My parents bought this house in 1985 and we've been living here ever since.* • *I've been working in a bank ever since I left school.* • *It was the first time they'd won since 1998.* • *I haven't seen him since last Tuesday.* • *She has had a number of jobs since leaving university.*

> **GRAMMAR** We use both **since** and **for** to talk about how long something has been happening. We use **since** when we are talking about the *beginning* of the period of time, and **for** when we are talking about the *length* of the period of time: *I've known her since 2009.* • *I've known him for three years.*

2 because; as □ *oleh sebab; memandangkan*: *Since they've obviously forgotten to phone me, I'll have to phone them.* **3** at a time after a particular time in the past □ *selepas itu*: *We were divorced two years ago and she has since married someone else.*

sincere /sɪnˈsɪə(r)/ adj (sincerest) [no comparative] **1** (used about sb's feelings, beliefs or behaviour) true; showing what you really mean or feel □ *ikhlas*: *Please accept our sincere thanks/ apologies.* SYN **genuine 2** (used about a person) really meaning or believing what you say; not pretending □ *ikhlas; jujur*: *Do you think she was being sincere when she said she admired me?* SYN **honest** OPP for both meanings **insincere** ▶ **sincerely** adv: *I am sincerely grateful to you for all your help.* • *Yours sincerely, …* (= at the end of a formal letter) ⊃ note at **dear**

WRITING TIP

How to end a letter

Use **Yours sincerely** at the end of a letter, if you know the name of the person you are writing to. If you do not know their name, use **Yours faithfully**. Use **Sincerely, Sincerely yours** or **Yours truly** in American English.

ⓘ For more help with writing, look at **Wordpower Writing Tutor** at the back of this dictionary. ▶ **sincerity** /sɪnˈserəti/ noun [U] OPP **insincerity**

sinful /ˈsɪnfl/ adj breaking a religious law; immoral □ *berdosa*

sing /sɪŋ/ verb [I,T] (pt **sang** /sæŋ/; pp **sung** /sʌŋ/) to make musical sounds with your voice □ *menyanyi*: He always sings when he's in the bath. ◆ The birds were singing outside my window. ◆ She sang all her most popular songs at the concert. ▶ **singing** noun [U]: singing lessons

singe /sɪndʒ/ verb [I,T] (**singeing**) to burn the surface of sth slightly, usually by accident; to be burned in this way □ *terbakar; hangus sedikit*

singer /ˈsɪŋə(r)/ noun [C] a person who sings, or whose job is singing, especially in public □ *penyanyi*: an opera singer

single¹ /ˈsɪŋɡl/ adj
▶ ONE **1** [only before a noun] only one □ *satu; se(kuntum, dsb)*: He gave her a single red rose. ◆ I managed to finish the whole job in a single afternoon. ◆ I went to a **single-sex school** (= for boys only or girls only).
▶ FOR EMPHASIS **2** [only before a noun] used to emphasize that you are talking about each individual item in a group or series □ *setiap*: You answered every single question correctly. Well done!
▶ NOT MARRIED **3** not married or in a relationship □ *bujang*: Are you married or single? ◆ a single man/woman
▶ FOR ONE PERSON **4** [only before a noun] for the use of only one person □ *bujang*: I'd like to book a single room, please. ⊃ note at **bed¹** ⊃ picture at **bed**
▶ TICKET **5** (AmE **one-ˈway**) [only before a noun] (used about a ticket or the price of a ticket for a journey to a particular place, but not back again □ *sehala*: How much is the single fare to York ⊃ look at **return**
IDM **in single file** in a line, one behind the other □ *sebaris; sederet*

single² /ˈsɪŋɡl/ noun
▶ TICKET **1** [C] a ticket for a journey to a particular place, but not back again □ *tiket (utk perjalanan) sehala*: Two singles to Hull, please. ⊃ look at **return**
▶ CD **2** [C] a piece of recorded music, usually popular music, that consists of one song; a CD that a **single** is recorded on □ *'single' (lagu dlm cakera padat, pita, dsb)*: Adele's new single ⊃ look at **album**
▶ ROOM **3** [C] a bedroom for one person in a hotel, etc. □ *bilik bujang* ⊃ look at **double**
▶ UNMARRIED PEOPLE **4** **singles** [pl] people who are not married and do not have a romantic relationship with sb else □ *orang bujang*
▶ IN SPORT **5** **singles** [pl] (in sports such as **tennis**) a game in which one player plays against one other player □ *perseorangan* ⊃ look at **double**

single³ /ˈsɪŋɡl/ verb
PHR V **single sb/sth out (for sth)** to give special attention or treatment to one person or thing from a group □ *memilih sso/sst (utk sst)*: She was singled out for criticism.

ˌsingle-ˈhanded adj, adv on your own with nobody helping you □ *seorang diri; sendirian*

ˌsingle-ˈminded adj having one clear aim or goal which you are determined to achieve □ *dgn satu tujuan*
▶ **single-ˈmindedness** noun [U]

ˌsingle ˈparent noun [C] a person who looks after their child or children without a husband, wife or partner □ *ibu/bapa tunggal*: a single-parent family

singly /ˈsɪŋɡli/ adv one at a time; alone □ *satu per satu; seorang demi seorang; satu-satu*: You can buy the pens either singly or in packs of three.
SYN **individually**

singular /ˈsɪŋɡjələ(r)/ adj **1** in the form that is used for talking about one person or thing only □ *mufrad; tunggal*: 'Table' is a singular noun; 'tables' is its plural. ⊃ look at **plural 2** (written) unusual □ *luar biasa* ▶ **singular** noun [sing]: The word 'clothes' has no singular. ◆ What's the singular of 'people'?

singularly /ˈsɪŋɡjələli/ adv (formal) very; in an unusual way □ *betul-betul; benar-benar; sungguh*: He chose a singularly inappropriate moment to make his request. ◆ singularly beautiful

sinister /ˈsɪnɪstə(r)/ adj seeming evil or dangerous; making you feel that sth bad will happen □ *jahat; menakutkan*: There's something sinister about him. He frightens me.

sink¹ /sɪŋk/ verb (pt **sank** /sæŋk/; pp **sunk** /sʌŋk/) **1** [I,T] to go down or make sth go down under the surface of liquid or a soft substance □ *tenggelam; terbenam*: If you throw a stone into water, it sinks. ◆ The boat sank to the bottom of the sea. ◆ My feet sank into the mud. ⊃ picture at **float 2** [I] (used about a person) to move downwards, usually by falling or sitting down □ *merebahkan diri*: I came home and sank into a chair, exhausted. **3** [I] to get lower; to fall to a lower position or level □ *jatuh; terbenam*: We watched the sun sink slowly below the horizon. **4** [I] to decrease in value, number, amount, strength, etc. □ *berkurang; susut; merendah*
IDM **your heart sinks** ⊃ **heart**
PHR V **sink in** (used about information, an event, an experience, etc.) to be completely understood or realized □ *betul-betul memahami/menyedari*: It took a long time for the terrible news to sink in.
sink in; sink into sth (used about a liquid) to go into sth solid; to be absorbed □ *menyerap/meresap ke dlm sst*

sink² /sɪŋk/ noun [C] a large open container in a kitchen or bathroom, with taps to supply water, where you wash things □ *sink* ⊃ look at **washbasin** ⊃ picture on **page P8**

sinus /ˈsaɪnəs/ noun [C, often plural] one of the spaces in the bones of your face that are connected to your nose □ *sinus*: I've got a terrible cold and my sinuses are blocked. ◆ a sinus infection

sip /sɪp/ verb [I,T] (**sipping**; **sipped**) to drink, taking only a very small amount of liquid into your

siphon → situation 798

mouth at a time □ *menghirup*: *We sat in the sun, sipping lemonade.* ▶ **sip** *noun* [C]

siphon (also **syphon**) /ˈsaɪfn/ *verb* [T] **1 siphon sth into/out of sth; siphon sth off/out** to remove a liquid from a container, often into another container, through a tube □ *mengalirkan keluar* **2 siphon sth off; siphon sth (from/out of sth)** to take money from a company illegally over a period of time □ *menyalurkan*

sir /sɜː(r)/ *noun* **1** [sing] used as a polite way of speaking to a man whose name you do not know, for example in a shop or restaurant, or to show respect □ *encik; tuan*: *I'm afraid we haven't got your size, sir.* ⊃ look at **madam 2 Sir** [C] used at the beginning of a formal letter to a male person or male people □ *Tuan*: *Dear Sir … ◆ Dear Sirs …* ⊃ look at **madam 3** /sə(r)/ [sing] the title that is used in front of the name of a man who has received one of the highest British honours □ *Sir*: *Sir Tom Jones*

siren /ˈsaɪrən/ *noun* [C] a device that makes a long, loud sound as a warning or signal □ *siren*: *an air-raid siren ◆ Three fire engines raced past, sirens wailing.*

sister /ˈsɪstə(r)/ *noun* [C] **1** a girl or woman who has the same parents as another person □ *kakak; adik perempuan*: *I've got one brother and two sisters. ◆ We're sisters.* ⊃ look at **half-sister, stepsister**

> **HELP** Siblings means 'both brothers and sisters' but it is very formal, so we usually say: *Have you got any brothers and sisters? ◆ I haven't got any brothers or sisters.*

2 (*informal*) a woman who you feel close to because she is a member of the same society, group, etc. as you □ *teman; saudara (seperjuangan)* **3** often **Sister** (*BrE*) a female nurse who has responsibility for part of a hospital □ *sister* **4 Sister** a nun (= a member of a religious group of women) □ *Sister (Biarawati)*: *Sister Mary-Theresa* **5** [usually used as an adjective] a thing that belongs to the same type or group as sth else □ *kembar; sekutu*: *We have a sister company in Japan.*

ˈsister-in-law *noun* [C] (*pl* **sisters-in-law**) **1** the sister of your husband or wife □ *kakak/adik ipar (perempuan)* **2** the wife of your brother □ *kakak/adik ipar (perempuan)*

sit /sɪt/ *verb* (**sitting**; *pt, pp* **sat** /sæt/)
➤ ON CHAIR, ETC. **1** [I] to rest your weight on your bottom, for example in a chair □ *duduk*: *We sat in the garden all afternoon. ◆ She was sitting on the sofa, talking to her mother.* **2** [T] **sit sb (down)** to put sb into a sitting position; to make sb sit down □ *mendudukkan; menyuruh (sso) duduk*: *He picked up his daughter and sat her down on a chair. ◆ She sat me down and offered me a cup of tea.*
➤ OF THINGS **3** [I] to be in a particular place or position □ *terletak*: *The letter sat on the table for several days before anybody opened it.*
➤ PARLIAMENT, ETC. **4** [I] (*formal*) (used about an official group of people) to have a meeting or series of meetings □ *bersidang*: *Parliament was still sitting at 3 o'clock in the morning.*
➤ EXAM **5** [T] (*BrE*) to take an exam □ *menduduki/mengambil peperiksaan*: *If I fail, will I be able to sit the exam again?*

IDM **sit on the fence** to avoid saying which side of an argument you support □ *tdk menyokong mana-mana pihak*

PHR V **sit about/around** (*informal*) to spend time doing nothing active or useful □ *duduk-duduk sahaja*: *We just sat around chatting all afternoon.*
sit back to relax and not take an active part in what other people are doing □ *berehat-rehat*: *Sit back and take it easy while I make dinner.*
sit down to lower your body into a sitting position □ *duduk*: *He sat down in an armchair.*
sit sth out 1 to stay in a place and wait for sth unpleasant or boring to finish □ *menunggu hingga tamat sst*: *We sat out the storm in a cafe.* **2** to not take part in a dance, game, etc. □ *tdk turut menari, mengambil bahagian, dsb*: *I think I'll sit this one out.*
sit through sth to stay in your seat until sth boring or long has finished □ *duduk (menonton, mendengar, dsb sst) hingga habis*
sit up 1 to move into a sitting position when you have been lying down, or to make your back straight □ *bangun duduk; duduk tegak*: *Sit up straight and concentrate!* **2** to not go to bed although it is very late □ *berjaga*: *We sat up all night talking.*

sitcom /ˈsɪtkɒm/ (also *formal* ˌsituation ˈcomedy) *noun* [C,U] a funny programme on TV that shows the same characters in different amusing situations each week □ *sitkom*

site /saɪt/ *noun* [C] **1** a piece of land where a building was, is or will be □ *tapak*: *a building/construction site ◆ The company is looking for a site for its new offices.* **2** a place where sth has happened or that is used for sth □ *tempat kejadian*: *the site of a famous battle* **3** = **website** ▶ **site** *verb* [T] (*formal*): *The castle is magnificently sited on top of the mountain.*

sitting /ˈsɪtɪŋ/ *noun* [C] **1** a period of time during which a court of law or a parliament meets and does its work □ *bersidang* **2** a time when a meal is served in a school, hotel, etc. to a number of people at the same time □ *waktu makanan dihidangkan*: *Dinner will be in two sittings.*

ˈsitting room (*BrE*) = **living room**

situated /ˈsɪtʃueɪtɪd/ *adj* [not before a noun] in a particular place or position □ *terletak*: *The hotel is conveniently situated close to the beach.*

situation /ˌsɪtʃuˈeɪʃn/ *noun* [C] **1** the things that are happening in a particular place or at a particular time □ *keadaan; situasi*: *The situation in the north of the country is extremely serious. ◆ Tim is **in a difficult situation** at the moment. ◆ the*

[I] **intransitive**, a verb which has no object: *He laughed.*   [T] **transitive**, a verb which has an object: *He ate an apple.*

economic/financial/political situation **2** (*formal*) the position of a building, town, etc. in relation to the area around it □ *kedudukan; tempat*: *The house is in a beautiful situation on the edge of a lake.* **3** *old-fashioned or formal*) a job □ *jawatan; pekerjaan*: *Situations Vacant* (= the part of a newspaper where jobs are advertised)

situation comedy (*formal*) = **sitcom**

sit-up *noun* [C] an exercise for the stomach muscles in which you lie on your back with your legs bent, then lift the top half of your body from the floor □ *senaman utk menguatkan otot perut*: *to do sit-ups* ◯ picture at **exercise**

six /sɪks/ *number* **1** 6 □ *enam*; *6* **2** **six-** [in compounds] having six of the thing mentioned □ *enam*: *She works a six-day week.*

> **HELP** Note how numbers are used in sentences: *The answers are on page six.* ◆ *There are six of us for dinner tonight.* ◆ *Sally has six cats.* ◆ *My son is six (years old) next month.* ◆ *She lives at 6 Elm Drive.* ◆ *a birthday card with a big six on it*

ℹ For more information about numbers, look at the section on using numbers at the back of this dictionary.

sixteen /ˌsɪks'tiːn/ *number* 16 □ *enam belas*; *16* ◯ note at **six** ▶ **sixteenth** /ˌsɪks'tiːnθ/ *ordinal number, noun* ◯ note at **sixth**

sixth¹ /sɪksθ/ *ordinal number* 6th □ *keenam*; *ke-6*

> **HELP** Note how ordinal numbers are used in sentences: *Today is March the sixth.* ◆ *My office is on the sixth floor.* ◆ *This is the sixth time I've tried to phone him.*

ℹ For more information about numbers, look at the section on using numbers at the back of this dictionary.

sixth² /sɪksθ/ *noun* [C] ⅙; one of six equal parts of sth □ *satu per enam*; ⅙

sixth form *noun* [C, with sing or pl verb] (in Britain) the final two years at secondary school for students from the age of 16 to 18 who are studying for A level exams □ *tingkatan enam* ▶ **sixth-former** *noun* [C]

sixty /'sɪksti/ *number* **1** 60 ◯ note at **six** □ *berenam puluh*; *60*

> **HELP** Note how numbers are used in sentences: *Sixty people went to the meeting.* ◆ *There are sixty pages in the book.* ◆ *He retired at (the age of) sixty.*

2 the sixties [pl] the numbers, years or temperatures between 60 and 69; the 60s □ *enam puluhan*; *60-an*: *I don't know the exact number of members, but it's in the sixties.* ◆ *The most famous pop group of the sixties was The Beatles.* ◆ *The temperature tomorrow will be in the high sixties.*

IDM in your sixties between the age of 60 and 69 □ *dlm lingkungan umur enam puluhan*: *I'm not sure how old she is but I should think she's in*

799 situation comedy → skateboard

her sixties. ◆ *in your early/mid/late sixties*
▶ **sixtieth** /'sɪkstiəθ/ *ordinal number, noun*
◯ note at **sixth**

size¹ /saɪz/ *noun* **1** [C,U] how big or small sth is □ *saiz; besar; besarnya*: *I was surprised at the size of the hotel. It was enormous!* ◆ *The planet Uranus is about four times the size of* (= as big as) *Earth.*

> **HELP** When we ask about the size of something, we usually say, 'How big ...?': *How big is your house?* We say, 'What size ...?' when we ask about the size of something that is produced in a number of fixed measurements: *What size shoes do you take?* ◆ *What size are you?* (= when buying clothes)

2 [C] one of a number of fixed measurements in which sth is made □ *saiz*: *Have you got this dress in a bigger size?* ◆ *I'm a size 12.* ◆ *What size pizza would you like? Medium or large?* **3** **-sized**; **-size** [in compounds] of the size mentioned □ *bersaiz*: *a medium-sized flat* ◆ *a king-size bed*

size² /saɪz/ *verb*

PHR V size sb/sth up to form an opinion or a judgement about sb/sth □ *menilai sso/sst*

sizeable (also **sizable**) /'saɪzəbl/ *adj* quite large □ *agak besar*: *a sizeable sum of money*

sizzle /'sɪzl/ *verb* [I] to make the sound of food frying in hot fat □ *berdesir*

skate¹ /skeɪt/ *verb* [I] **1** (also **'ice-skate**) to move on ice wearing **skates** □ *kasut luncur*: *Can you skate?* ◆ *They skated across the frozen lake.*

> **HELP Go skating** is a common way of talking about skating for pleasure.

2 = **roller skate** ▶ **skater** *noun* [C]

skates

ice skates   Rollerblades™   roller skates

skateboard

skate² /skeɪt/ *noun* [C] **1** (also **'ice skate**) a boot with a thin sharp metal part on the bottom that is used for moving on ice □ *kasut luncur* **2** = **roller skate 3** a large flat sea fish that you can eat □ *ikan pari*

skateboard /'skeɪtbɔːd/ *noun* [C] a short narrow board with small wheels at each end that you can stand on and ride as a sport □ *papan*

CONSONANTS   p **p**en   b **b**ad   t **t**ea   d **d**id   k **c**at   g **g**ot   tʃ **ch**in   dʒ **J**une   f **f**all   v **v**an   θ **th**in

selaju ⊃ picture at **skate** ▶**skateboarder** *noun* [C] ▶**skateboarding** *noun* [U]: *When we were children we used to* **go skateboarding** *in the park.*

skating /ˈskeɪtɪŋ/ *noun* [U] **1** (also ˈ**ice skating**) the activity or sport of moving on ice wearing special boots □ *meluncur; sukan luncur*: *Would you like to* **go skating** *this weekend?* ⊃ picture on **page P4 2** = **roller skating**

ˈ**skating rink** (also **rink**) **1** = **ice rink 2** an area or a building where you can **roller skate** (=move using a type of shoe with wheels on the bottom) □ *gelanggang luncur*

skeleton¹ /ˈskelɪtn/ *noun* [C] the structure formed by all the bones in a human or animal body □ *rangka*: *the human skeleton* ♦ *a dinosaur skeleton* ⊃ picture at **body**

skeleton² /ˈskelɪtn/ *adj* (used about an organization, a service, etc.) having the smallest number of people that is necessary for it to operate □ *(kakitangan) yg sedikit sekali*

skeptic, skepticism (*AmE*) = **sceptic, scepticism**

sketch /sketʃ/ *noun* [C] **1** a simple, quick drawing without many details □ *lakaran*: *He drew a* **rough sketch** *of the new building on the back of an envelope.* **2** a short funny scene on TV, in the theatre, etc. □ *sketsa; lakonan pendek*: *The drama group did a sketch about a couple buying a new house.* **3** a short description without any details □ *ringkasan* ▶**sketch** *verb* [I,T]: *I sat on the grass and sketched the castle.*

sketchy /ˈsketʃi/ *adj* (**sketchier**; **sketchiest**) not having many or enough details □ *tdk lengkap; terlalu ringkas*

skewer /ˈskjuːə(r)/ *noun* [C] a long thin pointed piece of metal or wood that is pushed through pieces of meat, vegetables, etc. to hold them together while they are cooking or to check that they are completely cooked □ *pencucuk* ⊃ picture on **page P16** ▶**skewer** *verb* [T]

ski¹ /skiː/ *verb* [I] (**skiing**; *pt*, *pp* **skied**) to move over snow on **skis** □ *bermain ski*: *When did you learn to ski?* ♦ *They* **go skiing** *every year.* ▶**ski** *adj* [only before a noun]: *a ski resort/instructor/slope/suit* ▶**skiing** *noun* [U]: *alpine/downhill/cross-country skiing* ⊃ picture on **page P4**

ski² /skiː/ *noun* [C] one of a pair of long, flat, narrow pieces of wood or plastic that are fastened to boots and used for sliding over snow □ *ski*: *a pair of skis*

skid /skɪd/ *verb* [I] (**skidding**; **skidded**) (often used about a vehicle) to suddenly slide forwards or sideways without any control □ *tergelincir*: *The lorry skidded to a halt just in time.* ▶**skid** *noun* [C]: *The car went into a skid and came off the road.*

skier /ˈskiːə(r)/ *noun* [C] a person who **skis** □ *pemain ski*: *Dita's a good skier.* ⊃ picture on **page P4**

skilful (*AmE* **skillful**) /ˈskɪlfl/ *adj* **1** (used about a person) very good at doing sth □ *cekap; mahir*: *a skilful painter/politician* ♦ *He's very skilful with his hands.* **2** done very well □ *cekap; mahir*: *skilful guitar playing* ▶**skilfully** /-fəli/ *adv*

skill /skɪl/ *noun* **1** [U] the ability to do sth well, especially because of training, practice, etc. □ *kemahiran; kepakaran*: *It takes great skill to make such beautiful jewellery.* ♦ *This is an easy game to play. No skill is required.* **2** [C] an ability that you need in order to do a job, an activity, etc. well □ *kemahiran*: *The course will help you to develop your reading and listening skills.* ♦ *management skills* ♦ *Typing is a skill I have never mastered.*

skilled /skɪld/ *adj* **1** (used about a person) having skill; skilful □ *mahir*: *a skilled worker* **2** (used about work, a job, etc.) needing skill or skills; done by people who have been trained □ *mahir; pakar; terlatih*: *a highly skilled job* ♦ *Skilled work is difficult to find in this area.* **OPP** for both meanings **unskilled**

skim /skɪm/ *verb* (**skimming**; **skimmed**) **1** [T] **skim sth (off/from sth)** to remove sth from the surface of a liquid □ *mengaup (dan membuang)*: *to skim the cream off the milk* **2** [I,T] to move quickly over or past sth, almost touching it or touching it slightly □ *melayap*: *The plane flew very low, skimming the tops of the buildings.* **3** [I,T] **skim (through/over) sth** to read sth quickly in order to get the main idea, without paying attention to the details and without reading every word □ *membaca sepintas lalu*: *I usually just skim through the newspaper in the morning.*

EXAM TIP

Skimming

For a **reading comprehension** it is a good idea to skim the text first, to get a general idea of what it is about. If you do this, it will be easier to understand when you read it for a second time. Next, read the questions, then **scan** the text (= read it quickly), looking only for the relevant information to answer the questions.

ˌ**skimmed** ˈ**milk** *noun* [U] milk from which the cream has been removed □ *susu skim*

skimp /skɪmp/ *verb* [I] **skimp (on sth)** to use or provide less of sth than is necessary □ *berjimat; berdikit-dikit*

skimpy /ˈskɪmpi/ *adj* (**skimpier**; **skimpiest**) using or having less than is necessary; too small or few □ *sedikit sangat; tdk cukup; (pakaian) pendek dan terdedah*

skin¹ /skɪn/ *noun* [C,U]
▶ ON BODY **1** the natural outer covering of a human or animal body □ *kulit*: *to have (a) fair/dark/sensitive skin* ♦ *skin cancer*
▶ -SKINNED **2** -**skinned** [in compounds] having the type of skin mentioned □ *berkulit*: *a dark-skinned/fair-skinned woman*
▶ OF DEAD ANIMAL **3** [in compounds] the skin of a dead animal, with or without its fur, used for

making things □ *kulit (binatang)*: *a sheepskin jacket* ◆ *a bag made of crocodile skin*
▶ OF FRUIT/VEGETABLES **4** the natural outer covering of some fruits or vegetables; the outer covering of a **sausage** (= meat formed in a long thin shape) □ *kulit*: *(a) banana/tomato skin* ➲ note at **rind** ➲ picture on **page P14**
▶ ON LIQUIDS **5** the thin solid layer that can form on a liquid □ *kepala (susu dsb)*: *A skin had formed on top of the milk.*

IDM **by the skin of your teeth** (*informal*) (used to show that sb almost failed to do sth) only just □ *nyaris-nyaris tdk sempat/dpt (membuat sst)*: *I ran into the airport and caught the plane by the skin of my teeth.*
have a thick skin ➲ **thick¹**

skin² /skɪn/ *verb* [T] (**skinning**; **skinned**) to remove the skin from sth □ *mengupas kulit; menguliti*
IDM **keep your eyes peeled/skinned (for sb/sth)** ➲ **eye¹**

skin-'deep *adj* (used about a feeling or an attitude) not as important or as strongly felt as it appears to be; only on the surface □ *pd zahirnya sahaja*: *His concern for me was only skin-deep.* **SYN** **superficial**

skinny /'skɪni/ *adj* (*informal*) (**skinnier**; **skinniest**) (used about a person) too thin □ *kurus kering* ➲ note at **thin**

skintight /skɪn'taɪt/ *adj* (used about a piece of clothing) fitting very tightly and showing the shape of the body □ *sendat; sangat ketat*

skip¹ /skɪp/ *verb* (**skipping**; **skipped**) **1** [I] to move along quickly and lightly in a way that is similar to dancing, with little jumps and steps, from one foot to the other □ *meloncat-loncat; melompat-lompat*: *A little girl came skipping along the road.* ◆ *Lambs were skipping about in the field.* **2** [I] to jump over a rope that you or two other people hold at each end, turning it round and round over your head and under your feet □ *bermain skip; lompat tali*: *Some girls were skipping in the playground.* **3** [T] to not do sth that you usually do or should do □ *tdk membuat sst; ponteng*: *I got up rather late, so I skipped breakfast.* **4** [T] to miss the next thing that you would normally read, do, etc. □ *melangkau*: *I accidentally skipped one of the questions in the test.*

skip² /skɪp/ *noun* [C] **1** a small jumping movement □ *loncatan; lompatan* **2** a large, open metal container for rubbish, often used during building work □ *tong pengangkut (sampah)*

skipper /'skɪpə(r)/ *noun* [C] (*informal*) the captain of a boat or ship, or of a sports team □ *kapten*

'skipping rope *noun* [C] a rope, often with handles at each end, that you turn over your head and then jump over, for fun or for exercise □ *tali skip*

skirmish /'skɜːmɪʃ/ *noun* [C] a short fight between groups of people □ *pertempuran kecil*

skirt¹ /skɜːt/ *noun* [C] a piece of clothing that is worn by women and girls and that hangs down from the waist □ *skirt* ➲ picture on **page P1**

skirt² /skɜːt/ *verb* [I,T] to go around the edge of sth □ *mengelilingi*: *The road skirts the lake.*

PHR V **skirt round sth** to avoid talking about sth in a direct way □ *mengelak drpd (bercakap ttg sst secara langsung)*: *The manager skirted round the subject of our pay increase.*

skittles /'skɪtlz/ *noun* [U] (in Britain) a game in which players roll a ball at nine **skittles** (= objects shaped like bottles) and try to knock over as many of them as possible □ *permainan 'skittles'*

skive /skaɪv/ *verb* [I] (*BrE informal*) **skive (off)** to not work when you should □ *mengelat; mencuri tulang*

skulk /skʌlk/ *verb* [I] to stay somewhere quietly and secretly, hoping that nobody will notice you, especially because you are planning to do sth bad □ *menghendap-hendap*: *He was skulking in the bushes.*

skull /skʌl/ *noun* [C] the bone structure of a human or animal head □ *tengkorak*: *She suffered a fractured skull in the fall.* ➲ picture at **body**

sky /skaɪ/ *noun* [C,U] (*pl* **skies**) the space that you can see when you look up from the earth, and where you can see the sun, moon and stars □ *langit*: *a cloudless sky* ◆ *a clear blue sky* ◆ *I saw a bit of blue sky between the clouds.* ◆ *I saw a plane high up in the sky.*

skydiving /'skaɪdaɪvɪŋ/ *noun* [U] a sport in which you jump from a plane and fall for as long as you safely can before opening your **parachute** (= a piece of thin cloth that opens and lets you fall to the ground slowly) □ *(sukan) terjun udara*: *to go skydiving* ▶ **skydiver** *noun* [C]

sky-'high *adj*, *adv* very high □ *tinggi melangit*

skylight /'skaɪlaɪt/ *noun* [C] a small window in a roof □ *jendela bumbung* ➲ picture on **page P8**

skyline /'skaɪlaɪn/ *noun* [C] the shape that is made by tall buildings, etc. against the sky □ *latar langit*: *the Manhattan skyline*

Skype™ /skaɪp/ *noun* [U] a telephone system that works by direct communication between users' computers on the Internet ▶ **skype** *verb* [I,T]: *When she was working in Turkey, Amy skyped her parents every week.*

skyscraper /'skaɪskreɪpə(r)/ *noun* [C] an extremely tall building □ *pencakar langit* ➲ picture on **page P11**

slab /slæb/ *noun* [C] a thick, flat piece of sth □ *kepingan tebal*: *huge concrete slabs*

slack /slæk/ *adj* (**slacker**; **slackest**) **1** loose; not tightly stretched □ *longgar; kendur*: *Leave the rope slack.* **2** (used about a period of business) not busy; not having many customers □ *tdk sibuk*: *Trade is very slack here in winter.* **3** not carefully or properly done □ *tdk teliti, rapi, ketat, dsb*: *Slack security made terrorist attacks possible.* **4** (used about a person) not doing sth carefully

slacken → slave

or properly □ *cuai; lalai*: *You've been rather slack about your homework lately.*

slacken /ˈslækən/ *verb* [I,T] **1** to become or make sth less tight □ *mengendur*: *The rope slackened and he pulled his hand free.* **2 slacken (sth) (off)** to become or make sth slower or less active □ *mula berkurang; memperlahan*: *He slackened off his pace towards the end of the race.*

slag¹ /slæg/ *noun* [U] the waste material that is left after metal has been removed from rock □ *sanga*

slag² /slæg/ *verb*
PHR V **slag sb off** (*slang*) to say cruel or critical things about sb □ *mengutuk sso*

ˈslag heap *noun* [C] a hill made of **slag** □ *timbunan sanga*

slain *past participle* of **slay**

slalom /ˈslɑːləm/ *noun* [C] (in sports such as skiing, canoeing, etc.) a race along a course on which you have to move from side to side between poles □ *slalom*

slam /slæm/ *verb* (**slamming**; **slammed**) **1** [I,T] to shut or make sth shut very loudly and with great force □ *menghempaskan; menutup (dgn kuat)*: *I heard the front door slam.* ♦ *She slammed her book shut and rushed out of the room.* **2** [T] to put sth somewhere very quickly and with great force □ *menghempaskan*: *He slammed the book down on the table and stormed out.* ➲ look at **grand slam**

slander /ˈslɑːndə(r)/ *noun* [C,U] a spoken statement about sb that is not true and that is intended to damage the good opinion that other people have of them; the legal offence of making this kind of statement □ *fitnah*; **slander** ▶**slander** *verb* [T] ▶**slanderous** /ˈslɑːndərəs/ *adj*

slang /slæŋ/ *noun* [U] very informal words and expressions that are more common in spoken than written language. Slang is sometimes used only by a particular group of people (for example students, young people or criminals) and often stays in fashion for a short time. Some slang is not polite □ *slanga*: *'Hop it!' is slang for 'Go away!'*

slant¹ /slɑːnt/ *verb* **1** [I] to be at an angle, not vertical or horizontal □ *condong; menyerong*: *My handwriting slants backwards.* ♦ *That picture isn't straight—it's slanting to the right.* **2** [T, usually passive] to describe information, events, etc. in a way that supports a particular group or opinion □ *mencondongkan; berat sebelah* ▶**slanting** *adj*: *She has beautiful slanting eyes.*

slant² /slɑːnt/ *noun* **1** [sing] a position at an angle, not horizontal or vertical □ *kecondongan; condong; senget*: *The sunlight fell on the table at a slant.* **2** [C] a way of thinking, writing, etc. about sth, that sees things from a particular point of view □ *sudut (pandangan)*

slap¹ /slæp/ *verb* [T] (**slapping**; **slapped**) **1** to hit sb/sth with the inside of your hand when it is flat □ *menampar; menepuk*: *She slapped her really hard across the face.* ♦ *People slapped him on the back and congratulated him on winning.* **2** to put sth onto a surface quickly and carelessly □ *menepek; menempelkan* ▶**slap** *noun* [C]: *I gave him a slap across the face.*

slap² /slæp/ (also ˌslap ˈbang) *adv* (*informal*) straight, and with great force □ *terus; tepat*: *I hurried round the corner and walked slap into someone coming the other way.*

slapdash /ˈslæpdæʃ/ *adj* careless, or done quickly and carelessly □ *semberono*: *slapdash building methods* ♦ *He's a bit slapdash about doing his homework on time.*

slapstick /ˈslæpstɪk/ *noun* [U] a type of humour that is based on simple physical jokes, for example people falling over or hitting each other □ *slapstik* ➲ note at **humour**

ˈslap-up *adj* (*BrE*) [only *before* a noun] (*informal*) (used about a meal) very large and very good □ *istimewa; spesial*

slash¹ /slæʃ/ *verb* [I,T] **slash (at) sb/sth** to make or try to make a long cut in sth with a violent movement □ *mengelar; menetak* **2** [T] (*informal*) to reduce an amount of money, etc. very much □ *memotong*: *The price of coffee has been slashed by 20%.*

slash² /slæʃ/ *noun* [C] **1** a sharp movement made with a knife, etc. in order to cut sb/sth □ *kelaran; tetakan; cantasan* **2** a long narrow wound or cut □ *luka panjang; kelar*: *a slash across his right cheek* **3** the symbol (/) used to show alternatives, as in *lunch and/or dinner*, and in Internet addresses to separate the different parts of the address □ *garis condong/miring* ➲ look at **forward slash, backslash**

slat /slæt/ *noun* [C] one of a series of long, narrow pieces of wood, metal or plastic, used in furniture, fences, etc. □ *bilah*

slate /sleɪt/ *noun* **1** [U] a type of dark grey rock that can easily be split into thin flat pieces □ *batu loh* **2** [C] one of the thin flat pieces of **slate** that are used for covering roofs □ *genting batu loh*

slaughter /ˈslɔːtə(r)/ *verb* [T] **1** to kill an animal, usually for food □ *menyembelih* **2** to kill a large number of people at one time, especially in a cruel way □ *membunuh beramai-ramai* ➲ note at **kill** ▶**slaughter** *noun* [U]

slaughterhouse /ˈslɔːtəhaʊs/ (*BrE also* abattoir) *noun* [C] a place where animals are killed for food □ *rumah sembelih*

slave¹ /sleɪv/ *noun* [C] (especially in past times) a person who was owned by another person and had to work for them □ *hamba abdi* ▶**slavery**

/ˈsleɪvəri/ noun [U]: *the abolition of slavery in America*

slave² /sleɪv/ verb [I] slave (away) to work very hard □ *bekerja bertungkus-lumus*

slay /sleɪ/ verb [T] (pt slew /sluː/; pp slain /sleɪn/) (*old-fashioned*) to kill sb/sth violently; to murder sb/sth □ *membunuh dgn kejam*

sleazy /ˈsliːzi/ adj (sleazier; sleaziest) (*informal*) (used about a place or a person) unpleasant and probably connected with criminal activities □ *kotor dan jelik*: *a sleazy nightclub*

sledge /sledʒ/ (also sled /sled/) noun [C] a vehicle without wheels that is used for travelling on snow. Large sledges are often pulled by dogs, and smaller ones are used for going down hills, for fun or as a sport □ *andur salji* ➪ look at bobsleigh, toboggan ➪ picture at sleigh
▶ sledge verb [I]

sleek /sliːk/ adj (sleeker; sleekest) 1 (used about hair or fur) smooth and shiny because it is healthy □ *licin berkilat* 2 (used about a vehicle) having an elegant, smooth shape □ *(berbentuk) anggun*: *a sleek new sports car*

sleep¹ /sliːp/ verb (pt, pp slept /slept/) 1 [I] to rest with your eyes closed and your mind and body not active □ *tidur*: *Did you sleep well?* ♦ *I only slept for a couple of hours last night.* ♦ *I slept solidly from 10 last night till 11 this morning.* ➪ note at **asleep, routine** 2 [T] (used about a place) to have enough beds for a particular number of people □ *memuatkan; menampung*: *an apartment that sleeps four people*
IDM live/sleep rough ➪ rough⁴
PHR V sleep in to sleep until later than usual in the morning because you do not have to get up □ *bangun lambat* ➪ look at **oversleep**
sleep together; sleep with sb to have sex with sb (usually when you are not married to or living with that person) □ *tidur dgn sso; berseketiduran*

TOPIC

Sleep

When we feel **tired** or **sleepy**, we usually **yawn** (= open our mouth wide and breathe in deeply). **Go to sleep** is the expression we use to mean 'start to sleep': *I was reading in bed last night, and I didn't go to sleep until about 1 o'clock.* Some people **snore** (= breathe noisily through their nose and mouth) when they are **asleep**. Most people **dream** (= see pictures in their mind). Frightening dreams are called **nightmares**. Some people **sleepwalk** (= get out of bed and move about while they are asleep). If you **wake up** later than you had planned to, you **oversleep**: *I'm sorry I'm late. I overslept.* Sometimes we don't have to **get up**, so we have a **lie-in** (= stay in bed longer than usual). A short sleep that you have in the day is called a **nap**.

---

sleep² /sliːp/ noun 1 [U] the natural condition of rest when your eyes are closed and your mind

803   **slave² → sleight of hand**

and body are not active or conscious □ *tidur*: *Most people need at least seven hours' sleep every night.* ♦ *I didn't get much sleep last night.* ♦ *Do you ever talk in your sleep?* ♦ *I couldn't get to sleep last night.* 2 [sing] a period of sleep □ *(jangka masa) tidur*: *You'll feel better after a good night's sleep.* ♦ *I sometimes have a short sleep in the afternoon.*
IDM go to sleep 1 to start sleeping □ *tidur*: *He got into bed and went to sleep.* 2 (used about an arm, a leg, etc.) to lose the sense of feeling in a part of your body □ *kebas*
put (an animal) to sleep to kill an animal that is ill or injured because you want to stop it suffering □ *membunuh binatang (kerana sakit atau cedera)*

sleeper /ˈsliːpə(r)/ noun [C] 1 [with an adjective] a person who sleeps in a particular way, for example if you are a **light sleeper** you wake up easily □ *jenis orang yg tidurnya (tidur-tidur ayam, tidur mati, dsb)*: *a light/heavy sleeper* 2 a bed on a train; a train with beds □ *tempat tidur dlm kereta api; kereta api yg ada tempat tidur*

'sleeping bag noun [C] a large soft bag that you use for sleeping in when you go camping, etc. □ *beg tidur*

'sleeping pill noun [C] a medicine in solid form that you swallow to help you sleep □ *pil tidur*: *to take a sleeping pill*

sleepless /ˈsliːpləs/ adj [only before a noun] (used about a period, usually the night) without sleep □ *tdk dpt tidur* ▶ sleeplessness noun [U] ➪ look at **insomnia**

sleepover /ˈsliːpəʊvə(r)/ (*AmE* also **'slumber party**) noun [C] a party for children or young people when a group of them spend the night at one house □ *pesta remaja*

sleepwalk /ˈsliːpwɔːk/ verb [I] to walk around while you are asleep □ *berjalan semasa tidur*

sleepy /ˈsliːpi/ adj (sleepier; sleepiest) 1 tired and ready to go to sleep □ *mengantuk*: *These pills might make you feel a bit sleepy.* 2 (used about a place) very quiet and not having much activity □ *sepi* ▶ sleepily adv: *She yawned sleepily.*

sleet /sliːt/ noun [U] a mixture of rain and snow □ *hujan beku* ➪ note at **weather**

sleeve /sliːv/ noun [C] 1 one of the two parts of a piece of clothing that cover the arms or part of the arms □ *lengan baju*: *a blouse with long sleeves* ➪ picture on page P1 2 -sleeved [in compounds] with sleeves of a particular kind □ *berlengan (pendek, dsb)*: *a short-sleeved shirt*

sleeveless /ˈsliːvləs/ adj without sleeves □ *tanpa lengan*: *a sleeveless sweater*

sleigh /sleɪ/ noun [C] a vehicle without wheels that is used for travelling on snow and that is usually pulled by horses □ *kereta luncur salji* ➪ look at **bobsleigh**

sleight of hand /ˌslaɪt əv ˈhænd/ noun [U] skilful movements of your hand that other

[C] **countable**, a noun with a plural form: *one book, two books*   [U] **uncountable**, a noun with no plural form: *some sugar*

people cannot see □ *gerakan tangan yg lincah*: *The trick is done simply by sleight of hand.*

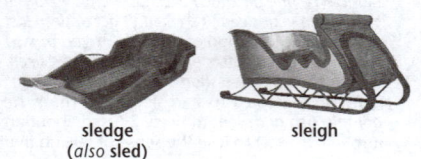

sledge
(*also* **sled**)

sleigh

slender /ˈslendə(r)/ *adj* (**slenderer**; **slenderest**) [You can also use **more slender** and **most slender**.] **1** (used about a person or part of sb's body) thin in an attractive way □ *langsing*: *long slender fingers* **2** smaller in amount or size than you would like □ *kecil*; *sedikit*: *My chances of winning are very slender.*

slept *past tense, past participle* of **sleep**[1]

slew *past tense* of **slay**

slice[1] /slaɪs/ *noun* [C] **1** a flat piece of food that is cut from a larger piece □ *keping*: *a thick/thin slice of bread* ♦ *Cut the meat into thin slices.* ⊃ picture at **cake 2** a part of sth □ *bahagian*: *The directors have taken a large slice of the profits.*

slice[2] /slaɪs/ *verb* **1** [T] to cut into thin flat pieces □ *menghiris*; *memotong*: *Peel and slice the apples.* ♦ *a loaf of sliced bread* **2** [I,T] to cut sth easily with sth sharp □ *memotong*: *He sliced through the rope with a knife.* ♦ *The glass sliced her hand.* **3** [T] (in ball sports) to hit the ball on the bottom or side so that it does not travel in a straight line □ *membuat pukulan cantas*

slick[1] /slɪk/ *adj* (**slicker**; **slickest**) **1** done smoothly and well, and seeming to be done without any effort □ *licin dan bagus* **2** clever at persuading people but perhaps not completely honest □ *licik*

slick[2] /slɪk/ = **oil slick**

slide[1] /slaɪd/ *verb* (*pt, pp* **slid** /slɪd/) **1** [I,T] to move or make sth move smoothly along a surface □ *menggelongsor*; *meluncur*; *tergelincir*: *She fell over and slid along the ice.* ♦ *The doors slide open automatically.* ♦ *You can slide the front seat forward* **2** [I,T] to move or make sth move quietly without being noticed □ *bergerak dgn senyap-senyap*: *I slid out of the room when nobody was looking.* ♦ *She slid her hand into her pocket and took out a sweet.* **3** [I] (used about prices, values, etc.) to go down slowly and continuously □ *merosot*; *menyusut*: *The Euro is sliding against the dollar.* **4** [I] to move gradually towards a worse situation □ *menjadi semakin teruk*: *The company slid into debt and eventually closed.*

slide[2] /slaɪd/ *noun* [C] **1** a continuous slow fall, for example of prices, values, levels, etc. □ *kemerosotan* **2** a large toy consisting of steps and a long piece of metal, plastic, etc. Children climb up the steps then slide down the other part. □ *gelongsor* ⊃ picture at **swing 3** one page of an electronic presentation that is usually viewed on a computer screen or projected onto a larger screen □ *paparan* **4** a small photograph on a piece of film in a frame that can be shown on a screen when you shine a light through it □ *slaid* ⊃ look at **transparency 5** a small piece of glass that you put sth on when you want to examine it under a **microscope** (= a piece of equipment that makes small objects look bigger) □ *slaid*; *sisip kaca* **6** = **hairslide**

'slide show (*also* **slideshow**) *noun* [C] **1** a number of **slides** (3) shown to an audience using a **slide projector**, often during a lecture □ *tayangan slaid* **2** a piece of software that shows a number of images on a computer screen in a particular order □ *pertunjukan slaid*: *a slide-show presentation*

slight /slaɪt/ *adj* (**slighter**; **slightest**) **1** very small; not important or serious □ *sedikit*: *I've got a slight problem, but it's nothing to be too worried about.* ♦ *a slight change/difference/increase/improvement* ♦ *I haven't the slightest idea* (= no idea at all) *what you're talking about.* **2** (used about sb's body) thin and light □ *kurus dan kecil*: *His slight frame is perfect for a long-distance runner.*
IDM **not in the slightest** not at all □ *sama sekali tdk*: *'Are you angry with me?' 'Not in the slightest.'*

slightly /ˈslaɪtli/ *adv* **1** a little □ *sedikit*; *agak*: *I'm slightly older than her.* **2** a **slightly built** person is small and thin □ *berbadan kecil dan kurus*

slim[1] /slɪm/ *adj* (**slimmer**; **slimmest**) **1** thin in an attractive way □ *langsing*: *a tall, slim woman* ⊃ note at **thin 2** not as big as you would like □ *tipis*: *Her chances of success are very slim.*

slim[2] /slɪm/ *verb* [I] (**slimming**; **slimmed**) to become or try to become thinner and lighter by eating less food, taking exercise, etc. □ *melangsingkan badan* ⊃ look at **diet**

slime /slaɪm/ *noun* [U] a thick unpleasant liquid □ *selut*; *lendir*: *The pond was covered with slime and had a horrible smell.* **SYN** **goo** ⊃ look at **sludge**

slimy /ˈslaɪmi/ *adj* (**slimier**; **slimiest**) **1** covered with **slime** □ *berselut*; *berlendir* **2** (*informal*) (used about a person) pretending to be friendly, in a way that you do not trust or like □ *bermuka-muka*

sling[1] /slɪŋ/ *verb* [T] (*pt, pp* **slung**) **1** to put or throw sth somewhere in a rough or careless way □ *menghumban*; *mencampakkan* **2** to put sth into a position where it hangs in a loose way □ *menyangkut*; *menyandang*

sling[2] /slɪŋ/ *noun* [C] a piece of cloth that you put under your arm and tie around your neck to support a broken arm, wrist, etc. □ *anduh* ⊃ picture at **plaster**

slingshot /ˈslɪŋʃɒt/ (*AmE*) = **catapult**[1]

slink /slɪŋk/ *verb* [I] (*pt, pp* **slunk**) to move somewhere slowly and quietly because you do not want anyone to see you, often when you feel guilty or embarrassed □ *bergerak takut-takut atau terhendap-hendap*

slip¹ /slɪp/ *verb* (**slipping**; **slipped**)
▶ SLIDE/FALL **1** [I] slip (over); slip (on sth) to slide accidentally and fall or nearly fall □ *tergelincir*: *She slipped over on the wet floor.* ♦ *His foot slipped on the top step and he fell down the stairs.*
▶ OUT OF POSITION **2** [I] to slide accidentally out of the correct position or out of your hand □ *melorot; terlucut; terlepas; teranjak*: *This hat's too big. It keeps slipping down over my eyes.* ♦ *The glass slipped out of my hand and smashed on the floor.*
▶ GO/PUT QUIETLY **3** [I] to move or go somewhere quietly, quickly, and often without being noticed □ *menyelinap*: *While everyone was dancing we slipped away and went home.* **4** [T] slip sth to sb/into sth; slip sb sth to put sth somewhere or give sth to sb quietly and often without being noticed □ *menyelitkan; memberi dgn senyap-senyap*: *She picked up the money and slipped it into her pocket.*
▶ CLOTHES **5** [I,T] slip into/out of sth; slip sth on/off to put on or take off a piece of clothing quickly and easily □ *menyarung; menanggalkan*: *I slipped off my shoes.*
▶ BECOME WORSE **6** [I] to fall a little in value, level, etc. □ *merosot*: *Sales have been slipping slightly over the last few months.*
IDM let sth slip to accidentally say sth that you should keep secret □ *terlepas cakap*
slip your mind to be forgotten □ *terlupa*: *I'm sorry, the meeting completely slipped my mind.*
PHR V slip out when sth slips out, you say it without really intending to □ *terlepas cakap*: *I'm sorry I said that. It just slipped out.*
slip up (*informal*) to make a mistake □ *membuat kesilapan*

slip² /slɪp/ *noun* [C] **1** a small mistake, usually made by being careless or not paying attention □ *kesilapan*: *to make a slip* **2** a small piece of paper □ *keratan penyata; slip* ➾ look at **payslip**: *I made a note of her name on a slip of paper.* **3** an act of sliding accidentally and falling or nearly falling □ *tergelincir* **4** a thin piece of clothing that is worn by a woman under a dress or skirt □ *kain dlm*
IDM give sb the slip (*informal*) to escape from sb who is following or trying to catch you □ *melepaskan diri (drpd orang yg mengekor atau mengejar)*
a slip of the tongue something that you say that you did not mean to say □ *tersilap sebut*

slipped disc *noun* [C] a painful injury caused when one of the **discs** (= flat things between the bones in your back) moves out of its correct position □ *cakera teranjak*

slipper /ˈslɪpə(r)/ *noun* [C] a light soft shoe that is worn inside the house □ *selipar*: *a pair of slippers* ➾ picture at **shoe**

slippery /ˈslɪpəri/ (also *informal* **slippy** /ˈslɪpi/) *adj* (used about a surface or an object) difficult to walk on or hold because it is smooth, wet, etc. □ *licin*: *a slippery floor*

slip road (*AmE* **ramp**) *noun* [C] a road that leads onto or off a large road such as a **motorway** □ *jalan susur*

slit¹ /slɪt/ *noun* [C] a long narrow cut or opening □ *belahan; belah*: *a long skirt with a slit up the back*

slit² /slɪt/ *verb* [T] (**slitting**; *pt, pp* **slit**) to make a long narrow cut in sth □ *mengelar; membuka (sampul surat, dll dgn pisau, dsb)*: *She slit the envelope open with a knife.*

slither /ˈslɪðə(r)/ *verb* [I] to move by sliding from side to side along the ground like a snake □ *menggelongsor*: *I saw a snake slithering down a rock.*

slob /slɒb/ *noun* [C] (*informal*) (used as an insult) a very lazy or untidy person □ *orang yg malas atau selekeh*

slog¹ /slɒɡ/ *verb* [I] (**slogging**; **slogged**) (*informal*) **1** slog (away) (at sth); slog (through sth) to work hard for a long period at sth difficult or boring □ *bertungkus-lumus*: *I've been slogging away at this homework for hours.* **2** slog down, up, along, etc. to walk or move in a certain direction with a lot of effort □ *berjalan atau bergerak dgn susah payah*

slog² /slɒɡ/ *noun* [sing] a period of long, hard, boring work or a long, tiring journey □ *tempoh membuat kerja yg teruk dan membosankan atau perjalanan yg jauh dan memenatkan*

slogan /ˈsləʊɡən/ *noun* [C] a short phrase that is easy to remember and that is used in politics or advertising □ *cogan kata; slogan*: *Anti-government slogans had been painted all over the walls.* ♦ *an advertising slogan*

slop /slɒp/ *verb* [I,T] (**slopping**; **slopped**) (used about a liquid) to pour over the edge of its container; to make a liquid do this □ *tumpah; tertumpah; melimpah*: *He filled his glass too full and beer slopped onto the table.*

slope /sləʊp/ *noun* **1** [C] a surface or piece of land that goes up or down □ *cerun; lereng*: *The village is built on a slope.* ♦ *a steep/gentle slope* ♦ *The best ski slopes are in the Alps.* ➾ picture on **page P10** **2** [sing] the amount that a surface is not level; the fact of not being level □ *kecerunan*: *The slope of the football pitch makes it quite difficult to play on.* ▶ **slope** *verb* [I]: *The road slopes down to the river.* ♦ *a sloping roof*

sloppy /ˈslɒpi/ *adj* (**sloppier**; **sloppiest**) **1** that shows a lack of care, thought or effort; untidy □ *cuai; cincai*: *a sloppy worker/writer/dresser* ♦ *a sloppy piece of work* **2** (used about clothes) not tight and without much shape □ *selekeh; serbah-serbih* **3** (*BrE informal*) showing emotions in a silly and embarrassing way □ *terlalu sentimental*: *I can't stand sloppy love songs.* ➾ A more formal word is **sentimental**.

slosh /slɒʃ/ *verb* (*informal*) **1** [I] (used about a liquid) to move around noisily inside a container □ *berkocak; mengocakkan* **2** [T] to pour or drop liquid somewhere in a careless way □ *menyimbah; mencurah*

sloshed /slɒʃt/ adj (slang) drunk □ *mabuk*

slot¹ /slɒt/ noun [C] **1** a straight narrow opening in a machine, etc. □ *slot; lubang selit*: Put your money into the slot and take the ticket. **2** a place in a list, a system, an organization, etc. □ *slot; tempat*: The single has occupied the Number One slot for the past two weeks.

slot² /slɒt/ verb [I,T] (**slotting; slotted**) to put sth into a particular space that is designed for it; to fit into such a space □ *memasukkan ke dlm slot/lubang selit*: He slotted a disc into the CD player. ◆ The disc slotted in easily.
IDM fall/slot into place ⊃ **place¹**

'slot machine noun [C] a machine with an opening for coins that sells drinks, cigarettes, etc., or on which you can play games □ *mesin slot*

slouch /slaʊtʃ/ verb [I] to sit, stand or walk in a lazy way, with your head and shoulders hanging down □ *membongkok*

slovenly /ˈslʌvnli/ adj (old-fashioned) lazy, careless and untidy □ *selekeh*

slow¹ /sləʊ/ adj (**slower; slowest**) adv
▶NOT FAST **1** moving, doing sth or happening without much speed; not fast □ *perlahan*: The traffic is always very slow in the city centre. ◆ Haven't you finished your homework yet? You're being very slow! ◆ Progress was slower than expected. ◆ a slow driver/walker/reader **OPP** fast

> **GRAMMAR** It is possible to use **slow** as an adverb, but **slowly** is much more common. However, **slow** is often used in compounds: *slow-moving traffic*. The comparative forms **slower** and **more slowly** are both common: *Could you drive a bit slower/more slowly, please?*

▶WITH DELAY **2** slow to do sth; slow (in/about) doing sth not doing sth immediately □ *lambat*: She was rather slow to realize what was going on. ◆ They've been rather slow in replying to my letter!
▶NOT CLEVER **3** not quick to learn or understand □ *lembap; tumpul*: He's the slowest student in the class.
▶NOT BUSY **4** not very busy; with little action □ *lembap*: Business is very slow at the moment.
▶WATCH/CLOCK **5** [not before a noun] showing a time that is earlier than the real time □ *lambat*: That clock is five minutes slow (= it says it is 8.55 when the correct time is 9.00). **OPP** fast
IDM quick/slow on the uptake ⊃ **uptake**
▶**slowness** noun [U]

slow² /sləʊ/ verb [I,T] to start to move, do sth or happen at a slower speed; to cause sth to do this □ *memperlahan*: He slowed his pace a little.
PHR V slow (sb/sth) down/up to start to move, do sth or happen at a slower speed; to cause sb/sth to do this □ *perlahankan; memperlahan*: Can't you slow down a bit? You're driving much too fast. ◆ These problems have slowed up the whole process.

slowly /ˈsləʊli/ adv at a slow speed; not quickly □ *dgn perlahan-lahan*: He walked slowly along the street.

,slow 'motion noun [U] (in a film or on TV) a method of making action appear much slower than in real life □ *gerak perlahan*: They showed the winning goal again, this time **in slow motion**.

sludge /slʌdʒ/ noun [U] thick, soft, wet mud or a substance that looks like it □ *selut; enapan* ⊃ look at **slime**

slug /slʌɡ/ noun [C] a small black or brown creature with a soft body and no legs, that moves slowly along the ground and eats garden plants □ *lintah bulan* ⊃ picture at **snail**

sluggish /ˈslʌɡɪʃ/ adj moving or working more slowly than normal in a way that seems lazy □ *lembap; bergerak perlahan-lahan*

slum /slʌm/ noun [C] an area of a city where living conditions are extremely bad, and where the buildings are dirty and have not been repaired for a long time □ *kawasan perumahan yg miskin*

slumber /ˈslʌmbə(r)/ noun [U,C] (formal) sleep; a time when sb is asleep □ *tidur*: She fell into a deep and peaceful slumber. ▶**slumber** verb [I]

'slumber party (AmE) = **sleepover**

slump¹ /slʌmp/ verb [I] **1** (used about economic activity, prices, etc.) to fall suddenly and by a large amount □ *merosot; jatuh*: Shares in BP slumped 33p to 181p yesterday. ◆ The newspaper's circulation has slumped by 30%. **SYN** drop **2** to fall or sit down suddenly when your body feels heavy and weak, usually because you are tired or ill □ *tersembam; merebahkan diri*

slump² /slʌmp/ noun [C] **1** a slump (in sth) a sudden large fall in sales, prices, the value of sth, etc □ *kejatuhan*: a slump in house prices **SYN** decline **2** a period when a country's economy is doing very badly and a lot of people do not have jobs □ *kemerosotan*: The car industry is in a slump. ⊃ look at **boom**

slung past tense, past participle of **sling¹**

slunk past tense, past participle of **slink**

slur¹ /slɜː(r)/ verb [T] (**slurring; slurred**) to pronounce words in a way that is not clear, often because you are drunk □ *menyebut perkataan dgn tdk jelas (selalunya kerana mabuk)*

slur² /slɜː(r)/ noun [C] a slur (on sb/sth) an unfair comment or an insult that could damage people's opinion of sb/sth □ *mencemarkan* **SYN** insult

slurp /slɜːp/ verb [I,T] (informal) to drink noisily □ *menghirup*

slush /slʌʃ/ noun [U] **1** snow that has been on the ground for a time and that is now a dirty mixture of ice and water □ *lecah salji* **2** (informal) films, books, feelings, etc. that are considered to be silly because they are too romantic and emotional □ *filem, buku, perasaan, dsb yg terlalu romantik atau sentimental* ▶**slushy** adj

sly /slaɪ/ *adj* **1** acting or done in a secret or dishonest way, often intending to trick people □ *licik* **SYN** **cunning** **2** suggesting that you know sth secret □ *bermakna; bermuslihat*: *a sly smile/look* ▶ **slyly** *adv*

smack /smæk/ *verb* [T] to hit sb with the inside of your hand when it is flat, especially as a punishment □ *menampar; menyepak*: *I never smack my children.* ⊃ note at **hit**
PHR V **smack of sth** to make you think that sb/sth has an unpleasant attitude or quality □ *bernada; berbau; membayangkan*
▶ **smack** *noun* [C]

small /smɔːl/ *adj* (**smaller**; **smallest**) **1** not large in size, number, amount, etc. □ *kecil*: *a small car/flat/town* ◆ *a small group of people* ◆ *a small amount of money* ◆ *That dress is too small for you.* **2** young □ *kecil*: *He has a wife and three small children.* ◆ *When I was small we lived in a big old house.* **3** not important or serious; slight □ *kecil; sedikit*: *Don't worry. It's only a small problem.*
IDM **in a big/small way** ⊃ **way¹**
▶ **small** *adv*: *She's painted the picture far too small.*

OTHER WORDS FOR

small

Small is the most usual opposite of **big** or **large**. **Little** is often used with another adjective to express an emotion, as well as the idea of smallness: *a horrible little man* ◆ *a lovely little girl* ◆ *a nice little house*. The comparative and superlative forms **smaller** and **smallest** are common, and small is often used with words like 'rather', 'quite' and 'very': *My flat is smaller than yours.* ◆ *The village is quite small.* ◆ *a very small car*. **Little** is not often used with these words and does not usually have a comparative or superlative form. **Tiny** and **minute** /maɪˈnjuːt/ both mean 'very small'.

'small ad (*BrE informal*) = **classified advertisement**

small 'change *noun* [U] coins that have a low value □ *duit syiling*

the 'small hours *noun* [pl] the early morning hours soon after midnight □ *dinihari*

smallpox /ˈsmɔːlpɒks/ *noun* [U] a serious infectious disease that causes a high temperature and leaves marks on the skin. In past times many people died from **smallpox**. □ *(penyakit) cacar*

the ,small 'print (*AmE* **the fine 'print**) *noun* [U] the important details of a legal document, contract, etc. that are usually printed in small type and are therefore easy to miss □ *butir-butir penting yg tdk ketara (kerana biasanya dicetak dgn tulisan kecil)*: *Make sure you read the small print before you sign anything.*

small-'scale *adj* (used about an organization or activity) not large; limited in what it does □ *kecil-kecilan*

'small talk *noun* [U] polite conversation, for example at a party, about unimportant things □ *omong kosong*: *We had to make small talk for half an hour.*

smart¹ /smɑːt/ *adj* (**smarter**; **smartest**) **1** (*especially BrE*) (used about a person) having a clean and tidy appearance □ *ranggi; segak dan kemas*: *You look smart. Are you going somewhere special?* **2** (*especially BrE*) (used about a piece of clothing, etc.) good enough to wear on a formal occasion □ *cantik; bergaya*: *a smart suit* **3** (*especially AmE*) clever; intelligent □ *pandai; bijak*: *He's not smart enough to be a politician.* ⊃ note at **intelligent 4** (*especially BrE*) fashionable and usually expensive □ *ada kelas; bergaya*: *a smart restaurant/hotel* **5** (used about a movement or action) quick and usually done with force □ *cepat dan kuat*: *We set off at a smart pace.* ▶ **smartly** *adv*: *She's always smartly dressed.*

smart² /smɑːt/ *verb* [I] **1** **smart (from sth)** to feel a stinging pain in your body □ *berasa pedih*: *Her cheek smarted from the blow.* **2** **smart (from/over sth)** to feel upset or offended because of a criticism, failure, etc. □ *terasa pedih*

'smart card *noun* [C] a small plastic card on which information can be stored in electronic form □ *kad pintar*

smarten /ˈsmɑːtn/ *verb*
PHR V **smarten (yourself/sb/sth) up** to make yourself/sb/sth look tidy and more attractive □ *memperkemas diri*

smartphone /ˈsmɑːtfəʊn/ *noun* [C] a mobile phone that also has some of the functions of a computer □ *telefon pintar*: *You can play games on your smartphone.*

TOPIC

Smartphones

You can use a smartphone to **access the Internet**, **browse web pages**, and **send and receive mail**. You can also **stream videos** and **music** (= view or listen via the Internet without buying or owning the files) to keep you entertained. There are **apps** (= special applications) that you can **download** that will make it possible to do more with your smartphone, such as play games, organize your **contacts** (= list of addresses, telephone numbers, etc. that belong to people you know), read books, etc. Don't forget to **charge the battery** using the **charger**, or your phone will **go dead** (= not work).

---

smash¹ /smæʃ/ *verb* **1** [I,T] to break sth, or to be broken violently and noisily into many pieces □ *pecah berkecai*: *The police had to smash the door open.* ◆ *The glass smashed into a thousand pieces.* **2** [I,T] **smash (sth) against, into, through, etc.** to move with great force in a particular direction; to hit sth very hard □ *merempuh; menghentam*: *The car smashed into a tree.* ◆ *He smashed his fist through the window.* **3** [T] **smash**

VOWELS iː see | i any | ɪ sit | e ten | æ hat | ɑː father | ɒ got | ɔː saw | ʊ put | uː too | u usual

smash → smooth 808

sth (up) to crash a vehicle, usually causing a lot of damage ▫ *berlanggar*: *I smashed up my father's car.* **4** [T] (in sports such as **tennis**) to hit a ball that is high in the air downwards very hard over the net ▫ *membuat smesy*

smash² /smæʃ/ *noun* **1** [sing] the action or the noise of sth breaking violently ▫ *perbuatan atau bunyi benda pecah berkecai*: *I heard the smash of breaking glass.* **2** [C] (in sports such as **tennis**) a way of hitting a ball that is high in the air downwards very hard over the net ▫ *smesy* **3** (also smash 'hit) [C] (*informal*) a song, play, film, etc. that is very successful ▫ *lagu, drama, filem, dsb yg amat berjaya*: *her latest chart smash*

smashing /'smæʃɪŋ/ *adj* (BrE old-fashioned informal) very good or enjoyable ▫ *hebat*: *We had a smashing time.*

smear¹ /smɪə(r)/ *verb* [T] smear sth on/over sth/sb; smear sth/sb with sth to spread a sticky substance across sth/sb ▫ *melumurkan; berlumur*: *Her face was smeared with blood.*

smear² /smɪə(r)/ *noun* [C] **1** a dirty mark made by spreading a substance across sth ▫ *palitan; bekas comot*: *a smear of oil* **2** something that is not true that is said or written about an important person and that is intended to damage people's opinion about them, especially in politics ▫ *sst yg memburuk-burukkan nama sso*: *He was the victim of a smear campaign.*

smell¹ /smel/ *verb* (*pt, pp* smelt /smelt/ or smelled /smeld/) **1** [I] smell (of sth) to have a particular smell ▫ *berbau*: *Dinner smells good!* ♦ *This perfume smells of roses.* ♦ *His breath smelt of whisky.* **2** [T] to notice or recognize sb/sth by using your nose ▫ *terbau; membaui*: *He could smell something burning.* ♦ *Can you smell gas?* ♦ *I could still smell her perfume in the room.*

> **HELP** Touch can be used in the continuous tenses, but the other verbs of the senses smell, taste, see and hear cannot. Instead we often use can: *I can smell smoke.*

3 [T] to put your nose near sth and breathe in so that you can discover or identify its smell ▫ *menghidu; mencium (bau)*: *I smelt the milk to see if it had gone off.* **4** [I] to have a bad smell ▫ *berbau (busuk)*: *Your feet smell.* **5** [I] to be able to smell ▫ *menghidu/mencium (bau)*: *I can't smell properly because I've got a cold.*

smell² /smel/ *noun* **1** [C] the impression that you get of sth by using your nose; the thing that you smell ▫ *bau*: *What's that smell?* ♦ *a sweet/musty/fresh/sickly smell* ♦ *a strong/faint smell of garlic* **2** [sing] an unpleasant smell ▫ *bau (busuk)*: *Ugh! What's that smell?* **3** [U] the ability to sense things with the nose ▫ *deria hidu*: *Dogs have a very good sense of smell.* **4** [C] the act of putting your nose near sth to smell it ▫ *(perbuatan) menghidu/mencium*: *Have a smell of this milk; is it all right?*

OTHER WORDS FOR

smell

Stink, stench, odour and pong (*slang*) are all words for unpleasant smells. Aroma, fragrance, perfume and scent refer to pleasant smells.

---

smelly /'smeli/ *adj* (smellier; smelliest) (*informal*) having a bad smell ▫ *berbau (busuk)*: *smelly feet*

smile¹ /smaɪl/ *verb* **1** [I] smile (at sb/sth) to make a smile appear on your face ▫ *senyum; tersenyum*: *to smile sweetly/faintly/broadly* ♦ *She smiled at the camera.* **2** [T] to say or express sth with a smile ▫ *menyatakan sst dgn senyuman*: *I smiled a greeting to them.*

smile² /smaɪl/ *noun* [C] an expression on your face in which the corners of your mouth turn up, showing happiness, pleasure, etc. ▫ *senyuman*: *to have a smile on your face* ♦ *'It's nice to see you,' he said with a smile.* ➲ look at beam, grin, smirk

smirk /smɜːk/ *noun* [C] an unpleasant smile which you have when you are pleased with yourself or think you are very clever ▫ *senyum sinis* ▸ smirk *verb* [I]

smog /smɒg/ (AmE also /) *noun* [U] dirty, poisonous air that can cover a whole city ▫ *asbut* ➲ note at fog

smoke¹ /sməʊk/ *noun* **1** [U] the grey, white or black gas that you can see in the air when sth is burning ▫ *asap*: *Thick smoke poured from the chimney.* ♦ *a room full of cigarette smoke* **2** [C, usually sing] an action of smoking a cigarette, etc. ▫ *(perbuatan) merokok*: *He went outside for a quick smoke.*

smoke² /sməʊk/ *verb* **1** [I,T] to breathe in smoke through a cigarette, etc. and let it out again; to use cigarettes, etc. in this way, as a habit ▫ *merokok*: *Do you mind if I smoke?* ♦ *I used to smoke 20 cigarettes a day.* **2** [I] to send out smoke ▫ *berasap*: *The oil in the pan started to smoke.* ▸ smoker *noun* [C]: *She's a chain smoker* (= she finishes one cigarette and then immediately lights another). **OPP** non-smoker ▸ smoking *noun* [U]: *My doctor has advised me to give up smoking.* ♦ *All our rooms are non-smoking.*

smoked /sməʊkt/ *adj* (used of certain types of food) given a special taste by being hung for a period of time in smoke from wood fires ▫ *salai*: *smoked salmon/ham/cheese*

smoky /'sməʊki/ *adj* (smokier; smokiest) **1** full of smoke; producing a lot of smoke ▫ *berasap*: *a smoky room/fire* **2** with the smell, taste or appearance of smoke ▫ *berbau, berasa atau spt asap*

smolder (AmE) = smoulder

smooth¹ /smuːð/ *adj* (smoother; smoothest) **1** having a completely flat surface with no lumps or holes or rough areas ▫ *licin; rata*: *smooth skin* ♦ *a smooth piece of wood* **OPP** rough **2** (used about a liquid mixture) without lumps ▫ *tdk*

ʌ cup   ɜː bird   ə ago   eɪ pay   əʊ go   aɪ my   aʊ now   ɔɪ boy   ɪə near   eə hair   ʊə pure

berbintil-bintil: *Stir the sauce until it is smooth.* **OPP** **lumpy** **3** without difficulties □ *licin; lancar*: *The transition from the old method to the new has been very smooth.* **4** (used about a journey in a car, etc.) with an even, comfortable movement □ *lancar*: *You get a very smooth ride in this car.* **OPP** **bumpy** **5** (used in a critical way, usually about a man) too pleasant or polite to be trusted □ *licin; licik*: *I don't like him. He's far too smooth.* **IDM** take the rough with the smooth ⊃ **rough²** ▶ **smoothness** *noun* [U]

smooth² /smuːð/ *verb* [T] **smooth sth (away, back, down, out, etc.)** to move your hands in the direction mentioned over a surface to make it smooth □ *dgn lancar*

smoothie /ˈsmuːði/ *noun* [C] a drink made of fruit or fruit juice, sometimes mixed with milk or ice cream □ *minuman yg dibuat drpd buah atau jus buah-buahan dan kadangkala dicampur susu atau aiskrim*

smoothly /ˈsmuːðli/ *adv* without any difficulty □ *meratakan; melicinkan*: *My work has been going quite smoothly.*

smother /ˈsmʌðə(r)/ *verb* [T] **1** **smother sb (with sth)** to kill sb by covering their face so that they cannot breathe □ *membunuh sso dgn menekap mukanya hingga lemas*: *She was smothered with a pillow.* **2** **smother sth/sb in/ with sth** to cover sth/sb with too much of sth □ *meliputi; mencurahkan (kasih sayang, dsb) banyak-banyak*: *The salad was smothered in oil.* **3** to stop a feeling, etc. from being expressed □ *menahan* **4** to stop sth burning by covering it □ *memadamkan*: *to smother the flames with a blanket*

smoulder (*AmE* **smolder**) /ˈsməʊldə(r)/ *verb* [I] to burn slowly without a flame □ *membara*: *The bonfire was still smouldering the next day.*

SMS /ˌes em ˈes/ *noun* [U] **short message service**; a system for sending short written messages from one mobile phone to another □ *sistem pesanan ringkas* **SYN** **text** ▶ **SMS** *verb* [I,T]

smudge /smʌdʒ/ *verb* **1** [I] to become untidy, without a clean line around it □ *menjadi comot*: *Her lipstick smudged when she kissed him.* **2** [T] to make sth dirty or untidy by touching it □ *mencomotkan*: *Leave your painting to dry or you'll smudge it.* ▶ **smudge** *noun* [C]

smug /smʌɡ/ *adj* too happy or satisfied with yourself □ *bangga diri*: *Don't look so smug.* ▶ **smugly** *adv*: *He smiled smugly as the results were announced.* ▶ **smugness** *noun* [U]

smuggle /ˈsmʌɡl/ *verb* [T] to take things into or out of a country secretly in a way that is not allowed by the law; to take a person or a thing secretly into or out of a place □ *menyeludup*: *The drugs had been smuggled through customs.* ▶ **smuggler** *noun* [C]: *a drug smuggler*

snack /snæk/ *noun* [C] food that you eat quickly between main meals □ *snek; makanan ringan*: *I had a snack on the train.* ⊃ note at **meal** ▶ **snack** *verb* [I] (*informal*) **snack (on sth)**

'snack bar *noun* [C] a place where you can buy a small quick meal, such as a **sandwich** (= two slices of bread with food between them) □ *snek bar*

snag¹ /snæɡ/ *noun* [C] a small difficulty or disadvantage that is often unexpected or hidden □ *masalah/halangan kecil*: *His offer is very generous—are you sure there isn't a snag?*

snag² /snæɡ/ *verb* [T] (**snagging**; **snagged**) to catch a piece of clothing, etc. on sth sharp and tear it □ *tersangkut lalu koyak*

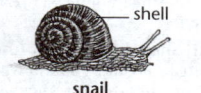

shell

snail   slug

snail /sneɪl/ *noun* [C] a type of animal with a soft body and no legs that is covered by a shell. **Snails** move very slowly. □ *siput*

'snail mail *noun* [U] (*informal*) used by people who use email to describe the system of sending letters by ordinary post □ *mel biasa*

snake¹ /sneɪk/ *noun* [C] a type of long thin animal with no legs that slides along the ground by moving its body from side to side □ *ular*: *a poisonous snake* ⊃ picture on **page P13**

snake² /sneɪk/ *verb* [I] (*written*) to move like a snake in long curves from side to side □ *membengkang-bengkok*

snap¹ /snæp/ *verb* (**snapping**; **snapped**)
▶ BREAK **1** [I,T] to break or be broken suddenly, usually with a sharp noise □ *patah (berderap); putus*: *The top has snapped off my pen.* ♦ *The branch snapped.* ♦ *He snapped a twig off a bush.*
▶ MOVE INTO POSITION **2** [I,T] to move or be moved into a particular position, especially with a sharp noise □ *berdetap; berderap*: *She snapped the bag shut and walked out.*
▶ SPEAK ANGRILY **3** [I,T] **snap (sth) (at sb)** to speak or say sth in a quick angry way □ *membentak*: *Why do you always snap at me?*
▶ OF ANIMAL **4** [I] to try to bite sb/sth □ *cuba menggigit*: *The dog snapped at the child's hand.*
▶ TAKE PHOTOGRAPH **5** [I,T] (*informal*) to take a quick photograph of sb/sth □ *menangkap gambar*: *A tourist snapped the plane as it crashed.*
▶ LOSE CONTROL **6** [I] to suddenly be unable to control your feelings any longer □ *tdk dpt mengawal perasaan*: *Suddenly something just snapped and I lost my temper with him.*
IDM **snap your fingers** to make a sharp noise by moving your middle finger quickly against your thumb, especially when you want to attract sb's attention □ *memetik jari*
PHR V **snap sth up** to buy or take sth quickly, especially because it is very cheap □ *berebut membeli atau mengambil sst*

snap² /snæp/ *noun* **1** [C] a sudden sharp sound of sth breaking □ *bunyi berderak; derakan; de-*

tapan **2** (*also* **snapshot** /'snæpʃɒt/) [C] a photograph that is taken quickly and in an informal way ▫ *gambar (foto)*: *I showed them some holiday snaps.* **3** [U] a card game where players call out 'Snap' when two cards that are the same are put down by different players ▫ *(permainan) snap* **4** [C] (*AmE*) = **press stud**

snap³ /snæp/ *adj* [only *before* a noun] (*informal*) done quickly and suddenly, often without any careful thought ▫ *kilat; cepat*: *a snap decision/ judgement*

snare /sneə(r)/ *noun* [C] a piece of equipment used to catch birds or small animals ▫ *jerat; perangkap* ▶ **snare** *verb* [T]

snarl /snɑːl/ *verb* [I] **snarl (sth) (at sb)** (used about an animal) to make an angry sound while showing its teeth ▫ *menderam dan menyeringai*: *The dog snarled at the stranger.* ▶ **snarl** *noun* [C, usually sing]

snatch¹ /snætʃ/ *verb* **1** [I,T] to take sth with a quick rough movement ▫ *merampas; merenggut; merentap*: *A boy snatched her handbag and ran off.*

> **MORE** Grab is similar in meaning.

2 [T] to take or get sth quickly using the only time or chance that you have ▫ *mencuri-curi masa utk membuat sst*: *I managed to snatch some sleep on the train.*

PHR V **snatch at sth** to try to take hold of sth suddenly ▫ *cuba menyambar/merampas sst*: *The man snatched at my wallet but I didn't let go of it.*

snatch² /snætʃ/ *noun* **1** [C, usually pl] a short part or period of sth ▫ *bahagian pendek; sedikit sahaja*: *I heard snatches of conversation from the next room.* **2** [sing] a sudden movement that sb makes when trying to take hold of sth ▫ *sambaran; rentapan; (perbuatan) merampas*

sneak¹ /sniːk/ *verb* **1** [I] **sneak into, out of, past, etc. sth**; **sneak in, out, away, etc.** to go very quietly in the direction mentioned, so that nobody can see or hear you ▫ *menyelinap*: *The prisoner sneaked past the guards.* ♦ *Instead of working, he sneaked out to play football.* **2** [T] (*informal*) to do or take sth secretly ▫ *mencuri-curi membuat sst*: *I tried to sneak a look at the test results in the teacher's bag.*

PHR V **sneak up (on sb/sth)** to go near sb very quietly, especially so that you can surprise them ▫ *menghampiri sso senyap-senyap*

sneak² /sniːk/ *noun* [C] (*informal*) (used in a critical way) a person, especially a child, who tells sb about the bad things sb else has done ▫ *orang yg suka mengadu; tukang repot*

sneaker /'sniːkə(r)/ (*AmE*) = **trainer**(1)

sneaking /'sniːkɪŋ/ *adj* [only *before* a noun] (used about feelings) not expressed; secret ▫ *(yg) terpendam; secara diam-diam*: *I've a sneaking suspicion that he's lying.*

sneer /snɪə(r)/ *verb* [I] **sneer (at sb/sth)** to show that you have no respect for sb/sth by the expression on your face or the way that you speak ▫ *mencemik; mencemuh*: *She sneered at his attempts to speak French.* ▶ **sneer** *noun* [C]

sneeze /sniːz/ *verb* [I] to make air come out of your nose suddenly and noisily in a way that you cannot control, for example because you have a cold ▫ *bersin*: *Dust makes me sneeze.* ⊃ picture at **cough** ▶ **sneeze** *noun* [C]

snide /snaɪd/ *adj* (*informal*) (used about an expression or a comment) critical in an unpleasant way ▫ *mencemuh*

sniff /snɪf/ *verb* **1** [I] to breathe air in through the nose in a way that makes a sound, especially because you have a cold or you are crying ▫ *menyenguk; menyedut nafas berbunyi (kerana selesema atau menangis)*: *Stop sniffing and blow your nose.* **2** [I,T] **sniff (at) sth** to smell sth by **sniffing** ▫ *menghidu*: *'I can smell gas,'* he said, sniffing the air. ♦ *The dog sniffed at the bone.* ▶ **sniff** *noun* [C]: *Have a sniff of this milk and tell me if it's still OK.*

sniffle /'snɪfl/ *verb* [I] to make noises by breathing air suddenly up your nose, especially because you have a cold or you are crying ▫ *menyenguk-nyenguk*

snigger /'snɪɡə(r)/ *verb* [I] **snigger (at sb/sth)** to laugh quietly and secretly in an unpleasant way ▫ *ketawa tertahan-tahan (kerana mengejek, dsb)* ▶ **snigger** *noun* [C]

snip¹ /snɪp/ *verb* [I,T] (**snipping**; **snipped**) **snip (sth) (off, out, in, etc.)** to cut using scissors, with a short quick action ▫ *menggunting; memotong*: *He sewed on the button and snipped off the ends of the cotton.* ♦ *to snip a hole in something*

snip² /snɪp/ *noun* **1** [C] a small cut made with scissors ▫ *guntingan*: *She made a row of small snips in the cloth.* **2** [sing] (*BrE informal*) something that is much cheaper than expected ▫ *harga murah*

sniper /'snaɪpə(r)/ *noun* [C] a person who shoots at sb from a hidden position ▫ *penembak hendap*

snippet /'snɪpɪt/ *noun* [C] a small piece of sth, especially information or news ▫ *cebisan*

snivel /'snɪvl/ *verb* [I] (**snivelling**; **snivelled**, (*AmE*) **sniveling**; **sniveled**) to keep crying quietly in a way that is annoying ▫ *teresak-esak*

snob /snɒb/ *noun* [C] a person who thinks they are better than people of a lower social class and who admires people who have a high social position ▫ *penyombong*: *He's such a snob—he looks down on all my friends.* ▶ **snobbish** *adj* ▶ **snobbishly** *adv* ▶ **snobbishness** *noun* [U]

snobbery /'snɒbəri/ *noun* [U] behaviour or attitudes typical of people who think they are better than other people in society, for example because they have more money, better education, etc. ▫ *kesombongan*: *To say that 'all pop music is rubbish' is just snobbery.*

snog /snɒg (AmE also) / verb [I,T] (snogging; snogged) (BrE informal) (used about a couple) to kiss each other for a long period of time □ *bercumbu-cumbuan* ▶ snog noun [sing]

snooker /'snu:kə(r)/ noun [U] a game in which two players try to hit a number of coloured balls into pockets at the edges of a large table using a **cue** (= a long thin stick) □ *snuker*: *to play snooker* ⊃ look at **billiards, pool**

snoop /snu:p/ verb [I] snoop (around); snoop (on sb) to look around secretly and without permission in order to find out information, etc. □ *mengintip*: *She suspected that her neighbours visited just to snoop on her.*

snooty /'snu:ti/ adj (snootier; snootiest) (informal) acting in a rude way because you think you are better than other people □ *sombong*

snooze /snu:z/ verb [I] (informal) to have a short sleep, especially during the day □ *tidur sekejap* ▶ snooze noun [C, usually sing]: *I had a bit of a snooze on the train.* ⊃ look at **nap**

snore /snɔ:(r)/ verb [I] to breathe noisily through your nose and mouth while you are asleep □ *berdengkur*: *She heard her father snoring in the next room.* ▶ snore noun [C]: *He has the loudest snore I've ever heard.*

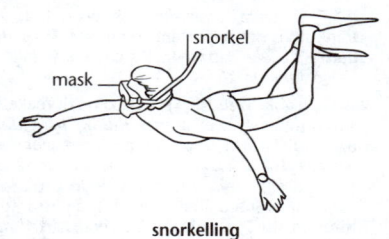

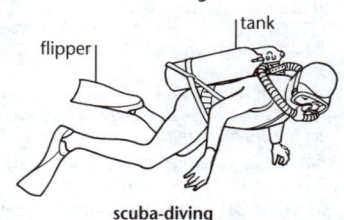

snorkel
mask

snorkelling

flipper
tank

scuba-diving

snorkel /'snɔ:kl/ noun [C] a short tube that a person swimming just below the surface of the water can use to breathe through □ *snorkel* ▶ snorkelling (AmE snorkeling) noun [U]: *to go snorkelling*

snort /snɔ:t/ verb [I] **1** (used about animals) to make a noise by blowing air through the nose and mouth □ *mendengus*: *The horse snorted in fear.* **2** (used about people) to blow out air noisily as a way of showing that you do not like sth, or that you are impatient □ *mendengus (kerana tdk suka atau tdk sabar)* ▶ snort noun [C]: *She gave a snort of disgust when I got the answer wrong.*

snot /snɒt/ noun [U] (informal) the liquid produced by the nose □ *hingus*

snout /snaʊt/ noun [C] the long nose of certain animals □ *muncung; jongor*: *a pig's snout* ⊃ picture at **badger**

snow¹ /snəʊ/ noun [U] small, soft, white pieces of frozen water that fall from the sky in cold weather □ *salji*: *Three inches of snow fell during the night.* ♦ *The snow melted before it could settle* (= stay on the ground). ⊃ note at **weather** ⊃ picture on **page P10**

snow² /snəʊ/ verb [I] (used about snow) to fall from the sky □ *salji turun*: *It snowed all night.*

snowball¹ /'snəʊbɔ:l/ noun [C] a lump of snow that is pressed into the shape of a ball and used by children for throwing □ *bola salji*

snowball² /'snəʊbɔ:l/ verb [I] to quickly grow bigger and bigger or more and more important □ *semakin besar, penting, dsb*

snowboard /'snəʊbɔ:d/ noun [C] a type of board that you fasten to both your feet and use for moving down mountains that are covered with snow □ *papan luncur salji* ▶ snowboarder noun [C] ▶ snowboarding noun [U]: *Have you ever been snowboarding?*

snowdrift /'snəʊdrɪft/ noun [C] a deep pile of snow that has been made by the wind □ *hanyutan salji*: *The car got stuck in a snowdrift.*

snowdrop /'snəʊdrɒp/ noun [C] a type of small white flower that appears at the end of winter □ *(bunga) snowdrop*

snowed in adj not able to leave home or travel because the snow is too deep □ *terkepung oleh salji*

snowed under adj with more work, etc. than you can deal with □ *kerja bertimbun*

snowfall /'snəʊfɔ:l/ noun **1** [C] the snow that falls on one occasion □ *curahan salji; salji yg turun*: *heavy snowfalls* **2** [U] the amount of snow that falls in a particular place □ *banyaknya salji yg turun*

snowflake /'snəʊfleɪk/ noun [C] one of the small, soft, white pieces of frozen water that fall together as snow □ *emping salji*

snowman /'snəʊmæn/ noun [C] (pl -men /-men/) the figure of a person made out of snow □ *orang-orang salji*

snowplough (AmE snowplow) /'snəʊplaʊ/ noun [C] a vehicle that is used to clear snow away from roads or railways □ *jentolak salji* ⊃ look at **plough**

snowstorm /'snəʊstɔ:m/ noun [C] a very heavy fall of snow, usually with a strong wind □ *ribut salji*

snowy /'snəʊi/ adj (snowier; snowiest) with a lot of snow □ *bersalji*: *snowy weather* ♦ *a snowy scene*

CONSONANTS   p **p**en   b **b**ad   t **t**ea   d **d**id   k **c**at   g **g**ot   tʃ **ch**in   dʒ **J**une   f **f**all   v **v**an   θ **th**in

Snr *abbr* (*especially AmE*) = **Senior**[1](2)

snub /snʌb/ *verb* [T] (**snubbing**; **snubbed**) to treat sb rudely, for example by refusing to look at or speak to them □ *tdk mempedulikan sso* ▶ **snub** *noun* [C]: *When they weren't invited to the party, they felt it was a snub.*

snuff /snʌf/ *noun* [U] **tobacco** (= the dried leaves used for making cigarettes) in the form of a powder which people breathe up into their noses □ *serbuk tembakau*

snuffle /'snʌfl/ *verb* [I] (used about people and animals) to make a noise through your nose □ *tersengguk-sengguk*: *The dog snuffled around the lamp post.*

snug /snʌg/ *adj* **1** warm and comfortable □ *selesa*: *a snug little room* ♦ *The children were snug in bed.* **2** fitting sb/sth closely □ *padan*: *Adjust the safety belt to give a snug fit.* ▶ **snugly** *adv*

snuggle /'snʌgl/ *verb* [I] **snuggle (up to sb)**; **snuggle (up/down)** to get into a position that makes you feel safe, warm and comfortable, usually next to another person □ *memeluk; mengerekot*: *She snuggled up to her mother.* ♦ *I snuggled down under the blanket to get warm.*

So. *abbr* (*AmE*) = **South**[1], **Southern**

so[1] /səʊ/ *adv* **1** used to emphasize an adjective or adverb, especially when this produces a particular result □ *begitu; sangat; betul-betul*: *She's so ill (that) she can't get out of bed.* ♦ *He was driving so fast that he couldn't stop.* ♦ *You've been so kind. How can I thank you?* ➔ note at **such 2** used in negative sentences for comparing people or things □ *begitu*: *She's not so clever as we thought.* **3** used in place of sth that has been said already, to avoid repeating it □ *begitu; begitulah*: *Are you coming by plane? If so,* (= if you are coming by plane) *I can meet you at the airport.* ♦ *'I failed, didn't I?' 'I'm afraid so.'* ♦ *'Did you lock the door?' 'I think so.'* ♦ *'Can you come out tonight?' 'I hope so.'*

> **HELP** In formal language, you can refer to actions that somebody has mentioned using **do** with **so**: *He asked me to write to him and **I did so** (= I wrote to him).*

4 [not with verbs in the negative; also; too] □ *begitu juga*: *He's a teacher and so is his wife.* ♦ *'I've been to New York.' 'So have I.'* ♦ *I like singing and so does Helen.*

> **HELP** In negative sentences we use **neither**: *I don't eat meat, and neither does Sarah.*

5 used to show that you agree that sth is true, especially when you are surprised □ *ya! ya tak ya*: *'It's getting late.' 'So it is. We'd better go.'* **6** (*formal*) (used when you are showing sb sth in this way; like this □ *spt ini*: *It was a black insect, about so big* (= using your hands to show the size). ♦ *Fold the paper in two diagonally, like so.*

IDM **and so on (and so forth)** used at the end of a list to show that it continues in the same way □ *dan seterusnya*: *They sell pens, pencils, paper and so on.*

I told you so ➔ **tell**

it (just) so happens (used to introduce a surprising fact) by chance □ *secara kebetulan*: *It just so happened that we were going the same way, so he gave me a lift.*

just so ➔ **just**[1]

or so (used to show that a number, time, etc. is not exact) approximately; about □ *lebih kurang*: *A hundred or so people came to the meeting.*

so as to do sth with the intention of doing sth; in order to do sth □ *supaya dpt membuat sst*

so much for used for saying that sth was not helpful or successful □ *sudahlah, tak guna punya...*: *So much for that diet! I didn't lose any weight at all.*

that is so (*formal*) that is true □ *itu benar*

so[2] /səʊ/ *conj* **1** **so (that)** with the purpose that; in order that □ *supaya; agar*: *She wore dark glasses so (that) nobody would recognize her.* **2** with the result that; therefore □ *oleh itu; jadi*: *She felt very tired, so she went to bed early.* ➔ note at **because, therefore 3** used to show how one part of a story follows another □ *jadi; habis*: *So what happened next?*

IDM **so what?** (*informal*) (showing that you think sth is not important) Who cares? □ *peduli apa?*: *'It's late.' 'So what? We don't have to go to school tomorrow.'*

soak /səʊk/ *verb* **1** [I,T] to become or make sb/sth completely wet □ *merendam; berendam; menjadi basah*: *Leave the dishes to soak for a while.* ♦ *The dog came out of the river and shook itself, soaking everyone.* **2** [I] **soak into/through sth**; **soak in** (used about a liquid) to pass into or through sth □ *meresap*: *Blood had soaked right through the bandage.*

PHR V **soak sth up** to take sth in (especially a liquid) □ *menyerap/mengelap sst*: *I soaked the water up with a cloth.*

soaked /səʊkt/ *adj* [not before a noun] extremely wet □ *basah kuyup*: *I got soaked waiting for my bus in the rain.*

soaking /'səʊkɪŋ/ (also ˌsoaking ˈwet) *adj* extremely wet □ *basah kuyup*

'so-and-so *noun* [C] (*pl* **so-and-sos**) (*informal*) **1** a person who is not named □ *si anu si anu*: *Imagine a Mrs So-and-so telephones. What would you say?* **2** a person that you do not like □ *si celaka, dsb itu*: *He's a bad-tempered old so-and-so.*

soap /səʊp/ *noun* **1** [U,C] a substance that you use for washing and cleaning □ *sabun*: *He washed his hands with soap.* ♦ *a bar of soap* ♦ *soap powder* (= for washing clothes) ➔ picture at **bar 2** [C] (*informal*) = **soap opera** ▶ **soapy** *adj*

'soap opera (also *informal* **soap** /səʊp/) *noun* [C] a story about the lives and problems of a group of people, which continues several times a week on TV or radio □ *drama lipur lara* ➔ look at **opera**

soar /sɔː(r)/ verb [I] **1** to rise very fast □ *naik melambung*: Prices are soaring because of inflation. **2** to fly high in the air □ *melayang tinggi*: an eagle soaring above us

sob /sɒb/ verb [I] (**sobbing**; **sobbed**) to cry when taking in sudden, sharp breaths; to speak while you are crying □ *menangis teresak-esak*: The child was sobbing because he'd lost his toy. ▶ **sob** noun [C]: It was heartbreaking to listen to her sobs.

sober¹ /ˈsəʊbə(r)/ adj **1** (used about a person) not affected by alcohol □ *tdk mabuk*: He'd been drunk the first time he'd met her, but this time he was **stone-cold sober**. **2** not funny; serious □ *serius*: a sober expression ♦ Her death is a sober reminder of just how dangerous drugs can be. ♦ Her death is a sober reminder of just how dangerous extreme sports can be. **3** (used about a colour) not bright or likely to be noticed □ *suram; tdk cerah*: a sober grey suit

sober² /ˈsəʊbə(r)/ verb
PHR V sober (sb) up to become or make sb become normal again after being affected by alcohol □ *menjadi atau membuat sso sedar drpd mabuk*: There's no point talking to him until he's sobered up.

sobering /ˈsəʊbərɪŋ/ adj making you feel serious □ *membuat sso berasa serius*: It is a sobering thought that over 25 million people have been killed in car accidents.

Soc. abbr = **Society**(2): the Amateur Dramatic Soc.

so-called adj **1** [only before a noun] used to show that the words you describe sb/sth with are not correct □ *yg kononnya*: She realized that her so-called friends only wanted her money. **2** used to show that a special name has been given to sb/sth □ *yg dinamakan/dipanggil*

soccer /ˈsɒkə(r)/ (especially AmE) = **football**(1)

sociable /ˈsəʊʃəbl/ adj enjoying being with other people; friendly □ *suka bergaul*

social /ˈsəʊʃl/ adj [only before a noun] **1** connected with society and the way it is organized □ *sosial; berkenaan dgn masyarakat*: social problems/issues/reforms **2** connected with the position of people in society □ *(kedudukan/taraf) sosial*: We share the same social background. **3** connected with meeting people and enjoying yourself □ *(aktiviti) sosial*: a social club ♦ She has a busy social life. ♦ Children have to develop their social skills when they start school. **4** (used about animals) living in groups □ *sosial; hidup berkumpulan*: Lions are social animals. ▶ **socially** /-ʃəli/ adv: We work together but I don't know him socially.

socialism /ˈsəʊʃəlɪzəm/ noun [U] the political idea that is based on the belief that everyone has an equal right to a share of a country's wealth and that the government should own and control the main industries □ *sosialisme* ⇒ look at **capitalism**, **communism**, **Marxism** ▶ **socialist** /-ɪst/ adj, noun [C]: socialist beliefs/policies/writers ♦ Tony was a socialist when he was younger.

socialize (also **-ise**) /ˈsəʊʃəlaɪz/ verb [I] **socialize (with sb)** to meet and spend time with people in a friendly way, in order to enjoy yourself □ *bergaul mesra*: I enjoy socializing with the other students. ⇒ look at **go out**

social networking noun [U] communication with people who share your interests using a website or other service on the Internet □ *rangkaian sosial*

TOPIC

Social networking

You can **access** social networking sites from your computer. First you need to **register**, then you can **create a personal profile** (= give details about yourself and your interests), and exchange messages with other **users**. If you are **on Facebook™**, you can **add** somebody **as a friend**, **post** photos and messages, **poke** somebody (= say hello) or **unfriend** somebody (= delete them from your list of contacts). Friends can post messages on your **wall** (= a space where you can share photos, messages, etc.) Your **status** tells people where you are and what you are doing. If you **like** a page on a website, you give positive feedback or make a connection with things you care about.

---

social science noun [C,U] the study of people in society □ *sains sosial*

social security (AmE **welfare**) noun [U] money paid regularly by the government to people who are poor, old, ill, or who have no job □ *bantuan kebajikan masyarakat*: to live on social security

social services noun [pl] a group of services organized by local government to help people who have money or family problems □ *perkhidmatan kebajikan masyarakat*

social work noun [U] work that involves giving help and advice to people with money or family problems □ *kerja sosial/kebajikan masyarakat* ▶ **social worker** noun [C]

society /səˈsaɪəti/ noun (pl **societies**) **1** [C,U] the people in a country or an area, thought of as a group, who have shared customs and laws □ *masyarakat*: a civilized society ♦ Society's attitude to women has changed considerably this century. ♦ The role of men **in society** is changing. **2** [C] (abbr **Soc.**) an organization of people who share a particular interest or purpose; a club □ *persatuan*: a drama society

sociologist /ˌsəʊsiˈɒlədʒɪst/ noun [C] a student of or an expert in **sociology** □ *pengkaji atau ahli sosiologi*

sociology /ˌsəʊsiˈɒlədʒi/ noun [U] the study of human societies and social behaviour □ *sosiologi* ▶ **sociological** /ˌsəʊsiəˈlɒdʒɪkl/ adj

sock /sɒk/ noun [C] a piece of clothing that you wear on your foot and lower leg, inside your shoe □ *stoking; sarung kaki*: *a pair of socks* **IDM** **pull your socks up** ➔ **pull¹**

socket /'sɒkɪt/ noun [C] **1** (also **power point**) (BrE) a place in a wall where a piece of electrical equipment can be connected to the electricity supply □ *soket* ➔ picture at **plug** **2** a hole in a piece of electrical equipment where another piece of equipment can be connected □ *soket* **3** a hole that sth fits into □ *rongga; lesung*: *your eye socket*

soda /'səʊdə/ noun **1** (also **soda water**) [U] water that has bubbles in it and is usually used for mixing with other drinks □ *soda (minuman)*: *a whisky and soda* **2** [C] (AmE) = **fizzy drink**

sodium /'səʊdiəm/ noun [U] (symbol Na) a chemical element that exists as a soft, silver-white metal and combines with other elements, for example to make salt □ *natrium*

sofa /'səʊfə/ noun [C] a comfortable seat with a back and arms for two or more people to sit on □ *sofa*: *a sofa bed* (= a sofa that you can open out to make a bed) **SYN** **settee** ➔ picture at **chair**

soft /sɒft/ adj (softer; softest)
▸ NOT HARD **1** not hard or firm □ *lembut; lembik*: *a soft bed/seat* ◆ *The ground is very soft after all that rain.* **OPP** **hard**
▸ NOT ROUGH **2** smooth and pleasant to touch □ *lembut*: *soft skin/hands* ◆ *a soft towel* **OPP** **rough**
▸ LIGHT/COLOURS **3** gentle and pleasant □ *lembut dan menarik*: *The room was decorated in soft pinks and greens.* **OPP** **bright**
▸ NOT LOUD **4** (used about sounds, voices, words, etc.) quiet or gentle; not angry □ *perlahan; lembut*: *She spoke in a soft whisper.* **OPP** **loud, harsh**
▸ NOT STRICT **5** (used about people) kind and gentle, sometimes too much so □ *lembut; baik hati*: *A good manager can't afford to be too soft.* **OPP** **hard, strict**
▸ DRUGS **6** less dangerous and serious than the type of illegal drugs which can kill people □ *kurang berbahaya*: *soft drugs such as marijuana* ➔ look at **hard drug**
IDM **have a soft spot for sb/sth** (informal) to have positive or loving feelings towards sb/sth □ *sayangkan sso/sst*
▸ **softly** adv: *He closed the door softly behind him.*
▸ **softness** noun [U]

softball /'sɒftbɔːl/ noun [U] a team game similar to baseball but played on a smaller field with a larger, softer ball □ *sofbol*

soft drink noun [C] a cold drink that contains no alcohol □ *minuman ringan* ➔ look at **alcoholic**

soften /'sɒfn/ verb **1** [I,T] to become softer or gentler; to make sb/sth softer or gentler □ *menjadi lembut; melembutkan*: *a lotion to soften the skin* **2** [T] to make sth less shocking and unpleasant □ *melembutkan; mengurangkan*: *Her letter sounded too angry so she softened the language.* ◆ *The airbag softened the impact of the crash.*

soft-hearted adj kind and good at understanding other people's feelings □ *lembut hati; baik hati* **OPP** **hard-hearted**

soft option noun [C] the easier thing to do of two or more possibilities, but not the best one □ *pilihan mudah*: *The government has taken the soft option of agreeing to their demands.*

soft-spoken (also **softly-spoken**) adj having a gentle, quiet voice □ *bersuara lembut*: *He was a kind, soft-spoken man.*

software /'sɒftweə(r)/ noun [U] the programs, etc. used to operate a computer □ *perisian*: *There's a lot of new educational software available now.* ◆ *to install/run a piece of software* ➔ look at **hardware**

soggy /'sɒgi/ adj (soggier; soggiest) very wet and soft and so unpleasant □ *basah dan lembik*

soil¹ /sɔɪl/ noun **1** [C,U] the substance that plants, trees, etc. grow in; earth □ *tanah*: *poor/dry/acid/sandy soil* ➔ note at **ground¹** **2** [U] (written) the land that is part of a country □ *tanah; bumi*: *to set foot on British soil* (= to arrive in Britain)

soil² /sɔɪl/ verb [T, often passive] (formal) to make sth dirty □ *mengotorkan*

solace /'sɒləs/ noun [U, sing] (formal) **solace (in sth)** a feeling of comfort when you are sad or disappointed; a person or thing that gives you this feeling □ *ketenangan ketika bersedih atau kecewa*: *to find/seek solace in somebody/something* **SYN** **comfort**

solar /'səʊlə(r)/ adj [only before a noun] **1** connected with the sun □ *(berkenaan dgn) matahari; suria*: *a solar eclipse* (= when the sun cannot be seen because the moon is passing in front of it) **2** using the sun's energy □ *suria*: *solar power* ➔ note at **environment**

the solar system noun [sing] the sun and the planets that move around it □ *sistem suria*

sold past tense, past participle of **sell**

soldier /'səʊldʒə(r)/ noun [C] a member of an army □ *askar*: *The soldiers marched past.*

sole¹ /səʊl/ adj [only before a noun] **1** only; single □ *satu-satunya; tunggal; hanyalah*: *His sole interest is football.* **2** belonging to one person only; not shared □ *satu-satunya; hanya*
▸ **solely** adv: *I agreed to come solely because of your mother.*

sole² /səʊl/ noun **1** [C] the bottom surface of your foot □ *tapak kaki* ➔ picture at **body, shoe** **2** [C] the part of a shoe or sock that covers the bottom surface of your foot □ *tapak kasut/stoking* **3** [C,U] (pl **sole**) a flat sea fish that we eat □ *ikan sisa Nabi*

solemn /'sɒləm/ adj **1** (used about a person) very serious; not happy or smiling □ *serius*: *Her solemn face told them that the news was bad.* **OPP** **cheerful** **2** sincere; done or said in a formal way □ *sungguh-sungguh; dgn penuh takzim*: *to make a solemn promise* **SYN** **serious** ▶**solemnity** /sə'lemnəti/ *noun* [U] ▶**solemnly** *adv*: *'I have something very important to tell you,'* she began solemnly.

solicit /sə'lɪsɪt/ *verb* **1** [T] (*formal*) to ask sb for money, help, support, etc. □ *meminta; mendapatkan*: *They tried to solicit support for the proposal.* **2** [I,T] (used about a person who has sex for money) to go to sb, especially in a public place, and offer sex in return for money □ *menawarkan seks*

solicitor /sə'lɪsɪtə(r)/ *noun* [C] (in Britain) a lawyer whose job is to give legal advice, prepare legal documents and arrange the buying and selling of land, etc. □ *peguam cara* ➲ note at **lawyer**

solid[1] /'sɒlɪd/ *adj*
▶NOT LIQUID/GAS **1** hard and firm; not in the form of liquid or gas □ *keras; pejal; pepejal*: *It was so cold that the village pond had frozen solid.*
▶WITHOUT HOLES **2** having no holes or empty spaces inside □ *padu; padat*: *a solid mass of rock*
▶STRONG **3** strong, firm and well made □ *tegap; teguh; kukuh*: *a solid little car* ♦ (*figurative*) *They built up a solid friendship over the years.*
▶STH YOU CAN TRUST **4** of good enough quality; that you can trust □ *kukuh; boleh dipercayai*: *The police cannot make an arrest without solid evidence.*
▶MATERIAL **5** [only *before* a noun] made completely of one substance, both on the inside and outside □ *padu*: *a solid gold chain*
▶PERIOD OF TIME **6** (*informal*) without a break or pause □ *terus-menerus; suntuk*: *I was so tired that I slept for twelve solid hours/twelve hours solid.* ▶**solidity** /sə'lɪdəti/ *noun* [U]

solid[2] /'sɒlɪd/ *noun* [C] **1** a substance or object that is hard; not a liquid or gas □ *pepejal*: *Liquids become solids when frozen.* ♦ *The baby is not yet on solids* (= solid food). **2** an object that has length, width and height, not a flat shape □ *bentuk padu*: *A cube is a solid.*

solidarity /ˌsɒlɪ'dærəti/ *noun* [U] **solidarity (with sb)** the support of one group of people for another, because they agree with their aims □ *perpaduan*: *Many local people expressed solidarity with the strikers.*

solidify /sə'lɪdɪfaɪ/ *verb* [I] (**solidifying**; **solidifies**; *pt*, *pp* **solidified**) to become hard or solid □ *membeku; menjadi keras/pepejal; mengeras; memejal*

solidly /'sɒlɪdli/ *adv* **1** strongly □ *dgn kukuh*: *a solidly built house* **2** without stopping □ *berterusan; tanpa henti-henti*: *It rained solidly all night.*

solitaire /ˌsɒlɪ'teə(r)/ *noun* [U] **1** (*BrE*) a game for one person in which you remove pieces from a special board by moving other pieces over them until you have only one piece left □ *permainan 'solitaire'* **2** (*AmE*) = **patience** (2)

solitary /'sɒlətri/ *adj* **1** done alone, without other people □ *bersendirian; seorang diri*: *Writ-*

815   **solicit → sombre**

ing novels is a solitary occupation. **2** (used about a person or an animal) enjoying being alone; often spending time alone □ *selalu bersendirian*: *She was always a solitary child.* **3** [only *before* a noun] alone; with no others around □ *seorang diri*: *a solitary figure walking up the hillside* **SYN** **lone** **4** [only *before* a noun] [usually in negative sentences or questions] only one; single □ *satu (apa pun)*: *I can't think of a solitary example* (= not even one).

ˌ**solitary con'finement** *noun* [U] a punishment in which a person in prison is kept completely alone in a separate cell away from the other prisoners □ *hukuman pengasingan diri dlm kurungan*

solitude /'sɒlɪtjuːd/ *noun* [U] the state of being alone, especially when you find this pleasant □ *(keadaan) bersendirian*: *She longed for peace and solitude.* ➲ look at **loneliness, isolation**

solo[1] /'səʊləʊ/ *adj* [only *before* a noun] *adv* **1** (done) alone; by yourself □ *seorang diri*: *a solo flight* ♦ *to fly solo* **2** connected with or played as a musical **solo** □ *solo*: *a solo artist* (= a singer who is not part of a group)

solo[2] /'səʊləʊ/ *noun* [C] (*pl* **solos**) a piece of music for only one person to play or sing □ *solo* ➲ look at **duet** ▶**soloist** /-ɪst/ *noun* [C]

solstice /'sɒlstɪs/ *noun* [C] the longest or the shortest day of the year □ *solstis*: *the summer/winter solstice*

soluble /'sɒljəbl/ *adj* **1 soluble (in sth)** that will dissolve in liquid □ *boleh larut*: *These tablets are soluble in water.* **2** (*formal*) (used about a problem, etc.) that has an answer; that can be solved □ *boleh diselesaikan* **OPP** for both meanings **insoluble**

solution /sə'luːʃn/ *noun* **1** [C] **a solution (to sth)** a way of solving a problem, dealing with a difficult situation, etc. □ *penyelesaian*: *a solution to the problem of unemployment* **2** [C] **the solution (to sth)** the answer (to a game, competition, etc.) □ *jawapan*: *The solution to the quiz will be published next week.* **3** [C,U] (a) liquid in which sth solid has been dissolved □ *larutan*: *saline solution*

solve /sɒlv/ *verb* [T] **1** to find a way of dealing with a problem or difficult situation □ *menyelesaikan*: *The government is trying to solve the problem of inflation.* **2** to find the correct answer or explanation for sth □ *mencari jawapan; menyelesaikan*: *to solve a puzzle/an equation/a riddle* ♦ *The police have not managed to solve the crime.* ♦ *to solve a mystery* ➲ *noun* **solution** ➲ *adjective* **soluble**

solvent /'sɒlvənt/ *noun* [C,U] a liquid that can dissolve another substance □ *pelarut*

sombre (*AmE* **somber**) /'sɒmbə(r)/ *adj* **1** dark in colour □ *suram; muram* **SYN** **dull** **2** sad and serious □ *muram; sayu*: *a sombre occasion* ▶**sombrely** *adv*

[C] **countable**, a noun with a plural form: *one book, two books*   [U] **uncountable**, a noun with no plural form: *some sugar*

some /səm; *strong form* sʌm/ *determiner, pron* **1** [before uncountable nouns and plural countable nouns] a certain amount of or a number of □ *sedikit; beberapa*: *We need some butter and some potatoes.* ♦ *I don't need any more money —I've still got some.*

HELP In negative sentences and in questions we use **any** instead of **some**: *Do we need any butter? I need some more money. I haven't got any.* Look at sense **2** for examples of questions where **some** is used.

2 used in questions when you expect or want the answer 'yes' □ *sedikit*: *Would you like some more cake?* ♦ *Can I take some of this paper?* **3** **some (of sb/sth)** used when you are referring to certain members of a group or certain types of a thing, but not all of them □ *sesetengah; sebahagian; ada antara*: *Some pupils enjoy this kind of work, some don't.* ♦ *Some of his books are very exciting.* ♦ *Some of us are going to the park.* **4** used with singular nouns for talking about a person or thing without saying any details □ *digunakan utk bercakap ttg sso atau sst tanpa memberikan butir-butirnya*: *I'll see you again some time, I expect.* ♦ *There must be some mistake.* ♦ *I read about it in some newspaper or other.*

somebody /'sʌmbədi/ (*also* someone) *pron* a person who is not known or not mentioned by name □ *sso; seorang; orang tertentu*: *How are you? Somebody said that you'd been ill.* ♦ *She's getting married to someone she met at work.* ♦ *There's somebody at the door.* ♦ *I think you should talk to someone else* (= another person) *about this problem.*

GRAMMAR Somebody, anybody and **everybody** are used with a singular verb but are often followed by a plural pronoun (except in formal language, where 'his/her' or 'him/ her' must be used): *Somebody has left their coat behind.* ♦ *Has anyone not brought their books?* ♦ *I'll see everybody concerned and tell them the news.*

The difference between **somebody** and **anybody** is the same as the difference between **some** and **any**.

some day (*also* someday) *adv* at a time in the future that is not yet known □ *suatu hari nanti*: *I hope you'll come and visit me some day.*

somehow /'sʌmhaʊ/ *adv* **1** in a way that is not known or certain □ *dgn sebarang cara*: *The car's broken down but I'll get to work somehow.* ♦ *Somehow we had got completely lost.* **2** for a reason you do not know or understand □ *entah kenapa*: *I somehow get the feeling that I've been here before.*

someone /'sʌmwʌn/ = somebody

someplace /'sʌmpleɪs/ (*AmE*) = somewhere

somersault /'sʌməsɔːlt/ *noun* [C] a movement in which you roll right over with your feet going over your head □ *balik kuang*

something /'sʌmθɪŋ/ *pron* **1** a thing that is not known or not named □ *sst*: *I've got something in my eye.* ♦ *Wait a minute—I've forgotten something.* ♦ *Would you like something else* (= another thing) *to drink?*

HELP The difference between **something** and **anything** is the same as the difference between **some** and **any**. Look at the note at **some**.

2 a thing that is important, useful or worth considering □ *sst (yg penting, bermakna, dsb)*: *There's something in what your mother says.* ♦ *I think you've got something there—I like that idea.* **3** (*informal*) used to show that a description, an amount, etc. is not exact □ *lebih kurang; lingkungan*: *a new comedy series aimed at thirty-somethings* (= people between 30 and 40 years old). ♦ *'What's his job?' 'I think he's a plumber, or something.'* ♦ *The cathedral took something like 200 years to build.* ♦ *A loganberry is something like a raspberry.* ♦ *The programme's something to do with* (= in some way about) *the environment.*

sometime (*also* some time) /'sʌmtaɪm/ *adv* at a time that you do not know exactly or have not yet decided □ *(suatu masa) nanti*: *I'll phone you sometime this evening.* ♦ *I must go and see her sometime.*

sometimes /'sʌmtaɪmz/ *adv* on some occasions; now and then □ *kadang-kadang*: *Sometimes I drive to work and sometimes I go by bus.* ♦ *I sometimes watch TV in the evenings.*

somewhat /'sʌmwɒt/ *adv* rather; to some degree □ *agak; sedikit sebanyak*: *We missed the train, which was somewhat unfortunate.*

somewhere /'sʌmweə(r)/ (*AmE also* someplace) *adv* at, in, or to a place that you do not know or do not mention by name □ *di suatu tempat*: *I've seen your glasses somewhere downstairs.* ♦ *'Have they gone to France?' 'No, I think they've gone somewhere else* (= to another place) *this year.'*

HELP The difference between **somewhere** and **anywhere** is the same as the difference between **some** and **any**. Look at the note at **some**.

IDM get somewhere/nowhere (with sb/sth) ⊃ get

somewhere along/down the line at some time; sooner or later □ *pd sst masa (cepat atau lambat)*

somewhere around used when you do not know an exact time, number, etc. □ *kira-kira; dlm lingkungan*: *Your ideal weight should probably be somewhere around 70 kilos.*

son /sʌn/ *noun* [C] a male child □ *anak lelaki* ⊃ look at **daughter**: *They have a son and two daughters.*

sonata /sə'nɑːtə/ *noun* [C] a piece of music written for the piano, or for another instrument together with the piano □ *sonata*

[I] **intransitive**, a verb which has no object: *He laughed.*   [T] **transitive**, a verb which has an object: *He ate an apple.*

song /sɒŋ/ noun **1** [C] a piece of music with words that you sing □ *lagu*: *a folk/love/pop song* ⊃ note at **pop 2** [U] songs in general; music for singing □ *lagu; nyanyian*: *to burst/break into song* (= to suddenly start singing) **3** [U,C] the musical sounds that birds make □ *bunyi burung*: *birdsong*

songwriter /ˈsɒŋraɪtə(r)/ noun [C] a person who writes songs □ *pencipta lagu*

sonic /ˈsɒnɪk/ adj (*technical*) connected with sound waves □ *(berkenaan dgn) gelombang bunyi; sonik*

son-in-law noun [C] (pl **sons-in-law**) the husband of your daughter □ *menantu lelaki*

sonnet /ˈsɒnɪt/ noun [C] a type of poem that has 14 lines that **rhyme** (= end with the same sound) in a fixed pattern □ *soneta*: *Shakespeare's sonnets*

soon /suːn/ adv **1** in a short time from now; a short time after sth else has happened □ *sebentar lagi; tdk lama lagi*: *It will soon be dark.* ◆ *He left soon after me.* ◆ *We should arrive at your house soon after twelve.* ◆ (*informal*) *See you soon.* **2** early; quickly □ *awal; cepat*: *Don't leave so soon. Stay for tea.* ◆ *How soon can you get here?*

IDM **as soon as** at the moment (that); when □ *sebaik sahaja; secepat (mungkin)*: *Phone me as soon as you hear some news.* ◆ *I'd like your reply as soon as possible* (= at the earliest possible moment).

no sooner ... than immediately when or after □ *sebaik sahaja*: *No sooner had I shut the door than I realized I'd left my keys inside.*

HELP Note the word order here. The verb follows immediately after 'No sooner', and the subject comes after that.

sooner or later at some time in the future; one day □ *lambat-laun*

the sooner the better very soon; as soon as possible □ *secepat mungkin*

soot /sʊt/ noun [U] black powder that is produced when wood, coal, etc. is burnt □ *jelaga*

soothe /suːð/ verb [T] **1** to make sb calmer or less upset □ *menenangkan* **SYN** **comfort 2** to make a part of the body or a feeling less painful □ *melegakan*: *The doctor gave me some skin cream to soothe the irritation.* ▶ **soothing** adj: *soothing music* ◆ *a soothing massage* ▶ **soothingly** adv

sophisticated /səˈfɪstɪkeɪtɪd/ adj **1** having or showing a lot of experience of the world and social situations; knowing about fashion, culture, etc. □ *canggih; sofistikated* **2** (used about machines, systems, etc.) advanced and complicated □ *canggih; rumit; kompleks* **3** able to understand difficult or complicated things □ *sofistikated; cerdik*: *Voters are much more sophisticated these days.* ▶ **sophistication** /səˌfɪstɪˈkeɪʃn/ noun [U]

817

song → sorry

soppy /ˈsɒpi/ adj (**soppier; soppiest**) (*informal*) full of unnecessary emotion; silly □ *terlalu sentimental*: *a soppy romantic film*

soprano /səˈprɑːnəʊ (AmE also) / noun [C] (pl **sopranos** /-nəʊz/) the highest singing voice; a woman, girl, or boy with this voice □ *soprano*

sordid /ˈsɔːdɪd/ adj **1** unpleasant; not honest or moral □ *keji; buruk*: *We discovered the truth about his sordid past.* **2** very dirty and unpleasant □ *menjijikkan; kotor*

sore¹ /sɔː(r)/ adj (used about a part of the body) painful and often red □ *sakit*: *to have a sore throat* ◆ *My feet were sore from walking so far.*

IDM **a sore point** a subject that is likely to make sb upset or angry when mentioned □ *perkara yg menyakitkan hati*

stand/stick out like a sore thumb to be extremely obvious, especially in a negative way □ *menonjol; terlalu ketara*: *A big new office block would stand out like a sore thumb in the old part of town.* ▶ **soreness** noun [U]: *a cream to reduce soreness and swelling*

sore² /sɔː(r)/ noun [C] a painful, often red place on your body where the skin is cut or infected □ *luka; kudis; tempat yg sakit*

sorely /ˈsɔːli/ adv (*formal*) very much; seriously □ *amat; sangat*: *You'll be sorely missed when you leave.*

sorrow /ˈsɒrəʊ (AmE also) / noun (*formal*) **1** [U] a feeling of great sadness because sth bad has happened □ *kesedihan; dukacita* **2** [C] a very sad event or situation □ *sst yg menyedihkan* ▶ **sorrowful** /-fl/ adj ▶ **sorrowfully** /-fəli/ adv

sorry¹ /ˈsɒri (AmE also) / adj (**sorrier; sorriest**) **1** [not before a noun] **sorry (to see, hear, etc.); sorry that ...** sad or disappointed □ *sedih; kecewa; kesal*: *I was sorry to hear that you've been ill.* ◆ *I am sorry that we have to leave so soon.* ◆ *'Simon's mother died last week.' 'Oh, I am sorry.'* **2** [not before a noun] **sorry (for/about sth); sorry (to do sth/that ...)** used for excusing yourself for sth that you have done □ *bermaksud meminta maaf*: *I'm awfully sorry for spilling that coffee.* ◆ *I'm sorry I've kept you all waiting.* ◆ *I'm sorry to disturb you so late in the evening, but I wonder if you can help me.* **3** [only before a noun] very bad □ *teruk*: *The house was in a sorry state when we first moved in.* ◆ *They were a sorry sight when they finally got home.*

IDM **be/feel sorry for sb** to feel sadness or pity for sb □ *berasa sedih atau kasihan terhadap sso*: *I feel very sorry for the families of the victims.* ◆ *Stop feeling sorry for yourself!*

I'm sorry used for politely saying 'no' to sth, disagreeing with sth or introducing bad news □ *bermaksud menolak, tdk bersetuju atau menyatakan rasa kesal*: *'Would you like to come to dinner on Friday?' 'I'm sorry, I'm busy that evening.'* ◆ *I'm sorry, I don't agree with you. I think we should accept the offer.* ◆ *I'm sorry to tell you that your application has been unsuccessful.*

sorry² /ˈsɒri/ (*AmE* also) / *exclam* **1** used for making excuses, apologizing, etc. □ *maaf*: *Sorry, I didn't see you standing behind me.* ♦ *Sorry I'm late—the bus didn't come on time.* ♦ *He didn't even* **say sorry** (= apologize). **2** (*especially BrE*) (used for asking sb to repeat sth that you have not heard correctly) □ *maaf (kerana tdk dengar)*: *'My name's Dave Harries.' 'Sorry? Dave who?'* **3** (used for correcting yourself when you have said sth wrong) □ *maaf (kerana salah cakap)*: *Take the second turning, sorry, the third turning on the right.*

sort¹ /sɔːt/ *noun* **1** [C] **a sort of sb/sth** a type or kind □ *jenis; macam*: *What sort of music do you like?* ♦ *She's got* **all sorts of** *problems at the moment.* ♦ *There were snacks—peanuts, olives,* **that sort of thing**. **2** [sing] (*especially BrE*) a particular type of character; a person □ *jenis (orangnya)*: *My brother would never cheat on his wife; he's not that sort.* **SYN** for both meanings **kind**
IDM **a sort of sth** (*informal*) a type of sth; something that is similar to sth □ *semacam*: *Can you hear a sort of ticking noise?*
sort of (*spoken*) rather; in a way □ *agak; lebih kurang; rasa macam*: *'Do you see what I mean?' 'Sort of.'* ♦ *I'd sort of like to go, but I'm not sure.*

sort² /sɔːt/ *verb* [T] **1 sort sth (into sth)** to put things into different groups or places, according to their type, etc.; to separate things of one type from others □ *mengisih; mengasing-asingkan*: *I'm just sorting these papers into the correct files.* ♦ *The computer will sort the words into alphabetical order.* **2** (often passive) (*especially BrE informal*) to find an answer to a problem or difficult situation; to organize sb/sth □ *menyelesaikan (masalah, dsb); mengaturkan*: *I'll have more time when I've* **got things sorted** *at home.*
PHR V **sort sth out 1** to tidy or organize sth □ *mengemaskan*: *The toy cupboard needs sorting out.* **2** to find an answer to a problem; to organize sth □ *menyelesaikan masalah; mengaturkan sst*: *I haven't found a flat yet but I hope to sort something out soon.*
sort through sth to look through a number of things, in order to find sth that you are looking for or to put them in order □ *memeriksa sebilangan benda utk mencari sst; menyusun sst*

so-so *adj, adv* (*informal*) all right but not particularly good/well □ *bolehlah tahan*: *'How are you feeling today?' 'So-so.'*

soufflé /ˈsuːfleɪ/ *noun* [C,U] a type of food made mainly from egg whites, flour and milk, beaten together and baked until it rises □ *'soufflé'*

sought *past tense, past participle* of **seek**

'sought after *adj* that people want very much, because it is of high quality or rare □ *yg diidam-idamkan*

soul /səʊl/ *noun*

▶ SPIRIT OF PERSON **1** [C] the spiritual part of a person that is believed to continue to exist after the body is dead □ *roh*: *Christians believe that your soul goes to heaven when you die.*
▶ INNER CHARACTER **2** [C] the inner part of a person containing their deepest thoughts and feelings □ *jiwa*: *There was a feeling of restlessness deep in her soul.* ⊃ look at **spirit**
▶ PERSON **3** [C] [used with adjectives] (*old-fashioned*) a particular type of person □ *orang yg*: *She's a kind old soul.* **4** [sing] [in negative sentences] a person □ *orang*: *There wasn't a soul in sight* (= there was nobody). ♦ *Promise me you won't tell a soul.*
▶ MUSIC **5** (also **'soul music**) [U] a type of music made popular by African American musicians □ *muzik soul*: *a soul singer*
IDM **heart and soul** ⊃ **heart**

soulful /ˈsəʊlfl/ *adj* having or showing deep feeling □ *penuh perasaan*: *a soulful expression*

soulless /ˈsəʊlləs/ *adj* without feeling, warmth or interest □ *tdk berperasaan; membosankan*: *They live in soulless concrete blocks.* **SYN** **depressing**

'soul music = **soul** (5)

sound¹ /saʊnd/ *noun* **1** [C,U] something that you hear or that can be heard □ *bunyi*: *the sound of voices* ♦ *a clicking/buzzing/scratching sound* ♦ *After that, he didn't* **make a sound**. ♦ *She opened the door without a sound.* ♦ *Light travels faster than sound.* ♦ *sound waves* **SYN** **noise** **2** [U] what you can hear coming from a TV, radio, etc. □ *bunyi*: *Can you turn the sound up/down* (= make it louder/quieter)?
IDM **by the sound of it/that/things** judging from what sb has said or what you have read about sb/sth □ *drpd apa yg didengar/diketahui*: *She must be an interesting person, by the sound of it.*
like the look/sound of sb/sth ⊃ **like²**

sound² /saʊnd/ *verb* **1** [I] [not usually used in the continuous tenses] to give a particular impression when heard or read about; to seem □ *berbunyi; bunyinya; kedengaran; nampaknya*: *That sounds like a child crying.* ♦ *He sounded upset and angry on the phone.* ♦ *You sound like your father when you say things like that!* ♦ *He sounds a very nice person from his letter.* ♦ *Does she sound like the right person for the job?* ♦ *It doesn't sound as if/though he's very reliable.*

> **HELP** In spoken English, people often use 'like' instead of 'as if' or 'as though', especially in American English. *It sounds like you had a great time.* This is considered incorrect in written British English.

2 -sounding [in compounds] seeming to be of the type mentioned, from what you have heard or read □ *berbunyi; kelihatan spt*: *a Spanish-sounding surname* ♦ *They had a very unromantic-sounding dinner at a fast food restaurant.* **3** [T] to cause sth to make a sound; to give a signal by making a sound □ *membunyikan*: *to* *sound the horn of your car* ♦ *A student on one of the upper floors sounded the alarm.*

PHR V **sound sb out (about sth)** to ask sb questions in order to find out what they think or intend to do □ *merisik-risik pendapat sso (ttg sst)*

sound³ /saʊnd/ *adj* (**sounder; soundest**) *adv* **1** sensible; that you can depend on and that will probably give good results □ *bijak; baik*: *sound advice* ♦ *a sound investment* **2** healthy and strong; in good condition □ *sihat; kukuh; teguh*: *The structure of the bridge is basically sound.* **OPP** for both meanings **unsound**

IDM **be sound asleep** to be deeply asleep □ *tidur nyenyak*

▶ **soundness** *noun* [U]

'**sound bite** *noun* [C] a short phrase or sentence taken from a longer speech, especially a speech made by a politician, that is particularly effective or appropriate □ *sedutan ucapan*

'**sound effect** *noun* [C, usually pl] a sound, for example the sound of the wind, that is made in an artificial way and used in a play, film or computer game to make it more realistic □ *kesan bunyi*

soundly /'saʊndli/ *adv* completely or deeply □ *betul-betul; dgn lena*: *The children were sleeping soundly.*

soundproof /'saʊndpruːf/ *adj* made so that no sound can get in or out □ *kalis bunyi*: *a soundproof room*

soundtrack /'saʊndtræk/ *noun* [C] the recorded sound and music from a film or computer game □ *runut bunyi* ⊃ note at **film** ⊃ look at **track**

ᵢ **soup** /suːp/ *noun* [U,C] liquid food made by cooking meat, vegetables, etc. in water □ *sup*: *a tin of chicken soup* ⊃ picture on page P16

ᵢ **sour** /'saʊə(r)/ *adj* **1** having a sharp taste like that of a lemon □ *masam*: *This sauce is quite sour.* ⊃ look at **bitter**, **sweet 2** (used especially about milk) tasting or smelling unpleasant because it is no longer fresh □ *masam; basi*: *This cream has gone sour.* **3** (used about people) angry and unpleasant □ *masam*: *a sour expression* ♦ *a sour-faced old woman*

IDM **go/turn sour** to stop being pleasant or friendly □ *menjadi buruk, dingin, dsb*: *Their relationship turned sour after a few months.*

sour grapes used to show that you think sb is jealous and is pretending that sth is not important □ *termengkelan*

▶ **sour** *verb* [T] (*formal*): *The disagreement over trade tariffs has soured relations between the two countries.* ▶ **sourly** *adv* ▶ **sourness** *noun* [U]

ᵢ **source** /sɔːs/ *noun* [C] a place, person or thing where sth comes or starts from or where sth is obtained □ *sumber*: *Tourism in Cornwall is an important source of income.* ♦ *The TV is a great source of entertainment.* ♦ *Police have refused to reveal the source of their information.* ♦ *He set out to discover the source of the river* ⊃ picture on page P10 ▶ **source** *verb* [T]

---

sound → southwards

ᵢ **south¹** /saʊθ/ *noun* [U, sing] (*abbr* S; So.) **1** (also **the south**) the direction that is on your right when you watch the sun rise; one of the **points of the compass** (= the main directions that we give names to) □ *selatan*: *warm winds from the south* ♦ *Which way is south?* ♦ *We live to the south of* (= further south than) *London.* ⊃ picture at **compass 2 the south; the South** the southern part of a country, a city, a region or the world □ *bahagian/kawasan selatan*: *Nice is in the South of France.* ⊃ look at **north, east, west**

ᵢ **south²** /saʊθ/ *adj, adv* **1** [only *before* a noun] in the south □ *(di) selatan*: *the south coast of Cornwall* **2** (used about a wind) coming from the south □ *(dr) selatan* **3** to or towards the south □ *(ke/ke arah) selatan*: *The house faces south.* ♦ *We live just south of Birmingham.*

southbound /'saʊθbaʊnd/ *adj* travelling or leading towards the south □ *menghala ke selatan*

ˌ**south-'east¹** (also **the ˌsouth-'east**) *noun* [sing] (*abbr* SE) the direction or a region that is an equal distance between south and east □ *(arah atau bahagian) tenggara* ⊃ picture at **compass**

ˌ**south-'east²** *adj, adv* in, from or to the **south-east** of a place or country □ *(di, dr atau ke) tenggara*: *the south-east coast of Spain*

ˌ**south-'easterly** *adj* **1** [only *before* a noun] towards the south-east □ *ke arah tenggara*: *in a south-easterly direction* **2** (used about a wind) coming from the south-east □ *(di, dr atau ke) tenggara*

ˌ**south-'eastern** *adj* (*abbr* SE) [only *before* a noun] connected with the south-east of a place or country □ *(berkaitan dgn bahagian) tenggara*: *the south-eastern states of the US*

ˌ**south-'eastwards** (also ˌsouth-'eastward) *adv* towards the south-east □ *ke arah tenggara*

southerly /'sʌðəli/ *adj* **1** [only *before* a noun] to, towards or in the south □ *(ke, ke arah atau di) selatan*: *Keep going in a southerly direction.* **2** (used about a wind) coming from the south □ *(dari) selatan*

ᵢ **southern** (also **Southern**) /'sʌðən/ *adj* (*abbr* S; So.) of, in or from the south of a place □ *(berkenaan dgn, di atau dr) selatan*: *a man with a southern accent* ♦ *Greece is in Southern Europe.*

southerner (also **Southerner**) /'sʌðənə(r)/ *noun* [C] a person who was born in or lives in the southern part of a country □ *orang selatan*

the ˌSouth 'Pole *noun* [sing] the point on the Earth's surface which is furthest south □ *Kutub Selatan* ⊃ picture at **earth**

southwards /'saʊθwədz/ (also **southward**) *adv* towards the south □ *ke arah selatan*: *We're flying southwards at the moment.* ▶ **southward** *adj*: *in a southward direction*

VOWELS iː: see i any ɪ sit e ten æ hat ɑː father ɒ got ɔː saw ʊ put uː too u usual

south-west → spacious

south-'west¹ (also **the South-West**) noun [sing] (abbr **SW**) the direction or a region that is an equal distance between south and west □ *(arah atau bahagian) barat daya* ⊃ picture at **compass**

south-'west² adj, adv in, from or to the south-west of a place or a country □ *(di, dr atau ke) barat daya*: *the south-west coast of France* ♦ *Our garden faces south-west.*

south-'westerly adj **1** [only before a noun] towards the south-west □ *ke arah barat daya*: *in a south-westerly direction* **2** (used about a wind) coming from the south-west □ *dr barat daya*

south-'western adj (abbr **SW**) [only before a noun] connected with the south-west of a place or country □ *(berkaitan dgn bahagian) barat daya*

south-'westwards (also **south-'westward**) adv towards the south-west □ *ke arah barat daya*: *Follow the B409 south-westwards for twenty miles.*

souvenir /ˌsuːvəˈnɪə(r) (AmE also) / noun [C] something that you buy or keep to remind you of somewhere you have been on holiday or of a special event □ *cenderamata*: *I brought back a menu as a souvenir of my trip.* **SYN** **memento**

sovereign¹ /ˈsɒvrɪn/ noun [C] a king or queen □ *raja; ratu*

sovereign² /ˈsɒvrɪn/ adj **1** [only before a noun] (used about a country) not controlled by any other country; independent □ *berdaulat* **2** having the highest possible authority □ *berdaulat; paling berkuasa*

sovereignty /ˈsɒvrənti/ noun [U] the power that a country has to control its own government □ *kedaulatan*

sow¹ /səʊ/ verb [T] (pt **sowed**; pp **sown** /səʊn/ or **sowed**) **sow A (in B); sow B (with A)** to plant seeds in the ground □ *menyemai*: *to sow seeds in pots* ♦ *to sow a field with wheat*

sow² /saʊ/ noun [C] an adult female pig □ *babi betina* ⊃ note at **pig**

soya bean /ˈsɔɪə biːn/ (AmE **soy bean**) noun [C] a type of **bean** (= a seed from a plant) that can be cooked and eaten or used to make many different types of food, for example flour, oil and a type of milk □ *kacang soya*

soy sauce /ˌsɔɪ ˈsɔːs/ (also **soya 'sauce**) noun [U] a dark brown sauce that is made from **soya beans** and that you add to food to make it taste better □ *kicap*

spa /spɑː/ noun [C] **1** a place where mineral water comes out of the ground and where people go to drink this water because it is considered to be healthy □ *spa; kolam air mineral* **2** a place where people can relax and improve their health □ *spa*: *a superb health spa which includes sauna, Turkish bath and fitness rooms*

space¹ /speɪs/ noun **1** [C,U] **space (for sb/sth) (to do sth)** a place or an area that is empty or not used □ *ruang; tempat*: *Is there enough space for me to park the car there?* ♦ *Shelves would take up less space than a cupboard.* ♦ *a parking space* ♦ *We're a bit short of space.* ♦ *There's a space here for you to write your name.* ♦ *Leave a space after the comma.* **SYN** **room** ⊃ note at **place¹** **2** [U] (also **outer 'space**) the area which surrounds the planet Earth and the other planets and stars □ *angkasa lepas*: *space travel* ♦ *a spaceman/spacewoman* (= a person who travels in space) **3** [C, usually sing] a period of time □ *tempoh; jangka masa*: *Priti had been ill three times in/within the space of four months.* ♦ *He's achieved a lot in a short space of time.* **4** [U] time and freedom to think and do what you want □ *masa*: *I need some space to think.*

TOPIC

Space

The **Earth** and other **planets** form the **solar system**. The Earth **orbits** (= goes round) the **sun**, and the **moon** orbits the Earth. Everything beyond the Earth's **atmosphere** is **outer space** and the Earth, the planets and the whole of space make up the **universe**. **Astronomers** study the sun, planets and stars; the subject is called **astronomy**. **Astronauts** travel into space in a **spaceship** or **space shuttle**. **Satellites** are **launched** (= sent) into space and are used to send back information, television pictures, etc.

Some people believe that there is life on other planets and that these **aliens** are trying to contact us. Some people who see **UFOs** (= unidentified flying objects) think that they may be alien **spaceships**.

space² /speɪs/ verb [T] **space sth (out)** to arrange things so that there are empty spaces between them □ *menjarakkan*

'space bar noun [C] a bar on the keyboard of a computer that you press to make spaces between words □ *palang penjarak* ⊃ picture at **computer**

spacecraft /ˈspeɪskrɑːft/ noun [C] (pl **spacecraft**) a vehicle that travels in space □ *kapal angkasa lepas; pesawat angkasa*

spaced 'out adj (informal) not completely conscious of what is happening around you, often because of taking drugs □ *mandam; tdk sedar sepenuhnya; berkhayal*

spaceship /ˈspeɪsʃɪp/ noun [C] a vehicle that travels in space, carrying people □ *kapal angkasa lepas*

'space shuttle noun [C] a vehicle that can travel into space and land like a plane when it returns to Earth □ *pesawat ulang-alik*

spacious /ˈspeɪʃəs/ adj having a lot of space; large in size □ *lapang; luas*: *a spacious flat* **SYN** **roomy** ▶ **spaciousness** noun [U]

spade /speɪd/ noun **1** [C] a tool that you use for digging □ *penyodok* ➲ look at **shovel** ➲ picture at **dig, garden 2 spades** [pl] in a pack of playing cards, the **suit** (= one of the four sets) with pointed black symbols on them □ *daun sped: the king of spades* ➲ note at **card** ➲ picture at **card 3** [C] one of the cards from this suit □ *daun sped: Have you got a spade?*

spaghetti /spəˈɡeti/ noun [U] a type of **pasta** (= Italian food made from flour and water) that looks like long strings □ *spageti: How long does spaghetti take to cook?* ➲ note at **pasta** ➲ picture on **page P16**

spam /spæm/ noun [U] advertising material sent by email to people who have not asked for it □ *spam; mel sampah* ➲ look at **junk mail**

span¹ /spæn/ noun [C] **1** the length of time that sth lasts or continues □ *tempoh; jangka: Young children have a short attention span.* **2** the length of sth from one end to the other □ *jarak; buka; depang; rentang: the wingspan of a bird*

span² /spæn/ verb [T] (**spanning; spanned**) **1** to form a bridge over sth □ *merentangi* **2** to last or continue for a particular period of time □ *menjangkau*

spank /spæŋk/ verb [T] to hit sb several times on their bottom with an open hand as a punishment □ *menampar; memukul*

spanner /ˈspænə(r)/ (*AmE* **wrench**) noun [C] a metal tool with an end shaped for turning **nuts** (= small metal rings) and **bolts** (= pins that are used for holding things together) □ *sepana* ➲ picture at **tool**

spare¹ /speə(r)/ adj **1** [only *before* a noun] not needed now but kept because it may be needed in the future □ *ganti: The spare tyre is kept in the boot.* ♦ *a spare room* **2** not being used; free □ *kosong: There were no seats spare so we had to stand.* **3** not used for work □ *luang; lapang: What do you do in your spare time?* ▶**spare** noun [C]: *The fuse has blown. Where do you keep your spares?*

spare² /speə(r)/ verb [T] **1** spare sth (for sb); spare (sb) sth to be able to give sth to sb □ *memberi; meluangkan: I suppose I can spare you a few minutes.* **2** spare sb (from) sth/doing sth to save sb from having an unpleasant experience □ *menyelamatkan; tdk payah membuat, menanggung, dsb sst: You could spare yourself waiting if you book in advance.* **3** spare sb/sth (from sth) to not hurt or damage sb/sth □ *tdk mencederakan, dsb sso/sst* **4** spare no effort, expense, etc. to do sth as well as possible without limiting the time, money, etc. involved □ *betul-betul; tanpa berkira: No expense was spared at the wedding.* ♦ *He spared no effort in trying to find a job.*

IDM to spare more than is needed □ *lebih: There's no time to spare. We must leave straight away.*

spare part noun [C] a part for a machine, an engine, etc. that you can use to replace an old part which is damaged or broken □ *alat/barang ganti*

sparing /ˈspeərɪŋ/ adj (*formal*) using only a little of sth; careful □ *berjimat* ▶**sparingly** adv

spark¹ /spɑːk/ noun **1** [C] a very small bright piece of burning material □ *bunga api: A spark set fire to the carpet.* **2** [C] a flash of light that is caused by electricity □ *percikan api: A spark ignites the fuel in a car engine.* **3** [C,U] an exciting quality that sb/sth has □ *sst yg menarik atau merangsangkan*

spark² /spɑːk/ verb [T] spark (sth) off to cause sth to start or develop □ *mencetuskan: Eric's comments sparked off a tremendous argument.*

sparkle /ˈspɑːkl/ verb [I] to shine with many small points of light □ *berkilau; bergemerlapan: The river sparkled in the sunlight.* ▶**sparkle** noun [C,U]

sparkler /ˈspɑːklə(r)/ noun [C] a type of small **firework** (= a small object that burns or explodes with coloured lights and loud sounds) that you hold in your hand and light. It burns with many bright **sparks**. □ *bunga api*

sparkling /ˈspɑːklɪŋ/ adj **1** shining with many small points of light □ *berkilau-kilau; bersinar-sinar: sparkling blue eyes* **2** (used about a drink) containing bubbles of gas □ *bergas: sparkling wine/mineral water* **SYN** **fizzy**

ˈspark plug noun [C] a small piece of equipment in an engine that produces a **spark** of electricity to make the fuel burn and start the engine □ *palam pencucuh*

sparrow /ˈspærəʊ/ noun [C] a small brown and grey bird that is common in many parts of the world □ *burung pipit*

sparse /spɑːs/ adj small in quantity or amount □ *jarang; tdk banyak/ramai: a sparse crowd* ♦ *He just had a few sparse hairs on his head.* ▶**sparsely** adv: *a sparsely populated area* ▶**sparseness** noun [U]

spartan /ˈspɑːtn/ adj (*formal*) very simple and not comfortable □ *terlalu sederhana dan tdk selesa: spartan living conditions*

spasm /ˈspæzəm/ noun [C,U] a sudden movement of a muscle that you cannot control □ *kekejangan otot: He had painful muscular spasms in his leg.*

spat past tense, past participle of **spit¹**

spate /speɪt/ noun [sing] a large number or amount of sth happening at one time □ *jumlah yg banyak: There has been a spate of burglaries in the area recently.*

spatial /ˈspeɪʃl/ adj (*formal*) connected with the size or position of sth □ *(berkenaan dgn) ruang*

spatter /ˈspætə(r)/ verb [T] spatter sb/sth (with sth); spatter sth (on sb/sth) to cover sb/sth with small drops of sth wet □ *memercikkan; terpercik*

spatula /'spætʃələ/ noun [C] a tool with a wide flat part, used in cooking for mixing and spreading things □ *sudip* ➔ picture at **kitchen**

speak /spi:k/ verb (pt **spoke** /spəʊk/; pp **spoken** /'spəʊkən/) 1 [I] **speak (to sb) (about sb/sth); speak (of sth)** to talk or say things □ *bercakap*: I'd like to speak to the manager, please. ♦ Could you speak more slowly? ♦ I was so angry I could hardly speak.

> **HELP** Speak or talk? Speak and talk have almost the same meaning but we use talk more informally, to show that two or more people are having a conversation, and speak to show that only one person is saying something, especially in a formal situation: *I'd like to speak to the manager, please.* ♦ *We talked all night.* ♦ *The head teacher spoke to the class about university courses.*

2 [I,T] [not used in the continuous tenses] to know and be able to use a language □ *bercakap; tahu berbahasa*: Does anyone here speak German? ♦ She speaks (in) Greek to her parents. ♦ a French-speaking guide 3 [I] **speak (on/about sth)** to make a speech to a group of people □ *berucap*: Professor Hurst has been invited to speak on American foreign policy.
IDM be on speaking terms (with sb) to be friendly with sb again after an argument □ *bertegur semula (dgn sso)*: Thankfully they are back on speaking terms again.
be speaking (to sb) (*informal*) to be friendly with sb again after an argument □ *bertegur semula*
so to speak used when you are describing sth in a way that sounds strange □ *lebih kurang begitulah*: She turned green, so to speak, after watching a TV programme about the environment.
speak for itself to be very clear so that no other explanation is needed □ *jelas dgn sendirinya*: The statistics speak for themselves.
speak/talk of the devil ➔ **devil**
speak your mind to say exactly what you think, even though you might offend sb □ *berterus terang*
strictly speaking ➔ **strictly**
PHR V speak for sb to express the thoughts or opinions of sb else □ *bercakap bagi pihak sso*
speak out (against sth) to say publicly that you think sth is bad or wrong □ *bersuara (menentang sst)*
speak up to speak louder □ *bercakap kuat sedikit*

speaker /'spi:kə(r)/ noun [C] 1 a person who makes a speech to a group of people □ *penceramah*: Tonight's speaker is a well-known writer and journalist. 2 a person who speaks a particular language □ *penutur*: She's a fluent Russian speaker. 3 (also **loudspeaker**) the part of a radio, computer or piece of musical equipment that the sound comes out of □ *pembesar suara*

spear /spɪə(r)/ noun [C] a long pole with a sharp point at one end, used for hunting or fighting □ *lembing* ➔ picture at **sword**

spearhead /'spɪəhed/ noun [C, usually sing] a person or group that begins or leads an attack □ *pasukan penggempur; peneraju tindakan, dsb* ▶ **spearhead** verb [T]

spearmint /'spɪəmɪnt/ noun [U] a type of leaf with a strong fresh taste that is used in sweets, etc. □ *permen*: spearmint chewing gum ➔ look at **peppermint**

special¹ /'speʃl/ adj 1 not usual or ordinary; important for some particular reason □ *istimewa*: a special occasion ♦ Please take special care of it. ♦ Are you doing anything special tonight? 2 [only before a noun] for a particular purpose □ *khas; khusus*: Andy goes to a special school for the deaf. ♦ There's a special tool for doing that.

special² /'speʃl/ noun [C] something that is not of the usual or ordinary type □ *rancangan khas; sst yg istimewa*: an all-night election special on TV ♦ I'm going to cook one of my specials tonight.

specialist /'speʃəlɪst/ noun [C] a person with special knowledge of a particular subject □ *pakar*: She's a specialist in diseases of cattle. ♦ I have to see a heart specialist. ♦ to give specialist advice

speciality /ˌspeʃi'æləti/ noun [C] (pl **specialities**) (*AmE* **specialty**, pl **specialties**) 1 something made by a person, place, business, etc. that is very good and that he/she/it is known for □ *keistimewaan*: The cheese is a speciality of the region. 2 an area of study or a subject that you know a lot about □ *bidang pengkhususan*

specialize (also **-ise**) /'speʃəlaɪz/ verb [I] **specialize (in sth)** to give most of your attention to one subject, type of product, etc. □ *mengkhusus*: This shop specializes in clothes for taller men. ▶ **specialization** (also **-isation**) /ˌspeʃəlaɪ'zeɪʃn/ noun [U]

specialized (also **-ised**) /'speʃəlaɪzd/ adj 1 to be used for a particular purpose □ *(yg) khusus*: a specialized system 2 having or needing special knowledge of a particular subject □ *(yg) pakar*: We have specialized staff to help you with any problems.

specially /'speʃəli/ (also **especially**) adv 1 for a particular purpose or reason □ *khas; istimewa*: I made this specially for you. 2 (*informal*) particularly; very; more than usual □ *begitu; sangat*: The restaurant has a great atmosphere but the food is not specially good. ♦ I hate homework. Specially history.

specialty /'speʃəlti/ (*AmE*) = **speciality**

species /'spi:ʃi:z/ noun [C] (pl **species**) a group of plants or animals that are all similar and that can breed together □ *spesies*: This conservation group aims to protect endangered species. ♦ a rare species of frog

specific /spə'sɪfɪk/ adj 1 **specific (about sth)** detailed or exact □ *khusus; tertentu; terperinci*: You must give the class specific instructions on what they have to do. ♦ Can you be more specific *about what the man was wearing?* **2** particular; not general □ *khusus; khas*: *Everyone has been given a specific job to do.* ▶ **specifically** /-kli/ *adv*: *a play written specifically for radio* ◆ *I specifically asked you to write in pencil, not pen.*

specification /ˌspesɪfɪˈkeɪʃn/ *noun* [C,U] detailed information about how sth is or should be built or made □ *spesifikasi; tentuan*

specify /ˈspesɪfaɪ/ *verb* [T] (**specifying**; **specifies**; *pt, pp* **specified**) to say or name sth clearly or in detail □ *menentukan; menetapkan*: *The fire regulations specify the maximum number of people allowed in.*

specimen /ˈspesɪmən/ *noun* [C] **1** a small amount of sth that is tested for medical or scientific purposes □ *spesimen*: *Specimens of the patient's blood were tested in the hospital laboratory.* **2** an example of a particular type of thing, especially sth intended to be studied by experts or scientists □ *spesimen; contoh* **SYN** for both meanings **sample**

speck /spek/ *noun* [C] a very small spot or mark □ *bintik; tompok*: *a speck of dust/dirt*

specs /speks/ (*informal*) = **glasses**

spectacle /ˈspektəkl/ *noun* [C] something that is impressive or shocking to look at □ *sst yg menakjubkan atau mengejutkan*

spectacles /ˈspektəklz/ (*formal*) = **glasses**

spectacular /spekˈtækjələ(r)/ *adj* very impressive to see □ *hebat; menakjubkan*: *The view from the top of the hill is quite spectacular.* ▶ **spectacularly** *adv*

spectator /spekˈteɪtə(r)/ *noun* [C] a person who is watching an event, especially a sports event □ *penonton*

spectre (*AmE* **specter**) /ˈspektə(r)/ *noun* [C] **1** something unpleasant that people are afraid might happen in the future □ *bayangan*: *the spectre of unemployment* **2** (*old-fashioned*) = **ghost**

spectrum /ˈspektrəm/ *noun* [C, usually sing] (*pl* **spectra** /ˈspektrə/) **1** the set of seven colours into which white light can be separated □ *spektrum*: *You can see the colours of the spectrum in a rainbow.* **2** all the possible varieties of sth □ *lingkungan; julat*: *The speakers represented the whole spectrum of political opinions.*

speculate /ˈspekjuleɪt/ *verb* **1** [I,T] **speculate (about/on sth)**; **speculate that …** to make a guess about sth □ *mengagak; meramal*: *to speculate about the result of the next election* **2** [I] to buy and sell with the aim of making money but with the risk of losing it □ *membuat spekulasi*: *to speculate on the stock market* ▶ **speculation** /ˌspekjuˈleɪʃn/ *noun* [U,C] ▶ **speculator** /ˈspekjuleɪtə(r)/ *noun* [C]

speculative /ˈspekjələtɪv/ *adj* **1** based on guessing or on opinions that have been formed without knowing all the facts □ *spekulatif* **2** (used in business) done in the hope of making money, but involving the risk of losing it □ *bersifat spekulasi*

specification → spell

sped *past tense, past participle* of **speed²**

speech /spiːtʃ/ *noun* **1** [C] a formal talk that you give to a group of people □ *ucapan*: *The Chancellor is going to make a speech to City businessmen.* **2** [U] the ability to speak □ *pertuturan*: *He lost the power of speech after the accident.* ◆ *freedom of speech* (= being allowed to express your opinions in an open way) **3** [U] the particular way of speaking of a person or group of people □ *gaya percakapan*: *She's doing a study of children's speech.* **4** [C] a group of words that one person must say in a play □ *dialog*: *This character has the longest speech in the play.*

speechless /ˈspiːtʃləs/ *adj* not able to speak, for example because you are shocked, angry, etc. □ *terdiam; bungkam*: *He was speechless with rage.*

speed¹ /spiːd/ *noun* **1** [U] fast movement □ *kelajuan; laju*: *She started the race slowly, but she gradually picked up speed.* ◆ *The bus was travelling at speed when it hit the wall.* **2** [C,U] the rate at which sb/sth moves or travels □ *kelajuan speed*: *The car was travelling at a speed of 140 kilometres an hour.* ◆ *to travel at top/high/full/maximum speed*

speed² /spiːd/ *verb* [I] (*pt, pp* **speeded** /ˈspiːdɪd/ *or* **sped** /sped/) **1** to go or move very quickly □ *memecut; bergerak laju*: *He sped round the corner on his bicycle.* **2** [only used in the continuous tenses] to drive a car, etc. faster than the legal speed limit □ *memandu melebihi had laju*: *The police said she had been speeding.*
PHR V **speed (sth) up** to go or make sth go faster □ *mempercepat (sst)*: *The new computer system should speed up production in the factory.*

speedboat /ˈspiːdbəʊt/ *noun* [C] a small fast boat with an engine □ *bot laju*

speeding /ˈspiːdɪŋ/ *noun* [U] driving a car, etc. faster than the legal speed limit □ *memandu melebihi had laju*

ˈ**speed limit** *noun* [C, usually sing] the highest speed that you are allowed to drive without breaking the law on a particular road □ *had laju*: *He was going way over the speed limit when the police stopped him.* ◆ *to break/exceed the speed limit* (= go faster than you are allowed to by law) ⊃ note at **driving**

speedometer /spiːˈdɒmɪtə(r)/ *noun* [C] a piece of equipment in a vehicle that tells you how fast you are travelling □ *meter laju* ⊃ picture at **car**

speedway /ˈspiːdweɪ/ *noun* [U] the sport of racing cars or motorbikes around a special track □ *lumba motosikal*

speedy /ˈspiːdi/ *adj* (**speedier**; **speediest**) fast; quick □ *cepat; pantas*: *a speedy response/reply* ▶ **speedily** *adv* ▶ **speediness** *noun* [U]

spell¹ /spel/ *verb* (*pt, pp* **spelled** /speld/ *or* **spelt** /spelt/) **1** [I,T] to write or say the letters of a word

spell → spin

in the correct order □ *mengeja*: *I could never spell very well at school.* ◆ *How do you spell your surname?* ◆ *His name is spelt P-H-I-L-I-P.* **2** [T] (used about a set of letters) to form a particular word □ *membentuk perkataan*: *If you add an 'e' to 'car' it spells 'care'.* **3** [T] to mean sth; to have sth as a result □ *bermakna; menandakan; mengakibatkan*: *Another poor harvest would spell disaster for the region.*

PHR V spell sth out **1** to express sth in a very clear and direct way □ *menyatakan dgn jelas*: *Although she didn't spell it out, it was obvious she wasn't happy.* **2** to write or say the letters of a word or name in the correct order □ *mengeja*: *I have an unusual name, so I always have to spell it out to people.*

spell² /spel/ *noun* [C] **1** a short period of time □ *tempoh; jangka waktu*: *a spell of cold weather* **2** (especially in stories) magic words that cause sb to be in a particular state or condition □ *jampi serapah; mantera*: *The witch put/cast a spell on the prince.*

spellchecker /'speltʃekə(r)/ (also **spellcheck**) *noun* [C] a computer program that checks your writing to see if your spelling is correct □ *penyemak ejaan*

spelling /'spelɪŋ/ *noun* **1** [U] the ability to write the letters of a word correctly □ *ejaan; (kebolehan) mengeja*: *Roger is very poor at spelling.* **2** [C,U] the way that letters are arranged to make a word □ *ejaan*: *'Center' is the American spelling of 'centre'.*

EXAM TIP

Spelling mistakes

Keep a list of all the words that you have got wrong more than once in your homework. Before the exam, go through your list and learn the correct spellings. Work with a friend and test each other.

---

spelt past tense, past participle of **spell¹**

spend /spend/ *verb* (*pt, pp* spent /spent/) **1** [I,T] spend (sth) (on sth) to give or pay money for sth □ *membelanjakan; berbelanja; membayar*: *You shouldn't go on spending like that.* ◆ *How much do you spend on food each week?* **2** [T] spend sth (on sth/doing sth) to pass time □ *menghabiskan (masa)*: *I spent a whole evening writing letters.* ◆ *I'm spending the weekend at my parents' house.* ◆ *He spent two years in Brno.* ◆ *I don't want to spend too much time on this project.*

spending /'spendɪŋ/ *noun* [U] the amount of money that is spent by a government or an organization □ *perbelanjaan*

spent past tense, past participle of **spend**

sperm /spɜːm/ *noun* **1** [C] (*pl* sperm *or* sperms) a cell that is produced in the sex organs of a male and that can join with a female egg to produce young □ *sperma* **2** [U] the liquid that contains sperms □ *mani* **SYN** semen

SPF /,es piː 'ef/ *abbr* sun protection factor; a number that tells you how much protection a particular cream or liquid gives you from the harmful effects of the sun □ *SPF (faktor perlindungan matahari)*

sphere /sfɪə(r)/ *noun* [C] **1** any round object shaped like a ball □ *sfera* ⊃ picture at **cube 2** an area of interest or activity □ *bidang* ▶ **spherical** /'sferɪkl/ *adj*

spice¹ /spaɪs/ *noun* **1** [C,U] a substance, especially a powder, that is made from a plant and used to give flavour to food □ *rempah*: *I use a lot of herbs and spices in my cooking.* ◆ *There isn't enough spice in the sauce.* ⊃ look at **herb** ⊃ picture on **page P14 2** [U] excitement and interest □ *keseronokan*: *to add spice to a situation* ▶ **spicy** *adj* (spicier; spiciest): *Do you like spicy food?*

spice² /spaɪs/ *verb* [T] spice sth (up) (with sth) **1** to add spice to food □ *membubuh rempah; merempahi*: *He always spices his cooking with lots of chilli powder.* **2** to add excitement to sth □ *menambah keseronokan; membumbui*

spider /'spaɪdə(r)/ *noun* [C] a small creature with eight thin legs □ *labah-labah*

spidergram /'spaɪdəɡræm/ = **mind map**

spike /spaɪk/ *noun* [C] a piece of metal, wood, etc. that has a sharp point at one end □ *pancang*

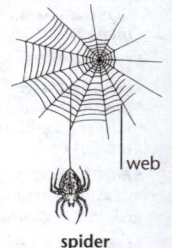

spill /spɪl/ *verb* (*pt, pp* spilt /spɪlt/ *or* spilled) **1** [I,T] (used especially about a liquid) to accidentally come out of a container; to make a liquid, etc. do this □ *tumpah; menumpahkan*: *Some water had spilled out of the bucket onto the floor.* ◆ *The bag split, and sugar spilled everywhere.* ◆ *I've spilt some coffee on the desk.* **2** [I] spill out, over, into, etc. to come out of a place suddenly and go in different directions □ *berpusu-pusu keluar*: *The train stopped and everyone spilled out.*

IDM spill the beans (*informal*) to tell a person about sth that should be a secret □ *membocorkan rahsia*

▶ **spill** *noun* [C]: *Many seabirds died as a result of the oil spill.*

spin¹ /spɪn/ *verb* (spinning; *pt, pp* spun /spʌn/) **1** [I,T] spin (sth) (round) to turn or to make sth turn round quickly □ *berputar; berpusing; memutarkan; memusingkan*: *Mary spun round when she heard someone call her name.* ◆ *to spin a ball/*

coin/wheel **2** [I,T] to make thread from a mass of wool, cotton, etc. □ *memintal*: *She spun and dyed the wool herself.* **3** [T] to remove water from clothes that have just been washed in a machine that turns them round and round very fast □ *memerah (kain dgn mesin)*

PHR V **spin sth out** to make sth last as long as possible □ *melanjutkan; menghematkan*

spin[2] /spɪn/ *noun* [C,U] **1** an act of making sth **spin**[1] (1) □ *putaran; pusingan*: *She put a lot of spin on the ball.* **2** (especially in politics) a way of talking publicly about a difficult situation, a mistake, etc. that makes it sound positive for you □ *cara memutarbelitkan (maklumat, dsb) supaya kelihatan lebih baik*

IDM **go/take sb for a spin** to go/take sb out in a car or other vehicle □ *pergi bersiar-siar (dgn kereta, dsb)*

spinach /ˈspɪnɪtʃ; -ɪdʒ/ *noun* [U] a plant with large dark green leaves that can be cooked and eaten as a vegetable □ *bayam* ⊃ picture on **page P15**

spinal /ˈspaɪnl/ *adj* connected with the **spine** (= the bones of your back) □ *(berkaitan dgn) tulang belakang*

ˈspin doctor *noun* [C] (especially in politics) a person who finds ways of talking about difficult situations, mistakes, etc. in a positive way □ *orang yg mengolah maklumat, dsb supaya sst keadaan, dll kelihatan lebih baik drpd sebenarnya*

ˌspin ˈdryer *noun* [C] (BrE) a machine that removes water from wet clothes by turning them round and round very fast □ *pengering putar* ⊃ look at **tumble dryer** ▶ **ˌspin-ˈdry** *verb* [T]

spine /spaɪn/ *noun* [C] **1** the row of small bones that are connected together down the middle of your back □ *tulang belakang* **SYN** **backbone** ⊃ picture at **body 2** one of the sharp points like needles on some plants and animals □ *duri*: *Porcupines use their spines to protect themselves.* ⊃ look at **prickle** ⊃ picture at **hedgehog 3** the narrow part of the cover of a book that you can see when it is on a shelf □ *tulang belakang*

spineless /ˈspaɪnləs/ *adj* weak and easily frightened □ *tdk bertulang belakang*

ˈspin-off *noun* [C] **a spin-off (from/of sth)** something unexpected and useful that develops from sth else □ *hasil sampingan*

spinster /ˈspɪnstə(r)/ *noun* [C] (old-fashioned) a woman, especially an older woman, who has never been married □ *wanita yg tdk berkahwin* ⊃ look at **bachelor**

MORE Nowadays **single** is the most usual word for describing a woman who is not married: *a single woman.*

spiral /ˈspaɪrəl/ *noun* [C] a long curved line that moves round and round away from a central point □ *pilin; lingkaran* ▶ **spiral** *adj*: *a spiral staircase* ▶ **spiral** *verb* [I] (spiralling; spiralled, (AmE) spiraling; spiraled): *The plane spiralled to the ground.*

spire /ˈspaɪə(r)/ *noun* [C] a tall pointed structure on the top of a building, especially a church □ *puncak menara*

spirit[1] /ˈspɪrɪt/ *noun*
▶ MIND/FEELINGS **1** [sing] the part of a person that is not physical; your thoughts and feelings, not your body □ *jiwa; semangat*: *the power of the human spirit to overcome difficulties* **2 spirits** [pl] the mood, attitude or state of mind of sb/sth □ *semangat; sikap*: *to be in high/low spirits* (= in a happy/sad mood)

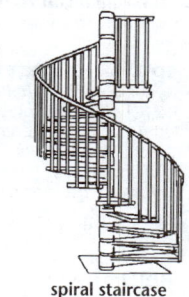

spiral staircase

▶ -SPIRITED **3** -spirited [in compounds] having the mood or attitude of mind mentioned □ *bersemangat*: *a group of high-spirited teenagers*

▶ DETERMINATION **4** [U] energy, strength of mind or determination □ *semangat; kecekalan; ketabahan*: *The group had plenty of team spirit.*

▶ QUALITY **5** [sing] the typical or most important quality of sth □ *semangat; suasana*: *the pioneer spirit* ♦ *The painting perfectly captures the spirit of the times.*

▶ SOUL **6** [C] a being without a body; the part of a person that many people believe still exists after their body is dead □ *roh*: *It was believed that people could be possessed by evil spirits.* ⊃ look at **ghost, soul**

▶ ALCOHOL **7 spirits** [pl] (especially BrE) strong alcoholic drinks □ *arak*: *She didn't drink whisky or brandy or any other spirits.*

spirit[2] /ˈspɪrɪt/ *verb*

PHR V **spirit sb/sth away/off** to take sb/sth away secretly □ *membawa sso/sst pergi dgn senyap-senyap*

spirited /ˈspɪrɪtɪd/ *adj* full of energy, determination and courage □ *bersemangat; lincah; giat*

spiritual /ˈspɪrɪtʃuəl/ *adj* **1** connected with deep thoughts, feelings or emotions rather than the body or physical things □ *rohaniah; batiniah*: *spiritual development/growth/needs* ⊃ look at **material 2** connected with religion □ *keagamaan*: *a spiritual leader* ▶ **spiritually** /-tʃuəli/ *adv*

spiritualism /ˈspɪrɪtʃuəlɪzəm/ *noun* [U] the belief that people who have died can send messages to living people, usually through a **medium** (= a person who has special powers) □ *spiritualisme; ilmu wasitah* ▶ **spiritualist** /-ɪst/ *noun* [C]

spit[1] /spɪt/ *verb* [I,T] (spitting; *pt*, *pp* **spat** /spæt/) **HELP** In American English the past tense and past participle can also be **spit**. **spit (sth) (out)**

spit → spoil

to force liquid, food, etc. out from your mouth □ *meludahkan (keluar); meluahkan*: He took one sip of the wine and spat it out. ◆ She spat in his face.

spit² /spɪt/ noun 1 [U] (*informal*) the liquid in your mouth □ *air liur/ludah* ⊃ look at **saliva** 2 [C] a long thin piece of land that sticks out into the sea, a lake, etc. □ *tetanjung* 3 [C] a long thin metal stick that you put through meat to hold it when you cook it over a fire □ *pencucuk; cucuk*: chicken roasted **on a spit**

spite /spaɪt/ noun [U] the desire to hurt or annoy sb □ *rasa busuk hati*: He stole her letters **out of spite**.
IDM in spite of used to show that sth happened although you did not expect it □ *walaupun; meskipun*: In spite of all her hard work, Sue failed her exam. ◆ I slept well in spite of the noise. ⊃ note at **despite**
▶ **spite** verb [T]

spiteful /ˈspaɪtfl/ adj behaving in a cruel or unkind way in order to hurt or upset sb □ *busuk hati*: He's been saying a lot of spiteful things about his ex-girlfriend. ▶ **spitefully** /-fəli/ adv

splash¹ /splæʃ/ verb [I,T] (used about a liquid) to fall or to make liquid fall noisily or fly in drops onto a person or thing □ *memercik; terpercik*: Rain splashed against the windows. ◆ The children were splashing each other with water. ◆ Be careful not to splash paint onto the floor.
PHR V splash out (on sth) (*BrE informal*) to spend money on sth that is expensive and that you do not really need □ *membelanjakan banyak wang (membeli sst)*

splash² /splæʃ/ noun [C] 1 the sound of liquid hitting sth or of sth hitting liquid □ *deburan*: Paul jumped into the pool with a big splash. 2 a small amount of liquid that falls onto sth □ *percikan; tompokan*: splashes of oil on the cooker ⊃ picture at **ripple** 3 a small bright area of colour □ *tompokan*: Flowers add **a splash of colour** to a room.

splatter /ˈsplætə(r)/ verb [I,T] (used about a liquid) to fly about in large drops and hit sb/sth noisily □ *merecik; memercik; bercucuran*: Heavy rain splattered on the roof. ◆ The paint was splattered all over the floor. ◆ The walls were splattered with blood.

splay /spleɪ/ verb [I,T] **splay (sth) (out)** (to cause sth) to spread out or become wide apart at one end □ *mengembangkan; mengepakkan*: splayed fingers

splendid /ˈsplendɪd/ adj (*old-fashioned*) 1 very good; excellent □ *sangat bagus*: What a splendid idea! **SYN** great 2 very impressive □ *hebat*: the splendid royal palace ▶ **splendidly** adv

splendour (*AmE* **splendor**) /ˈsplendə(r)/ noun [U] very impressive beauty □ *keindahan; kehebatan*

splint /splɪnt/ noun [C] a piece of wood or metal that is tied to a broken arm or leg to keep it in the right position □ *penganduh; splin*

splinter /ˈsplɪntə(r)/ noun [C] a small thin sharp piece of wood, metal or glass that has broken off a larger piece □ *selumbar; serpihan*: I've got a splinter in my finger. ▶ **splinter** verb [I,T]: The vase splintered into a thousand pieces.

split¹ /splɪt/ verb (**splitting**; pt, pp **split**) 1 [I,T] **split (sb) (up) (into sth)** to divide or to make a group of people divide into smaller groups □ *berpecah; membahagikan*: Let's split into two groups. ◆ A debate that has **split** the country **down the middle**. 2 [T] **split sth (between sb/sth); split sth (with sb)** to divide or share sth □ *membahagikan*: We split the cost of the meal between the six of us. 3 [I,T] **split (sth) (open)** to break or make sth break along a straight line □ *membelah; terkoyak*: My jeans have split.
IDM split the difference (used when discussing a price) to agree on an amount that is at an equal distance between the two amounts that have been suggested □ *membahagi dua beza antara harga (jumlah, dsb) yg diminta dgn harga (jumlah, dsb) yg ditawarkan*
split hairs (usually used in a critical way) to pay too much attention in an argument to details that are very small and not important □ *terlampau mengambil kira perkara-perkara yg remeh-temeh*
PHR V split up (with sb) to end a marriage or relationship □ *berpisah*: He's split up with his girlfriend.

split² /splɪt/ noun [C] 1 a disagreement that divides a group of people □ *perpecahan; pemisahan*: Disagreement about European policy led to a split within the Conservative party. 2 a long cut or hole in sth □ *rekahan; belahan*: There's a big split in the tent. 3 a division between two or more things □ *pembahagian*: He demanded a 50–50 split of the profits.

split ˈsecond noun [C] a very short period of time □ *sekelip mata*

splutter /ˈsplʌtə(r)/ verb 1 [I,T] to speak with difficulty, for example because you are very angry or embarrassed □ *tergagap-gagap (kerana marah atau malu)*: 'How dare you!' she spluttered indignantly. 2 [I] to make a series of sounds like a person coughing □ *tersedak-sedak* ▶ **splutter** noun [C]

spoil /spɔɪl/ verb [T] (pt, pp **spoilt** /spɔɪlt/ or **spoiled** /spɔɪld/) 1 to change sth good into sth bad, unpleasant, useless, etc.; to ruin sth □ *merosakkan*: The new office block will spoil the view. ◆ Our holiday was spoilt by bad weather. ◆ Eating between meals will spoil your appetite. 2 to do too much for sb, especially a child, so that you have a bad effect on their character □ *memanjakan; memberi muka*: a spoilt child 3 **spoil sb/yourself** to do sth special or nice to make sb/yourself happy □ *memanjakan*: Why not spoil yourself with one of our new range of beauty products? (= in an advertisement)

spoils /spɔɪlz/ noun [pl] (formal) things that have been stolen by thieves, or taken in a war or battle □ *barang curian; (harta) rampasan*: *the spoils of war*

spoilsport /ˈspɔɪlspɔːt/ noun [C] (informal) a person who tries to stop other people enjoying themselves, for example by not taking part in an activity □ *orang yg cuba merosakkan sst rancangan (kerana tdk mahu menyertainya, dsb)*

spoilt past tense, past participle of **spoil**

spoke¹ /spəʊk/ noun [C] one of the thin pieces of metal that connect the centre of a wheel to the outside edge □ *ruji; jejari; lidi basikal* ⊃ picture at **bicycle**

spoke² past tense of **speak**

spoken¹ /ˈspəʊkən/ adj involving speaking rather than writing; expressed in speech rather than in writing □ *lisan*: *spoken English* ⊃ look at **written**

spoken² past participle of **speak**

spokesman /ˈspəʊksmən/, **spokeswoman** /ˈspəʊkswʊmən/, **spokesperson** /ˈspəʊkspɜːsn/ noun [C] (pl -men /-mən/, -women /-wɪmɪn/, -persons or -people /-piːpl/) a person who is chosen to speak for a group or an organization □ *jurucakap*

> **MORE** Spokesperson is now often preferred to 'spokesman' or 'spokeswoman' because it can be used for a man or a woman.

sponge¹ /spʌndʒ/ noun [C,U] **1** a piece of artificial or natural material that is soft and light and full of holes and can hold water easily, used for washing yourself or cleaning sth □ *span* ⊃ picture at **bucket 2** = **sponge cake**

sponge² /spʌndʒ/ verb [T] to remove or clean sth with a wet **sponge¹**(1) or cloth □ *mengelap*
PHR V **sponge off sb** (informal) to get money, food, etc. from sb without paying or doing anything in return □ *menebeng; menenggek*

ˈsponge bag (BrE **ˈtoilet bag**; AmE **ˈtoiletry bag**) noun [C] a small bag that you use when travelling to carry the things you need to wash with, clean your teeth with, etc. □ *beg mandian*

ˈsponge cake (also **sponge**) noun [C,U] a light cake made from eggs, flour and sugar, with or without fat □ *kek span*

sponsor /ˈspɒnsə(r)/ noun [C] **1** a person or an organization that helps to pay for a special sports event, etc. (usually so that it can advertise its products) □ *penaja* ⊃ look at **patron 2** a person who agrees to pay money to a charity if sb else completes a particular activity □ *penaja* ▸**sponsor** verb [T]: *a sponsored walk to raise money for children in need* ▸**sponsorship** noun [U]: *Many theatres depend on industry for sponsorship.*

spontaneous /spɒnˈteɪniəs/ adj done or happening suddenly; not planned □ *spontan*: *a spontaneous burst of applause* ▸**spontaneously** adv ▸**spontaneity** /ˌspɒntəˈneɪəti/ noun [U]

spoof /spuːf/ noun [C] (informal) an amusing copy of a film, TV programme, etc. that exaggerates its main characteristics □ *olok-olokan; ajukan kelakar*: *It's a spoof on horror movies.*

spooky /ˈspuːki/ adj (**spookier; spookiest**) (informal) strange and frightening □ *menakutkan*: *It's spooky being in the house alone at night.* **SYN** **creepy**

spool /spuːl/ noun [C] a round object which thread, film, wire, etc. is put around □ *gelendong* ⊃ look at **reel**

spoon /spuːn/ noun [C] an object with a round end and a long handle that you use for eating, mixing or serving food □ *sudu*: *Give each person a knife, fork and spoon.* ♦ *a wooden spoon for cooking* ⊃ look at **cutlery** ▸**spoon** verb [T]: *Next, spoon the mixture onto a baking tray.*

spoonful /ˈspuːnfʊl/ noun [C] the amount that one spoon can hold □ *sesudu penuh*: *Add two spoonfuls of sugar.*

spoons

teaspoon

dessertspoon

soup spoon

tablespoon

sporadic /spəˈrædɪk/ adj not done or happening regularly □ *sekali-sekala* ▸**sporadically** /-kli/ adv

sport /spɔːt/ noun **1** [U] a physical game or activity that you do for exercise or because you enjoy it □ *sukan*: *John did a lot of sport when he was at school.* ♦ *Do you like sport?* ⊃ picture on **page P4 2** [C] a particular game or type of sport □ *sukan; permainan*: *What's your favourite sport?* ♦ *winter sports* (= skiing, skating, etc.) ♦ *team sports* ▸**sporting** adj [only before a noun]: *a major sporting event*

> **TOPIC**
>
> **Sport**
>
> You can **play** particular sports (without 'the'): *I play football every Saturday.* In **team sports**, one team **plays** or **plays against** another team: *Who are you playing against next week?* Other sports and activities can take the verbs **do** or **go**: *I do gymnastics and yoga.* ♦ *I go swimming twice a week.*
>
> Sports that are played outside on a grass field, like **football**, **cricket** and **rugby**, are played on a **pitch**. Some other sports, for example **tennis**

[C] **countable**, a noun with a plural form: *one book, two books*   [U] **uncountable**, a noun with no plural form: *some sugar*

and **basketball**, are played on a **court**. **Athletics** is made up of **track events** (= sports that involve running on a track, such as **sprinting** and **hurdling**) and **field events** (= sports that involve jumping and throwing, such as the **high jump** and **javelin**). Sports that take place on snow or ice, such as **skiing**, **snowboarding** and **skating**, are called **winter sports**. Dangerous activities, such as **bungee jumping**, are often called **extreme sports**.

A person who trains people to compete in certain sports is a **coach**. The person who controls a **match** and makes sure that players do not break the rules is a **referee** (in football, rugby, etc.) or an **umpire** (in tennis, cricket, etc.)

'sports car noun [C] a low, fast car often with a roof that you can open □ *kereta sport* ⊃ picture on page P7

sportsman /ˈspɔːtsmən/ noun [C] (pl **-men** /-mən/) a man who does a lot of sport or who is good at sport □ *ahli sukan (lelaki)*: *a keen sportsman*

sportsmanlike /ˈspɔːtsmənlaɪk/ adj behaving in a fair, generous and polite way when you are playing a game or doing sport □ *sikap kesukanan*

sportsmanship /ˈspɔːtsmənʃɪp/ noun [U] the quality of being fair, generous and polite when you are playing a game or doing sport □ *semangat kesukanan*

sportswoman /ˈspɔːtswʊmən/ noun [C] (pl **-women** /-wɪmɪn/) a woman who does a lot of sport or who is good at sport □ *ahli sukan (wanita)*

sporty /ˈspɔːti/ adj (**sportier**; **sportiest**) (*especially BrE informal*) liking or good at sport □ *gemar akan sukan*: *I'm not very sporty.*

spot¹ /spɒt/ noun [C]
▸SMALL MARK **1** a small round mark on a surface □ *bintik; tompok*: *Leopards have dark spots.* ♦ *a blue skirt with red spots on it* ⊃ adjective **spotted** **2** a small dirty mark on sth □ *tompok; tanda*: *grease/rust spots*
▸ON SKIN **3** a small red or yellow lump that appears on your skin □ *bintik; bintat; jerawat*: *Many teenagers get spots.* ⊃ adjective **spotty**
▸PLACE **4** a particular place or area □ *tempat*: *a quiet/lonely/secluded spot*
▸SMALL AMOUNT **5** [usually sing] (*BrE informal*) a spot of sth a small amount of sth □ *sedikit*: *Can you help me? I'm having a spot of trouble.*
▸LIGHT **6** = **spotlight**(1)
IDM **have a soft spot for sb/sth** ⊃ **soft**
on the spot 1 immediately □ *serta-merta*: *Paul was caught stealing money and was dismissed on the spot.* **2** at the place where sth happened or where sb/sth is needed □ *berada di tempat kejadian*: *The fire brigade were on the spot within five minutes.*

put sb on the spot to make sb answer a difficult question or make a difficult decision without having much time to think □ *menyebabkan sso berada dlm keadaan serba salah*

spot² /spɒt/ verb [T] (**spotting**; **spotted**) [not used in the continuous tenses] to see or notice sb/sth, especially suddenly or when it is not easy to do □ *nampak; melihat*: *I've spotted a couple of spelling mistakes.*

HELP Although this verb is not used in the continuous tenses, it is common to see the present participle (= *-ing* form): *Spotting a familiar face in the crowd, he began to push his way towards her.*

,spot 'check noun [C] a check that is made suddenly and without warning on a few things or people chosen from a group □ *pemeriksaan mengejut*

spotless /ˈspɒtləs/ adj perfectly clean □ *betul-betul bersih*

spotlight /ˈspɒtlaɪt/ noun **1** (also **spot**) [C] a lamp that can send a single line of bright light onto a small area. Spotlights are often used in theatres. □ *lampu sorot* **2 the spotlight** [U] the centre of public attention or interest □ *tumpuan utama*: *to be in the spotlight*

,spot 'on adj [not before a noun] (*BrE informal*) exactly right □ *betul-betul tepat*: *Your estimate was spot on.*

spotted /ˈspɒtɪd/ adj (used about clothes, cloth, etc.) having a regular pattern of round dots on it □ *berbintik-bintik*: *a red spotted blouse*

spotty /ˈspɒti/ adj having small red or yellow lumps on your skin □ *berjerawat*

spouse /spaʊs/ noun [C] (*formal*) your husband or wife □ *suami atau isteri*

HELP **Spouse** is a formal or official word, used on forms, documents, etc.

spout¹ /spaʊt/ noun [C] a tube or pipe through which liquid comes out □ *muncung; cerat*: *the spout of a teapot* ⊃ picture at **teapot**

spout² /spaʊt/ verb [I,T] **1** (of a liquid) to come out with great force; to make a liquid do this □ *memancut* **2** (*informal*) **spout (on/off) (about sth)** to say sth, using a lot of words, in a way that is boring or annoying □ *bercakap dgn panjang lebar dan membosankan*

sprain /spreɪn/ verb [T] to injure part of your body, especially your wrist or your ankle, by suddenly bending or turning it □ *tergeliat; terkehel*: *I've sprained my ankle.* ▸ **sprain** noun [C]

sprang past tense of **spring²**

sprawl /sprɔːl/ verb [I] **1** to sit or lie with your arms and legs spread out in an untidy way □ *tergelimpang; terbongkang*: *People lay sprawled out in the sun.* **2** to cover a large area of land □ *terbentang; berselerak* ▸ **sprawling** adj: *the sprawling city suburbs*

spray¹ /spreɪ/ noun 1 [U] liquid in very small drops that is sent through the air □ *percikan; semburan*: *clouds of spray from the waves* 2 [C,U] liquid in an **aerosol** (= a special container) that is forced out under pressure when you push a button □ *semburan*: *hairspray* ♦ *a body spray*

spray² /spreɪ/ verb spray [I,T] (used about a liquid) to be forced out of a container or sent through the air in very small drops; to send a liquid out in this way □ *menyembur; disembur*: *The crops are regularly sprayed with pesticide.*

aerosol

spread¹ /spred/ verb (pt, pp spread) 1 [T] spread sth (out) (on/over sth) to open sth that has been folded so that it covers a larger area; to move things so that they cover a larger area □ *membentangkan*: *Spread the map out on the table so we can all see it.* 2 [I,T] to affect a larger area or a bigger group of people; to make sth do this □ *merebak; menular*: *The fire spread rapidly because of the strong wind.* ♦ *Rats and flies spread disease.* ♦ *to spread rumours about somebody* 3 [T] spread A on/over B; spread B with A to cover a surface with a layer of a soft substance □ *menyapu*: *to spread jam on bread* ♦ *to spread bread with jam* 4 [T] spread sth (out) (over sth) to separate sth into parts and divide them between different times or people □ *mengagihkan*: *You can spread your repayments over a period of three years.*

PHR V spread (sb/yourself) out to move away from other people in a group in order to cover a larger area □ *berpecah*: *The police spread out to search the whole area.*

spread² /spred/ noun 1 [U] an increase in the amount or number of sth that there is, or in the area that is affected by sth □ *penyebaran; penularan*: *Dirty drinking water encourages the spread of disease.* 2 [C,U] a soft food that you put on bread □ *sapuan* 3 [C] a newspaper or magazine article that covers one or more pages □ *halaman penuh*: *a double-page spread* 4 [C] a range or variety of people or things □ *cakupan; liputan*: *a broad spread of opinion*

spreadsheet /ˈspredʃiːt/ noun [C] a computer program for working with rows of numbers, used especially for doing accounts □ *lembaran hamparan; 'spreadsheet'*

spree /spriː/ noun [C] (*informal*) a short time that you spend doing sth you enjoy, often doing too much of it □ *masa berhibur*: *to go on a shopping/spending spree*

sprig /sprɪɡ/ noun [C] a small piece of a plant with leaves on it □ *tangkai*

spring¹ /sprɪŋ/ noun 1 [C,U] the season of the year between winter and summer when the weather gets warmer and plants begin to grow □ *musim bunga*: *Daffodils bloom in spring.* 2 [C] a long piece of thin metal or wire that is bent round and round. After you push or pull a spring it goes back to its original shape and size □ *spring; pegas*: *bed springs* ⇒ picture at **coil** 3 [C] a place where water comes up naturally from under the ground □ *mata air*: *a hot spring* 4 [C] a sudden jump upwards or forwards □ *loncatan*

spring² /sprɪŋ/ verb [I] (*pt* sprang /spræŋ/; *pp* sprung /sprʌŋ/) 1 to jump or move quickly □ *melompat*: *When the alarm went off, Ray sprang out of bed.* ♦ *to spring to your feet* (= stand up suddenly) ♦ (*figurative*) *to spring to somebody's defence/assistance* (= to quickly defend or help sb) 2 (used about an object) to move suddenly and violently □ *melenting; membingkas; membidas*: *The branch sprang back and hit him in the face.* 3 to appear or come somewhere suddenly □ *muncul; timbul*: *Tears sprang to her eyes.* ♦ *Where did you just spring from?*

IDM come/spring to mind ⇒ **mind¹**

PHR V spring from sth (*formal*) to be the result of sth □ *berpunca drpd sst*: *The idea for the book sprang from an experience she had while travelling in India.*

spring sth on sb to do or say sth that sb is not expecting □ *membuat atau mengatakan sst yg tdk dijangka kpd sso*

spring up to appear or develop quickly or suddenly □ *muncul; tumbuh*: *Play areas for children are springing up everywhere.*

springboard /ˈsprɪŋbɔːd/ noun [C] 1 a low board that bends and that helps you jump higher, for example before you jump into a swimming pool □ *papan anjal* 2 a springboard (for/to sth) something that helps you start an activity, especially by giving you ideas □ *batu loncatan*

spring-ˈclean verb [T] to clean a house, room, etc. very well, including the parts that you do not usually clean □ *membersihkan (rumah, bilik, dll) habis-habis*

spring ˈonion noun [C,U] a type of small onion with a long green central part and leaves □ *daun bawang* ⇒ picture on **page P15**

springtime /ˈsprɪŋtaɪm/ noun [U] (*formal*) the season of spring □ *musim bunga*

springy /ˈsprɪŋi/ adj (springier; springiest) going quickly back to its original shape or size after being pushed, pulled, etc. □ *menganjal*: *soft springy grass*

sprinkle /ˈsprɪŋkl/ verb [T] sprinkle A (on/onto/over B); sprinkle B (with A) to throw drops of water or small pieces of sth over a surface □ *merenjiskan; menaburkan*: *to sprinkle sugar on a cake* ♦ *to sprinkle a cake with sugar*

sprinkler /ˈsprɪŋklə(r)/ noun [C] a device with holes in it that sends out water in small drops. Sprinklers are used in gardens to keep the grass green, and in buildings to stop fires from spreading. □ *perenjis*

sprint → square

sprint /sprɪnt/ verb [I,T] to run a short distance as fast as you can □ *lari pecut* ▶**sprint** noun [C]: *a 100-metre sprint* ▶**sprinter** noun [C]

sprout[1] /spraʊt/ verb [I,T] (used about a plant) to begin to grow or to produce new leaves □ *bertunas*: *The seeds are sprouting.*

sprout[2] /spraʊt/ noun [C] **1** = Brussels sprout **2** a new part that has grown on a plant □ *tunas*

spruce /spruːs/ verb
PHR V **spruce (sb/yourself) up** to make sb/yourself clean and tidy □ *mengemaskan diri*

sprung *past participle* of **spring**[2]

spud /spʌd/ noun [C] (*informal*) a potato □ *ubi kentang*

spun *past tense, past participle* of **spin**[1]

spur[1] /spɜː(r)/ noun [C] **1** a piece of metal that some riders wear on the back of their boots to encourage their horses to go faster □ *pacu* ⊃ picture at **horse 2 a spur (to sth)** something that encourages you to do sth or that makes sth happen more quickly □ *pendorong*: *My poor exam results acted as a spur to make me study harder.*
IDM **on the spur of the moment** without planning; suddenly □ *tanpa dirancang; tiba-tiba*

spur[2] /spɜː(r)/ verb [T] (**spurring; spurred**) **spur sb/sth (on/onto sth)** to encourage sb or make them work harder or faster □ *mendorong; menggalak*: *The letter spurred me into action.* ♦ *We were spurred on by the positive feedback from customers.*

spurn /spɜːn/ verb [T] (*formal*) to refuse sth that sb has offered to you □ *menolak*: *She spurned his offer of friendship.*

spurt /spɜːt/ verb **1** [I,T] (used about a liquid) to come out with great force; to make a liquid do this □ *memancut*: *Blood spurted from the wound.* **2** [I] to suddenly increase your speed or effort □ *memecut* ▶**spurt** noun [C]

spy[1] /spaɪ/ noun [C] (*pl* **spies**) a person who tries to get secret information about another country, person or organization □ *perisik; pengintip*

spy[2] /spaɪ/ verb (**spying; spies**; *pt, pp* **spied**) **1** [I] to try to get secret information about sb/sth □ *merisik; mengintip* ⊃ look at **espionage 2** [T] (*formal*) to see sb/sth □ *ternampak; nampak*
IDM **spy on sb/sth** to watch sb/sth secretly □ *mengintip sso/sst*: *The man next door is spying on us.*

sq *abbr* **1** = **square**[1](3): *10 sq cm* **2 Sq** = **square**[2](2): *6 Hanover Sq*

squabble /ˈskwɒbl/ verb [I] **squabble (over/about sth)** to argue in a noisy way about sth that is not very important □ *bergaduh; bertengkar* ▶**squabble** noun [C]

squad /skwɒd/ noun [C, with sing or pl verb] a group of people who work as a team □ *skuad; pasukan*: *He's a policeman with the fraud squad.*

squadron /ˈskwɒdrən/ noun [C, with sing or pl verb] a group of military aircraft or ships □ *skuadron*

squalid /ˈskwɒlɪd/ adj very dirty, untidy and unpleasant □ *sangat kotor*: *squalid housing conditions*

squall /skwɔːl/ noun [C] a sudden storm with strong winds □ *ribut; angin kencang*

squalor /ˈskwɒlə(r)/ noun [U] the state of being very dirty, untidy or unpleasant □ *keadaan kotor*: *to live in squalor*

squander /ˈskwɒndə(r)/ verb [T] **squander sth (on sth)** to waste time, money, etc. □ *membazirkan*: *He squanders his time on TV and computer games.*

square[1] /skweə(r)/ adj, adv
▶SHAPE **1** having four straight sides of the same length and corners of 90° □ *segi empat*: *a square tablecloth* **2** shaped like a square or forming an angle of about 90° □ *bersegi*: *a square face* ♦ *square shoulders*
▶MEASUREMENT **3** (*abbr* **sq**) used for talking about the area of sth □ *persegi*: *If a room is 5 metres long and 4 metres wide, its area is 20 square metres.* **4** (used about sth that is square in shape) having sides of a particular length □ *berukuran (sisi)*: *The picture is twenty centimetres square* (= each side is twenty centimetres long).
▶WITH MONEY **5** [not before a noun] (*informal*) not owing any money □ *tdk berhutang lagi; langsai*: *Here is the money I owe you. Now we're (all) square.*
▶IN SPORT **6** [not before a noun] having equal points (in a game, etc.) □ *seri*: *The teams were all square at half-time.*
▶HONEST **7** fair or honest, especially in business matters □ *adil; jujur*: *a square deal*
▶DIRECTLY **8** (also **squarely**) in an obvious and direct way □ *tepat*: *to look somebody square in the eye* ♦ *I think the blame falls squarely on her.*
IDM **a square meal** a good meal that makes you feel satisfied □ *hidangan makan yg cukup*

square[2] /skweə(r)/ noun [C] **1** a shape that has four sides of the same length and four **right angles** (= angles of 90°) □ *segi empat sama sisi*: *There are 64 squares on a chess board.* ⊃ picture at **shape 2** (also **Square**) (*abbr* **Sq**) an open space in a town or city that has buildings all around it □ *medan; dataran*: *Protesters gathered in the town square.* ♦ *Trafalgar Square* **3** the number that you get when you multiply another number by itself □ *kuasa dua*: *Four is the square of two.* ⊃ look at **square root**

square[3] /skweə(r)/ verb [I,T] **square (sth) with sb/sth** to agree with sth; to make sure that sb/sth agrees with sth □ *selaras; mendapatkan persetujuan*: *Your conclusion doesn't really square with the facts.* ♦ *If you want time off, you'll have to square it with the boss.*
PHR V **square up (with sb)** to pay sb the money that you owe them □ *membayar (hutang, bil, dsb)*

squared /skweəd/ adj (used about a number) multiplied by itself □ *dikuasaduakan; kuasa dua*: *Four squared is sixteen.* ➲ look at **square root**

squarely /'skweəli/ = **square¹**(8)

square 'root noun [C] a number that produces another particular number when it is multiplied by itself □ *punca kuasa dua*: *The square root of sixteen is four.* ➲ look at **square²**(3), **squared**, **root**

squash¹ /skwɒʃ (AmE also) / verb 1 [T] to press sth so that it is damaged, changes shape or becomes flat □ *memenyekkan; menjadi benyek; menghempap; menghimpit*: *The fruit at the bottom of the bag will get squashed.* ◆ *Move up—you're squashing me!* ➲ picture at **squeeze** 2 [I,T] to go into a place, or move sb/sth to a place, where there is not much space □ *mengasak-asak; berhimpit-himpit*: *We all squashed into the back of the car.* 3 [T] to destroy sth because it is a problem □ *menghancurkan; mematahkan; menolak*: *to squash somebody's suggestion/plan/idea*

squash² /skwɒʃ (AmE also) / noun 1 [C, usually sing] a lot of people in a small space □ *(keadaan) sesak; kesesakan*: *We can get ten people around the table, but it's a bit of a squash.* 2 [U,C] (BrE) a drink that is made from fruit juice and sugar. You add water to **squash** before you drink it □ *skuasy*: *orange squash* 3 [U] a game for two people, played in a area surrounded by four walls using **rackets** (= types of bat) and a small rubber ball □ *skuasy* 4 a type of vegetable that grows on the ground and has yellow, orange or green skin □ *sejenis sayur labu*

squat¹ /skwɒt/ verb [I] (**squatting**; **squatted**) 1 to rest with your weight on your feet, your legs bent and your bottom just above the ground □ *mencangkung* ➲ picture at **kneel** 2 to go and live in an empty building without permission from the owner □ *menduduki rumah kosong, dsb tanpa kebenaran; bersetinggan*

squat² /skwɒt/ adj short and fat or thick □ *dempak*: *a squat ugly building*

squatter /'skwɒtə(r)/ noun [C] a person who is living in an empty building without the owner's permission □ *setinggan*

squawk /skwɔːk/ verb [I,T] (used especially about a bird) to make a loud unpleasant noise □ *berkeok* ▸**squawk** noun [C]

squeak /skwiːk/ noun [C] a short high noise that is not very loud □ *berdecit; mendecit*: *the squeak of a mouse* ◆ *She gave a little squeak of surprise.* ▸**squeak** verb [I,T] ▸**squeaky** adj: *a squeaky floorboard* ◆ *a squeaky voice*

squeal /skwiːl/ verb [I,T] to make a loud high noise because of pain, fear or enjoyment □ *menjerit*: *The baby squealed in delight at the new toy.* ▸**squeal** noun [C]

squeamish /'skwiːmɪʃ/ adj easily upset by unpleasant sights, especially blood □ *mudah loya; cepat jijik*

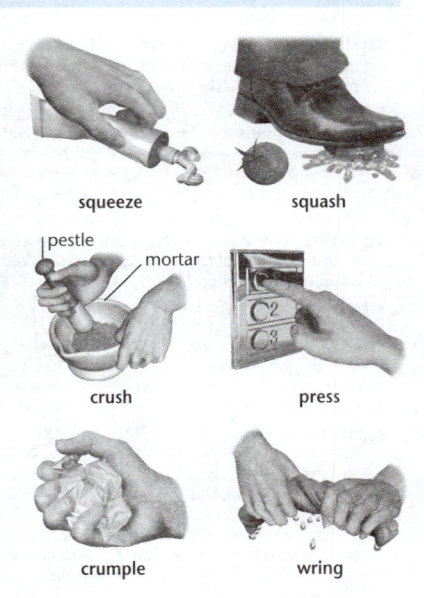

831

squared → squid

squeeze squash

pestle mortar

crush press

crumple wring

squeeze¹ /skwiːz/ verb 1 [T] **squeeze sth (out); squeeze sth (from/out of sth)** to press sth hard □ *memicit; menekan*: *She squeezed his hand as a sign of affection.* ◆ *to squeeze a tube of toothpaste* 2 [T] to get liquid out of sth by pressing it hard □ *memerah*: *Squeeze a lemon/the juice of a lemon into a glass.* ◆ *I squeezed the water out of the cloth.* 3 [I,T] **squeeze (sb/sth) into, through, etc. sth; squeeze (sb/sth) through, in, past, etc.** to force sb/sth into or through a small space □ *mengasak; berasak; menyelitkan; lolos; lepas lalu*: *We can squeeze another person into the back of the car.* ◆ *There was just room for the bus to squeeze past.*

squeeze² /skwiːz/ noun 1 [C] an act of pressing sth firmly □ *(perbuatan) memicit*: *He gave her hand a squeeze and told her he loved her.* 2 [C] the amount of liquid that you get from squeezing an orange, a lemon, etc. □ *perahan*: *a squeeze of lemon* 3 [sing] a situation where there is not much space □ *(keadaan) sesak/berhimpit-himpit*: *It was a tight squeeze to get twelve people around the table.* 4 [C, usually sing] a reduction in the amount of money, jobs, etc. available; a difficult situation caused by this □ *kekangan*: *a government squeeze on spending*

squelch /skweltʃ/ verb [I] to make a wet sucking sound □ *bunyi lecak-lecuk*: *The mud squelched as I walked through it.*

squid /skwɪd/ noun [C,U] (pl **squid** or **squids**) a sea animal that you can eat, with a long soft body, eight arms and two **tentacles** (= long thin parts like arms) □ *sotong* ➲ picture at **octopus**

VOWELS iː: see i any ɪ sit e ten æ hat ɑː father ɒ got ɔː saw ʊ put uː too u usual

squiggle /ˈskwɪɡl/ noun [C] (informal) a quickly drawn line that goes in all directions □ *(garis, tulisan, dsb) cakar ayam*

squint /skwɪnt/ verb [I] **1** squint (at sth) to look at sth with your eyes almost closed □ *mengecilkan mata*: *to squint in bright sunlight* **2** to have eyes that appear to look in different directions at the same time □ *(bermata) juling* ▶ squint noun [C]

squirm /skwɜːm/ verb [I] to move around a lot because you are nervous, uncomfortable, etc. □ *menggeletik; menggelisah*

squirrel /ˈskwɪrəl/ noun [C] a small animal with a long thick tail and red, grey or black fur, that lives in trees and eats nuts □ *tupai*

squirt /skwɜːt/ verb [I,T] If a liquid **squirts** or if you **squirt** it, it is suddenly forced out of sth in a particular direction □ *memancut; terpancut*: *I cut the orange and juice squirted out.* ♦ *She squirted water on the flames.* ♦ *He squirted me with water.* ▶ squirt noun [C]: *a squirt of lemon juice*

squirrel

Sr abbr = Senior¹(2)

St abbr **1** = street(2): *20 Swan St* **2** = saint(1): *St Peter*

st abbr = stone(5)

stab¹ /stæb/ verb [T] (stabbing; stabbed) to push a knife or other pointed object into sb/sth □ *menikam; menusuk; mencucuk*: *The man had been stabbed in the back.* ♦ *He stabbed a potato with his fork.*

stab² /stæb/ noun [C] **1** an injury that was caused by a knife, etc. □ *tikaman*: *He received stab wounds to his neck and back.* **2** a sudden sharp pain □ *rasa sakit yg mencucuk-cucuk* **IDM have a stab at sth/doing sth** (informal) to try to do sth □ *mencuba membuat sst*

stabbing¹ /ˈstæbɪŋ/ noun [C] an occasion when sb is injured or killed with a knife or other sharp object □ *kejadian menikam*

stabbing² /ˈstæbɪŋ/ adj [only before a noun] (used about a pain) sudden and strong □ *mencucuk-cucuk*

stability /stəˈbɪləti/ noun [U] the state or quality of being steady and not changing □ *kestabilan*: *After so much change we now need a period of stability.* ♦ *The ladder is slightly wider at the bottom for greater stability.* **OPP** instability ⊃ adjective **stable**

stabilize (also -ise) /ˈsteɪbəlaɪz/ verb [I,T] to become or to make sth firm, steady and unlikely to change □ *menstabilkan; menjadi stabil*: *The patient's condition has stabilized.* ⊃ look at **destabilize**

stable¹ /ˈsteɪbl/ adj steady, firm and unlikely to change □ *stabil*: *This ladder doesn't seem very stable.* ♦ *The patient is in a stable condition.* **OPP** unstable ⊃ noun **stability**

stable² /ˈsteɪbl/ noun [C] a building where horses are kept □ *kandang kuda* ⊃ picture on page P11

stack¹ /stæk/ noun [C] **1** a tidy pile of sth □ *susunan; timbunan; longgokan*: *a stack of plates/books/chairs* **2** [often plural] (informal) a lot of sth □ *banyak; bertimbun*: *I've still got stacks of work to do.*

stack² /stæk/ verb [T] stack sth (up) to put sth into a tidy pile □ *menyusun; melonggokkan*: *Could you stack those chairs?*

stacked /stækt/ adj full of piles of things □ *bertimbun*: *The room was stacked high with books.*

stadium /ˈsteɪdiəm/ noun [C] (pl stadiums or stadia /-diə/) a large structure, usually with no roof, where people can sit and watch sport □ *stadium*

staff /stɑːf/ noun [C, usually sing, U] the group of people who work for a particular organization □ *kakitangan; staf*: *hotel/library/medical staff* ♦ *Two members of staff will accompany the students on the school trip.* ♦ *The hotel has over 200 people on its staff.* ♦ *full-time/part-time staff*

> **GRAMMAR** We usually use **staff** in the singular but with a plural verb: *The staff are all English.*

▶ staff verb [T, usually passive]: *The office is staffed 24 hours a day.*

staffroom /ˈstɑːfruːm; -rʊm/ noun [C] (BrE) a room in a school where teachers can go when they are not teaching □ *bilik guru*

stag /stæɡ/ noun [C] a male **deer** (= a large wild animal) with **antlers** (= horns shaped like branches) on its head □ *rusa jantan* ⊃ note at **deer** ⊃ picture on page P8

stage¹ /steɪdʒ/ noun **1** [C] one part of the progress or development of sth □ *peringkat; tahap*: *The first stage of the course lasts for three weeks.* ♦ *I suggest we do the journey in two stages.* ♦ *At this stage it's too early to say what will happen.* **2** [C,U] a platform in a theatre, concert hall, etc. on which actors, musicians, etc. perform □ *pentas*: *There were more than 50 people on stage in one scene.* **3** [sing, U] the world of theatre; the profession of acting □ *(bidang) teater; bidang lakonan pentas*: *Her parents didn't want her to go on the stage.* ♦ *an actor of stage and screen*

stage² /steɪdʒ/ verb [T] **1** to organize a performance of a play, concert, etc. for the public □ *mementaskan* **2** to organize an event □ *mengadakan*: *They have decided to stage a 24-hour strike.*

,stage 'manager noun [C] the person who is responsible for the stage, lights, etc. during a theatre performance □ *pengurus pentas*

stagger /ˈstæɡə(r)/ verb [I] to walk with short steps as if you could fall at any moment, for example because you are ill, drunk or carrying sth heavy □ *berjalan terhuyung-hayang*: *He staggered across the finishing line and collapsed.*

staggered /ˈstægəd/ *adj* **1** [not before a noun] (*informal*) very surprised □ *terperanjat*: *I was absolutely staggered when I heard the news.* **2** (used about a set of times, payments, etc.) arranged so that they do not all happen at the same time □ *berperingkat-peringkat*: *staggered working hours* (= when people start and finish work at different times)

staggering /ˈstægərɪŋ/ *adj* that you find difficult to believe □ *memeranjatkan; mengagumkan* ▶ **staggeringly** *adv*

stagnant /ˈstægnənt/ *adj* **1** (used about water) not flowing and therefore dirty and having an unpleasant smell □ *bertakung; tergenang* **2** (used about business, etc.) not active; not developing □ *lembap; tdk giat*: *a stagnant economy*

stagnate /stægˈneɪt/ *verb* [I] **1** to stop developing, changing or being active □ *tdk berkembang; tdk aktif*: *a stagnating economy* **2** (used about water) to be or become **stagnant** □ *bertakung* ▶ **stagnation** /stægˈneɪʃn/ *noun* [U]

ˈ**stag night** (also ˈ**stag party**) *noun* [C] a party for men only that is given for a man just before his wedding day □ *parti utk bakal pengantin lelaki dan teman-teman lelakinya sahaja* ➔ look at **hen party**

staid /steɪd/ *adj* serious, old-fashioned and rather boring □ *serius dan membosankan; kolot*

stain /steɪn/ *verb* [I,T] to leave a mark that is difficult to remove □ *meninggalkan kesan (tompok kotor, dsb)*: *Don't spill any of that juice—it'll stain the carpet.* ▶ **stain** *noun* [C]: *The blood had left a stain on his shirt.*

ˌ**stained** ˈ**glass** *noun* [U] pieces of coloured glass that are used in church windows, etc. □ *kaca berwarna*: *a stained-glass window*

ˌ**stainless** ˈ**steel** *noun* [U] a type of steel that does not **rust** (= get damaged by water or air and change colour) □ *keluli tahan karat*: *a stainless steel pan*

stair /steə(r)/ *noun* **1 stairs** [pl] a series of steps inside a building that lead from one level to another □ *tangga*: *a flight of stairs* ♦ *I heard somebody coming down the stairs.* ♦ *She ran up the stairs.* ➔ picture on **page P8** ➔ look at **downstairs, upstairs**

> **HELP** Stairs or steps? Stairs or flights of stairs are usually inside buildings. Steps are usually outside buildings and made of stone or concrete.

2 [C] one of the steps in a series inside a building □ *anak tangga*: *She sat down on the bottom stair to read the letter.*

staircase /ˈsteəkeɪs/ (also **stairway** /ˈsteəweɪ/) *noun* [C] a set of stairs with rails on each side that you can hold on to □ *tangga* ➔ look at **escalator**

[C] **countable**, a noun with a plural form: *one book, two books*

833   **staggered → stall**

stake¹ /steɪk/ *noun* [C] **1** a wooden or metal pole with a point at one end that you push into the ground □ *pancang* **2** a part of a company, etc. that you own, usually because you have put money into it □ *kepentingan; hak*: *Foreign investors now have a 20% stake in the company.* **3** something, especially money, that you might win or lose in a game or in a particular situation □ *pertaruhan; taruhan*: *We play cards for money, but never for very high stakes.*
IDM **at stake** in danger of being lost; at risk □ *dipertaruhkan; menghadapi risiko*: *He thought very carefully about the decision because he knew his future was at stake.*

stake² /steɪk/ *verb* [T] **stake sth (on sth)** to put your future, etc. in danger by doing sth, because you hope that it will bring you a good result □ *mempertaruhkan*: *He is staking his political reputation on this issue.* **SYN** **bet**
IDM **stake a/your claim (to sth)** to say that you have a right to have sth □ *menuntut hak milik (terhadap sst)*
PHR V **stake sth out 1** to clearly mark an area of land that you are going to use □ *menandakan (dgn pancang, dsb)* **2** to make your position, opinion, etc. clear to everyone □ *menjelaskan kedudukan, pendapat, dsb*: *In his speech, the President staked out his position on tax reform.* **3** to watch a place secretly for a period of time □ *mengintip*: *The police had been staking out the house for months.*

stale /steɪl/ *adj* **1** (used about food or air) old and not fresh any more □ *basi; sudah masuk angin; hapak*: *The bread will go stale if you don't put it away.* **2** not interesting or exciting any more □ *basi; lapuk* ➔ look at **fresh**

stalemate /ˈsteɪlmeɪt/ *noun* [sing, U] **1** a situation in an argument in which neither side can win or make any progress □ *kebuntuan; titik buntu* **2** (in the game of **chess**) a position in which a game ends without a winner because neither side can move □ *kedudukan buntu*

stalk¹ /stɔːk/ *noun* [C] one of the long thin parts of a plant which the flowers, leaves or fruit grow on □ *batang; tangkai* ➔ picture at **plant** ➔ picture on **page P14**

stalk² /stɔːk/ *verb* **1** [T] to move slowly and quietly towards an animal in order to catch or kill it □ *menghendap*: *a lion stalking its prey* **2** [T] to follow a person over a period of time in a frightening or annoying way □ *mengekor sso dgn cara yg mengancam atau menyakitkan hati*: *The actress claimed the man had been stalking her for two years.* **3** [I] to walk in an angry way □ *berjalan dgn marah*

stall¹ /stɔːl/ *noun* **1** [C] a small shop with an open front or a table with things for sale □ *gerai*: *a market stall* ♦ *a bookstall at the station* ➔ picture on **page P11** **2 stalls** [pl] the seats nearest the front in a theatre or cinema □ *tempat duduk di depan pentas* **3** [C, usually sing] a situation in

[U] **uncountable**, a noun with no plural form: *some sugar*

stall → stand 834

which a vehicle's engine suddenly stops because it is not receiving enough power □ *(kejadian) enjin mati*: *The plane went into a stall and almost crashed.*

stall² /stɔ:l/ *verb* [I,T] **1** (used about a vehicle) to stop suddenly because the engine is not receiving enough power; to make a vehicle do this accidentally □ *enjin mati/terhenti*: *The bus often stalls on this hill.* ♦ *I kept stalling the car.* **2** to avoid doing sth or to try to stop sth happening until a later time □ *melengah-lengahkan; menangguhkan*

stallion /ˈstæliən/ *noun* [C] an adult male horse, especially one that is kept for breeding □ *kuda jantan* ⊃ note at **horse**

stalwart /ˈstɔ:lwət/ *adj* always loyal to the same organization, team, etc. □ *setia*: *a stalwart supporter of the club* ▶ **stalwart** *noun* [C]

stamen /ˈsteɪmən/ *noun* [C] a small thin male part in the middle of a flower that produces **pollen** (= a fine yellow powder) □ *stamen*

stamina /ˈstæmɪnə/ *noun* [U] the ability to do sth that involves a lot of physical or mental effort for a long time □ *stamina; daya; ketabahan*: *You need a lot of stamina to run long distances.*

stammer /ˈstæmə(r)/ *verb* [I,T] to speak with difficulty, repeating sounds and pausing before saying things correctly □ *gagap; tergagap-gagap*: *He stammered an apology and left quickly.* ▶ **stammer** *noun* [sing]: *to have a stammer*

stamp¹ /stæmp/ *noun* [C] **1** (also ˌpostage ˈstamp) a small piece of paper that you stick onto a letter or package to show that you have paid for it to be posted □ *setem*: *a first-class/second-class stamp* ♦ *John's hobby is collecting stamps.* ⊃ note at **post** ⊃ look at **first class** ⊃ picture at **letter** ⊃ picture on **page P3**

> **MORE** In the British postal system, there are two types of stamp for posting letters, etc. to other parts of Britain: **first-class** and **second-class** stamps. It costs more to send letters first-class, and they arrive more quickly.

2 a small object that prints some words, a design, the date, etc. when you press it onto a surface □ *cap; meterai*: *a date stamp* **3** the mark made by stamping sth onto a surface □ *cap; tanda; kesan*: *Have you got any visa stamps in your passport?* ♦ (*figurative*) *The government has given the project its stamp of approval.* **4** [usually sing] **the stamp of sth** something that shows a particular quality or that sth was done by a particular person □ *tanda; ciri*: *Her novels have the stamp of genius.*

stamp² /stæmp/ *verb* **1** [I,T] **stamp (on sth)** to put your foot down very heavily and noisily □ *menghentak; memijak-mijak*: *He stamped on the spider and squashed it.* ♦ *It was so cold that I had to stamp my feet to keep warm.* ♦ *She stamped her foot in anger.* **2** [I] to walk with loud heavy steps □ *berjalan dgn menghentak-hentakkan*

kaki: *She stamped around the room, shouting angrily.* **3** [T] **stamp A (on B); stamp B (with A)** to print some words, a design, the date, etc. by pressing a **stamp¹** (2) onto a surface □ *mengecapkan*: *to stamp a passport*

PHR V **stamp sth out** to put an end to sth completely □ *menghapuskan/membanteras sst*: *The police are trying to stamp out this kind of crime.*

ˌstamped adˌdressed ˈenvelope *noun* [C] (*abbr* **SAE**) an empty envelope with your own name and address and a stamp on it that you send to a company, etc. when you want sth to be sent back to you □ *sampul bersetem dan beralamat*

stampede /stæmˈpi:d/ *noun* [C] a situation in which a large number of animals or people start running in the same direction, for example because they are frightened or excited □ *rempuhan* ▶ **stampede** *verb* [I,T]

stance /stæns; stɑ:ns/ *noun* [C, usually sing] **1 stance (on sth)** the opinions that sb expresses publicly about sth □ *pendirian*: *the prime minister's stance on foreign affairs* **2** the position in which sb stands, especially when playing a sport □ *cara berdiri*

stand¹ /stænd/ *verb* (*pt, pp* **stood** /stʊd/)

▶ ON FEET **1** [I] to be on your feet, not sitting or lying down; to be in a vertical position □ *berdiri*: *He was standing near the window.* ♦ *Stand still—I'm trying to draw you!* ♦ *Only a few houses were left standing after the earthquake.* **2** [I] **stand (up)** to rise to your feet from another position □ *bangun berdiri*: *He stood up when I entered the room.*

▶ IN POSITION **3** [T] to put sb/sth in a particular place or position □ *meletakkan*: *We stood the mirror against the wall while we decided where to hang it.* **4** [I] to be or to stay in a particular position or situation □ *terletak*: *The castle stands on a hill.* ♦ *The house has stood empty for ten years.*

▶ HEIGHT, LEVEL, ETC. **5** [I] **stand (at sth)** to be of a particular height, level, amount, etc. □ *berada pd ketinggian, aras, jumlah, dsb tertentu*: *The world record stands at 6.59 metres.* ♦ *The building stands nearly 60 metres high.*

▶ STAY THE SAME **6** [I] to stay the same as before, without being changed □ *kekal; tdk berubah*: *Does your decision still stand?* ♦ *The world record has stood for ten years.*

▶ HAVE OPINION **7** [I] **stand (on sth)** to have an opinion or view about sth □ *berpendirian*: *Where do you stand on euthanasia?*

▶ BE LIKELY TO **8** [I] **stand to do sth** to be in a situation where you are likely to do sth □ *mungkin akan*: *If he has to sell the company, he stands to lose a lot of money.*

▶ NOT LIKE **9** [T] (in negative sentences and questions, with *can/could*) to not like sb/sth at all; to hate sb/sth □ *tahan; sanggup*: *I can't stand that woman—she's so rude.* ♦ *I couldn't stand the thought of waiting another two hours so I went home.* ⊃ note at **dislike**

▶ SURVIVE **10** [T] (used especially with *can/could*) to be able to survive difficult conditions □ *ta-*

[I] **intransitive**, a verb which has no object: *He laughed.*   [T] **transitive**, a verb which has an object: *He ate an apple.*

han; sanggup menghadapi: *Camels can stand extremely hot and cold temperatures.* **SYN** **bear, take**

➤IN ELECTION **11** [I] **stand (for/as sth)** to be one of the people who hopes to be chosen in an election □ *bertanding*: *She's standing for the European Parliament.* ❶ For idioms containing **stand**, look at the entries for the nouns, adjectives, etc. For example, **it stands to reason** is at **reason**.

PHR V **stand around** to stand somewhere not doing anything □ *berdiri-diri sahaja*: *A lot of people were just standing around outside.*

stand aside to move to one side □ *berdiri ke tepi*: *People stood aside to let the police pass.*

stand back to move back □ *berundur*: *The policeman told everybody to stand back.*

stand by 1 to be present, but do nothing in a situation □ *tengok saja*: *How can you stand by and let them treat their animals like that?* **2** to be ready to act □ *bersiap sedia*: *The police are standing by in case there's trouble.*

stand by sb to help sb or be friends with them, even in difficult times □ *membantu; menyokong*

stand for sth 1 to be a short form of sth □ *merupakan singkatan bagi sst*: *What does BBC stand for?* **2** to support sth (such as an idea or opinion) □ *menyokong sst*: *I hate everything that the party stands for.*

stand in (for sb) to take sb's place for a short time □ *mengambil tempat (sso); memangku*

stand out to be easily seen or noticed □ *jelas kelihatan; menonjol*

stand up to be or become vertical □ *berdiri tegak*: *You'll look taller if you stand up straight.*

stand sb up (*informal*) to not appear when you have arranged to meet sb, especially a boyfriend or girlfriend □ *tdk menepati janji temu*

stand up for sb/sth to say or do sth which shows that you support sb/sth □ *menyokong, mempertahankan atau membela sso/sst*: *I admire him. He really stands up for his rights.*

stand up to sb/sth to defend yourself against sb/sth that is stronger or more powerful □ *melawan sso/sst*

stand² /stænd/ *noun* [C] **1** [usually sing] **a stand (on/against sth)** a strong effort to defend yourself or sth that you have a strong opinion about □ *(mengambil) tindakan utk mempertahankan diri/sst*: *The head teacher has been praised for his tough stand on bullying.* ◆ *The workers have decided to take/make a stand against further job losses.* **2** a table or an object that holds or supports sth, often so that people can buy it or look at it □ *tempat letak; kaki; gerai*: *a newspaper/hamburger stand* ◆ *a company stand at a trade fair* **3** a large structure with rows where people sit or stand to watch a sports event □ *tempat duduk*

standard¹ /'stændəd/ *noun* **1** [C,U] a level of quality, especially that people think is acceptable □ *ukuran; standard*: *By European standards this is a very expensive city.* ◆ *He is a brilliant player by any standard.* ◆ *We complained about the low standard of service in the hotel.* **2** [pl] a level of behaviour that is morally acceptable □ *taraf moral*: *Many people are worried about falling standards in modern society.*

standard² /'stændəd/ *adj* **1** normal or average; not special or unusual □ *biasa; lazim*: *He's got long arms, so standard sizes of shirt don't fit him.* **2** that people generally accept as normal and correct □ *baku; standard*: *standard English*

'**standard class** = second class(1)

standardize (also **-ise**) /'stændədaɪz/ *verb* [T] to make things that are different the same □ *memiawaikan; menstandardkan*: *Safety tests on old cars have been standardized throughout Europe.* ▶ **standardization** (also **-isation**) /ˌstændədaɪ'zeɪʃn/ *noun* [U]

ˌ**standard of 'living** *noun* [C] (*pl* **standards of living**) the amount of money and level of comfort that a particular person or group has □ *taraf hidup*: *There is a higher standard of living in the north than in the south.*

> **MORE** An expression with a similar meaning is **living standards**. This is used in the plural: *Living standards have improved.*

standby /'stændbaɪ/ *noun* **1** [C] (*pl* **standbys**) a thing or person that can be used if needed, for example if sb/sth is not available or in an emergency □ *pengganti; persediaan*: *We always keep candles as a standby in case there is a power cut.* **2** [U] the state of being ready to do sth immediately if needed, or if a ticket becomes available □ *bersiap sedia; tunggu sedia*: *Ambulances were on standby along the route of the marathon.* ◆ *We were put on standby for the flight to Beirut.* ▶ **standby** *adj* [only *before* a noun]: *a standby ticket/passenger*

standing¹ /'stændɪŋ/ *adj* [only *before* a noun] that always exists; permanent □ *tetap; lazim*

standing² /'stændɪŋ/ *noun* [U] **1** the position that sb/sth has, or how people think of them or it □ *taraf; status*: *The agreement has no legal standing.* **SYN** **status 2** the amount of time during which sth has continued to exist □ *tempoh; jangka masa*

ˌ**standing 'order** *noun* [C] an instruction to your bank to make a regular payment to sb from your account □ *arahan tetap*

standpoint /'stændpɔɪnt/ *noun* [C] a particular way of thinking about sth □ *sudut pandangan* **SYN** **point of view**

standstill /'stændstɪl/ *noun* [sing] a situation when there is no movement, progress or activity □ *terhenti; tdk bergerak*: *The traffic is at/has come to a complete standstill.*
IDM **grind to a halt/standstill** ➔ **grind**¹

stank past tense of **stink**

stanza /ˈstænzə/ noun [C] a group of lines that form a unit in some types of poem □ *stanza; rangkap sajak* **SYN** verse

staple /ˈsteɪpl/ noun [C] a small thin piece of bent wire that you push through pieces of paper using a **stapler** (= a special tool) to fasten them together □ *(dawai) kokot* ▶ **staple** verb [T]: *Staple the letter to the application form.* ▶ **stapler** noun [C] ➲ picture at **stationery**

staple diet noun [C, usually sing] the main food that a person or an animal normally eats □ *makanan ruji: a staple diet of rice and fish*

star¹ /stɑː(r)/ noun
▶ IN SKY **1** [C] a large ball of burning gas in space that you see as a small point of light in the sky at night □ *bintang: It was a clear night and the stars were shining brightly.*
▶ SHAPE **2** [C] a shape, decoration, mark, etc. with five or six points sticking out in a regular pattern □ *bintang: I've marked the possible candidates on the list with a star.* ➲ picture at **shape**
▶ FOR HOTEL, ETC. **3** [C] a mark that represents a star that is used for telling you how good sth is, especially a hotel or restaurant □ *bintang: a five-star hotel*
▶ PERSON **4** [C] a famous person in acting, music or sport □ *bintang (pop) filem, dsb: a pop/rock/film/movie star* ♦ *a football/tennis star*
▶ BEST **5** [C] a person or thing that is the best □ *bintang pujaan: a star student* ♦ *She was the star of many popular television series.* ♦ *A green parrot was the star of the show.*
▶ PREDICTING SB'S FUTURE **6** stars [pl] = **horoscope**

star² /stɑː(r)/ verb (starring; starred) **1** [I] star (in sth) to be one of the main actors in a play, film, etc □ *berlakon; membintangi: Anne Hathaway is to star in a new romantic comedy.* **2** [T] to have sb as a star □ *dibintangi: The film stars Elio Germano as the son of a journalist.*

starboard /ˈstɑːbəd/ noun [U] the side of a ship that is on the right when you are facing towards the front of it □ *bahagian kanan kapal* **OPP** port ➲ note at **boat**

starch /stɑːtʃ/ noun **1** [C,U] a white substance that is found in foods such as potatoes, rice and bread □ *kanji* **2** [U] a substance that is used for making cloth stiff □ *tepung kanji*

stardom /ˈstɑːdəm/ noun [U] the state of being a famous person in acting, music or sport □ *(menjadi) bintang terkenal: She shot to stardom in a Broadway musical.*

stare /steə(r)/ verb [I] stare (at sb/sth) to look at sb/sth for a long time because you are surprised, shocked, etc. □ *merenung; tercengang memandang: Everybody stared at his hat.* ♦ *He didn't reply, he just stared into the distance.* ▶ **stare** noun [C]: *She gave him a blank stare.*

stark¹ /stɑːk/ adj (starker; starkest) **1** very empty and without decoration and therefore not attractive □ *gondol; tandus; kosong: a stark landscape* **2** unpleasant and impossible to avoid □ *tdk menyenangkan dan tdk dpt dielak: He now faces the stark reality of life in prison.* **3** very different to sth in a way that is easy to see □ *jelas berbeza*

stark² /stɑːk/ adv completely; extremely □ *betul-betul: stark naked* ♦ *Have you gone stark raving mad?*

starlight /ˈstɑːlaɪt/ noun [U] the light that is sent out by stars in the sky □ *cahaya bintang*

starry /ˈstɑːri/ adj full of stars □ *penuh bintang: a starry night*

star sign (also informal **sign**) one of the twelve divisions of the **zodiac** (= symbols which represent the positions of the sun, moon and planets) □ *lambang bintang: 'What's your star sign?' 'Leo.'*

start¹ /stɑːt/ verb
▶ BEGIN **1** [I,T] start (sth/to do sth/doing sth) to begin doing sth □ *mula; bermula; bertolak: Turn over your exam papers and start now.* ♦ *We'll have to start (= leave) early if we want to be in Dover by 10.30.* ♦ *Prices start at £5.* ♦ *After waiting for an hour, the customers started to complain.* ♦ *She started playing the piano when she was six.* ♦ *What time do you have to start work in the morning?* **2** [I,T] to begin or to make sth begin to happen □ *mula; bermula; memulakan: What time does the concert start?* ♦ *I'd like to start the meeting now.* ♦ *The police think a young woman may have started the fire.* ➲ note at **begin**
▶ MACHINE/VEHICLE **3** [I,T] start (sth) (up) to make an engine, a car, etc. begin to work □ *menghidupkan: The car won't start.* ♦ *We heard an engine starting up in the street.* ♦ *He got onto his motorbike, started the engine and rode away.*
▶ ORGANIZATION **4** [I,T] start (sth) (up) to create a company, an organization, etc.; to begin to exist □ *memulakan; menubuhkan: There are a lot of new companies starting up in that area now.* ♦ *They've decided to start their own business.*
▶ MOVE SUDDENLY **5** [I] to make a sudden, quick movement because you are surprised or afraid □ *tersentak: A loud noise outside made me start.*
IDM get/start off on the right/wrong foot (with sb) ➲ **foot¹**
set/start the ball rolling ➲ **ball**
to start (off) with **1** used for giving your first reason for sth □ *pertama-tamanya: 'Why are you so angry?' 'Well, to start off with, you're late, and secondly you've lied to me.'* **2** in the beginning; at first □ *pd mulanya: Everything was fine to start with, but the marriage quickly deteriorated.*
PHR V start off to begin in a particular way □ *memulakan; bermula: I'd like to start off by welcoming you all to Leeds.*
start on sth to begin doing sth that needs to be done □ *mula (membuat sst)*
start out (to do sth) to have a particular intention when you begin sth □ *mula-mula (bekerja, dsb): I started out to tidy my desk but ended up tidying the whole room.*
start over (AmE) to begin again □ *mula semula*

start² → statesman

start² /stɑ:t/ noun
▶BEGINNING **1** [C, usually sing] the point at which sth begins □ *permulaan; mula*: *The chairman made a short speech at the start of the meeting.* ◆ *I told you it was a bad idea from the start.* **2** [C, usually sing] the action or process of starting □ *(perbuatan/proses) memulakan*: *to make a fresh start* (= do sth again in a different way)
▶IN RACE **3 the start** [sing] the place where a race begins □ *garis permulaan*: *The athletes are now lining up at the start.* **4** [C, usually sing] an amount of time or distance that you give to a weaker person at the beginning of a race, game, etc. □ *manfaat mula*: *I gave the younger children a start.* ⊃ look at **head start**
▶SUDDEN MOVEMENT **5** [C, usually sing] a sudden quick movement that your body makes because you are surprised or afraid □ *tersentak*: *She woke up with a start.*
IDM **for a start** (*informal*) (used to emphasize your first reason for sth) □ *pertama-tamanya*: *'Why can't we go on holiday?' 'Well, for a start we can't afford it …'*
get off to a flying start ⊃ **flying**
get off to a good, bad, etc. start to start well, badly, etc. □ *bermula dgn baik; tdk bermula dgn baik, dsb*

starter /'stɑ:tə(r)/ (*AmE usually* **appetizer**) noun [C] a small amount of food that is served before the main course of a meal □ *pembuka selera* ⊃ note at **restaurant**

'starting point noun [C] **starting point (for sth) 1** an idea or a topic that you use to begin a discussion □ *titik permulaan* **2** the place where you begin a journey □ *tempat permulaan*

startle /'stɑ:tl/ verb [T] to surprise sb/sth in a way that slightly shocks or frightens them or it □ *mengejutkan; terkejut*: *The noise startled the horses.* ▶ **startled** adj ▶ **startling** adj

starvation /stɑ:'veɪʃn/ noun [U] suffering or death because there is not enough food □ *kebuluran*: *to die of starvation*

starve /stɑ:v/ verb [I,T] to suffer or die because you do not have enough food to eat; to make sb/sth suffer or die in this way □ *menderita atau mati kebuluran*: *Millions of people are starving in the poorer countries of the world.* ◆ *That winter many animals starved to death.*
IDM **be starved of sth** to suffer because you are not getting enough of sth that you need □ *dahaga akan sst*: *The children had been starved of love and affection for years.*
be starving (*informal*) to be extremely hungry □ *sangat lapar*

state¹ /steɪt/ noun
▶CONDITION **1** [C] the mental, emotional or physical condition that sb/sth is in at a particular time □ *keadaan*: *the state of the economy* ◆ *He is in a state of shock.* ◆ *The house is in a terrible state.*
▶COUNTRY **2** (also **State**) [C] a country considered as an organized political community controlled by one government □ *negara*: *Pakistan has been an independent state since 1947.* ⊃ note at **country**
▶PART OF COUNTRY **3** (also **State**) [C] an organized political community forming part of a country □ *negeri*: *the southern States of the US* ⊃ look at **county, province**
▶GOVERNMENT **4** often (**the**) **State** [U, sing] the government of a country □ *kerajaan*: *affairs/matters of state* ◆ *the relationship between the Church and the State* ◆ *a state-owned company* ◆ *heads of State* (= government leaders)
▶OFFICIAL CEREMONY **5** [U] the formal ceremonies connected with high levels of government or with the leaders of countries □ *rasmi*: *The president was driven in state through the streets.*
▶USA **6 the States** [pl] (*informal*) the United States of America □ *Amerika Syarikat*: *We lived in the States for about five years.*
IDM **be in/get into a state** (*especially BrE informal*) **1** to be or become very nervous or upset □ *menggelabah*: *Now don't get into a state! I'm sure everything will be all right.* **2** (*informal*) to be or become dirty or untidy □ *menjadi kotor*
state of affairs a situation □ *keadaan; situasi*: *This state of affairs must not be allowed to continue.*
state of mind mental condition □ *keadaan fikiran*: *She's in a very confused state of mind.*

state² adj /steɪt/ [only before a noun] **1** provided or controlled by the government of a country □ *bantuan/kawalan kerajaan*: *She went to a state school.* **2** connected with the leader of a country attending an official ceremony □ *rasmi*: *The Queen is on a state visit to Moscow.* **3** connected with a particular state of a country, especially in the US □ *negeri*: *a state prison/hospital/university*

state³ /steɪt/ verb [T] to say or write sth, especially formally □ *menyatakan*: *Your letter states that you sent the goods on 31 March, but we have not received them.*

stately /'steɪtli/ adj formal and impressive □ *tersergam; mengagumkan*: *a stately old building*

stately 'home noun [C] (*BrE*) a large old house that has historical interest and can be visited by the public □ *rumah besar yg tersergam dan bersejarah* ⊃ picture on page P9

statement /'steɪtmənt/ noun [C] **1** something that you say or write, especially formally □ *kenyataan; pernyataan*: *The Prime Minister will make a statement about the defence cuts today.* **2** = **bank statement**

state of the 'art adj using the most modern or advanced methods; as good as it can be at the present time □ *terkini; tercanggih*: *The system was state of the art.* ◆ *a state-of-the-art system*

statesman /'steɪtsmən/ noun [C] (*pl* **-men** /-mən/) an important and experienced politician who has earned public respect □ *negarawan*

static[1] /ˈstætɪk/ *adj* not moving, changing or developing □ *statik; pegun; tdk berubah-ubah*: *House prices are static.*

static[2] /ˈstætɪk/ *noun* [U] **1** sudden noises that disturb radio or TV signals, caused by electricity in the atmosphere □ *gangguan bunyi* **2** (also ˌstatic elecˈtricity) electricity that collects on a surface □ *elektrik statik*: *My hair gets full of static when I brush it.*

station[1] /ˈsteɪʃn/ *noun* [C] **1** a building on a railway line where trains stop so that passengers can get on and off □ *stesen (kereta api)*: *I get off at the next station.* ◆ *a railway station* ◆ *a train station* ◆ (*BrE*) *a tube/underground station* ◆ (*AmE*) *a subway station* ⊃ note at **train 2** [in compounds] a building from which buses begin and end journeys □ *stesen (bas)*: *The coach leaves the bus/coach station at 9.30 a.m.* **3** [in compounds] a building where a particular service or activity is based □ *balai; stesen; tempat pam minyak*: *a police/fire station* ◆ *a petrol station* ◆ *a power station* (= where electricity is produced) **4** [usually in compounds] a radio or TV company and the programmes it sends out □ *stesen; saluran*: *a local radio/TV station* ◆ *He tuned in to another station.* ⊃ look at **channel**

station[2] /ˈsteɪʃn/ *verb* [T, often passive] to send sb, especially a member of the armed forces, to work in a place for a period of time □ *dihantar bertugas*

stationary /ˈsteɪʃənri/ *adj* not moving □ *pegun; tdk bergerak; yg sedang berhenti*: *He crashed into the back of a stationary vehicle.*

stationer's /ˈsteɪʃənəz/ *noun* [sing] a shop that sells writing equipment, such as paper, pens, envelopes, etc. □ *kedai alat tulis*

stationery /ˈsteɪʃənri/ *noun* [U] writing equipment, for example pens, pencils, paper, envelopes, etc. □ *alat tulis*

ˈstation wagon (*AmE*) = **estate car**

statistics /stəˈtɪstɪks/ *noun* (also *informal* **stats**) **1** [pl] a piece or a collection of information shown in numbers □ *statistik; perangkaan*: *Statistics indicate that 90% of homes in this country have a TV.* ◆ *crime statistics* **2** [U] the science of collecting and studying these numbers □ *ilmu statistik/perangkaan* ▶ **statistical** /stəˈtɪstɪkl/ *adj*: *statistical* /-kli/ *adv*

stats (*informal*) = **statistics**

statue /ˈstætʃuː/ *noun* [C] a figure of a person or an animal that is made of stone or metal and usually put in a public place □ *patung*: *the Statue of Liberty in New York* ⊃ picture on page P11

stature /ˈstætʃə(r)/ *noun* [U] (*formal*) **1** the importance and respect that sb has because people have a high opinion of their skill or of what they have done □ *nama baik; keagungan; kaliber* **2** the height of a person □ *tinggi; ketinggian*: *He's quite small in stature.*

status /ˈsteɪtəs/ *noun* **1** [U] the legal position of a person, group or country □ *taraf; kedudukan*: *Please indicate your name, age and marital status* (= if you are married or single). ◆ *They were granted refugee status.* **2** [sing] your social or professional position in relation to other people □ *taraf; status*: *Teachers don't have a very high status in this country.* **3** [U] a high social position □ *taraf/kedudukan tinggi*: *The new job gave him much more status.*

the status quo /ˌsteɪtəs ˈkwəʊ/ *noun* [sing] the situation as it is now, or as it was before a recent change □ *status quo; keadaan spt yg wujud sekarang atau sebelum berlaku perubahan*

ˈstatus symbol *noun* [C] something that a person owns that shows that they have a high position in society and a lot of money □ *lambang taraf/status*

statute /ˈstætʃuːt/ *noun* [C] (*formal*) a law or a rule □ *statut; peraturan*

statutory /ˈstætʃətri/ *adj* (*formal*) decided by law □ *berkanun; mengikut undang-undang*: *a statutory right*

staunch /stɔːntʃ/ *adj* (**staunchest**) [no comparative] believing in sb/sth or supporting sb/sth very strongly; loyal □ *kuat; setia*

stave /steɪv/ *verb*
PHR V **stave sth off** to stop sth unpleasant from happening now, although it may happen at a later time; to delay sth □ *menghindarkan/mengelakkan sst*: *to stave off hunger/illness/inflation/bankruptcy*

stay[1] /steɪ/ *verb* [I] **1** to continue to be somewhere and not go away □ *tinggal; tunggu; duduk; berada di sst tempat*: *Patrick stayed in bed until 11 o'clock.* ◆ *I can't stay long.* ◆ *Stay on this road until you get to Wells.* ◆ *Pete's staying late at the office tonight.* ◆ *Can you stay for lunch?* **2** to continue to be in a particular state or situation without change □ *terus; kekal*: *I can't stay awake any longer.* ◆ *I don't know why they stay together* (= continue to be married or in a relationship).

HELP **Stay** or **remain**? **Remain** and **stay** are similar in meaning but **remain** is more formal.

3 to live in a place temporarily as a visitor or guest □ *menumpang; menginap; tinggal*: *We stayed with friends in France.* ◆ *Which hotel are you staying at?* ◆ *Why don't you stay the night?*
IDM **keep/stay/steer clear (of sb/sth)** ⊃ **clear**[3]
stay put (*informal*) to continue in one place; to not leave □ *tunggu; tdk ke mana-mana*
PHR V **stay behind** to not leave a place after other people have gone □ *tinggal; tdk balik*: *I'll stay behind and help you wash up.*
stay in to remain at home and not go out □ *tdk keluar rumah*: *I'm going to stay in and watch TV.*
stay on (at ...) to continue studying, working, etc. somewhere for longer than expected or

after other people have left □ *terus belajar, bekerja, dsb (di...)*

stay out to continue to be away from your house, especially late at night □ *keluar atau berada di luar (rumah)*

stay out of sth to avoid or not become involved in sth □ *menjauhkan; menghindarkan*: *to stay out of trouble*

stay up to go to bed later than usual □ *berjaga*: *I'm going to stay up to watch the late film.*

stay² /steɪ/ *noun* [C] a period of time that you spend somewhere as a visitor or guest □ *lawatan*: *Did you enjoy your stay in Crete?*

staycation /ˌsteɪˈkeɪʃn/ *noun* [C] a holiday that you spend at or near your home □ *percutian dekat dgn rumah sendiri*: *Turn off your phone and computer—you're on staycation, remember?*

STD /ˌes tiː ˈdiː/ *abbr* **1** sexually transmitted disease; any disease that is spread through having sex □ *penyakit yg berjangkit melalui hubungan seks* **2** (*BrE*) subscriber trunk dialling; the system by which you can make direct telephone calls over long distances □ *STD (sambung jauh terus dail)*

steady¹ /ˈstedi/ *adj* (**steadier**; **steadiest**) **1** developing, growing or happening gradually and at a regular rate □ *tetap; berterusan; mantap*: *a steady increase/decline* **2** staying the same; not changing and therefore safe □ *tetap*: *a steady job/income* ◆ *a steady boyfriend/girlfriend* (= one that has lasted a long time) **3** firmly fixed, supported or balanced; not shaking or likely to fall down □ *tegap; tdk goyang; kukuh*: *You need a steady hand to take good photographs.* ◆ *He held the ladder steady as she climbed up it.* ▶ **steadily** *adv*: *Unemployment has risen steadily since April 2011.*

steady² /ˈstedi/ *verb* [I,T] (**steadying**; **steadies**; *pt, pp* **steadied**) to stop yourself/sb/sth from moving, shaking or falling; to stop moving, shaking or falling □ *memantapkan; menetapkan*: *She thought she was going to fall, so she put out a hand to steady herself.* ◆ *He had to steady his nerves/voice before beginning his speech.*

steak /steɪk/ *noun* [C,U] a thick flat piece of meat or fish □ *stik*: *a piece of steak* ◆ *a cod/salmon steak* ⊃ look at **chop**

steal /stiːl/ *verb* (*pt* **stole** /stəʊl/; *pp* **stolen** /ˈstəʊlən/) **1** [I,T] **steal (sth) (from sb/sth)** to take sth from a person, shop, etc. without permission and without intending to return it or pay for it □ *mencuri*: *We found out she had been stealing from us for years.* ◆ *The terrorists were driving a stolen car.* ⊃ note at **thief**

stationery

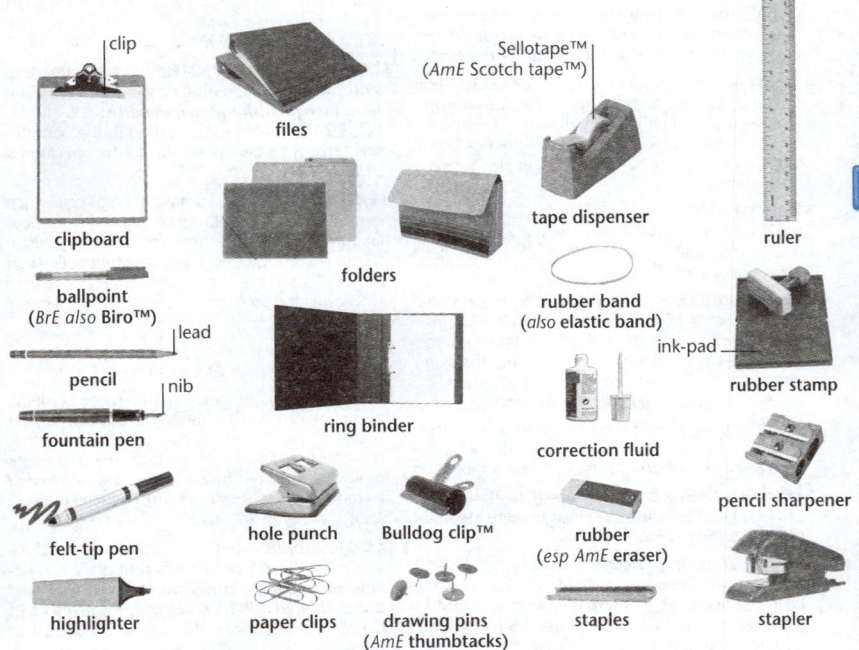

- clip
- files
- Sellotape™ (*AmE* Scotch tape™)
- tape dispenser
- ruler
- clipboard
- folders
- ballpoint (*BrE* also **Biro**™)
- lead
- pencil
- nib
- ring binder
- rubber band (also **elastic band**)
- ink-pad
- rubber stamp
- fountain pen
- correction fluid
- felt-tip pen
- hole punch
- Bulldog clip™
- rubber (*esp AmE* **eraser**)
- pencil sharpener
- highlighter
- paper clips
- drawing pins (*AmE* **thumbtacks**)
- staples
- stapler

[C] **countable**, a noun with a plural form: *one book, two books*   [U] **uncountable**, a noun with no plural form: *some sugar*

stealth → step

> **HELP** Steal or rob? You **steal** things, but you **rob** a person or place: *My camera has been stolen!* ♦ *I've been robbed!* ♦ *to rob a bank*

2 [I] **steal away, in, out,** etc. to move somewhere secretly and quietly □ *mencuri-curi (pergi, masuk, keluar, dsb)*: *She stole out of the room.*

stealth /stelθ/ *noun* [U] (*formal*) behaviour that is secret or quiet □ *cara diam-diam* ▶**stealthy** *adj*: *a stealthy approach/movement* ▶**stealthily** *adv*

steam¹ /sti:m/ *noun* [U] the hot gas that water changes into when it boils □ *wap; stim*: *Steam was rising from the coffee.* ♦ *a steam engine* (= that uses the power of steam)

IDM let off steam (*informal*) to get rid of energy or express strong feeling by behaving in a noisy or wild way □ *melepaskan geram, dsb*
run out of steam (*informal*) to gradually lose energy or enthusiasm □ *menjadi letih; semakin tdk bersemangat*

steam² /sti:m/ *verb* **1** [I] to send out steam □ *berwap*: *a bowl of steaming hot soup* **2** [I,T] to place food over boiling water so that it cooks in the steam; to cook in this way □ *mengukus*: *Leave the potatoes to steam for 30 minutes.* ♦ *steamed vegetables/fish* ➔ note at **cook**

IDM be/get steamed up (*informal*) to be or become very angry or worried about sth □ *naik marah atau risau*

PHR V steam (sth) up to cover sth or become covered with steam □ *diliputi wap; menjadikan berwap*: *As he walked in, his glasses steamed up.*

steamer /'sti:mə(r)/ *noun* [C] **1** a boat or ship driven by steam power □ *kapal stim; kapal wap* **2** a metal container with small holes in it that is used in cooking. You put it over a pan of boiling water in order to cook food in the steam. □ *pengukus*

steamroller /'sti:mrəʊlə(r)/ *noun* [C] a big heavy vehicle with wheels that is used for making the surface of a road flat □ *penggelek jalan*

steel¹ /sti:l/ *noun* [U] a very strong metal that is made from iron mixed with **carbon** (= another chemical element). Steel is used for making knives, tools, machines, etc. □ *keluli*: *the iron and steel industry* ♦ *a frame made of steel* ♦ *a bridge reinforced with huge steel girders*

steel² /sti:l/ *verb* [T] **steel yourself** to prepare yourself to deal with sth difficult or unpleasant □ *menabahkan hati*: *Steel yourself for a shock.*

steelworks /'sti:lwɜ:ks/ *noun* [C, with sing or pl verb] (*pl* **steelworks**) a factory where steel is made □ *kilang keluli*

steep /sti:p/ *adj* (**steeper**; **steepest**) **1** (used about a hill, mountain, street, etc.) rising or falling quickly; at a sharp angle □ *curam*: *I don't think I can cycle up that hill. It's too steep.* **2** (used about an increase or a fall in sth) very big

□ *(naik) melambung; (turun/jatuh) menjunam*: *a steep rise in unemployment* **3** (*informal*) too expensive □ *sangat mahal*: *£3 for a cup of coffee seems a little steep to me.* ▶**steeply** *adv*: *House prices have risen steeply this year.* ▶**steepness** *noun* [U]

steeped /sti:pt/ *adj* **steeped in sth** having a lot of sth; full of sth □ *penuh dgn*: *a city steeped in history*

steeple /'sti:pl/ *noun* [C] a tower on the roof of a church, often with a **spire** (= a tall pointed top) □ *menara gereja*

steer /stɪə(r)/ *verb* **1** [I,T] to control the direction that a vehicle is going in □ *memandu; mengendali; mengemudi*: *Can you push the car while I steer?* ♦ *to steer a boat/ship/bicycle/motorbike* **2** [T] to take control of a situation and try to influence the way it develops □ *mengarah; membawa*: *She tried to steer the conversation away from the subject of money.*

IDM keep/stay/steer clear (of sb/sth) ➔ **clear³**

steering /'stɪərɪŋ/ *noun* [U] the parts of a vehicle that control the direction that it moves in □ *stereng*: *the power steering in a car*

'steering wheel (also **wheel**) *noun* [C] the wheel that the driver turns in a vehicle to control the direction that it moves in □ *stereng* ➔ picture at **car**

stem¹ /stem/ *noun* [C] **1** the main central part of a plant above the ground from which the leaves or flowers grow □ *batang* ➔ picture at **plant** **2** the main part of a word onto which other parts are added □ *kata dasar*: '*Writ-*' is the stem of the words '*write*', '*writing*', '*written*' and '*writer*'.

stem² /stem/ *verb* [T] (**stemming**; **stemmed**) to stop sth that is increasing or spreading □ *menahan; menghentikan; membendung*

PHR V stem from sth [not used in the continuous tenses] to be the result of sth □ *berpunca drpd sst; akibat sst*

'stem cell *noun* [C] a basic type of cell which can divide and develop into cells with particular functions. All the different kinds of cells in the human body develop from stem cells □ *sel dasar*: *Tests suggest that stem cells could be used to regenerate damaged body parts.* ♦ *stem cell research*

stench /stentʃ/ *noun* [sing] a very unpleasant smell □ *bau busuk* ➔ note at **smell²**

stencil /'stensl/ *noun* [C] a thin piece of metal, plastic or card with a design cut out of it, that you put onto a surface and paint over so that the design is left on the surface; the pattern or design that is produced in this way □ *stensil* ▶**stencil** *verb* [I,T] (**stencilling**; **stencilled**, (*AmE* also) **stenciling**; **stenciled**)

step¹ /step/ *noun* [C] **1** the act of lifting one foot and putting it down in a different place □ *langkah; melangkah; bunyi tapak kaki*: *Nick took a step forward and then stopped.* ♦ *I heard steps outside the window.* ♦ *We were obviously lost so we decided to retrace our steps* (= go back the way we had come). **2** one action in a series of actions that you take in order to achieve sth □ *langkah*: *This will not solve the problem completely, but it is **a step in the right direction**.* **3** one of the surfaces on which you put your foot when you are going up or down stairs □ *anak tangga*: *on the top/bottom step* ➲ note at **stair** ➲ picture at **ladder** ➲ picture on **page P8**

IDM **in/out of step (with sb/sth)** moving/not moving your feet at the same time as other people when you are marching, dancing, etc. □ *sama/tdk sama langkah (dgn sso)*

step by step (used for talking about a series of actions) moving slowly and gradually from one action or stage to the next □ *langkah demi langkah*: *clear step-by-step instructions*

take steps to do sth to take action in order to achieve sth □ *mengambil langkah utk melakukan sst*

watch your step ➲ **watch¹**

step² /step/ *verb* [I] (**stepping**; **stepped**) **1** to lift one foot and put it down in a different place when you are walking □ *melangkah; memijak; terpijak*: *Be careful! Don't step in the mud.* ◆ *to step forward/back* ◆ *Ouch! You stepped on my foot!* **2** to move a short distance; to go somewhere □ *melangkah (keluar, masuk, turun, dsb); pergi (ke sst tempat)*: *Could you step out of the car please, sir?* ◆ *I stepped outside for a minute to get some air.*

PHR V **step down** to leave an important job or position and let sb else take your place □ *meletakkan jawatan*

step in to help sb in a difficult situation or to become involved in a disagreement □ *menolong; campur tangan*

step sth up to increase the amount, speed, etc. of sth □ *meningkatkan sst*: *The Army has decided to step up its security arrangements.*

step- /step-/ [in compounds] related as a result of one parent marrying again □ *(persaudaraan) tiri*

stepbrother /'stepbrʌðə(r)/ *noun* [C] the son from an earlier marriage of sb who has married your mother or father □ *abang/adik (lelaki) tiri* ➲ look at **half-brother**

stepchild /'steptʃaɪld/ *noun* [C] (*pl* **stepchildren**) the child from an earlier marriage of your husband or wife □ *anak tiri* ➲ note at **child**

stepdaughter /'stepdɔːtə(r)/ *noun* [C] the daughter from an earlier marriage of your husband or wife □ *anak (perempuan) tiri*

stepfather /'stepfɑːðə(r)/ *noun* [C] the man who has married your mother when your parents are divorced or your father is dead □ *bapa tiri*

stepladder /'steplædə(r)/ *noun* [C] a short **ladder** (= a piece of equipment that is used for climbing up sth) with two parts, one with steps. The parts are joined together at the top so that it can stand on its own and be folded up when you are not using it. □ *tangga tapak* ➲ picture at **ladder**

stepmother /'stepmʌðə(r)/ *noun* [C] the woman who has married your father when your parents are divorced or your mother is dead □ *ibu/emak tiri*

'stepping stone *noun* [C] **1** one of a line of flat stones that you can step on in order to cross a river □ *batu tempat berpijak* **2** something that allows you to make progress or helps you to achieve sth □ *batu loncatan*

stepsister /'stepsɪstə(r)/ *noun* [C] the daughter from an earlier marriage of sb who has married your mother or father □ *kakak/adik (perempuan) tiri* ➲ look at **half-sister**

stepson /'stepsʌn/ *noun* [C] the son from an earlier marriage of your husband or wife □ *anak (lelaki) tiri*

stereo /'steriəʊ/ *noun* (*pl* **stereos**) **1** (also **'stereo system**) [C] a machine that plays CDs, etc., sometimes with a radio, that has two separate speakers so that you hear sounds from each □ *alat stereo*: *a car/personal stereo* ➲ note at **listen 2** [U] the system for playing recorded music, speech, etc. in which the sound is divided into two parts □ *stereo*: *This programme is broadcast in stereo.* ➲ look at **mono** ▶ **stereo** *adj* [only before a noun]: *a stereo TV*

stereotype /'steriətaɪp/ *noun* [C] a fixed idea about a particular type of person or thing, which is often not true in reality □ *stereotaip; spt yg lazim kedapatan* ▶ **stereotype** *verb* [T]: *In advertisements, women are often stereotyped as housewives.* ▶ **stereotypical** /ˌsteriə'tɪpɪkl/ *adj*: *stereotypical views of accountants* ▶ **stereotypically** /-kli/ *adv*

sterile /'steraɪl/ *adj* **1** not able to produce young animals or babies □ *mandul* **2** completely clean and free from bacteria □ *steril; bersih drpd kuman*: *All equipment used during a medical operation must be sterile.* **3** not producing any useful result □ *tandus; tdk berfaedah*: *a sterile discussion/argument* ▶ **sterility** /stə'rɪləti/ *noun* [U]

sterilize (also **-ise**) /'sterəlaɪz/ *verb* [T] **1** to make sb/sth completely clean and free from bacteria □ *mensteril; membasmi kuman* **2** [usually passive] to perform an operation on a person or an animal so that they or it cannot have babies □ *memandulkan* ▶ **sterilization** (also **-isation**) /ˌsterəlaɪ'zeɪʃn/ *noun* [C,U]

sterling¹ /'stɜːlɪŋ/ *noun* [U] the system of money used in the UK, that uses the pound as its basic unit □ *sterling (mata wang UK)*

sterling² /'stɜːlɪŋ/ *adj* of very high quality □ *sangat bagus; bermutu tinggi*: *sterling work*

stern¹ /stɜːn/ *adj* (**sterner**; **sternest**) very serious; not smiling □ *garang; serius*: *a stern expression/warning* ▶ **sternly** *adv*

stern² /stɜːn/ *noun* [C] the back end of a ship or boat □ *buritan (kapal, bot, dsb)* **OPP** **bow** ➲ note at **boat** ➲ picture on **page P6**

steroid /ˈstɪərɔɪd/ noun [C] a chemical substance produced naturally in the body. There are many different **steroids** and they can be used to treat diseases and are sometimes used illegally by people playing sports. □ *steroid*

stethoscope /ˈsteθəskəʊp/ noun [C] the piece of equipment that a doctor uses for listening to your breathing and heart □ *stetoskop*

stew /stjuː/ noun [C,U] a type of food that you make by cooking meat and/or vegetables in liquid for a long time □ *stu* ▶ **stew** verb [I,T]

steward /ˈstjuːəd/ noun [C] **1** a man whose job is to look after passengers on an aircraft, a ship or a train □ *pramugara* **2** (BrE) a person who helps to organize a large public event, for example a race □ *pengelola*

stewardess /ˌstjuːəˈdes; ˈstjuːəˌ-/ noun [C] **1** (old-fashioned) a woman whose job is to look after passengers on an aircraft □ *pramugari* **2** a woman who looks after passengers on a ship or train □ *pramugari; pelayan*

⚑ stick¹ /stɪk/ verb (pt, pp stuck /stʌk/)
▶PUSH STH IN **1** [I,T] **stick (sth) in/into (sth)** to push a pointed object into sth; to be pushed into sth □ *mencucuk; menusuk*: I found a nail sticking in the tyre. ◆ Stick a fork into the meat to see if it's ready.
▶FIX **2** [I,T] to fix sth to sth else by using a sticky substance; to become fixed to sth else □ *melekatkan; menampal*: I stuck a stamp on the envelope. ◆ We used glue to stick the pieces together.
▶PUT **3** [T] (informal) to put sth somewhere, especially quickly or carelessly □ *meletakkan; menjengukkan (kepala)*: Stick your bags in the bedroom. ◆ Just at that moment James stuck his head round the door.
▶BECOME FIXED **4** [I] **stick (in sth)** (used about sth that can usually be moved) to become fixed in one position so that it cannot be moved □ *terlekat; tersangkut*: The car was stuck in the mud. ◆ This drawer keeps sticking.
▶DIFFICULT SITUATION **5** [T] [often in negative sentences and questions] (informal) to stay in a difficult or unpleasant situation □ *tahan*: I can't stick this job much longer.
IDM poke/stick your nose into sth ➪ **nose¹**
put/stick your tongue out ➪ **tongue**
stand/stick out like a sore thumb ➪ **sore¹**
PHR V stick around (informal) to stay somewhere, waiting for sth to happen or for sb to arrive □ *menunggu*
stick at sth (informal) to continue working at sth even when it is difficult □ *bertekun meneruskan sst*
stick by sb (informal) to continue to give sb help and support even in difficult times □ *menyokong atau terus membantu sso*
stick out (informal) to be very noticeable and easily seen □ *menonjol*: The new office block really sticks out from the older buildings around it.
stick out (of sth) to be further out than sth else □ *terjulur keluar*: The boy's head was sticking out of the window.
stick it/sth out (informal) to stay in a difficult or unpleasant situation until the end □ *bertahan; terus (menghadapi sst yg sukar hingga ke akhir)*
stick to sth (informal) to continue with sth and not change to anything else □ *tetap/terus dgn sst*
stick together (informal) (used about a group of people) to stay friendly and loyal to each other □ *bersatu padu; bersepakat*
stick up to point upwards □ *tegak (ke atas); tercacak*: You look funny. Your hair's sticking up!
stick up for yourself/sb/sth (informal) to support or defend yourself/sb/sth □ *menyokong atau mempertahankan diri/sso/sst*: Don't worry. I'll stick up for you if there's any trouble.

⚑ stick² /stɪk/ noun [C] **1** a small thin piece of wood from a tree □ *kayu; ranting*: We collected dry sticks to start a fire. **2** (especially BrE) = **walking stick 3** a long thin piece of wood that you use for hitting the ball in some sports □ *kayu*: a hockey stick ➪ note at **bat 4** a long thin piece of sth □ *batang*: a stick of celery/dynamite

sticker /ˈstɪkə(r)/ noun [C] a piece of paper with writing or a picture on one side that you can stick onto sth □ *pelekat*

'sticking plaster = **plaster¹(3)**

⚑ sticky /ˈstɪki/ adj (stickier; stickiest) **1** used for describing a substance that easily becomes joined to things that it touches, or sth that is covered with this kind of substance □ *melekit*: These sweets are very sticky. **2** (informal) (used about a situation) difficult or unpleasant □ *sukar*: There were a few sticky moments in the meeting.

'sticky tape = **Sellotape™**

⚑ stiff¹ /stɪf/ adj (stiffer; stiffest)
▶DIFFICULT TO BEND **1** (used about material, paper, etc.) firm and difficult to bend or move □ *keras; ketat*: My new shoes feel rather stiff. ◆ The door handle is stiff and I can't turn it.
▶PARTS OF BODY **2** if a person is stiff, their muscles hurt when they move them □ *kejang*: My arm feels really stiff after playing tennis yesterday.
▶LIQUID **3** very thick; almost solid □ *betul-betul pekat/likat; (telur) betul-betul kembang*: Beat the egg whites until they are stiff.
▶DIFFICULT/STRONG **4** more difficult or stronger than usual □ *sengit; hebat; kencang*: The firm faces stiff competition from its rivals. ◆ a stiff breeze/wind
▶BEHAVIOUR **5** not relaxed or friendly; formal □ *kaku; formal*: The speech he made to welcome them was stiff and formal.
▶ALCOHOLIC DRINK **6** [only before a noun] strong □ *arak keras*: a stiff whisky ▶ **stiffness** noun [U]

stiff² /stɪf/ adv (informal) extremely □ *betul-betul; sangat*: to be bored/frozen/scared/worried stiff

stiffen /ˈstɪfn/ verb **1** [I] (used about a person) to suddenly stop moving and hold your body very straight, usually because you are afraid or angry □ *mengejangkan; menjadi kaku* **2** [I,T] to become, or to make sth become, difficult to bend or move □ *mengeraskan*

stiffly /'stɪflɪ/ *adv* in an unfriendly formal way □ *dgn kaku; secara formal*: *He smiled stiffly*.

stifle /'staɪfl/ *verb* **1** [T] to stop sth happening, developing or continuing □ *menyekat; menahan; membendung*: *Her strict education had stifled her natural creativity.* ◆ *to stifle a yawn/cry/giggle* **2** [I,T] to be or to make sb unable to breathe because it is very hot and/or there is no fresh air □ *berasa lemas; melemaskan*: *Fergus was almost stifled by the smoke.* ▶ **stifling** *adj*: *The heat was stifling*.

stigma /'stɪgmə/ *noun* [C,U] bad and often unfair feelings that people in general have about a particular illness, way of behaving, etc. □ *aib; stigma*: *There is still a lot of stigma attached to being unemployed.*

stiletto /stɪ'letəʊ/ *noun* [C] (*pl* **-os** or **-oes**) **1** a woman's shoe with a very high narrow heel □ *kasut tumit tinggi* **2** (also ˌstiletto 'heel) the heel on such a shoe □ *tumit*

still¹ /stɪl/ *adv* **1** continuing until now or until the time you are talking about and not finishing □ *masih*: *Do you still live in London?* ◆ *It's still raining.* ◆ *I've eaten all the food but I'm still hungry.* ◆ *In 2009 Zoran was still a student.* **2** in spite of what has just been said □ *masih juga*: *He had a bad headache but he still went to the party.* **3** used for making a comparative adjective stronger □ *lagi*: *It was very cold yesterday, but today it's colder still.* ◆ *There was still more bad news to come.* **4** in addition; more □ *ada lagi; masih ada*: *There are still ten days to go until my holiday.*

still² /stɪl/ *adj* **1** not moving □ *(duduk) diam; tdk bergerak*: *Stand still! I want to take a photograph!* ◆ *Children find it hard to* **keep/stay still** *for long periods.* **2** quiet or calm □ *sunyi sepi; tenang*: *The water was perfectly still.* **3** (used about a drink) not containing gas □ *tdk bergas*: *still mineral water* ⊃ look at **fizzy, sparkling** ▶ **stillness** *noun* [U]

still³ /stɪl/ *noun* [C] a single photograph that is taken from a film or video □ *gambar pegun*

stillborn /'stɪlbɔːn/ *adj* (used about a baby) dead when it is born □ *lahir mati*

stilt /stɪlt/ *noun* [C] **1** one of two long pieces of wood, with places to rest your feet on, on which you can walk above the ground □ *jangkungan*: *Have you tried walking on stilts?* **2** one of a set of poles that supports a building above the ground or water □ *tiang; kaki bajang*

stilted /'stɪltɪd/ *adj* (used about a way of speaking or writing) not natural or relaxed; too formal □ *kaku dan kekok*

stimulant /'stɪmjələnt/ *noun* [C] a drug or medicine that makes you feel more active □ *(dadah, ubat, dsb) perangsang*

stimulate /'stɪmjuleɪt/ *verb* [T] **1** to make sth active or more active □ *merangsangkan*: *Exercise stimulates the blood circulation.* ◆ *The government has decided to cut taxes in order to stimulate the economy.* **2** to make sb feel interested and excited about sth □ *membangkitkan minat*: *The lessons don't really stimulate him.* ▶ **stimulation** /ˌstɪmju'leɪʃn/ *noun* [U]

stimulating /'stɪmjuleɪtɪŋ/ *adj* interesting and exciting □ *(yg) merangsangkan*: *a stimulating discussion*

stimulus /'stɪmjələs/ *noun* [C,U] (*pl* **stimuli** /-laɪ/) something that causes activity, development or interest □ *rangsangan*: *Books provide children with ideas and a stimulus for play.*

sting¹ /stɪŋ/ *verb* [I,T] (*pt, pp* **stung** /stʌŋ/) **1** (used about an insect, a plant, etc.) to make a person or an animal feel a sudden pain by pushing sth sharp into their skin and sending poison into them □ *menyengat; berduri bisa*: *Be careful. Those plants sting.* ◆ *Ow! I've been stung by a bee!* ⊃ look at **bite 2** to make sb/sth feel a sudden, sharp pain □ *berasa pedih; memedihkan*: *Soap stings if it gets in your eyes.* **3** to make sb feel very hurt and upset because of sth you say □ *memedihkan/menyakitkan hati*: *Kate was stung by her father's criticism.*

sting² /stɪŋ/ *noun* **1** [C] the sharp pointed part of some insects and animals that is used for pushing into the skin of a person or an animal and putting in poison □ *sengat*: *the sting of a bee* ⊃ picture at **scorpion** ⊃ picture on page **P13 2** [C] a wound that is made when an animal or insect pushes its sting into you □ *bisa sengat; sengatan*: *I got a wasp sting on the leg.* **3** [C,U] a sharp pain that feels like a sting □ *rasa pedih; kepedihan*: *the sting of soap in your eyes*

stink /stɪŋk/ *verb* [I] (*pt* **stank** /stæŋk/ *or* **stunk** /stʌŋk/; *pp* **stunk**) (*informal*) **stink (of sth) 1** to have a very strong and unpleasant smell □ *berbau busuk*: *It stinks in here—open a window!* ◆ *to stink of fish* ⊃ note at **smell² 2** to seem to be very bad, unpleasant or dishonest □ *teruk; tdk baik; berbau (rasuah, dll)*: *The whole business stinks of corruption.* ▶ **stink** *noun* [C]

stint /stɪnt/ *noun* [C] a fixed period of time that you spend doing sth □ *tempoh (melakukan sst)*: *He did a brief stint in the army after leaving school.*

stipulate /'stɪpjuleɪt/ *verb* [T] (*formal*) to say exactly and officially what must be done □ *mensyaratkan; menetapkan*: *The law stipulates that all schools must be inspected every three years.* ▶ **stipulation** /ˌstɪpju'leɪʃn/ *noun* [C,U]

stir¹ /stɜː(r)/ *verb* (**stirring; stirred**) **1** [T] to move a liquid, etc. round and round, using a spoon, etc. □ *mengacau*: *She stirred her coffee with a teaspoon.* **2** [I,T] to move or make sb/sth move slightly □ *bergerak; menggerakkan*: *She heard the baby stir in the next room.* **3** [T] to make sb feel a strong emotion □ *membangkitkan; menimbulkan; menyentuh (perasaan, dsb)*: *The story stirred Carol's imagination.* ◆ *a stirring speech*

stir → stomach

PHR V **stir sth up** to cause problems, or to make people feel strong emotions □ *menimbulkan/ mencetuskan (pergaduhan, dsb); membuat kacau*: *He's always trying to **stir up** trouble.* ♦ *The article stirred up a lot of anger among local residents.*

stir² /stɜː(r)/ *noun* **1** [sing] excitement, anger or shock that is felt by a number of people □ *kegemparan; keributan* **2** [C] the act of **stirring¹** (1) □ *kacau*: *Give the soup a stir.*

'stir-fry *verb* [T] to cook thin strips of vegetables or meat quickly in a small amount of very hot oil □ *menumis* ▶ **'stir-fry** *noun* [C]

stirrup /'stɪrəp/ *noun* [C] one of the two metal objects that you put your feet in when you are riding a horse □ *rakap* ⊃ picture at **horse**

stitch¹ /stɪtʃ/ *noun* [C] **1** one of the small lines of thread that you can see on a piece of cloth after it has been sewn □ *jahitan* ⊃ picture at **sew 2** one of the small circles of wool that you put round a needle when you are knitting □ *mata kaitan; gelungan* **3** one of the small pieces of thread that a doctor uses to sew your skin together if you cut yourself very badly, or after an operation □ *jahitan*: *How many stitches did you have in your leg?* **4** [usually sing] a sudden pain that you get in the side of your body when you are running □ *rasa sakit mencucuk-cucuk*
IDM **in stitches** (*informal*) laughing so much that you cannot stop □ *ketawa bagai nak pecah perut*

stitch² /stɪtʃ/ *verb* [I,T] to sew □ *menjahit*

stock¹ /stɒk/ *noun* [C,U] **1** the supply of things that a shop, etc. has for sale □ *stok*: *We'll have to order extra stock if we sell a lot more this week.* ♦ *I'm afraid that book's **out of stock** at the moment. Shall I order it for you?* ♦ *I'll see if we have your size **in stock**.* **2** an amount of sth that has been kept ready to be used □ *bekalan; simpanan*: *Food stocks in the village were very low.* **3** a share that sb has bought in a company, or the value of a company's shares □ *stok*: *to invest in stocks and shares* **4** a liquid that is made by boiling meat, bones, vegetables, etc. in water, used especially for making soups and sauces □ *air rebusan; kaldu*: *vegetable/chicken stock*
IDM **take stock (of sth)** to think about sth very carefully before deciding what to do next □ *membuat penilaian (ttg sst)*

stock² /stɒk/ *verb* [T] **1** (usually used about a shop) to have a supply of sth □ *ada menyimpan stok; ada menjual*: *They stock food from all over the world.* **2** to fill a place with sth □ *melengkapkan (dgn sst); ada (banyak buku, dll)*: *a well-stocked library*
PHR V **stock up (on/with sth)** to collect a large supply of sth for future use □ *menyimpan bekalan*: *to stock up with food for the winter*

stock³ /stɒk/ *adj* [only before a noun] (used for describing sth that sb says used so often that it does not have much meaning □ *biasa; basi*: *He always gives the same stock answers.*

stockbroker /'stɒkbrəʊkə(r)/ (also **broker**) *noun* [C] a person whose job is to buy and sell shares in companies for other people □ *broker saham*

'stock exchange *noun* [C] **1** a place where shares in companies are bought and sold □ *bursa saham*: *the Tokyo Stock Exchange* **2** (also **'stock market**) the business or activity of buying and selling shares in companies □ *pasaran saham* ⊃ note at **money** ⊃ look at **exchange**

stocking /'stɒkɪŋ/ *noun* [C] one of a pair of thin pieces of clothing that fit tightly over a woman's feet and legs □ *stoking*: *a pair of stockings* ⊃ look at **tights**

stockist /'stɒkɪst/ *noun* [C] a shop that sells goods made by a particular company □ *pembekal*

'stock market *noun* = **stock exchange** (2)

stockpile /'stɒkpaɪl/ *verb* [T] to collect and keep a large supply of sth □ *simpanan stok* ▶ **stockpile** *noun* [C]: *a stockpile of weapons*

stocktaking /'stɒkteɪkɪŋ/ *noun* [U] the activity of counting the total supply of things that a shop or business has at a particular time □ *pengiraan stok*: *They close for an hour a month to do the stocktaking.*

stocky /'stɒki/ *adj* (**stockier**; **stockiest**) (used about sb's body) short but strong and heavy □ *pendek dan gempal*

stoic /'stəʊɪk/ (also **stoical** /-kl/) *adj* (*formal*) suffering pain or difficulty without complaining □ *tabah* ▶ **stoically** /-kli/ *adv* ▶ **stoicism** /'stəʊɪsɪzəm/ *noun* [U]

stoke /stəʊk/ *verb* [T] **1 stoke sth (up) (with sth)** to add fuel to a fire □ *memarakkan api*: *to stoke up a fire with more coal* ♦ *to stoke a furnace* **2 stoke sth (up)** to make people feel sth more strongly □ *mengapi-apikan*: *to stoke up envy*

stole past tense of **steal**

stolen past participle of **steal**

stolid /'stɒlɪd/ *adj* (used about a person) showing very little emotion or excitement ▶ *tdk menunjukkan sebarang perasaan* ▶ **stolidly** *adv*

stomach¹ /'stʌmək/ (also *informal* **tummy**) *noun* [C] **1** the organ in your body where food goes after you have eaten it □ *(kantung) perut*: *He went to the doctor with stomach pains.* ⊃ picture at **body 2** the front part of your body below your chest and above your legs □ *perut*: *She turned over onto her stomach.* ⊃ picture at **body**

stomach² /'stʌmək/ *verb* [T] [usually in negative sentences and questions] (*informal*) to be able to watch, listen to, accept, etc. sth that you think is unpleasant □ *tahan; sanggup*: *I can't stomach too much violence in films.*

ʌ c**u**p ɜː b**i**rd ə **a**go eɪ p**ay** əʊ g**o** aɪ m**y** aʊ n**ow** ɔɪ b**oy** ɪə n**ear** eə h**air** ʊə p**ure**

stomach ache noun [C,U] a pain in your stomach □ *sakit perut*: *I've got terrible stomach ache.* ⊃ note at **ache**

stomp /stɒmp/ verb [I] (*informal*) to walk with heavy steps □ *berjalan menghentakkan kaki*

stone /stəʊn/ noun
▶HARD SUBSTANCE **1** [U] a hard solid substance that is found in the ground □ *batu*: *The house was built of grey stone.* ♦ *a stone wall* **2** [C] a small piece of rock □ *batu*: *The boy picked up a stone and threw it into the river.*
▶JEWEL **3** [C] = **precious stone**
▶IN FRUIT **4** (*AmE* **pit**) [C] the hard seed inside some types of fruit □ *biji*: *Peaches, plums, cherries and olives all have stones.* ⊃ picture on **page P14**
▶WEIGHT **5** [C] (*pl* **stone**) (*abbr* **st**) (in Britain) a measure of weight; 6.35 kilograms. There are 14 pounds in a stone □ *ston*: *I weigh eleven stone two* (= 2 pounds).
IDM **kill two birds with one stone** ⊃ **kill**[1]

stoned /stəʊnd/ adj (*slang*) not behaving or thinking normally because of drugs or alcohol □ *mabuk; khayal*

stony /ˈstəʊni/ adj (**stonier**; **stoniest**) **1** (used about the ground) having a lot of stones in it, or covered with stones □ *berbatu* **2** not friendly □ *dingin; tdk menunjukkan kemesraan atau simpati*: *There was a stony silence as he walked into the room.*

stood past tense, past participle of **stand**[1]

stool /stuːl/ noun [C] a seat that does not have a back or arms □ *bangku*: *a piano stool* ⊃ picture at **chair**, **piano**

stoop /stuːp/ verb [I] to bend your head and shoulders forwards and downwards □ *membongkok*: *He had to stoop to get through the low doorway.*
PHR V **stoop to sth/doing sth** to do sth bad or wrong that you would normally not do □ *sanggup melakukan sst (yg tdk baik, dsb)*
▶ **stoop** noun [sing]: *to walk with a stoop*

stop[1] /stɒp/ verb (**stopping**; **stopped**) **1** [I,T] to finish moving or make sb/sth finish moving □ *berhenti; memberhentikan; singgah; menahan*: *He walked along the road for a bit, and then stopped.* ♦ *Does this train stop at Didcot?* ♦ *My watch has stopped.* ♦ *I stopped someone in the street to ask the way to the station.* **2** [I,T] to no longer continue or to make sb/sth not continue □ *berhenti*: *I think the rain has stopped.* ♦ *It's stopped raining now.* ♦ *Stop making that terrible noise!* ♦ *The bus service stops at midnight.* ♦ *We tied a bandage round his arm to stop the bleeding.*

GRAMMAR If you **stop to do sth**, you stop in order to do it: *On the way home I stopped to buy a newspaper.* If you **stop doing sth**, you do not now do something that you did in the past: *I stopped smoking 3 months ago.*

3 [T] **stop sb/sth (from) doing sth** to make sb/sth end or finish an activity; to prevent sb/sth from doing sth □ *menghalang; menyekat*: *They've built a fence to stop the dog getting out.* ♦ *I'm going to go and you can't stop me.* **4** [I,T] **stop (for sth); stop (and do/to do sth)** to end an activity for a short time in order to do sth □ *berhenti*: *Shall we stop for lunch now?* ♦ *Let's stop and look at the map.* ♦ *We stopped for half an hour to have a cup of coffee.*
IDM **stop at nothing** to do anything to get what you want, even if it is wrong or dangerous □ *sanggup melakukan apa saja*
stop short of sth/doing sth to almost do sth, but then decide not to do it at the last minute □ *tdk sanggup sampai (membuat sst)*
PHR V **stop off (at/in ...)** to stop during a journey to do sth □ *berhenti/singgah sekejap (di...)*
stop over (at/in ...) to stay somewhere for a short time during a long journey □ *berhenti/singgah (di...)*

stop[2] /stɒp/ noun [C] **1** an act of stopping or the state of being stopped □ *(perbuatan/keadaan) berhenti atau menghentikan; tempat berhenti*: *Our first stop will be in Edinburgh.* ♦ *Production at the factory will come to a stop at midnight tonight.* ♦ *I managed to bring the car to a stop just in time.* **2** the place where a bus, train, etc. stops so that people can get on and off □ *perhentian*: *a bus stop* ♦ *I'm getting off at the next stop.* ⊃ picture on **page P11**
IDM **pull out all the stops** ⊃ **pull**[1]
put a stop to sth to prevent sth bad or unpleasant from continuing □ *menghentikan sst*

stopgap /ˈstɒpɡæp/ noun [C] a person or a thing that does a job for a short time until sb/sth permanent can be found □ *(pengganti) sementara*

stopover /ˈstɒpəʊvə(r)/ noun [C] a short stay between two parts of a journey □ *perhentian; persinggahan*

stoppage /ˈstɒpɪdʒ/ noun [C] **1** a situation in which people stop working as part of a protest □ *pemogokan* **2** (in sport) an interruption in a game for a particular reason □ *henti main*

stopper /ˈstɒpə(r)/ noun [C] an object that you put into the top of a bottle in order to close it □ *penyumbat*

stopwatch /ˈstɒpwɒtʃ/ noun [C] a watch which can be started and stopped by pressing a button, so that you can measure exactly how long sth takes □ *jam randik*

storage /ˈstɔːrɪdʒ/ noun [U] the process of keeping things until they are needed; the space where they are kept □ *penyimpanan; tempat simpanan*: *This room is being used for storage at the moment.*

store[1] /stɔː(r)/ noun [C] **1** a large shop □ *gedung*: *She's a sales assistant in a large department store.* ♦ *a furniture store* ⊃ look at **chain store 2** (*AmE*) = **shop**[1] **3** a supply of sth that you keep for future use; the place where it is kept □ *simpanan; bekalan; stor*: *a good store of food for the*

store → straight

winter ♦ *Police discovered a weapons store in the house.*
IDM **in store (for sb/sth)** going to happen in the future □ *sst (yg akan berlaku utk sso/sst)*: *There's a surprise in store for you when you get home!*
set ... store by sth to consider sth to be important □ *menganggap penting; mementingkan*: *Nick sets great store by his mother's opinion.*

store² /stɔː(r)/ *verb* [T] to keep sth or a supply of sth for future use □ *menyimpan*: *to store information on a computer*

storekeeper /'stɔːkiːpə(r)/ (*AmE*) = **shopkeeper**

storeroom /'stɔːruːm; -rʊm/ *noun* [C] a room where things are kept until they are needed □ *bilik stor*

storey (*AmE* **story**) /'stɔːri/ *noun* [C] (*pl* **storeys**, (*AmE*) **stories**) one floor or level of a building □ *tingkat*: *The building will be five storeys high.* ♦ *a two-storey house* ♦ *a multi-storey car park*

stork /stɔːk/ *noun* [C] a large black and white bird with a long beak, neck and legs. **Storks** often make their nests on the top of buildings. □ *burung botak*

storm¹ /stɔːm/ *noun* [C] very bad weather with strong winds and rain □ *ribut*: *Look at those black clouds. I think there's going to be a storm.* ♦ *a hailstorm* (= a storm when hail falls from the sky) ♦ *a sandstorm* (= a storm in the desert when sand is blown into the air) ➲ note at **weather**

OTHER WORDS FOR

storm

During a **thunderstorm** you hear **thunder** and see flashes of **lightning** in the sky. Large, violent storms with very strong winds are called **cyclones**. **Hurricanes** (or **typhoons**) are a type of cyclone. A storm with a very strong circular wind is called a **tornado**. A **blizzard** is a very bad **snowstorm**.

---

storm² /stɔːm/ *verb* **1** [T] to attack a building, town, etc. suddenly and violently in order to take control of it □ *menyerbu; menggempur* **2** [I] to enter or leave somewhere in a very angry and noisy way □ *menghentak-hentak (keluar, masuk sst kerana marah)*: *He threw down the book and stormed out of the room.*

stormy /'stɔːmi/ *adj* (**stormier**; **stormiest**) **1** used for talking about very bad weather, with strong winds, heavy rain, etc. □ *bercuaca buruk*: *a stormy night* ♦ *stormy weather* **2** involving a lot of angry argument and strong feeling □ *bergolak; penuh perbalahan, dsb*: *a stormy relationship*

story /'stɔːri/ *noun* [C] (*pl* **stories**) **1 a story (about sb/sth)** a description of people and events that are not real □ *cerita*: *I'll tell you a story about the animals that live in that forest.* ♦ *I always read the children **a bedtime story**.* ♦ *a detective/fairy/ghost/love story* ➲ note at **history** **2** an account, especially a spoken one, of sth that has happened □ *cerita*: *The police didn't believe his story.* **3** a description of true events that happened in the past □ *cerita; kisah*: *He's writing his life story.* **4** an article or a report in a newspaper or a magazine □ *cerita; laporan; kisah*: *The plane crash was the front-page story in most newspapers.* **5** (*AmE*) = **storey**

stout /staʊt/ *adj* (**stouter**; **stoutest**) **1** (used about a person) rather fat □ *gempal; agak gemuk* **2** strong and thick □ *kuat; kukuh*: *stout walking boots*

stove /stəʊv/ *noun* [C] **1** a piece of equipment that can burn wood, coal, etc. to heat a room □ *dapur*: *a wood-burning stove* **2** (especially *AmE*) = **cooker**: *He put a pan of water to boil on the stove.*

stovetop /'stəʊvtɒp/ (*AmE*) = **hob**

stow /stəʊ/ *verb* [T] **stow sth (away)** to put sth away in a particular place until it is needed □ *menyimpan*

stowaway /'stəʊəweɪ/ *noun* [C] a person who hides in a ship or plane so that they can travel without paying □ *penumpang gelap*

straddle /'strædl/ *verb* [T] **1** (used about a person) to sit or stand with your legs on each side of sth □ *mengangkangi*: *to straddle a chair* **2** (used about a building, bridge, etc.) to be on both sides of sth □ *merentang*

straggle /'strægl/ *verb* [I] **1** to grow, spread or move in an untidy way or in different directions □ *berselerak; bercelaru*: *Her wet hair straggled across her forehead.* **2** to walk, etc. more slowly than the rest of the group □ *berjalan lambat-lambat*: *The children straggled along behind their parents.* ▸ **straggler** *noun* [C] ▸ **straggly** *adj*: *long straggly hair*

straight¹ /streɪt/ *adv* (**straighter**; **straightest**) **1** not in a curve or at an angle; in a straight line □ *terus; lurus; tegak*: *Go straight on for about two miles until you come to some traffic lights.* ♦ *He was looking straight ahead.* ♦ *to sit up straight* (= with a straight back) **2** without stopping □ *terus*: *I took the children straight home after school.* ♦ *to walk straight past somebody/something* ♦ *I'm going straight to bed when I get home.* ♦ *He joined the army straight from school.* **3** in an honest and direct way □ *dgn terus terang*: *Tell me straight, doctor—is it serious?*
IDM **go straight** (*informal*) to become honest after being a criminal □ *hidup lurus menjadi (orang) baik*
right/straight away ➲ **away**
straight out (*informal*) in an honest and direct way □ *dgn terus terang*: *I told Asif straight out that I didn't want to see him any more.*

straight² /streɪt/ *adj* (**straighter**; **straightest**)
▸ WITHOUT BENDS **1** with no bends or curves; going in one direction only □ *lurus*: *a straight line* ♦ *He's got straight dark hair.* ♦ *Keep your back*

straight! ◆ He was so tired he couldn't walk **in a straight line**. ➔ picture at **hair**, **line**
▸HORIZONTAL/VERTICAL **2** [not before a noun] in an exactly horizontal or vertical position □ *tegak: That picture isn't straight.*
▸TIDY **3** tidy or organized as it should be □ *kemas; teratur: It took ages to put the room straight after we'd decorated it.*
▸HONEST **4** honest and direct □ *lurus; jujur: Politicians never give a straight answer.* ◆ *Are you being straight with me?*
▸ALCOHOLIC DRINK **5** (AmE) = **neat**(5)
▸BORING **6** (*informal*) used to describe a person who you think is too serious and boring □ *serius*
▸SEX **7** (*informal*) attracted to people of the opposite sex □ *heteroseksual; bukan homoseksual* **SYN** heterosexual **OPP** gay
IDM **get sth straight** to make sure that you understand sth completely □ *faham betul-betul*
keep a straight face to stop yourself from smiling or laughing □ *cuba menahan senyum atau ketawa*
put/set the record straight ➔ **record**[1]

straighten /ˈstreɪtn/ *verb* [I,T] **straighten (sth) (up/out)** to become straight or to make sth straight □ *meluruskan; menjadi lurus; membetulkan: The road straightens out at the bottom of the hill.* ◆ *to straighten your tie*
PHR V **straighten sth out** to remove the confusion or difficulties from a situation □ *menyelesaikan; membetulkan sst*
straighten up to make your body straight and vertical □ *meluruskan badan; duduk/berdiri tegak*

straightforward /ˌstreɪtˈfɔːwəd/ *adj* **1** easy to do or understand; simple □ *jelas; mudah: straightforward instructions* **2** honest and open □ *lurus; jujur: a straightforward person*

straightjacket = **straitjacket**

⚑ **strain**[1] /streɪn/ *noun*
▸WORRY **1** [C,U] worry or pressure caused by having too much to deal with □ *tekanan: to be under a lot of strain at work* **2** [C] something that makes you feel worried and tense □ *tekanan; beban: I always find exams a terrible strain.*
▸PRESSURE **3** [U] pressure that is put on sth when it is pulled or pushed by a physical force □ *ketegangan; tegang; bebanan; (perbuatan) membebankan: Running downhill puts strain on the knees.* ◆ *The rope finally broke under the strain.*
▸INJURY **4** [C,U] an injury to part of your body that is caused by using it too much □ *tegang otot: He is out of today's game with a back strain.*
▸TYPE OF ANIMAL, ETC. **5** [C] one type of animal, plant or disease that is slightly different from the other types □ *baka; jenis: This new strain of the disease is particularly dangerous.*

strain[2] /streɪn/ *verb* **1** [T] to injure a part of your body by using it too much □ *merosakkan; melemahkan; menegangkan: Don't read in the dark. You'll strain your eyes.* ◆ *I think I've strained a muscle in my neck.* **2** [I,T] to make a great effort to do sth □ *berusaha sedaya upaya: I was straining to see what was happening.* ◆ *Bend down*

847 **straighten → strap**

as far as you can without straining. **3** [T] to put a lot of pressure on sth □ *membebankan: Money problems have strained their relationship.* **4** [T] to separate a solid and a liquid by pouring them into a special container with small holes in it □ *menapis: to strain tea/vegetables/spaghetti*

strained /streɪnd/ *adj* **1** worried because of having too much to deal with □ *tegang: Martin looked tired and strained.* **2** not natural or friendly □ *dipaksa-paksa; tegang: Relations between the two countries are strained.*

strait /streɪt/ *noun* **1** [C] (also **straits** [pl]) a narrow piece of sea that joins two larger seas □ *selat: the Strait(s) of Gibraltar* **2** **straits** [pl] a very difficult situation, especially one caused by having no money □ *kesukaran: The company is in desperate financial straits.*
IDM **be in dire straits** ➔ **dire**

straitjacket (also **straightjacket**) /ˈstreɪtdʒækɪt/ *noun* [C] a piece of clothing like a jacket with long arms which are tied to prevent people who are considered dangerous from behaving violently □ *baju pasung*

strand /strænd/ *noun* [C] **1** a single piece of cotton, wool, hair, etc. □ *lembar* **2** one part of a story, a situation or an idea □ *bahagian; unsur*

stranded /ˈstrændɪd/ *adj* left in a place that you cannot get away from □ *terkandas: We were left stranded when our car broke down in the mountains.*

⚑ **strange** /streɪndʒ/ *adj* (**stranger**; **strangest**) **1** unusual or unexpected □ *aneh; ganjil; pelik: A very strange thing happened to me on the way home.* ◆ *a strange noise* **2** that you have not seen, visited, met, etc. before □ *belum pernah dilihat, dilawati, ditemui, dsb: a strange town* ◆ *Do not talk to strange men.* ➔ look at **foreign**

HELP **Strange** does not mean 'from another country'.

▸**strangely** *adv*: *The streets were strangely quiet.* ◆ *He's behaving very strangely at the moment.*
▸**strangeness** *noun* [U]

⚑ **stranger** /ˈstreɪndʒə(r)/ *noun* [C] **1** a person that you do not know □ *orang yg tdk dikenali: I had to ask a complete stranger to help me with my suitcase.* ➔ look at **foreigner**

HELP **Stranger** DOES NOT mean 'someone who comes from a different country'.

2 a person who is in a place that they do not know □ *orang asing; tdk biasa: I'm a stranger to this part of the country.*

strangle /ˈstræŋgl/ *verb* [T] **1** to kill sb by squeezing their neck or throat with your hands, a rope, etc. □ *mencekik; menjerut* **SYN** throttle ➔ look at **choke** **2** to prevent sth from developing □ *menyekat*

strap /stræp/ *noun* [C] a long narrow piece of leather, cloth, plastic, etc. that you use for carrying sth or for keeping sth in position □ *tali*: *a watch with a leather strap* ⊃ picture at **bag**, **clock** ▶**strap** *verb* [T] (**strapping**; **strapped**): *The racing driver was securely strapped into the car.*

strategic /strə'ti:dʒɪk/ (also **strategical** /-kl/) *adj* **1** helping you to achieve a plan; giving you an advantage □ *strategik; memanfaatkan; bermanfaat*: *They made a strategic decision to sell off part of the company.* **2** connected with a country's plans to achieve success in a war or in its defence system □ *strategik* **3** (used about bombs and other weapons) intended to be fired at the enemy's country rather than be used in battle □ *strategik* ▶**strategically** /-kli/ *adv*: *The island is strategically important.*

strategy /'strætədʒi/ *noun* (*pl* **strategies**) **1** [C] a plan that you use in order to achieve sth □ *strategi*: *What's your strategy for this exam?* **2** [U] the act of planning how to do or achieve sth □ *strategi; perancangan*: *military strategy*

straw /strɔ:/ *noun* **1** [U] the long thin parts of some plants, for example **wheat** (= a plant grown for its grain), which are dried and then used for animals to sleep on or for making hats, covering a roof, etc. □ *jerami*: *a straw hat* **2** [C] one piece of **straw** □ *jerami* **3** [C] a long plastic or paper tube that you can use for drinking through □ *straw*
IDM **the last/final straw** the last in a series of bad things that happen to you and that makes you decide that you cannot accept the situation any longer □ *habis sabar; tdk tahan/sanggup lagi*

strawberry /'strɔ:bəri/ *noun* [C] (*pl* **strawberries**) a small soft red fruit with small white seeds on it □ *strawberi*: *strawberries and cream* ⊃ picture on **page P14**

stray¹ /streɪ/ *verb* [I] **1** to go away from the place where you should be □ *melencong; merayau*: *The sheep had strayed onto the road.* **2** to not keep to the subject you should be thinking about or discussing □ *menyimpang*: *My thoughts strayed for a few moments.*

stray² /streɪ/ *noun* [C] a dog, cat, etc. that does not have a home □ *anjing, kucing, dsb yg tdk bertuan* ▶**stray** *adj* [only *before* a noun]: *a stray dog*

streak¹ /stri:k/ *noun* [C] **1 streak (of sth)** a thin line or mark □ *garis; jalur*: *The cat had brown fur with streaks of white in it.* **2** a part of sb's character that sometimes shows in the way they behave □ *unsur*: *Vesna's a very caring girl, but she does have a selfish streak.* **3** a continuous period of bad or good luck in a game or sport □ *tempoh; jangka masa*: *The team is on a losing/winning streak at the moment.*

streak² /stri:k/ *verb* [I] (*informal*) to run fast □ *memecut*

streaked /stri:kt/ *adj* **streaked (with sth)** having lines of a different colour □ *berjalur*: *black hair streaked with grey*

stream¹ /stri:m/ *noun* [C] **1** a small river □ *anak sungai*: *I waded across the shallow stream.* ⊃ picture on **page P10**, **page P11 2** the continuous movement of a liquid or gas □ *aliran; lelehan*: *a stream of blood* **3** a continuous movement of people or things □ *aliran; arus*: *a stream of traffic* **4** a large number of things which happen one after another □ *berduyun-duyun; banjiran*: *a stream of letters/telephone calls/questions*

stream² /stri:m/ *verb* **1** [I] (used about a liquid, gas or light) to flow in large amounts □ *mengalir*: *Tears were streaming down his face.* ♦ *Sunlight was streaming in through the windows.* **2** [I] (used about people or things) to move somewhere in a continuous flow □ *berduyun-duyun; berbondong-bondong*: *People were streaming out of the station.* **3** [T] to play video or sound on a computer by receiving it as a continuous stream, from the Internet for example □ *memainkan* ⊃ note at **touch screen**

streamer /'stri:mə(r)/ *noun* [C] a long piece of coloured paper that you use for decorating a room before a party, etc. □ *ular-ular*

streamline /'stri:mlaɪn/ *verb* [T] **1** to give a vehicle, etc. a long smooth shape so that it will move easily through air or water □ *menggaris arus* **2** to make an organization, a process, etc. work better by making it simpler □ *memperkemas* ▶**streamlined** *adj*

street /stri:t/ *noun* [C] **1** a public road in a city or town that has houses and buildings on one side or both sides □ *jalan*: *to walk along/down the street* ♦ *to cross the street* ♦ *I met Ian in the street this morning.* ♦ *a narrow street* ♦ *a street map of Oporto* ⊃ note at **road 2 Street** (*abbr* **St**) used in the names of streets □ *Jalan*: *64 High Street* ♦ *The post office is in Sheep Street.*
IDM **the man in the street** ⊃ **man¹**
streets ahead (of sb/sth) (*BrE informal*) much better than sb/sth □ *jauh lebih baik (drpd sso/sst)*
(right) up your street (*informal*) (used about an activity, a subject, etc.) exactly right for you because you know a lot about it, like it very much, etc. □ *betul-betul sesuai/bagus (utk sso)*

streetcar /'stri:tkɑ:(r)/ (*AmE*) = **tram**

'street light (*BrE also* **'street lamp**) *noun* [C] a light at the top of a tall post in the street □ *lampu jalan* ⊃ look at **lamp post**

strength /streŋθ/ *noun*
▶PHYSICAL POWER **1** [U] the quality of being physically strong; the amount of this quality that you have □ *kekuatan; tenaga*: *He pulled with all his strength but the rock would not move.* ♦ *I didn't have the strength to walk any further.* **2** [U] the ability of an object to hold heavy weights or to not break or be damaged easily □ *kekuatan; keteguhan*: *All our suitcases are tested for strength before they leave the factory.*
▶INFLUENCE **3** [U] the power and influence that sb has □ *kekuatan*: *Germany's economic strength*

strengthen → strife

▶OF FEELING/OPINION **4** [U] how strong a feeling or opinion is □ *kekuatan; kuatnya*: *The government has misjudged the strength of public feeling on this issue.*

▶GOOD QUALITY **5** [C,U] a good quality or ability that sb/sth has □ *kelebihan*: *His greatest strength is his ability to communicate with people.* ◆ *the strengths and weaknesses of a plan* ◆ *He showed great strength of character.* **OPP** weakness
IDM **at full strength** ⊃ **full¹**
below strength (used about a group) not having the number of people it needs or usually has □ *kekurangan anggota (pasukan, dsb)*
on the strength of as a result of information, advice, etc. □ *berdasarkan*

strengthen /ˈstreŋθən/ *verb* [I,T] to become stronger or to make sth stronger □ *menguatkan*: *exercises to strengthen your muscles* **OPP** weaken

strenuous /ˈstrenjuəs/ *adj* needing or using a lot of effort or energy □ *berat; memerlukan banyak tenaga*: *Don't do strenuous exercise after eating.* ▶**strenuously** *adv*

stress¹ /stres/ *noun* **1** [C,U] worry and pressure that is caused by problems and by having too much to deal with □ *tekanan*: *He's been under a lot of stress since his wife went into hospital.* ⊃ look at **trauma** **2** [C,U] a physical force that may cause sth to bend or break □ *tekanan; beban*: *Heavy lorries put too much stress on this bridge.* **3** [U] stress (on sth) the special attention that you give to sth because you think it is important □ *penekanan; pengutamaan*: *We should put more stress on preventing crime.* **4** [C,U] (a) stress (on sth) the force that you put on a particular word or part of a word when you speak □ *tekanan*: *In the word 'dictionary' the stress is on the first syllable, 'dic'.*

stress² /stres/ *verb* [T] to give sth special force or attention because it is important □ *menekankan*: *The minister stressed the need for a peaceful solution.* ◆ *You stress the first syllable in this word.* **SYN** emphasize

stressed /strest/ *adj* [not before a noun] (*informal*) (*also* ˌstressed ˈout) too anxious and tired to be able to relax □ *tertekan*: *He was feeling very stressed and tired.*

stressful /ˈstresfl/ *adj* causing worry and pressure □ *penuh tekanan*: *a stressful job*

stretch¹ /stretʃ/ *verb* **1** [I,T] to pull sth so that it becomes longer or wider; to become longer or wider in this way □ *meregang(kan); menegangkan*: *The artist stretched the canvas tightly over the frame.* ◆ *My T-shirt stretched when I washed it.* **2** [I,T] stretch (sth) (out) to push out your arms, legs, etc. as far as possible □ *menggeliat; meregangkan; menghulurkan; menjangkau*: *He switched off the alarm clock, yawned and stretched.* ◆ *She stretched out on the sofa and fell asleep.* ◆ *She stretched out her arm to take the book.* ⊃ picture at **exercise 3** [I] to cover a large area of land or a long period of time □ *terbentang; terus-menerus; berterusan*: *The long white beaches stretch for miles along the coast.* **4** [T] to make use of all the money, ability, time, etc. that sb has available for use □ *menggunakan sehabis-habisnya; mencabar*: *The test has been designed to really stretch students' knowledge.*
IDM **stretch your legs** (*informal*) to go for a walk after sitting down for a long time □ *bangun berjalan-jalan (setelah lama duduk)*

stretch² /stretʃ/ *noun* [C] **1 a stretch (of sth)** an area of land or water □ *bahagian*: *a dangerous stretch of road* **2** [usually sing] the act of making the muscles in your arms, legs, back, etc. as long as possible □ *menggeliat*: *Stand up, everybody, and have a good stretch.*
IDM **at full stretch** ⊃ **full¹**
at a stretch without stopping □ *tanpa berhenti*: *We travelled for six hours at a stretch.*

stretcher /ˈstretʃə(r)/ *noun* [C] a piece of cloth supported by two poles that is used for carrying a person who has been injured □ *usungan*

stretchy /ˈstretʃi/ *adj* (**stretchier**; **stretchiest**) that can easily be made longer or wider without tearing or breaking □ *anjal; boleh diregang dgn mudah; boleh ditarik*: *stretchy fabric*

strict /strɪkt/ *adj* (**stricter**; **strictest**) **1** that must be obeyed completely □ *tegas*: *I gave her strict instructions to be home before 9.00.* **2** not allowing people to break rules or behave badly □ *tegas; ketat*: *Samir's very strict with his children.* ◆ *I went to an extremely strict school.* **3** obeying the rules of a particular religion or belief exactly □ *tegas*: *a strict Muslim* **4** exactly correct; accurate □ *tepat; sebenarnya*: *a strict interpretation of the law*

strictly /ˈstrɪktli/ *adv* **1** with a lot of control and rules that must be obeyed □ *secara ketat/ tegas*: *She was brought up very strictly.* **2** used to emphasize that sth happens or must happen in all circumstances □ *secara tegas*: *Smoking is strictly forbidden.* ◆ *Chewing gum is strictly forbidden in the classroom.*
IDM **strictly speaking** to be exactly correct or accurate □ *sebenarnya*: *Strictly speaking, the tomato is not a vegetable. It's a fruit.*

stride¹ /straɪd/ *verb* [I] (*pt* **strode** /strəʊd/) [not used in the perfect tenses] to walk with long steps, often because you feel very confident or determined □ *berjalan dgn langkah panjang*: *He strode up to the house and knocked on the door.*

stride² /straɪd/ *noun* [C] a long step □ *langkah (panjang)*
IDM **get into your stride** to start to do sth well and in a confident way after an uncertain beginning □ *sudah lancar*
make great strides ⊃ **great¹**
take sth in your stride to deal with a new or difficult situation easily and without worrying □ *menerima/menghadapi sst dgn tenang*

strident /ˈstraɪdnt/ *adj* (used about a voice or a sound) loud and unpleasant □ *lantang*

strife /straɪf/ *noun* [U] (*formal*) trouble or fighting between people or groups □ *perbalahan; persengketaan*

| VOWELS | iː see | i any | ɪ sit | e ten | æ hat | ɑː father | ɒ got | ɔː saw | ʊ put | uː too | u usual |

strike¹ /straɪk/ verb (pt, pp struck /strʌk/)
▸HIT SB/STH **1** [T] (formal) to hit sb/sth □ *memukul; menghentam; melanggar*: *The stone struck her on the head.* ♦ *The boat struck a rock and began to sink.* ➲ note at **hit**
▸ATTACK **2** [I,T] to attack and harm sb/sth suddenly □ *melanda; menimpa; menyambar; disambar*: *The earthquake struck Haiti in 2010.* ♦ *The building had been struck by lightning.*
▸OF THOUGHT **3** [T] to come suddenly into sb's mind □ *terlintas dlm fikiran*: *It suddenly struck me that she would be the ideal person for the job.*
▸GIVE IMPRESSION **4** [T] **strike sb (as sth)** to give sb a particular impression □ *menimbulkan; rasa; nampaknya*: *Does anything here strike you as unusual?* ♦ *He strikes me as a very caring man.*
▸OF WORKERS **5** [I] to stop work as a protest □ *mogok*: *The workers voted to strike for more money.*
▸MAKE FIRE **6** [T] to produce fire by rubbing sth, especially a match, on a surface □ *menggores; memantikkan*: *She struck a match and lit the candle.*
▸OF CLOCK **7** [I,T] to ring a bell so that people know what time it is □ *berbunyi*: *The church clock struck three.*
▸GOLD, OIL, ETC. **8** [T] to discover gold, oil, etc. in the ground □ *menemui (emas, minyak, dll)*: *They had struck oil!*
IDM **strike a balance (between A and B)** to find a middle way between two extremes □ *mencari keseimbangan (antara A dgn B)*
strike a bargain (with sb) to make an agreement with sb □ *membuat perjanjian (dgn sso)*
within striking distance near enough to be reached or attacked easily □ *cukup dekat; sudah dekat*
PHR V **strike back** to attack sb/sth that has attacked you □ *menyerang balik*
strike up sth (with sb) to start a conversation or friendship with sb □ *memulakan perbualan atau berkenalan dgn sso*

strike² /straɪk/ noun [C] **1** a period of time when people refuse to go to work, usually because they want more money or better working conditions □ *mogok*: *a one-day strike* ♦ *Union members voted to **go on strike**.* **2** a sudden military attack, especially by aircraft □ *serangan*: *an air strike*

striker /ˈstraɪkə(r)/ noun [C] **1** a person who has stopped working as a protest □ *pemogok* **2** (in football) a player whose job is to score goals □ *penyerang*

striking /ˈstraɪkɪŋ/ adj very noticeable; making a strong impression □ *ketara; menarik*: *There was a striking similarity between the two men.* ▸**strikingly** adv: *She is strikingly beautiful.*

string¹ /strɪŋ/ noun
▸FOR TYING THINGS **1** [C,U] a piece of long, strong material like very thin rope, that you use for tying things □ *tali*: *a ball/piece/length of string* ♦ *The key is hanging on a string.* ➲ picture at **rope**
▸LINE OF THINGS **2** [C] **a string of sth** a line of things that are joined together on the same piece of thread □ *utas; untai*: *a string of beads*
▸SERIES **3** [C] **a string of sth** a series of people, things or events that follow one after another □ *rangkaian; deretan; rentetan*: *a string of visitors*
▸MUSICAL INSTRUMENTS **4** [C] one of the pieces of thin wire, etc. that produce the sound on some musical instruments □ *tali*: *A guitar has six strings.* ➲ picture at **music, piano 5 the strings** [pl] (in an **orchestra**) the instruments that have strings □ *alat tali*: *Listen to the melody in the strings.* ➲ note at **instrument** ➲ picture at **music**
▸ON RACKET **6** [C] one of the pieces of thin material that is stretched across a **racket** (= the thing you use to hit the ball in some sports) □ *tali*
IDM **(with) no strings attached; without strings** with no special conditions □ *tanpa sebarang syarat/ikatan*
pull strings ➲ **pull¹**

string² /strɪŋ/ verb [T] (pt, pp strung /strʌŋ/) **string sth (up)** to hang or tie sth in place, especially as a decoration □ *menggantung*: *Coloured lights were strung up along the front of the hotel.*
PHR V **string sb/sth out** to make people or things form a line with spaces between each person or thing □ *membariskan; berbaris*
string sth together to put words or phrases together to make a sentence, speech, etc. □ *merangkaikan sst*: *I can barely string two words together in Japanese.*

stringent /ˈstrɪndʒənt/ adj (used about a law, rule, etc.) very strict □ *ketat*

strip¹ /strɪp/ verb (stripping; stripped) **1** [I,T] **strip (sth) (off)** to take off your clothes; to take off sb else's clothes □ *menanggalkan/melucutkan pakaian*: *The doctor asked him to strip to the waist.* ♦ *She was stripped and searched at the airport by two customs officers.* **2** [T] **strip sth (off)** to remove sth that is covering a surface □ *menanggalkan; mengikis*: *to strip the paint off a door* ♦ *to strip wallpaper* **3** [T] **strip sb/sth (of sth)** to take sth away from sb/sth □ *melucutkan; mengambil; merampas*: *They stripped the house of all its furniture.*

strip² /strɪp/ noun [C] **1** a long narrow piece of sth □ *jalur*: *a strip of paper* ♦ *a tiny strip of garden* **2** the uniform that is worn by the members of a sports team when they are playing □ *pakaian seragam*

strip carˈtoon = comic strip

stripe /straɪp/ noun [C] a long narrow line of colour □ *belang*: *Zebras have black and white stripes.* ▸**striped** adj: *a red and white striped dress* ➲ picture on **page P1**

stripper /ˈstrɪpə(r)/ noun [C] a person whose job is to take off their clothes in order to entertain people □ *penari bogel*

striptease /ˈstrɪptiːz/ noun [C,U] entertainment in which sb takes off their clothes, usually to music □ *tarian bogel*

strive /straɪv/ *verb* [I] (*pt* **strove** /strəʊv/; *pp* **striven** /'strɪvn/) (*formal*) **strive (for sth/to do sth)** to try very hard to do or get sth □ *berusaha*: *to strive for perfection*

strode *past tense of* **stride**[1]

stroke[1] /strəʊk/ *noun*
▶IN SPORT **1** [C] one of the movements that you make when you are swimming, rowing (= in a boat), etc. □ *kuak; dayungan; pukulan*: *Rose won by three strokes* (= hits of the ball in golf). **2** [C,U] [in compounds] one of the styles of swimming □ *kuak; gaya*: *I can do backstroke and breaststroke, but not front crawl.* ⊃ look at **crawl** ⊃ picture at **swim**
▶WITH PEN/BRUSH **3** [C] one of the movements that you make when you are writing or painting □ *coret; calitan*: *a brush stroke*
▶LUCK **4** [sing] **a stroke of sth** a sudden successful action or event □ *sst (perbuatan atau peristiwa) yg berjaya atau bermanfaat; tuah*: *It was a stroke of luck finding your ring on the beach, wasn't it?*
▶ILLNESS **5** [C] a sudden illness which attacks the brain and can leave a person unable to move part of their body, speak clearly, etc. □ *strok; angin ahmar*: *to have a stroke*
IDM **at a/one stroke** with a single action □ *dgn satu tindakan (pukulan, dsb)*
not do a stroke (of work) to not do any work at all □ *tdk membuat apa-apa kerja pun*

stroke[2] /strəʊk/ *verb* [T] **1** to move your hand gently over sb/sth □ *mengusap; membelai*: *She stroked his hair affectionately.* ♦ *to stroke a dog* **2** to move sth somewhere with a smooth movement □ *membawa sst dgn gerakan yg licin dan lancar; memukul (bola, dsb) dgn licin dan baik*: *He stroked the ball just wide of the hole.*

stroke

He's stroking the dog.

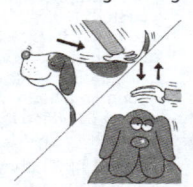

He's patting the dog.

stroll /strəʊl/ *noun* [C] a slow walk for pleasure □ *berjalan-jalan (mengambil angin, dsb)*: *to go for a stroll along the beach* ▶**stroll** *verb* [I]

stroller /'strəʊlə(r)/ (*AmE*) = **pushchair**

strong /strɒŋ/ *adj* (**stronger**; **strongest**)
▶POWERFUL **1** (used about a person) able to lift or carry heavy things □ *kuat; gagah*: *I need someone strong to help me move this bookcase.* ♦ *to have strong arms/muscles* **OPP** **weak 2** powerful □ *kuat; kencang*: *strong winds/currents/sunlight*
▶HAVING BIG EFFECT **3** having a big effect on the mind, body or senses □ *kuat; keras*: *a strong smell of garlic* ♦ *strong coffee* ♦ *a strong drink* (= with a lot of alcohol in it) ♦ *I have the strong impression that they don't like us.*
▶OPINION/BELIEF **4** difficult to fight against □ *tegas; kuat*: *There was strong opposition to the idea.* ♦ *strong support for the government's plan* **SYN** **firm**
▶NOT EASILY BROKEN **5** (used about an object) not easily broken or damaged □ *kuat; kukuh*: *That chair isn't strong enough for you to stand on.* ⊃ look at **fragile**
▶LIKELY TO SUCCEED **6** powerful and likely to succeed □ *kuat; berkemungkinan menang*: *She's a strong candidate for the job.* ♦ *a strong team* ♦ *He's got a very strong will.* **OPP** **weak**
▶NUMBER OF PEOPLE **7** [used after a noun] having a particular number of people □ *seramai bilangan tertentu*: *The army was 50 000 strong.* **8** great in number □ *bilangan yg besar*: *a strong police presence at the demonstration* ⊃ noun **strength**
IDM **going strong** (*informal*) continuing, even after a long time □ *masih kuat, cergas, aktif, dsb*: *The company was formed in 1851 and is still going strong.*
sb's strong point something that a person is good at □ *sst (perkara, dsb) yg sso itu pandai atau ada kelebihan*: *Maths is not my strong point.*
▶**strongly** *adv*: *The directors are strongly opposed to the idea.* ♦ *to feel very strongly about something*

'strong form *noun* [C] used to describe the way some words are pronounced when they have stress □ *bentuk tegas* **OPP** **weak form**

,strong-'minded *adj* having firm ideas or beliefs □ *bentuk tegas* **SYN** **determined**

stroppy /'strɒpi/ *adj* (**stroppier**; **stroppiest**) (*BrE informal*) (used about a person) easily annoyed and difficult to deal with □ *perengus*

strove *past tense of* **strive**

struck *past tense, past participle of* **strike**[1]

structure[1] /'strʌktʃə(r)/ *noun* **1** [C,U] the way that the parts of sth are put together or organized □ *struktur*: *the political and social structure of a country* ♦ *the grammatical structures of a language* **2** [C] a building or sth that has been built or made from a number of parts □ *binaan; bangunan*: *The old office block had been replaced by a modern glass structure.* **3** [C,U] the state of being well organized or planned; a careful plan □ *perancangan*: *Your essay needs (a) structure.* ▶**structural** /'strʌktʃərəl/ *adj*

structure[2] /'strʌktʃə(r)/ *verb* [T] to arrange sth in an organized way □ *menstrukturkan; mengatur; menyusun*: *a carefully structured English course*

struggle[1] /'strʌɡl/ *verb* [I] **1** **struggle (with sth/for sth/to do sth)** to try very hard to do sth, especially when it is difficult □ *berusaha sedaya upaya; bekerja keras*: *We struggled up the stairs with our heavy suitcases.* ♦ *Maria was struggling with her English homework.* ♦ *The country is struggling for independence.* ♦ *They struggled just to pay their bills.* **2** **struggle (with sb/sth); struggle (against sth)** to fight in order to prevent sth or to escape from sb/sth □ *bergelut; berjuang melawan*: *He shouted and struggled but he couldn't get free.* ♦ *A passer-by was struggling with one of the*

struggle → stuff 852

robbers on the ground. ◆ He has been struggling against cancer for years.
PHR V **struggle on** to continue to do sth although it is difficult □ *dgn susah payah meneruskan (sst yg sukar)*: I felt terrible but managed to struggle on to the end of the day.

struggle² /ˈstrʌgl/ noun 1 [C] a fight in which sb tries to do or get sth when this is difficult □ *pergelutan; perjuangan; berjuang*: All countries should join together in the struggle against terrorism. ◆ He will not give up the presidency without a struggle. ◆ a struggle for independence 2 [sing] something that is difficult to achieve □ *sst yg sukar*: It will be a struggle to get there on time. **SYN** effort

strum /strʌm/ verb [I,T] (**strumming**; **strummed**) to play a **guitar** (= a musical instrument with strings) by moving your hand up and down over the strings □ *memetik*

strung past tense, past participle of **string²**

strut /strʌt/ verb [I] (**strutting**; **strutted**) to walk in a proud way □ *berjalan dgn sombong*

stub /stʌb/ noun [C] the short piece of a cigarette or pencil that is left after the rest of it has been used □ *puntung*

stubble /ˈstʌbl/ noun [U] 1 the short parts of crops such as **wheat** (= a plant grown for its grain) that are left standing after the rest has been cut □ *tunggul jerami* 2 the short hairs that grow on a man's face when he has not shaved for some time □ *janggut yg baru tumbuh*

stubborn /ˈstʌbən/ adj not wanting to do what other people want you to do; refusing to change your plans or decisions □ *degil*: She's too stubborn to admit that she's wrong. **SYN** obstinate ⇨ look at **pig-headed** ▶**stubbornly** adv: He stubbornly refused to apologize so he was sacked. ▶**stubbornness** noun [U]

stuck¹ past tense, past participle of **stick²**

stuck² /stʌk/ adj [not before a noun] 1 not able to move □ *tersangkut; terlekat*: This drawer's stuck. I can't open it at all. ◆ We were stuck in traffic for over two hours. 2 not able to continue with an exercise, etc. because it is too difficult □ *tersangkut; menghadapi kesulitan*: If you get stuck, ask your teacher for help.

stud /stʌd/ noun 1 [C] a small, round, solid piece of metal that you wear through a hole in your ear or other part of the body □ *subang* 2 [C] a small piece of metal that sticks out from the rest of the surface that it is fixed to □ *tatah*: a black leather jacket with studs all over it 3 [C] one of the pieces of plastic or metal that stick out from the bottom of football boots, etc. and that help you stand up on wet ground □ *pepaku; stad* 4 [C,U] a number of high quality horses or other animals that are kept for breeding young animals; the place where these animals are kept □ *kuda bibit; pembaka; ladang pembaka*: a stud farm

studded /ˈstʌdɪd/ adj 1 covered or decorated with small pieces of metal that stick out from the rest of the surface □ *bertatah(kan)* 2 **studded (with sth)** containing a lot of sth □ *penuh dgn; bertaburan dgn*

student /ˈstjuːdnt/ noun [C] a person who is studying at a school, college or university □ *pelajar; penuntut*: Paola is a medical student at Bristol University. ◆ a full-time/part-time student ◆ a postgraduate/research student ◆ a first-year student at Cherwell School ⇨ note at **school, university** ⇨ look at **pupil, scholar**

studied /ˈstʌdɪd/ adj [only before a noun] (formal) carefully planned or done, especially when you are trying to give a particular impression □ *dgn sengaja; (yg) dibuat-buat*

studio /ˈstjuːdiəʊ/ noun [C] (pl **studios**) 1 a room or building where films or TV programmes are made, or where music, radio programmes, etc. are recorded □ *studio*: a film/TV/recording studio 2 a room where an artist or a photographer works □ *studio*: a sculptor's studio

studious /ˈstjuːdiəs/ adj (used about a person) spending a lot of time studying □ *rajin belajar*

studiously /ˈstjuːdiəsli/ adv with great care □ *dgn teliti*

study¹ /ˈstʌdi/ noun (pl **studies**) 1 [U] the activity of learning about sth □ *pembelajaran; kajian*: One hour every afternoon is left free for individual study. ◆ Physiology is the study of how living things work. 2 **studies** [pl] the subjects that you study □ *pengajian*: business/media/Japanese studies 3 [C] a piece of research that examines a question or a subject in detail □ *kajian*: They are doing a study of the causes of heart disease. 4 [C] a room in a house where you go to read, write or study □ *bilik telaah*

study² /ˈstʌdi/ verb (**studying**; **studies**; pt, pp **studied**) 1 [I,T] **study (sth/for sth)** to spend time learning about sth □ *menelaah; mempelajari; belajar*: Leon has been studying hard for his exams. ◆ to study French at university 2 [T] to look at sth very carefully □ *meneliti*: to study a map

---

TOPIC

Studying

If you want to **study** something or **learn about** something, you can **teach yourself** or you can take a **course**. This will be **full-time** or **part-time**, perhaps with **evening classes**. You will need to **take notes**, and you might have to **write essays** or **do a project**. You should **hand** these **in** to your **teacher/tutor** before the **deadline**. Before you take **exams**, you'll need to **revise** (= study again what you have learnt).

---

stuff¹ /stʌf/ noun [U] (informal) 1 used to refer to sth without using its name □ *benda; barang*: What's that green stuff at the bottom of the bottle? ◆ The shop was burgled and a lot of stuff was stolen. ◆ They sell stationery and stuff (like that). ◆ I'll put the swimming stuff in this bag. 2 used

[I] **intransitive**, a verb which has no object: *He laughed.*   [T] **transitive**, a verb which has an object: *He ate an apple.*

stuff → stylish

to refer in general to things that people do, say, think, etc. □ *benda, perkara, cerita, kerja, dll*: *I've got lots of stuff to do tomorrow so I'm going to get up early.* ♦ *I don't believe all that stuff about him being robbed.* ♦ *I like reading and stuff.*

stuff² /stʌf/ *verb* [T] **1** stuff sth (with sth) to fill sth with sth □ *menyumbat; mengisikan; berisi*: *The pillow was stuffed with feathers.* ♦ *red peppers stuffed with rice* **2** (*informal*) stuff sth into sth to put sth into sth else quickly or carelessly □ *menyumbat; memerosok*: *He quickly stuffed a few clothes into a suitcase.* **3** (*informal*) stuff yourself (with sth) to eat too much of sth □ *makan banyak-banyak; memolok*: *Barry just sat there stuffing himself with sandwiches.* **4** to fill the body of a dead bird or animal with special material so that it looks as if it is alive □ *menyumbat*: *They've got a stuffed crocodile in the museum.*

stuffing /'stʌfɪŋ/ *noun* [U] **1** a mixture of small pieces of food that you put inside a chicken, vegetable, etc. before you cook it □ *sarak* **2** the material that you put inside **cushions** (= soft bags which you put on chairs, etc. to make them more comfortable), soft toys, etc. □ *isi; bahan utk mengisi kusyen, mainan, dsb*

stuffy /'stʌfi/ *adj* (stuffier; stuffiest) **1** (used about a room) too warm and having no fresh air □ *pengap* **2** (*informal*) (used about a person) formal and old-fashioned □ *terlalu formal; kolot*

stumble /'stʌmbl/ *verb* [I] **1** stumble (over/on sth) to hit your foot against sth when you are walking or running and almost fall over □ *tersandung* **SYN** trip **2** stumble (over/through sth) to make a mistake when you are speaking, playing music, etc. □ *tersilap*: *The newsreader stumbled over the name of the Russian tennis player.*
PHR V stumble across/on sb/sth to meet or find sb/sth by chance □ *terjumpa sso/sst*

'stumbling block *noun* [C] something that causes trouble or a problem, so that you cannot achieve what you want □ *halangan*: *Money is still the stumbling block to settling the dispute.*

stump¹ /stʌmp/ *noun* [C] the part that is left after sth has been cut down, broken off, etc. □ *tunggul; puntung*: *a tree stump*

stump² /stʌmp/ *verb* [T] (*informal*) to cause sb to be unable to answer a question or find a solution to a problem □ *buntu fikiran*: *I was completely stumped by question 14.*

stun /stʌn/ *verb* [T] (stunning; stunned) **1** to make a person or an animal unconscious or confused by hitting them or it on the head □ *membuat orang atau binatang pengsan atau tergamam* **2** to make a person very surprised by telling them some unexpected news □ *memeranjatkan*: *His sudden death stunned his friends.* **SYN** astound ▶ stunned *adj*: *a stunned silence*

stung *past tense, past participle of* sting¹

stunk *past participle of* stink

stunning /'stʌnɪŋ/ *adj* (*informal*) very attractive, impressive or surprising □ *sangat cantik, indah, dsb; menakjubkan*: *a stunning view*

stunt¹ /stʌnt/ *noun* [C] **1** a very difficult or dangerous thing that sb does to entertain people or as part of a film □ *lakonan/lagak ngeri*: *Some actors do their own stunts; others use a stunt man.* **2** something that you do to get people's attention □ *daya penarik*: *a publicity stunt*

stunt² /stʌnt/ *verb* [T] to stop sb/sth growing or developing properly □ *membantutkan*: *A poor diet can stunt a child's growth.*

stuntman /'stʌntmæn/, **stuntwoman** /'stʌntwʊmən/ *noun* [C] (*pl* -men /-men/, -women /-wɪmɪn/) a person who does sth dangerous in a film in the place of an actor □ *pelagak ngeri*

stupendous /stjuː'pendəs/ *adj* very large or impressive □ *amat besar; hebat*: *a stupendous achievement*

stupid /'stjuːpɪd/ *adj* (stupider; stupidest) [More stupid and most stupid are also common.] **1** not intelligent or sensible □ *bodoh; tolol*: *Don't be so stupid.* ♦ *Don't help you!* ♦ *He was stupid to trust her.* ♦ *a stupid mistake/suggestion/question* **SYN** silly **2** [only *before* a noun] (*informal*) used to show that you are angry or do not like sb/sth □ *sial, celaka, tdk berguna, dsb*: *I'm tired of hearing about his stupid car.* ▶ **stupidity** /stjuː'pɪdəti/ *noun* [U] ▶ **stupidly** *adv*

stupor /'stjuːpə(r)/ *noun* [sing, U] the state of being nearly unconscious or being unable to think properly □ *keadaan hampir tdk sedar diri*

sturdy /'stɜːdi/ *adj* (sturdier; sturdiest) strong and healthy; that will not break easily □ *tegap; teguh; kukuh*: *sturdy legs* ♦ *sturdy shoes* ▶ **sturdily** *adv* ▶ **sturdiness** *noun* [U]

sturgeon /'stɜːdʒən/ *noun* [C,U] (*pl* sturgeon or sturgeons) a large fish that we eat. The eggs (called **caviar**) are also eaten. □ *sturgeon*

stutter /'stʌtə(r)/ *verb* [I,T] to have difficulty when you speak, so that you keep repeating the first sound of a word □ *tergagap-gagap* ▶ **stutter** *noun* [sing]: *to have a stutter*

sty /staɪ/ *noun* [C] **1** (*pl* sties) = pigsty **2** (also stye) (*pl* sties or styes) a painful spot on your **eyelid** (= the skin that covers your eye) □ *tembel; ketumbit*

style /staɪl/ *noun* **1** [C,U] the way that sth is done, built, etc. □ *gaya; cara*: *a new style of architecture* ♦ *The writer's style is very clear and simple.* ♦ *an American-style education system* **2** [C,U] the fashion, shape or design of sth □ *fesyen; reka bentuk*: *We stock all the latest styles.* ⊃ look at hairstyle **3** [U] the ability to do things in a way that other people admire □ *gaya; stail*: *He's got no sense of style.* ♦ *They don't have many parties but when they do, they do it in style.*

stylish /'staɪlɪʃ/ *adj* fashionable and attractive □ *bergaya*: *She's a stylish dresser.* ▶ **stylishly** *adv*

stylist /ˈstaɪlɪst/ noun [C] a person whose job is cutting and shaping people's hair ▢ *penggaya; pendandan rambut*

suave /swɑːv/ adj (usually used about a man) confident, elegant and polite, sometimes in a way that does not seem sincere ▢ *yakin, anggun dan bersopan*

subconscious /ˌsʌbˈkɒnʃəs/ noun the subconscious [sing] the hidden part of your mind that can affect the way that you behave without you realizing ▢ *fikiran bawah sedar* ▶ subconscious adj: *the subconscious mind* ◆ *Many advertisements work on a subconscious level.* ▶ subconsciously adv

subcontinent /ˌsʌbˈkɒntɪnənt/ noun [sing] a large area of land that forms part of a continent, especially the part of Asia that includes India, Pakistan and Bangladesh ▢ *benua kecil: the Indian subcontinent*

subdivide /ˌsʌbdɪˈvaɪd/ verb [I,T] to divide or be divided into smaller parts ▢ *membahagikan lagi; memecahbahagikan* ▶ subdivision /ˌsʌbdɪˈvɪʒn/ noun [C,U]

subdue /səbˈdjuː/ verb [T] to defeat sb/sth or bring sb/sth under control ▢ *menumpaskan; mengawal*

subdued /səbˈdjuːd/ adj 1 (used about a person) quieter and with less energy than usual ▢ *sugul; diam* 2 not very loud or bright ▢ *lembut; tdk kuat; malap: subdued laughter/lighting*

subject¹ /ˈsʌbdʒɪkt/ noun [C] 1 a person or thing that is being considered, shown or talked about ▢ *tajuk; perkara; hal: What subject is the lecture on?* ◆ *What are your views on this subject?* ◆ *I've tried several times to bring up/raise the subject of money.* 2 an area of knowledge that you study at school, university, etc. ▢ *mata pelajaran; subjek: My favourite subjects at school are Biology and French.* 3 the person or thing that does the action described by the verb in a sentence ▢ *subjek: In the sentence 'The cat sat on the mat', 'the cat' is the subject.* ➲ look at **object** 4 a person from a particular country, especially one with a king or queen; a citizen ▢ *rakyat: a British subject*

IDM change the subject ➲ change¹

subject² /ˈsʌbdʒekt/ adj subject to sth 1 likely to be affected by sth ▢ *mudah dilanda/diserang; mudah mendapat: The area is subject to regular flooding.* ◆ *Smokers are more subject to heart attacks than non-smokers.* ◆ *People who eat a lot of fatty foods are more subject to heart attacks.* 2 depending on sth as a condition ▢ *tertakluk kpd: The plan for new housing is still subject to approval by the minister.* 3 controlled by or having to obey sb/sth ▢ *di bawah kuasa*

subject³ /səbˈdʒekt/ verb

PHR V subject sb/sth to sth to make sb/sth experience sth unpleasant ▢ *terpaksa/dipaksa mengalami sst: He was subjected to verbal and physical abuse from the other boys.*

subjective /səbˈdʒektɪv/ adj based on your own tastes and opinions instead of on facts ▢ *subjektif: Try not to be so subjective in your essays.* **OPP** objective ▶ subjectively adv

ˈsubject matter noun [U] the ideas or information contained in a book, speech, painting, etc. ▢ *isi; perkara: I don't think the subject matter of this programme is suitable for children.*

subjunctive /səbˈdʒʌŋktɪv/ noun [sing] the form of a verb in certain languages that expresses doubt, possibility, a wish, etc. ▢ *subjunktif; sembawa* ▶ subjunctive adj

sublime /səˈblaɪm/ adj (formal) of extremely high quality that makes you admire sth very much ▢ *mengagumkan; sangat bagus* ▶ sublimely adv

submarine /ˌsʌbməˈriːn/ noun [C] a type of ship that can travel under the water as well as on the surface ▢ *kapal selam* ➲ picture on **page P6**

submerge /səbˈmɜːdʒ/ verb [I,T] to go or make sth go underwater ▢ *menenggelamkan: The fields were submerged by the floods.* ▶ submerged adj

submission /səbˈmɪʃn/ noun 1 [U] the accepting of sb else's power or control because they have defeated you ▢ *kepatuhan; berserah* 2 [U,C] the act of giving a plan, document, etc. to an official organization so that it can be studied and considered; the plan, document, etc. that you send ▢ *penyerahan; serahan*

submissive /səbˈmɪsɪv/ adj ready to obey other people and do whatever they want ▢ *patuh; submisif*

submit /səbˈmɪt/ verb (submitting; submitted) 1 [T] submit sth (to sb/sth) to give a plan, document, etc. to an official organization so that it can be studied and considered ▢ *menyerahkan: to submit an application/a complaint/a claim* 2 [I] submit (to sb/sth) to accept sb/sth's power or control because they have defeated you ▢ *menyerah; berserah*

subordinate¹ /səˈbɔːdɪnət/ adj subordinate (to sb/sth) having less power or authority than sb else; less important than sth else ▢ *bawahan; kurang penting* ▶ subordinate noun [C]: *the relationship between superiors and their subordinates*

subordinate² /səˈbɔːdɪneɪt/ verb [T] to treat one person or thing as less important than another ▢ *menganggap kurang penting*

suˌbordinate ˈclause noun [C] a group of words that is not a sentence but that adds information to the main part of the sentence ▢ *klausa subordinat: In the sentence 'We left early because it was raining', 'because it was raining' is the subordinate clause.*

subscribe /səbˈskraɪb/ verb [I] subscribe (to sth) to pay an amount of money regularly in order to receive or use sth ▢ *melanggan: Do you subscribe to 'Marie Claire'?* ◆ *We subscribe to several sports channels (= on TV).*

PHR V **subscribe to sth** to agree with an idea, a belief, etc □ *bersetuju; menerima*: *I don't subscribe to the view that all was wrong.*

subscriber /səbˈskraɪbə(r)/ *noun* [C] a person who pays to receive a newspaper or magazine regularly or to use a particular service □ *pelanggan*: *subscribers to satellite and cable TV*

subscription /səbˈskrɪpʃn/ *noun* [C] an amount of money that you pay, usually once a year, to receive a newspaper or magazine regularly or to belong to an organization □ *wang langganan*

subsequent /ˈsʌbsɪkwənt/ *adj* [only before a noun] (*formal*) coming after or later □ *berikutnya; kemudiannya*: *I thought that was the end of the matter but subsequent events proved me wrong.* ▶ **subsequently** *adv*: *The rumours were subsequently found to be untrue.*

subservient /səbˈsɜːviənt/ *adj* 1 **subservient (to sb/sth)** too ready to obey other people □ *mudah menurut perintah* 2 (*formal*) **subservient (to sth)** considered to be less important than sb/sth else □ *dianggap kurang penting* ▶ **subservience** *noun* [U]

subside /səbˈsaɪd/ *verb* [I] 1 to become calmer or quieter □ *reda; berkurang*: *The storm seems to be subsiding.* 2 (used about land, a building, etc.) to sink down into the ground □ *tenggelam; semakin turun* ▶ **subsidence** /ˈsʌbsɪdns; səbˈsaɪdns/ *noun* [U]: *The road was closed because of subsidence.*

subsidiary[1] /səbˈsɪdiəri/ *adj* connected with sth but less important than it □ *subsidiari; sampingan; kurang penting*

subsidiary[2] /səbˈsɪdiəri/ *noun* [C] (*pl* **subsidiaries**) a business company that belongs to and is controlled by another larger company □ *anak syarikat*

subsidize (also **-ise**) /ˈsʌbsɪdaɪz/ *verb* [T] to give money to sb or an organization to help pay for sth □ *memberi subsidi; bersubsidi*: *Public transport should be subsidized.*

subsidy /ˈsʌbsədi/ *noun* [C,U] (*pl* **subsidies**) money that the government, etc. pays to help an organization or to keep the cost of a service low □ *subsidi; bantuan kewangan*: *agricultural/state/housing subsidies*

subsist /səbˈsɪst/ *verb* [I] (*formal*) **subsist (on sth)** to manage to live with very little food or money □ *hidup (dgn amat sedikit wang atau makanan)* ▶ **subsistence** *noun* [U]

substance /ˈsʌbstəns/ *noun* 1 [C] a solid or liquid material □ *bahan*: *poisonous substances* ♦ *The cloth is coated in a new waterproof substance.* 2 [U] importance, value or truth □ *kepentingan; pentingnya; kebenaran; benarnya*: *The manager's report gives substance to these allegations.* ♦ *It was unkind gossip, completely without substance.* 3 [U] the most important or main part of sth □ *pokok; intipati; bahagian utama*: *What was the substance of his argument?*

substandard /ˌsʌbˈstændəd/ *adj* of poor quality; not as good as usual or as it should be □ *substandard; tdk bermutu*

substantial /səbˈstænʃl/ *adj* 1 large in amount □ *cukup besar; banyak*: *The storms caused substantial damage.* ♦ *a substantial sum of money* 2 large and/or strongly built □ *besar; teguh*: *The furniture was cheap and not very substantial.* **OPP** for both meanings **insubstantial**

substantially /səbˈstænʃəli/ *adv* 1 very much □ *agak banyak*: *House prices have fallen substantially.* **SYN** **greatly** 2 generally; in most points □ *pd umumnya*: *The landscape of Wales has remained substantially the same for centuries.*

substitute /ˈsʌbstɪtjuːt/ *noun* [C] **a substitute (for sb/sth)** a person or thing that takes the place of sb/sth else □ *pengganti*: *One player was injured so the substitute was sent on to play.* ▶ **substitute** *verb* [T] **substitute sb/sth (for sb/sth)**: *You can substitute margarine for butter.* ▶ **substitution** /ˌsʌbstɪˈtjuːʃn/ *noun* [C,U]

subterranean /ˌsʌbtəˈreɪniən/ *adj* (*formal*) under the ground □ *bawah tanah*: *a subterranean cave*

subtitle /ˈsʌbtaɪtl/ *noun* [C, usually pl] the words at the bottom of the picture on TV or at the cinema. The **subtitles** translate the words that are spoken, or show them to help people with hearing problems □ *sari kata*: *a Polish film with English subtitles* ⊃ look at **dub**

subtle /ˈsʌtl/ *adj* (**subtler**; **subtlest**) 1 not very noticeable; not very strong or bright □ *tdk ketara; lembut*: *subtle colours* ♦ *I noticed a subtle difference in her.* 2 very clever, and using indirect methods to achieve sth □ *licik; dgn cara yg tdk ketara*: *Advertisements persuade us to buy things in very subtle ways.* ▶ **subtlety** /ˈsʌtlti/ *noun* [C,U] (*pl* **subtleties**) ▶ **subtly** /ˈsʌtli/ *adv*

subtract /səbˈtrækt/ *verb* [T] **subtract sth (from sth)** to take one number or quantity away from another □ *(kira-kira) tolak*: *If you subtract five from nine, you get four.* **OPP** **add** ▶ **subtraction** /səbˈtrækʃn/ *noun* [C,U]

suburb /ˈsʌbɜːb/ *noun* [C] an area where people live that is outside the central part of a town or city □ *subbandar; pinggir bandar*: *Most people live in the suburbs and work in the centre of town.* ▶ **suburban** /səˈbɜːbən/ *adj*

> **MORE** People often think of life in the suburbs as dull, so **suburban** sometimes means 'uninteresting'.

▶ **suburbia** /səˈbɜːbiə/ *noun* [U]

subversive /səbˈvɜːsɪv/ *adj* trying to destroy or damage a government, religion or political system by attacking it secretly and in an indirect way □ *subversif*: *subversive literature* ▶ **subversive** *noun* [C]

subvert /səbˈvɜːt/ *verb* [T] (*formal*) to try to destroy or damage a government, religion or political system by attacking it secretly and in an

subway → sudden

indirect way □ *cuba menjatuhkan/menggulingkan* ▶**subversion** /səbˈvɜːʃn/ *noun* [U]

subway /ˈsʌbweɪ/ *noun* [C] **1** (*BrE*) a tunnel under a busy road or railway that people can walk through to cross to the other side □ *jalan bawah tanah* **2** (*AmE*) = **underground**³

succeed /səkˈsiːd/ *verb* **1** [I] **succeed (in sth/doing sth)** to manage to achieve what you want; to do well □ *berjaya; berhasil*: *Our plan succeeded.* ♦ *A good education will help you succeed in life.* ♦ *to succeed in passing an exam* **OPP** **fail** **2** [I,T] to have a job or important position after sb else □ *menggantikan; mengambil tempat*: *David Cameron succeeded Gordon Brown as British Prime Minister in 2010.*

success /səkˈses/ *noun* **1** [U] the fact that you have achieved what you want; doing well and becoming famous, rich, etc. □ *kejayaan; berjaya*: *Hard work is the key to success.* ♦ *Her attempts to get a job for the summer have not met with much success* (= she hasn't managed to do it). ♦ *What's the secret of your success?* **2** [C] the thing that you achieve; something that becomes very popular □ *kejayaan*: *He really tried to make a success of the business.* ♦ *The film 'War Horse' was a huge success.* **OPP** for both meanings **failure**

successful /səkˈsesfl/ *adj* having achieved what you wanted; having become popular, rich, etc. □ *berjaya*: *a successful attempt to climb Mount Everest* ♦ *a successful actor* **OPP** **unsuccessful** ▶**successfully** /-fəli/ *adv*

succession /səkˈseʃn/ *noun* **1** [C] a number of people or things that follow each other in time or order; a series □ *rentetan; berturut-turut*: *a succession of events/problems/visitors* **2** [U] the right to have an important position after sb else □ *pewarisan*
IDM **in succession** following one after another □ *satu demi satu; berturut-turut*: *There have been three deaths in the family in quick succession.*

successive /səkˈsesɪv/ *adj* [only before a noun] following immediately one after the other □ *berturut-turut; seterusnya*: *This was their fourth successive win.* ♦ *Successive governments have tried to tackle the problem.* **SYN** **consecutive**

successor /səkˈsesə(r)/ *noun* [C] a person or thing that comes after sb/sth else and takes their or its place □ *pengganti; waris* ⊃ look at **predecessor**

succinct /səkˈsɪŋkt/ *adj* said clearly, in a few words □ *ringkas dan jelas* ▶**succinctly** *adv*

succulent /ˈsʌkjələnt/ *adj* (used about fruit, vegetables and meat) containing a lot of juice and tasting very good □ *berjus dan enak*

succumb /səˈkʌm/ *verb* [I] (*formal*) **succumb (to sth)** to not be able to fight an attack, an illness, etc. □ *tewas; alah*

such /sʌtʃ/ *determiner, pron* **1** (used for referring to sb/sth that you mentioned earlier) of this or that type □ *spt itu/ini; sedemikian*: *I don't believe in ghosts. There's no such thing.* ♦ *The economic situation is such that we all have less money to spend.* **2** used to describe the result of sth □ *sebegitu; sedemikian*: *The statement was worded in such a way that it did not upset anyone.* **3** used for emphasizing the degree of sth □ *begitu; betul-betul; sungguh*: *It was such a fascinating book that I couldn't put it down.* ♦ *It seems such a long time since we last saw each other.*

GRAMMAR You use **such** before a noun or before a noun that has an adjective in front of it: *Simon is such a bore!* ♦ *Susan is such a boring woman.* You use **so** before an adjective that is used without a noun: *Don't be so boring.* Compare: *It was so cold that we stayed at home.* ♦ *It was such a cold night that we stayed at home.*

IDM **as such** as the word is usually understood; exactly □ *dlm erti kata yg sebenarnya*: *It's not a promotion as such, but it will mean more money.*
such as for example □ *misalnya*: *Fatty foods such as chips are bad for you.* ⊃ note at **example**

suck /sʌk/ *verb* **1** [I,T] to pull a liquid into your mouth □ *menghisap; menyedut*: *to suck milk up through a straw* ⊃ picture at **blow** **2** [I,T] to have sth in your mouth and keep touching it with your tongue □ *menghisap; mengulum*: *He was noisily sucking (on) a sweet.* **3** [T] to pull sth in a particular direction, using force □ *menyedut*: *Vacuum cleaners suck up the dirt.*

sucker /ˈsʌkə(r)/ *noun* [C] **1** (*informal*) a person who believes everything that you tell them and who is easy to trick or persuade to do sth □ *orang yg mudah ditipu* **2** a part of some plants, animals or insects that is used for helping them stick onto a surface □ *penghisap; sulur*

suction /ˈsʌkʃn/ *noun* [U] the act of removing air or liquid from a space or container so that sth else can be pulled into it or so that two surfaces can stick together □ *sedutan*: *A vacuum cleaner works by suction.*

sudden /ˈsʌdn/ *adj* done or happening quickly, or when you do not expect it □ *tiba-tiba*: *a sudden decision/change*
IDM **all of a sudden** quickly and unexpectedly □ *dgn tiba-tiba*: *All of a sudden the lights went out.*
sudden death a way of deciding who wins a game where the score is equal by continuing to play until one side gains the lead □ *kalah mati*
▶**suddenly** *adv*: *It all happened so suddenly.*
▶**suddenness** *noun* [U]

WRITING TIP

Using adverbs

If you are writing a story, use adverbs and phrases that make it lively and interesting. Here are some common adverbs: *Suddenly, everybody started shouting.* ♦ *All of a sudden, there was a bang.* ♦ *His new neighbours were amazingly helpful.* ◆ **Luckily**, *she escaped with only minor injuries.* ◆ **Unfortunately**, *no one heard her cries for help.*

ℹ️ For more help with writing, look at **Wordpower Writing Tutor** at the back of this dictionary.

sudoku /suˈdəʊkuː/ *noun* [U,C] a number puzzle with nine squares, each containing nine smaller squares in which you have to write the numbers 1 to 9 in a particular pattern □ *permainan sudoku*: *I'm addicted to sudoku.* ◆ *a sudoku puzzle* ⊃ picture at **crossword**

suds /sʌdz/ *noun* [pl] the bubbles that you get when you mix soap and water □ *buih sabun*

sue /suː/ *verb* [I,T] **sue (sb) (for sth)** to go to a court of law and ask for money from sb because they have done sth bad to you, or said sth bad about you □ *mendakwa; menyaman*: *to sue somebody for libel/breach of contract/damages*

suede /sweɪd/ *noun* [U] a type of soft leather which does not have a smooth surface and feels a little like cloth □ *suede*

suet /ˈsuːɪt/ *noun* [U] a type of hard animal fat that is used in cooking □ *lemak ginjal*

suffer /ˈsʌfə(r)/ *verb* 1 [I,T] **suffer (from sth); suffer (for sth)** to experience sth unpleasant, for example pain, sadness, difficulty, etc. □ *menderita; menghidap; mengalami*: *Mary often suffers from severe headaches.* ◆ *He made a rash decision and now he's suffering for it.* ◆ *Our troops suffered heavy losses.* 2 [I] to become worse in quality □ *terjejas*: *My work is suffering as a result of problems at home.* ▶ **sufferer** *noun* [C]: *asthma sufferers* ▶ **suffering** *noun* [U]: *The famine caused great hardship and suffering.*

sufficient /səˈfɪʃnt/ *adj (formal)* as much as is necessary; enough □ *cukup*: *We have sufficient oil reserves to last for three months.* **OPP** insufficient ▶ **sufficiently** *adv*

suffix /ˈsʌfɪks/ *noun* [C] a letter or group of letters that you add at the end of a word, and that changes the meaning of the word or the way it is used □ *akhiran*: *To form the noun from the adjective 'sad', add the suffix 'ness'.* ⊃ look at **prefix**

suffocate /ˈsʌfəkeɪt/ *verb* [I,T] to die because there is no air to breathe; to kill sb by not letting them breathe air □ *mati lemas; melemaskan* ▶ **suffocating** *adj* ▶ **suffocation** /ˌsʌfəˈkeɪʃn/ *noun* [U]

sugar /ˈʃʊɡə(r)/ *noun* 1 [U] a sweet substance that you get from certain plants □ *gula*: *Do you take sugar in tea?* 2 [C] (in a cup of tea, coffee, etc.) the amount of sugar that a small spoon can hold; a lump of sugar □ *sudu/ketul gula*: *Two sugars, please.*

sugary /ˈʃʊɡəri/ *adj* very sweet □ *bergula; sangat manis*

suggest /səˈdʒest/ *verb* [T] 1 **suggest sth (to sb); suggest doing sth; suggest that ...** to mention a plan or an idea that you have for sb to discuss or consider □ *mencadangkan; mengesyorkan*: *Can anybody suggest ways of raising more money?* ◆ *Kate suggested going out for a walk.* ◆ *Kate suggested (that) we go out for a walk.* ◆ *Kate suggested a walk.* 2 **suggest sb/sth (for/as sth)** to say that a person, thing or place is suitable □ *mencadangkan*: *Who would you suggest for the job?* **SYN** recommend

HELP You CANNOT say 'suggest sb sth'.

3 to say or show sth in an indirect way □ *mengatakan*: *Are you suggesting the accident was my fault?* 4 to put an idea into sb's mind; to make sb think that sth is true □ *menggambarkan; membayangkan*: *What do these results suggest to you?*

suggestion /səˈdʒestʃən/ *noun* 1 [C] a plan or idea that sb mentions for sb else to discuss and consider □ *cadangan; syor; saranan*: *May I make a suggestion?* ◆ *Has anyone got any suggestions for how to solve this problem?* 2 [sing] a slight amount or sign of sth □ *sedikit*: *He spoke with a suggestion of a Scottish accent.* **SYN** hint 3 [U] putting an idea into sb's mind; giving advice about what to do □ *cadangan; syor; (secara) implikasi*: *I came at Tim's suggestion* (= because he suggested it).

suggestive /səˈdʒestɪv/ *adj* 1 **suggestive (of sth)** making you think of sth; being a sign of sth □ *membayangkan; menandakan*: *Your symptoms are more suggestive of an allergy than a virus.* 2 making you think about sex □ *gatal; memberahikan*: *a suggestive dance/remark/posture* ▶ **suggestively** *adv*

suicidal /ˌsuːɪˈsaɪdl/ *adj* 1 people who are **suicidal** want to kill themselves □ *mahu membunuh diri*: *to be/feel suicidal* 2 likely to have a very bad result; extremely dangerous □ *sangat berbahaya; mencari nahas*: *Changing jobs at this point would be a suicidal career move.*

suicide /ˈsuːɪsaɪd/ *noun* [U,C] the act of killing yourself deliberately □ *(perbuatan) membunuh diri*: *Ben has tried to commit suicide several times.* ◆ *There have been three suicides by university students this year.*

suit¹ /suːt/ *noun* [C] 1 a formal set of clothes that are made of the same cloth, consisting of a jacket and either trousers or a skirt □ *suit*: *He always wears a suit and tie to work.* ⊃ picture on page P1 2 a piece of clothing or set of clothes that you wear for a particular activity □ *sut; pakaian/baju (utk sst aktiviti)*: *a diving suit* ◆ *a suit of armour* ⊃ look at **swimsuit, tracksuit** 3 one of the 4 sets of 13 playing cards that form a pack □ *(daun terup) sama bunga*: *The four suits are hearts, clubs, diamonds and spades.* ⊃ note at **card** ⊃ picture at **card**
IDM follow suit ⊃ **follow**

suit² /suːt/ *verb* [T] [not used in the continuous tenses] 1 to be convenient or useful for sb/sth □ *sesuai*: *Would Thursday at 9.30 suit you?* ◆ *He will help around the house, but only when it suits him.* 2 (used about clothes, colours, etc.) to

suitable → sun 858

make you look attractive □ *sesuai/padan/kena dgn*: *That dress really suits you.*

suitable /ˈsuːtəbl/ *adj* **suitable (for sb/sth); suitable (to do sth)** right or appropriate for sb/sth □ *sesuai*: *The film isn't suitable for children.* ◆ *I've got nothing suitable to wear for a wedding.* **OPP unsuitable** ▶ **suitability** /ˌsuːtəˈbɪləti/ *noun* [U] ▶ **suitably** /-əbli/ *adv*

suitcase /ˈsuːtkeɪs/ (also **case**) *noun* [C] a box with a handle that you use for carrying your clothes, etc. in when you are travelling □ *beg pakaian* ⊃ picture at **bag**: *to pack/unpack a suitcase* ◆ *The suitcase was too heavy to lift.*

suite /swiːt/ *noun* [C] **1** a set of rooms, especially in a hotel □ *bilik-bilik 'suite'*: *the honeymoon/penthouse suite* ◆ *a suite of rooms/offices* ⊃ look at **en suite 2** a set of two or more pieces of furniture of the same style or covered in the same material □ *set*: *a three-piece suite* (= a sofa and two armchairs)

suited /ˈsuːtɪd/ *adj* **suited (for/to sb/sth)** appropriate or right for sb/sth □ *sesuai*: *She and her husband are very well suited.*

sulk /sʌlk/ *verb* [I] to refuse to speak or smile because you want people to know that you are angry about sth □ *merajuk* ▶ **sulky** *adj* ▶ **sulkily** /-ɪli/ *adv*

sullen /ˈsʌlən/ *adj* looking bad-tempered and not wanting to speak to people □ *masam muka; merengus*: *a sullen face/expression/glare* ▶ **sullenly** *adv*

sulphur (*AmE* **sulfur**) /ˈsʌlfə(r)/ *noun* [U] (symbol **S**) a natural yellow substance with a strong unpleasant smell □ *sulfur; belerang*

sultan (also **Sultan**) /ˈsʌltən/ *noun* [C] the title of the ruler in some Muslim countries □ *sultan*

sultana /sʌlˈtɑːnə/ *noun* [C] a dried **grape** (= a small fruit that grows in bunches) with no seeds in it that is used in cooking □ *sultana* ⊃ look at **raisin**

sultry /ˈsʌltri/ *adj* (**sultrier; sultriest**) **1** (used about the weather) hot and uncomfortable □ *panas berlengas* **2** (used about a woman) behaving in a way that makes her sexually attractive □ *mengghairahkan*

sum¹ /sʌm/ *noun* [C] **1** an amount of money □ *jumlah/sejumlah wang*: *The industry has spent huge sums of money modernizing its equipment.* **2** [usually sing] **the sum (of sth)** the amount that you get when you add two or more numbers together □ *jumlah; hasil tambah*: *The sum of two and five is seven.* **3** a simple problem that involves calculating numbers □ *kira-kira*: *to do sums in your head*

sum² /sʌm/ *verb* (**summing; summed**)
PHR V **sum (sth) up** to describe in a few words the main ideas of what sb has said or written □ *menyimpulkan; merumuskan; menggulung*: *To sum up, there are three options here …*

sum sb/sth up to form an opinion about sb/sth □ *membuat penilaian; berpendapat*: *He summed the situation up immediately.*

summary¹ /ˈsʌməri/ *noun* [C] (*pl* **summaries**) a short description of the main ideas or points of sth but without any details □ *ringkasan*: *A brief summary of the experiment is given at the beginning of the report.* **SYN precis** ▶ **summarize** (also **-ise**) /ˈsʌməraɪz/ *verb* [T]: *Could you summarize the story so far?*

summary² /ˈsʌməri/ *adj* [only before a noun] (*formal*) done quickly and without taking time to consider if it is the right thing to do or following the right process □ *terus; tanpa banyak soal*: *a summary judgment*

summer /ˈsʌmə(r)/ *noun* [C,U] one of the four seasons of the year, after spring and before autumn. Summer is the warmest season of the year □ *musim panas*: *Is it very hot here in summer?* ◆ *a summer's day* ▶ **summery** /ˈsʌməri/ *adj*: *summery weather* ◆ *a summery dress*

summertime /ˈsʌmətaɪm/ *noun* [U] the season of summer □ *musim panas*: *It's busy here in the summertime.*

summing-up *noun* [C] (*pl* **summings-up**) a speech in which a judge gives a **summary** of what has been said in a court of law before a **verdict** (= a decision) is reached □ *penggulungan*

summit /ˈsʌmɪt/ *noun* [C] **1** the top of a mountain □ *puncak; mercu* **2** an important meeting or series of meetings between the leaders of two or more countries □ *sidang kemuncak*

summon /ˈsʌmən/ *verb* [T] **1** (*formal*) to order a person to come to a place □ *memerintah/diperintah utk menghadirkan diri*: *The boys were summoned to the head teacher's office.* **2 summon sth (up)** to find strength, courage or some other quality that you need even though it is difficult to do so □ *mengumpulkan tenaga, keberanian, dll (yg diperlukan)*: *She couldn't summon up the courage to leave him.*

summons /ˈsʌmənz/ *noun* [C] an order to appear in a court of law □ *saman*

sumptuous /ˈsʌmptʃuəs/ *adj* (*formal*) very expensive and looking very impressive □ *mewah; sangat bagus dan berharga; kelihatan mahal dan bagus*: *We dined in sumptuous surroundings.* ▶ **sumptuously** *adv*

Sun. *abbr* = **Sunday** □ *Ahad*: *Sun. 5 April*

sun¹ /sʌn/ *noun* **1 the Sun** [sing] the star that shines in the sky during the day and that gives the earth heat and light □ *matahari*: *The sun rises in the east and sets in the west.* ◆ *the rays of the sun* ⊃ note at **space** ⊃ picture at **eclipse 2** [sing, U] light and heat from the sun □ *(sinar) matahari*: *Don't sit in the sun too long.* ◆ *Too much sun can be harmful.*
IDM catch the sun ⊃ **catch¹**

sun² /sʌn/ *verb* [T] (**sunning; sunned**) **sun yourself** to sit or lie outside when the sun is shining in order to enjoy the heat □ *berjemur*

[I] **intransitive**, a verb which has no object: *He laughed.* [T] **transitive**, a verb which has an object: *He ate an apple.*

sunbathe /ˈsʌnbeɪð/ *verb* [I] to take off most of your clothes or lie in the sun in order to get a **tan** (= darker skin) □ *berjemur* ➔ look at **bathe**

sunbeam /ˈsʌnbiːm/ *noun* [C] a line of light from the sun □ *pancaran sinar matahari*

sunbed /ˈsʌnbed/ *noun* [C] a bed for lying on under a **sunlamp** (= a lamp that can turn the skin brown) □ *katil penjemuran* ➔ look at **sunlounger**

sunburn /ˈsʌnbɜːn/ *noun* [U] red painful skin caused by spending too long in the sun □ *selaran matahari* ▶**sunburned** (also **sunburnt**) *adj*

suncream /ˈsʌnkriːm/ *noun* [C,U] (*especially BrE*) cream that you put on your skin to protect it from the harmful effects of the sun □ *krim pelindung matahari*: Make sure the children have plenty of suncream on. ➔ look at **sunscreen**

Sunday /ˈsʌndeɪ; -di/ *noun* [C,U] (*abbr* **Sun.**) the day of the week after Saturday □ *Ahad* ➔ note at **Monday**

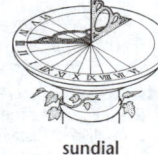

sundial /ˈsʌndaɪəl/ *noun* [C] a type of clock used in past times that uses the sun and the shadow from a pointed piece of metal to show what the time is □ *jam matahari*

sundial

sundry /ˈsʌndri/ *adj* [only *before* a noun] of various kinds that are not important enough to be named separately □ *berbagai-bagai*
IDM **all and sundry** (*informal*) everyone □ *semua orang*

sunflower /ˈsʌnflaʊə(r)/ *noun* [C] a very tall plant with large yellow flowers, often grown for its seeds and their oil which are used in cooking □ *bunga matahari*

sung *past participle* of **sing**

sunglasses /ˈsʌnglɑːsɪz/ (also ˌdark ˈglasses (*informal* **shades**) *noun* [pl] a pair of dark glasses which you wear to protect your eyes from bright sunlight □ *cermin mata hitam*

sunk *past participle* of **sink**¹

sunken /ˈsʌŋkən/ *adj* **1** [only *before* a noun] below the water □ *tenggelam*: a sunken ship **2** (used about cheeks or eyes) very far into the face as a result of illness or age □ *cengkung* **3** at a lower level than the surrounding area □ *terbenam*: a sunken bath/garden

sunlamp /ˈsʌnlæmp/ *noun* [C] a lamp that produces **ultraviolet** light that has the same effect as the sun and can turn the skin brown □ *lampu ultraungu*

sunlight /ˈsʌnlaɪt/ *noun* [U] the light from the sun □ *cahaya matahari*: a ray/pool of sunlight

sunlit /ˈsʌnlɪt/ *adj* having bright light from the sun □ *disinari cahaya matahari*: a sunlit terrace

sunlounger /ˈsʌnlaʊndʒə(r)/ *noun* [C] a chair with a long seat that supports your legs, used for sitting or lying on in the sun □ *kerusi penjemuran*

sunny /ˈsʌni/ *adj* (**sunnier**; **sunniest**) having a lot of light from the sun □ *cerah; terang*: a sunny garden ♦ a sunny day

sunrise /ˈsʌnraɪz/ *noun* [C,U] the time when the sun comes up in the morning □ *matahari terbit*: to get up at sunrise ➔ look at **dawn**, **sunset**

sunscreen /ˈsʌnskriːn/ *noun* [C,U] a cream or liquid that you put on your skin to protect it from the harmful effects of the sun □ *skrin pelindung matahari*: I need to put some sunscreen on or I'll burn. ♦ factor 10 sunscreen ➔ look at **suncream**

sunset /ˈsʌnset/ *noun* [C,U] the time when the sun goes down in the evening □ *matahari terbenam*: The park closes at sunset. ♦ a beautiful sunset

sunshine /ˈsʌnʃaɪn/ *noun* [U] heat and light from the sun □ *sinar/cahaya matahari*: We sat down in the sunshine and had lunch.

sunstroke /ˈsʌnstrəʊk/ *noun* [U] an illness that is caused by spending too much time in very hot, strong sun □ *strok matahari*: Keep your head covered or you'll get sunstroke.

suntan /ˈsʌntæn/ (also **tan**) *noun* [C] when you have a **suntan**, your skin is darker than usual because you have spent time in the sun □ *kulit perang*: to have/get a suntan ♦ suntan lotion ▶**suntanned** (also **tanned**) *adj*

super /ˈsuːpə(r)/ *adj* **1** (*old-fashioned*) very good; wonderful □ *sangat bagus; hebat*: We had a super time. **2** [in compounds] bigger, better, stronger, etc. than other things of the same type □ *super; lebih besar, baik, kuat drpd yg serupa dgnnya*: super-rich ♦ superglue

superb /suːˈpɜːb/ (*BrE also* sjuː-/ *adj* extremely good, excellent □ *sangat bagus* ▶**superbly** *adv*

supercilious /ˌsuːpəˈsɪliəs/ (*BrE also* ˌsjuː-/ *adj* showing that you think that you are better than other people □ *sombong; angkuh*: She gave a supercilious smile. ▶**superciliously** *adv*

superficial /ˌsuːpəˈfɪʃl/ *adj* **1** not studying or thinking about sth in a deep or complete way □ *dangkal; cetek; tdk mendalam*: a superficial knowledge of the subject **2** only on the surface, not deep □ *tdk dlm; di permukaan sahaja*: a superficial wound/cut/burn **3** (used about people) not caring about serious or important things □ *dangkal; cetek pemikiran*: He's a very superficial sort of person. ▶**superficiality** /ˌsuːpəˌfɪʃiˈæləti/ *noun* [U] ▶**superficially** /-ʃəli/ *adv*

superfluous /suːˈpɜːfluəs/ (*BrE also* sjuː-/ *adj* more than is wanted; not needed □ *berlebihan; tdk diperlukan*

superhuman /ˌsuːpəˈhjuːmən/ (*BrE also* ˌsjuː-/ *adj* much greater than is normal □ *sangat luar biasa*: superhuman strength

superimpose → support

superimpose /ˌsuːpərɪmˈpəʊz/ verb [T] superimpose sth (on sth) to put sth on top of sth else so that what is underneath can still be seen □ *menindan; ditindan*: *The old street plan was superimposed on a map of the modern city.*

superintendent /ˌsuːpərɪnˈtendənt/ noun [C] **1** a police officer with a high position □ *penguasa; superintenden*: *Detective Superintendent Waters* **2** (*AmE*) a person who looks after a large building □ *penyelia*

superior¹ /suːˈpɪəriə(r)/ adj **1** superior (to sb/sth) better than usual or than sb/sth else □ *lebih baik*: *He is clearly superior to all the other candidates.* **OPP** inferior **2** superior (to sb) having a more important position □ *kanan; lebih tinggi kedudukan/pangkatnya*: *his superior officer* **3** thinking that you are better than other people □ *meninggi diri; besar diri*: *There's no need to be so superior.* ▶ **superiority** /suːˌpɪəriˈɒrəti/ (*BrE also*) sju:- (*AmE also*) / noun [U]

superior² /suːˈpɪəriə(r)/ noun [C] a person of higher position □ *pegawai yg lebih tinggi*: *Report any accidents to your superior.* **OPP** inferior

superlative /suːˈpɜːlətɪv/ (*BrE also*) sju:- / noun [C] the form of an adjective or adverb that expresses its highest degree □ *superlatif; darjah kepalingan*: *'Most beautiful', 'best' and 'fastest' are all superlatives.*

supermarket /ˈsuːpəmɑːkɪt/ (*BrE also*) ˈsjuː- / noun [C] a very large shop that sells food, drink, goods used in the home, etc. □ *pasar raya*: *More and more of us are doing all our shopping in supermarkets.*

> **MORE** At a supermarket, you put your **shopping** in a **basket** or a **trolley**. Then you **queue** (/kjuːˈpɒlɒn:/) at the **checkout**, where you **pack** everything into **shopping bags** or **carrier bags** and pay.

supermodel /ˈsuːpəmɒdl/ noun [C] a very famous and highly paid fashion model □ *model/peragawati terunggul/terkenal/agung*

supernatural /ˌsuːpəˈnætʃrəl/ (*BrE also*) ˌsjuː- / adj **1** that cannot be explained by the laws of science □ *ghaib; luar biasa*: *a creature with supernatural powers* **2** the supernatural noun [sing] events, forces or powers that cannot be explained by the laws of science □ *kuasa ghaib*: *I don't believe in the supernatural.*

superpower /ˈsuːpəpaʊə(r)/ noun [C] one of the countries in the world that has very great military or economic power, for example the US □ *kuasa terbesar; bangsa atau negara yg amat kuat*

supersede /ˌsuːpəˈsiːd/ (*BrE also*) ˌsjuː- / verb [T] to take the place of sb/sth which existed or was used before and which has become old-fashioned □ *menggantikan; digantikan*: *The old software has been superseded by a new package.*

supersonic /ˌsuːpəˈsɒnɪk/ (*BrE also*) ˌsjuː- / adj faster than the speed of sound □ *supersonik*

superstar /ˈsuːpəstɑː(r)/ (*BrE also*) ˈsjuː- / noun [C] a singer, film star, etc. who is very famous and popular □ *superstar; bintang handalan*

superstition /ˌsuːpəˈstɪʃn/ (*BrE also*) ˌsjuː- / noun [C,U] a belief that cannot be explained by reason or science □ *tahayul; kepercayaan karut*: *According to superstition, it's unlucky to open an umbrella indoors.* ▶ **superstitious** /ˌsuːpəˈstɪʃəs/ (*BrE also*) ˌsjuː- / adj: *I never do anything important on Friday 13th—I'm superstitious.*

superstore /ˈsuːpəstɔː(r)/ (*BrE also*) ˈsjuː- / noun [C] a very large shop that sells food or a wide variety of one particular type of goods □ *gedung*

supervise /ˈsuːpəvaɪz/ (*BrE also*) ˈsjuː- / verb [I,T] to watch sb/sth to make sure that work is being done properly or that people are behaving correctly □ *menyelia; mengawasi*: *Your job is to supervise the building work.* ▶ **supervision** /ˌsuːpəˈvɪʒn/ (*BrE also*) ˌsjuː- / noun [U]: *Children should not play here without supervision.* ▶ **supervisor** /ˈsuːpəvaɪzə(r)/ noun [C]

supper /ˈsʌpə(r)/ noun [C,U] the last meal of the day, either the main meal of the evening or a small meal that you eat quite late, not long before you go to bed □ *makan malam; makan lewat malam* ⊃ note at **meal**

supple /ˈsʌpl/ adj that bends or moves easily; not stiff □ *lembut; mudah lentur*: *Children are generally far more supple than adults.* ▶ **suppleness** noun [U]

supplement /ˈsʌplɪmənt/ noun [C] something that is added to sth else □ *tambahan*: *You have to pay a small supplement if you travel on a Saturday.* ♦ *I take a vitamin supplement every day.* ▶ **supplement** /ˈsʌplɪment/ verb [T] supplement sth (with sth): *to supplement your diet with vitamins* ▶ **supplementary** /ˌsʌplɪˈmentri/ adj: *supplementary exercises at the back of the book*

supplier /səˈplaɪə(r)/ noun [C] a person or company that supplies goods □ *pembekal*

supply¹ /səˈplaɪ/ noun [C,U] (*pl* supplies) a store or an amount of sth that is provided or available to be used □ *bekalan*: *The water supply was contaminated.* ♦ *Food supplies were dropped by helicopter.* ♦ *In many parts of the country water is in short supply* (= there is not much of it).

supply² /səˈplaɪ/ verb [T] (supplying; supplies; *pt, pp* supplied) supply sth (to sb); supply sb (with sth) to give or provide sth □ *membekal*: *The farmer supplies eggs to the surrounding villages.* ♦ *He supplies the surrounding villages with eggs.*

support¹ /səˈpɔːt/ verb [T]
▶ HELP SB/STH **1** to help sb/sth by saying that you agree with them or it, and sometimes giving practical help such as money □ *menyokong; membantu*: *Several large companies are supporting the project.* ♦ *Which political party do you support?*

▶GIVE MONEY **2** to give sb the money they need for food, clothes, etc. □ *menyara; membiayai*: *Jim has to support two children from his previous marriage.*
▶CARRY WEIGHT **3** to carry the weight of sb/sth □ *menyokong; menopang*: *Large columns support the roof.*
▶SHOW STH IS TRUE **4** to show that sth is true or correct □ *menyokong*: *What evidence do you have to support what you say?*
▶SPORTS TEAM **5** to have a particular sports team that you like more than any other □ *menyokong; sokong*: *Which football team do you support?*

support² /sə'pɔːt/ *noun* **1** [U] **support (for sb/sth)** help and confidence that you give, especially in order to encourage a person or thing □ *sokongan; bantuan*: *public support for the campaign* ◆ *Steve spoke in support of the proposal.* **2** [U] money to buy food, clothes, etc. □ *wang sara diri*: *She has no home and no means of support.* **3** [C,U] something that carries the weight of sb/sth or holds sth firmly in place □ *tiang; topang*: *a roof support* ◆ *She held on to his arm for support.* **4** a band or singer who performs in a concert before the main performer □ *persembahan sampingan*
IDM moral support ➲ moral¹

supporter /sə'pɔːtə(r)/ *noun* [C] a person who supports a political party, sports team, etc. □ *penyokong*: *football supporters*

supportive /sə'pɔːtɪv/ *adj* giving help or support to sb in a difficult situation □ *memberikan bantuan; menyokong*: *Everyone was very supportive when I lost my job.*

suppose /sə'pəʊz/ *verb* [T] **1** to think that sth is probable □ *agak; rasa; kira; jangka*: *What do you suppose could have happened?* ◆ *I don't suppose that they're coming now.* **2** to pretend that sth will happen or is true □ *andainya; katakanlah*: *Suppose you won the lottery. What would you do?* **3** used to make a suggestion, request or statement less strong □ *agaknya; rasanya; mungkin*: *I don't suppose you'd lend me your car tonight, would you?* **4** used when you agree with sth, but are not very happy about it □ *agaknya*: *'Can we give Andy a lift?' 'Yes, I suppose so, if we must.'*
IDM **be supposed to do sth 1** to be expected to do sth or to have to do sth □ *sepatutnya*: *The train was supposed to arrive ten minutes ago.* ◆ *This is secret and I'm not supposed to talk about it.* **2** (*informal*) to be considered or thought to be sth □ *dikatakan; dipercayai*: *This is supposed to be the oldest building in the city.*
not supposed to do sth to not be allowed to do sth □ *ditegah; dilarang*: *This is secret and I'm not supposed to talk about it.*

supposedly /sə'pəʊzɪdli/ *adv* according to what many people believe □ *dikatakan; kononnya*

supposing /sə'pəʊzɪŋ/ *conj* if sth happens or is true; what if □ *sekiranya*: *Supposing the plan goes wrong, what will we do then?*

supposition /ˌsʌpə'zɪʃn/ *noun* [C,U] (*formal*) an idea that a person thinks is true but which has not been shown to be true □ *anggapan; sangkaan*

suppress /sə'pres/ *verb* [T] **1** to stop sth by using force □ *menindas; menumpaskan* **2** to stop sth from being seen or known □ *memendamkan; menyembunyikan*: *to suppress the truth* **3** to stop yourself from expressing your feelings, etc. □ *menahan*: *to suppress laughter/a yawn* ▶**suppression** /sə'preʃn/ *noun* [U]

supremacy /suː'preməsi/ *noun* [U] **supremacy (over sb/sth)** the state of being the most powerful □ *keulungan; kekuasaan*

supreme /suː'priːm/ *adj* the highest or greatest possible □ *tertinggi; paling agung*

supremely /suː'priːmli/ *adv* extremely □ *amat; sangat*

surcharge /'sɜːtʃɑːdʒ/ *noun* [C] an extra amount of money that you have to pay for sth □ *surcaj; bayaran tambahan*

sure /ʃʊə(r)/ (*BrE also*) /ʃɔː(r)/ *adj* (**surer; surest**) [You can also use **more sure** and **most sure**, especially in sense 1.] *adv* **1** [not before a noun] having no doubt about sth; certain □ *pasti*: *You must be sure of your facts before you make an accusation.* ◆ *I'm not sure what to do next.* ◆ *Craig was sure that he'd made the right decision.* ◆ *I think I had my bag when I got off the bus but I'm not sure.*
OPP unsure

HELP **Sure** or **certain**? **Sure** and **certain** are very similar in meaning but are used differently: *It is certain that there will be an election next year.* ◆ *There is sure to be an election next year.*

2 [not before a noun] **sure of sth**; **sure to do sth** certain that you will receive sth or that sth will happen □ *pasti; sudah tentu*: *If you go and see them you can be sure of a warm welcome.* ◆ *If you work hard you are sure to pass the exam.* **3** that you can be certain of □ *pasti; mesti*: *A noise like that is a sure sign of engine trouble.* **4** (*informal*) used to say 'yes' to sb □ *sudah tentu; ya*: *'Can I have a look at your newspaper?' 'Sure.'*
IDM **be sure to do sth** (used for telling sb to do sth) do not forget to do sth □ *jangan lupa (membuat sst)*: *Be sure to text and tell me what happens.*
for sure without doubt □ *(memang) pasti*: *Nobody knows for sure what happened.* ◆ (*especially AmE*) *'Will you be there?' 'For sure!'*
make sure 1 to take the action that is necessary □ *pastikan; memastikan*: *Make sure you are back home by 11 o'clock.* **2** to check that sth is in a particular state or has been done □ *memastikan*: *I must go back and make sure I closed the window.*
sure thing (*AmE informal*) yes □ *sudah tentu*: *'Can I borrow this book?' 'Sure thing.'*
sure enough as was expected □ *memang betul pun*: *I expected him to be early, and sure enough he arrived five minutes before the others.*

surely → surprised

sure of yourself confident about your opinions, or about what you can do □ *yakin betul (pd diri sendiri)*

surely /'ʃʊəli/ (BrE also) /'ʃɔːli/ adv **1** without doubt □ *pastinya; sudah tentu*: *This will surely cause problems.* **2** used for expressing surprise at sb else's opinions, plans, actions, etc. □ *tentu; takkanlah*: *Surely you're not going to walk home in this rain?* ◆ *'Jo's looking for another job.' 'Surely not!'* **3** (AmE old-fashioned informal) yes; of course □ *sudah tentu*

surf¹ /sɜːf/ noun [U] the white part on the top of waves in the sea □ *buih ombak*

surf² /sɜːf/ verb [I] **1** to stand or lie on a **surfboard** and ride on a wave towards the beach □ *meluncur ombak* ⊃ picture on **page P11**

> **HELP Go surfing** is a common way of talking about this activity: *Let's go surfing in Cornwall this weekend.*

2 surf the net/ Internet to use the Internet □ *melayari Internet*

surface¹ /'sɜːfɪs/ noun **1 the surface** [sing] the top part of an area of water □ *permukaan*: *leaves floating on the surface of a pond* **2** [C] the outside part of sth □ *permukaan*: *the earth's surface* ◆ *Teeth have a hard surface called enamel.* ◆ *This tennis court has a very uneven surface.* **3** [C] the flat top part of a piece of furniture, used for working on □ *permukaan; bahagian atas*: *a work surface* ◆ *kitchen surfaces* **4** [sing] the qualities of sb/sth that you see or notice, that are not hidden □ *zahirnya; luaran*: *Everybody seems very friendly but there are a lot of tensions* **below/beneath the surface**.

surface² /'sɜːfɪs/ verb **1** [I] to come up to the surface of water □ *timbul* **2** [I] to appear again □ *timbul; muncul*: *All the old arguments surfaced again in the discussion.* **3** [T] to put a surface on a road, etc. □ *melapisi; menurap*

'surface mail noun [U] letters, packages, etc. that go by road, rail or sea, not by air □ *mel biasa* ⊃ look at **airmail**

surfboard /'sɜːfbɔːd/ noun [C] a long narrow board used for **surfing** □ *papan luncur* ⊃ picture on **page P5**

surfeit /'sɜːfɪt/ noun [sing] (formal) **a surfeit (of sth)** too much of sth □ *terlalu banyak; banyak sangat*

surfer /'sɜːfə(r)/ noun [C] **1** a person who rides on waves standing on a special board □ *peluncur air* ⊃ picture on **page P5 2** (informal) a person who spends a lot of time using the Internet □ *pelayar Internet*

surfing /'sɜːfɪŋ/ noun [U] **1** the sport of riding on waves while standing or lying on a **surfboard** □ *bermain luncur ombak; meluncur ombak*: *to go surfing* ⊃ picture on **page P5 2** the activity of looking at different things on the Internet, or of looking quickly at different TV programmes, in order to find sth interesting □ *melayari* ⊃ picture on **page P3**

surge /sɜːdʒ/ noun [C, usually sing] **a surge (of/ in sth) 1** a sudden strong movement in a particular direction by a large number of people or things □ *gerakan meluru, menerpa, dsb; pertambahan*: *a surge of interest* ◆ *a surge* (= an increase) *in the demand for electricity* **2** a sudden strong feeling □ *perasaan yg meluap* ▶ **surge** verb [I]: *The crowd surged forward.*

surgeon /'sɜːdʒən/ noun [C] a doctor who performs medical operations □ *pakar bedah*: *a brain surgeon*

surgery /'sɜːdʒəri/ noun (pl **surgeries**) **1** [U] medical treatment in which your body is cut open so that part of it can be removed or repaired □ *pembedahan*: *to undergo surgery* ⊃ look at **operation, plastic surgery 2** [C,U] the place or time when a doctor or dentist sees patients □ *bilik rawatan*: *Surgery hours are from 9.00 to 11.30.* ⊃ note at **doctor**

surgical /'sɜːdʒɪkl/ adj [only before a noun] connected with medical operations □ *(berkenaan dgn) pembedahan*: *surgical instruments* ▶ **surgically** /-kli/ adv

surly /'sɜːli/ adj (**surlier; surliest**) unfriendly and rude □ *masam; tdk mesra*: *a surly expression*

surmount /sə'maʊnt/ verb [T] (formal) to deal successfully with a problem or difficulty □ *mengatasi* ⊃ look at **insurmountable**

surname /'sɜːneɪm/ (also **'last name; 'second name**) noun [C] the name that you share with other people in your family □ *nama keluarga*: *'What's your surname?' 'Jones.'* ⊃ note at **name**

surpass /sə'pɑːs/ verb [T] (formal) to do sth better than sb/sth else or better than expected □ *mengatasi; melebihi*: *The success of the film surpassed all expectations.*

surplus /'sɜːpləs/ noun [C,U] an amount that is extra or more than you need □ *lebihan*: *the food surplus in Western Europe* ▶ **surplus** adj: *They sell their surplus grain to other countries.*

surprise¹ /sə'praɪz/ noun **1** [C] something that you did not expect or know about □ *sst yg mengejutkan/memeranjatkan*: *What a pleasant surprise to see you again!* ◆ *The news came as a complete surprise.* ◆ *a surprise visit/attack/party* **2** [U] the feeling that you have when sth happens that you do not expect □ *kehairanan; rasa hairan/terkejut*: *They looked up* **in surprise** *when she walked in.* ◆ **To my surprise** *they all agreed with me.*

> **IDM take sb by surprise** to happen or do sth when sb is not expecting it □ *secara mengejut; tdk disangka-sangka*

surprise² /sə'praɪz/ verb [T] **1** to make sb feel surprised □ *mengejutkan; memeranjatkan*: *It wouldn't surprise me if you get the job.* **2** to attack or find sb suddenly and unexpectedly □ *secara mengejut*

surprised /sə'praɪzd/ adj feeling or showing surprise □ *mengejutkan; memeranjatkan*: *I was* very surprised to see Cara there. I thought she was still abroad.

surprising /sə'praɪzɪŋ/ adj that causes surprise □ *terkejut; terperanjat*: *It's surprising how many adults can't read or write.* ▶**surprisingly** adv: *Surprisingly few people got the correct answer.*

surreal /sə'riːəl/ (also **surrealistic** /sə,riːə'lɪstɪk/) adj very strange; with images mixed together in a strange way like in a dream □ *di luar alam nyata*: *a surreal film/painting/situation*

surrender /sə'rendə(r)/ verb 1 [I,T] surrender (yourself) (to sb) to stop fighting and admit that you have lost □ *menyerah kalah; mengalah* SYN **yield** 2 [T] (formal) surrender sb/sth (to sb) to give sb/sth to sb else when you are forced to □ *menyerahkan (senjata, dll)*: *The police ordered them to surrender their weapons.* ▶**surrender** noun [C,U]

surreptitious /,sʌrəp'tɪʃəs/ adj done secretly □ *secara curi-curi/diam-diam*: *I had a surreptitious look at what she was writing.* ▶**surreptitiously** adv

surrogate /'sʌrəgət/ noun [C], adj (a person or thing) that takes the place of sb/sth else □ *pengganti*: *a surrogate mother* (= a woman who has a baby and gives it to another woman who cannot have children)

surround /sə'raʊnd/ verb [T] surround sb/sth (by/with sth) to be or go all around sb/sth □ *mengelilingi; mengepung*: *The garden is surrounded by a high wall.* ◆ *Troops have surrounded the parliament building.*

surrounding /sə'raʊndɪŋ/ adj [only before a noun] that is near or around sth □ *sekeliling; sekitar*: *Oxford and the surrounding area*

surroundings /sə'raʊndɪŋz/ noun [pl] everything that is near or around you; the place where you live □ *persekitaran*: *to live in pleasant surroundings* ◆ *animals living in their natural surroundings* (= not in zoos) ➔ look at **environment**

surveillance /sɜː'veɪləns/ noun [U] the careful watching of sb who may have done sth wrong □ *pengawasan; pemerhatian rapi*: *The building is protected by surveillance cameras.*

survey¹ /'sɜːveɪ/ noun [C] 1 a study of the opinions, behaviour, etc. of a group of people □ *tinjauan*: *Surveys have shown that more and more people are getting into debt.* ◆ *to carry out/conduct/do a survey* 2 the act of examining an area of land and making a map of it □ *kerja-kerja mengukur*: *a geological survey* 3 the act of examining a building in order to find out if it is in good condition □ *pemeriksaan*

survey² /sə'veɪ/ verb [T] 1 to look carefully at the whole of sth □ *meninjau; memerhatikan*: *We stood at the top of the hill and surveyed the countryside.* 2 to carefully measure and make a map of an area of land □ *mengukur* 3 to examine a building carefully in order to find out if it is in good condition □ *memeriksa*

surveyor /sə'veɪə(r)/ noun [C] 1 a person whose job is to examine and record the details of a piece of land □ *juruukur* 2 (AmE **inspector**) a person whose job is to examine a building to make sure it is in good condition, usually done for sb who wants to buy it □ *pemeriksa; peninjau*

survive /sə'vaɪv/ verb 1 [I,T] to continue to live or exist in or after a difficult or dangerous situation □ *terus hidup; terselamat; bertahan*: *More than a hundred people were killed in the crash and only five passengers survived.* ◆ *How can she survive on such a small salary?* ◆ *to survive a plane crash* ◆ *Not many buildings survived the bombing.* 2 [T] to live longer than sb/sth □ *hidup lebih lama*: *The old man survived all his children.* ▶**survival** /sə'vaɪvl/ noun [U]: *A heart transplant was his only chance of survival.* ▶**survivor** /sə'vaɪvə(r)/ noun [C]: *There were five survivors of the crash.*

susceptible /sə'septəbl/ adj [not before a noun] susceptible to sth easily influenced, damaged or affected by sb/sth □ *mudah dipengaruhi/dijangkiti/kena*: *The young are susceptible to advertising.* ◆ *Some of these plants are more susceptible to frost damage than others.*

suspect¹ /sə'spekt/ verb [T] 1 to believe that sth may happen or be true, especially sth bad □ *menjangka; dijangka; mengesyaki*: *The situation is worse than we first suspected.* ◆ *Nobody suspected that she was thinking of leaving.* ➔ look at **unsuspecting** 2 to not be sure that you can trust sb or believe sth □ *mencurigai*: *I rather suspect his motives for offering to help.* 3 suspect sb (of sth/of doing sth) to believe that sb is guilty of sth, although you do not have any proof □ *mengesyaki*: *I suspect Laura of taking the money.* ◆ *She strongly suspected that he was lying.* ▶**suspected** adj: *suspected terrorists* ➔ noun **suspicion**

suspect² /'sʌspekt/ noun [C] a person who is thought to be guilty of a crime □ *orang yg disyaki*: *The suspects are being questioned by police.* ➔ note at **crime**

suspect³ /'sʌspekt/ adj possibly not true or not to be trusted □ *disyaki; dicurigai*: *to have suspect motives* ◆ *a suspect package* (= that may contain a bomb)

suspend /sə'spend/ verb [T] 1 suspend sth (from sth) (by/on sth) to hang sth from sth else □ *menggantung; tergantung*: *The huge skeleton is suspended from the museum's ceiling on chains.* 2 to stop or delay sth for a time □ *menangguhkan*: *Some rail services were suspended during the strike.* ◆ *The young man was given a suspended sentence* (= he will go to prison only if he commits another crime). 3 suspend sb (from sth) to send sb away from their school, job, position, etc. for a period of time, usually as a punishment □ *menggantung; digantung*: *He was suspended from school for a week for stealing.* ➔ noun **suspension**

suspender /səˈspendə(r)/ noun 1 [C, usually pl] (BrE) a short piece of **elastic** (= material that can stretch) that women use to hold up their **stockings** (= thin pieces of clothing that fit closely over a woman's legs and feet) □ *tali pinggang garter* 2 **suspenders** [pl] (AmE) = **brace**[1](2)

suspense /səˈspens/ noun [U] the feeling of excitement or worry that you have when you feel sth is going to happen, when you are waiting for news, etc. □ *kegelisahan menunggu sst; suspen: Don't keep us in suspense. Tell us what happened.*

suspension /səˈspenʃn/ noun 1 [C,U] not being allowed to do your job or go to school for a period of time, usually as a punishment □ *penggantungan: suspension on full pay* 2 [U] delaying sth for a period of time □ *penangguhan* ⊃ verb **suspend** 3 the **suspension** [U] the parts that are connected to the wheels of a car, etc. that make it more comfortable to ride in □ *sistem (ampaian)*

⚑ suspicion /səˈspɪʃn/ noun 1 [C,U] a feeling or belief that sth is wrong or that sb has done sth wrong □ *rasa sangsi; syak; kecurigaan: I always treat smiling politicians with suspicion.* ♦ *She was arrested on suspicion of murder.* ♦ *He is under suspicion of being involved in organized crime.* ♦ *It's time to confront him with our suspicions.* 2 [C] a feeling that sth may happen or be true □ *agak: I have a suspicion that he's forgotten he invited us.* ⊃ verb **suspect**

⚑ suspicious /səˈspɪʃəs/ adj 1 **suspicious (of/about sb/sth)** feeling that sb has done sth wrong, dishonest or illegal □ *berasa syak/curiga: We became suspicious of his behaviour and alerted the police.* 2 that makes you feel that sth is wrong, dishonest or illegal □ *mencurigakan; menimbulkan kecurigaan: The old man died in suspicious circumstances.* ♦ *It's very suspicious that she was not at home on the evening of the murder.* ♦ *a suspicious-looking person* ▶**suspiciously** adv: *to behave suspiciously*

sustain /səˈsteɪn/ verb [T] 1 to keep sb/sth alive or healthy □ *mengekalkan; meneruskan; membolehkan sso/sst terus hidup: Oxygen sustains life.* 2 to make sth continue for a long period of time without becoming less □ *dpt mengekalkan: It's hard to sustain interest for such a long time.* 3 (formal) to experience sth bad □ *mengalami; menderita: to sustain damage/an injury/a defeat*

sustainable /səˈsteɪnəbl/ adj 1 involving the use of natural products and energy in a way that does not harm the environment □ *secara jimat: sustainable forest management* 2 that can continue or be continued for a long time □ *mapan: sustainable economic growth* ▶**sustainability** /səˌsteɪnəˈbɪləti/ noun [U]: *environmental sustainability*

SW abbr = **south-west**[1], **south-western** □ *barat daya: SW Australia*

swab /swɒb/ noun [C] 1 a piece of soft material used by a doctor, nurse, etc. for cleaning wounds or taking a small amount of a substance from sb's body for testing □ *kapas kesat* 2 an act of taking a small amount of a substance from sb's body, with a **swab** □ *pengambilan spesimen drpd sso dgn kapas kesat: to take a throat swab* ▶**swab** verb [T] (**swabbing**; **swabbed**)

swagger /ˈswæɡə(r)/ verb [I] to walk in a way that shows that you are too confident or proud □ *berjalan dgn angkuh; berlagak* ▶**swagger** noun [sing]

⚑ swallow /ˈswɒləʊ/ verb
▶FOOD/DRINK 1 [T] to make food, drink, etc. go down your throat to your stomach □ *menelan: It's easier to swallow pills if you take them with water.* ⊃ picture at **lick**
▶IN FEAR, ETC. 2 [I] to make a movement in your throat, often because you are afraid or surprised, etc. □ *meneguk; menelan: She swallowed hard and tried to speak, but nothing came out.*
▶USE ALL 3 [T] **swallow sth (up)** to use all of sth, especially money □ *menelan; menghabiskan: The rent swallows up most of our monthly income.*
▶ACCEPT/BELIEVE 4 [T] to accept or believe sth too easily □ *menerima bulat-bulat: You shouldn't swallow everything they tell you!* 5 [T] to accept an insult, etc. without complaining □ *menelan; menerima: I find her criticisms very hard to swallow.* ▶**swallow** noun [C]

swam past tense of **swim**

swamp[1] /swɒmp/ noun [C,U] an area of soft wet land □ *paya*

swamp[2] /swɒmp/ verb [T] 1 [usually passive] **swamp sb/sth (with sth)** to give sb so much of sth that they cannot deal with it □ *membanjiri: We've been swamped with applications for the job.* **SYN** **inundate** 2 to cover or fill sth with water □ *menenggelami: The fishing boat was swamped by enormous waves.*

swan /swɒn/ noun [C] a large, usually white, bird with a very long neck that lives on lakes and rivers □ *(burung) swan*

swap (also **swop**) /swɒp/ verb [I,T] (**swapping**; **swapped**) **swap (sth) (with sb)**; **swap A for B** to give sth for sth else; to exchange □ *bertukar-tukar; menukar: When we finish these books shall we swap (= you have my book and I'll have yours)?* ♦ *Would you swap seats with me?* ♦ *I'd swap my job for hers any day.*
IDM **change/swap places (with sb)** ⊃ **place**[1]
▶**swap** (also **swop**) noun [sing]: *Let's do a swap.*

swan

goose

swarm¹ /swɔːm/ noun [C] **1** a large group of insects moving around together □ *kawan, kawanan sst (serangga, dll)*: *a swarm of bees/locusts/flies* **2** a large number of people together □ *kumpulan besar orang*

swarm² /swɔːm/ verb [I] to fly or move in large numbers □ *terbang berkawan*
PHR V **swarm with sb/sth** to be full of people or things □ *mengerumuni; memenuhi*

swat /swɒt/ verb [T] (**swatting**; **swatted**) to hit sth, especially an insect, with sth flat □ *memukul*

sway /sweɪ/ verb **1** [I] to move slowly from side to side □ *bergoyang-goyang; berbuai-buai*: *The trees were swaying in the wind.* **2** [T] to influence sb □ *mempengaruhi*: *Many people were swayed by his convincing arguments.*

swear /sweə(r)/ verb (pt **swore** /swɔː(r)/; pp **sworn** /swɔːn/) **1** [I] **swear (at sb/sth)** to use rude or bad language □ *memaki; menyumpah*: *He hit his thumb with the hammer and swore loudly.* ♦ *There's no point in swearing at the car just because it won't start!* ➔ look at **curse 2** [I,T] **swear (to do sth); swear that …** to make a serious promise □ *bersumpah; mengangkat sumpah*: *When you give evidence in court you have to swear to tell the truth.* ♦ *Will you swear not to tell anyone?*
PHR V **swear by sth** to believe completely in the value of sth □ *yakin/percaya akan keandalan atau baiknya sst*
swear sb in [usually passive] to make sb say officially that they will accept the responsibility of a new position □ *mengangkat sumpah*: *The President will be sworn in next week.*

swearing /'sweərɪŋ/ noun [U] rude language that may offend people □ *makian; sumpah seranah*: *I was shocked at the swearing.*

'swear word (also old-fashioned **oath**) noun [C] a word that is considered rude or bad and that may offend people □ *kata sumpah*

sweat /swet/ verb [I] **1** to produce liquid through your skin because you are hot, ill or afraid □ *berpeluh*: *to sweat heavily* **2 sweat (over sth)** to work hard □ *bekerja kuat/keras*: *I've been sweating over that problem all day.* ▶ **sweat** noun [C,U]: *He stopped digging and wiped the sweat from his forehead.* ♦ *He woke up in a sweat.* ➔ look at **perspiration**

sweater /'swetə(r)/ noun [C] a warm piece of clothing with long sleeves, often made of wool, which you wear on the top half of your body □ *baju panas/sejuk* ➔ picture on **page P1**

OTHER WORDS FOR

sweater

In British English, **sweater**, **jumper**, **pullover** and **jersey** are all words for the same piece of clothing. A **cardigan** is similar but fastens at the front. A **fleece** is made from a type of soft warm cloth that feels like sheep's wool.

---

865 **swarm → sweep**

A **sweatshirt** is made from thick cotton and is often worn for sports.

sweatshirt /'swetʃɜːt/ noun [C] a piece of cotton clothing with long sleeves, which you wear on the top half of your body □ *baju panas kain kapas; kemeja peluh* ➔ note at **sweater**

sweatshop /'swetʃɒp/ noun [C] a place where people work for low wages in poor conditions □ *kilang peras tenaga*

sweaty /'sweti/ adj (**sweatier**; **sweatiest**) **1** wet with sweat □ *berpeluh-peluh*: *I was hot and sweaty after the match and needed a shower.* **2** [only before a noun] causing you to sweat □ *berlengas*: *a hot sweaty day*

swede /swiːd/ noun [C,U] a large, round, yellow vegetable that grows under the ground □ *'swede'; sejenis sayuran ubi spt lobak tetapi bulat*

sweep¹ /swiːp/ verb (pt, pp **swept** /swept/)
▶WITH BRUSH **1** [I,T] to clean the floor, etc. by moving dust, dirt, etc. away with a brush □ *menyapu; membersihkan*: *to sweep the floor* ♦ *I'm going to sweep the leaves off the path.* ➔ note at **clean²**
▶WITH HAND **2** [T] to remove sth from a surface using your hand, etc. □ *menolak*: *He swept the books angrily off the table.*
▶MOVE WITH FORCE **3** [T] to move or push sb/sth with a lot of force □ *menghanyutkan; menolak; tertolak*: *The huge waves swept her overboard.* ♦ *He was swept along by the huge crowd.*
▶MOVE FAST **4** [I,T] to move quickly and smoothly over the area or in the direction mentioned □ *melanda; merebak*: *Fire swept through the building.* **5** [I] to move in a way that impresses or is intended to impress people □ *bergerak dgn megah; meluncur*: *Five big black Mercedes swept past us.*
▶SEARCH **6** [I,T] to move over an area, especially in order to look for sth □ *meninjau*: *His eyes swept quickly over the page.* ♦ *The army were sweeping the fields for mines.*
PHR V **sweep sb/sth aside** to not allow sb/sth to affect your progress or plans □ *mengetepikan; menolak ke tepi*
sweep sth out to remove dirt and dust from the floor of a room or building using a brush □ *menyapu sst*
sweep over sb (used about a feeling) to suddenly affect sb very strongly □ *melanda; menguasai*
sweep (sth) up/away to remove dirt, dust, leaves, etc. using a brush □ *menyapu*

sweep² /swiːp/ noun [C] **1** [usually sing] the act of moving dirt and dust from a floor or surface using a brush □ *(perbuatan) menyapu/disapu*: *I'd better give the floor a sweep.* **2** a long, curving shape or movement □ *ayunan*: *He showed us which way to go with a sweep of his arm.* **3** a movement over an area, especially in order to

CONSONANTS p **p**en b **b**ad t **t**ea d **d**id k **c**at g **g**ot tʃ **ch**in dʒ **J**une f **f**all v **v**an θ **th**in

sweeper → swim

look for sth □ *penggeledahan; pencarian* **4** = chimney sweep
IDM a clean sweep ⊃ clean¹

sweeper /'swiːpə(r)/ *noun* [C] **1** a person or thing that cleans surfaces with a brush □ *tukang/alat sapu; penyapu*: *He's a road sweeper.* ◆ *Do you sell carpet sweepers?* **2** (in football) the defending player who plays behind the other defending players □ *pemain pertahanan yg terakhir*

sweeping /'swiːpɪŋ/ *adj* **1** having a great and important effect □ *secara meluas/menyeluruh*: *sweeping reforms* **2** (used about statements, etc.) too general and not accurate enough □ *umum; terlalu am*: *He made a sweeping statement about all politicians being dishonest.*

sweet¹ /swiːt/ *adj* (**sweeter**; **sweetest**) **1** containing, or tasting as if it contains, a lot of sugar □ *manis*: *Children usually like sweet things.* ◆ *This cake's too sweet.* ⊃ look at **savoury**, **sour** **2** (used about a smell or a sound) pleasant □ *wangi; harum; merdu*: *the sweet sound of children singing* **3** (used especially about children and small things) attractive □ *comel; manis; cantik*: *a sweet little kitten* ◆ *Isn't that little girl sweet?* **SYN** cute **4** having or showing a kind character □ *manis; baik*: *a sweet smile*
IDM have a sweet tooth (*informal*) to like eating sweet things □ *suka makan benda-benda manis*
▶**sweetness** *noun* [U]

sweet² /swiːt/ *noun* **1** [C, usually pl] (*AmE* **candy**) a small piece of boiled sugar, chocolate, etc., eaten between meals □ *gula-gula*: *He was sucking a sweet.* ◆ *a sweet shop* **2** [C,U] sweet food served at the end of a meal □ *pencuci mulut; manisan*: *As a sweet/For sweet there is ice cream or chocolate mousse.* ⊃ look at **pudding**, **dessert**

sweetcorn /'swiːtkɔːn/ (*AmE* **corn**) *noun* [U] the yellow grains of a type of **maize** (= a tall plant) that you cook and eat as a vegetable □ *jagung manis*: *tinned sweetcorn* ⊃ picture on page P15

sweeten /'swiːtn/ *verb* [T] to make sth sweet by adding sugar, etc. □ *memaniskan*

sweetener /'swiːtnə(r)/ *noun* [C,U] a substance used instead of sugar for making food or drink sweet □ *bahan pemanis*: *artificial sweeteners*

sweetheart /'swiːthɑːt/ *noun* **1** [sing] used when speaking to sb, especially a child, in a very friendly way □ *sayang*: *Do you want a drink, sweetheart?* **2** [C] (*old-fashioned*) a boyfriend or girlfriend □ *buah hati; kekasih*

sweetly /'swiːtli/ *adv* in an attractive, kind or pleasant way □ *dgn cara yg manis/menawan; dgn harumnya*: *She smiled sweetly.* ◆ *sweetly scented flowers*

swell¹ /swel/ *verb* (*pt* **swelled** /sweld/; *pp* **swollen** /'swəʊlən/ *or* **swelled**) **1** [I,T] swell (up) to become or to make sth bigger, fuller or thicker □ *menjadi bengkak; mengembung; melimpah*: *After the fall her ankle began to swell up.* ◆ *Heavy rain had swollen the rivers.* **2** [I,T] to increase or make sth increase in number or size □ *bertambah (banyak, besar, dsb)*: *The crowd swelled to 600 by the end of the evening.* **3** [I] (*formal*) (used about feelings or sound) to suddenly become stronger or louder □ *memuncak; semakin meninggi*: *Hatred swelled inside him.*

swell² /swel/ *noun* [sing] the slow movement up and down of the surface of the sea □ *gelombang; ombak besar*

swelling /'swelɪŋ/ *noun* **1** [U] the process of becoming swollen □ *menjadi bengkak; membengkak*: *The disease often causes swelling of the ankles and knees.* **2** [C] a place on your body that is bigger or fatter than usual because of an injury or illness □ *bengkak*: *I've got a nasty swelling under my eye.*

sweltering /'sweltərɪŋ/ *adj* (*informal*) much too hot □ *sangat panas*: *It was sweltering in the office today.*

swept *past tense, past participle of* **sweep¹**

swerve /swɜːv/ *verb* [I] to change direction suddenly □ *membelok dgn tiba-tiba*: *The car swerved to avoid the child.* ▶**swerve** *noun* [C]

swift /swɪft/ *adj* (**swifter**; **swiftest**) happening without delay; quick □ *pantas; deras*: *a swift reaction/decision/movement* ◆ *a swift runner*
▶**swiftly** *adv*

swig /swɪɡ/ *verb* [I,T] (**swigging**; **swigged**) (*informal*) to take a quick drink of sth □ *meneguk; menggogok* ▶**swig** *noun* [C]

swill /swɪl/ *verb* [T] swill sth (out/down) to wash sth by pouring large amounts of water, etc. into, over or through it □ *menyimbah; membilas*

swim /swɪm/ *verb* (**swimming**; *pt* **swam** /swæm/; *pp* **swum** /swʌm/) **1** [I,T] to move your body through water □ *berenang*: *How far can you swim?* ◆ *Hundreds of tiny fish swam past.* ◆ *I swam 25 lengths of the pool.*

> **HELP** Go swimming is a common way of talking about swimming for pleasure: *We go swimming every Saturday.* We can also say go for a swim when we are talking about one particular occasion: *I went for a swim this morning.*

2 [I] be swimming (in/with sth) to be covered with a lot of liquid □ *tergenang*: *The salad was swimming in oil.* **3** [I] to seem to be moving or turning □ *kelihatan berpusing-pusing*: *The floor began to swim before my eyes and I fainted.* **4** [I] (used about your head) to feel confused □ *rasa berpusing; rasa pening*: *My head was swimming with so much new information.* ▶**swim** *noun* [sing]: *to go for/have a swim* ▶**swimmer** *noun* [C]: *a strong/weak swimmer*

diving

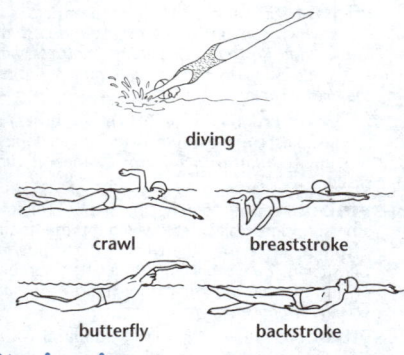

crawl — *breaststroke*

butterfly — *backstroke*

swimming /ˈswɪmɪŋ/ *noun* [U] the sport or activity of swimming □ *sukan atau aktiviti renang*: *Swimming is a good form of exercise.*

swimming bath *noun* [C] (also **swimming baths** [pl]) (*old-fashioned*) a public swimming pool, usually inside a building □ *kolam renang dlm bangunan*

swimming costume (*BrE*) = **swimsuit**

swimming pool (also **pool**) *noun* [C] a pool that is built especially for people to swim in; the building that contains this pool □ *kolam renang*: *an indoor/outdoor/open-air swimming pool*

swimming trunks *noun* [pl] a piece of clothing like short trousers that a man wears to go swimming □ *seluar mandi*: *a pair of swimming trunks*

swimsuit /ˈswɪmsuːt/ (*BrE* also **swimming costume**; **costume**) *noun* [C] a piece of clothing that a woman wears to go swimming □ *baju mandi/renang* ➪ look at **bikini**

swindle /ˈswɪndl/ *verb* [T] **swindle sb/sth (out of sth)** to trick sb in order to get money, etc. □ *menipu* ▶ **swindle** *noun* [C]: *a tax swindle*

swine /swaɪn/ *noun* **1** [C] (*informal*) a very unpleasant person □ *org yg dibenci; celaka; babi* **2** [pl] (*old-fashioned*) pigs □ *babi; khinzir*

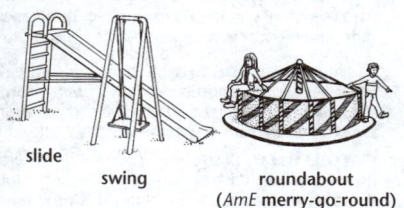

slide

swing — *roundabout* (*AmE* **merry-go-round**)

swing¹ /swɪŋ/ *verb* (*pt, pp* **swung** /swʌŋ/) **1** [I,T] to move backwards and forwards or from side to side while hanging from sth; to make sb/sth move in this way □ *berayun; mengayun; membuai*: *The rope was swinging from a branch.* ♦ *She sat on the wall, swinging her legs.* **2** [I] to move or change from one position or situation towards the opposite one □ *berpaling; beru-*

bah: *She swung round when she heard the door open.* ♦ *His moods swing from one extreme to the other.* **3** [I,T] to move or make sb/sth move in a curve □ *mengayun*: *The door swung open and Rudi walked in.* ♦ *He swung the child up onto his shoulders.* **4** [I,T] **swing (sth) (at sb/sth)** to try to hit sb/sth □ *melibas/cuba memukul sso/sst*: *He swung violently at the other man but missed.*

swing² /swɪŋ/ *noun* **1** [sing] a **swinging** movement or rhythm □ *ayunan; gerakan mengayun kayu pemukul utk memukul bola, dsb*: *He took a swing at the ball.* **2** [C] a change from one position or situation towards the opposite one □ *perubahan; pertukaran*: *Opinion polls indicate a significant swing towards the right.* **3** [C] a seat, a piece of rope, etc. that is hung from above so that you can **swing** backwards and forwards on it □ *buaian*: *Some children were playing on the swings.*

IDM **in full swing** ➪ **full¹**

swipe /swaɪp/ *verb* **1** [I,T] (*informal*) **swipe (at) sb/sth** to hit or try to hit sb/sth by moving your arm in a curve □ *memukul*: *He swiped at the wasp with a newspaper but missed.* **2** [T] (*informal*) to steal sth □ *mencuri; mengebas* **3** [T] to pass the part of a plastic card on which information is stored through a special machine for reading it □ *mengimbas*: *The cash register only opens once the card has been swiped.* **4** [I] (on some small computer devices) to move content across a screen using your finger □ *menggerakkan* ➪ note at **touch screen** ▶ **swipe** *noun* [C]: *She took a swipe at him with her handbag.*

swipe card *noun* [C] a small plastic card on which information is stored which can be read by an electronic machine □ *kad imbas*

swirl /swɜːl/ *verb* [I,T] to move or to make sth move around quickly in a circle □ *berpusar; berolak*: *Her long skirt swirled round her legs as she danced.* ♦ *He swirled some water round in his mouth and spat it out.* ▶ **swirl** *noun* [C]: *a pattern of blue swirls*

switch¹ /swɪtʃ/ *noun* [C] **1** a small button or sth similar that you press up or down in order to turn on electricity □ *perubahan/pertukaran mendadak*: *a light switch* **2** a sudden change □ *suis*: *a switch in policy*

switch² /swɪtʃ/ *verb* [I,T] **1 switch (sth) (over) (from sth) (to sth); switch (between A and B)** to change or be changed from one thing to another □ *beralih; bertukar*: *I'm fed up with my glasses—I'm thinking of switching over to contact lenses.* ♦ *Press these two keys to switch between documents on screen.* ♦ *The match has been switched from Saturday to Sunday.* **2 switch (sth) (with sb/sth); switch (sth) (over/round)** to exchange positions, activities, etc. □ *bertukar tempat; mengubah*: *This week you can have the car and I'll go on the bus, and next week we'll switch over.* ♦ *Someone switched the signs round and everyone went the wrong way.*

VOWELS iː **see** i **any** ɪ **sit** e **ten** æ **hat** ɑː **father** ɒ **got** ɔː **saw** ʊ **put** uː **too** u **usual**

switchboard → sympathizer

PHR V **switch off** to stop thinking about sth or paying attention to sth □ *mengalihkan tumpuan*: When I hear the word 'football', I switch off (= because I'm not interested in it).
switch (sth) off/on to press a switch in order to stop/start electric power □ *memadam/memasang suis*: Don't forget to switch off the cooker.
switch (sth) over to change to a different TV programme □ *menukar saluran*

switchboard /'swɪtʃbɔːd/ noun [C] the place in a large company, etc. where all the telephone calls are connected □ *papan suis*

swivel /'swɪvl/ verb [I,T] (swivelling; swivelled, AmE swiveling; swiveled) swivel (sth) (round) to turn around a central point; to make sth do this □ *berpusing; memusingkan*: She swivelled round to face me. ♦ He swivelled his chair towards the door.

swollen¹ past participle of swell¹

swollen² /'swəʊlən/ adj thicker or wider than usual □ *bengkak*: Her ankle was badly swollen after she twisted it.

swoop /swuːp/ verb [I] **1** to fly or move down suddenly □ *melayah; turun menjunam (lalu menyambar sst)*: The bird swooped down on its prey. **2** (used especially about the police or the army) to visit or capture sb/sth without warning □ *menyerbu; menyergap*: Police swooped at dawn and arrested the man at his home. ▶ swoop noun [C] a swoop (on sb/sth)

swop = swap

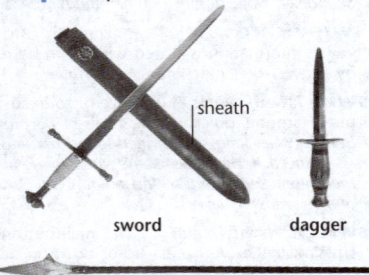

sheath

sword   dagger

spear

sword /sɔːd/ noun [C] a long, very sharp metal weapon, like a large knife □ *pedang*

swore past tense of swear

sworn past participle of swear

swot¹ /swɒt/ noun [C] (informal) a person who studies too hard □ *kaki belajar/studi*

swot² /swɒt/ verb [I,T] (informal) (swotting; swotted) swot (up) (for/on sth); swot sth up to study sth very hard, especially to prepare for an exam □ *belajar/menelaah dgn tekun*: She's swotting for her final exams.

swum past participle of swim

swung past tense, past participle of swing¹

syllable /'sɪləbl/ noun [C] a word or part of a word which contains one vowel sound □ *suku kata*: 'Mat' has one syllable and 'mattress' has two syllables. ♦ The stress in 'international' is on the third syllable.

syllabus /'sɪləbəs/ noun [C] (pl syllabuses) a list of subjects, etc. that are included in a course of study □ *sukatan pelajaran* ⊃ look at curriculum

symbol /'sɪmbl/ noun [C] **1** a symbol (of sth) a person, sign, object, etc. which represents sth □ *tanda; lambang*: The cross is the symbol of Christianity. **2** a symbol (for sth) a letter, number or sign that has a particular meaning □ *simbol*: O is the symbol for oxygen.

symbolic /sɪm'bɒlɪk/ (also symbolical /-kl/) adj used or seen to represent sth □ *(merupakan) lambang*: The white dove is symbolic of peace. ▶ symbolically /-kli/ adv

symbolism /'sɪmbəlɪzəm/ noun [U] the use of symbols to represent things, especially in art and literature □ *perlambangan; simbolisme*

symbolize (also -ise) /'sɪmbəlaɪz/ verb [T] to represent sth □ *melambangkan*: The deepest notes in music are often used to symbolize danger or despair.

symmetric /sɪ'metrɪk/ (also symmetrical /-rɪkl/) adj having two halves that match each other exactly in size, shape, etc. □ *bersimetri* ▶ symmetrically /-kli/ adv

symmetry /'sɪmətri/ noun [U] the state of having two halves that match each other exactly in size, shape, etc. □ *simetri; kedua-dua belahnya betul-betul sama dr segi ukuran, bentuk, dsb*

sympathetic /ˌsɪmpə'θetɪk/ adj **1** sympathetic (to/towards sb) showing that you understand other people's feelings, especially their problems □ *(sikap) bersimpati*: When Suki was ill, everyone was very sympathetic. ♦ I felt very sympathetic towards him.

HELP Be careful. **Sympathetic** does not mean 'friendly and pleasant'. If you want to express this meaning, you say a person is **nice** or **pleasant**: I met Alex's sister yesterday. She's very nice.

2 sympathetic (to sb/sth) being in agreement with or supporting sb/sth □ *bersetuju; menyokong*: I explained our ideas but she wasn't sympathetic to them. ▶ sympathetically /-kli/ adv

sympathize (also -ise) /'sɪmpəθaɪz/ verb [I] sympathize (with sb/sth) **1** to feel sorry for sb; to show that you understand sb's problems □ *berasa/menunjukkan simpati; bersimpati*: I sympathize with her, but I don't know what I can do to help. **2** to support sb/sth □ *bersetuju dgn; menyokong*: I find it difficult to sympathize with his opinions.

sympathizer (also -iser) /'sɪmpəθaɪzə(r)/ noun [C] a person who agrees with and supports an idea or aim □ *penyokong*

sympathy /ˈsɪmpəθi/ noun (pl **sympathies**) **1** [U] sympathy (for/towards sb) an understanding of other people's feelings, especially their problems □ *rasa simpati*: *Everyone feels great sympathy for the victims of the attack.* ◆ *I don't expect any sympathy from you.* ◆ *I have no sympathy for Mark—it's his own fault.* **2** sympathies [pl] feelings of support or agreement □ *sokongan*: *Some members of the party have nationalist sympathies.*

IDM in sympathy (with sb/sth) in agreement, showing that you support or approve of sb/sth □ *sbg menyokong (sso/sst)*: *Train drivers stopped work in sympathy with the striking bus drivers.*

symphony /ˈsɪmfəni/ noun [C] (pl **symphonies**) a long piece of music written for a large **orchestra** (= a group of musicians who play together) □ *simfoni*

symptom /ˈsɪmptəm/ noun [C] **1** a change in your body that is a sign of illness □ *gejala; tanda*: *The symptoms of flu include a headache, a high temperature and aches in the body.* ➔ note at **ill 2** a sign (that sth bad is happening or exists) □ *petanda* ▸ symptomatic /ˌsɪmptəˈmætɪk/ adj

synagogue /ˈsɪnəgɒg/ noun [C] a building where Jewish people go to worship or to study their religion □ *saumaah*

synchronize (also -ise) /ˈsɪŋkrənaɪz/ verb [T] to make sth happen or work at the same time or speed □ *menyelaraskan; menyamakan*: *We synchronized our watches to make sure we agreed what the time was.*

syndicate /ˈsɪndɪkət/ noun [C] a group of people or companies that work together in order to achieve a particular aim □ *sindiket*

syndrome /ˈsɪndrəʊm/ noun [C] **1** a group of signs or changes in the body that are typical of an illness □ *sindrom*: *Down's syndrome* ◆ *Acquired Immune Deficiency Syndrome (AIDS)* **2** a set of opinions or a way of behaving that is typical of a particular type of person, attitude or social problem □ *sindrom*

synonym /ˈsɪnənɪm/ noun [C] a word or phrase that has the same meaning as another word or phrase in the same language □ *sinonim; perkataan seerti*: *'Big' and 'large' are synonyms.* ▸ synonymous /sɪˈnɒnɪməs/ adj synonymous (with sth) (figurative): *Wealth is not always synonymous with happiness.* ➔ look at **antonym**

EXAM TIP

Synonyms

In an exam, your writing will be more interesting and you will make a better impression if you avoid repeating the same words again and again. Look at the **Other words for** notes in the dictionary to build up a good choice of words that you can use. In some exams, one of the tasks may be to find other words to express something.

---

synopsis /sɪˈnɒpsɪs/ noun [C] (pl **synopses** /-siːz/) a short description of a piece of writing, a play, etc □ *sinopsis; ringkasan*: *The programme gives a brief synopsis of the plot.* **SYN** **summary**

syntax /ˈsɪntæks/ noun [U] the system of rules for the structure of sentences in a language □ *sintaksis*

synthesis /ˈsɪnθəsɪs/ noun (pl **syntheses** /-siːz/) **1** [C,U] synthesis (of sth) the act of combining separate ideas, beliefs, styles, etc.; a mixture or combination of ideas, beliefs, styles, etc. □ *sintesis (penggabungan bahagian-bahagian, unsur dsb yg berasingan utk membentuk satu keseluruhan)*: *the synthesis of art with everyday life* ◆ *a synthesis of traditional and modern values* **2** [U] (*technical*) the natural chemical production of a substance in animals and plants, or the artificial production of such a substance □ *sintesis (penghasilan secara kimia tabii sst bahan dlm haiwan dan tumbuhan atau penghasilan buatan bahan berkenaan)*: *protein synthesis* **3** [U] (*technical*) the production of sounds, music or speech using electronic equipment □ *sintesis (penghasilan bunyi, muzik atau ucapan secara elektronik)*: *speech synthesis* ▸ synthesize (also -ise) /ˈsɪnθəsaɪz/ verb [T]

synthesizer (also -iser) /ˈsɪnθəsaɪzə(r)/ noun [C] an electronic musical instrument that can produce a wide variety of different sounds □ *alat sintesis*

synthetic /sɪnˈθetɪk/ adj made by a chemical process; not natural □ *tiruan; sintetik*: *synthetic materials/fibres* ▸ synthetically /-kli/ adv

syphon = siphon

syringe /sɪˈrɪndʒ/ noun [C] a plastic or glass tube with a needle that is used for taking a small amount of blood out of the body or for putting drugs into the body □ *picagari* ➔ picture at **medicine**

syrup /ˈsɪrəp/ noun [U] a thick sweet liquid, often made by boiling sugar with water or fruit juice □ *sirap*: *peaches in syrup* ➔ look at **treacle**

system /ˈsɪstəm/ noun **1** [C] a set of ideas or rules for organizing sth; a particular way of doing sth □ *sistem; kaedah*: *a new system for assessing tax bills* ◆ *The government is planning to reform the education system.* **2** [C] a group of things or parts that work together □ *sistem*: *a central heating system* ◆ *a transport system* ◆ *a computer operating system* **3** [C] the body of a person or an animal; parts of the body that work together □ *sistem*: *the central nervous system* **4** the system [sing] (*informal*) the traditional methods and rules of a society □ *sistem pentadbiran, tradisi, kelaziman masyarakat, dsb*: *You can't beat the system* (= you must accept these rules).

IDM get sth out of your system (*informal*) to do sth to free yourself of a strong feeling or emotion □ *(membuat sst utk) melupakan sst perkara atau perasaan*

systematic /ˌsɪstəˈmætɪk/ adj done using a fixed plan or method □ *sistematik; teratur;*

bersistem: *a systematic search* ▶**systematically** /-kli/ *adv*

'system unit *noun* [C] the main part of a computer, separate from the keyboard, monitor and mouse, that contains all the other parts of the system □ *unit sistem* ⊃ picture at **computer**

T, t /tiː/ *noun* [C,U] (*pl* **Ts**; **T's**; **t's** /tiːz/) the 20th letter of the English alphabet □ *T, t (huruf)*: *'Table' begins with (a) 'T'.*

t *abbr* = **ton**(1), **tonne** □ *tan; tan metrik; tonne*: *5t coal*

ta /tɑː/ *exclam* (*BrE informal*) thank you □ *terima kasih*

tab /tæb/ *noun* [C] **1** a small piece of cloth, metal or paper that is fixed to the edge of sth to help you open, hold or identify it □ *tab; penanda*: *You open the tin by pulling the metal tab.* **2** the money that you owe for food, drink, etc. that you receive in a bar, restaurant, etc. but pay for later □ *bil* **3** one of a number of small areas at the edge of a computer window that allows you to change the section of the website or piece of software that you are looking at □ *petak kecil di sisi tetingkap komputer utk menukar halaman laman web*: *Click on the tab at the top of this window to see another section of today's paper.* ♦ *Use the tab key.*

IDM **keep tabs on sb/sth** (*informal*) to watch sb/sth carefully; to check sth □ *mengawas sso/sst*

table /'teɪbl/ *noun* [C] **1** a piece of furniture with a flat top supported by legs □ *meja*: *a dining/bedside/coffee/kitchen table* ♦ *Could you lay/set the table for lunch?* (= put the knives, forks, plates, etc. on it) ♦ *Let me help you clear the table* (= remove the dirty plates, etc. at the end of a meal). ♦ *Can I reserve a table, please* (= in a restaurant)*?* ⊃ picture on **page P8**

HELP We put things **on the table** but we sit **at the table** (= around the table).

2 a list of facts or figures, usually arranged in rows and columns down a page □ *jadual; sifir*: *Table 3 shows the results.*

tablecloth /'teɪblklɒθ/ *noun* [C] a piece of cloth that you use for covering a table, especially when having a meal □ *alas meja*

'table manners *noun* [pl] behaviour that is considered correct while you are having a meal at a table with other people □ *adab semasa makan*

tablespoon /'teɪblspuːn/ *noun* [C] **1** a large spoon used for serving or measuring food □ *sudu besar* **2** (*also* **tablespoonful** /-fʊl/) (*abbr* **tbsp**) the amount that a **tablespoon** holds □ *se-*

sudu besar: *Add two tablespoons of sugar.* ⊃ picture at **spoon**

tablet /'tæblət/ *noun* [C] **1** a small amount of medicine in solid form that you swallow □ *tablet (ubat dlm bentuk biji)*: *Take two tablets with water before meals.* **SYN** **pill** ⊃ picture at **medicine** **2** a small amount of a substance in solid form □ *tablet (ketulan kecil sst)*: *dishwasher tablets* **3** (*also* ˌTablet P'C™) a very small, flat computer that you can carry with you and that you work by touching the screen □ *tablet (komputer mudah alih kecil)*

'table tennis (*also informal* **ping-pong**) *noun* [U] a game with rules like **tennis** in which you hit a light plastic ball across a table with a small round **bat** (= a piece of wood) □ *pingpong* ⊃ picture on **page P5**

tabloid /'tæblɔɪd/ *noun* [C] a newspaper with small pages, often with a lot of pictures and short articles, especially ones about famous people □ *tabloid* ⊃ note at **newspaper**

taboo /tə'buː/ *noun* [C] (*pl* **taboos**) something that you must not say or do because it might shock, offend or embarrass people □ *larangan; tabu* ▶**taboo** *adj*: *a taboo subject/word*

tacit /'tæsɪt/ *adj* (*formal*) understood but not actually said □ *dimengerti tanpa perlu disebutkan* ▶**tacitly** *adv*

tack¹ /tæk/ *noun* **1** [sing] a way of dealing with a particular situation □ *jalan; kaedah; cara*: *If people won't listen we'll have to try a different tack.* **2** [C] a small nail with a sharp point and a flat head □ *paku payung*

tack² /tæk/ *verb* [T] **1** to fasten sth in place with **tacks¹**(2) □ *melekatkan (sst) dgn paku payung* **2** to fasten cloth together temporarily with long **stitches** (= lines of thread) that can be removed easily □ *menjelujur*

PHR V **tack sth on (to sth)** to add sth extra on the end of sth □ *menambah sst*

tackle¹ /'tækl/ *verb* **1** [T] to make an effort to deal with a difficult situation or problem □ *menangani; menghadapi*: *The government must tackle the problem of rising unemployment.* ♦ *Firemen were brought in to tackle the blaze.* **2** [T] **tackle sb about sth** to speak to sb about a difficult subject □ *bercakap (dgn sso ttg sst)*: *I'm going to tackle Henry about the money he owes me.* **3** [I,T] (in football, etc.) to try to take the ball from sb in the other team □ *merebut/merampas bola*: *He was tackled just outside the penalty area.* **4** [T] to stop sb running away by pulling them down □ *menumbangkan (orang yg sedang melarikan diri)*: *The police officer tackled one of the robbers as he ran out.*

tackle² /'tækl/ *noun* [C] **1** the act of trying to get the ball from another player in football, etc. □ *(perbuatan) merebut/merampas bola* **2** [U] the equipment you use in some sports, especially fishing □ *kelengkapan*: *fishing tackle*

tacky /'tæki/ *adj* (**tackier**; **tackiest**) (*informal*) **1** cheap and of poor quality and/or not in good taste ◻ *kodi; tdk bermutu: a shop selling tacky souvenirs* **2** (used about paint, etc.) not quite dry; sticky ◻ *melekit*

tact /tækt/ *noun* [U] the ability to deal with people without offending or upsetting them ◻ *kebijaksanaan: She handled the situation with great tact and diplomacy.*

tactful /'tæktfl/ *adj* careful not to say or do things that could offend people ◻ *bijaksana* **SYN** diplomatic **OPP** tactless ▶**tactfully** /-fəli/ *adv*

tactic /'tæktɪk/ *noun* **1** [C, usually pl] the particular method you use to achieve sth ◻ *taktik; kaedah; muslihat: We must decide what our tactics are going to be at the next meeting.* ◆ *I don't think this tactic will work.* **2 tactics** [pl] the skilful arrangement and use of military forces in order to win a battle ◻ *taktik*

tactical /'tæktɪkl/ *adj* **1** connected with the particular method you use to achieve sth ◻ *taktikal: I made a tactical error.* ◆ *tactical planning* **2** designed to bring a future advantage ◻ *taktikal; yg dirancang dgn bijak: a tactical decision* ▶**tactically** /-kli/ *adv*

tactless /'tæktləs/ *adj* saying and doing things that are likely to offend and upset other people ◻ *tdk bijaksana: It was rather tactless of you to ask her how old she was.* **OPP** tactful ▶**tactlessly** *adv*

tadpole /'tædpəʊl/ *noun* [C] a young form of a **frog** (= a small animal that lives in or near water, with long back legs that it uses for jumping) with a black head and a long tail ◻ *berudu* ⊃ picture on **page P13**

tag¹ /tæg/ *noun* [C] **1** [in compounds] a small piece of card, cloth, etc. fastened to sth to give information about it ◻ *tag; tanda: How much is this dress? There isn't a price tag on it.* ⊃ picture at **label 2** = **question tag**

tag² /tæg/ *verb* [T] (**tagging**; **tagged**) to fasten a **tag** onto sb/sth ◻ *meletakkan tag/tanda* **PHR V** **tag along** to follow or go somewhere with sb, especially when you have not been invited ◻ *mengikut; mengekor*

tail¹ /teɪl/ *noun*
▶OF ANIMAL, BIRD **1** [C] the part at the end of the body of an animal, bird, fish, etc. ◻ *ekor: The dog barked and wagged its tail.* ⊃ picture on **page P12, page P13**
▶OF PLANE **2** [C] the back part of an aircraft, etc. ◻ *ekor; hujung: the tail wing*
▶JACKET **3 tails** [pl] a man's formal coat that is short at the front but with a long, divided piece at the back, worn especially at weddings ◻ *kot formal yg pendek di depan dgn bahagian belakang yg panjang dan berbelah: The men all wore top hat and tails.*
▶SIDE OF COIN **4 tails** [U] the side of a coin that does not have the head of a person on it ◻ *bunga (muka duit syiling): 'We'll toss a coin to decide,' said my father. 'Heads or tails?'*
▶PERSON **5** [C] (*informal*) a person who is sent to follow sb secretly to get information about them ◻ *pengekor: The police have put a tail on him.*

IDM **make head or tail of sth** ⊃ **head¹**

tail² /teɪl/ *verb* [T] to follow sb closely, especially to watch where they go ◻ *mengekori*
PHR V **tail away/off** (*especially BrE*) to become less or weaker ◻ *menjadi semakin kecil, kurang, lemah, dsb*

tailor¹ /'teɪlə(r)/ *noun* [C] a person whose job is to make clothes, especially for men ◻ *tukang jahit*

tailor² /'teɪlə(r)/ *verb* [T, usually passive] **1 tailor sth to/for sb/sth** to make or design sth for a particular person or purpose ◻ *disesuaikan; dibina/dibuat khas: programmes tailored to the needs of specific groups* **2** to make clothes ◻ *menjahit (pakaian): a well-tailored coat*

ˌtailor-ˈmade *adj* **tailor-made (for sb/sth)** made for a particular person or purpose and therefore very suitable ◻ *dibuat khas*

tailpipe /'teɪlpaɪp/ (*AmE*) = **exhaust¹**(2)

taint /teɪnt/ *noun* [C, usually sing] (*formal*) the effect of sth bad or unpleasant that spoils the quality of sb/sth ◻ *kesan sst yg buruk; kecelaan: the taint of corruption.* ▶**taint** *verb* [T, usually passive]: *Her reputation was tainted by the scandal.*

take /teɪk/ *verb* [T] (*pt* **took** /tʊk/; *pp* **taken** /'teɪkən/)
▶CARRY/MOVE **1** to carry or move sb/sth; to go with sb from one place to another ◻ *membawa: Take your coat with you—it's cold.* ◆ *Could you take this letter home to your parents?* ◆ *The ambulance took him to hospital.* ◆ *I'm taking the children swimming this afternoon.* ◆ *Her energy and talent took her to the top of her profession.* ⊃ picture at **bring**
▶IN YOUR HAND **2** to put your hand round sth and hold it (and move it towards you) ◻ *mengambil; memegang: She held out the keys, and I took them.* ◆ *He took a sweater out of the drawer.* ◆ *She took my hand/me by the hand* (= held my hand).
▶REMOVE **3** to remove sth from a place or a person, often without permission ◻ *mengambil; mencuri; memotong (nama drpd senarai, dsb): Who's taken my pen?* ◆ *My name had been taken off the list.* ◆ *The burglars took all my jewellery.*
▶CONTROL **4** to capture a place by force; to get control of sb/sth ◻ *menawan; mengambil alih; menguasai: The state will take control of the company.*
▶EAT/DRINK **5** to swallow sth ◻ *ambil; makan; telan: Take two tablets four times a day.* ◆ *Do you take sugar in tea?*
▶WRITE DOWN **6** to write or record sth ◻ *mencatat: She took notes during the lecture.* ◆ *The police officer took my name and address.*
▶PHOTOGRAPH **7** to photograph sth ◻ *mengambil (gambar): I took some nice photos of the wedding.*
▶MEASUREMENT **8** to measure sth ◻ *mengambil (ukuran, dsb): The doctor took my temperature/pulse/blood pressure.*
▶ACCEPT **9** to accept or receive sth ◻ *mengambil; menerima; menanggung: If you take my advice you'll forget all about him.* ◆ *Do you take credit*

cards? ♦ What coins does the machine take? ♦ I'm not going to **take the blame** for the accident. ♦ She's not going to **take the job**. ♦ We took a room at the hotel for two nights. **10** to understand sth or react to sth in a particular way □ *menganggap; menyangka*: She took what he said as a compliment. ♦ I wish you would **take** things more seriously.

▶DEAL WITH STH BAD **11** to be able to deal with sth difficult or unpleasant □ *menanggung*: I can't take much more of this heat. **SYN** stand

▶HAVE FEELING **12** to get a particular feeling from sth □ *berasa*: He takes great pleasure in his grandchildren. ♦ When she failed the exam she **took comfort from** the fact that it was only by a few marks.

▶ACTION **13** used with nouns to say that sb is performing an action □ *digunakan dgn kn utk menyatakan perbuatan tertentu*: Take a look at this article (= look at it). ♦ We have to **take a decision** (= decide).

▶NEED **14** to need sth/sb □ *memerlukan*: How long did the journey take? ♦ It took a lot of courage to say that. ♦ It took three people to move the piano.

▶SIZE **15** [not used in the continuous tenses] to have a certain size of shoes or clothes □ *memakai/menggunakan (saiz tertentu bagi kasut atau pakaian)*: What size shoes do you take?

▶CONTAIN **16** [not used in the continuous tenses] to have enough space for sb/sth □ *muat*: How many passengers can this bus take?

▶TEACH **17** take sb (for sth) to give lessons to sb □ *mengajar*: Who takes you for History (= who is your teacher)?

▶EXAM **18** to study a subject for an exam; to do an exam □ *mengambil; menduduki*: I'm taking the advanced exam this summer.

▶TRANSPORT **19** to use a form of transport; to use a particular route □ *naik (kenderaan); ikut/ mengikut (jalan tertentu)*: I always **take** the train to York. ♦ Which road do you take to Lille? ♦ Take the second turning on the right.

▶GRAMMAR **20** [not used in the continuous tenses] to have or need a word to go with it in a sentence or other structure □ *memerlukan*: The verb 'depend' takes the preposition 'on'.

IDM **be taken with sb/sth** to find sb/sth attractive or interesting □ *suka/tertarik pd sso/sst*

I take it (that …) (used to show that you understand sth from a situation, even though you have not been told) I suppose □ *Saya kira/andaikan (bahawa)*: I take it that you're not coming?

take it from me believe me □ *percayalah*

take a lot of/some doing to need a lot of work or effort □ *memerlukan banyak kerja atau tenaga*

take a lot out of sb to make sb very tired □ *meletihkan sso* ⓘ For other idioms containing **take**, look at the entries for the nouns, adjectives, etc. For example, **take place** is at **place**.

PHR V **take sb aback** to surprise or shock sb □ *(membuat sso) terkejut*

take after sb [not used in the continuous tenses] to look or behave like an older member of your family, especially a parent □ *serupa dgn sso*

take sth apart to separate sth into the different parts it is made of □ *merungkai sst*

take away (used in sums) less □ *tolak*: Six take away two is four (6—2 = 4).

take sb/sth away (from sb) to remove sb/sth □ *membawa sso pergi atau mengambil sst (drpd sso)*: She took the scissors away from the child.

take sth away **1** to cause a feeling, etc. to disappear □ *menghilangkan/melegakan sst*: These aspirins will take the pain away. **2** (*AmE* **take sth out**) to buy cooked food at a restaurant, etc. and carry it out to eat somewhere else, for example at home □ *bungkus atau bawa balik (ttg makanan yg dibeli)* ⊃ noun **takeaway**

take sth back **1** to return sth to the place that you got it from □ *memulangkan/meletakkan balik sst*: I took the dress back because it didn't go with my shoes. ⊃ note at **shopping** **2** to admit that sth you said was wrong □ *menarik balik kata-kata*

take sth down **1** to remove a structure by separating it into the pieces it is made of □ *menanggalkan/membuka sst*: They took the tent down and started the journey home. **2** to write down sth that is said □ *mencatat sst*

take sb in **1** to invite sb who has no home to live with you □ *mengajak (membenarkan) sso menumpang (di rumah kita)*: Her parents were killed in a crash so she was taken in by her grandparents. **2** to make sb believe sth that is not true □ *memperdayakan sso; membuat sso terpedaya*: I was completely taken in by her story.

take sth in to understand what you see, hear or read □ *memahami/menyerap sst*: There was too much in the museum to take in at one go.

take off **1** (used about an aircraft) to leave the ground and start flying □ *berlepas*: The plane took off an hour late. **OPP** **land** **2** (used about an idea, a product, etc.) to become successful or popular very quickly or suddenly □ *menjadi laku/popular sekali*

take sb off to copy the way sb speaks or behaves in an amusing way □ *mengajuk sso*

take sth off **1** to remove sth, especially clothes □ *menanggalkan sst*: Come in and take your coat off. **OPP** **put sth on** **2** to have the period of time mentioned as a holiday □ *bercuti*: I'm going to take a week off.

take sb on to start to employ sb □ *mengambil (sso) bekerja*: The firm is taking on new staff.

take sth on to accept a responsibility or decide to do sth □ *mengambil atau menerima (tanggungjawab, kerja, dsb)*: He's taken on a lot of extra work.

take sb out to go out with sb (for a social occasion) □ *membawa sso keluar*: I'm taking Angela out for a meal tonight.

take sth out **1** to remove sth from inside a person's body □ *membuang sst; mencabut (gigi)*: He's having two teeth taken out. **2** to obtain a service □ *memperoleh; mengambil*: to take out a mortgage/loan

take sth out (of sth) to remove sth from sth □ *mengeluarkan sst (drpd sst)*: *He took a notebook out of his pocket.* ♦ *I need to take some money out of the bank.*

take it out on sb to behave badly towards sb because you are angry or upset about sth, even though it is not this person's fault □ *melepaskan geram pd sso*

take (sth) over to get control of sth or responsibility for sth □ *mengambil alih*: *The firm is being taken over by a large company.* ♦ *Who's going to take over as assistant when Tim leaves?*

take to sb/sth to start liking sb/sth or doing sth well □ *suka kpd sso/sst*

take to sth/doing sth to begin doing sth regularly as a habit □ *mula suka (membuat sst)*

take sth up to start doing sth regularly (for example as a hobby) □ *mula membuat sst sebagai hobi*: *I've taken up yoga recently.*

take up sth to use or fill an amount of time or space □ *mengambil/memakan (ruang atau masa)*: *All her time is taken up looking after the new baby.* **SYN** occupy

take sb up on sth 1 to say that you disagree with sth that sb has just said, and ask them to explain it □ *meminta penjelasan drpd sso ttg sst yg kita tdk setuju*: *I must take you up on that last point.* 2 (*informal*) to accept an offer that sb has made □ *menerima tawaran drpd sso*: 'Come and stay with us any time.' 'We'll take you up on that!'

take sth up with sb to ask or complain about sth □ *membangkitkan/mengemukakan sst kpd sso*: *I'll take the matter up with my MP.*

takeaway /'teɪkəweɪ/ (*AmE* **takeout**; **carry-out**) *noun* [C] 1 a restaurant that sells food that you can eat somewhere else □ *restoran yg menjual makanan bungkus (iaitu yg dibawa pulang)* 2 the food that such a restaurant sells □ *makanan bungkus*: *Let's have a takeaway.* ⊃ note at **meal**

taken past participle of **take**

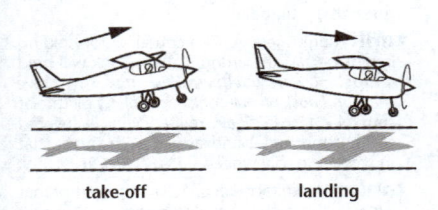

take-off

landing

'take-off *noun* [U,C] the moment when an aircraft leaves the ground and starts to fly □ *berlepas*: *The plane is ready for take-off.* **OPP** landing

takeout /'teɪkaʊt/ (*AmE*) = **takeaway**

takeover /'teɪkəʊvə(r)/ *noun* [C] the act of taking control of sth □ *pengambilalihan*: *They made a takeover bid for the company.* ♦ *a military takeover of the government*

'take-up *noun* [U, sing] the rate at which people accept sth that is offered or made available to them □ *penerimaan; pengambilan*: *The take-up of foreign language courses has been disappointing.* ♦ *The take-up rate rose to 80%.*

takings /'teɪkɪŋz/ *noun* [pl] the amount of money that a shop, theatre, etc. gets from selling goods, tickets, etc. □ *hasil kutipan*

talcum powder /'tælkəm paʊdə(r)/ (also **talc** /tælk/) *noun* [U] a soft powder which smells nice. People often put it on their skin after a bath. □ *bedak talkum*

tale /teɪl/ *noun* [C] 1 a story about events that are not real □ *cerita dongeng*: *fairy tales* 2 a report or description of sb/sth that may not be true □ *cerita*: *I've heard tales of people seeing ghosts in that house.*

talent /'tælənt/ *noun* [C,U] **(a) talent (for sth)** a natural skill or ability □ *bakat*: *She has a talent for painting.* ♦ *His work shows great talent.* ♦ *a talent show* ▶ **talented** *adj*: *a talented musician*

talk¹ /tɔːk/ *verb* 1 [I] **talk (to/with sb) (about/of sb/sth)** to say things; to speak in order to give information or to express feelings, ideas, etc. □ *bercakap*: *The baby is just starting to talk.* ♦ *I could hear them talking downstairs.* ♦ *Can I talk to you for a minute?* ♦ *Nasreen is not an easy person to talk to.* ♦ *We need to talk about the plans for the weekend.* ♦ *He's been talking of going to Australia for some time now.* ♦ *Dr Impey will be talking about Japanese Art in his lecture.* ⊃ note at **speak** 2 [I,T] to discuss sth serious or important □ *berbincang; membincangkan*: *We can't go on like this. We need to talk.* ♦ *Could we talk business after dinner?* 3 [I] to discuss people's private lives □ *mengata; menjadi buah mulut orang*: *His strange lifestyle and appearance started the local people talking.* **SYN** gossip 4 [I] to give information to sb, especially when you do not want to □ *memberi maklumat*: *The police questioned him for hours but he refused to talk.*

IDM **know what you are talking about** ⊃ **know**¹
speak/talk of the devil ⊃ **devil**

talk sense to say things that are correct or sensible □ *bercakap perkara yg betul atau munasabah*: *He's the only politician who talks any sense.*

talk shop to talk about your work with the people you work with, outside working hours □ *bercakap ttg kerja*

PHR V **talk down to sb** to talk to sb as if they are less intelligent or important than you □ *bercakap secara merendahkan orang lain*

talk sb into/out of doing sth to persuade sb to do/not to do sth □ *memujuk sso supaya membuat/tdk membuat sst*: *She tried to talk him into buying a new car.*

talk sth over (with sb) to discuss sth with sb, especially in order to reach an agreement or make a decision □ *membincangkan sst dgn sso*

talk² /tɔːk/ *noun* 1 [C] **a talk (with sb) (about sth)** a conversation or discussion □ *perbualan;*

talkative → tantalizing

perbincangan: Charles and Anne had a long talk about the problem. **2 talks** [pl] formal discussions between governments □ *rundingan*: The Foreign Ministers of the two countries will meet for talks next week. ♦ *arms/peace talks* **3** [C] **a talk (on sth)** a formal speech on a particular subject □ *ceramah*: He's giving a talk on 'Our changing world'. **SYN** lecture **4** [U] (*informal*) things that people say that are not based on facts or reality □ *cakap saja*: He says he's going to resign but it's just talk. ⊃ look at **small talk**

talkative /ˈtɔːkətɪv/ *adj* liking to talk a lot □ *suka/kuat bercakap*

tall /tɔːl/ *adj* (**taller**; **tallest**) **1** (used about people or things) of more than average height; not short □ *tinggi*: *a tall young man* ♦ *a tall tree/tower/chimney* ♦ *Nick is taller than his brother.* **OPP** short **2** used to describe the height of sb/sth □ *tinggi*: *Claire is five feet tall.* ♦ *How tall are you?* ⊃ *noun* **height**

> **HELP** Tall or high? **Tall** and **high** have similar meanings. We use **tall** to describe the height of people, trees and other narrow objects: *He is six foot three inches tall.* ♦ *A tall oak tree stands in the garden.* ♦ *I saw the tall skyscrapers of Manhattan.* We use **high** to describe things that are not narrow: *high mountains* ♦ *The wall is two metres high.* and the distance of something from the ground: *a room with high ceilings*

talon /ˈtælən/ *noun* [C] a long sharp curved nail on the feet of some birds, used to catch other animals for food □ *cakar; kuku burung pemangsa* ⊃ picture on **page P12**

tambourine /ˌtæmbəˈriːn/ *noun* [C] a musical instrument that has a round frame covered with plastic or skin, with small flat pieces of metal around the edge. To play it, you hit it or shake it with your hand. □ *tamborin* ⊃ picture at **music**

tame¹ /teɪm/ *adj* (**tamer**; **tamest**) **1** (used about animals or birds) not wild or afraid of people □ *jinak*: *The birds are so tame they will eat from your hand.* **2** boring; not interesting or exciting □ *membosankan; tdk menarik*: *After the big city, you must find village life very tame.*

tame² /teɪm/ *verb* [T] to bring a wild animal under your control; to make sth easy to control □ *menguasai; menjinakkan*

tamper /ˈtæmpə(r)/ *verb*
PHR V tamper with sth to make changes to sth without permission, especially in order to damage it □ *mengusik; mengubah*

tampon /ˈtæmpɒn/ *noun* [C] a piece of cotton material that a woman puts inside her body to absorb the blood that she loses once a month □ *tampon* ⊃ look at **sanitary towel**

tan¹ /tæn/ *verb* [I,T] (**tanning**; **tanned**) (used about sb's skin) to become brown as a result of spending time in the sun □ *menjadi perang/sawo matang*: *Do you tan easily?* ▶ **tanned** *adj*: *You're looking very tanned—have you been on holiday?*

tan² /tæn/ *noun* **1** [U] a colour between yellow and brown □ *(warna) sawo matang/perang* **2** [C] = **suntan** ▶ **tan** *adj*

tandem /ˈtændəm/ *noun* [C] a bicycle with seats for two people, one behind the other □ *basikal tandem (iaitu ada pengayuh utk dua orang)*
IDM in tandem (with sb/sth) working together with sth/sb else; happening at the same time as sth else □ *seiring (dgn sso/sst); serentak (dgn sst)*

tangent /ˈtændʒənt/ *noun* [C] a straight line that touches a curve but does not cross it □ *tangen*
IDM go off at a tangent; (*AmE*) **go off on a tangent** to suddenly start saying or doing sth that seems to have no connection with what has gone before □ *menyimpang; menyeleweng*

tangerine /ˌtændʒəˈriːn/ *noun* **1** [C] a fruit like a small sweet orange with a skin that is easy to take off □ *(limau) tangerin* **2** [U] a deep orange colour □ *(warna) jingga tua* ▶ **tangerine** *adj*

tangible /ˈtændʒəbl/ *adj* that can be clearly seen to exist □ *nyata; yg nyata wujud*: *There are tangible benefits in the new system.* **OPP** intangible

tangle /ˈtæŋgl/ *noun* [C] a confused mass, especially of threads, hair, branches, etc. that cannot easily be separated from each other □ *kusut; gumpalan*: *My hair's full of tangles.* ♦ *This string's in a tangle.* ▶ **tangled** *adj*: *The wool was all tangled up.*

tango /ˈtæŋgəʊ/ *noun* [C] (*pl* **tangos** /-gəʊz/) a fast South American dance with a strong beat, in which two people hold each other closely; a piece of music for this dance □ *tarian tango; muzik tango* ▶ **tango** *verb* [I] (**tangoing**; **tangoes**; *pt, pp* **tangoed**)

tank /tæŋk/ *noun* [C] **1** a container for holding liquids or gas; the amount that a tank will hold □ *tangki*: *a water/fuel/petrol/fish tank* ♦ *We drove there and back on one tank of petrol.* ⊃ picture at **snorkel** **2** a large, heavy military vehicle covered with strong metal and armed with guns, that moves on special wheels □ *kereta kebal*

tanker /ˈtæŋkə(r)/ *noun* [C] a ship or lorry that carries oil, petrol, etc. in large amounts □ *kapal/lori tangki*: *an oil tanker* ⊃ picture on **page P6**

Tannoy™ /ˈtænɔɪ/ *noun* [C] a system used for giving spoken information in a public place □ *Tannoy™; sejenis sistem siar raya/pemakluman umum*: *They announced over the Tannoy that our flight was delayed.*

tantalizing (*also* **-ising**) /ˈtæntəlaɪzɪŋ/ *adj* making you want sth that you cannot have or do □ *menggoda*: *A tantalizing aroma of cooking was coming from the kitchen next door.* ▶ **tantalizingly** (*also* **-isingly**) *adv*

tantrum /ˈtæntrəm/ noun [C] a sudden explosion of anger, especially in a child □ *buat perangai*

tap¹ /tæp/ verb (tapping; tapped) 1 [I,T] tap (at/on sth); tap sb/sth (on/with sth) to touch or hit sb/sth quickly and lightly □ *menepuk; mengetuk-ngetuk*: *He tapped at the window.* ♦ *Their feet were tapping in time to the music.* ♦ *She tapped me on the shoulder.* 2 [I,T] tap (into) sth to make use of a source of energy, knowledge, etc. that already exists □ *memanfaati*: *to tap the skills of young people* 3 [T] to fit a device to sb's telephone so that their calls can be listened to secretly □ *memasang alat pd telefon sso utk mendengar perbualannya secara rahsia*: *She was convinced that the police had tapped her phone.*

tap² /tæp/ noun [C] 1 (AmE faucet) a type of handle that you turn to let water, gas, etc. out of a pipe or container □ *kepala paip*: *Turn the hot/cold tap on/off.* ⊃ picture at **plug** 2 a light hit with your hand or fingers □ *tepukan; ketukan*: *a tap on the shoulder* 3 a device that is fitted to sb's telephone so that their calls can be listened to secretly □ *alat utk mendengar perbualan telefon orang secara rahsia*: *a phone tap*

tap dance noun [C] a style of dancing in which you tap the rhythm of the music with your feet, wearing special shoes with pieces of metal on them □ *tarian tap* ▶ **tap dance** verb [I] ▶ **tap-dancing** (also **tap**) noun [U]

tape¹ /teɪp/ noun
▷FOR MUSIC 1 [U] a long thin band of plastic material used for recording sound, pictures or information □ *pita rakaman*: *I've got the whole concert on tape* (= recorded). 2 [C] a small flat plastic case containing tape for playing or recording music or sound □ *pita; kaset; pita video*: *a blank tape* (= a tape which is empty) ♦ *to rewind a tape*
▷FOR STICKING 3 [U] a long narrow band of plastic, etc. with a sticky substance on one side that is used for sticking things together, covering electric wires, etc □ *pita perekat*: *sticky/adhesive tape* ⊃ look at **Sellotape™** ⊃ picture at **roll**
▷FOR TYING 4 [C,U] a narrow piece of cloth that is used for tying things together □ *pita*: *The papers were in a pile, bound with blue tape.* ⊃ look at **red tape**
▷IN RACE 5 [C] a piece of material stretched across a race track to mark where the race finishes □ *pita penamat*: *the finishing tape*

tape² /teɪp/ verb [T] 1 to record sound, music, TV programmes, etc. using tape □ *merakamkan (ke dlm pita)* 2 tape sth (up) to fasten sth by sticking or tying sth with **tape**(3) □ *melekatkan/mengikat sst dgn pita perekat*

tape measure (also **measuring tape**) noun [C] a long thin piece of plastic, cloth or metal with centimetres, etc. marked on it. It is used for measuring things. □ *pita ukur* ⊃ picture at **sewing**

tape recorder noun [C] a machine that is used for recording and playing sounds on tape □ *perakam pita*

tapestry /ˈtæpəstri/ noun [C,U] (pl **tapestries**) a piece of heavy cloth with pictures or designs sewn on it in coloured thread □ *tapestri*

tap water noun [U] water that comes through pipes and out of taps, not water sold in bottles □ *air paip*

tar /tɑː(r)/ noun [U] 1 a thick black sticky liquid that becomes hard when it is cold. Tar is obtained from coal and is used for making roads, etc. □ *tar* ⊃ look at **Tarmac™** 2 a similar substance formed by burning **tobacco** (= the dried leaves used for making cigarettes) □ *tar; candu tembakau*: *low-tar cigarettes*

tarantula /təˈræntʃələ/ noun [C] a large spider covered with hair that lives in hot countries □ *tarantula; sejenis labah-labah besar*

target¹ /ˈtɑːgɪt/ noun [C] 1 a result that you try to achieve □ *matlamat; sasaran*: *Our target is to finish the job by Friday.* ♦ *So far we're right on target* (= making the progress we expected). ♦ *a target area/audience/group* (= the particular area, audience, etc. that a product, programme, etc. is aimed at) 2 a person, place or thing that you try to hit when shooting or attacking □ *sasaran*: *They bombed military and civilian targets.* ♦ *Doors and windows are an easy target for burglars.* 3 a person or thing that people criticize, laugh at, etc. □ *sasaran*: *The education system has been the target of heavy criticism.* 4 an object, often a round board with circles on it, that you try to hit in shooting practice □ *sasaran*: *to aim at/hit/miss a target*

target² /ˈtɑːgɪt/ verb [T, usually passive] target sb/sth; target sth at/on sb/sth to try to have an effect on a particular group of people; to try to attack sb/sth □ *ditujukan; dijadikan sasaran*: *The advertising campaign is targeted at teenagers.*

tariff /ˈtærɪf/ noun [C] 1 a tax that has to be paid on goods coming into a country □ *tarif; cukai import* 2 a list of prices, especially in a hotel □ *tarif; senarai harga*

Tarmac™ /ˈtɑːmæk/ noun 1 [U] a black material used for making the surfaces of roads □ *Tarmac™ (tarmak)* ⊃ look at **tar** 2 **the tarmac** [sing] an area covered with a **Tarmac** surface, especially at an airport □ *kawasan yg diturap dgn tarmak; landasan terbang*

tarnish /ˈtɑːnɪʃ/ verb 1 [I,T] (used about metal, etc.) to become or to make sth less bright and shiny □ *menjadi kusam* 2 [T] to spoil the good opinion people have of sb/sth □ *mencemarkan; merosakkan*

tarpaulin /tɑːˈpɔːlɪn/ noun [C,U] a piece of strong material that water cannot pass through, which is used for covering things to protect them from the rain □ *kain terpal*

tart¹ /tɑːt/ noun [C,U] an open **pie** (= a type of baked food) filled with sweet food such as fruit

tart → taxi 876

or jam □ *tart* **2** [C] (*BrE informal*) a woman who dresses or behaves in a way that people think is immoral □ *perempuan sundal*

tart² /tɑːt/ *verb*
PHR V **tart sb/sth up** (*BrE informal*) to decorate and improve the appearance of sb/sth □ *menghias sso/sst*

tartan /'tɑːtn/ *noun* [U,C] **1** a traditional Scottish pattern of coloured squares and lines that cross each other □ *corak tartan* **2** cloth made from wool with this pattern on it □ *kain tartan*

task /tɑːsk/ *noun* [C] a piece of work that has to be done, especially an unpleasant or difficult one □ *tugas; kerja*: *Your first task will be to type these letters.* ◆ *to perform/carry out/undertake a task*

tassel /'tæsl/ *noun* [C] a bunch of threads that are tied together at one end and hang from curtains, clothes, etc. as a decoration □ *rambu; rumbai; jumbai*

taste¹ /teɪst/ *noun*
▶FLAVOUR **1** [C,U] the particular quality of different foods or drinks that allows you to recognize them when you put them in your mouth; flavour □ *rasa*: *I don't like the taste of this coffee.* ◆ *a sweet/bitter/sour/salty taste*
▶SENSE **2** [U] the ability to recognize the flavour of food or drink □ *deria rasa*: *I've got such a bad cold that I seem to have lost my sense of taste.*
▶SMALL QUANTITY **3** [C, usually sing] a taste (of sth) a small amount of sth to eat or drink that you have in order to see what it is like □ *rasa*: *Have a taste of this cheese to see if you like it.*
▶SHORT EXPERIENCE **4** [sing] a short experience of sth □ *rasa; mengecap; kecapi*: *That was my first taste of success.*
▶RECOGNIZING QUALITY **5** [U] the ability to decide if things are suitable, of good quality, etc. □ *cita rasa*: *He has excellent taste in music.*
▶WHAT YOU LIKE **6** [sing] a taste (for sth) what a person likes or prefers □ *kecenderungan; minat; kesukaan*: *She has developed a taste for modern art.*
IDM **(be) in bad, poor, etc. taste** (used about sb's behaviour) (to be) unpleasant and not suitable □ *tdk senonoh; tdk baik*: *Some of his comments were in very bad taste.*

taste² /teɪst/ *verb* **1** [I] taste (of sth) to have a particular flavour □ *berasa*: *The pudding tasted of oranges.* ◆ *to taste sour/sweet/delicious* **2** [T] to notice or recognize the flavour of food or drink □ *merasa*: *Can you taste the garlic in this soup?* ⊃ note at **smell¹** **3** [T] to try a small amount of food and drink; to test the flavour of sth □ *merasa*: *Can I taste a piece of that cheese to see what it's like?*

tasteful /'teɪstfl/ *adj* (used especially about clothes, furniture, decorations, etc.) attractive and well chosen □ *menarik; sangat elok cita rasanya* **OPP** tasteless ▶tastefully /-fəli/ *adv*

tasteless /'teɪstləs/ *adj* **1** having little or no flavour □ *tawar; hambar*: *This sauce is rather tasteless.* **OPP** tasty **2** likely to offend people □ *tdk senonoh; tdk bersopan*: *His joke about the funeral was particularly tasteless.* **3** (used especially about clothes, furniture, decorations, etc.) not attractive; not well chosen □ *tdk menarik; tdk cantik* **OPP** tasteful

tasty /'teɪsti/ *adj* (tastier; tastiest) having a good flavour □ *lazat*: *spaghetti with a tasty sauce*

tattered /'tætəd/ *adj* old and torn; in bad condition □ *koyak rabak*: *a tattered coat*

tatters /'tætəz/ *noun*
IDM **in tatters** badly torn or damaged □ *koyak rabak*: *Her dress was in tatters.*

tattoo /tə'tuː/ *noun* [C] (*pl* tattoos) a picture or pattern that is marked permanently with ink on sb's skin □ *gambar cacah; tatu* ▶tattoo *verb* [T] (tattooing; tattoos; *pt, pp* tattooed): *She had a butterfly tattooed on her back.*

tatty /'tæti/ *adj* (tattier; tattiest) (*informal*) in bad condition □ *lusuh; buruk*: *tatty old clothes*

taught *past tense, past participle* of **teach**

taunt /tɔːnt/ *verb* [T] to try to make sb angry or upset by saying unpleasant or cruel things □ *mengejek; mencemuh* ▶taunt *noun* [C]

Taurus /'tɔːrəs/ *noun* [C,U] the 2nd sign of the **zodiac** (= 12 signs which represent the positions of the sun, moon and planets), the Bull; a person born under this sign □ *Taurus*: *I'm a Taurus.* ⊃ picture at **zodiac**

taut /tɔːt/ *adj* (used about rope, wire, etc.) stretched very tight; not loose □ *tegang*

tavern /'tævən/ *noun* [C] (*old-fashioned*) a pub or bar □ *kedai arak; pub*

tax /tæks/ *noun* [C,U] (a) tax (on sth) the money that you have to pay to the government so that it can provide public services □ *cukai*: *income tax* ◆ *There used to be a tax on windows.* ▶tax *verb* [T, often passive]: *Petrol is heavily taxed.*

taxable /'tæksəbl/ *adj* on which you have to pay tax □ *boleh dicukai*: *taxable income*

taxation /tæk'seɪʃn/ *noun* [U] **1** the amount of money that people have to pay in tax □ *cukai*: *to increase/reduce taxation* ◆ *high/low taxation* **2** the system by which a government takes money from people so that it can pay for public services □ *pencukaian*: *direct/indirect taxation*

tax-'free *adj* on which you do not have to pay tax □ *bebas cukai*: *a tax-free allowance*

taxi¹ /'tæksi/ (also **taxicab** /'tæksikæb/ (*especially AmE* cab) *noun* [C] (*pl* taxis) a car with a driver whose job is to take you somewhere in exchange for money □ *teksi*: *Shall we go by bus or get/take a taxi?* ⊃ picture on **page P7**

MORE You **hail** a taxi to stop it so that you can get in. The amount of money that you have to pay (your **fare**) is shown on a **meter**.

[I] **intransitive**, a verb which has no object: *He laughed.* [T] **transitive**, a verb which has an object: *He ate an apple.*

taxi² /'tæksi/ (taxiing; taxies; pt, pp taxied) verb [I] (used about an aircraft) to move slowly along the ground before or after flying □ *bergerak perlahan-lahan (pesawat)*

taxing /'tæksɪŋ/ adj difficult; needing a lot of effort □ *sukar; memeras otak*: *a taxing exam*

'taxi rank noun [C] a place where taxis park while they are waiting for customers □ *perhentian teksi*

taxpayer /'tækspeɪə(r)/ noun [C] a person who pays tax to the government, especially on the money that they earn □ *pembayar cukai*

TB /ˌti:ˈbi:/ abbr = **tuberculosis**

tbsp abbr = **tablespoon**(2) □ *sudu besar*: Add 3 tbsp sugar.

tea /ti:/ noun **1** [U] the dried leaves of the tea plant □ *(serbuk) teh*: *a packet of tea* **2** [C,U] a hot drink made by pouring boiling water onto the dried leaves of the tea plant or of some other plants; a cup of this drink □ *(air/minuman) teh*: *a cup/pot of tea* ♦ *weak/strong tea* ♦ *herbal/mint/camomile tea* ♦ *Three teas and one coffee, please.* ⊃ picture on **page P16 3** [C,U] (especially BrE) a small afternoon meal of **sandwiches** (= two slices of bread with food between them), cakes, etc. and tea to drink, or a cooked meal eaten at 5 or 6 o'clock □ *minum petang; makan lewat petang*: *The kids have their tea as soon as they get home from school.* ⊃ note at **meal**
IDM **not sb's cup of tea** ⊃ **cup¹**

'tea bag noun [C] a small paper bag with tea leaves in it, that you use for making tea □ *uncang teh* ⊃ picture on **page P10**

teach /ti:tʃ/ verb (pt, pp **taught** /tɔ:t/) **1** [I,T] **teach (sb/sth/ to do sth)**; **teach sth (to sb)** to give sb lessons or instructions so that they know how to do sth □ *mengajar*: *My mother taught me to play the piano.* ♦ *He is teaching his son how to ride a bike.* ♦ *Jeremy teaches English to foreign students.* ♦ *I teach in a primary school.* **2** [T] to make sb believe sth or behave in a certain way □ *mengajar*: *The story teaches us that history often repeats itself.* ♦ *My parents taught me always to tell the truth.* **3** [T] to make sb have a bad experience so that they are careful not to do the thing that caused it again □ *mengajar; memberi/mendapat pengajaran*: *Lost all your money? That'll teach you to gamble!* ♦ *The accident taught me a lesson I'll never forget.*

teacher /'ti:tʃə(r)/ noun [C] a person whose job is to teach, especially in a school or college □ *guru; cikgu*: *He's a teacher at a primary school.* ♦ *a chemistry/music teacher* ♦ *She's a head teacher* (= the teacher in charge of a school) *who knows the name of every student.* ⊃ note at **school** ⊃ look at **head¹**(5) ⊃ picture on **page P2**

teaching /'ti:tʃɪŋ/ noun **1** [U] the work of a teacher □ *(kerja) mengajar*: *My son went into teaching.* ♦ *teaching methods* **2** [C, usually pl] ideas and beliefs that are taught by sb/sth □ *ajaran*: *the teachings of Gandhi*

'tea cloth = **tea towel**

teacup /'ti:kʌp/ noun [C] a cup that you drink tea from □ *cawan teh*

teak /ti:k/ noun [U] the strong hard wood of a tall Asian tree, used for making furniture □ *kayu jati*

'tea leaves noun [pl] the small leaves that are left in a cup after you have drunk the tea □ *daun teh*

team¹ /ti:m/ noun [C, with sing or pl verb] **1** a group of people who play a sport or game together against another group □ *pasukan*: *a football team* ♦ *Are you in/on the team?* **2** a group of people who work together □ *kumpulan*: *a team of doctors*

GRAMMAR In the singular, **team** is used with a singular or plural verb: *The team play/plays two matches every week.*

team² /ti:m/ verb
PHR V **team up (with sb)** to join sb in order to do sth together □ *bekerja bersama-sama; bekerjasama*: *I teamed up with Irena to plan the project.*

teammate /'ti:mmeɪt/ noun [C] a member of the same team or group as yourself □ *teman sepasukan*

teamwork /'ti:mwɜ:k/ noun [U] the ability of people to work together □ *kerjasama berpasukan*: *Teamwork is a key feature of the training programme.*

teapot /'ti:pɒt/ noun [C] a container that you use for making tea in and for serving it □ *teko teh*

tear¹ /tɪə(r)/ noun [C, usually pl] a drop of water that comes from your eye when you are crying, etc □ *air mata; menangis*: *I was in tears* (= crying) *at the end of the film.* ♦ *The little girl burst into tears* (= suddenly started to cry).
IDM **shed tears** ⊃ **shed²**

tear² /teə(r)/ verb (pt **tore** /tɔ:(r)/; pp **torn** /tɔ:n/) **1** [T,I] to damage sth by pulling it apart or into pieces; to become damaged in this way □ *mengoyakkan; terkoyak*: *I tore my shirt on that nail.* ♦ *She tore the letter in half.* ♦ *I tore a page out of my notebook.* ♦ *This material doesn't tear easily.* **SYN** **rip 2** [T] to make a hole in sth by force □ *memecahkan; berlubang*: *The explosion tore a hole in the wall.* **SYN** **rip 3** [T] to remove sth by pulling violently and quickly □ *mengoyakkan; merampas*: *Paul tore the poster down from the wall.* ♦ *He tore the bag out of her hands.* **SYN** **rip 4** [I] **tear along, up, down, past, etc.** to move very quickly in a particular direction □ *meluru; berkejar*: *An ambulance went tearing past.*
IDM **wear and tear** ⊃ **wear²**

tearful → teething troubles

PHR V **tear sth apart** 1 to pull sth violently into pieces □ *menyiat-nyiat sst*: *The bird was torn apart by the two dogs.* 2 to destroy sth completely □ *menghancurkan; memusnahkan*: *The country has been torn apart by the war.*

tear yourself away (from sb/sth) to make yourself leave sb/sth or stop doing sth □ *memaksa diri meninggalkan sso/sst atau berhenti membuat sst*

be torn between A and B to find it difficult to choose between two things or people □ *berbelah hati*

tear sth down to pull or knock down a building, wall, etc. □ *merobohkan sst*: *They tore down the old houses and built a shopping centre.*

tear sth up to pull sth into pieces, especially sth made of paper □ *mengoyak-ngoyakkan sst*: *'I hate this photograph,' she said, tearing it up.*

▶ **tear** noun [C]: *You've got a tear in the back of your trousers.*

tearful /ˈtɪəfl/ adj crying or nearly crying □ *menangis; bergenang air mata*

tear gas /ˈtɪə gæs/ noun [U] a type of gas that hurts the eyes and throat, and is used by the police, etc. to control large groups of people □ *gas pemedih mata*

tease /tiːz/ verb [I,T] to laugh at sb either in a friendly way or in order to upset them □ *mengusik; mengejek*: *Don't pay any attention to those boys. They're only teasing.* ♦ *They teased her about being fat.*

teaspoon /ˈtiːspuːn/ noun [C] 1 a small spoon used for putting sugar in tea, coffee, etc. □ *sudu kecil* 2 (also **teaspoonful** /-fʊl/) (abbr **tsp**) the amount that a **teaspoon** can hold □ *sesudu kecil* ⊃ picture at **spoon**

teat /tiːt/ noun [C] 1 (AmE **nipple**) the soft rubber part at the end of a baby's bottle □ *puting getah* 2 one of the parts of a female animal's body that the young animals suck in order to get milk □ *puting tetek* ⊃ look at **nipple**

ˈtea towel (also **ˈtea cloth**) (BrE) noun [C] a small piece of cloth that is used for drying plates, knives, forks, etc. □ *kain lap pinggan*

technical /ˈteknɪkl/ adj 1 connected with the practical use of machines, methods, etc. in science and industry □ *teknikal*: *The train was delayed due to a technical problem.* ♦ *All our software licences include technical support.* 2 connected with the skills involved in a particular activity or subject □ *teknikal*: *All the Brazilian team play with great technical skill.*

technicality /ˌteknɪˈkæləti/ noun [C] (pl **technicalities**) one of the details of a particular subject or activity □ *butir-butir teknikal*

technically /ˈteknɪkli/ adv 1 according to the exact meaning, facts, etc. □ *sebenarnya*: *Technically, you should pay by August 1st, but it doesn't matter if it's a few days late.* 2 used about sb's practical ability in a particular activity □ *dari segi teknik*: *He's a technically brilliant dancer.* 3 in a way that involves detailed knowledge of the machines, etc. that are used in industry or science □ *dr segi teknik*: *The country is technically not very advanced.*

technician /tekˈnɪʃn/ noun [C] a person whose work involves practical skills, especially in industry or science □ *juruteknik*: *a laboratory technician*

technique /tekˈniːk/ noun 1 [C] a particular way of doing sth □ *teknik; kaedah*: *new techniques for teaching languages* ♦ *marketing/management techniques* 2 [U] the practical skill that sb has in a particular activity □ *teknik*: *He's a naturally talented runner, but he needs to work on his technique.*

technology /tekˈnɒlədʒi/ noun [C,U] (pl **technologies**) the scientific knowledge and/or equipment that is needed for a particular industry, etc. □ *teknologi*: *developments in computer technology* ▶ **technological** /ˌteknəˈlɒdʒɪkl/ adj: *technological developments* ▶ **technologist** /tekˈnɒlədʒɪst/ noun [C]: *Technologists are developing a computer that can perform surgery.*

tectonic /tekˈtɒnɪk/ adj [only before a noun] connected with the structure of the earth's surface □ *tektonik*

ˈteddy bear /ˈtedi beə(r)/ (also **teddy**; pl **teddies**) noun [C] a soft toy that looks like a bear (= a large brown wild animal) □ *anak patung beruang*

tedious /ˈtiːdiəs/ adj boring and lasting for a long time □ *menjemukan; membosankan*: *a tedious train journey* **SYN** **boring**

tee /tiː/ noun [C] (in the game of **golf**) a flat area where a player stands to hit the ball □ *tempat rata utk memukul bola (dlm permainan golf)*

teem /tiːm/ verb [I] **teem with sth** (used about a place) to have a lot of people or things moving about in it □ *penuh dgn*: *The streets were teeming with people.*

teenage /ˈtiːneɪdʒ/ adj [only before a noun] 1 between 13 and 19 years old □ *(berusia) belasan tahun*: *teenage children* 2 typical of or suitable for people between 13 and 19 years old □ *remaja*: *teenage magazines/fashion*

teenager /ˈtiːneɪdʒə(r)/ noun [C] a person aged between 13 and 19 years old □ *(budak-budak) belasan tahun/remaja*: *The group's music is very popular with teenagers.* ⊃ look at **adolescent**

teens /tiːnz/ noun [pl] the period of sb's life between the ages of 13 and 19 □ *usia belasan tahun; remaja*: *to be in your early/late teens*

ˈtee shirt = **T-shirt**

teeth plural of **tooth**

teethe /tiːð/ verb [I] (usually in the -*ing* forms) (used about a baby) to start growing its first teeth □ *baru tumbuh gigi*

ˈteething troubles (also **ˈteething problems**) noun [pl] the problems that can develop when a person, system, etc. is new □ *masalah awal*: *We've just installed this new software and are having a few teething troubles with it.*

teetotal /ˌtiːˈtəʊtl/ *adj* [not before a noun] (used about a person) never drinking alcohol □ *tdk minum arak* ▶**teetotaller** (*AmE* **teetotaler**) *noun* [C] ⊃ look at **alcoholic**

TEFL /ˈtefl/ *abbr* Teaching English as a Foreign Language □ *TEFL (Pengajaran Bahasa Inggeris Sebagai Bahasa Asing)*

tel. (also **Tel.**) *abbr* telephone (number) □ *tel. (telefon)*: *tel. 01865 56767*

telecommunications /ˌtelikəˌmjuːnɪˈkeɪʃnz/ *noun* [pl] the technology of sending signals, images and messages over long distances by radio, telephone, TV, etc. □ *telekomunikasi*

telegram /ˈtelɪɡræm/ *noun* [C] (in the past) a message that is sent by a system that uses electrical signals and that is then printed and given to sb □ *telegram*

telegraph /ˈtelɪɡrɑːf/ *noun* [U] a method of sending messages over long distances, using wires that carry electrical signals □ *telegraf*

telegraph pole *noun* [C] a tall wooden pole that is used for supporting telephone wires □ *tiang telegraf/telefon*

telemarketing /ˈtelimɑːkɪtɪŋ/ = telesales

telepathy /təˈlepəθi/ *noun* [U] the communication of thoughts between people's minds without using speech, writing or other normal methods □ *telepati*

telephone /ˈtelɪfəʊn/ (also *informal* **phone**) *noun* **1** [U] an electrical system for talking to sb in another place by speaking into a special piece of equipment □ *telefon*: *Can I contact you by telephone?* ♦ *to make a telephone call* ♦ *What's your telephone number?* **2** [C] the piece of equipment that you use when you talk to sb by telephone □ *telefon*: *Could I use your telephone?* ♦ *Where's the nearest public telephone?*

HELP It is more common to use **phone** rather than **telephone**, especially when you are speaking.

IDM on the phone/telephone ⊃ phone ⊃ note at mobile phone
▶**telephone** (also **phone**) *verb* [I,T]: *He telephoned to say he'd be late.*

TOPIC

Using the telephone

When you **call** somebody or **phone** somebody (NOT *to* somebody), his/her phone **rings** and he/she **answers** it. Sometimes the phone is **engaged** (= he/she is already talking to somebody on it) or there is **no answer**. You might need to **leave a message**, either on an **answering machine**, or with somebody else: *Could you please ask her to call me back?* Introduce yourself by saying '**It's** ...' or '**This**

879

teetotal → television

is ...' (NOT '*Here is* ...'). If you phone somebody by mistake you can say, 'I'm sorry, I've **dialled** the **wrong number**.' The number that you dial before the telephone number if you are telephoning a different area or country is called the **code**: *'What's the code for Spain?'* When you finish speaking you **put the phone down/hang up**. You can use a telephone line to send a copy of a letter, etc. using a **fax machine**.

telephone box (also ˈphone box; ˈcall box) *noun* [C] a small covered place in a street, etc. that contains a telephone for public use □ *pondok telefon*

telephone directory (also ˈphone book) *noun* [C] a book or website that gives a list of the names, addresses and telephone numbers of the people in a particular area □ *buku panduan telefon*

telephone exchange (also **exchange**) *noun* [C] a place belonging to a telephone company where telephone lines are connected to each other □ *ibu sawat telefon*

telesales /ˈteliseɪlz/ (also **telemarketing**) *noun* [U] a method of selling things by telephone □ *telejual*: *He works in telesales.*

telescope /ˈtelɪskəʊp/ *noun* [C] an instrument in the shape of a tube with **lenses** (= special pieces of glass) inside it. You look through it to make things that are far away appear bigger and nearer. □ *teleskop* ⊃ picture at **binoculars**

televise /ˈtelɪvaɪz/ *verb* [T] to show sth on TV □ *menyiarkan melalui televisyen*: *a televised concert*

television /ˈtelɪvɪʒn/ (also **TV**) *noun* **1** (also ˈtelevision set) (*BrE informal* **telly**) [C] a piece of electrical equipment with a screen on which you can watch programmes with moving pictures and sounds □ *(peti) televisyen*: *to switch/turn the television on/off* ♦ *a plasma/flat-screen television* ⊃ picture on **page P8 2** (*BrE informal* **telly**) [U] the programmes that are shown on a television set □ *(siaran) televisyen*: *Paul's watching television.* **3** [U] the system, process or business of sending out television programmes □ *televisyen*: *a television presenter/series/documentary* ♦ *cable/satellite/digital television* ♦ *She works in television.*
IDM on television being shown by television; appearing in a television programme □ *di televisyen*: *What's on television tonight?* ⊃ look at **media**

TOPIC

Television

If you have **digital**, **cable** or **satellite TV**, you can watch **programmes** on lots of different **channels**. You use the **remote control** to change channels without having to leave your seat. **Independent** TV channels have a

VOWELS   iː see   i any   ɪ sit   e ten   æ hat   ɑː father   ɒ got   ɔː saw   ʊ put   uː too   u usual

tell → tempo 880

lot of **commercials/adverts** (= advertisements). They **broadcast** programmes that get good **ratings** (= have a lot of viewers). These include **dramas**, **quiz programmes** and **soap operas**. A TV **serial** has a number of **episodes** (= parts) which tell one story over a period of time.

tell /tel/ *verb* (*pt, pp* **told** /təʊld/)
▶GIVE INFORMATION **1** [T] **tell sb (sth/that ...)**; **tell sb (about sth)**; **tell sth to sb** to give information to sb by speaking or writing □ *memberitahu; menceritakan: She told me her address but I've forgotten it.* ♦ *He wrote to tell me that his mother had died.* ♦ *Tell us about your holiday.* ♦ *to tell the truth/a lie* ♦ *to tell a story* ♦ *Excuse me, could you tell me where the station is?* ♦ *He tells that story to everyone he sees.* ⊃ note at **say 2** [T] (used about a thing) to give information to sb □ *memberitahu; memberi maklumat: This book will tell you all you need to know.*
▶SECRET **3** [I] to not keep a secret □ *membocorkan rahsia: Promise you won't tell!*
▶ORDER **4** [T] **tell sb to do sth** to order or advise sb to do sth □ *menyuruh: The policewoman told us to get out of the car.*
▶KNOW **5** [I,T] to know, see or judge (sth) correctly □ *kata; cakap; tahu; membezakan: 'What do you think Jenny will do next?' 'It's hard to tell.'* ♦ *I could tell that he had enjoyed the evening.* ♦ *You can never tell what he's going to say next.* ♦ *I can't tell the difference between Dan's sisters.*
▶HAVE EFFECT **6** [I] **tell (on sb/sth)** to have a noticeable effect □ *mendatangkan kesan: I can't run as fast as I could—my age is beginning to tell!*
▶SEE DIFFERENCE **7** [T] **tell A and B apart**; **tell A from B** to see the difference between one thing or person and another □ *membezakan: It's very difficult to tell Tom and James apart.* ♦ *Can you tell Tom from his twin brother?*

IDM **all told** with everyone or everything counted and included □ *semuanya*
(I'll) tell you what (*informal*) used to introduce a suggestion □ *apa kata: I'll tell you what—let's ask Diane to take us.*
I told you so (*informal*) I warned you that this would happen □ *kan dah saya katakan: 'I missed the bus.' 'I told you so. I said you needed to leave earlier.'*
tell the time to read the time from a clock or watch □ *pandai tengok jam*

PHR V **tell sb off (for sth/for doing sth)** to speak to sb angrily because they have done sth wrong □ *memarahi sso (kerana sst/kerana membuat sst): The teacher told me off for not doing my homework.*
tell on sb to tell a parent, teacher, etc. about sth bad that sb has done □ *mengadu ttg sso*

telling /'telɪŋ/ *adj* **1** having a great effect □ *berkesan: That's quite a telling argument.* **2** showing, without intending to, what sb/sth is really like □ *penuh makna: The number of homeless people is a telling comment on today's society.*

telltale /'telteɪl/ *adj* [only before a noun] giving information about sth secret or private □ *yg menunjukkan/menandakan (sst): He said he was fine, but there were telltale signs of worry on his face.*

telly /'teli/ *noun* (*pl* **tellies**) (*BrE informal*) = **television**

temp[1] /temp/ *noun* [C] (*informal*) a temporary employee, especially in an office, who works somewhere for a short period of time when sb else is ill or on holiday □ *kakitangan sementara* ▶ **temp** *verb* [I]

temp[2] (also **temp.**) *abbr* = **temperature** □ *suhu: temp 15°C*

temper /'tempə(r)/ *noun* **1** [C,U] if you have a **temper**, you get angry very easily □ *(sifat) pemarah; panas baran: Be careful of Paul. He's got quite a temper!* ♦ *You must learn to control your temper.* **2** [C] the way you are feeling at a particular time □ *keadaan perasaan: It's no use talking to him when he's in a bad temper.* **SYN** **mood**

IDM **in a temper** feeling very angry and not controlling your behaviour □ *menjadi marah*
keep/lose your temper to stay calm/to become angry □ *dpt/tdk dpt mengawal perasaan marah* ⊃ look at **bad-tempered**

temperament /'temprəmənt/ *noun* [C,U] a person's character, especially as it affects the way they behave and feel □ *pembawaan; perangai: to have an artistic/a fiery/a calm temperament* **SYN** **disposition**

temperamental /ˌtemprə'mentl/ *adj* often and suddenly changing the way you behave or feel □ *ada angin: a temperamental character*

temperate /'tempərət/ *adj* (used about a climate) not very hot and not very cold □ *beriklim sederhana*

temperature /'temprətʃə(r)/ *noun* (*abbr* **temp**) **1** [C,U] how hot or cold sth is □ *suhu: Heat the oven to a temperature of 200°C.* ♦ *a high/low temperature* ♦ *an increase in temperature* ⊃ note at **cold 2** [C] how hot or cold sb's body is □ *suhu badan: to take somebody's temperature* (= measure the temperature of sb's body)

IDM **have a temperature** to be hotter than normal because you are ill □ *panas badan; demam*

MORE In American English you can take sb's temperature, but in the other examples the word **fever** is used.

⊃ look at **fever** ⊃ note at **ill**

tempest /'tempɪst/ *noun* [C] (*formal*) a violent storm □ *ribut*

temple /'templ/ *noun* [C] **1** a building where people worship □ *kuil; tokong: a Buddhist/Hindu temple* **2** one of the flat parts on each side of your head, at the same level as your eyes and higher □ *pelipis* ⊃ picture at **body**

tempo /'tempəʊ/ *noun* (*pl* **tempos** /'tempəʊz/) **1** [C,U] the speed of a piece of music □ *tempo;*

ʌ c**u**p ɜː b**ir**d ə **a**go eɪ p**ay** əʊ g**o** aɪ m**y** aʊ n**ow** ɔɪ b**oy** ɪə n**ear** eə h**air** ʊə p**ure**

rentak: a fast/slow tempo **2** [sing, U] the speed of an activity or event ⇒ *rentak*

temporary /ˈtemprəri/ *adj* lasting for a short time □ *sementara: a temporary job* ♦ *This arrangement is only temporary.* **OPP** **permanent**
▶temporarily /ˈtemprərəli/ *adv*

tempt /tempt/ *verb* [T] **tempt sb (into sth/into doing sth); tempt sb (to do sth)** to try to persuade or attract sb to do sth, even if it is wrong □ *menggoda; cuba mempengaruhi; membuat sso teringin: His dream of riches had tempted him into a life of crime.* ♦ *She was tempted to stay in bed all day.*

temptation /tempˈteɪʃn/ *noun* **1** [U] a feeling that you want to do sth, even if you know that it is wrong □ *keinginan: I managed to resist the temptation to tell him what I really thought.* ♦ *She wanted a cream cake badly, but didn't give in to temptation.* **2** [C] a thing that attracts you to do sth wrong or silly □ *godaan: All that money is certainly a big temptation.*

tempting /ˈtemptɪŋ/ *adj* attractive in a way that makes you want to do or have sth □ *menarik: a tempting offer*

ten /ten/ *number* 10 □ *sepuluh; 10* ⇒ note at **six**

tenacious /təˈneɪʃəs/ *adj* (*formal*) not likely to give up or let sth go; determined □ *memegang dgn kuat (tdk mahu lepas); bertekad* ▶tenacity /təˈnæsəti/ *noun* [U]

tenancy /ˈtenənsi/ *noun* [C,U] (*pl* **tenancies**) the use of a room, flat, building or piece of land, for which you pay rent to the owner □ *penyewaan: a six-month tenancy* ♦ *It says in the tenancy agreement that you can't keep pets.*

tenant /ˈtenənt/ *noun* [C] a person who pays rent to the owner of a room, flat, building or piece of land so that they can live in it or use it □ *penyewa* ⇒ look at **landlord**

tend /tend/ *verb* **1** [I] **tend to do sth** to usually do or be sth □ *cenderung; biasanya: Women tend to live longer than men.* ♦ *There tends to be a lot of heavy traffic on that road.* ♦ *My brother tends to talk a lot when he's nervous.* **2** [I] used for giving your opinion in a polite way □ *rasa: I tend to think that we shouldn't interfere.* **3** [I,T] (*formal*) **tend (to) sb/sth** to look after sb/sth □ *menjaga; merawat; melayani: Paramedics tended (to) the injured.*

tendency /ˈtendənsi/ *noun* [C] (*pl* **tendencies**) **a tendency (to do sth/towards sth)** something that a person or thing usually does; a way of behaving □ *selalu; kecenderungan: They both have a tendency to be late for appointments.* ♦ *The dog began to show vicious tendencies.* ♦ *She seems to have a tendency towards depression.*

tender¹ /ˈtendə(r)/ *adj* (**tenderer; tenderest**) [More **tender** and most **tender** are also common.] **1** kind and loving □ *penyayang; lembut: tender words/looks/kisses* **2** (used about food) soft and easy to cut or bite □ *lembut; empuk: The meat should be nice and tender.* **OPP** **tough**

3 (used about a part of the body) painful when you touch it □ *mudah terasa sakit*
IDM **at a tender age; at the tender age of …** when still young and without much experience □ *pd usia yg masih muda: She went to live in London at the tender age of 15.*
▶tenderly *adv*
▶tenderness *noun* [U]

tender² /ˈtendə(r)/ *verb* [I,T] (*formal*) to offer or give sth formally □ *menawarkan; mengemukakan; menyerahkan: After the scandal the Foreign Minister was forced to tender her resignation.* ♦ *Five different companies tendered for the building contract* (= stated a price for doing the work). ▶tender (*especially AmE* **bid**) *noun* [C]: *Several firms submitted a tender for the catering contract.*

tendon /ˈtendən/ *noun* [C] a strong, thin part inside the body that joins a muscle to a bone □ *tendon* ⇒ look at **ligament**

tenement /ˈtenəmənt/ *noun* [C] a large building that is divided into small flats, especially in a poor area of a city □ *rumah pangsa murah*

tenner /ˈtenə(r)/ *noun* [C] (*BrE informal*) £10 or a ten-pound note □ *£10; wang kertas £10: You can have it for a tenner.*

tennis /ˈtenɪs/ *noun* [U] a game for two or four players who hit a ball over a net using a **racket** (= a piece of equipment that is held in the hand) □ *tenis: Let's play tennis.* ♦ *to have a game of tennis* ♦ *a tennis match* ♦ *a tennis court* ⇒ note at **sport** ⇒ picture on **page P4**

MORE In tennis you can play **singles** (a game between two people) or **doubles** (a game between two teams of two people).

tenor /ˈtenə(r)/ *noun* [C] a fairly high singing voice for a man; a man with this voice □ *(suara) tenor; penyanyi tenor: José Carreras is a famous tenor.*

MORE Tenor is between **alto** and **baritone**.

▶tenor *adj* [only before a noun]: *a tenor saxophone/trombone*

tenpin bowling /ˌtenpɪn ˈbəʊlɪŋ/ *noun* [U] a game in which you roll a heavy ball towards ten **tenpins** (= objects shaped like bottles) and try to knock them down □ *boling sepuluh pin* ⇒ picture on **page P3**

tense¹ /tens/ *adj* **1** (used about a person) not able to relax because you are worried or nervous □ *tegang; cemas: She looked pale and tense.* **2** (used about an atmosphere or a situation) in which people feel worried and not relaxed □ *tegang; kejang* **3** (used about a muscle or a part of the body) tight; not relaxed □ *tegang*

tense² /tens/ *noun* [C,U] a form of a verb that shows if sth happens in the past, present or future □ *kala*

tense → termite 882

EXAM TIP

Irregular verb forms

Remember that the dictionary tells you when the past tense and past participle of a verb are irregular. There is a list in the back of the dictionary that you can work through, learning a few each day before the exam.

ℹ️ For more information about verb tenses, look at the **Reference Section** at the back of this dictionary.

tense³ /tens/ verb [I,T] **tense (up)** to have muscles that have become hard and not relaxed □ *menjadi tegang; menegang*

tension /'tenʃn/ noun 1 [C,U] bad feeling and lack of trust between people, countries, etc. □ *ketegangan*: *There are signs of growing tensions between the two countries.* 2 [U] the condition of not being able to relax because you are worried or nervous □ *perasaan cemas*: *I could hear the tension in her voice as she spoke.* 3 [U] (used about a rope, muscle, etc.) the state of being stretched tight; how tightly sth is stretched □ *ketegangan; tegangan*: *The massage relieved the tension in my neck.*

tent /tent/ noun [C] a small structure made of cloth that is held up by poles and ropes. You use a tent to sleep in when you go camping □ *khemah*: *to put up/take down a tent* ➲ picture at **camping**

tentacle /'tentəkl/ noun [C] one of the long thin soft parts like legs that some sea animals have □ *sesungut; tentakel*: *An octopus has eight tentacles.* ➲ picture at **octopus**

tentative /'tentətɪv/ adj 1 (used about plans, etc.) uncertain; not definite □ *belum pasti; tdk muktamad; tentatif* 2 (used about a person or their behaviour) not confident about what you are saying or doing □ *teragak-agak*: *a tentative smile/suggestion* ▶ **tentatively** adv

tenterhooks /'tentəhʊks/ noun
IDM **(be) on tenterhooks** (to be) in a very nervous or excited state because you are waiting to find out what is going to happen □ *dlm keadaan tertanya-tanya/berdebar-debar*

tenth¹ /tenθ/ ordinal number 10th □ *kesepuluh; ke-10* ➲ note at **sixth**

tenth² /tenθ/ noun [C] ¹⁄₁₀; one of ten equal parts of sth □ *satu per sepuluh*; ¹⁄₁₀

'tent peg = **peg¹(2)**

tenuous /'tenjuəs/ adj very weak or uncertain □ *lemah; tdk kukuh*: *The connection between Joe's story and what actually happened was tenuous.*

tenure /'tenjə(r)/ noun [U] a legal right to live in a place, hold a job, use land, etc. for a certain time □ *hak utk tinggal di sst tempat, memegang sst jawatan, menggunakan tanah, dsb utk tempoh tertentu*

tepid /'tepɪd/ adj (used about liquids) only slightly warm □ *suam*

term¹ /tɜːm/ noun 1 [C] a word or group of words with a particular meaning □ *perkataan; kata-kata; istilah*: *What exactly do you mean by the term 'racist'?* ♦ *a technical term in computing* 2 **terms** [pl] **in terms of ...; in ... terms** used for showing which particular way you are thinking about sth or from which point of view □ *dr segi*: *The flat would be ideal in terms of size, but it is very expensive.* ♦ *I'll explain in simple terms.* 3 **terms** [pl] the conditions of an agreement □ *syarat*: *Under the terms of the contract you must give a week's notice.* ♦ *Both sides agreed to the peace terms.* 4 [C] a period of time that the school or university year is divided into □ *penggal*: *the autumn/spring/summer term* ♦ *an end-of-term test* ➲ look at **semester** 5 [C] a period of time for which sth lasts □ *tempoh*: *He faces a prison term of 25 years.* ♦ *The US President is now in his second term of office.*

IDM **be on equal terms (with sb)** ➲ **equal¹**
be on good, friendly, etc. terms (with sb) to have a friendly relationship with sb □ *baik, mesra, dsb (dgn sso)*
be on speaking terms (with sb) ➲ **speak**
come to terms with sth to accept sth unpleasant or difficult □ *menerima hakikat sst*
in the long/short term over a long/short period of time in the future □ *dlm jangka panjang/pendek*

term² /tɜːm/ verb [T] to describe sb/sth by using a particular word or expression □ *mengatakan; disebut; dinamakan*: *the period of history that is often termed the 'Dark Ages'*

terminal¹ /'tɜːmɪnl/ noun [C] 1 a large railway station, bus station or building at an airport where journeys begin and end □ *perhentian; terminal*: *the bus terminal* ♦ *Which terminal are you flying from?* 2 the computer that one person uses for getting information from a central computer or for putting information into it □ *terminal*

terminal² /'tɜːmɪnl/ adj (used about an illness) slowly causing death □ *yg tdk dpt diubat lagi; yg membawa maut*: *terminal cancer* ▶ **terminally** /-nəli/ adv: *a terminally ill patient*

terminate /'tɜːmɪneɪt/ verb [I,T] (formal) to end or to make sth end □ *menamatkan*: *This train terminates at London Victoria.* ♦ *to terminate a contract/an agreement* ▶ **termination** /ˌtɜːmɪ'neɪʃn/ noun [U]

terminology /ˌtɜːmɪ'nɒlədʒi/ noun [U] the special words and expressions that are used in a particular profession, subject or activity □ *istilah*

terminus /'tɜːmɪnəs/ noun [C] the last stop or station at the end of a bus route or railway line □ *perhentian penghabisan*

termite /'tɜːmaɪt/ noun [C] an insect that lives in hot countries and does a lot of damage by eating the wood of trees and buildings □ *anai-anai*

[I] **intransitive**, a verb which has no object: *He laughed.*   [T] **transitive**, a verb which has an object: *He ate an apple.*

terrace /ˈterəs/ noun 1 (BrE) [C] a line of similar houses that are all joined together □ *deretan rumah* 2 [C] a flat area of stone next to a restaurant or large house where people can have meals, sit in the sun, etc. □ *teres* ➔ look at **patio**, **veranda** 3 **terraces** [pl] the wide steps that people stand on to watch a football match □ *teres* 4 [C, usually pl] one of a series of steps that are cut into the side of a hill so that crops can be grown there □ *teres*

terraced /ˈterəst/ adj 1 (BrE) (used about a house) forming part of a line of similar houses that are all joined together □ *rumah teres/deret* ➔ picture on **page P9** 2 (used about a hill) having steps cut out of it so that crops can be grown there □ *berteres*

terrain /təˈreɪn/ noun [U] land of the type mentioned □ *rupa bumi*: *mountainous/steep/rocky terrain*

terrestrial /təˈrestriəl/ adj 1 connected with, or living on, the earth □ *berkaitan dgn bumi* 2 (used about television, etc.) operating on earth rather than from a **satellite** (= an electronic device that is sent into space) □ *daratan; berkenaan dgn bumi*

terrible /ˈterəbl/ adj 1 ill or very upset □ *teruk; sangat kesal*: *I feel terrible. I think I'm going to be sick.* ♦ *He felt terrible when he realized what he had done.* 2 very unpleasant; causing great shock or injury □ *teruk; dahsyat*: *a terrible accident* ♦ *terrible news* ♦ *What a terrible thing to do!* 3 very bad; of poor quality □ *teruk*: *a terrible hotel/book/memory/driver* ➔ note at **bad** 4 [only before a noun] used to emphasize how bad sth is □ *teruk*: *in terrible pain/trouble* ♦ *The room was in a terrible mess.*

terribly /ˈterəbli/ adv 1 very □ *sangat; amat; betul-betul*: *I'm terribly sorry.* 2 very badly □ *dgn (sangat) teruk; dgn dahsyat*: *I played terribly.* ♦ *The experiment went terribly wrong.*

terrier /ˈteriə(r)/ noun [C] a type of small dog □ *anjing terrier*

terrific /təˈrɪfɪk/ adj (informal) 1 extremely nice or good; excellent □ *sangat bagus; hebat*: *You're doing a terrific job!* ➔ note at **good** 2 [only before a noun] very great □ *sangat banyak*: *I've got a terrific amount of work to do.* ▶**terrifically** /-kli/ adv: *terrifically expensive*

terrified /ˈterɪfaɪd/ adj **terrified (of sb/sth)** very afraid □ *amat ketakutan*: *I'm absolutely terrified of snakes.* ♦ *What's the matter? You look terrified.*

terrify /ˈterɪfaɪ/ verb [T] (**terrifying**; **terrifies**; *pt, pp* **terrified**) to frighten sb very much □ *menakutkan*

territorial /ˌterəˈtɔːriəl/ adj [only before a noun] connected with the land or area of sea that belongs to a country □ *(berkenaan dgn) wilayah*: *territorial waters*

territory /ˈterətri/ noun (pl **territories**) 1 [C,U] an area of land that belongs to one country □ *wilayah*: *to fly over enemy territory* 2 [C,U] an area that an animal has as its own □ *kawasan* 3 [U] an area of knowledge or responsibility □ *bidang*: *Computer programming is Frank's territory.*

terror /ˈterə(r)/ noun 1 [U] very great fear □ *ketakutan yg amat sangat*: *He screamed in terror as the rats came towards him.* 2 [C] a person or thing that makes you feel afraid □ *orang atau benda yg menakutkan*: *the terrors of the night* 3 [U] violence and the killing of ordinary people for political purposes □ *keganasan*: *a campaign of terror* 4 [C] (*informal*) a person (especially a child) or an animal that is difficult to control □ *budak yg sangat nakal; binatang yg sukar dikawal*: *Joey's a little terror.*

terrorism /ˈterərɪzəm/ noun [U] the use of violence for political purposes □ *keganasan*: *an act of terrorism* ▶**terrorist** /-ɪst/ noun [C], adj: *a terrorist attack/bomb/group* ➔ note at **crime**

terrorize (also **-ise**) /ˈterəraɪz/ verb [T] to make sb feel frightened by using or threatening to use violence against them □ *menakutkan*: *The gang has terrorized the neighbourhood for months.*

terse /tɜːs/ adj said in few words and in a not very friendly way □ *ringkas dan kasar*: *a terse reply*

tertiary /ˈtɜːʃəri/ (*AmE* also) / adj (*BrE*) (used about education) at university or college level □ *pd peringkat tinggi*: *a tertiary college*

TESL /ˈtesl/ abbr Teaching English as a Second Language □ *Pengajaran Bahasa Inggeris Sebagai Bahasa Kedua*

test¹ /test/ noun [C] 1 a short exam to measure sb's knowledge or skill in sth □ *ujian*: *We have a spelling test every Friday.* ➔ note at **exam** ➔ look at **driving** 2 a short medical examination of a part of your body □ *pemeriksaan*: *to have an eye test* 3 an experiment to find out if sth works or to find out more information about it □ *ujian; kajian*: *Tests show that the new drug is safe and effective.* ♦ *to carry out/perform/do a test* 4 a situation or event that shows how good, strong, etc. sb/sth is □ *ujian*: *The local elections will be a good test of the government's popularity.*

IDM **put sb/sth to the test** to do sth to find out how good, strong, etc. sb/sth is □ *menguji sso/sst*

test² /test/ verb [T] 1 **test sb (on sth)** to examine sb's knowledge or skill in sth □ *menguji; memberi ujian*: *We're being tested on irregular verbs this morning.* 2 to examine a part of the body to find out if it is healthy □ *memeriksa*: *to have your eyes tested* 3 **test sb/sth (for sth); test sth (on sb/sth)** to try, use or examine sth carefully to find out if it is working properly or what it is like □ *menguji; mencuba*: *These cars have all been tested for safety.* ♦ *Do you think it's right to test cosmetics on animals?*

testament → thanks 884

> **EXAM TIP**
>
> **Test yourself**
>
> If you just read through a list of words, it is difficult to be sure whether or not you really know them. Before an exam, test yourself and your friends. Can you write the words without making a spelling mistake? Do you know what they mean? Can you put them into a sentence correctly?

testament /'testəmənt/ *noun* [C, usually sing] (*formal*) **a testament (to sth)** something that shows that sth exists or is true □ *bukti*

testicle /'testɪkl/ *noun* [C] one of the two male sex organs that produce **sperm** (= the seed necessary for making babies) □ *testikel; buah zakar*

testify /'testɪfaɪ/ *verb* [I,T] (**testifying**; **testifies**; *pt, pp* **testified**) to make a formal statement that sth is true, especially in a court of law □ *memberi keterangan*

testimony /'testɪməni/ *noun* (*pl* **testimonies**) **1** [U, sing] (*formal*) something that shows that sth else exists or is true □ *bukti* **2** [C,U] a formal statement that sth is true, especially one that is made in a court of law □ *penyataan rasmi; testimoni*

testing /'testɪŋ/ *noun* [U] the activity of testing sb/sth in order to find sth out, see if it works, etc. □ *pengujian*: *testing and assessment in education*

'test tube *noun* [C] a thin glass tube that is used in chemical experiments □ *tabung uji*

tetanus /'tetənəs/ *noun* [U] a serious disease that makes your muscles, especially the muscles of your face, hard and impossible to move. You can get **tetanus** by cutting yourself on sth dirty. □ *kancing gigi; tetanus*

tether¹ /'teðə(r)/ *verb* [T] to tie an animal to sth with a rope, etc. □ *menambat; mengikat*

tether² /'teðə(r)/ *noun*
IDM **at the end of your tether** ⊃ **end¹**

text¹ /tekst/ *noun* **1** [U] the main written part of a book, newspaper, etc. (not the pictures, notes, etc.) □ *teks*: *My job is to lay out the text on the page.* **2** [C] the written form of a speech, etc. □ *teks*: *The newspaper printed the complete text of the interview.* **3** [C] = **text message 4** [C] a book or a short piece of writing that people study as part of a literature or language course: *a set text* (= one that has to be studied for an examination) □ *teks; buku yg ditetapkan*

text² /tekst/ (also **'text-message**) *verb* [T,I] to send sb a written message using a mobile phone □ *menghantar mesej melalui telefon bimbit*: *I texted him to say we were home.* ⊃ look at **SMS** ⊃ note at **mobile phone**

textbook /'tekstbʊk/ *noun* [C] a book that teaches a particular subject and that is used especially in schools □ *buku teks*: *a history textbook*

textile /'tekstaɪl/ *noun* [C] any cloth made in a factory □ *tekstil*: *cotton textiles* ♦ *the textile industry*

'text message (also **text**) *noun* [C] a written message that you send using a mobile phone □ *mesej teks; mesej bertulis yg dihantar melalui telefon bimbit*: *Send a text message to this number to vote for the winner.* ⊃ look at **SMS** ⊃ note at **mobile phone** ▸ **'text-messaging** (also **texting** /'tekstɪŋ/) *noun* [U]

texture /'tekstʃə(r)/ *noun* [C,U] the way that sth feels when you touch it □ *tekstur; rasa*: *a rough/smooth/coarse texture* ♦ *cheese with a very creamy texture*

than /ðən; *strong form* ðæn/ *conj, prep* **1** used when you are comparing two things □ *drpd*: *He's taller than me.* ♦ *He's taller than I am.* ♦ *London is more expensive than Madrid.* ♦ *You speak French much better than she does/than her.* ♦ *I'd rather play tennis than football.* **2** used with 'more' and 'less' before numbers, expressions of time, distances, etc. □ *drpd*: *I've worked here for more than three years.*

thank /θæŋk/ *verb* [T] **thank sb (for sth/for doing sth)** to tell sb that you are grateful □ *mengucapkan terima kasih*: *I'm writing to thank you for the present you sent me.* ♦ *I'll go and thank him for offering to help.*

> **HELP** **Thank you** and **thanks** are both used for telling somebody that you are grateful for something. **Thanks** is more informal: *Thank you very much for your letter.* ♦ '*How are you, Rachel?*' '*Much better, thanks.*' You can also use **thank you** and **thanks** to accept something that somebody has offered to you: '*Stay for dinner.*' '*Thank you. That would be nice.*' When you want to refuse something you can say **no, thank you** or **no, thanks**: '*Would you like some more tea?*' '*No, thanks.*'

IDM **thank God, goodness, heavens**, etc. used for expressing happiness that sth unpleasant has stopped or will not happen □ *syukur*: *Thank goodness it's stopped raining!* ⊃ note at **god**

thankful /'θæŋkfl/ *adj* [not before a noun] **thankful (for sth/to do sth/that …)** pleased and grateful □ *berterima kasih*: *I was thankful to hear that you got home safely.* ♦ *I was thankful for my thick coat when it started to snow.*

thankfully /'θæŋkfəli/ *adv* **1** used for expressing happiness that sth unpleasant did not or will not happen □ *mujurlah; nasib baik* **SYN** **fortunately**: *Thankfully, no one was injured in the accident.* **2** in a pleased or grateful way □ *dgn penuh rasa terima kasih*: *I accepted her offer thankfully.* **SYN** **gratefully**

thankless /'θæŋkləs/ *adj* involving hard work that other people do not notice or thank you for □ *tdk dihargai*

thanks /θæŋks/ *noun* [pl] **1** words which show that you are grateful □ *ucapan terima kasih*: *I'd like to express my thanks to all of you for coming*

ð **th**en s **s**o z **z**oo ʃ **sh**e ʒ vi**s**ion h **h**ow m **m**an n **n**o ŋ si**ng** l **l**eg r **r**ed j **y**es w **w**et

here today. ◆ Thanks! **2** no thanks a polite way of refusing sth that sb has offered you □ *cara sopan utk menolak sst*: 'Would you like some more cake?' 'No thanks.'
IDM thanks to sb/sth because of sb/sth □ *kerana sso/sst*: We're late, thanks to you!
a vote of thanks ⊃ vote¹

Thanksgiving (Day) /ˌθæŋksˈɡɪvɪŋ deɪ/ noun [U,C] a public holiday in the US and in Canada □ *Hari Kesyukuran*

CULTURE

Thanksgiving Day is on the fourth Thursday in November in the US and on the second Monday in October in Canada. It was originally a day when people thanked God for the **harvest** (= food from the land or sea, especially that which is produced by farmers).

ʔ 'thank you noun [C] an expression of thanks □ *terima kasih*: Thank you! ◆ 'How are you?' 'I'm fine, thank you.' ◆ I'd like to say a big thank you to everybody who worked so hard.

ʔ that /ðæt/ determiner, pron, conj, adv **1** (pl those /ðəʊz/) used to refer to a person or thing, especially when he/she/it is not near the person speaking □ *itu*: I like that house over there. ◆ What's that in the road? ◆ 'Could you pass me the book?' 'This one?' 'No, that one over there.' ◆ How much are those apples at the back? **2** (pl those) used for talking about a person or thing already known or mentioned □ *itu*: That was the year we went to Spain, wasn't it? ◆ Can you give me back that money I lent you last week? **3** /ðət; strong form ðæt/ [used for introducing a relative clause] the person or thing already mentioned □ *yg*: I'm reading the book that won the Booker prize. ◆ The people that live next door are French. ⊃ note at **which**

GRAMMAR When **that** is the object of the verb in the relative clause, it is often left out: I want to see the doctor (that) I saw last week. ◆ She wore the dress (that) she bought in Paris.

4 /ðət; strong form ðæt/ used after certain verbs, nouns and adjectives to introduce a new part of the sentence □ *bahawa*: She told me that she was leaving. ◆ I hope that you feel better soon. ◆ I'm certain that he will come. ◆ It's funny that you should say that.

GRAMMAR **That** is often left out in this type of sentence: I thought you would like it.

5 [used with adjectives and adverbs] as much as that □ *itu*: 30 miles? I can't walk that far.
IDM that is (to say) used when you are giving more information about sb/sth □ *iaitu; yakni*: I'm on holiday next week. That's to say, from Tuesday.
that's that there is nothing more to say or do □ *itu saja; habis cerita*: I'm not going and that's that.

thatched /θætʃt/ adj (used about a building) having a roof made of **straw** (= dried grass)

885 **Thanksgiving (Day)** → **theatre**

□ *beratap jerami* ⊃ picture on **page P9**

thaw /θɔː/ verb [I,T] thaw (sth) (out) to become or to make sth become soft or liquid again after freezing □ *menjadi cair; tdk beku lagi*: Is the snow thawing? ◆ Always thaw chicken thoroughly before you cook it. ⊃ look at **melt** ▶thaw noun [C, usually sing]

ʔ the /ðə; ði; strong form ðiː/ definite article **1** used for talking about a person or thing that is already known or that has already been mentioned □ *itu; ini; yg; tersebut*: I took the children to the dentist. ◆ We met the man who bought your house. ◆ The milk is in the fridge. **2** used when there is only one of sth □ *digunakan utk benda yg ada satu sahaja*: The sun is very strong today. ◆ Who won the World Cup? ◆ the government **3** used with numbers and dates □ *digunakan dgn bilangan dan tarikh*: This is the third time I've seen this film. ◆ Friday the thirteenth ◆ I grew up in the 1980s. **4** (formal) used with a singular noun when you are talking generally about sth □ *digunakan dgn kn tunggal apabila bercakap secara umum ttg sst*: The dolphin is an intelligent animal. **5** with musical instruments □ *digunakan dgn nama alat muzik*: Do you play the piano? **6** used with adjectives to name a group of people □ *digunakan dgn adjektif utk menyebut nama sst kumpulan orang*: the French ◆ the poor **7** with units of measurement, meaning 'every' □ *setiap; tiap-tiap*: Our car does forty miles to the gallon. **8** the well-known or important that □ *yg terkenal atau penting itu*: 'My best friend at school was Adele.' 'You mean **the** Adele?'

HELP 'The' is pronounced /ðiːpcolon:/ in this sense.

9 the … the … used for saying that the way in which two things change is connected □ *digunakan utk menyatakan bahawa cara dua perkara itu berubah ada kaitannya*: The more you eat, the fatter you get. ❶ For more information about articles, look at the **Reference Section** at the back of this dictionary.

ʔ theatre (AmE theater) /ˈθɪətə(r)/ noun **1** [C] a building where you go to see plays, shows, etc. □ *panggung*: How often do you **go to the theatre**? **2** [U] plays in general □ *teater*: He's studying modern Russian theatre. **SYN** drama **3** [sing, U] the work of acting in or producing plays □ *(bidang) teater*: He's worked in (the) theatre for thirty years. **4** [C,U] = operating theatre: He's still **in theatre**. ◆ a theatre nurse (= a nurse with special training who helps during operations)

TOPIC

Theatre

A **play** is performed in a **theatre**, on a flat area called **the stage**. The furniture, etc. on the stage is the **scenery**. If an **actor/actress** wants a **part** in a play, he/she must have an **audition**, so the **director** can decide if he/she is suit-

VOWELS iː: see i any ɪ sit e ten æ hat ɑː father ɒ got ɔː saw ʊ put uː too u usual

theatrical → therapy 886

able. Before they **put on** a play, **the cast** (= all of the actors) practise by having **rehearsals**. If the **audience** like the play, they **clap/applaud** (= hit their hands together) at the end of the **performance**.

theatrical /θiˈætrɪkl/ *adj* **1** [only *before* a noun] connected with the theatre □ *(berkaitan dgn) teater* **2** (used about behaviour) exaggerated or showing feelings, etc. in a very obvious way because you want people to notice you □ *berlebih-lebih; dibuat-buat*

theft /θeft/ *noun* [C,U] the crime of stealing sth □ *pencurian; mencuri*: There have been a lot of thefts in this area recently. ◆ The woman was arrested for theft. ⊃ note at **thief**

ℹ their /ðeə(r)/ *determiner* **1** of or belonging to them □ *(mengenai atau milik) mereka*: The children picked up their books and left. **2** used instead of *his* or *her* □ *-nya; masing-masing*: Has everyone got their book? ⊃ note at **he**

ℹ theirs /ðeəz/ *pron* of or belonging to them □ *(milik) mereka*: Our flat isn't as big as theirs.

ℹ them /ðəm; *strong form* ðem/ *pron* [the object of a verb or preposition] **1** the people or things mentioned earlier □ *mereka; -nya*: I'll phone them now. ◆ 'I've got the keys here.' 'Oh good. Give them to me.' ◆ We have students from several countries but *most of them* are Italian. ◆ They asked for your address so I gave it to them. **2** him or her □ *dia*: If anyone phones, tell them I'm busy. ⊃ note at **he**

ℹ theme /θi:m/ *noun* [C] the subject of a talk, a piece of writing or a work of art □ *tema*: The theme of today's discussion will be 'Our changing cities'.

'theme park *noun* [C] a park where people go to enjoy themselves, for example by riding on **roller coasters** (= large machines that go very fast), and where much of the entertainment is connected with one subject or idea □ *taman tema*

ℹ themselves /ðəmˈselvz/ *pron* **1** used when the people or things who do an action are also affected by it □ *diri mereka (sendiri) – kadangkala tdk diterjemahkan*: Susie and Angela seem to be enjoying themselves. ◆ People often talk to themselves when they are worried. **2** used to emphasize the people who do the action □ *(mereka) sendiri*: They themselves say that the situation cannot continue. ◆ Did they paint the house themselves? (= or did sb else do it for them?)
IDM (all) by themselves **1** alone □ *sendirian*: The boys are too young to go out by themselves. ⊃ note at **alone 2** without help □ *sendiri*: The children cooked the dinner all by themselves.

ℹ then /ðen/ *adv* **1** (at) that time □ *(pd) masa itu; lepas itu; sejak itu; hingga itu*: In 2009? I was at university then. ◆ I spoke to him on Wednesday, but I haven't seen him since then. ◆ They met in 1961 and remained close friends from then on. ◆ I'm going tomorrow. Can you wait until then? ◆ Phone me tomorrow—I will have decided by then. **2** next; after that □ *selepas itu; kemudian*: I'll have a shower and get changed, then we'll go out. ◆ There was silence for a minute. Then he replied. **3** used to show the logical result of a statement or situation □ *jadi; kalau begitu*: 'I don't feel at all well.' 'Why don't you go to the doctor, then?' ◆ If you don't do any work then you'll fail the exam. **4** used after words like *now, right, well*, etc. to show the beginning or end of a conversation or statement □ *baiklah; kalau begitu*: Now then, are we all ready to go? ◆ OK then, I'll see you tomorrow.
IDM then/there again ⊃ **again**
there and then; then and there ⊃ **there**

WRITING TIP

Order of events

When you tell a story, you need to show how events follow one another. It is better not to use **then** every time: *I watched TV for a bit, and then I went to bed.* ◆ *After a while, I heard a strange noise.* ◆ *Next, somebody turned on the lights.* ◆ *After that, I heard people talking.* ◆ *Later on, everything went quiet.*

ℹ For more help with writing, look at **Wordpower Writing Tutor** at the back of this dictionary.

thence /ðens/ *adv* (*old-fashioned*) from there □ *dr situ; selepas itu*

theology /θiˈɒlədʒi/ *noun* [U] the study of religion □ *teologi* ▶**theological** /ˌθiːəˈlɒdʒɪkl/ *adj*

theoretical /ˌθɪəˈretɪkl/ *adj* **1** based on ideas and principles, not on practical experience □ *(bersifat) teori*: A lot of university courses are still far too theoretical. **2** that may possibly exist or happen, although it is unlikely □ *dr segi teori*: There is a theoretical possibility that the world will end tomorrow. ⊃ look at **practical** ▶**theoretically** /-kli/ *adv*

ℹ theory /ˈθɪəri/ (*AmE also*) / *noun* (pl **theories**) **1** [C] an idea or set of ideas that try to explain sth □ *teori*: the theory about how life on earth began **2** [U] the general idea or principles of a particular subject □ *teori*: political theory ◆ the theory and practice of language teaching **3** [C] an opinion or a belief that has not been shown to be true □ *teori; pendapat*: He has this theory that drinking tea helps you live longer.
IDM in theory as a general idea which may not be true in reality □ *dr segi teori*: Your plan sounds fine in theory, but I don't know if it'll work in practice. ⊃ look at **practice**

therapeutic /ˌθerəˈpjuːtɪk/ *adj* **1** helping to cure an illness □ *terapeutik; mengubat penyakit*: therapeutic drugs **2** helping you to relax and feel better □ *terapeutik; merehatkan*: I find listening to music very therapeutic.

therapy /ˈθerəpi/ *noun* [U] treatment to help or cure a mental or physical illness, often without

ʌ **c**u**p** ɜː **b**i**rd** ə **a**g**o** eɪ **p**ay əʊ g**o** aɪ m**y** aʊ n**ow** ɔɪ b**oy** ɪə n**ear** eə h**air** ʊə p**ure**

drugs or medical operations □ *terapi*: *to have/undergo therapy* ◆ *She's in therapy* (= having psychotherapy). ▶**therapist** /-pɪst/ *noun* [C]: *a speech therapist*

there /ðeə(r)/ *adv, pron* **1** used as the subject of 'be', 'seem', 'appear', etc. to say that sth exists □ *ada*: *Is there a god?* ◆ *There's a man at the door.* ◆ *There wasn't much to eat.* ◆ *There's somebody singing outside our house.* ◆ *There seems to be a mistake here.* **2** in, at or to that place □ *di atau ke situ/sana*: *Could you put the table there, please?* ◆ *I like Milan. My husband and I met there.* ◆ *Have you been to Bonn? We're going there next week.* ◆ *Have you looked under there?* **3** available if needed □ *ada (jika perlu)*: *Her parents are always there if she needs help.* **4** at that point (in a conversation, story, etc.) □ *di sini*; *dlm hal ini*: *Could I interrupt you there for a minute?* **5** used for calling attention to sth □ *digunakan utk menarik perhatian kpd sst*: *Oh look, there's Kate!* ◆ *Hello there! Can anyone hear me?*
IDM **be there for sb** to be available to help and support sb when they have a problem □ *ada utk memberi bantuan dan sokongan*: *Whenever I'm in trouble, my sister is always there for me.*
then/there again ⊃ **again**
there and then; then and there at that time and place; immediately □ *pd masa itu juga*
there you are; there you go 1 used when you give sth to sb □ *ini dia; nah*: *There you are. I've bought you a newspaper.* **2** used when you are explaining sth to sb □ *dah pun jadi, dsb (digunakan apabila menunjuk ajar sso ttg sst)*: *Just press the switch and there you are!*

thereabouts /ˌðeərəˈbaʊts/ *adv* [usually after *or*] somewhere near a number, time or place □ *lebih kurang; kira-kira*: *There are 100 students, or thereabouts.* ◆ *She lives in Sydney, or thereabouts.*

thereafter /ˌðeərˈɑːftə(r)/ *adv (formal)* after that □ *selepas itu*

thereby /ˌðeəˈbaɪ/ *adv (formal)* in that way □ *dan dgn itu; oleh itu*

therefore /ˈðeəfɔː(r)/ *adv* for that reason □ *oleh itu; oleh sebab itu*: *The new trains have more powerful engines and are therefore faster.*

WRITING TIP
Describing results

In formal writing you can use **therefore**, **as a result** or **consequently** to talk about the result of an action: *No one provided any money, and therefore the youth club closed.* ◆ *There was no money, and as a result, the youth club closed.* ◆ *The money ran out, and consequently, the youth club closed.* A very formal way of saying **therefore** is **thus**: *There was no money, and thus the youth club could continue no longer.* In spoken and informal English it is more common to use **so**: *There was no money, so the youth club closed.*

ⓘ For more help with writing, look at **Wordpower Writing Tutor** at the back of this dictionary.

therein /ˌðeərˈɪn/ *adv (formal)* because of sth that has just been mentioned □ *di situlah*

thereupon /ˌðeərəˈpɒn/ *adv (formal)* immediately after that and often as the result of sth □ *terus; dgn segera*

thermal[1] /ˈθɜːml/ *adj* [only *before* a noun] **1** connected with heat □ *(berkenaan dgn) haba*: *thermal energy* **2** (used about clothes) made to keep you warm in cold weather □ *panas*: *thermal underwear*

thermal[2] /ˈθɜːml/ *noun* **1** [C] a flow of rising warm air □ *arus udara panas* **2 thermals** [pl] clothes, especially underwear, made to keep you warm in cold weather □ *baju, seluar (dsb) panas*

thermometer /θəˈmɒmɪtə(r)/ *noun* [C] an instrument for measuring the temperature of the air or of sb's body □ *termometer; jangka suhu*

Thermos™ /ˈθɜːməs/ (also ˈThermos flask; BrE also flask) *noun* [C] a type of container used for keeping a liquid hot or cold □ *Thermos*™; *termos* ⊃ look at **vacuum**

thermostat /ˈθɜːməstæt/ *noun* [C] a device that controls the temperature in a house or machine by switching the heat on and off as necessary □ *termostat*

thesaurus /θɪˈsɔːrəs/ *noun* [C] a book that contains lists of words with similar meanings in groups □ *tesaurus*

these plural of **this**

thesis /ˈθiːsɪs/ *noun* [C] (*pl* **theses** /ˈθiːsiːz/) **1** a long piece of writing on a particular subject that you do as part of a university degree □ *tesis*: *He did his thesis on Japanese investment in Europe.* ⊃ look at **dissertation** **2** an idea that is discussed and presented with evidence in order to show that it is true □ *tesis*

they /ðeɪ/ *pron* [the subject of a verb] **1** the people or things that have been mentioned □ *mereka; dia*: *We've got two children. They're both boys.* ◆ *'Have you seen my keys?' 'Yes, they are on the table.'* **2** used instead of *he* or *she* □ *dia*: *Somebody phoned for you but they didn't leave their name.* ⊃ note at **he** **3** people in general or people whose identity is not known or stated □ *mereka; orang*: *They say it's going to be a mild winter.*

they'd /ðeɪd/ *short for* **they had; they would**

they'll /ðeɪl/ *short for* **they will**

they're /ðeə(r)/ *short for* **they are**

they've /ðeɪv/ *short for* **they have**

thick[1] /θɪk/ *adj* (**thicker**; **thickest**)
▶NOT THIN **1** (used about sth solid) having a large distance between its opposite sides; not thin □ *tebal*: *a thick black line* ◆ *a thick coat/book* ◆ *These walls are very thick.* **OPP** **thin** **2** used for saying what the distance is between the two

opposite sides of sth □ *tebalnya*: *The ice was six centimetres thick.*

▶TREES/HAIR **3** growing closely together in large numbers □ *tebal; lebat*: *a thick forest* ♦ *thick hair* **OPP** thin

▶LIQUID **4** that does not flow easily □ *pekat*: *thick cream* ♦ *This paint is too thick.* **OPP** thin

▶CLOUD, FOG, ETC. **5** difficult to see through □ *tebal*: *There'll be a thick fog tonight.* ♦ *thick clouds of smoke*

▶WITH LARGE AMOUNT **6 thick (with sth)** containing a lot of sth/sb close together □ *penuh dgn; banyak*: *The air was thick with dust.* ♦ *The streets were thick with shoppers.*

▶STUPID **7** (*informal*) slow to learn or understand; stupid □ *bebal*: *Are you thick, or what?*

▶ACCENT **8** easily recognized as being from a particular country or area □ *pekat*: *a thick Brooklyn accent* **SYN** strong

IDM **have a thick skin** to be not easily upset or worried by what other people say about you □ *tebal kulit; tdk tahu malu*

▶**thick** *adv*: *Snow lay thick on the ground.* ▶**thickly** *adv*: *Spread the butter thickly.* ♦ *a thickly wooded area*

thick² /θɪk/ *noun*
IDM **in the thick of sth** in the most active or crowded part of sth; very involved in sth □ *sedang sibuk*
through thick and thin all the time, even when there are difficult times and situations □ *susah senang*

thicken /'θɪkən/ *verb* [I,T] to become or to make sth thicker □ *menjadi lebih pekat/tebal*

thickness /'θɪknəs/ *noun* [C,U] the quality of being thick or how thick sth is □ *kepekatan; ketebalan* ⊃ look at **width**

thick-'skinned *adj* not easily worried or upset by what other people say about you □ *tebal kulit*: *Politicians have to be thick-skinned.*

thief /θiːf/ *noun* [C] (*pl* **thieves** /θiːvz/) a person who steals things from another person □ *pencuri* ⊃ note at **steal**: *'Stop thief!' she cried.* ♦ *A thief snatched her handbag containing her wages.*

OTHER WORDS FOR

thief

A **thief** is a general word for a person who steals things, usually secretly and without violence. The name of the crime is **theft**. A **robber** steals from a bank, shop, etc. and often uses violence or threats. A **burglar** steals things by breaking into a house, shop, etc., often at night, and a **shoplifter** goes into a shop when it is open and takes things without paying. A **mugger** steals from somebody in the street and uses violence or threats.

---

thigh /θaɪ/ *noun* [C] the top part of your leg, above your knee □ *paha* ⊃ picture at **body**

thimble /'θɪmbl/ *noun* [C] a small metal or plastic object that you wear on the end of your finger to protect it when you are sewing □ *jidal* ⊃ picture at **sewing**

thin¹ /θɪn/ *adj* (**thinner**; **thinnest**) **1** (used about sth solid) having a small distance between the opposite sides □ *nipis*: *a thin book/shirt* ♦ *a thin slice of meat* **OPP** thick **2** having very little fat on the body □ *kurus*: *You need to eat more. You're too thin!* **OPP** fat **3** that flows easily; not thick □ *nipis*: *a thin sauce* **OPP** thick **4** not growing closely together or in large amounts □ *jarang*: *thin grey hair* **OPP** thick **5** not difficult to see through □ *nipis*: *They fought their way through where the smoke was thinner.* **OPP** thick

IDM **thin on the ground** difficult to find; not common □ *sukar didapati*: *Jobs for people with my skills are fairly thin on the ground these days.*
through thick and thin ⊃ **thick**
vanish, etc. into thin air to disappear completely □ *lenyap sama sekali*
wear thin ⊃ **wear¹**

OTHER WORDS FOR

thin

Thin is the most general word for describing people who have very little fat on their bodies. **Slim** is used about people who are thin in an attractive way: *You're so slim! How do you do it?* If you say a person is **skinny**, you mean that he/she is too thin and not attractive. **Underweight** is a formal word, and is often used in a medical context: *The doctor says I'm underweight.*

▶**thin** *adv*: *Don't slice the onion too thin.*
▶**thinly** *adv*: *thinly sliced bread* ♦ *thinly populated areas*

thin² /θɪn/ *verb* [I,T] (**thinning**; **thinned**) **thin (sth) (out)** to become thinner or fewer in number; to make sth thinner □ *menjadi semakin cair, jarang atau kurang*: *The trees thin out towards the edge of the forest.* ♦ *Thin the sauce by adding milk.*

thing /θɪŋ/ *noun*
▶OBJECT **1** [C] an object that is not named □ *benda*: *What's that red thing on the table?* ♦ *A pen is a thing you use for writing with.* ♦ *I need to get a few things at the shops.*
▶EQUIPMENT **2 things** [pl] clothes or tools that belong to sb or are used for a particular purpose □ *barang; pakaian; perkakas*: *I'll just go and pack my things.* ♦ *We keep all the cooking things in this cupboard.*
▶ACTION/EVENT **3** [C] an action, event or statement □ *perkara; hal*: *When I get home the first thing I do is have a cup of tea.* ♦ *A strange thing happened to me yesterday.* ♦ *What a nice thing to say!*
▶FACT **4** [C] a fact, subject, etc. □ *perkara*: *He told me a few things that I didn't know before.*
▶QUALITY/STATE **5** [C] a quality or state □ *benda; perkara*: *There's no such thing as a ghost* (= it doesn't exist). ♦ *The best thing about my job is the way it changes all the time.*
▶YOUR LIFE **6 things** [pl] the situation or conditions of your life □ *keadaan; kehidupan*: *How are things with you?*

▶WHAT IS NEEDED **7** the thing [sing] exactly what is wanted or needed □ *benda (yg betul-betul dikehendaki atau diperlukan)*: *That's just the thing I was looking for!*

▶PERSON/ANIMAL **8** [C] used for expressing how you feel about a person or an animal □ *digunakan utk menyatakan perasaan ttg sso atau sst binatang*: *You've broken your finger? You poor thing!*

IDM a close shave/thing ➔ close³

be a good thing (that) to be lucky that □ *mujur; nasib baik*: *It's a good thing you remembered your umbrella.*

do your own thing (*informal*) to do what you want to do, without thinking about other people □ *membuat sst mengikut kesukaan sendiri*: *I like to spend time alone, just doing my own thing.*

first/last thing as early/late as possible □ *pagi-pagi; lewat petang*: *I'll phone her first thing tomorrow morning.* ◆ *I saw him last thing on Friday evening.*

for one thing used for introducing a reason for sth □ *pertamanya; lagipun*: *I think we should go by train. For one thing it's cheaper.*

have a thing about sb/sth (*informal*) to have strong feelings about sb/sth □ *tergila-gila akan sso/sst; benci akan sso/sst*

to make matters/things worse ➔ worse

the real thing ➔ real¹

take it/things easy ➔ easy²

think /θɪŋk/ *verb* (*pt, pp* thought /θɔːt/)

▶HAVE OPINION **1** [I,T] think (sth) (of/about sb/sth); think that ... to have a particular idea or opinion about sth/sb; to believe sth □ *fikir; rasa; ingat; berpendapat; pendapat*: *'Do you think (that) we'll win?' 'No, I don't think so.'* ◆ *'Jay's coming tomorrow, isn't he?' 'Yes, I think so.'* ◆ *I think (that) they've moved to York but I'm not sure.* ◆ *What did you think of the film?* ◆ *What do you think about going out tonight?*

▶USE MIND **2** [I] think (about sth) to use your mind to consider sth or to form connected ideas □ *berfikir*: *Think before you speak.* ◆ *What are you thinking about?* ◆ *He had to think hard* (= a lot) *about the question.*

▶IMAGINE **3** [T] to form an idea of sth; to imagine sth □ *memikirkan; fikirkan; membayangkan; bayangkan*: *Just think what we could do with all that money!*

▶EXPECT **4** [T] to expect sth □ *menjangka; dijangka*: *I never thought that I'd see her again.*

▶IN A PARTICULAR WAY **5** [I] to think in a particular way □ *berfikir*: *If you want to be successful, you have to think big.* ◆ *We've got to think positive.*

▶INTEND **6** [I,T] think of/about doing sth; think (that)... to intend or plan to do sth □ *bercadang; rasa*: *We're thinking of moving house.* ◆ *I think (that) I'll go for a swim.*

▶REMEMBER **7** [T] to remember sth; to have sth come into your mind □ *mengingati; ingat; teringat; terfikir*: *Can you think where you left the keys?* ◆ *I didn't think to ask him his name.*

IDM think better of (doing) sth to decide not to do sth; to change your mind □ *tdk jadi (membuat sst)*

think highly, a lot, not much, etc. of sb/sth to have a good, bad, etc. opinion of sb/sth □ *memandang tinggi, rendah, dll akan sso/sst*: *I didn't think much of that film.*

think the world of sb/sth to love and admire sb/sth very much □ *sangat kasih dan memandang tinggi akan sso*

PHR V think about/of sb to consider the feelings of sb else □ *memikirkan (ttg orang lain)*: *She never thinks about anyone but herself.*

think of sth to create an idea in your imagination □ *memikirkan sst*: *Who first thought of the plan?*

think sth out to consider carefully all the details of a plan, idea, etc □ *memikirkan sst dgn teliti*: *a well-thought-out scheme*

think sth over to consider sth carefully □ *memikirkan; mempertimbangkan*: *I'll think your offer over and let you know tomorrow.*

think sth through to consider every detail of sth carefully □ *memikirkan masak-masak*: *He made a bad decision because he didn't think it through.*

think sth up (*informal*) to create sth in your mind; to invent sth □ *memikirkan/mereka sst*: *to think up a new advertising slogan*

OTHER WORDS FOR

think

If you want to give your opinion, you can say '**I think** (that)…', or '**Personally, I think** (that)…', or use another phrase: *In my opinion/As far as I'm concerned/It seems to me that ...* In informal conversation we often use **reckon** to say that something is true or possible: *I reckon (that) I'm going to get that job.* You can use **believe** to talk about something that you feel is morally right or wrong: *She believes (that) killing animals is wrong.* In a formal discussion with somebody you can ask '**What is your opinion of/on/about** ...?', or '**How do you feel about** ...?'.

▶think *noun* (*informal*): *I'm not sure. I'll have to have a think about it.*

thinker /ˈθɪŋkə(r)/ *noun* [C] **1** a person who thinks about serious and important subjects □ *ahli fikir* **2** a person who thinks in a particular way □ *pemikir*: *a quick/creative/clear thinker*

thinking¹ /ˈθɪŋkɪŋ/ *noun* [U] **1** using your mind to think about sth □ *berfikir*: *We're going to have to do some quick thinking.* **2** ideas or opinions about sth □ *pemikiran*: *This accident will make them change their thinking on safety matters.* ➔ look at **wishful thinking**

thinking² /ˈθɪŋkɪŋ/ *adj* [only *before* a noun] intelligent and using your mind to think about important subjects □ *berfikiran*

ˈthink tank *noun* [C] a group of experts who provide advice and ideas on political, social or economic matters □ *kumpulan pemikir dan penasihat*

third¹ /θɜːd/ ordinal number 3rd □ *ketiga; ke-3* ➜ note at **sixth**

third² /θɜːd/ noun [C] **1** ⅓; one of three equal parts of sth □ *satu per tiga;* ⅓ **2** (BrE) a result in final university exams, below first and second class degrees □ *(kelas) tiga*

thirdly /ˈθɜːdli/ adv used to introduce the third point in a list □ *yg ketiga*: *We have made savings in three areas: firstly, defence, secondly, education and thirdly, health.*

third 'party noun [C] a person who is involved in a situation in addition to the two main people involved □ *pihak ketiga*

the Third 'World noun [sing] a way of referring to the poorer countries of Asia, Africa and South America, which is sometimes considered offensive □ *Negara-negara Dunia Ketiga*

> **MORE** Many people now prefer to talk about **developing countries** or **the developing world**.

thirst /θɜːst/ noun **1** [U, sing] the feeling that you have when you want or need a drink □ *(rasa) haus/dahaga; kehausan; kedahagaan*: *Iced tea really quenches your thirst.* ◆ *to die of thirst* **2** [sing] **a thirst for sth** a strong desire for sth □ *haus; dahaga* ➜ look at **hunger**

thirsty /ˈθɜːsti/ adj (**thirstier; thirstiest**) wanting or needing a drink □ *haus; dahaga*: *I'm thirsty. Can I have a drink of water, please?* ➜ look at **hungry** ▸**thirstily** adv

thirteen /ˌθɜːˈtiːn/ number 13 □ *tiga belas; 13* ➜ note at **six** ▸**thirteenth** /ˌθɜːˈtiːnθ/ ordinal number, noun □ *ketiga belas; ke-13* ➜ note at **sixth**

thirty /ˈθɜːti/ number 30 □ *tiga puluh; 30* ➜ note at **sixty** ▸**thirtieth** /ˈθɜːtiəθ/ ordinal number, noun □ *ketiga puluh; ke-30* ➜ note at **sixth**

this /ðɪs/ determiner, pron (pl **these** /ðiːz/) **1** used for talking about sb/sth that is close to you in time or space □ *ini*: *Have a look at this photo.* ◆ *These boots are really comfortable. My old ones weren't.* ◆ *Is this the book you asked for?* ◆ *These are the letters to be filed, not those over there.* ◆ *This chair's softer than that one, so I'll sit here.* **2** used for talking about sth that was mentioned or talked about earlier □ *ini*: *Where did you hear about this?* **3** used for introducing sb or showing sb sth □ *ini*: *This is my wife, Claudia, and these are our children, David and Vicky.* ◆ *It's easier if you do it like this.* **4** (used with days of the week or periods of time) of today or the present week, year, etc. □ *ini*: *Are you busy this afternoon?* ◆ *this Friday* (= the Friday of this week) **5** (informal) (used when you are telling a story) a certain □ *itu (sso/sst tertentu)*: *Then this woman said …* **IDM** **this and that; this, that and the other** (informal) various things □ *itu ini; macam-macam*: *We chatted about this and that.*
▸**this** adv: *The road is not usually this busy.*

thistle /ˈθɪsl/ noun [C] a wild plant with purple flowers and sharp points on its leaves, which is the national symbol of Scotland □ *'thistle'; sejenis pokok dgn bunga berwarna ungu dan daunnya berduri*

thong /θɒŋ/ (AmE) = **flip-flop**

thorn /θɔːn/ noun [C] one of the hard sharp points on some plants and bushes, for example on rose bushes □ *duri* ➜ picture at **plant**

thorny /ˈθɔːni/ adj (**thornier; thorniest**) **1** causing difficulty or disagreement □ *bermasalah*: *a thorny problem/question* **2** having thorns □ *berduri*

thorough /ˈθʌrə/ adj **1** careful and complete □ *teliti dan lengkap*: *The police made a thorough search of the house.* **2** doing things in a very careful way, making sure that you look at every detail □ *teliti*: *Pam is slow but she is very thorough.* ▸**thoroughness** noun [U]: *I admire his thoroughness.*

thoroughbred /ˈθʌrəbred/ noun [C] an animal, especially a horse, of high quality, that has parents that are both of the same breed □ *baka sejati; belima (kuda)* ▸**thoroughbred** adj: *a thoroughbred mare*

thoroughly /ˈθʌrəli/ adv **1** completely; very much □ *betul-betul*: *We thoroughly enjoyed our holiday.* **2** in a careful and complete way □ *dgn teliti*: *to study a subject thoroughly*

those plural of **that**

though /ðəʊ/ conj, adv **1** in spite of the fact that □ *sungguhpun; meskipun*: *Though he had very little money, Neil always managed to dress smartly.* ◆ *She still loved him* **even though** *he had treated her so badly.* **SYN** **although** **2** but □ *tetapi*: *I'll come as soon as I can, though I can't promise to be on time.* **3** however □ *bagaimanapun; tetapi*: *I quite like him. I don't like his wife, though.* ➜ note at **although**
IDM **as though** ➜ **as**

thought¹ past tense, past participle of **think**

thought² /θɔːt/ noun
▸IDEA/OPINION **1** [C] an idea or opinion □ *fikiran; idea; pendapat*: *What are your thoughts on this subject?* ◆ *I've just had a thought* (= an idea).
▸MIND **2 thoughts** [pl] a person's mind and all the ideas that are in it □ *fikiran*: *You are always in my thoughts.*
▸ACT OF THINKING **3** [U] the power or process of thinking □ *berfikir*: *I need to* **give** *this problem* **some thought.** ◆ *You haven't put enough thought into this work.*
▸FEELING OF CARE **4** [C] a feeling of care or worry □ *fikiran; perasaan (baik hati, bimbang, dll)*: *They sent me flowers. What a kind thought!*
▸IN POLITICS, SCIENCE ETC. **5** [U] particular ideas or a particular way of thinking □ *pemikiran*: *a change in medical thought on the subject*
IDM **deep in thought/conversation** ➜ **deep¹**
a school of thought ➜ **school**
second thoughts ➜ **second¹**

ð **t**hen   s **s**o   z **z**oo   ʃ **sh**e   ʒ vi**s**ion   h **h**ow   m **m**an   n **n**o   ŋ si**ng**   l **l**eg   r **r**ed   j **y**es   w **w**et

thoughtful /ˈθɔːtfl/ adj **1** thinking deeply □ *(sedang) berfikir*: *a thoughtful expression* **2** thinking about what other people want or need □ *bertimbang rasa; baik hati*: *It was very thoughtful of you to send her some flowers.* **SYN** kind ▶**thoughtfully** /-fəli/ adv ▶**thoughtfulness** noun [U]

thoughtless /ˈθɔːtləs/ adj not thinking about what other people want or need or what the result of your actions will be □ *tdk berfikir; tdk bertimbang rasa*: *a thoughtless remark* **SYN** inconsiderate ▶**thoughtlessly** adv ▶**thoughtlessness** noun [U]

thousand /ˈθaʊznd/ number 1 000 □ *ribu; seribu; 1000*

> **HELP** Notice that you use **thousand** in the singular when you are talking about a number. You use **thousands** when you mean 'a lot': *There were over seventy thousand spectators at the match.* ◆ *Thousands of people took part in the protest march.*

ⓘ For more information about numbers, look at the section on using numbers at the back of this dictionary.

thousandth¹ /ˈθaʊznθ/ ordinal number 1 000th □ *keseribu; ke-1000*: *the city's thousandth anniversary*

thousandth² /ˈθaʊznθ/ noun [C] 1/1000; one of a thousand equal parts of sth □ *satu per seribu; (¹/₁₀₀₀)*: *one thousandth of a second*

thrash /θræʃ/ verb **1** [T] to hit sb/sth many times with a stick, etc. as a punishment □ *membelasah; menyebat* **2** [I,T] **thrash (sth) (about/around)** to move or make sth move in a wild way without any control □ *meronta-ronta* **3** [T] (*informal*) to defeat sb easily in a game, competition, etc. □ *membelasah; mengalahkan (sso/sst) dgn teruk*: *I thrashed Leo at tennis yesterday.* **PHR V thrash sth out** to talk about sth with sb until you reach an agreement □ *membincangkan sst utk mencapai persetujuan*

thrashing /ˈθræʃɪŋ/ noun [C] **1** the act of hitting sb/sth many times with a stick, etc. as a punishment □ *kena belasah* **2** (*informal*) a bad defeat in a game □ *kalah teruk*

thread¹ /θred/ noun **1** [C,U] a long thin piece of cotton, wool, etc. that you use for sewing or making cloth □ *benang*: *a needle and thread* ➪ picture at **rope, sew, sewing 2** [C] the connection between ideas, the parts of a story, etc. □ *aliran; urutan*: *I've lost the thread of this argument.* **3** [C] a series of connected messages on a **message board** (= a place where a user can write or read messages) on the Internet, which have been sent by different people □ *rentetan; jaringan*

thread² /θred/ verb [T] **1** to put sth long and thin, especially thread, through a narrow opening or hole □ *memasukkan benang, tali pinggang, dll*: *to thread a needle* ◆ *He threaded the belt through the loops on his trousers.* **2** to join things together by putting them onto a string, etc. □ *mengarang; menguntai*: *to thread beads onto a string*

IDM thread your way through sth to move through sth with difficulty, going around things or people that are in your way □ *berjalan dgn susah payah mencelah-celah orang, benda, dsb*

threadbare /ˈθredbeə(r)/ adj (used about cloth or clothes) old and very thin □ *lusuh*

threat /θret/ noun **1** [C] a warning that sb may hurt, kill or punish you if you do not do what they want □ *ugutan; ancaman*: *to make threats against somebody* ◆ *He keeps saying he'll resign, but he won't carry out his threat.* **2** [U, sing] the possibility of trouble or danger □ *terancam*: *The forest is under threat from building developments.* **3** [C] a person or thing that may damage sth or hurt sb; something that indicates future danger □ *ancaman*: *a threat to national security*

threaten /ˈθretn/ verb **1** [T] **threaten sb (with sth); threaten (to do sth)** to warn that you may hurt, kill or punish sb if they do not do what you want □ *mengugut; mengancam*: *The boy threatened him with a knife.* ◆ *She was threatened with dismissal.* ◆ *The man threatened to kill her if she didn't tell him where the money was.* **2** [I,T] to seem likely to do sth unpleasant □ *mengancam; mungkin akan*: *The strong wind was threatening to destroy the bridge.* ▶**threatening** adj: *threatening behaviour* ◆ *I found a threatening message on my answering machine.* ▶**threateningly** adv

three /θriː/ number **1** 3 □ *tiga*; 3 ➪ note at **six 2** [in compounds] having three of the thing mentioned □ *tiga*: *a three-legged stool* ➪ look at **third**

three-diˈmensional (also ˌ3-ˈD) adj having, or appearing to have, length, width and height □ *tiga dimensi/matra*: *a three-dimensional model* ◆ *These glasses allow you to see the film in 3-D.*

threshold /ˈθreʃhəʊld/ noun [C] **1** the ground at the entrance to a room or building □ *ambang* **2** the level at which sth starts to happen □ *had; tahap*: *Young children have a low boredom threshold.* **3** the time when you are just about to start sth or find sth □ *ambang*: *We could be on the threshold of a scientific breakthrough.*

threw past tense of **throw**

thrift /θrɪft/ noun [U] the quality of being careful not to spend too much money □ *berjimat cermat* ▶**thrifty** adj

thrill /θrɪl/ noun [C] a sudden strong feeling of pleasure or excitement □ *keseronokan* ▶**thrill** verb [T]: *His singing thrilled the audience.* ▶**thrilled** adj: *He was thrilled with my present.* ▶**thrilling** adj

thriller /ˈθrɪlə(r)/ noun [C] a play, film, book, etc. with a very exciting story, often about a crime □ *cerita saspens (drama, filem, buku, dsb)*

thrive → throw 892

thrive /θraɪv/ verb [I] to grow or develop well □ *berkembang maju* ▶**thriving** adj: *a thriving industry*

throat /θrəʊt/ noun [C] **1** the front part of your neck □ *leher*: *The attacker grabbed the man by the throat.* ⊃ picture at **body 2** the back part of your mouth and the passage down your neck through which air and food pass □ *tekak; kerongkong*: *She got a piece of bread stuck in her throat.* ♦ *I've got a sore throat.* ⊃ picture at **body** **IDM** clear your throat ⊃ clear² have/feel a lump in your throat ⊃ lump¹

throb /θrɒb/ verb [I] (**throbbing; throbbed**) to make strong regular movements or noises; to beat strongly □ *berdenyut-denyut*: *Her finger throbbed with pain.* ▶**throb** noun [C]

thrombosis /θrɒmˈbəʊsɪs/ noun [C,U] (pl **thromboses** /-siːz/) a serious condition caused by a blood **clot** (= a thick mass of blood) forming in the heart or in a tube that carries blood □ *trombosis* ⊃ look at **deep vein thrombosis**

throne /θrəʊn/ noun **1** [C] the special chair where a king or queen sits □ *singgahsana* **2** the **throne** [sing] the position of being king or queen □ *takhta*

throng¹ /θrɒŋ/ (*AmE* usually /) noun [C] (formal) a large crowd of people □ *kumpulan orang ramai*

throng² /θrɒŋ/ (*AmE* usually /) verb [I,T] (formal) (used about a crowd of people) to move into or fill a particular place □ *berpusu-pusu; penuh sesak*: *Crowds were thronging into the square, keen to catch a glimpse of the band.*

throttle¹ /ˈθrɒtl/ verb [T] to hold sb tightly by the throat and stop them breathing □ *mencekik* **SYN** strangle

throttle² /ˈθrɒtl/ noun [C] the part in a vehicle that controls the speed by controlling how much fuel goes into the engine □ *pendikit*

through /θruː/ prep, adv **1** from one end or side of sth to the other □ *melalui; menembusi*: *We drove through the centre of London.* ♦ *to look through a telescope* ♦ *She cut through the rope.* ♦ *to push through a crowd of people* **2** from the beginning to the end of sth □ *sepanjang; dr awal hingga akhir*: *Food supplies will not last through the winter.* ♦ *We're halfway through the book.* ♦ *He read the letter through and handed it back.* **3** past a limit, stage or test □ *lalu; lulus*: *He lifted the rope to let us through.* ♦ *She didn't get through the first interview.* **4** (also informal **thru**) (*AmE*) until, and including □ *hingga; sampai*: *They are staying Monday through Friday.* **5** because of; with the help of □ *kerana; melalui*: *Errors were made through bad organization.* ♦ *David got the job through his uncle.* **6** (*BrE*) connected by telephone □ *menyambung*: *Can you put me through to extension 5678, please?*
PHR V be through (with sb/sth) to have finished with sb/sth □ *putus (hubungan, dsb dgn sso/sst)*

throughout /θruːˈaʊt/ adv, prep **1** in every part of sth □ *seluruhnya*: *The house is beautifully decorated throughout.* ♦ *The match can be watched live on TV throughout the world.* **2** from the beginning to the end of sth □ *sepanjang (masa, dll)*: *We didn't enjoy the holiday, because it rained throughout.*

throw /θrəʊ/ verb (pt **threw** /θruː/; pp **thrown** /θrəʊn/)
▶WITH HAND **1** [I,T] **throw** (sth) (to/at sb); **throw sb sth** to send sth from your hand through the air by moving your hand or arm quickly □ *membaling; melontar*: *How far can you throw?* ♦ *Throw the ball to me.* ♦ *Throw me the ball.* ♦ *Don't throw stones at people.*
▶PUT CARELESSLY **2** [T] to put sth somewhere quickly or carelessly □ *mencampakkan; menghumban; melemparkan*: *He threw his bag down in a corner.* ♦ *She threw on a sweater and ran out of the door.*
▶MOVE WITH FORCE **3** [T] to move your body or part of it quickly or suddenly □ *menghempaskan diri; mendongakkan kepala*: *Jenny threw herself onto the bed and sobbed.* ♦ *Lee threw back his head and roared with laughter.*
▶MAKE SB FALL **4** [T] to cause sb to fall down quickly or violently □ *menghumban; terhumban*: *The bus braked and we were thrown to the floor.*
▶PUT IN SITUATION **5** [T] to put sb in a particular (usually unpleasant) situation □ *menjadi; menyebabkan*: *We were thrown into confusion by the news.*
▶UPSET/CONFUSE **6** [T] (informal) to make sb feel upset, confused or surprised □ *membuat sso terganggu, bingung atau terkejut*: *The question threw me and I didn't know what to reply.*
▶LIGHT/SHADE **7** [T] to send light or shade onto sth □ *melemparkan (cahaya atau bayang-bayang)*: *The tree threw a long shadow across the lawn in the late afternoon.*
PHR V throw sth away **1** (also throw sth out) to get rid of rubbish or sth that you do not want □ *membuang sst*: *I threw his letters away.* **2** to waste or not use sth useful □ *mensia-siakan*: *to throw away an opportunity*

throw sth in (informal) to include sth extra without increasing the price □ *sst (barang tambahan) yg diberi secara percuma*

throw sb out to force sb to leave a place □ *mengusir/menghalau sso*

throw sth out **1** to decide not to accept sb's idea or suggestion □ *menolak sst* **2** = throw sth away (1)

throw up (informal) to be sick □ *muntah* **SYN** vomit

throw sth up **1** (informal) to be sick □ *memuntahkan*: *The baby's thrown up her dinner.* **SYN** vomit **2** to produce or show sth □ *menghasilkan*: *Our research has thrown up some interesting facts.* **3** to leave your job, career, studies, etc. □ *melepaskan* ▶**throw** noun [C]: *It's your turn to throw (= it's your turn to throw the dice in a board game, etc.).* ♦ *a throw of 97 metres*

thru (*AmE*) = **through** (4)

thrust¹ /θrʌst/ *verb* [I,T] (*pt, pp* thrust) **1** to push sb/sth suddenly or violently; to move quickly and suddenly in a particular direction □ *menolak; memasukkan; merempuh; meredah*: *The man thrust his hands deeper into his pockets.* ♦ *She thrust past him and ran out of the room.* **2** to make a sudden forward movement with a knife, etc. □ *merodok*

PHR V **thrust sb/sth upon sb** to force sb to accept or deal with sb/sth □ *memaksa sso menerima atau berurusan dgn sso/sst*

thrust² /θrʌst/ *noun* **1** the thrust [sing] the main part or point of an argument, policy, etc. □ *teras; inti sari* **2** [C] a sudden strong movement forward □ *tolakan; tujahan*

thud /θʌd/ *noun* [C] the low sound that is made when a heavy object hits sth else □ *bunyi berdebap*: *She fell to the ground and her head hit the floor with a dull thud.* ▶ **thud** *verb* [I] (thudding; thudded)

thug /θʌɡ/ *noun* [C] a violent person who may harm other people □ *samseng; penjahat*

thumb¹ /θʌm/ *noun* [C] **1** the short thick finger at the side of each hand □ *ibu jari*: *She sucks her thumb.* ➲ note at **finger** ➲ picture at **body** **2** the part of a glove, etc. that covers your thumb □ *bahagian ibu jari*

IDM **have green fingers/a green thumb** ➲ **green¹**

a rule of thumb ➲ **rule¹**

stand/stick out like a sore thumb ➲ **sore¹**

the thumbs up/down a sign or an expression that shows approval/disapproval □ *isyarat atau ungkapan yg menandakan persetujuan/tdk bersetuju*

under sb's thumb (used about a person) completely controlled by sb □ *di bawah telunjuk sso*: *She's got him under her thumb.*

thumb² /θʌm/ *verb* [I,T] **thumb (through) sth** to turn the pages of a book, etc. quickly □ *menyelak-nyelak muka surat buku, dsb*

IDM **thumb a lift/ride** to hold out your thumb to cars going past, to ask sb to give you a free ride □ *meminta tumpang* ➲ note at **hitchhike**

thumbtack /ˈθʌmtæk/ (*AmE*) = **drawing pin**

thump /θʌmp/ *verb* **1** [T] to hit sb/sth hard with sth, usually your **fist** (= closed hand) □ *mendebuk; memukul*: *He started coughing and Jo thumped him on the back.* **2** [I,T] to make a loud sound by hitting sth or by beating hard □ *berdebak-debuk*: *His heart was thumping with excitement.* ▶ **thump** *noun* [C]

thunder¹ /ˈθʌndə(r)/ *noun* [U] the loud noise in the sky that you can hear when there is a storm □ *guruh; petir*: *a clap/crash/roll of thunder* ➲ note at **storm** ➲ look at **lightning**

thunder² /ˈθʌndə(r)/ *verb* [I] **1** when it thunders, there is a loud noise in the sky during a storm □ *guruh berbunyi*: *The rain poured down and it started to thunder.* **2** to make a loud deep noise like **thunder** □ *bergemuruh*: *Traffic thundered across the bridge.*

thunderstorm /ˈθʌndəstɔːm/ *noun* [C] a storm with thunder and **lightning** (= flashes of light in the sky) □ *ribut petir* ➲ note at **storm**

Thur. (also **Thurs.**) *abbr* = **Thursday** □ *Khamis*: *Thur. 26 September*

Thursday /ˈθɜːzdeɪ; -di/ *noun* [C,U] (*abbr* **Thur.; Thurs.**) the day of the week after Wednesday □ *Khamis* ➲ note at **Monday**

thus /ðʌs/ *adv* (*formal*) **1** like this; in this way □ *begini; demikian*: *Thus began the series of incidents which changed her life.* **2** because of or as a result of this □ *oleh itu; dgn demikian*: *He is the eldest son and thus heir to the throne.* ➲ note at **therefore**

thwart /θwɔːt/ *verb* [T] **thwart sth; thwart sb (in sth)** to stop sb doing what they planned to do; to prevent sth happening □ *mencegah; menghalang*: *to thwart somebody's plans/ambitions/efforts* ♦ *She was thwarted in her attempt to gain control.*

thyme /taɪm/ *noun* [U] a **herb** (= a type of plant) that is used in cooking and has small leaves and a sweet smell □ *'thyme' (sejenis herba)* ➲ picture on page P14

tic /tɪk/ *noun* [C] a sudden quick movement of a muscle, especially in your face or head, that you cannot control □ *gerenyet*: *He has a nervous tic.*

tick¹ /tɪk/ *verb* **1** [I] (used about a clock or watch) to make regular short sounds □ *berdetik* **2** (*AmE* **check**) [T] to put a mark (✓) next to a name, an item on a list, etc. to show that sb/sth has been dealt with or chosen, or that sth is correct □ *membubuh tanda rait; menandakan*: *Please tick the appropriate box.*

IDM **what makes sb/sth tick** the reasons why sb behaves or sth works in the way he/she/it does □ *apa yg membuat sso berperilaku tertentu; mengapa sst berfungsi, dsb sedemikian*: *He has a strong interest in people and what makes them tick.*

PHR V **tick away/by** (used about time) to pass □ *(masa) berlalu*

tick sb/sth off to put a mark (✓) next to a name, an item on a list, etc. to show that sth has been done or sb has been dealt with □ *membubuh tanda rait pd nama sso/sst (dlm senarai, dsb)*

tick over [usually used in the continuous tenses] (*informal*) **1** (used about an engine) to run slowly while the vehicle is not moving □ *(berkenaan dgn enjin) hidup* **2** to keep working slowly without producing or achieving very much □ *terus berjalan ala kadar*

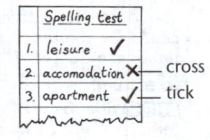

tick

Spelling test	
1. leisure	✓
2. accomodation	✗ — cross
3. apartment	✓ — tick

tick² /tɪk/ noun 1 [C] (AmE check mark; check) a mark (✓) next to an item on a list that shows that sth has been done or next to an answer to show that it is correct □ *tanda rait*: *Put a tick after each correct answer.* 2 [U] (also **ticking**) the regular short sound that a watch or clock makes when it is working □ *bunyi detik; detikan* 3 (BrE informal) a moment □ *detik; sebentar*

ticket /'tɪkɪt/ noun [C] 1 a ticket (for/to sth) a piece of paper or card that shows you have paid for a journey, or allows you to enter a theatre, cinema, etc. □ *tiket*: *two tickets for the Cup Final* ♦ *I'd like a single/return ticket to London.* ♦ *a ticket office/machine/collector* ♦ *I always buy a lottery ticket* ⇒ look at **season ticket** ⇒ picture at **label** 2 a piece of paper fastened to sth in a shop that shows its price, size, etc. □ *label* 3 an official piece of paper that you get when you have parked illegally or driven too fast telling you that you must pay money as a punishment □ *surat saman*: *a parking ticket*
IDM just the job/ticket ⇒ **job**

ticking /'tɪkɪŋ/ = tick²(2)

tickle /'tɪkl/ verb 1 [T] to touch sb lightly with your fingers or with sth soft so that they laugh □ *menggeletek*: *She tickled the baby's toes.* 2 [I,T] to produce or to have an uncomfortable feeling in a part of your body □ *membuat rasa geli atau gatal*: *The woollen scarf tickled her neck.* ♦ *My nose tickles/is tickling.* 3 [T] (informal) to amuse and interest sb □ *menggelikan hati*: *That joke really tickled me.* ▶ **tickle** noun [C]

ticklish /'tɪklɪʃ/ adj if a person is **ticklish**, they laugh when sb tickles them □ *mudah geli*: *Are you ticklish?*

tic-tac-toe /ˌtɪk tæk 'təʊ/ (AmE) = **noughts and crosses**

tidal /'taɪdl/ adj connected with the **tides** of the sea □ *(berkenaan dgn) pasang surut*: *tidal forces* ♦ *a tidal river*

'tidal wave noun [C] a very large wave in the sea which destroys things when it reaches the land, and is often caused by an **earthquake** (= a violent movement of the earth's surface) □ *ombak gadang* ⇒ look at **tsunami**

tidbit /'tɪdbɪt/ (AmE) = **titbit**

tide¹ /taɪd/ noun 1 [C,U] the regular change in the level of the sea caused by the moon and the sun. At **high tide** the sea is closer to the land, at **low tide** it is further away and more of the beach can be seen □ *(air) pasang surut*: *The tide is coming in/going out.* ⇒ note at **ebb** 2 [C, usually sing] the way that most people think or feel about sth at a particular time □ *aliran/arus pendapat umum*: *It appears that the tide has turned in the government's favour.*

tide² /taɪd/ verb
PHR V tide sb over to give sb sth to help them through a difficult time □ *menolong sso utk sementara waktu*

tidy¹ /'taɪdi/ adj (**tidier; tidiest**) 1 (especially BrE) arranged with everything in good order □ *kemas; rapi; teratur*: *If you keep your room tidy, it is easier to find things.* 2 (used about a person) liking to keep things in good order □ *kemas; teratur*: *Mark is a very tidy boy.* **SYN** for both meanings **neat** **OPP** for both meanings **untidy** ▶ **tidily** adv ▶ **tidiness** noun [U]

tidy² /'taɪdi/ verb [I,T] (**tidying; tidies**; pt, pp **tidied**) **tidy (sth) (up)** to make sth look in order and well arranged □ *mengemaskan; berkemas*: *We must tidy this room up before the visitors arrive.*
PHR V tidy sth away to put sth into the drawer, cupboard, etc. where it is kept so that it cannot be seen □ *menyimpan sst (supaya kemas)*

tie¹ /taɪ/ verb (**tying; ties**; pt, pp **tied**) 1 [T] to fasten sb/sth or fix sb/sth in position with rope, string, etc.; to make a knot in sth □ *mengikat; diikat*: *The prisoner was tied to a chair.* ♦ *Kay tied her hair back with a ribbon.* ♦ *to tie something in a knot* ♦ *to tie your shoelaces* **OPP** **untie** 2 [T, usually passive] **tie sb (to sth/to doing sth)** to limit sb's freedom and make them unable to do everything they want to □ *terikat*: *I don't want to be tied to staying in this country permanently.* 3 [I] **tie (with sb) (for sth)** to have the same number of points as another player or team at the end of a game or competition □ *seri*: *England tied with Italy for third place.*
IDM your hands are tied ⇒ **hand¹**
PHR V tie sb/yourself down to limit sb's/your freedom □ *membuat sso terikat*: *Having young children really ties you down.*
tie in (with sth) to agree with other facts or information that you have; to match □ *selaras/bersesuaian (dgn sst)*: *The new evidence seems to tie in with your theory.*
tie sb/sth up 1 to fix sb/sth in position with rope, string, etc. □ *mengikat sso/sst*: *The dog was tied up in the back garden.* **OPP** **untie** 2 [usually passive] to keep sb busy □ *sibuk*: *Mr Jones is tied up in a meeting.*

tie² /taɪ/ noun [C] 1 (AmE also **necktie**) a long thin piece of cloth worn round the neck, especially by men, with a knot at the front. A tie is usually worn with a shirt □ *tali leher*: *a striped silk tie* ⇒ look at **bow tie** ⇒ picture on page **P1** 2 [usually pl] a strong connection between people or organizations □ *pertalian; hubungan*: *personal/emotional ties* ♦ *family ties* 3 something that limits your freedom □ *ikatan; terikat*: *He never married because he didn't want any ties.* 4 a situation in a game or competition in which two or more teams or players get the same score □ *(keputusan) seri*: *There was a tie for first place.*

tier /tɪə(r)/ noun [C] one of a number of levels □ *tingkat*: *The seating is arranged in tiers.* ♦ *a wedding cake with three tiers*

tiger /'taɪgə(r)/ noun [C] a large wild cat that has yellow fur with black lines. **Tigers** live in parts of Asia. □ *harimau* ⇒ picture at **lion**

MORE A female tiger is called a **tigress** and a baby is called a **cub**.

tight /taɪt/ adj (tighter; tightest) adv

▸FIRM **1** fixed firmly in position and difficult to move or open □ *ketat: a tight knot* ◆ *Keep a tight grip/hold on this rope.* ◆ *Hold tight so that you don't fall off.*

HELP **Tightly**, not **tight**, is used before a past participle: *The van was tightly packed with boxes.* ◆ *The van was packed tight with boxes.*

▸CLOTHES **2** fitting very closely in a way that is often uncomfortable □ *ketat; sendat; sempit: These shoes hurt. They're too tight.* ◆ *a tight-fitting skirt* **OPP** loose

▸CONTROL **3** controlled very strictly and firmly □ *ketat: Security is very tight at the airport.*

▸STRETCHED **4** stretched or pulled hard so that it cannot be stretched further □ *tegang: The rope was stretched tight.*

▸BUSY/FULL **5** not having much free time or space □ *ketat; sibuk: My schedule this week is very tight.*

▸-TIGHT **6** -tight [in compounds] not allowing sth to get in or out □ *kedap: an airtight/watertight container* ▸**tightly** adv: *Screw the lid on tightly.* ◆ *She kept her eyes tightly closed.* ▸**tightness** noun [U]

tighten /ˈtaɪtn/ verb [I,T] tighten (sth) (up)

to become or to make sth tight or tighter □ *menge-tatkan: His grip on her arm tightened.* ◆ *He tightened the screws as far as they would go.*

IDM **tighten your belt** to spend less money because you have less than usual available □ *mengikat perut; berjimat*

PHR V **tighten up (on) sth** to cause sth to become stricter □ *memperketat/mengetatkan sst: to tighten up security/a law*

tightrope /ˈtaɪtrəʊp/ noun [C]

a rope or wire that is stretched high above the ground on which people walk, especially as a form of entertainment □ *tali yg direntang tegang*

tights /taɪts/ (AmE pantyhose) noun [pl]

a piece of thin clothing, usually worn by women, that fits tightly from the waist over the legs and feet □ *tait; seluar sendat: a pair of tights* ⇨ look at **stocking** ⇨ picture on **page P1**

tile /taɪl/ noun [C]

one of the flat, usually square, objects that are arranged in rows to cover roofs, floors, bathroom walls, etc. □ *jubin* ⇨ picture on **page P8** ▸**tile** verb [T]: *a tiled bathroom*

till¹ /tɪl/ (informal) = until: *We're open till 6 o'clock.* ◆ *Just wait till you see it. It's great.*

till² /tɪl/ (also ˈcash register) noun [C]

the machine or drawer where money is kept in a shop, etc. □ *mesin daftar tunai; laci duit: Please pay at the till.*

tilt /tɪlt/ verb [I,T]

to move, or make sth move, into a position with one end or side higher than the other □ *menyengetkan; menyendengkan: The front seats of the car tilt forward.* ◆ *She tilted her head to one side.* ▸**tilt** noun [sing]

timber /ˈtɪmbə(r)/ noun

1 (especially AmE **lumber**) [U] wood that is going to be used for building □ *kayu (papan, dsb)* **2** [C] a large piece of wood □ *kayu: roof timbers*

time¹ /taɪm/ noun

▸HOURS, YEARS, ETC. **1** [U, sing] a period of minutes, hours, days, etc. □ *masa: As time passed and there was still no news, we got more worried.* ◆ *You're wasting time—get on with your work!* ◆ *I'll go by car to save time.* ◆ *free/spare time* ◆ *We haven't got time to stop now.* ◆ *I've been waiting a long time.* ◆ *Learning a language takes time.* **2** [U,C] **time (to do sth); time (for sth)** the time in hours and minutes shown on a clock; the moment when sth happens or should happen □ *pukul; jam; waktu; masa: What's the time?/What time is it?* ◆ *Can you tell me the times of trains to Mumbai, please?* ◆ *It's time to go home.* ◆ *By the time I get home, Mark will have cooked the dinner.* ◆ *This time tomorrow I'll be on the plane.* ◆ *It's time for lunch.* ◆ *He never takes any time off* (= time spent not working). **3** [U] a system for measuring time in a particular part of the world □ *waktu: 11 o'clock local time*

▸PERIOD **4** [C] a period in the past; a part of history □ *zaman; masa: In Shakespeare's times, few people could read.* ◆ *The 19th century was a time of great industrial change.*

▸OCCASION/EVENT **5** [C] an occasion when you do sth or when sth happens □ *kali: I phoned them three times.* ◆ *I'll do it better next time.* ◆ *Last time I saw him, he looked ill.* ◆ *How many times have I told you not to touch that?* **6** [C] an event or an occasion that you experience in a certain way □ *masa: Have a good time tonight.* ◆ *We had a terrible time at the hospital.*

▸FOR RACE **7** [C,U] the number of minutes, etc., taken to complete a race or an event □ *masa: What was his time in the hundred metres?*

IDM **(and) about time (too); (and) not before time** (informal) used to say that sth should already have happened □ *sudah tiba masanya*

ahead of your time ⇨ **ahead**

all the time/the whole time during the period that sb was doing sth or that sth was happening □ *sepanjang masa; selama ini; sentiasa: I searched everywhere for my keys and they were in the door all the time.*

at the same time ⇨ **same**

at a time on each occasion □ *setiap kali; sekali: The lift can hold six people at a time.* ◆ *She ran down the stairs two at a time.*

at one time in the past □ *pd suatu masa dahulu* **SYN** previously

at the time at a particular moment or period in the past; then □ *pd masa itu: I agreed at the time but later changed my mind.*

at times sometimes □ *ada masanya; kadangkala: At times I wish we'd never moved house.* **SYN** occasionally

before your time before you were born, or before you lived, worked, etc. somewhere □ *sebelum zaman sso*

behind the times not modern or fashionable ▫ *ketinggalan zaman*
bide your time ➪ **bide**
buy time ➪ **buy¹**
for the time being just for the present; not for long ▫ *buat masa ini; buat sementara ini*
from time to time sometimes; not often ▫ *dr semasa ke semasa; sekali-sekala*
give sb a hard time ➪ **hard¹**
have a hard time doing sth ➪ **hard¹**
have no time for sb/sth to not like sb/sth ▫ *tdk ada masa utk sso/sst*: *I have no time for lazy people.*
have the time of your life (*informal*) to enjoy yourself very much ▫ *betul-betul seronok*
in the course of time ➪ **course**
in good time early; at the right time ▫ *awal; cepat*
in the nick of time ➪ **nick¹**
in time (for sth/to do sth) not late; with enough time to be able to do sth ▫ *sempat; tepat pd waktunya*: *Don't worry. We'll get to the station in time for your train.*
it's about/high time (*informal*) used to say that you think sb should do sth very soon ▫ *memang masanya pun*: *It's about time you told him what's going on.*
on time not too late or too early ▫ *tepat pd masanya*: *The train left the station on time.*

> **HELP** **In time** or **on time**? If you arrive **in time**, you arrive either before or at the correct time. If you arrive **on time**, you arrive at exactly the correct time: *I arrived at the station at 6.55, in time for the train, which left on time, at 7.00.*

once upon a time ➪ **once**
one at a time ➪ **one¹**
take your time to do sth without hurrying ▫ *tdk perlu terburu-buru*
tell the time ➪ **tell**
time after time; time and (time) again again and again ▫ *berkali-kali; banyak kali* SYN **repeatedly**

time² /taɪm/ *verb* [T] **1** [often passive] to arrange to do sth or arrange for sth to happen at a particular time ▫ *menjadualkan; mengatur/menetapkan/memilih masa*: *Their request was badly timed* (= *it came at the wrong time*). ◆ *She timed her arrival for shortly after three.* **2** to measure how long sb/sth takes ▫ *mengukur masa*: *Try timing yourself when you write your essay.*

EXAM TIP

Time yourself

A sure way to get a poor mark in an exam is not to answer enough questions. Make sure that you read through all the instructions at the beginning to find out how many questions you have to answer. Then you can work out how much time you can spend on each part.

'time-consuming *adj* that takes or needs a lot of time ▫ *memakan banyak masa*

'time lag = **lag²**

timeless /'taɪmləs/ *adj* (*formal*) that does not seem to be changed by time or affected by changes in fashion ▫ *tdk lapuk dek zaman*

'time limit *noun* [C] a time during which sth must be done ▫ *had masa*: *We have to set a time limit for the work.*

timely /'taɪmli/ *adj* happening at exactly the right time ▫ *tepat pd masanya*

timer /'taɪmə(r)/ *noun* [C] a person or machine that measures time ▫ *penjaga masa; penentu masa; pemasa*: *an oven timer*

times¹ /taɪmz/ *prep* (*symbol* ×) used when you are multiplying one figure by another ▫ *kali; darab*: *Three times four is twelve.*

times² /taɪmz/ *noun* [pl] used for comparing amounts ▫ *kali*: *Cherries are three times more expensive in England than in Spain.*

timetable /'taɪmteɪbl/ (*AmE* **schedule**) *noun* [C] **1** a list that shows the times at which sth happens ▫ *jadual waktu*: *a bus/train/school timetable* **2** a plan of when you hope or expect particular events to happen ▫ *jadual*: *I have a busy timetable this week* (= *I have planned to do many things*).

timid /'tɪmɪd/ *adj* easily frightened; shy and nervous ▫ *mudah takut; pemalu*: *as timid as a rabbit* ▶ **timidity** /tɪ'mɪdəti/ *noun* [U] ▶ **timidly** *adv*

timing /'taɪmɪŋ/ *noun* [U] **1** the time when sth is planned to happen ▫ *(pengaturan) masa; mengaturkan masa*: *The manager was careful about the timing of his announcement.* **2** the skill of doing sth at exactly the right time ▫ *penentuan masa*: *The timing of her speech was perfect.*

timpani /'tɪmpəni/ *noun* [pl] a set of large metal drums (also called **kettledrums**) ▫ *timpani (gendang)* ▶ **timpanist** /-nɪst/ *noun* [C]

tin /tɪn/ *noun* **1** [U] (*symbol* Sn) a soft silver-white metal that is often mixed with other metals ▫ *timah*: *a tin mine* **2** (also ,tin 'can; especially *AmE* can) [C] a closed metal container in which food, paint, etc. is stored and sold; the contents of one of these containers ▫ *tin; setin*: *a tin of peas/beans/soup* ◆ *a tin of paint/varnish* ➪ note at **can²** ➪ picture at **container 3** [C] a metal container with a lid for keeping food in ▫ *tin*: *a biscuit/cake tin* ▶ **tinned** *adj*: *tinned peaches/peas/soup*

tinfoil /'tɪnfɔɪl/ = **foil¹**

tinge /tɪndʒ/ *noun* [C, usually sing] a small amount of a colour or a feeling ▫ *sedikit*: *a tinge of sadness* ▶ **tinged** *adj* **tinged (with sth)**: *Her joy at leaving was tinged with regret.*

tingle /'tɪŋgl/ *verb* [I] (used about a part of the body) to feel as if a lot of small sharp points are pushing into it ▫ *menggelenyar*: *His cheeks tingled as he came in from the cold.* ▶ **tingle** *noun*

tinker /ˈtɪŋkə(r)/ verb [I] **tinker (with sth)** to try to repair or improve sth without having the proper skill or knowledge □ *menggodek-godek; cuba-cuba membaiki sst*

tinkle /ˈtɪŋkl/ verb [I] to make a light high ringing sound, like that of a small bell □ *berkelenting* ▶ **tinkle** noun [C, usually sing]

ˈtin opener (especially AmE ˈcan opener) noun [C] a tool that you use for opening a tin of food □ *pembuka tin* ⊃ picture at **kitchen**

tinsel /ˈtɪnsl/ noun [U] long strings of material like metal, used as a decoration to hang on a Christmas tree □ *jurai kertas berkilat utk hiasan pokok Krismas*

tint /tɪnt/ noun [C] a shade or a small amount of a colour □ *seri warna*: *white paint with a pinkish tint* ▶ **tint** verb [T]: *tinted glasses* ♦ *She had her hair tinted.*

tiny /ˈtaɪni/ adj (tinier; tiniest) very small □ *sangat kecil*: *the baby's tiny fingers*

tip¹ /tɪp/ noun [C]
▶END OF STH **1** the thin or pointed end of sth □ *hujung*: *the tips of your toes/fingers* ♦ *the tip of your nose* ♦ *the southernmost tip of South America*
▶ADVICE **2 a tip (on/for sth/doing sth)** a small piece of useful advice about sth practical □ *petua*: *useful tips on how to save money*
▶MONEY **3** a small amount of extra money that you give to sb who serves you, for example in a restaurant □ *tip; saguhati*: *to leave a tip for the waiter* ♦ *I gave the porter a $5 tip.*
▶FOR RUBBISH **4** (BrE) (also ˈrubbish tip) a place where you can take rubbish and leave it □ *tempat buang sampah*: *We took the old furniture to the tip.* **SYN** dump
▶UNTIDY PLACE **5** (BrE informal) a place that is very dirty or untidy □ *tempat yg kotor atau selekeh*: *The house was a tip!*
IDM **on the tip of your tongue** if a word or name is **on the tip of your tongue**, you are sure that you know it but you cannot remember it □ *memang tahu tetapi tdk ingat*
the tip of the iceberg only a small part of a much larger problem □ *bahagian kecil drpd sst yg jauh lebih besar*

tip² /tɪp/ verb (tipping; tipped) **1** [I,T] **tip (sth) (up)** to move so that one side is higher than the other; to make sth move in this way □ *menjongketkan; terjongket; mencondongkan*: *When I stood up, the bench tipped up and the person on the other end fell off.* **2** [T] to make sth come out of a container by holding or lifting it at an angle □ *mencurahkan*: *Tip the dirty water down the drain.* ♦ *The child tipped all the toys onto the floor.* **3** [I,T] to give sb a small amount of extra money (in addition to the normal charge) to thank them for a service □ *memberi tip/sagu hati*: *She tipped the taxi driver generously.* **4** [T] **tip sb/sth (as sth/to do sth)** to think or say that sb/sth is likely to do sth □ *meramalkan; menelah*: *This horse is tipped to win the race.* ♦ *He is widely tipped as the next leader of the Labour Party.*
PHR V **tip sb off** (informal) to give sb secret information □ *memberi maklumat sulit ttg sst*
tip (sth) up/over to fall or turn over; to make sth do this □ *menterbalikkan sst*: *An enormous wave crashed into the little boat and it tipped over.*

ˈtip-off noun [C] secret information that sb gives, for example to the police, about an illegal activity that is going to happen □ *maklumat sulit*: *Acting on a tip-off, the police raided the house.*

tiptoe¹ /ˈtɪptəʊ/ noun
IDM **on tiptoe(s)** standing or walking on the ends of your toes with the back part of your foot off the ground, in order not to make any noise or to reach sth high up □ *berjengket-jengket*

tiptoe² /ˈtɪptəʊ/ verb [I] to walk on your toes with the back part of your foot off the ground □ *berjalan berjengket-jengket*

tire¹ /ˈtaɪə(r)/ verb [I,T] to feel that you need to rest or sleep; to make sb feel like this □ *berasa/menjadi penat; memenatkan*: *Now that he's over 60, he tires easily.*
PHR V **tire of sth/sb** to become bored or not interested in sth/sb any more □ *bosan/jemu akan sst/sso*: *I'll never tire of living here.*
tire sb/yourself out to make sb/yourself very tired □ *memenatkan sso/diri sendiri*: *The long country walk tired us all out.* **SYN** exhaust

tire² /ˈtaɪə(r)/ (AmE) = tyre

tired /ˈtaɪəd/ adj feeling that you need to rest or sleep □ *berasa penat*: *She was tired after a hard day's work.* ♦ *They were cold, hungry and tired out* (= very tired). ⊃ note at **sleep**
IDM **be tired of sb/sth/doing sth** to be bored with or annoyed by sb/sth/doing sth □ *bosan atau jemu dgn sso/sst/melakukan sst*: *I'm tired of this game. Let's play something else.* ♦ *I'm sick and tired of listening to the same thing again and again.*
▶ **tiredness** noun [U]

tireless /ˈtaɪələs/ adj putting a lot of hard work and energy into sth over a long period of time without stopping or losing interest □ *bersungguh-sungguh; tdk henti-henti; tdk mengenal penat*

tiresome /ˈtaɪəsəm/ adj (formal) that makes you angry or bored; annoying □ *menjemukan; menyusahkan; menyakitkan hati*

tiring /ˈtaɪərɪŋ/ adj making you want to rest or sleep □ *meletihkan; memenatkan*: *a tiring journey/job* **SYN** exhausting

tissue /ˈtɪʃuː/ (BrE also) /ˈtɪsjuː/ noun **1** (also tissues) [U, pl] the mass of cells that form the bodies of humans, animals and plants □ *tisu*: *muscle/brain/nerve/scar tissue* ♦ *Radiation can destroy the body's tissues.* **2** [C] a thin piece of soft paper that you use to clean your nose and throw away after you have used it □ *kertas tisu*: *a box of tissues*

➲ note at **handkerchief** **3** (also ˈ**tissue paper**) [U] thin soft paper that you use for putting around things that may break □ *kertas tisu*

tit /tɪt/ *noun* [C] (*slang*) a woman's breast □ *tetek*

> **HELP** Be careful. Some people find this word offensive.

> **IDM** **tit for tat** something unpleasant that you do to sb because they have done sth to you □ *balas balik*

titbit /ˈtɪtbɪt/ (*AmE* **tidbit**) *noun* [C] **1** a small but very nice piece of food □ *kudap-kudapan; makanan ringan yg enak* **2** an interesting piece of information □ *berita/desas-desus yg menarik*

⚡ **title** /ˈtaɪtl/ *noun* [C] **1** the name of a book, play, film, picture, etc. □ *tajuk; judul*: *I know the author's name but I can't remember the title of the book.* **2** a word that shows sb's position, profession, etc. □ *gelaran*: *'Lord', 'Doctor', 'Reverend', 'Mrs' and 'General' are all titles.* **3** the position of being the winner of a competition, especially a sports competition □ *kejuaraan*: *Sue is playing this match to defend her title* (= to remain the winner).

titled /ˈtaɪtld/ *adj* having a word, for example 'Lord', 'Lady', etc. before your name that shows that your family has an important position in society □ *ada gelaran*

ˈ**title-holder** *noun* [C] the person or team who won a sports competition the last time it took place □ *penyandang kejuaraan; juara*

ˈ**title role** *noun* [C] the main role in a film, book, etc. whose name is the same as the title □ *watak tajuk*

titter /ˈtɪtə(r)/ *verb* [I] to laugh quietly, especially in an embarrassed or nervous way □ *ketawa kecil yg tertahan-tahan* ▸ **titter** *noun* [C]

ˈ**T-junction** *noun* [C] a place where two roads join to form the shape of a T □ *simpang tiga* ➲ picture at **roundabout**

TM /ˌtiː ˈem/ *abbr* = **trademark**

⚡ **to** /tə; *before vowels* tu:; tu; *strong form* tu:/ *prep, adv* **1** in the direction of; as far as □ *ke*: *She's going to London.* ♦ *Turn to the left.* ♦ *Pisa is to the west of Florence.* ♦ *He has gone to school.* **2** reaching a particular state □ *hingga; sampai ke; setakat*: *The meat was cooked to perfection.* ♦ *His speech reduced her to tears* (= made her cry). **3** used to show the end or limit of a series of things or period of time □ *hingga; sampai*: *from Monday to Friday* ♦ *from beginning to end* **4** used to say what time it is) before □ *sebelum; lagi*: *It's ten to three* (= ten minutes before 3 o'clock). **5** used to show the person or thing that receives sth or is affected by an action □ *kpd; pd; dgn*: *Give that to me.* ♦ *I am very grateful to my parents.* ♦ *What have you done to your hair?* ♦ *Sorry, I didn't realize you were talking to me.* **6** (nearly) touching sth; directed towards sth □ *ke; kpd*: *He put his hands to his ears.* ♦ *They sat back to back.* ♦ *She made no reference to her personal problems.* **7** used to introduce the second part of a comparison □ *drpd; berbanding dgn*: *I prefer theatre to opera.* **8** (used for expressing quantity) for each unit of money, measurement, etc. □ *per; se*: *How many dollars are there to the euro?* **9** used for expressing a reaction or attitude to sth □ *digunakan utk menyatakan reaksi atau sikap terhadap sst*: *To my surprise, I saw two strangers coming out of my house.* ♦ *His paintings aren't really to my taste.* **10** used to express sb's opinion or feeling about sth □ *bagi saya/dia, dll*: *To me, it was the wrong decision.* ♦ *It sounded like a good idea to me.* ♦ *I don't think our friendship means anything to him.* **11** used with verbs to form the infinitive □ *digunakan utk membentuk infinitif*: *I want to go home now.* ♦ *Don't forget to write.* ♦ *I didn't know what to do.* **12** /tu:/ (used about a door) in or into a closed position □ *(berkenaan dgn pintu) tutup*: *Push the door to.*

> **IDM** **to and fro** backwards and forwards □ *ke depan ke belakang; pergi balik*

toad /təʊd/ *noun* [C] a small animal with rough skin and long back legs that it uses for jumping, that lives both on land and in water □ *kodok; katak puru* ➲ picture on **page P13**

toadstool /ˈtəʊdstuːl/ *noun* [C] a plant without leaves, flowers or green colouring, with a flat or curved top. Toadstools are usually poisonous. □ *cendawan berbentuk payung dan lazimnya beracun* ➲ note at **mushroom** ➲ look at **fungus**

toast /təʊst/ *noun* **1** [U] a thin piece of bread that is heated on both sides to make it brown □ *roti bakar*

> **GRAMMAR** **Toast** in this meaning is uncountable. We say **a piece/slice of toast** (not 'a toast').

2 [C] **a toast (to sb/sth)** an occasion at which a group of people wish sb happiness, success, etc., by drinking a glass of wine, etc. at the same time □ *minum ucap selamat*: *I'd like to propose a toast to the happy couple.* ♦ *The committee drank a toast to the new project.* ➲ look at **drink** ▸ **toast** *verb* [T]

toaster /ˈtəʊstə(r)/ *noun* [C] an electrical machine for making bread turn brown by heating it on both sides □ *pembakar roti*

tobacco /təˈbækəʊ/ *noun* [U] the dried leaves of the **tobacco** plant that some people smoke in cigarettes and pipes □ *tembakau*

tobacconist /təˈbækənɪst/ *noun* **1** [C] a person who sells cigarettes, matches, etc. □ *penjual rokok, mancis, dsb* **2** (also **the tobacconist's**) [sing] a shop where you can buy cigarettes, matches, etc. □ *kedai rokok, mancis, dsb*

toboggan /təˈbɒɡən/ *noun* [C] a type of plastic or board with flat pieces of metal underneath, that people use for travelling down hills on snow for fun □ *tobogan; sejenis kereta luncur salji* ➲ look at **bobsleigh**, **sledge**

⚡ **today** /təˈdeɪ/ *noun* [U], *adv* **1** (on) this day □ *hari ini*: *Today is Monday.* ♦ *What shall we do* today? ♦ *School ends **a week today*** (= on this day next week). ♦ *Where is today's paper?* **2** (in) the present age; these days □ *pd masa sekarang; zaman ini*: *Young people today have far more freedom.* **SYN** nowadays

toddle /'tɒdl/ *verb* [I] **1** to walk with short, unsteady steps like a very young child □ *bertatih-tatih* **2** (*informal*) to walk or go somewhere □ *berjalan*

toddler /'tɒdlə(r)/ *noun* [C] A young child who has only just learnt to walk □ *anak kecil yg baru belajar berjalan*

toe¹ /təʊ/ *noun* [C] **1** one of the small parts like fingers at the end of each foot □ *jari kaki*: *the big/little toe* (= largest/smallest toe) ➔ note at **finger** ➔ picture at **body** ➔ picture on **page P12** **2** the part of a sock, shoe, etc. that covers your toes □ *bahagian jari kaki pd kasut atau stoking* ➔ picture at **shoe**

toe² /təʊ/ *verb* (toeing; toed)
IDM **toe the line** to do what sb in authority tells you to do, even if you do not agree with them □ *mengikut perintah/arahan*

TOEFL /'təʊfl/ *abbr* Test of English as a Foreign Language; the examination for foreign students who want to study at an American university □ *TOEFL (Ujian Bahasa Inggeris Sebagai Bahasa Asing)*

toenail /'təʊneɪl/ *noun* [C] one of the hard flat parts that cover the end of your toes □ *kuku jari kaki* ➔ picture at **body**

toffee /'tɒfi/ (*AmE* also) / *noun* [C,U] a hard sticky sweet that is made by cooking sugar and butter together □ *tofi*

together¹ /tə'geðə(r)/ *adv* **1** with or near each other □ *sama; bersama; bersama-sama*: *Can we have lunch together?* ♦ *They walked home together.* ♦ *I'll get all my things together tonight because I want to leave early.* ♦ *Stand with your feet together.* **2** so that two or more things are mixed or joined to each other □ *sekali*: *Mix the butter and sugar together.* ♦ *Tie the two ends together.* ♦ *Add these numbers together to find the total.* **3** at the same time □ *serentak*: *Don't all talk together.*
IDM **get your act together** ➔ **act¹**
put together [used after a noun or nouns referring to a group of people or things] combined; in total □ *sama-sama*: *You got more presents than the rest of the family put together.*
put/get your heads together ➔ **head¹**
together with in addition to; as well as □ *bersama/berserta dgn*: *I enclose my order together with a cheque for £15.*

together² /tə'geðə(r)/ *adj* (*informal*) (used about a person) organized, capable □ *teratur; terkelola; berkemampuan*: *I'm not very together this morning.*

togetherness /tə'geðənəs/ *noun* [U] a feeling of friendship □ *kesetiakawanan*

toggle /'tɒgl/ *noun* [C] **1** a short piece of wood, plastic, etc. that is put through a **loop** (= round piece) of thread to fasten sth, such as a coat or bag, instead of a button □ *pengikat; pembebat* **2** (also 'toggle switch) a key on a computer that you press to change from one style or operation to another, and back again □ *butang penukar fungsi operasi (pd papan kekunci komputer*
▶ **toggle** *verb* [I,T] toggle (between A and B); toggle sth: *He toggled between the two windows.*

toil /tɔɪl/ *verb* [I] (*formal*) to work very hard or for a long time at sth □ *bekerja keras* ▶ **toil** *noun* [U]

toilet /'tɔɪlət/ *noun* [C] a large bowl with a seat, connected to a water pipe, that you use when you need to get rid of waste material from your body; the room containing this □ *jamban; tandas*: *I need to go to the toilet* (= use the toilet). ➔ picture on **page P8**

MORE In their houses, people usually refer to the **toilet** or, informally, the **loo**. **Lavatory** and **WC** are formal and old-fashioned words. In public places the toilets are called the **Ladies** or the **Gents**. In American English, people talk about the **bathroom** in their houses and the **restroom**, **ladies' room** or **men's room** in public places.

'toilet bag (*BrE*) = sponge bag

'toilet paper (also 'toilet tissue) *noun* [U] soft, thin paper that you use to clean yourself after going to the toilet □ *kertas tandas*

toiletries /'tɔɪlətriz/ *noun* [pl] things such as soap or toothpaste that you use for washing, cleaning your teeth, etc. □ *kelengkapan dandanan diri* ➔ look at **sponge bag, toilet bag**

'toilet roll *noun* [C] (*BrE*) a long piece of toilet paper rolled round a tube □ *gulungan kertas tandas* ➔ picture at **roll**

'toiletry bag (*AmE*) = sponge bag

'toilet tissue = toilet paper

token¹ /'təʊkən/ *noun* [C] **1** a round piece of metal, plastic, etc. that you use instead of money to operate some machines or as a form of payment □ *token* **2** (*BrE*) a piece of paper that you can use to buy sth of a certain value in a particular shop. **Tokens** are often given as presents □ *baucar hadiah*: *a £10 book/CD/gift token* ➔ look at **voucher** **3** something that represents or is a symbol of sth □ *tanda*: *We would like you to accept this gift **as a token of** our gratitude.*

token² /'təʊkən/ *adj* [only *before* a noun] **1** done, chosen, etc. in a very small quantity, and only in order not to be criticized □ *sedikit; buat syarat sahaja*: *There is a token woman on the board of directors.* **2** small, but done or given to show that you are serious about sth and will keep a promise or an agreement □ *sedikit; sebagai tanda*: *a token payment*

told past tense, past participle of **tell**

tolerable /'tɒlərəbl/ adj (formal) **1** quite good, but not of the best quality □ *agak baik; memadai* **2** of a level that you can accept or deal with, although unpleasant or painful □ *dpt ditahan*: Drugs can reduce the pain to a tolerable level. **OPP** intolerable

tolerant /'tɒlərənt/ adj tolerant (of/towards sb/sth) able to allow or accept sth that you do not like or agree with □ *bersifat sabar; bertoleransi; boleh tahan*: As a society, we've become less tolerant of cruelty. **OPP** intolerant ▶**tolerance** (also **toleration**) noun [U] tolerance (of/for sb/sth): religious/racial tolerance **OPP** intolerance

tolerate /'tɒləreɪt/ verb [T] **1** to allow or accept sth that you do not like or agree with □ *menerima; bersabar menanggung*: In a democracy we must tolerate opinions that are different from our own. **2** to accept or be able to deal with sb/sth unpleasant without complaining □ *menahan; menanggung*: The noise was more than she could tolerate. ▶**toleration** /ˌtɒləˈreɪʃn/ = tolerance

toll /təʊl/ noun **1** [C] money that you pay to use a road or bridge □ *bayaran tol*: motorway tolls ◆ a toll bridge **2** [C, usually sing] the amount of damage done or the number of people who were killed or injured by sth □ *jumlah kerugian, kematian atau yg cedera*: The official death toll has now reached 5 000. **IDM** take a heavy toll/take its toll (on sth) to cause great loss, damage, suffering, etc. □ *menyebabkan kerugian, kerosakan atau penderitaan yg besar*

tom /tɒm/ noun = tomcat

tomato /təˈmɑːtəʊ/ noun [C] (pl **tomatoes**) a soft red fruit that is often eaten without being cooked in salads, or cooked as a vegetable □ *tomato*: tomato juice/soup/sauce ➜ picture on page P15

tomb /tuːm/ noun [C] a large grave, especially one built of stone above or below the ground □ *makam*: the tombs of the Pharaohs ➜ look at **grave**

tomboy /'tɒmbɔɪ/ noun [C] a young girl who likes games and activities that are traditionally considered to be for boys □ *budak perempuan yg berkelakuan spt lelaki*

tombstone /'tuːmstəʊn/ noun [C] a large flat stone that lies on or stands at one end of the place where sb is buried and shows the name, dates, etc. of the dead person □ *batu nisan* **SYN** gravestone, headstone

tomcat /'tɒmkæt/ (also **tom**) noun [C] a male cat □ *kucing jantan* ➜ note at **cat**

tomorrow /təˈmɒrəʊ/ (AmE also) / noun [C] U], adv **1** (on) the day after today □ *besok; esok*: Today is Friday so tomorrow is Saturday. ◆ See you tomorrow. ◆ I'm going to bed. I've got to get up early tomorrow morning. ◆ a week tomorrow (= a week from tomorrow) ➜ note at **morning**

HELP Notice that we say 'tomorrow morning', 'tomorrow afternoon', etc. NOT 'tomorrow in the morning', etc.

2 the future □ *masa depan*: The schoolchildren of today are tomorrow's workers.

ton /tʌn/ noun **1** [C] (informal) (abbr **t**) a measure of weight; 2 240 pounds □ *tan*: What have you got in this bag? It weighs a ton!

HELP Do not confuse **ton** and **tonne**. A ton is 1 016.04 kilograms and a tonne is 1 000 kilograms. In British English, a ton is 2 240 pounds in the non-metric system, but in American English, a ton is 2 000 pounds.

2 tons [pl] (informal) a lot □ *bertimbun-timbun; terlalu banyak*: I've got tons of homework to do.

tone¹ /təʊn/ noun **1** [C,U] the quality of a sound or of sb's voice, especially expressing a particular emotion □ *nada suara*: 'Do you know each other?' she asked in a casual tone of voice. **2** [sing] the general quality or style of sth □ *suasana; nada*: The tone of the meeting was optimistic. **3** [C] a shade of a colour □ *warna*: warm tones of red and orange **4** [C] a sound that you hear on the telephone □ *nada*: Please speak after the tone (= an instruction on an answering machine).

tone² /təʊn/ verb [T] tone sth (up) to make your muscles, skin, etc. firmer, especially by doing exercise □ *menguatkan otot, dsb*
PHR V tone sth down to change sth that you have said, written, etc., to make it less likely to offend □ *melembutkan nada, bahasa, dsb sst*

tone-ˈdeaf adj not able to sing or hear the difference between notes in music □ *pekak ton*

tongs /tɒŋz/ (AmE also) / noun [pl] a tool with two long parts that are joined at one end, that you use for picking up and holding things □ *penyepit*

tongue /tʌŋ/ noun **1** [C] the soft part inside your mouth that you can move. You use your tongue for speaking, tasting things, etc. □ *lidah*: He ran his tongue nervously over his lips. ➜ picture at **body 2** [C,U] the tongue of some animals, cooked and eaten □ *lidah (makanan)*: a slice of ox tongue **3** [C] (formal) a language □ *bahasa*: your mother tongue (= the language you learnt as a child)
IDM on the tip of your tongue ➜ **tip¹**
put/stick your tongue out to put your tongue outside your mouth as a rude sign to sb □ *menjelirkan lidah sebagai tanda mengejek, dll*
a slip of the tongue ➜ **slip²**
(with) tongue in cheek done or said as a joke; not intended seriously □ *secara bergurau*

tongue-tied adj not saying anything because you are shy or nervous □ *kelu (lidah)*

tongue-twister noun [C] a phrase or sentence with many similar sounds that is difficult to say correctly when you are speaking quickly □ *ungkapan pembelit lidah*: 'Red lorry, yellow lorry' is a tongue-twister.

tonic /ˈtɒnɪk/ noun 1 (also ˈtonic water) [U,C] a type of water with bubbles in it and a rather bitter taste that is often added to alcoholic drinks □ *air tonik: a gin and tonic* 2 [C,U] a medicine or sth you do that makes you feel stronger, healthier, etc., especially when you are very tired □ *tonik; penyegar: A relaxing holiday is a wonderful tonic.*

tonight /təˈnaɪt/ noun [U], adv (on) the evening or night of today □ *malam ini: Tonight is the last night of our holiday.* ◆ *What's on TV tonight?* ◆ *We are staying with friends tonight and going home tomorrow.*

tonne /tʌn/ noun [C] (abbr t) a measure of weight; 1 000 kilograms □ *tonne; tan metrik* ➔ look at **ton**

tonsil /ˈtɒnsl/ noun [C] one of the two small soft parts in your throat at the back of your mouth: *She had to have her tonsils out* (= removed in a medical operation). □ *anak tekak; tonsil*

tonsillitis /ˌtɒnsəˈlaɪtɪs/ noun [U] an illness in which the **tonsils** become very sore and swollen □ *radang tonsil*

Tom's sweater is not big enough.

Kevin's sweater is too big.

too /tuː/ adv 1 [used before adjectives and adverbs] more than is good, allowed, possible, etc □ *terlampau; terlalu: These boots are too small.* ◆ *It's far too cold to go out without a coat.* ◆ *It's too long a journey for you to make alone.*

HELP Notice that you cannot say 'It's a too long journey'.

2 [not with negative statements] in addition; also □ *juga: Red is my favourite colour but I like blue, too.* ◆ *Phil thinks you're right and I do too.* ➔ note at **also**

HELP Notice that at the end of a clause you use **too** for agreement with positive statements and **either** for agreement with negative statements: *I like eating out and Rakesh does too.* ◆ *I don't like cooking and Rakesh doesn't either.*

3 used to add sth which makes a situation even worse □ *juga: Her purse was stolen. And on her birthday, too.* 4 [usually used in negative sentences] very □ *begitu: The weather is not too bad today.*

IDM **be too much (for sb)** to need more ability than you have; to be more difficult than you can bear □ *di luar kemampuan sso*

took past tense of **take**

tools

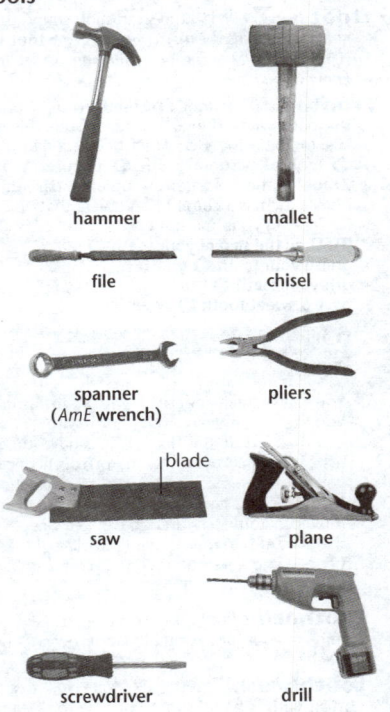

hammer   mallet

file   chisel

spanner   pliers
(AmE wrench)

                  blade
saw   plane

screwdriver   drill

tool /tuːl/ noun [C] a piece of equipment such as a hammer, that you hold in your hand(s) and use to do a particular job □ *alat; perkakas: Hammers, screwdrivers and saws are all carpenter's tools.* ◆ *garden tools* ◆ *a tool kit* (= a set of tools in a box or a bag)

OTHER WORDS FOR

tool

A **tool** is usually something you can hold in your hand, for example a spanner or hammer. An **implement** is often used outside, for example for farming or gardening. A **machine** has moving parts and works by electricity, with an engine, etc. An **instrument** is often used for technical or delicate work: *a dentist's instruments*. A **device** is a more general word for a

CONSONANTS p **p**en b **b**ad t **t**ea d **d**id k **c**at g **g**ot tʃ **ch**in dʒ **J**une f **f**all v **v**an θ **th**in

toolbar → top

piece of equipment that you consider to be useful and that is designed to do one particular task: *The machine has a safety device which switches the power off if there is a fault.*

toolbar /'tu:lbɑ:(r)/ *noun* [C] a row of symbols on a computer screen that show the different things that the computer can do □ *'tool bar'*

toot /tu:t/ *noun* [C] the short high sound that a car horn makes □ *bunyi hon kereta* ▶**toot** *verb* [I,T] (*especially BrE*): *Toot your horn to let them know we're here.*

tooth /tu:θ/ *noun* [C] (*pl* **teeth** /ti:θ/) **1** one of the hard white things in your mouth that you use for biting □ *gigi*: *She's got beautiful teeth.* ➔ look at **wisdom tooth** ➔ picture at **body 2** one of the long narrow pointed parts of an object such as a **comb** (= an object that you use for making your hair tidy) □ *gigi*
IDM **by the skin of your teeth** ➔ **skin**[1]
gnash your teeth ➔ **gnash**
grit your teeth ➔ **grit**[2]
have a sweet tooth ➔ **sweet**[1]

TOPIC

Teeth

You **brush/clean** your teeth with a **toothbrush**. You clean between your teeth with special string called **dental floss**. If you have **toothache** (= pain in your teeth) or **tooth decay**, you should see a **dentist**. You might need a **filling**, or you can **have the tooth out** (= removed). Some children have a **brace** (= a metal frame) to make their teeth straight, and people who have had their teeth out can have **false teeth**.

toothache /'tu:θeɪk/ *noun* [U,C, usually sing] a pain in your tooth or teeth □ *sakit gigi* ➔ note at **ache**

toothbrush /'tu:θbrʌʃ/ *noun* [C] a small brush with a handle that you use for cleaning your teeth □ *berus gigi* ➔ picture at **brush**

toothpaste /'tu:θpeɪst/ *noun* [U] a substance that you put on a brush and use for cleaning your teeth □ *ubat gigi*

toothpick /'tu:θpɪk/ *noun* [C] a short pointed piece of wood or plastic that you use for getting pieces of food out from between your teeth □ *pencungkil gigi*

top[1] /tɒp/ *noun*
▶HIGHEST PART **1** [C] the highest part or point of sth □ *(bahagian) atas; puncak*: *The flat is at the top of the stairs.* ♦ *Snow was falling on the mountain tops.* ♦ *Start reading at the top of the page.* **OPP** **foot**
▶FARTHEST POINT **2** [sing] the end of a street, table, etc. that is farthest away from you or from where you usually come to it □ *hujung*: *I'll meet you at the top of Broad Street.*
▶FLAT SURFACE **3** [C] the flat upper surface of sth

□ *permukaan*: *a desk/table/bench top*
▶HIGHEST POSITION **4** [sing] **the top (of sth)** the highest or most important position □ *paling tinggi/penting*: *to be at the top of your profession*
▶FOR PEN, ETC. **5** [C] the cover that you put onto sth in order to close it □ *penutup; tudung*: *Put the tops back on the pens or they will dry out.* ➔ picture at **container**

HELP **Top, cap** or **lid**? A **top** or a **cap** is often small and round. You often take it off by turning: *a bottle top* ♦ *Unscrew cap to open.* A **lid** may be larger. You can lift it off: *a saucepan lid* ♦ *Put the lid back on the box.*

▶CLOTHING **6** [C] a piece of clothing that you wear on the upper part of your body □ *baju, blaus, kemeja, dsb*: *a tracksuit/bikini/pyjama top* ♦ *I need a top to match my new skirt.* ➔ picture on page P1
▶TOY **7** [C] a child's toy that turns round very quickly on a point □ *gasing*: *a spinning top*
IDM **at the top of your voice** as loudly as possible □ *sekuat-kuatnya*
get on top of sb (*informal*) to be too much for sb to manage or deal with □ *memberatkan/ membebankan sso*: *I've got so much work to do. It's really getting on top of me.*
off the top of your head (*informal*) just guessing or using your memory without preparing or thinking about sth first □ *dgn meneka sahaja; sejauh mana yg dpt diingat*
on top 1 on or onto the highest point □ *di atas; di puncak*: *a mountain with snow on top* **2** in control; in a leading position □ *menguasai; di hadapan*: *Josie always seems to come out on top.*
on top of sb/sth 1 on, over or covering sth else □ *di atas sso/sst; bertindan-tindih*: *Books were piled on top of one another.* ♦ *The remote control is on top of the TV.* **2** in addition to sb/sth else □ *selain; di samping itu*: *On top of everything else, the car's broken down.* **3** (*informal*) very close to sb/sth □ *bersesak-sesak; berhimpit-himpit*: *We were all living on top of each other in that tiny flat.*
over the top; OTT /ˌəʊ ti:'ti:/ (*especially BrE spoken*) exaggerated or done with too much effort □ *melebih-lebih*

top[2] /tɒp/ *adj* highest in position or degree □ *paling tinggi, atas, dsb; terkemuka*: *one of Britain's top businessmen* ♦ *at top speed* ♦ *the top floor of the building* ♦ *She got top marks for her essay.*

top[3] /tɒp/ *verb* [T] (**topping; topped**) **1** to be higher or greater than a particular amount □ *melebihi* **2** to be in the highest position on a list because you are the most important, successful, etc. □ *berada di tempat paling atas; mendahului* **3** [usually passive] **top sth (with sth)** to put sth on the top of sth □ *membubuh sst di atas sst*: *cauliflower topped with cheese sauce*
IDM **to top it all** (*informal*) used to introduce the final piece of information that is worse than the other bad things that you have just mentioned

□ *yg teruk/buruk sekali*: *And then, to top it all, it started to rain!*
PHR V **top (sth) up** to fill sth that is partly empty □ *menambah*: *I need to top up my phone* (= pay more money so I can make more calls).

top ˈhat *noun* [C] the tall black or grey hat that a man wears on formal occasions □ *topi tinggi* ➲ picture at **hat**

ˌtop-ˈheavy *adj* heavier at the top than the bottom and likely to fall over □ *berat di bahagian atas*

topic /ˈtɒpɪk/ *noun* [C] a subject that you talk, write or learn about □ *tajuk; topik*: *The main topic of conversation was Tim's new girlfriend.* ♦ *The topic for today's discussion is …*

EXAM TIP

Topics

Revise vocabulary in related themes. The dictionary is a complete alphabetical list of words, but when you learn words, you will want to look at groups that belong together. Use the **Topic** notes to make sure you know the important words about each subject. If you have the **Wordpower CD-ROM**, choose a topic a day from the **Topic Dictionary** until you have revised all the topics you need to know for your exam.

---

topical /ˈtɒpɪkl/ *adj* connected with sth that is happening now; that people are interested in at the present time □ *semasa; merujuk kpd kejadian semasa*

topless /ˈtɒpləs/ *adj, adv* (used about a woman) not wearing any clothes on the upper part of the body so that her breasts are not covered □ *separuh bogel*

topmost /ˈtɒpməʊst/ *adj* [only before a noun] highest □ *tertinggi; paling atas*: *the topmost branches of the tree*

topping /ˈtɒpɪŋ/ *noun* [C,U] something such as cream or a sauce that is put on the top of food to decorate it or make it taste nicer □ *krim atau sos yg dituang di atas makanan sebagai hiasan atau utk menyedapkannya*

topple /ˈtɒpl/ *verb* **1** [I] **topple (over)** to become less steady and fall down □ *tumbang; rebah*: *Don't add another book to the pile or it will topple over.* **2** [T] to cause a leader of a country, etc. to lose his or her position of power or authority □ *menggulingkan; menjatuhkan*

ˌtop ˈsecret *adj* that must be kept very secret, especially from other governments □ *rahsia besar (terutamanya rahsia kerajaan); sangat sulit*

ˈtop-up *noun* [C] (*BrE*) **1** a payment that you make to increase the amount of money, etc. to the level that is needed □ *tambah nilai (wang)*: *a phone top-up* **2** (*informal*) an amount of a drink that you add to a cup or glass in order to fill it again □ *tambah isian (minuman)*: *Can I give anyone a top-up?*

903   **top hat → torture**

the Torah *noun* [sing] (in the Jewish religion) the law of God as given to Moses and recorded in the first five books of the Bible □ *Torah*

torch /tɔːtʃ/ *noun* [C] **1** (*AmE* **flashlight**) a small electric light that you carry in your hand □ *lampu suluh/picit*: *Shine the torch under the sofa and see if you can find my ring.* **2** a long piece of wood with burning material at the end that you carry to give light □ *obor; jamung*: *the Olympic torch*

tore past tense of **tear**²

torment /ˈtɔːment/ *noun* [U,C] (*formal*) great pain and suffering in your mind or body; a person or thing that causes this □ *seksaan; punca seksaan*: *to be in torment* ▶**torment** /tɔːˈment/ *verb* [T]

torn past participle of **tear**²

tornado /tɔːˈneɪdəʊ/ *noun* [C] (*pl* **tornados** or **tornadoes**) a violent storm with very strong winds that move in a circle. **Tornadoes** form a tall column of air which is narrower at the bottom than at the top. □ *tornado; puting beliung* ➲ note at **storm**

torpedo /tɔːˈpiːdəʊ/ *noun* [C] (*pl* **torpedoes**) a long narrow bomb that is fired under the water from a ship or **submarine** (= a type of ship that travels under the water) and explodes when it hits another ship □ *torpedo*

torrent /ˈtɒrənt/ (*AmE* also) / *noun* [C] a strong fast flow of sth, especially water □ *curahan; hujan yg mencurah-curah*: *The rain was coming down in torrents.*

torrential /təˈrenʃl/ *adj* (used about rain) very great in amount □ *lebat; mencurah-curah*

torso /ˈtɔːsəʊ/ *noun* [C] (*pl* **torsos**) the main part of your body, not your head, arms and legs □ *badan; torso*

tortoise /ˈtɔːtəs/ (*AmE* also **turtle**) *noun* [C] a small animal with a hard shell that moves very slowly. A **tortoise** can pull its head and legs into its shell to protect them. □ *kura-kura* ➲ picture on **page P13**

tortuous /ˈtɔːtʃuəs/ *adj* (*formal*) **1** complicated, not clear and simple □ *berbelit-belit* **2** (used about a road, etc.) with many bends □ *berliku-liku*

torture /ˈtɔːtʃə(r)/ *noun* [U,C] **1** the act of causing sb great pain either as a punishment or to make them say or do sth □ *penyeksaan*: *a confession extracted under torture* **2** mental or physical suffering □ *kesengsaraan; seksaan*: *It's torture having to sit here and listen to him complaining.* ▶**torture** *verb* [T]: *Prisoners were tortured into making confessions.* ♦ *She was tortured by the thought that the accident was her fault.* ▶**torturer** *noun* [C]

VOWELS   i: see   i any   ɪ sit   e ten   æ hat   ɑ: father   ɒ got   ɔ: saw   ʊ put   u: too   u usual

Tory → touch pad

Tory /ˈtɔːri/ noun [C] (pl **Tories**) adj a member of, or sb who supports, the British Conservative Party; connected with this party □ *ahli atau penyokong Parti Konservatif British; berkaitan dgn parti ini*: the Tory Party conference

toss /tɒs/ verb **1** [T] to throw sth lightly and carelessly □ *mencampakkan*: Rhodri opened the letter and tossed the envelope into the bin. **2** [T] to move your head back quickly, especially to show you are annoyed or impatient □ *mengangkat kepala/muka*: I tried to apologize but she just tossed her head and walked away. **3** [I,T] to move, or make sb/sth move, up and down or from side to side □ *beralih-alih; berpusing ke kiri ke kanan; terumbang-ambing*: He lay tossing and turning in bed, unable to sleep. ◆ The ship was tossed about by huge waves. **4** [I,T] **toss (up) (for sth)** to throw a coin into the air in order to decide sth, by guessing which side of the coin will land facing upwards □ *melambung duit*: to toss a coin

> **MORE** Look at **heads** and **tails**. These are the names of the two sides of a coin. We ask 'Heads or tails?' when we want someone to guess which side will face upwards.

▶ **toss** noun [C]
IDM **win/lose the toss** to guess correctly/wrongly which side of a coin will face upwards when it lands □ *menang/kalah lambungan duit*: Ms Kvitova won the toss and chose to serve first.

tot¹ /tɒt/ noun [C] **1** (informal) a very small child □ *anak kecil* **2** (especially BrE) a small glass of a strong alcoholic drink □ *sedikit atau segelas kecil arak*

tot² /tɒt/ verb (**totting; totted**)
PHR V **tot (sth) up** (informal) to add numbers together to form a total □ *menjumlahkan*

total¹ /ˈtəʊtl/ adj **1** being the amount after everyone or everything is counted or added together □ *jumlah*: What was the total number of people there? **2** complete □ *jumlah sepenuhnya*: a total failure ◆ The couple ate in total silence.

total² /ˈtəʊtl/ noun [C] the number that you get when you add two or more numbers or amounts together □ *jumlah*
IDM **in total** when you add two or more numbers or amounts together □ *jumlah keseluruhannya*: The appeal raised £4 million in total.
▶ **total** verb [T] (**totalling; totalled**, (AmE) **totaling; totaled**): His debts totalled more than £10 000.

totally /ˈtəʊtəli/ adv completely □ *sepenuhnya; betul-betul*: I totally agree with you.

totter /ˈtɒtə(r)/ verb [I] to stand or move in a way that is not steady, as if you are going to fall, especially because you are drunk, ill or weak □ *berjalan terhuyung-hayang*

touch¹ /tʌtʃ/ verb **1** [T] to put your hand or fingers onto sb/sth □ *menyentuh*: It's very delicate so don't touch it. ◆ He touched her gently on the cheek. ◆ The police asked us not to touch anything. **2** [I,T] (used about two or more things, surfaces, etc.) to be or move so close together that there is no space between them □ *bersentuhan; menyentuh; mencecah*: They were sitting so close that their shoulders touched. ◆ This bicycle is too big. My feet don't touch the ground. **3** [T] to make sb feel sad, sorry for sb, grateful, etc. □ *mengharukan; menyentuh perasaan sso* ⊃ look at **touched 4** [T] [in negative sentences] to be as good as sb/sth in skill, quality, etc. □ *menandingi; menyamai*: He's a much better player than all the others. No one else can touch him.
IDM **knock on wood; touch wood** ⊃ **wood**
PHR V **touch down** (used about an aircraft) to land □ *mendarat (kapal terbang)*
touch on/upon sth to mention or refer to a subject for only a short time □ *menyentuh atau merujuk secara ringkas kpd sst perkara*

touch² /tʌtʃ/ noun
▶SENSE **1** [U] one of the five senses: the ability to feel things and know what they are like by putting your hands or fingers on them □ *deria sentuh/rasa*: The sense of touch is very important to blind people.
▶WITH HAND **2** [C, usually sing] the act of putting your hands or fingers onto sb/sth □ *sentuhan*: I felt the touch of her hand on my arm. ⊃ picture at **exercise**
▶WAY STH FEELS **3** [U] the way sth feels when you touch it □ *rasa*: Marble is cold to the touch.
▶DETAIL **4** [C] a small detail that is added to improve sth □ *sentuhan; tambahan; perapian*: The flowers in our room were a nice touch. ◆ She's just putting the finishing touches to the cake.
▶WAY OF DOING STH **5** [sing] a way or style of doing sth □ *gaya; sentuhan*: She prefers to write her letters by hand for a more personal touch.
▶SMALL AMOUNT **6** [sing] **a touch (of sth)** a small amount of sth □ *sedikit*: He's not very ill. It's just a touch of flu.
IDM **in/out of touch (with sb)** being/not being in contact with sb by speaking or writing to them □ *berhubung/tdk berhubung dgn sso*: During the year she was abroad, they kept in touch by email.
in/out of touch with sth having/not having recent information about sth □ *mengikuti/tdk mengikuti (perkembangan terbaharu, dsb ttg sst)*: We're out of touch with what's going on.
lose touch ⊃ **lose**
lose your touch ⊃ **lose**

touched /tʌtʃt/ adj [not before a noun] **touched (by sth); touched that ...** made to feel sad, sorry for sb, grateful, etc. □ *terharu*: We were very touched by the plight of the refugees. ◆ I was touched that he offered to help.

touching /ˈtʌtʃɪŋ/ adj that makes you feel sad, sorry for sb, grateful, etc. □ *mengharukan; menyayat hati* **SYN** moving

'touch pad (also **trackpad**) noun [C] a device which you touch in different places in order to operate a computer □ *pad sentuh*: *I use the touch pad on my laptop much more than the mouse.* ➲ picture at **computer**

touch screen *noun* [C] a computer screen which shows information when you touch it □ *skrin sentuh*: *My satnav has a touch screen.* ♦ *a touch-screen phone*

> **TOPIC**
>
> **Touch screens**
>
> With a **touch-screen phone** you can send and receive emails, **browse web pages** (= look for information), **stream music** and **videos** (= listen to them or view them via the Internet without buying or owning the files) or **download content**, as well as making calls. On a **touch-screen computer** you **swipe** to move across the screen, **zoom** to make the screen larger and see the details, and **pinch in** to make the screen smaller.

touchy /'tʌtʃi/ *adj* (**touchier**; **touchiest**) **1** touchy (about sth) easily upset or made angry □ *mudah tersinggung*: *He's a bit touchy about his weight.* **2** (used about a subject, situation, etc.) that may easily upset people or make them angry □ *sensitif; mudah menyinggung perasaan*: *Don't mention the exam. It's a very touchy subject.* **SYN** for both meanings **sensitive**

tough /tʌf/ *adj* (**tougher**; **toughest**)
▶DIFFICULT **1** having or causing problems □ *sukar; susah*: *It will be a tough decision to make.* ♦ *He's had a tough time of it* (= a lot of problems) *recently.*
▶STRICT **2** tough (on/with sb/sth) not feeling sorry for anyone □ *tegas; keras*: *Don't be too tough on them — they were trying to help.* ♦ *The government plans to get tough with people who drink and drive.*
▶STRONG **3** strong enough to deal with difficult conditions or situations □ *tahan lasak*: *You need to be tough to go climbing in winter.* **4** not easily broken, torn or cut; very strong □ *kuat; tahan*: *a tough pair of boots*
▶MEAT **5** difficult to cut and eat □ *liat*
▶BAD LUCK **6** (*informal*) tough (on sb) unfortunate for sb in a way that seems unfair □ *malang (bagi sso)*: *It's tough on her that she lost her job.*
▶**toughness** *noun* [U]

toughen /'tʌfn/ *verb* [I,T] toughen (sb/sth) (up) to make sb/sth tough □ *menguatkan; menjadikan tahan lasak*

toupee /'tu:peɪ/ *noun* [C] a small section of artificial hair, worn by a man to cover an area of his head where hair no longer grows □ *rambut palsu (utk lelaki)*

tour /tʊə(r)/ (*BrE also*) tɔ:(r)/ *noun* **1** [C] a tour (of/round/around sth) a journey that you make for pleasure during which you visit many places □ *perjalanan; pelancongan; melancong*: *to go on a ten-day coach tour of/around Scotland* ♦ *a sightseeing tour* ♦ *a tour operator* (= a person or company that organizes tours) ➲ note at **travel** **2** [C] a short visit around a city, famous building, etc. □ *lawatan; kunjungan*: *a guided tour round St Paul's Cathedral* **3** [C,U] an official series of visits that singers, musicians, sports players, etc. make to different places to perform, play, etc. □ *lawatan*: *The band is currently on tour in America.* ♦ *a concert/cricket tour* ▶**tour** *verb* [I,T]: *We toured southern Spain for three weeks.*

tourism /'tʊərɪzəm (*BrE also*) 'tɔ:r-/ *noun* [U] the business of providing and arranging holidays and services for people who are visiting a place □ *pelancongan*: *The country's economy relies heavily on tourism.*

tourist /'tʊərɪst (*BrE also*) 'tɔ:r-/ *noun* [C] a person who visits a place for pleasure □ *pelancong*: *The city is full of tourists in summer.* ♦ *You can get more information at the local tourist office.* ➲ look at **sightseer**

tournament /'tʊənəmənt (*BrE also*) 'tɔ:n-(*AmE also*) / *noun* [C] a competition in which many players or teams play games against each other □ *pertandingan; kejohanan*

tourniquet /'tʊənɪkeɪ/ *noun* [C] a band of cloth that is tied tightly around an arm or a leg to stop the loss of blood from a wound □ *turnikuet; kain pembalut yg diikat pd lengan atau kaki utk menghentikan pengaliran darah*

tousled /'taʊzld/ *adj* (used about hair) untidy, often in an attractive way □ *kusut; tdk terurus*

tow /təʊ/ *verb* [T] to pull a car or boat behind another vehicle, using a rope or chain □ *menunda; menarik*: *My car was towed away by the police.*
IDM **in tow** (*informal*) following closely behind □ *mengekor di belakang*: *He arrived with his wife and five children in tow.*
▶**tow** *noun* [sing]

towards /təˈwɔːdz/ (*also* **toward** /təˈwɔːd/) *prep* **1** in the direction of sb/sth □ *ke arah*: *I saw Ken walking towards the station.* ♦ *She had her back towards me.* ♦ *a first step towards world peace* **2** near or nearer a time or date □ *menjelang; hampir*: *It gets cool towards evening.* ♦ *The shops get very busy towards Christmas.* **3** (used when you are talking about your feelings about sb/sth) in relation to □ *terhadap*: *Patti felt very protective towards her younger brother.* ♦ *What is your attitude towards this government?* **4** as part of the payment for sth □ *utk; bagi*: *The money will go towards the cost of a new minibus.*

towel /'taʊəl/ *noun* [C] a piece of cloth or paper that you use for drying sb/sth/yourself □ *tuala*: *a bath/hand/beach towel* ♦ *kitchen/paper towels* ➲ look at **sanitary towel**, **tea towel**

tower /'taʊə(r)/ *noun* [C] a tall narrow building or part of a building such as a church or castle □ *menara*: *the Eiffel Tower* ♦ *a church tower* ▶**tower** *verb* [T]
PHR V **tower over/above sb/sth** to be much higher or taller than the people or things that are near □ *mengatasi; melebihi*: *The cliffs towered above them.* ♦ *He towers over all his classmates.*

tower block → trade

'tower block noun [C] (BrE) a very tall building consisting of flats or offices □ *blok menara*

town /taʊn/ noun 1 [C] a place with many streets and buildings. A town is larger than a village but smaller than a city □ *bandar*: *Romsey is a small market town.* ♦ *After ten years away, she decided to move back to her home town* (= the town where she was born and lived when she was a child). 2 **the town** [sing] all the people who live in a town □ *semua orang (di sesebuah bandar atau tempat)*: *The whole town is talking about it.* 3 [U] the main part of a town, where the shops, etc. are □ *pusat bandar*: *I've got to go into town this afternoon.*

IDM go to town (on sth) (informal) to do sth with a lot of energy and enthusiasm; to spend a lot of money on sth □ *membuat sst dgn bersungguh-sungguh; berhabis-habisan*
(out) on the town (informal) going to restaurants, theatres, clubs, etc. for entertainment, especially at night □ *pergi ke tempat-tempat hiburan*

town 'council noun [C] (in the UK) a group of people who are responsible for the local government of a town □ *majis bandaran*

town 'hall noun [C] a large building that contains the local government offices and often a large room for public meetings, concerts, etc. □ *dewan bandaran* ⊃ look at **hall**

toxic /'tɒksɪk/ adj poisonous □ *bertoksin; beracun*

toy¹ /tɔɪ/ noun [C] an object for a child to play with □ *mainan*: *The children were playing happily with their toys.* ♦ *a toyshop* ▶ **toy** adj [only before a noun]: *a toy soldier/farm*

toy² /tɔɪ/ verb
PHR V toy with sth 1 to think about doing sth, perhaps not very seriously □ *berfikir-fikir; berangan-angan*: *She's toying with the idea of going abroad for a year.* 2 to move sth about without thinking about what you are doing, often because you are nervous or upset □ *mengusik-usik; bermain-main dgn sst*: *He toyed with his food but hardly ate any of it.*

trace¹ /treɪs/ verb [T] 1 **trace sb/sth (to sth)** to find out where sb/sth is by following marks, signs or other information □ *mengesan; menjejaki*: *The wanted man was traced to an address in Amsterdam.* 2 **trace sth (back) (to sth)** to find out where sth came from or what caused it; to describe the development of sth □ *menyusurgalur; memerikan*: *She traced her family tree back to the 16th century.* 3 to make a copy of a map, plan, etc. by placing a piece of **tracing paper** (= transparent paper) over it and drawing over the lines □ *menekap*

trace² /treɪs/ noun 1 [C,U] a mark, an object or a sign that shows that sb/sth existed or happened □ *kesan*: *traces of an earlier civilization*
♦ *The man disappeared/vanished without trace.*
2 [C] **a trace (of sth)** a very small amount of sth □ *kesan; tanda*: *Traces of blood were found under her fingernails.*

track¹ /træk/ noun
▶ PATH 1 [C] a natural path or rough road □ *runut; denai*: *Follow the dirt track through the forest.* ⊃ picture on **page P10**
▶ MARKS ON GROUND 2 [C, usually pl] marks that are left on the ground by a person, an animal or a moving vehicle □ *jejak; bekas (tapak kaki, tayar, dll)*: *The hunter followed the tracks of a deer.*
♦ *tyre tracks* ⊃ look at **footprint**
▶ FOR TRAIN 3 [C,U] the two metal rails on which a train runs □ *rel; landasan*: *The train stopped because there was a tree across the track.*
▶ FOR RACE 4 [C] a piece of ground, often in a circle, for people, cars, etc. to have races on □ *trek; balapan*: *a running track*
▶ MUSIC 5 [C] one song or piece of music on a CD, record, etc. □ *lagu*: *the first track from her latest album* ⊃ look at **soundtrack**
IDM keep/lose track of sb/sth to have/not have information about what is happening or where sb/sth is □ *mengikut/tdk mengikuti perkembangan sso/sst*
off the beaten track ⊃ **beat¹**
on the right/wrong track having the right/wrong idea about sth □ *berada di jalan yg betul/salah*: *That's not the answer but you're on the right track.*

track² /træk/ verb [T] to follow the movements of sb/sth □ *mengesan; menjejaki*: *to track enemy planes on a radar screen*
PHR V track sb/sth down to find sb/sth after searching for them or it □ *menjumpai sso/sst yg dicari*

'track event noun [C] a sports event that consists of running round a track in a race, rather than throwing sth or jumping □ *acara balapan*
⊃ look at **field event**

trackpad /'trækpæd/ = **touch pad**

'track record noun [sing] all the past successes or failures of a person or an organization □ *rekod prestasi*

tracksuit /'træksuːt/ noun [C] a warm pair of soft trousers and a matching jacket that you wear for sports practice □ *sut balapan*

tractor /'træktə(r)/ noun [C] a large vehicle that is used on farms for pulling heavy pieces of machinery □ *traktor*

tractor

trade¹ /treɪd/ noun 1 [U] the buying or selling of goods or services between people or countries □ *perdagangan; perniagaan*: *an international trade agreement*
♦ *Trade is not very good* (= not many goods are sold) *at this time of year.* 2 [C] a particular type of business □ *perniagaan; industri*: *the tourist/building/retail trade* 3 [C,U] a job for which you need special skill, especially with your hands

[I] **intransitive**, a verb which has no object: *He laughed.*   [T] **transitive**, a verb which has an object: *He ate an apple.*

□ *pekerjaan*: *Jeff is a plumber by trade.* ♦ *to learn a trade* ⊃ note at **work**

trade² /treɪd/ *verb* **1** [I] **trade (in sth) (with sb)** to buy or sell goods or services □ *berdagang; berniaga*: *We no longer trade with that country.* ♦ *to trade in luxury goods* ♦ *to trade in stocks and shares* **2** [T] **trade sth (for sth)** to exchange sth for sth else □ *menukar*: *He traded his iPod for some concert tickets.*
PHR V **trade sth in (for sth)** to give sth old in part payment for sth new or newer □ *menukar beli sst (dgn sst)*: *We traded in our old car for a van.*
▶ **trading** *noun* [U]

trademark /'treɪdmɑːk/ *noun* [C] (*abbr* **TM**) a special symbol, design or name that a company puts on its products and that cannot be used by any other company □ *cap dagang; tanda niaga*

trader /'treɪdə(r)/ *noun* [C] a person who buys and sells things, especially goods in a market or company shares □ *pedagang; peniaga* ⊃ picture on **page P11**

tradesman /'treɪdzmən/ *noun* [C] (*pl* **-men** /-mən/) a person who brings goods or services to people's homes or who has a shop □ *penjaja; peniaga*

trade 'union = **union**

tradition /trə'dɪʃn/ *noun* [C,U] a custom, belief or way of doing sth that has continued from the past to the present □ *tradisi*: *religious/cultural/literary traditions* ♦ *By tradition, the bride's family pays the costs of the wedding.*
▶ **traditional** /-ʃənl/ *adj*: *It is traditional in Britain to eat turkey at Christmas.* ▶ **traditionally** /-ʃənəli/ *adv*

traffic /'træfɪk/ *noun* [U] **1** all the vehicles that are on a road at a particular time □ *lalu lintas*: *heavy/light traffic* ♦ *We got stuck in traffic and were late for the meeting.* **2** the movement of ships, aircraft, etc. □ *pergerakan kapal, kapal terbang, dll*: *air traffic control* **3 traffic (in sth)** the illegal buying and selling of sth □ *perniagaan haram*: *the traffic in drugs/firearms*

'traffic island (*BrE* **island**) *noun* [C] a higher area in the middle of the road, where you can stand and wait for the traffic to pass when you want to cross □ *pembahagi jalan*

'traffic jam *noun* [C] a long line of cars, etc. that cannot move or that can only move very slowly □ *kesesakan lalu lintas*: *We were stuck in a terrible traffic jam.* ⊃ note at **driving**

trafficking /'træfɪkɪŋ/ *noun* [U] the activity of buying and selling sth illegally □ *perdagangan atau perniagaan haram*: *drug trafficking* ▶ **trafficker** *noun* [C]: *a drugs trafficker*

'traffic light *noun* [C, usually pl] a sign with red, orange and green lights that is used for controlling the traffic where two or more roads meet □ *lampu isyarat* ⊃ picture at **roundabout**

'traffic warden *noun* [C] (*BrE*) a person whose job is to check that cars are not parked in the wrong place or for longer than is allowed □ *penguat kuasa lalu lintas* ⊃ note at **parking**

tragedy /'trædʒədi/ *noun* (*pl* **tragedies**) [C,U] **1** a very sad event or situation, especially one that involves death □ *tragedi*: *It's a tragedy that he died so young.* **2** a serious play that has a sad ending; plays of this type □ *drama/cerita tragedi*: *Shakespeare's 'King Lear' is a tragedy.* ⊃ look at **comedy**

tragic /'trædʒɪk/ *adj* **1** that makes you very sad, especially because it involves death □ *tragik; penuh tragedi*: *It's tragic that she lost her only child.* ♦ *a tragic accident* **2** [only *before* a noun] (used about literature) in the style of **tragedy** □ *(berkaitan dgn sastera) tragedi*: *a tragic actor/hero* ▶ **tragically** /-kli/ *adv*

trail¹ /treɪl/ *noun* [C] **1** a series of marks in a long line that is left by sb/sth as he/she/it moves □ *tanda; kesan*: *a trail of blood/footprints* **2** a track, sign or smell that is left behind and that you follow when you are hunting sb/sth □ *jejak*: *The dogs ran off on the trail of the fox.* **3** a path through the country □ *denai*

trail² /treɪl/ *verb* **1** [I,T] to pull or be pulled along behind sb/sth □ *meleret; menyeret*: *The skirt was too long and trailed along the ground.* **2** [I] to move or walk slowly behind sb/sth else, usually because you are tired or bored □ *berjalan mengheret kaki*: *It was impossible to do any shopping with the kids trailing around after me.* **3** [I,T] [usually used in the continuous tenses] **trail (by/in sth)** to be in the process of losing a game or a competition □ *tertinggal; ketinggalan*: *At half-time Liverpool were trailing by two goals to three.* **4** [I] (used about plants or sth long and thin) to grow over sth and hang downwards; to lie across a surface □ *menjalar*: *Computer wires trailed across the floor.*
PHR V **trail away/off** (used about sb's voice) to gradually become quieter and then stop □ *beransur-ansur lenyap*

trailer /'treɪlə(r)/ *noun* [C] **1** a type of container with wheels that is pulled by a vehicle □ *treler*: *a car towing a trailer with a boat on it* **2** (*AmE*) = **caravan**(1) **3** (*especially BrE*) a series of short pieces taken from a film and used to advertise it □ *treler; sedutan filem utk mengiklan* ⊃ look at **clip**

train¹ /treɪn/ *noun* [C] **1** a type of transport that is pulled by an engine along a railway line. A train is divided into **carriages** and **coaches** (= sections for people) and **wagons** (= for goods) □ *kereta api*: *a passenger/goods/freight train* ♦ *a fast/slow/express train* ♦ *to catch/take/get the train to London* ♦ *the 12 o'clock train to Bristol* ♦ *to get on/off a train* ♦ *Hurry up or we'll miss the train.* ♦ *You have to change trains at Reading.* ⊃ picture on **page P7**

HELP Note that we say **by train** when speaking in general. To talk about one particular train journey we say **on the train**: *Victoria travels to work by train.* ◆ *Yesterday she left her scarf on the train.*

2 [usually sing] a series of thoughts or events that are connected □ *aliran*: *A knock at the door interrupted my train of thought.*

TOPIC

Travelling by train

You go to the **station** to **catch** a train. You can buy a **single** (= to your destination but not back) or a **return** (= to your destination and back). In American English these are called a **one-way ticket** and a **round-trip ticket**. A **first-class** ticket is the most expensive type of ticket. A **timetable** is the list that shows the times when trains **arrive** and **depart** (= leave). You wait on the **platform** to get on your train. Sometimes it might be **delayed** (= late) or even **cancelled**. If you are late and the train is **on time**, you will **miss** it. If there is no **direct** service, you will have to **change** (= get off your train and get on another in order to continue your journey).

---

train² /treɪn/ *verb* **1** [T] **train sb (as sth/to do sth)** to teach a person to do sth which is difficult or which needs practice □ *melatih*: *The organization trains guide dogs for the blind.* ◆ *There is a shortage of trained teachers.* **2** [I,T] **train (as/in sth) (to do sth)** to learn how to do a job □ *menjalani latihan*: *She trained as an engineer.* ◆ *He's not trained in anything.* ◆ *He's training to be a doctor.* **3** [I,T] **train (for sth)** to prepare yourself, especially for a sports event, by practising; to help a person or an animal to do this □ *berlatih; melatih*: *I'm training for the London Marathon.* ◆ *to train racehorses*

PHR V **train sth at/on sb/sth** to point a gun, camera, etc. at sb/sth □ *menghalakan; mengarahkan*

'train driver = engine driver

trainee /ˌtreɪˈniː/ *noun* [C] a person who is being taught how to do a particular job □ *pelatih*

trainer /ˈtreɪnə(r)/ *noun* [C] **1** (*AmE* **sneaker**) [usually pl] a shoe that you wear for doing sport or as informal clothing □ *kasut utk bersukan* ➲ look at **plimsoll** ➲ picture at **shoe** ➲ picture on **page P1 2** a person who teaches people or animals a skill or how to do a particular job well, or to do a particular sport □ *jurulatih*: *teacher trainers* ◆ *a racehorse trainer*

training /ˈtreɪnɪŋ/ *noun* [U] **1 training (in sth/in doing sth)** the process of learning the skills that you need to do a job □ *latihan*: *Few candidates had received any training in management.* ◆ *a training course* **2** the process of preparing to take part in a sports competition by doing physical exercises □ *latihan*: *to be in training for the Olympics*

trainspotter /ˈtreɪnspɒtə(r)/ *noun* [C] (*BrE*) **1** a person who collects the numbers of railway engines as a hobby □ *orang yg memerhatikan kereta api dan mencatat nombor enjinnya sebagai hobi* **2** a person who has a boring hobby or who is interested in the details of a subject that other people find boring □ *orang yg mempunyai hobi yg pd orang lain sungguh membosankan* ▶ **trainspotting** *noun* [U]

trait /treɪt/ *noun* [C] a quality that forms part of your character □ *sifat; ciri*

traitor /ˈtreɪtə(r)/ *noun* [C] **a traitor (to sb/sth)** a person who is not loyal to their country, friends, etc. □ *pengkhianat; pembelot*

MORE A traitor **betrays** his/her friends, country, etc. and the crime against his/her country is called **treason**.

tram /træm/ (*AmE* **streetcar**; **trolley**) *noun* [C] a type of bus that works by electricity and that moves along special rails in the road carrying passengers □ *trem* ➲ picture on **page P7**

tramp¹ /træmp/ *noun* **1** [C] a person who has no home or job and who moves from place to place □ *kutu rayau; orang yg tdk ada tempat tinggal atau pekerjaan* **2** [sing] the sound of people walking with heavy or noisy steps □ *bunyi langkah yg berat; berdetap*

tramp² /træmp/ *verb* [I,T] to walk with slow heavy steps, especially for a long time □ *berjalan dgn langkah yg berat*

trample /ˈtræmpl/ *verb* [I,T] **trample on/over sb/sth** to walk on sb/sth and damage or hurt them or it □ *memijak-mijak; melanyak*: *The boys trampled on the flowers.*

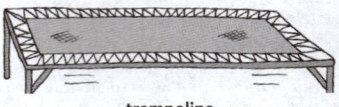

trampoline

trampoline /ˈtræmpəliːn/ *noun* [C] a piece of equipment for jumping up and down on, made of a piece of strong cloth fixed to a metal frame by springs □ *trampolin* ▶ **trampoline** *verb* [I] ▶ **trampolining** *noun* [U]

trance /trɑːns/ noun [C] a mental state in which you do not notice what is going on around you □ *keadaan bersawai/khayal*: *to go/fall into a trance*

tranquil /'træŋkwɪl/ adj (formal) calm and quiet □ *tenang; damai; tenteram*

tranquillizer (also -iser; AmE tranquilizer) /'træŋkwəlaɪzə(r)/ noun [C] a drug that is used for making people or animals calm or unconscious □ *ubat penenang/penenteram* ➔ look at **sedative** ▶**tranquillize** (also -ise; AmE tranquilize) verb [T]

transaction /træn'zækʃn/ noun [C] a piece of business that is done between people □ *urus niaga*: *financial transactions*

transatlantic /ˌtrænzət'læntɪk/ adj [only before a noun] to or from the other side of the Atlantic Ocean; across the Atlantic □ *rentas Atlantik*: *a transatlantic flight/voyage*

transcend /træn'send/ verb [T] (formal) to go further than the usual limits of sth □ *menjangkaui; mengatasi; melebihi*

transcribe /træn'skraɪb/ verb [T] **transcribe sth (into sth)** to record thoughts, speech or data in a written form, or in a different written form from the original □ *mentranskripsikan; menyalin*: *The interview was recorded and then transcribed.*

transcript /'trænskrɪpt/ (also **transcription** /træn'skrɪpʃn/) noun [C] a written or printed copy of what sb has said □ *transkrip; salinan bertulis ucapan, temu bual, dsb*: *a transcript of the interview/trial*

transfer¹ /træns'fɜː(r)/ verb (**transferring**; **transferred**) 1 [I,T] **transfer (sb/sth) (from ...) (to ...)** to move, or to make sb/sth move, from one place to another □ *memindahkan; berpindah; bertukar*: *He's transferring to our Tokyo branch next month.* ◆ *I'd like to transfer £1 000 from my deposit account* (= in a bank). ◆ *Transfer the data onto a disk.* 2 [T] to officially arrange for sth to belong to, or be controlled by, sb else □ *memindah milik*: *She transferred the property to her son.* ▶**transferable** adj: *This ticket is not transferable* (= may only be used by the person who bought it).

transfer² /'trænsfɜː(r)/ noun 1 [C,U] moving or being moved from one place, job or state to another □ *pemindahan; pertukaran; bertukar*: *Paul is not happy here and has asked for a transfer.* 2 [U] changing to a different vehicle or route during a journey □ *pengangkutan; perjalanan*: *Transfer from the airport to the hotel is included.* 3 [C] (AmE) a ticket that allows you to continue your journey on another bus or train □ *tiket lanjutan* 4 [C] (especially BrE) a piece of paper with a picture or writing on it that you can stick onto another surface by pressing or heating it □ *gambar lekat alih*

transform /træns'fɔːm/ verb [T] **transform sb/sth (from sth) (into sth)** to change sb/sth completely, especially in a way which improves sb/sth □ *mengubah; menukar*: *Having a baby has transformed my life.* ▶**transformation** /ˌtrænsfə'meɪʃn/ noun [C,U]: *Our lifestyles have undergone a complete transformation in the past decade.*

transformer /træns'fɔːmə(r)/ noun [C] a device for reducing or increasing the strength of a supply of electricity, usually to allow a particular piece of electrical equipment to be used □ *transformer*

transfusion /træns'fjuːʒn/ noun [C] the act of putting new blood into sb's body because they are ill □ *transfusi; pemindahan darah*: *a blood transfusion*

transistor /træn'zɪstə(r); -'sɪstə(r)/ noun [C] a small piece of electronic equipment that is used in computers, radios, TVs, etc. □ *transistor*

transit /'trænzɪt; -sɪt/ noun [U] 1 the act of being moved or carried from one place to another □ *transit; pengangkutan; pemindahan*: *The goods had been damaged in transit.* 2 going through a place on the way to somewhere else □ *transit; persinggahan*

transition /træn'zɪʃn; -'sɪʃn/ noun [C,U] **(a) transition (from sth) (to sth)** a change from one state or form to another □ *peralihan*: *the transition from childhood to adolescence* ▶**transitional** /-ʃənl/ adj: *a transitional stage/period*

transitive /'trænsətɪv/ adj (used about a verb) that has a direct object. Transitive verbs are marked '[T]' in this dictionary. □ *transitif* **OPP** intransitive ❶ For more information about transitive verbs, look at the **Reference Section** at the back of this dictionary.

translate /træns'leɪt; trænz-/ verb [I,T] **translate (sth) (from sth) (into sth)** to change sth written or spoken from one language to another □ *menterjemahkan*: *This book has been translated from Czech into English.* ➔ look at **interpret** ▶**translation** /træns'leɪʃn; trænz-/ noun [C,U]: *a word-for-word translation* ◆ *The book loses something in translation.*

translator /træns'leɪtə(r); trænz-/ noun [C] a person who changes sth that has been written or spoken from one language to another □ *penterjemah* ➔ look at **interpreter**

translucent /træns'luːsnt; trænz-/ adj (formal) that light can pass through □ *lut cahaya* ➔ look at **opaque, transparent** ▶**translucence** (also **translucency** /-snsi/) noun [U]

transmission /træns'mɪʃn; trænz-/ noun 1 [U] sending sth out or passing sth on from one person, place or thing to another □ *penghantaran; penyiaran; pemancaran; penjangkitan*: *the transmission of TV pictures by satellite* ◆ *the transmission of a disease/virus* 2 [C] a TV or radio programme □ *siaran* 3 [U,C] the system in a car, etc. by which power is passed from the engine to the wheels □ *sistem gear*

transmit /træns'mɪt; trænz-/ *verb* [T] (**transmitting; transmitted**) **1** to send out TV or radio programmes, electronic signals, etc. □ *menyiarkan; memancarkan*: *The match was transmitted live all over the world.* **2** to send or pass sth from one person or place to another □ *menyampaikan; menjangkitkan*: *a sexually transmitted disease*

transmitter /træns'mɪtə(r); trænz-/ *noun* [C] a piece of equipment that sends out electronic signals, TV or radio programmes, etc. □ *alat pemancar*

transparency /træns'pærənsi/ *noun* [C] (*pl* **transparencies**) a picture printed on a piece of film, usually in a frame, that can be shown on a screen by shining light through the film □ *transparensi*: *a transparency for the overhead projector* ⊃ look at **slide**

transparent /træns'pærənt/ *adj* that you can see through □ *lut sinar; jernih*: *Glass is transparent.* **OPP** opaque ⊃ look at **translucent**

transplant¹ /træns'plɑːnt; trænz-/ *verb* [T] **1** to take out an organ or other part of sb's body and put it into another person's body □ *memindahkan* **2** to move a growing plant and plant it somewhere else □ *memindahkan; mengalih; mengubah* ⊃ look at **graft**

transplant² /'trænsplɑːnt; 'trænz-/ *noun* [C] a medical operation in which an organ, etc. is taken out of sb's body and put into another person's body □ *pemindahan*: *to have a heart/kidney transplant*

transport /'trænspɔːt/ (*AmE usually* **transportation** /ˌtrænspɔː'teɪʃn/) *noun* [U] **1** the act of carrying or taking people or goods from one place to another □ *pengangkutan*: *road/rail/sea transport* **2** vehicles that you travel in; a method of transport □ *kenderaan*: *Do you have your own transport (for example a car)?* ♦ *I travel to school by public transport.* ♦ *His bike is his only means of transport.* ⊃ picture on **page P6** ▶**transport** /træn'spɔːt/ *verb* [T]

transvestite /trænz'vestaɪt/ *noun* [C] a person, especially a man, who enjoys dressing like a member of the opposite sex □ *transvestit; pondan*

trap¹ /træp/ *noun* [C] **1** a piece of equipment that you use for catching animals □ *jerat; perangkap*: *a mousetrap* ♦ *The rabbit's leg was caught in the trap.* **2** a clever plan that is designed to trick sb □ *perangkap; jebak*: *She walked straight into the trap.* **3** an unpleasant situation from which it is hard to escape □ *jebak; perangkap*: *He thought of marriage as a trap.*

trap² /træp/ *verb* [T] (**trapping; trapped**) **1** [often passive] to keep sb in a dangerous place or a bad situation from which they cannot escape □ *terperangkap; terjebak*: *The door closed behind them and they were trapped.* ♦ *Many people are trapped in low-paid jobs.* **2** to catch and keep or store sth □ *memerangkap*: *Special glass panels trap heat from the sun.* **3** to force sb/sth into a place or situation from which they or it cannot escape □ *memerangkap*: *Police believe this new evidence could help trap the killer.* **4** to catch an animal, etc. in a trap □ *menjerat; memerangkap*: *Raccoons used to be trapped for their fur.* **5 trap sb (into sth/into doing sth)** to make sb do sth by tricking them □ *memperdaya; memerangkap*: *She had been trapped into revealing her true identity.*

trapdoor /'træpdɔː(r)/ *noun* [C] a small door in a floor or ceiling □ *pintu kolong; pintu di lantai atau siling*

trapeze /trə'piːz/ *noun* [C] a wooden or metal bar hanging from two ropes high above the ground, used by **acrobats** (= people who amuse an audience by performing difficult acts) □ *trapez; buai utk ahli akrobat bergayut*

trappings /'træpɪŋz/ *noun* [pl] (*formal*) clothes, possessions, etc. which are signs of a particular social position □ *perhiasan; benda-benda yg melambangkan taraf sosial sso*

trash /træʃ/ (*AmE*) = rubbish

trash can (*AmE*) = dustbin, litter bin

trashy /'træʃi/ *adj* (*informal*) (**trashier; trashiest**) of poor quality □ *tdk bermutu; picisan*: *trashy novels*

trauma /'trɔːmə/ *noun* [C,U] (an event that causes) a state of great shock or sadness □ *trauma; renjatan emosi*: *the trauma of losing your parents* ⊃ look at **stress** ▶**traumatic** /trɔː'mætɪk/ *adj*

travel¹ /'trævl/ *verb* (**travelling; travelled**, (*AmE*) **traveling; traveled**) **1** [I] to go from one place to another, especially over a long distance □ *mengembara; berpergian; pergi berjalan-jalan; pergi (ke sst tempat)*: *Charles travels a lot on business.* ♦ *to travel abroad* ♦ *to travel by sea/air/car* ♦ *to travel to work* ♦ *travelling expenses* ⊃ note at **plane, train 2** [I] to go or move at/in a particular speed, direction or distance □ *bergerak; beralih*: *News travels fast these days.* **3** [T] to make a journey of a particular distance □ *membuat perjalanan; berjalan*: *They travelled 60 kilometres to come and see us.*

IDM **travel light** to take very few things with you when you travel □ *tdk banyak membawa barang utk sst perjalanan*

travel² /'trævl/ *noun* **1** [U] the act of going from one place to another □ *perjalanan*: *air/rail/space travel* ♦ *a travel bag/clock/iron* (= designed to be used when travelling) **2 travels** [pl] time spent travelling, especially to places that are far away □ *perjalanan; pengembaraan*

OTHER WORDS FOR

travel

The word **travel** is uncountable and you can only use it to talk about the general activity of moving from place to place: *Foreign travel is very popular these days.* When you talk about going from one particular place to another, you use **journey**. A journey can be long: *the journey across Canada* or short but repeated: *the journey to work*. A **tour** is a circular journey or walk during which you visit several places. You often use **trip** when you are thinking about the whole visit (including your stay in a place and the journeys there and back): *We're just back from a trip to Japan. We had a wonderful time.* A trip may be short: *a day trip*, or longer: *a trip round the world*, and can be for business or pleasure. An **excursion** is a short organized trip with a group of people. You **go on** a journey/tour/trip/excursion.

'travel agency noun [C] (pl **travel agencies**) a company that makes travel arrangements for people (arranging tickets, flights, hotels, etc.) □ *agensi pelancongan/perjalanan*

'travel agent noun **1** [C] a person whose job is to make travel arrangements for people □ *ejen pelancongan/perjalanan* **2 travel agent's** [sing] the shop where you can go to make travel arrangements, buy tickets, etc. □ *pejabat ejen pelancongan/perjalanan* ⊃ note at **holiday**

traveller (*AmE* **traveler**) /'trævələ(r)/ noun [C] **1** a person who is travelling or who often travels □ *pengembara; orang yg sering membuat perjalanan*: *She is a frequent traveller to Belgium.* **2** (*BrE*) a person who travels around the country in a large vehicle and does not have a permanent home anywhere □ *orang yg hidup mengembara*: *New Age travellers* ⊃ note at **Gypsy**

'traveller's cheque (*AmE* **'traveler's check**) noun [C] a cheque that you can change into foreign money when you are travelling in other countries □ *cek kembara*

'travel-sick adj (*BrE*) feeling sick or **vomiting** (= bringing up food from the stomach) because of the movement of the vehicle you are travelling in □ *mabuk perjalanan* ⊃ look at **airsick, carsick, seasick**

trawl /trɔːl/ verb **1** [I,T] **trawl (through sth) (for sth/sb); trawl sth (for sth/sb)** to search through a large amount of information or a large number of people, places, etc. looking for a particular thing or person □ *meneliti; memerhatikan; mencari*: *The police are trawling through their files for similar cases.* ◆ *She trawled the shops for bargains.* **2** [I] **trawl (for sth)** to try to catch fish by pulling a large net with a wide opening through the water □ *berpukat tunda*

trawler /'trɔːlə(r)/ noun [C] a fishing boat that uses large nets that it pulls through the sea behind it □ *kapal pukat tunda*

tray /treɪ/ noun [C] **1** a flat piece of wood, plastic, metal, etc. with slightly higher edges that you use for carrying food, drink, etc. on □ *dulang* **2** a shallow plastic box, used for various purposes □ *bakul*

treacherous /'tretʃərəs/ adj **1** (used about a person) that you cannot trust and who may do sth to harm you □ *khianat; tdk jujur*: *He was cowardly and treacherous.* **2** dangerous, although seeming safe □ *berbahaya*: *The roads are treacherous this morning. There are icy patches.*

treachery /'tretʃəri/ noun [U] the act of causing harm to sb who trusts you □ *pengkhianatan*

treacle /'triːkl/ (*AmE* **molasses**) noun [U] a thick, dark, sticky liquid that is made from sugar □ *sirap pekat hitam* ⊃ look at **syrup**

tread¹ /tred/ verb (pt **trod** /trɒd/; pp **trodden** /'trɒdn/) **1** [I] (*especially BrE*) **tread (on/in/over sb/sth)** to put your foot down while you are walking □ *memijak*: *Don't tread in the puddle!* ◆ *He trod on my foot and didn't even say sorry!* **2** [T] **tread sth (in/into/down)** to press down on sth with your foot □ *memijak; menginjak*: *This wine is still made by treading grapes in the traditional way.*

tread² /tred/ noun **1** [sing] the sound you make when you walk; the way you walk □ *bunyi tapak kaki; cara berjalan* **2** [C,U] the pattern on the surface of a tyre on a vehicle which is slightly higher than the rest of the surface □ *bunga*

treason /'triːzn/ noun [U] the criminal act of causing harm to your country, for example by helping its enemies □ *penderhakaan; derhaka; pengkhianatan; khianat* ⊃ note at **traitor**

treasure¹ /'treʒə(r)/ noun **1** [U] a collection of very valuable objects, for example gold, silver, jewellery, etc. □ *harta kekayaan; barang-barang berharga*: *to find buried treasure* **2** [C, usually pl] something that is very valuable □ *sst yg amat berharga*

treasure² /'treʒə(r)/ verb [T] to consider sb/sth to be very special or valuable □ *menghargai*: *I will treasure those memories forever.*

'treasure hunt noun [C] a game in which people try to find a hidden prize by answering a series of questions that have been left in different places □ *permainan mencari harta karun*

treasurer /'treʒərə(r)/ noun [C] the person who looks after the money and accounts of a club or an organization □ *bendahari*

the Treasury /'treʒəri/ noun [sing, with sing or pl verb] the government department that controls public money □ *Perbendaharaan*

treat¹ /triːt/ verb [T]
▶BEHAVE TOWARDS SB/STH **1 treat sb/sth (with/as/like sth)** to act or behave towards sb/sth in a particular way □ *memperlakukan; buat*: *Teenagers hate being treated like children.* ◆ *They treat their workers like dirt* (= very badly). ◆ *You should treat older people with respect.* ◆ *to treat somebody badly/fairly/well*
▶CONSIDER STH **2 treat sth as sth** to consider sth in a particular way □ *menganggap; menyifatkan*: *I decided to treat his comment as a joke.* **3** to deal with or discuss sth in a particular way □ *mengolah; membincangkan*: *The article treats this question in great detail.*

treat → tremendous

▶ GIVE MEDICAL CARE **4 treat sb (for sth)** to use medicine or medical care to try to make a sick or injured person well again □ *merawat; mengubati: The boy was treated for burns at the hospital.*

▶ USE CHEMICAL **5 treat sth (with sth)** to put a chemical substance onto sth in order to protect it from damage, clean it, etc. □ *mengawet; merawat: Most vegetables are treated with insecticide.*

▶ PAY FOR STH SPECIAL **6 treat sb/yourself (to sth)** to pay for sth or give sb/yourself sth that is very special or enjoyable □ *membelanjai: Clare treated the children to ice creams* (= she paid for them).

treat² /triːt/ *noun* [C] something special or enjoyable that you pay for or give to sb/yourself □ *sst yg istimewa atau menyeronokkan: I've brought some cream cakes as a treat.* ◆ *It's a real treat for me to stay in bed late.*
IDM trick or treat ⇨ **trick**

treatment /ˈtriːtmənt/ *noun* **1** [U,C] **treatment (for sth)** the use of medicine or medical care to cure an illness or injury; something that is done to make sb feel and look good □ *rawatan: to require hospital/medical treatment* ◆ *The spa offers a wide range of beauty treatments.* **2** [U] the way that you behave towards sb or deal with sth □ *layanan; perlakuan: The treatment of the prisoners of war was very harsh.* **3** [U,C] **treatment (for sth)** a process by which sth is cleaned, protected from damage, etc. □ *perawatan; pengawetan: an effective treatment for dry rot*

treaty /ˈtriːti/ *noun* [C] (*pl* **treaties**) a written agreement between two or more countries □ *perjanjian; triti:* to sign a peace treaty

treble¹ /ˈtrebl/ *noun* [C] **1** a high singing voice, especially that of a young boy □ *trebel* **2** a boy who has a high singing voice □ *penyanyi suara trebel*

treble² /ˈtrebl/ *verb* [I,T] to become or to make sth three times bigger □ *menjadi tiga kali ganda: Prices have trebled in the past ten years.*
▶ **treble** *determiner: This figure is treble the number five years ago.*

tree /triː/ *noun* [C] a tall plant that can live for a long time. Trees have a thick wooden central part from which branches grow □ *pokok; pohon: an oak/apple/elm tree*

trek /trek/ *noun* [C] **1** a long hard walk, lasting several days or weeks, usually in the mountains □ *perjalanan jauh (dgn berjalan kaki)* **2** (*informal*) a long walk □ *berjalan kaki jauh: It's quite a trek to the shops from here.* ▶ **trek** *verb* [I] (**trekking**; **trekked**)

HELP We use **go trekking** to talk about walking long distances for pleasure.

trellis /ˈtrelɪs/ *noun* [C,U] a light wooden frame used to support climbing plants □ *junjung; jalaran; para-para*

tremble /ˈtrembl/ *verb* [I] **tremble (with sth)** to shake, for example because you are cold, frightened, etc. □ *menggeletar: She was pale and trembling with shock.* ◆ *His hand was trembling as he picked up his pen to sign.* ▶ **tremble** *noun* [C, usually sing]

tremendous /trəˈmendəs/ *adj* **1** very large or great □ *amat besar/banyak: a tremendous*

tree

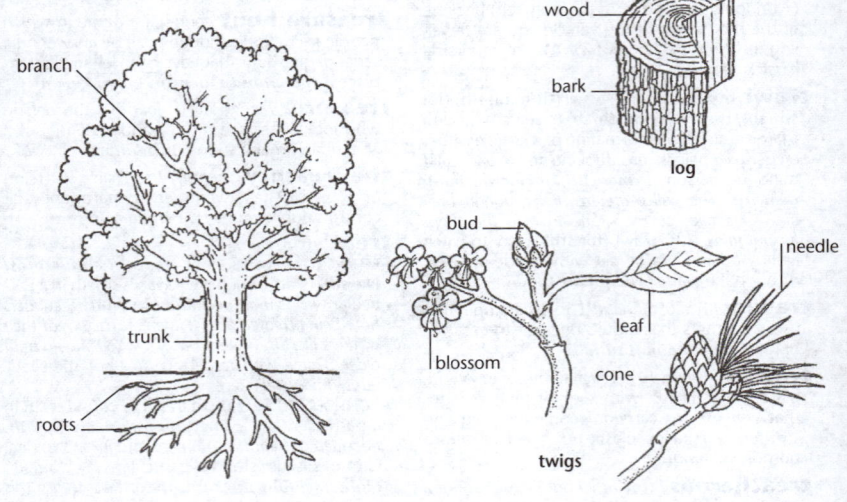

(labels: branch, trunk, roots, wood, bark, log, bud, blossom, leaf, needle, cone, twigs, tree)

[I] **intransitive**, a verb which has no object: *He laughed.*

[T] **transitive**, a verb which has an object: *He ate an apple.*

amount of work SYN **huge** **2** very good □ *hebat; sangat bagus*: *It was a tremendous experience.* SYN **great**

tremendously /trə'mendəsli/ *adv* very; very much □ *amat; sangat*: *tremendously exciting* ♦ *Prices vary tremendously from one shop to another.*

tremor /'tremə(r)/ *noun* [C] a slight shaking movement □ *getaran; gementar*: *There was a tremor in his voice.* ♦ *an earth tremor* (= a small earthquake)

trench /trentʃ/ *noun* [C] **1** a long narrow hole dug in the ground for water to flow along □ *parit* **2** a long deep hole dug in the ground for soldiers to hide in during enemy attacks □ *parit (pelindung)*: *life in the trenches during the First World War*

trend /trend/ *noun* [C] a trend (towards sth) a general change or development □ *trend; gaya; arah aliran*: *The current trend is towards smaller families.* ♦ *He always followed the latest trends in fashion.*
IDM **set a/the trend** to start a new style or fashion □ *memulakan trend, gaya atau fesyen baharu*
▶ **trend** *verb* [I] **be trending**: *Find out what's trending on Twitter right now.*

trendy /'trendi/ *adj* (**trendier**; **trendiest**) (*informal*) fashionable □ *mengikut fesyen/aliran baharu; bergaya*

trespass /'trespəs/ *verb* [I] to go onto sb's land or property without permission □ *menceroboh*
▶ **trespasser** *noun* [C]

trial /'traɪəl/ *noun* [C,U] **1** the process in a court of law where a judge, and often a jury, listens to evidence and decides if sb is guilty of a crime or not □ *perbicaraan*: *a fair trial* ♦ *He was on trial for murder.* ⊃ note at **court** **2** an act of testing sb/sth □ *ujian*: *New drugs must go through extensive trials.* ♦ *a trial period of three months*
IDM **trial and error** trying different ways of doing sth until you find the best one □ *cuba-cuba*

trial run *noun* [C] an occasion when you practise doing sth in order to make sure you can do it correctly later on □ *ujian percubaan*

triangle /'traɪæŋgl/ *noun* [C] **1** a shape that has three straight sides □ *segi tiga*: *a right-angled triangle* ⊃ picture at **shape** **2** a metal musical instrument in the shape of a triangle that you play by hitting it with a metal stick □ *kerincing* ⊃ picture at **music** **3** (*AmE*) = **set square**

triangular /traɪ'æŋgjələ(r)/ *adj* shaped like a triangle □ *berbentuk segi tiga*

triathlon /traɪ'æθlən/ *noun* [C] a sports competition in which you have to take part in three different events, usually swimming, cycling and running □ *triatlon* ⊃ look at **pentathlon**

tribe /traɪb/ *noun* [C] a group of people who have the same language and customs and who live in a particular area, often with one of the group as an official leader □ *suku kaum; puak*: *tribes living in the Amazonian rainforest* ▶ **tribal**

tremendously → trickle

/'traɪbl/ *adj*: *tribal art*

tribunal /traɪ'bjuːnl/ *noun* [C] a type of court with the authority to decide who is right in particular types of disagreement □ *tribunal*: *an industrial tribunal*

tributary /'trɪbjətri/ *noun* [C] (*pl* **tributaries**) a small river that flows into a larger river □ *cabang/cawang sungai*

tribute /'trɪbjuːt/ *noun* **1** [C,U] tribute (to sb/sth) something that you say or do to show that you respect or admire sb/sth, especially sb who has died □ *penghargaan; penghormatan*: *A special concert was held as a tribute to the composer.* **2** [sing] a tribute to sb/sth a sign of how good sb/sth is □ *tanda*: *The success of the festival is a tribute to the organizers.*
IDM **pay tribute to sb/sth** ⊃ **pay**[1]

trick /trɪk/ *noun* [C] **1** something that you do to make sb believe sth that is not true or a joke that you play to annoy sb □ *penipuan; tipu daya*: *The thieves used a trick to get past the security guards.* **2** something that confuses you so that you see, remember, understand, etc. things in the wrong way □ *muslihat*: *It was a trick question* (= one in which the answer looks easy, but actually is not). **3** an action that uses special skills to make people believe sth which is not true or real as a form of entertainment □ *silap mata; muslihat*: *The magician performed a trick in which he made a rabbit disappear.* ♦ *a card trick* **4** [usually sing] a clever or the best way of doing sth □ *teknik; cara*: *I can't get the top off this jar. Is there a trick to it?*
IDM **do the job/trick** ⊃ **job**
play a joke/trick on sb ⊃ **joke**[1]

trick or treat a custom in which children dress up in special clothes and go to people's houses on Halloween (= the evening of October 31st) and threaten to do sth bad to them if they do not give them sweets, etc □ *tradisi ugut-ugutan main-main yg dibuat oleh kanak-kanak pd waktu malam hari 'Hallowe'en'*: *to go trick or treating*
PHR V **trick sb into sth/doing sth** to persuade sb to do sth by making them believe sth that is not true □ *memperdaya atau menipu sso supaya berbuat sst*: *He tricked me into lending him money.*
trick sb out of sth to get sth from sb by making them believe sth that is not true □ *menipu sso utk mendapatkan sst*: *Stella was tricked out of her share of the money.*
▶ **trick** *verb* [T]: *I'd been tricked and I felt like a fool.*

trickery /'trɪkəri/ *noun* [U] the use of dishonest methods to trick sb in order to get what you want □ *penipuan*

trickle /'trɪkl/ *verb* [I] **1** (used about a liquid) to flow in a thin line □ *menitis*: *Raindrops trickled down the window.* **2** to go somewhere slowly and gradually □ *(pergi, datang, masuk, dsb ke sst tempat) secara beransur-ansur* ▶ **trickle** *noun* [C, usually sing]: *a trickle of water*

tricky /ˈtrɪki/ *adj* (**trickier**; **trickiest**) difficult to do or deal with □ *rumit*: *a tricky situation*

tricycle /ˈtraɪsɪkl/ *noun* [C] a bicycle that has one wheel at the front and two at the back □ *basikal roda tiga*

trifle /ˈtraɪfl/ *noun* **1 a trifle** [sing] [used as an adverb] (*formal*) slightly; rather □ *sedikit*; *agak* **2** [C] something that is of little value or importance □ *sst yg remeh-temeh* **3** [C,U] (*BrE*) a type of cold **dessert** (= a sweet food) made from cake and fruit covered with **custard** (= a sweet yellow sauce) and cream □ *trifel*

trifling /ˈtraɪflɪŋ/ *adj* (*formal*) very unimportant or small □ *remeh*; *tdk penting* **SYN** trivial

trigger¹ /ˈtrɪɡə(r)/ *noun* [C] **1** the part of a gun that you press to fire it □ *picu*; *pemetik*: *to pull the trigger* **2** the cause of a particular reaction or event, especially a bad one □ *pencetus*

trigger² /ˈtrɪɡə(r)/ *verb* [T] **trigger sth (off)** to make sth happen suddenly □ *mencetuskan*: *Smoke from the kitchen triggered off the fire alarm.*

trillion /ˈtrɪljən/ *number* one million million □ *trilion* ❶ For more information about numbers, look at the section on using numbers at the back of this dictionary.

trilogy /ˈtrɪlədʒi/ *noun* [C] (*pl* **trilogies**) a group of three novels, plays, films, etc. that form a set □ *trilogi*

trim¹ /trɪm/ *verb* [T] (**trimming**; **trimmed**) **1** to cut a small amount off sth so that it is tidy □ *menggunting sedikit*; *memangkas*: *to trim your hair/fringe/beard* ◆ *The hedge needs trimming.* **2 trim sth (off sth)** to cut sth off because you do not need it □ *memotong (buang)*; *mengurangkan*: *Trim the fat off the meat.* **3 trim sth (with sth)** to decorate the edge of sth with sth □ *menghias* ▸**trim** *noun* [C, usually sing]: *My hair needs a trim.*

trim² /trɪm/ *adj* **1** (used about a person) looking thin, healthy and attractive □ *langsing* **2** well cared for; tidy □ *kemas*; *rapi*

trimming /ˈtrɪmɪŋ/ *noun* **1 trimmings** [pl] extra things which you add to sth to improve its appearance, taste, etc. □ *alat tambahan* **2** [C,U] material that you use for decorating the edge of sth □ *hiasan*

the Trinity /ˈtrɪnəti/ *noun* [sing] (in Christianity) the union of Father, Son and Holy Spirit as one God □ *Triniti*; *Trinitas*

trinket /ˈtrɪŋkɪt/ *noun* [C] a piece of jewellery or an attractive small object that is not worth much money □ *barang perhiasan yg kodi dan murah*

trio /ˈtriːəʊ/ *noun* (*pl* **trios**) **1** [C, with sing or pl verb] a group of three people □ *trio*; *tiga serangkai* **2** [C] a piece of music for three people to play or sing □ *trio*

trip¹ /trɪp/ *noun* [C] a journey to a place and back again, either for pleasure or for a particular purpose □ *perjalanan*; *lawatan*: *How was your trip to Turkey?* ◆ *We had to make several trips to move all the furniture.* ◆ *to go on a business/shopping trip* ⊃ note at **travel** ▸**tripper** *noun* [C] (*BrE*): *Brighton was full of* **day trippers** (= people on trips that last for one day) *from London.*

trip² /trɪp/ *verb* (**tripping**; **tripped**) **1** [I] **trip (over/up)**; **trip (over/on sth)** to catch your foot on sth when you are walking and fall or nearly fall □ *tersandung*: *Don't leave your bag on the floor. Someone might trip over it.* ◆ *She tripped up on a loose paving stone.* **2** [T] **trip sb (up)** to catch sb's foot and make them fall or nearly fall □ *menyandung*: *Linda stuck out her foot and tripped Barry up.*

PHR V **trip (sb) up** to make a mistake; to make sb say sth that they did not want to say □ *cuba memerangkap sso (supaya dia menyatakan sst yg tdk mahu dinyatakannya)*: *The journalist asked a difficult question to try to trip the politician up.*

triple /ˈtrɪpl/ *adj* [only *before* a noun] having three parts, happening three times or containing three times as much as usual □ *tiga bahagian*, *kali atau kali ganda*: *You'll receive triple pay if you work over the New Year.* ▸**triple** *verb* [I,T]

the ˈtriple jump *noun* [sing] a sporting event in which people try to jump as far forward as possible with three jumps. The first jump lands on one foot, the second on the other, and the third on both feet. □ *lompat kijang*

triplet /ˈtrɪplət/ *noun* [C] one of three children or animals that are born to one mother at the same time □ *kembar tiga* ⊃ look at **twin**

tripod /ˈtraɪpɒd/ *noun* [C] a piece of equipment with three legs that you use for putting a camera, etc. on □ *tripod*; *kaki tiga* ⊃ picture at **camera**

triumph¹ /ˈtraɪʌmf/ *noun* [C,U] a great success or victory; the feeling of happiness that you have because of this □ *kejayaan*; *kemenangan*: *The team returned home in triumph.* ◆ *The new programme was a triumph with the public.*

triumph² /ˈtraɪʌmf/ *verb* [I] **triumph (over sb/sth)** to achieve success; to defeat sb/sth □ *berjaya*; *menang*; *mengalahkan*: *France triumphed over Brazil in the final.*

triumphant /traɪˈʌmfənt/ *adj* feeling or showing great happiness because you have won or succeeded at sth □ *(yg) menang/berjaya*: *a triumphant cheer* ▸**triumphantly** *adv*

trivial /ˈtrɪviəl/ *adj* of little importance; not worth considering □ *remeh-temeh*; *tdk penting*: *a trivial detail/problem* ▸**triviality** /ˌtrɪviˈæləti/ *noun* [C,U] (*pl* **trivialities**)

trivialize (also **-ise**) /ˈtrɪviəlaɪz/ *verb* [T] to make sth seem less important, serious, etc. than it really is □ *memperkecil-kecilkan*; *memandang ringan*

trod past tense of **tread¹**

trodden past participle of **tread¹**

troll /trɒl; trəʊl/ noun [C] (informal) a message to a discussion group on the Internet that sb sends to make other people angry; a person who sends a message like this □ *mesej hasut; orang yg menghantar mesej itu* ⊃ note at **chat room**

trolleys

shopping trolley
(*AmE* **shopping cart**)

luggage trolley
(*AmE* **baggage cart**)

trolley /'trɒli/ noun [C] **1** (*AmE* **cart**) a piece of equipment on wheels that you use for carrying things □ *troli*: *a supermarket/shopping/luggage trolley* **2** (*BrE*) a small table with wheels that is used for carrying or serving food and drinks □ *troli*: *a tea/sweet/drinks trolley* **3** (*AmE*) = **tram**

trombone /trɒmˈbəʊn/ noun [C] a large musical instrument made of **brass** (= a yellow metal) that you play by blowing into it and moving a long tube backwards and forwards □ *trombon* ⊃ picture at **music**

troop /truːp/ noun **1 troops** [pl] soldiers □ *askar* **2** [C] a large group of people or animals □ *kumpulan* ▸**troop** verb [I]: *When the bell rang everyone trooped into the hall.*

trophy /'trəʊfi/ noun [C] (pl **trophies**) a large silver cup, etc. that you get for winning a competition or race □ *piala* ⊃ picture at **medal**

tropic /'trɒpɪk/ noun **1** [C, usually sing] one of the two imaginary lines around the earth that are 23° 26′ north and south of the **equator** (= the line around the middle of the earth). The lines are called the Tropic of Cancer (= north) and the Tropic of Capricorn (= south). □ *garisan (Sartan atau Jadi)* ⊃ picture at **earth 2 the tropics** [pl] the part of the world that is between these two lines, where the climate is hot and wet □ *kawasan tropika* ▸**tropical** /-kl/ adj: *tropical fruit* ◆ *tropical fish* ◆ *a tropical island*

trot¹ /trɒt/ verb [I] (**trotting**; **trotted**) **1** (used about a horse and its rider) to move forward at a speed that is faster than a walk □ *meligas* ⊃ look at **canter**, **gallop 2** (used about a person or an animal) to walk fast, taking short quick steps □ *berlari-lari anak*

PHR V **trot sth out** (*informal*) to repeat an old idea rather than thinking of sth new to say □ *berturut-turut; berterusan*: *to trot out the same old story*

trot² /trɒt/ noun [sing] a speed that is faster than a walk □ *meligas*
IDM **on the trot** (*BrE informal*) one after another; without stopping □ *berturut-turut;* *berterusan*: *We worked for six hours on the trot.*

trouble¹ /'trʌbl/ noun **1** [U,C] **trouble (with sb/sth)** (a situation that causes) a problem, difficulty or worry □ *masalah; (mendapat) susah*: *If I don't get home by 11 o'clock I'll be in trouble.* ◆ *I'm having trouble getting the car started.* ◆ *I'm having trouble with my car.* ◆ *financial troubles* ◆ *Marie is clever. The trouble is she's very lazy.* **2** [U] illness or pain □ *sakit*: *back/heart trouble* **3** [U] a situation where people are fighting or arguing with each other □ *kekacauan*: *There's often trouble in town on Saturday night after the bars have closed.* **4** [U] extra work or effort □ *kesusahan; susah payah; menyusahkan*: *Let's eat out tonight. It will save you the trouble of cooking.* ◆ *Why don't you stay the night with us? It's no trouble.* ◆ *I'm sorry to put you to so much trouble.*
IDM **ask for trouble/it** ⊃ **ask**
get into trouble to get into a situation which is dangerous or in which you may be punished □ *mendapat susah*
go to a lot of trouble (to do sth) to put a lot of work or effort into sth □ *bersusah payah (membuat sst)*: *They went to a lot of trouble to make us feel welcome.*
take trouble over/with sth; take trouble to do sth/doing sth to do sth with care □ *membuat sst dgn teliti*
take the trouble to do sth to do sth even though it means extra work or effort □ *bersusah payah membuat sst*

trouble² /'trʌbl/ verb [T] **1** to make sb worried, upset, etc. □ *menyusahkan*: *Is there something troubling you?* **2** (*formal*) **trouble sb (for sth)** (used when you are politely asking sb for sth or to do sth) to disturb sb □ *menyusahkan; mengganggu*: *Sorry to trouble you, but would you mind answering a few questions?* **SYN** for both meanings **bother**

troublemaker /'trʌblmeɪkə(r)/ noun [C] a person who often deliberately causes trouble □ *pengacau*

troubleshoot /'trʌblʃuːt/ verb [I,T] **1** to analyse and solve serious problems for a company or other organization □ *menyelesaikan masalah* **2** to identify and correct faults in a computer system □ *membaiki kerosakan* ▸**troubleshooter** noun [C] ▸**troubleshooting** noun [U]

troublesome /'trʌblsəm/ adj causing trouble, pain, etc. over a long period of time □ *menyusahkan* **SYN** annoying

trough /trɒf/ noun [C] **1** a long narrow container from which farm animals eat or drink □ *palung* **2** a low area or point between two higher areas □ *jurang*

trousers /'traʊzəz/ (*AmE* **pants**) noun [pl] a piece of clothing that covers the body from the waist down and is divided into two parts to cover each leg separately □ *seluar panjang* ⊃ picture on page P1

trout → trust

GRAMMAR Trousers are plural, so we cannot say, for example, 'a new trouser'. The following are possible: *I need some trousers/a pair of trousers.* • *These trousers are too tight.* Before another noun the form **trouser** is used: *a trouser suit* (= a woman's suit consisting of a jacket and trousers).

trout /traʊt/ *noun* [C,U] (*pl* trout) a type of fish that lives in rivers and that we eat □ *ikan trout*

trowel /ˈtraʊəl/ *noun* [C] **1** a small garden tool used for lifting plants, digging small holes, etc. □ *kulir; sudip* ⊃ picture at **garden 2** a small tool with a flat blade, used in building □ *kulir; sudip*

truant /ˈtruːənt/ *noun* [C] a child who stays away from school without permission □ *budak yg ponteng sekolah*
IDM **play truant**; (*AmE*) **play hooky** to stay away from school without permission □ *ponteng sekolah*
▶ **truancy** /-ənsi/ *noun* [U]

truce /truːs/ *noun* [C] an agreement to stop fighting for a period of time □ *perdamaian sementara* ⊃ look at **ceasefire**

truck /trʌk/ *noun* [C] **1** (*especially AmE*) = **lorry**: *a truck driver* **2** (*AmE* **car**) a section of a train that is used for carrying goods or animals □ *gerabak barang*: *a cattle truck*

trudge /trʌdʒ/ *verb* [I] to walk with slow, heavy steps, for example because you are very tired □ *berjalan dgn susah payah*

true /truː/ *adj* (**truer**; **truest**) **1** right or correct □ *benar; betul*: *Is it true that Adam is leaving?* • *I didn't think the film was at all true to life* (= it didn't show life as it really is). • *Read the statements and decide if they are true or false.* **OPP** **untrue, false 2** real or genuine, often when this is different from how sth seems □ *benar*: *The novel was based on a true story.* **OPP** **false 3** having all the typical qualities of the thing mentioned □ *sebenar*: *How do you know when you have found true love?* **4 true (to sb/sth)** behaving as expected or as promised □ *menepati janji; setia*: *He was true to his word* (= he did what he had promised). • *She has been a true friend to me.* ⊃ *noun* **truth**
IDM **come true** to happen in the way you hoped or dreamed □ *menjadi kenyataan*: *Winning was like a dream come true!*
too good to be true used to say that you cannot believe that sth is as good as it seems □ *terlalu baik, dsb hingga sukar dipercayai*
true to form typical; as usual □ *spt biasa/kebiasaannya*

truly /ˈtruːli/ *adv* **1** (used to emphasize a feeling or statement) really; completely □ *benar-benar; sungguh-sungguh*: *We are truly grateful to you for your help.* • *I'm really and truly sorry.* **2** used to emphasize that sth is correct or accurate □ *sebenarnya; dgn benar*: *I cannot truly say that I was surprised at the news.*

MORE **Yours truly** is often used at the end of a formal letter in American English.

⊃ note at **sincere**
IDM **well and truly** ⊃ **well¹**

trump /trʌmp/ *noun* [C] (in some card games) a card of the chosen **suit** (= one of the four sets) that has a higher value than cards of the other three suits during a particular game □ *daun terup yg lebih nilainya*: *Spades are trumps.*

ˈtrump card *noun* [C] a special advantage you have over other people that you keep secret until you can surprise them with it □ *kelebihan yg dirahsiakan*: *It was time for her to play her trump card.*

trumpet /ˈtrʌmpɪt/ *noun* [C] a musical instrument made of **brass** (= a yellow metal) that you play by blowing into it. There are three buttons on it which you press to make different notes. □ *trompet* ⊃ note at **music** ⊃ picture at **music**

truncheon /ˈtrʌntʃən/ *noun* [C] (*especially BrE*) (also **baton**) a short thick stick that a police officer carries as a weapon □ *cota; tongkat waran*

trundle /ˈtrʌndl/ *verb* [I,T] to move, or make sth heavy move, slowly and noisily □ *bergerak dgn berat, perlahan-lahan serta bising*: *A lorry trundled down the hill.*

trunk /trʌŋk/ *noun*
▶ TREE **1** [C] the thick central part of a tree that the branches grow from □ *batang* ⊃ picture at **tree**
▶ CAR **2** [C] (*AmE*) = **boot¹**(2)
▶ ELEPHANT **3** [C] the long nose of an **elephant** (= a very large grey animal) □ *belalai gajah* ⊃ picture at **elephant** ⊃ picture on **page P12**
▶ CLOTHING **4 trunks** [pl] = **swimming trunks**
▶ LARGE BOX **5** [C] a large box that you use for storing or transporting things □ *peti besar* ⊃ picture on **page P8**
▶ BODY **6** [usually sing] the main part of your body (not including your head, arms and legs) □ *badan; tubuh*

trust¹ /trʌst/ *noun* **1** [U] **trust (in sb/sth)** the belief that sb/sth is good, honest, sincere, etc. and will not try to harm or trick you □ *kepercayaan; saling mempercayai*: *Our marriage is based on love and trust.* • *I should never have put my trust in him.* ⊃ look at **distrust, mistrust 2** [C,U] a legal arrangement by which a person or an organization looks after money and property for sb else, usually until that person is old enough to control it □ *amanah*: *The money was put into (a) trust for the children.*
IDM **take sth on trust** to believe what sb says without having proof that it is true □ *mempercayai sst tanpa bukti*: *I can't prove it. You must take it on trust.*

trust² /trʌst/ *verb* [T] **trust sb (to do sth)**; **trust sb (with sth)** to believe that sb/sth is good, sincere, honest, etc. and that they will not trick you or try to harm you □ *mempercayai*: *He said the car was safe but I just don't trust him.* • *You can't*

trust her with money. ♦ You can trust Penny to do the job well. ⊃ look at **distrust**, **mistrust**
IDM **trust you, him, her, etc. (to do sth)** (*spoken*) it is typical of sb to do sth □ *Memang biasalah (bagi sso berbuat begitu)*: Trust Alice to be late. She's never on time!

trustee /trʌˈstiː/ noun [C] a person who looks after money or property for sb else □ *pemegang amanah*

trusting /ˈtrʌstɪŋ/ adj believing that other people are good, sincere, honest, etc. □ *mudah percaya (pd orang)*

trustworthy /ˈtrʌstwɜːði/ adj that you can depend on to be good, sincere, honest, etc. □ *boleh dipercayai*

truth /truːθ/ noun (pl truths /truːðz/) **1 the truth** [sing] what is true; the facts □ *sebenarnya*: Please tell me the truth. ♦ Are you telling me **the whole truth** about what happened? ♦ **The truth is**, we can't afford to live here any more. **2** [U] the state or quality of being true □ *kebenaran*: There's a lot of truth in what she says. **3** [C] a fact or an idea that is believed by most people to be true □ *hakikat*: scientific/universal truths ⊃ adjective **true**

truthful /ˈtruːθfl/ adj **1 truthful (about sth)** (used about a person) who tells the truth □ *jujur; terus terang*: He was less than truthful about his part in the crime. ♦ I don't think you're being truthful with me. **SYN** honest **2** (used about a statement) true or correct □ *sebenar; benar*: a truthful account ▶ **truthfully** /-fəli/ adv

try¹ /traɪ/ verb (trying; tries; pt, pp tried) **1** [I,T] **try (to do sth)** to make an effort to do sth □ *mencuba; cuba*: I tried to phone you but I couldn't get through. ♦ She was **trying hard** not to laugh. ♦ She'll **try her best** to help you. ♦ I'm sure you can do it if you try.

HELP **Try and** is more informal than **try to**. It cannot be used in the past tense: *I'll try and get there on time*. ♦ *I tried to get there on time, but I was late.*

2 [T] **try (doing) sth** to do, use or test sth in order to see how good or successful it is □ *mencuba; cuba*: 'I've tried everything but I can't get the baby to sleep.' 'Have you tried taking her out in the car?' ♦ Have you ever tried raw fish? ♦ We tried the door but it was locked.

GRAMMAR Compare **try to do sth** with **try doing sth**: *I tried to pick up the box, but it was too heavy* (= I attempted to pick it up, but I couldn't.) ♦ *'I've got a sore throat.' 'You should try taking some medicine.'* (= Medicine might help you feel better.)

3 [T] **try sb (for sth)** to examine sb in a court of law in order to decide if they are guilty of a crime or not □ *membicarakan; dibicarakan*: He was tried for murder.
IDM **try your hand at sth** to do sth such as an activity or a sport for the first time □ *mencuba membuat sst*

PHR V **try sth on** to put on a piece of clothing to see if it fits you properly □ *mencuba sst*: Can I try these jeans on, please? ⊃ note at **clothes**
try sb/sth out to test sb/sth to find out if he/she/it is good enough □ *mencuba*

try² /traɪ/ noun [C] (pl tries) an occasion when you try to do sth □ *percubaan*: I don't know if I can move it by myself, but I'll **give it a try**. **SYN** attempt

trying /ˈtraɪɪŋ/ adj that makes you tired or angry □ *meletihkan; memanaskan hati*: a trying journey

tsar (also **czar**, **tzar**) /zɑː(r)/ noun [C] **1** the title of the ruler of Russia in the past □ *Tsar*: Tsar Nicholas II **2** an expert, usually chosen by a government, with responsibility for sth important □ *tsar; pakar*: the Government's social media tsar

tsarina (also **czarina**, **tzarina**) /zɑːˈriːnə/ noun [C] the title of the female ruler of Russia in the past □ *Tsarina*

ˈT-shirt (also **teeshirt**) noun [C] a shirt with short sleeves and without buttons or a **collar** (= a folded part around the neck) □ *kemeja-T*

tsp abbr = **teaspoon** (2) □ *sudu kecil*: Add 1 tsp salt.

tsunami /tsuːˈnɑːmi/ noun [C] a very large wave in the sea caused, for example, by an **earthquake** (= a violent movement of the earth's surface) □ *tsunami* ⊃ look at **tidal wave**

tub /tʌb/ noun [C] **1** a large round container □ *besen; pasu*: On the terrace there were several tubs with flowers in them. **2** a small plastic container with a lid that is used for holding food □ *tab*: a tub of margarine/ice cream **3** (especially AmE informal) = **bath¹** (1) ⊃ picture at **container**

tuba /ˈtjuːbə/ noun [C] a large musical instrument made of **brass** (= a yellow metal) that makes a low sound □ *tuba* ⊃ picture at **music**

tube /tjuːb/ noun **1** [C] a long empty pipe □ *tiub*: Blood flowed along the tube into the bottle. ♦ the inner tube of a bicycle tyre ⊃ look at **test tube 2** [C] **a tube (of sth)** a long thin container with a lid at one end made of soft plastic or metal. Tubes are used for holding thick liquids that can be squeezed out of them □ *tiub*: a tube of toothpaste ⊃ picture at **container 3** **the tube** (also **the Tube**™) [sing] (*BrE informal*) = **underground³**: We came by tube.

tuberculosis /tjuːˌbɜːkjuˈləʊsɪs/ noun [U] (abbr **TB**) a serious disease that affects the lungs □ *TB; tuberkulosis; batuk kering*

tubing /ˈtjuːbɪŋ/ noun [U] a long piece of metal, rubber, etc. in the shape of a tube □ *tetiub*

TUC /ˌtiː juː ˈsiː/ abbr the **Trades Union Congress**; the association of British **trade unions** (= organizations for people who work in the same industry) □ *TUC (Kongres Kesatuan Sekerja)*

[C] **countable**, a noun with a plural form: *one book, two books* [U] **uncountable**, a noun with no plural form: *some sugar*

tuck /tʌk/ verb [T] **1 tuck sth in, under, round, etc. (sth)** to put or fold the ends or edges of sth into or round sth else so that it looks tidy □ *melipatkan; memasukkan; menyelitkan*: *Tuck your shirt in—it looks untidy like that.* **2 tuck sth (away)** to put sth into a small space, especially to hide it or to keep it safe □ *menyelitkan*: *The letter was tucked behind a pile of books.*
PHR V **tuck sth away 1** [only in the passive form] to be hidden □ *tersorok*: *The house was tucked away among the trees.* **2** to hide sth somewhere; to keep sth in a safe place □ *menyembunyikan atau menyimpan dgn selamat*: *He tucked his wallet away in his inside pocket.*
tuck sb in/up to make sb feel comfortable in bed by pulling the covers up around them □ *menyelimutkan sso (supaya tidur selesa)*
tuck in; tuck into sth (*BrE informal*) to eat with pleasure □ *makan dgn penuh selera*

Tue. (also **Tues.**) abbr = **Tuesday** □ *Selasa*: *Tue. 9 March*

Tuesday /ˈtjuːzdeɪ; -di/ noun [C,U] (abbr **Tue.; Tues.**) the day of the week after Monday □ *Selasa* ⊃ note at **Monday**

tuft /tʌft/ noun [C] a small amount of hair, grass, etc. growing together □ *jambul; jumbai; jambak*

tug¹ /tʌɡ/ verb [I,T] (**tugging; tugged**) **tug (at/on sth)** to pull sth hard and quickly, often several times □ *menarik-narik; menyentap*: *The boy tugged at his father's trouser leg.*

tug² /tʌɡ/ noun [C] **1** (also **tugboat** /ˈtʌɡbəʊt/) a small powerful boat that is used for pulling ships into a port, etc. □ *bot tunda* **2** a sudden hard pull □ *tarikan; sentapan*: *She gave the rope a tug.*

tuition /tjuˈɪʃn/ noun [U] **tuition (in sth)** teaching, especially to a small group of people □ *tuisyen*: *private tuition in Italian* ♦ *tuition fees* (= the money that you pay to be taught, especially in a college or university)

tulip /ˈtjuːlɪp/ noun [C] a brightly coloured flower, shaped like a cup, that grows in the spring □ *bunga tulip*

tumble /ˈtʌmbl/ verb [I] **1** to fall down suddenly but without serious injury □ *jatuh bergolek*: *He tripped and tumbled all the way down the steps.* **2** to fall suddenly in value or amount □ *jatuh menjunam*: *House prices have tumbled.* **3** to move or fall somewhere in an untidy way □ *tunggang-langgang*: *She opened her bag and all her things tumbled out of it.*
PHR V **tumble down** to fall down □ *roboh; runtuh*: *The walls of the old house were tumbling down.*
▶ **tumble** noun [C, usually sing]

tumble 'dryer (also **tumble-drier**) noun [C] (*BrE*) a machine that dries clothes by moving them about in hot air □ *mesin pengering*

tumbler /ˈtʌmblə(r)/ noun [C] a glass for drinking out of with straight sides and no handle □ *gelas* ⊃ picture at **glass**

tummy /ˈtʌmi/ (pl **tummies**) (*informal*) = **stomach¹**

tumour (*AmE* **tumor**) /ˈtjuːmə(r)/ noun [C] a mass of cells growing in or on a part of the body where they should not, usually causing medical problems □ *tumor; ketumbuhan*: *a brain tumour*

tumultuous /tjuːˈmʌltʃuəs/ adj very noisy, because people are excited □ *gamat; riuh-rendah*: *a tumultuous welcome* ♦ *tumultuous applause*

tuna /ˈtjuːnə/ (also **ˈtuna fish**) noun [C,U] (pl **tuna**) a large sea fish that we eat □ *tuna*: *a tin of tuna*

tune¹ /tjuːn/ noun [C,U] a series of musical notes that are sung or played to form a piece of music □ *lagu; melodi; tiun*: *The children played us a tune on their recorders.*
IDM **call the shots/tune** ⊃ **call¹**
change your tune ⊃ **change¹**
in/out of tune 1 (not) singing or playing the correct musical notes to sound pleasant □ *serentak atau senada; berbunyi sumbang atau salah nada*: *You're singing out of tune.* **2** having/ not having the same opinions, interests, feelings, etc. as sb/sth □ *secocok atau serasi; tdk secocok atau serasi*: *The President doesn't seem to be in tune with what ordinary people are thinking.*

tune² /tjuːn/ verb [T] **1** to make small changes to the sound a musical instrument makes so that it plays the correct notes □ *menala*: *to tune a piano/guitar* **2** to make small changes to an engine so that it runs well □ *menala* **3** [usually passive] **tune sth (in) (to sth)** to move the controls on a radio or TV so that you can receive a particular station □ *menala; mengikuti*: *Stay tuned to this station for the latest news.*
PHR V **tune in (to sth)** to listen to a radio programme or watch a TV programme □ *memasang/mengikuti (sst saluran radio atau televisyen)*
tune sth up to make small changes to a group of musical instruments so that they sound pleasant when played together □ *menalakan*

tuneful /ˈtjuːnfl/ adj (used about music) nice or pleasant to listen to □ *merdu*

tunic /ˈtjuːnɪk/ noun [C] **1** a piece of women's clothing, usually without sleeves, that is long and not tight □ *tunik* **2** (*BrE*) the jacket that is part of the uniform of police officers, soldiers, etc. □ *baju*

tunnel /ˈtʌnl/ noun [C] a passage built underground □ *terowong*: *The train disappeared into a tunnel.* ▶ **tunnel** verb [I,T] (**tunnelling; tunnelled**, (*AmE*) **tunneling; tunneled**)

turban /ˈtɜːbən/ noun [C] a covering for the head worn especially by Muslim and Sikh men. A **turban** is made by folding a long piece of cloth around the head. □ *serban*

turbine /ˈtɜːbaɪn/ noun [C] a machine or an engine that receives its power from a wheel that is turned by the pressure of water, air or gas ☐ *turbin*

turbulent /ˈtɜːbjələnt/ adj **1** in which there is a lot of sudden change, confusion, disagreement and sometimes violence ☐ *bergolak; bergelora* **2** (used about water or air) moving in a violent way ☐ *bergelora* ▶ **turbulence** noun [U]

turf¹ /tɜːf/ noun [U,C] (a piece of) short thick grass and the layer of soil underneath it ☐ *kepingan tanah berumput*

turf² /tɜːf/ verb [T] to cover ground with turf ☐ *menanam rumput*
PHR V **turf sb out (of sth)** (BrE informal) to force sb to leave a place ☐ *menghalau sso (dr sst tempat)*

turkey /ˈtɜːki/ noun [C,U] a large bird that is kept on farms for its meat. Turkeys are usually eaten at Christmas in Britain and at Thanksgiving in the US. ☐ *ayam belanda*
IDM **cold turkey** ⊃ **cold¹**

Turkish delight /ˌtɜːkɪʃ dɪˈlaɪt/ noun [U,C] a sweet made from a substance like jelly that is flavoured with fruit and covered with fine white sugar ☐ *sejenis gula-gula*

turmoil /ˈtɜːmɔɪl/ noun [U, sing] a state of great noise or confusion ☐ *kekacauan; kebingungan*: *Her mind was in (a) turmoil.* ♦ *His statement threw the court into turmoil.*

turn¹ /tɜːn/ verb
➤MOVE ROUND **1** [I,T] to move or make sth move round a fixed central point ☐ *berpusing; memusingkan; berputar; memutarkan*: *The wheels turned faster and faster.* ♦ *She turned the key in the lock.* ♦ *Turn the steering wheel to the right.*
➤CHANGE POSITION/DIRECTION **2** [I,T] to move your body, or part of your body, so that you are facing in a different direction ☐ *berpaling; menoleh*: *He turned round when he heard my voice.* ♦ *She turned her back on me* (= she deliberately moved her body to face away from me). **3** [T] to change the position of sth ☐ *membalikkan; menterbalikkan; menyelak; membuka*: *I turned the box upside down.* ♦ *He turned the page and started the next chapter.* **4** [I,T] to change direction when you are moving ☐ *membelok; belok; memusing*: *Go straight on and* **turn left** *at the church.* ♦ *The car* **turned the corner.**
➤AIM **5** [T] to point or aim sth in a particular direction ☐ *beralih; mengalihkan*: *She turned her attention back to me.*
➤BECOME **6** [I,T] (to cause) to become ☐ *berubah; bertukar*: *He* **turned** *very red when I asked him about the money.* ♦ *These caterpillars will turn into butterflies.*
➤AGE/TIME **7** [T] [not used in the continuous tenses] to reach or pass a particular age or time ☐ *sudah*: *It's turned midnight.*

919 **turbine → turn**

ℹ For idioms containing **turn**, look at the entries for the nouns, adjectives, etc. For example **turn a blind eye** is at **blind**.

PHR V **turn (sth) around/round** to change position or direction in order to face the opposite way, or to return the way you came; to make sth do this ☐ *memusingkan; berpusing; pusing balik; berpatah balik*: *This road is a dead end. We'll have to turn round and go back to the main road.* ♦ *He turned the car around and drove off.*

turn away to stop looking at sb/sth ☐ *berpaling*: *She turned away in horror at the sight of the blood.*

turn sb away to refuse to allow a person to go into a place ☐ *menolak/tdk menerima sso*

turn back to return the same way that you came ☐ *berpatah balik*: *We've come so far already, we can't turn back now.*

turn sb/sth down to refuse an offer, etc. or the person who makes it ☐ *menolak sso/sst*: *Why did you turn that job down?* ♦ *He asked her to marry him, but she turned him down.*

turn sth down to reduce the sound or heat that sth produces ☐ *mengecilkan/memperlahankan sst*: *Turn the TV down!*

turn off (sth) to leave one road and go on another ☐ *membelok; menyimpang*

turn sth off to stop the flow of electricity, water, etc. by moving a switch, tap, etc. ☐ *menutup/memadamkan sst*: *He turned the TV off.*

turn sth on to start the flow of electricity, water, etc. by moving a switch, tap, etc. ☐ *membuka/memasang sst*: *to turn the lights on*

turn out (for sth) to be present at an event ☐ *datang/keluar (menghadiri sst)*

turn out (to be sth) to be in the end ☐ *menjadi; rupanya*: *The weather turned out fine.* ♦ *The house that they had promised us turned out to be a tiny flat.*

turn sth out to move the switch, etc. on a light or a source of heat to stop it ☐ *memadamkan/menutup sst*: *Turn the lights out before you go to bed.*

turn over 1 to change position so that the other side is facing out or upwards ☐ *berpaling*: *He turned over and went back to sleep.* **2** (used about an engine) to start or to continue to run ☐ *menghidupkan enjin atau membiarkannya berjalan* **3** (BrE) to change to another programme when you are watching TV ☐ *menukar*: *This film's awful. Shall I turn over?*

turn sth over 1 to make sth change position so that the other side is facing out or upwards ☐ *membalikkan; menterbalikkan*: *You may now turn over your exam papers and begin.* **2** to keep thinking about sth carefully ☐ *memikir-mikirkan*: *She kept turning over what he'd said in her mind.*

turn to sb/sth to go to sb/sth to get help, advice, etc. ☐ *meminta nasihat, bantuan, dsb drpd sso/sst*

CONSONANTS   p **p**en   b **b**ad   t **t**ea   d **d**id   k **c**at   g **g**ot   tʃ **ch**in   dʒ **J**une   f **f**all   v **v**an   θ **th**in

turn → twang 920

turn up 1 to arrive; to appear □ *tiba; muncul*: *What time did they finally turn up?* **2** to be found, especially by chance □ *dijumpai*: *I lost my glasses a week ago and they haven't turned up yet.*

turn sth up to increase the sound or heat that sth produces □ *membesarkan atau menguatkan sst*: *Turn the heating up—I'm cold.*

ʔ turn² /tɜːn/ *noun* [C]
▶MOVEMENT **1** the act of turning sb/sth round □ *pusingan; putaran*: *Give the screw another couple of turns to make sure it is really tight.*
▶IN VEHICLE **2** a change of direction in a vehicle □ *pusingan*: *to make a left/right turn* ♦ *a U-turn* (= when you turn round in a vehicle and go back in the opposite direction)
▶IN ROAD **3** (*BrE also* **turning**) a bend or corner in a road, river, etc. □ *selekoh; belokan*: *Take the next turn on the left.*
▶TIME **4** [usually sing] the time when sb in a group of people should or is allowed to do sth □ *giliran*: *When it's your turn, take another card.* ♦ *Please wait in the queue until it is your turn.* ♦ *Whose turn is it to do the cleaning?*
▶CHANGE **5** an unusual or unexpected change □ *perubahan; berubah (menjadi lebih teruk, baik, dsb)*: *The patient's condition has taken a turn for the worse* (= suddenly got worse).
IDM **(do sb) a good turn** (to do) sth that helps sb □ *menolong sso*: *Well, that's my good turn for today.*
in turn one after the other □ *satu demi satu; seorang demi seorang*: *I spoke to each of the children in turn.*
take turns (at sth); take it in turns to do sth one after the other to make sure it is fair □ *bergilir-gilir (membuat sst)*
the turn of the century/year the time when a new century/year starts □ *peralihan abad; bermulanya abad/tahun baharu*
wait your turn ⇨ **wait¹**

turning /ˈtɜːnɪŋ/ (*BrE* **turn**) *noun* [C] a place where one road leads off from another □ *belokan; simpang*: *We must have taken a wrong turning.*

ˈturning point *noun* [C] **a turning point (in sth)** a time when an important change happens, usually a good one □ *titik perubahan*

turnip /ˈtɜːnɪp/ *noun* [C,U] a round white vegetable that grows under the ground □ *turnip*

ˈturn-off *noun* [C] the place where a road leads away from a larger or more important road □ *jalan susur*: *This is the turn-off for York.*

turnout /ˈtɜːnaʊt/ *noun* [C, usually sing] the number of people who go to a meeting, sports event, etc. □ *jumlah hadirin, penonton, dsb*: *There was a good turnout despite the rain.*

turnover /ˈtɜːnəʊvə(r)/ *noun* [C, usually sing] **a turnover (of sth) 1** the amount of business that a company does in a particular period of time □ *pusing ganti*: *The firm has an annual turnover of $50 million.* **2** the rate at which workers leave a company and are replaced by new ones □ *pusing ganti kakitangan/pekerja*: *a high turnover of staff*

ˈturn signal (*AmE*) = **indicator** (2)

turnstile /ˈtɜːnstaɪl/ *noun* [C] a metal gate that moves round in a circle when it is pushed, and allows one person at a time to enter a place □ *lawang putar*

turntable /ˈtɜːnteɪbl/ *noun* [C] the round surface on a record player that you place the record on to be played □ *piring putar; alat pemain/pemutar piring hitam*

turpentine /ˈtɜːpəntaɪn/ *noun* [U] a clear liquid with a strong smell that you use for removing paint or for making paint thinner □ *turpentin*

turquoise /ˈtɜːkwɔɪz/ *noun* **1** [C,U] a blue or greenish-blue **precious stone** (= one that is rare and valuable) □ *batu firus* **2** [U] a greenish-blue colour □ *warna firus; biru kehijau-hijauan*
▶**turquoise** *adj*

turret /ˈtʌrət/ *noun* [C] a small tower on the top of a large building □ *menara kecil*

turtle /ˈtɜːtl/ *noun* [C] **1** an animal with a thick shell and a skin covered in scales that lives in the sea □ *penyu* ⇨ picture on **page P13 2** (*AmE*) = **tortoise**

tusk /tʌsk/ *noun* [C] one of the two very long pointed teeth of an **elephant** (= a large grey animal with a long nose), etc. **Elephants' tusks** are made of **ivory** (= a hard white substance like bone). □ *gading; taring* ⇨ picture at **elephant** ⇨ picture on **page P12**

tussle /ˈtʌsl/ *noun* [C] (*informal*) **a tussle (for/over sth)** a fight, for example between two or more people who want to have the same thing □ *pergelutan*

tut /tʌt/ (*also* tut-ˈtut) *exclam* the way of writing the sound that people make to show disapproval of sb/sth □ *isy (kata seruan)*

tutor /ˈtjuːtə(r)/ *noun* [C] **1** a private teacher who teaches one person or a very small group □ *guru peribadi; tutor* **2** (*BrE*) a teacher who is responsible for a small group of students at school, college or university. A **tutor** advises students on their work or helps them if they have problems in their private life. □ *tutor*

tutorial /tjuːˈtɔːriəl/ *noun* [C] a lesson at a college or university for an individual student or a small group of students □ *tutorial*

tuxedo /tʌkˈsiːdəʊ/ *noun* (*pl* **tuxedos** /-dəʊz/) (*also informal* **tux** /tʌks/) (*especially AmE*) □ *(baju) tuksedo* = **dinner jacket**

ʔ TV /ˌtiː ˈviː/ = **television**: *What's on TV tonight?* ♦ *cable/digital/satellite TV* ♦ *a TV programme/series/show*

twang /twæŋ/ *noun* [C] the sound that is made when you pull a tight string or wire, etc. and then let it go suddenly □ *dentingan* ▶**twang** *verb* [I,T]

ð **then**   s **so**   z **zoo**   ʃ **she**   ʒ **vi**sion   h **how**   m **man**   n **no**   ŋ **si**ng   l **leg**   r **red**   j **yes**   w **wet**

tweed /twi:d/ noun [U] a type of thick rough cloth that is made from wool and used for making clothes □ *(kain) tweed*

tweet /twi:t/ noun [C] **1** the short high sound made by a small bird □ *bunyi nyaring sejenis burung* **2** (also **twitter**) a message sent using the Twitter™ **social networking, service** (= short communications with people who share your interests using the Internet) □ *mesej yg dihantar melalui Twitter*: *I've just sent a tweet about the match.* ▶**tweet** verb [I,T] = **twitter**

tweezers /'twi:zəz/ noun [pl] a small tool consisting of two pieces of metal that are joined at one end. You use tweezers for picking up or pulling out very small things □ *penyepit kecil*: *a pair of tweezers*

twelve /twelv/ number 12 □ *dua belas*; 12 ⊃ note at **six** ⊃ look at **dozen** ▶**twelfth** /twelfθ/ ordinal number, noun ⊃ note at **sixth**

twenty /'twenti/ number 20 □ *dua puluh*; 20 ⊃ note at **sixty** ▶**twentieth** /'twentiəθ/ ordinal number, noun ⊃ note at **sixth**

twice /twaɪs/ adv two times □ *dua kali*: *I've been to Egypt twice—once last year and once in 1994.* ◆ *The film will be shown twice daily.* ◆ *Take the medicine twice a day.* ◆ *Prices have risen twice as fast in this country as in Japan.*

twiddle /'twɪdl/ verb [I,T] (BrE) **twiddle (with) sth** to keep turning or moving sth with your fingers, often because you are nervous or bored □ *memutar-mutar sst*; *memusing-musing sst*

twig /twɪɡ/ noun [C] a small thin branch on a tree or bush □ *ranting* ⊃ picture at **tree**

twilight /'twaɪlaɪt/ noun [U] the time after the sun has set and before it gets completely dark; the faint light at this time □ *senja*; *senjakala* ⊃ look at **dusk**

twin /twɪn/ noun [C] **1** one of two children or animals that are born to one mother at the same time □ *kembar (dua)*: *They're very alike. Are they twins?* ◆ *a twin brother/sister* ◆ *identical twins* ⊃ look at **triplet** **2** one of a pair of things that are the same or very similar □ *kembar*: *twin engines* ◆ *twin beds* ⊃ note at **bed**[1] ▶**twin** verb [T]: *Oxford is twinned with Bonn in Germany.*

twinge /twɪndʒ/ noun [C] **1** a sudden short pain □ *rasa mencucuk atau pedih*: *He kicked the ball and suddenly felt a twinge in his back.* **2** **a twinge (of sth)** a sudden short feeling of an unpleasant emotion □ *perasaan yg tdk menyenangkan*

twinkle /'twɪŋkl/ verb [I] **1** to shine with a light that seems to go on and off □ *berkelip-kelip*; *berkerlipan*: *Stars twinkled in the sky.* **2** (used about your eyes) to look bright because you are happy □ *bersinar-sinar* ▶**twinkle** noun [sing]

twin town noun [C] one of two towns in different countries that have a special relationship □ *bandar kembar*: *Bonn is Oxford's twin town.*

twirl /twɜ:l/ verb [I,T] **twirl (sb/sth) (around/**

921   **tweed → Twitter™**

round) to turn round and round quickly; to make sb/sth do this □ *berputar*; *memutarkan*; *berpusing-pusing*; *memusing-musingkan*

twist[1] /twɪst/ verb
▶BEND **1** [I,T] to bend or turn sth into a particular shape, often one it does not go in naturally; to be bent in this way □ *memintal*; *mengherotkan*; *tergeliat*: *She twisted her long hair into a knot.* ◆ *Her face twisted in anger.* ◆ *He twisted his ankle while he was playing squash.*
▶TURN **2** [I,T] to turn a part of your body while the rest stays still □ *memusingkan*; *berpusing*: *She twisted round to see where the noise was coming from.* ◆ *He kept twisting his head from side to side.* **3** [T] to turn sth around in a circle with your hand □ *memutar-mutar*; *memusing-musing*: *She twisted the ring on her finger nervously.*
▶OF ROAD/RIVER **4** [I] to change direction often □ *bengkang-bengkok*: *a narrow twisting lane* ◆ *The road twists and turns along the coast.*
▶PUT ROUND STH **5** [I,T] **twist (sth) (round/around sth)** to put sth round another object; to be bound to another object □ *membelitkan*; *terbelit*; *melilitkan*: *The telephone wire has got twisted round the table leg.*
▶WORDS/FACTS **6** [T] to change the meaning of what sb has said □ *memutarbelitkan*: *Journalists often twist your words.*
IDM **twist sb's arm** (informal) to force or persuade sb to do sth □ *memaksa/mendesak sso*

twist[2] /twɪst/ noun [C] **1** the act of turning sth with your hand, or of turning part of your body □ *putaran*; *pusingan*; *pintalan*: *She killed the chicken with one twist of its neck.* **2** an unexpected change or development in a story or situation □ *perubahan/perkembangan yg tdk dijangka*: *There's a brilliant twist at the end of the film.* **3** a place where a road, river, etc. bends or changes direction □ *bengkang-bengkok*: *the twists and turns of the river* **4** something that has become or been bent into a particular shape □ *pintalan*; *bengkok*: *Straighten out the wire so that there are no twists in it.*

twisted /'twɪstɪd/ adj **1** bent or turned so that the original shape is lost □ *berpintal*; *bengkang-bengkok*: *After the crash the car was a mass of twisted metal.* ◆ *a twisted ankle* (= injured by being turned suddenly) **2** (used about a person's mind or behaviour) not normal; strange in an unpleasant way □ *fikiran atau tingkah laku tdk normal*: *Her experiences had left her bitter and twisted.*

twit /twɪt/ noun [C] (especially BrE informal) a stupid or annoying person □ *orang yg bodoh*

twitch /twɪtʃ/ verb [I,T] to make a quick sudden movement, often one that you cannot control; to cause sth to make a sudden movement □ *berkernyut*; *bergerak-gerak*: *The rabbit twitched and then lay still.* ◆ *He twitched his nose.* ▶**twitch** noun [C]: *He has a nervous twitch.*

Twitter™ /'twɪtə(r)/ noun [U] a service on the Internet that lets people send short mes-

VOWELS   i: see   i any   ɪ sit   e ten   æ hat   ɑ: father   ɒ got   ɔ: saw   ʊ put   u: too   u usual

twitter → ugh 922

sages to lots of people at the same time ➲ look at **microblogging, tweet**

twitter /ˈtwɪtə(r)/ verb [I] (also **tweet**) **1** (used about birds) to make a series of short high sounds □ *berciap-ciap; menciap; berkicau* **2** to send a message using **Twitter™** □ *hantar mesej melalui Twitter*

two /tuː/ number **1** 2 □ *dua; 2* ➲ note at **six** ➲ look at **second 2 two-** [in compounds] having two of the thing mentioned □ *dua; 2: a two-week holiday*
IDM be in two minds (about sth/doing sth) to not feel sure of sth □ *teragak-agak: I'm in two minds about leaving Will alone in the house while we're away.*
in two in or into two pieces □ *(menjadi) dua: The plate fell on the floor and broke in two.*

tycoon /taɪˈkuːn/ noun [C] a person who is very successful in business or industry and who has become rich and powerful □ *taikun; hartawan: a business/property/media tycoon*

type¹ /taɪp/ noun **1** [C] **a type (of sth)** a group of people or things that share certain qualities and that are part of a larger group □ *jenis: Which type of paint should you use on metal?* • *Spaniels are a type of dog.* • *You meet all types of people in this job.* • *the first building of its type in the world* • *I love this type/these types of movie.* **SYN kind, sort 2** [C] a person of a particular kind □ *jenis: He's the careful type.* • *She's not the type to do anything silly.* ➲ look at **typical 3 -type** [in compounds] having the qualities, etc. of the group, person or thing mentioned □ *jenis: a continental-type cafe* • *a police-type badge* **4** [U] letters that are printed or typed □ *huruf taip: The type is too small to read.*

type² /taɪp/ verb [I,T] to write sth using a computer or **typewriter** □ *menaip: How fast can you type?* • *Type (in) the filename, then press 'Return'.*
▶ **typing** noun [U]: *typing skills*

typewriter /ˈtaɪpraɪtə(r)/ noun [C] a machine that you use for writing in print □ *mesin taip*

typewritten /ˈtaɪprɪtn/ adj written using a **typewriter** or computer □ *bertaip*

typhoid /ˈtaɪfɔɪd/ noun [U] a serious disease that can cause death. People get **typhoid** from bad food or water. □ *demam kepialu; tifoid*

typhoon /taɪˈfuːn/ noun [C] a violent tropical storm with very strong winds □ *taufan* ➲ note at **storm**

typical /ˈtɪpɪkl/ adj **typical (of sb/sth) 1** having or showing the usual qualities of a particular person, thing or type □ *tipikal: a typical Italian village* • *There's no such thing as a typical American* (= they are all different). **SYN representative OPP atypical 2** happening in the usual way; showing what sth is usually like □ *biasa: On a typical day, I receive about 50 emails.* **SYN normal OPP untypical 3** behaving in the way you

expect □ *biasa; lazim: It was absolutely typical of him not to reply to my letter.*

typically /ˈtɪpɪkli/ adv **1** in a typical case; that usually happens in this way □ *spt biasa: Typically it is the girls who offer to help, not the boys.* **2** in a way that shows the usual qualities of a particular person, type or thing □ *(yg) tipikal: typically British humour*

typify /ˈtɪpɪfaɪ/ verb [T] (**typifying; typifies;** pt, pp **typified**) to be a typical mark or example of sb/sth □ *merupakan contoh tipikal: This film typified the Hollywood westerns of that time.*

typist /ˈtaɪpɪst/ noun [C] a person who uses a computer keyboard to type letters, etc., especially sb who works in an office □ *jurutaip*

tyranny /ˈtɪrəni/ noun [U] the cruel and unfair use of power by a person or small group to control a country or state □ *kezaliman; penindasan* ▶ **tyrannical** /tɪˈrænɪkl/ adj: *a tyrannical ruler* ▶ **tyrannize** (also **-ise**) /ˈtɪrənaɪz/ verb [I,T]

tyrant /ˈtaɪrənt/ noun [C] a cruel ruler who has complete power over the people in his or her country □ *orang yg zalim; penindas* ➲ look at **dictator**

tyre (AmE **tire**) /ˈtaɪə(r)/ noun [C] the thick rubber ring that fits around the outside of a wheel □ *tayar: a flat tyre* (= a tyre with no air in it) ➲ picture at **bicycle** ➲ picture on **page P7**

tzar, tzarina = **tsar, tsarina**

U u

U, u /juː/ noun [C,U] (pl **Us; U's; u's** /juːz/) the 21st letter of the English alphabet □ *U, u (huruf): 'Understand' begins with (a) 'U'.*

U /juː/ abbr (BrE) (used about films that are suitable for anyone, including children) **universal** □ *pengelasan filem yg sesuai utk tontonan semua*

ubiquitous /juːˈbɪkwɪtəs/ adj (formal) seeming to be everywhere or in several places at the same time; very common □ *sentiasa ada; terdapat di mana-mana: the ubiquitous mobile phone*

udder /ˈʌdə(r)/ noun [C] the part of a female cow, etc. that hangs under its body and produces milk □ *tetek (binatang)* ➲ picture at **cow**

UEFA /juˈeɪfə/ abbr the **Union of European Football Associations** □ *UEFA (Gabungan Kesatuan Bola Sepak Eropah): the UEFA cup*

UFO (also **ufo**) /ˌjuː ef ˈəʊ; ˈjuːfəʊ/ abbr (pl **UFOs**) an **unidentified flying object**; a strange object that some people claim to have seen in the sky and believe is a **spacecraft** (= a vehicle from another planet) □ *UFO (objek terbang yg tdk dpt dikenal pasti)* ➲ look at **flying saucer**

ugh /ɜː/ exclam used in writing to express the sound that you make when you think sth is disgusting □ *ceh; e...!*

| ʌ cup | ɜː bird | ə ago | eɪ pay | əʊ go | aɪ my | aʊ now | ɔɪ boy | ɪə near | eə hair | ʊə pure |

ugly /'ʌgli/ adj (**uglier**; **ugliest**) **1** unpleasant to look at or listen to □ *hodoh; buruk*: *The burn left an ugly scar on her face.* ♦ *an ugly modern office block* SYN **unattractive 2** (used about a situation) dangerous or threatening □ *membahayakan; mengancam*: *The situation turned ugly when people started throwing stones.* ▶**ugliness** noun [U]

UHT /ˌjuː eɪtʃ 'tiː/ abbr **ultra heat treated**; used about foods such as milk that are treated to last longer □ *UHT (perlakuan ultrahaba)*: *UHT milk*

UK /ˌjuː 'keɪ/ abbr = **United Kingdom** □ *UK (United Kingdom)*: *She is Kenyan by birth but is now a UK citizen*

ulcer /'ʌlsə(r)/ noun [C] a painful area on your skin or inside your body, which may lose blood or produce a poisonous substance □ *ulser; borok*: *a mouth/stomach ulcer*

ulterior /ʌl'tɪəriə(r)/ adj [only before a noun] that you keep hidden or secret □ *tersembunyi; terselindung*: *Why is he suddenly being so nice to me? He must have an ulterior motive.*

ultimate¹ /'ʌltɪmət/ adj [only before a noun] **1** being or happening at the end; last or final □ *yg terakhir; muktamad*: *Our ultimate goal is complete independence.* **2** the greatest, best or worst □ *paling – hebat, baik atau buruk*: *For me the ultimate luxury is to stay in bed till 10 o'clock on a Sunday.*

ultimate² /'ʌltɪmət/ noun [sing] (informal) **the ultimate (in sth)** the greatest or best □ *(sst) yg terunggul/terbaik*: *This new car is the ultimate in comfort.*

ultimately /'ʌltɪmətli/ adv **1** in the end □ *akhirnya*: *Ultimately, the decision is yours.* **2** at the most basic level; most importantly □ *pada asasnya/dasarnya; paling pentingnya*: *Ultimately, this discussion is not about quality but about money.*

ultimatum /ˌʌltɪ'meɪtəm/ noun [C] (pl **ultimatums**) a final warning to sb that, if they do not do what you ask, you will use force or take action against them □ *kata dua*: *I gave him an ultimatum—either he paid his rent or he was out.*

ultra- /'ʌltrə/ [in compounds] extremely □ *ultra-; lampau*: *ultra-modern*

ultrasound /'ʌltrəsaʊnd/ noun **1** [U] sound that is higher than humans can hear □ *lampau bunyi; ultrabunyi; bunyi berfrekuensi ultrasonik* **2** [U,C] a medical process that produces an image of what is inside your body □ *ultrabunyi*: *Ultrasound showed she was expecting twins.*

ultraviolet /ˌʌltrə'vaɪələt/ adj (used about light) that causes your skin to turn darker and that can be dangerous in large amounts □ *ultraungu; ultralembayung*: *ultraviolet radiation* ⊃ look at **infrared**

umbilical cord /ʌmˌbɪlɪkl 'kɔːd/ noun [C] the tube that connects a baby to its mother before it is born □ *tali pusat*

[C] **countable**, a noun with a plural form: *one book, two books*

ugly → unanimous

umbrella /ʌm'brelə/ (BrE informal **brolly**) noun [C] an object that you open and hold over your head to keep yourself dry when it is raining □ *payung*: *to put an umbrella up/down*

umpire /'ʌmpaɪə(r)/ noun [C] a person who watches a game such as **tennis** or **cricket** to make sure that the players obey the rules □ *pengadil* ⊃ look at **referee** ⊃ picture on page P4 ▶**umpire** verb [I,T]

umpteen /ˌʌmp'tiːn/ pron, determiner (informal) very many; a lot □ *banyak; kesekian (kalinya)* ▶**umpteenth** /ˌʌmp'tiːnθ/ determiner: *For the umpteenth time—phone if you're going to be late!*

UN /ˌjuː 'en/ abbr = **United Nations**

unable /ʌn'eɪbl/ adj **unable to do sth** not having the time, knowledge, skill, etc. to do sth; not able to do sth □ *tdk mampu/berupaya; tdk dpt*: *She lay there, unable to move.* OPP **able** ⊃ noun **inability**

unacceptable /ˌʌnək'septəbl/ adj that you cannot accept or allow □ *tdk dpt diterima*: *Noise from the factory has reached unacceptable levels.* ♦ *Her behaviour was quite unacceptable.* OPP **acceptable** ▶**unacceptably** /-əbli/ adv

unaccompanied /ˌʌnə'kʌmpənid/ adj alone, without sb/sth else with you □ *tdk ditemani*: *Unaccompanied children are not allowed in the building.*

unadulterated /ˌʌnə'dʌltəreɪtɪd/ adj **1** used to emphasize that sth is complete or total □ *betul-betul; benar-benar; sepenuhnya*: *For me, the holiday was sheer unadulterated pleasure.* **2** not mixed with other substances □ *tdk lancung; sejati; tulen*: *unadulterated foods* SYN **pure**

unaffected /ˌʌnə'fektɪd/ adj **1** not changed by sth □ *tdk terjejas* **2** behaving in a natural way without trying to impress anyone □ *tdk berpura-pura; ikhlas* OPP for both meanings **affected**

unaffordable /ˌʌnə'fɔːdəbl/ adj costing so much that people do not have enough money to pay for it □ *di luar kemampuan*: *Holidays abroad are unaffordable for many people.* OPP **affordable**

unafraid /ˌʌnə'freɪd/ adj [not before a noun] (formal) not afraid or nervous; not worried about what might happen □ *tdk takut*: *She's unafraid of conflict.* ♦ *He's unafraid to speak his mind.* OPP **afraid**

unaided /ʌn'eɪdɪd/ adv without any help □ *tanpa pertolongan/bantuan*

unanimous /ju'nænɪməs/ adj **1** (used about a decision, etc.) agreed by everyone □ *sebulat suara*: *The jury reached a unanimous verdict of guilty.* **2** (used about a group of people) all agreeing about sth □ *bersepakat; sebulat suara*: *The*

[U] **uncountable**, a noun with no plural form: *some sugar*

judges were unanimous in their decision. ▶**unanimously** adv

unarmed /ˌʌnˈɑːmd/ adj having no guns, knives, etc.; not armed □ *tdk bersenjata* **OPP** armed

unashamed /ˌʌnəˈʃeɪmd/ adj not feeling sorry or embarrassed about sth bad that you have done □ *tanpa segan silu; tanpa berasa malu* **OPP** ashamed ▶**unashamedly** /ˌʌnəˈʃeɪmɪdli/ adv

unassuming /ˌʌnəˈsjuːmɪŋ/ adj not wanting people to notice how good, important, etc. you are □ *rendah hati; tdk berlagak* **SYN** modest

unattached /ˌʌnəˈtætʃt/ adj 1 not married; without a regular partner □ *bujang; belum berkahwin; tdk berteman* **SYN** single 2 not connected to sb/sth else □ *tdk terikat*

unattended /ˌʌnəˈtendɪd/ adj not watched or looked after □ *tdk diawasi/dijaga*: *Do not leave bags unattended.*

unattractive /ˌʌnəˈtræktɪv/ adj 1 not attractive or pleasant to look at □ *tdk menarik* 2 not good, interesting or pleasant □ *tdk menarik/baik/bagus* **OPP** for both meanings **attractive**

unauthorized /ʌnˈɔːθəraɪzd/ adj done without permission □ *tanpa izin/kebenaran*

unavoidable /ˌʌnəˈvɔɪdəbl/ adj that cannot be avoided or prevented □ *tdk dpt dielakkan* **OPP** avoidable ▶**unavoidably** /-əbli/ adv

unaware /ˌʌnəˈweə(r)/ adj [not before a noun] **unaware (of sb/sth)** not knowing about or not noticing sb/sth □ *tdk sedar/menyedari*: *She seemed unaware of all the trouble she had caused.* **OPP** aware

unawares /ˌʌnəˈweəz/ adv by surprise; without expecting sth or being prepared for it □ *tdk diduga; tdk disangka-sangka*: *I was taken completely unawares by his suggestion.*

unbalanced /ˌʌnˈbælənst/ adj 1 (used about a person) slightly crazy □ *tdk waras* 2 not fair to all ideas or sides of an argument □ *tdk seimbang* **OPP** balanced

unbearable /ʌnˈbeərəbl/ adj too unpleasant, painful, etc. for you to accept □ *tdk tertahan* **SYN** intolerable **OPP** bearable ▶**unbearably** /-əbli/ adv: *It was unbearably hot.*

unbeatable /ʌnˈbiːtəbl/ adj that cannot be defeated or improved on □ *tdk dpt dikalahkan; tdk dpt diatasi*: *unbeatable prices*

unbeaten /ʌnˈbiːtn/ adj that has not been beaten or improved on □ *tdk pernah tewas; belum diatasi*

unbelievable /ˌʌnbɪˈliːvəbl/ adj very surprising; difficult to believe □ *menghairankan; sukar dipercayai; dahsyat betul* **OPP** believable ⊃ look at **incredible** ▶**unbelievably** /-əbli/ adj: *His work was unbelievably bad.*

unbiased (also **unbiassed**) /ʌnˈbaɪəst/ adj fair and not influenced by your own or sb else's opinions, desires, etc. □ *tdk berat sebelah*: *unbiased advice* ♦ *an unbiased judge* **OPP** biased

unblemished /ʌnˈblemɪʃt/ adj (formal) not spoiled, damaged or marked in any way □ *tdk rosak; tdk tercela*: *The new party leader has an unblemished reputation.*

unborn /ˌʌnˈbɔːn/ adj not yet born □ *belum lahir*: *She hasn't decided on a name for her unborn baby yet.*

unbroken /ʌnˈbrəʊkən/ adj 1 continuous; not interrupted □ *terus-menerus; berterusan*: *a period of unbroken silence* 2 that has not been beaten □ *belum dpt diatasi*: *His record for the 1500 metres remains unbroken.*

uncalled for /ʌnˈkɔːld fɔː(r)/ adj (used about sth sb says or does) not fair or appropriate □ *tdk wajar; tdk patut*: *His comments were uncalled for.* ♦ *uncalled-for comments* **SYN** unnecessary

uncanny /ʌnˈkæni/ adj very strange; that you cannot easily explain □ *luar biasa*: *an uncanny coincidence*

uncertain /ʌnˈsɜːtn/ adj 1 **uncertain (about/of sth)** not sure; not able to decide □ *tdk pasti*: *She was still uncertain of his true feelings for her.* 2 not known exactly or not decided □ *tdk menentu; tdk tetap*: *He's lost his job and his future seems very uncertain.* **OPP** for both meanings **certain** ▶**uncertainly** adv ▶**uncertainty** noun [C,U] (pl **uncertainties**): *Today's decision will put an end to all the uncertainty.* **OPP** certainty

unchanged /ʌnˈtʃeɪndʒd/ adj staying the same; not changed □ *tdk berubah*

uncharacteristic /ˌʌnˌkærəktəˈrɪstɪk/ adj not typical or usual □ *tdk spt sifat lazim sso* **OPP** characteristic ▶**uncharacteristically** /-kli/ adv

uncheck /ʌnˈtʃek/ verb [T] to click on a mark beside an answer or option on a computer in order to delete that mark □ *mengklik tanda pd skrin komputer utk menghilangkan tanda itu*: *Uncheck the box at the bottom of the page if you do not wish to receive our advertising material.*

unchecked /ʌnˈtʃekt/ adj (used about sth harmful) not controlled or stopped from getting worse □ *tdk terhalang/tersekat; tanpa diperiksa; tanpa disekat/dihalang*: *The fire was allowed to burn unchecked.* ♦ *The rise in violent crime must not go unchecked.* ♦ *The plant will soon choke ponds and waterways if left unchecked.*

uncle /ˈʌŋkl/ noun [C] the brother of your father or mother; the husband of your aunt □ *bapa saudara*: *Uncle Steven*

uncomfortable /ʌnˈkʌmftəbl/ adj 1 not pleasant to wear, sit in, lie on, etc □ *tdk selesa*: *uncomfortable shoes* 2 not able to sit, lie, etc. in a position that is pleasant □ *tdk selesa*: *I was very uncomfortable for most of the journey.* 3 feeling or causing worry or embarrassment □ *tdk selesa; malu*: *I felt very uncomfortable when they started arguing in front of me.* **OPP** for all meanings **comfortable** ▶**uncomfortably** /-əbli/ adv

uncommon /ʌnˈkɒmən/ adj unusual □ *luar biasa* SYN **rare** OPP **common**

uncomplicated /ʌnˈkɒmplɪkeɪtɪd/ adj simple and without difficulties or problems □ *mudah*: *an easy, uncomplicated routine*

uncompromising /ʌnˈkɒmprəmaɪzɪŋ/ adj refusing to discuss or change a decision □ *tetap; tdk mahu berkompromi atau bertolak ansur*

unconcerned /ˌʌnkənˈsɜːnd/ adj **unconcerned (about/by/with sth)** not interested in sth or not worried about it □ *tdk mengambil berat; tdk risau; tdk peduli* OPP **concerned**

unconditional /ˌʌnkənˈdɪʃənl/ adj without limits or conditions □ *tdk bersyarat; tanpa syarat*: *the unconditional surrender of military forces* OPP **conditional** ▶ **unconditionally** /-ʃənəli/ adv

unconscious /ʌnˈkɒnʃəs/ adj **1** in a state that is like sleep, for example because of injury or illness □ *tdk sedar; pengsan*: *He was found lying unconscious on the kitchen floor.* **2 unconscious of sb/sth** not knowing about or not noticing sb/sth □ *tdk sedar*: *He seemed unconscious of everything that was going on around him.* SYN **unaware 3** done, spoken, etc. without you thinking about it or realizing it □ *tdk disengajakan*: *The article was full of unconscious humour.* OPP for all meanings **conscious 4** **the unconscious** noun [sing] = **subconscious** ▶ **unconsciously** adv ▶ **unconsciousness** noun [U]

uncontrollable /ˌʌnkənˈtrəʊləbl/ adj that you cannot control □ *tdk terkawal; tdk dpt dikawal*: *I had an uncontrollable urge to laugh.* ▶ **uncontrollably** /-əbli/ adv

uncontrolled /ˌʌnkənˈtrəʊld/ adj **1** (used about emotions, behaviour, etc.) that sb cannot control or stop □ *tdk tertahan/terkawal*: *uncontrolled anger* **2** that is not limited or managed by law or rules □ *tdk terkawal*: *the uncontrolled growth of cities* ◆ *uncontrolled dumping of toxic waste* ➔ look at **controlled**

uncountable /ʌnˈkaʊntəbl/ (also **noncount, uncount**) adj an uncountable noun cannot be counted and so does not have a plural. In this dictionary uncountable nouns are marked '[U]' □ *kn tak terhitung*: *'Water', 'bread' and 'information' are all uncountable nouns.* OPP **countable** ❶ For more information about uncountable nouns, look at the **Reference Section** at the back of this dictionary.

uncouth /ʌnˈkuːθ/ adj rude or socially unacceptable □ *kasar; kurang sopan; biadab*: *an uncouth young man*

uncover /ʌnˈkʌvə(r)/ verb [T] **1** to remove the cover from sth □ *membuka tudung, tutup, dsb* OPP **cover 2** to find out or discover sth □ *mendedahkan; menemui*: *Police have uncovered a plot to murder a top politician.*

undecided /ˌʌndɪˈsaɪdɪd/ adj **1** not having made a decision □ *belum membuat keputusan*: *I'm still undecided about whether to take the job or not.* **2** without any result or decision □ *belum diputuskan*

undeniable /ˌʌndɪˈnaɪəbl/ adj clear, true or certain □ *tdk dpt dinafikan/disangkal* ▶ **undeniably** /-əbli/ adv

under /ˈʌndə(r)/ prep, adv **1** in or to a position that is below sth □ *di bawah*: *We found him hiding under the table.* ◆ *The dog crawled under the gate and ran into the road.* **2** below the surface of sth; covered by sth □ *di bawah; di sebalik*: *Most of an iceberg is under the water.* ◆ *He was wearing a vest under his shirt.* **3** less than a certain number; younger than a certain age □ *kurang drpd; di bawah*: *People working under 20 hours a week will pay no extra tax.* ◆ *Nobody under eighteen is allowed in the club.* **4** governed or controlled by sb/sth □ *di bawah*: *The country is now under martial law.* **5** according to a law, an agreement, a system, etc. □ *di bawah; menurut*: *Under English law you are innocent until you are proved guilty.* **6** experiencing a particular feeling, process or effect □ *semasa; sedang; mengalami; beranggapan*: *She's been under a lot of stress recently.* ◆ *a building under construction* ◆ *The manager is under pressure to resign.* ◆ *I was under the impression that Bill was not very happy there.* **7** using a particular name □ *dgn menggunakan*: *to travel under a false name* **8** found in a particular part of a book, list, etc. □ *di bawah*: *You'll find some information on rugby under 'team sports'.*

OTHER WORDS FOR

under

You use **under** to say that one thing is directly under another thing. There may be a space between the two things: *The cat is asleep under the table* or one thing may be touching or covered by the other thing: *I think your letter is under that book.* You can use **below** to say that one thing is in a lower position than another thing: *They live on the floor below us.* ◆ *The skirt comes down to just below the knee.* You use **under** (not below) to talk about movement from one side of something to the other side: *We swam under the bridge.* You can use **beneath** in formal writing to say that one thing is directly under another thing, but **under** is more common. You can use **underneath** in place of **under** when you want to emphasize that something is being covered or hidden by another thing: *Have you looked underneath the sofa as well as behind it?*

---

under- /ˈʌndə(r)/ [in compounds] **1** lower in level or position □ *(imbuhan dlm kata majmuk) bermaksud berpangkat lebih rendah*: *an under-secretary* **2** not enough □ *kurang*: *undercooked food*

underarm /ˈʌndərɑːm/ adj [only before a noun] connected with the part of the body under the arm where it meets the shoulder □ *ketiak*: *underarm deodorant* ➔ look at **armpit**

undercarriage /ˈʌndəkærɪdʒ/ (also **landing gear**) noun [C] the part of an aircraft, including the wheels, that supports it when it is landing and taking off □ *peralatan pendaratan pesawat udara* ⊃ picture on page P6

underclothes /ˈʌndəkləʊðz/ noun [pl] (formal) = **underwear**

undercover /ˌʌndəˈkʌvə(r)/ adj working or happening secretly □ *secara sulit/rahsia: an undercover reporter/detective*

undercurrent /ˈʌndəkʌrənt/ noun [C] **undercurrent (of sth)** a feeling, especially a negative one, that is hidden but whose effects are felt □ *perasaan yg tersembunyi atau tersorok: I detect an undercurrent of resentment towards the new proposals.*

undercut /ˌʌndəˈkʌt/ verb [T] (**undercutting**; pt, pp **undercut**) to sell sth at a lower price than other shops, etc. □ *menjual lebih murah*

underdeveloped /ˌʌndədɪˈveləpt/ adj (used about a country, society, etc.) having few industries and a low standard of living □ *kurang maju; kurang membangun* ⊃ look at **developed**, **developing** ▸**underdevelopment** noun [U]

underdog /ˈʌndədɒɡ/ noun [C] a person, team, etc. who is weaker than others and not expected to be successful □ *orang/pasukan yg dijangka lebih lemah: San Marino were the underdogs, but managed to win the game 2-1.*

underestimate /ˌʌndərˈestɪmeɪt/ verb [T] **1** to guess that the amount, etc. of sth will be less than it really is □ *menganggar kurang drpd sebenar* **2** to think that sb/sth is not as strong, good, etc. as he/she/it really is □ *memandang rendah: Don't underestimate your opponent. He's a really good player.* **OPP** for both meanings **overestimate** ▸**underestimate** /-mət/ noun [C]

underfoot /ˌʌndəˈfʊt/ adv under your feet; where you are walking □ *di bawah tapak kaki; di tempat yg dipijak (tanah, dsb): It's very wet underfoot.*

undergo /ˌʌndəˈɡəʊ/ verb [T] (**undergoing**; **undergoes** /-ˈɡəʊz/; pt **underwent** /-ˈwent/; pp **undergone** /-ˈɡɒn/) (AmE also /-ˈɡɔːn/) to have a difficult or an unpleasant experience □ *menjalani; mengalami; mengharungi: She underwent a five-hour operation.*

undergraduate /ˌʌndəˈɡrædʒuət/ noun [C] a student at college or university who is studying for their first degree □ *mahasiswa; mahasiswi* ⊃ look at **graduate**, **postgraduate**

underground¹ /ˈʌndəɡraʊnd/ adj [only before a noun] **1** under the surface of the ground □ *bawah tanah: an underground car park* **2** secret or illegal □ *haram; bawah tanah: an underground radio station*

underground² /ˌʌndəˈɡraʊnd/ adv **1** under the surface of the ground □ *di bawah tanah: The cables all run underground.* **2** into a secret place □ *bawah tanah; bersembunyi: She went underground to escape from the police.*

underground³ /ˈʌndəɡraʊnd/ (AmE **subway**) noun [sing] a railway system under the ground □ *sistem kereta api bawah tanah* ⊃ picture on page P7

CULTURE

In London the underground railway is called **the underground** or **the tube**.

undergrowth /ˈʌndəɡrəʊθ/ noun [U] bushes and plants that grow around and under trees □ *semak; belukar*

underhand /ˌʌndəˈhænd/ adj secret or not honest □ *secara sembunyi-sembunyi dan tdk jujur; dgn menipu*

underlie /ˌʌndəˈlaɪ/ verb [T] (**underlying**; **underlies**; pt **underlay** /ˌʌndəˈleɪ/; pp **underlain** /-ˈleɪn/) (formal) to be the reason for or cause of sth □ *menjadi dasar; merupakan asas/sebab: It is a principle that underlies all the party's policies.*

underline /ˌʌndəˈlaɪn/ (especially AmE **underscore**) verb [T] **1** to draw a line under a word, etc. □ *menggariskan* **2** to show sth clearly or to emphasize sth □ *menekankan; menegaskan: This accident underlines the need for greater care.*

EXAM TIP

Underline key words

Underline the key words in questions to help you to focus on exactly what the question is asking you. When you are reading a text, underline words and phrases where you find answers. This way you can easily find these parts of the text again when you are checking your answers.

underlying /ˌʌndəˈlaɪɪŋ/ adj [only before a noun] important but hidden □ *di sebalik; mendasari: the underlying causes of the disaster*

undermine /ˌʌndəˈmaɪn/ verb [T] to make sth weaker □ *melemahkan; dilemahkan: The public's confidence in the government has been undermined by the crisis.*

underneath /ˌʌndəˈniːθ/ prep, adv under; below □ *bawah: The coin rolled underneath the chair.* ⊃ note at **under**

the underneath /ˌʌndəˈniːθ/ noun [sing] the bottom or lowest part of something □ *di bahagian bawah: There is a lot of rust on the underneath of the car.*

undernourished /ˌʌndəˈnʌrɪʃt/ adj in bad health because you do not have enough food or enough of the right type of food □ *kurang zat makanan*

underpaid past tense, past participle of **underpay**

underpants /ˈʌndəpænts/ (BrE also **pants**) noun [pl] a piece of clothing that men or boys wear under their trousers □ *seluar dlm (lelaki)*

underpass /'ʌndəpɑːs/ noun [C] a road or path that goes under another road, railway, etc. □ *jalan bawah*

underpay /ˌʌndə'peɪ/ verb [T] (pt, pp **underpaid**) to pay sb too little □ *membayar gaji, upah, dsb yg kurang drpd sepatutnya* **OPP** **overpay**

underprivileged /ˌʌndə'prɪvəlɪdʒd/ adj having less money and fewer rights, opportunities, etc. than other people in society □ *kurang bernasib* **OPP** **privileged**

underrate /ˌʌndə'reɪt/ verb [T] to think that sb/sth is less clever, important, good, etc. than he/she/it really is □ *menganggap sso/sst kurang pandai, penting dll drpd sebenarnya* **OPP** **overrate**

underscore¹ /ˌʌndə'skɔː(r)/ verb [T] (especially AmE) = **underline**

underscore² /'ʌndəskɔː(r)/ noun [C] the symbol (_) that is used to draw a line under a letter or word and used in computer commands and in Internet addresses □ *garis bawah*

undershirt /'ʌndəʃɜːt/ (AmE) = **vest**(1)

underside /'ʌndəsaɪd/ noun [C] the side or surface of sth that is underneath □ *sebelah bawah; permukaan bawah* **SYN** **bottom**

understand /ˌʌndə'stænd/ verb (pt, pp **understood** /-'stʊd/) **1** [I,T] to know or realize the meaning of sth □ *memahami; faham*: I'm not sure that I really understand. ♦ I didn't understand the instructions. ♦ Please speak more slowly. I can't understand you. ♦ Do you understand what I'm asking you? **2** [T] to know how or why sth happens or why it is important □ *tahu; faham*: I can't understand why the engine won't start. ♦ As far as I understand it, the changes won't affect us. **3** [T] to know sb's character and why they behave in a particular way □ *memahami*: It's easy to understand why she felt so angry. **4** [T] (formal) to have heard or been told sth □ *mendapat tahu; diberitahu; difahamkan*: I understand that you have decided to leave.

IDM **give sb to believe/understand (that)** ⊃ **believe**

make yourself understood to make your meaning clear □ *membuat org lain faham (apa yg dituturkan atau dikatakan)*: I can just about make myself understood in Russian.

understandable /ˌʌndə'stændəbl/ adj that you can understand □ *boleh/dpt difahami*: It was an understandable mistake to make. ▶**understandably** /-əbli/ adv: She was understandably angry at the decision.

understanding¹ /ˌʌndə'stændɪŋ/ noun **1** [U, sing] the knowledge that sb has of a particular subject or situation □ *pemahaman; kefahaman*: A basic understanding of physics is necessary for this course. ♦ He has little understanding of how computers work. **2** [C, usually sing] an informal agreement □ *kata sepakat; persetujuan*: I'm sure we can **come to/reach an understanding** about the money I owe him. **3** [U] the ability to know why people behave in a particular way and to forgive them if they do sth wrong or bad □ *sifat bertimbang rasa*: She apologized for her actions and her boss showed great understanding. **4** [U] the way in which you think sth is meant □ *(mengikut apa yg) difahamkan*: My understanding of the arrangement is that he will only phone if there is a problem.

IDM **on the understanding that …** (formal) only if …; because it was agreed that … □ *dgn syarat*: We let them stay in our house on the understanding that it was only for a short period.

understanding² /ˌʌndə'stændɪŋ/ adj showing kind feelings towards sb □ *bertimbang rasa* **SYN** **sympathetic**

understate /ˌʌndə'steɪt/ verb [T] to say that sth is smaller or less important than it really is □ *menyatakan sst lebih kecil atau kurang penting drpd yg sebenarnya; memperkecil* **OPP** **overstate** ▶**understatement** noun [C]: 'Is she pleased?' 'That's an understatement. She's delighted.'

understood past tense, past participle of **understand**

understudy /'ʌndəstʌdi/ noun [C] (pl **understudies**) an actor who learns the role of another actor and replaces them if they are ill □ *pelakon ganti*

undertake /ˌʌndə'teɪk/ verb [T] (pt **undertook** /-'tʊk/; pp **undertaken** /-'teɪkən/) **1** to decide to do sth and start doing it □ *memulakan; menjalankan*: The company is undertaking a major programme of modernization. **2** to agree or promise to do sth □ *berjanji*

undertaker /'ʌndəteɪkə(r)/ (also **'funeral director**; AmE also **mortician**) noun [C] a person whose job is to prepare dead bodies to be buried and to arrange funerals □ *pengurus mayat*

undertaking /ˌʌndə'teɪkɪŋ/ noun [C, usually sing] **1** a piece of work or business □ *kerja; tugas; usaha*: Buying the company would be a very risky undertaking. **2 an undertaking (that …/to do sth)** a formal or legal promise to do sth □ *perjanjian; persetujuan*

undertone /'ʌndətəʊn/ noun [C] a feeling, quality or meaning that is not expressed in a direct way □ *perasaan atau maksud yg terpendam/tersembunyi; berbau*

IDM **in an undertone**; **in undertones** in a quiet voice □ *dgn suara yg rendah/perlahan*

undertook past tense of **undertake**

undervalue /ˌʌndə'væljuː/ verb [T] to place too low a value on sb/sth □ *menilai kurang; kurang menghargai*

underwater /ˌʌndə'wɔːtə(r)/ adj, adv (existing, happening or used) below the surface of water □ *dlm air*: underwater exploration ♦ an underwater camera ♦ Can you swim underwater?

underwear → unexpected

underwear /ˈʌndəweə(r)/ noun [U] clothing that is worn next to the skin under other clothes □ *pakaian dlm*: She packed *a change of underwear*. ♦ *Your clean underwear is in the top drawer*.

> **MORE** The word **underclothes** has the same meaning, but is more formal and is a plural noun.

underweight /ˌʌndəˈweɪt/ adj weighing less than is normal or correct □ *kurang beratnya* **OPP** overweight ⊃ note at **thin**

underwent past tense of **undergo**

the underworld /ˈʌndəwɜːld/ noun [sing] people who are involved in organized crime □ *golongan yg terlibat dlm jenayah terancang; dunia jenayah*

undesirable /ˌʌndɪˈzaɪərəbl/ adj unpleasant or not wanted; likely to cause problems □ *tdk diingini* **OPP** desirable

undid past tense of **undo**

undignified /ʌnˈdɪɡnɪfaɪd/ adj causing you to look silly and to lose the respect of other people □ *tdk senonoh; tdk sopan* **OPP** dignified

undiscovered /ˌʌndɪsˈkʌvəd/ adj that has not been found or noticed; that has not been discovered □ *belum disedari/ditemukan*: *a previously undiscovered talent*

undivided /ˌʌndɪˈvaɪdɪd/ adj
IDM get/have sb's undivided attention to receive all sb's attention □ *mendapat perhatian yg tdk berbelah bahagi*
give your undivided attention (to sb/sth) to give all your attention to sb/sth □ *menumpukan sepenuh perhatian (kpd sso/sst)*

undo /ʌnˈduː/ verb [T] (undoing; undoes /ʌnˈdʌz/; pt undid /ʌnˈdɪd/; pp undone /ʌnˈdʌn/) 1 to open sth that was tied or fastened □ *membuka; merungkai*: *to undo a knot/zip/button* 2 to destroy the effect of sth that has already happened □ *merosakkan; memusnahkan; membatalkan*: *His mistake has undone all our good work*.

undone /ʌnˈdʌn/ adj 1 open; not fastened or tied □ *terbuka; terungkai*: *I realized that my zip was undone*. 2 not done □ *tdk dibuat; tdk disiapkan*: *I left the housework undone*.

undoubted /ʌnˈdaʊtɪd/ adj definite; accepted as being true □ *pasti; tdk syak; tdk diragui* ▶ undoubtedly adv

undress /ʌnˈdres/ verb 1 [I] to take off your clothes □ *menanggalkan pakaian (sendiri)* ⊃ **Get undressed** is more common than **undress**. 2 [T] to take off sb's clothes □ *menanggalkan pakaian* **OPP** for both meanings dress ▶ undressed adj

undue /ʌnˈdjuː/ adj (formal) [only before a noun] more than is necessary or reasonable □ *berlebih-lebih; tdk wajar*: *The police try not to use undue force when arresting a person*. ▶ unduly

adv: *She didn't seem unduly worried by their unexpected arrival*.

unearth /ʌnˈɜːθ/ verb [T] to dig sth up out of the ground; to discover sth that was hidden □ *menggali; membongkar*: *Archaeologists have unearthed a Roman tomb*.

unearthly /ʌnˈɜːθli/ adj strange or frightening □ *luar biasa; mengerikan; menakutkan*: *an unearthly scream*
IDM at an unearthly hour (informal) extremely early in the morning □ *pagi-pagi buta*

unease /ʌnˈiːz/ (also **uneasiness** /ʌnˈiːzinəs/) noun [U] a worried or an uncomfortable feeling □ *perasaan resah, risau atau tdk sedap hati* **SYN** anxiety **OPP** ease

uneasy /ʌnˈiːzi/ adj 1 uneasy (about sth/doing sth) worried; not feeling relaxed or comfortable □ *risau; tdk sedap hati* 2 not settled; unlikely to last □ *tdk menyenangkan; tdk berapa teguh*: *an uneasy compromise* ▶ uneasily adv

uneconomic /ˌʌnˌiːkəˈnɒmɪk; ˌʌnˌek-/ adj (used about a company, etc.) not making or likely to make a profit □ *tdk menguntungkan* **OPP** economic

uneconomical /ˌʌnˌiːkəˈnɒmɪkl; ˌʌnˌek-/ adj wasting money, time, materials, etc. □ *tdk menjimatkan* **OPP** economical ▶ uneconomically /-kli/ adv

unemployed /ˌʌnɪmˈplɔɪd/ adj 1 not able to find a job; out of work □ *menganggur*: *She has been unemployed for over a year*. **SYN** jobless **OPP** employed ⊃ look at **work** 2 the unemployed noun [pl] people who cannot find a job □ *penganggur*: *the long-term unemployed*

unemployment /ˌʌnɪmˈplɔɪmənt/ noun [U] 1 the number of people who are unemployed □ *bilangan orang yg menganggur*: *The economy is doing very badly and unemployment is rising*. **SYN** joblessness ⊃ look at **the dole** 2 the situation of not being able to find a job □ *pengangguran*: *If the factory closes, many people face unemployment*. ♦ *The number of people claiming unemployment benefit* (= money given by the state) *has gone up*. **OPP** employment

unending /ʌnˈendɪŋ/ adj having or seeming to have no end □ *tdk henti-henti; tdk berkesudahan*

unequal /ʌnˈiːkwəl/ adj 1 not fair or balanced □ *tdk saksama; tdk sama rata; tdk seimbang*: *an unequal distribution of power* 2 different in size, amount, level, etc. □ *tdk sama* **OPP** for both meanings equal ▶ unequally /ʌnˈiːkwəli/ adv

uneven /ʌnˈiːvn/ adj 1 not completely smooth, level or regular □ *tdk rata; tdk sekata*: *The sign was painted in rather uneven letters*. **OPP** even 2 not always of the same level or quality □ *tdk sama taraf atau kualiti* ▶ unevenly adv: *The country's wealth is unevenly distributed*.

unexpected /ˌʌnɪkˈspektɪd/ adj not expected and therefore causing surprise □ *tdk disangka; tdk diduga*: *His death was completely* unexpected. ▶**unexpectedly** adv: *I got there late because I was unexpectedly delayed.*

unfailing /ʌnˈfeɪlɪŋ/ adj that you can be sure will always be there and always be the same □ *berterusan; tdk putus-putus*: *unfailing support* ▶**unfailingly** adv

unfair /ʌnˈfeə(r)/ adj **1 unfair (on/to sb)** not dealing with people as they deserve; not treating each person equally □ *tdk adil; tdk sama rata*: *This law is unfair to women.* ♦ *The tax is unfair on people with low incomes.* **2** not following the rules and therefore giving an advantage to one person, team, etc. □ *tdk adil; tdk wajar*: *The referee warned him for unfair play.* **OPP** for both meanings **fair** ▶**unfairly** adv ▶**unfairness** noun [U]

unfaithful /ʌnˈfeɪθfl/ adj **unfaithful (to sb/sth)** having a sexual relationship with sb who is not your husband, wife or partner □ *tdk setia; curang* **OPP faithful** ▶**unfaithfulness** noun [U]

unfamiliar /ˌʌnfəˈmɪliə(r)/ adj **1 unfamiliar (to sb)** that you do not know well □ *tdk biasa; tdk dikenali*: *an unfamiliar part of town* **2 unfamiliar (with sb/sth)** not having knowledge or experience of sth □ *tdk mengetahui*: *I'm unfamiliar with this author.* **OPP** for both meanings **familiar**

unfashionable /ʌnˈfæʃnəbl/ adj that was popular in the past but is not popular now □ *tdk mengikut zaman atau fesyen*: *unfashionable ideas/clothes* **OPP fashionable** ⊃ look at **old-fashioned**

unfasten /ʌnˈfɑːsn/ verb [T] to open sth that is fastened □ *membuka; merungkai ikatan; menanggalkan*: *to unfasten a belt/button, etc.* **OPP fasten**

unfavourable (AmE **unfavorable**) /ʌnˈfeɪvərəbl/ adj **1** not good and likely to cause problems or make sth difficult □ *tdk baik; boleh menimbulkan masalah* **2** showing that you do not like or approve of sb/sth □ *tdk suka; tdk menyenangi* **OPP** for both meanings **favourable** ⊃ look at **adverse**

unfinished /ʌnˈfɪnɪʃt/ adj not complete; not finished □ *belum siap; tdk sempurna; tdk habis/dihabiskan*: *We have some unfinished business to settle.*

unfit /ʌnˈfɪt/ adj **1 unfit (for sth/to do sth)** not suitable or not good enough for sth □ *tdk sesuai; tdk layak*: *His criminal past makes him unfit to be a politician.* **2** not in good physical health, especially because you do not get enough exercise □ *tdk betul-betul kuat dan sihat* **OPP** for both meanings **fit**

unfold /ʌnˈfəʊld/ verb [I,T] **1** to open out and become flat; to open out sth that was folded □ *membuka; membentangkan*: *The sofa unfolds into a spare bed.* ♦ *I unfolded the letter and read it.* **OPP fold (up)** **2** to become known, or to allow sth to become known, a little at a time □ *mendedahkan; terbongkar*

unforeseen /ˌʌnfɔːˈsiːn/ adj not expected □ *tdk dpt dijangka atau diduga*: *an unforeseen problem*

unforgettable /ˌʌnfəˈɡetəbl/ adj making such a strong impression that you cannot forget it □ *tdk dpt dilupakan* **SYN memorable**

unfortunate /ʌnˈfɔːtʃənət/ adj **1** not lucky □ *tdk bernasib baik; malang*: *The unfortunate people who lived near the river lost their homes in the flood.* **SYN unlucky 2** that you feel sorry about □ *malang; dikesali*: *I would like to apologize for this unfortunate mistake.* ▶**unfortunately** adv: *I'd like to help you but unfortunately there's nothing I can do.* ⊃ note at **sudden**

unfounded /ʌnˈfaʊndɪd/ adj not based on or supported by facts □ *tdk berasas*: *unfounded allegations*

unfriend /ʌnˈfrend/ verb [T] to remove sb from your list of friends on a **social networking, site** (= a website for people who share your interests) □ *mengeluarkan nama sso drpd senarai kawan dlm rangkaian sosial* ⊃ note at **social networking**

unfriendly /ʌnˈfrendli/ adj **unfriendly (to/towards sb)** unpleasant or not polite to sb □ *tdk mesra*: *There was an unfriendly atmosphere in the room.* **OPP friendly**

ungainly /ʌnˈɡeɪnli/ adj moving in a way that is not smooth or elegant □ *canggung; kekok*

ungrateful /ʌnˈɡreɪtfl/ adj not feeling or showing thanks to sb □ *tdk mengenang budi* **OPP grateful** ▶**ungratefully** /-fəli/ adv

unguarded /ʌnˈɡɑːdɪd/ adj **1** not protected or guarded □ *tdk dijaga; tdk berkawal* **2** saying more than you wanted to □ *tdk berhati-hati; terlepas cakap* **OPP** for both meanings **guarded**

unhappily /ʌnˈhæpɪli/ adv **1** in a sad way □ *dgn sedihnya* **SYN sadly 2** unfortunately □ *malangnya* **OPP** for both meanings **happily**

unhappy /ʌnˈhæpi/ adj (**unhappier; unhappiest**) **1 unhappy (about sth)** sad □ *tdk gembira; tdk bahagia; sedih*: *She's terribly unhappy about losing her job.* ♦ *He had a very unhappy childhood.* ⊃ note at **sad** **2 unhappy (about/at/with sth)** not satisfied or pleased; worried □ *tdk puas hati; tdk gembira*: *They're unhappy at being left out of the team.* **OPP** for both meanings **happy** ▶**unhappiness** noun [U]

unhealthy /ʌnˈhelθi/ adj **1** not having or showing good health □ *tdk sihat*: *He looks pale and unhealthy.* **2** likely to cause illness or poor health □ *tdk menyihatkan*: *unhealthy conditions* **3** not natural □ *tdk sihat; tdk normal*: *an unhealthy interest in death* **OPP** for all meanings **healthy**

unheard /ʌnˈhɜːd/ adj [not before a noun] not listened to or given any attention □ *tdk diberi perhatian; tdk dipedulikan*: *My suggestions went unheard.*

unˈheard-of adj not known; never having happened before □ *tdk pernah diketahui; tdk pernah berlaku*

unhygienic /ˌʌnhaɪˈdʒiːnɪk/ *adj* not clean and therefore likely to cause disease or infection □ *kotor*: *The animals were kept in cramped and unhygienic conditions* **OPP** hygienic

unicorn /ˈjuːnɪkɔːn/ *noun* [C] (in stories) an animal that looks like a white horse with a long straight horn on its head □ *unikorn; sejenis kuda khayalan yg bertanduk satu*

unidentified /ˌʌnaɪˈdentɪfaɪd/ *adj* whose identity is not known □ *tdk dpt dikenal pasti*: *An unidentified body has been found in the river.*

uniform¹ /ˈjuːnɪfɔːm/ *noun* [C,U] the set of clothes worn at work by the members of an organization or a group, or by children at school □ *pakaian seragam*: *I didn't know he was a policeman because he wasn't in uniform.* ➔ note at **clothes** ▶**uniformed** *adj*

uniform² /ˈjuːnɪfɔːm/ *adj* not varying; the same in all cases or at all times □ *tetap; nalar; seragam; sekata*: *uniform rates of pay* ▶**uniformity** /ˌjuːnɪˈfɔːməti/ *noun* [U]

unify /ˈjuːnɪfaɪ/ *verb* [T] (**unifying**; **unifies**; *pt, pp* **unified**) to join separate parts together to make one unit, or to make them similar to each other □ *menyatukan* ▶**unification** /ˌjuːnɪfɪˈkeɪʃn/ *noun* [U]

unilateral /ˌjuːnɪˈlætrəl/ *adj* done or made by one person, group or organization that is involved in sth without the agreement of the other person, group, etc. □ *unilateral; melibatkan satu pihak sahaja*: *a unilateral declaration of independence* ➔ look at **multilateral** ▶**unilaterally** /-rəli/ *adv*

unimportant /ˌʌnɪmˈpɔːtnt/ *adj* not important □ *tdk penting*: *unimportant details* ♦ *They dismissed the problem as unimportant.*

uninhabitable /ˌʌnɪnˈhæbɪtəbl/ *adj* not fit or possible to live in □ *tdk dpt atau tdk layak utk didiami* **OPP** habitable

uninhabited /ˌʌnɪnˈhæbɪtɪd/ *adj* (used about a place or a building) with nobody living in it □ *tdk didiami; tdk berpenghuni*

uninhibited /ˌʌnɪnˈhɪbɪtɪd/ *adj* behaving in a free and natural way, without worrying what other people think of you □ *bersikap bebas; tdk segan-segan* **OPP** inhibited

uninstall /ˌʌnɪnˈstɔːl/ *verb* [T] to remove a program from a computer □ *menghapuskan sst program drpd komputer*: *Uninstall any programs that you no longer need.* **OPP** install

unintelligible /ˌʌnɪnˈtelɪdʒəbl/ *adj* impossible to understand □ *tdk dpt difahami* **OPP** intelligible

unintentional /ˌʌnɪnˈtenʃənl/ *adj* not done deliberately, but happening by accident □ *tdk sengaja* **OPP** intentional ▶**unintentionally** /-ʃənəli/ *adv*: *He had unintentionally written the wrong date.*

[I] **intransitive**, a verb which has no object: *He laughed.*

uninterested /ʌnˈɪntrəstɪd/ *adj* **uninterested (in sb/sth)** having or showing no interest in sb/sth □ *tdk berminat; bersikap bebas; tdk segan-segan*: *She seemed uninterested in anything I had to say.* **OPP** interested

HELP Be careful. **Disinterested** has a different meaning.

union /ˈjuːniən/ *noun* **1** (also ˌtrade ˈunion, ˌtrades ˈunion) [C] an organization for people who all work in a particular industry. Unions try to get better pay and working conditions for their members. □ *kesatuan sekerja* **2** [C] an organization for a particular group of people □ *persatuan*: *the Athletics Union* **3** [C] a group of states or countries that have joined together to form one country or group □ *kesatuan*: *the European Union* **4** [U, sing] the act of joining or the situation of being joined □ *penyatuan; percantuman*: *the union of the separate groups into one organization*

the ˌUnion ˈJack *noun* [sing] the national flag of the United Kingdom, with red and white crosses on a dark blue background □ *Union Jack (bendera United Kingdom)*

unique /juˈniːk/ *adj* **1** not like anything else; being the only one of its type □ *unik; lain drpd yg lain; unggul*: *Everyone's fingerprints are unique.* **2** very unusual □ *unik; luar biasa*: *There's nothing unique about that sort of crime.* **3** **unique to sb/sth** connected with only one place, person or thing □ *khusus*: *This dance is unique to this region.*

unisex /ˈjuːnɪseks/ *adj* designed for and used by both sexes □ *uniseks*: *unisex fashions*

unison /ˈjuːnɪsn/ *noun*
IDM **in unison** saying, singing or doing the same thing at the same time as sb else □ *serentak; bersama-sama*: *'No, thank you,' they said in unison.*

unit /ˈjuːnɪt/ *noun* [C]
▶SINGLE THING **1** a single thing which is complete in itself, although it can be part of sth larger □ *unit*: *The book is divided into ten units.*
▶GROUP OF PEOPLE **2** a group of people who perform a certain function within a larger organization □ *unit; pasukan; bahagian*: *army/military units*
▶MEASUREMENT **3** a fixed amount or number used as a standard of measurement □ *unit*: *a unit of currency*
▶FURNITURE **4** a piece of furniture that fits with other pieces of furniture and has a particular use □ *unit*: *kitchen units*
▶SMALL MACHINE **5** a small machine that performs a particular task or that is part of a larger machine □ *unit; bahagian*: *The heart of a computer is the central processing unit.*
▶DEPARTMENT **6** a department, especially in a hospital, that provides a particular type of care or treatment □ *unit; bahagian*: *a maternity unit* ♦ *the intensive care unit*

unite /juˈnaɪt/ *verb* **1** [I] **unite (in sth/in doing sth)** to join together for a particular purpose

[T] **transitive**, a verb which has an object: *He ate an apple.*

□ *bersatu*: We should all unite in seeking a solution to this terrible problem. **2** [I,T] to join together and act in agreement; to make this happen □ *bersatu; berpadu*: Unless we unite, our enemies will defeat us. ♦ *Italy was united in 1861.*

united /juːˈnaɪtɪd/ *adj* joined together by a common feeling or aim □ *bersatu*: *Throughout the crisis, the whole country remained united.*

the U͵nited ˈKingdom *noun* [sing] (*abbr* (the) **UK**) England, Scotland, Wales and Northern Ireland (considered as a political unit) □ *United Kingdom*

CULTURE

The UK consists of England, Scotland, Wales and Northern Ireland, but *not* the Republic of Ireland (Eire), which is a separate country. **Great Britain** is England, Scotland and Wales only. **The British Isles** are a geographical unit including the Republic of Ireland and the UK.

the U͵nited ˈNations *noun* [sing, with sing or pl verb] (*abbr* **UN**) the organization formed to encourage peace in the world and to deal with problems between countries □ *Pertubuhan Bangsa-Bangsa Bersatu*

the U͵nited ˈStates (of Aˈmerica) *noun* [sing, with sing or pl verb] (*abbr* **US; USA**) a large country in North America made up of 50 states and the District of Columbia □ *Amerika Syarikat*

unity /ˈjuːnəti/ *noun* [U] the situation in which people are in agreement and working together □ *perpaduan*

universal /ˌjuːnɪˈvɜːsl/ *adj* connected with, done by or affecting everyone in the world or everyone in a particular group □ *sejagat; universal*: *The environment is a universal issue.* ▶**universally** /-səli/ *adv*

the universe /ˈjuːnɪvɜːs/ *noun* [sing] everything that exists, including the planets, stars, space, etc. □ *alam semesta*: *There are many theories of how the universe began.*

university /ˌjuːnɪˈvɜːsəti/ *noun* [C] (*pl* **universities**) an institution that provides the highest level of education, in which students study for degrees and in which academic research is done □ *universiti*: *Which university did you go to?* ♦ *I did History* **at university**. ♦ *a university lecturer* ⊃ note at **study**

HELP We use the expressions **at university** and **go to university** without *a* or *the* when we mean that somebody attends the university as a student: *He's hoping to go to university next year* but not if somebody goes there for any other reason: *I'm going to a conference at the university in July.*

TOPIC

University

People who want to **go to university** in Britain have to **apply** and they often have to go for an interview. Some also apply for a **scholarship** in order to pay their **tuition fees**. University **students** attend classes such as **lectures, seminars** and **tutorials**. They are taught by **professors, lecturers** and **tutors**. They may have to **do research** and **write a thesis** (= a long piece of writing). People studying for their first degree are called **undergraduates** and those doing further studies after their first degree are called **postgraduates**. If undergraduates pass their **finals** (= final exams), they will **graduate** (/ˈɡrædʒueɪt/) with a **degree**. A person who has graduated is called a **graduate** (/ˈɡrædʒuət/).

unkempt /ˌʌnˈkempt/ *adj* (especially of sb's hair or general appearance) not well cared for; not tidy □ *selekeh; kusut-masai; tdk terpelihara*: *greasy, unkempt hair* **SYN** **dishevelled**

unkind /ˌʌnˈkaɪnd/ *adj* unpleasant and not friendly □ *tdk bertimbang rasa; tdk menaruh belas kasihan*: *That was an unkind thing to say.* ♦ *It would be unkind to go without him.* **OPP** **kind** ▶**unkindly** *adv* ▶**unkindness** *noun* [U]

unknown[1] /ˌʌnˈnəʊn/ *adj* **1 unknown (to sb)** that sb does not know; without sb knowing □ *tanpa diketahui*: *Unknown to the boss, she went home early.* **2** not famous or familiar to other people □ *tdk terkenal*: *an unknown actress* **OPP** **well known, famous**

IDM **an unknown quantity** a person or thing that you know very little about □ *sso/sst yg tdk atau belum dikenali/diketahui*

unknown[2] /ˌʌnˈnəʊn/ *noun* **1** usually **the unknown** [sing] a place or thing that you know nothing about □ *tempat yg biasa atau tdk diketahui*: *a fear of the unknown* **2** [C] a person who is not well known □ *orang yg tdk terkenal*

unleaded /ˌʌnˈledɪd/ *adj* not containing lead □ *tanpa plumbum*: *unleaded petrol*

unleash /ʌnˈliːʃ/ *verb* [T] **unleash sth (on/ upon sb/sth)** to suddenly let a strong force, emotion, etc., be felt or have an effect □ *melepaskan; membebaskan drpd kawalan; menghamburkan*: *The new government proposals unleashed a storm of protest in the press.*

unless /ənˈles/ *conj* if ... not; except if □ *jika... tdk; kecuali*: *I was told that unless my work improved, I would lose the job.* ♦ *'Would you like a cup of coffee?' 'Not unless you've already made some.'* ♦ *Unless anyone has anything else to say, the meeting is closed.* ♦ *Don't switch that on unless I'm here.*

unlike /ˌʌnˈlaɪk/ *adj* [not before a noun] *prep* **1** in contrast to; different from □ *berbeza; berlainan drpd*: *He's extremely ambitious, unlike me.* ♦ *She's unlike anyone else I've ever met.* ♦ *This is an exciting place to live, unlike my home town.* ⊃ note at **difference 2** not typical of; unusual for □ *tdk spt lazim; tdk biasa*: *It's unlike him to*

unlikely → unprovoked 932

be so rude—he's usually very polite. **OPP** for both meanings **like**

unlikely /ʌnˈlaɪkli/ adj (**unlikelier; unlikeliest**) **1 unlikely (to do sth/that ...)** not likely to happen; not expected; not probable □ *tdk mungkin atau tdk dijangka akan berlaku*: *I suppose she might win but I think it's very unlikely.* ♦ *It's highly unlikely that I'll have any free time next week.* **OPP** **likely 2** [only before a noun] difficult to believe □ *mustahil; sukar diterima*: *an unlikely excuse* **SYN** for both meanings **improbable**

unlimited /ʌnˈlɪmɪtɪd/ adj without limit; as much or as great as you want □ *tdk terhad* **OPP** **limited**

unload /ʌnˈləʊd/ verb **1** [I,T] **unload (sth) (from sth)** to remove things from a vehicle or ship after it has taken them somewhere □ *memunggah barang dr; mengeluarkan*: *We unloaded the boxes from the back of the van.* ♦ *Parking here is restricted to vehicles that are loading or unloading.* **OPP** **load 2** [T] (*informal*) **unload sb/sth (on/onto sb)** to get rid of sth you do not want or to pass it to sb else □ *meluahkan; melepaskan*: *He shouldn't try and unload the responsibility onto you.*

unlock /ʌnˈlɒk/ verb [I,T] to open the lock on sth using a key; to be opened with a key □ *membuka kunci; membuka dgn kunci*: *I can't unlock this door.* ♦ *This door won't unlock.* **OPP** **lock**

unlucky /ʌnˈlʌki/ adj (**unluckier; unluckiest**) having or causing bad luck □ *kurang bernasib baik*: *They were unlucky to lose because they played so well.* ♦ *Thirteen is often thought to be an unlucky number.* **OPP** **lucky** ▶ **unluckily** adv

unmanned /ʌnˈmænd/ adj if a machine, a vehicle, a place or an activity is unmanned, it does not have or need a person to control or operate it □ *dikelolakan tanpa manusia*: *an unmanned spacecraft*

unmarried /ʌnˈmærid/ adj not married □ *tdk berkahwin; bujang* **SYN** **single** **OPP** **married**

unmistakable (also **unmistakeable**) /ˌʌnmɪˈsteɪkəbl/ adj that cannot be confused with anything else; easy to recognize □ *memang jelas; tdk dpt disangsi lagi*: *She had an unmistakable French accent.* ▶ **unmistakably** (also **unmistakeably**) /-əbli/ adv

unmoved /ʌnˈmuːvd/ adj not affected in an emotional way □ *tdk terharu*: *The judge was unmoved by the man's sad story, and sent him to jail.*

unnatural /ʌnˈnætʃrəl/ adj different from what is normal or expected □ *tdk normal; luar biasa* **OPP** **natural** ▶ **unnaturally** /-rəli/ adv: *It's unnaturally quiet in here.*

unnecessary /ʌnˈnesəsəri/ adj more than is needed or acceptable □ *tdk perlu; lebih drpd yg perlu*: *We should try to avoid all unnecessary expense.* **OPP** **necessary** ▶ **unnecessarily** /ʌnˈnesəsərəli; ˌʌnˌnesəˈserəli/ adv: *His explan-* *ation was unnecessarily complicated.*

unnerve /ʌnˈnɜːv/ verb [T] to make sb feel nervous or frightened or lose confidence □ *menggentarkan; melemahkan semangat*: *His silence unnerved us.* ▶ **unnerving** adj

unnoticed /ʌnˈnəʊtɪst/ adj [not before a noun] not noticed or seen □ *tdk dilihat; tanpa disedari*: *He didn't want his hard work to go unnoticed.*

unobtrusive /ˌʌnəbˈtruːsɪv/ adj (*formal*) avoiding being noticed; not attracting attention □ *tdk menonjol; tdk ketara* ▶ **unobtrusively** adv: *He tried to leave as unobtrusively as possible.*

unofficial /ˌʌnəˈfɪʃl/ adj not accepted or approved by a person in authority □ *tdk rasmi*: *an unofficial strike* ♦ *Unofficial reports say that four people died in the explosion.* **OPP** **official** ▶ **unofficially** /-ʃəli/ adv

unorthodox /ʌnˈɔːθədɒks/ adj different from what is generally accepted, usual or traditional □ *tdk ortodoks; tdk spt yg lazim diterima umum* **OPP** **orthodox**

unpack /ʌnˈpæk/ verb [I,T] to take out the things that were in a bag, suitcase, etc. □ *mengeluarkan barang*: *When we arrived at the hotel we unpacked and went to the beach.* **OPP** **pack**

unpaid /ʌnˈpeɪd/ adj **1** not yet paid □ *belum berbayar*: *an unpaid bill* **2** (used about work) done without payment □ *tdk dibayar*: *unpaid overtime* **3** not receiving money for work done □ *tdk dibayar gaji; tdk mendapat upah*: *an unpaid assistant*

unpleasant /ʌnˈpleznt/ adj **1** not pleasant or comfortable □ *tdk menyenangkan*: *This news has come as an unpleasant surprise.* **OPP** **pleasant 2** unfriendly; not polite □ *bersikap kasar; menunjukkan rasa tdk suka*: *There's no need to get unpleasant; we can discuss this in a friendly way.* ▶ **unpleasantly** adv

unplug /ʌnˈplʌɡ/ verb [T] (**unplugging; unplugged**) to remove a piece of electrical equipment from the electricity supply □ *mencabut palam (alat elektrik)*: *Could you unplug the printer, please?* **OPP** **plug sth in**

unpopular /ʌnˈpɒpjələ(r)/ adj **unpopular (with sb)** not liked by many people □ *tdk popular; tdk disukai*: *Her methods made her very unpopular with the staff.* **OPP** **popular** ▶ **unpopularity** /ʌnˌpɒpjuˈlærəti/ noun [U]

unprecedented /ʌnˈpresɪdentɪd/ adj never having happened or existed before □ *tdk pernah berlaku/wujud* ➲ look at **precedent**

unpredictable /ˌʌnprɪˈdɪktəbl/ adj that cannot be predicted because it changes a lot or depends on too many different things □ *tdk dpt diduga/diramalkan*: *unpredictable weather* ♦ *The result is entirely unpredictable.* **OPP** **predictable** ▶ **unpredictability** /ˌʌnprɪˌdɪktəˈbɪləti/ noun [U] ▶ **unpredictably** /ˌʌnprɪˈdɪktəbli/ adv

unprovoked /ˌʌnprəˈvəʊkt/ adj (used especially about an attack) not caused by anything

unqualified → unsound

the person who is attacked has said or done □ *tanpa dirangsang; tanpa bersebab* **OPP** provoked

unqualified /ˌʌnˈkwɒlɪfaɪd/ *adj* **1** not having the knowledge or not having passed the exams that you need for sth □ *tdk berkelayakan*: *I'm unqualified to offer an opinion on this matter.* **OPP** qualified **2** complete; total □ *benar-benar; betul-betul*: *an unqualified success*

unquestionable /ʌnˈkwestʃənəbl/ *adj* certain; that cannot be doubted □ *pasti; tdk dpt dipertikaikan* **OPP** questionable ▶**unquestionably** /-əbli/ *adv*: *She is unquestionably the most famous opera singer in the world.*

unravel /ʌnˈrævl/ *verb* [I,T] (unravelling; unravelled, (*AmE*) unraveling; unraveled) **1** if you unravel threads that are twisted or they unravel, you separate them □ *menguraikan*: *I unravelled the tangled string and wound it into a ball.* **2** (used about a complicated story, etc.) to become or to make sth become clear □ *merungkaikan; menjadi jelas*: *Eventually the mystery unravelled and the truth came out.*

unreal /ˌʌnˈrɪəl/ *adj* **1** very strange and seeming more like a dream than reality □ *spt khayalan; aneh*: *Her voice had an unreal quality about it.* **2** not connected with reality □ *tdk berasaskan kenyataan*: *Some people have unreal expectations of marriage.*

unrealistic /ˌʌnrɪəˈlɪstɪk/ *adj* not showing or accepting things as they are □ *tdk realistik*: *unrealistic expectations* ♦ *It is unrealistic to expect them to be able to solve the problem immediately.* **OPP** realistic ▶**unrealistically** /-kli/ *adv*

unreasonable /ʌnˈriːznəbl/ *adj* unfair; expecting too much □ *tdk munasabah; keterlaluan*: *I think she is being totally unreasonable about it.* ♦ *He makes unreasonable demands on his students.* **OPP** reasonable ▶**unreasonably** /-əbli/ *adv*

unrelenting /ˌʌnrɪˈlentɪŋ/ *adj* (*formal*) continuously strong, not becoming weaker or less severe or stopping □ *tdk henti-henti; berterusan*

unreliable /ˌʌnrɪˈlaɪəbl/ *adj* that cannot be trusted or depended on □ *tdk boleh diharap; tdk boleh dipercayai*: *The trains are notoriously unreliable.* ♦ *an unreliable witness* ♦ *He's totally unreliable as a source of information.* **OPP** reliable ▶**unreliability** /ˌʌnrɪˌlaɪəˈbɪləti/ *noun* [U]

unreserved /ˌʌnrɪˈzɜːvd/ *adj* **1** (used about seats in a theatre, etc.) not kept for the use of a particular person □ *tdk ditempah* **OPP** reserved **2** (*formal*) without limit; complete □ *tanpa had; sepenuhnya*: *The government's action received the unreserved support of all parties.* ▶**unreservedly** /ˌʌnrɪˈzɜːvɪdli/ *adv*: *We apologize unreservedly for our mistake and will refund your money.*

unrest /ʌnˈrest/ *noun* [U] a situation in which people are angry or not happy and likely to protest or fight □ *pergolakan; kekacauan*: *political and social unrest*

unrivalled (*AmE* unrivaled) /ʌnˈraɪvld/ *adj* much better than any other of the same type □ *tdk ada tandingannya*: *His knowledge of Greek theology is unrivalled.*

unroll /ʌnˈrəʊl/ *verb* [I,T] to open from a rolled position □ *membuka (gulungan sst)*: *He unrolled the poster and stuck it on the wall.* **OPP** roll up

unruly /ʌnˈruːli/ *adj* difficult to control; without discipline □ *tdk terkawal; tdk berdisiplin*: *an unruly crowd* ▶**unruliness** *noun* [U]

unsavoury (*AmE* unsavory) /ʌnˈseɪvəri/ *adj* unpleasant; not morally acceptable □ *tdk menyenangkan; tdk baik*: *His friends are all unsavoury characters.*

unscathed /ʌnˈskeɪðd/ *adj* [not before a noun] not hurt, without injury □ *tdk tercedera; tanpa cedera*: *He came out of the fight unscathed.*

unscrew /ˌʌnˈskruː/ *verb* [T] **1** to open or remove sth by turning it □ *membuka dgn memutar*: *Could you unscrew the top of this bottle for me?* **2** to remove the screws from sth □ *membuka/menanggalkan skru*

unscrupulous /ʌnˈskruːpjələs/ *adj* being dishonest, cruel or unfair in order to get what you want □ *tdk berprinsip; tdk jujur* **OPP** scrupulous

unselfish /ʌnˈselfɪʃ/ *adj* giving more time or importance to other people's needs or wishes than to your own □ *tdk mementingkan diri; bertimbang rasa* **OPP** selfish ⇨ look at selfless

unsettled /ʌnˈsetld/ *adj* **1** (used about a situation) that may change; making people uncertain about what might happen □ *tdk stabil; berubah-ubah*: *These were difficult and unsettled times.* ♦ *The weather has been very unsettled* (= it has changed a lot). **2** not calm or relaxed □ *tdk tenang/tenteram*: *They all felt restless and unsettled.* **3** (used about an argument, etc.) that continues without any agreement being reached □ *tdk selesai; belum selesai; belum mencapai kata sepakat/persetujuan* **4** (used about a bill, etc.) not yet paid □ *belum lunas/dilangsaikan/dibayar*

unsettling /ʌnˈsetlɪŋ/ *adj* making you feel upset, nervous or worried □ *rasa tdk senang hati*

unsightly /ʌnˈsaɪtli/ *adj* very unpleasant to look at □ *hodoh*: *an unsightly new building* **SYN** ugly

unskilled /ˌʌnˈskɪld/ *adj* not having or needing special skill or training □ *tdk mahir*: *an unskilled job/worker* **OPP** skilled

unsolicited /ˌʌnsəˈlɪsɪtɪd/ *adj* not asked for □ *tanpa diminta*: *unsolicited praise/advice*

unsound /ˌʌnˈsaʊnd/ *adj* **1** based on wrong ideas and therefore not correct or sensible □ *tdk wajar* **2** in poor condition; weak □ *tdk teguh; tdk kukuh; lemah*: *The building is structurally unsound.* **OPP** for both meanings sound

unstable /ʌnˈsteɪbl/ *adj* **1** likely to change or fail □ *tdk stabil; tdk tetap*: *a period of unstable government* **2** (used about sb's moods or behaviour) likely to change suddenly or often □ *tdk menentu; tdk stabil* **3** likely to fall down or move; not firmly fixed □ *tdk kukuh; tdk tegap* **OPP** stable ⊃ *noun* **instability**

unsteady /ʌnˈstedi/ *adj* **1** not completely in control of your movements so that you might fall □ *terhuyung-hayang; tdk stabil*: *She is still a little unsteady on her feet after the operation.* **2** shaking or moving in a way that is not controlled □ *terketar-ketar*: *His writing is untidy because he has an unsteady hand.* **OPP** for both meanings **steady** ▶ **unsteadily** *adv*

unstuck /ˌʌnˈstʌk/ *adj* no longer stuck together or stuck down □ *tertanggal*: *The label on the parcel is about to come unstuck.*
IDM **come unstuck** (*informal*) to fail badly; to go wrong □ *gagal; tdk berjaya*: *His plan came unstuck when he realized he didn't have enough money.*

unsubscribe /ˌʌnsəbˈskraɪb/ *verb* [I,T] **unsubscribe (from sth)** to remove your email address from an Internet **mailing list** (= a list of the names and addresses of people to whom sth is sent) □ *mengeluarkan nama drpd senarai mel Internet*

unsuccessful /ˌʌnsəkˈsesfl/ *adj* not successful; not achieving what you wanted to □ *tdk berjaya; tdk berhasil; gagal*: *His efforts to get a job proved unsuccessful.* ◆ *She made several unsuccessful attempts to see him.* **OPP** successful ▶ **unsuccessfully** /-fəli/ *adv*

unsuitable /ʌnˈsuːtəbl/ *adj* not right or appropriate for sb/sth □ *tdk sesuai*: *This film is unsuitable for children under 12.* **OPP** suitable

unsure /ʌnˈʃʊə(r)/ (*BrE also*) -ˈʃɔː(r)/ *adj* **1 unsure (about/of sth)** not certain; having doubts □ *tdk pasti*: *I didn't argue because I was unsure of the facts.* **2 unsure of yourself** not feeling confident about yourself □ *tdk yakin*: *He's young and still quite unsure of himself.* **OPP** for both meanings **sure**

unsuspecting /ˌʌnsəˈspektɪŋ/ *adj* not realizing that there is danger □ *tdk menyangka* ⊃ look at **suspect**, **suspicious**

untangle /ʌnˈtæŋgl/ *verb* [T] to separate threads which have become tied together in a confused way □ *menguraikan*: *The wires got mixed up and it took me ages to untangle them.*

unthinkable /ʌnˈθɪŋkəbl/ *adj* impossible to imagine or accept □ *tdk dpt dibayangkan/ diterima; tdk sanggup difikirkan*: *It was unthinkable that he would never see her again.*

unthinking /ʌnˈθɪŋkɪŋ/ *adj* (*formal*) done, said, etc. without thinking carefully □ *melulu; tdk berfikir panjang* ▶ **unthinkingly** *adv*

untidy /ʌnˈtaɪdi/ *adj* (untidier; untidiest) **1** not tidy or well arranged □ *tdk kemas*: *an untidy bedroom* ◆ *untidy hair* **2** (used about a person) not keeping things tidy or in good order □ *selekeh*: *My flatmate is so untidy!* **OPP** for both meanings **tidy, neat** ▶ **untidily** *adv* ▶ **untidiness** *noun* [U]

untie /ʌnˈtaɪ/ *verb* [T] (untying; unties; *pt*, *pp* untied) to remove a knot; to free sb/sth that is tied by a rope, etc. □ *membuka ikatan; menguraikan* **OPP** tie, tie up, fasten

until /ənˈtɪl/ (*also informal* **till**) *prep, conj* up to the time or the event mentioned □ *sehingga*: *The restaurant is open until midnight.* ◆ *Until that moment she had been happy.* ◆ *She waited until he had finished.* ◆ *We won't leave until the police get here* (= we won't leave before they come).

> **OTHER WORDS FOR**
>
> **until**
>
> We can use **until** in both formal and informal English. **Till** is more common in informal English and is not usually used at the beginning of a sentence. **Till/until** are used to talk about a time. We use **as far as** to talk about distance: *I walked as far as the shops.* We use **up to** to talk about a number: *You can take up to 20 kilos of luggage.*

untold /ˌʌnˈtəʊld/ *adj* [only *before* a noun] very great; so big, etc. that you cannot count or measure it □ *amat banyak; tdk terkira; sangat teruk*: *untold suffering*

untoward /ˌʌntəˈwɔːd/ *adj* (used about an event, etc.) unexpected and unpleasant □ *tdk dijangka; ganjil*: *The security guard noticed nothing untoward.*

untrue /ʌnˈtruː/ *adj* not true; not based on facts □ *tdk benar/betul/sah* **SYN** false **OPP** true

untruth /ʌnˈtruːθ/ *noun* [C] (*pl* untruths /ʌnˈtruːðz/) (*formal*) something that is not true; a lie □ *sst yg tdk benar; dusta* ▶ **untruthful** /-fl/ *adj* ▶ **untruthfully** /-fəli/ *adv*

untypical /ʌnˈtɪpɪkl/ *adj* not typical or usual □ *tdk tipikal; bukan lazim*: *an untypical example* **OPP** typical ⊃ look at **atypical**

unused¹ /ˌʌnˈjuːzd/ *adj* that has not been used □ *belum pernah digunakan*

unused² /ʌnˈjuːst/ *adj* **unused to sth/to doing sth** not having any experience of sth □ *tdk biasa dgn sst*: *She was unused to getting such a lot of attention.*

unusual /ʌnˈjuːʒuəl; -ʒəl/ *adj* **1** not expected or normal □ *luar biasa*: *It's unusual for Joe to be late.* **OPP** usual **2** interesting because it is different □ *lain drpd yg lain*: *What an unusual hat!*

unusually /ʌnˈjuːʒuəli; -ʒəli/ *adv* **1** more than is common; extremely □ *amat*: *an unusually hot summer* **2** in a way that is not normal or typical of sb/sth □ *luar biasa*: *Unusually for her, she forgot his birthday.* **OPP** usually

unveil /ʌnˈveɪl/ *verb* [T] to show sth new to the public for the first time □ *menunjukkan/*

mendedahkan sst yg belum pernah ditunjuk-kan atau diberitahu: *The President unveiled a memorial to those who died in the war.*

unwanted /ˌʌnˈwɒntɪd/ *adj* not wanted □ *tdk diingini*: *an unwanted gift*

unwarranted /ʌnˈwɒræntɪd/ (*AmE* also) /*adj* (*formal*) that is not deserved or for which there is no good reason □ *tdk wajar*: *unwarranted criticism*

unwell /ʌnˈwel/ *adj* [not before a noun] ill; sick □ *tdk sihat; uzur*: *to feel unwell* **OPP** **well**

unwieldy /ʌnˈwiːldi/ *adj* difficult to move or carry because it is too big, heavy, etc. □ *sukar dialih atau dibawa kerana terlalu besar, berat, dsb*

unwilling /ʌnˈwɪlɪŋ/ *adj* not wanting to do sth but often forced to do it by other people □ *tdk rela; tdk sudi*: *She was unwilling to give me any further details.* **OPP** **willing** ▶**unwillingly** *adv*: *He handed over the money unwillingly.*

unwind /ˌʌnˈwaɪnd/ *verb* (*pt, pp* **unwound** /ˌʌnˈwaʊnd/) **1** [I,T] to undo sth that has been wrapped into a ball or around sth □ *menguraikan; terurai*: *to unwind a ball of string* ◆ *The bandage had unwound.* **2** [I] (*informal*) to relax, especially after working hard □ *bersantai; bersenang-senang*: *After a busy day, it takes me a while to unwind.* ➔ look at **wind**

unwise /ˌʌnˈwaɪz/ *adj* showing a lack of good judgement; silly □ *tdk bijak*: *I think it would be unwise to tell anyone about our plan yet.* **OPP** **wise** ▶**unwisely** *adv*

unwitting /ʌnˈwɪtɪŋ/ *adj* [only before a noun] not realizing sth; not intending to do sth □ *tanpa disedari; tdk sengaja*: *an unwitting accomplice to the crime* ▶**unwittingly** *adv*

unwound *past tense, past participle of* **unwind**

unwrap /ʌnˈræp/ *verb* [T] (**unwrapping**; **unwrapped**) to take off the paper, etc. that covers or protects sth □ *membuka bungkusan*

unzip /ˌʌnˈzɪp/ *verb* [I,T] (**unzipping**; **unzipped**) if a bag, piece of clothing, etc. **unzips**, or you **unzip** it, you open it by pulling on the **zip** (= the device that fastens the opening, with two rows of metal or plastic teeth) □ *membuka zip* **OPP** **zip sth (up)**

up /ʌp/ *prep, adv* **1** at or to a high or higher place or position □ *di/ke atas; naik; angkat*: *The monkey climbed up the tree.* ◆ *I carried her suitcase up to the third floor.* ◆ *Put your hand up if you know the answer.* ◆ *I walked up the hill.* **2** in or into a vertical position □ *tegak; bangun; tdk tidur*: *Stand up, please.* ◆ *Is he up (= out of bed) yet?* **3** used for showing an increase in sth □ *naik; meningkat*: *Prices have gone up.* ◆ *Turn the volume up.* **4** to the place where sb/sth is □ *ke; di*: *She ran up to her mother and kissed her.* ◆ *A car drove up and two men got out.* **5** in or to the north of □ *di/ke utara*: *My parents have just moved up north.* ◆ *When are you going up to Scotland?* **6** into pieces □ *bermaksud menghancurkan atau menjadi kepingan-kepingan kecil*: *We chopped the old table up and used it for firewood.* ◆ *She tore up the letter and threw it away.* **7** used for showing that an action continues until it is completed □ *digunakan dgn maksud sst perbuatan itu berterusan hingga habis atau tamat*: *Eat up, everybody, I want you to finish everything on the table.* ◆ *Can you help me clean up the kitchen?* **8** coming or being put together □ *mengumpulkan; bersama; bergabung*: *The teacher collected up our exam papers.* ◆ *Keiko and Jos teamed up in the doubles competition.* **9** (used about a period of time) finished □ *(utk waktu) cukup/habis*: *Stop writing. Your time's up.* **10** used with verbs of closing or covering □ *digunakan dgn kk yg membawa maksud menutup atau melitupi*: *Do up your coat. It's cold.* ◆ *She tied the parcel up with string.* ◆ *I found some wood to cover up the hole.* **11** in a particular direction □ *dlm arah tertentu*: *I live just up the road.* ◆ *Move up a little and let me sit down.* **12** (used about computers) working; in operation □ *berjalan; berfungsi*: *Are the computers back up yet?* **13** (*informal*) used for showing that sth is spoiled □ *bermaksud merosakkan*: *I really messed up when I told the interviewer I liked sleeping.* ❶ For special uses with many verbs, for example **pick sth up**, look at the verb entries.

IDM **be up for sth 1** to be available to be bought or chosen □ *ditawarkan*: *That house is up for sale.* ◆ *How many candidates are up for election?* **2** (*informal*) to be willing to take part in an activity □ *hendak/suka membuat sst*: *Is anyone up for a swim?*

be up to sb to be sb's responsibility □ *terpulang kpd sso*: *I can't take the decision. It's not up to me.*

not up to much (*informal*) not very good □ *tdk begitu baik*: *The programme wasn't up to much.*

up against sth/sb (*informal*) facing sth/sb that causes problems □ *menghadapi masalah (dr sso/sst)*

up and down backwards and forwards, or rising and falling □ *mundar-mandir; turun naik*: *He was nervously walking up and down outside the interview room.*

up and running (used about sth new) working; being used □ *berjalan dgn baik*

ups and downs ➔ **ups**

up to sth 1 as much/many as □ *hingga (sebanyak)*: *We're expecting up to 100 people at the meeting.* **2** as far as now □ *sehingga kini*: *Up to now, things have been easy.* **3** capable of sth □ *larat; berdaya*: *I don't feel up to cooking this evening. I'm too tired.* **4** (*informal*) doing sth secret and perhaps bad □ *membuat sst (mungkin yg tdk baik) secara diam-diam*: *What are the children up to? Go and see.*

what's up? (*informal*) what's the matter? □ *apa halnya?*

ˌup-and-ˈcoming *adj* likely to be successful and popular in the future □ *bakal berjaya dan popular*: *up-and-coming young actors*

upbringing /ˈʌpbrɪŋɪŋ/ *noun* [sing] the way a child is treated and taught how to behave by their parents □ *didikan; asuhan*: *a strict upbringing*

update /ˌʌpˈdeɪt/ *verb* [T] **1** to make sth more modern □ *menjadikan lebih moden/terkini* **2** to put the most recent information into sth; to give sb the most recent information □ *mengemaskinikan*: *Our database of addresses is updated regularly.* ▶**update** /ˈʌpdeɪt/ *noun* [C]: *an update on a news story* (= the latest information) ♦ *a computer update* (= the most recent improvements sent to a user of a program)

upgrade /ˌʌpˈɡreɪd/ *verb* [T] to change sth so that it is of a higher standard □ *menaikkan taraf*: *Upgrading your computer software can be expensive.* ▶**upgrade** /ˈʌpɡreɪd/ *noun* [C]

upheaval /ʌpˈhiːvl/ *noun* [C,U] a sudden big change, especially one that causes a lot of trouble □ *pergolakan*

upheld *past tense, past participle* of **uphold**

uphill /ˌʌpˈhɪl/ *adj, adv* **1** going towards the top of a hill □ *ke atas bukit* **OPP** **downhill** **2** needing a lot of effort □ *sukar; mencabar*: *It was an uphill struggle to find a job.*

uphold /ʌpˈhəʊld/ *verb* [T] (*pt, pp* **upheld** /-ˈheld/) to support a decision, etc. especially when other people are against it □ *menegakkan; menyokong*

upholstered /ʌpˈhəʊlstəd/ *adj* (used about a chair, etc.) covered with a soft thick material □ *berbalut dgn kain tebal lembut*

upholstery /ʌpˈhəʊlstəri/ *noun* [U] the thick soft materials used to cover chairs, car seats, etc. □ *upholsteri; kusyen*

upkeep /ˈʌpkiːp/ *noun* [U] **1** the cost or process of keeping sth in a good condition □ *senggaraan; kos senggaraan*: *The landlord pays for the upkeep of the building.* **2** the cost or process of providing children or animals with what they need to live □ *pembiayaan hidup; senggaraan*

upland /ˈʌplənd/ *adj* [only *before* a noun] consisting of hills and mountains □ *tanah tinggi* ▶**upland** *noun* [C, usually pl]

uplifting /ʌpˈlɪftɪŋ/ *adj* producing a feeling of hope and happiness □ *memberangsangkan; menaikkan semangat*: *an uplifting speech*

upload /ˌʌpˈləʊd/ *verb* [T] to move data to a larger computer system from a smaller one □ *muat naik* **OPP** **download** ▶**upload** /ˈʌpləʊd/ *noun* [C]

upmarket /ˌʌpˈmɑːkɪt/ *adj, adv* smart or expensive □ *mewah*: *an upmarket restaurant* **OPP** **downmarket**

upon /əˈpɒn/ (*formal*) = **on**(1): *a castle upon a hill* ♦ *row upon row of seats* ♦ *Once upon a time there lived an old woman in the middle of a forest.*

upper /ˈʌpə(r)/ *adj* [only *before* a noun] in a higher position than sth else; above sth □ *atas; atasan*: *He had a cut on his upper lip.* **OPP** **lower**

[I] **intransitive**, a verb which has no object: *He laughed.*

IDM **get, have, etc. the upper hand** to get into a stronger position than another person; to gain control over sb □ *berkedudukan lebih baik; menguasai keadaan*

ˌupper ˈcase *noun* [U] letters that are written or printed in their large form □ *huruf besar*: *'BBC' is written in upper case.* **SYN** **capital letters** **OPP** **lower case**

the ˌupper ˈclass *noun* [sing, with sing or pl verb] (also **the ˌupper ˈclasses** [pl]) the groups of people that are considered to have the highest social position and that have more money and/or power than other people in society □ *golongan/kelas atasan*: *a member of the upper class/upper classes* ⊃ look at **middle class, working class**
▶**ˌupper ˈclass** *adj*: *Her family is very upper class.* ♦ *an upper-class accent*

uppermost /ˈʌpəməʊst/ *adj* in the highest or most important position □ *paling atas/penting*: *Concern for her family was uppermost in her mind.*

upright /ˈʌpraɪt/ *adj, adv* **1** in or into a vertical position □ *menegak*: *I was so tired I could hardly stay upright.* **SYN** **erect** **2** honest and responsible □ *jujur dan bertanggungjawab*
IDM **bolt upright** ⊃ **bolt**³

uprising /ˈʌpraɪzɪŋ/ *noun* [C] a situation in which a group of people start to fight against the people in power in their country □ *pemberontakan*

uproar /ˈʌprɔː(r)/ *noun* [U, sing] a lot of noise, confusion, anger, etc.; an angry discussion about sth □ *kegemparan; kekecohan*: *The meeting ended in uproar.*

uproot /ˌʌpˈruːt/ *verb* [T] to pull up a plant by the roots □ *mencabut*: *Strong winds had uprooted the tree.*

ups /ʌps/ *noun*
IDM **ups and downs** both good times and bad times □ *suka duka*: *We're happy together but we've had our ups and downs.*

upset¹ /ˌʌpˈset/ *verb* [T] (**upsetting**; *pt, pp* **upset**) **1** to make sb worry or feel unhappy □ *merunsingkan; menyedihkan*: *The pictures of starving children upset her.* ⊃ note at **sad 2** to make sth go wrong □ *mengganggu; mengacau*: *to upset someone's plans* **3** to make sb ill in the stomach □ *menyebabkan sakit perut*: *Rich food usually upsets me.* **4** to knock sth over □ *terlanggar sst hingga terlungkup atau terbalik*: *I upset a cup of tea all over the tablecloth.*

upset² /ʌpˈset/ *adj* **1** [not *before* a noun] worried and unhappy □ *susah hati*: *She was looking very upset about something.* ⊃ note at **sad 2** slightly ill □ *sakit*: *I've got an upset stomach.*

HELP Note that the adjective is pronounced /ˈʌpset/ when it comes before a noun and /ˌʌpˈset/ in other positions in the sentence.

upset³ /ˈʌpset/ *noun* **1** [U] a situation in which there are unexpected problems or difficulties □ *gangguan*: *The company survived the recent*

[T] **transitive**, a verb which has an object: *He ate an apple.*

upset in share prices. **2** [C,U] a situation that causes worry and sadness □ *gangguan perasaan*: *She's had a few upsets recently.* ♦ *It had been the cause of much emotional upset.* **3** [C] a slight illness in your stomach □ *sakit*: *a stomach upset*

upshot /'ʌpʃɒt/ *noun* [sing] the upshot (of sth) the final result, especially of a conversation or an event □ *kesudahan*

The painting is upside down.

upside down /ˌʌpsaɪd 'daʊn/ *adv* with the top part turned to the bottom □ *terbalik*: *You're holding the picture upside down.*
IDM turn sth upside down **1** (*informal*) to make a place untidy when looking for sth □ *tunggang-langgang; lintang-pukang*: *I had to turn the house upside down looking for my keys.* **2** to cause large changes and confusion in sb's life □ *berada di dlm atau menjadi kacau-bilau*: *His sudden death turned her world upside down.*
▶ upside down *adj*: *The painting is upside down.*

upstairs /ˌʌp'steəz/ *adv* to or on a higher floor of a building □ *ke/di tingkat atas*: *to go upstairs* ♦ *She's sleeping upstairs.* **OPP** downstairs
▶ upstairs /ˌʌp'steəz/ *adj* [only before a noun]: *an upstairs window* ▶ upstairs *noun* [sing]: *We're going to paint the upstairs.*

upstream /ˌʌp'striːm/ *adv, adj* in the direction that a river flows from □ *(ke) hulu sungai*: *He found it hard work swimming upstream.* **OPP** downstream

upsurge /'ʌpsɜːdʒ/ *noun* [C, usually sing] an upsurge (in sth) a sudden increase of sth □ *kenaikan mendadak*

uptake /'ʌpteɪk/ *noun*
IDM quick/slow on the uptake (*informal*) quick/slow to understand the meaning of sth □ *cepat/lambat faham*: *I gave him a hint but he's slow on the uptake.*

uptight /ˌʌp'taɪt/ *adj* (*informal*) nervous and not relaxed □ *gemuruh; berdebar; mudah melenting*: *He gets uptight before an exam.*

ˌup to 'date *adj* **1** modern □ *moden*: *up-to-date fashions* **2** having the most recent information □ *terkini; mutakhir*: *Is this information up to date?* ⊃ look at out of date

ˌup-to-the-'minute *adj* having the most recent information possible □ *terkini; mutak-*

hir; terbaharu

upturn /'ʌptɜːn/ *noun* [C] an upturn (in sth) an improvement in sth □ *peningkatan*: *an upturn in support for the government* **OPP** downturn

upturned /ˌʌp'tɜːnd/ *adj* **1** pointing upwards □ *terjongket; terdongak*: *an upturned nose* **2** with the top part turned to the bottom □ *terbalik; terlungkup*

upward /'ʌpwəd/ *adj* [only before a noun] moving or directed towards a higher place □ *menaik; meningkat*: *an upward trend in exports* (= an increase) **OPP** downward ▶ upwards /'ʌpwədz/ (also upward) *adv*: *I looked upwards.*

'**upwards of** *prep* more than the number mentioned □ *lebih drpd*: *They've invited upwards of a hundred guests.*

uranium /ju'reɪniəm/ *noun* [U] (*symbol* U) a metal that can be used to produce nuclear energy □ *(simbol U) uranium*: *Uranium is highly radioactive.*

Uranus /'jʊərənəs; ju'reɪnəs/ *noun* [sing] the planet that is 7th in order from the sun □ *Uranus*

urban /'ɜːbən/ *adj* connected with a town or city □ *bandar*: *urban development* ⊃ look at rural

urge¹ /ɜːdʒ/ *verb* [T] **1** urge sb (to do sth); urge sth to advise or try hard to persuade sb to do sth □ *menggesa; menggalakkan*: *I urged him to fight the decision.* ♦ *Drivers are urged to take care on icy roads.* ♦ *Police urge caution on the icy roads.* **2** to force sb/sth to go in a certain direction □ *memacu; mendesak*: *He urged his horse over the fence.*
PHR V urge sb on to encourage sb □ *menggalakkan/merangsang sso*: *The captain urged his team on.*

urge² /ɜːdʒ/ *noun* [C] a strong need or desire □ *dorongan; keinginan*: *sexual/creative urges*

urgent /'ɜːdʒənt/ *adj* needing immediate attention □ *penting; perlu disegerakan*: *an urgent message* ▶ urgency /'ɜːdʒənsi/ *noun* [U]: *a matter of the greatest urgency* ▶ urgently *adv*: *I must see you urgently.*

urinate /'jʊərɪneɪt/ *verb* [I] (*formal*) to pass urine from the body □ *kencing; buang air kecil*

urine /'jʊərɪn; -raɪn/ *noun* [U] the yellowish liquid that is passed from your body when you go to the toilet □ *air kencing*

URL /ˌjuː ɑːr 'el/ *abbr* uniform/universal resource locator; the address of a World Wide Web page □ *URL; alamat laman World Wide Web* ⊃ note at Internet

urn /ɜːn/ *noun* [C] **1** a special container, used especially to hold the **ashes** (= the powder) that is left when a dead person has been **cremated** (= burnt) □ *bekas simpan abu mayat* **2** a large metal container used for making a large quantity of tea or coffee and for keeping it hot □ *kendi besar*

US → usher

US (also U.S.) /ˌjuː ˈes/ abbr the **United States** (of America) □ *AS (Amerika Syarikat)*

us /əs; strong form ʌs/ pron [used as the object of a verb, or after be] me and another person or other people; me and you □ *kami*: *Come with us.* ♦ *Leave us alone.* ♦ *Will you write to us?*

USA (also U.S.A.) /ˌjuː es ˈeɪ/ abbr = **the United States of America** □ *AS (Amerika Syarikat)*

usable /ˈjuːzəbl/ adj that can be used □ *boleh digunakan*

usage /ˈjuːsɪdʒ/ noun **1** [U] the way that sth is used; the amount that sth is used □ *penggunaan* **2** [C,U] the way that words are normally used in a language □ *penggunaan*: *a guide to English grammar and usage*

USB /ˌjuː es ˈbiː/ abbr **universal serial bus**; the system for connecting other pieces of equipment to a computer □ *USB; bas bersiri universal*: *All new PCs now have USB sockets.* ♦ *a USB port* ➾ picture at **computer**

ˈUSB drive (also informal ˌUSB ˈstick) = **flash drive**

use¹ /juːz/ verb [T] (**using**; pt, pp **used** /juːzd/) **1 use sth (as/for sth); use sth (to do sth)** to do sth with a machine, an object, a method, etc. for a particular purpose □ *menggunakan*: *Could I use your phone?* ♦ *The building was used as a shelter for homeless people.* ♦ *A pen is used for writing with.* ♦ *What's this used for?* ♦ *We used the money to buy a house.* ♦ *Use your imagination!* ♦ *That's a word I never use.* **2** to need or to take sth □ *menggunakan; mengambil*: *Don't use all the milk.* ♦ *The heater uses a lot of electricity.* **3** to treat sb/sth in an unfair way in order to get sth that you want □ *memperguna; memperalat*: *I felt used.*

PHR V use sth up to use sth until no more is left □ *menghabiskan; menggunakan sampai habis*

use² /juːs/ noun **1** [U] the act of using sth or of being used □ *penggunaan*: *The use of car share schemes is now widespread.* ♦ *She kept the money for use in an emergency.* **2** [C,U] the purpose for which sth is used □ *guna; penggunaan*: *This machine has many uses.* **3** [U] the ability or permission to use sth □ *keupayaan; kebenaran menggunakan*: *He lost the use of his hand after the accident.* ♦ *She offered them the use of her car.* **4** [U] the advantage of sth; how useful sth is □ *faedahnya; guna*: *It's no use studying for an exam at the last minute.* ♦ *What's the use of trying?* ♦ *Will this jumper be of use to you or should I get rid of it?*

IDM come into/go out of use to start/stop being used regularly or by a lot of people □ *mula digunakan/tdk digunakan*: *When did this word come into common use?*

make use of sth/sb to use sth/sb in a way that will give you an advantage □ *memperguna atau memperalat sst/sso*

used¹ /juːzd/ adj that has had another own-er before □ *terpakai*: *a garage selling used cars* **SYN second-hand**

used² /juːst/ adj **used to sth/to doing sth** familiar with sth because you do it or experience it often □ *biasa dgn*: *He's used to the heat.* ♦ *I'll never get used to getting up so early.*

used to /ˈjuːst tə; before a vowel and in final position tu/ modal verb used for talking about sth that happened often or continuously in the past or about a situation which existed in the past □ *pernah; dulunya*: *She used to live with her parents, but she doesn't any more.* ♦ *You used to live in Glasgow, didn't you?* ♦ *Did you use to smoke?* ♦ *Did you use to believe in Father Christmas?* ♦ *He didn't use to speak to me.* ➾ look at **would** (8)

> **GRAMMAR** To form questions we use **did** with **use to**: *Did she use to be in your class?* We form negatives with **didn't use to** or **never used to**: *I never used to like jazz.* Do not confuse **used to** + infinitive, which refers only to the past, with **be used to (doing) sth**: *I used to live with my parents, but now I live on my own.* ♦ *I'm used to living on my own* (= I am familiar with it), *so I don't feel lonely.* **Get used to (doing) sth** is for new situations that you are not yet familiar with: *I'm still getting used to my new job.*

useful /ˈjuːsfl/ adj having some practical use; helpful □ *berguna*: *a useful tool* ♦ *useful advice*

IDM come in useful to be of practical help in a certain situation □ *ada gunanya*: *Don't throw that box away—it might come in useful for something.*

▶ **usefully** /-fəli/ adv ▶ **usefulness** noun [U]

useless /ˈjuːsləs/ adj **1** that does not work well, that does not achieve anything □ *tdk berguna*: *This new machine is useless.* ♦ *It's useless complaining/to complain—you won't get your money back.* **2** (informal) **useless (at sth/at doing sth)** (used about a person) weak or not successful at sth □ *lemah; tdk pandai*: *I'm useless at sport.*

▶ **uselessly** adv ▶ **uselessness** noun [U]

user /ˈjuːzə(r)/ noun [C] [in compounds] a person who uses a service, machine, place, etc. □ *pengguna*: *users of public transport* ♦ *computer software users*

ˌuser-ˈfriendly adj (used about computers, books, machines, etc.) easy to understand and use □ *mesra pengguna*

username /ˈjuːzəneɪm/ noun [C] the name you use in order to be able to use a computer program or system □ *nama pengguna*: *Please enter your username.*

usher¹ /ˈʌʃə(r)/ noun [C] a person who shows people to their seats in a theatre, church, etc. □ *penunjuk tempat duduk*

usher² /ˈʌʃə(r)/ verb [T] to take or show sb where to go □ *mengiringi; menunjukkan (tempat duduk atau ke mana hendak pergi)*: *I was ushered into an office.*

PHR V usher sth in (formal) to be the beginning of sth new or to make sth new begin □ *menan-*

usual /ˈjuːʒuəl; -ʒəl/ *adj* **usual (for sb/sth) (to do sth)** happening or used most often □ *biasa; lazim*: *It's usual for her to work at weekends.* ♦ *He got home later than usual.* ♦ *I sat in my usual seat.* **OPP unusual**
IDM as usual in the way that has often happened before □ *seperti biasa*: *Here's Dylan, late as usual!*

usually /ˈjuːʒuəli; -ʒəli/ *adv* in the way that is usual; most often □ *biasanya; lazimnya*: *She's usually home by six.* ♦ *Usually, we go out on Saturdays.*

usurp /juːˈzɜːp/ *verb* [T] (*formal*) to take sb's position and put yourself or power without having the right to do this □ *merampas; merebut kuasa* ▶ **usurper** *noun* [C]

UTC /ˌjuː tiː ˈsiː/ *abbr* = **Coordinated Universal Time**

utensil /juːˈtensl/ *noun* [C] a type of tool that is used in the home □ *perkakas; alat*: *kitchen/cooking utensils* ➲ picture at **kitchen**

uterus /ˈjuːtərəs/ *noun* [C] (*pl* **uteruses**; *in scientific use* **uteri** /-raɪ/) the part of a woman or female animal where a baby develops before it is born □ *uterus; rahim* ➲ In everyday English we say **womb**.

utility /juːˈtɪləti/ *noun* (*pl* **utilities**) **1** [C] a service provided for the public, such as a water, gas or electricity supply □ *kemudahan awam*: *the administration of public utilities* **2** [U] (*formal*) the quality of being useful □ *kebergunaan* **3** [C] a computer program or part of a program that does a particular task □ *utiliti; program utk tugas tertentu*: *a utility program*

uˈtility room *noun* [C] a small room in some houses, often next to the kitchen, where people keep large pieces of kitchen equipment, such as a washing machine □ *bilik serba guna*

utilize (also **-ise**) /ˈjuːtəlaɪz/ *verb* [T] (*formal*) to make use of sth □ *menggunakan; memanfaatkan*: *to utilize natural resources*

utmost¹ /ˈʌtməʊst/ *adj* [only before a noun] (*formal*) greatest □ *paling; sangat*: *a message of the utmost importance*

utmost² /ˈʌtməʊst/ *noun* [sing] the greatest amount possible □ *sebanyak yg mungkin; betul-betul; sedaya upaya*: *Resources have been exploited to the utmost.* ♦ *I will do my utmost* (= try as hard as possible) *to help.*

utopia (also **Utopia**) /juːˈtəʊpiə/ *noun* [C,U] a place or state that exists only in the imagination, where everything is perfect □ *Utopia* ▶ **utopian** (also **Utopian**) /juːˈtəʊpiən/ *adj*

utter¹ /ˈʌtə(r)/ *adj* [only before a noun] complete; total □ *benar-benar*: *He felt an utter fool.* ▶ **utterly** *adv*: *It's utterly impossible.*

utter² /ˈʌtə(r)/ *verb* [T] to say sth or make a sound with your voice □ *melafazkan; menyebut; berkata*: *She did not utter a word* (= she did not say anything) *in the meeting.* ▶ **utterance** /ˈʌtərəns/ *noun* [C] (*formal*)

U-turn /ˈjuː tɜːn/ *noun* [C] **1** a type of movement where a car, etc. turns round so that it goes back in the direction it came from □ *pusingan U* **2** (*informal*) a sudden change from one plan or policy to a completely different or opposite one □ *perubahan yg sebaliknya* ➲ look at **about-turn**

V v

V, v /viː/ *noun* [C,U] (*pl* **V's**; **v's** /viːz/) **1** the 22nd letter of the English alphabet □ *V, v (huruf)*: *'Velvet' begins with (a) 'V'.* **2** the shape of a V □ *bentuk V*: *a V-neck sweater* ➲ picture on page P1

v *abbr* **1** (also **vs**) = **versus**(1) □ *lwn (lawan)*: *Liverpool v Everton* **2 V** = **volt** □ *volt*: *a 9V battery* **3** = **verse**(2) □ *bentuk V* **4** (*informal*) = **very**(1) □ *sangat; amat*: *v good*

vacancy /ˈveɪkənsi/ *noun* [C] (*pl* **vacancies**) **1 a vacancy (for sb/sth)** a job that is available for sb to do □ *kekosongan; jawatan kosong*: *We have a vacancy for a secretary.* **2** a room in a hotel, etc. that is available □ *bilik kosong*: *The sign outside the hotel said 'No Vacancies'.*

vacant /ˈveɪkənt/ *adj* **1** (used about a house, hotel room, seat, etc.) not being used; empty □ *kosong; tdk ada orang* **2** (used about a job in a company, etc.) that is available for sb to take □ *kosong*: *the 'Situations Vacant' page* (= the page of a British newspaper where jobs are advertised) **3** showing no sign of intelligence or understanding □ *kosong*: *a vacant expression* ▶ **vacantly** *adv*: *She stared at him vacantly.*

vacate /vəˈkeɪt; veɪˈk-/ *verb* [T] (*formal*) to leave a building, a seat, a job, a hotel room, etc. so that it is available for sb else □ *mengosongkan; meninggalkan*

vacation /vəˈkeɪʃn/ *noun* **1** [C] (*BrE*) any of the periods of time when universities or courts of law are closed □ *cuti; percutian*: *the Christmas/Easter vacation* **2** (*AmE*) = **holiday**(1) □ *cuti*: *The boss is on vacation.*

vaccinate /ˈvæksɪneɪt/ *verb* [T, often passive] **vaccinate sb (against sth)** to give a person or an animal a **vaccine**, especially by **injecting** (= putting a substance under the skin using a needle) it, in order to protect them against a disease □ *menyuntik vaksin; menanam cacar*: *I was vaccinated against tetanus.* ➲ look at **immunize, inoculate** ▶ **vaccination** /ˌvæksɪˈneɪʃn/ *noun* [C,U]

vaccine /ˈvæksiːn/ *noun* [C,U] a substance that is put into the blood and that protects the body from a disease □ *vaksin*: *The polio vaccine has saved millions of lives.*

vacuum → value

vacuum¹ /ˈvækjuəm/ noun [C] **1** a space that is completely empty of all substances, including air or other gases □ *vakum; ruang hampa gas*: *vacuum-packed foods* (= in a pack from which most of the air has been removed) ♦ *a vacuum flask* (= a bottle used for keeping liquids hot or cold) **2** [usually sing] a situation from which sth is missing or lacking □ *kekosongan* **3** (*informal*) = **vacuum cleaner 4** [usually sing] the act of cleaning sth with a vacuum cleaner □ *(perbuatan) memvakum*: *to give a room a quick vacuum*

vacuum² /ˈvækjuəm/ verb [I,T] to clean sth using a **vacuum cleaner** □ *memvakum; membersihkan dgn pembersih vakum*

ˈvacuum cleaner (also *informal* **vacuum**) noun [C] an electric machine that cleans carpets, etc. by sucking up dirt □ *pembersih vakum* ⊃ look at **cleaner**, **Hoover™**

vagina /vəˈdʒaɪnə/ noun [C] the passage in the body of a woman or female animal that connects the outer sex organs to the **womb** (= the part where a baby grows) □ *vagina; faraj*

vacuum cleaner

vagrant /ˈveɪɡrənt/ noun [C] a person who has no home and no job, especially one who asks people for money □ *gelandangan*

vague /veɪɡ/ adj (**vaguer**; **vaguest**) **1** not clear or definite □ *samar-samar; tdk jelas; kabur*: *He was very vague about how much money he'd spent.* ♦ *a vague shape in the distance* **2** (used about a person) not thinking or understanding clearly □ *terpinga-pinga; agak bingung*: *She looked a bit vague when I tried to explain.* ▶ **vagueness** noun [U]

vaguely /ˈveɪɡli/ adv **1** in a way that is not clear; slightly □ *dgn kabur; secara samar-samar; agak*: *Her name is vaguely familiar.* **2** without thinking about what is happening □ *dgn fikiran yg melayang ke tempat lain*: *He smiled vaguely and walked away.*

vain /veɪn/ adj **1** failing to produce the result you want □ *sia-sia; tdk berjaya*: *She turned away in a vain attempt to hide her tears.* **SYN** **useless 2** (used about a person) too proud of your own appearance, abilities, etc □ *bangga diri*: *He's so vain—he looks in every mirror he passes.* ⊃ noun **vanity**

IDM **in vain** without success □ *dgn sia-sia*: *The firemen tried in vain to put out the fire.*
▶ **vainly** adv

valentine /ˈvæləntaɪn/ noun [C] **1** (also **ˈvalentine card**) a card that you send, usually without putting your name on it, to sb you love □ *kad valentine*

CULTURE

It is traditional to send these cards on **St Valentine's Day** (14 February).

2 the person you send this card to □ *kekasih (orang yg dikirim kad valentine)*

valiant /ˈvæliənt/ adj (*formal*) full of courage and not afraid □ *berani* ▶ **valiantly** adv

valid /ˈvælɪd/ adj **1 valid (for sth)** legally or officially acceptable □ *sah*: *This passport is valid for one year only.* **2** based on what is logical or true; acceptable □ *munasabah; wajar*: *I could raise no valid objections to the plan.* ♦ *Jeff's making a perfectly valid point.* **OPP** for both meanings **invalid** ▶ **validity** /vəˈlɪdəti/ noun [U]

validate /ˈvælɪdeɪt/ verb [T] (*formal*) **1** to prove that sth is true □ *mewajarkan; mensahihkan*: *to validate a theory* **OPP** **invalidate 2** to make sth legally or officially valid or acceptable □ *mengesahkan*: *to validate a contract* **OPP** **invalidate 3** to state officially that sth is useful and of an acceptable standard □ *membuat/memberi pengesahan*: *Check that their courses have been validated by a reputable organization.* ▶ **validation** /ˌvælɪˈdeɪʃn/ noun [C,U]

valley /ˈvæli/ noun [C] the low land between two mountains or hills, which often has a river flowing through it □ *lembah*: *a small town set in a valley* ⊃ picture on page P10

valour (*AmE* **valor**) /ˈvælə(r)/ noun [U] (*formal, old-fashioned*) great courage, especially in war □ *keberanian*

valuable /ˈvæljuəbl/ adj **1** very useful □ *bernilai; berguna*: *a valuable piece of information* **2** worth a lot of money □ *berharga*: *Is this ring valuable?* **OPP** for both meanings **valueless**, **worthless**

HELP Be careful. **Invaluable** means 'very useful'.

valuables /ˈvæljuəblz/ noun [pl] the small things that you own that are worth a lot of money, such as jewellery, etc. □ *barang-barang berharga*: *Please put your valuables in the hotel safe.*

valuation /ˌvæljuˈeɪʃn/ noun [C] a professional judgement about how much money sth is worth □ *penilaian*

value¹ /ˈvæljuː/ noun **1** [U,C] the amount of money that sth is worth □ *nilai; harga*: *to go up/down in value* ♦ *The thieves stole goods with a total value of $10 000.* ⊃ look at **face value 2** [U] (*BrE*) how much sth is worth compared with its price □ *nilai*: *The hotel was good/excellent value* (= well worth the money it cost). ♦ *Package holidays give the best value for money.* **3** [U] the importance of sth □ *nilai*: *to be of great/little/no value to somebody* ♦ *This bracelet is of great sentimental value to me.* **4 values** [pl] beliefs about what is the right and wrong way for people to behave; moral principles □ *nilai; prinsip*: *a return to traditional values* ♦ *Young people have a completely different set of values and expectations.*

value² /'vælju:/ *verb* [T] (**valuing**) **1 value sb/sth (as sth)** to think sb/sth is very important □ *menghargai*: *Sandra has always valued his independence.* ♦ *I really value her as a friend.* **2** [usually passive] **value sth (at sth)** to decide the amount of money that sth is worth □ *menilai; bernilai*: *The house was valued at $150 000.*

valueless /'vælju:ləs/ *adj* (*formal*) without value or use □ *tdk berharga* SYN **worthless** OPP **valuable**

valve /vælv/ *noun* [C] a device in a pipe or tube which controls the flow of air, liquid or gas, letting it move in one direction only □ *injap*: *a radiator valve* ♦ *the valve on a bicycle tyre* ➔ picture at **bicycle**

vampire /'væmpaɪə(r)/ *noun* [C] (in stories) a dead person who comes out at night and drinks the blood of living people □ *puntianak*

van /væn/ *noun* [C] a road vehicle that is used for transporting things □ *van*: *a delivery van* ♦ *a van driver* ➔ picture on **page P7**

HELP **Van** or **lorry**? A **van** is smaller than a **lorry** and is always covered.

vandal /'vændl/ *noun* [C] a person who damages sb else's property on purpose and for no reason □ *pelaku musnah* ▶**vandalism** /'vændəlɪzəm/ *noun* [U]: *acts of vandalism* ▶**vandalize** (also -**ise**) /'vændəlaɪz/ *verb* [T, usually passive]: *All the garages in this area have been vandalized.* ➔ note at **crime**

vanilla /və'nɪlə/ *noun* [U] a substance from a plant that is used for giving flavour to sweet food □ *vanila*: *vanilla ice cream*

vanish /'vænɪʃ/ *verb* [I] **1** to disappear suddenly or in a way that you cannot explain □ *lesap; menghilang*: *When he turned round, the two men had vanished without trace.* **2** to stop existing □ *lenyap; pupus*: *This species of plant is vanishing from our countryside.*

vanity /'vænəti/ *noun* [U] the quality of being too proud of your appearance or abilities □ *sifat megah/bangga diri; keangkuhan* ➔ *adjective* **vain**

vantage point /'vɑ:ntɪdʒ pɔɪnt/ *noun* [C] a place from which you have a good view of sth □ *kedudukan yg baik; sudut pandangan*: (*figurative*) *From our modern vantage point, we can see why the Roman Empire collapsed.*

vapour (*AmE* **vapor**) /'veɪpə(r)/ *noun* [C,U] a mass of very small drops of liquid in the air, for example steam □ *wap*: *water vapour*

variable /'veəriəbl/ (*AmE* also) / *adj* not staying the same; often changing □ *berubah-ubah* ▶**variable** *noun* [C] ▶**variability** /,veəriə'bɪləti/ (*AmE* also) / *noun* [U]

variant /'veəriənt/ (*AmE* also) / *noun* [C] a slightly different form or type of sth □ *varian; kelainan*

variation /,veəri'eɪʃn/ *noun* **1** [C,U] (**a**) **variation (in sth)** a change or difference in the amount or level of sth □ *perbezaan*: *There was a lot of variation in the examination results.* ♦ *There may be a slight variation in price from shop to shop.* **2** [C] **a variation (on/of sth)** a thing that is slightly different from another thing in the same general group □ *variasi; sst yg hanya berbeza sedikit drpd yg lain*: *All her films are just variations on a basic theme.*

varied /'veərid/ (*AmE* also) / *adj* having many different kinds of things or activities □ *berbagai-bagai; penuh kepelbagaian*: *I try to make my classes as varied as possible.*

variety /və'raɪəti/ *noun* (*pl* **varieties**) **1** [sing] **a variety (of sth)** a number of different types of the same thing □ *berbagai-bagai*: *There is a wide variety of dishes to choose from.* **2** [U] the quality of not being or doing the same all the time □ *kepelbagaian*: *There's so much variety in my new job. I do something different every day!* **3** [C] **a variety (of sth)** a type of sth □ *jenis*: *a new variety of apple called 'Perfection'*

various /'veəriəs/ (*AmE* also) / *adj* several different □ *pelbagai*: *I decided to leave London for various reasons.*

varnish /'vɑ:nɪʃ/ *noun* [U] a clear liquid that you paint onto hard surfaces, especially wood, to protect them and make them shine □ *varnis* ➔ look at **nail polish** ▶**varnish** *verb* [T]

vary /'veəri/ (*AmE* also) / *verb* (**varying**; **varies**; *pt, pp* **varied**) **1** [I] **vary (in sth)** (used about a group of similar things) to be different from each other □ *berbeza*: *The hotel bedrooms vary in size from medium to very large.* **2** [I] **vary (from ... to ...)** to be different or to change according to the situation, etc. □ *berubah-ubah*: *The price of the holiday varies from £500 to £1 200, depending on the time of year.* **3** [T] to make sth different by changing it often in some way □ *mempelbagaikan*: *I try to vary my work as much as possible so I don't get bored.*

vase /vɑ:z/ *noun* [C] a container that is used for holding cut flowers □ *pasu bunga; jambangan* ➔ picture on **page P8**

vasectomy /və'sektəmi/ *noun* [C] (*pl* **vasectomies**) a medical operation to stop a man being able to make a woman pregnant □ *vasektomi*

vast /vɑ:st/ *adj* extremely big □ *amat besar, banyak, luas, dsb*: *a vast sum of money* ♦ *a vast country* SYN **huge** ▶**vastly** *adv*: *a vastly improved traffic system*

VAT (also **Vat**) /,vi: eɪ 'ti:; væt/ *abbr* **value added tax**; a tax that is added to the price of goods and services □ *VAT (cukai nilai tambahan)*: *prices include VAT*

[C] **countable**, a noun with a plural form: *one book, two books*   [U] **uncountable**, a noun with no plural form: *some sugar*

vault → vengeance

vault¹ /vɔːlt/ noun [C] **1** a room with a strong door and thick walls in a bank, etc. that is used for keeping money and other valuable things safe □ *bilik kebal* **2** a room under a church where dead people are buried □ *makam*: *a family vault* **3** a high roof or ceiling in a church, etc., made from a number of **arches** (= curved structures) joined together at the top □ *kekubah* **4** a jump made by vaulting □ *lombol bergalah*

vault² /vɔːlt/ verb [I,T] **vault (over) sth** to jump over or onto sth in one movement, using your hands or a pole to help you □ *melompat; melombol*: *The boy vaulted over the wall.*

VCR /ˌviː siː ˈɑː(r)/ abbr = **video cassette recorder**

VDU /ˌviː diː ˈjuː/ noun [C] **visual display unit**; a screen on which you can see information from a computer □ *unit paparan video*

veal /viːl/ noun [U] the meat from a **calf** (= a young cow) □ *daging anak lembu* ➔ note at **meat**

veer /vɪə(r)/ verb [I] (used about vehicles) to change direction suddenly □ *melencong tiba-tiba*: *The car veered across the road and hit a tree.*

veg¹ /vedʒ/ (BrE informal) = **vegetable** □ *sayur-sayuran*: *a fruit and veg stall*

veg² /vedʒ/ verb (**vegging**; **vegged**)
PHR V **veg out** (informal) to relax and do nothing that needs thought or effort □ *melepak*: *I'm just going to go home and veg out in front of the telly.*

vegan /ˈviːɡən/ noun [C] a person who does not eat meat or any other animal products at all □ *vegan; pemakan sayur yg tdk langsung makan sebarang benda drpd binatang* ➔ look at **vegetarian** ▶ **vegan** adj

vegetable /ˈvedʒtəbl/ (also informal **veg**, **veggie**) noun [C] a plant or part of a plant that we eat □ *sayur-sayuran*: *Potatoes, beans and onions are all vegetables.* ♦ *vegetable soup* ➔ picture on **page P15**

vegetarian /ˌvedʒəˈteəriən/ (also informal **veggie**) noun [C] a person who does not eat meat or fish □ *vegetarian; pemakan sayur* ➔ look at **vegan** ▶ **vegetarian** adj: *a vegetarian cookery book*

vegetation /ˌvedʒəˈteɪʃn/ noun [U] (formal) plants in general; all the plants that are found in a particular place □ *tumbuh-tumbuhan*: *tropical vegetation*

veggie /ˈvedʒi/ noun [C] (informal) **1** = **vegetarian 2** = **vegetable** ▶ **veggie** adj: *a veggie burger*

vehement /ˈviːəmənt/ adj showing very strong (often negative) feelings, especially anger □ *keras; hebat; bersungguh-sungguh*: *a vehement attack on the government*

vehicle /ˈviːəkl/ noun [C] **1** something which transports people or things from place to place, especially on land, for example cars, bicycles, lorries and buses □ *kenderaan*: *Are you the owner of this vehicle?* **2** something which is used for communicating particular ideas or opinions □ *wahana; alat*: *This newspaper has become a vehicle for Conservative opinion.*

veil /veɪl/ noun [C] a piece of thin material for covering the head and face of a woman □ *tudung; kelubung; vel*: *a bridal veil*

vein /veɪn/ noun **1** [C] one of the tubes which carry blood from all parts of your body to your heart □ *vena; salur darah; urat* ➔ look at **artery 2** [sing, U] a particular style or quality □ *nada; unsur*: *After a humorous beginning, the programme continued in a more serious vein.*

Velcro™ /ˈvelkrəʊ/ noun [U] a material for fastening parts of clothes together. Velcro™ is made of **nylon** (= a strong material) and is used in small pieces, one rough and one smooth, that can stick together and be pulled apart. □ *Velcro™ (velkro)*

velocity /vəˈlɒsəti/ noun [U] (technical) the speed at which sth moves □ *halaju*

velvet /ˈvelvɪt/ noun [U] a type of cloth made of cotton or other material, with a soft thick surface on one side only □ *(kain) baldu*: *black velvet trousers*

vendetta /venˈdetə/ noun [C] a serious argument or disagreement between two people or groups which lasts for a long time □ *permusuhan*

'vending machine noun [C] a machine from which you can buy drinks, sweets, etc. by putting coins in it □ *mesin layan diri*

vendor /ˈvendə(r)/ noun [C] (formal) a person who is selling sth □ *penjual* ➔ look at **purchaser**

veneer /vəˈnɪə(r)/ noun **1** [C,U] a thin layer of wood or plastic that is stuck onto the surface of cheaper wood, to give it a better appearance □ *venier; lapisan* **2** [sing] (formal) **a veneer (of sth)** a part of sb's behaviour or of a situation which hides what it is really like underneath □ *(sifat/perlakuan) yg pd zahirnya; topeng*: *a thin veneer of politeness*

venetian blind /vəˌniːʃn ˈblaɪnd/ noun [C] a covering for a window that is made of horizontal pieces of flat plastic, etc. which can be turned to let in as much light as you want □ *bidai venetian* ➔ picture at **curtain**

vengeance /ˈvendʒəns/ noun [U] (formal) **vengeance (on sb)** the act of punishing or harming sb in return for sth bad they have done to you, your friends or family □ *balas dendam*: *He felt a terrible desire for vengeance on the people who had destroyed his career.* ➔ look at **revenge**
IDM **with a vengeance** to a greater degree than is expected or usual □ *dgn lebih hebat, teruk, dll*: *After a week of good weather winter returned with a vengeance.*

[I] **intransitive**, a verb which has no object: *He laughed.* [T] **transitive**, a verb which has an object: *He ate an apple.*

venison /ˈvenɪsn/ noun [U] the meat from a **deer** (= a large wild animal that eats grass) □ *daging rusa* ➔ note at **deer**

venom /ˈvenəm/ noun [U] **1** the poisonous liquid that some snakes, spiders, etc. produce when they bite or sting you □ *bisa* **2** (*formal*) extreme anger or hatred and a desire to hurt sb □ *kebencian yg keterlaluan*: *a look of pure venom* ▸**venomous** /ˈvenəməs/ adj

vent /vent/ noun [C] an opening in the wall of a room or machine which allows air to come in, and smoke, steam or smells to go out □ *lubang udara/angin*: *an air vent* ♦ *a heating vent*

ventilate /ˈventɪleɪt/ verb [T] to allow air to move freely in and out of a room or building □ *mengalih udara*: *The office is badly ventilated.* ▸**ventilation** /ˌventɪˈleɪʃn/ noun [U]: *There was no ventilation in the room except for one tiny window.*

venture¹ /ˈventʃə(r)/ noun [C] a project which is new and possibly dangerous, because you cannot be sure that it will succeed □ *usaha; usaha niaga*: *a business venture*

venture² /ˈventʃə(r)/ verb [I] to do sth or go somewhere new and dangerous, when you are not sure what will happen □ *pergi/keluar mengharung (sst keadaan yg berbahaya, dsb); berani menceburi (sst bidang, dsb)*: *He ventured out into the storm to look for the lost child.* ♦ *The company has decided to venture into computer production as well as design.*

venue /ˈvenjuː/ noun [C] the place where people meet for an organized event, for example a concert or a sports event □ *tempat*

Venus /ˈviːnəs/ noun [sing] the planet that is second in order from the sun and nearest to the earth □ *Zuhrah*

veranda (also **verandah**) /vəˈrændə/ (*AmE* also **porch**) noun [C] a platform joined to the side of a house, with a roof and floor but no outside wall □ *beranda; serambi* ➔ look at **patio**, **terrace**

verb /vɜːb/ noun [C] a word or group of words that expresses an action (such as *eat*), an event (such as *happen*) or a state (such as *exist*) □ *kata kerja*: *What's the main verb of the sentence?* ♦ *In this essay he has used the same verbs over and over again.* ➔ look at **phrasal verb**

verbal /ˈvɜːbl/ adj **1** connected with words or the use of words □ *(berkenaan dgn) kata-kata*: *verbal skills* **2** spoken, not written □ *lisan*: *a verbal agreement/warning* ▸**verbally** /ˈvɜːbəli/ adv

verdict /ˈvɜːdɪkt/ noun [C] **1** the decision that is made by the **jury** (= a group of members of the public) in a court of law, which states if a person is guilty of a crime or not □ *keputusan (mahkamah)*: *The jury returned a verdict of 'not guilty'.* ♦ *Has the jury reached a verdict?* ➔ note at **court 2** a **verdict (on sb/sth)** a decision that you make or an opinion that you give after testing sth or considering sth carefully □ *pendapat*: *The general verdict was that the restaurant was too expensive.*

verge¹ /vɜːdʒ/ noun [C] (*BrE*) the narrow piece of land at the side of a road, railway line, etc. that is usually covered in grass □ *bahu jalan*

IDM on the verge of sth/doing sth very near to doing sth, or to sth happening □ *hampir-hampir (berlaku sst/membuat sst)*: *He was on the verge of a nervous breakdown.* ♦ *Scientists are on the verge of discovering a cure.*

verge² /vɜːdʒ/ verb

PHR V verge on sth to be very close to an extreme state or condition □ *hampir-hampir merupakan*: *What they are doing verges on the illegal.*

verify /ˈverɪfaɪ/ verb [T] (*verifying*; *verifies*; pt, pp *verified*) (*formal*) to check or state that sth is true □ *mengesahkan*: *to verify a statement* ▸**verification** /ˌverɪfɪˈkeɪʃn/ noun [U]

veritable /ˈverɪtəbl/ adj [only before a noun] (*formal*) used to emphasize that sb/sth can be compared to sb/sth else that is more exciting, more impressive, etc. □ *benar-benar; betul-betul; sesungguhnya*: *The meal he cooked was a veritable banquet.*

vermin /ˈvɜːmɪn/ noun [pl] small wild animals (for example mice) that carry disease and destroy plants and food □ *haiwan perosak*

vernacular /vəˈnækjələ(r)/ noun [C] **the vernacular** [sing] the language spoken in a particular area or by a particular group, especially one that is not the official or written language □ *bahasa vernakular*

versatile /ˈvɜːsətaɪl/ adj **1** (used about a person) able to do many different things □ *serba boleh*: *Gloria is so versatile! She can dance, sing, act and play the guitar!* **2** (used about an object) having many different uses □ *serba guna*: *a versatile tool that drills, cuts or polishes*

verse /vɜːs/ noun **1** [U] writing arranged in lines which have a definite rhythm and often **rhyme** (= end with the same sound) □ *rangkap; puisi*: *He wrote his valentine's message in verse.* **SYN poetry 2** [C] (*abbr* v) a group of lines which form one part of a song or poem □ *rangkap*: *This song has five verses.* ➔ look at **chorus**

version /ˈvɜːʃn; -ʒn/ noun [C] **1** a thing which has the same basic content as sth else but which is presented in a different way □ *versi*: *Have you heard the live version of this song?* **2** a person's description of sth that has happened □ *cerita, laporan, dsb dr sudut pandangan sso*: *The two drivers gave very different versions of the accident.*

versus /ˈvɜːsəs/ prep **1** (*abbr* v; vs) used in sport for showing that two teams or people are playing against each other □ *lawan*: *England versus Argentina* **2** used for showing that two ideas or things are opposite to each other, especially when you are trying to choose one of them □ *antara... dgn*: *It's a question of quality versus price.*

vertebra → vicinity

vertebra /ˈvɜːtɪbrə/ noun [C] (pl **vertebrae** /-reɪ; -riː/) any of the small bones that are connected together in a row down the middle of your back □ *vertebra* ⇒ look at **spine**

vertical /ˈvɜːtɪkl/ adj going straight up at an angle of 90° from the ground □ *tegak*: *a vertical line* ◆ *The cliff was almost vertical.* ⇒ look at **horizontal, perpendicular** ⇒ picture at **line** ▶**vertically** /-kli/ adv

very /ˈveri/ adv, adj 1 (abbr v) used with an adjective or adverb to make it stronger □ *amat; sangat*: *very small* ◆ *very slowly* ◆ *I don't like milk very much.* ◆ *'Are you hungry?' 'No, not very.'*

> **GRAMMAR** We use **very** with superlative adjectives: *the very best, youngest, etc.* but with comparative adjectives we use **much** or **very much**: *much better; very much younger*

2 used to emphasize a noun □ *paling; betul-betul*: *We climbed to the very top of the mountain* (= right to the top). ◆ *You're the very person I wanted to talk to* (= exactly the right person).

vessel /ˈvesl/ noun [C] **1** (formal) a ship or large boat □ *kapal* **2** (old-fashioned) a container for liquids, for example a bottle, cup or bowl □ *bekas*: *ancient drinking vessels* ⇒ look at **blood vessel**

vest /vest/ noun [C] **1** (AmE **undershirt**) a piece of clothing that you wear under your other clothes, on the top part of your body □ *anak baju* **2** (AmE) = **waistcoat**

vested interest /ˌvestɪd ˈɪntrəst/ noun [C] a strong and often secret reason for doing sth that will bring you an advantage of some kind, for example more money or power □ *kepentingan diri*

vestige /ˈvestɪdʒ/ noun [C] a small part of sth that is left after the rest of it has gone □ *kesan; bekas; sisa; sekelumit*: *the last vestige of the old system* **SYN** trace

vet[1] /vet/ (BrE formal **veterinary surgeon**; AmE **veterinarian**) noun [C] a doctor for animals □ *doktor haiwan*: *We took the cat to the vet/to the vet's.* ⇒ note at **pet**

vet[2] /vet/ verb [T] (**vetting**; **vetted**) to do careful and secret checks before deciding if sb/sth can be accepted or not □ *memeriksa dgn teliti*: *All new employees at the Ministry of Defence are carefully vetted* (= sb examines the details of their past lives).

veteran /ˈvetərən/ noun [C] **1** a person who has very long experience of a particular job or activity □ *veteran* **2** a person who has served in the army, navy or air force, especially during a war □ *bekas perajurit; veteran*

veterinarian /ˌvetərɪˈneəriən/ (AmE) = **vet**[1]

veterinary /ˈvetnri; ˈvetrənəri/ adj [only before a noun] connected with the medical treatment of sick or injured animals □ *veterinar;* berkenaan dgn rawatan perubatan utk haiwan: *a veterinary practice* ⇒ look at **vet**

veterinary surgeon (BrE formal) = **vet**[1]

veto /ˈviːtəʊ/ verb [T] (**vetoing**; **vetoes**; pt, pp **vetoed**) to refuse to give official permission for an action or a plan, when other people have agreed to it □ *memveto; menolak*: *The Prime Minister vetoed the proposal to reduce taxation.* ▶**veto** noun [C,U] (pl **vetoes**): *the right of veto*

vexed /vekst/ adj causing difficulty, worry and a lot of discussion □ *menyusahkan; membimbangkan; rumit*: *the vexed question of our growing prison population*

via /ˈvaɪə/ prep **1** going through a place □ *melalui*: *We flew from Paris to Sydney via Bangkok.* **2** by means of sth; using sth □ *melalui*: *These pictures come to you via our satellite link.*

viable /ˈvaɪəbl/ adj that can be done; that will be successful □ *boleh dibuat; berkemungkinan berjaya*: *I'm afraid your idea is not commercially viable.* ▶**viability** /ˌvaɪəˈbɪləti/ noun [U]

viaduct /ˈvaɪədʌkt/ noun [C] a long, high bridge which carries a railway or road across a valley □ *jejambat*

vibrant /ˈvaɪbrənt/ adj **1** full of life and energy □ *bersemangat; lincah*: *a vibrant city/ atmosphere/personality* **SYN** exciting **2** (used about colours) bright and strong □ *terang; ceria*

vibrate /vaɪˈbreɪt/ verb [I] to make continuous very small and fast movements from side to side □ *bergetar*: *When a guitar string vibrates it makes a sound.* ▶**vibration** /vaɪˈbreɪʃn/ noun [C,U]

vicar /ˈvɪkə(r)/ noun [C] a priest of the Anglican church. A **vicar** looks after a church and its **parish** (= the area around the church and the people in it). □ *vikar* ⇒ look at **minister**

vicarage /ˈvɪkərɪdʒ/ noun [C] the house where a **vicar** lives □ *kediaman vikar*

vice /vaɪs/ noun **1** [U] criminal activities involving sex or drugs □ *maksiat; kejahatan* **2** [C] a moral weakness or bad habit □ *tabiat buruk; kelemahan*: *Greed and envy are terrible vices.* ◆ *My only vice is smoking.* ⇒ look at **virtue 3** (AmE **vise**) [C] a tool that you use to hold a piece of wood, metal, etc. firmly while you are working on it □ *ragum*: (figurative) *He held my arm in a vice-like* (= very firm) *grip*.

vice- /vaɪs/ [in compounds] having a position second in importance to the position mentioned □ *naib*: *Vice President* ◆ *the vice-captain*

vice versa /ˌvaɪs ˈvɜːsə; ˌvaɪsi/ adv in the opposite way to what has just been said □ *dan sebaliknya*: *Anna ordered fish and Maria chicken—or was it vice versa?*

vicinity /vəˈsɪnəti/ noun
IDM **in the vicinity (of sth)** in the surrounding area □ *di sekitar (sst)*: *There's no bank in the immediate vicinity.*

vicious /'vɪʃəs/ adj **1** cruel; done in order to hurt sb/sth □ *kejam; jahat*: *a vicious attack* **2** (used about an animal) dangerous; likely to hurt sb □ *garang; ganas*: *a vicious dog*
IDM **a vicious circle** a situation in which one problem leads to another and the new problem makes the first problem worse □ *lingkaran ganas*
▶**viciously** adv

victim /'vɪktɪm/ noun [C] a person or an animal that is injured, killed or hurt by sb/sth □ *mangsa*: *a murder victim* ◆ *The children are often the innocent victims of a divorce.*

victimize (also **-ise**) /'vɪktɪmaɪz/ verb [T] to punish or make sb suffer unfairly □ *menjadikan mangsa* ▶**victimization** (also **-isation**) /ˌvɪktɪmaɪˈzeɪʃn/ noun [U]

victor /'vɪktə(r)/ noun [C] (*formal*) the person who wins a game, competition, battle, etc. □ *pemenang*

Victorian /vɪkˈtɔːriən/ adj **1** connected with the time of the British queen Victoria (1837–1901) □ *zaman Victoria*: *Victorian houses* **2** having attitudes that were typical in the time of Queen Victoria □ *ala zaman Victoria* ▶**Victorian** noun [C]

victory /'vɪktəri/ noun [C,U] (*pl* **victories**) success in winning a battle, a game, a competition, an election, etc. □ *kemenangan*: *Moyes led his team to victory in the final.*
IDM **romp home/to victory** ⊃ **romp**
▶**victorious** /vɪkˈtɔːriəs/ adj: *the victorious team*

video /'vɪdiəʊ/ noun (*pl* **videos**) **1** (also ˌvideo casˈsette, **videotape**) [C] a tape used for recording moving pictures and sound; a plastic case containing this tape □ *(pita/kaset) video*: *Have you got a blank video?* **2** = **video cassette recorder** **3** [U] a system of recording moving pictures and sound; a method of storing data □ *rakaman video*: *My parents recorded their wedding on video.* ◆ *a music video* (= a short film made by a band to be shown with a song) **4** (also ˈvideo clip) a short film or recording of an event that you watch on a computer □ *filem video*: *Upload your videos and share them with friends and family online.* ▶**video** verb [T] (**videoing**; **videos**; *pt, pp* **videoed**)

ˌvideo casˈsette recorder (also **video**, ˈvideo recorder) noun [C] (*abbr* **VCR**) a machine that is connected to a TV on which you can record or play back a film or TV programme □ *perakam kaset video*

videoconferencing /'vɪdiəʊkɒnfərənsɪŋ/ noun [U] a system that people in different parts of the world can use to have a meeting, by watching and listening to each other using video screens □ *sidang video* ▶**videoconference** noun [C] an official meeting conducted using **videoconferencing**: *We're having a videoconference this afternoon to discuss the budget.*

videotape /'vɪdiəʊteɪp/ noun [C] = **video**(1)

view¹ /vjuː/ noun **1** [C] **a view (about/on sth)** an opinion or a particular way of thinking about sth □ *pendapat*: *He expressed the view that standards were falling.* ◆ **In my view**, *she has done nothing wrong.* ◆ *She has* **strong views** *on the subject.* **2** [U, sing] the ability to see sth or to be seen from a particular place □ *pandangan*: *The garden was hidden from view behind a high wall.* ◆ *to come into view* ◆ *to disappear from view* **3** [C] what you can see from a particular place □ *pemandangan*: *There are* **breathtaking views** *from the top of the mountain.* ◆ *a room with* **a sea view** ⊃ note at **scenery**
IDM **have, etc. sth in view** (*formal*) to have sth as a plan or idea in your mind □ *sst (rancangan, idea, dsb) yg difikirkan*
in full view (of sb/sth) ⊃ **full¹**
in view of sth (*formal*) because of sth; as a result of sth □ *memandangkan*: *In view of her apology, we decided to take no further action.*
point of view ⊃ **point¹**
with a view to doing sth (*formal*) with the aim or intention of doing sth □ *dgn tujuan membuat sst*

view² /vjuː/ verb [T] **1 view sb/sth (as sth)** to think about sb/sth in a particular way □ *melihat; menganggap*: *She viewed holidays as a waste of time.* **2** to watch or look at sth □ *melihat; dilihat*: *Viewed from this angle, the building looks much taller than it really is.*

viewer /'vjuːə(r)/ noun [C] a person who watches TV □ *penonton (TV)*

viewpoint /'vjuːpɔɪnt/ noun [C] a way of looking at a situation; an opinion □ *sudut pandangan*: *Let's look at this problem from the customer's viewpoint.* **SYN** **point of view**

vigil /'vɪdʒɪl/ noun [C,U] a period when you stay awake all night for a special purpose □ *tempoh tdk tidur utk tujuan tertentu*: *All night she kept vigil over the sick child.*

vigilant /'vɪdʒɪlənt/ adj (*formal*) careful and looking out for danger □ *berjaga-jaga* ▶**vigilance** noun [U]: *the need for constant vigilance*

vigilante /ˌvɪdʒɪˈlænti/ noun [C] a member of a group of people who try to prevent crime or punish criminals in a community, especially because they believe the police are not doing this □ *sukarelawan yg mengawasi keselamatan kawasan mereka; anggota rukun tetangga*

vigour (*AmE* **vigor**) /'vɪɡə(r)/ noun [U] strength or energy □ *kekuatan; tenaga*: *After the break we started work again with renewed vigour.* ▶**vigorous** /'vɪɡərəs/ adj: *vigorous exercise* ▶**vigorously** adv

vile /vaɪl/ adj (**viler**; **vilest**) very bad or unpleasant □ *keji; teruk; dahsyat; (bau) busuk*: *She's in a vile mood.* ◆ *a vile smell* **SYN** **terrible**

villa /'vɪlə/ noun [C] **1** a house that people rent and stay in on holiday □ *vila* **2** a large house in the country, especially in Southern Europe □ *vila*

village /'vɪlɪdʒ/ noun **1** [C] a group of houses with other buildings, for example a shop, school,

villager → virility 946

etc., in a country area. A village is smaller than a town □ *kampung: a small fishing village* ♦ *the village shop* ➲ picture on **page P11** **2** [sing, with sing or pl verb] all the people who live in a village □ *(semua orang) kampung: All the village is/are taking part in the carnival.*

villager /ˈvɪlɪdʒə(r)/ *noun* [C] a person who lives in a village □ *penduduk kampung; orang desa*

villain /ˈvɪlən/ *noun* [C] **1** an evil person, especially in a book or play □ *penjahat; penyangak: In most of his films he has played villains, but in this one he's a good guy.* ➲ look at **hero 2** (*informal*) a criminal □ *penjenayah: The police caught the villains who robbed the bank.*

vindicate /ˈvɪndɪkeɪt/ *verb* [T] (*formal*) **1** to prove that sth is true or that you were right to do sth, especially when other people had a different opinion □ *mengesahkan/membuktikan kebenaran: I have every confidence that this decision will be fully vindicated.* **2** to prove that sb is not guilty when they have been accused of doing sth wrong or illegal □ *menyangkal tuduhan terhadap sso; membersihkan nama sso: New evidence emerged, vindicating him completely.*

vindictive /vɪnˈdɪktɪv/ *adj* wanting or trying to hurt sb without good reason □ *berhasad dengki: a vindictive comment/person* ▶**vindictiveness** *noun* [U]

vine /vaɪn/ *noun* [C] the climbing plant that **grapes** (= small green or purple fruit that grow in bunches) grow on □ *pokok anggur*

vinegar /ˈvɪnɪɡə(r)/ *noun* [U] a liquid with a strong sharp taste that is made from wine. Vinegar is often mixed with oil and put onto salads. □ *cuka*

vineyard /ˈvɪnjəd/ *noun* [C] a piece of land where **grapes** (= small green or purple fruit that grow in bunches) are grown in order to produce wine □ *ladang anggur*

vintage¹ /ˈvɪntɪdʒ/ *noun* [C] the wine that was made in a particular year □ *vintaj; wain yg dihasilkan pd tahun tertentu: 2010 was an excellent vintage.*

vintage² /ˈvɪntɪdʒ/ *adj* [only *before* a noun] **1** vintage wine is of very good quality and has been stored for several years □ *vintaj; (wain) yg dihasilkan beberapa tahun dahulu: a bottle of vintage champagne* **2** of very high quality □ *terbaik: a vintage performance by Robert De Niro*

vinyl /ˈvaɪnl/ *noun* [U] a strong plastic that can bend easily and is used to cover walls, floors, furniture, books, etc. □ *vinil*

viola /viˈəʊlə/ *noun* [C] a musical instrument with strings, that you hold under your chin and play with a **bow** (= a long thin piece of wood with hair stretched across it) □ *viola: A viola is like a large violin.* ➲ picture at **music**

violate /ˈvaɪəleɪt/ *verb* [T] (*formal*) **1** to break a rule, an agreement, etc. □ *melanggar: to violate a peace treaty* **2** to not respect sth; to spoil or damage sth □ *mencabuli; mengganggu: to violate somebody's privacy/rights* ▶**violation** /ˌvaɪəˈleɪʃn/ *noun* [C,U]: *(a) violation of human rights*

violence /ˈvaɪələns/ *noun* [U] **1** behaviour which harms or damages sb/sth physically □ *keganasan; ganas: They threatened to use violence if we didn't give them the money.* ♦ *an act of violence* **2** great force or energy □ *keganasan: the violence of the storm*

violent /ˈvaɪələnt/ *adj* **1** using physical strength to hurt or kill sb; caused by this behaviour □ *ganas: The demonstration started peacefully but later turned violent.* ♦ *a violent death* ♦ *violent crime* **2** very strong and impossible to control □ *kuat; teruk; hebat; dahsyat: He has a violent temper.* ♦ *a violent storm/collision* ▶**violently** *adv*: *The ground shook violently and buildings collapsed in the earthquake.*

violet /ˈvaɪələt/ *noun* **1** [C] a small plant that grows wild or in gardens and has purple or white flowers and a pleasant smell □ *(pokok bunga) violet* **2** [U] a bluish-purple colour □ *(warna) ungu* ▶**violet** *adj*

violin /ˌvaɪəˈlɪn/ *noun* [C] a musical instrument with strings, that you hold under your chin and play with a **bow** (= a long thin piece of wood with hair stretched across it) □ *biola; violin* ➲ An informal word is **fiddle**. ➲ note at **music** ➲ picture at **music**

VIP /ˌviː aɪ ˈpiː/ *abbr* **very important person** □ *VIP (orang kenamaan): the VIP lounge at the airport* ♦ *give someone the VIP treatment* (= treat sb especially well)

viral /ˈvaɪrəl/ *adj* like or caused by a virus □ *seperti atau disebabkan oleh virus: a viral infection* ♦ *a viral email* (= that is sent on from one person to others, who then send it on again)

virgin¹ /ˈvɜːdʒɪn/ *noun* [C] a person who has never had sex □ *anak dara; orang yg belum pernah mengadakan hubungan seks*

virgin² /ˈvɜːdʒɪn/ *adj* that has not yet been used, touched, damaged, etc. □ *dara; murni; belum pernah digunakan, diterokai, diusik, dicemar, dsb: virgin forest*

virginity /vəˈdʒɪnəti/ *noun* [U] the state of never having had sex □ *kedaraan; dara: to lose your virginity*

Virgo /ˈvɜːɡəʊ/ *noun* [C,U] (*pl* **Virgos**) the 6th sign of the **zodiac** (= 12 signs which represent the positions of the sun, moon and planets), the **Virgin**; a person born under this sign □ *Virgo: I'm a Virgo.* ➲ picture at **zodiac**

virile /ˈvɪraɪl/ *adj* (used about a man) strong and having great sexual energy □ *bersifat kejantanan; berdaya seks yg kuat*

virility /vəˈrɪləti/ *noun* [U] a man's sexual power and energy □ *kejantanan; kekuatan daya seks*

virtual /ˈvɜːtʃuəl/ adj [only before a noun] **1** being almost or nearly sth □ *hampir*: *The country is in a state of virtual civil war.* **2** made to appear to exist by the use of computer software, for example on the Internet □ *maya*: *virtual reality* ▶**virtually** /-ʃuəli/ adv: *The building is virtually finished.*

virtue /ˈvɜːtʃuː/ noun **1** [U] behaviour which shows high moral standards □ *kebaikan; kemuliaan akhlak*: *to lead a life of virtue* **SYN** **goodness** **2** [C] a good quality or habit □ *sifat baik*: *Patience is a great virtue.* ➜ look at **vice 3** [C,U] **the virtue (of sth/of being/doing sth)** an advantage or a useful quality of sth □ *kelebihan; kebaikan*: *This new material has the virtue of being strong as well as very light.*
IDM **by virtue of sth** (*formal*) by means of sth or because of sth □ *oleh sebab*

virtuoso /ˌvɜːtʃuˈəʊsəʊ; -ˈəʊzəʊ/ noun [C] (pl **virtuosos** or **virtuosi** /-siː; -ziː/) a person who is extremely skilful at sth, especially playing a musical instrument □ *orang (pemuzik, dll) yg luar biasa bakatnya*

virtuous /ˈvɜːtʃuəs/ adj behaving in a morally good way □ *berakhlak mulia*

virulent /ˈvɪrələnt; -rjəl-/ adj **1** (used about a poison or a disease) very strong and dangerous □ *sangat berbahaya*: *a particularly virulent form of influenza* **2** (*formal*) very strong and full of anger □ *sangat tajam/pedas*: *a virulent attack on the leader*

ʔ virus /ˈvaɪrəs/ noun [C] **1** a living thing, too small to be seen without a **microscope** (= a piece of equipment that makes small objects look bigger), that causes disease in people, animals and plants □ *virus (kuman)*: *HIV, the virus that can cause AIDS* ◆ *to catch a virus* ➜ look at **bacteria, germ 2** a disease caused by a **virus** □ *virus (penyakit)*: *The doctor said I had a virus.* **3** instructions that are put into a computer program in order to stop it working properly and destroy information □ *virus (komputer)* ➜ note at **cybercrime**

visa /ˈviːzə/ noun [C] an official mark or piece of paper that shows you are allowed to enter, leave or travel through a country □ *visa*: *His passport was full of visa stamps.* ◆ *a tourist/work/student visa*

vise (*AmE*) = **vice**(3)

visibility /ˌvɪzəˈbɪləti/ noun [U] the distance that you can see in particular light or weather conditions □ *jarak penglihatan*: *In the fog visibility was down to 50 metres.* ◆ *poor/good visibility*

ʔ visible /ˈvɪzəbl/ adj that can be seen or noticed □ *dpt dilihat; tampak*: *The church tower was visible from the other side of the valley.* ◆ *a visible improvement in his work* **OPP** **invisible** ▶**visibly** /-əbli/ adv: *Rosa was visibly upset.*

ʔ vision /ˈvɪʒn/ noun
▶SIGHT **1** [U] the ability to see; sight □ *penglihatan*: *to have good/poor/normal/perfect vision*
▶PICTURE IN MIND **2** [C] a picture in your imagination □ *visi; bayangan; gambaran*: *They have a vision of a world without weapons.* ◆ *I had visions of being left behind, but in fact the others had waited for me.*
▶DREAM **3** [C] a dream or similar experience often connected with religion □ *visi; bayangan*: *God appeared to Paul in a vision.*
▶PLANS FOR FUTURE **4** [U] the ability to make great plans for the future □ *wawasan; visi*: *a leader of great vision*
▶TV/CINEMA **5** [U] the picture on a TV or cinema screen □ *gambar*: *a temporary loss of vision*

visionary /ˈvɪʒənri/ adj having great plans for the future □ *orang yg berwawasan*: *He was a visionary leader.* ▶**visionary** noun [C] (pl **visionaries**)

ʔ visit /ˈvɪzɪt/ verb [I,T] **1** to go to see a person or place for a period of time □ *melawat; menziarahi; mengunjungi; pergi berjumpa/melihat*: *I don't live here. I'm just visiting.* ◆ *We often visit relatives at the weekend.* ◆ *She's going to visit her son in hospital.* ◆ *When you go to London you must visit the Science Museum.* **2** to go to a website on the Internet □ *melayari*: *For more information, visit our website.* ▶**visit** noun [C]: *The Prime Minister is on a visit to Germany.* ◆ *We had a flying (= very short) visit from Richard on Sunday.*

ʔ visitor /ˈvɪzɪtə(r)/ noun [C] a person who visits sb/sth □ *pelawat; pengunjung*: *visitors to London from overseas*

visor /ˈvaɪzə(r)/ noun [C] **1** the part of a **helmet** (= a hard hat) that you can pull down to protect your eyes or face □ *visor* **2** a piece of plastic, cloth, etc. on a hat or in a car, which stops the sun shining into your eyes □ *visor* ➜ picture at **hat**

vista /ˈvɪstə/ noun [C] (*formal, written*) a beautiful view, for example of the countryside, a city, etc. □ *pemandangan indah*

visual /ˈvɪʒuəl/ adj connected with seeing □ *visual; (berkaitan dgn) melihat/penglihatan*: *the visual arts* (= painting, sculpture, cinema, etc.) ▶**visually** /ˈvɪʒuəli/ adv: *The film is visually stunning.*

visual ˈaid noun [C] a picture, film, map, etc. that helps a student to learn sth □ *alat bantu pandang*

visualize (also **-ise**) /ˈvɪʒuəlaɪz/ verb [T] to imagine or have a picture in your mind of sb/sth □ *membayangkan; menggambarkan*: *It's hard to visualize what this place looked like before the factory was built.*

ʔ vital /ˈvaɪtl/ adj **1** very important or necessary □ *amat penting*: *Practice is vital if you want to speak a language well.* ◆ *vital information* ➜ note at **important 2** full of energy □ *bertenaga; cergas; lincah* **SYN** **lively** ▶**vitally** /-təli/ adv: *vitally important*

vitality /vaɪˈtæləti/ noun [U] the state of being full of energy □ *kecergasan; kelincahan*

vitamin → volcano

vitamin /ˈvɪtəmɪn/ noun [C] one of several natural substances in certain types of food that are important to help humans and animals grow and stay healthy □ *vitamin*: *Oranges are rich in vitamin C.*

vivacious /vɪˈveɪʃəs/ adj (used about a person, usually a woman) full of energy; happy □ *lincah dan menarik* SYN **lively**

vivid /ˈvɪvɪd/ adj **1** having or producing a strong, clear picture in your mind □ *amat jelas*: *vivid dreams/memories* **2** (used about light or a colour) strong and very bright □ *terang*: *the vivid reds and yellows of the flowers* ▶ **vividly** adv

vivisection /ˌvɪvɪˈsekʃn/ noun [U] doing scientific experiments on live animals □ *viviseksi; pembedahan haiwan hidup utk kajian sains*

vixen /ˈvɪksn/ noun [C] a female **fox** (= a wild animal like a dog, with reddish fur and a thick tail) □ *rubah betina* ⊃ note at **fox**

viz. /vɪz/ abbr (often read out as 'namely') used to introduce a list of things that explain sth more clearly or are given as examples □ *iaitu; dgn perkataan lain*: *four major colleges of surgery, viz. London, Glasgow, Edinburgh and Dublin*

VLE /ˌviː el ˈiː/ noun [C] (BrE) **virtual learning environment**; a software system for teaching and learning on the Internet □ *VLE; persekitaran pembelajaran maya*

vocabulary /vəˈkæbjələri/ noun (pl **vocabularies**) **1** [C,U] all the words that sb knows or that are used in a particular book, subject, etc. □ *perbendaharaan kata*: *He has an amazing vocabulary for a five-year-old.* ◆ *Reading will increase your English vocabulary.* **2** [sing] all the words in a language □ *perbendaharaan kata*: *New words are always entering the vocabulary.*

vocal /ˈvəʊkl/ adj **1** [only before a noun] connected with the voice □ *(berkenaan dgn) suara*: *vocal cords* (= the thin strips in the back of your throat that move to produce the voice) **2** expressing your ideas or opinions loudly or freely □ *lantang bersuara*: *a small but vocal group of protesters*

vocalist /ˈvəʊkəlɪst/ noun [C] a singer, especially in a band □ *penyanyi*: *a lead/backing vocalist*

vocation /vəʊˈkeɪʃn/ noun [C,U] a type of work or a way of life that you believe to be especially suitable for you □ *kerjaya; cara hidup*: *Peter has finally found his vocation in life.*

vocational /vəʊˈkeɪʃənl/ adj connected with the skills, knowledge, etc. that you need to do a particular job □ *vokasional*: *vocational training*

vociferous /vəˈsɪfərəs/ adj (formal) expressing your opinions or feelings in a loud and confident way □ *lantang dan tegas menyuarakan pendapat, dsb* ▶ **vociferously** adv

vodka /ˈvɒdkə/ noun [C] a strong clear alcoholic drink originally from Russia □ *vodka*

vogue /vəʊɡ/ noun [C,U] **a vogue (for sth)** a fashion for sth □ *fesyen semasa*: *a vogue for large cars* ◆ *That hairstyle is in vogue at the moment.*

voice¹ /vɔɪs/ noun
▶ SOUND FROM MOUTH **1** [C] the sounds that you make when you speak or sing; the ability to make these sounds □ *suara*: *He had a bad cold and lost his voice* (= could not speak for a period of time). ◆ *to speak in a loud/soft/low/hoarse voice* ◆ *to lower/raise your voice* (= speak more quietly/loudly) ◆ *Shh! Keep your voice down!* ◆ *Alan is 13 and his voice is breaking* (= becoming deep and low like a man's).
▶ -VOICED **2** **-voiced** [in compounds] having a voice of the type mentioned □ *bersuara*: *husky-voiced*
▶ OPINION **3** [sing] **a voice (in sth)** (the right to express) your ideas or opinions □ *hak bersuara*: *The workers want more of a voice in the running of the company.* **4** [C] a particular feeling, attitude or opinion that you have or express □ *suara; bisikan; seruan*: *You should listen to the voice of reason and apologize.*
▶ GRAMMAR **5** [sing] the form of a verb that shows if a sentence is active or passive □ *ragam ayat*: *'Keats wrote this poem' is in the **active voice**.* ◆ *'This poem was written by Keats' is in the **passive voice**.* ❶ For more information about the passive voice, look at the **Reference Section** at the back of this dictionary.
IDM **at the top of your voice** ⊃ **top¹**

voice² /vɔɪs/ verb [T] to express your opinions or feelings □ *menyuarakan*: *to voice complaints/criticisms*

voicemail /ˈvɔɪsmeɪl/ noun [U] an electronic system which can store telephone messages, so that you can listen to them later □ *mel suara* ⊃ note at **mobile phone**

void¹ /vɔɪd/ noun [C, usually sing] (formal) a large empty space □ *ruang kosong; kekosongan*: *Her death left a void in their lives.*

void² /vɔɪd/ adj **1** (formal) **void (of sth)** completely lacking sth □ *tdk langsung*: *The sky was void of stars.* **2** (used about a ticket, contract, decision, etc.) that can no longer be accepted or used □ *terbatal; mansuh*: *The agreement was declared void.*

vol. abbr (pl **vols**) = **volume**(1)(4) □ *isi padu*: *The Complete Works of Byron, Vol. 2*

volatile /ˈvɒlətaɪl/ adj **1** that can change suddenly and unexpectedly □ *sentiasa bergolak; mudah berubah*: *a highly volatile situation which could easily develop into rioting* ◆ *a volatile personality* **2** (used about a liquid) that can easily change into a gas □ *mudah meruap*

volcano /vɒlˈkeɪnəʊ/ noun [C] (pl **volcanoes**; **volcanos**) a mountain with a **crater** (= a hole) at the top through which steam, **lava** (= hot melted rock), fire, etc. sometimes come out □ *gunung berapi*: *an active/dormant/extinct volcano* ◆ *When did the volcano last erupt?* ▶ **volcanic** /vɒlˈkænɪk/ adj: *volcanic rock/ash*

[I] **intransitive**, a verb which has no object: *He laughed.* [T] **transitive**, a verb which has an object: *He ate an apple.*

volition /vəˈlɪʃn/ noun [U] (formal) the power to choose sth freely or to make your own decisions □ *kerelaan; dgn kehendak sendiri*: They left entirely **of their own volition** (= because they wanted to).

volley /ˈvɒli/ noun [C] **1** (in sports such as football, tennis, etc.) a hit or kick of the ball before it touches the ground □ *voli; pukulan (tendangan, dsb) sangga*: a forehand/backhand volley **2** a number of stones, bullets, etc. that are thrown or shot at the same time □ *tembakan (balingan, dsb) serentak*: The soldiers fired a volley over the heads of the crowd. **3** a lot of questions, insults, etc. that are directed at one person very quickly, one after the other □ *hamburan (soalan, sumpah seranah, dll)*: a volley of abuse ▶**volley** verb [I,T]: Murray volleyed the ball into the net.

volleyball /ˈvɒlibɔːl/ noun [U] a game in which two teams of six players hit a ball over a high net with their hands while trying not to let the ball touch the ground on their own side □ *bola tampar*

volt /vəʊlt/ (BrE also) vɒlt/ noun [C] (abbr V) a measure of electric force □ *volt*

voltage /ˈvəʊltɪdʒ/ noun [C,U] an electrical force measured in **volts** □ *voltan*

? volume /ˈvɒljuːm/ noun **1** [U,C] (abbr vol.) the amount of space that sth contains or fills □ *isi padu*: What is the volume of this sphere? ⊃ look at **area 2** [C,U] the large quantity or amount of sth □ *amat banyak*: the **sheer volume** (= the large amount) of traffic on the roads ◆ I've got volumes of work to get through. **3** [U, sing] how loud a sound is □ *(kuat atau perlahannya) bunyi*: to turn the volume on a radio up/down ◆ a low/high volume ⊃ note at **listen 4** [C] (abbr vol.) a book, especially one of a set or series □ *jilid*: The dictionary comes in three volumes.

voluminous /vəˈluːmɪnəs/ adj (formal) (used about clothing, furniture, etc.) very large; having plenty of space □ *sangat besar; kembang; banyak ruang*: a voluminous skirt

voluntary /ˈvɒləntri/ adj **1** done or given because you want to do it, not because you have to do it □ *secara sukarela*: He took voluntary redundancy and left the firm last year. **OPP** compulsory **2** done or working without payment □ *sukarela*: She does some **voluntary work** at the hospital. **3** (used about movements of the body) that you can control □ *voluntari* **OPP** involuntary ▶**voluntarily** /ˈvɒləntrəli/ adv: She left the job voluntarily; she wasn't sacked.

volunteer¹ /ˌvɒlənˈtɪə(r)/ noun [C] **1** a person who offers or agrees to do sth without being forced or paid to do it □ *sukarelawan*: Are there any volunteers to do the washing-up? **2** a person who joins the armed forces without being ordered to □ *askar sukarelawan* ⊃ look at **conscript**

volunteer² /ˌvɒlənˈtɪə(r)/ verb **1** [I,T] **volunteer (sth); volunteer (to do sth)** to offer sth or to do sth which you do not have to do or for which you will not be paid □ *bersukarela; menawarkan (diri/sst) secara sukarela*: They volunteered their services free. ◆ She frequently volunteers for extra work because she really likes her job. ◆ One of my friends volunteered to take us all in his car. **2** [T] to give information, etc. or to make a comment or suggestion without being asked to □ *memberi maklumat, dll tanpa diminta*: I volunteered a few helpful suggestions. **3** [I] **volunteer (for sth)** to join the armed forces without being ordered □ *memasuki tentera secara sukarela*

vomit /ˈvɒmɪt/ verb [I,T] to bring food, etc. up from the stomach and out of the mouth □ *muntah* ⊃ In everyday British English we say **be sick**. ▶**vomit** noun [U]

? vote¹ /vəʊt/ noun **1** [C] **a vote (for/against sb/ sth)** a formal choice in an election or at a meeting in order to choose sb or decide sth □ *undi*: The votes are still being counted. ◆ There were 10 votes for, and 25 against, the motion. **2** [C] **a vote (on sth)** a method of deciding sth by asking people to express their choice and finding out what most people want □ *pengundian; undi; mengundi*: The democratic way to decide this would be to **take a vote**. ◆ Let's have a vote/**put it to the vote**. **3 the vote** [sing] the total number of votes in an election □ *undi*: She obtained 30% of the vote. **4 the vote** [sing] the legal right to vote in political elections □ *hak mengundi*: Women did not get the vote in this country until the 1920s. **IDM cast a/your vote** ⊃ **cast¹**

a vote of thanks a short speech to thank sb, usually a guest at a meeting, etc. □ *ucapan terima kasih*: The club secretary proposed a vote of thanks to the guest speaker.

? vote² /vəʊt/ verb **1** [I,T] **vote (for/against sb/sth); vote (on sth); vote to do sth** to show formally a choice or an opinion, for example by marking a piece of paper or by holding up your hand □ *mengundi; membuang undi*: Who did you vote for in the last general election? ◆ 46% **voted in favour of** (= for) the proposed change. ◆ Very few MPs voted against the new law. ◆ After the debate we'll vote on the motion. ◆ They voted to change the rules of the club. ◆ I voted Liberal Democrat. ⊃ note at **politics 2** [T, usually passive] to choose sb for a particular position or prize □ *dipilih*: He was voted best actor at the Oscars. ▶**voter** noun [C]

vouch /vaʊtʃ/ verb
PHR V vouch for sb/sth to say that a person is honest or good or that sth is true or genuine □ *menjamin*: I can vouch for her ability to work hard.

voucher /ˈvaʊtʃə(r)/ noun [C] a piece of paper that you can use instead of money to pay for all or part of sth □ *baucar* ⊃ look at **token**

vow /vaʊ/ noun [C] a formal and serious promise (especially in a religious ceremony) □ *ikrar; sumpah*: to keep/break your **marriage vows** ▶**vow** verb [T]: We vowed never to discuss the subject again.

vowel /ˈvaʊəl/ noun [C] a letter that represents a **vowel** sound. In English the vowels are *a, e, i, o* or *u*. □ *vokal* ⊃ look at **consonant**

voyage /ˈvɔɪɪdʒ/ noun [C] a long journey by sea or in space □ *pelayaran; pengembaraan: a voyage to Jupiter* ⊃ note at **journey** ▶**voyager** noun [C]

vs abbr = **versus**(1)

VSO /ˌviː es ˈəʊ/ abbr **Voluntary Service Overseas**; a British organization that sends people to go to work in developing countries □ *VSO (khidmat sukarela di luar negeri)*

vulgar /ˈvʌlɡə(r)/ adj **1** not having or showing good judgement about what is attractive or appropriate; not polite or well behaved □ *tdk bercita rasa; tdk beradab: vulgar furnishings* ♦ *a vulgar man/woman* **2** rude or likely to offend people □ *biadab; tdk sopan; lucah: a vulgar joke* ▶**vulgarity** /vʌlˈɡærəti/ noun [C,U] (pl **vulgarities**)

vulnerable /ˈvʌlnərəbl/ adj **vulnerable (to sth/sb)** weak and easy to hurt in a physical or an emotional way □ *lemah dan mudah cedera: Poor organization left the troops vulnerable to enemy attack.* ▶**vulnerability** /ˌvʌlnərəˈbɪləti/ noun [U]

vulture /ˈvʌltʃə(r)/ noun [C] a large bird with no feathers on its head or neck that eats the flesh of animals that are already dead □ *burung hering*

vuvuzela™ /ˌvuːvuːˈzeɪlə/ noun [C] a long plastic instrument in the shape of a **trumpet** (= a musical instrument), that makes a very loud noise when you blow it and is popular with football fans in South Africa □ *sejenis alat muzik*

W, w /ˈdʌbljuː/ noun [C,U] (pl **Ws; W's; w's** /ˈdʌbljuːz/) the 23rd letter of the English alphabet □ *W, w (huruf): 'Water' begins with (a) 'W'.*

W abbr **1** = **watt** □ *W (watt): a 60W light bulb* **2** = **west**[1], **western**[1](1) □ *Barat: W Africa*

wacky (also **whacky**) /ˈwæki/ adj (**wackier; wackiest**) (informal) amusing or funny in a slightly crazy way □ *gila-gila*

wad /wɒd/ noun [C] **1** a large number of papers, paper money, etc. folded or rolled together □ *gulungan; segulung: He pulled a wad of £20 notes out of his pocket.* **2** a mass of soft material that is used for blocking sth or keeping sth in place □ *gumpalan: The nurse used a wad of cotton wool to stop the bleeding.*

waddle /ˈwɒdl/ verb [I] to walk with short steps, moving the weight of your body from one side to the other, like a **duck** (= a common bird that lives near water) □ *berjalan terkedek-kedek*

wade /weɪd/ verb [I] to walk with difficulty through fairly deep water, mud, etc. □ *mengharung; meranduk*

PHR V **wade through sth** to deal with or read sth that is boring and takes a long time □ *dgn susah payah membaca (menyemak, dsb) sst yg membosankan*

wafer /ˈweɪfə(r)/ noun [C] a very thin, dry biscuit often eaten with ice cream □ *wafer; keropok aiskrim*

waffle[1] /ˈwɒfl/ noun **1** [C] a flat cake with a pattern of squares on it that is often eaten warm with **syrup** (= a sweet sauce) □ *wafel* ⊃ picture on page P16 **2** [U] (BrE informal) language that uses a lot of words but that does not say anything important or interesting □ *cakap kosong: The last two paragraphs of your essay are just waffle.*

waffle[2] /ˈwɒfl/ verb [I] (BrE informal) **waffle (on) (about sth)** to talk or write for much longer than necessary without saying anything important or interesting □ *bercakap kosong*

waft /wɒft (AmE also) / verb [I,T] to move, or make sth move, gently through the air □ *dibawa angin; semerbak: The smell of her perfume wafted across the room.*

wag /wæɡ/ verb [I,T] (**wagging; wagged**) to shake up and down or move from side to side; to make sth do this □ *menggoyang-goyangkan: The dog wagged its tail.*

wage[1] /weɪdʒ/ noun [sing] (also **wages** [pl]) the regular amount of money that you earn for a week's work □ *upah; gaji: a weekly wage of £200* ♦ *What's the national minimum wage* (= the lowest wage that an employer is allowed to pay by law)? ⊃ note at **pay**[2]

HELP **Wage** in the singular is mainly used to talk about the amount of money paid, or when the word is combined with another, for example 'wage packet', 'wage rise', etc. **Wages** in the plural means the money itself: *I have to pay the rent out of my wages.*

wage[2] /weɪdʒ/ verb [T] **wage sth (against/on sb/sth)** to begin and then continue a war, battle, etc. □ *memulakan peperangan; berperang: to wage war on your enemy*

waggle /ˈwæɡl/ verb [I,T] (informal) to move up and down or from side to side with quick, short movements; to make sth do this □ *menggoyang-goyangkan*

wagon /ˈwæɡən/ noun [C] **1** (AmE ˈfreight car) an open section of a train, used for carrying goods or animals □ *gerabak: coal transported in goods wagons* ⊃ look at **truck** **2** (BrE also **waggon**) a vehicle with four wheels pulled by animals and used for carrying heavy loads □ *kereta sorong*

waif /weɪf/ noun [C] a small thin person, usually a child, who looks as if they do not have enough to eat □ *orang terbuang; budak terbiar*

wail /weɪl/ *verb* **1** [I,T] to cry or complain in a loud, high voice, especially because you are sad or in pain □ *meraung* **2** [I] (used about things) to make a sound like this □ *melaung-laung*: *sirens wailing in the streets outside* ▶ **wail** *noun* [C]: *a wail of anguish/despair/distress* ♦ *the wail of sirens*

waist /weɪst/ *noun* [C, usually sing] **1** the narrowest part around the middle of your body □ *pinggang*: *She put her arms around his waist.* ⊃ picture at **body 2** the part of a piece of clothing that goes round the waist □ *(bahagian) pinggang*: *The trousers are too baggy round the waist.*

waistband /ˈweɪstbænd/ *noun* [C] the narrow piece of cloth at the waist of a piece of clothing, especially trousers or a skirt □ *ikat pinggang*

waistcoat /ˈweɪskəʊt/ (*AmE* **vest**) *noun* [C] a piece of clothing with buttons down the front and no sleeves that is often worn over a shirt and under a jacket as part of a man's suit □ *weskot*

waistline /ˈweɪstlaɪn/ *noun* [C, usually sing] **1** (used to talk about how fat or thin a person is) the measurement or size of the body around the waist □ *ukuran pinggang* **2** the place on a piece of clothing where your waist is □ *(garis) pinggang*

wait¹ /weɪt/ *verb* [I] **1 wait (for sb/sth) (to do sth)** to stay in a particular place and not do anything until sb/sth arrives or until sth happens □ *tunggu; menunggu; menanti*: *Wait here. I'll be back in a few minutes.* ♦ *Have you been waiting long?* ♦ *If I'm a bit late, can you wait for me?* ♦ *I'm waiting to see the doctor.*

> **MORE** Compare **wait** and **expect**: *I was expecting him to be there at 7.30 but at 8 I was still waiting.* ♦ *I'm waiting for the exam results but I'm not expecting to pass.* If you **wait for** somebody or something, you stay in one place and pass the time until somebody arrives or something happens: *I waited outside the theatre until they arrived.* If you **expect** something, you think that it will happen or is likely to happen: *I'm expecting you to get a good grade in your exam.* You use **hope**, not **expect**, to say that you want sth to happen: *I hope you have a good party.* You use **look forward to** when you are feeling happy and excited about something that you expect to happen: *I'm looking forward to your visit.*

2 to be left or delayed until a later time □ *ditangguhkan*: *Is this matter urgent or can it wait?* **IDM can't wait/can hardly wait** used when you are emphasizing that sb is very excited and enthusiastic about doing sth □ *tdk sabar-sabar*: *The kids can't wait to see their father again.*
keep sb waiting to make sb wait or be delayed, especially because you arrive late □ *membuat sso terpaksa menunggu*: *I'm sorry if I've kept you waiting.*
wait and see to be patient and find out what will happen later (perhaps before deciding to do sth) □ *tunggu dan lihat*: *We'll just have to wait and see—there's nothing more we can do.*

951 **wail → wake**

wait your turn to wait until the time when you are allowed to do sth □ *tunggu giliran awak, kamu, dsb*
PHR V wait behind to stay in a place after others have left it □ *menunggu sehingga orang lain habis balik*: *She waited behind after class to speak to her teacher.*
wait in to stay at home because you are expecting sb to come or sth to happen □ *menunggu di rumah*
wait on sb to act as a servant to sb, especially by serving food to them □ *melayan sso*
wait up (for sb) to not go to bed because you are waiting for sb to come home □ *berjaga menunggu sehingga sso pulang*

wait² /weɪt/ *noun* [C, usually sing] **a wait (for sth/sb)** a period of time when you wait □ *penantian; (tempoh) menunggu*
IDM lie in wait (for sb) ⊃ **lie²**

waiter /ˈweɪtə(r)/ *noun* [C] a man whose job is to serve customers at their tables in a restaurant, etc. □ *pelayan (lelaki)*: *I'll ask the waiter for the bill.* ⊃ picture on **page P2**

waiting list *noun* [C] a list of people who are waiting for sth, for example a service or medical treatment, that will be available in the future □ *senarai menunggu*: *to put your name on a waiting list*

waiting room *noun* [C] a room where people can sit while they are waiting, for example for a train, or to see a doctor or dentist □ *bilik menunggu*

waitress /ˈweɪtrəs/ *noun* [C] a woman whose job is to serve customers at their tables in a restaurant, etc. □ *pelayan (wanita)*

waive /weɪv/ *verb* [T] to say officially that a rule, etc. need not be obeyed; to say officially that you no longer have a right to sth □ *mengetepikan*: *In your case, we will waive your tuition fees.*

wake¹ /weɪk/ *verb* [I,T] (*pt* **woke** /wəʊk/; *pp* **woken** /ˈwəʊkən/) **wake (sb) (up)** to stop sleeping; to make sb stop sleeping □ *bangun (tidur); terjaga; mengejutkan*: *I woke early in the morning and got straight out of bed.* ♦ *Wake up! It's nearly 8 o'clock!* ♦ *Could you wake me at 7.30, please?* ⊃ note at **sleep** ⊃ adjective **awake**
PHR V wake sb up to make sb become more active or full of energy □ *mencergaskan sso; menghilangkan rasa mengantuk*: *She always has a coffee to wake her up when she gets to work.*
wake up to sth to realize sth; to notice sth □ *menyedari*

wake² /weɪk/ *noun* [C] **1** an occasion before or after a funeral when people meet to remember the dead person, traditionally held in order to watch over the body before it is buried □ *upacara berjaga di sisi mayat sebelum dikebumikan* **2** the track that a moving ship leaves behind on the surface of the water □ *olak buri* ⊃ picture on **page P10**

VOWELS i: **see** i **any** ɪ **sit** e **ten** æ **hat** ɑ: **father** ɒ **got** ɔ: **saw** ʊ **put** u: **too** u **usual**

waken → wall-to-wall 952

IDM **in the wake of sb/sth** following or coming after sb/sth □ *berikutan sso/sst*: *The earthquake left a trail of destruction in its wake.*

waken /'weɪkən/ *verb* [I,T] (*old-fashioned, formal*) to stop sleeping or to make sb/sth stop sleeping □ *terjaga*: *She wakened from a deep sleep.*

walk¹ /wɔːk/ *verb* **1** [I,T] to move or go somewhere by putting one foot in front of the other on the ground, but without running □ *berjalan*: *The door opened and Billy walked in.* ◆ *I walk to work every day.* ◆ *He walks with a limp.* ◆ *I've walked miles today.* ◆ *Are the shops **within walking distance** (= near enough to walk to)?* **2** [I,T] to move in this way for exercise or pleasure □ *berjalan*: *I walked across Scotland with a friend.* ⊃ note at **walk²** **3** [T] to go somewhere with sb/sth on foot, especially to make sure they get there safely □ *berjalan (bersama sso); menemani; mengiringi*: *I'll walk you home if you don't want to go on your own.* ◆ *He walked me to my car.* **4** [T] to take a dog out for exercise □ *membawa berjalan*: *I'm just going to walk the dog.*

PHR V **walk off with sth** (*informal*) **1** to win sth easily □ *menang/menggondol (hadiah, dsb)*: *She walked off with all the prizes.* **2** to steal sth; to take sth that does not belong to you by mistake □ *mencuri sst; terbawa pulang sst*: *When I got home I realized that I had walked off with her pen.*
walk out (of sth) to leave suddenly and angrily □ *meninggalkan sst dgn rasa marah*: *She walked out of the meeting in disgust.*
walk out on sb (*informal*) to leave sb for ever □ *meninggalkan sso*: *He walked out on his wife and children after 15 years of marriage.*
walk (all) over sb (*informal*) **1** to treat sb badly, without considering their needs or feelings □ *bersikap kasar, dsb terhadap sso*: *I don't know why she lets her husband walk all over her like that.* **2** to defeat sb completely □ *mengalahkan sso dgn teruk*: *He played brilliantly and walked all over his opponent.*
walk up (to sb/sth) to walk towards sb/sth, especially in a confident way □ *mendekati; menghampiri (sso/sst)*: *He walked up to her and asked her if she wanted to dance.*

▶ **walker** *noun* [C]: *She's a fast walker.* ◆ *This area is very popular with walkers.*

walk² /wɔːk/ *noun* **1** [C] an occasion when you go somewhere on foot for pleasure, exercise, etc. □ *berjalan; berjalan-jalan*: *We went for a walk in the country.* ◆ *I'm just going to take the dog for a walk.* ◆ *The beach is five minutes' walk/a five-minute walk from the hotel.*

HELP We use **go for a walk** when we are talking about a short walk that we take for pleasure. We use **go walking** to talk about a long walk that may last several hours or days.

2 [C] a path or route for walking for pleasure; an organized event when people walk for pleasure □ *jalan; lorong*: *From here there's a lovely walk through the woods.* ◆ *a charity walk* **3** [sing] a way or style of walking □ *cara/gaya berjalan*: *He has a funny walk.* **4** [sing] the speed of walking □ *berjalan*: *She slowed to a walk.*

IDM **a walk of life** a person's job or position in society □ *lapisan/golongan masyarakat*: *She has friends from all walks of life.*

walkie-talkie /ˌwɔːki ˈtɔːki/ *noun* [C] (*informal*) a small radio that you can carry with you to send or receive messages □ *walkie-talkie*

walking *noun* [U] the activity of going for walks in the countryside for exercise or pleasure □ *perihal berjalan-jalan*: *to go walking* ◆ *walking boots* ◆ *We like to go walking in the Alps in the summer.*

'walking stick (*especially BrE* **stick**) *noun* [C] a stick that you carry and use as a support to help you walk □ *tongkat* ⊃ look at **crutch**

walkover /ˈwɔːkəʊvə(r)/ *noun* [C] an easy win or victory in a game or competition □ *kemenangan mudah*

wall /wɔːl/ *noun* [C] **1** a solid, vertical structure made of stone, brick, etc. that is built round an area of land to protect it or to divide it □ *tembok*: *There is a high wall all around the prison.* **2** one of the sides of a room or building joining the ceiling and the floor □ *dinding*: *He put the picture up **on the wall**.* ⊃ picture at **fence**

IDM **up the wall** (*informal*) crazy or angry □ *membuat sso berasa marah atau nak gila*: *That noise is driving me up the wall.*

walled /wɔːld/ *adj* surrounded by a wall □ *bertembok*

wallet /ˈwɒlɪt/ (*AmE also*) / (*AmE* **billfold**) *noun* [C] a small, flat, folding case in which you keep paper money, plastic cards, etc. □ *dompet; beg duit*: *Don't forget your wallet and keys.* ⊃ look at **purse** ⊃ picture at **bag**

wallop /ˈwɒləp/ *verb* [T] (*informal*) to hit sb/sth very hard □ *membelasah; membantai*

wallow /ˈwɒləʊ/ *verb* [I] **wallow (in sth)** **1** (used about people and large animals) to lie and roll around in water, etc. in order to keep cool or for pleasure □ *berendam; berkubang*: *I spent an hour wallowing in the bath.* **2** to take great pleasure in sth (a feeling, situation, etc.) □ *suka melayan sst perasaan*: *to wallow in self-pity* (= to think about your unhappiness all the time and seem to be enjoying it)

wallpaper /ˈwɔːlpeɪpə(r)/ *noun* [U] **1** paper that you stick to the walls of a room to decorate or cover them □ *kertas hias dinding* **2** the background pattern or picture that you choose to have on your computer screen □ *kertas hias*
▶ **wallpaper** *verb* [I,T]

wall-to-ˈwall *adj* [only *before* a noun] **1** (used especially about a carpet) covering the floor of a room completely □ *dr dinding ke dinding* **2** (*informal*) continuous; happening all the time □ *berterusan*: *wall-to-wall TV sports coverage*

wally /ˈwɒli/ noun [C] (pl **wallies**) (BrE slang) a silly or stupid person □ *(orang) bodoh*

walnut /ˈwɔːlnʌt/ noun **1** [C] a nut that we eat, with a rough surface and a hard brown shell that is in two halves □ *walnut (kekeras)* ⊃ picture at **nut 2** (also **'walnut tree**) [C] the tree on which these nuts grow □ *(pokok) walnut* **3** [U] the wood from the **walnut** tree, used in making furniture □ *(kayu) walnut*

walrus /ˈwɔːlrəs/ noun [C] a large animal with two **tusks** (= long teeth) that lives in or near the sea in Arctic regions □ *walrus*

waltz¹ /wɔːls/ noun [C] an elegant dance that you do with a partner to music which has a rhythm of three beats; the music for this dance □ *(tarian) waltz: a Strauss waltz*

waltz² /wɔːls/ verb **1** [I,T] to dance a **waltz** □ *menari waltz: They waltzed around the floor.* ♦ *He waltzed her round the room.* **2** [I] (informal) to go somewhere in a confident way □ *berjalan senang-senang: You can't just waltz in and expect your meal to be ready for you.*

WAN /wæn/ abbr **wide area network**; a system in which computers in different places are connected, usually over a large area □ *rangkaian kawasan luas* ⊃ look at **LAN**

wan /wɒn/ adj looking pale and ill or tired □ *pucat dan lesu*

wand /wɒnd/ noun [C] a thin stick that people hold when they are doing magic tricks □ *tongkat sakti: I wish I could wave a magic wand and make everything better.*

wander /ˈwɒndə(r)/ verb **1** [I,T] to walk somewhere slowly with no particular sense of direction or purpose □ *berjalan-jalan: We spent a pleasant day wandering around the town.* ♦ *He was found in a confused state, wandering the streets.* **2** [I] **wander (away/off) (from sb/sth)** to walk away from a place where you ought to be or the people you were with □ *merayau-rayau: We must stay together while visiting the town so I don't want anybody to wander off.* ♦ *Don't wander away from the main road.* **3** [I] (used about sb's mind, thoughts, etc.) to stop paying attention to sth; to be unable to stay on one subject □ *melayang: The lecture was so boring that my attention began to wander.* ▶ **wander** noun [sing]: *I went to the park for a wander.*

wane¹ /weɪn/ verb [I] **1** (formal) to become gradually weaker or less important □ *surut: My enthusiasm was waning rapidly.* **2** (used about the moon) to appear slightly smaller each day after being full and round □ *berkurang; merosot*

wane² /weɪn/ noun
IDM **on the wane** (formal) becoming smaller, less important or less common □ *semakin berkurang/merosot: The singer's popularity seems to be on the wane these days.*

wangle /ˈwæŋgl/ verb [T] (informal) to get sth that you want by persuading sb or by having a clever plan □ *merujuk; membuat helah supaya mendapat sst: Somehow he wangled a day off to meet me.*

wanna /ˈwɒnə/ (AmE also) / a way of writing 'want to' or 'want a' to show that sb is speaking in an informal way □ *hendak; mahu: I wanna go home now.* ⊃ note at **contraction**

EXAM TIP

Do not write 'wanna' yourself (unless you are copying somebody's accent) because it might be marked as a mistake.

wannabe /ˈwɒnəbi/ (AmE also) / noun [C] (informal) a person who behaves, dresses, etc. like a famous person because they want to be like them □ *orang yg meniru kelakuan, pakaian, dsb orang terkenal kerana mahu menjadi spt mereka*

want¹ /wɒnt/ (AmE also) / verb [T] [not used in the continuous tenses]
➤WISH **1 want sth (for sth); want (sb) to do sth; want sth (to be) done** to have a desire or a wish for sth □ *mahu; hendak: He wants a new bike.* ♦ *What do they want for breakfast?* ♦ *I don't want to discuss it now.* ♦ *I want you to stop worrying about it.* ♦ *The boss wants this letter typed.* ♦ *I don't want Emma going out on her own at night.* ♦ *They want Bhanot as captain.*

HELP **Want** or **would like**? **Want** and **would like** are similar in meaning, but 'would like' is more polite: *'I want a drink!' screamed the child.* ♦ *'Would you like some more tea, Mrs Atwal?'*

➤NEED **2** (informal) used to say that sth needs to be done □ *perlu; memerlukan: The button on my shirt wants sewing on.* ♦ *The house wants a new coat of paint.* **3** [usually passive] to need sb to be in a particular place or for a particular reason □ *dikehendaki: Mrs Dawson, you are wanted on the phone.* ♦ *She is wanted by the police* (= the police are looking for her because she may have committed a crime).
➤SHOULD/OUGHT TO **4** (informal) (used to give advice to sb) should or ought to □ *patut; harus: He wants to be more careful about what he tells people.*
➤SEXUAL DESIRE **5** to feel sexual desire for sb □ *berasa berahi*

HELP Although this verb is not used in the continuous tenses, it is common to see the present participle (= -ing form): *She kept her head down, not wanting to attract attention.*

IDM **what do you want?** used to ask sb in a rude or angry way why they are there or what they want you to do □ *menanyakan sst secara kasar*

want² /wɒnt/ (AmE also) / noun (formal) **1 wants** [pl] something you need or want □ *keperluan; kemahuan: All our wants were satisfied.* **2** [U, sing] a lack of sth □ *kekurangan; ketiadaan: a want of clean water*

IDM for (the) want of sth because of a lack of sth; because sth is not available ◻ *kerana tdk ada (sst)*: *I took the job for want of a better offer.*

wanting /ˈwɒntɪŋ (AmE also) / adj (formal) [not before a noun] **wanting (in sth) 1** not having enough of sth; lacking ◻ *kekurangan*: *The children were certainly not wanting in enthusiasm.* **2** not good enough ◻ *ada kekurangannya*: *The new system was found wanting.*

wanton /ˈwɒntən (AmE also) / adj (formal) (used about an action) done in order to hurt sb or damage sth for no good reason ◻ *disengajakan*: *wanton vandalism*

WAP /wæp/ abbr wireless application protocol; a technology that connects devices such as mobile phones to the Internet ◻ *Protokol Aplikasi Wayarles*: *a WAP-enabled phone*

🔑 **war** /wɔː(r)/ noun **1** [U,C] a state of fighting between different countries or groups within countries using armies and weapons ◻ *perang; peperangan*: *The Prime Minister announced that the country was at war.* ◆ *to declare war on another country* (= say officially that a war has started) ◆ *When war broke out* (= started), *thousands of men volunteered for the army.* ◆ *a civil war* (= fighting between different groups in one country) ◆ *to go to war against somebody* ◆ *to fight a war* **2** [C,U] aggressive competition between groups of people, companies, countries, etc. ◻ *perang*: *a price war among oil companies* **3** [U,sing] **war (against/on sb/sth)** efforts to end or get rid of sth ◻ *usaha membasmi/memerangi*: *We seem to be winning the war against organized crime.*

TOPIC

War

The three main parts of a country's **armed forces** are the **army**, the **navy** and the **air force**. **Officers** in the forces give orders to their **troops**. When a war **breaks out** (= starts), two or more countries are **at war**. A war between different groups in the same country is called a **civil war**. A country's **enemies** are the countries it is fighting against and its **allies** are countries which support it. If armed forces from one country enter another country, they **invade** it. If they stay there and take control of the country they **occupy** it. A country will try to **defend** itself against **attack** from another country. At the end of a war one country is **defeated** and **surrenders** (= stops fighting and says that it has lost).

ˈ**war crime** noun [C] a cruel act that is committed during a war and that is against the international rules of war ◻ *jenayah perang*

ward¹ /wɔːd/ noun [C] **1** a separate part or room in a hospital for patients with the same kind of medical condition ◻ *wad*: *the maternity/psychiatric/surgical ward* **2** one of the sections into which a town is divided for elections ◻ *kawasan pilihan raya* **3** a child who is under the protection of a court of law; a child whose parents are dead and who is cared for by a **guardian** (= sb who is legally responsible for their care) ◻ *(anak) jagaan*: *The child was made a ward of court.*

ward² /wɔːd/ verb
PHR V **ward sb/sth off** to protect or defend yourself against danger, illness, attack, etc. ◻ *mencegah sso/sst*

warden /ˈwɔːdn/ noun [C] **1** a person whose job is to check that rules are obeyed or to look after a particular place ◻ *pengawas; warden*: *a traffic warden* (= a person who checks that cars are not parked in the wrong place) **2** (*especially AmE*) the person in charge of a prison ◻ *warden; penjaga penjara*

warder /ˈwɔːdə(r)/ noun [C] (BrE) a person whose job is to guard prisoners in a prison ◻ *wadar; penjaga penjara* ➔ look at **guard**

wardrobe /ˈwɔːdrəʊb/ noun [C] **1** a large cupboard in which you can hang your clothes ◻ *almari pakaian* ➔ picture on page P8 **2** [usually sing] a person's collection of clothes ◻ *(koleksi) pakaian*: *I need a whole new summer wardrobe.*

ware /weə(r)/ noun **1** [U] [in compounds] things made from a particular type of material or suitable for a particular use ◻ *barang-barang*: *glassware* ◆ *kitchenware* ➔ look at **hardware** **2 wares** [pl] (old-fashioned) goods offered for sale ◻ *barang-barang jualan*

warehouse /ˈweəhaʊs/ noun [C] a building where large quantities of goods are stored before being sent to shops ◻ *gudang*

warfare /ˈwɔːfeə(r)/ noun [U] the activity of fighting a war; types of war ◻ *(cara/jenis) perang*: *guerrilla warfare*

warily, wariness ➔ **wary**

warlike /ˈwɔːlaɪk/ adj liking to fight or good at fighting ◻ *suka berperang*: *a warlike nation*

🔑 **warm**¹ /wɔːm/ adj (warmer; warmest) **1** having a pleasant temperature that is fairly high, between cool and hot ◻ *sederhana panas*: *It's quite warm in the sunshine.* ◆ *I jumped up and down to keep my feet warm.* ➔ note at **cold**¹ **2** (used about clothes) preventing you from getting cold ◻ *(pakaian) panas*: *Take plenty of warm clothes.* **3** friendly, kind and pleasant ◻ *mesra; baik hati*: *I was given a very warm welcome.* **4** creating a pleasant, comfortable feeling ◻ *selesa*: *warm colours* ▶ **the warm** noun [sing]: *It's awfully cold out here—I want to go back into the warm.* ▶ **warmly** adv: *warmly dressed* ◆ *She thanked him warmly for his help.*

🔑 **warm**² /wɔːm/ verb [I,T] **warm (sb/sth) (up)** to become or to make sb/sth become warm or warmer ◻ *memanaskan; menjadi panas*: *It was cold earlier but it's beginning to warm up now.* ◆ *I sat by the fire to warm up.*
PHR V **warm to/towards sb** to begin to like sb that you did not like at first ◻ *mulai suka/mesra dgn sso*

warm to sth to become more interested in sth □ *mula menyukai sst*

warm up to prepare to do an activity or sport by practising gently □ *gerakan utk memanaskan badan*: *The team warmed up before the match.*

warm-blooded *adj* (used about animals) having a warm blood temperature that does not change if the temperature around them changes □ *berdarah panas* ⊃ look at **cold-blooded**

warm-hearted *adj* kind and friendly □ *baik hati*

warmth /wɔːmθ/ *noun* [U] **1** a fairly high temperature or the effect created by this, especially when it is pleasant □ *kepanasan; rasa panas*: *She felt the warmth of the sun on her face.* **2** the quality of being kind and friendly □ *kemesraan*: *I was touched by the warmth of their welcome.*

warn /wɔːn/ *verb* [T] **1 warn sb (of sth); warn sb (about sb/sth)** to tell sb about sth unpleasant or dangerous that exists or might happen, so that they can avoid it □ *memberi amaran*: *When I saw the car coming I tried to warn him, but it was too late.* ♦ *The government is warning the public of possible terrorist attacks.* ♦ *He warned me about the danger of walking home alone at night.* **2 warn (sb) against doing sth; warn sb (not to do sth)** to advise sb not to do sth □ *mengingatkan; menasihatkan; memberi amaran*: *The government warned people against going out during the storm.* ♦ *I warned you not to trust him.*

warning /ˈwɔːnɪŋ/ *noun* [C,U] something that tells you to be careful or tells you about sth, usually sth bad, before it happens □ *amaran*: *Your employers can't dismiss you without warning.* ♦ *You could have given me some warning that your parents were coming to visit.*

warp /wɔːp/ *verb* **1** [I,T] to become bent into the wrong shape, for example as a result of getting hot or wet; to make sth become like this □ *meleding*: *The window frame was badly warped and wouldn't shut.* **2** [T] to influence sb so that they start behaving in an unusual or shocking way □ *menjejaskan; merosakkan*: *His experiences in the war had warped him.* ►**warped** *adj*

warpath /ˈwɔːpɑːθ/ *noun*
IDM **(be/go) on the warpath** (*informal*) to be very angry and want to fight or punish sb □ *tengah marah*

warrant¹ /ˈwɒrənt/ (*AmE* also) / *noun* [C] an official written statement that gives sb permission to do sth □ *waran*: *a search warrant* (= a document that allows the police to search a house)

warrant² /ˈwɒrənt/ (*AmE* also) / *verb* [T] (*formal*) to make sth seem right or necessary; to deserve sth □ *mewajarkan; patut*: *Her behaviour does not warrant such criticism.*

warranty /ˈwɒrənti/ (*AmE* also) / *noun* [C,U] (*pl* **warranties**) a written statement that you get when you buy sth, which promises to re-

955 **warm-blooded → wash**

pair or replace it if it is broken or does not work □ *waranti; jaminan*: *Fortunately my washing machine is still under warranty.* ⊃ look at **guarantee**

warren /ˈwɒrən/ (*AmE* also) / = **rabbit warren**

warrior /ˈwɒriə(r)/ (*AmE* also) / *noun* [C] (*old-fashioned*) a person who fights in a battle; a soldier □ *pahlawan*

warship /ˈwɔːʃɪp/ *noun* [C] a ship for use in war □ *kapal perang*

wart /wɔːt/ *noun* [C] a small hard dry lump that sometimes grows on the face or body □ *kutil; ketuat*

wartime /ˈwɔːtaɪm/ *noun* [U] a period of time during which there is a war □ *masa perang*

wary /ˈweəri/ *adj* (**warier** ; *no superlative*) **wary (of sb/sth)** careful because you are uncertain or afraid of sb/sth □ *berhati-hati*: *Since becoming famous, she has grown wary of journalists.* ►**warily** *adv* ►**wariness** *noun* [U]

was /wəz; *strong form* wɒz/ ⊃ **be**

wash¹ /wɒʃ/ (*AmE* also) / *verb* **1** [I,T] to clean sb/sth/yourself with water and often soap □ *membasuh*: *to wash your hands/face/hair* ♦ *That shirt needs washing.* ♦ *Wash and dress quickly or you'll be late!* ♦ *I'll wash* (= wash the dishes), *you dry.* ⊃ note at **clean²** **2** [I] to be able to be washed without being damaged □ *boleh dibasuh*: *Does this material wash well, or does the colour come out?* **3** [I,T] (used about water) to flow or carry sth/sb in the direction mentioned □ *mengalir; memukul; menghanyutkan*: *I let the waves wash over my feet.* ♦ *The current washed the ball out to sea.*

IDM **wash your hands of sb/sth** to refuse to be responsible for sb/sth any longer □ *cuci tangan; enggan terlibat lagi dlm hal sso/sst*: *They washed their hands of their son when he was sent to prison.*

PHR V **wash sb/sth away** (used about water) to carry sb/sth away □ *menghanyutkan sso/sst*: *The floods had washed away the path.*

wash (sth) off (to make sth) disappear by washing □ *hilang kerana dibasuh atau kena air; membersihkan*: *The writing has washed off and now I can't read it.* ♦ *Go and wash that make-up off!*

wash out to be removed from a material by washing □ *hilang/tanggal apabila dibasuh*: *These grease marks won't wash out.*

wash sth out to wash sth or the inside of sth in order to remove dirt □ *membasuh*: *I'll just wash out this bowl and then we can use it.*

wash (sth) up 1 (*BrE*) to wash the plates, knives, forks, etc. after a meal □ *membasuh pinggan mangkuk*: *Whose turn is it to wash up?* **2** (*AmE*) to wash your face and hands □ *membasuh muka dan tangan*: *Go and wash up quickly and put on some clean clothes.* **3** [*often passive*] (used about water) to carry sth to land and leave it there □ *terdampar*: Police found the girl's body washed up on the beach.

wash² /wɒʃ (AmE also) / noun **1** [C, usually sing] an act of cleaning or being cleaned with water □ *bercuci; mandi*: I'd better go and **have a wash** before we go out. **2** [sing] the waves caused by the movement of a ship through water □ *olak air*

IDM **in the wash** (used about clothes) being washed □ *sedang dibasuh*: 'Where's my red T-shirt?' 'It's in the wash.'

washable /ˈwɒʃəbl (AmE also) / adj that can be washed without being damaged □ *boleh dibasuh*

washbasin /ˈwɒʃbeɪsn (AmE also) / (also **basin**) noun [C] a large bowl for water that has taps and is fixed to a wall in a bathroom, etc. □ *singki cuci tangan* ⊃ look at **sink** ⊃ picture at **plug** ⊃ picture on **page P8**

washed out adj tired and pale □ *pucat dan lesu*: They arrived looking washed out after their long journey.

washer /ˈwɒʃə(r) (AmE also) / noun [C] a small flat ring placed between two surfaces to make a connection tight □ *sesendal; relang pelapik* ⊃ picture at **bolt**

washing /ˈwɒʃɪŋ (AmE also) / noun [U] **1** the act of cleaning clothes, etc. with water □ *(perbuatan) membasuh kain*: I usually **do the washing** on Mondays. **2** clothes that need to be washed or are being washed □ *basuhan; cucian*: Could you put the washing in the machine? ◆ a pile of dirty washing

washing machine noun [C] an electric machine for washing clothes □ *mesin basuh* ⊃ picture on **page P8**

washing powder noun [U] soap in the form of powder for washing clothes □ *serbuk pencuci*

washing-up noun [U] **1** the work of washing the plates, knives, forks, etc. after a meal □ *(kerja) membasuh pinggan mangkuk*: I'll **do the washing-up**. ◆ washing-up liquid **2** plates, etc. that need washing after a meal □ *pinggan mangkuk kotor*: Put the washing-up next to the sink.

washout /ˈwɒʃaʊt (AmE also) / noun [C] (informal) an event that is a complete failure, especially because of rain □ *sst yg gagal*

washroom /ˈwɒʃruːm; -rʊm (AmE also) / noun [C] (AmE) a toilet, especially in a public building □ *tandas*

wasn't /ˈwɒznt/ short for **was not**

wasp /wɒsp (AmE also) / noun [C] a small black and yellow flying insect that can sting □ *penyengat* ⊃ look at **bee** ⊃ picture on **page P13**

wastage /ˈweɪstɪdʒ/ noun [U] (formal) using too much of sth in a careless way; the amount of sth that is wasted □ *pembaziran*

waste¹ /weɪst/ verb [T] **1 waste sth (on sb/sth); waste sth (in doing sth)** to use or spend sth in a careless way or for sth that is not necessary □ *membazirkan; membuang; mensia-siakan*: She wastes a lot of money on magazines. ◆ He wasted his time at university because he didn't work hard. ◆ She wasted no time in decorating her new room (= she did it immediately). **2** [usually passive] to give sth to sb who does not value it □ *sia-sia*: Expensive wine is wasted on me. I don't even like it.

waste² /weɪst/ noun **1** [sing] **a waste (of sth)** using sth in a careless and unnecessary way □ *pembaziran; membazir; membuang*: The seminar was **a waste of time**—I'd heard it all before. ◆ It seems a waste to throw away all these old newspapers. **2** [U] material, food, etc. that is not needed and is therefore thrown away □ *bahan buangan*: nuclear waste ◆ A lot of household waste can be recycled and reused. ⊃ look at **rubbish 3 wastes** [pl] (formal) large areas of land that are not lived in and not used □ *kawasan tandus*: the wastes of the Sahara desert

IDM **go to waste** to not be used and so thrown away and wasted □ *terbuang*: I can't bear to see good food going to waste!

waste³ /weɪst/ adj [only before a noun] **1** (used about land) not used or not suitable for use; not looked after □ *terbiar*: There's an area of waste ground outside the town where people dump their rubbish. **2** no longer useful; that is thrown away □ *buangan*: waste paper ◆ waste material

wasted /ˈweɪstɪd/ adj **1** [only before a noun] not necessary or successful □ *sia-sia*: a wasted journey **2** very thin, especially because of illness □ *cengkung; susut* **3** (slang) suffering from the effects of drugs or alcohol □ *mabuk; khayal*

wasteful /ˈweɪstfl/ adj using more of sth than necessary; causing waste □ *membazir*

waste-paper basket noun [C] a container in which you put paper, etc. that is to be thrown away □ *bakul sampah*

watch¹ /wɒtʃ/ verb **1** [I,T] to look at sb/sth for a time, paying attention to what happens □ *melihat; memerhatikan; menonton*: I watched in horror as the car swerved and crashed. ◆ I'm watching to see how you do it. ◆ We watch TV most evenings. ◆ Watch what she does next. ◆ I watched him open the door and walk away. ⊃ note at **look 2** [T] **watch sb/sth (for sth)** to take care of sth for a short time □ *menjaga; mengawasi*: Could you watch my bag for a second while I go and get a drink? **3** [T] to be careful about sb/sth; to pay careful attention to sth/sb □ *berhati-hati*: You'd better watch what you say to her. She gets upset very easily. ◆ Watch that boy—he's acting suspiciously.

IDM **watch your step 1** to be careful about where you are walking □ *berhati-hati*: The path's very slippery here so watch your step. **2** to be careful about how you behave □ *berhati-hati*

PHR V **watch out** to be careful because of possible danger or trouble □ *jaga-jaga; berjaga-jaga*: Watch out! There's a car coming. ♦ If you don't watch out you'll lose your job.

watch out for sb/sth to look carefully and be ready for sb/sth □ *tengok-tengok/jaga-jaga (kalau-kalau ada sso/sst)*: Watch out for snakes if you walk through the fields.

watch over sb/sth to look after or protect sb/sth □ *menjaga sso/sst*: For two weeks she watched over the sick child.

watch² /wɒtʃ/ noun **1** [C] a type of small clock that you usually wear around your wrist □ *jam tangan*: a digital watch ♦ My watch is a bit fast/slow (= shows a time that is later/earlier than the correct time). ⊃ look at **clock** ⊃ picture at **clock** **2** [sing, U] the act of watching sb/sth in case of possible danger or problems □ *(perbuatan) mengawasi atau berjaga-jaga*: Tour companies have to keep a close watch on the political situation in the region.

watchdog /'wɒtʃdɒg/ noun [C] a person or group whose job is to make sure that large companies respect people's rights □ *pemerhati; pengawas*: a consumer watchdog

watchful /'wɒtʃfl/ adj careful to notice things □ *mengawasi/memerhati dgn teliti*

water¹ /'wɔːtə(r)/ noun **1** [U] the clear liquid that falls as rain and is in rivers, seas and lakes □ *air*: a glass of water ♦ All the rooms have hot and cold running water. ♦ drinking water ♦ tap water ⊃ look at **freeze**, **steam** **2** [U] a large amount of water, especially the water in a lake, river or sea □ *air*: Don't go too near the edge or you'll fall in the water! ♦ After the heavy rain several fields were under water. **3** waters [pl] the water in a particular sea, lake, etc. or near a particular country □ *perairan*: The ship was still in British waters. **4** [U] the surface of an area of water □ *air*: Can you swim **under water**? ♦ I can see my reflection in the water.

IDM **keep your head above water** ⊃ **head¹**
pass water ⊃ **pass¹**

water² /'wɔːtə(r)/ verb **1** [T] to give water to plants □ *menyiram; menjirus* **2** [I] (used about the eyes or mouth) to fill with liquid □ *menjirus*: The smoke in the room was starting to **make my eyes water**. ♦ Chopping onions **makes my eyes water**. ♦ These menus will really **make your mouth water**.

PHR V **water sth down** **1** to add water to a liquid in order to make it weaker □ *mencairkan* **2** to change a statement, report, etc. so that the meaning is less strong or direct □ *melembutkan; mengurangkan*

watercolour /'wɔːtəkʌlə(r)/ noun **1** watercolours [pl] paints that are mixed with water, not oil □ *cat air* **2** [C] a picture that has been painted with **watercolours** □ *lukisan cat air*

watercress /'wɔːtəkres/ noun [U] a type of plant with small round green leaves which have a strong taste and are often eaten in salads □ *selada air*

957 **watch → wave**

waterfall /'wɔːtəfɔːl/ noun [C] a river that falls from a high place, for example over a rock, etc. □ *air terjun* ⊃ picture on page P10

waterhole /'wɔːtəhəʊl/ (also 'watering hole) noun [C] a place in a hot country, where animals go to drink □ *lopak berair tempat minum utk binatang*

'watering can noun [C] a container with a long tube on one side which is used for pouring water on plants □ *penyiram* ⊃ picture at **garden**

waterlogged /'wɔːtəlɒgd/ (AmE also) / adj **1** (used about the ground) extremely wet □ *bertakung air*: Our boots sank into the waterlogged ground. **2** (used about a boat) full of water and likely to sink □ *dipenuhi air*

watermelon /'wɔːtəmelən/ noun [C,U] a large, round fruit with a thick, green skin. It is pink or red inside with a lot of black seeds. □ *tembikai* ⊃ picture on page P14

'water polo noun [U] a game played by two teams of people swimming in a swimming pool. Players try to throw a ball into the other team's goal. □ *polo air*

waterproof /'wɔːtəpruːf/ adj that does not let water go through □ *kalis air*: a waterproof jacket

watershed /'wɔːtəʃed/ noun [C] an event or a time which is important because it marks the beginning of sth new or different □ *titik perubahan*

waterski /'wɔːtəskiː/ verb [I] to move across the surface of water standing on **waterskis** (= narrow boards) and being pulled by a boat □ *meluncur air* ⊃ picture on page P5

watertight /'wɔːtətaɪt/ adj **1** made so that water cannot get in or out □ *kedap air*: Store in a watertight container. **2** (used about an excuse, opinion, etc.) impossible to prove wrong; without any faults □ *tdk dpt disangkal/dipertikaikan*: His alibi was absolutely watertight.

waterway /'wɔːtəweɪ/ noun [C] a river, **canal** (= an artificial river), etc. along which boats can travel □ *jalan air*

watery /'wɔːtəri/ adj **1** containing mostly water □ *cair; berair*: watery soup ♦ A watery liquid came out of the wound. **2** weak and pale □ *malap; pudar*: watery sunshine ♦ a watery smile

watt /wɒt/ noun [C] (abbr W) a unit of electric power □ *watt*: a 60-watt light bulb

wave¹ /weɪv/ noun [C]
▶WATER **1** a line of water moving across the surface of water, especially the sea, that is higher than the rest of the surface □ *ombak; gelombang*: We watched the waves roll in and break on the shore. ⊃ look at **tidal wave** ⊃ picture on page P10
▶FEELING/BEHAVIOUR **2** a sudden increase or spread of a feeling or type of behaviour □ *gelombang; (sst) yg meningkat; bertubi-tubi*: There has been a wave of sympathy for the refugees. ♦ a

crime wave ♦ The pain came in waves. ➲ look at heatwave

▸LARGE NUMBER **3** a large number of people or things suddenly moving or appearing somewhere □ *gelombang; kumpulan*: There is normally a wave of tourists in August.

▸MOVEMENT OF HAND **4** a movement of sth, especially your hand, from side to side in the air □ *lambaian; melambai*: With a wave of his hand, he said goodbye and left.

▸SOUND/LIGHT/HEAT **5** the form that some types of energy such as sound, heat, light, etc. take when they move □ *gelombang*: sound waves ♦ shock waves from the earthquake ➲ look at LW, MW

▸HAIR **6** a gentle curve in your hair □ *berombak; ketak-ketak* ➲ look at perm

wave² /weɪv/ verb

1 [I,T] to move your hand from side to side in the air, usually to attract sb's attention or as you meet or leave sb □ *melambai*: She waved to her friends. ♦ He leant out of the window and waved goodbye to her as the train left the station. **2** [T] wave sb/sth away, on, through, etc. to move your hand in a particular direction to show sb/sth which way to go □ *mengisyaratkan dgn tangan*: There was a policeman in the middle of the road, waving us on. **3** [T] wave sth (at sb); wave sth (about) to hold sth in the air and move it from side to side □ *melambai-lambaikan; mengibar-ngibarkan*: The crowd waved flags as the President came out. ♦ She was talking excitedly and waving her arms about. **4** [I] to move gently up and down or from side to side □ *melambai-lambai; bergoyang*: The branches of the trees waved gently in the breeze.

They waved goodbye.

PHR V wave sth aside to decide not to pay attention to sb/sth because you think he/she/it is not important □ *mengetepikan (sso/sst)*

wave sb off to wave to sb who is leaving □ *melambai sso pergi*

waveband /ˈweɪvbænd/ (also **band**) noun [C] a set of radio waves of similar length □ *jalur gelombang*

wavelength /ˈweɪvleŋθ/ noun [C] **1** the distance between two sound waves □ *jarak gelombang* **2** the length of wave on which a radio station sends out its programmes □ *jarak gelombang*

IDM on the same wavelength able to understand sb because you have similar ideas and opinions □ *sebulu; secocok*

waver /ˈweɪvə(r)/ verb [I] **1** to become weak or uncertain, especially when making a decision or choice □ *teragak-agak; goyah*: He never wavered in his support. **2** to move in a way that is not firm or steady □ *tdk tetap; bergoyang; ter-*

ketar-ketar: His hand wavered as he reached for the money.

wavy /ˈweɪvi/ adj (**wavier**; **waviest**) having curves; not straight □ *berketak-ketak; berombak-ombak; tdk lurus*: wavy hair ♦ a wavy line ➲ picture at hair, line

wax /wæks/ noun [U] **1** a substance made from fat or oil that melts easily and is used for making polish, **candles** (= tall sticks that you burn to give light), etc. □ *lilin* **2** a yellow substance that is found in your ears □ *tahi telinga*

waxwork /ˈwækswɜːk/ noun [C] **1** a model of sb/sth, especially of a famous person, that is made of **wax** □ *patung lilin* **2 waxworks** [sing] a place where **wax** models of famous people are shown to the public □ *tempat pameran patung lilin*

way¹ /weɪ/ noun

▸METHOD/STYLE **1** [C] a way (to do sth/of doing sth) a particular method, style or manner of doing sth □ *cara*: What is the best way to learn a language? ♦ I've discovered a brilliant way of saving paper! ♦ They'll have to find the money one way or another. ♦ He always does things his own way. ♦ She smiled in a friendly way.

▸ROUTE **2** [C, usually sing] the route you take to reach somewhere; the route you would take if nothing were stopping you □ *jalan*: Can you tell me the way to James Street? ♦ Which way should I go to get to the town centre? ♦ If you lose your way, phone me. ♦ We stopped on the way to Leeds for a meal. ♦ Can I drive you home? It's on my way. ♦ Get out of my way! ♦ Can you move that box—it's in my/the way. **3** [C] a path, road, route, etc. that you can travel along □ *jalan*: There's a way across the fields. ➲ look at highway, motorway, railway

▸DIRECTION **4** [sing] a direction or position □ *bermaksud arah atau kedudukan*: Look this way! ♦ That painting is the wrong way up (= with the wrong edge at the top). ♦ Shouldn't you be wearing that hat the other way round? (= facing in the other direction) ♦ He thought I was older than my sister but in fact it's the other way round (= the opposite of what he thought). ➲ look at back to front

▸DISTANCE **5** [sing] a distance in space or time □ *jauh; lama*: It's a long way from London to Edinburgh. ♦ The exams are still a long way off. ♦ We came all this way to see him and he's not at home!

IDM be set in your ways to be unable to change your habits, attitudes, etc. □ *sudah biasa dgn sst tabiat, sikap, dsb (oleh itu sukar mengubahnya)*

bluff your way in, out, through, etc. sth ➲ bluff¹

by the way (used for adding sth to the conversation) on a new subject □ *Oh ya*: Oh, by the way, I saw Mario in town yesterday.

change your ways ➲ change¹

get/have your own way to get or do what you want, although others may want sth else □ *ikut kehendak sendiri*

give way to break or fall down □ *patah; runtuh*: The branch of the tree suddenly gave way and he fell.

give way (to sb/sth) 1 to stop or to allow sb/sth to go first □ *memberi laluan*: *Give way to traffic coming from the right.* ➲ picture at **roundabout** **2** to allow sb to have what they want although you did not at first agree with it □ *mengalah; menurut kehendak sso/sst*: *We shall not give way to the terrorists' demands.*

go a long way ➲ **long¹**

go out of your way (to do sth) to make a special effort to do sth □ *bersusah payah (membuat sst)*

have a long way to go ➲ **long¹**

in a/one/any way; in some ways to a certain degree but not completely □ *dr satu/beberapa segi*: *In some ways I prefer working in a small office.*

in a big/small way used for expressing the size or importance of an activity □ *secara besar-besaran/kecil-kecilan; banyak/sedikit*: '*Have you done any acting before?*' '*Yes, but in a very small way* (= not very much).'

in the way 1 blocking the road or path □ *menghalang; merintang*: *I can't get past. There's a big lorry in the way.* **2** not needed or wanted □ *mengganggu*: *I felt rather in the way at my daughter's party.*

learn the hard way ➲ **learn**

no way (*informal*) definitely not □ *sama sekali tdk; jangan harap*: '*Can I borrow your car?*' '*No way!*'

on your/the/its ˈway coming or going □ *beredar*: *I'd better be on my way* (= I must leave) *soon.*

the other way round ➲ **other**

out of harm's way ➲ **harm¹**

out of the way no longer stopping sb from moving or doing sth □ *mengalihkan*: *I moved my legs out of the way so that she could get past.*

thread your way through sth ➲ **thread²**

under way having started and making progress □ *sudah bermula*: *Discussions between the two sides are now under way.*

a/sb's way of life the behaviour and customs that are typical of a person or group of people □ *cara hidup*

way² /weɪ/ *adv* (*informal*) very far; very much □ *jauh; jauh lebih*: *I finally found his name way down the list.* ◆ *Matt's got way more experience than me.*

WC /ˌdʌblju: ˈsi:/ *abbr* **water closet**; toilet □ *tandas*

we /wi:/ *pron* the subject of a verb; used for talking about the speaker and one or more other people □ *kami; kita*: *We're going to the cinema.* ◆ *We are both going to the party.*

weak /wi:k/ *adj* (**weaker**; **weakest**)
▶NOT STRONG **1** (used about the body) having little strength or energy □ *lemah*: *The child was weak with hunger.* ◆ *Her legs felt weak.* **2** that cannot support a lot of weight; likely to break □ *lemah; tdk kuat/kukuh*: *That bridge is too weak to take heavy traffic.*
▶NOT POWERFUL **3** easy to influence; not firm □ *lemah; tdk tegas*: *He is too weak to be a good leader.* ◆ *a weak character*
▶ECONOMY **4** not having economic success □ *lemah*: *a weak currency/economy/market*
▶NOT GOOD AT STH **5** **weak (at/in/on sth)** not very good at sth □ *lemah; tdk pandai*: *He's weak at maths.* ◆ *His maths is weak.* ◆ *a weak team* **OPP** **strong**
▶ARGUMENT/EXCUSE **6** not easy to believe □ *lemah*: *She made some weak excuse about washing her hair tonight.*
▶VOICE/SMILE **7** not easy to see or hear; not definite or strong □ *lemah*: *a weak voice* ◆ *She gave a weak smile.*
▶LIQUID **8** containing a lot of water, not strong in taste □ *cair*: *weak coffee* ◆ *I like my tea quite weak.*
▶**weakly** *adv*

weaken /ˈwi:kən/ *verb* [I,T] **1** to become less strong; to make sb/sth less strong □ *menjadi lemah; melemahkan*: *The illness had left her weakened.* ◆ *The building had been weakened by the earthquake.* **OPP** **strengthen** **2** to become, or make sb become, less certain or firm about sth □ *mengalah*: *She eventually weakened and allowed him to stay.*

ˈweak form *noun* [C] a way of pronouncing a word when there is no stress on that word □ *bentuk lemah*: *In the phrase 'bread and butter', 'and' is a weak form.* **OPP** **strong form**

weakness /ˈwi:knəs/ *noun* **1** [U] the state of being weak □ *kelemahan*: *He thought that crying was a sign of weakness.* **OPP** **strength** **2** [C] a fault or lack of strength, especially in sb's character □ *kelemahan; kekurangan*: *It's important to know your own strengths and weaknesses.* **OPP** **strength** **3** [C, usually sing] **a weakness for sth/sb** a particular and often silly liking for sth/sb □ *kegemaran; sangat suka*: *I have a weakness for chocolate.*

wealth /welθ/ *noun* **1** [U] a lot of money, property, etc. that sb owns; the state of being rich □ *kekayaan; harta benda*: *They were a family of enormous wealth.* **SYN** **riches** **2** [sing] **a wealth of sth** a large number or amount of sth □ *banyak*: *a wealth of information/experience/talent*

wealthy /ˈwelθi/ *adj* (**wealthier**; **wealthiest**) having a lot of money, property, etc. □ *kaya* **SYN** **rich, well-to-do** **OPP** **poor**

wean /wi:n/ *verb* [T] to gradually stop feeding a baby or young animal with its mother's milk and start giving it solid food □ *mencerai susu*

weapon /ˈwepən/ *noun* [C] an object which is used for fighting or for killing people, such as a gun, knife, bomb, etc. □ *senjata*

wear¹ /weə(r)/ *verb* (*pt* **wore** /wɔ:(r)/; *pp* **worn** /wɔ:n/)
▶CLOTHES **1** [T] to have clothes, jewellery, etc. on your body □ *memakai*: *He was wearing a suit and tie.* ◆ *I wear glasses for reading.* ➲ note at **carry**
▶EXPRESSION ON FACE **2** [T] to have a certain look on your face □ *menunjukkan*: *His face wore a puzzled look.*
▶DAMAGE WITH USE **3** [I,T] to become or make sth become thinner, smoother or weaker because of being used or rubbed a lot □ *menjadi lu-*

suh; menghauskan: *These tyres are badly worn.* ◆ *The soles of his shoes had worn smooth.* **4** [T] to make a hole, path, etc. in sth by rubbing, walking, etc. □ *menjadi haus, berlubang, dll*: *Put some slippers on or you'll wear a hole in your socks!*

▶STAY IN GOOD CONDITION **5** [I] to last for a long time without becoming thinner or damaged □ *tahan*: *This material wears well.*

IDM **wear thin** to have less effect because of being used too much □ *sudah tdk berkesan, dsb (kerana terlalu kerap digunakan)*: *We've heard that excuse so often that it's beginning to wear thin.*

PHR V **wear (sth) away** to damage sth or to make it disappear over a period of time, by using or touching it a lot; to disappear or become damaged in this way □ *menghauskan/menghakis sst*: *The wind had worn the soil away.*
wear (sth) down to become or to make sth smaller or smoother □ *menghauskan sst; menjadi haus*: *The heels on these shoes have worn right down.*
wear sb/sth down to make sb/sth weaker by attacking, persuading, etc. □ *membuat sso/sst lemah atau mengalah akhirnya*: *They wore him down with constant arguments until he changed his mind.*
wear off to become less strong or to disappear completely □ *hilang; tdk berkesan lagi*: *The effects of the drug wore off after a few hours.*
wear (sth) out to become too thin or damaged to use any more; to cause sth to do this □ *menjadi haus; menghauskan*: *Children's shoes wear out very quickly.*
wear sb/yourself out to make sb/yourself very tired □ *meletihkan sso*: *She wore herself out walking home with the heavy bags.* ➔ look at **worn out**

wear² /weə(r)/ *noun* [U] **1** wearing or being worn; use as clothing □ *dipakai*: *You'll need jeans and jumpers for everyday wear.* **2** [in compounds] used especially in shops to describe clothes for a particular purpose or occasion □ *pakaian*: *casual/evening/sports wear* ◆ *children's wear* **3** long use which damages the quality or appearance of sth □ *kelusuhan; haus*: *The engine is checked regularly for signs of wear.*

IDM **wear and tear** the damage caused by ordinary use □ *haus dan lusuh*
the worse for wear ➔ **worse**

weary /'wɪəri/ *adj* (**wearier**; **weariest**) very tired, especially after you have been doing sth for a long time □ *letih; penat*: *He gave a weary sigh.* ▶**wearily** *adv* ▶**weariness** *noun* [U]

weasel /'wiːzl/ *noun* [C] a small wild animal with reddish-brown fur, a long thin body and short legs □ *wesel; sejenis cerpelai*

weather¹ /'weðə(r)/ *noun* [U] the condition of the atmosphere at a particular place and time, including how much wind, rain, sun, etc. there is, and how hot or cold it is □ *cuaca*: *What's the weather like where you are?* ◆ *hot/warm/sunny/fine weather* ◆ *cold/wet/windy/wintry weather* ◆ *I'm not going for a run in this weather!* ➔ note at **cold**, **fog**, **storm**

IDM **make heavy weather of sth** ➔ **heavy**
under the weather (*informal*) not very well □ *tdk berapa sihat*

TOPIC

Weather

Drops of water that fall from the sky are called **rain**. When it is raining a lot, it is **pouring**. When it is only raining slightly, it is **drizzling**. **Snow** is frozen rain that is soft and white. **Sleet** is rain that is not completely frozen. Small balls of ice that fall like rain are called **hail**. **Fog** is like a cloud close to the ground and is difficult to see through. When we talk about the weather, we often say 'It's a **lovely/beautiful/horrible/terrible** day (= the weather is good/bad), isn't it?' If you want to know what the weather is going to be like, you can watch or listen to the **weather forecast**.

---

weather² /'weðə(r)/ *verb* **1** [I,T] to change or make sth change in appearance because of the effect of the sun, air or wind □ *meluluhawa; diluluhawakan; kering, berkedut, dsb kerana dimakan hari*: *The farmer's face was weathered by the sun.* **2** [T] to come safely through a difficult time or experience □ *selamat menempuhi*: *Their company managed to weather the recession and recover.*

'weather-beaten *adj* (used especially about sb's face or skin) made rough and damaged by the sun and wind □ *dimakan hari (muka atau kulit)*

'weather forecast (also **forecast**) *noun* [C] a description of the weather that is expected for the next day or next few days □ *ramalan cuaca*

weave /wiːv/ *verb* [I,T] (*pt* **wove** /wəʊv/ or *in sense 2* **weaved**; *pp* **woven** /'wəʊvn/ or *in sense 2* **weaved**) **1** to make cloth, etc. by passing threads under and over a set of threads that is fixed to a **loom** (= a special frame or machine) □ *menenun*: *woven cloth* **2** to change direction often when you are moving so that you are not stopped by anything □ *menyelit-nyelit; mencelah-celah*: *The cyclist weaved in and out of the traffic.*

web /web/ *noun* **1** [C] a type of fine net that a spider makes in order to catch small insects □ *sarang labah-labah*: *A spider spins webs.* ➔ look at **cobweb** ➔ picture at **spider 2 the Web** [sing] = **World Wide Web**: *I looked it up on the Web.*

webbed /webd/ *adj* [only *before* a noun] (used about the feet of some birds or animals) having the toes connected by pieces of skin □ *kaki berselaput* ➔ picture on **page P12**

webcam (*AmE* **Webcam™**) /'webkæm/ *noun* [C] a video camera that is connected to a computer so that what it records can be seen on a website as it happens □ *kamera web*

webcast /ˈwebkɑːst/ noun [C] a live broadcast that is sent out on the Internet □ *siaran langsung melalui Internet*: *We were able to watch a live webcast of the eclipse.*

webinar /ˈwebɪnɑː(r)/ noun [C] a live lecture, presentation, etc. that is sent out on the Internet and in which you can take part □ *persembahan langsung melalui Internet*

weblog /ˈweblɒg (AmE also) / = **blog**

'web page noun [C] a document connected to the World Wide Web, usually forming part of a website, that anyone with an Internet connection can see □ *laman web*: *We learned how to create and register a new web page.*

website /ˈwebsaɪt/ (also **site**) noun [C] a place connected to the Internet where a company, an organization or an individual person puts information □ *tapak web*: *I found it on their website.* ♦ *Visit our website to learn more.* ⊃ note at **Internet**

Wed. (also **Weds.**) abbr = **Wednesday** □ *Rabu*: *Wed. 4 May*

we'd /wiːd/ short for **we had; we would**

wedding /ˈwedɪŋ/ noun [C] a marriage ceremony and often the **reception** (= the party that follows it) □ *(majlis) perkahwinan*: *I've been invited to their wedding.* ♦ *a wedding dress* ♦ *a wedding ring* (= one that is worn on the third finger to show that sb is married) ♦ *a wedding present*

TOPIC

Weddings

At a **wedding**, two people **get married**. The woman is called the **bride** and the man is the **groom** (or **bridegroom**). They are helped during the **wedding ceremony** by the **best man** and the **bridesmaids**. A wedding can take place in church (a **church wedding**) or in a **registry office**. After the ceremony there is usually a **wedding reception** (= a formal party). Many couples go on a **honeymoon** (= holiday) after getting married. **Marriage** refers to the relationship between a **husband** and **wife**: *They have a happy marriage.* A couple celebrate their **silver wedding anniversary** when they have been married for 25 years, their **golden wedding** after 50 years and their **diamond wedding** after 60.

---

wedge¹ /wedʒ/ noun [C] a piece of wood, etc. with one thick and one thin pointed end that you can push into a small space, for example to keep things apart □ *sendal; baji*: *The door was kept open with a wedge.*

wedge² /wedʒ/ verb [T] **1** to force sth/sb to fit into a small space □ *mengasak; menyumbat*: *The cupboard was wedged between the table and the door.* **2** to force sth apart or to prevent sth from moving by using a **wedge** □ *menyendal*: *to wedge a door open*

Wednesday /ˈwenzdeɪ; -di/ noun [C,U] (abbr **Wed.**) the day of the week after Tuesday □ *Rabu* ⊃ note at **Monday**

wee /wiː/ (also **ˈwee-wee**) noun [C,U] (informal) (used by young children or when you are talking to them) water that you pass from your body □ *kencing* **SYN** **urine** ▶ **wee** (also **ˈwee-wee**) verb [I]

weed¹ /wiːd/ noun **1** [C] a wild plant that is not wanted in a garden because it prevents other plants from growing properly □ *rumpai* **2** [U] a mass of very small green plants that floats on the surface of an area of water □ *rumpair*

weed² /wiːd/ verb [I,T] to remove **weeds** from a piece of ground, etc. □ *merumpai*
PHR V **weed sth/sb out** to remove the things or people that you do not think are good enough □ *membuang; menyisihkan; mengetepikan*: *He weeded out all the letters with spelling mistakes in them.*

weedy /ˈwiːdi/ adj (**weedier**; **weediest**) (informal) small and weak □ *kurus dan lemah*: *a small weedy man*

week /wiːk/ noun [C] **1** (abbr **wk**) a period of seven days, especially from Monday to Sunday or from Sunday to Saturday □ *minggu*: *We arrived last week.* ♦ *He left two weeks ago.* ♦ *I haven't seen her for a week.* ♦ *I go there twice a week.* ♦ *They'll be back in a week/in a week's time.*

MORE In British English, a period of two weeks is usually called a **fortnight**.

2 the part of the week when people go to work, etc. usually from Monday to Friday □ *minggu (hari Isnin hingga Jumaat); hari biasa (bukan hujung minggu)*: *She works hard during the week so that she can enjoy herself at the weekend.* ♦ *I work a 40-hour week.*
IDM **today, tomorrow, Monday, etc. week** seven days after today, tomorrow, Monday, etc. □ *seminggu dr hari ini, esok, Isnin, dsb*
week in, week out every week without a rest or change □ *minggu demi minggu; dr minggu ke minggu*: *He's played for the same team week in, week out for 20 years.*
a week yesterday, last Monday, etc. seven days before yesterday, Monday, etc. □ *seminggu yg lalu dr semalam, Isnin lepas, dsb*

weekday /ˈwiːkdeɪ/ noun [C] any day except Saturday or Sunday □ *hari biasa; hari kerja (bukan Sabtu atau Ahad)*: *I only work on weekdays.* ⊃ note at **routine**

weekend /ˌwiːkˈend/ noun [C] Saturday and Sunday □ *hujung minggu*: *What are you doing at the weekend?*

HELP **At the weekend** is used in British English. In American English you say **on the weekend**.

weekly¹ /ˈwiːkli/ adj, adv happening or appearing once a week or every week □ *minggu-*

weekly → welfare 962

an; setiap minggu: *a weekly report* ♦ *We are paid weekly.*

weekly² /'wi:kli/ *noun* [C] (*pl* **weeklies**) a newspaper or magazine that is published every week □ *(akhbar atau majalah) mingguan*

weep /wi:p/ *verb* [I,T] (*pt, pp* **wept** /wept/) (*formal*) to let tears fall because of strong emotion; to cry □ *menangis: She wept at the news of his death.*

weigh /weɪ/ *verb* **1** [T] to have or show a certain weight □ *berat: I weigh 56 kilos.* ♦ *How much does this weigh?* **2** [T] to measure how heavy sth is, especially by using **scales** (= a piece of equipment designed for this) □ *menimbang: I weigh myself every week.* ♦ *Can you weigh this parcel for me, please?* **3** [T] **weigh sth (up)** to consider sth carefully □ *menimbangkan: You need to weigh up your chances of success.* **4** [T] **weigh sth (against sb/sth)** to consider if one thing is better, more important, etc. than another or not □ *mempertimbangkan: We shall weigh the advantages of the plan against the risks.* **5** [I] **weigh against (sb/sth)** to be considered as a disadvantage when sb/sth is being judged □ *dianggap sebagai kelemahan/kekurangan: She didn't get the job because her lack of experience weighed against her.*
PHRV **weigh sb down** to make sb feel worried and sad □ *membebani sso; (sso itu) berasa dibebankan: He felt weighed down by all his responsibilities.*
weigh sb/sth down to make it difficult for sb/sth to move (by being heavy) □ *membebankan sso/sst; dibebani: I was weighed down by heavy shopping.*
weigh on sb/sth to make sb worry □ *merisaukan sso: The responsibilities weigh heavily on him.* ♦ *That problem has been weighing on my mind for a long time.*
weigh sb/sth up to consider sb/sth carefully and form an opinion □ *menilai sso; mempertimbangkan sst: I weighed up my chances and decided it was worth applying.*

weight¹ /weɪt/ *noun* (*abbr* **wt**) **1** [U] how heavy sth/sb is; the fact of being heavy □ *berat; berat badan: The doctor advised him to lose weight* (= become thinner and less heavy). ♦ *He's put on weight* (= got fatter). ♦ *The weight of the snow broke the branch.* **2** [C] a heavy object □ *benda berat: The doctor has told me not to lift heavy weights.* **3** [C] a piece of metal that weighs a known amount that can be used to measure an amount of sth, or that can be lifted as a form of exercise □ *batu timbang; pemberat; (angkat) berat: a 500-gram weight* ♦ *She lifts weights in the gym as part of her daily training.* **4** [sing] something that you are worried about □ *beban: Telling her the truth took a weight off his mind.*
IDM **carry weight** ⊃ **carry**
pull your weight ⊃ **pull¹**

weight² /weɪt/ *verb* [T] **1** **weight sth (down) (with sth)** to hold sth down with a heavy object or objects □ *memberati; diberati: to weight down a fishing net* **2** [usually passive] to organize sth so that a particular person or group has an advantage/disadvantage □ *berat sebelah (memihak kpd/menentang): The system is weighted in favour of/against people with children.*

weightless /'weɪtləs/ *adj* having no weight, for example when travelling in space □ *nirberat* ▶ **weightlessness** *noun* [U]

weightlifting /'weɪtlɪftɪŋ/ *noun* [U] a sport in which heavy metal objects are lifted □ *(sukan) angkat berat* ⊃ picture on **page P4** ▶ **weightlifter** *noun* [C]

'weight training *noun* [U] the activity of lifting **weights** as a form of exercise □ *senaman angkat berat: I do weight training to keep fit.*

weighty /'weɪti/ *adj* (**weightier; weightiest**) serious and important □ *penting dan serius: a weighty question*

weir /wɪə(r)/ *noun* [C] a type of wall that is built across a river to stop or change the direction of the flow of water □ *tebat*

weird /wɪəd/ *adj* (**weirder; weirdest**) strange and unusual □ *pelik; aneh: a weird noise/experience* **SYN** **bizarre, strange** ▶ **weirdly** *adv*

weirdo /'wɪədəʊ/ *noun* [C] (*pl* **weirdos** /-əʊz/) (*informal*) a person who looks strange and/or behaves in a strange way □ *orang yg berkelakuan aneh: I wouldn't go into that bar—it's full of weirdos.*

welcome¹ /'welkəm/ *verb* [T] **1** to be friendly to sb when they arrive somewhere □ *menyambut; mengalu-alukan: Everyone came to the door to welcome us.* **2** to be pleased to receive or accept sth □ *mengalu-alukan: I've no idea what to do next, so I'd welcome any suggestions.* ▶ **welcome** *noun* [C]: *Let's give a warm welcome to our next guest.*

welcome² /'welkəm/ *adj* **1** received with pleasure; giving pleasure □ *dialu-alukan: You're always welcome here.* ♦ *welcome news* **2** **welcome to sth/to do sth** allowed to do sth □ *dipersilakan; boleh gunakan/pakai, dsb: You're welcome to use my bicycle.* **3** used to say that sb can have sth that you do not want yourself □ *ambil terus sahajalah: Take the car if you want. You're welcome to it. It's always breaking down.*
IDM **make sb welcome** to receive sb in a friendly way □ *mengalu-alukan sso*
you're welcome (*spoken*) you do not need to thank me □ *ungkapan balas bagi ucapan terima kasih; sama-sama: 'Thank you for your help.' 'You're welcome.'*
▶ **welcome** *exclam*: *Welcome to London!* ♦ *Welcome home!*

weld /weld/ *verb* [I,T] to join pieces of metal by heating them and pressing them together □ *mengimpal*

welfare /'welfeə(r)/ *noun* [U] **1** the general health, happiness safety of a person, an animal or a group □ *kebajikan: The doctor is concerned* about the child's welfare. **SYN** well-being 2 the help and care that is given to people who have problems with health, money, etc. □ *kebajikan*: *education and welfare services* 3 (*AmE*) = **social security**

welfare state *noun* [sing] a system organized by a government to provide free services and money for people who have no job, who are ill, etc.; a country that has this system □ *negara kebajikan*

we'll /wiːl/ short for **we shall; we will**

well¹ /wel/ *adv* (**better; best**) 1 in a good way □ *baik; bagus*: *You speak English very well.* ♦ *I hope your work is going well.* ♦ *You passed your exam! Well done!* ♦ *He took it well when I told him he wasn't on the team.* **OPP** **badly** 2 completely or fully □ *betul-betul*: *Shake the bottle well before opening.* ♦ *How well do you know Henry?* 3 very much □ *jauh; lebih*: *They arrived home well past midnight.* ♦ *She says she's 32 but I'm sure she's well over 40.* ♦ *This book is well worth reading.* 4 [used with **can, could, may** or **might**] probably or possibly □ *mungkin*: *He might well be right.* 5 [used with **can, could, may** or **might**] with good reason □ *digunakan utk membawa maksud wajar*: *I can't very well refuse to help them after all they've done for me.* ♦ *'Where's Bill?' 'You may well ask!'* (= I don't know either)*
IDM **as well (as sb/sth)** in addition to sb/sth □ *juga; selain drpd*: *Can I come as well?* ♦ *He's worked in Japan as well as Italy.* ⊃ note at **also**
augur well/ill for sb/sth ⊃ **augur**
bode well/ill (for sb/sth) ⊃ **bode**
do well 1 to be successful □ *berjaya*: *Their daughter has done well at university.* 2 to be getting better after an illness □ *semakin sihat*: *Mr Singh is doing well after his operation.*
do well to do sth used to say that sth is the right and sensible thing to do □ *ada baiknya atau lebih baik (sso membuat sst)*: *He would do well to check the facts before accusing people.*
it is just as well (that ...) ⊃ **just¹**
may/might as well (do sth) used for saying that sth is the best thing you can do in the situation, even though you may not want to do it □ *lebih baiklah*: *I may as well tell you the truth—you'll find out anyway.*
mean well ⊃ **mean¹**
well and truly completely □ *betul-betul*: *We were well and truly lost.*
well/badly off ⊃ **off¹**

well² /wel/ *adj* (**better** /ˈbetə(r)/, **best** /best/) [not before a noun] 1 in good health □ *sihat*: *'How are you?' 'I'm very well, thanks.'* ♦ *This medicine will make you feel better.* ♦ *Get well soon* (= written in a card that you send to sb who is ill)*. 2 in a good state □ *baik*: *I hope all is well with you.*
IDM **all very well (for sb)** (*informal*) used for showing that you are not happy or do not agree with sth □ *memang senang (bagi sso mengatakan sst, dsb)*: *It's all very well for her to criticize* (= it's easy for her to criticize) *but it doesn't help the situation.*
be (just) as well (to do sth) to be sensible; to be a good idea □ *baik; baik juga*: *It would be just as well to ask his permission.*

OTHER WORDS FOR

well

There are various answers to the question 'How are you?'. The most positive replies are: *I'm* **very well**. ♦ *I'm* **great**. ♦ *I'm* **good**. Other ways to say 'I'm well' are: *I'm* **OK**. ♦ *I'm* **fine**. If you are not feeling so well you can say: *I'm* **not (too) bad**. ♦ **So-so**.

well³ /wel/ *exclam* 1 used for showing surprise □ *digunakan utk menyatakan rasa hairan*: *Well, thank goodness you've arrived.* 2 (also **oh well**) used for showing that you know there is nothing you can do to change a situation □ *digunakan utk menyatakan tdk ada apa yg boleh dibuat ttg sst keadaan itu*: *Oh well, there's nothing we can do.* 3 used when you begin the next part of a story or when you are thinking about what to say next □ *digunakan apabila menyambung cerita atau apabila sedang memikirkan apa yg hendak dikatakan berikutnya*: *Well, the next thing that happened was ...* ♦ *Well now, let me see ...* 4 used when you feel uncertain about sth □ *digunakan utk menyatakan rasa tdk pasti*: *'Do you like it?' 'Well, I'm not really sure.'* 5 used to show that you are waiting for sb to say sth □ *digunakan utk menunjukkan yg anda menunggu utk sso itu berkata sst*: *Well? Are you going to tell us what happened?* 6 used to show that you want to finish a conversation □ *baiklah (utk menamatkan perbualan)*: *Well, it's been nice talking to you.*

well⁴ /wel/ *noun* [C] 1 a deep hole in the ground from which water is obtained □ *perigi; telaga*: *to draw water from a well* 2 = **oil well**

well⁵ /wel/ *verb* [I] **well (out/up)** (used about a liquid) to come to the surface □ *bergenang*: *Tears welled up in her eyes.*

well balanced *adj* 1 (used about a meal, etc.) containing enough of the healthy types of food your body needs □ *seimbang*: *a well-balanced diet* 2 (used about a person) calm and sensible □ *waras*: *His response was well balanced.*

well behaved *adj* behaving in a way that most people think is correct □ *berkelakuan baik*

well-being *noun* [U] a state of being healthy and happy □ *kesejahteraan*

well done *adj* (used about meat, etc.) cooked for a long time □ *betul-betul masak* ⊃ look at **rare, medium**

well dressed *adj* wearing attractive and fashionable clothes □ *berpakaian kemas dan bergaya*

well earned *adj* that you deserve, especially because you have been working hard □ *sepatutnya; sewajarnya*: *She's having a well-earned holiday.*

well fed *adj* having good food regularly □ *cukup makan*

well informed *adj* knowing a lot about one or several subjects □ *berpengetahuan*

wellington /ˈwelɪŋtən/ (also informal **welly**, *AmE* **rubber boot**) *noun* [C] (*BrE*) one of a pair of long rubber boots that you wear to keep your feet and the lower part of your legs dry □ *but wellington: a pair of wellingtons* ♦ *It's very muddy—you'll need your wellingtons.* ⊃ picture at **shoe**

well kept *adj* looked after very carefully so that it has a tidy appearance □ *dijaga dgn baik: a well-kept garden*

well known *adj* known by a lot of people □ *terkenal; dikenali ramai* **SYN** **famous** **OPP** **unknown**

well meaning *adj* (used about a person) wanting to be kind or helpful, but often not having this effect □ *berniat baik*

well meant *adj* intended to be kind or helpful but not having this result □ *berniat baik*

well paid *adj* earning or providing a lot of money □ *berpendapatan tinggi: well-paid doctors* ♦ *This job is not very well paid.*

well-to-do *adj* having a lot of money, property, etc. □ *berada* **SYN** **rich, wealthy**

well-wisher *noun* [C] a person who hopes that sb/sth will be successful □ *orang yg mengucap selamat: She received lots of letters from well-wishers.*

welly /ˈweli/ (*pl* **wellies**) (*BrE informal*) = **wellington**

Welsh /welʃ/ *adj* from Wales □ *dr Wales*
ⓘ For more information, look at the section on geographical names at the back of this dictionary.

went *past tense* of **go**[1]

wept *past tense, past participle* of **weep**

were /wə(r); *strong form* wɜː(r)/ ⊃ **be**

we're /wɪə(r)/ *short for* **we are**

weren't /wɜːnt/ *short for* **were not**

W

west[1] /west/ *noun* [U, sing] (*abbr* **W**) 1 (also **the west**) the direction you look towards in order to see the sun go down; one of the four **points of the compass** (= the main directions that we give names to) □ *barat: Which way is west?* ♦ *Rain is spreading from the west.* ♦ *There's a road to the west of* (= further west than) *here.* ⊃ picture at **compass** 2 **the West** the part of any country, city, etc. that is further to the west than other parts □ *bahagian barat: I live in the west of Scotland.* ♦ *The climate in the West is much wetter than the East.* 3 **the West** [sing] the countries of North America and Western Europe □ *negara-negara Barat: I was born in Japan, but I've lived in the West for some years now.*

west[2] /west/ *adj, adv* 1 (also **West**) [only before a noun] in the west □ *di barat: West London* 2 (used about a wind) coming from the west □ *datang dr barat* 3 to or towards the west □ *ke barat: to travel west* ♦ *The island is five miles west of here.*

westbound /ˈwestbaʊnd/ *adj* travelling or leading towards the west □ *menghala ke barat: the westbound carriageway of the motorway*

westerly /ˈwestəli/ *adj* 1 [only before a noun] to, towards or in the west □ *(ke, ke arah atau di) barat: in a westerly direction* 2 (used about winds) coming from the west □ *(dr) barat*

western[1] (also **Western**) /ˈwestən/ *adj* 1 [only before a noun] (*abbr* **W**) in or of the west □ *(di atau berkenaan dgn) barat: western France* 2 from or connected with the western part of the world, especially Europe or North America □ *(dr atau berkaitan dgn) negara-negara Barat: Western art*

western[2] /ˈwestən/ *noun* [C] a film or book about life in the past in the west of the United States □ *filem/cerita koboi*

westerner /ˈwestənə(r)/ *noun* [C] a person who was born or who lives in the western part of the world, especially Europe or North America □ *orang Barat: Westerners arriving in China usually experience culture shock.*

westernize (also **-ise**) /ˈwestənaɪz/ *verb* [T, usually passive] to make a country or people more like Europe and North America □ *membaratkan: Young people in our country are becoming westernized through watching American TV programmes.*

the West Indies *noun* [pl] a group of islands in the Caribbean Sea that consists of the Bahamas, the Antilles and the Leeward and Windward Islands □ *Hindia Barat* ▶ **West Indian** *noun* [C]: *The West Indians won their match against Australia.* ▶ **West Indian** *adj*

westwards /ˈwestwədz/ (also **westward**) *adv* towards the west □ *ke arah barat: to fly westwards* ▶ **westward** *adj*: *in a westward direction*

wet[1] /wet/ *adj* (**wetter**; **wettest**) 1 covered in a liquid, especially water □ *basah: wet clothes/hair/grass/roads* ♦ *Don't get your feet wet.* **OPP** **dry**

MORE **Moist** means slightly wet. **Damp** is used to describe things that are slightly wet and feel unpleasant because of it: *Don't sit on the grass. It's damp.* **Humid** is used about weather or the air when it feels warm and damp.

2 (used about the weather, etc.) with a lot of rain □ *lembap; hujan: a wet day* **OPP** **dry** 3 (used about paint, etc.) not yet dry or hard □ *basah; belum kering: The ink is still wet.* **OPP** **dry** 4 (used about a person) without energy or enthusiasm □ *lembik; tdk bersemangat: 'Don't be so wet,' she laughed.*

IDM **a wet blanket** (*informal*) a person who spoils other people's fun, especially because they

refuse to take part in sth □ *orang yg merosakkan rancangan atau kemeriahan orang lain (kerana tdk mahu turut serta)*
wet through extremely wet □ *basah kuyup*
▶ **the wet** noun [sing]: *Come in out of the wet* (= the rain).

wet² /wet/ verb [T] (**wetting**; pt, pp **wet** or **wetted**) **1** to make sth wet □ *membasahkan* **2** (used especially of young children) to make yourself or your bed, clothes, etc. wet by letting *urine* (= waste liquid) escape from your body □ *basah (kerana kencing)*

wetsuit /ˈwetsuːt/ noun [C] a piece of clothing made of rubber that fits the whole body closely, worn by people swimming underwater or sailing □ *sut basah; baju getah utk sukan air, menyelam, dsb*

wetted past tense, past participle of **wet²**

we've /wiːv/ short for **we have**

whack /wæk/ verb [T] (*informal*) to hit sb/sth hard □ *memukul*

whacky = **wacky**

whale /weɪl/ noun [C] a very large animal that lives in the sea and looks like a very large fish □ *(ikan) paus* ➲ picture on page P12

whaling /ˈweɪlɪŋ/ noun [U] the hunting of whales □ *pemburuan (ikan) paus*

wharf /wɔːf/ noun [C] (pl **wharves** /wɔːvz/) a platform made of stone or wood at the side of a river where ships and boats can be tied up □ *dermaga*

what /wɒt/ (*AmE also*) / determiner, pron **1** used for asking for information about sb/sth □ *apa; apakah; berapa*: *What time is it?* ◆ *What kind of music do you like?* ◆ *She asked him what he was doing.* ◆ *What's their phone number?* ➲ note at **which 2** the thing or things that have been mentioned or said □ *apa*: *What he says is true.* ◆ *I haven't got much, but you can borrow what money I have.* **3** used for emphasizing sth □ *digunakan utk menegaskan sst; alangkah anehnya, baiknya, dll*: *What strange eyes she's got!* ◆ *What a kind thing to do!* ◆ *What awful weather!*

IDM **how/what about …?** ➲ **about²**

what! used to express surprise or to tell sb to say or repeat sth □ *apa*: *'I've asked Alice to marry me.' 'What?'*

what for? for what purpose or reason □ *apa gunanya; kenapa*: *What's this little switch for?* ◆ *What did you say that for* (= why did you say that)?

what if …? what would happen if …? □ *macam mana/bagaimana kalau*: *What if the car breaks down?*

what's up? ➲ **up**

whatever /wɒtˈevə(r) (*AmE also*) / determiner, pron, adv **1** any or every; anything or everything □ *apa sahaja*: *You can say whatever you like.* ◆ *He took whatever help he could get.* **2** used to say that it does not matter what happens or what sb does, because the result will be the same □ *walau apa pun*: *I still love you, whatever you may think.* ◆ *Whatever she says, she doesn't really mean it.* **3** (used for expressing surprise or worry) what □ *apa; entah apa agaknya*: *Whatever could have happened to them?* **4** (also **whatsoever** /ˌwɒtsəʊˈevə(r)/) at all □ *apa pun*: *I've no reason whatever to doubt him.* ◆ *'Any questions?' 'None whatsoever.'*

IDM **or whatever** (*informal*) or any other or others of a similar kind □ *apa-apa sahaja (yg serupa itu)*: *You don't need to wear anything smart—jeans and a sweater or whatever.*

whatever you do used to emphasize that sb must not do sth □ *walau apa sekalipun*: *Don't touch the red switch, whatever you do.*

wheat /wiːt/ noun [U] **1** a type of grain which can be made into flour □ *gandum* **2** the plant which produces this grain □ *pokok gandum*: *a field of wheat* ➲ picture at **ear**

wheel¹ /wiːl/ noun [C] **1** one of the round objects under a car, bicycle, etc. that turns when it moves □ *roda*: *His favourite toy is a dog on wheels.* ◆ *By law, you have to carry a spare wheel in your car.* ➲ picture at **bicycle** ➲ picture on page **P7 2** [usually sing] = **steering wheel** □ *stereng*: *Her husband was at the wheel* (= he was driving) *when the accident happened.* **3** a flat round part in a machine □ *roda*: *gear wheels*

wheel² /wiːl/ verb **1** [T] to push along an object that has wheels; to move sb about in/on a vehicle with wheels □ *menyorong*: *He wheeled his bicycle up the hill.* ◆ *She was wheeled back to her bed on a trolley.* **2** [I] to fly round in circles □ *berpusing-pusing*: *Birds wheeled above the ship.* **3** [I] to turn round suddenly □ *berpusing/berpaling tiba-tiba*: *Eleanor wheeled round, with a look of horror on her face.*

wheelbarrow /ˈwiːlbærəʊ/ (also **barrow**) noun [C] a type of small open container with one wheel and two handles that you use outside for carrying things □ *kereta sorong* ➲ picture at **garden**

wheelchair /ˈwiːltʃeə(r)/ noun [C] a chair with large wheels that a person who cannot walk can move or be pushed about in □ *kerusi roda* ➲ picture at **chair**

'wheel clamp = **clamp²**(2)

wheeze /wiːz/ verb [I] to breathe noisily, for example if you have a chest illness □ *mendehit; berdehit*

when /wen/ adv, conj **1** at what time □ *bila; bilakah*: *When did she arrive?* ◆ *I don't know when she arrived.* **2** used for talking about the time at which sth happens or happened □ *apabila*: *Sunday is the day when I can relax.* ◆ *I last saw her in May, when she was in London.* ◆ *He jumped up when the phone rang.*

GRAMMAR Notice that we use the present tense after **when** if we are talking about a future time: *I'll call you when I'm ready.*

[C] **countable**, a noun with a plural form: *one book, two books*   [U] **uncountable**, a noun with no plural form: *some sugar*

3 since; as; considering that □ *sedangkan*: *Why do you want more money when you've got enough already?*

> **GRAMMAR** **When** is used for talking about something that you think or know will happen, but **if** is used for something you are not sure will happen. Compare: *I'll ask her when she comes* (= you are sure that she will come). ◆ *I'll ask her if she comes* (= you are not sure if she will come or not).

whenever /wen'evə(r)/ *conj, adv* **1** at any time; no matter when □ *bila-bila masa sahaja*: *You can borrow my car whenever you want.* ◆ *Don't worry. You can give it back the next time you see me, or whenever.* **2** (used in questions when you are showing that you are surprised or impatient) when □ *bila pula*: *Whenever did you find time to do all that cooking?*

where /weə(r)/ *adv, conj* **1** in or to what place or position □ *(di/ke) mana*: *Where can I buy a paper?* ◆ *I asked him where he lived.* **2** in or to the place or situation mentioned □ *tempat; (di/ke) mana*: *the town where you were born* ◆ *She ran to where they were standing.* ◆ *Where possible, you should travel by bus, not taxi.* ◆ *We came to a village, where we stopped for lunch.* ◆ *Where maths is concerned, I'm hopeless.*

whereabouts¹ /'weərəbauts/ *noun* [U, with sing or pl verb] the place where sb/sth is □ *di mana sso/sst berada*: *The whereabouts of the stolen painting is unknown.*

whereabouts² /ˌweərə'bauts/ *adv* where; in or near what place □ *di mana*: *Whereabouts did you lose your purse?*

whereas /ˌweər'æz/ *conj* used for showing a fact that is different □ *sedangkan*: *He eats meat, whereas she's a vegetarian.* **SYN** while

whereby /weə'baɪ/ *adv* (formal) by which; because of which □ *yg dgnnya*: *These countries have an agreement whereby foreign visitors can have free medical care.*

whereupon /ˌweərə'pɒn/ *conj* (formal) after which □ *lalu; maka*: *He fell asleep, whereupon she walked quietly from the room.*

wherever /weər'evə(r)/ *conj, adv* **1** in or to any place □ *(di/ke) mana sahaja*: *You can sit wherever you like.* ◆ *She comes from Omiya, wherever that is* (= I do not know where it is). **2** everywhere, in all places that □ *(di/ke) mana-mana sahaja*: *Wherever I go, he goes.* **3** used in questions for showing surprise □ *di mana*: *Wherever did you learn to cook like that?*

IDM **or wherever** or any other place □ *atau mana-mana*: *The students might be from Sweden, Denmark or wherever.*

whet /wet/ *verb* (whetting; whetted)
IDM **whet sb's appetite** to make sb want more of sth □ *membangkitkan/merangsangkan minat sso*: *Our short stay in Prague whetted our ap-*

petite to spend more time there.

whether /'weðə(r)/ *conj* **1** [used after verbs like ask, doubt, know, etc.] if □ *sama ada*: *He asked me whether we would be coming to the party.* **2** used for expressing a choice or doubt between two or more possibilities □ *sama ada*: *I can't make up my mind whether to go or not.*

> **GRAMMAR** **Whether** and **if** can both be used in sense 1. Only **whether** can be used before 'to' + verb: *Have you decided whether to accept the offer yet?* Only **whether** can be used after a preposition: *the problem of whether to accept the offer.*

IDM **whether or not** used to say that sth will be true in either of the situations that are mentioned □ *sama ada; tdk kira*: *We shall play on Saturday whether it rains or not.* ◆ *Whether or not it rains, we shall play on Saturday.*

which /wɪtʃ/ *determiner, pron* **1** used in questions to ask sb to be exact, when there are a number of people or things to choose from □ *yg mana*: *Which hand do you write with?* ◆ *Which is your bag?* ◆ *She asked me which book I preferred.* ◆ *I can't remember which of the boys is the older.*

> **GRAMMAR** **Which** or **what**? We use **which** when there is only a limited group or number to choose from: *Which car is yours? The Toyota or the BMW?* (= there are only two cars there). We use **what** when the group is not limited: *What car would you choose* (= of all the makes of car that exist), *if you could have any one you wanted?* ◆ *What is your name?*

2 used for saying exactly what thing or things you are talking about □ *yg*: *Cars which use unleaded petrol are more eco-friendly.* ◆ *The situation which he found himself in was very difficult.*

> **HELP** In formal English we write: *The situation in which he found himself was very difficult.*

> **GRAMMAR** In the example above, the words 'which use unleaded petrol' give us *essential* (= necessary) information about the cars. This part of the sentence after **which** is called a **defining relative clause**. We can also use **that**: *Cars that use unleaded petrol …* There is NO comma before **which** or **that** in these sentences.

ⓘ For more information about defining relative clauses, look at the **Reference Section** at the back of this dictionary. **3** used for giving more information about a thing or an animal □ *yg*: *My first car, which I bought as a student, was a Renault.*

> **GRAMMAR** In the example above, the words 'which I bought as a student' give us *extra* information about the car. This part of the sentence after **which** is called a **non-defining relative clause**. We CANNOT use **that** in sentences like this. Note that there is a comma (,) before 'which' and at the end of the part of the sentence which it introduces.

[I] **intransitive**, a verb which has no object: *He laughed.* [T] **transitive**, a verb which has an object: *He ate an apple.*

ⓘ For more information about non-defining relative clauses, look at the **Reference Section** at the back of this dictionary. **4** used for making a comment on what has just been said □ *yg; dan ini*: *We had to wait 16 hours for our plane, which was really annoying.*

HELP Note that there is a comma before 'which'.

whichever /wɪtʃˈevə(r)/ *determiner, pron* **1** used to say what feature or quality is important in deciding sth □ *yg mana sahaja*: *Whichever song gets the most votes will win.* ◆ *Pensions should be increased annually in line with earnings or prices, whichever is the higher.* **2** used to say that it does not matter which, as the result will be the same □ *yg mana-mana pun*: *It takes three hours, whichever route you take.* **3** (used for expressing surprise) which □ *yg mana*: *You're very late. Whichever way did you come?*

whiff /wɪf/ *noun* [usually sing] **a whiff (of sth)** a smell, especially one which only lasts for a short time □ *bau*: *He caught a whiff of her perfume.*

while¹ /waɪl/ (also formal **whilst** /waɪlst/) *conj* **1** during the time that; when □ *semasa; ketika*: *He always phones while we're having lunch.* **2** at the same time as □ *sambil*: *He always listens to the radio while he's driving to work.* **3** (formal) used when you are contrasting two ideas □ *sementara; manakala; sedangkan*: *Some countries are rich, while others are extremely poor.* **SYN** **whereas** ⊃ note at **difference**

while² /waɪl/ *noun* [sing] a (usually short) period of time □ *sebentar; seketika*: *Let's sit down here for a while.*
IDM **once in a while** ⊃ **once**
worth sb's while ⊃ **worth¹**

while³ /waɪl/ *verb*
PHR V **while sth away** to pass time in a lazy or relaxed way □ *menghabiskan masa*: *We whiled away the evening chatting and listening to music.*

whim /wɪm/ *noun* [C] a sudden idea or desire to do sth (often sth that is unusual or not necessary) □ *kerenah; (kerana) teragak*: *I bought a guitar on a whim.*

whimper /ˈwɪmpə(r)/ *verb* [I] to make weak crying sounds, especially with fear or pain □ *merengek* ▶**whimper** *noun* [C]

whine /waɪn/ *verb* **1** [I,T] to complain about sth in an annoying, crying voice □ *merungut; merengek*: *The children were whining all afternoon.* **2** [I] to make a long high unpleasant sound because you are in pain or unhappy □ *memeking*: *The dog is whining to go out.* ▶**whine** *noun* [C]

whip¹ /wɪp/ *noun* [C] **1** a long thin piece of leather, etc. with a handle, that is used for making animals go faster and for hitting people as a punishment □ *cemeti; cambuk*: *He cracked the whip and the horse leapt forward.* **2** (in Britain and the US) an official of a political party who makes sure that all members vote in parliament on important matters □ *ahli parti politik di parlimen*

yg memastikan semua ahli partinya mengundi mengikut kehendak parti

whip² /wɪp/ *verb* (whipping; whipped)
▶HIT PERSON/ANIMAL **1** [T] to hit a person or an animal hard with a **whip**, as a punishment or to make them or it go faster or work harder □ *menyebat*
▶MOVE QUICKLY **2** [I] (*informal*) to move quickly, suddenly or violently □ *meluru; kelencong; berpusing*: *She whipped round to see what had made the noise behind her.* **3** [T] to remove or pull sth quickly and suddenly □ *mengeluarkan*: *He whipped out a pen and made a note of the number.*
▶MIX **4** [T] **whip sth (up)** to mix the white part of an egg, cream, etc. until it is stiff □ *memukul; memutar*: *whipped cream*
▶STEAL **5** [T] (*BrE informal*) to steal sth □ *mengebas; mencuri*: *Who's whipped my pen?*
PHR V **whip through sth** (*informal*) to do or finish sth very quickly □ *membuat atau menyiapkan sst cepat-cepat*: *I whipped through my homework in ten minutes.*
whip sb/sth up to deliberately try to make people excited or feel strongly about sth □ *merangsangkan sso; membangkitkan sst*: *to whip up excitement*
whip sth up (*informal*) to prepare food quickly □ *menyediakan makanan dgn cepat*: *to whip up a quick snack*

whir (*especially AmE*) = **whirr**

whirl¹ /wɜːl/ *verb* [I,T] to move, or to make sb/sth move, round and round very quickly in a circle □ *berpusing-pusing; memusing-musingkan*: *The dancers whirled round the room.* ◆ (*figurative*) *I couldn't sleep. My mind was whirling after all the excitement.*

whirl² /wɜːl/ *noun* [sing] **1** the action or sound of sth moving round and round very quickly □ *putaran; pusaran*: *the whirl of the helicopter's blades* **2** a state of confusion or excitement □ *pusing*: *My head's in a whirl—I'm so excited.* **3** a number of events or activities happening one after the other □ *kesibukan*: *The next few days passed in a whirl of activity.*
IDM **give sth a whirl** (*informal*) to try sth to see if you like it or can do it □ *mencuba sst*

whirlpool /ˈwɜːlpuːl/ *noun* [C] a place in a river or the sea where currents in the water move very quickly round in a circle □ *lubuk pusar*

whirlwind /ˈwɜːlwɪnd/ *noun* [C] a very strong wind that moves very fast in a circle □ *angin puting beliung* **SYN** **tornado**

whirr (*especially AmE* **whir**) /wɜː(r)/ *verb* [I] to make a continuous low sound like the parts of a machine moving □ *deruan; dengung*: *The noise of the fan whirring kept me awake.* ▶**whirr** (*especially AmE* **whir**) *noun* [C, usually sing]

whisk¹ /wɪsk/ *verb* [T] **1** to beat or mix eggs, cream, etc. together fast using a fork or a **whisk** □ *memutar; memukul*: *Whisk the egg whites un-*

whisk → who

...til stiff. **SYN** beat 2 to take sb/sth somewhere very quickly □ *membawa pergi dgn cepat*: *The prince was whisked away in a black limousine.*

whisk² /wɪsk/ noun [C] a tool that you use for beating eggs, cream, etc. very fast □ *pemutar* ⊃ picture at **kitchen**, **mixer**

whisker /ˈwɪskə(r)/ noun [C] one of the long thick hairs that grow near the mouth of some animals such as a mouse, cat, etc. □ *misai (binatang)* ⊃ picture on **page P12**

whisky /ˈwɪski/ noun (pl whiskies) **HELP** In the US and Ireland the spelling is **whiskey**. 1 [U] a strong alcoholic drink that is made from grain and is sometimes drunk with water and/or ice □ *wiski*: *Scotch whisky* 2 [C] a glass of **whisky** □ *segelas wiski*

whisper /ˈwɪspə(r)/ verb [I,T] to speak very quietly into sb's ear, so that other people cannot hear what you are saying □ *membisikkan; berbisik*: *She whispered something in his ear.* ◆ *What are you two whispering about?* ▶**whisper** noun [C]: *to speak in a whisper*

whistle¹ /ˈwɪsl/ noun [C] 1 a small metal or plastic tube that you blow into to make a long high sound □ *wisel*: *The referee blew his whistle to stop the game.* 2 the sound made by blowing a **whistle** or by blowing air out between your lips □ *(bunyi) wisel; siulan*: *United scored just moments before the final whistle.* ◆ *He gave a low whistle of surprise.* 3 a sound made by air or steam being forced through a small opening, or by sth moving quickly through the air □ *siulan (cerek)*: *the whistle of a boiling kettle*

whistle

whistle² /ˈwɪsl/ verb 1 [I,T] to make a musical or a high sound by forcing air out between your lips or by blowing a **whistle** □ *bersiul*: *He whistled a tune to himself.* 2 [I] to move somewhere quickly making a sound like a **whistle** □ *berdesing*: *A bullet whistled past his head.*

white¹ /waɪt/ adj (whiter; whitest) 1 having the very light colour of fresh snow or milk □ *putih*: *a white shirt* ◆ *white coffee* (= with milk) ◆ *white bread* 2 (used about a person) belonging to or connected with a race of people who have pale skin □ *(orang) kulit putih*: *white middle-class families* 3 **white (with sth)** (used about a person) very pale because you are ill, afraid, etc. □ *pucat*: *to be white with shock/anger/fear* ◆ *She went white as a sheet when they told her the news.*
IDM black and white ⊃ **black¹**

white² /waɪt/ noun 1 [U] the very light colour of fresh snow or milk □ *(warna) putih*: *She was dressed in white.* 2 [C, usually pl] a member of a race of people with pale skin □ *orang kulit putih* 3 [C,U] the part of an egg that surrounds the **yolk** (= the yellow part) and that becomes white when it is cooked □ *putih telur*: *Beat the whites of four eggs.* ⊃ picture at **egg** 4 [C] the white part of the eye □ *bahagian putih (mata)*: *The whites of her eyes were bloodshot.*
IDM in black and white ⊃ **black²**

whiteboard /ˈwaɪtbɔːd/ noun [C] a large board with a smooth white surface that teachers, etc. write on with special pens □ *papan putih* ⊃ look at **interactive whiteboard**

ˌwhite-ˈcollar adj (used about work) done in an office not a factory; (used about people) who work in an office □ *kolar putih* ⊃ look at **blue-collar**

ˌwhite ˈelephant noun [usually sing] something that you no longer need and that is not useful any more, although it cost a lot of money □ *spt gajah putih (sst yg tdk berguna lagi)*

the ˌWhite ˈHouse noun [sing] 1 the large house in Washington D.C. where the US president lives and works □ *Rumah Putih (kediaman Presiden AS)* 2 used to refer to the US president and the other people in the government who work with him or her □ *Rumah Putih (Presiden AS dan kakitangan kerajaan yg bekerja dgnnya)*

ˌwhite ˈlie noun [C] a lie that is not very harmful or serious, especially one that you tell because the truth would hurt sb □ *bohong sunat*

whitewash¹ /ˈwaɪtwɒʃ/ (AmE also) / noun 1 [U] a white liquid that you use for painting walls □ *cat kapur* 2 [sing] an attempt to try to hide unpleasant facts about sb/sth □ *usaha utk mengelabui mata orang*: *The opposition say the report is a whitewash.*

whitewash² /ˈwaɪtwɒʃ/ (AmE also) / verb [T] 1 to paint **whitewash** onto a wall □ *menyapu cat kapur* 2 to try to hide sth bad or wrong that you have done □ *mengelabui mata orang*

ˌwhite-water ˈrafting noun [U] the sport of travelling in a rubber boat down a section of a river where water is moving very fast □ *merakit redah jeram* ⊃ picture on **page P5**

whizz¹ (especially AmE whiz) /wɪz/ verb [I] (informal) to move very quickly, often making a high continuous sound □ *meluru; berdesing; bersiung*: *The racing cars went whizzing past.*

whizz² (especially AmE whiz) /wɪz/ noun [C] (informal) a person who is very good and successful at sth □ *orang yg pandai/handal (ttg sst)*: *She's a whizz at crosswords.* ◆ *He's our new marketing whizz-kid* (= a young person who is very good at sth).

who /huː/ pron 1 used in questions to ask sb's name, identity, position, etc. □ *siapa*: *Who was on the phone?* ◆ *Who's that woman in the grey suit?* ◆ *She wondered who he was.* 2 used for saying exactly which person or what kind of person you are talking about □ *yg*: *I like people who say what they think.* ◆ *That's the man who I met at Ann's party.* ◆ *The woman who I work for is very nice.*

ð **th**en s **s**o z **z**oo ʃ **sh**e ʒ vi**s**ion h **h**ow m **m**an n **n**o ŋ si**ng** l **l**eg r **r**ed j **y**es w **w**et

who'd → why

GRAMMAR In the last two examples (= when 'who' is the object, or when it is used with a preposition) 'who' is usually left out: *That's the man I met at Ann's party.* ◆ *The woman I work for is very nice.*

3 used for giving extra information about sb □ *yg*: *My grandmother, who's over 80, still drives a car.* ⊃ note at **whom**

GRAMMAR Note that the extra information you give is separated from the main clause by commas.

who'd /huːd/ short for **who had**; **who would**

whoever /huːˈevə(r)/ *pron* **1** the person or people who; any person who □ *siapa-siapa sahaja*: *I want to speak to whoever is in charge.* **2** it does not matter who □ *walau siapa-siapa pun*: *She doesn't want to see anybody—whoever it is.* **3** (used for expressing surprise) who □ *siapa*: *Whoever could have done that?*

whole¹ /həʊl/ *adj* **1** [only *before* a noun] complete; full □ *kesemua; seluruh; penuh*: *I drank a whole bottle of water.* ◆ *Let's just forget the whole thing.* ◆ *She wasn't telling me the whole truth.* **2** not broken or cut □ *bulat-bulat; sebiji-sebiji; tdk pecah*: *Snakes swallow their prey whole* (= in one piece). ⊃ adverb **wholly**

whole² /həʊl/ *noun* [C] **1** a thing that is complete or full in itself □ *keseluruhan; sst yg lengkap*: *Two halves make a whole.* **2 the whole of sth** all that there is of sth □ *seluruh; sepanjang*: *I spent the whole of the morning cooking.*

IDM **as a whole** as one complete thing or unit and not as separate parts □ *secara keseluruhannya*: *This is true in Britain, but also in Europe as a whole.*

on the whole generally, but not true in every case □ *umumnya; pd keseluruhannya*: *On the whole I think it's a very good idea.*

wholefood /ˈhəʊlfuːd/ *noun* [U] (also [pl] **wholefoods**) food that is considered healthy because it does not contain artificial substances and is produced as naturally as possible □ *makanan lengkap/asli*

wholehearted /ˌhəʊlˈhɑːtɪd/ *adj* complete and enthusiastic □ *sepenuh hati; bersungguh-sungguh*: *to give somebody your wholehearted support* ▶ **wholeheartedly** *adv*

wholemeal /ˈhəʊlmiːl/ (also **wholewheat** /ˈhəʊlwiːt/) *adj* (made from flour) that contains all the grain including the outside layer □ *mil penuh; gandum tulen*: *wholemeal bread/flour*

wholesale /ˈhəʊlseɪl/ *adv, adj* [only *before* a noun] **1** connected with buying and selling goods in large quantities, especially in order to sell them again and make a profit □ *borong*: *They get all their building materials wholesale.* ◆ *wholesale goods/prices* ⊃ look at **retail 2** (usually about sth bad) very great; on a very large scale □ *secara besar-besaran*: *the wholesale slaughter of wildlife*

wholesome /ˈhəʊlsəm/ *adj* **1** good for your health □ *selamat dimakan; yg menyegarkan/ menyihatkan*: *simple wholesome food* **2** having a moral effect that is good □ *sihat; baik*: *clean wholesome fun*

who'll /huːl/ short for **who will**

wholly /ˈhəʊlli/ *adv* (*formal*) completely; fully □ *sepenuhnya*: *George is not wholly to blame for the situation.*

whom /huːm/ *pron* (*formal*) used instead of 'who' as the object of a verb or preposition □ *siapa*: *Whom did you meet there?* ◆ *He asked me whom I had met.* ◆ *To whom am I speaking?*

HELP In very formal English we say 'He asked me **with whom** I had discussed it'. We usually say 'He asked me **who** I had discussed it **with**'.

whooping cough /ˈhuːpɪŋ kɒf/ *noun* [U] a serious disease, especially of children, which makes them cough loudly and not be able to breathe easily □ *batuk kokol*

whoops /wʊps/ *exclam* used when you have, or nearly have, a small accident, or say or do sth embarrassing □ *op; alamak!*: *Whoops! I nearly dropped the cup.*

whoosh /wʊʃ/ *noun* [C, usually sing] (*informal*) the sudden movement and sound of air or water going past very fast □ *desiran* ▶ **whoosh** *verb* [I]

who're /ˈhuːə(r)/ short for **who are**

who's /huːz/ short for **who is**; **who has**

whose /huːz/ *determiner, pron* **1** (used in questions to ask who sth belongs to) of whom? □ *siapa punya*: *Whose car is that?* ◆ *Whose is that car?* ◆ *Those are nice shoes—I wonder whose they are.* **2** (used to say exactly which person or thing you mean, or to give extra information about a person or thing) of whom; of which □ *yg ...-nya*: *That's the boy whose mother I met.* ◆ *My neighbours, whose house is up for sale, are splitting up.*

GRAMMAR When using 'whose' to give extra information about a person or thing, you should separate that part of the sentence from the main clause with commas.

who've /huːv/ short for **who have**

why /waɪ/ *adv* **1** for what reason □ *mengapa; kenapa*: *Why was she so late?* ◆ *I wonder why they went.* ◆ *'I'm not staying any longer.' 'Why not?'* **2** used for giving or talking about a reason for sth □ *mengapa; kenapa; sebab*: *The reason why I'm leaving you is obvious.* ◆ *I'm tired and that's why I'm in such a bad mood.*

IDM **why ever** used to show that you are surprised or angry □ *mengapa; entah mengapalah*: *Why ever didn't you phone?*

why not? used for making or agreeing to a suggestion □ *mengapa tdk; digunakan dgn maksud 'ya' atau 'baiklah'*: *Why not phone her tonight?* ◆ *'Shall we go out tonight?' 'Yes, why not?'*

VOWELS iː see i any ɪ sit e ten æ hat ɑː father ɒ got ɔː saw ʊ put uː too u usual

wick /wɪk/ noun [C] the piece of string that burns in the middle of a **candle** (= a tall stick that you burn to give light) □ *sumbu* ⮞ picture at **candle**

wicked /ˈwɪkɪd/ adj (**wickeder**; **wickedest**) [You can also use **more wicked** and **most wicked**.] **1** morally bad; evil □ *sangat jahat; kejam* **2** (*informal*) slightly bad but in a way that is amusing and/or attractive □ *nakal*: *a wicked sense of humour* **3** (*slang*) very good □ *sangat baik*: *This song's wicked.* ▶**wickedly** adv ▶**wickedness** noun [U]

wicker /ˈwɪkə(r)/ noun [U] thin sticks of wood that bend easily and are crossed over and under each other to make furniture and other objects □ *rotan yg dianyam utk membuat bakul atau perabot*: *a wicker basket* ⮞ picture at **basket**

wicket /ˈwɪkɪt/ noun [C] **1** (in the sport of **cricket**) either of the two sets of three vertical sticks that the player throwing the ball tries to hit □ *wiket* ⮞ picture on **page P4 2** (in the sport of **cricket**) the area of ground between the two **wickets** □ *wiket*

wide /waɪd/ adj (**wider**; **widest**)
▶MEASUREMENT **1** measuring a lot from one side to the other □ *lebar; luas*: *The road was not wide enough for two cars to pass.* ♦ *a wide river* OPP **narrow** ⮞ note at **broad 2** measuring a particular distance from one side to the other □ *lebar; lebarnya*: *The box was only 20 centimetres wide.* ♦ *How wide is the river?* ⮞ noun **width**
▶LARGE NUMBER/AMOUNT **3** including a large number or variety of different people or things; covering a large area □ *luas; pelbagai; beraneka*: *You're the nicest person in the whole wide world!* ♦ *a wide range/choice/variety of goods* ♦ *a manager with wide experience of industry*
▶OPEN **4** fully open □ *luas*: *The children's eyes were wide with excitement.*
▶NOT NEAR **5** not near what you wanted to touch or hit □ *tersasar; tdk kena sasaran*: *His first serve was wide* (for example in tennis). ▶**wide** adv: *Open your mouth wide.* ♦ *It was late but she was still wide awake.*

widely /ˈwaɪdli/ adv by a lot of people; in or to many places □ *secara meluas*: *Steve travelled widely in his youth.* ♦ *Her books are widely read* (= a lot of people read them). ♦ *He's an educated, widely-read man* (= he has read a lot of books).

widen /ˈwaɪdn/ verb [I,T] to become wider; to make sth wider □ *meluaskan; melebarkan; menjadi lebar*: *The road widens just up ahead.*

wide-ranging adj covering a large area or many subjects □ *berbagai-bagai; beraneka*: *a wide-ranging discussion*

widespread /ˈwaɪdspred/ adj found or happening over a large area; affecting a large number of people □ *meluas*: *The storm has caused widespread damage.*

widget /ˈwɪdʒɪt/ noun [C] **1** (*informal*) used to refer to any small device that you do not know the name of □ *widget; peranti kecil* **2** a small box on a web page that gives changing information, such as news items or weather reports, while the rest of the page remains the same □ *widget; kotak kecil pd laman web yg berganti-ganti maklumatnya*: *This widget is a link to the latest news headlines.*

widow /ˈwɪdəʊ/ noun [C] a woman whose husband has died and who has not married again □ *balu* ▶**widowed** adj: *She's been widowed for ten years now.*

widower /ˈwɪdəʊə(r)/ noun [C] a man whose wife has died and who has not married again □ *duda*

width /wɪdθ/ noun **1** [C,U] the amount that sth measures from one side or edge to the other □ *lebar; lebarnya; kelebaran*: *The room is eight metres in width.* ♦ *The carpet is available in two different widths.* ⮞ adjective **wide** ⮞ picture at **length 2** [C] the distance from one side of a swimming pool to the other □ *lebar kolam renang*: *How many widths can you swim?* ⮞ look at **length, breadth**

wield /wiːld/ verb [T] **1** to have and use power, authority, etc. □ *mempunyai; memiliki*: *She wields enormous power in the company.* **2** to hold and be ready to use a weapon □ *mengacu-acukan (senjata, dsb)*: *Some of the men were wielding knives.*

wiener /ˈwiːnə(r)/ (*AmE*) = **frankfurter**

wife /waɪf/ noun [C] (*pl* **wives** /waɪvz/) the woman to whom a man is married □ *isteri*: *She's his second wife.* ♦ *a doctor's wife* ♦ *husband and wife*

Wi-Fi™ /ˈwaɪ faɪ/ noun [U] **wireless fidelity**; a system for sending data over computer networks using radio waves instead of wires □ *Wi-Fi; sistem penghantaran data wayarles*: *Wi-Fi Internet access* ♦ *a Wi-Fi connection*

wig /wɪɡ/ noun [C] a covering made of real or false hair that you wear on your head □ *rambut palsu*

wiggle /ˈwɪɡl/ verb [I,T] (*informal*) to move from side to side with small quick movements; to make sth do this □ *menggoyang-goyangkan; bergoyang-goyang*: *You have to wiggle your hips in time to the music.* ▶**wiggle** noun [C] ▶**wiggly** /ˈwɪɡli/ adj: *She drew a wiggly line.* SYN **wavy**

wigwam /ˈwɪɡwæm/ noun [C] a type of tent that was used by some Native Americans in past times □ *khemah kaum peribumi Amerika*

wiki /ˈwɪki/ noun [C] a website that allows any user to change or add to the information it contains □ *laman web yg membenarkan pengguna mengubah atau menambah maklumat pd laman itu*: *The company has a wiki where we can share ideas and information.* ♦ *a wiki page*

wild¹ /waɪld/ adj (**wilder**; **wildest**)
▶ANIMAL/PLANT **1** living or growing in natural conditions, not looked after by people □ *liar;*

wild → wily

(*pokok/tumbuhan*) *hutan*: *wild animals/ flowers/strawberries*
►LAND **2** in its natural state; not changed by people □ *tdk dihuni manusia*: *the wild plains of Siberia*
►WITHOUT CONTROL **3** (used about a person or their behaviour or emotions) without control or discipline; slightly crazy □ *liar; tdk dikawal*: *The crowd went wild with excitement.* ♦ *They let their children run wild* (= behave in a free way, without enough control).
►NOT SENSIBLE **4** not carefully planned; not sensible or accurate □ *secara rambang; melulu*: *She made a wild guess.* ♦ *wild accusations/rumours*
►LIKING STH/SB **5** (*informal*) **wild (about sb/sth)** liking sb/sth very much □ *tergila-gila; suka sangat*: *I'm not wild about the band's new album.*
►WEATHER **6** with strong winds or storms □ (*ada*) *ribut; bergelora*: *It was a wild night last night.*
►**wildly** *adv* ►**wildness** *noun* [U]

wild² /waɪld/ *noun* **1 the wild** [sing] a natural environment that is not controlled by people □ *hutan; persekitaran tabii*: *the thrill of seeing elephants in the wild* **2 the wilds** [pl] places that are far away from towns, where few people live □ *kawasan terpencil*: *They live somewhere out in the wilds.*

wilderness /ˈwɪldənəs/ *noun* [C, usually sing] **1** a large area of land that has never been used for building on or for growing things □ *tanah gersang; kawasan liar; hutan*: *The Antarctic is the world's last great wilderness.* **2** a place that people do not take care of or control □ *kawasan terbiar; semak*: *Their garden is a wilderness.*

wildlife /ˈwaɪldlaɪf/ *noun* [U] animals, birds, insects, etc. that are wild and live in a natural environment □ *hidupan liar*

wilful (*AmE also* **willful**) /ˈwɪlfl/ *adj* **1** done deliberately although the person doing it knows that it is wrong □ *yg sengaja; disengajakan*: *wilful damage/neglect* **2** doing exactly what you want, no matter what other people think or say □ *keras kepala*: *a wilful child* ►**wilfully** /-fəli/ *adv*

will¹ /wɪl/ *modal verb* (*short form* '**ll** /l/; *negative will not*; *short form* **won't** /wəʊnt/; *pt* **would** /wəd/; *short form* '**d** /d/; *negative would not*; *short form* **wouldn't** /ˈwʊdnt/) **1** used in forming the future tenses □ *akan*: *He'll be here soon.* ♦ *I'm sure you'll pass your exam.* ♦ *I'll be sitting on the beach this time next week.* ♦ *Next Sunday, they will have been in England for a year.* **2** used for showing that sb is offering sth or wants to do sth, or that sth is able to do sth □ *akan; hendak*: '*We need some more milk.*' '*OK, I'll get it.*' ♦ *Why won't you tell me where you were last night?* ♦ *My car won't start.* **3** used for asking sb to do sth □ *tolong; bolehkah*: *Will you sit down, please?* **4** used for ordering sb to do sb □ *tolong; minta; hendaklah*: *Will you all be quiet!* **5** used for saying that you think sth is probably true □ *agaknya*: *That'll be the postman at the door.* ♦ *He'll have left work by now, I suppose.* **6** [only in positive sentences] used for talking about habits □ *digunakan utk menyatakan sst yg menyakitkan hati yg biasa atau sering dibuat oleh sso*: *She'll listen to music, alone in her room, for hours.*

HELP If you put extra stress on 'will' in this meaning, it shows that the habit annoys you: *He **will** keep interrupting me when I'm trying to work.*

ℹ For more information about modal verbs, look at the **Reference Section** at the back of this dictionary.

will² /wɪl/ *verb* [T] to use the power of your mind to do sth or to make sth happen □ *memaksa diri*: *He willed himself to carry on to the end of the race.*

will³ /wɪl/ *noun* **1** [C,U] the power of the mind to choose what to do; a feeling of strong determination □ *semangat; keinginan*: *Both her children have got very strong wills.* ♦ *My father seems to have lost the will to live.* **2** [sing] what sb wants to happen in a particular situation □ *kehendak*: *My mother doesn't want to sell the house and I don't want to go against her will.* **3** [C] a legal document in which you write down who should have your money and property after your death □ *wasiat*: *You really ought to make a will.* ♦ *Gran left us some money in her will.* **4 -willed** [in compounds] having the type of will mentioned □ *semangat*: *a strong-willed/weak-willed person*

IDM **of your own free will** ➔ **free¹**

willing /ˈwɪlɪŋ/ *adj* [not before a noun] **1 willing (to do sth)** happy to do sth; having no reason for not doing sth □ *sanggup; bersedia*: *Are you willing to help us?* ♦ *She's perfectly willing to lend me her car.* ♦ *I'm not willing to take any risks.* **2** ready or pleased to help and not needing to be persuaded; enthusiastic □ *rela; mahu; bersedia*: *a willing helper/volunteer* **OPP** for both meanings **unwilling** ►**willingly** *adv* ►**willingness** *noun* [U, sing]

willow /ˈwɪləʊ/ (*also* **ˈwillow tree**) *noun* [C] a tree with long thin branches that hang down. Willows grow near water. □ *pokok 'willow'*

willpower /ˈwɪlpaʊə(r)/ *noun* [U] determination to do sth; strength of mind □ *keazaman; kekuatan semangat; tekad*: *It takes a lot of willpower to give up smoking.* ♦ *It takes a lot of willpower to lose weight.*

willy /ˈwɪli/ *noun* [C] (*pl* **willies**) (*informal*) a word used by children to refer to the **penis** (= the male sexual organ) □ *kotek; burung; pipit*

willy-nilly /ˌwɪli ˈnɪli/ *adv* (*informal*) **1** if you want to or not □ *mahu tak mahu* **2** in a careless way without planning □ *sesuka hati*: *Don't spend your money willy-nilly.*

wilt /wɪlt/ *verb* [I,T] (used about a plant or person) to bend and become weak, often because of heat or a lack of water □ (*menjadi*) *layu*

wily /ˈwaɪli/ *adj* (**wilier**; **wiliest**) clever at getting what you want □ *licik* **SYN** cunning

wimp /wɪmp/ noun [C] (informal) a weak person who has no courage or confidence □ *orang yg bacul; penakut*: *Don't be such a wimp!* ▶ **wimpish** adj

win /wɪn/ verb (winning; pt, pp won /wʌn/) 1 [I,T] to be the best, first or strongest in a race, game, competition, etc. □ *menang; memenangi*: *to win a game/match/championship* ◆ *I never win at table tennis.* ◆ *Which party do you think will win the next election?* 2 [T] to get money, a prize, etc. as a result of success in a competition, race, etc. □ *memenangi*: *We won a trip to Australia.* ◆ *Who won the gold medal?* ◆ *He won the jackpot in the lottery.*

> **HELP** Note that we **earn** (not **win**) money at our job: *I earn £15 000 a year.*

3 [T] to get sth by hard work, great effort, etc. □ *mendapat; mendapatkan*: *Her brilliant performance won her a great deal of praise.* ◆ *to win support for a plan*
IDM you can't win (informal) there is no way of being completely successful or of pleasing everyone □ *macam mana sekalipun memang tak akan berjaya atau ada saja yg tak kena, tak setuju, tak puas hati, dsb*: *Whatever you do you will upset somebody. You can't win.*
win/lose the toss ⊃ **toss**
PHR V win sb over/round (to sth) to persuade sb to support or agree with you □ *berjaya memujuk atau menawan hati sso*: *They're against the proposal at the moment, but I'm sure we can win them over.*
▶ **win** noun [C]: *We have had two wins and a draw so far this season.* ⊃ **winning**

wince /wɪns/ verb [I] to make a sudden quick movement (usually with a part of your face) to show you are feeling pain or embarrassment □ *menggerenyet*

winch /wɪntʃ/ noun [C] a machine that lifts or pulls heavy objects using a thick chain, rope, etc. □ *kapi; kerekan; takal* ▶ **winch** verb [T]: *The injured climber was winched up into a helicopter.*

winch

wind¹ /wɪnd/ noun 1 [C,U] air that is moving across the surface of the earth □ *angin*: *There was a strong wind blowing.* ◆ *A gust of wind blew his hat off.* ◆ *gale-force/strong/high winds* ◆ *Listen to the wind.* 2 [U] gas that is formed in your stomach □ *angin; kembung perut*: *The baby cries when he has wind.* 3 [U] the breath that you need for doing exercise or playing a musical instrument □ *nafas*: *She stopped running to get her wind back.* 4 [U] (in an **orchestra**) the group of instruments that you play by blowing into them □ *alat tiup*: *the wind section*
IDM get wind of sth (informal) to hear about sth that is secret □ *mendapat tahu sst rahsia*

wind² /wɪnd/ verb [T] 1 to cause sb to have difficulty in breathing □ *menyebabkan sesak nafas; tdk dpt bernafas*: *The punch in the stomach winded her.* 2 to help a baby get rid of painful gas in the stomach by rubbing or gently hitting its back □ *mengurut perut atau menepuk belakang bayi supaya tdk kembung*

wind³ /waɪnd/ verb (pt, pp wound /waʊnd/) 1 [I] (used about a road, path, etc.) to have a lot of bends or curves in it □ *berliku-liku*: *The path winds down the cliff to the sea.* 2 [T] to put sth long round sth else several times □ *melilit; membelit*: *She wound the bandage around his arm.* 3 [T] to make sth work or move by turning a key, handle, etc. □ *memutar; memusing; mengunci (jam)*: *He wound the car window down.* ◆ *He had forgotten to wind his watch.*
PHR V wind down (about a person) to rest and relax after a period of hard work, worry, etc. □ *berehat-rehat* ⊃ look at **unwind**
wind up (informal) to find yourself in a place or situation that you did not intend to be in □ *akhirnya sampai/berada di*: *We got lost and wound up in a dangerous-looking part of town.*
wind sb up to annoy sb until they become angry □ *menyakitkan hati sso*
wind sth up to finish, stop or close sth □ *menamatkan sst; menutup (perniagaan, dsb)*: *The company was losing money and had to be wound up.*

windfall /'wɪndfɔːl/ noun [C] an amount of money that you win or receive unexpectedly □ *durian runtuh; wang yg didapati tanpa disangka-sangka*

'wind farm noun [C] an area of land on which there are a lot of **windmills** or **wind turbines** (= modern windmills) for producing electricity □ *kawasan kincir angin*

winding /'waɪndɪŋ/ adj with bends or curves in it □ *berliku-liku; berpilin-pilin*: *a winding road through the hills*

'wind instrument noun [C] a musical instrument that you play by blowing through it □ *alat tiup*

windmill /'wɪndmɪl/ noun [C] a tall building or structure with long parts called **sails** that turn in the wind. In past times windmills were used for making flour from grain. □ *kincir angin* ⊃ look at **wind turbine**

sail

windmill

window /'wɪndəʊ/ noun [C] 1 the opening in a building, car, etc. that you can see through and that lets light in. A window usually has glass in it □ *tingkap*: *Open the window. It's hot in here.* ◆ *a shop window* ◆ *These windows need cleaning.* ⊃ picture on

window box → winning

page P8 2 an area on a computer screen that has a particular type of information in it □ *tetingkap*: *to open/close a window* 3 a time when you have not arranged to do anything and so are free to meet sb, etc. □ *masa luang*: *I'm busy all Tuesday morning, but I've got a window from 2 until 3.*

'**window box** *noun* a long narrow box outside a window, in which plants are grown □ *kotak bunga di luar tingkap* ⊃ picture on **page P8**

'**window ledge** = windowsill

windowpane /'wɪndəʊpeɪn/ *noun* [C] one piece of glass in a window □ *kaca tingkap*

'**window-shopping** *noun* [U] looking at things in shop windows without intending to buy anything □ *menjamu mata (melihat-lihat barang) di kedai*

windowsill /'wɪndəʊsɪl/ (also '**window ledge**) *noun* [C] the narrow shelf at the bottom of a window, either inside or outside □ *ambang tingkap* ⊃ picture at **curtain** ⊃ picture on **page P8**

windpipe /'wɪndpaɪp/ *noun* [C] the tube that takes air from the throat to the lungs □ *salur udara*

windscreen /'wɪndskriːn/ (*AmE* **windshield**) *noun* [C] the window in the front of a vehicle □ *cermin depan* ⊃ picture on **page P7**

'**windscreen wiper** (also **wiper**, (*AmE*) '**windshield wiper**) *noun* [C] one of the two blades with rubber edges that move across a **windscreen** to make it clear of water, snow, etc. □ *pengelap cermin depan* ⊃ picture at **car**

windshield /'wɪndʃiːld/ (*AmE*) = windscreen

'**windshield wiper** (*AmE*) = windscreen wiper

windsurf /'wɪndsɜːf/ *verb* [I] to move over water standing on a special board with a sail □ *meluncur angin*

HELP We usually say **go windsurfing**: *Have you ever been windsurfing?*

▸windsurfing *noun* [U] ⊃ picture on **page P5**

windsurfer /'wɪndsɜːfə(r)/ *noun* [C] 1 (also **sailboard**) a board with a sail that you stand on as it moves over the surface of the water, pushed by the wind □ *papan peluncur angin* 2 a person who rides on a board like this □ *peluncur angin*

windswept /'wɪndswept/ *adj* 1 (used about a place) that often has strong winds □ *terdedah kpd angin*: *a windswept coastline* 2 looking untidy because you have been in a strong wind □ *ditiup angin (rambut, dsb yg tdk kemas)*: *windswept hair*

'**wind turbine** *noun* [C] a type of modern **windmill** (= a tall building with sails that turn in the wind) used for producing electricity □ *turbin angin*

windy /'wɪndi/ *adj* (**windier**; **windiest**) with a lot of wind □ *berangin*: *a windy day*

wine /waɪn/ *noun* [C,U] an alcoholic drink that is made from **grapes** (= small green or purple fruit that grow in bunches), or sometimes other fruit □ *wain*: *sweet/dry wine* ◆ *German wines* ⊃ look at **beer**

MORE Wine is made in three colours: **red**, **white** and **rosé**. The grapes are grown in a **vineyard** (/'vɪnjəd/).

wing /wɪŋ/ *noun*
▸OF BIRD/INSECT 1 [C] one of the two parts that a bird, an insect, etc. uses for flying □ *sayap; kepak*: *The goose ran around flapping its wings.* ⊃ picture on **page P12**, **page P13**
▸OF PLANE 2 [C] one of the two long parts that stick out from the side of a plane and support it in the air □ *sayap* ⊃ picture on **page P6**
▸OF BUILDING 3 [C] a part of a building that sticks out from the main part or that was added on to the main part □ *sayap; bahagian*: *the maternity wing of the hospital*
▸OF CAR 4 (*AmE* **fender**) [C] the part of the outside of a car that covers the top of the wheels □ *dapra*: *There was a dent in the wing.*
▸OF POLITICAL PARTY 5 [C, usually sing] a group of people in a political party that have particular beliefs or opinions □ *sayap; haluan*: *He's on the right wing of the Conservative Party.* ⊃ look at **left wing**, **right wing**
▸IN FOOTBALL, ETC. 6 [C] the part at each side of the area where the game is played □ *sayap*: *to play on the wing* 7 (also **winger** /'wɪŋə(r)/) [C] a person who plays in an attacking position at one of the sides of the field □ *pemain sayap*
▸IN THEATRE 8 **the wings** [pl] the area at the sides of the stage where the actors cannot be seen by the audience □ *sayap pentas*
IDM **take sb under your wing** to take care of and help sb who has less experience than you □ *menjaga dan membantu sso*

wink /wɪŋk/ *verb* [I] **wink (at sb)** to close and open one eye very quickly, usually as a signal to sb □ *mengenyit* ⊃ picture at **blink**
IDM **forty winks** ⊃ **forty**
▸wink *noun* [C]: *He smiled and gave the little girl a wink.* ◆ *I didn't sleep a wink* (= not at all).

winner /'wɪnə(r)/ *noun* [C] 1 a person or an animal that wins a competition, game, race, etc. □ *pemenang*: *The winner of the competition will be announced next week.* 2 (*informal*) something that is likely to be successful □ *sst yg berjaya*: *I think your idea is a winner.* 3 (in sport) a goal that wins a match, a hit that wins a point, etc. □ *gol, mata, dsb kemenangan*: *Henry scored the winner in the last minute.*

winning /'wɪnɪŋ/ *adj* [only before a noun] that wins or has won sth, for example a race or competition □ *memenangi*: *The winning ticket is number 65.* ◆ *He scored the winning goal in the final.*

winnings /ˈwɪnɪŋz/ noun [pl] money that you win in a competition or game □ *wang kemenangan*

winter /ˈwɪntə(r)/ noun [C,U] the coldest season of the year between autumn and spring □ *musim sejuk*: *It snows a lot here in winter.* ♦ *a cold winter's day* ♦ *We went skiing in France last winter.* ▶ **wintry** /ˈwɪntri/ adj: *wintry weather*

winter ˈsports noun [pl] sports which take place on snow or ice, for example skiing and skating □ *sukan musim sejuk*

wintertime /ˈwɪntətaɪm/ noun [U] the period or season of winter □ *(waktu) musim sejuk*

wipe¹ /waɪp/ verb [T] **1** to clean or dry sth by rubbing it with a cloth, etc. □ *mengelap; mengesat*: *She stopped crying and wiped her eyes with a tissue.* ♦ *Could you wipe the table, please?* ⇒ note at **clean²** **2** wipe sth from/off sth; wipe sth away/off/up to remove sth by rubbing it □ *menyapu; menyapu*: *He wiped the sweat from his forehead.* ♦ *Wipe up the milk you spilled.* **3** wipe sth (off) (sth) to remove sound, information or images from sth □ *memadamkan; menghilangkan; melupakan*: *I accidentally wiped the file.* ♦ *I tried to wipe the memory from my mind.*

PHR V wipe sth out to destroy sth completely □ *memusnahkan; menghapuskan*: *Whole villages were wiped out in the bombing raids.*

wipe² /waɪp/ noun [C] **1** the act of wiping □ *(perbuatan) mengelap/mengesat*: *He gave the table a quick wipe.* **2** a piece of paper or thin cloth that has been made wet with a special liquid and is used for cleaning sth □ *kertas atau kain lap/kesat*: *a box of baby wipes*

wiper /ˈwaɪpə(r)/ = windscreen wiper

wire¹ /ˈwaɪə(r)/ noun [C,U] **1** metal in the form of thin thread; a piece of this □ *dawai; kawat*: *a piece of wire* ♦ *Twist those two wires together.* ♦ *a wire fence* **2** a piece of wire that is used to carry electricity □ *wayar*: *telephone wires*

wire² /ˈwaɪə(r)/ verb [T] **1** wire sth (up) (to sth) to connect sth to a supply of electricity or to a piece of electrical equipment by using wires □ *mendawaikan; memasang wayar (pd sst)*: *to wire a plug* ♦ *The microphone was wired up to a loudspeaker.* **2** wire sth (to sb); wire sb sth to send money to sb's bank account using an electronic system □ *mengirim (wang) melalui sistem elektronik*: *The bank's going to wire me the money.* **3** to join two things together using wire □ *menyambung dgn dawai*

wireless /ˈwaɪələs/ adj not using wires □ *wayarles; tanpa wayar*: *wireless technology/communications*

wiring /ˈwaɪərɪŋ/ noun [U] the system of wires that supplies electricity to rooms in a building or to parts of a machine □ *pendawaian*

wiry /ˈwaɪəri/ adj (wirier; wiriest) (used about a person) small and thin but strong □ *kurus tetapi kuat*

wisdom /ˈwɪzdəm/ noun [U] the ability to make sensible decisions and judgements because of your knowledge or experience □ *kebijaksanaan; kearifan*: *I don't see the wisdom of this plan* (= I do not think that it is a good idea). ⇒ adjective **wise**

ˈwisdom tooth noun [C] one of the four teeth at the back of your mouth that do not grow until you are an adult □ *gigi bongsu*

wise /waɪz/ adj (wiser; wisest) **1** (used about people) able to make sensible decisions and give good advice because of the experience and knowledge that you have □ *bijak; arif*: *a wise old man* **2** (used about actions) sensible; based on good judgement □ *bijak; arif*: *a wise decision* ♦ *It would be wiser to wait for a few days.*
IDM none the wiser/worse ⇒ **none²**
▶ **wisely** adv

wish¹ /wɪʃ/ verb **1** [T] [often with a verb in the past tense] wish (that) to want sth that cannot now happen or that probably will not happen □ *kalaulah; hendaknya*: *I wish I had listened more carefully.* ♦ *I wish that I knew what was going to happen.* ♦ *I wish I was taller.* ♦ *I wish I could help you.*

HELP In formal English we use **were** instead of **was** with 'I' or 'he/she': *I wish I were rich.* ♦ *She wishes she were in a different class.*

2 [I,T] (formal) wish (to do sth) to want to do sth □ *ingin; mahu*: *I wish to make a complaint about one of the doctors.* **3** [I] wish for sth to think very hard that you want sth, especially sth that can only be achieved by good luck or magic □ *mengharapkan; menginginkan*: *She shut her eyes and wished for him to get better.* ♦ *It's no use wishing for the impossible.* **4** [T] to say that you hope sb will have sth □ *mengucapkan*: *I rang him up to wish him a happy birthday.* ♦ *We wish you all the best for your future career.*

wish² /wɪʃ/ noun **1** [C] a feeling that you want to have sth or that sth should happen □ *hasrat; keinginan; kemahuan; harapan*: *I have no wish to see her ever again.* ♦ *Doctors should respect the patient's wishes.* **2** [C] a try at making sth happen by thinking hard about it, especially in stories when it often happens by magic □ *keinginan; hajat*: *Throw a coin into the fountain and make a wish.* ♦ *My wish came true* (= I got what I asked for). **3** wishes [pl] a hope that sb will be happy or have good luck □ *ucap selamat*: *Please give your parents my best wishes.* ♦ *Best Wishes* (= at the end of a letter)

ˌwishful ˈthinking noun [U] ideas that are based on what you would like, not on facts □ *angan-angan* ⇒ look at **thinking**

wisp /wɪsp/ noun [C] **1** a small, thin piece of hair, grass, etc. □ *sedikit/beberapa helai rambut* **2** a small amount of smoke □ *jaluran; kepulan* ▶ **wispy** adj

wistful /ˈwɪstfl/ adj feeling or showing sadness because you cannot have what you want □ *sayu*: *a wistful sigh* ▶ **wistfully** /-fəli/ adv

wit /wɪt/ noun [U] **1** the ability to use words in a clever and amusing way □ *kebolehan berjenaka pintar* ⊃ adjective **witty 2 wits** [pl] your ability to think quickly and clearly and to make good decisions □ *kepintaran*: *The game of chess is essentially a battle of wits.* **3 -witted** [in compounds] having a particular type of intelligence □ *digunakan dlm kata majmuk dgn maksud mempunyai jenis atau taraf kecerdasan yg disebutkan*: *quick-witted ◆ slow-witted*
IDM **at your wits' end** not knowing what to do or say because you are very worried □ *mati akal* **keep your wits about you** to be ready to act in a difficult situation □ *berwaspada; berhati-hati*

witch /wɪtʃ/ noun [C] (in past times and in stories) a woman who is thought to have magic powers □ *perempuan sihir* ⊃ look at **wizard**

witchcraft /ˈwɪtʃkrɑːft/ noun [U] the use of magic powers, especially evil ones □ *ilmu sihir; ilmu hitam*

with /wɪð; wɪθ/ prep **1** in the company of sb/sth; in or to the same place as sb/sth □ *bersama; dgn*: *I live with my parents. ◆ Are you coming with us? ◆ I talked about the problem with my tutor.* **2** having or carrying sth □ *mempunyai; membawa*: *a girl with red hair ◆ a house with a garden ◆ the man with the suitcase* **3** using sth □ *dgn (menggunakan sst)*: *Cut it with a knife. ◆ I did it with his help.* **4** used for saying what fills, covers, etc. sth □ *dgn; berisi*: *Fill the bowl with water. ◆ His hands were covered with oil.* **5** in competition with sb/sth; against sb/sth □ *dgn*: *He's always arguing with his brother. ◆ I usually play tennis with my sister.* **6** towards, concerning or compared with sb/sth □ *dgn; pd*: *Is he angry with us? ◆ There's a problem with my visa. ◆ Compared with Canada, England has mild winters.* **7** including sth □ *termasuk*: *The price is for two people with all meals.* **8** used to say how sth happens or is done □ *dgn*: *Open this parcel with care. ◆ to greet somebody with a smile* **9** because of sth; as a result of sth □ *kerana; oleh sebab*: *We were shivering with cold. ◆ With all the problems we've got, we're not going to finish on time.* **10** in the care of sb □ *bersama; dgn; di bawah jagaan*: *We left the keys with the neighbours.* **11** agreeing with or supporting sb/sth □ *bersama; menyokong*: *We've got everybody with us on this issue.* **OPP against 12** at the same time as sth □ *dgn; kerana*: *I can't concentrate with you watching me all the time.*
IDM **be with me/you** (informal) to be able to follow what sb is saying □ *faham (apa yg dikatakan oleh sso)*: *I'm not quite with you. Say it again.*

withdraw /wɪðˈdrɔː; wɪθˈd-/ verb (pt **withdrew** /-ˈdruː/; pp **withdrawn** /-ˈdrɔːn/) **1** [I,T] **withdraw (sb/sth) (from sth)** to move back or away from a place or order sb to move back or away from a place □ *mengundurkan; berundur; menarik balik*: *The troops withdrew from the town.* **2** [T] to remove sth or take sth away □ *menarik balik*: *to withdraw an offer/a statement* **3** [I] to decide not to take part in sth □ *menarik diri*: *Jackson withdrew from the race at the last minute.* **4** [T] to take money out of a bank account □ *mengeluarkan*: *How much would you like to withdraw?* ⊃ note at **money** ⊃ look at **deposit**

withdrawal /wɪðˈdrɔːəl; wɪθˈd-/ noun **1** [C,U] moving or being moved back or away from a place □ *pengunduran*: *the withdrawal of troops from the war zone* **2** [C] taking money out of your bank account; the amount of money that you take out □ *pengeluaran wang*: *to make a withdrawal* **3** [U] the act of stopping doing sth, especially taking a drug □ *pemberhentian (dadah/alkohol)*: *When he gave up alcohol he suffered severe withdrawal symptoms.*

withdrawn¹ past participle of **withdraw**

withdrawn² /wɪðˈdrɔːn; wɪθˈd-/ adj (used about a person) very quiet and not wanting to talk to other people □ *suka menyendiri; menyisihkan diri*

withdrew past tense of **withdraw**

wither /ˈwɪðə(r)/ verb **1** [I,T] **wither (sth) (away)** (used about plants) to become dry and die; to make a plant do this □ *layu; melayukan*: *The plants withered in the hot sun.* **2** [I] **wither (away)** to become weaker then disappear □ *pudar; lenyap*: *This type of industry will wither away in the years to come.*

withering /ˈwɪðərɪŋ/ adj done to make sb feel silly or embarrassed □ *menghina; mencemuh*: *a withering look*

withhold /wɪðˈhəʊld; wɪθˈh-/ verb [T] (pt, pp **withheld** /-ˈheld/) (formal) **withhold sth (from sb/sth)** to refuse to give sth to sb □ *menahan; enggan memberikan*: *to withhold information from the police*

within /wɪˈðɪn/ prep, adv **1** in a period not longer than a particular length of time □ *dlm masa*: *I'll be back within an hour. ◆ She got married, found a job and moved house, all within a month.* **2 within sth (of sth)** not further than a particular distance from sth □ *dlm jarak*: *The house is within a kilometre of the station.* **3** not outside the limits of sb/sth □ *dlm (lingkungan)*: *Each department must keep within its budget.* **4** (formal) inside sb/sth □ *di dlm diri*: *The anger was still there deep within him. ◆ Cleaner required. Apply within* (= come in and ask).

without /wɪˈðaʊt/ prep, adv **1** not having or showing sth □ *tanpa*: *Don't go out without a coat on. ◆ He spoke without much enthusiasm. ◆ If there's no salt, we'll have to manage without.* **2** not using or being with sb/sth □ *tanpa*: *I drink my coffee without milk. ◆ I can't see a thing without my glasses. ◆ Don't leave without me.* **3** used with a verb in the -ing form to mean 'not' □ *tanpa*: *She left without saying goodbye. ◆ I used her phone without her knowing.*

withstand /wɪð'stænd/ verb [T] (pt, pp **withstood** /-'stʊd/) (formal) to be strong enough not to break, give up, be damaged, etc. □ *tahan; dpt bertahan*: *These animals can withstand very high temperatures.*

witness¹ /'wɪtnəs/ noun [C] **1** (also **eyewitness**) a witness (to sth) a person who sees sth happen and who can tell other people about it later □ *saksi; orang yg melihat*: *There were two witnesses to the accident.* **2** a person who appears in a court of law to say what they have seen or what they know about sb/sth □ *saksi*: *a witness for the defence/prosecution* ➔ note at **court 3** a person who sees sb sign an official document and who then signs it himself or herself □ *saksi*: *Mary was one of the witnesses at our wedding.*
IDM bear witness (to sth) ➔ **bear¹**

witness² /'wɪtnəs/ verb [T] **1** to see sth happen and be able to tell other people about it later □ *menyaksikan; melihat*: *to witness a murder* **2** to see sb sign an official document and then sign it yourself □ *menjadi saksi*: *to witness a will*

'witness box (AmE **'witness stand**) noun [C] the place in a court of law where a **witness** stands when he or she is giving evidence □ *kandang saksi*

witty /'wɪti/ adj (**wittier**; **wittiest**) clever and amusing; using words in a clever way □ *pandai berjenaka pintar; lucu*: *a very witty speech* ➔ note at **humour** ➔ noun **wit**

wives plural of **wife**

wizard /'wɪzəd/ noun [C] **1** (in stories) a man who is believed to have magic powers □ *ahli sihir lelaki* ➔ look at **witch, magician 2** a person who is especially good at sth □ *pakar*: *a computer/financial wizard*

wk abbr (pl **wks**) = **week**(1)

wobble /'wɒbl/ verb [I,T] to move from side to side in a way that is not steady; to make sb/sth do this □ *terhuyung-hayang; bergoyang; menggoyang-goyangkan*: *Put something under the leg of the table. It's wobbling.* ◆ *Stop wobbling the desk. I can't write.* ▶ **wobbly** /'wɒbli/ adj

woe /wəʊ/ noun (formal) **1** woes [pl] the problems that sb has □ *kesusahan* **2** [U] (old-fashioned) great unhappiness □ *duka lara; nestapa*
IDM woe betide sb used as a warning that there will be trouble if sb does/does not do a particular thing □ *malanglah nasib nanti*: *Woe betide anyone who yawns while the boss is talking.*

wok /wɒk/ noun [C] a large pan that is shaped like a bowl and used for cooking Chinese food □ *kuali*

woke past tense of **wake¹**

woken past participle of **wake¹**

wolf /wʊlf/ noun [C] (pl **wolves** /wʊlvz/) a wild animal that looks like a dog and that lives and hunts in a group called a **pack** □ *serigala* ➔ picture on **page P12**

woman /'wʊmən/ noun [C] (pl **women** /'wɪmɪn/) **1** an adult female person □ *wanita; orang perempuan*: *men, women and children* ◆ *Would you prefer to see a woman doctor?* **2** -woman [in compounds] a woman who does a particular activity □ *wanita*: *a businesswoman*

womanhood /'wʊmənhʊd/ noun [U] (formal) the state of being a woman □ *(keadaan sebagai) wanita; kewanitaan*

womanly /'wʊmənli/ adj having qualities considered typical of a woman □ *sifat kewanitaan*

womb /wuːm/ noun [C] the part of a woman or female animal where a baby grows before it is born □ *rahim* ➔ A more formal word is **uterus**.

won past tense, past participle of **win**

wonder¹ /'wʌndə(r)/ verb **1** [I,T] wonder (about sth) to want to know sth; to ask yourself questions about sth □ *tertanya-tanya; ingin tahu*: *I wonder what the new teacher will be like.* ◆ *Vesna's been gone a long time—I wonder if she's all right.* ◆ *It was something that she had been wondering about for a long time.* **2** [T] used as a polite way of asking a question or of asking sb to do sth □ *bolehkah; sudikah*: *I wonder if you could help me.* ◆ *I was wondering if you'd like to come to dinner at our house.* **3** [I,T] wonder (at sth) to feel great surprise or admiration □ *berasa hairan; kagum*: *We wondered at the speed with which he worked.* ◆ *'She was very angry.' 'I don't wonder (= I'm not surprised). She had a right to be.'*

wonder² /'wʌndə(r)/ noun **1** [U] a feeling of surprise and admiration □ *kekaguman; kehairanan; (rasa) takjub*: *The children just stared in wonder at the acrobats.* **2** [C] something that causes you to feel surprise or admiration □ *keajaiban*: *the wonders of modern technology*
IDM do wonders (for sb/sth) to have a very good effect on sb/sth □ *sangat berkesan/sangat baik (bagi sso/sst)*: *Working in Mexico did wonders for my Spanish.*
it's a wonder (that)... it's surprising that ... □ *hairan juga...*: *It's a wonder we managed to get here on time, with all the traffic.*
no wonder it is not surprising □ *tak hairanlah; patutlah*: *You've been out every evening this week. No wonder you're tired.*

wonderful /'wʌndəfl/ adj extremely good; great □ *sangat baik; mengagumkan; hebat; seronok*: *What wonderful weather!* ◆ *It's wonderful to see you again.* ➔ note at **good, nice** ▶ **wonderfully** /-fəli/ adv

won't short for **will not**

wood /wʊd/ noun **1** [U,C] the hard substance that trees are made of □ *kayu*: *He chopped some wood for the fire.* ◆ *Pine is a soft wood.* ➔ picture at **tree 2** [C, often plural] an area of land that is covered with trees. A **wood** is smaller than a **forest** □ *hutan kecil*: *a walk in the woods* ➔ note at **forest** ➔ picture on **page P11**

IDM **touch wood**; (*AmE*) **knock on wood** an expression that people use (often while touching a piece of wood) to prevent bad luck □ *minta simpang; semoga dijauhkan (Tuhan)*: *I've been driving here for 20 years and I haven't had an accident yet—touch wood!*

wooded /ˈwʊdɪd/ *adj* (used about an area of land) having a lot of trees growing on it □ *berhutan; banyak pokok*

wooden /ˈwʊdn/ *adj* made of wood □ *(diperbuat drpd) kayu*: *The toys are kept in a wooden box.*

woodland /ˈwʊdlənd/ *noun* [C,U] land that has a lot of trees growing on it □ *kawasan pepohonan*: *The village is surrounded by woodland.*
♦ *woodland birds*

woodwind /ˈwʊdwɪnd/ *noun* [U, with sing or pl verb] the group of musical instruments that you play by blowing into them □ *alat tiup (yg dahulunya dibuat drpd kayu)*: *the woodwind section of the orchestra* ⊃ note at **instrument** ⊃ picture at **music**

woodwork /ˈwʊdwɜːk/ *noun* [U] **1** the parts of a building that are made of wood such as the doors, stairs, etc. □ *bahagian kayu* **2** the activity or skill of making things out of wood □ *pertukangan kayu*

woof /wʊf/ *noun* [C] (*informal*) used for describing the sound that a dog makes □ *kungkung; bunyi salakan anjing* ⊃ look at **bark**

wool /wʊl/ *noun* [U] **1** the soft thick hair of sheep □ *bulu biri-biri* **2** thick thread or cloth that is made from wool □ *benang/kain drpd bulu biri-biri*: *The sweater is 50% wool and 50% acrylic.* ⊃ look at **cotton wool** ⊃ picture at **sew**

woollen (*AmE* **woolen**) /ˈwʊlən/ *adj* made of wool □ *sakhlat; (diperbuat drpd) bulu biri-biri*: *a warm woollen jumper*

woolly (*AmE* **wooly**) /ˈwʊli/ *adj* (**woollier**; **woolliest**; *AmE* **woolier**; **wooliest**) like wool or made of wool □ *(spt atau diperbuat drpd) bulu biri-biri*: *The dog had a thick woolly coat.*
♦ *a warm woolly hat* ⊃ picture at **hat**

word[1] /wɜːd/ *noun* **1** [C] a single unit of language that expresses a particular meaning □ *perkataan; kata*: *What's the Greek word for 'mouth'?* ♦ *What does this word mean?* **2** [C] a thing that you say; a short statement or comment □ *bercakap; cakap; komen, dll*: *Could I have a word with you in private?* ♦ *Don't say a word about this to anyone.* **3** [sing] a promise □ *janji*: *I give you my word that I won't tell anyone.* ♦ *I kept my word to her and lent her the money.* ♦ *I trust him not to go back on his word.*
IDM **a dirty word** ⊃ **dirty**[1]
(not) breathe a word (of/about sth) (to sb) ⊃ **breathe**
not get a word in edgeways to not be able to interrupt when sb else is talking so that you can say sth yourself □ *tdk dpt mencelah pun*
have, etc. the last word ⊃ **last**[1]
in other words ⊃ **other**

977   **wooded → work**

lost for words ⊃ **lost**[2]
put in a (good) word for sb to say sth good about sb to sb else □ *menyokong sso*: *If you could put in a good word for me I might stand a better chance of getting the job.*
take sb's word for it to believe what sb says without any proof □ *menerima/percaya sahaja akan kata-kata sso*
word for word 1 repeating sth exactly □ *mengulangi sepatah demi sepatah*: *Sharon repeated word for word what he had told her.* **2** translating each word separately, not looking at the general meaning □ *menterjemah secara harfiah*: *a word-for-word translation*

word[2] /wɜːd/ *verb* [T, often passive] to write or say sth using particular words □ *menyusun kata-kata*: *The statement was carefully worded so that nobody would be offended by it.*

wording /ˈwɜːdɪŋ/ *noun* [sing] the words that you use to express sth □ *susunan kata-kata*: *The wording of the contract was vague.*

ˌword-ˈperfect *adj* able to say sth that you have learnt from memory, without making a mistake □ *hafaz; lancar*

ˈword processor *noun* [C] (*abbr* **WP**) a type of computer that you can use for writing letters, reports, etc. You can correct or change what you have written before you print it out. □ *pemproses(an) kata* ▶ **ˈword processing** *noun* [U]

wordsearch /ˈwɜːdsɜːtʃ/ *noun* [C] a game consisting of letters arranged in a square, containing several hidden words that you must find □ *carian kata*: *The CD-ROM includes a wordsearch to help you learn new vocabulary.*

wore past tense of **wear**[1]

work[1] /wɜːk/ *verb*
▶DO JOB/TASK **1** [I,T] **work (as sth) (for sb)**; **work (at/on sth)**; **work (to do sth)** to do sth which needs physical or mental effort, in order to earn money or to achieve sth □ *bekerja; membuat sst*: *She's working for a large firm in Glasgow.* ♦ *I'd like to work as a newspaper reporter.* ♦ *Doctors often work extremely long hours.* ♦ *My teacher said that I wouldn't pass the exam unless I worked harder.* ♦ *I hear she's working on a new novel.*
♦ *I'm going to stay in tonight and work at my project.* ⊃ note at **job**, **office**
▶MAKE EFFORT **2** [T] to make yourself/sb work, especially very hard □ *bekerja; menyuruh/mendera sso supaya bekerja*: *The coach works the players very hard in training.*
▶MACHINE **3** [I,T] to function; to make sth function; to operate □ *berfungsi; berjalan; menggunakan*: *Our telephone hasn't been working for several days.* ♦ *We still don't really understand how the brain works.* ♦ *Can you show me how to work the photocopier?*
▶HAVE RESULT **4** [I] to have the result or effect that you want; to be successful □ *berhasil; berjaya*: *Your idea sounds good but I don't think it will really*

[C] **countable**, a noun with a plural form: *one book, two books*   [U] **uncountable**, a noun with no plural form: *some sugar*

work. ◆ *The heat today could work in favour of the African runners.*
▶USE MATERIALS **5** [I,T] to use materials to make a model, a picture, etc. □ *menggunakan*: *He worked the clay into the shape of a horse.* ◆ *She usually works in/with oils or acrylics.*
▶MOVE GRADUALLY **6** [I,T] to move gradually to a new position or state □ *menjadi*: *Engineers check the plane daily, because nuts and screws can work loose.* ◆ *I watched the snail work its way up the wall.*
IDM work/perform miracles ➲ miracle
work to rule to follow the rules of your job in a very strict way in order to cause delay, as a form of protest against your employer or your working conditions □ *kerja ikut peraturan*
PHR V work out **1** to develop or progress, especially in a good way □ *berhasil*: *I hope things work out for you.* **2** to do physical exercises in order to keep your body fit □ *bersenam*: *We work out to music at my exercise class.*
work out (at) to come to a particular result or total after everything has been calculated □ *jumlahnya; hasilnya*: *If we divide the work between us, it'll work out at about four hours each.*
work sb out to understand sb □ *memahami sso*: *I've never been able to work her out.*
work sth out **1** to find the answer to sth; to solve sth □ *mencari penyelesaian; menyelesaikan*: *I can't work out how to do this.* **2** to calculate sth □ *mengira sst*: *I worked out the total cost.* **3** to plan sth □ *merancangkan/mengatur sst*: *Have you worked out the route through France?*
work sth up to develop or improve sth with effort □ *mengusahakan sst*: *I'm trying to work up the energy to go out.*
work sb/yourself up (into sth) to make sb/yourself become angry, excited, upset, etc. □ *menyebabkan sso/diri sendiri berasa sakit hati, terlalu suka, marah, risau, dll*: *He had worked himself up into a state of anxiety about his interview.*
work up to sth to develop or progress to sth □ *meningkat sampai*: *Start with 15 minutes' exercise and gradually work up to 30.*

work² /wɜːk/ noun
▶JOB **1** [U] the job that you do, especially in order to earn money; the place where you do your job □ *pekerjaan; tempat kerja*: *It is very difficult to find work in this city.* ◆ *He's been out of work* (= without a job) *for six months.* ◆ *When do you start work?* ◆ *I'll ask if I can leave work early today.* ◆ *I go to work at 8 o'clock.* ◆ *The people at work gave me some flowers for my birthday.* ◆ *Police work is not as exciting as it looks on TV.* ➲ note at job, routine ➲ look at employment ➲ picture on page P2

OTHER WORDS FOR

work

Work is uncountable in this meaning, so you CANNOT say 'a work' or 'works': *I've found work at the hospital.* **Job** is countable: *I've got a new job at the hospital.* **Employment** is the state of having a paid job and is more formal and official than **work** or **job**: *Many married women are in part-time employment.* **Occupation** is the word used on forms to ask what you are or what job you do: *Occupation—bus driver.* A **profession** is a job that needs special training and higher education: *the medical profession.* A **trade** is a job that you do with your hands and that needs special skill: *He's a carpenter by trade.*

▶EFFORT **2** [U] something that needs physical or mental effort that you do in order to achieve sth □ *kerja; usaha*: *Her success is due to sheer hard work.* ◆ *I've got a lot of work to do today.* ◆ *We hope to start work on the project next week.*
▶PRODUCT OF WORK **3** [U] something that you are working on or have produced □ *hasil kerja/usaha*: *a piece of written work* ◆ *The teacher marked their work.* ◆ *Is this all your own work?*
▶ART **4** [C] a book, painting, piece of music, etc. □ *karya; hasil ciptaan*: *an early work by Picasso* ◆ *the complete works of Shakespeare*
▶BUILDING/REPAIRING **5** works [pl] the act of building or repairing sth □ *kerja pembinaan, membaiki jalan, dsb*: *The roadworks are causing long traffic jams.*
▶FACTORY **6** works [C, with sing or pl verb] [in compounds] a factory □ *kilang*: *The steelworks is/are closing down.*
IDM get/go/set to work (on sth) to begin; to make a start (on sth) □ *memulakan; mula mengerjakan sst*

workable /ˈwɜːkəbl/ *adj* that can be used successfully □ *dpt dilaksanakan; praktikal*: *a workable idea/plan/solution* **SYN** practical

workaholic /ˌwɜːkəˈhɒlɪk/ (*AmE* also) / noun [C] (*informal*) a person who loves work and does too much of it □ *mabuk/gila kerja*

workbench /ˈwɜːkbentʃ/ noun [C] a long heavy table used for doing practical jobs, working with tools, etc. □ *meja kerja (utk mekanik / tukang kayu dsb)*

workbook /ˈwɜːkbʊk/ noun [C] a book with questions and exercises in it that you use when you are studying sth □ *buku kerja*

worker /ˈwɜːkə(r)/ noun [C] **1** [in compounds] a person who works, especially one who does a particular kind of work □ *pekerja*: *factory/office/farm workers* ◆ *skilled/manual workers* **2** a person who is employed to do physical work rather than organizing things or managing people □ *buruh; pekerja*: *Workers' representatives will meet management today to discuss the pay dispute.* **3** a person who works in a particular way □ *pekerja*: *a slow/fast worker*

work experience noun [U] the knowledge and skills that you get from working in a particular job for a short period of time; the process of gaining this □ *pengalaman kerja*: *Students do unpaid work experience in local firms.*

• *Jill is **on work experience** at the local newspaper's offices for a month.*

workforce /ˈwɜːkfɔːs/ noun [C, with sing or pl verb] **1** the total number of people who work in a company, factory, etc. □ *bilangan pekerja* **2** the total number of people in a country who are able to work □ *tenaga kerja*: *Ten per cent of the workforce is/are unemployed.*

working /ˈwɜːkɪŋ/ adj [only before a noun] **1** employed; having a job □ *yg bekerja*: *the problems of childcare for working mothers* **2** connected with your job □ *kerja*: *He stayed with the same company for the whole of his working life.*
• *The company offers excellent working conditions.*
3 good enough to be used, although it could be improved □ *memadai/cukup (utk tujuan tertentu)*: *We are looking for someone with a working knowledge of French.*

IDM **in working order** (used about machines, etc.) working properly, not broken □ *berfungsi; berjalan dgn baik*

the ˌworking ˈclass noun [sing, with sing or pl verb] (also **the ˌworking ˈclasses** [pl]) the group of people in society who do not have much money or power and who usually do physical work, especially in industry □ *kelas; golongan pekerja (buruh)*: *unemployment among the working class* ➲ look at **middle class**, **upper class**
▶ ˌworking-ˈclass adj: *a working-class area/family*

workings /ˈwɜːkɪŋz/ noun [pl] the way in which a machine, an organization, etc. operates □ *cara sst berfungsi*: *It's very difficult to understand the workings of the legal system.*

workload /ˈwɜːkləʊd/ noun [C] the amount of work that you have to do □ *beban kerja; kerja*: *She often gets home late when she has a heavy workload.*

workman /ˈwɜːkmən/ noun [C] (pl **-men** /-mən/) a man who works with his hands, especially at building or making things □ *pekerja mahir/buruh*

workmanlike /ˈwɜːkmənlaɪk/ adj done, made, etc. very well, but not original or exciting □ *cekap; baik buatannya, dsb tetapi tdk ada keaslian atau keistimewaannya*: *a workmanlike performance*

workmanship /ˈwɜːkmənʃɪp/ noun [U] the skill with which sth is made □ *kemahiran; kecekapan*

workmate /ˈwɜːkmeɪt/ noun [C] (especially BrE) a person that you work with, often doing the same job, in an office, a factory, etc. □ *teman sekerja* **SYN** colleague

ˌwork of ˈart noun [C] (pl **works of art**) a painting, book, piece of music, etc., usually one that is well-made □ *karya seni* ➲ look at **art**

workout /ˈwɜːkaʊt/ noun [C] a period of physical exercise, for example when you are training for a sport or keeping fit □ *sesi senaman/latihan*: *She does a twenty-minute workout every morning.*

979   **workforce → world-famous**

workplace /ˈwɜːkpleɪs/ noun [C] often **the workplace** [sing] the office, factory, etc. where people work □ *tempat kerja*: *new technology in the workplace*

worksheet /ˈwɜːkʃiːt/ noun [C] a piece of paper with questions or exercises on it that you use when you are studying sth □ *lembaran kerja*

workshop /ˈwɜːkʃɒp/ noun [C] **1** a place where things are made or repaired □ *bengkel* **2** a period of discussion and practical work on a particular subject, when people share their knowledge and experience □ *bengkel*: *a drama/writing workshop*

workstation /ˈwɜːksteɪʃn/ noun [C] the desk and computer at which a person works; one computer that is part of a system of computers □ *stesen kerja (dgn kelengkapan meja dan komputer)*

worktop /ˈwɜːktɒp/ (also **work surface**, AmE **counter**) noun [C] a flat surface in a kitchen, etc. that you use for preparing food, etc. on □ *permukaan utk kerja dapur* ➲ picture on **page P8**

world /wɜːld/ noun
▶THE EARTH **1 the world** [sing] the earth with all its countries and people □ *dunia*: *a map of the world*
• *the most beautiful place in the world* • *I took a year off work to travel round the world.* • *She is famous all over the world.*
▶COUNTRIES **2** [sing] a particular part of the earth or a group of countries □ *dunia*: *the western world* • *the Arab world* • *the Third World*
▶ANOTHER PLANET **3** [C] a planet with life on it □ *dunia; planet yg ada hidupan*: *Do you believe there are other worlds out there, like ours?*
▶AREA OF ACTIVITY **4** [C] [in compounds] a particular area of activity or group of people or things □ *dunia; alam*: *the world of sport/fashion/politics* • *the medical/business/animal/natural world*
▶LIFE **5** [sing] the life and activities of people; their experience □ *dunia; dunia luar*: *It's time you learned something about the real world!* • *the modern world*
▶PEOPLE **6** [sing] the people in the world □ *seluruh dunia; semua orang*: *The whole world was waiting for news of the astronauts.*

IDM **do sb a/the world of good** (*informal*) to have a very good effect on sb □ *baik utk sso*: *The holiday has done her the world of good.*

in the world used to emphasize what you are saying □ *digunakan utk menegaskan apa yg dikatakan*: *Everyone else is stressed but he doesn't seem to have a care in the world.* • *There's no need to rush—we've got all the time in the world.* • *What in the world are you doing?*

the outside world ➲ **outside²**
think the world of sb/sth ➲ **think**

ˌworld-ˈclass adj as good as the best in the world □ *taraf dunia*: *a world-class athlete*

ˌworld-ˈfamous adj known all over the world □ *terkenal di seluruh dunia*

worldly /'wɜːldli/ adj **1** [only before a noun] connected with ordinary life, not with the spirit □ *duniawi; berkaitan dgn kebendaan*: *He left all his worldly possessions to his nephew.* **2** having a lot of experience and knowledge of life and people □ *berpengalaman; sudah banyak makan asam garam*: *a sophisticated and worldly man*

world 'war noun [C] a war that involves a lot of different countries □ *perang dunia*: *the First World War/World War One* ♦ *the Second World War/World War Two*

worldwide /'wɜːldwaɪd/ adj happening in the whole world □ *di seluruh dunia; sedunia*: *The situation has caused worldwide concern.*
▶ **worldwide** adv /ˌwɜːldˈwaɪd/: *The product will be marketed worldwide.*

the World Wide 'Web (also **the Web**) noun [sing] (abbr **WWW**) the system for finding information on the Internet, in which documents are connected to other documents using special links □ *Web Sedunia* ➡ look at **the Internet**

worm¹ /wɜːm/ noun [C] **1** a small creature with a long thin body and no eyes, bones or legs □ *cacing*: *an earthworm* **2 worms** [pl] one or more **worms** that live inside a person or an animal and may cause disease □ *cacing*: *He's got worms.*

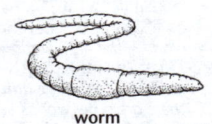

maggot   worm

worm² /wɜːm/ verb [T] **worm your way/yourself along, through, etc.** to move slowly or with difficulty in the direction mentioned □ *menyusup; bergerak perlahan-lahan*: *I managed to worm my way through the crowd.*
PHR V worm your way/yourself into sth to make sb like you or trust you, in order to dishonestly gain an advantage for yourself □ *berjinak-jinak dgn sso dgn tujuan utk mendapat sst*

worn past participle of **wear¹**

worn 'out adj **1** too old or damaged to use any more □ *lusuh; betul-betul lusuh/haus*: *My shoes are completely worn out.* **2** extremely tired □ *lesu; terlalu penat*: *I'm absolutely worn out. I think I'll go to bed early.* ➡ look at **wear**

worried /'wʌrid/ adj **worried (about sb/sth); worried (that …)** thinking that sth bad might happen or has happened □ *runsing; risau; bimbang*: *Don't look so worried. Everything will be all right.* ♦ *I'm worried sick about the exam.* ♦ *We were worried stiff* (= extremely worried) *that you might have had an accident.*

worry¹ /'wʌri/ verb (worrying; worries; pt, pp worried) **1** [I] **worry (about sb/sth)** to think that sth bad might happen or has happened □ *berasa runsing, khuatir atau risau*: *Don't worry—I'm sure everything will be all right.* ♦ *There's nothing to worry about.* ♦ *He worries if I don't phone every weekend.* **2** [T] **worry sb/yourself (about sb/sth)** to make sb/yourself think that sth bad might happen or has happened □ *merunsingkan; mengkhuatirkan; merisaukan*: *What worries me is how are we going to get home?* ♦ *She worried herself sick when he was away in the army.* **3** [T] **worry sb (with sth)** to disturb sb □ *mengganggu; menyusahkan*: *Don't keep worrying him with questions.* **SYN bother**
IDM not to worry it is not important; it does not matter □ *tdk penting; tdk mengapa*
▶ **worrying** adj /'wʌriɪŋ/: *It was a worrying time for us all.*

worry² /'wʌri/ noun (pl worries) **1** [U] the state of worrying about sth □ *kerisauan; kekhuatiran; kebimbangan; kesusahan*: *His son has caused him a lot of worry recently.* **2** [C] something that makes you worry; a problem □ *masalah*: *Crime is a real worry for old people.* ♦ *financial worries*

worse /wɜːs/ adj, adv [the comparative of **bad** or of **badly**] **1** not as good or as well as sth else □ *teruk; lebih buruk*: *My exam results were far/much worse than I thought they would be.* ♦ *She speaks German even worse than I do.* **2** [not before a noun] more ill; less well □ *semakin teruk*: *If you get any worse, we'll call the doctor.*
IDM a change for the better/worse ➡ **change²**
none the wiser/worse ➡ **none²**
to make matters/things worse to make a situation, problem, etc. even more difficult or dangerous than before □ *utk memburukkan keadaan lagi*
the worse for wear (*informal*) damaged; not in good condition □ *lusuh; rosak; tdk berkeadaan baik*: *This suitcase looks a bit the worse for wear.*
worse luck (*spoken*) unfortunately □ *malangnya nasib*: *The dentist says I need three fillings, worse luck!*
▶ **worse** noun [U]: *The situation was already bad but there was worse to come.*

worsen /'wɜːsn/ verb [I,T] to become worse or to make sth worse □ *memburukkan lagi*: *Relations between the two countries have worsened.*

worship /'wɜːʃɪp/ verb (worshipping; worshipped; *AmE* worshiping; worshiped) **1** [I,T] to show respect for God or a god, by saying prayers, singing with others, etc. □ *menyembah; bersembahyang*: *People travel from all over the world to worship at this shrine.* **2** [T] to love or admire sb/sth very much □ *memuji; memuja; mengagung-agungkan*: *She worshipped her husband.* ▶ **worship** noun [U]: *Different religions have different forms of worship.* ▶ **worshipper** (*AmE* **worshiper**) noun [C]

worst¹ /wɜːst/ adj, adv [the superlative of **bad** or of **badly**] the least pleasant or suitable; the least well □ *paling buruk/teruk*: *It's been the worst winter that I can remember.* ♦ *A lot of the children behaved badly but my son behaved worst of all!*

worst² /wɜːst/ noun [sing] **the worst** the most serious or unpleasant thing that could happen □ *(keadaan) yg paling buruk/teruk*: *My parents always expect the worst if I'm late.*
IDM **at (the) worst** if the worst happens or if you consider sb/sth in the worst way □ *paling-paling buruk/teruk; seburuk-buruknya*: *The problem doesn't look too serious. At worst we'll have to make a few small changes.*
bring out the best/worst in sb ➔ **best³**
if the worst comes to the worst if the worst possible situation happens □ *dlm keadaan yg benar-benar teruk*

worth¹ /wɜːθ/ adj [not before a noun] **1** having a particular value (in money) □ *bernilai; berharga*: *How much do you think that house is worth?* **2 worth doing, etc.** used as a way of recommending or advising □ *berbaloi; ada baiknya*: *That museum's well worth visiting if you have time.* ◆ *The library closes in 5 minutes—it's not worth going in.*

HELP We can say either *It isn't worth repairing the car* or *The car isn't worth repairing.*

3 enjoyable or useful to do or have, even if it means extra cost, effort, etc. □ *berbaloi; berfaedah*: *It takes a long time to walk to the top of the hill but it's worth the effort.* ◆ *Don't bother cooking a big meal. It isn't worth it—we're not hungry.*
IDM **get your money's worth** ➔ **money**
worth sb's while helpful, useful or interesting to sb □ *berbaloi, berfaedah atau berguna (bagi sso)*

worth² /wɜːθ/ noun [U] **1** the amount of sth that the money mentioned will buy □ *sebanyak; bernilai*: *twenty pounds' worth of petrol* **2** the amount of sth that will last for the time mentioned □ *cukup utk*: *two days' worth of food* **3** the value of sb/sth; how useful sb/sth is □ *nilai*: *She has proved her worth as a member of the team.*

worthless /ˈwɜːθləs/ adj **1** having no value or use □ *tdk berharga/bernilai*: *It's worthless—it's only a bit of plastic!* **2** (used about a person) having bad qualities □ *tdk berguna* ➔ look at **priceless, valuable, invaluable**

worthwhile /ˌwɜːθˈwaɪl/ adj important, enjoyable or interesting enough to be worth the cost or effort □ *berfaedah; berbaloi*: *Working for so little money just isn't worthwhile.*

worthy /ˈwɜːði/ adj (**worthier**; **worthiest**) **1** (formal) **worthy of sth/to do sth** good enough for sth or to have sth □ *wajar; layak*: *He felt he was not worthy to accept such responsibility.* **2** that should receive respect, support or attention □ *wajar/patut disanjung*: *a worthy leader* ◆ *a worthy cause*

would /wəd/ *strong form* /wʊd/ modal verb (*short form* **'d**; *negative* **would not**; *short form* **wouldn't** /ˈwʊdnt/) **1** used as the past form of 'will' when you report what sb says or thinks □ *digunakan sebagai bentuk kala lampau bagi 'will'*: *They said that they would help us.*

◆ *She didn't think that he would do a thing like that.* **2** used when talking about the result of an event that you imagine □ *akan; tentu*: *He would be delighted if you went to see him.* ◆ *She'd be stupid not to accept.* ◆ *I would have done more, if I'd had the time.* **3** used to describe sth that could have happened but did not □ *akan*: *If I had seen the advertisement in time, I would have applied for the job.* **4** used after 'wish' □ *digunakan selepas perkataan 'wish' (bermaksud ingin, harap, dsb)*: *I wish the sun would come out.* **5** to agree or be ready to do sth □ *mahu; bersetuju*: *She just wouldn't do what I asked her.* **6** used when you are giving your opinion but are not certain that you are right □ *digunakan utk memberi pendapat atau membuat andaian*: *I'd say she's about 40.* **7** used for asking sb politely to do sth □ *bolehkah*: *Would you come this way, please?* **8** used with 'like' or 'love' as a way of asking or saying what sb wants □ *ingin; mahu*: *Would you like to come with us?* ◆ *I'd love a piece of cake.* ➔ note at **want**

GRAMMAR **Would like** and **would love** are followed by the infinitive, not by the *-ing* form.

9 used for talking about things that often happened in the past □ *digunakan utk bercakap ttg perkara yg sering berlaku pd masa lalu*: *When he was young he would often walk in these woods.* ➔ look at **used to 10** used for commenting on behaviour that is typical of sb □ *spt yg dijangkakan*: *You would say that. You always support him.* ❶ For more information about modal verbs, look at the **Reference Section** at the back of this dictionary.

ˈwould-be adj [only before a noun] used to describe sb who is hoping to become the type of person mentioned □ *bakal*: *a would-be actor* ◆ *advice for would-be parents*

wound¹ /wuːnd/ noun [C] an injury to part of your body, especially a cut, often one received in fighting □ *luka; kecederaan*: *a bullet wound*
IDM **rub salt into the wound/sb's wounds** ➔ **rub**

wound² /wuːnd/ verb [T, usually passive] **1** to injure sb's body with a weapon □ *mencederakan; melukakan; mendapat (cedera)*: *He was wounded in the leg during the war.* ➔ note at **hurt 2** to hurt sb's feelings deeply □ *menyinggung perasaan; menyakitkan hati sso*: *I was wounded by his criticism.* ▸**wounded** adj: *a wounded soldier* ▸**the wounded** noun [pl]: *Soldiers moved the wounded away from the battlefield.*

wound³ past tense, past participle of **wind³**

wove past tense of **weave**

woven past participle of **weave**

wow /waʊ/ exclam (informal) used for showing that you find sth impressive or surprising □ *wau; wah*: *Wow! What a fantastic boat!*

WP abbr = word processor, word processing

wrangle /'ræŋgl/ noun [C] a noisy or complicated argument □ *pertengkaran; perkelahian*: The company is involved in **a legal wrangle** over copyright. ▶ **wrangle** verb [I]

wrap

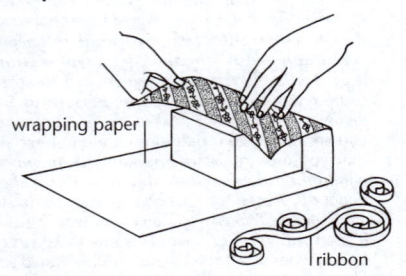

wrapping paper

ribbon

wrap /ræp/ verb [T] (**wrapping; wrapped**) 1 **wrap sth (up) (in sth)** to put paper or cloth around sb/sth as a cover □ *membalut; membungkus*: to wrap up a present ♦ The baby was found wrapped in a blanket. 2 **wrap sth round/around sb/sth** to tie sth such as paper or cloth around an object or a part of the body □ *membalut; dibalut; melilit*: The man had a bandage wrapped round his head.
IDM **be wrapped up in sb/sth** to be very involved and interested in sb/sth □ *asyik/leka membuat sst*: They were completely wrapped up in each other. They didn't notice I was there.
PHR V **wrap (sb/yourself) up** to put warm clothes on sb/yourself □ *memakai/mengenakan pakaian tebal*

wrapper /'ræpə(r)/ noun [C] the piece of paper or plastic which covers sth when you buy it □ *pembalut; pembungkus*: a sweet/chocolate wrapper

wrapping /'ræpɪŋ/ noun [U] (also [pl] **wrappings**) paper, plastic, etc. that is used for covering sth in order to protect it □ *pembalut*: She tore off the wrapping.

'wrapping paper noun [U] paper which is used for putting round presents □ *kertas pembalut* ⊃ picture at **wrap**

wrath /rɒθ/ noun [U] (formal) very great anger □ *kemurkaan; kemarahan*

wreak /riːk/ verb [T] (formal) **wreak sth (on sb/sth)** to cause great damage or harm to sb/sth □ *mengakibatkan kemusnahan; memusnahkan*: Fierce storms **wreak havoc** at this time of year.

wreath /riːθ/ noun [C] (pl **wreaths** /riːðz/) a circle of flowers and leaves placed on a grave, etc. as a sign of respect for sb who has died □ *kalungan/lingkaran bunga*

wreck /rek/ noun 1 [C] a ship that has sunk or been badly damaged at sea □ *bangkai kapal; kapal karam*: Divers searched the wreck. 2 [C] a car, plane, etc. which has been badly damaged, especially in an accident □ *kenderaan yg ranap dlm kemalangan*: The car was a wreck but the lorry escaped almost without damage. 3 [C, usually sing] (informal) a person or thing that is in a very bad condition □ *orang atau sst yg berada dlm keadaan yg teruk*: He drove so badly I was a nervous wreck when we got there. ▶ **wreck** verb [T]: Vandals had wrecked the school hall. ♦ The strike wrecked all our holiday plans.

wreckage /'rekɪdʒ/ noun [U] the broken pieces of sth that has been damaged or destroyed □ *bangkai kapal, pesawat, dll yg ranap*: They searched the wreckage of the plane for evidence.

wrench¹ /rentʃ/ verb [T] 1 **wrench sb/sth (away, off, etc.)** to pull or turn sb/sth strongly and suddenly □ *merenggut; merentap; memaksa diri beredar atau pergi*: They had to wrench the door off the car to get the driver out. ♦ (figurative) The film was so exciting that I could hardly wrench myself away. 2 to injure part of your body by turning it suddenly □ *terseliuh; terkehel*

wrench² /rentʃ/ noun 1 [C] (AmE) = **spanner** 2 [sing] the sadness you feel because you have to leave sb/sth □ *kesedihan; kesayuan* 3 [C, usually sing] a sudden, violent pull or turn □ *renggutan; sentakan*: With a wrench I managed to open the door.

wrestle /'resl/ verb [I] 1 **wrestle (with) sb** to fight by trying to get hold of your opponent's body and throw them to the ground. People **wrestle** as a sport □ *bergelut; bergusti*: He managed to wrestle the man to the ground and take the knife from him. 2 **wrestle (with sth)** to try hard to deal with sth that is difficult □ *bersusah payah; bergelut*

wrestling /'reslɪŋ/ noun [U] a sport in which two people fight and try to throw each other to the ground □ *perlawanan gusti*: a wrestling match ▶ **wrestler** noun [C]

wretch /retʃ/ noun [C] a poor, unhappy person □ *si malang*: The poor wretch was clearly starving.

wretched /'retʃɪd/ adj 1 (of a person) very unhappy or ill □ *muram; sugul* **SYN** awful 2 [only before a noun] (informal) used for expressing anger □ *celaka; bedebah*: That wretched dog has chewed up my slippers again!

wriggle /'rɪgl/ verb [I,T] 1 **wriggle (sth) (about/around)** to move about, or to move a part of your body, with short, quick movements, especially from side to side □ *menggeliang-geliut; meliuk-liukkan*: The baby was wriggling around on my lap. ♦ She wriggled her fingers about in the hot sand. 2 to move in the direction mentioned by making quick turning movements □ *menggeliang-geliut*: The worm wriggled back into the soil.
PHR V **wriggle out of sth/doing sth** (informal) to avoid sth by making clever excuses □ *mengelak drpd sst/membuat sst*: It's your turn to wash up—you can't wriggle out of it this time!

wring /rɪŋ/ verb [T] (pt, pp **wrung** /rʌŋ/) **wring sth (out)** to press and squeeze sth in order to remove water from it □ *memerah; memulas* ⊃ picture at **squeeze**

wrinkle¹ /'rɪŋkl/ noun [C] a small line in sth, especially one on the skin of your face which you get as you grow older □ *kedut; kedutan; kerut*: *She's got fine wrinkles around her eyes.* ♦ *Smooth out the wrinkles in the fabric.* ⊃ look at **furrow**

wrinkle² /'rɪŋkl/ verb [I,T] **wrinkle (sth) (up)** to form small lines and folds in sth □ *menjadi berkedut; mengedutkan; mengerutkan*: *She wrinkled her nose at the nasty smell.* ♦ *My skirt had wrinkled up on the journey.* ▶ **wrinkled** adj

He wrinkled his forehead.

wrist /rɪst/ noun [C] the narrow part at the end of your arm where it joins your hand □ *pergelangan tangan* ⊃ picture at **body**: *She wore a silver bracelet on her wrist.*

wristband /'rɪstbænd/ noun [C] a strip of material worn around the wrist as a decoration, to absorb sweat during exercise or to show support for sth □ *bebat pergelangan tangan*: *He was wearing an anti-nuclear wristband.*

wristwatch /'rɪstwɒtʃ/ (*AmE* also) / noun [C] a watch that you wear on your wrist □ *jam tangan*

writ /rɪt/ noun [C] a legal order to do or not to do sth, given by a court of law □ *writ; surat dakwa*

write /raɪt/ verb (pt **wrote** /rəʊt/; pp **written** /'rɪtn/) [I,T] **1** to make words, letters, etc., especially on paper using a pen or pencil □ *menulis*: *I can't write with this pen.* ♦ *Write your name and address on the form.* **2** to create a book, story, song, etc. in written form for people to read or use □ *mengarang; mencipta; menulis*: *Tolstoy wrote 'War and Peace'.* ♦ *He wrote his wife a poem.* ♦ *Who wrote the music for that film?* **3** **write (sth) (to sb); write (sb) sth** to write and send a letter, an email, etc. to sb □ *menulis surat*: *She wrote that they were all well and would be home soon.* ♦ *She phones every week and writes occasionally.* ♦ *I've written a letter to my son./I've written my son a letter.* ♦ *I've written to him.*

HELP In American English we can say: *I've written him.*

4 [T] **write sth (out) (for sb)** to fill or complete a form, document, etc. with the necessary information □ *menulis*: *I wrote out a receipt for £10.*

PHR V **write back (to sb)** to send a reply to sb □ *membalas surat* **SYN** reply

write sth down to write sth on paper, especially so that you can remember it □ *mencatat sst*: *Did you write down Jon's address?*

write in (to sb/sth) (for sth) to write a letter to an organization, etc. to ask for sth, give an opinion, etc. □ *menulis surat kpd sso utk meminta sst, menyatakan pendapat, dll*

write off/away (to sb/sth) (for sth) to write a letter to an organization, etc. to order sth or ask for sth □ *menulis surat kpd sso utk memesan atau meminta sst*

write sb/sth off to accept or decide that sb/sth will not be successful or useful □ *mengetepikan sso/sst*: *Don't write him off yet. He could still win.*

write sth off to accept that you will not get back an amount of money you have lost or spent □ *mengira hangus hutang atau perbelanjaan*: *to write off a debt*

write sth out to write the whole of sth on paper □ *menuliskan sst (resipi, dll)*: *Can you write out that recipe for me?*

write sth up to write sth in a complete and final form, often using notes that you have made □ *menulis semula sst*: *to write up lecture notes*

'write-off noun [C] a thing, especially a vehicle, that is so badly damaged that it is not worth repairing □ *(kenderaan) yg dikira tdk boleh digunakan lagi*

writer /'raɪtə(r)/ noun [C] a person who writes, especially one whose job is to write books, articles, stories, etc. □ *penulis*: *Charles Dickens was a famous writer.*

'write-up noun [C] an article in a newspaper or magazine in which sb writes what they think about a new book, play, product, etc. □ *sorotan; liputan; pemerian; ulasan*: *The performance got a good write-up in the local paper.*

writhe /raɪð/ verb [I] to turn and roll your body about □ *bergolek-golek; menggeliang-geliut; menggeletik*: *She was writhing in pain.*

writing /'raɪtɪŋ/ noun [U] **1** the skill or activity of writing words □ *penulisan; menulis*: *He had problems with his reading and writing at school.* **2** the activity or job of writing books, etc. □ *menulis; mengarang*: *It's difficult to earn much money from writing.* **3** the books, etc. that sb has written or the style in which sb writes □ *penulisan; karya; karangan*: *Love is a common theme in his early writing.* **4** words that have been written or printed; the way a person writes □ *tulisan*: *This card's got no writing inside. You can put your own message.* ♦ *I can't read your writing, it's too small.*

IDM **in writing** in written form □ *secara bertulis*: *I'll confirm the offer in writing next week.*

'writing paper noun [U] paper for writing letters on □ *kertas tulis*

written¹ /'rɪtn/ adj expressed in writing; not just spoken □ *bertulis*: *a written agreement* ♦ *Some expressions are only used in written English.* ♦ *a written test and an oral test* ⊃ look at **spoken**

written² past participle of **write**

wrong¹ /rɒŋ/ adj, adv **1** not correct; in a way that is not correct □ *salah; silap*: *the wrong answer* ◆ *I always pronounce that word wrong.* ◆ *You've got the wrong number* (= on the telephone). ◆ *I think you're wrong about Nicola—she's not lazy.* OPP **right 2** [not before a noun] **wrong (with sb/sth)** causing problems or difficulties; not as it should be □ *tdk kena*: *You look upset. Is something wrong?* ◆ *What's wrong with the car this time?* ◆ *She's got something wrong with her leg.* **3** not the best; not suitable □ *salah; tdk sesuai*: *That's the wrong way to hold the bat.* ◆ *I think she married the wrong man.* ◆ *I like him—I just think he's wrong for the job.* OPP **right 4 wrong (to do sth)** not morally right or honest □ *salah; tdk baik*: *It's wrong to tell lies.* ◆ *The man said that he had done nothing wrong.* OPP **right**

IDM **get/start off on the right/wrong foot (with sb)** ➔ **foot¹**
get on the right/wrong side of sb ➔ **side¹**
get sb wrong (*informal*) to not understand sb □ *salah faham*: *Don't get me wrong! I don't dislike him.*
go wrong 1 to make a mistake □ *tersilap*: *I'm afraid we've gone wrong. We should have taken the other road.* **2** to stop working properly or to stop developing well □ *rosak; tdk berjalan/berkembang dgn baik*: *My computer keeps going wrong.*
on the right/wrong track ➔ **track¹**

wrong² /rɒŋ/ noun **1** [U] things that are morally bad or dishonest □ *kesalahan; salah*: *Children quickly learn the difference between right and wrong.* **2** [C] an action or a situation which is not fair □ *ketidakadilan*: *A terrible wrong has been done. Those men should never have gone to prison.* IDM **in the wrong** (used about a person) having made a mistake □ *bersalah*
right a wrong ➔ **right⁴**

wrong³ /rɒŋ/ verb [T] (*formal*) to do sth to sb which is bad or unfair □ *berlaku tdk adil (terhadap sso)*: *I wronged her when I said she was lying.*

wrongful /'rɒŋfl/ adj [only before a noun] (*formal*) not fair, not legal or not moral □ *tdk adil; tdk bermoral; menyalahi undang-undang*: *He sued the company for wrongful dismissal.*

wrongly /'rɒŋli/ adv in a way that is wrong or not correct □ *salah; secara tdk tepat*: *He was wrongly accused of stealing money.*

HELP **Wrongly** or **wrong**? The adverb **wrong** is used after a verb or the object of a verb, especially in conversation: *He's spelt my name wrong.* The adverb **wrongly** is especially used before a past participle or a 'that' clause: *My name's been wrongly spelt.*

wrote past tense of **write**

wrought iron /ˌrɔːt 'aɪən/ noun [U] a form of iron used to make fences, gates, etc. □ *besi tempa*: *The gates were made of wrought iron.*
◆ **wrought-iron gates** ➔ look at **cast iron**

wrung past tense, past participle of **wring**

wry /raɪ/ adj showing that you are both disappointed and amused □ *yg membayangkan kekecewaan di samping rasa agak lucu sedikit*: *'Never mind,' she said with a wry grin. 'At least we got one vote.'* ▶ **wryly** adv

wt abbr = **weight¹** □ *berat*: *net wt 500g*

WWW /ˌdʌblju: dʌblju: 'dʌblju:/ abbr = **World Wide Web**

X, x /eks/ noun [C,U] (pl **Xs**; **X's**; **x's** /'eksɪz/) the 24th letter of the English alphabet □ *X, x (huruf)*: *'Xylophone' begins with (an) 'X'.*

HELP **X** is used by teachers to show that an answer is wrong. It is also used instead of the name of a person if you do not know or do not want to say his/her name: *Mr and Mrs X*. At the end of a letter it represents a kiss: *Lots of love, Mary XX.*

xenophobia /ˌzenə'fəʊbiə/ noun [U] a fear or hatred of foreign people and cultures □ *xenofobia; takut atau benci akan orang dan budaya asing* ▶ **xenophobic** adj

Xerox™ /'zɪərɒks/ noun **1** [U] a process for producing copies of letters, documents, etc. using a special machine □ *Xerox™ (mesin zeroks)* **2** [C] a copy produced by Xerox™ or a similar process □ *salinan zeroks; fotokopi* SYN **photocopy** ▶ **xerox** verb [T]

X factor /'eks fæktə(r)/ noun [sing] a special quality, especially one that you need for success and that is difficult to describe □ *kelebihan khusus*: *She certainly has the X factor that all great singers have.*

XL abbr **extra large**; used for sizes of things, especially clothes □ *XL (ekstra besar)*

Xmas /'krɪsməs; 'eksməs/ noun [C,U] (*informal*) (used as a short form in writing) Christmas □ *Krismas*: *Happy Xmas* (= written message in a Christmas card)

'X-ray noun [C] **1** [usually pl] a type of light that makes it possible to see inside solid objects, for example the human body, so that they can be examined and a photograph of them can be made □ *X-ray; sinar X* **2** a photograph that is made with an **X-ray** machine □ *(gambar) X-ray*: *The X-ray showed that the bone was not broken.* ➔ look at **ray** ▶ **X-ray** verb [T]: *She had her chest X-rayed.*

xylophone /'zaɪləfəʊn/ noun [C] a musical instrument that consists of two rows of wooden bars of different lengths. You play it by hitting these bars with a small hammer. □ *zilofon* ➔ picture at **music**

Y, y

Y, y /waɪ/ noun [C,U] (pl **Ys**; **Y's**; **y's** /waɪz/) the 25th letter of the English alphabet □ *Y, y (huruf)*: 'Yesterday' begins with (a) 'Y'.

yacht /jɒt/ noun [C] **1** a boat with sails, often used for pleasure trips and racing □ *kapal layar*: *a yacht race* ➔ note at **boat** ➔ picture on page **P6 2** a large boat with a motor, used for pleasure □ *kapal persiaran* ➔ look at **dinghy**

yachting /'jɒtɪŋ/ noun [U] the activity or sport of sailing or racing yachts □ *sukan kapal layar*

yachtsman /'jɒtsmən/, **yachtswoman** /'jɒtswʊmən/ noun [C] (pl **-men** /-mən/, **-women** /-wɪmɪn/) a person who sails a **yacht** in races or for pleasure □ *pelayar kapal layar (lelaki/ wanita)*

yank /jæŋk/ verb [I,T] (*informal*) to pull sth suddenly, quickly and hard □ *menyentap; merentap*: *She yanked at the door handle.* ▶**yank** noun [C]

yap /jæp/ verb [I] (**yapping**; **yapped**) (used about dogs, especially small ones) to make short, loud noises in an excited way □ *menyalak*

yard /jɑːd/ noun [C] **1** an area outside a building, usually with a hard surface and a wall or fence around it □ *laman; pekarangan*: *a school/ prison yard* ➔ look at **courtyard**, **churchyard** **2** (*AmE*) = **garden¹**(1) **3** [in compounds] an area, usually without a roof, used for a particular type of work or purpose □ *tempat utk membuat sst kerja, misalnya limbungan kapal*: *a shipyard/ boatyard* ◆ *a builder's yard*

> **HELP** In British English the piece of land belonging to a house is a **garden** if it has grass, flowers, etc., and a **yard** if it is made of concrete or stone. In American English this piece of land is a **yard** whether it has grass or is made of concrete or stone.

4 (*abbr* **yd**) a measure of length; 0.914 of a metre or 36 inches. There are 3 feet in a yard □ *ela*: *Our house is 100 yards from the supermarket.* ❶ For more information about measurements, look at the section on using numbers at the back of this dictionary.

yardstick /'jɑːdstɪk/ noun [C] a standard with which things can be compared □ *kayu ukur*: *Exam results should not be the only yardstick by which pupils are judged.*

yarn /jɑːn/ noun **1** [C,U] thread (usually of wool or cotton) that is used for knitting, etc. □ *yarn; benang* **2** [C] (*informal*) a long story that sb tells, especially one that is invented or exaggerated □ *cerita*

yawn /jɔːn/ verb [I] to open your mouth wide and breathe in deeply, especially when you are tired or bored □ *menguap; sangap*: *I kept yawning all through the lecture.* ▶**yawn** noun [C]: 'How much longer will it take?' he said with a yawn.

yay /jeɪ/ exclam (*especially AmE informal*) used to show that you are very pleased about sth □ *kata seru utk menyatakan rasa gembira*: *I won! Yay!*

yd abbr (pl **yds**) = **yard**(4)

yeah /jeə/ exclam (*informal*) yes □ *ya*: *Yeah, that's right.*

year /jɪə(r)/ (*BrE also*) jɜː(r)/ noun (*abbr* **yr**)
▶12 MONTHS **1** [C] (*also* **calendar year**) the period from 1 January to 31 December, 365 or 366 days divided into 12 months or 52 weeks □ *tahun*: *last year/this year/next year* ◆ *The population of the country will be 70 million by the year 2014.* ◆ *Interest is paid on this account once a year.* ◆ *a leap year* (= one that has 366 days) ◆ *the New Year* (= the first days of January) **2** [C] any period of 12 months, measured from any date □ *tahun*: *She worked here for twenty years.* ◆ *He left school just over a year ago.* ◆ *In a year's time, you'll be old enough to vote.* **3** [C] a period of 12 months in connection with schools, the business world, etc. □ *tahun*: *the academic/school year* ◆ *the tax/ financial year*
▶IN SCHOOL/UNIVERSITY **4** [C] (*especially BrE*) the level that a particular student is at □ *tahun*: *My son is in year ten now.* ◆ *The first years* (= students in their first year at school/university, etc.) *do French as a compulsory subject.* ◆ *He was a year below me at school.*
▶AGE **5** [C, usually pl] (used in connection with the age of sb/sth) a period of 12 months □ *tahun*: *He's ten years old today.* ◆ *a six-year-old daughter* ◆ *This car is nearly five years old.* ◆ *The company is now in its fifth year.* ➔ note at **age**

> **HELP** Note that you say *He is ten*, *He's ten* or *He's ten years old*. You CANNOT say *He has ten years*, *He's ten years* or *a ten-years-old boy*.

▶LONG TIME **6** years [pl] a long time □ *lama; bertahun-tahun*: *It happened years ago.* ◆ *I haven't seen him for years.*
IDM **all year round** for the whole year □ *sepanjang tahun*
donkey's years ➔ **donkey**
the turn of the century/year ➔ **turn²**
year after year; year in year out every year for many years □ *tahun demi tahun; tahun berganti tahun*

yearbook /'jɪəbʊk/ noun [C] **1** a book published once a year, giving details of events, etc. of the previous year, especially those connected with a particular area of activity □ *buku tahunan* **2** a book that is produced by students in their final year of school or college, containing photographs of students and details of school activities □ *buku tahunan*

yearly /'jɪəli/ (*BrE also*) 'jɜːli/ adj, adv (happening) every year or once a year □ *tahunan*: *The conference is held yearly.*

yearn /jɜːn/ verb [I] (*formal*) **yearn (for sb/sth)**; **yearn (to do sth)** to want sb/sth very much, es-

yeast → yield

pecially sb/sth that you cannot have □ *sangat mengingini* SYN long ▶yearning noun [C,U]

yeast /jiːst/ noun [U] a substance used for making bread rise and for making beer, wine, etc. □ *ragi*

yell /jel/ verb [I,T] yell (out) (sth); yell (sth) (at sb/sth) to shout very loudly, often because you are angry, excited or in pain □ *memekik; melaung: She yelled out his name.* ♦ *There's no need to yell at me; I can hear you perfectly well.* ▶yell noun [C]

yellow /ˈjeləʊ/ adj (yellower; yellowest) noun [C,U] (of) the colour of lemons or butter □ *kuning: a pale/light yellow dress* ♦ *a bright shade of yellow* ♦ *the yellows and browns of the autumn leaves*

yellow card noun [C] (in football) a card that is shown to a player as a warning that he or she will be sent off the field if he or she behaves badly again □ *kad kuning* ⊃ look at **red card**

yellowish /ˈjeləʊɪʃ/ adj (also yellowy) slightly yellow in colour □ *kekuning-kuningan*

yellow line noun [C] (in Britain) a yellow line at the side of a road to show that you can only park there for a limited time □ *garis kuning: double yellow lines* (= you must not park there at all)

Yellow Pages™ noun [pl] a website or telephone book (on yellow paper) that lists all the business companies, etc. in a certain area in sections according to the goods or services they provide □ *Halaman Kuning*

yellowy /ˈjeləʊi/ = yellowish

yelp /jelp/ verb [I] to give a sudden short cry, especially of pain □ *mendengking; menjerit* ▶yelp noun [C]

yes /jes/ exclam 1 used to give a positive answer to a question, for saying that sth is true or correct or for saying that you want sth □ *ya: 'Are you having a good time?' 'Yes, thank you.'* ♦ *'You're married, aren't you?' 'Yes, I am.'* ♦ *'May I sit here?' 'Yes, of course.'* ♦ *'More coffee?' 'Yes, please.'* OPP **no** 2 used when saying that a negative statement that sb has made is not true □ *digunakan utk menafikan sst pernyataan yg negatif: 'You don't care about anyone but yourself.' 'Yes I do.'* OPP **no** 3 used for showing you have heard sb or will do what they ask □ *ya: 'Waiter!' 'Yes, madam.'* ▶yes noun [C] (pl yesses or yeses): *Was that a yes or a no?*

yesterday /ˈjestədeɪ, -di/ adv, noun [U] (on) the day before today □ *semalam; kelmarin: Did you watch the film on TV yesterday?* ♦ *yesterday morning/afternoon/evening* ♦ *I posted the form the day before yesterday* (= if I am speaking on Wednesday, I posted it on Monday). ♦ *Have you still got yesterday's paper?* ♦ *I spent the whole of yesterday walking round the shops.*

yet /jet/ adv 1 used with negative verbs or in questions for talking about sth that has not happened but that you expect to happen □ *lagi; belum...lagi: Has it stopped raining yet?* ♦ *I haven't finished yet.* ♦ *I haven't seen that film yet.*

HELP In American English you can say: *I didn't see that film yet.*

2 [used with negative verbs] now; as early as this □ *dulu; lagi: You don't have to leave yet—your train isn't for another hour.* 3 from now until the period of time mentioned has passed □ *lagi: She isn't that old; she'll live for years yet.* 4 [used especially with may or might] at some time in the future □ *masih: With a bit of luck, they may yet win.* 5 [used with superlatives] until now/until then; so far □ *setakat ini: This is her best film yet.* 6 used with comparatives to emphasize an increase in the degree of sth □ *lagi: a recent and yet more improbable theory*

IDM **as yet** until now □ *setakat ini: As yet little is known about the disease.*

yet again (used for expressing surprise or anger that sth happens again) once more; another time □ *sekali lagi: I found out that he had lied to me yet again.*

yet another used for expressing surprise that there is one more of sth □ *satu lagi: They're opening yet another fast food restaurant in the square.*

yet to do, etc. that has not been done and is still to do in the future □ *masih belum (dibuat, dsb): The final decision has yet to be made.*

▶yet conj but; in spite of that □ *tetapi; namun: He seems pleasant, yet there's something about him I don't like.*

yew /juː/ noun 1 [C,U] (also 'yew tree) a tree with dark green leaves and small round red fruit which are poisonous □ *pokok yew* 2 [U] the wood from the yew tree □ *kayu pokok yew*

Y-fronts™ noun [pl] (BrE) a type of men's underwear with an opening in the front sewn in the shape of a Y upside-down □ *seluar dlm lelaki dgn bukaan berbentuk Y pd bahagian hadapan*

YHA /ˌwaɪ eɪtʃ ˈeɪ/ abbr Youth Hostels Association; an organization that provides cheap, simple accommodation □ *Persatuan Asrama Belia*

yield¹ /jiːld/ verb
▶PRODUCE STH 1 [T] to produce or provide crops, profits or results □ *menghasilkan: How much wheat does each field yield?* ♦ *Did the experiment yield any new information?*
▶STOP REFUSING 2 [I] (formal) yield (to sb/sth) to stop refusing to do sth or to obey sb □ *tunduk; mengalah: The government refused to yield to the hostage-takers' demands.* ⊃ A less formal expression is **give in**.
▶GIVE CONTROL 3 [T] yield sb/sth (up) (to sb/sth) to allow sb to have control of sth that you were controlling □ *menyerahkan: The army has yielded power to the rebels.*
▶MOVE UNDER PRESSURE 4 [I] (formal) to move, bend or break because of pressure □ *berganjak, bengkok, melendut, pecah, roboh, dll: The dam*

finally yielded under the weight of the water. ⊃ A less formal expression is **give way**.
➤IN VEHICLE **5** [I] (*AmE*) **yield (to sb/sth)** to allow other vehicles on a bigger road to go first □ *memberi laluan*: *You have to yield to traffic from the left here.*

HELP Give way is used in British English.

PHR V **yield to sth** (*formal*) to be replaced by sth, especially sth newer □ *digantikan dgn/ oleh*: *Old-fashioned methods have yielded to new technology.* ⊃ A less formal expression is **give way**.

yield² /jiːld/ *noun* [C] the amount that is produced □ *hasil*: *Wheat yields were down 5% this year.* ♦ *This investment has an annual yield of 12%.*

yo /jəʊ/ *exclam* (*especially AmE slang*) used by some people when they see a friend; hello □ *kata utk menyapa sso*

yob /jɒb/ *noun* [C] (*BrE informal*) a boy or young man who is rude, loud and sometimes violent or aggressive □ *penyangak* ⊃ look at **hooligan, lout** ▸**yobbish** *adj* [usually before a noun]: *yobbish behaviour*

yoga /ˈjəʊɡə/ *noun* [U] a system of exercises for the body that helps you control and relax both your mind and your body □ *yoga*

yogurt (also **yoghurt**) /ˈjɒɡət/ *noun* [C,U] a slightly sour, thick liquid food made from milk □ *tairu*: *plain/banana/strawberry yogurt*

yoke /jəʊk/ *noun* **1** [C] a long piece of wood fixed across the necks of two animals so that they can pull heavy loads together □ *kuk* **2** [sing] (*formal*) something that limits your freedom and makes your life difficult □ *belenggu*: *the yoke of parental control*

yolk /jəʊk/ *noun* [C,U] the yellow part in the middle of an egg □ *kuning telur* ⊃ picture at **egg**

ʔ **you** /ju; *strong form* juː/ *pron* **1** used as the subject or object of a verb, or after a preposition to refer to the person or people being spoken or written to □ *anda; awak; engkau, kamu, dsb*: *You can play the guitar, can't you?* ♦ *I've told you about this before.* ♦ *Bring all your photos with you.* **2** used with a noun, adjective or phrase when calling sb sth □ *kau*: *You idiot! What do you think you're doing?* **3** used for referring to people in general □ *kita; anda*: *The more you earn, the more tax you pay.*

you'd /juːd/ *short for* **you had; you would**

you'll /juːl/ *short for* **you will**

ʔ **young¹** /jʌŋ/ *adj* (**younger** /ˈjʌŋɡə(r)/, **youngest** /ˈjʌŋɡɪst/) not having lived or existed for very long; not old □ *muda; kecil; adik*: *They have two young children.* ♦ *I'm a year younger than her.* ♦ *My father was the youngest of eight children.* ♦ *my younger brothers* **OPP** **old**
IDM **young at heart** behaving or thinking like a young person, although you are old □ *muda di hati*

young² /jʌŋ/ *noun* [pl] **1** **the young** young people considered as a group □ *orang muda; muda-mudi*: *The young of today are more ambitious than their parents.* **2** young animals □ *anak*: *Swans will attack to protect their young.*

youngish /ˈjʌŋɪʃ/ *adj* quite young □ *agak muda*

youngster /ˈjʌŋstə(r)/ *noun* [C] a young person □ *budak; anak muda*: *There is very little entertainment for youngsters in this town.*

ʔ **your** /jɔː(r); jə(r)/ *determiner* **1** of or belonging to the person or people being spoken to □ *(berkenaan dgn atau milik) anda, awak, engkau, kamu, dsb*: *What's your flat like?* ♦ *Thanks for all your help.* ♦ *How old are your children now?* **2** belonging to or connected with people in general □ *kita; anda*: *When your life is as busy as mine, you have little time to relax.* **3** (*informal*) used for saying that sth is well known to people in general □ *awak; kau*: *So this is your typical English summer, is it?* **4** (also **Your**) used in some titles □ *digunakan dlm gelaran tertentu*: *your Highness*

you're /jʊə(r) (*BrE also*) jɔː(r) (*AmE also*) / *short for* **you are**

ʔ **yours** /jɔːz (*AmE also*) / *pron* **1** of or belonging to you □ *(berkenaan dgn atau milik) anda, awak, engkau, kamu, dsb*: *Is this bag yours or mine?* ♦ *I was talking to a friend of yours the other day.* **2** **Yours** used at the end of a letter □ *Yg (digunakan pd akhir surat)*: *Yours sincerely .../ faithfully ...* ♦ *Yours ...* ⊃ note at **sincere**

ʔ **yourself** /jɔːˈself; *weak form* jəˈself (*AmE also*) / *pron* (*pl* **yourselves** /-ˈselvz/) **1** used when the person or people being spoken to both do an action and are also affected by the action □ *dirimu sendiri*: *Be careful or you'll hurt yourself.* ♦ *Here's some money. Buy yourselves a present.* ♦ *You're always talking about yourself!* ♦ *You don't look yourself today* (= you do not look well or do not look as happy as usual). **2** used to emphasize the person or people who do the action □ *(anda, awak, engkau, kamu, dsb) sendiri*: *You yourself told me there was a problem last week.* ♦ *Did you repair the car yourself?* (= or did sb else do it for you?) **3** (*informal*) you □ *anda, awak, engkau, kamu, dsb*: *'How are you?' 'Not too bad, thanks. And yourself?'*
IDM **(all) by yourself/yourselves** **1** alone □ *seorang diri; sendirian*: *Do you live by yourself?* ⊃ note at **alone** **2** without help □ *sendiri*: *You can't cook dinner for ten people by yourself.*

EXAM TIP

Talking about yourself

In a **speaking exam** you will be expected to talk about yourself. This could include talking about your daily routine, sports you like, travel and holidays, work experience or your hopes

---

VOWELS   iː see   i any   ɪ sit   e ten   æ hat   ɑː father   ɒ got   ɔː saw   ʊ put   uː too   u usual

for the future. Before the exam, prepare some ideas and vocabulary for each of these topics, but do not be tempted to memorize complete answers. It is important to show that you can hold a conversation with someone.

youth /juːθ/ noun (pl **youths** /juːðz/) **1** [U] the period of your life when you are young, especially the time before a child becomes an adult □ *masa muda*: *He was quite a good sportsman in his youth.* **2** [U] the fact or state of being young □ *muda; usia muda*: *I think that her youth will be a disadvantage in this job.* **3** [C] a young person (usually a young man, and often one that you do not have a good opinion of) □ *budak muda*: *a gang of youths* **4 the youth** [U] young people considered as a group □ *belia*: *the youth of today* ⊃ look at **age**, **old age**

youth club noun [C] a club where young people can meet each other and take part in various activities □ *kelab belia*

youthful /'juːθfl/ adj **1** typical of young people □ *muda; orang muda*: *youthful enthusiasm* **2** seeming younger than you are □ *kelihatan muda*: *She's a youthful fifty-year-old.*

youth hostel noun [C] a cheap and simple place to stay, especially for young people when they are travelling □ *asrama belia*

you've /juːv/ short for **you have**

Yo Yo™ (also **yo-yo**) noun [C] (pl **Yo Yos**; **yo-yos**) a toy which is a round piece of wood or plastic with a string round the middle. You put the string round your finger and can make the yo-yo go up and down it. □ *yoyo*

yr (also **yr.**) abbr (pl **yrs**) = **year**

yuck (also **yuk**) /jʌk/ exclam (informal) used for saying that you think sth is disgusting or very unpleasant □ *ceh*: *It's filthy! Yuck!* ▶**yucky** (also **yukky**) adj: *a yucky colour*

yummy /'jʌmi/ adj (informal) tasting very good □ *lazat/sedap betul*: *a yummy cake* SYN **delicious**

yuppie (also **yuppy**) /'jʌpi/ noun [C] (pl **yuppies**) a successful young professional person who lives in a city, earns a lot of money and spends it on fashionable things □ *orang profesional muda yg berwang dan bergaya*

Z z

Z, z /zed/ noun [C,U] (pl **Zs**; **Z's**; **z's** /zedz/) the 26th letter of the English alphabet □ *Z, z (huruf)*: *'Zero' begins with (a) 'Z'.*

zany /'zeɪni/ adj (informal) (**zanier**; **zaniest**) funny in an unusual and crazy way □ *lucu dgn cara yg agak aneh atau luar biasa*: *a zany comedian*

zap /zæp/ verb (**zapping**; **zapped**) (informal) **1** [T] **zap sb/sth (with sth)** to destroy, hit or kill sb, usually with a gun or other weapon □ *memusnahkan; menembak; menghentam, dll*: *It's a computer game where you have to zap aliens with a laser.* **2** [I,T] to change TV programmes very quickly using a **remote control** (= an electronic device) □ *menukar saluran televisyen cepat-cepat*

zeal /ziːl/ noun [U] (formal) great energy or enthusiasm □ *semangat; minat besar*: *religious zeal*

zealous /'zeləs/ adj using great energy and enthusiasm □ *bersemangat* ▶**zealously** adv

zebra /'zebrə/ noun [C] (pl **zebra** or **zebras**) an African wild animal that looks like a horse, with black and white lines all over its body □ *kuda belang*

zebra

zebra crossing noun [C] (in Britain) a place where the road is marked with black and white lines and people can cross safely because cars must stop to let them do this □ *lintasan zebra* ⊃ look at **pedestrian crossing** ⊃ picture at **roundabout**

zenith /'zenɪθ/ noun [sing] **1** the highest point that the sun or moon reaches in the sky, directly above you □ *puncak langit; kerubung langit*: *The sun rose towards its zenith.* **2** (formal) the time when sth is strongest and most successful □ *kemuncak*

zero[1] /'zɪərəʊ/ (AmE also) / number (pl **zeros**) **1** [C] the figure 0 □ *kosong; sifar*; *0* ⊃ note at **six 2** [U] freezing point in the Celsius system; 0°C □ *takat beku; 0°C*: *The temperature is likely to fall to five degrees below zero* (= −5°C). **3** [U] the lowest possible amount or level; nothing at all □ *kosong; sifar*: *My chances of passing the exam are zero.* ♦ *zero growth/inflation/profit*

OTHER WORDS FOR

zero

The figure **0** has several different names in British English. **Zero** is most commonly used in scientific or technical contexts. **Nil** is most commonly used in scores in sport, especially football (when spoken). **Nought** is used when referring to the figure **0** as part of a larger number: *a million is one followed by six noughts*. **O** (pronounced /əʊ/) is most commonly used when saying numbers such as telephone or flight numbers.

zero[2] /'zɪərəʊ/ (AmE also) / verb [T] (**zeroing**; **zeroes**; pt, pp **zeroed**) to turn an instrument, a control, etc. to zero □ *mengubah/memutar/memusing kpd sifar atau kosong*

PHR V **zero in on sb/sth 1** to fix all your attention on the person or thing mentioned

☐ *menumpukan/menentukan perhatian*: *They zeroed in on the key issues.* **2** to aim guns, etc. at the person or thing mentioned ☐ *menghala kpd sasaran tertentu*

,zero-'carbon *adj* in which the amount of **carbon dioxide** (= a gas) produced has been reduced to nothing or is balanced by actions that protect the environment ☐ *karbon sifar*: *a zero-carbon house that uses no energy from external sources* SYN **carbon neutral**

,zero 'tolerance *noun* [U] the policy of applying laws very strictly so that people are punished even for offences that are not very serious ☐ *tiada langsung toleransi; dasar tiada toleransi*

zest /zest/ *noun* [U, sing] **zest (for sth)** a feeling of enjoyment, excitement and enthusiasm ☐ *keseronokan*: *She has a great zest for life.*

zigzag /'zɪgzæg/ *noun* [C], *adj* [only before a noun] (consisting of) a line with left and right turns, like a lot of letter Ws, one after the other ☐ *zig zag; berliku-liku; bengkang-bengkok*: *The skier came down the slope in a series of zigzags.* ♦ *a zigzag pattern/line* ➪ picture at **line** ➪ picture on **page P1** ▶**zigzag** *verb* [I] (**zigzagging; zigzagged**): *We took a road that zigzagged through the mountains.*

zilch /zɪltʃ/ *noun* [U] (*informal*) nothing ☐ *tiada apa-apa; tanpa apa-apa; kosong*: *I arrived in this country with zilch.*

zillion /'zɪljən/ *noun* [C] (*especially AmE informal*) a very large number ☐ *zilion; jumlah besar yg tdk pasti*: *There were zillions of people waiting outside the theatre.*

zinc /zɪŋk/ *noun* [U] (*symbol* **Zn**) a silver-grey metal, often put on the surface of iron and steel as protection against water ☐ *zink*: *Brass is made from copper and zinc.*

zip /zɪp/ (*AmE* **zipper**) *noun* [C] a device consisting of two rows of metal or plastic teeth, that you use for fastening clothes, bags, etc. ☐ *zip*: *to do up/undo a zip* ➪ picture at **button** ➪ picture on **page P1** ▶**zip** *verb* [T] (**zipping; zipped**) **zip sth (up)**: *There was so much in the bag that it was difficult to zip it up.* OPP **unzip**

'zip code (also **ZIP code**) (*AmE*) = **postcode**

zipper /'zɪpə(r)/ (*AmE*) = **zip**

zit /zɪt/ *noun* [C] (*informal*) a spot on the skin, especially on the face ☐ *bintik/tompok kecil pd kulit (muka)*

the zodiac /'zəʊdɪæk/ *noun* [sing] a diagram of the positions of the sun, moon and planets, which is divided into twelve equal parts, each with a special name and symbol called a **sign of the zodiac** ☐ *zodiak*

MORE The signs of the zodiac are used in **astrology** and **horoscopes** (often called **the stars**) in newspapers and magazines. People often refer to the signs and to the influence that they think these have on a person's personality and future: *Which sign (of the zodiac) are you?*

the zodiac

the signs of the zodiac

zombie /'zɒmbi/ *noun* [C] (*informal*) a person who seems only partly alive, without any feeling or interest in what is happening ☐ *orang yg tdk bermaya dan tdk berminat dlm apa-apa pun*

zone /zəʊn/ *noun* [C] an area that is different from those around it, for example because sth special happens there ☐ *zon*: *a war zone* ♦ *a flight crossing several* **time zones** (= one of the 24 areas that the world is divided into, each with its own time)

zoo /zu:/ *noun* [C] (*pl* **zoos**) a park where many kinds of wild animals are kept so that people can look at them and where they are bred, studied and protected ☐ *zoo*

zookeeper /'zu:ki:pə(r)/ *noun* [C] a person who works in a **zoo**, taking care of the animals ☐ *penjaga zoo/penjaga binatang di zoo*

zoology /zu'ɒlədʒi/ *noun* [U] the scientific study of animals ☐ *zoologi* ➪ look at **biology**, **botany** ▶**zoological** /,zu:ə'lɒdʒɪkl/ *adj*: *zoological illustrations* ▶**zoologist** /-dʒɪst/ *noun* [C]

zoom /zu:m/ *verb* [I] **1** to move or go somewhere very fast ☐ *bergerak pantas; menderum*: *Traffic zoomed past us.* **2** on some small computer devices) to make the screen larger using your fingers, in order to see more detail ☐ *membesarkan imej pd skrin peranti komputer kecil dgn jari* OPP **pinch in** ➪ note at **touch screen** PHR V **zoom in (on sb/sth)** (when taking a photograph) to give a closer view of the object/person being photographed by using a **zoom lens** on the camera ☐ *memfokus (pd sso/sst) dlm jarak dekat*: *The camera zoomed in on the actor's face.*

,zoom 'lens (also **zoom**) *noun* [C] a device on a camera that makes an object being photographed appear gradually bigger or smaller so that it seems to be getting closer or further away ☐ *kanta zum* ➪ picture at **camera**

zucchini /zu'ki:ni/ (*pl* **zucchini** or **zucchinis**) (*AmE*) = **courgette** ☐ *zukini*

Study section

WT1–WT16 **Writing Tutor**
- WT1 Using the Writing Tutor
- WT4 Writing an argument essay
- WT6 Writing a comparison essay
- WT8 Writing a report
- WT10 Writing a book or film review
- WT12 Writing formal letters: a letter of complaint
- WT14 Applying for a job 1: writing a CV
- WT15 Applying for a job 2: writing a covering letter
- WT16 Writing an informal email

P1–P16 **Colour pages**
- P1 Clothes
- P2 Work and jobs
- P3 Leisure activities
- P4 Sports
- P6 Transport
- P8 House
- P9 Homes
- P10 Landscape
- P12 Animals
- P14 Fruit
- P15 Vegetables
- P16 Food and drink

R1–R41 **Reference section**
- R2 Grammar
- R21 Other reference

R42–R55 **Wordpower Workout**
- R56 Workout key
- R60 List of illustrations in the dictionary
- R62 List of notes in the dictionary

Writing Tutor

Using the Writing Tutor to improve your writing

In the Writing Tutor you will find examples of essays, letters and emails to help you with your writing in class and in exams. You will also find advice about planning and organizing your work, and tips about checking your writing.

The writing model
Look carefully at:
- the **content** (what is being said)
- the **language** and **style**
- the **layout** (the way the text is arranged on the page)

Before you write
This section will help you to think of ideas, to plan and organize your own writing.

Language Bank
This section gives you some useful words and phrases that you can use in each type of writing.

Notes in the dictionary
You can find notes in the main part of the dictionary to give you more help with your writing.

Checklist
Use this section to check and improve your work and correct mistakes.

Formal and informal writing

Your writing should not be informal unless you are writing an informal letter or email. When you check your work, think about these things:

Have you used any words that are too informal?
If you are not sure, check in the dictionary and do not use anything marked *informal*, *slang* or *spoken*.

Avoid short forms
For example, do not write *I'm* or *haven't*, but use *I am* or *have not*.

Sentences
Too many short sentences can sound very informal. To express your ideas you will need to use words like *which*, *that* (relative pronouns), *and*, *but*, *or* and *although*, *because*, *if* to join parts of sentences. Avoid very long sentences, as these can be difficult to understand.

Using 'I'
Try not to use 'I' too much in essays unless you are asked to give your own opinion. For example, instead of *I find my smartphone very useful*, write *Many people find smartphones very useful*.

Contents	
Using the Writing Tutor	WT 1
Argument essay	WT 4
Comparison essay	WT 6
Report	WT 8
Book and film review	WT 10
Formal letters	WT 12
Applying for a job: CV and covering letter	WT 14
Email	WT 16

How to write well

When you have to write an essay, a letter or an email, whether it is for class, for an exam, or in real life, you will be more successful if you plan and write in an organized way.

1. Think

Before you start, ask yourself:
Who will read it?
Am I writing for a teacher or an examiner, other students, an employer? The answer will help you to decide what information to include and how formal or informal your language should be.

2. Plan

Brainstorm
Think of as many ideas as possible about the topic. You can make lists, use a table or draw a mind map.

Organize
Choose your best ideas and organize them into paragraphs. Think about how many words you are asked to use.

Vocabulary and language
Additional notes in the dictionary, such as Topic and Writing Tips, will help you choose appropriate language. There is a list of notes on page R62.

3. Write

You are now ready to start writing.

Use your plan
Try to keep to your plan. Think about the content, the paragraphs and the sentences at this stage.

Language and style
Is this a formal or in informal piece of writing? You can use informal, slang or spoken words and phrases if you are writing to a friend, but you do not usually use them in an essay.

Layout
If you are writing a letter or an email, make sure you put names and addresses in the right place.

4. Check

Find and correct mistakes
It is very important to re-read your work and check it very carefully. If you make a lot of mistakes, people may find it difficult to understand and you can lose marks in an exam.

Check that you have used the right number of words
If you are told to write, for example, 170 – 200 words, you must not use fewer than 170 or more than 200.
If you do, you may lose marks in an exam.

Checking your work

Using your dictionary
The main part of the dictionary can help you choose the right language to use. You can also use it to check that you have used the correct grammar and spelling.

Ask yourself:

Have I used the right word?
The dictionary has notes and illustrations that explain confusing words, for example *borrow/lend* (look at **borrow**) and *sympathetic/nice* (look at **sympathetic**). Sometimes learners choose the wrong word because they translate from their own language. Check any words that you are not sure about.

What about language and style?
Have you used any words that are too formal or informal in this type of writing? Check in the dictionary if you're not sure. The labels *formal*, *informal*, *spoken* and *slang* will help you.

Have I used the same word or phrase too many times?
Try to find different ways to say things. Use the **Other words for** notes in the dictionary. (For example, look at the note at **nice**.) See if there is a synonym for a word you use a lot.

Have I used the right words together?
Is it *make homework* or *do homework*? Look up the main word in the dictionary (**homework**) and see which word it is used with in the examples.

What about prepositions?
Is it *close to* or *close from*? Check prepositions after nouns, verbs or adjectives very carefully.

Spelling test	
1.	leisure ✓
2.	accomodation ✗
3.	apartment ✓

Have I used the correct verb patterns?
Is it *enjoy to do something* or *enjoy doing something*? Look at the example sentences for **enjoy**.

What about spelling?
Check the spelling of plurals, past tenses, -ing forms and comparative and superlative adjectives and adverbs. Words that are similar to words in your language may be spelled differently. You can find the names of countries, cities and nationalities in the list at the back of the dictionary.

Is the grammar correct?
Have you checked whether the nouns are countable or uncountable? Are the verbs irregular? There is a list of irregular verbs at the back of the dictionary.

Make your own checklist
Look carefully at the mistakes your teacher marks in your written work and make a list of the mistakes you often make. Use this list to check each piece of work you do – *before* you give it to the teacher.

Writing an argument essay

An argument essay needs to be clearly organized. You should give points for and against the argument. Use formal language and avoid using **I** too much.

A smartphone is an essential possession in modern society. Discuss. (170–200 words)

Today's mobile devices allow us to receive email, chat online, and look at websites wherever we are. Smartphones offer a number of benefits, but they also have several disadvantages.

Paragraph 1 – Introduction
Show why the topic is important or interesting and give a basic plan for the rest of the essay.

Smartphones certainly have many advantages. For example, users can work, access information, and use services such as banking or shopping at any time. In addition, special software can provide directions and help if you get lost. Many people also like to play games, surf the web or watch videos while waiting for a bus or an appointment.

Paragraph 2 – Advantages
You may support your points with examples from your own experience.

However, smartphones also have their drawbacks. First of all, many consumers cannot afford to buy them, and secondly, the monthly fees for service plans are quite high. Moreover, some people depend too much on their smartphones and feel uncomfortable when they are not able to use them.

Paragraph 3 – Disadvantages
Try to balance the number of positive and negative points.

In short, smartphones are not an essential part of modern life for everyone. Nevertheless, if you can afford one, and if you think you can control the amount of time you spend online, then a smartphone might be a convenient and enjoyable option for you.

Paragraph 4 – Conclusion
Summarize the main points. Give your own opinion on the topic.

Linking words and phrases help the reader to move easily from one point to the next.

Use formal language. *Allow* is more formal than *let*, and *receive* is more formal than *get*.

Use synonyms to avoid repeating key words and phrases. *Benefits* is a synonym for *advantages*, and *drawbacks* is a synonym for *disadvantages*.

Before you write

- Read the question carefully and make sure that you understand what it is asking before you begin to write.
- **Brainstorm:** Think of points for and against smartphones. For example:

advantages	disadvantages
• info and services whenever you need them (transfer money, etc.) • entertainment when bored (while waiting, etc.) …	• expensive to buy • monthly fees are high …

- Look again at your notes and choose the best points to include.
- Organize your ideas into paragraphs.
  1 Introduction 2 Advantages 3 Disadvantages 4 Conclusion

Language Bank: Linking expressions

You use all these words or phrases at the start of a sentence, except for *also* and *as well*.

Introduction
Today, Nowadays, These days,…

More information
In addition, Furthermore, Moreover, What is more, First of all, Firstly/Secondly, Finally/Lastly, also, as well,…
➲ See NOTE at **also**

Contrast
However, Nevertheless, Despite this, In spite of this, Although, On the other hand,…
➲ See WRITING TIP at **contrast**

Consequences
Therefore, As a result, For this Reason, Consequently, So,…
➲ See WRITING TIP at **therefore**

Opinions
In my opinion, From my point of view,…
➲ See NOTE at **think**

Conclusion
In short, To sum up, In conclusion, To conclude,…

Checklist

Have I

- written about *exactly* what the task asked me to discuss? ☐
- written about both sides of the argument? ☐
- organized my ideas into logical paragraphs? ☐
- used linking words to help the reader follow what I've said? ☐
- given my opinion in the conclusion? ☐

Writing a comparison essay

When you are asked to compare two things, you should think about how they are similar to each other, as well as what makes them different.

Compare life for young people today with life before the invention of the Internet. Is it better to be a teenager today, or was it better in the past? (180–200 words)

Paragraph 1 – Introduction
General comment about the two things

The Internet has brought important changes to the lives of young people. Teenagers today have a very different way of life from their parents, both at school and in their leisure time.

Paragraph 2
Differences and similarities at school

While their parents used to visit libraries and read books to research a school project, today's teenagers do research at home on their computers. They can find a much wider variety of up-to-date information. However, books are still used in lessons, so methods of teaching today are often quite similar to what their parents knew.

Paragraph 3
Differences and similarities in social life

Outside school, differences are greater. With the Internet, teenagers can chat to their friends more easily than when they had to use the family phone. They are also likely to have a wider circle of friends through social networking sites, although there is a danger that they may spend too much time alone with their computers. On the other hand, like their parents, teenagers today still enjoy spending time together.

Paragraph 4 – Conclusion
Summary and writer's opinion about which is better

In conclusion, the Internet has made life more interesting for today's teenagers. While any new technology should always be used with care, most of these changes have made life easier and more exciting.

Linking words and phrases help the reader to move easily from one point to the next.

These words and phrases show the reader the differences between the two things. Try to use a variety of ways of showing differences.

These words and phrases show the reader the similarities between the two things. Try to use a variety of phrases.

Before you write

- Make notes about the differences and similarities between the two things you are comparing:

Before Internet	Today	Similar or different?
• School: research in libraries for essays • teaching with books	• School: research on Internet • teaching mainly with books	• Different • Similar
• Social: used the family phone • Teenagers like to get together in person	• Social: chat via text/email • Social networking • Teenagers like to get together	• Different • Different • Similar

- Choose the best points to include.
- Choose a structure (A or B) and organize your ideas into paragraphs.
  - A 1 Introduction   2 Differences and similarities of one aspect
     3 Differences and similarities of a second aspect
     4 Summary and your opinion
  - B 1 Introduction   2 Similarities   3 Differences   4 Summary and opinion

Language Bank: Comparing two things

Similarities
as + adjective or adverb + as
X is as good/strong/fast as Y.
Both X and Y…
Both boys and girls follow fashion and music.
Like X, Y…
Like their parents, they enjoy meeting their friends.
➲ See WRITING TIP at similarity

Differences
Comparative adjectives and adverbs
X is better/stronger/faster than Y.
Unlike X, Y…
Unlike their parents, most teenagers have grown up using computers.
X is different from Y (in that…)
X…, while Y… / While X…, Y…
➲ See WRITING TIP at difference

Checklist

Have I

- written about *exactly* what the task asked me to discuss? ☐
- written about both similarities and differences? ☐
- organized my ideas into logical paragraphs? ☐
- used linking words to help the reader follow what I've said? ☐
- given my opinion in the conclusion? ☐

Writing a report

A report describes a project or a study of a situation or problem. It includes facts or the results of your research. It may also include your suggestions or opinions on these facts. The language in reports should be clear, accurate and formal. *We* and *I* are often used in reports, for example to describe research that you have carried out.

> **Your town council wants to improve the sports facilities for teenagers in your area. Your head teacher has asked you to write a report to describe the current situation and make suggestions on how improvements can be made.**
> (180 - 200 words)
>
> **Local Sports Facilities for Teenagers**
>
> The purpose of this report is to examine our town's sports facilities for teenagers and make suggestions for their improvement. I visited each of our five sports centres and conducted a survey of students at my school.
>
> According to my survey, basketball and football are the most popular sports for boys, while swimming and tennis are the most popular for girls. Each centre has an indoor sports hall and swimming pool, as well as outdoor tennis courts, basketball courts and grass fields.
>
> However, most students said that they do not visit the centres because they are in such poor condition. For example:
>
> - All the outdoor courts need new fences and ground surfaces.
> - The indoor facilities require new paint and flooring.
> - The changing rooms are in poor condition and often dirty.
> - Damaged equipment should be repaired.
> - Each of the facilities is regularly short of equipment such as balls and nets.
>
> From the evidence, I conclude that if the facilities were in a better state, they would be used more often. It is recommended that the council consider investing in these centres to make them safer and more appealing to young people.

Paragraph 1 – Introduction
Explains the purpose of the report and how you did your research.

Paragraph 2 and 3 – Results
Give the results of the research.

Paragraph 4 – Conclusion
Gives a general conclusion and makes some suggestions.

Before you write

Think about the reader:
   Who will read this report and why?

Structure your writing
Title: Your title should tell the reader exactly what the report is about.
Introduction: This paragraph will give the reader some background.
   Why are you writing this report?
   What topics does it cover?
   How did you get the information?
Results: Give precise information about your research and what you have learned from it. It is important to give facts here rather than opinions.
Conclusion: Make suggestions and give your opinion.

Language Bank: Useful phrases for reports

Stating the purpose of the report
The purpose/aim of this report is to…
This report aims to…

Outlining research
I visited…
I asked 10 students to…
We examined/looked at (e.g. several centres)
I conducted a survey (of)…

Presenting findings
According to my survey…
We found that, on the whole,…
Overall, people preferred…
50% of those surveyed said that…

Giving conclusions
From the evidence, I conclude that…
In conclusion,…
The research shows/demonstrates that…

Making suggestions
It is recommended that…
We recommend/suggest that…
The best solution is/would be to…

Checklist

Have I
- made the purpose of my report clear? ☐
- included the information asked for? ☐
- made suggestions in the conclusion? ☐
- used clear formal language? ☐

Writing a review of a book or a film

The main purpose of a review is to give information about the book or film so that your readers can decide if they would like to read it or see it. Many student magazines and websites use an informal tone. However, for exams it is best to use more formal vocabulary and sentence structures.

> Your teacher has asked you to write a review for a film you have seen recently, to go on the school's website. Review the film, giving your opinion and saying whether or not you would recommend it.
> (180 - 200 words)
>
> ### Harry Potter and the Deathly Hallows: Part 2
>
> Millions of people have watched the earlier Harry Potter films. Will the final film of this famous story live up to expectations? *Harry Potter and the Deathly Hallows: Part 2* is set in both modern Britain and a fantasy world. Although it is much darker than previous films in the series, fans will leave the cinema feeling satisfied.
>
> Harry and his friends, Hermione and Ron, continue their search for the last three special objects hidden by the evil Voldemort, which they must destroy. As they fight their enemies for the last time, they learn some surprising secrets about several of the other characters and Harry finally discovers what he must do.
>
> The three friends have now grown up, like the actors playing the parts. This makes these characters very convincing. In fact, the acting is as usual of a very high standard. Alan Rickman, playing the role of Severus Snape, skilfully shows us a hidden side of the wicked headmaster.
>
> The battle scenes are thrilling, and the audience will laugh and cry with Harry and his friends as the story comes to its emotional end. I thoroughly recommend this exciting and enjoyable film.

Paragraph 1 – Introduction
General comments about the film and your opinion.

Paragraph 2 – Plot or story
A summary of what happens. Do not spoil it for your readers by telling them the end of the story.

Paragraph 3 – Characters
A comment on the characters in the film.

Paragraph 4 – Conclusion
Giving your opinion
Your conclusion and whether you think people should see the film or not.

- Starting with a question makes your readers interested.
- Include the title in the first paragraph and the name of the author, if it is a book.
- Use a variety of adjectives to make your review interesting.
- Use the present tense to describe the story.

Before you write

- Think about the film or look at the book again.
- Make notes about: the **type** of book or film it is
  the **setting** (the time and place of the story)
  the **plot** (what happens)
  the **characters** (and the **acting**, if it is a film)
  your **opinion**, positive or negative, with reasons
- Choose the best points to include in your review.
- Organize your ideas into paragraphs.

TIP
Remember that the person who reads the review has NOT seen the film or read the book.

Language Bank: Adjectives

Try to use a good variety of adjectives in your review. Use your dictionary to find synonyms for words like 'interesting'.

*This is an **exciting**/a **fast-moving**/
  gripping story…*
*This **dark**/**frightening** tale takes
  place in …*
*A **funny**/an **amusing** scene shows …*
*This **moving** account of… (e.g. a
  young man's experiences)*
*a **violent** film*
*an **interesting** situation*
*an **imaginary** world*
*a **romantic** relationship*
*a **tragic**/an **emotional** ending*

*The **principal**/My **favourite**
  characters are …*
*an **unpleasant**/a **strange**/
  sympathetic character*
*an **action**/a **battle**/**love**/**fight** scene*
*I thoroughly enjoyed this **rewarding**
  book.*
*I highly recommend this **action-
  packed** film.*

➲ See NOTE at **book**
➲ See NOTE at **film**

Checklist

Have I

- given the name of the film or book in the first paragraph? ☐
- written about the story without telling readers the ending? ☐
- written about the characters? ☐
- organized my ideas into logical paragraphs? ☐
- given my opinion in the conclusion? ☐

Writing formal letters: a letter of complaint

When you write a formal letter, think about **layout**, **style** and **content**.
Layout: how your letter looks on the page, where you put the addresses, etc.
Style: be polite. Avoid using 'you' or 'you didn't'.
Content: state the facts and say what you want to happen.

You have just returned from an English language course in England. You were not happy with the accommodation or activities arranged. Write a letter to the company complaining about this, and ask for compensation.
(120–150 words)

Carrer de Dali, 18
43740 Móra d'Ebre
Tarragona

Mrs Brigit Deakins
LearnFun Language Centres Ltd.
13 Erebos Road
London SW11 2AG
30th July 2012

Dear Mrs Deakins

I am writing to complain about the English language course I took in Worcester from July 1st –22nd, organised by LearnFun Language Centres Ltd.

Firstly, I was very dissatisfied with the accommodation. The advertisement promised that each student would have 'their own private room with study facilities'. Not only did I have to share a room with two other students, but it was not possible for me to study. Furthermore, your advertisement mentioned that 'exciting excursions and activities' would be available every week. In fact there were only two trips, both to a nearby town where there was very little to do.

I had been looking forward to my course. However, although the teaching was good, it was spoiled by these problems. I would therefore appreciate a refund of part of the cost of the course in compensation for my disappointment.

I look forward to hearing from you.

Yours sincerely

Natalio Hidalgo

Mr N Hidalgo

Paragraph 1 – Reason for writing
Explain clearly why you are writing.

Paragraph 2 – Complaint
Explain the problem and how you were affected.

Paragraph 3 – Demand for action
State clearly what action you want the company to take.

Paragraph 4 – Comment
A general comment saying you would like a quick reply.

Your address on the right.

The name and address of the person you are writing to on the left.

Date: usually under this address

Formal greeting and closing. If you do not know the person's name, use *Dear Sir or Madam* and finish with *Yours faithfully*.

Formal language. Do not use contractions or abbreviations.

Linking words and phrases to help the reader move from one point to the next.

Before you write
- Make notes about the details you need to include.
- Organize your points into 3 or 4 paragraphs.
- Plan the layout.
- Think about the beginning and ending and the language you will use.

TIP
If you are writing for an exam, you do not usually need to include addresses.

Language Bank: Formal letters

Openings and closings
Dear Sir/Madam... ...Yours faithfully
Dear Mrs Dawson... ...Yours sincerely

Introducing the topic
I am writing to complain about...
I am writing to express my dissatisfaction with...

Describing the problem
Strong adjectives:
I am/was appalled, distressed, disgusted, shocked...
Less strong adjectives:
I am/was unhappy, disappointed, dissatisfied...

Consequences
Therefore, As a result, For this Reason, Consequently, So
⊃ See NOTE at **therefore**

Listing items
Firstly,... Secondly,...
To begin with,...
In addition to this,...
Furthermore,...

What do you want?
A full/partial refund, a replacement, an apology, compensation

Endings
I look forward to your swift reply.
I look forward to hearing/ I hope to hear from you soon.

Checklist

Have I
- used the appropriate layout for a formal letter? ☐
- used a suitable greeting and close? ☐
- arranged my points into clear paragraphs? ☐
- explained the problem and the action I would like? ☐
- used formal, polite, clear language? ☐

Applying for a job 1: Writing a CV

A CV (*AmE résumé*) is a brief description of your education, work experience, skills and interests.

A good CV should be set out clearly so that the important facts and information are easy to find.

Name Nicholas Woodward
Address 8 St Peter's Close, Bromyard, Herefordshire HR7 4PS
Telephone 01632 960531   Mobile 07700 900420
Email nickw@zapmail.co.uk
Objective To find a temporary position that will help me to gain work experience in the hotel business.
Profile An outgoing and hard-working student.

Education and qualifications

2011– The King's School, Hereford. Taking A levels in: German; History; Social Studies

2007–2011 Queen Mary High School, Bromyard. 9 GCSEs: English Language (A*); English Literature (A); German (A); ICT (B); History (B); Physics (B); Social Studies (B); Geography (C); Mathematics (C)

Work experience

July 2011-September 2011: Activities Assistant at Worton Sports Centre. Assisted with the summer programme for young people. Responsibilities included teaching football and swimming.

August 2010-July 2012: Saturday morning shop assistant at Pinsley News, Hereford. Served customers, handled money, and checked stock, often working alone.

Skills

Languages: German - good

IT: Good keyboard skills. Familiarity with Word and Excel.

First Aid: Junior First Aid Certificate (March 2010)

Interests

Football (I was captain of the school team last year), photography, Scouts (I have been a member of the local Scout group since 2008)

References – attached

You can omit these labels. You do not need to include other information or send a photo.

These sections are optional, but are useful for employers.

Put your most recent education first.
Put your most recent work experience first. You do not need to use full sentences.

Your practical abilities. Mention any exams you have passed.

Keep this section short. Give the details of 2 people who know you well.

See NOTE at **job**
See NOTE at **reference**

Applying for a job 2: Writing a covering letter

When you apply for a job, you should send a covering letter (*AmE cover letter*) with your CV. Pay particular attention to the **layout**, **style** and **content**.

You have seen an advertisement for a hotel receptionist during the summer. Write to the hotel manager to apply for the job. Explain why you think you would be suitable. Give details of your skills and experience. (120 - 150 words)

---

8 St Peter's Close
Bromyard
Herefordshire HR7 4PS

Mrs Rachel Adams
The Lion Hotel
23 High Street
Hereford HR1 2LR

4th July 2012

Dear Mrs Adams

Paragraph 1: Give your reason for writing. Say why you are interested in the job.

I am writing to apply for the post of temporary receptionist, which I saw advertised in the local newspaper on 1st July. I enclose a copy of my CV. I have just finished the first year of my A level studies and am interested in gaining work experience within the hotel business during the summer, as I hope to apply to university to study Hotel Management.

Paragraph 2: Say what you can bring to the job.

As you will see from my CV, I have some experience in dealing with people. Although I lack direct experience as a receptionist, as a shop assistant I have dealt with all types of customers in a polite and helpful way. In addition, I can offer skills in IT, German and First Aid.

Paragraph 3: Say when you will be available for interview.

I would very much like to be a part of your team. I am available for interview next week, and I look forward to hearing from you.

Yours sincerely

N Woodward

Nick Woodward

Your address, but not your name, on the right. The name and address of the person you are writing to on the left. The date: usually under the address

See NOTE at dear
See NOTE at sincere

Formal greeting and closing. If you do not know the person's name, use *Dear Sir or Madam* and finish with *Yours faithfully*.

Use formal language and full sentences. Do not use contractions or abbreviations.

Writing an informal email

Emails can vary a lot in style. An email can be very informal if you are writing to somebody you know well. If you are writing about something serious, or if you do not know the person very well, you will need to use more formal language.

You have received an email from a friend who has moved to a new city and is very homesick. Reply to your friend and give her some advice about how she can make new friends and settle into her new surroundings. (120 – 150 words)

From: miguel@unimail.es

To: jules@informail.com

Subject: **Feeling homesick**

Hi Juliet

It was great to get your email, but I'm sorry to hear you're feeling homesick and missing us all. We miss you too!

I know it's lonely for you being in a new place – it was the same for me – but it takes time to make new friends. Why don't you try joining some local clubs or societies? You may be able to find people who have the same interests as you. I know you love rock climbing – maybe you can find some fellow climbers!

Another thing you should do is introduce yourself to your neighbours. It's always good to get to know the people who live around you. They may be able to help you settle in and find your way around.

I hope you'll start to feel better soon. Remember that you can always email me if you have any problems or just need to chat.

Love

Miguel

Write a subject line that says clearly what your email is about. You can use an informal greeting and close.

Use informal but polite language. You can use contractions and abbreviations. You do not need to use long or full sentences.

You can use exclamation marks, but not too many.

TIP
Do not use slang, emoticons (such as :-)) or texting abbreviations (such as **2nite** instead of **tonight**).

Language Bank: Informal emails

Opening
Dear, Hi , Hello + first name

Closing
Best wishes, All the best (friends and acquaintances)
Love, Take care, Speak to you soon (close friends)

Clothes

- cap
- V-neck
- sweater (*BrE also* jumper)
- backpack (*BrE also* rucksack)
- trainer (*AmE* sneaker)
- coat
- zip (*AmE* zipper)
- glove
- jeans
- button
- top
- denim jacket
- shoulder bag
- skirt
- tights (*AmE* pantyhose)
- tie
- jacket
- suit
- trousers (*AmE* pants)
- briefcase
- shoe
- hoody
- fly (*also* flies)
- pocket
- cargo pants
- collar
- shirt
- sleeve
- cuff
- buckle
- belt
- pyjamas (*AmE* pajamas)

MORE TO EXPLORE

bag
button
cardigan
dress
hat
lace
overall
raincoat
sari
scarf
shoe
sock
sweater
swimsuit
underwear

patterns

- zigzag
- patterned
- plain
- flowery
- checked
- striped

Work and jobs

farmer

carpenter

plumber

pilot

teacher

police officer

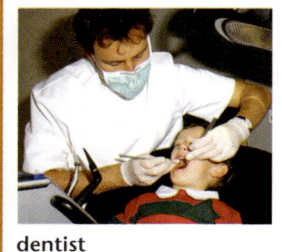

dentist

doctor

nurse

waiter

cook

shop assistant (*AmE* **sales clerk**)

MORE TO EXPLORE

accountant	engineer	journalist	pay
chef	firefighter	lawyer	politician
chemist	hairdresser	office	programmer
electrician	job	optician	secretary

Leisure activities

painting

tenpin bowling

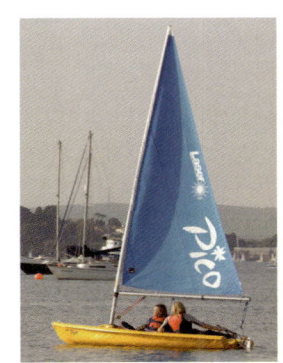

sailing

playing computer games

model making

going to the gym

sewing

photography

surfing the Internet

stamp collecting

acting

climbing

MORE TO EXPLORE

aerobics	domino	pool
card	hiking	snooker
chess	jigsaw	

Sports

rugby

baseball

cricket
- umpire
- bowler
- batsman
- wicket

tennis
- net
- court
- racket

ice hockey (*AmE* hockey)
- goal

hockey (*AmE* field hockey)

basketball
- basket

weightlifting

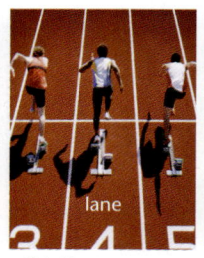

athletics
- lane

gymnastics
- gymnast

skating

skiing
- skier

P5

Sports

horse racing — jockey

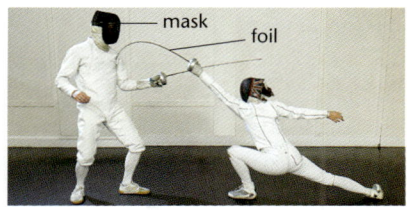

fencing — mask, foil

table tennis

karate

boxing — boxer

golf — golf club, golfer

MORE TO EXPLORE

badminton	skate	amateur
football	sport	professional
horse	squash	exercise
martial arts	swim	score
netball	trampoline	
parachute	volleyball	

Extreme sports

waterskiing

bungee jumping

surfing — surfer, surfboard

abseiling (*AmE* **rappelling**)

white-water rafting

windsurfing

Transport

aircraft

plane | undercarriage

helicopter — blade

glider — wing

boats

oil tanker

liner — stern | bow

lifeboat

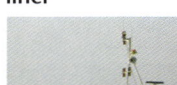

hovercraft

ferry

yacht — mast, sail

submarine

MORE TO EXPLORE

barge	bus	engine	sail
bicycle	car	motor	raft
bike	cruiser	parking	train
boat	driving	plane	travel

P7 Transport

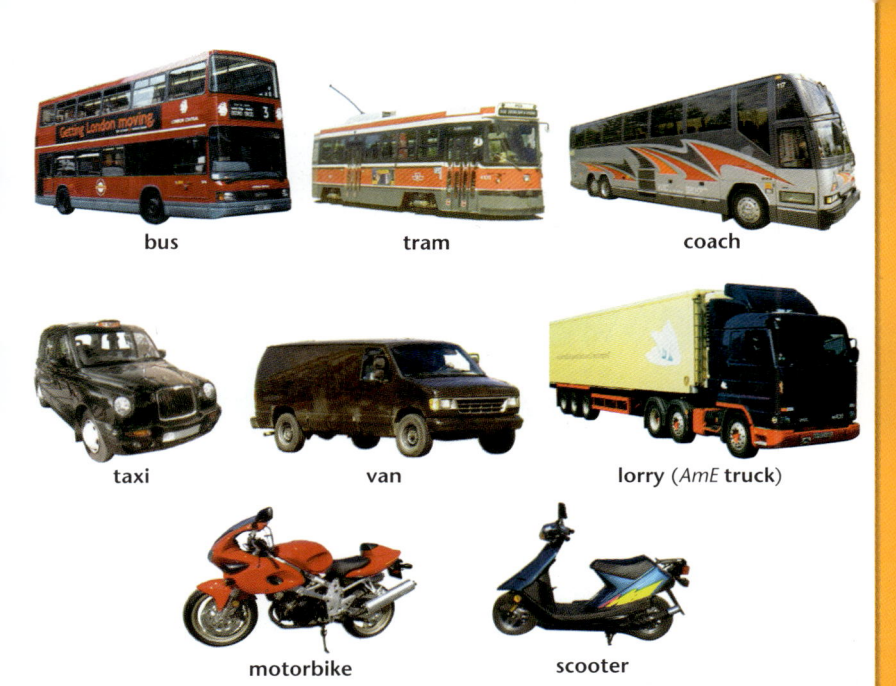

bus   **tram**   **coach**

taxi   **van**   **lorry** (*AmE* **truck**)

motorbike   **scooter**

cars

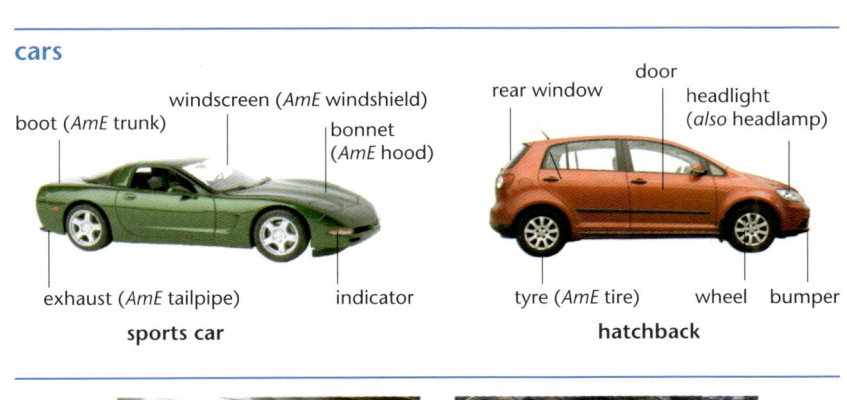

boot (*AmE* trunk) — windscreen (*AmE* windshield) — bonnet (*AmE* hood) — exhaust (*AmE* tailpipe) — indicator

sports car

rear window — door — headlight (*also* headlamp) — tyre (*AmE* tire) — wheel — bumper

hatchback

carriage

underground (*AmE* **subway**)    **train**

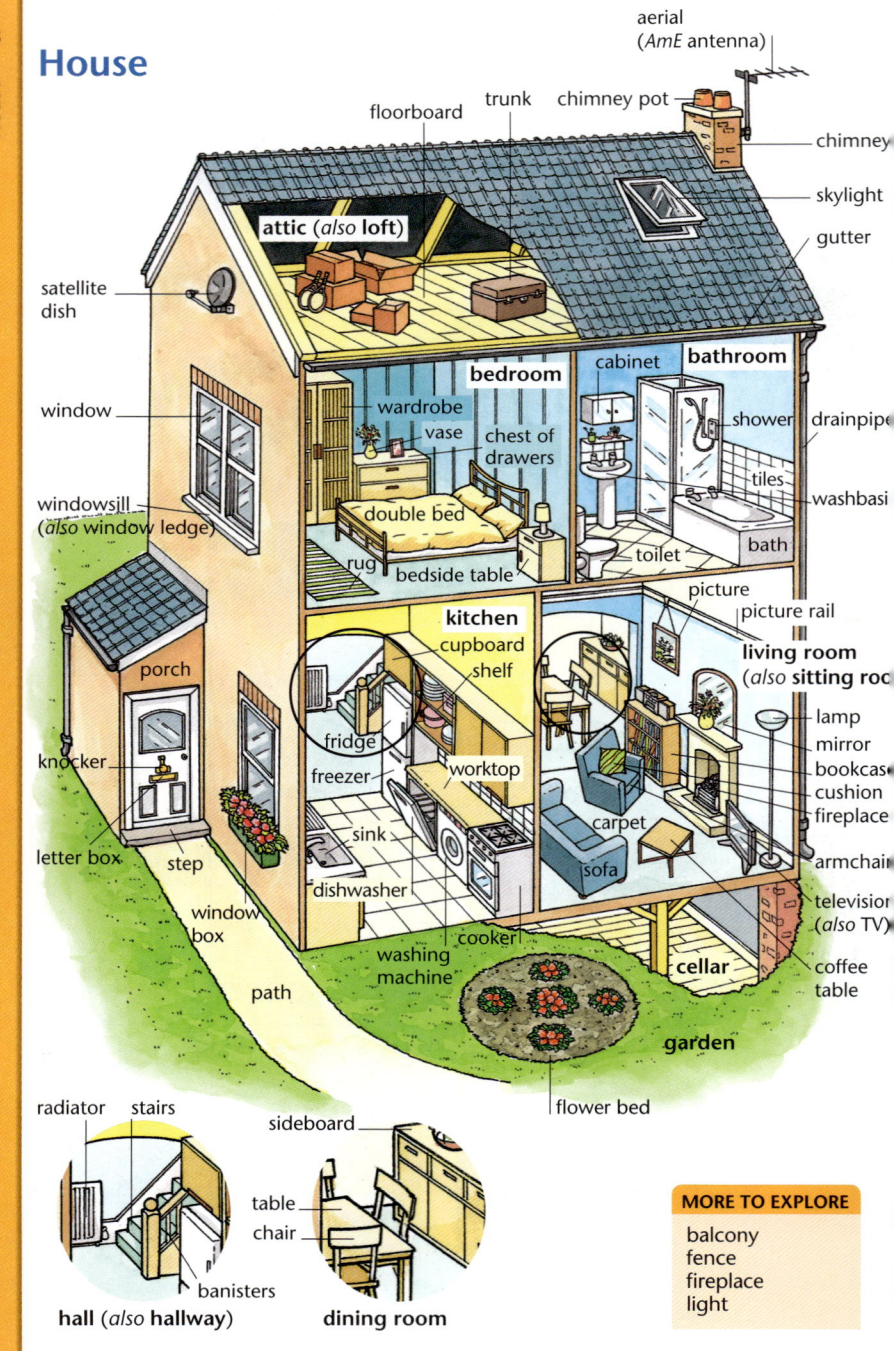

House

A labeled illustration of a house with the following parts identified:

- aerial (AmE antenna)
- floorboard
- trunk
- chimney pot
- chimney
- skylight
- gutter
- attic (also loft)
- satellite dish
- window
- windowsill (also window ledge)
- bedroom
- wardrobe
- vase
- chest of drawers
- cabinet
- bathroom
- shower
- drainpipe
- tiles
- washbasin
- double bed
- rug
- bedside table
- bath
- toilet
- picture
- picture rail
- porch
- kitchen
- cupboard
- shelf
- living room (also sitting room)
- knocker
- fridge
- freezer
- worktop
- lamp
- mirror
- bookcase
- cushion
- fireplace
- letter box
- step
- sink
- dishwasher
- carpet
- sofa
- armchair
- television (also TV)
- window box
- cooker
- cellar
- coffee table
- washing machine
- path
- garden
- flower bed
- radiator
- stairs
- sideboard
- table
- chair
- banisters
- hall (also hallway)
- dining room

MORE TO EXPLORE

balcony
fence
fireplace
light

Homes

terraced houses

block of flats (*AmE* apartment block)

detached house

semi-detached houses (bay window)

bungalow (roof, lawn)

thatched cottage (thatch)

farm

stately home

MORE TO EXPLORE			
castle	estate	palace	yard
chalet	flat	property	

Landscape

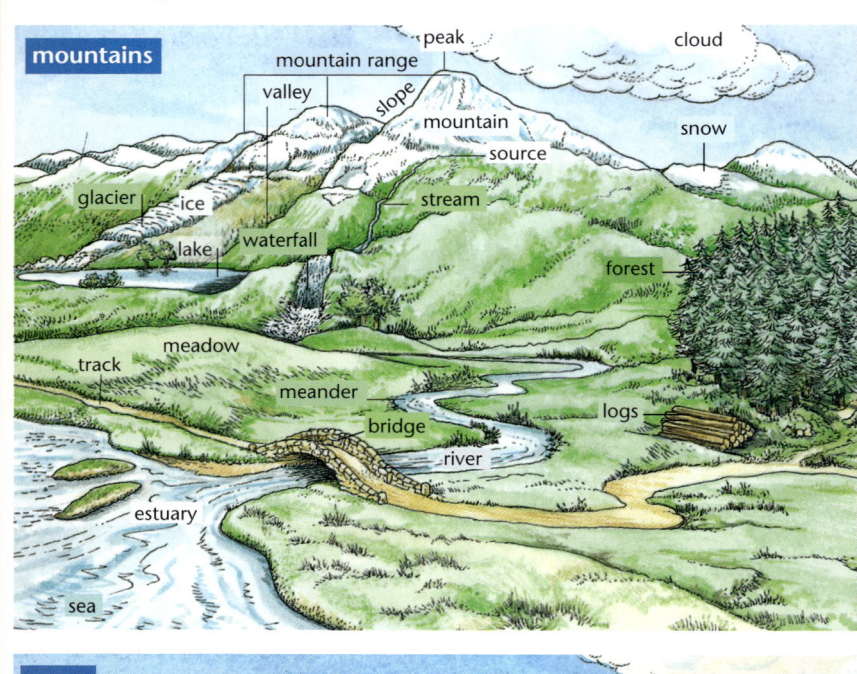

mountains

- peak
- mountain range
- valley
- slope
- mountain
- snow
- cloud
- source
- stream
- glacier
- ice
- lake
- waterfall
- forest
- track
- meadow
- meander
- logs
- bridge
- river
- estuary
- sea

coast

- lighthouse
- harbour (AmE harbor)
- headland
- horizon
- island
- cave
- cliff
- rock
- sea
- wake
- rock pool
- shore
- bay
- waves
- sand dune
- beach
- pebble
- sand
- shell
- seaweed

Landscape

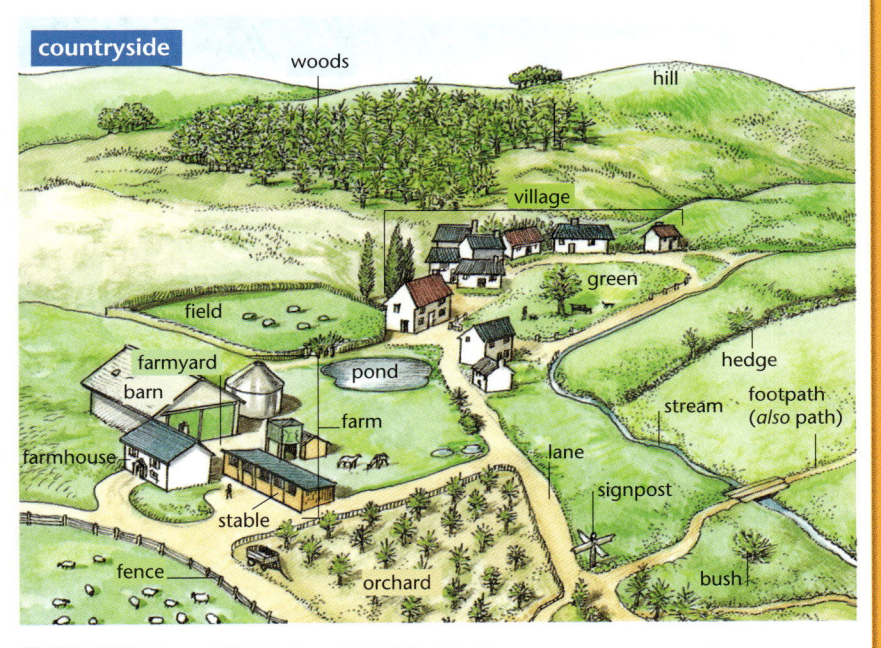

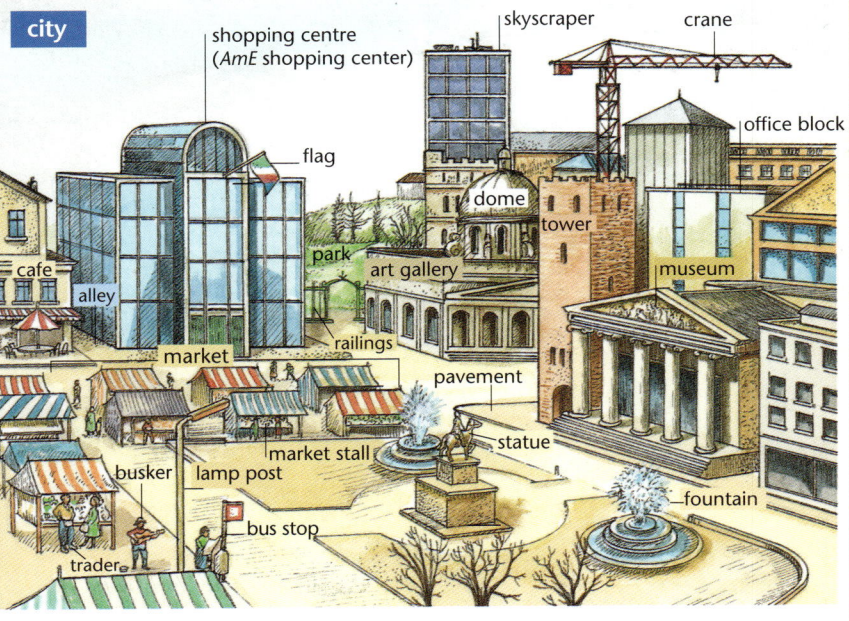

countryside

- woods
- hill
- village
- green
- field
- hedge
- farmyard
- pond
- footpath (*also* path)
- barn
- farm
- stream
- farmhouse
- lane
- stable
- signpost
- fence
- orchard
- bush

city

- shopping centre (*AmE* shopping center)
- skyscraper
- crane
- flag
- office block
- dome
- park
- tower
- cafe
- art gallery
- museum
- alley
- market
- railings
- pavement
- statue
- busker
- market stall
- lamp post
- fountain
- trader
- bus stop

P11

Animals

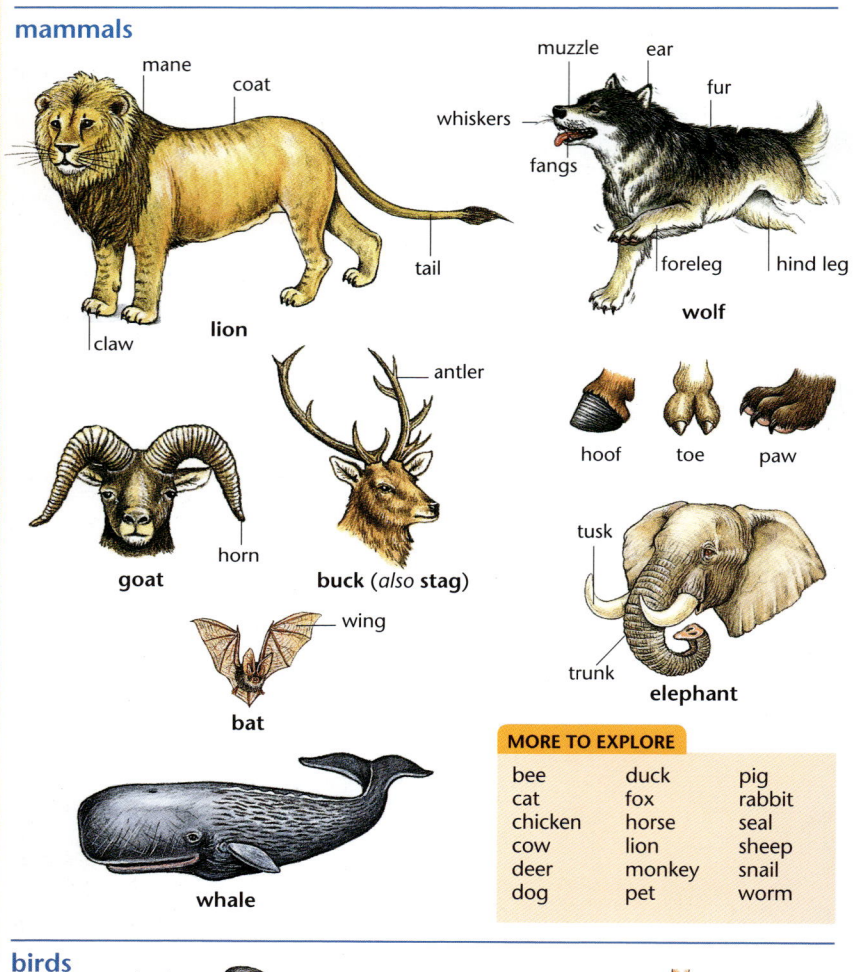

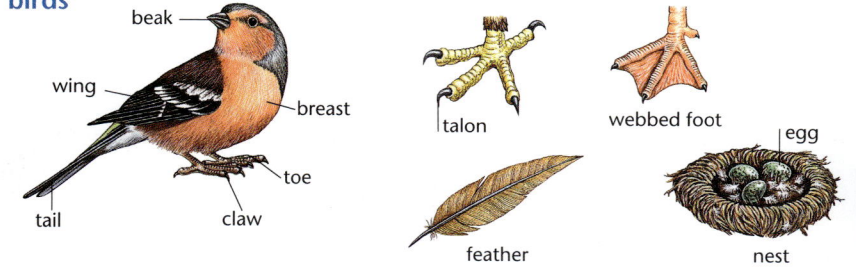

mammals

lion — mane, coat, tail, claw

wolf — muzzle, ear, fur, whiskers, fangs, foreleg, hind leg

goat — horn

buck (*also* **stag**) — antler

hoof, toe, paw

elephant — tusk, trunk

bat — wing

whale

MORE TO EXPLORE

bee	duck	pig
cat	fox	rabbit
chicken	horse	seal
cow	lion	sheep
deer	monkey	snail
dog	pet	worm

birds

beak, wing, breast, tail, claw, toe

talon, webbed foot, feather, egg, nest

reptiles

snake

shell — tortoise (*AmE* turtle)

turtle — flipper

amphibians

tadpole   frogspawn

toad   frog

insects

butterfly

eggs

caterpillar

chrysalis

moth

flea

mosquito

dragonfly

antenna, wing, sting — bee

wasp

fly   ant

beetle   larva

ladybird (*AmE* ladybug)   grasshopper

shellfish

antenna — prawn (*AmE* shrimp)

claw/pincer, shell — crab

fish

fin, tail, gill

Fruit

- lime
- lemon
- orange
- grapefruit (segment)
- apple (pip, core)
- pear
- plum
- peach (stone)
- papaya (*also* pawpaw) (skin, flesh)
- fig
- apricot
- coconut (shell, milk)
- mango
- kiwi fruit
- pomegranate (seeds)
- banana (peel)
- watermelon
- melon
- pineapple
- cherries (stalk)
- strawberries
- gooseberries
- avocado
- grapes
- raspberries
- blackberries

herbs and spices

- thyme
- parsley
- basil
- mint
- ginger
- cloves
- cinnamon

Vegetables

- asparagus
- Brussels sprouts
- parsnip
- carrot
- sweetcorn (*AmE* corn)
- potato
- broccoli
- artichoke
- aubergine (*AmE* eggplant)
- cabbage
- spinach
- cauliflower
- celery
- pumpkin
- marrow
- leek
- courgette (*AmE* zucchini)
- spring onions
- mushrooms
- peas (pod)
- beans
- onion
- peppers
- radishes
- lettuce
- garlic
- chilli (*AmE* chili)
- tomato
- cucumber

Food and drink

burger
noodles
salad
filling
sandwich
soup
hot dog
pizza
skewer
kebab
pasta
fish and chips
sauce
roast beef
spaghetti
quiche
jacket potato (*also* baked potato)
apple pie
ice cream
pancake
cheese
bowl
cereal
cream
jam (*AmE* jelly)
eggs
waffle
honey
milkshake
cup of tea
black coffee

MORE TO EXPLORE

cake	nuts
coffee	porridge
drink	pudding
fish	sausage
fizzy	shellfish
meat	takeaway

Reference section

Contents

Grammar

- R2 Irregular verbs
- R5 Be, do, have
- R6 The tenses of regular verbs
- R8 Talking about the present, past and future
- R10 Conditionals
- R11 Modal verbs
- R12 The passive
- R13 Reported speech
- R14 Verb patterns
- R16 Phrasal verbs
- R17 Nouns
- R19 Adjectives
- R20 Relative clauses

Other reference

- R21 Prefixes
- R22 Suffixes
- R23 Expressions using numbers
- R27 British and American English
- R28 Map of the British Isles
- R30 Map of Canada and the United States
- R32 Geographical names
- R37 Telephoning and texting
- R38 Learning vocabulary
- R40 Punctuation
- R41 Pronunciation

Irregular verbs

In this list you will find the infinitive form of the verb followed by the past tense and the past participle. Where two forms are given, look up the verb in the main part of the dictionary to see whether there is a difference in the meaning.

Infinitive	Past tense	Past participle	Infinitive	Past tense	Past participle
arise	arose	arisen	dive	dived;	dived
awake	awoke	awoken		(AmE) dove	
babysit	babysat	babysat	do	did	done
be	was/were	been	draw	drew	drawn
bear	bore	borne	dream	dreamt,	dreamt,
beat	beat	beaten		dreamed	dreamed
become	became	become	drink	drank	drunk
befall	befell	befallen	drive	drove	driven
begin	began	begun	dwell	dwelt,	dwelt,
bend	bent	bent		dwelled	dwelled
beset	beset	beset	eat	ate	eaten
bet	bet, betted	bet, betted	fall	fell	fallen
bid	bid	bid	feed	fed	fed
bind	bound	bound	feel	felt	felt
bite	bit	bitten	fight	fought	fought
bleed	bled	bled	find	found	found
blow	blew	blown	flee	fled	fled
break	broke	broken	fling	flung	flung
breastfeed	breastfed	breastfed	fly	flew	flown
breed	bred	bred	forbid	forbade,	forbidden
bring	brought	brought		forbad	
broadcast	broadcast	broadcast	forecast	forecast	forecast
browbeat	browbeat	browbeaten	foresee	foresaw	foreseen
build	built	built	forget	forgot	forgotten
burn	burnt,	burnt,	forgive	forgave	forgiven
	burned	burned	forgo	forwent	forgone
burst	burst	burst	forsake	forsook	forsaken
bust	bust,	bust,	freeze	froze	frozen
	busted	busted	get	got	got;
buy	bought	bought			(AmE) gotten
cast	cast	cast	give	gave	given
catch	caught	caught	go	went	gone
choose	chose	chosen	grind	ground	ground
cling	clung	clung	grow	grew	grown
come	came	come	hang	hung,	hung,
cost	cost	cost		hanged	hanged
creep	crept	crept	have	had	had
cut	cut	cut	hear	heard	heard
deal	dealt	dealt	hide	hid	hidden
dig	dug	dug	hit	hit	hit

Irregular verbs

Infinitive	Past tense	Past participle
hold	held	held
hurt	hurt	hurt
input	input, inputted	input, inputted
keep	kept	kept
kneel	knelt; (esp AmE) kneeled	knelt; (esp AmE) kneeled
know	knew	known
lay	laid	laid
lead	led	led
lean	leant, leaned	leant, leaned
leap	leapt, leaped	leapt, leaped
learn	learnt, learned	learnt, learned
leave	left	left
lend	lent	lent
let	let	let
lie	lay	lain
light	lighted, lit	lighted, lit
lose	lost	lost
make	made	made
mean	meant	meant
meet	met	met
mislay	mislaid	mislaid
mislead	misled	misled
misread	misread	misread
misspell	misspelt, misspelled	misspelt, misspelled
mistake	mistook	mistaken
misunderstand	misunderstood	misunderstood
mow	mowed	mown, mowed
outdo	outdid	outdone
outgrow	outgrew	outgrown
overcome	overcame	overcome
overdo	overdid	overdone
overhang	overhung	overhung
overhear	overheard	overheard
overpay	overpaid	overpaid
override	overrode	overridden
overrun	overran	overrun
oversee	oversaw	overseen
oversleep	overslept	overslept
overtake	overtook	overtaken
overthrow	overthrew	overthrown
pay	paid	paid
prove	proved	proved; (AmE) proven

Infinitive	Past tense	Past participle
put	put	put
quit	quit	quit
read	read	read
rebuild	rebuilt	rebuilt
repay	repaid	repaid
rethink	rethought	rethought
rewind	rewound	rewound
rewrite	rewrote	rewritten
rid	rid	rid
ride	rode	ridden
ring	rang	rung
rise	rose	risen
run	ran	run
saw	sawed	sawn; (AmE) sawed
say	said	said
see	saw	seen
seek	sought	sought
sell	sold	sold
send	sent	sent
set	set	set
sew	sewed	sewn, sewed
shake	shook	shaken
shear	sheared	shorn, sheared
shed	shed	shed
shine	shone	shone
shoe	shod	shod
shoot	shot	shot
show	showed	shown, showed
shrink	shrank, shrunk	shrunk
shut	shut	shut
sing	sang	sung
sink	sank	sunk
sit	sat	sat
slay	slew	slain
sleep	slept	slept
slide	slid	slid
sling	slung	slung
slink	slunk	slunk
slit	slit	slit
smell	smelt, smelled	smelt, smelled
sow	sowed	sown, sowed
speak	spoke	spoken
speed	sped, speeded	sped, speeded
spell	spelt, spelled	spelt, spelled

Irregular verbs

Infinitive	Past tense	Past participle	Infinitive	Past tense	Past participle
spend	spent	spent	think	thought	thought
spill	spilt, spilled	spilt, spilled	thrive	thrived, throve	thrived
spin	spun	spun	throw	threw	thrown
spit	spat; (AmE also) spit	spat; (AmE also) spit	thrust	thrust	thrust
			tread	trod	trodden
split	split	split	undercut	undercut	undercut
spoil	spoilt, spoiled	spoilt, spoiled	undergo	underwent	undergone
			underlie	underlay	underlain
spread	spread	spread	underpay	underpaid	underpaid
spring	sprang	sprung	understand	understood	understood
stand	stood	stood	undertake	undertook	undertaken
steal	stole	stolen	undo	undid	undone
stick	stuck	stuck	unwind	unwound	unwound
sting	stung	stung	uphold	upheld	upheld
stink	stank, stunk	stunk	upset	upset	upset
			wake	woke	woken
stride	strode	—	wear	wore	worn
strike	struck	struck	weave	wove, weaved	woven, weaved
string	strung	strung			
strive	strove	striven	weep	wept	wept
swear	swore	sworn	wet	wet, wetted	wet, wetted
sweep	swept	swept			
swell	swelled	swollen, swelled	win	won	won
swim	swam	swum	wind	wound	wound
swing	swung	swung	withdraw	withdrew	withdrawn
take	took	taken	withhold	withheld	withheld
teach	taught	taught	withstand	withstood	withstood
tear	tore	torn	wring	wrung	wrung
tell	told	told	write	wrote	written

Be, do, have

Full forms	Short forms	Negative short forms

be present tense

I am	I'm	I'm not
you are	you're	you're not/you aren't
he is	he's	he's not/he isn't
she is	she's	she's not/she isn't
it is	it's	it's not/it isn't
we are	we're	we're not/we aren't
you are	you're	you're not/you aren't
they are	they're	they're not/they aren't

be past tense

I was	—	I wasn't
you were	—	you weren't
he was	—	he wasn't
she was	—	she wasn't
it was	—	it wasn't
we were	—	we weren't
you were	—	you weren't
they were	—	they weren't

have present tense

I have	I've	I haven't/I've not
you have	you've	you haven't/you've not
he has	he's	he hasn't/he's not
she has	she's	she hasn't/she's not
it has	it's	it hasn't/it's not
we have	we've	we haven't/we've not
you have	you've	you haven't/you've not
they have	they've	they haven't/they've not

have past tense (all persons)

| had | I'd you'd etc. | hadn't |

do present tense

I do	—	I don't
you do	—	you don't
he does	—	he doesn't
she does	—	she doesn't
it does	—	it doesn't
we do	—	we don't
you do	—	you don't
they do	—	they don't

do past tense (all persons)

| did | — | didn't |

	be	*do*	*have*
present participle	being	doing	having
past participle	been	done	had

- The negative full forms are formed by adding **not**.

- Questions in the present and past are formed by placing the verb before the subject:
  - ▶ am I?   isn't he?
  - was I?   weren't we?
  - do I?   didn't I?
  - have I?   hadn't they?
  - etc.

Auxiliary verbs

- **Do** is used to form questions and negatives in the present and past simple. Note that the auxiliary verb and not the main verb shows the negative past tense:
  - ▶ *She washed.*
  - ▶ *She didn't wash.*

- **Have** is used to form the perfect tenses:
  - ▶ *I haven't finished.*
  - ▶ *Has he arrived yet?*
  - ▶ *They hadn't seen each other for a long time.*

- **Be** is used to form the continuous tenses and the passive:
  - ▶ *I'm studying Italian.*
  - ▶ *We were watching TV.*
  - ▶ *It was painted by a famous artist.*

Verbs

Regular verbs: the simple tenses

Present simple

I/we/you/they work	do not work (don't work)	Do **I** work?
he/she/it works	does not work (doesn't work)	Does **he** work?

Past simple

I/we/you/they/he/she/it worked	did not work (didn't work)	Did **they** work?

Future simple

I/we/you/they/he/she/it will work (**he'**ll work)	will not work (won't work)	Will **he** work?

Present perfect

I/we/you/they have worked (**I'**ve worked)	have not worked (haven't worked)	Have **you** worked?
he/she/it has worked (**she'**s worked)	has not worked (hasn't worked)	Has **she** worked?

Past perfect

I/we/you/they/he/she/it had worked (**they'**d worked)	had not worked (hadn't worked)	Had **they** worked?

Future perfect

I/we/you/they/he/she/it will have worked (**we'**ll have worked)	will not have worked (won't have worked)	Will **we** have worked?

Conditional

I/we/you/they/he/she/it would work (**I'**d work)	would not work (wouldn't work)	Would **you** work?

Conditional perfect

I/we/you/they/he/she/it would have worked (**would'**ve worked)	would not have worked (wouldn't have worked)	Would **she** have worked?

Regular verbs: the continuous tenses

NOTE The continuous tenses are sometimes called the progressive tenses.

Present continuous

I am working (I'm working)	am not working (I'm not working)	Am I working?
you/we/they are working (you're working)	are not working (aren't working)	Are you working?
he/she/it is working (he's working)	is not working (isn't working)	Is he working?

Past continuous

I/he/she/it was working	was not working (wasn't working)	Was he working?
we/you/they were working	were not working (weren't working)	Were you working?

Future continuous

I/we/you/they/he/she/it will be working (he'll be working)	will not be working (won't be working)	Will he be working?

Present perfect continuous

I/we/you/they have been working (you've been working)	have not been working (haven't been working)	Have I been working?
he/she/it has been working (she's been working)	has not been working (hasn't been working)	Has she been working?

Past perfect continuous

I/we/you/they/he/she/it had been working (he'd been working)	had not been working (hadn't been working)	Had he been working?

Future perfect continuous

I/we/you/they/he/she/it will have been working (she'll have been working)	will not have been working (won't have been working)	Will she have been working?

Conditional continuous

I/we/you/they/he/she/it would be working (he'd be working)	would not be working (wouldn't be working)	Would he be working?

Conditional perfect continuous

I/we/you/they/he/she/it would have been working (would've been working)	would not have been working (wouldn't have been working)	Would she have been working?

Talking about the present

You use the **present continuous**

- to talk about an action that is happening now:
  - ▶ We're **waiting** for a train.
  - ▶ What **are** you **doing**?
  - ▶ She's **listening** to the radio.
- to talk about something that is not yet finished, even if you are not doing it at the moment when you are talking:
  - ▶ I'm **learning** the guitar.
  - ▶ He's **writing** a book about fashion.
- with **always**, to talk about something that happens often, and that you find annoying:
  - ▶ He's always **asking** to borrow money.
  - ▶ She's always **phoning** her friends late at night.

  NOTE Some verbs are not used in the continuous tenses, for example **need, want, know, hear, smell, agree, seem, appear, understand**, etc. These verbs refer to a state, not an action:
  - ▶ I **need** a holiday.
  - ▶ She **hates** the new house.
  - ▶ They **love** Indian food.
  - ▶ He **wants** to be alone.
  - ▶ Do you **know** Lucy Johnston?

Other verbs are used in the present continuous when they refer to an action, and the present simple when they refer to a state:
  - ▶ She's **tasting** the cheese.
  - ▶ The cheese **tastes** salty.
  - ▶ He's **being** noisy today.
  - ▶ He's a noisy dog.
  - ▶ What **are** you **thinking** about?
  - ▶ Do you **think** I should leave?

You use the **present simple**

- to talk about a permanent situation:
  - ▶ He **lives** in Scotland.
  - ▶ She **works** in local government.
- to talk about something that is always true:
  - ▶ Oranges **don't grow** this far north.
  - ▶ What temperature **does** water **freeze** at?
- to talk about things that happen regularly:
  - ▶ She **goes** to yoga every Monday.
  - ▶ We **don't** often **go** to the theatre.

Talking about the past

You use the **past simple**

- to talk about an action that took place in the past:
  - ▶ He **turned** round, **dropped** the bag and **ran** away.
  - ▶ I **didn't write** to her, but I **rang** her.
  - ▶ Where **did** you **stay** in Glasgow?

  NOTE Often a specific time is mentioned:
  - ▶ **Did** you **see** Rory yesterday?

- to talk about a state that continued for some time, but that is now finished:
  - ▶ I **went** to school in Ireland.
  - ▶ **Did** she really **work** there for ten years?

- to talk about actions that happened regularly in the past:
  - ▶ They often **played** chess together. She always **won**.
  - ▶ We always **went** to Devon for our summer holidays when I was a child.

You use the **present perfect**

- to talk about something that happened during a period of time that is not yet finished:
  - ▶ The train **has been** late three times this week.
  - ▶ He still **hasn't visited** her.

- when the time is not mentioned, or is not important:
  - *He's **written** a book.*
  - (BUT *He **wrote** a book last year.*)
  - *I've **bought** a bike.*
  - (BUT *I **bought** a bike on Saturday.*)
- when the action finished in the past, but the effect is still felt in the present:
  - *He's **lost** his wallet*
  - (and he still hasn't found it).
- with **for** and **since** to show the duration of an action or state up until the present:
  - *She **hasn't bought** any new clothes for ages.*
  - *They **have lived** here for ten years, and they don't want to move.*
  - *I've **worked** here since 1998.*
- in British English with **just**, **ever**, **already** and **yet**:
  - *I've just **arrived**.*
  - *Have you ever **been** here before?*
  - *He's already **packed** his suitcases.*
  - *Haven't you **finished** yet?*

You use the **present perfect continuous**

- with **for** and **since** to talk about an activity that started in the past and is still happening:
  - *I've **been waiting** since ten o'clock.*
  - *They **haven't been learning** English for very long.*

- to talk about an activity that has finished and whose results are visible now:
  - *My hands are dirty because I've **been digging** the garden.*

You use the **past continuous**

- to talk about something that was already in progress when something else happened:
  - *The telephone rang while we **were having** dinner.*
  - ***Was** it **raining** when you left the house?*

  NOTE As with the present continuous, this tense cannot be used with 'state' verbs:
  - *Jamie's cake tasted delicious.*
  - (NOT *was tasting*)

You use the **past perfect**

- to talk about something that happened before another action in the past:
  - *When I got to the airport, the plane **had** already **left**.*
  - *They **had** just **bought** a flat when Joe lost his job.*

You use the **past perfect continuous**

- to talk about an activity that went on for a period of time further back in the past than something else:
  - *My hands were dirty because I **had been digging** the garden.*
  - *She **hadn't been working** at the shop very long when they sacked her.*

Talking about the future

There are several ways of talking about the future.

You use **be going to** with the **infinitive**

- to talk about what you intend to do in the future:
  - *I'm **going to see** a film tonight.*
  - *What **are you going to do** when you leave school?*
  - *I'm not **going to play** tennis this Saturday.*

You use the **future simple**
(**will** with the **infinitive**)

- to talk about a decision that you make as you are speaking:
  - *It's warm in here. I'**ll open** a window.*
  - *I'**ll have** the salad, please.*
- to talk about what you know or think will happen in the future (but not about your own intentions or plans):
  - *She'**ll be** 25 on her next birthday.*
  - ***Will** he **pass** the exam, do you think?*
  - *This job **won't take** long.*

- for requests, promises, and offers:
  - ▶ *Will* you *buy* some milk on your way home?
  - ▶ *We'll be* back soon, don't worry.
  - ▶ *I'll help* you with your homework.

You use the present continuous

- to talk about future plans where the time is mentioned:
  - ▶ *He's flying* to Thailand in June.
  - ▶ What *are* you *doing* this weekend?
  - ▶ *I'm* not *starting* my new job till next Monday.

You use the present simple

- to talk about future plans where something has been officially arranged, for example on a timetable or programme:
  - ▶ We *leave* Prague at 10 and *arrive* in London at 11.50.
  - ▶ School *starts* on 3rd September.
- to refer to a future time after when, as soon as, before, until, etc.:
  - ▶ Ring me as soon as you *hear* any news.
  - ▶ I'll look after Tim until you *get* back.
  - ▶ You'll remember Dita when you *see* her.

You use about to with the infinitive

- to talk about the very near future:
  - ▶ Hurry up! The train is *about to leave*.

You use the future continuous

- to talk about actions that will continue for a period of time in the future:
  - ▶ *I'll be waiting* near the ticket office. *I'll be wearing* a red scarf.
  - ▶ This time next week you*'ll be relaxing* in the sun!
- to ask somebody about their plans or intentions:
  - ▶ How many nights *will* you *be staying*?
  - ▶ *Will* you *be returning* by bus or by train?

You use the future perfect:

- to talk about something that will be finished at a particular time in the future:
  - ▶ *I will have finished* this work by 3 o'clock.
  - ▶ *They'll have lived* here for four years in May.

Conditionals

Sentences with if express possibilities. There are three main types:

1 possible – it might happen in the future:
- ▶ If I *win* £1000, I *will take* you to Paris.
- ▶ If I *pass* the exam, I*'ll go* to medical school.

Present tense after *if*, **future tense** in the main clause.

2 improbable – it is unlikely to happen in the future:
- ▶ If I *won* £1000, I *would take* you to Paris.
- ▶ If I *passed* the exam, I *would go* to medical school.

Past simple after *if*, **conditional tense** in the main clause.

3 impossible – it didn't happen in the past:
- ▶ If I *had won* £1000, I *would have taken* you to Paris.
- ▶ If I *had passed* the exam, I *would have gone* to medical school.

Past perfect after *if*, **conditional perfect** in the main clause.

Another type of *if* sentence expresses something that is always true or was always true in the past:
- ▶ If you *pour* oil on water, it *floats*.

Present simple in both parts of the sentence.
- ▶ If I *asked* her to come with us, she always *said* no.

Past simple in both parts of the sentence.

Modal verbs

Ability
can • could • be able to
- **Can** he swim?
- My sister **could** read when she was four.
- I **couldn't** find my shoes this morning.
- I **could have** run faster, but I didn't want to get tired.
- She **has** not **been able to** walk since the accident.
- He **was able to** speak to Tracey before she left.
- **Will** people **be able to** live on the moon one day?

➲ For the difference between 'could' and 'managed to', look at the note at the entry for **could**.

Possibility
could • may • might • can
- **Could/Might** you **have** left it on the bus?
- She **may/might/could** be ill. I'll phone her.
- I **may have/might have** left my purse in the shop.
- Liz **might/may** know where it is.
- I **might/may** not go if I'm tired.
- He **might have** enjoyed the party if he'd gone.
- His wife **can** be very difficult at times.

Permission
can • could • may
- **Can** we come in?
- **Could** we possibly stay at your flat?
- Staff **may** take their break between 12 and 2. (*formal*)
- **May** I sit here? (*formal*)

Prohibition
cannot • may not • must not
- You **can't** get up until you're better.
- You **mustn't** tell anyone I'm here.
- Crockery **may not** be taken out of the canteen. (*written*)
- You **must not** begin until I tell you. (*formal*)

Obligation
have (got) to • must
- All visitors **must** report to reception on arrival.
- I **must** get that letter written today.
- Do you **have to** write your age on the form?
- She **had to** wait an hour for the bus.
- You **will have to** ring back later, I'm afraid.

Advice and criticism
ought to • should
- **Ought** I **to/Should** I wear a jacket?
- She **ought to/should** get her hair cut.
- You **ought to/should have** gone to bed earlier.
- You **ought not to/shouldn't** borrow the car without asking.
- I **ought to/should** go on a diet.
- I **ought to have/should have** asked her first.

No necessity
don't have to • shouldn't have
didn't need to • needn't have
- You **don't have to** cook, we can get a takeaway.
- They **didn't have to** show their passports.
- You **shouldn't have** bought me a present.
- He **didn't need to** have any fillings at the dentist's.
- They **needn't have** waited.

➲ For the difference between 'didn't need to' and 'needn't have', look at the note at **need¹**.

Assumptions and deductions
will • should • must • can't
- That **will** be Tanya – she's often early.
- The book **should** be interesting.
- There **must** be a leak – the floor's wet.
- You **must have** dialled the wrong number – there's no one called Pat living here.
- You **can't have** finished already!

Requests
can • could • will • would

- ***Can** you help me lift this box?*
- ***Could** you pass me the salt?*
- ***Will** you buy me a puppy, Dad?*
- ***Would** you post this letter for me, please?*

Could and **would** are more formal than **can** and **will**.

Offers and suggestions
shall • will • can

- *Shall I make you a sandwich?*
- *I'll (I **will**) drive you to the station.*
- ***Shall** we go now?*
- ***Can** I help you?*

The passive

In an active sentence, the subject is the person or thing that performs the action:
- ***Masked thieves** stole a valuable painting from the museum last night.*

When you make this into a passive sentence, the object of the verb becomes the subject:
- ***A valuable painting** was stolen from the museum last night.*

The passive is made with the auxiliary verb **to be** and the **past participle** of the verb:

present simple	*The painting **is valued** by experts at 2 million dollars.*
present continuous	*The theft **is being investigated** by the police.*
present perfect	*Other museums **have been warned** to take extra care.*
past simple	*The painting **was kept** in a special room.*
past perfect	*The lock **had been broken**.*
past continuous	*This morning everything possible **was being done** to find the thieves.*
future	*Staff at the museum **will be questioned** tomorrow.*

You use the **passive**

- when you want to save new information until the end of the sentence for emphasis:
  - *The picture **was painted** by Turner.*
- when you do not know who performed the action, or when this information is not important. It is common in formal writing, for example scientific writing:
  - *The liquid **is heated** to 60° and then filtered.*

If you want to say who performed the action, you use **by** at the end of the sentence:
- *The painting was stolen **by** masked thieves.*

It is possible to put a verb that has two objects into the passive:
- *An American millionaire gave the museum the painting.*
- *The museum **was given** the painting by an American millionaire.*

↪ Some verbs cannot be used in the passive, and this is shown at the entries.

Reported speech

Reported (or indirect) speech is the term used for the words that are used to report what someone has said.

If the reporting verb (say, ask, etc.) is in the present or present perfect, then the tense of the sentence does not change:
- *'I'm going home.'*
- Bob says he's going home.
- Bob's just told me he's going home.

Reporting statements in the past

When you report somebody's words using said, asked, etc., you usually change the tense to one further back in the past:

present simple	*'I **don't know** whether Nell **wants** an ice cream.'*
past simple	He said he **didn't know** whether Nell **wanted** an ice cream.
present continuous	*'She **is hoping** to rent a car tomorrow.'*
past continuous	He said she **was hoping** to rent a car the following day.
present perfect	*'**Have** you **brought** your licence?'*
past perfect	He asked whether she **had brought** her licence.
past simple	*'I **passed** my driving test yesterday.'*
past perfect	He said he **had passed** his driving test the day before.
will	*'I**'ll ring** from the airport.'*
would	She told me she **would ring** from the airport.
can	*'I **can play** the flute.'*
could	He said he **could play** the flute.

- Other changes:
  I/you/we becomes **he/she/they**,
  my/your becomes **his/her**, etc.

- Time references change:
  tomorrow becomes **the following day**,
  yesterday becomes **the day before**,
  last week becomes **the week before/the previous week**, etc.

- The modal verbs **should, would, might, could, must,** and **ought to** are not usually changed:
  - *'We **might** get a dog.'*
  - They said they **might** get a dog.

- The modal verb **may** changes to **might**.

Reporting requests and commands

When you report a request or an order, you usually use a to-infinitive:
- *'Please will you wash the dishes?'*
- She asked me **to wash** the dishes.
- *'Don't eat all the cake!'*
- She told the children **not to eat** all the cake.

Reporting questions

Notice that you use **if** or **whether** to report yes/no questions:
- *'Are you ready?'*
- She asked **if/whether** I was ready.

With **wh-** questions, the **wh-** word stays in the sentence:
- *'When are you leaving?'*
- She asked me **when** I was leaving.

The word order in these sentences is the same as a normal statement, not as in a question:
- *'Did you see them?'*
- He asked me if I had seen them.

Reporting verbs

Here are some useful reporting verbs. Look them up in the dictionary to see how you can use them:

admit	apologize	recommend
advise	complain	suggest
agree	deny	

Verb patterns

When one verb is followed by another, you need to know what form the second verb should take. Look at the entry for **promise** to see how this information is shown:

> **promise¹** /ˈprɒmɪs/ *verb* **1** [I,T] promise (to do sth); promise (sb) that ... to say definitely that you will do or not do sth or that sth will happen: *She promised to phone every week.* ♦ *She promised (me) that she would write.*

Every time you learn a new verb, write it down with the pattern that it uses. You will soon come to know which pattern looks or sounds right.

The meaning of the verb can sometimes make one pattern more likely than another. The following points can help you to make a good guess:

Many verbs that suggest that **an action will follow, or will be completed successfully**, are followed by **to do**:

(can) afford to do sth
agree to do sth
decide to do sth
hope to do sth
intend to do sth
manage to do sth
offer to do sth
plan to do sth
remember to do sth
try to do sth
(or try doing sth)
volunteer to do sth
ask (sb) to do sth
expect (sb) to do sth
help (sb) to do sth
need (sb) to do sth
wait (for sb) to do sth
want (sb) to do sth
would like (sb) to do sth
advise sb to do sth
allow sb to do sth
enable sb to do sth
encourage sb to do sth
get sb to do sth
persuade sb to do sth
remind sb to do sth
teach sb to do sth
tell sb to do sth

But note these verbs, which have a similar meaning but a different pattern:

let sb do sth
make sb do sth
consider doing sth
think about doing sth
suggest doing sth
recommend doing sth
look forward to doing sth
succeed in doing sth

Several verbs that suggest that **an action is unlikely to follow, or to be completed successfully**, are followed by an **-ing** form, sometimes with a preposition too:

avoid doing sth
resist doing sth
put sb off doing sth
save sb (from) doing sth
prevent sb from doing sth
dissuade sb from doing sth
advise sb against doing sth
(or advise sb not to do sth)

But note these verbs:

fail to do sth
forget to do sth
refuse to do sth

Several verbs that refer to **past events or actions** are followed by an **-ing** form, sometimes with a **preposition**:

admit doing sth
celebrate doing sth
miss doing sth
regret doing sth
remember doing sth
thank sb for doing sth

Verbs that refer to **starting, stopping or continuing** are often followed by an **-ing** form:

begin doing sth
continue doing sth
carry on doing sth
finish doing sth
go on doing sth
put off doing sth
start doing sth

But note that you can also say:

begin to do sth
continue to do sth
start to do sth

Verbs meaning **like** and **dislike** are usually followed by an **-ing** form:

like doing sth
love doing sth
prefer doing sth
hate doing sth
dread doing sth

But note that you can also say:

like to do sth
prefer to do sth
hate to do sth

Look at the entries for these verbs to see the slight difference in meaning that this pattern gives.

Transitive and intransitive

▶ *We arrived.*
▶ *He bought a jacket.*

Each of these sentences has a **subject** (we, he) and a **verb** (arrive, buy).

In the first sentence **arrive** stands alone. Verbs like this are called **intransitive**. They are marked [I] in this dictionary. In the second sentence **bought** has an object (a jacket). Verbs like this are called **transitive**. They are marked [T] in this dictionary.

Compare the following sentences:

▶ *Nobody spoke.*
▶ *Patrick speaks Japanese.*

In the first sentence the verb **speak** is used intransitively, without an object. In the second it is used transitively with the noun **Japanese** as the object. Many verbs can be both intransitive and transitive. In this dictionary they are marked [I,T]

Many verbs can have two objects, an **indirect object** and a **direct object**. The thing that is given, bought, etc. is the direct object and the person who receives it is the indirect object. The indirect object usually comes first.

Look up the verb **give** and notice the structures that are shown there:
give sb sth; give sth to sb
In a sentence you can say:

▶ *He gave his mother the eggs.*
▶ *He gave the eggs to his mother.*

Either or both of the objects can be pronouns:

▶ *He gave her the eggs.*
▶ *He gave the eggs to her.*
▶ *He gave them to his mother.*
▶ *He gave her them.*
▶ *He gave them to her.*

Phrasal verbs

Phrasal verbs are verbs that have two parts – a **verb** (sit, give, look, get, etc.) and a **particle** (down, up, after, etc.). Some phrasal verbs (come down with, put up with, etc.) have two particles.

sit down	give up
look after	get along with

Many phrasal verbs are easy to understand. For example, if you know the words **sit** and **down**, you can guess the meaning of **sit down**. But some phrasal verbs are more difficult because they have special meanings. For example, "**give up** smoking" means "stop smoking", but you can't guess this, even if you know the words **give** and **up**.

In Wordpower, phrasal verbs are listed after the ordinary meanings of the verb, in the sections marked **PHR V** (for example, to find **give up**, see **give**). The phrasal verbs are arranged alphabetically according to the particle (after, along, at, etc.).

The four types

There are four main types of phrasal verb:

Type 1
Phrasal verbs without an object

- Please **sit down**.
- I have to **get up** early tomorrow.

In the dictionary, these verbs are written like this: sit down; get up.

Type 2
Phrasal verbs that can be separated by an object

If the object is a noun, it can go either *after* both parts of the phrasal verb or *between* them:

- She **tried on** the red sweater.
- She **tried** the red sweater **on**.

If the object is a pronoun, it must go between the two parts of the phrasal verb:

- She **tried** it **on**. (NOT ~~She tried on it.~~)

In the dictionary, this verb is written like this: try sth on. When you see **sth** or **sb** between the two parts of the phrasal verb, you know that they can be separated by an object.

Type 3
Phrasal verbs that cannot be separated by an object

The two parts of the phrasal verb must go together:

- Could you **look after** my dog while I'm on holiday? (NOT ~~Could you look my dog after while I'm on holiday?~~)
- Could you **look after** it while I'm on holiday? (NOT ~~Could you look it after while I'm on holiday?~~)

In the dictionary, this verb is written like this: look after sb/sth. When you see **sb** or **sth** *after* the two parts of the phrasal verb, you know that they *cannot* be separated by an object.

Type 4
Phrasal verbs with three parts

The three parts of the phrasal verb must go together:

- I can't **put up with** this noise anymore.

In the dictionary, this verb is written like this: put up with sb/sth. Again, when you see **sb** or **sth** after the three parts of the phrasal verb, you know that they *cannot* be separated by an object.

Nouns

Countable and uncountable nouns

[C]

Countable nouns can be singular or plural:
- *a friend/two friends*
- *one book/five books*

In this dictionary they are marked [C].

[U]

Uncountable nouns cannot have a plural and are not used with **a/an**. They cannot be counted. In this dictionary they are marked [U].

⮕ Look up the entries for:

advice	money
furniture	rice
information	water

It is possible to say **some rice** but not **a rice** or **two rices**.

Abstract nouns like **happiness**, **importance** and **luck**, are usually uncountable.

[C,U]

Some nouns have both countable and uncountable meanings. In this dictionary they are marked [C,U] or [U,C].

Look up the entries for:

cheese coffee friendship paper

- [U] *Have some cheese!*
- [C] *They sell a variety of cheeses.*
  (= types of cheese)
- [U] *I don't drink much coffee.*
- [C] *She ordered two coffees.*
  (= cups of coffee)
- [U] *Friendship is more important than wealth.*
- [C] *None of these were lasting friendships.*
  (= relationships)
- [U] *I haven't got any more paper.*
- [C] *Can you buy me a paper?*
  (= a newspaper)

[sing]

Some nouns are only singular. They cannot be used in the plural. In this dictionary they are marked [sing].

⮕ Look up the entries for:

the countryside   the doctor's   a laugh

- *We love walking in the countryside.*
- *I'm going to the doctor's today.*
- *The party was a good laugh.*

[pl]

Other words are only plural.
In this dictionary they are marked [pl].

⮕ Look up the entries for:

jeans scissors sunglasses

You cannot say ~~a sunglasses~~. To talk about individual items, you say **a pair**:
- *a pair of sunglasses*
- *two pairs of sunglasses*

Words like **clothes**, **goods** and **headphones** can only be used in the plural:
- *I need to buy some new clothes.*

Nouns which describe groups of people, such as **the poor** are plural:
- *The poor are getting poorer and the rich are getting richer.*

Articles

The definite article

You use the definite article, **the**, when you expect the person who is listening to know which person or thing you are talking about:
- *Thank you for **the** flowers*
  (= the ones that you brought me).
- ***The** teacher said my essay was the best*
  (= our teacher).

You use **the** with the names of rivers and groups of islands:
- *Which is longer, **the** Rhine or **the** Danube?*
- *Where are **the** Seychelles?*
- *Menorca is one of **the** Balearic Islands.*

R17

Nouns

The indefinite article

You use the indefinite article, **a** (**an** before a vowel sound), when the other person does not know which person or thing you are talking about or when you are not referring to a particular thing or person:
- *He's got **a** new bike.*
  (I haven't mentioned it before.)
- *Can I borrow **a** pen?*
  (Any pen will be okay.)

You also use **a/an** to talk about a type or class of people or things, such as when you describe a person's job:
- *She's **an** accountant.*

You use **a/an** in prices, speeds, etc:
- *$100 **a** day*
- *50 cents **a** pack*
- *70 kilometres **an** hour*
- *three times **a** week*

No article

You do not use an article when you are talking in general:
- *I love flowers (all flowers).*
- *Honey is sweet (all honey).*
- *Lawyers are well paid (lawyers in general).*

You do not use **the** with most names of countries, counties, states, streets, or lakes:
- *I'm going to Turkey.*
- *a house in Walton Street*
- *She's from Yorkshire.*
- *Lake Louise*
- *They live in Iowa.*

or with a person's title when the name is mentioned:
- *President Kennedy*
  BUT *the President of the United States*

⮕ Look at the entries for **school**, **university**, **college**, **hospital**, **prison** and **music** for more information about the use of articles.

The possessive with 's

You can add **'s** to a word or a name to show possession. It is most often used with words for people, countries and animals:
- *Ann**'s** job*
- *the children**'s** clothes*
- *the manager**'s** secretary*
- *the dog**'s** basket*
- *my brother**'s** computer*
- *Spain**'s** beaches*

When the word already ends in a plural s, you add an apostrophe after it:
- *the boys**'** rooms*
- *the Smiths**'** house*

much, many, a lot, a little, a few

Much is used with **uncountable nouns**, usually in negative sentences and questions:
- *I haven't got **much** money left.*
- *Did you watch **much** television?*

Much is very formal in affirmative sentences:
- *There will be **much** discussion before a decision is made.*

Many is used with **countable nouns**, usually in negative sentences and questions:
- *There aren't **many** tourists here in December.*
- *Are there **many** opportunities for young people?*

In affirmative sentences, it is more formal than **a lot of**:
- ***Many** people prefer to stay at home.*

A lot of or (*informal*) **lots of** is used with countable and uncountable nouns:
- ***A lot of** tourists visit the castle.*
- *He's been here **lots of** times.*
- *I've spent **a lot of** money.*
- *You need **lots of** patience to make model aircraft.*

A little is used with **uncountable nouns**:
- *Add **a little** salt.*

A few is used with **countable nouns**:
- *I've got **a few** letters to write.*

Note that in these sentences, the meaning is positive. **Few** and **little** without **a** have a negative meaning.

Adjectives

Comparatives and superlatives

Look at this text. It contains several comparatives and superlatives.

▶ *Temperatures yesterday were **highest** in the south-east. The **sunniest** place was Brighton, and the **wettest** was Glasgow. Tomorrow will be **cooler** than today, but in Scotland it will be a **drier** day. **Better** weather is expected for the weekend, but it will become **more changeable** again next week.*

To form comparatives and superlatives:

- Adjectives of **one syllable** add **-er**, **est**:
  | cool | cooler | coolest |
  | high | higher | highest |

- Adjectives that already end in **-e** only add **-r**, **-st**:
  | nice | nicer | nicest |

- Some words double the last letter:
  | wet | wetter | wettest |
  | big | bigger | biggest |

- Adjectives of three syllables or more take **more**, **most**:
changeable	more changeable
	most changeable
interesting	more interesting
	most interesting

- Some adjectives of **two syllables** are like **cool**, especially those that end in **-er**, **-y**, or **-ly**:
  | clever | cleverer | cleverest |

- Words that end in **-y** change it to **-i**:
  | sunny | sunnier | sunniest |
  | friendly | friendlier | friendliest |

- Other adjectives of **two syllables** are like **interesting**:
  | harmful | more harmful |
  | | most harmful |

- Some adjectives have **irregular forms**:
  | good | better | best |
  | bad | worse | worst |

Adjectives with nouns

Most adjectives can be used **before** the noun that they describe or **after** a linking verb:

▶ *I need a **new** bike.*
▶ *This bike isn't **new**.*
▶ *It's an **interesting** book.*
▶ *She said the film sounded **interesting**.*

Some adjectives **cannot** come **before** a noun. ⊃ Look at the entry for **asleep** and notice how this information is given in the dictionary. You can say:

▶ *Don't wake him – he's **asleep**.*
   BUT NOT: *an asleep child*

⊃ Look up the entries for **afraid** and **pleased**.

Some adjectives can **only** be used **before** a noun. ⊃ Look at the entry for the adjective **chief** and notice how this information is given in the dictionary. You can say:

▶ *That was the **chief** disadvantage.*
   BUT NOT: *This disadvantage was chief.*

⊃ Look up the entries for **former** and **main**.

Relative clauses

Defining relative clauses

These phrases **define** or **identify** which person or thing we are talking about:
- *'Which of them is the boss?' 'The man **who** came in late is the boss.'*

When the **subject** is a person:
- *the man **who** came in late*
  OR *the man **that** came in late*

When the **object** is a person:
- *the girl **that** I saw*
  OR *the girl I saw*
  OR *the girl **who** I saw*
  OR *the girl **whom** I saw (formal)*

When the **subject** is a thing:
- *the chair **that** is in the corner*
  OR *the chair **which** is in the corner*

When the **object** is a thing:
- *the book **that** I'm reading*
  OR *the book I'm reading*
  OR *the book **which** I'm reading*

whose shows that something belongs to somebody:
- *the woman **whose** car broke down*
- *the people **whose** house was burgled*

Whose is not usually used to refer to a thing:
- NOT *the chair whose leg is broken*

It is more natural to say:
- *the chair with the broken leg*

Non-defining relative clauses

These phrases **add extra information** about somebody or something which could be left out and the sentence would still make sense. This extra information is separated from the main clause by commas:
- *The film, which was shot in Mexico, has won an Oscar.*

The pronouns that can be used in non-defining relative clauses are **who** for a person; **which** for a thing; **whose** to show belonging
- *My sister, who is a vegetarian, ordered a cheese salad.*
- *The tickets, which can be bought at the station, are valid for one day.*
- *Lucy, whose car had broken down, arrived by bus.*

Prefixes

a- not: *atypical*

ante- before: *antenatal* (= before birth)

anti- against: *anti-American, antisocial*

auto- self: *autobiography* (= the story of the writer's own life)

bi- two: *bicycle, bilingual* (= using two languages), *bimonthly* (= twice a month or every two months)

cent-, centi- hundred: *centenary* (= the hundredth anniversary), *centimetre* (= one hundredth of a metre)

circum- around: *circumnavigate* (= sail around)

co- with; together: *co-pilot, coexist, cooperation*

con- with; together: *context* (= the words or sentences that come before and after a particular word or sentence)

contra- against; opposite: *contradict* (= say the opposite)

counter- against; opposite: *counter-revolution, counterproductive* (= producing the opposite of the desired effect)

de- taking sth away; the opposite: *defrost* (= removing the layers of ice from a fridge, etc.), *decentralize*

deca- ten: *decathlon* (= a competition involving ten different sports)

deci- one tenth: *decilitre*

dis- reverse or opposite: *displeasure, disembark, discomfort*

e- using electronic communication: *e-commerce*

ex- former: *ex-wife, ex-president*

extra- 1 very; more than usual: *extra-thin, extra-special* **2** outside; beyond: *extraordinary, extraterrestrial* (= coming from somewhere beyond the earth)

fore- 1 before; in advance: *foreword* (= at the beginning of a book) **2** front: *foreground* (= the front part of a picture), *forehead*

hexa- six: *hexagon* (= a shape with six sides)

in-, il-, im-, ir- not: *incorrect, invalid, illegal, illegible, immoral, impatient, impossible, irregular, irrelevant*

inter- between; from one to another: *international, interracial*

kilo- thousand: *kilogram, kilowatt*

maxi- most; very large: *maximum*

mega- million; very large: *megabyte, megabucks* (= a lot of money)

micro- very small: *microchip*

mid- in the middle of: *mid-afternoon, mid-air*

milli- thousandth: *millisecond, millimetre*

mini- small: *miniskirt, miniseries*

mis- bad or wrong; not: *misbehave, miscalculate, misunderstand*

mono- one; single: *monolingual* (= using one language), *monorail*

multi- many: *multinational* (= involving many countries)

non- not: *non-alcoholic, nonsense, non-smoker, non-stop*

octa- eight: *octagon* (= a shape with eight sides)

out- more; to a greater degree: *outdo, outrun* (= run faster or better than sb)

over- more than normal; too much: *overeat, oversleep* (= sleep too long)

penta- five: *pentagon* (= a shape with five sides), *pentathlon* (= a competition involving five different sports)

post- after: *post-war*

pre- before: *pre-pay, preview*

pro- for; in favour of: *pro-democracy, pro-hunting*

quad- four: *quadruple* (= multiply by four), *quadruplet* (= one of four babies born at the same time)

re- again: *rewrite, rebuild*

self- of, to or by yourself: *self-taught*

semi- half: *semicircle, semiconscious*

sub- 1 below; less than: *sub-zero* **2** under: *subway, subtitles* (= translations under the pictures of a film)

super- extremely; more than: *superhuman* (= having greater power than humans normally have), *supersonic* (= faster than the speed of sound)

tele- far; over a long distance: *telecommunications, telephoto lens*

trans- across; through: *transatlantic, transcontinental*

tri- three: *triangle, tricycle*

ultra- extremely; beyond a certain limit: *ultra-modern*

un- not; opposite; taking sth away: *uncertain, uncomfortable, unsure, undo, undress*

under- not enough: *undercooked*

uni- one; single: *uniform* (= having the same form)

vice- the second most important: *vice-president*

Suffixes

-able, -ible, -ble (to make adjectives) possible to: *acceptable, noticeable, convertible, divisible* (= possible to divide), *irresistible* (= that you cannot resist)

-age (to make nouns) a process or state: *storage, shortage*

-al (to make adjectives) connected with: *experimental, accidental, environmental*

-ance, -ence, -ancy, -ency (to make nouns) an action, process or state: *appearance, performance, existence, intelligence, pregnancy, efficiency*

-ant, -ent (to make nouns) a person who does sth: *assistant, immigrant, student*

-ation (to make nouns) a state or an action: *examination, imagination, organization*

-ble → **-able**

-ed (to make adjectives) having a particular state or quality: *bored, patterned*

-ee (to make nouns) a person to whom sth is done: *employee* (= sb who is employed), *trainee* (= sb who is being trained)

-en (to make verbs) to give sth a particular quality; to make sth more ~: *shorten, widen, blacken, sharpen, loosen,* (but note: *lengthen*)

ence (-ency) → **-ance**

-ent → **-ant**

-er (to make nouns) a person who does sth: *rider, painter, banker, driver, teacher*

-ese (to make adjectives) from a place: *Japanese, Chinese, Viennese*

-ess (to make nouns) a woman who does sth as a job: *waitress, actress*

-ful (to make adjectives) having a particular quality: *helpful, useful, beautiful*

-hood (to make nouns) **1** a state, often during a particular period of time: *childhood, motherhood* **2** a group with sth in common: *sisterhood, neighbourhood*

-ian (to make nouns) a person who does sth as a job or hobby: *historian, comedian, politician*

-ible → **-able**

-ical (to make adjectives from nouns ending in -y or -ics) connected with: *economical, mathematical, physical*

-ify (to make verbs) to produce a state or quality: *beautify, simplify, purify*

-ing (to make adjectives) producing a particular state or effect: *interesting*

-ish (to make adjectives) **1** describing nationality or language: *English, Swedish, Polish* **2** like sth: *babyish, foolish* **3** fairly; sort of: *longish, youngish, brownish*

-ist (to make nouns) **1** a person who has studied sth or does sth as a job: *artist, scientist, economist* **2** a person who believes in sth or belongs to a particular group: *capitalist, pacifist, feminist*

-ion (to make nouns) a state or process: *action, connection, exhibition*

-ive (to make adjectives) having a particular quality: *attractive, effective*

-ize, -ise (to make verbs) producing a particular state: *magnetize, standardize, modernize, generalize*

-less (to make adjectives) not having sth: *hopeless, friendless*

-like (to make adjectives) similar to: *childlike*

-ly (to make adverbs) in a particular way: *badly, beautifully, completely*

-ment (to make nouns) a state, an action or a quality: *development, arrangement, excitement, achievement*

-ness (to make nouns) a state or quality: *kindness, happiness, weakness*

-ology (to make nouns) the study of a subject: *biology, psychology, zoology*

-or (to make nouns) a person who does sth, often as a job: *actor, conductor, sailor*

-ous (to make adjectives) having a particular quality: *dangerous, religious, ambitious*

-ship (to make nouns) showing status: *friendship, membership, citizenship*

-ward, -wards (to make adverbs) in a particular direction: *backward, upwards*

-wise (to make adverbs) in a particular way: *clockwise, edgewise*

-y (to make adjectives) having the quality of the thing mentioned: *cloudy, rainy, fatty, thirsty*

Expressions using numbers

The numbers

1	one	1st	first
2	two	2nd	second
3	three	3rd	third
4	four	4th	fourth
5	five	5th	fifth
6	six	6th	sixth
7	seven	7th	seventh
8	eight	8th	eighth
9	nine	9th	ninth
10	ten	10th	tenth
11	eleven	11th	eleventh
12	twelve	12th	twelfth
13	thirteen	13th	thirteenth
14	fourteen	14th	fourteenth
15	fifteen	15th	fifteenth
16	sixteen	16th	sixteenth
17	seventeen	17th	seventeenth
18	eighteen	18th	eighteenth
19	nineteen	19th	nineteenth
20	twenty	20th	twentieth
21	twenty-one	21st	twenty-first
22	twenty-two	22nd	twenty-second
30	thirty	30th	thirtieth
40	forty	40th	fortieth
50	fifty	50th	fiftieth
60	sixty	60th	sixtieth
70	seventy	70th	seventieth
80	eighty	80th	eightieth
90	ninety	90th	ninetieth
100	a/one hundred*	100th	hundredth
101	a/one hundred and one*	101st	hundred and first
200	two hundred	200th	two hundredth
1 000	a/one thousand*	1 000th	thousandth
10 000	ten thousand	10 000th	ten thousandth
100 000	a/one hundred thousand*	100 000th	hundred thousandth
1 000 000	a/one million*	1 000 000th	millionth

Examples
- 697: *six hundred and ninety-seven*
- 3 402: *three thousand, four hundred and two*
- 80 534: *eighty thousand, five hundred and thirty-four*

*You use **one hundred**, **one thousand**, etc., instead of **a hundred**, **a thousand**, when it is important to stress that you mean one (not two, for example). In numbers over a thousand, you use a comma or a small space: **1,200** or **1 200**

Telephone numbers

In telephone numbers you say each number separately, often with a pause after two or three numbers:
- 509236 *five oh nine – two three six*

You can say **six six** or **double six** for **66**:
- 02166 *oh two one – six six* or *oh two one – double six*

Expressions using numbers

If you are phoning a number in a different town, you have to use the **area code** before the number:
▶ *01865 is the code for Oxford.*

If you are phoning somebody in a large firm, you can ask for their extension number.
▶ *(01865) 56767 x 4840 (extension 4840)*

Fractions and decimals

½	a half	⅓	a/one third
¼	a quarter	⅖	two fifths
⅛	an/one eighth	7/12	seven twelfths
1/10	a/one tenth	1½	one and a half
1/16	a/one sixteenth	2⅜	two and three eighths

0.1 (nought) point one
0.25 (nought) point two five
0.33 (nought) point three three
1.75 one point seven five
3.976 three point nine seven six

Percentages and proportions

▶ *90% of all households have a television.*
▶ *Nine out of ten households have a television.*
▶ *Nine tenths of all households have a television.*

Mathematical expressions

+ plus
− minus
× times or multiplied by
÷ divided by
= equals
% per cent
3^2 three squared
5^3 five cubed
6^{10} six to the power of ten

Examples $7 + 6 = 13$ *seven plus six equals (or is) thirteen*
$5 \times 8 = 40$ *five times eight equals forty*
  or *five eights are forty*
  or *five multiplied by eight is forty*

Temperature

In Britain, temperatures are now usually given in **degrees Celsius**, (although many people are still more familiar with **Fahrenheit**). In the United States, **Fahrenheit** is used, except in science.

To convert **Fahrenheit** to **Celsius**, subtract 32 from the number, then multiply by 5 and divide by 9:

  68 °F −
  32
= 36 ×
  5
= 180 ÷ 9
= **20 °C**

Examples
▶ *Water freezes at 32°F and boils at 212°F.*
▶ *The maximum temperature this afternoon will be 15°, and the minimum tonight may reach −5° (minus five).*
▶ *She had a temperature of 102° last night, and it's still above normal.*

Weight

	Non-metric	Metric
	1 ounce (oz)	= 28.35 grams (g)
16 ounces =	1 pound (lb)	= 0.454 kilogram (kg)
14 pounds =	1 stone (st)	= 6.356 kilograms
8 stone =	1 hundredweight (cwt)	= 50.8 kilograms
20 hundredweight =	1 ton (t)	= 1 016.04 kilograms

Examples
- The baby weighed 8 lb 2oz (eight pounds two ounces).
- For this recipe you need 750g (seven hundred and fifty grams) of flour.

Length and height

	Non-metric	Metric
	1 inch (in)	= 25.4 millimetres (mm)
12 inches =	1 foot (ft)	= 30.48 centimetres (cm)
3 feet =	1 yard (yd)	= 0.914 metre (m)
1 760 yards =	1 mile	= 1.609 kilometres (km)

Examples
- flying at 7 000 feet
- The speed limit is 30 mph (thirty miles per/an hour).
- The room is 11'x 9'6" (eleven feet by nine feet six or eleven foot by nine foot six).
- She's five feet four (inches).
- He's one metre sixty (centimetres).

Area

	Non-metric	Metric
	1 square inch (sq in)	= 6.452 square centimetres (cm²)
144 square inches =	1 square foot (sq ft)	= 929.03 square centimetres
9 square feet =	1 square yard (sq yd)	= 0.836 square metre (m²)
4 840 square yards =	1 acre	= 0.405 hectare
640 acres =	1 square mile	= 2.59 square kilometres (km²) or 259 hectares

Examples
- an 80-acre country park
- 160 000 square miles of the jungle have been destroyed.

Cubic measurements

	Non-metric	Metric
	1 cubic inch (cu in)	= 16.39 cubic centimetres (cc)
1 728 cubic inches =	1 cubic foot (cu ft)	= 0.028 cubic metre
27 cubic feet =	1 cubic yard (cu yd)	= 0.765 cubic metre

Example
- a car with a 1500 cc engine

Capacity

	GB	US	Metric
20 fluid ounces (fl oz) =	1 pint (pt)	= 1.201 pints	= 0.568 litre (l)
2 pints =	1 quart (qt)	= 1.201 quarts	= 1.136 litres
4 quarts =	1 gallon (gall)	= 1.201 gallons	= 4.546 litres

Examples
- I drink a litre of water a day.
- a quart of orange juice

Expressions using numbers

Dates
- *8 April 2005* or *8th April 2005 (8/4/05) (BrE)*
- *Her birthday is on the thirteenth of July.*
- *Her birthday is on July the thirteenth.*
- *April 8, 2005 (4/8/05) (AmE)*
- *Her birthday is July 13th. (AmE)*

Years
1999 *nineteen ninety-nine*
1608 *sixteen oh eight*
1700 *seventeen hundred*
2000 *(the year) two thousand*
2002 *two thousand and two*
2015 *twenty fifteen*

Age
When saying a person's age, use only numbers:
- *Sue is ten and Tom is six.*
- *She left home at sixteen.*

You can say a ... year-old/month-old/ week-old, etc.:
- *Youth training is available to all sixteen-year-olds.*
- *a ten-week-old baby*

To give the approximate age of a person:
13–19 *in his/her teens*
21–29 *in his/her twenties*
31–33 *in his/her early thirties*
34–36 *in his/her mid-thirties*
37–39 *in his/her late thirties*

Times
There is often more than one way of telling the time:

Half hours

6:30 *six thirty*
half past six
half six (informal)

Other times

5:45 *five forty-five* *(a) quarter to six*
2:15 *two fifteen* *(a) quarter past two*
1:10 *one ten* *ten past one*
3:05 *three oh five* *five past three*
1:55 *one fifty-five* *five to two*

In American English, *after* is sometimes used instead of *past*, and *of* instead of *to*.

with 5, 10, 20 and 25 the word *minutes* is not necessary, but it is used with other numbers:
10.25 *twenty-five past ten*
10.17 *seventeen minutes past ten*

use *o'clock* only for whole hours:
- *It's three o'clock.*

Twenty-four hour clock
The twenty-four hour clock is used in official language:
13:52 *thirteen fifty-two (1:52 p.m.)*
22:30 *twenty-two thirty (10.30 p.m.)*

British and American English

There are some important differences between British and American English.

Vocabulary

Many everyday words are different in British and American English. For example:
- items of clothing:
  dressing gown (*AmE* **bathrobe**), **trainers** (*AmE* **sneakers**)
- words connected with cars:
  boot (*AmE* **trunk**), **motorway** (*AmE* **expressway**), **petrol** (*AmE* **gasoline**)

Some words have different meanings in British and American English. For example:
- *AmE* **pants** = a piece of clothing that covers the whole of both your legs (*BrE* **trousers**)
- *BrE* **pants** = a piece of clothing that men or boys wear under their trousers

Spelling

- Words which end in *-tre* are spelt *-ter* in American English: **centre** (*AmE* **center**)
- Words which end in *-our* are usually spelt *-or* in American English: **colour** (*AmE* **color**)
- Words which end in *-ogue* are usually spelt *-og* in American English: **dialogue** (*AmE* **dialog**)
- In British English many verbs can be spelt with either *-ize* or *-ise*. In American English only the spelling with *-ize* is possible: **realize, -ise**; (*AmE* **realize**)
- In verbs which end in *-l* and are not stressed on the final syllable, there is only one *-l-* in the *-ing* and *-ed* forms in American English: **cancelling** (*AmE* **canceling**)

Grammar

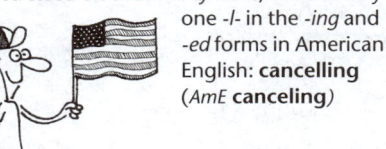

Past simple/Present perfect

American English often uses the past simple tense where British English uses the present perfect:
- (BrE) I've just seen her.
- (AmE) I just saw her.
- (BrE) Have you heard the news?
- (AmE) Did you hear the news?

Have/Have got

In American English **have** is always used instead of **have got** in questions and negative sentences:
- (BrE) Have you got a dog?
- (BrE and AmE) Do you have a dog?
- (BrE) I haven't got a dog.
- (BrE and AmE) I don't have a dog.

Prepositions and adverbs

Some prepositions and adverbs are used differently in British and American English, for example:
- stay at home (AmE stay home)
- at the weekend (AmE on the weekend)

Irregular verbs

In British English the past simple and past participle of many verbs can be formed with *-ed* or *-t*, for example **learned/learnt**. In American English only the forms ending in *-ed* are used:
- (BrE) I learned/learnt English at school.
- (AmE) I learned English at school.

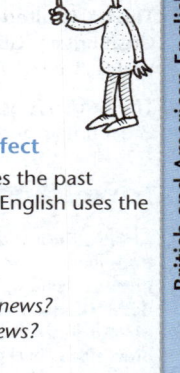

Britain and Ireland

The UK (United Kingdom) consists of Great Britain and Northern Ireland. Great Britain (GB) is **England** /ˈɪŋglənd/, **Scotland** /ˈskɒtlənd/ and **Wales** /weɪlz/. The Republic of Ireland is a separate country.

The British Isles is a geographical term which includes the islands of Great Britain and Ireland, and the smaller islands around them.

Towns and cities in the UK and Ireland

Aberdeen /ˌæbəˈdiːn/
Bath /bɑːθ/
Belfast /ˈbelfɑːst; ˌbelˈfɑːst/
Berwick-upon-Tweed /ˌberɪk əpɒn ˈtwiːd/
Birmingham /ˈbɜːmɪŋəm/
Blackpool /ˈblækpuːl/
Bournemouth /ˈbɔːnməθ/
Bradford /ˈbrædfəd/
Brighton /ˈbraɪtn/
Bristol /ˈbrɪstl/
Caernarfon /kəˈnɑːvn/
Cambridge /ˈkeɪmbrɪdʒ/
Canterbury /ˈkæntəbəri/
Cardiff /ˈkɑːdɪf/
Carlisle /kɑːˈlaɪl/
Chester /ˈtʃestə(r)/
Colchester /ˈkəʊltʃɪstə(r)/
Cork /kɔːk/
Coventry /ˈkɒvəntri/
Derby /ˈdɑːbi/
Douglas /ˈdʌɡləs/
Dover /ˈdəʊvə(r)/
Dublin /ˈdʌblɪn/
Dundee /dʌnˈdiː/
Durham /ˈdʌrəm/
Eastbourne /ˈiːstbɔːn/
Edinburgh /ˈedɪnbrə/
Ely /ˈiːli/
Exeter /ˈeksɪtə(r)/
Galway /ˈɡɔːlweɪ/
Glasgow /ˈɡlɑːzɡəʊ/
Gloucester /ˈɡlɒstə(r)/
Hastings /ˈheɪstɪŋz/
Hereford /ˈherɪfəd/
Holyhead /ˈhɒlihed/
Inverness /ˌɪnvəˈnes/
Ipswich /ˈɪpswɪtʃ/

Keswick /ˈkezɪk/
Kingston upon Hull /ˌkɪŋstən əpɒn ˈhʌl/
Leeds /liːdz/
Leicester /ˈlestə(r)/
Limerick /ˈlɪmərɪk/
Lincoln /ˈlɪŋkən/
Liverpool /ˈlɪvəpuːl/
London /ˈlʌndən/
Londonderry /ˈlʌndənderi/
Luton /ˈluːtn/
Manchester /ˈmæntʃɪstə(r)/
Middlesbrough /ˈmɪdlzbrə/
Newcastle upon Tyne /ˌnjuːkɑːsl əpɒn ˈtaɪn/
Norwich /ˈnɒrɪdʒ/
Nottingham /ˈnɒtɪŋəm/
Oxford /ˈɒksfəd/
Plymouth /ˈplɪməθ/
Poole /puːl/
Portsmouth /ˈpɔːtsməθ/
Ramsgate /ˈræmzɡeɪt/
Reading /ˈredɪŋ/
Salisbury /ˈsɔːlzbəri/
Sheffield /ˈʃefiːld/
Shrewsbury /ˈʃrəʊzbəri/
Southampton /saʊˈθæmptən/
St Andrews /snt ˈændruːz/
Stirling /ˈstɜːlɪŋ/
Stoke-on-Trent /ˌstəʊk ɒn ˈtrent/
Stratford-upon-Avon /ˌstrætfəd əpɒn ˈeɪvn/
Swansea /ˈswɒnzi/
Taunton /ˈtɔːntən/
Warwick /ˈwɒrɪk/
Worcester /ˈwʊstə(r)/
York /jɔːk/

Map of Britain and Ireland

The United States of America and Canada

The provinces and territories of Canada

Alberta /ælˈbɜːtə/
British Columbia /ˌbrɪtɪʃ kəˈlʌmbiə/
Manitoba /ˌmænɪˈtəʊbə/
New Brunswick /ˌnjuːˈbrʌnzwɪk/
Newfoundland and Labrador
 /ˌnjuːfəndlənd ən ˈlæbrədɔː(r)/
Northwest Territories /ˌnɔːθwest ˈterətriz/
Nova Scotia /ˌnəʊvə ˈskəʊʃə/
Nunavut /ˈnʊnəvʊt/
Ontario /ɒnˈteəriəʊ/
Prince Edward Island /ˌprɪns ˈedwəd aɪlənd/
Quebec /kwɪˈbek/
Saskatchewan /səˈskætʃəwən/
Yukon Territory /ˈjuːkɒn terətri/

The states of the USA

Alabama /ˌæləˈbæmə/
Alaska /əˈlæskə/
Arizona /ˌærɪˈzəʊnə/
Arkansas /ˈɑːkənsɔː/
California /ˌkæləˈfɔːniə/
Colorado /ˌkɒləˈrɑːdəʊ/
Connecticut /kəˈnetɪkət/
Delaware /ˈdeləweə(r)/
Florida /ˈflɒrɪdə/
Georgia /ˈdʒɔːdʒə/
Hawaii /həˈwaɪi/
Idaho /ˈaɪdəhəʊ/
Illinois /ˌɪləˈnɔɪ/
Indiana /ˌɪndiˈænə/
Iowa /ˈaɪəwə/
Kansas /ˈkænzəs/
Kentucky /kenˈtʌki/
Louisiana /luˌiːziˈænə/
Maine /meɪn/
Maryland /ˈmeərilənd/
Massachusetts
 /ˌmæsəˈtʃuːsɪts/
Michigan /ˈmɪʃɪɡən/
Minnesota /ˌmɪnɪˈsəʊtə/
Mississippi /ˌmɪsɪˈsɪpi/
Missouri /mɪˈzʊəri/
Montana /mɒnˈtænə/
Nebraska /nəˈbræskə/
Nevada /nəˈvɑːdə/
New Hampshire
 /ˌnjuːˈhæmpʃə(r)/
New Jersey /ˌnjuːˈdʒɜːzi/
New Mexico /ˌnjuːˈmeksɪkəʊ/
New York /ˌnjuːˈjɔːk/
North Carolina
 /ˌnɔːθ kærəˈlaɪnə/
North Dakota /ˌnɔːθ dəˈkəʊtə/
Ohio /əʊˈhaɪəʊ/
Oklahoma /ˌəʊkləˈhəʊmə/
Oregon /ˈɒrɪɡən/
Pennsylvania /ˌpenslˈveɪniə/
Rhode Island /ˌrəʊd ˈaɪlənd/
South Carolina
 /ˌsaʊθ kærəˈlaɪnə/
South Dakota
 /ˌsaʊθ dəˈkəʊtə/
Tennessee /ˌtenəˈsiː/
Texas /ˈteksəs/
Utah /ˈjuːtɑː/
Vermont /vəˈmɒnt/
Virginia /vəˈdʒɪniə/
Washington /ˈwɒʃɪŋtən/
West Virginia
 /ˌwest vəˈdʒɪniə/
Wisconsin /wɪsˈkɒnsɪn/
Wyoming /waɪˈəʊmɪŋ/

Cities in Canada and the USA

Anchorage /ˈæŋkərɪdʒ/
Atlanta /ətˈlæntə/
Baltimore /ˈbɔːltɪmɔː(r)/
Boston /ˈbɒstən/
Chicago /ʃɪˈkɑːɡəʊ/
Cincinnati /ˌsɪnsɪˈnæti/
Cleveland /ˈkliːvlənd/
Dallas /ˈdæləs/
Denver /ˈdenvə(r)/
Detroit /dɪˈtrɔɪt/
Honolulu /ˌhɒnəˈluːluː/
Houston /ˈhjuːstən/
Indianapolis /ˌɪndiəˈnæpəlɪs/
Kansas City /ˌkænzəs ˈsɪti/
Los Angeles /ˌlɒs ˈændʒəliːz/
Miami /maɪˈæmi/
Milwaukee /mɪlˈwɔːki/
Minneapolis /ˌmɪniˈæpəlɪs/
Montreal /ˌmɒntriˈɔːl/
New Orleans /ˌnjuː ɔːˈliːənz/
New York /ˌnjuːˈjɔːk/
Ottawa /ˈɒtəwə/
Philadelphia /ˌfɪləˈdelfiə/
Pittsburgh /ˈpɪtsbɜːɡ/
Quebec City /kwɪˌbek ˈsɪti/
San Diego /ˌsæn diˈeɪɡəʊ/
San Francisco
 /ˌsæn frənˈsɪskəʊ/
Seattle /siˈætl/
St Louis /ˌsnt ˈluːɪs/
Toronto /təˈrɒntəʊ/
Vancouver /vænˈkuːvə(r)/
Washington D.C.
 /ˌwɒʃɪŋtən diː ˈsiː/
Winnipeg /ˈwɪnɪpeɡ/

Map of the United States of America and Canada

Geographical names

This list shows the English spelling and pronunciation of geographical names and the adjectives that go with them.

To talk in general about the people from a country, you can use the word **people**:
▶ Moroccan people, French people, Italian people, Japanese people, etc.

You can also add an **-s** to the adjective:
▶ Moroccans, Italians, etc.

If the adjective ends in a /s/, /z/ or /ʃ/ sound, use **the** and no **-s**:
▶ the Swiss, the Chinese, the French, etc.

To talk about a number of people from one country, add an **-s** to the adjective, unless it ends in an /s/, /z/ or /ʃ/ sound:
▶ two Germans, some Pakistanis, a group of Japanese, a few Swiss, etc.

Sometimes there is a special word for a person from a country, in which case this is shown after the adjective, for example **Denmark: Danish, a Dane**:
▶ two Danes, several Turks, a roomful of Dutchwomen, etc.

Inclusion in this list does not imply status as a sovereign nation.

Afghanistan /æfˈgænɪstɑːn/	**Afghan** /ˈæfgæn/
Africa /ˈæfrɪkə/	**African** /ˈæfrɪkən/
Albania /ælˈbeɪniə/	**Albanian** /ælˈbeɪniən/
Algeria /ælˈdʒɪəriə/	**Algerian** /ælˈdʒɪəriən/
America /əˈmerɪkə/	**American** /əˈmerɪkən/
Andorra /ænˈdɔːrə/	**Andorran** /ænˈdɔːrən/
Angola /æŋˈgəʊlə/	**Angolan** /æŋˈgəʊlən/
Antarctica /ænˈtɑːktɪkə/	**Antarctic** /ænˈtɑːktɪk/
Antigua and Barbuda /ænˌtiːgə ən bɑːˈbjuːdə/	**Antiguan** /ænˈtiːgən/ **Barbudan** /bɑːˈbjuːdən/
(the) Arctic /ˌɑːktɪk/	**Arctic** /ˈɑːktɪk/
Argentina /ˌɑːdʒənˈtiːnə/	**Argentinian** /ˌɑːdʒənˈtɪniən/
	Argentine /ˈɑːdʒəntaɪn/
Armenia /ɑːˈmiːniə/	**Armenian** /ɑːˈmiːniən/
Asia /ˈeɪʒə/	**Asian** /ˈeɪʒn/
Australia /ɒˈstreɪliə/	**Australian** /ɒˈstreɪliən/
Austria /ˈɒstriə/	**Austrian** /ˈɒstriən/
Azerbaijan /ˌæzəbaɪˈdʒɑːn/	**Azerbaijani** /ˌæzəbaɪˈdʒɑːni/ **Azeri** /əˈzeəri/
(the) Bahamas /bəˈhɑːməz/	**Bahamian** /bəˈheɪmiən/
Bahrain /bɑːˈreɪn/	**Bahraini** /bɑːˈreɪni/
Bangladesh /ˌbæŋgləˈdeʃ/	**Bangladeshi** /ˌbæŋgləˈdeʃi/
Barbados /bɑːˈbeɪdɒs/	**Barbadian** /bɑːˈbeɪdiən/
Belarus /ˌbeləˈruːs/	**Belarusian** /ˌbeləˈruːsiən/ **Belorussian** /ˌbeləˈrʌʃn/
Belgium /ˈbeldʒəm/	**Belgian** /ˈbeldʒən/
Belize /bəˈliːz/	**Belizean** /bəˈliːziən/
Benin /beˈniːn/	**Beninese** /ˌbenɪˈniːz/
Bhutan /buːˈtɑːn/	**Bhutani** /buːˈtɑːni/
	Bhutanese /ˌbuːtəˈniːz/
Bolivia /bəˈlɪviə/	**Bolivian** /bəˈlɪviən/
Bosnia and Herzegovina /ˌbɒzniə ən ˌhɜːtsəgəˈviːnə/	**Bosnian** /ˈbɒzniən/ **Herzegovinian** /ˌhɜːtsəgəˈvɪniən/
Botswana /bɒtˈswɑːnə/	**Botswanan** /bɒtˈswɑːnən/
	person: a **Motswana** /mɒtˈswɑːnə/
	people: **Batswana** /bætˈswɑːnə/

Geographical names

Brazil /brəˈzɪl/	**Brazilian** /brəˈzɪliən/
Brunei /bruːˈnaɪ/	**Bruneian** /bruːˈnaɪən/
Bulgaria /bʌlˈɡeəriə/	**Bulgarian** /bʌlˈɡeəriən/
Burkina /bɜːˈkiːnə/	**Burkinan** /ˌbɜːˈkiːnən/
	Burkinabe /bɜːˌkiːnəˈbeɪ/
Burma /ˈbɜːmə/ (see also **Myanmar**)	**Burmese** /bɜːˈmiːz/
Burundi /bʊˈrʊndi/	**Burundian** /bʊˈrʊndiən/
Cambodia /kæmˈbəʊdiə/	**Cambodian** /kæmˈbəʊdiən/
Cameroon /ˌkæməˈruːn/	**Cameroonian** /ˌkæməˈruːniən/
Canada /ˈkænədə/	**Canadian** /kəˈneɪdiən/
Cape Verde /ˌkeɪp ˈvɜːd/	**Cape Verdean** /ˌkeɪp ˈvɜːdiən/
Central African Republic /ˌsentrəl ˌæfrɪkən rɪˈpʌblɪk/	**Central African** /ˌsentrəl ˈæfrɪkən/
Chad /tʃæd/	**Chadian** /ˈtʃædiən/
Chile /ˈtʃɪli/	**Chilean** /ˈtʃɪliən/
China /ˈtʃaɪnə/	**Chinese** /tʃaɪˈniːz/
Colombia /kəˈlɒmbiə/	**Colombian** /kəˈlɒmbiən/
Comoros /ˈkɒmərəʊz/	**Comoran** /kəˈmɔːrən/
Congo /ˈkɒŋɡəʊ/	**Congolese** /ˌkɒŋɡəˈliːz/
(the) Democratic Republic of the Congo (DR Congo) /ˌdeməˌkrætɪk rɪˌpʌblɪk əv ðə ˈkɒŋɡəʊ/	**Congolese** /ˌkɒŋɡəˈliːz/
Costa Rica /ˌkɒstə ˈriːkə/	**Costa Rican** /ˌkɒstə ˈriːkən/
Côte d'Ivoire /ˌkəʊt diːˈvwɑː(r)/ (see also **Ivory Coast**)	**Ivorian** /aɪˈvɔːriən/
Croatia /krəʊˈeɪʃə/	**Croatian** /krəʊˈeɪʃn/
Cuba /ˈkjuːbə/	**Cuban** /ˈkjuːbən/
Cyprus /ˈsaɪprəs/	**Cypriot** /ˈsɪpriət/
(the) Czech Republic /ˌtʃek rɪˈpʌblɪk/	**Czech** /tʃek/
Denmark /ˈdenmɑːk/	**Danish** /ˈdeɪnɪʃ/ a **Dane** /deɪn/
Djibouti /dʒɪˈbuːti/	**Djiboutian** /dʒɪˈbuːtiən/
Dominica /ˌdɒmɪˈniːkə/	**Dominican** /ˌdɒmɪˈniːkən/
(the) Dominican Republic /dəˌmɪnɪkən rɪˈpʌblɪk/	**Dominican** /dəˈmɪnɪkən/
East Timor /ˌiːst ˈtiːmɔː(r)/	**East Timorese** /ˌiːst tɪməˈriːz/
Ecuador /ˈekwədɔː(r)/	**Ecuadorian Ecuadorean** /ˌekwəˈdɔːriən/
Egypt /ˈiːdʒɪpt/	**Egyptian** /iˈdʒɪpʃn/
El Salvador /ˌel ˈsælvədɔː(r)/	**Salvadorean** /ˌsælvəˈdɔːriən/
England /ˈɪŋɡlənd/	**English** /ˈɪŋɡlɪʃ/
	an **Englishman** /ˈɪŋɡlɪʃmən/
	an **Englishwoman** /ˈɪŋɡlɪʃwʊmən/
Equatorial Guinea /ˌekwətɔːriəl ˈɡɪni/	**Equatorial Guinean** /ˌekwətɔːriəl ˈɡɪniən/
Eritrea /ˌerɪˈtreɪə/	**Eritrean** /ˌerɪˈtreɪən/
Estonia /eˈstəʊniə/	**Estonian** /eˈstəʊniən/
Ethiopia /ˌiːθiˈəʊpiə/	**Ethiopian** /ˌiːθiˈəʊpiən/
Europe /ˈjʊərəp/	**European** /ˌjʊərəˈpiːən/
Fiji /ˈfiːdʒiː/	**Fijian** /fiːˈdʒiːən/
Finland /ˈfɪnlənd/	**Finnish** /ˈfɪnɪʃ/ a **Finn** /fɪn/
France /frɑːns/	**French** /frentʃ/
	a **Frenchman** /ˈfrentʃmən/
	a **Frenchwoman** /ˈfrentʃwʊmən/

R33

Geographical names

FYROM /ˈfaɪrɒm/ **(the) Former Yugoslav Republic of Macedonia** /ˌfɔːmə ˌjuːgəslɑːv rɪˌpʌblɪk əv ˌmæsəˈdəʊniə/	**Macedonian** /ˌmæsəˈdəʊniən/
Gabon /ɡæˈbɒn/	**Gabonese** /ˌɡæbəˈniːz/
(the) Gambia /ˈɡæmbiə/	**Gambian** /ˈɡæmbiən/
Georgia /ˈdʒɔːdʒə/	**Georgian** /ˈdʒɔːdʒən/
Germany /ˈdʒɜːməni/	**German** /ˈdʒɜːmən/
Ghana /ˈɡɑːnə/	**Ghanaian** /ɡɑːˈneɪən/
Great Britain /ˌɡreɪt ˈbrɪtn/	**British** /ˈbrɪtɪʃ/ **a Briton** /ˈbrɪtn/
Greece /ɡriːs/	**Greek** /ɡriːk/
Grenada /ɡrəˈneɪdə/	**Grenadian** /ɡrəˈneɪdiən/
Guatemala /ˌɡwɑːtəˈmɑːlə/	**Guatemalan** /ˌɡwɑːtəˈmɑːlən/
Guinea /ˈɡɪni/	**Guinean** /ˈɡɪniən/
Guinea-Bissau /ˌɡɪni bɪˈsaʊ/	**Guinean** /ˈɡɪniən/
Guyana /ɡaɪˈænə/	**Guyanese** /ˌɡaɪəˈniːz/
Haiti /ˈheɪti/	**Haitian** /ˈheɪʃn/
Honduras /hɒnˈdjʊərəs/	**Honduran** /hɒnˈdjʊərən/
Hungary /ˈhʌŋɡəri/	**Hungarian** /hʌŋˈɡeəriən/
Iceland /ˈaɪslənd/	**Icelandic** /aɪsˈlændɪk/ **an Icelander** /ˈaɪsləndə(r)/
India /ˈɪndiə/	**Indian** /ˈɪndiən/
Indonesia /ˌɪndəˈniːʒə/	**Indonesian** /ˌɪndəˈniːʒn/
Iran /ɪˈrɑːn/	**Iranian** /ɪˈreɪniən/
Iraq /ɪˈrɑːk/	**Iraqi** /ɪˈrɑːki/
(the) Republic of Ireland /rɪˌpʌblɪk əv ˈaɪələnd/	**Irish** /ˈaɪrɪʃ/ **an Irishman** /ˈaɪrɪʃmən/ **an Irishwoman** /ˈaɪrɪʃwʊmən/
Israel /ˈɪzreɪl/	**Israeli** /ɪzˈreɪli/
Italy /ˈɪtəli/	**Italian** /ɪˈtæliən/
(the) Ivory Coast /ˌaɪvəri ˈkəʊst/ (*see also* **Côte d'Ivoire**)	**Ivorian** /aɪˈvɔːriən/
Jamaica /dʒəˈmeɪkə/	**Jamaican** /dʒəˈmeɪkən/
Japan /dʒəˈpæn/	**Japanese** /ˌdʒæpəˈniːz/
Jordan /ˈdʒɔːdn/	**Jordanian** /dʒɔːˈdeɪniən/
Kazakhstan /ˌkæzəkˈstɑːn/	**Kazakh** /kəˈzæk/
Kenya /ˈkenjə/	**Kenyan** /ˈkenjən/
Kiribati /ˌkɪrɪˈbɑːti/	**Kiribati** /ˌkɪrɪˈbɑːti/
Kuwait /kʊˈweɪt/	**Kuwaiti** /kʊˈweɪti/
Kyrgyzstan /ˌkɜːɡɪˈstɑːn/	**Kyrgyz** /ˈkɜːɡɪz/
Laos /laʊs/	**Laotian** /ˈlaʊʃn/
Latvia /ˈlætviə/	**Latvian** /ˈlætviən/
Lebanon /ˈlebənən/	**Lebanese** /ˌlebəˈniːz/
Lesotho /ləˈsuːtuː/	person: **a Mosotho** /məˈsuːtuː/ people: **Basotho** /bəˈsuːtuː/
Liberia /laɪˈbɪəriə/	**Liberian** /laɪˈbɪəriən/
Libya /ˈlɪbiə/	**Libyan** /ˈlɪbiən/
Liechtenstein /ˈlɪktənstaɪn/	**Liechtenstein a Liechtensteiner** /ˈlɪktənstaɪnə(r)/
Lithuania /ˌlɪθjuˈeɪniə/	**Lithuanian** /ˌlɪθjuˈeɪniən/
Luxembourg /ˈlʌksəmbɜːɡ/	**Luxembourg a Luxembourger** /ˈlʌksəmbɜːɡə(r)/
Madagascar /ˌmædəˈɡæskə(r)/	**Madagascan** /ˌmædəˈɡæskən/ **Malagasy** /ˌmæləˈɡæsi/

Malawi /məˈlɑːwi/	**Malawian** /məˈlɑːwiən/
Malaysia /məˈleɪʒə/	**Malaysian** /məˈleɪʒn/
(the) Maldives /ˈmɔːldiːvz/	**Maldivian** /mɔːlˈdɪviən/
Mali /ˈmɑːli/	**Malian** /ˈmɑːliən/
Malta /ˈmɔːltə/	**Maltese** /mɔːlˈtiːz/
Mauritania /ˌmɒrɪˈteɪniə/	**Mauritanian** /ˌmɒrɪˈteɪniən/
Mauritius /məˈrɪʃəs/	**Mauritian** /məˈrɪʃn/
Mexico /ˈmeksɪkəʊ/	**Mexican** /ˈmeksɪkən/
Moldova /mɒlˈdəʊvə/	**Moldovan** /mɒlˈdəʊvn/
Monaco /ˈmɒnəkəʊ/	**Monégasque** /ˌmɒnɪˈgæsk/
Mongolia /mɒŋˈgəʊliə/	**Mongolian** /mɒŋˈgəʊliən/ **Mongol** /ˈmɒŋgl/
Montenegro /ˌmɒntɪˈniːgrəʊ/	**Montenegrin** /ˌmɒntɪˈniːgrɪn/
Morocco /məˈrɒkəʊ/	**Moroccan** /məˈrɒkən/
Mozambique /ˌməʊzæmˈbiːk/	**Mozambican** /ˌməʊzæmˈbiːkən/
Myanmar /miˌænˈmɑː(r)/ (*see also* **Burma**)	
Namibia /nəˈmɪbiə/	**Namibian** /nəˈmɪbiən/
Nauru /ˈnaʊruː/	**Nauruan** /naʊˈruːən/
Nepal /nəˈpɔːl/	**Nepalese** /ˌnepəˈliːz/
(the) Netherlands /ˈneðələndz/	**Dutch** /dʌtʃ/ a **Dutchman** /ˈdʌtʃmən/ a **Dutchwoman** /ˈdʌtʃwʊmən/
New Zealand /ˌnjuːˈziːlənd/	**New Zealand** a **New Zealander** /ˌnjuːˈziːləndə(r)/
Nicaragua /ˌnɪkəˈrægjuə/	**Nicaraguan** /ˌnɪkəˈrægjuən/
Niger /niːˈʒeə(r)/	**Nigerien** /niːˈʒeəriən/
Nigeria /naɪˈdʒɪəriə/	**Nigerian** /naɪˈdʒɪəriən/
Northern Ireland /ˌnɔːðən ˈaɪələnd/	**Northern Irish** /ˌnɔːðən ˈaɪrɪʃ/
North Korea /ˌnɔːθ kəˈriə/	**North Korean** /ˌnɔːθ kəˈriən/
Norway /ˈnɔːweɪ/	**Norwegian** /nɔːˈwiːdʒən/
Oman /əʊˈmɑːn/	**Omani** /əʊˈmɑːni/
Pakistan /ˌpaːkɪˈstɑːn/	**Pakistani** /ˌpɑːkɪˈstɑːni/
Panama /ˈpænəmɑː/	**Panamanian** /ˌpænəˈmeɪniən/
Papua New Guinea /ˌpæpjuə ˌnjuː ˈgɪni/	**Papua New Guinean** /ˌpæpjuə ˌnjuː ˈgɪniən/
Paraguay /ˈpærəgwaɪ/	**Paraguayan** /ˌpærəˈgwaɪən/
Peru /pəˈruː/	**Peruvian** /pəˈruːviən/
(the) Philippines /ˈfɪlɪpiːnz/	**Philippine** /ˈfɪlɪpiːn/ a **Filipino** /ˌfɪlɪˈpiːnəʊ/ a **Filipina** /ˌfɪlɪˈpiːnə/
Poland /ˈpəʊlənd/	**Polish** /ˈpəʊlɪʃ/ a **Pole** /pəʊl/
Portugal /ˈpɔːtʃʊgl/	**Portuguese** /ˌpɔːtʃʊˈgiːz/
Qatar /ˈkʌtɑː(r)/	**Qatari** /kʌˈtɑːri/
Romania /ruˈmeɪniə/	**Romanian** /ruˈmeɪniən/
Russia /ˈrʌʃə/	**Russian** /ˈrʌʃn/
Rwanda /ruˈændə/	**Rwandan** /ruˈændən/
Samoa /səˈməʊə/	**Samoan** /səˈməʊən/
San Marino /ˌsæn məˈriːnəʊ/	
São Tomé and Príncipe /ˌsaʊ təˌmeɪ ən ˈprɪnsɪpeɪ/	
Saudi Arabia /ˌsaʊdi əˈreɪbiə/	**Saudi** /ˈsaʊdi/ **Saudi Arabian** /ˌsaʊdi əˈreɪbiən/
Scotland /ˈskɒtlənd/	**Scottish** /ˈskɒtɪʃ/ **Scots** /skɒts/ a **Scot** /skɒt/ a **Scotsman** /ˈskɒtsmən/ a **Scotswoman** /ˈskɒtswʊmən/
Senegal /ˌsenɪˈgɔːl/	**Senegalese** /ˌsenɪgəˈliːz/

Geographical names

Geographical names

Serbia /ˈsɜːbiə/	**Serbian** /ˈsɜːbiən/ **a Serb** /sɜːb/
(the) Seychelles /seɪˈʃelz/	**Seychellois** /ˌseɪʃelˈwɑː/
Sierra Leone /siˌerə liˈəʊn/	**Sierra Leonean** /siˌerə liˈəʊniən/
Singapore /ˌsɪŋəˈpɔː(r)/	**Singaporean** /ˌsɪŋəˈpɔːriən/
Slovakia /sləˈvækiə/	**Slovak** /ˈsləʊvæk/ **Slovakian** /sləˈvækiən/
Slovenia /sləˈviːniə/	**Slovene** /ˈsləʊviːn/ **Slovenian** /sləˈviːniən/
(the) Solomon Islands /ˈsɒləmən aɪləndz/	**a Solomon Islander** /ˈsɒləmən aɪləndə(r)/
Somalia /səˈmɑːliə/	**Somali** /səˈmɑːli/
South Africa /ˌsaʊθ ˈæfrɪkə/	**South African** /ˌsaʊθ ˈæfrɪkən/
South Korea /ˌsaʊθ kəˈriə/	**South Korean** /ˌsaʊθ kəˈriən/
South Sudan /ˌsaʊθ suˈdɑːn/	**South Sudanese** /ˌsaʊθ suːdəˈniːz/
Spain /speɪn/	**Spanish** /ˈspænɪʃ/ **a Spaniard** /ˈspæniəd/
Sri Lanka /ˌsri ˈlæŋkə/	**Sri Lankan** /ˌsri ˈlæŋkən/
St Kitts and Nevis /snt ˌkɪts ən ˈniːvɪs/	**Kittitian** /kɪˈtɪʃn/, **Nevisian** /niːˈvɪsiən/
St Lucia /ˌsnt ˈluːʃə/	**St Lucian** /ˌsnt ˈluːʃən/
St Vincent and the Grenadines /snt ˌvɪnsnt ən ðə ˈɡrenədiːnz/	**Vincentian** /vɪnˈsenʃn/
Sudan /suˈdɑːn/	**Sudanese** /ˌsuːdəˈniːz/
Suriname /ˌsʊərɪˈnɑːm/	**Surinamese** /ˌsʊərɪnəˈmiːz/
Swaziland /ˈswɑːzilænd/	**Swazi** /ˈswɑːzi/
Sweden /ˈswiːdn/	**Swedish** /ˈswiːdɪʃ/ **a Swede** /swiːd/
Switzerland /ˈswɪtsələnd/	**Swiss** /swɪs/
Syria /ˈsɪriə/	**Syrian** /ˈsɪriən/
Tajikistan /tæˌdʒiːkɪˈstɑːn/	**Tajik** /tæˈdʒiːk/
Tanzania /ˌtænzəˈniːə/	**Tanzanian** /ˌtænzəˈniːən/
Thailand /ˈtaɪlænd/	**Thai** /taɪ/
Togo /ˈtəʊɡəʊ/	**Togolese** /ˌtəʊɡəˈliːz/
Tonga /ˈtɒŋə/	**Tongan** /ˈtɒŋən/
Trinidad and Tobago /ˌtrɪnɪdæd ən təˈbeɪɡəʊ/	**Trinidadian** /ˌtrɪnɪˈdædiən/ **Tobagan** /təˈbeɪɡən/ **Tobagonian** /ˌtəʊbəˈɡəʊniən/
Tunisia /tjuˈnɪziə/	**Tunisian** /tjuˈnɪziən/
Turkey /ˈtɜːki/	**Turkish** /ˈtɜːkɪʃ/ **a Turk** /tɜːk/
Turkmenistan /tɜːkˌmenɪˈstɑːn/	**Turkmen** /ˈtɜːkmen/
Tuvalu /tuːˈvɑːluː/	**Tuvaluan** /ˌtuːvɑːˈluːən/
Uganda /juːˈɡændə/	**Ugandan** /juːˈɡændən/
Ukraine /juːˈkreɪn/	**Ukrainian** /juːˈkreɪniən/
(the) United Arab Emirates (UAE) /juˌnaɪtɪd ˌærəb ˈemɪrəts/	**Emirati** /emɪˈrɑːti/
(the) United Kingdom (UK) /juˌnaɪtɪd ˈkɪŋdəm/	**British** /ˈbrɪtɪʃ/ **a Briton** /ˈbrɪtn/
(the) United States of America (USA) /juˌnaɪtɪd ˌsteɪts əv əˈmerɪkə/	**American** /əˈmerɪkən/
Uruguay /ˈjʊərəɡwaɪ/	**Uruguayan** /ˌjʊərəˈɡwaɪən/
Uzbekistan /ʊzˌbekɪˈstɑːn/	**Uzbek** /ˈʊzbek/
Vanuatu /ˌvænuˈɑːtuː/	**Vanuatuan** /ˌvænwɑːˈtuːən/
Venezuela /ˌvenəˈzweɪlə/	**Venezuelan** /ˌvenəˈzweɪlən/
Vietnam /ˌvjetˈnæm/	**Vietnamese** /ˌvjetnəˈmiːz/
Wales /weɪlz/	**Welsh** /welʃ/ **a Welshman** /ˈwelʃmən/ **a Welshwoman** /ˈwelʃwʊmən/
Yemen /ˈjemən/	**Yemeni** /ˈjeməni/
Zambia /ˈzæmbiə/	**Zambian** /ˈzæmbiən/
Zimbabwe /zɪmˈbɑːbwi/	**Zimbabwean** /zɪmˈbɑːbwiən/

Telephoning

Making an informal call

— Hi, can I speak to Martin, please?
— *Sorry, he's out at the moment.*
  Can I take a message?
— Can you tell him that Natasha called?
— *OK, Natasha.*
  I'll let him know when he gets back.

— Hello?
— *Hi, is that Tanya? It's Amy here.*
— Hi Amy! Sorry, the battery on my mobile is about to run out.
  Can you call me on the landline?
— *Sure, what's the number?*
— It's 258 440.
  (= two five eight, double four oh)

Finishing an informal call

…
— OK, then. So I'll see you next Saturday at 7 o'clock. I'm looking forward to it.
— *Yeah, me too. See you on Saturday, then. Thanks for calling.*
— No problem. Bye!
…
— Right, then, I'll find out how much the tickets cost and get back to you.
— *Thanks, that would be great. Speak to you later. Bye!*

Making a formal call

— Good morning, could I speak to Dr. McSweeney, please?
— *Yes, of course. May I ask who's calling?*
— It's Nigel Briggs.
— *OK, just a moment, please.*
  I'll put you through.
  …
— *Hello, Mr Briggs? I'm afraid she's on the other line at the moment.*
  Shall I ask her to call you back?
— No, that's OK. I'll phone again later. Thank you. Goodbye.

— Good morning, this is Helen Randall. Could I talk to Simon Hooper, please?
— *I'm afraid he's away from his desk at the moment. Would you like to leave a message?*
— Yes, please. Could you ask him to call me when he gets back?
  My number is…

To find out more about telephoning, look at **mobile phone** and **telephone** in the dictionary.

Text messages

Mobile phone text messages, chat room messages and sometimes emails can be written using the smallest number of letters possible. These are some examples of how words might be shown in a message:

thx 4
gr8 party!
c u 2moro?

2day today
2moro tomorrow
2nite tonight
asap as soon as possible
b4 before
b4n bye for now
btw by the way

c see
cul8r see you later
gr8 great
ilu i love you
lol laughing out loud
msg message
pls please

soz sorry
spk speak
thx thanks
u you
wan2 want to
wknd weekend
x kiss

Learning vocabulary

You can easily remember a large number of new words if you organize your vocabulary learning.

Recording the meaning of new words

You can draw a picture:
- snake

You can explain the word in English:
- salary = *the money you receive from your job*

You can copy an example:
- I've known her **since** 1997.

And you can use the dictionary example sentence to help you write your own personal sentence:
- I've been studying English **since** 2001.

Vocabulary cards

You can record important new words on **cards**:

pronunciation | **grammar information**

happy /ˈhæpi/ (adjective)
happy to do sth
OPP *sad / unhappy*
happiness (noun)

meaning → = *feeling pleasure; pleased*
example sentence → *I was really _____ to see my family again.*
related words
OPP _____ / _____
_____ (noun)

(front of card)   (back of card)

Carry the cards in your pocket or bag. When you have a few minutes, test yourself. Look at one side of the card and try to remember what is written on the other side.

Vocabulary notebooks

Write new vocabulary in a **notebook**:

Write the English words on the left, and the meaning, explanation, picture, etc. on the right. Then you can cover the left side and test yourself.

JOBS

employee   *sb who works for an employer*
/ɪmˈplɔɪiː/

part-time (adj)   OPP *full-time*
                         She's got a ___ job.

'What do you do?'   *'I'm a doctor.'*

Organizing words

You will remember new words more easily if you organize them into groups:
- topics
  ('*jobs*', '*the environment*', '*holidays*')
- word families
  (*happy, unhappy, happiness, happily*)
- opposite pairs (*happy/sad, rich/poor*)
- words with a similar meaning
  (*very good, great, wonderful, fantastic*)
- key words (*get up, get on well with sb, get your hair cut*)

Here are two more ways of grouping words:

Word tables

sport	person	place
football	footballer	pitch
athletics	athlete	track
golf	golfer	course
tennis	tennis player	court

Word diagrams

doing homework

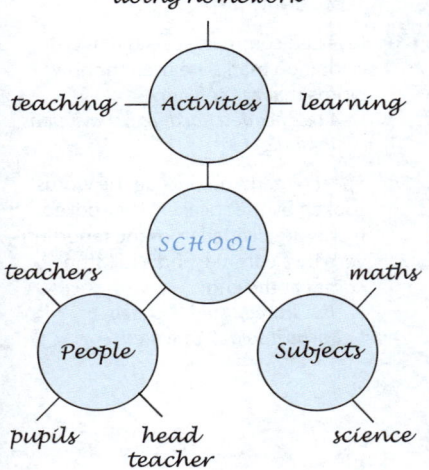

teaching — Activities — *learning*

SCHOOL

teachers *maths*

People   Subjects

pupils *head teacher* *science*

The most important words – The Oxford 3000™

There are thousands and thousands of words and phrases in this dictionary – you can't learn them all!

Start by learning the most important words. These are the **Oxford 3000™**. They are marked in the dictionary with a 🔑.

> 🔑 **progress** /ˈprəʊɡres/ *noun* [U] movement forwards or towards achieving sth: *Anna's **making progress** at school.*

Remembering words

You will not remember words if you only write them down. You must also:
- **try** to remember them
- look at them **again** and **again**
- **start using** them when you speak or write English

Connecting words

One trick for remembering words is to connect the English word with a word in your language.
- For example, if a French student learning English wants to remember the verb **to chat** (= to talk to somebody in a friendly way), he/she can connect it to the French word **chat**, which means 'cat'. *Imagine a cat talking to its friends.*

It doesn't matter if the words are not exactly the same.
- For example, the Japanese verb *oyogu* (= swim) sounds a little like the English word *yogurt*. How could an English student remember this Japanese word? *Imagine a person swimming in a very big pot of yogurt.*

These connections may seem silly. But the sillier they are, the easier they will be to remember!

Punctuation

A A capital letter is used at the start of each new sentence. You also use capitals for proper nouns; names of people and places; titles of books, films, etc.:
> Tessa and Don saw Finding Neverland at the Ritzy Cinema, Brixton when they were in England.

. A full stop shows the end of a sentence. It is also often used after initials and abbreviations:
> Peter Pan was written by J. M. Barrie.

! An exclamation mark is used at the end of a sentence to show surprise, joy, anger or shock:
> Don't speak to me like that!' she shouted.
> What a glorious day for a wedding!

? A question mark is used at the end of a direct question:
> 'Can you drive?' asked Laura.

, A comma separates parts of a sentence or words in a list, or shows additional information:
> Peter refuses to leave Neverland, but Wendy returns to her family.
> It's a play about children, fairies and pirates.
> The crocodile, which was large and hungry, swam close to the ship.

' An apostrophe replaces a missing letter or letters in contracted forms: I'd (= I had), isn't (= is not), we'll (= we will), won't (= will not).

We also use apostrophes before or after the possessive with **s** (see Grammar Section R18).

( ) Brackets are used when the writer adds information, an explanation, a comment, etc. to something in the text. The text would still make sense if the information in brackets was removed:
> Captain Hook (usually played by the same actor as Wendy's father) terrifies the children.

— A dash is used when an additional comment or additional information is added to a sentence:
> Peter is usually – but not always – played by a woman.

- A hyphen is used in many cases where two words have been joined together to form one: *self-service*. It is also used to separate long words that will not fit on one line. As there are complicated rules about where you can correctly divide words, it is safer to start the word on the next line.

: A colon tells the reader that something is coming next, for example a list:
> People go to the theatre for many reasons: to meet friends, to be entertained, to be educated.

; A semicolon is used to divide two parts of a sentence:
> She looked up and frowned; the boy ran away.

" " Inverted commas, speech marks or quotation marks are used to show words that are spoken:
> A teacher described his behaviour as 'infantile'.

Speech marks go outside the words spoken by the speaker. The spoken words are divided from the reporting verb by a comma, and a full stop comes at the end.
> 'I'm scared,' said Michael.
> Michael said, 'I'm scared.'

Pronunciation

If two pronunciations for one word are given, both are acceptable. The first form given is considered to be more common.

/-/ A hyphen is used in alternative pronunciations when only part of the pronunciation changes. The part that remains the same is replaced by the hyphen.

accent /ˈæksent; -sənt/

/ˈ/ This mark shows that the syllable after it is said with more force (stress) than other syllables in the word or group of words. For example **any** /ˈeni/ has a stress on the first syllable; **depend** /dɪˈpend/ has a stress on the second syllable.

/ˌ/ This mark shows that a syllable is said with more force than other syllables in a word but with a stress that is not as strong as for those syllables marked /ˈ/. So in the word **pronunciation** /prəˌnʌnsiˈeɪʃn/ the main stress is on the syllable /ˈeɪ/ and the secondary stress is on the syllable /ˌnʌn/.

Strong and weak forms

Some very common words, for example **an**, **as**, **that**, **of**, have two or more pronunciations: a **strong** form and one or more **weak** forms. In speech the weak forms are more common. For example **from** is /frəm/ in *He comes from Spain*. The strong form occurs when the word comes at the end of a sentence or when it is given special emphasis. For example **from** is /frɒm/ in *Where are you from?* and in *The present's not from John, it's for him.*

Pronunciation in derivatives and compounds

Many **derivatives** are formed by adding a suffix to the end of a word. These are pronounced by simply saying the suffix after the word. For example **slowly** /ˈsləʊli/ is said by adding the suffix -**ly** /-li/ to the word **slow** /sləʊ/.

However, where there is doubt about how a derivative is pronounced, the phonetic spelling is given. The part that remains the same is represented by a hyphen.

accidental /ˌæksɪˈdentl/

accidentally /-təli/

In **compounds** (made up of two or more words) the pronunciation of the individual words is not repeated. The dictionary shows how the compound is stressed using the marks /ˈ/ and /ˌ/. In ˈ**air force** the stress is on the first word. In ˌ**air ˌtraffic conˈtroller** there are secondary stresses on **air** and on the first syllable of **traffic**, and the main stress is on the second syllable of **controller**.

Wordpower Workout

What is a Workout?

The **Wordpower Workout** will train you to use this dictionary in the best way. It will also help you to learn new vocabulary.

> **workout** /'wɜːkaʊt/ noun [C] a period of physical exercise, for example when you are training for a sport or keeping fit: *She does a twenty-minute workout every morning.*

How to find words
The alphabet

A Put the words below into alphabetical order (a, b, c, etc.) by writing a number:

____ glasses ____ jellyfish

____ zodiac ____ windmill

____ ripple ____ sneeze

____ volcano ____ snorkel

_2_ blow _1_ arch

____ puddle ____ robot

____ snail ____ eclipse

____ duck ____ lick

____ hat ____ zebra

B Most of these words are **illustrations** (= pictures) in this dictionary. Do you know what these words mean? Check by looking at the illustrations.

C Two of these words are **not** illustrations in the dictionary. Which two?

Choosing the right meaning

Many words have more than one meaning.

A Look at the **bold** words below. They are all *nouns*. Find them in the dictionary and read the different meanings. Are these sentences true (T) or false (F)?

1 _F_ A **mouse** is an animal and a piece of sports equipment. (*A mouse is an animal and a piece of computer equipment.*)

2 ____ You can find a **mole** underground, or on your body.

3 ____ You can eat a Christmas **cracker**.

4 ____ Something that 'costs a **bomb**' is very cheap.

5 ____ It is polite to call somebody a **dummy**.

6 ____ A **school** is a large group of dogs.

7 ____ In British English, the season after summer and before winter is called **fall**.

8 ____ A piece of clothing that a man wears to go swimming is called **a trunk**.

9 ____ You can see **scenery** in the countryside and in the theatre.

B Fill the gaps with a verb in the correct form and write the sense number (= the number that shows which meaning of the verb it is). Each verb is used twice.

break	cut	drop	face
freeze	play	turn	

1 It's so cold that even the river has _frozen_ . (sense _1_)

2 Tommy _____ the glass and it shattered on the floor. (sense ____)

© Oxford Fajar Sdn. Bhd. Photocopiable

3 He _____ the key in the lock. (*sense* ___)

4 Where do you get your hair _____? (*sense* ___)

5 When Jill _____ her leg it was in plaster for six weeks. (*sense* ___)

6 The hotel rooms all _____ the sea. (*sense* ___)

7 My favourite song was _____ on the radio. (*sense* ___)

8 The government wants to _____ taxes before the election. (*sense* ___)

9 She _____ the silence by coughing. (*sense* ___)

10 The weather has _____ cold. (*sense* ___)

11 She had to _____ the fact that her life had changed forever. (*sense* ___)

12 Can you _____ me near the station, please? (*sense* ___)

13 Parents _____ a vital role in their children's education. (*sense* ___)

14 She _____ with terror as the door slowly opened. (*sense* ___)

Finding phrasal verbs – fast!

Find **go** in the dictionary and look at the PHR V (= phrasal verbs) section.

A Complete the phrasal verbs by filling each gap with one word.

1 go ___*away*___ = leave home for a period of time, especially for a holiday

2 go _____ with an illness = become ill

3 go _____ about sth = talk about sth for a long time in an annoying way

4 go _____ with sth = continue doing sth

5 go _____ for a meal / a walk

6 go _____ / _____ sth = look at sth carefully, from beginning to end

7 go _____ to sb's (*home*) = visit sb

8 go _____ = become higher in price, level, etc.

9 go _____ sth = look good with sth else

B Complete the sentences using the verbs in part A.

1 Do you fancy going ___*out*___ for dinner tonight?

2 I went _____ with the flu when I was on holiday.

3 No, that shirt doesn't go _____ those trousers.

4 Let's go _____ / _____ your homework and correct the mistakes.

5 That's enough for now – let's go _____ with it tomorrow.

6 We went _____ to his house for dinner last night.

7 Prices in the shops keep going _____!

8 We're going _____ to the seaside for a week.

9 He's always going _____ about his health problems.

10 'Where's Tom?' 'He went _____ for a walk.'

Parts of speech (= nouns, verbs, etc.)

A Which **part of speech** is the word light in each of these sentences?
noun verb adjective adverb
1 Modern cameras are light and easy to carry. _adjective_
2 This room has big windows so there is lots of light. _____
3 We had to light candles because there was no electricity. _____
4 I always travel light. _____

B Look at the **bold** words. Are they nouns, verbs, adjectives or adverbs? Find the word in the dictionary. Write the number of the part of speech.
1 What time is it? I don't have a **watch**. _noun_
  WATCH _2_
2 Do you **watch** much television? _____ WATCH ___
3 We walked in the **park**. _____ PARK ___
4 Where can I **park** my car? _____ PARK ___
5 Do you live in a house or a **flat**? _____ FLAT ___
6 People used to think the earth was **flat**. _____ FLAT ___
7 I like travelling by **train**. _____ TRAIN ___
8 You have to **train** to be a teacher. _____ TRAIN ___
9 The exam was very **hard**. _____ HARD ___
10 Students should work **hard**. _____ HARD ___

C Use the words in part B to make your own sentences. They should include both parts of speech. Don't worry if they are funny or strange!

▶ I **watched** a television programme about **watches**.

▶ You can't **park** your car in the **park**! You should **park** it in the car **park**.

Finding the right word

The large blue words in the dictionary are called **headwords**.

Not all words are headwords. For example, if you want to find the word **happiness**, you should look at **happy**.

Types of words that may not be headwords include:
- derivatives (**happiness**, from **happy**)
- plural forms of nouns (**women**, from **woman**)
- comparative/superlative forms of adjectives (**noisier/noisiest**, from **noisy**)
- verb forms ending in -ing, -s, -ed (**studying, studies, studied**, from **study**)

Where can you find the words below?
1 inspection _inspect_
2 luckily _____
3 spies _____
4 thieves _____
5 limo _____
6 the jeweller's _____
7 greedier _____
8 clumsiest _____
9 digging _____
10 burgled _____

Understanding words

Defining vocabulary

The **definitions** (= the meanings of words) in this dictionary are easy to understand because they use simple words. These 3 000 simple words are called the *defining vocabulary*.

When a word that is not in the defining vocabulary is used in a definition, it is written in **bold** letters and explained with (= ...). For example:

> **octopus** /ˈɒktəpəs/ *noun* [C] a sea animal with a soft body and eight **tentacles** (= long thin parts like arms)

A Definitions puzzle

Look at the definitions. Which word is being defined? Write the word on the correct line in the puzzle below.

If you need help, look in your dictionary at the words in brackets.

1. a musical instrument with strings (Help? Look at *strum*)
2. a large wild animal with horns on its head (*stag*)
3. dried leaves used for making cigarettes (*cigarette*)
4. a mixture of flour, fat and water (*quiche*)
5. a vehicle that travels in space (*lift-off*)
6. a piece of equipment that makes small objects look bigger (*bacteria*)
7. small green or purple fruit that grow in bunches (*wine*)

When you have finished 1–6, read downwards to find the answer to 7

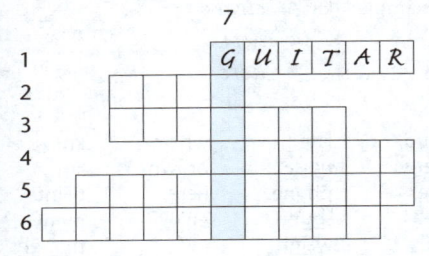

```
        7
1     | G | U | I | T | A | R |
2 | _ | _ | _ | _ | _ |
3         | _ | _ | _ | _ | _ | _ |
4     | _ | _ | _ | _ | _ | _ |
5 | _ | _ | _ | _ | _ |
6 | _ | _ | _ | _ |
```

B Which word is different?

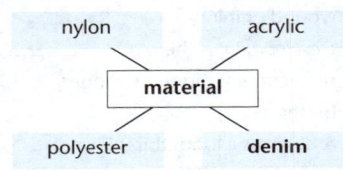

nylon — acrylic
↘   ↙
material
↗   ↘
polyester — **denim**

(*Denim is a material made from **cotton**. The others are **artificial materials**.*)

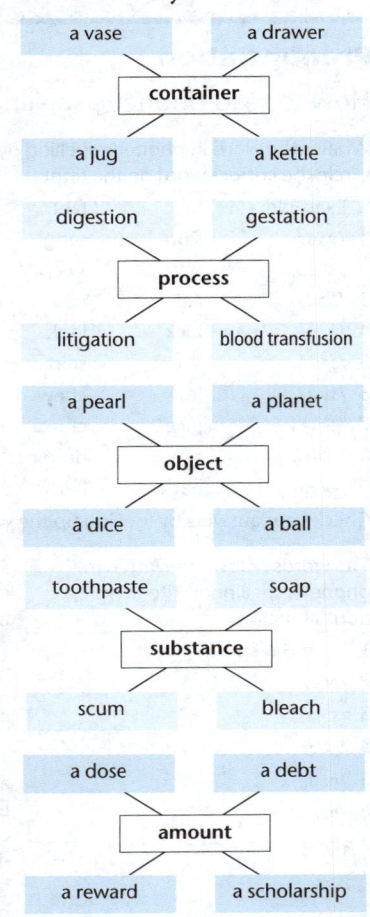

a vase — a drawer
↘   ↙
container
↗   ↘
a jug — a kettle

digestion — gestation
↘   ↙
process
↗   ↘
litigation — blood transfusion

a pearl — a planet
↘   ↙
object
↗   ↘
a dice — a ball

toothpaste — soap
↘   ↙
substance
↗   ↘
scum — bleach

a dose — a debt
↘   ↙
amount
↗   ↘
a reward — a scholarship

© Oxford Fajar Sdn. Bhd.   Photocopiable

R45

Wordpower Workout

C Fill each space with one of the **bold** words from part B.

1 A *bandage* is a long piece of soft white _material_ that you tie round a wound or injury.
2 *Development* is the _____ of becoming bigger, stronger, better, etc.
3 A *ribbon* is a long, thin piece of _____ that is used for tying or decorating something.
4 *Pocket money* is an _____ of money that parents give a child to spend, usually every week.
5 A *waste-paper basket* is a _____ in which you put paper, etc. that is to be thrown away.
6 *Salt* is a common white _____ that is found in sea water and the earth.
7 A *pencil* is an _____ that you use for writing or drawing.

Pronunciation
How to read phonetic spelling

A What is the word in phonetic spelling on the left? Circle the correct word on the right.

▶ Example: /fɑː/   fair   (far)   four   fur
1 /sʌŋ/   sing   sang   sung   song
2 /slæp/   slap   sleep   slip   slurp
3 /kɔːt/   cat   cut   kit   caught
4 /lʊk/   luck   look   lack   lick
5 /ʃɜːt/   sheet   shirt   shoot   feet
6 /tʃuː/   Jew   chew   dew   shoe
7 /dʒəʊk/ joke   choke   yolk   yoke
8 /ðəʊ/   sew   dough   toe   though
9 /bɑːθ/   bath   barn   bathe   back

Check your answers by looking up the words in the dictionary.

B The words below are written in phonetic spelling. Write them in normal spelling.

1 /klɪə/ = *clear*
2 /heə/
3 /steɪ/
4 /gəʊ/
5 /maɪ/
6 /bɔɪ/
7 /haʊ/

C How do we pronounce the words below? Put them into the correct group in part B according to the sound of the underlined part.

▶ Example: /klɪə/ = *clear*
    deer
    here
    beer

aloud	late	where	know
beer	noise	brown	lie
care	phone	here	paint
deer	sound	enjoy	point
fair	weigh	five	though
high			

Stress

Word stress is shown in the dictionary like this:

Italy /ˈɪtəli/

The stress comes on the sound after '. You can also mark stress like this:

İtaly

The adjective from *Italy* is *Italian*. The stress is like this:

Italian /ɪˈtaeliən/ Itàlian

A Write the adjectives. Mark the stress on the country and the adjective.

1 Italy   *Italian*
2 Egypt
3 Peru
4 Canada
5 Brazil
6 Argentina
7 Turkey
8 Indonesia
9 Portugal
10 Japan

B Check your answers by looking at the list of **Geographical names** in the Reference Section.

C How is the name of your country pronounced in English? Is it the same in your language?

How to use words

Examples

Wordpower gives you lots of information in **examples**.

> **medal** /ˈmedl/ noun [C] a small flat piece of metal, usually with a design and words on it, which is given to sb who has shown courage or as a prize in a sport: *to win a gold/silver/bronze medal in the Olympics*

Try to answer these questions *without* using the dictionary!

1 The best athlete usually wins a gold **medal**. What are the 2 other types of medal? *silver, bronze*

2 Name 3 sports that are played on a **court**, and 3 that are played on a **pitch**.

3 A place where a lot of people can go on holiday in order to **ski** is called a ski _____

4 Skating and skiing are types of _____ **sport**.

5 Is this example correct? *My brother is a very **sporting** person.*

6 Which is correct? He is in **training** *to / for / of* the Olympics.

7 Complete the sentence: *Students are encouraged to **participate** _____ sporting activities.*

8 Where might you find a water **chute**?

9 Do these sentences mean the same thing?
*He **windsurfs** every summer.*
*He **goes windsurfing** every summer.*
Which is more usual?

10 In a sports match, who uses a **whistle**? What might he/she do with it?

11 Correct the mistake in this sentence: *This city has excellent sports **facility**.*

Now find the **bold** words in the dictionary and look at the examples. Were your answers correct?

© Oxford Fajar Sdn. Bhd.   Photocopiable

Collocation – Words that go together

Which is the correct word in these sentences?
- I have to do / make an exam tomorrow.
- I'm sorry, I've done / made a mistake.

Find the answers by looking at the examples in *Wordpower*.

We say **do an exam** and **make a mistake**. We never say *make an exam* or *do a mistake*.

Words which often go together (like **do** + **an exam**, and **make** + **a mistake**) are called **collocations**. They are very important in English.

exam /ɪgˈzæm/ (also *formal* examination) *noun* [C] a written, spoken or practical test of what you know or can do: *an English exam* ◆ *the exam results* ◆ *to do/take/sit an exam* ◆ *to pass/fail an exam* ◆ *to revise for an exam* ⊃ note at **pass**, **study**

mistake /mɪˈsteɪk/ *noun* [C] something that you think or do that is wrong: *Try not to **make** any **mistakes** in your essays.*

Verb + noun collocations

A Match the verbs and nouns that usually go together.

do — weight
draw — on holiday
fall — money
go — a story
have — your homework
lose — TV
save — pictures
tell — in love
watch — a good time

B Correct the mistakes below using a verb from the list in part A in the appropriate form.
1 Why haven't you ~~written~~ your homework? *done*
2 She became in love with him the moment she saw him.
3 If you hadn't seen so much TV, your eyes wouldn't be hurting now.
4 You look fabulous! Have you put off weight?
5 'Where is Eva?' 'She has left on holiday.'
6 The children love writing pictures.
7 I wish he wouldn't say the same stories over and over again.
8 Did you enjoy a good time at the party?
9 We need to keep more money if we want to buy a car.

Adjective + noun collocations

A Make collocations connected with **health** by matching the nouns from the box with the adjectives below. Use each noun only once.

headache	throat	~~back~~	recovery
ankle	illness	tooth	leg
nose	diet	disease	eye

1 a bad *back*
2 a balanced
3 a black
4 a broken
5 a contagious
6 a decayed
7 a runny
8 a serious
9 a sore
10 a speedy
11 a splitting
12 a twisted

B 10 of these expressions are types of illness or injury. In your opinion, which of the 10 is the most serious? Put them in order by writing a number from 1 (the most serious) to 10 (the least serious).

Prepositions

Wordpower gives you lots of information about **prepositions**.

> **good** /gʊd/ *adj* good at sth; good with sb/sth able to do sth or deal with sb/sth well

A Find the **bold** words in the dictionary. Fill the gaps below with the correct preposition.
1 Do you know anyone who is **afraid** ___of___ snakes, spiders, heights, etc?
2 Can you think of anything you have done that you are **proud** _____?
3 Are there any songs or smells that **remind** you _____ something?
4 Is there anything that you **dream** _____ / _____ doing one day?
5 Have you ever done something that you were **embarrassed** _____?
6 What kinds of things did you **worry** _____ when you were a teenager?
7 When you were at school, which subjects were you **bad** _____?
8 Do you **believe** _____ ghosts?
9 When did you last **receive** a present _____ somebody? What was it?

B Now answer the questions!

Verb patterns

A Find the **bold** words in the dictionary. Cross out the incorrect verb pattern.
1 What do you **enjoy** do / doing in your free time?
2 What are you **planning** doing / to do on your next holiday?
3 When you were a child, what did your parents / teachers **make** you to do / do? What were you not **allowed** do / to do?
4 Describe something that you are **looking forward** to do / to doing soon.
5 Do you know anyone who usually **puts off** doing / to do things that he / she **should** to do / do?
6 Have you ever **forgotten** to do / doing something important?
7 Describe something nice / terrible that you **remember** doing / to do when you were a child.

B Now answer the questions!

Irregular verbs

If you want to check the form of an irregular verb, look at the list of **Irregular verbs** at the back of this dictionary.

Complete the puzzle by writing the past tense and past participle forms of these irregular verbs. 'Sing' is already done for you as an example.

break	eat	take
do	fall	find
drink	run	write

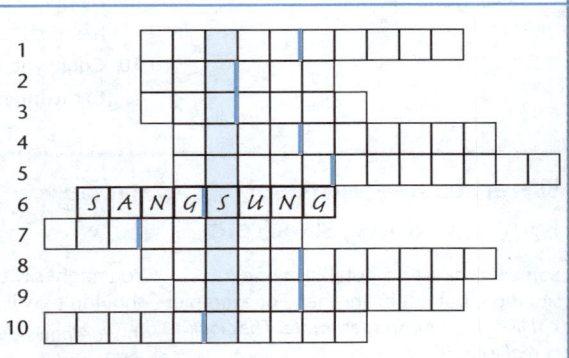

6 S A N G S U N G

The letters in the blue boxes will reveal another word. Of which verb is it the irregular past tense and past participle?

© Oxford Fajar Sdn. Bhd.   Photocopiable

R49

Wordpower Workout

GRAMMAR notes

These notes help you to avoid mistakes by explaining difficult or confusing grammar points.

Each of these sentences contains a mistake. Use the word in **bold** to help you find the GRAMMAR note in the dictionary. Then correct the sentence.

1 I never watch the **news** on TV because ~~they are~~ so depressing.
   it is
2 Thank you, it's delicious, but I can't eat **some** more.
3 I've been studying English **since** four years.
4 When I was a child I **must** to help my mother with the housework.
5 Could you give me some **informations** about your English courses, please?
6 **When** the weather will be good tomorrow, we can play tennis.
7 My twin brother **who** lives in Germany is called John.
8 I have a **so** boring teacher that I always fall asleep in lessons.
9 'Nice to meet you. When did you arrive in Oxford?' 'Two days **before**.'
10 I've visited Korea and Japan, but I've never **gone** to China.

HELP notes

These notes help you to avoid mistakes by explaining the difference between similar words.

Look up the words in brackets. Read the HELP notes and write the correct words in each sentence below. Change the form of the verb if necessary.

1 He drives ___*like*___ a maniac! (as/like)
2 My dog was sick so I stayed at home to _____ it. (care about/take care of)
3 I'm sorry, but I _____ my books at home this morning. (forget/leave)
4 Tom's jokes are not very _____ (fun/funny)
5 Could you _____ me some money? (lend/borrow)
6 I _____ my towel on the sand, _____ down on it and went to sleep. (lie/lay)
7 I like my colleagues. They are really _____ people. (nice/sympathetic)
8 _____ your hand if you know the answer. (rise/raise)
9 Help! I've been _____! Somebody has _____ my wallet! (rob/steal)
10 Could you _____ me how to get to the Internet cafe, please? (say/tell)

When to use words
Formal, informal, slang, etc.

Some words are acceptable in one situation, but not in another. For example:
▶ '*I like your new **shades**, **mate**. They look really **cool**!*'

You might say this to a friend, but you shouldn't say it to your boss or your teacher.

In *Wordpower*, words or phrases that are only used in particular situations are marked using the terms *formal*, *informal*, etc.

© Oxford Fajar Sdn. Bhd. Photocopiable

Are the sentences true or false? Mark them with a ✓ or a ✗. Decide if the word in **bold** is *formal, informal, slang, figurative* or *spoken*. The first one has been done for you.

1 You wear a pair of **spectacles** on your feet.
   ✗   *formal*

2 'I beg your **pardon**' is another way of saying 'Thank you'.
   ___   _____

3 You give your friend a present. She says, 'This is **wicked**!' This means she doesn't like it.
   ___   _____

4 A **loony** is somebody who is **crazy**.
   ___   _____

5 A **half-baked** scheme is a type of dessert that you can buy in a bakery.
   ___   _____

6 Your **spouse** is the person to whom you are married.
   ___   _____

7 If somebody asks you, 'What is your **occupation**?', you should tell him/her where you live.
   ___   _____

8 If a person is **catapulted** to fame, he/she becomes famous very quickly.
   ___   _____

9 If an American says, 'Don't give me that **baloney**!', he/she thinks you are not telling the truth.
   ___   _____

10 You ask a friend if he wants to go to the cinema with you. He replies, 'You **bet**!' This means he doesn't want to go.
   ___   _____

British and American English

Wordpower shows you the difference between *British* and *American* words. For example:

boot /buːt/ *noun* [C] (*AmE* trunk) the part of a car where you put luggage, usually at the back

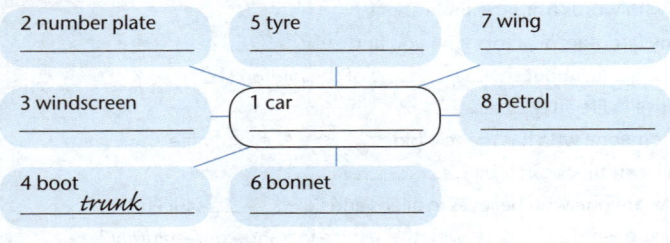

Complete the balloons with the *British* or *American* words that mean the same:

A Write the *American* words.

1 car
2 number plate _____
3 windscreen _____
4 boot *trunk*
5 tyre _____
6 bonnet _____
7 wing _____
8 petrol _____

B Write the *British* words.

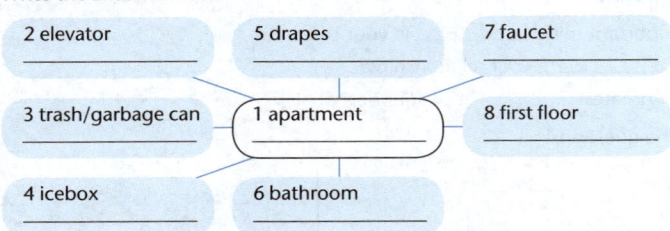

1 apartment _____
2 elevator _____
3 trash/garbage can _____
4 icebox _____
5 drapes _____
6 bathroom _____
7 faucet _____
8 first floor _____

© Oxford Fajar Sdn. Bhd.   Photocopiable

Build your vocabulary
Word families

You can improve your vocabulary fast by learning **word families** (for example, **happy, unhappy, happiness, happily**, etc.).

A Use the dictionary to fill in the missing words.

verb	noun	adjective
attract	*attraction*	(un) attractive
deepen		
	destruction	
		dead
differ		
	education	educated /
fly		
	fright	frightened /
	hope	(OPP)
satisfy		(dis)
		successful
		strong
	worry	/

B Fill the blanks with words from the table above.

1 Are there any film stars or actors who you find *attractive*?
2 Do you _____ about the _____ of the rainforests?
3 Do you believe in life after _____?
4 Talk about someone who has made a big _____ to your life.
5 Is television harmful, or can it be _____?
6 Do you know anyone who believes in aliens and _____ saucers?
7 Have you ever been _____ with the service in a shop or restaurant? Did you complain?
8 Is it more important to be _____ in your career, or to have _____ in your relationships?
9 What is your greatest _____ (= your best quality?)

C Now answer the questions!

© Oxford Fajar Sdn. Bhd. Photocopiable

MORE notes

Look up the **bold** words in the dictionary. Use the MORE notes to find the answers.

Across

1 A **bruise** on your eye (5,3)
3 The children's word for a **rabbit** (5)
5 A **shirt** usually has one of these at the neck (6)
10 The opposite of a **saltwater** fish is a ___ fish (10)
11 A type of **jam** that is made from oranges or lemons (9)
13 If you ___ a **meeting**, you arrange that it will happen at a later time than you had planned (8)
14 Something that you have to do at the checkout in a **supermarket** (5)
15 The place where an **ambassador** lives and works (7)
17 A day when you choose to have a **holiday** and not go to work (3,3)
18 Things that **birds** build (5)

Down

2 Trees (such as the **pine**) which do not lose their leaves in winter are called ___ trees (9)
4 Cotton and wool are types of ___ **fibre** (7)
5 There are 100 of these in a **dollar** (5)
6 A **mirror** ___ images (8)
7 An **argument** or disagreement (7)
8 Another name for non-**alcoholic** drinks (4,6)
9 A type of ape, although people sometimes call it a **monkey** (10)
12 The signs of the **zodiac** are used in ___ (9)
13 The area of **science** concerned with natural forces such light, electricity, etc. (7)
16 When you close both **eyes** and open them again quickly, you ___ (5)

OTHER WORDS FOR notes

These notes help you to improve your vocabulary. They group similar words, and explain the differences between them.

A Choose the correct word in each sentence below. Find the **OTHER WORDS FOR** note that you need, and use it to help you.

1 It was his **mistake/error/fault/responsibility** that we were late. (*Note at* **mistake**)
2 Tom and his sister are both very **pretty/good-looking/handsome/beautiful**.
3 If he wins this match, he will become the **largest/biggest/greatest/fattest** tennis player this country has ever known.
4 In our office, the lunch **interval/break/intermission/recess** is from 12.30 – 13.30.
5 If you look carefully, you can just **see/watch/look/witness** our house from here.
6 There was a terrible **aroma/fragrance/scent/stench** coming from the bin.
7 Come inside and get out of the snow. It's nice and **humid/warm/hot/cool** in here.
8 The skiers were caught in a **hurricane/blizzard/tornado/typhoon**.
9 Your sister is so beautifully **thin/skinny/slim/obese**.
10 Are you enjoying your new **occupation/profession/trade/job**?

B Improve the vocabulary in this essay. Replace the underlined words with a word or phrase from an **OTHER WORDS FOR** note.

▶ Example: (1) *In my opinion, Croatia .../ Personally, I think that Croatia ...*(*Note at* **think**)

(1) <u>I think that</u> Croatia is a (2) <u>very good</u> place for a holiday. I had a (3) <u>very good</u> time there. When I arrived at my hotel, I was (4) <u>very happy</u> to discover that I had a (5) <u>very good</u> view of the sea. (6) <u>I like</u> swimming and (7) <u>I also like</u> water sports, so I went to the beach every day. I (8) <u>also</u> spent a lot of time looking at the scenery, because the (9) <u>scenery</u> in Croatia is so beautiful. The weather is also (10) <u>nice</u>. The restaurants served (11) <u>good</u> food. The breakfast in the hotel was also really (12) <u>good</u>, and the waitress was (13) <u>nice</u>. Nearly all of the Croatians I met were (14) <u>nice</u>. The only (15) <u>bad</u> experience I had was when I lost my backpack. That was (16) <u>very bad</u>! I felt (17) <u>very sad</u> because my camera was in it and I lost all my (18) <u>nice</u> photos.

TOPIC notes

These notes give you lots of words that you can use to talk about everyday topics.

Look up the bold words. Read the **TOPIC** notes and answer the questions below.

1 What do we usually do before we buy new **clothes**?
2 What is the difference between slapstick **humour** and satire?
3 We say 'Good will soon!' to somebody who is **ill** – true or false?
4 If I want to buy a house, do I probably need a debt, a mortgage or a **loan**?
5 What type of **newspaper** is a tabloid?
6 The **recipe** for *shepherd's pie* includes apples and honey – true or false?
7 Name three things that people sometimes do when they **sleep**.
8 What are three problems you might have with your **teeth**?
9 Which of these is not a type of **weather**? *hail, muzzle, sleet, drizzle*
10 Name four different people you might find at a **wedding**.

Colour pages

These pages are full of useful vocabulary arranged according to topic.

A Look at the definitions below. Find the words on the colour pages.

1 a sweet brown powder that is used as a spice in cooking
2 a plant with a strong taste and smell that looks like a small onion and is used in cooking
3 trousers made of denim (= a strong, usually blue, cotton cloth)
4 a style of fighting originally from Japan in which the hands and feet are used as weapons
5 a small insect that is red or yellow with black spots
6 a person whose job is to put in or repair water pipes, baths, toilets etc.
7 a bag that you use for carrying things on your back
8 a piece of thick material that covers a small part of a floor
9 a mixture of vegetables, usually not cooked, that you often eat together with other foods
10 a light motorbike with a small engine
11 a type of animal, such as a crab or prawn, that lives in water
12 an extremely tall building
13 using a needle and thread to make or repair things
14 a male deer
15 a small river
16 flat, square objects that are arranged in rows to cover roofs, floors, bathroom walls, etc.
17 a tall narrow building or part of a building such as a church or castle
18 the long nose of an elephant
19 a river that falls from a high place, for example over a rock
20 a boat with sails, used for pleasure

B Circle the words in the wordsearch.

T	P	L	U	M	B	E	R	W	S	R	C
I	K	A	R	A	T	E	U	A	T	U	I
L	M	D	T	S	L	B	C	T	A	K	N
E	E	Y	A	C	H	T	K	E	G	S	N
S	O	B	K	O	R	O	S	R	P	H	A
K	W	I	S	O	G	W	A	F	O	E	M
S	Y	R	E	T	A	E	C	A	S	L	O
J	T	D	W	E	R	R	K	L	A	L	N
E	R	P	I	R	L	E	M	L	L	F	Y
A	U	U	N	D	I	J	A	P	A	I	A
N	N	T	G	E	C	L	F	M	D	S	R
S	K	Y	S	C	R	A	P	E	R	H	G

Workout key

How to find words

The alphabet

A
- **5** glasses
- **18** zodiac
- **10** ripple
- **15** volcano
- **2** blow
- **9** puddle
- **12** snail
- **3** duck
- **6** hat
- **7** jellyfish
- **16** windmill
- **13** sneeze
- **14** snorkel
- **1** arch
- **11** robot
- **4** eclipse
- **8** lick
- **17** zebra

Puddle and *robot* are not illustrations in *Wordpower*.

Choosing the right meaning

A
1 F
2 T
3 F A Christmas cracker is a cardboard tube covered in coloured paper.
4 F If something 'costs a bomb', it is expensive.
5 F A dummy is a stupid person.
6 F A school is a large group of fish.
7 F The season after summer and before winter is called **fall** in American English.
8 F A man wears trunks to go swimming.
9 T

B
1 frozen   sense 1
2 dropped   sense 1
3 turned   sense 1
4 cut   sense 4
5 broke   sense 1
6 faced/face sense 1
7 playing   sense 4
8 cut   sense 6
9 broke   sense 5
10 turned   sense 6
11 face   sense 3
12 drop   sense 4
13 play   sense 5
14 froze   sense 4

Finding phrasal verbs – fast!

A
1 away
2 down
3 on
4 on
5 out
6 over/through
7 round
8 up
9 with

B
1 out
2 down
3 with
4 over/through
5 on
6 round
7 up
8 away
9 on
10 out

Parts of speech (= nouns, verbs, etc.)

A
1 adjective
2 noun
3 verb
4 adverb

B
1 noun   watch   2
2 verb   watch   1
3 noun   park   1
4 verb   park   2
5 noun   flat   2
6 adjective flat   1
7 noun   train   1
8 verb   train   2
9 adjective hard   1
10 adverb hard   2

Finding the right word

1 inspect
2 lucky
3 spy
4 thief
5 limousine
6 jeweller
7 greedy
8 clumsy
9 dig
10 burglar

Understanding words

Defining vocabulary

A Definitions puzzle
1 guitar
2 deer
3 tobacco
4 pastry
5 spacecraft
6 microscope
7 grapes

B Which word is different?

drawer — not a container for water
litigation — not a process in the body
dice — not a round object
scum — not a substance used for cleaning
dose — not an amount of money

C
1 material
2 process
3 material
4 amount
5 container
6 substance
7 object

Pronunciation

How to read phonetic spelling

A
1 sung
2 slap
3 caught
4 look
5 shirt
6 chew
7 joke
8 though
9 bath

B
1 clear
2 hair
3 stay
4 go
5 my
6 boy
7 how

C hair care fair where
stay late paint weigh
go know phone though
my five high lie
boy enjoy noise point
how aloud brown sound

Stress

A Check your answers by looking at the list of **Geographical names** at the back of the dictionary.

How to use words

Examples

2 court = badminton squash tennis
pitch = football hockey cricket
3 ski resort
4 winter sport
5 No. You cannot use **sporting** to describe people.
6 to be in training for
7 participate in
8 at a swimming pool
9 Yes, they do.
Goes windsurfing is more usual.
10 A referee. He/She blows it.
11 sports facilities

Collocation – Words that go together

Verb + noun collocations

A do your homework   lose weight
draw pictures   save money
fall in love   tell a story
go on holiday   watch TV
have a good time

B done your homework?
She fell in love with him…
If you hadn't watched so much…
Have you lost weight?
She has gone on holiday.
love drawing pictures.
tell the same stories…
have a good time…
save more money…

Adjective + noun collocations

1 a bad back
2 a balanced diet
3 a black eye
4 a broken leg
5 a contagious disease
6 a decayed tooth
7 a runny nose
8 a serious illness
9 a sore throat
10 a speedy recovery
11 a splitting headache
12 a twisted ankle

Prepositions

1 afraid of
2 proud of
3 remind you of
4 dream of/about
5 embarrassed about
6 worry about
7 bad at
8 believe in
9 receive a present from

Verb patterns

1 enjoy doing
2 planning to do
3 make you do/not allowed to do
4 looking forward to doing
5 puts off doing/should do
6 forgotten to do
7 remember doing

Irregular verbs

fou**n**d / found
ra**n** / run
did / done
f**e**ll / fallen
w**r**ote / written
sang /**s**ung
ate / eat**e**n
br**o**ke / broken
t**o**ok / taken
drank / **d**runk

mystery word = understood (past tense and past participle of understand)

GRAMMAR notes

1 it is so depressing (note at **news**)
2 I can't eat any more (note at **some**)
3 I've been studying English for four years (note at **since**)
4 I had to help (note at **must**)
5 some information about (note at **information**)
6 If the weather is good tomorrow (note at **when**)
7 My twin brother, who lives in Germany, is called (note at **who**)
8 I have such a boring teacher (note at **such**)
9 Two days ago (note at **ago**)
10 I've never been to China (note at **go**)

HELP notes

1 like	7 nice
2 take care of	8 raise
3 left	9 robbed, stolen
4 funny	10 tell
5 lend	
6 laid (= past simple of lay), lay (= past simple of lie)	

When to use words

Formal, informal, slang, etc.

1 ✗	formal	6 ✔	formal
2 ✗	formal	7 ✗	formal
3 ✗	slang	8 ✔	figurative
4 ✔	slang	9 ✔	informal
5 ✗	informal	10 ✗	spoken

British and American English

American words

1	automobile	5	tire
2	license plate	6	hood
3	windshield	7	fender
4	trunk	8	gas/gasoline

British words

1	flat	5	curtains
2	lift	6	toilet
3	dustbin/litter bin	7	tap
4	fridge	8	ground floor

Build your vocabulary

Word families

A

verb	noun	adjective
attract	**attraction**	(un)attractive
deepen	**depth**	**deep**
destroy	destruction	**destructive**
die	**death**	dead
differ	**difference**	**different**
educate	education	educated / **educational**
fly	**flight**	**flying**
frighten	fright	frightened / **frightening**
hope	hope	**hopeful** / (OPP **hopeless**)
satisfy	**satisfaction**	(dis)**satisfied**
succeed	**success**	successful
strengthen	**strength**	strong
worry	worry	**worried / worrying**

B
1 attractive
2 worry, destruction
3 death
4 difference
5 educational
6 flying
7 dissatisfied
8 successful, success
9 strength

MORE notes

across
1. black eye
3. bunny
5. collar
10. freshwater
11. marmalade
13. postpone
14. queue
15. embassy
17. day off
18. nests

down
2. evergreen
4. natural
5. cents
6. reflects
7. quarrel
8. soft drinks
9. chimpanzee
12. astrology
13. physics
16. blink

OTHER WORDS FOR notes

A
1. fault (note at **mistake**)
2. good-looking (note at **beautiful**)
3. greatest (note at **big**)
4. break (note at **interval**)
5. see (note at **look**)
6. stench (note at **smell**)
7. warm (note at **cold**)
8. blizzard (note at **storm**)
9. slim (note at **fat**)
10. job (note at **work**)

B Possible answers:

2 + 3 brilliant / an excellent / fantastic / great / wonderful
4 very glad / very pleased / delighted
5 brilliant / an excellent / fantastic / great / wonderful
6 I enjoy / I love / I'm really keen on / I'm really into
7 I also enjoy / I also love / I'm also really keen on / I'm also really into
8 spent a lot of time looking at the scenery as well / too
9 countryside
10 lovely
11 + 12 delicious / tasty
13 + 14 lovely / friendly
15 unpleasant
16 awful / dreadful / horrible / terrible
17 miserable / unhappy / upset
18 great / lovely / wonderful

TOPIC notes

1. We try them on to see if they fit.
2. **Slapstick** is the type of humour where people (such as clowns) fall over or cover other people with water. **Satire** is the type of humour which makes fun of people such as politicians.
3. False. We say 'Get well soon!'
4. You probably need a mortgage.
5. Tabloid newspapers have small pages. Some of them have shocking stories and reports about famous people's lives.
6. False. The recipe for shepherd's pie includes potatoes, butter, milk, an onion, minced meat, chopped tomatoes, herbs and cheese.
7. snore, dream, have nightmares or sleepwalk
8. You might have toothache, tooth decay, and you might need a brace to straighten your teeth. Some people need false teeth.
9. muzzle
10. the bride, the bridegroom, the bridesmaids and the best man

Colour pages

A
1. cinnamon
2. garlic
3. jeans
4. karate
5. ladybird
6. plumber
7. rucksack
8. rug
9. salad
10. scooter
11. shellfish
12. skyscraper
13. sewing
14. stag
15. stream
16. tiles
17. tower
18. trunk
19. waterfall
20. yacht

B

```
T P L U M B E R W S R C
I K A R A T E U A T U I
L M D T S L B C T A K N
E E Y A C H T K E G S N
S O B K O R O S R P H A
K W I S O G W A F O E M
S Y R E T A E C A S L O
J T D W E R R K L A L N
E R P I R L E M L L F Y
A U U N D I J A P A I A
N N T G E C L F M D S R
S K Y S C R A P E R H G
```

List of illustrations in the dictionary

At or near these words in the dictionary, you will find pictures to help you to understand words and expand your vocabulary. Many of these pictures have different parts labelled, for example the picture at *egg* includes the items *eggshell*, *white* and *yolk*.

accordion	catapult	earth
angle	chair	eclipse
antelope	chess	egg
arch	chicken	elbow
arm	chip[1]	elephant
back	chip[2]	elk
badge	circle	exercise
badger	clock	fan
badminton	cog	fence
bag	coil	fireplace
bagpipes	compass	firework
balcony	computer	fist
ballet	concave	flick
bar	concentric	float
basket	container	football
beaver	corner	footprint
bed	corrugated	forklift
bend	cough	fox
between	cow	frown
bicycle	crawl	garden
bin	crinkle	glass
binoculars	cross-legged	glasses
blink	crossword	glove
blow	cube	goat
boat	cup	graffiti
body	curtain	graph
bolt	cutlery	hair
borrow	deer	handle
bread	dice	harmonica
bring	dig	hat
brush	dimple	hedgehog
bucket	dolphin	hinge
bulldozer	domino	hippopotamus
button	donkey	hold
cake	drawer	hook
camel	drop	hop
camera	duck[1]	horse
camp	duck[2]	iron
candle	dummy	jellyfish
car	each other	jewellery
card	eagle	jug
castle	ear	juggler

List of illustrations

kangaroo
kayak
kettle
key
kitchen
kneel
koala
label
lace
ladder
lamp
lean
leapfrog
length
letter
lick
lighthouse
line
lion
lizard
loop
magnet
magnify
medal
medicine
merry-go-round
mixer
money
monkey
music
nod
noughts and crosses
nut
nutcracker
octopus
opposite
optical illusion
otter
overall
overflow
overlap
owl
padlock

panda
parachute
peg
penguin
penknife
piano
pier
pin
pinch
placard
plant
plaster
plug
poke
pool
postbox
pram
pull
pulley
punch
QR code
rabbit
rack
reindeer
ripple
roll
rope
roundabout
sari
scale
scissors
scorpion
seal
seashell
sew
sewing
shadow
shake
shallow
shape
shellfish
shoe
shrink

shrug
skate
slap
sleigh
snail
snorkel
spider
spill
spiral
spoon
spray
squeeze
squirrel
stationery
stroke
sundial
swan
swim
swing
sword
take-off
teapot
tick
too
tool
torch
tractor
trampoline
tree
trolley
turkey
upside down
vacuum
volcano
wave
whistle
winch
windmill
worm
wrap
wrinkle
zebra
zodiac

List of notes in the dictionary

Different types of note in the dictionary give you extra help with key aspects of English and support you with your studies. The words in blue show you where to find notes:

Culture

April Fool's Day
Bonfire Night
breakfast
cafe
clover
congress – US Congress
election – British elections
English – English, Scots, Welsh, British
fish – fish and chips
the Foreign and Commonwealth Office
form – the sixth form
Halloween
independence – Independence Day
May Day
mistletoe
pantomime
parliament – UK parliament
party – political parties
Pluto – the solar system
public school – types of school
Shrove Tuesday
Thanksgiving (Day)
underground – railway system
the United Kingdom
valentine – St. Valentine's Day

Exam tips

check	Checking your work	plan	Planning your answer
cloze test	Doing a cloze test	predict	Predicting listening
collocation	Collocations	pronunciation	Pronunciation
contraction	Using contractions	relevant	Relevant information
copy	Copying	revision	Revision
family	Word families	skim	Skimming
format	Exam format	spelling	Spelling mistakes
gonna	gonna	synonym	Synonyms
last-minute	Last-minute learning	tense	Irregular verb forms
limit	Word limit	test	Test yourself
mock	Mock exams	time	Time yourself
multiple-choice	Multiple-choice	topic	Topics
note	Revision notes	underline	Underline key words
oral	Oral/Speaking exams	wanna	wanna
paragraph	Paragraphs	yourself	Talking about yourself
part	Parts of speech		

Other words for

allow	permit, let
alone	lonely, on your own, by yourself
also	too, as well
answer	reply, respond
area	district, region, part
bad	awful, dreadful, terrible, horrible
beautiful	pretty, good-looking, attractive, handsome, gorgeous
big	large, great
border	frontier, boundary
clean	wash, wipe, dust, brush, sweep, do the housework
cold	cool, freezing
country	nation, state, land

dislike	don't like, don't spend much time doing sth, not keen on, not interested in, hate, can't stand
fat	large, overweight, chubby, obese
good	brilliant, fantastic, great, excellent, wonderful, delicious, tasty, talented, outstanding
ground	the Earth, land, floor, earth, soil
happen	occur, take place
happy	glad, pleased, delighted, cheerful
hit	strike, beat, punch, smack
hurt	wounded, injured
important	essential, vital, play a vital/key role in…, historic
intelligent	bright, clever, smart
interval	intermission, break, recess, interlude, pause
kill	murder, assassinate, slaughter, massacre
lake	pond, pool, puddle
like	enjoy/spend a lot of time doing sth, keen on sth, be into sth, interested in
mistake	error, do sth wrong, fault
nice	great, lovely, wonderful, friendly, cosy, attractive, beautiful, expensive, fashionable, smart
price	charge, cost
road	street, motorway, freeway, expressway, lane
sad	upset, unhappy, miserable, depressed, depressing
scenery	country, countryside, landscape, view
small	little, tiny, minute
smell	stink, stench, odour, pong, aroma, fragrance, perfume, scent
storm	thunderstorm, cyclone, hurricane, typhoon, tornado, blizzard, snowstorm
sweater	jumper, pullover, cardigan, fleece, sweatshirt
thief	robber, burglar, shoplifter, mugger
thin	slim, skinny, underweight
think	In my opinion/As far as I'm concerned/It seems to me that…, reckon, believe
tool	implement, machine, instrument, device
travel	journey, tour, trip, excursion
under	below, beneath, underneath
until	till, as far as, up to
well	great, good, OK, fine, I'm not (too) bad
work	job, employment, occupation, profession, trade
zero	nil, nought, O

Topic notes

art	Art	clothes	Clothes
baby	Babies	coffee	Coffee
bed	Beds	computer	Computers
birthday	Birthdays	cook	Cooking
blog	Blogs	court	Court
boat	Boats	crime	Crime
book	Books	cybercrime	Cybercrime
bus	Travelling by bus	degree	Qualifications
camera	Cameras	direction	Asking for and giving directions
car	Cars		
card	Playing cards	doctor	Going to the doctor
chat	Chat room	dog	Dogs
child	Children	driving	Driving
city	City life	eBay™	eBay

List of notes

e-book	E-books	office	Office work
email	Email	online	Online
environment	The environment	pay	Pay
film	Films	pet	Pets
flat	Living in a flat	plane	Travelling by plane
friend	Friends	podcast	Podcasts
hair	Hair	politics	Politics
hard drive	Hard drive	pop	Pop music
holiday	Holidays	post	Posting letters
hospital	Hospitals	recipe	A recipe
hotel	Hotels	reference	References
house	Houses	restaurant	Restaurants
humour	Humour	routine	Daily routine
ill	Feeling ill	school	Schools
instant messaging	Instant messaging	shop	Shops
instrument	Musical instruments	shopping	Shopping
Internet	The Internet	sleep	Sleep
introduce	Introducing people	smartphone	Smartphones
iPod™	iPods	social networking	Social networking
job	Jobs	space	Space
job	Leaving a job	sport	Sport
listen	Listening to music	study	Studying
literature	Literature	telephone	Using the telephone
loan	Loans	television	Television
meal	Meals	theatre	Theatre
meat	Meat	tooth	Teeth
mobile phone	Mobile phones	touch screen	Touch screens
money	Money	train	Travelling by train
music	Music	university	University
name	Names	war	War
netiquette	Netiquette	weather	Weather
newspaper	Newspapers	wedding	Weddings

Writing tips

because	Giving a reason	mind map	Preparing to write
contrast	How to show contrast 1	similarity	How to compare similar things
despite	How to show contrast 2	sincere	How to end a letter
difference	How to compare different things	sudden	Using adverbs
		then	Order of events
example	Giving examples	therefore	Describing results